The Directory of

Local Court and County Record Retrievers

The Definitive Guide to Searching for Public Record Information at the State Level

2005 Edition

BRB Publications, Inc.
www.brbpub.com

Dedicated to the Searching & Understanding of Public Records

BRB Publications

THE DIRECTORY OF LOCAL COURT AND COUNTY RECORD RETRIEVERS

2005 Edition

Edited by: Peter J. Weber, Annette Jackson, and Michael Sankey

Post Office Box 27869 206 W Julie Dr. #2
Tempe, AZ 85285 U.S.A. Tempe, AZ 85283 U.S.A.
Tele.: 800-929-3811 Fax: 800-929-3810

www.brbpub.com

ISBN 1-879792-80-X

The directory of local court and county record retrievers : The definitive guide to searching for public record information at the state level / [editors, Michael L. Sankey, Annette Talley, Peter J. Weber]. -- 2005 ed.
p. cm.
Includes index.
ISBN 1-879792-80-X

1. Court records--Research--United States--Directories. 2. Public records--Research--United States --Directories. 3. Legal research--United States--Directories. I. Sankey, Michael L., 1949- II. Talley, Annette. III. Weber, Peter J. (Peter Julius), 1952- IV. BRB Publications.

KF8700.A19D572 2005 342.73'0662'02573
QBI04-200527

This Sourcebook includes elements of *The Public Record Retriever Network (PRRN)*

Contents

Introduction

Simply put, this directory is a resource of local, hands-on document retrievers who research public record information.

Who Are These Firms?

Local Document Retrievers physically visit government agencies—such as a courthouse or recorder's office—to search specific requested categories of public records. Usually the purpose is to obtain documentation for legal compliance (e.g., incorporations), for lending, for hiring, or for litigation. Document Retriever is considered a profession. The retriever or their personnel go directly to the agency to "look up" the information. Retrievers do *not* review or interpret the results or issue reports in the sense that investigators do, but rather return existing documents as the results of searches.

The act of retrieving public record documents can also be a function or service offered by a private investigator, public record search firm, a screening company, title company, or even a genealogist. Document Retrievers may also be known as **abstractors.** In many states, abstractors perform services commonly associated with real estate title and ownership research.

In this directory, these types of local document retrievers are indexed and profiled, with only one qualification: that they provide hands-on document retrieval. Each year, they are contacted by us to verify their geographical coverage areas and the types of records they retrieve.

These Record Retrievers Are Experts

Remember that the public record retrievers and vendors found in this directory are experts. Based on the information they've provided about themselves, we feel they can fulfill your particular public record searching needs in an accurate and legal manner. We highly recommend the PRRN members indicated by the icon.

How This Book is Organized

This directory consists of two main sections. To help you know "who" has access to "what" public record information, see **the Local Retriever County Index**. This is a county-by-county index showing which firm visits the courthouse or recorder's office within a particular county.

To learn more about a particular retriever, review **the Local Document Retriever Profiles** section. Also, we strongly urge readers to read the text found the front portion of this Directory. We have included proven hints and suggestions that will make your public record searching tasks easier.

This Directory is Based on Surveys

All of the information contained in this directory is based upon responses to surveys conducted by our staff. The geographic coverage and profile information listed for each entry is based upon that company's or that individual's own responses to our survey. While trying to reflect these responses correctly, we are not responsible for the accuracy of their answers. Keeping in mind that not all inaccuracies are readily apparent, when conflicts have been noticed, our staff has conducted phone interviews. In some instances, to complete the profile, information was taken from company websites. And, we have removed companies profiled in previous works when multiple complaints of their services have been brought to our attention. Thus, this directory can be considered more comprehensive and "cleaner" than pay-per-listing directories or in the highly limited lists that you may find online.

What is out there? Keep in Mind Where Public Records Come From

Retrievers are your link to public records, but the public record search process is complicated by the degree of restrictions placed by government agencies on their access. Consider the following:

- Very little of what you may perceive as government record information is truly open to the general public. Even seemingly harmless information is subject to restrictions somewhere in the United States.
- And, what you may think is highly confidential information could be public information, depending on the rules of a state or a jurisdiction.

So, simply because your state or county has certain rules, regulations, and practices regarding the accessibility and content of its records, that does not mean that another state or county adheres to the same rules.

How To Be Listed In This Directory

If you or your firm provides the service of hands-on record retrieval service at the county level, you are eligible to be listed in the next edition. There is no charge to be listed in this directory. But, there are membership fees involved if you choose to join the Public Record Retriever Network (PRRN). You may be listed immediately on our web sites if join as a PRRN member (see the PRRN Member information starting at the rear of this book).

You can call BRB Publications at 800-929-3811 to obtain a questionnaire form and information about PRRN membership. We would be glad to answer any questions you might have.

You can also visit www.brbpub.com/prrn/join.asp to download the retriever and abstractor questionnaire and the PRRN member application.

Be aware that we can list your firm in other publications and on the web if you qualify as a public record search firm, pre-employment screening firm, tenant screening firm, a public record gateway, publisher, or distributor. These types of public record providers are examined in the Introduction.

It is the policy at BRB Publications not to include a company in this book if we have received complaints about the company. Also, our editors may, at their discretion, cancel the listing of any company that, in their opinion, is not conducting business in a highly ethical manner.

A Quick Primer on Public Records and Vendors

Definition of Public Records

The strict **definition of public records is**—

"*Those records maintained by government agencies that are open without restriction to public inspection, either by statute or by tradition.*"

If access to a record that is held by a government agency is restricted in some way, then it is not a public record.

Accessibility Paradox

Adding to the mystique of government records is the accessibility paradox. For example, in some states a specific category of records is severely restricted, and therefore those records are not "public," while the very same category of records may be 100% open in other states. Among these categories are criminal histories, vehicle ownership records and workers' compensation records.

Public vs. Private vs. Personal

Before reading further, let us define types of records held by government or by private industry. Of course, not all information about a company or individual is public. The boundaries between public and private information are not well understood, and continually undergo intense scrutiny. The following is an introduction to the subject from a viewpoint of a professional record searcher.

Public Record

Public records are records of incidents or actions filed or recorded with a government agency for the purpose of notifying others about the matter — the "public." The deed to your house recorded at the county recorder's office is a public record — it is a legal requirement that you record with the county recorder. Anyone requiring details about your property may review or copy the documents.

Public Information

Your telephone listing in the phone book is public information; that is, you freely furnished the information to ease the flow of commercial and private communications.

Personal Information

Any information about a person or business that the person or business might consider private and confidential in nature, such as your Social Security Number, is personal information. Such information will remain private to a limited extent unless it is disclosed to some outside entity that could make it public. Personal information may be found in either public records or in public information.

How Personal Information Enters the Public Domain

Many people confuse the three categories above, lump them into one and wonder how "big brother" accumulated so much information about them. Therefore, these distinctions are important. The reality is that much of this information is given willingly.

Actually, there are two ways that personal information can enter the public domain — statutory and voluntary. The confusion of terms used today feeds the increasing conflict between privacy advocates and commercial interests. This, in turn, is driving legislation towards more and more restrictions on the dissemination of personal information — the same personal information that, in fact, is willingly shared by most people and companies in order to participate in our market economy.

Voluntary vs. Statutory—Shared vs. Disclosed

As mentioned above, there are two ways that personal information can enter the public domain—voluntary and statutory. In a **voluntary** transaction, you **share** personal information of your own free will. Examples of voluntary sharing include: your telephone number in the phone book; your Social Security Number on an application to obtain a credit card; and your estimated annual income on a magazine subscription form.

In a **statutory** transaction, you **disclose** personal information because the law **requires** it. Examples of statutory disclosure include: your height, weight, eye color and date of birth on a driver's license application; your Social Security Number, income, and children's names and ages on your tax return; and your address on a deed.

Disclosure by Statue or Usage

Disclosure of information by government agencies is controlled by either statute or usage by traditional practice. An example of control by usage by historical tradition is that most civil and criminal court records are open to public inspection. Disclosure of information by private companies is either unregulated or regulated by statute.

The increasing conflict between privacy advocates and commercial interests is driving legislation that applies more and more **restrictions** on the **dissemination of personal information**—the same personal information which, in fact, is willingly shared by most people and companies in order to participate in our market economy. Some of the legislative mandates have come from the federal government, such as the Driver's Privacy Protection Act, which restricts the states from determining their own policies of selling motor vehicle records. Other mandates typically come from the states and local authorities. All of these entities are trying to find the balance between protection of privacy and the protection of legitimate business interests.

Where Public Records are Held

There are two places you can find public records—

- at a government agency
- within the database of a private company

Government agencies maintain records in a variety of ways. While many state agencies and highly populated county agencies are computerized, many others use microfiche, microfilm, and paper to store files and indexes. Agencies that have converted to computer will not necessarily place complete file records on their system; they are more apt to include only an index, pointer or summary data to the files.

Private enterprises develop their databases in one of two ways: they buy the records in bulk from government agencies; or they send personnel to the agencies and compile this information by using a copy machine or keying information into a laptop computer. The database is then available for internal use or for resale purposes. An example of such a company is Superior Information (800 848-0489). Superior maintains a very comprehensive database of civil judgments, tax liens, Uniform Commercial Code filings, and bankruptcy data gathered from the Mid-Atlantic States.

Categories of Professional Public Record Vendors

We define six main categories of professional public record vendors: 1. local document retrievers; 2. distributors and gateways; 3. search firms; 4. screening firms; 5. investigators; and, 6. application specialists. This directory is devoted to the first category—Local Document Retrievers.

In the interest of presenting an all-encompassing overview, all six categories with subcategories are described as follows—

1. Local Document Retrievers

Local Document Retrievers physically visit government agencies—such as a courthouse or recorder's office—to search specific requested categories of public records. Usually, the purpose is to obtain documentation for legal compliance (e.g., incorporations), for lending, for hiring, and for litigation—basically for verifying or finding. The retriever or his/her personnel go directly to the agency to "look up" the information you request. Retrievers do *not* review or interpret the results or issue reports in the sense that investigators do, but rather return existing documents as the results of searches. Document Retrievers may also be known as **abstractors.** In most states, abstractors perform services commonly associated with real estate title and ownership research.

For best results, the members of the **Public Record Retriever Network (PRRN),** shown by the icon, are recommended. Also, PRRN members firms can be found, by state and counties served, at www.brbpub.com/prrn. This organization has set industry standards for the retrieval of public record documents and operates under a Code of Professional Conduct. For more information regarding PRRN, turn to the rear of this directory.

Local Retrievers as search firms. A retriever may be relied upon for strong knowledge in a local area, whereas a search firm (described below) has a breadth of knowledge and experience in a wider geographic range, usually statewide or regionally. Many of the local retrievers listed in this directory do offer statewide services, often retrieving records via electronic means in addition to their local hands-on services, which we have listed by county. When contacting a record retriever, and that retriever carries the **Public Record Retriever Network (PRRN) designation,** , ask them if they offer statewide or regional services. For instance, a retrieval firm may be listed for criminal records in eight counties in their state, but they may be capable of retrieving from the statewide criminal records repository, or from state UCC or MVR records sources.

Correspondents. While document retrievers tend to be localized, there are many retrieval companies that offer a state or national network of other retrievers. Keep in mind that, often, larger retrieval companies will hire other local retrievers as independent contractors, or under some sort of trade agreement. A retriever company's "other retrievers" are commonly referred to as **correspondents**. Thus, many of the retrievers found in this directory may act as correspondents for larger firms, covering a certain geographic area. Some entries in the directory prefer to work as correspondents on an ongoing basis in a "wholesale" manner, while others prefer to only work the "retail" side of the business for the true end users of the records. Accordingly, fees retrievers charge can vary.

Editor's Tip: In the interest of compiling a concise index with less than 5,000 pages, the Local Retrievers County Index does not indicate counties where a firm provides document retrieval services using hired correspondents and non-employees. However, the *correspondent coverage* of a firm is indicated in that retriever's profile in the Local Retrievers Profile section.

2. Search Firms

Search firms are companies that furnish public record search services and document retrieval services through outside online services and/or through a network of specialists that may include their own employees or correspondents (see Local Document Retrievers). Search firms may obtain public record information from distributors or gateways, or obtain their records direct from government agencies.

There are two types of Search Firms:

Search Generalists offer a full range of search capabilities in many public record categories over a wide geographic region. They may rely on gateways, primary distributors and/or networks of retrievers. They combine online proficiency with document retrieval expertise.

Search Specialists specialize in one or a few types of records. They may also be limited to a specific geographic area. Examples include a firm that specializes in only searching criminal records in New England, or a firm that only searches real estate records in Iowa.

While many of the local document retriever companies in the Retrievers County Index are also search firms, there is an additional short list of search firms listed at the back of this directory in the PRRN section. On this short list are **Associate Members of PRRN**, and they are not listed in this directory's Local Retrievers County Index and Retriever Profile sections.

To find additional search firms, we suggest searching at www.publicrecordsources.com.

3. Distributors and Gateways (Proprietary Database Vendors)

Distributors are automated public record firms that combine public sources of bulk data and/or online access to develop their own database products. Primary Distributors include companies that collect or buy public record information from its source and have reformatted that information in some useful way. Distributors tend to focus on one or a limited number of types of information, although a few firms offer access to a number of information categories.

Gateways are companies that provide a sophisticated, automated gateway to Primary Distributors or government sources. Usually the transaction is interactive and immediate. Thus, Gateways provide "one-stop shopping" for multiple geographic areas and/or categories of information.

Companies can be **both** Primary Distributors and Gateways. For example, an online database companies may be a Primary Distributor, say, of corporate information, and may also act as a Gateway to real estate or other information from other Primary Distributors.

Another interesting characteristic about Distributors and Gateway is that they tend to be either **horizontal or vertical.** In other words, they specialize in either a geographic area or in a specific type or record. A *horizontal* company provides a wide range of public record categories including criminal, civil, corporate, and UCC records, among others, but may only do so for one area, the Pacific Northwest. A *vertical* company offers one type of nationwide data, such as vehicle history database.

To find a proprietary database vendor, we suggest the *Public Record Online* book by Facts on Demand Press or visit www.publicrecordsources.com.

4. Screening Companies

Screening Companies are hired to perform backgrounds checks on individuals or companies for hiring or property leasing purposes, generally. For our purposes, these companies are referred to as **Pre-employment Screening Firms** and **Tenant Screening Firms**. They search many of the categories of public records in order to prepare an overall report about a person or business. Since Screening companies are experts in public record information, they should be immediately knowledgeable on legal issues and limits such as the Fair Credit Reporting Act, and compliant. Typically, Screening Firms can customize their information packages to fit a client's needs. To find a screening company, we suggest searching at www.publicrecordsources.com.

Most professional Pre-employment Screening Firms are national in scope and have the ability to provide quality background checks for all sizes of companies. Most Tenant Screening Companies are geographic specialist in nature and are hired, in part, because of their location.

Background checking—or screening—is certainly a common function of a private investigator (see below). It is important to note that many states require a screening company to have a licensed investigator on staff, and there are also states that do not.

While many of the local document retriever companies are also screening firms, there is a short list of screening firms listed in the PRRN section. On this short list are **Associate Members of PRRN**, and they are not listed in this directory's Local Retrievers County Index and Retriever Profile sections.

5. Private Investigation Firms

Investigators perform the types of services traditionally thought of as detective work, such as surveillance, but they are also called upon to perform some of the same functions as a Search Firm or Screening Company. By using public records as tools rather than as ends in themselves, an Investigator creates an overall, comprehensive "picture" of an individual or company for a client's particular purpose. Additionally, the Investigator interprets the information they have gathered in order to identify further investigation tracks. They summarize their results in a report compiled from all the sources used. To find a reputable investigator, we suggest going to www.publicrecordsources.com and review the excellent link list resources there.

6. Application Specialists

Application Specialists focus on unique services—using public records—geared to a client's specific needs. Three of the most common types of Application Specialists are listed below.

Information Brokers (IB) gather information that will help their clients make informed business decisions. Their work is usually done on a custom basis, with each project being unique. IBs are extremely knowledgeable in online research of full-text databases. Most IBs specialize in a particular subject area such as patent searching or competitive intelligence. The Association of Independent Information Professionals (AIIP), at www.aiip.org, has professional information specialist members from twenty-one countries. Many small search firms and investigative firms refer to themselves as information brokers, but that is not necessarily true. The term **Information Brokers** was coined in the 1970s by the founders of AIIP and is recognized as a professional designation within that organization.

Competitive Intelligence (CI) involves "the legal and ethical collection of information, analysis that doesn't avoid unwelcome conclusions, and controlled dissemination of actionable intelligence to decision makers." CI professionals enable businesses to make informed decisions about everything from marketing, R&D, and investing tactics to long-term business strategies. The Society of Competitive Intelligence Professionals, at www.scip.org, has members in over forty-five countries.

Genealogists work with public records, primarily at the local or county level. They may research and access vital records and probate records from "current" government databases, but much of their work involves research of archived records. A number of Genealogists may be found in this directory. They may be identifiable by the type of records they retrieve: Vital records and Probate courts.

Which Type of Vendor is Right for You?

With all the variations of vendors and the many categories of public record information, the obvious question is, "How do I find the right retriever to go to for the public record information I need?" Before you start calling every interesting vendor that catches your eye, you need to narrow your search to the **type of records** you need. Answer the following questions—

What Information Does the Retriever Specialize In or Offer?

Do you need a local search, a statewide search, or is your record need national in scope? Must documents be retrieved by hand? This directory is meant to be especially useful for locating hands-on document retrievers. To determine if you need a local retriever or online vendor/gateway, see page 9.

What is the Frequency of Usage?

If you have ongoing, recurring requests for a particular type of information, it may be best to choose a different vendor then if you have infrequent requests. Setting up an account with a primary distributor will give you an inexpensive per search fee, but the monthly minimum requirements will be prohibitive to the casual requester. In the latter instance, we suggest going to www.publicrecordresources.com to find a vendor who accesses a distributor or gateway on a regular basis. Also, we suggest that you always *ask* the local retriever if they offer regional or national services beyond what is listed in the county index section.

What is the Complexity of the Search?

The importance of hiring a vendor who understands and can interpret the information in the final format increases with the complexity of the search. Pulling a corporation record in Maryland is not difficult, but doing an online criminal record search in Maryland, when only a portion of the felony records are online, is not so easy.

A good source of information about what is available from over 20,000 government offices—including costs, restrictions, turnaround times, and access methods—is BRB Publication's annual *Sourcebook to Public Record Information.* This is also available as a CD-Rom or an online subscription service.

What are the Geographic Boundaries of the Search?

A search of local records close to you may require little assistance, but a search of records nationally or in a state 2,000 miles away will require seeking a vendor who covers the search area you need. If your record searching is narrowed by a region or locality, a local record retriever may be a wise alternative to a national vendor. If you are considering a vendor with online access, keep in mind that many national firms allow you to order a search online even though results cannot be delivered immediately. If some hands-on local searching is required, then expect an answer in a few days or more.

Of course, you may want to use a government agency online system—if it's available—for the kind of information you need. An excellent source for finding online government records in the book *Public Records Online*, available from BRB Publications.

Not sure of the geographic boundaries of your search? If you have a zip code, then BRB Publication's *Ultimate County Locator* will tell you what county or counties the zip code falls in. Additionally, the *Ultimate County Locator* - which is available on CD-rom - is a handy reference for matching zip codes to place names, and place names to counties.

How to Choose a Competent Retriever

The four most significant attributes of the kind of Retriever you want on your side are:

1. Local Experience and Expertise

Knows exactly where to go to obtain the information you need

Knows personally the people who work at the government agency

Knows exactly what the records look like and what the contents mean

2. Searching Time Frame

Knows just how long the project will take

Knows whether it is possible to expedite the project

Completes the project as promised

3. Delivery of Document

Can deliver the document when and where required

Can guarantee the search will be legal

Knows and explains the possible pitfalls involved in obtaining the information you need

4. Cost

Knows the basis for the costs—copy fee, certification fee, etc.

Can estimate the total fee

Other Research Tools

Having knowledge about a jurisdiction's record-keeping policies and retrieval procedures is always a plus when you need to obtain information from that office. For example, if you already know facts about the office—such as that the records in a court are indexed only by defendant, or that a public terminal is available at the court office—you can better tell if the retriever really knows what they're talking about. BRB Publications maintains databases that feature this kind of information about state agencies, state and federal courts, county recorders' offices, and other public and private institutions you may want to search in. This useful directory information is brought together in the *Public Record Research System*, as mentioned previously, a subscription web product updated weekly. BRB also offers an annual publication, titled *The Sourcebook to Public Record Information*.

13 Questions to Ask a Retriever

The **Thirteen Questions to Ask a Retriever** illustrates the kinds of questions you want answered before committing your project to a Retriever. Information provided by Retrievers—who are experienced and who do the searches themselves as is frequently the case in court and real estate searching—is often more complete and accurate than that jurisdiction clerk's information would be. In fact, fewer government offices are performing searches of their records, so use of an outside Retriever in these offices is required.

The following questions will help you determine the quality of a Retriever.

	Questions to Ask:			
1.	What is your expertise in the type of information I need?	**HIGH**	**MEDIUM**	**LOW**
2.	What is your expertise in dealing with the agency where the information is stored?	**HIGH**	**MEDIUM**	**LOW**
3.	How frequently do you access the agency where the information I need is stored?	**DAILY**	**WEEKLY**	**OTHER**
4.	How frequently do you access the specific information I need?	**DAILY**	**WEEKLY**	**OTHER**
5.	Are the original documents stored at this agency?	**YES**	**NO**	**DON'T KNOW**
6.	Do you access the information yourself or through a third party?	**SELF**		**THIRD PARTY**
7.	Who does the actual search for the information?	***See*: Note**	***See*: Note**	
8.	How long before some results are known?	**1-2 DAYS**	**LESS THAN A WEEK**	**OTHER**
9.	In what form will I receive the information?	**AS YOU WISH**	**VERBAL**	**DOCS ONLY**
10.	Will you interpret the information for me?	**YES**	**NO**	
11.	Will my search be legal and remain confidential?	**YES**		**DON'T KNOW**
12.	What are all the costs I will (may) incur to obtain the information?	**EXPLAINED**	**NOT FULLY EXPLAINED**	**DON'T KNOW**
13.	Do you serve other clients who have needs like mine and may I talk to a few of them?	**YES**		**NO**
	If you circled a preponderance of answers in one column, you should—	**Consider This Retriever**	**Consider Other Retrievers**	**Do Not Use This Retriever**

Note—Some jurisdictions only perform searches themselves, while other jurisdictions do no searching themselves instead leaving that to local record retrievers. However, in many jurisdictions where the government office either performs searches themselves or allows the public to perform them, you must decide which type of search—by the office *or* by the retriever—best meets your needs.

Retriever or Online Service/Gateway?

Here is a handy chart to help you decide whether to use a Local Document Retriever or an Online Service/Gateway to perform your public record search project.

Circle your answer to each of the seven questions, and choose the course of action that makes the most sense for you.

	Questions to Ask:			
1.	What is my level of expertise in the type of information I need?	**HIGH**	**MODERATE**	**LOW**
2.	Do I know where the information is located?	**YES**	**NOT SURE**	**NO**
3.	Do I know how to search for the information?	**YES**	**NOT SURE**	**NO**
4.	Can I obtain the information directly?	**YES**	**DON'T KNOW**	**NO**
5.	What is the age of the information that is accessible?	**KNOW**	**DON'T KNOW**	
6.	Does the information in its final form need interpretation?	**YES**	**DON'T KNOW**	**NO**
7.	What is my budget to obtain the information?	**LOW**	**MEDIUM**	**HIGH**

If you circled a preponderance of answers in one column, you should . . .	**Call a Retriever**	**Consider a Gateway**	**Call a Gateway**

Suggestions on How to Use This Book

Six Items to Keep in Mind

The County Index is based on physical visitation by retrieval company employees. The retriever entries found in the County Index are based on physical document retrieval—or hands-on record searching—at the county courthouse or recorder's office or at state agencies. This retrieval is performed either by the individual listed, or by employees working exclusively for that retrieval company (and not as independent contractors or correspondents who work for other search firms).

Coverage and Correspondents. In the interest of compiling a concise index with less than 5,000 pages, the Local Retriever County Index does not indicate counties where a firm provides document retrieval services using hired correspondents and non-employees. However, the **correspondent coverage** of a retrieval firm is indicated in its profile in the Local Document Retrievers Profile Section.

Public Record Retriever Network. Throughout this section you will see an icon ▣. This designates the retriever as being a member of the **Public Record Retriever Network (PRRN)**. This organization has set industry standards for the retrieval of public record documents. Members operate under a Code of Professional Conduct. Also, PRRN members firms can be found, by state and counties served, at www.brbpub.com/prrn. More information regarding PRRN can be found at the rear of this directory.

This directory is based on surveys of local retrievers. All of the information contained in this directory is based upon responses to surveys conducted by our staff. The geographic coverage and profile information listed for each retriever is based on their own responses to our survey. We have tried to reflect these responses accurately, but we are not responsible for the accuracy of the answers. Companies do not pay a fee for their listings.

Ask about their services. As some of the firms listed do offer statewide or regional retrieval services beyond those listed in this directory's index, or they offer electronic document retrieval, we recommend that you *ask* the retriever what additional services they offer. If their company profile includes a web site address, we recommend that visit their web site to learn more about their services.

We want your feedback. At the rear of this Directory is "The Retriever Satisfaction Survey." We would like to hear from you concerning your experiences with public record retrievers. Our policy is to remove retrievers from future editions if we receive numerous or serious complaints regarding their services or business practices.

How to Use The County Index

Retrievers Shown County by County

Each of the 4,266 counties, parishes, independent cities and equivalent jurisdictions in the United States are listed here in alphabetical order within their state. Note that there are entries for North America (Canada and Bermuda) in the front of the Index. You will find Puerto Rico and the Virgin Islands listed alphabetically among the states.

Icons and Bullet Items

Each retriever that accesses government offices in a county is listed under that county name with a bullet to signify each category of data the company retrieves.

Retrievers who **serve process**, usually for litigation purposes, are indicated with the designation "[SOP]". Retrievers that are members of the **Public Record Retriever Network (PRRN)** are indicated by the PRRN logo.

Nine Types of Data Included

Each county heading indicates the types of records available in that jurisdiction. The left side of the page indicates records available from the county or municipal court system. The right side of the page indicates records available from the recorder or other courthouse offices.

On the following page, the **Summary of Codes** explains the meaning of each abbreviation used.

State Agencies

Often, the expertise of retrievers located in or near state capitol cities is primarily in dealing with state offices where, for example, corporate and UCC records are located. To find these firms you need to know the county where the state offices are located. It is always a wise practice to ask a retriever if they retrieve records from state agencies in addition to the county records listed in this directory.

Coverage Claimed in the County Index

Entries in this publication are based on the responses of each retrieval company. An entry is included because the company states to us that, in that area, county or city, they have an employee – and not a friend, networker, or correspondent. That employee goes to the covered agency on a regular basis, offering "hands-on" service. Companies that offer only online indexing to these counties have been excluded, to the best of our knowledge, although there are many companies that offer both hands-on and electronic retrieval. Do keep in mind that many companies do service areas beyond the counties listed, which is indicated in their company profile in the Local Retrievers Profiles section.

Coverage By Correspondents or Networks

When a company uses a friend, network, or correspondent, this is indicated in its Retriever Profile under **Correspondent Relationships**.

If You Solicit Firms in this Directory, Some Advice if You Fax

One of the objectives of this Directory is to promote the vendors. A stated objective of PRRN is to promote improved marketing and sales practices within the industry. So entries in this book do expect to receive faxes.

However, if you fax to someone in this book, we urge you pre-qualify the entity and be careful with the wording of your message. If you wish to let a company know that you provide retrieval services in a certain geographic area and want to see if they may be interested in using you, consider the following:

- Does the firm use outsides sources? (outside sources are called "Correspondents" in the profile)
- Does this firm offer to its own clientele the type for public record you wish to provide?

For example, if you provide criminal record searches, do not fax an information sheet about your services to a firm in the book that only does real estate records in three counties. When you do wish to see if a firm is interested in your services, we suggest to call them first and ask if you can fax them your information

FYI - The Telephone Consumer Protection Act of 1991 (A Federal Law) states .... "It shall be unlawful for any person within the U.S. to use a (c) telephone facsimile machine, computer, or other device to send an unsolicited advertisement to a telephone facsimile machine....." and " A person or entity may.....bring in an appropriate Court of that State (B) an action to recover..... or to receive $500 in damages for each violation" .....plus up to three times that amount..... etc.

Summary of Codes

Court Records

CODE	GOVERNMENT AGENCY	TYPE OF INFORMATION
DT	US District Court	Federal civil and criminal cases
BK	Bankruptcy Court	United States bankruptcy cases
CV	Civil Court	Municipal, county and state level civil cases
CR	Criminal Court	Municipal, county and state level criminal cases
PR	Probate Court	Wills and estate cases

County Records

CODE	GOVERNMENT AGENCY	TYPE OF INFORMATION
UC	UCC Filing Office	Uniform Commercial Code and other personal property liens
RE	Recorder of Deeds	Real property transactions and liens
TX	Tax Filing Office(s)	Federal and state tax liens, judgment liens
VS	Vital Records Office	Vital statistics—birth, death, marriage, divorce

- "CODE" designates the agency and type of information obtainable in each county from a retriever.
- —This symbol designates a Public Record Retriever Network member.
- "[SOP]" after the retriever name designates Service of Process.
- Individual retrievers without a company name are listed in order of their last name.
- Companies that retrieve state MVR records are listed at the beginning of that state's section.

North America

Canada

COURT RECORDS RETRIEVED — **RECORDING RECORDS RETRIEVED**

DT	BK	CV	CR	PR	←COURTS ALBERTA	RECORDING→	UC	RE	TX	VS
		•	•		Accurate Source.com Inc	800-978-8950				
	•	•	•		Bison Security Group [SOP]	800-661-2245		•	•	•
		•	•		Shepp Johnman & Associates Inv [SOP]	877-258-9073				

DT	BK	CV	CR	PR	←COURTS BRITISH COLUMBIA	RECORDING→	UC	RE	TX	VS
		•	•		Accurate Source.com Inc	800-978-8950				
•	•	•		•	Mercury Service Inc	604-228-9993	•	•		
	•	•	•	•	Sterling Pacific Inv Ltd [SOP]	250-652-0541				

DT	BK	CV	CR	PR	←COURTS MANITOBA - SASKATCHEWAN	RECORDING→	UC	RE	TX	VS
		•	•		Accurate Source.com Inc	800-978-8950				

DT	BK	CV	CR	PR	←COURTS NEW BRUNSWICK-NEWFOUNDLAND-NOVA SCOTIA	RECORDING→	UC	RE	TX	VS
		•	•		Accurate Source.com Inc	800-978-8950				

DT	BK	CV	CR	PR	←COURTS NORTHWEST TERRITORIES - YUKON	RECORDING→	UC	RE	TX	VS
		•	•		Accurate Source.com Inc	800-978-8950				

DT	BK	CV	CR	PR	←COURTS ONTARIO	RECORDING→	UC	RE	TX	VS
		•		•	Aberdeen Inv, Inc [SOP]	807-626-4074		•	•	
		•	•		Accurate Source.com Inc	800-978-8950				
	•	•			Idealogic [SOP]	866-506-9900	•	•	•	•
•	•	•		•	King-Reed & Assoc Ltd	877-695-6575	•		•	•

DT	BK	CV	CR	PR	←COURTS PRINCE EDWARD	RECORDING→	UC	RE	TX	VS
		•	•		Accurate Source.com Inc	800-978-8950				

Bermuda

DT	BK	CV	CR	PR	←COURTS BERMUDA	RECORDING→	UC	RE	TX	VS
	•	•	•	•	Caribbean Investigative Network [SOP]	441-292-2626		•		•

Note: Puerto Rico and the Virgin Islands are listed with the US States, which follow alphabetically.

Alabama

COURT RECORDS RETRIEVED — **RECORDING RECORDS RETRIEVED**

DT	BK	CV	CR	PR	←COURTS **AUTAUGA**	RECORDING→	UC	RE	TX	VS
				•	AlaDocs Inc	205-251-8200	•	•	•	
				•	Autauga Abstract	334-361-0606	•	•	•	
•	•	•	•	•	McDaniel & Associates Inc [SOP]	334-312-0781	•	•	•	
•	•	•	•	•	Public Record Services [SOP]	334-262-0350	•	•	•	•

DT	BK	CV	CR	PR	←COURTS **BALDWIN**	RECORDING→	UC	RE	TX	VS
•	•	•	•	•	A & A Screening Solutions LLC [SOP]	877-999-9318	•		•	
				•	AlaDocs Inc	205-251-8200	•	•	•	
•	•	•	•	•	Brabston Legal Inv Inc [SOP]	251-666-5666	•	•	•	
•	•	•	•	•	Charles F Edgar & Associates Inc [SOP]	256-539-7761	•	•	•	
•	•	•	•	•	Ike L Hoy PE (Control Systems)	850-259-4650	•	•	•	•
•	•	•	•	•	Legal Research Service LLC [SOP]	251-432-1006	•		•	•
•	•	•	•	•	Alice S Mosley [SOP]	251-937-8468	•	•	•	
•	•	•	•	•	Parker Legal Services [SOP]	251-476-7464	•	•	•	•
•	•	•	•	•	Parrish Research	850-936-1240	•	•	•	•
•	•	•	•	•	Public Record Services [SOP]	334-262-0350	•	•	•	•
•	•	•	•		Vinson Detective Agency AL [SOP]	800-438-6072				

DT	BK	CV	CR	PR	←COURTS **BARBOUR**	RECORDING→	UC	RE	TX	VS
				•	AlaDocs Inc	205-251-8200	•	•	•	
•	•	•	•		Attorneys Services & Legal Inv [SOP]	706-322-3554	•	•		•
•	•	•	•	•	Charles F Edgar & Associates Inc [SOP]	256-539-7761	•	•	•	
•	•	•	•	•	Public Record Services [SOP]	334-262-0350	•	•	•	•

DT	BK	CV	CR	PR	←COURTS **BIBB**	RECORDING→	UC	RE	TX	VS
				•	AlaDocs Inc	205-251-8200	•	•	•	
				•	Capstone Title Services	205-759-1105	•	•	•	
•	•	•	•	•	Public Record Services [SOP]	334-262-0350	•	•	•	•

DT	BK	CV	CR	PR	←COURTS **BLOUNT**	RECORDING→	UC	RE	TX	VS
				•	AlaDocs Inc	205-251-8200	•	•	•	
•	•	•	•	•	Charles F Edgar & Associates Inc [SOP]	256-539-7761	•	•	•	
•	•	•	•	•	Public Record Services [SOP]	334-262-0350	•	•	•	•

DT	BK	CV	CR	PR	←COURTS **BULLOCK**	RECORDING→	UC	RE	TX	VS
				•	AlaDocs Inc	205-251-8200	•	•	•	
•	•	•	•	•	Public Record Services [SOP]	334-262-0350	•	•	•	•

DT	BK	CV	CR	PR	←COURTS **BUTLER**	RECORDING→	UC	RE	TX	VS
				•	AlaDocs Inc	205-251-8200	•	•	•	
•	•	•	•	•	Public Record Services [SOP]	334-262-0350	•	•	•	•

DT	BK	CV	CR	PR	←COURTS **CALHOUN**	RECORDING→	UC	RE	TX	VS
				•	AlaDocs Inc	205-251-8200	•	•	•	
•	•	•	•	•	B & B Reporting Inc [SOP]	256-574-2524	•	•	•	•
•	•	•	•	•	Charles F Edgar & Associates Inc [SOP]	256-539-7761	•	•	•	
•	•	•	•	•	Public Record Services [SOP]	334-262-0350	•	•	•	•
•	•	•		•	Southern Land & Title LLC	256-543-1361	•	•	•	

DT	BK	CV	CR	PR	←Courts	CHAMBERS	Recording→	UC	RE	TX	VS
				•	AlaDocs Inc	205-251-8200		•	•	•	
•	•	•	•		Attorneys Services & Legal Inv [SOP]	706-322-3554		•	•		•
•	•	•	•	•	Public Record Services [SOP]	334-262-0350		•	•	•	•

DT	BK	CV	CR	PR	←Courts	CHEROKEE	Recording→	UC	RE	TX	VS
				•	AlaDocs Inc	205-251-8200		•	•	•	
•	•	•	•	•	Charles F Edgar & Associates Inc [SOP]	256-539-7761		•	•	•	
•	•	•	•	•	Public Record Services [SOP]	334-262-0350		•	•	•	•
•	•	•		•	Southern Land & Title LLC	256-543-1361		•	•	•	
•	•	•		•	Title Guaranty & Trust of Chattanooga	423-266-5751		•	•	•	

DT	BK	CV	CR	PR	←Courts	CHILTON	Recording→	UC	RE	TX	VS
				•	AlaDocs Inc	205-251-8200		•	•	•	
•	•	•	•	•	Public Record Services [SOP]	334-262-0350		•	•	•	•

DT	BK	CV	CR	PR	←Courts	CHOCTAW	Recording→	UC	RE	TX	VS
				•	AlaDocs Inc	205-251-8200		•	•	•	
•	•	•	•	•	Public Record Services [SOP]	334-262-0350		•	•	•	•

DT	BK	CV	CR	PR	←Courts	CLARKE	Recording→	UC	RE	TX	VS
				•	AlaDocs Inc	205-251-8200		•	•	•	
•	•	•	•	•	Brabston Legal Inv Inc [SOP]	251-666-5666		•	•	•	
•	•	•	•	•	Legal Research Service LLC [SOP]	251-432-1006		•			•
•		•		•	Deloris Presley	888-544-8006		•	•	•	•
•	•	•	•	•	Public Record Services [SOP]	334-262-0350		•	•	•	•
•	•	•	•		Vinson Detective Agency AL [SOP]	800-438-6072					

DT	BK	CV	CR	PR	←Courts	CLAY	Recording→	UC	RE	TX	VS
				•	AlaDocs Inc	205-251-8200		•	•	•	
•	•	•	•	•	Public Record Services [SOP]	334-262-0350		•	•	•	•

DT	BK	CV	CR	PR	←Courts	CLEBURNE	Recording→	UC	RE	TX	VS
				•	AlaDocs Inc	205-251-8200		•	•	•	
•	•	•	•	•	Public Record Services [SOP]	334-262-0350		•	•	•	•
•	•	•		•	Southern Land & Title LLC	256-543-1361		•	•	•	

DT	BK	CV	CR	PR	←Courts	COFFEE	Recording→	UC	RE	TX	VS
				•	AlaDocs Inc	205-251-8200		•	•	•	
•	•	•	•	•	Charles F Edgar & Associates Inc [SOP]	256-539-7761		•	•	•	
•	•	•	•	•	Parrish Research	850-936-1240		•	•	•	•
•	•	•	•	•	Public Record Services [SOP]	334-262-0350		•	•	•	•
				•	V & A Research LLC	334-774-7092		•	•	•	

DT	BK	CV	CR	PR	←Courts	COLBERT	Recording→	UC	RE	TX	VS
				•	AlaDocs Inc	205-251-8200		•	•	•	
•	•	•	•	•	ASAP Process Services [SOP]	256-766-9805		•	•		•
•	•	•	•	•	Charles F Edgar & Associates Inc [SOP]	256-539-7761		•	•	•	
•	•	•	•	•	Freelance Abstracting Svc [SOP]	662-424-3636		•	•	•	•
•	•	•		•	Maureen H Poole	931-294-2988		•	•	•	
•	•	•	•	•	Public Record Services [SOP]	334-262-0350		•	•	•	•
•	•	•	•	•	Risk Mitigation Services Inc [SOP]	866-633-9339		•	•	•	•

DT	BK	CV	CR	PR	←Courts	CONECUH	Recording→	UC	RE	TX	VS
				•	AlaDocs Inc	205-251-8200		•	•	•	
		•		•	Melissa F Morris	334-222-1986		•	•	•	
•		•		•	Deloris Presley	888-544-8006		•	•	•	•
•	•	•	•	•	Public Record Services [SOP]	334-262-0350		•	•	•	•
•	•	•	•		Vinson Detective Agency AL [SOP]	800-438-6072					

DT	BK	CV	CR	PR	←Courts	COOSA	Recording→	UC	RE	TX	VS
				•	AlaDocs Inc		205-251-8200	•	•	•	
•	•	•	•	•	Public Record Services [SOP]		334-262-0350	•	•	•	•

DT	BK	CV	CR	PR	←Courts	COVINGTON	Recording→	UC	RE	TX	VS
				•	AlaDocs Inc		205-251-8200	•	•	•	
•	•	•	•	•	Ike L Hoy PE (Control Systems)		850-259-4650	•	•	•	•
		•		•	Melissa F Morris		334-222-1986	•	•	•	
•		•		•	Deloris Presley		888-544-8006	•	•	•	•
•	•	•	•	•	Public Record Services [SOP]		334-262-0350	•	•	•	•

DT	BK	CV	CR	PR	←Courts	CRENSHAW	Recording→	UC	RE	TX	VS
				•	AlaDocs Inc		205-251-8200	•	•	•	
•	•	•	•	•	Public Record Services [SOP]		334-262-0350	•	•	•	•

DT	BK	CV	CR	PR	←Courts	CULLMAN	Recording→	UC	RE	TX	VS
				•	AlaDocs Inc		205-251-8200	•	•	•	
•	•	•	•	•	ASAP Process Services [SOP]		256-766-9805	•	•		•
•	•	•	•	•	Charles F Edgar & Associates Inc [SOP]		256-539-7761	•	•	•	
•	•	•		•	Maureen H Poole		931-294-2988	•	•	•	
•	•	•	•	•	Public Record Services [SOP]		334-262-0350	•	•	•	•
•	•	•	•	•	Risk Mitigation Services Inc [SOP]		866-633-9339	•	•	•	•

DT	BK	CV	CR	PR	←Courts	DALE	Recording→	UC	RE	TX	VS
				•	AlaDocs Inc		205-251-8200	•	•	•	
•	•	•	•	•	Charles F Edgar & Associates Inc [SOP]		256-539-7761	•	•	•	
•	•	•	•	•	Parrish Research		850-936-1240	•	•	•	•
•	•	•	•	•	Public Record Services [SOP]		334-262-0350	•	•	•	•
				•	V & A Research LLC		334-774-7092	•	•	•	

DT	BK	CV	CR	PR	←Courts	DALLAS	Recording→	UC	RE	TX	VS
				•	AlaDocs Inc		205-251-8200	•	•	•	
				•	Capstone Title Services		205-759-1105	•	•	•	
•	•	•	•	•	Public Record Services [SOP]		334-262-0350	•	•	•	•

DT	BK	CV	CR	PR	←Courts	DE KALB	Recording→	UC	RE	TX	VS
•	•	•	•	•	A All State Tracers Company		423-605-0155	•	•	•	•
				•	AlaDocs Inc		205-251-8200	•	•	•	
•	•	•	•	•	B & B Reporting Inc [SOP]		256-574-2524	•	•	•	•
•	•	•	•	•	Charles F Edgar & Associates Inc [SOP]		256-539-7761	•	•	•	
•	•	•	•	•	Public Record Services [SOP]		334-262-0350	•	•	•	•
•	•	•		•	Southern Land & Title LLC		256-543-1361	•	•	•	
•	•	•		•	Title Guaranty & Trust of Chattanooga		423-266-5751	•	•	•	

DT	BK	CV	CR	PR	←Courts	ELMORE	Recording→	UC	RE	TX	VS
				•	AlaDocs Inc		205-251-8200	•	•	•	
				•	Autauga Abstract		334-361-0606	•	•	•	
•	•	•	•	•	McDaniel & Associates Inc [SOP]		334-312-0781	•	•	•	
•	•	•	•	•	Public Record Services [SOP]		334-262-0350	•	•	•	•

DT	BK	CV	CR	PR	←Courts	ESCAMBIA	Recording→	UC	RE	TX	VS
				•	AlaDocs Inc		205-251-8200	•	•	•	
•	•	•	•	•	Ike L Hoy PE (Control Systems)		850-259-4650	•	•	•	•
•	•	•	•	•	Legal Research Service LLC [SOP]		251-432-1006	•	•	•	•
		•		•	Melissa F Morris		334-222-1986	•	•	•	
•		•		•	Deloris Presley		888-544-8006	•	•	•	•
•	•	•	•	•	Public Record Services [SOP]		334-262-0350	•	•	•	•
•	•	•	•		Vinson Detective Agency AL [SOP]		800-438-6072				

DT	BK	CV	CR	PR	←Courts	ETOWAH	Recording→	UC	RE	TX	VS
				•	AlaDocs Inc		205-251-8200	•	•	•	

DT	BK	CV	CR	PR	←COURTS		RECORDING→	UC	RE	TX	VS
•	•	•	•	•	Charles F Edgar & Associates Inc [SOP]		256-539-7761	•	•	•	
•	•	•	•	•	Johnston & Associates		256-572-4967	•	•	•	
•	•	•	•	•	Public Record Services [SOP]		334-262-0350	•	•	•	•
•	•	•		•	Southern Land & Title LLC		256-543-1361	•	•	•	
DT	**BK**	**CV**	**CR**	**PR**	**←COURTS**	**FAYETTE**	**RECORDING→**	**UC**	**RE**	**TX**	**VS**
				•	AlaDocs Inc		205-251-8200	•	•	•	
				•	Capstone Title Services		205-759-1105	•	•	•	
•	•	•	•	•	Charles F Edgar & Associates Inc [SOP]		256-539-7761	•	•	•	
•	•	•	•	•	Public Record Services [SOP]		334-262-0350	•	•	•	•
DT	**BK**	**CV**	**CR**	**PR**	**←COURTS**	**FRANKLIN**	**RECORDING→**	**UC**	**RE**	**TX**	**VS**
				•	AlaDocs Inc		205-251-8200	•	•	•	
•	•	•	•	•	ASAP Process Services [SOP]		256-766-9805	•	•		•
•	•	•	•	•	Charles F Edgar & Associates Inc [SOP]		256-539-7761	•	•	•	
•	•	•		•	Maureen H Poole		931-294-2988	•	•	•	
•	•	•	•	•	Public Record Services [SOP]		334-262-0350	•	•	•	•
•	•	•	•	•	Risk Mitigation Services Inc [SOP]		866-633-9339	•	•	•	•
DT	**BK**	**CV**	**CR**	**PR**	**←COURTS**	**GENEVA**	**RECORDING→**	**UC**	**RE**	**TX**	**VS**
				•	AlaDocs Inc		205-251-8200	•	•	•	
•	•	•	•	•	Charles F Edgar & Associates Inc [SOP]		256-539-7761	•	•	•	
•	•	•	•	•	Ike L Hoy PE (Control Systems)		850-259-4650	•	•	•	•
•	•	•	•	•	Parrish Research		850-936-1240	•	•	•	•
•	•	•	•	•	Public Record Services [SOP]		334-262-0350	•	•	•	•
				•	V & A Research LLC		334-774-7092	•	•	•	
DT	**BK**	**CV**	**CR**	**PR**	**←COURTS**	**GREENE**	**RECORDING→**	**UC**	**RE**	**TX**	**VS**
				•	AlaDocs Inc		205-251-8200	•	•	•	
				•	Capstone Title Services		205-759-1105	•	•	•	
•	•	•	•	•	Public Record Services [SOP]		334-262-0350	•	•	•	•
DT	**BK**	**CV**	**CR**	**PR**	**←COURTS**	**HALE**	**RECORDING→**	**UC**	**RE**	**TX**	**VS**
				•	AlaDocs Inc		205-251-8200	•	•	•	
				•	Capstone Title Services		205-759-1105	•	•	•	
•	•	•	•	•	Public Record Services [SOP]		334-262-0350	•	•	•	•
DT	**BK**	**CV**	**CR**	**PR**	**←COURTS**	**HENRY**	**RECORDING→**	**UC**	**RE**	**TX**	**VS**
				•	AlaDocs Inc		205-251-8200	•	•	•	
•	•	•	•	•	Charles F Edgar & Associates Inc [SOP]		256-539-7761	•	•	•	
•	•	•	•	•	Parrish Research		850-936-1240	•	•	•	•
•	•	•	•	•	Public Record Services [SOP]		334-262-0350	•	•	•	•
				•	V & A Research LLC		334-774-7092	•	•	•	
DT	**BK**	**CV**	**CR**	**PR**	**←COURTS**	**HOUSTON**	**RECORDING→**	**UC**	**RE**	**TX**	**VS**
				•	AlaDocs Inc		205-251-8200	•	•	•	
•	•	•	•	•	Charles F Edgar & Associates Inc [SOP]		256-539-7761	•	•	•	
•	•	•	•	•	Parrish Research		850-936-1240	•	•	•	•
•	•	•		•	Maureen H Poole		931-294-2988	•	•	•	
•	•	•	•	•	Public Record Services [SOP]		334-262-0350	•	•	•	•
•	•	•		•	Title Guaranty & Trust of Chattanooga		423-266-5751	•	•	•	
				•	V & A Research LLC		334-774-7092	•	•	•	
DT	**BK**	**CV**	**CR**	**PR**	**←COURTS**	**JACKSON**	**RECORDING→**	**UC**	**RE**	**TX**	**VS**
•	•	•	•	•	A All State Tracers Company		423-605-0155	•	•	•	•
				•	AlaDocs Inc		205-251-8200	•	•	•	
•	•	•	•	•	B & B Reporting Inc [SOP]		256-574-2524	•	•	•	•
•	•	•	•	•	Charles F Edgar & Associates Inc [SOP]		256-539-7761	•	•	•	
•	•	•	•	•	Public Record Services [SOP]		334-262-0350	•	•	•	•

DT	BK	CV	CR	PR	←Courts JEFFERSON	Recording→	UC	RE	TX	VS
•	•	•	•		A Wright Resource	478-757-9371				
•	•		•		ADM & Associates Inc	800-242-5999				
				•	AlaDocs Inc	205-251-8200	•	•	•	
•	•	•	•	•	ASAP Process Services [SOP]	256-766-9805	•	•		•
•	•	•	•	•	Charles F Edgar & Associates Inc [SOP]	256-539-7761	•	•	•	
•	•	•	•	•	Confidential Background Services [SOP]	205-853-4535	•	•	•	•
•	•	•	•	•	Johnston & Associates	256-572-4967	•	•	•	
•	•	•	•	•	Mid-South Legal Services [SOP]	205-326-0900	•		•	•
•	•	•	•	•	Public Record Services [SOP]	334-262-0350	•	•	•	•
				•	Faith Simpson	205-381-0788	•	•	•	
•	•	•		•	Southern Land & Title LLC	256-543-1361	•	•	•	
•	•	•	•		Vinson Detective Agency AL [SOP]	800-438-6072				

DT	BK	CV	CR	PR	←Courts LAMAR	Recording→	UC	RE	TX	VS
				•	AlaDocs Inc	205-251-8200	•	•	•	
•	•	•	•	•	Aldridge & Associates [SOP]	662-651-7376	•	•	•	•
•	•	•	•	•	Charles F Edgar & Associates Inc [SOP]	256-539-7761	•	•	•	
•	•	•	•	•	Public Record Services [SOP]	334-262-0350	•	•	•	•

DT	BK	CV	CR	PR	←Courts LAUDERDALE	Recording→	UC	RE	TX	VS
				•	AlaDocs Inc	205-251-8200	•	•	•	
•	•	•	•	•	ASAP Process Services [SOP]	256-766-9805	•	•		•
•	•	•	•	•	Charles F Edgar & Associates Inc [SOP]	256-539-7761	•	•	•	
•	•	•		•	Maureen H Poole	931-294-2988	•	•	•	
•	•	•	•	•	Public Record Services [SOP]	334-262-0350	•	•	•	•
•	•	•	•	•	Risk Mitigation Services Inc [SOP]	866-633-9339	•	•	•	•

DT	BK	CV	CR	PR	←Courts LAWRENCE	Recording→	UC	RE	TX	VS
				•	AlaDocs Inc	205-251-8200	•	•	•	
•	•	•	•	•	ASAP Process Services [SOP]	256-766-9805	•	•		•
•	•	•	•	•	Charles F Edgar & Associates Inc [SOP]	256-539-7761	•	•	•	
•	•	•	•	•	Public Record Services [SOP]	334-262-0350	•	•	•	•
•	•	•	•	•	Risk Mitigation Services Inc [SOP]	866-633-9339	•	•	•	•

DT	BK	CV	CR	PR	←Courts LEE	Recording→	UC	RE	TX	VS
				•	AlaDocs Inc	205-251-8200	•	•	•	
•	•	•	•		Attorneys Services & Legal Inv [SOP]	706-322-3554	•	•		•
•	•	•	•	•	Public Record Services [SOP]	334-262-0350	•	•	•	•

DT	BK	CV	CR	PR	←Courts LIMESTONE	Recording→	UC	RE	TX	VS
				•	AlaDocs Inc	205-251-8200	•	•	•	
•	•	•	•	•	ASAP Process Services [SOP]	256-766-9805	•	•		•
•	•	•	•	•	Charles F Edgar & Associates Inc [SOP]	256-539-7761	•	•	•	
•	•	•		•	Maureen H Poole	931-294-2988	•	•	•	
•	•	•	•	•	Public Record Services [SOP]	334-262-0350	•	•	•	•
•	•	•	•	•	Risk Mitigation Services Inc [SOP]	866-633-9339	•	•	•	•

DT	BK	CV	CR	PR	←Courts LOWNDES	Recording→	UC	RE	TX	VS
				•	AlaDocs Inc	205-251-8200	•	•	•	
•	•	•	•	•	Public Record Services [SOP]	334-262-0350	•	•	•	•

DT	BK	CV	CR	PR	←Courts MACON	Recording→	UC	RE	TX	VS
				•	AlaDocs Inc	205-251-8200	•	•	•	
•	•	•	•	•	Public Record Services [SOP]	334-262-0350	•	•	•	•

DT	BK	CV	CR	PR	←Courts MADISON	Recording→	UC	RE	TX	VS
				•	AlaDocs Inc	205-251-8200	•	•	•	
•	•	•	•	•	B & B Reporting Inc [SOP]	256-574-2524	•	•	•	•
•	•	•	•	•	Charles F Edgar & Associates Inc [SOP]	256-539-7761	•	•	•	
•	•	•	•	•	Johnston & Associates	256-572-4967	•	•	•	

DT	BK	CV	CR	PR	←Courts	Recording→	UC	RE	TX	VS
•	•	•		•	Maureen H Poole	931-294-2988	•	•	•	
•	•	•	•	•	Public Record Services [SOP]	334-262-0350	•	•	•	•
•	•	•	•	•	Risk Mitigation Services Inc [SOP]	866-633-9339	•	•	•	•
•	•	•		•	Southern Land & Title LLC	256-543-1361	•	•	•	

DT	BK	CV	CR	PR	←Courts **MARENGO**	Recording→	UC	RE	TX	VS
				•	AlaDocs Inc	205-251-8200	•	•	•	
•	•	•	•	•	Public Record Services [SOP]	334-262-0350	•	•	•	•

DT	BK	CV	CR	PR	←Courts **MARION**	Recording→	UC	RE	TX	VS
				•	AlaDocs Inc	205-251-8200	•	•	•	
•	•	•	•	•	ASAP Process Services [SOP]	256-766-9805	•	•		•
•	•	•	•	•	Charles F Edgar & Associates Inc [SOP]	256-539-7761	•	•	•	
•	•	•		•	Maureen H Poole	931-294-2988	•	•	•	
•	•	•	•	•	Public Record Services [SOP]	334-262-0350	•	•	•	•

DT	BK	CV	CR	PR	←Courts **MARSHALL**	Recording→	UC	RE	TX	VS
				•	AlaDocs Inc	205-251-8200	•	•	•	
•	•	•	•	•	B & B Reporting Inc [SOP]	256-574-2524	•	•	•	•
•	•	•	•	•	Charles F Edgar & Associates Inc [SOP]	256-539-7761	•	•	•	
•	•	•	•	•	Johnston & Associates	256-572-4967	•	•	•	
•	•	•	•	•	Public Record Services [SOP]	334-262-0350	•	•	•	•
•	•	•		•	Southern Land & Title LLC	256-543-1361	•	•	•	

DT	BK	CV	CR	PR	←Courts **MOBILE**	Recording→	UC	RE	TX	VS
•	•	•	•	•	A & A Screening Solutions LLC [SOP]	877-999-9318	•		•	
				•	AlaDocs Inc	205-251-8200	•	•	•	
•	•	•	•	•	Brabston Legal Inv Inc [SOP]	251-666-5666	•	•	•	
•	•	•	•	•	Charles F Edgar & Associates Inc [SOP]	256-539-7761	•	•	•	
•	•	•	•	•	Ike L Hoy PE (Control Systems)	850-259-4650	•	•	•	•
•	•	•	•	•	Legal Research Service LLC [SOP]	251-432-1006	•		•	•
•	•	•	•	•	Parker Legal Services [SOP]	251-476-7464	•	•	•	•
•	•	•	•	•	Parrish Research	850-936-1240	•	•	•	•
•	•	•	•	•	Public Record Services [SOP]	334-262-0350	•	•	•	•
•	•	•	•		Vinson Detective Agency AL [SOP]	800-438-6072				

DT	BK	CV	CR	PR	←Courts **MONROE**	Recording→	UC	RE	TX	VS
				•	AlaDocs Inc	205-251-8200	•	•	•	
•	•	•	•	•	Legal Research Service LLC [SOP]	251-432-1006	•		•	•
•		•		•	Deloris Presley	888-544-8006	•	•	•	•
•	•	•	•	•	Public Record Services [SOP]	334-262-0350	•	•	•	•
•	•	•	•		Vinson Detective Agency AL [SOP]	800-438-6072				

DT	BK	CV	CR	PR	←Courts **MONTGOMERY**	Recording→	UC	RE	TX	VS
				•	AlaDocs Inc	205-251-8200	•	•	•	
•	•	•	•	•	McDaniel & Associates Inc [SOP]	334-312-0781	•	•	•	
•	•	•	•	•	Public Record Services [SOP]	334-262-0350	•	•	•	•

DT	BK	CV	CR	PR	←Courts **MORGAN**	Recording→	UC	RE	TX	VS
				•	AlaDocs Inc	205-251-8200	•	•	•	
•	•	•	•	•	ASAP Process Services [SOP]	256-766-9805	•	•		•
•	•	•	•	•	Charles F Edgar & Associates Inc [SOP]	256-539-7761	•	•	•	
•	•	•		•	Maureen H Poole	931-294-2988	•	•	•	
•	•	•	•	•	Public Record Services [SOP]	334-262-0350	•	•	•	•
•	•	•	•	•	Risk Mitigation Services Inc [SOP]	866-633-9339	•	•	•	•

DT	BK	CV	CR	PR	←Courts **PERRY**	Recording→	UC	RE	TX	VS
				•	AlaDocs Inc	205-251-8200	•	•	•	
		•	•	•	James M Barnes Jr [SOP]	334-683-6060	•	•	•	•
•	•	•	•	•	Public Record Services [SOP]	334-262-0350	•	•	•	•

DT	BK	CV	CR	PR	←Courts PICKENS	Recording→	UC	RE	TX	VS
				•	AlaDocs Inc	205-251-8200	•	•	•	
				•	Capstone Title Services	205-759-1105	•	•	•	
•	•	•	•	•	Charles F Edgar & Associates Inc [SOP]	256-539-7761	•	•	•	
•	•	•	•	•	Public Record Services [SOP]	334-262-0350	•	•	•	•

DT	BK	CV	CR	PR	←Courts PIKE	Recording→	UC	RE	TX	VS
				•	AlaDocs Inc	205-251-8200	•	•	•	
•	•	•	•	•	Public Record Services [SOP]	334-262-0350	•	•	•	•

DT	BK	CV	CR	PR	←Courts RANDOLPH	Recording→	UC	RE	TX	VS
				•	AlaDocs Inc	205-251-8200	•	•	•	
•	•	•	•	•	Public Record Services [SOP]	334-262-0350	•	•	•	•
•	•	•		•	Southern Land & Title LLC	256-543-1361	•	•	•	

DT	BK	CV	CR	PR	←Courts RUSSELL	Recording→	UC	RE	TX	VS
				•	AlaDocs Inc	205-251-8200	•	•	•	
•	•	•	•		Attorneys Services & Legal Inv [SOP]	706-322-3554	•	•		•
•	•	•	•	•	Public Record Services [SOP]	334-262-0350	•	•	•	•

DT	BK	CV	CR	PR	←Courts SHELBY	Recording→	UC	RE	TX	VS
				•	AlaDocs Inc	205-251-8200	•	•	•	
•	•	•	•	•	ASAP Process Services [SOP]	256-766-9805	•	•		•
•	•	•	•	•	Charles F Edgar & Associates Inc [SOP]	256-539-7761	•	•	•	
•	•	•	•	•	Confidential Background Services [SOP]	205-853-4535	•	•	•	•
•	•	•	•	•	Mid-South Legal Services [SOP]	205-326-0900	•		•	•
•	•	•	•	•	Public Record Services [SOP]	334-262-0350	•	•	•	•
•	•	•		•	Southern Land & Title LLC	256-543-1361	•	•	•	

DT	BK	CV	CR	PR	←Courts ST CLAIR	Recording→	UC	RE	TX	VS
				•	AlaDocs Inc	205-251-8200	•	•	•	
•	•		•		ADM & Associates Inc	800-242-5999				
•	•	•	•	•	Charles F Edgar & Associates Inc [SOP]	256-539-7761	•	•	•	
•	•	•	•	•	Confidential Background Services [SOP]	205-853-4535	•	•	•	•
•	•	•	•	•	Mid-South Legal Services [SOP]	205-326-0900	•		•	•
•	•	•	•	•	Public Record Services [SOP]	334-262-0350	•	•	•	•
•	•	•		•	Southern Land & Title LLC	256-543-1361	•	•	•	

DT	BK	CV	CR	PR	←Courts SUMTER	Recording→	UC	RE	TX	VS
				•	AlaDocs Inc	205-251-8200	•	•	•	
•	•	•	•	•	Public Record Services [SOP]	334-262-0350	•	•	•	•

DT	BK	CV	CR	PR	←Courts TALLADEGA	Recording→	UC	RE	TX	VS
				•	AlaDocs Inc	205-251-8200	•	•	•	
•	•	•	•	•	Charles F Edgar & Associates Inc [SOP]	256-539-7761	•	•	•	
•	•	•	•	•	Mid-South Legal Services [SOP]	205-326-0900	•		•	•
•	•	•	•	•	Public Record Services [SOP]	334-262-0350	•	•	•	•
•	•	•		•	Southern Land & Title LLC	256-543-1361	•	•	•	

DT	BK	CV	CR	PR	←Courts TALLAPOOSA	Recording→	UC	RE	TX	VS
				•	AlaDocs Inc	205-251-8200	•	•	•	
•	•	•	•	•	Public Record Services [SOP]	334-262-0350	•	•	•	•

DT	BK	CV	CR	PR	←Courts TUSCALOOSA	Recording→	UC	RE	TX	VS
				•	AlaDocs Inc	205-251-8200	•	•	•	
				•	Capstone Title Services	205-759-1105	•	•	•	
•	•	•	•	•	Charles F Edgar & Associates Inc [SOP]	256-539-7761	•	•	•	
•	•	•	•	•	Mid-South Legal Services [SOP]	205-326-0900	•		•	•
•	•	•	•	•	Public Record Services [SOP]	334-262-0350	•	•	•	•

DT	BK	CV	CR	PR	←Courts WALKER	Recording→	UC	RE	TX	VS
				•	AlaDocs Inc	205-251-8200	•	•	•	
				•	Capstone Title Services	205-759-1105	•	•	•	
•	•	•	•	•	Charles F Edgar & Associates Inc [SOP]	256-539-7761	•	•	•	
•	•	•	•	•	Mid-South Legal Services [SOP]	205-326-0900	•		•	•
•	•	•	•	•	Public Record Services [SOP]	334-262-0350	•	•	•	•

DT	BK	CV	CR	PR	←Courts WASHINGTON	Recording→	UC	RE	TX	VS
				•	AlaDocs Inc	205-251-8200	•	•	•	
•	•	•	•	•	Legal Research Service LLC [SOP]	251-432-1006	•		•	•
•	•	•	•	•	Public Record Services [SOP]	334-262-0350	•	•	•	•
•	•	•	•		Vinson Detective Agency AL [SOP]	800-438-6072				

DT	BK	CV	CR	PR	←Courts WILCOX	Recording→	UC	RE	TX	VS
				•	AlaDocs Inc	205-251-8200	•	•	•	
•	•	•	•	•	Public Record Services [SOP]	334-262-0350	•	•	•	•

DT	BK	CV	CR	PR	←Courts WINSTON	Recording→	UC	RE	TX	VS
				•	AlaDocs Inc	205-251-8200	•	•	•	
•	•	•	•	•	ASAP Process Services [SOP]	256-766-9805	•	•		•
•	•	•	•	•	Charles F Edgar & Associates Inc [SOP]	256-539-7761	•	•	•	
•	•	•		•	Maureen H Poole	931-294-2988	•	•	•	
•	•	•	•	•	Public Record Services [SOP]	334-262-0350	•	•	•	•

[SOP] = Performs Service of Process

Court Records

CODE	Government Agency	Type of Information
DT	US District Court	Federal civil and criminal cases
BK	Bankruptcy Court	United States bankruptcy cases
CV	Civil Court	Municipal, county and state level civil cases
CR	Criminal Court	Municipal, county and state level criminal cases
PR	Probate Court	Wills and estate cases

County Records - Recordings

CODE	Government Agency	Type of Information
UC	UCC Filing Office	Uniform Commercial Code and other personal property liens
RE	Real Estate Recording Office	Real property transactions and liens
TX	Tax Filing Office(s)	Federal and state tax liens, judgment liens
VS	Vital Records Office	Vital statistics—birth, death, marriage, divorce

Alaska

COURT RECORDS RETRIEVED — **RECORDING RECORDS RETRIEVED**

Aleutian Islands, East

DT	BK	CV	CR	PR	<Courts / Recording>	Phone	UC	RE	TX	VS
•	•	•	•		Alaska Public Records Search LLC [SOP]	800-808-5105	•	•	•	

Aleutian Islands, West

DT	BK	CV	CR	PR	←Courts / Recording→	Phone	UC	RE	TX	VS
•	•	•	•		Alaska Public Records Search LLC [SOP]	800-808-5105	•	•	•	

Anchorage

DT	BK	CV	CR	PR	←Courts / Recording→	Phone	UC	RE	TX	VS
•	•	•	•		Alaska Public Records Search LLC [SOP]	800-808-5105	•	•	•	
	•	•	•	•	Anchorage & Matzu Process Svc [SOP]	907-258-3211	•			
•	•	•	•	•	Complete Corporate Services of Alaska [SOP]	907-790-4956	•	•	•	
•	•	•	•	•	Freelance Legal Secretary	907-278-8855		•		•
•	•	•	•	•	InQuest Agency Inc [SOP]	907-272-2201	•	•	•	•
•	•	•	•	•	North Country Process Inc [SOP]	907-274-2023	•	•	•	
					Pacific NW Title of Alaska	907-561-5122		•	•	

Bethel

DT	BK	CV	CR	PR	←Courts / Recording→	Phone	UC	RE	TX	VS
					Pacific NW Title of Alaska	907-561-5122		•	•	

Bristol Bay

DT	BK	CV	CR	PR	←Courts / Recording→	Phone	UC	RE	TX	VS
•	•	•	•		Alaska Public Records Search LLC [SOP]	800-808-5105	•	•	•	
					Pacific NW Title of Alaska	907-561-5122		•	•	

Denali

DT BK CV CR PR ←Courts — Recording→ UC RE TX VS

See adjoining counties for retrievers or contact court or recording office.

Dillingham

DT BK CV CR PR ←Courts — Recording→ UC RE TX VS

See adjoining counties for retrievers or contact court or recording office.

Fairbanks North Star

DT	BK	CV	CR	PR	←Courts / Recording→	Phone	UC	RE	TX	VS
•	•	•	•		Alaska Public Records Search LLC [SOP]	800-808-5105	•	•	•	
	•	•	•	•	Anchorage & Matzu Process Svc [SOP]	907-258-3211	•			
•	•	•	•	•	Credit Services LLC [SOP]	907-456-1749		•		
					Fairbanks Title Agency	907-456-6626		•	•	
•	•	•	•	•	Fort Enterprises Process Srv & Investigation [SOP]	907-488-7766	•	•	•	•
•	•	•	•	•	InQuest Agency Inc [SOP]	907-272-2201	•	•	•	•
•	•	•	•	•	North Country Process Inc [SOP]	907-274-2023	•	•	•	

Haines

DT	BK	CV	CR	PR	←Courts / Recording→	Phone	UC	RE	TX	VS
•	•	•	•	•	Civil Claims Service [SOP]	907-364-2714	•	•	•	
•	•	•	•	•	Complete Corporate Services of Alaska [SOP]	907-790-4956	•	•	•	

Juneau

DT	BK	CV	CR	PR	←Courts / Recording→	Phone	UC	RE	TX	VS
•	•	•	•		Alaska Public Records Search LLC [SOP]	800-808-5105	•	•	•	
•	•	•	•	•	Civil Claims Service [SOP]	907-364-2714	•	•	•	
•	•	•	•	•	Complete Corporate Services of Alaska [SOP]	907-790-4956	•	•	•	

Kenai Peninsula

DT	BK	CV	CR	PR	←Courts / Recording→	Phone	UC	RE	TX	VS
•	•	•	•		Alaska Public Records Search LLC [SOP]	800-808-5105	•	•	•	
	•	•	•	•	Anchorage & Matzu Process Svc [SOP]	907-258-3211	•			
•	•	•	•	•	North Country Process Inc [SOP]	907-274-2023	•	•	•	
					South Central Title Agency Inc	907-262-4494		•	•	

DT	BK	CV	CR	PR	←Courts **Ketchikan Gateway** Recording→	UC	RE	TX	VS
•	•	•	•	•	Civil Claims Service [SOP]....907-364-2714	•	•	•	
•	•	•	•	•	Complete Corporate Services of Alaska [SOP]....907-790-4956	•	•	•	
•	•	•	•	•	North Country Process Inc [SOP]....907-274-2023	•	•	•	

DT	BK	CV	CR	PR	←Courts **Kodiak Island** Recording→	UC	RE	TX	VS
	•	•	•	•	Anchorage & Matzu Process Svc [SOP]....907-258-3211	•			

DT	BK	CV	CR	PR	←Courts **Lake And Peninsula** Recording→	UC	RE	TX	VS
•	•	•	•		Alaska Public Records Search LLC [SOP]....800-808-5105	•	•	•	

DT	BK	CV	CR	PR	←Courts **Matanuska Susitna** Recording→	UC	RE	TX	VS
•	•	•	•		Alaska Public Records Search LLC [SOP]....800-808-5105	•	•	•	
•	•	•	•	•	InQuest Agency Inc [SOP]....907-272-2201	•	•	•	•
•	•	•	•	•	North Country Process Inc [SOP]....907-274-2023	•	•	•	

DT	BK	CV	CR	PR	←Courts **Nome** Recording→	UC	RE	TX	VS
					Fairbanks Title Agency....907-456-6626		•	•	

DT	BK	CV	CR	PR	←Courts **North Slope** Recording→	UC	RE	TX	VS
•	•	•	•		Alaska Public Records Search LLC [SOP]....800-808-5105	•	•	•	

DT	BK	CV	CR	PR	←Courts **Northwest Arctic** Recording→	UC	RE	TX	VS
					See adjoining counties for retrievers or contact court or recording office.				

DT	BK	CV	CR	PR	←Courts **Prince of Wales-Outer Ketchikan** Recording→	UC	RE	TX	VS
•	•	•	•	•	Complete Corporate Services of Alaska [SOP]....907-790-4956	•	•	•	

DT	BK	CV	CR	PR	←Courts **Sitka** Recording→	UC	RE	TX	VS
•	•	•	•	•	Civil Claims Service [SOP]....907-364-2714	•	•	•	
•	•	•	•	•	Complete Corporate Services of Alaska [SOP]....907-790-4956	•	•	•	

DT	BK	CV	CR	PR	←Courts **Skagway-Hoonah-Angoon** Recording→	UC	RE	TX	VS
•	•	•	•	•	Civil Claims Service [SOP]....907-364-2714	•	•	•	
•	•	•	•	•	Complete Corporate Services of Alaska [SOP]....907-790-4956	•	•	•	

DT	BK	CV	CR	PR	←Courts **Southeast Fairbanks** Recording→	UC	RE	TX	VS
					See adjoining counties for retrievers or contact court or recording office.				

DT	BK	CV	CR	PR	←Courts **Valdez-Cordova** Recording→	UC	RE	TX	VS
•	•	•	•		Alaska Public Records Search LLC [SOP]....800-808-5105	•	•	•	
	•	•	•	•	Anchorage & Matzu Process Svc [SOP]....907-258-3211	•			
					Pacific NW Title of Alaska....907-561-5122		•	•	

DT	BK	CV	CR	PR	←Courts **Wade Hampton** Recording→	UC	RE	TX	VS
					See adjoining counties for retrievers or contact court or recording office.				

DT	BK	CV	CR	PR	←Courts **Wrangell-Petersburg** Recording→	UC	RE	TX	VS
•	•	•	•	•	Civil Claims Service [SOP]....907-364-2714	•	•	•	
•	•	•	•	•	Complete Corporate Services of Alaska [SOP]....907-790-4956	•	•	•	

DT	BK	CV	CR	PR	←Courts **Yakutat** Recording→	UC	RE	TX	VS
					See adjoining counties for retrievers or contact court or recording office.				

DT	BK	CV	CR	PR	←Courts **Yukon-Koyukuk** Recording→	UC	RE	TX	VS
					See adjoining counties for retrievers or contact court or recording office.				

Arizona

COURT RECORDS RETRIEVED — **RECORDING RECORDS RETRIEVED**

DT	BK	CV	CR	PR	←COURTS	APACHE	RECORDING→	UC	RE	TX	VS
•	•	•	•	•		Arizona Research & Retrieval Services Inc	888-500-7767	•	•	•	•
		•	•			Attorney Service New Mexico [SOP]	505-326-7486				
•	•	•	•			PDQ Legal Services Inc [SOP]	480-556-6660	•	•	•	
	•	•	•	•		Raban's Record Search & Inv [SOP]	928-337-4250	•	•	•	
		•	•	•		The Public Record Source	623-773-3997	•		•	•

DT	BK	CV	CR	PR	←COURTS	COCHISE	RECORDING→	UC	RE	TX	VS
•	•	•	•	•		ACMS Process Service [SOP]	520-629-0303	•	•	•	•
		•	•			Katie Anderson	520-405-8737				
•	•	•	•	•		Arizona Research & Retrieval Services Inc	888-500-7767	•	•	•	•
•	•	•	•	•		E-Z Messenger Attorney Service Inc [SOP]	800-264-8436	•	•	•	
		•	•	•		Holifield Investigation Agency	800-427-1294		•	•	
•	•	•	•	•		MacIntire & Associates (Tucson)	800-641-2737	•		•	
•	•	•	•			PDQ Legal Services Inc [SOP]	480-556-6660	•	•	•	
•	•	•	•	•		Research Unlimited LLC	520-624-7024	•	•	•	•
		•	•	•		Southeast Arizona Legal Support	520-432-9032	•	•	•	
		•	•	•		The Public Record Source	623-773-3997	•		•	•
		•	•			Valley Security Inc [SOP]	928-428-2142				

DT	BK	CV	CR	PR	←COURTS	COCONINO	RECORDING→	UC	RE	TX	VS
•	•	•	•	•		Arizona Research & Retrieval Services Inc	888-500-7767	•	•	•	•
		•	•	•		Frontier Private Process Service (Flagstaff) [SOP]	800-711-8511	•	•	•	
•	•	•	•	•		The Information Super Store	800-774-6585	•		•	•
						Nationwide Environmental Title Research	800-324-4956		•		
		•	•	•		Northern Arizona Inv [SOP]	800-657-2747	•	•	•	
•	•	•	•			PDQ Legal Services Inc [SOP]	480-556-6660	•	•	•	
		•	•			Public Records Info Service	520-321-8015				
		•	•	•		The Public Record Source	623-773-3997	•		•	•

DT	BK	CV	CR	PR	←COURTS	GILA	RECORDING→	UC	RE	TX	VS
		•	•			Katie Anderson	520-405-8737				
•	•	•	•	•		Arizona Research & Retrieval Services Inc	888-500-7767	•	•	•	•
		•	•	•		Barnone Bailbonds & Investigations [SOP]	800-607-8200	•	•	•	•
•	•	•	•			PDQ Legal Services Inc [SOP]	480-556-6660	•	•	•	
		•	•	•		The Public Record Source	623-773-3997	•		•	•

DT	BK	CV	CR	PR	←COURTS	GRAHAM	RECORDING→	UC	RE	TX	VS
•	•	•	•	•		ACMS Process Service [SOP]	520-629-0303	•	•	•	•
		•	•			Katie Anderson	520-405-8737				
•	•	•	•	•		Arizona Research & Retrieval Services Inc	888-500-7767	•	•	•	•
•	•	•	•			PDQ Legal Services Inc [SOP]	480-556-6660	•	•	•	
		•	•	•		The Public Record Source	623-773-3997	•		•	•
		•	•			Valley Security Inc [SOP]	928-428-2142				

DT	BK	CV	CR	PR	←COURTS	GREENLEE	RECORDING→	UC	RE	TX	VS
•	•	•	•	•		Arizona Research & Retrieval Services Inc	888-500-7767	•	•	•	•
•	•	•	•			PDQ Legal Services Inc [SOP]	480-556-6660	•	•	•	
		•	•	•		The Public Record Source	623-773-3997	•		•	•
		•	•			Valley Security Inc [SOP]	928-428-2142				

DT	BK	CV	CR	PR	←Courts **La Paz**	Recording→	UC	RE	TX	VS
•	•	•	•	•	Arizona Research & Retrieval Services Inc	888-500-7767	•	•	•	•
		•	•	•	The Public Record Source	623-773-3997	•		•	•
•	•	•	•		PDQ Legal Services Inc [SOP]	480-556-6660	•	•	•	

DT	BK	CV	CR	PR	←Courts **Maricopa**	Recording→	UC	RE	TX	VS
•	•	•	•		Accurate Background Inc	800-784-3911	•		•	
•	•	•	•	•	AccuSearch Inc	800-462-7019	•	•	•	
		•	•		Katie Anderson	520-405-8737				
					Arizona Abstractors	602-989-3428	•	•	•	
•	•	•	•	•	Arizona Express Attorney Services [SOP]	602-616-1715	•	•	•	•
•	•	•	•	•	Arizona Research & Retrieval Services Inc	888-500-7767	•	•	•	•
•	•	•	•	•	Capital City Assurance Group	602-728-0100		•	•	•
•	•	•		•	Capitol Corporate Services Inc (AZ)	800-255-4052	•		•	
		•	•		Clarifacts Inc	800-318-0553				
•	•	•	•	•	DL Inv & Attorney Support [SOP]	602-285-9901	•	•	•	•
					Document Research Service	480-947-5493	•	•	•	•
•	•	•	•	•	E-Z Messenger Attorney Service Inc [SOP]	800-380-8081	•			•
•	•	•	•	•	Fleming Attorney Service [SOP]	800-776-3301	•	•	•	
•	•	•	•	•	Frontier Private Process Service (Phoenix) [SOP]	800-860-0858	•	•	•	•
•	•	•	•	•	Guardian Inv & Doc Svcs, TPI Court Svcs, dba L & L Paper Chase	888-268-6162	•	•	•	
•	•	•	•	•	Guardian Investigations & Document Svc Inc	602-257-0897	•	•	•	
•	•	•	•	•	Hawkins & Campbell Inc [SOP]	602-452-1800	•	•	•	•
					HK Partners Research	808-291-2071	•	•	•	•
•	•	•	•	•	The Information Super Store	800-774-6585	•		•	•
•	•	•	•		Infotrack Information Services Inc	800-275-5594	•	•	•	
•	•	•	•	•	MacIntire & Associates (Tucson)	800-641-2737	•		•	
	•	•			Maricopa Research	623-935-0572	•	•	•	•
•	•	•	•	•	National Document Filing & Retrieval Inc	800-829-5578	•	•	•	
					Nationwide Environmental Title Research	800-324-4956		•		
•	•	•	•	•	NU West Investigations [SOP]	623-937-9676	•	•	•	•
•	•	•	•		PDQ Legal Services Inc [SOP]	480-556-6660	•	•	•	
•	•	•	•	•	Phelps Investigation & Employer Services	800-347-9918	•	•	•	
		•	•		Public Records Info Service	520-321-8015				
	•	•	•	•	Records Research & Retrieval	602-574-2781	•	•	•	•
					Reliance Abstract Company AZ	800-207-1523	•	•	•	
			•		Risk Assessment Group	866-777-1114				
			•		Screencorp Inc	602-739-7289				
•		•	•	•	Slover Investigations	480-917-3708	•		•	
		•	•	•	The Public Record Source	623-773-3997	•		•	•
•	•	•	•	•	Trace Unlimited [SOP]	520-299-0015	•	•	•	•
			•		Universal Background Screening	602-263-8033				

DT	BK	CV	CR	PR	←Courts **Mohave**	Recording→	UC	RE	TX	VS
		•	•	•	ABC Inv [SOP]	928-757-4370	•	•	•	
•	•	•	•	•	Arizona Research & Retrieval Services Inc	888-500-7767	•	•	•	•
•	•	•	•	•	Bodo PI [SOP]	877-381-7009	•	•	•	•
		•	•		Mohave County Process Service [SOP]	800-692-5881			•	
					Nationwide Environmental Title Research	800-324-4956		•		
•	•	•	•		PDQ Legal Services Inc [SOP]	480-556-6660	•	•	•	
					Reliance Abstract Company AZ	800-207-1523	•	•	•	
		•	•	•	The Public Record Source	623-773-3997	•		•	•

DT	BK	CV	CR	PR	←Courts **Navajo**	Recording→	UC	RE	TX	VS
•	•	•	•	•	Arizona Research & Retrieval Services Inc	888-500-7767	•	•	•	•
		•	•	•	Northern Arizona Inv [SOP]	800-657-2747	•	•	•	
•	•	•	•		PDQ Legal Services Inc [SOP]	480-556-6660	•	•	•	
		•	•	•	The Public Record Source	623-773-3997	•		•	•

DT	BK	CV	CR	PR	←Courts	PIMA	Recording→	UC	RE	TX	VS
•	•	•	•	•		ACMS Process Service [SOP]	520-629-0303	•	•	•	•
		•	•			Katie Anderson	520-405-8737				
•	•	•	•	•		Arizona Research & Retrieval Services Inc	888-500-7767	•	•	•	•
•	•	•	•	•		Diablo Consulting Services	520-323-1951	•	•	•	•
•	•	•	•	•		E-Z Messenger Attorney Service Inc [SOP]	800-264-8436	•	•	•	
•	•	•	•	•		Linda Gonzales	520-603-6360	•	•	•	•
•	•	•	•	•		Hawkins & Ezinessenger Tucson Inc [SOP]	520-628-9737	•	•	•	•
•	•	•	•	•		The Information Super Store	800-774-6585	•		•	•
•	•	•	•			Infotrack Information Services Inc	800-275-5594	•	•	•	
•	•	•	•	•		Kroes Detective Agency [SOP]	800-249-0694	•	•	•	
•	•	•	•	•		MacIntire & Associates (Tucson)	800-641-2737	•		•	
•	•	•	•	•		Malloy & Company Inc dba Judicial Courier [SOP]	520-792-0250	•	•	•	•
						Nationwide Environmental Title Research	800-324-4956		•		
•	•	•	•			PDQ Legal Services Inc [SOP]	480-556-6660	•	•	•	
		•	•			Public Records Info Service	520-321-8015				
						Reliance Abstract Company AZ	800-207-1523	•	•	•	
•	•	•	•	•		Research Unlimited LLC	520-624-7024	•	•	•	•
•	•	•	•	•		Securitech Inc	800-805-4473	•		•	•
		•	•	•		The Public Record Source	623-773-3997	•		•	•
•	•	•	•	•		Trace Unlimited [SOP]	520-299-0015	•	•	•	•
•	•	•	•	•		Kathy Wolken	520-544-4228			•	

DT	BK	CV	CR	PR	←Courts	PINAL	Recording→	UC	RE	TX	VS
•	•	•	•	•		ACMS Process Service [SOP]	520-629-0303	•	•	•	•
		•	•			Katie Anderson	520-405-8737				
•	•	•	•	•		Arizona Research & Retrieval Services Inc	888-500-7767	•	•	•	•
•	•	•	•			Infotrack Information Services Inc	800-275-5594	•	•	•	
						Nationwide Environmental Title Research	800-324-4956		•		
•	•	•	•			PDQ Legal Services Inc [SOP]	480-556-6660	•	•	•	
						Reliance Abstract Company AZ	800-207-1523	•	•	•	
		•	•	•		The Public Record Source	623-773-3997	•		•	•

DT	BK	CV	CR	PR	←Courts	SANTA CRUZ	Recording→	UC	RE	TX	VS
•	•	•	•	•		ACMS Process Service [SOP]	520-629-0303	•	•	•	•
		•	•			Katie Anderson	520-405-8737				
•	•	•	•	•		Arizona Research & Retrieval Services Inc	888-500-7767	•	•	•	•
•	•	•	•	•		E-Z Messenger Attorney Service Inc [SOP]	800-264-8436	•	•	•	
•	•	•	•			PDQ Legal Services Inc [SOP]	480-556-6660	•	•	•	
•	•	•	•	•		Research Unlimited LLC	520-624-7024	•	•	•	•
		•	•	•		The Public Record Source	623-773-3997	•		•	•

DT	BK	CV	CR	PR	←Courts	YAVAPAI	Recording→	UC	RE	TX	VS
•	•	•	•	•		Arizona Research & Retrieval Services Inc	888-500-7767	•	•	•	•
		•	•	•		Kim Estrada	928-443-0779	•	•	•	
•	•	•	•	•		The Information Super Store	800-774-6585	•		•	•
						Nationwide Environmental Title Research	800-324-4956		•		
•	•	•	•	•		Palmer Inv Services [SOP]	800-280-2951	•	•	•	
•	•	•	•			PDQ Legal Services Inc [SOP]	480-556-6660	•	•	•	
						Reliance Abstract Company AZ	800-207-1523	•	•	•	
		•	•	•		The Public Record Source	623-773-3997	•		•	•

DT	BK	CV	CR	PR	←Courts	YUMA	Recording→	UC	RE	TX	VS
		•	•			Katie Anderson	520-405-8737				
•	•	•	•	•		Arizona Research & Retrieval Services Inc	888-500-7767	•	•	•	•
•	•	•	•	•		Certified Process & Information Services [SOP]	928-341-0756	•	•	•	•
•	•	•	•	•		The Information Super Store	800-774-6585	•		•	•
•	•	•	•			JRW Documents & Lien Services LLC	928-314-3993	•	•	•	
•	•	•	•			PDQ Legal Services Inc [SOP]	480-556-6660	•	•	•	
		•	•	•		The Public Record Source	623-773-3997	•		•	•

Arkansas

COURT RECORDS RETRIEVED | **RECORDING RECORDS RETRIEVED**

DT	BK	CV	CR	PR	←Courts **ARKANSAS**	Recording→	UC	RE	TX	VS
•		•	•		Advantage Research Corporation [SOP]	501-262-5575	•	•		
•	•	•	•	•	CourthouseData	479-582-0900	•	•	•	•
•	•	•	•	•	Quest Research (Arkansas)	501-374-4712	•	•	•	•
•	•	•		•	Record Data Inc (Arkansas)	501-223-0949	•	•	•	

DT	BK	CV	CR	PR	←Courts **ASHLEY**	Recording→	UC	RE	TX	VS
•		•	•		Advantage Research Corporation [SOP]	501-262-5575	•	•		
•	•	•	•	•	CourthouseData	479-582-0900	•	•	•	•
•	•	•	•	•	Quest Research (Arkansas)	501-374-4712	•	•	•	•
•	•	•		•	Record Data Inc (Arkansas)	501-223-0949	•	•	•	

DT	BK	CV	CR	PR	←Courts **BAXTER**	Recording→	UC	RE	TX	VS
•		•	•		Advantage Research Corporation [SOP]	501-262-5575	•	•		
				•	Baxter County Abstract Co	870-425-8989		•		
•	•	•	•	•	CourthouseData	479-582-0900	•	•	•	•
•	•	•		•	Record Data Inc (Arkansas)	501-223-0949	•	•	•	

DT	BK	CV	CR	PR	←Courts **BENTON**	Recording→	UC	RE	TX	VS
•		•	•		Advantage Research Corporation [SOP]	501-262-5575	•	•		
•		•	•	•	AL McLeroy Inv [SOP]	479-484-0444	•	•		•
•	•	•	•	•	Courthouse Concepts Inc	877-750-3660	•	•	•	•
•	•	•	•	•	CourthouseData	479-582-0900	•	•	•	•
•	•	•	•	•	North Winds Inv Inc [SOP]	800-530-4514	•	•	•	•
•	•	•		•	Record Data Inc (Arkansas)	501-223-0949	•	•	•	
•	•	•	•		Ridgerunner Record Search Inc	479-443-4928	•		•	
		•		•	Stewart Title of Arkansas	479-273-2111	•	•	•	
•	•	•	•	•	Triad Inv [SOP]	800-400-7582	•	•	•	•

DT	BK	CV	CR	PR	←Courts **BOONE**	Recording→	UC	RE	TX	VS
•		•	•		Advantage Research Corporation [SOP]	501-262-5575	•	•		
•	•	•	•	•	CourthouseData	479-582-0900	•	•	•	•
•	•	•		•	Record Data Inc (Arkansas)	501-223-0949	•	•	•	

DT	BK	CV	CR	PR	←Courts **BRADLEY**	Recording→	UC	RE	TX	VS
•		•	•		Advantage Research Corporation [SOP]	501-262-5575	•	•		
•	•	•	•	•	CourthouseData	479-582-0900	•	•	•	•
		•	•	•	Martin Abstract Co (Warren)	870-226-7487	•	•	•	
•	•	•	•	•	Quest Research (Arkansas)	501-374-4712	•	•	•	•
•	•	•		•	Record Data Inc (Arkansas)	501-223-0949	•	•	•	

DT	BK	CV	CR	PR	←Courts **CALHOUN**	Recording→	UC	RE	TX	VS
•		•	•		Advantage Research Corporation [SOP]	501-262-5575	•	•		
•	•	•	•	•	CourthouseData	479-582-0900	•	•	•	•
•	•	•	•	•	Quest Research (Arkansas)	501-374-4712	•	•	•	•
•	•	•		•	Record Data Inc (Arkansas)	501-223-0949	•	•	•	

DT	BK	CV	CR	PR	←Courts **CARROLL**	Recording→	UC	RE	TX	VS
•		•	•		Advantage Research Corporation [SOP]	501-262-5575	•	•		
•		•	•	•	AL McLeroy Inv [SOP]	479-484-0444	•	•		•
•	•	•	•	•	Courthouse Concepts Inc	877-750-3660	•	•	•	•

DT	BK	CV	CR	PR	←Courts		Recording→	UC	RE	TX	VS
•	•	•	•	•	CourthouseData		479-582-0900	•	•	•	•
•	•	•		•	Record Data Inc (Arkansas)		501-223-0949	•	•	•	
•	•	•	•	•	Triad Inv [SOP]		800-400-7582	•	•	•	•

DT	BK	CV	CR	PR	←Courts	**Chicot**	Recording→	UC	RE	TX	VS
•		•	•		Advantage Research Corporation [SOP]		501-262-5575	•	•		
•	•	•	•	•	CourthouseData		479-582-0900	•	•	•	•
•	•	•	•	•	Quest Research (Arkansas)		501-374-4712	•	•	•	•
•	•	•		•	Record Data Inc (Arkansas)		501-223-0949	•	•	•	

DT	BK	CV	CR	PR	←Courts	**Clark**	Recording→	UC	RE	TX	VS
•		•	•		Advantage Research Corporation [SOP]		501-262-5575	•	•		
		•	•	•	Clark County Abstract & Title Co Inc		870-246-2821	•	•	•	
•	•	•	•	•	CourthouseData		479-582-0900	•	•	•	•
•	•	•	•	•	Quest Research (Arkansas)		501-374-4712	•	•	•	•
•	•	•		•	Record Data Inc (Arkansas)		501-223-0949	•	•	•	

DT	BK	CV	CR	PR	←Courts	**Clay**	Recording→	UC	RE	TX	VS
•		•	•		Advantage Research Corporation [SOP]		501-262-5575	•	•		
•	•	•	•	•	CourthouseData		479-582-0900	•	•	•	•
•	•	•		•	Record Data Inc (Arkansas)		501-223-0949	•	•	•	

DT	BK	CV	CR	PR	←Courts	**Cleburne**	Recording→	UC	RE	TX	VS
•		•	•		Advantage Research Corporation [SOP]		501-262-5575	•	•		
•	•	•	•	•	CourthouseData		479-582-0900	•	•	•	•
•	•	•		•	Record Data Inc (Arkansas)		501-223-0949	•	•	•	
				•	Search Arkansas		888-875-2553	•	•	•	

DT	BK	CV	CR	PR	←Courts	**Cleveland**	Recording→	UC	RE	TX	VS
•		•	•		Advantage Research Corporation [SOP]		501-262-5575	•	•		
•	•	•	•	•	CourthouseData		479-582-0900	•	•	•	•
		•	•	•	Martin Abstract Co (Warren)		870-226-7487	•	•	•	
•	•	•	•	•	Quest Research (Arkansas)		501-374-4712	•	•	•	•
•	•	•		•	Record Data Inc (Arkansas)		501-223-0949	•	•	•	

DT	BK	CV	CR	PR	←Courts	**Columbia**	Recording→	UC	RE	TX	VS
•		•	•		Advantage Research Corporation [SOP]		501-262-5575	•	•		
•	•	•	•	•	CourthouseData		479-582-0900	•	•	•	•
•	•	•			Joe Gillenwater [SOP]		870-772-2923	•	•	•	
•	•	•	•	•	Quest Research (Arkansas)		501-374-4712	•	•	•	•
•	•	•		•	Record Data Inc (Arkansas)		501-223-0949	•	•	•	
		•		•	Security Abstract Co (Arkansas)		870-234-1291	•	•	•	

DT	BK	CV	CR	PR	←Courts	**Conway**	Recording→	UC	RE	TX	VS
•		•	•		Advantage Research Corporation [SOP]		501-262-5575	•	•		
•	•	•	•	•	Courthouse Concepts Inc		877-750-3660	•	•	•	•
•	•	•	•	•	CourthouseData		479-582-0900	•	•	•	•
		•		•	Morrilton Abstract Co		501-354-2611	•	•	•	
•	•	•	•	•	Quest Research (Arkansas)		501-374-4712	•	•	•	•
•	•	•		•	Record Data Inc (Arkansas)		501-223-0949	•	•	•	

DT	BK	CV	CR	PR	←Courts	**Craighead**	Recording→	UC	RE	TX	VS
•		•	•		Advantage Research Corporation [SOP]		501-262-5575	•	•		
•	•	•	•	•	CourthouseData		479-582-0900	•	•	•	•
•	•	•		•	Record Data Inc (Arkansas)		501-223-0949	•	•	•	

DT	BK	CV	CR	PR	←Courts	**Crawford**	Recording→	UC	RE	TX	VS
•		•	•		Advantage Research Corporation [SOP]		501-262-5575	•	•		
•		•	•	•	AL McLeroy Inv [SOP]		479-484-0444	•	•		•
•	•	•	•	•	Courthouse Concepts Inc		877-750-3660	•	•	•	•
•	•	•	•	•	CourthouseData		479-582-0900	•	•	•	•

DT	BK	CV	CR	PR	←Courts	Recording→	UC	RE	TX	VS
		•	•	•	Crawford County Abstract Co Inc (Arkansas)	479-474-2711		•	•	
		•		•	Hebert Land Services	918-647-9524	•	•	•	•
					Mosley Abstract & Title Insurance Co.	479-782-3054		•	•	
•	•	•	•	•	North Winds Inv Inc [SOP]	800-530-4514	•	•	•	•
•	•	•		•	Record Data Inc (Arkansas)	501-223-0949	•	•	•	
•	•	•	•	•	Triad Inv [SOP]	800-400-7582	•	•	•	•

DT	BK	CV	CR	PR	←Courts **CRITTENDEN**	Recording→	UC	RE	TX	VS
•		•	•		Advantage Research Corporation [SOP]	501-262-5575	•	•		
			•		Blue Line Investigations	901-266-7100				
•	•	•	•	•	CourthouseData	479-582-0900	•	•	•	•
•	•	•	•	•	National Background Reports Inc	901-526-4654	•	•	•	•
•	•	•		•	Record Data Inc (Arkansas)	501-223-0949	•	•	•	
•	•	•	•	•	Schaeffer Papers [SOP]	800-848-6119	•	•	•	•
•	•	•	•	•	The Discovery Group Inc [SOP]	662-280-1576	•		•	•

DT	BK	CV	CR	PR	←Courts **CROSS**	Recording→	UC	RE	TX	VS
•		•	•		Advantage Research Corporation [SOP]	501-262-5575	•	•		
•	•	•	•	•	CourthouseData	479-582-0900	•	•	•	•
•	•	•		•	Record Data Inc (Arkansas)	501-223-0949	•	•	•	

DT	BK	CV	CR	PR	←Courts **DALLAS**	Recording→	UC	RE	TX	VS
•		•	•		Advantage Research Corporation [SOP]	501-262-5575	•	•		
•	•	•	•	•	CourthouseData	479-582-0900	•	•	•	•
•	•	•	•	•	Quest Research (Arkansas)	501-374-4712	•	•	•	•
•	•	•		•	Record Data Inc (Arkansas)	501-223-0949	•	•	•	

DT	BK	CV	CR	PR	←Courts **DESHA**	Recording→	UC	RE	TX	VS
•		•	•		Advantage Research Corporation [SOP]	501-262-5575	•	•		
•	•	•	•	•	CourthouseData	479-582-0900	•	•	•	•
		•	•	•	Desha Abstract & Title Co LLC	870-222-5001	•	•	•	
•	•	•	•	•	Quest Research (Arkansas)	501-374-4712	•	•	•	•
•	•	•		•	Record Data Inc (Arkansas)	501-223-0949	•	•	•	

DT	BK	CV	CR	PR	←Courts **DREW**	Recording→	UC	RE	TX	VS
•		•	•		Advantage Research Corporation [SOP]	501-262-5575	•	•		
•	•	•	•	•	CourthouseData	479-582-0900	•	•	•	•
					Drew County Abstract & Title Co	870-367-6607	•	•	•	
•	•	•	•	•	Quest Research (Arkansas)	501-374-4712	•	•	•	•
•	•	•		•	Record Data Inc (Arkansas)	501-223-0949	•	•	•	

DT	BK	CV	CR	PR	←Courts **FAULKNER**	Recording→	UC	RE	TX	VS
•		•	•		Advantage Research Corporation [SOP]	501-262-5575	•	•		
•	•	•	•		Arkansas Corporate Research & Service Co	501-374-3843	•			
•	•	•	•	•	Courthouse Concepts Inc	877-750-3660	•	•	•	•
•	•	•	•	•	CourthouseData	479-582-0900	•	•	•	•
•	•	•	•		Data-Search of Arkansas	501-868-4814	•			
•	•	•	•		Pro Facto Inc	501-988-5340	•	•	•	
•	•	•	•	•	Quest Research (Arkansas)	501-374-4712	•	•	•	•
•	•	•		•	Record Data Inc (Arkansas)	501-223-0949	•	•	•	
				•	Search Arkansas	888-875-2553	•	•	•	

DT	BK	CV	CR	PR	←Courts **FRANKLIN**	Recording→	UC	RE	TX	VS
•		•	•		Advantage Research Corporation [SOP]	501-262-5575	•	•		
•	•	•	•	•	Courthouse Concepts Inc	877-750-3660	•	•	•	•
•	•	•	•	•	CourthouseData	479-582-0900	•	•	•	•
		•		•	Hebert Land Services	918-647-9524	•	•	•	•
					Mosley Abstract & Title Insurance Co.	479-782-3054		•	•	
•	•	•		•	Record Data Inc (Arkansas)	501-223-0949	•	•	•	

DT	BK	CV	CR	PR	←Courts FULTON	Recording→	UC	RE	TX	VS
•		•	•		Advantage Research Corporation [SOP]	501-262-5575	•	•		
•	•	•	•	•	CourthouseData	479-582-0900	•	•	•	•
•	•	•		•	Record Data Inc (Arkansas)	501-223-0949	•	•	•	

DT	BK	CV	CR	PR	←Courts GARLAND	Recording→	UC	RE	TX	VS
•		•	•		Advantage Research Corporation [SOP]	501-262-5575	•	•		
•	•	•	•	•	CourthouseData	479-582-0900	•	•	•	•
•	•	•	•		Data-Search of Arkansas	501-868-4814	•			
•	•	•	•	•	Quest Research (Arkansas)	501-374-4712	•	•	•	•
•	•	•		•	Record Data Inc (Arkansas)	501-223-0949	•	•	•	

DT	BK	CV	CR	PR	←Courts GRANT	Recording→	UC	RE	TX	VS
•		•	•		Advantage Research Corporation [SOP]	501-262-5575	•	•		
•	•	•	•	•	CourthouseData	479-582-0900	•	•	•	•
•	•	•	•	•	Quest Research (Arkansas)	501-374-4712	•	•	•	•
•	•	•		•	Record Data Inc (Arkansas)	501-223-0949	•	•	•	
		•	•	•	Spears & Jones Attorneys	501-315-5335	•	•	•	

DT	BK	CV	CR	PR	←Courts GREENE	Recording→	UC	RE	TX	VS
•		•	•		Advantage Research Corporation [SOP]	501-262-5575	•	•		
•	•	•	•	•	CourthouseData	479-582-0900	•	•	•	•
•	•	•		•	Record Data Inc (Arkansas)	501-223-0949	•	•	•	

DT	BK	CV	CR	PR	←Courts HEMPSTEAD	Recording→	UC	RE	TX	VS
•		•	•		Advantage Research Corporation [SOP]	501-262-5575	•	•		
•	•	•	•	•	CourthouseData	479-582-0900	•	•	•	•
•	•	•			Joe Gillenwater [SOP]	870-772-2923	•	•	•	
		•	•	•	Hempstead County Abstract & Title	870-777-2351	•	•	•	
•	•	•		•	Record Data Inc (Arkansas)	501-223-0949	•	•	•	

DT	BK	CV	CR	PR	←Courts HOT SPRING	Recording→	UC	RE	TX	VS
•		•	•		Advantage Research Corporation [SOP]	501-262-5575	•	•		
					Central Arkansas Title	501-332-3770	•	•	•	•
•	•	•	•	•	CourthouseData	479-582-0900	•	•	•	•
•	•	•	•		Pro Facto Inc	501-988-5340	•	•	•	
•	•	•	•	•	Quest Research (Arkansas)	501-374-4712	•	•	•	•
•	•	•		•	Record Data Inc (Arkansas)	501-223-0949	•	•	•	

DT	BK	CV	CR	PR	←Courts HOWARD	Recording→	UC	RE	TX	VS
•		•	•		Advantage Research Corporation [SOP]	501-262-5575	•	•		
•	•	•	•	•	CourthouseData	479-582-0900	•	•	•	•
•	•	•			Joe Gillenwater [SOP]	870-772-2923	•	•	•	
•	•	•	•	•	Quest Research (Arkansas)	501-374-4712	•	•	•	•
•	•	•		•	Record Data Inc (Arkansas)	501-223-0949	•	•	•	

DT	BK	CV	CR	PR	←Courts INDEPENDENCE	Recording→	UC	RE	TX	VS
•		•	•		Advantage Research Corporation [SOP]	501-262-5575	•	•		
•	•	•	•	•	CourthouseData	479-582-0900	•	•	•	•
				•	Independence County Abstract Co	870-793-3333	•	•	•	
•	•	•		•	Record Data Inc (Arkansas)	501-223-0949	•	•	•	
				•	Search Arkansas	888-875-2553	•	•	•	

DT	BK	CV	CR	PR	←Courts IZARD	Recording→	UC	RE	TX	VS
•		•	•		Advantage Research Corporation [SOP]	501-262-5575	•	•		
•	•	•	•	•	CourthouseData	479-582-0900	•	•	•	•
				•	Izard County Abstract Co	870-368-4818	•	•	•	
•	•	•		•	Record Data Inc (Arkansas)	501-223-0949	•	•	•	

DT	BK	CV	CR	PR	←Courts JACKSON	Recording→	UC	RE	TX	VS
•		•	•		Advantage Research Corporation [SOP]	501-262-5575	•	•		

DT	BK	CV	CR	PR	←Courts	Recording→	UC	RE	TX	VS
•	•	•	•	•	CourthouseData	479-582-0900	•	•	•	•
•	•	•	•		Data-Search of Arkansas	501-868-4814	•			
		•		•	Jackson County Land Title Services, Inc	870-523-8976	•	•	•	
•	•	•		•	Record Data Inc (Arkansas)	501-223-0949	•	•	•	

DT	BK	CV	CR	PR	←Courts **JEFFERSON**	Recording→	UC	RE	TX	VS
•		•	•		Advantage Research Corporation [SOP]	501-262-5575	•	•		
•	•	•	•	•	CourthouseData	479-582-0900	•	•	•	•
•	•	•	•		Data-Search of Arkansas	501-868-4814	•			
		•	•	•	Molly Ply Investigations	501-397-2620	•		•	
•	•	•	•	•	Quest Research (Arkansas)	501-374-4712	•	•	•	•
•	•	•		•	Record Data Inc (Arkansas)	501-223-0949	•	•	•	

DT	BK	CV	CR	PR	←Courts **JOHNSON**	Recording→	UC	RE	TX	VS
•		•	•		Advantage Research Corporation [SOP]	501-262-5575	•	•		
•	•	•	•	•	Courthouse Concepts Inc	877-750-3660	•	•	•	•
•	•	•	•	•	CourthouseData	479-582-0900	•	•	•	•
•	•	•		•	Record Data Inc (Arkansas)	501-223-0949	•	•	•	

DT	BK	CV	CR	PR	←Courts **LAFAYETTE**	Recording→	UC	RE	TX	VS
•		•	•		Advantage Research Corporation [SOP]	501-262-5575	•	•		
•	•	•	•	•	CourthouseData	479-582-0900	•	•	•	•
•	•	•			Joe Gillenwater [SOP]	870-772-2923	•	•	•	
		•	•	•	Lafayette County Abstract & Title Inc	870-921-4263	•	•	•	•
•	•	•	•	•	Quest Research (Arkansas)	501-374-4712	•	•	•	•
•	•	•		•	Record Data Inc (Arkansas)	501-223-0949	•	•	•	

DT	BK	CV	CR	PR	←Courts **LAWRENCE**	Recording→	UC	RE	TX	VS
•		•	•		Advantage Research Corporation [SOP]	501-262-5575	•	•		
•	•	•	•	•	CourthouseData	479-582-0900	•	•	•	•
		•	•	•	Mullen Abstract Co	870-886-2452	•	•	•	
•	•	•		•	Record Data Inc (Arkansas)	501-223-0949	•	•	•	

DT	BK	CV	CR	PR	←Courts **LEE**	Recording→	UC	RE	TX	VS
•		•	•		Advantage Research Corporation [SOP]	501-262-5575	•	•		
•	•	•	•	•	CourthouseData	479-582-0900	•	•	•	•
		•	•	•	Daggett Abstract Co	870-295-3434	•	•	•	
•	•	•	•		Data-Search of Arkansas	501-868-4814	•			
•	•	•	•	•	Quest Research (Arkansas)	501-374-4712	•	•	•	•
•	•	•		•	Record Data Inc (Arkansas)	501-223-0949	•	•	•	

DT	BK	CV	CR	PR	←Courts **LINCOLN**	Recording→	UC	RE	TX	VS
•		•	•		Advantage Research Corporation [SOP]	501-262-5575	•	•		
•	•	•	•	•	CourthouseData	479-582-0900	•	•	•	•
					Lincoln Abstract Co	870-628-3144	•	•	•	
•	•	•	•	•	Quest Research (Arkansas)	501-374-4712	•	•	•	•
•	•	•		•	Record Data Inc (Arkansas)	501-223-0949	•	•	•	

DT	BK	CV	CR	PR	←Courts **LITTLE RIVER**	Recording→	UC	RE	TX	VS
•		•	•		Advantage Research Corporation [SOP]	501-262-5575	•	•		
•	•	•	•	•	CourthouseData	479-582-0900	•	•	•	•
•	•	•			Joe Gillenwater [SOP]	870-772-2923	•	•	•	
					McIver Abstract & Title Co	870-898-3502		•		
•	•	•	•	•	Quest Research (Arkansas)	501-374-4712	•	•	•	•
•	•	•		•	Record Data Inc (Arkansas)	501-223-0949	•	•	•	

DT	BK	CV	CR	PR	←Courts **LOGAN**	Recording→	UC	RE	TX	VS
•		•	•		Advantage Research Corporation [SOP]	501-262-5575	•	•		
•	•	•	•	•	CourthouseData	479-582-0900	•	•	•	•
		•		•	Hebert Land Services	918-647-9524	•	•	•	•
•	•	•		•	Record Data Inc (Arkansas)	501-223-0949	•	•	•	

DT	BK	CV	CR	PR	←COURTS LONOKE RECORDING→		UC	RE	TX	VS
•		•	•		Advantage Research Corporation [SOP]	501-262-5575	•	•		
•	•	•	•		Arkansas Corporate Research & Service Co	501-374-3843	•			
•	•	•	•	•	CourthouseData	479-582-0900	•	•	•	•
•	•	•	•		Data-Search of Arkansas	501-868-4814	•			
		•		•	First State Abstract	501-676-2486	•	•	•	
•	•	•	•		Pro Facto Inc	501-988-5340	•	•	•	
•	•	•	•	•	Quest Research (Arkansas)	501-374-4712	•	•	•	•
•	•	•		•	Record Data Inc (Arkansas)	501-223-0949	•	•	•	

DT	BK	CV	CR	PR	←COURTS MADISON RECORDING→		UC	RE	TX	VS
•		•	•		Advantage Research Corporation [SOP]	501-262-5575	•	•		
•		•	•	•	AL McLeroy Inv [SOP]	479-484-0444	•	•		•
•	•	•	•	•	Courthouse Concepts Inc	877-750-3660	•	•	•	•
•	•	•	•	•	CourthouseData	479-582-0900	•	•	•	•
•	•	•		•	Record Data Inc (Arkansas)	501-223-0949	•	•	•	
				•	Town & Country Abstract Co (Arkansas)	479-738-2055	•	•	•	
•	•	•	•	•	Triad Inv [SOP]	800-400-7582	•	•	•	•

DT	BK	CV	CR	PR	←COURTS MARION RECORDING→		UC	RE	TX	VS
•		•	•		Advantage Research Corporation [SOP]	501-262-5575	•	•		
•	•	•	•	•	CourthouseData	479-582-0900	•	•	•	•
		•	•	•	Marion County Abstract Co (Arkansas)	870-449-4218	•	•	•	
•	•	•		•	Record Data Inc (Arkansas)	501-223-0949	•	•	•	

DT	BK	CV	CR	PR	←COURTS MILLER RECORDING→		UC	RE	TX	VS
•		•	•		Advantage Research Corporation [SOP]	501-262-5575	•	•		
•	•	•	•	•	CourthouseData	479-582-0900	•	•	•	•
•	•	•			Joe Gillenwater [SOP]	870-772-2923	•	•	•	
•	•	•	•	•	Quest Research (Arkansas)	501-374-4712	•	•	•	•
•	•	•		•	Record Data Inc (Arkansas)	501-223-0949	•	•	•	

DT	BK	CV	CR	PR	←COURTS MISSISSIPPI RECORDING→		UC	RE	TX	VS
•		•	•		Advantage Research Corporation [SOP]	501-262-5575	•	•		
•	•	•	•	•	CourthouseData	479-582-0900	•	•	•	•
		•		•	Prewitt-Rogers Abstract Co	870-563-2137	•	•	•	
•	•	•		•	Record Data Inc (Arkansas)	501-223-0949	•	•	•	

DT	BK	CV	CR	PR	←COURTS MONROE RECORDING→		UC	RE	TX	VS
•		•	•		Advantage Research Corporation [SOP]	501-262-5575	•	•		
•	•	•	•	•	CourthouseData	479-582-0900	•	•	•	•
		•	•	•	Menard Title & Abstract Co Inc	870-747-3712		•	•	•
•	•	•	•	•	Quest Research (Arkansas)	501-374-4712	•	•	•	•
•	•	•		•	Record Data Inc (Arkansas)	501-223-0949	•	•	•	

DT	BK	CV	CR	PR	←COURTS MONTGOMERY RECORDING→		UC	RE	TX	VS
•		•	•		Advantage Research Corporation [SOP]	501-262-5575	•	•		
•	•	•	•	•	CourthouseData	479-582-0900	•	•	•	•
•	•	•	•	•	Quest Research (Arkansas)	501-374-4712	•	•	•	•
•	•	•		•	Record Data Inc (Arkansas)	501-223-0949	•	•	•	

DT	BK	CV	CR	PR	←COURTS NEVADA RECORDING→		UC	RE	TX	VS
•		•	•		Advantage Research Corporation [SOP]	501-262-5575	•	•		
•	•	•	•	•	CourthouseData	479-582-0900	•	•	•	•
•	•	•			Joe Gillenwater [SOP]	870-772-2923	•	•	•	
•	•	•	•	•	Quest Research (Arkansas)	501-374-4712	•	•	•	•
•	•	•		•	Record Data Inc (Arkansas)	501-223-0949	•	•	•	

DT	BK	CV	CR	PR	←COURTS NEWTON RECORDING→		UC	RE	TX	VS
•		•	•		Advantage Research Corporation [SOP]	501-262-5575	•	•		
•	•	•	•	•	CourthouseData	479-582-0900	•	•	•	•

DT	BK	CV	CR	PR	←Courts		Recording→	UC	RE	TX	VS
•	•	•		•	Record Data Inc (Arkansas)		501-223-0949	•	•	•	
DT	**BK**	**CV**	**CR**	**PR**	**←Courts**	**Ouachita**	**Recording→**	**UC**	**RE**	**TX**	**VS**
•		•	•		Advantage Research Corporation [SOP]		501-262-5575	•	•		
•	•	•	•	•	CourthouseData		479-582-0900	•	•	•	•
•	•	•	•		Data-Search of Arkansas		501-868-4814	•			
•	•	•	•	•	Quest Research (Arkansas)		501-374-4712	•	•	•	•
•	•	•		•	Record Data Inc (Arkansas)		501-223-0949	•	•	•	
DT	**BK**	**CV**	**CR**	**PR**	**←Courts**	**Perry**	**Recording→**	**UC**	**RE**	**TX**	**VS**
•		•	•		Advantage Research Corporation [SOP]		501-262-5575	•	•		
•	•	•	•	•	CourthouseData		479-582-0900	•	•	•	•
•	•	•	•	•	Quest Research (Arkansas)		501-374-4712	•	•	•	•
•	•	•		•	Record Data Inc (Arkansas)		501-223-0949	•	•	•	
DT	**BK**	**CV**	**CR**	**PR**	**←Courts**	**Phillips**	**Recording→**	**UC**	**RE**	**TX**	**VS**
•		•	•		Advantage Research Corporation [SOP]		501-262-5575	•	•		
•	•	•	•	•	CourthouseData		479-582-0900	•	•	•	•
		•		•	East Arkansas Title Co		870-338-8306	•	•	•	
•	•	•		•	Record Data Inc (Arkansas)		501-223-0949	•	•	•	
DT	**BK**	**CV**	**CR**	**PR**	**←Courts**	**Pike**	**Recording→**	**UC**	**RE**	**TX**	**VS**
•		•	•		Advantage Research Corporation [SOP]		501-262-5575	•	•		
•	•	•	•	•	CourthouseData		479-582-0900	•	•	•	•
•	•	•	•	•	Quest Research (Arkansas)		501-374-4712	•	•	•	•
•	•	•		•	Record Data Inc (Arkansas)		501-223-0949	•	•	•	
DT	**BK**	**CV**	**CR**	**PR**	**←Courts**	**Poinsett**	**Recording→**	**UC**	**RE**	**TX**	**VS**
•		•	•		Advantage Research Corporation [SOP]		501-262-5575	•	•		
•	•	•	•	•	CourthouseData		479-582-0900	•	•	•	•
		•	•	•	Poinsett County Abstract Co		870-578-5914	•	•	•	
•	•	•		•	Record Data Inc (Arkansas)		501-223-0949	•	•	•	
DT	**BK**	**CV**	**CR**	**PR**	**←Courts**	**Polk**	**Recording→**	**UC**	**RE**	**TX**	**VS**
•		•	•		Advantage Research Corporation [SOP]		501-262-5575	•	•		
•	•	•	•	•	CourthouseData		479-582-0900	•	•	•	•
		•	•	•	Martin Title & Closing Services		479-394-1963	•	•	•	
•	•	•	•	•	Quest Research (Arkansas)		501-374-4712	•	•	•	•
•	•	•		•	Record Data Inc (Arkansas)		501-223-0949	•	•	•	
DT	**BK**	**CV**	**CR**	**PR**	**←Courts**	**Pope**	**Recording→**	**UC**	**RE**	**TX**	**VS**
•		•	•		Advantage Research Corporation [SOP]		501-262-5575	•	•		
•	•	•	•	•	Courthouse Concepts Inc		877-750-3660	•	•	•	•
•	•	•	•	•	CourthouseData		479-582-0900	•	•	•	•
•	•	•	•	•	Hebert Land Services		918-647-9524	•	•	•	•
•	•	•		•	Record Data Inc (Arkansas)		501-223-0949	•	•	•	
DT	**BK**	**CV**	**CR**	**PR**	**←Courts**	**Prairie**	**Recording→**	**UC**	**RE**	**TX**	**VS**
•		•	•		Advantage Research Corporation [SOP]		501-262-5575	•	•		
•	•	•	•	•	CourthouseData		479-582-0900	•	•	•	•
•	•	•	•	•	Quest Research (Arkansas)		501-374-4712	•	•	•	•
•	•	•		•	Record Data Inc (Arkansas)		501-223-0949	•	•	•	
DT	**BK**	**CV**	**CR**	**PR**	**←Courts**	**Pulaski**	**Recording→**	**UC**	**RE**	**TX**	**VS**
•		•	•		Advantage Research Corporation [SOP]		501-262-5575	•	•		
•	•	•	•		Arkansas Corporate Research & Service Co		501-374-3843	•			
•	•	•	•	•	Attorney's Services Inc [SOP]		888-376-6267	•	•	•	•
			•		Blue Line Investigations		901-266-7100				
•	•	•	•	•	Courthouse Concepts Inc		877-750-3660	•	•	•	•
•	•	•	•	•	CourthouseData		479-582-0900	•	•	•	•
•	•	•	•		Data-Search of Arkansas		501-868-4814	•			

		•	•	•	Molly Ply Investigations	501-397-2620	•		•	
•	•	•	•	•	North Winds Inv Inc [SOP]	800-530-4514	•	•	•	•
•	•	•	•		Pro Facto Inc	501-988-5340	•	•	•	
•	•	•	•	•	Quest Research (Arkansas)	501-374-4712	•	•	•	•
•	•	•		•	Record Data Inc (Arkansas)	501-223-0949	•	•	•	

DT	BK	CV	CR	PR	←Courts **Randolph**	Recording→	UC	RE	TX	VS
•		•	•		Advantage Research Corporation [SOP]	501-262-5575	•	•		
•	•	•	•	•	CourthouseData	479-582-0900	•	•	•	•
•	•	•		•	Record Data Inc (Arkansas)	501-223-0949	•	•	•	
		•	•	•	Service Abstract Company of Randolph County [SOP]	870-892-4538	•	•	•	•

DT	BK	CV	CR	PR	←Courts **Saline**	Recording→	UC	RE	TX	VS
•		•	•		Advantage Research Corporation [SOP]	501-262-5575	•	•		
•	•	•	•		Arkansas Corporate Research & Service Co	501-374-3843	•			
•	•	•	•	•	CourthouseData	479-582-0900	•	•	•	•
•	•	•	•		Data-Search of Arkansas	501-868-4814	•			
•	•	•	•		Pro Facto Inc	501-988-5340	•	•	•	
•	•	•	•	•	Quest Research (Arkansas)	501-374-4712	•	•	•	•
•	•	•		•	Record Data Inc (Arkansas)	501-223-0949	•	•	•	
		•	•	•	Spears & Jones Attorneys	501-315-5335	•	•	•	

DT	BK	CV	CR	PR	←Courts **Scott**	Recording→	UC	RE	TX	VS
•		•	•		Advantage Research Corporation [SOP]	501-262-5575	•	•		
•	•	•	•	•	CourthouseData	479-582-0900	•	•	•	•
		•		•	Hebert Land Services	918-647-9524	•	•	•	•
•	•	•		•	Record Data Inc (Arkansas)	501-223-0949	•	•	•	

DT	BK	CV	CR	PR	←Courts **Searcy**	Recording→	UC	RE	TX	VS
•		•	•		Advantage Research Corporation [SOP]	501-262-5575	•	•		
•	•	•	•	•	CourthouseData	479-582-0900	•	•	•	•
•	•	•		•	Record Data Inc (Arkansas)	501-223-0949	•	•	•	

DT	BK	CV	CR	PR	←Courts **Sebastian**	Recording→	UC	RE	TX	VS
•		•	•		Advantage Research Corporation [SOP]	501-262-5575	•	•		
•		•	•	•	AL McLeroy Inv [SOP]	479-484-0444	•	•		•
•	•	•	•	•	Courthouse Concepts Inc	877-750-3660	•	•	•	•
•	•	•	•	•	CourthouseData	479-582-0900	•	•	•	•
		•		•	Hebert Land Services	918-647-9524	•	•	•	•
					Mosley Abstract & Title Insurance Co.	479-782-3054		•	•	
•	•	•	•	•	North Winds Inv Inc [SOP]	800-530-4514	•	•	•	•
•	•	•		•	Record Data Inc (Arkansas)	501-223-0949	•	•	•	
•	•	•	•	•	Triad Inv [SOP]	800-400-7582	•	•	•	•

DT	BK	CV	CR	PR	←Courts **Sevier**	Recording→	UC	RE	TX	VS
•		•	•		Advantage Research Corporation [SOP]	501-262-5575	•	•		
•	•	•	•	•	CourthouseData	479-582-0900	•	•	•	•
•	•	•	•	•	Quest Research (Arkansas)	501-374-4712	•	•	•	•
•	•	•		•	Record Data Inc (Arkansas)	501-223-0949	•	•	•	

DT	BK	CV	CR	PR	←Courts **Sharp**	Recording→	UC	RE	TX	VS
•		•	•		Advantage Research Corporation [SOP]	501-262-5575	•	•		
•	•	•	•	•	CourthouseData	479-582-0900	•	•	•	•
•	•	•		•	Record Data Inc (Arkansas)	501-223-0949	•	•	•	
		•	•	•	Sharp County Abstract Co Inc	870-994-7314	•	•	•	

DT	BK	CV	CR	PR	←Courts **St Francis**	Recording→	UC	RE	TX	VS
•		•	•		Advantage Research Corporation [SOP]	501-262-5575	•	•		
•	•	•	•	•	CourthouseData	479-582-0900	•	•	•	•
•	•	•		•	Record Data Inc (Arkansas)	501-223-0949	•	•	•	

DT	BK	CV	CR	PR	←COURTS	STONE	RECORDING→	UC	RE	TX	VS
•		•	•		Advantage Research Corporation [SOP]		501-262-5575	•	•		
•	•	•	•	•	CourthouseData		479-582-0900	•	•	•	•
		•		•	Mountain View Abstract Co		870-269-8410	•	•	•	
•	•	•		•	Record Data Inc (Arkansas)		501-223-0949	•	•	•	
				•	Search Arkansas		888-875-2553	•	•	•	

DT	BK	CV	CR	PR	←COURTS	UNION	RECORDING→	UC	RE	TX	VS
•		•	•		Advantage Research Corporation [SOP]		501-262-5575	•	•		
•	•	•	•	•	CourthouseData		479-582-0900	•	•	•	•
•	•	•	•	•	Quest Research (Arkansas)		501-374-4712	•	•	•	•
•	•	•		•	Record Data Inc (Arkansas)		501-223-0949	•	•	•	
		•		•	Union Abstract Co		870-863-6053	•	•	•	

DT	BK	CV	CR	PR	←COURTS	VAN BUREN	RECORDING→	UC	RE	TX	VS
•		•	•		Advantage Research Corporation [SOP]		501-262-5575	•	•		
•	•	•	•	•	CourthouseData		479-582-0900	•	•	•	•
•	•	•		•	Record Data Inc (Arkansas)		501-223-0949	•	•	•	

DT	BK	CV	CR	PR	←COURTS	WASHINGTON	RECORDING→	UC	RE	TX	VS
•		•	•		Advantage Research Corporation [SOP]		501-262-5575	•	•		
•		•	•	•	AL McLeroy Inv [SOP]		479-484-0444	•	•		•
•	•	•	•	•	Courthouse Concepts Inc		877-750-3660	•	•	•	•
•	•	•	•	•	CourthouseData		479-582-0900	•	•	•	•
•	•	•	•	•	North Winds Inv Inc [SOP]		800-530-4514	•	•	•	•
•	•	•		•	Record Data Inc (Arkansas)		501-223-0949	•	•	•	
•	•	•	•		Ridgerunner Record Search Inc		479-443-4928	•		•	
		•		•	Stewart Title of Arkansas		479-273-2111	•	•	•	
•	•	•	•	•	Triad Inv [SOP]		800-400-7582	•	•	•	•

DT	BK	CV	CR	PR	←COURTS	WHITE	RECORDING→	UC	RE	TX	VS
•		•	•		Advantage Research Corporation [SOP]		501-262-5575	•	•		
		•	•	•	Citizen's Title Co		501-268-5571	•	•	•	
•	•	•	•	•	CourthouseData		479-582-0900	•	•	•	•
•	•	•	•		Data-Search of Arkansas		501-868-4814	•			
•	•	•		•	Record Data Inc (Arkansas)		501-223-0949	•	•	•	
				•	Search Arkansas		888-875-2553	•	•	•	
		•		•	Strother-Wilbourn Land Title Co		501-268-8273	•	•	•	

DT	BK	CV	CR	PR	←COURTS	WOODRUFF	RECORDING→	UC	RE	TX	VS
•		•	•		Advantage Research Corporation [SOP]		501-262-5575	•	•		
•	•	•	•	•	CourthouseData		479-582-0900	•	•	•	•
•	•	•		•	Record Data Inc (Arkansas)		501-223-0949	•	•	•	

DT	BK	CV	CR	PR	←COURTS	YELL	RECORDING→	UC	RE	TX	VS
•		•	•		Advantage Research Corporation [SOP]		501-262-5575	•	•		
•	•	•	•	•	CourthouseData		479-582-0900	•	•	•	•
		•		•	Hebert Land Services		918-647-9524	•	•	•	•
•	•	•		•	Record Data Inc (Arkansas)		501-223-0949	•	•	•	

California

COURT RECORDS RETRIEVED — **RECORDING RECORDS RETRIEVED**

DT	BK	CV	CR	PR	←COURTS ALAMEDA	RECORDING→	UC	RE	TX	VS
•	•	•	•	•	A & A Legal Service Inc [SOP]	650-697-9431	•	•	•	•
•		•	•		A-1 Unisource Screening & Information	800-525-6972				
•	•	•	•	•	Access Research	800-456-9613	•		•	•
		•	•	•	AD Services (ADS) [SOP]	800-827-9101		•	•	•
•		•	•		Advantage Background Services Inc	800-355-2650				
•	•	•	•	•	Attorney's Aid Inc of Sacramento [SOP]	888-443-3915	•	•		•
•	•	•	•	•	Attorney's Diversified Services-Oakland [SOP]	800-800-6788	•	•	•	•
•	•	•	•	•	Attorneys' Service Limited [SOP]	408-293-9111	•	•	•	•
•	•	•	•		Timothy & Sara Baxter	415-333-5402				
•	•	•	•	•	Bay Area Records [SOP]	888-934-3848	•	•	•	
					Birthcertificate.com	888-934-3848				•
•	•	•	•	•	C & S Research	530-415-3161	•	•	•	•
•	•	•	•	•	Cal Search	858-488-7572	•		•	•
•	•	•	•	•	Court Record Consultants [SOP]	818-366-1906	•	•	•	
•	•	•	•		Laura Cross	510-336-0865			•	•
		•	•	•	Equity Title Search [SOP]	323-965-0759		•		•
		•	•		Huffman Research	510-537-4261				
		•	•		Inquest	408-395-1300				
•	•	•	•	•	Lone Star Legal	415-255-8550	•	•	•	•
					Models with Brains	925-838-3899	•	•	•	
•	•	•	•	•	One Legal [SOP]	800-938-8815	•	•	•	•
•	•	•		•	Pacific Corporate & Title Services (Sacramento)	800-230-4988	•	•	•	•
•	•	•	•	•	Pacific Research & Retrieval Inc [SOP]	800-222-7040	•	•	•	•
•	•	•	•	•	PFC Information Services Inc	510-653-5061	•	•	•	•
•	•	•	•	•	Probus Research [SOP]	888-934-3848	•	•	•	•
•	•	•		•	Quest Discovery Service [SOP]	408-441-7000	•	•	•	•
•	•	•	•	•	Rapid Document Service	209-745-0999	•	•	•	•
		•	•		Rapid Research	510-883-1602				
•	•	•	•	•	RJI Services Inc [SOP]	800-344-4754	•	•	•	•
		•	•		Sumpter & Associates LLC	925-671-7755	•	•	•	•
•	•	•	•	•	Swift Attorney Service [SOP]	800-987-9438	•	•	•	•
•	•	•	•	•	The Amherst Group	800-521-0237	•	•	•	•
•	•	•		•	Title Court Service	510-763-0975	•	•	•	•
	•	•	•		Total Access	559-325-1169	•		•	•
		•	•		Triad Consultants	415-332-4400				
•	•	•	•	•	Universal Information Research [SOP]	800-363-9813	•	•		•
•	•	•	•	•	W P Mortensen & Associates [SOP]	925-828-6440	•	•	•	•
•	•	•	•	•	Wakeman Process Service Inc [SOP]	510-886-7667	•	•	•	•
•	•	•	•	•	Western Attorney Services	415-487-4140				
•	•	•	•	•	Wheels of Justice Inc [SOP]	800-649-1198	•	•	•	•
•	•	•	•	•	Zook Search Inc	415-387-1029	•	•	•	

DT	BK	CV	CR	PR	←COURTS ALPINE	RECORDING→	UC	RE	TX	VS
•	•	•	•	•	Attorney's Diversified Services-Sacramento [SOP]	800-266-4624	•	•	•	•
•	•	•		•	Quest Discovery Service [SOP]	408-441-7000	•	•	•	•
•	•	•		•	Title Court Service	510-763-0975	•	•	•	•

DT	BK	CV	CR	PR	←COURTS AMADOR	RECORDING→	UC	RE	TX	VS
•	•	•	•	•	Attorney's Diversified Services-Stockton [SOP]	800-343-2108	•	•	•	•
		•	•		M L Cozart Copy Service (dba: Quality Business Information)	916-691-9685				
•	•	•		•	Quest Discovery Service [SOP]	408-441-7000	•	•	•	•
•	•	•	•	•	Rapid Document Service	209-745-0999	•	•	•	•
•	•	•		•	Title Court Service	510-763-0975	•	•	•	•

DT	BK	CV	CR	PR	←COURTS BUTTE	RECORDING→	UC	RE	TX	VS
		•	•	•	A.D.I. Investigative [SOP]	530-743-4245		•	•	•
•	•	•	•	•	Attorney's Diversified Services-Redding [SOP]	800-473-1228	•	•	•	•
•	•	•	•		Business Connections [SOP]	530-527-6262	•		•	•
•	•	•	•	•	C & S Research	530-415-3161	•	•	•	•
•	•	•	•	•	Cal Search	858-488-7572	•		•	•
		•	•	•	Nina N Cooper	707-428-5712	•		•	•
		•	•		Nor-Cal Court Research	530-865-3525				
•	•	•		•	Quest Discovery Service [SOP]	408-441-7000	•	•	•	•
		•	•		The Legal Source Attorney Services	800-786-8163				
•	•	•		•	Title Court Service	510-763-0975	•	•	•	•

DT	BK	CV	CR	PR	←COURTS CALAVERAS	RECORDING→	UC	RE	TX	VS
•	•	•	•	•	Ahern Research	209-754-9709	•	•	•	•
•	•	•	•	•	Attorney's Diversified Services-Stockton [SOP]	800-343-2108	•	•	•	•
		•	•		M L Cozart Copy Service (dba: Quality Business Information)	916-691-9685				
•	•	•		•	Quest Discovery Service [SOP]	408-441-7000	•	•	•	•
•	•	•	•	•	Rapid Document Service	209-745-0999	•	•	•	•
•	•	•		•	Title Court Service	510-763-0975	•	•	•	•

DT	BK	CV	CR	PR	←COURTS COLUSA	RECORDING→	UC	RE	TX	VS
		•	•	•	A.D.I. Investigative [SOP]	530-743-4245		•	•	•
•	•	•	•	•	Attorney's Diversified Services-Sacramento [SOP]	800-266-4624	•	•	•	•
•	•	•	•	•	C & S Research	530-415-3161	•	•	•	•
•	•	•		•	Quest Discovery Service [SOP]	408-441-7000	•	•	•	•
		•	•		The Legal Source Attorney Services	800-786-8163				
•	•	•		•	Title Court Service	510-763-0975	•	•	•	•

DT	BK	CV	CR	PR	←COURTS CONTRA COSTA	RECORDING→	UC	RE	TX	VS
•	•	•	•	•	A & A Legal Service Inc [SOP]	650-697-9431	•	•	•	•
		•	•	•	AD Services (ADS) [SOP]	800-827-9101		•	•	•
•	•	•	•	•	Attorney's Aid Inc of Sacramento [SOP]	888-443-3915	•	•		•
•	•	•	•	•	Attorney's Diversified Services-Oakland [SOP]	800-800-6788	•	•	•	•
•	•	•	•		Timothy & Sara Baxter	415-333-5402				
•	•	•	•	•	Bay Area Records [SOP]	888-934-3848	•	•	•	
					Birthcertificate.com	888-934-3848				•
•	•	•	•	•	C & S Research	530-415-3161	•	•	•	•
•	•	•	•	•	Cal Search	858-488-7572	•		•	•
•	•	•	•	•	Court Record Consultants [SOP]	818-366-1906	•	•	•	
•	•	•	•		Laura Cross	510-336-0865			•	•
		•	•		Inquest	408-395-1300				
					Models with Brains	925-838-3899	•	•	•	
•	•	•	•	•	One Legal [SOP]	800-938-8815	•	•	•	•
•	•	•		•	Pacific Corporate & Title Services (Sacramento)	800-230-4988	•	•	•	•
•	•	•	•	•	Probus Research [SOP]	888-934-3848	•	•	•	•
•	•	•		•	Quest Discovery Service [SOP]	408-441-7000	•	•	•	•
•	•	•	•	•	Rapid Document Service	209-745-0999	•	•	•	•
•	•	•	•	•	RJI Services Inc [SOP]	800-344-4754	•	•	•	•
		•	•		Sumpter & Associates LLC	925-671-7755	•	•	•	•
•	•	•	•	•	Swift Attorney Service [SOP]	800-987-9438	•	•	•	•
•	•	•	•	•	The Amherst Group	800-521-0237	•	•	•	•
•	•	•		•	Title Court Service	510-763-0975	•	•	•	•

DT	BK	CV	CR	PR	←Courts	Recording→	UC	RE	TX	VS
•	•	•	•	•	W P Mortensen & Associates [SOP]	925-828-6440	•	•	•	•
•	•	•	•	•	Wakeman Process Service Inc [SOP]	510-886-7667	•	•	•	•
•	•	•	•	•	West Coast MCI [SOP]	925-372-8909	•	•	•	•
•	•	•	•	•	Western Attorney Services	415-487-4140				
•	•	•	•	•	Wheels of Justice Inc [SOP]	800-649-1198	•	•	•	•

DT	BK	CV	CR	PR	←Courts **Del Norte**	Recording→	UC	RE	TX	VS
•	•	•	•	•	Attorney's Diversified Services-Redding [SOP]	800-473-1228	•	•	•	•
•	•	•		•	Quest Discovery Service [SOP]	408-441-7000	•	•	•	•
		•	•	•	Red's Rapid Research	707-764-8836	•	•	•	•
		•	•	•	Research & Investigative Associates [SOP]	707-444-8767	•	•	•	•
•	•	•		•	Title Court Service	510-763-0975	•	•	•	•

DT	BK	CV	CR	PR	←Courts **El Dorado**	Recording→	UC	RE	TX	VS
•		•	•		A-1 Unisource Screening & Information	800-525-6972				
•	•	•	•	•	Abess/Cyberdix [SOP]	877-594-0498	•		•	•
•	•	•	•	•	Attorney's Aid Inc of Sacramento [SOP]	888-443-3915	•	•		•
•	•	•	•	•	Attorney's Diversified Services-Sacramento [SOP]	800-266-4624	•	•	•	•
•	•	•	•	•	C & S Research	530-415-3161	•	•	•	•
•	•	•	•	•	DataSearch Inc	800-452-3282	•	•	•	•
•	•	•	•	•	Legalese [SOP]	916-453-2860	•	•	•	•
		•	•		M L Cozart Copy Service (dba: Quality Business Information)	916-691-9685				
					Nisonger Abstracting Services	916-965-6544	•	•	•	
•	•	•		•	Pacific Corporate & Title Services (Sacramento)	800-230-4988	•	•	•	•
•	•	•	•		Quality Business Information	916-684-0444		•	•	•
•	•	•		•	Quest Discovery Service [SOP]	408-441-7000	•	•	•	•
•	•	•	•	•	Rapid Document Service	209-745-0999	•	•	•	•
•					Reliable Document Retrieval Inc	916-438-3000				
•	•	•	•	•	Seyfried Support Services	916-359-5275	•	•	•	•
					Leslie or Mike Sosa	916-984-7654	•	•	•	
•	•	•		•	Title Court Service	510-763-0975	•	•	•	•
•	•	•	•	•	William Olmsted Inv	916-484-6465	•	•	•	•

DT	BK	CV	CR	PR	←Courts **Fresno**	Recording→	UC	RE	TX	VS
•	•	•	•	•	Access Research	800-456-9613	•		•	•
•	•	•	•	•	Accessible Document Retrieval	559-779-5491	•	•	•	•
•	•	•	•	•	Action Legal Support Services [SOP]	559-432-3337				
			•		Alpha Information Inc	800-900-1471				
•		•	•		Atlas Research Services Inc	818-362-0140				
•	•	•	•	•	Attorney's Aid Inc of Sacramento [SOP]	888-443-3915	•	•		•
•	•	•	•	•	Attorney's Diversified Services-Fresno [SOP]	800-842-2695	•	•	•	•
•	•	•	•		Bonafide Research Services	818-349-3955	•		•	•
•	•	•	•		Business Connections [SOP]	530-527-6262	•		•	•
•	•	•	•	•	Cal Search	858-488-7572	•		•	•
			•		California Backgrounds	559-274-9784				
•	•	•	•	•	Court Record Consultants [SOP]	818-366-1906	•	•	•	
			•		InVision Research	559-432-3053				
•	•	•	•		Keppler Legal Research	559-431-1358				
•	•	•	•	•	One Legal [SOP]	800-938-8815	•	•	•	•
•	•	•	•	•	Dora Orum	559-251-5193	•	•	•	•
•	•	•		•	Pacific Corporate & Title Services (Sacramento)	800-230-4988	•	•	•	•
•	•	•		•	Quest Discovery Service [SOP]	408-441-7000	•	•	•	•
•	•	•	•	•	Rapid Document Service	209-745-0999	•	•	•	•
•	•	•		•	Title Court Service	510-763-0975	•	•	•	•
	•	•	•		Total Access	559-325-1169	•		•	•
•	•	•	•	•	Vio-Com-Data Research	559-438-1058	•	•	•	•

DT	BK	CV	CR	PR	←Courts **Glenn**	Recording→	UC	RE	TX	VS
•		•	•		A-1 Unisource Screening & Information	800-525-6972				
•	•	•	•	•	Attorney's Diversified Services-Redding [SOP]	800-473-1228	•	•	•	•

DT	BK	CV	CR	PR			UC	RE	TX	VS
•	•	•	•		Business Connections [SOP]	530-527-6262	•		•	•
		•	•		Nor-Cal Court Research	530-865-3525				
•	•	•		•	Quest Discovery Service [SOP]	408-441-7000	•	•	•	•
		•	•		The Legal Source Attorney Services	800-786-8163				
•	•	•		•	Title Court Service	510-763-0975	•	•	•	•

Humboldt

DT	BK	CV	CR	PR	←Courts	Recording→	UC	RE	TX	VS
•	•	•	•	•	Attorney's Diversified Services-Santa Rosa [SOP]	800-473-5455	•	•	•	•
		•	•		Nor-Cal Court Research	530-865-3525				
		•	•	•	Jerome Nye	707-442-9542	•	•	•	•
•	•	•		•	Quest Discovery Service [SOP]	408-441-7000	•	•	•	•
		•	•	•	Red's Rapid Research	707-764-8836	•	•	•	•
		•	•	•	Research & Investigative Associates [SOP]	707-444-8767	•	•	•	•
•	•	•		•	Title Court Service	510-763-0975	•	•	•	•

Imperial

DT	BK	CV	CR	PR	←Courts	Recording→	UC	RE	TX	VS
•	•	•	•	•	Attorney's Diversified Services-San Diego [SOP]	800-566-9501	•	•	•	•
		•	•	•	Bollinger Attorney Service [SOP]	760-329-2504	•	•	•	•
•	•	•	•	•	One Legal [SOP]	800-938-8815	•	•	•	•
•	•	•		•	Quest Discovery Service [SOP]	408-441-7000	•	•	•	•
•	•	•	•	•	The Amherst Group	800-521-0237	•	•	•	•
•	•	•		•	Title Court Service	510-763-0975	•	•	•	•

Inyo

DT	BK	CV	CR	PR	←Courts	Recording→	UC	RE	TX	VS
		•	•	•	Sharron Andrews	760-878-2038	•	•	•	•
•	•	•	•	•	Attorney's Diversified Services-Fresno [SOP]	800-842-2695	•	•	•	•
•	•	•		•	Quest Discovery Service [SOP]	408-441-7000	•	•	•	•
•	•	•		•	Title Court Service	510-763-0975	•	•	•	•
	•	•	•		W.E. Works Office/Attorney Support [SOP]	760-873-3788		•	•	•

Kern

DT	BK	CV	CR	PR	←Courts	Recording→	UC	RE	TX	VS
•		•	•		A-1 Unisource Screening & Information	800-525-6972				
•	•	•	•	•	Access Research	800-456-9613	•		•	•
•	•	•	•	•	Action Legal Support Services [SOP]	559-432-3337				
•	•	•	•	•	APSCREEN Inc	800-277-2733	•	•	•	•
•		•	•		Atlas Research Services Inc	818-362-0140				
•	•	•	•	•	Attorney's Diversified Services-Bakersfield [SOP]	800-842-6334	•		•	
			•		California Backgrounds	559-274-9784				
•	•	•	•	•	Court Record Consultants [SOP]	818-366-1906	•	•	•	
		•		•	For The Record Title & Court Services	661-703-9610	•	•	•	•
			•		InVision Research	559-432-3053				
•	•	•	•	•	One Legal [SOP]	800-938-8815	•	•	•	•
•	•	•		•	Quest Discovery Service [SOP]	408-441-7000	•	•	•	•
	•	•	•	•	Select Research	661-301-7979	•	•	•	•
	•	•		•	The Daily Report	800-803-6127	•	•	•	•
•	•	•		•	Title Court Service	510-763-0975	•	•	•	•
•	•	•	•	•	Vio-Com-Data Research	559-438-1058	•	•	•	•

Kings

DT	BK	CV	CR	PR	←Courts	Recording→	UC	RE	TX	VS
•	•	•	•	•	Attorney's Diversified Services-Fresno [SOP]	800-842-2695	•	•	•	•
			•		California Backgrounds	559-274-9784				
			•		InVision Research	559-432-3053				
•	•	•	•		Keppler Legal Research	559-431-1358				
		•	•		Mike Moore Inv [SOP]	559-636-1057	•	•	•	•
•	•	•	•	•	One Legal [SOP]	800-938-8815	•	•	•	•
		•	•	•	Marilyn Peterson [SOP]	800-401-5356	•	•	•	•
•	•	•		•	Quest Discovery Service [SOP]	408-441-7000	•	•	•	•
•	•	•		•	Title Court Service	510-763-0975	•	•	•	•
	•	•	•		Total Access	559-325-1169	•	•	•	•
•	•	•	•	•	Vio-Com-Data Research	559-438-1058	•	•	•	•

DT	BK	CV	CR	PR	←Courts	LAKE	Recording→	UC	RE	TX	VS
•	•	•	•	•		Attorney's Diversified Services-Santa Rosa [SOP]	800-473-5455	•	•	•	•
		•	•	•		Mendo-Lake Paralegals	707-263-8755	•	•	•	•
•	•	•		•		Quest Discovery Service [SOP]	408-441-7000	•	•	•	•
•	•	•		•		Title Court Service	510-763-0975	•	•	•	•

DT	BK	CV	CR	PR	←Courts	LASSEN	Recording→	UC	RE	TX	VS
•	•	•	•	•		Attorney's Diversified Services-Redding [SOP]	800-473-1228	•	•	•	•
		•	•			Lassen Inv Services [SOP]	530-251-2399				
•	•	•		•		Quest Discovery Service [SOP]	408-441-7000	•	•	•	•
		•	•			The Legal Source Attorney Services	800-786-8163				
•	•	•		•		Title Court Service	510-763-0975	•	•	•	•

DT	BK	CV	CR	PR	←Courts	LOS ANGELES	Recording→	UC	RE	TX	VS
•	•	•	•	•		A & M Attorney Services Inc [SOP]	562-426-8306				
•	•	•	•	•		A California Process & Attorney Svc [SOP]	909-381-5185	•	•	•	•
•		•	•			A-1 Unisource Screening & Information	800-525-6972				
•		•	•	•		AAABackgroundchex.com - Eleda Luther	661-250-8254		•		
•	•	•	•	•		Access Research	800-456-9613	•		•	•
•	•	•	•			Accurate Background Inc	800-784-3911	•		•	
•	•	•	•	•		Accurate Source.com Inc [SOP]	800-978-8950	•	•	•	•
•	•	•	•	•		All-American Attorney Services [SOP]	800-838-9044	•	•	•	•
			•			Alpha Information Inc	800-900-1471				
•	•	•	•	•		Alpha Record Search & Retrieval	323-851-5701	•	•	•	•
•	•	•	•	•		Alternative Investigative & Attorney Services [SOP]	888-457-1314	•	•	•	•
•	•	•	•	•		APSCREEN Inc	800-277-2733	•	•	•	•
•	•	•	•	•		Assist Investigations	310-451-2204	•	•	•	•
•		•	•			Atlas Research Services Inc	818-362-0140				
•	•	•	•	•		Attorney's Diversified Services-Ventura [SOP]	800-933-8014	•	•	•	•
	•					Banko Document Retrieval	800-969-2377				
•	•	•	•	•		Bergman Records Access [SOP]	323-939-1632	•	•	•	•
•	•	•	•			Bonafide Research Services	818-349-3955	•		•	•
•	•	•	•	•		Cal Info Inc	213-537-8901	•	•	•	•
•	•	•	•	•		Cal Search	858-488-7572	•		•	•
			•			California Criminal Research [SOP]	909-445-7288				
•	•	•	•	•		Collective Intelligence Inc	800-436-1969				•
•	•	•	•	•		Confidential Service Group	877-799-9197	•	•	•	•
•	•	•	•	•		Corporate Research Solutions Inc	800-486-0757	•	•	•	•
•	•	•	•	•		Court Record Consultants [SOP]	818-366-1906	•	•	•	
•	•	•	•	•		CourtEXPRESS (CA)	800-766-3320	•	•	•	•
•	•	•	•			CourtEXPRESS (DC) [SOP]	800-542-3320				
		•	•			Crutchfield & Associates [SOP]	818-349-4836	•	•	•	
•	•	•	•	•		Daily Journal Corporation	800-952-5232	•	•		•
•	•	•	•	•		DataSearch Inc	800-452-3282	•	•	•	•
•	•	•	•	•		DCW & Associates [SOP]	800-899-0442	•	•	•	•
						Document Depot Express	562-860-2907, 706-2031		•	•	•
•	•	•	•	•		Docu-Search California	800-466-9450	•	•	•	•
						Dr Dave's Docs	818-246-3087		•		
•	•	•		•		EAGLE i Communications	702-658-3912	•	•	•	
•	•	•	•	•		English Research Services	951-328-9995	•	•	•	•
		•	•	•		Equity Title Search [SOP]	323-965-0759			•	•
•	•	•	•	•		Executive Attorney Service Inc [SOP]	213-482-6680				
•	•	•	•	•		First Investigative Consultants, PI# 6949 [SOP]	800-900-4342	•	•	•	•
			•			Fleischmann Research	714-229-5938				
		•	•			General Services [SOP]	310-859-1122				
•	•	•		•		Howard Glass	310-827-8473				
•	•	•	•			GSB Communications & Inv [SOP]	866-472-2666	•	•	•	•
•	•	•	•	•		Kern Attorney Service Inc [SOP]	213-483-4900		•	•	•
•	•	•		•		Patrick King [SOP]	626-452-0838	•	•	•	•

DT	BK	CV	CR	PR	←Courts		Recording→	UC	RE	TX	VS
•	•	•	•	•	Legal Research Associates Inc [SOP]		714-734-9337	•	•	•	•
•	•	•	•	•	LegalNet Inc [SOP]		888-530-3100	•	•	•	•
					Los Angeles County Document Services Inc		818-241-1990		•	•	
•	•	•	•	•	Loss Prevention Associates Inc		714-593-2323				
•	•	•	•		Metropolis Group		818-240-1332				
•	•	•	•	•	Net Check Investigations		888-638-2432	•	•		
•	•	•	•	•	One Legal [SOP]		800-938-8815	•	•	•	•
•	•	•		•	Pacific Corporate & Title Services (Sacramento)		800-230-4988	•	•	•	•
•	•	•	•	•	Pacificsearch & Information		619-702-3334	•	•	•	•
•	•	•	•	•	Parasec (California) [SOP]		800-533-7272	•	•	•	•
•	•	•	•	•	Process Service Network [SOP]		800-417-7623		•	•	•
•	•	•		•	Quest Discovery Service [SOP]		408-441-7000	•	•	•	•
•	•	•	•	•	Record Access		888-621-1491	•		•	
•	•	•	•	•	Research & Retrieval Inc		800-707-8771	•	•	•	
•	•	•	•	•	Research For You		626-974-4484	•	•	•	•
•	•	•	•	•	RJI Services Inc [SOP]		800-344-4754	•	•	•	•
•	•	•	•	•	San Diego Attorney Service Inc [SOP]		619-236-9585	•	•	•	•
•	•	•	•	•	Southern California Strategic Research		323-257-4472	•	•	•	•
•	•	•	•	•	Specialized Investigations [SOP]		800-714-3728	•	•	•	•
•	•	•	•		Star Group Services		909-625-8810	•	•	•	•
•	•	•	•	•	The Amherst Group		800-521-0237	•	•	•	•
•	•	•	•		The Wright Group [SOP]		877-847-0431	•	•	•	•
•	•	•		•	Title Court Service		510-763-0975	•	•	•	•
•	•	•	•	•	Triwest Investigative Services [SOP]		323-254-5151			•	•
•	•	•	•	•	Universal Information Research [SOP]		800-363-9813	•	•		•
		•	•		US Background Screening Inc		866-777-1322				
•	•		•		Welliver & Associates LLC [SOP]		800-569-5677				
•	•	•	•	•	XL Professional Services Inc [SOP]		619-232-7874	•	•	•	•

DT	BK	CV	CR	PR	←Courts	**Madera**	Recording→	UC	RE	TX	VS
•	•	•	•	•	Accessible Document Retrieval		559-779-5491	•	•	•	•
•	•	•	•	•	Action Legal Support Services [SOP]		559-432-3337				
•	•	•	•	•	Attorney Service of Merced [SOP]		209-383-3233	•	•	•	•
•	•	•	•	•	Attorney's Diversified Services-Fresno [SOP]		800-842-2695	•	•	•	•
			•		California Backgrounds		559-274-9784				
			•		InVision Research		559-432-3053				
•	•	•	•		Keppler Legal Research		559-431-1358				
•	•	•	•	•	One Legal [SOP]		800-938-8815	•	•	•	•
•	•	•		•	Quest Discovery Service [SOP]		408-441-7000	•	•	•	•
•	•	•	•	•	Rapid Document Service		209-745-0999	•	•	•	•
•	•	•		•	Title Court Service		510-763-0975	•	•	•	•
	•	•	•		Total Access		559-325-1169	•		•	•
•	•	•	•	•	Vio-Com-Data Research		559-438-1058	•	•	•	•

DT	BK	CV	CR	PR	←Courts	**Marin**	Recording→	UC	RE	TX	VS
•	•	•	•	•	A & A Legal Service Inc [SOP]		650-697-9431	•	•	•	•
			•		Alpha Information Inc		800-900-1471				
•	•	•	•	•	Attorney's Diversified Services-Santa Rosa [SOP]		800-473-5455	•		•	•
•	•	•	•		Timothy & Sara Baxter		415-333-5402				
•	•	•	•	•	Bay Area Records [SOP]		888-934-3848	•	•	•	
					Birthcertificate.com		888-934-3848				•
•	•	•	•	•	Cal Search		858-488-7572	•		•	•
•	•	•	•	•	Court Record Consultants [SOP]		818-366-1906	•	•	•	
		•	•	•	Jean Randall Process Service [SOP]		415-897-2361	•	•	•	
•	•	•	•	•	One Legal [SOP]		800-938-8815	•	•	•	•
•	•	•		•	Pacific Corporate & Title Services (Sacramento)		800-230-4988	•	•	•	•
•	•	•	•	•	Probus Research [SOP]		888-934-3848	•	•	•	•
•	•	•		•	Quest Discovery Service [SOP]		408-441-7000	•	•	•	•
•	•	•	•	•	Rapid Document Service		209-745-0999	•	•	•	•

DT	BK	CV	CR	PR	←COURTS		RECORDING→	UC	RE	TX	VS
					Leslie or Mike Sosa	916-984-7654		•	•	•	
•	•	•	•	•	The Amherst Group	800-521-0237		•	•	•	•
•	•	•		•	Title Court Service	510-763-0975		•	•	•	•
•	•	•	•	•	Universal Information Research [SOP]	800-363-9813		•	•		•
•	•	•	•	•	Wakeman Process Service Inc [SOP]	510-886-7667		•	•	•	•
•	•	•	•	•	Western Attorney Services	415-487-4140					
•	•	•	•	•	Wheels of Justice Inc [SOP]	800-649-1198		•	•	•	•

DT	BK	CV	CR	PR	←COURTS	MARIPOSA	RECORDING→	UC	RE	TX	VS
•	•	•	•	•	Attorney Service of Merced [SOP]	209-383-3233		•	•	•	•
•	•	•	•	•	Attorney's Diversified Services-Fresno [SOP]	800-842-2695		•	•	•	•
•	•	•	•		DLS Background Services Inc	951-301-8584		•		•	
•	•	•		•	Quest Discovery Service [SOP]	408-441-7000		•	•	•	•
•	•	•		•	Title Court Service	510-763-0975		•	•	•	•

DT	BK	CV	CR	PR	←COURTS	MENDOCINO	RECORDING→	UC	RE	TX	VS
•	•	•	•	•	Attorney's Diversified Services-Santa Rosa [SOP]	800-473-5455		•	•	•	•
•	•	•	•	•	C & S Research	530-415-3161		•	•	•	•
		•	•	•	Frazier & Associates	707-462-8559		•		•	•
		•	•	•	Kamber Agency	707-961-5464			•	•	•
•	•	•		•	Quest Discovery Service [SOP]	408-441-7000		•	•	•	•
•	•	•		•	Title Court Service	510-763-0975		•	•	•	•

DT	BK	CV	CR	PR	←COURTS	MERCED	RECORDING→	UC	RE	TX	VS
•	•	•	•	•	Action Legal Support Services [SOP]	559-432-3337					
•	•	•	•	•	Attorney Service of Merced [SOP]	209-383-3233		•	•	•	•
•	•	•	•	•	Attorney's Diversified Services-Fresno [SOP]	800-842-2695		•	•	•	•
•	•	•	•		Business Connections [SOP]	530-527-6262		•		•	•
•	•	•	•	•	Cal Search	858-488-7572		•		•	•
	•	•	•		Central Valley Records Service Inc	209-524-3849		•		•	•
•	•	•	•	•	One Legal [SOP]	800-938-8815		•	•	•	•
•	•	•		•	Quest Discovery Service [SOP]	408-441-7000		•	•	•	•
•	•	•	•	•	Rapid Document Service	209-745-0999		•	•	•	•
					Leslie or Mike Sosa	916-984-7654		•	•	•	
•	•	•		•	Title Court Service	510-763-0975		•	•	•	•

DT	BK	CV	CR	PR	←COURTS	MODOC	RECORDING→	UC	RE	TX	VS
•	•	•	•	•	Attorney's Diversified Services-Redding [SOP]	800-473-1228		•	•	•	•
•	•	•	•		Business Connections [SOP]	530-527-6262		•		•	•
		•	•		Lassen Inv Services [SOP]	530-251-2399					
•	•	•		•	Quest Discovery Service [SOP]	408-441-7000		•	•	•	•
•	•	•		•	Title Court Service	510-763-0975		•	•	•	•

DT	BK	CV	CR	PR	←COURTS	MONO	RECORDING→	UC	RE	TX	VS
•	•	•	•	•	Attorney's Diversified Services-Fresno [SOP]	800-842-2695		•	•	•	•
•	•	•		•	Quest Discovery Service [SOP]	408-441-7000		•	•	•	•
•	•	•		•	Title Court Service	510-763-0975		•	•	•	•
	•	•	•		W.E. Works Office/Attorney Support [SOP]	760-873-3788			•	•	•

DT	BK	CV	CR	PR	←COURTS	MONTEREY	RECORDING→	UC	RE	TX	VS
		•	•	•	Attorney Service of California-Monterey [SOP]	888-306-2194		•	•	•	•
		•	•	•	Attorney Service of California-Salinas [SOP]	888-306-2194		•	•	•	•
		•	•	•	Attorney Service of California-Santa Cruz [SOP]	888-306-2194		•	•	•	•
•	•	•	•	•	Attorney's Diversified Services-Fresno [SOP]	800-842-2695		•	•	•	•
•	•	•	•		Timothy & Sara Baxter	415-333-5402					
		•	•		Bit O' Blarney	831-663-6945					
•	•	•	•	•	Cal Search	858-488-7572		•		•	•
•	•	•	•	•	Court Record Consultants [SOP]	818-366-1906		•	•	•	
		•	•	•	Lincoln Inv Inc DBA Bay Point Legal Svc [SOP]	831-422-3007		•	•	•	•
•	•	•	•	•	One Legal [SOP]	800-938-8815		•	•	•	•

DT	BK	CV	CR	PR	Name	Phone	UC	RE	TX	VS
•	•	•		•	Pacific Corporate & Title Services (Sacramento)	800-230-4988	•	•	•	•
•	•	•		•	Quest Discovery Service [SOP]	408-441-7000	•	•	•	•
					🏛Leslie or Mike Sosa	916-984-7654	•	•	•	
		•	•	•	🏛Stan Duby Investigations [SOP]	800-953-0435	•		•	•
•	•	•		•	Title Court Service	510-763-0975	•	•	•	•
		•	•	•	🏛Tri County Inv	831-758-3124	•	•	•	•
•	•	•	•	•	Western Attorney Services	415-487-4140				

DT	BK	CV	CR	PR	←Courts **NAPA**	Recording→	UC	RE	TX	VS
		•	•	•	🏛A David Research	707-479-2779	•	•	•	•
		•	•		🏛Annette Sanders Research	707-449-3620				
•	•	•	•	•	Attorney's Diversified Services-Santa Rosa [SOP]	800-473-5455	•	•	•	•
		•	•	•	🏛Nina N Cooper	707-428-5712	•		•	•
		•	•		🏛M L Cozart Copy Service (dba: Quality Business Information)	916-691-9685				
•	•	•	•	•	One Legal [SOP]	800-938-8815	•	•	•	•
•	•	•		•	Pacific Corporate & Title Services (Sacramento)	800-230-4988	•	•	•	•
•	•	•		•	Quest Discovery Service [SOP]	408-441-7000	•	•	•	•
•	•	•	•	•	🏛Rapid Document Service	209-745-0999	•	•	•	•
•	•	•	•	•	The Amherst Group	800-521-0237	•	•	•	•
•	•	•		•	Title Court Service	510-763-0975	•	•	•	•
	•	•	•		🏛Total Access	559-325-1169	•		•	•

DT	BK	CV	CR	PR	←Courts **NEVADA**	Recording→	UC	RE	TX	VS
•	•	•	•	•	Attorney's Diversified Services-Sacramento [SOP]	800-266-4624	•	•	•	•
•	•	•	•	•	🏛C & S Research	530-415-3161	•	•	•	•
		•	•	•	🏛Nina N Cooper	707-428-5712	•		•	•
		•	•		🏛Norcal Public Records Service	800-252-0910	•	•	•	
•	•	•	•		🏛Quality Business Information	916-684-0444		•	•	•
•	•	•		•	Quest Discovery Service [SOP]	408-441-7000	•	•	•	•
		•	•		The Legal Source Attorney Services	800-786-8163				
•	•	•		•	Title Court Service	510-763-0975	•	•	•	•

DT	BK	CV	CR	PR	←Courts **ORANGE**	Recording→	UC	RE	TX	VS
		•	•		A & C Research	951-301-6956				
•	•	•	•	•	A & M Attorney Services Inc [SOP]	562-426-8306				
•	•	•	•	•	A California Process & Attorney Svc [SOP]	909-381-5185	•	•	•	•
•		•	•		A-1 Unisource Screening & Information	800-525-6972				
•	•	•	•	•	🏛Access Research	800-456-9613	•		•	•
•	•	•	•		🏛Accurate Background Inc	800-784-3911	•		•	
•	•	•	•	•	🏛Accurate Source.com Inc [SOP]	800-978-8950	•	•	•	•
			•		🏛Alpha Information Inc	800-900-1471				
•	•	•	•	•	Alternative Investigative & Attorney Services [SOP]	888-457-1314	•	•	•	•
•	•	•	•	•	🏛APSCREEN Inc	800-277-2733	•	•	•	•
•	•	•	•	•	🏛Assist Investigations	310-451-2204	•	•	•	•
•		•	•		Atlas Research Services Inc	818-362-0140				
•	•	•	•	•	Attorney's Diversified Services-San Diego [SOP]	800-566-9501	•	•	•	•
•	•	•	•	•	🏛Bergman Records Access [SOP]	323-939-1632	•	•	•	•
•	•	•	•		Bonafide Research Services	818-349-3955	•		•	•
		•	•	•	Bosic & Bosic [SOP]	951-788-1988		•	•	•
•	•	•	•	•	Cal Info Inc	213-537-8901	•	•	•	•
•	•	•	•	•	🏛Cal Search	858-488-7572	•		•	•
			•		🏛California Criminal Research [SOP]	909-445-7288				
•	•	•	•	•	🏛Collective Intelligence Inc	800-436-1969				•
•	•	•	•		🏛Corporate Research Solutions Inc	800-486-0757	•	•	•	•
•	•	•	•	•	Court Record Consultants [SOP]	818-366-1906	•	•	•	
•	•	•	•	•	CourtEXPRESS (CA)	800-766-3320	•	•	•	•
		•	•		Crutchfield & Associates [SOP]	818-349-4836	•	•	•	
	•	•	•	•	Crystal Clear Copy Service [SOP]	760-947-5699				•
•	•	•	•	•	Daily Journal Corporation	800-952-5232	•	•		•

DT	BK	CV	CR	PR	←Courts	Recording→	UC	RE	TX	VS
•	•	•	•	•	DataSearch Inc	800-452-3282	•	•	•	•
•	•	•	•	•	DCW & Associates [SOP]	800-899-0442	•	•	•	•
					Document Depot Express	562-860-2907, 706-2031		•	•	•
•	•	•	•	•	Docu-Search California	800-466-9450	•	•	•	•
					Dr Dave's Docs	818-246-3087		•		
•	•	•		•	EAGLE i Communications	702-658-3912	•	•	•	
•	•	•	•	•	English Research Services	951-328-9995	•	•	•	•
		•	•	•	Equity Title Search [SOP]	323-965-0759		•		•
•	•	•	•	•	Executive Attorney Service Inc [SOP]	213-482-6680				
•	•	•	•	•	First Investigative Consultants, PI# 6949 [SOP]	800-900-4342	•	•	•	•
			•		Fleischmann Research	714-229-5938				
		•	•		General Services [SOP]	310-859-1122				
•	•	•	•	•	Howard Glass	310-827-8473				
•	•	•	•		GSB Communications & Inv [SOP]	866-472-2666	•	•	•	•
•	•	•	•	•	Kern Attorney Service Inc [SOP]	213-483-4900		•	•	•
		•	•		Deborah Labhart	714-993-0185				
•	•	•	•	•	Legal Research Associates Inc [SOP]	714-734-9337	•	•	•	•
•	•	•	•	•	LegalNet Inc [SOP]	888-530-3100	•	•	•	•
					Los Angeles County Document Services Inc	818-241-1990		•	•	
•	•	•	•	•	Loss Prevention Associates Inc	714-593-2323				
•	•	•	•	•	Net Check Investigations	888-638-2432	•	•		
•	•	•	•	•	Theresa Olaires	714-595-4729	•	•	•	•
•	•	•	•	•	One Legal [SOP]	800-938-8815	•	•	•	•
•	•	•		•	Pacific Corporate & Title Services (Sacramento)	800-230-4988	•	•	•	•
•	•	•	•	•	Pacificsearch & Information	619-702-3334	•	•	•	•
•	•	•	•	•	Parasec (California) [SOP]	800-533-7272	•	•	•	•
•	•	•	•	•	Process Service Network [SOP]	800-417-7623		•	•	•
•	•	•		•	Quest Discovery Service [SOP]	408-441-7000	•	•	•	•
•	•	•		•	RAM Services [SOP]	714-792-2860	•	•	•	•
•	•	•	•	•	Record Access	888-621-1491	•		•	
•	•	•	•	•	Research & Retrieval Inc	800-707-8771	•	•	•	
•	•	•	•	•	Research For You	626-974-4484	•	•	•	•
•	•	•	•	•	RJI Services Inc [SOP]	800-344-4754	•	•	•	•
•	•	•	•	•	Rogers Inv & Research [SOP]	800-935-6654	•	•	•	•
•	•	•	•	•	San Diego Attorney Service Inc [SOP]	619-236-9585	•	•	•	•
•	•	•	•	•	Southern California Strategic Research	323-257-4472	•	•	•	•
•	•	•	•		Star Group Services	909-625-8810	•	•	•	•
•	•	•	•	•	The Amherst Group	800-521-0237	•	•	•	•
•	•	•	•		The Wright Group [SOP]	877-847-0431	•	•	•	•
•	•	•		•	Title Court Service	510-763-0975	•	•	•	•
•	•	•	•	•	Universal Information Research [SOP]	800-363-9813	•	•		•
•	•		•		Welliver & Associates LLC [SOP]	800-569-5677				

DT	BK	CV	CR	PR	←Courts **Placer**	Recording→	UC	RE	TX	VS
•	•	•	•	•	A Data Source	916-726-4636	•	•		•
•	•	•	•	•	Abess/Cyberdix [SOP]	877-594-0498	•		•	•
		•	•		Alpha Omega USA Information Brokers LLC [SOP]	866-636-6342				
		•	•		AlphaOmega USA Info Brokers LLC	866-636-6342				
•	•	•	•	•	Attorney's Aid Inc of Sacramento [SOP]	888-443-3915	•	•		•
•	•	•	•	•	Attorney's Diversified Services-Sacramento [SOP]	800-266-4624	•	•	•	•
•	•	•	•	•	C & S Research	530-415-3161	•	•	•	•
•	•	•	•		DLS Background Services Inc	951-301-8584	•		•	
			•		InVision Research	559-432-3053				
•	•	•	•	•	Legalese [SOP]	916-453-2860	•	•	•	•
		•	•		M L Cozart Copy Service (dba: Quality Business Information)	916-691-9685				
					Models with Brains	925-838-3899	•	•	•	
					Nisonger Abstracting Services	916-965-6544	•	•	•	
		•	•		Norcal Public Records Service	800-252-0910	•	•	•	
•	•	•	•	•	One Legal [SOP]	800-938-8815	•	•	•	•

DT	BK	CV	CR	PR			UC	RE	TX	VS
•	•	•		•	Pacific Corporate & Title Services (Sacramento)	800-230-4988	•	•	•	•
•	•	•	•		Quality Business Information	916-684-0444		•	•	•
•	•	•		•	Quest Discovery Service [SOP]	408-441-7000	•	•	•	•
•	•	•	•	•	Rapid Document Service	209-745-0999	•	•	•	•
•					Reliable Document Retrieval Inc	916-438-3000				
•	•	•	•	•	Seyfried Support Services	916-359-5275	•	•	•	•
					Leslie or Mike Sosa	916-984-7654	•	•	•	
•	•	•		•	Title Court Service	510-763-0975	•	•	•	•
•	•	•	•	•	United Attorneys' Services	916-457-3000	•	•	•	•
•	•	•	•	•	William Olmsted Inv	916-484-6465	•	•	•	•

DT	BK	CV	CR	PR	←COURTS PLUMAS	RECORDING→	UC	RE	TX	VS
•	•	•	•	•	Attorney's Diversified Services-Redding [SOP]	800-473-1228	•	•	•	•
•	•	•	•	•	C & S Research	530-415-3161	•	•	•	•
•	•	•	•		DLS Background Services Inc	951-301-8584	•		•	
		•	•		Lassen Inv Services [SOP]	530-251-2399				
•	•	•		•	Quest Discovery Service [SOP]	408-441-7000	•	•	•	•
		•	•		The Legal Source Attorney Services	800-786-8163				
•	•	•		•	Title Court Service	510-763-0975	•	•	•	•

DT	BK	CV	CR	PR	←COURTS RIVERSIDE	RECORDING→	UC	RE	TX	VS
		•	•		A & C Research	951-301-6956				
•	•	•	•	•	A California Process & Attorney Svc [SOP]	909-381-5185	•	•	•	•
•		•	•		A-1 Unisource Screening & Information	800-525-6972				
•	•	•	•	•	Access Research	800-456-9613	•		•	•
•	•	•	•		Accurate Background Inc	800-784-3911	•		•	
•	•	•	•	•	Accurate Source.com Inc [SOP]	800-978-8950	•	•	•	•
			•		Alpha Information Inc	800-900-1471				
•	•	•	•	•	Alternative Investigative & Attorney Services [SOP]	888-457-1314	•	•	•	•
•	•	•	•	•	American Legal Services [SOP]	760-323-5445		•	•	
•	•	•	•	•	APSCREEN Inc	800-277-2733	•	•	•	•
•		•	•		Atlas Research Services Inc	818-362-0140				
•	•	•	•	•	Attorney's Diversified Services-San Diego [SOP]	800-566-9501	•	•	•	•
		•	•	•	Bollinger Attorney Service [SOP]	760-329-2504	•	•	•	•
		•	•	•	Bosic & Bosic [SOP]	951-788-1988		•	•	•
•	•	•	•	•	Cal Search	858-488-7572	•		•	•
•	•	•	•	•	Collective Intelligence Inc	800-436-1969				•
•	•	•	•	•	Court Record Consultants [SOP]	818-366-1906	•	•	•	
	•	•	•	•	Crystal Clear Copy Service [SOP]	760-947-5699				•
•	•	•	•	•	Daily Journal Corporation	800-952-5232	•	•	•	•
•	•	•	•	•	DataSearch Inc	800-452-3282	•	•	•	•
•	•	•	•	•	DCW & Associates [SOP]	800-899-0442	•	•	•	•
					Document Depot Express	562-860-2907, 706-2031		•	•	•
•	•	•	•	•	Docu-Search California	800-466-9450	•	•	•	•
					Dr Dave's Docs	818-246-3087		•		
•	•	•	•	•	English Research Services	951-328-9995	•	•	•	•
		•	•	•	Equity Title Search [SOP]	323-965-0759		•		•
•	•	•	•	•	Executive Attorney Service Inc [SOP]	213-482-6680				
•	•	•	•	•	First Investigative Consultants, PI# 6949 [SOP]	800-900-4342	•	•	•	•
			•		Fleischmann Research	714-229-5938				
		•	•		General Services [SOP]	310-859-1122				
•	•	•	•	•	Howard Glass	310-827-8473				
	•	•	•	•	Grissom & Associates [SOP]	800-861-6483	•	•	•	•
•	•	•	•	•	Kern Attorney Service Inc [SOP]	213-483-4900		•	•	•
•	•	•	•	•	Legal Research Associates Inc [SOP]	714-734-9337	•	•	•	•
					Los Angeles County Document Services Inc	818-241-1990		•	•	
•	•	•	•	•	Loss Prevention Associates Inc	714-593-2323				
•	•	•	•	•	Joe Y Nerio	909-824-9358				•
•	•	•	•		New Information Court Research	909-514-1595	•		•	

DT	BK	CV	CR	PR	←Courts	Recording→	UC	RE	TX	VS
•	•	•	•	•	One Legal [SOP]	800-938-8815	•	•	•	•
•	•	•		•	Pacific Corporate & Title Services (Sacramento)	800-230-4988	•	•	•	•
•	•	•	•	•	Precision Research & Information	951-244-8118	•		•	•
•	•	•	•	•	Process Service Network [SOP]	800-417-7623		•	•	•
•	•	•		•	Quest Discovery Service [SOP]	408-441-7000	•	•	•	•
		•		•	RASCAL [SOP]	951-693-0165		•	•	
•	•	•	•	•	Research & Retrieval Inc	800-707-8771	•	•	•	
•	•	•	•	•	RJI Services Inc [SOP]	800-344-4754	•	•	•	•
•	•	•	•	•	San Diego Attorney Service Inc [SOP]	619-236-9585	•	•	•	•
•	•	•	•	•	Southern California Strategic Research	323-257-4472	•	•	•	•
•	•	•	•	•	The Amherst Group	800-521-0237	•	•	•	•
•	•	•	•		The Wright Group [SOP]	877-847-0431	•	•	•	•
•	•	•		•	Title Court Service	510-763-0975	•	•	•	•
•	•	•	•	•	Universal Information Research [SOP]	800-363-9813	•	•		•
•	•		•		Welliver & Associates LLC [SOP]	800-569-5677				
•	•	•	•	•	XL Professional Services Inc [SOP]	619-232-7874	•	•	•	•

DT	BK	CV	CR	PR	←Courts **SACRAMENTO**	Recording→	UC	RE	TX	VS
•	•	•	•	•	A Data Source	916-726-4636	•	•		•
•		•	•		A-1 Unisource Screening & Information	800-525-6972				
•	•	•	•	•	Abess/Cyberdix [SOP]	877-594-0498	•		•	•
•	•	•	•	•	Access Research	800-456-9613	•		•	•
		•	•		AlphaOmega USA Info Brokers LLC	866-636-6342				
•	•	•	•	•	Attorney's Aid Inc of Sacramento [SOP]	888-443-3915	•	•		•
•	•	•	•	•	Attorney's Diversified Services-Sacramento [SOP]	800-266-4624	•	•	•	•
•	•	•	•	•	C & S Research	530-415-3161	•	•	•	•
•	•	•	•	•	Cal Search	858-488-7572	•		•	•
•	•	•		•	Cal Title-Search Inc	800-482-1497	•	•	•	•
•	•	•	•	•	Capitol City Network	916-395-2917	•	•	•	•
•	•	•			Capitol Corporate Services Inc (California)	800-327-4842	•		•	
					Capitol Services (California)	916-443-0657	•			
•	•	•	•	•	Confi-Chek	800-821-7404	•	•	•	•
		•	•	•	Nina N Cooper	707-428-5712	•		•	•
•	•	•	•	•	Court Record Consultants [SOP]	818-366-1906	•	•	•	
•	•	•	•	•	CourtEXPRESS (CA)	800-766-3320	•	•	•	•
•	•	•	•	•	DataSearch Inc	800-452-3282	•	•	•	•
		•	•		Inquest	408-395-1300				
			•		InVision Research	559-432-3053				
•	•	•	•	•	Legalese [SOP]	916-453-2860	•	•	•	•
					Logan Registration Service Inc	916-457-5787	•			
		•	•		M L Cozart Copy Service (dba: Quality Business Information)	916-691-9685				
•	•	•	•		McCoy Investigations (CAPI# 18621)	800-287-6789				
					Models with Brains	925-838-3899	•	•	•	
					Nisonger Abstracting Services	916-965-6544	•	•	•	
•	•	•	•	•	One Legal [SOP]	800-938-8815	•	•	•	•
•	•	•		•	Pacific Corporate & Title Services (Sacramento)	800-230-4988	•	•	•	•
•	•	•	•	•	Parasec (California) [SOP]	800-533-7272	•	•	•	•
•	•	•	•		Quality Business Information	916-684-0444		•	•	•
•	•	•		•	Quest Discovery Service [SOP]	408-441-7000	•	•	•	•
•	•	•	•	•	Rapid Document Service	209-745-0999	•	•	•	•
		•	•		Records Research Inc (California)	800-952-5766	•	•	•	
•					Reliable Document Retrieval Inc	916-438-3000				
•	•	•	•	•	Research & Retrieval Inc	800-707-8771	•	•	•	
					Searching Registration Service	800-488-0238	•	•		•
•	•	•	•	•	Seyfried Support Services	916-359-5275	•	•	•	•
	•	•	•		Parri Shebley [SOP]	707-448-5018				•
					Leslie or Mike Sosa	916-984-7654	•	•	•	
•	•	•	•	•	The Amherst Group	800-521-0237	•	•	•	•
		•	•		The Legal Source Attorney Services	800-786-8163				

DT	BK	CV	CR	PR	Courts		UC	RE	TX	VS
•	•	•		•	Title Court Service	510-763-0975	•	•	•	•
•	•	•	•		Unisearch Inc (California)	800-769-1864	•		•	
•	•	•	•	•	United Attorneys' Services	916-457-3000	•	•	•	•
•	•	•	•	•	William Olmsted Inv	916-484-6465	•	•	•	•

DT	BK	CV	CR	PR	←Courts **San Benito**	Recording→	UC	RE	TX	VS
•	•	•	•	•	Attorney's Diversified Services-Fresno [SOP]	800-842-2695	•	•	•	•
•	•	•	•	•	Court Record Consultants [SOP]	818-366-1906	•	•	•	
•	•	•		•	Quest Discovery Service [SOP]	408-441-7000	•	•	•	•
					Leslie or Mike Sosa	916-984-7654	•	•	•	
		•	•	•	Stan Duby Investigations [SOP]	800-953-0435	•		•	•
•	•	•		•	Title Court Service	510-763-0975	•	•	•	•
		•	•	•	Tri County Inv	831-758-3124	•	•	•	•

DT	BK	CV	CR	PR	←Courts **San Bernardino**	Recording→	UC	RE	TX	VS
		•	•		A & C Research	951-301-6956				
•	•	•	•	•	A California Process & Attorney Svc [SOP]	909-381-5185	•	•	•	•
•		•	•		A-1 Unisource Screening & Information	800-525-6972				
•	•	•	•	•	Access Research	800-456-9613	•		•	•
•	•	•	•		Accurate Background Inc	800-784-3911	•		•	
•	•	•	•	•	Accurate Source.com Inc [SOP]	800-978-8950	•	•	•	•
			•		Alpha Information Inc	800-900-1471				
•	•	•	•	•	Alternative Investigative & Attorney Services [SOP]	888-457-1314	•	•	•	•
•	•	•	•	•	APSCREEN Inc	800-277-2733	•	•	•	•
•		•	•		Atlas Research Services Inc	818-362-0140				
		•	•	•	Bollinger Attorney Service [SOP]	760-329-2504	•	•	•	•
		•	•	•	Bosic & Bosic [SOP]	951-788-1988		•	•	•
•	•	•	•	•	Cal Search	858-488-7572	•		•	•
•	•	•	•	•	Collective Intelligence Inc	800-436-1969				•
•	•	•	•	•	Court Record Consultants [SOP]	818-366-1906	•	•	•	
		•	•		Crutchfield & Associates [SOP]	818-349-4836	•	•	•	
	•	•	•	•	Crystal Clear Copy Service [SOP]	760-947-5699				•
•	•	•	•	•	Daily Journal Corporation	800-952-5232	•	•		•
•	•	•	•	•	DataSearch Inc	800-452-3282	•	•	•	•
•	•	•	•	•	DCW & Associates [SOP]	800-899-0442	•	•	•	•
•	•	•	•		DLS Background Services Inc	951-301-8584	•		•	
					Document Depot Express	562-860-2907, 706-2031		•	•	•
•	•	•	•	•	Docu-Search California	800-466-9450	•	•	•	•
					Dr Dave's Docs	818-246-3087		•		
		•	•		DRS Information Services	909-792-6466				
•	•	•	•	•	English Research Services	951-328-9995	•	•	•	•
•	•	•	•	•	Executive Attorney Service Inc [SOP]	213-482-6680				
•	•	•	•	•	First Investigative Consultants, PI# 6949 [SOP]	800-900-4342	•	•	•	•
			•		Fleischmann Research	714-229-5938				
		•	•		General Services [SOP]	310-859-1122				
	•	•	•	•	Grissom & Associates [SOP]	800-861-6483	•	•	•	•
•	•	•	•	•	Kern Attorney Service Inc [SOP]	213-483-4900		•	•	•
•	•	•	•	•	Legal Research Associates Inc [SOP]	714-734-9337	•	•	•	•
					Los Angeles County Document Services Inc	818-241-1990		•	•	
•	•	•	•	•	Loss Prevention Associates Inc	714-593-2323				
•	•	•	•	•	Joe Y Nerio	909-824-9358				•
•	•	•	•		New Information Court Research	909-514-1595	•		•	
•	•	•	•	•	One Legal [SOP]	800-938-8815	•	•	•	•
•	•	•		•	Pacific Corporate & Title Services (Sacramento)	800-230-4988	•	•	•	•
•	•	•	•	•	Precision Research & Information	951-244-8118	•		•	•
•	•	•	•	•	Process Service Network [SOP]	800-417-7623		•	•	•
•	•	•		•	Quest Discovery Service [SOP]	408-441-7000	•	•	•	•
•	•	•	•	•	Research & Retrieval Inc	800-707-8771	•	•	•	
•	•	•	•	•	San Diego Attorney Service Inc [SOP]	619-236-9585	•	•	•	•

DT	BK	CV	CR	PR	Courts	Recording	UC	RE	TX	VS
•	•	•	•	•	Southern California Strategic Research	323-257-4472	•	•	•	•
•	•	•	•		Star Group Services	909-625-8810	•	•	•	•
•	•	•	•	•	The Amherst Group	800-521-0237	•	•	•	•
•	•	•	•		The Wright Group [SOP]	877-847-0431	•	•	•	•
•	•	•		•	Title Court Service	510-763-0975	•	•	•	•
•	•	•	•	•	Universal Information Research [SOP]	800-363-9813	•	•		•
•	•		•		Welliver & Associates LLC [SOP]	800-569-5677				

DT	BK	CV	CR	PR	←Courts San Diego	Recording→	UC	RE	TX	VS
•		•	•		A-1 Unisource Screening & Information	800-525-6972				
•	•	•	•		Aaron Anderson Agency	760-751-0101			•	
•	•	•	•	•	Access Research	800-456-9613	•		•	•
•	•	•	•		Accurate Background Inc	800-784-3911	•		•	
•	•	•	•	•	Accurate Source.com Inc [SOP]	800-978-8950	•	•	•	•
•	•	•	•	•	AccuTech Legal Support Services [SOP]	800-275-7189	•	•	•	•
•	•	•	•	•	Alpha Attorney Service [SOP]	619-235-8008	•	•	•	•
			•		Alpha Information Inc	800-900-1471				
•	•	•	•	•	APSCREEN Inc	800-277-2733	•	•	•	•
•		•	•		Atlas Research Services Inc	818-362-0140				
•	•	•	•	•	Attorney's Diversified Services-San Diego [SOP]	800-566-9501	•	•	•	•
	•				Banko Document Retrieval	800-969-2377				
•	•	•	•		Budget Document Retrieval & Information Service	866-805-6288	•	•	•	•
•	•	•	•	•	Cal Search	858-488-7572	•		•	•
			•		California Criminal Research [SOP]	909-445-7288				
•	•	•	•	•	Collective Intelligence Inc	800-436-1969				•
•	•	•	•	•	Court Record Consultants [SOP]	818-366-1906	•	•	•	
•	•	•	•	•	CourtEXPRESS (CA)	800-766-3320	•	•	•	•
•	•	•	•	•	Courthouse Connections	619-692-3538	•	•	•	•
		•	•		Crutchfield & Associates [SOP]	818-349-4836	•	•	•	
•	•	•	•	•	Daily Journal Corporation	800-952-5232	•	•		•
•	•	•	•	•	DataSearch Inc	800-452-3282	•	•	•	•
•	•	•	•	•	DCW & Associates [SOP]	800-899-0442	•	•	•	•
•	•	•	•		DLS Background Services Inc	951-301-8584	•		•	
					Document Depot Express	562-860-2907, 706-2031		•	•	•
•	•	•	•	•	Docu-Search California	800-466-9450	•	•	•	•
					Dr Dave's Docs	818-246-3087		•		
•	•	•	•	•	First Investigative Consultants, PI# 6949 [SOP]	800-900-4342	•	•	•	•
•		•	•	•	Fred Phillips Research Inc	858-735-3431				
•	•	•	•	•	Hire Screening Inc	619-656-6068	•	•	•	•
•	•	•	•	•	Kern Attorney Service Inc [SOP]	213-483-4900		•	•	•
•	•	•	•		L & J Research	619-829-2083	•		•	•
•	•	•	•	•	Law In Motion [SOP]	619-232-1291	•	•	•	•
					Los Angeles County Document Services Inc	818-241-1990		•	•	
•	•	•	•	•	Loss Prevention Associates Inc	714-593-2323				
•	•	•	•		Metropolis Group	818-240-1332				
•	•	•	•	•	One Legal [SOP]	800-938-8815	•	•	•	•
•	•	•	•	•	Owens & Associates Inv [SOP]	800-297-1343	•	•	•	•
•	•	•		•	Pacific Corporate & Title Services (Sacramento)	800-230-4988	•	•	•	•
•	•	•	•	•	Pacificsearch & Information	619-702-3334	•	•	•	•
•	•	•		•	Quest Discovery Service [SOP]	408-441-7000	•	•	•	•
		•		•	RASCAL [SOP]	951-693-0165		•	•	
•	•	•	•	•	Research & Retrieval Inc	800-707-8771	•	•	•	
•	•	•	•	•	RJI Services Inc [SOP]	800-344-4754	•	•	•	•
•	•	•	•	•	Rogers Inv & Research [SOP]	800-935-6654	•	•	•	•
•	•	•	•	•	San Diego Attorney Service Inc [SOP]	619-236-9585	•	•	•	•
•	•	•	•	•	Seva Services	858-490-9009		•	•	•
•	•	•	•	•	Sutherlin Associated Services	800-217-1555	•	•	•	
•	•	•	•	•	The Amherst Group	800-521-0237	•	•	•	•
•	•	•	•		The Wright Group [SOP]	877-847-0431	•	•	•	•

DT	BK	CV	CR	PR	←Courts	Recording→	UC	RE	TX	VS
•	•	•		•	Title Court Service	510-763-0975	•	•	•	•
•	•	•	•	•	Universal Information Research [SOP]	800-363-9813	•	•		•
•	•		•		Welliver & Associates LLC [SOP]	800-569-5677				
•	•	•	•	•	XL Professional Services Inc [SOP]	619-232-7874	•	•	•	•

DT	BK	CV	CR	PR	←Courts San Francisco	Recording→	UC	RE	TX	VS
•	•	•	•	•	A & A Legal Service Inc [SOP]	650-697-9431	•	•	•	•
•		•	•		A-1 Unisource Screening & Information	800-525-6972				
•	•	•	•	•	Access Research	800-456-9613	•		•	•
•	•	•	•		Accurate Background Inc	800-784-3911	•		•	
•		•	•		Advantage Background Services Inc	800-355-2650				
•	•	•	•	•	Attorney's Diversified Services-San Francisco [SOP]	800-775-3455	•	•	•	•
•	•	•	•	•	Attorneys' Service Limited [SOP]	408-293-9111	•	•	•	•
•	•	•	•		Timothy & Sara Baxter	415-333-5402				
•	•	•	•	•	Bay Area Records [SOP]	888-934-3848	•	•	•	
					Birthcertificate.com	888-934-3848				•
•	•	•	•	•	Cal Search	858-488-7572	•		•	•
•	•	•	•	•	Court Record Consultants [SOP]	818-366-1906	•	•	•	
•	•	•	•	•	CourtEXPRESS (CA)	800-766-3320	•	•	•	•
•		•	•	•	Edith Wiggins & Marvin Singer	415-771-9369	•		•	
		•	•	•	Equity Title Search [SOP]	323-965-0759		•		•
			•		InVision Research	559-432-3053				
•	•	•	•	•	Lone Star Legal	415-255-8550	•	•	•	•
					Models with Brains	925-838-3899	•	•	•	
•	•	•	•	•	One Legal [SOP]	800-938-8815	•	•	•	•
•	•	•		•	Pacific Corporate & Title Services (Sacramento)	800-230-4988	•	•	•	•
•	•	•	•	•	Pacific Research & Retrieval Inc [SOP]	800-222-7040	•	•	•	•
•	•	•	•	•	PFC Information Services Inc	510-653-5061	•	•	•	•
•	•	•	•	•	Probus Research [SOP]	888-934-3848	•	•	•	•
•	•	•		•	Quest Discovery Service [SOP]	408-441-7000	•	•	•	•
•	•	•	•	•	Rapid Document Service	209-745-0999	•	•	•	•
•	•	•	•	•	Research & Retrieval Inc	800-707-8771	•	•	•	
•	•	•	•	•	RJI Services Inc [SOP]	800-344-4754	•	•	•	•
					Leslie or Mike Sosa	916-984-7654	•	•	•	
•	•	•	•	•	Swift Attorney Service [SOP]	800-987-9438	•	•	•	•
•	•	•	•	•	The Amherst Group	800-521-0237	•	•	•	•
•	•	•		•	Title Court Service	510-763-0975	•	•	•	•
		•	•		Triad Consultants	415-332-4400				
•	•	•	•	•	Universal Information Research [SOP]	800-363-9813	•	•		•
•	•	•	•	•	Wakeman Process Service Inc [SOP]	510-886-7667	•	•	•	•
•	•	•	•	•	Western Attorney Services	415-487-4140				
•	•	•	•	•	Wheels of Justice Inc [SOP]	800-649-1198	•	•	•	•
•	•	•	•	•	Zook Search Inc	415-387-1029	•	•	•	

DT	BK	CV	CR	PR	←Courts San Joaquin	Recording→	UC	RE	TX	VS
•	•	•	•	•	Abess/Cyberdix [SOP]	877-594-0498	•		•	•
•	•	•	•	•	Access Research	800-456-9613	•		•	•
		•	•	•	AD Services (ADS) [SOP]	800-827-9101		•	•	•
•	•	•	•	•	Attorney Service of Merced [SOP]	209-383-3233	•	•	•	•
•	•	•	•	•	Attorney's Aid Inc of Sacramento [SOP]	888-443-3915	•	•		•
•	•	•	•	•	Attorney's Diversified Services-Stockton [SOP]	800-343-2108	•	•	•	•
			•		California Backgrounds	559-274-9784				
	•	•	•		Central Valley Records Service Inc	209-524-3849	•		•	•
			•		InVision Research	559-432-3053				
•	•	•	•	•	Legalese [SOP]	916-453-2860	•	•	•	•
		•	•		M L Cozart Copy Service (dba: Quality Business Information)	916-691-9685				
•	•	•	•	•	One Legal [SOP]	800-938-8815	•	•	•	•
•	•	•		•	Pacific Corporate & Title Services (Sacramento)	800-230-4988	•	•	•	•
•	•	•		•	Quest Discovery Service [SOP]	408-441-7000	•	•	•	•

DT	BK	CV	CR	PR	Courts	Recording	UC	RE	TX	VS
•	•	•	•	•	Rapid Document Service	209-745-0999	•	•	•	•
•	•	•		•	Title Court Service	510-763-0975	•	•	•	•
•	•	•	•	•	United Attorneys' Services	916-457-3000	•	•	•	•
•	•	•	•	•	William Olmsted Inv	916-484-6465	•	•	•	•

DT	BK	CV	CR	PR	←Courts **San Luis Obispo**	Recording→	UC	RE	TX	VS
•	•	•	•	•	Abstrax	805-965-9858	•	•	•	•
•	•	•	•	•	Access Research	800-456-9613	•		•	•
•	•	•	•	•	Attorney Service of San Luis Obispo [SOP]	850-543-8919	•	•	•	•
•	•	•	•	•	Attorney's Diversified Services-Ventura [SOP]	800-933-8014	•	•	•	•
		•	•	•	Leslie Bearce	805-541-2615	•	•	•	•
		•	•		Coastal Research	805-710-4926		•	•	
•	•	•	•	•	Collective Intelligence Inc	800-436-1969				•
•	•	•	•	•	Court Record Consultants [SOP]	818-366-1906	•	•	•	
•	•	•	•	•	CourtCheckers [SOP]	805-898-7084	•	•	•	•
•	•	•	•	•	One Legal [SOP]	800-938-8815	•	•	•	•
•	•	•		•	Quest Discovery Service [SOP]	408-441-7000	•	•	•	•
•	•	•		•	Title Court Service	510-763-0975	•	•	•	•

DT	BK	CV	CR	PR	←Courts **San Mateo**	Recording→	UC	RE	TX	VS
•	•	•	•	•	A & A Legal Service Inc [SOP]	650-697-9431	•	•	•	•
•		•	•		A-1 Unisource Screening & Information	800-525-6972				
•	•	•	•	•	Access Research	800-456-9613	•		•	•
•	•	•	•		Accurate Background Inc	800-784-3911	•		•	
		•	•	•	AD Services (ADS) [SOP]	800-827-9101		•	•	•
•	•	•	•	•	Attorney's Diversified Services-San Francisco [SOP]	800-775-3455	•	•	•	•
•	•	•	•	•	Attorneys' Service Limited [SOP]	408-293-9111	•	•	•	•
•	•	•	•		Timothy & Sara Baxter	415-333-5402				
•	•	•	•	•	Bay Area Records [SOP]	888-934-3848	•	•	•	
•	•	•	•	•	Bayshore Research & Retrieval [SOP]	408-776-1544	•	•	•	•
					Birthcertificate.com	888-934-3848				•
•	•	•	•	•	Cal Search	858-488-7572	•		•	•
•	•	•	•	•	CourtEXPRESS (CA)	800-766-3320	•	•	•	•
•		•	•	•	Edith Wiggins & Marvin Singer	415-771-9369	•		•	
		•	•		Incognito Services [SOP]	650-363-9100		•		
		•	•		Inquest	408-395-1300				
			•		InVision Research	559-432-3053				
		•	•		Legal Document Search & Signing Services [SOP]	408-483-0061			•	•
•	•	•	•	•	Lone Star Legal	415-255-8550	•	•	•	•
					Models with Brains	925-838-3899	•	•	•	
•	•	•	•	•	One Legal [SOP]	800-938-8815	•	•	•	•
•	•	•		•	Pacific Corporate & Title Services (Sacramento)	800-230-4988	•	•	•	•
•	•	•	•	•	Pacific Research & Retrieval Inc [SOP]	800-222-7040	•	•	•	•
•	•	•	•	•	Probus Research [SOP]	888-934-3848	•	•	•	•
•	•	•		•	Quest Discovery Service [SOP]	408-441-7000	•	•	•	•
•	•	•	•	•	Rapid Document Service	209-745-0999	•	•	•	•
		•	•		Rapid Research	510-883-1602				
					Leslie or Mike Sosa	916-984-7654	•	•	•	
•	•	•	•	•	Swift Attorney Service [SOP]	800-987-9438	•	•	•	•
•	•	•		•	Title Court Service	510-763-0975	•	•	•	•
		•	•		Triad Consultants	415-332-4400				
•	•	•	•	•	Wakeman Process Service Inc [SOP]	510-886-7667	•	•	•	•
•	•	•	•	•	Western Attorney Services	415-487-4140				
•	•	•	•	•	Wheels of Justice Inc [SOP]	800-649-1198	•	•	•	•

DT	BK	CV	CR	PR	←Courts **Santa Barbara**	Recording→	UC	RE	TX	VS
•		•	•		A-1 Unisource Screening & Information	800-525-6972				
•	•	•	•	•	Abstrax	805-965-9858	•	•	•	•
•	•	•	•	•	Access Research	800-456-9613	•		•	•

DT	BK	CV	CR	PR	Retriever	Phone	UC	RE	TX	VS
•	•	•	•	•	APSCREEN Inc	800-277-2733	•	•	•	•
•	•	•	•	•	Associated Attorney Services [SOP]	805-898-0022	•	•	•	•
•		•	•		Atlas Research Services Inc	818-362-0140				
•	•	•	•	•	Attorney Service of San Luis Obispo [SOP]	850-543-8919	•	•	•	•
•	•	•	•	•	Attorney's Diversified Services-Ventura [SOP]	800-933-8014	•	•	•	•
		•	•		Todd Boehr	805-452-7579				
•	•	•	•		Bonafide Research Services	818-349-3955	•		•	•
•	•	•	•	•	Cal Search	858-488-7572	•		•	•
		•	•		Coastal Research	805-710-4926		•	•	
•	•	•	•	•	Collective Intelligence Inc	800-436-1969				•
	•	•	•	•	Commercial Process Serving Inc [SOP]	800-382-0088				
•	•	•	•	•	Court Record Consultants [SOP]	818-366-1906	•	•	•	
•	•	•	•	•	CourtCheckers [SOP]	805-898-7084	•	•	•	•
•	•	•	•	•	DCW & Associates [SOP]	800-899-0442	•	•	•	•
					Dr Dave's Docs	818-246-3087		•		
		•	•		General Services [SOP]	310-859-1122				
			•		InVision Research	559-432-3053				
•	•	•	•	•	One Legal [SOP]	800-938-8815	•	•	•	•
•	•	•		•	Quest Discovery Service [SOP]	408-441-7000	•	•	•	•
•	•	•	•	•	Southern California Strategic Research	323-257-4472	•	•	•	•
•	•	•	•	•	The Amherst Group	800-521-0237	•	•	•	•
•	•	•		•	Title Court Service	510-763-0975	•	•	•	•
	•				Title Runners	805-569-6939	•	•	•	•

DT	BK	CV	CR	PR	←COURTS SANTA CLARA	RECORDING→	UC	RE	TX	VS
•	•	•	•	•	A & A Legal Service Inc [SOP]	650-697-9431	•	•	•	•
•	•	•	•		Accurate Background Inc	800-784-3911	•		•	
•	•	•	•	•	Accurate Source.com Inc [SOP]	800-978-8950	•	•	•	•
		•	•	•	AD Services (ADS) [SOP]	800-827-9101		•	•	•
•		•	•		Advantage Background Services Inc	800-355-2650				
			•		Alpha Information Inc	800-900-1471				
•	•	•	•	•	Attorney's Diversified Services-San Francisco [SOP]	800-775-3455	•	•	•	•
•	•	•	•	•	Attorneys' Service Limited [SOP]	408-293-9111	•	•	•	•
•	•	•	•		Timothy & Sara Baxter	415-333-5402				
•	•	•	•	•	Bay Area Records [SOP]	888-934-3848	•	•	•	
•	•	•	•	•	Bayshore Research & Retrieval [SOP]	408-776-1544	•	•	•	•
					Birthcertificate.com	888-934-3848				•
•	•	•	•	•	Cal Search	858-488-7572	•		•	•
•	•	•	•	•	Court Record Consultants [SOP]	818-366-1906	•	•	•	
•	•	•	•	•	CourtEXPRESS (CA)	800-766-3320	•	•	•	•
•	•	•	•		DLS Background Services Inc	951-301-8584	•		•	
•	•	•	•	•	Haber Investigations [SOP]	800-382-6333	•	•	•	•
		•	•		Inquest	408-395-1300				
		•	•		Legal Document Search & Signing Services [SOP]	408-483-0061			•	•
					Models with Brains	925-838-3899	•	•	•	
•	•	•	•	•	One Legal [SOP]	800-938-8815	•	•	•	•
•	•	•	•		PAC Research	831-475-7780	•		•	•
•	•	•		•	Pacific Corporate & Title Services (Sacramento)	800-230-4988	•	•	•	•
•	•	•	•	•	Pacific Research & Retrieval Inc [SOP]	800-222-7040	•	•	•	•
•	•	•	•	•	Probus Research [SOP]	888-934-3848	•	•	•	•
•	•	•		•	Quest Discovery Service [SOP]	408-441-7000	•	•	•	•
•	•	•	•	•	Rapid Document Service	209-745-0999	•	•	•	•
•	•	•	•	•	Research & Retrieval Inc	800-707-8771	•	•	•	
					Leslie or Mike Sosa	916-984-7654	•	•	•	
•	•	•	•	•	Swift Attorney Service [SOP]	800-987-9438	•	•	•	•
•	•	•	•	•	The Amherst Group	800-521-0237	•	•	•	•
•	•	•		•	Title Court Service	510-763-0975	•	•	•	•
		•	•		Triad Consultants	415-332-4400				
•	•	•	•	•	Universal Information Research [SOP]	800-363-9813	•	•		•

DT	BK	CV	CR	PR			UC	RE	TX	VS
•	•	•	•	•	Wakeman Process Service Inc [SOP]	510-886-7667	•	•	•	•
•	•	•	•	•	Western Attorney Services	415-487-4140				
•	•	•	•	•	Wheels of Justice Inc [SOP]	800-649-1198	•	•	•	•

DT	BK	CV	CR	PR	←COURTS **SANTA CRUZ**	RECORDING→	UC	RE	TX	VS
		•	•	•	Attorney Service of California-Salinas [SOP]	888-306-2194	•	•	•	•
		•	•	•	Attorney Service of California-Santa Cruz [SOP]	888-306-2194	•	•	•	•
•	•	•	•	•	Attorney's Diversified Services-Fresno [SOP]	800-842-2695	•	•	•	•
•	•	•	•		Timothy & Sara Baxter	415-333-5402				
•	•	•	•	•	Cal Search	858-488-7572	•		•	•
		•	•		Inquest	408-395-1300				
•	•	•	•	•	One Legal [SOP]	800-938-8815	•	•	•	•
•	•	•	•		PAC Research	831-475-7780	•		•	•
•	•	•		•	Pacific Corporate & Title Services (Sacramento)	800-230-4988	•	•	•	•
•	•	•	•	•	Pacific Research & Retrieval Inc [SOP]	800-222-7040	•	•	•	•
•	•	•		•	Quest Discovery Service [SOP]	408-441-7000	•	•	•	•
					Leslie or Mike Sosa	916-984-7654	•	•	•	
		•	•	•	Stan Duby Investigations [SOP]	800-953-0435	•		•	•
•	•	•		•	Title Court Service	510-763-0975	•	•	•	•
		•	•	•	Tri County Inv	831-758-3124	•	•	•	•

DT	BK	CV	CR	PR	←COURTS **SHASTA**	RECORDING→	UC	RE	TX	VS
•	•	•	•	•	Ahern Research	209-754-9709	•	•	•	•
•	•	•	•	•	Attorney's Aid Inc of Sacramento [SOP]	888-443-3915	•	•		•
•	•	•	•	•	Attorney's Diversified Services-Redding [SOP]	800-473-1228	•	•	•	•
•	•	•	•		Business Connections [SOP]	530-527-6262	•		•	•
•	•	•	•	•	C & S Research	530-415-3161	•	•	•	•
		•	•		Carmona & Associates [SOP]	530-246-1010	•	•	•	•
•	•	•	•		DLS Background Services Inc	951-301-8584	•		•	
		•	•		Nor-Cal Court Research	530-865-3525				
•	•	•		•	Quest Discovery Service [SOP]	408-441-7000	•	•	•	•
		•	•		The Legal Source Attorney Services	800-786-8163				
•	•	•		•	Title Court Service	510-763-0975	•	•	•	•

DT	BK	CV	CR	PR	←COURTS **SIERRA**	RECORDING→	UC	RE	TX	VS
•	•	•	•	•	Attorney's Diversified Services-Sacramento [SOP]	800-266-4624	•	•	•	•
•	•	•	•	•	C & S Research	530-415-3161	•	•	•	•
		•	•	•	Nina N Cooper	707-428-5712	•		•	•
		•	•		Lassen Inv Services [SOP]	530-251-2399				
•	•	•		•	Quest Discovery Service [SOP]	408-441-7000	•	•	•	•
•	•	•		•	Title Court Service	510-763-0975	•	•	•	•

DT	BK	CV	CR	PR	←COURTS **SISKIYOU**	RECORDING→	UC	RE	TX	VS
•		•	•		Atlas Research Services Inc	818-362-0140				
•	•	•	•	•	Attorney's Diversified Services-Redding [SOP]	800-473-1228	•	•	•	•
		•	•		Carmona & Associates [SOP]	530-246-1010	•	•	•	•
•	•	•	•	•	Cleveland & Carl Inv [SOP]	800-888-6629	•	•	•	•
•	•	•		•	Quest Discovery Service [SOP]	408-441-7000	•	•	•	•
		•	•		Shaw Investigations [SOP]	530-841-0255				
•	•	•		•	Title Court Service	510-763-0975	•	•	•	•

DT	BK	CV	CR	PR	←COURTS **SOLANO**	RECORDING→	UC	RE	TX	VS
		•	•		Annette Sanders Research	707-449-3620				
•	•	•	•	•	Attorney's Diversified Services-Sacramento [SOP]	800-266-4624	•	•	•	•
•	•	•	•	•	Bay Area Records [SOP]	888-934-3848	•	•	•	
		•	•	•	Nina N Cooper	707-428-5712	•	•	•	•
		•	•		M L Cozart Copy Service (dba: Quality Business Information)	916-691-9685				
					Models with Brains	925-838-3899	•	•	•	
•	•	•	•	•	One Legal [SOP]	800-938-8815	•	•	•	•
•	•	•		•	Pacific Corporate & Title Services (Sacramento)	800-230-4988	•	•	•	•

DT	BK	CV	CR	PR	Courts	Recording	UC	RE	TX	VS
•	•	•		•	Quest Discovery Service [SOP]	408-441-7000	•	•	•	•
•	•	•	•	•	Rapid Document Service	209-745-0999	•	•	•	•
	•	•	•		Parri Shebley [SOP]	707-448-5018				•
					Leslie or Mike Sosa	916-984-7654	•	•	•	
		•	•		Sumpter & Associates LLC	925-671-7755	•	•	•	•
•	•	•		•	Title Court Service	510-763-0975	•	•	•	•
•	•	•	•	•	Wakeman Process Service Inc [SOP]	510-886-7667	•	•	•	•
•	•	•	•	•	West Coast MCI [SOP]	925-372-8909	•	•	•	•
•	•	•	•	•	Western Attorney Services	415-487-4140				

DT	BK	CV	CR	PR	←Courts **Sonoma**	Recording→	UC	RE	TX	VS
		•	•	•	A David Research	707-479-2779	•	•	•	•
		•	•		Alpha Omega USA Information Brokers LLC [SOP]	866-636-6342				
		•	•		AlphaOmega USA Info Brokers LLC	866-636-6342				
•	•	•	•	•	Attorney's Aid Inc of Sacramento [SOP]	888-443-3915	•	•		•
•	•	•	•	•	Attorney's Diversified Services-Santa Rosa [SOP]	800-473-5455	•	•	•	•
•	•	•	•		Timothy & Sara Baxter	415-333-5402				
•	•	•			Maggie M & Associates	707-778-7304	•	•	•	
		•	•		Norcal Public Records Service	800-252-0910	•	•	•	
•	•	•	•	•	One Legal [SOP]	800-938-8815	•	•	•	•
•	•	•		•	Pacific Corporate & Title Services (Sacramento)	800-230-4988	•	•	•	•
•	•	•		•	Quest Discovery Service [SOP]	408-441-7000	•	•	•	•
		•	•	•	SRS Private Inv Inc [SOP]	707-537-1091	•	•	•	•
•	•	•	•	•	The Amherst Group	800-521-0237	•	•	•	•
•	•	•		•	Title Court Service	510-763-0975	•	•	•	•
	•	•	•		Total Access	559-325-1169	•		•	•
•	•	•	•	•	Western Attorney Services	415-487-4140				

DT	BK	CV	CR	PR	←Courts **Stanislaus**	Recording→	UC	RE	TX	VS
•	•	•	•	•	Action Legal Support Services [SOP]	559-432-3337				
		•	•	•	AD Services (ADS) [SOP]	800-827-9101		•	•	•
•	•	•	•	•	Attorney Service of Merced [SOP]	209-383-3233	•	•	•	•
•	•	•	•	•	Attorney's Aid Inc of Sacramento [SOP]	888-443-3915	•	•		•
•	•	•	•	•	Attorney's Diversified Services-Modesto [SOP]	800-473-0273	•	•	•	•
•	•	•	•	•	Cal Search	858-488-7572	•		•	•
	•	•	•		Central Valley Records Service Inc	209-524-3849	•		•	•
•	•	•	•	•	Court Record Consultants [SOP]	818-366-1906	•	•	•	
		•	•		M L Cozart Copy Service (dba: Quality Business Information)	916-691-9685				
•	•	•	•	•	One Legal [SOP]	800-938-8815	•	•	•	•
•	•	•		•	Pacific Corporate & Title Services (Sacramento)	800-230-4988	•	•	•	•
•	•	•		•	Quest Discovery Service [SOP]	408-441-7000	•	•	•	•
•	•	•	•	•	Rapid Document Service	209-745-0999	•	•	•	•
•	•	•		•	Title Court Service	510-763-0975	•	•	•	•

DT	BK	CV	CR	PR	←Courts **Sutter**	Recording→	UC	RE	TX	VS
		•	•	•	A.D.I. Investigative [SOP]	530-743-4245		•	•	•
•	•	•	•	•	Attorney's Aid Inc of Sacramento [SOP]	888-443-3915	•	•		•
•	•	•	•	•	Attorney's Diversified Services-Sacramento [SOP]	800-266-4624	•	•	•	•
•	•	•	•	•	C & S Research	530-415-3161	•	•	•	•
		•	•	•	Nina N Cooper	707-428-5712	•		•	•
•	•	•	•	•	Legalese [SOP]	916-453-2860	•	•	•	•
•	•	•		•	Quest Discovery Service [SOP]	408-441-7000	•	•	•	•
•	•	•	•	•	Rapid Document Service	209-745-0999	•	•	•	•
•	•	•	•	•	Seyfried Support Services	916-359-5275	•	•	•	•
		•	•		The Legal Source Attorney Services	800-786-8163				
•	•	•		•	Title Court Service	510-763-0975	•	•	•	•
•	•	•	•	•	William Olmsted Inv	916-484-6465	•	•	•	•

DT	BK	CV	CR	PR	←Courts **Tehama**	Recording→	UC	RE	TX	VS
•	•	•	•	•	Attorney's Diversified Services-Redding [SOP]	800-473-1228	•	•	•	•

DT	BK	CV	CR	PR	Name	Phone	UC	RE	TX	VS
•	•	•	•		Business Connections [SOP]	530-527-6262	•		•	•
•	•	•	•	•	C & S Research	530-415-3161	•	•	•	•
		•	•		Carmona & Associates [SOP]	530-246-1010	•	•	•	•
•	•	•	•		DLS Background Services Inc	951-301-8584	•		•	
		•	•		Nor-Cal Court Research	530-865-3525				
•	•	•		•	Quest Discovery Service [SOP]	408-441-7000	•	•	•	•
		•	•		The Legal Source Attorney Services	800-786-8163				
•	•	•		•	Title Court Service	510-763-0975	•	•	•	•

DT	BK	CV	CR	PR	←COURTS TRINITY	RECORDING→	UC	RE	TX	VS
•	•	•	•	•	Attorney's Diversified Services-Redding [SOP]	800-473-1228	•	•	•	•
•	•	•		•	Quest Discovery Service [SOP]	408-441-7000	•	•	•	•
•	•	•		•	Title Court Service	510-763-0975	•	•	•	•

DT	BK	CV	CR	PR	←COURTS TULARE	RECORDING→	UC	RE	TX	VS
•	•	•	•	•	Action Legal Support Services [SOP]	559-432-3337				
•	•	•	•	•	Attorney's Diversified Services-Fresno [SOP]	800-842-2695	•	•	•	•
			•		California Backgrounds	559-274-9784				
•	•	•	•		DLS Background Services Inc	951-301-8584	•		•	
			•		InVision Research	559-432-3053				
•	•	•	•		Keppler Legal Research	559-431-1358				
		•	•		Mike Moore Inv [SOP]	559-636-1057	•	•	•	•
•	•	•	•	•	One Legal [SOP]	800-938-8815	•	•	•	•
		•	•	•	Marilyn Peterson [SOP]	800-401-5356	•	•	•	•
•	•	•		•	Quest Discovery Service [SOP]	408-441-7000	•	•	•	•
•	•	•		•	Title Court Service	510-763-0975	•	•	•	•
	•	•	•		Total Access	559-325-1169	•		•	•
•	•	•	•	•	Vio-Com-Data Research	559-438-1058	•	•	•	•

DT	BK	CV	CR	PR	←COURTS TUOLUMNE	RECORDING→	UC	RE	TX	VS
•	•	•	•	•	Attorney's Diversified Services-Modesto [SOP]	800-473-0273	•	•	•	•
•	•	•	•		DLS Background Services Inc	951-301-8584	•		•	
•	•	•		•	Quest Discovery Service [SOP]	408-441-7000	•	•	•	•
•	•	•		•	Title Court Service	510-763-0975	•	•	•	•

DT	BK	CV	CR	PR	←COURTS VENTURA	RECORDING→	UC	RE	TX	VS
•		•	•		A-1 Unisource Screening & Information	800-525-6972				
•		•	•	•	AAABackgroundchex.com - Eleda Luther	661-250-8254		•		
•	•	•	•	•	Abstrax	805-965-9858	•	•	•	•
•	•	•	•	•	Access Research	800-456-9613	•		•	•
•	•	•	•		Accurate Background Inc	800-784-3911	•		•	
•	•	•	•	•	Accurate Source.com Inc [SOP]	800-978-8950	•	•	•	•
			•		Alpha Information Inc	800-900-1471				
•	•	•	•	•	Alternative Investigative & Attorney Services [SOP]	888-457-1314	•	•	•	•
•	•	•	•	•	APSCREEN Inc	800-277-2733	•	•	•	•
•		•	•		Atlas Research Services Inc	818-362-0140				
•	•	•	•	•	Attorney's Diversified Services-Ventura [SOP]	800-933-8014	•	•	•	•
		•	•		Todd Boehr	805-452-7579				
•	•	•	•		Bonafide Research Services	818-349-3955	•		•	•
•	•	•	•	•	Cal Search	858-488-7572	•		•	•
•	•	•	•	•	Collective Intelligence Inc	800-436-1969				•
	•	•	•	•	Commercial Process Serving Inc [SOP]	800-382-0088				
•	•	•	•	•	Court Record Consultants [SOP]	818-366-1906	•	•	•	
•	•	•	•	•	CourtCheckers [SOP]	805-898-7084	•	•	•	•
		•	•		Crutchfield & Associates [SOP]	818-349-4836	•	•	•	
•	•	•	•	•	Daily Journal Corporation	800-952-5232	•	•		•
					Dr Dave's Docs	818-246-3087		•		
•	•	•	•	•	Executive Attorney Service Inc [SOP]	213-482-6680				
•	•	•	•	•	First Investigative Consultants, PI# 6949 [SOP]	800-900-4342	•	•	•	•
		•	•		General Services [SOP]	310-859-1122				

DT	BK	CV	CR	PR	Name	Phone	UC	RE	TX	VS
			•		InVision Research	559-432-3053				
•	•	•	•	•	Kern Attorney Service Inc [SOP]	213-483-4900		•	•	•
					Los Angeles County Document Services Inc	818-241-1990		•	•	
•	•	•	•		Metropolis Group	818-240-1332				
•	•	•	•	•	One Legal [SOP]	800-938-8815	•	•	•	•
•	•	•	•	•	Process Service Network [SOP]	800-417-7623		•	•	•
•	•	•		•	Quest Discovery Service [SOP]	408-441-7000	•	•	•	•
•	•	•	•	•	RJI Services Inc [SOP]	800-344-4754	•	•	•	•
•	•	•	•	•	Southern California Strategic Research	323-257-4472	•	•	•	•
•	•	•	•	•	The Amherst Group	800-521-0237	•	•	•	•
•	•	•		•	Title Court Service	510-763-0975	•	•	•	•
	•				Title Runners	805-569-6939	•	•	•	•
•	•	•	•	•	Universal Information Research [SOP]	800-363-9813	•	•		•
•	•	•	•	•	Vio-Com-Data Research	559-438-1058	•	•	•	•

Yolo

DT	BK	CV	CR	PR	←Courts — Yolo — Recording→		UC	RE	TX	VS
•	•	•	•	•	Abess/Cyberdix [SOP]	877-594-0498	•		•	•
•	•	•	•	•	Attorney's Aid Inc of Sacramento [SOP]	888-443-3915	•	•		•
•	•	•	•	•	Attorney's Diversified Services-Sacramento [SOP]	800-266-4624	•	•	•	•
•	•	•	•	•	C & S Research	530-415-3161	•	•	•	•
		•	•	•	Nina N Cooper	707-428-5712	•		•	•
			•		InVision Research	559-432-3053				
•	•	•	•	•	Legalese [SOP]	916-453-2860	•	•	•	•
		•	•		M L Cozart Copy Service (dba: Quality Business Information)	916-691-9685				
					Nisonger Abstracting Services	916-965-6544	•	•	•	
•	•	•	•	•	One Legal [SOP]	800-938-8815	•	•	•	•
•	•	•		•	Pacific Corporate & Title Services (Sacramento)	800-230-4988	•	•	•	•
•	•	•	•		Quality Business Information	916-684-0444		•	•	•
•	•	•		•	Quest Discovery Service [SOP]	408-441-7000	•	•	•	•
•	•	•	•	•	Rapid Document Service	209-745-0999	•	•	•	•
•					Reliable Document Retrieval Inc	916-438-3000				
•	•	•	•	•	Seyfried Support Services	916-359-5275	•	•	•	•
	•	•	•		Parri Shebley [SOP]	707-448-5018				•
•	•	•		•	Title Court Service	510-763-0975	•	•	•	•
•	•	•	•	•	United Attorneys' Services	916-457-3000	•	•	•	•
•	•	•	•	•	William Olmsted Inv	916-484-6465	•	•	•	•

Yuba

DT	BK	CV	CR	PR	←Courts — Yuba — Recording→		UC	RE	TX	VS
		•	•	•	A.D.I. Investigative [SOP]	530-743-4245		•	•	•
•	•	•	•	•	Abess/Cyberdix [SOP]	877-594-0498	•		•	•
•	•	•	•	•	Attorney's Diversified Services-Sacramento [SOP]	800-266-4624	•	•	•	•
•	•	•	•	•	C & S Research	530-415-3161	•	•	•	•
		•	•	•	Nina N Cooper	707-428-5712	•		•	•
•	•	•	•	•	Legalese [SOP]	916-453-2860	•	•	•	•
•	•	•		•	Quest Discovery Service [SOP]	408-441-7000	•	•	•	•
•	•	•	•	•	Seyfried Support Services	916-359-5275	•	•	•	•
		•	•		The Legal Source Attorney Services	800-786-8163				
•	•	•		•	Title Court Service	510-763-0975	•	•	•	•
•	•	•	•	•	William Olmsted Inv	916-484-6465	•	•	•	•

Colorado

Court Records Retrieved							Recording Records Retrieved			
DT	BK	CV	CR	PR	←Courts **Adams**	Recording→	UC	RE	TX	VS
•	•	•	•	•	AAA Process Servers Inc	800-293-6098	•	•		
•	•	•	•		ABA Services	720-344-1259	•	•	•	
•	•	•	•	•	Business Maven LLC	303-725-2668	•	•	•	•
•	•	•	•	•	Centennial Coverages Inc (Colorado)	800-338-8221	•	•	•	•
•	•	•	•	•	Colorado Records Search Inc [SOP]	800-645-7712	•	•	•	•
•	•	•			Colorado Records Sooner	303-494-2132	•	•	•	•
•	•	•	•	•	Condello Associates, Accusearch [SOP]	888-756-9687	•	•	•	•
•	•	•	•	•	Court Process Service & Investigations [SOP]	800-898-8662	•	•	•	•
•	•	•	•	•	DIG Research Inc	720-941-9959	•	•	•	•
					Documents 5280	303-438-8967	•	•	•	
•	•	•	•	•	FOX Investigations, Research & Legal Services [SOP]	877-369-3698	•	•	•	•
•	•	•	•	•	Franklin Investigations LLC	720-371-0212	•	•	•	•
•	•	•	•	•	Barbara K Henritze	303-499-3750	•	•	•	•
•	•	•	•	•	Independent Research LLC	303-969-8608	•	•	•	•
•	•	•	•	•	Peregrine Investigation & Research [SOP]	303-324-7442	•	•	•	•
•	•	•	•	•	R A Heales & Associates Ltd	800-225-7043	•	•	•	•
					Records Quest	303-369-0693	•	•	•	•
•		•	•		RIQ and Associates Inc	720-529-5736	•	•	•	•
•	•	•	•	•	Search Company International [SOP]	800-727-2120	•	•	•	
•	•	•	•	•	Snoop For You	303-985-5521	•	•	•	•
•	•	•	•	•	The Paper Chase - CO [SOP]	970-350-1008	•	•	•	•
					Title Company of Denver	303-369-5443		•	•	
•	•	•		•	Zook Search Inc	303-292-5138	•	•	•	

DT	BK	CV	CR	PR	←Courts **Alamosa**	Recording→	UC	RE	TX	VS
•	•	•	•	•	Independent Research LLC	303-969-8608	•	•	•	•

DT	BK	CV	CR	PR	←Courts **Arapahoe**	Recording→	UC	RE	TX	VS
					A Total Search Solution	303-738-9955	•	•	•	
•	•	•	•	•	AAA Process Servers Inc	800-293-6098	•	•		
•	•	•	•		ABA Services	720-344-1259	•	•	•	
•	•	•	•	•	Access Information	800-827-7607	•	•	•	•
•	•	•	•	•	Centennial Coverages Inc (Colorado)	800-338-8221	•	•	•	•
•	•	•	•	•	Colorado Records Search Inc [SOP]	800-645-7712	•	•	•	•
•	•	•			Colorado Records Sooner	303-494-2132	•	•	•	•
•	•	•	•	•	Condello Associates, Accusearch [SOP]	888-756-9687	•	•	•	•
•	•	•	•	•	Court Process Service & Document Retrieval [SOP]	800-898-8662	•	•	•	•
•	•	•	•	•	DIG Research Inc	720-941-9959	•	•	•	•
					Documents 5280	303-438-8967	•	•	•	
•	•	•	•	•	FOX Investigations, Research & Legal Services [SOP]	877-369-3698	•	•	•	•
•	•	•	•	•	Franklin Investigations LLC	720-371-0212	•	•	•	•
•	•	•	•	•	Independent Research LLC	303-969-8608	•	•	•	•
					Paragon Property Services	866-697-6156	•	•	•	
•	•	•	•	•	Peregrine Investigation & Research [SOP]	303-324-7442	•	•	•	•
•	•	•	•	•	R A Heales & Associates Ltd	800-225-7043	•	•	•	•
					Records Quest	303-369-0693	•	•	•	•
•		•	•		RIQ and Associates Inc	720-529-5736	•	•	•	•
•	•	•	•	•	Search Company International [SOP]	800-727-2120	•	•	•	
•	•	•	•	•	Snoop For You	303-985-5521	•	•	•	•

DT	BK	CV	CR	PR	Name	Phone	UC	RE	TX	VS
					Title Company of Denver	303-369-5443		•	•	
•	•	•		•	Zook Search Inc	303-292-5138	•	•	•	

DT	BK	CV	CR	PR	←Courts ARCHULETA Recording→		UC	RE	TX	VS
		•	•		Attorney Service New Mexico [SOP]	505-326-7486				
•	•	•	•	•	Colorado Records Search Inc [SOP]	800-645-7712	•	•	•	•
•		•	•	•	Finney Land Co	970-259-5691	•	•	•	•
				•	Great Divide Title	970-731-7700	•	•	•	
•	•	•	•	•	Independent Research LLC	303-969-8608	•	•	•	•

DT	BK	CV	CR	PR	←Courts BACA Recording→		UC	RE	TX	VS
•	•	•	•	•	Colorado Records Search Inc [SOP]	800-645-7712	•	•	•	•
•	•	•	•	•	Independent Research LLC	303-969-8608	•	•	•	•

DT	BK	CV	CR	PR	←Courts BENT Recording→		UC	RE	TX	VS
					Bent County Abstract & Title	719-456-0381		•		
				•	Guaranty Abstract Co (Colorado)	719-336-3261	•	•	•	
•	•	•	•	•	Independent Research LLC	303-969-8608	•	•	•	•

DT	BK	CV	CR	PR	←Courts BOULDER Recording→		UC	RE	TX	VS
•	•	•	•	•	A Judicial Process Inc [SOP]	800-317-9221	•	•	•	•
•	•	•	•	•	AAA Process Servers Inc	800-293-6098	•	•		
•	•	•	•		ABA Services	720-344-1259	•	•	•	
•	•	•	•	•	Access Information	800-827-7607	•	•	•	•
•	•	•	•	•	Alpha-Omega Investigations [SOP]	866-510-8200	•	•	•	•
•		•	•		Background Information Services	303-442-3960	•			
•	•	•	•	•	Business Maven LLC	303-725-2668	•	•	•	•
•	•	•	•	•	Centennial Coverages Inc (Colorado)	800-338-8221	•	•	•	•
•	•	•	•	•	Colorado Records Search Inc [SOP]	800-645-7712	•	•	•	•
•	•	•			Colorado Records Sooner	303-494-2132	•	•	•	•
•	•	•	•	•	Condello Associates, Accusearch [SOP]	888-756-9687	•	•	•	•
•	•	•	•	•	Court Process Service & Investigations [SOP]	800-898-8662	•	•	•	•
					Documents 5280	303-438-8967	•	•	•	
•	•	•	•	•	FOX Investigations, Research & Legal Services [SOP]	877-369-3698	•	•	•	•
•	•	•	•	•	Barbara K Henritze	303-499-3750	•	•	•	•
•	•	•	•	•	Independent Research LLC	303-969-8608	•	•	•	•
					Paragon Property Services	866-697-6156	•	•	•	
•	•	•	•	•	Peregrine Investigation & Research [SOP]	303-324-7442	•	•	•	•
•	•	•	•	•	R A Heales & Associates Ltd	800-225-7043	•	•	•	•
					Records Quest	303-369-0693	•	•	•	•
•		•	•		RIQ and Associates Inc	720-529-5736	•	•	•	•
•	•	•	•	•	Search Company International [SOP]	800-727-2120	•	•	•	
•	•	•	•	•	Snoop For You	303-985-5521	•	•	•	•
•	•	•	•	•	The Paper Chase - CO [SOP]	970-350-1008	•	•	•	•
					Title Company of Denver	303-369-5443		•	•	
•	•	•		•	Zook Search Inc	303-292-5138	•	•	•	

DT	BK	CV	CR	PR	←Courts BROOMFIELD Recording→		UC	RE	TX	VS
•	•	•	•	•	Access Information	800-827-7607	•	•	•	•
•	•	•	•	•	Business Maven LLC	303-725-2668	•	•	•	•
•	•	•	•	•	Colorado Records Search Inc [SOP]	800-645-7712	•	•	•	•
•	•	•			Colorado Records Sooner	303-494-2132	•	•	•	•
•	•	•	•	•	Condello Associates, Accusearch [SOP]	888-756-9687	•	•	•	•
•	•	•	•	•	DIG Research Inc	720-941-9959	•	•	•	•
					Documents 5280	303-438-8967	•	•	•	
•	•	•	•	•	FOX Investigations, Research & Legal Services [SOP]	877-369-3698	•	•	•	•
•	•	•	•	•	Barbara K Henritze	303-499-3750	•	•	•	•
•	•	•	•	•	Independent Research LLC	303-969-8608	•	•	•	•
					Records Quest	303-369-0693	•	•	•	•
•		•	•		RIQ and Associates Inc	720-529-5736	•	•	•	•

DT	BK	CV	CR	PR	Courts / Recording	Phone	UC	RE	TX	VS
•	•	•	•	•	Search Company International [SOP]	800-727-2120	•	•	•	
					Title Company of Denver	303-369-5443		•	•	

DT	BK	CV	CR	PR	←COURTS CHAFFEE RECORDING→		UC	RE	TX	VS
					Chaffee Title-Abstract Co	719-539-2215	•	•	•	
•	•	•	•	•	Court Process Service & Investigations [SOP]	800-898-8662	•	•	•	•
					Credit Bureau of Connecticut Inc	800-922-0002		•	•	
•	•	•	•	•	Independent Research LLC	303-969-8608	•	•	•	•

DT	BK	CV	CR	PR	←COURTS CHEYENNE RECORDING→		UC	RE	TX	VS
				•	Cheyenne County Abstract Co	719-767-5585	•	•	•	
•	•	•	•	•	Colorado Records Search Inc [SOP]	800-645-7712	•	•	•	•
•	•	•	•	•	Independent Research LLC	303-969-8608	•	•	•	•

DT	BK	CV	CR	PR	←COURTS CLEAR CREEK RECORDING→		UC	RE	TX	VS
				•	Clear Creek-Gelpin Abstract & Title Corp	303-569-2391		•		
•	•	•	•	•	Colorado Records Search Inc [SOP]	800-645-7712	•	•	•	•
•	•	•	•	•	Court Process Service & Investigations [SOP]	800-898-8662	•	•	•	•
					Documents 5280	303-438-8967	•	•	•	
•	•	•	•	•	Independent Research LLC	303-969-8608	•	•	•	•
		•	•		McCormick Detective Agency [SOP]	970-453-6378	•	•	•	
•		•	•		RIQ and Associates Inc	720-529-5736	•	•	•	•
•	•	•	•	•	Snoop For You	303-985-5521	•	•	•	•

DT	BK	CV	CR	PR	←COURTS CONEJOS RECORDING→		UC	RE	TX	VS
•	•	•	•	•	Independent Research LLC	303-969-8608	•	•	•	•

DT	BK	CV	CR	PR	←COURTS COSTILLA RECORDING→		UC	RE	TX	VS
•	•	•	•	•	Independent Research LLC	303-969-8608	•	•	•	•

DT	BK	CV	CR	PR	←COURTS CROWLEY RECORDING→		UC	RE	TX	VS
•	•	•	•	•	Independent Research LLC	303-969-8608	•	•	•	•

DT	BK	CV	CR	PR	←COURTS CUSTER RECORDING→		UC	RE	TX	VS
•	•	•	•	•	Independent Research LLC	303-969-8608	•	•	•	•
					Security Title Canon City	800-526-7805		•		•

DT	BK	CV	CR	PR	←COURTS DELTA RECORDING→		UC	RE	TX	VS
•	•	•	•	•	Colorado Records Search Inc [SOP]	800-645-7712	•	•	•	•
					Comparable Sales Research	970-249-2118	•	•	•	
					First American Title Co (Colorado)	970-874-8286	•	•	•	
		•	•	•	Grand Valley Associates [SOP]	970-256-9300	•	•	•	
•	•	•	•	•	Independent Research LLC	303-969-8608	•	•	•	•
•	•	•	•	•	Search Company International [SOP]	800-727-2120	•	•	•	

DT	BK	CV	CR	PR	←COURTS DENVER RECORDING→		UC	RE	TX	VS
•	•	•	•	•	A Judicial Process Inc [SOP]	800-317-9221	•	•	•	•
					A Total Search Solution	303-738-9955	•	•	•	
•	•	•	•	•	AAA Process Servers Inc	800-293-6098	•	•		
•	•	•	•		ABA Services	720-344-1259	•	•	•	
•	•	•	•	•	Access Information	800-827-7607	•	•	•	•
•	•	•	•	•	Business Maven LLC	303-725-2668	•	•	•	•
•	•	•	•	•	Centennial Coverages Inc (Colorado)	800-338-8221	•	•	•	•
•	•	•	•	•	Colorado Records Search Inc [SOP]	800-645-7712	•	•	•	•
•	•	•			Colorado Records Sooner	303-494-2132	•	•	•	•
•	•	•	•	•	Condello Associates, Accusearch [SOP]	888-756-9687	•	•	•	•
•	•	•	•	•	Court Process Service & Document Retrieval [SOP]	800-898-8662	•	•	•	•
•		•	•	•	Kathleen Demmitt	303-781-0605				•
•	•	•	•	•	DIG Research Inc	720-941-9959	•	•	•	•
					Documents 5280	303-438-8967	•	•	•	
•	•	•	•	•	FOX Investigations, Research & Legal Services [SOP]	877-369-3698	•	•	•	•

DT	BK	CV	CR	PR	Courts / Recording	Phone	UC	RE	TX	VS
•	•	•	•	•	Franklin Investigations LLC	720-371-0212	•	•	•	•
•	•	•	•	•	Barbara K Henritze	303-499-3750	•	•	•	•
			•		HR Plus	800-332-7587				
•	•	•	•	•	Independent Research LLC	303-969-8608	•	•	•	•
	•				NACM/Colorado	800-451-7868	•			
					Paragon Property Services	866-697-6156	•	•	•	
•	•	•	•	•	Peregrine Investigation & Research [SOP]	303-324-7442	•	•	•	•
•	•	•	•	•	R A Heales & Associates Ltd	800-225-7043	•	•	•	•
					Records Quest	303-369-0693	•	•	•	•
•		•	•		RIQ and Associates Inc	720-529-5736	•	•	•	•
•	•	•	•	•	Search Company International [SOP]	800-727-2120	•	•	•	
•	•	•	•	•	Snoop For You	303-985-5521	•	•	•	•
					Title Company of Denver	303-369-5443		•	•	
•	•	•		•	Zook Search Inc	303-292-5138	•	•	•	

DT	BK	CV	CR	PR	←Courts **Dolores** Recording→	Phone	UC	RE	TX	VS
•	•	•	•	•	Independent Research LLC	303-969-8608	•	•	•	•
					Montezuma-Dolores Title Co	970-565-8491	•	•	•	

DT	BK	CV	CR	PR	←Courts **Douglas** Recording→	Phone	UC	RE	TX	VS
					A Total Search Solution	303-738-9955	•	•	•	
•	•	•	•	•	AAA Process Servers Inc	800-293-6098	•	•		
•	•	•	•		ABA Services	720-344-1259	•	•	•	
•	•	•	•	•	Access Information	800-827-7607	•	•	•	•
•	•	•	•	•	Centennial Coverages Inc (Colorado)	800-338-8221	•	•	•	•
•	•	•	•	•	Colorado Records Search Inc [SOP]	800-645-7712	•	•	•	•
•	•	•			Colorado Records Sooner	303-494-2132	•	•	•	•
•	•	•	•	•	Court Process Service & Investigations [SOP]	800-898-8662	•	•	•	•
•	•	•	•	•	DIG Research Inc	720-941-9959	•	•	•	•
					Documents 5280	303-438-8967	•	•	•	
•	•	•	•	•	FOX Investigations, Research & Legal Services [SOP]	877-369-3698	•	•	•	•
•	•	•	•	•	Franklin Investigations LLC	720-371-0212	•	•	•	•
•	•	•	•	•	Independent Research LLC	303-969-8608	•	•	•	•
					Paragon Property Services	866-697-6156	•	•	•	
•	•	•	•	•	Peregrine Investigation & Research [SOP]	303-324-7442	•	•	•	•
•	•	•	•	•	R A Heales & Associates Ltd	800-225-7043	•	•	•	•
					Records Quest	303-369-0693	•	•	•	•
•		•	•		RIQ and Associates Inc	720-529-5736	•	•	•	•
•	•	•	•	•	Search Company International [SOP]	800-727-2120	•	•	•	
•	•	•	•	•	Snoop For You	303-985-5521	•	•	•	•
					Title Company of Denver	303-369-5443		•	•	

DT	BK	CV	CR	PR	←Courts **Eagle** Recording→	Phone	UC	RE	TX	VS
•	•	•	•	•	Colorado Records Search Inc [SOP]	800-645-7712	•	•	•	•
•	•	•	•	•	Court Process Service & Investigations [SOP]	800-898-8662	•	•	•	•
•	•	•	•	•	Independent Research LLC	303-969-8608	•	•	•	•
•	•	•	•	•	Research Specialists & Investigators [SOP]	970-331-7712	•	•	•	•
•	•	•	•	•	Search Company International [SOP]	800-727-2120	•	•	•	

DT	BK	CV	CR	PR	←Courts **El Paso** Recording→	Phone	UC	RE	TX	VS
•	•	•	•	•	AAA Process Servers Inc	800-293-6098	•	•		
		•	•	•	Broadmoor Research Consultants [SOP]	719-205-1177	•	•	•	•
•	•	•	•	•	Centennial Coverages Inc (Colorado)	800-338-8221	•	•	•	•
•	•	•	•	•	Colorado Records Search Inc [SOP]	800-645-7712	•	•	•	•
•	•	•			Colorado Records Sooner	303-494-2132	•	•	•	•
•	•	•	•	•	Court Process Service & Document Retrieval [SOP]	800-898-8662	•	•	•	•
					Documents 5280	303-438-8967	•	•	•	
•	•	•	•	•	Independent Research LLC	303-969-8608	•	•	•	•
		•	•	•	Legal Express [SOP]	719-578-0407		•	•	•
		•	•	•	PreSearch Background Services	719-533-1880	•	•	•	

DT	BK	CV	CR	PR	←Courts	Recording→	UC	RE	TX	VS
•	•	•	•	•	R A Heales & Associates Ltd	800-225-7043	•	•	•	•
					Records Quest	303-369-0693	•	•	•	•
•		•	•		RIQ and Associates Inc	720-529-5736	•	•	•	•
•	•	•	•	•	Search Company International [SOP]	800-727-2120	•	•	•	
					Title Company of Denver	303-369-5443		•	•	

DT	BK	CV	CR	PR	←Courts **ELBERT**	Recording→	UC	RE	TX	VS
•	•	•	•		ABA Services	720-344-1259	•	•	•	
•	•	•	•	•	Centennial Coverages Inc (Colorado)	800-338-8221	•	•	•	•
•	•	•	•	•	Colorado Records Search Inc [SOP]	800-645-7712	•	•	•	•
					Documents 5280	303-438-8967	•	•	•	
•	•	•	•	•	Independent Research LLC	303-969-8608	•	•	•	•
•		•	•		RIQ and Associates Inc	720-529-5736	•	•	•	•
•	•	•	•	•	Search Company International [SOP]	800-727-2120	•	•	•	
					Title Company of Denver	303-369-5443		•	•	

DT	BK	CV	CR	PR	←Courts **FREMONT**	Recording→	UC	RE	TX	VS
		•	•	•	Broadmoor Research Consultants [SOP]	719-205-1177	•	•	•	•
•	•	•	•	•	Colorado Records Search Inc [SOP]	800-645-7712	•	•	•	•
•	•	•	•	•	Independent Research LLC	303-969-8608	•	•	•	•
•		•	•		RIQ and Associates Inc	720-529-5736	•	•	•	•
•	•	•	•	•	Search Company International [SOP]	800-727-2120	•	•	•	
					Security Title Canon City	800-526-7805		•		•

DT	BK	CV	CR	PR	←Courts **GARFIELD**	Recording→	UC	RE	TX	VS
•	•	•	•	•	Colorado Records Search Inc [SOP]	800-645-7712	•	•	•	•
		•	•	•	Grand Valley Associates [SOP]	970-256-9300	•	•	•	
•	•	•	•	•	Independent Research LLC	303-969-8608	•	•	•	•
•	•	•	•	•	Search Company International [SOP]	800-727-2120	•	•	•	

DT	BK	CV	CR	PR	←Courts **GILPIN**	Recording→	UC	RE	TX	VS
				•	Clear Creek-Gelpin Abstract & Title Corp	303-569-2391		•		
•	•	•	•	•	Colorado Records Search Inc [SOP]	800-645-7712	•	•	•	•
					Documents 5280	303-438-8967	•	•	•	
•	•	•	•	•	Independent Research LLC	303-969-8608	•	•	•	•
•		•	•		RIQ and Associates Inc	720-529-5736	•	•	•	•

DT	BK	CV	CR	PR	←Courts **GRAND**	Recording→	UC	RE	TX	VS
•	•	•			Colorado Records Sooner	303-494-2132	•	•	•	•
•	•	•	•	•	Independent Research LLC	303-969-8608	•	•	•	•

DT	BK	CV	CR	PR	←Courts **GUNNISON**	Recording→	UC	RE	TX	VS
•	•	•	•	•	Colorado Records Search Inc [SOP]	800-645-7712	•	•	•	•
•	•	•	•	•	Court Process Service & Investigations [SOP]	800-898-8662	•	•	•	•
					First Gunnison Title & Escrow	800-530-9598		•	•	
•	•	•	•	•	Independent Research LLC	303-969-8608	•	•	•	•

DT	BK	CV	CR	PR	←Courts **HINSDALE**	Recording→	UC	RE	TX	VS
					First Gunnison Title & Escrow	800-530-9598		•	•	
				•	Hinsdale Title Co	970-944-2614		•	•	
•	•	•	•	•	Independent Research LLC	303-969-8608	•	•	•	•

DT	BK	CV	CR	PR	←Courts **HUERFANO**	Recording→	UC	RE	TX	VS
					Dotter Abstract & Associates	719-738-1730	•	•	•	•
•	•	•	•	•	Independent Research LLC	303-969-8608	•	•	•	•

DT	BK	CV	CR	PR	←Courts **JACKSON**	Recording→	UC	RE	TX	VS
•	•	•	•	•	Independent Research LLC	303-969-8608	•	•	•	•

DT	BK	CV	CR	PR	←Courts **JEFFERSON**	Recording→	UC	RE	TX	VS
					A Total Search Solution	303-738-9955	•	•	•	
•	•	•	•	•	AAA Process Servers Inc	800-293-6098	•	•		

DT	BK	CV	CR	PR	←Courts	Recording→	UC	RE	TX	VS
•	•	•	•		ABA Services	720-344-1259	•	•	•	
•	•	•	•	•	Access Information	800-827-7607	•	•	•	•
•	•	•	•	•	Business Maven LLC	303-725-2668	•	•	•	•
•	•	•	•	•	Centennial Coverages Inc (Colorado)	800-338-8221	•	•	•	•
•	•	•	•	•	Colorado Records Search Inc [SOP]	800-645-7712	•	•	•	•
•	•	•			Colorado Records Sooner	303-494-2132	•	•	•	•
•	•	•	•	•	Condello Associates, Accusearch [SOP]	888-756-9687	•	•	•	•
•	•	•	•	•	Court Process Service & Investigations [SOP]	800-898-8662	•	•	•	•
•	•	•	•	•	DIG Research Inc	720-941-9959	•	•	•	•
					Documents 5280	303-438-8967	•	•	•	
•	•	•	•	•	FOX Investigations, Research & Legal Services [SOP]	877-369-3698	•	•	•	•
•	•	•	•	•	Franklin Investigations LLC	720-371-0212	•	•	•	•
•	•	•	•	•	Barbara K Henritze	303-499-3750	•	•	•	•
•	•	•	•	•	Independent Research LLC	303-969-8608	•	•	•	•
					Paragon Property Services	866-697-6156	•	•	•	
•	•	•	•	•	Peregrine Investigation & Research [SOP]	303-324-7442	•	•	•	•
•	•	•	•	•	R A Heales & Associates Ltd	800-225-7043	•	•	•	•
					Records Quest	303-369-0693	•	•	•	•
•		•	•		RIQ and Associates Inc	720-529-5736	•	•	•	•
•	•	•	•	•	Search Company International [SOP]	800-727-2120	•	•	•	
•	•	•	•	•	Snoop For You	303-985-5521	•	•	•	•
					Title Company of Denver	303-369-5443		•	•	
•	•	•		•	Zook Search Inc	303-292-5138	•	•	•	

DT	BK	CV	CR	PR	←Courts	**Kiowa**	Recording→	UC	RE	TX	VS
•	•	•	•	•	Independent Research LLC		303-969-8608	•	•	•	•
					Kiowa County Abstract Co		719-438-5811	•	•	•	

DT	BK	CV	CR	PR	←Courts	**Kit Carson**	Recording→	UC	RE	TX	VS
•	•	•	•	•	Independent Research LLC		303-969-8608	•	•	•	•

DT	BK	CV	CR	PR	←Courts	**La Plata**	Recording→	UC	RE	TX	VS
		•	•		Attorney Service New Mexico [SOP]		505-326-7486				
•	•	•	•	•	Colorado Records Search Inc [SOP]		800-645-7712	•	•	•	•
•		•	•	•	Finney Land Co		970-259-5691	•	•	•	•
•	•	•	•	•	Independent Research LLC		303-969-8608	•	•	•	•
					Information Services (Colorado)		877-385-4897	•	•	•	•

DT	BK	CV	CR	PR	←Courts	**Lake**	Recording→	UC	RE	TX	VS
•	•	•	•	•	Court Process Service & Investigations [SOP]		800-898-8662	•	•	•	•
•	•	•	•	•	Independent Research LLC		303-969-8608	•	•	•	•
				•	Lake County Abstract Co		719-486-2688	•	•	•	•
		•	•		McCormick Detective Agency [SOP]		970-453-6378	•	•	•	

DT	BK	CV	CR	PR	←Courts	**Larimer**	Recording→	UC	RE	TX	VS
•	•	•	•	•	Alpha-Omega Investigations [SOP]		866-510-8200	•	•	•	•
•	•	•	•	•	Centennial Coverages Inc (Colorado)		800-338-8221	•	•	•	•
•	•	•	•	•	Colorado Records Search Inc [SOP]		800-645-7712	•	•	•	•
•	•	•			Colorado Records Sooner		303-494-2132	•	•	•	•
•	•	•	•	•	Condello Associates, Accusearch [SOP]		888-756-9687	•	•	•	•
					Documents 5280		303-438-8967	•	•	•	
			•		HR Plus		800-332-7587				
•	•	•	•	•	Independent Research LLC		303-969-8608	•	•	•	•
•	•	•		•	Daniel E Peel		970-484-1542	•	•	•	
					Records Quest		303-369-0693	•	•	•	•
		•			Research & Revisions Etc		970-484-0176		•	•	
•		•	•		RIQ and Associates Inc		720-529-5736	•	•	•	•
•	•	•	•	•	Search Company International [SOP]		800-727-2120	•	•	•	
•	•	•	•	•	The Paper Chase - CO [SOP]		970-350-1008	•	•	•	•
					Title Company of Denver		303-369-5443		•	•	

DT	BK	CV	CR	PR	←Courts **Las Animas**	Recording→	UC	RE	TX	VS
•	•	•	•	•	Colorado Records Search Inc [SOP]	800-645-7712	•	•	•	•
					Dotter Abstract & Associates	719-738-1730	•	•	•	•
•	•	•	•	•	Independent Research LLC	303-969-8608	•	•	•	•

DT	BK	CV	CR	PR	←Courts **Lincoln**	Recording→	UC	RE	TX	VS
		•			Hedlund Abstract	719-743-2353	•	•	•	
•	•	•	•	•	Independent Research LLC	303-969-8608	•	•	•	•

DT	BK	CV	CR	PR	←Courts **Logan**	Recording→	UC	RE	TX	VS
•	•	•	•	•	Independent Research LLC	303-969-8608	•	•	•	•
		•	•		Northeast Colorado Title Co LLC	970-522-7130	•	•	•	
•	•	•	•	•	The Paper Chase - CO [SOP]	970-350-1008	•	•	•	•

DT	BK	CV	CR	PR	←Courts **Mesa**	Recording→	UC	RE	TX	VS
•	•	•	•	•	Colorado Records Search Inc [SOP]	800-645-7712	•	•	•	•
		•	•	•	Grand Valley Associates [SOP]	970-256-9300	•	•	•	
•	•	•	•	•	Independent Research LLC	303-969-8608	•	•	•	•
					Information Services (Colorado)	877-385-4897	•	•	•	•
					Records Quest	303-369-0693	•	•	•	•
•	•	•	•	•	Records Research of Mesa County [SOP]	866-321-6611	•	•	•	•
•	•	•	•	•	Search Company International [SOP]	800-727-2120	•	•	•	

DT	BK	CV	CR	PR	←Courts **Mineral**	Recording→	UC	RE	TX	VS
•	•	•	•	•	Independent Research LLC	303-969-8608	•	•	•	•
					Rio Grande Mineral Title	719-657-3366	•	•	•	

DT	BK	CV	CR	PR	←Courts **Moffat**	Recording→	UC	RE	TX	VS
•	•	•	•	•	Independent Research LLC	303-969-8608	•	•	•	•
					Quality Research Service Inc	970-824-4144 (Cell 970-629-0388)	•	•	•	

DT	BK	CV	CR	PR	←Courts **Montezuma**	Recording→	UC	RE	TX	VS
		•	•		Attorney Service New Mexico [SOP]	505-326-7486				
•	•	•	•	•	Colorado Records Search Inc [SOP]	800-645-7712	•	•	•	•
•		•	•	•	Finney Land Co	970-259-5691	•	•	•	•
•	•	•	•	•	Independent Research LLC	303-969-8608	•	•	•	•
					Montezuma-Dolores Title Co	970-565-8491	•	•	•	

DT	BK	CV	CR	PR	←Courts **Montrose**	Recording→	UC	RE	TX	VS
•	•	•	•	•	Colorado Records Search Inc [SOP]	800-645-7712	•	•	•	•
					Comparable Sales Research	970-249-2118	•	•	•	
					First American Title Co (Colorado)	970-874-8286	•	•	•	
		•	•	•	Grand Valley Associates [SOP]	970-256-9300	•	•	•	
•	•	•	•	•	Independent Research LLC	303-969-8608	•	•	•	•

DT	BK	CV	CR	PR	←Courts **Morgan**	Recording→	UC	RE	TX	VS
•	•	•	•	•	Colorado Records Search Inc [SOP]	800-645-7712	•	•	•	•
					Documents 5280	303-438-8967	•	•	•	
•	•	•	•	•	Independent Research LLC	303-969-8608	•	•	•	•
•	•	•	•	•	The Paper Chase - CO [SOP]	970-350-1008	•	•	•	•

DT	BK	CV	CR	PR	←Courts **Otero**	Recording→	UC	RE	TX	VS
•	•	•	•	•	Independent Research LLC	303-969-8608	•	•	•	•

DT	BK	CV	CR	PR	←Courts **Ouray**	Recording→	UC	RE	TX	VS
•	•	•	•	•	Colorado Records Search Inc [SOP]	800-645-7712	•	•	•	•
					Comparable Sales Research	970-249-2118	•	•	•	
					First American Title Co (Colorado)	970-874-8286	•	•	•	
•	•	•	•	•	Independent Research LLC	303-969-8608	•	•	•	•

DT	BK	CV	CR	PR	←Courts **Park**	Recording→	UC	RE	TX	VS
•	•	•	•	•	Colorado Records Search Inc [SOP]	800-645-7712	•	•	•	•

DT	BK	CV	CR	PR	Retriever	Phone	UC	RE	TX	VS
•	•	•	•	•	Court Process Service & Investigations [SOP]	800-898-8662	•	•	•	•
•	•	•	•	•	Independent Research LLC	303-969-8608	•	•	•	•
		•	•		McCormick Detective Agency [SOP]	970-453-6378	•	•	•	

DT	BK	CV	CR	PR	←Courts **PHILLIPS**	Recording→	UC	RE	TX	VS
•	•	•	•	•	Independent Research LLC	303-969-8608	•	•	•	•

DT	BK	CV	CR	PR	←Courts **PITKIN**	Recording→	UC	RE	TX	VS
•	•	•	•	•	Colorado Records Search Inc [SOP]	800-645-7712	•	•	•	•
•	•	•	•	•	Independent Research LLC	303-969-8608	•	•	•	•
					Land Title Guarantee Co	970-925-1678	•	•	•	•

DT	BK	CV	CR	PR	←Courts **PROWERS**	Recording→	UC	RE	TX	VS
					Bent County Abstract & Title	719-456-0381		•		
				•	Guaranty Abstract Co (Colorado)	719-336-3261	•	•	•	
•	•	•	•	•	Independent Research LLC	303-969-8608	•	•	•	•

DT	BK	CV	CR	PR	←Courts **PUEBLO**	Recording→	UC	RE	TX	VS
•	•	•	•	•	Colorado Records Search Inc [SOP]	800-645-7712	•	•	•	•
•	•	•	•	•	Court Process Service & Document Retrieval [SOP]	800-898-8662	•	•	•	•
•	•	•	•	•	Independent Research LLC	303-969-8608	•	•	•	•
•		•	•		RIQ and Associates Inc	720-529-5736	•	•	•	•
•	•	•	•	•	Search Company International [SOP]	800-727-2120	•	•	•	

DT	BK	CV	CR	PR	←Courts **RIO BLANCO**	Recording→	UC	RE	TX	VS
•	•	•	•	•	Independent Research LLC	303-969-8608	•	•	•	•
					Quality Research Service Inc	970-824-4144 (Cell 970-629-0388)	•	•	•	

DT	BK	CV	CR	PR	←Courts **RIO GRANDE**	Recording→	UC	RE	TX	VS
•	•	•	•	•	Colorado Records Search Inc [SOP]	800-645-7712	•	•	•	•
•	•	•	•	•	Independent Research LLC	303-969-8608	•	•	•	•
					Rio Grande Mineral Title	719-657-3366	•	•	•	

DT	BK	CV	CR	PR	←Courts **ROUTT**	Recording→	UC	RE	TX	VS
•	•	•	•	•	Colorado Records Search Inc [SOP]	800-645-7712	•	•	•	•
•	•	•	•	•	Independent Research LLC	303-969-8608	•	•	•	•
					Quality Research Service Inc	970-824-4144 (Cell 970-629-0388)	•	•	•	

DT	BK	CV	CR	PR	←Courts **SAGUACHE**	Recording→	UC	RE	TX	VS
•	•	•	•	•	Independent Research LLC	303-969-8608	•	•	•	•
•	•	•	•	•	Saguache County Abstract & Investment	719-655-2611	•	•	•	•

DT	BK	CV	CR	PR	←Courts **SAN JUAN**	Recording→	UC	RE	TX	VS
•	•	•	•	•	Independent Research LLC	303-969-8608	•	•	•	•

DT	BK	CV	CR	PR	←Courts **SAN MIGUEL**	Recording→	UC	RE	TX	VS
•	•	•	•	•	Colorado Records Search Inc [SOP]	800-645-7712	•	•	•	•
•	•	•	•	•	Independent Research LLC	303-969-8608	•	•	•	•

DT	BK	CV	CR	PR	←Courts **SEDGWICK**	Recording→	UC	RE	TX	VS
•	•	•	•	•	Independent Research LLC	303-969-8608	•	•	•	•
					Sedgwick County Title Co	970-474-2696	•	•	•	

DT	BK	CV	CR	PR	←Courts **SUMMIT**	Recording→	UC	RE	TX	VS
•	•	•	•	•	Colorado Records Search Inc [SOP]	800-645-7712	•	•	•	•
•	•	•	•	•	Court Process Service & Investigations [SOP]	800-898-8662	•	•	•	•
•	•	•	•	•	Independent Research LLC	303-969-8608	•	•	•	•
		•	•		McCormick Detective Agency [SOP]	970-453-6378	•	•	•	•
•	•	•	•	•	Snoop For You	303-985-5521	•	•	•	•

DT	BK	CV	CR	PR	←Courts **TELLER**	Recording→	UC	RE	TX	VS
		•	•	•	Broadmoor Research Consultants [SOP]	719-205-1177	•	•	•	•
•	•	•	•	•	Colorado Records Search Inc [SOP]	800-645-7712	•	•	•	•

DT	BK	CV	CR	PR	Retriever	Phone	UC	RE	TX	VS
•	•	•	•	•	Court Process Service & Document Retrieval [SOP]	800-898-8662	•	•	•	•
•	•	•	•	•	Independent Research LLC	303-969-8608	•	•	•	•
		•	•	•	Legal Express [SOP]	719-578-0407		•	•	•
•		•	•		RIQ and Associates Inc	720-529-5736	•	•	•	•
•	•	•	•	•	Search Company International [SOP]	800-727-2120	•	•	•	

DT	BK	CV	CR	PR	←COURTS **WASHINGTON**	RECORDING→	UC	RE	TX	VS
•	•	•	•	•	Independent Research LLC	303-969-8608	•	•	•	•
					Washington County Title Co	970-345-2256	•	•	•	

DT	BK	CV	CR	PR	←COURTS **WELD**	RECORDING→	UC	RE	TX	VS
•	•	•	•	•	Alpha-Omega Investigations [SOP]	866-510-8200	•	•	•	•
•	•	•	•	•	Colorado Records Search Inc [SOP]	800-645-7712	•	•	•	•
•	•	•			Colorado Records Sooner	303-494-2132	•	•	•	•
•	•	•	•	•	Condello Associates, Accusearch [SOP]	888-756-9687	•	•	•	•
					Documents 5280	303-438-8967	•	•	•	
•	•	•	•	•	Independent Research LLC	303-969-8608	•	•	•	•
•	•	•		•	Daniel E Peel	970-484-1542	•	•	•	
•	•	•	•	•	Peregrine Investigation & Research [SOP]	303-324-7442	•	•	•	•
					Records Quest	303-369-0693	•	•	•	•
		•			Research & Revisions Etc	970-484-0176		•	•	
•		•	•		RIQ and Associates Inc	720-529-5736	•	•	•	•
•	•	•	•	•	Search Company International [SOP]	800-727-2120	•	•	•	
•	•	•	•	•	Snoop For You	303-985-5521	•	•	•	•
•	•	•	•	•	The Paper Chase - CO [SOP]	970-350-1008	•	•	•	•
					Title Company of Denver	303-369-5443		•	•	

DT	BK	CV	CR	PR	←COURTS **YUMA**	RECORDING→	UC	RE	TX	VS
•	•	•	•	•	Independent Research LLC	303-969-8608	•	•	•	•

[SOP] = PERFORMS SERVICE OF PROCESS

COURT RECORDS

CODE	GOVERNMENT AGENCY	TYPE OF INFORMATION
DT	US District Court	Federal civil and criminal cases
BK	Bankruptcy Court	United States bankruptcy cases
CV	Civil Court	Municipal, county and state level civil cases
CR	Criminal Court	Municipal, county and state level criminal cases
PR	Probate Court	Wills and estate cases

COUNTY RECORDS - RECORDINGS

CODE	GOVERNMENT AGENCY	TYPE OF INFORMATION
UC	UCC Filing Office	Uniform Commercial Code and other personal property liens
RE	Real Estate Recording Office	Real property transactions and liens
TX	Tax Filing Office(s)	Federal and state tax liens, judgment liens
VS	Vital Records Office	Vital statistics—birth, death, marriage, divorce

Connecticut

COURT RECORDS RETRIEVED — **RECORDING RECORDS RETRIEVED**

DT	BK	CV	CR	PR	←COURTS FAIRFIELD RECORDING→		UC	RE	TX	VS
•	•	•	•	•	ATT Loss Prevention Inc	860-496-1472	•	•	•	•
•	•	•			Business Services Group of CT LLC	203-758-2493	•	•	•	
•	•	•	•		CN Search LLC	860-349-3772	•		•	
					Credit Bureau of Connecticut Inc	800-922-0002		•	•	
•	•	•	•	•	Data Reporting Corp [SOP]	800-570-7750	•	•	•	
					Horizons Unlimited	617-696-6397		•	•	
•	•	•	•	•	Information Management Systems Inc [SOP]	888-403-8347	•	•	•	•
•	•	•	•	•	National Research Associates Inc	860-529-3006	•	•	•	•
•		•	•	•	New England Abstract LLC	203-265-0256	•	•	•	•
					Pro Search Inc	203-348-6994	•	•	•	
•	•	•	•	•	Professional Process Service LLC [SOP]	888-712-7378	•	•	•	•
•	•	•	•	•	The Docket Clerk	866-758-2683	•	•	•	•
•	•	•	•	•	TJM & Associates	800-749-4254	•	•	•	•

DT	BK	CV	CR	PR	←COURTS HARTFORD RECORDING→		UC	RE	TX	VS
					Advanced Title & Closing Services (CT)	888-443-4592 (Pager)	•	•	•	•
•	•	•	•	•	ATT Loss Prevention Inc	860-496-1472	•	•	•	•
•	•	•			Business Services Group of CT LLC	203-758-2493	•	•	•	
•	•	•	•		CN Search LLC	860-349-3772	•		•	
					Credit Bureau of Connecticut Inc	800-922-0002		•	•	
•	•	•	•	•	Data Reporting Corp [SOP]	800-570-7750	•	•	•	
					Horizons Unlimited	617-696-6397		•	•	
•	•	•	•	•	Information Management Systems Inc [SOP]	888-403-8347	•	•	•	•
•		•	•		Lutek Investigations LLC [SOP]	860-729-3310	•	•	•	•
•	•	•	•		National Data Retrieval	860-589-6716	•	•	•	
•	•	•	•	•	National Research Associates Inc	860-529-3006	•	•	•	•
•		•	•	•	New England Abstract LLC	203-265-0256	•	•	•	•
•	•	•	•	•	Professional Process Service LLC [SOP]	888-712-7378	•	•	•	•
•	•	•	•	•	The Docket Clerk	866-758-2683	•	•	•	•
•	•	•	•	•	TJM & Associates	800-749-4254	•	•	•	•

DT	BK	CV	CR	PR	←COURTS LITCHFIELD RECORDING→		UC	RE	TX	VS
•	•	•	•	•	ATT Loss Prevention Inc	860-496-1472	•	•	•	•
•	•	•			Business Services Group of CT LLC	203-758-2493	•	•	•	
•	•	•	•		CN Search LLC	860-349-3772	•		•	
					Credit Bureau of Connecticut Inc	800-922-0002		•	•	
•	•	•	•	•	Data Reporting Corp [SOP]	800-570-7750	•	•	•	
					Horizons Unlimited	617-696-6397		•	•	
•	•	•	•	•	Information Management Systems Inc [SOP]	888-403-8347	•	•	•	•
•	•	•	•	•	National Research Associates Inc	860-529-3006	•	•	•	•
•		•	•	•	New England Abstract LLC	203-265-0256	•	•	•	•
•	•	•	•	•	Professional Process Service LLC [SOP]	888-712-7378	•	•	•	•
•	•	•	•	•	The Docket Clerk	866-758-2683	•	•	•	•
•	•	•	•	•	TJM & Associates	800-749-4254	•	•	•	•

DT	BK	CV	CR	PR	←COURTS MIDDLESEX RECORDING→		UC	RE	TX	VS
					Advanced Title & Closing Services (CT)	888-443-4592 (Pager)	•	•	•	•
•	•	•	•	•	ATT Loss Prevention Inc	860-496-1472	•	•	•	•
•	•	•			Business Services Group of CT LLC	203-758-2493	•	•	•	
•	•	•	•		CN Search LLC	860-349-3772	•		•	
					Credit Bureau of Connecticut Inc	800-922-0002		•	•	
•	•	•	•	•	Data Reporting Corp [SOP]	800-570-7750	•	•	•	
					Horizons Unlimited	617-696-6397		•	•	
•	•	•	•	•	Information Management Systems Inc [SOP]	888-403-8347	•	•	•	•
•		•	•		Lutek Investigations LLC [SOP]	860-729-3310	•	•	•	•
•	•	•	•	•	National Research Associates Inc	860-529-3006	•	•	•	•
•		•	•	•	New England Abstract LLC	203-265-0256	•	•	•	•
•	•	•	•	•	Professional Process Service LLC [SOP]	888-712-7378	•	•	•	•
		•		•	Valerie Shickel	860-767-2269	•	•	•	•
•	•	•	•	•	The Docket Clerk	866-758-2683	•	•	•	•
•	•	•	•	•	TJM & Associates	800-749-4254	•	•	•	•

DT	BK	CV	CR	PR	←COURTS NEW HAVEN RECORDING→		UC	RE	TX	VS
					Advanced Title & Closing Services (CT)	888-443-4592 (Pager)	•	•	•	•
•	•	•	•	•	ATT Loss Prevention Inc	860-496-1472	•	•	•	•
•	•	•			Business Services Group of CT LLC	203-758-2493	•	•	•	
•	•	•	•		CN Search LLC	860-349-3772	•		•	
					Credit Bureau of Connecticut Inc	800-922-0002		•	•	
•	•	•	•	•	Data Reporting Corp [SOP]	800-570-7750	•	•	•	
					Horizons Unlimited	617-696-6397		•	•	
•	•	•	•	•	Information Management Systems Inc [SOP]	888-403-8347	•	•	•	•
•	•	•	•	•	National Research Associates Inc	860-529-3006	•	•	•	•
•		•	•	•	New England Abstract LLC	203-265-0256	•	•	•	•
•	•	•	•	•	Professional Process Service LLC [SOP]	888-712-7378	•	•	•	•
		•		•	Valerie Shickel	860-767-2269	•	•	•	•
•	•	•	•	•	The Docket Clerk	866-758-2683	•	•	•	•
•	•	•	•	•	TJM & Associates	800-749-4254	•	•	•	•

DT	BK	CV	CR	PR	←COURTS NEW LONDON RECORDING→		UC	RE	TX	VS
•	•	•	•	•	ATT Loss Prevention Inc	860-496-1472	•	•	•	•
•	•	•			Business Services Group of CT LLC	203-758-2493	•	•	•	
•	•	•	•		CN Search LLC	860-349-3772	•		•	
					Credit Bureau of Connecticut Inc	800-922-0002		•	•	
•	•	•	•	•	Data Reporting Corp [SOP]	800-570-7750	•	•	•	
					Horizons Unlimited	617-696-6397		•	•	
•	•	•	•	•	Information Management Systems Inc [SOP]	888-403-8347	•	•	•	•
•	•	•	•	•	National Research Associates Inc	860-529-3006	•	•	•	•
•		•	•	•	New England Abstract LLC	203-265-0256	•	•	•	•
•	•	•	•	•	Professional Process Service LLC [SOP]	888-712-7378	•	•	•	•
		•		•	Valerie Shickel	860-767-2269	•	•	•	•
•	•	•	•	•	The Docket Clerk	866-758-2683	•	•	•	•

DT	BK	CV	CR	PR	←COURTS TOLLAND RECORDING→		UC	RE	TX	VS
•	•	•	•	•	ATT Loss Prevention Inc	860-496-1472	•	•	•	•
•	•	•			Business Services Group of CT LLC	203-758-2493	•	•	•	
•	•	•	•		CN Search LLC	860-349-3772	•		•	
					Credit Bureau of Connecticut Inc	800-922-0002		•	•	
•	•	•	•	•	Data Reporting Corp [SOP]	800-570-7750	•	•	•	
					Horizons Unlimited	617-696-6397		•	•	
•	•	•	•	•	Information Management Systems Inc [SOP]	888-403-8347	•	•	•	•
•		•	•		Lutek Investigations LLC [SOP]	860-729-3310	•	•	•	•
•	•	•	•	•	National Research Associates Inc	860-529-3006	•	•	•	•
•		•	•	•	New England Abstract LLC	203-265-0256	•	•	•	•
•	•	•	•	•	Professional Process Service LLC [SOP]	888-712-7378	•	•	•	•

DT	BK	CV	CR	PR	←Courts		Recording→	UC	RE	TX	VS
•	•	•	•	•	The Docket Clerk		866-758-2683	•	•	•	•

DT	BK	CV	CR	PR	←Courts	Windham	Recording→	UC	RE	TX	VS
•	•	•	•	•	ATT Loss Prevention Inc		860-496-1472	•	•	•	•
•	•	•	•		CN Search LLC		860-349-3772	•		•	
					Credit Bureau of Connecticut Inc		800-922-0002		•	•	
•	•	•	•	•	Data Reporting Corp [SOP]		800-570-7750	•	•	•	
					Horizons Unlimited		617-696-6397		•	•	
•	•	•	•	•	Information Management Systems Inc [SOP]		888-403-8347	•	•	•	•
•	•	•	•	•	National Research Associates Inc		860-529-3006	•	•	•	•
•		•	•	•	New England Abstract LLC		203-265-0256	•	•	•	•
•	•	•	•	•	Professional Process Service LLC [SOP]		888-712-7378	•	•	•	•
•	•	•	•	•	The Docket Clerk		866-758-2683	•	•	•	•

= PRRN Member. *A retriever you can trust!*

[SOP] = Performs Service of Process

Court Records

CODE	Government Agency	Type of Information
DT	US District Court	Federal civil and criminal cases
BK	Bankruptcy Court	United States bankruptcy cases
CV	Civil Court	Municipal, county and state level civil cases
CR	Criminal Court	Municipal, county and state level criminal cases
PR	Probate Court	Wills and estate cases

County Records - Recordings

CODE	Government Agency	Type of Information
UC	UCC Filing Office	Uniform Commercial Code and other personal property liens
RE	Real Estate Recording Office	Real property transactions and liens
TX	Tax Filing Office(s)	Federal and state tax liens, judgment liens
VS	Vital Records Office	Vital statistics—birth, death, marriage, divorce

Delaware

COURT RECORDS RETRIEVED / **RECORDING RECORDS RETRIEVED**

DT	BK	CV	CR	PR	←COURTS KENT RECORDING→	Phone	UC	RE	TX	VS
•	•	•	•		Blue Marble Logistics LLC [SOP]	302-661-4390	•	•	•	
		•	•		CorpAmerica Inc	888-736-4300	•	•	•	
•	•	•	•	•	Corporation Service Company - CSC	800-927-9800	•	•	•	•
•	•	•	•	•	DDR (Delaware Document Retrieval) [SOP]	800-343-1742	•	•	•	
•	•	•	•		Delaware Attorney Services [SOP]	800-457-9560	•	•	•	•
•	•	•	•		Employmentscreening.com	215-234-0700	•	•	•	•
•	•	•	•	•	Hylind Search Company Inc (Delaware) [SOP]	888-243-6857	•	•	•	•
•	•	•			Incorporating Services Ltd	800-346-4646	•	•	•	•
		•	•		InfoRetrieval Services [SOP]	302-337-0548				
		•	•		Know It All Background Research Services Inc	888-281-9535				
		•	•		Legal Research Services	302-672-9411	•	•	•	•
•	•	•	•		National Background Inv Inc	800-798-0079			•	
•	•	•			National Corporate Research Ltd	800-483-1140	•	•	•	
•	•	•	•		Research Specialists Inc	610-358-2507	•		•	

DT	BK	CV	CR	PR	←COURTS NEW CASTLE RECORDING→	Phone	UC	RE	TX	VS
•	•	•	•	•	Assured Inquiries LLC [SOP]	888-644-0004				
•	•	•	•		Blue Marble Logistics LLC [SOP]	302-661-4390	•	•	•	
		•	•		CorpAmerica Inc	888-736-4300	•	•	•	
•	•	•	•	•	Corporation Service Company - CSC	800-927-9800	•	•	•	•
•	•	•	•	•	DDR (Delaware Document Retrieval) [SOP]	800-343-1742	•	•	•	
•	•	•	•		Delaware Attorney Services [SOP]	800-457-9560	•	•	•	•
•	•	•	•		Employmentscreening.com	215-234-0700	•	•	•	•
•	•	•	•	•	Hylind Search Company Inc (Delaware) [SOP]	888-243-6857	•	•	•	•
•	•	•			Incorporating Services Ltd	800-346-4646	•	•	•	•
		•	•		InfoRetrieval Services [SOP]	302-337-0548				
		•	•		Know It All Background Research Services Inc	888-281-9535				
•	•	•	•	•	Lawyers Filing Services of Southeastern PA Inc	888-490-0409	•	•	•	•
•	•	•	•	•	Legal Beagles Inc [SOP]	800-743-9897	•	•	•	•
		•	•		Legal Research Services	302-672-9411	•	•	•	•
•	•	•	•		National Background Inv Inc	800-798-0079			•	
•	•	•	•		Research Specialists Inc	610-358-2507	•		•	
•	•	•			Security Search & Abstract Co Inc	800-345-9494	•	•	•	
•	•	•	•	•	TriState Courier [SOP]	800-783-0945	•	•	•	

DT	BK	CV	CR	PR	←COURTS SUSSEX RECORDING→	Phone	UC	RE	TX	VS
		•	•		CorpAmerica Inc	888-736-4300	•	•	•	
•	•	•	•	•	Corporation Service Company - CSC	800-927-9800	•	•	•	•
•	•	•	•	•	DDR (Delaware Document Retrieval) [SOP]	800-343-1742	•	•	•	
•	•	•	•		Delaware Attorney Services [SOP]	800-457-9560	•	•	•	•
•	•	•	•		Employmentscreening.com	215-234-0700	•	•	•	•
•	•	•	•	•	Hylind Search Company Inc (Delaware) [SOP]	888-243-6857	•	•	•	•
•	•	•			Incorporating Services Ltd	800-346-4646	•	•	•	•
		•	•		InfoRetrieval Services [SOP]	302-337-0548				
		•	•		Know It All Background Research Services Inc	888-281-9535				
		•	•		Legal Research Services	302-672-9411	•	•	•	•
•	•	•	•		National Background Inv Inc	800-798-0079			•	
•	•	•	•		Research Specialists Inc	610-358-2507	•		•	
		•	•	•	Researchers Ltd	302-238-7442	•	•	•	

District of Columbia

DT	BK	CV	CR	PR	←Courts District of Columbia	Recording→	UC	RE	TX	VS
•	•	•	•	•	ALIASS [SOP]	800-747-0820	•	•	•	•
•	•	•	•		Asset Control Inc	877-277-3812	•	•	•	•
•	•	•	•	•	Cal Info Inc	202-537-8901				
•	•	•	•		Capitol District Information [SOP]	800-494-5225	•		•	
•	•	•	•	•	CorpAssist Inc - DC Office	800-438-2996	•	•	•	•
•	•	•	•	•	Corporation Service Company - CSC	800-927-9800	•	•	•	•
•	•	•	•		CourtEXPRESS (DC) [SOP]	800-542-3320				
•	•	•	•	•	Document Services	202-637-0362	•	•	•	•
•	•	•	•	•	Docu-Search of Washington DC	202-737-5707	•	•	•	•
•	•	•	•	•	Enterprise Title Company Inc	703-351-8066	•	•	•	•
					Estate Title & Escrow Inc	703-385-5850	•	•	•	
•	•	•		•	Federal Research Corporation [SOP]	800-846-3190	•	•	•	•
					First Choice Title Service LLC	410-252 3803		•		
•	•	•	•	•	Fitzgerald Servaites Inc	202-257-7775	•	•	•	•
•	•	•	•	•	Global Securities Information	202-628-1155				
•	•	•	•	•	Hylind Search Company Inc (Maryland) [SOP]	888-449-5463	•	•	•	•
•	•	•	•	•	Infoline Inc	888-284-4581	•	•	•	•
•	•	•	•	•	Investigative Consultants Inc	202-237-1500	•	•	•	•
•	•	•		•	M & M Search Service	301-251-9545	•	•	•	•
•	•	•	•	•	MLQ Attorney Services [SOP]	800-446-8794	•	•	•	•
•	•	•	•	•	Mohr Information Services LLC	540-678-8775	•	•	•	
•	•	•	•		National Background Inv Inc	800-798-0079			•	
•	•	•	•		OneSource, Inc	540-450-2250		•	•	
•	•	•	•		Pat's Information Services	202-285-2116			•	
•		•			ResearchSource for Hard-to-Find Information	202-778-0002				
•	•	•	•	•	Richmond Group International [SOP]	703-494-4645			•	•
•	•	•	•		Security Consultants Inc	202-686-3953			•	
•	•	•	•	•	Torri's Legal Services [SOP]	800-990-7378				
	•	•		•	Tri-County Title Abstracts Inc	202-737-6116	•	•	•	
•	•	•	•	•	Washington Document Service (DC)	800-728-5201	•	•	•	•

Florida

COURT RECORDS RETRIEVED — **RECORDING RECORDS RETRIEVED**

DT	BK	CV	CR	PR	←COURTS ALACHUA	RECORDING→	UC	RE	TX	VS
•	•	•	•	•	Accurate Background Check	877-611-2277		•	•	•
•	•	•	•	•	Direct Corporate Services Inc	800-783-7904	•	•	•	
•	•	•	•	•	First Choice Research	954-964-1260	•	•	•	
•		•	•	•	Lehr's Process Service [SOP]	352-331-1010	•	•	•	•
•	•	•			Phoenix Document Service Inc	727-581-2552	•	•	•	
					The Searchers	352-493-0101	•	•	•	
		•	•	•	Twin Oaks Research	352-465-7844	•	•	•	

DT	BK	CV	CR	PR	←COURTS BAKER	RECORDING→	UC	RE	TX	VS
•	•	•	•	•	Accurate Background Check	877-611-2277		•	•	•
•	•	•	•	•	First Choice Research	954-964-1260	•	•	•	
•	•	•	•	•	Mulholland Investigations & Security [SOP]	904-354-7989	•	•	•	•
•	•	•	•	•	Pacific Photocopy & Research (Jacksonville) [SOP]	904-355-1062	•	•	•	•
•	•	•			Phoenix Document Service Inc	727-581-2552	•	•	•	

DT	BK	CV	CR	PR	←COURTS BAY	RECORDING→	UC	RE	TX	VS
		•		•	AAA Search Excellence Inc	352-688-6751	•	•	•	
•	•	•	•	•	Accurate Background Check	877-611-2277		•	•	•
•	•	•	•	•	Corporate Access Inc [SOP]	800-969-1666	•	•	•	•
•	•	•	•	•	Direct Corporate Services Inc	800-783-7904	•	•	•	
•	•	•	•	•	Emerald Coast Protective Services Inc [SOP]	877-234-6252	•	•	•	•
•	•	•	•	•	First Choice Research	954-964-1260	•	•	•	
•	•	•	•	•	Ike L Hoy PE (Control Systems)	850-259-4650	•	•	•	•
•	•	•	•	•	Pacific Photocopy & Research (Pensacola) [SOP]	850-435-3183	•	•	•	•
•	•	•	•	•	Parrish Research	850-936-1240	•	•	•	•
		•	•		Pasco Records Check Inc	813-991-5719				
•	•	•			Phoenix Document Service Inc	727-581-2552	•	•	•	
					Research Express	850-926-5665		•		

DT	BK	CV	CR	PR	←COURTS BRADFORD	RECORDING→	UC	RE	TX	VS
•	•	•	•	•	Accurate Background Check	877-611-2277		•	•	•
•	•	•	•	•	First Choice Research	954-964-1260	•	•	•	
		•		•	Dudley P Hardy PA (Bradford Title Service)	904-964-4747	•	•	•	
•	•	•	•	•	Pacific Photocopy & Research (Jacksonville) [SOP]	904-355-1062	•	•	•	•
					The Searchers	352-493-0101	•	•	•	

DT	BK	CV	CR	PR	←COURTS BREVARD	RECORDING→	UC	RE	TX	VS
•	•	•	•	•	A Very Private Eye Inc [SOP]	407-273-6646	•	•	•	•
•	•	•	•	•	Accurate Background Check	877-611-2277		•	•	•
•	•	•	•	•	Andrews Agency Inc [SOP]	407-649-2085	•	•	•	•
•	•	•	•	•	Bell Investigative Services Inc	954-454-4859	•	•	•	•
		•	•	•	Crummey Investigations Inc [SOP]	321-724-0518	•	•	•	•
•	•	•	•	•	Direct Corporate Services Inc	800-783-7904	•	•	•	
•	•	•		•	First American Title Ins Co	407-740-7131	•	•	•	•
•	•	•	•	•	First Choice Research	954-964-1260	•	•	•	
•	•	•	•	•	Hale Investigative Services/Process [SOP]	800-882-5137	•	•	•	•
•	•	•		•	ICDI Inc	407-622-2532	•	•	•	
•	•	•		•	Independent Research Assoc	407-832-8580	•	•	•	
					L L Lesko Inc	772-879-2625	•	•	•	

DT	BK	CV	CR	PR	←Courts	Recording→	UC	RE	TX	VS
•	•	•	•	•	Merlins Data Research	888-434-6337	•	•	•	•
	•	•	•	•	National Information Agency [SOP]	321-543-9381	•	•	•	•
•	•	•			Phoenix Document Service Inc	727-581-2552	•	•	•	
					Source Documents & Information Inc	727-447-8844	•	•	•	
		•	•	•	World Class Inv [SOP]	321-728-0641	•	•	•	

DT	BK	CV	CR	PR	←Courts BROWARD	Recording→	UC	RE	TX	VS
•	•	•	•	•	Accurate Background Check	877-611-2277		•	•	•
•	•	•	•	•	Accurate Confidential Research Inc	305-386-6677	•	•	•	•
•	•	•	•	•	All American Document Services	954-761-7292	•	•	•	•
•	•	•	•	•	American Legal Solution Inc	954-986-5442	•	•	•	•
•	•	•	•	•	ATT Investigations Inc	800-733-4405	•	•	•	•
•	•	•	•	•	Bell Investigative Services Inc	954-454-4859	•	•	•	•
•	•	•	•	•	Bill Greenberg Special Services Inc [SOP]	888-770-9008	•	•	•	•
•	•	•	•	•	Compass Investigations [SOP]	954-527-5722	•	•	•	•
		•	•		Deception Control Inc	800-776-1660		•	•	•
•	•	•	•	•	Direct Corporate Services Inc	800-783-7904	•	•	•	
•	•	•	•	•	Esquire Express Inc [SOP]	800-439-8744	•	•	•	•
•	•	•	•	•	First Choice Research	954-964-1260	•	•	•	
•	•	•		•	FLA Search Company	561-969-6594	•	•	•	•
					Fort Lauderdale-Miami Courthouse Research Inc	954-434-6819	•	•	•	
•	•	•	•	•	Ken Haave PI	305-710-7409	•	•	•	•
•	•	•	•	•	IGB Associates Inc	813-226-8810	•	•	•	•
•	•	•	•		Infotrack Information Services Inc	800-275-5594	•	•	•	
•	•	•	•	•	Intracoastal Detective Agency Inc	954-564-5455	•	•	•	•
•	•	•	•	•	JM Search Services Inc	800-393-7563	•	•	•	•
•	•	•	•	•	Judicial Research & Retrieval Svcs (Ft Lauderdale)	954-832-0111	•	•	•	•
•	•	•	•	•	Legal 1 Document Retrieval [SOP]	954-733-8934	•	•	•	•
•	•	•		•	Johanna E Malki	305-899-0273	•	•	•	
•	•	•	•	•	Medina Retrieval Service	954-560-9077		•		
•	•	•	•	•	Pacific Photocopy & Research (Ft. Lauderdale)	954-764-5646	•	•	•	•
•	•	•	•	•	Patrick Investigative Services Inc	800-700-2958	•	•	•	•
•	•	•	•	•	Premiere Investigations [SOP]	954-974-1139	•	•	•	•
•	•	•	•	•	Research & Abstract Associates	239-337-5354	•	•	•	•
					Source Documents & Information Inc	727-447-8844	•	•	•	
					South Florida Title Research Inc dba SFTR	866-398-7387	•	•	•	
•	•	•	•	•	Sugarbaker Investigations	800-720-2567	•			•
•	•	•	•	•	The Records Reviewer Inc	305-934-4920	•	•	•	•
		•	•		VeriQuest Inc	813-948-4889				

DT	BK	CV	CR	PR	←Courts CALHOUN	Recording→	UC	RE	TX	VS
•	•	•	•	•	Accurate Background Check	877-611-2277		•	•	•
•	•	•	•	•	Corporate Access Inc [SOP]	800-969-1666	•	•	•	•
•	•	•	•	•	First Choice Research	954-964-1260	•	•	•	
					Research Express	850-926-5665		•		

DT	BK	CV	CR	PR	←Courts CHARLOTTE	Recording→	UC	RE	TX	VS
•	•	•	•	•	A Public Record Expert Inc	941-504-7734	•	•		•
•	•	•	•	•	Accurate Background Check	877-611-2277		•	•	•
•	•	•	•	•	Bill Greenberg Special Services Inc [SOP]	888-770-9008	•	•	•	•
•	•	•	•	•	Direct Corporate Services Inc	800-783-7904	•	•	•	
•	•	•	•	•	First Choice Research	954-964-1260	•	•	•	
					Guzman Title Research Inc	941-423-5310	•	•	•	
•	•	•	•		Infotrack Information Services Inc	800-275-5594	•	•	•	
•	•	•	•	•	Pacific Photocopy & Research (Tampa)	813-221-6828	•	•	•	•
		•	•	•	Palo Verde Research	239-481-9434	•	•	•	•
•	•	•			Phoenix Document Service Inc	727-581-2552	•	•	•	
•	•	•	•	•	Research & Abstract Associates	239-337-5354	•	•	•	•
•	•	•	•	•	South Florida Legal Services of Naples [SOP]	239-332-7000		•	•	•

DT	BK	CV	CR	PR	Name	Phone	UC	RE	TX	VS
		•	•	•	SWF Private Inv [SOP]	941-764-9156	•	•	•	•
DT	**BK**	**CV**	**CR**	**PR**	**←COURTS CITRUS**	**RECORDING→**	**UC**	**RE**	**TX**	**VS**
		•		•	AAA Search Excellence Inc	352-688-6751	•	•	•	
•	•	•	•	•	Accurate Background Check	877-611-2277		•	•	•
				•	Coast to Coast Abstracting	352-442-1500	•	•	•	
•	•	•		•	First Choice Research	954-964-1260	•	•	•	
•	•	•	•		GPS & Assoc (Florida)	866-813-8131	•		•	•
•	•	•	•	•	Pacific Photocopy & Research (Jacksonville) [SOP]	904-355-1062	•	•	•	•
•	•	•			Phoenix Document Service Inc	727-581-2552	•	•	•	
•	•	•	•	•	Prestige Legal Services [SOP]	800-784-7572	•	•	•	•
					The Searchers	352-493-0101	•	•	•	
		•	•	•	Twin Oaks Research	352-465-7844	•	•	•	
DT	**BK**	**CV**	**CR**	**PR**	**←COURTS CLAY**	**RECORDING→**	**UC**	**RE**	**TX**	**VS**
•	•	•	•	•	Accurate Background Check	877-611-2277		•	•	•
•	•	•	•	•	First Choice Research	954-964-1260	•	•	•	
•	•	•	•	•	First Coast Inv [SOP]	904-398-4076			•	•
					Fort Lauderdale-Miami Courthouse Research Inc	954-434-6819	•	•	•	
•	•	•	•		G & L Research Associates	904-743-4116	•	•	•	
				•	Land Title of America Group	904-797-9600	•	•	•	•
•	•	•	•	•	Millennial Investigative Agency	888-299-7574	•	•	•	•
•	•	•	•	•	Mulholland Investigations & Security [SOP]	904-354-7989	•	•	•	•
•	•	•	•	•	Pacific Photocopy & Research (Jacksonville) [SOP]	904-355-1062	•	•	•	•
					The Searchers	352-493-0101	•	•	•	
DT	**BK**	**CV**	**CR**	**PR**	**←COURTS COLLIER**	**RECORDING→**	**UC**	**RE**	**TX**	**VS**
•	•	•	•	•	Accurate Background Check	877-611-2277		•	•	•
		•			Attorney's Title Ins. Fund Inc	239-774-2627	•	•	•	•
•	•	•	•	•	Bell Investigative Services Inc	954-454-4859	•	•	•	•
•	•	•	•	•	Direct Corporate Services Inc	800-783-7904	•	•	•	
•	•	•	•	•	First Choice Research	954-964-1260	•	•	•	
•	•	•	•	•	Florida Records Research	239-435-1189	•	•	•	•
•	•	•	•		Infotrack Information Services Inc	800-275-5594	•	•	•	
•	•	•	•	•	MEM Consulting [SOP]	239-394-2893	•	•	•	•
•	•	•	•	•	Pacific Photocopy & Research (Tampa)	813-221-6828	•	•	•	•
		•	•	•	Palo Verde Research	239-481-9434	•	•	•	•
•	•	•			Phoenix Document Service Inc	727-581-2552	•	•	•	
•	•	•	•	•	Research & Abstract Associates	239-337-5354	•	•	•	•
•	•	•	•	•	South Florida Legal Services of Naples [SOP]	239-332-7000		•	•	•
DT	**BK**	**CV**	**CR**	**PR**	**←COURTS COLUMBIA**	**RECORDING→**	**UC**	**RE**	**TX**	**VS**
•	•	•	•	•	Accurate Background Check	877-611-2277		•	•	•
•	•	•	•	•	First Choice Research	954-964-1260	•	•	•	
•	•	•	•	•	Pacific Photocopy & Research (Jacksonville) [SOP]	904-355-1062	•	•	•	•
		•	•		Pasco Records Check Inc	813-991-5719				
					Research Express	850-926-5665		•		
DT	**BK**	**CV**	**CR**	**PR**	**←COURTS DADE (MIAMI-DADE)**	**RECORDING→**	**UC**	**RE**	**TX**	**VS**
•	•	•	•	•	Accurate Background Check	877-611-2277		•	•	•
•	•	•	•	•	Accurate Confidential Research Inc	305-386-6677	•	•	•	•
•	•	•	•	•	All American Document Services	954-761-7292	•	•	•	•
•	•	•	•	•	American Legal Solution Inc	954-986-5442	•	•	•	•
•	•	•	•	•	ATT Investigations Inc	800-733-4405	•	•	•	•
	•				Banko Document Retrieval	800-969-2377				
•	•	•	•	•	Bell Investigative Services Inc	954-454-4859	•	•	•	•
•	•	•	•	•	Bill Greenberg Special Services Inc [SOP]	888-770-9008	•	•	•	•
•	•	•	•	•	Compass Investigations [SOP]	954-527-5722	•	•	•	•
		•	•		Deception Control Inc	800-776-1660		•	•	•
•	•	•	•	•	Direct Corporate Services Inc	800-783-7904	•	•	•	

DT	BK	CV	CR	PR	←Courts	Recording→	UC	RE	TX	VS
•	•	•	•	•	Esquire Express Inc [SOP]	800-439-8744	•	•	•	•
•	•	•	•	•	First Choice Research	954-964-1260	•	•	•	
•	•	•		•	FLA Search Company	561-969-6594	•	•	•	•
•	•	•	•		GPS & Assoc (Florida)	866-813-8131	•	•	•	•
•	•	•	•	•	Ken Haave PI	305-710-7409	•	•	•	•
•	•	•	•	•	IGB Associates Inc	813-226-8810	•	•	•	•
•	•	•	•		Infotrack Information Services Inc	800-275-5594	•	•	•	
•	•	•	•	•	Intracoastal Detective Agency Inc	954-564-5455	•	•	•	•
•	•	•	•	•	JM Search Services Inc	800-393-7563	•	•	•	
•	•	•	•	•	Judicial Research & Retrieval Svcs (Miami) [SOP]	800-529-6226	•	•	•	•
•	•	•	•	•	Legal 1 Document Retrieval [SOP]	954-733-8934	•	•	•	•
•	•	•		•	Johanna E Malki	305-899-0273	•	•	•	
•	•	•	•	•	Medina Retrieval Service	954-560-9077		•		
•	•	•	•	•	Pacific Photocopy & Research (Miami)	305-371-7694	•	•	•	•
•	•	•	•	•	Patrick Investigative Services Inc	800-700-2958	•	•	•	•
•	•	•			Phoenix Document Service Inc	727-581-2552	•	•	•	
•	•	•	•	•	Premiere Investigations [SOP]	954-974-1139	•	•	•	•
					Source Documents & Information Inc	727-447-8844	•	•	•	
					South Florida Title Research Inc dba SFTR	866-398-7387	•	•	•	
•	•	•	•	•	Sugarbaker Investigations	800-720-2567	•			•
•	•	•	•	•	The Records Reviewer Inc	305-934-4920	•	•	•	•
		•	•		VeriQuest Inc	813-948-4889				
•	•	•	•	•	Robert Vollrath [SOP]	305-343-9344	•	•	•	•

DT	BK	CV	CR	PR	←Courts **De Soto**	Recording→	UC	RE	TX	VS
•	•	•	•	•	A Public Record Expert Inc	941-504-7734	•	•		•
•	•	•	•	•	Accurate Background Check	877-611-2277		•	•	•
		•	•	•	DeSoto Abstract & Title Co (FL)	863-494-3656	•	•	•	•
•	•	•	•	•	Direct Corporate Services Inc	800-783-7904	•	•	•	
•	•	•	•	•	First Choice Research	954-964-1260	•	•	•	
					Guzman Title Research Inc	941-423-5310	•	•	•	
•	•	•	•	•	Pacific Photocopy & Research (Tampa)	813-221-6828	•	•	•	•
•	•	•	•	•	Research & Abstract Associates	239-337-5354	•	•	•	•
		•	•	•	SWF Private Inv [SOP]	941-764-9156	•	•	•	•

DT	BK	CV	CR	PR	←Courts **Dixie**	Recording→	UC	RE	TX	VS
•	•	•	•	•	Accurate Background Check	877-611-2277		•	•	•
•	•	•	•	•	First Choice Research	954-964-1260	•	•	•	
					Research Express	850-926-5665		•		

DT	BK	CV	CR	PR	←Courts **Duval**	Recording→	UC	RE	TX	VS
•	•	•	•	•	Accurate Background Check	877-611-2277		•	•	•
•	•	•		•	First American Title Ins Co	407-740-7131	•	•	•	•
•	•	•	•	•	First Choice Research	954-964-1260	•	•	•	
•	•	•	•	•	First Coast Inv [SOP]	904-398-4076			•	•
•	•	•	•		G & L Research Associates	904-743-4116	•	•	•	
•	•	•	•	•	IGB Associates Inc	813-226-8810	•	•	•	•
•	•	•	•		Infotrack Information Services Inc	800-275-5594	•	•	•	
•	•	•	•	•	Judicial Research & Retrieval Svcs (Jacksonville)	904-356-9110	•	•	•	•
				•	Land Title of America Group	904-797-9600	•	•	•	•
•	•	•	•	•	Millennial Investigative Agency	888-299-7574	•	•	•	•
•	•	•	•	•	Mulholland Investigations & Security [SOP]	904-354-7989	•	•	•	•
•	•	•	•	•	Pacific Photocopy & Research (Jacksonville) [SOP]	904-355-1062	•	•	•	•
		•	•		SingleSource Services Corp	800-713-3412	•		•	
		•	•		VeriQuest Inc	813-948-4889				

DT	BK	CV	CR	PR	←Courts **Escambia**	Recording→	UC	RE	TX	VS
•	•	•	•	•	Accurate Background Check	877-611-2277		•	•	•
•	•	•	•	•	Bill Greenberg Special Services Inc [SOP]	888-770-9008	•	•	•	•
•	•	•	•	•	Coastal Office Dimensions	850-484-8098	•	•	•	•

DT	BK	CV	CR	PR	←Courts	Recording→	UC	RE	TX	VS
•	•	•	•	•	Direct Corporate Services Inc	800-783-7904	•	•	•	
•	•	•	•	•	First Choice Research	954-964-1260	•	•	•	
•	•	•	•		Infotrack Information Services Inc	800-275-5594	•	•	•	
•	•	•	•	•	Judicial Research & Retrieval Svcs (Miami) [SOP]	800-529-6226	•	•	•	•
•	•	•	•	•	Pacific Photocopy & Research (Pensacola) [SOP]	850-435-3183	•	•	•	•
•	•	•	•	•	Parker Legal Services [SOP]	251-476-7464	•	•	•	•
•	•	•	•	•	Parrish Research	850-936-1240	•	•	•	•
•	•	•			Phoenix Document Service Inc	727-581-2552	•	•	•	

DT	BK	CV	CR	PR	←Courts **Flagler**	Recording→	UC	RE	TX	VS
•	•	•	•	•	Accurate Background Check	877-611-2277		•	•	•
•	•	•	•	•	Direct Corporate Services Inc	800-783-7904	•	•	•	
•	•	•		•	First American Title Ins Co	407-740-7131	•	•	•	•
•	•	•	•	•	First Choice Research	954-964-1260	•	•	•	
				•	Flagler County Abstract Co [SOP]	386-437-4151	•	•	•	
				•	Land Title of America Group	904-797-9600	•	•	•	•
		•	•	•	Lowry Document Service	386-789-6193	•	•	•	•
•	•	•	•	•	Pacific Photocopy & Research (Jacksonville) [SOP]	904-355-1062	•	•	•	•
•	•	•			Phoenix Document Service Inc	727-581-2552	•	•	•	
•	•		•	•	XpertSearch Inc	732-229-6688	•	•	•	•

DT	BK	CV	CR	PR	←Courts **Franklin**	Recording→	UC	RE	TX	VS
•	•	•	•	•	Accurate Background Check	877-611-2277		•	•	•
•	•	•	•	•	Advanced Investigations Inc [SOP]	850-863-3997	•	•	•	•
•	•	•	•	•	Corporate Access Inc [SOP]	800-969-1666	•	•	•	•
•	•	•	•	•	First Choice Research	954-964-1260	•	•	•	
					Research Express	850-926-5665		•		

DT	BK	CV	CR	PR	←Courts **Gadsden**	Recording→	UC	RE	TX	VS
•	•	•	•	•	Accurate Background Check	877-611-2277		•	•	•
•	•	•	•	•	Advanced Investigations Inc [SOP]	850-863-3997	•	•	•	•
•	•	•	•		Capital Connection [SOP]	850-224-8870	•	•	•	
•	•	•	•	•	Corporate Access Inc [SOP]	800-969-1666	•	•	•	•
•	•	•	•	•	First Choice Research	954-964-1260	•	•	•	
•	•	•			Florida Filing & Search Services Inc	800-435-9371	•		•	
		•		•	Gadsden Abstract Co	850-627-6811		•	•	
•	•	•	•	•	Judicial Research & Retrieval Svcs (Miami) [SOP]	800-529-6226	•	•	•	•
					Research Express	850-926-5665		•		
•	•	•	•	•	State Information Bureau	800-881-1742	•	•	•	
•	•	•			Sunstate Research Associates Inc	800-621-7234	•		•	

DT	BK	CV	CR	PR	←Courts **Gilchrist**	Recording→	UC	RE	TX	VS
•	•	•	•	•	Accurate Background Check	877-611-2277		•	•	•
•	•	•	•	•	First Choice Research	954-964-1260	•	•	•	
					Research Express	850-926-5665		•		

DT	BK	CV	CR	PR	←Courts **Glades**	Recording→	UC	RE	TX	VS
•	•	•	•	•	Accurate Background Check	877-611-2277		•	•	•
•	•	•	•	•	First Choice Research	954-964-1260	•	•	•	
		•	•	•	Okeechobee Abstract & Title Ins Inc	863-763-3710	•	•	•	
•	•	•	•	•	Pacific Photocopy & Research (Tampa)	813-221-6828	•	•	•	•
•	•	•	•	•	Research & Abstract Associates	239-337-5354	•	•	•	•

DT	BK	CV	CR	PR	←Courts **Gulf**	Recording→	UC	RE	TX	VS
•	•	•	•	•	Accurate Background Check	877-611-2277		•	•	•
•	•	•	•	•	Corporate Access Inc [SOP]	800-969-1666	•	•	•	•
•	•	•	•	•	Emerald Coast Protective Services Inc [SOP]	877-234-6252	•	•	•	•
•	•	•	•	•	First Choice Research	954-964-1260	•	•	•	
					Research Express	850-926-5665		•		

DT	BK	CV	CR	PR	←COURTS **HAMILTON** RECORDING→	Phone	UC	RE	TX	VS
•	•	•	•	•	Accurate Background Check	877-611-2277		•	•	•
•	•	•	•	•	First Choice Research	954-964-1260	•	•	•	
•	•	•	•	•	Pacific Photocopy & Research (Jacksonville) [SOP]	904-355-1062	•	•	•	•
					Research Express	850-926-5665		•		

DT	BK	CV	CR	PR	←COURTS **HARDEE** RECORDING→	Phone	UC	RE	TX	VS
•	•	•	•	•	A Public Record Expert Inc	941-504-7734	•	•		•
•	•	•	•	•	Accurate Background Check	877-611-2277		•	•	•
		•	•	•	Al Smith Private Inv [SOP]	863-295-1375	•	•	•	•
•	•	•	•	•	First Choice Research	954-964-1260	•	•	•	
•	•	•	•	•	Pacific Photocopy & Research (Tampa)	813-221-6828	•	•	•	•
•	•	•	•	•	Research & Abstract Associates	239-337-5354	•	•	•	•

DT	BK	CV	CR	PR	←COURTS **HENDRY** RECORDING→	Phone	UC	RE	TX	VS
•	•	•	•	•	Accurate Background Check	877-611-2277		•	•	•
•	•	•	•	•	Direct Corporate Services Inc	800-783-7904	•	•	•	
•	•	•	•	•	First Choice Research	954-964-1260	•	•	•	
•	•	•	•	•	Florida Records Research	239-435-1189	•	•	•	•
•	•	•	•	•	Pacific Photocopy & Research (Tampa)	813-221-6828	•	•	•	•
		•	•	•	Palo Verde Research	239-481-9434	•	•	•	•
•	•	•	•	•	Research & Abstract Associates	239-337-5354	•	•	•	•
•	•	•	•	•	South Florida Legal Services of Naples [SOP]	239-332-7000		•	•	•

DT	BK	CV	CR	PR	←COURTS **HERNANDO** RECORDING→	Phone	UC	RE	TX	VS
		•		•	AAA Search Excellence Inc	352-688-6751	•	•	•	
•	•	•	•	•	Accurate Background Check	877-611-2277		•	•	•
				•	Coast to Coast Abstracting	352-442-1500	•	•	•	
•	•	•	•	•	Direct Corporate Services Inc	800-783-7904	•	•	•	
•	•	•	•	•	First Choice Research	954-964-1260	•	•	•	
•	•	•	•		GPS & Assoc (Florida)	866-813-8131	•		•	•
•	•	•	•	•	Gulf Coast Records	727-580-4873	•	•	•	•
•	•	•	•	•	Mohr Information Services LLC	540-678-8775	•	•	•	•
•	•	•	•	•	Pacific Photocopy & Research (Tampa)	813-221-6828	•	•	•	•
•	•	•			Phoenix Document Service Inc	727-581-2552	•	•	•	
•	•	•	•	•	Prestige Legal Services [SOP]	800-784-7572	•	•	•	•
•	•	•	•	•	Research & Abstract Associates	239-337-5354	•	•	•	•
					Source Documents & Information Inc	727-447-8844	•	•	•	
•	•	•	•	•	Sugarbaker Investigations	800-720-2567	•			•
					The Searchers	352-493-0101	•	•	•	
		•	•		VeriQuest Inc	813-948-4889				

DT	BK	CV	CR	PR	←COURTS **HIGHLANDS** RECORDING→	Phone	UC	RE	TX	VS
•	•	•	•	•	Accurate Background Check	877-611-2277		•	•	•
					Advanced Title	863-471-6334		•		
		•	•	•	Al Smith Private Inv [SOP]	863-295-1375	•	•	•	•
•	•	•	•	•	First Choice Research	954-964-1260	•	•	•	
•	•	•	•	•	Pacific Photocopy & Research (Miami)	305-371-7694	•	•	•	•
•	•	•			Phoenix Document Service Inc	727-581-2552	•	•	•	
•	•	•	•	•	Research & Abstract Associates	239-337-5354	•	•	•	•
		•		•	South Ridge Abstract & Title Co	863-385-2521	•	•	•	

DT	BK	CV	CR	PR	←COURTS **HILLSBOROUGH** RECORDING→	Phone	UC	RE	TX	VS
•	•	•	•	•	A Public Record Expert Inc	941-504-7734	•	•		•
•	•	•	•	•	Accurate Background Check	877-611-2277		•	•	•
•	•	•	•		Ace Data Service [SOP]	727-735-9311	•	•	•	•
•	•	•	•	•	All American Research LLC	800-215-7958	•	•	•	•
•		•	•	•	All Phase Reports [SOP]	813-885-9822		•		•
•	•	•	•	•	ATT Investigations Inc	800-733-4405	•	•	•	•
•	•	•	•	•	Bay Area Search Inc	727-724-5995	•	•	•	•

DT	BK	CV	CR	PR	←Courts	Recording→	UC	RE	TX	VS
•	•	•	•	•	Bell Investigative Services Inc	954-454-4859	•	•	•	•
•	•	•	•	•	Bill Greenberg Special Services Inc [SOP]	888-770-9008	•	•	•	•
				•	Coast to Coast Abstracting	352-442-1500	•	•	•	
•	•	•	•	•	Colton & Associates Inc [SOP]	800-704-6699	•	•	•	•
•	•	•	•	•	Direct Corporate Services Inc	800-783-7904	•	•	•	
					Doc Hunters	727-518-6700	•	•	•	
•	•	•	•	•	EX-CEL Inv [SOP]	800-317-7626	•	•	•	•
•	•	•	•	•	First Choice Research	954-964-1260	•	•	•	
•	•	•	•	•	Gietzen & Associates Inc [SOP]	813-223-3233		•	•	
•	•	•	•		GPS & Assoc (Florida)	866-813-8131	•		•	•
•	•	•	•	•	Gulf Coast Records	727-580-4873	•	•	•	•
•	•	•	•	•	IGB Associates Inc	813-226-8810	•	•	•	•
•	•	•	•		Infotrack Information Services Inc	800-275-5594	•	•	•	
•	•	•	•	•	Judicial Research & Retrieval Svcs (Tampa)	813-228-7200	•	•	•	•
•	•	•	•	•	Mohr Information Services LLC	540-678-8775	•	•	•	
•	•	•	•	•	Pacific Photocopy & Research (Tampa)	813-221-6828	•	•	•	•
		•	•		Pasco Records Check Inc	813-991-5719				
•	•	•			Phoenix Document Service Inc	727-581-2552	•	•	•	
•	•	•	•	•	Prestige Legal Services [SOP]	800-784-7572	•	•	•	•
•	•	•	•	•	Research & Abstract Associates	239-337-5354	•	•	•	•
					Source Documents & Information Inc	727-447-8844	•	•	•	
•	•	•	•	•	Sugarbaker Investigations	800-720-2567	•			•
•		•	•		Sunshine Research Inc	888-786-1242	•			
		•	•		VeriQuest Inc	813-948-4889				

DT	BK	CV	CR	PR	←Courts **Holmes**	Recording→	UC	RE	TX	VS
•	•	•	•	•	Accurate Background Check	877-611-2277		•	•	•
•	•	•	•	•	First Choice Research	954-964-1260	•	•	•	
•	•	•	•	•	Ike L Hoy PE (Control Systems)	850-259-4650	•	•	•	•
•	•	•	•	•	Parrish Research	850-936-1240	•	•	•	•
					Research Express	850-926-5665		•		

DT	BK	CV	CR	PR	←Courts **Indian River**	Recording→	UC	RE	TX	VS
•	•	•	•	•	Accurate Background Check	877-611-2277		•	•	•
		•	•	•	Crummey Investigations Inc [SOP]	321-724-0518	•	•	•	•
•	•	•	•	•	Direct Corporate Services Inc	800-783-7904	•	•	•	
•	•	•	•	•	First Choice Research	954-964-1260	•	•	•	
•	•	•	•		Infotrack Information Services Inc	800-275-5594	•	•	•	
					L L Lesko Inc	772-879-2625	•	•	•	
•	•	•	•	•	Merlins Data Research	888-434-6337	•	•	•	•
•	•	•	•	•	Pacific Photocopy & Research (Miami)	305-371-7694	•	•	•	•
•	•	•			Phoenix Document Service Inc	727-581-2552	•	•	•	
					Reliable Title Search Inc	772-489-9650	•	•	•	
				•	Treasure Coast Abstract & Title Ins Co	772-461-7190	•	•	•	

DT	BK	CV	CR	PR	←Courts **Jackson**	Recording→	UC	RE	TX	VS
•	•	•	•	•	Accurate Background Check	877-611-2277		•	•	•
•	•	•	•	•	Emerald Coast Protective Services Inc [SOP]	877-234-6252	•	•	•	•
•	•	•	•	•	First Choice Research	954-964-1260	•	•	•	
•	•	•	•	•	Parrish Research	850-936-1240	•	•	•	•
					Research Express	850-926-5665		•		

DT	BK	CV	CR	PR	←Courts **Jefferson**	Recording→	UC	RE	TX	VS
•	•	•	•	•	Accurate Background Check	877-611-2277		•	•	•
•	•	•	•	•	Advanced Investigations Inc [SOP]	850-863-3997	•	•	•	•
•	•	•	•		Capital Connection [SOP]	850-224-8870	•	•	•	
•	•	•	•	•	Corporate Access Inc [SOP]	800-969-1666	•	•	•	•
•	•	•	•	•	First Choice Research	954-964-1260	•	•	•	
•	•	•			Florida Filing & Search Services Inc	800-435-9371	•		•	
		•	•	•	North Florida Abstract & Title Company	850-997-2670	•	•	•	•

DT	BK	CV	CR	PR	Retriever	Phone	UC	RE	TX	VS
					Research Express	850-926-5665		•		
•	•	•	•	•	State Information Bureau	800-881-1742	•	•	•	
•	•	•			Sunstate Research Associates Inc	800-621-7234	•		•	

DT	BK	CV	CR	PR	←COURTS LAFAYETTE	RECORDING→	UC	RE	TX	VS
•	•	•	•	•	Accurate Background Check	877-611-2277		•	•	•
•	•	•	•	•	First Choice Research	954-964-1260	•	•	•	
					Research Express	850-926-5665		•		

DT	BK	CV	CR	PR	←COURTS LAKE	RECORDING→	UC	RE	TX	VS
•	•	•	•	•	A Very Private Eye Inc [SOP]	407-273-6646	•	•	•	•
•	•	•	•	•	Accurate Background Check	877-611-2277		•	•	•
•	•	•	•	•	Andrews Agency Inc [SOP]	407-649-2085	•	•	•	•
•	•	•	•	•	ATT Investigations Inc	800-733-4405	•	•	•	•
•	•	•	•	•	Direct Corporate Services Inc	800-783-7904	•	•	•	
		•	•		Elman Resources	407-834-5344				
•	•	•		•	First American Title Ins Co	407-740-7131	•	•	•	•
•	•	•	•	•	First Choice Research	954-964-1260	•	•	•	
•	•	•	•	•	Hale Investigative Services/Process [SOP]	800-882-5137	•	•	•	•
•	•	•	•		Infotrack Information Services Inc	800-275-5594	•	•	•	
•	•	•	•	•	Investigative Legal Services Inc [SOP]	888-426-7436	•	•	•	•
•	•	•	•	•	Merlins Data Research	888-434-6337	•	•	•	•
•	•	•			Phoenix Document Service Inc	727-581-2552	•	•	•	
					The Searchers	352-493-0101	•	•	•	

DT	BK	CV	CR	PR	←COURTS LEE	RECORDING→	UC	RE	TX	VS
•	•	•	•	•	Accurate Background Check	877-611-2277		•	•	•
•	•	•	•	•	Bell Investigative Services Inc	954-454-4859	•	•	•	•
•	•	•	•	•	Direct Corporate Services Inc	800-783-7904	•	•	•	
•	•	•	•	•	First Choice Research	954-964-1260	•	•	•	
•	•	•	•	•	Florida Records Research	239-435-1189	•	•	•	•
					Guzman Title Research Inc	941-423-5310	•	•	•	
•	•	•	•		Infotrack Information Services Inc	800-275-5594	•	•	•	
•	•	•	•	•	Judicial Research & Retrieval Svcs (Miami) [SOP]	800-529-6226	•	•	•	•
•	•	•	•	•	Pacific Photocopy & Research (Tampa)	813-221-6828	•	•	•	•
		•	•	•	Palo Verde Research	239-481-9434	•	•	•	•
•	•	•			Phoenix Document Service Inc	727-581-2552	•	•	•	
•	•	•	•	•	Research & Abstract Associates	239-337-5354	•	•	•	•
•	•	•	•	•	South Florida Legal Services of Naples [SOP]	239-332-7000		•	•	•
		•	•	•	SWF Private Inv [SOP]	941-764-9156	•	•	•	•

DT	BK	CV	CR	PR	←COURTS LEON	RECORDING→	UC	RE	TX	VS
•	•	•	•	•	Accurate Background Check	877-611-2277		•	•	•
•	•	•	•	•	Advanced Investigations Inc [SOP]	850-863-3997	•	•	•	•
•	•	•	•		Capital Connection [SOP]	850-224-8870	•	•	•	
•	•	•	•	•	Corporate Access Inc [SOP]	800-969-1666	•	•	•	•
•	•	•	•	•	Corporation Service Company - CSC	800-927-9800	•	•	•	•
•	•	•	•	•	Direct Corporate Services Inc	800-783-7904	•	•	•	
•	•	•	•	•	First Choice Research	954-964-1260	•	•	•	
•	•	•			Florida Filing & Search Services Inc	800-435-9371	•		•	
•	•	•			Florida Information Associates Inc	850-878-0188				
•	•	•			Florida Research & Filing Services Inc	850-656-6446	•	•	•	
•	•	•	•		Infotrack Information Services Inc	800-275-5594	•	•	•	
			•		International Research Bureau Inc (IRB)	866-620-4636	•	•		
•	•	•	•	•	Judicial Research & Retrieval Svcs (Miami) [SOP]	800-529-6226	•	•	•	•
•	•	•			Phoenix Document Service Inc	727-581-2552	•	•	•	
					Research Express	850-926-5665		•		
•	•	•	•	•	State Information Bureau	800-881-1742	•	•	•	
•	•	•			Sunstate Research Associates Inc	800-621-7234	•		•	
		•	•		VeriQuest Inc	813-948-4889				

DT	BK	CV	CR	PR	←Courts	LEVY	Recording→ UC	RE	TX	VS
•	•	•	•	•	Accurate Background Check	877-611-2277		•	•	•
•	•	•	•	•	First Choice Research	954-964-1260	•	•	•	
					The Searchers	352-493-0101	•	•	•	
		•	•	•	Twin Oaks Research	352-465-7844	•	•	•	

DT	BK	CV	CR	PR	←Courts	LIBERTY	Recording→ UC	RE	TX	VS
•	•	•	•	•	Accurate Background Check	877-611-2277		•	•	•
•	•	•	•	•	Advanced Investigations Inc [SOP]	850-863-3997	•	•	•	•
•	•	•	•	•	Corporate Access Inc [SOP]	800-969-1666	•	•	•	•
•	•	•	•	•	First Choice Research	954-964-1260	•	•	•	
					Research Express	850-926-5665		•		

DT	BK	CV	CR	PR	←Courts	MADISON	Recording→ UC	RE	TX	VS
•	•	•	•	•	Accurate Background Check	877-611-2277		•	•	•
•	•	•	•	•	First Choice Research	954-964-1260	•	•	•	
					Research Express	850-926-5665		•		

DT	BK	CV	CR	PR	←Courts	MANATEE	Recording→ UC	RE	TX	VS
•	•	•	•	•	A Public Record Expert Inc	941-504-7734	•	•		•
•	•	•	•	•	Accurate Background Check	877-611-2277		•	•	•
		•	•	•	Chambers Investigations [SOP]	800-792-1107	•	•	•	•
•	•	•	•	•	Direct Corporate Services Inc	800-783-7904	•	•	•	
		•	•	•	Employee Screening Inc	727-581 1147		•	•	
•	•	•	•	•	First Choice Research	954-964-1260	•	•	•	
•	•	•	•	•	Gulf Coast Records	727-580-4873	•	•	•	•
•	•	•	•	•	IGB Associates Inc	813-226-8810	•	•	•	•
•	•	•	•		Infotrack Information Services Inc	800-275-5594	•	•	•	
•	•	•	•	•	Pacific Photocopy & Research (Tampa)	813-221-6828	•	•	•	•
•	•	•			Phoenix Document Service Inc	727-581-2552	•	•	•	
•	•	•	•	•	Research & Abstract Associates	239-337-5354	•	•	•	•
					Source Documents & Information Inc	727-447-8844	•	•	•	
		•	•	•	Steele Investigation Agency [SOP]	941-758-5890	•	•	•	•
•	•	•	•	•	Sugarbaker Investigations	800-720-2567	•			•
•		•	•		Sunshine Research Inc	888-786-1242	•			
		•	•		VeriQuest Inc	813-948-4889				

DT	BK	CV	CR	PR	←Courts	MARION	Recording→ UC	RE	TX	VS
•	•	•	•	•	Accurate Background Check	877-611-2277		•	•	•
•	•	•	•	•	ATT Investigations Inc	800-733-4405	•	•	•	•
•	•	•	•	•	Direct Corporate Services Inc	800-783-7904	•	•	•	
		•	•		Elman Resources	407-834-5344				
•	•	•		•	First American Title Ins Co.	407-740-7131	•	•	•	•
•	•	•	•	•	First Choice Research	954-964-1260	•	•	•	
•		•	•	•	Lehr's Process Service [SOP]	352-331-1010	•	•	•	•
•	•	•	•	•	Pacific Photocopy & Research (Jacksonville) [SOP]	904-355-1062	•	•	•	•
•	•	•			Phoenix Document Service Inc	727-581-2552	•	•	•	
•	•	•	•	•	Sugarbaker Investigations	800-720-2567	•			•
					The Searchers	352-493-0101	•	•	•	

DT	BK	CV	CR	PR	←Courts	MARTIN	Recording→ UC	RE	TX	VS
•	•	•	•	•	Accurate Background Check	877-611-2277		•	•	•
•	•	•	•	•	Bell Investigative Services Inc	954-454-4859	•	•	•	•
•	•	•	•	•	Direct Corporate Services Inc	800-783-7904	•	•	•	
•	•	•	•	•	First Choice Research	954-964-1260	•	•	•	
•	•	•		•	FLA Search Company	561-969-6594	•	•	•	•
•	•	•	•	•	Information Search Inc [SOP]	561-624-5115	•	•	•	•
					L L Lesko Inc	772-879-2625	•	•	•	
•	•	•	•	•	Merlins Data Research	888-434-6337	•	•	•	•
•	•	•	•	•	Pacific Photocopy & Research (Miami)	305-371-7694	•	•	•	•

DT	BK	CV	CR	PR	←Courts	Recording→	UC	RE	TX	VS
		•	•		Pasco Records Check Inc	813-991-5719				
•	•	•			Phoenix Document Service Inc	727-581-2552	•	•	•	
					Reliable Title Search Inc	772-489-9650	•	•	•	
					South Florida Title Research Inc dba SFTR	866-398-7387	•	•	•	
				•	Treasure Coast Abstract & Title Ins Co	772-461-7190	•	•	•	

DT	BK	CV	CR	PR	←Courts **Monroe**	Recording→	UC	RE	TX	VS
•	•	•	•	•	Accurate Background Check	877-611-2277		•	•	•
•	•	•	•	•	Coastal Office Dimensions	850-484-8098	•	•	•	•
•	•	•	•	•	Direct Corporate Services Inc	800-783-7904	•	•	•	
•	•	•	•	•	First Choice Research	954-964-1260	•	•	•	
		•	•	•	Independent Abstract & Title	305-294-5105	•	•	•	
•	•	•	•	•	Pacific Photocopy & Research (Miami)	305-371-7694	•	•	•	•
•	•	•			Phoenix Document Service Inc	727-581-2552	•	•	•	

DT	BK	CV	CR	PR	←Courts **Nassau**	Recording→	UC	RE	TX	VS
•	•	•	•	•	Accurate Background Check	877-611-2277		•	•	•
•	•	•	•	•	First Choice Research	954-964-1260	•	•	•	
•	•	•	•	•	First Coast Inv [SOP]	904-398-4076			•	•
					Fort Lauderdale-Miami Courthouse Research Inc	954-434-6819	•	•	•	
•	•	•	•		G & L Research Associates	904-743-4116	•	•	•	
•	•	•	•		Infotrack Information Services Inc	800-275-5594	•	•	•	
•	•	•	•	•	Judicial Research & Retrieval Svcs (Jacksonville)	904-356-9110	•	•	•	•
				•	Land Title of America Group	904-797-9600	•	•	•	
•	•	•	•	•	Mulholland Investigations & Security [SOP]	904-354-7989	•	•	•	•
•	•	•	•	•	Pacific Photocopy & Research (Jacksonville) [SOP]	904-355-1062	•	•	•	•
		•	•		Pasco Records Check Inc	813-991-5719				
•	•	•			Phoenix Document Service Inc	727-581-2552	•	•	•	

DT	BK	CV	CR	PR	←Courts **Okaloosa**	Recording→	UC	RE	TX	VS
		•		•	AAA Search Excellence Inc	352-688-6751	•	•	•	
•	•	•	•	•	Accurate Background Check	877-611-2277		•	•	•
•	•	•	•	•	Advanced Investigations Inc [SOP]	850-863-3997	•	•	•	•
•	•	•	•	•	Direct Corporate Services Inc	800-783-7904	•	•	•	
•	•	•	•	•	First Choice Research	954-964-1260	•	•	•	
•	•	•	•	•	Ike L Hoy PE (Control Systems)	850-259-4650	•	•	•	•
•	•	•	•		Infotrack Information Services Inc	800-275-5594	•	•	•	
•	•	•	•	•	Pacific Photocopy & Research (Pensacola) [SOP]	850-435-3183	•	•	•	•
•	•	•	•	•	Parrish Research	850-936-1240	•	•	•	•
•	•	•			Phoenix Document Service Inc	727-581-2552	•	•	•	

DT	BK	CV	CR	PR	←Courts **Okeechobee**	Recording→	UC	RE	TX	VS
•	•	•	•	•	Accurate Background Check	877-611-2277		•	•	•
•	•	•	•	•	Direct Corporate Services Inc	800-783-7904	•	•	•	
•	•	•	•	•	First Choice Research	954-964-1260	•	•	•	
		•	•	•	Okeechobee Abstract & Title Ins Co	863-763-3710	•	•	•	
•	•	•	•	•	Pacific Photocopy & Research (Miami)	305-371-7694	•	•	•	•
					Reliable Title Search Inc	772-489-9650	•	•	•	
				•	Treasure Coast Abstract & Title Ins Co	772-461-7190	•	•	•	

DT	BK	CV	CR	PR	←Courts **Orange**	Recording→	UC	RE	TX	VS
•	•	•	•	•	A Very Private Eye Inc [SOP]	407-273-6646	•	•	•	•
•	•	•	•	•	Accurate Background Check	877-611-2277		•	•	•
•	•	•	•	•	Andrews Agency Inc [SOP]	407-649-2085	•	•	•	•
•	•	•	•	•	ATT Investigations Inc	800-733-4405	•	•	•	•
•	•	•	•	•	Bell Investigative Services Inc	954-454-4859	•	•	•	•
		•	•	•	Crummey Investigations Inc [SOP]	321-724-0518	•	•	•	•
•	•	•	•	•	Direct Corporate Services Inc	800-783-7904	•	•	•	
		•	•		Elman Resources	407-834-5344				
•	•	•		•	First American Title Ins Co	407-740-7131	•	•	•	•

DT	BK	CV	CR	PR	←Courts	Recording→	UC	RE	TX	VS
•	•	•	•	•	First Choice Research	954-964-1260	•	•	•	
					Fort Lauderdale-Miami Courthouse Research Inc	954-434-6819	•	•	•	
•	•	•	•		GPS & Assoc (Florida)	866-813-8131	•		•	•
•	•	•	•	•	Hale Investigative Services/Process [SOP]	800-882-5137	•	•	•	•
•	•	•		•	ICDI Inc	407-622-2532	•	•	•	
•	•	•	•	•	IGB Associates Inc	813-226-8810	•	•	•	•
•	•	•		•	Independent Research Assoc	407-832-8580	•	•	•	
•	•	•	•		Infotrack Information Services Inc	800-275-5594	•	•	•	
•	•	•	•	•	Investigative Legal Services Inc [SOP]	888-426-7436	•	•	•	•
		•	•		Jackson Research Associates	877-654-9988				
•	•	•	•	•	Judicial Research & Retrieval Svcs (Orlando)	407-999-7717	•	•	•	•
•	•	•	•	•	Legal 1 Document Retrieval [SOP]	954-733-8934	•	•	•	•
•	•	•	•	•	Liquori Investigations	386-423-4235	•	•	•	•
		•	•	•	Lowry Document Service	386-789-6193	•	•	•	•
•	•	•	•	•	Merlins Data Research	888-434-6337	•	•	•	•
•	•	•	•	•	Pacific Photocopy & Research (Orlando)	407-425-7234	•	•	•	•
		•	•		Pasco Records Check Inc	813-991-5719				
•	•	•			Phoenix Document Service Inc	727-581-2552	•	•	•	
					Source Documents & Information Inc	727-447-8844	•	•	•	
•	•	•	•	•	Sugarbaker Investigations	800-720-2567	•			•
		•	•		VeriQuest Inc	813-948-4889				
•	•		•	•	XpertSearch Inc	732-229-6688	•	•	•	•

DT	BK	CV	CR	PR	←Courts **Osceola**	Recording→	UC	RE	TX	VS
•	•	•	•	•	A Very Private Eye Inc [SOP]	407-273-6646	•	•	•	•
•	•	•	•	•	Accurate Background Check	877-611-2277		•	•	•
•	•	•	•	•	Andrews Agency Inc [SOP]	407-649-2085	•	•	•	•
•	•	•	•	•	ATT Investigations Inc	800-733-4405	•	•	•	•
•	•	•	•	•	Direct Corporate Services Inc	800-783-7904	•	•	•	
		•	•		Elman Resources	407-834-5344				
•	•	•		•	First American Title Ins Co	407-740-7131	•	•	•	•
•	•	•	•	•	First Choice Research	954-964-1260	•	•	•	
•	•	•	•	•	Hale Investigative Services/Process [SOP]	800-882-5137	•	•	•	•
•	•	•		•	ICDI Inc	407-622-2532	•	•	•	
•	•	•		•	Independent Research Assoc	407-832-8580	•	•	•	
•	•	•	•		Infotrack Information Services Inc	800-275-5594	•	•	•	
•	•	•	•	•	Investigative Legal Services Inc [SOP]	888-426-7436	•	•	•	•
		•	•		Jackson Research Associates	877-654-9988				
•	•	•	•	•	Judicial Research & Retrieval Svcs (Orlando)	407-999-7717	•	•	•	•
•	•	•	•	•	Merlins Data Research	888-434-6337	•	•	•	•
•	•	•	•	•	Pacific Photocopy & Research (Orlando)	407-425-7234	•	•	•	•
•	•	•			Phoenix Document Service Inc	727-581-2552	•	•	•	

DT	BK	CV	CR	PR	←Courts **Palm Beach**	Recording→	UC	RE	TX	VS
•	•	•	•	•	Accurate Background Check	877-611-2277		•	•	•
•	•	•	•	•	Accurate Confidential Research Inc	305-386-6677	•	•	•	•
•	•	•	•	•	All American Document Services	954-761-7292	•	•	•	•
•	•	•	•	•	American Legal Solution Inc	954-986-5442	•	•	•	•
•	•	•	•	•	ATT Investigations Inc	800-733-4405	•	•	•	•
•	•	•	•	•	Barry Shuster Information Services, A Div of Search-It Inc	877-852-2507	•	•	•	•
•	•	•	•	•	Bell Investigative Services Inc	954-454-4859	•	•	•	•
•	•	•	•	•	Bill Greenberg Special Services Inc [SOP]	888-770-9008	•	•	•	•
•	•	•	•	•	Compass Investigations [SOP]	954-527-5722	•	•	•	•
		•	•		Deception Control Inc	800-776-1660		•	•	•
•	•	•	•	•	Direct Corporate Services Inc	800-783-7904	•	•	•	
•	•	•	•	•	Esquire Express Inc [SOP]	800-439-8744	•	•	•	•
•	•	•	•	•	First Choice Research	954-964-1260	•	•	•	
•	•	•		•	FLA Search Company	561-969-6594	•	•	•	•
					Fort Lauderdale-Miami Courthouse Research Inc	954-434-6819	•	•	•	

DT	BK	CV	CR	PR	←Courts	Recording→	UC	RE	TX	VS
•	•	•	•		GPS & Assoc (Florida)	866-813-8131	•		•	•
•	•	•	•	•	Ken Haave PI	305-710-7409	•	•	•	•
•	•	•	•	•	Information Search Inc [SOP]	561-624-5115	•	•	•	•
•	•	•	•		Infotrack Information Services Inc	800-275-5594	•	•	•	
•	•	•	•	•	Intracoastal Detective Agency Inc	954-564-5455	•	•	•	•
•	•	•	•	•	JM Search Services Inc	800-393-7563	•	•	•	
•	•	•	•	•	Judicial Research & Retrieval Svcs (Palm Beach)	561-659-7677	•	•	•	•
					L L Lesko Inc	772-879-2625	•	•	•	
•	•	•	•	•	Legal 1 Document Retrieval [SOP]	954-733-8934	•	•	•	•
•	•	•		•	Johanna E Malki	305-899-0273	•	•	•	
•	•	•	•	•	Medina Retrieval Service	954-560-9077		•		
•	•	•	•	•	David Mulberry [SOP]	800-704-1287	•	•	•	•
•	•	•	•	•	Pacific Photocopy & Research (West Palm Beach)	561-832-3878	•	•	•	•
•	•	•	•	•	Paralegal Field Research Service [SOP]	800-256-7459	•	•	•	•
		•	•		Pasco Records Check Inc	813-991-5719				
•	•	•	•	•	Patrick Investigative Services Inc	800-700-2958	•	•	•	•
•	•	•			Phoenix Document Service Inc	727-581-2552	•	•	•	
•	•	•	•	•	Premiere Investigations [SOP]	954-974-1139	•	•	•	•
•	•	•	•	•	Public Records Research Inc (Florida)	561-746-0850	•	•	•	
					Reliable Title Search Inc	772-489-9650	•	•	•	
•	•	•	•	•	Paul Scholtes [SOP]	561-385-8163	•	•	•	•
					Source Documents & Information Inc	727-447-8844	•	•	•	
					South Florida Title Research Inc dba SFTR	866-398-7387	•	•	•	
•	•	•	•	•	The Records Reviewer Inc	305-934-4920	•	•	•	•

DT	BK	CV	CR	PR	←Courts **Pasco**	Recording→	UC	RE	TX	VS
		•		•	AAA Search Excellence Inc	352-688-6751	•	•	•	
•	•	•	•	•	Accurate Background Check	877-611-2277		•	•	•
•	•	•	•		Ace Data Service [SOP]	727-735-9311	•	•	•	•
•	•	•	•	•	All American Research LLC	800-215-7958	•	•	•	•
•		•	•	•	All Phase Reports [SOP]	813-885-9822		•		•
•	•	•	•		Applicant Insight Ltd	800-771-7703	•			
•	•	•	•	•	ATT Investigations Inc	800-733-4405	•	•	•	•
•	•	•	•	•	Bay Area Search Inc	727-724-5995	•	•	•	•
•	•	•	•	•	Bill Greenberg Special Services Inc [SOP]	888-770-9008	•	•	•	•
				•	Coast to Coast Abstracting	352-442-1500	•	•	•	
•	•	•	•	•	Colton & Associates Inc [SOP]	800-704-6699	•	•	•	•
•	•	•	•	•	Direct Corporate Services Inc	800-783-7904	•	•	•	
•	•	•	•	•	First Choice Research	954-964-1260	•	•	•	
•	•	•	•	•	Gietzen & Associates Inc [SOP]	813-223-3233		•	•	
•	•	•	•		GPS & Assoc (Florida)	866-813-8131	•		•	•
•	•	•	•	•	Gulf Coast Records	727-580-4873	•	•	•	•
•	•	•	•	•	IGB Associates Inc	813-226-8810	•	•	•	•
•	•	•	•		Infotrack Information Services Inc	800-275-5594	•	•	•	
•	•	•	•	•	Judicial Research & Retrieval Svcs (Tampa)	813-228-7200	•	•	•	•
•	•	•	•	•	Mohr Information Services LLC	540-678-8775	•	•	•	
•	•	•	•	•	Pacific Photocopy & Research (Tampa)	813-221-6828	•	•	•	•
		•	•		Pasco Records Check Inc	813-991-5719				
•	•	•			Phoenix Document Service Inc	727-581-2552	•	•	•	
•	•	•	•	•	Prestige Legal Services [SOP]	800-784-7572	•	•	•	•
•	•	•	•	•	Research & Abstract Associates	239-337-5354	•	•	•	•
					Source Documents & Information Inc	727-447-8844	•	•	•	
•	•	•	•	•	Sugarbaker Investigations	800-720-2567	•			•
•		•	•		Sunshine Research Inc	888-786-1242	•			
					The Searchers	352-493-0101	•	•	•	
		•	•		VeriQuest Inc	813-948-4889				

DT	BK	CV	CR	PR	←Courts **Pinellas**	Recording→	UC	RE	TX	VS
•	•	•	•	•	A Public Record Expert Inc	941-504-7734	•	•		•

DT	BK	CV	CR	PR	←Courts	Recording→	UC	RE	TX	VS
•	•	•	•	•	Accurate Background Check	877-611-2277		•	•	•
•	•	•	•		Ace Data Service [SOP]	727-735-9311	•	•	•	•
•	•	•	•	•	All American Research LLC	800-215-7958	•	•	•	•
•	•	•	•	•	All Phase Reports [SOP]	813-885-9822		•		•
•	•	•	•		Applicant Insight Ltd	800-771-7703	•			
•	•	•	•	•	ATT Investigations Inc	800-733-4405	•	•	•	•
•	•	•	•	•	Bay Area Search Inc	727-724-5995	•	•	•	•
•	•	•	•	•	Bell Investigative Services Inc	954-454-4859	•	•	•	•
•	•	•	•	•	Bill Greenberg Special Services Inc [SOP]	888-770-9008	•	•	•	•
•	•	•	•	•	Colton & Associates Inc [SOP]	800-704-6699	•	•	•	•
•	•	•	•	•	Direct Corporate Services Inc	800-783-7904	•	•	•	
					Doc Hunters	727-518-6700	•	•	•	
		•	•	•	Employee Screening Inc	727-581 1147		•	•	
•	•	•	•	•	EX-CEL Inv [SOP]	800-317-7626	•	•	•	•
•	•	•	•	•	First Choice Research	954-964-1260	•	•	•	
•	•	•	•	•	Gietzen & Associates Inc [SOP]	813-223-3233		•	•	
•	•	•	•		GPS & Assoc (Florida)	866-813-8131	•		•	•
•	•	•	•	•	Gulf Coast Records	727-580-4873	•	•	•	•
•	•	•	•	•	IGB Associates Inc	813-226-8810	•	•	•	•
•	•	•	•		Infotrack Information Services Inc	800-275-5594	•	•	•	
•	•	•	•	•	Judicial Research & Retrieval Svcs (Tampa)	813-228-7200	•	•	•	•
•	•	•	•	•	Mohr Information Services LLC	540-678-8775	•	•	•	
•	•	•	•	•	Pacific Photocopy & Research (Tampa)	813-221-6828	•	•	•	•
		•	•		Pasco Records Check Inc	813-991-5719				
•	•	•			Phoenix Document Service Inc	727-581-2552	•	•	•	
•	•	•	•	•	Prestige Legal Services [SOP]	800-784-7572	•	•	•	•
•	•	•	•	•	Research & Abstract Associates	239-337-5354	•	•	•	•
					Source Documents & Information Inc	727-447-8844	•	•	•	
•	•	•	•	•	Sugarbaker Investigations	800-720-2567	•			•
•		•	•		Sunshine Research Inc	888-786-1242	•			
		•	•		VeriQuest Inc	813-948-4889				

DT	BK	CV	CR	PR	←Courts **POLK**	Recording→	UC	RE	TX	VS
•	•	•	•	•	A Very Private Eye Inc [SOP]	407-273-6646	•	•	•	•
•	•	•	•	•	Accurate Background Check	877-611-2277		•	•	•
		•	•	•	Al Smith Private Inv [SOP]	863-295-1375	•	•	•	•
•		•	•	•	All Phase Reports [SOP]	813-885-9822		•		•
•	•	•	•	•	Bill Greenberg Special Services Inc [SOP]	888-770-9008	•	•	•	•
				•	Coast to Coast Abstracting	352-442-1500	•	•	•	
•	•	•	•	•	Direct Corporate Services Inc	800-783-7904	•	•	•	
•	•	•		•	First American Title Ins Co	407-740-7131	•	•	•	•
•	•	•	•	•	First Choice Research	954-964-1260	•	•	•	
•	•	•	•	•	Gietzen & Associates Inc [SOP]	813-223-3233		•	•	
		•	•	•	John Gordon [SOP]	863-224-4377	•	•	•	•
•	•	•	•		GPS & Assoc (Florida)	866-813-8131	•		•	•
•	•	•	•	•	Gulf Coast Records	727-580-4873	•	•	•	•
•	•	•	•	•	Hale Investigative Services/Process [SOP]	800-882-5137	•	•	•	•
•	•	•	•	•	IGB Associates Inc	813-226-8810	•	•	•	•
•	•	•	•		Infotrack Information Services Inc	800-275-5594	•	•	•	
•	•	•	•	•	Judicial Research & Retrieval Svcs (Tampa)	813-228-7200	•	•	•	•
•	•	•	•	•	Mohr Information Services LLC	540-678-8775	•	•	•	
•	•	•	•	•	Pacific Photocopy & Research (Tampa)	813-221-6828	•	•	•	•
•	•	•			Phoenix Document Service Inc	727-581-2552	•	•	•	
					Source Documents & Information Inc	727-447-8844	•	•	•	
•	•	•	•	•	Sugarbaker Investigations	800-720-2567	•			•
		•	•		VeriQuest Inc	813-948-4889				

DT	BK	CV	CR	PR	←Courts **PUTNAM**	Recording→	UC	RE	TX	VS
•	•	•	•	•	Accurate Background Check	877-611-2277		•	•	•

DT	BK	CV	CR	PR	←Courts	Recording→	UC	RE	TX	VS
•	•	•	•	•	First Choice Research	954-964-1260	•	•	•	
				•	Land Title of America Group	904-797-9600	•	•	•	•
•	•	•	•	•	Pacific Photocopy & Research (Jacksonville) [SOP]	904-355-1062	•	•	•	•
•	•	•			Phoenix Document Service Inc	727-581-2552	•	•	•	

DT	BK	CV	CR	PR	←Courts **Santa Rosa**	Recording→	UC	RE	TX	VS
•	•	•	•	•	Accurate Background Check	877-611-2277		•	•	•
•	•	•	•	•	Advanced Investigations Inc [SOP]	850-863-3997	•	•	•	•
•	•	•	•	•	Coastal Office Dimensions	850-484-8098	•	•	•	•
•	•	•	•	•	Direct Corporate Services Inc	800-783-7904	•	•	•	
•	•	•	•	•	First Choice Research	954-964-1260	•	•	•	
•	•	•	•	•	Ike L Hoy PE (Control Systems)	850-259-4650	•	•	•	•
•	•	•	•	•	Pacific Photocopy & Research (Pensacola) [SOP]	850-435-3183	•	•	•	•
•	•	•	•	•	Parrish Research	850-936-1240	•	•	•	•
•	•	•			Phoenix Document Service Inc	727-581-2552	•	•	•	

DT	BK	CV	CR	PR	←Courts **Sarasota**	Recording→	UC	RE	TX	VS
•	•	•	•	•	A Public Record Expert Inc	941-504-7734	•	•		•
•	•	•	•	•	Accurate Background Check	877-611-2277		•	•	•
		•	•	•	Chambers Investigations [SOP]	800-792-1107	•	•	•	•
•	•	•	•	•	Colton & Associates Inc [SOP]	800-704-6699	•	•	•	•
•	•	•	•	•	Direct Corporate Services Inc	800-783-7904	•	•	•	
•	•	•	•	•	First Choice Research	954-964-1260	•	•	•	
•	•	•	•	•	Gulf Coast Records	727-580-4873	•	•	•	•
					Guzman Title Research Inc	941-423-5310	•	•	•	
•	•	•	•	•	IGB Associates Inc	813-226-8810	•	•	•	•
•	•	•	•		Infotrack Information Services Inc	800-275-5594	•	•	•	
•	•	•	•	•	Pacific Photocopy & Research (Tampa)	813-221-6828	•	•	•	•
•	•	•			Phoenix Document Service Inc	727-581-2552	•	•	•	
•	•	•	•	•	Research & Abstract Associates	239-337-5354	•	•	•	•
					Source Documents & Information Inc	727-447-8844	•	•	•	
		•	•	•	Steele Investigation Agency [SOP]	941-758-5890	•	•	•	•
•	•	•	•	•	Sugarbaker Investigations	800-720-2567	•			•
		•	•	•	SWF Private Inv [SOP]	941-764-9156	•	•	•	•
		•	•		VeriQuest Inc	813-948-4889				

DT	BK	CV	CR	PR	←Courts **Seminole**	Recording→	UC	RE	TX	VS
•	•	•	•	•	A Very Private Eye Inc [SOP]	407-273-6646	•	•	•	•
•	•	•	•	•	Accurate Background Check	877-611-2277		•	•	•
•	•	•	•	•	Andrews Agency Inc [SOP]	407-649-2085	•	•	•	•
•	•	•	•	•	ATT Investigations Inc	800-733-4405	•	•	•	•
•	•	•	•	•	Bell Investigative Services Inc	954-454-4859	•	•	•	•
•	•	•	•	•	Bill Greenberg Special Services Inc [SOP]	888-770-9008	•	•	•	•
•	•	•	•	•	Direct Corporate Services Inc	800-783-7904	•	•	•	
		•	•		Elman Resources	407-834-5344				
•	•	•		•	First American Title Ins Co	407-740-7131	•	•	•	•
•	•	•	•	•	First Choice Research	954-964-1260	•	•	•	
•	•	•	•	•	Hale Investigative Services/Process [SOP]	800-882-5137	•	•	•	•
•	•	•		•	ICDI Inc	407-622-2532	•	•	•	
•	•	•		•	Independent Research Assoc	407-832-8580	•	•	•	
•	•	•	•	•	Investigative Legal Services Inc [SOP]	888-426-7436	•	•	•	•
•	•	•	•	•	Judicial Research & Retrieval Svcs (Orlando)	407-999-7717	•	•	•	•
•	•	•	•	•	Legal 1 Document Retrieval [SOP]	954-733-8934	•	•	•	•
•	•	•	•	•	Liquori Investigations	386-423-4235	•	•	•	•
		•	•	•	Lowry Document Service	386-789-6193	•	•	•	•
•	•	•	•	•	Merlins Data Research	888-434-6337	•	•	•	•
•	•	•	•	•	Pacific Photocopy & Research (Orlando)	407-425-7234	•	•	•	•
•	•	•			Phoenix Document Service Inc	727-581-2552	•	•	•	
•	•	•	•	•	Sugarbaker Investigations	800-720-2567	•			•

DT	BK	CV	CR	PR	Retriever	Phone	UC	RE	TX	VS
•	•		•	•	XpertSearch Inc	732-229-6688	•	•	•	•

DT	BK	CV	CR	PR	←Courts **ST. JOHNS**	Recording→	UC	RE	TX	VS
•	•	•	•	•	Accurate Background Check	877-611-2277		•	•	•
•	•	•	•	•	First Choice Research	954-964-1260	•	•	•	
				•	Flagler County Abstract Co [SOP]	386-437-4151	•	•	•	
•	•	•	•		G & L Research Associates	904-743-4116	•	•	•	
				•	Land Title of America Group	904-797-9600	•	•	•	•
•	•	•	•	•	Millennial Investigative Agency	888-299-7574	•	•	•	•
•	•	•	•	•	Mulholland Investigations & Security [SOP]	904-354-7989	•	•	•	•
•	•	•	•	•	Pacific Photocopy & Research (Jacksonville) [SOP]	904-355-1062	•	•	•	•
•	•	•			Phoenix Document Service Inc	727-581-2552	•	•	•	
•	•		•	•	XpertSearch Inc	732-229-6688	•	•	•	•

DT	BK	CV	CR	PR	←Courts **ST. LUCIE**	Recording→	UC	RE	TX	VS
•	•	•	•	•	Accurate Background Check	877-611-2277		•	•	•
•	•	•	•	•	Bell Investigative Services Inc	954-454-4859	•	•	•	•
•	•	•	•	•	Direct Corporate Services Inc	800-783-7904	•	•	•	
•	•	•	•	•	First Choice Research	954-964-1260	•	•	•	
•	•	•		•	FLA Search Company	561-969-6594	•	•	•	•
•	•	•	•	•	Information Search Inc [SOP]	561-624-5115	•	•	•	•
					L L Lesko Inc	772-879-2625	•	•	•	
•	•	•	•	•	Merlins Data Research	888-434-6337	•	•	•	•
•	•	•	•	•	Pacific Photocopy & Research (Miami)	305-371-7694	•	•	•	•
		•	•		Pasco Records Check Inc	813-991-5719				
•	•	•			Phoenix Document Service Inc	727-581-2552	•	•	•	
					Reliable Title Search Inc	772-489-9650	•	•	•	
				•	Treasure Coast Abstract & Title Ins Co	772-461-7190	•	•	•	

DT	BK	CV	CR	PR	←Courts **SUMTER**	Recording→	UC	RE	TX	VS
•	•	•	•	•	Accurate Background Check	877-611-2277		•	•	•
				•	Coast to Coast Abstracting	352-442-1500	•	•	•	
•	•	•	•	•	Direct Corporate Services Inc	800-783-7904	•	•	•	
•	•	•	•	•	First Choice Research	954-964-1260	•	•	•	
•	•	•	•	•	Pacific Photocopy & Research (Jacksonville) [SOP]	904-355-1062	•	•	•	•
•	•	•	•	•	Prestige Legal Services [SOP]	800-784-7572	•	•	•	•
					The Searchers	352-493-0101	•	•	•	

DT	BK	CV	CR	PR	←Courts **SUWANNEE**	Recording→	UC	RE	TX	VS
•	•	•	•	•	Accurate Background Check	877-611-2277		•	•	•
•	•	•	•	•	First Choice Research	954-964-1260	•	•	•	
•	•	•	•	•	Pacific Photocopy & Research (Jacksonville) [SOP]	904-355-1062	•	•	•	•
					Research Express	850-926-5665		•		

DT	BK	CV	CR	PR	←Courts **TAYLOR**	Recording→	UC	RE	TX	VS
•	•	•	•	•	Accurate Background Check	877-611-2277		•	•	•
•	•	•	•	•	First Choice Research	954-964-1260	•	•	•	
					Research Express	850-926-5665		•		

DT	BK	CV	CR	PR	←Courts **UNION**	Recording→	UC	RE	TX	VS
•	•	•	•	•	Accurate Background Check	877-611-2277		•	•	•
•	•	•	•	•	First Choice Research	954-964-1260	•	•	•	
•	•	•	•	•	Pacific Photocopy & Research (Jacksonville) [SOP]	904-355-1062	•	•	•	•
		•	•		Pasco Records Check Inc	813-991-5719				
					Research Express	850-926-5665		•		

DT	BK	CV	CR	PR	←Courts **VOLUSIA**	Recording→	UC	RE	TX	VS
•	•	•	•	•	Accurate Background Check	877-611-2277		•	•	•
•	•	•	•	•	Andrews Agency Inc [SOP]	407-649-2085	•	•	•	•
•	•	•	•	•	ATT Investigations Inc	800-733-4405	•	•	•	•

DT	BK	CV	CR	PR	Retriever	Phone	UC	RE	TX	VS
•	•	•	•	•	Bell Investigative Services Inc	954-454-4859	•	•	•	•
•	•	•	•	•	Bill Greenberg Special Services Inc [SOP]	888-770-9008	•	•	•	•
•	•	•	•	•	Direct Corporate Services Inc	800-783-7904	•	•	•	
		•	•		Elman Resources	407-834-5344				
•	•	•		•	First American Title Ins Co	407-740-7131	•	•	•	•
•	•	•	•	•	First Choice Research	954-964-1260	•	•	•	
				•	Flagler County Abstract Co [SOP]	386-437-4151	•	•	•	
•	•	•	•	•	Hale Investigative Services/Process [SOP]	800-882-5137	•	•	•	•
•	•	•		•	ICDI Inc	407-622-2532	•	•	•	
•	•	•		•	Independent Research Assoc	407-832-8580	•	•	•	
•	•	•	•		Infotrack Information Services Inc	800-275-5594	•	•	•	
•	•	•	•	•	Legal 1 Document Retrieval [SOP]	954-733-8934	•	•	•	•
•	•	•	•	•	Liquori Investigations	386-423-4235	•	•	•	•
		•	•	•	Lowry Document Service	386-789-6193	•	•	•	•
•		•	•	•	Marx Information Service Inc	386-740-7122	•	•	•	•
•	•	•	•	•	Merlins Data Research	888-434-6337	•	•	•	•
•	•	•			Phoenix Document Service Inc	727-581-2552	•	•	•	
					Property Research Associates	386-423-0258	•	•	•	
•	•	•	•	•	Sugarbaker Investigations	800-720-2567	•			•
					The Searchers	352-493-0101	•	•	•	
•	•		•	•	XpertSearch Inc	732-229-6688	•	•	•	•

DT	BK	CV	CR	PR	←Courts **WAKULLA**	Recording→	UC	RE	TX	VS
•	•	•	•	•	Accurate Background Check	877-611-2277		•	•	•
•	•	•	•	•	Advanced Investigations Inc [SOP]	850-863-3997	•	•	•	•
•	•	•	•		Capital Connection [SOP]	850-224-8870	•	•	•	
•	•	•	•	•	Corporate Access Inc [SOP]	800-969-1666	•	•	•	•
•	•	•	•	•	First Choice Research	954-964-1260	•	•	•	
•	•	•			Florida Filing & Search Services Inc	800-435-9371	•		•	
					Research Express	850-926-5665		•		
•	•	•	•	•	State Information Bureau	800-881-1742	•	•	•	
•	•	•			Sunstate Research Associates Inc	800-621-7234	•		•	

DT	BK	CV	CR	PR	←Courts **WALTON**	Recording→	UC	RE	TX	VS
		•		•	AAA Search Excellence Inc	352-688-6751	•	•	•	
•	•	•	•	•	Accurate Background Check	877-611-2277		•	•	•
•	•	•	•	•	Advanced Investigations Inc [SOP]	850-863-3997	•	•	•	•
•	•	•	•	•	Direct Corporate Services Inc	800-783-7904	•	•	•	
•	•	•	•	•	Emerald Coast Protective Services Inc [SOP]	877-234-6252	•	•	•	•
•	•	•	•	•	First Choice Research	954-964-1260	•	•	•	
•	•	•	•	•	Ike L Hoy PE (Control Systems)	850-259-4650	•	•	•	•
•	•	•	•		Infotrack Information Services Inc	800-275-5594	•	•	•	
•	•	•	•	•	Pacific Photocopy & Research (Pensacola) [SOP]	850-435-3183	•	•	•	•
•	•	•	•	•	Parrish Research	850-936-1240	•	•	•	•
		•	•		Pasco Records Check Inc	813-991-5719				
•	•	•			Phoenix Document Service Inc	727-581-2552	•	•	•	

DT	BK	CV	CR	PR	←Courts **WASHINGTON**	Recording→	UC	RE	TX	VS
•	•	•	•	•	Accurate Background Check	877-611-2277		•	•	•
•	•	•	•	•	First Choice Research	954-964-1260	•	•	•	
•	•	•	•	•	Ike L Hoy PE (Control Systems)	850-259-4650	•	•	•	•
•	•	•	•	•	Pacific Photocopy & Research (Pensacola) [SOP]	850-435-3183	•	•	•	•
•	•	•	•	•	Parrish Research	850-936-1240	•	•	•	•
					Research Express	850-926-5665		•		

Georgia

COURT RECORDS RETRIEVED — **RECORDING RECORDS RETRIEVED**

Appling

DT	BK	CV	CR	PR	←Courts / Recording→	Phone	UC	RE	TX	VS
		•	•	•	Background Research Agency Inc	770-788-1885	•		•	
		•	•		National Pre-Employment Research [SOP]	770-389-6607				
•	•	•	•	•	Origin Information & Services Inc (GA)	800-315-3492	•	•	•	

Atkinson

DT	BK	CV	CR	PR	←Courts / Recording→	Phone	UC	RE	TX	VS
•	•	•	•	•	Origin Information & Services Inc (GA)	800-315-3492	•	•	•	

Bacon

DT	BK	CV	CR	PR	←Courts / Recording→	Phone	UC	RE	TX	VS
		•	•	•	Background Research Agency Inc	770-788-1885	•		•	
•	•	•	•	•	Origin Information & Services Inc (GA)	800-315-3492	•	•	•	

Baker

DT	BK	CV	CR	PR	←Courts / Recording→	Phone	UC	RE	TX	VS
		•	•	•	Background Research Agency Inc	770-788-1885	•		•	
•	•	•	•	•	Origin Information & Services Inc (GA)	800-315-3492	•	•	•	
	•	•	•		Vinson Detective Agency [SOP]	800-404-6698	•	•	•	•

Baldwin

DT	BK	CV	CR	PR	←Courts / Recording→	Phone	UC	RE	TX	VS
		•	•	•	Background Research Agency Inc	770-788-1885	•		•	
				•	M V Bostick Jr	478-781-9344		•	•	
		•	•		National Pre-Employment Research [SOP]	770-389-6607				
•	•	•	•	•	Origin Information & Services Inc (GA)	800-315-3492	•	•	•	
		•	•		Professional Paralegal Services Inc [SOP]	706-310-1166				
	•	•			Southern Courthouse Ventures	678-413-4697	•	•	•	

Banks

DT	BK	CV	CR	PR	←Courts / Recording→	Phone	UC	RE	TX	VS
		•	•	•	Background Research Agency Inc	770-788-1885	•		•	
•	•	•	•	•	EL-RU Inc	770-963-8023	•	•	•	•
•	•	•	•	•	Origin Information & Services Inc (GA)	800-315-3492	•	•	•	
	•	•			Southern Courthouse Ventures	678-413-4697	•	•	•	

Barrow

DT	BK	CV	CR	PR	←Courts / Recording→	Phone	UC	RE	TX	VS
		•	•		Able Atlanta Research	404-502-2024	•		•	
•	•	•		•	Atlanta Title Abstractors	770-267-2727	•	•	•	
		•	•	•	Background Research Agency Inc	770-788-1885	•		•	
•	•	•	•	•	Excel Search Inc	770-844-1201	•	•	•	•
•	•	•	•	•	Origin Information & Services Inc (GA)	800-315-3492	•	•	•	
		•	•		Professional Paralegal Services Inc [SOP]	706-310-1166				
	•	•			Southern Courthouse Ventures	678-413-4697	•	•	•	

Bartow

DT	BK	CV	CR	PR	←Courts / Recording→	Phone	UC	RE	TX	VS
•	•	•	•	•	A All State Tracers Company	423-605-0155	•	•	•	•
•	•	•	•	•	Axis Research Inc [SOP]	678-795-1005	•	•	•	•
		•	•	•	Background Research Agency Inc	770-788-1885	•		•	
•	•	•			Courthouse Abstractors	770-271-9002	•	•	•	
		•	•	•	Euchner Research LLC	678-614-1816	•	•	•	•
		•	•	•	Lighthouse Information Service LLC [SOP]	912-367-5900; 678-574-5795	•	•	•	•
					Majestic Research Services Inc	678-355-5393	•	•	•	
•	•	•	•	•	Origin Information & Services Inc (GA)	800-315-3492	•	•	•	
•	•	•	•		Public Chex Inc	770-889-5662	•	•	•	
	•	•			Southern Courthouse Ventures	678-413-4697	•	•	•	

DT	BK	CV	CR	PR	Retriever	Phone	UC	RE	TX	VS
•	•	•	•	•	Southern Research Enterprises	770-387-9439	•	•	•	•

DT	BK	CV	CR	PR	←Courts **BEN HILL**	Recording→	UC	RE	TX	VS
		•	•	•	Background Research Agency Inc	770-788-1885	•		•	
•	•	•	•	•	Origin Information & Services Inc (GA)	800-315-3492	•	•	•	

DT	BK	CV	CR	PR	←Courts **BERRIEN**	Recording→	UC	RE	TX	VS
		•	•	•	Background Research Agency Inc	770-788-1885	•		•	
•	•	•	•	•	Origin Information & Services Inc (GA)	800-315-3492	•	•	•	

DT	BK	CV	CR	PR	←Courts **BIBB**	Recording→	UC	RE	TX	VS
•	•	•	•		A Wright Resource	478-757-9371				
•	•	•			Advanced Data Technology Inc	800-426-5265		•	•	
		•	•	•	Background Research Agency Inc	770-788-1885	•		•	
				•	M V Bostick Jr	478-781-9344		•	•	
•	•	•	•	•	Excel Search Inc	770-844-1201	•	•	•	•
•	•				Georgia Bankruptcy Services	770-908-9133				
•	•	•	•	•	Graystone Investigations Inc [SOP]	478-743-5551	•	•	•	•
		•	•		National Pre-Employment Research [SOP]	770-389-6607				
•	•	•	•	•	Origin Information & Services Inc (GA)	800-315-3492	•	•	•	
	•	•			Southern Courthouse Ventures	678-413-4697	•	•	•	

DT	BK	CV	CR	PR	←Courts **BLECKLEY**	Recording→	UC	RE	TX	VS
		•	•	•	Background Research Agency Inc	770-788-1885	•		•	
				•	M V Bostick Jr	478-781-9344		•	•	
		•	•		National Pre-Employment Research [SOP]	770-389-6607				
•	•	•	•	•	Origin Information & Services Inc (GA)	800-315-3492	•	•	•	

DT	BK	CV	CR	PR	←Courts **BRANTLEY**	Recording→	UC	RE	TX	VS
		•	•	•	Background Research Agency Inc	770-788-1885	•		•	
					Michael's Legal Research	912-269-5532		•		
		•	•		National Pre-Employment Research [SOP]	770-389-6607				
•	•	•	•	•	Origin Information & Services Inc (GA)	800-315-3492	•	•	•	
		•		•	Betty M Rowell, CLA	912-449-0849	•	•	•	

DT	BK	CV	CR	PR	←Courts **BROOKS**	Recording→	UC	RE	TX	VS
		•	•	•	Background Research Agency Inc	770-788-1885	•		•	
•	•	•	•	•	Origin Information & Services Inc (GA)	800-315-3492	•	•	•	

DT	BK	CV	CR	PR	←Courts **BRYAN**	Recording→	UC	RE	TX	VS
		•	•	•	Background Research Agency Inc	770-788-1885	•		•	
•	•	•	•	•	Crisp & Associates [SOP]	912-898-9973	•		•	
		•	•		National Pre-Employment Research [SOP]	770-389-6607				
•	•	•	•	•	Origin Information & Services Inc (GA)	800-315-3492	•	•	•	

DT	BK	CV	CR	PR	←Courts **BULLOCH**	Recording→	UC	RE	TX	VS
		•	•	•	Background Research Agency Inc	770-788-1885	•		•	
		•	•		National Pre-Employment Research [SOP]	770-389-6607				
•	•	•	•	•	Origin Information & Services Inc (GA)	800-315-3492	•	•	•	

DT	BK	CV	CR	PR	←Courts **BURKE**	Recording→	UC	RE	TX	VS
		•	•	•	Background Research Agency Inc	770-788-1885	•		•	
•	•	•	•	•	CSRA Background Verification Inc	706-869-8882	•	•	•	
•	•	•	•	•	David Smith Detective Agency [SOP]	877-793-9426	•		•	
		•	•		National Pre-Employment Research [SOP]	770-389-6607				
•	•	•	•	•	Origin Information & Services Inc (GA)	800-315-3492	•	•	•	
					David V Weber, Attorney	706-860-8160		•		

DT	BK	CV	CR	PR	←Courts **BUTTS**	Recording→	UC	RE	TX	VS
		•	•	•	Background Research Agency Inc	770-788-1885	•		•	
•	•	•	•	•	Excel Search Inc	770-844-1201	•	•	•	•
		•	•		National Pre-Employment Research [SOP]	770-389-6607				

DT	BK	CV	CR	PR	←Courts	Recording→	UC	RE	TX	VS
•	•	•	•	•	Origin Information & Services Inc (GA)	800-315-3492	•	•	•	
		•		•	Reliable Abstract	678-614-0715		•	•	
	•	•			Southern Courthouse Ventures	678-413-4697	•	•	•	
DT	**BK**	**CV**	**CR**	**PR**	**←Courts — CALHOUN**	**Recording→**	**UC**	**RE**	**TX**	**VS**
•	•	•	•	•	Origin Information & Services Inc (GA)	800-315-3492	•	•	•	
DT	**BK**	**CV**	**CR**	**PR**	**←Courts — CAMDEN**	**Recording→**	**UC**	**RE**	**TX**	**VS**
		•	•	•	Background Research Agency Inc	770-788-1885	•		•	
					Michael's Legal Research	912-269-5532		•		
		•	•		National Pre-Employment Research [SOP]	770-389-6607				
•	•	•	•	•	Origin Information & Services Inc (GA)	800-315-3492	•	•	•	
DT	**BK**	**CV**	**CR**	**PR**	**←Courts — CANDLER**	**Recording→**	**UC**	**RE**	**TX**	**VS**
		•	•	•	Background Research Agency Inc	770-788-1885	•		•	
•	•			•	John E Jones Jr Land Title & Appraisal	912-685-3047	•	•	•	•
•	•	•	•	•	Origin Information & Services Inc (GA)	800-315-3492	•	•	•	
DT	**BK**	**CV**	**CR**	**PR**	**←Courts — CARROLL**	**Recording→**	**UC**	**RE**	**TX**	**VS**
		•	•	•	Background Research Agency Inc	770-788-1885	•		•	
		•	•		Carson & Associates Research, Inc [SOP]	404-610-7181 or 608-8300				
•	•	•	•	•	Origin Information & Services Inc (GA)	800-315-3492	•	•	•	
		•	•		Sheila Pettit	770-832-9273	•		•	
	•	•			Southern Courthouse Ventures	678-413-4697	•	•	•	
•	•	•	•		Specialty Services [SOP]	770-942-8264	•	•	•	
DT	**BK**	**CV**	**CR**	**PR**	**←Courts — CATOOSA**	**Recording→**	**UC**	**RE**	**TX**	**VS**
•	•	•	•	•	A All State Tracers Company	423-605-0155	•	•	•	•
		•	•	•	Background Research Agency Inc	770-788-1885	•		•	
•	•	•	•	•	Origin Information & Services Inc (GA)	800-315-3492	•	•	•	
		•	•		Search & Find	706-884-9801			•	
	•	•			Southern Courthouse Ventures	678-413-4697	•	•	•	
•	•	•	•	•	Southern Research Enterprises	770-387-9439	•	•	•	•
•	•	•		•	Title Guaranty & Trust of Chattanooga	423-266-5751	•	•	•	
DT	**BK**	**CV**	**CR**	**PR**	**←Courts — CHARLTON**	**Recording→**	**UC**	**RE**	**TX**	**VS**
		•	•	•	Background Research Agency Inc	770-788-1885	•		•	
•	•	•	•	•	Origin Information & Services Inc (GA)	800-315-3492	•	•	•	
DT	**BK**	**CV**	**CR**	**PR**	**←Courts — CHATHAM**	**Recording→**	**UC**	**RE**	**TX**	**VS**
•	•	•			Advanced Data Technology Inc	800-426-5265		•	•	
		•	•	•	Background Research Agency Inc	770-788-1885	•		•	
•	•	•	•	•	Crisp & Associates [SOP]	912-898-9973	•		•	
•	•	•	•		R L Ferrelle	912-786-6577				
		•	•		National Pre-Employment Research [SOP]	770-389-6607				
•	•	•	•	•	Origin Information & Services Inc (GA)	800-315-3492	•	•	•	
DT	**BK**	**CV**	**CR**	**PR**	**←Courts — CHATTAHOOCHEE**	**Recording→**	**UC**	**RE**	**TX**	**VS**
•	•	•	•		Attorneys Services & Legal Inv [SOP]	706-322-3554	•	•		•
		•	•	•	Background Research Agency Inc	770-788-1885	•		•	
•	•	•	•	•	Origin Information & Services Inc (GA)	800-315-3492	•	•	•	
DT	**BK**	**CV**	**CR**	**PR**	**←Courts — CHATTOOGA**	**Recording→**	**UC**	**RE**	**TX**	**VS**
•	•	•	•	•	A All State Tracers Company	423-605-0155	•	•	•	•
		•	•	•	Background Research Agency Inc	770-788-1885	•		•	
					DocuSearch Services	423-894-2425	•	•	•	
•	•	•	•	•	Origin Information & Services Inc (GA)	800-315-3492	•	•	•	
	•	•			Southern Courthouse Ventures	678-413-4697	•	•	•	
•	•	•	•	•	Southern Research Enterprises	770-387-9439	•	•	•	•
•	•	•		•	Title Guaranty & Trust of Chattanooga	423-266-5751	•	•	•	

DT	BK	CV	CR	PR	←COURTS CHEROKEE RECORDING→	UC	RE	TX	VS
•	•	•	•	•	A All State Tracers Company 423-605-0155	•	•	•	•
•	•	•	•	•	Archives Retrieval Service of GA....770-252-5510	•	•	•	•
•	•	•	•	•	Axis Research Inc [SOP]....678-795-1005	•	•	•	•
		•	•	•	Background Research Agency Inc 770-788-1885	•		•	
		•	•		Carson & Associates Research, Inc [SOP].... 404-610-7181 or 608-8300				
•	•	•			Courthouse Abstractors....770-271-9002	•	•	•	
•	•	•	•	•	Excel Search Inc....770-844-1201	•	•	•	•
		•	•	•	Lighthouse Information Service LLC [SOP].... 912-367-5900; 678-574-5795	•	•	•	•
					Majestic Research Services Inc 678-355-5393	•	•	•	
•	•	•	•	•	Origin Information & Services Inc (GA) 800-315-3492	•	•	•	
•	•	•	•		Public Chex Inc....770-889-5662	•	•	•	
	•	•			Southern Courthouse Ventures....678-413-4697	•	•	•	
•	•	•	•	•	Southern Research Enterprises....770-387-9439	•	•	•	•

DT	BK	CV	CR	PR	←COURTS CLARKE RECORDING→	UC	RE	TX	VS
•	•	•		•	Atlanta Title Abstractors....770-267-2727	•	•	•	
		•	•	•	Background Research Agency Inc 770-788-1885	•		•	
•	•	•	•	•	Excel Search Inc....770-844-1201	•	•	•	•
		•	•		National Pre-Employment Research [SOP] 770-389-6607				
•	•	•	•	•	Origin Information & Services Inc (GA) 800-315-3492	•	•	•	
		•	•		Professional Paralegal Services Inc [SOP]....706-310-1166				
	•	•			Southern Courthouse Ventures....678-413-4697	•	•	•	
		•	•	•	Taya Gordon Research....706-546-6598	•	•	•	
		•	•	•	John Wilmot....706-546-7411	•	•	•	•

DT	BK	CV	CR	PR	←COURTS CLAY RECORDING→	UC	RE	TX	VS
•	•	•	•	•	Origin Information & Services Inc (GA) 800-315-3492	•	•	•	

DT	BK	CV	CR	PR	←COURTS CLAYTON RECORDING→	UC	RE	TX	VS
•	•	•	•	•	A All State Tracers Company 423-605-0155	•	•	•	•
		•	•		Able Atlanta Research....404-502-2024	•		•	
		•	•		ACS Legal Search....770-474-3195				
•	•	•	•	•	Archives Retrieval Service of GA....770-252-5510	•	•	•	•
•	•	•	•	•	Atlanta Attorney Services [SOP] 800-804-4078	•		•	
•	•	•	•	•	Atlanta Legal Services Inc [SOP] 877-302-4136	•	•	•	•
•	•	•		•	Atlanta Title Abstractors....770-267-2727	•	•	•	
•	•	•	•	•	Attorneys' Personal Services [SOP] 800-245-0122	•	•	•	•
•	•	•	•	•	Axis Research Inc [SOP]....678-795-1005	•	•	•	•
		•	•	•	Background Research Agency Inc 770-788-1885	•		•	
		•	•		Carson & Associates Research, Inc [SOP].... 404-610-7181 or 608-8300				
•	•	•			Courthouse Abstractors....770-271-9002	•	•	•	
•	•	•	•		Ed Knight Information Service 800-282-6418	•	•	•	
•	•	•	•	•	Excel Search Inc....770-844-1201	•	•	•	•
•	•	•	•	•	John Roberson Inv [SOP]....800-325-0914	•	•	•	•
•	•		•	•	Judicial Research & Retrieval Svcs (Georgia) 800-529-1338	•	•	•	•
					Majestic Research Services Inc....678-355-5393	•	•	•	
		•	•		Minor Services Inc - Excel Legal Search.... 770-987-0942, 770-789-8543	•		•	
•	•	•	•	•	Origin Information & Services Inc (GA) 800-315-3492	•	•	•	
•	•	•	•	•	Orion Research Services Inc 800-975-0865	•		•	•
		•	•		Search & Find 706-884-9801			•	
	•	•			Southern Courthouse Ventures....678-413-4697	•	•	•	
		•	•	•	The TarTec Corporation....678-479-0942	•	•	•	
		•	•		TPQ Associates 770-475-0743		•	•	

DT	BK	CV	CR	PR	←COURTS CLINCH RECORDING→	UC	RE	TX	VS
		•	•	•	Background Research Agency Inc 770-788-1885	•		•	
•	•	•	•	•	Origin Information & Services Inc (GA) 800-315-3492	•	•	•	

DT	BK	CV	CR	PR	←Courts	Cobb	Recording→	UC	RE	TX	VS
•	•	•	•	•		A All State Tracers Company	423-605-0155	•	•	•	•
•	•	•	•	•		Atlanta Attorney Services [SOP]	800-804-4078	•		•	
•	•	•	•	•		Atlanta Legal Services Inc [SOP]	877-302-4136	•	•	•	•
•	•	•		•		Atlanta Title Abstractors	770-267-2727	•	•	•	
•	•	•	•	•		Attorneys' Personal Services [SOP]	800-245-0122	•	•	•	•
•	•	•	•	•		Axis Research Inc [SOP]	678-795-1005	•	•	•	•
		•	•	•		Background Research Agency Inc	770-788-1885	•		•	
		•	•			Carson & Associates Research, Inc [SOP]	404-610-7181 or 608-8300				
•	•	•				Courthouse Abstractors	770-271-9002	•	•	•	
						Docx	866-729-8099	•	•		
•	•	•	•	•		Excel Search Inc	770-844-1201	•	•	•	•
•	•	•	•	•		John Roberson Inv [SOP]	800-325-0914	•	•	•	•
•	•		•	•		Judicial Research & Retrieval Svcs (Georgia)	800-529-1338	•	•	•	•
•	•	•	•	•		JV & Associates [SOP]	877-716-6668	•	•	•	•
		•	•	•		Lighthouse Information Service LLC [SOP]	912-367-5900; 678-574-5795	•	•	•	•
						Majestic Research Services Inc	678-355-5393	•	•	•	
•	•	•	•	•		MLQ Attorney Services [SOP]	800-446-8794	•	•	•	•
•	•	•	•	•		Origin Information & Services Inc (GA)	800-315-3492	•	•	•	
•	•	•	•	•		Orion Research Services Inc	800-975-0865	•		•	•
	•	•	•	•		PRP Research	770-769-9794	•	•	•	
•	•	•	•			Public Chex Inc	770-889-5662	•	•	•	
	•	•				Southern Courthouse Ventures	678-413-4697	•	•	•	
•	•	•	•	•		Southern Research Enterprises	770-387-9439	•	•	•	•
•	•	•	•			Specialty Services [SOP]	770-942-8264	•	•	•	
		•	•			TPQ Associates	770-475-0743		•	•	

DT	BK	CV	CR	PR	←Courts	Coffee	Recording→	UC	RE	TX	VS
		•	•	•		Background Research Agency Inc	770-788-1885	•		•	
•	•	•	•	•		Origin Information & Services Inc (GA)	800-315-3492	•	•	•	

DT	BK	CV	CR	PR	←Courts	Colquitt	Recording→	UC	RE	TX	VS
		•	•	•		Background Research Agency Inc	770-788-1885	•		•	
•	•	•	•	•		Origin Information & Services Inc (GA)	800-315-3492	•	•	•	
	•	•	•			Vinson Detective Agency [SOP]	800-404-6698	•	•	•	•

DT	BK	CV	CR	PR	←Courts	Columbia	Recording→	UC	RE	TX	VS
•	•	•				Advanced Data Technology Inc	800-426-5265		•	•	
		•	•	•		Background Research Agency Inc	770-788-1885	•		•	
•	•	•	•	•		CSRA Background Verification Inc	706-869-8882	•	•	•	
•	•	•	•	•		David Smith Detective Agency [SOP]	877-793-9426	•		•	
		•	•			National Pre-Employment Research [SOP]	770-389-6607				
•	•	•	•	•		Origin Information & Services Inc (GA)	800-315-3492	•	•	•	
						David V Weber, Attorney	706-860-8160		•		

DT	BK	CV	CR	PR	←Courts	Cook	Recording→	UC	RE	TX	VS
		•	•	•		Background Research Agency Inc	770-788-1885	•		•	
•	•	•	•	•		Origin Information & Services Inc (GA)	800-315-3492	•	•	•	

DT	BK	CV	CR	PR	←Courts	Coweta	Recording→	UC	RE	TX	VS
•	•	•	•	•		Archives Retrieval Service of GA	770-252-5510	•	•	•	•
		•	•	•		Background Research Agency Inc	770-788-1885	•		•	
•	•	•	•	•		John Roberson Inv [SOP]	800-325-0914	•	•	•	•
						Majestic Research Services Inc	678-355-5393	•	•	•	
		•	•			National Pre-Employment Research [SOP]	770-389-6607				
•	•	•	•	•		Origin Information & Services Inc (GA)	800-315-3492	•	•	•	
		•	•			Sheila Pettit	770-832-9273	•	•	•	
		•	•			Search & Find	706-884-9801			•	
	•	•				Southern Courthouse Ventures	678-413-4697	•	•	•	
•	•	•	•	•		Southern Research Enterprises	770-387-9439	•	•	•	•

DT	BK	CV	CR	PR	←Courts		Recording→	UC	RE	TX	VS
•	•	•	•		Specialty Services [SOP]		770-942-8264	•	•	•	

DT	BK	CV	CR	PR	←Courts	CRAWFORD	Recording→	UC	RE	TX	VS
		•	•	•	Background Research Agency Inc		770-788-1885	•		•	
				•	M V Bostick Jr		478-781-9344		•	•	
•	•	•	•	•	Graystone Investigations Inc [SOP]		478-743-5551	•	•	•	•
•	•	•	•	•	Origin Information & Services Inc (GA)		800-315-3492	•	•	•	
	•	•			Southern Courthouse Ventures		678-413-4697	•	•	•	

DT	BK	CV	CR	PR	←Courts	CRISP	Recording→	UC	RE	TX	VS
		•	•	•	Background Research Agency Inc		770-788-1885	•		•	
•	•	•	•	•	Origin Information & Services Inc (GA)		800-315-3492	•	•	•	

DT	BK	CV	CR	PR	←Courts	DADE	Recording→	UC	RE	TX	VS
		•	•	•	Background Research Agency Inc		770-788-1885	•		•	
•	•	•	•	•	Origin Information & Services Inc (GA)		800-315-3492	•	•	•	
	•	•			Southern Courthouse Ventures		678-413-4697	•	•	•	
•	•	•	•	•	Southern Research Enterprises		770-387-9439	•	•	•	•
•	•	•		•	Title Guaranty & Trust of Chattanooga		423-266-5751	•	•	•	

DT	BK	CV	CR	PR	←Courts	DAWSON	Recording→	UC	RE	TX	VS
•	•	•	•	•	A All State Tracers Company		423-605-0155	•	•	•	•
		•	•	•	Background Research Agency Inc		770-788-1885	•		•	
•	•	•			Courthouse Abstractors		770-271-9002	•	•	•	
•	•	•	•	•	Excel Search Inc		770-844-1201	•	•	•	•
			•		Intricate Solutions Inc		866-640-5210				
•	•	•	•	•	Origin Information & Services Inc (GA)		800-315-3492	•	•	•	
•	•	•	•		Public Chex Inc		770-889-5662	•	•	•	
	•	•			Southern Courthouse Ventures		678-413-4697	•	•	•	
•	•	•	•	•	Southern Research Enterprises		770-387-9439	•	•	•	•

DT	BK	CV	CR	PR	←Courts	DE KALB	Recording→	UC	RE	TX	VS
•	•	•	•	•	A All State Tracers Company		423-605-0155	•	•	•	•
		•	•		Able Atlanta Research		404-502-2024	•		•	
		•	•		ACS Legal Search		770-474-3195				
•	•	•	•	•	Archives Retrieval Service of GA		770-252-5510	•	•	•	•
•	•	•	•	•	Atlanta Attorney Services [SOP]		800-804-4078	•		•	
•	•	•	•	•	Atlanta Legal Services Inc [SOP]		877-302-4136	•	•	•	•
•	•	•		•	Atlanta Title Abstractors		770-267-2727	•	•	•	
•	•	•	•	•	Atlantic Investigations [SOP]		800-216-9877	•	•	•	•
•	•	•	•	•	Attorneys' Personal Services [SOP]		800-245-0122	•	•	•	•
•	•	•	•	•	Axis Research Inc [SOP]		678-795-1005	•	•	•	•
		•	•	•	Background Research Agency Inc		770-788-1885	•		•	
		•	•		Carson & Associates Research, Inc [SOP]		404-610-7181 or 608-8300				
•	•	•			Courthouse Abstractors		770-271-9002	•	•	•	
					Docx		866-729-8099	•	•		
•	•	•	•	•	EL-RU Inc		770-963-8023	•	•	•	•
•	•	•	•	•	Excel Search Inc		770-844-1201	•	•	•	•
•	•	•	•	•	John Roberson Inv [SOP]		800-325-0914	•	•	•	•
•	•		•	•	Judicial Research & Retrieval Svcs (Georgia)		800-529-1338	•	•	•	•
•	•	•	•	•	JV & Associates [SOP]		877-716-6668	•	•	•	•
					Majestic Research Services Inc		678-355-5393	•	•	•	
		•	•		Minor Services Inc - Excel Legal Search		770-987-0942, 770-789-8543	•		•	
•	•	•	•	•	MLQ Attorney Services [SOP]		800-446-8794	•	•	•	•
•	•	•	•	•	Origin Information & Services Inc (GA)		800-315-3492	•	•	•	
•	•	•	•	•	Orion Research Services Inc		800-975-0865	•		•	•
•	•	•	•		Public Chex Inc		770-889-5662	•	•	•	
	•	•			Southern Courthouse Ventures		678-413-4697	•	•	•	
•	•	•	•		Specialty Services [SOP]		770-942-8264	•	•	•	
		•	•		TPQ Associates		770-475-0743		•	•	

DT	BK	CV	CR	PR	←COURTS	DECATUR	RECORDING→	UC	RE	TX	VS
		•	•	•		Background Research Agency Inc	770-788-1885	•		•	
•	•	•	•	•		Origin Information & Services Inc (GA)	800-315-3492	•	•	•	

DT	BK	CV	CR	PR	←COURTS	DODGE	RECORDING→	UC	RE	TX	VS
		•	•	•		Background Research Agency Inc	770-788-1885	•		•	
•	•	•	•	•		Origin Information & Services Inc (GA)	800-315-3492	•	•	•	

DT	BK	CV	CR	PR	←COURTS	DOOLY	RECORDING→	UC	RE	TX	VS
		•	•	•		Background Research Agency Inc	770-788-1885	•		•	
•	•	•	•	•		Origin Information & Services Inc (GA)	800-315-3492	•	•	•	

DT	BK	CV	CR	PR	←COURTS	DOUGHERTY	RECORDING→	UC	RE	TX	VS
		•	•	•		Background Research Agency Inc	770-788-1885	•		•	
•	•	•	•	•		Origin Information & Services Inc (GA)	800-315-3492	•	•	•	
	•	•	•			Vinson Detective Agency [SOP]	800-404-6698	•	•	•	•

DT	BK	CV	CR	PR	←COURTS	DOUGLAS	RECORDING→	UC	RE	TX	VS
•	•	•	•	•		A All State Tracers Company	423-605-0155	•	•	•	•
•	•	•	•	•		Atlanta Legal Services Inc [SOP]	877-302-4136	•	•	•	•
•	•	•		•		Atlanta Title Abstractors	770-267-2727	•	•	•	
•	•	•	•	•		Axis Research Inc [SOP]	678-795-1005	•	•	•	•
		•	•	•		Background Research Agency Inc	770-788-1885	•		•	
		•	•			Carson & Associates Research, Inc [SOP]	404-610-7181 or 608-8300				
•	•	•				Courthouse Abstractors	770-271-9002	•	•	•	
		•	•	•		Terri Irwin	770-920-9957			•	
						Majestic Research Services Inc	678-355-5393	•	•	•	
•	•	•	•	•		Origin Information & Services Inc (GA)	800-315-3492	•	•	•	
	•	•				Southern Courthouse Ventures	678-413-4697	•	•	•	
•	•	•	•	•		Southern Research Enterprises	770-387-9439	•	•	•	•
•	•	•	•			Specialty Services [SOP]	770-942-8264	•	•	•	

DT	BK	CV	CR	PR	←COURTS	EARLY	RECORDING→	UC	RE	TX	VS
		•	•	•		Background Research Agency Inc	770-788-1885	•		•	
•	•	•	•	•		Origin Information & Services Inc (GA)	800-315-3492	•	•	•	

DT	BK	CV	CR	PR	←COURTS	ECHOLS	RECORDING→	UC	RE	TX	VS
•	•	•	•	•		Origin Information & Services Inc (GA)	800-315-3492	•	•	•	

DT	BK	CV	CR	PR	←COURTS	EFFINGHAM	RECORDING→	UC	RE	TX	VS
		•	•	•		Background Research Agency Inc	770-788-1885	•		•	
•	•	•	•	•		Crisp & Associates [SOP]	912-898-9973	•		•	
•	•	•	•			R L Ferrelle	912-786-6577				
		•	•			National Pre-Employment Research [SOP]	770-389-6607				
•	•	•	•	•		Origin Information & Services Inc (GA)	800-315-3492	•	•	•	

DT	BK	CV	CR	PR	←COURTS	ELBERT	RECORDING→	UC	RE	TX	VS
		•	•	•		Background Research Agency Inc	770-788-1885	•		•	
•	•	•	•	•		Origin Information & Services Inc (GA)	800-315-3492	•	•	•	
		•	•			Professional Paralegal Services Inc [SOP]	706-310-1166				
	•	•				Southern Courthouse Ventures	678-413-4697	•	•	•	

DT	BK	CV	CR	PR	←COURTS	EMANUEL	RECORDING→	UC	RE	TX	VS
		•	•	•		Background Research Agency Inc	770-788-1885	•		•	
•	•	•	•	•		Origin Information & Services Inc (GA)	800-315-3492	•	•	•	

DT	BK	CV	CR	PR	←COURTS	EVANS	RECORDING→	UC	RE	TX	VS
		•	•	•		Background Research Agency Inc	770-788-1885	•		•	
		•	•			National Pre-Employment Research [SOP]	770-389-6607				
•	•	•	•	•		Origin Information & Services Inc (GA)	800-315-3492	•	•	•	

DT	BK	CV	CR	PR	←COURTS FANNIN	RECORDING→	UC	RE	TX	VS
•	•	•	•	•	Origin Information & Services Inc (GA)	800-315-3492	•	•	•	
	•	•			Southern Courthouse Ventures	678-413-4697	•	•	•	
•	•	•	•	•	Southern Research Enterprises	770-387-9439	•	•	•	•
•	•	•		•	Title Guaranty & Trust of Chattanooga	423-266-5751	•	•	•	

DT	BK	CV	CR	PR	←COURTS FAYETTE	RECORDING→	UC	RE	TX	VS
•	•	•	•	•	Archives Retrieval Service of GA	770-252-5510	•	•	•	•
•	•	•		•	Atlanta Title Abstractors	770-267-2727	•	•	•	
•	•	•	•	•	Axis Research Inc [SOP]	678-795-1005	•	•	•	•
		•	•	•	Background Research Agency Inc	770-788-1885	•		•	
		•	•		Carson & Associates Research, Inc [SOP]	404-610-7181 or 608-8300				
•	•	•			Courthouse Abstractors	770-271-9002	•	•	•	
•	•	•	•	•	John Roberson Inv [SOP]	800-325-0914	•	•	•	•
					Majestic Research Services Inc	678-355-5393	•	•	•	
•	•	•	•	•	Origin Information & Services Inc (GA)	800-315-3492	•	•	•	
		•	•		Search & Find	706-884-9801			•	
	•	•			Southern Courthouse Ventures	678-413-4697	•	•	•	

DT	BK	CV	CR	PR	←COURTS FLOYD	RECORDING→	UC	RE	TX	VS
•	•	•	•	•	A All State Tracers Company	423-605-0155	•	•	•	•
		•	•	•	Background Research Agency Inc	770-788-1885	•		•	
		•	•	•	Euchner Research LLC	678-614-1816	•	•	•	•
•	•	•	•	•	Origin Information & Services Inc (GA)	800-315-3492	•	•	•	
	•	•			Southern Courthouse Ventures	678-413-4697	•	•	•	
•	•	•	•	•	Southern Research Enterprises	770-387-9439	•	•	•	•

DT	BK	CV	CR	PR	←COURTS FORSYTH	RECORDING→	UC	RE	TX	VS
•	•	•	•	•	A All State Tracers Company	423-605-0155	•	•	•	•
•	•	•	•	•	Atlanta Attorney Services [SOP]	800-804-4078	•		•	
•	•	•	•	•	Atlanta Legal Services Inc [SOP]	877-302-4136	•	•	•	•
•	•	•	•	•	Axis Research Inc [SOP]	678-795-1005	•	•	•	•
		•	•	•	Background Research Agency Inc	770-788-1885	•		•	
•	•	•			Courthouse Abstractors	770-271-9002	•	•	•	
•	•	•	•	•	Excel Search Inc	770-844-1201	•	•	•	•
•	•	•	•	•	Graystone Investigations Inc [SOP]	478-743-5551	•	•	•	•
•	•	•	•	•	Origin Information & Services Inc (GA)	800-315-3492	•	•	•	
•	•	•	•		Public Chex Inc	770-889-5662	•	•	•	
	•	•			Southern Courthouse Ventures	678-413-4697	•	•	•	
		•	•		TPQ Associates	770-475-0743		•	•	

DT	BK	CV	CR	PR	←COURTS FRANKLIN	RECORDING→	UC	RE	TX	VS
		•	•	•	Background Research Agency Inc	770-788-1885	•		•	
•	•	•	•	•	Origin Information & Services Inc (GA)	800-315-3492	•	•	•	
	•	•			Southern Courthouse Ventures	678-413-4697	•	•	•	

DT	BK	CV	CR	PR	←COURTS FULTON	RECORDING→	UC	RE	TX	VS
•	•	•	•	•	A All State Tracers Company	423-605-0155	•	•	•	•
		•	•		Able Atlanta Research	404-502-2024	•		•	
•	•	•	•	•	Archives Retrieval Service of GA	770-252-5510	•	•	•	•
•	•	•	•	•	Atlanta Attorney Services [SOP]	800-804-4078	•		•	
•	•	•	•	•	Atlanta Legal Services Inc [SOP]	877-302-4136	•	•	•	•
•	•	•		•	Atlanta Title Abstractors	770-267-2727	•	•	•	
•	•	•	•	•	Attorneys' Personal Services [SOP]	800-245-0122	•	•	•	•
•	•	•	•	•	Axis Research Inc [SOP]	678-795-1005	•	•	•	•
		•	•	•	Background Research Agency Inc	770-788-1885	•		•	
		•	•		Carson & Associates Research, Inc [SOP]	404-610-7181 or 608-8300				
•	•	•			Courthouse Abstractors	770-271-9002	•	•	•	
					Docx	866-729-8099	•		•	
•	•	•	•	•	EL-RU Inc	770-963-8023	•	•	•	•

DT	BK	CV	CR	PR	Retriever	Phone	UC	RE	TX	VS
•	•	•	•	•	Excel Search Inc	770-844-1201	•	•	•	•
•	•				Georgia Bankruptcy Services	770-908-9133				
•	•	•	•	•	John Roberson Inv [SOP]	800-325-0914	•	•	•	•
•	•		•	•	Judicial Research & Retrieval Svcs (Georgia)	800-529-1338	•	•	•	•
•	•	•	•	•	JV & Associates [SOP]	877-716-6668	•	•	•	•
		•	•	•	Lighthouse Information Service LLC [SOP]	912-367-5900; 678-574-5795	•	•	•	•
					Majestic Research Services Inc	678-355-5393	•	•	•	
		•	•		Minor Services Inc - Excel Legal Search	770-987-0942, 770-789-8543	•		•	
•	•	•	•	•	MLQ Attorney Services [SOP]	800-446-8794	•	•	•	•
•	•	•	•	•	Origin Information & Services Inc (GA)	800-315-3492	•	•	•	
•	•	•	•	•	Orion Research Services Inc	800-975-0865	•		•	•
	•	•	•	•	PRP Research	770-769-9794	•	•	•	
•	•	•	•		Public Chex Inc	770-889-5662	•	•	•	
	•	•			Southern Courthouse Ventures	678-413-4697	•	•	•	
•	•	•	•	•	Southern Research Enterprises	770-387-9439	•	•	•	•
•	•	•	•		Specialty Services [SOP]	770-942-8264	•	•	•	
		•	•	•	The TarTec Corporation	678-479-0942	•	•	•	
		•	•		TPQ Associates	770-475-0743		•	•	

DT	BK	CV	CR	PR	←COURTS GILMER RECORDING→		UC	RE	TX	VS
•	•	•	•	•	A All State Tracers Company	423-605-0155	•	•	•	•
		•	•	•	Background Research Agency Inc	770-788-1885	•		•	
•	•	•	•	•	Origin Information & Services Inc (GA)	800-315-3492	•	•	•	
	•	•			Southern Courthouse Ventures	678-413-4697	•	•	•	
•	•	•	•	•	Southern Research Enterprises	770-387-9439	•	•	•	•
•	•	•		•	Title Guaranty & Trust of Chattanooga	423-266-5751	•	•	•	

DT	BK	CV	CR	PR	←COURTS GLASCOCK RECORDING→		UC	RE	TX	VS
		•	•		National Pre-Employment Research [SOP]	770-389-6607				
•	•	•	•	•	Origin Information & Services Inc (GA)	800-315-3492	•	•	•	

DT	BK	CV	CR	PR	←COURTS GLYNN RECORDING→		UC	RE	TX	VS
		•	•	•	Background Research Agency Inc	770-788-1885	•		•	
					Michael's Legal Research	912-269-5532		•		
		•	•		National Pre-Employment Research [SOP]	770-389-6607				
•	•	•	•	•	Origin Information & Services Inc (GA)	800-315-3492	•	•	•	

DT	BK	CV	CR	PR	←COURTS GORDON RECORDING→		UC	RE	TX	VS
•	•	•	•	•	A All State Tracers Company	423-605-0155	•	•	•	•
		•	•	•	Background Research Agency Inc	770-788-1885	•		•	
•	•	•			Courthouse Abstractors	770-271-9002	•	•	•	
		•	•	•	Euchner Research LLC	678-614-1816	•	•	•	•
•	•	•	•	•	Origin Information & Services Inc (GA)	800-315-3492	•	•	•	
	•	•			Southern Courthouse Ventures	678-413-4697	•	•	•	
•	•	•	•	•	Southern Research Enterprises	770-387-9439	•	•	•	•
•	•	•		•	Title Guaranty & Trust of Chattanooga	423-266-5751	•	•	•	

DT	BK	CV	CR	PR	←COURTS GRADY RECORDING→		UC	RE	TX	VS
		•	•	•	Background Research Agency Inc	770-788-1885	•		•	
•	•	•	•	•	Origin Information & Services Inc (GA)	800-315-3492	•	•	•	

DT	BK	CV	CR	PR	←COURTS GREENE RECORDING→		UC	RE	TX	VS
•	•	•	•	•	Excel Search Inc	770-844-1201	•	•	•	•
		•	•	•	Merritt & Henry LLC	706-342-9668	•	•	•	
		•	•		National Pre-Employment Research [SOP]	770-389-6607				
•	•	•	•	•	Origin Information & Services Inc (GA)	800-315-3492	•	•	•	
		•	•		Professional Paralegal Services Inc [SOP]	706-310-1166				
	•	•			Southern Courthouse Ventures	678-413-4697	•	•	•	

DT	BK	CV	CR	PR	←COURTS GWINNETT RECORDING→		UC	RE	TX	VS
•	•	•	•	•	A All State Tracers Company	423-605-0155	•	•	•	•

DT	BK	CV	CR	PR	←Courts	Recording→	UC	RE	TX	VS
		•	•		Able Atlanta Research	404-502-2024	•		•	
•	•	•	•	•	Archives Retrieval Service of GA	770-252-5510	•	•	•	•
•	•	•	•	•	Atlanta Attorney Services [SOP]	800-804-4078	•		•	
•	•	•	•	•	Atlanta Legal Services Inc [SOP]	877-302-4136	•	•	•	•
•	•	•		•	Atlanta Title Abstractors	770-267-2727	•	•	•	
•	•	•	•	•	Attorneys' Personal Services [SOP]	800-245-0122	•	•	•	•
•	•	•	•	•	Axis Research Inc [SOP]	678-795-1005	•	•	•	•
		•	•	•	Background Research Agency Inc	770-788-1885	•		•	
		•	•		Carson & Associates Research, Inc [SOP]	404-610-7181 or 608-8300				
•	•	•			Courthouse Abstractors	770-271-9002	•	•	•	
•	•	•	•	•	EL-RU Inc	770-963-8023	•	•	•	•
•	•	•	•	•	Excel Search Inc	770-844-1201	•	•	•	•
•	•	•	•	•	John Roberson Inv [SOP]	800-325-0914	•	•	•	•
•	•		•	•	Judicial Research & Retrieval Svcs (Georgia)	800-529-1338	•	•	•	•
					Majestic Research Services Inc	678-355-5393	•	•	•	
		•	•		Minor Services Inc - Excel Legal Search	770-987-0942, 770-789-8543	•		•	
•	•	•	•	•	MLQ Attorney Services [SOP]	800-446-8794	•	•	•	•
•	•	•	•	•	Origin Information & Services Inc (GA)	800-315-3492	•	•	•	
•	•	•	•	•	Orion Research Services Inc	800-975-0865	•		•	•
•	•	•	•		Public Chex Inc	770-889-5662	•	•	•	
	•	•			Southern Courthouse Ventures	678-413-4697	•	•	•	
		•	•		TPQ Associates	770-475-0743		•	•	

DT	BK	CV	CR	PR	←Courts **HABERSHAM**	Recording→	UC	RE	TX	VS
		•	•	•	Background Research Agency Inc	770-788-1885	•		•	
		•	•		National Pre-Employment Research [SOP]	770-389-6607				
•	•	•	•	•	Origin Information & Services Inc (GA)	800-315-3492	•	•	•	
	•	•			Southern Courthouse Ventures	678-413-4697	•	•	•	

DT	BK	CV	CR	PR	←Courts **HALL**	Recording→	UC	RE	TX	VS
		•	•		Able Atlanta Research	404-502-2024	•		•	
•	•	•		•	Atlanta Title Abstractors	770-267-2727	•	•	•	
•	•	•	•	•	Axis Research Inc [SOP]	678-795-1005	•	•	•	•
		•	•	•	Background Research Agency Inc	770-788-1885	•		•	
•	•	•			Courthouse Abstractors	770-271-9002	•	•	•	
•	•	•	•	•	Excel Search Inc	770-844-1201	•	•	•	•
		•	•		Minor Services Inc - Excel Legal Search	770-987-0942, 770-789-8543	•		•	
•	•	•	•	•	Origin Information & Services Inc (GA)	800-315-3492	•	•	•	
•	•	•	•		Public Chex Inc	770-889-5662	•	•	•	
	•	•			Southern Courthouse Ventures	678-413-4697	•	•	•	
		•	•		TPQ Associates	770-475-0743		•	•	

DT	BK	CV	CR	PR	←Courts **HANCOCK**	Recording→	UC	RE	TX	VS
		•	•	•	Background Research Agency Inc	770-788-1885	•		•	
•	•	•	•	•	Origin Information & Services Inc (GA)	800-315-3492	•	•	•	
		•	•		Professional Paralegal Services Inc [SOP]	706-310-1166				
	•	•			Southern Courthouse Ventures	678-413-4697	•	•	•	

DT	BK	CV	CR	PR	←Courts **HARALSON**	Recording→	UC	RE	TX	VS
		•	•	•	Background Research Agency Inc	770-788-1885	•		•	
•	•	•	•	•	Origin Information & Services Inc (GA)	800-315-3492	•	•	•	
		•	•		Sheila Pettit	770-832-9273	•	•	•	
	•	•			Southern Courthouse Ventures	678-413-4697	•	•	•	

DT	BK	CV	CR	PR	←Courts **HARRIS**	Recording→	UC	RE	TX	VS
•	•	•	•		Attorneys Services & Legal Inv [SOP]	706-322-3554	•	•		•
		•	•	•	Background Research Agency Inc	770-788-1885	•		•	
•	•	•	•	•	Origin Information & Services Inc (GA)	800-315-3492	•	•	•	
		•	•		Search & Find	706-884-9801			•	
	•	•			Southern Courthouse Ventures	678-413-4697	•	•	•	

DT	BK	CV	CR	PR	←Courts HART	Recording→	UC	RE	TX	VS
		•	•	•	Background Research Agency Inc	770-788-1885	•		•	
•	•	•	•	•	Origin Information & Services Inc (GA)	800-315-3492	•	•	•	
	•	•			Southern Courthouse Ventures	678-413-4697	•	•	•	

DT	BK	CV	CR	PR	←Courts HEARD	Recording→	UC	RE	TX	VS
		•	•	•	Background Research Agency Inc	770-788-1885	•		•	
•	•	•	•	•	Origin Information & Services Inc (GA)	800-315-3492	•	•	•	
		•	•		Sheila Pettit	770-832-9273	•	•	•	
		•	•		Search & Find	706-884-9801			•	
	•	•			Southern Courthouse Ventures	678-413-4697	•	•	•	

DT	BK	CV	CR	PR	←Courts HENRY	Recording→	UC	RE	TX	VS
•	•	•	•	•	A All State Tracers Company	423-605-0155	•	•	•	•
		•	•		Able Atlanta Research	404-502-2024	•		•	
		•	•		ACS Legal Search	770-474-3195				
•	•	•	•	•	Archives Retrieval Service of GA	770-252-5510	•	•	•	•
•	•	•	•	•	Axis Research Inc [SOP]	678-795-1005	•	•	•	•
		•	•	•	Background Research Agency Inc	770-788-1885	•		•	
•	•	•	•		Ed Knight Information Service	800-282-6418	•	•	•	
•	•	•	•	•	Excel Search Inc	770-844-1201	•	•	•	•
•	•	•	•	•	John Roberson Inv [SOP]	800-325-0914	•	•	•	•
					Majestic Research Services Inc	678-355-5393	•	•	•	
		•	•		Minor Services Inc - Excel Legal Search	770-987-0942, 770-789-8543	•		•	
		•	•		National Pre-Employment Research [SOP]	770-389-6607				
•	•	•	•	•	Origin Information & Services Inc (GA)	800-315-3492	•	•	•	
		•		•	Reliable Abstract	678-614-0715		•	•	
		•	•		Search & Find	706-884-9801			•	
	•	•			Southern Courthouse Ventures	678-413-4697	•	•	•	

DT	BK	CV	CR	PR	←Courts HOUSTON	Recording→	UC	RE	TX	VS
		•	•	•	Background Research Agency Inc	770-788-1885	•		•	
•	•	•	•	•	Graystone Investigations Inc [SOP]	478-743-5551	•	•	•	•
•	•	•	•	•	Origin Information & Services Inc (GA)	800-315-3492	•	•	•	
	•	•			Southern Courthouse Ventures	678-413-4697	•	•	•	

DT	BK	CV	CR	PR	←Courts IRWIN	Recording→	UC	RE	TX	VS
		•	•	•	Background Research Agency Inc	770-788-1885	•		•	
•	•	•	•	•	Origin Information & Services Inc (GA)	800-315-3492	•	•	•	

DT	BK	CV	CR	PR	←Courts JACKSON	Recording→	UC	RE	TX	VS
•	•	•		•	Atlanta Title Abstractors	770-267-2727	•	•	•	
		•	•	•	Background Research Agency Inc	770-788-1885	•		•	
•	•	•	•	•	Excel Search Inc	770-844-1201	•	•	•	•
•	•	•	•	•	Origin Information & Services Inc (GA)	800-315-3492	•	•	•	
	•	•			Southern Courthouse Ventures	678-413-4697	•	•	•	
		•	•	•	Taya Gordon Research	706-546-6598	•	•	•	

DT	BK	CV	CR	PR	←Courts JASPER	Recording→	UC	RE	TX	VS
		•	•	•	Background Research Agency Inc	770-788-1885	•		•	
•	•	•	•	•	Excel Search Inc	770-844-1201	•	•	•	•
		•	•		National Pre-Employment Research [SOP]	770-389-6607				
•	•	•	•	•	Origin Information & Services Inc (GA)	800-315-3492	•	•	•	
		•	•		Professional Paralegal Services Inc [SOP]	706-310-1166				
		•		•	Reliable Abstract	678-614-0715		•	•	
	•	•			Southern Courthouse Ventures	678-413-4697	•	•	•	

DT	BK	CV	CR	PR	←Courts JEFF DAVIS	Recording→	UC	RE	TX	VS
•	•	•	•	•	Origin Information & Services Inc (GA)	800-315-3492	•	•	•	

DT	BK	CV	CR	PR	←COURTS **JEFFERSON**	RECORDING→	UC	RE	TX	VS
		•	•	•	Background Research Agency Inc	770-788-1885	•		•	
•	•	•	•	•	David Smith Detective Agency [SOP]	877-793-9426	•		•	
•	•	•	•	•	Origin Information & Services Inc (GA)	800-315-3492	•	•	•	

DT	BK	CV	CR	PR	←COURTS **JENKINS**	RECORDING→	UC	RE	TX	VS
		•	•	•	Background Research Agency Inc	770-788-1885	•		•	
•	•	•	•	•	Origin Information & Services Inc (GA)	800-315-3492	•	•	•	

DT	BK	CV	CR	PR	←COURTS **JOHNSON**	RECORDING→	UC	RE	TX	VS
		•	•	•	Background Research Agency Inc	770-788-1885	•		•	
•	•	•	•	•	Origin Information & Services Inc (GA)	800-315-3492	•	•	•	

DT	BK	CV	CR	PR	←COURTS **JONES**	RECORDING→	UC	RE	TX	VS
		•	•	•	Background Research Agency Inc	770-788-1885	•		•	
				•	M V Bostick Jr	478-781-9344		•	•	
•	•	•	•	•	Graystone Investigations Inc [SOP]	478-743-5551	•	•	•	•
•	•	•	•	•	Origin Information & Services Inc (GA)	800-315-3492	•	•	•	
		•	•		Professional Paralegal Services Inc [SOP]	706-310-1166				
	•	•			Southern Courthouse Ventures	678-413-4697	•	•	•	

DT	BK	CV	CR	PR	←COURTS **LAMAR**	RECORDING→	UC	RE	TX	VS
		•	•	•	Background Research Agency Inc	770-788-1885	•		•	
				•	M V Bostick Jr	478-781-9344		•	•	
•	•	•	•	•	Excel Search Inc	770-844-1201	•	•	•	•
		•	•		National Pre-Employment Research [SOP]	770-389-6607				
•	•	•	•	•	Origin Information & Services Inc (GA)	800-315-3492	•	•	•	
	•	•			Southern Courthouse Ventures	678-413-4697	•	•	•	

DT	BK	CV	CR	PR	←COURTS **LANIER**	RECORDING→	UC	RE	TX	VS
•	•	•	•	•	Origin Information & Services Inc (GA)	800-315-3492	•	•	•	

DT	BK	CV	CR	PR	←COURTS **LAURENS**	RECORDING→	UC	RE	TX	VS
		•	•	•	Background Research Agency Inc	770-788-1885	•		•	
		•	•		National Pre-Employment Research [SOP]	770-389-6607				
•	•	•	•	•	Origin Information & Services Inc (GA)	800-315-3492	•	•	•	

DT	BK	CV	CR	PR	←COURTS **LEE**	RECORDING→	UC	RE	TX	VS
		•	•	•	Background Research Agency Inc	770-788-1885	•		•	
•	•	•	•	•	Origin Information & Services Inc (GA)	800-315-3492	•	•	•	
	•	•	•		Vinson Detective Agency [SOP]	800-404-6698	•	•	•	•

DT	BK	CV	CR	PR	←COURTS **LIBERTY**	RECORDING→	UC	RE	TX	VS
		•	•	•	Background Research Agency Inc	770-788-1885	•		•	
•	•	•	•	•	Crisp & Associates [SOP]	912-898-9973	•		•	
		•	•		National Pre-Employment Research [SOP]	770-389-6607				
•	•	•	•	•	Origin Information & Services Inc (GA)	800-315-3492	•	•	•	

DT	BK	CV	CR	PR	←COURTS **LINCOLN**	RECORDING→	UC	RE	TX	VS
•	•	•	•	•	David Smith Detective Agency [SOP]	877-793-9426	•		•	
•	•	•	•	•	Origin Information & Services Inc (GA)	800-315-3492	•	•	•	
	•	•			Southern Courthouse Ventures	678-413-4697	•	•	•	

DT	BK	CV	CR	PR	←COURTS **LONG**	RECORDING→	UC	RE	TX	VS
		•	•	•	Background Research Agency Inc	770-788-1885	•		•	
					Michael's Legal Research	912-269-5532		•		
•	•	•	•	•	Origin Information & Services Inc (GA)	800-315-3492	•	•	•	

DT	BK	CV	CR	PR	←COURTS **LOWNDES**	RECORDING→	UC	RE	TX	VS
		•	•	•	Background Research Agency Inc	770-788-1885	•		•	
•	•	•	•	•	Origin Information & Services Inc (GA)	800-315-3492	•	•	•	

DT	BK	CV	CR	PR	←Courts	**Lumpkin**	Recording→	UC	RE	TX	VS
		•	•	•		Background Research Agency Inc	770-788-1885	•		•	
•	•	•				Courthouse Abstractors	770-271-9002	•	•	•	
•	•	•	•	•		EL-RU Inc	770-963-8023	•	•	•	•
			•			Intricate Solutions Inc	866-640-5210				
•	•	•	•	•		Origin Information & Services Inc (GA)	800-315-3492	•	•	•	
	•	•				Southern Courthouse Ventures	678-413-4697	•	•	•	
•	•	•	•	•		Southern Research Enterprises	770-387-9439	•	•	•	•

DT	BK	CV	CR	PR	←Courts	**Macon**	Recording→	UC	RE	TX	VS
				•		M V Bostick Jr	478-781-9344		•	•	
•	•	•	•	•		Origin Information & Services Inc (GA)	800-315-3492	•	•	•	

DT	BK	CV	CR	PR	←Courts	**Madison**	Recording→	UC	RE	TX	VS
•	•	•		•		Atlanta Title Abstractors	770-267-2727	•	•	•	
		•	•	•		Background Research Agency Inc	770-788-1885	•		•	
•	•	•	•	•		Excel Search Inc	770-844-1201	•	•	•	•
		•	•			National Pre-Employment Research [SOP]	770-389-6607				
•	•	•	•	•		Origin Information & Services Inc (GA)	800-315-3492	•	•	•	
		•	•			Professional Paralegal Services Inc [SOP]	706-310-1166				
	•	•				Southern Courthouse Ventures	678-413-4697	•	•	•	
		•	•	•		Taya Gordon Research	706-546-6598	•	•	•	

DT	BK	CV	CR	PR	←Courts	**Marion**	Recording→	UC	RE	TX	VS
•	•	•	•			Attorneys Services & Legal Inv [SOP]	706-322-3554	•	•		•
		•	•	•		Background Research Agency Inc	770-788-1885	•		•	
		•	•			National Pre-Employment Research [SOP]	770-389-6607				
•	•	•	•	•		Origin Information & Services Inc (GA)	800-315-3492	•	•	•	

DT	BK	CV	CR	PR	←Courts	**McDuffie**	Recording→	UC	RE	TX	VS
		•	•	•		Background Research Agency Inc	770-788-1885	•		•	
•	•	•	•	•		CSRA Background Verification Inc	706-869-8882	•	•	•	
•	•	•	•	•		David Smith Detective Agency [SOP]	877-793-9426	•		•	
		•	•			National Pre-Employment Research [SOP]	770-389-6607				
•	•	•	•	•		Origin Information & Services Inc (GA)	800-315-3492	•	•	•	

DT	BK	CV	CR	PR	←Courts	**McIntosh**	Recording→	UC	RE	TX	VS
		•	•	•		Background Research Agency Inc	770-788-1885	•		•	
						Michael's Legal Research	912-269-5532		•		
		•	•			National Pre-Employment Research [SOP]	770-389-6607				
•	•	•	•	•		Origin Information & Services Inc (GA)	800-315-3492	•	•	•	

DT	BK	CV	CR	PR	←Courts	**Meriwether**	Recording→	UC	RE	TX	VS
		•	•	•		Background Research Agency Inc	770-788-1885	•		•	
		•	•			National Pre-Employment Research [SOP]	770-389-6607				
•	•	•	•	•		Origin Information & Services Inc (GA)	800-315-3492	•	•	•	
	•	•				Southern Courthouse Ventures	678-413-4697	•	•	•	

DT	BK	CV	CR	PR	←Courts	**Miller**	Recording→	UC	RE	TX	VS
		•	•	•		Background Research Agency Inc	770-788-1885	•		•	
•	•	•	•	•		Origin Information & Services Inc (GA)	800-315-3492	•	•	•	

DT	BK	CV	CR	PR	←Courts	**Mitchell**	Recording→	UC	RE	TX	VS
		•	•	•		Background Research Agency Inc	770-788-1885	•		•	
•	•	•	•	•		Origin Information & Services Inc (GA)	800-315-3492	•	•	•	

DT	BK	CV	CR	PR	←Courts	**Monroe**	Recording→	UC	RE	TX	VS
		•	•	•		Background Research Agency Inc	770-788-1885	•		•	
				•		M V Bostick Jr	478-781-9344		•	•	
•	•	•	•	•		Excel Search Inc	770-844-1201	•	•	•	•
•	•	•	•	•		Graystone Investigations Inc [SOP]	478-743-5551	•	•	•	•

DT	BK	CV	CR	PR	Retriever	Phone	UC	RE	TX	VS
		•	•		National Pre-Employment Research [SOP]	770-389-6607				
•	•	•	•	•	Origin Information & Services Inc (GA)	800-315-3492	•	•	•	
	•	•			Southern Courthouse Ventures	678-413-4697	•	•	•	

MONTGOMERY

DT	BK	CV	CR	PR	←COURTS / RECORDING→	Phone	UC	RE	TX	VS
		•	•	•	Background Research Agency Inc	770-788-1885	•		•	
•	•	•	•	•	Origin Information & Services Inc (GA)	800-315-3492	•	•	•	

MORGAN

DT	BK	CV	CR	PR	←COURTS / RECORDING→	Phone	UC	RE	TX	VS
•	•	•		•	Atlanta Title Abstractors	770-267-2727	•	•	•	
		•	•	•	Background Research Agency Inc	770-788-1885	•		•	
•	•	•	•	•	Excel Search Inc	770-844-1201	•	•	•	•
		•	•	•	Merritt & Henry LLC	706-342-9668	•	•	•	
		•	•		National Pre-Employment Research [SOP]	770-389-6607				
•	•	•	•	•	Origin Information & Services Inc (GA)	800-315-3492	•	•	•	
		•	•		Professional Paralegal Services Inc [SOP]	706-310-1166				
	•	•			Southern Courthouse Ventures	678-413-4697	•	•	•	

MURRAY

DT	BK	CV	CR	PR	←COURTS / RECORDING→	Phone	UC	RE	TX	VS
•	•	•	•	•	A All State Tracers Company	423-605-0155	•	•	•	•
		•	•	•	Background Research Agency Inc	770-788-1885	•		•	
					DocuSearch Services	423-894-2425	•	•	•	
•	•	•	•	•	Origin Information & Services Inc (GA)	800-315-3492	•	•	•	
	•	•			Southern Courthouse Ventures	678-413-4697	•	•	•	
•	•	•	•	•	Southern Research Enterprises	770-387-9439	•	•	•	•
•	•	•		•	Title Guaranty & Trust of Chattanooga	423-266-5751	•	•	•	

MUSCOGEE

DT	BK	CV	CR	PR	←COURTS / RECORDING→	Phone	UC	RE	TX	VS
•	•	•	•		Attorneys Services & Legal Inv [SOP]	706-322-3554	•	•		•
		•	•	•	Background Research Agency Inc	770-788-1885	•		•	
		•	•		Carson & Associates Research, Inc [SOP]	404-610-7181 or 608-8300				
•	•				Georgia Bankruptcy Services	770-908-9133				
		•	•		National Pre-Employment Research [SOP]	770-389-6607				
•	•	•	•	•	Origin Information & Services Inc (GA)	800-315-3492	•	•	•	
		•	•		Search & Find	706-884-9801			•	
	•	•			Southern Courthouse Ventures	678-413-4697	•	•	•	

NEWTON

DT	BK	CV	CR	PR	←COURTS / RECORDING→	Phone	UC	RE	TX	VS
•	•	•		•	Atlanta Title Abstractors	770-267-2727	•	•	•	
		•	•	•	Background Research Agency Inc	770-788-1885	•		•	
•	•	•	•	•	Excel Search Inc	770-844-1201	•	•	•	•
		•	•	•	Roger Gladden Law Office [SOP]	404-550-0749	•	•	•	
		•	•		National Pre-Employment Research [SOP]	770-389-6607				
•	•	•	•	•	Origin Information & Services Inc (GA)	800-315-3492	•	•	•	
	•	•			Southern Courthouse Ventures	678-413-4697	•	•	•	

OCONEE

DT	BK	CV	CR	PR	←COURTS / RECORDING→	Phone	UC	RE	TX	VS
•	•	•		•	Atlanta Title Abstractors	770-267-2727	•	•	•	
		•	•	•	Background Research Agency Inc	770-788-1885	•		•	
•	•	•	•	•	Excel Search Inc	770-844-1201	•	•	•	•
		•	•		National Pre-Employment Research [SOP]	770-389-6607				
•	•	•	•	•	Origin Information & Services Inc (GA)	800-315-3492	•	•	•	
		•	•		Professional Paralegal Services Inc [SOP]	706-310-1166				
	•	•			Southern Courthouse Ventures	678-413-4697	•	•	•	
		•	•	•	Taya Gordon Research	706-546-6598	•	•	•	

OGLETHORPE

DT	BK	CV	CR	PR	←COURTS / RECORDING→	Phone	UC	RE	TX	VS
•	•	•		•	Atlanta Title Abstractors	770-267-2727	•	•	•	
		•	•	•	Background Research Agency Inc	770-788-1885	•		•	
•	•	•	•	•	Excel Search Inc	770-844-1201	•	•	•	•
•	•	•	•	•	Origin Information & Services Inc (GA)	800-315-3492	•	•	•	

DT	BK	CV	CR	PR	Retriever	Phone	UC	RE	TX	VS
		•	•		Professional Paralegal Services Inc [SOP]	706-310-1166				
	•	•			Southern Courthouse Ventures	678-413-4697	•	•	•	
		•	•	•	Taya Gordon Research	706-546-6598	•	•	•	

DT	BK	CV	CR	PR	←COURTS PAULDING	RECORDING→	UC	RE	TX	VS
•	•	•	•	•	A All State Tracers Company	423-605-0155	•	•	•	•
•	•	•	•	•	Atlanta Legal Services Inc [SOP]	877-302-4136	•	•	•	•
•	•	•	•	•	Axis Research Inc [SOP]	678-795-1005	•	•	•	•
		•	•	•	Background Research Agency Inc	770-788-1885	•		•	
•	•	•			Courthouse Abstractors	770-271-9002	•	•	•	
					Majestic Research Services Inc	678-355-5393	•	•	•	
•	•	•	•	•	Origin Information & Services Inc (GA)	800-315-3492	•	•	•	
	•	•			Southern Courthouse Ventures	678-413-4697	•	•	•	
•	•	•	•	•	Southern Research Enterprises	770-387-9439	•	•	•	•
•	•	•	•		Specialty Services [SOP]	770-942-8264	•	•	•	

DT	BK	CV	CR	PR	←COURTS PEACH	RECORDING→	UC	RE	TX	VS
		•	•	•	Background Research Agency Inc	770-788-1885	•		•	
				•	M V Bostick Jr	478-781-9344		•	•	
•	•	•	•	•	Graystone Investigations Inc [SOP]	478-743-5551	•	•	•	•
		•	•		National Pre-Employment Research [SOP]	770-389-6607				
•	•	•	•	•	Origin Information & Services Inc (GA)	800-315-3492	•	•	•	
	•	•			Southern Courthouse Ventures	678-413-4697	•	•	•	

DT	BK	CV	CR	PR	←COURTS PICKENS	RECORDING→	UC	RE	TX	VS
•	•	•	•	•	A All State Tracers Company	423-605-0155	•	•	•	•
•	•	•	•	•	Axis Research Inc [SOP]	678-795-1005	•	•	•	•
		•	•	•	Background Research Agency Inc	770-788-1885	•		•	
•	•	•			Courthouse Abstractors	770-271-9002	•	•	•	
•	•	•	•	•	EL-RU Inc	770-963-8023	•	•	•	•
		•	•	•	Lighthouse Information Service LLC [SOP]	912-367-5900; 678-574-5795	•	•	•	•
•	•	•	•	•	Origin Information & Services Inc (GA)	800-315-3492	•	•	•	
	•	•			Southern Courthouse Ventures	678-413-4697	•	•	•	
•	•	•	•	•	Southern Research Enterprises	770-387-9439	•	•	•	•

DT	BK	CV	CR	PR	←COURTS PIERCE	RECORDING→	UC	RE	TX	VS
		•	•	•	Background Research Agency Inc	770-788-1885	•		•	
		•	•		National Pre-Employment Research [SOP]	770-389-6607				
•	•	•	•	•	Origin Information & Services Inc (GA)	800-315-3492	•	•	•	
		•		•	Betty M Rowell, CLA	912-449-0849	•	•	•	

DT	BK	CV	CR	PR	←COURTS PIKE	RECORDING→	UC	RE	TX	VS
		•	•	•	Background Research Agency Inc	770-788-1885	•		•	
		•	•		National Pre-Employment Research [SOP]	770-389-6607				
•	•	•	•	•	Origin Information & Services Inc (GA)	800-315-3492	•	•	•	
	•	•			Southern Courthouse Ventures	678-413-4697	•	•	•	

DT	BK	CV	CR	PR	←COURTS POLK	RECORDING→	UC	RE	TX	VS
•	•	•	•	•	A All State Tracers Company	423-605-0155	•	•	•	•
		•	•	•	Background Research Agency Inc	770-788-1885	•		•	
•	•	•	•	•	Origin Information & Services Inc (GA)	800-315-3492	•	•	•	
	•	•			Southern Courthouse Ventures	678-413-4697	•	•	•	

DT	BK	CV	CR	PR	←COURTS PULASKI	RECORDING→	UC	RE	TX	VS
		•	•	•	Background Research Agency Inc	770-788-1885	•		•	
				•	M V Bostick Jr	478-781-9344		•	•	
•	•	•	•	•	Origin Information & Services Inc (GA)	800-315-3492	•	•	•	

DT	BK	CV	CR	PR	←COURTS PUTNAM	RECORDING→	UC	RE	TX	VS
		•	•	•	Background Research Agency Inc	770-788-1885	•		•	
•	•	•	•	•	Excel Search Inc	770-844-1201	•	•	•	•

DT	BK	CV	CR	PR	Retriever	Phone	UC	RE	TX	VS
				•	M V Bostick Jr	478-781-9344		•	•	
		•	•	•	Merritt & Henry LLC	706-342-9668	•	•	•	
		•	•		National Pre-Employment Research [SOP]	770-389-6607				
•	•	•	•	•	Origin Information & Services Inc (GA)	800-315-3492	•	•	•	
		•	•		Professional Paralegal Services Inc [SOP]	706-310-1166				
		•		•	Reliable Abstract	678-614-0715		•	•	
	•	•			Southern Courthouse Ventures	678-413-4697	•	•	•	

DT	BK	CV	CR	PR	←Courts **QUITMAN**	Recording→	UC	RE	TX	VS
		•	•	•	Background Research Agency Inc	770-788-1885	•		•	
•	•	•	•	•	Origin Information & Services Inc (GA)	800-315-3492	•	•	•	

DT	BK	CV	CR	PR	←Courts **RABUN**	Recording→	UC	RE	TX	VS
•	•	•	•	•	Origin Information & Services Inc (GA)	800-315-3492	•	•	•	
	•	•			Southern Courthouse Ventures	678-413-4697	•	•	•	

DT	BK	CV	CR	PR	←Courts **RANDOLPH**	Recording→	UC	RE	TX	VS
•	•	•	•	•	Origin Information & Services Inc (GA)	800-315-3492	•	•	•	

DT	BK	CV	CR	PR	←Courts **RICHMOND**	Recording→	UC	RE	TX	VS
•	•	•			Advanced Data Technology Inc	800-426-5265		•	•	
		•	•	•	Background Research Agency Inc	770-788-1885	•		•	
•	•	•	•	•	CSRA Background Verification Inc	706-869-8882	•	•	•	
•	•	•	•	•	David Smith Detective Agency [SOP]	877-793-9426	•		•	
		•	•		National Pre-Employment Research [SOP]	770-389-6607				
•	•	•	•	•	Origin Information & Services Inc (GA)	800-315-3492	•	•	•	
					David V Weber, Attorney	706-860-8160		•		

DT	BK	CV	CR	PR	←Courts **ROCKDALE**	Recording→	UC	RE	TX	VS
		•	•		Able Atlanta Research	404-502-2024	•		•	
•	•	•	•	•	Atlanta Legal Services Inc [SOP]	877-302-4136	•	•	•	•
•	•	•		•	Atlanta Title Abstractors	770-267-2727	•	•	•	
		•	•	•	Background Research Agency Inc	770-788-1885	•		•	
•	•	•	•	•	Excel Search Inc	770-844-1201	•	•	•	•
		•	•	•	Roger Gladden Law Office [SOP]	404-550-0749	•	•	•	
		•	•		Minor Services Inc - Excel Legal Search	770-987-0942, 770-789-8543	•		•	
		•	•		National Pre-Employment Research [SOP]	770-389-6607				
•	•	•	•	•	Origin Information & Services Inc (GA)	800-315-3492	•	•	•	
		•	•		Search & Find	706-884-9801			•	
	•	•			Southern Courthouse Ventures	678-413-4697	•	•	•	

DT	BK	CV	CR	PR	←Courts **SCHLEY**	Recording→	UC	RE	TX	VS
•	•	•	•	•	Origin Information & Services Inc (GA)	800-315-3492	•	•	•	

DT	BK	CV	CR	PR	←Courts **SCREVEN**	Recording→	UC	RE	TX	VS
•	•	•	•	•	Origin Information & Services Inc (GA)	800-315-3492	•	•	•	

DT	BK	CV	CR	PR	←Courts **SEMINOLE**	Recording→	UC	RE	TX	VS
		•	•	•	Background Research Agency Inc	770-788-1885	•		•	
•	•	•	•	•	Origin Information & Services Inc (GA)	800-315-3492	•	•	•	

DT	BK	CV	CR	PR	←Courts **SPALDING**	Recording→	UC	RE	TX	VS
•	•	•		•	Atlanta Title Abstractors	770-267-2727	•	•	•	
•	•	•	•	•	Axis Research Inc [SOP]	678-795-1005	•	•	•	•
		•	•	•	Background Research Agency Inc	770-788-1885	•		•	
•	•	•	•	•	Excel Search Inc	770-844-1201	•	•	•	•
•	•	•	•	•	John Roberson Inv [SOP]	800-325-0914	•	•	•	•
		•	•		National Pre-Employment Research [SOP]	770-389-6607				
•	•	•	•	•	Origin Information & Services Inc (GA)	800-315-3492	•	•	•	
		•		•	Reliable Abstract	678-614-0715		•	•	
	•	•			Southern Courthouse Ventures	678-413-4697	•	•	•	

DT	BK	CV	CR	PR	←Courts STEPHENS	Recording→	UC	RE	TX	VS
		•	•	•	Background Research Agency Inc	770-788-1885	•		•	
•	•	•	•	•	Origin Information & Services Inc (GA)	800-315-3492	•	•	•	
	•	•			Southern Courthouse Ventures	678-413-4697	•	•	•	

DT	BK	CV	CR	PR	←Courts STEWART	Recording→	UC	RE	TX	VS
•	•	•	•	•	Origin Information & Services Inc (GA)	800-315-3492	•	•	•	

DT	BK	CV	CR	PR	←Courts SUMTER	Recording→	UC	RE	TX	VS
		•	•	•	Background Research Agency Inc	770-788-1885	•		•	
•	•	•	•	•	Origin Information & Services Inc (GA)	800-315-3492	•	•	•	

DT	BK	CV	CR	PR	←Courts TALBOT	Recording→	UC	RE	TX	VS
•	•	•	•		Attorneys Services & Legal Inv [SOP]	706-322-3554	•	•		•
		•	•	•	Background Research Agency Inc	770-788-1885	•		•	
		•	•		National Pre-Employment Research [SOP]	770-389-6607				
•	•	•	•	•	Origin Information & Services Inc (GA)	800-315-3492	•	•	•	

DT	BK	CV	CR	PR	←Courts TALIAFERRO	Recording→	UC	RE	TX	VS
		•	•	•	Background Research Agency Inc	770-788-1885	•		•	
		•	•		National Pre-Employment Research [SOP]	770-389-6607				
•	•	•	•	•	Origin Information & Services Inc (GA)	800-315-3492	•	•	•	
	•	•			Southern Courthouse Ventures	678-413-4697	•	•	•	

DT	BK	CV	CR	PR	←Courts TATTNALL	Recording→	UC	RE	TX	VS
		•	•	•	Background Research Agency Inc	770-788-1885	•		•	
		•	•		National Pre-Employment Research [SOP]	770-389-6607				
•	•	•	•	•	Origin Information & Services Inc (GA)	800-315-3492	•	•	•	

DT	BK	CV	CR	PR	←Courts TAYLOR	Recording→	UC	RE	TX	VS
•	•	•	•		Attorneys Services & Legal Inv [SOP]	706-322-3554	•	•		•
		•	•	•	Background Research Agency Inc	770-788-1885	•		•	
				•	M V Bostick Jr	478-781-9344		•	•	
		•	•		National Pre-Employment Research [SOP]	770-389-6607				
•	•	•	•	•	Origin Information & Services Inc (GA)	800-315-3492	•	•	•	

DT	BK	CV	CR	PR	←Courts TELFAIR	Recording→	UC	RE	TX	VS
		•	•	•	Background Research Agency Inc	770-788-1885	•		•	
•	•	•	•	•	Origin Information & Services Inc (GA)	800-315-3492	•	•	•	

DT	BK	CV	CR	PR	←Courts TERRELL	Recording→	UC	RE	TX	VS
		•	•	•	Background Research Agency Inc	770-788-1885	•		•	
•	•	•	•	•	Origin Information & Services Inc (GA)	800-315-3492	•	•	•	

DT	BK	CV	CR	PR	←Courts THOMAS	Recording→	UC	RE	TX	VS
		•	•	•	Background Research Agency Inc	770-788-1885	•		•	
•	•	•	•	•	Corporate Access Inc [SOP]	800-969-1666	•	•	•	•
•	•	•	•	•	Origin Information & Services Inc (GA)	800-315-3492	•	•	•	
	•	•	•		Vinson Detective Agency [SOP]	800-404-6698	•	•	•	•

DT	BK	CV	CR	PR	←Courts TIFT	Recording→	UC	RE	TX	VS
		•	•	•	Background Research Agency Inc	770-788-1885	•		•	
•	•	•	•	•	Origin Information & Services Inc (GA)	800-315-3492	•	•	•	
	•	•	•		Vinson Detective Agency [SOP]	800-404-6698	•	•	•	•

DT	BK	CV	CR	PR	←Courts TOOMBS	Recording→	UC	RE	TX	VS
		•	•	•	Background Research Agency Inc	770-788-1885	•		•	
•	•	•	•	•	Origin Information & Services Inc (GA)	800-315-3492	•	•	•	

DT	BK	CV	CR	PR	←Courts TOWNS	Recording→	UC	RE	TX	VS
•	•	•	•	•	Origin Information & Services Inc (GA)	800-315-3492	•	•	•	
	•	•			Southern Courthouse Ventures	678-413-4697	•	•	•	

DT	BK	CV	CR	PR	←Courts	TREUTLEN	Recording→	UC	RE	TX	VS
		•	•	•	Background Research Agency Inc		770-788-1885	•		•	
•	•	•	•	•	Origin Information & Services Inc (GA)		800-315-3492	•	•	•	

DT	BK	CV	CR	PR	←Courts	TROUP	Recording→	UC	RE	TX	VS
		•	•	•	Background Research Agency Inc		770-788-1885	•		•	
		•	•		National Pre-Employment Research [SOP]		770-389-6607				
•	•	•	•	•	Origin Information & Services Inc (GA)		800-315-3492	•	•	•	
		•	•		Search & Find		706-884-9801			•	
	•	•			Southern Courthouse Ventures		678-413-4697	•	•	•	

DT	BK	CV	CR	PR	←Courts	TURNER	Recording→	UC	RE	TX	VS
		•	•	•	Background Research Agency Inc		770-788-1885	•		•	
•	•	•	•	•	Origin Information & Services Inc (GA)		800-315-3492	•	•	•	

DT	BK	CV	CR	PR	←Courts	TWIGGS	Recording→	UC	RE	TX	VS
		•	•	•	Background Research Agency Inc		770-788-1885	•		•	
				•	M V Bostick Jr		478-781-9344		•	•	
		•	•		National Pre-Employment Research [SOP]		770-389-6607				
•	•	•	•	•	Origin Information & Services Inc (GA)		800-315-3492	•	•	•	
	•	•			Southern Courthouse Ventures		678-413-4697	•	•	•	

DT	BK	CV	CR	PR	←Courts	UNION	Recording→	UC	RE	TX	VS
		•	•	•	Background Research Agency Inc		770-788-1885	•		•	
•	•	•	•	•	Origin Information & Services Inc (GA)		800-315-3492	•	•	•	
	•	•			Southern Courthouse Ventures		678-413-4697	•	•	•	

DT	BK	CV	CR	PR	←Courts	UPSON	Recording→	UC	RE	TX	VS
		•	•	•	Background Research Agency Inc		770-788-1885	•		•	
				•	M V Bostick Jr		478-781-9344		•	•	
		•	•		National Pre-Employment Research [SOP]		770-389-6607				
•	•	•	•	•	Origin Information & Services Inc (GA)		800-315-3492	•	•	•	
	•	•			Southern Courthouse Ventures		678-413-4697	•	•	•	

DT	BK	CV	CR	PR	←Courts	WALKER	Recording→	UC	RE	TX	VS
		•	•	•	Background Research Agency Inc		770-788-1885	•		•	
					DocuSearch Services		423-894-2425	•	•	•	
•	•	•	•	•	Origin Information & Services Inc (GA)		800-315-3492	•	•	•	
		•	•		Search & Find		706-884-9801			•	
	•	•			Southern Courthouse Ventures		678-413-4697	•	•	•	
•	•	•	•	•	Southern Research Enterprises		770-387-9439	•	•	•	•
•	•	•		•	Title Guaranty & Trust of Chattanooga		423-266-5751	•	•	•	

DT	BK	CV	CR	PR	←Courts	WALTON	Recording→	UC	RE	TX	VS
		•	•		Able Atlanta Research		404-502-2024	•		•	
		•	•	•	Background Research Agency Inc		770-788-1885	•		•	
•	•	•	•	•	Excel Search Inc		770-844-1201	•	•	•	•
		•	•	•	Roger Gladden Law Office [SOP]		404-550-0749	•	•	•	
		•	•		National Pre-Employment Research [SOP]		770-389-6607				
•	•	•	•	•	Origin Information & Services Inc (GA)		800-315-3492	•	•	•	
		•	•		Professional Paralegal Services Inc [SOP]		706-310-1166				
	•	•			Southern Courthouse Ventures		678-413-4697	•	•	•	

DT	BK	CV	CR	PR	←Courts	WARE	Recording→	UC	RE	TX	VS
		•	•	•	Background Research Agency Inc		770-788-1885	•		•	
		•	•		National Pre-Employment Research [SOP]		770-389-6607				
•	•	•	•	•	Origin Information & Services Inc (GA)		800-315-3492	•	•	•	
		•		•	Betty M Rowell, CLA		912-449-0849	•	•	•	

DT	BK	CV	CR	PR	←Courts	WARREN	Recording→	UC	RE	TX	VS
		•	•	•	Background Research Agency Inc		770-788-1885	•		•	

DT	BK	CV	CR	PR			UC	RE	TX	VS
•	•	•	•	•	Origin Information & Services Inc (GA)	800-315-3492	•	•	•	

DT	BK	CV	CR	PR	←Courts **WASHINGTON**	Recording→	UC	RE	TX	VS
		•	•	•	Background Research Agency Inc	770-788-1885	•		•	
•	•	•	•	•	Origin Information & Services Inc (GA)	800-315-3492	•	•	•	

DT	BK	CV	CR	PR	←Courts **WAYNE**	Recording→	UC	RE	TX	VS
		•	•	•	Background Research Agency Inc	770-788-1885	•		•	
		•	•		National Pre-Employment Research [SOP]	770-389-6607				
•	•	•	•	•	Origin Information & Services Inc (GA)	800-315-3492	•	•	•	

DT	BK	CV	CR	PR	←Courts **WEBSTER**	Recording→	UC	RE	TX	VS
		•	•	•	Background Research Agency Inc	770-788-1885	•		•	
•	•	•	•	•	Origin Information & Services Inc (GA)	800-315-3492	•	•	•	

DT	BK	CV	CR	PR	←Courts **WHEELER**	Recording→	UC	RE	TX	VS
		•	•	•	Background Research Agency Inc	770-788-1885	•		•	
•	•	•	•	•	Origin Information & Services Inc (GA)	800-315-3492	•	•	•	

DT	BK	CV	CR	PR	←Courts **WHITE**	Recording→	UC	RE	TX	VS
		•	•	•	Background Research Agency Inc	770-788-1885	•		•	
•	•	•	•	•	EL-RU Inc	770-963-8023	•	•	•	•
•	•	•	•	•	Origin Information & Services Inc (GA)	800-315-3492	•	•	•	
	•	•			Southern Courthouse Ventures	678-413-4697	•	•	•	

DT	BK	CV	CR	PR	←Courts **WHITFIELD**	Recording→	UC	RE	TX	VS
•	•	•	•	•	A All State Tracers Company	423-605-0155	•	•	•	•
		•	•	•	Background Research Agency Inc	770-788-1885	•		•	
•	•	•			Courthouse Abstractors	770-271-9002	•	•	•	
•	•	•	•	•	Origin Information & Services Inc (GA)	800-315-3492	•	•	•	
	•	•			Southern Courthouse Ventures	678-413-4697	•	•	•	
•	•	•	•	•	Southern Research Enterprises	770-387-9439	•	•	•	•
•	•	•		•	Title Guaranty & Trust of Chattanooga	423-266-5751	•	•	•	

DT	BK	CV	CR	PR	←Courts **WILCOX**	Recording→	UC	RE	TX	VS
•	•	•	•	•	Origin Information & Services Inc (GA)	800-315-3492	•	•	•	

DT	BK	CV	CR	PR	←Courts **WILKES**	Recording→	UC	RE	TX	VS
		•	•	•	Background Research Agency Inc	770-788-1885	•		•	
•	•	•	•	•	Origin Information & Services Inc (GA)	800-315-3492	•	•	•	
	•	•			Southern Courthouse Ventures	678-413-4697	•	•	•	

DT	BK	CV	CR	PR	←Courts **WILKINSON**	Recording→	UC	RE	TX	VS
		•	•	•	Background Research Agency Inc	770-788-1885	•		•	
				•	M V Bostick Jr	478-781-9344				
•	•	•	•	•	Origin Information & Services Inc (GA)	800-315-3492	•	•	•	
		•	•		Professional Paralegal Services Inc [SOP]	706-310-1166				

DT	BK	CV	CR	PR	←Courts **WORTH**	Recording→	UC	RE	TX	VS
		•	•	•	Background Research Agency Inc	770-788-1885	•		•	
•	•	•	•	•	Origin Information & Services Inc (GA)	800-315-3492	•	•	•	
	•	•	•		Vinson Detective Agency [SOP]	800-404-6698	•	•	•	•

Hawaii

COURT RECORDS RETRIEVED / **RECORDING RECORDS RETRIEVED**

DT	BK	CV	CR	PR	←COURTS HAWAII RECORDING→	UC	RE	TX	VS
•	•	•	•		Doc-U-Search Hawaii [SOP] 808-523-1200	•	•	•	
•	•	•	•	•	Judith A Fitzgerald 808-263-2120	•	•	•	
•	•			•	Hawaii Real Property Research 808-396-7581	•	•	•	•
•	•	•	•	•	Honolulu Information Service, Inc [SOP] 808-524-4488	•	•	•	•
•	•	•	•	•	Wood & Tait Inc [SOP] 800-774-8585		•		

DT	BK	CV	CR	PR	←COURTS HONOLULU RECORDING→	UC	RE	TX	VS
•	•	•	•		Doc-U-Search Hawaii [SOP] 808-523-1200	•	•	•	
•	•	•	•	•	Judith A Fitzgerald 808-263-2120	•	•	•	
•	•			•	Hawaii Real Property Research 808-396-7581	•	•	•	•
•	•	•	•	•	Honolulu Information Service, Inc [SOP] 808-524-4488	•	•	•	•
•	•	•	•		National Information Access Bureau (NIAB) 800-787-6422		•		•
•	•	•	•	•	Wood & Tait Inc [SOP] 800-774-8585		•		

DT	BK	CV	CR	PR	←COURTS KALAWAO RECORDING→	UC	RE	TX	VS
•	•	•	•		Doc-U-Search Hawaii [SOP] 808-523-1200	•	•	•	
•	•			•	Hawaii Real Property Research 808-396-7581	•	•	•	•

DT	BK	CV	CR	PR	←COURTS KAUAI RECORDING→	UC	RE	TX	VS
•	•	•	•		Doc-U-Search Hawaii [SOP] 808-523-1200	•	•	•	
•	•	•	•	•	Judith A Fitzgerald 808-263-2120	•	•	•	
•	•			•	Hawaii Real Property Research 808-396-7581	•	•	•	•
•	•	•	•	•	Honolulu Information Service, Inc [SOP] 808-524-4488	•	•	•	•
•	•	•	•	•	Wood & Tait Inc [SOP] 800-774-8585		•		

DT	BK	CV	CR	PR	←COURTS MAUI RECORDING→	UC	RE	TX	VS
•	•	•	•		Doc-U-Search Hawaii [SOP] 808-523-1200	•	•	•	
•	•	•	•	•	Judith A Fitzgerald 808-263-2120	•	•	•	
•	•			•	Hawaii Real Property Research 808-396-7581	•	•	•	•
•	•	•	•	•	Honolulu Information Service, Inc [SOP] 808-524-4488	•	•	•	•
•	•	•	•	•	Wood & Tait Inc [SOP] 800-774-8585		•		

Editor's Tip: Simply because your state or county has certain rules, regulations and practices regarding the accessibility and content of public records, does not mean those same rules apply elsewhere.

Idaho

COURT RECORDS RETRIEVED — **RECORDING RECORDS RETRIEVED**

DT	BK	CV	CR	PR	←COURTS ADA	RECORDING→	UC	RE	TX	VS
•		•	•		Accurate Records Research LLC	208-888-2857	•	•	•	
•	•	•	•	•	Attorneys Messenger Svc [SOP]	208-345-2905	•	•	•	•
•	•	•	•		Cory Brooks [SOP]	208-376-3312	•		•	
•	•	•	•	•	Burr Investigation [SOP]	800-582-5441	•	•	•	•
•	•	•	•	•	Integrity Check LLC	877-887-1226	•	•	•	•
•	•	•	•	•	Lord Investigations, LLC [SOP]	208-939-4040	•			
•	•			•	Record Search America Inc	208-375-1906	•	•	•	
•	•	•	•		Shadow Trackers Investigative Svcs Inc [SOP]	208-895-0074			•	
•	•	•	•	•	Tri-County Process Serving [SOP]	800-473-3454	•	•	•	
		•	•	•	Wright Research	208-455-2450	•		•	•

DT	BK	CV	CR	PR	←COURTS ADAMS	RECORDING→	UC	RE	TX	VS
•	•	•	•	•	Burr Investigation [SOP]	800-582-5441	•	•	•	•
•	•			•	Record Search America Inc	208-375-1906	•	•	•	

DT	BK	CV	CR	PR	←COURTS BANNOCK	RECORDING→	UC	RE	TX	VS
•		•	•		Accurate Records Research LLC	208-888-2857	•	•	•	
•	•	•	•	•	Carter Investigations [SOP]	208-232-3592	•	•	•	•
•	•			•	Record Search America Inc	208-375-1906	•	•	•	
•	•	•	•		Shadow Trackers Investigative Svcs Inc [SOP]	208-895-0074			•	

DT	BK	CV	CR	PR	←COURTS BEAR LAKE	RECORDING→	UC	RE	TX	VS
•		•	•		Accurate Records Research LLC	208-888-2857	•	•	•	
		•		•	First Idaho Title Co	208-847-1300	•	•	•	
•	•			•	Record Search America Inc	208-375-1906	•	•	•	

DT	BK	CV	CR	PR	←COURTS BENEWAH	RECORDING→	UC	RE	TX	VS
•	•	•	•	•	Gem State Inv [SOP]	208-746-4152	•	•	•	•
•	•			•	Record Search America Inc	208-375-1906	•	•	•	

DT	BK	CV	CR	PR	←COURTS BINGHAM	RECORDING→	UC	RE	TX	VS
•		•	•		Accurate Records Research LLC	208-888-2857	•	•	•	
•	•	•	•	•	Carter Investigations [SOP]	208-232-3592	•	•	•	•
•	•			•	Record Search America Inc	208-375-1906	•	•	•	

DT	BK	CV	CR	PR	←COURTS BLAINE	RECORDING→	UC	RE	TX	VS
•		•	•		Accurate Records Research LLC	208-888-2857	•	•	•	
•	•	•	•	•	Burr Investigation [SOP]	800-582-5441	•	•	•	•
		•	•	•	Mower Services [SOP]	888-317-7458	•	•	•	
		•	•	•	Northern Intermountain Security Inc [SOP]	208-726-2705	•	•	•	•
•	•			•	Record Search America Inc	208-375-1906	•	•	•	

DT	BK	CV	CR	PR	←COURTS BOISE	RECORDING→	UC	RE	TX	VS
•		•	•		Accurate Records Research LLC	208-888-2857	•	•	•	
•	•	•	•	•	Burr Investigation [SOP]	800-582-5441	•	•	•	•
•	•	•	•	•	Integrity Check LLC	877-887-1226	•	•	•	•
•	•	•	•	•	Lord Investigations, LLC [SOP]	208-939-4040	•			
•	•	•	•	•	Record Search America Inc	208-375-1906	•	•	•	
•	•	•	•	•	Tri-County Process Serving [SOP]	800-473-3454	•	•	•	

DT	BK	CV	CR	PR	←Courts	Bonner	Recording→	UC	RE	TX	VS
•		•	•			Accurate Records Research LLC	208-888-2857	•	•	•	
						Rat Dog Research LLC	208-765-4598	•	•	•	
•	•			•		Record Search America Inc	208-375-1906	•	•	•	

DT	BK	CV	CR	PR	←Courts	Bonneville	Recording→	UC	RE	TX	VS
•		•	•			Accurate Records Research LLC	208-888-2857	•	•	•	
•	•	•	•	•		Carter Investigations [SOP]	208-232-3592	•	•	•	•
•	•			•		Record Search America Inc	208-375-1906	•	•	•	

DT	BK	CV	CR	PR	←Courts	Boundary	Recording→	UC	RE	TX	VS
•		•	•			Accurate Records Research LLC	208-888-2857	•	•	•	
						Rat Dog Research LLC	208-765-4598	•	•	•	
•	•			•		Record Search America Inc	208-375-1906	•	•	•	

DT	BK	CV	CR	PR	←Courts	Butte	Recording→	UC	RE	TX	VS
		•		•		Idaho Title & Trust Co [SOP]	208-527-8517	•	•	•	
•	•			•		Record Search America Inc	208-375-1906	•	•	•	

DT	BK	CV	CR	PR	←Courts	Camas	Recording→	UC	RE	TX	VS
•	•			•		Record Search America Inc	208-375-1906	•	•	•	

DT	BK	CV	CR	PR	←Courts	Canyon	Recording→	UC	RE	TX	VS
•		•	•			Accurate Records Research LLC	208-888-2857	•	•	•	
•	•	•	•	•		Attorneys Messenger Svc [SOP]	208-345-2905	•	•	•	•
•	•	•	•			Cory Brooks [SOP]	208-376-3312	•		•	
•	•	•	•	•		Burr Investigation [SOP]	800-582-5441	•	•	•	•
•	•	•	•	•		Integrity Check LLC	877-887-1226	•	•	•	•
•	•	•	•	•		Lord Investigations, LLC [SOP]	208-939-4040	•			
•	•			•		Record Search America Inc	208-375-1906	•	•	•	
•	•	•	•			Shadow Trackers Investigative Svcs Inc [SOP]	208-895-0074			•	
•	•	•	•	•		Tri-County Process Serving [SOP]	800-473-3454	•	•	•	
		•	•	•		Wright Research	208-455-2450	•		•	•

DT	BK	CV	CR	PR	←Courts	Caribou	Recording→	UC	RE	TX	VS
•	•			•		Record Search America Inc	208-375-1906	•	•	•	

DT	BK	CV	CR	PR	←Courts	Cassia	Recording→	UC	RE	TX	VS
•		•	•			Accurate Records Research LLC	208-888-2857	•	•	•	
•	•	•	•	•		Burr Investigation [SOP]	800-582-5441	•	•	•	•
				•		Cassia County Abstract Co	208-678-8347	•	•	•	
•	•			•		Record Search America Inc	208-375-1906	•	•	•	

DT	BK	CV	CR	PR	←Courts	Clark	Recording→	UC	RE	TX	VS
•	•			•		Record Search America Inc	208-375-1906	•	•	•	

DT	BK	CV	CR	PR	←Courts	Clearwater	Recording→	UC	RE	TX	VS
•		•	•			Accurate Records Research LLC	208-888-2857	•	•	•	
•	•	•	•	•		Gem State Inv [SOP]	208-746-4152	•	•	•	•
						Rat Dog Research LLC	208-765-4598	•	•	•	
•	•			•		Record Search America Inc	208-375-1906	•	•	•	

DT	BK	CV	CR	PR	←Courts	Custer	Recording→	UC	RE	TX	VS
•	•			•		Record Search America Inc	208-375-1906	•	•	•	

DT	BK	CV	CR	PR	←Courts	Elmore	Recording→	UC	RE	TX	VS
•	•	•	•	•		Attorneys Messenger Svc [SOP]	208-345-2905	•	•	•	•
•	•	•	•	•		Burr Investigation [SOP]	800-582-5441	•	•	•	•
•	•	•	•	•		Integrity Check LLC	877-887-1226	•	•	•	•
•	•	•	•	•		Lord Investigations, LLC [SOP]	208-939-4040	•			
•	•			•		Record Search America Inc	208-375-1906	•	•	•	
•	•	•	•	•		Tri-County Process Serving [SOP]	800-473-3454	•	•	•	

DT	BK	CV	CR	PR	←Courts	Franklin	Recording→	UC	RE	TX	VS
		•		•		First American Title of Preston	208-852-2810	•	•	•	•
•	•			•		Record Search America Inc	208-375-1906	•	•	•	

DT	BK	CV	CR	PR	←Courts	Fremont	Recording→	UC	RE	TX	VS
•		•	•			Accurate Records Research LLC	208-888-2857	•	•	•	
•	•			•		Record Search America Inc	208-375-1906	•	•	•	

DT	BK	CV	CR	PR	←Courts	Gem	Recording→	UC	RE	TX	VS
•		•	•			Accurate Records Research LLC	208-888-2857	•	•	•	
•	•	•	•	•		Attorneys Messenger Svc [SOP]	208-345-2905	•	•	•	•
•	•	•	•	•		Burr Investigation [SOP]	800-582-5441	•	•	•	•
•	•	•	•	•		Integrity Check LLC	877-887-1226	•	•	•	•
•	•	•	•	•		Lord Investigations, LLC [SOP]	208-939-4040	•			
•	•			•		Record Search America Inc	208-375-1906	•	•	•	
•	•	•	•			Shadow Trackers Investigative Svcs Inc [SOP]	208-895-0074			•	
•	•	•	•	•		Tri-County Process Serving [SOP]	800-473-3454	•	•	•	

DT	BK	CV	CR	PR	←Courts	Gooding	Recording→	UC	RE	TX	VS
•		•	•			Accurate Records Research LLC	208-888-2857	•	•	•	
•	•	•	•	•		Burr Investigation [SOP]	800-582-5441	•	•	•	•
•	•			•		Record Search America Inc	208-375-1906	•	•	•	

DT	BK	CV	CR	PR	←Courts	Idaho	Recording→	UC	RE	TX	VS
•		•	•			Accurate Records Research LLC	208-888-2857	•	•	•	
•	•	•	•	•		Gem State Inv [SOP]	208-746-4152	•	•	•	•
•	•			•		Record Search America Inc	208-375-1906	•	•	•	

DT	BK	CV	CR	PR	←Courts	Jefferson	Recording→	UC	RE	TX	VS
•		•	•			Accurate Records Research LLC	208-888-2857	•	•	•	
•	•			•		Record Search America Inc	208-375-1906	•	•	•	

DT	BK	CV	CR	PR	←Courts	Jerome	Recording→	UC	RE	TX	VS
•		•	•			Accurate Records Research LLC	208-888-2857	•	•	•	
•	•			•		Record Search America Inc	208-375-1906	•	•	•	

DT	BK	CV	CR	PR	←Courts	Kootenai	Recording→	UC	RE	TX	VS
•		•	•			Accurate Records Research LLC	208-888-2857	•	•	•	
						Rat Dog Research LLC	208-765-4598	•	•	•	
•	•			•		Record Search America Inc	208-375-1906	•	•	•	
	•	•	•			Alice E Sackman	208-964-0209	•	•	•	

DT	BK	CV	CR	PR	←Courts	Latah	Recording→	UC	RE	TX	VS
•		•	•			Accurate Records Research LLC	208-888-2857	•	•	•	
•	•	•	•	•		Gem State Inv [SOP]	208-746-4152	•	•	•	•
•	•	•	•			Carrie J Myers	208-883-7963	•	•	•	
						Rat Dog Research LLC	208-765-4598	•	•	•	
•	•			•		Record Search America Inc	208-375-1906	•	•	•	
•	•	•	•			Shadow Trackers Investigative Svcs Inc [SOP]	208-895-0074			•	

DT	BK	CV	CR	PR	←Courts	Lemhi	Recording→	UC	RE	TX	VS
•	•			•		Record Search America Inc	208-375-1906	•	•	•	

DT	BK	CV	CR	PR	←Courts	Lewis	Recording→	UC	RE	TX	VS
•		•	•			Accurate Records Research LLC	208-888-2857	•	•	•	
•	•	•	•	•		Gem State Inv [SOP]	208-746-4152	•	•	•	•
		•	•	•		Lewis County Abstract (Idaho) d/b/a Lewis County Title	208-937-2621		•	•	
•	•			•		Record Search America Inc	208-375-1906	•	•	•	

DT	BK	CV	CR	PR	←Courts	Lincoln	Recording→	UC	RE	TX	VS
•		•	•			Accurate Records Research LLC	208-888-2857	•	•	•	
•	•			•		Record Search America Inc	208-375-1906	•	•	•	

DT	BK	CV	CR	PR	←Courts	Madison	Recording→	UC	RE	TX	VS
•		•	•		Accurate Records Research LLC		208-888-2857	•	•	•	
•	•			•	Record Search America Inc		208-375-1906	•	•	•	

DT	BK	CV	CR	PR	←Courts	Minidoka	Recording→	UC	RE	TX	VS
•		•	•		Accurate Records Research LLC		208-888-2857	•	•	•	
•	•	•	•	•	Burr Investigation [SOP]		800-582-5441	•	•	•	•
•	•			•	Record Search America Inc		208-375-1906	•	•	•	

DT	BK	CV	CR	PR	←Courts	Nez Perce	Recording→	UC	RE	TX	VS
•		•	•		Accurate Records Research LLC		208-888-2857	•	•	•	
•	•	•	•	•	Gem State Inv [SOP]		208-746-4152	•	•	•	•
•	•	•	•		Ryan Myers		208-882-6678	•	•	•	
					Rat Dog Research LLC		208-765-4598	•	•	•	
•	•			•	Record Search America Inc		208-375-1906	•	•	•	

DT	BK	CV	CR	PR	←Courts	Oneida	Recording→	UC	RE	TX	VS
•	•			•	Record Search America Inc		208-375-1906	•	•	•	

DT	BK	CV	CR	PR	←Courts	Owyhee	Recording→	UC	RE	TX	VS
•	•	•	•	•	Attorneys Messenger Svc [SOP]		208-345-2905	•	•	•	•
•	•	•	•	•	Burr Investigation [SOP]		800-582-5441	•	•	•	•
•	•			•	Record Search America Inc		208-375-1906	•	•	•	

DT	BK	CV	CR	PR	←Courts	Payette	Recording→	UC	RE	TX	VS
•		•	•		Accurate Records Research LLC		208-888-2857	•	•	•	
•	•			•	Record Search America Inc		208-375-1906	•	•	•	
•	•	•	•		Shadow Trackers Investigative Svcs Inc [SOP]		208-895-0074			•	
•	•	•	•	•	Tri-County Process Serving [SOP]		800-473-3454	•	•	•	

DT	BK	CV	CR	PR	←Courts	Power	Recording→	UC	RE	TX	VS
•	•	•	•	•	Carter Investigations [SOP]		208-232-3592	•	•	•	•
•	•			•	Record Search America Inc		208-375-1906	•	•	•	

DT	BK	CV	CR	PR	←Courts	Shoshone	Recording→	UC	RE	TX	VS
•	•			•	Record Search America Inc		208-375-1906	•	•	•	

DT	BK	CV	CR	PR	←Courts	Teton	Recording→	UC	RE	TX	VS
•	•				Alliance Title & Escrow Corp		800-214-1418	•	•	•	
•	•			•	Record Search America Inc		208-375-1906	•	•	•	

DT	BK	CV	CR	PR	←Courts	Twin Falls	Recording→	UC	RE	TX	VS
•		•	•		Accurate Records Research LLC		208-888-2857	•	•	•	
•	•	•	•	•	Burr Investigation [SOP]		800-582-5441	•	•	•	•
		•	•	•	Northern Intermountain Security Inc [SOP]		208-726-2705	•	•	•	•
•	•			•	Record Search America Inc		208-375-1906	•	•	•	

DT	BK	CV	CR	PR	←Courts	Valley	Recording→	UC	RE	TX	VS
•	•	•	•	•	Burr Investigation [SOP]		800-582-5441	•	•	•	•
•	•	•	•	•	Lord Investigations, LLC [SOP]		208-939-4040	•			
•	•			•	Record Search America Inc		208-375-1906	•	•	•	
•	•	•	•	•	Tri-County Process Serving [SOP]		800-473-3454	•	•	•	

DT	BK	CV	CR	PR	←Courts	Washington	Recording→	UC	RE	TX	VS
•		•	•		Accurate Records Research LLC		208-888-2857	•	•	•	
•	•	•	•	•	Lord Investigations, LLC [SOP]		208-939-4040	•			
•	•			•	Record Search America Inc		208-375-1906	•	•	•	

Illinois

COURT RECORDS RETRIEVED — **RECORDING RECORDS RETRIEVED**

DT	BK	CV	CR	PR	←COURTS ADAMS	RECORDING→	UC	RE	TX	VS
		•	•		Ferret Diversified Services Inc	847-266-7666				
		•	•		Teresa L Godman	217-223-4186				
•	•	•	•		Infotrack Information Services Inc	800-275-5594	•	•	•	
		•	•	•	Marion County Abstract Co (Missouri)	800-952-5314	•	•	•	•
•	•	•	•	•	PII Inc [SOP]	217-483-8845	•	•	•	•
•	•	•	•	•	Woelfel & Assoc Inc [SOP]	888-297-7180	•	•	•	

DT	BK	CV	CR	PR	←COURTS ALEXANDER	RECORDING→	UC	RE	TX	VS
		•	•	•	Abstract & Title Co	618-445-2554	•	•	•	

DT	BK	CV	CR	PR	←COURTS BOND	RECORDING→	UC	RE	TX	VS
			•	•	Bi-State Title Search (Div of Bi-State Ind.)	866-450-7399	•	•	•	
		•		•	Bond Title	618-664-1872	•	•	•	•
•	•	•	•		Infotrack Information Services Inc	800-275-5594	•	•	•	
•	•	•	•	•	Woelfel & Assoc Inc [SOP]	888-297-7180	•	•	•	

DT	BK	CV	CR	PR	←COURTS BOONE	RECORDING→	UC	RE	TX	VS
•	•	•	•	•	Gregg Inv, Inc of Rockford [SOP]	800-377-1976	•		•	•
•	•	•	•		Infotrack Information Services Inc	800-275-5594	•	•	•	
	•	•	•	•	Security First Title Co	815-235-2900	•	•	•	
•	•	•	•	•	Stewart & Associates Inc [SOP]	800-442-3807	•	•	•	•
		•	•		Julie L Thomas	815-234-4172				

DT	BK	CV	CR	PR	←COURTS BROWN	RECORDING→	UC	RE	TX	VS
•	•	•	•		Infotrack Information Services Inc	800-275-5594	•	•	•	

DT	BK	CV	CR	PR	←COURTS BUREAU	RECORDING→	UC	RE	TX	VS
		•	•	•	Associated Title Company Inc	800-713-4224	•	•	•	•
•	•	•	•		Infotrack Information Services Inc	800-275-5594	•	•	•	
		•	•		RBI Inc Ottawa [SOP]	815-228-3694				

DT	BK	CV	CR	PR	←COURTS CALHOUN	RECORDING→	UC	RE	TX	VS
•	•	•	•		Infotrack Information Services Inc	800-275-5594	•	•	•	
•	•	•	•	•	Woelfel & Assoc Inc [SOP]	888-297-7180	•	•	•	

DT	BK	CV	CR	PR	←COURTS CARROLL	RECORDING→	UC	RE	TX	VS
		•	•		Ferret Diversified Services Inc	847-266-7666				
•	•	•	•		Infotrack Information Services Inc	800-275-5594	•	•	•	
	•	•	•	•	Security First Title Co	815-235-2900	•	•	•	
•	•	•	•	•	Stewart & Associates Inc [SOP]	800-442-3807	•	•	•	•

DT	BK	CV	CR	PR	←COURTS CASS	RECORDING→	UC	RE	TX	VS
		•		•	First American Title Insurance Company (IL)	309-347-6126	•	•	•	•
•	•	•	•		Infotrack Information Services Inc	800-275-5594	•	•	•	
•	•	•	•	•	PII Inc [SOP]	217-483-8845	•	•	•	•

DT	BK	CV	CR	PR	←COURTS CHAMPAIGN	RECORDING→	UC	RE	TX	VS
•	•	•	•	•	Diligent Detective Agency Inc [SOP]	877-694-3332		•	•	•
		•	•		Ferret Diversified Services Inc	847-266-7666				
•	•	•	•		Infotrack Information Services Inc	800-275-5594	•	•	•	
•	•	•	•	•	Jacobs & Associates CPD Inc [SOP]	800-445-1675	•	•	•	•

DT	BK	CV	CR	PR	←Courts	Recording→	UC	RE	TX	VS
•	•	•	•	•	Kellerman Investigations Ltd [SOP]	888-402-6662				

DT	BK	CV	CR	PR	←Courts **CHRISTIAN**	Recording→	UC	RE	TX	VS
•	•	•	•		Infotrack Information Services Inc	800-275-5594	•	•	•	
•	•	•	•	•	PII Inc [SOP]	217-483-8845	•	•	•	•

DT	BK	CV	CR	PR	←Courts **CLARK**	Recording→	UC	RE	TX	VS
		•	•	•	Abstract & Title Co	618-445-2554	•	•	•	
					Everhart & Everhart Abstractors	217-849-2671	•	•	•	

DT	BK	CV	CR	PR	←Courts **CLAY**	Recording→	UC	RE	TX	VS
		•	•	•	Abstract & Title Co	618-445-2554	•	•	•	
•	•	•	•	•	Nancy Durbin Process Service [SOP]	618-548-8296	•	•	•	•
•	•	•	•	•	Woelfel & Assoc Inc [SOP]	888-297-7180	•	•	•	

DT	BK	CV	CR	PR	←Courts **CLINTON**	Recording→	UC	RE	TX	VS
		•	•	•	Abstract & Title Co	618-445-2554	•	•	•	
		•		•	Bond Title	618-664-1872	•	•	•	•
•	•	•	•		Infotrack Information Services Inc	800-275-5594	•	•	•	
•	•	•	•	•	Kevin W McClain Inv Ltd [SOP]	877-532-1152	•	•	•	•
•	•	•	•	•	Nancy Durbin Process Service [SOP]	618-548-8296	•	•	•	•
•	•	•	•	•	Woelfel & Assoc Inc [SOP]	888-297-7180	•	•	•	

DT	BK	CV	CR	PR	←Courts **COLES**	Recording→	UC	RE	TX	VS
		•	•	•	Abstract & Title Co	618-445-2554	•	•	•	
					Everhart & Everhart Abstractors	217-849-2671	•	•	•	
		•	•		Ferret Diversified Services Inc	847-266-7666				
•	•	•	•	•	Folks Finders Ltd	800-277-3318	•	•	•	•
•	•	•	•		Infotrack Information Services Inc	800-275-5594	•	•	•	
•	•	•	•	•	Jacobs & Associates CPD Inc [SOP]	800-445-1675	•	•	•	•
•	•	•	•	•	PII Inc [SOP]	217-483-8845	•	•	•	•

DT	BK	CV	CR	PR	←Courts **COOK**	Recording→	UC	RE	TX	VS
•	•	•	•	•	AAA VTS Investigations [SOP]	800-203-4160	•	•	•	•
		•	•	•	Stephen J Addison	708-335-9179	•	•	•	•
					AIM3 Research	630-631-6531		•		
					ARC Document Research Inc	312-346-4895	•	•	•	
•	•	•	•	•	Argus Services Inc [SOP]	800-297-3377			•	•
•	•	•	•		Asset Control Inc	877-277-3812	•	•	•	•
•	•	•	•	•	Aurico Inv LLC [SOP]	847-255-1852	•	•	•	•
•	•	•	•	•	Chicagoland Detective Services Inc [SOP]	877-426-4278	•	•	•	•
					Concord Commercial Services	972-931-7431		•		
•	•	•	•	•	Corporation Service Company - CSC	800-927-9800	•	•	•	•
•	•	•	•		George L Dickinson	708-307-4792				
		•	•		Ferret Diversified Services Inc	847-266-7666				
•	•	•	•		Infotrack Information Services Inc	800-275-5594	•	•	•	
		•	•		Investigative Research Consultants Inc [SOP]	888-578-8600				
•	•	•	•	•	JG Weiss Research & Retrieval	773-241-6923	•	•	•	•
•	•	•	•	•	Kevin W McClain Inv Ltd [SOP]	877-532-1152	•	•	•	•
•	•	•	•	•	LaSalle Process Servers LP [SOP]	800-815-3801	•	•	•	•
•	•	•	•	•	Legal Data Resources [SOP]	800-735-9207	•	•	•	•
•	•	•	•	•	Lynne J Cox Paralegal	800-510-3009	•	•	•	
•	•	•	•	•	Metro Clerking Inc	312-263-2977	•	•	•	•
			•		Professional Services of America Inc	304-485-1278				
					R & B Research & Recording Inc	847-477-7510	•	•		
•	•	•	•	•	RBI Inc Joliet [SOP]	800-724-8366	•	•	•	•
•	•	•	•	•	Record Information Services	630-557-1000	•	•	•	•
•	•	•	•		SPI [SOP]	773-581-1400				
•	•	•	•	•	Spyglass Pre-Employment Specialist [SOP]	773-581-0180	•	•	•	•
•	•	•		•	Title Search	773-655-4142	•	•	•	•

DT	BK	CV	CR	PR	←Courts	Recording→	UC	RE	TX	VS
•	•	•	•	•	Tyler-McLennon Choicepoint	512-334-6244	•	•	•	•
					The Wilki Group Inc	847-356-8546	•	•	•	

DT	BK	CV	CR	PR	←Courts CRAWFORD	Recording→	UC	RE	TX	VS
		•	•	•	Abstract & Title Co	618-445-2554	•	•	•	
		•	•	•	Lawrence County Title	618-943-4464	•	•	•	•

DT	BK	CV	CR	PR	←Courts CUMBERLAND	Recording→	UC	RE	TX	VS
		•	•	•	Abstract & Title Co	618-445-2554	•	•	•	
					Everhart & Everhart Abstractors	217-849-2671	•	•	•	
•	•	•	•	•	Folks Finders Ltd	800-277-3318	•	•	•	•
•	•	•	•		Infotrack Information Services Inc	800-275-5594	•	•	•	

DT	BK	CV	CR	PR	←Courts DE KALB	Recording→	UC	RE	TX	VS
•	•	•	•	•	AAA VTS Investigations [SOP]	800-203-4160	•	•	•	•
•	•	•	•	•	Argus Services Inc [SOP]	800-297-3377			•	•
		•	•		Ferret Diversified Services Inc	847-266-7666				
•	•	•	•		Infotrack Information Services Inc	800-275-5594	•	•	•	
•	•	•	•	•	Kellerman Investigations Ltd [SOP]	888-402-6662				
		•	•	•	Cynthia Potthoff	815-895-9527				
		•	•		RBI Inc Ottawa [SOP]	815-228-3694				
•	•		•		Reality Check Inc	309-699-1846		•		
•	•	•	•	•	Record Information Services	630-557-1000	•	•	•	•
•	•	•	•	•	Stewart & Associates Inc [SOP]	800-442-3807	•	•	•	•
		•	•		Julie L Thomas	815-234-4172				
					The Wilki Group Inc	847-356-8546	•	•	•	
		•	•	•	Yahnke Professional Srvs & Inv [SOP]	800-203-4160	•	•	•	•

DT	BK	CV	CR	PR	←Courts DE WITT	Recording→	UC	RE	TX	VS
		•	•		Margaret Flowers	217-877-2105				
•	•	•	•		Infotrack Information Services Inc	800-275-5594	•	•	•	
•	•	•	•	•	Jacobs & Associates CPD Inc [SOP]	800-445-1675	•	•	•	•

DT	BK	CV	CR	PR	←Courts DOUGLAS	Recording→	UC	RE	TX	VS
				•	Douglas County Abstract Co Inc	217-253-3214	•	•	•	
•	•	•	•		Infotrack Information Services Inc	800-275-5594	•	•	•	
•	•	•	•	•	Jacobs & Associates CPD Inc [SOP]	800-445-1675	•	•	•	•

DT	BK	CV	CR	PR	←Courts DU PAGE	Recording→	UC	RE	TX	VS
•	•	•	•	•	AAA VTS Investigations [SOP]	800-203-4160	•	•	•	•
					AIM3 Research	630-631-6531		•		
					ARC Document Research Inc	312-346-4895	•	•	•	
•	•	•	•	•	Argus Services Inc [SOP]	800-297-3377			•	•
•	•	•	•	•	Aurico Inv LLC [SOP]	847-255-1852	•	•	•	•
		•	•	•	AV Investigations Inc [SOP]	630-443-3617	•	•	•	•
•	•	•	•	•	Chicagoland Detective Services Inc [SOP]	877-426-4278	•	•	•	•
		•	•		Ferret Diversified Services Inc	847-266-7666				
•	•	•	•		Infotrack Information Services Inc	800-275-5594	•	•	•	
		•	•		Investigative Research Consultants Inc [SOP]	888-578-8600				
•	•	•	•	•	JG Weiss Research & Retrieval	773-241-6923	•	•	•	•
•	•	•	•	•	LaSalle Process Servers LP [SOP]	800-815-3801	•	•	•	•
•	•	•	•	•	Legal Data Resources [SOP]	800-735-9207	•	•	•	•
•	•	•	•	•	Metro Clerking Inc	312-263-2977	•	•	•	•
			•		Professional Services of America Inc	304-485-1278				
					R & B Research & Recording Inc	847-477-7510	•	•		
•	•	•	•	•	RBI Inc Joliet [SOP]	800-724-8366	•	•	•	•
•	•	•	•	•	Record Information Services	630-557-1000	•	•	•	•
•	•	•	•		SPI [SOP]	773-581-1400	•	•	•	•
•	•	•	•	•	Spyglass Pre-Employment Specialist [SOP]	773-581-0180	•	•	•	•
					The Wilki Group Inc	847-356-8546	•	•	•	

DT	BK	CV	CR	PR	Name	Phone	UC	RE	TX	VS
		•	•		Wisestart Information Services	262-723-7881				
		•	•	•	Yahnke Professional Srvs & Inv [SOP]	800-203-4160	•	•	•	•

DT	BK	CV	CR	PR	←Courts **Edgar** Recording→		UC	RE	TX	VS
		•	•	•	Abstract & Title Co	618-445-2554	•	•	•	
		•		•	Edgar County Title Co	217-465-5821	•	•	•	•
•	•	•	•		Infotrack Information Services Inc	800-275-5594	•	•	•	

DT	BK	CV	CR	PR	←Courts **Edwards** Recording→		UC	RE	TX	VS
		•	•	•	Abstract & Title Co	618-445-2554	•	•	•	

DT	BK	CV	CR	PR	←Courts **Effingham** Recording→		UC	RE	TX	VS
		•	•	•	Abstract & Title Co	618-445-2554	•	•	•	
					Everhart & Everhart Abstractors	217-849-2671	•	•	•	
•	•	•	•	•	Folks Finders Ltd	800-277-3318	•	•	•	•
•	•	•	•		Infotrack Information Services Inc	800-275-5594	•	•	•	
•	•	•	•	•	Kevin W McClain Inv Ltd [SOP]	877-532-1152	•	•	•	•
•	•	•	•	•	PII Inc [SOP]	217-483-8845	•	•	•	•

DT	BK	CV	CR	PR	←Courts **Fayette** Recording→		UC	RE	TX	VS
		•		•	Bond Title	618-664-1872	•	•	•	•
					Burtschi Bros & Co	618-283-2102	•	•	•	
•	•	•	•		Infotrack Information Services Inc	800-275-5594	•	•	•	
•	•	•	•	•	Nancy Durbin Process Service [SOP]	618-548-8296	•	•	•	•
•	•	•	•	•	Woelfel & Assoc Inc [SOP]	888-297-7180	•	•	•	

DT	BK	CV	CR	PR	←Courts **Ford** Recording→		UC	RE	TX	VS
•	•	•	•	•	Diligent Detective Agency Inc [SOP]	877-694-3332		•	•	•
		•	•		Margaret Fiorillo [SOP]	217-379-3359	•	•	•	•
•	•	•	•		Infotrack Information Services Inc	800-275-5594	•	•	•	

DT	BK	CV	CR	PR	←Courts **Franklin** Recording→		UC	RE	TX	VS
		•	•	•	Abstract & Title Co	618-445-2554	•	•	•	
•	•	•	•	•	Heartland Inv Inc [SOP]	618-687-4900	•	•	•	•
•	•	•	•		Infotrack Information Services Inc	800-275-5594	•	•	•	
•	•	•	•	•	Kevin W McClain Inv Ltd [SOP]	877-532-1152	•	•	•	•
•	•		•		Midwest Backgrounds Inc	618-942-8808				
•	•	•	•	•	William J O'Shea, PI [SOP]	618-937-3895	•	•	•	•
		•	•	•	Palmer & Murrie Abstract Co Inc	618-993-3866	•	•	•	•
		•		•	Real Estate Data Inc	618-964-1907	•	•	•	
	•				Sharp Law Office	618-242-0246		•	•	

DT	BK	CV	CR	PR	←Courts **Fulton** Recording→		UC	RE	TX	VS
		•		•	First American Title Insurance Company (IL)	309-347-6126	•	•	•	•
•	•	•	•		Infotrack Information Services Inc	800-275-5594	•	•	•	
•	•	•	•		Security Services Inc (SSI) [SOP]	800-383-4312				
				•	Wilson Abstract Co	309-833-2049	•	•	•	•

DT	BK	CV	CR	PR	←Courts **Gallatin** Recording→		UC	RE	TX	VS
		•	•	•	Abstract & Title Co	618-445-2554	•	•	•	

DT	BK	CV	CR	PR	←Courts **Greene** Recording→		UC	RE	TX	VS
•	•	•	•		Infotrack Information Services Inc	800-275-5594	•	•	•	
		•	•	•	O H Vivell Title Co	217-942-3733	•	•	•	•

DT	BK	CV	CR	PR	←Courts **Grundy** Recording→		UC	RE	TX	VS
•	•	•	•		Infotrack Information Services Inc	800-275-5594	•	•	•	
•	•	•	•	•	RBI Inc Joliet [SOP]	800-724-8366	•	•	•	•
					The Wilki Group Inc	847-356-8546	•	•	•	

DT	BK	CV	CR	PR	←Courts **Hamilton** Recording→		UC	RE	TX	VS
		•	•	•	Abstract & Title Co	618-445-2554	•	•	•	

DT	BK	CV	CR	PR	←COURTS HANCOCK	RECORDING→	UC	RE	TX	VS
•	•	•	•		Infotrack Information Services Inc	800-275-5594	•	•	•	
		•	•	•	Marion County Abstract Co (Missouri)	800-952-5314	•	•	•	•
				•	Wilson Abstract Co	309-833-2049	•	•	•	•

DT	BK	CV	CR	PR	←COURTS HARDIN	RECORDING→	UC	RE	TX	VS
		•	•	•	Hardin County Abstract Company	618-287-7944	•	•	•	•

DT	BK	CV	CR	PR	←COURTS HENDERSON	RECORDING→	UC	RE	TX	VS
•	•	•	•		Infotrack Information Services Inc	800-275-5594	•	•	•	
				•	Wilson Abstract Co	309-833-2049	•	•	•	•

DT	BK	CV	CR	PR	←COURTS HENRY	RECORDING→	UC	RE	TX	VS
		•	•		Ferret Diversified Services Inc	847-266-7666				
•	•	•	•		Infotrack Information Services Inc	800-275-5594	•	•	•	
•	•	•	•	•	SAS Associates Inc [SOP]	800-373-0727	•		•	

DT	BK	CV	CR	PR	←COURTS IROQUOIS	RECORDING→	UC	RE	TX	VS
•	•	•	•	•	Diligent Detective Agency Inc [SOP]	877-694-3332		•	•	•
•	•	•	•		Infotrack Information Services Inc	800-275-5594	•	•	•	

DT	BK	CV	CR	PR	←COURTS JACKSON	RECORDING→	UC	RE	TX	VS
		•	•	•	Abstract & Title Co	618-445-2554	•	•	•	
		•	•		Ferret Diversified Services Inc	847-266-7666				
•	•	•	•	•	Heartland Inv Inc [SOP]	618-687-4900	•	•	•	•
•	•	•	•		Infotrack Information Services Inc	800-275-5594	•	•	•	
		•	•	•	Search & Genealogy Services	618-529-1024	•	•	•	•

DT	BK	CV	CR	PR	←COURTS JASPER	RECORDING→	UC	RE	TX	VS
		•	•	•	Abstract & Title Co	618-445-2554	•	•	•	
		•	•	•	Eaton Abstract Company	618-783-8474	•	•	•	

DT	BK	CV	CR	PR	←COURTS JEFFERSON	RECORDING→	UC	RE	TX	VS
		•	•	•	Abstract & Title Co	618-445-2554	•	•	•	
•	•	•	•	•	Heartland Inv Inc [SOP]	618-687-4900	•	•	•	•
•	•	•	•		Infotrack Information Services Inc	800-275-5594	•	•	•	
•	•	•	•	•	Kevin W McClain Inv Ltd [SOP]	877-532-1152	•	•	•	•
•	•	•	•	•	Nancy Durbin Process Service [SOP]	618-548-8296	•	•	•	•
		•	•	•	Palmer & Murrie Abstract Co Inc	618-993-3866	•	•	•	•
	•				Sharp Law Office	618-242-0246		•	•	

DT	BK	CV	CR	PR	←COURTS JERSEY	RECORDING→	UC	RE	TX	VS
			•	•	Bi-State Title Search (Div of Bi-State Ind.)	866-450-7399	•	•	•	
•	•	•	•		Infotrack Information Services Inc	800-275-5594	•	•	•	
•	•	•	•	•	Woelfel & Assoc Inc [SOP]	888-297-7180	•	•	•	

DT	BK	CV	CR	PR	←COURTS JO DAVIESS	RECORDING→	UC	RE	TX	VS
		•	•		Ferret Diversified Services Inc	847-266-7666				
•	•	•	•		Infotrack Information Services Inc	800-275-5594	•	•	•	
	•	•	•	•	Security First Title Co	815-235-2900	•	•	•	
•	•	•	•	•	Stewart & Associates Inc [SOP]	800-442-3807	•	•	•	•
		•	•		Julie L Thomas	815-234-4172				

DT	BK	CV	CR	PR	←COURTS JOHNSON	RECORDING→	UC	RE	TX	VS
		•	•	•	Abstract & Title Co	618-445-2554	•	•	•	
•	•	•	•		Infotrack Information Services Inc	800-275-5594	•	•	•	
		•		•	Johnson County Abstract	618-658-3721	•	•	•	•
		•	•	•	Palmer & Murrie Abstract Co Inc	618-993-3866	•	•	•	•
		•		•	Real Estate Data Inc	618-964-1907	•	•	•	

DT	BK	CV	CR	PR	←COURTS KANE	RECORDING→	UC	RE	TX	VS
•	•	•	•	•	AAA VTS Investigations [SOP]	800-203-4160	•	•	•	•

DT	BK	CV	CR	PR	←Courts	Recording→	UC	RE	TX	VS
					AIM3 Research	630-631-6531		•		
					ARC Document Research Inc	312-346-4895	•	•	•	
•	•	•	•	•	Argus Services Inc [SOP]	800-297-3377			•	•
		•	•	•	AV Investigations Inc [SOP]	630-443-3617	•	•	•	•
•	•	•	•	•	Chicagoland Detective Services Inc [SOP]	877-426-4278	•	•	•	•
		•	•		Ferret Diversified Services Inc	847-266-7666				
•	•	•	•		Infotrack Information Services Inc	800-275-5594	•	•	•	
•	•	•	•	•	JG Weiss Research & Retrieval	773-241-6923	•	•	•	•
•	•	•	•	•	LaSalle Process Servers LP [SOP]	800-815-3801	•	•	•	•
•	•	•	•	•	Metro Clerking Inc	312-263-2977	•	•	•	•
		•	•	•	Cynthia Potthoff	815-895-9527				
					R & B Research & Recording Inc	847-477-7510	•	•		
•	•	•	•	•	RBI Inc Joliet [SOP]	800-724-8366	•	•	•	•
•	•		•		Reality Check Inc	309-699-1846		•		
•	•	•	•	•	Record Information Services	630-557-1000	•	•	•	•
•	•	•	•	•	Spyglass Pre-Employment Specialist [SOP]	773-581-0180	•	•	•	•
		•	•		Julie L Thomas	815-234-4172				
					The Wilki Group Inc	847-356-8546	•	•	•	
		•	•		Wisestart Information Services	262-723-7881				
		•	•	•	Yahnke Professional Srvs & Inv [SOP]	800-203-4160	•	•	•	•

DT	BK	CV	CR	PR	←Courts **Kankakee**	Recording→	UC	RE	TX	VS
		•	•	•	Stephen J Addison	708-335-9179	•	•	•	•
•	•	•	•	•	Diligent Detective Agency Inc [SOP]	877-694-3332		•	•	•
•	•	•	•		Infotrack Information Services Inc	800-275-5594	•	•	•	
•	•	•	•	•	RBI Inc Joliet [SOP]	800-724-8366	•	•	•	•
•	•		•		Reality Check Inc	309-699-1846		•		
		•	•	•	Skimerhorn Inv [SOP]	815-933-0843	•	•	•	•

DT	BK	CV	CR	PR	←Courts **Kendall**	Recording→	UC	RE	TX	VS
•	•	•	•	•	AAA VTS Investigations [SOP]	800-203-4160	•	•	•	•
					AIM3 Research	630-631-6531		•		
•	•	•	•	•	Argus Services Inc [SOP]	800-297-3377			•	•
		•	•	•	AV Investigations Inc [SOP]	630-443-3617	•	•	•	•
		•	•		Ferret Diversified Services Inc	847-266-7666				
•	•	•	•		Infotrack Information Services Inc	800-275-5594	•	•	•	
•	•	•	•	•	Kellerman Investigations Ltd [SOP]	888-402-6662				
		•	•	•	Cynthia Potthoff	815-895-9527				
•	•		•		Reality Check Inc	309-699-1846		•		
•	•	•	•	•	Record Information Services	630-557-1000	•	•	•	•
		•	•		Julie L Thomas	815-234-4172				
					The Wilki Group Inc	847-356-8546	•	•	•	
		•	•	•	Yahnke Professional Srvs & Inv [SOP]	800-203-4160	•	•	•	•

DT	BK	CV	CR	PR	←Courts **Knox**	Recording→	UC	RE	TX	VS
•	•	•	•		Infotrack Information Services Inc	800-275-5594	•	•	•	
•	•	•	•		Security Services Inc (SSI) [SOP]	800-383-4312				

DT	BK	CV	CR	PR	←Courts **La Salle**	Recording→	UC	RE	TX	VS
•	•	•	•		Infotrack Information Services Inc	800-275-5594	•	•	•	
•	•	•	•	•	RBI Inc Joliet [SOP]	800-724-8366	•	•	•	•

DT	BK	CV	CR	PR	←Courts **Lake**	Recording→	UC	RE	TX	VS
•	•	•	•	•	AAA VTS Investigations [SOP]	800-203-4160	•	•	•	•
					ARC Document Research Inc	312-346-4895	•	•	•	
•	•	•	•	•	Argus Services Inc [SOP]	800-297-3377			•	•
•	•	•	•	•	Chicagoland Detective Services Inc [SOP]	877-426-4278	•	•	•	•
		•	•		Ferret Diversified Services Inc	847-266-7666				
•	•	•	•		Infotrack Information Services Inc	800-275-5594	•	•	•	
•	•	•	•	•	JG Weiss Research & Retrieval	773-241-6923	•	•	•	•

DT	BK	CV	CR	PR	←Courts	Recording→	UC	RE	TX	VS
•	•	•	•	•	LaSalle Process Servers LP [SOP]	800-815-3801	•	•	•	•
		•	•	•	Lawyer's Resource	888-909-7112	•	•	•	•
•	•	•	•	•	Legal Data Resources [SOP]	800-735-9207	•	•	•	•
•	•	•	•	•	Metro Clerking Inc	312-263-2977	•	•	•	•
		•	•	•	PeopleSearch	877-835-1983	•	•	•	•
		•	•	•	R & B Research & Recording Inc	847-477-7510	•	•		
•	•	•	•	•	RBI Inc Joliet [SOP]	800-724-8366	•	•	•	•
•	•	•	•	•	Record Information Services	630-557-1000	•	•	•	•
•	•	•	•	•	Spyglass Pre-Employment Specialist [SOP]	773-581-0180	•	•	•	•
		•	•	•	Dona Szymaszek	847-540-7425	•	•	•	•
•	•	•	•	•	Tyler-McLennon Choicepoint	512-334-6244	•	•	•	•
					The Wilki Group Inc	847-356-8546	•	•	•	
		•	•		Wisestart Information Services	262-723-7881				

DT	BK	CV	CR	PR	←Courts **Lawrence**	Recording→	UC	RE	TX	VS
		•	•	•	Abstract & Title Co	618-445-2554	•	•	•	
		•	•	•	Lawrence County Title	618-943-4464	•	•	•	•

DT	BK	CV	CR	PR	←Courts **Lee**	Recording→	UC	RE	TX	VS
		•	•		Ferret Diversified Services Inc	847-266-7666				
•	•	•	•		Infotrack Information Services Inc	800-275-5594	•	•	•	
		•	•		RBI Inc Ottawa [SOP]	815-228-3694				
	•	•	•	•	Security First Title Co	815-235-2900	•	•	•	
•	•	•	•	•	Stewart & Associates Inc [SOP]	800-442-3807	•	•	•	•

DT	BK	CV	CR	PR	←Courts **Livingston**	Recording→	UC	RE	TX	VS
•	•	•	•		Infotrack Information Services Inc	800-275-5594	•	•	•	

DT	BK	CV	CR	PR	←Courts **Logan**	Recording→	UC	RE	TX	VS
		•	•		Ferret Diversified Services Inc	847-266-7666				
		•	•		Margaret Flowers	217-877-2105				
•	•	•	•		Infotrack Information Services Inc	800-275-5594	•	•	•	
•	•	•	•	•	Jacobs & Associates CPD Inc [SOP]	800-445-1675	•	•	•	•
•	•	•	•	•	PII Inc [SOP]	217-483-8845	•	•	•	•

DT	BK	CV	CR	PR	←Courts **Macon**	Recording→	UC	RE	TX	VS
		•	•		Margaret Flowers	217-877-2105				
•	•	•	•		Infotrack Information Services Inc	800-275-5594	•	•	•	
•	•	•	•	•	Jacobs & Associates CPD Inc [SOP]	800-445-1675	•	•	•	•
•	•	•	•	•	PII Inc [SOP]	217-483-8845	•	•	•	•

DT	BK	CV	CR	PR	←Courts **Macoupin**	Recording→	UC	RE	TX	VS
		•		•	Bond Title	618-664-1872	•	•	•	•
•	•	•	•		Infotrack Information Services Inc	800-275-5594	•	•	•	
•	•	•	•	•	Jess Barker Document Research/Retrieval	888-316-3773	•	•	•	•
•	•	•	•	•	PII Inc [SOP]	217-483-8845	•	•	•	•
•	•	•	•	•	Woelfel & Assoc Inc [SOP]	888-297-7180	•	•	•	

DT	BK	CV	CR	PR	←Courts **Madison**	Recording→	UC	RE	TX	VS
•	•	•	•	•	AAA Process Service Inc [SOP]	888-350-5809	•	•	•	•
			•	•	Bi-State Title Search (Div of Bi-State Ind.)	866-450-7399	•	•	•	
		•		•	Bond Title	618-664-1872	•	•	•	•
•	•	•	•	•	Brad Clarkson	618-344-0656	•	•	•	•
		•	•	•	Compu-Fact Research Inc	636-477-1115, 618-239-0677	•	•	•	
		•	•		Ferret Diversified Services Inc	847-266-7666				
					GHI Abstracting Inc	618-971-5780 or 618-654-7253	•	•	•	
•	•	•	•		Infotrack Information Services Inc	800-275-5594	•	•	•	
•	•	•	•	•	Jess Barker Document Research/Retrieval	888-316-3773	•	•	•	•
•	•	•	•	•	Kellerman Investigations Ltd [SOP]	888-402-6662				
•	•	•	•	•	Kevin W McClain Inv Ltd [SOP]	877-532-1152	•	•	•	•
•	•	•		•	Master File Inc [SOP]	866-242-0469	•	•	•	

DT	BK	CV	CR	PR	←Courts	Recording→	UC	RE	TX	VS
•	•	•	•	•	Services Rendered Inc [SOP]	888-434-8200	•		•	•
•	•	•	•	•	Woelfel & Assoc Inc [SOP]	888-297-7180	•	•	•	

DT	BK	CV	CR	PR	←Courts **MARION**	Recording→	UC	RE	TX	VS
		•	•	•	Abstract & Title Co	618-445-2554	•	•	•	
•	•	•	•		Infotrack Information Services Inc	800-275-5594	•	•	•	
•	•	•	•	•	Kevin W McClain Inv Ltd [SOP]	877-532-1152	•	•	•	•
•	•	•	•	•	Nancy Durbin Process Service [SOP]	618-548-8296	•	•	•	•
	•				Sharp Law Office	618-242-0246		•	•	
•	•	•	•	•	Woelfel & Assoc Inc [SOP]	888-297-7180	•	•	•	

DT	BK	CV	CR	PR	←Courts **MARSHALL**	Recording→	UC	RE	TX	VS
•	•	•	•		Infotrack Information Services Inc	800-275-5594	•	•	•	
		•	•		RBI Inc Ottawa [SOP]	815-228-3694				
•	•	•	•		Security Services Inc (SSI) [SOP]	800-383-4312				

DT	BK	CV	CR	PR	←Courts **MASON**	Recording→	UC	RE	TX	VS
		•		•	First American Title Insurance Company (IL)	309-347-6126	•	•	•	•
•	•	•	•		Infotrack Information Services Inc	800-275-5594	•	•	•	
•	•	•	•	•	Jacobs & Associates CPD Inc [SOP]	800-445-1675	•	•	•	•
•	•	•	•	•	PII Inc [SOP]	217-483-8845	•	•	•	•

DT	BK	CV	CR	PR	←Courts **MASSAC**	Recording→	UC	RE	TX	VS
		•	•	•	Abstract & Title Co	618-445-2554	•	•	•	
•	•	•	•	•	Heartland Inv Inc [SOP]	618-687-4900	•	•	•	•
		•	•	•	Palmer & Murrie Abstract Co Inc	618-993-3866	•	•	•	•

DT	BK	CV	CR	PR	←Courts **MCDONOUGH**	Recording→	UC	RE	TX	VS
•	•	•	•		Infotrack Information Services Inc	800-275-5594	•	•	•	
				•	Wilson Abstract Co	309-833-2049	•	•	•	•

DT	BK	CV	CR	PR	←Courts **MCHENRY**	Recording→	UC	RE	TX	VS
•	•	•	•	•	AAA VTS Investigations [SOP]	800-203-4160	•	•	•	•
					ARC Document Research Inc	312-346-4895	•	•	•	
•	•	•	•	•	Argus Services Inc [SOP]	800-297-3377			•	•
•	•	•	•		Infotrack Information Services Inc	800-275-5594	•	•	•	
•	•	•	•	•	JG Weiss Research & Retrieval	773-241-6923	•	•	•	•
•	•	•	•	•	LaSalle Process Servers LP [SOP]	800-815-3801	•	•	•	•
•	•	•	•	•	Metro Clerking Inc	312-263-2977	•	•	•	•
		•	•	•	PeopleSearch	877-835-1983	•	•	•	•
			•		Quickfacts	815-236-8874				
					R & B Research & Recording Inc	847-477-7510	•	•		
•	•		•		Reality Check Inc	309-699-1846		•		
•	•	•	•	•	Record Information Services	630-557-1000	•	•	•	•
		•	•	•	Dona Szymaszek	847-540-7425	•	•	•	•
					The Wilki Group Inc	847-356-8546	•	•	•	
		•	•		Wisestart Information Services	262-723-7881				

DT	BK	CV	CR	PR	←Courts **MCLEAN**	Recording→	UC	RE	TX	VS
		•	•	•	Foster Inv [SOP]	800-526-0307	•	•	•	•
•	•	•	•		Infotrack Information Services Inc	800-275-5594	•	•	•	
•	•	•	•	•	Jacobs & Associates CPD Inc [SOP]	800-445-1675	•	•	•	•
•	•	•	•		Security Services Inc (SSI) [SOP]	800-383-4312				

DT	BK	CV	CR	PR	←Courts **MENARD**	Recording→	UC	RE	TX	VS
		•		•	First American Title Insurance Company (IL)	309-347-6126	•	•	•	•
•	•	•	•		Infotrack Information Services Inc	800-275-5594	•	•	•	
•	•	•	•	•	PII Inc [SOP]	217-483-8845	•	•	•	•

DT	BK	CV	CR	PR	←Courts **MERCER**	Recording→	UC	RE	TX	VS
		•	•		Ferret Diversified Services Inc	847-266-7666				

DT	BK	CV	CR	PR	Retriever	Phone	UC	RE	TX	VS
•	•	•	•		Infotrack Information Services Inc	800-275-5594	•	•	•	
•	•	•	•	•	SAS Associates Inc [SOP]	800-373-0727	•		•	

DT	BK	CV	CR	PR	←COURTS MONROE	RECORDING→	UC	RE	TX	VS
•	•	•	•	•	AAA Process Service Inc [SOP]	888-350-5809	•	•	•	•
			•	•	Bi-State Title Search (Div of Bi-State Ind.)	866-450-7399	•	•	•	
•	•	•	•		Infotrack Information Services Inc	800-275-5594	•	•	•	
					Monroe County Title Co	618-939-8292		•		
•	•	•	•	•	Services Rendered Inc [SOP]	888-434-8200	•		•	•

DT	BK	CV	CR	PR	←COURTS MONTGOMERY	RECORDING→	UC	RE	TX	VS
		•		•	Bond Title	618-664-1872	•	•	•	•
•	•	•	•		Infotrack Information Services Inc	800-275-5594	•	•	•	
•	•	•	•	•	PII Inc [SOP]	217-483-8845	•	•	•	•

DT	BK	CV	CR	PR	←COURTS MORGAN	RECORDING→	UC	RE	TX	VS
•	•	•	•		Infotrack Information Services Inc	800-275-5594	•	•	•	
•	•	•	•	•	PII Inc [SOP]	217-483-8845	•	•	•	•

DT	BK	CV	CR	PR	←COURTS MOULTRIE	RECORDING→	UC	RE	TX	VS
		•	•		Margaret Flowers	217-877-2105				
•	•	•	•	•	Folks Finders Ltd	800-277-3318	•	•	•	•
•	•	•	•		Infotrack Information Services Inc	800-275-5594	•	•	•	
•	•	•	•	•	Jacobs & Associates CPD Inc [SOP]	800-445-1675	•	•	•	•
•	•	•	•	•	PII Inc [SOP]	217-483-8845	•	•	•	•

DT	BK	CV	CR	PR	←COURTS OGLE	RECORDING→	UC	RE	TX	VS
		•	•		Ferret Diversified Services Inc	847-266-7666				
•	•	•	•		Infotrack Information Services Inc	800-275-5594	•	•	•	
	•	•	•	•	Security First Title Co	815-235-2900	•	•	•	
•	•	•	•	•	Stewart & Associates Inc [SOP]	800-442-3807	•	•	•	•
		•	•		Julie L Thomas	815-234-4172				

DT	BK	CV	CR	PR	←COURTS PEORIA	RECORDING→	UC	RE	TX	VS
•	•	•	•	•	Dana Caughey Document Retrieval Svc	309-694-4407	•	•	•	
•	•	•	•		Infotrack Information Services Inc	800-275-5594	•	•	•	
•	•		•		Reality Check Inc	309-699-1846		•		
•	•	•	•		Security Services Inc (SSI) [SOP]	800-383-4312				

DT	BK	CV	CR	PR	←COURTS PERRY	RECORDING→	UC	RE	TX	VS
		•	•	•	Abstract & Title Co	618-445-2554	•	•	•	
•	•	•	•		Infotrack Information Services Inc	800-275-5594	•	•	•	
		•	•	•	Search & Genealogy Services	618-529-1024	•	•	•	•

DT	BK	CV	CR	PR	←COURTS PIATT	RECORDING→	UC	RE	TX	VS
•	•	•	•		Infotrack Information Services Inc	800-275-5594	•	•	•	
•	•	•	•	•	Jacobs & Associates CPD Inc [SOP]	800-445-1675	•	•	•	•

DT	BK	CV	CR	PR	←COURTS PIKE	RECORDING→	UC	RE	TX	VS
		•	•		Ferret Diversified Services Inc	847-266-7666				
•	•	•	•		Infotrack Information Services Inc	800-275-5594	•	•	•	
		•	•	•	Marion County Abstract Co (Missouri)	800-952-5314	•	•	•	•

DT	BK	CV	CR	PR	←COURTS POPE	RECORDING→	UC	RE	TX	VS
		•	•	•	Abstract & Title Co	618-445-2554	•	•	•	

DT	BK	CV	CR	PR	←COURTS PULASKI	RECORDING→	UC	RE	TX	VS
		•	•	•	Abstract & Title Co	618-445-2554	•	•	•	
		•		•	Pulaski County Abstract Company	618-748-9233	•	•	•	•

DT	BK	CV	CR	PR	←COURTS PUTNAM	RECORDING→	UC	RE	TX	VS
		•	•	•	Associated Title Company Inc	800-713-4224	•	•	•	•

DT	BK	CV	CR	PR	←Courts	Recording→	UC	RE	TX	VS
•	•	•	•		Infotrack Information Services Inc	800-275-5594	•	•	•	

DT	BK	CV	CR	PR	←Courts **RANDOLPH**	Recording→	UC	RE	TX	VS
		•	•	•	Abstract & Title Co	618-445-2554	•	•	•	
•	•	•	•	•	Heartland Inv Inc [SOP]	618-687-4900	•	•	•	•
•	•	•	•		Infotrack Information Services Inc	800-275-5594	•	•	•	
•	•	•	•	•	Woelfel & Assoc Inc [SOP]	888-297-7180	•	•	•	

DT	BK	CV	CR	PR	←Courts **RICHLAND**	Recording→	UC	RE	TX	VS
		•	•	•	Abstract & Title Co	618-445-2554	•	•	•	
		•	•	•	Lawrence County Title	618-943-4464	•	•	•	•

DT	BK	CV	CR	PR	←Courts **ROCK ISLAND**	Recording→	UC	RE	TX	VS
•	•	•	•	•	DocumentServe Express [SOP]	309-786-2220	•	•	•	•
		•	•		Ferret Diversified Services Inc	847-266-7666				
•	•	•	•	•	FYII Acct [SOP]	563-299-5683	•	•	•	•
•	•	•	•		Infotrack Information Services Inc	800-275-5594	•	•	•	
•	•	•	•	•	James M Sweeney & Associates Inc [SOP]	800-494-5922	•		•	•
•	•	•	•	•	SAS Associates Inc [SOP]	800-373-0727	•		•	

DT	BK	CV	CR	PR	←Courts **SALINE**	Recording→	UC	RE	TX	VS
		•	•	•	Abstract & Title Co	618-445-2554	•	•	•	
•	•	•	•	•	Heartland Inv Inc [SOP]	618-687-4900	•	•	•	•
		•		•	Kotner Abstract & Title	618-273-7611	•	•	•	
		•	•	•	Palmer & Murrie Abstract Co Inc	618-993-3866	•	•	•	•

DT	BK	CV	CR	PR	←Courts **SANGAMON**	Recording→	UC	RE	TX	VS
					ARC Document Research Inc	312-346-4895	•	•	•	
•	•	•	•	•	Corporation Service Company - CSC	800-927-9800	•	•	•	•
•	•	•	•	•	Faxxon Legal Information Services Inc	800-932-9966	•	•	•	•
		•	•		Ferret Diversified Services Inc	847-266-7666				
		•	•		Margaret Flowers	217-877-2105				
•	•	•	•		Infotrack Information Services Inc	800-275-5594	•	•	•	
•	•	•	•	•	Jacobs & Associates CPD Inc [SOP]	800-445-1675	•	•	•	•
•	•	•	•	•	Jess Barker Document Research/Retrieval	888-316-3773	•	•	•	•
•	•	•	•	•	Kellerman Investigations Ltd [SOP]	888-402-6662				
•	•	•	•	•	PII Inc [SOP]	217-483-8845	•	•	•	•
•	•	•	•	•	ProCom Services Corp	217-744-4013	•		•	•

DT	BK	CV	CR	PR	←Courts **SCHUYLER**	Recording→	UC	RE	TX	VS
		•		•	First American Title Insurance Company (IL)	309-347-6126	•	•	•	•
•	•	•	•		Infotrack Information Services Inc	800-275-5594	•	•	•	
				•	Wilson Abstract Co	309-833-2049	•	•	•	•

DT	BK	CV	CR	PR	←Courts **SCOTT**	Recording→	UC	RE	TX	VS
•	•	•	•		Infotrack Information Services Inc	800-275-5594	•	•	•	
•	•	•	•	•	PII Inc [SOP]	217-483-8845	•	•	•	•

DT	BK	CV	CR	PR	←Courts **SHELBY**	Recording→	UC	RE	TX	VS
•	•	•	•	•	Folks Finders Ltd	800-277-3318	•		•	•
•	•	•	•		Infotrack Information Services Inc	800-275-5594	•	•	•	
•	•	•	•	•	Jacobs & Associates CPD Inc [SOP]	800-445-1675	•	•	•	•
•	•	•	•	•	PII Inc [SOP]	217-483-8845	•	•	•	•
		•	•	•	Shelby County Land Title Corp	217-774-2623	•	•	•	•

DT	BK	CV	CR	PR	←Courts **ST. CLAIR**	Recording→	UC	RE	TX	VS
•	•	•	•	•	AAA Process Service Inc [SOP]	888-350-5809	•	•	•	•
			•	•	Bi-State Title Search (Div of Bi-State Ind.)	866-450-7399	•	•	•	
		•		•	Bond Title	618-664-1872	•	•	•	•
•	•	•	•	•	Brad Clarkson	618-344-0656	•	•	•	•
		•	•	•	Compu-Fact Research Inc	636-477-1115, 618-239-0677	•	•	•	

DT	BK	CV	CR	PR	←Courts	Recording→	UC	RE	TX	VS
					GHI Abstracting Inc	618-971-5780 or 618-654-7253	•	•	•	
•	•	•	•		Infotrack Information Services Inc	800-275-5594	•	•	•	
•	•	•	•	•	Jess Barker Document Research/Retrieval	888-316-3773	•	•	•	•
•	•	•	•	•	Kellerman Investigations Ltd [SOP]	888-402-6662				
•	•	•	•	•	Kevin W McClain Inv Ltd [SOP]	877-532-1152	•	•	•	•
•	•	•	•	•	KLK Research	636-366-7055				•
•	•	•		•	Master File Inc [SOP]	866-242-0469	•	•	•	
•	•	•	•	•	Services Rendered Inc [SOP]	888-434-8200	•	•	•	•
•	•	•	•	•	Woelfel & Assoc Inc [SOP]	888-297-7180	•	•	•	

DT	BK	CV	CR	PR	←Courts **Stark**	Recording→	UC	RE	TX	VS
•	•	•	•		Infotrack Information Services Inc	800-275-5594	•	•	•	
•	•	•	•		Security Services Inc (SSI) [SOP]	800-383-4312				

DT	BK	CV	CR	PR	←Courts **Stephenson**	Recording→	UC	RE	TX	VS
		•	•		Ferret Diversified Services Inc	847-266-7666				
•	•	•	•	•	Gregg Inv, Inc of Rockford [SOP]	800-377-1976	•		•	•
•	•	•	•		Infotrack Information Services Inc	800-275-5594	•	•	•	
	•	•	•	•	Security First Title Co	815-235-2900	•	•	•	
•	•	•	•	•	Stewart & Associates Inc [SOP]	800-442-3807	•	•	•	•
		•	•		Julie L Thomas	815-234-4172				

DT	BK	CV	CR	PR	←Courts **Tazewell**	Recording→	UC	RE	TX	VS
•	•	•	•	•	Dana Caughey Document Retrieval Svc	309-694-4407	•	•	•	
•	•	•	•		Infotrack Information Services Inc	800-275-5594	•	•	•	
•	•		•		Reality Check Inc	309-699-1846		•		
		•	•		Secretarial Outsource Services	309-347-3736				
•	•	•	•		Security Services Inc (SSI) [SOP]	800-383-4312				

DT	BK	CV	CR	PR	←Courts **Union**	Recording→	UC	RE	TX	VS
		•	•	•	Abstract & Title Co	618-445-2554	•	•	•	
		•	•		Ferret Diversified Services Inc	847-266-7666				
•	•	•	•	•	Heartland Inv Inc [SOP]	618-687-4900	•	•	•	•
•	•	•	•		Infotrack Information Services Inc	800-275-5594	•	•	•	
		•	•	•	Palmer & Murrie Abstract Co Inc	618-993-3866	•	•	•	•
		•	•	•	Search & Genealogy Services	618-529-1024	•	•	•	•

DT	BK	CV	CR	PR	←Courts **Vermilion**	Recording→	UC	RE	TX	VS
•	•	•	•	•	Diligent Detective Agency Inc [SOP]	877-694-3332		•	•	•
•	•	•	•		Infotrack Information Services Inc	800-275-5594	•	•	•	

DT	BK	CV	CR	PR	←Courts **Wabash**	Recording→	UC	RE	TX	VS
		•	•	•	Abstract & Title Co	618-445-2554	•	•	•	
		•	•	•	Lawrence County Title	618-943-4464	•	•	•	•

DT	BK	CV	CR	PR	←Courts **Warren**	Recording→	UC	RE	TX	VS
•	•	•	•		Infotrack Information Services Inc	800-275-5594	•	•	•	
				•	Wilson Abstract Co	309-833-2049	•	•	•	•

DT	BK	CV	CR	PR	←Courts **Washington**	Recording→	UC	RE	TX	VS
		•	•	•	Abstract & Title Co	618-445-2554	•	•	•	
•	•	•	•		Infotrack Information Services Inc	800-275-5594	•	•	•	
•	•	•	•	•	Kevin W McClain Inv Ltd [SOP]	877-532-1152	•	•	•	•

DT	BK	CV	CR	PR	←Courts **Wayne**	Recording→	UC	RE	TX	VS
		•	•	•	Abstract & Title Co	618-445-2554	•	•	•	

DT	BK	CV	CR	PR	←Courts **White**	Recording→	UC	RE	TX	VS
		•	•	•	Abstract & Title Co	618-445-2554	•	•	•	

DT	BK	CV	CR	PR	←Courts **Whiteside**	Recording→	UC	RE	TX	VS
		•	•		Ferret Diversified Services Inc	847-266-7666				

DT	BK	CV	CR	PR	←Courts	Recording→	UC	RE	TX	VS
•	•	•	•		Infotrack Information Services Inc	800-275-5594	•	•	•	
•	•	•	•	•	SAS Associates Inc [SOP]	800-373-0727	•		•	
	•	•	•	•	Security First Title Co	815-235-2900	•	•	•	
•	•	•	•	•	Stewart & Associates Inc [SOP]	800-442-3807	•	•	•	•

DT	BK	CV	CR	PR	←Courts **Will**	Recording→	UC	RE	TX	VS
•	•	•	•	•	AAA VTS Investigations [SOP]	800-203-4160	•	•	•	•
					ARC Document Research Inc	312-346-4895	•	•	•	
•	•	•	•	•	Argus Services Inc [SOP]	800-297-3377			•	•
			•		Jo Ann Entwisle	815-838-2871				
		•	•		Ferret Diversified Services Inc	847-266-7666				
•	•	•	•		Infotrack Information Services Inc	800-275-5594	•	•	•	
•	•	•	•	•	JG Weiss Research & Retrieval	773-241-6923	•	•	•	•
•	•	•	•	•	Kellerman Investigations Ltd [SOP]	888-402-6662				
•	•	•	•	•	LaSalle Process Servers LP [SOP]	800-815-3801	•	•	•	•
•	•	•	•	•	Legal Data Resources [SOP]	800-735-9207	•	•	•	•
•	•	•	•	•	Metro Clerking Inc	312-263-2977	•	•	•	•
					R & B Research & Recording Inc	847-477-7510	•	•		
•	•	•	•	•	RBI Inc Joliet [SOP]	800-724-8366	•	•	•	•
•	•		•		Reality Check Inc	309-699-1846		•		
•	•	•	•	•	Record Information Services	630-557-1000	•	•	•	•
•	•	•	•		SPI [SOP]	773-581-1400				
•	•	•	•	•	Spyglass Pre-Employment Specialist [SOP]	773-581-0180	•	•	•	•
•	•	•	•	•	Tyler-McLennon Choicepoint	512-334-6244	•	•	•	•
					The Wilki Group Inc	847-356-8546	•	•	•	

DT	BK	CV	CR	PR	←Courts **Williamson**	Recording→	UC	RE	TX	VS
		•	•	•	Abstract & Title Co	618-445-2554	•	•	•	
•	•	•	•	•	Heartland Inv Inc [SOP]	618-687-4900	•	•	•	•
•	•	•	•		Infotrack Information Services Inc	800-275-5594	•	•	•	
•	•	•	•	•	Kevin W McClain Inv Ltd [SOP]	877-532-1152	•	•	•	•
•	•		•		Midwest Backgrounds Inc	618-942-8808				
•	•	•	•	•	William J O'Shea, PI [SOP]	618-937-3895	•	•	•	•
		•	•	•	Palmer & Murrie Abstract Co Inc	618-993-3866	•	•	•	•
		•		•	Real Estate Data Inc	618-964-1907	•	•	•	
	•				Sharp Law Office	618-242-0246		•	•	

DT	BK	CV	CR	PR	←Courts **Winnebago**	Recording→	UC	RE	TX	VS
					ARC Document Research Inc	312-346-4895	•	•	•	
•	•	•	•	•	Argus Services Inc [SOP]	800-297-3377			•	•
		•	•		Ferret Diversified Services Inc	847-266-7666				
•	•	•	•	•	Gregg Inv, Inc of Rockford [SOP]	800-377-1976	•		•	•
•	•	•	•		Infotrack Information Services Inc	800-275-5594	•	•	•	
•	•	•	•	•	Kellerman Investigations Ltd [SOP]	888-402-6662				
	•	•	•	•	Security First Title Co	815-235-2900	•	•	•	
•	•	•	•	•	Stewart & Associates Inc [SOP]	800-442-3807	•	•	•	•
		•	•		Julie L Thomas	815-234-4172				

DT	BK	CV	CR	PR	←Courts **Woodford**	Recording→	UC	RE	TX	VS
•	•	•	•	•	Dana Caughey Document Retrieval Svc	309-694-4407	•	•	•	
•	•	•	•		Infotrack Information Services Inc	800-275-5594	•	•	•	
•	•	•	•		Security Services Inc (SSI) [SOP]	800-383-4312				

Indiana

COURT RECORDS RETRIEVED — **RECORDING RECORDS RETRIEVED**

Adams

DT	BK	CV	CR	PR	←Courts	Recording→	UC	RE	TX	VS
		•	•		Document Hunters LLC	260-760-5703		•		
•	•	•			McGinley Search & File Service Corp	317-807-0760	•	•	•	
		•		•	Tri-County Land Title	260-589-3139	•	•	•	•
•	•	•	•	•	We Search ReSearch Inc	800-251-8167	•	•	•	

Allen

DT	BK	CV	CR	PR	←Courts	Recording→	UC	RE	TX	VS
•	•	•	•		Advanced Background Services	317-884-4600		•	•	
		•	•		Document Hunters LLC	260-760-5703		•		
		•		•	Kings Title & Closing Services	800-860-2990	•	•	•	
•	•	•			McGinley Search & File Service Corp	317-807-0760	•	•	•	
•	•	•	•	•	We Search ReSearch Inc	800-251-8167	•	•	•	

Bartholomew

DT	BK	CV	CR	PR	←Courts	Recording→	UC	RE	TX	VS
		•			Hotopp Public Record Searches	812-342-2163	•	•	•	
•	•	•			McGinley Search & File Service Corp	317-807-0760	•	•	•	
		•	•		Myers Investigations Inc [SOP]	800-788-8018	•		•	•
		•			Parsley Enterprises Inc	317-878-9979		•	•	
		•		•	Three Rivers Title Co	260-424-2929	•	•	•	•

Benton

DT	BK	CV	CR	PR	←Courts	Recording→	UC	RE	TX	VS
		•		•	Benton County Abstract & Title Co Inc	765-884-1140	•	•	•	
		•	•	•	County Courthouse Retrieval	765-485-0233	•	•	•	•
		•	•	•	Held Abstract & Title Co Inc	765-762-2457	•	•	•	
•	•	•			McGinley Search & File Service Corp	317-807-0760	•	•	•	
				•	Tippecanoe Title Services Inc	888-423-2457	•	•	•	
•	•	•	•	•	We Search ReSearch Inc	800-251-8167	•	•	•	

Blackford

DT	BK	CV	CR	PR	←Courts	Recording→	UC	RE	TX	VS
		•		•	Kings Title & Closing Services	800-860-2990	•	•	•	
•	•	•			McGinley Search & File Service Corp	317-807-0760	•	•	•	
		•		•	Tri-County Land Title	260-589-3139	•	•	•	•
•	•	•	•	•	We Search ReSearch Inc	800-251-8167	•	•	•	

Boone

DT	BK	CV	CR	PR	←Courts	Recording→	UC	RE	TX	VS
		•	•		Checkered Past Inc	765-474-3905	•	•	•	
		•	•	•	County Courthouse Retrieval	765-485-0233	•	•	•	•
•	•	•	•	•	International Investigators Inc [SOP]	800-403-8111	•	•	•	•
•	•	•			McGinley Search & File Service Corp	317-807-0760	•	•	•	
					Mill Creek Title Service	317-714-7190	•	•	•	•
		•	•		Myers Investigations Inc [SOP]	800-788-8018	•		•	•
•	•	•	•	•	National Service Information Inc (Indiana) [SOP]	317-266-0040	•	•	•	•
		•	•		Paper Trail Information Services Inc	765-471-4999	•	•	•	
		•	•		Royal Title Services	800-773-7279	•	•	•	•
•	•	•	•	•	Special Inv Inc [SOP]	317-773-7900	•	•	•	•
		•		•	Three Rivers Title Co	260-424-2929	•	•	•	•
				•	Tippecanoe Title Services Inc	888-423-2457	•	•	•	
•	•	•	•	•	We Search ReSearch Inc	800-251-8167	•	•	•	

Brown

DT	BK	CV	CR	PR	←Courts	Recording→	UC	RE	TX	VS
		•			Hotopp Public Record Searches	812-342-2163	•	•	•	

DT	BK	CV	CR	PR	←COURTS	RECORDING→	UC	RE	TX	VS
•	•	•			McGinley Search & File Service Corp	317-807-0760	•	•	•	
		•			Parsley Enterprises Inc	317-878-9979		•	•	

DT	BK	CV	CR	PR	←COURTS CARROLL	RECORDING→	UC	RE	TX	VS
•	•	•			McGinley Search & File Service Corp	317-807-0760	•	•	•	
					Mill Creek Title Service	317-714-7190	•	•	•	•
				•	Tippecanoe Title Services Inc	888-423-2457	•	•	•	
•	•	•	•	•	We Search ReSearch Inc	800-251-8167	•	•	•	

DT	BK	CV	CR	PR	←COURTS CASS	RECORDING→	UC	RE	TX	VS
		•	•		Don Martin & Assoc. [SOP]	765-452-1760				
•	•	•			McGinley Search & File Service Corp	317-807-0760	•	•	•	
				•	Tippecanoe Title Services Inc	888-423-2457	•	•	•	
•	•	•	•	•	We Search ReSearch Inc	800-251-8167	•	•	•	

DT	BK	CV	CR	PR	←COURTS CLARK	RECORDING→	UC	RE	TX	VS
					Virginia Balentine	812-737-2871		•		
•	•	•	•	•	Rick Hessig [SOP]	502-583-2453	•		•	•
•	•	•			KY Data Search Inc	502-637-4658	•	•	•	
•	•	•			McGinley Search & File Service Corp	317-807-0760	•	•	•	
					Salem Title Corporation	812-883-5806	•	•	•	
		•	•		Tracy Cuevas Record Retrieval	502-957-6459			•	

DT	BK	CV	CR	PR	←COURTS CLAY	RECORDING→	UC	RE	TX	VS
•	•	•			McGinley Search & File Service Corp	317-807-0760	•	•	•	

DT	BK	CV	CR	PR	←COURTS CLINTON	RECORDING→	UC	RE	TX	VS
•	•	•			McGinley Search & File Service Corp	317-807-0760	•	•	•	
					Mill Creek Title Service	317-714-7190	•	•	•	•
		•		•	Three Rivers Title Co	260-424-2929	•	•	•	•
				•	Tippecanoe Title Services Inc	888-423-2457	•	•	•	
•	•	•	•	•	We Search ReSearch Inc	800-251-8167	•	•	•	

DT	BK	CV	CR	PR	←COURTS CRAWFORD	RECORDING→	UC	RE	TX	VS
•	•	•			McGinley Search & File Service Corp	317-807-0760	•	•	•	
					Salem Title Corporation	812-883-5806	•	•	•	

DT	BK	CV	CR	PR	←COURTS DAVIESS	RECORDING→	UC	RE	TX	VS
		•		•	James F Havill Attorney at Law PC	812-254-0050	•	•	•	•
•	•	•			McGinley Search & File Service Corp	317-807-0760	•	•	•	
		•	•		Priority Process Service [SOP]	866-464-2192	•	•	•	

DT	BK	CV	CR	PR	←COURTS DE KALB	RECORDING→	UC	RE	TX	VS
		•	•		Document Hunters LLC	260-760-5703		•		
•	•	•			McGinley Search & File Service Corp	317-807-0760	•	•	•	
		•		•	Three Rivers Title Co	260-424-2929	•	•	•	•
•	•	•	•	•	We Search ReSearch Inc	800-251-8167	•	•	•	

DT	BK	CV	CR	PR	←COURTS DEARBORN	RECORDING→	UC	RE	TX	VS
		•	•	•	AM Search & Retrieve	812-689-0672	•	•	•	
•	•	•	•	•	DDI Inc [SOP]	866-954-3000	•	•	•	•
•	•	•			McGinley Search & File Service Corp	317-807-0760	•	•	•	
			•		Phoenix Research Inc	800-260-1092				

DT	BK	CV	CR	PR	←COURTS DECATUR	RECORDING→	UC	RE	TX	VS
		•		•	Ford Abstract Corp	812-663-2190	•	•	•	
		•		•	Kings Title & Closing Services	800-860-2990	•	•	•	
•	•	•			McGinley Search & File Service Corp	317-807-0760	•	•	•	
		•			Parsley Enterprises Inc	317-878-9979		•	•	

DT	BK	CV	CR	PR	←COURTS DELAWARE	RECORDING→	UC	RE	TX	VS
		•		•	Kings Title & Abstract Co (Muncie)	800-294-1566	•	•	•	

DT	BK	CV	CR	PR	←Courts	Recording→	UC	RE	TX	VS
		•		•	Kings Title & Closing Services	800-860-2990	•	•	•	
•	•	•			McGinley Search & File Service Corp	317-807-0760	•	•	•	
		•	•		Myers Investigations Inc [SOP]	800-788-8018	•	•	•	•
•	•	•	•	•	We Search ReSearch Inc	800-251-8167	•	•	•	

DT	BK	CV	CR	PR	←Courts DUBOIS	Recording→	UC	RE	TX	VS
•	•	•			McGinley Search & File Service Corp	317-807-0760	•	•	•	

DT	BK	CV	CR	PR	←Courts ELKHART	Recording→	UC	RE	TX	VS
•	•	•			Abstract & Data Search Services	888-457-5344	•	•	•	
			•		Acme Research	219-878-9950				
•	•	•	•		ASK Services Inc (Indiana)	888-416-1313	•	•	•	
•	•	•	•	•	Case Services Inc [SOP]	877-291-6868	•	•	•	•
•	•	•		•	Land Grant Title Group Inc	888-563-4768	•	•	•	
•	•	•			McGinley Search & File Service Corp	317-807-0760	•	•	•	
					McKesson Title Corp	800-261-8437	•	•	•	
		•			Michiana Searches Inc	574-266-4652, 574-536-7135	•	•	•	
•	•	•	•		MJT Research	219-326-7637	•	•	•	•
•	•	•	•	•	We Search ReSearch Inc	800-251-8167	•	•	•	

DT	BK	CV	CR	PR	←Courts FAYETTE	Recording→	UC	RE	TX	VS
		•		•	Kings Title & Closing Services	800-860-2990	•	•	•	
•	•	•			McGinley Search & File Service Corp	317-807-0760	•	•	•	
		•			Union County Title Co	765-458-7148	•	•	•	
•	•	•	•	•	We Search ReSearch Inc	800-251-8167	•	•	•	

DT	BK	CV	CR	PR	←Courts FLOYD	Recording→	UC	RE	TX	VS
					Virginia Balentine	812-737-2871		•		
•	•	•	•	•	Rick Hessig [SOP]	502-583-2453	•		•	•
•	•	•			KY Data Search Inc	502-637-4658	•	•	•	
•	•	•			McGinley Search & File Service Corp	317-807-0760	•	•	•	
					Salem Title Corporation	812-883-5806	•	•	•	
		•	•		Tracy Cuevas Record Retrieval	502-957-6459			•	

DT	BK	CV	CR	PR	←Courts FOUNTAIN	Recording→	UC	RE	TX	VS
		•	•	•	Held Abstract & Title Co Inc	765-762-2457	•	•	•	
		•		•	Massey Abstract Inc	765-793-3451	•	•	•	
•	•	•			McGinley Search & File Service Corp	317-807-0760	•	•	•	
					Mill Creek Title Service	317-714-7190	•	•	•	•
				•	Tippecanoe Title Services Inc	888-423-2457	•	•	•	
•	•	•	•	•	We Search ReSearch Inc	800-251-8167	•	•	•	

DT	BK	CV	CR	PR	←Courts FRANKLIN	Recording→	UC	RE	TX	VS
		•		•	Kings Title & Closing Services	800-860-2990	•	•	•	
•	•	•			McGinley Search & File Service Corp	317-807-0760	•	•	•	
		•			Union County Title Co	765-458-7148	•	•	•	
•	•	•	•	•	We Search ReSearch Inc	800-251-8167	•	•	•	

DT	BK	CV	CR	PR	←Courts FULTON	Recording→	UC	RE	TX	VS
•	•	•			McGinley Search & File Service Corp	317-807-0760	•	•	•	
					McKesson Title Corp	800-261-8437	•	•	•	
•	•	•	•	•	We Search ReSearch Inc	800-251-8167	•	•	•	

DT	BK	CV	CR	PR	←Courts GIBSON	Recording→	UC	RE	TX	VS
•	•	•	•		D.G.I. LLC [SOP]	812-853-3222	•		•	•
•	•	•	•		Hi-Tech Investigative [SOP]	812-477-1400				
•	•	•			McGinley Search & File Service Corp	317-807-0760	•	•	•	

DT	BK	CV	CR	PR	←Courts GRANT	Recording→	UC	RE	TX	VS
		•	•		Don Martin & Assoc. [SOP]	765-452-1760				
		•		•	Grant County Abstract Co (Indiana)	765-664-7371	•	•	•	

DT	BK	CV	CR	PR	←COURTS	RECORDING→	UC	RE	TX	VS
		•		•	Kings Title & Abstract Co (Marion)	800-662-1299	•	•	•	
		•		•	Kings Title & Closing Services	800-860-2990	•	•	•	
•	•	•			McGinley Search & File Service Corp	317-807-0760	•	•	•	
•	•	•	•	•	We Search ReSearch Inc	800-251-8167	•	•	•	

DT	BK	CV	CR	PR	←COURTS GREENE	RECORDING→	UC	RE	TX	VS
•	•	•			McGinley Search & File Service Corp	317-807-0760	•	•	•	
		•	•		Priority Process Service [SOP]	866-464-2192	•	•	•	

DT	BK	CV	CR	PR	←COURTS HAMILTON	RECORDING→	UC	RE	TX	VS
•	•	•	•		ASK Services Inc (Indiana)	888-416-1313	•	•	•	
		•	•		Checkered Past Inc	765-474-3905	•	•	•	
		•	•	•	County Courthouse Retrieval	765-485-0233	•	•	•	•
•	•	•	•	•	Info Search Inc	317-251-6290	•	•	•	•
•	•	•	•	•	International Investigators Inc [SOP]	800-403-8111	•	•	•	•
•	•	•			McGinley Search & File Service Corp	317-807-0760	•	•	•	
		•	•		Myers Investigations Inc [SOP]	800-788-8018	•		•	•
•	•	•	•	•	National Service Information Inc (Indiana) [SOP]	317-266-0040	•	•	•	•
		•	•		Paper Trail Information Services Inc	765-471-4999	•	•	•	
•	•	•	•	•	Special Inv Inc [SOP]	317-773-7900	•	•	•	•
		•		•	Three Rivers Title Co	260-424-2929	•	•	•	•
				•	Tippecanoe Title Services Inc	888-423-2457	•	•	•	
•	•	•	•	•	We Search ReSearch Inc	800-251-8167	•	•	•	

DT	BK	CV	CR	PR	←COURTS HANCOCK	RECORDING→	UC	RE	TX	VS
•	•	•	•	•	International Investigators Inc [SOP]	800-403-8111	•	•	•	•
		•		•	Kings Title & Abstract Co (Shelbyville)	317-398-0424	•	•	•	
•	•	•			McGinley Search & File Service Corp	317-807-0760	•	•	•	
		•	•		Myers Investigations Inc [SOP]	800-788-8018	•		•	•
•	•	•	•	•	National Service Information Inc (Indiana) [SOP]	317-266-0040	•	•	•	•
		•			Parsley Enterprises Inc	317-878-9979		•	•	
		•		•	Three Rivers Title Co	260-424-2929	•	•	•	•
•	•	•	•	•	We Search ReSearch Inc	800-251-8167	•	•	•	

DT	BK	CV	CR	PR	←COURTS HARRISON	RECORDING→	UC	RE	TX	VS
					Virginia Balentine	812-737-2871		•		
•	•	•			McGinley Search & File Service Corp	317-807-0760	•	•	•	
					Salem Title Corporation	812-883-5806	•	•	•	

DT	BK	CV	CR	PR	←COURTS HENDRICKS	RECORDING→	UC	RE	TX	VS
•	•	•	•		ASK Services Inc (Indiana)	888-416-1313	•	•	•	
		•	•		Checkered Past Inc	765-474-3905	•	•	•	
		•	•	•	County Courthouse Retrieval	765-485-0233	•	•	•	•
•	•	•	•	•	Info Search Inc	317-251-6290	•	•	•	•
•	•	•	•	•	International Investigators Inc [SOP]	800-403-8111	•	•	•	•
•	•	•			McGinley Search & File Service Corp	317-807-0760	•	•	•	
					Mill Creek Title Service	317-714-7190	•	•	•	•
		•	•		Myers Investigations Inc [SOP]	800-788-8018	•		•	•
•	•	•	•	•	National Service Information Inc (Indiana) [SOP]	317-266-0040	•	•	•	•
		•	•		Paper Trail Information Services Inc	765-471-4999	•	•	•	
				•	Tippecanoe Title Services Inc	888-423-2457	•	•	•	
•	•	•	•	•	We Search ReSearch Inc	800-251-8167	•	•	•	

DT	BK	CV	CR	PR	←COURTS HENRY	RECORDING→	UC	RE	TX	VS
		•		•	Kings Title & Closing Services	800-860-2990	•	•	•	
•	•	•			McGinley Search & File Service Corp	317-807-0760	•	•	•	
		•		•	Three Rivers Title Co	260-424-2929	•	•	•	•
•	•	•	•	•	We Search ReSearch Inc	800-251-8167	•	•	•	

DT	BK	CV	CR	PR	←COURTS HOWARD	RECORDING→	UC	RE	TX	VS
		•	•		Don Martin & Assoc. [SOP]	765-452-1760				

DT	BK	CV	CR	PR	←COURTS	RECORDING→	UC	RE	TX	VS
•	•	•			McGinley Search & File Service Corp	317-807-0760	•	•	•	
		•		•	Moore Title & Escrow Inc	888-289-1301	•	•	•	•
				•	Tippecanoe Title Services Inc	888-423-2457	•	•	•	
•	•	•	•	•	We Search ReSearch Inc	800-251-8167	•	•	•	

DT	BK	CV	CR	PR	←COURTS **HUNTINGTON**	RECORDING→	UC	RE	TX	VS
		•	•		Document Hunters LLC	260-760-5703		•		
		•		•	Jones Abstract & Title Co Inc	866-356-5663	•	•	•	
•	•	•			McGinley Search & File Service Corp	317-807-0760	•	•	•	
		•		•	Three Rivers Title Co	260-424-2929	•	•	•	•
•	•	•	•	•	We Search ReSearch Inc	800-251-8167	•	•	•	

DT	BK	CV	CR	PR	←COURTS **JACKSON**	RECORDING→	UC	RE	TX	VS
					Virginia Balentine	812-737-2871		•		
		•			Hotopp Public Record Searches	812-342-2163	•	•	•	
•	•	•			McGinley Search & File Service Corp	317-807-0760	•	•	•	
		•			Parsley Enterprises Inc	317-878-9979		•	•	
					Salem Title Corporation	812-883-5806	•	•	•	

DT	BK	CV	CR	PR	←COURTS **JASPER**	RECORDING→	UC	RE	TX	VS
•	•	•			McGinley Search & File Service Corp	317-807-0760	•	•	•	
•	•	•	•		Star Security & Inv [SOP]	219-554-0100	•	•	•	•
				•	Tippecanoe Title Services Inc	888-423-2457	•	•	•	
•	•	•	•	•	We Search ReSearch Inc	800-251-8167	•	•	•	

DT	BK	CV	CR	PR	←COURTS **JAY**	RECORDING→	UC	RE	TX	VS
		•		•	Jay County Abstract Company Inc	260-726-4303	•	•	•	•
		•		•	Jay Portland Abstract Inc Co	260-726-6466	•	•	•	•
		•		•	Kings Title & Closing Services	800-860-2990	•	•	•	
•	•	•			McGinley Search & File Service Corp	317-807-0760	•	•	•	
		•		•	Tri-County Land Title	260-589-3139	•	•	•	•
•	•	•	•	•	We Search ReSearch Inc	800-251-8167	•	•	•	

DT	BK	CV	CR	PR	←COURTS **JEFFERSON**	RECORDING→	UC	RE	TX	VS
		•	•	•	AM Search & Retrieve	812-689-0672	•	•	•	
					Virginia Balentine	812-737-2871		•		
•	•	•			McGinley Search & File Service Corp	317-807-0760	•	•	•	

DT	BK	CV	CR	PR	←COURTS **JENNINGS**	RECORDING→	UC	RE	TX	VS
					Virginia Balentine	812-737-2871		•		
•	•	•			McGinley Search & File Service Corp	317-807-0760	•	•	•	
		•		•	North Vernon Abstract Co Inc	812-346-2259	•	•	•	
		•			Parsley Enterprises Inc	317-878-9979		•	•	

DT	BK	CV	CR	PR	←COURTS **JOHNSON**	RECORDING→	UC	RE	TX	VS
•	•	•	•		Advanced Background Services	317-884-4600		•	•	
•	•	•	•		ASK Services Inc (Indiana)	888-416-1313	•	•	•	
		•			Hotopp Public Record Searches	812-342-2163	•	•	•	
•	•	•	•	•	International Investigators Inc [SOP]	800-403-8111	•	•	•	•
•	•	•			McGinley Search & File Service Corp	317-807-0760	•	•	•	
					Mill Creek Title Service	317-714-7190	•	•	•	•
		•	•		Myers Investigations Inc [SOP]	800-788-8018	•		•	•
•	•	•	•	•	National Service Information Inc (Indiana) [SOP]	317-266-0040	•	•	•	•
		•			Parsley Enterprises Inc	317-878-9979		•	•	
		•		•	Three Rivers Title Co	260-424-2929	•	•	•	•
•	•	•	•	•	We Search ReSearch Inc	800-251-8167	•	•	•	

DT	BK	CV	CR	PR	←COURTS **KNOX**	RECORDING→	UC	RE	TX	VS
		•		•	L Fay Hedden Abstract Office Inc	812-882-5273	•	•	•	•
•	•	•			McGinley Search & File Service Corp	317-807-0760	•	•	•	
		•	•		Priority Process Service [SOP]	866-464-2192	•	•	•	

Kosciusko

DT	BK	CV	CR	PR	←Courts / Recording→	Phone	UC	RE	TX	VS
•	•	•		•	Land Grant Title Group Inc	888-563-4768	•	•	•	
•	•	•			McGinley Search & File Service Corp	317-807-0760	•	•	•	
					McKesson Title Corp	800-261-8437	•	•	•	
		•		•	Three Rivers Title Co	260-424-2929	•	•	•	•
•	•	•	•	•	We Search ReSearch Inc	800-251-8167	•	•	•	

La Porte

DT	BK	CV	CR	PR	←Courts / Recording→	Phone	UC	RE	TX	VS
•	•	•			Abstract & Data Search Services	888-457-5344	•	•	•	
•	•	•	•		ASK Services Inc (Indiana)	888-416-1313	•	•	•	
•	•	•	•	•	Case Services Inc [SOP]	877-291-6868	•	•	•	•
		•	•	•	Divine Eye Investigations [SOP]	219-872-5204	•	•	•	•
•	•	•			McGinley Search & File Service Corp	317-807-0760	•	•	•	
					McKesson Title Corp	800-261-8437	•	•	•	
•	•	•	•		Merola Services (Indiana)	219-878-9699	•	•	•	•
•	•	•	•		MJT Research	219-326-7637	•	•	•	•
•	•	•	•		Star Security & Inv [SOP]	219-554-0100	•	•	•	•
•	•	•	•	•	We Search ReSearch Inc	800-251-8167	•	•	•	

LaGrange

DT	BK	CV	CR	PR	←Courts / Recording→	Phone	UC	RE	TX	VS
		•		•	LaGrange Title Company	260-463-3232	•	•	•	
•	•	•		•	Land Grant Title Group Inc	888-563-4768	•	•	•	
•	•	•			McGinley Search & File Service Corp	317-807-0760	•	•	•	
		•		•	Three Rivers Title Co	260-424-2929	•	•	•	•
•	•	•	•	•	We Search ReSearch Inc	800-251-8167	•	•	•	

Lake

DT	BK	CV	CR	PR	←Courts / Recording→	Phone	UC	RE	TX	VS
•	•	•	•		Advanced Background Services	317-884-4600		•	•	
•	•	•	•		ASK Services Inc (Indiana)	888-416-1313	•	•	•	
•	•	•	•	•	Lynne J Cox Paralegal	800-510-3009	•	•	•	
•	•	•			McGinley Search & File Service Corp	317-807-0760	•	•	•	
•	•	•	•		MJT Research	219-326-7637	•	•	•	•
•	•	•	•		Star Security & Inv [SOP]	219-554-0100	•	•	•	•
•	•	•	•	•	We Search ReSearch Inc	800-251-8167	•	•	•	

Lawrence

DT	BK	CV	CR	PR	←Courts / Recording→	Phone	UC	RE	TX	VS
•	•	•			McGinley Search & File Service Corp	317-807-0760	•	•	•	
		•	•		Priority Process Service [SOP]	866-464-2192	•	•	•	
					Salem Title Corporation	812-883-5806	•	•	•	

Madison

DT	BK	CV	CR	PR	←Courts / Recording→	Phone	UC	RE	TX	VS
		•		•	Kings Title & Abstract Co (Anderson)	800-317-1515	•	•	•	
		•		•	Kings Title & Closing Services	800-860-2990	•	•	•	
•	•	•			McGinley Search & File Service Corp	317-807-0760	•	•	•	
		•	•		Myers Investigations Inc [SOP]	800-788-8018	•		•	•
•	•	•	•	•	National Service Information Inc (Indiana) [SOP]	317-266-0040	•	•	•	•
		•		•	Three Rivers Title Co	260-424-2929	•	•	•	•
•	•	•	•	•	We Search ReSearch Inc	800-251-8167	•	•	•	

Marion

DT	BK	CV	CR	PR	←Courts / Recording→	Phone	UC	RE	TX	VS
•	•	•			Abstract & Data Search Services	888-457-5344	•	•	•	
•	•	•	•		Advanced Background Services	317-884-4600		•	•	
•	•	•	•		ASK Services Inc (Indiana)	888-416-1313	•	•	•	
•	•	•		•	Central Indiana Paralegal Service Inc	317-636-1311	•		•	
•	•	•	•	•	Info Search Inc	317-251-6290	•	•	•	•
•	•	•	•	•	International Investigators Inc [SOP]	800-403-8111	•	•	•	•
•	•	•			McGinley Search & File Service Corp	317-807-0760	•	•	•	
		•	•		Myers Investigations Inc [SOP]	800-788-8018	•		•	•
•	•	•	•	•	National Service Information Inc (Indiana) [SOP]	317-266-0040	•	•	•	•
		•			Parsley Enterprises Inc	317-878-9979		•	•	

DT	BK	CV	CR	PR	←Courts	Recording→	UC	RE	TX	VS
•	•	•	•	•	Record Retrieval of Indianapolis [SOP]	317-383-1306	•	•	•	•
•	•	•	•	•	Special Inv Inc [SOP]	317-773-7900	•	•	•	•
		•		•	Three Rivers Title Co	260-424-2929	•	•	•	•
				•	Tippecanoe Title Services Inc	888-423-2457	•	•	•	
•	•	•	•	•	We Search ReSearch Inc	800-251-8167	•	•	•	

DT	BK	CV	CR	PR	←Courts	Marshall / Recording→	UC	RE	TX	VS
•	•	•			Abstract & Data Search Services	888-457-5344	•	•	•	
			•		Acme Research	219-878-9950				
•	•	•	•	•	Case Services Inc [SOP]	877-291-6868	•	•	•	•
•	•	•		•	Land Grant Title Group Inc	888-563-4768	•	•	•	
•	•	•			McGinley Search & File Service Corp	317-807-0760	•	•	•	
					McKesson Title Corp	800-261-8437	•	•	•	
•	•	•	•		MJT Research	219-326-7637	•	•	•	•
•	•	•	•	•	We Search ReSearch Inc	800-251-8167	•	•	•	

DT	BK	CV	CR	PR	←Courts	Martin / Recording→	UC	RE	TX	VS
•	•	•			McGinley Search & File Service Corp	317-807-0760	•	•	•	
		•	•		Priority Process Service [SOP]	866-464-2192	•	•	•	

DT	BK	CV	CR	PR	←Courts	Miami / Recording→	UC	RE	TX	VS
		•	•		Don Martin & Assoc. [SOP]	765-452-1760				
•	•	•			McGinley Search & File Service Corp	317-807-0760	•	•	•	
		•		•	Wabash Valley Abstract Co Inc	765-472-4351	•	•	•	
•	•	•	•	•	We Search ReSearch Inc	800-251-8167	•	•	•	

DT	BK	CV	CR	PR	←Courts	Monroe / Recording→	UC	RE	TX	VS
					Applecheeks Research Ltd	765-349-8371	•	•	•	
		•	•	•	Daniel E Gardner, dba SCIPRIS	812-335-0746	•	•	•	•
		•			Hotopp Public Record Searches	812-342-2163	•	•	•	
•	•	•			McGinley Search & File Service Corp	317-807-0760	•	•	•	
					Mill Creek Title Service	317-714-7190	•	•	•	•
		•	•		Myers Investigations Inc [SOP]	800-788-8018	•		•	•
		•	•		Becky Petro	812-335-1185	•			
		•	•		Priority Process Service [SOP]	866-464-2192	•	•	•	
		•	•	•	Trace Investigations [SOP]	812-334-8857	•	•	•	•

DT	BK	CV	CR	PR	←Courts	Montgomery / Recording→	UC	RE	TX	VS
		•	•	•	County Courthouse Retrieval	765-485-0233	•	•	•	•
•	•	•			McGinley Search & File Service Corp	317-807-0760	•	•	•	
					Mill Creek Title Service	317-714-7190	•	•	•	•
				•	Tippecanoe Title Services Inc	888-423-2457	•	•	•	
•	•	•	•	•	We Search ReSearch Inc	800-251-8167	•	•	•	

DT	BK	CV	CR	PR	←Courts	Morgan / Recording→	UC	RE	TX	VS
					Applecheeks Research Ltd	765-349-8371	•	•	•	
•	•	•	•		ASK Services Inc (Indiana)	888-416-1313	•	•	•	
•	•	•			McGinley Search & File Service Corp	317-807-0760	•	•	•	
					Mill Creek Title Service	317-714-7190	•	•	•	•
•	•	•	•	•	National Service Information Inc (Indiana) [SOP]	317-266-0040	•	•	•	•
		•		•	Three Rivers Title Co	260-424-2929	•	•	•	•

DT	BK	CV	CR	PR	←Courts	Newton / Recording→	UC	RE	TX	VS
•	•	•			McGinley Search & File Service Corp	317-807-0760	•	•	•	
•	•	•	•		Star Security & Inv [SOP]	219-554-0100	•	•	•	•
				•	Tippecanoe Title Services Inc	888-423-2457	•	•	•	
•	•	•	•	•	We Search ReSearch Inc	800-251-8167	•	•	•	

DT	BK	CV	CR	PR	←Courts	Noble / Recording→	UC	RE	TX	VS
		•	•		Document Hunters LLC	260-760-5703		•		
•	•	•			McGinley Search & File Service Corp	317-807-0760	•	•	•	

DT	BK	CV	CR	PR	Retriever	Phone	UC	RE	TX	VS
		•		•	Three Rivers Title Co	260-424-2929	•	•	•	•
•	•	•	•	•	We Search ReSearch Inc	800-251-8167	•	•	•	

DT	BK	CV	CR	PR	←Courts **Ohio** Recording→		UC	RE	TX	VS
		•	•	•	AM Search & Retrieve	812-689-0672	•	•	•	
•	•	•			McGinley Search & File Service Corp	317-807-0760	•	•	•	

DT	BK	CV	CR	PR	←Courts **Orange** Recording→		UC	RE	TX	VS
•	•	•			McGinley Search & File Service Corp	317-807-0760	•	•	•	
		•		•	Orange County Abstract & Title Co Inc	812-723-3044	•	•	•	
					Salem Title Corporation	812-883-5806	•	•	•	

DT	BK	CV	CR	PR	←Courts **Owen** Recording→		UC	RE	TX	VS
•	•	•			McGinley Search & File Service Corp	317-807-0760	•	•	•	
					Mill Creek Title Service	317-714-7190	•	•	•	•
		•	•		Priority Process Service [SOP]	866-464-2192	•	•	•	

DT	BK	CV	CR	PR	←Courts **Parke** Recording→		UC	RE	TX	VS
•	•	•			McGinley Search & File Service Corp	317-807-0760	•	•	•	
					Mill Creek Title Service	317-714-7190	•	•	•	•
				•	Tippecanoe Title Services Inc	888-423-2457	•	•	•	

DT	BK	CV	CR	PR	←Courts **Perry** Recording→		UC	RE	TX	VS
•	•	•			McGinley Search & File Service Corp	317-807-0760	•	•	•	
•	•	•	•	•	Summit Documents	270-281-5406	•	•	•	•

DT	BK	CV	CR	PR	←Courts **Pike** Recording→		UC	RE	TX	VS
•	•	•			McGinley Search & File Service Corp	317-807-0760	•	•	•	

DT	BK	CV	CR	PR	←Courts **Porter** Recording→		UC	RE	TX	VS
•	•	•			Abstract & Data Search Services	888-457-5344	•	•	•	
•	•	•	•		ASK Services Inc (Indiana)	888-416-1313	•	•	•	
		•	•	•	Divine Eye Investigations [SOP]	219-872-5204	•	•	•	•
•	•	•			McGinley Search & File Service Corp	317-807-0760	•	•	•	
•	•	•	•		MJT Research	219-326-7637	•	•	•	•
•	•	•	•		Star Security & Inv [SOP]	219-554-0100	•	•	•	•
•	•	•	•	•	We Search ReSearch Inc	800-251-8167	•	•	•	

DT	BK	CV	CR	PR	←Courts **Posey** Recording→		UC	RE	TX	VS
•	•	•	•		D.G.I. LLC [SOP]	812-853-3222	•		•	•
•	•	•	•		Hi-Tech Investigative [SOP]	812-477-1400				
•	•	•			McGinley Search & File Service Corp	317-807-0760	•	•	•	

DT	BK	CV	CR	PR	←Courts **Pulaski** Recording→		UC	RE	TX	VS
•	•	•			McGinley Search & File Service Corp	317-807-0760	•	•	•	
					McKesson Title Corp	800-261-8437	•	•	•	
•	•	•	•	•	We Search ReSearch Inc	800-251-8167	•	•	•	

DT	BK	CV	CR	PR	←Courts **Putnam** Recording→		UC	RE	TX	VS
•	•	•			McGinley Search & File Service Corp	317-807-0760	•	•	•	
					Mill Creek Title Service	317-714-7190	•	•	•	•
		•	•		Myers Investigations Inc [SOP]	800-788-8018	•	•	•	•
		•	•		Paper Trail Information Services Inc	765-471-4999	•	•	•	

DT	BK	CV	CR	PR	←Courts **Randolph** Recording→		UC	RE	TX	VS
		•		•	Kings Title & Abstract Co (Winchester)	800-280-6322	•	•	•	
		•		•	Kings Title & Closing Services	800-860-2990	•	•	•	
•	•	•			McGinley Search & File Service Corp	317-807-0760	•	•	•	
•	•	•	•	•	We Search ReSearch Inc	800-251-8167	•	•	•	

DT	BK	CV	CR	PR	←Courts **Ripley** Recording→		UC	RE	TX	VS
		•	•	•	AM Search & Retrieve	812-689-0672	•	•	•	

DT	BK	CV	CR	PR	←Courts	Recording→	UC	RE	TX	VS
•	•	•			McGinley Search & File Service Corp	317-807-0760	•	•	•	
DT	**BK**	**CV**	**CR**	**PR**	**←COURTS — RUSH**	**RECORDING→**	**UC**	**RE**	**TX**	**VS**
		•		•	Kings Title & Abstract Co (Rushville)	877-932-5757	•	•	•	
		•		•	Kings Title & Closing Services	800-860-2990	•	•	•	
•	•	•			McGinley Search & File Service Corp	317-807-0760	•	•	•	
•	•	•	•	•	We Search ReSearch Inc	800-251-8167	•	•	•	
DT	**BK**	**CV**	**CR**	**PR**	**←COURTS — SCOTT**	**RECORDING→**	**UC**	**RE**	**TX**	**VS**
					Virginia Balentine	812-737-2871		•		
•	•	•			McGinley Search & File Service Corp	317-807-0760	•	•	•	
		•			Parsley Enterprises Inc	317-878-9979		•	•	
					Salem Title Corporation	812-883-5806	•	•	•	
DT	**BK**	**CV**	**CR**	**PR**	**←COURTS — SHELBY**	**RECORDING→**	**UC**	**RE**	**TX**	**VS**
•	•	•	•	•	International Investigators Inc [SOP]	800-403-8111	•	•	•	•
		•		•	Kings Title & Abstract Co (Shelbyville)	317-398-0424	•	•	•	
		•		•	Kings Title & Closing Services	800-860-2990	•	•	•	
•	•	•			McGinley Search & File Service Corp	317-807-0760	•	•	•	
		•	•		Myers Investigations Inc [SOP]	800-788-8018	•		•	•
•	•	•	•	•	National Service Information Inc (Indiana) [SOP]	317-266-0040	•	•	•	•
		•			Parsley Enterprises Inc	317-878-9979		•	•	
•	•	•	•	•	We Search ReSearch Inc	800-251-8167	•	•	•	
DT	**BK**	**CV**	**CR**	**PR**	**←COURTS — SPENCER**	**RECORDING→**	**UC**	**RE**	**TX**	**VS**
•	•	•	•		D.G.I. LLC [SOP]	812-853-3222	•		•	•
•	•	•	•		Hi-Tech Investigative [SOP]	812-477-1400				
•	•	•			McGinley Search & File Service Corp	317-807-0760	•	•	•	
•	•	•	•	•	Summit Documents	270-281-5406	•	•	•	•
		•	•	•	Wetherill Law Office	812-649-2221	•	•	•	•
DT	**BK**	**CV**	**CR**	**PR**	**←COURTS — ST JOSEPH**	**RECORDING→**	**UC**	**RE**	**TX**	**VS**
•	•	•			Abstract & Data Search Services	888-457-5344	•	•	•	
			•		Acme Research	219-878-9950				
•	•	•	•		Advanced Background Services	317-884-4600		•	•	
•	•	•	•		ASK Services Inc (Indiana)	888-416-1313	•	•	•	
•	•	•	•	•	Case Services Inc [SOP]	877-291-6868	•	•	•	•
•	•	•		•	Land Grant Title Group Inc	888-563-4768	•	•	•	
•	•	•			McGinley Search & File Service Corp	317-807-0760	•	•	•	
					McKesson Title Corp	800-261-8437	•	•	•	
		•			Michiana Searches Inc	574-266-4652, 574-536-7135	•	•	•	
•	•	•	•		MJT Research	219-326-7637	•	•	•	•
•	•	•	•	•	We Search ReSearch Inc	800-251-8167	•	•	•	
DT	**BK**	**CV**	**CR**	**PR**	**←COURTS — STARKE**	**RECORDING→**	**UC**	**RE**	**TX**	**VS**
•	•	•			McGinley Search & File Service Corp	317-807-0760	•	•	•	
					McKesson Title Corp	800-261-8437	•	•	•	
		•	•	•	Starke County Abstract Title & Guaranty	574-772-3733	•	•	•	
•	•	•	•	•	We Search ReSearch Inc	800-251-8167	•	•	•	
DT	**BK**	**CV**	**CR**	**PR**	**←COURTS — STEUBEN**	**RECORDING→**	**UC**	**RE**	**TX**	**VS**
•	•	•			McGinley Search & File Service Corp	317-807-0760	•	•	•	
		•		•	Three Rivers Title Co	260-424-2929	•	•	•	•
•	•	•	•	•	We Search ReSearch Inc	800-251-8167	•	•	•	
DT	**BK**	**CV**	**CR**	**PR**	**←COURTS — SULLIVAN**	**RECORDING→**	**UC**	**RE**	**TX**	**VS**
•	•	•			McGinley Search & File Service Corp	317-807-0760	•	•	•	
		•	•		Priority Process Service [SOP]	866-464-2192	•	•	•	
DT	**BK**	**CV**	**CR**	**PR**	**←COURTS — SWITZERLAND**	**RECORDING→**	**UC**	**RE**	**TX**	**VS**
•	•	•			McGinley Search & File Service Corp	317-807-0760	•	•	•	

		•		•	Valley Title Services Inc	812-427-2135	•	•	•	

DT	BK	CV	CR	PR	←COURTS TIPPECANOE	RECORDING→	UC	RE	TX	VS
		•	•		Checkered Past Inc	765-474-3905	•	•	•	
		•	•	•	County Courthouse Retrieval	765-485-0233	•	•	•	•
•	•	•			McGinley Search & File Service Corp	317-807-0760	•	•	•	
					Mill Creek Title Service	317-714-7190	•	•	•	•
		•	•		Paper Trail Information Services Inc	765-471-4999	•	•	•	
				•	Tippecanoe Title Services Inc	888-423-2457	•	•	•	
•	•	•	•	•	We Search ReSearch Inc	800-251-8167	•	•	•	

DT	BK	CV	CR	PR	←COURTS TIPTON	RECORDING→	UC	RE	TX	VS
		•	•		Don Martin & Assoc. [SOP]	765-452-1760				
•	•	•			McGinley Search & File Service Corp	317-807-0760	•	•	•	
		•		•	Moore Title & Escrow Inc	888-289-1301	•	•	•	•
•	•	•	•	•	We Search ReSearch Inc	800-251-8167	•	•	•	

DT	BK	CV	CR	PR	←COURTS UNION	RECORDING→	UC	RE	TX	VS
•	•	•			McGinley Search & File Service Corp	317-807-0760	•	•	•	
		•			Union County Title Co	765-458-7148	•	•	•	
•	•	•	•	•	We Search ReSearch Inc	800-251-8167	•	•	•	

DT	BK	CV	CR	PR	←COURTS VANDERBURGH	RECORDING→	UC	RE	TX	VS
•	•	•	•		D.G.I. LLC [SOP]	812-853-3222	•		•	•
•	•	•	•		Hi-Tech Investigative [SOP]	812-477-1400				
•	•	•			McGinley Search & File Service Corp	317-807-0760	•	•	•	

DT	BK	CV	CR	PR	←COURTS VERMILLION	RECORDING→	UC	RE	TX	VS
		•		•	Massey Abstract Inc	765-793-3451	•	•	•	
•	•	•			McGinley Search & File Service Corp	317-807-0760	•	•	•	
					Mill Creek Title Service	317-714-7190	•	•	•	•
				•	Tippecanoe Title Services Inc	888-423-2457	•	•	•	

DT	BK	CV	CR	PR	←COURTS VIGO	RECORDING→	UC	RE	TX	VS
•	•	•			McGinley Search & File Service Corp	317-807-0760	•	•	•	

DT	BK	CV	CR	PR	←COURTS WABASH	RECORDING→	UC	RE	TX	VS
		•	•		Don Martin & Assoc. [SOP]	765-452-1760				
•	•	•			McGinley Search & File Service Corp	317-807-0760	•	•	•	
		•		•	Three Rivers Title Co	260-424-2929	•	•	•	•
•	•	•	•	•	We Search ReSearch Inc	800-251-8167	•	•	•	

DT	BK	CV	CR	PR	←COURTS WARREN	RECORDING→	UC	RE	TX	VS
		•	•	•	Held Abstract & Title Co Inc	765-762-2457	•	•	•	
		•		•	Massey Abstract Inc	765-793-3451	•	•	•	
•	•	•			McGinley Search & File Service Corp	317-807-0760	•	•	•	
					Mill Creek Title Service	317-714-7190	•	•	•	•
				•	Tippecanoe Title Services Inc	888-423-2457	•	•	•	
•	•	•	•	•	We Search ReSearch Inc	800-251-8167	•	•	•	

DT	BK	CV	CR	PR	←COURTS WARRICK	RECORDING→	UC	RE	TX	VS
•	•	•	•		D.G.I. LLC [SOP]	812-853-3222	•		•	•
•	•	•	•		Hi-Tech Investigative [SOP]	812-477-1400				
•	•	•			McGinley Search & File Service Corp	317-807-0760	•	•	•	
•	•	•	•	•	Summit Documents	270-281-5406	•	•	•	•

DT	BK	CV	CR	PR	←COURTS WASHINGTON	RECORDING→	UC	RE	TX	VS
•	•	•			McGinley Search & File Service Corp	317-807-0760	•	•	•	
					Salem Title Corporation	812-883-5806	•	•	•	

DT	BK	CV	CR	PR	←COURTS WAYNE	RECORDING→	UC	RE	TX	VS
		•		•	Kings Title & Abstract Co (Richmond)	800-757-7762	•	•	•	

DT	BK	CV	CR	PR	Retriever	Phone	UC	RE	TX	VS
		•		•	Kings Title & Closing Services	800-860-2990	•	•	•	
•	•	•			McGinley Search & File Service Corp	317-807-0760	•	•	•	
		•			Union County Title Co	765-458-7148	•	•	•	
•	•	•	•	•	We Search ReSearch Inc	800-251-8167	•	•	•	

DT	BK	CV	CR	PR	←COURTS WELLS	RECORDING→	UC	RE	TX	VS
		•	•		Document Hunters LLC	260-760-5703		•		
•	•	•			McGinley Search & File Service Corp	317-807-0760	•	•	•	
		•		•	Three Rivers Title Co	260-424-2929	•	•	•	•
		•		•	Tri-County Land Title	260-589-3139	•	•	•	•
•	•	•	•	•	We Search ReSearch Inc	800-251-8167	•	•	•	

DT	BK	CV	CR	PR	←COURTS WHITE	RECORDING→	UC	RE	TX	VS
•	•	•			McGinley Search & File Service Corp	317-807-0760	•	•	•	
				•	Tippecanoe Title Services Inc	888-423-2457	•	•	•	
•	•	•	•	•	We Search ReSearch Inc	800-251-8167	•	•	•	

DT	BK	CV	CR	PR	←COURTS WHITLEY	RECORDING→	UC	RE	TX	VS
		•	•		Document Hunters LLC	260-760-5703		•		
		•		•	Gates Land Title Corp	260-244-5127	•	•	•	•
•	•	•			McGinley Search & File Service Corp	317-807-0760	•	•	•	
		•		•	Three Rivers Title Co	260-424-2929	•	•	•	•
•	•	•	•	•	We Search ReSearch Inc	800-251-8167	•	•	•	

[SOP] = PERFORMS SERVICE OF PROCESS

COURT RECORDS

CODE	GOVERNMENT AGENCY	TYPE OF INFORMATION
DT	US District Court	Federal civil and criminal cases
BK	Bankruptcy Court	United States bankruptcy cases
CV	Civil Court	Municipal, county and state level civil cases
CR	Criminal Court	Municipal, county and state level criminal cases
PR	Probate Court	Wills and estate cases

COUNTY RECORDS - RECORDINGS

CODE	GOVERNMENT AGENCY	TYPE OF INFORMATION
UC	UCC Filing Office	Uniform Commercial Code and other personal property liens
RE	Real Estate Recording Office	Real property transactions and liens
TX	Tax Filing Office(s)	Federal and state tax liens, judgment liens
VS	Vital Records Office	Vital statistics—birth, death, marriage, divorce

Iowa

COURT RECORDS RETRIEVED | **RECORDING RECORDS RETRIEVED**

DT	BK	CV	CR	PR	←Courts	Adair	Recording→	UC	RE	TX	VS
		•		•	Adair County Abstract Company		800-798-6129	•	•	•	
•	•	•	•	•	Applicant Profile Services		515-727-7964	•	•	•	
		•			Court Services of Iowa Inc		515-965-5722	•	•	•	
•	•			•	The Title Co Inc (Prairie Du Chien WI)		888-918-4853	•	•	•	
				•	Williamson Abstract Co		641-743-2175	•	•	•	•

DT	BK	CV	CR	PR	←Courts	Adams	Recording→	UC	RE	TX	VS
•	•	•	•	•	Applicant Profile Services		515-727-7964	•	•	•	
		•			Court Services of Iowa Inc		515-965-5722	•	•	•	
•	•			•	The Title Co Inc (Prairie Du Chien WI)		888-918-4853	•	•	•	

DT	BK	CV	CR	PR	←Courts	Allamakee	Recording→	UC	RE	TX	VS
•	•	•	•	•	Applicant Profile Services		515-727-7964	•	•	•	
		•			Court Services of Iowa Inc		515-965-5722	•	•	•	
		•	•	•	Palmer Abstract Inc		563-568-3488	•	•	•	•
•	•			•	The Title Co Inc (Prairie Du Chien WI)		888-918-4853	•	•	•	

DT	BK	CV	CR	PR	←Courts	Appanoose	Recording→	UC	RE	TX	VS
•	•	•	•	•	Applicant Profile Services		515-727-7964	•	•	•	
		•			Court Services of Iowa Inc		515-965-5722	•	•	•	
•	•	•	•	•	Meier Inv [SOP]		515-205-2738	•	•	•	•
•	•			•	The Title Co Inc (Prairie Du Chien WI)		888-918-4853	•	•	•	

DT	BK	CV	CR	PR	←Courts	Audubon	Recording→	UC	RE	TX	VS
•	•	•	•	•	Applicant Profile Services		515-727-7964	•	•	•	
		•			Court Services of Iowa Inc		515-965-5722	•	•	•	
•	•			•	The Title Co Inc (Prairie Du Chien WI)		888-918-4853	•	•	•	

DT	BK	CV	CR	PR	←Courts	Benton	Recording→	UC	RE	TX	VS
•	•	•	•	•	Applicant Profile Services		515-727-7964	•	•	•	
•	•	•	•	•	ASAP Process Service [SOP]		877-455-2490		•		•
		•	•	•	Benton County Title Co		319-472-2369	•	•	•	
		•			Court Services of Iowa Inc		515-965-5722	•	•	•	
•	•			•	The Title Co Inc (Prairie Du Chien WI)		888-918-4853	•	•	•	

DT	BK	CV	CR	PR	←Courts	Black Hawk	Recording→	UC	RE	TX	VS
•	•	•	•	•	Applicant Profile Services		515-727-7964	•	•	•	
•	•	•	•	•	ASAP Process Service [SOP]		877-455-2490		•		•
		•		•	Black Hawk County Abstract Co		319-291-4000	•	•	•	
		•	•		Bob Prins Associates		319-232-4752		•	•	
		•			Court Services of Iowa Inc		515-965-5722	•	•	•	
•	•			•	The Title Co Inc (Prairie Du Chien WI)		888-918-4853	•	•	•	

DT	BK	CV	CR	PR	←Courts	Boone	Recording→	UC	RE	TX	VS
•	•	•	•	•	Applicant Profile Services		515-727-7964	•	•	•	
		•	•	•	Boone County Abstract Co		515-432-3633	•	•	•	•
		•			Court Services of Iowa Inc		515-965-5722	•	•	•	
•	•			•	The Title Co Inc (Prairie Du Chien WI)		888-918-4853	•	•	•	

DT	BK	CV	CR	PR	←Courts	Bremer	Recording→	UC	RE	TX	VS
•	•	•	•	•	Applicant Profile Services		515-727-7964	•	•	•	

DT	BK	CV	CR	PR	←Courts	Recording→	UC	RE	TX	VS
•		•		•	Bremer County Abstract Co	319-352-2710	•	•	•	•
		•			Court Services of Iowa Inc	515-965-5722	•	•	•	
•	•			•	The Title Co Inc (Prairie Du Chien WI)	888-918-4853	•	•	•	
DT	**BK**	**CV**	**CR**	**PR**	**←Courts BUCHANAN**	**Recording→**	**UC**	**RE**	**TX**	**VS**
•	•	•	•	•	Applicant Profile Services	515-727-7964	•	•	•	
•	•	•	•	•	ASAP Process Service [SOP]	877-455-2490		•		•
		•			Court Services of Iowa Inc	515-965-5722	•	•	•	
•	•			•	The Title Co Inc (Prairie Du Chien WI)	888-918-4853	•	•	•	
DT	**BK**	**CV**	**CR**	**PR**	**←Courts BUENA VISTA**	**Recording→**	**UC**	**RE**	**TX**	**VS**
•	•	•	•	•	Applicant Profile Services	515-727-7964	•	•	•	
		•			Court Services of Iowa Inc	515-965-5722	•	•	•	
•		•	•	•	Fritcher Abstract Co	712-732-2732	•	•	•	•
•		•	•	•	R & D Research Services [SOP]	712-737-8741	•	•	•	•
•	•			•	The Title Co Inc (Prairie Du Chien WI)	888-918-4853	•	•	•	
DT	**BK**	**CV**	**CR**	**PR**	**←Courts BUTLER**	**Recording→**	**UC**	**RE**	**TX**	**VS**
•	•	•	•	•	Applicant Profile Services	515-727-7964	•	•	•	
		•			Court Services of Iowa Inc	515-965-5722	•	•	•	
•	•			•	The Title Co Inc (Prairie Du Chien WI)	888-918-4853	•	•	•	
DT	**BK**	**CV**	**CR**	**PR**	**←Courts CALHOUN**	**Recording→**	**UC**	**RE**	**TX**	**VS**
•	•	•	•	•	Applicant Profile Services	515-727-7964	•	•	•	
		•			Court Services of Iowa Inc	515-965-5722	•	•	•	
•	•			•	The Title Co Inc (Prairie Du Chien WI)	888-918-4853	•	•	•	
DT	**BK**	**CV**	**CR**	**PR**	**←Courts CARROLL**	**Recording→**	**UC**	**RE**	**TX**	**VS**
•	•	•	•	•	Applicant Profile Services	515-727-7964	•	•	•	
		•			Court Services of Iowa Inc	515-965-5722	•	•	•	
•	•			•	The Title Co Inc (Prairie Du Chien WI)	888-918-4853	•	•	•	
DT	**BK**	**CV**	**CR**	**PR**	**←Courts CASS**	**Recording→**	**UC**	**RE**	**TX**	**VS**
•	•	•	•	•	Applicant Profile Services	515-727-7964	•	•	•	
		•	•	•	Cass County Abstract Co Inc (Iowa)	712-243-2136	•	•	•	•
		•			Court Services of Iowa Inc	515-965-5722	•	•	•	
•	•			•	The Title Co Inc (Prairie Du Chien WI)	888-918-4853	•	•	•	
			•		Beth Young	712-767-2510		•	•	
DT	**BK**	**CV**	**CR**	**PR**	**←Courts CEDAR**	**Recording→**	**UC**	**RE**	**TX**	**VS**
•	•	•	•	•	Applicant Profile Services	515-727-7964	•	•	•	
•	•	•	•	•	ASAP Process Service [SOP]	877-455-2490		•		•
		•			Court Services of Iowa Inc	515-965-5722	•	•	•	
•	•	•	•	•	FYII Acct [SOP]	563-299-5683	•	•	•	•
		•	•	•	Land Title Corp	563-886-6915	•	•	•	•
•	•			•	The Title Co Inc (Prairie Du Chien WI)	888-918-4853	•	•	•	
DT	**BK**	**CV**	**CR**	**PR**	**←Courts CERRO GORDO**	**Recording→**	**UC**	**RE**	**TX**	**VS**
•	•	•	•	•	Applicant Profile Services	515-727-7964	•	•	•	
•	•	•	•	•	Cerro Gordo Abstract Co	641-423-1145	•	•	•	•
		•			Court Services of Iowa Inc	515-965-5722	•	•	•	
•	•			•	The Title Co Inc (Prairie Du Chien WI)	888-918-4853	•	•	•	
DT	**BK**	**CV**	**CR**	**PR**	**←Courts CHEROKEE**	**Recording→**	**UC**	**RE**	**TX**	**VS**
•	•	•	•	•	Applicant Profile Services	515-727-7964	•	•	•	
		•			Court Services of Iowa Inc	515-965-5722	•	•	•	
		•	•	•	First Abstract & Loan Co	712-225-3612	•	•	•	
•		•	•	•	R & D Research Services [SOP]	712-737-8741	•	•	•	•
•	•			•	The Title Co Inc (Prairie Du Chien WI)	888-918-4853	•	•	•	
DT	**BK**	**CV**	**CR**	**PR**	**←Courts CHICKASAW**	**Recording→**	**UC**	**RE**	**TX**	**VS**
•	•	•	•	•	Applicant Profile Services	515-727-7964	•	•	•	

DT	BK	CV	CR	PR	←COURTS	RECORDING→	UC	RE	TX	VS
		•			Court Services of Iowa Inc	515-965-5722	•	•	•	
•	•			•	The Title Co Inc (Prairie Du Chien WI)	888-918-4853	•	•	•	

DT	BK	CV	CR	PR	←COURTS CLARKE	RECORDING→	UC	RE	TX	VS
•	•	•	•	•	Applicant Profile Services	515-727-7964	•	•	•	
					Banta Abstract Co	641-342-2029		•	•	
		•			Court Services of Iowa Inc	515-965-5722	•	•	•	
•	•			•	The Title Co Inc (Prairie Du Chien WI)	888-918-4853	•	•	•	

DT	BK	CV	CR	PR	←COURTS CLAY	RECORDING→	UC	RE	TX	VS
•	•	•	•	•	Applicant Profile Services	515-727-7964	•	•	•	
		•			Court Services of Iowa Inc	515-965-5722	•	•	•	
•		•	•	•	R & D Research Services [SOP]	712-737-8741	•	•	•	•
		•	•	•	Security Land Title Co	712-262-1074	•	•	•	
•	•			•	The Title Co Inc (Prairie Du Chien WI)	888-918-4853	•	•	•	

DT	BK	CV	CR	PR	←COURTS CLAYTON	RECORDING→	UC	RE	TX	VS
•	•	•	•	•	Applicant Profile Services	515-727-7964	•	•	•	
		•	•	•	Clayton County Abstract Co	563-245-1430	•	•	•	•
		•			Court Services of Iowa Inc	515-965-5722	•	•	•	
•	•			•	The Title Co Inc (Prairie Du Chien WI)	888-918-4853	•	•	•	

DT	BK	CV	CR	PR	←COURTS CLINTON	RECORDING→	UC	RE	TX	VS
		•	•	•	Abstract & Title Guaranty Co	563-243-2027	•	•	•	•
•	•	•	•	•	Applicant Profile Services	515-727-7964	•	•	•	
•	•	•	•	•	ASAP Process Service [SOP]	877-455-2490		•		•
		•			Court Services of Iowa Inc	515-965-5722	•	•	•	
•	•	•	•	•	SAS Associates Inc [SOP]	800-373-0727	•		•	
•	•			•	The Title Co Inc (Prairie Du Chien WI)	888-918-4853	•	•	•	

DT	BK	CV	CR	PR	←COURTS CRAWFORD	RECORDING→	UC	RE	TX	VS
•	•	•	•	•	Applicant Profile Services	515-727-7964	•	•	•	
		•			Court Services of Iowa Inc	515-965-5722	•	•	•	
		•	•	•	Crawford County Abstract Co (Iowa)	712-263-5626	•	•	•	•
•	•			•	The Title Co Inc (Prairie Du Chien WI)	888-918-4853	•	•	•	

DT	BK	CV	CR	PR	←COURTS DALLAS	RECORDING→	UC	RE	TX	VS
•	•	•	•	•	Adams Investigations [SOP]	888-844-0624	•	•	•	•
•	•	•	•	•	Applicant Profile Services	515-727-7964	•	•	•	
		•			Court Services of Iowa Inc	515-965-5722	•	•	•	
			•		Page-Hawkeye Legal Services [SOP]	515-276-3984				
•	•			•	The Title Co Inc (Prairie Du Chien WI)	888-918-4853	•	•	•	

DT	BK	CV	CR	PR	←COURTS DAVIS	RECORDING→	UC	RE	TX	VS
•	•	•	•	•	Applicant Profile Services	515-727-7964	•	•	•	
		•			Court Services of Iowa Inc	515-965-5722	•	•	•	
		•	•	•	Lynch Abstracting	641-664-3188		•	•	•
•	•			•	The Title Co Inc (Prairie Du Chien WI)	888-918-4853	•	•	•	

DT	BK	CV	CR	PR	←COURTS DECATUR	RECORDING→	UC	RE	TX	VS
•	•	•	•	•	Applicant Profile Services	515-727-7964	•	•	•	
		•			Court Services of Iowa Inc	515-965-5722	•	•	•	
		•	•	•	Elson & Fulton Abstractors	641-446-4621	•	•	•	•

DT	BK	CV	CR	PR	←COURTS DELAWARE	RECORDING→	UC	RE	TX	VS
•	•	•	•	•	Applicant Profile Services	515-727-7964	•	•	•	
•	•	•	•	•	ASAP Process Service [SOP]	877-455-2490		•		•
		•			Court Services of Iowa Inc	515-965-5722	•	•	•	
		•	•	•	Delaware County Abstract Co (Iowa)	563-927-4858	•	•	•	•
•	•			•	The Title Co Inc (Prairie Du Chien WI)	888-918-4853	•	•	•	

DT	BK	CV	CR	PR	←Courts	Des Moines	Recording→	UC	RE	TX	VS
•	•	•	•	•	Applicant Profile Services		515-727-7964	•	•	•	
•	•	•	•	•	ASAP Process Service [SOP]		877-455-2490		•		•
		•			Court Services of Iowa Inc		515-965-5722	•	•	•	
•	•			•	The Title Co Inc (Prairie Du Chien WI)		888-918-4853	•	•	•	

DT	BK	CV	CR	PR	←Courts	Dickinson	Recording→	UC	RE	TX	VS
•	•	•	•	•	Applicant Profile Services		515-727-7964	•	•	•	
				•	Cornell Abstract Co		712-336-3845	•	•	•	
		•			Court Services of Iowa Inc		515-965-5722	•	•	•	
•		•	•	•	R & D Research Services [SOP]		712-737-8741	•	•	•	•
•	•			•	The Title Co Inc (Prairie Du Chien WI)		888-918-4853	•	•	•	

DT	BK	CV	CR	PR	←Courts	Dubuque	Recording→	UC	RE	TX	VS
		•		•	Abeln Abstract & Title Co		563-582-7148		•	•	•
•	•	•	•	•	Applicant Profile Services		515-727-7964	•	•	•	
•	•	•	•	•	ASAP Process Service [SOP]		877-455-2490		•		•
		•			Court Services of Iowa Inc		515-965-5722	•	•	•	
•	•			•	The Title Co Inc (Prairie Du Chien WI)		888-918-4853	•	•	•	

DT	BK	CV	CR	PR	←Courts	Emmet	Recording→	UC	RE	TX	VS
•	•	•	•	•	Applicant Profile Services		515-727-7964	•	•	•	
		•			Court Services of Iowa Inc		515-965-5722	•	•	•	
		•	•	•	Estherville Abstract Co		712-362-3148	•	•	•	•
•	•			•	The Title Co Inc (Prairie Du Chien WI)		888-918-4853	•	•	•	

DT	BK	CV	CR	PR	←Courts	Fayette	Recording→	UC	RE	TX	VS
•	•	•	•	•	Applicant Profile Services		515-727-7964	•	•	•	
		•			Court Services of Iowa Inc		515-965-5722	•	•	•	
•	•			•	The Title Co Inc (Prairie Du Chien WI)		888-918-4853	•	•	•	

DT	BK	CV	CR	PR	←Courts	Floyd	Recording→	UC	RE	TX	VS
•	•	•	•	•	Applicant Profile Services		515-727-7964	•	•	•	
		•			Court Services of Iowa Inc		515-965-5722	•	•	•	
				•	Iowa Title & Realty Co		641-228-1515	•	•	•	•
•	•			•	The Title Co Inc (Prairie Du Chien WI)		888-918-4853	•	•	•	

DT	BK	CV	CR	PR	←Courts	Franklin	Recording→	UC	RE	TX	VS
•	•	•	•	•	Applicant Profile Services		515-727-7964	•	•	•	
		•			Court Services of Iowa Inc		515-965-5722	•	•	•	
		•	•	•	Franklin County Abstract Co (Iowa)		641-456-4551	•	•	•	•
•	•			•	The Title Co Inc (Prairie Du Chien WI)		888-918-4853	•	•	•	

DT	BK	CV	CR	PR	←Courts	Fremont	Recording→	UC	RE	TX	VS
•	•	•	•	•	Applicant Profile Services		515-727-7964	•	•	•	
		•			Court Services of Iowa Inc		515-965-5722	•	•	•	

DT	BK	CV	CR	PR	←Courts	Greene	Recording→	UC	RE	TX	VS
•	•	•	•	•	Applicant Profile Services		515-727-7964	•	•	•	
		•			Court Services of Iowa Inc		515-965-5722	•	•	•	
		•	•	•	Greene County Abstract Company Inc		515-386-2191	•	•	•	•
			•		Page-Hawkeye Legal Services [SOP]		515-276-3984				
•	•			•	The Title Co Inc (Prairie Du Chien WI)		888-918-4853	•	•	•	

DT	BK	CV	CR	PR	←Courts	Grundy	Recording→	UC	RE	TX	VS
•	•	•	•	•	Applicant Profile Services		515-727-7964	•	•	•	
		•			Court Services of Iowa Inc		515-965-5722	•	•	•	
•	•			•	The Title Co Inc (Prairie Du Chien WI)		888-918-4853	•	•	•	

DT	BK	CV	CR	PR	←Courts	Guthrie	Recording→	UC	RE	TX	VS
•	•	•	•	•	Applicant Profile Services		515-727-7964	•	•	•	

DT	BK	CV	CR	PR	←Courts	Recording→	UC	RE	TX	VS
		•			Court Services of Iowa Inc	515-965-5722	•	•	•	
		•		•	Guthrie County Abstract	641-332-2339	•	•	•	•
•	•			•	The Title Co Inc (Prairie Du Chien WI)	888-918-4853	•	•	•	
DT	**BK**	**CV**	**CR**	**PR**	**←Courts HAMILTON**	**Recording→**	**UC**	**RE**	**TX**	**VS**
•	•	•	•	•	Applicant Profile Services	515-727-7964	•	•	•	
		•			Court Services of Iowa Inc	515-965-5722	•	•	•	
		•	•	•	Tim Neuroth	515-832-3156	•	•	•	•
•	•			•	The Title Co Inc (Prairie Du Chien WI)	888-918-4853	•	•	•	
DT	**BK**	**CV**	**CR**	**PR**	**←Courts HANCOCK**	**Recording→**	**UC**	**RE**	**TX**	**VS**
•	•	•	•	•	Applicant Profile Services	515-727-7964	•	•	•	
		•			Court Services of Iowa Inc	515-965-5722	•	•	•	
				•	Hancock County Abstract Co	641-923-2454	•	•	•	
•	•			•	The Title Co Inc (Prairie Du Chien WI)	888-918-4853	•	•	•	
DT	**BK**	**CV**	**CR**	**PR**	**←Courts HARDIN**	**Recording→**	**UC**	**RE**	**TX**	**VS**
•	•	•	•	•	Applicant Profile Services	515-727-7964	•	•	•	
		•			Court Services of Iowa Inc	515-965-5722	•	•	•	
•	•			•	The Title Co Inc (Prairie Du Chien WI)	888-918-4853	•	•	•	
DT	**BK**	**CV**	**CR**	**PR**	**←Courts HARRISON**	**Recording→**	**UC**	**RE**	**TX**	**VS**
•	•	•	•	•	Applicant Profile Services	515-727-7964	•	•	•	
		•			Court Services of Iowa Inc	515-965-5722	•	•	•	
		•	•	•	Harrison County Title & Guaranty	712-644-2703		•	•	
•	•			•	The Title Co Inc (Prairie Du Chien WI)	888-918-4853	•	•	•	
•	•	•	•		Thomas Research Services (Donna Thomas) [SOP]	402-339-7291	•		•	
DT	**BK**	**CV**	**CR**	**PR**	**←Courts HENRY**	**Recording→**	**UC**	**RE**	**TX**	**VS**
•	•	•	•	•	Applicant Profile Services	515-727-7964	•	•	•	
•	•	•	•	•	ASAP Process Service [SOP]	877-455-2490		•		•
		•			Court Services of Iowa Inc	515-965-5722	•	•	•	
		•	•	•	Henry County Abstract Co (Iowa)	319-385-9017	•	•	•	•
•	•			•	The Title Co Inc (Prairie Du Chien WI)	888-918-4853	•	•	•	
DT	**BK**	**CV**	**CR**	**PR**	**←Courts HOWARD**	**Recording→**	**UC**	**RE**	**TX**	**VS**
•	•	•	•	•	Applicant Profile Services	515-727-7964	•	•	•	
		•			Court Services of Iowa Inc	515-965-5722	•	•	•	
		•	•	•	Howard County Abstract & Title Co	563-547-4944	•	•	•	•
•	•			•	The Title Co Inc (Prairie Du Chien WI)	888-918-4853	•	•	•	
DT	**BK**	**CV**	**CR**	**PR**	**←Courts HUMBOLDT**	**Recording→**	**UC**	**RE**	**TX**	**VS**
•	•	•	•	•	Applicant Profile Services	515-727-7964	•	•	•	
		•			Court Services of Iowa Inc	515-965-5722	•	•	•	
		•	•	•	Olson & Humboldt County Abstract	515-332-1593	•	•	•	•
•	•			•	The Title Co Inc (Prairie Du Chien WI)	888-918-4853	•	•	•	
DT	**BK**	**CV**	**CR**	**PR**	**←Courts IDA**	**Recording→**	**UC**	**RE**	**TX**	**VS**
•	•	•	•	•	Applicant Profile Services	515-727-7964	•	•	•	
		•			Court Services of Iowa Inc	515-965-5722	•	•	•	
•	•			•	The Title Co Inc (Prairie Du Chien WI)	888-918-4853	•	•	•	
DT	**BK**	**CV**	**CR**	**PR**	**←Courts IOWA**	**Recording→**	**UC**	**RE**	**TX**	**VS**
•	•	•	•	•	Applicant Profile Services	515-727-7964	•	•	•	
•	•	•	•	•	ASAP Process Service [SOP]	877-455-2490		•		•
		•			Court Services of Iowa Inc	515-965-5722	•	•	•	
		•	•	•	Iowa County Abstract Company	319-642-7321	•	•	•	
•	•			•	The Title Co Inc (Prairie Du Chien WI)	888-918-4853	•	•	•	
DT	**BK**	**CV**	**CR**	**PR**	**←Courts JACKSON**	**Recording→**	**UC**	**RE**	**TX**	**VS**
		•	•	•	Abstract & Title Guaranty Co	563-243-2027	•	•	•	•
•	•	•	•	•	Applicant Profile Services	515-727-7964	•	•	•	

DT	BK	CV	CR	PR			UC	RE	TX	VS
•	•	•	•	•	ASAP Process Service [SOP]	877-455-2490		•		•
		•			Court Services of Iowa Inc	515-965-5722	•	•	•	
		•		•	Iowa Title & Guaranty Co	563-652-6081	•	•	•	•
•	•	•	•	•	SAS Associates Inc [SOP]	800-373-0727	•		•	
•	•			•	The Title Co Inc (Prairie Du Chien WI)	888-918-4853	•	•	•	

DT	BK	CV	CR	PR	←Courts **JASPER**	Recording→	UC	RE	TX	VS
•	•	•	•	•	Applicant Profile Services	515-727-7964	•	•	•	
		•			Court Services of Iowa Inc	515-965-5722	•	•	•	
•	•	•	•	•	JR Investigations [SOP]	515-288-4682	•	•	•	•
			•		Page-Hawkeye Legal Services [SOP]	515-276-3984				
•	•			•	The Title Co Inc (Prairie Du Chien WI)	888-918-4853	•	•	•	

DT	BK	CV	CR	PR	←Courts **JEFFERSON**	Recording→	UC	RE	TX	VS
•	•	•	•	•	Applicant Profile Services	515-727-7964	•	•	•	
•	•	•	•	•	ASAP Process Service [SOP]	877-455-2490		•		•
		•			Court Services of Iowa Inc	515-965-5722	•	•	•	
		•	•	•	Jefferson County Abstract	641-472-5052	•	•	•	•
•	•			•	The Title Co Inc (Prairie Du Chien WI)	888-918-4853	•	•	•	

DT	BK	CV	CR	PR	←Courts **JOHNSON**	Recording→	UC	RE	TX	VS
•	•	•	•	•	Applicant Profile Services	515-727-7964	•	•	•	
•	•	•	•	•	ASAP Process Service [SOP]	877-455-2490		•		•
		•			Court Services of Iowa Inc	515-965-5722	•	•	•	
•	•	•	•	•	FYII Acct [SOP]	563-299-5683	•	•	•	•
		•	•	•	Reliance Title Services	319-354-6505	•	•	•	•
•	•	•	•	•	SAS Associates Inc [SOP]	800-373-0727	•		•	
•	•			•	The Title Co Inc (Prairie Du Chien WI)	888-918-4853	•	•	•	

DT	BK	CV	CR	PR	←Courts **JONES**	Recording→	UC	RE	TX	VS
		•	•	•	Abstract & Title Services Inc	319-462-4828	•	•	•	•
•	•	•	•	•	Applicant Profile Services	515-727-7964	•	•	•	
•	•	•	•	•	ASAP Process Service [SOP]	877-455-2490		•		•
		•			Court Services of Iowa Inc	515-965-5722	•	•	•	
•	•			•	The Title Co Inc (Prairie Du Chien WI)	888-918-4853	•	•	•	

DT	BK	CV	CR	PR	←Courts **KEOKUK**	Recording→	UC	RE	TX	VS
•	•	•	•	•	Applicant Profile Services	515-727-7964	•	•	•	
		•			Court Services of Iowa Inc	515-965-5722	•	•	•	
•	•			•	The Title Co Inc (Prairie Du Chien WI)	888-918-4853	•	•	•	

DT	BK	CV	CR	PR	←Courts **KOSSUTH**	Recording→	UC	RE	TX	VS
•	•	•	•	•	Applicant Profile Services	515-727-7964	•	•	•	
		•			Court Services of Iowa Inc	515-965-5722	•	•	•	
		•		•	Kossuth Abstract & Title Co	515-295-3745		•	•	
•	•			•	The Title Co Inc (Prairie Du Chien WI)	888-918-4853	•	•	•	

DT	BK	CV	CR	PR	←Courts **LEE**	Recording→	UC	RE	TX	VS
		•		•	American Abstract & Title	319-372-8110	•	•	•	•
•	•	•	•	•	Applicant Profile Services	515-727-7964	•	•	•	
		•			Court Services of Iowa Inc	515-965-5722	•	•	•	
•	•			•	The Title Co Inc (Prairie Du Chien WI)	888-918-4853	•	•	•	

DT	BK	CV	CR	PR	←Courts **LINN**	Recording→	UC	RE	TX	VS
•	•	•	•	•	Applicant Profile Services	515-727-7964	•	•	•	
•	•	•	•	•	ASAP Process Service [SOP]	877-455-2490		•		•
		•			Court Services of Iowa Inc	515-965-5722	•	•	•	
•	•	•	•	•	FYII Acct [SOP]	563-299-5683	•	•	•	•
•	•	•	•	•	Iowa Title Co	319-365-1478	•	•	•	•
•	•	•	•	•	SAS Associates Inc [SOP]	800-373-0727	•		•	
•	•			•	The Title Co Inc (Prairie Du Chien WI)	888-918-4853	•	•	•	

DT	BK	CV	CR	PR	←Courts	LOUISA	Recording→	UC	RE	TX	VS
•	•	•	•	•	Applicant Profile Services		515-727-7964	•	•	•	
		•			Court Services of Iowa Inc		515-965-5722	•	•	•	
•	•			•	The Title Co Inc (Prairie Du Chien WI)		888-918-4853	•	•	•	

DT	BK	CV	CR	PR	←Courts	LUCAS	Recording→	UC	RE	TX	VS
•	•	•	•	•	Applicant Profile Services		515-727-7964	•	•	•	
		•			Court Services of Iowa Inc		515-965-5722	•	•	•	
•	•			•	The Title Co Inc (Prairie Du Chien WI)		888-918-4853	•	•	•	

DT	BK	CV	CR	PR	←Courts	LYON	Recording→	UC	RE	TX	VS
•	•	•	•	•	Applicant Profile Services		515-727-7964	•	•	•	
		•			Court Services of Iowa Inc		515-965-5722	•	•	•	
				•	Lyon County Title Co Inc		712-472-3758		•	•	
•		•	•	•	R & D Research Services [SOP]		712-737-8741	•	•	•	•

DT	BK	CV	CR	PR	←Courts	MADISON	Recording→	UC	RE	TX	VS
•	•	•	•	•	Applicant Profile Services		515-727-7964	•	•	•	
		•			Court Services of Iowa Inc		515-965-5722	•	•	•	
•	•	•	•	•	JR Investigations [SOP]		515-288-4682	•	•	•	•
			•		Page-Hawkeye Legal Services [SOP]		515-276-3984				
		•	•	•	Security Abstract & Title Inc		515-462-1691	•	•	•	•
•	•			•	The Title Co Inc (Prairie Du Chien WI)		888-918-4853	•	•	•	

DT	BK	CV	CR	PR	←Courts	MAHASKA	Recording→	UC	RE	TX	VS
•	•	•	•	•	Applicant Profile Services		515-727-7964	•	•	•	
		•			Court Services of Iowa Inc		515-965-5722	•	•	•	
		•	•	•	Mahaska Title - Johnson Abstract Co		641-673-5666	•	•	•	•
			•		Page-Hawkeye Legal Services [SOP]		515-276-3984				
•	•			•	The Title Co Inc (Prairie Du Chien WI)		888-918-4853	•	•	•	

DT	BK	CV	CR	PR	←Courts	MARION	Recording→	UC	RE	TX	VS
•	•	•	•	•	Applicant Profile Services		515-727-7964	•	•	•	
		•			Court Services of Iowa Inc		515-965-5722	•	•	•	
		•	•	•	Marion County Title Services		641-842-3518	•	•	•	•
			•		Page-Hawkeye Legal Services [SOP]		515-276-3984				
•	•			•	The Title Co Inc (Prairie Du Chien WI)		888-918-4853	•	•	•	

DT	BK	CV	CR	PR	←Courts	MARSHALL	Recording→	UC	RE	TX	VS
•	•	•	•	•	Applicant Profile Services		515-727-7964	•	•	•	
		•			Court Services of Iowa Inc		515-965-5722	•	•	•	
•	•	•	•	•	Marshall County Abstract Company		641-752-5358	•	•	•	•
•	•			•	The Title Co Inc (Prairie Du Chien WI)		888-918-4853	•	•	•	

DT	BK	CV	CR	PR	←Courts	MILLS	Recording→	UC	RE	TX	VS
•	•	•	•	•	Applicant Profile Services		515-727-7964	•	•	•	
•	•	•	•	•	Coit Enterprises		402-451-0462		•	•	
		•			Court Services of Iowa Inc		515-965-5722	•	•	•	
•	•			•	The Title Co Inc (Prairie Du Chien WI)		888-918-4853	•	•	•	
•	•	•	•		Thomas Research Services (Donna Thomas) [SOP]		402-339-7291	•		•	

DT	BK	CV	CR	PR	←Courts	MITCHELL	Recording→	UC	RE	TX	VS
•	•	•	•	•	Applicant Profile Services		515-727-7964	•	•	•	
		•			Court Services of Iowa Inc		515-965-5722	•	•	•	
		•	•	•	Mitchell County Abstract Co		641-732-4571	•	•	•	
•	•			•	The Title Co Inc (Prairie Du Chien WI)		888-918-4853	•	•	•	

DT	BK	CV	CR	PR	←Courts	MONONA	Recording→	UC	RE	TX	VS
•	•	•	•	•	Applicant Profile Services		515-727-7964	•	•	•	
		•			Court Services of Iowa Inc		515-965-5722	•	•	•	
•	•	•	•	•	Intra-Lex Investigations Inc [SOP]		712-233-1639	•	•	•	•

DT	BK	CV	CR	PR	Name	Phone	UC	RE	TX	VS
•	•			•	The Title Co Inc (Prairie Du Chien WI)	888-918-4853	•	•	•	
DT	**BK**	**CV**	**CR**	**PR**	**←COURTS — MONROE**	**RECORDING→**	**UC**	**RE**	**TX**	**VS**
•	•	•	•	•	Applicant Profile Services	515-727-7964	•	•	•	
		•			Court Services of Iowa Inc	515-965-5722	•	•	•	
		•	•	•	Graham Abstract Co	641-932-7156	•	•	•	•
•	•	•	•	•	Meier Inv [SOP]	515-205-2738	•	•	•	•
•	•			•	The Title Co Inc (Prairie Du Chien WI)	888-918-4853	•	•	•	
DT	**BK**	**CV**	**CR**	**PR**	**←COURTS — MONTGOMERY**	**RECORDING→**	**UC**	**RE**	**TX**	**VS**
•	•	•	•	•	Applicant Profile Services	515-727-7964	•	•	•	
		•			Court Services of Iowa Inc	515-965-5722	•	•	•	
•	•			•	The Title Co Inc (Prairie Du Chien WI)	888-918-4853	•	•	•	
			•		Beth Young	712-767-2510		•	•	
DT	**BK**	**CV**	**CR**	**PR**	**←COURTS — MUSCATINE**	**RECORDING→**	**UC**	**RE**	**TX**	**VS**
•	•	•	•	•	Applicant Profile Services	515-727-7964	•	•	•	
•	•	•	•	•	ASAP Process Service [SOP]	877-455-2490		•		•
		•			Court Services of Iowa Inc	515-965-5722	•	•	•	
•	•	•	•	•	FYII Acct [SOP]	563-299-5683	•	•	•	•
		•		•	Legal Abstract Co	563-263-3171	•	•	•	•
•	•	•	•	•	SAS Associates Inc [SOP]	800-373-0727	•		•	
•	•			•	The Title Co Inc (Prairie Du Chien WI)	888-918-4853	•	•	•	
DT	**BK**	**CV**	**CR**	**PR**	**←COURTS — O'BRIEN**	**RECORDING→**	**UC**	**RE**	**TX**	**VS**
•	•	•	•	•	Applicant Profile Services	515-727-7964	•	•	•	
		•			Court Services of Iowa Inc	515-965-5722	•	•	•	
•		•	•	•	R & D Research Services [SOP]	712-737-8741	•	•	•	•
DT	**BK**	**CV**	**CR**	**PR**	**←COURTS — OSCEOLA**	**RECORDING→**	**UC**	**RE**	**TX**	**VS**
•	•	•	•	•	Applicant Profile Services	515-727-7964	•	•	•	
					Court Services of Iowa Inc	515-965-5722	•	•	•	
•		•	•	•	R & D Research Services [SOP]	712-737-8741	•	•	•	•
•				•	The Title Co Inc (Iowa)	712-754-2284	•	•	•	
DT	**BK**	**CV**	**CR**	**PR**	**←COURTS — PAGE**	**RECORDING→**	**UC**	**RE**	**TX**	**VS**
•	•	•	•	•	Applicant Profile Services	515-727-7964	•	•	•	
		•			Court Services of Iowa Inc	515-965-5722	•	•	•	
		•		•	Page County Abstract & Title Company	712-542-3613	•	•	•	
DT	**BK**	**CV**	**CR**	**PR**	**←COURTS — PALO ALTO**	**RECORDING→**	**UC**	**RE**	**TX**	**VS**
•	•	•	•	•	Applicant Profile Services	515-727-7964	•	•	•	
		•			Court Services of Iowa Inc	515-965-5722	•	•	•	
		•	•	•	Palo Alto County Abstract Co	712-852-4313	•	•	•	•
•	•			•	The Title Co Inc (Prairie Du Chien WI)	888-918-4853	•	•	•	
DT	**BK**	**CV**	**CR**	**PR**	**←COURTS — PLYMOUTH**	**RECORDING→**	**UC**	**RE**	**TX**	**VS**
•	•	•	•	•	Applicant Profile Services	515-727-7964	•	•	•	
		•			Court Services of Iowa Inc	515-965-5722	•	•	•	
•	•	•	•	•	Intra-Lex Investigations Inc [SOP]	712-233-1639	•	•	•	•
				•	Plymouth County Abstract	712-546-4564	•	•	•	
•		•	•	•	R & D Research Services [SOP]	712-737-8741	•	•	•	•
•	•			•	The Title Co Inc (Prairie Du Chien WI)	888-918-4853	•	•	•	
DT	**BK**	**CV**	**CR**	**PR**	**←COURTS — POCAHONTAS**	**RECORDING→**	**UC**	**RE**	**TX**	**VS**
•	•	•	•	•	Applicant Profile Services	515-727-7964	•	•	•	
		•			Court Services of Iowa Inc	515-965-5722	•	•	•	
•	•			•	The Title Co Inc (Prairie Du Chien WI)	888-918-4853	•	•	•	
DT	**BK**	**CV**	**CR**	**PR**	**←COURTS — POLK**	**RECORDING→**	**UC**	**RE**	**TX**	**VS**
•	•	•	•	•	Adams Investigations [SOP]	888-844-0624	•	•	•	•
•	•	•	•	•	Applicant Profile Services	515-727-7964	•	•	•	

DT	BK	CV	CR	PR	←Courts	Name	Recording→	UC	RE	TX	VS
		•				Court Services of Iowa Inc	515-965-5722	•	•	•	
•	•	•	•	•		FYII Acct [SOP]	563-299-5683	•	•	•	•
•	•	•	•	•		JR Investigations [SOP]	515-288-4682	•	•	•	•
•	•	•	•	•		Meier Inv [SOP]	515-205-2738	•	•	•	•
			•			Page-Hawkeye Legal Services [SOP]	515-276-3984				
•	•	•	•	•		SAS Associates Inc [SOP]	800-373-0727	•		•	
•	•	•				Search Network Ltd (Iowa)	800-383-5050	•	•	•	
•	•			•		The Title Co Inc (Prairie Du Chien WI)	888-918-4853	•	•	•	
DT	**BK**	**CV**	**CR**	**PR**	**←Courts**	**POTTAWATTAMIE**	**Recording→**	**UC**	**RE**	**TX**	**VS**
•	•	•	•	•		Applicant Profile Services	515-727-7964	•	•	•	
•	•	•	•	•		Coit Enterprises	402-451-0462		•	•	
		•				Court Services of Iowa Inc	515-965-5722	•	•	•	
•	•	•	•	•		Legal Eagle Inc / Eagle Search & Service [SOP]	402-342-4427	•	•	•	•
•	•			•		The Title Co Inc (Prairie Du Chien WI)	888-918-4853	•	•	•	
•	•	•	•			Thomas Research Services (Donna Thomas) [SOP]	402-339-7291	•		•	
DT	**BK**	**CV**	**CR**	**PR**	**←Courts**	**POWESHIEK**	**Recording→**	**UC**	**RE**	**TX**	**VS**
•	•	•	•	•		Applicant Profile Services	515-727-7964	•	•	•	
		•				Court Services of Iowa Inc	515-965-5722	•	•	•	
•	•	•	•	•		Poweshiek Abstract Co Inc	641-236-8668	•	•	•	•
•	•			•		The Title Co Inc (Prairie Du Chien WI)	888-918-4853	•	•	•	
DT	**BK**	**CV**	**CR**	**PR**	**←Courts**	**RINGGOLD**	**Recording→**	**UC**	**RE**	**TX**	**VS**
•	•	•	•	•		Applicant Profile Services	515-727-7964	•	•	•	
		•				Court Services of Iowa Inc	515-965-5722	•	•	•	
		•	•	•		Ringgold County Abstract Co Inc	641-464-3902	•	•	•	•
•	•			•		The Title Co Inc (Prairie Du Chien WI)	888-918-4853	•	•	•	
DT	**BK**	**CV**	**CR**	**PR**	**←Courts**	**SAC**	**Recording→**	**UC**	**RE**	**TX**	**VS**
•	•	•	•	•		Applicant Profile Services	515-727-7964	•	•	•	
		•				Court Services of Iowa Inc	515-965-5722	•	•	•	
		•	•	•		Sac County Abstract Co	712-662-7317	•	•	•	•
•	•			•		The Title Co Inc (Prairie Du Chien WI)	888-918-4853	•	•	•	
DT	**BK**	**CV**	**CR**	**PR**	**←Courts**	**SCOTT**	**Recording→**	**UC**	**RE**	**TX**	**VS**
•	•	•	•	•		Applicant Profile Services	515-727-7964	•	•	•	
•	•	•	•	•		ASAP Process Service [SOP]	877-455-2490		•		•
		•	•	•		Bettendorf Abstract Co [SOP]	563-359-3646	•	•	•	•
		•				Court Services of Iowa Inc	515-965-5722	•	•	•	
•	•	•	•	•		DocumentServe Express [SOP]	309-786-2220	•	•	•	•
•	•	•	•	•		FYII Acct [SOP]	563-299-5683	•	•	•	•
•	•	•	•	•		James M Sweeney & Associates Inc [SOP]	800-494-5922	•		•	•
•	•	•	•	•		SAS Associates Inc [SOP]	800-373-0727	•		•	
•	•			•		The Title Co Inc (Prairie Du Chien WI)	888-918-4853	•	•	•	
DT	**BK**	**CV**	**CR**	**PR**	**←Courts**	**SHELBY**	**Recording→**	**UC**	**RE**	**TX**	**VS**
•	•	•	•	•		Applicant Profile Services	515-727-7964	•	•	•	
		•				Court Services of Iowa Inc	515-965-5722	•	•	•	
				•		Ouren Title Inc	712-755-2174		•	•	•
•	•			•		The Title Co Inc (Prairie Du Chien WI)	888-918-4853	•	•	•	
DT	**BK**	**CV**	**CR**	**PR**	**←Courts**	**SIOUX**	**Recording→**	**UC**	**RE**	**TX**	**VS**
•	•	•	•	•		Applicant Profile Services	515-727-7964	•	•	•	
		•				Court Services of Iowa Inc	515-965-5722	•	•	•	
•	•	•	•	•		Intra-Lex Investigations Inc [SOP]	712-233-1639	•	•	•	•
•		•	•	•		R & D Research Services [SOP]	712-737-8741	•	•	•	•
DT	**BK**	**CV**	**CR**	**PR**	**←Courts**	**STORY**	**Recording→**	**UC**	**RE**	**TX**	**VS**
•	•	•	•	•		Applicant Profile Services	515-727-7964	•	•	•	
						Batman-Sayers Abstract & Title Co	515-382-4127	•	•	•	

DT	BK	CV	CR	PR			UC	RE	TX	VS
		•			Court Services of Iowa Inc	515-965-5722	•	•	•	
			•		Page-Hawkeye Legal Services [SOP]	515-276-3984				
•	•			•	The Title Co Inc (Prairie Du Chien WI)	888-918-4853	•	•	•	

DT	BK	CV	CR	PR	←Courts **TAMA**	Recording→	UC	RE	TX	VS
•	•	•	•	•	Applicant Profile Services	515-727-7964	•	•	•	
		•			Court Services of Iowa Inc	515-965-5722	•	•	•	
•		•	•	•	Tama County Abstract	888-561-9061	•	•	•	•
•	•			•	The Title Co Inc (Prairie Du Chien WI)	888-918-4853	•	•	•	

DT	BK	CV	CR	PR	←Courts **TAYLOR**	Recording→	UC	RE	TX	VS
•	•	•	•	•	Applicant Profile Services	515-727-7964	•	•	•	
		•			Court Services of Iowa Inc	515-965-5722	•	•	•	

DT	BK	CV	CR	PR	←Courts **UNION**	Recording→	UC	RE	TX	VS
•	•	•	•	•	Applicant Profile Services	515-727-7964	•	•	•	
		•			Court Services of Iowa Inc	515-965-5722	•	•	•	
•	•			•	The Title Co Inc (Prairie Du Chien WI)	888-918-4853	•	•	•	

DT	BK	CV	CR	PR	←Courts **VAN BUREN**	Recording→	UC	RE	TX	VS
•	•	•	•	•	Applicant Profile Services	515-727-7964	•	•	•	
		•			Court Services of Iowa Inc	515-965-5722	•	•	•	
•	•			•	The Title Co Inc (Prairie Du Chien WI)	888-918-4853	•	•	•	
		•	•	•	Van Buren Abstract Co	319-293-7760	•	•	•	•

DT	BK	CV	CR	PR	←Courts **WAPELLO**	Recording→	UC	RE	TX	VS
•	•	•	•	•	Applicant Profile Services	515-727-7964	•	•	•	
		•			Court Services of Iowa Inc	515-965-5722	•	•	•	
•	•			•	The Title Co Inc (Prairie Du Chien WI)	888-918-4853	•	•	•	

DT	BK	CV	CR	PR	←Courts **WARREN**	Recording→	UC	RE	TX	VS
•	•	•	•	•	Applicant Profile Services	515-727-7964	•	•	•	
		•			Court Services of Iowa Inc	515-965-5722	•	•	•	
•	•	•	•	•	JR Investigations [SOP]	515-288-4682	•	•	•	•
•	•	•	•	•	Meier Inv [SOP]	515-205-2738	•	•	•	•
			•		Page-Hawkeye Legal Services [SOP]	515-276-3984				
•	•			•	The Title Co Inc (Prairie Du Chien WI)	888-918-4853	•	•	•	
				•	Warren County Abstract Company	515-961-7479	•	•	•	•

DT	BK	CV	CR	PR	←Courts **WASHINGTON**	Recording→	UC	RE	TX	VS
•	•	•	•	•	Applicant Profile Services	515-727-7964	•	•	•	
		•			Court Services of Iowa Inc	515-965-5722	•	•	•	
•	•			•	The Title Co Inc (Prairie Du Chien WI)	888-918-4853	•	•	•	

DT	BK	CV	CR	PR	←Courts **WAYNE**	Recording→	UC	RE	TX	VS
•	•	•	•	•	Applicant Profile Services	515-727-7964	•	•	•	
		•			Court Services of Iowa Inc	515-965-5722	•	•	•	
		•	•	•	John H Rider Abstracts of Title	641-872-1966	•	•	•	
•	•			•	The Title Co Inc (Prairie Du Chien WI)	888-918-4853	•	•	•	

DT	BK	CV	CR	PR	←Courts **WEBSTER**	Recording→	UC	RE	TX	VS
•	•	•	•	•	Applicant Profile Services	515-727-7964	•	•	•	
		•			Court Services of Iowa Inc	515-965-5722	•	•	•	
•	•			•	The Title Co Inc (Prairie Du Chien WI)	888-918-4853	•	•	•	
		•	•	•	Webster County-Butler & Rhodes Abstract	515-573-3341	•	•	•	•

DT	BK	CV	CR	PR	←Courts **WINNEBAGO**	Recording→	UC	RE	TX	VS
•	•	•	•	•	Applicant Profile Services	515-727-7964	•	•	•	
		•			Court Services of Iowa Inc	515-965-5722	•	•	•	
•	•			•	The Title Co Inc (Prairie Du Chien WI)	888-918-4853	•	•	•	

DT	BK	CV	CR	PR	←COURTS WINNESHIEK RECORDING→		UC	RE	TX	VS
•	•	•	•	•	Applicant Profile Services	515-727-7964	•	•	•	
		•			Court Services of Iowa Inc	515-965-5722	•	•	•	
•	•			•	The Title Co Inc (Prairie Du Chien WI)	888-918-4853	•	•	•	

DT	BK	CV	CR	PR	←COURTS WOODBURY RECORDING→		UC	RE	TX	VS
•	•	•	•	•	Applicant Profile Services	515-727-7964	•	•	•	
		•			Court Services of Iowa Inc	515-965-5722	•	•	•	
•	•	•	•	•	Intra-Lex Investigations Inc [SOP]	712-233-1639	•	•	•	•
•		•	•	•	R & D Research Services [SOP]	712-737-8741	•	•	•	•
•	•			•	The Title Co Inc (Prairie Du Chien WI)	888-918-4853	•	•	•	

DT	BK	CV	CR	PR	←COURTS WORTH RECORDING→		UC	RE	TX	VS
•	•	•	•	•	Applicant Profile Services	515-727-7964	•	•	•	
		•			Court Services of Iowa Inc	515-965-5722	•	•	•	
•	•			•	The Title Co Inc (Prairie Du Chien WI)	888-918-4853	•	•	•	
		•	•	•	Worth County Abstract Co Inc	641-324-1761		•	•	•

DT	BK	CV	CR	PR	←COURTS WRIGHT RECORDING→		UC	RE	TX	VS
•	•	•	•	•	Applicant Profile Services	515-727-7964	•	•	•	
		•			Court Services of Iowa Inc	515-965-5722	•	•	•	
•	•			•	The Title Co Inc (Prairie Du Chien WI)	888-918-4853	•	•	•	

[SOP] = PERFORMS SERVICE OF PROCESS

COURT RECORDS

CODE	GOVERNMENT AGENCY	TYPE OF INFORMATION
DT	US District Court	Federal civil and criminal cases
BK	Bankruptcy Court	United States bankruptcy cases
CV	Civil Court	Municipal, county and state level civil cases
CR	Criminal Court	Municipal, county and state level criminal cases
PR	Probate Court	Wills and estate cases

COUNTY RECORDS - RECORDINGS

CODE	GOVERNMENT AGENCY	TYPE OF INFORMATION
UC	UCC Filing Office	Uniform Commercial Code and other personal property liens
RE	Real Estate Recording Office	Real property transactions and liens
TX	Tax Filing Office(s)	Federal and state tax liens, judgment liens
VS	Vital Records Office	Vital statistics—birth, death, marriage, divorce

Kansas

COURT RECORDS RETRIEVED — **RECORDING RECORDS RETRIEVED**

DT	BK	CV	CR	PR	←Courts	County / Retriever	Recording→	UC	RE	TX	VS
						ALLEN					
•	•	•	•			Research Information Services LLC	800-522-3884	•		•	
		•	•	•		Street Abstract Co	620-625-2421	•	•	•	
						ANDERSON					
•	•	•	•			Research Information Services LLC	800-522-3884	•		•	
						ATCHISON					
			•	•		Bi-State Title Search (Div of Bi-State Ind.)	866-450-7399	•	•	•	
•	•	•	•			Research Information Services LLC	800-522-3884	•		•	
						BARBER					
•	•	•	•			Research Information Services LLC	800-522-3884	•		•	
						BARTON					
		•		•		Barton County Abstract & Title Co	620-793-3781	•	•	•	
•	•	•	•			Research Information Services LLC	800-522-3884	•		•	
						BOURBON					
•	•	•	•	•		American Research Unlimited Inc [SOP]	417-358-6494	•	•	•	•
•	•	•	•			Research Information Services LLC	800-522-3884	•		•	
						BROWN					
		•	•	•		Brown County Title Co	785-742-4194	•	•	•	
•	•	•	•			Research Information Services LLC	800-522-3884	•		•	
						BUTLER					
•	•	•	•	•		Branda Agency [SOP]	800-310-8174	•	•	•	•
•	•	•	•	•		Investigations LLC [SOP]	800-658-1688				
•	•	•	•	•		Kansas Investigative Services Inc [SOP]	888-889-3340	•	•	•	•
•	•	•	•			Research Information Services LLC	800-522-3884	•		•	
						CHASE					
•	•	•	•			Research Information Services LLC	800-522-3884	•		•	
						CHAUTAUQUA					
		•	•	•		Chautauqua County Abstract Co inc	620-725-3215	•	•	•	•
•	•	•	•			Research Information Services LLC	800-522-3884	•		•	
						CHEROKEE					
•	•	•	•	•		American Research Unlimited Inc [SOP]	417-358-6494	•	•	•	•
		•	•	•		Barrett Title Co	620-856-3531	•	•	•	•
•	•	•	•			Research Information Services LLC	800-522-3884	•		•	
						CHEYENNE					
		•	•	•		Patsy Maranville	785-426-2725				
•	•	•	•			Research Information Services LLC	800-522-3884	•		•	
•		•	•	•		The R M Jaqua Abstract Co	785-332-3041	•	•	•	
						CLARK					
		•		•		Meade County Title Co	800-725-7802	•	•	•	•
•	•	•	•			Research Information Services LLC	800-522-3884	•		•	

DT	BK	CV	CR	PR	←COURTS	CLAY	RECORDING→	UC	RE	TX	VS
		•	•	•	Attorney's Title Co		785-243-1357	•	•	•	
•	•	•	•		Research Information Services LLC		800-522-3884	•		•	

DT	BK	CV	CR	PR	←COURTS	CLOUD	RECORDING→	UC	RE	TX	VS
		•	•	•	Attorney's Title Co		785-243-1357	•	•	•	
•	•	•	•		Research Information Services LLC		800-522-3884	•		•	

DT	BK	CV	CR	PR	←COURTS	COFFEY	RECORDING→	UC	RE	TX	VS
•	•	•	•		Research Information Services LLC		800-522-3884	•		•	
		•	•	•	Street Abstract Co		620-625-2421	•	•	•	

DT	BK	CV	CR	PR	←COURTS	COMANCHE	RECORDING→	UC	RE	TX	VS
		•	•	•	Comanche Abstract & Title Co		620-582-2125	•	•	•	
•	•	•	•		Research Information Services LLC		800-522-3884	•		•	

DT	BK	CV	CR	PR	←COURTS	COWLEY	RECORDING→	UC	RE	TX	VS
		•	•	•	Barbour Title Co		866-379-0430	•	•	•	•
•	•	•	•		Research Information Services LLC		800-522-3884	•		•	

DT	BK	CV	CR	PR	←COURTS	CRAWFORD	RECORDING→	UC	RE	TX	VS
•	•	•	•	•	American Research Unlimited Inc [SOP]		417-358-6494	•	•	•	•
•	•	•	•		Research Information Services LLC		800-522-3884	•		•	

DT	BK	CV	CR	PR	←COURTS	DECATUR	RECORDING→	UC	RE	TX	VS
		•	•	•	Decatur County Abstract		785-626-3885	•	•	•	•
•		•	•	•	First Insurance Agency of Hoxie Inc		800-569-0198	•	•	•	
•	•	•	•		Research Information Services LLC		800-522-3884	•		•	

DT	BK	CV	CR	PR	←COURTS	DICKINSON	RECORDING→	UC	RE	TX	VS
		•	•		Al Bernardi Backgrounds Process Svc [SOP]		785-456-8821	•	•	•	
		•	•		Capital Inv Services Inc		800-633-7136				
•	•	•	•		Research Information Services LLC		800-522-3884	•		•	

DT	BK	CV	CR	PR	←COURTS	DONIPHAN	RECORDING→	UC	RE	TX	VS
		•	•	•	Euler Abstract & Title Co [SOP]		785-985-3562		•	•	
•	•	•	•		Research Information Services LLC		800-522-3884	•		•	

DT	BK	CV	CR	PR	←COURTS	DOUGLAS	RECORDING→	UC	RE	TX	VS
			•	•	Bi-State Title Search (Div of Bi-State Ind.)		866-450-7399	•	•	•	
		•	•		Capital Inv Services Inc		800-633-7136				
		•	•	•	Credit Bureau of Eudora Inc (CBE) [SOP]		785-542-1771	•	•	•	
•	•	•	•		Executive Investigative Services [SOP]		800-764-9484	•	•	•	
•	•	•	•		Future Security Concepts		800-398-3051	•		•	
•	•	•	•	•	Hatfield Process Service [SOP]		816-842-9800	•	•	•	•
					Heartland Document Retrieval		888-221-2778 orders only	•	•	•	
•	•		•		LLG Enterprises		816-443-2396				
•	•	•	•		Research Information Services LLC		800-522-3884	•		•	
•	•	•			SearchWorks Inc		913-383-0940	•	•	•	

DT	BK	CV	CR	PR	←COURTS	EDWARDS	RECORDING→	UC	RE	TX	VS
•	•	•	•		Research Information Services LLC		800-522-3884	•		•	
		•	•	•	Richardson Abstract Co Inc		620-659-2592	•	•	•	

DT	BK	CV	CR	PR	←COURTS	ELK	RECORDING→	UC	RE	TX	VS
		•	•	•	Elk County Abstract & Title Co		620-374-2500	•	•	•	•
•	•	•	•		Research Information Services LLC		800-522-3884	•		•	

DT	BK	CV	CR	PR	←COURTS	ELLIS	RECORDING→	UC	RE	TX	VS
		•	•	•	Ellis County Abstract & Title Co		785-625-2316	•	•	•	•
•	•	•	•		Research Information Services LLC		800-522-3884	•		•	

DT	BK	CV	CR	PR	←Courts **ELLSWORTH**	Recording→	UC	RE	TX	VS
		•	•		Capital Inv Services Inc	800-633-7136				
		•	•	•	G & H Abstract	800-640-7390			•	
•	•	•	•		Research Information Services LLC	800-522-3884	•		•	

DT	BK	CV	CR	PR	←Courts **FINNEY**	Recording→	UC	RE	TX	VS
		•		•	Campbell Abstract Inc	620-275-7441	•	•	•	
•	•	•	•		Research Information Services LLC	800-522-3884	•		•	

DT	BK	CV	CR	PR	←Courts **FORD**	Recording→	UC	RE	TX	VS
•	•	•	•		Research Information Services LLC	800-522-3884	•		•	

DT	BK	CV	CR	PR	←Courts **FRANKLIN**	Recording→	UC	RE	TX	VS
			•	•	Bi-State Title Search (Div of Bi-State Ind.)	866-450-7399	•	•	•	
		•	•		Capital Inv Services Inc	800-633-7136				
•	•	•	•		Executive Investigative Services [SOP]	800-764-9484	•	•	•	
		•	•	•	Haley Title Co Inc	785-242-2457	•	•	•	
					Heartland Document Retrieval	888-221-2778 orders only	•	•	•	
•	•	•	•		Research Information Services LLC	800-522-3884	•		•	

DT	BK	CV	CR	PR	←Courts **GEARY**	Recording→	UC	RE	TX	VS
		•	•		Al Bernardi Backgrounds Process Svc [SOP]	785-456-8821	•	•	•	
		•	•		Capital Inv Services Inc	800-633-7136				
•	•	•	•		Research Information Services LLC	800-522-3884	•		•	

DT	BK	CV	CR	PR	←Courts **GOVE**	Recording→	UC	RE	TX	VS
•		•	•	•	First Insurance Agency of Hoxie Inc	800-569-0198	•	•	•	
•	•	•	•		Research Information Services LLC	800-522-3884	•		•	

DT	BK	CV	CR	PR	←Courts **GRAHAM**	Recording→	UC	RE	TX	VS
•		•	•	•	First Insurance Agency of Hoxie Inc	800-569-0198	•	•	•	
•	•	•	•		Research Information Services LLC	800-522-3884	•		•	

DT	BK	CV	CR	PR	←Courts **GRANT**	Recording→	UC	RE	TX	VS
		•	•	•	Frazee Abstract & Title Co	800-736-7832	•	•	•	•
•	•	•	•		Research Information Services LLC	800-522-3884	•		•	

DT	BK	CV	CR	PR	←Courts **GRAY OR GREELEY**	Recording→	UC	RE	TX	VS
•	•	•	•		Research Information Services LLC	800-522-3884	•		•	

DT	BK	CV	CR	PR	←Courts **GREENWOOD**	Recording→	UC	RE	TX	VS
•	•	•	•		Research Information Services LLC	800-522-3884	•		•	
		•	•	•	Street Abstract Co	620-625-2421	•	•	•	

DT	BK	CV	CR	PR	←Courts **HAMILTON**	Recording→	UC	RE	TX	VS
		•	•	•	Frazee Abstract & Title Co	800-736-7832	•	•	•	•
•	•	•	•		Research Information Services LLC	800-522-3884	•		•	

DT	BK	CV	CR	PR	←Courts **HARPER**	Recording→	UC	RE	TX	VS
•	•	•	•		Research Information Services LLC	800-522-3884	•		•	

DT	BK	CV	CR	PR	←Courts **HARVEY**	Recording→	UC	RE	TX	VS
•	•	•	•	•	Branda Agency [SOP]	800-310-8174	•	•	•	•
		•	•		Capital Inv Services Inc	800-633-7136				
•	•	•	•	•	Investigations LLC [SOP]	800-658-1688				
		•		•	Regier Title Co	316-283-2750	•	•	•	
•	•	•	•		Research Information Services LLC	800-522-3884	•		•	
•	•	•	•	•	SumData	620-241-5448	•	•	•	

DT	BK	CV	CR	PR	←Courts **HASKELL**	Recording→	UC	RE	TX	VS
		•	•	•	American Title & Abstract Specialists Inc	620-624-9111	•	•	•	•
		•	•	•	Haskell County Abstract & Title	620-675-2322	•	•	•	•

DT	BK	CV	CR	PR	←Courts	Recording→	UC	RE	TX	VS
•	•	•	•		Research Information Services LLC	800-522-3884	•		•	

DT	BK	CV	CR	PR	←Courts **HODGEMAN**	Recording→	UC	RE	TX	VS
		•	•	•	Hodgeman County Abstract & Title	620-357-8328	•	•	•	
•	•	•	•		Research Information Services LLC	800-522-3884	•		•	

DT	BK	CV	CR	PR	←Courts **JACKSON**	Recording→	UC	RE	TX	VS
		•	•		Capital Inv Services Inc	800-633-7136				
•	•	•	•		Research Information Services LLC	800-522-3884	•		•	

DT	BK	CV	CR	PR	←Courts **JEFFERSON**	Recording→	UC	RE	TX	VS
			•	•	Bi-State Title Search (Div of Bi-State Ind.)	866-450-7399	•	•	•	
		•	•		Capital Inv Services Inc	800-633-7136				
		•		•	Finley Abstract & Title Co	785-863-2271	•	•	•	
•	•	•	•		Research Information Services LLC	800-522-3884	•		•	

DT	BK	CV	CR	PR	←Courts **JEWELL**	Recording→	UC	RE	TX	VS
		•	•	•	Gail L Miller	785-378-3128			•	
•	•	•	•		Research Information Services LLC	800-522-3884	•		•	
		•	•	•	Weltner Law Office	785-378-3172	•	•	•	

DT	BK	CV	CR	PR	←Courts **JOHNSON**	Recording→	UC	RE	TX	VS
•	•	•	•		Armstrong Document Retrieval	913-341-1991	•	•	•	
			•	•	Bi-State Title Search (Div of Bi-State Ind.)	866-450-7399	•	•	•	
•	•	•	•	•	D & B Legal Services Inc [SOP]	913-963-1279	•	•	•	•
•	•	•	•		Executive Investigative Services [SOP]	800-764-9484	•	•	•	
•	•	•	•		Future Security Concepts	800-398-3051	•		•	
•	•	•	•	•	Hatfield Process Service [SOP]	816-842-9800	•	•	•	•
					Heartland Document Retrieval	888-221-2778 orders only	•	•	•	
•	•	•	•	•	KC Court Research Inc	913-239-8995	•	•	•	
•	•		•		LLG Enterprises	816-443-2396				
•		•		•	M & J Abstractors	913-727-3588	•	•	•	
•	•	•	•	•	Medlin Research Company	913-206-4615	•	•	•	
•	•	•	•		Research Information Services LLC	800-522-3884	•		•	
		•	•		Rigoli Searches	913-908-8863	•	•	•	
•	•	•			SearchWorks Inc	913-383-0940	•	•	•	

DT	BK	CV	CR	PR	←Courts **KEARNY**	Recording→	UC	RE	TX	VS
		•	•	•	Frazee Abstract & Title Co	800-736-7832	•	•	•	•
•	•	•	•		Research Information Services LLC	800-522-3884	•		•	

DT	BK	CV	CR	PR	←Courts **KINGMAN**	Recording→	UC	RE	TX	VS
•	•	•	•	•	Branda Agency [SOP]	800-310-8174	•	•	•	•
•	•	•	•	•	Investigations LLC [SOP]	800-658-1688				
		•		•	Kingman Abstract & Title Co Inc	620-532-2011		•	•	
•	•	•	•		Research Information Services LLC	800-522-3884	•		•	

DT	BK	CV	CR	PR	←Courts **KIOWA**	Recording→	UC	RE	TX	VS
•	•	•	•		Research Information Services LLC	800-522-3884	•		•	

DT	BK	CV	CR	PR	←Courts **LABETTE**	Recording→	UC	RE	TX	VS
•	•	•	•	•	American Research Unlimited Inc [SOP]	417-358-6494	•	•	•	•
•	•	•	•		Research Information Services LLC	800-522-3884	•		•	

DT	BK	CV	CR	PR	←Courts **LANE**	Recording→	UC	RE	TX	VS
•	•	•	•		Research Information Services LLC	800-522-3884	•		•	

DT	BK	CV	CR	PR	←Courts **LEAVENWORTH**	Recording→	UC	RE	TX	VS
			•	•	Bi-State Title Search (Div of Bi-State Ind.)	866-450-7399	•	•	•	
		•	•	•	Credit Bureau of Eudora Inc (CBE) [SOP]	785-542-1771	•	•	•	
•	•	•	•		Executive Investigative Services [SOP]	800-764-9484	•	•	•	
					Heartland Document Retrieval	888-221-2778 orders only	•	•	•	

DT	BK	CV	CR	PR	←Courts		Recording→	UC	RE	TX	VS
•	•		•		LLG Enterprises		816-443-2396				
•		•		•	M & J Abstractors		913-727-3588	•	•	•	
•	•	•	•		Research Information Services LLC		800-522-3884	•		•	
		•	•		Rigoli Searches		913-908-8863	•	•	•	
DT	**BK**	**CV**	**CR**	**PR**	**←Courts**	**LINCOLN**	**Recording→**	**UC**	**RE**	**TX**	**VS**
		•		•	Lincoln Home Title (KS)		785-524-4228	•	•	•	
•	•	•	•		Research Information Services LLC		800-522-3884	•		•	
DT	**BK**	**CV**	**CR**	**PR**	**←Courts**	**LINN**	**Recording→**	**UC**	**RE**	**TX**	**VS**
		•	•	•	Linn County Abstract Co		888-795-2949	•	•	•	
•	•	•	•		Research Information Services LLC		800-522-3884	•		•	
DT	**BK**	**CV**	**CR**	**PR**	**←Courts**	**LOGAN**	**Recording→**	**UC**	**RE**	**TX**	**VS**
•	•	•	•		Research Information Services LLC		800-522-3884	•		•	
DT	**BK**	**CV**	**CR**	**PR**	**←Courts**	**LYON**	**Recording→**	**UC**	**RE**	**TX**	**VS**
		•	•		Capital Inv Services Inc		800-633-7136				
		•		•	Moon Abstract Co		620-342-1917	•	•	•	
•	•	•	•		Research Information Services LLC		800-522-3884	•		•	
DT	**BK**	**CV**	**CR**	**PR**	**←Courts**	**MARION**	**Recording→**	**UC**	**RE**	**TX**	**VS**
		•	•		Capital Inv Services Inc		800-633-7136				
		•	•	•	Hannaford Abstract & Title Co		620-382-2130	•	•	•	•
•	•	•	•		Research Information Services LLC		800-522-3884	•		•	
•	•	•	•	•	SumData		620-241-5448	•	•	•	
DT	**BK**	**CV**	**CR**	**PR**	**←Courts**	**MARSHALL**	**Recording→**	**UC**	**RE**	**TX**	**VS**
•	•	•	•		Research Information Services LLC		800-522-3884	•		•	
DT	**BK**	**CV**	**CR**	**PR**	**←Courts**	**MCPHERSON**	**Recording→**	**UC**	**RE**	**TX**	**VS**
•	•	•	•	•	Branda Agency [SOP]		800-310-8174	•	•	•	•
		•	•		Capital Inv Services Inc		800-633-7136				
•	•	•	•		Research Information Services LLC		800-522-3884	•		•	
•	•	•	•	•	SumData		620-241-5448	•	•	•	
DT	**BK**	**CV**	**CR**	**PR**	**←Courts**	**MEADE**	**Recording→**	**UC**	**RE**	**TX**	**VS**
		•		•	Meade County Title		620-873-2756	•	•	•	
•	•	•	•		Research Information Services LLC		800-522-3884	•		•	
DT	**BK**	**CV**	**CR**	**PR**	**←Courts**	**MIAMI**	**Recording→**	**UC**	**RE**	**TX**	**VS**
			•	•	Bi-State Title Search (Div of Bi-State Ind.)		866-450-7399	•	•	•	
•	•	•	•		Executive Investigative Services [SOP]		800-764-9484	•	•	•	
					Heartland Document Retrieval		888-221-2778 orders only	•	•	•	
•	•	•	•	•	Medlin Research Company		913-206-4615	•	•	•	
•	•	•	•		Research Information Services LLC		800-522-3884	•		•	
DT	**BK**	**CV**	**CR**	**PR**	**←Courts**	**MITCHELL**	**Recording→**	**UC**	**RE**	**TX**	**VS**
		•	•	•	Attorney's Title Co		785-243-1357	•	•	•	
•	•	•	•		Research Information Services LLC		800-522-3884	•		•	
DT	**BK**	**CV**	**CR**	**PR**	**←Courts**	**MONTGOMERY**	**Recording→**	**UC**	**RE**	**TX**	**VS**
		•		•	Montgomery County Abstract Co		620-331-1440	•	•	•	
•	•	•	•		Research Information Services LLC		800-522-3884	•		•	
DT	**BK**	**CV**	**CR**	**PR**	**←Courts**	**MORRIS OR MORTON**	**Recording→**	**UC**	**RE**	**TX**	**VS**
•	•	•	•		Research Information Services LLC		800-522-3884	•		•	
DT	**BK**	**CV**	**CR**	**PR**	**←Courts**	**NEMAHA**	**Recording→**	**UC**	**RE**	**TX**	**VS**
		•		•	Nemaha County Abstract & Title Co		785-336-2137	•	•	•	•
•	•	•	•		Research Information Services LLC		800-522-3884	•		•	

DT	BK	CV	CR	PR	←Courts	Neosho Recording→	UC	RE	TX	VS
		•		•	Locke-Neosho Abstracts Inc	620-244-3641	•	•	•	
•	•	•	•		Research Information Services LLC	800-522-3884	•		•	
		•	•	•	Street Abstract Co	620-625-2421	•	•	•	

DT	BK	CV	CR	PR	←Courts	Ness Recording→	UC	RE	TX	VS
•	•	•	•		Research Information Services LLC	800-522-3884	•		•	

DT	BK	CV	CR	PR	←Courts	Norton Recording→	UC	RE	TX	VS
•	•	•	•		Research Information Services LLC	800-522-3884	•		•	
		•	•	•	Security Abstract Company	785-877-2141	•	•	•	•

DT	BK	CV	CR	PR	←Courts	Osage Recording→	UC	RE	TX	VS
		•	•		Capital Inv Services Inc	800-633-7136				
•	•	•	•		Research Information Services LLC	800-522-3884	•		•	

DT	BK	CV	CR	PR	←Courts	Osborne Recording→	UC	RE	TX	VS
		•	•	•	Gregory Abstract & Title Co Inc	785-346-5445	•	•	•	
•	•	•	•		Research Information Services LLC	800-522-3884	•		•	

DT	BK	CV	CR	PR	←Courts	Ottawa Recording→	UC	RE	TX	VS
		•	•	•	Attorney's Title Co	785-243-1357	•	•	•	
•	•	•	•		Research Information Services LLC	800-522-3884	•		•	

DT	BK	CV	CR	PR	←Courts	Pawnee Recording→	UC	RE	TX	VS
•	•	•	•		Research Information Services LLC	800-522-3884	•		•	
		•	•	•	Taylor Abstract & Title Inc	620-285-2026	•	•	•	

DT	BK	CV	CR	PR	←Courts	Phillips Recording→	UC	RE	TX	VS
•	•	•	•		Research Information Services LLC	800-522-3884	•		•	

DT	BK	CV	CR	PR	←Courts	Pottawatomie Recording→	UC	RE	TX	VS
		•	•		Capital Inv Services Inc	800-633-7136				
		•		•	Pottawatomie County Abstract Co	785-457-3441	•	•	•	•
•	•	•	•		Research Information Services LLC	800-522-3884	•		•	

DT	BK	CV	CR	PR	←Courts	Pratt Recording→	UC	RE	TX	VS
		•		•	Centennial Abstract of Pratt	620-672-5928	•	•	•	
•	•	•	•		Research Information Services LLC	800-522-3884	•		•	

DT	BK	CV	CR	PR	←Courts	Rawlins Recording→	UC	RE	TX	VS
		•	•	•	Decatur County Abstract	785-626-3885	•	•	•	•
•	•	•	•		Research Information Services LLC	800-522-3884	•		•	

DT	BK	CV	CR	PR	←Courts	Reno Recording→	UC	RE	TX	VS
•	•	•	•	•	Branda Agency [SOP]	800-310-8174	•	•	•	•
•	•	•	•	•	Investigations LLC [SOP]	800-658-1688				
•	•	•	•	•	Kansas Investigative Services Inc [SOP]	888-889-3340	•	•	•	•
•	•	•	•		Research Information Services LLC	800-522-3884	•		•	
•	•	•	•	•	SumData	620-241-5448	•	•	•	

DT	BK	CV	CR	PR	←Courts	Republic Recording→	UC	RE	TX	VS
		•	•	•	Attorney's Title Co	785-243-1357	•	•	•	
		•	•	•	Gail L Miller	785-378-3128			•	
•	•	•	•		Research Information Services LLC	800-522-3884	•		•	

DT	BK	CV	CR	PR	←Courts	Rice Recording→	UC	RE	TX	VS
		•	•		Capital Inv Services Inc	800-633-7136				
•	•	•	•		Research Information Services LLC	800-522-3884	•		•	

DT	BK	CV	CR	PR	←Courts	Riley Recording→	UC	RE	TX	VS
		•	•		Al Bernardi Backgrounds Process Svc [SOP]	785-456-8821	•	•	•	
		•	•		Capital Inv Services Inc	800-633-7136				

DT	BK	CV	CR	PR	←Courts		Recording→	UC	RE	TX	VS
		•		•	Charlson & Wilson Bonded Abstractors	785-537-2900		•	•	•	
•	•	•	•		Research Information Services LLC	800-522-3884		•		•	
					Rooks						
		•	•	•	Ellis County Abstract & Title Co	785-625-2316		•	•	•	•
•	•	•	•		Research Information Services LLC	800-522-3884		•		•	
					Rush						
		•	•	•	LaCrosse Abstract & Title LLC	800-256-6911		•	•	•	
•	•	•	•		Research Information Services LLC	800-522-3884		•		•	
					Russell						
•	•	•	•		Research Information Services LLC	800-522-3884		•		•	
					Saline						
		•		•	C W Lynn Abstract Co Inc	785-823-3706		•	•	•	
		•	•		Capital Inv Services Inc	800-633-7136					
•	•	•	•		Research Information Services LLC	800-522-3884		•		•	
•	•	•	•	•	SumData	620-241-5448		•	•	•	
					Scott						
•	•	•	•		Research Information Services LLC	800-522-3884		•		•	
•		•		•	Scott County Abstract & Title Co Inc	620-872-3470		•	•	•	•
					Sedgwick						
•	•	•	•	•	Branda Agency [SOP]	800-310-8174		•	•	•	•
•	•	•	•		Future Security Concepts	800-398-3051		•		•	
•	•	•	•	•	Investigations LLC [SOP]	800-658-1688					
•	•	•	•	•	Kansas Investigative Services Inc [SOP]	888-889-3340		•	•	•	•
•	•		•		LLG Enterprises	816-443-2396					
•	•	•	•		Research Information Services LLC	800-522-3884		•		•	
					Seward						
		•	•	•	American Title & Abstract Specialists Inc	620-624-9111		•	•	•	•
•	•	•	•		Research Information Services LLC	800-522-3884		•		•	
					Shawnee						
		•	•		Capital Inv Services Inc	800-633-7136					
		•	•	•	Credit Bureau of Eudora Inc (CBE) [SOP]	785-542-1771		•	•	•	
•	•	•	•		Future Security Concepts	800-398-3051		•		•	
•	•	•	•	•	Hatfield Process Service [SOP]	816-842-9800		•	•	•	•
					Heartland Document Retrieval	888-221-2778 orders only		•	•	•	
•	•		•		LLG Enterprises	816-443-2396					
•	•	•	•		Research Information Services LLC	800-522-3884		•		•	
•	•	•			Search Network Ltd (Kansas)	800-338-3618		•	•	•	•
					Sheridan						
•		•	•	•	First Insurance Agency of Hoxie Inc	800-569-0198		•	•	•	
•	•	•	•		Research Information Services LLC	800-522-3884		•		•	
					Sherman						
•	•	•	•		Research Information Services LLC	800-522-3884		•		•	
		•		•	Teeters Abstract & Title Co	785-890-7138		•	•	•	
					Smith						
		•		•	Collier Abstracts Inc	785-282-3351		•	•	•	
•	•	•	•		Research Information Services LLC	800-522-3884		•		•	
					Stafford						
•	•	•	•		Research Information Services LLC	800-522-3884		•		•	
		•		•	Stafford County Abstract & Title Co	620-549-3579		•	•	•	•
		•	•	•	Taylor Abstract & Title Inc	620-285-2026		•	•	•	

DT	BK	CV	CR	PR	←Courts STANTON	Recording→	UC	RE	TX	VS
		•	•	•	Frazee Abstract & Title Co	800-736-7832	•	•	•	•
•	•	•	•		Research Information Services LLC	800-522-3884	•		•	

DT	BK	CV	CR	PR	←Courts STEVENS	Recording→	UC	RE	TX	VS
		•	•	•	American Title & Abstract Specialists Inc	620-624-9111	•	•	•	•
		•	•	•	McQueen Abstract Company	620-544-2311		•	•	
•	•	•	•		Research Information Services LLC	800-522-3884	•		•	

DT	BK	CV	CR	PR	←Courts SUMNER	Recording→	UC	RE	TX	VS
		•	•	•	Barbour Title Co	866-379-0430	•	•	•	•
•	•	•	•	•	Branda Agency [SOP]	800-310-8174	•	•	•	•
•	•	•	•	•	Investigations LLC [SOP]	800-658-1688				
•	•	•	•		Research Information Services LLC	800-522-3884	•		•	

DT	BK	CV	CR	PR	←Courts THOMAS	Recording→	UC	RE	TX	VS
•		•	•	•	First Insurance Agency of Hoxie Inc	800-569-0198	•	•	•	
•	•	•	•		Research Information Services LLC	800-522-3884	•		•	
		•	•	•	The Gordon Company of Colby	785-462-7555	•	•	•	

DT	BK	CV	CR	PR	←Courts TREGO	Recording→	UC	RE	TX	VS
		•	•	•	Fowler Abstract & Title Inc	785-743-6422	•	•	•	•
•	•	•	•		Research Information Services LLC	800-522-3884	•		•	

DT	BK	CV	CR	PR	←Courts WABAUNSEE	Recording→	UC	RE	TX	VS
		•	•		Capital Inv Services Inc	800-633-7136				
•	•	•	•		Research Information Services LLC	800-522-3884	•		•	

DT	BK	CV	CR	PR	←Courts WALLACE	Recording→	UC	RE	TX	VS
•	•	•	•		Research Information Services LLC	800-522-3884	•		•	

DT	BK	CV	CR	PR	←Courts WASHINGTON	Recording→	UC	RE	TX	VS
		•	•	•	Attorney's Title Co	785-243-1357	•	•	•	
•	•	•	•		Research Information Services LLC	800-522-3884	•		•	

DT	BK	CV	CR	PR	←Courts WICHITA	Recording→	UC	RE	TX	VS
•	•	•	•		Research Information Services LLC	800-522-3884	•		•	

DT	BK	CV	CR	PR	←Courts WILSON	Recording→	UC	RE	TX	VS
		•		•	Fink Abstract Co	620-378-2351	•	•	•	•
•	•	•	•		Research Information Services LLC	800-522-3884	•		•	
		•	•	•	Street Abstract Co	620-625-2421	•	•	•	

DT	BK	CV	CR	PR	←Courts WOODSON	Recording→	UC	RE	TX	VS
•	•	•	•		Research Information Services LLC	800-522-3884	•		•	
		•	•	•	Street Abstract Co	620-625-2421	•	•	•	

DT	BK	CV	CR	PR	←Courts WYANDOTTE	Recording→	UC	RE	TX	VS
•	•	•	•		Armstrong Document Retrieval	913-341-1991	•	•	•	
			•	•	Bi-State Title Search (Div of Bi-State Ind.)	866-450-7399	•	•	•	
•	•	•	•	•	D & B Legal Services Inc [SOP]	913-963-1279	•	•	•	•
•	•	•	•		Executive Investigative Services [SOP]	800-764-9484	•	•	•	
•	•	•	•		Future Security Concepts	800-398-3051	•		•	
•	•	•		•	Connie Giandalia	816-217-1849	•	•	•	
•	•	•	•	•	Hatfield Process Service [SOP]	816-842-9800	•	•	•	•
					Heartland Document Retrieval	888-221-2778 orders only	•	•	•	
•	•	•	•	•	KC Court Research Inc	913-239-8995	•	•	•	
•	•		•		LLG Enterprises	816-443-2396				
•	•	•	•		Research Information Services LLC	800-522-3884	•		•	
•	•	•			SearchWorks Inc	913-383-0940	•	•	•	

Kentucky

COURT RECORDS RETRIEVED — **RECORDING RECORDS RETRIEVED**

DT	BK	CV	CR	PR	←COURTS		RECORDING→	UC	RE	TX	VS
						ADAIR					
					A & S Abstracting		270-250-1203		•	•	
DT	BK	CV	CR	PR	←COURTS	**ALLEN**	RECORDING→	UC	RE	TX	VS
		•	•		Hayes Inv [SOP]		270-781-7488				
DT	BK	CV	CR	PR	←COURTS	**ANDERSON**	RECORDING→	UC	RE	TX	VS
•	•	•			Equisearch		859-268-1206	•	•	•	
•	•	•			KY Search & Retrieval Services		859-252-6874	•	•	•	
DT	BK	CV	CR	PR	←COURTS	**BALLARD**	RECORDING→	UC	RE	TX	VS
					Western Kentucky Title		270-898-9666		•	•	
DT	BK	CV	CR	PR	←COURTS	**BARREN**	RECORDING→	UC	RE	TX	VS
					Jeanetta, Conner		270-746-4465		•	•	
		•	•		Hayes Inv [SOP]		270-781-7488				
		•		•	Attorney Reed Moore Jr		270-487-6262	•	•	•	
DT	BK	CV	CR	PR	←COURTS	**BATH**	RECORDING→	UC	RE	TX	VS
					All Search Title Co		606-474-4253		•	•	
DT	BK	CV	CR	PR	←COURTS	**BELL**	RECORDING→	UC	RE	TX	VS
					See adjoining counties for retrievers or contact court or recording office.						
DT	BK	CV	CR	PR	←COURTS	**BOONE**	RECORDING→	UC	RE	TX	VS
•	•	•	•	•	Active Detective Bureau Inc [SOP]		800-405-4006		•	•	•
		•	•		Criminal Information Network Inc		888-923-0271				
•	•	•	•	•	DDI Inc [SOP]		866-954-3000	•	•	•	•
					Document Retrieval Network Inc		859-654-2890	•	•	•	
					FarVision Consulting Title Co		304-733-5086		•	•	
•	•	•	•	•	General Corporate Inv - GCI [SOP]		800-735-7992	•	•	•	•
•	•	•			KY Search & Retrieval Services		859-252-6874	•	•	•	
			•		Phoenix Research Inc		800-260-1092				
		•	•		Real Land Abstract Inc		859-291-1140		•	•	
•	•	•	•		Search International Inc		859-342-0456	•	•	•	
•		•	•		Xpedite Wholesale Criminal Research		800-325-3609				
DT	BK	CV	CR	PR	←COURTS	**BOURBON**	RECORDING→	UC	RE	TX	VS
•	•	•			Equisearch		859-268-1206	•	•	•	
•	•	•			KY Search & Retrieval Services		859-252-6874	•	•	•	
DT	BK	CV	CR	PR	←COURTS	**BOYD**	RECORDING→	UC	RE	TX	VS
					All Search Title Co		606-474-4253		•	•	
•		•	•	•	Daniel Agency		606-324-6029	•	•	•	•
•	•	•	•	•	McBrayer McGinnis Leslie & Kirkland		606-473-7303	•	•	•	•
DT	BK	CV	CR	PR	←COURTS	**BOYLE**	RECORDING→	UC	RE	TX	VS
•	•	•			Equisearch		859-268-1206	•	•	•	
•	•	•			KY Search & Retrieval Services		859-252-6874	•	•	•	
DT	BK	CV	CR	PR	←COURTS	**BRACKEN**	RECORDING→	UC	RE	TX	VS
					FarVision Consulting Title Co		304-733-5086		•	•	
		•	•		Real Land Abstract Inc		859-291-1140		•	•	

DT	BK	CV	CR	PR	←Courts	County	Recording→	UC	RE	TX	VS
						BREATHITT					
					Irene Friend		606-464-2638	•	•	•	
						BRECKENRIDGE					
				•	Jerry Guffey		270-259-4828	•	•	•	•
						BULLITT					
•	•	•	•	•	Attorney Services of Kentucky [SOP]		502-327-6677	•	•	•	•
•	•	•			KY Data Search Inc		502-637-4658	•	•	•	
		•	•		Tracy Cuevas Record Retrieval		502-957-6459			•	
						BUTLER					
				•	Jerry Guffey		270-259-4828	•	•	•	•
		•	•		Hayes Inv [SOP]		270-781-7488				
						CALDWELL					
		•	•		Global Inv Agency [SOP]		800-597-2812				
						CALLOWAY					
					Western Kentucky Title		270-898-9666		•	•	
						CAMPBELL					
•	•	•	•	•	Active Detective Bureau Inc [SOP]		800-405-4006		•	•	•
		•	•		Criminal Information Network Inc		888-923-0271				
•	•	•	•	•	DDI Inc [SOP]		866-954-3000	•	•	•	•
					Document Retrieval Network Inc		859-654-2890	•	•	•	
•	•	•	•	•	General Corporate Inv - GCI [SOP]		800-735-7992	•	•	•	•
•	•	•			KY Search & Retrieval Services		859-252-6874	•	•	•	
			•		Phoenix Research Inc		800-260-1092				
		•	•		Real Land Abstract Inc		859-291-1140		•	•	
•	•	•	•		Search International Inc		859-342-0456	•	•	•	
•		•	•		Xpedite Wholesale Criminal Research		800-325-3609				
						CARLISLE					
					Dawn Curran Letcher		859-289-3745		•	•	
					Western Kentucky Title		270-898-9666		•	•	
						CARROLL					
		•	•		Real Land Abstract Inc		859-291-1140		•	•	
						CARTER					
					All Search Title Co		606-474-4253		•	•	
•		•	•	•	Daniel Agency		606-324-6029	•	•	•	•
•	•	•	•	•	McBrayer McGinnis Leslie & Kirkland		606-473-7303	•	•	•	•
						CASEY					
					See adjoining counties for retrievers or contact court or recording office.						
						CHRISTIAN					
		•	•		Global Inv Agency [SOP]		800-597-2812				
						CLARK					
•	•	•			Equisearch		859-268-1206	•	•	•	
•	•	•			KY Search & Retrieval Services		859-252-6874	•	•	•	
						CLAY					
					See adjoining counties for retrievers or contact court or recording office.						
						CLINTON					
		•	•		David Cross		606-387-6638		•	•	
						CRITTENDEN					
		•	•		Global Inv Agency [SOP]		800-597-2812				

DT	BK	CV	CR	PR	←COURTS	CUMBERLAND	RECORDING→	UC	RE	TX	VS
					Judd Law Office		270-864-3144		•	•	

DT	BK	CV	CR	PR	←COURTS	DAVIESS	RECORDING→	UC	RE	TX	VS
		•		•	Attorney John O Hicks III		270-273-5749	•	•	•	
•		•	•	•	Lindsey and Suyak Inv LLC [SOP]		270-281-0213	•	•	•	
•	•	•	•	•	Summit Documents		270-281-5406	•	•	•	•

DT	BK	CV	CR	PR	←COURTS	EDMONSON	RECORDING→	UC	RE	TX	VS
				•	Jerry Guffey		270-259-4828	•	•	•	•
		•	•		Hayes Inv [SOP]		270-781-7488				

DT	BK	CV	CR	PR	←COURTS	ELLIOTT	RECORDING→	UC	RE	TX	VS
					All Search Title Co		606-474-4253		•	•	
•		•	•	•	Daniel Agency		606-324-6029	•	•	•	•

DT	BK	CV	CR	PR	←COURTS	ESTILL	RECORDING→	UC	RE	TX	VS
					Irene Friend		606-464-2638	•	•	•	

DT	BK	CV	CR	PR	←COURTS	FAYETTE	RECORDING→	UC	RE	TX	VS
•	•	•	•	•	Attorney Services of Kentucky [SOP]		502-327-6677	•	•	•	•
					Document Retrieval Network Inc		859-654-2890	•	•	•	
•	•	•			Equisearch		859-268-1206	•	•	•	
•	•	•			KY Search & Retrieval Services		859-252-6874	•	•	•	
•	•	•	•	•	McBrayer McGinnis Leslie & Kirkland		606-473-7303	•	•	•	•
		•	•		Tracy Cuevas Record Retrieval		502-957-6459			•	
			•		VeriCORP, Inc		800-416-2769				

DT	BK	CV	CR	PR	←COURTS	FLEMING	RECORDING→	UC	RE	TX	VS
					All Search Title Co		606-474-4253		•	•	
•	•	•			KY Search & Retrieval Services		859-252-6874	•	•	•	

DT	BK	CV	CR	PR	←COURTS	FLOYD	RECORDING→	UC	RE	TX	VS
					All Search Title Co		606-474-4253		•	•	
•		•	•	•	Daniel Agency		606-324-6029	•	•	•	•

DT	BK	CV	CR	PR	←COURTS	FRANKLIN	RECORDING→	UC	RE	TX	VS
•	•	•	•	•	Attorney Services of Kentucky [SOP]		502-327-6677	•	•	•	•
•	•	•			Equisearch		859-268-1206	•	•	•	
•	•	•			KY Data Search Inc		502-637-4658	•	•	•	
•	•	•			KY Search & Retrieval Services		859-252-6874	•	•	•	
•	•	•	•	•	McBrayer McGinnis Leslie & Kirkland		606-473-7303	•	•	•	•
•	•	•	•	•	National Service Information Inc (Ohio)		800-235-0337	•		•	•

DT	BK	CV	CR	PR	←COURTS	FULTON	RECORDING→	UC	RE	TX	VS
•	•	•		•	Helen Lattus		731-884-9994	•	•	•	

DT	BK	CV	CR	PR	←COURTS	GALLATIN	RECORDING→	UC	RE	TX	VS
				•	Huddleston & Huddleston Law Firm		859-567-2818	•	•	•	

DT	BK	CV	CR	PR	←COURTS	GARRARD	RECORDING→	UC	RE	TX	VS
•	•	•			Equisearch		859-268-1206	•	•	•	
•	•	•			KY Search & Retrieval Services		859-252-6874	•	•	•	

DT	BK	CV	CR	PR	←COURTS	GRANT	RECORDING→	UC	RE	TX	VS
					Document Retrieval Network Inc		859-654-2890	•	•	•	
•	•	•			KY Search & Retrieval Services		859-252-6874	•	•	•	
		•	•		Real Land Abstract Inc		859-291-1140		•	•	
•	•	•	•		Search International Inc		859-342-0456	•	•	•	

DT	BK	CV	CR	PR	←COURTS	GRAVES	RECORDING→	UC	RE	TX	VS
					Western Kentucky Title		270-898-9666		•	•	

DT	BK	CV	CR	PR	←COURTS GRAYSON RECORDING→	UC	RE	TX	VS
				•	Jerry Guffey 270-259-4828	•	•	•	•

DT	BK	CV	CR	PR	←COURTS GREEN RECORDING→	UC	RE	TX	VS
					See adjoining counties for retrievers or contact court or recording office.				

DT	BK	CV	CR	PR	←COURTS GREENUP RECORDING→	UC	RE	TX	VS
					All Search Title Co 606-474-4253		•	•	
•		•	•	•	Daniel Agency 606-324-6029	•	•	•	•
•	•	•	•	•	McBrayer McGinnis Leslie & Kirkland....606-473-7303	•	•	•	•

DT	BK	CV	CR	PR	←COURTS HANCOCK RECORDING→	UC	RE	TX	VS
•		•	•	•	Lindsey and Suyak Inv LLC [SOP] 270-281-0213	•	•	•	
•	•	•	•	•	Summit Documents....270-281-5406	•	•	•	•

DT	BK	CV	CR	PR	←COURTS HARDIN RECORDING→	UC	RE	TX	VS
•	•	•	•	•	Attorney Services of Kentucky [SOP] 502-327-6677	•	•	•	•
				•	Jerry Guffey 270-259-4828	•	•	•	•
•	•	•			KY Data Search Inc 502-637-4658	•	•	•	
		•		•	Lincoln Trail Title Services Inc 270-765-5566	•	•	•	
		•	•		Tracy Cuevas Record Retrieval 502-957-6459	•	•	•	

DT	BK	CV	CR	PR	←COURTS HARLAN RECORDING→	UC	RE	TX	VS
					Laura Vance .... 606-574-1912, 606-273-2460 cell		•	•	

DT	BK	CV	CR	PR	←COURTS HARRISON RECORDING→	UC	RE	TX	VS
					Document Retrieval Network Inc....859-654-2890	•	•	•	
		•		•	Hood & Whalen 859-234-4321	•	•	•	•
•	•	•			KY Search & Retrieval Services 859-252-6874	•	•	•	

DT	BK	CV	CR	PR	←COURTS HART RECORDING→	UC	RE	TX	VS
				•	Jerry Guffey 270-259-4828	•	•	•	•

DT	BK	CV	CR	PR	←COURTS HENDERSON RECORDING→	UC	RE	TX	VS
•	•	•	•		D.G.I. LLC [SOP] 812-853-3222	•		•	•
		•	•		Global Inv Agency [SOP] 800-597-2812				
•	•	•	•	•	Summit Documents....270-281-5406	•	•	•	•

DT	BK	CV	CR	PR	←COURTS HENRY RECORDING→	UC	RE	TX	VS
•	•	•			KY Data Search Inc 502-637-4658	•	•	•	

DT	BK	CV	CR	PR	←COURTS HICKMAN RECORDING→	UC	RE	TX	VS
•	•	•		•	Helen Lattus 731-884-9994	•	•	•	

DT	BK	CV	CR	PR	←COURTS HOPKINS RECORDING→	UC	RE	TX	VS
		•	•		Global Inv Agency [SOP] 800-597-2812				

DT	BK	CV	CR	PR	←COURTS JACKSON RECORDING→	UC	RE	TX	VS
					Tommy Hayes....606-287-8891		•		

DT	BK	CV	CR	PR	←COURTS JEFFERSON RECORDING→	UC	RE	TX	VS
•	•	•	•	•	Attorney Services of Kentucky [SOP] 502-327-6677	•	•	•	•
					Document Retrieval Network Inc....859-654-2890	•	•	•	
•	•	•	•	•	Rick Hessig [SOP] 502-583-2453	•		•	•
•	•	•			KY Data Search Inc 502-637-4658	•	•	•	
		•	•		Tracy Cuevas Record Retrieval 502-957-6459			•	
			•		VeriCORP, Inc 800-416-2769				

DT	BK	CV	CR	PR	←COURTS JESSAMINE RECORDING→	UC	RE	TX	VS
•	•	•			Equisearch....859-268-1206	•	•	•	
•	•	•			KY Search & Retrieval Services....859-252-6874	•	•	•	

DT	BK	CV	CR	PR	←Courts **Johnson** Recording→		UC	RE	TX	VS
					All Search Title Co	606-474-4253		•	•	
•		•	•	•	Daniel Agency	606-324-6029	•	•	•	•

DT	BK	CV	CR	PR	←Courts **Kenton** Recording→		UC	RE	TX	VS
•	•	•	•	•	Active Detective Bureau Inc [SOP]	800-405-4006		•	•	•
•	•	•	•	•	Attorney Services of Kentucky [SOP]	502-327-6677	•	•	•	•
		•	•		Criminal Information Network Inc	888-923-0271				
•	•	•	•	•	DDI Inc [SOP]	866-954-3000	•	•	•	•
					Document Retrieval Network Inc	859-654-2890	•	•	•	
•	•	•	•	•	General Corporate Inv - GCI [SOP]	800-735-7992	•	•	•	•
•	•	•			KY Search & Retrieval Services	859-252-6874	•	•	•	
			•		Phoenix Research Inc	800-260-1092				
		•	•		Real Land Abstract Inc	859-291-1140		•	•	
•	•	•	•		Search International Inc	859-342-0456	•	•	•	
•		•	•		Xpedite Wholesale Criminal Research	800-325-3609				

DT	BK	CV	CR	PR	←Courts **Knott** Recording→	UC	RE	TX	VS

See adjoining counties for retrievers or contact court or recording office.

DT	BK	CV	CR	PR	←Courts **Knox** Recording→		UC	RE	TX	VS
					William Patrick Hauser	606-546-3811		•	•	

DT	BK	CV	CR	PR	←Courts **Larue** Recording→		UC	RE	TX	VS
					Lincoln Trail Title	270-765-5566		•	•	

DT	BK	CV	CR	PR	←Courts **Laurel** Recording→		UC	RE	TX	VS
•	•	•			KY Search & Retrieval Services	859-252-6874	•	•	•	

DT	BK	CV	CR	PR	←Courts **Lawrence** Recording→		UC	RE	TX	VS
					All Search Title Co	606-474-4253		•	•	
•		•	•	•	Daniel Agency	606-324-6029	•	•	•	•
•	•	•	•	•	McBrayer McGinnis Leslie & Kirkland	606-473-7303	•	•	•	•

DT	BK	CV	CR	PR	←Courts **Lee** Recording→		UC	RE	TX	VS
					Irene Friend	606-464-2638	•	•	•	

DT	BK	CV	CR	PR	←Courts **Leslie** Recording→		UC	RE	TX	VS
		•	•	•	Attorney Leonard Brashear	606-672-3577	•	•	•	

DT	BK	CV	CR	PR	←Courts **Letcher** Recording→	UC	RE	TX	VS

See adjoining counties for retrievers or contact court or recording office.

DT	BK	CV	CR	PR	←Courts **Lewis** Recording→		UC	RE	TX	VS
					All Search Title Co	606-474-4253		•	•	
•	•	•	•	•	McBrayer McGinnis Leslie & Kirkland	606-473-7303	•	•	•	•

DT	BK	CV	CR	PR	←Courts **Lincoln** Recording→		UC	RE	TX	VS
•	•	•			Equisearch	859-268-1206	•	•	•	
•	•	•			KY Search & Retrieval Services	859-252-6874	•	•	•	

DT	BK	CV	CR	PR	←Courts **Livingston** Recording→		UC	RE	TX	VS
					Richard Peek Jr Attny	270-928-4523		•	•	

DT	BK	CV	CR	PR	←Courts **Logan** Recording→		UC	RE	TX	VS
		•	•		Hayes Inv [SOP]	270-781-7488				

DT	BK	CV	CR	PR	←Courts **Lyon** Recording→		UC	RE	TX	VS
		•	•	•	William R Young	270-388-0807		•	•	

DT	BK	CV	CR	PR	←Courts **Madison** Recording→		UC	RE	TX	VS
•	•	•			Equisearch	859-268-1206	•	•	•	
•	•	•			KY Search & Retrieval Services	859-252-6874	•	•	•	

DT	BK	CV	CR	PR	←Courts	Magoffin	Recording→	UC	RE	TX	VS
					See adjoining counties for retrievers or contact court or recording office.						

DT	BK	CV	CR	PR	←Courts	Marion	Recording→	UC	RE	TX	VS
		•		•	Avritt & Avritt		270-692-4270	•	•	•	•

DT	BK	CV	CR	PR	←Courts	Marshall	Recording→	UC	RE	TX	VS
					Western Kentucky Title		270-898-9666		•	•	

DT	BK	CV	CR	PR	←Courts	Martin	Recording→	UC	RE	TX	VS
					All Search Title Co		606-474-4253		•	•	
•		•	•	•	Daniel Agency		606-324-6029	•	•	•	•

DT	BK	CV	CR	PR	←Courts	Mason	Recording→	UC	RE	TX	VS
					All Search Title Co		606-474-4253		•	•	
		•	•		Real Land Abstract Inc		859-291-1140		•	•	

DT	BK	CV	CR	PR	←Courts	Mc Cracken	Recording→	UC	RE	TX	VS
					Western Kentucky Title		270-898-9666		•	•	

DT	BK	CV	CR	PR	←Courts	Mc Creary	Recording→	UC	RE	TX	VS
					Vickie King Paralegal		606-376-5931		•		

DT	BK	CV	CR	PR	←Courts	Mc Lean	Recording→	UC	RE	TX	VS
		•	•		Global Inv Agency [SOP]		800-597-2812				
		•		•	Attorney John O Hicks III		270-273-5749	•	•	•	

DT	BK	CV	CR	PR	←Courts	Meade	Recording→	UC	RE	TX	VS
•	•	•	•	•	Attorney Services of Kentucky [SOP]		502-327-6677	•	•	•	•
•	•	•			KY Data Search Inc		502-637-4658	•	•	•	

DT	BK	CV	CR	PR	←Courts	Menifee	Recording→	UC	RE	TX	VS
					All Search Title Co		606-474-4253		•	•	

DT	BK	CV	CR	PR	←Courts	Mercer	Recording→	UC	RE	TX	VS
•	•	•			Equisearch		859-268-1206	•	•	•	
•	•	•			KY Search & Retrieval Services		859-252-6874	•	•	•	

DT	BK	CV	CR	PR	←Courts	Metcalfe	Recording→	UC	RE	TX	VS
					Jeanetta, Conner		270-746-4465		•	•	

DT	BK	CV	CR	PR	←Courts	Monroe	Recording→	UC	RE	TX	VS
		•		•	Attorney Reed Moore Jr		270-487-6262	•	•	•	

DT	BK	CV	CR	PR	←Courts	Montgomery	Recording→	UC	RE	TX	VS
					All Search Title Co		606-474-4253		•	•	
•	•	•			Equisearch		859-268-1206	•	•	•	
•	•	•			KY Search & Retrieval Services		859-252-6874	•	•	•	

DT	BK	CV	CR	PR	←Courts	Morgan	Recording→	UC	RE	TX	VS
					All Search Title Co		606-474-4253		•	•	
•		•	•	•	Daniel Agency		606-324-6029	•	•	•	•

DT	BK	CV	CR	PR	←Courts	Muhlenberg	Recording→	UC	RE	TX	VS
		•	•		Global Inv Agency [SOP]		800-597-2812				
		•		•	Attorney John O Hicks III		270-273-5749	•	•	•	

DT	BK	CV	CR	PR	←Courts	Nelson	Recording→	UC	RE	TX	VS
•	•	•	•	•	Attorney Services of Kentucky [SOP]		502-327-6677	•	•	•	•
•	•	•			KY Data Search Inc		502-637-4658	•	•	•	
		•	•		Tracy Cuevas Record Retrieval		502-957-6459			•	

DT	BK	CV	CR	PR	←Courts	Nicholas	Recording→	UC	RE	TX	VS
					See adjoining counties for retrievers or contact court or recording office.						

DT	BK	CV	CR	PR	←Courts	Ohio	Recording→	UC	RE	TX	VS
				•	Jerry Guffey		270-259-4828	•	•	•	•
•		•	•	•	Lindsey and Suyak Inv LLC [SOP]		270-281-0213	•	•	•	
•	•	•	•	•	Summit Documents		270-281-5406	•	•	•	•

DT	BK	CV	CR	PR	←Courts	Oldham	Recording→	UC	RE	TX	VS
•	•	•	•	•	Attorney Services of Kentucky [SOP]		502-327-6677	•	•	•	•
•	•	•			KY Data Search Inc		502-637-4658	•	•	•	
		•	•		Tracy Cuevas Record Retrieval		502-957-6459			•	
			•		VeriCORP, Inc		800-416-2769				

DT	BK	CV	CR	PR	←Courts	Owen	Recording→	UC	RE	TX	VS
		•	•		Real Land Abstract Inc		859-291-1140		•	•	

DT	BK	CV	CR	PR	←Courts	Owsley	Recording→	UC	RE	TX	VS
					Irene Friend		606-464-2638	•	•	•	

DT	BK	CV	CR	PR	←Courts	Pendleton	Recording→	UC	RE	TX	VS
					Document Retrieval Network Inc		859-654-2890	•	•	•	
		•	•		Real Land Abstract Inc		859-291-1140		•	•	
•	•	•	•		Search International Inc		859-342-0456	•	•	•	

DT	BK	CV	CR	PR	←Courts	Perry	Recording→	UC	RE	TX	VS

See adjoining counties for retrievers or contact court or recording office.

DT	BK	CV	CR	PR	←Courts	Pike	Recording→	UC	RE	TX	VS
•		•	•	•	Daniel Agency		606-324-6029	•	•	•	•

DT	BK	CV	CR	PR	←Courts	Powell	Recording→	UC	RE	TX	VS
					Irene Friend		606-464-2638	•	•	•	

DT	BK	CV	CR	PR	←Courts	Pulaski	Recording→	UC	RE	TX	VS
					Robin Fisher Paralegal		606-219-1700		•		

DT	BK	CV	CR	PR	←Courts	Robertson	Recording→	UC	RE	TX	VS
					Jesse Melcher, Attny		606-724-5322		•	•	

DT	BK	CV	CR	PR	←Courts	Rockcastle	Recording→	UC	RE	TX	VS
					Adams Freelance Title		606-365-8108		•	•	

DT	BK	CV	CR	PR	←Courts	Rowan	Recording→	UC	RE	TX	VS
					All Search Title Co		606-474-4253		•	•	
•		•	•	•	Daniel Agency		606-324-6029	•	•	•	•

DT	BK	CV	CR	PR	←Courts	Russell	Recording→	UC	RE	TX	VS
					Courtesy Title		270-343-4486		•	•	

DT	BK	CV	CR	PR	←Courts	Scott	Recording→	UC	RE	TX	VS
•	•	•			Equisearch		859-268-1206	•	•	•	
•	•	•			KY Search & Retrieval Services		859-252-6874	•	•	•	

DT	BK	CV	CR	PR	←Courts	Shelby	Recording→	UC	RE	TX	VS
•	•	•	•	•	Attorney Services of Kentucky [SOP]		502-327-6677	•	•	•	•
•	•	•			KY Data Search Inc		502-637-4658	•	•	•	
			•		VeriCORP, Inc		800-416-2769				

DT	BK	CV	CR	PR	←Courts	Simpson	Recording→	UC	RE	TX	VS
		•	•		Hayes Inv [SOP]		270-781-7488				

DT	BK	CV	CR	PR	←Courts	Spencer	Recording→	UC	RE	TX	VS
•	•	•			KY Data Search Inc		502-637-4658	•	•	•	

DT	BK	CV	CR	PR	←Courts	Taylor	Recording→	UC	RE	TX	VS
					Cumberland Title		606-787-8743		•	•	

DT	BK	CV	CR	PR	←Courts	TODD	Recording→	UC	RE	TX	VS
		•	•			Global Inv Agency [SOP]	800-597-2812				

DT	BK	CV	CR	PR	←Courts	TRIGG	Recording→	UC	RE	TX	VS
						Quinn and Woodall Attnys	270-522-3481		•	•	

DT	BK	CV	CR	PR	←Courts	TRIMBLE	Recording→	UC	RE	TX	VS
		•	•			Real Land Abstract Inc	859-291-1140		•	•	

DT	BK	CV	CR	PR	←Courts	UNION	Recording→	UC	RE	TX	VS
			•			Phoenix Research Inc	800-260-1092				

DT	BK	CV	CR	PR	←Courts	WARREN	Recording→	UC	RE	TX	VS
						Jeanetta, Conner	270-746-4465		•	•	
		•	•			Hayes Inv [SOP]	270-781-7488				

DT	BK	CV	CR	PR	←Courts	WASHINGTON	Recording→	UC	RE	TX	VS
						Theresa Marrinan	859-336-5425		•	•	

DT	BK	CV	CR	PR	←Courts	WAYNE	Recording→	UC	RE	TX	VS
						Terry Kirkland	606-348-8645				

DT	BK	CV	CR	PR	←Courts	WEBSTER	Recording→	UC	RE	TX	VS
		•	•			Global Inv Agency [SOP]	800-597-2812				
•	•	•	•	•		Summit Documents	270-281-5406	•	•	•	•

DT	BK	CV	CR	PR	←Courts	WHITLEY	Recording→	UC	RE	TX	VS
						South Eastern Data	606-679-1688		•	•	

DT	BK	CV	CR	PR	←Courts	WOLFE	Recording→	UC	RE	TX	VS
						Irene Friend	606-464-2638	•	•	•	

DT	BK	CV	CR	PR	←Courts	WOODFORD	Recording→	UC	RE	TX	VS
•	•	•				Equisearch	859-268-1206	•	•	•	
•	•	•				KY Search & Retrieval Services	859-252-6874	•	•	•	

Editor's Tip: Sending an unsolicited fax is not recommended, and it is not legal. So, before faxing to a potential new retriever contact, we recommend that you first make a courtesy call, and ask for permission to fax to them.

Louisiana

COURT RECORDS RETRIEVED							RECORDING RECORDS RETRIEVED			
DT	BK	CV	CR	PR	←COURTS **ACADIA**	RECORDING→	UC	RE	TX	VS
•	•	•	•	•	ABC Investigators Inc [SOP]	800-738-7300	•	•	•	
•	•	•			Bayou Investigations Inc [SOP]	800-256-9009	•			
•	•	•	•	•	TENSTAR Corporation (Crowley) [SOP]	800-960-2214	•	•	•	•
DT	BK	CV	CR	PR	←COURTS **ALLEN**	RECORDING→	UC	RE	TX	VS
•	•	•	•	•	Abstracting & Legal Research Inc	318-473-9979	•	•	•	•
•	•	•	•	•	TENSTAR Corporation (Main Office) [SOP]	800-960-2214	•	•	•	•
DT	BK	CV	CR	PR	←COURTS **ASCENSION**	RECORDING→	UC	RE	TX	VS
•	•	•		•	Abstracts by Godail	800-660-7318	•	•	•	
		•		•	Ascension Title Services Inc	225-647-8051	•	•	•	
•	•	•	•	•	Bombet Cashio & Associates [SOP]	800-256-5333	•	•	•	•
•		•	•	•	Kerry H Callahan [SOP]	225-752-8750	•			•
•	•	•	•	•	Faith to Faith Legal Productions	225-685-0008	•	•	•	
•	•	•	•		P & A Research Service [SOP]	225-268-2777	•	•	•	
•	•	•	•	•	TENSTAR Corporation (Baton Rouge) [SOP]	800-864-5154	•	•	•	•
•	•	•	•		Vinson Detective Agency [SOP]	800-441-7899	•	•	•	
DT	BK	CV	CR	PR	←COURTS **ASSUMPTION**	RECORDING→	UC	RE	TX	VS
•	•	•		•	Abstracts by Godail	800-660-7318	•	•	•	
•	•	•	•	•	Faith to Faith Legal Productions	225-685-0008	•	•	•	
•	•	•	•	•	TENSTAR Corporation (New Orleans) [SOP]	800-856-8515	•	•	•	•
DT	BK	CV	CR	PR	←COURTS **AVOYELLES**	RECORDING→	UC	RE	TX	VS
•	•	•	•	•	Abstracting & Legal Research Inc	318-473-9979	•	•	•	•
•	•	•	•	•	TENSTAR Corporation (Baton Rouge) [SOP]	800-864-5154	•	•	•	•
DT	BK	CV	CR	PR	←COURTS **BEAUREGARD**	RECORDING→	UC	RE	TX	VS
				•	Beauregard Abstract Co	337-463-7090	•	•	•	
•	•	•	•	•	Pelican Land & Abstract Co Inc	337-436-3419	•	•	•	•
•	•	•	•	•	TENSTAR Corporation (Main Office) [SOP]	800-960-2214	•	•	•	•
DT	BK	CV	CR	PR	←COURTS **BIENVILLE**	RECORDING→	UC	RE	TX	VS
•	•	•		•	Access Louisiana Inc	800-489-5620	•	•	•	•
		•		•	M & M Title / Mitchell Co	318-798-1198	•	•	•	
•	•	•	•	•	North Louisiana Title Co Inc	800-515-7715	•	•	•	
•	•	•	•	•	TENSTAR Corporation (Shreveport)	800-960-2214	•	•	•	•
DT	BK	CV	CR	PR	←COURTS **BOSSIER**	RECORDING→	UC	RE	TX	VS
•	•	•		•	Access Louisiana Inc	800-489-5620	•	•	•	•
•	•	•	•	•	All The Facts [SOP]	866-401-5676	•	•	•	•
•	•	•	•	•	Bradley Enterprises LLC	318-868-4906	•	•	•	
•	•	•	•		J & J Research	318-686-3109	•			
		•		•	M & M Title / Mitchell Co	318-798-1198	•	•	•	
•	•	•	•	•	North Louisiana Title Co Inc	800-515-7715	•	•	•	
•	•	•	•	•	Southern Research Company [SOP]	888-772-6953	•	•	•	
•	•	•	•	•	TENSTAR Corporation (Shreveport)	800-960-2214	•	•	•	•
•	•	•	•		Vinson Detective Agency [SOP]	800-441-7899	•	•	•	
DT	BK	CV	CR	PR	←COURTS **CADDO**	RECORDING→	UC	RE	TX	VS
•	•	•		•	Access Louisiana Inc	800-489-5620	•	•	•	•

DT	BK	CV	CR	PR	←Courts	Recording→	UC	RE	TX	VS
•	•	•	•	•	All The Facts [SOP]	866-401-5676	•	•	•	•
•	•	•	•	•	Bradley Enterprises LLC	318-868-4906	•	•	•	
•	•	•	•		J & J Research	318-686-3109	•			
		•		•	M & M Title / Mitchell Co	318-798-1198	•	•	•	
•	•	•	•	•	North Louisiana Title Co Inc	800-515-7715	•	•	•	
•	•	•	•	•	Southern Research Company [SOP]	888-772-6953	•	•	•	
•	•	•	•	•	TENSTAR Corporation (Shreveport)	800-960-2214	•	•	•	•
•	•	•	•		Vinson Detective Agency [SOP]	800-441-7899	•	•	•	

DT	BK	CV	CR	PR	←Courts **Calcasieu**	Recording→	UC	RE	TX	VS
			•		Donna Eccles	337-558-6627				
•	•	•	•	•	Pelican Land & Abstract Co Inc	337-436-3419	•	•	•	•
•	•	•	•	•	Tactical Private Inv [SOP]	800-779-4893	•	•	•	•
•	•	•	•	•	TENSTAR Corporation (Main Office) [SOP]	800-960-2214	•	•	•	•
•	•	•	•		Vinson Detective Agency [SOP]	800-441-7899	•	•	•	

DT	BK	CV	CR	PR	←Courts **Caldwell**	Recording→	UC	RE	TX	VS
•	•	•	•	•	North Louisiana Title Co Inc	800-515-7715	•	•	•	
•	•	•	•	•	TENSTAR Corporation (Main Office) [SOP]	800-960-2214	•	•	•	•

DT	BK	CV	CR	PR	←Courts **Cameron**	Recording→	UC	RE	TX	VS
•	•	•	•	•	Pelican Land & Abstract Co Inc	337-436-3419	•	•	•	•
•	•	•	•	•	TENSTAR Corporation (Main Office) [SOP]	800-960-2214	•	•	•	•

DT	BK	CV	CR	PR	←Courts **Catahoula**	Recording→	UC	RE	TX	VS
•	•	•	•	•	North Louisiana Title Co Inc	800-515-7715	•	•	•	
•	•	•	•	•	TENSTAR Corporation (Main Office) [SOP]	800-960-2214	•	•	•	•

DT	BK	CV	CR	PR	←Courts **Claiborne**	Recording→	UC	RE	TX	VS
•	•	•		•	Access Louisiana Inc	800-489-5620	•	•	•	•
		•		•	M & M Title / Mitchell Co	318-798-1198	•	•	•	
•	•	•	•	•	North Louisiana Title Co Inc	800-515-7715	•	•	•	
•	•	•	•	•	TENSTAR Corporation (Shreveport)	800-960-2214	•	•	•	•

DT	BK	CV	CR	PR	←Courts **Concordia**	Recording→	UC	RE	TX	VS
•	•	•	•	•	North Louisiana Title Co Inc	800-515-7715	•	•	•	
•	•	•	•	•	TENSTAR Corporation (Baton Rouge) [SOP]	800-864-5154	•	•	•	•

DT	BK	CV	CR	PR	←Courts **DeSoto**	Recording→	UC	RE	TX	VS
•	•	•		•	Access Louisiana Inc	800-489-5620	•	•	•	•
		•		•	M & M Title / Mitchell Co	318-798-1198	•	•	•	
•	•	•			Mary Lindsey Research	225-654-6576				
•	•	•	•	•	TENSTAR Corporation (Shreveport)	800-960-2214	•	•	•	•

DT	BK	CV	CR	PR	←Courts **East Baton Rouge**	Recording→	UC	RE	TX	VS
•	•	•		•	Abstracts by Godail	800-660-7318	•	•	•	
		•	•		AccuScreen Systems [SOP]	800-383-6476				
	•	•	•	•	Judy J Badon/Public Records Specialists	225-291-5537	•	•	•	
•	•	•	•	•	Bombet Cashio & Associates [SOP]	800-256-5333	•	•	•	•
•		•	•	•	Kerry H Callahan [SOP]	225-752-8750	•			•
•		•			Capitol Corporate Services Inc (Louisiana)	800-408-1262	•		•	
•	•	•	•	•	Faith to Faith Legal Productions	225-685-0008	•	•	•	
•	•	•	•	•	Genco Services [SOP]	225-216-9595	•	•	•	•
•	•	•	•	•	Hollingsworth Court Reporting Inc	225-769-3386		•	•	
•	•	•	•	•	TENSTAR Corporation (Baton Rouge) [SOP]	800-864-5154	•	•	•	•
•	•	•	•		Vinson Detective Agency [SOP]	800-441-7899	•	•	•	

DT	BK	CV	CR	PR	←Courts **East Carroll**	Recording→	UC	RE	TX	VS
•	•	•	•	•	North Louisiana Title Co Inc	800-515-7715	•	•	•	
•	•	•	•	•	TENSTAR Corporation (Main Office) [SOP]	800-960-2214	•	•	•	•

DT	BK	CV	CR	PR	←Courts	East Feliciana	Recording→	UC	RE	TX	VS
•	•	•	•	•		TENSTAR Corporation (Baton Rouge) [SOP]	800-864-5154	•	•	•	•

DT	BK	CV	CR	PR	←Courts	Evangeline	Recording→	UC	RE	TX	VS
•	•	•	•	•		Abstracting & Legal Research Inc	318-473-9979	•	•	•	•
•	•	•	•			Bayou Investigations Inc [SOP]	800-256-9009	•			
•	•	•	•	•		TENSTAR Corporation (Main Office) [SOP]	800-960-2214	•	•	•	•

DT	BK	CV	CR	PR	←Courts	Franklin	Recording→	UC	RE	TX	VS
•	•	•	•	•		North Louisiana Title Co Inc	800-515-7715	•	•	•	
•	•	•	•	•		TENSTAR Corporation (Main Office) [SOP]	800-960-2214	•	•	•	•

DT	BK	CV	CR	PR	←Courts	Grant	Recording→	UC	RE	TX	VS
•	•	•	•	•		Abstracting & Legal Research Inc	318-473-9979	•	•	•	•
•	•	•	•	•		North Louisiana Title Co Inc	800-515-7715	•	•	•	
•	•	•	•	•		TENSTAR Corporation (Main Office) [SOP]	800-960-2214	•	•	•	•

DT	BK	CV	CR	PR	←Courts	Iberia	Recording→	UC	RE	TX	VS
•	•	•	•			Bayou Investigations Inc [SOP]	800-256-9009	•			
•	•	•	•	•		TENSTAR Corporation (Main Office) [SOP]	800-960-2214	•	•	•	•
•	•	•	•			Vinson Detective Agency [SOP]	800-441-7899	•	•	•	

DT	BK	CV	CR	PR	←Courts	Iberville	Recording→	UC	RE	TX	VS
		•		•		Ascension Title Services Inc	225-647-8051	•	•	•	
•	•	•	•	•		Bombet Cashio & Associates [SOP]	800-256-5333	•	•	•	•
•		•	•	•		Kerry H Callahan [SOP]	225-752-8750	•			•
•	•	•	•	•		Faith to Faith Legal Productions	225-685-0008	•	•	•	
•	•	•	•	•		Genco Services [SOP]	225-216-9595	•	•	•	•
•	•	•	•	•		TENSTAR Corporation (Baton Rouge) [SOP]	800-864-5154	•	•	•	•
•	•	•	•			Vinson Detective Agency [SOP]	800-441-7899	•	•	•	

DT	BK	CV	CR	PR	←Courts	Jackson	Recording→	UC	RE	TX	VS
•	•	•	•	•		North Louisiana Title Co Inc	800-515-7715	•	•	•	
•	•	•	•	•		TENSTAR Corporation (Main Office) [SOP]	800-960-2214	•	•	•	•

DT	BK	CV	CR	PR	←Courts	Jefferson	Recording→	UC	RE	TX	VS
•	•	•	•			Analytical Inspection Services	504-832-0869	•	•		
•	•	•	•	•		Bombet Cashio & Associates [SOP]	800-256-5333	•	•	•	•
•	•	•				Darren J Harper & Associates [SOP]	800-962-4907		•	•	
•		•	•			Powell's Backtracking [SOP]	504-242-7700				
•	•	•	•	•		TENSTAR Corporation (New Orleans) [SOP]	800-856-8515	•	•	•	•
•	•	•	•			Vinson Detective Agency [SOP]	800-441-7899	•	•	•	

DT	BK	CV	CR	PR	←Courts	Jefferson Davis	Recording→	UC	RE	TX	VS
•	•	•	•	•		ABC Investigators Inc [SOP]	800-738-7300	•	•	•	
•	•	•	•			Bayou Investigations Inc [SOP]	800-256-9009	•			
•	•	•	•	•		Pelican Land & Abstract Co Inc	337-436-3419	•	•	•	•
•	•	•	•	•		TENSTAR Corporation (Crowley) [SOP]	800-960-2214	•	•	•	•

DT	BK	CV	CR	PR	←Courts	La Salle	Recording→	UC	RE	TX	VS
•	•	•	•	•		North Louisiana Title Co Inc	800-515-7715	•	•	•	
•	•	•	•	•		TENSTAR Corporation (Main Office) [SOP]	800-960-2214	•	•	•	•

DT	BK	CV	CR	PR	←Courts	Lafayette	Recording→	UC	RE	TX	VS
•	•	•	•	•		ABC Investigators Inc [SOP]	800-738-7300	•	•	•	
•	•	•	•			Bayou Investigations Inc [SOP]	800-256-9009	•			
•	•	•	•	•		TENSTAR Corporation (Main Office) [SOP]	800-960-2214	•	•	•	•
•	•	•	•			Vinson Detective Agency [SOP]	800-441-7899	•	•	•	

DT	BK	CV	CR	PR	←Courts	Lafourche	Recording→	UC	RE	TX	VS
		•	•	•		Jerry M Braud	985-447-1227	•	•	•	
•	•	•	•			P & A Research Service [SOP]	225-268-2777	•	•	•	

DT	BK	CV	CR	PR			UC	RE	TX	VS
•	•	•	•	•	TENSTAR Corporation (New Orleans) [SOP]	800-856-8515	•	•	•	•
•	•	•	•		Vinson Detective Agency [SOP]	800-441-7899	•	•	•	

DT	BK	CV	CR	PR	←COURTS LINCOLN	RECORDING→	UC	RE	TX	VS
		•		•	M & M Title / Mitchell Co	318-798-1198	•	•	•	
•	•	•	•	•	North Louisiana Title Co Inc	800-515-7715	•	•	•	
•		•	•		Princess McDonald Process & Record Retrieval [SOP]	318-323-8566				•
•	•	•	•	•	TENSTAR Corporation (Main Office) [SOP]	800-960-2214	•	•	•	•

DT	BK	CV	CR	PR	←COURTS LIVINGSTON	RECORDING→	UC	RE	TX	VS
•	•	•		•	Abstracts by Godail	800-660-7318	•	•	•	
•		•	•	•	Kerry H Callahan [SOP]	225-752-8750	•			•
•	•	•	•	•	Faith to Faith Legal Productions	225-685-0008	•	•	•	
		•	•	•	Professional Choice Services	225-294-3703	•	•	•	•
•	•	•	•	•	TENSTAR Corporation (Baton Rouge) [SOP]	800-864-5154	•	•	•	•

DT	BK	CV	CR	PR	←COURTS MADISON	RECORDING→	UC	RE	TX	VS
•	•	•	•	•	North Louisiana Title Co Inc	800-515-7715	•	•	•	
•		•	•		Princess McDonald Process & Record Retrieval [SOP]	318-323-8566				•
•	•	•	•	•	TENSTAR Corporation (Main Office) [SOP]	800-960-2214	•	•	•	•

DT	BK	CV	CR	PR	←COURTS MOREHOUSE	RECORDING→	UC	RE	TX	VS
•	•	•	•	•	North Louisiana Title Co Inc	800-515-7715	•	•	•	
•		•	•		Princess McDonald Process & Record Retrieval [SOP]	318-323-8566				•
•	•	•	•	•	TENSTAR Corporation (Main Office) [SOP]	800-960-2214	•	•	•	•

DT	BK	CV	CR	PR	←COURTS NATCHITOCHES	RECORDING→	UC	RE	TX	VS
•	•	•	•	•	Abstracting & Legal Research Inc	318-473-9979	•	•	•	•
•	•	•	•	•	TENSTAR Corporation (Shreveport)	800-960-2214	•	•	•	•

DT	BK	CV	CR	PR	←COURTS ORLEANS	RECORDING→	UC	RE	TX	VS
•	•	•	•		Analytical Inspection Services	504-832-0869	•	•		
•	•	•	•	•	Bombet Cashio & Associates [SOP]	800-256-5333	•	•	•	•
•	•	•			Darren J Harper & Associates [SOP]	800-962-4907		•	•	
•		•	•		Powell's Backtracking [SOP]	504-242-7700				
•	•	•	•	•	TENSTAR Corporation (New Orleans) [SOP]	800-856-8515	•	•	•	•
•	•	•	•		Vinson Detective Agency [SOP]	800-441-7899	•	•	•	

DT	BK	CV	CR	PR	←COURTS OUACHITA	RECORDING→	UC	RE	TX	VS
•	•	•	•	•	North Louisiana Title Co Inc	800-515-7715	•	•	•	
•		•	•		Princess McDonald Process & Record Retrieval [SOP]	318-323-8566				•
•	•	•	•	•	TENSTAR Corporation (Main Office) [SOP]	800-960-2214	•	•	•	•
•	•	•	•		Vinson Detective Agency [SOP]	800-441-7899	•	•	•	

DT	BK	CV	CR	PR	←COURTS PLAQUEMINES	RECORDING→	UC	RE	TX	VS
		•	•		Glenn A Fleming	504-393-0988	•	•	•	
•	•	•	•	•	TENSTAR Corporation (New Orleans) [SOP]	800-856-8515	•	•	•	•
•	•	•	•		Vinson Detective Agency [SOP]	800-441-7899	•	•	•	

DT	BK	CV	CR	PR	←COURTS POINTE COUPEE	RECORDING→	UC	RE	TX	VS
•	•	•		•	Abstracts by Godail	800-660-7318	•	•	•	
•	•	•	•	•	Faith to Faith Legal Productions	225-685-0008	•	•	•	
•	•	•	•	•	TENSTAR Corporation (Baton Rouge) [SOP]	800-864-5154	•	•	•	•

DT	BK	CV	CR	PR	←COURTS RAPIDES	RECORDING→	UC	RE	TX	VS
•	•	•	•	•	Abstracting & Legal Research Inc	318-473-9979	•	•	•	•
•	•	•		•	Abstracts by Godail	800-660-7318	•	•	•	
•	•	•	•	•	North Louisiana Title Co Inc	800-515-7715	•	•	•	
•	•	•	•	•	TENSTAR Corporation (Main Office) [SOP]	800-960-2214	•	•	•	•
•	•	•	•		Vinson Detective Agency [SOP]	800-441-7899	•	•	•	

DT	BK	CV	CR	PR	←COURTS RED RIVER RECORDING→		UC	RE	TX	VS
•	•	•		•	Access Louisiana Inc	800-489-5620	•	•	•	•
•	•	•	•	•	TENSTAR Corporation (Shreveport)	800-960-2214	•	•	•	•

DT	BK	CV	CR	PR	←COURTS RICHLAND RECORDING→		UC	RE	TX	VS
•	•	•	•	•	North Louisiana Title Co Inc	800-515-7715	•	•	•	
•		•	•		Princess McDonald Process & Record Retrieval [SOP]	318-323-8566				•
•	•	•	•	•	TENSTAR Corporation (Main Office) [SOP]	800-960-2214	•	•	•	•

DT	BK	CV	CR	PR	←COURTS SABINE RECORDING→		UC	RE	TX	VS
•	•	•	•	•	Abstracting & Legal Research Inc	318-473-9979	•	•	•	•
•	•	•	•	•	TENSTAR Corporation (Shreveport)	800-960-2214	•	•	•	•

DT	BK	CV	CR	PR	←COURTS ST. BERNARD RECORDING→		UC	RE	TX	VS
•		•	•		Powell's Backtracking [SOP]	504-242-7700				
•	•	•	•	•	TENSTAR Corporation (New Orleans) [SOP]	800-856-8515	•	•	•	•
•	•	•	•		Vinson Detective Agency [SOP]	800-441-7899	•	•	•	

DT	BK	CV	CR	PR	←COURTS ST. CHARLES RECORDING→		UC	RE	TX	VS
•	•	•	•	•	Bombet Cashio & Associates [SOP]	800-256-5333	•	•	•	•
•	•	•	•	•	TENSTAR Corporation (New Orleans) [SOP]	800-856-8515	•	•	•	•
•	•	•	•		Vinson Detective Agency [SOP]	800-441-7899	•	•	•	

DT	BK	CV	CR	PR	←COURTS ST. HELENA RECORDING→		UC	RE	TX	VS
•	•	•	•	•	TENSTAR Corporation (Baton Rouge) [SOP]	800-864-5154	•	•	•	•

DT	BK	CV	CR	PR	←COURTS ST. JAMES RECORDING→		UC	RE	TX	VS
		•		•	Ascension Title Services Inc	225-647-8051	•	•	•	
•	•	•	•	•	TENSTAR Corporation (New Orleans) [SOP]	800-856-8515	•	•	•	•

DT	BK	CV	CR	PR	←COURTS ST. JOHN THE BAPTIST RECORDING→		UC	RE	TX	VS
•	•	•	•	•	Bombet Cashio & Associates [SOP]	800-256-5333	•	•	•	•
•	•	•	•	•	TENSTAR Corporation (New Orleans) [SOP]	800-856-8515	•	•	•	•
•	•	•	•		Vinson Detective Agency [SOP]	800-441-7899	•	•	•	

DT	BK	CV	CR	PR	←COURTS ST. LANDRY RECORDING→		UC	RE	TX	VS
•	•	•	•	•	ABC Investigators Inc [SOP]	800-738-7300	•	•	•	
•	•	•	•	•	Abstracting & Legal Research Inc	318-473-9979	•	•	•	•
•	•	•	•	•	Abstracts by Godail	800-660-7318	•	•	•	
•	•	•	•		Bayou Investigations Inc [SOP]	800-256-9009	•			
•	•	•	•	•	TENSTAR Corporation (Main Office) [SOP]	800-960-2214	•	•	•	•
•	•	•	•		Vinson Detective Agency [SOP]	800-441-7899	•	•	•	

DT	BK	CV	CR	PR	←COURTS ST. MARTIN RECORDING→		UC	RE	TX	VS
•	•	•	•		Bayou Investigations Inc [SOP]	800-256-9009	•			
•	•	•	•	•	TENSTAR Corporation (Main Office) [SOP]	800-960-2214	•	•	•	•

DT	BK	CV	CR	PR	←COURTS ST. MARY RECORDING→		UC	RE	TX	VS
•	•	•	•		Bayou Investigations Inc [SOP]	800-256-9009	•			
•	•	•	•	•	TENSTAR Corporation (Main Office) [SOP]	800-960-2214	•	•	•	•
•	•	•	•		Vinson Detective Agency [SOP]	800-441-7899	•	•	•	

DT	BK	CV	CR	PR	←COURTS ST. TAMMANY RECORDING→		UC	RE	TX	VS
		•	•	•	A Public Record Search Inc	985-892-5194	•	•	•	
•	•	•	•	•	Bombet Cashio & Associates [SOP]	800-256-5333	•	•	•	•
•		•	•		Powell's Backtracking [SOP]	504-242-7700				
		•	•	•	Professional Choice Services	225-294-3703	•	•	•	•
		•	•	•	Kathy Swenson, PI	985-863-8151	•	•	•	
•	•	•	•	•	TENSTAR Corporation (New Orleans) [SOP]	800-856-8515	•	•	•	•
•	•	•	•		Vinson Detective Agency [SOP]	800-441-7899	•	•	•	

Tangipahoa

DT	BK	CV	CR	PR	←Courts / Recording→	Phone	UC	RE	TX	VS
		•	•	•	Professional Choice Services	225-294-3703	•	•	•	•
•	•	•	•	•	TENSTAR Corporation (New Orleans) [SOP]	800-856-8515	•	•	•	•

Tensas

DT	BK	CV	CR	PR	←Courts / Recording→	Phone	UC	RE	TX	VS
•	•	•	•	•	North Louisiana Title Co Inc	800-515-7715	•	•	•	
•	•	•	•	•	TENSTAR Corporation (Main Office) [SOP]	800-960-2214	•	•	•	•

Terrebonne

DT	BK	CV	CR	PR	←Courts / Recording→	Phone	UC	RE	TX	VS
•	•	•	•	•	TENSTAR Corporation (New Orleans) [SOP]	800-856-8515	•	•	•	•
•	•	•	•		Vinson Detective Agency [SOP]	800-441-7899	•	•	•	

Union

DT	BK	CV	CR	PR	←Courts / Recording→	Phone	UC	RE	TX	VS
•	•	•	•	•	North Louisiana Title Co Inc	800-515-7715	•	•	•	
•		•	•		Princess McDonald Process & Record Retrieval [SOP]	318-323-8566				•
•	•	•	•	•	TENSTAR Corporation (Main Office) [SOP]	800-960-2214	•	•	•	•

Vermilion

DT	BK	CV	CR	PR	←Courts / Recording→	Phone	UC	RE	TX	VS
•	•	•	•	•	ABC Investigators Inc [SOP]	800-738-7300	•	•	•	
•	•	•	•		Bayou Investigations Inc [SOP]	800-256-9009	•			
•	•	•	•	•	TENSTAR Corporation (Main Office) [SOP]	800-960-2214	•	•	•	•

Vernon

DT	BK	CV	CR	PR	←Courts / Recording→	Phone	UC	RE	TX	VS
•	•	•	•	•	Abstracting & Legal Research Inc	318-473-9979	•	•	•	•
•	•	•	•	•	TENSTAR Corporation (Main Office) [SOP]	800-960-2214	•	•	•	•

Washington

DT	BK	CV	CR	PR	←Courts / Recording→	Phone	UC	RE	TX	VS
•	•	•	•	•	TENSTAR Corporation (New Orleans) [SOP]	800-856-8515	•	•	•	•

Webster

DT	BK	CV	CR	PR	←Courts / Recording→	Phone	UC	RE	TX	VS
•	•	•		•	Access Louisiana Inc	800-489-5620	•	•	•	•
		•		•	M & M Title / Mitchell Co	318-798-1198	•	•	•	
•	•	•	•	•	North Louisiana Title Co Inc	800-515-7715	•	•	•	
•	•	•	•	•	TENSTAR Corporation (Shreveport)	800-960-2214	•	•	•	•

West Baton Rouge

DT	BK	CV	CR	PR	←Courts / Recording→	Phone	UC	RE	TX	VS
•	•	•		•	Abstracts by Godail	800-660-7318	•	•	•	
		•	•		AccuScreen Systems [SOP]	800-383-6476				
	•	•	•	•	Judy J Badon/Public Records Specialists	225-291-5537	•	•	•	
•	•	•	•	•	Bombet Cashio & Associates [SOP]	800-256-5333	•	•	•	•
•		•	•	•	Kerry H Callahan [SOP]	225-752-8750	•			•
•	•	•	•	•	Faith to Faith Legal Productions	225-685-0008	•	•	•	
•	•	•	•	•	Genco Services [SOP]	225-216-9595	•	•	•	•
•	•	•			Mary Lindsey Research	225-654-6576				
•	•	•	•	•	TENSTAR Corporation (Baton Rouge) [SOP]	800-864-5154	•	•	•	•
•	•	•	•		Vinson Detective Agency [SOP]	800-441-7899	•	•	•	

West Carroll

DT	BK	CV	CR	PR	←Courts / Recording→	Phone	UC	RE	TX	VS
•	•	•	•	•	North Louisiana Title Co Inc	800-515-7715	•	•	•	
•	•	•	•	•	TENSTAR Corporation (Main Office) [SOP]	800-960-2214	•	•	•	•

West Feliciana

DT	BK	CV	CR	PR	←Courts / Recording→	Phone	UC	RE	TX	VS
•	•	•			Mary Lindsey Research	225-654-6576				
•	•	•	•	•	TENSTAR Corporation (Baton Rouge) [SOP]	800-864-5154	•	•	•	•

Winn

DT	BK	CV	CR	PR	←Courts / Recording→	Phone	UC	RE	TX	VS
•	•	•	•	•	North Louisiana Title Co Inc	800-515-7715	•	•	•	
•	•	•	•	•	TENSTAR Corporation (Main Office) [SOP]	800-960-2214	•	•	•	•

Maine

COURT RECORDS RETRIEVED — **RECORDING RECORDS RETRIEVED**

DT	BK	CV	CR	PR	←COURTS ANDROSCOGGIN RECORDING→	Phone	UC	RE	TX	VS
					Horizons Unlimited	617-696-6397		•	•	
•	•	•	•	•	Lawyers Investigating Svc [SOP]	888-244-5685	•	•	•	•
•	•	•	•	•	Pearl Information Services	207-775-5889	•	•	•	•
•	•	•	•	•	Public Information Resource	800-675-6350	•	•	•	•
		•	•	•	Surette Investigations [SOP]	207-268-3419	•	•	•	•
•	•	•	•	•	Toby Nason Detective & Security Agency [SOP]	207-873-7512				

DT	BK	CV	CR	PR	←COURTS AROOSTOOK RECORDING→	Phone	UC	RE	TX	VS
					Horizons Unlimited	617-696-6397		•	•	
•	•	•	•	•	Toby Nason Detective & Security Agency [SOP]	207-873-7512				

DT	BK	CV	CR	PR	←COURTS CUMBERLAND RECORDING→	Phone	UC	RE	TX	VS
•					A/M Investigations [SOP]	207-838-3111				
					Horizons Unlimited	617-696-6397		•	•	
•	•	•	•	•	Lawyers Investigating Svc [SOP]	888-244-5685	•	•	•	•
•		•	•	•	Maine Public Record Services	207-646-9065	•	•	•	
•	•	•	•	•	NR&C	207-791-2852	•	•	•	
•	•	•	•	•	Pearl Information Services	207-775-5889	•	•	•	•
•	•	•	•	•	Public Information Resource	800-675-6350	•	•	•	•
		•	•		Serunian Inv [SOP]	207-773-2660				
•	•	•	•	•	Toby Nason Detective & Security Agency [SOP]	207-873-7512				

DT	BK	CV	CR	PR	←COURTS FRANKLIN RECORDING→	Phone	UC	RE	TX	VS
					Horizons Unlimited	617-696-6397		•	•	
•	•	•	•	•	NR&C	207-791-2852	•	•	•	
•	•	•	•	•	Public Information Resource	800-675-6350	•	•	•	•
•	•	•	•	•	Toby Nason Detective & Security Agency [SOP]	207-873-7512				

DT	BK	CV	CR	PR	←COURTS HANCOCK RECORDING→	Phone	UC	RE	TX	VS
•	•	•	•	•	Acadia Legal Support [SOP]	207-223-5285		•	•	
				•	Fraser Abstracting	207-947-6344	•	•	•	
					Horizons Unlimited	617-696-6397		•	•	
•	•	•	•	•	Toby Nason Detective & Security Agency [SOP]	207-873-7512				

DT	BK	CV	CR	PR	←COURTS KENNEBEC RECORDING→	Phone	UC	RE	TX	VS
•	•	•	•	•	Axess Maine Co [SOP]	207-594-2641	•	•	•	•
					Horizons Unlimited	617-696-6397		•	•	
•	•	•	•	•	Lawyers Investigating Svc [SOP]	888-244-5685	•	•	•	•
•	•	•	•	•	NR&C	207-791-2852	•	•	•	
•	•	•	•	•	Pearl Information Services	207-775-5889	•	•	•	•
					Pro-Serv Process Service [SOP]	207-453-2331				
•	•	•	•	•	Public Information Resource	800-675-6350	•	•	•	•
		•	•	•	Surette Investigations [SOP]	207-268-3419	•	•	•	•
•	•	•	•	•	Toby Nason Detective & Security Agency [SOP]	207-873-7512				

DT	BK	CV	CR	PR	←COURTS KNOX RECORDING→	Phone	UC	RE	TX	VS
•	•	•	•	•	Axess Maine Co [SOP]	207-594-2641	•	•	•	•
					Horizons Unlimited	617-696-6397		•	•	
•	•	•	•	•	Pearl Information Services	207-775-5889	•	•	•	•
•	•	•	•	•	Public Information Resource	800-675-6350	•	•	•	•
•	•	•	•	•	Toby Nason Detective & Security Agency [SOP]	207-873-7512				

DT	BK	CV	CR	PR	←COURTS LINCOLN RECORDING→	Phone	UC	RE	TX	VS
•	•	•	•	•	Axess Maine Co [SOP]	207-594-2641	•	•	•	•
					Horizons Unlimited	617-696-6397		•	•	

DT	BK	CV	CR	PR	←Courts	Recording→	UC	RE	TX	VS
•	•	•	•	•	Lawyers Investigating Svc [SOP]	888-244-5685	•	•	•	•
•	•	•	•	•	Public Information Resource	800-675-6350	•	•	•	•
		•	•	•	Surette Investigations [SOP]	207-268-3419	•	•	•	•
•	•	•	•	•	Toby Nason Detective & Security Agency [SOP]	207-873-7512				

DT	BK	CV	CR	PR	←Courts **Oxford**	Recording→	UC	RE	TX	VS
					Horizons Unlimited	617-696-6397		•	•	
•	•	•	•	•	Lawyers Investigating Svc [SOP]	888-244-5685	•	•	•	•
•	•	•	•	•	NR&C	207-791-2852	•	•	•	
•	•	•	•	•	Public Information Resource	800-675-6350	•	•	•	•
•	•	•	•	•	Toby Nason Detective & Security Agency [SOP]	207-873-7512				

DT	BK	CV	CR	PR	←Courts **Penobscot**	Recording→	UC	RE	TX	VS
•	•	•	•	•	Acadia Legal Support [SOP]	207-223-5285		•	•	
				•	Fraser Abstracting	207-947-6344	•	•	•	
					Horizons Unlimited	617-696-6397		•	•	
•	•	•	•	•	Public Information Resource	800-675-6350	•	•	•	•
•	•	•	•	•	Toby Nason Detective & Security Agency [SOP]	207-873-7512				

DT	BK	CV	CR	PR	←Courts **Piscataquis**	Recording→	UC	RE	TX	VS
				•	Fraser Abstracting	207-947-6344	•	•	•	
					Horizons Unlimited	617-696-6397		•	•	
•	•	•	•	•	Toby Nason Detective & Security Agency [SOP]	207-873-7512				

DT	BK	CV	CR	PR	←Courts **Sagadahoc**	Recording→	UC	RE	TX	VS
					Horizons Unlimited	617-696-6397		•	•	
•	•	•	•	•	Lawyers Investigating Svc [SOP]	888-244-5685	•	•	•	•
•	•	•	•	•	Pearl Information Services	207-775-5889	•	•	•	•
•	•	•	•	•	Public Information Resource	800-675-6350	•	•	•	•
		•	•	•	Surette Investigations [SOP]	207-268-3419	•	•	•	•
•	•	•	•	•	Toby Nason Detective & Security Agency [SOP]	207-873-7512				

DT	BK	CV	CR	PR	←Courts **Somerset**	Recording→	UC	RE	TX	VS
•	•	•	•	•	Axess Maine Co [SOP]	207-594-2641	•	•	•	•
					Horizons Unlimited	617-696-6397		•	•	
					Pro-Serv Process Service [SOP]	207-453-2331				
•	•	•	•	•	Public Information Resource	800-675-6350	•	•	•	•
•	•	•	•	•	Toby Nason Detective & Security Agency [SOP]	207-873-7512				

DT	BK	CV	CR	PR	←Courts **Waldo**	Recording→	UC	RE	TX	VS
•	•	•	•	•	Acadia Legal Support [SOP]	207-223-5285		•	•	
•	•	•	•	•	Axess Maine Co [SOP]	207-594-2641	•	•	•	•
				•	Fraser Abstracting	207-947-6344	•	•	•	
					Horizons Unlimited	617-696-6397		•	•	
•	•	•	•	•	Public Information Resource	800-675-6350	•	•	•	•
•	•	•	•	•	Toby Nason Detective & Security Agency [SOP]	207-873-7512				

DT	BK	CV	CR	PR	←Courts **Washington**	Recording→	UC	RE	TX	VS
					Horizons Unlimited	617-696-6397		•	•	
•	•	•	•	•	Toby Nason Detective & Security Agency [SOP]	207-873-7512				

DT	BK	CV	CR	PR	←Courts **York**	Recording→	UC	RE	TX	VS
					Horizons Unlimited	617-696-6397		•	•	
•	•	•	•	•	Lawyers Investigating Svc [SOP]	888-244-5685	•	•	•	•
•		•	•	•	Maine Public Record Services	207-646-9065	•	•	•	
•	•	•	•	•	NR&C	207-791-2852	•	•	•	
•	•	•	•	•	Pearl Information Services	207-775-5889	•	•	•	•
•	•	•	•	•	Public Information Resource	800-675-6350	•	•	•	•
		•	•		Serunian Inv [SOP]	207-773-2660				
•	•	•	•	•	Toby Nason Detective & Security Agency [SOP]	207-873-7512				

Maryland

COURT RECORDS RETRIEVED | **RECORDING RECORDS RETRIEVED**

DT	BK	CV	CR	PR	←COURTS ALLEGANY RECORDING→		UC	RE	TX	VS
•	•	•	•		Employmentscreening.com	215-234-0700	•	•	•	•
					First Choice Title Service LLC	410-252 3803		•		
•	•	•	•	•	Hylind Search Company Inc (Maryland) [SOP]	888-449-5463	•	•	•	•
•	•	•	•		National Background Inv Inc	800-798-0079			•	

DT	BK	CV	CR	PR	←COURTS ANNE ARUNDEL RECORDING→		UC	RE	TX	VS
•	•	•	•	•	A P Legal Support Services [SOP]	800-273-9928	•	•	•	•
•	•	•	•		Arrow Background Svcs LLC	410-243-8301			•	
		•	•	•	Chesapeake Services [SOP]	800-834-7938	•	•	•	•
•	•	•	•		CorpAssist Inc - Baltimore	800-536-9778	•	•	•	
					Document Retrieval Inc [SOP]	443-995-7488		•		
•	•	•	•		Employmentscreening.com	215-234-0700	•	•	•	•
•	•	•		•	Federal Research Corporation [SOP]	800-846-3190	•	•	•	•
					First Choice Title Service LLC	410-252 3803		•		
•	•	•		•	Harbor City Research Inc	800-445-6029	•	•	•	
•	•	•	•	•	Hylind Search Company Inc (Maryland) [SOP]	888-449-5463	•	•	•	•
•	•	•	•	•	Infoline Inc	888-284-4581	•	•	•	•
		•			Maryland Abstract Services LLC	410-641-2298	•	•	•	
•	•	•	•	•	MLQ Attorney Services [SOP]	800-446-8794	•	•	•	•
•	•	•	•	•	Mohr Information Services LLC	540-678-8775	•	•	•	
•	•	•	•		National Background Inv Inc	800-798-0079			•	
•	•	•	•	•	Rosemary O'Brien [SOP]	301-434-4044; Cell-301-807-1809	•	•	•	•
•	•	•	•		Security Consultants Inc	202-686-3953			•	
•	•	•	•		Wieder Young & Assoc Inc	301-681-7206	•		•	

DT	BK	CV	CR	PR	←COURTS BALTIMORE COUNTY RECORDING→		UC	RE	TX	VS
•	•	•	•	•	A P Legal Support Services [SOP]	800-273-9928	•	•	•	•
					Action Abstracts	410-358-7162 or 410-493-6344		•	•	
•	•	•	•		Arrow Background Svcs LLC	410-243-8301			•	
•	•	•	•		CorpAssist Inc - Baltimore	800-536-9778	•	•	•	
					Document Retrieval Inc [SOP]	443-995-7488		•		
•	•	•	•		Employmentscreening.com	215-234-0700	•	•	•	•
•	•	•		•	Federal Research Corporation [SOP]	800-846-3190	•	•	•	•
					First Choice Title Service LLC	410-252 3803		•		
•	•	•		•	Harbor City Research Inc	800-445-6029	•	•	•	
•	•	•	•	•	Hylind Search Company Inc (Maryland) [SOP]	888-449-5463	•	•	•	•
•	•	•	•	•	Infoline Inc	888-284-4581	•	•	•	•
			•		Kroll Background America	800-697-7189		•	•	
		•			Maryland Abstract Services LLC	410-641-2298	•	•	•	
		•		•	Maryland Research & Abstract Co	410-823-1944	•	•		
•	•	•	•	•	Mohr Information Services LLC	540-678-8775	•	•	•	
•	•	•	•		National Background Inv Inc	800-798-0079			•	
					Runnymeade Research Inc	410-998-9886	•	•		
•	•	•	•		Security Consultants Inc	202-686-3953			•	
•	•	•	•		Wieder Young & Assoc Inc	301-681-7206	•		•	

DT	BK	CV	CR	PR	←COURTS BALTIMORE CITY RECORDING→		UC	RE	TX	VS
•	•	•	•	•	A P Legal Support Services [SOP]	800-273-9928	•	•	•	•
•	•	•	•		Arrow Background Svcs LLC	410-243-8301			•	

DT	BK	CV	CR	PR	←Courts	Recording→	UC	RE	TX	VS
•	•	•	•		CorpAssist Inc - Baltimore	800-536-9778	•	•	•	
					Document Retrieval Inc [SOP]	443-995-7488		•		
•	•	•	•		Employmentscreening.com	215-234-0700	•	•	•	•
•	•	•		•	Federal Research Corporation [SOP]	800-846-3190	•	•	•	•
					First Choice Title Service LLC	410-252 3803		•		
•	•	•		•	Harbor City Research Inc	800-445-6029	•	•	•	
•	•	•	•	•	Hylind Search Company Inc (Maryland) [SOP]	888-449-5463	•	•	•	•
•	•	•	•	•	Infoline Inc	888-284-4581	•	•	•	•
			•		Kroll Background America	800-697-7189		•	•	
		•			Maryland Abstract Services LLC	410-641-2298	•	•	•	
•	•	•	•	•	Mohr Information Services LLC	540-678-8775	•	•	•	
•	•	•	•		National Background Inv Inc	800-798-0079			•	
					Runnymeade Research Inc	410-998-9886	•	•		
•	•	•	•	•	Torri's Legal Services [SOP]	800-990-7378				
•	•	•	•		Wieder Young & Assoc Inc	301-681-7206	•		•	
DT	**BK**	**CV**	**CR**	**PR**	**←Courts CALVERT**	**Recording→**	**UC**	**RE**	**TX**	**VS**
					Document Retrieval Inc [SOP]	443-995-7488		•		
•	•	•	•		Employmentscreening.com	215-234-0700	•	•	•	•
					First Choice Title Service LLC	410-252 3803		•		
•	•	•	•	•	Hylind Search Company Inc (Maryland) [SOP]	888-449-5463	•	•	•	•
•	•	•	•	•	Infoline Inc	888-284-4581	•	•	•	•
		•			Maryland Abstract Services LLC	410-641-2298	•	•	•	
•	•	•	•		National Background Inv Inc	800-798-0079			•	
•	•	•	•		Wieder Young & Assoc Inc	301-681-7206	•		•	
DT	**BK**	**CV**	**CR**	**PR**	**←Courts CAROLINE**	**Recording→**	**UC**	**RE**	**TX**	**VS**
		•	•	•	Chesapeake Services [SOP]	800-834-7938	•	•	•	•
		•	•	•	Delmarva Abstractors [SOP]	410-228-6044	•	•	•	
•	•	•	•		Employmentscreening.com	215-234-0700	•	•	•	•
					First Choice Title Service LLC	410-252 3803		•		
•	•	•	•	•	Hylind Search Company Inc (Maryland) [SOP]	888-449-5463	•	•	•	•
		•			Maryland Abstract Services LLC	410-641-2298	•	•	•	
•	•	•	•		National Background Inv Inc	800-798-0079			•	
		•	•	•	Shore One Title Abstract Services	410-943-8637	•	•	•	
DT	**BK**	**CV**	**CR**	**PR**	**←Courts CARROLL**	**Recording→**	**UC**	**RE**	**TX**	**VS**
•	•	•	•	•	A P Legal Support Services [SOP]	800-273-9928	•	•	•	•
•	•	•	•		Arrow Background Svcs LLC	410-243-8301			•	
					Document Retrieval Inc [SOP]	443-995-7488		•		
•	•	•	•		Employmentscreening.com	215-234-0700	•	•	•	•
					First Choice Title Service LLC	410-252 3803		•		
•	•	•	•	•	Hylind Search Company Inc (Maryland) [SOP]	888-449-5463	•	•	•	•
			•		Kroll Background America	800-697-7189		•	•	
		•			Maryland Abstract Services LLC	410-641-2298	•	•	•	
•	•	•	•		National Background Inv Inc	800-798-0079			•	
•	•	•	•		Wieder Young & Assoc Inc	301-681-7206	•		•	
DT	**BK**	**CV**	**CR**	**PR**	**←Courts CECIL**	**Recording→**	**UC**	**RE**	**TX**	**VS**
					Document Retrieval Inc [SOP]	443-995-7488		•		
•	•	•	•		Employmentscreening.com	215-234-0700	•	•	•	•
					First Choice Title Service LLC	410-252 3803		•		
•	•	•	•	•	Hylind Search Company Inc (Maryland) [SOP]	888-449-5463	•	•	•	•
		•			Maryland Abstract Services LLC	410-641-2298	•	•	•	
•	•	•	•		National Background Inv Inc	800-798-0079			•	
DT	**BK**	**CV**	**CR**	**PR**	**←Courts CHARLES**	**Recording→**	**UC**	**RE**	**TX**	**VS**
					Document Retrieval Inc [SOP]	443-995-7488		•		
•	•	•	•		Employmentscreening.com	215-234-0700	•	•	•	•
					First Choice Title Service LLC	410-252 3803		•		

DT	BK	CV	CR	PR	←Courts	Recording→	UC	RE	TX	VS
•	•	•	•	•	Hylind Search Company Inc (Maryland) [SOP]	888-449-5463	•	•	•	•
•	•	•	•	•	Infoline Inc	888-284-4581	•	•	•	•
		•			Maryland Abstract Services LLC	410-641-2298	•	•	•	
•	•	•	•		National Background Inv Inc	800-798-0079			•	
•	•	•	•		Wieder Young & Assoc Inc	301-681-7206	•		•	
DT	**BK**	**CV**	**CR**	**PR**	**←Courts** **Dorchester**	**Recording→**	**UC**	**RE**	**TX**	**VS**
		•	•	•	Delmarva Abstractors [SOP]	410-228-6044	•	•	•	
•	•	•	•		Employmentscreening.com	215-234-0700	•	•	•	•
					First Choice Title Service LLC	410-252 3803		•		
•	•	•	•	•	Hylind Search Company Inc (Maryland) [SOP]	888-449-5463	•	•	•	•
		•			Maryland Abstract Services LLC	410-641-2298	•	•	•	
•	•	•	•		National Background Inv Inc	800-798-0079			•	
		•	•	•	Shore One Title Abstract Services	410-943-8637	•	•	•	
DT	**BK**	**CV**	**CR**	**PR**	**←Courts** **Frederick**	**Recording→**	**UC**	**RE**	**TX**	**VS**
					Document Retrieval Inc [SOP]	443-995-7488		•		
•	•	•	•		Employmentscreening.com	215-234-0700	•	•	•	•
					First Choice Title Service LLC	410-252 3803		•		
•	•	•	•	•	Hylind Search Company Inc (Maryland) [SOP]	888-449-5463	•	•	•	•
•	•	•	•	•	Infoline Inc	888-284-4581	•	•	•	•
		•			Maryland Abstract Services LLC	410-641-2298	•	•	•	
•	•	•	•	•	Mohr Information Services LLC	540-678-8775	•	•	•	
•	•	•	•		National Background Inv Inc	800-798-0079			•	
		•	•	•	Quality Abstractors Inc	301-695-9329	•	•	•	
•	•	•	•	•	Resource Reporting Ltd [SOP]	877-279-0298	•	•	•	
•	•	•	•		Wieder Young & Assoc Inc	301-681-7206	•		•	
DT	**BK**	**CV**	**CR**	**PR**	**←Courts** **Garrett**	**Recording→**	**UC**	**RE**	**TX**	**VS**
•	•	•	•		Employmentscreening.com	215-234-0700	•	•	•	•
					First Choice Title Service LLC	410-252 3803		•		
•	•	•	•	•	Hylind Search Company Inc (Maryland) [SOP]	888-449-5463	•	•	•	•
•	•	•	•		National Background Inv Inc	800-798-0079			•	
DT	**BK**	**CV**	**CR**	**PR**	**←Courts** **Harford**	**Recording→**	**UC**	**RE**	**TX**	**VS**
•	•	•	•	•	A P Legal Support Services [SOP]	800-273-9928	•	•	•	•
•	•	•	•		Arrow Background Svcs LLC	410-243-8301			•	
					Document Retrieval Inc [SOP]	443-995-7488		•		
•	•	•	•		Employmentscreening.com	215-234-0700	•	•	•	•
•	•	•		•	Federal Research Corporation [SOP]	800-846-3190	•	•	•	•
					First Choice Title Service LLC	410-252 3803		•		
•	•	•		•	Harbor City Research Inc	800-445-6029	•	•	•	
•	•	•	•	•	Hylind Search Company Inc (Maryland) [SOP]	888-449-5463	•	•	•	•
			•		Kroll Background America	800-697-7189		•	•	
		•			Maryland Abstract Services LLC	410-641-2298	•	•	•	
		•		•	Maryland Research & Abstract Co	410-823-1944	•	•		
•	•	•	•		National Background Inv Inc	800-798-0079			•	
•	•	•	•		Security Consultants Inc	202-686-3953			•	
•	•	•	•		Wieder Young & Assoc Inc	301-681-7206	•		•	
DT	**BK**	**CV**	**CR**	**PR**	**←Courts** **Howard**	**Recording→**	**UC**	**RE**	**TX**	**VS**
•	•	•	•	•	A P Legal Support Services [SOP]	800-273-9928	•	•	•	•
•	•	•	•		Arrow Background Svcs LLC	410-243-8301			•	
•	•	•	•		CorpAssist Inc - Baltimore	800-536-9778	•	•	•	
					Document Retrieval Inc [SOP]	443-995-7488		•		
•	•	•	•		Employmentscreening.com	215-234-0700	•	•	•	•
•	•	•		•	Federal Research Corporation [SOP]	800-846-3190	•	•	•	•
					First Choice Title Service LLC	410-252 3803		•		
•	•	•		•	Harbor City Research Inc	800-445-6029	•	•	•	
•	•	•	•	•	Hylind Search Company Inc (Maryland) [SOP]	888-449-5463	•	•	•	•

DT	BK	CV	CR	PR	←Courts	Recording→	UC	RE	TX	VS
•	•	•	•	•	Infoline Inc	888-284-4581	•	•	•	•
•	•	•	•	•	Investigative Consultants Inc	202-237-1500	•	•	•	•
		•			Maryland Abstract Services LLC	410-641-2298	•	•	•	
•	•	•	•	•	Mohr Information Services LLC	540-678-8775	•	•	•	
•	•	•	•		National Background Inv Inc	800-798-0079			•	
•	•	•	•		Pat's Information Services	202-285-2116			•	
					Runnymeade Research Inc	410-998-9886	•	•		
•	•	•	•		Security Consultants Inc	202-686-3953			•	
•	•	•	•		Wieder Young & Assoc Inc	301-681-7206	•		•	

DT	BK	CV	CR	PR	←Courts **Kent**	Recording→	UC	RE	TX	VS
		•	•	•	Chesapeake Services [SOP]	800-834-7938	•	•	•	•
•	•	•	•		Employmentscreening.com	215-234-0700	•	•	•	•
					First Choice Title Service LLC	410-252 3803		•		
•	•	•	•	•	Hylind Search Company Inc (Maryland) [SOP]	888-449-5463	•	•	•	•
		•			Maryland Abstract Services LLC	410-641-2298	•	•	•	
•	•	•	•		National Background Inv Inc	800-798-0079			•	

DT	BK	CV	CR	PR	←Courts **Montgomery**	Recording→	UC	RE	TX	VS
•	•	•	•	•	A P Legal Support Services [SOP]	800-273-9928	•	•	•	•
•	•	•	•	•	ALIASS [SOP]	800-747-0820	•	•	•	•
•	•	•	•		Arrow Background Svcs LLC	410-243-8301			•	
•	•	•	•		Capitol District Information [SOP]	800-494-5225	•		•	
•	•	•	•	•	CorpAssist Inc - DC Office	800-438-2996	•	•	•	•
•	•	•	•		CourtEXPRESS (DC) [SOP]	800-542-3320				
					Document Retrieval Inc [SOP]	443-995-7488		•		
•	•	•	•	•	Docu-Search of Washington DC	202-737-5707	•	•	•	•
•	•	•	•	•	Elder & Ryan Abstracts LLC	301-854-1200	•	•	•	•
•	•	•	•		Employmentscreening.com	215-234-0700	•	•	•	•
					First Choice Title Service LLC	410-252 3803		•		
•	•	•	•	•	Fitzgerald Servaites Inc	202-257-7775	•	•	•	•
•	•	•		•	Harbor City Research Inc	800-445-6029	•	•	•	
•	•	•	•	•	Hylind Search Company Inc (Maryland) [SOP]	888-449-5463	•	•	•	•
•	•	•	•	•	Infoline Inc	888-284-4581	•	•	•	•
•	•	•	•	•	Investigative Consultants Inc	202-237-1500	•	•	•	•
•	•	•		•	M & M Search Service	301-251-9545	•	•	•	•
		•			Maryland Abstract Services LLC	410-641-2298	•	•	•	
•	•	•	•	•	MLQ Attorney Services [SOP]	800-446-8794	•	•	•	•
•	•	•	•	•	Mohr Information Services LLC	540-678-8775	•	•	•	
•	•	•	•		Montgomery Investigative Services [SOP]	800-410-4404		•		
•	•	•	•		National Background Inv Inc	800-798-0079			•	
•	•	•	•	•	Rosemary O'Brien [SOP]	301-434-4044; Cell-301-807-1809	•	•	•	•
•	•	•	•		Pat's Information Services	202-285-2116			•	
		•		•	Boyd F Plumley, BA, M.S.L.S.	703-522-4363		•		•
•	•	•	•	•	Prudential Associates [SOP]	800-726-7723	•	•		•
•	•	•	•	•	Resource Reporting Ltd [SOP]	877-279-0298	•	•	•	
•	•	•	•		Security Consultants Inc	202-686-3953			•	
•	•	•	•	•	Washington Document Service (DC)	800-728-5201	•	•	•	•
•	•	•	•		Wieder Young & Assoc Inc	301-681-7206	•		•	

DT	BK	CV	CR	PR	←Courts **Prince George's**	Recording→	UC	RE	TX	VS
•	•	•	•	•	A P Legal Support Services [SOP]	800-273-9928	•	•	•	•
•	•	•	•	•	ALIASS [SOP]	800-747-0820	•	•	•	•
•	•	•	•		Arrow Background Svcs LLC	410-243-8301			•	
•	•	•	•		Capitol District Information [SOP]	800-494-5225	•		•	
•	•	•	•	•	CorpAssist Inc - DC Office	800-438-2996	•	•	•	•
•	•	•	•		CourtEXPRESS (DC) [SOP]	800-542-3320				
					Document Retrieval Inc [SOP]	443-995-7488		•		
•	•	•	•		Employmentscreening.com	215-234-0700	•	•	•	•

DT	BK	CV	CR	PR	←Courts	Recording→	UC	RE	TX	VS
					First Choice Title Service LLC	410-252 3803		•		
•	•	•	•	•	Fitzgerald Servaites Inc	202-257-7775	•	•	•	•
•	•	•		•	Harbor City Research Inc	800-445-6029	•	•	•	
•	•	•	•	•	Hylind Search Company Inc (Maryland) [SOP]	888-449-5463	•	•	•	•
•	•	•	•	•	Infoline Inc	888-284-4581	•	•	•	•
•	•	•	•	•	Investigative Consultants Inc	202-237-1500	•	•	•	•
•	•	•		•	M & M Search Service	301-251-9545	•	•	•	•
		•			Maryland Abstract Services LLC	410-641-2298	•	•	•	
•	•	•	•	•	MLQ Attorney Services [SOP]	800-446-8794	•	•	•	•
•	•	•	•	•	Mohr Information Services LLC	540-678-8775	•	•	•	
•	•	•	•		Montgomery Investigative Services [SOP]	800-410-4404		•		
•	•	•	•		National Background Inv Inc	800-798-0079			•	
•	•	•	•	•	Rosemary O'Brien [SOP]	301-434-4044; Cell-301-807-1809	•	•	•	•
•	•	•	•		Pat's Information Services	202-285-2116			•	
•	•	•	•	•	Prudential Associates [SOP]	800-726-7723	•	•		•
•	•	•	•		Security Consultants Inc	202-686-3953			•	
•	•	•	•		Wieder Young & Assoc Inc	301-681-7206	•		•	

DT	BK	CV	CR	PR	←Courts **QUEEN ANNE'S**	Recording→	UC	RE	TX	VS
		•	•	•	Chesapeake Services [SOP]	800-834-7938	•	•	•	•
		•	•	•	Delmarva Abstractors [SOP]	410-228-6044	•	•	•	
					Document Retrieval Inc [SOP]	443-995-7488		•		
•	•	•	•		Employmentscreening.com	215-234-0700	•	•	•	•
					First Choice Title Service LLC	410-252 3803		•		
		•			Maryland Abstract Services LLC	410-641-2298	•	•	•	
•	•	•	•		National Background Inv Inc	800-798-0079			•	

DT	BK	CV	CR	PR	←Courts **SOMERSET**	Recording→	UC	RE	TX	VS
		•	•	•	Judith Ayres	757-336-5313	•	•	•	•
•	•	•	•		Employmentscreening.com	215-234-0700	•	•	•	•
					First Choice Title Service LLC	410-252 3803		•		
		•			Maryland Abstract Services LLC	410-641-2298	•	•	•	
•	•	•	•		National Background Inv Inc	800-798-0079			•	

DT	BK	CV	CR	PR	←Courts **ST. MARY'S**	Recording→	UC	RE	TX	VS
					Document Retrieval Inc [SOP]	443-995-7488		•		
•	•	•	•		Employmentscreening.com	215-234-0700	•	•	•	•
					First Choice Title Service LLC	410-252 3803		•		
•	•	•	•	•	Hylind Search Company Inc (Maryland) [SOP]	888-449-5463	•	•	•	•
		•			Maryland Abstract Services LLC	410-641-2298	•	•	•	
•	•	•	•		National Background Inv Inc	800-798-0079			•	

DT	BK	CV	CR	PR	←Courts **TALBOT**	Recording→	UC	RE	TX	VS
		•	•	•	Chesapeake Services [SOP]	800-834-7938	•	•	•	•
		•	•	•	Delmarva Abstractors [SOP]	410-228-6044	•	•	•	
•	•	•	•		Employmentscreening.com	215-234-0700	•	•	•	•
					First Choice Title Service LLC	410-252 3803		•		
•	•	•	•	•	Hylind Search Company Inc (Maryland) [SOP]	888-449-5463	•	•	•	•
		•			Maryland Abstract Services LLC	410-641-2298	•	•	•	
•	•	•	•		National Background Inv Inc	800-798-0079			•	
		•	•	•	Shore One Title Abstract Services	410-943-8637	•	•	•	

DT	BK	CV	CR	PR	←Courts **WASHINGTON**	Recording→	UC	RE	TX	VS
•	•	•	•		Employmentscreening.com	215-234-0700	•	•	•	•
					First Choice Title Service LLC	410-252 3803		•		
•	•	•	•	•	Hylind Search Company Inc (Maryland) [SOP]	888-449-5463	•	•	•	•
		•			Maryland Abstract Services LLC	410-641-2298	•	•	•	
•	•	•	•	•	Mohr Information Services LLC	540-678-8775	•	•	•	
•	•	•	•		National Background Inv Inc	800-798-0079			•	
•	•	•	•	•	Prudential Associates [SOP]	800-726-7723	•	•		•

DT	BK	CV	CR	PR	←Courts	Recording→	UC	RE	TX	VS
		•	•	•	Quality Abstractors Inc	301-695-9329	•	•	•	
•	•	•	•	•	Resource Reporting Ltd [SOP]	877-279-0298	•	•	•	
•	•	•	•		Wieder Young & Assoc Inc	301-681-7206	•		•	

DT	BK	CV	CR	PR	←Courts WICOMICO	Recording→	UC	RE	TX	VS
		•	•	•	Judith Ayres	757-336-5313	•	•	•	•
•	•	•	•		Employmentscreening.com	215-234-0700	•	•	•	•
					First Choice Title Service LLC	410-252 3803		•		
•	•	•	•	•	Hylind Search Company Inc (Maryland) [SOP]	888-449-5463	•	•	•	•
		•			Maryland Abstract Services LLC	410-641-2298	•	•	•	
•	•	•	•		National Background Inv Inc	800-798-0079			•	

DT	BK	CV	CR	PR	←Courts WORCESTER	Recording→	UC	RE	TX	VS
		•	•	•	Judith Ayres	757-336-5313	•	•	•	•
•	•	•	•		Employmentscreening.com	215-234-0700	•	•	•	•
					First Choice Title Service LLC	410-252 3803		•		
•	•	•	•	•	Hylind Search Company Inc (Maryland) [SOP]	888-449-5463	•	•	•	•
		•			Maryland Abstract Services LLC	410-641-2298	•	•	•	
•	•	•	•		National Background Inv Inc	800-798-0079			•	

[SOP] = PERFORMS SERVICE OF PROCESS

COURT RECORDS

CODE	GOVERNMENT AGENCY	TYPE OF INFORMATION
DT	US District Court	Federal civil and criminal cases
BK	Bankruptcy Court	United States bankruptcy cases
CV	Civil Court	Municipal, county and state level civil cases
CR	Criminal Court	Municipal, county and state level criminal cases
PR	Probate Court	Wills and estate cases

COUNTY RECORDS - RECORDINGS

CODE	GOVERNMENT AGENCY	TYPE OF INFORMATION
UC	UCC Filing Office	Uniform Commercial Code and other personal property liens
RE	Real Estate Recording Office	Real property transactions and liens
TX	Tax Filing Office(s)	Federal and state tax liens, judgment liens
VS	Vital Records Office	Vital statistics—birth, death, marriage, divorce

Editor's Tip: Remember the first rule about public record searching-- Simply because your state or county has certain rules, regulations and practices regarding the accessibility and content of public records, does not mean that another state or county adheres to the same rules.

Massachusetts

COURT RECORDS RETRIEVED | **RECORDING RECORDS RETRIEVED**

DT	BK	CV	CR	PR	←COURTS BARNSTABLE	RECORDING→	UC	RE	TX	VS
•	•	•	•	•	Associated Professional Services [SOP]	800-849-7870	•	•	•	•
•	•	•	•	•	Attorney Subpoena Services [SOP]	877-786-5374	•	•	•	•
•	•	•	•	•	Badzmierowski Services [SOP]	508-498-3583	•	•	•	•
•	•	•	•	•	Barry Shuster Information Services, A Div of Search-It Inc	877-852-2507	•	•	•	•
•	•	•	•	•	Bearak Reports	800-331-5677	•	•	•	•
		•	•	•	Brenda L Gaskill	508-759-3156	•	•	•	•
•	•	•	•	•	Len Page Paralegal/Research Services	508-967-2504	•	•	•	•
•	•	•	•	•	Northshore Paralegal Services Inc	800-883-6020	•	•	•	•
•	•	•	•	•	R & R Search Inc	508-359-2400	•	•	•	•
		•	•		Rapid Record Retrieval	508-759-8622				
•	•	•	•	•	Simmons Agency Inc	800-237-8230	•	•	•	•

DT	BK	CV	CR	PR	←COURTS BERKSHIRE	RECORDING→	UC	RE	TX	VS
•	•	•	•	•	Attorney Subpoena Services [SOP]	877-786-5374	•	•	•	•
•	•	•	•	•	Badzmierowski Services [SOP]	508-498-3583	•	•	•	•
•	•	•	•	•	Barry Shuster Information Services, A Div of Search-It Inc	877-852-2507	•	•	•	•
•	•	•	•	•	Bearak Reports	800-331-5677	•	•	•	•
•	•	•			Forbes Public Research Inc	518-732-2841	•	•	•	
					Horizons Unlimited	617-696-6397		•	•	
•	•	•	•	•	Northshore Paralegal Services Inc	800-883-6020	•	•	•	•
•	•	•	•	•	R & R Search Inc	508-359-2400	•	•	•	•
				•	Registry Research	413-528-3919		•		

DT	BK	CV	CR	PR	←COURTS BRISTOL	RECORDING→	UC	RE	TX	VS
•	•	•	•	•	Associated Professional Services [SOP]	800-849-7870	•	•	•	•
•	•	•	•	•	Attorney Subpoena Services [SOP]	877-786-5374	•	•	•	•
•	•	•	•	•	Badzmierowski Services [SOP]	508-498-3583	•	•	•	•
•	•	•	•	•	Barry Shuster Information Services, A Div of Search-It Inc	877-852-2507	•	•	•	•
•	•	•	•	•	Bearak Reports	800-331-5677	•	•	•	•
		•	•	•	Brenda L Gaskill	508-759-3156	•	•	•	•
					Horizons Unlimited	617-696-6397		•	•	
•	•	•	•	•	LegalTrieve Information Services	508-238-4227	•	•	•	
•	•	•	•	•	Len Page Paralegal/Research Services	508-967-2504	•	•	•	•
•	•	•	•	•	Northshore Paralegal Services Inc	800-883-6020	•	•	•	•
•	•	•	•	•	R & R Search Inc	508-359-2400	•	•	•	•
		•	•		Rapid Record Retrieval	508-759-8622				

DT	BK	CV	CR	PR	←COURTS DUKES	RECORDING→	UC	RE	TX	VS
•	•	•	•	•	Attorney Subpoena Services [SOP]	877-786-5374	•	•	•	•
•	•	•	•	•	Badzmierowski Services [SOP]	508-498-3583	•	•	•	•
•	•	•	•	•	Barry Shuster Information Services, A Div of Search-It Inc	877-852-2507	•	•	•	•
					Horizons Unlimited	617-696-6397		•	•	
•	•	•	•	•	R & R Search Inc	508-359-2400	•	•	•	•

DT	BK	CV	CR	PR	←COURTS ESSEX	RECORDING→	UC	RE	TX	VS
•	•	•	•	•	A Scott Broadhurst Associates	617-536-3486	•	•	•	
•	•	•			Access Information & Retrievals	617-306-1547	•	•	•	
•	•	•	•	•	Attorney Subpoena Services [SOP]	877-786-5374	•	•	•	•
•	•	•	•	•	Badzmierowski Services [SOP]	508-498-3583	•	•	•	•

DT	BK	CV	CR	PR	Retriever	Phone	UC	RE	TX	VS
•	•	•	•	•	Barry Shuster Information Services, A Div of Search-It Inc	877-852-2507	•	•	•	•
•	•	•	•	•	Bearak Reports	800-331-5677	•	•	•	•
•	•	•		•	Essex County Paralegals Inc	800-922-4752	•	•	•	
					Horizons Unlimited	617-696-6397		•	•	
•	•	•	•	•	LegalTrieve Information Services	508-238-4227	•	•	•	
•	•	•	•	•	Michael B Fixman & Associates [SOP]	800-434-9626	•	•	•	•
•	•	•	•	•	Northshore Paralegal Services Inc	800-883-6020	•	•	•	•
•	•	•	•	•	P.S.P.S. Legal Support Services Inc [SOP]	617-846-7130	•	•	•	•
•	•	•	•	•	Paralegal Resource Center Inc	866-742-1939	•	•	•	•
•	•	•	•	•	Pickard & Associates Inc	978-468-4118	•	•	•	•
		•	•		Primetime Research Inc	866-737-2714				
•	•	•	•	•	R & R Search Inc	508-359-2400	•	•	•	•
•	•	•	•	•	Suburban Record Research	617-536-3486	•	•	•	
		•	•	•	Surette Investigations [SOP]	207-268-3419	•	•	•	•

DT	BK	CV	CR	PR	←COURTS **FRANKLIN**	RECORDING→	UC	RE	TX	VS
•	•	•	•	•	Attorney Subpoena Services [SOP]	877-786-5374	•	•	•	•
•	•	•	•	•	Badzmierowski Services [SOP]	508-498-3583	•	•	•	•
•	•	•	•	•	Barry Shuster Information Services, A Div of Search-It Inc	877-852-2507	•	•	•	•
•	•	•	•	•	Bearak Reports	800-331-5677	•	•	•	•
					Horizons Unlimited	617-696-6397		•	•	
				•	M & M Title Services	413-374-0158	•	•	•	
•	•	•	•	•	Northshore Paralegal Services Inc	800-883-6020	•	•	•	•
		•	•		Primetime Research Inc	866-737-2714				
•	•	•	•	•	R & R Search Inc	508-359-2400	•	•	•	•
•		•	•		Seyler Retrieval	413-782-9907/348-3667				
•	•	•	•	•	Worcester Record Search	508-842-7282	•	•	•	•

DT	BK	CV	CR	PR	←COURTS **HAMPDEN**	RECORDING→	UC	RE	TX	VS
•	•	•	•	•	Attorney Subpoena Services [SOP]	877-786-5374	•	•	•	•
•	•	•	•	•	Badzmierowski Services [SOP]	508-498-3583	•	•	•	•
•	•	•	•	•	Barry Shuster Information Services, A Div of Search-It Inc	877-852-2507	•	•	•	•
•	•	•			Forbes Public Research Inc	518-732-2841	•	•	•	
					Horizons Unlimited	617-696-6397		•	•	
				•	M & M Title Services	413-374-0158	•	•	•	
•	•	•	•	•	Northshore Paralegal Services Inc	800-883-6020	•	•	•	•
		•	•		Primetime Research Inc	866-737-2714				
•	•	•	•	•	R & R Search Inc	508-359-2400	•	•	•	•
•		•	•		Seyler Retrieval	413-782-9907/348-3667				
•	•	•	•	•	Worcester Record Search	508-842-7282	•	•	•	•

DT	BK	CV	CR	PR	←COURTS **HAMPSHIRE**	RECORDING→	UC	RE	TX	VS
•	•	•	•	•	Attorney Subpoena Services [SOP]	877-786-5374	•	•	•	•
•	•	•	•	•	Badzmierowski Services [SOP]	508-498-3583	•	•	•	•
•	•	•	•	•	Barry Shuster Information Services, A Div of Search-It Inc	877-852-2507	•	•	•	•
•	•	•	•	•	Bearak Reports	800-331-5677	•	•	•	•
•	•	•			Forbes Public Research Inc	518-732-2841	•	•	•	
					Horizons Unlimited	617-696-6397		•	•	
				•	M & M Title Services	413-374-0158	•	•	•	
•	•	•	•	•	Northshore Paralegal Services Inc	800-883-6020	•	•	•	•
		•	•		Primetime Research Inc	866-737-2714				
•	•	•	•	•	R & R Search Inc	508-359-2400	•	•	•	•
•		•	•		Seyler Retrieval	413-782-9907/348-3667				
•	•	•	•	•	Worcester Record Search	508-842-7282	•	•	•	•

DT	BK	CV	CR	PR	←COURTS **MIDDLESEX**	RECORDING→	UC	RE	TX	VS
•	•	•	•	•	A Scott Broadhurst Associates	617-536-3486	•	•	•	
•	•	•			Access Information & Retrievals	617-306-1547	•	•	•	
•	•	•	•	•	Attorney Subpoena Services [SOP]	877-786-5374	•	•	•	•
•	•	•	•	•	Badzmierowski Services [SOP]	508-498-3583	•	•	•	•

DT	BK	CV	CR	PR	←Courts	Recording→	UC	RE	TX	VS
•	•	•	•	•	Barry Shuster Information Services, A Div of Search-It Inc	877-852-2507	•	•	•	•
•	•	•	•	•	Bearak Reports	800-331-5677	•	•	•	•
•	•	•		•	Essex County Paralegals Inc	800-922-4752	•	•	•	
					Horizons Unlimited	617-696-6397		•	•	
•	•	•	•	•	LegalTrieve Information Services	508-238-4227	•	•	•	
				•	Massachusetts Document Retrieval	617-249-0323				•
•	•	•	•		Masscourtresearch	617-696-2178			•	
•	•	•	•	•	Michael B Fixman & Associates [SOP]	800-434-9626	•	•	•	•
•	•	•	•	•	NH Background Investigations LLC	603-598-4106	•	•	•	•
•	•	•	•	•	Northshore Paralegal Services Inc	800-883-6020	•	•	•	•
•	•	•	•	•	P.S.P.S. Legal Support Services Inc [SOP]	617-846-7130	•	•	•	•
		•	•		Walter J Pace	617-389-6730				
•	•	•	•	•	Paralegal Resource Center Inc	866-742-1939	•	•	•	•
		•	•		Primetime Research Inc	866-737-2714				
				•	Quirk Associates	781-326-1202	•	•	•	•
•	•	•	•	•	R & R Search Inc	508-359-2400	•	•	•	•
•	•	•	•	•	RCC & Associates Inc	508-839-3234			•	
•	•	•	•	•	Simmons Agency Inc	800-237-8230	•	•	•	•
•	•	•	•	•	Suburban Record Research	617-536-3486	•	•	•	
		•	•	•	Surette Investigations [SOP]	207-268-3419	•	•	•	•
					Veritas Information Services	781-643-7811		•		

DT	BK	CV	CR	PR	←Courts **Nantucket**	Recording→	UC	RE	TX	VS
•	•	•	•	•	Attorney Subpoena Services [SOP]	877-786-5374	•	•	•	•
•	•	•	•	•	Badzmierowski Services [SOP]	508-498-3583	•	•	•	•
•	•	•	•	•	Barry Shuster Information Services, A Div of Search-It Inc	877-852-2507	•	•	•	•
					Horizons Unlimited	617-696-6397		•	•	
•	•	•	•	•	Northshore Paralegal Services Inc	800-883-6020	•	•	•	•
•	•	•	•	•	R & R Search Inc	508-359-2400	•	•	•	•

DT	BK	CV	CR	PR	←Courts **Norfolk**	Recording→	UC	RE	TX	VS
•	•	•	•	•	A Scott Broadhurst Associates	617-536-3486	•	•	•	
•	•	•			Access Information & Retrievals	617-306-1547	•	•	•	
•	•	•	•	•	Attorney Subpoena Services [SOP]	877-786-5374	•	•	•	•
•	•	•	•	•	Badzmierowski Services [SOP]	508-498-3583	•	•	•	•
•	•	•	•	•	Barry Shuster Information Services, A Div of Search-It Inc	877-852-2507	•	•	•	•
•	•	•	•	•	Bearak Reports	800-331-5677	•	•	•	•
					Horizons Unlimited	617-696-6397		•	•	
•	•	•	•	•	LegalTrieve Information Services	508-238-4227	•	•	•	•
•	•	•	•	•	Len Page Paralegal/Research Services	508-967-2504	•	•	•	•
•	•	•	•	•	Northshore Paralegal Services Inc	800-883-6020	•	•	•	•
•	•	•	•	•	Paralegal Resource Center Inc	866-742-1939	•	•	•	•
		•	•		Primetime Research Inc	866-737-2714				
				•	Quirk Associates	781-326-1202	•	•	•	•
•	•	•	•	•	R & R Search Inc	508-359-2400	•	•	•	•
		•	•		Rapid Record Retrieval	508-759-8622				
•	•	•	•	•	Simmons Agency Inc	800-237-8230	•	•	•	•
•	•	•	•	•	Suburban Record Research	617-536-3486	•	•	•	
					Veritas Information Services	781-643-7811		•		

DT	BK	CV	CR	PR	←Courts **Plymouth**	Recording→	UC	RE	TX	VS
•	•	•			Access Information & Retrievals	617-306-1547	•	•	•	
•	•	•	•	•	Associated Professional Services [SOP]	800-849-7870	•	•	•	•
•	•	•	•	•	Attorney Subpoena Services [SOP]	877-786-5374	•	•	•	•
•	•	•	•	•	Badzmierowski Services [SOP]	508-498-3583	•	•	•	•
•	•	•	•	•	Barry Shuster Information Services, A Div of Search-It Inc	877-852-2507	•	•	•	•
•	•	•	•	•	Bearak Reports	800-331-5677	•	•	•	•
		•	•	•	Brenda L Gaskill	508-759-3156	•	•	•	•
					Horizons Unlimited	617-696-6397		•	•	

DT	BK	CV	CR	PR	Name	Phone	UC	RE	TX	VS
•	•	•	•	•	LegalTrieve Information Services	508-238-4227	•	•	•	
•	•	•	•	•	Len Page Paralegal/Research Services	508-967-2504	•	•	•	•
•	•	•	•	•	Northshore Paralegal Services Inc	800-883-6020	•	•	•	•
•	•	•	•	•	Paralegal Resource Center Inc	866-742-1939	•	•	•	•
•	•	•	•	•	R & R Search Inc	508-359-2400	•	•	•	•
		•	•		Rapid Record Retrieval	508-759-8622				
•	•	•	•	•	Simmons Agency Inc	800-237-8230	•	•	•	•

DT	BK	CV	CR	PR	←Courts — **Suffolk**	Recording→	UC	RE	TX	VS
•	•	•	•	•	A Scott Broadhurst Associates	617-536-3486	•	•	•	
•	•	•			Access Information & Retrievals	617-306-1547	•	•	•	
•	•	•	•	•	Attorney Subpoena Services [SOP]	877-786-5374	•	•	•	•
•	•	•	•	•	Badzmierowski Services [SOP]	508-498-3583	•	•	•	•
•	•	•	•	•	Barry Shuster Information Services, A Div of Search-It Inc	877-852-2507	•	•	•	•
•	•	•		•	Bay State Corporate Services Inc	617-742-8484	•	•	•	•
•	•	•	•	•	Bearak Reports	800-331-5677	•	•	•	•
•	•	•	•	•	Corporation Service Company - CSC	800-927-9800	•	•	•	•
•	•	•		•	Essex County Paralegals Inc	800-922-4752	•	•	•	
					Horizons Unlimited	617-696-6397		•	•	
•	•	•	•	•	LegalTrieve Information Services	508-238-4227	•	•	•	
				•	Massachusetts Document Retrieval	617-249-0323				•
•	•	•	•		Masscourtresearch	617-696-2178			•	
•	•	•	•	•	Michael B Fixman & Associates [SOP]	800-434-9626	•	•	•	•
•	•	•	•	•	NH Background Investigations LLC	603-598-4106	•	•	•	•
•	•	•	•	•	Northshore Paralegal Services Inc	800-883-6020	•	•	•	•
•	•	•	•	•	P.S.P.S. Legal Support Services Inc [SOP]	617-846-7130	•	•	•	•
		•	•		Walter J Pace	617-389-6730				
•	•	•	•	•	Paralegal Resource Center Inc	866-742-1939	•	•	•	•
		•	•		Primetime Research Inc	866-737-2714				
				•	Quirk Associates	781-326-1202	•	•	•	•
•	•	•	•	•	R & R Search Inc	508-359-2400	•	•	•	•
•	•	•	•	•	RCC & Associates Inc	508-839-3234			•	
•	•	•	•	•	Simmons Agency Inc	800-237-8230	•	•	•	•
•	•	•	•	•	Suburban Record Research	617-536-3486	•	•	•	
					Veritas Information Services	781-643-7811		•		

DT	BK	CV	CR	PR	←Courts — **Worcester**	Recording→	UC	RE	TX	VS
•	•	•	•	•	A Scott Broadhurst Associates	617-536-3486	•	•	•	
•	•	•	•	•	Attorney Subpoena Services [SOP]	877-786-5374	•	•	•	•
•	•	•	•	•	Badzmierowski Services [SOP]	508-498-3583	•	•	•	•
•	•	•	•	•	Barry Shuster Information Services, A Div of Search-It Inc	877-852-2507	•	•	•	•
•	•	•	•	•	Bearak Reports	800-331-5677	•	•	•	•
•	•	•		•	Essex County Paralegals Inc	800-922-4752	•	•	•	
•	•	•		•	Marcia A Gazoorian	508-754-9503	•	•	•	
					Horizons Unlimited	617-696-6397		•	•	
				•	M & M Title Services	413-374-0158	•	•	•	
•	•	•	•	•	Northshore Paralegal Services Inc	800-883-6020	•	•	•	•
•	•	•	•	•	Paralegal Resource Center Inc	866-742-1939	•	•	•	•
		•	•		Primetime Research Inc	866-737-2714				
•	•	•	•	•	R & R Search Inc	508-359-2400	•	•	•	•
•	•	•	•	•	RCC & Associates Inc	508-839-3234			•	
•	•	•	•	•	Suburban Record Research	617-536-3486	•	•	•	
•	•	•	•	•	Worcester Record Search	508-842-7282	•	•	•	•

Michigan

COURT RECORDS RETRIEVED — **RECORDING RECORDS RETRIEVED**

DT	BK	CV	CR	PR	←Courts	ALCONA	Recording→	UC	RE	TX	VS
•	•	•	•		ASK Services Inc (Michigan)		888-416-1313	•	•	•	•

DT	BK	CV	CR	PR	←Courts	ALGER	Recording→	UC	RE	TX	VS
•	•	•	•		ASK Services Inc (Michigan)		888-416-1313	•	•	•	•

DT	BK	CV	CR	PR	←Courts	ALLEGAN	Recording→	UC	RE	TX	VS
•	•	•	•		ASK Services Inc (Michigan)		888-416-1313	•	•	•	•
				•	Lake Michigan Title Co		269-637-8595	•	•	•	
•	•	•			Michigan Search Company		734-427-7224	•	•	•	
•	•	•	•	•	ProSearch		888-585-6473	•	•	•	•
•	•	•	•	•	SWP Searches [SOP]		616-847-6989	•	•	•	•

DT	BK	CV	CR	PR	←Courts	ALPENA	Recording→	UC	RE	TX	VS
•	•	•	•		ASK Services Inc (Michigan)		888-416-1313	•	•	•	•
				•	Huron Shores Abstract & Title		989-734-3344	•	•	•	
•	•	•	•	•	Research North Inc of Alpena [SOP]		888-876-1010	•	•	•	•

DT	BK	CV	CR	PR	←Courts	ANTRIM	Recording→	UC	RE	TX	VS
•	•	•	•		ASK Services Inc (Michigan)		888-416-1313	•	•	•	•

DT	BK	CV	CR	PR	←Courts	ARENAC	Recording→	UC	RE	TX	VS
		•	•	•	Arenae Abstract & Title Co		989-846-6560	•	•	•	•
•	•	•	•		ASK Services Inc (Michigan)		888-416-1313	•	•	•	•
				•	Bay County Abstract Co		989-895-9910	•	•	•	
		•	•	•	Ogemaw Title Co		989-345-7240	•	•	•	•

DT	BK	CV	CR	PR	←Courts	BARAGA	Recording→	UC	RE	TX	VS
•	•	•	•		ASK Services Inc (Michigan)		888-416-1313	•	•	•	•

DT	BK	CV	CR	PR	←Courts	BARRY	Recording→	UC	RE	TX	VS
•	•	•	•		ASK Services Inc (Michigan)		888-416-1313	•	•	•	•
		•	•	•	Magic P I & Security Inc [SOP]		800-362-4388	•	•	•	•
		•	•	•	Metropolitan Title Co (Hastings)		269-945-9447	•	•	•	•
•	•	•			Michigan Search Company		734-427-7224	•	•	•	
•	•	•	•	•	The Fatman Intl Private Detective Svc [SOP]		616-949-1790	•	•	•	•

DT	BK	CV	CR	PR	←Courts	BAY	Recording→	UC	RE	TX	VS
•	•	•	•		ASK Services Inc (Michigan)		888-416-1313	•	•	•	•
				•	Bay County Abstract Co		989-895-9910	•	•	•	
				•	Gladwin County Abstract Company		989-426-7411	•	•	•	
•	•	•	•	•	Paul Maisano Designs		248-625-6366	•	•	•	
•	•	•	•	•	Records Retrieval Service		810-220-0810	•	•	•	•
•	•	•	•	•	Teter Security Assoc Inc		800-726-5959			•	

DT	BK	CV	CR	PR	←Courts	BENZIE	Recording→	UC	RE	TX	VS
•	•	•	•		ASK Services Inc (Michigan)		888-416-1313	•	•	•	•

DT	BK	CV	CR	PR	←Courts	BERRIEN	Recording→	UC	RE	TX	VS
•	•	•	•		ASK Services Inc (Michigan)		888-416-1313	•	•	•	•
•	•	•	•	•	Case Services Inc [SOP]		877-291-6868	•	•	•	•
		•	•		Independent Research Inc		269-429-9873				

DT	BK	CV	CR	PR	←Courts	Recording→	UC	RE	TX	VS
		•	•	•	Magic P I & Security Inc [SOP]	800-362-4388	•	•	•	•
•	•	•			Michigan Search Company	734-427-7224	•	•	•	
•	•	•	•	•	ProSearch	888-585-6473	•	•	•	•

DT	BK	CV	CR	PR	←Courts **Branch**	Recording→	UC	RE	TX	VS
•	•	•	•		ASK Services Inc (Michigan)	888-416-1313	•	•	•	•
				•	Hillsdale Title Co - Mid-State Title	517-437-7345		•	•	•
•	•	•			Michigan Search Company	734-427-7224	•	•	•	

DT	BK	CV	CR	PR	←Courts **Calhoun**	Recording→	UC	RE	TX	VS
•	•	•	•		ASK Services Inc (Michigan)	888-416-1313	•	•	•	•
		•	•	•	Magic P I & Security Inc [SOP]	800-362-4388	•	•	•	•
•	•	•			Michigan Search Company	734-427-7224	•	•	•	
•	•	•	•	•	Paul Maisano Designs	248-625-6366	•	•	•	
•	•	•	•	•	Records Retrieval Service	810-220-0810	•	•	•	•
•	•	•	•	•	The Fatman Intl Private Detective Svc [SOP]	616-949-1790	•	•	•	•

DT	BK	CV	CR	PR	←Courts **Cass**	Recording→	UC	RE	TX	VS
•	•	•	•		ASK Services Inc (Michigan)	888-416-1313	•	•	•	•
•	•	•	•	•	Case Services Inc [SOP]	877-291-6868	•	•	•	•
		•	•	•	Magic P I & Security Inc [SOP]	800-362-4388	•	•	•	•
•	•	•			Michigan Search Company	734-427-7224	•	•	•	
•	•	•	•	•	ProSearch	888-585-6473	•	•	•	•
		•	•	•	St Joseph County Abstract Office Inc	269-467-6075	•	•	•	•

DT	BK	CV	CR	PR	←Courts **Charlevoix**	Recording→	UC	RE	TX	VS
•	•	•	•		ASK Services Inc (Michigan)	888-416-1313	•	•	•	•
•	•	•	•	•	Research North Inc of Petoskey [SOP]	888-876-1010	•	•	•	•

DT	BK	CV	CR	PR	←Courts **Cheboygan**	Recording→	UC	RE	TX	VS
•	•	•	•		ASK Services Inc (Michigan)	888-416-1313	•	•	•	•
					Cheboygan Title	866-627-7150	•	•	•	•

DT	BK	CV	CR	PR	←Courts **Chippewa**	Recording→	UC	RE	TX	VS
•	•	•	•		ASK Services Inc (Michigan)	888-416-1313	•	•	•	•
				•	Mackinac Abstract & Title	906-643-7452		•	•	

DT	BK	CV	CR	PR	←Courts **Clare**	Recording→	UC	RE	TX	VS
•	•	•	•		ASK Services Inc (Michigan)	888-416-1313	•	•	•	•
				•	Bay County Abstract Co	989-895-9910	•	•	•	
				•	Gladwin County Abstract Company	989-426-7411	•	•	•	
					Isabella County Abstract	989-773-3241		•	•	•
				•	Land Title & Abstract	989-426-0011	•	•	•	•
		•		•	Mt Pleasant Abstract & Title Inc	989-773-3651	•	•	•	

DT	BK	CV	CR	PR	←Courts **Clinton**	Recording→	UC	RE	TX	VS
•	•	•	•		ASK Services Inc (Michigan)	888-416-1313	•	•	•	•
•	•	•	•	•	Paul Maisano Designs	248-625-6366	•	•	•	

DT	BK	CV	CR	PR	←Courts **Crawford**	Recording→	UC	RE	TX	VS
•	•	•	•		ASK Services Inc (Michigan)	888-416-1313	•	•	•	•
					AuSable Valley Abstract & Title Co.	989-826-3385	•	•	•	
					Crawford Cty Title, Roscommon Cty Title	989-348-9832	•	•	•	

DT	BK	CV	CR	PR	←Courts **Delta**	Recording→	UC	RE	TX	VS
•	•	•	•		ASK Services Inc (Michigan)	888-416-1313	•	•	•	•
•	•	•	•	•	Research North Inc of Marquette [SOP]	888-876-1010	•	•	•	•

DT	BK	CV	CR	PR	←Courts **Dickinson**	Recording→	UC	RE	TX	VS
•	•	•	•		ASK Services Inc (Michigan)	888-416-1313	•	•	•	•
•	•	•			Michigan Search Company	734-427-7224	•	•	•	
		•	•		Superior Title & Abstract	906-774-9010	•	•	•	

DT	BK	CV	CR	PR	←Courts	EATON	Recording→	UC	RE	TX	VS
•	•	•	•			ASK Services Inc (Michigan)	888-416-1313	•	•	•	•
•	•	•				Michigan Search Company	734-427-7224	•	•	•	
•	•	•	•	•		Paul Maisano Designs	248-625-6366	•	•	•	

DT	BK	CV	CR	PR	←Courts	EMMET	Recording→	UC	RE	TX	VS
•	•	•	•			ASK Services Inc (Michigan)	888-416-1313	•	•	•	•
•	•	•	•	•		Research North Inc of Petoskey [SOP]	888-876-1010	•	•	•	•

DT	BK	CV	CR	PR	←Courts	GENESEE	Recording→	UC	RE	TX	VS
•	•	•	•	•		Advanced Surveillance Group Inc [SOP]	888-677-9700	•	•		•
•	•	•	•			ASK Services Inc (Michigan)	888-416-1313	•	•	•	•
						Centennial Title & Abstract Co.	810-238-5100		•	•	
		•	•	•		Huffmaster Associates Inc [SOP]	800-446-1515	•	•	•	•
		•	•			Independent Research Inc	269-429-9873				
		•	•			Investigative Information Inc	586-491-6125		•	•	
•	•	•				Michigan Search Company	734-427-7224	•	•	•	
•	•	•	•	•		Paul Maisano Designs	248-625-6366	•	•	•	
			•			Pure Again	586-465-4359	•	•	•	
•	•	•	•	•		Records Retrieval Service	810-220-0810	•	•	•	•
						Sargents Title Co.	810-767-2355		•		

DT	BK	CV	CR	PR	←Courts	GLADWIN	Recording→	UC	RE	TX	VS
•	•	•	•			ASK Services Inc (Michigan)	888-416-1313	•	•	•	•
				•		Bay County Abstract Co	989-895-9910	•	•	•	
				•		Gladwin County Abstract Company	989-426-7411	•	•	•	
				•		Land Title & Abstract	989-426-0011	•	•	•	•
		•		•		Mt Pleasant Abstract & Title Inc.	989-773-3651	•	•	•	

DT	BK	CV	CR	PR	←Courts	GOGEBIC	Recording→	UC	RE	TX	VS
•	•	•	•			ASK Services Inc (Michigan)	888-416-1313	•	•	•	•
		•		•		Iron Title & Abstract Co	906-932-6340	•	•	•	

DT	BK	CV	CR	PR	←Courts	GRAND TRAVERSE	Recording→	UC	RE	TX	VS
•	•	•	•			ASK Services Inc (Michigan)	888-416-1313	•	•	•	•
				•		Grand Traverse Title Co.	231-946-5686	•	•	•	
•	•	•				Michigan Search Company	734-427-7224	•	•	•	
		•	•	•		Research North Inc of Traverse City [SOP]	888-876-1010	•	•	•	•

DT	BK	CV	CR	PR	←Courts	GRATIOT	Recording→	UC	RE	TX	VS
				•		Alma Abstract & Title Co	989-463-8325	•	•	•	•
•	•	•	•			ASK Services Inc (Michigan)	888-416-1313	•	•	•	•
		•		•		Mt Pleasant Abstract & Title Inc.	989-773-3651	•	•	•	

DT	BK	CV	CR	PR	←Courts	HILLSDALE	Recording→	UC	RE	TX	VS
•	•	•	•			ASK Services Inc (Michigan)	888-416-1313	•	•	•	•
				•		Hillsdale Title Co - Mid-State Title	517-437-7345		•	•	•
•	•	•				Michigan Search Company	734-427-7224	•	•	•	

DT	BK	CV	CR	PR	←Courts	HOUGHTON	Recording→	UC	RE	TX	VS
•	•	•	•			ASK Services Inc (Michigan)	888-416-1313	•	•	•	•
				•		Copper Range Abstract & Title Co	906-482-7903	•	•	•	•

DT	BK	CV	CR	PR	←Courts	HURON	Recording→	UC	RE	TX	VS
•	•	•	•			ASK Services Inc (Michigan)	888-416-1313	•	•	•	•
				•		Bay County Abstract Co	989-895-9910	•	•	•	

DT	BK	CV	CR	PR	←Courts	INGHAM	Recording→	UC	RE	TX	VS
•	•	•	•			ASK Services Inc (Michigan)	888-416-1313	•	•	•	•
		•	•			Independent Research Inc	269-429-9873				
•	•	•				Michigan Search Company	734-427-7224	•	•	•	

DT	BK	CV	CR	PR	←COURTS	RECORDING→	UC	RE	TX	VS
•	•	•	•	•	Paul Maisano Designs	248-625-6366	•	•	•	
•	•	•	•	•	Records Retrieval Service	810-220-0810	•	•	•	•

DT	BK	CV	CR	PR	←COURTS IONIA	RECORDING→	UC	RE	TX	VS
•	•	•	•		ASK Services Inc (Michigan)	888-416-1313	•	•	•	•

DT	BK	CV	CR	PR	←COURTS IOSCO	RECORDING→	UC	RE	TX	VS
•	•	•	•		ASK Services Inc (Michigan)	888-416-1313	•	•	•	•
		•		•	Iosco County Abstract Office Ltd	989-362-3231	•	•	•	•

DT	BK	CV	CR	PR	←COURTS IRON	RECORDING→	UC	RE	TX	VS
•	•	•	•		ASK Services Inc (Michigan)	888-416-1313	•	•	•	•
					Penninsula Title & Abstract Corp	906-875-6618	•	•	•	

DT	BK	CV	CR	PR	←COURTS ISABELLA	RECORDING→	UC	RE	TX	VS
•	•	•	•		ASK Services Inc (Michigan)	888-416-1313	•	•	•	•
				•	Bay County Abstract Co	989-895-9910	•	•	•	
					Isabella County Abstract	989-773-3241		•	•	•
•	•	•			Michigan Search Company	734-427-7224	•	•	•	
•	•	•		•	Midland Title and Abstract Co	989-839-1003	•	•	•	•
		•		•	Mt Pleasant Abstract & Title Inc	989-773-3651	•	•	•	

DT	BK	CV	CR	PR	←COURTS JACKSON	RECORDING→	UC	RE	TX	VS
•	•	•	•		ASK Services Inc (Michigan)	888-416-1313	•	•	•	•
•	•	•			Michigan Search Company	734-427-7224	•	•	•	
•	•	•	•	•	Paul Maisano Designs	248-625-6366	•	•	•	

DT	BK	CV	CR	PR	←COURTS KALAMAZOO	RECORDING→	UC	RE	TX	VS
•	•	•	•		ASK Services Inc (Michigan)	888-416-1313	•	•	•	•
		•	•		Independent Research Inc	269-429-9873				
		•	•	•	Magic P I & Security Inc [SOP]	800-362-4388	•	•	•	•
•	•	•			Michigan Search Company	734-427-7224	•	•	•	
•	•	•	•	•	Paul Maisano Designs	248-625-6366	•	•	•	
•	•	•	•	•	ProSearch	888-585-6473	•	•	•	•
•	•	•	•	•	Records Retrieval Service	810-220-0810	•	•	•	•

DT	BK	CV	CR	PR	←COURTS KALKASKA	RECORDING→	UC	RE	TX	VS
•	•	•	•		ASK Services Inc (Michigan)	888-416-1313	•	•	•	•

DT	BK	CV	CR	PR	←COURTS KENT	RECORDING→	UC	RE	TX	VS
•	•	•	•		ASK Services Inc (Michigan)	888-416-1313	•	•	•	•
		•	•		Independent Research Inc	269-429-9873				
		•	•		InfoQuest of West Michigan LLC	616-581-2820				
•	•	•			Michigan Search Company	734-427-7224	•	•	•	
•	•	•	•	•	Paul Maisano Designs	248-625-6366	•	•	•	
•	•	•	•		Professional Courier Service	616-451-4445	•			•
•	•	•	•	•	ProSearch	888-585-6473	•	•	•	•
•	•	•	•	•	Records Retrieval Service	810-220-0810	•	•	•	•
•	•			•	Special Private Inv Inc [SOP]	800-577-3783				
•	•			•	SPI [SOP]	800-577-3783				
•	•	•	•	•	SWP Searches [SOP]	616-847-6989	•	•	•	•
•	•	•	•	•	The Fatman Intl Private Detective Svc [SOP]	616-949-1790	•	•	•	•

DT	BK	CV	CR	PR	←COURTS KEWEENAW	RECORDING→	UC	RE	TX	VS
•	•	•	•		ASK Services Inc (Michigan)	888-416-1313	•	•	•	•
				•	Copper Range Abstract & Title Co	906-482-7903	•	•	•	•

DT	BK	CV	CR	PR	←COURTS LAKE	RECORDING→	UC	RE	TX	VS
•	•	•	•		ASK Services Inc (Michigan)	888-416-1313	•	•	•	•
		•	•	•	Lake County Abstract Co Inc	231-745-3432	•	•	•	•

DT	BK	CV	CR	PR	←Courts	LAPEER	Recording→	UC	RE	TX	VS
•	•	•	•		ASK Services Inc (Michigan)		888-416-1313	•	•	•	•
				•	Bay County Abstract Co		989-895-9910	•	•	•	
		•	•	•	Huffmaster Associates Inc [SOP]		800-446-1515	•	•	•	•
				•	LaPeer County Abstract & Title Co Inc		810-664-9951	•	•	•	•
•	•	•	•	•	Paul Maisano Designs		248-625-6366	•	•	•	
			•		Pure Again		586-465-4359	•	•	•	

DT	BK	CV	CR	PR	←Courts	LEELANAU	Recording→	UC	RE	TX	VS
•	•	•	•		ASK Services Inc (Michigan)		888-416-1313	•	•	•	•
				•	Leelanau Title Co		231-271-6191	•	•	•	
		•	•	•	Research North Inc of Traverse City [SOP]		888-876-1010	•	•	•	•

DT	BK	CV	CR	PR	←Courts	LENAWEE	Recording→	UC	RE	TX	VS
					American Title Company of Lenawee		517-263-4040	•	•	•	•
•	•	•	•		ASK Services Inc (Michigan)		888-416-1313	•	•	•	•
				•	Hillsdale Title Co - Mid-State Title		517-437-7345		•	•	•

DT	BK	CV	CR	PR	←Courts	LIVINGSTON	Recording→	UC	RE	TX	VS
•	•	•	•		ASK Services Inc (Michigan)		888-416-1313	•	•	•	•
		•	•	•	Huffmaster Associates Inc [SOP]		800-446-1515	•	•	•	•
•			•		Infocite		734-665-6484		•	•	•
		•		•	Landmark Title Service		810-227-1733	•	•	•	•
•	•	•	•	•	Michael Anderson Company		800-992-9936	•	•	•	•
•	•	•			Michigan Search Company		734-427-7224	•	•	•	
•	•	•	•	•	Paul Maisano Designs		248-625-6366	•	•	•	
			•		Pure Again		586-465-4359	•	•	•	
•	•	•	•	•	Records Retrieval Service		810-220-0810	•	•	•	•

DT	BK	CV	CR	PR	←Courts	LUCE	Recording→	UC	RE	TX	VS
•	•	•	•		ASK Services Inc (Michigan)		888-416-1313	•	•	•	•
				•	Mackinac Abstract & Title		906-643-7452		•	•	

DT	BK	CV	CR	PR	←Courts	MACKINAC	Recording→	UC	RE	TX	VS
•	•	•	•		ASK Services Inc (Michigan)		888-416-1313	•	•	•	•
				•	Mackinac Abstract & Title		906-643-7452		•	•	
				•	Whiteside Abstract & Title Insurance		906-643-9292	•	•	•	

DT	BK	CV	CR	PR	←Courts	MACOMB	Recording→	UC	RE	TX	VS
•	•	•		•	Abstractor Associates Inc		586-778-7554	•	•	•	•
•	•	•	•	•	Advanced Surveillance Group Inc [SOP]		888-677-9700	•	•		•
•	•	•	•		ASK Services Inc (Michigan)		888-416-1313	•	•	•	•
		•	•	•	Huffmaster Associates Inc [SOP]		800-446-1515	•	•	•	•
		•	•		Independent Research Inc		269-429-9873				
•			•		Infocite		734-665-6484		•	•	•
		•	•		Investigative Information Inc		586-491-6125		•	•	
•	•	•	•	•	Michael Anderson Company		800-992-9936	•	•	•	•
•	•	•			Michigan Search Company		734-427-7224	•	•	•	
•	•	•	•	•	Paul Maisano Designs		248-625-6366	•	•	•	
			•		Pure Again		586-465-4359	•	•	•	
•	•	•	•	•	Records Retrieval Service		810-220-0810	•	•	•	•
•	•	•	•	•	VISTA Inc [SOP]		248-559-3500	•	•	•	•

DT	BK	CV	CR	PR	←Courts	MANISTEE	Recording→	UC	RE	TX	VS
•	•	•	•		ASK Services Inc (Michigan)		888-416-1313	•	•	•	•
		•	•	•	Manistee Abstract & Title Co		231-723-3397	•	•	•	•

DT	BK	CV	CR	PR	←Courts	MARQUETTE	Recording→	UC	RE	TX	VS
•	•	•	•		ASK Services Inc (Michigan)		888-416-1313	•	•	•	•
				•	Great Northern Title & Abstract Inc		906-228-6100	•	•	•	
•	•	•	•	•	Research North Inc of Marquette [SOP]		888-876-1010	•	•	•	•

DT	BK	CV	CR	PR	←Courts	MASON	Recording→	UC	RE	TX	VS
•	•	•	•			ASK Services Inc (Michigan)	888-416-1313	•	•	•	•
						Mason County Abstract & Title Inc	231-843-2645	•	•	•	

DT	BK	CV	CR	PR	←Courts	MECOSTA	Recording→	UC	RE	TX	VS
•	•	•	•			ASK Services Inc (Michigan)	888-416-1313	•	•	•	•
						Isabella County Abstract	989-773-3241		•	•	•
		•		•		Mt Pleasant Abstract & Title Inc	989-773-3651	•	•	•	

DT	BK	CV	CR	PR	←Courts	MENOMINEE	Recording→	UC	RE	TX	VS
•	•	•	•			ASK Services Inc (Michigan)	888-416-1313	•	•	•	•
		•	•	•		Associated Peninsula Title & Abstract Co	906-863-7871	•	•	•	•
		•	•			Superior Title & Abstract	906-774-9010	•	•	•	

DT	BK	CV	CR	PR	←Courts	MIDLAND	Recording→	UC	RE	TX	VS
•	•	•	•			ASK Services Inc (Michigan)	888-416-1313	•	•	•	•
				•		Bay County Abstract Co	989-895-9910	•	•	•	
				•		Gladwin County Abstract Company	989-426-7411	•	•	•	
•	•	•				Michigan Search Company	734-427-7224	•	•	•	
•	•	•		•		Midland Title and Abstract Co	989-839-1003	•	•	•	•
		•		•		Mt Pleasant Abstract & Title Inc	989-773-3651	•	•	•	
•	•	•	•	•		Records Retrieval Service	810-220-0810	•	•	•	•
•	•	•	•	•		Teter Security Assoc Inc	800-726-5959			•	

DT	BK	CV	CR	PR	←Courts	MISSAUKEE	Recording→	UC	RE	TX	VS
•	•	•	•			ASK Services Inc (Michigan)	888-416-1313	•	•	•	•
						Missaukee Title Co	231-839-4563		•		

DT	BK	CV	CR	PR	←Courts	MONROE	Recording→	UC	RE	TX	VS
•	•	•	•			ASK Services Inc (Michigan)	888-416-1313	•	•	•	•
		•	•	•		Huffmaster Associates Inc [SOP]	800-446-1515	•	•	•	•
•	•	•	•	•		Paul Maisano Designs	248-625-6366	•	•	•	
•	•	•	•	•		Records Retrieval Service	810-220-0810	•	•	•	•
•	•	•	•	•		VISTA Inc [SOP]	248-559-3500	•	•	•	•

DT	BK	CV	CR	PR	←Courts	MONTCALM	Recording→	UC	RE	TX	VS
				•		Alma Abstract & Title Co	989-463-8325	•	•	•	•
•	•	•	•			ASK Services Inc (Michigan)	888-416-1313	•	•	•	•
						Isabella County Abstract	989-773-3241		•	•	•
		•		•		Mt Pleasant Abstract & Title Inc	989-773-3651	•	•	•	

DT	BK	CV	CR	PR	←Courts	MONTMORENCY	Recording→	UC	RE	TX	VS
•	•	•	•			ASK Services Inc (Michigan)	888-416-1313	•	•	•	•

DT	BK	CV	CR	PR	←Courts	MUSKEGON	Recording→	UC	RE	TX	VS
•	•	•	•			ASK Services Inc (Michigan)	888-416-1313	•	•	•	•
		•	•			InfoQuest of West Michigan LLC	616-581-2820				
•	•	•	•	•		SWP Searches [SOP]	616-847-6989	•	•	•	•

DT	BK	CV	CR	PR	←Courts	NEWAYGO	Recording→	UC	RE	TX	VS
•	•	•	•			ASK Services Inc (Michigan)	888-416-1313	•	•	•	•
		•		•		Mt Pleasant Abstract & Title Inc	989-773-3651	•	•	•	

DT	BK	CV	CR	PR	←Courts	OAKLAND	Recording→	UC	RE	TX	VS
•	•	•	•	•		Advanced Surveillance Group Inc [SOP]	888-677-9700	•	•		•
•	•	•	•			ASK Services Inc (Michigan)	888-416-1313	•	•	•	•
		•	•	•		Huffmaster Associates Inc [SOP]	800-446-1515	•	•	•	•
		•	•			Independent Research Inc	269-429-9873				
•			•			Infocite	734-665-6484		•	•	•
		•	•			Investigative Information Inc	586-491-6125		•	•	
		•		•		Landmark Title Service	810-227-1733	•	•	•	•

DT	BK	CV	CR	PR	Courts / Recording	Phone	UC	RE	TX	VS
•					Lightning Records Inc	734-285-2495	•	•	•	
•	•		•		LT Marketing LLC	313-361-2468				
•	•	•	•	•	Michael Anderson Company	800-992-9936	•	•	•	•
•	•	•			Michigan Search Company	734-427-7224	•	•	•	
•	•	•	•	•	Paul Maisano Designs	248-625-6366	•	•	•	
			•		Pure Again	586-465-4359	•	•	•	
•	•	•	•	•	Records Retrieval Service	810-220-0810	•	•	•	•
•	•	•	•	•	VISTA Inc [SOP]	248-559-3500	•	•	•	•

Oceana

DT	BK	CV	CR	PR	←Courts	Recording→	UC	RE	TX	VS
•	•	•	•		ASK Services Inc (Michigan)	888-416-1313	•	•	•	•

Ogemaw

DT	BK	CV	CR	PR	←Courts	Recording→	UC	RE	TX	VS
•	•	•	•		ASK Services Inc (Michigan)	888-416-1313	•	•	•	•
					AuSable Valley Abstract & Title Co	989-826-3385	•	•	•	
				•	Gladwin County Abstract Company	989-426-7411	•	•	•	
					Ogemaw County Abstract Co	989-345-0110		•	•	
		•	•	•	Ogemaw Title Co	989-345-7240	•	•	•	•

Ontonagon

DT	BK	CV	CR	PR	←Courts	Recording→	UC	RE	TX	VS
•	•	•	•		ASK Services Inc (Michigan)	888-416-1313	•	•	•	•
					Penninsula Title & Abstract Corp	906-875-6618	•	•	•	

Osceola

DT	BK	CV	CR	PR	←Courts	Recording→	UC	RE	TX	VS
•	•	•	•		ASK Services Inc (Michigan)	888-416-1313	•	•	•	•
		•	•	•	Lake County Abstract Co Inc	231-745-3432	•	•	•	•
		•		•	Mt Pleasant Abstract & Title Inc	989-773-3651	•	•	•	

Oscoda

DT	BK	CV	CR	PR	←Courts	Recording→	UC	RE	TX	VS
•	•	•	•		ASK Services Inc (Michigan)	888-416-1313	•	•	•	•
					AuSable Valley Abstract & Title Co	989-826-3385	•	•	•	
		•		•	Oscoda County Abstract Inc	989-826-5832	•	•	•	

Otsego

DT	BK	CV	CR	PR	←Courts	Recording→	UC	RE	TX	VS
•	•	•	•		ASK Services Inc (Michigan)	888-416-1313	•	•	•	•
		•	•	•	Otsego County Abstract Co	989-732-5765	•	•	•	•

Ottawa

DT	BK	CV	CR	PR	←Courts	Recording→	UC	RE	TX	VS
•	•	•	•		ASK Services Inc (Michigan)	888-416-1313	•	•	•	•
		•	•		InfoQuest of West Michigan LLC	616-581-2820				
•	•	•			Michigan Search Company	734-427-7224	•	•	•	
•	•	•	•	•	Paul Maisano Designs	248-625-6366	•	•	•	
•	•	•	•	•	ProSearch	888-585-6473	•	•	•	•
•	•	•	•	•	Records Retrieval Service	810-220-0810	•	•	•	•
•	•	•	•	•	SWP Searches [SOP]	616-847-6989	•	•	•	•
•	•	•	•	•	The Fatman Intl Private Detective Svc [SOP]	616-949-1790	•	•	•	•

Presque Isle

DT	BK	CV	CR	PR	←Courts	Recording→	UC	RE	TX	VS
•	•	•	•		ASK Services Inc (Michigan)	888-416-1313	•	•	•	•
				•	Huron Shores Abstract & Title	989-734-3344	•	•	•	
		•		•	Presque Isle Title Inc	989-734-2816	•	•	•	
•	•	•	•	•	Research North Inc of Alpena [SOP]	888-876-1010	•	•	•	•

Roscommon

DT	BK	CV	CR	PR	←Courts	Recording→	UC	RE	TX	VS
•	•	•	•		ASK Services Inc (Michigan)	888-416-1313	•	•	•	•
					Crawford Cty Title, Roscommon Cty Title	989-348-9832	•	•	•	
				•	Gladwin County Abstract Company	989-426-7411	•	•	•	

Saginaw

DT	BK	CV	CR	PR	←Courts	Recording→	UC	RE	TX	VS
•	•	•	•		ASK Services Inc (Michigan)	888-416-1313	•	•	•	•
				•	Bay County Abstract Co	989-895-9910	•	•	•	
		•	•		Independent Research Inc	269-429-9873				

DT	BK	CV	CR	PR	←Courts	Recording→	UC	RE	TX	VS
		•	•		Investigative Information Inc	586-491-6125		•	•	
•	•	•			Michigan Search Company	734-427-7224	•	•	•	
•	•	•	•	•	Paul Maisano Designs	248-625-6366	•	•	•	
•	•	•	•	•	Records Retrieval Service	810-220-0810	•	•	•	•
•	•	•	•	•	Teter Security Assoc Inc	800-726-5959			•	

DT	BK	CV	CR	PR	←Courts Sanilac	Recording→	UC	RE	TX	VS
•	•	•	•		ASK Services Inc (Michigan)	888-416-1313	•	•	•	•
				•	Bay County Abstract Co	989-895-9910	•	•	•	

DT	BK	CV	CR	PR	←Courts Schoolcraft	Recording→	UC	RE	TX	VS
•	•	•	•		ASK Services Inc (Michigan)	888-416-1313	•	•	•	•

DT	BK	CV	CR	PR	←Courts Shiawassee	Recording→	UC	RE	TX	VS
•	•	•	•		ASK Services Inc (Michigan)	888-416-1313	•	•	•	•
•	•	•	•	•	Paul Maisano Designs	248-625-6366	•	•	•	

DT	BK	CV	CR	PR	←Courts St. Clair	Recording→	UC	RE	TX	VS
•	•	•		•	Abstractor Associates Inc	586-778-7554	•	•	•	•
•	•	•	•		ASK Services Inc (Michigan)	888-416-1313	•	•	•	•
		•	•	•	Huffmaster Associates Inc [SOP]	800-446-1515	•	•	•	•
		•		•	Huron Title Co (Michigan)	800-878-4853	•	•	•	
		•	•		Investigative Information Inc	586-491-6125		•	•	
•	•	•	•	•	Paul Maisano Designs	248-625-6366	•	•	•	

DT	BK	CV	CR	PR	←Courts St. Joseph	Recording→	UC	RE	TX	VS
•	•	•	•		ASK Services Inc (Michigan)	888-416-1313	•	•	•	•
		•	•	•	Magic P I & Security Inc [SOP]	800-362-4388	•	•	•	•
•	•	•			Michigan Search Company	734-427-7224	•	•	•	
•	•	•	•	•	ProSearch	888-585-6473	•	•	•	•
		•	•	•	St Joseph County Abstract Office Inc	269-467-6075	•	•	•	•

DT	BK	CV	CR	PR	←Courts Tuscola	Recording→	UC	RE	TX	VS
•	•	•	•		ASK Services Inc (Michigan)	888-416-1313	•	•	•	•
				•	Bay County Abstract Co	989-895-9910	•	•	•	

DT	BK	CV	CR	PR	←Courts Van Buren	Recording→	UC	RE	TX	VS
•	•	•	•		ASK Services Inc (Michigan)	888-416-1313	•	•	•	•
				•	Lake Michigan Title Co	269-637-8595	•	•	•	
		•	•	•	Magic P I & Security Inc [SOP]	800-362-4388	•	•	•	•
•	•	•			Michigan Search Company	734-427-7224	•	•	•	
•	•	•	•	•	ProSearch	888-585-6473	•	•	•	•
		•	•	•	Van Buren County Abstract Office	269-657-4250	•	•	•	•

DT	BK	CV	CR	PR	←Courts Washtenaw	Recording→	UC	RE	TX	VS
•	•	•		•	Abstractor Associates Inc	586-778-7554	•	•	•	•
•	•	•	•		ASK Services Inc (Michigan)	888-416-1313	•	•	•	•
		•	•	•	Huffmaster Associates Inc [SOP]	800-446-1515	•	•	•	•
		•	•		Independent Research Inc	269-429-9873				
•			•		Infocite	734-665-6484		•	•	•
		•		•	Landmark Title Service	810-227-1733	•	•	•	•
•					Lightning Records Inc	734-285-2495	•	•	•	
•	•	•	•	•	Michael Anderson Company	800-992-9936	•	•	•	•
•	•	•			Michigan Search Company	734-427-7224	•	•	•	
•	•	•	•	•	Paul Maisano Designs	248-625-6366	•	•	•	
			•		Pure Again	586-465-4359	•	•	•	
•	•	•	•	•	Records Retrieval Service	810-220-0810	•	•	•	•
•	•	•	•	•	VISTA Inc [SOP]	248-559-3500	•	•	•	•

DT	BK	CV	CR	PR	←COURTS WAYNE RECORDING→	Phone	UC	RE	TX	VS
•	•	•		•	Abstractor Associates Inc	586-778-7554	•	•	•	•
•	•	•	•	•	Advanced Surveillance Group Inc [SOP]	888-677-9700	•	•		•
•	•	•	•		ASK Services Inc (Michigan)	888-416-1313	•	•	•	•
		•	•	•	Huffmaster Associates Inc [SOP]	800-446-1515	•	•	•	•
		•	•		Independent Research Inc	269-429-9873				
•			•		Infocite	734-665-6484		•	•	•
		•	•		Investigative Information Inc	586-491-6125		•	•	
•					Lightning Records Inc	734-285-2495	•	•	•	
•	•		•		LT Marketing LLC	313-361-2468				
•	•	•	•	•	Michael Anderson Company	800-992-9936	•	•	•	•
•	•	•			Michigan Search Company	734-427-7224	•	•	•	
•	•	•	•	•	Paul Maisano Designs	248-625-6366	•	•	•	
			•		Pure Again	586-465-4359	•	•	•	
•	•	•	•	•	Records Retrieval Service	810-220-0810	•	•	•	•
•	•	•	•	•	VISTA Inc [SOP]	248-559-3500	•	•	•	•

DT	BK	CV	CR	PR	←COURTS WEXFORD RECORDING→	Phone	UC	RE	TX	VS
•	•	•	•		ASK Services Inc (Michigan)	888-416-1313	•	•	•	•
•	•	•			Michigan Search Company	734-427-7224	•	•	•	

[SOP] = PERFORMS SERVICE OF PROCESS

COURT RECORDS

CODE	GOVERNMENT AGENCY	TYPE OF INFORMATION
DT	US District Court	Federal civil and criminal cases
BK	Bankruptcy Court	United States bankruptcy cases
CV	Civil Court	Municipal, county and state level civil cases
CR	Criminal Court	Municipal, county and state level criminal cases
PR	Probate Court	Wills and estate cases

COUNTY RECORDS - RECORDINGS

CODE	GOVERNMENT AGENCY	TYPE OF INFORMATION
UC	UCC Filing Office	Uniform Commercial Code and other personal property liens
RE	Real Estate Recording Office	Real property transactions and liens
TX	Tax Filing Office(s)	Federal and state tax liens, judgment liens
VS	Vital Records Office	Vital statistics—birth, death, marriage, divorce

Editor's Tip: Only Call a Retriever For the Records They Retrieve.
If you call for a criminal record from a retriever who only does work at the recorder's office, then you are wasting your time and the retriever's time.

Minnesota

COURT RECORDS RETRIEVED — **RECORDING RECORDS RETRIEVED**

DT	BK	CV	CR	PR	←Courts **AITKIN** Recording→	Phone	UC	RE	TX	VS
•	•	•	•		ABC Services Inc	507-357-6320	•	•	•	
•	•	•	•	•	Abstract & Title Services of Carlton Inc [SOP]	888-331-3966	•	•	•	•
•	•	•	•	•	Capitol Lien Records & Research [SOP]	800-845-4077	•	•	•	•
•		•	•		GHS Inc - Record Research	763-566-2125		•	•	
•		•	•		Omni Data Retrieval Inc	952-985-7220			•	

DT	BK	CV	CR	PR	←Courts **ANOKA** Recording→	Phone	UC	RE	TX	VS
•	•	•	•		ABC Services Inc	507-357-6320	•	•	•	
•	•	•	•	•	Accountable Process Servers Inc [SOP]	763-689-4190		•	•	
•	•	•	•	•	Adit Research Inc	888-721-5220	•	•	•	•
•	•	•	•		Alpha Court Records & Research	651-699-2222	•		•	
•	•	•			Associated Abstracting Services of MN	612-819-6115	•	•	•	
	•	•	•		Avalon Information Services	715-554-0890	•	•	•	•
•	•	•	•	•	Capitol Lien Records & Research [SOP]	800-845-4077	•	•	•	•
•		•	•		GHS Inc - Record Research	763-566-2125		•	•	
•	•	•	•	•	Heartland Information Services [SOP]	800-967-1882	•	•	•	•
		•	•		Horvath Enterprises Inc	320-982-3253			•	
	•			•	Independent Abstracting Service Inc	763-792-6800	•	•	•	•
•	•	•	•	•	Information Reporting Services Inc [SOP]	612-870-8770			•	
	•	•			Land Title Inc	651-638-1900	•	•	•	
•	•	•	•	•	Metro Legal Services [SOP]	800-488-8994	•	•	•	•
					Midwest Data Search	952-475-2002	•	•	•	
•		•	•		Omni Data Retrieval Inc	952-985-7220			•	
•	•	•	•	•	Paragon Document Research Inc [SOP]	800-892-4235	•	•	•	•
	•	•	•		T D Wolfson & Associates [SOP]	952-920-9645	•		•	
•	•	•	•	•	Twin Cities Research	651-714-0002	•	•	•	•
•	•	•		•	US Corporate Services	800-327-1886	•	•	•	•
•	•	•	•	•	Verified Credentials Inc	800-473-4934	•	•	•	•

DT	BK	CV	CR	PR	←Courts **BECKER** Recording→	Phone	UC	RE	TX	VS
•	•	•	•		ABC Services Inc	507-357-6320	•	•	•	
•	•	•	•	•	Capitol Lien Records & Research [SOP]	800-845-4077	•	•	•	•
•		•	•		GHS Inc - Record Research	763-566-2125		•	•	
		•	•		Horvath Enterprises Inc	320-982-3253			•	
•		•	•		Omni Data Retrieval Inc	952-985-7220			•	

DT	BK	CV	CR	PR	←Courts **BELTRAMI** Recording→	Phone	UC	RE	TX	VS
•	•	•	•		ABC Services Inc	507-357-6320	•	•	•	
•	•	•	•	•	ACME Research [SOP]	218-224-3239	•	•	•	•
•	•	•	•	•	Capitol Lien Records & Research [SOP]	800-845-4077	•	•	•	•
•		•	•		GHS Inc - Record Research	763-566-2125		•	•	
•		•	•		Omni Data Retrieval Inc	952-985-7220			•	
					Sathre Title & Abstracting Inc	218-751-4565	•	•	•	

DT	BK	CV	CR	PR	←Courts **BENTON** Recording→	Phone	UC	RE	TX	VS
•	•	•	•		ABC Services Inc	507-357-6320	•	•	•	
•	•	•	•		Alpha Court Records & Research	651-699-2222	•		•	
•	•	•			Associated Abstracting Services of MN	612-819-6115	•	•	•	
•		•		•	Benton County Abstract Co	320-968-7278	•	•	•	•
•	•	•	•	•	Capitol Lien Records & Research [SOP]	800-845-4077	•	•	•	•

DT	BK	CV	CR	PR	←Courts	Recording→	UC	RE	TX	VS
•		•	•		GHS Inc - Record Research	763-566-2125		•	•	
		•	•		Horvath Enterprises Inc	320-982-3253			•	
•		•	•		Omni Data Retrieval Inc	952-985-7220			•	
		•	•	•	Scott Investigation [SOP]	800-357-7862	•	•	•	•
					Tri-County Abstract & Title Guaranty	800-892-2399	•	•	•	

DT	BK	CV	CR	PR	←Courts **Big Stone**	Recording→	UC	RE	TX	VS
•	•	•	•		ABC Services Inc	507-357-6320	•	•	•	
•	•	•	•	•	Capitol Lien Records & Research [SOP]	800-845-4077	•	•	•	•
•		•	•		GHS Inc - Record Research	763-566-2125		•	•	
•		•	•		Omni Data Retrieval Inc	952-985-7220			•	

DT	BK	CV	CR	PR	←Courts **Blue Earth**	Recording→	UC	RE	TX	VS
•	•	•	•		ABC Services Inc	507-357-6320	•	•	•	
•	•	•	•		Alpha Court Records & Research	651-699-2222	•		•	
•	•	•			Associated Abstracting Services of MN	612-819-6115	•	•	•	
•	•	•	•	•	Capitol Lien Records & Research [SOP]	800-845-4077	•	•	•	•
•		•	•		GHS Inc - Record Research	763-566-2125		•	•	
•	•	•	•	•	Information Reporting Services Inc [SOP]	612-870-8770			•	
•		•	•		Omni Data Retrieval Inc	952-985-7220			•	

DT	BK	CV	CR	PR	←Courts **Brown**	Recording→	UC	RE	TX	VS
•	•	•	•		ABC Services Inc	507-357-6320	•	•	•	
•	•	•	•		Alpha Court Records & Research	651-699-2222	•		•	
•	•	•	•	•	Capitol Lien Records & Research [SOP]	800-845-4077	•	•	•	•
•		•	•		GHS Inc - Record Research	763-566-2125		•	•	
•		•	•		Omni Data Retrieval Inc	952-985-7220			•	

DT	BK	CV	CR	PR	←Courts **Carlton**	Recording→	UC	RE	TX	VS
•	•	•	•		ABC Services Inc	507-357-6320	•	•	•	
•	•	•	•	•	Abstract & Title Services of Carlton Inc [SOP]	888-331-3966	•	•	•	•
•	•	•	•		Alpha Court Records & Research	651-699-2222	•		•	
•	•	•	•	•	Capitol Lien Records & Research [SOP]	800-845-4077	•	•	•	•
•		•	•		GHS Inc - Record Research	763-566-2125		•	•	
•		•	•		Omni Data Retrieval Inc	952-985-7220			•	

DT	BK	CV	CR	PR	←Courts **Carver**	Recording→	UC	RE	TX	VS
•	•	•	•		ABC Services Inc	507-357-6320	•	•	•	
•	•	•	•	•	Adit Research Inc	888-721-5220	•	•	•	•
•	•	•	•		Alpha Court Records & Research	651-699-2222	•		•	
•	•	•			Associated Abstracting Services of MN	612-819-6115	•	•	•	
	•	•	•		Avalon Information Services	715-554-0890	•	•	•	•
•	•	•	•	•	Capitol Lien Records & Research [SOP]	800-845-4077	•	•	•	•
•		•	•		GHS Inc - Record Research	763-566-2125		•	•	
•	•	•	•	•	Heartland Information Services [SOP]	800-967-1882	•	•	•	•
	•			•	Independent Abstracting Service Inc	763-792-6800	•	•	•	•
•	•	•	•	•	Information Reporting Services Inc [SOP]	612-870-8770			•	
•	•	•	•		INPRO [SOP]	952-891-3617	•		•	•
•	•	•	•	•	Metro Legal Services [SOP]	800-488-8994	•	•	•	•
					Midwest Data Search	952-475-2002	•	•	•	
•		•	•		Omni Data Retrieval Inc	952-985-7220			•	
•	•	•	•	•	Paragon Document Research Inc [SOP]	800-892-4235	•	•	•	•
	•	•	•		T D Wolfson & Associates [SOP]	952-920-9645	•		•	
•	•	•	•	•	Twin Cities Research	651-714-0002	•	•	•	•
•	•	•		•	US Corporate Services	800-327-1886	•	•	•	•
•	•	•	•	•	Verified Credentials Inc	800-473-4934	•	•	•	•

DT	BK	CV	CR	PR	←Courts **Cass**	Recording→	UC	RE	TX	VS
•	•	•	•		ABC Services Inc	507-357-6320	•	•	•	
•	•	•	•	•	ACME Research [SOP]	218-224-3239	•	•	•	•

DT	BK	CV	CR	PR	←Courts	Recording→	UC	RE	TX	VS
•	•	•	•	•	Capitol Lien Records & Research [SOP]	800-845-4077	•	•	•	•
			•	•	Cygneture Title Inc	218-828-0122	•	•	•	
•		•	•		GHS Inc - Record Research	763-566-2125		•	•	
•		•	•		Omni Data Retrieval Inc	952-985-7220			•	

DT	BK	CV	CR	PR	←Courts **CHIPPEWA**	Recording→	UC	RE	TX	VS
•	•	•	•		ABC Services Inc	507-357-6320	•	•	•	
•	•	•	•	•	Capitol Lien Records & Research [SOP]	800-845-4077	•	•	•	•
•		•	•		GHS Inc - Record Research	763-566-2125		•	•	
•		•	•		Omni Data Retrieval Inc	952-985-7220			•	

DT	BK	CV	CR	PR	←Courts **CHISAGO**	Recording→	UC	RE	TX	VS
•	•	•	•		ABC Services Inc	507-357-6320	•	•	•	
•	•	•	•	•	Accountable Process Servers Inc [SOP]	763-689-4190		•	•	
•	•	•	•	•	Adit Research Inc	888-721-5220	•	•	•	•
•	•	•	•		Alpha Court Records & Research	651-699-2222	•		•	
•	•	•			Associated Abstracting Services of MN	612-819-6115	•	•	•	
•	•	•	•	•	Capitol Lien Records & Research [SOP]	800-845-4077	•	•	•	•
•		•	•		GHS Inc - Record Research	763-566-2125		•	•	
		•	•		Horvath Enterprises Inc	320-982-3253			•	
	•			•	Independent Abstracting Service Inc	763-792-6800	•	•	•	•
	•	•			Land Title Inc	651-638-1900	•	•	•	
•		•	•		Omni Data Retrieval Inc	952-985-7220			•	
•	•	•	•	•	Twin Cities Research	651-714-0002	•	•	•	•
•	•	•	•	•	Verified Credentials Inc	800-473-4934	•	•	•	•

DT	BK	CV	CR	PR	←Courts **CLAY**	Recording→	UC	RE	TX	VS
•	•	•	•		ABC Services Inc	507-357-6320	•	•	•	
•	•	•	•	•	Butcher & Associates Ltd [SOP]	701-224-1541	•	•	•	•
•	•	•	•	•	C.C.I. [SOP]	701-235-4842	•	•	•	
•	•	•	•	•	Capitol Lien Records & Research [SOP]	800-845-4077	•	•	•	•
					Cass County Abstract Co (North Dakota)	701-232-3341	•	•	•	
				•	Clay County Abstract Co [SOP]	218-233-1358	•	•	•	
•		•	•		GHS Inc - Record Research	763-566-2125		•	•	
		•	•		Horvath Enterprises Inc	320-982-3253			•	
•		•	•		Omni Data Retrieval Inc	952-985-7220			•	

DT	BK	CV	CR	PR	←Courts **CLEARWATER**	Recording→	UC	RE	TX	VS
•	•	•	•		ABC Services Inc	507-357-6320	•	•	•	
•	•	•	•	•	Capitol Lien Records & Research [SOP]	800-845-4077	•	•	•	•
•		•	•		GHS Inc - Record Research	763-566-2125		•	•	
•		•	•		Omni Data Retrieval Inc	952-985-7220			•	

DT	BK	CV	CR	PR	←Courts **COOK**	Recording→	UC	RE	TX	VS
•	•	•	•		ABC Services Inc	507-357-6320	•	•	•	
•	•	•	•	•	Capitol Lien Records & Research [SOP]	800-845-4077	•	•	•	•
•		•	•		GHS Inc - Record Research	763-566-2125		•	•	
•		•	•		Omni Data Retrieval Inc	952-985-7220			•	

DT	BK	CV	CR	PR	←Courts **COTTONWOOD**	Recording→	UC	RE	TX	VS
•	•	•	•		ABC Services Inc	507-357-6320	•	•	•	
•	•	•	•	•	Capitol Lien Records & Research [SOP]	800-845-4077	•	•	•	•
					Cottonwood County Abstract Company	507-831-1504		•	•	
•		•	•		GHS Inc - Record Research	763-566-2125		•	•	
•		•	•		Omni Data Retrieval Inc	952-985-7220			•	

DT	BK	CV	CR	PR	←Courts **CROW WING**	Recording→	UC	RE	TX	VS
•	•	•	•		ABC Services Inc	507-357-6320	•	•	•	
•	•	•	•	•	Capitol Lien Records & Research [SOP]	800-845-4077	•	•	•	•
					Crow Wing County Abstract Co	218-829-7368	•	•	•	
			•	•	Cygneture Title Inc	218-828-0122	•	•	•	

DT	BK	CV	CR	PR	←COURTS	RECORDING→	UC	RE	TX	VS
•		•	•		GHS Inc - Record Research	763-566-2125		•	•	
•		•	•		Omni Data Retrieval Inc	952-985-7220			•	

DT	BK	CV	CR	PR	←COURTS **DAKOTA**	RECORDING→	UC	RE	TX	VS
•	•	•	•		ABC Services Inc	507-357-6320	•	•	•	
•	•	•	•	•	Adit Research Inc	888-721-5220	•	•	•	•
•	•	•	•		Alpha Court Records & Research	651-699-2222	•		•	
	•	•	•		Avalon Information Services	715-554-0890	•	•	•	•
•	•	•	•	•	Capitol Lien Records & Research [SOP]	800-845-4077	•	•	•	•
				•	Dakota County Abstract Co	651-437-5600	•	•	•	
•		•	•		GHS Inc - Record Research	763-566-2125		•	•	
•	•	•	•	•	Heartland Information Services [SOP]	800-967-1882	•	•	•	•
	•			•	Independent Abstracting Service Inc	763-792-6800	•	•	•	•
•	•	•	•	•	Information Reporting Services Inc [SOP]	612-870-8770			•	
•	•	•	•		INPRO [SOP]	952-891-3617	•		•	•
	•	•			Land Title Inc	651-638-1900	•	•	•	
•	•	•	•	•	Metro Legal Services [SOP]	800-488-8994	•	•	•	•
•		•	•		Omni Data Retrieval Inc	952-985-7220			•	
•	•	•	•	•	Paragon Document Research Inc [SOP]	800-892-4235	•	•	•	•
	•	•	•		T D Wolfson & Associates [SOP]	952-920-9645	•		•	
•	•	•	•	•	The McDowell Agency Inc [SOP]	651-644-3880	•	•	•	•
•	•	•	•	•	Twin Cities Research	651-714-0002	•	•	•	•
•	•	•		•	US Corporate Services	800-327-1886	•	•	•	•
•	•	•	•	•	Verified Credentials Inc	800-473-4934	•	•	•	•

DT	BK	CV	CR	PR	←COURTS **DODGE**	RECORDING→	UC	RE	TX	VS
•	•	•	•		ABC Services Inc	507-357-6320	•	•	•	
•	•	•	•		Alpha Court Records & Research	651-699-2222	•		•	
•	•	•	•	•	Capitol Lien Records & Research [SOP]	800-845-4077	•	•	•	•
•		•	•		GHS Inc - Record Research	763-566-2125		•	•	
•		•	•		Omni Data Retrieval Inc	952-985-7220			•	

DT	BK	CV	CR	PR	←COURTS **DOUGLAS**	RECORDING→	UC	RE	TX	VS
•	•	•	•		ABC Services Inc	507-357-6320	•	•	•	
•	•	•	•	•	Capitol Lien Records & Research [SOP]	800-845-4077	•	•	•	•
•	•	•	•	•	CJRS	866-758-7903	•	•	•	•
		•		•	Douglas County Abstract Co	320-763-3426		•	•	
•		•	•		GHS Inc - Record Research	763-566-2125		•	•	
		•	•		Horvath Enterprises Inc	320-982-3253			•	
•		•	•		Omni Data Retrieval Inc	952-985-7220			•	

DT	BK	CV	CR	PR	←COURTS **FARIBAULT**	RECORDING→	UC	RE	TX	VS
•	•	•	•		ABC Services Inc	507-357-6320	•	•	•	
•	•	•	•		Alpha Court Records & Research	651-699-2222	•		•	
•	•	•	•	•	Capitol Lien Records & Research [SOP]	800-845-4077	•	•	•	•
•		•	•		GHS Inc - Record Research	763-566-2125		•	•	
					Sharon K Hannaman Abstracter	507-526-5144		•	•	
•		•	•		Omni Data Retrieval Inc	952-985-7220			•	

DT	BK	CV	CR	PR	←COURTS **FILLMORE**	RECORDING→	UC	RE	TX	VS
•	•	•	•		ABC Services Inc	507-357-6320	•	•	•	
•	•	•	•	•	Capitol Lien Records & Research [SOP]	800-845-4077	•	•	•	•
•		•	•		GHS Inc - Record Research	763-566-2125		•	•	
•		•	•		Omni Data Retrieval Inc	952-985-7220			•	

DT	BK	CV	CR	PR	←COURTS **FREEBORN**	RECORDING→	UC	RE	TX	VS
•	•	•	•		ABC Services Inc	507-357-6320	•	•	•	
				•	Albert Lea Abstract Co	507-373-9001	•	•	•	•
•	•	•	•	•	Capitol Lien Records & Research [SOP]	800-845-4077	•	•	•	•
•		•	•		GHS Inc - Record Research	763-566-2125		•	•	

DT	BK	CV	CR	PR			UC	RE	TX	VS
•		•	•		Omni Data Retrieval Inc	952-985-7220			•	

DT	BK	CV	CR	PR	←Courts GOODHUE	Recording→	UC	RE	TX	VS
•	•	•	•		ABC Services Inc	507-357-6320	•	•	•	
•	•	•	•		Alpha Court Records & Research	651-699-2222	•		•	
•	•	•	•	•	Capitol Lien Records & Research [SOP]	800-845-4077	•	•	•	•
•		•	•		GHS Inc - Record Research	763-566-2125		•	•	
•	•	•	•	•	Information Reporting Services Inc [SOP]	612-870-8770			•	
•		•	•		Omni Data Retrieval Inc	952-985-7220			•	
•	•	•	•	•	Twin Cities Research	651-714-0002	•	•	•	•
•	•	•	•	•	Verified Credentials Inc	800-473-4934	•	•	•	•

DT	BK	CV	CR	PR	←Courts GRANT	Recording→	UC	RE	TX	VS
•	•	•	•		ABC Services Inc	507-357-6320	•	•	•	
•	•	•	•	•	Capitol Lien Records & Research [SOP]	800-845-4077	•	•	•	•
•		•	•		GHS Inc - Record Research	763-566-2125		•	•	
•		•	•		Omni Data Retrieval Inc	952-985-7220			•	

DT	BK	CV	CR	PR	←Courts HENNEPIN	Recording→	UC	RE	TX	VS
•	•	•	•		ABC Services Inc	507-357-6320	•	•	•	
•	•	•	•	•	Accountable Process Servers Inc [SOP]	763-689-4190		•	•	
•	•	•	•	•	Adit Research Inc	888-721-5220	•	•	•	•
•	•	•	•		Alpha Court Records & Research	651-699-2222	•		•	
•	•	•			Associated Abstracting Services of MN	612-819-6115	•	•	•	
	•	•	•		Avalon Information Services	715-554-0890	•	•	•	•
•	•	•	•	•	Capitol Lien Records & Research [SOP]	800-845-4077	•	•	•	•
•		•	•		GHS Inc - Record Research	763-566-2125		•	•	
•	•	•	•	•	Heartland Information Services [SOP]	800-967-1882	•	•	•	•
	•			•	Independent Abstracting Service Inc	763-792-6800	•	•	•	•
•	•	•	•	•	Information Reporting Services Inc [SOP]	612-870-8770			•	
•	•	•	•		INPRO [SOP]	952-891-3617	•		•	•
	•	•			Land Title Inc	651-638-1900	•	•	•	
•	•	•	•	•	Metro Legal Services [SOP]	800-488-8994	•	•	•	•
					Midwest Data Search	952-475-2002	•	•	•	
•		•	•		Omni Data Retrieval Inc	952-985-7220			•	
•	•	•	•	•	Paragon Document Research Inc [SOP]	800-892-4235	•	•	•	•
•	•	•			Premier Corporate Services MN	800-227-1256	•	•	•	
	•	•	•		T D Wolfson & Associates [SOP]	952-920-9645	•		•	
•	•	•	•	•	The McDowell Agency Inc [SOP]	651-644-3880	•	•	•	•
•	•	•	•	•	Twin Cities Research	651-714-0002	•	•	•	•
•	•	•		•	US Corporate Services	800-327-1886	•	•	•	•
•	•	•	•	•	Verified Credentials Inc	800-473-4934	•	•	•	•

DT	BK	CV	CR	PR	←Courts HOUSTON	Recording→	UC	RE	TX	VS
•	•	•	•		ABC Services Inc	507-357-6320	•	•	•	
•	•	•	•	•	Capitol Lien Records & Research [SOP]	800-845-4077	•	•	•	•
•		•	•		GHS Inc - Record Research	763-566-2125		•	•	
•		•	•		Omni Data Retrieval Inc	952-985-7220			•	
•	•			•	The Title Co Inc (La Crosse)	800-788-4853	•	•	•	

DT	BK	CV	CR	PR	←Courts HUBBARD	Recording→	UC	RE	TX	VS
•	•	•	•		ABC Services Inc	507-357-6320	•	•	•	
•	•	•	•	•	ACME Research [SOP]	218-224-3239	•	•	•	•
•	•	•	•	•	Capitol Lien Records & Research [SOP]	800-845-4077	•	•	•	•
•		•	•		GHS Inc - Record Research	763-566-2125		•	•	
•		•	•		Omni Data Retrieval Inc	952-985-7220			•	

DT	BK	CV	CR	PR	←Courts ISANTI	Recording→	UC	RE	TX	VS
•	•	•	•		ABC Services Inc	507-357-6320	•	•	•	
•	•	•	•	•	Accountable Process Servers Inc [SOP]	763-689-4190		•	•	
•	•	•	•		Alpha Court Records & Research	651-699-2222	•		•	
•	•	•			Associated Abstracting Services of MN	612-819-6115	•	•	•	
•	•	•	•	•	Capitol Lien Records & Research [SOP]	800-845-4077	•	•	•	•

DT	BK	CV	CR	PR	←Courts		Recording→	UC	RE	TX	VS
•		•	•			GHS Inc - Record Research	763-566-2125		•	•	
		•	•			Horvath Enterprises Inc	320-982-3253			•	
	•			•		Independent Abstracting Service Inc	763-792-6800	•	•	•	•
•		•	•			Omni Data Retrieval Inc	952-985-7220			•	
•	•	•	•	•		Twin Cities Research	651-714-0002	•	•	•	•

DT	BK	CV	CR	PR	←Courts	Itasca	Recording→	UC	RE	TX	VS
•	•	•	•			ABC Services Inc	507-357-6320	•	•	•	
•	•	•	•			Alpha Court Records & Research	651-699-2222	•		•	
•	•	•	•	•		Capitol Lien Records & Research [SOP]	800-845-4077	•	•	•	•
•		•	•			GHS Inc - Record Research	763-566-2125		•	•	
		•		•		Itasca County Abstract Co	218-326-9601	•	•	•	•
•		•	•			Omni Data Retrieval Inc	952-985-7220			•	

DT	BK	CV	CR	PR	←Courts	Jackson	Recording→	UC	RE	TX	VS
•	•	•	•			ABC Services Inc	507-357-6320	•	•	•	
•	•	•	•	•		Capitol Lien Records & Research [SOP]	800-845-4077	•	•	•	•
•		•	•			GHS Inc - Record Research	763-566-2125		•	•	
•		•	•			Omni Data Retrieval Inc	952-985-7220			•	

DT	BK	CV	CR	PR	←Courts	Kanabec	Recording→	UC	RE	TX	VS
•	•	•	•			ABC Services Inc	507-357-6320	•	•	•	
•	•	•	•			Alpha Court Records & Research	651-699-2222	•		•	
•	•	•	•	•		Capitol Lien Records & Research [SOP]	800-845-4077	•	•	•	•
•		•	•			GHS Inc - Record Research	763-566-2125		•	•	
		•	•			Horvath Enterprises Inc	320-982-3253			•	
•		•	•			Omni Data Retrieval Inc	952-985-7220			•	
•	•	•	•	•		Twin Cities Research	651-714-0002	•	•	•	•

DT	BK	CV	CR	PR	←Courts	Kandiyohi	Recording→	UC	RE	TX	VS
•	•	•	•			ABC Services Inc	507-357-6320	•	•	•	
•	•	•	•			Alpha Court Records & Research	651-699-2222	•		•	
•	•	•	•	•		Capitol Lien Records & Research [SOP]	800-845-4077	•	•	•	•
•		•	•			GHS Inc - Record Research	763-566-2125		•	•	
•		•	•			Omni Data Retrieval Inc	952-985-7220			•	

DT	BK	CV	CR	PR	←Courts	Kittson	Recording→	UC	RE	TX	VS
•	•	•	•			ABC Services Inc	507-357-6320	•	•	•	
•	•	•	•	•		Capitol Lien Records & Research [SOP]	800-845-4077	•	•	•	•
•		•	•			GHS Inc - Record Research	763-566-2125		•	•	
•		•	•			Omni Data Retrieval Inc	952-985-7220			•	

DT	BK	CV	CR	PR	←Courts	Koochiching	Recording→	UC	RE	TX	VS
•	•	•	•			ABC Services Inc	507-357-6320	•	•	•	
•	•	•	•	•		Capitol Lien Records & Research [SOP]	800-845-4077	•	•	•	•
•		•	•			GHS Inc - Record Research	763-566-2125		•	•	
•		•	•			Omni Data Retrieval Inc	952-985-7220			•	

DT	BK	CV	CR	PR	←Courts	Lac qui Parle	Recording→	UC	RE	TX	VS
•	•	•	•			ABC Services Inc	507-357-6320	•	•	•	
•	•	•	•	•		Capitol Lien Records & Research [SOP]	800-845-4077	•	•	•	•
•		•	•			GHS Inc - Record Research	763-566-2125		•	•	
•		•	•			Omni Data Retrieval Inc	952-985-7220			•	

DT	BK	CV	CR	PR	←Courts	Lake	Recording→	UC	RE	TX	VS
•	•	•	•			ABC Services Inc	507-357-6320	•	•	•	
•	•	•	•	•		Capitol Lien Records & Research [SOP]	800-845-4077	•	•	•	•
•		•	•			GHS Inc - Record Research	763-566-2125		•	•	
•		•	•			Omni Data Retrieval Inc	952-985-7220			•	

DT	BK	CV	CR	PR	←Courts	Lake of the Woods	Recording→	UC	RE	TX	VS
•	•	•	•			ABC Services Inc	507-357-6320	•	•	•	
•	•	•	•	•		Capitol Lien Records & Research [SOP]	800-845-4077	•	•	•	•
•		•	•			GHS Inc - Record Research	763-566-2125		•	•	
•		•	•			Omni Data Retrieval Inc	952-985-7220			•	

DT	BK	CV	CR	PR	←Courts	Le Sueur	Recording→	UC	RE	TX	VS
•	•	•	•			ABC Services Inc	507-357-6320	•	•	•	
•	•	•	•			Alpha Court Records & Research	651-699-2222	•		•	
•	•	•				Associated Abstracting Services of MN	612-819-6115	•	•	•	
•	•	•	•	•		Capitol Lien Records & Research [SOP]	800-845-4077	•	•	•	•
•		•	•			GHS Inc - Record Research	763-566-2125		•	•	
•		•	•			Omni Data Retrieval Inc	952-985-7220			•	
•	•	•	•	•		Twin Cities Research	651-714-0002	•	•	•	•

DT	BK	CV	CR	PR	←Courts	Lincoln	Recording→	UC	RE	TX	VS
•	•	•	•			ABC Services Inc	507-357-6320	•	•	•	
•	•	•	•	•		Capitol Lien Records & Research [SOP]	800-845-4077	•	•	•	•
•		•	•			GHS Inc - Record Research	763-566-2125		•	•	
•		•	•			Omni Data Retrieval Inc	952-985-7220			•	

DT	BK	CV	CR	PR	←Courts	Lyon	Recording→	UC	RE	TX	VS
•	•	•	•			ABC Services Inc	507-357-6320	•	•	•	
•	•	•	•	•		Capitol Lien Records & Research [SOP]	800-845-4077	•	•	•	•
•		•	•			GHS Inc - Record Research	763-566-2125		•	•	
•		•	•			Omni Data Retrieval Inc	952-985-7220			•	

DT	BK	CV	CR	PR	←Courts	Mahnomen	Recording→	UC	RE	TX	VS
•	•	•	•			ABC Services Inc	507-357-6320	•	•	•	
•	•	•	•	•		Capitol Lien Records & Research [SOP]	800-845-4077	•	•	•	•
•		•	•			GHS Inc - Record Research	763-566-2125		•	•	
						Mahnomen County Abstract Co	218-935-5227		•		
•		•	•			Omni Data Retrieval Inc	952-985-7220			•	

DT	BK	CV	CR	PR	←Courts	Marshall	Recording→	UC	RE	TX	VS
•	•	•	•			ABC Services Inc	507-357-6320	•	•	•	
•	•	•	•	•		Capitol Lien Records & Research [SOP]	800-845-4077	•	•	•	•
•		•	•			GHS Inc - Record Research	763-566-2125		•	•	
•		•	•			Omni Data Retrieval Inc	952-985-7220			•	

DT	BK	CV	CR	PR	←Courts	Martin	Recording→	UC	RE	TX	VS
•	•	•	•			ABC Services Inc	507-357-6320	•	•	•	
•	•	•	•			Alpha Court Records & Research	651-699-2222	•		•	
•	•	•	•	•		Capitol Lien Records & Research [SOP]	800-845-4077	•	•	•	•
•		•	•			GHS Inc - Record Research	763-566-2125		•	•	
•		•	•			Omni Data Retrieval Inc	952-985-7220			•	

DT	BK	CV	CR	PR	←Courts	McLeod	Recording→	UC	RE	TX	VS
•	•	•	•			ABC Services Inc	507-357-6320	•	•	•	
•	•	•	•			Alpha Court Records & Research	651-699-2222	•		•	
•	•	•				Associated Abstracting Services of MN	612-819-6115	•	•	•	
•	•	•	•	•		Capitol Lien Records & Research [SOP]	800-845-4077	•	•	•	•
•		•	•			GHS Inc - Record Research	763-566-2125		•	•	
•		•	•			Omni Data Retrieval Inc	952-985-7220			•	
•	•	•	•	•		Twin Cities Research	651-714-0002	•	•	•	•

DT	BK	CV	CR	PR	←Courts	Meeker	Recording→	UC	RE	TX	VS
•	•	•	•			ABC Services Inc	507-357-6320	•	•	•	
•	•	•	•	•		Capitol Lien Records & Research [SOP]	800-845-4077	•	•	•	•
•		•	•			GHS Inc - Record Research	763-566-2125		•	•	
•		•	•			Omni Data Retrieval Inc	952-985-7220			•	

DT	BK	CV	CR	PR	←Courts	Mille Lacs	Recording→	UC	RE	TX	VS
•	•	•	•			ABC Services Inc	507-357-6320	•	•	•	
•	•	•	•			Alpha Court Records & Research	651-699-2222	•		•	
•	•	•				Associated Abstracting Services of MN	612-819-6115	•	•	•	
•	•	•	•	•		Capitol Lien Records & Research [SOP]	800-845-4077	•	•	•	•
•		•	•			GHS Inc - Record Research	763-566-2125		•	•	
		•	•			Horvath Enterprises Inc	320-982-3253			•	
•		•	•			Omni Data Retrieval Inc	952-985-7220			•	
						Tri-County Abstract & Title Guaranty	800-892-2399	•	•	•	

DT	BK	CV	CR	PR	←Courts	Morrison	Recording→	UC	RE	TX	VS
•	•	•	•			ABC Services Inc	507-357-6320	•	•	•	
•	•	•	•	•		Capitol Lien Records & Research [SOP]	800-845-4077	•	•	•	•
			•	•		Cygneture Title Inc	218-828-0122	•	•	•	
•		•	•			GHS Inc - Record Research	763-566-2125		•	•	
		•	•			Horvath Enterprises Inc	320-982-3253			•	
				•		Larson Abstract Co	320-632-5667	•	•	•	•
•		•	•			Omni Data Retrieval Inc	952-985-7220			•	
						Tri-County Abstract & Title Guaranty	800-892-2399	•	•	•	

DT	BK	CV	CR	PR	←Courts	Mower	Recording→	UC	RE	TX	VS
•	•	•	•			ABC Services Inc	507-357-6320	•	•	•	
				•		Albert Lea Abstract Co	507-373-9001	•	•	•	•
•	•	•	•	•		Capitol Lien Records & Research [SOP]	800-845-4077	•	•	•	•
•		•	•			GHS Inc - Record Research	763-566-2125		•	•	
•		•	•			Omni Data Retrieval Inc	952-985-7220			•	

DT	BK	CV	CR	PR	←Courts	Murray	Recording→	UC	RE	TX	VS
•	•	•	•			ABC Services Inc	507-357-6320	•	•	•	
•	•	•	•	•		Capitol Lien Records & Research [SOP]	800-845-4077	•	•	•	•
•		•	•			GHS Inc - Record Research	763-566-2125		•	•	
•		•	•			Omni Data Retrieval Inc	952-985-7220			•	

DT	BK	CV	CR	PR	←Courts	Nicollet	Recording→	UC	RE	TX	VS
•	•	•	•			ABC Services Inc	507-357-6320	•	•	•	
•	•	•	•			Alpha Court Records & Research	651-699-2222	•		•	
•	•	•				Associated Abstracting Services of MN	612-819-6115	•	•	•	
•	•	•	•	•		Capitol Lien Records & Research [SOP]	800-845-4077	•	•	•	•
•		•	•			GHS Inc - Record Research	763-566-2125		•	•	
•		•	•			Omni Data Retrieval Inc	952-985-7220			•	

DT	BK	CV	CR	PR	←Courts	Nobles	Recording→	UC	RE	TX	VS
•	•	•	•			ABC Services Inc	507-357-6320	•	•	•	
•	•	•	•	•		Capitol Lien Records & Research [SOP]	800-845-4077	•	•	•	•
•		•	•			GHS Inc - Record Research	763-566-2125		•	•	
•		•	•			Omni Data Retrieval Inc	952-985-7220			•	

DT	BK	CV	CR	PR	←Courts	Norman	Recording→	UC	RE	TX	VS
•	•	•	•			ABC Services Inc	507-357-6320	•	•	•	
•	•	•	•	•		Capitol Lien Records & Research [SOP]	800-845-4077	•	•	•	•
•		•	•			GHS Inc - Record Research	763-566-2125		•	•	
•		•	•			Omni Data Retrieval Inc	952-985-7220			•	

DT	BK	CV	CR	PR	←Courts	Olmsted	Recording→	UC	RE	TX	VS
•	•	•	•			ABC Services Inc	507-357-6320	•	•	•	
•	•	•	•	•		Capitol Lien Records & Research [SOP]	800-845-4077	•	•	•	•
•		•	•			GHS Inc - Record Research	763-566-2125		•	•	
•	•	•	•	•		Information Reporting Services Inc [SOP]	612-870-8770			•	
•		•	•			Omni Data Retrieval Inc	952-985-7220			•	

DT	BK	CV	CR	PR	←Courts	Otter Tail	Recording→	UC	RE	TX	VS
•	•	•	•			ABC Services Inc	507-357-6320	•	•	•	
•	•	•	•	•		Capitol Lien Records & Research [SOP]	800-845-4077	•	•	•	•
•		•	•			GHS Inc - Record Research	763-566-2125		•	•	
		•	•			Horvath Enterprises Inc	320-982-3253			•	
		•		•		N F Field Abstract Co	218-736-6844	•	•	•	
•		•	•			Omni Data Retrieval Inc	952-985-7220			•	
				•		West Central Abstracting Co	218-736-5685	•	•	•	•

DT	BK	CV	CR	PR	←Courts	Pennington	Recording→	UC	RE	TX	VS
•	•	•	•			ABC Services Inc	507-357-6320	•	•	•	
•	•	•	•	•		Capitol Lien Records & Research [SOP]	800-845-4077	•	•	•	•
•		•	•			GHS Inc - Record Research	763-566-2125		•	•	
		•				Grand Forks Abstract & Title Co	701-772-3484	•	•	•	
•		•	•			Omni Data Retrieval Inc	952-985-7220			•	
		•	•	•		Pennington County Abstract Co	218-681-2527		•	•	•

DT	BK	CV	CR	PR	←Courts	Pine	Recording→	UC	RE	TX	VS
•	•	•	•			ABC Services Inc	507-357-6320	•	•	•	
•	•	•	•			Alpha Court Records & Research	651-699-2222	•		•	
•	•	•	•	•		Capitol Lien Records & Research [SOP]	800-845-4077	•	•	•	•
•		•	•			GHS Inc - Record Research	763-566-2125		•	•	
		•	•			Horvath Enterprises Inc	320-982-3253			•	
•		•	•			Omni Data Retrieval Inc	952-985-7220			•	
•	•	•	•	•		Twin Cities Research	651-714-0002	•	•	•	•

DT	BK	CV	CR	PR	←Courts	Pipestone	Recording→	UC	RE	TX	VS
•	•	•	•			ABC Services Inc	507-357-6320	•	•	•	
•	•	•	•	•		Capitol Lien Records & Research [SOP]	800-845-4077	•	•	•	•
•		•	•			GHS Inc - Record Research	763-566-2125		•	•	
•		•	•			Omni Data Retrieval Inc	952-985-7220			•	
		•	•	•		Pipestone County Abstract Co LLC	507-825-5833	•	•	•	

DT	BK	CV	CR	PR	←Courts	Polk	Recording→	UC	RE	TX	VS
•	•	•	•			ABC Services Inc	507-357-6320	•	•	•	
•	•	•	•	•		Capitol Lien Records & Research [SOP]	800-845-4077	•	•	•	•
•		•	•			GHS Inc - Record Research	763-566-2125		•	•	
•		•	•			Omni Data Retrieval Inc	952-985-7220			•	
		•				Strander Abstract Inc	218-281-1191	•	•	•	

DT	BK	CV	CR	PR	←Courts	Pope	Recording→	UC	RE	TX	VS
•	•	•	•			ABC Services Inc	507-357-6320	•	•	•	
•	•	•	•	•		Capitol Lien Records & Research [SOP]	800-845-4077	•	•	•	•
		•		•		Douglas County Abstract Co	320-763-3426	•	•	•	
•		•	•			GHS Inc - Record Research	763-566-2125		•	•	
•		•	•			Omni Data Retrieval Inc	952-985-7220			•	

DT	BK	CV	CR	PR	←Courts	Ramsey	Recording→	UC	RE	TX	VS
•	•	•	•			ABC Services Inc	507-357-6320	•	•	•	
•	•	•	•	•		Accountable Process Servers Inc [SOP]	763-689-4190		•	•	
•	•	•	•	•		Adit Research Inc	888-721-5220	•	•	•	•
•	•	•	•			Alpha Court Records & Research	651-699-2222	•		•	
•	•	•				Associated Abstracting Services of MN	612-819-6115	•	•	•	
	•	•	•			Avalon Information Services	715-554-0890	•	•	•	•
•	•	•	•	•		Capitol Lien Records & Research [SOP]	800-845-4077	•	•	•	•
•		•	•			GHS Inc - Record Research	763-566-2125		•	•	
•	•	•	•	•		Heartland Information Services [SOP]	800-967-1882	•	•	•	•
	•			•		Independent Abstracting Service Inc	763-792-6800	•	•	•	•
•	•	•	•	•		Information Reporting Services Inc [SOP]	612-870-8770			•	
•	•	•	•			INPRO [SOP]	952-891-3617	•		•	•
	•	•				Land Title Inc	651-638-1900	•	•	•	

DT	BK	CV	CR	PR	←Courts	Recording→	UC	RE	TX	VS
•	•	•	•	•	Metro Legal Services [SOP]	800-488-8994	•	•	•	•
•		•	•		Omni Data Retrieval Inc	952-985-7220			•	
•	•	•	•	•	Paragon Document Research Inc [SOP]	800-892-4235	•	•	•	•
•	•	•			Premier Corporate Services MN	800-227-1256	•	•	•	
	•	•	•		T D Wolfson & Associates [SOP]	952-920-9645	•		•	
•	•	•	•	•	The McDowell Agency Inc [SOP]	651-644-3880	•	•	•	•
•	•	•	•	•	Twin Cities Research	651-714-0002	•	•	•	•
•	•	•		•	US Corporate Services	800-327-1886	•	•	•	•
•	•	•	•	•	Verified Credentials Inc	800-473-4934	•	•	•	•

DT	BK	CV	CR	PR	←Courts **Red Lake**	Recording→	UC	RE	TX	VS
•	•	•	•		ABC Services Inc	507-357-6320	•	•	•	
•	•	•	•	•	Capitol Lien Records & Research [SOP]	800-845-4077	•	•	•	•
•		•	•		GHS Inc - Record Research	763-566-2125		•	•	
•		•	•		Omni Data Retrieval Inc	952-985-7220			•	

DT	BK	CV	CR	PR	←Courts **Redwood**	Recording→	UC	RE	TX	VS
•	•	•	•		ABC Services Inc	507-357-6320	•	•	•	
•	•	•	•	•	Capitol Lien Records & Research [SOP]	800-845-4077	•	•	•	•
•		•	•		GHS Inc - Record Research	763-566-2125		•	•	
•		•	•		Omni Data Retrieval Inc	952-985-7220			•	
				•	Renville County Abstract Co	320-523-5328		•	•	•

DT	BK	CV	CR	PR	←Courts **Renville**	Recording→	UC	RE	TX	VS
•	•	•	•		ABC Services Inc	507-357-6320	•	•	•	
•	•	•	•		Alpha Court Records & Research	651-699-2222	•		•	
•	•	•	•	•	Capitol Lien Records & Research [SOP]	800-845-4077	•	•	•	•
•		•	•		GHS Inc - Record Research	763-566-2125		•	•	
•		•	•		Omni Data Retrieval Inc	952-985-7220			•	
				•	Renville County Abstract Co	320-523-5328		•	•	•

DT	BK	CV	CR	PR	←Courts **Rice**	Recording→	UC	RE	TX	VS
•	•	•	•		ABC Services Inc	507-357-6320	•	•	•	
•	•	•			Associated Abstracting Services of MN	612-819-6115	•	•	•	
•	•	•	•	•	Capitol Lien Records & Research [SOP]	800-845-4077	•	•	•	•
•		•	•		GHS Inc - Record Research	763-566-2125		•	•	
•		•	•		Omni Data Retrieval Inc	952-985-7220			•	
•	•	•	•	•	Verified Credentials Inc	800-473-4934	•	•	•	•

DT	BK	CV	CR	PR	←Courts **Rock**	Recording→	UC	RE	TX	VS
•	•	•	•		ABC Services Inc	507-357-6320	•	•	•	
•	•	•	•	•	Capitol Lien Records & Research [SOP]	800-845-4077	•	•	•	•
•		•	•		GHS Inc - Record Research	763-566-2125		•	•	
•		•	•		Omni Data Retrieval Inc	952-985-7220			•	

DT	BK	CV	CR	PR	←Courts **Roseau**	Recording→	UC	RE	TX	VS
•	•	•	•		ABC Services Inc	507-357-6320	•	•	•	
•	•	•	•	•	Capitol Lien Records & Research [SOP]	800-845-4077	•	•	•	•
•		•	•		GHS Inc - Record Research	763-566-2125		•	•	
•		•	•		Omni Data Retrieval Inc	952-985-7220			•	

DT	BK	CV	CR	PR	←Courts **Scott**	Recording→	UC	RE	TX	VS
•	•	•	•		ABC Services Inc	507-357-6320	•	•	•	
•	•	•	•	•	Adit Research Inc	888-721-5220	•	•	•	•
•	•	•	•		Alpha Court Records & Research	651-699-2222	•		•	
•	•	•			Associated Abstracting Services of MN	612-819-6115	•	•	•	
	•	•	•		Avalon Information Services	715-554-0890	•	•	•	•
•	•	•	•	•	Capitol Lien Records & Research [SOP]	800-845-4077	•	•	•	•
•		•	•		GHS Inc - Record Research	763-566-2125		•	•	
•	•	•	•	•	Heartland Information Services [SOP]	800-967-1882	•	•	•	•
	•			•	Independent Abstracting Service Inc	763-792-6800	•	•	•	•
•	•	•	•	•	Information Reporting Services Inc [SOP]	612-870-8770			•	

DT	BK	CV	CR	PR	←Courts	Recording→	UC	RE	TX	VS
•	•	•	•		INPRO [SOP]	952-891-3617	•		•	•
•	•	•	•	•	Metro Legal Services [SOP]	800-488-8994	•	•	•	•
					Midwest Data Search	952-475-2002	•	•	•	
•		•	•		Omni Data Retrieval Inc	952-985-7220			•	
•	•	•	•	•	Paragon Document Research Inc [SOP]	800-892-4235	•	•	•	•
	•	•	•		T D Wolfson & Associates [SOP]	952-920-9645	•		•	
•	•	•	•	•	Twin Cities Research	651-714-0002	•	•	•	•
•	•	•		•	US Corporate Services	800-327-1886	•	•	•	•
•	•	•	•	•	Verified Credentials Inc	800-473-4934	•	•	•	•

DT	BK	CV	CR	PR	←Courts	**Sherburne** Recording→	UC	RE	TX	VS
•	•	•	•		ABC Services Inc	507-357-6320	•	•	•	
•	•	•	•	•	Accountable Process Servers Inc [SOP]	763-689-4190		•	•	
•	•	•	•	•	Adit Research Inc	888-721-5220	•	•	•	•
•	•	•	•		Alpha Court Records & Research	651-699-2222	•		•	
•	•	•			Associated Abstracting Services of MN	612-819-6115	•	•	•	
	•	•	•		Avalon Information Services	715-554-0890	•	•	•	•
•	•	•	•	•	Capitol Lien Records & Research [SOP]	800-845-4077	•	•	•	•
•		•	•		GHS Inc - Record Research	763-566-2125		•	•	
		•	•		Horvath Enterprises Inc	320-982-3253			•	
	•			•	Independent Abstracting Service Inc	763-792-6800	•	•	•	•
•	•	•	•	•	Metro Legal Services [SOP]	800-488-8994	•	•	•	•
					Midwest Data Search	952-475-2002	•	•	•	
•		•	•		Omni Data Retrieval Inc	952-985-7220			•	
					Tri-County Abstract & Title Guaranty	800-892-2399	•	•	•	
•	•	•	•	•	Twin Cities Research	651-714-0002	•	•	•	•
•	•	•		•	US Corporate Services	800-327-1886	•	•	•	•
•	•	•	•	•	Verified Credentials Inc	800-473-4934	•	•	•	•

DT	BK	CV	CR	PR	←Courts	**Sibley** Recording→	UC	RE	TX	VS
•	•	•	•		ABC Services Inc	507-357-6320	•	•	•	
•	•	•	•		Alpha Court Records & Research	651-699-2222	•		•	
•	•	•	•	•	Capitol Lien Records & Research [SOP]	800-845-4077	•	•	•	•
•		•	•		GHS Inc - Record Research	763-566-2125		•	•	
•		•	•		Omni Data Retrieval Inc	952-985-7220			•	
•	•	•	•	•	Twin Cities Research	651-714-0002	•	•	•	•

DT	BK	CV	CR	PR	←Courts	**St. Louis** Recording→	UC	RE	TX	VS
•	•	•	•		ABC Services Inc	507-357-6320	•	•	•	
•	•	•	•	•	Abstract & Title Services of Carlton Inc [SOP]	888-331-3966	•	•	•	•
•	•	•	•	•	Capitol Lien Records & Research [SOP]	800-845-4077	•	•	•	•
•	•	•	•	•	CJRS	866-758-7903	•	•	•	•
•		•	•		GHS Inc - Record Research	763-566-2125		•	•	
•		•	•		Omni Data Retrieval Inc	952-985-7220			•	
•	•	•	•	•	Paragon Document Research Inc [SOP]	800-892-4235	•	•	•	•

DT	BK	CV	CR	PR	←Courts	**Stearns** Recording→	UC	RE	TX	VS
•	•	•	•		ABC Services Inc	507-357-6320	•	•	•	
•	•	•	•	•	Adit Research Inc	888-721-5220	•	•	•	•
•	•	•			Associated Abstracting Services of MN	612-819-6115	•	•	•	
•	•	•	•	•	Capitol Lien Records & Research [SOP]	800-845-4077	•	•	•	•
•		•	•		GHS Inc - Record Research	763-566-2125		•	•	
		•	•		Horvath Enterprises Inc	320-982-3253			•	
•		•	•		Omni Data Retrieval Inc	952-985-7220			•	
•	•	•	•	•	Paragon Document Research Inc [SOP]	800-892-4235	•	•	•	•
•	•	•	•	•	Scott Investigation [SOP]	800-357-7862	•	•	•	•
					Tri-County Abstract & Title Guaranty	800-892-2399	•	•	•	
•	•	•	•	•	Verified Credentials Inc	800-473-4934	•	•	•	•

DT	BK	CV	CR	PR	←COURTS	STEELE	RECORDING→	UC	RE	TX	VS
•	•	•	•			ABC Services Inc	507-357-6320	•	•	•	
•	•	•				Associated Abstracting Services of MN	612-819-6115	•	•	•	
•	•	•	•	•		Capitol Lien Records & Research [SOP]	800-845-4077	•	•	•	•
•		•	•			GHS Inc - Record Research	763-566-2125		•	•	
•		•	•			Omni Data Retrieval Inc	952-985-7220			•	
		•	•			Steele County Abstract Co	507-451-6487	•	•	•	

DT	BK	CV	CR	PR	←COURTS	STEVENS	RECORDING→	UC	RE	TX	VS
•	•	•	•			ABC Services Inc	507-357-6320	•	•	•	
•	•	•	•	•		Capitol Lien Records & Research [SOP]	800-845-4077	•	•	•	•
•		•	•			GHS Inc - Record Research	763-566-2125		•	•	
•		•	•			Omni Data Retrieval Inc	952-985-7220			•	

DT	BK	CV	CR	PR	←COURTS	SWIFT	RECORDING→	UC	RE	TX	VS
•	•	•	•			ABC Services Inc	507-357-6320	•	•	•	
•	•	•	•	•		Capitol Lien Records & Research [SOP]	800-845-4077	•	•	•	•
•		•	•			GHS Inc - Record Research	763-566-2125		•	•	
•		•	•			Omni Data Retrieval Inc	952-985-7220			•	

DT	BK	CV	CR	PR	←COURTS	TODD	RECORDING→	UC	RE	TX	VS
•	•	•	•			ABC Services Inc	507-357-6320	•	•	•	
•	•	•	•	•		Capitol Lien Records & Research [SOP]	800-845-4077	•	•	•	•
			•	•		Cygneture Title Inc	218-828-0122	•	•	•	
•		•	•			GHS Inc - Record Research	763-566-2125		•	•	
		•	•			Horvath Enterprises Inc	320-982-3253			•	
•		•	•			Omni Data Retrieval Inc	952-985-7220			•	

DT	BK	CV	CR	PR	←COURTS	TRAVERSE	RECORDING→	UC	RE	TX	VS
•	•	•	•			ABC Services Inc	507-357-6320	•	•	•	
•	•	•	•	•		Capitol Lien Records & Research [SOP]	800-845-4077	•	•	•	•
•		•	•			GHS Inc - Record Research	763-566-2125		•	•	
•		•	•			Omni Data Retrieval Inc	952-985-7220			•	

DT	BK	CV	CR	PR	←COURTS	WABASHA	RECORDING→	UC	RE	TX	VS
•	•	•	•			ABC Services Inc	507-357-6320	•	•	•	
•	•	•	•	•		Capitol Lien Records & Research [SOP]	800-845-4077	•	•	•	•
•		•	•			GHS Inc - Record Research	763-566-2125		•	•	
•		•	•			Omni Data Retrieval Inc	952-985-7220			•	
•	•	•		•		Wabasha County Abstract Co	651-565-3391	•	•	•	•

DT	BK	CV	CR	PR	←COURTS	WADENA	RECORDING→	UC	RE	TX	VS
•	•	•	•			ABC Services Inc	507-357-6320	•	•	•	
•	•	•	•	•		Capitol Lien Records & Research [SOP]	800-845-4077	•	•	•	•
			•	•		Cygneture Title Inc	218-828-0122	•	•	•	
•		•	•			GHS Inc - Record Research	763-566-2125		•	•	
		•	•			Horvath Enterprises Inc	320-982-3253			•	
•		•	•			Omni Data Retrieval Inc	952-985-7220			•	

DT	BK	CV	CR	PR	←COURTS	WASECA	RECORDING→	UC	RE	TX	VS
•	•	•	•			ABC Services Inc	507-357-6320	•	•	•	
•	•	•				Associated Abstracting Services of MN	612-819-6115	•	•	•	
•	•	•	•	•		Capitol Lien Records & Research [SOP]	800-845-4077	•	•	•	•
•		•	•			GHS Inc - Record Research	763-566-2125		•	•	
•		•	•			Omni Data Retrieval Inc	952-985-7220			•	

DT	BK	CV	CR	PR	←COURTS	WASHINGTON	RECORDING→	UC	RE	TX	VS
•	•	•	•			ABC Services Inc	507-357-6320	•	•	•	
•	•	•	•	•		Accountable Process Servers Inc [SOP]	763-689-4190		•	•	
•	•	•	•	•		Adit Research Inc	888-721-5220	•	•	•	•
•	•	•	•			Alpha Court Records & Research	651-699-2222	•		•	

DT	BK	CV	CR	PR	←Courts	Recording→	UC	RE	TX	VS
	•	•	•		Avalon Information Services	715-554-0890	•	•	•	•
•	•	•	•	•	Capitol Lien Records & Research [SOP]	800-845-4077	•	•	•	•
•		•	•		GHS Inc - Record Research	763-566-2125		•	•	
•	•	•	•	•	Heartland Information Services [SOP]	800-967-1882	•	•	•	•
		•	•		Horvath Enterprises Inc	320-982-3253			•	
	•			•	Independent Abstracting Service Inc	763-792-6800	•	•	•	•
•	•	•	•	•	Information Reporting Services Inc [SOP]	612-870-8770			•	
	•	•			Land Title Inc	651-638-1900	•	•	•	
•	•	•	•	•	Metro Legal Services [SOP]	800-488-8994	•	•	•	•
•		•	•		Omni Data Retrieval Inc	952-985-7220			•	
•	•	•	•	•	Paragon Document Research Inc [SOP]	800-892-4235	•	•	•	•
	•	•	•		T D Wolfson & Associates [SOP]	952-920-9645	•		•	
•	•	•	•	•	The McDowell Agency Inc [SOP]	651-644-3880	•	•	•	•
•	•	•	•	•	Twin Cities Research	651-714-0002	•	•	•	•
•	•	•		•	US Corporate Services	800-327-1886	•	•	•	•
•	•	•	•	•	Verified Credentials Inc	800-473-4934	•	•	•	•

DT	BK	CV	CR	PR	←Courts	**Watonwan** — Recording→	UC	RE	TX	VS
•	•	•	•		ABC Services Inc	507-357-6320	•	•	•	
•	•	•	•	•	Capitol Lien Records & Research [SOP]	800-845-4077	•	•	•	•
•		•	•		GHS Inc - Record Research	763-566-2125		•	•	
•		•	•		Omni Data Retrieval Inc	952-985-7220			•	

DT	BK	CV	CR	PR	←Courts	**Wilkin** — Recording→	UC	RE	TX	VS
•	•	•	•		ABC Services Inc	507-357-6320	•	•	•	
•	•	•	•	•	Capitol Lien Records & Research [SOP]	800-845-4077	•	•	•	•
•		•	•		GHS Inc - Record Research	763-566-2125		•	•	
•		•	•		Omni Data Retrieval Inc	952-985-7220			•	
		•	•	•	Richland County Abstract Co	701-642-3781	•	•	•	•
		•	•	•	Wilkin County Abstract	701-642-3781	•	•	•	

DT	BK	CV	CR	PR	←Courts	**Winona** — Recording→	UC	RE	TX	VS
•	•	•	•		ABC Services Inc	507-357-6320	•	•	•	
•	•	•	•	•	Capitol Lien Records & Research [SOP]	800-845-4077	•	•	•	•
•		•	•		GHS Inc - Record Research	763-566-2125		•	•	
•	•	•	•	•	Information Reporting Services Inc [SOP]	612-870-8770			•	
•		•	•		Omni Data Retrieval Inc	952-985-7220			•	

DT	BK	CV	CR	PR	←Courts	**Wright** — Recording→	UC	RE	TX	VS
•	•	•	•		ABC Services Inc	507-357-6320	•	•	•	
•	•	•	•	•	Adit Research Inc	888-721-5220	•	•	•	•
•	•	•	•		Alpha Court Records & Research	651-699-2222	•		•	
•	•	•			Associated Abstracting Services of MN	612-819-6115	•	•	•	
•	•	•		•	Campbell Abstract Co	763-682-1252	•	•	•	
•	•	•	•	•	Capitol Lien Records & Research [SOP]	800-845-4077	•	•	•	•
•		•	•		GHS Inc - Record Research	763-566-2125		•	•	
		•	•		Horvath Enterprises Inc	320-982-3253			•	
	•			•	Independent Abstracting Service Inc	763-792-6800	•	•	•	•
•	•	•	•	•	Information Reporting Services Inc [SOP]	612-870-8770			•	
•	•	•	•	•	Metro Legal Services [SOP]	800-488-8994	•	•	•	•
					Midwest Data Search	952-475-2002	•	•	•	
•		•	•		Omni Data Retrieval Inc	952-985-7220			•	
•	•	•	•	•	Paragon Document Research Inc [SOP]	800-892-4235	•	•	•	•
					Tri-County Abstract & Title Guaranty	800-892-2399	•	•	•	
•	•	•	•	•	Twin Cities Research	651-714-0002	•	•	•	•
•	•	•		•	US Corporate Services	800-327-1886	•	•	•	•
•	•	•	•	•	Verified Credentials Inc	800-473-4934	•	•	•	•

DT	BK	CV	CR	PR	←Courts	**Yellow Medicine** — Recording→	UC	RE	TX	VS
•	•	•	•		ABC Services Inc	507-357-6320	•	•	•	
•	•	•	•	•	Capitol Lien Records & Research [SOP]	800-845-4077	•	•	•	•
•		•	•		GHS Inc - Record Research	763-566-2125		•	•	
•		•	•		Omni Data Retrieval Inc	952-985-7220			•	

Mississippi

COURT RECORDS RETRIEVED — **RECORDING RECORDS RETRIEVED**

ADAMS

DT	BK	CV	CR	PR	←Courts	Recording→	UC	RE	TX	VS

See adjoining counties for retrievers or contact court or recording office.

ALCORN

DT	BK	CV	CR	PR	←Courts	Recording→	UC	RE	TX	VS
		•		•	Carly J Carman Abstracting Service [SOP]	662-423-5923	•	•	•	
•	•	•	•	•	Freelance Abstracting Svc [SOP]	662-424-3636	•	•	•	•
•	•	•		•	Mitchell McNutt & Sams PA	662-842-3871	•	•	•	•
		•	•	•	Segars & Holly [SOP]	662-423-1006	•	•	•	•

AMITE

DT	BK	CV	CR	PR	←Courts	Recording→	UC	RE	TX	VS

See adjoining counties for retrievers or contact court or recording office.

ATTALA

DT	BK	CV	CR	PR	←Courts	Recording→	UC	RE	TX	VS
		•	•		Newell & Associates Inc [SOP]	601-693-7700	•	•	•	

BENTON

DT	BK	CV	CR	PR	←Courts	Recording→	UC	RE	TX	VS
•	•	•	•	•	Freelance Abstracting Svc [SOP]	662-424-3636	•	•	•	•
•	•	•	•	•	Record-Check Services Inc	800-530-7226	•	•	•	•

BOLIVAR

DT	BK	CV	CR	PR	←Courts	Recording→	UC	RE	TX	VS
•	•	•	•	•	CourthouseData	479-582-0900	•	•	•	•
		•	•	•	Barbara Tweedle	662-759-3048, 662-759-3762	•	•	•	

CALHOUN

DT	BK	CV	CR	PR	←Courts	Recording→	UC	RE	TX	VS
•	•	•	•	•	Aldridge & Associates [SOP]	662-651-7376	•	•	•	•

CARROLL

DT	BK	CV	CR	PR	←Courts	Recording→	UC	RE	TX	VS

See adjoining counties for retrievers or contact court or recording office.

CHICKASAW

DT	BK	CV	CR	PR	←Courts	Recording→	UC	RE	TX	VS
•	•	•	•	•	Aldridge & Associates [SOP]	662-651-7376	•	•	•	•
•	•	•	•	•	TENSTAR Corporation (Tupelo) [SOP]	800-864-5154	•	•	•	•

CHOCTAW

DT	BK	CV	CR	PR	←Courts	Recording→	UC	RE	TX	VS
		•	•	•	Joe C Griffin	662-285-6080	•	•	•	•

CLAIBORNE

DT	BK	CV	CR	PR	←Courts	Recording→	UC	RE	TX	VS

See adjoining counties for retrievers or contact court or recording office.

CLARKE

DT	BK	CV	CR	PR	←Courts	Recording→	UC	RE	TX	VS
		•	•		Newell & Associates Inc [SOP]	601-693-7700	•	•	•	
•	•	•	•	•	Pro-Tech Investigations LLC	877-685-5655	•	•	•	
		•	•	•	George Williams	601-776-2111	•	•	•	

CLAY

DT	BK	CV	CR	PR	←Courts	Recording→	UC	RE	TX	VS
•	•	•	•	•	Aldridge & Associates [SOP]	662-651-7376	•	•	•	•
		•	•		Newell & Associates Inc [SOP]	601-693-7700	•	•	•	

COAHOMA

DT	BK	CV	CR	PR	←Courts	Recording→	UC	RE	TX	VS
•	•	•	•	•	CourthouseData	479-582-0900	•	•	•	•

COPIAH

DT	BK	CV	CR	PR	←Courts	Recording→	UC	RE	TX	VS
•	•	•	•	•	TENSTAR Corporation (Jackson) [SOP]	800-864-5154	•	•	•	•

DT	BK	CV	CR	PR	←Courts	Covington	Recording→	UC	RE	TX	VS
					B Scott Buffington		601-849-4267	●	●	●	
●	●	●	●	●	Pro-Tech Investigations LLC		877-685-5655	●	●	●	
		●	●	●	TSI - Title Services Inc		800-736-9331	●	●	●	

DT	BK	CV	CR	PR	←Courts	De Soto	Recording→	UC	RE	TX	VS
			●		Blue Line Investigations		901-266-7100				
				●	Landmark Abstract & Information Svcs		901-268-3200	●	●	●	
●	●	●	●	●	Lenow International Inc [SOP]		901-726-0735	●		●	●
		●	●	●	Mid-America Reporting Co LLC		662-487-0932	●	●	●	●
●	●	●	●	●	National Background Reports Inc		901-526-4654	●	●	●	●
●	●	●	●	●	Record-Check Services Inc		800-530-7226	●	●	●	●
●	●	●	●	●	Schaeffer Papers [SOP]		800-848-6119	●	●	●	●
●	●	●	●	●	The Discovery Group Inc [SOP]		662-280-1576	●		●	●

DT	BK	CV	CR	PR	←Courts	DeSoto	Recording→	UC	RE	TX	VS
●	●	●	●	●	CourthouseData		479-582-0900	●	●	●	●

DT	BK	CV	CR	PR	←Courts	Forrest	Recording→	UC	RE	TX	VS
					B Scott Buffington		601-849-4267	●	●	●	
●	●	●	●	●	Pro-Tech Investigations LLC		877-685-5655	●	●	●	
		●	●	●	TSI - Title Services Inc		800-736-9331	●	●	●	

DT	BK	CV	CR	PR	←Courts	Franklin	Recording→	UC	RE	TX	VS
		●	●	●	K Maxwell Graves Jr [SOP]		601-384-2733	●	●	●	

DT	BK	CV	CR	PR	←Courts	George	Recording→	UC	RE	TX	VS
		●	●	●	Jerry Axton [SOP]		228-475-1739	●	●	●	
●	●	●	●	●	Recon Investigative Services [SOP]		228-452-0120	●		●	●
		●	●		SRA Inv Inc [SOP]		800-530-7115 x4197				
●	●	●	●	●	TENSTAR Corporation (Jackson) [SOP]		800-864-5154	●	●	●	●

DT	BK	CV	CR	PR	←Courts	Greene	Recording→	UC	RE	TX	VS
●	●	●	●	●	Pro-Tech Investigations LLC		877-685-5655	●	●	●	
		●	●	●	TSI - Title Services Inc		800-736-9331	●	●	●	

DT	BK	CV	CR	PR	←Courts	Grenada	Recording→	UC	RE	TX	VS
					See adjoining counties for retrievers or contact court or recording office.						

DT	BK	CV	CR	PR	←Courts	Hancock	Recording→	UC	RE	TX	VS
		●	●	●	Jerry Axton [SOP]		228-475-1739	●	●	●	
●	●	●	●	●	Pro-Tech Investigations LLC		877-685-5655	●	●	●	
●	●	●	●	●	Recon Investigative Services [SOP]		228-452-0120	●		●	●
		●	●		SRA Inv Inc [SOP]		800-530-7115 x4197				
●	●	●	●	●	TENSTAR Corporation (Jackson) [SOP]		800-864-5154	●	●	●	●

DT	BK	CV	CR	PR	←Courts	Harrison	Recording→	UC	RE	TX	VS
		●	●	●	Jerry Axton [SOP]		228-475-1739	●	●	●	
●	●	●	●	●	Pro-Tech Investigations LLC		877-685-5655	●	●	●	
●	●	●	●	●	Recon Investigative Services [SOP]		228-452-0120	●		●	●
		●	●		SRA Inv Inc [SOP]		800-530-7115 x4197				
●	●	●	●	●	TENSTAR Corporation (Jackson) [SOP]		800-864-5154	●	●	●	●

DT	BK	CV	CR	PR	←Courts	Hinds	Recording→	UC	RE	TX	VS
●	●	●	●	●	McAllister & Associates Inc [SOP]		601-977-0406	●	●	●	●
●	●	●	●	●	Mr Holmes Inv [SOP]		601-859-7955	●	●	●	●
●	●	●	●	●	TENSTAR Corporation (Jackson) [SOP]		800-864-5154	●	●	●	●

DT	BK	CV	CR	PR	←Courts	Holmes	Recording→	UC	RE	TX	VS
					See adjoining counties for retrievers or contact court or recording office.						

DT	BK	CV	CR	PR	←Courts	**HUMPHREYS** Recording→	UC	RE	TX	VS
					See adjoining counties for retrievers or contact court or recording office.					

DT	BK	CV	CR	PR	←Courts	**ISSAQUENA** Recording→	UC	RE	TX	VS
		•	•	•	Weissinger & Hunter	662-873-6258	•	•	•	•

DT	BK	CV	CR	PR	←Courts	**ITAWAMBA** Recording→	UC	RE	TX	VS
•	•	•	•	•	Aldridge & Associates [SOP]	662-651-7376	•	•	•	•
•	•	•	•	•	Freelance Abstracting Svc [SOP]	662-424-3636	•	•	•	•
•	•	•	•	•	TENSTAR Corporation (Tupelo) [SOP]	800-864-5154	•	•	•	•

DT	BK	CV	CR	PR	←Courts	**JACKSON** Recording→	UC	RE	TX	VS
		•	•	•	Jerry Axton [SOP]	228-475-1739	•	•	•	
•	•	•	•	•	Parker Legal Services [SOP]	251-476-7464	•	•	•	•
•	•	•	•	•	Recon Investigative Services [SOP]	228-452-0120	•		•	•
		•	•		SRA Inv Inc [SOP]	800-530-7115 x4197				
•	•	•	•	•	TENSTAR Corporation (Jackson) [SOP]	800-864-5154	•	•	•	•

DT	BK	CV	CR	PR	←Courts	**JASPER** Recording→	UC	RE	TX	VS
		•	•		Newell & Associates Inc [SOP]	601-693-7700	•	•	•	
•	•	•	•	•	Pro-Tech Investigations LLC	877-685-5655	•	•	•	

DT	BK	CV	CR	PR	←Courts	**JEFFERSON** Recording→	UC	RE	TX	VS
					See adjoining counties for retrievers or contact court or recording office.					

DT	BK	CV	CR	PR	←Courts	**JEFFERSON DAVIS** Recording→	UC	RE	TX	VS
					B Scott Buffington	601-849-4267	•	•	•	
•	•	•	•	•	Pro-Tech Investigations LLC	877-685-5655	•	•	•	
		•	•	•	TSI - Title Services Inc	800-736-9331	•	•	•	

DT	BK	CV	CR	PR	←Courts	**JONES** Recording→	UC	RE	TX	VS
•	•	•	•	•	Pro-Tech Investigations LLC	877-685-5655	•	•	•	
•	•	•	•	•	TENSTAR Corporation (Jackson) [SOP]	800-864-5154	•	•	•	•
		•	•	•	TSI - Title Services Inc	800-736-9331	•	•	•	

DT	BK	CV	CR	PR	←Courts	**KEMPER** Recording→	UC	RE	TX	VS
		•	•		Newell & Associates Inc [SOP]	601-693-7700	•	•	•	

DT	BK	CV	CR	PR	←Courts	**LAFAYETTE** Recording→	UC	RE	TX	VS
•	•	•	•	•	Freelance Abstracting Svc [SOP]	662-424-3636	•	•	•	•
•	•	•		•	Mitchell McNutt & Sams PA	662-842-3871	•	•	•	•
•	•	•	•	•	The Discovery Group Inc [SOP]	662-280-1576	•		•	•

DT	BK	CV	CR	PR	←Courts	**LAMAR** Recording→	UC	RE	TX	VS
					B Scott Buffington	601-849-4267	•	•	•	
•	•	•	•	•	Pro-Tech Investigations LLC	877-685-5655	•	•	•	
		•	•	•	TSI - Title Services Inc	800-736-9331	•	•	•	

DT	BK	CV	CR	PR	←Courts	**LAUDERDALE** Recording→	UC	RE	TX	VS
•	•	•	•	•	ASAP Process Services [SOP]	256-766-9805	•	•		•
		•	•		Newell & Associates Inc [SOP]	601-693-7700	•	•	•	

DT	BK	CV	CR	PR	←Courts	**LAWRENCE** Recording→	UC	RE	TX	VS
					See adjoining counties for retrievers or contact court or recording office.					

DT	BK	CV	CR	PR	←Courts	**LEAKE** Recording→	UC	RE	TX	VS
		•	•		Newell & Associates Inc [SOP]	601-693-7700	•	•	•	

DT	BK	CV	CR	PR	←Courts	**LEE** Recording→	UC	RE	TX	VS
•	•	•	•	•	Aldridge & Associates [SOP]	662-651-7376	•	•	•	•
•	•	•	•	•	Freelance Abstracting Svc [SOP]	662-424-3636	•	•	•	•
•	•	•		•	Mitchell McNutt & Sams PA	662-842-3871	•	•	•	•
		•	•		Newell & Associates Inc [SOP]	601-693-7700	•	•	•	

DT	BK	CV	CR	PR			UC	RE	TX	VS
•	•	•	•	•	TENSTAR Corporation (Tupelo) [SOP]	800-864-5154	•	•	•	•

DT	BK	CV	CR	PR	←Courts	LEFLORE Recording→	UC	RE	TX	VS
					See adjoining counties for retrievers or contact court or recording office.					

DT	BK	CV	CR	PR	←Courts	LINCOLN Recording→	UC	RE	TX	VS
					See adjoining counties for retrievers or contact court or recording office.					

DT	BK	CV	CR	PR	←Courts	LOWNDES Recording→	UC	RE	TX	VS
•	•	•	•	•	Aldridge & Associates [SOP]	662-651-7376	•	•	•	•
•	•	•		•	Mitchell McNutt & Sams PA	662-842-3871	•	•	•	•
		•	•		Newell & Associates Inc [SOP]	601-693-7700	•	•	•	

DT	BK	CV	CR	PR	←Courts	MADISON Recording→	UC	RE	TX	VS
•	•	•	•	•	McAllister & Associates Inc [SOP]	601-977-0406	•	•	•	•
•	•	•	•	•	Mr Holmes Inv [SOP]	601-859-7955	•	•	•	•
•	•	•	•	•	TENSTAR Corporation (Jackson) [SOP]	800-864-5154	•	•	•	•

DT	BK	CV	CR	PR	←Courts	MARION Recording→	UC	RE	TX	VS
•	•	•	•	•	Pro-Tech Investigations LLC	877-685-5655	•	•	•	
		•	•	•	TSI - Title Services Inc	800-736-9331	•	•	•	

DT	BK	CV	CR	PR	←Courts	MARSHALL Recording→	UC	RE	TX	VS
			•		Blue Line Investigations	901-266-7100				
•	•	•	•	•	Freelance Abstracting Svc [SOP]	662-424-3636	•	•	•	•
•	•	•	•	•	Record-Check Services Inc	800-530-7226	•	•	•	•
•	•	•	•	•	The Discovery Group Inc [SOP]	662-280-1576	•		•	•

DT	BK	CV	CR	PR	←Courts	MONROE Recording→	UC	RE	TX	VS
•	•	•	•	•	Aldridge & Associates [SOP]	662-651-7376	•	•	•	•
•	•	•	•	•	Freelance Abstracting Svc [SOP]	662-424-3636	•	•	•	•
		•	•		Newell & Associates Inc [SOP]	601-693-7700	•	•	•	
•	•	•	•	•	TENSTAR Corporation (Tupelo) [SOP]	800-864-5154	•	•	•	•
•	•	•			The Copy Shop of Aberdeen	662-369-4428				

DT	BK	CV	CR	PR	←Courts	MONTGOMERY Recording→	UC	RE	TX	VS
					See adjoining counties for retrievers or contact court or recording office.					

DT	BK	CV	CR	PR	←Courts	NESHOBA Recording→	UC	RE	TX	VS
		•	•		Newell & Associates Inc [SOP]	601-693-7700	•	•	•	

DT	BK	CV	CR	PR	←Courts	NEWTON Recording→	UC	RE	TX	VS
		•	•		Newell & Associates Inc [SOP]	601-693-7700	•	•	•	

DT	BK	CV	CR	PR	←Courts	NOXUBEE Recording→	UC	RE	TX	VS
		•	•		Newell & Associates Inc [SOP]	601-693-7700	•	•	•	

DT	BK	CV	CR	PR	←Courts	OKTIBBEHA Recording→	UC	RE	TX	VS
			•		Blue Line Investigations	901-266-7100				
		•	•		Newell & Associates Inc [SOP]	601-693-7700	•	•	•	

DT	BK	CV	CR	PR	←Courts	PANOLA Recording→	UC	RE	TX	VS
			•		Blue Line Investigations	901-266-7100				
		•	•	•	Mid-America Reporting Co LLC	662-487-0932	•	•	•	•

DT	BK	CV	CR	PR	←Courts	PEARL RIVER Recording→	UC	RE	TX	VS
•	•	•	•	•	Pro-Tech Investigations LLC	877-685-5655	•	•	•	
•	•	•	•	•	Recon Investigative Services [SOP]	228-452-0120	•		•	•
		•	•		SRA Inv Inc [SOP]	800-530-7115 x4197				
		•	•	•	TSI - Title Services Inc	800-736-9331	•	•	•	

DT	BK	CV	CR	PR	←Courts	PERRY Recording→	UC	RE	TX	VS
•	•	•	•	•	Pro-Tech Investigations LLC	877-685-5655	•	•	•	

DT	BK	CV	CR	PR	Courts	Recording	UC	RE	TX	VS
		●	●	●	TSI - Title Services Inc	800-736-9331	●	●	●	

DT	BK	CV	CR	PR	←Courts **PIKE**	Recording→	UC	RE	TX	VS
		●	●	●	Conrad Mord	601-876-2611	●	●	●	●

DT	BK	CV	CR	PR	←Courts **PONTOTOC**	Recording→	UC	RE	TX	VS
●	●	●	●	●	Aldridge & Associates [SOP]	662-651-7376	●	●	●	●
●	●	●	●	●	Freelance Abstracting Svc [SOP]	662-424-3636	●	●	●	●
●	●	●		●	Mitchell McNutt & Sams PA	662-842-3871	●	●	●	●
●	●	●	●	●	TENSTAR Corporation (Tupelo) [SOP]	800-864-5154	●	●	●	●

DT	BK	CV	CR	PR	←Courts **PRENTISS**	Recording→	UC	RE	TX	VS
		●		●	Carly J Carman Abstracting Service [SOP]	662-423-5923	●	●	●	
●	●	●	●	●	Freelance Abstracting Svc [SOP]	662-424-3636	●	●	●	●
		●	●	●	Attorney John A Hatcher [SOP]	662-728-9444	●	●	●	●
		●	●	●	Segars & Holly [SOP]	662-423-1006	●	●	●	●
●	●	●	●	●	TENSTAR Corporation (Tupelo) [SOP]	800-864-5154	●	●	●	●

DT	BK	CV	CR	PR	←Courts **QUITMAN**	Recording→	UC	RE	TX	VS
					See adjoining counties for retrievers or contact court or recording office.					

DT	BK	CV	CR	PR	←Courts **RANKIN**	Recording→	UC	RE	TX	VS
●	●	●	●	●	McAllister & Associates Inc [SOP]	601-977-0406	●	●	●	●
●	●	●	●	●	Mr Holmes Inv [SOP]	601-859-7955	●	●	●	●
●	●	●	●	●	TENSTAR Corporation (Jackson) [SOP]	800-864-5154	●	●	●	●

DT	BK	CV	CR	PR	←Courts **SCOTT**	Recording→	UC	RE	TX	VS
		●	●	●	Thompson & Hollingsworth PA	601-469-3411	●	●	●	●

DT	BK	CV	CR	PR	←Courts **SHARKEY**	Recording→	UC	RE	TX	VS
		●	●	●	Weissinger & Hunter	662-873-6258	●	●	●	●

DT	BK	CV	CR	PR	←Courts **SIMPSON**	Recording→	UC	RE	TX	VS
					B Scott Buffington	601-849-4267	●	●	●	
●	●	●	●	●	TENSTAR Corporation (Jackson) [SOP]	800-864-5154	●	●	●	●

DT	BK	CV	CR	PR	←Courts **SMITH**	Recording→	UC	RE	TX	VS
					B Scott Buffington	601-849-4267	●	●	●	
●	●	●	●	●	Pro-Tech Investigations LLC	877-685-5655	●	●	●	
		●	●	●	Thompson & Hollingsworth PA	601-469-3411	●	●	●	●

DT	BK	CV	CR	PR	←Courts **STONE**	Recording→	UC	RE	TX	VS
●	●	●	●	●	Pro-Tech Investigations LLC	877-685-5655	●	●	●	
●	●	●	●	●	Recon Investigative Services [SOP]	228-452-0120	●		●	●
		●	●		SRA Inv Inc [SOP]	800-530-7115 x4197				
		●	●	●	TSI - Title Services Inc	800-736-9331	●	●	●	

DT	BK	CV	CR	PR	←Courts **SUNFLOWER**	Recording→	UC	RE	TX	VS
					See adjoining counties for retrievers or contact court or recording office.					

DT	BK	CV	CR	PR	←Courts **TALLAHATCHIE**	Recording→	UC	RE	TX	VS
					See adjoining counties for retrievers or contact court or recording office.					

DT	BK	CV	CR	PR	←Courts **TATE**	Recording→	UC	RE	TX	VS
			●		Blue Line Investigations	901-266-7100				
●	●	●	●	●	CourthouseData	479-582-0900	●	●	●	●
		●	●	●	Mid-America Reporting Co LLC	662-487-0932	●	●	●	●
●	●	●	●	●	The Discovery Group Inc [SOP]	662-280-1576	●		●	●

DT	BK	CV	CR	PR	←Courts **TIPPAH**	Recording→	UC	RE	TX	VS
●	●	●	●	●	Freelance Abstracting Svc [SOP]	662-424-3636	●	●	●	●
●	●	●	●	●	TENSTAR Corporation (Tupelo) [SOP]	800-864-5154	●	●	●	●

DT	BK	CV	CR	PR	←Courts	**Tishomingo**	Recording→	UC	RE	TX	VS
•	•	•	•	•		ASAP Process Services [SOP]	256-766-9805	•	•		•
		•		•		Carly J Carman Abstracting Service [SOP]	662-423-5923	•	•	•	
•	•	•	•	•		Freelance Abstracting Svc [SOP]	662-424-3636	•	•	•	•
		•	•	•		Segars & Holly [SOP]	662-423-1006	•	•	•	•

DT	BK	CV	CR	PR	←Courts	**Tunica**	Recording→	UC	RE	TX	VS
			•			Blue Line Investigations	901-266-7100				
•	•	•	•	•		CourthouseData	479-582-0900	•	•	•	•
		•	•	•		Mid-America Reporting Co LLC	662-487-0932	•	•	•	•
•	•	•	•	•		Schaeffer Papers [SOP]	800-848-6119	•	•	•	•
•	•	•	•	•		The Discovery Group Inc [SOP]	662-280-1576	•		•	•

DT	BK	CV	CR	PR	←Courts	**Union**	Recording→	UC	RE	TX	VS
•	•	•	•	•		Aldridge & Associates [SOP]	662-651-7376	•	•	•	•
•	•	•	•	•		Freelance Abstracting Svc [SOP]	662-424-3636	•	•	•	•
•	•	•		•		Mitchell McNutt & Sams PA	662-842-3871	•	•	•	•
•	•	•		•		TENSTAR Corporation (Tupelo) [SOP]	800-864-5154	•	•	•	•

DT	BK	CV	CR	PR	←Courts	**Walthall**	Recording→	UC	RE	TX	VS
		•	•	•		Conrad Mord	601-876-2611	•	•	•	•
		•	•	•		TSI - Title Services Inc	800-736-9331	•	•	•	

DT	BK	CV	CR	PR	←Courts	**Warren**	Recording→	UC	RE	TX	VS
•	•	•	•	•		McAllister & Associates Inc [SOP]	601-977-0406	•	•	•	•
•	•	•	•	•		TENSTAR Corporation (Jackson) [SOP]	800-864-5154	•	•	•	•

DT	BK	CV	CR	PR	←Courts	**Washington**	Recording→	UC	RE	TX	VS
						See adjoining counties for retrievers or contact court or recording office.					

DT	BK	CV	CR	PR	←Courts	**Wayne**	Recording→	UC	RE	TX	VS
•	•	•	•	•		Pro-Tech Investigations LLC	877-685-5655	•	•	•	
		•	•	•		TSI - Title Services Inc	800-736-9331	•	•	•	

DT	BK	CV	CR	PR	←Courts	**Webster**	Recording→	UC	RE	TX	VS
		•	•			Newell & Associates Inc [SOP]	601-693-7700	•	•	•	

DT	BK	CV	CR	PR	←Courts	**Wilkinson**	Recording→	UC	RE	TX	VS
						See adjoining counties for retrievers or contact court or recording office.					

DT	BK	CV	CR	PR	←Courts	**Winston**	Recording→	UC	RE	TX	VS
		•	•			Newell & Associates Inc [SOP]	601-693-7700	•	•	•	
		•		•		Taylor Tucker	662-773-9254	•	•	•	•

DT	BK	CV	CR	PR	←Courts	**Yalobusha**	Recording→	UC	RE	TX	VS
						See adjoining counties for retrievers or contact court or recording office.					

DT	BK	CV	CR	PR	←Courts	**Yazoo**	Recording→	UC	RE	TX	VS
•	•	•	•	•		TENSTAR Corporation (Jackson) [SOP]	800-864-5154	•	•	•	•

= PRRN Member. *A retriever you can trust!*

Missouri

DT	BK	CV	CR	PR	←Courts	Recording→	UC	RE	TX	VS
COURT RECORDS RETRIEVED						**RECORDING RECORDS RETRIEVED**				
					ADAIR					
					North Missouri Title	660-665-4711		•	•	
					ANDREW					
•	•	•	•	•	NW Missouri Information Services [SOP]	816-233-4779	•	•	•	•
					ATCHISON					
•	•	•	•	•	NW Missouri Information Services [SOP]	816-233-4779	•	•	•	•
					AUDRAIN					
		•		•	Audrain County Title Co	573-581-5136	•	•	•	
		•		•	Guaranty Land Title	573-874-4912	•	•	•	•
	•	•			Real Data	573-893-4898		•	•	
		•	•	•	Wells Abstract Co	573-221-0644	•	•	•	
					BARRY					
				•	Barry County Abstract & Title	417-847-3224	•	•	•	
•	•	•	•	•	National Inv Services Inc [SOP]	417-831-2500	•	•	•	•
					BARTON					
•	•	•	•	•	American Research Unlimited Inc [SOP]	417-358-6494	•	•	•	•
		•	•	•	Barton County Title Co	417-682-3100	•	•	•	•
•	•		•		LLG Enterprises	816-443-2396				
•	•	•	•	•	National Inv Services Inc [SOP]	417-831-2500	•	•	•	•
					BATES					
•	•	•	•	•	American Research Unlimited Inc [SOP]	417-358-6494	•	•	•	•
			•	•	Bi-State Title Search (Div of Bi-State Ind.)	866-450-7399	•	•	•	
					BENTON					
		•	•	•	Drake Land Title Co	660-438-5188	•	•	•	
		•	•	•	General Investigations LLC [SOP]	660-747-8900	•	•	•	•
		•	•		Ozark Inv [SOP]	888-685-5366				
•	•	•	•	•	The Right Search Inc	417-852-7097	•	•	•	•
					BOLLINGER					
		•		•	American Heritage Abstract	573-431-1359	•	•	•	
		•	•	•	Bollinger County Abstract Co	573-238-2823	•	•	•	
					Collier Connections	573-833-6349		•	•	
		•	•		Services Rendered Inc [SOP]	314-644-3955				
					BOONE					
		•		•	Guaranty Land Title	573-874-4912	•	•	•	•
•			•		Harmon Legal Process Service [SOP]	573-635-6690				
•		•	•		J & J Enterprises - MO [SOP]	573-395-4205	•	•	•	
•	•		•		LLG Enterprises	816-443-2396				
	•	•			Real Data	573-893-4898		•	•	
					BUCHANAN					
			•	•	Bi-State Title Search (Div of Bi-State Ind.)	866-450-7399	•	•	•	
•	•	•	•	•	Hatfield Process Service [SOP]	816-842-9800	•	•	•	•
•	•		•		LLG Enterprises	816-443-2396				

DT	BK	CV	CR	PR	←Courts	Recording→	UC	RE	TX	VS
•	•	•	•	•	NW Missouri Information Services [SOP]	816-233-4779	•	•	•	•
DT	**BK**	**CV**	**CR**	**PR**	**←Courts BUTLER**	**Recording→**	**UC**	**RE**	**TX**	**VS**
		•		•	Butler County Abstract & Title Inc	573-686-1495	•	•	•	
		•	•		Services Rendered Inc [SOP]	314-644-3955				
DT	**BK**	**CV**	**CR**	**PR**	**←Courts CALDWELL**	**Recording→**	**UC**	**RE**	**TX**	**VS**
		•		•	Daviess County Land Title LLC	660-663-2155	•	•	•	
		•		•	Guaranty Land Title	573-874-4912	•	•	•	•
DT	**BK**	**CV**	**CR**	**PR**	**←Courts CALLAWAY**	**Recording→**	**UC**	**RE**	**TX**	**VS**
		•		•	Guaranty Land Title	573-874-4912	•	•	•	•
•			•		Harmon Legal Process Service [SOP]	573-635-6690				
•		•	•		J & J Enterprises - MO [SOP]	573-395-4205	•	•	•	
•	•		•		LLG Enterprises	816-443-2396				
	•	•			Real Data	573-893-4898		•	•	
DT	**BK**	**CV**	**CR**	**PR**	**←Courts CAMDEN**	**Recording→**	**UC**	**RE**	**TX**	**VS**
		•		•	Guaranty Land Title	573-874-4912	•	•	•	•
		•	•	•	Mozark Investigations [SOP]	866-308-1411	•	•	•	•
		•	•		Ozark Inv [SOP]	888-685-5366				
	•	•			Real Data	573-893-4898		•	•	
•	•	•	•	•	The Right Search Inc	417-852-7097	•	•	•	•
DT	**BK**	**CV**	**CR**	**PR**	**←Courts CAPE GIRARDEAU**	**Recording→**	**UC**	**RE**	**TX**	**VS**
•		•		•	Cape Girardeau County Abstract & Title	573-335-5890	•	•	•	
					Collier Connections	573-833-6349		•	•	
•	•	•	•		Interquest Information Services	800-455-1655	•	•	•	•
		•	•		Services Rendered Inc [SOP]	314-644-3955				
DT	**BK**	**CV**	**CR**	**PR**	**←Courts CARROLL**	**Recording→**	**UC**	**RE**	**TX**	**VS**
		•	•	•	Carroll Abstract Co	660-542-1364		•	•	
DT	**BK**	**CV**	**CR**	**PR**	**←Courts CARTER**	**Recording→**	**UC**	**RE**	**TX**	**VS**
		•	•	•	Mozark Investigations [SOP]	866-308-1411	•	•	•	•
DT	**BK**	**CV**	**CR**	**PR**	**←Courts CASS**	**Recording→**	**UC**	**RE**	**TX**	**VS**
					Arbuckle Searches	816-550-9106		•		
•	•	•		•	ASAP Services	816-540-2901		•	•	
			•	•	Bi-State Title Search (Div of Bi-State Ind.)	866-450-7399	•	•	•	
•	•	•	•	•	D & B Legal Services Inc [SOP]	913-963-1279	•	•	•	•
•	•	•	•	•	Hatfield Process Service [SOP]	816-842-9800	•	•	•	•
•	•	•	•	•	Medlin Research Company	913-206-4615	•	•	•	
•	•	•			SearchWorks Inc	913-383-0940	•	•	•	
DT	**BK**	**CV**	**CR**	**PR**	**←Courts CEDAR**	**Recording→**	**UC**	**RE**	**TX**	**VS**
•	•	•	•	•	American Research Unlimited Inc [SOP]	417-358-6494	•	•	•	•
•	•	•	•	•	National Inv Services Inc [SOP]	417-831-2500	•	•	•	•
•	•	•	•	•	The Right Search Inc	417-852-7097	•	•	•	•
DT	**BK**	**CV**	**CR**	**PR**	**←Courts CHARITON**	**Recording→**	**UC**	**RE**	**TX**	**VS**
		•		•	Guaranty Land Title	573-874-4912	•	•	•	•
DT	**BK**	**CV**	**CR**	**PR**	**←Courts CHRISTIAN**	**Recording→**	**UC**	**RE**	**TX**	**VS**
•	•	•	•	•	American Research Unlimited Inc [SOP]	417-358-6494	•	•	•	•
		•		•	Hogan Land Title Co	417-882-3000		•	•	
•	•	•	•		Kolling & Associates	417-889-4092				
					Lincoln-Evans Advanced Land & Title	417-581-8251	•	•	•	
		•			MO Data Inc	417-299-2469	•	•	•	
•	•	•	•	•	National Inv Services Inc [SOP]	417-831-2500	•	•	•	•
					Sparks Searches	417-725-4851		•	•	
•	•	•	•	•	The Right Search Inc	417-852-7097	•	•	•	•

DT	BK	CV	CR	PR	←Courts CLARK	Recording→	UC	RE	TX	VS
		•	•	•	Marion County Abstract Co (Missouri)	800-952-5314	•	•	•	•
				•	Scotland County Abstract & Title Inc	660-465-7052		•	•	

DT	BK	CV	CR	PR	←Courts CLAY	Recording→	UC	RE	TX	VS
•	•	•	•		Armstrong Document Retrieval	913-341-1991	•	•	•	
•	•	•		•	ASAP Services	816-540-2901		•	•	
			•	•	Bi-State Title Search (Div of Bi-State Ind.)	866-450-7399	•	•	•	
•	•	•	•	•	D & B Legal Services Inc [SOP]	913-963-1279	•	•	•	•
•	•	•	•		Executive Investigative Services [SOP]	800-764-9484	•	•	•	
•	•	•		•	Connie Giandalia	816-217-1849	•	•	•	
•	•	•	•	•	Hatfield Process Service [SOP]	816-842-9800	•	•	•	•
•	•		•		LLG Enterprises	816-443-2396				
•		•		•	M & J Abstractors	913-727-3588	•	•	•	
•	•	•	•	•	NW Missouri Information Services [SOP]	816-233-4779	•	•	•	•
		•	•		Rigoli Searches	913-908-8863	•	•	•	
•	•	•			SearchWorks Inc	913-383-0940	•	•	•	

DT	BK	CV	CR	PR	←Courts CLINTON	Recording→	UC	RE	TX	VS
			•	•	Bi-State Title Search (Div of Bi-State Ind.)	866-450-7399	•	•	•	
		•		•	Daviess County Land Title LLC	660-663-2155	•	•	•	
		•		•	Guaranty Land Title	573-874-4912	•	•	•	•
•	•	•	•	•	NW Missouri Information Services [SOP]	816-233-4779	•	•	•	•

DT	BK	CV	CR	PR	←Courts COLE	Recording→	UC	RE	TX	VS
		•		•	Guaranty Land Title	573-874-4912	•	•	•	•
•			•		Harmon Legal Process Service [SOP]	573-635-6690				
•		•	•		J & J Enterprises - MO [SOP]	573-395-4205	•	•	•	
		•	•	•	Jeff City Filing Inc [SOP]	573-634-3894	•	•	•	•
•	•		•		LLG Enterprises	816-443-2396				
	•	•			Real Data	573-893-4898		•	•	

DT	BK	CV	CR	PR	←Courts COOPER	Recording→	UC	RE	TX	VS
		•		•	Guaranty Land Title	573-874-4912	•	•	•	•
	•	•			Real Data	573-893-4898		•	•	

DT	BK	CV	CR	PR	←Courts CRAWFORD	Recording→	UC	RE	TX	VS
			•	•	Bi-State Title Search (Div of Bi-State Ind.)	866-450-7399	•	•	•	
					Crawford County Title Co	573-885-6470		•	•	
		•		•	Guaranty Land Title	573-874-4912	•	•	•	•
		•	•	•	Mozark Investigations [SOP]	866-308-1411	•	•	•	•
	•	•			Real Data	573-893-4898		•	•	

DT	BK	CV	CR	PR	←Courts DADE	Recording→	UC	RE	TX	VS
•	•	•	•	•	National Inv Services Inc [SOP]	417-831-2500	•	•	•	•
				•	Russell Abstract	417-637-2414		•	•	

DT	BK	CV	CR	PR	←Courts DALLAS	Recording→	UC	RE	TX	VS
		•		•	Hogan Land Title Co	417-882-3000		•	•	
•	•	•	•	•	National Inv Services Inc [SOP]	417-831-2500	•	•	•	•
		•	•		Ozark Inv [SOP]	888-685-5366				
•	•	•	•	•	The Right Search Inc	417-852-7097	•	•	•	•

DT	BK	CV	CR	PR	←Courts DAVIESS	Recording→	UC	RE	TX	VS
		•		•	Daviess County Land Title LLC	660-663-2155	•	•	•	
		•		•	Guaranty Land Title	573-874-4912	•	•	•	•
					Trenton Abstract	660-359-2100		•	•	

DT	BK	CV	CR	PR	←Courts DEKALB	Recording→	UC	RE	TX	VS
		•		•	Daviess County Land Title LLC	660-663-2155	•	•	•	
		•		•	Guaranty Land Title	573-874-4912	•	•	•	•

DT	BK	CV	CR	PR	Retriever	Phone	UC	RE	TX	VS
•	•	•	•	•	NW Missouri Information Services [SOP]	816-233-4779	•	•	•	•

DT	BK	CV	CR	PR	←COURTS **DENT**	RECORDING→	UC	RE	TX	VS
		•		•	Guaranty Land Title	573-874-4912	•	•	•	•
		•	•	•	Mozark Investigations [SOP]	866-308-1411	•	•	•	•
		•		•	Steelman Abstracting Co	573-729-6183		•	•	

DT	BK	CV	CR	PR	←COURTS **DOUGLAS**	RECORDING→	UC	RE	TX	VS
		•	•	•	Douglas County Abstract & Title Co	417-683-4701		•	•	
•	•	•	•	•	National Inv Services Inc [SOP]	417-831-2500	•	•	•	•
					Sparks Searches	417-725-4851		•	•	
		•		•	Wright County Title Co	417-926-6163	•	•	•	

DT	BK	CV	CR	PR	←COURTS **DUNKLIN**	RECORDING→	UC	RE	TX	VS
		•	•		Services Rendered Inc [SOP]	314-644-3955				

DT	BK	CV	CR	PR	←COURTS **FRANKLIN**	RECORDING→	UC	RE	TX	VS
•	•	•	•	•	AAA Process Service Inc [SOP]	888-350-5809	•	•	•	•
			•	•	Bi-State Title Search (Div of Bi-State Ind.)	866-450-7399	•	•	•	
		•	•		David Lung & Assoc [SOP]	888-477-2664				
•	•	•	•		Infotrack Information Services Inc	800-275-5594	•	•	•	
		•		•	Integrity Abstracting	314-807-6359	•	•	•	
•	•	•	•	•	Lenmark Personal Services [SOP]	636-677-3831		•		
•	•		•		LLG Enterprises	816-443-2396				
		•	•	•	Mozark Investigations [SOP]	866-308-1411	•	•	•	•
•	•	•	•	•	Services Rendered Inc [SOP]	888-434-8200	•		•	•
•	•	•	•	•	St Vrain Resources [SOP]	314-645-1710		•	•	•
		•	•	•	TRI-County Title LLC	636-239-7800	•	•	•	

DT	BK	CV	CR	PR	←COURTS **GASCONADE**	RECORDING→	UC	RE	TX	VS
			•	•	Bi-State Title Search (Div of Bi-State Ind.)	866-450-7399	•	•	•	
•		•	•		J & J Enterprises - MO [SOP]	573-395-4205	•	•	•	
		•	•	•	Mozark Investigations [SOP]	866-308-1411	•	•	•	•
		•	•	•	Donna Mundwiller	573-486-2925	•	•	•	•
	•	•			Real Data	573-893-4898		•	•	

DT	BK	CV	CR	PR	←COURTS **GENTRY**	RECORDING→	UC	RE	TX	VS
		•		•	Holden Abstract Co	660-726-3417	•	•	•	

DT	BK	CV	CR	PR	←COURTS **GREENE**	RECORDING→	UC	RE	TX	VS
•	•	•	•	•	American Research Unlimited Inc [SOP]	417-358-6494	•	•	•	•
		•	•	•	Compu-Fact Research Inc	636-477-1115, 618-239-0677	•	•	•	
		•		•	Hogan Land Title Co	417-882-3000		•	•	
					J & A Land Searching	417-887-1049		•		
•	•	•	•		Kolling & Associates	417-889-4092				
					Lincoln-Evans Advanced Land & Title	417-581-8251	•	•	•	
•	•		•		LLG Enterprises	816-443-2396				
		•			MO Data Inc	417-299-2469	•	•	•	
•	•	•	•	•	National Inv Services Inc [SOP]	417-831-2500	•	•	•	•
			•		Jacqueline Schoeneberg	417-889-6390				
					Sparks Searches	417-725-4851		•	•	
•	•	•	•	•	The Right Search Inc	417-852-7097	•	•	•	•

DT	BK	CV	CR	PR	←COURTS **GRUNDY**	RECORDING→	UC	RE	TX	VS
					Trenton Abstract	660-359-2100		•	•	

DT	BK	CV	CR	PR	←COURTS **HARRISON**	RECORDING→	UC	RE	TX	VS
		•		•	Harrison County Title	660-425-3523	•	•	•	

DT	BK	CV	CR	PR	←COURTS **HENRY**	RECORDING→	UC	RE	TX	VS
			•	•	Bi-State Title Search (Div of Bi-State Ind.)	866-450-7399	•	•	•	
		•	•	•	General Investigations LLC [SOP]	660-747-8900	•	•	•	•

DT	BK	CV	CR	PR	←COURTS		RECORDING→	UC	RE	TX	VS
		•		•	Henry County Abstract Co (Missouri)		800-748-7985	•	•	•	
DT	**BK**	**CV**	**CR**	**PR**	**←COURTS**	**HICKORY**	**RECORDING→**	**UC**	**RE**	**TX**	**VS**
					Bentley Title Co		417-745-6626	•	•	•	
•	•	•	•	•	National Inv Services Inc [SOP]		417-831-2500	•	•	•	•
		•	•		Ozark Inv [SOP]		888-685-5366				
•	•	•	•	•	The Right Search Inc		417-852-7097	•	•	•	•
DT	**BK**	**CV**	**CR**	**PR**	**←COURTS**	**HOLT**	**RECORDING→**	**UC**	**RE**	**TX**	**VS**
•	•	•	•	•	NW Missouri Information Services [SOP]		816-233-4779	•	•	•	•
DT	**BK**	**CV**	**CR**	**PR**	**←COURTS**	**HOWARD**	**RECORDING→**	**UC**	**RE**	**TX**	**VS**
		•	•	•	Geo G Smith & Son Inc		660-248-2467	•	•	•	•
		•		•	Guaranty Land Title		573-874-4912	•	•	•	•
DT	**BK**	**CV**	**CR**	**PR**	**←COURTS**	**HOWELL**	**RECORDING→**	**UC**	**RE**	**TX**	**VS**
		•		•	Brill Title Company		417-256-2951	•	•	•	
•	•		•		LLG Enterprises		816-443-2396				
DT	**BK**	**CV**	**CR**	**PR**	**←COURTS**	**IRON**	**RECORDING→**	**UC**	**RE**	**TX**	**VS**
		•		•	American Heritage Abstract		573-431-1359	•	•	•	
		•	•	•	Mozark Investigations [SOP]		866-308-1411	•	•	•	•
DT	**BK**	**CV**	**CR**	**PR**	**←COURTS**	**JACKSON**	**RECORDING→**	**UC**	**RE**	**TX**	**VS**
•	•	•	•		Armstrong Document Retrieval		913-341-1991	•	•	•	
•	•	•		•	ASAP Services		816-540-2901		•	•	
			•	•	Bi-State Title Search (Div of Bi-State Ind.)		866-450-7399	•	•	•	
					Kathy Coonts		816-833-0417		•	•	
•	•	•	•	•	D & B Legal Services Inc [SOP]		913-963-1279	•	•	•	•
•	•	•		•	Connie Giandalia		816-217-1849	•	•	•	
•	•	•	•	•	Hatfield Process Service [SOP]		816-842-9800	•	•	•	•
•	•	•	•	•	Jess Barker Document Research/Retrieval		888-316-3773	•	•	•	•
•	•	•	•	•	KC Court Research Inc		913-239-8995	•	•	•	
•		•		•	M & J Abstractors		913-727-3588	•	•	•	
•	•	•	•	•	NW Missouri Information Services [SOP]		816-233-4779	•	•	•	•
•	•	•			SearchWorks Inc		913-383-0940	•	•	•	
DT	**BK**	**CV**	**CR**	**PR**	**←COURTS**	**JASPER**	**RECORDING→**	**UC**	**RE**	**TX**	**VS**
•	•	•	•	•	American Research Unlimited Inc [SOP]		417-358-6494	•	•	•	•
•	•	•	•	•	National Inv Services Inc [SOP]		417-831-2500	•	•	•	•
DT	**BK**	**CV**	**CR**	**PR**	**←COURTS**	**JEFFERSON**	**RECORDING→**	**UC**	**RE**	**TX**	**VS**
•	•	•	•	•	AAA Process Service Inc [SOP]		888-350-5809	•	•	•	•
			•	•	Bi-State Title Search (Div of Bi-State Ind.)		866-450-7399	•	•	•	
		•	•		David Lung & Assoc [SOP]		888-477-2664				
	•				G-Docs Inc		636 937 9440	•	•	•	
•	•	•	•		Infotrack Information Services Inc		800-275-5594	•	•	•	
		•		•	Integrity Abstracting		314-807-6359	•	•	•	
•	•	•	•	•	Lenmark Personal Services [SOP]		636-677-3831		•		
•	•	•		•	Master File Inc [SOP]		866-242-0469	•	•	•	
•	•	•	•	•	Services Rendered Inc [SOP]		888-434-8200	•		•	•
•	•	•	•	•	St Vrain Resources [SOP]		314-645-1710		•	•	•
DT	**BK**	**CV**	**CR**	**PR**	**←COURTS**	**JOHNSON**	**RECORDING→**	**UC**	**RE**	**TX**	**VS**
					Arbuckle Searches		816-550-9106		•		
			•	•	Bi-State Title Search (Div of Bi-State Ind.)		866-450-7399	•	•	•	
		•	•	•	General Investigations LLC [SOP]		660-747-8900	•	•	•	•
•	•	•			SearchWorks Inc		913-383-0940	•	•	•	
DT	**BK**	**CV**	**CR**	**PR**	**←COURTS**	**KNOX**	**RECORDING→**	**UC**	**RE**	**TX**	**VS**
				•	Scotland County Abstract & Title Inc		660-465-7052		•	•	
		•	•	•	Wells Abstract Co		573-221-0644	•	•	•	

DT	BK	CV	CR	PR	←COURTS LACLEDE RECORDING→		UC	RE	TX	VS
		•		•	Guaranty Land Title	573-874-4912	•	•	•	•
•		•	•		J & J Enterprises - MO [SOP]	573-395-4205	•	•	•	
•	•	•	•	•	National Inv Services Inc [SOP]	417-831-2500	•	•	•	•
		•	•		Ozark Inv [SOP]	888-685-5366				
•	•	•	•	•	The Right Search Inc	417-852-7097	•	•	•	•

DT	BK	CV	CR	PR	←COURTS LAFAYETTE RECORDING→		UC	RE	TX	VS
			•	•	Bi-State Title Search (Div of Bi-State Ind.)	866-450-7399	•	•	•	
				•	Lafayette County Land Title Co	660-259-4631		•		

DT	BK	CV	CR	PR	←COURTS LAWRENCE RECORDING→		UC	RE	TX	VS
•	•	•	•	•	American Research Unlimited Inc [SOP]	417-358-6494	•	•	•	•
•	•	•	•	•	National Inv Services Inc [SOP]	417-831-2500	•	•	•	•
•	•	•	•	•	The Right Search Inc	417-852-7097	•	•	•	•

DT	BK	CV	CR	PR	←COURTS LEWIS RECORDING→		UC	RE	TX	VS
				•	Lewis County Abstract (Missouri)	573-288-4461	•	•	•	
		•	•	•	Marion County Abstract Co (Missouri)	800-952-5314	•	•	•	•
		•	•	•	Wells Abstract Co	573-221-0644	•	•	•	

DT	BK	CV	CR	PR	←COURTS LINCOLN RECORDING→		UC	RE	TX	VS
		•	•	•	Assured Title Company	636-240-0833	•	•	•	
			•	•	Bi-State Title Search (Div of Bi-State Ind.)	866-450-7399	•	•	•	
		•	•		David Lung & Assoc [SOP]	888-477-2664				
	•				G-Docs Inc	636 937 9440	•	•	•	
•	•	•	•		Infotrack Information Services Inc	800-275-5594	•	•	•	
		•		•	Troy Title Co LLC	636-528-2220		•	•	

DT	BK	CV	CR	PR	←COURTS LINN RECORDING→		UC	RE	TX	VS
					Linn County Title	660-258-2260		•	•	

DT	BK	CV	CR	PR	←COURTS LIVINGSTON RECORDING→		UC	RE	TX	VS
		•		•	Guaranty Land Title	573-874-4912	•	•	•	•
		•		•	Staton Abstract & Title Co	660-646-1421	•	•	•	•
					Trenton Abstract	660-359-2100		•	•	

DT	BK	CV	CR	PR	←COURTS MACON RECORDING→		UC	RE	TX	VS
		•		•	Guaranty Land Title	573-874-4912	•	•	•	•
		•		•	Macon County Title	660-385-6474	•	•	•	•
		•	•	•	Marion County Abstract Co (Missouri)	800-952-5314	•	•	•	•
		•	•	•	Wells Abstract Co	573-221-0644	•	•	•	

DT	BK	CV	CR	PR	←COURTS MADISON RECORDING→		UC	RE	TX	VS
		•		•	American Heritage Abstract	573-431-1359	•	•	•	
				•	Preferred Land Title	800-310-6721	•	•	•	

DT	BK	CV	CR	PR	←COURTS MARIES RECORDING→		UC	RE	TX	VS
		•		•	Guaranty Land Title	573-874-4912	•	•	•	•
				•	Hollenbeck Title Co	573-422-3633	•	•	•	
•		•	•		J & J Enterprises - MO [SOP]	573-395-4205	•	•	•	
		•	•	•	Mozark Investigations [SOP]	866-308-1411	•	•	•	•
	•	•			Real Data	573-893-4898		•	•	

DT	BK	CV	CR	PR	←COURTS MARION RECORDING→		UC	RE	TX	VS
		•	•	•	Marion County Abstract Co (Missouri)	800-952-5314	•	•	•	•
	•	•			Real Data	573-893-4898	•	•	•	
		•	•	•	Wells Abstract Co	573-221-0644	•	•	•	

DT	BK	CV	CR	PR	←COURTS MCDONALD RECORDING→		UC	RE	TX	VS
•	•	•	•	•	American Research Unlimited Inc [SOP]	417-358-6494	•	•	•	•
•	•	•	•	•	National Inv Services Inc [SOP]	417-831-2500	•	•	•	•

DT	BK	CV	CR	PR	←COURTS	MERCER	RECORDING→	UC	RE	TX	VS
					Trenton Abstract		660-359-2100		•	•	

DT	BK	CV	CR	PR	←COURTS	MILLER	RECORDING→	UC	RE	TX	VS
		•		•	Guaranty Land Title		573-874-4912	•	•	•	•
•			•		Harmon Legal Process Service [SOP]		573-635-6690				
•		•	•		J & J Enterprises - MO [SOP]		573-395-4205	•	•	•	
		•	•	•	Mozark Investigations [SOP]		866-308-1411	•	•	•	•
•	•	•	•	•	National Inv Services Inc [SOP]		417-831-2500	•	•	•	•
		•	•		Ozark Inv [SOP]		888-685-5366				

DT	BK	CV	CR	PR	←COURTS	MISSISSIPPI	RECORDING→	UC	RE	TX	VS
		•		•	Mississippi County Abstract & Loan Co		573-683-4671		•	•	
		•	•		Services Rendered Inc [SOP]		314-644-3955				

DT	BK	CV	CR	PR	←COURTS	MONITEAU	RECORDING→	UC	RE	TX	VS
		•		•	Guaranty Land Title		573-874-4912	•	•	•	•

DT	BK	CV	CR	PR	←COURTS	MONROE	RECORDING→	UC	RE	TX	VS
		•		•	Guaranty Land Title		573-874-4912	•	•	•	•
		•	•	•	Marion County Abstract Co (Missouri)		800-952-5314	•	•	•	•
		•	•	•	Monroe County Abstract & Title Co Inc		660-327-4109	•	•	•	
		•	•	•	Wells Abstract Co		573-221-0644	•	•	•	

DT	BK	CV	CR	PR	←COURTS	MONTGOMERY	RECORDING→	UC	RE	TX	VS
		•	•	•	Assured Title Company		636-240-0833	•	•	•	
			•	•	Bi-State Title Search (Div of Bi-State Ind.)		866-450-7399	•	•	•	
•	•		•		LLG Enterprises		816-443-2396				
		•	•	•	Montgomery County Abstract & Title Co		573-564-2298	•	•	•	
		•		•	Troy Title Co LLC		636-528-2220		•	•	

DT	BK	CV	CR	PR	←COURTS	MORGAN	RECORDING→	UC	RE	TX	VS
		•		•	Guaranty Land Title		573-874-4912	•	•	•	•
•			•		Harmon Legal Process Service [SOP]		573-635-6690				
		•		•	Hubbard-Kavanaugh Title Co		573-378-4411	•	•	•	•
		•	•		Ozark Inv [SOP]		888-685-5366				
	•	•			Real Data		573-893-4898		•	•	

DT	BK	CV	CR	PR	←COURTS	NEW MADRID	RECORDING→	UC	RE	TX	VS
		•	•	•	Security Abstract Co (Missouri)		573-748-2372		•	•	•
		•	•		Services Rendered Inc [SOP]		314-644-3955				

DT	BK	CV	CR	PR	←COURTS	NEWTON	RECORDING→	UC	RE	TX	VS
•	•	•	•	•	American Research Unlimited Inc [SOP]		417-358-6494	•	•	•	•
•	•	•	•	•	National Inv Services Inc [SOP]		417-831-2500	•	•	•	•

DT	BK	CV	CR	PR	←COURTS	NODAWAY	RECORDING→	UC	RE	TX	VS
		•		•	Nodaway County Abstract Co		660-582-2332	•	•	•	•
•	•	•	•	•	NW Missouri Information Services [SOP]		816-233-4779	•	•	•	•

DT	BK	CV	CR	PR	←COURTS	OREGON	RECORDING→	UC	RE	TX	VS
					Allen Abstract & Title		417-778-6665		•	•	

DT	BK	CV	CR	PR	←COURTS	OSAGE	RECORDING→	UC	RE	TX	VS
		•		•	Guaranty Land Title		573-874-4912	•	•	•	•
•			•		Harmon Legal Process Service [SOP]		573-635-6690				
•		•	•		J & J Enterprises - MO [SOP]		573-395-4205	•	•	•	
•	•		•		LLG Enterprises		816-443-2396				
	•	•			Real Data		573-893-4898		•	•	

DT	BK	CV	CR	PR	←COURTS	OZARK	RECORDING→	UC	RE	TX	VS
•	•	•	•	•	National Inv Services Inc [SOP]		417-831-2500	•	•	•	•

DT	BK	CV	CR	PR	←Courts **Pemiscot**	Recording→	UC	RE	TX	VS
		•		•	DeReign & DeReign Attorneys at Law	573-333-4666	•	•	•	
		•	•		Services Rendered Inc [SOP]	314-644-3955				

DT	BK	CV	CR	PR	←Courts **Perry**	Recording→	UC	RE	TX	VS
					Collier Connections	573-833-6349		•	•	
				•	Kiefer Title Co	573-547-7755		•	•	
•	•		•		LLG Enterprises	816-443-2396				
		•	•		Services Rendered Inc [SOP]	314-644-3955				

DT	BK	CV	CR	PR	←Courts **Pettis**	Recording→	UC	RE	TX	VS
		•	•	•	General Investigations LLC [SOP]	660-747-8900	•	•	•	•
		•		•	Guaranty Land Title	573-874-4912	•	•	•	•
	•	•			Real Data	573-893-4898		•	•	

DT	BK	CV	CR	PR	←Courts **Phelps**	Recording→	UC	RE	TX	VS
		•		•	Guaranty Land Title	573-874-4912	•	•	•	•
•		•	•		J & J Enterprises - MO [SOP]	573-395-4205	•	•	•	
		•	•	•	Mozark Investigations [SOP]	866-308-1411	•	•	•	•
•	•	•	•	•	National Inv Services Inc [SOP]	417-831-2500	•	•	•	•
	•	•			Real Data	573-893-4898		•	•	

DT	BK	CV	CR	PR	←Courts **Pike**	Recording→	UC	RE	TX	VS
			•	•	Bi-State Title Search (Div of Bi-State Ind.)	866-450-7399	•	•	•	
		•	•	•	Marion County Abstract Co (Missouri)	800-952-5314	•	•	•	•
		•		•	Troy Title Co LLC	636-528-2220		•	•	

DT	BK	CV	CR	PR	←Courts **Platte**	Recording→	UC	RE	TX	VS
•	•	•	•		Armstrong Document Retrieval	913-341-1991	•	•	•	
			•	•	Bi-State Title Search (Div of Bi-State Ind.)	866-450-7399	•	•	•	
•	•	•	•	•	D & B Legal Services Inc [SOP]	913-963-1279	•	•	•	•
•	•	•	•		Executive Investigative Services [SOP]	800-764-9484	•	•	•	
•	•	•	•	•	Hatfield Process Service [SOP]	816-842-9800	•	•	•	•
•	•		•		LLG Enterprises	816-443-2396				
•		•		•	M & J Abstractors	913-727-3588	•	•	•	
•	•	•	•	•	NW Missouri Information Services [SOP]	816-233-4779	•	•	•	•
		•	•		Rigoli Searches	913-908-8863	•	•	•	
•	•	•			SearchWorks Inc	913-383-0940	•	•	•	

DT	BK	CV	CR	PR	←Courts **Polk**	Recording→	UC	RE	TX	VS
•	•	•	•	•	National Inv Services Inc [SOP]	417-831-2500	•	•	•	•
•	•	•	•	•	The Right Search Inc	417-852-7097	•	•	•	•

DT	BK	CV	CR	PR	←Courts **Pulaski**	Recording→	UC	RE	TX	VS
	•				G-Docs Inc	636 937 9440	•	•	•	
		•		•	Guaranty Land Title	573-874-4912	•	•	•	•
•		•	•		J & J Enterprises - MO [SOP]	573-395-4205	•	•	•	
		•	•	•	Mozark Investigations [SOP]	866-308-1411	•	•	•	•
		•	•		Ozark Inv [SOP]	888-685-5366				
	•	•			Real Data	573-893-4898		•	•	

DT	BK	CV	CR	PR	←Courts **Putnam**	Recording→	UC	RE	TX	VS
•	•	•	•	•	Meier Inv [SOP]	515-205-2738	•	•	•	•
					Putnam County Abstract	660-947-3105	•	•	•	

DT	BK	CV	CR	PR	←Courts **Ralls**	Recording→	UC	RE	TX	VS
		•	•	•	Marion County Abstract Co (Missouri)	800-952-5314	•	•	•	•
	•	•			Real Data	573-893-4898		•	•	
		•	•	•	Wells Abstract Co	573-221-0644	•	•	•	

DT	BK	CV	CR	PR	←Courts RANDOLPH	Recording→	UC	RE	TX	VS
		•		•	Guaranty Land Title	573-874-4912	•	•	•	•
	•	•			Real Data	573-893-4898		•	•	
		•		•	Town & Country Abstract Co (Missouri)	660-277-3467	•	•	•	
		•	•	•	Wells Abstract Co	573-221-0644	•	•	•	

DT	BK	CV	CR	PR	←Courts RAY	Recording→	UC	RE	TX	VS
			•	•	Bi-State Title Search (Div of Bi-State Ind.)	866-450-7399	•	•	•	
					Ray County Land Title	816-470-6500		•	•	

DT	BK	CV	CR	PR	←Courts REYNOLDS	Recording→	UC	RE	TX	VS
		•	•	•	Mozark Investigations [SOP]	866-308-1411	•	•	•	•

DT	BK	CV	CR	PR	←Courts RIPLEY	Recording→	UC	RE	TX	VS
					Current River Abstract	573-996-2907		•	•	

DT	BK	CV	CR	PR	←Courts SALINE	Recording→	UC	RE	TX	VS
		•	•	•	General Investigations LLC [SOP]	660-747-8900	•	•	•	•
		•		•	Guaranty Land Title	573-874-4912	•	•	•	•

DT	BK	CV	CR	PR	←Courts SCHUYLER	Recording→	UC	RE	TX	VS
				•	Scotland County Abstract & Title Inc	660-465-7052		•	•	

DT	BK	CV	CR	PR	←Courts SCOTLAND	Recording→	UC	RE	TX	VS
				•	Scotland County Abstract & Title Inc	660-465-7052		•	•	

DT	BK	CV	CR	PR	←Courts SCOTT	Recording→	UC	RE	TX	VS
					Collier Connections	573-833-6349		•	•	
		•	•		Services Rendered Inc [SOP]	314-644-3955				

DT	BK	CV	CR	PR	←Courts SHANNON	Recording→	UC	RE	TX	VS
		•	•	•	Mozark Investigations [SOP]	866-308-1411	•	•	•	•
		•		•	Shannon County Abstract Co	573-226-3331	•	•	•	

DT	BK	CV	CR	PR	←Courts SHELBY	Recording→	UC	RE	TX	VS
		•	•	•	Marion County Abstract Co (Missouri)	800-952-5314	•	•	•	•
		•	•	•	Wells Abstract Co	573-221-0644	•	•	•	

DT	BK	CV	CR	PR	←Courts ST. CHARLES	Recording→	UC	RE	TX	VS
•	•	•	•	•	AAA Process Service Inc [SOP]	888-350-5809	•	•	•	•
		•	•	•	Assured Title Company	636-240-0833	•	•	•	
			•	•	Bi-State Title Search (Div of Bi-State Ind.)	866-450-7399	•	•	•	
•	•	•	•	•	Brad Clarkson	618-344-0656	•	•	•	•
		•	•		David Lung & Assoc [SOP]	888-477-2664				
	•				G-Docs Inc	636 937 9440	•	•	•	
•	•	•	•		Infotrack Information Services Inc	800-275-5594	•	•	•	
		•		•	Integrity Abstracting	314-807-6359	•	•	•	
•	•	•	•	•	Jess Barker Document Research/Retrieval	888-316-3773	•	•	•	•
•	•	•	•	•	KLK Research	636-366-7055				•
•	•	•	•	•	Kyle & Kyle (Michelle Kyle)	314-846-7728	•	•	•	
•	•	•	•	•	Lenmark Personal Services [SOP]	636-677-3831		•		
•	•		•		LLG Enterprises	816-443-2396				
•	•	•		•	Master File Inc [SOP]	866-242-0469	•	•	•	
•	•	•	•	•	Quick Search Title Services	636-723-1888		•	•	•
•	•	•	•	•	Services Rendered Inc [SOP]	888-434-8200	•		•	•
•	•	•	•	•	SMS Searches	314-691-1593	•	•	•	•
•	•	•	•	•	St Vrain Resources [SOP]	314-645-1710		•	•	•
•	•	•	•	•	Woelfel & Assoc Inc [SOP]	888-297-7180	•	•	•	

DT	BK	CV	CR	PR	←Courts ST. CLAIR	Recording→	UC	RE	TX	VS
•	•	•	•	•	The Right Search Inc	417-852-7097	•	•	•	•

DT	BK	CV	CR	PR	←COURTS ST. FRANCOIS	RECORDING→	UC	RE	TX	VS
		•		•	American Heritage Abstract	573-431-1359	•	•	•	
			•	•	Bi-State Title Search (Div of Bi-State Ind.)	866-450-7399	•	•	•	
					Collier Connections	573-833-6349		•	•	
		•	•	•	Mozark Investigations [SOP]	866-308-1411	•	•	•	•
				•	Preferred Land Title	800-310-6721	•	•	•	

DT	BK	CV	CR	PR	←COURTS ST. LOUIS COUNTY	RECORDING→	UC	RE	TX	VS
•	•	•	•	•	AAA Process Service Inc [SOP]	888-350-5809	•	•	•	•
			•	•	Bi-State Title Search (Div of Bi-State Ind.)	866-450-7399	•	•	•	
•	•	•	•	•	Brad Clarkson	618-344-0656	•	•	•	•
		•	•		David Lung & Assoc [SOP]	888-477-2664				
	•				G-Docs Inc	636 937 9440	•	•	•	
		•		•	Guaranty Land Title	573-874-4912	•	•	•	•
•	•	•	•		Infotrack Information Services Inc	800-275-5594	•	•	•	
		•		•	Integrity Abstracting	314-807-6359	•	•	•	
•	•	•	•	•	Jess Barker Document Research/Retrieval	888-316-3773	•	•	•	•
•	•	•	•	•	KLK Research	636-366-7055				•
•	•	•	•	•	Kyle & Kyle (Michelle Kyle)	314-846-7728	•	•	•	
•	•	•	•	•	Lenmark Personal Services [SOP]	636-677-3831		•		
•	•	•	•	•	Lueken Document Research Inc	314-631-5928	•	•	•	•
•	•	•		•	Master File Inc [SOP]	866-242-0469	•	•	•	
•	•	•	•	•	Quick Search Title Services	636-723-1888		•	•	•
•	•	•	•	•	Services Rendered Inc [SOP]	888-434-8200	•		•	•
•	•	•	•	•	SMS Searches	314-691-1593	•	•	•	•
•	•	•	•	•	St Vrain Resources [SOP]	314-645-1710		•	•	•
•	•	•	•	•	Tyler-McLennon Choicepoint	512-334-6244	•	•	•	•
•	•	•	•	•	Woelfel & Assoc Inc [SOP]	888-297-7180	•	•	•	
•	•	•	•	•	Elaine Wolf	314-731-1839				

DT	BK	CV	CR	PR	←COURTS ST. LOUIS CITY	RECORDING→	UC	RE	TX	VS
•	•	•	•	•	AAA Process Service Inc [SOP]	888-350-5809	•	•	•	•
			•	•	Bi-State Title Search (Div of Bi-State Ind.)	866-450-7399	•	•	•	
•	•	•	•	•	Brad Clarkson	618-344-0656	•	•	•	•
	•				G-Docs Inc	636 937 9440	•	•	•	
		•		•	Guaranty Land Title	573-874-4912	•	•	•	•
•	•	•	•		Infotrack Information Services Inc	800-275-5594	•	•	•	
		•		•	Integrity Abstracting	314-807-6359	•	•	•	
•	•	•	•	•	KLK Research	636-366-7055				•
•	•	•	•	•	Kyle & Kyle (Michelle Kyle)	314-846-7728	•	•	•	
•	•	•	•	•	Lueken Document Research Inc	314-631-5928	•	•	•	•
•	•	•		•	Master File Inc [SOP]	866-242-0469	•	•	•	
•	•	•	•	•	Quick Search Title Services	636-723-1888		•	•	•
•	•	•	•	•	Services Rendered Inc [SOP]	888-434-8200	•		•	•
•	•	•	•	•	SMS Searches	314-691-1593	•	•	•	•
•	•	•	•	•	St Vrain Resources [SOP]	314-645-1710		•	•	•
•	•	•	•	•	Tyler-McLennon Choicepoint	512-334-6244	•	•	•	•
•	•	•	•	•	Elaine Wolf	314-731-1839				

DT	BK	CV	CR	PR	←COURTS STE. GENEVIEVE	RECORDING→	UC	RE	TX	VS
			•	•	Bi-State Title Search (Div of Bi-State Ind.)	866-450-7399	•	•	•	
					Collier Connections	573-833-6349		•	•	
				•	Preferred Land Title	800-310-6721	•	•	•	

DT	BK	CV	CR	PR	←COURTS STODDARD	RECORDING→	UC	RE	TX	VS
					Collier Connections	573-833-6349		•	•	
				•	County Wide Abstract & Title Co Inc	573-624-2436	•	•	•	
		•	•		Services Rendered Inc [SOP]	314-644-3955				

DT	BK	CV	CR	PR	←COURTS STONE	RECORDING→	UC	RE	TX	VS
		•		•	Hogan Land Title Co	417-882-3000		•	•	
		•			MO Data Inc	417-299-2469	•	•	•	

DT	BK	CV	CR	PR	Retriever	Phone	UC	RE	TX	VS
•	•	•	•	•	National Inv Services Inc [SOP]	417-831-2500	•	•	•	•
					Sparks Searches	417-725-4851		•	•	
•	•	•	•	•	The Right Search Inc	417-852-7097	•	•	•	•

DT	BK	CV	CR	PR	←Courts **SULLIVAN** Recording→		UC	RE	TX	VS
					Putnam County Abstract	660-947-3105	•	•	•	
•	•	•	•	•	Sullivan County Abstract Co	660-265-3744	•	•	•	•

DT	BK	CV	CR	PR	←Courts **TANEY** Recording→		UC	RE	TX	VS
		•		•	Hogan Land Title Co	417-882-3000		•	•	
					Lincoln-Evans Advanced Land & Title	417-581-8251	•	•	•	
•	•		•		LLG Enterprises	816-443-2396				
		•			MO Data Inc	417-299-2469	•	•	•	
•	•	•	•	•	National Inv Services Inc [SOP]	417-831-2500	•	•	•	•
					Sparks Searches	417-725-4851		•	•	
•	•	•	•	•	The Right Search Inc	417-852-7097	•	•	•	•

DT	BK	CV	CR	PR	←Courts **TEXAS** Recording→		UC	RE	TX	VS
		•	•	•	Mozark Investigations [SOP]	866-308-1411	•	•	•	•

DT	BK	CV	CR	PR	←Courts **VERNON** Recording→		UC	RE	TX	VS
•	•	•	•	•	American Research Unlimited Inc [SOP]	417-358-6494	•	•	•	•
•	•		•		LLG Enterprises	816-443-2396				
•	•	•	•	•	National Inv Services Inc [SOP]	417-831-2500	•	•	•	•

DT	BK	CV	CR	PR	←Courts **WARREN** Recording→		UC	RE	TX	VS
		•	•	•	Assured Title Company	636-240-0833	•	•	•	
			•	•	Bi-State Title Search (Div of Bi-State Ind.)	866-450-7399	•	•	•	
		•	•		David Lung & Assoc [SOP]	888-477-2664				
•	•	•	•		Infotrack Information Services Inc	800-275-5594	•	•	•	
		•		•	Troy Title Co LLC	636-528-2220		•	•	

DT	BK	CV	CR	PR	←Courts **WASHINGTON** Recording→		UC	RE	TX	VS
		•		•	American Heritage Abstract	573-431-1359	•	•	•	
			•	•	Bi-State Title Search (Div of Bi-State Ind.)	866-450-7399	•	•	•	
	•				G-Docs Inc	636 937 9440	•	•	•	
		•	•	•	Mozark Investigations [SOP]	866-308-1411	•	•	•	•
				•	Preferred Land Title	800-310-6721	•	•	•	

DT	BK	CV	CR	PR	←Courts **WAYNE** Recording→		UC	RE	TX	VS
					Wayne County Abstract	573-224-3616		•	•	

DT	BK	CV	CR	PR	←Courts **WEBSTER** Recording→		UC	RE	TX	VS
		•		•	D D Hamilton Title Co	417-859-2078	•	•	•	
		•			MO Data Inc	417-299-2469	•	•	•	
•	•	•	•	•	National Inv Services Inc [SOP]	417-831-2500	•	•	•	•
•	•	•	•	•	The Right Search Inc	417-852-7097	•	•	•	•

DT	BK	CV	CR	PR	←Courts **WORTH** Recording→		UC	RE	TX	VS
		•		•	Nodaway County Abstract Co	660-582-2332	•	•	•	

DT	BK	CV	CR	PR	←Courts **WRIGHT** Recording→		UC	RE	TX	VS
		•		•	D D Hamilton Title Co	417-859-2078	•	•	•	
•	•	•	•	•	National Inv Services Inc [SOP]	417-831-2500	•	•	•	•
		•		•	Wright County Title Co	417-926-6163	•	•	•	

Montana

COURT RECORDS RETRIEVED — **RECORDING RECORDS RETRIEVED**

DT	BK	CV	CR	PR	←Courts	BEAVERHEAD	Recording→	UC	RE	TX	VS
		•	•	•	J B Data & Research, LLC		406-585-3323	•	•	•	
		•		•	Southern Montana Abstract & Title		406-683-4445	•	•	•	•
•	•	•	•	•	Washington Court Records Svc		509-448-5012	•	•	•	•

DT	BK	CV	CR	PR	←Courts	BIG HORN	Recording→	UC	RE	TX	VS
		•		•	American Title & Escrow of Big Horn County		406-665-3797	•	•	•	

DT	BK	CV	CR	PR	←Courts	BLAINE	Recording→	UC	RE	TX	VS
		•	•	•	Blaine County Title Co		406-357-3884	•	•	•	•
•	•	•	•	•	Washington Court Records Svc		509-448-5012	•	•	•	•

DT	BK	CV	CR	PR	←Courts	BROADWATER	Recording→	UC	RE	TX	VS
•	•	•	•	•	AEGIS Consulting & Inv Inc		888-742-3447	•		•	•
		•	•	•	J B Data & Research, LLC		406-585-3323	•	•	•	
		•	•		Mountain States Title Services		406-443-0521	•	•	•	
•	•	•	•	•	MT Corporate Services		406-227-7665	•	•	•	•
		•			Titleworks		406-442-4450	•	•	•	
•	•	•	•	•	Washington Court Records Svc		509-448-5012	•	•	•	•

DT	BK	CV	CR	PR	←Courts	CARBON	Recording→	UC	RE	TX	VS
					Carbon County Abstract & Title		406-446-1090	•	•	•	
•	•	•	•	•	Washington Court Records Svc		509-448-5012	•	•	•	•

DT	BK	CV	CR	PR	←Courts	CARTER	Recording→	UC	RE	TX	VS
					Security Title Miles City		800-728-5022		•	•	
•	•	•	•	•	Washington Court Records Svc		509-448-5012	•	•	•	•

DT	BK	CV	CR	PR	←Courts	CASCADE	Recording→	UC	RE	TX	VS
•	•	•	•	•	AEGIS Consulting & Inv Inc		888-742-3447	•		•	•
•	•	•	•	•	Equity Process Management [SOP]		888-721-3337	•		•	•
		•	•	•	J B Data & Research, LLC		406-585-3323	•	•	•	
•		•	•	•	Statewide Recovery Inc [SOP]		406-761-4843	•	•	•	•
		•	•		Statewide Recovery Inc [SOP]		406-761-4843				
		•			Titleworks		406-442-4450	•	•	•	
•	•	•	•	•	Washington Court Records Svc		509-448-5012	•	•	•	•

DT	BK	CV	CR	PR	←Courts	CHOUTEAU	Recording→	UC	RE	TX	VS
		•		•	Chouteau County Abstract Co		406-622-3221	•	•	•	
		•	•		Statewide Recovery Inc [SOP]		406-761-4843				

DT	BK	CV	CR	PR	←Courts	CUSTER	Recording→	UC	RE	TX	VS
		•		•	Security Abstract & Title Co		406-234-3415	•	•	•	
					Security Title Miles City		800-728-5022		•	•	

DT	BK	CV	CR	PR	←Courts	DANIELS	Recording→	UC	RE	TX	VS
•	•	•		•	Montana Abstract Co Inc		406-487-5961		•	•	•
					Jake Nichols		406-765-1651, 406-765-1806		•	•	

DT	BK	CV	CR	PR	←Courts	DAWSON	Recording→	UC	RE	TX	VS
		•		•	First American Title Co of Montana Inc		406-365-5482	•	•	•	
•	•	•	•	•	Washington Court Records Svc		509-448-5012	•	•	•	•

DT	BK	CV	CR	PR	←COURTS DEER LODGE RECORDING→		UC	RE	TX	VS
•	•	•	•	•	Equity Process Management [SOP]	888-721-3337	•		•	•
•	•	•	•	•	Montana Abstract & Title Co	406-533-0433	•	•	•	•
		•			Titleworks	406-442-4450	•	•	•	

DT	BK	CV	CR	PR	←COURTS FALLON RECORDING→		UC	RE	TX	VS
					Fallon County Abstractor	406-778-2422		•	•	

DT	BK	CV	CR	PR	←COURTS FERGUS RECORDING→		UC	RE	TX	VS
		•	•	•	J B Data & Research, LLC	406-585-3323	•	•	•	
		•	•	•	Realty Title Co Inc	406-538-8176	•	•	•	•
•	•	•	•	•	Washington Court Records Svc	509-448-5012	•	•	•	•

DT	BK	CV	CR	PR	←COURTS FLATHEAD RECORDING→		UC	RE	TX	VS
•	•	•	•	•	Equity Process Management [SOP]	888-721-3337	•		•	•
		•	•	•	J B Data & Research, LLC	406-585-3323	•	•	•	
		•	•		Statewide Recovery Inc [SOP]	406-761-4843				
•	•	•	•	•	Washington Court Records Svc	509-448-5012	•	•	•	•

DT	BK	CV	CR	PR	←COURTS GALLATIN RECORDING→		UC	RE	TX	VS
•	•	•	•	•	AEGIS Consulting & Inv Inc	888-742-3447	•		•	•
•	•	•	•	•	Equity Process Management [SOP]	888-721-3337	•		•	•
		•	•	•	J B Data & Research, LLC	406-585-3323	•	•	•	
		•	•	•	Madrona Research Inc	360-647-8126	•	•	•	•
•	•	•	•	•	Washington Court Records Svc	509-448-5012	•	•	•	•

DT	BK	CV	CR	PR	←COURTS GARFIELD RECORDING→		UC	RE	TX	VS
					Security Title Miles City	800-728-5022		•	•	

DT	BK	CV	CR	PR	←COURTS GLACIER RECORDING→		UC	RE	TX	VS
		•	•		Statewide Recovery Inc [SOP]	406-761-4843				

DT	BK	CV	CR	PR	←COURTS GOLDEN VALLEY RECORDING→		UC	RE	TX	VS
		•		•	Sweet Grass Title Co	406-932-4888		•	•	

DT	BK	CV	CR	PR	←COURTS GRANITE RECORDING→		UC	RE	TX	VS
•	•	•	•	•	Montana Abstract & Title Co	406-533-0433	•	•	•	•

DT	BK	CV	CR	PR	←COURTS HILL RECORDING→		UC	RE	TX	VS
•	•	•	•	•	Equity Process Management [SOP]	888-721-3337	•		•	•
		•		•	Hill County Title Co	406-265-7624	•	•	•	•
		•	•		Statewide Recovery Inc [SOP]	406-761-4843				

DT	BK	CV	CR	PR	←COURTS JEFFERSON RECORDING→		UC	RE	TX	VS
•	•	•	•	•	AEGIS Consulting & Inv Inc	888-742-3447	•		•	•
		•	•		Mountain States Title Services	406-443-0521	•	•	•	
		•			Titleworks	406-442-4450	•	•	•	

DT	BK	CV	CR	PR	←COURTS JUDITH BASIN RECORDING→		UC	RE	TX	VS
		•	•	•	Realty Title Co Inc	406-538-8176	•	•	•	•

DT	BK	CV	CR	PR	←COURTS LAKE RECORDING→		UC	RE	TX	VS
•	•	•	•	•	Equity Process Management [SOP]	888-721-3337	•		•	•
		•	•	•	First American Title & Escrow (Polson)	800-331-2349	•	•	•	
		•		•	Lake County Abstract & Title Co	800-823-6225	•	•	•	•

DT	BK	CV	CR	PR	←COURTS LEWIS AND CLARK RECORDING→		UC	RE	TX	VS
•	•	•	•	•	AEGIS Consulting & Inv Inc	888-742-3447	•		•	•
•	•	•	•	•	Equity Process Management [SOP]	888-721-3337	•		•	•
•	•	•		•	Helena Abstract & Title Co	406-442-5080	•	•	•	•
		•	•	•	J B Data & Research, LLC	406-585-3323	•	•	•	
		•	•		Mountain States Title Services	406-443-0521	•	•	•	
•	•	•	•	•	MT Corporate Services	406-227-7665	•	•	•	•

DT	BK	CV	CR	PR	Retriever	Phone	UC	RE	TX	VS
•		•	•	•	Statewide Recovery Inc [SOP]	406-761-4843	•	•	•	•
		•			Titleworks	406-442-4450	•	•	•	

DT	BK	CV	CR	PR	←COURTS **LIBERTY**	RECORDING→	UC	RE	TX	VS
		•		•	Marias Title Company	406-434-5156	•	•	•	•

DT	BK	CV	CR	PR	←COURTS **LINCOLN**	RECORDING→	UC	RE	TX	VS
					First American Title & Escrow (Libby)	800-282-5630		•	•	

DT	BK	CV	CR	PR	←COURTS **MADISON**	RECORDING→	UC	RE	TX	VS
					First American Title Co	800-570-5337		•		
		•	•	•	J B Data & Research, LLC	406-585-3323	•	•	•	

DT	BK	CV	CR	PR	←COURTS **MCCONE**	RECORDING→	UC	RE	TX	VS
		•		•	First American Title Co of Montana Inc	406-365-5482	•	•	•	

DT	BK	CV	CR	PR	←COURTS **MEAGHER**	RECORDING→	UC	RE	TX	VS
		•	•	•	Potter & Co	406-547-3355	•	•	•	•

DT	BK	CV	CR	PR	←COURTS **MINERAL**	RECORDING→	UC	RE	TX	VS
					First American Title Mineral County	406-822-3391		•	•	

DT	BK	CV	CR	PR	←COURTS **MISSOULA**	RECORDING→	UC	RE	TX	VS
•	•	•	•	•	🏛AEGIS Consulting & Inv Inc	888-742-3447	•		•	•
•	•	•	•	•	Equity Process Management [SOP]	888-721-3337	•		•	•
				•	Insured Titles Inc	406-728-7900	•	•	•	
		•	•	•	J B Data & Research, LLC	406-585-3323	•	•	•	
•	•	•	•	•	USIS - Commercial Services	800-331-9175 x2433	•	•	•	•

DT	BK	CV	CR	PR	←COURTS **MUSSELSHELL**	RECORDING→	UC	RE	TX	VS
					American Title & Escrow of Musselshell County	406-323-3165	•	•	•	

DT	BK	CV	CR	PR	←COURTS **PARK**	RECORDING→	UC	RE	TX	VS
		•	•	•	J B Data & Research, LLC	406-585-3323	•	•	•	

DT	BK	CV	CR	PR	←COURTS **PETROLEUM**	RECORDING→	UC	RE	TX	VS
		•	•	•	Realty Title Co Inc	406-538-8176	•	•	•	•

DT	BK	CV	CR	PR	←COURTS **PHILLIPS**	RECORDING→	UC	RE	TX	VS
					Phillips County Abstract Co.	406-654-1413		•	•	

DT	BK	CV	CR	PR	←COURTS **PONDERA**	RECORDING→	UC	RE	TX	VS
		•	•		Statewide Recovery Inc [SOP]	406-761-4843				

DT	BK	CV	CR	PR	←COURTS **POWDER RIVER**	RECORDING→	UC	RE	TX	VS
		•	•	•	Sherry McDowell	406-436-2885				

DT	BK	CV	CR	PR	←COURTS **POWELL**	RECORDING→	UC	RE	TX	VS
•	•	•	•	•	Equity Process Management [SOP]	888-721-3337	•		•	•
		•	•		Mountain States Title Services	406-443-0521	•	•	•	
		•			Titleworks	406-442-4450	•	•	•	

DT	BK	CV	CR	PR	←COURTS **PRAIRIE**	RECORDING→	UC	RE	TX	VS
		•	•	•	Prairie Abstract & Title	406-635-5472	•	•	•	•

DT	BK	CV	CR	PR	←COURTS **RAVALLI**	RECORDING→	UC	RE	TX	VS
					🏛Bitterroot Research	406-363-4408	•	•	•	
•	•	•	•	•	Equity Process Management [SOP]	888-721-3337	•		•	•
		•	•	•	J B Data & Research, LLC	406-585-3323	•	•	•	

DT	BK	CV	CR	PR	←COURTS **RICHLAND**	RECORDING→	UC	RE	TX	VS

See adjoining counties for retrievers or contact court or recording office.

DT	BK	CV	CR	PR	←COURTS	ROOSEVELT	RECORDING→	UC	RE	TX	VS
					Jake Nichols		406-765-1651, 406-765-1806		•	•	
		•		•	Roosevelt County Abstract Co Inc		406-653-2800	•	•	•	

DT	BK	CV	CR	PR	←COURTS	ROSEBUD	RECORDING→	UC	RE	TX	VS
					First Montana Title		406-356-2011		•	•	

DT	BK	CV	CR	PR	←COURTS	SANDERS	RECORDING→	UC	RE	TX	VS
		•		•	First American Title Co (Thomspon Falls)		406-827-3591	•	•	•	
		•	•	•	J B Data & Research, LLC		406-585-3323	•	•	•	

DT	BK	CV	CR	PR	←COURTS	SHERIDAN	RECORDING→	UC	RE	TX	VS
					Jake Nichols		406-765-1651, 406-765-1806		•	•	

DT	BK	CV	CR	PR	←COURTS	SILVER BOW	RECORDING→	UC	RE	TX	VS
•	•	•	•	•	Equity Process Management [SOP]		888-721-3337	•		•	•
		•	•	•	J B Data & Research, LLC		406-585-3323	•	•	•	
•	•	•	•	•	Montana Abstract & Title Co		406-533-0433	•	•	•	•

DT	BK	CV	CR	PR	←COURTS	STILLWATER	RECORDING→	UC	RE	TX	VS
		•		•	Stillwater Abstract		406-322-5216	•	•	•	

DT	BK	CV	CR	PR	←COURTS	SWEET GRASS	RECORDING→	UC	RE	TX	VS
		•		•	Sweet Grass Title Co		406-932-4888		•	•	

DT	BK	CV	CR	PR	←COURTS	TETON	RECORDING→	UC	RE	TX	VS
		•	•		Statewide Recovery Inc [SOP]		406-761-4843				

DT	BK	CV	CR	PR	←COURTS	TOOLE	RECORDING→	UC	RE	TX	VS
		•		•	Marias Title Company		406-434-5156	•	•	•	•
		•	•		Statewide Recovery Inc [SOP]		406-761-4843				

DT	BK	CV	CR	PR	←COURTS	TREASURE	RECORDING→	UC	RE	TX	VS
					First Montana Title		406-356-2011		•	•	

DT	BK	CV	CR	PR	←COURTS	VALLEY	RECORDING→	UC	RE	TX	VS
		•	•	•	Valley County Abstract Company		406-228-2350	•	•	•	•

DT	BK	CV	CR	PR	←COURTS	WHEATLAND	RECORDING→	UC	RE	TX	VS
		•		•	Sweet Grass Title Co		406-932-4888		•	•	

DT	BK	CV	CR	PR	←COURTS	WIBAUX	RECORDING→	UC	RE	TX	VS
•	•	•	•	•	Washington Court Records Svc		509-448-5012	•	•	•	•

DT	BK	CV	CR	PR	←COURTS	YELLOWSTONE	RECORDING→	UC	RE	TX	VS
•	•	•	•	•	AEGIS Consulting & Inv Inc		888-742-3447	•		•	•
		•		•	Deister Ward & Witcher		800-443-7874	•	•	•	•
		•	•	•	J B Data & Research, LLC		406-585-3323	•	•	•	
•		•	•	•	PHB Minerals		406-248-8838	•	•	•	•

DT	BK	CV	CR	PR	←COURTS	YELLOWSTONE NATIONAL PARK (PART)	RECORDING→	UC	RE	TX	VS

See adjoining counties for retrievers or contact court or recording office. The Park is largely in Wyoming.

Nebraska

COURT RECORDS RETRIEVED							RECORDING RECORDS RETRIEVED			
DT	BK	CV	CR	PR	←COURTS	**ADAMS**	RECORDING→	UC	RE	TX	VS

DT	BK	CV	CR	PR	←Courts: ADAMS	Recording→	UC	RE	TX	VS
•				•	Adams Land Title (Hastings)	402-463-4198		•	•	
		•	•	•	Fact Finders of Nebraska	308-534-8956	•	•	•	•
•				•	St Paul Abstract & Title	308-754-4922		•	•	

DT	BK	CV	CR	PR	←Courts: ANTELOPE	Recording→	UC	RE	TX	VS
		•	•		Susan K Rosenbaum	888-459-8700			•	

DT	BK	CV	CR	PR	←Courts: ARTHUR	Recording→	UC	RE	TX	VS
•	•	•		•	Thalken Title Co	308-284-3972	•	•	•	

DT	BK	CV	CR	PR	←Courts: BANNER	Recording→	UC	RE	TX	VS
					City Abstract	308-632-4021		•	•	

DT	BK	CV	CR	PR	←Courts: BLAINE	Recording→	UC	RE	TX	VS
		•		•	Brown County Abstract Co (Nebraska)	402-387-2718	•	•	•	

DT	BK	CV	CR	PR	←Courts: BOONE	Recording→	UC	RE	TX	VS
		•	•		Susan K Rosenbaum	888-459-8700			•	

DT	BK	CV	CR	PR	←Courts: BOX BUTTE	Recording→	UC	RE	TX	VS
					See adjoining counties for retrievers or contact court or recording office.					

DT	BK	CV	CR	PR	←Courts: BOYD	Recording→	UC	RE	TX	VS
				•	McCarthy Abstract Co	402-336-2860	•	•	•	

DT	BK	CV	CR	PR	←Courts: BROWN	Recording→	UC	RE	TX	VS
		•		•	Brown County Abstract Co (Nebraska)	402-387-2718	•	•	•	
		•	•	•	Sandhills Title	402-376-2639		•	•	

DT	BK	CV	CR	PR	←Courts: BUFFALO	Recording→	UC	RE	TX	VS
•				•	Adams Land Title (Hastings)	402-463-4198				
		•		•	Barney Abstract & Title Co	308-234-5548	•	•	•	•
		•	•	•	Fact Finders of Nebraska	308-534-8956	•	•	•	•
		•	•		Susan K Rosenbaum	888-459-8700			•	
•				•	St Paul Abstract & Title	308-754-4922		•	•	

DT	BK	CV	CR	PR	←Courts: BURT	Recording→	UC	RE	TX	VS
		•	•	•	Anderson Abstract Co	402-374-1476	•	•	•	

DT	BK	CV	CR	PR	←Courts: BUTLER	Recording→	UC	RE	TX	VS
		•		•	Colfax County Title & Abstract Co	402-352-2027	•	•	•	
		•	•		Susan K Rosenbaum	888-459-8700			•	

DT	BK	CV	CR	PR	←Courts: CASS	Recording→	UC	RE	TX	VS
		•	•	•	Otoe County Title Co	402-873-5501	•	•	•	
•	•	•	•	•	Street Legal Research	402-476-9505				
•	•	•	•		Thomas Research Services (Donna Thomas) [SOP]	402-339-7291	•		•	

DT	BK	CV	CR	PR	←Courts: CEDAR	Recording→	UC	RE	TX	VS
•				•	Merkel Abstract & Title	402-254-3547		•		

DT	BK	CV	CR	PR	←Courts: CHASE	Recording→	UC	RE	TX	VS
		•	•	•	Patsy Maranville	785-426-2725				

DT	BK	CV	CR	PR	Name	Phone	UC	RE	TX	VS
		•	•	•	Southwestern Title & Abstract Co	308-423-2611	•	•	•	•
•	•	•		•	Thalken Title Co	308-284-3972	•	•	•	

DT	BK	CV	CR	PR	←COURTS CHERRY	RECORDING→	UC	RE	TX	VS
		•	•	•	Sandhills Abstracting	308-282-0715	•	•	•	•
		•	•	•	Sandhills Title	402-376-2639		•	•	
•	•	•		•	Thalken Title Co	308-284-3972	•	•	•	

DT	BK	CV	CR	PR	←COURTS CHEYENNE	RECORDING→	UC	RE	TX	VS
•	•	•		•	Cheyenne County Abstract	308-254-5636	•	•	•	
		•		•	Deuel County Abstract Co (Nebraska) [SOP]	308-874-2212		•	•	
		•	•	•	Fact Finders of Nebraska	308-534-8956	•	•	•	•

DT	BK	CV	CR	PR	←COURTS CLAY	RECORDING→	UC	RE	TX	VS
					Abstract & Title Inc	402-729-2771	•	•	•	
•				•	Adams Land Title (Hastings)	402-463-4198		•	•	

DT	BK	CV	CR	PR	←COURTS COLFAX	RECORDING→	UC	RE	TX	VS
		•		•	Colfax County Title & Abstract Co	402-352-2027	•	•	•	
		•	•		Susan K Rosenbaum	888-459-8700			•	

DT	BK	CV	CR	PR	←COURTS CUMING	RECORDING→	UC	RE	TX	VS
		•	•	•	Northeast Nebraska Court Research	402-439-2469		•	•	•

DT	BK	CV	CR	PR	←COURTS CUSTER	RECORDING→	UC	RE	TX	VS
		•	•		Western Nebraska Inv [SOP]	308-534-9003				

DT	BK	CV	CR	PR	←COURTS DAKOTA	RECORDING→	UC	RE	TX	VS
•	•	•	•	•	Intra-Lex Investigations Inc [SOP]	712-233-1639	•	•	•	•

DT	BK	CV	CR	PR	←COURTS DAWES	RECORDING→	UC	RE	TX	VS
				•	Dawes County Abstract Co	308-432-4840	•	•	•	

DT	BK	CV	CR	PR	←COURTS DAWSON	RECORDING→	UC	RE	TX	VS
		•	•	•	Fact Finders of Nebraska	308-534-8956	•	•	•	•
		•	•		Western Nebraska Inv [SOP]	308-534-9003				

DT	BK	CV	CR	PR	←COURTS DEUEL	RECORDING→	UC	RE	TX	VS
		•		•	Deuel County Abstract Co (Nebraska) [SOP]	308-874-2212		•	•	
•	•	•		•	Thalken Title Co	308-284-3972	•	•	•	

DT	BK	CV	CR	PR	←COURTS DIXON	RECORDING→	UC	RE	TX	VS
•	•	•	•	•	Intra-Lex Investigations Inc [SOP]	712-233-1639	•	•	•	•

DT	BK	CV	CR	PR	←COURTS DODGE	RECORDING→	UC	RE	TX	VS
•	•	•	•	•	Coit Enterprises	402-451-0462		•	•	
		•	•	•	Northeast Nebraska Court Research	402-439-2469		•	•	•
		•	•	•	Jean Peck [SOP]	402-721-4143	•	•	•	•
		•	•		Susan K Rosenbaum	888-459-8700			•	

DT	BK	CV	CR	PR	←COURTS DOUGLAS	RECORDING→	UC	RE	TX	VS
•	•	•	•	•	Coit Enterprises	402-451-0462		•	•	
•	•	•	•	•	Intra-Lex Investigations Inc [SOP]	712-233-1639	•	•	•	•
•	•	•	•	•	Legal Eagle Inc / Eagle Search & Service [SOP]	402-342-4427	•	•	•	•
			•		Resource Management Specialists	877-476-3337				
•	•	•	•	•	Street Legal Research	402-476-9505				
•	•	•	•		Thomas Research Services (Donna Thomas) [SOP]	402-339-7291	•		•	

DT	BK	CV	CR	PR	←COURTS DUNDY	RECORDING→	UC	RE	TX	VS
		•	•	•	Patsy Maranville	785-426-2725				
		•	•	•	Southwestern Title & Abstract Co	308-423-2611	•	•	•	•

DT	BK	CV	CR	PR	←COURTS FILLMORE	RECORDING→	UC	RE	TX	VS
					Abstract & Title Inc	402-729-2771	•	•	•	

DT	BK	CV	CR	PR	←COURTS FRANKLIN	RECORDING→	UC	RE	TX	VS

See adjoining counties for retrievers or contact court or recording office.

DT	BK	CV	CR	PR	←COURTS FRONTIER	RECORDING→	UC	RE	TX	VS
		•	•	•	Scott Abstract	308-532-8535	•	•	•	•

DT	BK	CV	CR	PR	←COURTS FURNAS	RECORDING→	UC	RE	TX	VS
					Furnas Valley Title	308-824-3304		•	•	

DT	BK	CV	CR	PR	←COURTS GAGE	RECORDING→	UC	RE	TX	VS
					Abstract & Title Inc	402-729-2771	•	•	•	
•		•		•	Nebraska Title Company	402-228-2233	•	•	•	

DT	BK	CV	CR	PR	←COURTS GARDEN	RECORDING→	UC	RE	TX	VS
		•		•	Deuel County Abstract Co (Nebraska) [SOP]	308-874-2212		•	•	
•	•	•		•	Thalken Title Co	308-284-3972	•	•	•	

DT	BK	CV	CR	PR	←COURTS GARFIELD	RECORDING→	UC	RE	TX	VS

See adjoining counties for retrievers or contact court or recording office.

DT	BK	CV	CR	PR	←COURTS GOSPER	RECORDING→	UC	RE	TX	VS
		•	•	•	Todd Wilson PC	308-785-2550		•	•	

DT	BK	CV	CR	PR	←COURTS GRANT	RECORDING→	UC	RE	TX	VS
•	•	•		•	Thalken Title Co	308-284-3972	•	•	•	

DT	BK	CV	CR	PR	←COURTS GREELEY	RECORDING→	UC	RE	TX	VS
		•		•	Janke Abstract Co	308-754-4251	•	•	•	

DT	BK	CV	CR	PR	←COURTS HALL	RECORDING→	UC	RE	TX	VS
•				•	Adams Land Title (Hastings)	402-463-4198		•	•	
		•	•	•	Fact Finders of Nebraska	308-534-8956	•	•	•	•
		•		•	Janke Abstract Co	308-754-4251	•	•	•	
		•	•		Susan K Rosenbaum	888-459-8700			•	
•				•	St Paul Abstract & Title	308-754-4922		•	•	

DT	BK	CV	CR	PR	←COURTS HAMILTON	RECORDING→	UC	RE	TX	VS
		•	•	•	First Securities Corp in Aurora	402-694-6926	•	•	•	•
		•	•		Susan K Rosenbaum	888-459-8700			•	

DT	BK	CV	CR	PR	←COURTS HARLAN	RECORDING→	UC	RE	TX	VS
					Harlan County Abstract	308-928-2343		•	•	

DT	BK	CV	CR	PR	←COURTS HAYES	RECORDING→	UC	RE	TX	VS
		•	•	•	Scott Abstract	308-532-8535	•	•	•	•

DT	BK	CV	CR	PR	←COURTS HITCHCOCK	RECORDING→	UC	RE	TX	VS
		•	•	•	Patsy Maranville	785-426-2725				
		•	•	•	Southwestern Title & Abstract Co	308-423-2611	•	•	•	•

DT	BK	CV	CR	PR	←COURTS HOLT	RECORDING→	UC	RE	TX	VS
				•	McCarthy Abstract Co	402-336-2860	•	•	•	

DT	BK	CV	CR	PR	←COURTS HOOKER	RECORDING→	UC	RE	TX	VS
		•	•	•	Scott Abstract	308-532-8535	•	•	•	•

DT	BK	CV	CR	PR	←COURTS HOWARD	RECORDING→	UC	RE	TX	VS
		•		•	Janke Abstract Co	308-754-4251	•	•	•	
		•	•		Susan K Rosenbaum	888-459-8700			•	
•				•	St Paul Abstract & Title	308-754-4922		•	•	

DT	BK	CV	CR	PR	←Courts JEFFERSON	Recording→	UC	RE	TX	VS
					Abstract & Title Inc	402-729-2771	•	•	•	

DT	BK	CV	CR	PR	←Courts JOHNSON	Recording→	UC	RE	TX	VS
					Morrissey Morrissey & Dalluge	402-335-3344		•		

DT	BK	CV	CR	PR	←Courts KEARNEY	Recording→	UC	RE	TX	VS
•				•	Adams Land Title (Hastings)	402-463-4198		•	•	
		•	•	•	Fact Finders of Nebraska	308-534-8956	•	•	•	•
				•	Miller Abstract & Title Co	308-832-0969	•	•	•	

DT	BK	CV	CR	PR	←Courts KEITH	Recording→	UC	RE	TX	VS
		•		•	Deuel County Abstract Co (Nebraska) [SOP]	308-874-2212		•	•	
		•	•	•	Southwestern Title & Abstract Co	308-423-2611	•	•	•	•
•	•	•		•	Thalken Title Co	308-284-3972	•	•	•	
		•	•		Western Nebraska Inv [SOP]	308-534-9003				

DT	BK	CV	CR	PR	←Courts KEYA PAHA	Recording→	UC	RE	TX	VS
		•		•	Brown County Abstract Co (Nebraska)	402-387-2718	•	•	•	
		•	•	•	Sandhills Title	402-376-2639		•	•	

DT	BK	CV	CR	PR	←Courts KIMBALL	Recording→	UC	RE	TX	VS
		•		•	Deuel County Abstract Co (Nebraska) [SOP]	308-874-2212		•	•	

DT	BK	CV	CR	PR	←Courts KNOX	Recording→	UC	RE	TX	VS
		•		•	Northeast Nebraska Title & Escrow	402-371-1221	•	•	•	•
		•	•		Susan K Rosenbaum	888-459-8700			•	
		•	•	•	Valverde Abstract Co Inc	402-288-4466		•	•	

DT	BK	CV	CR	PR	←Courts LANCASTER	Recording→	UC	RE	TX	VS
•	•	•			Records Research Inc (Neb.) [SOP]	402-476-3869, 402-323-3828 (direct line)	•	•	•	
		•	•		Susan K Rosenbaum	888-459-8700			•	
•		•	•		Searches by SKW	402-786-2184			•	
•	•	•	•	•	Street Legal Research	402-476-9505				

DT	BK	CV	CR	PR	←Courts LINCOLN	Recording→	UC	RE	TX	VS
		•	•	•	Fact Finders of Nebraska	308-534-8956	•	•	•	•
		•	•	•	Scott Abstract	308-532-8535	•	•	•	•
		•	•		Western Nebraska Inv [SOP]	308-534-9003				

DT	BK	CV	CR	PR	←Courts LOGAN	Recording→	UC	RE	TX	VS
		•	•	•	Scott Abstract	308-532-8535	•	•	•	•

DT	BK	CV	CR	PR	←Courts LOUP	Recording→	UC	RE	TX	VS
					See adjoining counties for retrievers or contact court or recording office.					

DT	BK	CV	CR	PR	←Courts MADISON	Recording→	UC	RE	TX	VS
		•	•	•	Northeast Nebraska Court Research	402-439-2469		•	•	•
		•		•	Northeast Nebraska Title & Escrow	402-371-1221		•	•	•
		•	•		Susan K Rosenbaum	888-459-8700			•	
		•	•	•	Stanton Co Abstract	402-439-2142	•	•	•	•

DT	BK	CV	CR	PR	←Courts MCPHERSON	Recording→	UC	RE	TX	VS
		•	•	•	Scott Abstract	308-532-8535	•	•	•	•

DT	BK	CV	CR	PR	←Courts MERRICK	Recording→	UC	RE	TX	VS
		•		•	Janke Abstract Co	308-754-4251	•	•	•	
		•	•		Susan K Rosenbaum	888-459-8700			•	

DT	BK	CV	CR	PR	←Courts MORRILL	Recording→	UC	RE	TX	VS
		•		•	Deuel County Abstract Co (Nebraska) [SOP]	308-874-2212		•	•	

DT	BK	CV	CR	PR	←Courts NANCE	Recording→	UC	RE	TX	VS
		•		•	Janke Abstract Co	308-754-4251	•	•	•	
		•	•		Susan K Rosenbaum	888-459-8700			•	

DT	BK	CV	CR	PR	←Courts NEMAHA	Recording→	UC	RE	TX	VS
				•	Auburn Abstract & Title Company LLC	402-274-4321	•	•	•	
		•	•	•	Otoe County Title Co	402-873-5501	•	•	•	

DT	BK	CV	CR	PR	←Courts NUCKOLLS	Recording→	UC	RE	TX	VS
•				•	Adams Land Title (Hastings)	402-463-4198		•	•	

DT	BK	CV	CR	PR	←Courts OTOE	Recording→	UC	RE	TX	VS
		•	•	•	Otoe County Title Co	402-873-5501	•	•	•	
•	•	•	•		Thomas Research Services (Donna Thomas) [SOP]	402-339-7291	•		•	

DT	BK	CV	CR	PR	←Courts PAWNEE	Recording→	UC	RE	TX	VS
		•	•	•	Pawnee County Abstract Co	402-852-2035	•	•	•	
		•	•	•	Stehlik Law Office	402-852-2973	•	•	•	

DT	BK	CV	CR	PR	←Courts PERKINS	Recording→	UC	RE	TX	VS
•	•	•		•	Thalken Title Co	308-284-3972	•	•	•	
		•	•		Western Nebraska Inv [SOP]	308-534-9003				

DT	BK	CV	CR	PR	←Courts PHELPS	Recording→	UC	RE	TX	VS
				•	Dealey Abstract & Title Company	308-995-4622	•	•	•	
		•	•	•	Fact Finders of Nebraska	308-534-8956	•	•	•	•

DT	BK	CV	CR	PR	←Courts PIERCE	Recording→	UC	RE	TX	VS
				•	Chilvers Abstract & Title Co	402-329-4525	•	•	•	
		•	•	•	Northeast Nebraska Court Research	402-439-2469		•	•	•
		•		•	Northeast Nebraska Title & Escrow	402-371-1221	•	•	•	•
		•	•		Susan K Rosenbaum	888-459-8700			•	
		•	•	•	Stanton Co Abstract	402-439-2142	•	•	•	•

DT	BK	CV	CR	PR	←Courts PLATTE	Recording→	UC	RE	TX	VS
		•	•	•	Platte County Title & Escrow Co	402-563-4519	•	•	•	•
		•	•		Susan K Rosenbaum	888-459-8700			•	
•				•	Tri County Title & Escrow Co	402-747-2141	•	•	•	

DT	BK	CV	CR	PR	←Courts POLK	Recording→	UC	RE	TX	VS
		•	•		Susan K Rosenbaum	888-459-8700			•	
•				•	Tri County Title & Escrow Co	402-747-2141	•	•	•	

DT	BK	CV	CR	PR	←Courts RED WILLOW	Recording→	UC	RE	TX	VS
		•	•	•	Fact Finders of Nebraska	308-534-8956	•	•	•	•
		•	•	•	Southwestern Title & Abstract Co	308-423-2611	•	•	•	•

DT	BK	CV	CR	PR	←Courts RICHARDSON	Recording→	UC	RE	TX	VS
		•	•	•	Southeast Nebraska Abstract	402-245-4222	•	•	•	

DT	BK	CV	CR	PR	←Courts ROCK	Recording→	UC	RE	TX	VS
		•		•	Brown County Abstract Co (Nebraska)	402-387-2718	•	•	•	

DT	BK	CV	CR	PR	←Courts SALINE	Recording→	UC	RE	TX	VS
					Abstract & Title Inc	402-729-2771	•	•	•	

DT	BK	CV	CR	PR	←Courts SARPY	Recording→	UC	RE	TX	VS
•	•	•	•	•	Coit Enterprises	402-451-0462		•	•	
•	•	•	•	•	Intra-Lex Investigations Inc [SOP]	712-233-1639	•	•	•	•
•	•	•	•	•	Legal Eagle Inc / Eagle Search & Service [SOP]	402-342-4427	•	•	•	•
			•		Resource Management Specialists	877-476-3337				
•	•	•	•		Thomas Research Services (Donna Thomas) [SOP]	402-339-7291	•		•	

DT	BK	CV	CR	PR	←COURTS SAUNDERS RECORDING→	UC	RE	TX	VS
				•	Hamilton & Johnson Abstract Inc 402-443-3081	•	•	•	
		•	•	•	Northeast Nebraska Court Research....402-439-2469		•	•	•
		•	•	•	Jean Peck [SOP]....402-721-4143	•	•	•	•
		•	•		Susan K Rosenbaum 888-459-8700			•	

DT	BK	CV	CR	PR	←COURTS SCOTTS BLUFF RECORDING→	UC	RE	TX	VS
					City Abstract 308-632-4021		•	•	
		•		•	Deuel County Abstract Co (Nebraska) [SOP]....308-874-2212		•	•	

DT	BK	CV	CR	PR	←COURTS SEWARD RECORDING→	UC	RE	TX	VS
					Abstract & Title Inc 402-729-2771	•	•	•	
		•	•		Susan K Rosenbaum 888-459-8700			•	

DT	BK	CV	CR	PR	←COURTS SHERIDAN RECORDING→	UC	RE	TX	VS
				•	Dawes County Abstract Co....308-432-4840	•	•	•	
		•	•	•	Sandhills Abstracting....308-282-0715	•	•	•	•
•	•	•		•	Thalken Title Co 308-284-3972	•	•	•	

DT	BK	CV	CR	PR	←COURTS SHERMAN RECORDING→	UC	RE	TX	VS
		•		•	Janke Abstract Co 308-754-4251	•	•	•	

DT	BK	CV	CR	PR	←COURTS SIOUX RECORDING→	UC	RE	TX	VS
				•	Dawes County Abstract Co....308-432-4840	•	•	•	

DT	BK	CV	CR	PR	←COURTS STANTON RECORDING→	UC	RE	TX	VS
		•	•	•	Northeast Nebraska Court Research....402-439-2469		•	•	•
		•	•	•	Stanton Co Abstract 402-439-2142	•	•	•	•

DT	BK	CV	CR	PR	←COURTS THAYER RECORDING→	UC	RE	TX	VS
					Abstract & Title Inc 402-729-2771	•	•	•	

DT	BK	CV	CR	PR	←COURTS THOMAS RECORDING→	UC	RE	TX	VS
		•	•	•	Sandhills Title....402-376-2639		•	•	
		•	•	•	Scott Abstract....308-532-8535	•	•	•	•

DT	BK	CV	CR	PR	←COURTS THURSTON RECORDING→	UC	RE	TX	VS
•	•	•	•	•	Intra-Lex Investigations Inc [SOP] 712-233-1639	•	•	•	•

DT	BK	CV	CR	PR	←COURTS VALLEY RECORDING→	UC	RE	TX	VS
					Springdale Realty....308-728-3569		•	•	

DT	BK	CV	CR	PR	←COURTS WASHINGTON RECORDING→	UC	RE	TX	VS
•	•	•	•	•	Coit Enterprises....402-451-0462		•	•	
		•	•	•	Jean Peck [SOP]....402-721-4143	•	•	•	•
•	•	•	•		Thomas Research Services (Donna Thomas) [SOP] 402-339-7291	•		•	

DT	BK	CV	CR	PR	←COURTS WAYNE RECORDING→	UC	RE	TX	VS
		•	•		Heartland Recovery....866-375-1730				
		•	•	•	Northeast Nebraska Court Research....402-439-2469		•	•	•

DT	BK	CV	CR	PR	←COURTS WEBSTER RECORDING→	UC	RE	TX	VS
•				•	Adams Land Title (Hastings) 402-463-4198		•	•	

DT	BK	CV	CR	PR	←COURTS WHEELER RECORDING→	UC	RE	TX	VS
				•	McCarthy Abstract Co 402-336-2860	•	•	•	

DT	BK	CV	CR	PR	←COURTS YORK RECORDING→	UC	RE	TX	VS
		•	•		Susan K Rosenbaum 888-459-8700			•	
		•	•	•	York County Title Co 402-362-4405	•	•	•	

Nevada

COURT RECORDS RETRIEVED **RECORDING RECORDS RETRIEVED**

DT	BK	CV	CR	PR	←COURTS CARSON CITY	RECORDING→	UC	RE	TX	VS
•	•	•	•	•	Avalon/Tracy Bowers	775-853-3003	•	•	•	•
					Capitol Corporate Services Inc (Nevada)	800-899-0490	•		•	
•	•	•	•	•	Corporation Service Company - CSC	800-927-9800	•	•	•	•
•	•	•	•	•	High Sierra Courier Service [SOP]	877-812-8444	•		•	•
		•			Parasec (Nevada)	888-972-7273	•		•	•
•	•	•	•	•	Reno/Carson Messenger Service Inc [SOP]	800-222-4249	•	•	•	•
•	•	•	•	•	Top Flight Solutions	775-887-6645	•	•	•	•
•	•	•	•	•	Unisearch Inc (Nevada)	800-260-1131	•		•	•

DT	BK	CV	CR	PR	←COURTS CHURCHILL	RECORDING→	UC	RE	TX	VS
•	•	•	•	•	Avalon/Tracy Bowers	775-853-3003	•	•	•	•
					Nevada Land Services	800-233-4999	•	•	•	
		•			Parasec (Nevada)	888-972-7273	•		•	•
•	•	•	•	•	Reno/Carson Messenger Service Inc [SOP]	800-222-4249	•	•	•	•
•	•	•	•	•	Top Flight Solutions	775-887-6645	•	•	•	•

DT	BK	CV	CR	PR	←COURTS CLARK	RECORDING→	UC	RE	TX	VS
•	•	•	•		Accurate Background Inc	800-784-3911	•		•	
•	•	•	•	•	Arizona Research & Retrieval Services Inc	888-500-7767	•	•	•	•
•	•	•	•	•	Bodo PI [SOP]	877-381-7009	•	•	•	•
•	•	•	•	•	Deines Inc	702-453-9859	•	•	•	
					Document Recording & Retrieval Services	702-558-6207	•	•	•	•
•	•	•		•	EAGLE i Communications	702-658-3912	•	•	•	
					Global Title Reporting Services Inc	702-248-0593	•	•	•	
•	•	•	•	•	Infotrackers Inc	702-948-7055	•	•	•	
•	•	•	•	•	Integrity Records Access	702-296-9145	•	•	•	•
					National Search Solutions LLC	702-431-9100	•	•	•	•
		•			Parasec (Nevada)	888-972-7273	•		•	•
•	•	•	•	•	Pete Costanzo Private Inv	702-459-1640	•	•	•	
		•	•		Public Records Info Service	520-321-8015				

DT	BK	CV	CR	PR	←COURTS DOUGLAS	RECORDING→	UC	RE	TX	VS
•	•	•	•	•	Avalon/Tracy Bowers	775-853-3003	•	•	•	•
•	•	•	•	•	High Sierra Courier Service [SOP]	877-812-8444	•		•	•
		•			Parasec (Nevada)	888-972-7273	•		•	•
•	•	•	•	•	Reno/Carson Messenger Service Inc [SOP]	800-222-4249	•	•	•	•
•	•	•	•	•	Top Flight Solutions	775-887-6645	•	•	•	•
•	•	•	•	•	Unisearch Inc (Nevada)	800-260-1131	•		•	•

DT	BK	CV	CR	PR	←COURTS ELKO	RECORDING→	UC	RE	TX	VS
		•			Parasec (Nevada)	888-972-7273	•		•	•

DT	BK	CV	CR	PR	←COURTS ESMERALDA	RECORDING→	UC	RE	TX	VS
					Nevada Land Services	800-233-4999	•	•	•	
		•			Parasec (Nevada)	888-972-7273	•		•	•

DT	BK	CV	CR	PR	←COURTS EUREKA	RECORDING→	UC	RE	TX	VS
					Nevada Land Services	800-233-4999	•	•	•	
		•			Parasec (Nevada)	888-972-7273	•		•	•

DT	BK	CV	CR	PR	←Courts	Humboldt	Recording→	UC	RE	TX	VS
•	•	•	•	•		Avalon/Tracy Bowers	775-853-3003	•	•	•	•
						Nevada Land Services	800-233-4999	•	•	•	
		•				Parasec (Nevada)	888-972-7273	•		•	•

DT	BK	CV	CR	PR	←Courts	Lander	Recording→	UC	RE	TX	VS
						Nevada Land Services	800-233-4999	•	•	•	
		•				Parasec (Nevada)	888-972-7273	•		•	•

DT	BK	CV	CR	PR	←Courts	Lincoln	Recording→	UC	RE	TX	VS
						Nevada Land Services	800-233-4999	•	•	•	
		•				Parasec (Nevada)	888-972-7273	•		•	•

DT	BK	CV	CR	PR	←Courts	Lyon	Recording→	UC	RE	TX	VS
•	•	•	•	•		Avalon/Tracy Bowers	775-853-3003	•	•	•	•
		•				Parasec (Nevada)	888-972-7273	•		•	•
•	•	•	•	•		Reno/Carson Messenger Service Inc [SOP]	800-222-4249	•	•	•	•

DT	BK	CV	CR	PR	←Courts	Mineral	Recording→	UC	RE	TX	VS
						Nevada Land Services	800-233-4999	•	•	•	
		•				Parasec (Nevada)	888-972-7273	•		•	•

DT	BK	CV	CR	PR	←Courts	Nye	Recording→	UC	RE	TX	VS
						Nevada Land Services	800-233-4999	•	•	•	
		•				Parasec (Nevada)	888-972-7273	•		•	•

DT	BK	CV	CR	PR	←Courts	Pershing	Recording→	UC	RE	TX	VS
•	•	•	•	•		Avalon/Tracy Bowers	775-853-3003	•	•	•	•
						Nevada Land Services	800-233-4999	•	•	•	
		•				Parasec (Nevada)	888-972-7273	•		•	•

DT	BK	CV	CR	PR	←Courts	Storey	Recording→	UC	RE	TX	VS
•	•	•	•	•		Avalon/Tracy Bowers	775-853-3003	•	•	•	•
		•				Parasec (Nevada)	888-972-7273	•		•	•
•	•	•	•	•		Reno/Carson Messenger Service Inc [SOP]	800-222-4249	•	•	•	•
•	•	•	•	•		Top Flight Solutions	775-887-6645	•	•	•	•

DT	BK	CV	CR	PR	←Courts	Washoe	Recording→	UC	RE	TX	VS
•	•	•	•	•		Avalon/Tracy Bowers	775-853-3003	•	•	•	•
•	•					Coyote	775-972-6530	•	•	•	
						Document Recording & Retrieval Services	702-558-6207	•	•	•	•
•	•	•	•	•		High Sierra Courier Service [SOP]	877-812-8444	•		•	•
		•	•			M L Cozart Copy Service (dba: Quality Business Information)	916-691-9685				
		•				Parasec (Nevada)	888-972-7273	•		•	•
•	•	•	•			Quality Business Information	916-684-0444		•	•	•
•	•	•	•	•		Reno/Carson Messenger Service Inc [SOP]	800-222-4249	•	•	•	•
•	•	•	•	•		Top Flight Solutions	775-887-6645	•	•	•	•
•	•	•	•	•		Unisearch Inc (Nevada)	800-260-1131	•		•	•

DT	BK	CV	CR	PR	←Courts	White Pine	Recording→	UC	RE	TX	VS
		•				Parasec (Nevada)	888-972-7273	•		•	•

Editor's Tip: At the back of this directory is a short list of search firms who are Public Record Retriever Network "Associate Members." These Associate Members utilize retrievers to obtain documents outside their local area of coverage. The Associate Members are statewide, regional, or national in scope, and are not listed in the county sections.

New Hampshire

COURT RECORDS RETRIEVED — **RECORDING RECORDS RETRIEVED**

DT	BK	CV	CR	PR	←COURTS **BELKNAP** RECORDING→		UC	RE	TX	VS
•	•	•	•	•	Coast to Coast Research Network	603-783-8034	•	•	•	•
•	•	•	•	•	Concord Search & Retrieval Inc	877-273-1119	•	•	•	•
•	•	•	•	•	Doc*U*Search Inc	800-332-3034	•	•	•	•
					Horizons Unlimited	617-696-6397		•	•	
		•	•		MSI Inv [SOP]	603-298-8060				
		•	•		Primetime Research Inc	866-737-2714				
•	•	•	•		The Research Connection Inc of NH [SOP]	800-540-5064	•	•	•	•

DT	BK	CV	CR	PR	←COURTS **CARROLL** RECORDING→		UC	RE	TX	VS
•	•	•	•	•	Coast to Coast Research Network	603-783-8034	•	•	•	•
•	•	•	•	•	Doc*U*Search Inc	800-332-3034	•	•	•	•
					Horizons Unlimited	617-696-6397		•	•	
•	•	•	•	•	NR&C	207-791-2852	•	•	•	
•	•	•	•		The Research Connection Inc of NH [SOP]	800-540-5064	•	•	•	•

DT	BK	CV	CR	PR	←COURTS **CHESHIRE** RECORDING→		UC	RE	TX	VS
•	•	•	•	•	Coast to Coast Research Network	603-783-8034	•	•	•	•
•	•	•	•	•	Doc*U*Search Inc	800-332-3034	•	•	•	•
					Horizons Unlimited	617-696-6397		•	•	
		•	•		MSI Inv [SOP]	603-298-8060				
•	•	•	•	•	NR&C	207-791-2852	•	•	•	
		•	•		Primetime Research Inc	866-737-2714				
•	•	•	•		The Research Connection Inc of NH [SOP]	800-540-5064	•	•	•	•

DT	BK	CV	CR	PR	←COURTS **COOS** RECORDING→		UC	RE	TX	VS
•	•	•	•	•	Coast to Coast Research Network	603-783-8034	•	•	•	•
•	•	•	•	•	Doc*U*Search Inc	800-332-3034	•	•	•	•
					Horizons Unlimited	617-696-6397		•	•	
•	•	•	•		The Research Connection Inc of NH [SOP]	800-540-5064	•	•	•	•

DT	BK	CV	CR	PR	←COURTS **GRAFTON** RECORDING→		UC	RE	TX	VS
•	•	•	•	•	Coast to Coast Research Network	603-783-8034	•	•	•	•
•	•	•	•	•	Doc*U*Search Inc	800-332-3034	•	•	•	•
					Horizons Unlimited	617-696-6397		•	•	
		•	•		MSI Inv [SOP]	603-298-8060				
•	•	•	•		The Research Connection Inc of NH [SOP]	800-540-5064	•	•	•	•

DT	BK	CV	CR	PR	←COURTS **HILLSBOROUGH** RECORDING→		UC	RE	TX	VS
•	•	•	•	•	Coast to Coast Research Network	603-783-8034	•	•	•	•
•	•	•	•	•	Concord Search & Retrieval Inc	877-273-1119	•	•	•	•
•	•	•	•	•	Doc*U*Search Inc	800-332-3034	•	•	•	•
					Horizons Unlimited	617-696-6397		•	•	
•	•	•	•	•	NH Background Investigations LLC	603-598-4106	•	•	•	•
•	•	•	•	•	NR&C	207-791-2852	•	•	•	
		•	•		Primetime Research Inc	866-737-2714				
•	•	•	•		The Research Connection Inc of NH [SOP]	800-540-5064	•	•	•	•
	•	•	•	•	S & S Public Record Retrievers	603-672-7179	•	•	•	•

DT	BK	CV	CR	PR	←Courts	Merrimack	Recording→	UC	RE	TX	VS
•	•	•	•	•		Coast to Coast Research Network	603-783-8034	•	•	•	•
•	•	•	•	•		Concord Search & Retrieval Inc	877-273-1119	•	•	•	•
•	•	•	•	•		Doc*U*Search Inc	800-332-3034	•	•	•	•
						Horizons Unlimited	617-696-6397		•	•	
•	•	•	•	•		NH Background Investigations LLC	603-598-4106	•	•	•	•
•	•	•	•	•		NR&C	207-791-2852	•	•	•	
		•	•			Primetime Research Inc	866-737-2714				
•	•	•	•			The Research Connection Inc of NH [SOP]	800-540-5064	•	•	•	•
	•	•	•	•		S & S Public Record Retrievers	603-672-7179	•	•	•	•

DT	BK	CV	CR	PR	←Courts	Rockingham	Recording→	UC	RE	TX	VS
•	•	•	•	•		Coast to Coast Research Network	603-783-8034	•	•	•	•
•	•	•	•	•		Concord Search & Retrieval Inc	877-273-1119	•	•	•	•
•	•	•	•	•		Doc*U*Search Inc	800-332-3034	•	•	•	•
						Horizons Unlimited	617-696-6397		•	•	
•	•	•	•	•		NR&C	207-791-2852	•	•	•	
		•	•			Primetime Research Inc	866-737-2714				
				•		Reliable Title Co of NH	603-798-5230	•	•	•	
•	•	•	•			The Research Connection Inc of NH [SOP]	800-540-5064	•	•	•	•

DT	BK	CV	CR	PR	←Courts	Strafford	Recording→	UC	RE	TX	VS
•	•	•	•	•		Coast to Coast Research Network	603-783-8034	•	•	•	•
•	•	•	•	•		Doc*U*Search Inc	800-332-3034	•	•	•	•
						Horizons Unlimited	617-696-6397		•	•	
•		•	•	•		Maine Public Record Services	207-646-9065	•	•	•	
		•	•			Primetime Research Inc	866-737-2714				
•	•	•	•			The Research Connection Inc of NH [SOP]	800-540-5064	•	•	•	•

DT	BK	CV	CR	PR	←Courts	Sullivan	Recording→	UC	RE	TX	VS
•	•	•	•	•		Coast to Coast Research Network	603-783-8034	•	•	•	•
•	•	•	•	•		Doc*U*Search Inc	800-332-3034	•	•	•	•
						Horizons Unlimited	617-696-6397		•	•	
		•	•			MSI Inv [SOP]	603-298-8060				
•	•	•	•			The Research Connection Inc of NH [SOP]	800-540-5064	•	•	•	•

Editor's Tip: Only Call a Retriever For the Records They Retrieve. If you call for a criminal record from a retriever who only does work at the recorder's office, then you are wasting your time and the retriever's time.

New Jersey

COURT RECORDS RETRIEVED — **RECORDING RECORDS RETRIEVED**

DT	BK	CV	CR	PR	←COURTS ATLANTIC RECORDING→		UC	RE	TX	VS
●	●	●		●	Charles Jones Inc	800-792-8888	●	●	●	
●	●	●	●		County House Research Inc	866-594-1177			●	
			●		Detailed Investigations	609-338-3088				
●	●	●	●		Employmentscreening.com	215-234-0700	●	●	●	●
●	●	●	●	●	Fidelifacts	800-678-0007	●	●	●	●
●	●	●	●		Flink Findzum Lawyers Service [SOP]	800-380-5434	●	●	●	●
					Peg Fuoti	609-625-9401	●	●	●	
●	●	●	●	●	Inquisitive Research Corporation	732-321-0041	●	●	●	●
		●		●	Liberty Record Search of NJ Inc	973-887-8808	●	●	●	
●	●	●	●		National Background Inv Inc	800-798-0079			●	
●	●	●	●	●	Searcher Girls	800-292-2757	●	●	●	●
●	●	●			Superior Information Services, LLC	800-848-0489	●		●	
●	●	●	●	●	US Document Retrieval Service Inc	800-595-0145		●	●	●
●	●	●	●	●	Washington Document Services (NY)	800-422-2776	●		●	

DT	BK	CV	CR	PR	←COURTS BERGEN RECORDING→		UC	RE	TX	VS
●	●	●	●	●	Callahan Lawyers Service [SOP]	877-767-2245				●
●	●	●		●	Charles Jones Inc	800-792-8888	●	●	●	
●	●	●	●		County House Research Inc	866-594-1177			●	
●	●	●	●		Court Data Search	973-770-1170				
●	●				Credit Lenders Service Agency Inc	856-787-9005	●	●	●	
			●		Detailed Investigations	609-338-3088				
●	●	●	●	●	DLS (Demovsky Lawyer Service - New York) [SOP]	800-443-1058	●	●	●	●
				●	Dolores Dios Title Abstractor	201-207-0628	●	●	●	
●	●	●	●		Employmentscreening.com	215-234-0700	●	●	●	●
●	●	●	●	●	Fidelifacts	800-678-0007	●	●	●	●
●	●	●	●		Flink Findzum Lawyers Service [SOP]	800-380-5434	●	●	●	●
●	●	●	●	●	Gamma Investigative Research Inc [SOP]	800-878-9393	●	●	●	●
●	●	●	●	●	In Search of Inc	201-224-3063	●	●	●	●
●	●	●	●	●	Inquisitive Research Corporation	732-321-0041	●	●	●	●
●	●	●	●	●	Landlord Secure Assoc (LSA) Process Serve & Legal Svcs[SOP]	973-332-4016	●	●	●	●
		●		●	Liberty Record Search of NJ Inc	973-887-8808	●	●	●	
●	●	●	●		National Background Inv Inc	800-798-0079			●	
●	●	●			Phoenix Document Service Inc	727-581-2552	●	●	●	
●	●	●	●	●	Searcher Girls	800-292-2757	●	●	●	●
●	●	●			Superior Information Services, LLC	800-848-0489	●		●	
●	●	●	●	●	US Document Retrieval Service Inc	800-595-0145		●	●	●
●	●	●	●	●	Washington Document Services (NY)	800-422-2776	●		●	

DT	BK	CV	CR	PR	←COURTS BURLINGTON RECORDING→		UC	RE	TX	VS
●	●	●	●		Best Legal Services Inc [SOP]	800-562-9620	●	●	●	●
●	●	●		●	Charles Jones Inc	800-792-8888	●	●	●	
●	●	●	●	●	Coyne Search Service Inc	215-781-3722	●	●	●	●
●	●				Credit Lenders Service Agency Inc	856-787-9005	●	●	●	
			●		Detailed Investigations	609-338-3088				
●	●	●	●		Employmentscreening.com	215-234-0700	●	●	●	●
●	●	●	●	●	Fidelifacts	800-678-0007	●	●	●	●
●	●	●	●		Flink Findzum Lawyers Service [SOP]	800-380-5434	●	●	●	●
					Infiniti Title Agency Inc	609-727-0818		●	●	
●	●	●	●	●	Inquisitive Research Corporation	732-321-0041	●	●	●	●
		●	●		Know It All Background Research Services Inc	888-281-9535	●	●	●	
		●		●	Liberty Record Search of NJ Inc	973-887-8808	●	●	●	
●	●	●	●		National Background Inv Inc	800-798-0079			●	
●	●	●	●	●	Searcher Girls	800-292-2757	●	●	●	●

DT	BK	CV	CR	PR	Retriever	Phone	UC	RE	TX	VS
•	•	•		•	Searchtec	877-2SEARCH	•	•	•	
•	•	•			Superior Information Services, LLC	800-848-0489	•		•	
•	•	•	•	•	Talone & Associates [SOP]	800-553-5189	•	•	•	•
•	•	•	•	•	Washington Document Services (NY)	800-422-2776	•		•	

DT	BK	CV	CR	PR	←Courts CAMDEN	Recording→	UC	RE	TX	VS
		•	•		Eileen Augatis	609-472-6513	•	•	•	
•	•	•	•		Best Legal Services Inc [SOP]	800-562-9620	•	•	•	•
•	•	•		•	Charles Jones Inc	800-792-8888	•	•	•	
•	•	•	•		County House Research Inc	866-594-1177			•	
•	•	•	•	•	Coyne Search Service Inc	215-781-3722	•	•	•	•
•	•				Credit Lenders Service Agency Inc	856-787-9005	•	•	•	
			•		Detailed Investigations	609-338-3088				
•	•	•	•		Employmentscreening.com	215-234-0700	•	•	•	•
•	•	•	•	•	Fidelifacts	800-678-0007	•	•	•	•
•	•	•	•		Flink Findzum Lawyers Service [SOP]	800-380-5434	•	•	•	•
•	•	•	•	•	Inquisitive Research Corporation	732-321-0041	•	•	•	•
•	•	•	•	•	Keystone Intelligence Network Inc	215-545-1111	•	•	•	•
		•	•		Know It All Background Research Services Inc	888-281-9535				
		•		•	Liberty Record Search of NJ Inc	973-887-8808	•	•	•	
•	•	•	•		National Background Inv Inc	800-798-0079			•	
•	•	•	•	•	Searcher Girls	800-292-2757	•	•	•	•
•	•	•		•	Searchtec	877-2SEARCH	•	•	•	
•	•	•			Superior Information Services, LLC	800-848-0489	•		•	
•	•	•	•	•	Talone & Associates [SOP]	800-553-5189	•	•	•	•
•	•	•	•	•	US Document Retrieval Service Inc	800-595-0145	•	•	•	•
•	•	•	•	•	Washington Document Services (NY)	800-422-2776	•		•	

DT	BK	CV	CR	PR	←Courts CAPE MAY	Recording→	UC	RE	TX	VS
•	•	•		•	Charles Jones Inc	800-792-8888	•	•	•	
			•		Detailed Investigations	609-338-3088				
•	•	•	•		Employmentscreening.com	215-234-0700	•	•	•	•
•	•	•	•	•	Fidelifacts	800-678-0007	•	•	•	•
•	•	•	•		Flink Findzum Lawyers Service [SOP]	800-380-5434	•	•	•	•
•	•	•	•	•	Inquisitive Research Corporation	732-321-0041	•	•	•	•
		•		•	Liberty Record Search of NJ Inc	973-887-8808	•	•	•	
•	•	•	•		National Background Inv Inc	800-798-0079			•	
•	•	•	•	•	Searcher Girls	800-292-2757	•	•	•	•
•	•	•			Superior Information Services, LLC	800-848-0489	•		•	
•	•	•	•	•	Washington Document Services (NY)	800-422-2776	•		•	

DT	BK	CV	CR	PR	←Courts CUMBERLAND	Recording→	UC	RE	TX	VS
•	•	•		•	Charles Jones Inc	800-792-8888	•	•	•	
			•		Detailed Investigations	609-338-3088				
•	•	•	•		Employmentscreening.com	215-234-0700	•	•	•	•
•	•	•	•	•	Fidelifacts	800-678-0007	•	•	•	•
•	•	•	•		Flink Findzum Lawyers Service [SOP]	800-380-5434	•	•	•	•
•	•	•	•	•	Inquisitive Research Corporation	732-321-0041	•	•	•	•
		•	•		Know It All Background Research Services Inc	888-281-9535				
		•		•	Liberty Record Search of NJ Inc	973-887-8808	•	•	•	
•	•	•	•		National Background Inv Inc	800-798-0079			•	
•	•	•	•	•	Searcher Girls	800-292-2757	•	•	•	•
•	•	•			Superior Information Services, LLC	800-848-0489	•		•	
•	•	•	•	•	Washington Document Services (NY)	800-422-2776	•		•	

DT	BK	CV	CR	PR	←Courts ESSEX	Recording→	UC	RE	TX	VS
		•	•		B & B Investigative Services	732-446-7482				
•	•	•	•	•	Callahan Lawyers Service [SOP]	877-767-2245				•
•	•	•		•	Charles Jones Inc	800-792-8888	•	•	•	
•	•	•	•		County House Research Inc	866-594-1177			•	
•	•	•	•		Court Data Search	973-770-1170				
			•		Detailed Investigations	609-338-3088				
•	•	•	•	•	DLS (Demovsky Lawyer Service - New York) [SOP]	800-443-1058	•	•	•	•
				•	Dolores Dios Title Abstractor	201-207-0628	•	•	•	
•	•	•	•		Employmentscreening.com	215-234-0700	•	•	•	•

DT	BK	CV	CR	PR	Courts / Recording	Phone	UC	RE	TX	VS
•	•	•	•	•	Fidelifacts	800-678-0007	•	•	•	•
•	•	•	•		Flink Findzum Lawyers Service [SOP]	800-380-5434	•	•	•	•
•	•	•	•	•	In Search of Inc	201-224-3063	•	•	•	•
•	•	•	•	•	Inquisitive Research Corporation	732-321-0041	•	•	•	•
		•	•		Know It All Background Research Services Inc	888-281-9535				
•	•	•	•	•	Landlord Secure Assoc (LSA) Process Serve & Legal Svcs[SOP]	973-332-4016	•	•	•	•
		•		•	Liberty Record Search of NJ Inc	973-887-8808	•	•	•	
•	•	•	•		National Background Inv Inc	800-798-0079			•	
•	•	•			Phoenix Document Service Inc	727-581-2552	•	•	•	
•	•	•	•	•	Searcher Girls	800-292-2757	•	•	•	•
•	•	•			Superior Information Services, LLC	800-848-0489	•		•	
•	•	•	•	•	Superior Subpoena Service [SOP]	800-862-5660	•	•	•	
•	•	•	•	•	US Document Retrieval Service Inc	800-595-0145		•	•	•
•	•	•	•	•	Washington Document Services (NY)	800-422-2776	•		•	

DT	BK	CV	CR	PR	←Courts **GLOUCESTER** Recording→		UC	RE	TX	VS
		•	•		Eileen Augatis	609-472-6513	•	•	•	
•	•	•	•		Best Legal Services Inc [SOP]	800-562-9620	•	•	•	•
•	•	•		•	Charles Jones Inc	800-792-8888	•	•	•	
			•		Detailed Investigations	609-338-3088				
•	•	•	•		Employmentscreening.com	215-234-0700	•	•	•	•
•	•	•	•	•	Fidelifacts	800-678-0007	•	•	•	•
•	•	•	•		Flink Findzum Lawyers Service [SOP]	800-380-5434	•	•	•	•
•	•	•	•	•	Inquisitive Research Corporation	732-321-0041	•	•	•	•
•	•	•	•	•	Keystone Intelligence Network Inc	215-545-1111	•	•	•	•
		•		•	Liberty Record Search of NJ Inc	973-887-8808	•	•	•	
•	•	•	•		National Background Inv Inc	800-798-0079			•	
•	•	•	•	•	Searcher Girls	800-292-2757	•	•	•	•
•	•	•		•	Searchtec	877-2SEARCH	•	•		
•	•	•			Superior Information Services, LLC	800-848-0489	•		•	
•	•	•	•	•	Talone & Associates [SOP]	800-553-5189	•	•	•	•
•	•	•	•	•	Washington Document Services (NY)	800-422-2776	•		•	

DT	BK	CV	CR	PR	←Courts **HUDSON** Recording→		UC	RE	TX	VS
		•	•		B & B Investigative Services	732-446-7482				
•	•	•	•	•	Callahan Lawyers Service [SOP]	877-767-2245				•
•	•	•		•	Charles Jones Inc	800-792-8888	•	•	•	
•	•	•	•		Court Data Search	973-770-1170				
			•		Detailed Investigations	609-338-3088				
				•	Dolores Dios Title Abstractor	201-207-0628	•	•	•	
•	•	•	•		Employmentscreening.com	215-234-0700	•	•	•	•
•	•	•	•	•	Fidelifacts	800-678-0007	•	•	•	•
•	•	•	•		Flink Findzum Lawyers Service [SOP]	800-380-5434	•	•	•	•
•	•	•	•	•	Gamma Investigative Research Inc [SOP]	800-878-9393	•	•	•	
•	•	•	•	•	In Search of Inc	201-224-3063	•	•	•	•
•	•	•	•	•	Inquisitive Research Corporation	732-321-0041	•	•	•	•
•	•	•	•	•	Landlord Secure Assoc (LSA) Process Serve & Legal Svcs[SOP]	973-332-4016	•	•	•	•
		•		•	Liberty Record Search of NJ Inc	973-887-8808	•	•	•	
•	•	•	•		National Background Inv Inc	800-798-0079			•	
•	•	•	•	•	Searcher Girls	800-292-2757	•	•	•	•
•	•	•			Superior Information Services, LLC	800-848-0489	•		•	
•	•	•	•	•	Superior Subpoena Service [SOP]	800-862-5660	•	•	•	
•	•	•	•	•	US Document Retrieval Service Inc	800-595-0145		•	•	•
•	•	•	•	•	Washington Document Services (NY)	800-422-2776	•		•	

DT	BK	CV	CR	PR	←Courts **HUNTERDON** Recording→		UC	RE	TX	VS
		•	•	•	Dan & Jackie Buck	908-537-2475	•	•	•	•
•	•	•		•	Charles Jones Inc	800-792-8888	•	•	•	
			•		Detailed Investigations	609-338-3088				
•	•	•	•		Employmentscreening.com	215-234-0700	•	•	•	•
•	•	•	•	•	Fidelifacts	800-678-0007	•	•	•	•
•	•	•	•		Flink Findzum Lawyers Service [SOP]	800-380-5434	•	•	•	•
•	•	•	•	•	Inquisitive Research Corporation	732-321-0041	•	•	•	•
		•		•	Liberty Record Search of NJ Inc	973-887-8808	•	•	•	
•	•	•	•		National Background Inv Inc	800-798-0079			•	

DT	BK	CV	CR	PR	←Courts		Recording→	UC	RE	TX	VS
•	•	•	•	•	Searcher Girls		800-292-2757	•	•	•	•
•	•	•			Superior Information Services, LLC		800-848-0489	•		•	
•	•	•	•	•	Washington Document Services (NY)		800-422-2776	•		•	

DT	BK	CV	CR	PR	←Courts	**Mercer**	Recording→	UC	RE	TX	VS
		•	•		B & B Investigative Services		732-446-7482				
•	•	•		•	Charles Jones Inc		800-792-8888	•	•	•	
•	•	•	•	•	Corporation Service Company - CSC		800-927-9800	•	•	•	•
•	•	•	•	•	Coyne Search Service Inc		215-781-3722	•	•	•	•
•	•				Credit Lenders Service Agency Inc		856-787-9005	•	•	•	
			•		Detailed Investigations		609-338-3088				
•	•	•	•		Employmentscreening.com		215-234-0700	•	•	•	•
•	•	•	•	•	Fidelifacts		800-678-0007	•	•	•	•
•	•	•	•		Flink Findzum Lawyers Service [SOP]		800-380-5434	•	•	•	•
•	•	•	•	•	Inquisitive Research Corporation		732-321-0041	•	•	•	•
		•	•		Intelysis Corp (Ziegler & Assoc.)		800-489-1239	•	•		•
•	•	•			Kaufman Information Resources Inc.		732-438-1967	•	•	•	•
•	•	•	•	•	Landlord Secure Assoc (LSA) Process Serve & Legal Svcs[SOP]		973-332-4016	•	•	•	•
		•		•	Liberty Record Search of NJ Inc		973-887-8808	•	•	•	
•	•	•	•		National Background Inv Inc		800-798-0079			•	
•	•	•	•	•	Searcher Girls		800-292-2757	•	•	•	•
•	•	•		•	Searchtec		877-2SEARCH	•	•	•	
•	•				State Capital Title & Abstract Co		800-876-8994				
•	•	•			Superior Information Services, LLC		800-848-0489	•		•	
•	•	•	•	•	Washington Document Services (NY)		800-422-2776	•		•	

DT	BK	CV	CR	PR	←Courts	**Middlesex**	Recording→	UC	RE	TX	VS
		•	•		B & B Investigative Services		732-446-7482				
•	•	•		•	Charles Jones Inc		800-792-8888	•	•	•	
•	•	•	•		Court Data Search		973-770-1170				
•	•				Credit Lenders Service Agency Inc		856-787-9005	•	•	•	
			•		Detailed Investigations		609-338-3088				
				•	Dolores Dios Title Abstractor		201-207-0628	•	•	•	
•	•	•	•		Employmentscreening.com		215-234-0700	•	•	•	•
•	•	•	•	•	Fidelifacts		800-678-0007	•	•	•	•
•	•	•	•		Flink Findzum Lawyers Service [SOP]		800-380-5434	•	•	•	•
•	•	•	•	•	Inquisitive Research Corporation		732-321-0041	•	•	•	•
•	•	•			Kaufman Information Resources Inc.		732-438-1967	•	•	•	•
•	•	•	•	•	Landlord Secure Assoc (LSA) Process Serve & Legal Svcs[SOP]		973-332-4016	•	•	•	•
		•		•	Liberty Record Search of NJ Inc		973-887-8808	•	•	•	
•	•	•	•		National Background Inv Inc		800-798-0079			•	
•	•	•			Phoenix Document Service Inc		727-581-2552	•	•	•	
•	•	•	•	•	Searcher Girls		800-292-2757	•	•	•	•
•	•	•			Superior Information Services, LLC		800-848-0489	•		•	
•	•	•	•	•	Superior Subpoena Service [SOP]		800-862-5660	•	•	•	
•	•	•	•	•	US Document Retrieval Service Inc		800-595-0145		•	•	•
•	•	•	•	•	Washington Document Services (NY)		800-422-2776	•		•	

DT	BK	CV	CR	PR	←Courts	**Monmouth**	Recording→	UC	RE	TX	VS
		•	•		B & B Investigative Services		732-446-7482				
•	•	•		•	Charles Jones Inc		800-792-8888	•	•	•	
•	•	•	•		Court Data Search		973-770-1170				
			•		Detailed Investigations		609-338-3088				
				•	Dolores Dios Title Abstractor		201-207-0628	•	•	•	
•	•	•	•		Employmentscreening.com		215-234-0700	•	•	•	•
•	•	•	•	•	Fidelifacts		800-678-0007	•	•	•	•
•	•	•	•		Flink Findzum Lawyers Service [SOP]		800-380-5434	•	•	•	•
•	•	•	•	•	Inquisitive Research Corporation		732-321-0041	•	•	•	•
•	•	•			Kaufman Information Resources Inc.		732-438-1967	•	•	•	•

DT	BK	CV	CR	PR	←Courts	Recording→	UC	RE	TX	VS
		•		•	Liberty Record Search of NJ Inc	973-887-8808	•	•	•	
				•	M R Search Co LLC	732 462 6108	•	•		
•	•	•	•		National Background Inv Inc	800-798-0079			•	
•	•	•			Phoenix Document Service Inc	727-581-2552	•	•	•	
•	•	•	•	•	Searcher Girls	800-292-2757	•	•	•	•
•	•	•			Security Search & Abstract Co Inc	800-345-9494	•	•	•	
•	•	•			Superior Information Services, LLC	800-848-0489	•		•	
•	•	•	•	•	US Document Retrieval Service Inc	800-595-0145		•	•	•
•	•	•	•	•	Washington Document Services (NY)	800-422-2776	•		•	
•	•		•	•	XpertSearch Inc	732-229-6688	•	•	•	•

DT	BK	CV	CR	PR	←Courts MORRIS	Recording→	UC	RE	TX	VS
				•	Ronald J Axelrod	973-538-4606	•	•	•	
		•	•	•	Dan & Jackie Buck	908-537-2475	•	•	•	•
•	•	•	•	•	Callahan Lawyers Service [SOP]	877-767-2245				•
•	•	•		•	Charles Jones Inc	800-792-8888	•	•	•	
•	•	•	•		Court Data Search	973-770-1170				
•	•				Credit Lenders Service Agency Inc	856-787-9005	•	•	•	
			•		Detailed Investigations	609-338-3088				
				•	Dolores Dios Title Abstractor	201-207-0628	•	•	•	
•	•	•	•		Employmentscreening.com	215-234-0700	•	•	•	•
•	•	•	•	•	Fidelifacts	800-678-0007	•	•	•	•
•	•	•	•		Flink Findzum Lawyers Service [SOP]	800-380-5434	•	•	•	•
•	•	•	•	•	Inquisitive Research Corporation	732-321-0041	•	•	•	•
•	•	•	•	•	Landlord Secure Assoc (LSA) Process Serve & Legal Svcs[SOP]	973-332-4016	•	•	•	•
		•		•	Liberty Record Search of NJ Inc	973-887-8808	•	•	•	
				•	Morris Hills Abstract Co	973-267-0450	•	•	•	
•	•	•	•		National Background Inv Inc	800-798-0079			•	
•	•	•			Phoenix Document Service Inc	727-581-2552	•	•	•	
•	•	•	•	•	Searcher Girls	800-292-2757	•	•	•	•
•	•	•			Superior Information Services, LLC	800-848-0489	•		•	
•	•	•	•	•	US Document Retrieval Service Inc	800-595-0145		•	•	•
•	•	•	•	•	Washington Document Services (NY)	800-422-2776	•		•	

DT	BK	CV	CR	PR	←Courts OCEAN	Recording→	UC	RE	TX	VS
		•	•		B & B Investigative Services	732-446-7482				
•	•	•		•	Charles Jones Inc	800-792-8888	•	•	•	
•	•				Credit Lenders Service Agency Inc	856-787-9005	•	•	•	
			•		Detailed Investigations	609-338-3088				
				•	Dolores Dios Title Abstractor	201-207-0628	•	•	•	
			•		Edna Yerks Abstracts	732-349-9747				
•	•	•	•		Employmentscreening.com	215-234-0700	•	•	•	•
		•		•	Faithful Abstract	908-351-9398	•	•	•	
•	•	•	•	•	Fidelifacts	800-678-0007	•	•	•	•
•	•	•	•		Flink Findzum Lawyers Service [SOP]	800-380-5434	•	•	•	•
•	•	•	•	•	Inquisitive Research Corporation	732-321-0041	•	•	•	•
				•	Margaret Laratta	732-349-1301	•	•	•	
		•		•	Liberty Record Search of NJ Inc	973-887-8808	•	•	•	
				•	M R Search Co LLC	732 462 6108	•	•		
•	•	•	•		National Background Inv Inc	800-798-0079			•	
•	•	•			Phoenix Document Service Inc	727-581-2552	•	•	•	
•	•	•	•	•	Searcher Girls	800-292-2757	•	•	•	•
•	•	•			Security Search & Abstract Co Inc	800-345-9494	•	•	•	
•	•	•			Superior Information Services, LLC	800-848-0489	•		•	
•	•	•	•	•	US Document Retrieval Service Inc	800-595-0145		•	•	•
•	•	•	•	•	Washington Document Services (NY)	800-422-2776	•		•	
•	•	•	•	•	XpertSearch Inc	732-229-6688	•	•	•	•

DT	BK	CV	CR	PR	←COURTS PASSAIC	RECORDING→	UC	RE	TX	VS
•	•	•	•	•	Callahan Lawyers Service [SOP]	877-767-2245				•
•	•	•		•	Charles Jones Inc	800-792-8888	•	•	•	
•	•	•	•		County House Research Inc	866-594-1177			•	
•	•	•	•		Court Data Search	973-770-1170				
			•		Detailed Investigations	609-338-3088				
				•	Dolores Dios Title Abstractor	201-207-0628	•	•	•	
•	•	•	•		Employmentscreening.com	215-234-0700	•	•	•	•
•	•	•	•	•	Fidelifacts	800-678-0007	•	•	•	•
•	•	•	•		Flink Findzum Lawyers Service [SOP]	800-380-5434	•	•	•	•
•	•	•	•	•	Gamma Investigative Research Inc [SOP]	800-878-9393	•	•	•	•
•	•	•	•	•	In Search of Inc	201-224-3063	•	•	•	•
•	•	•	•	•	Inquisitive Research Corporation	732-321-0041	•	•	•	•
•	•	•	•	•	Landlord Secure Assoc (LSA) Process Serve & Legal Svcs[SOP]	973-332-4016	•	•	•	•
		•		•	Liberty Record Search of NJ Inc	973-887-8808	•	•	•	
•	•	•	•		National Background Inv Inc	800-798-0079			•	
•	•	•			Phoenix Document Service Inc	727-581-2552	•	•	•	
•	•	•	•	•	Searcher Girls	800-292-2757	•	•	•	•
•	•	•			Superior Information Services, LLC	800-848-0489	•		•	
•	•	•	•	•	Washington Document Services (NY)	800-422-2776	•		•	

DT	BK	CV	CR	PR	←COURTS SALEM	RECORDING→	UC	RE	TX	VS
•	•	•		•	Charles Jones Inc	800-792-8888	•	•	•	
			•		Detailed Investigations	609-338-3088				
•	•	•	•		Employmentscreening.com	215-234-0700	•	•	•	•
•	•	•	•	•	Fidelifacts	800-678-0007	•	•	•	•
•	•	•	•		Flink Findzum Lawyers Service [SOP]	800-380-5434	•	•	•	•
•	•	•	•	•	Inquisitive Research Corporation	732-321-0041	•	•	•	•
		•		•	Liberty Record Search of NJ Inc	973-887-8808	•	•	•	
•	•	•	•		National Background Inv Inc	800-798-0079			•	
•	•	•	•	•	Searcher Girls	800-292-2757	•	•	•	•
•	•	•			Superior Information Services, LLC	800-848-0489	•		•	
•	•	•	•	•	Washington Document Services (NY)	800-422-2776	•		•	

DT	BK	CV	CR	PR	←COURTS SOMERSET	RECORDING→	UC	RE	TX	VS
				•	Ronald J Axelrod	973-538-4606	•	•	•	
		•	•		B & B Investigative Services	732-446-7482				
		•	•	•	Dan & Jackie Buck	908-537-2475	•	•	•	•
•	•	•		•	Charles Jones Inc	800-792-8888	•	•	•	
				•	CMT Abstract	908-722-6565	•	•	•	
•	•	•	•		Court Data Search	973-770-1170				
•	•				Credit Lenders Service Agency Inc	856-787-9005	•	•	•	
			•		Detailed Investigations	609-338-3088				
				•	Dolores Dios Title Abstractor	201-207-0628	•	•	•	
•	•	•	•		Employmentscreening.com	215-234-0700	•	•	•	•
•	•	•	•	•	Fidelifacts	800-678-0007	•	•	•	•
•	•	•	•		Flink Findzum Lawyers Service [SOP]	800-380-5434	•	•	•	•
•	•	•	•	•	Inquisitive Research Corporation	732-321-0041	•	•	•	•
•	•	•			Kaufman Information Resources Inc	732-438-1967	•	•	•	•
					KJK Abstract Co	908-725-6336	•	•	•	
		•		•	Liberty Record Search of NJ Inc	973-887-8808	•	•	•	
•	•	•	•		National Background Inv Inc	800-798-0079			•	
•	•	•	•	•	Searcher Girls	800-292-2757	•	•	•	•
•	•	•			Superior Information Services, LLC	800-848-0489	•		•	
•	•	•	•	•	Washington Document Services (NY)	800-422-2776	•		•	

DT	BK	CV	CR	PR	←COURTS SUSSEX	RECORDING→	UC	RE	TX	VS
•	•	•	•	•	Callahan Lawyers Service [SOP]	877-767-2245				•
•	•	•		•	Charles Jones Inc	800-792-8888	•	•	•	

DT	BK	CV	CR	PR	←Courts	Recording→	UC	RE	TX	VS
•	•	•	•		Court Data Search	973-770-1170				
			•		Detailed Investigations	609-338-3088				
				•	Dolores Dios Title Abstractor	201-207-0628	•	•	•	
•	•	•	•		Employmentscreening.com	215-234-0700	•	•	•	•
•	•	•	•	•	Fidelifacts	800-678-0007	•	•	•	•
•	•	•	•		Flink Findzum Lawyers Service [SOP]	800-380-5434	•	•	•	•
•	•	•	•	•	Gamma Investigative Research Inc [SOP]	800-878-9393	•	•	•	
•	•	•	•	•	Inquisitive Research Corporation	732-321-0041	•	•	•	•
		•		•	Liberty Record Search of NJ Inc	973-887-8808	•	•	•	
•	•	•	•		National Background Inv Inc	800-798-0079			•	
•	•	•	•	•	Searcher Girls	800-292-2757	•	•	•	•
•	•	•			Superior Information Services, LLC	800-848-0489	•		•	
•	•	•	•	•	Washington Document Services (NY)	800-422-2776	•		•	

DT	BK	CV	CR	PR	←Courts Union	Recording→	UC	RE	TX	VS
		•	•		B & B Investigative Services	732-446-7482				
•	•	•		•	Charles Jones Inc	800-792-8888	•	•	•	
•	•	•	•		Court Data Search	973-770-1170				
			•		Detailed Investigations	609-338-3088				
				•	Dolores Dios Title Abstractor	201-207-0628	•	•	•	
•	•	•	•		Employmentscreening.com	215-234-0700	•	•	•	•
		•		•	Faithful Abstract	908-351-9398	•	•	•	
•	•	•	•	•	Fidelifacts	800-678-0007	•	•	•	•
•	•	•	•		Flink Findzum Lawyers Service [SOP]	800-380-5434	•	•	•	•
•	•	•	•	•	Gamma Investigative Research Inc [SOP]	800-878-9393	•	•	•	
•	•	•	•	•	In Search of Inc	201-224-3063	•	•	•	•
•	•	•	•	•	Inquisitive Research Corporation	732-321-0041	•	•	•	•
•	•	•			Kaufman Information Resources Inc	732-438-1967	•	•	•	•
		•	•		Know It All Background Research Services Inc	888-281-9535				
•	•	•	•	•	Landlord Secure Assoc (L.S.A.) Process Serve & Legal Svcs [SOP]	973-332-4016	•	•	•	•
		•		•	Liberty Record Search of NJ Inc	973-887-8808	•	•	•	
•	•	•	•		National Background Inv Inc	800-798-0079			•	
•	•	•			Phoenix Document Service Inc	727-581-2552	•	•	•	
•	•	•	•	•	Searcher Girls	800-292-2757	•	•	•	•
•	•	•			Superior Information Services, LLC	800-848-0489	•		•	
•	•	•	•	•	Superior Subpoena Service [SOP]	800-862-5660	•	•	•	
•	•	•	•	•	US Document Retrieval Service Inc	800-595-0145	•	•	•	•
•	•	•	•	•	Washington Document Services (NY)	800-422-2776	•		•	

DT	BK	CV	CR	PR	←Courts Warren	Recording→	UC	RE	TX	VS
•	•	•		•	Charles Jones Inc	800-792-8888	•	•	•	
			•		Detailed Investigations	609-338-3088				
•	•	•	•		Employmentscreening.com	215-234-0700	•	•	•	•
•	•	•	•	•	Fidelifacts	800-678-0007	•	•	•	•
•	•	•	•		Flink Findzum Lawyers Service [SOP]	800-380-5434	•	•	•	•
•	•	•	•	•	Gamma Investigative Research Inc [SOP]	800-878-9393	•	•	•	
•	•	•	•	•	Inquisitive Research Corporation	732-321-0041	•	•	•	•
		•			JAK Abstract	908-475-3344		•		
		•		•	Liberty Record Search of NJ Inc	973-887-8808	•	•	•	
•	•	•	•		National Background Inv Inc	800-798-0079			•	
•	•	•	•	•	Searcher Girls	800-292-2757	•	•	•	•
•	•	•			Superior Information Services, LLC	800-848-0489	•		•	
•	•	•	•	•	Washington Document Services (NY)	800-422-2776	•		•	

New Mexico

COURT RECORDS RETRIEVED — **RECORDING RECORDS RETRIEVED**

DT	BK	CV	CR	PR	←COURTS **BERNALILLO** RECORDING→	UC	RE	TX	VS
•	•	•	•	•	Apex Research 505-275-0848	•	•	•	
•	•	•	•	•	Casa De Search Inc 800-757-0220	•	•	•	•
•	•	•	•	•	Duke City Process Service & Inv [SOP] 505-275-0994		•	•	•
•	•	•	•	•	Infomax 505-994-0370	•	•	•	•
					Sue Ellen Lagneaux 505-466-4061		•		
•	•		•	•	Professional Services of New Mexico Inc 505-271-2291				
•	•	•	•	•	R Miller & Associates LLC [SOP] 800-395-1992	•	•	•	•
		•		•	Real Property Resources 505-232-3555	•	•	•	
•	•	•			Carol Seewald 505-831-5713	•	•	•	

DT	BK	CV	CR	PR	←COURTS **CATRON** RECORDING→	UC	RE	TX	VS
					See adjoining counties for retrievers or contact court or recording office.				

DT	BK	CV	CR	PR	←COURTS **CHAVES** RECORDING→	UC	RE	TX	VS
		•		•	Landmark Title Roswell 505-622-5340	•	•	•	

DT	BK	CV	CR	PR	←COURTS **CIBOLA** RECORDING→	UC	RE	TX	VS
		•	•		Attorney Service New Mexico [SOP] 505-326-7486				
		•		•	Real Property Resources 505-232-3555	•	•	•	

DT	BK	CV	CR	PR	←COURTS **COLFAX** RECORDING→	UC	RE	TX	VS
					See adjoining counties for retrievers or contact court or recording office.				

DT	BK	CV	CR	PR	←COURTS **CURRY** RECORDING→	UC	RE	TX	VS
•		•	•	•	Clovis Title & Abstract Ltd 505-762-4403	•	•	•	
•	•	•	•	•	Davick Services 800-658-6656	•	•	•	
		•		•	Landmark Title Inc (Clovis NM) 505-763-3904	•	•	•	

DT	BK	CV	CR	PR	←COURTS **DE BACA** RECORDING→	UC	RE	TX	VS
		•		•	De Baca Abstract Inc 505-355-2431	•	•		

DT	BK	CV	CR	PR	←COURTS **DEBACA** RECORDING→	UC	RE	TX	VS
•	•	•	•	•	Davick Services 800-658-6656	•	•	•	

DT	BK	CV	CR	PR	←COURTS **DONA ANA** RECORDING→	UC	RE	TX	VS
		•	•	•	A.G.O. Legal Process Service [SOP] 505-526-4303	•	•	•	•
•	•	•	•	•	Casa De Search Inc 800-757-0220	•	•	•	•
•		•	•		Nancy Harris [SOP] 877-461-6700	•	•	•	
•	•	•	•	•	Legal Net Process Service [SOP] 915-532-7871	•		•	•

DT	BK	CV	CR	PR	←COURTS **EDDY** RECORDING→	UC	RE	TX	VS
		•		•	Caprock Title Co 432-687-3232		•	•	
		•		•	Currier Abstract Company 505-746-9823	•	•	•	
		•	•		Lorina Dominquez 505-887-3489				
		•		•	Eddy County Abstract Co 800-348-1232	•	•	•	
		•		•	Guaranty Title Co (New Mexico) 505-887-3593	•	•	•	

DT	BK	CV	CR	PR	←COURTS **GRANT** RECORDING→	UC	RE	TX	VS
		•	•	•	A.G.O. Legal Process Service [SOP] 505-526-4303	•	•	•	•

DT	BK	CV	CR	PR	←COURTS **GUADALUPE** RECORDING→	UC	RE	TX	VS
				•	Territorial Title 505-425-3563	•	•	•	•

DT	BK	CV	CR	PR	←Courts	**Harding**	Recording→	UC	RE	TX	VS
					See adjoining counties for retrievers or contact court or recording office.						

DT	BK	CV	CR	PR	←Courts	**Hidalgo**	Recording→	UC	RE	TX	VS
		•	•	•	A.G.O. Legal Process Service [SOP]		505-526-4303	•	•	•	•
					Hidalgo County Abstract		505-542-9181		•	•	

DT	BK	CV	CR	PR	←Courts	**Lea**	Recording→	UC	RE	TX	VS
		•		•	Caprock Title Co		432-687-3232		•	•	
•	•	•	•	•	Davick Services		800-658-6656	•	•	•	
		•		•	Elliott & Waldron Title & Abstract		505-393-7706	•	•	•	

DT	BK	CV	CR	PR	←Courts	**Lincoln**	Recording→	UC	RE	TX	VS
		•	•	•	A.G.O. Legal Process Service [SOP]		505-526-4303	•	•	•	•
		•		•	Lincoln County Abstract & Title Co (NM)		800-635-4692	•	•	•	

DT	BK	CV	CR	PR	←Courts	**Los Alamos**	Recording→	UC	RE	TX	VS
•	•	•	•	•	Casa De Search Inc		800-757-0220	•	•	•	•
•		•	•		Nancy Harris [SOP]		877-461-6700	•	•	•	
•	•	•	•	•	Infomax		505-994-0370	•	•	•	•
		•		•	Real Property Resources		505-232-3555	•	•	•	

DT	BK	CV	CR	PR	←Courts	**Luna**	Recording→	UC	RE	TX	VS
		•	•	•	A.G.O. Legal Process Service [SOP]		505-526-4303	•	•	•	•
		•	•	•	Mimbres Valley Abstract & Title Co		505-546-8896	•	•	•	•

DT	BK	CV	CR	PR	←Courts	**McKinley**	Recording→	UC	RE	TX	VS
		•	•		Attorney Service New Mexico [SOP]		505-326-7486				
		•		•	Real Property Resources		505-232-3555	•	•	•	

DT	BK	CV	CR	PR	←Courts	**Mora**	Recording→	UC	RE	TX	VS
				•	Territorial Title		505-425-3563	•	•	•	•

DT	BK	CV	CR	PR	←Courts	**Otero**	Recording→	UC	RE	TX	VS
					See adjoining counties for retrievers or contact court or recording office.						

DT	BK	CV	CR	PR	←Courts	**Quay**	Recording→	UC	RE	TX	VS
•	•	•	•	•	Davick Services		800-658-6656	•	•	•	

DT	BK	CV	CR	PR	←Courts	**Rio Arriba**	Recording→	UC	RE	TX	VS
		•	•		Attorney Service New Mexico [SOP]		505-326-7486				
		•		•	Espanola Abstract Co		505-753-2248	•	•	•	•
•		•	•		Nancy Harris [SOP]		877-461-6700	•	•	•	

DT	BK	CV	CR	PR	←Courts	**Roosevelt**	Recording→	UC	RE	TX	VS
•	•	•	•	•	Davick Services		800-658-6656	•	•	•	
•	•	•		•	Graham Abstract Co		505-356-8505	•	•	•	

DT	BK	CV	CR	PR	←Courts	**San Juan**	Recording→	UC	RE	TX	VS
		•	•		Attorney Service New Mexico [SOP]		505-326-7486				
•	•	•	•	•	Casa De Search Inc		800-757-0220	•	•	•	•
		•	•	•	San Juan County Abstract & Title		505-325-2808	•	•	•	•

DT	BK	CV	CR	PR	←Courts	**San Miguel**	Recording→	UC	RE	TX	VS
•		•	•		Nancy Harris [SOP]		877-461-6700	•	•	•	
				•	Territorial Title		505-425-3563	•	•	•	•

DT	BK	CV	CR	PR	←Courts	**Sandoval**	Recording→	UC	RE	TX	VS
•	•	•	•	•	Apex Research		505-275-0848	•	•	•	
•	•	•	•	•	Casa De Search Inc		800-757-0220	•	•	•	•
•	•	•	•	•	Duke City Process Service & Inv [SOP]		505-275-0994		•	•	•
•	•	•	•	•	Infomax		505-994-0370	•	•	•	•
					Sue Ellen Lagneaux		505-466-4061		•		

DT	BK	CV	CR	PR	Retriever	Phone	UC	RE	TX	VS
•	•		•	•	Professional Services of New Mexico Inc	505-271-2291				
•	•	•	•	•	R Miller & Associates LLC [SOP]	800-395-1992	•	•	•	•
		•		•	Real Property Resources	505-232-3555	•	•	•	
•	•	•			Carol Seewald	505-831-5713	•	•	•	

DT	BK	CV	CR	PR	←Courts **Santa Fe**	Recording→	UC	RE	TX	VS
•	•	•	•	•	Apex Research	505-275-0848	•	•	•	
•	•	•	•	•	Casa De Search Inc	800-757-0220	•	•	•	•
•		•	•		Nancy Harris [SOP]	877-461-6700	•	•	•	
•	•	•	•	•	Infomax	505-994-0370	•	•	•	•
					Sue Ellen Lagneaux	505-466-4061		•		
		•		•	Real Property Resources	505-232-3555	•	•	•	
•	•	•			Carol Seewald	505-831-5713	•	•	•	
•	•	•	•		UCC Search Inc	800-453-9404	•	•	•	

DT	BK	CV	CR	PR	←Courts **Sierra**	Recording→	UC	RE	TX	VS
					See adjoining counties for retrievers or contact court or recording office.					

DT	BK	CV	CR	PR	←Courts **Socorro**	Recording→	UC	RE	TX	VS
					See adjoining counties for retrievers or contact court or recording office.					

DT	BK	CV	CR	PR	←Courts **Taos**	Recording→	UC	RE	TX	VS
		•	•	•	PLM Court Research [SOP]	505-758-4467				

DT	BK	CV	CR	PR	←Courts **Torrance**	Recording→	UC	RE	TX	VS
					See adjoining counties for retrievers or contact court or recording office.					

DT	BK	CV	CR	PR	←Courts **Union**	Recording→	UC	RE	TX	VS
		•		•	Clayton Title Services Inc	505-374-9789	•	•	•	•

DT	BK	CV	CR	PR	←Courts **Valencia**	Recording→	UC	RE	TX	VS
•	•	•	•	•	Apex Research	505-275-0848	•	•	•	
•	•	•	•	•	Duke City Process Service & Inv [SOP]	505-275-0994		•	•	•
•	•	•	•	•	R Miller & Associates LLC [SOP]	800-395-1992	•	•	•	•
		•		•	Real Property Resources	505-232-3555	•	•	•	
•	•	•			Carol Seewald	505-831-5713	•	•	•	

Editor's Tip: Only Call a Retriever For the Records They Retrieve.
If you call for a criminal record from a retriever who only does work at the recorder's office, then you are wasting your time and the retriever's time.

New York

COURT RECORDS RETRIEVED — **RECORDING RECORDS RETRIEVED**

DT	BK	CV	CR	PR	←COURTS ALBANY RECORDING→		UC	RE	TX	VS
•	•	•	•		Access Information Services Inc [SOP]	800-388-1598	•	•	•	
•	•	•			Attorney's Process & Research Service Inc [SOP]	800-640-7863	•	•	•	•
•	•	•	•	•	Blumberg Excelsior Corporate Services Inc [SOP]	800-999-0850	•	•	•	•
•	•				Capitol Services Inc (New York)	800-662-0171	•		•	
•	•	•	•	•	CMS (Consumer Marketing Services)	800-388-1365	•	•	•	
•	•	•	•	•	Corporation Service Company - CSC	800-927-9800	•	•	•	•
•	•	•	•	•	Credit Control Inc/Resource Confidential [SOP]	800-886-7407	•	•	•	•
•	•	•	•	•	DLS (Demovsky Lawyer Service - Albany) [SOP]	518-449-8411	•	•	•	
•	•	•			Forbes Public Research Inc	518-732-2841	•	•	•	
				•	Four Corners Abstract	800-724-3668	•	•	•	
•	•			•	Lightning Legal Services LLC [SOP]	518-463-1049	•		•	•
•	•	•	•		Merola Services	219-878-9699	•	•	•	•
•	•				Monroe Title Insurance Corp (Albany)	800-966-6763	•	•	•	
•	•			•	Monroe Title Insurance Corp (Rochester)	800-966-6763	•	•	•	
•	•	•	•	•	Nationwide Information Services Inc [SOP]	800-873-3482	•	•	•	•
•	•	•	•	•	Northeast Investigations Inc [SOP]	888-796-1051	•	•	•	•
•	•	•	•	•	Relyea Services Inc [SOP]	800-854-4111	•	•	•	•
•	•	•	•	•	SearchLink LLC	716-873-8315	•	•	•	
•	•	•	•	•	Servico Inc [SOP]	518-463-4179	•	•	•	
•	•	•	•	•	Tracers International (Albany) [SOP]	800-872-2377	•	•	•	•
•	•	•			UCC Direct Services	800-342-3676	•	•	•	
•	•	•			Zap! Courier Service	518-449-3361				

DT	BK	CV	CR	PR	←COURTS ALLEGANY RECORDING→		UC	RE	TX	VS
•	•			•	Monroe Title Insurance Corp (Rochester)	800-966-6763	•	•	•	
•	•	•	•	•	SearchLink LLC	716-873-8315	•	•	•	

DT	BK	CV	CR	PR	←COURTS BRONX RECORDING→		UC	RE	TX	VS
•	•	•			Accurate Search Corporation	212-228-1850	•	•	•	
•	•	•	•	•	Alstate Process Service Inc [SOP]	631-667-1800	•	•	•	•
•	•				American Abstract	631-262-1826	•	•	•	•
•	•	•	•	•	ASSIST International [SOP]	800-382-7747	•	•	•	•
	•				Blumberg Excelsior Corporate Svcs Inc (NYC, NY)	800-221-2972	•		•	
•	•	•		•	Bridge Service Corp	800-225-2736	•	•	•	•
•	•	•	•	•	Court Explorers Inc [SOP]	212-608-1585	•	•	•	•
•	•	•	•	•	DLS (Demovsky Lawyer Service - New York) [SOP]	800-443-1058	•	•	•	•
					Document Retrieval Network Inc	859-654-2890	•	•	•	
•	•	•	•	•	Fidelifacts	800-678-0007	•	•	•	•
•	•	•	•		G.A. Public Record Services Inc	800-760-2468	•	•	•	
•	•	•	•	•	Inquisitive Research Corporation	732-321-0041	•	•	•	•
•	•	•	•		Investigative Resources [SOP]	718-317-0043. 212-571-2500	•	•	•	
•	•	•		•	Keating & Walker [SOP]	800-466-2730	•	•	•	
•	•	•		•	LegalEase Inc [SOP]	800-393-1277			•	
	•				Mutual Abstract Corporation	212-964-4686	•	•	•	
•	•	•	•	•	Nationwide Court Services Inc [SOP]	888-941-1234	•	•	•	•
•	•	•	•	•	Pallorium Inc [SOP]	212-969-0286	•	•	•	•
•	•	•	•	•	Search NY Inc [SOP]	212-608-2546	•	•	•	•
•	•	•	•	•	SearchLink LLC	716-873-8315	•	•	•	
					Deborah W Thompson	917-309-4830	•	•	•	

DT	BK	CV	CR	PR	←Courts		Recording→	UC	RE	TX	VS
•	•	•	•	•	Tracers International (New York) [SOP]	800-872-2377		•	•	•	•
•	•	•	•	•	US Document Retrieval Service Inc	800-595-0145			•	•	•
•	•	•	•	•	Washington Document Services (NY)	800-422-2776		•		•	

DT	BK	CV	CR	PR	←Courts	Broome	Recording→	UC	RE	TX	VS
•	•	•	•	•	CMS (Consumer Marketing Services)	800-388-1365		•	•	•	
•	•	•	•	•	Credit Control Inc/Resource Confidential [SOP]	800-886-7407		•	•	•	•
				•	Four Corners Abstract	800-724-3668		•	•	•	
•	•			•	Monroe Title Insurance Corp (Rochester)	800-966-6763		•	•	•	
•	•	•	•	•	Northeast Investigations Inc [SOP]	888-796-1051		•	•	•	•
•	•	•	•	•	SearchLink LLC	716-873-8315		•	•	•	

DT	BK	CV	CR	PR	←Courts	Cattaraugus	Recording→	UC	RE	TX	VS
		•		•	Cattaraugus Abstract Corp	800-559-1242		•	•	•	
					Thomas E Corsi	716-863-7797			•		
•	•	•	•	•	SearchLink LLC	716-873-8315		•	•	•	

DT	BK	CV	CR	PR	←Courts	Cayuga	Recording→	UC	RE	TX	VS
		•		•	Central New York Abstract Corp	315-724-1614		•	•	•	
•	•	•	•	•	CMS (Consumer Marketing Services)	800-388-1365		•	•	•	
				•	Four Corners Abstract	800-724-3668		•	•	•	
•	•			•	Monroe Title Insurance Corp (Rochester)	800-966-6763		•	•	•	
•	•	•	•	•	Northeast Investigations Inc [SOP]	888-796-1051		•	•	•	•
•	•	•	•	•	SearchLink LLC	716-873-8315		•	•	•	
	•	•	•	•	Twenty Four Hour Record Retriever & Abstract Inc [SOP]	800-294-3740		•	•	•	

DT	BK	CV	CR	PR	←Courts	Chautauqua	Recording→	UC	RE	TX	VS
					Thomas E Corsi	716-863-7797			•		
•	•	•	•	•	SearchLink LLC	716-873-8315		•	•	•	

DT	BK	CV	CR	PR	←Courts	Chemung	Recording→	UC	RE	TX	VS
•	•	•	•	•	CMS (Consumer Marketing Services)	800-388-1365		•	•	•	
•	•			•	Monroe Title Insurance Corp (Rochester)	800-966-6763		•	•	•	
•	•	•	•	•	SearchLink LLC	716-873-8315		•	•	•	

DT	BK	CV	CR	PR	←Courts	Chenango	Recording→	UC	RE	TX	VS
•	•	•	•	•	CMS (Consumer Marketing Services)	800-388-1365		•	•	•	
				•	Four Corners Abstract	800-724-3668		•	•	•	
•	•	•	•	•	New Road Research	607-432-8911		•	•	•	
•	•	•	•	•	SearchLink LLC	716-873-8315		•	•	•	

DT	BK	CV	CR	PR	←Courts	Clinton	Recording→	UC	RE	TX	VS
•	•	•	•	•	SearchLink LLC	716-873-8315		•	•	•	

DT	BK	CV	CR	PR	←Courts	Columbia	Recording→	UC	RE	TX	VS
•	•	•			Attorney's Process & Research Service Inc [SOP]	800-640-7863		•	•	•	•
•	•	•	•	•	Blumberg Excelsior Corporate Services Inc [SOP]	800-999-0850		•	•	•	•
•	•	•	•	•	CMS (Consumer Marketing Services)	800-388-1365		•	•	•	
				•	Four Corners Abstract	800-724-3668		•	•	•	
		•	•	•	Onistagrawa Abstracting Corp	518-827-8088		•	•	•	
•	•	•	•	•	SearchLink LLC	716-873-8315		•	•	•	
•	•	•	•	•	Walsh Inv Services [SOP]	888-438-9757		•	•	•	•

DT	BK	CV	CR	PR	←Courts	Cortland	Recording→	UC	RE	TX	VS
•	•	•	•	•	CMS (Consumer Marketing Services)	800-388-1365		•	•	•	
•	•	•	•	•	Northeast Investigations Inc [SOP]	888-796-1051		•	•	•	•
•	•	•	•	•	SearchLink LLC	716-873-8315		•	•	•	

DT	BK	CV	CR	PR	←Courts	Delaware	Recording→	UC	RE	TX	VS
•	•	•	•	•	CMS (Consumer Marketing Services)	800-388-1365		•	•	•	
				•	Four Corners Abstract	800-724-3668		•	•	•	
•	•	•		•	Harry W Hawley Inc	607-746-3860		•	•	•	

DT	BK	CV	CR	PR	←Courts	Recording→	UC	RE	TX	VS
•	•	•	•	•	New Road Research	607-432-8911		•	•	
		•	•	•	Onistagrawa Abstracting Corp	518-827-8088	•	•	•	
•	•	•	•	•	SearchLink LLC	716-873-8315	•	•	•	

DT	BK	CV	CR	PR	←Courts **Dutchess**	Recording→	UC	RE	TX	VS
•	•	•	•	•	CMS (Consumer Marketing Services)	800-388-1365	•	•	•	
•	•	•	•	•	Court Explorers Inc [SOP]	212-608-1585	•	•	•	•
•	•	•	•	•	Fidelifacts	800-678-0007	•	•	•	•
		•	•	•	LaPrade Services Inc [SOP]	845-473-0468	•	•	•	•
•	•	•	•		Mills & Associates	845-744-4243	•	•	•	
•	•	•	•	•	Nationwide Court Services Inc [SOP]	888-941-1234	•	•	•	•
		•	•	•	Orange Paper Placers Inc [SOP]	845-294-7810	•	•	•	•
		•	•		PC Abstracting	845-699-6107	•	•	•	
•	•	•	•	•	Search NY Inc [SOP]	212-608-2546	•	•	•	•
•	•	•	•	•	SearchLink LLC	716-873-8315	•	•	•	
•	•	•	•	•	Walsh Inv Services [SOP]	888-438-9757	•	•	•	•
•	•	•	•	•	Washington Document Services (NY)	800-422-2776	•		•	

DT	BK	CV	CR	PR	←Courts **Erie**	Recording→	UC	RE	TX	VS
•	•	•	•	•	Action Services & Research Inc [SOP]	877-553-7504	•	•	•	•
•	•	•			Attorney's Process & Research Service Inc [SOP]	800-640-7863	•	•	•	•
•	•	•	•	•	CMS (Consumer Marketing Services)	800-388-1365	•	•	•	
					CMS Information Services	716-812-2587	•	•	•	•
					Thomas E Corsi	716-863-7797		•		
				•	Four Corners Abstract	800-724-3668	•	•	•	
•	•	•	•		G.A. Public Record Services Inc	800-760-2468				
•	•	•	•	•	Investigate-Claims.com [SOP]	716-689-6577	•	•	•	•
•	•	•	•		Mills & Associates	845-744-4243	•	•	•	
•	•			•	Monroe Title Insurance Corp (Rochester)	800-966-6763	•	•	•	
•	•	•	•	•	Northeast Investigations Inc [SOP]	888-796-1051	•	•	•	•
•	•	•	•	•	Paralegal Services of Buffalo	716-822-3279	•	•	•	•
	•		•		Past Records Inc	716-805-0418				
•	•	•	•		Philip D Smith & Associates [SOP]	716-631-2100	•		•	
•	•	•	•	•	SearchLink LLC	716-873-8315	•	•	•	
			•		Synerfax Inc	800-245-3013				
•	•	•	•	•	Tracers International (Albany) [SOP]	800-872-2377	•	•	•	•

DT	BK	CV	CR	PR	←Courts **Essex**	Recording→	UC	RE	TX	VS
•	•	•	•	•	SearchLink LLC	716-873-8315	•	•	•	

DT	BK	CV	CR	PR	←Courts **Franklin**	Recording→	UC	RE	TX	VS
				•	Etna Abstract Corp	518-483-7204	•	•	•	
•	•	•	•	•	SearchLink LLC	716-873-8315	•	•	•	

DT	BK	CV	CR	PR	←Courts **Fulton**	Recording→	UC	RE	TX	VS
•	•	•	•	•	CMS (Consumer Marketing Services)	800-388-1365	•	•	•	
		•	•	•	County Seat Abstract	518-762-3011	•	•	•	
•	•	•	•	•	Credit Control Inc/Resource Confidential [SOP]	800-886-7407	•	•	•	•
				•	Four Corners Abstract	800-724-3668	•	•	•	
•	•			•	Monroe Title Insurance Corp (Rochester)	800-966-6763	•	•	•	
		•	•	•	Onistagrawa Abstracting Corp	518-827-8088	•	•	•	
				•	Sacandaga Abstract Corp	518-773-2828	•	•	•	
•	•	•	•	•	SearchLink LLC	716-873-8315	•	•	•	

DT	BK	CV	CR	PR	←Courts **Genesee**	Recording→	UC	RE	TX	VS
•	•	•	•	•	CMS (Consumer Marketing Services)	800-388-1365	•	•	•	
					Thomas E Corsi	716-863-7797		•		
				•	Four Corners Abstract	800-724-3668	•	•	•	
•	•			•	Monroe Title Insurance Corp (Rochester)	800-966-6763	•	•	•	
•	•	•	•	•	SearchLink LLC	716-873-8315	•	•	•	

DT	BK	CV	CR	PR	←Courts	Greene	Recording→	UC	RE	TX	VS
●	●	●				Attorney's Process & Research Service Inc [SOP]	800-640-7863	●	●	●	●
●	●	●	●	●		Blumberg Excelsior Corporate Services Inc [SOP]	800-999-0850	●	●	●	●
●	●	●	●	●		CMS (Consumer Marketing Services)	800-388-1365	●	●	●	
				●		Four Corners Abstract	800-724-3668	●	●	●	
		●	●	●		Onistagrawa Abstracting Corp	518-827-8088	●	●	●	
●	●	●	●	●		SearchLink LLC	716-873-8315	●	●	●	

DT	BK	CV	CR	PR	←Courts	Hamilton	Recording→	UC	RE	TX	VS
		●	●	●		County Seat Abstract	518-762-3011	●	●	●	
●	●	●	●	●		SearchLink LLC	716-873-8315	●	●	●	

DT	BK	CV	CR	PR	←Courts	Herkimer	Recording→	UC	RE	TX	VS
		●		●		Central New York Abstract Corp	315-724-1614	●	●	●	
●	●	●	●	●		CMS (Consumer Marketing Services)	800-388-1365	●	●	●	
●	●	●	●	●		Credit Control Inc/Resource Confidential [SOP]	800-886-7407	●	●	●	●
				●		Four Corners Abstract	800-724-3668	●	●	●	
●	●	●	●	●		LegalWorks Inc [SOP]	800-853-6756	●	●	●	●
●	●			●		Monroe Title Insurance Corp (Rochester)	800-966-6763	●	●	●	
●	●	●	●	●		Northeast Investigations Inc [SOP]	888-796-1051	●	●	●	●
●	●	●	●	●		SearchLink LLC	716-873-8315	●	●	●	

DT	BK	CV	CR	PR	←Courts	Jefferson	Recording→	UC	RE	TX	VS
●	●	●	●	●		CMS (Consumer Marketing Services)	800-388-1365	●	●	●	
●	●	●	●	●		MS Document Services Inc	800-292-3868	●	●	●	●
●	●	●	●	●		Northeast Investigations Inc [SOP]	888-796-1051	●	●	●	●
●	●	●	●	●		SearchLink LLC	716-873-8315	●	●	●	
	●	●	●	●		Twenty Four Hour Record Retriever & Abstract Inc [SOP]	800-294-3740	●	●	●	

DT	BK	CV	CR	PR	←Courts	Kings	Recording→	UC	RE	TX	VS
●	●	●				Accurate Search Corporation	212-228-1850	●	●	●	
●	●	●	●	●		Alstate Process Service Inc [SOP]	631-667-1800	●	●	●	●
●	●					American Abstract	631-262-1826	●	●	●	●
●	●	●	●	●		ASSIST International [SOP]	800-382-7747	●	●	●	●
	●					Blumberg Excelsior Corporate Svcs Inc (NYC, NY)	800-221-2972	●		●	
●	●	●		●		Bridge Service Corp	800-225-2736	●	●	●	
●	●	●	●	●		Business Intelligence Inc [SOP]	516-938-1525 x107	●	●	●	●
●	●	●	●	●		Corporation Service Co - CSC (New York City)	800-221-0770	●	●	●	●
●	●	●	●	●		Court Explorers Inc [SOP]	212-608-1585	●	●	●	●
●	●	●	●	●		DLS (Demovsky Lawyer Service - New York) [SOP]	800-443-1058	●	●	●	●
						Document Retrieval Network Inc	859-654-2890	●	●	●	
●	●	●	●	●		Fidelifacts	800-678-0007	●	●	●	●
●	●	●	●			G.A. Public Record Services Inc	800-760-2468				
●	●	●	●	●		Inquisitive Research Corporation	732-321-0041	●	●	●	●
●	●	●	●	●		Introspect Investigations USA Inc [SOP]	800-847-7177	●	●	●	
●	●	●	●			Investigative Resources [SOP]	718-317-0043. 212-571-2500	●	●	●	
●	●	●		●		Keating & Walker [SOP]	800-466-2730				
●	●	●		●		LegalEase Inc [SOP]	800-393-1277			●	
	●					Mutual Abstract Corporation	212-964-4686	●	●	●	
●	●	●	●	●		Nationwide Court Services Inc [SOP]	888-941-1234	●	●	●	●
		●	●	●		Pallorium Inc [SOP]	212-969-0286		●	●	●
●	●	●	●	●		Search NY Inc [SOP]	212-608-2546	●	●	●	●
●	●	●	●	●		SearchLink LLC	716-873-8315	●	●	●	
						Deborah W Thompson	917-309-4830	●	●	●	
●	●	●	●	●		Tracers International (New York) [SOP]	800-872-2377	●	●	●	●
●	●	●	●	●		US Document Retrieval Service Inc	800-595-0145		●	●	●
●	●	●	●	●		Washington Document Services (NY)	800-422-2776	●		●	
●	●	●	●	●		Zook Search Inc	718-369-3879	●	●	●	

DT	BK	CV	CR	PR	←COURTS LEWIS RECORDING→		UC	RE	TX	VS
	•	•		•	National Abstract	800-535-3477	•	•	•	
•	•	•	•	•	Northeast Investigations Inc [SOP]	888-796-1051	•	•	•	•
•	•	•	•	•	SearchLink LLC	716-873-8315	•	•	•	

DT	BK	CV	CR	PR	←COURTS LIVINGSTON RECORDING→		UC	RE	TX	VS
•	•	•	•	•	CMS (Consumer Marketing Services)	800-388-1365	•	•	•	
					Thomas E Corsi	716-863-7797		•		
				•	Four Corners Abstract	800-724-3668	•	•	•	
•	•			•	Monroe Title Insurance Corp (Rochester)	800-966-6763	•	•	•	
•	•	•	•	•	SearchLink LLC	716-873-8315	•	•	•	

DT	BK	CV	CR	PR	←COURTS MADISON RECORDING→		UC	RE	TX	VS
		•		•	Central New York Abstract Corp	315-724-1614	•	•	•	
•	•	•	•	•	CMS (Consumer Marketing Services)	800-388-1365	•	•	•	
•	•	•	•	•	Credit Control Inc/Resource Confidential [SOP]	800-886-7407	•	•	•	•
				•	Four Corners Abstract	800-724-3668	•	•	•	
•	•	•	•	•	LegalWorks Inc [SOP]	800-853-6756	•	•	•	•
•	•			•	Monroe Title Insurance Corp (Rochester)	800-966-6763	•	•	•	
•	•	•	•	•	Northeast Investigations Inc [SOP]	888-796-1051	•	•	•	•
				•	Oneida Valley Abstract	315-363-1444	•	•	•	
•	•	•	•	•	SearchLink LLC	716-873-8315	•	•	•	

DT	BK	CV	CR	PR	←COURTS MONROE RECORDING→		UC	RE	TX	VS
•	•	•			Attorney's Process & Research Service Inc [SOP]	800-640-7863	•	•	•	•
•	•	•	•	•	Balkin Library & Information Services	585-482-1506	•	•	•	
•	•	•	•	•	CMS (Consumer Marketing Services)	800-388-1365	•	•	•	
					CMS Information Services	716-812-2587	•	•	•	•
				•	Four Corners Abstract	800-724-3668	•	•	•	
•	•	•	•	•	Legal Recording of Rochester Inc	585-232-6710	•	•	•	
•	•			•	Monroe Title Insurance Corp (Rochester)	800-966-6763	•	•	•	
•	•	•	•	•	MS Document Services Inc	800-292-3868	•	•	•	•
•	•	•	•	•	Northeast Investigations Inc [SOP]	888-796-1051	•	•	•	•
•	•	•	•		Philip D Smith & Associates [SOP]	716-631-2100	•		•	
•	•	•	•	•	SearchLink LLC	716-873-8315	•	•	•	
			•		Synerfax Inc	800-245-3013				
•	•	•	•	•	Tracers International (Albany) [SOP]	800-872-2377	•	•	•	•
	•	•	•	•	Twenty Four Hour Record Retriever & Abstract Inc [SOP]	800-294-3740	•	•	•	

DT	BK	CV	CR	PR	←COURTS MONTGOMERY RECORDING→		UC	RE	TX	VS
•	•	•	•	•	CMS (Consumer Marketing Services)	800-388-1365	•	•	•	
		•	•	•	County Seat Abstract	518-762-3011	•	•	•	
				•	Four Corners Abstract	800-724-3668	•	•	•	
•	•			•	Monroe Title Insurance Corp (Rochester)	800-966-6763	•	•	•	
		•	•	•	Onistagrawa Abstracting Corp	518-827-8088	•	•	•	
				•	Sacandaga Abstract Corp	518-773-2828	•	•	•	
•	•	•	•	•	SearchLink LLC	716-873-8315	•	•	•	

DT	BK	CV	CR	PR	←COURTS NASSAU RECORDING→		UC	RE	TX	VS
•	•	•	•	•	Alstate Process Service Inc [SOP]	631-667-1800	•	•	•	•
•	•				American Abstract	631-262-1826	•	•	•	•
•	•	•	•	•	Business Intelligence Inc [SOP]	516-938-1525 x107	•	•	•	•
					Contemporary Realty Solutions Inc	631-979-5677	•	•	•	
•	•	•	•	•	Court Explorers Inc [SOP]	212-608-1585	•	•	•	•
•	•	•	•	•	DLS (Demovsky Lawyer Service - New York) [SOP]	800-443-1058	•	•	•	•
					Document Retrieval Network Inc	859-654-2890	•	•	•	
•	•	•	•	•	Fidelifacts	800-678-0007	•	•	•	•
•	•	•	•	•	Gotcha Legal Process Service Inc [SOP]	800-698-2748	•	•	•	
•	•	•	•	•	Inquisitive Research Corporation	732-321-0041	•	•	•	•
•	•	•	•	•	Introspect Investigations USA Inc [SOP]	800-847-7177	•	•	•	

DT	BK	CV	CR	PR	Retriever	Phone	UC	RE	TX	VS
•	•	•	•		Investigative Resources [SOP]	718-317-0043. 212-571-2500	•	•	•	
•	•	•		•	Keating & Walker [SOP]	800-466-2730				
•	•	•		•	LegalEase Inc [SOP]	800-393-1277			•	
•	•	•	•	•	LIDA Credit Agency Inc [SOP]	516-678-4600	•	•	•	•
•	•	•	•		Mills & Associates	845-744-4243	•	•	•	
	•				Mutual Abstract Corporation	212-964-4686	•	•	•	
•	•	•	•	•	Nationwide Court Services Inc [SOP]	888-941-1234	•	•	•	•
		•	•	•	Pallorium Inc [SOP]	212-969-0286		•	•	•
•	•	•		•	PST Abstracting Inc	631-744-0759	•	•	•	
•	•	•	•	•	Search NY Inc [SOP]	212-608-2546	•	•	•	•
•	•	•	•	•	SearchLink LLC	716-873-8315	•	•	•	
•	•	•	•	•	Security Enforcement Inc [SOP]	800-924-2896 (NY)	•	•	•	•
•	•	•	•	•	Tracers International (New York) [SOP]	800-872-2377	•	•	•	•
•	•	•	•	•	US Document Retrieval Service Inc	800-595-0145		•	•	•
•	•	•	•	•	Washington Document Services (NY)	800-422-2776	•		•	

DT	BK	CV	CR	PR	←COURTS NEW YORK (MANHATTAN)	RECORDING→	UC	RE	TX	VS
•	•	•			Accurate Search Corporation	212-228-1850	•	•	•	
•	•	•	•	•	Alstate Process Service Inc [SOP]	631-667-1800	•	•	•	•
•	•				American Abstract	631-262-1826	•	•	•	•
•	•	•	•	•	ASSIST International [SOP]	800-382-7747	•	•	•	•
	•				Blumberg Excelsior Corporate Svcs Inc (NYC, NY)	800-221-2972	•		•	
•	•	•		•	Bridge Service Corp	800-225-2736	•	•	•	
•	•	•	•	•	Business Intelligence Inc [SOP]	516-938-1525 x107	•	•	•	•
•	•	•	•	•	Corporation Service Co - CSC (New York City)	800-221-0770	•	•	•	•
•	•	•	•	•	Court Explorers Inc [SOP]	212-608-1585	•	•	•	•
•	•	•	•	•	CourtEXPRESS (DC) [SOP]	800-542-3320				
•	•	•	•	•	DLS (Demovsky Lawyer Service - New York) [SOP]	800-443-1058	•	•	•	•
•	•	•	•	•	EHS Research Services [SOP]	914-472-5848	•	•	•	
•	•	•	•	•	Fidelifacts	800-678-0007	•	•	•	•
•	•	•	•		G.A. Public Record Services Inc	800-760-2468				
•	•	•	•	•	Inquisitive Research Corporation	732-321-0041	•	•	•	•
•	•	•	•	•	Introspect Investigations USA Inc [SOP]	800-847-7177	•	•	•	
•	•	•	•		Investigative Resources [SOP]	718-317-0043. 212-571-2500	•	•	•	
•	•	•		•	Keating & Walker [SOP]	800-466-2730				
•	•	•		•	LegalEase Inc [SOP]	800-393-1277			•	
	•				Mutual Abstract Corporation	212-964-4686	•	•	•	
•	•	•	•	•	Nationwide Court Services Inc [SOP]	888-941-1234	•	•	•	•
		•	•	•	Pallorium Inc [SOP]	212-969-0286		•	•	•
•	•	•	•	•	Search NY Inc [SOP]	212-608-2546	•	•	•	•
•	•	•	•	•	SearchLink LLC	716-873-8315	•	•	•	
					Deborah W Thompson	917-309-4830	•	•	•	
•	•	•	•	•	Tracers International (New York) [SOP]	800-872-2377	•	•	•	•
•	•	•	•	•	Washington Document Services (NY)	800-422-2776	•		•	
•	•	•	•	•	Zook Search Inc	718-369-3879	•	•	•	

DT	BK	CV	CR	PR	←COURTS NIAGARA	RECORDING→	UC	RE	TX	VS
•	•	•	•	•	Action Services & Research Inc [SOP]	877-553-7504	•	•	•	•
•	•	•	•	•	CMS (Consumer Marketing Services)	800-388-1365	•	•	•	
					CMS Information Services	716-812-2587	•	•	•	•
					Thomas E Corsi	716-863-7797		•		
				•	Four Corners Abstract	800-724-3668	•	•	•	
•	•	•	•	•	Investigate-Claims.com [SOP]	716-689-6577	•	•	•	•
•	•			•	Monroe Title Insurance Corp (Rochester)	800-966-6763	•	•	•	
•	•	•	•	•	Paralegal Services of Buffalo	716-822-3279	•	•	•	•
	•		•		Past Records Inc	716-805-0418				
•	•	•	•		Philip D Smith & Associates [SOP]	716-631-2100	•		•	
•	•	•	•	•	SearchLink LLC	716-873-8315	•	•	•	
			•		Synerfax Inc	800-245-3013				

DT	BK	CV	CR	PR	←Courts	ONEIDA	Recording→	UC	RE	TX	VS
		•		•		Central New York Abstract Corp	315-724-1614	•	•	•	
•	•	•	•	•		CMS (Consumer Marketing Services)	800-388-1365	•	•	•	
•	•	•	•	•		Credit Control Inc/Resource Confidential [SOP]	800-886-7407	•	•	•	•
				•		Four Corners Abstract	800-724-3668	•	•	•	
•	•	•	•	•		LegalWorks Inc [SOP]	800-853-6756	•	•	•	•
•	•	•	•	•		Midstate Legal Support Services [SOP]	315-797-8609	•	•	•	•
•	•			•		Monroe Title Insurance Corp (Rochester)	800-966-6763	•	•	•	
•	•	•	•	•		Northeast Investigations Inc [SOP]	888-796-1051	•	•	•	•
•	•	•	•	•		Shirley Perrone	315-733-6126			•	
•	•	•	•	•		SearchLink LLC	716-873-8315	•	•	•	

DT	BK	CV	CR	PR	←Courts	ONONDAGA	Recording→	UC	RE	TX	VS
•	•	•				Attorney's Process & Research Service Inc [SOP]	800-640-7863	•	•	•	•
•	•	•	•	•		CMS (Consumer Marketing Services)	800-388-1365	•	•	•	
•	•	•	•	•		Credit Control Inc/Resource Confidential [SOP]	800-886-7407	•	•	•	•
				•		Four Corners Abstract	800-724-3668	•	•	•	
•	•	•	•			Merola Services	219-878-9699	•	•	•	•
•	•			•		Monroe Title Insurance Corp (Rochester)	800-966-6763	•	•	•	
•	•	•	•	•		MS Document Services Inc	800-292-3868	•	•	•	•
•	•	•	•	•		Northeast Investigations Inc [SOP]	888-796-1051	•	•	•	•
	•			•		Ryco Information Services Inc	800-240-7926	•	•	•	
•	•	•	•	•		SearchLink LLC	716-873-8315	•	•	•	
			•			Synerfax Inc	800-245-3013				
•	•	•	•	•		Tracers International (Albany) [SOP]	800-872-2377	•	•	•	•
	•	•	•	•		Twenty Four Hour Record Retriever & Abstract Inc [SOP]	800-294-3740	•	•	•	

DT	BK	CV	CR	PR	←Courts	ONTARIO	Recording→	UC	RE	TX	VS
•	•	•	•	•		CMS (Consumer Marketing Services)	800-388-1365	•	•	•	
				•		Four Corners Abstract	800-724-3668	•	•	•	
•	•			•		Monroe Title Insurance Corp (Rochester)	800-966-6763	•	•	•	
•	•	•	•	•		SearchLink LLC	716-873-8315	•	•	•	
			•			Synerfax Inc	800-245-3013				

DT	BK	CV	CR	PR	←Courts	ORANGE	Recording→	UC	RE	TX	VS
•	•	•	•	•		ASSIST International [SOP]	800-382-7747	•	•	•	•
•	•	•	•	•		Attorney Service Bureau [SOP]	845-638-1323	•	•	•	•
•	•	•	•	•		CMS (Consumer Marketing Services)	800-388-1365	•	•	•	
•	•	•	•	•		Court Explorers Inc [SOP]	212-608-1585	•	•	•	•
•	•	•	•	•		Fidelifacts	800-678-0007	•	•	•	•
						Hill-N-Dale Abstracters Inc	845-294-5110		•		
		•	•	•		LaPrade Services Inc [SOP]	845-473-0468	•	•	•	•
•	•	•	•	•		Mills & Associates	845-744-4243	•	•	•	
•	•	•	•	•		Nationwide Court Services Inc [SOP]	888-941-1234	•	•	•	•
•	•	•	•	•		Orange Abstractor Services Co	845-294-3331	•	•	•	
		•	•	•		Orange Paper Placers Inc [SOP]	845-294-7810	•	•	•	•
		•	•			PC Abstracting	845-699-6107	•	•	•	
•	•	•	•	•		Search NY Inc [SOP]	212-608-2546	•	•	•	•
•	•	•	•	•		SearchLink LLC	716-873-8315	•	•	•	
•	•	•	•	•		US Document Retrieval Service Inc	800-595-0145		•	•	•
•	•	•	•	•		Walsh Inv Services [SOP]	888-438-9757	•	•	•	•

DT	BK	CV	CR	PR	←Courts	ORLEANS	Recording→	UC	RE	TX	VS
•	•	•	•	•		CMS (Consumer Marketing Services)	800-388-1365	•	•	•	
						Thomas E Corsi	716-863-7797		•		
				•		Four Corners Abstract	800-724-3668	•	•	•	
•	•			•		Monroe Title Insurance Corp (Rochester)	800-966-6763	•	•	•	
•	•	•	•	•		SearchLink LLC	716-873-8315	•	•	•	

DT	BK	CV	CR	PR	←Courts OSWEGO Recording→		UC	RE	TX	VS
•	•	•	•	•	CMS (Consumer Marketing Services)	800-388-1365	•	•	•	
•	•	•	•	•	Credit Control Inc/Resource Confidential [SOP]	800-886-7407	•	•	•	•
				•	Four Corners Abstract	800-724-3668	•	•	•	
•	•			•	Monroe Title Insurance Corp (Rochester)	800-966-6763	•	•	•	
•	•	•	•	•	MS Document Services Inc	800-292-3868	•	•	•	•
•	•	•	•	•	Northeast Investigations Inc [SOP]	888-796-1051	•	•	•	•
•	•	•	•	•	SearchLink LLC	716-873-8315	•	•	•	
	•	•	•	•	Twenty Four Hour Record Retriever & Abstract Inc [SOP]	800-294-3740	•	•	•	

DT	BK	CV	CR	PR	←Courts OTSEGO Recording→		UC	RE	TX	VS
•	•	•	•	•	CMS (Consumer Marketing Services)	800-388-1365	•	•	•	
•	•			•	Monroe Title Insurance Corp (Rochester)	800-966-6763	•	•	•	
•	•	•	•	•	New Road Research	607-432-8911		•	•	
		•	•	•	Onistagrawa Abstracting Corp	518-827-8088	•	•	•	
•	•	•	•	•	SearchLink LLC	716-873-8315	•	•	•	

DT	BK	CV	CR	PR	←Courts PUTNAM Recording→		UC	RE	TX	VS
•	•	•	•	•	ASSIST International [SOP]	800-382-7747	•	•	•	•
•	•	•	•	•	CMS (Consumer Marketing Services)	800-388-1365	•	•	•	
•	•	•	•	•	EHS Research Services [SOP]	914-472-5848	•	•	•	
•	•	•	•	•	Fidelifacts	800-678-0007	•	•	•	•
		•	•	•	LaPrade Services Inc [SOP]	845-473-0468	•	•	•	•
•	•	•	•		Mills & Associates	845-744-4243	•	•	•	
•	•	•	•	•	Nationwide Court Services Inc [SOP]	888-941-1234	•	•	•	•
		•	•	•	Orange Paper Placers Inc [SOP]	845-294-7810	•	•	•	•
•	•	•	•	•	SearchLink LLC	716-873-8315	•	•	•	
•	•	•	•	•	Tracers International (New York) [SOP]	800-872-2377	•	•	•	•
•	•	•	•	•	Walsh Inv Services [SOP]	888-438-9757	•	•	•	•

DT	BK	CV	CR	PR	←Courts QUEENS Recording→		UC	RE	TX	VS
•	•	•			Accurate Search Corporation	212-228-1850	•	•	•	
•	•	•	•	•	Alstate Process Service Inc [SOP]	631-667-1800	•	•	•	•
•	•				American Abstract	631-262-1826	•	•	•	•
•	•	•	•	•	ASSIST International [SOP]	800-382-7747	•	•	•	•
	•				Blumberg Excelsior Corporate Svcs Inc (NYC, NY)	800-221-2972	•		•	
•	•	•		•	Bridge Service Corp	800-225-2736	•	•	•	
•	•	•	•	•	Business Intelligence Inc [SOP]	516-938-1525 x107	•	•	•	•
•	•	•	•	•	Corporation Service Co - CSC (New York City)	800-221-0770	•	•	•	•
•	•	•	•	•	Court Explorers Inc [SOP]	212-608-1585	•	•	•	•
•	•	•	•	•	DLS (Demovsky Lawyer Service - New York) [SOP]	800-443-1058	•	•	•	•
					Document Retrieval Network Inc	859-654-2890	•	•	•	
•	•	•	•	•	Fidelifacts	800-678-0007	•	•	•	•
•	•	•	•		G.A. Public Record Services Inc	800-760-2468				
•	•	•	•	•	Inquisitive Research Corporation	732-321-0041	•	•	•	•
•	•	•	•	•	Introspect Investigations USA Inc [SOP]	800-847-7177	•	•	•	
•	•	•	•		Investigative Resources [SOP]	718-317-0043. 212-571-2500	•	•	•	
•	•	•		•	Keating & Walker [SOP]	800-466-2730				
•	•	•		•	LegalEase Inc [SOP]	800-393-1277			•	
•	•	•	•	•	LIDA Credit Agency Inc [SOP]	516-678-4600	•	•	•	•
	•				Mutual Abstract Corporation	212-964-4686	•	•	•	
•	•	•	•	•	Nationwide Court Services Inc [SOP]	888-941-1234	•	•	•	•
		•	•	•	Pallorium Inc [SOP]	212-969-0286	•	•	•	•
•	•	•	•	•	Search NY Inc [SOP]	212-608-2546	•	•	•	•
•	•	•	•	•	SearchLink LLC	716-873-8315	•	•	•	
					Deborah W Thompson	917-309-4830	•	•	•	
•	•	•	•	•	Tracers International (New York) [SOP]	800-872-2377	•	•	•	•
•	•	•	•	•	US Document Retrieval Service Inc	800-595-0145		•	•	•
•	•	•	•	•	Washington Document Services (NY)	800-422-2776	•		•	

DT	BK	CV	CR	PR	←Courts	Recording→	UC	RE	TX	VS
•	•	•	•	•	Zook Search Inc	718-369-3879	•	•	•	

DT	BK	CV	CR	PR	←Courts RENSSELAER	Recording→	UC	RE	TX	VS
•	•	•	•		Access Information Services Inc [SOP]	800-388-1598	•	•	•	
•	•	•			Attorney's Process & Research Service Inc [SOP]	800-640-7863	•	•	•	•
•	•	•	•	•	Blumberg Excelsior Corporate Services Inc [SOP]	800-999-0850	•	•	•	•
•	•				Capitol Services Inc (New York)	800-662-0171	•		•	
•	•	•	•	•	CMS (Consumer Marketing Services)	800-388-1365	•	•	•	
•	•	•	•	•	Credit Control Inc/Resource Confidential [SOP]	800-886-7407	•	•	•	•
•	•	•	•	•	DLS (Demovsky Lawyer Service - Albany) [SOP]	518-449-8411	•	•	•	
•	•	•			Forbes Public Research Inc	518-732-2841	•	•	•	
				•	Four Corners Abstract	800-724-3668	•	•	•	
•	•			•	Lightning Legal Services LLC [SOP]	518-463-1049	•		•	•
•	•				Monroe Title Insurance Corp (Albany)	800-966-6763	•	•	•	
•	•			•	Monroe Title Insurance Corp (Rochester)	800-966-6763	•	•	•	
•	•	•	•	•	Relyea Services Inc [SOP]	800-854-4111	•	•	•	•
•	•	•	•	•	SearchLink LLC	716-873-8315	•	•	•	
•	•	•	•	•	Tracers International (Albany) [SOP]	800-872-2377	•	•	•	•
•	•	•	•	•	Tracers International (Schenectady) [SOP]	800-872-2377	•	•	•	•
•	•	•			Zap! Courier Service	518-449-3361				

DT	BK	CV	CR	PR	←Courts RICHMOND	Recording→	UC	RE	TX	VS
•	•	•			Accurate Search Corporation	212-228-1850	•	•	•	
•	•	•	•	•	Alstate Process Service Inc [SOP]	631-667-1800	•	•	•	•
•	•				American Abstract	631-262-1826	•	•	•	•
•	•	•	•	•	ASSIST International [SOP]	800-382-7747	•	•	•	•
	•				Blumberg Excelsior Corporate Svcs Inc (NYC, NY)	800-221-2972	•		•	
•	•	•	•	•	Court Explorers Inc [SOP]	212-608-1585	•	•	•	•
•	•	•	•	•	DLS (Demovsky Lawyer Service - New York) [SOP]	800-443-1058	•	•	•	•
•	•	•	•	•	Fidelifacts	800-678-0007	•	•	•	•
•	•	•	•	•	Inquisitive Research Corporation	732-321-0041	•	•	•	•
•	•	•	•		Investigative Resources [SOP]	718-317-0043. 212-571-2500	•	•	•	
•	•	•		•	Keating & Walker [SOP]	800-466-2730				
•	•	•	•	•	Nationwide Court Services Inc [SOP]	888-941-1234	•	•	•	•
		•	•	•	Pallorium Inc [SOP]	212-969-0286		•	•	•
•	•	•	•	•	Search NY Inc [SOP]	212-608-2546	•	•	•	•
•	•	•	•	•	SearchLink LLC	716-873-8315	•	•	•	
•	•	•	•	•	Tracers International (New York) [SOP]	800-872-2377	•	•	•	•
•	•	•	•	•	US Document Retrieval Service Inc	800-595-0145		•	•	•
•	•	•	•	•	Washington Document Services (NY)	800-422-2776	•		•	

DT	BK	CV	CR	PR	←Courts ROCKLAND	Recording→	UC	RE	TX	VS
•	•	•	•	•	ASSIST International [SOP]	800-382-7747	•	•	•	•
•	•	•	•	•	Attorney Service Bureau [SOP]	845-638-1323	•	•	•	•
•	•	•	•	•	DLS (Demovsky Lawyer Service - New York) [SOP]	800-443-1058	•	•	•	•
•	•	•	•	•	EHS Research Services [SOP]	914-472-5848	•	•	•	
•	•	•	•	•	Fidelifacts	800-678-0007	•	•	•	•
		•	•	•	Marilyn Smolinsky & Associates	845-634-5770	•	•		
•	•	•	•		Mills & Associates	845-744-4243	•	•	•	
•	•	•	•	•	Nationwide Court Services Inc [SOP]	888-941-1234	•	•	•	•
		•	•	•	Orange Paper Placers Inc [SOP]	845-294-7810	•	•	•	•
		•	•		PC Abstracting	845-699-6107	•	•	•	
•	•	•	•	•	Search NY Inc [SOP]	212-608-2546	•	•	•	•
•	•	•	•	•	SearchLink LLC	716-873-8315	•	•	•	
•	•	•	•	•	Tracers International (New York) [SOP]	800-872-2377	•	•	•	•
•	•	•	•	•	US Document Retrieval Service Inc	800-595-0145		•	•	•
•	•	•	•	•	Walsh Inv Services [SOP]	888-438-9757	•	•	•	•
•	•	•	•	•	Washington Document Services (NY)	800-422-2776	•		•	
•	•	•	•	•	Westchester Court Services-Fox Advertising Inc [SOP]	914-948-5200	•		•	

DT	BK	CV	CR	PR	←Courts — SARATOGA	Recording→	UC	RE	TX	VS
•	•	•	•		Access Information Services Inc [SOP]	800-388-1598	•	•	•	
•	•	•	•	•	CMS (Consumer Marketing Services)	800-388-1365	•	•	•	
•	•	•	•	•	Credit Control Inc/Resource Confidential [SOP]	800-886-7407	•	•	•	•
•	•	•			Forbes Public Research Inc	518-732-2841	•	•	•	
				•	Four Corners Abstract	800-724-3668	•	•	•	
•	•			•	Lightning Legal Services LLC [SOP]	518-463-1049	•		•	•
•	•			•	Monroe Title Insurance Corp (Rochester)	800-966-6763	•	•	•	
•	•	•	•	•	Relyea Services Inc [SOP]	800-854-4111	•	•	•	•
•	•	•	•	•	SearchLink LLC	716-873-8315	•	•	•	
•	•	•	•	•	Tracers International (Albany) [SOP]	800-872-2377	•	•	•	•
•	•	•	•	•	Tracers International (Schenectady) [SOP]	800-872-2377	•	•	•	•
•	•	•			Zap! Courier Service	518-449-3361				

DT	BK	CV	CR	PR	←Courts — SCHENECTADY	Recording→	UC	RE	TX	VS
•	•	•	•		Access Information Services Inc [SOP]	800-388-1598	•	•	•	
•	•	•			Attorney's Process & Research Service Inc [SOP]	800-640-7863	•	•	•	•
•	•	•	•	•	Blumberg Excelsior Corporate Services Inc [SOP]	800-999-0850	•	•	•	•
•	•	•	•	•	CMS (Consumer Marketing Services)	800-388-1365	•	•	•	
•	•	•	•	•	Credit Control Inc/Resource Confidential [SOP]	800-886-7407	•	•	•	•
•	•	•	•	•	DLS (Demovsky Lawyer Service - Albany) [SOP]	518-449-8411	•	•	•	
•	•	•			Forbes Public Research Inc	518-732-2841	•	•	•	
				•	Four Corners Abstract	800-724-3668	•	•	•	
•	•			•	Lightning Legal Services LLC [SOP]	518-463-1049	•		•	•
•	•			•	Monroe Title Insurance Corp (Rochester)	800-966-6763	•	•	•	
		•	•	•	Onistagrawa Abstracting Corp	518-827-8088	•	•	•	
•	•	•	•	•	Relyea Services Inc [SOP]	800-854-4111	•	•	•	•
•	•	•	•	•	SearchLink LLC	716-873-8315	•	•	•	
		•	•	•	Servico Inc [SOP]	518-463-4179	•		•	
•	•	•	•	•	Tracers International (Schenectady) [SOP]	800-872-2377	•	•	•	•
•	•	•			Zap! Courier Service	518-449-3361				

DT	BK	CV	CR	PR	←Courts — SCHOHARIE	Recording→	UC	RE	TX	VS
•	•	•	•	•	CMS (Consumer Marketing Services)	800-388-1365	•	•	•	
•	•			•	Monroe Title Insurance Corp (Rochester)	800-966-6763	•	•	•	
		•	•	•	Onistagrawa Abstracting Corp	518-827-8088	•	•	•	
•	•	•	•	•	SearchLink LLC	716-873-8315	•	•	•	
•	•	•	•	•	Tracers International (Schenectady) [SOP]	800-872-2377	•	•	•	•

DT	BK	CV	CR	PR	←Courts — SCHUYLER	Recording→	UC	RE	TX	VS
•	•	•	•	•	CMS (Consumer Marketing Services)	800-388-1365	•	•	•	
•	•			•	Monroe Title Insurance Corp (Rochester)	800-966-6763	•	•	•	
•	•	•	•	•	SearchLink LLC	716-873-8315	•	•	•	

DT	BK	CV	CR	PR	←Courts — SENECA	Recording→	UC	RE	TX	VS
•	•	•	•	•	CMS (Consumer Marketing Services)	800-388-1365	•	•	•	
				•	Four Corners Abstract	800-724-3668	•	•	•	
•	•			•	Monroe Title Insurance Corp (Rochester)	800-966-6763	•	•	•	
•	•	•	•	•	SearchLink LLC	716-873-8315	•	•	•	

DT	BK	CV	CR	PR	←Courts — ST. LAWRENCE	Recording→	UC	RE	TX	VS
•	•	•	•	•	CMS (Consumer Marketing Services)	800-388-1365	•	•	•	
•	•	•	•	•	SearchLink LLC	716-873-8315	•	•	•	

DT	BK	CV	CR	PR	←Courts — STEUBEN	Recording→	UC	RE	TX	VS
•	•	•	•	•	CMS (Consumer Marketing Services)	800-388-1365	•	•	•	
•	•			•	Monroe Title Insurance Corp (Rochester)	800-966-6763	•	•	•	
•	•	•	•	•	SearchLink LLC	716-873-8315	•	•	•	

DT	BK	CV	CR	PR	←Courts	SUFFOLK	Recording→	UC	RE	TX	VS
•	•	•	•	•	Alstate Process Service Inc [SOP]		631-667-1800	•	•	•	•
•	•				American Abstract		631-262-1826	•	•	•	•
•	•	•	•	•	ASSIST International [SOP]		800-382-7747	•	•	•	•
•	•	•	•	•	Business Intelligence Inc [SOP]		516-938-1525 x107	•	•	•	•
					Contemporary Realty Solutions Inc		631-979-5677	•	•	•	
•	•	•	•	•	Court Explorers Inc [SOP]		212-608-1585	•	•	•	•
					Document Retrieval Network Inc		859-654-2890	•	•	•	
•	•	•	•	•	Fidelifacts		800-678-0007	•	•	•	•
•	•	•	•		G.A. Public Record Services Inc		800-760-2468				
•	•	•	•	•	Gotcha Legal Process Service Inc [SOP]		800-698-2748	•	•	•	
•	•	•	•	•	Inquisitive Research Corporation		732-321-0041	•	•	•	•
•	•	•	•		Investigative Resources [SOP]		718-317-0043. 212-571-2500	•	•	•	
•	•	•	•	•	LIDA Credit Agency Inc [SOP]		516-678-4600	•	•	•	•
•	•	•	•		Mills & Associates		845-744-4243	•	•	•	
•	•	•	•	•	Nationwide Court Services Inc [SOP]		888-941-1234	•	•	•	•
		•	•	•	Pallorium Inc [SOP]		212-969-0286		•	•	•
•	•	•		•	PST Abstracting Inc		631-744-0759	•	•	•	
					Reda's Attorney Service		631-331-0700	•	•	•	
•	•	•	•	•	Search NY Inc [SOP]		212-608-2546	•	•	•	•
•	•	•	•	•	SearchLink LLC		716-873-8315	•	•	•	
•	•	•	•	•	Security Enforcement Inc [SOP]		800-924-2896 (NY)	•	•	•	•
		•	•		Donna Stovall [SOP]		631-744-5834	•	•	•	
•	•	•	•	•	Tracers International (New York) [SOP]		800-872-2377	•	•	•	•
•	•	•	•	•	US Document Retrieval Service Inc		800-595-0145		•	•	•
•	•	•	•	•	Washington Document Services (NY)		800-422-2776	•		•	

DT	BK	CV	CR	PR	←Courts	SULLIVAN	Recording→	UC	RE	TX	VS
•	•	•	•	•	CMS (Consumer Marketing Services)		800-388-1365	•	•	•	
					Hill-N-Dale Abstracters Inc		845-294-5110		•		
		•	•	•	Orange Paper Placers Inc [SOP]		845-294-7810	•	•	•	•
		•	•		PC Abstracting		845-699-6107	•	•	•	
•	•	•	•	•	SearchLink LLC		716-873-8315	•	•	•	
•	•	•	•	•	Walsh Inv Services [SOP]		888-438-9757	•	•	•	•

DT	BK	CV	CR	PR	←Courts	TIOGA	Recording→	UC	RE	TX	VS
•	•	•	•	•	CMS (Consumer Marketing Services)		800-388-1365	•	•	•	
				•	Four Corners Abstract		800-724-3668	•	•	•	
•	•			•	Monroe Title Insurance Corp (Rochester)		800-966-6763	•	•	•	
•	•	•	•	•	SearchLink LLC		716-873-8315	•	•	•	

DT	BK	CV	CR	PR	←Courts	TOMPKINS	Recording→	UC	RE	TX	VS
•	•	•	•	•	CMS (Consumer Marketing Services)		800-388-1365	•	•	•	
•	•			•	Monroe Title Insurance Corp (Rochester)		800-966-6763	•	•	•	
•	•	•	•	•	SearchLink LLC		716-873-8315	•	•	•	

DT	BK	CV	CR	PR	←Courts	ULSTER	Recording→	UC	RE	TX	VS
•	•	•	•	•	CMS (Consumer Marketing Services)		800-388-1365	•	•	•	
		•	•	•	Data-Find		845-246-3263	•	•	•	
•	•	•	•	•	Fidelifacts		800-678-0007	•	•	•	•
					Hill-N-Dale Abstracters Inc		845-294-5110		•		
		•	•	•	LaPrade Services Inc [SOP]		845-473-0468	•	•	•	•
		•	•	•	Orange Paper Placers Inc [SOP]		845-294-7810	•	•	•	•
		•	•		PC Abstracting		845-699-6107	•	•	•	
		•	•	•	Ranger Recovery [SOP]		845-679-2957	•	•	•	•
•	•	•	•	•	SearchLink LLC		716-873-8315	•	•	•	
•	•	•	•	•	Walsh Inv Services [SOP]		888-438-9757	•	•	•	•

DT	BK	CV	CR	PR	←Courts	WARREN	Recording→	UC	RE	TX	VS
•	•	•			Attorney's Process & Research Service Inc [SOP]		800-640-7863	•	•	•	•

DT	BK	CV	CR	PR	Retriever	Phone	UC	RE	TX	VS
•	•	•	•	•	Credit Control Inc/Resource Confidential [SOP]	800-886-7407	•	•	•	•
•	•	•			Forbes Public Research Inc	518-732-2841	•	•	•	
•	•			•	Monroe Title Insurance Corp (Rochester)	800-966-6763	•	•	•	
•	•	•	•	•	SearchLink LLC	716-873-8315	•	•	•	
•	•	•	•	•	Tracers International (Albany) [SOP]	800-872-2377	•	•	•	•

DT	BK	CV	CR	PR	←Courts **Washington**	Recording→	UC	RE	TX	VS
•	•	•			Attorney's Process & Research Service Inc [SOP]	800-640-7863	•	•	•	•
•	•	•	•	•	Credit Control Inc/Resource Confidential [SOP]	800-886-7407	•	•	•	•
•	•			•	Monroe Title Insurance Corp (Rochester)	800-966-6763	•	•	•	
•	•	•	•	•	SearchLink LLC	716-873-8315	•	•	•	
•	•	•	•	•	Tracers International (Albany) [SOP]	800-872-2377	•	•	•	•

DT	BK	CV	CR	PR	←Courts **Wayne**	Recording→	UC	RE	TX	VS
•	•	•	•	•	CMS (Consumer Marketing Services)	800-388-1365	•	•	•	
				•	Four Corners Abstract	800-724-3668	•	•	•	
•	•			•	Monroe Title Insurance Corp (Rochester)	800-966-6763	•	•	•	
•	•	•	•	•	SearchLink LLC	716-873-8315	•	•	•	
			•		Synerfax Inc	800-245-3013				

DT	BK	CV	CR	PR	←Courts **Westchester**	Recording→	UC	RE	TX	VS
•	•				American Abstract	631-262-1826	•	•	•	•
•	•	•	•	•	ASSIST International [SOP]	800-382-7747	•	•	•	•
•	•	•	•	•	Attorney Service Bureau [SOP]	845-638-1323	•	•	•	•
•	•	•	•	•	Business Intelligence Inc [SOP]	516-938-1525 x107	•	•	•	•
•	•	•	•	•	CMS (Consumer Marketing Services)	800-388-1365	•	•	•	
•	•	•	•	•	Court Explorers Inc [SOP]	212-608-1585	•	•	•	•
•	•	•	•	•	DLS (Demovsky Lawyer Service - New York) [SOP]	800-443-1058	•	•	•	•
•	•	•	•	•	EHS Research Services [SOP]	914-472-5848	•	•	•	
•	•	•	•	•	Fidelifacts	800-678-0007	•	•	•	•
•	•	•	•	•	Inquisitive Research Corporation	732-321-0041	•	•	•	•
•	•	•	•		Investigative Resources [SOP]	718-317-0043, 212-571-2500	•	•	•	
•	•	•		•	Keating & Walker [SOP]	800-466-2730				
•	•	•		•	LegalEase Inc [SOP]	800-393-1277			•	
•	•	•	•		Mills & Associates	845-744-4243	•	•	•	
	•				Mutual Abstract Corporation	212-964-4686	•	•	•	
•	•	•	•	•	Nationwide Court Services Inc [SOP]	888-941-1234	•	•	•	•
		•	•	•	Pallorium Inc [SOP]	212-969-0286		•	•	•
		•	•		PC Abstracting	845-699-6107	•	•	•	
•	•	•	•	•	Search NY Inc [SOP]	212-608-2546	•	•	•	•
•	•	•	•	•	SearchLink LLC	716-873-8315	•	•	•	
					Deborah W Thompson	917-309-4830	•	•	•	
•	•	•	•	•	Tracers International (New York) [SOP]	800-872-2377	•	•	•	•
•	•	•	•	•	US Document Retrieval Service Inc	800-595-0145		•	•	•
•	•	•	•	•	Walsh Inv Services [SOP]	888-438-9757	•	•	•	•
•	•	•	•	•	Washington Document Services (NY)	800-422-2776	•		•	
•	•	•	•	•	Westchester Court Services-Fox Advertising Inc [SOP]	914-948-5200	•		•	

DT	BK	CV	CR	PR	←Courts **Wyoming**	Recording→	UC	RE	TX	VS
•	•	•	•	•	CMS (Consumer Marketing Services)	800-388-1365	•	•	•	
					Thomas E Corsi	716-863-7797		•		
•	•			•	Monroe Title Insurance Corp (Rochester)	800-966-6763	•	•	•	
•	•	•	•	•	SearchLink LLC	716-873-8315	•	•	•	

DT	BK	CV	CR	PR	←Courts **Yates**	Recording→	UC	RE	TX	VS
•	•	•	•	•	CMS (Consumer Marketing Services)	800-388-1365	•	•	•	
				•	Four Corners Abstract	800-724-3668	•	•	•	
•	•			•	Monroe Title Insurance Corp (Rochester)	800-966-6763	•	•	•	
•	•	•	•	•	SearchLink LLC	716-873-8315	•	•	•	

North Carolina

COURT RECORDS RETRIEVED						RECORDING RECORDS RETRIEVED				
DT	BK	CV	CR	PR	←COURTS **ALAMANCE**	RECORDING→	UC	RE	TX	VS
•	•	•	•	•	Central Carolina Process Service [SOP]	919-776-7584	•	•	•	•
		•	•		Intercoastal Research & Inv	843-280-4461				
•	•	•	•	•	NC Corporate Connection Inc	888-844-8360	•	•	•	•
•	•	•	•		Origin Information & Services Inc (NC)	800-940-1755	•	•	•	
•	•	•	•	•	Paralegal Services of North Carolina Inc [SOP]	919-821-7762	•	•	•	•
•	•	•	•	•	Searchtec (Carolinas) [SOP]	800-528-8790	•	•	•	•
DT	BK	CV	CR	PR	←COURTS **ALEXANDER**	RECORDING→	UC	RE	TX	VS
•	•	•	•		Origin Information & Services Inc (NC)	800-940-1755	•	•	•	
•	•	•	•	•	Track' Um Private Investigations [SOP]	336-903-1700	•	•		•
DT	BK	CV	CR	PR	←COURTS **ALLEGHANY**	RECORDING→	UC	RE	TX	VS
•	•	•	•		Origin Information & Services Inc (NC)	800-940-1755	•	•	•	
•	•	•	•	•	Searchtec (Carolinas) [SOP]	800-528-8790	•	•	•	•
•	•	•	•	•	Track' Um Private Investigations [SOP]	336-903-1700	•	•	•	•
DT	BK	CV	CR	PR	←COURTS **ANSON**	RECORDING→	UC	RE	TX	VS
•	•	•	•	•	Central Carolina Process Service [SOP]	919-776-7584	•	•	•	•
•	•	•	•		Origin Information & Services Inc (NC)	800-940-1755	•	•	•	
•	•	•	•	•	Searchtec (Carolinas) [SOP]	800-528-8790	•	•	•	•
DT	BK	CV	CR	PR	←COURTS **ASHE**	RECORDING→	UC	RE	TX	VS
		•		•	Miller & Johnson PLLC	828-264-1125	•	•	•	
•	•	•	•		Origin Information & Services Inc (NC)	800-940-1755	•	•	•	
•	•	•	•	•	Searchtec (Carolinas) [SOP]	800-528-8790	•	•	•	•
•	•	•	•	•	Track' Um Private Investigations [SOP]	336-903-1700	•	•	•	•
DT	BK	CV	CR	PR	←COURTS **AVERY**	RECORDING→	UC	RE	TX	VS
		•		•	Miller & Johnson PLLC	828-264-1125	•	•	•	
•	•	•	•		Origin Information & Services Inc (NC)	800-940-1755	•	•	•	
DT	BK	CV	CR	PR	←COURTS **BEAUFORT**	RECORDING→	UC	RE	TX	VS
		•			Sue P Hamm	252-322-5015	•	•	•	•
•	•	•	•		Origin Information & Services Inc (NC)	800-940-1755	•	•	•	
•	•	•	•	•	Searchtec (Carolinas) [SOP]	800-528-8790	•	•	•	•
DT	BK	CV	CR	PR	←COURTS **BERTIE**	RECORDING→	UC	RE	TX	VS
•	•	•	•		Origin Information & Services Inc (NC)	800-940-1755	•	•	•	
•	•	•	•	•	Searchtec (Carolinas) [SOP]	800-528-8790	•	•	•	•
DT	BK	CV	CR	PR	←COURTS **BLADEN**	RECORDING→	UC	RE	TX	VS
•	•	•	•		Origin Information & Services Inc (NC)	800-940-1755	•	•	•	
•	•	•	•	•	Searchtec (Carolinas) [SOP]	800-528-8790	•	•	•	•
DT	BK	CV	CR	PR	←COURTS **BRUNSWICK**	RECORDING→	UC	RE	TX	VS
		•	•		Intercoastal Research & Inv	843-280-4461				
•	•	•	•		Origin Information & Services Inc (NC)	800-940-1755	•	•	•	
•	•	•	•	•	Searchtec (Carolinas) [SOP]	800-528-8790	•	•	•	•
DT	BK	CV	CR	PR	←COURTS **BUNCOMBE**	RECORDING→	UC	RE	TX	VS
		•	•	•	Carolina Investigative Research Inc [SOP]	800-328-8981	•	•	•	•

DT	BK	CV	CR	PR	←COURTS	RECORDING→	UC	RE	TX	VS
•	•	•	•		Origin Information & Services Inc (NC)	800-940-1755	•	•	•	
•	•	•	•	•	Paralegal Services Inc	828-606-8297	•	•	•	•
•	•	•	•	•	Ramsey Paralegal/Process [SOP]	828-687-9974	•	•	•	•
•	•	•	•		WNC Search Service	828-768-0062	•	•	•	

DT	BK	CV	CR	PR	←COURTS **BURKE**	RECORDING→	UC	RE	TX	VS
•	•	•	•		Origin Information & Services Inc (NC)	800-940-1755	•	•	•	
•	•	•	•	•	Ramsey Paralegal/Process [SOP]	828-687-9974	•	•	•	•

DT	BK	CV	CR	PR	←COURTS **CABARRUS**	RECORDING→	UC	RE	TX	VS
					Victoria J Armes	704-663-4085	•	•	•	
•	•	•	•	•	ASK Services Inc (North Carolina)	888-416-1313	•	•	•	•
•	•	•	•	•	Axis Research Inc [SOP]	678-795-1005	•	•	•	•
•	•	•	•	•	NC Corporate Connection Inc	888-844-8360	•	•	•	•
•	•	•	•		Origin Information & Services Inc (NC)	800-940-1755	•	•	•	
•	•	•	•	•	Priority Plus Investigations	704-857-7222	•	•	•	•
•	•	•	•		Reynolds Professional Service Inc [SOP]	800-814-8662				•
•	•	•	•	•	Searchtec (Carolinas) [SOP]	800-528-8790	•	•	•	•
•		•	•	•	The Henry Agency [SOP]	704-526-5030	•	•	•	•

DT	BK	CV	CR	PR	←COURTS **CALDWELL**	RECORDING→	UC	RE	TX	VS
•	•	•	•		Origin Information & Services Inc (NC)	800-940-1755	•	•	•	
•	•	•	•	•	Track' Um Private Investigations [SOP]	336-903-1700	•	•	•	•

DT	BK	CV	CR	PR	←COURTS **CAMDEN**	RECORDING→	UC	RE	TX	VS
•	•	•	•	•	Hornthal Riley Ellis & Maland	252-335-0871	•	•	•	•
•	•	•	•		Origin Information & Services Inc (NC)	800-940-1755	•	•	•	
•	•	•	•	•	Searchtec (Carolinas) [SOP]	800-528-8790	•	•	•	•

DT	BK	CV	CR	PR	←COURTS **CARTERET**	RECORDING→	UC	RE	TX	VS
•	•	•	•		Origin Information & Services Inc (NC)	800-940-1755	•	•	•	
•	•	•	•	•	Searchtec (Carolinas) [SOP]	800-528-8790	•	•	•	•

DT	BK	CV	CR	PR	←COURTS **CASWELL**	RECORDING→	UC	RE	TX	VS
•	•	•	•	•	Central Carolina Process Service [SOP]	919-776-7584	•	•	•	•
•	•	•	•		Origin Information & Services Inc (NC)	800-940-1755	•	•	•	
•	•	•	•	•	Searchtec (Carolinas) [SOP]	800-528-8790	•	•	•	•

DT	BK	CV	CR	PR	←COURTS **CATAWBA**	RECORDING→	UC	RE	TX	VS
					Victoria J Armes	704-663-4085	•	•	•	
•	•	•	•	•	Axis Research Inc [SOP]	678-795-1005	•	•	•	•
•	•	•	•	•	NC Corporate Connection Inc	888-844-8360	•	•	•	•
•	•	•	•		Origin Information & Services Inc (NC)	800-940-1755	•	•	•	
•	•	•	•	•	Track' Um Private Investigations [SOP]	336-903-1700	•	•	•	•

DT	BK	CV	CR	PR	←COURTS **CHATHAM**	RECORDING→	UC	RE	TX	VS
•	•	•	•	•	ASK Services Inc (North Carolina)	888-416-1313	•	•	•	•
		•	•	•	Carolina Investigative Research Inc [SOP]	800-328-8981	•	•	•	•
•	•	•	•	•	Central Carolina Process Service [SOP]	919-776-7584	•	•	•	•
•	•	•	•	•	NC Corporate Connection Inc	888-844-8360	•	•	•	•
•	•	•	•		Origin Information & Services Inc (NC)	800-940-1755	•	•	•	
•	•	•	•	•	Paralegal Services of North Carolina Inc [SOP]	919-821-7762	•	•	•	•
•	•	•	•	•	Poindexter & Associates Inc [SOP]	800-373-2804	•	•	•	•
•	•	•	•	•	Searchtec (Carolinas) [SOP]	800-528-8790	•	•	•	•
		•	•		Title Professionals Inc	919-779-7065	•	•	•	•

DT	BK	CV	CR	PR	←COURTS **CHEROKEE**	RECORDING→	UC	RE	TX	VS
•	•	•	•		Origin Information & Services Inc (NC)	800-940-1755	•	•	•	
•	•	•	•	•	Ramsey Paralegal/Process [SOP]	828-687-9974	•	•	•	•

DT	BK	CV	CR	PR	←COURTS **CHOWAN**	RECORDING→	UC	RE	TX	VS
•	•	•	•	•	Hornthal Riley Ellis & Maland	252-335-0871	•	•	•	•

DT	BK	CV	CR	PR	←Courts	Recording→	UC	RE	TX	VS
•	•	•	•		Origin Information & Services Inc (NC)	800-940-1755	•	•	•	
•	•	•	•	•	Searchtec (Carolinas) [SOP]	800-528-8790	•	•	•	•

DT	BK	CV	CR	PR	←Courts **Clay**	Recording→	UC	RE	TX	VS
•	•	•	•		Origin Information & Services Inc (NC)	800-940-1755	•	•	•	

DT	BK	CV	CR	PR	←Courts **Cleveland**	Recording→	UC	RE	TX	VS
•	•	•	•		Origin Information & Services Inc (NC)	800-940-1755	•	•	•	
•	•	•	•	•	Ramsey Paralegal/Process [SOP]	828-687-9974	•	•	•	•
•	•	•	•		Reynolds Professional Service Inc [SOP]	800-814-8662				•

DT	BK	CV	CR	PR	←Courts **Columbus**	Recording→	UC	RE	TX	VS
		•	•		Intercoastal Research & Inv	843-280-4461				
•	•	•	•		Origin Information & Services Inc (NC)	800-940-1755	•	•	•	
•	•	•	•	•	Searchtec (Carolinas) [SOP]	800-528-8790	•	•	•	•

DT	BK	CV	CR	PR	←Courts **Craven**	Recording→	UC	RE	TX	VS
		•			Sue P Hamm	252-322-5015	•	•	•	•
•	•	•	•		Origin Information & Services Inc (NC)	800-940-1755	•	•	•	
•	•	•	•	•	Searchtec (Carolinas) [SOP]	800-528-8790	•	•	•	•
					Cheryl Smith	252-633-3890	•	•		

DT	BK	CV	CR	PR	←Courts **Cumberland**	Recording→	UC	RE	TX	VS
					Abstract Art Inc	910-592-2972	•	•	•	•
•	•	•	•	•	ASK Services Inc (North Carolina)	888-416-1313	•	•	•	•
		•	•	•	Carolina Investigative Research Inc [SOP]	800-328-8981	•	•	•	•
•	•	•	•	•	Central Carolina Process Service [SOP]	919-776-7584	•	•	•	•
•	•	•	•		Origin Information & Services Inc (NC)	800-940-1755	•	•	•	
•	•	•	•	•	Paralegal Services of North Carolina Inc [SOP]	919-821-7762	•	•	•	•
•	•	•	•	•	Poindexter & Associates Inc [SOP]	800-373-2804	•	•	•	•
•	•	•	•	•	Searchtec (Carolinas) [SOP]	800-528-8790	•	•	•	•

DT	BK	CV	CR	PR	←Courts **Currituck**	Recording→	UC	RE	TX	VS
•	•	•	•		Origin Information & Services Inc (NC)	800-940-1755	•	•	•	
•	•	•	•	•	Searchtec (Carolinas) [SOP]	800-528-8790	•	•	•	•

DT	BK	CV	CR	PR	←Courts **Dare**	Recording→	UC	RE	TX	VS
•	•	•	•	•	Hornthal Riley Ellis & Maland	252-335-0871	•	•	•	•
•	•	•	•		Origin Information & Services Inc (NC)	800-940-1755	•	•	•	
•	•	•	•	•	Searchtec (Carolinas) [SOP]	800-528-8790	•	•	•	•

DT	BK	CV	CR	PR	←Courts **Davidson**	Recording→	UC	RE	TX	VS
•		•	•		Agency-One Inv [SOP]	800-557-5500	•	•	•	•
•	•	•	•		Origin Information & Services Inc (NC)	800-940-1755	•	•	•	
•	•	•	•	•	Priority Plus Investigations	704-857-7222	•	•	•	•
•	•	•	•		Reynolds Professional Service Inc [SOP]	800-814-8662				•
•	•	•	•	•	Searchtec (Carolinas) [SOP]	800-528-8790	•	•	•	•

DT	BK	CV	CR	PR	←Courts **Davie**	Recording→	UC	RE	TX	VS
•		•	•		Agency-One Inv [SOP]	800-557-5500	•	•	•	•
•	•	•	•		Origin Information & Services Inc (NC)	800-940-1755	•	•	•	
•	•	•	•	•	Priority Plus Investigations	704-857-7222	•	•	•	•
•	•	•	•	•	Searchtec (Carolinas) [SOP]	800-528-8790	•	•	•	•

DT	BK	CV	CR	PR	←Courts **Duplin**	Recording→	UC	RE	TX	VS
•	•	•	•		Origin Information & Services Inc (NC)	800-940-1755	•	•	•	
•	•	•	•	•	Searchtec (Carolinas) [SOP]	800-528-8790	•	•	•	•

DT	BK	CV	CR	PR	←Courts **Durham**	Recording→	UC	RE	TX	VS
•	•	•	•	•	ASK Services Inc (North Carolina)	888-416-1313	•	•	•	•
		•	•	•	Carolina Investigative Research Inc [SOP]	800-328-8981	•	•	•	•
•	•	•	•	•	Central Carolina Process Service [SOP]	919-776-7584	•	•	•	•

DT	BK	CV	CR	PR	←Courts	Recording→	UC	RE	TX	VS
		•	•		Intercoastal Research & Inv	843-280-4461				
•	•	•	•	•	NC Corporate Connection Inc	888-844-8360	•	•	•	•
•	•	•	•		Origin Information & Services Inc (NC)	800-940-1755	•	•	•	
•	•	•	•	•	Paralegal Services of North Carolina Inc [SOP]	919-821-7762	•	•	•	•
•	•	•	•	•	Poindexter & Associates Inc [SOP]	800-373-2804	•	•	•	•
•	•	•			Search Services [SOP]	919-781-9997	•	•	•	•
•	•	•	•	•	Searchtec (Carolinas) [SOP]	800-528-8790	•	•	•	•
		•	•		Title Professionals Inc	919-779-7065	•	•	•	•
DT	BK	CV	CR	PR	←Courts **EDGECOMBE**	Recording→	UC	RE	TX	VS
•	•	•	•		Origin Information & Services Inc (NC)	800-940-1755	•	•	•	
•	•	•	•	•	Searchtec (Carolinas) [SOP]	800-528-8790	•	•	•	•
DT	BK	CV	CR	PR	←Courts **FORSYTH**	Recording→	UC	RE	TX	VS
•		•	•		Agency-One Inv [SOP]	800-557-5500	•	•	•	•
•	•	•	•		Origin Information & Services Inc (NC)	800-940-1755	•	•	•	
•	•	•	•	•	Priority Plus Investigations	704-857-7222	•	•	•	•
•	•	•	•	•	Searchtec (Carolinas) [SOP]	800-528-8790	•	•	•	•
DT	BK	CV	CR	PR	←Courts **FRANKLIN**	Recording→	UC	RE	TX	VS
•	•	•	•	•	Central Carolina Process Service [SOP]	919-776-7584	•	•	•	•
•	•	•	•	•	NC Corporate Connection Inc	888-844-8360	•	•	•	•
•	•	•	•		Origin Information & Services Inc (NC)	800-940-1755	•	•	•	
•	•	•	•	•	Paralegal Services of North Carolina Inc [SOP]	919-821-7762	•	•	•	•
•	•	•	•	•	Poindexter & Associates Inc [SOP]	800-373-2804	•	•	•	•
•	•	•	•	•	Searchtec (Carolinas) [SOP]	800-528-8790	•	•	•	•
		•	•		Title Professionals Inc	919-779-7065	•	•	•	•
DT	BK	CV	CR	PR	←Courts **GASTON**	Recording→	UC	RE	TX	VS
•	•	•	•	•	Axis Research Inc [SOP]	678-795-1005	•	•	•	•
•	•	•	•	•	Barefoot Private Investigations [SOP]	704-377-1000	•	•	•	
•	•	•	•	•	NC Corporate Connection Inc	888-844-8360	•	•	•	•
•	•	•	•		Origin Information & Services Inc (NC)	800-940-1755	•	•	•	
•	•	•	•		Reynolds Professional Service Inc [SOP]	800-814-8662				•
•	•	•	•	•	Searchtec (Carolinas) [SOP]	800-528-8790	•	•	•	•
•		•	•	•	The Henry Agency [SOP]	704-526-5030	•	•	•	•
DT	BK	CV	CR	PR	←Courts **GATES**	Recording→	UC	RE	TX	VS
•	•	•	•	•	Hornthal Riley Ellis & Maland	252-335-0871	•	•	•	•
•	•	•	•		Origin Information & Services Inc (NC)	800-940-1755	•	•	•	
•	•	•	•	•	Searchtec (Carolinas) [SOP]	800-528-8790	•	•	•	•
DT	BK	CV	CR	PR	←Courts **GRAHAM**	Recording→	UC	RE	TX	VS
•	•	•	•		Origin Information & Services Inc (NC)	800-940-1755	•	•	•	
DT	BK	CV	CR	PR	←Courts **GRANVILLE**	Recording→	UC	RE	TX	VS
•	•	•	•	•	Central Carolina Process Service [SOP]	919-776-7584	•	•	•	•
		•	•		Intercoastal Research & Inv	843-280-4461				
•	•	•	•	•	NC Corporate Connection Inc	888-844-8360	•	•	•	•
•	•	•	•		Origin Information & Services Inc (NC)	800-940-1755	•	•	•	
•	•	•	•	•	Poindexter & Associates Inc [SOP]	800-373-2804	•	•	•	•
•	•	•	•	•	Searchtec (Carolinas) [SOP]	800-528-8790	•	•	•	•
		•	•		Title Professionals Inc	919-779-7065	•	•	•	•
DT	BK	CV	CR	PR	←Courts **GREENE**	Recording→	UC	RE	TX	VS
•	•	•	•		Origin Information & Services Inc (NC)	800-940-1755	•	•	•	
		•		•	Paralegal Enterprises Inc	252-758-6622	•	•	•	•
•	•	•	•	•	Searchtec (Carolinas) [SOP]	800-528-8790	•	•	•	•
DT	BK	CV	CR	PR	←Courts **GUILFORD**	Recording→	UC	RE	TX	VS
•		•	•		Agency-One Inv [SOP]	800-557-5500	•	•	•	•

DT	BK	CV	CR	PR	←Courts	Recording→	UC	RE	TX	VS
•	•	•	•	•	ASK Services Inc (North Carolina)	888-416-1313	•	•	•	•
•	•	•	•	•	Central Carolina Process Service [SOP]	919-776-7584	•	•	•	•
•	•	•	•		Origin Information & Services Inc (NC)	800-940-1755	•	•	•	
•	•	•	•	•	Paralegal Services of North Carolina Inc [SOP]	919-821-7762	•	•	•	•
•	•	•	•	•	Searchtec (Carolinas) [SOP]	800-528-8790	•	•	•	•

DT	BK	CV	CR	PR	←Courts **HALIFAX**	Recording→	UC	RE	TX	VS
•	•	•	•		Origin Information & Services Inc (NC)	800-940-1755	•	•	•	
•	•	•	•	•	Searchtec (Carolinas) [SOP]	800-528-8790	•	•	•	•
		•	•	•	Ward Abstracting Svcs	252-535-3440	•	•	•	•

DT	BK	CV	CR	PR	←Courts **HARNETT**	Recording→	UC	RE	TX	VS
					Abstract Art Inc	910-592-2972	•	•	•	•
•	•	•	•	•	ASK Services Inc (North Carolina)	888-416-1313	•	•	•	•
		•	•	•	Carolina Investigative Research Inc [SOP]	800-328-8981	•	•	•	•
•	•	•	•	•	Central Carolina Process Service [SOP]	919-776-7584	•	•	•	•
•	•	•	•	•	NC Corporate Connection Inc	888-844-8360	•	•	•	•
•	•	•	•		Origin Information & Services Inc (NC)	800-940-1755	•	•	•	
•	•	•	•	•	Paralegal Services of North Carolina Inc [SOP]	919-821-7762	•	•	•	•
•	•	•	•	•	Poindexter & Associates Inc [SOP]	800-373-2804	•	•	•	•
•	•	•	•	•	Searchtec (Carolinas) [SOP]	800-528-8790	•	•	•	•
		•	•		Title Professionals Inc	919-779-7065	•	•	•	•

DT	BK	CV	CR	PR	←Courts **HAYWOOD**	Recording→	UC	RE	TX	VS
•	•	•	•		Origin Information & Services Inc (NC)	800-940-1755	•	•	•	
•	•	•	•	•	Ramsey Paralegal/Process [SOP]	828-687-9974	•	•	•	•
		•	•	•	Kathi Watson	828-648-5830	•	•	•	•
•	•	•	•		WNC Search Service	828-768-0062	•	•	•	

DT	BK	CV	CR	PR	←Courts **HENDERSON**	Recording→	UC	RE	TX	VS
•	•	•	•		Origin Information & Services Inc (NC)	800-940-1755	•	•	•	
•	•	•	•	•	Paralegal Services Inc	828-606-8297	•	•	•	•
•	•	•	•	•	Ramsey Paralegal/Process [SOP]	828-687-9974	•	•	•	•
•	•	•	•		WNC Search Service	828-768-0062	•	•	•	

DT	BK	CV	CR	PR	←Courts **HERTFORD**	Recording→	UC	RE	TX	VS
•	•	•	•	•	Hornthal Riley Ellis & Maland	252-335-0871	•	•	•	•
•	•	•	•		Origin Information & Services Inc (NC)	800-940-1755	•	•	•	
•	•	•	•	•	Searchtec (Carolinas) [SOP]	800-528-8790	•	•	•	•

DT	BK	CV	CR	PR	←Courts **HOKE**	Recording→	UC	RE	TX	VS
		•	•	•	Carolina Investigative Research Inc [SOP]	800-328-8981	•	•	•	•
•	•	•	•	•	Central Carolina Process Service [SOP]	919-776-7584	•	•	•	•
•	•	•	•		Origin Information & Services Inc (NC)	800-940-1755	•	•	•	
•	•	•	•	•	Searchtec (Carolinas) [SOP]	800-528-8790	•	•	•	•

DT	BK	CV	CR	PR	←Courts **HYDE**	Recording→	UC	RE	TX	VS
•	•	•	•		Origin Information & Services Inc (NC)	800-940-1755	•	•	•	
•	•	•	•	•	Searchtec (Carolinas) [SOP]	800-528-8790	•	•	•	•

DT	BK	CV	CR	PR	←Courts **IREDELL**	Recording→	UC	RE	TX	VS
					Victoria J Armes	704-663-4085	•	•	•	
•	•	•	•		Origin Information & Services Inc (NC)	800-940-1755	•	•	•	
•	•	•	•	•	Priority Plus Investigations	704-857-7222	•	•	•	•
•	•	•	•		Reynolds Professional Service Inc [SOP]	800-814-8662				•
•	•	•	•	•	Searchtec (Carolinas) [SOP]	800-528-8790	•	•	•	•
•		•	•	•	The Henry Agency [SOP]	704-526-5030	•	•	•	•
•	•	•	•	•	Track' Um Private Investigations [SOP]	336-903-1700	•	•	•	•

DT	BK	CV	CR	PR	←Courts **JACKSON**	Recording→	UC	RE	TX	VS
•	•	•	•		Origin Information & Services Inc (NC)	800-940-1755	•	•	•	

DT	BK	CV	CR	PR	←Courts		Recording→	UC	RE	TX	VS
•	•	•	•	•	Ramsey Paralegal/Process [SOP]		828-687-9974	•	•	•	•
		•	•	•	Kathi Watson		828-648-5830	•	•	•	•

DT	BK	CV	CR	PR	←Courts	Johnston	Recording→	UC	RE	TX	VS
					Abstract Art Inc		910-592-2972	•	•	•	•
•	•	•	•	•	ASK Services Inc (North Carolina)		888-416-1313	•	•	•	•
		•	•	•	Carolina Investigative Research Inc [SOP]		800-328-8981	•	•	•	•
•	•	•	•	•	Central Carolina Process Service [SOP]		919-776-7584	•	•	•	•
		•	•		Intercoastal Research & Inv		843-280-4461				
•	•	•	•	•	NC Corporate Connection Inc		888-844-8360	•	•	•	•
•	•	•	•		Origin Information & Services Inc (NC)		800-940-1755	•	•	•	
•	•	•	•	•	Paralegal Services of North Carolina Inc [SOP]		919-821-7762	•	•	•	•
•	•	•	•	•	Poindexter & Associates Inc [SOP]		800-373-2804	•	•	•	•
•	•	•	•	•	Searchtec (Carolinas) [SOP]		800-528-8790	•	•	•	•
		•	•		Title Professionals Inc		919-779-7065	•	•	•	•

DT	BK	CV	CR	PR	←Courts	Jones	Recording→	UC	RE	TX	VS
•	•	•	•		Origin Information & Services Inc (NC)		800-940-1755	•	•	•	
•	•	•	•	•	Searchtec (Carolinas) [SOP]		800-528-8790	•	•	•	•
					Cheryl Smith		252-633-3890	•	•		

DT	BK	CV	CR	PR	←Courts	Lee	Recording→	UC	RE	TX	VS
		•	•	•	Carolina Investigative Research Inc [SOP]		800-328-8981	•	•	•	•
•	•	•	•	•	Central Carolina Process Service [SOP]		919-776-7584	•	•	•	•
•	•	•	•		Origin Information & Services Inc (NC)		800-940-1755	•	•	•	
•	•	•	•	•	Searchtec (Carolinas) [SOP]		800-528-8790	•	•	•	•

DT	BK	CV	CR	PR	←Courts	Lenoir	Recording→	UC	RE	TX	VS
		•			Sue P Hamm		252-322-5015	•	•	•	•
•	•	•	•		Origin Information & Services Inc (NC)		800-940-1755	•	•	•	
•	•	•	•	•	Searchtec (Carolinas) [SOP]		800-528-8790	•	•	•	•

DT	BK	CV	CR	PR	←Courts	Lincoln	Recording→	UC	RE	TX	VS
					Victoria J Armes		704-663-4085	•	•	•	
•	•	•	•	•	Axis Research Inc [SOP]		678-795-1005	•	•	•	•
•	•	•	•	•	NC Corporate Connection Inc		888-844-8360	•	•	•	•
•	•	•	•		Origin Information & Services Inc (NC)		800-940-1755	•	•	•	
•	•	•	•		Reynolds Professional Service Inc [SOP]		800-814-8662				•
•		•	•	•	The Henry Agency [SOP]		704-526-5030	•	•	•	•

DT	BK	CV	CR	PR	←Courts	Macon	Recording→	UC	RE	TX	VS
•	•	•	•		Origin Information & Services Inc (NC)		800-940-1755	•	•	•	
•	•	•	•	•	Ramsey Paralegal/Process [SOP]		828-687-9974	•	•	•	•

DT	BK	CV	CR	PR	←Courts	Madison	Recording→	UC	RE	TX	VS
•	•	•	•		Origin Information & Services Inc (NC)		800-940-1755	•	•	•	
•	•	•	•	•	Ramsey Paralegal/Process [SOP]		828-687-9974	•	•	•	•
•	•	•	•		WNC Search Service		828-768-0062	•	•	•	

DT	BK	CV	CR	PR	←Courts	Martin	Recording→	UC	RE	TX	VS
•	•	•	•		Origin Information & Services Inc (NC)		800-940-1755	•	•	•	
•	•	•	•	•	Searchtec (Carolinas) [SOP]		800-528-8790	•	•	•	•

DT	BK	CV	CR	PR	←Courts	McDowell	Recording→	UC	RE	TX	VS
•	•	•	•		Origin Information & Services Inc (NC)		800-940-1755	•	•	•	
•	•	•	•	•	Paralegal Services Inc		828-606-8297	•	•	•	•
•	•	•	•	•	Ramsey Paralegal/Process [SOP]		828-687-9974	•	•	•	•
•	•	•	•		WNC Search Service		828-768-0062	•	•	•	

DT	BK	CV	CR	PR	←Courts	Mecklenburg	Recording→	UC	RE	TX	VS
•	•	•	•	•	ASK Services Inc (North Carolina)		888-416-1313	•	•	•	•
•	•	•	•	•	Axis Research Inc [SOP]		678-795-1005	•	•	•	•

DT	BK	CV	CR	PR	Retriever	Phone	UC	RE	TX	VS
•	•	•	•	•	Barefoot Private Investigations [SOP]	704-377-1000	•	•	•	
		•		•	DiSearch	704-846-6335	•	•	•	•
		•	•		Intercoastal Research & Inv	843-280-4461				
•	•	•	•	•	NC Corporate Connection Inc	888-844-8360	•	•	•	•
•	•	•	•		Origin Information & Services Inc (NC)	800-940-1755	•	•	•	
•	•	•	•	•	Priority Plus Investigations	704-857-7222	•	•	•	•
•	•	•	•		Reynolds Professional Service Inc [SOP]	800-814-8662				•
•	•	•	•	•	Searchtec (Carolinas) [SOP]	800-528-8790	•	•	•	•
•		•	•	•	The Henry Agency [SOP]	704-526-5030	•	•	•	•

DT	BK	CV	CR	PR	←COURTS **MITCHELL**	RECORDING→	UC	RE	TX	VS
		•	•		Asset Protection Associates Inc	828-765-9359		•		
•	•	•	•		Origin Information & Services Inc (NC)	800-940-1755	•	•	•	
•	•	•	•	•	Paralegal Services Inc	828-606-8297	•	•	•	•
•	•	•	•	•	Searchtec (Carolinas) [SOP]	800-528-8790	•	•	•	•

DT	BK	CV	CR	PR	←COURTS **MONTGOMERY**	RECORDING→	UC	RE	TX	VS
•	•	•	•	•	Central Carolina Process Service [SOP]	919-776-7584	•	•	•	•
•	•	•	•		Origin Information & Services Inc (NC)	800-940-1755	•	•	•	
•	•	•	•	•	Searchtec (Carolinas) [SOP]	800-528-8790	•	•	•	•

DT	BK	CV	CR	PR	←COURTS **MOORE**	RECORDING→	UC	RE	TX	VS
		•	•	•	Carolina Investigative Research Inc [SOP]	800-328-8981	•	•	•	•
•	•	•	•	•	Central Carolina Process Service [SOP]	919-776-7584	•	•	•	•
•	•	•	•		Origin Information & Services Inc (NC)	800-940-1755	•	•	•	
•	•	•	•	•	Searchtec (Carolinas) [SOP]	800-528-8790	•	•	•	•

DT	BK	CV	CR	PR	←COURTS **NASH**	RECORDING→	UC	RE	TX	VS
•	•	•	•	•	NC Corporate Connection Inc	888-844-8360	•	•	•	•
•	•	•	•		Origin Information & Services Inc (NC)	800-940-1755	•	•	•	
•	•	•	•	•	Paralegal Services of North Carolina Inc [SOP]	919-821-7762	•	•	•	•
•	•	•	•	•	Searchtec (Carolinas) [SOP]	800-528-8790	•	•	•	•

DT	BK	CV	CR	PR	←COURTS **NEW HANOVER**	RECORDING→	UC	RE	TX	VS
		•	•		Intercoastal Research & Inv	843-280-4461				
•	•	•	•		Origin Information & Services Inc (NC)	800-940-1755	•	•	•	
•	•	•	•	•	Searchtec (Carolinas) [SOP]	800-528-8790	•	•	•	•

DT	BK	CV	CR	PR	←COURTS **NORTHAMPTON**	RECORDING→	UC	RE	TX	VS
•	•	•	•		Origin Information & Services Inc (NC)	800-940-1755	•	•	•	
•	•	•	•	•	Searchtec (Carolinas) [SOP]	800-528-8790	•	•	•	•
		•	•	•	Ward Abstracting Svcs	252-535-3440	•	•	•	•

DT	BK	CV	CR	PR	←COURTS **ONSLOW**	RECORDING→	UC	RE	TX	VS
•	•	•	•		Origin Information & Services Inc (NC)	800-940-1755	•	•	•	
•	•	•	•	•	Searchtec (Carolinas) [SOP]	800-528-8790	•	•	•	•

DT	BK	CV	CR	PR	←COURTS **ORANGE**	RECORDING→	UC	RE	TX	VS
•	•	•	•	•	ASK Services Inc (North Carolina)	888-416-1313	•	•	•	•
•	•	•	•	•	Central Carolina Process Service [SOP]	919-776-7584	•	•	•	•
		•	•		Intercoastal Research & Inv	843-280-4461				
•	•	•	•	•	NC Corporate Connection Inc	888-844-8360	•	•	•	•
•	•	•	•		Origin Information & Services Inc (NC)	800-940-1755	•	•	•	
•	•	•	•	•	Paralegal Services of North Carolina Inc [SOP]	919-821-7762	•	•	•	•
•	•	•	•	•	Searchtec (Carolinas) [SOP]	800-528-8790	•	•	•	•
		•	•		Title Professionals Inc	919-779-7065	•	•	•	•

DT	BK	CV	CR	PR	←COURTS **PAMLICO**	RECORDING→	UC	RE	TX	VS
		•			Sue P Hamm	252-322-5015	•	•	•	•
•	•	•	•		Origin Information & Services Inc (NC)	800-940-1755	•	•	•	
•	•	•	•	•	Searchtec (Carolinas) [SOP]	800-528-8790	•	•	•	•

DT	BK	CV	CR	PR	←Courts	Recording→	UC	RE	TX	VS
					Cheryl Smith	252-633-3890	•	•		

DT	BK	CV	CR	PR	←Courts **Pasquotank**	Recording→	UC	RE	TX	VS
•	•	•	•	•	Hornthal Riley Ellis & Maland	252-335-0871	•	•	•	•
•	•	•	•		Origin Information & Services Inc (NC)	800-940-1755	•	•	•	
•	•	•	•	•	Searchtec (Carolinas) [SOP]	800-528-8790	•	•	•	•

DT	BK	CV	CR	PR	←Courts **Pender**	Recording→	UC	RE	TX	VS
•	•	•	•		Origin Information & Services Inc (NC)	800-940-1755	•	•	•	
•	•	•	•	•	Searchtec (Carolinas) [SOP]	800-528-8790	•	•	•	•

DT	BK	CV	CR	PR	←Courts **Perquimans**	Recording→	UC	RE	TX	VS
•	•	•	•	•	Hornthal Riley Ellis & Maland	252-335-0871	•	•	•	•
•	•	•	•		Origin Information & Services Inc (NC)	800-940-1755	•	•	•	
•	•	•	•	•	Searchtec (Carolinas) [SOP]	800-528-8790	•	•	•	•

DT	BK	CV	CR	PR	←Courts **Person**	Recording→	UC	RE	TX	VS
•	•	•	•	•	Central Carolina Process Service [SOP]	919-776-7584	•	•	•	•
•	•	•	•		Origin Information & Services Inc (NC)	800-940-1755	•	•	•	
•	•	•	•	•	Searchtec (Carolinas) [SOP]	800-528-8790	•	•	•	•

DT	BK	CV	CR	PR	←Courts **Pitt**	Recording→	UC	RE	TX	VS
		•			Sue P Hamm	252-322-5015	•	•	•	•
•	•	•	•		Origin Information & Services Inc (NC)	800-940-1755	•	•	•	
		•		•	Paralegal Enterprises Inc	252-758-6622	•	•	•	•
•	•	•	•	•	Searchtec (Carolinas) [SOP]	800-528-8790	•	•	•	•

DT	BK	CV	CR	PR	←Courts **Polk**	Recording→	UC	RE	TX	VS
•	•	•	•		Origin Information & Services Inc (NC)	800-940-1755	•	•	•	
•	•	•	•	•	Paralegal Services Inc	828-606-8297	•	•	•	•
•	•	•	•	•	Ramsey Paralegal/Process [SOP]	828-687-9974	•	•	•	•
•	•	•	•		WNC Search Service	828-768-0062	•	•	•	

DT	BK	CV	CR	PR	←Courts **Randolph**	Recording→	UC	RE	TX	VS
•	•	•	•	•	Central Carolina Process Service [SOP]	919-776-7584	•	•	•	•
•	•	•	•		Origin Information & Services Inc (NC)	800-940-1755	•	•	•	
•	•	•	•	•	Searchtec (Carolinas) [SOP]	800-528-8790	•	•	•	•

DT	BK	CV	CR	PR	←Courts **Richmond**	Recording→	UC	RE	TX	VS
•	•	•	•	•	Central Carolina Process Service [SOP]	919-776-7584	•	•	•	•
•	•	•	•		Origin Information & Services Inc (NC)	800-940-1755	•	•	•	
•	•	•	•	•	Searchtec (Carolinas) [SOP]	800-528-8790	•	•	•	•

DT	BK	CV	CR	PR	←Courts **Robeson**	Recording→	UC	RE	TX	VS
•	•	•	•	•	Central Carolina Process Service [SOP]	919-776-7584	•	•	•	•
•	•	•	•		Origin Information & Services Inc (NC)	800-940-1755	•	•	•	
•	•	•	•	•	Searchtec (Carolinas) [SOP]	800-528-8790	•	•	•	•

DT	BK	CV	CR	PR	←Courts **Rockingham**	Recording→	UC	RE	TX	VS
•		•	•		Agency-One Inv [SOP]	800-557-5500	•	•	•	•
•	•	•	•	•	Central Carolina Process Service [SOP]	919-776-7584	•	•	•	•
•	•	•	•		Origin Information & Services Inc (NC)	800-940-1755	•	•	•	
•	•	•	•	•	Searchtec (Carolinas) [SOP]	800-528-8790	•	•	•	•

DT	BK	CV	CR	PR	←Courts **Rowan**	Recording→	UC	RE	TX	VS
•		•	•		Agency-One Inv [SOP]	800-557-5500	•	•	•	•
					Victoria J Armes	704-663-4085	•	•	•	
•	•	•	•	•	Axis Research Inc [SOP]	678-795-1005	•	•	•	•
•	•	•	•	•	NC Corporate Connection Inc	888-844-8360	•	•	•	•
•	•	•	•		Origin Information & Services Inc (NC)	800-940-1755	•	•	•	
•	•	•	•	•	Poindexter & Associates Inc [SOP]	800-373-2804	•	•	•	•
•	•	•	•	•	Priority Plus Investigations	704-857-7222	•	•	•	•

DT	BK	CV	CR	PR	←Courts	Recording→	UC	RE	TX	VS
•	•	•	•		Reynolds Professional Service Inc [SOP]	800-814-8662				•
•	•	•	•	•	Searchtec (Carolinas) [SOP]	800-528-8790	•	•	•	•

DT	BK	CV	CR	PR	←Courts **Rutherford**	Recording→	UC	RE	TX	VS
•	•	•	•		Origin Information & Services Inc (NC)	800-940-1755	•	•	•	
•	•	•	•	•	Paralegal Services Inc	828-606-8297	•	•	•	•
•	•	•	•	•	Ramsey Paralegal/Process [SOP]	828-687-9974	•	•	•	•
•	•	•	•		WNC Search Service	828-768-0062	•	•	•	

DT	BK	CV	CR	PR	←Courts **Sampson**	Recording→	UC	RE	TX	VS
					Abstract Art Inc	910-592-2972	•	•	•	•
•	•	•	•	•	Central Carolina Process Service [SOP]	919-776-7584	•	•	•	•
•	•	•	•		Origin Information & Services Inc (NC)	800-940-1755	•	•	•	
•	•	•	•	•	Searchtec (Carolinas) [SOP]	800-528-8790	•	•	•	•

DT	BK	CV	CR	PR	←Courts **Scotland**	Recording→	UC	RE	TX	VS
•	•	•	•	•	Central Carolina Process Service [SOP]	919-776-7584	•	•	•	•
•	•	•	•		Origin Information & Services Inc (NC)	800-940-1755	•	•	•	
•	•	•	•	•	Searchtec (Carolinas) [SOP]	800-528-8790	•	•	•	•

DT	BK	CV	CR	PR	←Courts **Stanly**	Recording→	UC	RE	TX	VS
•	•	•	•	•	Central Carolina Process Service [SOP]	919-776-7584	•	•	•	•
•	•	•	•		Origin Information & Services Inc (NC)	800-940-1755	•	•	•	
•	•	•	•	•	Priority Plus Investigations	704-857-7222	•	•	•	•
•	•	•	•		Reynolds Professional Service Inc [SOP]	800-814-8662				•
•	•	•	•	•	Searchtec (Carolinas) [SOP]	800-528-8790	•	•	•	•
•		•	•	•	The Henry Agency [SOP]	704-526-5030	•	•	•	•

DT	BK	CV	CR	PR	←Courts **Stokes**	Recording→	UC	RE	TX	VS
•		•	•		Agency-One Inv [SOP]	800-557-5500	•	•	•	•
•	•	•	•		Origin Information & Services Inc (NC)	800-940-1755	•	•	•	
•	•	•	•	•	Searchtec (Carolinas) [SOP]	800-528-8790	•	•	•	•

DT	BK	CV	CR	PR	←Courts **Surry**	Recording→	UC	RE	TX	VS
•		•	•		Agency-One Inv [SOP]	800-557-5500	•	•	•	•
•	•	•	•		Origin Information & Services Inc (NC)	800-940-1755	•	•	•	
•	•	•	•	•	Searchtec (Carolinas) [SOP]	800-528-8790	•	•	•	•
•	•	•	•	•	Track' Um Private Investigations [SOP]	336-903-1700	•	•	•	•

DT	BK	CV	CR	PR	←Courts **Swain**	Recording→	UC	RE	TX	VS
•	•	•	•		Origin Information & Services Inc (NC)	800-940-1755	•	•	•	
•	•	•	•	•	Ramsey Paralegal/Process [SOP]	828-687-9974	•	•	•	•

DT	BK	CV	CR	PR	←Courts **Transylvania**	Recording→	UC	RE	TX	VS
•	•	•	•		Origin Information & Services Inc (NC)	800-940-1755	•	•	•	
•	•	•	•	•	Ramsey Paralegal/Process [SOP]	828-687-9974	•	•	•	•
•	•	•	•		WNC Search Service	828-768-0062	•	•	•	

DT	BK	CV	CR	PR	←Courts **Tyrrell**	Recording→	UC	RE	TX	VS
•	•	•	•	•	Hornthal Riley Ellis & Maland	252-335-0871	•	•	•	•
•	•	•	•		Origin Information & Services Inc (NC)	800-940-1755	•	•	•	
•	•	•	•	•	Searchtec (Carolinas) [SOP]	800-528-8790	•	•	•	•

DT	BK	CV	CR	PR	←Courts **Union**	Recording→	UC	RE	TX	VS
•	•	•	•	•	Axis Research Inc [SOP]	678-795-1005	•	•	•	•
		•		•	DiSearch	704-846-6335	•	•	•	•
•	•	•	•	•	NC Corporate Connection Inc	888-844-8360	•	•	•	•
•	•	•	•		Origin Information & Services Inc (NC)	800-940-1755	•	•	•	
•	•	•	•	•	Searchtec (Carolinas) [SOP]	800-528-8790	•	•	•	•
•		•	•	•	The Henry Agency [SOP]	704-526-5030	•	•	•	•

DT	BK	CV	CR	PR	←COURTS VANCE	RECORDING→	UC	RE	TX	VS
•	•	•	•	•	Central Carolina Process Service [SOP]	919-776-7584	•	•	•	•
•	•	•	•		Origin Information & Services Inc (NC)	800-940-1755	•	•	•	
•	•	•	•	•	Poindexter & Associates Inc [SOP]	800-373-2804	•	•	•	•
•	•	•	•	•	Searchtec (Carolinas) [SOP]	800-528-8790	•	•	•	•
		•	•		Title Professionals Inc	919-779-7065	•	•	•	•

DT	BK	CV	CR	PR	←COURTS WAKE	RECORDING→	UC	RE	TX	VS
•	•	•	•	•	ASK Services Inc (North Carolina)	888-416-1313	•	•	•	•
		•	•	•	Carolina Investigative Research Inc [SOP]	800-328-8981	•	•	•	•
•	•	•	•	•	Central Carolina Process Service [SOP]	919-776-7584	•	•	•	•
•	•	•	•		For The Record Inc	919-783-7766				
		•	•		Intercoastal Research & Inv	843-280-4461				
•	•	•	•	•	NC Corporate Connection Inc	888-844-8360	•	•	•	•
•	•	•	•		Origin Information & Services Inc (NC)	800-940-1755	•	•	•	
•	•	•	•	•	Paralegal Services of North Carolina Inc [SOP]	919-821-7762	•	•	•	•
•	•	•	•	•	Poindexter & Associates Inc [SOP]	800-373-2804	•	•	•	•
•	•	•			Search Services [SOP]	919-781-9997	•		•	
•	•	•	•	•	Searchtec (Carolinas) [SOP]	800-528-8790	•	•	•	•
		•	•		Title Professionals Inc	919-779-7065	•	•	•	•

DT	BK	CV	CR	PR	←COURTS WARREN	RECORDING→	UC	RE	TX	VS
•	•	•	•	•	Central Carolina Process Service [SOP]	919-776-7584	•	•	•	•
•	•	•	•		Origin Information & Services Inc (NC)	800-940-1755	•	•	•	
•	•	•	•	•	Poindexter & Associates Inc [SOP]	800-373-2804	•	•	•	•
•	•	•	•	•	Searchtec (Carolinas) [SOP]	800-528-8790	•	•	•	•
		•	•	•	Ward Abstracting Svcs	252-535-3440	•	•	•	•

DT	BK	CV	CR	PR	←COURTS WASHINGTON	RECORDING→	UC	RE	TX	VS
•	•	•	•	•	Hornthal Riley Ellis & Maland	252-335-0871	•	•	•	•
•	•	•	•		Origin Information & Services Inc (NC)	800-940-1755	•	•	•	
•	•	•	•	•	Searchtec (Carolinas) [SOP]	800-528-8790	•	•	•	•

DT	BK	CV	CR	PR	←COURTS WATAUGA	RECORDING→	UC	RE	TX	VS
		•		•	Miller & Johnson PLLC	828-264-1125	•	•	•	
•	•	•	•		Origin Information & Services Inc (NC)	800-940-1755	•	•	•	
•	•	•	•	•	Searchtec (Carolinas) [SOP]	800-528-8790	•	•	•	•
•	•	•	•	•	Track' Um Private Investigations [SOP]	336-903-1700	•	•	•	•

DT	BK	CV	CR	PR	←COURTS WAYNE	RECORDING→	UC	RE	TX	VS
					Abstract Art Inc	910-592-2972	•	•	•	•
•	•	•	•	•	ASK Services Inc (North Carolina)	888-416-1313	•	•	•	•
•	•	•	•	•	Central Carolina Process Service [SOP]	919-776-7584	•	•	•	•
•	•	•	•		Origin Information & Services Inc (NC)	800-940-1755	•	•	•	
•	•	•	•	•	Paralegal Services of North Carolina Inc [SOP]	919-821-7762	•	•	•	•
•	•	•	•	•	Searchtec (Carolinas) [SOP]	800-528-8790	•	•	•	•

DT	BK	CV	CR	PR	←COURTS WILKES	RECORDING→	UC	RE	TX	VS
•	•	•	•		Origin Information & Services Inc (NC)	800-940-1755	•	•	•	
•	•	•	•	•	Searchtec (Carolinas) [SOP]	800-528-8790	•	•	•	•
•	•	•	•	•	Track' Um Private Investigations [SOP]	336-903-1700	•	•	•	•

DT	BK	CV	CR	PR	←COURTS WILSON	RECORDING→	UC	RE	TX	VS
•	•	•	•	•	Central Carolina Process Service [SOP]	919-776-7584	•	•	•	•
•	•	•	•		Origin Information & Services Inc (NC)	800-940-1755	•	•	•	
•	•	•	•	•	Searchtec (Carolinas) [SOP]	800-528-8790	•	•	•	•

DT	BK	CV	CR	PR	←COURTS YADKIN	RECORDING→	UC	RE	TX	VS
•		•	•		Agency-One Inv [SOP]	800-557-5500	•	•	•	•
•	•	•	•		Origin Information & Services Inc (NC)	800-940-1755	•	•	•	
•	•	•	•	•	Priority Plus Investigations	704-857-7222	•	•	•	•

DT	BK	CV	CR	PR	Retriever	Phone	UC	RE	TX	VS
•	•	•	•	•	Searchtec (Carolinas) [SOP]	800-528-8790	•	•	•	•
•	•	•	•	•	Track' Um Private Investigations [SOP]	336-903-1700	•	•	•	•

DT	BK	CV	CR	PR ←Courts	Yancey	Recording→	UC	RE	TX	VS
		•	•		Asset Protection Associates Inc	828-765-9359		•		
•	•	•	•		Origin Information & Services Inc (NC)	800-940-1755	•	•	•	
•	•	•	•	•	Ramsey Paralegal/Process [SOP]	828-687-9974	•	•	•	•
•	•	•	•		WNC Search Service	828-768-0062	•	•	•	

[SOP] = Performs service of process

Court Records

CODE	Government Agency	Type of Information
DT	US District Court	Federal civil and criminal cases
BK	Bankruptcy Court	United States bankruptcy cases
CV	Civil Court	Municipal, county and state level civil cases
CR	Criminal Court	Municipal, county and state level criminal cases
PR	Probate Court	Wills and estate cases

County Records - Recordings

CODE	Government Agency	Type of Information
UC	UCC Filing Office	Uniform Commercial Code and other personal property liens
RE	Real Estate Recording Office	Real property transactions and liens
TX	Tax Filing Office(s)	Federal and state tax liens, judgment liens
VS	Vital Records Office	Vital statistics—birth, death, marriage, divorce

Editor's Tip: In the interest of compiling a concise index with less than 5,000 pages, the Local Retrievers County Index does not indicate counties where a firm provides document retrieval services using hired correspondents and non-employees. Correspondent Relationships are indicated in a Retriever's Profile.

North Dakota

COURT RECORDS RETRIEVED | **RECORDING RECORDS RETRIEVED**

DT	BK	CV	CR	PR	←COURTS	RECORDING→	UC	RE	TX	VS
					ADAMS					
					Adams County Abstract Co	701-567-2224	•	•	•	
		•	•	•	Gion Law Office	701-563-4354	•	•	•	•
					BARNES					
		•	•	•	Credit Bureau of Valley City	701-845-3912	•	•	•	•
		•	•		Hons Investigations [SOP]	800-450-4667				
					BENSON					
		•		•	Surety Title Co	701-947-2446	•	•	•	
					BILLINGS					
					Billings County Abstract	701-623-4344		•	•	
					BOTTINEAU					
		•	•		Hons Investigations [SOP]	800-450-4667				
					BOWMAN					
		•	•	•	Gion Law Office	701-563-4354	•	•	•	•
		•	•		Hons Investigations [SOP]	800-450-4667				
•		•		•	Southwest Abstract & Title Company	701-523-2922	•	•	•	
					BURKE					
•	•	•		•	Mountrail County Abstract & Title Co	701-628-2886	•	•	•	
		•			Northwest Abstract & Title Inc	800-798-6723	•	•	•	
					BURLEIGH					
		•	•	•	Bismarck Title Co	701-222-4247	•	•	•	
•	•	•	•	•	Butcher & Associates Ltd [SOP]	701-224-1541	•	•	•	•
		•	•		Hons Investigations [SOP]	800-450-4667				
•	•	•	•	•	Search Company of North Dakota LLC [SOP]	701-223-1848	•	•	•	•
					CASS					
•	•	•	•	•	Butcher & Associates Ltd [SOP]	701-224-1541	•	•	•	•
•	•	•	•	•	C.C.I. [SOP]	701-235-4842	•	•	•	
					Cass County Abstract Co (North Dakota)	701-232-3341	•	•	•	
•	•	•		•	Clay County Abstract Co [SOP]	218-233-1358	•	•	•	
		•	•		Hons Investigations [SOP]	800-450-4667				
•	•	•	•	•	Search Company of North Dakota LLC [SOP]	701-223-1848	•	•	•	•
					CAVALIER					
		•	•		Hons Investigations [SOP]	800-450-4667				
•	•	•			McHugh Abstract Co	701-256-2851	•	•	•	•
		•	•	•	Welch & Ekman	701-284-7833	•	•	•	•
					DICKEY					
•	•	•	•	•	Dickey County Abstract & Title	701-349-3450	•	•	•	•
		•	•		Hons Investigations [SOP]	800-450-4667				
					DIVIDE					
					Divide Abstract Co	701-965-6352, 701-965-2222		•	•	

DT	BK	CV	CR	PR	←Courts	Dunn	Recording→	UC	RE	TX	VS
		•	•		Hons Investigations [SOP]		800-450-4667				
		•			Northwest Abstract & Title Inc		800-798-6723	•	•	•	

DT	BK	CV	CR	PR	←Courts	Eddy	Recording→	UC	RE	TX	VS
		•	•		Hons Investigations [SOP]		800-450-4667				
		•		•	Surety Title Co		701-947-2446	•	•	•	

DT	BK	CV	CR	PR	←Courts	Emmons	Recording→	UC	RE	TX	VS
					Emmons County Abstract & Title		701-254-4261	•	•	•	
		•	•		Hons Investigations [SOP]		800-450-4667				

DT	BK	CV	CR	PR	←Courts	Foster	Recording→	UC	RE	TX	VS
		•		•	Foster County Abstract & Title		701-652-3164	•	•	•	•

DT	BK	CV	CR	PR	←Courts	Golden Valley	Recording→	UC	RE	TX	VS
	•	•	•	•	Abstract & Title Co		701-872-4531	•	•	•	

DT	BK	CV	CR	PR	←Courts	Grand Forks	Recording→	UC	RE	TX	VS
		•			Grand Forks Abstract & Title Co		701-772-3484	•	•	•	
		•	•		Hons Investigations [SOP]		800-450-4667				

DT	BK	CV	CR	PR	←Courts	Grant	Recording→	UC	RE	TX	VS
		•	•	•	Gion Law Office		701-563-4354	•	•	•	•

DT	BK	CV	CR	PR	←Courts	Griggs	Recording→	UC	RE	TX	VS
		•		•	Surety Title Co		701-947-2446	•	•	•	

DT	BK	CV	CR	PR	←Courts	Hettinger	Recording→	UC	RE	TX	VS
		•	•	•	Gion Law Office		701-563-4354	•	•	•	•
•	•	•			Hettinger-Sioux County Abstractors Inc		701-824-3148	•	•	•	•

DT	BK	CV	CR	PR	←Courts	Kidder	Recording→	UC	RE	TX	VS
					Kidder County Abstract Co		701-475-2432	•	•	•	

DT	BK	CV	CR	PR	←Courts	La Moure	Recording→	UC	RE	TX	VS
					LaMoure County Abstract Co		701-883-4246	•	•	•	
					Stutsman County Abstract		701-252-4870	•	•	•	

DT	BK	CV	CR	PR	←Courts	Logan	Recording→	UC	RE	TX	VS
		•			Logan County Abstract Co		701-754-2200	•	•	•	

DT	BK	CV	CR	PR	←Courts	McHenry	Recording→	UC	RE	TX	VS
•		•	•	•	McHenry County Abstract & Title Co		701-537-5723	•	•	•	

DT	BK	CV	CR	PR	←Courts	McIntosh	Recording→	UC	RE	TX	VS
		•	•	•	Abstracts of McIntosh County Inc		701-288-3618	•	•	•	•
		•			Ashley Abstract Co		701-288-3584	•	•	•	•

DT	BK	CV	CR	PR	←Courts	McKenzie	Recording→	UC	RE	TX	VS
		•		•	Abstract &Title Co		701-842-3366	•	•	•	
•	•	•		•	Mountrail County Abstract & Title Co		701-628-2886	•	•	•	

DT	BK	CV	CR	PR	←Courts	McLean	Recording→	UC	RE	TX	VS
		•	•		Hons Investigations [SOP]		800-450-4667				
•	•	•	•	•	McLean County Abstract Inc		701-462-3244	•	•	•	•

DT	BK	CV	CR	PR	←Courts	Mercer	Recording→	UC	RE	TX	VS
		•	•		Hons Investigations [SOP]		800-450-4667				
		•			Mercer County Abstract Co Inc		701-748-2190		•	•	

DT	BK	CV	CR	PR	←Courts	Morton	Recording→	UC	RE	TX	VS
		•	•	•	Bismarck Title Co		701-222-4247	•	•	•	
•	•	•	•	•	Butcher & Associates Ltd [SOP]		701-224-1541	•	•	•	•

DT	BK	CV	CR	PR	←Courts		Recording→	UC	RE	TX	VS
		•	•		Hons Investigations [SOP]		800-450-4667				
•	•	•	•	•	Search Company of North Dakota LLC [SOP]		701-223-1848	•	•	•	•
DT	**BK**	**CV**	**CR**	**PR**	**←Courts**	**Mountrail**	**Recording→**	**UC**	**RE**	**TX**	**VS**
		•	•		Hons Investigations [SOP]		800-450-4667				
•	•	•		•	Mountrail County Abstract & Title Co		701-628-2886	•	•	•	
DT	**BK**	**CV**	**CR**	**PR**	**←Courts**	**Nelson**	**Recording→**	**UC**	**RE**	**TX**	**VS**
					Nelson County Abstract		701-247-2221		•	•	
DT	**BK**	**CV**	**CR**	**PR**	**←Courts**	**Oliver**	**Recording→**	**UC**	**RE**	**TX**	**VS**
•	•	•		•	Oliver County Abstract		701-794-3496	•	•	•	
DT	**BK**	**CV**	**CR**	**PR**	**←Courts**	**Pembina**	**Recording→**	**UC**	**RE**	**TX**	**VS**
					A Short Abstract Co		701-265-4176		•	•	
		•	•		Hons Investigations [SOP]		800-450-4667				
DT	**BK**	**CV**	**CR**	**PR**	**←Courts**	**Pierce**	**Recording→**	**UC**	**RE**	**TX**	**VS**
		•	•		Hons Investigations [SOP]		800-450-4667				
		•		•	Pierce County Abstract		701-776-7777	•	•	•	
DT	**BK**	**CV**	**CR**	**PR**	**←Courts**	**Ramsey**	**Recording→**	**UC**	**RE**	**TX**	**VS**
		•	•		Hons Investigations [SOP]		800-450-4667				
DT	**BK**	**CV**	**CR**	**PR**	**←Courts**	**Ransom**	**Recording→**	**UC**	**RE**	**TX**	**VS**
					Ransom County Title Co		701-683-5511		•	•	
DT	**BK**	**CV**	**CR**	**PR**	**←Courts**	**Renville**	**Recording→**	**UC**	**RE**	**TX**	**VS**
					Myaer & Co Inc		701-756-6487	•	•	•	
DT	**BK**	**CV**	**CR**	**PR**	**←Courts**	**Richland**	**Recording→**	**UC**	**RE**	**TX**	**VS**
		•	•		Hons Investigations [SOP]		800-450-4667				
		•	•	•	Richland County Abstract Co		701-642-3781	•	•	•	•
DT	**BK**	**CV**	**CR**	**PR**	**←Courts**	**Rolette**	**Recording→**	**UC**	**RE**	**TX**	**VS**
		•	•	•	Rolette County Abstract Inc		701-477-3149	•	•	•	•
DT	**BK**	**CV**	**CR**	**PR**	**←Courts**	**Sargent**	**Recording→**	**UC**	**RE**	**TX**	**VS**
		•	•	•	Richland County Abstract Co		701-642-3781	•	•	•	•
DT	**BK**	**CV**	**CR**	**PR**	**←Courts**	**Sheridan**	**Recording→**	**UC**	**RE**	**TX**	**VS**
•		•	•	•	McHenry County Abstract & Title Co		701-537-5723	•	•	•	
DT	**BK**	**CV**	**CR**	**PR**	**←Courts**	**Sioux**	**Recording→**	**UC**	**RE**	**TX**	**VS**
•	•	•			Hettinger-Sioux County Abstractors Inc		701-824-3148	•	•	•	•
DT	**BK**	**CV**	**CR**	**PR**	**←Courts**	**Slope**	**Recording→**	**UC**	**RE**	**TX**	**VS**
		•	•	•	Gion Law Office		701-563-4354	•	•	•	•
•		•		•	Southwest Abstract & Title Company		701-523-2922	•	•	•	
DT	**BK**	**CV**	**CR**	**PR**	**←Courts**	**Stark**	**Recording→**	**UC**	**RE**	**TX**	**VS**
		•	•	•	Bismarck Title Co		701-222-4247	•	•	•	
		•	•	•	Gion Law Office		701-563-4354	•	•	•	•
		•	•		Hons Investigations [SOP]		800-450-4667				
DT	**BK**	**CV**	**CR**	**PR**	**←Courts**	**Steele**	**Recording→**	**UC**	**RE**	**TX**	**VS**
		•			M B Cassell		701-524-1961		•	•	
DT	**BK**	**CV**	**CR**	**PR**	**←Courts**	**Stutsman**	**Recording→**	**UC**	**RE**	**TX**	**VS**
		•	•		Hons Investigations [SOP]		800-450-4667				
					Stutsman County Abstract		701-252-4870	•	•	•	
DT	**BK**	**CV**	**CR**	**PR**	**←Courts**	**Towner**	**Recording→**	**UC**	**RE**	**TX**	**VS**
					Towner County Abstract Co		701-968-3006		•	•	

DT	BK	CV	CR	PR	←COURTS **TRAILL**	RECORDING→	UC	RE	TX	VS
					Traill County Abstract	701-636-4880		•	•	

DT	BK	CV	CR	PR	←COURTS **WALSH**	RECORDING→	UC	RE	TX	VS
		•	•		Hons Investigations [SOP]	800-450-4667				
		•	•	•	Welch & Ekman	701-284-7833	•	•	•	•

DT	BK	CV	CR	PR	←COURTS **WARD**	RECORDING→	UC	RE	TX	VS
•				•	Devine & Co Inc	701-852-6800		•	•	
		•	•		Hons Investigations [SOP]	800-450-4667				
•	•	•		•	Mountrail County Abstract & Title Co	701-628-2886	•	•	•	

DT	BK	CV	CR	PR	←COURTS **WELLS**	RECORDING→	UC	RE	TX	VS
					Wells County Abstract	701-547-3433		•	•	

DT	BK	CV	CR	PR	←COURTS **WILLIAMS**	RECORDING→	UC	RE	TX	VS
		•	•		Hons Investigations [SOP]	800-450-4667				
•	•	•		•	Mountrail County Abstract & Title Co	701-628-2886	•	•	•	
		•			Northwest Abstract & Title Inc	800-798-6723	•	•	•	

[SOP] = PERFORMS SERVICE OF PROCESS

COURT RECORDS

CODE	GOVERNMENT AGENCY	TYPE OF INFORMATION
DT	US District Court	Federal civil and criminal cases
BK	Bankruptcy Court	United States bankruptcy cases
CV	Civil Court	Municipal, county and state level civil cases
CR	Criminal Court	Municipal, county and state level criminal cases
PR	Probate Court	Wills and estate cases

COUNTY RECORDS - RECORDINGS

CODE	GOVERNMENT AGENCY	TYPE OF INFORMATION
UC	UCC Filing Office	Uniform Commercial Code and other personal property liens
RE	Real Estate Recording Office	Real property transactions and liens
TX	Tax Filing Office(s)	Federal and state tax liens, judgment liens
VS	Vital Records Office	Vital statistics—birth, death, marriage, divorce

Editor's Tip: Remember the first rule about public record searching-- Simply because your state or county has certain rules, regulations and practices regarding the accessibility and content of public records, does not mean that another state or county adheres to the same rules.

Ohio

COURT RECORDS RETRIEVED **RECORDING RECORDS RETRIEVED**

DT	BK	CV	CR	PR	←COURTS	RECORDING→	UC	RE	TX	VS
					ADAMS					
•	•	•	•		Ace Background Check Inc	800-731-9221	•	•	•	•
					ALLEN					
		•	•		A1 Inv [SOP]	419-229-1955				
•	•	•	•		Ace Background Check Inc	800-731-9221	•	•	•	•
					ASHLAND					
•	•	•	•		Ace Background Check Inc	800-731-9221	•	•	•	•
•	•	•	•	•	Investigative Solutions	330-947-2911	•		•	•
•	•	•	•	•	On the Record Inc	330-652-4109	•	•	•	•
		•	•	•	Urban Title Search Services	419-289-0437	•	•	•	•
					ASHTABULA					
•	•	•	•		Ace Background Check Inc	800-731-9221	•	•	•	•
•	•	•	•	•	Allington International [SOP]	866-729-8555	•	•	•	•
•	•	•	•	•	Eagle Communications [SOP]	216-297-3200	•	•	•	•
•	•	•	•	•	Investigative Solutions	330-947-2911	•		•	•
•		•	•		Management Information Services	216-241-4282				
•	•	•	•	•	On the Record Inc	330-652-4109	•	•	•	•
•		•	•		Pre-Check, The Pre-Check Company	800-268-2435				
					ATHENS					
•	•	•	•	•	Accu-Check Information Services	304-375-4802	•		•	•
•	•	•	•		Ace Background Check Inc	800-731-9221	•	•	•	•
•	•	•	•	•	Boerger Investigative Services LLC [SOP]	877-754-8295	•	•	•	•
•	•	•	•	•	Confidential Services [SOP]	800-752-4581	•	•	•	•
•	•	•	•		Dennis S Carley and Associates Inc [SOP]	1-866-689-6899				
					Liberty Record Search Inc	304-863-5542	•	•	•	
					AUGLAIZE					
		•	•		A1 Inv [SOP]	419-229-1955				
•	•	•	•		Ace Background Check Inc	800-731-9221	•	•	•	•
		•	•	•	Steven P Mielke	419-586-2323	•	•	•	
					BELMONT					
•	•	•	•		Ace Background Check Inc	800-731-9221	•	•	•	•
		•	•	•	Dora Doty	740-695-4917	•	•	•	•
•	•	•	•	•	On the Record Inc	330-652-4109	•	•	•	•
					BROWN					
•	•	•	•		Ace Background Check Inc	800-731-9221	•	•	•	•
					BUTLER					
•	•	•	•		Ace Background Check Inc	800-731-9221	•	•	•	•
•	•	•	•	•	Active Detective Bureau Inc [SOP]	800-405-4006		•	•	•
•	•	•	•	•	Advanced Background Check Inc	888-264-4018	•	•	•	•
•		•	•		Advantage Background Services Inc	800-355-2650				
		•			Cynthia H Miller, Paralegal	513-368-2855	•	•	•	
					Document Retrieval Network Inc	859-654-2890	•	•	•	
•	•	•	•	•	General Corporate Inv - GCI [SOP]	800-735-7992	•	•	•	•
			•		Phoenix Research Inc	800-260-1092				

DT	BK	CV	CR	PR	←Courts	Recording→	UC	RE	TX	VS
		•			Union County Title Co	765-458-7148	•	•	•	
		•		•	Urban Abstract Inc	513-755-8527	•	•		
•		•	•		Xpedite Wholesale Criminal Research	800-325-3609				

DT	BK	CV	CR	PR	←Courts CARROLL	Recording→	UC	RE	TX	VS
•	•	•	•		Ace Background Check Inc	800-731-9221	•	•	•	•
					Liberty Record Search Inc	304-863-5542	•	•	•	
•	•	•	•	•	On the Record Inc	330-652-4109	•	•	•	•
	•	•	•	•	David M Rumancik	330-837-7737	•	•	•	
		•	•	•	Woodard & Bohse Law Office [SOP]	330-343-8848 or 8849	•	•	•	•

DT	BK	CV	CR	PR	←Courts CHAMPAIGN	Recording→	UC	RE	TX	VS
•	•	•	•		Ace Background Check Inc	800-731-9221	•	•	•	•
		•	•	•	Ginger Galloway	937-241-8442	•	•	•	

DT	BK	CV	CR	PR	←Courts CLARK	Recording→	UC	RE	TX	VS
•	•	•	•		Ace Background Check Inc	800-731-9221	•	•	•	•
•	•	•	•	•	Docutech Information Services Inc	800-361-3310	•	•	•	•
		•	•	•	Ginger Galloway	937-241-8442	•	•	•	
•	•	•	•		North American Security Solutions	888-898-6277		•	•	

DT	BK	CV	CR	PR	←Courts CLERMONT	Recording→	UC	RE	TX	VS
•	•	•	•		Ace Background Check Inc	800-731-9221	•	•	•	•
•	•	•	•	•	Active Detective Bureau Inc [SOP]	800-405-4006		•	•	•
•	•	•	•	•	Confidential Services [SOP]	800-752-4581	•	•	•	•
		•	•		Criminal Information Network Inc	888-923-0271				
		•			Cynthia H Miller, Paralegal	513-368-2855	•	•	•	
					Document Retrieval Network Inc	859-654-2890	•	•	•	
•	•	•	•	•	General Corporate Inv - GCI [SOP]	800-735-7992	•	•	•	•
•	•	•	•	•	Legal Ease Inc [SOP]	800-519-6331	•	•	•	•
			•		Phoenix Research Inc	800-260-1092				
		•			Queen City Paralegal	513-984-4345				
•	•	•	•		Search International Inc	859-342-0456	•	•	•	
•		•	•		Xpedite Wholesale Criminal Research	800-325-3609				

DT	BK	CV	CR	PR	←Courts CLINTON	Recording→	UC	RE	TX	VS
•	•	•	•		Ace Background Check Inc	800-731-9221	•	•	•	•
		•	•	•	Ginger Galloway	937-241-8442	•	•	•	

DT	BK	CV	CR	PR	←Courts COLUMBIANA	Recording→	UC	RE	TX	VS
•	•	•	•		Ace Background Check Inc	800-731-9221	•	•	•	•
		•	•	•	Applied Research & Investigation	800-594-0008				
•	•	•	•	•	Investigative Solutions	330-947-2911	•		•	•
					Liberty Record Search Inc	304-863-5542	•	•	•	
•	•	•	•	•	On the Record Inc	330-652-4109	•	•	•	•

DT	BK	CV	CR	PR	←Courts COSHOCTON	Recording→	UC	RE	TX	VS
•	•	•	•		Ace Background Check Inc	800-731-9221	•	•	•	•
		•	•	•	Woodard & Bohse Law Office [SOP]	330-343-8848 or 8849	•	•	•	•

DT	BK	CV	CR	PR	←Courts CRAWFORD	Recording→	UC	RE	TX	VS
•	•	•	•		Ace Background Check Inc	800-731-9221	•	•	•	•
		•		•	Oberdier Search Services	740-225-3057	•	•	•	
		•	•	•	Precision Quest [SOP]	740-383-3753	•	•	•	

DT	BK	CV	CR	PR	←Courts CUYAHOGA	Recording→	UC	RE	TX	VS
•	•	•	•	•	A1 Cleveland Service Agency Inc [SOP]	888-212-5614	•	•	•	•
•	•	•	•		Ace Background Check Inc	800-731-9221	•	•	•	•
•	•	•	•	•	Advanced Background Check Inc	888-264-4018	•	•	•	•
•		•	•		Advantage Background Services Inc	800-355-2650				
•	•	•	•	•	Allington International [SOP]	866-729-8555	•	•	•	•

DT	BK	CV	CR	PR	←Courts	Recording→	UC	RE	TX	VS
•	•	•	•		ASK Services Inc	888-416-1313	•	•	•	
•	•	•	•	•	Attorney Services of Northeast Ohio [SOP]	800-804-7787		•	•	
•	•	•	•	•	Boerger Investigative Services LLC [SOP]	877-754-8295	•	•	•	•
•	•	•	•	•	Confidential Services [SOP]	800-752-4581	•	•	•	•
•	•	•	•	•	Corporate Screening Services	800-229-8606	•			
•	•	•	•	•	Eagle Communications [SOP]	216-297-3200	•	•	•	•
•	•	•	•	•	Investigative Solutions	330-947-2911	•		•	•
•	•	•	•		J H L Enterprises	440-845-2823	•		•	
	•	•		•	KasparNet LLC	800-886-7534	•	•	•	
		•		•	Lorain County Title Co	440-284-5100	•	•	•	•
•		•	•		Management Information Services	216-241-4282				
•	•	•	•	•	National Service Information Inc (Ohio)	800-235-0337	•		•	•
•	•	•	•	•	On the Record Inc	330-652-4109	•	•	•	•
•		•	•		Pre-Check, The Pre-Check Company	800-268-2435				
•	•	•	•	•	Research Associates	800-225-9693	•	•	•	•
•	•	•			Search One Services	614-834-5603	•	•	•	
•	•	•	•		Security Essentials LLC	216-839-0700			•	
•	•	•	•	•	Sherlock Research	330-882-4690	•	•	•	•

DT	BK	CV	CR	PR	←Courts **Darke**	Recording→	UC	RE	TX	VS
•	•	•	•		Ace Background Check Inc	800-731-9221	•	•	•	•
•	•	•	•	•	Legal Ease Inc [SOP]	800-519-6331	•	•	•	•
•	•	•	•		North American Security Solutions	888-898-6277		•	•	

DT	BK	CV	CR	PR	←Courts **Defiance**	Recording→	UC	RE	TX	VS
•	•	•	•		Ace Background Check Inc	800-731-9221	•	•	•	•

DT	BK	CV	CR	PR	←Courts **Delaware**	Recording→	UC	RE	TX	VS
•	•	•	•		Ace Background Check Inc	800-731-9221	•	•	•	•
•	•	•	•	•	Advanced Background Check Inc	888-264-4018	•	•	•	•
•	•	•	•		ASK Services Inc	888-416-1313	•	•	•	
•	•	•	•	•	Boerger Investigative Services LLC [SOP]	877-754-8295	•	•	•	•
•	•	•	•	•	Confidential Services [SOP]	800-752-4581	•	•	•	•
•	•	•	•	•	InfoCorp Investigative Services LLC [SOP]	866-657-8003	•		•	•
•	•	•	•	•	M C Associates [SOP]	740-366-1922	•	•	•	•
		•		•	G Scott Miller	740-363-1324	•	•	•	
•	•	•	•	•	National Service Information Inc (Ohio)	800-235-0337	•		•	•
		•		•	Oberdier Search Services	740-225-3057	•	•	•	
		•	•	•	Precision Quest [SOP]	740-383-3753	•	•	•	
		•	•	•	Research Information Consultants	614-286-6303	•	•	•	
•	•	•			Search One Services	614-834-5603	•	•	•	

DT	BK	CV	CR	PR	←Courts **Erie**	Recording→	UC	RE	TX	VS
•	•	•	•		Ace Background Check Inc	800-731-9221	•	•	•	•
•	•	•	•	•	Investigative Solutions	330-947-2911	•		•	•
		•		•	Lorain County Title Co	440-284-5100	•	•	•	•
•	•	•	•	•	On the Record Inc	330-652-4109	•	•	•	•

DT	BK	CV	CR	PR	←Courts **Fairfield**	Recording→	UC	RE	TX	VS
•	•	•	•		Ace Background Check Inc	800-731-9221	•	•	•	•
•	•	•	•		ASK Services Inc	888-416-1313	•	•	•	
•	•	•	•	•	Boerger Investigative Services LLC [SOP]	877-754-8295	•	•	•	•
•	•	•	•		Dennis S Carley and Associates Inc [SOP]	1-866-689-6899				
•	•	•	•	•	Docutech Information Services Inc	800-361-3310	•	•	•	•
•	•	•	•	•	M C Associates [SOP]	740-366-1922	•	•	•	•
•	•	•			Search One Services	614-834-5603	•	•	•	

DT	BK	CV	CR	PR	←Courts **Fayette**	Recording→	UC	RE	TX	VS
•	•	•	•		Ace Background Check Inc	800-731-9221	•	•	•	•
•	•	•	•	•	Docutech Information Services Inc	800-361-3310	•	•	•	•

DT	BK	CV	CR	PR	←Courts		UC	RE	TX	VS
		•	•	•	Ginger Galloway	937-241-8442	•	•	•	

DT	BK	CV	CR	PR	←Courts	FRANKLIN Recording→	UC	RE	TX	VS
•	•	•	•		Ace Background Check Inc	800-731-9221	•	•	•	•
•	•	•	•	•	Advanced Background Check Inc	888-264-4018	•	•	•	•
•	•	•	•		ASK Services Inc	888-416-1313	•	•	•	
•	•	•	•	•	Boerger Investigative Services LLC [SOP]	877-754-8295	•	•	•	•
•	•	•	•	•	Confidential Services [SOP]	800-752-4581	•	•	•	•
•	•	•	•		Dennis S Carley and Associates Inc [SOP]	1-866-689-6899				
•	•	•	•	•	Docutech Information Services Inc	800-361-3310	•	•	•	•
•	•	•	•	•	Eagle Communications [SOP]	216-297-3200	•	•	•	•
			•		FYI Screening Inc	800-809-2419				
•	•	•	•	•	InfoCorp Investigative Services LLC [SOP]	866-657-8003	•		•	•
•	•	•	•	•	M C Associates [SOP]	740-366-1922	•	•	•	•
•	•			•	MBK Consulting	614-239-8977	•	•	•	•
•	•	•	•	•	National Service Information Inc (Ohio)	800-235-0337	•		•	•
•		•	•		Pre-Check, The Pre-Check Company	800-268-2435				
		•	•	•	Precision Quest [SOP]	740-383-3753	•	•	•	
		•		•	RecordSearch Inc	614-457-6836	•	•	•	
		•	•	•	Research Information Consultants	614-286-6303	•	•	•	
•	•	•			Search One Services	614-834-5603	•	•	•	
•	•	•			Unisearch Inc (Ohio)	877-208-7783	•		•	
•		•	•		Xpedite Wholesale Criminal Research	800-325-3609				

DT	BK	CV	CR	PR	←Courts	FULTON Recording→	UC	RE	TX	VS
•	•	•	•		Ace Background Check Inc	800-731-9221	•	•	•	•

DT	BK	CV	CR	PR	←Courts	GALLIA Recording→	UC	RE	TX	VS
•	•	•	•	•	Accu-Check Information Services	304-375-4802	•		•	•
•	•	•	•		Ace Background Check Inc	800-731-9221	•	•	•	•
					Liberty Record Search Inc	304-863-5542	•	•	•	

DT	BK	CV	CR	PR	←Courts	GEAUGA Recording→	UC	RE	TX	VS
•	•	•	•		Ace Background Check Inc	800-731-9221	•	•	•	•
•		•	•		Advantage Background Services Inc	800-355-2650				
•	•	•	•	•	Allington International [SOP]	866-729-8555	•	•	•	•
•	•	•	•	•	Attorney Services of Northeast Ohio [SOP]	800-804-7787		•	•	
•	•	•	•	•	Chreyton Research	440-354-0316	•	•	•	•
•	•	•	•	•	Eagle Communications [SOP]	216-297-3200	•	•	•	•
•	•	•	•	•	Investigative Solutions	330-947-2911	•		•	•
•		•	•		Management Information Services	216-241-4282				
•	•	•	•	•	On the Record Inc	330-652-4109	•	•	•	•
•	•	•	•		Security Essentials LLC	216-839-0700			•	

DT	BK	CV	CR	PR	←Courts	GREENE Recording→	UC	RE	TX	VS
•	•	•	•		Ace Background Check Inc	800-731-9221	•	•	•	•
•	•	•	•	•	Allen J Blazinski	937-475-4370	•	•	•	•
		•	•	•	Ginger Galloway	937-241-8442	•	•	•	
•	•	•	•	•	Legal Ease Inc [SOP]	800-519-6331	•	•	•	•
•	•	•	•		Midwest Investigative Services Inc [SOP]	800-227-9740				•
•	•	•	•		North American Security Solutions	888-898-6277		•	•	
•	•	•			Search One Services	614-834-5603	•	•	•	

DT	BK	CV	CR	PR	←Courts	GUERNSEY Recording→	UC	RE	TX	VS
•	•	•	•		Ace Background Check Inc	800-731-9221	•	•	•	•
		•	•	•	Dora Doty	740-695-4917	•	•	•	•

DT	BK	CV	CR	PR	←Courts	HAMILTON Recording→	UC	RE	TX	VS
•	•	•	•		Ace Background Check Inc	800-731-9221	•	•	•	•
•	•	•	•	•	Active Detective Bureau Inc [SOP]	800-405-4006		•	•	•
•	•	•	•	•	Advanced Background Check Inc	888-264-4018	•	•	•	•

DT	BK	CV	CR	PR	←Courts	Recording→	UC	RE	TX	VS
•		•	•		Advantage Background Services Inc	800-355-2650				
•	•	•	•		ASK Services Inc	888-416-1313	•	•	•	
•	•	•	•	•	Confidential Services [SOP]	800-752-4581	•	•	•	•
		•	•		Criminal Information Network Inc	888-923-0271				
		•			Cynthia H Miller, Paralegal	513-368-2855	•	•	•	
•	•	•	•	•	DDI Inc [SOP]	866-954-3000	•	•	•	•
					Document Retrieval Network Inc	859-654-2890	•	•	•	
•	•	•	•	•	Eagle Communications [SOP]	216-297-3200	•	•	•	•
•	•	•	•	•	General Corporate Inv - GCI [SOP]	800-735-7992	•	•	•	•
•	•	•	•	•	Legal Ease Inc [SOP]	800-519-6331	•	•	•	•
•	•	•	•	•	M C Associates [SOP]	740-366-1922	•	•	•	•
•	•	•	•	•	National Service Information Inc (Ohio)	800-235-0337	•		•	•
			•		Phoenix Research Inc	800-260-1092				
•		•	•		Pre-Check, The Pre-Check Company	800-268-2435				
		•			Queen City Paralegal	513-984-4345				
•	•	•	•		Search International Inc	859-342-0456	•	•	•	
•	•	•			Search One Services	614-834-5603	•	•	•	
		•		•	Urban Abstract Inc	513-755-8527	•	•		
•		•	•		Xpedite Wholesale Criminal Research	800-325-3609				
DT	**BK**	**CV**	**CR**	**PR**	**←Courts — HANCOCK**	**Recording→**	**UC**	**RE**	**TX**	**VS**
		•	•		A1 Inv [SOP]	419-229-1955				
•	•	•	•		Ace Background Check Inc	800-731-9221	•	•	•	•
DT	**BK**	**CV**	**CR**	**PR**	**←Courts — HARDIN**	**Recording→**	**UC**	**RE**	**TX**	**VS**
		•	•		A1 Inv [SOP]	419-229-1955				
•	•	•	•		Ace Background Check Inc	800-731-9221	•	•	•	•
		•		•	Oberdier Search Services	740-225-3057	•	•	•	
DT	**BK**	**CV**	**CR**	**PR**	**←Courts — HARRISON**	**Recording→**	**UC**	**RE**	**TX**	**VS**
•	•	•	•		Ace Background Check Inc	800-731-9221	•	•	•	•
		•	•	•	Dora Doty	740-695-4917	•	•	•	•
•	•	•	•	•	On the Record Inc	330-652-4109	•	•	•	•
		•	•	•	Woodard & Bohse Law Office [SOP]	330-343-8848 or 8849	•	•	•	•
DT	**BK**	**CV**	**CR**	**PR**	**←Courts — HENRY**	**Recording→**	**UC**	**RE**	**TX**	**VS**
•	•	•	•		Ace Background Check Inc	800-731-9221	•	•	•	•
DT	**BK**	**CV**	**CR**	**PR**	**←Courts — HIGHLAND**	**Recording→**	**UC**	**RE**	**TX**	**VS**
•	•	•	•		Ace Background Check Inc	800-731-9221	•	•	•	•
		•	•	•	Ginger Galloway	937-241-8442	•	•	•	
DT	**BK**	**CV**	**CR**	**PR**	**←Courts — HOCKING**	**Recording→**	**UC**	**RE**	**TX**	**VS**
•	•	•	•		Ace Background Check Inc	800-731-9221	•	•	•	•
•	•	•	•		Dennis S Carley and Associates Inc [SOP]	1-866-689-6899				
DT	**BK**	**CV**	**CR**	**PR**	**←Courts — HOLMES**	**Recording→**	**UC**	**RE**	**TX**	**VS**
•	•	•	•		Ace Background Check Inc	800-731-9221	•	•	•	•
•	•	•	•	•	Investigative Solutions	330-947-2911	•		•	•
•	•	•	•	•	On the Record Inc	330-652-4109	•	•	•	•
	•	•	•	•	David M Rumancik	330-837-7737	•	•	•	
		•	•	•	Urban Title Search Services	419-289-0437	•	•	•	•
		•	•	•	Woodard & Bohse Law Office [SOP]	330-343-8848 or 8849	•	•	•	•
DT	**BK**	**CV**	**CR**	**PR**	**←Courts — HURON**	**Recording→**	**UC**	**RE**	**TX**	**VS**
•	•	•	•		Ace Background Check Inc	800-731-9221	•	•	•	•
•	•	•	•	•	Investigative Solutions	330-947-2911	•		•	•
•	•	•	•	•	On the Record Inc	330-652-4109	•	•	•	•
DT	**BK**	**CV**	**CR**	**PR**	**←Courts — JACKSON**	**Recording→**	**UC**	**RE**	**TX**	**VS**
•	•	•	•		Ace Background Check Inc	800-731-9221	•	•	•	•

DT	BK	CV	CR	PR	Name	Phone	UC	RE	TX	VS
•	•	•	•	•	Docutech Information Services Inc	800-361-3310	•	•	•	•
		•	•	•	Salyer & Assoc.	740-596-5291	•	•	•	•

DT	BK	CV	CR	PR	←Courts	Jefferson Recording→	UC	RE	TX	VS
•	•	•	•		Ace Background Check Inc	800-731-9221	•	•	•	•
		•	•	•	Dora Doty	740-695-4917	•	•	•	•
					Liberty Record Search Inc	304-863-5542	•	•	•	
•	•	•	•	•	On the Record Inc	330-652-4109	•	•	•	•

DT	BK	CV	CR	PR	←Courts	Knox Recording→	UC	RE	TX	VS
•	•	•	•		Ace Background Check Inc	800-731-9221	•	•	•	•
•	•	•	•	•	M C Associates [SOP]	740-366-1922	•	•	•	•

DT	BK	CV	CR	PR	←Courts	Lake Recording→	UC	RE	TX	VS
•	•	•	•	•	A1 Cleveland Service Agency Inc [SOP]	888-212-5614	•	•	•	•
•	•	•	•		Ace Background Check Inc	800-731-9221	•	•	•	•
		•			Adams Title Agency	440-951-8296	•	•	•	
•		•	•		Advantage Background Services Inc	800-355-2650				
•	•	•	•	•	Allington International [SOP]	866-729-8555	•	•	•	•
•	•	•	•	•	Attorney Services of Northeast Ohio [SOP]	800-804-7787		•	•	
•	•	•	•	•	Boerger Investigative Services LLC [SOP]	877-754-8295	•	•	•	•
•	•	•	•	•	Chreyton Research	440-354-0316	•	•	•	•
•	•	•	•	•	Corporate Screening Services	800-229-8606	•			
•	•	•	•	•	Eagle Communications [SOP]	216-297-3200	•	•	•	•
•	•	•	•	•	Investigative Solutions	330-947-2911	•		•	•
•		•	•		Management Information Services	216-241-4282				
•	•	•	•	•	On the Record Inc	330-652-4109	•	•	•	•
•		•	•		Pre-Check, The Pre-Check Company	800-268-2435				
•	•	•	•	•	Research Associates	800-225-9693	•	•	•	•
•	•	•	•		Security Essentials LLC	216-839-0700			•	

DT	BK	CV	CR	PR	←Courts	Lawrence Recording→	UC	RE	TX	VS
•	•	•	•		Ace Background Check Inc	800-731-9221	•	•	•	•

DT	BK	CV	CR	PR	←Courts	Licking Recording→	UC	RE	TX	VS
•	•	•	•		Ace Background Check Inc	800-731-9221	•	•	•	•
•	•	•	•		ASK Services Inc	888-416-1313	•	•	•	
•	•	•	•	•	Boerger Investigative Services LLC [SOP]	877-754-8295	•	•	•	•
•	•	•	•		Dennis S Carley and Associates Inc [SOP]	1-866-689-6899				
•	•	•	•	•	Docutech Information Services Inc	800-361-3310	•	•	•	•
•	•	•	•	•	M C Associates [SOP]	740-366-1922	•	•	•	•
•	•	•			Search One Services	614-834-5603	•	•	•	

DT	BK	CV	CR	PR	←Courts	Logan Recording→	UC	RE	TX	VS
•	•	•	•		Ace Background Check Inc	800-731-9221	•	•	•	•

DT	BK	CV	CR	PR	←Courts	Lorain Recording→	UC	RE	TX	VS
•	•	•	•		Ace Background Check Inc	800-731-9221	•	•	•	•
•	•	•	•	•	Advanced Background Check Inc	888-264-4018	•	•	•	•
•	•	•	•	•	Allington International [SOP]	866-729-8555	•	•	•	•
•	•	•	•	•	Attorney Services of Northeast Ohio [SOP]	800-804-7787		•	•	
•	•	•	•	•	Corporate Screening Services	800-229-8606	•			
•	•	•	•	•	Eagle Communications [SOP]	216-297-3200	•	•	•	•
•	•	•	•	•	Investigative Solutions	330-947-2911	•		•	•
		•		•	Lorain County Title Co	440-284-5100	•	•	•	•
•		•	•		Management Information Services	216-241-4282				
•	•	•	•	•	On the Record Inc	330-652-4109	•	•	•	•
•		•	•		Pre-Check, The Pre-Check Company	800-268-2435				
•	•	•	•	•	Research Associates	800-225-9693	•	•	•	•

DT	BK	CV	CR	PR	←Courts LUCAS Recording→	UC	RE	TX	VS
•	•	•	•		Ace Background Check Inc....800-731-9221	•	•	•	•
•	•	•	•	•	Advanced Background Check Inc....888-264-4018	•	•	•	•
•	•	•	•		ASK Services Inc....888-416-1313	•	•	•	
•	•	•	•	•	Confidential Services [SOP]....800-752-4581	•	•	•	•
•	•	•	•	•	M & D Records Research....419-693-5649	•	•	•	•
•	•	•	•	•	National Service Information Inc (Ohio)....800-235-0337	•		•	•
•		•	•		Pre-Check, The Pre-Check Company....800-268-2435				

DT	BK	CV	CR	PR	←Courts MADISON Recording→	UC	RE	TX	VS
•	•	•	•		Ace Background Check Inc....800-731-9221	•	•	•	•
•	•	•	•		ASK Services Inc....888-416-1313	•	•	•	
•	•	•	•	•	Boerger Investigative Services LLC [SOP]....877-754-8295	•	•	•	•
		•	•	•	Ginger Galloway....937-241-8442	•	•	•	
		•	•	•	Research Information Consultants....614-286-6303	•	•	•	

DT	BK	CV	CR	PR	←Courts MAHONING Recording→	UC	RE	TX	VS
•	•	•	•		Ace Background Check Inc....800-731-9221	•	•	•	•
•	•	•	•	•	Attorney Services of Northeast Ohio [SOP]....800-804-7787		•	•	
•	•	•	•	•	Eagle Communications [SOP]....216-297-3200	•	•	•	•
•	•	•	•	•	Investigative Solutions....330-947-2911	•		•	•
•	•	•	•	•	On the Record Inc....330-652-4109	•	•	•	•
•		•	•		Pre-Check, The Pre-Check Company....800-268-2435				

DT	BK	CV	CR	PR	←Courts MARION Recording→	UC	RE	TX	VS
•	•	•	•		Ace Background Check Inc....800-731-9221	•	•	•	•
•	•	•	•	•	Boerger Investigative Services LLC [SOP]....877-754-8295	•	•	•	•
•	•	•	•	•	National Service Information Inc (Ohio)....800-235-0337	•		•	•
		•		•	Oberdier Search Services....740-225-3057	•	•	•	
		•	•	•	Precision Quest [SOP]....740-383-3753	•	•	•	
		•	•	•	Research Information Consultants....614-286-6303	•	•	•	

DT	BK	CV	CR	PR	←Courts MEDINA Recording→	UC	RE	TX	VS
•	•	•	•		Ace Background Check Inc....800-731-9221	•	•	•	•
•	•	•	•	•	Allington International [SOP]....866-729-8555	•	•	•	•
•	•	•	•	•	Attorney Services of Northeast Ohio [SOP]....800-804-7787	•	•	•	
•	•	•	•	•	Confidential Services [SOP]....800-752-4581	•	•	•	•
•	•	•	•	•	Corporate Screening Services....800-229-8606	•			
•	•	•	•	•	Investigative Solutions....330-947-2911	•		•	•
•	•	•	•		J H L Enterprises....440-845-2823	•		•	
	•	•		•	KasparNet LLC....800-886-7534	•	•	•	
•	•	•	•	•	On the Record Inc....330-652-4109	•	•	•	•
•	•	•	•	•	Sherlock Research....330-882-4690	•	•	•	•

DT	BK	CV	CR	PR	←Courts MEIGS Recording→	UC	RE	TX	VS
•	•	•	•	•	Accu-Check Information Services....304-375-4802	•		•	•
•	•	•	•		Ace Background Check Inc....800-731-9221	•	•	•	•
					Liberty Record Search Inc....304-863-5542	•	•	•	

DT	BK	CV	CR	PR	←Courts MERCER Recording→	UC	RE	TX	VS
		•	•		A1 Inv [SOP]....419-229-1955				
•	•	•	•		Ace Background Check Inc....800-731-9221	•	•	•	•
		•	•	•	Steven P Mielke....419-586-2323	•	•	•	

DT	BK	CV	CR	PR	←Courts MIAMI Recording→	UC	RE	TX	VS
•	•	•	•		Ace Background Check Inc....800-731-9221	•	•	•	•
•	•	•	•	•	Allen J Blazinski....937-475-4370	•	•	•	•
•	•	•	•		Midwest Investigative Services Inc [SOP]....800-227-9740				•
•	•	•	•		North American Security Solutions....888-898-6277		•	•	
•	•	•			Search One Services....614-834-5603	•	•	•	

DT	BK	CV	CR	PR	←Courts	MONROE	Recording→	UC	RE	TX	VS
•	•	•	•	•		Accu-Check Information Services	304-375-4802	•		•	•
•	•	•	•			Ace Background Check Inc	800-731-9221	•	•	•	•
		•	•	•		Dora Doty	740-695-4917	•	•	•	•

DT	BK	CV	CR	PR	←Courts	MONTGOMERY	Recording→	UC	RE	TX	VS
•	•	•	•			Ace Background Check Inc	800-731-9221	•	•	•	•
•	•	•	•	•		Advanced Background Check Inc	888-264-4018	•	•	•	•
•		•	•			Advantage Background Services Inc	800-355-2650				
•	•	•	•	•		Allen J Blazinski	937-475-4370	•	•	•	•
						Document Retrieval Network Inc	859-654-2890	•	•	•	
•	•	•	•	•		Docutech Information Services Inc	800-361-3310	•	•	•	•
•	•	•	•	•		General Corporate Inv - GCI [SOP]	800-735-7992	•	•	•	•
•	•	•	•	•		Legal Ease Inc [SOP]	800-519-6331	•	•	•	•
•	•	•	•	•		M C Associates [SOP]	740-366-1922	•	•	•	•
						Midwest Abstract Co	800-606-9488	•	•	•	
•	•	•	•			Midwest Investigative Services Inc [SOP]	800-227-9740				•
•	•	•	•	•		National Service Information Inc (Ohio)	800-235-0337	•		•	•
•	•	•	•			North American Security Solutions	888-898-6277		•	•	
•		•	•			Pre-Check, The Pre-Check Company	800-268-2435				
		•				Queen City Paralegal	513-984-4345				

DT	BK	CV	CR	PR	←Courts	MORGAN	Recording→	UC	RE	TX	VS
•	•	•	•	•		Accu-Check Information Services	304-375-4802	•		•	•
•	•	•	•			Ace Background Check Inc	800-731-9221	•	•	•	•

DT	BK	CV	CR	PR	←Courts	MORROW	Recording→	UC	RE	TX	VS
•	•	•	•			Ace Background Check Inc	800-731-9221	•	•	•	•
		•		•		Oberdier Search Services	740-225-3057	•	•	•	
		•	•	•		Precision Quest [SOP]	740-383-3753	•	•	•	
		•	•	•		Research Information Consultants	614-286-6303	•	•	•	

DT	BK	CV	CR	PR	←Courts	MUSKINGUM	Recording→	UC	RE	TX	VS
•	•	•	•			Ace Background Check Inc	800-731-9221	•	•	•	•
•	•	•	•	•		Docutech Information Services Inc	800-361-3310	•	•	•	•
•	•	•	•	•		M C Associates [SOP]	740-366-1922	•	•	•	•

DT	BK	CV	CR	PR	←Courts	NOBLE	Recording→	UC	RE	TX	VS
•	•	•	•	•		Accu-Check Information Services	304-375-4802	•		•	•
•	•	•	•			Ace Background Check Inc	800-731-9221	•	•	•	•
		•	•	•		Dora Doty	740-695-4917	•	•	•	•

DT	BK	CV	CR	PR	←Courts	OTTAWA	Recording→	UC	RE	TX	VS
•	•	•	•			Ace Background Check Inc	800-731-9221	•	•	•	•
•	•	•	•	•		Investigative Solutions	330-947-2911	•		•	•

DT	BK	CV	CR	PR	←Courts	PAULDING	Recording→	UC	RE	TX	VS
•	•	•	•			Ace Background Check Inc	800-731-9221	•	•	•	•

DT	BK	CV	CR	PR	←Courts	PERRY	Recording→	UC	RE	TX	VS
•	•	•	•			Ace Background Check Inc	800-731-9221	•	•	•	•
•	•	•	•			Dennis S Carley and Associates Inc [SOP]	1-866-689-6899				

DT	BK	CV	CR	PR	←Courts	PICKAWAY	Recording→	UC	RE	TX	VS
•	•	•	•			Ace Background Check Inc	800-731-9221	•	•	•	•
•	•	•	•			Dennis S Carley and Associates Inc [SOP]	1-866-689-6899				
•	•	•	•	•		Docutech Information Services Inc	800-361-3310	•	•	•	•
•	•	•	•	•		M C Associates [SOP]	740-366-1922	•	•	•	•
•	•	•				Search One Services	614-834-5603	•	•	•	

DT	BK	CV	CR	PR	←Courts **Pike**	Recording→	UC	RE	TX	VS
•	•	•	•		Ace Background Check Inc	800-731-9221	•	•	•	•
•	•	•	•	•	Docutech Information Services Inc	800-361-3310	•	•	•	•

DT	BK	CV	CR	PR	←Courts **Portage**	Recording→	UC	RE	TX	VS
•	•	•	•		Ace Background Check Inc	800-731-9221	•	•	•	•
•	•	•	•	•	Attorney Services of Northeast Ohio [SOP]	800-804-7787		•	•	
•	•	•	•	•	Check - Pointe, Inc	330-923-5930	•		•	
•	•	•	•	•	Eagle Communications [SOP]	216-297-3200	•	•	•	•
•	•	•	•	•	Investigative Solutions	330-947-2911	•		•	•
	•	•		•	KasparNet LLC	800-886-7534	•	•	•	
		•		•	Ohio Title	330-297-7003	•	•	•	•
•	•	•	•	•	On the Record Inc	330-652-4109	•	•	•	•
•	•	•	•	•	Sherlock Research	330-882-4690	•	•	•	•

DT	BK	CV	CR	PR	←Courts **Preble**	Recording→	UC	RE	TX	VS
•	•	•	•		Ace Background Check Inc	800-731-9221	•	•	•	•
•	•	•	•	•	Allen J Blazinski	937-475-4370	•	•	•	•
•	•	•	•	•	Legal Ease Inc [SOP]	800-519-6331	•	•	•	•
•	•	•	•		North American Security Solutions	888-898-6277		•	•	
		•			Union County Title Co	765-458-7148	•	•	•	

DT	BK	CV	CR	PR	←Courts **Putnam**	Recording→	UC	RE	TX	VS
		•	•		A1 Inv [SOP]	419-229-1955				
•	•	•	•	•	Accu-Check Information Services	304-375-4802	•		•	•
•	•	•	•		Ace Background Check Inc	800-731-9221	•	•	•	•

DT	BK	CV	CR	PR	←Courts **Richland**	Recording→	UC	RE	TX	VS
•	•	•	•		Ace Background Check Inc	800-731-9221	•	•	•	•
•	•	•	•	•	Boerger Investigative Services LLC [SOP]	877-754-8295	•	•	•	•
		•	•	•	Lori A Day	419-544-4740	•	•	•	
•	•	•	•	•	On the Record Inc	330-652-4109	•	•	•	•
		•	•	•	Urban Title Search Services	419-289-0437	•	•	•	•

DT	BK	CV	CR	PR	←Courts **Ross**	Recording→	UC	RE	TX	VS
•	•	•	•		Ace Background Check Inc	800-731-9221	•	•	•	•
•	•	•	•	•	Docutech Information Services Inc	800-361-3310	•	•	•	•
•	•	•	•	•	M C Associates [SOP]	740-366-1922	•	•	•	•

DT	BK	CV	CR	PR	←Courts **Sandusky**	Recording→	UC	RE	TX	VS
•	•	•	•		Ace Background Check Inc	800-731-9221	•	•	•	•
•	•	•	•	•	Investigative Solutions	330-947-2911	•		•	•

DT	BK	CV	CR	PR	←Courts **Scioto**	Recording→	UC	RE	TX	VS
•	•	•	•		Ace Background Check Inc	800-731-9221	•	•	•	•

DT	BK	CV	CR	PR	←Courts **Seneca**	Recording→	UC	RE	TX	VS
•	•	•	•		Ace Background Check Inc	800-731-9221	•	•	•	•

DT	BK	CV	CR	PR	←Courts **Shelby**	Recording→	UC	RE	TX	VS
•	•	•	•		Ace Background Check Inc	800-731-9221	•	•	•	•

DT	BK	CV	CR	PR	←Courts **Stark**	Recording→	UC	RE	TX	VS
•	•	•	•		Ace Background Check Inc	800-731-9221	•	•	•	•
•	•	•	•	•	Allington International [SOP]	866-729-8555	•	•	•	•
•	•	•	•	•	Attorney Services of Northeast Ohio [SOP]	800-804-7787		•	•	
•	•	•	•	•	Boerger Investigative Services LLC [SOP]	877-754-8295	•	•	•	•
•	•	•	•	•	Eagle Communications [SOP]	216-297-3200	•	•	•	•
•	•	•	•	•	Investigative Solutions	330-947-2911	•		•	•
•	•	•	•	•	On the Record Inc	330-652-4109	•	•	•	•
	•	•	•	•	David M Rumancik	330-837-7737	•	•	•	

DT	BK	CV	CR	PR	←Courts		Recording→	UC	RE	TX	VS
•	•	•	•	•	Sherlock Research	330-882-4690		•	•	•	•

DT	BK	CV	CR	PR	←Courts	**SUMMIT**	Recording→	UC	RE	TX	VS
•	•	•	•		Ace Background Check Inc	800-731-9221		•	•	•	•
•	•	•	•	•	Advanced Background Check Inc	888-264-4018		•	•	•	•
•		•	•		Advantage Background Services Inc	800-355-2650					
•	•	•	•	•	Allington International [SOP]	866-729-8555		•	•	•	•
•	•	•	•	•	Attorney Services of Northeast Ohio [SOP]	800-804-7787			•	•	
•	•	•	•	•	Boerger Investigative Services LLC [SOP]	877-754-8295		•	•	•	•
•	•	•	•	•	Check - Pointe, Inc	330-923-5930		•		•	
•	•	•	•	•	Eagle Communications [SOP]	216-297-3200		•	•	•	•
•	•	•	•	•	Investigative Solutions	330-947-2911		•		•	•
	•	•		•	KasparNet LLC	800-886-7534		•	•	•	
•	•	•	•	•	National Service Information Inc (Ohio)	800-235-0337		•		•	•
•	•	•	•	•	On the Record Inc	330-652-4109		•	•	•	•
•		•	•		Pre-Check, The Pre-Check Company	800-268-2435					
•	•	•	•	•	Research Associates	800-225-9693		•	•	•	•
	•	•	•	•	David M Rumancik	330-837-7737		•	•	•	
•	•	•	•		Security Essentials LLC	216-839-0700				•	
•	•	•	•	•	Sherlock Research	330-882-4690		•	•	•	•

DT	BK	CV	CR	PR	←Courts	**TRUMBULL**	Recording→	UC	RE	TX	VS
•	•	•	•		Ace Background Check Inc	800-731-9221		•	•	•	•
•	•	•	•	•	Allington International [SOP]	866-729-8555		•	•	•	•
•	•	•	•	•	Attorney Services of Northeast Ohio [SOP]	800-804-7787			•	•	
•	•	•	•	•	Eagle Communications [SOP]	216-297-3200		•	•	•	•
•	•	•	•	•	Investigative Solutions	330-947-2911		•		•	•
•	•	•	•	•	On the Record Inc	330-652-4109		•	•	•	•
	•	•	•	•	David M Rumancik	330-837-7737		•	•	•	
				•	Trumbull County Abstract Co	330-399-1891			•	•	

DT	BK	CV	CR	PR	←Courts	**TUSCARAWAS**	Recording→	UC	RE	TX	VS
•	•	•	•		Ace Background Check Inc	800-731-9221		•	•	•	•
•	•	•	•	•	Investigative Solutions	330-947-2911		•		•	•
•	•	•	•	•	On the Record Inc	330-652-4109		•	•	•	•
	•	•	•	•	David M Rumancik	330-837-7737		•	•	•	
		•	•	•	Woodard & Bohse Law Office [SOP]	330-343-8848 or 8849		•	•	•	•

DT	BK	CV	CR	PR	←Courts	**UNION**	Recording→	UC	RE	TX	VS
•	•	•	•		Ace Background Check Inc	800-731-9221		•	•	•	•
•	•	•	•	•	Boerger Investigative Services LLC [SOP]	877-754-8295		•	•	•	•
•	•	•	•	•	M C Associates [SOP]	740-366-1922		•	•	•	•
		•		•	Oberdier Search Services	740-225-3057		•	•	•	
		•	•	•	Precision Quest [SOP]	740-383-3753		•	•	•	
		•	•	•	Research Information Consultants	614-286-6303		•	•	•	

DT	BK	CV	CR	PR	←Courts	**VAN WERT**	Recording→	UC	RE	TX	VS
		•	•		A1 Inv [SOP]	419-229-1955					
•	•	•	•		Ace Background Check Inc	800-731-9221		•	•	•	•
		•	•	•	Steven P Mielke	419-586-2323		•	•	•	

DT	BK	CV	CR	PR	←Courts	**VINTON**	Recording→	UC	RE	TX	VS
•	•	•	•		Ace Background Check Inc	800-731-9221		•	•	•	•
		•	•	•	Salyer & Assoc.	740-596-5291		•	•	•	•

DT	BK	CV	CR	PR	←Courts	**WARREN**	Recording→	UC	RE	TX	VS
•	•	•	•		Ace Background Check Inc	800-731-9221		•	•	•	•
•	•	•	•	•	Active Detective Bureau Inc [SOP]	800-405-4006			•	•	•
•	•	•	•	•	Advanced Background Check Inc	888-264-4018		•	•	•	•
		•			Cynthia H Miller, Paralegal	513-368-2855		•	•	•	
					Document Retrieval Network Inc	859-654-2890		•	•	•	

DT	BK	CV	CR	PR			UC	RE	TX	VS
•	•	•	•	•	General Corporate Inv - GCI [SOP]	800-735-7992	•	•	•	•
•	•	•	•	•	Legal Ease Inc [SOP]	800-519-6331	•	•	•	•
•	•	•	•		Midwest Investigative Services Inc [SOP]	800-227-9740				•
			•		Phoenix Research Inc	800-260-1092				
		•			Queen City Paralegal	513-984-4345				
		•		•	Urban Abstract Inc	513-755-8527	•	•		
•		•	•		Xpedite Wholesale Criminal Research	800-325-3609				

DT	BK	CV	CR	PR	←COURTS **WASHINGTON**	RECORDING→	UC	RE	TX	VS
•	•	•	•	•	Accu-Check Information Services	304-375-4802	•		•	•
•	•	•	•		Ace Background Check Inc	800-731-9221	•	•	•	•
					Liberty Record Search Inc	304-863-5542	•	•	•	

DT	BK	CV	CR	PR	←COURTS **WAYNE**	RECORDING→	UC	RE	TX	VS
•	•	•	•		Ace Background Check Inc	800-731-9221	•	•	•	•
•	•	•	•	•	Attorney Services of Northeast Ohio [SOP]	800-804-7787		•	•	
•	•	•	•	•	Investigative Solutions	330-947-2911	•		•	•
•	•	•	•		J H L Enterprises	440-845-2823	•		•	
•	•	•	•	•	On the Record Inc	330-652-4109	•	•	•	•
	•	•	•	•	David M Rumancik	330-837-7737	•	•	•	
•	•	•	•	•	Sherlock Research	330-882-4690	•	•	•	•
		•	•	•	Urban Title Search Services	419-289-0437	•	•	•	•

DT	BK	CV	CR	PR	←COURTS **WILLIAMS**	RECORDING→	UC	RE	TX	VS
•	•	•	•		Ace Background Check Inc	800-731-9221	•	•	•	•

DT	BK	CV	CR	PR	←COURTS **WOOD**	RECORDING→	UC	RE	TX	VS
•	•	•	•		Ace Background Check Inc	800-731-9221	•	•	•	•
•	•	•	•	•	M & D Records Research	419-693-5649	•	•	•	•

DT	BK	CV	CR	PR	←COURTS **WYANDOT**	RECORDING→	UC	RE	TX	VS
•	•	•	•		Ace Background Check Inc	800-731-9221	•	•	•	•
•	•	•	•	•	Boerger Investigative Services LLC [SOP]	877-754-8295	•	•	•	•
		•		•	Oberdier Search Services	740-225-3057	•	•	•	

[SOP] = PERFORMS SERVICE OF PROCESS

COURT RECORDS

CODE	GOVERNMENT AGENCY	TYPE OF INFORMATION
DT	US District Court	Federal civil and criminal cases
BK	Bankruptcy Court	United States bankruptcy cases
CV	Civil Court	Municipal, county and state level civil cases
CR	Criminal Court	Municipal, county and state level criminal cases
PR	Probate Court	Wills and estate cases

COUNTY RECORDS - RECORDINGS

CODE	GOVERNMENT AGENCY	TYPE OF INFORMATION
UC	UCC Filing Office	Uniform Commercial Code and other personal property liens
RE	Real Estate Recording Office	Real property transactions and liens
TX	Tax Filing Office(s)	Federal and state tax liens, judgment liens
VS	Vital Records Office	Vital statistics—birth, death, marriage, divorce

Oklahoma

COURT RECORDS RETRIEVED — **RECORDING RECORDS RETRIEVED**

DT	BK	CV	CR	PR	←COURTS **ADAIR** RECORDING→		UC	RE	TX	VS
•	•	•	•	•	AAA Abstract Co Inc (Oklahoma)	918-696-2770	•	•	•	•
•	•	•	•	•	CourthouseData	479-582-0900	•	•	•	•
•	•	•	•		Document Retrieval Service	877-902-9377	•	•	•	•
•	•			•	Records Search & Report Svc	918-885-4724	•	•	•	•

DT	BK	CV	CR	PR	←COURTS **ALFALFA** RECORDING→		UC	RE	TX	VS
		•		•	Alfalfa Guaranty Abstract Co	580-596-3394	•	•	•	•
•	•	•	•		Document Retrieval Service	877-902-9377	•	•	•	•

DT	BK	CV	CR	PR	←COURTS **ATOKA** RECORDING→		UC	RE	TX	VS
					Atoka Abstract Co Inc	580-889-7316	•	•	•	
•	•	•	•		Document Retrieval Service	877-902-9377	•	•	•	•
					Moore Mowdy & Youngblood	580-889-5656				

DT	BK	CV	CR	PR	←COURTS **BEAVER** RECORDING→		UC	RE	TX	VS
		•		•	Beaver County Abstract Co	580-625-4423	•	•	•	•
•	•	•	•		Document Retrieval Service	877-902-9377	•	•	•	•

DT	BK	CV	CR	PR	←COURTS **BECKHAM** RECORDING→		UC	RE	TX	VS
		•	•	•	Beckham County Abstract	580-928-3143	•	•	•	•
•	•	•	•		Document Retrieval Service	877-902-9377	•	•	•	•
		•	•		Redi-Info Information Services	888-320-6805				

DT	BK	CV	CR	PR	←COURTS **BLAINE** RECORDING→		UC	RE	TX	VS
		•		•	Blaine County Abstract	580-623-7248 or 7257	•	•	•	
•	•	•	•		Document Retrieval Service	877-902-9377	•	•	•	•
		•	•		Redi-Info Information Services	888-320-6805				

DT	BK	CV	CR	PR	←COURTS **BRYAN** RECORDING→		UC	RE	TX	VS
•	•	•	•	•	Clarke Investigations Inc [SOP]	405-844-7300	•	•	•	•
•	•	•	•		Document Retrieval Service	877-902-9377	•	•	•	•
					Moore Mowdy & Youngblood	580-889-5656		•		
		•	•		Redi-Info Information Services	888-320-6805				
					Pat Stephens	903-583-5215		•	•	

DT	BK	CV	CR	PR	←COURTS **CADDO** RECORDING→		UC	RE	TX	VS
•	•	•	•	•	Clarke Investigations Inc [SOP]	405-844-7300	•	•	•	•
•	•	•	•		Document Retrieval Service	877-902-9377	•	•	•	•
		•	•	•	Lacey Pioneer Abstract Company Inc	405-247-5152	•	•	•	•
•	•	•	•		Tammy L Listen Investigations [SOP]	405-340-4843	•	•	•	•

DT	BK	CV	CR	PR	←COURTS **CANADIAN** RECORDING→		UC	RE	TX	VS
•	•	•	•	•	American Detective Agency [SOP]	800-219-9120	•	•	•	•
•	•	•	•	•	Clarke Investigations Inc [SOP]	405-844-7300	•	•	•	•
•	•	•	•		Document Retrieval Service	877-902-9377	•	•	•	•
					Noel D Law Jr	918-599-0988	•	•		
•	•	•	•	•	Mid-West Investigations [SOP]	800-359-5410	•	•	•	•
		•	•		Redi-Info Information Services	888-320-6805				
•		•	•	•	Rus B Robison & Associates Inc [SOP]	877-721-2295	•	•	•	•
•	•	•	•		Tammy L Listen Investigations [SOP]	405-340-4843	•	•	•	•
•	•	•	•	•	United Legal Services [SOP]	888-232-8432	•	•	•	

DT	BK	CV	CR	PR	←Courts	CARTER	Recording→	UC	RE	TX	VS
•	•	•	•	•		Clarke Investigations Inc [SOP]	405-844-7300	•	•	•	•
•	•	•	•			Document Retrieval Service	877-902-9377	•	•	•	•
						Marshall County Abstract Co	580-795-7388		•		

DT	BK	CV	CR	PR	←Courts	CHEROKEE	Recording→	UC	RE	TX	VS
		•	•	•		Cherokee Capitol Abstract Title & Closing	918-456-8851	•	•	•	•
•	•	•	•	•		Clarke Investigations Inc [SOP]	405-844-7300	•	•	•	•
•	•	•	•	•		CourthouseData	479-582-0900	•	•	•	•
•	•	•	•			Document Retrieval Service	877-902-9377	•	•	•	•
						Noel D Law Jr	918-599-0988	•	•		
•	•	•	•	•		Oklahoma Court Explorers	918-360-4798	•	•	•	
•	•			•		Records Search & Report Svc	918-885-4724	•	•	•	•
		•	•			Redi-Info Information Services	888-320-6805				

DT	BK	CV	CR	PR	←Courts	CHOCTAW	Recording→	UC	RE	TX	VS
		•		•		Choctaw County Abstract & Title	580-326-9616	•	•	•	
•	•	•	•			Document Retrieval Service	877-902-9377	•	•	•	•
•		•	•			Kota Cornelius Kruse & Assoc	903-783-1883		•	•	

DT	BK	CV	CR	PR	←Courts	CIMARRON	Recording→	UC	RE	TX	VS
•	•	•	•			Document Retrieval Service	877-902-9377	•	•	•	•

DT	BK	CV	CR	PR	←Courts	CLEVELAND	Recording→	UC	RE	TX	VS
•	•	•	•	•		American Detective Agency [SOP]	800-219-9120	•	•	•	•
		•		•		American-First Abstract Co	405-321-7577	•	•	•	
•	•	•	•	•		Clarke Investigations Inc [SOP]	405-844-7300	•	•	•	•
•	•	•	•	•		CourthouseData	479-582-0900	•	•	•	•
•	•	•	•			Document Retrieval Service	877-902-9377	•	•	•	•
						Noel D Law Jr	918-599-0988	•	•		
•	•	•	•	•		Mid-West Investigations [SOP]	800-359-5410	•	•	•	•
		•	•			Redi-Info Information Services	888-320-6805				
•		•	•	•		Rus B Robison & Associates Inc [SOP]	877-721-2295	•	•	•	•
•	•	•	•			Tammy L Listen Investigations [SOP]	405-340-4843	•	•	•	•
•	•	•	•	•		United Legal Services [SOP]	888-232-8432	•	•	•	

DT	BK	CV	CR	PR	←Courts	COAL	Recording→	UC	RE	TX	VS
•	•	•	•			Document Retrieval Service	877-902-9377	•	•	•	•
						Moore Mowdy & Youngblood	580-889-5656		•		

DT	BK	CV	CR	PR	←Courts	COMANCHE	Recording→	UC	RE	TX	VS
•	•	•	•	•		H Ray Anderson	580-355-4450	•	•	•	
•	•	•	•	•		Clarke Investigations Inc [SOP]	405-844-7300	•	•	•	•
•	•	•	•			Document Retrieval Service	877-902-9377	•	•	•	•
		•	•	•		King Investigations Inc	580-477-1676	•	•	•	•
•	•	•	•	•		Mendenhall Information Services	940-696-0758	•	•	•	•
		•	•			Redi-Info Information Services	888-320-6805				
		•		•		Southwest Abstract & Title Co	405-355-3680	•	•	•	•
		•	•	•		T.A.B.B.S. Inv & Process Service [SOP]	580-477-3292	•	•	•	•

DT	BK	CV	CR	PR	←Courts	COTTON	Recording→	UC	RE	TX	VS
•	•	•	•	•		H Ray Anderson	580-355-4450	•	•	•	
•	•	•	•			Document Retrieval Service	877-902-9377	•	•	•	•
•	•	•	•	•		Mendenhall Information Services	940-696-0758	•	•	•	•
		•	•			Redi-Info Information Services	888-320-6805				

DT	BK	CV	CR	PR	←Courts	CRAIG	Recording→	UC	RE	TX	VS
•	•	•	•	•		CourthouseData	479-582-0900	•	•	•	•
		•	•			Davis and Assoc. [SOP]	918-825-5223				
•	•	•	•			Document Retrieval Service	877-902-9377	•	•	•	•
						Noel D Law Jr	918-599-0988	•	•		

DT	BK	CV	CR	PR			UC	RE	TX	VS
•	•			•	Records Search & Report Svc	918-885-4724	•	•	•	•
		•	•		Redi-Info Information Services	888-320-6805				
					Vinita Title Co	918-256-2617	•	•	•	•

DT	BK	CV	CR	PR	←Courts **CREEK**	Recording→	UC	RE	TX	VS
•	•	•	•	•	Clarke Investigations Inc [SOP]	405-844-7300	•	•	•	•
•	•	•	•	•	CourthouseData	479-582-0900	•	•	•	•
					Docu-File Inc	877-742-4994	•	•	•	•
•	•	•	•		Document Retrieval Service	877-902-9377	•	•	•	•
					Noel D Law Jr	918-599-0988	•	•		
•	•			•	Records Search & Report Svc	918-885-4724	•	•	•	•
		•	•		Redi-Info Information Services	888-320-6805				
•	•	•	•	•	SRT Investigations	800-499-0472	•	•	•	
		•		•	Union-Speer Abstract Co	918-224-4540	•	•	•	
•	•	•	•	•	Zero Investigations Inc [SOP]	866-400-9376	•	•	•	•

DT	BK	CV	CR	PR	←Courts **CUSTER**	Recording→	UC	RE	TX	VS
•	•	•	•	•	Clarke Investigations Inc [SOP]	405-844-7300	•	•	•	•
		•		•	Clinton Abstract Co Inc	580-323-3025	•	•	•	
•	•	•	•		Document Retrieval Service	877-902-9377	•	•	•	•
		•	•		Redi-Info Information Services	888-320-6805				

DT	BK	CV	CR	PR	←Courts **DELAWARE**	Recording→	UC	RE	TX	VS
•	•	•	•	•	Clarke Investigations Inc [SOP]	405-844-7300	•	•	•	•
•	•	•	•	•	CourthouseData	479-582-0900	•	•	•	•
		•	•		Davis and Assoc. [SOP]	918-825-5223				
		•		•	Delaware County Abstract Co (Oklahoma)	918-253-4425	•	•	•	
•	•	•	•		Document Retrieval Service	877-902-9377	•	•	•	•
					Noel D Law Jr	918-599-0988	•	•		
•	•			•	Records Search & Report Svc	918-885-4724	•	•	•	•
		•	•		Redi-Info Information Services	888-320-6805				

DT	BK	CV	CR	PR	←Courts **DEWEY**	Recording→	UC	RE	TX	VS
•	•	•	•	•	Clarke Investigations Inc [SOP]	405-844-7300	•	•	•	•
•	•	•	•	•	Dewey County Abstract Co	580-328-5556	•	•	•	•
•	•	•	•		Document Retrieval Service	877-902-9377	•	•	•	•

DT	BK	CV	CR	PR	←Courts **ELLIS**	Recording→	UC	RE	TX	VS
•	•	•	•	•	Clarke Investigations Inc [SOP]	405-844-7300	•	•	•	•
•	•	•	•		Document Retrieval Service	877-902-9377	•	•	•	•

DT	BK	CV	CR	PR	←Courts **GARFIELD**	Recording→	UC	RE	TX	VS
•	•	•	•	•	Clarke Investigations Inc [SOP]	405-844-7300	•	•	•	•
•	•	•	•		Document Retrieval Service	877-902-9377	•	•	•	•
		•		•	J C Humphrey Abstract Co	580-237-3136	•	•	•	
		•	•		Redi-Info Information Services	888-320-6805				

DT	BK	CV	CR	PR	←Courts **GARVIN**	Recording→	UC	RE	TX	VS
•	•	•	•	•	Clarke Investigations Inc [SOP]	405-844-7300	•	•	•	•
•	•	•	•		Document Retrieval Service	877-902-9377	•	•	•	•
		•	•		Redi-Info Information Services	888-320-6805				

DT	BK	CV	CR	PR	←Courts **GRADY**	Recording→	UC	RE	TX	VS
•	•	•	•	•	Clarke Investigations Inc [SOP]	405-844-7300	•	•	•	•
•	•	•	•		Document Retrieval Service	877-902-9377	•	•	•	•
					Noel D Law Jr	918-599-0988	•	•		
•	•	•	•		Tammy L Listen Investigations [SOP]	405-340-4843	•	•	•	•
•	•	•	•	•	United Legal Services [SOP]	888-232-8432	•	•	•	
		•		•	Washita Valley Abstract Co	405-224-6111	•	•	•	

DT	BK	CV	CR	PR	←COURTS	GRANT	RECORDING→	UC	RE	TX	VS
•	•	•	•		Document Retrieval Service		877-902-9377	•	•	•	•
		•		•	Grant County Abstract Co (Oklahoma)		580-395-2854	•	•	•	
		•	•		Redi-Info Information Services		888-320-6805				

DT	BK	CV	CR	PR	←COURTS	GREER	RECORDING→	UC	RE	TX	VS
•	•	•	•	•	Clarke Investigations Inc [SOP]		405-844-7300	•	•	•	•
•	•	•	•		Document Retrieval Service		877-902-9377	•	•	•	•
		•		•	Greer Guaranty Abstract Co		580-782-3121	•	•	•	•
		•	•	•	King Investigations Inc		580-477-1676	•	•	•	
		•	•	•	T.A.B.B.S. Inv & Process Service [SOP]		580-477-3292	•	•	•	•

DT	BK	CV	CR	PR	←COURTS	HARMON	RECORDING→	UC	RE	TX	VS
•	•	•	•	•	Clarke Investigations Inc [SOP]		405-844-7300	•	•	•	•
•	•	•	•		Document Retrieval Service		877-902-9377	•	•	•	•
		•	•	•	King Investigations Inc		580-477-1676	•	•	•	
		•	•	•	T.A.B.B.S. Inv & Process Service [SOP]		580-477-3292	•	•	•	•

DT	BK	CV	CR	PR	←COURTS	HARPER	RECORDING→	UC	RE	TX	VS
•	•	•	•	•	Clarke Investigations Inc [SOP]		405-844-7300	•	•	•	•
•	•	•	•		Document Retrieval Service		877-902-9377	•	•	•	•
		•		•	Woodward County Abstract Co		580-256-3344	•	•	•	

DT	BK	CV	CR	PR	←COURTS	HASKELL	RECORDING→	UC	RE	TX	VS
•	•	•	•		Document Retrieval Service		877-902-9377	•	•	•	•
		•		•	Guaranty Abstract of Stigler		918-967-8876	•	•	•	
		•		•	Hebert Land Services		918-647-9524	•	•	•	•
•	•			•	Records Search & Report Svc		918-885-4724	•	•	•	•
		•	•		Redi-Info Information Services		888-320-6805				

DT	BK	CV	CR	PR	←COURTS	HUGHES	RECORDING→	UC	RE	TX	VS
		•		•	Atlas Abstract Co		405-379-3311	•	•	•	
•	•	•	•		Document Retrieval Service		877-902-9377	•	•	•	•
		•	•		Redi-Info Information Services		888-320-6805				

DT	BK	CV	CR	PR	←COURTS	JACKSON	RECORDING→	UC	RE	TX	VS
•	•	•	•	•	Clarke Investigations Inc [SOP]		405-844-7300	•	•	•	•
•	•	•	•		Document Retrieval Service		877-902-9377	•	•	•	•
		•		•	Jackson County Abstract Co		580-482-1235	•	•	•	
		•	•	•	King Investigations Inc		580-477-1676	•	•	•	
•	•	•	•	•	Mendenhall Information Services		940-696-0758	•	•	•	•
		•	•	•	T.A.B.B.S. Inv & Process Service [SOP]		580-477-3292	•	•	•	•

DT	BK	CV	CR	PR	←COURTS	JEFFERSON	RECORDING→	UC	RE	TX	VS
•	•	•	•	•	H Ray Anderson		580-355-4450	•	•	•	
•	•	•	•		Document Retrieval Service		877-902-9377	•	•	•	•

DT	BK	CV	CR	PR	←COURTS	JOHNSTON	RECORDING→	UC	RE	TX	VS
		•		•	Buffalo Land Abstract Inc		800-631-1880	•	•	•	
•	•	•	•		Document Retrieval Service		877-902-9377	•	•	•	•
					Marshall County Abstract Co		580-795-7388		•		
					Moore Mowdy & Youngblood		580-889-5656		•		

DT	BK	CV	CR	PR	←COURTS	KAY	RECORDING→	UC	RE	TX	VS
		•		•	Albright Abstract & Title Guaranty		800-522-1251		•	•	
•	•	•	•	•	Clarke Investigations Inc [SOP]		405-844-7300	•	•	•	•
•	•	•	•		Document Retrieval Service		877-902-9377	•	•	•	•
•	•			•	Records Search & Report Svc		918-885-4724	•	•	•	•
		•	•		Redi-Info Information Services		888-320-6805				

DT	BK	CV	CR	PR	←Courts	Kingfisher	Recording→	UC	RE	TX	VS
•	•	•	•	•	Clarke Investigations Inc [SOP]		405-844-7300	•	•	•	•
•	•	•	•		Document Retrieval Service		877-902-9377	•	•	•	•
		•	•		Redi-Info Information Services		888-320-6805				

DT	BK	CV	CR	PR	←Courts	Kiowa	Recording→	UC	RE	TX	VS
•	•	•	•	•	Clarke Investigations Inc [SOP]		405-844-7300	•	•	•	•
•	•	•	•		Document Retrieval Service		877-902-9377	•	•	•	•
		•	•	•	King Investigations Inc		580-477-1676	•	•	•	
		•		•	Kiowa County Abstract Company		580-726-5283	•	•	•	
		•	•	•	T.A.B.B.S. Inv & Process Service [SOP]		580-477-3292	•	•	•	•

DT	BK	CV	CR	PR	←Courts	Latimer	Recording→	UC	RE	TX	VS
•	•	•	•		Document Retrieval Service		877-902-9377	•	•	•	•
		•		•	Hebert Land Services		918-647-9524	•	•	•	•

DT	BK	CV	CR	PR	←Courts	Le Flore	Recording→	UC	RE	TX	VS
•	•	•	•		Document Retrieval Service		877-902-9377	•	•	•	•
		•		•	Hebert Land Services		918-647-9524	•	•	•	•

DT	BK	CV	CR	PR	←Courts	Lincoln	Recording→	UC	RE	TX	VS
		•		•	Abstract & Guaranty Co.		405-258-1244	•	•	•	
•	•	•	•	•	Clarke Investigations Inc [SOP]		405-844-7300	•	•	•	•
•	•	•	•	•	CourthouseData		479-582-0900	•	•	•	•
•	•	•	•		Document Retrieval Service		877-902-9377	•	•	•	•
					Noel D Law Jr		918-599-0988	•	•		
•	•			•	Records Search & Report Svc		918-885-4724	•	•	•	•
		•	•		Redi-Info Information Services		888-320-6805				
•	•	•	•		Tammy L Listen Investigations [SOP]		405-340-4843	•	•	•	•
•	•	•	•	•	United Legal Services [SOP]		888-232-8432	•	•	•	

DT	BK	CV	CR	PR	←Courts	Logan	Recording→	UC	RE	TX	VS
•	•	•	•	•	Clarke Investigations Inc [SOP]		405-844-7300	•	•	•	•
•	•	•	•		Document Retrieval Service		877-902-9377	•	•	•	•
					Noel D Law Jr		918-599-0988	•	•		
•	•			•	Records Search & Report Svc		918-885-4724	•	•	•	•
•	•	•	•	•	SRT Investigations		800-499-0472	•	•	•	•
•	•	•	•		Tammy L Listen Investigations [SOP]		405-340-4843	•	•	•	•
•	•	•	•	•	United Legal Services [SOP]		888-232-8432	•	•	•	

DT	BK	CV	CR	PR	←Courts	Love	Recording→	UC	RE	TX	VS
•	•	•	•		Document Retrieval Service		877-902-9377	•	•	•	•
		•		•	Marietta Abstract Co		580-276-2231	•	•	•	•

DT	BK	CV	CR	PR	←Courts	Major	Recording→	UC	RE	TX	VS
•	•	•	•		Document Retrieval Service		877-902-9377	•	•	•	•
		•	•	•	Fairview Abstract Co		580-227-4524	•	•	•	•

DT	BK	CV	CR	PR	←Courts	Marshall	Recording→	UC	RE	TX	VS
•	•	•	•		Document Retrieval Service		877-902-9377	•	•	•	•
					Marshall County Abstract Co		580-795-7388		•		

DT	BK	CV	CR	PR	←Courts	Mayes	Recording→	UC	RE	TX	VS
•	•	•	•	•	Clarke Investigations Inc [SOP]		405-844-7300	•	•	•	•
•	•	•	•	•	CourthouseData		479-582-0900	•	•	•	•
		•	•		Davis and Assoc. [SOP]		918-825-5223				
•	•	•	•		Document Retrieval Service		877-902-9377	•	•	•	•
					Noel D Law Jr		918-599-0988	•	•		
		•		•	Mayes County Abstract		918-825-3074	•	•	•	•
•	•	•	•	•	Oklahoma Court Explorers		918-360-4798	•	•	•	
•	•			•	Records Search & Report Svc		918-885-4724	•	•	•	•

DT	BK	CV	CR	PR	←COURTS	RECORDING→	UC	RE	TX	VS
		•	•		Redi-Info Information Services	888-320-6805				

DT	BK	CV	CR	PR	←COURTS MCCLAIN	RECORDING→	UC	RE	TX	VS
		•		•	American Abstract Company	405-527-7575	•	•	•	
•	•	•	•	•	Clarke Investigations Inc [SOP]	405-844-7300	•	•	•	•
•	•	•	•		Document Retrieval Service	877-902-9377	•	•	•	•
					Noel D Law Jr	918-599-0988	•	•		
		•	•		Redi-Info Information Services	888-320-6805				
•		•	•	•	Rus B Robison & Associates Inc [SOP]	877-721-2295	•	•	•	•
•	•	•	•		Tammy L Listen Investigations [SOP]	405-340-4843	•	•	•	•
•	•	•	•	•	United Legal Services [SOP]	888-232-8432	•	•	•	

DT	BK	CV	CR	PR	←COURTS MCCURTAIN	RECORDING→	UC	RE	TX	VS
•	•	•	•		Document Retrieval Service	877-902-9377	•	•	•	•
		•		•	Southern Abstract & Title Co	580-286-2288	•	•	•	•

DT	BK	CV	CR	PR	←COURTS MCINTOSH	RECORDING→	UC	RE	TX	VS
•	•	•	•	•	CourthouseData	479-582-0900	•	•	•	•
•	•	•	•		Document Retrieval Service	877-902-9377	•	•	•	•
					Eufaula Abstract & Title Co Inc	918-689-2241	•	•	•	
•	•	•	•	•	Oklahoma Court Explorers	918-360-4798	•	•	•	
•	•			•	Records Search & Report Svc	918-885-4724	•	•	•	•

DT	BK	CV	CR	PR	←COURTS MURRAY	RECORDING→	UC	RE	TX	VS
•	•	•	•		Document Retrieval Service	877-902-9377	•	•	•	•
		•		•	Murray County Abstract Inc	800-687-2988	•	•	•	

DT	BK	CV	CR	PR	←COURTS MUSKOGEE	RECORDING→	UC	RE	TX	VS
•	•	•	•	•	Clarke Investigations Inc [SOP]	405-844-7300	•	•	•	•
•	•	•	•	•	CourthouseData	479-582-0900	•	•	•	•
•	•	•	•		Document Retrieval Service	877-902-9377	•	•	•	•
					Noel D Law Jr	918-599-0988	•	•		
•	•	•	•	•	Oklahoma Court Explorers	918-360-4798	•	•	•	
•	•			•	Records Search & Report Svc	918-885-4724	•	•	•	•
		•	•		Redi-Info Information Services	888-320-6805				
•	•	•	•	•	SRT Investigations	800-499-0472	•	•	•	

DT	BK	CV	CR	PR	←COURTS NOBLE	RECORDING→	UC	RE	TX	VS
•	•	•	•	•	Clarke Investigations Inc [SOP]	405-844-7300	•	•	•	•
•	•	•	•		Document Retrieval Service	877-902-9377	•	•	•	•
					Noel D Law Jr	918-599-0988	•	•		
•		•	•	•	Powers Abstract Co Inc	580-336-4068	•	•	•	
•	•			•	Records Search & Report Svc	918-885-4724	•	•	•	•
		•	•		Redi-Info Information Services	888-320-6805				

DT	BK	CV	CR	PR	←COURTS NOWATA	RECORDING→	UC	RE	TX	VS
•	•	•	•	•	CourthouseData	479-582-0900	•	•	•	•
•	•	•	•		Document Retrieval Service	877-902-9377	•	•	•	•
					Noel D Law Jr	918-599-0988	•	•		
•	•			•	Records Search & Report Svc	918-885-4724	•	•	•	•
•	•	•	•	•	SRT Investigations	800-499-0472	•	•	•	

DT	BK	CV	CR	PR	←COURTS OKFUSKEE	RECORDING→	UC	RE	TX	VS
•	•	•	•	•	CourthouseData	479-582-0900	•	•	•	•
•	•	•	•		Document Retrieval Service	877-902-9377	•	•	•	•
		•		•	Okfusee Abstract & Title Co	918-623-0565	•	•	•	•
•	•			•	Records Search & Report Svc	918-885-4724	•	•	•	•

DT	BK	CV	CR	PR	←COURTS OKLAHOMA	RECORDING→	UC	RE	TX	VS
•	•	•	•	•	American Detective Agency [SOP]	800-219-9120	•	•	•	•
•	•	•	•	•	Clarke Investigations Inc [SOP]	405-844-7300	•	•	•	•

DT	BK	CV	CR	PR	Retriever	Phone	UC	RE	TX	VS
•	•	•	•	•	CourthouseData	479-582-0900	•	•	•	•
•	•	•	•		Document Retrieval Service	877-902-9377	•	•	•	•
•	•	•	•		Hart & Associates Inc	866-429-4044			•	•
					Noel D Law Jr	918-599-0988	•	•		
•	•	•	•	•	Mid-West Investigations [SOP]	800-359-5410	•	•	•	•
		•	•		Redi-Info Information Services	888-320-6805				
•		•	•	•	Rus B Robison & Associates Inc [SOP]	877-721-2295	•	•	•	•
•	•	•	•	•	SRT Investigations	800-499-0472	•	•	•	
•	•	•	•	•	Tammy L Listen Investigations [SOP]	405-340-4843	•	•	•	•
•	•	•	•	•	United Legal Services [SOP]	888-232-8432	•	•	•	

DT	BK	CV	CR	PR	←COURTS OKMULGEE RECORDING→		UC	RE	TX	VS
•	•	•	•	•	Clarke Investigations Inc [SOP]	405-844-7300	•	•	•	•
•	•	•	•	•	CourthouseData	479-582-0900	•	•	•	•
•	•	•	•		Document Retrieval Service	877-902-9377	•	•	•	•
					Noel D Law Jr	918-599-0988	•	•		
•	•			•	Records Search & Report Svc	918-885-4724	•	•	•	•
•	•	•	•	•	SRT Investigations	800-499-0472	•	•	•	

DT	BK	CV	CR	PR	←COURTS OSAGE RECORDING→		UC	RE	TX	VS
•	•	•	•	•	CourthouseData	479-582-0900	•	•	•	•
•	•	•	•		Document Retrieval Service	877-902-9377	•	•	•	•
					Noel D Law Jr	918-599-0988	•	•		
•	•			•	Records Search & Report Svc	918-885-4724	•	•	•	•
•	•	•	•	•	SRT Investigations	800-499-0472	•	•	•	

DT	BK	CV	CR	PR	←COURTS OTTAWA RECORDING→		UC	RE	TX	VS
•	•	•	•	•	CourthouseData	479-582-0900	•	•	•	•
•	•	•	•		Document Retrieval Service	877-902-9377	•	•	•	•
					Noel D Law Jr	918-599-0988	•	•		
		•		•	Photo Abstract Co	918-542-1871	•	•	•	•
•	•			•	Records Search & Report Svc	918-885-4724	•	•	•	•
		•	•		Redi-Info Information Services	888-320-6805				

DT	BK	CV	CR	PR	←COURTS PAWNEE RECORDING→		UC	RE	TX	VS
•	•	•	•	•	CourthouseData	479-582-0900	•	•	•	•
•	•	•	•		Document Retrieval Service	877-902-9377	•	•	•	•
					Noel D Law Jr	918-599-0988	•	•		
•	•			•	Records Search & Report Svc	918-885-4724	•	•	•	•
		•	•		Redi-Info Information Services	888-320-6805				

DT	BK	CV	CR	PR	←COURTS PAYNE RECORDING→		UC	RE	TX	VS
•	•	•	•	•	Clarke Investigations Inc [SOP]	405-844-7300	•	•	•	•
•	•	•	•	•	CourthouseData	479-582-0900	•	•	•	•
•	•	•	•		Document Retrieval Service	877-902-9377	•	•	•	•
					Noel D Law Jr	918-599-0988	•	•		
•	•			•	Records Search & Report Svc	918-885-4724	•	•	•	•
		•	•		Redi-Info Information Services	888-320-6805				

DT	BK	CV	CR	PR	←COURTS PITTSBURG RECORDING→		UC	RE	TX	VS
•	•	•	•	•	CourthouseData	479-582-0900	•	•	•	•
•	•	•	•		Document Retrieval Service	877-902-9377	•	•	•	•
		•		•	Hebert Land Services	918-647-9524	•	•	•	•
		•		•	Pioneer Abstract Co of McAlester Inc	918-423-0817		•	•	

DT	BK	CV	CR	PR	←COURTS PONTOTOC RECORDING→		UC	RE	TX	VS
•	•	•	•		Document Retrieval Service	877-902-9377	•	•	•	•

DT	BK	CV	CR	PR	←COURTS POTTAWATOMIE RECORDING→		UC	RE	TX	VS
•	•	•	•		Document Retrieval Service	877-902-9377	•	•	•	•
		•	•		Redi-Info Information Services	888-320-6805				

DT	BK	CV	CR	PR	Name	Phone	UC	RE	TX	VS
•	•	•	•		Tammy L Listen Investigations [SOP]	405-340-4843	•	•	•	•
•	•	•	•	•	United Legal Services [SOP]	888-232-8432	•	•	•	

DT	BK	CV	CR	PR	←Courts PUSHMATAHA	Recording→	UC	RE	TX	VS
•	•	•	•		Document Retrieval Service	877-902-9377	•	•	•	•
					Moore Mowdy & Youngblood	580-889-5656		•		
		•		•	Pushmataha County Abstract Co	580-298-3189		•	•	

DT	BK	CV	CR	PR	←Courts ROGER MILLS	Recording→	UC	RE	TX	VS
•	•	•	•	•	Clarke Investigations Inc [SOP]	405-844-7300	•	•	•	•
•	•	•	•		Document Retrieval Service	877-902-9377	•	•	•	•

DT	BK	CV	CR	PR	←Courts ROGERS	Recording→	UC	RE	TX	VS
•	•	•	•	•	Clarke Investigations Inc [SOP]	405-844-7300	•	•	•	•
•	•	•	•	•	Court Data Research Services	918-745-2231	•	•	•	
•	•	•	•	•	CourthouseData	479-582-0900	•	•	•	•
		•	•		Davis and Assoc. [SOP]	918-825-5223				
					Docu-File Inc	877-742-4994	•	•	•	•
•	•	•	•		Document Retrieval Service	877-902-9377	•	•	•	•
					Noel D Law Jr	918-599-0988	•	•		
•	•	•	•	•	Oklahoma Court Explorers	918-360-4798	•	•	•	
•	•			•	Records Search & Report Svc	918-885-4724	•	•	•	•
		•	•		Redi-Info Information Services	888-320-6805				
		•		•	Rogers County Abstract Co	918-341-0525	•	•	•	•
•	•	•	•	•	SRT Investigations	800-499-0472	•	•	•	
•	•	•	•	•	Zero Investigations Inc [SOP]	866-400-9376	•	•	•	•

DT	BK	CV	CR	PR	←Courts SEMINOLE	Recording→	UC	RE	TX	VS
•	•	•	•		Document Retrieval Service	877-902-9377	•	•	•	•
		•	•	•	Pioneer Abstract Co	405-257-3351	•	•	•	•
		•	•		Redi-Info Information Services	888-320-6805				

DT	BK	CV	CR	PR	←Courts SEQUOYAH	Recording→	UC	RE	TX	VS
•	•	•	•		Document Retrieval Service	877-902-9377	•	•	•	•
		•		•	Hebert Land Services	918-647-9524	•	•	•	•
•	•			•	Records Search & Report Svc	918-885-4724	•	•	•	•
		•	•		Redi-Info Information Services	888-320-6805				

DT	BK	CV	CR	PR	←Courts STEPHENS	Recording→	UC	RE	TX	VS
•	•	•	•	•	H Ray Anderson	580-355-4450	•	•	•	
•	•	•	•		Document Retrieval Service	877-902-9377	•	•	•	•
•	•	•	•	•	Mendenhall Information Services	940-696-0758	•	•	•	•
		•		•	Stephens County Abstract Co	580-255-2525	•	•	•	

DT	BK	CV	CR	PR	←Courts TEXAS	Recording→	UC	RE	TX	VS
•	•	•	•	•	Clarke Investigations Inc [SOP]	405-844-7300	•	•	•	•
•	•	•	•		Document Retrieval Service	877-902-9377	•	•	•	•
		•	•		Redi-Info Information Services	888-320-6805				

DT	BK	CV	CR	PR	←Courts TILLMAN	Recording→	UC	RE	TX	VS
•	•	•	•	•	H Ray Anderson	580-355-4450	•	•	•	
•	•	•	•	•	Clarke Investigations Inc [SOP]	405-844-7300	•	•	•	•
•	•	•	•		Document Retrieval Service	877-902-9377	•	•	•	•
		•	•	•	King Investigations Inc	580-477-1676	•	•	•	
•	•	•	•	•	Mendenhall Information Services	940-696-0758	•	•	•	•
		•	•	•	T.A.B.B.S. Inv & Process Service [SOP]	580-477-3292	•	•	•	•

DT	BK	CV	CR	PR	←Courts TULSA	Recording→	UC	RE	TX	VS
•	•	•	•	•	Clarke Investigations Inc [SOP]	405-844-7300	•	•	•	•
•	•	•	•	•	Court Data Research Services	918-745-2231	•	•	•	
•	•	•	•	•	CourthouseData	479-582-0900	•	•	•	•

DT	BK	CV	CR	PR	←Courts	Recording→	UC	RE	TX	VS
					Docu-File Inc	877-742-4994	•	•	•	•
•	•	•	•		Document Retrieval Service	877-902-9377	•	•	•	•
•	•	•	•		Indepth Profiles Inc	800-364-8319				
•	•	•	•	•	Jones & Associates Inc [SOP]	918-583-4779	•	•	•	
					Noel D Law Jr	918-599-0988	•	•		
•	•	•	•	•	Oklahoma Court Explorers	918-360-4798	•	•	•	
•	•			•	Records Search & Report Svc	918-885-4724	•	•	•	•
		•	•		Redi-Info Information Services	888-320-6805				
•	•	•	•	•	SRT Investigations	800-499-0472	•	•	•	
•	•	•	•	•	Zero Investigations Inc [SOP]	866-400-9376	•	•	•	•

DT	BK	CV	CR	PR	←Courts	**Wagoner** Recording→	UC	RE	TX	VS
•	•	•	•	•	Clarke Investigations Inc [SOP]	405-844-7300	•	•	•	•
•	•	•	•	•	CourthouseData	479-582-0900	•	•	•	•
•	•	•	•		Document Retrieval Service	877-902-9377	•	•	•	•
					Noel D Law Jr	918-599-0988	•	•		
•	•	•	•	•	Oklahoma Court Explorers	918-360-4798	•	•	•	
•	•			•	Records Search & Report Svc	918-885-4724	•	•	•	•
		•	•		Redi-Info Information Services	888-320-6805				
•	•	•	•	•	SRT Investigations	800-499-0472	•	•	•	
		•		•	Wagoner County Abstract Co	918-485-2215	•	•	•	

DT	BK	CV	CR	PR	←Courts	**Washington** Recording→	UC	RE	TX	VS
•	•	•	•	•	Clarke Investigations Inc [SOP]	405-844-7300	•	•	•	•
•	•	•	•	•	CourthouseData	479-582-0900	•	•	•	•
•	•	•	•		Document Retrieval Service	877-902-9377	•	•	•	•
					Noel D Law Jr	918-599-0988	•	•		
		•		•	Musselman Abstract Co	918-336-6410	•	•	•	
•	•			•	Records Search & Report Svc	918-885-4724	•	•	•	•
•	•	•	•	•	SRT Investigations	800-499-0472	•	•	•	

DT	BK	CV	CR	PR	←Courts	**Washita** Recording→	UC	RE	TX	VS
•	•	•	•		Document Retrieval Service	877-902-9377	•	•	•	•
		•	•		Redi-Info Information Services	888-320-6805				

DT	BK	CV	CR	PR	←Courts	**Woods** Recording→	UC	RE	TX	VS
•	•	•	•		Document Retrieval Service	877-902-9377	•	•	•	•
		•	•	•	Woods County Abstract Corp	580-327-1746	•	•	•	

DT	BK	CV	CR	PR	←Courts	**Woodward** Recording→	UC	RE	TX	VS
•	•	•	•	•	Clarke Investigations Inc [SOP]	405-844-7300	•	•	•	•
•	•	•	•		Document Retrieval Service	877-902-9377	•	•	•	•
		•		•	Woodward County Abstract Co	580-256-3344	•	•	•	

Editor's Tip: Sending an unsolicited fax is not recommended, and it is not legal. So, before faxing to a potential new retriever contact, we recommend that you first make a courtesy call and ask for permission to fax to them.

Oregon

DT	BK	CV	CR	PR	←Courts		Recording→	UC	RE	TX	VS
					BAKER						
		•	•	•	M & M Legal Services [SOP]		541-963-8219		•	•	•
•	•	•	•	•	Washington Court Records Svc		509-448-5012	•	•	•	•
					BENTON						
			•		Buffalo Employment Screening LLC		888-884-6860				
•	•	•	•	•	Data Research Inc (Oregon)		800-992-1983	•	•	•	
•	•	•	•	•	Quik Check Records		503-876-6477	•	•	•	•
•	•	•	•	•	Washington Court Records Svc		509-448-5012	•	•	•	•
					CLACKAMAS						
•	•	•	•	•	Barrister Support Service [SOP]		503-246-8934				
			•		Buffalo Employment Screening LLC		888-884-6860				
•	•	•	•	•	Burton Professional Services [SOP]		360-254-0878	•	•	•	•
•	•	•	•	•	CICS Employment Services LLC [SOP]		800-660-0507	•	•	•	
•	•	•	•	•	Data Research Inc (Oregon)		800-992-1983	•	•	•	
•	•	•	•	•	Lawyer's Legal Service LLC [SOP]		800-224-7911	•	•	•	•
•	•	•	•	•	Quik Check Records		503-876-6477	•	•	•	•
		•		•	Timely Documents		360-944-1082	•	•	•	
•	•	•	•		Vancouver Legal Messengers Inc [SOP]		888-695-3654	•	•	•	•
•	•	•	•	•	Washington Court Records Svc		509-448-5012	•	•	•	•
					CLATSOP						
•	•	•	•	•	Lawyer's Legal Service LLC [SOP]		800-224-7911	•	•	•	•
•	•	•	•	•	Washington Court Records Svc		509-448-5012	•	•	•	•
					COLUMBIA						
•	•	•	•	•	Data Research Inc (Oregon)		800-992-1983	•	•	•	
•	•	•	•	•	Lawyer's Legal Service LLC [SOP]		800-224-7911	•	•	•	•
•	•	•	•	•	Washington Court Records Svc		509-448-5012	•	•	•	•
					COOS						
•	•	•	•	•	Data Research Inc (Oregon)		800-992-1983	•	•	•	
		•		•	First American Title Insurance of Oregon		800-235-0119	•	•	•	•
		•	•	•	North Pacific Legal [SOP]		541-888-5118				
•	•	•	•	•	Washington Court Records Svc		509-448-5012	•	•	•	•
					CROOK						
		•	•	•	Central Legal Services [SOP]		800-599-8133	•	•	•	•
•	•	•	•	•	Data Research Inc (Oregon)		800-992-1983	•	•	•	
		•	•		Tri-County Legal Process Service [SOP]		800-600-6315				
•	•	•	•	•	Washington Court Records Svc		509-448-5012	•	•	•	•
					CURRY						
•	•	•	•	•	Data Research Inc (Oregon)		800-992-1983	•	•	•	
•	•	•	•	•	Washington Court Records Svc		509-448-5012	•	•	•	•
					DESCHUTES						
		•	•	•	Central Legal Services [SOP]		800-599-8133	•	•	•	•
•	•	•	•	•	Data Research Inc (Oregon)		800-992-1983	•	•	•	
		•	•		Tri-County Legal Process Service [SOP]		800-600-6315				
•	•	•	•	•	Washington Court Records Svc		509-448-5012	•	•	•	•

DT	BK	CV	CR	PR	←Courts	DOUGLAS	Recording→	UC	RE	TX	VS
•	•	•	•	•	Data Research Inc (Oregon)		800-992-1983	•	•	•	
		•	•	•	Douglas County Title Co (Oregon)		541-672-3388	•	•	•	•
		•	•	•	Ticor Title Roseburg		800-660-1146	•	•	•	
•	•	•	•	•	Washington Court Records Svc		509-448-5012	•	•	•	•

DT	BK	CV	CR	PR	←Courts	GILLIAM	Recording→	UC	RE	TX	VS
•	•	•	•	•	Washington Court Records Svc		509-448-5012	•	•	•	•

DT	BK	CV	CR	PR	←Courts	GRANT	Recording→	UC	RE	TX	VS
•	•	•	•	•	Washington Court Records Svc		509-448-5012	•	•	•	•

DT	BK	CV	CR	PR	←Courts	HARNEY	Recording→	UC	RE	TX	VS
•	•	•	•	•	Washington Court Records Svc		509-448-5012	•	•	•	•

DT	BK	CV	CR	PR	←Courts	HOOD RIVER	Recording→	UC	RE	TX	VS
•	•	•	•	•	Data Research Inc (Oregon)		800-992-1983	•	•	•	
•	•	•	•	•	Lawyer's Legal Service LLC [SOP]		800-224-7911	•	•	•	•
•	•	•	•	•	Washington Court Records Svc		509-448-5012	•	•	•	•

DT	BK	CV	CR	PR	←Courts	JACKSON	Recording→	UC	RE	TX	VS
•	•	•	•	•	Cleveland & Carl Inv [SOP]		800-888-6629	•	•	•	•
•	•	•	•	•	Data Research Inc (Oregon)		800-992-1983	•	•	•	
•	•	•	•	•	Washington Court Records Svc		509-448-5012	•	•	•	•

DT	BK	CV	CR	PR	←Courts	JEFFERSON	Recording→	UC	RE	TX	VS
		•	•	•	Central Legal Services [SOP]		800-599-8133	•	•	•	•
•	•	•	•	•	Data Research Inc (Oregon)		800-992-1983	•	•	•	
		•	•		Tri-County Legal Process Service [SOP]		800-600-6315				
•	•	•	•	•	Washington Court Records Svc		509-448-5012	•	•	•	•

DT	BK	CV	CR	PR	←Courts	JOSEPHINE	Recording→	UC	RE	TX	VS
•	•	•	•	•	Cleveland & Carl Inv [SOP]		800-888-6629	•	•	•	•
•	•	•	•	•	Washington Court Records Svc		509-448-5012	•	•	•	•

DT	BK	CV	CR	PR	←Courts	KLAMATH	Recording→	UC	RE	TX	VS
•	•	•	•	•	Cleveland & Carl Inv [SOP]		800-888-6629	•	•	•	•
•	•	•	•	•	Data Research Inc (Oregon)		800-992-1983	•	•	•	
•	•	•	•	•	Washington Court Records Svc		509-448-5012	•	•	•	•

DT	BK	CV	CR	PR	←Courts	LAKE	Recording→	UC	RE	TX	VS
•	•	•	•	•	Washington Court Records Svc		509-448-5012	•	•	•	•

DT	BK	CV	CR	PR	←Courts	LANE	Recording→	UC	RE	TX	VS
•	•	•	•	•	B & J/Barristers' Aide Inc [SOP]		541-687-0747				•
			•		Buffalo Employment Screening LLC		888-884-6860				
•	•	•	•	•	CICS Employment Services LLC [SOP]		800-660-0507	•	•	•	
•	•	•	•	•	Cleveland & Carl Inv [SOP]		800-888-6629	•	•	•	•
•	•	•	•	•	Data Research Inc (Oregon)		800-992-1983	•	•	•	
•	•	•	•	•	Quik Check Records		503-876-6477	•	•	•	•
		•	•		Thomas Legal Support Service [SOP]		541-265-2233				
•	•	•	•	•	Washington Court Records Svc		509-448-5012	•	•	•	•

DT	BK	CV	CR	PR	←Courts	LINCOLN	Recording→	UC	RE	TX	VS
•	•	•	•	•	CICS Employment Services LLC [SOP]		800-660-0507	•	•	•	
•	•	•	•	•	Data Research Inc (Oregon)		800-992-1983	•	•	•	
•	•	•	•	•	Quik Check Records		503-876-6477	•	•	•	•
		•	•		Thomas Legal Support Service [SOP]		541-265-2233				
•	•	•	•	•	Washington Court Records Svc		509-448-5012	•	•	•	•

DT	BK	CV	CR	PR	←Courts	LINN	Recording→	UC	RE	TX	VS
			•		Buffalo Employment Screening LLC		888-884-6860				

DT	BK	CV	CR	PR	←Courts	Recording→	UC	RE	TX	VS
•	•	•	•	•	Data Research Inc (Oregon)	800-992-1983	•	•	•	
•	•	•	•	•	Quik Check Records	503-876-6477	•	•	•	•
•	•	•	•	•	Washington Court Records Svc	509-448-5012	•	•	•	•

DT	BK	CV	CR	PR	←Courts **Malheur**	Recording→	UC	RE	TX	VS
•	•	•	•	•	Washington Court Records Svc	509-448-5012	•	•	•	•

DT	BK	CV	CR	PR	←Courts **Marion**	Recording→	UC	RE	TX	VS
			•		Buffalo Employment Screening LLC	888-884-6860				
•	•	•	•	•	CICS Employment Services LLC [SOP]	800-660-0507	•	•	•	
•	•	•	•	•	Corporation Service Company - CSC	800-927-9800	•	•	•	•
•	•	•	•	•	Data Research Inc (Oregon)	800-992-1983	•	•	•	
•	•	•	•	•	Lawyer's Legal Service LLC [SOP]	800-224-7911	•	•	•	•
		•	•	•	Mill Creek Investigation Agency PC	877-378-1581		•		
•	•	•	•	•	Quik Check Records	503-876-6477	•	•	•	•
		•			Unisearch Inc (Oregon)	800-554-3113	•		•	
•	•	•	•	•	Washington Court Records Svc	509-448-5012	•	•	•	•

DT	BK	CV	CR	PR	←Courts **Morrow**	Recording→	UC	RE	TX	VS
•	•	•	•	•	Washington Court Records Svc	509-448-5012	•	•	•	•

DT	BK	CV	CR	PR	←Courts **Multnomah**	Recording→	UC	RE	TX	VS
•	•	•	•	•	Barrister Support Service [SOP]	503-246-8934				
			•		Buffalo Employment Screening LLC	888-884-6860				
•	•	•	•	•	Burton Professional Services [SOP]	360-254-0878	•	•	•	•
•	•	•	•	•	CICS Employment Services LLC [SOP]	800-660-0507	•	•	•	
•	•	•	•	•	Data Research Inc (Oregon)	800-992-1983	•	•	•	
•	•	•	•	•	Lawyer's Legal Service LLC [SOP]	800-224-7911	•	•	•	•
		•	•		Prospective Renters Verification Svc	503-655-0888	•	•	•	•
•	•	•	•	•	Quik Check Records	503-876-6477	•	•	•	•
		•		•	Timely Documents	360-944-1082	•	•	•	
•	•	•	•		Vancouver Legal Messengers Inc [SOP]	888-695-3654	•	•	•	•
•	•	•	•	•	Washington Court Records Svc	509-448-5012	•	•	•	•

DT	BK	CV	CR	PR	←Courts **Polk**	Recording→	UC	RE	TX	VS
			•		Buffalo Employment Screening LLC	888-884-6860				
•	•	•	•	•	Cleveland & Carl Inv [SOP]	800-888-6629	•	•	•	•
•	•	•	•	•	Data Research Inc (Oregon)	800-992-1983	•	•	•	
		•	•	•	Mill Creek Investigation Agency PC	877-378-1581		•		
•	•	•	•	•	Quik Check Records	503-876-6477	•	•	•	•
•	•	•	•	•	Washington Court Records Svc	509-448-5012	•	•	•	•

DT	BK	CV	CR	PR	←Courts **Sherman**	Recording→	UC	RE	TX	VS
•	•	•	•	•	Washington Court Records Svc	509-448-5012	•	•	•	•

DT	BK	CV	CR	PR	←Courts **Tillamook**	Recording→	UC	RE	TX	VS
•	•	•	•	•	Quik Check Records	503-876-6477	•	•	•	•
		•	•		Thomas Legal Support Service [SOP]	541-265-2233				
•	•	•	•	•	Washington Court Records Svc	509-448-5012	•	•	•	•

DT	BK	CV	CR	PR	←Courts **Umatilla**	Recording→	UC	RE	TX	VS
•	•	•	•	•	Washington Court Records Svc	509-448-5012	•	•	•	•

DT	BK	CV	CR	PR	←Courts **Union**	Recording→	UC	RE	TX	VS
		•	•		Eastern Oregon Title Inc	541-963-8561	•	•	•	
		•	•	•	M & M Legal Services [SOP]	541-963-8219		•	•	•
•	•	•	•	•	Washington Court Records Svc	509-448-5012	•	•	•	•

DT	BK	CV	CR	PR	←Courts **Wallowa**	Recording→	UC	RE	TX	VS
		•	•	•	M & M Legal Services [SOP]	541-963-8219		•	•	•
•	•	•	•	•	Washington Court Records Svc	509-448-5012	•	•	•	•

DT	BK	CV	CR	PR	←Courts	Wasco	Recording→	UC	RE	TX	VS
•	•	•	•	•	Data Research Inc (Oregon)		800-992-1983	•	•	•	

DT	BK	CV	CR	PR	←Courts	Washington	Recording→	UC	RE	TX	VS
•	•	•	•	•	Barrister Support Service [SOP]		503-246-8934				
			•		Buffalo Employment Screening LLC		888-884-6860				
•	•	•	•	•	Burton Professional Services [SOP]		360-254-0878	•	•	•	•
•	•	•	•	•	CICS Employment Services LLC [SOP]		800-660-0507	•	•	•	
•	•	•	•	•	Data Research Inc (Oregon)		800-992-1983	•	•	•	
•	•	•	•	•	Lawyer's Legal Service LLC [SOP]		800-224-7911	•	•	•	•
•	•	•	•	•	Quik Check Records		503-876-6477	•	•	•	•
		•		•	Timely Documents		360-944-1082	•	•	•	
•	•	•	•		Vancouver Legal Messengers Inc [SOP]		888-695-3654	•	•	•	•
•	•	•	•	•	Washington Court Records Svc		509-448-5012	•	•	•	•

DT	BK	CV	CR	PR	←Courts	Wheeler	Recording→	UC	RE	TX	VS
•	•	•	•	•	Washington Court Records Svc		509-448-5012	•	•	•	•

DT	BK	CV	CR	PR	←Courts	Yamhill	Recording→	UC	RE	TX	VS
			•		Buffalo Employment Screening LLC		888-884-6860				
•	•	•	•	•	Data Research Inc (Oregon)		800-992-1983	•	•	•	
•	•	•	•	•	Lawyer's Legal Service LLC [SOP]		800-224-7911	•	•	•	•
•	•	•	•	•	Quik Check Records		503-876-6477	•	•	•	•
•	•	•	•	•	Washington Court Records Svc		509-448-5012	•	•	•	•

Editor's Tip: This section of the directory is not organized to promote search firms that are statewide, regional, or national in coverage.

An expanded resource of search firms, distributors, and screening firms is BRB Publication's website at www.brbpub.com. Click the "Find A Vendor" tab. Both sources contain information on firms that use online resources to obtain public record index information.

Pennsylvania

COURT RECORDS RETRIEVED — **RECORDING RECORDS RETRIEVED**

DT	BK	CV	CR	PR	←COURTS	ADAMS	RECORDING→	UC	RE	TX	VS
		•				Advance Real Estate Services LLC	717-328-5062	•	•	•	
						Colonial Valley Abstract Co	717-848-2871	•	•	•	
•	•	•	•	•		Credit Plus Solutions Group [SOP]	800-344-3125	•	•	•	
•	•	•	•			Employmentscreening.com	215-234-0700	•	•	•	•
•	•	•	•	•		Franklin Civil Process [SOP]	717-263-0041	•	•	•	•

DT	BK	CV	CR	PR	←COURTS	ALLEGHENY	RECORDING→	UC	RE	TX	VS
		•	•	•		Applied Research & Investigation	800-594-0008				
•	•	•		•		Cfacts	800-233-4747	•	•	•	
•	•	•	•			County House Research Inc	866-594-1177			•	
•	•	•	•			Employmentscreening.com	215-234-0700	•	•	•	•
•	•	•	•			Financial Dimensions	800-858-9808	•	•	•	
•	•	•	•	•		Hawk Investigations [SOP]	412-487-9274	•	•	•	•
		•	•			Justifacts Credential Verification Inc	800-356-6885				
		•	•			Know It All Background Research Services Inc	888-281-9535				
•	•	•	•	•		Miller Abstracts	412-607-4952	•	•	•	•
•	•	•	•	•		Pittsburgh Information & Research Co [SOP]	412-766-3832	•	•	•	•
•	•	•	•	•		Quest & Assoc Inc	412-563-1007	•	•	•	

DT	BK	CV	CR	PR	←COURTS	ARMSTRONG	RECORDING→	UC	RE	TX	VS
•	•	•	•			Employmentscreening.com	215-234-0700	•	•	•	•
	•	•	•	•		Falcon Research & Settlement	800-828-4081	•	•	•	
•	•	•	•	•		Hawk Investigations [SOP]	412-487-9274	•	•	•	•
•	•	•	•	•		ILS Research [SOP]	570-454-3535	•	•	•	•
		•		•		Jireh Business Information Solutions Inc	724-863-7270		•	•	
		•	•			Justifacts Credential Verification Inc	800-356-6885				
		•		•		Lawyers' Abstract Co	724-283-3510	•	•	•	
•	•	•	•	•		Pittsburgh Information & Research Co [SOP]	412-766-3832	•	•	•	•

DT	BK	CV	CR	PR	←COURTS	BEAVER	RECORDING→	UC	RE	TX	VS
		•	•	•		Applied Research & Investigation	800-594-0008				
•	•	•		•		Cfacts	800-233-4747	•	•	•	
•	•	•	•			County House Research Inc	866-594-1177			•	
•	•	•	•			Employmentscreening.com	215-234-0700	•	•	•	•
•	•	•	•	•		Hawk Investigations [SOP]	412-487-9274	•	•	•	•
•	•	•	•	•		ILS Research [SOP]	570-454-3535	•	•	•	•
		•		•		Jireh Business Information Solutions Inc	724-863-7270		•	•	
		•	•			Know It All Background Research Services Inc	888-281-9535				
•	•	•	•	•		Pittsburgh Information & Research Co [SOP]	412-766-3832	•	•	•	•

DT	BK	CV	CR	PR	←COURTS	BEDFORD	RECORDING→	UC	RE	TX	VS
		•	•	•		B & G Ltd of Hollidaysburg	814-695-8414	•	•	•	
•	•	•	•			Employmentscreening.com	215-234-0700	•	•	•	•
•	•	•	•			Excel Abstract Services	814-623-5213	•	•	•	
•	•	•	•	•		ILS Research [SOP]	570-454-3535	•	•	•	•
		•		•		Jireh Business Information Solutions Inc	724-863-7270		•	•	

DT	BK	CV	CR	PR	←COURTS	BERKS	RECORDING→	UC	RE	TX	VS
				•		Abstract Associates of Lancaster Inc [SOP]	717-581-5841	•	•	•	•
						ATACO Inc	800-220-2039		•		
•	•	•	•			Best Legal Services Inc [SOP]	800-562-9620	•	•	•	•

DT	BK	CV	CR	PR	←Courts	Recording→	UC	RE	TX	VS
•	•	•	•	•	Commonwealth Inv Agency [SOP]	610-433-2325	•	•	•	•
•	•	•	•		Confidential Investigations [SOP]	610-821-9112	•	•	•	•
•	•	•	•		County House Research Inc	866-594-1177			•	
•	•	•	•	•	Credit Plus Solutions Group [SOP]	800-344-3125	•	•	•	
•	•	•	•		Employmentscreening.com	215-234-0700	•	•	•	•
•	•	•	•	•	Lawyers Filing Services of Southeastern PA Inc	888-490-0409	•	•	•	•
			•		MBE	610-395-2202				
•	•	•	•		Public Records Abstract	484-256-6416	•	•	•	•
•	•	•			Security Search & Abstract Co Inc	800-345-9494	•	•	•	
		•	•	•	William C Brown & Co	610-373-1516	•	•	•	

DT	BK	CV	CR	PR	←Courts **Blair**	Recording→	UC	RE	TX	VS
		•	•	•	B & G Ltd of Hollidaysburg	814-695-8414	•	•	•	
•	•	•	•		Employmentscreening.com	215-234-0700	•	•	•	•
•	•	•	•		Excel Abstract Services	814-623-5213	•	•	•	
		•		•	Jireh Business Information Solutions Inc	724-863-7270		•	•	
•	•	•	•	•	Pittsburgh Information & Research Co [SOP]	412-766-3832	•	•	•	•

DT	BK	CV	CR	PR	←Courts **Bradford**	Recording→	UC	RE	TX	VS
					Deeds Plus Abstract Services Inc	570-746-3844	•	•	•	
•	•	•	•		Employmentscreening.com	215-234-0700	•	•	•	•
		•	•		Krayer Detective Agency Inc [SOP]	800-249-3704				

DT	BK	CV	CR	PR	←Courts **Bucks**	Recording→	UC	RE	TX	VS
					ATACO Inc	800-220-2039		•		
•	•	•	•	•	B & R Services for Professionals [SOP]	800-503-7400	•	•	•	•
•	•	•	•		Best Legal Services Inc [SOP]	800-562-9620	•	•	•	•
•	•	•	•	•	Bucks Legal Services Inc [SOP]	888-512-8257	•	•	•	•
•	•	•	•	•	Commonwealth Inv Agency [SOP]	610-433-2325	•	•	•	•
•	•	•	•	•	Coyne Search Service Inc	215-781-3722	•	•	•	•
•	•	•	•		Employmentscreening.com	215-234-0700	•	•	•	•
•	•	•	•	•	Inquisitive Research Corporation	732-321-0041	•	•	•	•
		•	•		Know It All Background Research Services Inc	888-281-9535				
•	•	•	•	•	Lawyers Filing Services of Southeastern PA Inc	888-490-0409	•	•	•	•
			•		MBE	610-395-2202				
•	•	•		•	Searchtec	877-2SEARCH	•	•	•	
•	•	•			Security Search & Abstract Co Inc	800-345-9494	•	•	•	
•	•	•	•	•	Talone & Associates [SOP]	800-553-5189	•	•	•	•

DT	BK	CV	CR	PR	←Courts **Butler**	Recording→	UC	RE	TX	VS
•	•	•		•	Cfacts	800-233-4747	•	•	•	
•	•	•	•		Employmentscreening.com	215-234-0700	•	•	•	•
	•	•	•	•	Falcon Research & Settlement	800-828-4081	•	•	•	
•	•	•	•	•	Hawk Investigations [SOP]	412-487-9274	•	•	•	•
•	•	•	•	•	ILS Research [SOP]	570-454-3535	•	•	•	•
		•		•	Jireh Business Information Solutions Inc	724-863-7270		•	•	
		•	•		Justifacts Credential Verification Inc	800-356-6885				
		•		•	Lawyers' Abstract Co	724-283-3510	•	•	•	
•	•	•	•	•	Pittsburgh Information & Research Co [SOP]	412-766-3832	•	•	•	•

DT	BK	CV	CR	PR	←Courts **Cambria**	Recording→	UC	RE	TX	VS
		•	•	•	B & G Ltd of Hollidaysburg	814-695-8414	•	•	•	
			•		Criminal Record Research Services	717-249-7053				
•	•	•	•		Employmentscreening.com	215-234-0700	•	•	•	•
•	•	•	•	•	ILS Research [SOP]	570-454-3535	•	•	•	•
		•		•	Jireh Business Information Solutions Inc	724-863-7270		•	•	
		•	•		Mainline Researchers Inc	814-472-7913	•	•	•	
•	•	•	•	•	Pittsburgh Information & Research Co [SOP]	412-766-3832	•	•	•	•

DT	BK	CV	CR	PR	←COURTS CAMERON	RECORDING→	UC	RE	TX	VS
•	•	•	•		Employmentscreening.com	215-234-0700	•	•	•	•
	•	•	•	•	Falcon Research & Settlement	800-828-4081	•	•	•	
•	•	•	•	•	ILS Research [SOP]	570-454-3535	•	•	•	•
		•	•	•	David Reed [SOP]	814-486-9327	•	•	•	•

DT	BK	CV	CR	PR	←COURTS CARBON	RECORDING→	UC	RE	TX	VS
		•	•		ACBS	866-530-2227	•	•	•	
•	•	•	•		Confidential Investigations [SOP]	610-821-9112	•	•	•	•
•	•	•	•		Employmentscreening.com	215-234-0700	•	•	•	•
		•		•	Fidelity Home Abstract Inc	800-224-5601	•	•	•	
•	•	•	•	•	ILS Research [SOP]	570-454-3535	•	•	•	•
		•		•	Toma Abstract Inc	570-454-7899	•	•	•	

DT	BK	CV	CR	PR	←COURTS CENTRE	RECORDING→	UC	RE	TX	VS
		•	•	•	B & G Ltd of Hollidaysburg	814-695-8414	•	•	•	
•	•	•	•		Employmentscreening.com	215-234-0700	•	•	•	•
•	•	•	•	•	Pittsburgh Information & Research Co [SOP]	412-766-3832	•	•	•	•

DT	BK	CV	CR	PR	←COURTS CHESTER	RECORDING→	UC	RE	TX	VS
				•	Abstract Associates of Lancaster Inc [SOP]	717-581-5841	•	•	•	•
•	•	•	•	•	American Abstractors Inc [SOP]	610-353-5375	•	•	•	•
					ATACO Inc	800-220-2039		•		
•	•	•	•	•	B & R Services for Professionals [SOP]	800-503-7400	•	•	•	•
•	•	•	•		Best Legal Services Inc [SOP]	800-562-9620	•	•	•	•
•	•	•	•		Blue Marble Logistics LLC [SOP]	302-661-4390	•	•	•	•
•	•	•	•	•	Coyne Search Service Inc	215-781-3722	•	•	•	•
•	•	•	•		Employmentscreening.com	215-234-0700	•	•	•	•
•	•	•	•	•	Inquisitive Research Corporation	732-321-0041	•	•	•	•
•	•	•	•	•	Lawyers Filing Services of Southeastern PA Inc	888-490-0409	•	•	•	•
•	•	•	•		Research Specialists Inc	610-358-2507	•		•	
•	•	•		•	Searchtec	877-2SEARCH	•	•	•	
•	•	•			Security Search & Abstract Co Inc	800-345-9494	•	•	•	
•	•	•	•	•	Services For Lawyers [SOP]	610-566-9165		•	•	•
•	•	•	•	•	Talone & Associates [SOP]	800-553-5189	•	•	•	•

DT	BK	CV	CR	PR	←COURTS CLARION	RECORDING→	UC	RE	TX	VS
•	•	•	•		County House Research Inc	866-594-1177			•	
•	•	•	•		Employmentscreening.com	215-234-0700	•	•	•	•
	•	•	•	•	Falcon Research & Settlement	800-828-4081	•	•	•	
•	•	•	•	•	ILS Research [SOP]	570-454-3535	•	•	•	•
•	•	•	•	•	Pittsburgh Information & Research Co [SOP]	412-766-3832	•	•	•	•

DT	BK	CV	CR	PR	←COURTS CLEARFIELD	RECORDING→	UC	RE	TX	VS
		•	•	•	B & G Ltd of Hollidaysburg	814-695-8414	•	•	•	
•	•	•	•		Employmentscreening.com	215-234-0700	•	•	•	•
	•	•	•	•	Falcon Research & Settlement	800-828-4081	•	•	•	

DT	BK	CV	CR	PR	←COURTS CLINTON	RECORDING→	UC	RE	TX	VS
•	•	•	•		Employmentscreening.com	215-234-0700	•	•	•	•

DT	BK	CV	CR	PR	←COURTS COLUMBIA	RECORDING→	UC	RE	TX	VS
•	•	•	•		Employmentscreening.com	215-234-0700	•	•	•	•
•	•	•	•	•	ILS Research [SOP]	570-454-3535	•	•	•	•
		•	•		Krayer Detective Agency Inc [SOP]	800-249-3704				
		•		•	Toma Abstract Inc	570-454-7899	•	•	•	

DT	BK	CV	CR	PR	←COURTS CRAWFORD	RECORDING→	UC	RE	TX	VS
•	•	•	•		Employmentscreening.com	215-234-0700	•	•	•	•
	•	•	•	•	Falcon Research & Settlement	800-828-4081	•	•	•	
•	•	•	•	•	ILS Research [SOP]	570-454-3535	•	•	•	•

DT	BK	CV	CR	PR	←Courts	Recording→	UC	RE	TX	VS
•	•	•	•	•	Pittsburgh Information & Research Co [SOP]	412-766-3832	•	•	•	•
		•			Realty Settlement Inc	814-336-1802	•	•	•	
	•	•	•	•	David M Rumancik	330-837-7737	•	•	•	

DT	BK	CV	CR	PR	←Courts **CUMBERLAND**	Recording→	UC	RE	TX	VS
		•			Advance Real Estate Services LLC	717-328-5062	•	•	•	
•	•	•	•		Associated Services [SOP]	717-938-1550	•	•	•	
•	•	•	•		County House Research Inc	866-594-1177			•	
•	•	•	•	•	Credit Plus Solutions Group [SOP]	800-344-3125	•	•	•	
			•		Criminal Record Research Services	717-249-7053				
•	•	•	•		Employmentscreening.com	215-234-0700	•	•	•	•
•	•	•	•	•	Franklin Civil Process [SOP]	717-263-0041	•	•	•	•
•	•	•	•	•	ILS Research [SOP]	570-454-3535	•	•	•	•
•	•	•	•	•	Information Network Associates Inc [SOP]	800-443-0824	•	•	•	•
•	•	•		•	Penncorp Service Group Inc	800-544-9050	•	•	•	•
•	•	•	•		Priority One Messenger Service [SOP]	800-444-1365	•	•	•	

DT	BK	CV	CR	PR	←Courts **DAUPHIN**	Recording→	UC	RE	TX	VS
				•	Abstract Associates of Lancaster Inc [SOP]	717-581-5841	•	•	•	•
•	•	•	•		Associated Services [SOP]	717-938-1550	•	•	•	
•	•	•	•		Best Legal Services Inc [SOP]	800-562-9620	•	•	•	•
•	•	•	•	•	Corporation Service Company - CSC	800-927-9800	•	•	•	•
•	•	•	•		County House Research Inc	866-594-1177			•	
•	•	•	•	•	Credit Plus Solutions Group [SOP]	800-344-3125	•	•	•	
•	•	•	•		Employmentscreening.com	215-234-0700	•	•	•	•
•	•	•	•	•	Esquire Assist Ltd	717-232-9398	•	•	•	•
•	•	•	•	•	Information Network Associates Inc [SOP]	800-443-0824	•	•	•	•
•	•	•		•	Penncorp Service Group Inc	800-544-9050	•	•	•	•
•	•	•	•	•	Pittsburgh Information & Research Co [SOP]	412-766-3832	•	•	•	•
•	•	•	•		Priority One Messenger Service [SOP]	800-444-1365	•	•	•	

DT	BK	CV	CR	PR	←Courts **DELAWARE**	Recording→	UC	RE	TX	VS
•	•	•	•	•	American Abstractors Inc [SOP]	610-353-5375	•	•	•	•
					ATACO Inc	800-220-2039		•		
•	•	•	•	•	B & R Services for Professionals [SOP]	800-503-7400	•	•	•	•
•	•	•	•		Best Legal Services Inc [SOP]	800-562-9620	•	•	•	•
•	•	•	•		Blue Marble Logistics LLC [SOP]	302-661-4390	•	•	•	
•	•	•	•		County House Research Inc	866-594-1177			•	
•	•	•	•	•	Coyne Search Service Inc	215-781-3722	•	•	•	•
•	•	•	•		Employmentscreening.com	215-234-0700	•	•	•	•
•	•	•	•	•	Inquisitive Research Corporation	732-321-0041	•	•	•	•
		•	•		Know It All Background Research Services Inc	888-281-9535				
•	•	•	•	•	Lawyers Filing Services of Southeastern PA Inc	888-490-0409	•	•	•	•
•	•	•	•		Research Specialists Inc	610-358-2507	•		•	
•	•	•		•	Searchtec	877-2SEARCH	•	•	•	
•	•	•			Security Search & Abstract Co Inc	800-345-9494	•	•	•	
•	•	•	•	•	Services For Lawyers [SOP]	610-566-9165		•	•	•
•	•	•	•	•	Talone & Associates [SOP]	800-553-5189	•	•	•	•

DT	BK	CV	CR	PR	←Courts **ELK**	Recording→	UC	RE	TX	VS
•	•	•	•		Employmentscreening.com	215-234-0700	•	•	•	•
	•	•	•	•	Falcon Research & Settlement	800-828-4081	•	•	•	
•	•	•	•	•	ILS Research [SOP]	570-454-3535	•	•	•	•
		•	•	•	David Reed [SOP]	814-486-9327	•	•	•	•

DT	BK	CV	CR	PR	←Courts **ERIE**	Recording→	UC	RE	TX	VS
•	•	•	•		Darlene Chiota	814-454-7589	•	•	•	
•	•	•	•		Employmentscreening.com	215-234-0700	•	•	•	•
•	•	•	•	•	Pittsburgh Information & Research Co [SOP]	412-766-3832	•	•	•	•

DT	BK	CV	CR	PR	←Courts **FAYETTE**	Recording→	UC	RE	TX	VS
•	•	•	•		Employmentscreening.com	215-234-0700	•	•	•	•
					Fayette Professional Services	412-439-1450	•	•	•	
•	•	•	•	•	Hawk Investigations [SOP]	412-487-9274	•	•	•	•
		•	•	•	Heather L Gilbert Title Abstract & Closing Svc	724-998-5954	•	•	•	•
•	•	•	•	•	ILS Research [SOP]	570-454-3535	•	•	•	•
		•		•	Jireh Business Information Solutions Inc	724-863-7270		•	•	
•	•	•	•	•	Pittsburgh Information & Research Co [SOP]	412-766-3832	•	•	•	•

DT	BK	CV	CR	PR	←Courts **FOREST**	Recording→	UC	RE	TX	VS
•	•	•	•		Employmentscreening.com	215-234-0700	•	•	•	•
	•	•	•	•	Falcon Research & Settlement	800-828-4081	•	•	•	
•	•	•	•	•	ILS Research [SOP]	570-454-3535	•	•	•	•

DT	BK	CV	CR	PR	←Courts **FRANKLIN**	Recording→	UC	RE	TX	VS
		•			Advance Real Estate Services LLC	717-328-5062	•	•	•	
					Colonial Valley Abstract Co	717-848-2871	•	•	•	
•	•	•	•	•	Credit Plus Solutions Group [SOP]	800-344-3125	•	•	•	
			•		Criminal Record Research Services	717-249-7053				
•	•	•	•		Employmentscreening.com	215-234-0700	•	•	•	•
•	•	•	•	•	Franklin Civil Process [SOP]	717-263-0041	•	•	•	•

DT	BK	CV	CR	PR	←Courts **FULTON**	Recording→	UC	RE	TX	VS
		•			Advance Real Estate Services LLC	717-328-5062	•	•	•	
•	•	•	•	•	Credit Plus Solutions Group [SOP]	800-344-3125	•	•	•	
•	•	•	•		Employmentscreening.com	215-234-0700	•	•	•	•
•	•	•	•		Excel Abstract Services	814-623-5213	•	•	•	
•	•	•	•	•	Franklin Civil Process [SOP]	717-263-0041	•	•	•	•

DT	BK	CV	CR	PR	←Courts **GREENE**	Recording→	UC	RE	TX	VS
•	•	•	•		Employmentscreening.com	215-234-0700	•	•	•	•
					Fayette Professional Services	412-439-1450	•	•	•	
		•	•	•	Heather L Gilbert Title Abstract & Closing Svc	724-998-5954	•	•	•	•
•	•	•	•	•	ILS Research [SOP]	570-454-3535	•	•	•	•
		•		•	Jireh Business Information Solutions Inc	724-863-7270		•	•	
•	•	•	•	•	Pittsburgh Information & Research Co [SOP]	412-766-3832	•	•	•	•

DT	BK	CV	CR	PR	←Courts **HUNTINGDON**	Recording→	UC	RE	TX	VS
		•	•	•	B & G Ltd of Hollidaysburg	814-695-8414	•	•	•	
•	•	•	•		Employmentscreening.com	215-234-0700	•	•	•	•
•	•	•	•		Excel Abstract Services	814-623-5213	•	•	•	
•	•	•	•	•	Franklin Civil Process [SOP]	717-263-0041	•	•	•	•

DT	BK	CV	CR	PR	←Courts **INDIANA**	Recording→	UC	RE	TX	VS
•	•	•	•		Employmentscreening.com	215-234-0700	•	•	•	•
	•	•	•	•	Falcon Research & Settlement	800-828-4081	•	•	•	
•	•	•	•	•	Hawk Investigations [SOP]	412-487-9274	•	•	•	•
•	•	•	•	•	ILS Research [SOP]	570-454-3535	•	•	•	•
		•		•	Jireh Business Information Solutions Inc	724-863-7270		•	•	
•	•	•	•	•	Pittsburgh Information & Research Co [SOP]	412-766-3832	•	•	•	•
		•	•	•	Schillinger & Keith Abstract & Settlement	800-275-2959	•	•	•	

DT	BK	CV	CR	PR	←Courts **JEFFERSON**	Recording→	UC	RE	TX	VS
•	•	•	•		Employmentscreening.com	215-234-0700	•	•	•	•
	•	•	•	•	Falcon Research & Settlement	800-828-4081	•	•	•	
•	•	•	•	•	ILS Research [SOP]	570-454-3535	•	•	•	•

DT	BK	CV	CR	PR	←Courts **JUNIATA**	Recording→	UC	RE	TX	VS
•	•	•	•	•	Credit Plus Solutions Group [SOP]	800-344-3125	•	•	•	
•	•	•	•		Employmentscreening.com	215-234-0700	•	•	•	•
•	•	•	•	•	Franklin Civil Process [SOP]	717-263-0041	•	•	•	•

DT	BK	CV	CR	PR	←COURTS LACKAWANNA	RECORDING→	UC	RE	TX	VS
		•		•	Abstract Enterprises Inc	570-963-5290	•	•	•	•
•	•				Credit Lenders Service Agency Inc	856-787-9005	•	•	•	
•	•	•	•		Employmentscreening.com	215-234-0700	•	•	•	•
•	•	•	•	•	ILS Research [SOP]	570-454-3535	•	•	•	•
		•	•		Krayer Detective Agency Inc [SOP]	800-249-3704				
					Marge Strein	570-457-3939				

DT	BK	CV	CR	PR	←COURTS LANCASTER	RECORDING→	UC	RE	TX	VS
				•	Abstract Associates of Lancaster Inc [SOP]	717-581-5841	•	•	•	•
•	•	•	•	•	American Abstractors Inc [SOP]	610-353-5375	•	•	•	•
•	•	•	•		Best Legal Services Inc [SOP]	800-562-9620	•	•	•	•
					Colonial Valley Abstract Co	717-848-2871	•	•	•	
•	•	•	•	•	Credit Plus Solutions Group [SOP]	800-344-3125	•	•	•	
•	•	•	•		Employmentscreening.com	215-234-0700	•	•	•	•
•	•	•	•	•	Information Network Associates Inc [SOP]	800-443-0824	•	•	•	•
•	•	•			Security Search & Abstract Co Inc	800-345-9494	•	•	•	
•	•	•	•	•	Talone & Associates [SOP]	800-553-5189	•	•	•	•

DT	BK	CV	CR	PR	←COURTS LAWRENCE	RECORDING→	UC	RE	TX	VS
•	•	•	•		Employmentscreening.com	215-234-0700	•	•	•	•
•	•	•	•	•	Hawk Investigations [SOP]	412-487-9274	•	•	•	•
•	•	•	•	•	ILS Research [SOP]	570-454-3535	•	•	•	•
		•		•	Jireh Business Information Solutions Inc	724-863-7270		•	•	
•	•	•	•	•	Pittsburgh Information & Research Co [SOP]	412-766-3832	•	•	•	•

DT	BK	CV	CR	PR	←COURTS LEBANON	RECORDING→	UC	RE	TX	VS
				•	Abstract Associates of Lancaster Inc [SOP]	717-581-5841	•	•	•	•
•	•	•	•	•	Credit Plus Solutions Group [SOP]	800-344-3125	•	•	•	
•	•	•	•		Employmentscreening.com	215-234-0700	•	•	•	•
•	•	•	•	•	Information Network Associates Inc [SOP]	800-443-0824	•	•	•	•

DT	BK	CV	CR	PR	←COURTS LEHIGH	RECORDING→	UC	RE	TX	VS
		•	•		ACBS	866-530-2227	•	•	•	
•	•	•	•	•	Associated Investigative Services Inc [SOP]	610-351-9911	•	•	•	
•	•	•	•	•	Commonwealth Inv Agency [SOP]	610-433-2325	•	•	•	•
•	•	•	•		Confidential Investigations [SOP]	610-821-9112	•	•	•	•
•	•	•	•	•	Credit Plus Solutions Group [SOP]	800-344-3125	•	•	•	
•	•	•	•		Employmentscreening.com	215-234-0700	•	•	•	•
		•	•		Know It All Background Research Services Inc	888-281-9535				
			•		MBE	610-395-2202				
•	•	•			Security Search & Abstract Co Inc	800-345-9494	•	•	•	
•	•	•	•	•	Talone & Associates [SOP]	800-553-5189	•	•	•	•
		•		•	John A Zapf II	610-868-5101	•	•	•	

DT	BK	CV	CR	PR	←COURTS LUZERNE	RECORDING→	UC	RE	TX	VS
				•	All Penn Abstract Co	570-823-5410	•	•	•	
•	•	•	•		Employmentscreening.com	215-234-0700	•	•	•	•
•	•	•	•	•	ILS Research [SOP]	570-454-3535	•	•	•	•
		•	•		Know It All Background Research Services Inc	888-281-9535				
		•	•		Krayer Detective Agency Inc [SOP]	800-249-3704				
					Marge Strein	570-457-3939				
		•		•	Toma Abstract Inc	570-454-7899	•	•	•	

DT	BK	CV	CR	PR	←COURTS LYCOMING	RECORDING→	UC	RE	TX	VS
•	•	•	•		Employmentscreening.com	215-234-0700	•	•	•	•

DT	BK	CV	CR	PR	←COURTS MCKEAN	RECORDING→	UC	RE	TX	VS
•	•	•	•		Employmentscreening.com	215-234-0700	•	•	•	•
	•	•	•	•	Falcon Research & Settlement	800-828-4081	•	•	•	

DT	BK	CV	CR	PR	←Courts	Recording→	UC	RE	TX	VS
		•	•	•	David Reed [SOP]	814-486-9327	•	•	•	•

DT	BK	CV	CR	PR	←Courts **Mercer**	Recording→	UC	RE	TX	VS
•	•	•	•		County House Research Inc	866-594-1177			•	
•	•	•	•		Employmentscreening.com	215-234-0700	•	•	•	•
	•	•	•	•	Falcon Research & Settlement	800-828-4081	•	•	•	
		•	•	•	DeAnne Fisher	724-699-5528	•	•	•	
•	•	•	•	•	Pittsburgh Information & Research Co [SOP]	412-766-3832	•	•	•	•
		•			Realty Settlement Inc	814-336-1802	•	•	•	
	•	•	•	•	David M Rumancik	330-837-7737	•	•	•	

DT	BK	CV	CR	PR	←Courts **Mifflin**	Recording→	UC	RE	TX	VS
•	•	•	•	•	Credit Plus Solutions Group [SOP]	800-344-3125	•	•	•	
•	•	•	•		Employmentscreening.com	215-234-0700	•	•	•	•
•	•	•	•	•	Franklin Civil Process [SOP]	717-263-0041	•	•	•	•

DT	BK	CV	CR	PR	←Courts **Monroe**	Recording→	UC	RE	TX	VS
•	•	•	•	•	Associated Investigative Services Inc [SOP]	610-351-9911	•	•	•	
•	•	•	•		Confidential Investigations [SOP]	610-821-9112	•	•	•	•
•	•	•	•		County House Research Inc	866-594-1177			•	
•	•				Credit Lenders Service Agency Inc	856-787-9005	•	•	•	
•		•	•		Richard Demoody	570-350-0105			•	
•	•	•	•		Employmentscreening.com	215-234-0700	•	•	•	•
		•		•	Fidelity Home Abstract Inc	800-224-5601	•	•	•	
		•	•		Krayer Detective Agency Inc [SOP]	800-249-3704				
		•		•	Toma Abstract Inc	570-454-7899	•	•	•	

DT	BK	CV	CR	PR	←Courts **Montgomery**	Recording→	UC	RE	TX	VS
•	•	•	•	•	American Abstractors Inc [SOP]	610-353-5375	•	•	•	•
•	•	•	•	•	B & R Services for Professionals [SOP]	800-503-7400	•	•	•	•
•	•	•	•		Best Legal Services Inc [SOP]	800-562-9620	•	•	•	•
•	•	•	•	•	Bucks Legal Services Inc [SOP]	888-512-8257	•	•	•	•
•	•	•	•	•	Coyne Search Service Inc	215-781-3722	•	•	•	•
•	•	•	•	•	Credit Plus Solutions Group [SOP]	800-344-3125	•	•	•	
•	•	•	•		Employmentscreening.com	215-234-0700	•	•	•	•
•	•	•	•	•	Inquisitive Research Corporation	732-321-0041	•	•	•	•
•	•	•	•	•	Keystone Intelligence Network Inc	215-545-1111	•	•	•	•
•	•	•	•	•	Lawyers Filing Services of Southeastern PA Inc	888-490-0409	•	•	•	•
			•		MBE	610-395-2202				
•	•	•	•		Research Specialists Inc	610-358-2507	•		•	
•	•	•		•	Searchtec	877-2SEARCH	•	•	•	
•	•	•			Security Search & Abstract Co Inc	800-345-9494	•	•	•	
•	•	•	•	•	Services For Lawyers [SOP]	610-566-9165		•	•	•
•	•	•	•	•	Talone & Associates [SOP]	800-553-5189	•	•	•	•

DT	BK	CV	CR	PR	←Courts **Montour**	Recording→	UC	RE	TX	VS
•	•	•	•		Employmentscreening.com	215-234-0700	•	•	•	•
		•	•	•	ST Sayers & MS Chiarkas	570-286-9831		•	•	
		•		•	Toma Abstract Inc	570-454-7899	•	•	•	

DT	BK	CV	CR	PR	←Courts **Northampton**	Recording→	UC	RE	TX	VS
		•	•		ACBS	866-530-2227	•	•	•	
•	•	•	•	•	Associated Investigative Services Inc [SOP]	610-351-9911	•	•	•	
•	•	•	•	•	Commonwealth Inv Agency [SOP]	610-433-2325	•	•	•	•
•	•	•	•		Confidential Investigations [SOP]	610-821-9112	•	•	•	•
•	•	•	•		County House Research Inc	866-594-1177			•	
•	•	•	•		Employmentscreening.com	215-234-0700	•	•	•	•
		•		•	Fidelity Home Abstract Inc	800-224-5601	•	•	•	
•	•	•	•	•	Inquisitive Research Corporation	732-321-0041	•	•	•	•
		•	•		Know It All Background Research Services Inc	888-281-9535				

DT	BK	CV	CR	PR	Retriever	Phone	UC	RE	TX	VS
			•		MBE	610-395-2202				
•	•	•			Security Search & Abstract Co Inc	800-345-9494	•	•	•	
		•		•	John A Zapf II	610-868-5101	•	•	•	

DT	BK	CV	CR	PR	←Courts NORTHUMBERLAND	Recording→	UC	RE	TX	VS
•	•	•	•		Employmentscreening.com	215-234-0700	•	•	•	•
		•	•	•	ST Sayers & MS Chiarkas	570-286-9831		•	•	

DT	BK	CV	CR	PR	←Courts PERRY	Recording→	UC	RE	TX	VS
•	•	•	•	•	Credit Plus Solutions Group [SOP]	800-344-3125	•	•	•	
•	•	•	•		Employmentscreening.com	215-234-0700	•	•	•	•
•	•	•	•	•	Franklin Civil Process [SOP]	717-263-0041	•	•	•	•

DT	BK	CV	CR	PR	←Courts PHILADELPHIA	Recording→	UC	RE	TX	VS
•	•	•	•	•	American Abstractors Inc [SOP]	610-353-5375	•	•	•	•
•	•	•	•	•	B & R Services for Professionals [SOP]	800-503-7400	•	•	•	•
•	•	•	•		Best Legal Services Inc [SOP]	800-562-9620	•	•	•	•
•	•	•	•		Blue Marble Logistics LLC [SOP]	302-661-4390	•	•	•	
•	•	•	•		County House Research Inc	866-594-1177			•	
•	•	•	•	•	Coyne Search Service Inc	215-781-3722	•	•	•	•
•	•	•	•		Employmentscreening.com	215-234-0700	•	•	•	•
			•		Iles & Bond Inc	856-854-9580	•	•		
•	•	•	•	•	Inquisitive Research Corporation	732-321-0041	•	•	•	•
•	•	•	•	•	Keystone Intelligence Network Inc	215-545-1111	•	•	•	•
		•	•		Know It All Background Research Services Inc	888-281-9535				
•	•	•	•	•	Lawyers Filing Services of Southeastern PA Inc	888-490-0409	•	•	•	•
			•		MBE	610-395-2202				
•	•	•		•	Searchtec	877-2SEARCH	•	•	•	
•	•	•			Security Search & Abstract Co Inc	800-345-9494	•	•	•	
•	•	•	•	•	Talone & Associates [SOP]	800-553-5189	•	•	•	•

DT	BK	CV	CR	PR	←Courts PIKE	Recording→	UC	RE	TX	VS
		•	•	•	Arbor Abstracting Co	570-253-0472	•	•	•	
•	•				Credit Lenders Service Agency Inc	856-787-9005	•	•	•	
•		•	•		Richard Demoody	570-350-0105			•	
•	•	•	•		Employmentscreening.com	215-234-0700	•	•	•	•
		•		•	Fidelity Home Abstract Inc	800-224-5601	•	•	•	
		•	•		Krayer Detective Agency Inc [SOP]	800-249-3704				

DT	BK	CV	CR	PR	←Courts POTTER	Recording→	UC	RE	TX	VS
•	•	•	•		Employmentscreening.com	215-234-0700	•	•	•	•
	•	•	•	•	Falcon Research & Settlement	800-828-4081	•	•	•	
		•	•	•	David Reed [SOP]	814-486-9327	•	•	•	•

DT	BK	CV	CR	PR	←Courts SCHUYLKILL	Recording→	UC	RE	TX	VS
		•	•		ACBS	866-530-2227	•	•	•	
		•		•	Assured Realty	570-622-1366	•	•	•	
•	•	•	•		Employmentscreening.com	215-234-0700	•	•	•	•
•	•	•	•	•	ILS Research [SOP]	570-454-3535	•	•	•	•
		•	•	•	Pellish & Pellish Attorneys at Law	570-622-2338	•	•	•	•
•	•	•			Security Search & Abstract Co Inc	800-345-9494	•	•	•	
		•		•	Toma Abstract Inc	570-454-7899	•	•	•	

DT	BK	CV	CR	PR	←Courts SNYDER	Recording→	UC	RE	TX	VS
•	•	•	•		Employmentscreening.com	215-234-0700	•	•	•	•

DT	BK	CV	CR	PR	←Courts SOMERSET	Recording→	UC	RE	TX	VS
•	•	•	•		Employmentscreening.com	215-234-0700	•	•	•	•
		•		•	Jireh Business Information Solutions Inc	724-863-7270		•	•	
•	•	•	•	•	Pittsburgh Information & Research Co [SOP]	412-766-3832	•	•	•	•
		•			Somerset Abstract Co Ltd	814-445-9525	•	•	•	

DT	BK	CV	CR	PR	←Courts	SULLIVAN	Recording→	UC	RE	TX	VS
•	•	•	•		Employmentscreening.com		215-234-0700	•	•	•	•

DT	BK	CV	CR	PR	←Courts	SUSQUEHANNA	Recording→	UC	RE	TX	VS
				•	Cindy Bartkis		570-756-3093	•	•	•	•
•	•	•	•		Employmentscreening.com		215-234-0700	•	•	•	•
		•	•		Krayer Detective Agency Inc [SOP]		800-249-3704				

DT	BK	CV	CR	PR	←Courts	TIOGA	Recording→	UC	RE	TX	VS
•	•	•	•		County House Research Inc		866-594-1177			•	
•	•	•	•		Employmentscreening.com		215-234-0700	•	•	•	•

DT	BK	CV	CR	PR	←Courts	UNION	Recording→	UC	RE	TX	VS
•	•	•	•		Employmentscreening.com		215-234-0700	•	•	•	•
		•	•	•	ST Sayers & MS Chiarkas		570-286-9831		•	•	

DT	BK	CV	CR	PR	←Courts	VENANGO	Recording→	UC	RE	TX	VS
•	•	•	•		County House Research Inc		866-594-1177			•	
•	•	•	•		Employmentscreening.com		215-234-0700	•	•	•	•
	•	•	•	•	Falcon Research & Settlement		800-828-4081	•	•	•	
•	•	•	•	•	ILS Research [SOP]		570-454-3535	•	•	•	•
•	•	•	•	•	Pittsburgh Information & Research Co [SOP]		412-766-3832	•	•	•	•
		•			Realty Settlement Inc		814-336-1802	•	•	•	
	•	•	•	•	David M Rumancik		330-837-7737	•	•	•	

DT	BK	CV	CR	PR	←Courts	WARREN	Recording→	UC	RE	TX	VS
•	•	•	•		Employmentscreening.com		215-234-0700	•	•	•	•
	•	•	•	•	Falcon Research & Settlement		800-828-4081	•	•	•	

DT	BK	CV	CR	PR	←Courts	WASHINGTON	Recording→	UC	RE	TX	VS
•	•	•		•	Cfacts		800-233-4747	•	•	•	
•	•	•	•		Employmentscreening.com		215-234-0700	•	•	•	•
					Fayette Professional Services		412-439-1450	•	•	•	
•	•	•	•	•	Hawk Investigations [SOP]		412-487-9274	•	•	•	•
		•	•	•	Heather L Gilbert Title Abstract & Closing Svc		724-998-5954	•	•	•	•
		•		•	Jireh Business Information Solutions Inc		724-863-7270		•	•	
•	•	•	•	•	Miller Abstracts		412-607-4952	•	•	•	•
•	•	•	•	•	Pittsburgh Information & Research Co [SOP]		412-766-3832	•	•	•	•

DT	BK	CV	CR	PR	←Courts	WAYNE	Recording→	UC	RE	TX	VS
		•	•	•	Arbor Abstracting Co		570-253-0472	•	•	•	
•	•				Credit Lenders Service Agency Inc		856-787-9005	•	•	•	
•	•	•	•		Employmentscreening.com		215-234-0700	•	•	•	•
		•		•	Fidelity Home Abstract Inc		800-224-5601	•	•	•	
					Inter-County Abstract		570-253-4734	•	•	•	
		•	•		Krayer Detective Agency Inc [SOP]		800-249-3704				
		•	•		Kathleen Schloesser		570-253-5368	•	•	•	

DT	BK	CV	CR	PR	←Courts	WESTMORELAND	Recording→	UC	RE	TX	VS
•	•	•		•	Cfacts		800-233-4747	•	•	•	
•	•	•	•		County House Research Inc		866-594-1177			•	
			•		Criminal Record Research Services		717-249-7053				
•	•	•	•		Employmentscreening.com		215-234-0700	•	•	•	•
					Fayette Professional Services		412-439-1450	•	•	•	
•	•	•	•	•	Hawk Investigations [SOP]		412-487-9274	•	•	•	•
•	•	•	•	•	ILS Research [SOP]		570-454-3535	•	•	•	•
		•		•	Jireh Business Information Solutions Inc		724-863-7270		•	•	
		•	•		Justifacts Credential Verification Inc		800-356-6885	•	•	•	•
		•		•	Lawyers' Abstract Co		724-283-3510	•	•	•	
•	•	•	•	•	Miller Abstracts		412-607-4952	•	•	•	•
•	•	•	•	•	Pittsburgh Information & Research Co [SOP]		412-766-3832	•	•	•	•

DT	BK	CV	CR	PR	←Courts	Wyoming	Recording→	UC	RE	TX	VS
•	•	•	•			Employmentscreening.com	215-234-0700	•	•	•	•
		•	•	•		Catherine J Garbus	570-836-6749	•	•	•	•
		•	•			Krayer Detective Agency Inc [SOP]	800-249-3704				

DT	BK	CV	CR	PR	←Courts	York	Recording→	UC	RE	TX	VS
				•		Abstract Associates of Lancaster Inc [SOP]	717-581-5841	•	•	•	•
		•	•	•		Abstract One	302-732-9027	•	•	•	•
•	•	•	•			Associated Services [SOP]	717-938-1550	•	•	•	
						Colonial Valley Abstract Co	717-848-2871	•	•	•	
•	•	•	•			County House Research Inc	866-594-1177			•	
•	•	•	•	•		Credit Plus Solutions Group [SOP]	800-344-3125	•	•	•	
•	•	•	•			Employmentscreening.com	215-234-0700	•	•	•	•
•	•	•	•	•		Information Network Associates Inc [SOP]	800-443-0824	•	•	•	•
		•	•			Know It All Background Research Services Inc	888-281-9535				
•	•	•	•			Priority One Messenger Service [SOP]	800-444-1365	•	•	•	

[SOP] = Performs service of process

Court Records

CODE	Government Agency	Type of Information
DT	US District Court	Federal civil and criminal cases
BK	Bankruptcy Court	United States bankruptcy cases
CV	Civil Court	Municipal, county and state level civil cases
CR	Criminal Court	Municipal, county and state level criminal cases
PR	Probate Court	Wills and estate cases

County Records - Recordings

CODE	Government Agency	Type of Information
UC	UCC Filing Office	Uniform Commercial Code and other personal property liens
RE	Real Estate Recording Office	Real property transactions and liens
TX	Tax Filing Office(s)	Federal and state tax liens, judgment liens
VS	Vital Records Office	Vital statistics—birth, death, marriage, divorce

Editor's Tip: Only Call a Retriever For the Records They Retrieve.
If you call for a criminal record from a retriever who only does work at the recorder's office, then you are wasting your time and the retriever's time.

Puerto Rico

COURT RECORDS RETRIEVED							RECORDING RECORDS RETRIEVED				
DT	BK	CV	CR	PR	←COURTS	PUERTO RICO	RECORDING→	UC	RE	TX	VS
•	•	•	•	•		Cestero & Co Inc [SOP]	888-764-7229	•		•	
•	•	•	•			GPS & Assoc (Florida)	866-813-8131	•		•	•
•	•	•	•			Rucar Business Information Center	787-645-1659	•	•	•	•

Editor's Tip: At the back of this directory is a short list of search firms who are Public Record Retriever Network "Associate Members." These Associate Members utilize retrievers to obtain documents outside their local area of coverage. The Associate Members are statewide, regional, or national in scope, and are not listed in the county sections.

[SOP] = PERFORMS SERVICE OF PROCESS

COURT RECORDS

CODE	GOVERNMENT AGENCY	TYPE OF INFORMATION
DT	US District Court	Federal civil and criminal cases
BK	Bankruptcy Court	United States bankruptcy cases
CV	Civil Court	Municipal, county and state level civil cases
CR	Criminal Court	Municipal, county and state level criminal cases
PR	Probate Court	Wills and estate cases

COUNTY RECORDS - RECORDINGS

CODE	GOVERNMENT AGENCY	TYPE OF INFORMATION
UC	UCC Filing Office	Uniform Commercial Code and other personal property liens
RE	Real Estate Recording Office	Real property transactions and liens
TX	Tax Filing Office(s)	Federal and state tax liens, judgment liens
VS	Vital Records Office	Vital statistics—birth, death, marriage, divorce

Rhode Island

COURT RECORDS RETRIEVED | **RECORDING RECORDS RETRIEVED**

DT	BK	CV	CR	PR	←COURTS **BRISTOL** RECORDING→		UC	RE	TX	VS
•	•	•	•	•	Access RI Public Information	877-999-7474	•		•	•
•	•	•	•	•	Barry Shuster Information Services, A Div of Search-It Inc	877-852-2507	•	•	•	•
			•		Creative Services Inc	800-227-0002				
					Horizons Unlimited	617-696-6397		•	•	
•	•	•	•	•	Hughes Legal Support [SOP]	800-783-7690	•	•	•	
•	•	•	•	•	McGuire Research Associates	401-647-7881	•	•	•	
		•	•		Primetime Research Inc	866-737-2714				
		•	•		Rapid Record Retrieval	508-759-8622				
•	•	•	•	•	Trax [SOP]	401-245-3004	•	•	•	•
		•	•		Vin Lunney Inv	401-253-6052		•		•

DT	BK	CV	CR	PR	←COURTS **KENT** RECORDING→		UC	RE	TX	VS
•	•	•	•	•	Access RI Public Information	877-999-7474	•		•	•
•	•	•	•	•	Barry Shuster Information Services, A Div of Search-It Inc	877-852-2507	•	•	•	•
			•		Creative Services Inc	800-227-0002				
					Horizons Unlimited	617-696-6397		•	•	
•	•	•	•	•	Hughes Legal Support [SOP]	800-783-7690	•	•	•	
•	•	•	•	•	McGuire Research Associates	401-647-7881	•	•	•	
•	•	•	•	•	Parasearch Inc	401-732-2490	•	•	•	
		•	•		Primetime Research Inc	866-737-2714				
		•	•		Rapid Record Retrieval	508-759-8622				
•	•	•	•	•	Trax [SOP]	401-245-3004	•	•	•	•
		•	•		Vin Lunney Inv	401-253-6052		•		•

DT	BK	CV	CR	PR	←COURTS **NEWPORT** RECORDING→		UC	RE	TX	VS
•	•	•	•	•	Access RI Public Information	877-999-7474	•		•	•
•	•	•	•	•	Barry Shuster Information Services, A Div of Search-It Inc	877-852-2507	•	•	•	•
			•		Creative Services Inc	800-227-0002				
					Horizons Unlimited	617-696-6397		•	•	
•	•	•	•	•	Hughes Legal Support [SOP]	800-783-7690	•	•	•	
•	•	•	•	•	McGuire Research Associates	401-647-7881	•	•	•	
•	•	•	•	•	Parasearch Inc	401-732-2490	•	•	•	
		•	•		Primetime Research Inc	866-737-2714				
		•	•		Rapid Record Retrieval	508-759-8622				
•	•	•	•	•	Trax [SOP]	401-245-3004	•	•	•	•
		•	•		Vin Lunney Inv	401-253-6052		•		•

DT	BK	CV	CR	PR	←COURTS **PROVIDENCE** RECORDING→		UC	RE	TX	VS
•	•	•	•	•	Access RI Public Information	877-999-7474	•		•	•
•	•	•	•	•	Barry Shuster Information Services, A Div of Search-It Inc	877-852-2507	•	•	•	•
			•		Creative Services Inc	800-227-0002				
					Horizons Unlimited	617-696-6397		•	•	
•	•	•	•	•	Hughes Legal Support [SOP]	800-783-7690	•	•	•	
•	•	•	•	•	McGuire Research Associates	401-647-7881	•	•	•	
•	•	•	•	•	Parasearch Inc	401-732-2490	•	•	•	
		•	•		Primetime Research Inc	866-737-2714				
		•	•		Rapid Record Retrieval	508-759-8622				
•	•	•	•	•	Trax [SOP]	401-245-3004	•	•	•	•
		•	•		Vin Lunney Inv	401-253-6052		•		•

DT	BK	CV	CR	PR	←COURTS WASHINGTON	RECORDING→	UC	RE	TX	VS
•	•	•	•	•	Access RI Public Information	877-999-7474	•		•	•
•	•	•	•	•	Barry Shuster Information Services, A Div of Search-It Inc	877-852-2507	•	•	•	•
			•		Creative Services Inc	800-227-0002				
					Horizons Unlimited	617-696-6397		•	•	
•	•	•	•	•	Hughes Legal Support [SOP]	800-783-7690	•	•	•	
•	•	•	•	•	McGuire Research Associates	401-647-7881	•	•	•	
•	•	•	•	•	Parasearch Inc	401-732-2490	•	•	•	
		•	•		Primetime Research Inc	866-737-2714				
		•	•		Rapid Record Retrieval	508-759-8622				
•	•	•	•	•	Trax [SOP]	401-245-3004	•	•	•	•
		•	•		Vin Lunney Inv	401-253-6052		•		•

[SOP] = PERFORMS SERVICE OF PROCESS

COURT RECORDS

CODE	GOVERNMENT AGENCY	TYPE OF INFORMATION
DT	US District Court	Federal civil and criminal cases
BK	Bankruptcy Court	United States bankruptcy cases
CV	Civil Court	Municipal, county and state level civil cases
CR	Criminal Court	Municipal, county and state level criminal cases
PR	Probate Court	Wills and estate cases

COUNTY RECORDS - RECORDINGS

CODE	GOVERNMENT AGENCY	TYPE OF INFORMATION
UC	UCC Filing Office	Uniform Commercial Code and other personal property liens
RE	Real Estate Recording Office	Real property transactions and liens
TX	Tax Filing Office(s)	Federal and state tax liens, judgment liens
VS	Vital Records Office	Vital statistics—birth, death, marriage, divorce

Editor's Tip: Remember the first rule about public record searching-- Simply because your state or county has certain rules, regulations and practices regarding the accessibility and content of public records, does not mean that another state or county adheres to the same rules.

South Carolina

COURT RECORDS RETRIEVED / **RECORDING RECORDS RETRIEVED**

DT	BK	CV	CR	PR	←COURTS ABBEVILLE	RECORDING→	UC	RE	TX	VS
•	•	•	•	•	Carolina Investigative Research (SC)	800-328-8981	•	•	•	•
•	•	•		•	Liberty Corporate Services Inc	888-875-1280	•	•	•	
•	•	•	•	•	Searchtec (Carolinas) [SOP]	800-528-8790	•	•	•	•
				•	Upper State Title Corp	864-260-4649	•	•	•	•
		•	•		Upstate Investigations [SOP]	864-277-0757			•	

DT	BK	CV	CR	PR	←COURTS AIKEN	RECORDING→	UC	RE	TX	VS
•	•	•			Advanced Data Technology Inc	800-426-5265		•	•	
•	•	•	•	•	CSRA Background Verification Inc	706-869-8882	•	•	•	
•	•	•	•	•	David Smith Detective Agency [SOP]	877-793-9426	•		•	
		•		•	Lexington Title Corp	803-957-1243	•	•	•	
•	•	•		•	Liberty Corporate Services Inc	888-875-1280	•	•	•	
		•		•	SCC Information Services Inc	803-957-1243	•	•	•	
•	•	•	•	•	Searchtec (Carolinas) [SOP]	800-528-8790	•	•	•	•
•	•	•	•	•	Title Abstracts & Document Services	803-649-2500	•	•	•	•

DT	BK	CV	CR	PR	←COURTS ALLENDALE	RECORDING→	UC	RE	TX	VS
•	•	•	•	•	Searchtec (Carolinas) [SOP]	800-528-8790	•	•	•	•

DT	BK	CV	CR	PR	←COURTS ANDERSON	RECORDING→	UC	RE	TX	VS
		•	•		Allied Inv Services [SOP]	800-302-0861				
•	•	•	•	•	Carolina Investigative Research (SC)	800-328-8981	•	•	•	•
•	•	•		•	Liberty Corporate Services Inc	888-875-1280	•	•	•	
•	•	•	•	•	Searchtec (Carolinas) [SOP]	800-528-8790	•	•	•	•
				•	Upper State Title Corp	864-260-4649	•	•	•	•

DT	BK	CV	CR	PR	←COURTS BAMBERG	RECORDING→	UC	RE	TX	VS
•	•	•		•	Horger Barnwell & Reid LLP	803-531-3000	•	•	•	•
•	•	•	•	•	Searchtec (Carolinas) [SOP]	800-528-8790	•	•	•	•

DT	BK	CV	CR	PR	←COURTS BARNWELL	RECORDING→	UC	RE	TX	VS
•	•	•	•	•	Searchtec (Carolinas) [SOP]	800-528-8790	•	•	•	•
•	•	•	•	•	Title Abstracts & Document Services	803-649-2500	•	•	•	•

DT	BK	CV	CR	PR	←COURTS BEAUFORT	RECORDING→	UC	RE	TX	VS
		•	•	•	Amma H General Ltd	843-263-5677 or 843-525-9890	•	•	•	
		•	•	•	Asset Protection Inv, Inc [SOP]	843-525-9664		•	•	
•	•	•		•	Liberty Corporate Services Inc	888-875-1280	•	•	•	
•	•	•	•	•	Searchtec (Carolinas) [SOP]	800-528-8790	•	•	•	•

DT	BK	CV	CR	PR	←COURTS BERKELEY	RECORDING→	UC	RE	TX	VS
•	•	•		•	Liberty Corporate Services Inc	888-875-1280	•	•	•	
•		•	•		Process Serving Unlimited [SOP]	843-728-2732				
•	•	•	•	•	Searchtec (Carolinas) [SOP]	800-528-8790	•	•	•	•
•	•	•	•	•	Seve Company	843-762-4520	•	•	•	•

DT	BK	CV	CR	PR	←COURTS CALHOUN	RECORDING→	UC	RE	TX	VS
•	•	•		•	Horger Barnwell & Reid LLP	803-531-3000	•	•	•	•
		•		•	Lexington Title Corp	803-957-1243	•	•	•	
•	•	•		•	Liberty Corporate Services Inc	888-875-1280	•	•	•	
•	•	•	•	•	Searchtec (Carolinas) [SOP]	800-528-8790	•	•	•	•

DT	BK	CV	CR	PR	←Courts CHARLESTON	Recording→	UC	RE	TX	VS
•	•	•			Advanced Data Technology Inc	800-426-5265		•	•	
•	•	•		•	Liberty Corporate Services Inc	888-875-1280	•	•	•	
•		•	•		Process Serving Unlimited [SOP]	843-728-2732				
•	•	•	•	•	Searchtec (Carolinas) [SOP]	800-528-8790	•	•	•	•
•	•	•	•	•	Seve Company	843-762-4520	•	•	•	•

DT	BK	CV	CR	PR	←Courts CHEROKEE	Recording→	UC	RE	TX	VS
•	•	•	•	•	Carolina Investigative Research (SC)	800-328-8981	•	•	•	•
•	•	•		•	Liberty Corporate Services Inc	888-875-1280	•	•	•	
•	•	•	•	•	Searchtec (Carolinas) [SOP]	800-528-8790	•	•	•	•

DT	BK	CV	CR	PR	←Courts CHESTER	Recording→	UC	RE	TX	VS
•	•	•		•	Liberty Corporate Services Inc	888-875-1280	•	•	•	
•	•	•	•	•	Searchtec (Carolinas) [SOP]	800-528-8790	•	•	•	•

DT	BK	CV	CR	PR	←Courts CHESTERFIELD	Recording→	UC	RE	TX	VS
•	•	•		•	Liberty Corporate Services Inc	888-875-1280	•	•	•	
•	•	•	•	•	Searchtec (Carolinas) [SOP]	800-528-8790	•	•	•	•

DT	BK	CV	CR	PR	←Courts CLARENDON	Recording→	UC	RE	TX	VS
•	•	•	•	•	Searchtec (Carolinas) [SOP]	800-528-8790	•	•	•	•

DT	BK	CV	CR	PR	←Courts COLLETON	Recording→	UC	RE	TX	VS
		•	•	•	Asset Protection Inv, Inc [SOP]	843-525-9664		•	•	
•	•	•		•	Liberty Corporate Services Inc	888-875-1280	•	•	•	
•	•	•	•	•	Searchtec (Carolinas) [SOP]	800-528-8790	•	•	•	•

DT	BK	CV	CR	PR	←Courts DARLINGTON	Recording→	UC	RE	TX	VS
•	•	•		•	Liberty Corporate Services Inc	888-875-1280	•	•	•	
•	•	•	•	•	Searchtec (Carolinas) [SOP]	800-528-8790	•	•	•	•

DT	BK	CV	CR	PR	←Courts DILLON	Recording→	UC	RE	TX	VS
•	•	•	•	•	Searchtec (Carolinas) [SOP]	800-528-8790	•	•	•	•

DT	BK	CV	CR	PR	←Courts DORCHESTER	Recording→	UC	RE	TX	VS
•	•	•		•	Horger Barnwell & Reid LLP	803-531-3000	•	•	•	•
•	•	•		•	Liberty Corporate Services Inc	888-875-1280	•	•	•	
•	•	•	•	•	Searchtec (Carolinas) [SOP]	800-528-8790	•	•	•	•
•	•	•	•	•	Seve Company	843-762-4520	•	•	•	•

DT	BK	CV	CR	PR	←Courts EDGEFIELD	Recording→	UC	RE	TX	VS
•	•	•	•	•	David Smith Detective Agency [SOP]	877-793-9426	•		•	
		•		•	Lexington Title Corp	803-957-1243	•	•	•	
		•		•	SCC Information Services Inc	803-957-1243	•	•	•	
•	•	•	•	•	Searchtec (Carolinas) [SOP]	800-528-8790	•	•	•	•
•	•	•	•	•	Title Abstracts & Document Services	803-649-2500	•	•	•	•

DT	BK	CV	CR	PR	←Courts FAIRFIELD	Recording→	UC	RE	TX	VS
		•		•	Lexington Title Corp	803-957-1243	•	•	•	
•	•	•		•	Liberty Corporate Services Inc	888-875-1280	•	•	•	
•	•	•	•	•	Searchtec (Carolinas) [SOP]	800-528-8790	•	•	•	•

DT	BK	CV	CR	PR	←Courts FLORENCE	Recording→	UC	RE	TX	VS
•	•	•	•	•	Carolina Investigative Research (SC)	800-328-8981	•	•	•	•
•	•	•		•	Liberty Corporate Services Inc	888-875-1280	•	•	•	
•	•	•	•	•	Searchtec (Carolinas) [SOP]	800-528-8790	•	•	•	•

DT	BK	CV	CR	PR	←Courts GEORGETOWN	Recording→	UC	RE	TX	VS
	•				Info Quest Inc	800-507-9628				•
•	•	•		•	Liberty Corporate Services Inc	888-875-1280	•	•	•	
•	•	•	•	•	Searchtec (Carolinas) [SOP]	800-528-8790	•	•	•	•

DT	BK	CV	CR	PR	←Courts GREENVILLE	Recording→	UC	RE	TX	VS
•	•	•			Advanced Data Technology Inc	800-426-5265		•	•	
•	•	•	•	•	Carolina Investigative Research (SC)	800-328-8981	•	•	•	•
•	•	•		•	Liberty Corporate Services Inc	888-875-1280	•	•	•	
•	•	•	•	•	Searchtec (Carolinas) [SOP]	800-528-8790	•	•	•	•
				•	Upper State Title Corp	864-260-4649	•	•	•	•

DT	BK	CV	CR	PR	←Courts GREENWOOD	Recording→	UC	RE	TX	VS
•	•	•	•	•	Carolina Investigative Research (SC)	800-328-8981	•	•	•	•
•	•	•		•	Liberty Corporate Services Inc	888-875-1280	•	•	•	
•	•	•	•	•	Searchtec (Carolinas) [SOP]	800-528-8790	•	•	•	•
				•	Upper State Title Corp	864-260-4649	•	•	•	•
		•	•		Upstate Investigations [SOP]	864-277-0757			•	

DT	BK	CV	CR	PR	←Courts HAMPTON	Recording→	UC	RE	TX	VS
		•	•	•	Amma H General Ltd	843-263-5677 or 843-525-9890	•	•	•	
		•	•	•	Asset Protection Inv, Inc [SOP]	843-525-9664		•	•	
•	•	•		•	Liberty Corporate Services Inc	888-875-1280	•	•	•	
•	•	•	•	•	Searchtec (Carolinas) [SOP]	800-528-8790	•	•	•	•

DT	BK	CV	CR	PR	←Courts HORRY	Recording→	UC	RE	TX	VS
	•				Info Quest Inc	800-507-9628				•
		•	•		Intercoastal Research & Inv	843-280-4461				
•	•	•		•	Liberty Corporate Services Inc	888-875-1280	•	•	•	
•	•	•	•	•	Searchtec (Carolinas) [SOP]	800-528-8790	•	•	•	•

DT	BK	CV	CR	PR	←Courts JASPER	Recording→	UC	RE	TX	VS
		•	•	•	Amma H General Ltd	843-263-5677 or 843-525-9890	•	•	•	
		•	•	•	Asset Protection Inv, Inc [SOP]	843-525-9664		•	•	
•	•	•		•	Liberty Corporate Services Inc	888-875-1280	•	•	•	
•	•	•	•	•	Searchtec (Carolinas) [SOP]	800-528-8790	•	•	•	•

DT	BK	CV	CR	PR	←Courts KERSHAW	Recording→	UC	RE	TX	VS
		•		•	Lexington Title Corp	803-957-1243	•	•	•	
•	•	•		•	Liberty Corporate Services Inc	888-875-1280	•	•	•	
•	•	•	•	•	Searchtec (Carolinas) [SOP]	800-528-8790	•	•	•	•

DT	BK	CV	CR	PR	←Courts LANCASTER	Recording→	UC	RE	TX	VS
•	•	•	•	•	Carolina Investigative Research (SC)	800-328-8981	•	•	•	•
•	•	•		•	Liberty Corporate Services Inc	888-875-1280	•	•	•	
•	•	•	•	•	Searchtec (Carolinas) [SOP]	800-528-8790	•	•	•	•

DT	BK	CV	CR	PR	←Courts LAURENS	Recording→	UC	RE	TX	VS
•	•	•	•	•	Carolina Investigative Research (SC)	800-328-8981	•	•	•	•
•	•	•		•	Liberty Corporate Services Inc	888-875-1280	•	•	•	
•	•	•	•	•	Searchtec (Carolinas) [SOP]	800-528-8790	•	•	•	•
				•	Upper State Title Corp	864-260-4649	•	•	•	•

DT	BK	CV	CR	PR	←Courts LEE	Recording→	UC	RE	TX	VS
•	•	•		•	Liberty Corporate Services Inc	888-875-1280	•	•	•	
•	•	•	•	•	Searchtec (Carolinas) [SOP]	800-528-8790	•	•	•	•

DT	BK	CV	CR	PR	←Courts LEXINGTON	Recording→	UC	RE	TX	VS
		•	•		Corley Research	803-951-3350				
•	•	•	•	•	Charles M Kneisley	803-936-1200	•	•	•	
		•		•	Lexington Title Corp	803-957-1243	•	•	•	
•	•	•		•	Liberty Corporate Services Inc	888-875-1280	•	•	•	
		•		•	SCC Information Services Inc	803-957-1243	•	•	•	
•	•	•	•	•	Searchtec (Carolinas) [SOP]	800-528-8790	•	•	•	•
		•	•		Bobbie Slice	803-932-7013	•	•	•	

DT	BK	CV	CR	PR	←Courts MARION	Recording→	UC	RE	TX	VS
•	•	•		•	Liberty Corporate Services Inc	888-875-1280	•	•	•	
•	•	•	•	•	Searchtec (Carolinas) [SOP]	800-528-8790	•	•	•	•

DT	BK	CV	CR	PR	←Courts MARLBORO	Recording→	UC	RE	TX	VS
•	•	•	•	•	Searchtec (Carolinas) [SOP]	800-528-8790	•	•	•	•

DT	BK	CV	CR	PR	←Courts MCCORMICK	Recording→	UC	RE	TX	VS
•	•	•		•	Liberty Corporate Services Inc	888-875-1280	•	•	•	
•	•	•	•	•	Searchtec (Carolinas) [SOP]	800-528-8790	•	•	•	•
				•	Upper State Title Corp	864-260-4649	•	•	•	•
		•	•		Upstate Investigations [SOP]	864-277-0757			•	

DT	BK	CV	CR	PR	←Courts NEWBERRY	Recording→	UC	RE	TX	VS
		•		•	Lexington Title Corp	803-957-1243	•	•	•	
•	•	•		•	Liberty Corporate Services Inc	888-875-1280	•	•	•	
		•		•	SCC Information Services Inc	803-957-1243	•	•	•	
•	•	•	•	•	Searchtec (Carolinas) [SOP]	800-528-8790	•	•	•	•
		•	•		Bobbie Slice	803-932-7013	•	•	•	

DT	BK	CV	CR	PR	←Courts OCONEE	Recording→	UC	RE	TX	VS
•	•	•		•	Liberty Corporate Services Inc	888-875-1280	•	•	•	
•	•	•	•	•	Searchtec (Carolinas) [SOP]	800-528-8790	•	•	•	•
				•	Upper State Title Corp	864-260-4649	•	•	•	•

DT	BK	CV	CR	PR	←Courts ORANGEBURG	Recording→	UC	RE	TX	VS
•	•	•		•	Horger Barnwell & Reid LLP	803-531-3000	•	•	•	•
		•		•	Lexington Title Corp	803-957-1243	•	•	•	
•	•	•		•	Liberty Corporate Services Inc	888-875-1280	•	•	•	
•	•	•	•	•	Searchtec (Carolinas) [SOP]	800-528-8790	•	•	•	•

DT	BK	CV	CR	PR	←Courts PICKENS	Recording→	UC	RE	TX	VS
•	•	•		•	Liberty Corporate Services Inc	888-875-1280	•	•	•	
•	•	•	•	•	Searchtec (Carolinas) [SOP]	800-528-8790	•	•	•	•
				•	Upper State Title Corp	864-260-4649	•	•	•	•

DT	BK	CV	CR	PR	←Courts RICHLAND	Recording→	UC	RE	TX	VS
•	•	•			Advanced Data Technology Inc	800-426-5265		•	•	
•	•	•	•	•	Carolina Investigative Research (SC)	800-328-8981	•	•	•	•
		•	•		Corley Research	803-951-3350				
•	•	•	•	•	Charles M Kneisley	803-936-1200	•	•	•	
		•		•	Lexington Title Corp	803-957-1243	•	•	•	
•	•	•		•	Liberty Corporate Services Inc	888-875-1280	•	•	•	
•	•	•	•	•	Searchtec (Carolinas) [SOP]	800-528-8790	•	•	•	•
		•	•		Bobbie Slice	803-932-7013	•	•	•	

DT	BK	CV	CR	PR	←Courts SALUDA	Recording→	UC	RE	TX	VS
•	•	•	•	•	David Smith Detective Agency [SOP]	877-793-9426	•		•	
		•		•	Lexington Title Corp	803-957-1243	•	•	•	
•	•	•		•	Liberty Corporate Services Inc	888-875-1280	•	•	•	
		•		•	SCC Information Services Inc	803-957-1243	•	•	•	
•	•	•	•	•	Searchtec (Carolinas) [SOP]	800-528-8790	•	•	•	•

DT	BK	CV	CR	PR	←Courts SPARTANBURG	Recording→	UC	RE	TX	VS
•	•	•	•	•	Carolina Investigative Research (SC)	800-328-8981	•	•	•	•
•	•	•		•	Liberty Corporate Services Inc	888-875-1280	•	•	•	
•	•	•	•	•	Searchtec (Carolinas) [SOP]	800-528-8790	•	•	•	•
				•	Upper State Title Corp	864-260-4649	•	•	•	•

DT	BK	CV	CR	PR	←Courts SUMTER	Recording→	UC	RE	TX	VS
•	•	•		•	Liberty Corporate Services Inc	888-875-1280	•	•	•	

DT	BK	CV	CR	PR	Retriever	Phone	UC	RE	TX	VS
•	•	•	•	•	Searchtec (Carolinas) [SOP]	800-528-8790	•	•	•	•

DT	BK	CV	CR	PR	←COURTS UNION RECORDING→		UC	RE	TX	VS
•	•	•	•	•	Searchtec (Carolinas) [SOP]	800-528-8790	•	•	•	•

DT	BK	CV	CR	PR	←COURTS WILLIAMSBURG RECORDING→		UC	RE	TX	VS
•	•	•	•	•	Searchtec (Carolinas) [SOP]	800-528-8790	•	•	•	•

DT	BK	CV	CR	PR	←COURTS YORK RECORDING→		UC	RE	TX	VS
•	•	•	•	•	Carolina Investigative Research (SC)	800-328-8981	•	•	•	•
•	•	•		•	Liberty Corporate Services Inc	888-875-1280	•	•	•	
•	•	•	•		Reynolds Professional Service Inc [SOP]	800-814-8662				•
•	•	•	•	•	Searchtec (Carolinas) [SOP]	800-528-8790	•	•	•	•

COURT RECORDS

CODE	GOVERNMENT AGENCY	TYPE OF INFORMATION
DT	US District Court	Federal civil and criminal cases
BK	Bankruptcy Court	United States bankruptcy cases
CV	Civil Court	Municipal, county and state level civil cases
CR	Criminal Court	Municipal, county and state level criminal cases
PR	Probate Court	Wills and estate cases

COUNTY RECORDS - RECORDINGS

CODE	GOVERNMENT AGENCY	TYPE OF INFORMATION
UC	UCC Filing Office	Uniform Commercial Code and other personal property liens
RE	Real Estate Recording Office	Real property transactions and liens
TX	Tax Filing Office(s)	Federal and state tax liens, judgment liens
VS	Vital Records Office	Vital statistics—birth, death, marriage, divorce

Editor's Tip: This section of the directory is not organized to promote search firms that are statewide, regional, or national in coverage.

An expanded resource of search firms, distributors, and screening firms is BRB Publication's website at www.brbpub.com. Click the "Find A Vendor" tab. Both sources contain information on firms that use online resources to obtain public record index information.

South Dakota

DT	BK	CV	CR	PR	←Courts	County / Retriever	Recording→	UC	RE	TX	VS
DT	BK	CV	CR	PR	←Courts	**Aurora**	Recording→	UC	RE	TX	VS
						Aurora County Abstract	605-942-7558		•	•	
DT	BK	CV	CR	PR	←Courts	**Beadle**	Recording→	UC	RE	TX	VS
		•		•		Huron Title Co	605-352-6157	•	•	•	
DT	BK	CV	CR	PR	←Courts	**Bennett**	Recording→	UC	RE	TX	VS
		•	•			Home Abstract Co	605-685-6525		•	•	
DT	BK	CV	CR	PR	←Courts	**Bon Homme**	Recording→	UC	RE	TX	VS
						Bon Homme Title Co	605-589-3572		•	•	
DT	BK	CV	CR	PR	←Courts	**Brookings**	Recording→	UC	RE	TX	VS
•	•	•	•	•		Decker Document Retrieval	605-336-8402	•	•	•	•
DT	BK	CV	CR	PR	←Courts	**Brown**	Recording→	UC	RE	TX	VS
•	•	•	•	•		Legal Support Services-II	800-583-0365	•	•	•	•
DT	BK	CV	CR	PR	←Courts	**Brule**	Recording→	UC	RE	TX	VS
		•		•		Brule County Abstract Co	605-734-4275		•	•	
DT	BK	CV	CR	PR	←Courts	**Buffalo**	Recording→	UC	RE	TX	VS
						Buffalo County Abstract	605-734-6891		•	•	
DT	BK	CV	CR	PR	←Courts	**Butte**	Recording→	UC	RE	TX	VS
•	•	•	•	•		Legal Support Services-II	800-583-0365	•	•	•	•
•	•	•	•	•		Webster's Research Inc	605-718-5472	•	•	•	•
DT	BK	CV	CR	PR	←Courts	**Campbell**	Recording→	UC	RE	TX	VS
						Campbell County Abstract & Title	605-437-2222		•	•	
DT	BK	CV	CR	PR	←Courts	**Charles Mix**	Recording→	UC	RE	TX	VS
						Platte Title Co	605-337-3824		•	•	
DT	BK	CV	CR	PR	←Courts	**Clark**	Recording→	UC	RE	TX	VS
				•		Clark Abstract & Title Co	605-532-3812	•	•	•	•
DT	BK	CV	CR	PR	←Courts	**Clay**	Recording→	UC	RE	TX	VS
						Clay County Title	605-624-2068		•	•	
DT	BK	CV	CR	PR	←Courts	**Codington**	Recording→	UC	RE	TX	VS
				•		Watertown Title & Escrow Co	605-886-8406	•	•	•	•
DT	BK	CV	CR	PR	←Courts	**Corson**	Recording→	UC	RE	TX	VS
						Corson County Land and Title	605-273-4513		•	•	
DT	BK	CV	CR	PR	←Courts	**Custer**	Recording→	UC	RE	TX	VS
•	•	•	•	•		Webster's Research Inc	605-718-5472	•	•	•	•
DT	BK	CV	CR	PR	←Courts	**Davison**	Recording→	UC	RE	TX	VS
		•				The Title Company	605-996-4900		•	•	
DT	BK	CV	CR	PR	←Courts	**Day**	Recording→	UC	RE	TX	VS
		•		•		Grue Abstract Co	605-345-3891	•	•	•	•

DT	BK	CV	CR	PR	←Courts	County / Retriever	Recording→	UC	RE	TX	VS
						DEUEL					
		•	•	•		Deuel County Abstract Co (South Dakota)	605-874-8597	•	•	•	•
						DEWEY					
		•	•	•		Titles of Dakota Inc (Dupree)	605-365-5247	•	•	•	
		•	•	•		Titles of Dakota Inc (Timber Lake)	605-365-5247	•	•	•	•
						DOUGLAS					
		•		•		Douglas County Title Inc (South Dakota)	605-724-2235		•	•	
						EDMUNDS					
		•		•		Edmunds County Abstract Co	605-426-6041		•	•	
						FALL RIVER					
				•		Fall River Abstract Co	605-745-5187		•	•	
•	•	•	•	•		Webster's Research Inc	605-718-5472	•	•	•	•
						FAULK					
						See adjoining counties for retrievers or contact court or recording office.					
						GRANT					
		•		•		Grant County Abstract & Title Co	605-432-5461	•	•	•	
						GREGORY					
		•	•	•		Gregory County Title Co	605-775-2943	•	•	•	•
						HAAKON					
						Haakon County Abstract Co	605-859-2461	•	•	•	
						HAMLIN					
						See adjoining counties for retrievers or contact court or recording office.					
						HAND					
						Hand County Abstract & Title Co	605-853-2194	•	•	•	
						HANSON					
		•				The Title Company	605-996-4900		•	•	
						HARDING					
						Harding County Abstract	605-375-3422		•	•	
						HUGHES					
•	•	•	•	•		Marilyn Person	605-224-8168	•		•	•
						HUTCHINSON					
		•	•	•		Oplinger Abstract & Title Inc	605-387-2335	•	•	•	•
						HYDE					
						See adjoining counties for retrievers or contact court or recording office.					
						JACKSON					
		•		•		Brule County Abstract Co	605-734-4275		•	•	
						JERAULD					
		•		•		Jerauld County Abstract Co Inc	605-539-1541	•	•	•	•
						KINGSBURY					
						Purintun Abstract	605-854-3401		•	•	
						LAKE					
		•		•		Weber Abstract Co	605-256-4640	•	•	•	•
						LAWRENCE					
•	•	•	•	•		Legal Support Services-II	800-583-0365	•	•	•	•
•	•	•	•	•		Webster's Research Inc	605-718-5472	•	•	•	•

DT	BK	CV	CR	PR	←Courts / Recording→	Phone	UC	RE	TX	VS
					LINCOLN					
		●	●		Action Professional Services [SOP]	888-335-3090	●	●	●	
●	●	●	●	●	Decker Document Retrieval	605-336-8402	●	●	●	●
					LYMAN					
		●		●	Brule County Abstract Co	605-734-4275		●	●	
		●		●	Lyman County Title Co	605-869-2269	●	●	●	
					MARSHALL					
●		●	●	●	Marshall Land & Title Co Inc	605-448-5796	●	●	●	●
					MCCOOK					
		●	●	●	McCook County Abstract & Title Ins	605-425-2612	●	●	●	●
					MCPHERSON					
					See adjoining counties for retrievers or contact court or recording office.					
					MEADE					
●	●	●	●	●	Legal Support Services-II	800-583-0365	●	●	●	●
●	●	●	●	●	Webster's Research Inc	605-718-5472	●	●	●	●
					MELLETTE					
					See adjoining counties for retrievers or contact court or recording office.					
					MINER					
		●		●	Fidelity Abstract & Title Co	605-772-5632	●	●	●	
					MINNEHAHA					
		●	●		Action Professional Services [SOP]	888-335-3090	●	●	●	
●	●	●	●	●	Decker Document Retrieval	605-336-8402	●	●	●	●
●	●	●	●	●	Legal Support Services-II	800-583-0365	●	●	●	●
					MOODY					
		●		●	Moody County Abstract Co	605-997-3723	●	●	●	
					MURDO					
					Jones County Abstract	605-669-3004		●	●	
					PENNINGTON					
●	●	●	●	●	Legal Support Services-II	800-583-0365	●	●	●	●
●	●	●	●	●	Webster's Research Inc	605-718-5472	●	●	●	●
					PERKINS					
		●	●	●	Perkins County Abstract Co	605-244-5544	●	●	●	
					POTTER					
		●	●	●	Potter County Land & Abstract Inc	605-765-2858		●	●	●
					ROBERTS					
					Roberts County Title	605-698-7272		●	●	
					SANBORN					
		●		●	Sanborn County Realty & Title	605-796-4417		●	●	
					SHANNON					
				●	Fall River Abstract Co	605-745-5187		●	●	
					SPINK					
					Spink County Abstract	605-472-2011		●	●	
					STANLEY					
●	●	●	●	●	Marilyn Person	605-224-8168	●		●	●
				●	Titles of Dakota Inc (Fort Pierre)	800-794-2725	●	●	●	

DT	BK	CV	CR	PR	←Courts	Recording→	UC	RE	TX	VS
					SULLY					
•	•	•	•	•	Marilyn Person	605-224-8168	•		•	•
				•	Titles of Dakota Inc (Fort Pierre)	800-794-2725	•	•	•	
					Titles of Dakota Inc (Onida)	605-258-2291		•	•	
					TODD					
		•		•	Tripp & Todd Title Company	605-842-0334	•	•	•	•
					TRIPP					
		•		•	Tripp & Todd Title Company	605-842-0334	•	•	•	•
					TURNER					
					Turner County Abstract	605-297-5555		•	•	
					UNION					
•	•	•	•	•	Intra-Lex Investigations Inc [SOP]	712-233-1639	•	•	•	•
		•	•	•	Union County Abstract & Title Co	605-356-3180	•	•	•	•
					WALWORTH					
		•		•	Walworth County Abstract & Title	605-649-7772	•	•	•	
					YANKTON					
					See adjoining counties for retrievers or contact court or recording office.					
					ZIEBACH					
		•	•	•	Titles of Dakota Inc (Dupree)	605-365-5247	•	•	•	

[SOP] = Performs service of process

Court Records

CODE	GOVERNMENT AGENCY	TYPE OF INFORMATION
DT	US District Court	Federal civil and criminal cases
BK	Bankruptcy Court	United States bankruptcy cases
CV	Civil Court	Municipal, county and state level civil cases
CR	Criminal Court	Municipal, county and state level criminal cases
PR	Probate Court	Wills and estate cases

County Records - Recordings

CODE	GOVERNMENT AGENCY	TYPE OF INFORMATION
UC	UCC Filing Office	Uniform Commercial Code and other personal property liens
RE	Real Estate Recording Office	Real property transactions and liens
TX	Tax Filing Office(s)	Federal and state tax liens, judgment liens
VS	Vital Records Office	Vital statistics—birth, death, marriage, divorce

= PRRN Member. *A retriever you can trust!*

Tennessee

COURT RECORDS RETRIEVED — RECORDING RECORDS RETRIEVED

DT	BK	CV	CR	PR	←COURTS ANDERSON	RECORDING→	UC	RE	TX	VS
				•	Thomas E Ewinger Jr	423-614-5290	•	•	•	•
•	•	•	•		Gamble Legal Research	865-966-3364	•		•	
•	•	•	•	•	IPS Investigations Inc [SOP]	865-689-7732	•		•	
				•	NNBS Inc	865-633-5079	•	•		•
•	•	•		•	Record Data Inc (Tennessee)	615-221-0021	•	•	•	
•	•	•	•		Records Research of Knoxville	865-693-3589	•	•	•	
•	•				Jamie D Stallings	615-781-2323	•	•	•	
•	•	•	•	•	Vinson Detective Agency TN [SOP]	888-525-5047	•	•	•	•

DT	BK	CV	CR	PR	←COURTS BEDFORD	RECORDING→	UC	RE	TX	VS
•	•	•	•	•	A All State Tracers Company	423-605-0155	•	•	•	•
•	•	•	•	•	Charles F Edgar & Associates Inc [SOP]	256-539-7761	•	•	•	
•	•	•		•	Maureen H Poole	931-294-2988	•	•	•	
•	•	•		•	Record Data Inc (Tennessee)	615-221-0021	•	•	•	

DT	BK	CV	CR	PR	←COURTS BENTON	RECORDING→	UC	RE	TX	VS
•	•	•		•	D K Abstract	731-686-9373/9363	•	•	•	•
•	•	•		•	Helen Lattus	731-884-9994	•	•	•	
•	•	•		•	Record Data Inc (Tennessee)	615-221-0021	•	•	•	

DT	BK	CV	CR	PR	←COURTS BLEDSOE	RECORDING→	UC	RE	TX	VS
•	•	•	•	•	A All State Tracers Company	423-605-0155	•	•	•	•
				•	Thomas E Ewinger Jr	423-614-5290	•	•	•	•
		•		•	Real Estate Loan Services	423-855-0581	•	•	•	
•	•	•		•	Record Data Inc (Tennessee)	615-221-0021	•	•	•	
•	•	•		•	Title Guaranty & Trust of Chattanooga	423-266-5751	•	•	•	

DT	BK	CV	CR	PR	←COURTS BLOUNT	RECORDING→	UC	RE	TX	VS
•	•	•	•	•	A All State Tracers Company	423-605-0155	•	•	•	•
				•	Thomas E Ewinger Jr	423-614-5290	•	•	•	•
•	•	•	•		Gamble Legal Research	865-966-3364	•		•	
•	•	•	•	•	IPS Investigations Inc [SOP]	865-689-7732	•		•	
					William (Bill) H Maynard	423-472-9858	•	•	•	
				•	NNBS Inc	865-633-5079	•	•		•
•	•	•	•	•	Profile Information Services	512-472-9380	•	•	•	•
•	•	•		•	Record Data Inc (Tennessee)	615-221-0021	•	•	•	
•	•	•	•		Records Research of Knoxville	865-693-3589	•	•	•	
•	•	•	•	•	Schaeffer Papers [SOP]	800-848-6119	•	•	•	•
•	•	•	•	•	Vinson Detective Agency TN [SOP]	888-525-5047	•	•	•	•

DT	BK	CV	CR	PR	←COURTS BRADLEY	RECORDING→	UC	RE	TX	VS
•	•	•	•	•	A All State Tracers Company	423-605-0155	•	•	•	•
•	•	•	•		Botts & Assoc [SOP]	423-595-2692	•	•	•	•
				•	Thomas E Ewinger Jr	423-614-5290	•	•	•	•
					William (Bill) H Maynard	423-472-9858	•	•	•	
		•		•	Real Estate Loan Services	423-855-0581	•	•	•	
•	•	•		•	Record Data Inc (Tennessee)	615-221-0021	•	•	•	
•	•	•		•	Title Guaranty & Trust of Chattanooga	423-266-5751	•	•	•	

DT	BK	CV	CR	PR	←Courts	**Campbell**	Recording→	UC	RE	TX	VS
•	•	•		•	Record Data Inc (Tennessee)		615-221-0021	•	•	•	

DT	BK	CV	CR	PR	←Courts	**Cannon**	Recording→	UC	RE	TX	VS
•	•	•	•	•	A All State Tracers Company		423-605-0155	•	•	•	•
•	•	•		•	Real Estate Loan Services of TN Inc		800-475-2334	•	•	•	
•	•	•		•	Record Data Inc (Tennessee)		615-221-0021	•	•	•	

DT	BK	CV	CR	PR	←Courts	**Carroll**	Recording→	UC	RE	TX	VS
•	•	•		•	D K Abstract		731-686-9373/9363	•	•	•	•
•	•	•		•	Helen Lattus		731-884-9994	•	•	•	
•	•				Jamie D Stallings		615-781-2323	•	•	•	
•	•	•		•	Record Data Inc (Tennessee)		615-221-0021	•	•	•	

DT	BK	CV	CR	PR	←Courts	**Carter**	Recording→	UC	RE	TX	VS
		•	•		Shelly and James Dobler		423-753-4885				
		•	•		National Pre-Employment Research [SOP]		770-389-6607				
•	•	•		•	Record Data Inc (Tennessee)		615-221-0021	•	•	•	

DT	BK	CV	CR	PR	←Courts	**Cheatham**	Recording→	UC	RE	TX	VS
			•		DataSearch		931-645-2562			•	
•	•	•	•	•	Kroll Document Filing & Retrieval Services [SOP]		800-324-2050	•	•	•	•
•	•	•		•	Real Estate Loan Services of TN Inc		800-475-2334	•	•	•	
•	•	•		•	Record Data Inc (Tennessee)		615-221-0021	•	•	•	
					Right On Time Documents Inc		615-885-8672	•	•		
•	•				Jamie D Stallings		615-781-2323	•	•	•	

DT	BK	CV	CR	PR	←Courts	**Chester**	Recording→	UC	RE	TX	VS
•	•	•		•	D K Abstract		731-686-9373/9363	•	•	•	•
•	•	•		•	Record Data Inc (Tennessee)		615-221-0021	•	•	•	

DT	BK	CV	CR	PR	←Courts	**Claiborne**	Recording→	UC	RE	TX	VS
•	•	•		•	Record Data Inc (Tennessee)		615-221-0021	•	•	•	
		•	•	•	Title Express Inc		423-587-9886	•	•	•	

DT	BK	CV	CR	PR	←Courts	**Clay**	Recording→	UC	RE	TX	VS
					Jimmie Kirby		931-858-8786				
•	•	•		•	Record Data Inc (Tennessee)		615-221-0021	•	•	•	
			•		Larry M Warner		931-484-1611		•	•	

DT	BK	CV	CR	PR	←Courts	**Cocke**	Recording→	UC	RE	TX	VS
		•	•		Datalink Investigative Services [SOP]		865-674-0030				
•	•	•		•	Record Data Inc (Tennessee)		615-221-0021	•	•	•	
		•	•	•	Title Express Inc		423-587-9886	•	•	•	

DT	BK	CV	CR	PR	←Courts	**Coffee**	Recording→	UC	RE	TX	VS
•	•	•	•	•	A All State Tracers Company		423-605-0155	•	•	•	•
•	•	•	•	•	Charles F Edgar & Associates Inc [SOP]		256-539-7761	•	•	•	
•	•	•		•	Maureen H Poole		931-294-2988	•	•	•	
•	•	•		•	Record Data Inc (Tennessee)		615-221-0021	•	•	•	
•	•	•		•	Title Guaranty & Trust of Chattanooga		423-266-5751	•	•	•	

DT	BK	CV	CR	PR	←Courts	**Crockett**	Recording→	UC	RE	TX	VS
•	•	•		•	D K Abstract		731-686-9373/9363	•	•	•	•
•	•	•		•	Helen Lattus		731-884-9994	•	•	•	
•	•	•		•	Record Data Inc (Tennessee)		615-221-0021	•	•	•	
•	•	•	•	•	RFYI (Research For Your Information)		901-475-1276	•	•	•	•

DT	BK	CV	CR	PR	←Courts	**Cumberland**	Recording→	UC	RE	TX	VS
		•	•		National Pre-Employment Research [SOP]		770-389-6607				
•	•	•	•	•	Public Records Research		931-520-8902	•	•	•	•
•	•	•		•	Real Estate Loan Services of TN Inc		800-475-2334	•	•	•	

DT	BK	CV	CR	PR	←Courts	Recording→	UC	RE	TX	VS
•	•	•		•	Record Data Inc (Tennessee)	615-221-0021	•	•	•	
•	•	•	•	•	Source [SOP]	800-678-8774	•	•	•	
			•		Larry M Warner	931-484-1611		•	•	
DT	**BK**	**CV**	**CR**	**PR**	**←Courts DAVIDSON**	**Recording→**	**UC**	**RE**	**TX**	**VS**
•	•	•	•	•	A All State Tracers Company	423-605-0155	•	•	•	•
•	•	•	•	•	ASAP Process Services [SOP]	256-766-9805	•	•		•
•		•	•	•	Information Inc	615-884-8000			•	•
•	•	•	•	•	Investigative Consultant Service	615-885-1126	•			•
•	•	•	•	•	Investigative Surveillance Group	615-895-0268	•	•	•	•
					Judi Knecht	615-832-8255		•		
			•		Kroll Background America	800-697-7189		•	•	
•	•	•	•	•	Kroll Document Filing & Retrieval Services [SOP]	800-324-2050	•	•	•	•
		•	•		National Pre-Employment Research [SOP]	770-389-6607				
•	•	•		•	Maureen H Poole	931-294-2988	•	•	•	
•	•	•		•	Real Estate Loan Services of TN Inc	800-475-2334	•	•	•	
•	•	•		•	Record Data Inc (Tennessee)	615-221-0021	•	•	•	
					Right On Time Documents Inc	615-885-8672	•	•		
•	•	•	•	•	Schaeffer Papers [SOP]	800-848-6119	•	•	•	•
•	•				Jamie D Stallings	615-781-2323	•	•	•	
DT	**BK**	**CV**	**CR**	**PR**	**←Courts DECATUR**	**Recording→**	**UC**	**RE**	**TX**	**VS**
•	•	•		•	D K Abstract	731-686-9373/9363	•	•	•	•
•	•	•		•	Record Data Inc (Tennessee)	615-221-0021	•	•	•	
DT	**BK**	**CV**	**CR**	**PR**	**←Courts DEKALB**	**Recording→**	**UC**	**RE**	**TX**	**VS**
•	•	•	•	•	A All State Tracers Company	423-605-0155	•	•	•	•
•	•	•	•	•	Public Records Research	931-520-8902	•	•	•	•
•	•	•		•	Real Estate Loan Services of TN Inc	800-475-2334	•	•	•	
•	•	•		•	Record Data Inc (Tennessee)	615-221-0021	•	•	•	
•	•	•	•	•	Source [SOP]	800-678-8774	•	•	•	
DT	**BK**	**CV**	**CR**	**PR**	**←Courts DICKSON**	**Recording→**	**UC**	**RE**	**TX**	**VS**
•	•	•		•	Real Estate Loan Services of TN Inc	800-475-2334	•	•	•	
•	•	•		•	Record Data Inc (Tennessee)	615-221-0021	•	•	•	
					Right On Time Documents Inc	615-885-8672	•	•		
•	•				Jamie D Stallings	615-781-2323	•	•	•	
DT	**BK**	**CV**	**CR**	**PR**	**←Courts DYER**	**Recording→**	**UC**	**RE**	**TX**	**VS**
			•		Blue Line Investigations	901-266-7100				
•	•	•		•	D K Abstract	731-686-9373/9363	•	•	•	•
•	•	•		•	Helen Lattus	731-884-9994	•	•	•	
•	•	•		•	Record Data Inc (Tennessee)	615-221-0021	•	•	•	
•	•	•	•	•	Schaeffer Papers [SOP]	800-848-6119	•	•	•	•
DT	**BK**	**CV**	**CR**	**PR**	**←Courts FAYETTE**	**Recording→**	**UC**	**RE**	**TX**	**VS**
			•		Blue Line Investigations	901-266-7100				
•	•	•		•	D K Abstract	731-686-9373/9363	•	•	•	•
•	•	•	•	•	Mid-South Subpoena Service [SOP]	800-737-8542				
•	•	•	•	•	National Background Reports Inc	901-526-4654	•	•	•	•
		•	•		National Pre-Employment Research [SOP]	770-389-6607				
•	•	•		•	Record Data Inc (Tennessee)	615-221-0021	•	•	•	
•	•	•	•	•	Record-Check Services Inc	800-530-7226	•	•	•	•
•	•	•	•	•	RFYI (Research For Your Information)	901-475-1276	•	•	•	•
•	•	•	•	•	Schaeffer Papers [SOP]	800-848-6119	•	•	•	•
DT	**BK**	**CV**	**CR**	**PR**	**←Courts FENTRESS**	**Recording→**	**UC**	**RE**	**TX**	**VS**
					Jimmie Kirby	931-858-8786				
•	•	•		•	Real Estate Loan Services of TN Inc	800-475-2334	•	•	•	
•	•	•		•	Record Data Inc (Tennessee)	615-221-0021	•	•	•	
			•		Larry M Warner	931-484-1611		•	•	

DT	BK	CV	CR	PR	←Courts FRANKLIN	Recording→	UC	RE	TX	VS
●	●	●	●	●	A All State Tracers Company	423-605-0155	●	●	●	●
		●	●	●	J Stephen Broadway	931-433-5979	●	●	●	●
●	●	●	●	●	Charles F Edgar & Associates Inc [SOP]	256-539-7761	●	●	●	
		●	●		National Pre-Employment Research [SOP]	770-389-6607				
●	●	●		●	Maureen H Poole	931-294-2988	●	●	●	
●	●	●		●	Record Data Inc (Tennessee)	615-221-0021	●	●	●	
●	●	●		●	Title Guaranty & Trust of Chattanooga	423-266-5751	●	●	●	

DT	BK	CV	CR	PR	←Courts GIBSON	Recording→	UC	RE	TX	VS
●	●	●		●	D K Abstract	731-686-9373/9363	●	●	●	●
●	●	●		●	Helen Lattus	731-884-9994	●	●	●	
●	●	●		●	Record Data Inc (Tennessee)	615-221-0021	●	●	●	
●	●	●	●	●	RFYI (Research For Your Information)	901-475-1276	●	●	●	●

DT	BK	CV	CR	PR	←Courts GILES	Recording→	UC	RE	TX	VS
●	●	●	●	●	ASAP Process Services [SOP]	256-766-9805	●	●		●
		●	●	●	J Stephen Broadway	931-433-5979	●	●	●	●
●	●	●	●	●	Charles F Edgar & Associates Inc [SOP]	256-539-7761	●	●	●	
		●	●		National Pre-Employment Research [SOP]	770-389-6607				
●	●	●		●	Maureen H Poole	931-294-2988	●	●	●	
●	●	●		●	Real Estate Loan Services of TN Inc	800-475-2334	●	●	●	
●	●	●		●	Record Data Inc (Tennessee)	615-221-0021	●	●	●	

DT	BK	CV	CR	PR	←Courts GRAINGER	Recording→	UC	RE	TX	VS
●	●	●		●	Record Data Inc (Tennessee)	615-221-0021	●	●	●	

DT	BK	CV	CR	PR	←Courts GREENE	Recording→	UC	RE	TX	VS
●	●	●		●	Record Data Inc (Tennessee)	615-221-0021	●	●	●	
		●	●	●	Title Express Inc	423-587-9886	●	●	●	

DT	BK	CV	CR	PR	←Courts GRUNDY	Recording→	UC	RE	TX	VS
●	●	●	●	●	A All State Tracers Company	423-605-0155	●	●	●	●
		●	●	●	Earlene Y Speer Law Offices	931-692-2368	●	●	●	●
		●		●	Real Estate Loan Services	423-855-0581	●	●	●	
●	●	●		●	Record Data Inc (Tennessee)	615-221-0021	●	●	●	
●	●	●		●	Title Guaranty & Trust of Chattanooga	423-266-5751	●	●	●	

DT	BK	CV	CR	PR	←Courts HAMBLEN	Recording→	UC	RE	TX	VS
		●	●		Datalink Investigative Services [SOP]	865-674-0030				
●	●	●		●	Record Data Inc (Tennessee)	615-221-0021	●	●	●	
		●	●	●	Title Express Inc	423-587-9886	●	●	●	

DT	BK	CV	CR	PR	←Courts HAMILTON	Recording→	UC	RE	TX	VS
●	●	●	●	●	A All State Tracers Company	423-605-0155	●	●	●	●
				●	Thomas E Ewinger Jr	423-614-5290	●	●	●	●
					William (Bill) H Maynard	423-472-9858	●	●	●	
		●		●	Real Estate Loan Services	423-855-0581	●	●	●	
●	●	●		●	Record Data Inc (Tennessee)	615-221-0021	●	●	●	
					Right On Time Documents Inc	615-885-8672	●	●		
●	●				Jamie D Stallings	615-781-2323	●	●	●	
●	●	●		●	Title Guaranty & Trust of Chattanooga	423-266-5751	●	●	●	

DT	BK	CV	CR	PR	←Courts HANCOCK	Recording→	UC	RE	TX	VS
●	●	●		●	Record Data Inc (Tennessee)	615-221-0021	●	●	●	
		●	●	●	Title Express Inc	423-587-9886	●	●	●	

DT	BK	CV	CR	PR	←Courts HARDEMAN	Recording→	UC	RE	TX	VS
●	●	●		●	D K Abstract	731-686-9373/9363	●	●	●	●
●	●	●	●	●	Mid-South Subpoena Service [SOP]	800-737-8542				
●	●	●		●	Record Data Inc (Tennessee)	615-221-0021	●	●	●	

DT	BK	CV	CR	PR	←Courts	HARDIN	Recording→	UC	RE	TX	VS
•	•	•	•	•	ASAP Process Services [SOP]		256-766-9805	•	•		•
•	•	•		•	D K Abstract		731-686-9373/9363	•	•	•	•
•	•	•	•	•	Freelance Abstracting Svc [SOP]		662-424-3636	•	•	•	•
•	•	•		•	Record Data Inc (Tennessee)		615-221-0021	•	•	•	

DT	BK	CV	CR	PR	←Courts	HAWKINS	Recording→	UC	RE	TX	VS
		•	•		National Pre-Employment Research [SOP]		770-389-6607				
•	•	•		•	Record Data Inc (Tennessee)		615-221-0021	•	•	•	
		•	•	•	Title Express Inc		423-587-9886	•	•	•	

DT	BK	CV	CR	PR	←Courts	HAYWOOD	Recording→	UC	RE	TX	VS
•	•	•		•	D K Abstract		731-686-9373/9363	•	•	•	•
•	•	•		•	Helen Lattus		731-884-9994	•	•	•	
		•	•		National Pre-Employment Research [SOP]		770-389-6607				
•	•	•		•	Record Data Inc (Tennessee)		615-221-0021	•	•	•	
•	•	•	•	•	RFYI (Research For Your Information)		901-475-1276	•	•	•	•

DT	BK	CV	CR	PR	←Courts	HENDERSON	Recording→	UC	RE	TX	VS
			•		Blue Line Investigations		901-266-7100				
•	•	•		•	D K Abstract		731-686-9373/9363	•	•	•	•
•	•	•		•	Record Data Inc (Tennessee)		615-221-0021	•	•	•	

DT	BK	CV	CR	PR	←Courts	HENRY	Recording→	UC	RE	TX	VS
•	•	•		•	D K Abstract		731-686-9373/9363	•	•	•	•
•	•	•		•	Helen Lattus		731-884-9994	•	•	•	
•	•	•		•	Record Data Inc (Tennessee)		615-221-0021	•	•	•	

DT	BK	CV	CR	PR	←Courts	HICKMAN	Recording→	UC	RE	TX	VS
					Larry R Dorning PC		931-796-5959	•	•	•	
•	•	•		•	Maureen H Poole		931-294-2988	•	•	•	
•	•	•		•	Real Estate Loan Services of TN Inc		800-475-2334	•	•	•	
•	•	•		•	Record Data Inc (Tennessee)		615-221-0021	•	•	•	

DT	BK	CV	CR	PR	←Courts	HOUSTON	Recording→	UC	RE	TX	VS
•	•	•		•	Real Estate Loan Services of TN Inc		800-475-2334	•	•	•	
•	•	•		•	Record Data Inc (Tennessee)		615-221-0021	•	•	•	

DT	BK	CV	CR	PR	←Courts	HUMPHREYS	Recording→	UC	RE	TX	VS
•	•	•		•	D K Abstract		731-686-9373/9363	•	•	•	•
•	•	•		•	Real Estate Loan Services of TN Inc		800-475-2334	•	•	•	
•	•	•		•	Record Data Inc (Tennessee)		615-221-0021	•	•	•	

DT	BK	CV	CR	PR	←Courts	JACKSON	Recording→	UC	RE	TX	VS
					Jimmie Kirby		931-858-8786				
•	•	•		•	Real Estate Loan Services of TN Inc		800-475-2334	•	•	•	
•	•	•		•	Record Data Inc (Tennessee)		615-221-0021	•	•	•	
•	•	•	•	•	Source [SOP]		800-678-8774	•	•	•	

DT	BK	CV	CR	PR	←Courts	JEFFERSON	Recording→	UC	RE	TX	VS
		•	•		Datalink Investigative Services [SOP]		865-674-0030				
				•	NNBS Inc		865-633-5079	•	•		•
•	•	•		•	Record Data Inc (Tennessee)		615-221-0021	•	•	•	
		•	•	•	Title Express Inc		423-587-9886	•	•	•	
•	•	•	•	•	Vinson Detective Agency TN [SOP]		888-525-5047	•	•	•	•

DT	BK	CV	CR	PR	←Courts	JOHNSON	Recording→	UC	RE	TX	VS
•	•	•		•	Record Data Inc (Tennessee)		615-221-0021	•	•	•	

DT	BK	CV	CR	PR	←Courts	KNOX	Recording→	UC	RE	TX	VS
•	•	•	•	•	A All State Tracers Company		423-605-0155	•	•	•	•
•	•	•	•	•	Business Research Services		800-608-4636	•	•	•	•

DT	BK	CV	CR	PR	←Courts		Recording→	UC	RE	TX	VS
				•	Thomas E Ewinger Jr		423-614-5290	•	•	•	•
•	•	•	•		Gamble Legal Research		865-966-3364	•		•	
•	•	•	•	•	IPS Investigations Inc [SOP]		865-689-7732	•		•	
•	•	•	•	•	Legal Investigations [SOP]		865-970-4444	•	•		
					William (Bill) H Maynard		423-472-9858	•	•	•	
				•	NNBS Inc		865-633-5079	•	•		•
•	•	•	•	•	Profile Information Services		512-472-9380	•	•	•	•
•	•	•		•	Record Data Inc (Tennessee)		615-221-0021	•	•	•	
•	•	•	•		Records Research of Knoxville		865-693-3589	•	•	•	
					Right On Time Documents Inc		615-885-8672	•	•		
•	•	•	•	•	Schaeffer Papers [SOP]		800-848-6119	•	•	•	•
•	•	•	•	•	Southern Process Service [SOP]		865-525-3124		•		
•	•				Jamie D Stallings		615-781-2323	•	•	•	
•	•	•	•	•	Vinson Detective Agency TN [SOP]		888-525-5047	•	•	•	•

DT	BK	CV	CR	PR	←Courts	Lake	Recording→	UC	RE	TX	VS
•	•	•		•	D K Abstract		731-686-9373/9363	•	•	•	•
•	•	•		•	Helen Lattus		731-884-9994	•	•	•	
•	•	•		•	Record Data Inc (Tennessee)		615-221-0021	•	•	•	

DT	BK	CV	CR	PR	←Courts	Lauderdale	Recording→	UC	RE	TX	VS
			•		Blue Line Investigations		901-266-7100				
•	•	•		•	D K Abstract		731-686-9373/9363	•	•	•	•
•	•	•		•	Helen Lattus		731-884-9994	•	•	•	
•	•	•	•	•	Mid-South Subpoena Service [SOP]		800-737-8542				
		•	•		National Pre-Employment Research [SOP]		770-389-6607				
•	•	•		•	Record Data Inc (Tennessee)		615-221-0021	•	•	•	
•	•	•	•	•	RFYI (Research For Your Information)		901-475-1276	•	•	•	•

DT	BK	CV	CR	PR	←Courts	Lawrence	Recording→	UC	RE	TX	VS
•	•	•	•	•	ASAP Process Services [SOP]		256-766-9805	•	•		•
		•	•	•	J Stephen Broadway		931-433-5979	•	•	•	•
•	•	•	•	•	Charles F Edgar & Associates Inc [SOP]		256-539-7761	•	•	•	
					Larry R Dorning PC		931-796-5959	•	•	•	
		•	•		National Pre-Employment Research [SOP]		770-389-6607				
•	•	•		•	Maureen H Poole		931-294-2988	•	•	•	
•	•	•		•	Real Estate Loan Services of TN Inc		800-475-2334	•	•	•	
•	•	•		•	Record Data Inc (Tennessee)		615-221-0021	•	•	•	

DT	BK	CV	CR	PR	←Courts	Lewis	Recording→	UC	RE	TX	VS
					Larry R Dorning PC		931-796-5959	•	•	•	
		•	•		National Pre-Employment Research [SOP]		770-389-6607				
•	•	•		•	Maureen H Poole		931-294-2988	•	•	•	
•	•	•		•	Real Estate Loan Services of TN Inc		800-475-2334	•	•	•	
•	•	•		•	Record Data Inc (Tennessee)		615-221-0021	•	•	•	

DT	BK	CV	CR	PR	←Courts	Lincoln	Recording→	UC	RE	TX	VS
•	•	•	•	•	A All State Tracers Company		423-605-0155	•	•	•	•
		•	•	•	J Stephen Broadway		931-433-5979	•	•	•	•
•	•	•	•	•	Charles F Edgar & Associates Inc [SOP]		256-539-7761	•	•	•	
•	•	•		•	Maureen H Poole		931-294-2988	•	•	•	
•	•	•		•	Record Data Inc (Tennessee)		615-221-0021	•	•	•	

DT	BK	CV	CR	PR	←Courts	Loudon	Recording→	UC	RE	TX	VS
•	•	•	•	•	A All State Tracers Company		423-605-0155	•	•	•	•
•	•	•	•		Botts & Assoc [SOP]		423-595-2692	•	•	•	•
				•	Thomas E Ewinger Jr		423-614-5290	•	•	•	•
•	•	•	•		Gamble Legal Research		865-966-3364	•		•	
•	•	•	•	•	IPS Investigations Inc [SOP]		865-689-7732	•		•	
					William (Bill) H Maynard		423-472-9858	•	•	•	

DT	BK	CV	CR	PR	←Courts	Recording→	UC	RE	TX	VS
				•	NNBS Inc	865-633-5079	•	•		•
•	•	•	•	•	Profile Information Services	512-472-9380	•	•	•	•
•	•	•		•	Record Data Inc (Tennessee)	615-221-0021	•	•	•	
•	•	•		•	Title Guaranty & Trust of Chattanooga	423-266-5751	•	•	•	

DT	BK	CV	CR	PR	←Courts **Macon**	Recording→	UC	RE	TX	VS
		•	•		Cumberland Research	615-735-6558	•	•	•	
•	•	•		•	Real Estate Loan Services of TN Inc	800-475-2334	•	•	•	
•	•	•		•	Record Data Inc (Tennessee)	615-221-0021	•	•	•	
•	•	•	•	•	Source [SOP]	800-678-8774	•	•	•	

DT	BK	CV	CR	PR	←Courts **Madison**	Recording→	UC	RE	TX	VS
•	•	•		•	D K Abstract	731-686-9373/9363	•	•	•	•
					Judi Knecht	615-832-8255		•		
•	•	•		•	Helen Lattus	731-884-9994	•	•	•	
•	•	•	•	•	Mid-South Subpoena Service [SOP]	800-737-8542				
•	•	•		•	Record Data Inc (Tennessee)	615-221-0021	•	•	•	
•	•	•	•	•	Schaeffer Papers [SOP]	800-848-6119	•	•	•	•

DT	BK	CV	CR	PR	←Courts **Marion**	Recording→	UC	RE	TX	VS
•	•	•	•	•	A All State Tracers Company	423-605-0155	•	•	•	•
•	•	•	•	•	Charles F Edgar & Associates Inc [SOP]	256-539-7761	•	•	•	
					DocuSearch Services	423-894-2425	•	•	•	
				•	Thomas E Ewinger Jr	423-614-5290	•	•	•	•
		•	•		National Pre-Employment Research [SOP]	770-389-6607				
		•		•	Real Estate Loan Services	423-855-0581	•	•	•	
•	•	•		•	Record Data Inc (Tennessee)	615-221-0021	•	•	•	
•	•	•		•	Title Guaranty & Trust of Chattanooga	423-266-5751	•	•	•	

DT	BK	CV	CR	PR	←Courts **Marshall**	Recording→	UC	RE	TX	VS
		•	•	•	J Stephen Broadway	931-433-5979	•	•	•	•
•	•	•	•	•	Charles F Edgar & Associates Inc [SOP]	256-539-7761	•	•	•	
•	•	•		•	Maureen H Poole	931-294-2988	•	•	•	
•	•	•		•	Real Estate Loan Services of TN Inc	800-475-2334	•	•	•	
•	•	•		•	Record Data Inc (Tennessee)	615-221-0021	•	•	•	

DT	BK	CV	CR	PR	←Courts **Maury**	Recording→	UC	RE	TX	VS
•	•	•	•	•	Charles F Edgar & Associates Inc [SOP]	256-539-7761	•	•	•	
					Larry R Dorning PC	931-796-5959	•	•	•	
		•	•		National Pre-Employment Research [SOP]	770-389-6607				
•	•	•		•	Maureen H Poole	931-294-2988	•	•	•	
•	•	•		•	Real Estate Loan Services of TN Inc	800-475-2334	•	•	•	
•	•	•		•	Record Data Inc (Tennessee)	615-221-0021	•	•	•	

DT	BK	CV	CR	PR	←Courts **McMinn**	Recording→	UC	RE	TX	VS
•	•	•	•	•	A All State Tracers Company	423-605-0155	•	•	•	•
•	•	•	•		Botts & Assoc [SOP]	423-595-2692	•	•	•	•
				•	Thomas E Ewinger Jr	423-614-5290	•	•	•	•
					William (Bill) H Maynard	423-472-9858	•	•	•	
		•	•		National Pre-Employment Research [SOP]	770-389-6607				
		•		•	Real Estate Loan Services	423-855-0581	•	•	•	
•	•	•		•	Record Data Inc (Tennessee)	615-221-0021	•	•	•	
•	•	•		•	Title Guaranty & Trust of Chattanooga	423-266-5751	•	•	•	

DT	BK	CV	CR	PR	←Courts **McNairy**	Recording→	UC	RE	TX	VS
•	•	•		•	D K Abstract	731-686-9373/9363	•	•	•	•
•	•	•		•	Record Data Inc (Tennessee)	615-221-0021	•	•	•	

DT	BK	CV	CR	PR	←Courts **Meigs**	Recording→	UC	RE	TX	VS
•	•	•	•	•	A All State Tracers Company	423-605-0155	•	•	•	•
•	•	•	•		Botts & Assoc [SOP]	423-595-2692	•	•	•	•

DT	BK	CV	CR	PR	←Courts	Recording→	UC	RE	TX	VS
				•	Thomas E Ewinger Jr	423-614-5290	•	•	•	•
					William (Bill) H Maynard	423-472-9858	•	•	•	
		•	•		National Pre-Employment Research [SOP]	770-389-6607				
		•		•	Real Estate Loan Services	423-855-0581	•	•	•	
•	•	•		•	Record Data Inc (Tennessee)	615-221-0021	•	•	•	
•	•	•		•	Title Guaranty & Trust of Chattanooga	423-266-5751	•	•	•	

DT	BK	CV	CR	PR	←Courts **Monroe**	Recording→	UC	RE	TX	VS
•	•	•	•	•	A All State Tracers Company	423-605-0155	•	•	•	•
•	•	•	•		Botts & Assoc [SOP]	423-595-2692	•	•	•	•
				•	Thomas E Ewinger Jr	423-614-5290	•	•	•	•
					William (Bill) H Maynard	423-472-9858	•	•	•	
•	•	•	•	•	Profile Information Services	512-472-9380	•	•	•	•
		•		•	Real Estate Loan Services	423-855-0581	•	•	•	
•	•	•		•	Record Data Inc (Tennessee)	615-221-0021	•	•	•	
•	•	•		•	Title Guaranty & Trust of Chattanooga	423-266-5751	•	•	•	

DT	BK	CV	CR	PR	←Courts **Montgomery**	Recording→	UC	RE	TX	VS
			•		DataSearch	931-645-2562			•	
					Judi Knecht	615-832-8255				
•	•	•		•	Real Estate Loan Services of TN Inc	800-475-2334	•	•	•	
•	•	•		•	Record Data Inc (Tennessee)	615-221-0021	•	•	•	
					Right On Time Documents Inc	615-885-8672	•	•		
•	•				Jamie D Stallings	615-781-2323	•	•	•	

DT	BK	CV	CR	PR	←Courts **Moore**	Recording→	UC	RE	TX	VS
		•	•	•	J Stephen Broadway	931-433-5979	•	•	•	•
•	•	•	•	•	Charles F Edgar & Associates Inc [SOP]	256-539-7761	•	•	•	
•	•	•		•	Maureen H Poole	931-294-2988	•	•	•	
•	•	•		•	Record Data Inc (Tennessee)	615-221-0021	•	•	•	

DT	BK	CV	CR	PR	←Courts **Morgan**	Recording→	UC	RE	TX	VS
		•	•		National Pre-Employment Research [SOP]	770-389-6607				
•	•	•		•	Record Data Inc (Tennessee)	615-221-0021	•	•	•	

DT	BK	CV	CR	PR	←Courts **Obion**	Recording→	UC	RE	TX	VS
			•		Blue Line Investigations	901-266-7100				
•	•	•		•	D K Abstract	731-686-9373/9363	•	•	•	•
•	•	•		•	Helen Lattus	731-884-9994	•	•	•	
•	•	•		•	Record Data Inc (Tennessee)	615-221-0021	•	•	•	
•	•	•	•	•	RFYI (Research For Your Information)	901-475-1276	•	•	•	•

DT	BK	CV	CR	PR	←Courts **Overton**	Recording→	UC	RE	TX	VS
					Jimmie Kirby	931-858-8786				
•	•	•	•	•	Public Records Research	931-520-8902	•	•	•	•
•	•	•		•	Real Estate Loan Services of TN Inc	800-475-2334	•	•	•	
•	•	•		•	Record Data Inc (Tennessee)	615-221-0021	•	•	•	
•	•	•	•	•	Source [SOP]	800-678-8774	•	•	•	
			•		Larry M Warner	931-484-1611		•	•	

DT	BK	CV	CR	PR	←Courts **Perry**	Recording→	UC	RE	TX	VS
•	•	•		•	D K Abstract	731-686-9373/9363	•	•	•	•
					Larry R Dorning PC	931-796-5959	•	•	•	
•	•	•		•	Real Estate Loan Services of TN Inc	800-475-2334	•	•	•	
•	•	•		•	Record Data Inc (Tennessee)	615-221-0021	•	•	•	

DT	BK	CV	CR	PR	←Courts **Pickett**	Recording→	UC	RE	TX	VS
•	•	•		•	Real Estate Loan Services of TN Inc	800-475-2334	•	•	•	
•	•	•		•	Record Data Inc (Tennessee)	615-221-0021	•	•	•	
			•		Larry M Warner	931-484-1611		•	•	

DT	BK	CV	CR	PR	←COURTS POLK	RECORDING→	UC	RE	TX	VS
•	•	•	•		Botts & Assoc [SOP]	423-595-2692	•	•	•	•
					DocuSearch Services	423-894-2425	•	•	•	
				•	Thomas E Ewinger Jr	423-614-5290	•	•	•	•
					William (Bill) H Maynard	423-472-9858	•	•	•	
		•	•		National Pre-Employment Research [SOP]	770-389-6607				
		•		•	Real Estate Loan Services	423-855-0581	•	•	•	
•	•	•		•	Record Data Inc (Tennessee)	615-221-0021	•	•	•	
•	•	•		•	Title Guaranty & Trust of Chattanooga	423-266-5751	•	•	•	

DT	BK	CV	CR	PR	←COURTS PUTNAM	RECORDING→	UC	RE	TX	VS
					Jimmie Kirby	931-858-8786				
•	•	•	•	•	Public Records Research	931-520-8902	•	•	•	•
		•	•	•	Rapid Documents	931-372-6948		•	•	•
•	•	•		•	Real Estate Loan Services of TN Inc	800-475-2334	•	•	•	
•	•	•		•	Record Data Inc (Tennessee)	615-221-0021	•	•	•	
•	•	•	•	•	Source [SOP]	800-678-8774	•	•	•	
			•		Larry M Warner	931-484-1611		•	•	

DT	BK	CV	CR	PR	←COURTS RHEA	RECORDING→	UC	RE	TX	VS
•	•	•	•		Botts & Assoc [SOP]	423-595-2692	•	•	•	•
				•	Thomas E Ewinger Jr	423-614-5290	•	•	•	•
					William (Bill) H Maynard	423-472-9858	•	•	•	
		•		•	Real Estate Loan Services	423-855-0581	•	•	•	
•	•	•		•	Record Data Inc (Tennessee)	615-221-0021	•	•	•	
•	•	•		•	Title Guaranty & Trust of Chattanooga	423-266-5751	•	•	•	

DT	BK	CV	CR	PR	←COURTS ROANE	RECORDING→	UC	RE	TX	VS
•	•	•	•	•	A All State Tracers Company	423-605-0155	•	•	•	•
				•	Thomas E Ewinger Jr	423-614-5290	•	•	•	•
•	•	•	•		Gamble Legal Research	865-966-3364	•	•	•	
					William (Bill) H Maynard	423-472-9858	•	•	•	
				•	NNBS Inc	865-633-5079	•	•		•
•	•	•	•	•	Profile Information Services	512-472-9380	•	•	•	•
•	•	•		•	Record Data Inc (Tennessee)	615-221-0021	•	•	•	
•	•	•	•	•	Source [SOP]	800-678-8774	•	•	•	

DT	BK	CV	CR	PR	←COURTS ROBERTSON	RECORDING→	UC	RE	TX	VS
			•		DataSearch	931-645-2562			•	
•	•	•	•	•	Kroll Document Filing & Retrieval Services [SOP]	800-324-2050	•	•	•	•
•	•	•		•	Real Estate Loan Services of TN Inc	800-475-2334	•	•	•	
•	•	•		•	Record Data Inc (Tennessee)	615-221-0021	•	•	•	
					Right On Time Documents Inc	615-885-8672	•	•		
•	•				Jamie D Stallings	615-781-2323	•	•	•	

DT	BK	CV	CR	PR	←COURTS RUTHERFORD	RECORDING→	UC	RE	TX	VS
•	•	•	•	•	A All State Tracers Company	423-605-0155	•	•	•	•
		•	•		Crime Checkers	615-735-0010	•		•	
•	•	•	•	•	Investigative Survelliance Group	615-895-0268	•	•	•	•
					Judi Knecht	615-832-8255		•		
			•		Kroll Background America	800-697-7189		•	•	
•	•	•	•	•	Kroll Document Filing & Retrieval Services [SOP]	800-324-2050	•	•	•	•
•	•	•		•	Maureen H Poole	931-294-2988	•	•	•	
•	•	•		•	Real Estate Loan Services of TN Inc	800-475-2334	•	•	•	
•	•	•		•	Record Data Inc (Tennessee)	615-221-0021	•	•	•	
					Right On Time Documents Inc	615-885-8672	•	•		
•	•				Jamie D Stallings	615-781-2323	•	•	•	

DT	BK	CV	CR	PR	←COURTS SCOTT	RECORDING→	UC	RE	TX	VS
•	•	•		•	Record Data Inc (Tennessee)	615-221-0021	•	•	•	

DT	BK	CV	CR	PR	←Courts **SEQUATCHIE** Recording→		UC	RE	TX	VS
•	•	•	•	•	A All State Tracers Company	423-605-0155	•	•	•	•
				•	Thomas E Ewinger Jr	423-614-5290	•	•	•	•
		•		•	Real Estate Loan Services	423-855-0581	•	•	•	
•	•	•		•	Record Data Inc (Tennessee)	615-221-0021	•	•	•	
•	•	•		•	Title Guaranty & Trust of Chattanooga	423-266-5751	•	•	•	

DT	BK	CV	CR	PR	←Courts **SEVIER** Recording→		UC	RE	TX	VS
•	•	•	•		Gamble Legal Research	865-966-3364	•		•	
•	•	•	•	•	IPS Investigations Inc [SOP]	865-689-7732	•		•	
		•	•		National Pre-Employment Research [SOP]	770-389-6607				
				•	NNBS Inc	865-633-5079	•	•		•
•	•	•		•	Record Data Inc (Tennessee)	615-221-0021	•	•	•	
•	•	•	•		Records Research of Knoxville	865-693-3589	•	•	•	
		•	•	•	Title Express Inc	423-587-9886	•	•	•	
•	•	•	•	•	Vinson Detective Agency TN [SOP]	888-525-5047	•	•	•	

DT	BK	CV	CR	PR	←Courts **SHELBY** Recording→		UC	RE	TX	VS
•	•	•	•	•	B & B Reporting Inc [SOP]	256-574-2524	•	•	•	•
•	•	•	•		Backgrounds Express LLC [SOP]	888-811-4667				
			•		Blue Line Investigations	901-266-7100				
			•		DJ Records	901-795-6450				
•	•	•	•	•	Lenow International Inc [SOP]	901-726-0735	•		•	•
•	•	•	•	•	Mid-South Subpoena Service [SOP]	800-737-8542				
•	•	•	•	•	National Background Reports Inc	901-526-4654	•	•	•	•
		•	•		Pinnacle Records	901-324-9163				
•	•	•		•	Record Data Inc (Tennessee)	615-221-0021	•	•	•	
•	•	•	•	•	Record-Check Services Inc	800-530-7226	•	•	•	•
•	•	•	•	•	RFYI (Research For Your Information)	901-475-1276	•	•	•	•
					Right On Time Documents Inc	615-885-8672	•	•		
•	•	•	•	•	Schaeffer Papers [SOP]	800-848-6119	•	•	•	•
•	•				Jamie D Stallings	615-781-2323	•	•	•	
•	•	•	•	•	The Discovery Group Inc [SOP]	662-280-1576	•		•	•

DT	BK	CV	CR	PR	←Courts **SMITH** Recording→		UC	RE	TX	VS
		•	•		Cumberland Research	615-735-6558	•	•	•	
					Jimmie Kirby	931-858-8786				
•	•	•		•	Real Estate Loan Services of TN Inc	800-475-2334	•	•	•	
•	•	•		•	Record Data Inc (Tennessee)	615-221-0021	•	•	•	
•	•	•	•	•	Source [SOP]	800-678-8774	•	•	•	

DT	BK	CV	CR	PR	←Courts **STEWART** Recording→		UC	RE	TX	VS
•	•	•		•	D K Abstract	731-686-9373/9363	•	•	•	•
			•		DataSearch	931-645-2562			•	
•	•	•		•	Helen Lattus	731-884-9994	•	•	•	
•	•	•		•	Real Estate Loan Services of TN Inc	800-475-2334	•	•	•	
•	•	•		•	Record Data Inc (Tennessee)	615-221-0021	•	•	•	

DT	BK	CV	CR	PR	←Courts **SULLIVAN** Recording→		UC	RE	TX	VS
		•	•		Shelly and James Dobler	423-753-4885				
•	•	•		•	Record Data Inc (Tennessee)	615-221-0021	•	•	•	
					Right On Time Documents Inc	615-885-8672	•	•		

DT	BK	CV	CR	PR	←Courts **SUMNER** Recording→		UC	RE	TX	VS
		•	•		Cumberland Research	615-735-6558	•	•	•	
•	•	•	•	•	Lisa Farris [SOP]	615-859-7135	•	•	•	•
					Judi Knecht	615-832-8255		•		
•	•	•	•	•	Kroll Document Filing & Retrieval Services [SOP]	800-324-2050	•	•	•	•
•	•	•		•	Real Estate Loan Services of TN Inc	800-475-2334	•	•	•	
•	•	•		•	Record Data Inc (Tennessee)	615-221-0021	•	•	•	

DT	BK	CV	CR	PR	Retriever	Phone	UC	RE	TX	VS
					Right On Time Documents Inc	615-885-8672	•	•		
•	•	•	•	•	Schaeffer Papers [SOP]	800-848-6119	•	•	•	•
•	•				Jamie D Stallings	615-781-2323	•	•	•	

DT	BK	CV	CR	PR	←COURTS TIPTON	RECORDING→	UC	RE	TX	VS
			•		Blue Line Investigations	901-266-7100				
•	•	•		•	D K Abstract	731-686-9373/9363	•	•	•	•
•	•	•		•	Helen Lattus	731-884-9994	•	•	•	
•	•	•	•	•	Mid-South Subpoena Service [SOP]	800-737-8542				
•	•	•	•	•	National Background Reports Inc	901-526-4654	•	•	•	•
		•	•		National Pre-Employment Research [SOP]	770-389-6607				
•	•	•		•	Record Data Inc (Tennessee)	615-221-0021	•	•	•	
•	•	•	•	•	Record-Check Services Inc	800-530-7226	•	•	•	•
•	•	•	•	•	RFYI (Research For Your Information)	901-475-1276	•	•	•	•
•	•	•	•	•	Schaeffer Papers [SOP]	800-848-6119	•	•	•	•

DT	BK	CV	CR	PR	←COURTS TROUSDALE	RECORDING→	UC	RE	TX	VS
		•	•		Cumberland Research	615-735-6558	•	•	•	
•	•	•		•	Real Estate Loan Services of TN Inc	800-475-2334	•	•	•	
•	•	•		•	Record Data Inc (Tennessee)	615-221-0021	•	•	•	

DT	BK	CV	CR	PR	←COURTS UNICOI	RECORDING→	UC	RE	TX	VS
		•	•		Shelly and James Dobler	423-753-4885				
•	•	•		•	Record Data Inc (Tennessee)	615-221-0021	•	•	•	

DT	BK	CV	CR	PR	←COURTS UNION	RECORDING→	UC	RE	TX	VS
		•	•		National Pre-Employment Research [SOP]	770-389-6607				
				•	NNBS Inc	865-633-5079	•	•		•
•	•	•		•	Record Data Inc (Tennessee)	615-221-0021	•	•	•	
•	•	•	•		Records Research of Knoxville	865-693-3589	•	•	•	

DT	BK	CV	CR	PR	←COURTS VAN BUREN	RECORDING→	UC	RE	TX	VS
•	•	•	•	•	A All State Tracers Company	423-605-0155	•	•	•	•
•	•	•		•	Record Data Inc (Tennessee)	615-221-0021	•	•	•	
•	•	•		•	Title Guaranty & Trust of Chattanooga	423-266-5751	•	•	•	

DT	BK	CV	CR	PR	←COURTS WARREN	RECORDING→	UC	RE	TX	VS
•	•	•	•	•	A All State Tracers Company	423-605-0155	•	•	•	•
•	•	•		•	Record Data Inc (Tennessee)	615-221-0021	•	•	•	

DT	BK	CV	CR	PR	←COURTS WASHINGTON	RECORDING→	UC	RE	TX	VS
		•	•		Shelly and James Dobler	423-753-4885				
•	•	•		•	Record Data Inc (Tennessee)	615-221-0021	•	•	•	
•	•				Jamie D Stallings	615-781-2323	•	•	•	

DT	BK	CV	CR	PR	←COURTS WAYNE	RECORDING→	UC	RE	TX	VS
					Larry R Dorning PC	931-796-5959	•	•	•	
•	•	•		•	Maureen H Poole	931-294-2988	•	•	•	
•	•	•		•	Real Estate Loan Services of TN Inc	800-475-2334	•	•	•	
•	•	•		•	Record Data Inc (Tennessee)	615-221-0021	•	•	•	

DT	BK	CV	CR	PR	←COURTS WEAKLEY	RECORDING→	UC	RE	TX	VS
			•		Blue Line Investigations	901-266-7100				
•	•	•		•	D K Abstract	731-686-9373/9363	•	•	•	•
•	•	•		•	Helen Lattus	731-884-9994	•	•	•	
•	•	•		•	Record Data Inc (Tennessee)	615-221-0021	•	•	•	

DT	BK	CV	CR	PR	←COURTS WHITE	RECORDING→	UC	RE	TX	VS
•	•	•	•	•	A All State Tracers Company	423-605-0155	•	•	•	•
					Jimmie Kirby	931-858-8786				
		•	•	•	Rapid Documents	931-372-6948		•	•	•
•	•	•		•	Real Estate Loan Services of TN Inc	800-475-2334	•	•	•	

DT	BK	CV	CR	PR	←Courts		Recording→	UC	RE	TX	VS
•	•	•		•	Record Data Inc (Tennessee)		615-221-0021	•	•	•	
•	•	•	•	•	Source [SOP]		800-678-8774	•	•	•	
			•		Larry M Warner		931-484-1611		•	•	

DT	BK	CV	CR	PR	←Courts	Williamson	Recording→	UC	RE	TX	VS
•	•	•	•	•	A All State Tracers Company		423-605-0155	•	•	•	•
		•	•		Information Consultants Inc		866-473-9149				
					Judi Knecht		615-832-8255		•		
•	•	•	•	•	Kroll Document Filing & Retrieval Services [SOP]		800-324-2050	•	•	•	•
•	•	•		•	Maureen H Poole		931-294-2988	•	•	•	
•	•	•		•	Real Estate Loan Services of TN Inc		800-475-2334	•	•	•	
•	•	•		•	Record Data Inc (Tennessee)		615-221-0021	•	•	•	
					Right On Time Documents Inc		615-885-8672	•	•		
•	•				Jamie D Stallings		615-781-2323	•	•	•	

DT	BK	CV	CR	PR	←Courts	Wilson	Recording→	UC	RE	TX	VS
		•	•		Crime Checkers		615-735-0010	•		•	
•	•	•	•	•	Investigative Consultant Service		615-885-1126	•			•
•	•	•	•	•	Investigative Survelliance Group		615-895-0268	•	•	•	•
					Jimmie Kirby		931-858-8786				
					Judi Knecht		615-832-8255		•		
•	•	•	•	•	Kroll Document Filing & Retrieval Services [SOP]		800-324-2050	•	•	•	•
•	•	•		•	Maureen H Poole		931-294-2988	•	•	•	
•	•	•		•	Real Estate Loan Services of TN Inc		800-475-2334	•	•	•	
•	•	•		•	Record Data Inc (Tennessee)		615-221-0021	•	•	•	
					Right On Time Documents Inc		615-885-8672	•	•		
•	•				Jamie D Stallings		615-781-2323	•	•	•	

Court Records

CODE	Government Agency	Type of Information
DT	US District Court	Federal civil and criminal cases
BK	Bankruptcy Court	United States bankruptcy cases
CV	Civil Court	Municipal, county and state level civil cases
CR	Criminal Court	Municipal, county and state level criminal cases
PR	Probate Court	Wills and estate cases

County Records - Recordings

CODE	Government Agency	Type of Information
UC	UCC Filing Office	Uniform Commercial Code and other personal property liens
RE	Real Estate Recording Office	Real property transactions and liens
TX	Tax Filing Office(s)	Federal and state tax liens, judgment liens
VS	Vital Records Office	Vital statistics—birth, death, marriage, divorce

Texas

COURT RECORDS RETRIEVED | **RECORDING RECORDS RETRIEVED**

DT	BK	CV	CR	PR	←COURTS	ANDERSON	RECORDING→	UC	RE	TX	VS
•	•	•		•	Abstracts/Trustees of Texas		888-452-0331	•	•	•	
					Anderson County Abstract Co		903-729-5871	•	•	•	
			•		Dataprompt Corporation		214-390-2530				
•	•	•	•	•	East Texas Professional Svcs [SOP]		903-928-0117			•	•
•	•	•	•	•	Investigative Concepts		903-677-9473				
	•	•		•	Land Records of Texas		800-678-8016	•	•	•	
•	•	•	•	•	Tyler-McLennon Choicepoint		512-334-6244	•	•	•	•

DT	BK	CV	CR	PR	←COURTS	ANDREWS	RECORDING→	UC	RE	TX	VS
•	•	•		•	Abstracts/Trustees of Texas		888-452-0331	•	•	•	
•	•	•	•	•	Davick Services		800-658-6656	•	•	•	
	•	•		•	Land Records of Texas		800-678-8016	•	•	•	

DT	BK	CV	CR	PR	←COURTS	ANGELINA	RECORDING→	UC	RE	TX	VS
•	•	•		•	Abstracts/Trustees of Texas		888-452-0331	•	•	•	
		•	•	•	Community Title Co		936-559-7900	•	•	•	•
		•	•		Crimecheck Research Services		281-288-6930				
•		•	•	•	East Tex Records Research		936-824-3724	•	•	•	
					East Texas Public Records		936-632-7385		•		
	•	•		•	Land Records of Texas		800-678-8016	•	•	•	
					Record Time Research		936-632-5150		•		

DT	BK	CV	CR	PR	←COURTS	ARANSAS	RECORDING→	UC	RE	TX	VS
•	•	•		•	Abstracts/Trustees of Texas		888-452-0331	•	•	•	
•	•	•	•	•	Condor Inv [SOP]		361-881-8977	•	•	•	•
•	•	•	•	•	Corpus Christi Court Services		361-887-8122	•	•	•	•
•	•	•	•	•	Brenda Kolle/Title Abstractor		361-852-8236	•	•	•	
	•	•		•	Land Records of Texas		800-678-8016	•	•	•	
•	•	•	•	•	Shawver & Associates		800-364-2333	•	•	•	•
•	•	•	•	•	Texas Civil Process [SOP]		800-976-9595	•	•	•	•
•	•	•	•	•	Tyler-McLennon Choicepoint		512-334-6244	•	•	•	•

DT	BK	CV	CR	PR	←COURTS	ARCHER	RECORDING→	UC	RE	TX	VS
•	•	•		•	Abstracts/Trustees of Texas		888-452-0331	•	•	•	
	•	•		•	Land Records of Texas		800-678-8016	•	•	•	
•	•	•	•	•	Mendenhall Information Services		940-696-0758	•	•	•	•
•	•	•		•	Superior Process Svc [SOP]		888-230-2663		•	•	•
•	•	•	•	•	Texas Detective.com [SOP]		940-592-7000	•	•	•	•

DT	BK	CV	CR	PR	←COURTS	ARMSTRONG	RECORDING→	UC	RE	TX	VS
•	•	•		•	Abstracts/Trustees of Texas		888-452-0331	•	•	•	
•	•	•	•	•	Davick Services		800-658-6656	•	•	•	
	•	•		•	Land Records of Texas		800-678-8016	•	•	•	
•	•	•		•	Rollins Research Ltd		806-353-7886	•	•	•	
		•	•	•	Security Abstract Co		806-874-3511	•	•	•	•

DT	BK	CV	CR	PR	←COURTS	ATASCOSA	RECORDING→	UC	RE	TX	VS
•	•	•		•	Abstracts/Trustees of Texas		888-452-0331	•	•	•	
		•	•		Crimecheck Research Services		281-288-6930				
	•	•		•	Land Records of Texas		800-678-8016	•	•	•	

DT	BK	CV	CR	PR	←COURTS	RECORDING→	UC	RE	TX	VS
•	•	•	•	•	Property Research & Documentation Service Inc	210-520-7884	•	•	•	•
•	•	•	•	•	Morris Todd [SOP]	210-673-4690	•	•	•	•

DT	BK	CV	CR	PR	←COURTS **AUSTIN**	RECORDING→	UC	RE	TX	VS
•	•	•		•	Abstracts/Trustees of Texas	888-452-0331	•	•	•	
•	•	•			All State Document Services	888-246-8180	•	•	•	•
				•	Botts Title Co	254-697-6962	•	•	•	•
	•	•		•	Land Records of Texas	800-678-8016	•	•	•	
•	•	•	•	•	Professional Civil Process (Austin) [SOP]	800-950-7493	•	•	•	•
•	•	•	•	•	The Research Staff Inc	800-822-3584	•	•	•	
•	•	•	•	•	Tyler-McLennon Choicepoint	512-334-6244	•	•	•	•

DT	BK	CV	CR	PR	←COURTS **BAILEY**	RECORDING→	UC	RE	TX	VS
•	•	•		•	Abstracts/Trustees of Texas	888-452-0331	•	•	•	
•	•	•	•	•	Davick Services	800-658-6656	•	•	•	
		•	•	•	Farwell Abstract Co Inc	806-481-9992		•	•	
	•	•		•	Land Records of Texas	800-678-8016	•	•	•	

DT	BK	CV	CR	PR	←COURTS **BANDERA**	RECORDING→	UC	RE	TX	VS
•	•	•		•	Abstracts/Trustees of Texas	888-452-0331	•	•	•	
		•	•		Crimecheck Research Services	281-288-6930				
	•	•		•	Land Records of Texas	800-678-8016	•	•	•	
•	•	•	•	•	Property Research & Documentation Service Inc	210-520-7884	•	•	•	•
•	•	•	•	•	Morris Todd [SOP]	210-673-4690	•	•	•	•
•	•	•	•	•	Tyler-McLennon Choicepoint	512-334-6244	•	•	•	•

DT	BK	CV	CR	PR	←COURTS **BASTROP**	RECORDING→	UC	RE	TX	VS
•	•	•		•	Abstracts/Trustees of Texas	888-452-0331	•	•	•	
•	•	•	•	•	Americorp Research Inc	877-989-6850	•	•	•	•
•	•	•			Carma Austin	254-634-1701	•		•	
•	•	•		•	Central Tejas Research & Title Services	512-469-6062	•	•	•	
•	•	•	•	•	John C Dunaway & Company [SOP]	512-835-5888	•	•	•	•
	•	•		•	Land Records of Texas	800-678-8016	•	•	•	
•	•	•	•	•	MS Document Services Inc	800-292-3868	•	•	•	•
•	•	•	•	•	Promesa Enterprises Inc	800-474-4420	•	•	•	•
•	•	•	•	•	Research Network	512-469-1740	•	•	•	•
•	•	•	•	•	Tyler-McLennon Choicepoint	512-334-6244	•	•	•	•

DT	BK	CV	CR	PR	←COURTS **BAYLOR**	RECORDING→	UC	RE	TX	VS
•	•	•		•	Abstracts/Trustees of Texas	888-452-0331	•	•	•	
	•	•		•	Land Records of Texas	800-678-8016	•	•	•	
•	•	•	•	•	Mendenhall Information Services	940-696-0758	•	•	•	•
•	•	•		•	Superior Process Svc [SOP]	888-230-2663		•	•	•

DT	BK	CV	CR	PR	←COURTS **BEE**	RECORDING→	UC	RE	TX	VS
•	•	•		•	Abstracts/Trustees of Texas	888-452-0331	•	•	•	
•	•	•	•	•	Condor Inv [SOP]	361-881-8977	•	•	•	•
			•		Dataprompt Corporation	214-390-2530				
	•	•		•	Land Records of Texas	800-678-8016	•	•	•	
•	•	•	•	•	Shawver & Associates	800-364-2333	•	•	•	•
•	•	•	•	•	Texas Civil Process [SOP]	800-976-9595	•	•	•	•
•	•	•	•	•	Tyler-McLennon Choicepoint	512-334-6244	•	•	•	•

DT	BK	CV	CR	PR	←COURTS **BELL**	RECORDING→	UC	RE	TX	VS
•	•	•		•	Abstracts/Trustees of Texas	888-452-0331	•	•	•	
		•		•	American Abstract & Title Co Inc	254-526-9525	•	•	•	•
•	•	•	•	•	Americorp Research Inc	877-989-6850	•	•	•	•
•	•	•	•	•	Attorney Civil Process Service [SOP]	254-755-6447				
•	•	•			Carma Austin	254-634-1701	•		•	
•		•	•	•	Bar Nunn Research Specialists	512-497-5584		•	•	
•	•	•	•	•	BG Criminal Research	254-755-6808	•		•	

DT	BK	CV	CR	PR			UC	RE	TX	VS
•		•		•	John Blackburn	210-867-0399	•	•	•	
		•	•		Crimecheck Research Services	281-288-6930				
•	•			•	DeedSearcher Title Research Services	281-375-8480	•	•	•	
•	•	•	•	•	Harvey Public Records Inc	254-662-6265	•	•	•	•
	•	•		•	Land Records of Texas	800-678-8016	•	•	•	
•	•	•	•	•	Research N More	512-868-5828	•	•	•	•
					Search Enterprises	254-752-2057		•	•	
•	•	•	•	•	Sterling Research	512-670-9334	•	•	•	•
•	•	•	•	•	Taylor Research & Investigations [SOP]	972-991-5045	•	•	•	•
•	•	•	•		Texsearch #A09479 [SOP]	903-786-4636	•	•	•	
•	•	•	•	•	Tyler-McLennon Choicepoint	512-334-6244	•	•	•	•

DT	BK	CV	CR	PR	←COURTS **BEXAR**	RECORDING→	UC	RE	TX	VS
•	•	•		•	Abstracts/Trustees of Texas	888-452-0331	•	•	•	
		•	•		Accu-Source Inc	214-637-4064				
•	•	•	•		Asset Control Inc	877-277-3812	•	•	•	•
		•	•		Background Information Systems Inc	800-687-0894				
•	•	•	•	•	Bexar Professional [SOP]	210-228-0083	•	•	•	•
•		•		•	John Blackburn	210-867-0399	•	•	•	
		•	•	•	Cornerstone Title Research	210-661-2357	•	•	•	•
•	•	•	•	•	Court & Public Records Service Inc	800-856-0585	•	•	•	•
			•		Dataprompt Corporation	214-390-2530				
•	•	•	•	•	DFW Court Services [SOP]	800-436-0516	•	•	•	
•	•	•	•		Hart & Associates Inc	866-429-4044			•	•
	•	•		•	Land Records of Texas	800-678-8016	•	•	•	
•	•			•	Morgan/Brooks Resources Inc	210-476-0500	•	•	•	
•	•	•	•	•	MS Document Services Inc	800-292-3868	•	•	•	•
			•		PI Inc	800-359-5131				
•	•	•	•	•	Professional Civil Process (Austin) [SOP]	800-950-7493	•	•	•	•
•	•	•	•	•	Property Research & Documentation Service Inc	210-520-7884	•	•	•	•
		•	•		Spearhead Research - On Target Information	512-295-7298				
•	•	•	•		Spectrum Screening Inc	800-222-8199	•		•	
•	•	•	•	•	Texas Industrial Security Inc	214-634-2791			•	
		•	•	•	TexDirect	512-353-4257	•	•	•	
•	•	•	•		Texsearch #A09479 [SOP]	903-786-4636	•	•	•	
•	•	•	•	•	Morris Todd [SOP]	210-673-4690	•	•	•	•
•	•	•	•	•	Tyler-McLennon Choicepoint	512-334-6244	•	•	•	•
		•	•		Your Information Source Inc	800-644-9668				

DT	BK	CV	CR	PR	←COURTS **BLANCO**	RECORDING→	UC	RE	TX	VS
•	•	•		•	Abstracts/Trustees of Texas	888-452-0331	•	•	•	
	•	•		•	Land Records of Texas	800-678-8016	•	•	•	
•	•	•	•	•	MS Document Services Inc	800-292-3868	•	•	•	•

DT	BK	CV	CR	PR	←COURTS **BORDEN**	RECORDING→	UC	RE	TX	VS
•	•	•		•	Abstracts/Trustees of Texas	888-452-0331	•	•	•	
•	•	•	•	•	Davick Services	800-658-6656	•	•	•	
	•	•		•	Land Records of Texas	800-678-8016	•	•	•	
•				•	Snyder Abstract & Title Co Inc	325-573-6339	•	•	•	

DT	BK	CV	CR	PR	←COURTS **BOSQUE**	RECORDING→	UC	RE	TX	VS
•	•	•		•	Abstracts/Trustees of Texas	888-452-0331	•	•	•	
•	•	•	•	•	Attorney Civil Process Service [SOP]	254-755-6447				
		•	•		B & B Info Search	817-774-1310				
•		•		•	John Blackburn	210-867-0399	•	•	•	
		•	•		Crimecheck Research Services	281-288-6930				
	•	•		•	Land Records of Texas	800-678-8016	•	•	•	
					Search Enterprises	254-752-2057		•	•	

DT	BK	CV	CR	PR	←COURTS BOWIE	RECORDING→	UC	RE	TX	VS
•	•	•		•	Abstracts/Trustees of Texas	888-452-0331	•	•	•	
			•		Dataprompt Corporation	214-390-2530				
•	•	•			Joe Gillenwater [SOP]	870-772-2923	•	•	•	
	•	•		•	Land Records of Texas	800-678-8016	•	•	•	
		•		•	Twin City Title Co Inc	903-793-7671	•	•	•	
•	•	•	•	•	Tyler-McLennon Choicepoint	512-334-6244	•	•	•	•

DT	BK	CV	CR	PR	←COURTS BRAZORIA	RECORDING→	UC	RE	TX	VS
•	•	•		•	Abstracts/Trustees of Texas	888-452-0331	•	•	•	
•	•	•			All State Document Services	888-246-8180	•	•	•	•
•	•	•		•	Ameritile Abstract & Research Inc	800-856-1228	•	•	•	
•	•	•	•	•	Asset Research Group	713-864-2536	•	•	•	•
•	•	•		•	BAST Research Services Inc	713-721-7077	•	•	•	
•	•	•	•	•	Court Record Research Inc	800-552-3353	•	•	•	•
	•	•	•	•	Courthouse Specialists	800-925-4225	•	•	•	
		•	•		Criminal Background Investigations	979-848-0632				
•	•			•	DeedSearcher Title Research Services	281-375-8480	•	•	•	
					Fox Hunt	713-772-8018	•	•	•	
•	•	•	•	•	Garza-McNamee Agency Inc	888-262-6221	•	•	•	
•	•	•	•	•	Houston Court Services Inc [SOP]	713-655-0555	•	•	•	•
•	•	•	•	•	John V Eriksson Group Inc	281-488-0018	•	•	•	•
•	•	•	•	•	Kimmons Security Services Inc [SOP]	281-679-0070	•	•	•	•
	•	•		•	Land Records of Texas	800-678-8016	•	•	•	
•	•	•			Mach 5 Couriers Inc [SOP]	800-593-2023				
•	•	•	•	•	PM Clinton International Investigation	866-686-6864	•	•	•	
•	•	•	•	•	The Research Staff Inc	800-822-3584	•	•	•	
•	•	•	•	•	Tyler-McLennon Choicepoint	512-334-6244	•	•	•	•

DT	BK	CV	CR	PR	←COURTS BRAZOS	RECORDING→	UC	RE	TX	VS
•	•	•		•	Abstracts/Trustees of Texas	888-452-0331	•	•	•	
•	•	•	•	•	Airborn Civil Process & Inv [SOP]	888-933-6863	•	•	•	•
•	•	•			All State Document Services	888-246-8180	•	•	•	•
•	•	•			Carma Austin	254-634-1701	•		•	
		•	•		Crimecheck Research Services	281-288-6930				
			•		Dataprompt Corporation	214-390-2530				
•	•			•	DeedSearcher Title Research Services	281-375-8480	•	•	•	
•	•	•	•	•	Houston Court Services Inc [SOP]	713-655-0555	•	•	•	•
	•	•		•	Land Records of Texas	800-678-8016	•	•	•	
•	•	•	•	•	Matrix Info Services [SOP]	979-846-3593	•	•	•	•
•	•	•	•	•	The Research Staff Inc	800-822-3584	•	•	•	
•	•	•	•	•	Tyler-McLennon Choicepoint	512-334-6244	•	•	•	•

DT	BK	CV	CR	PR	←COURTS BREWSTER	RECORDING→	UC	RE	TX	VS
•	•	•		•	Abstracts/Trustees of Texas	888-452-0331	•	•	•	
		•		•	Ellyson Abstract & Title Co of Brewster	432-837-5801	•	•	•	•
	•	•		•	Land Records of Texas	800-678-8016	•	•	•	

DT	BK	CV	CR	PR	←COURTS BRISCOE	RECORDING→	UC	RE	TX	VS
•	•	•		•	Abstracts/Trustees of Texas	888-452-0331	•	•	•	
•	•	•	•	•	Davick Services	800-658-6656	•	•	•	
				•	Guaranty Abstract Co (Silverton)	806-823-2354	•	•	•	
	•	•		•	Land Records of Texas	800-678-8016	•	•	•	

DT	BK	CV	CR	PR	←COURTS BROOKS	RECORDING→	UC	RE	TX	VS
•	•	•		•	Abstracts/Trustees of Texas	888-452-0331	•	•	•	
					Border Title Group	956-791-5810	•	•	•	
•	•	•	•	•	Condor Inv [SOP]	361-881-8977	•	•	•	•
	•	•		•	Land Records of Texas	800-678-8016	•	•	•	
•	•	•	•	•	Shawver & Associates	800-364-2333	•	•	•	•

DT	BK	CV	CR	PR	←COURTS	BROWN	RECORDING→	UC	RE	TX	VS
•	•	•		•	Abstracts/Trustees of Texas		888-452-0331	•	•	•	
		•		•	Brown County Abstract Co (Texas)		325-646-6591	•	•	•	
				•	Heartland Title Company		325-646-0509		•	•	
	•	•		•	Land Records of Texas		800-678-8016	•	•	•	
•	•	•	•	•	MS Document Services Inc		800-292-3868	•	•	•	•
		•	•	•	Texas Research		325-646-2890	•	•	•	

DT	BK	CV	CR	PR	←COURTS	BURLESON	RECORDING→	UC	RE	TX	VS
•	•	•		•	Abstracts/Trustees of Texas		888-452-0331	•	•	•	
•	•	•			Carma Austin		254-634-1701	•		•	
				•	Botts Title Co		254-697-6962	•	•	•	•
	•	•		•	Land Records of Texas		800-678-8016	•	•	•	

DT	BK	CV	CR	PR	←COURTS	BURNET	RECORDING→	UC	RE	TX	VS
•	•	•		•	Abstracts/Trustees of Texas		888-452-0331	•	•	•	
•	•	•	•	•	Americorp Research Inc		877-989-6850	•	•	•	•
•	•	•			Carma Austin		254-634-1701	•		•	
	•	•		•	Land Records of Texas		800-678-8016	•	•	•	
•	•	•	•	•	MS Document Services Inc		800-292-3868	•	•	•	•
•	•	•	•	•	Research N More		512-868-5828	•	•	•	•
•	•	•	•	•	Tyler-McLennon Choicepoint		512-334-6244	•	•	•	•

DT	BK	CV	CR	PR	←COURTS	CALDWELL	RECORDING→	UC	RE	TX	VS
•	•	•		•	Abstracts/Trustees of Texas		888-452-0331	•	•	•	
•	•	•	•	•	Americorp Research Inc		877-989-6850	•	•	•	•
•	•	•			Carma Austin		254-634-1701	•		•	
•	•	•		•	Central Tejas Research & Title Services		512-469-6062	•	•	•	
		•	•		Crimecheck Research Services		281-288-6930				
	•	•		•	Land Records of Texas		800-678-8016	•	•	•	
•	•	•	•	•	MS Document Services Inc		800-292-3868	•	•	•	•
			•		PI Inc		800-359-5131				
•	•	•	•	•	Property Research & Documentation Service Inc		210-520-7884	•	•	•	•
		•	•	•	TexDirect		512-353-4257	•	•	•	
•	•	•	•	•	Tyler-McLennon Choicepoint		512-334-6244	•	•	•	•

DT	BK	CV	CR	PR	←COURTS	CALHOUN	RECORDING→	UC	RE	TX	VS
•	•	•		•	Abstracts/Trustees of Texas		888-452-0331	•	•	•	
•	•	•			All State Document Services		888-246-8180	•	•	•	•
		•		•	Bedgood Abstract & Title Co (Port Lavaca)		361-552-6761	•	•	•	
•	•	•	•	•	Condor Inv [SOP]		361-881-8977	•	•	•	•
•	•			•	DeedSearcher Title Research Services		281-375-8480	•	•	•	
	•	•		•	Land Records of Texas		800-678-8016	•	•	•	
•	•	•	•	•	Tyler-McLennon Choicepoint		512-334-6244	•	•	•	•

DT	BK	CV	CR	PR	←COURTS	CALLAHAN	RECORDING→	UC	RE	TX	VS
•	•	•		•	Abstracts/Trustees of Texas		888-452-0331	•	•	•	
				•	Big Country Title		325-698-9195	•	•	•	•
	•	•		•	Land Records of Texas		800-678-8016	•	•	•	
•	•	•	•	•	MS Document Services Inc		800-292-3868	•	•	•	•
		•	•	•	Russell-Surles Title Inc		325-854-1115	•	•	•	

DT	BK	CV	CR	PR	←COURTS	CAMERON	RECORDING→	UC	RE	TX	VS
•	•	•		•	Abstracts/Trustees of Texas		888-452-0331	•	•	•	
	•	•		•	Land Records of Texas		800-678-8016	•	•	•	
•	•	•	•	•	Professional Civil Process (Austin) [SOP]		800-950-7493	•	•	•	•
•	•	•	•	•	Professional Civil Process (McAllen) [SOP]		800-880-4223	•	•	•	•
•	•	•	•	•	Record Finders		956-571-5378	•	•	•	•
•	•	•	•	•	Shawver & Associates		800-364-2333	•	•	•	•
					South Texas Title and Trustee Services		956-412-3413	•	•	•	

DT	BK	CV	CR	PR	←COURTS		RECORDING→	UC	RE	TX	VS
•	•	•	•		Texsearch #A09479 [SOP]		903-786-4636	•	•	•	
•	•	•	•	•	Tyler-McLennon Choicepoint		512-334-6244	•	•	•	•
•	•	•		•	Valley Abstract & Trustee Services		956-571-1119	•	•	•	
DT	**BK**	**CV**	**CR**	**PR**	**←COURTS**	**CAMP**	**RECORDING→**	**UC**	**RE**	**TX**	**VS**
•	•	•		•	Abstracts/Trustees of Texas		888-452-0331	•	•	•	
		•		•	Camp County Land Abstract Co		903-856-3676	•	•		•
	•	•		•	Land Records of Texas		800-678-8016	•	•	•	
•	•	•	•	•	Tyler-McLennon Choicepoint		512-334-6244	•	•	•	•
DT	**BK**	**CV**	**CR**	**PR**	**←COURTS**	**CARSON**	**RECORDING→**	**UC**	**RE**	**TX**	**VS**
•	•	•		•	Abstracts/Trustees of Texas		888-452-0331	•	•	•	
	•	•		•	Land Records of Texas		800-678-8016	•	•	•	
•	•	•		•	Rollins Research Ltd		806-353-7886	•	•	•	
DT	**BK**	**CV**	**CR**	**PR**	**←COURTS**	**CASS**	**RECORDING→**	**UC**	**RE**	**TX**	**VS**
•	•	•		•	Abstracts/Trustees of Texas		888-452-0331	•	•	•	
•	•	•			Joe Gillenwater [SOP]		870-772-2923	•	•	•	
	•	•		•	Land Records of Texas		800-678-8016	•	•	•	
		•		•	M & M Title / Mitchell Co.		318-798-1198	•	•	•	
•	•	•	•	•	Tyler-McLennon Choicepoint		512-334-6244	•	•	•	•
DT	**BK**	**CV**	**CR**	**PR**	**←COURTS**	**CASTRO**	**RECORDING→**	**UC**	**RE**	**TX**	**VS**
•	•	•		•	Abstracts/Trustees of Texas		888-452-0331	•	•	•	
•	•	•	•	•	Davick Services		800-658-6656	•	•	•	
	•	•		•	Land Records of Texas		800-678-8016	•	•	•	
•	•	•		•	Rollins Research Ltd		806-353-7886	•	•	•	
DT	**BK**	**CV**	**CR**	**PR**	**←COURTS**	**CHAMBERS**	**RECORDING→**	**UC**	**RE**	**TX**	**VS**
•	•	•		•	Abstracts/Trustees of Texas		888-452-0331	•	•	•	
•	•	•			All State Document Services		888-246-8180	•	•	•	•
		•	•		Don W Caskey		281-422-7527	•		•	
	•	•	•	•	Courthouse Specialists		800-925-4225	•	•	•	
•	•	•	•	•	ELH Contracting Inc Independent Land & Title Abstractor		409-832-5793	•	•	•	•
•	•	•	•	•	Garza-McNamee Agency Inc		888-262-6221	•	•	•	
	•	•		•	Land Records of Texas		800-678-8016	•	•	•	
•	•	•		•	Mach 5 Couriers Inc [SOP]		800-593-2023	•	•	•	
•	•	•	•	•	PM Clinton International Investigation		866-686-6864	•	•	•	
•	•	•	•	•	The Research Staff Inc		800-822-3584	•	•	•	
DT	**BK**	**CV**	**CR**	**PR**	**←COURTS**	**CHEROKEE**	**RECORDING→**	**UC**	**RE**	**TX**	**VS**
•	•	•		•	Abstracts/Trustees of Texas		888-452-0331	•	•	•	
•	•	•	•	•	East Texas Professional Svcs [SOP]		903-928-0117			•	•
	•	•		•	Land Records of Texas		800-678-8016	•	•	•	
•	•	•	•	•	Tyler-McLennon Choicepoint		512-334-6244	•	•	•	•
DT	**BK**	**CV**	**CR**	**PR**	**←COURTS**	**CHILDRESS**	**RECORDING→**	**UC**	**RE**	**TX**	**VS**
•	•	•		•	Abstracts/Trustees of Texas		888-452-0331	•	•	•	
		•		•	H S Black Abstractor Inc		940-937-3681	•	•	•	•
	•	•		•	Land Records of Texas		800-678-8016	•	•	•	
•	•	•	•	•	Mendenhall Information Services		940-696-0758	•	•	•	•
DT	**BK**	**CV**	**CR**	**PR**	**←COURTS**	**CLAY**	**RECORDING→**	**UC**	**RE**	**TX**	**VS**
•	•	•		•	Abstracts/Trustees of Texas		888-452-0331	•	•	•	
	•	•		•	Land Records of Texas		800-678-8016	•	•	•	
•	•	•	•	•	Mendenhall Information Services		940-696-0758	•	•	•	•
•	•	•		•	Superior Process Svc [SOP]		888-230-2663	•	•	•	•
•	•	•	•	•	Texas Detective.com [SOP]		940-592-7000	•	•	•	•
DT	**BK**	**CV**	**CR**	**PR**	**←COURTS**	**COCHRAN**	**RECORDING→**	**UC**	**RE**	**TX**	**VS**
•	•	•		•	Abstracts/Trustees of Texas		888-452-0331	•	•	•	

DT	BK	CV	CR	PR	←COURTS	RECORDING→	UC	RE	TX	VS
•	•	•	•	•	Davick Services	800-658-6656	•	•	•	
	•	•		•	Land Records of Texas	800-678-8016	•	•	•	
DT	**BK**	**CV**	**CR**	**PR**	**←COURTS — COKE**	**RECORDING→**	**UC**	**RE**	**TX**	**VS**
•	•	•		•	Abstracts/Trustees of Texas	888-452-0331	•	•	•	
		•	•	•	Coke County Abstract Co	325-453-2049	•	•	•	•
	•	•		•	Land Records of Texas	800-678-8016	•	•	•	
DT	**BK**	**CV**	**CR**	**PR**	**←COURTS — COLEMAN**	**RECORDING→**	**UC**	**RE**	**TX**	**VS**
•	•	•		•	Abstracts/Trustees of Texas	888-452-0331	•	•	•	
				•	Coleman County Title Co	325-625-4628	•	•	•	
	•	•		•	Land Records of Texas	800-678-8016	•	•	•	
•	•	•	•	•	MS Document Services Inc	800-292-3868	•	•	•	•
DT	**BK**	**CV**	**CR**	**PR**	**←COURTS — COLLIN**	**RECORDING→**	**UC**	**RE**	**TX**	**VS**
				•	A & J Research Inc	972-221-7744	•	•	•	
•	•	•		•	Abstracts/Trustees of Texas	888-452-0331	•	•	•	
		•	•		Accu-Source Inc	214-637-4064				
		•		•	Ameristar Information Network	800-920-9270		•	•	•
•	•	•		•	Ameritile Abstract & Research Inc	800-856-1228	•	•	•	
•	•	•	•	•	ASA (Attorney Service Associates) [SOP]	972-394-1175	•	•	•	•
•	•	•	•		Asset Control Inc	877-277-3812	•	•	•	•
•	•	•	•	•	Attorney's Service Bureau of Texas [SOP]	888-522-5297	•	•	•	•
		•	•		Background Information Systems Inc	800-687-0894				
					David C Bayoud	214-824-9944		•		
•	•	•	•	•	Bray & Freeman LP [SOP]	817-596-9255	•	•	•	•
					Concord Commercial Services	972-931-7431		•		
•	•	•	•	•	Court & Public Records Service Inc	800-856-0585	•	•	•	•
		•	•		Crimecheck Research Services	281-288-6930				
•	•	•	•	•	CRRG Inc	800-687-9030	•	•	•	•
			•		Dataprompt Corporation	214-390-2530				
•	•	•	•	•	DFW Court Services [SOP]	800-436-0516	•	•	•	
•		•	•		FP Resources	866-989-8999				
•	•	•	•		G.A. Public Record Services Inc	800-760-2468				
•	•	•	•		General Information Services	800-447-0798	•	•		
•	•	•	•		Hart & Associates Inc	866-429-4044			•	•
•	•	•	•	•	Info2go	817-656-1997	•	•	•	•
		•	•		Inquest Investigations, LLC	903-893-2020	•	•	•	
	•	•		•	Land Records of Texas	800-678-8016	•	•	•	
•	•	•	•		Lone Star Inv & Recovery Inc	800-887-3890	•	•	•	•
•	•	•	•	•	Mendenhall Information Services	940-696-0758	•	•	•	•
•	•	•	•	•	MS Document Services Inc	800-292-3868	•	•	•	•
•	•	•	•	•	PADIC Inc [SOP]	940-665-6130	•	•	•	•
			•		Princeton Data Search Inc	469-474-1025		•	•	
•	•	•	•	•	Quick Search	214-358-2840	•	•	•	•
		•	•		Record Retrieval Services Inc	877-527-5355		•		
•	•	•	•	•	Security Information Service Inc [SOP]	800-525-5747	•	•	•	•
•	•	•	•	•	Segovia & Associates [SOP]	877-573-7833		•		•
•	•	•	•		Spectrum Screening Inc	800-222-8199	•		•	
			•		Pat Stephens	903-583-5215		•	•	
•	•	•	•	•	Super Search Inc [SOP]	800-687-5553	•	•	•	
•	•	•	•	•	Taylor Research & Investigations [SOP]	972-991-5045	•	•	•	•
		•	•		Tex Research	817-472-5997				
•	•	•	•	•	Texas Subpoena & Process Svc [SOP]	800-717-3463	•	•	•	•
•	•	•	•		Texsearch #A09479 [SOP]	903-786-4636	•	•	•	
				•	Title Info	817-244-7757		•	•	
					TOB Public Records Research	214-358-4744	•	•	•	
•	•	•	•	•	Tyler-McLennon Choicepoint	512-334-6244	•	•	•	•

DT	BK	CV	CR	PR	←Courts **COLLINGSWORTH** Recording→		UC	RE	TX	VS
•	•	•		•	Abstracts/Trustees of Texas	888-452-0331	•	•	•	
	•	•		•	Land Records of Texas	800-678-8016	•	•	•	

DT	BK	CV	CR	PR	←Courts **COLORADO** Recording→		UC	RE	TX	VS
•	•	•		•	Abstracts/Trustees of Texas	888-452-0331	•	•	•	
•	•	•			All State Document Services	888-246-8180	•	•	•	•
				•	Botts Title Co	254-697-6962	•	•	•	•
					Colorado County Abstract Co	979-732-2213	•	•	•	
•	•			•	DeedSearcher Title Research Services	281-375-8480	•	•	•	
	•	•		•	Land Records of Texas	800-678-8016	•	•	•	

DT	BK	CV	CR	PR	←Courts **COMAL** Recording→		UC	RE	TX	VS
•	•	•		•	Abstracts/Trustees of Texas	888-452-0331	•	•	•	
•	•	•	•	•	Americorp Research Inc	877-989-6850	•	•	•	•
		•	•	•	Cornerstone Title Research	210-661-2357	•	•	•	•
		•	•		Crimecheck Research Services	281-288-6930				
	•	•		•	Land Records of Texas	800-678-8016	•	•	•	
•	•			•	Morgan/Brooks Resources Inc	210-476-0500	•	•	•	
•	•	•	•	•	MS Document Services Inc	800-292-3868	•	•	•	•
			•		PI Inc	800-359-5131				
•	•	•	•	•	Property Research & Documentation Service Inc	210-520-7884	•	•	•	•
		•	•	•	TexDirect	512-353-4257	•	•	•	
•	•	•	•		Texsearch #A09479 [SOP]	903-786-4636	•	•	•	
•	•	•	•	•	Morris Todd [SOP]	210-673-4690	•	•	•	•
•	•	•	•	•	Tyler-McLennon Choicepoint	512-334-6244	•	•	•	•

DT	BK	CV	CR	PR	←Courts **COMANCHE** Recording→		UC	RE	TX	VS
•	•	•		•	Abstracts/Trustees of Texas	888-452-0331	•	•	•	
		•	•	•	Comanche County Abstract Co	325-356-2564	•	•	•	•
	•	•		•	Land Records of Texas	800-678-8016	•	•	•	
•	•	•	•	•	MS Document Services Inc	800-292-3868	•	•	•	•

DT	BK	CV	CR	PR	←Courts **CONCHO** Recording→		UC	RE	TX	VS
•	•	•		•	Abstracts/Trustees of Texas	888-452-0331	•	•	•	
	•	•		•	Land Records of Texas	800-678-8016	•	•	•	
		•	•	•	Surety Title Co of Eden	325-869-7081	•	•	•	•

DT	BK	CV	CR	PR	←Courts **COOKE** Recording→		UC	RE	TX	VS
•	•	•		•	Abstracts/Trustees of Texas	888-452-0331	•	•	•	
•	•	•	•	•	Court & Public Records Service Inc	800-856-0585	•	•	•	•
			•		Dataprompt Corporation	214-390-2530				
	•	•		•	Land Records of Texas	800-678-8016	•	•	•	
•	•	•	•	•	Mendenhall Information Services	940-696-0758	•	•	•	•
•	•	•	•	•	PADIC Inc [SOP]	940-665-6130	•	•	•	•
•	•	•	•	•	Security Information Service Inc [SOP]	800-525-5747	•	•	•	•
•	•	•	•		Texsearch #A09479 [SOP]	903-786-4636	•	•	•	

DT	BK	CV	CR	PR	←Courts **CORYELL** Recording→		UC	RE	TX	VS
•	•	•		•	Abstracts/Trustees of Texas	888-452-0331	•	•	•	
		•		•	American Abstract & Title Co Inc	254-526-9525	•	•	•	•
•	•	•			Carma Austin	254-634-1701	•		•	
•	•	•	•	•	BG Criminal Research	254-755-6808	•		•	
			•		Dataprompt Corporation	214-390-2530				
•	•			•	DeedSearcher Title Research Services	281-375-8480	•	•	•	
	•	•		•	Land Records of Texas	800-678-8016	•	•	•	
					Search Enterprises	254-752-2057		•	•	
•	•	•	•	•	Tyler-McLennon Choicepoint	512-334-6244	•	•	•	•

DT	BK	CV	CR	PR	←Courts	Cottle	Recording→	UC	RE	TX	VS
•	•	•		•	Abstracts/Trustees of Texas		888-452-0331	•	•	•	
•	•	•	•	•	Davick Services		800-658-6656	•	•	•	
				•	Jones & Renfrow Abstracters		806-492-3573	•	•	•	•
	•	•		•	Land Records of Texas		800-678-8016	•	•	•	

DT	BK	CV	CR	PR	←Courts	Crane	Recording→	UC	RE	TX	VS
•	•	•		•	Abstracts/Trustees of Texas		888-452-0331	•	•	•	
	•	•		•	Land Records of Texas		800-678-8016	•	•	•	

DT	BK	CV	CR	PR	←Courts	Crockett	Recording→	UC	RE	TX	VS
•	•	•		•	Abstracts/Trustees of Texas		888-452-0331	•	•	•	
					Crockett County Abstract Co		325-392-2232	•	•	•	
	•	•		•	Land Records of Texas		800-678-8016	•	•	•	

DT	BK	CV	CR	PR	←Courts	Crosby	Recording→	UC	RE	TX	VS
•	•	•		•	Abstracts/Trustees of Texas		888-452-0331	•	•	•	
•	•	•	•	•	Davick Services		800-658-6656	•	•	•	
	•	•		•	Land Records of Texas		800-678-8016	•	•	•	

DT	BK	CV	CR	PR	←Courts	Culberson	Recording→	UC	RE	TX	VS
•	•	•		•	Abstracts/Trustees of Texas		888-452-0331	•	•	•	
	•	•		•	Land Records of Texas		800-678-8016	•	•	•	
•	•	•		•	Stewart Title of Midland Inc		432-687-3355		•		

DT	BK	CV	CR	PR	←Courts	Dallam	Recording→	UC	RE	TX	VS
•	•	•		•	Abstracts/Trustees of Texas		888-452-0331	•	•	•	
		•		•	Hunter & Oelke		800-350-1288		•	•	
	•	•		•	Land Records of Texas		800-678-8016	•	•	•	
•	•	•		•	Rollins Research Ltd		806-353-7886	•	•	•	

DT	BK	CV	CR	PR	←Courts	Dallas	Recording→	UC	RE	TX	VS
					A & J Research Inc		972-221-7744	•	•	•	
•	•	•		•	Abstracts/Trustees of Texas		888-452-0331	•	•	•	
		•	•		Accu-Source Inc		214-637-4064				
•	•	•	•	•	All-American Attorney Services [SOP]		800-838-9044	•	•	•	•
		•		•	Ameristar Information Network		800-920-9270		•	•	•
•	•	•		•	Amerititle Abstract & Research Inc		800-856-1228	•	•	•	
•	•	•	•	•	ASA (Attorney Service Associates) [SOP]		972-394-1175	•	•	•	•
•	•	•	•		Asset Control Inc		877-277-3812	•	•	•	•
•	•	•	•	•	Atlantis Agency [SOP]		817-896-9337			•	•
•	•	•	•	•	Attorney's Service Bureau of Texas [SOP]		888-522-5297	•	•	•	•
		•	•		Background Information Systems Inc		800-687-0894				
					David C Bayoud		214-824-9944		•		
•	•	•	•	•	Bray & Freeman LP [SOP]		817-596-9255	•	•	•	•
•	•	•			Capitol Services Inc (Texas)		800-345-4647	•		•	
•		•	•		CLUSO Inc		866-30-CLUSO			•	
					Concord Commercial Services		972-931-7431		•		
•	•	•	•	•	Court & Public Records Service Inc		800-856-0585	•	•	•	•
•	•	•	•	•	CRRG Inc		800-687-9030	•	•	•	•
			•		Dataprompt Corporation		214-390-2530				
•	•			•	DeedSearcher Title Research Services		281-375-8480	•	•	•	
•	•	•	•	•	DFW Court Services [SOP]		800-436-0516	•	•	•	
•		•	•		FP Resources		866-989-8999				
•	•	•	•		G.A. Public Record Services Inc		800-760-2468				
•	•	•	•		General Information Services		800-447-0798	•	•		
•	•	•	•		Hart & Associates Inc		866-429-4044			•	•
•	•	•	•	•	Info2go		817-656-1997	•	•	•	•
		•	•		Inquest Investigations, LLC		903-893-2020	•	•	•	
•	•	•	•	•	Kimmons Security Services Inc [SOP]		281-679-0070	•	•	•	•

DT	BK	CV	CR	PR	Retriever	Phone	UC	RE	TX	VS
	•	•		•	Land Records of Texas	800-678-8016	•	•	•	
•	•	•	•		Lone Star Inv & Recovery Inc	800-887-3890	•	•	•	•
•	•	•	•	•	Mendenhall Information Services	940-696-0758	•	•	•	•
•	•	•	•	•	MS Document Services Inc	800-292-3868	•	•	•	•
•	•	•	•	•	Nell Watkins & Associates	972-226-8811	•	•	•	•
•	•	•	•	•	PADIC Inc [SOP]	940-665-6130	•	•	•	•
			•		Princeton Data Search Inc	469-474-1025		•	•	
•	•	•	•	•	Professional Civil Process (Austin) [SOP]	800-950-7493	•	•	•	•
•	•	•	•	•	Quick Search	214-358-2840	•	•	•	•
		•	•		Record Retrieval Services Inc	877-527-5355		•		
•	•	•	•	•	Reliable Courier [SOP]	214-637-4800			•	•
•	•	•	•		Research Specialists [SOP]	800-771-7547				
•	•	•	•	•	Richmond Group International [SOP]	703-494-4645			•	•
•	•	•	•	•	Secrest Legal Services	214-696-3959	•	•	•	
•	•	•	•	•	Security Information Service Inc [SOP]	800-525-5747	•	•	•	•
•	•	•	•	•	Segovia & Associates [SOP]	877-573-7833		•		•
•	•	•	•		Spectrum Screening Inc	800-222-8199	•		•	
•	•	•	•	•	Super Search Inc [SOP]	800-687-5553	•	•	•	
•	•	•	•	•	Taylor Research & Investigations [SOP]	972-991-5045	•	•	•	•
•	•	•	•	•	Texas Industrial Security Inc	214-634-2791			•	
•	•	•	•	•	Texas Subpoena & Process Svc [SOP]	800-717-3463	•	•	•	•
•	•	•	•		Texsearch #A09479 [SOP]	903-786-4636	•	•	•	
				•	Title Info	817-244-7757		•	•	
					TOB Public Records Research	214-358-4744	•	•	•	
•	•	•	•	•	Tyler-McLennon Choicepoint	512-334-6244	•	•	•	•
		•	•	•	Watkins Investigations [SOP]	972-926-6011	•	•	•	
		•	•		Your Information Source Inc	800-644-9668				

DT	BK	CV	CR	PR	←COURTS DAWSON	RECORDING→	UC	RE	TX	VS
•	•	•		•	Abstracts/Trustees of Texas	888-452-0331	•	•	•	
•	•	•	•	•	Davick Services	800-658-6656	•	•	•	
	•	•		•	Land Records of Texas	800-678-8016	•	•	•	
					South Plains Abstract Co	806-872-3023	•	•	•	

DT	BK	CV	CR	PR	←COURTS DE WITT	RECORDING→	UC	RE	TX	VS
•	•	•		•	Abstracts/Trustees of Texas	888-452-0331	•	•	•	
	•	•		•	Land Records of Texas	800-678-8016	•	•	•	
•	•	•	•	•	Property Research & Documentation Service Inc	210-520-7884	•	•	•	•

DT	BK	CV	CR	PR	←COURTS DEAF SMITH	RECORDING→	UC	RE	TX	VS
•	•	•		•	Abstracts/Trustees of Texas	888-452-0331	•	•	•	
•	•	•	•	•	Davick Services	800-658-6656	•	•	•	
	•	•		•	Land Records of Texas	800-678-8016	•	•	•	
•	•	•	•	•	Patricia Chambers Inv [SOP]	806-359-5989	•	•	•	
•	•	•		•	Rollins Research Ltd	806-353-7886	•	•	•	

DT	BK	CV	CR	PR	←COURTS DELTA	RECORDING→	UC	RE	TX	VS
•	•	•		•	Abstracts/Trustees of Texas	888-452-0331	•	•	•	
		•	•	•	Delta County Title Co [SOP]	903-395-4116	•	•	•	•
•		•	•		Kota Cornelius Kruse & Assoc	903-783-1883		•	•	
	•	•		•	Land Records of Texas	800-678-8016	•	•	•	
•	•	•	•	•	Tyler-McLennon Choicepoint	512-334-6244	•	•	•	•

DT	BK	CV	CR	PR	←COURTS DENTON	RECORDING→	UC	RE	TX	VS
					A & J Research Inc	972-221-7744	•	•	•	
•	•	•		•	Abstracts/Trustees of Texas	888-452-0331	•	•	•	
		•	•		Accu-Source Inc	214-637-4064				
		•		•	Ameristar Information Network	800-920-9270		•	•	•
•	•	•		•	Ameritittle Abstract & Research Inc	800-856-1228	•	•	•	
•	•	•	•	•	ASA (Attorney Service Associates) [SOP]	972-394-1175	•	•	•	•

DT	BK	CV	CR	PR	←Courts	Recording→	UC	RE	TX	VS
•	•	•	•		Asset Control Inc	877-277-3812	•	•	•	•
•	•	•	•	•	Attorney's Service Bureau of Texas [SOP]	888-522-5297	•	•	•	•
		•	•		Background Information Systems Inc	800-687-0894				
					David C Bayoud	214-824-9944		•		
•	•	•	•	•	Bray & Freeman LP [SOP]	817-596-9255	•	•	•	•
•	•	•	•	•	Court & Public Records Service Inc	800-856-0585	•	•	•	•
•	•	•	•	•	CRRG Inc	800-687-9030	•	•	•	•
			•		Dataprompt Corporation	214-390-2530				
•	•	•	•	•	DFW Court Services [SOP]	800-436-0516	•	•	•	
•		•	•		FP Resources	866-989-8999				
•	•	•	•		G.A. Public Record Services Inc	800-760-2468				
•	•	•	•		General Information Services	800-447-0798	•	•		
•	•	•	•		Hart & Associates Inc	866-429-4044			•	•
•	•	•	•	•	Info2go	817-656-1997	•	•	•	•
		•	•		Inquest Investigations, LLC	903-893-2020	•	•	•	
	•	•		•	Land Records of Texas	800-678-8016	•	•	•	
•	•	•	•		Lone Star Inv & Recovery Inc	800-887-3890	•	•	•	•
•	•	•	•	•	Mendenhall Information Services	940-696-0758	•	•	•	•
•	•	•	•	•	MS Document Services Inc	800-292-3868	•	•	•	•
•	•	•	•	•	PADIC Inc [SOP]	940-665-6130	•	•	•	•
•	•	•	•	•	Professional Civil Process (Austin) [SOP]	800-950-7493	•	•	•	•
•	•	•	•	•	Quick Search	214-358-2840	•	•	•	•
•	•	•	•	•	Security Information Service Inc [SOP]	800-525-5747	•	•	•	•
•	•	•	•	•	Segovia & Associates [SOP]	877-573-7833		•		•
•	•	•	•		Spectrum Screening Inc	800-222-8199	•		•	
•	•	•	•	•	Super Search Inc [SOP]	800-687-5553	•	•	•	
•	•	•	•	•	Taylor Research & Investigations [SOP]	972-991-5045	•	•	•	•
•	•	•	•		Texsearch #A09479 [SOP]	903-786-4636	•	•	•	
				•	Title Info	817-244-7757		•	•	
					TOB Public Records Research	214-358-4744	•	•	•	
•	•	•	•	•	Tyler-McLennon Choicepoint	512-334-6244	•	•	•	•
		•	•		Your Information Source Inc	800-644-9668				

DT	BK	CV	CR	PR	←Courts **DICKENS**	Recording→	UC	RE	TX	VS
•	•	•		•	Abstracts/Trustees of Texas	888-452-0331	•	•	•	
		•		•	Caprock Title Co	432-687-3232		•	•	
•	•	•	•	•	Davick Services	800-658-6656	•	•	•	
	•	•		•	Land Records of Texas	800-678-8016	•	•	•	

DT	BK	CV	CR	PR	←Courts **DIMMIT**	Recording→	UC	RE	TX	VS
•	•	•		•	Abstracts/Trustees of Texas	888-452-0331	•	•	•	
		•	•	•	Border Legal Services [SOP]	830-773-0525			•	•
					Border Title Group	956-791-5810	•	•	•	
					Border Title Group, FKA Elliott & Waldron Abstract	830-876-2926	•	•	•	
	•	•		•	Land Records of Texas	800-678-8016	•	•	•	

DT	BK	CV	CR	PR	←Courts **DONLEY**	Recording→	UC	RE	TX	VS
•	•	•		•	Abstracts/Trustees of Texas	888-452-0331	•	•	•	
	•	•		•	Land Records of Texas	800-678-8016	•	•	•	
•	•	•		•	Rollins Research Ltd	806-353-7886	•	•	•	
		•	•	•	Security Abstract Co	806-874-3511	•	•	•	•

DT	BK	CV	CR	PR	←Courts **DUVAL**	Recording→	UC	RE	TX	VS
•	•	•		•	Abstracts/Trustees of Texas	888-452-0331	•	•	•	
•	•	•	•	•	Condor Inv [SOP]	361-881-8977	•	•	•	•
•	•	•	•	•	Corpus Christi Court Services	361-887-8122	•	•	•	•
	•	•		•	Land Records of Texas	800-678-8016	•	•	•	
•	•	•	•	•	Shawver & Associates	800-364-2333	•	•	•	•
•	•	•	•	•	Texas Civil Process [SOP]	800-976-9595	•	•	•	•

DT	BK	CV	CR	PR	←Courts	Eastland	Recording→	UC	RE	TX	VS
•	•	•		•		Abstracts/Trustees of Texas	888-452-0331	•	•	•	
	•	•		•		Land Records of Texas	800-678-8016	•	•	•	
•	•	•	•	•		MS Document Services Inc	800-292-3868	•	•	•	•

DT	BK	CV	CR	PR	←Courts	Ector	Recording→	UC	RE	TX	VS
•	•	•		•		Abstracts/Trustees of Texas	888-452-0331	•	•	•	
•	•	•	•	•		Davick Services	800-658-6656	•	•	•	
	•	•		•		Land Records of Texas	800-678-8016	•	•	•	
•	•	•	•			Permian Court Reporters Inc [SOP]	432-683-3032				
•	•	•	•			Texsearch #A09479 [SOP]	903-786-4636	•	•	•	
•	•	•	•	•		Tyler-McLennon Choicepoint	512-334-6244	•	•	•	•

DT	BK	CV	CR	PR	←Courts	Edwards	Recording→	UC	RE	TX	VS
•	•	•		•		Abstracts/Trustees of Texas	888-452-0331	•	•	•	
	•	•		•		Land Records of Texas	800-678-8016	•	•	•	
		•		•		Rocksprings Abstract & Title Co	830-683-2185	•	•	•	•

DT	BK	CV	CR	PR	←Courts	El Paso	Recording→	UC	RE	TX	VS
		•	•	•		A.G.O. Legal Process Service [SOP]	505-526-4303	•	•	•	•
•	•	•		•		Abstracts/Trustees of Texas	888-452-0331	•	•	•	
•	•	•	•			Human Arts Consulting	800-493-2641				
	•	•		•		Land Records of Texas	800-678-8016	•	•	•	
•	•	•	•	•		Legal Net Process Service [SOP]	915-532-7871	•		•	•
•	•	•	•	•		Professional Civil Process (Austin) [SOP]	800-950-7493	•	•	•	•
•	•	•	•	•		Quick Search	214-358-2840	•	•	•	•
•	•	•	•	•		Tyler-McLennon Choicepoint	512-334-6244	•	•	•	•

DT	BK	CV	CR	PR	←Courts	Ellis	Recording→	UC	RE	TX	VS
•	•	•		•		Abstracts/Trustees of Texas	888-452-0331	•	•	•	
		•	•			B & B Info Search	817-774-1310				
						David C Bayoud	214-824-9944		•		
		•	•			Sallie Blount	972-824-1414				
•	•	•	•	•		Court & Public Records Service Inc	800-856-0585	•	•	•	•
		•	•			Crimecheck Research Services	281-288-6930				
•	•	•	•	•		CRRG Inc	800-687-9030	•	•	•	•
•	•	•	•	•		Info2go	817-656-1997	•	•	•	•
	•	•		•		Land Records of Texas	800-678-8016	•	•	•	
•	•	•	•	•		PADIC Inc [SOP]	940-665-6130	•	•	•	•
			•			Princeton Data Search Inc	469-474-1025		•	•	
•	•	•	•	•		Quick Search	214-358-2840	•	•	•	•
•	•	•	•	•		Reliable Courier [SOP]	214-637-4800			•	•
•	•	•	•	•		Security Information Service Inc [SOP]	800-525-5747	•	•	•	•
•	•	•	•	•		Segovia & Associates [SOP]	877-573-7833		•		•
•	•	•	•	•		Super Search Inc [SOP]	800-687-5553	•	•	•	
•	•	•	•	•		Taylor Research & Investigations [SOP]	972-991-5045	•	•	•	•
						TOB Public Records Research	214-358-4744	•	•	•	
•	•	•	•	•		Tyler-McLennon Choicepoint	512-334-6244	•	•	•	•

DT	BK	CV	CR	PR	←Courts	Erath	Recording→	UC	RE	TX	VS
•	•	•		•		Abstracts/Trustees of Texas	888-452-0331	•	•	•	
		•	•			B & B Info Search	817-774-1310				
			•			Dataprompt Corporation	214-390-2530				
	•	•		•		Land Records of Texas	800-678-8016	•	•	•	
•	•	•	•	•		Mendenhall Information Services	940-696-0758	•	•	•	•
•	•	•	•	•		Super Search Inc [SOP]	800-687-5553	•	•	•	

DT	BK	CV	CR	PR	←Courts	Falls	Recording→	UC	RE	TX	VS
•	•	•		•		Abstracts/Trustees of Texas	888-452-0331	•	•	•	
•	•	•	•	•		Attorney Civil Process Service [SOP]	254-755-6447				

DT	BK	CV	CR	PR	←Courts	Recording→	UC	RE	TX	VS
•	•	•			Carma Austin	254-634-1701	•		•	
		•		•	Falls County Title Co Inc	254-883-2112	•	•	•	•
	•	•		•	Land Records of Texas	800-678-8016	•	•	•	
					Search Enterprises	254-752-2057		•	•	

DT	BK	CV	CR	PR	←Courts **FANNIN**	Recording→	UC	RE	TX	VS
•	•	•		•	Abstracts/Trustees of Texas	888-452-0331	•	•	•	
•	•	•	•	•	Court & Public Records Service Inc	800-856-0585	•	•	•	•
			•		Dataprompt Corporation	214-390-2530				
•		•	•		Kota Cornelius Kruse & Assoc	903-783-1883		•	•	
	•	•		•	Land Records of Texas	800-678-8016	•	•	•	
•	•	•	•	•	Quick Search	214-358-2840	•	•	•	•
					Pat Stephens	903-583-5215		•	•	
•	•	•	•		Texsearch #A09479 [SOP]	903-786-4636	•	•	•	

DT	BK	CV	CR	PR	←Courts **FAYETTE**	Recording→	UC	RE	TX	VS
•	•	•		•	Abstracts/Trustees of Texas	888-452-0331	•	•	•	
				•	Botts Title Co	254-697-6962	•	•	•	•
		•	•	•	Clear Title Co	979-968-5885	•	•	•	•
	•	•		•	Land Records of Texas	800-678-8016	•	•	•	

DT	BK	CV	CR	PR	←Courts **FISHER**	Recording→	UC	RE	TX	VS
•	•	•		•	Abstracts/Trustees of Texas	888-452-0331	•	•	•	
•	•	•	•	•	Davick Services	800-658-6656	•	•	•	
		•		•	Fisher/Jones Title Co (Roby)	325-776-2471	•	•	•	•
	•	•		•	Land Records of Texas	800-678-8016	•	•	•	
•	•	•	•	•	MS Document Services Inc	800-292-3868	•	•	•	•

DT	BK	CV	CR	PR	←Courts **FLOYD**	Recording→	UC	RE	TX	VS
•	•	•		•	Abstracts/Trustees of Texas	888-452-0331	•	•	•	
•	•	•	•	•	Davick Services	800-658-6656	•	•	•	
	•	•		•	Land Records of Texas	800-678-8016	•	•	•	

DT	BK	CV	CR	PR	←Courts **FOARD**	Recording→	UC	RE	TX	VS
•	•	•		•	Abstracts/Trustees of Texas	888-452-0331	•	•	•	
	•	•		•	Land Records of Texas	800-678-8016	•	•	•	
•	•	•	•	•	Mendenhall Information Services	940-696-0758	•	•	•	•
•	•	•		•	Superior Process Svc [SOP]	888-230-2663		•	•	•

DT	BK	CV	CR	PR	←Courts **FORT BEND**	Recording→	UC	RE	TX	VS
•	•	•		•	Abstracts/Trustees of Texas	888-452-0331	•	•	•	
•	•	•	•	•	Airborn Civil Process & Inv [SOP]	888-933-6863	•	•	•	•
•	•	•			All State Document Services	888-246-8180	•	•	•	•
•	•	•		•	Ameritiltle Abstract & Research Inc	800-856-1228	•	•	•	
•	•	•	•	•	Asset Research Group	713-864-2536	•	•	•	•
•	•	•		•	BAST Research Services Inc	713-721-7077	•	•	•	
•	•	•	•	•	Compex Legal Services [SOP]	713-861-3900				•
•	•	•	•	•	Court Record Research Inc	800-552-3353	•	•	•	•
	•	•	•	•	Courthouse Specialists	800-925-4225	•	•	•	
•	•			•	DeedSearcher Title Research Services	281-375-8480	•	•	•	
					Fox Hunt	713-772-8018	•	•	•	
•	•	•	•	•	Garza-McNamee Agency Inc	888-262-6221	•	•	•	
•	•	•	•	•	Houston Court Services Inc [SOP]	713-655-0555	•	•	•	•
		•	•	•	Information Protective Services Inc (IPS) [SOP]	888-720-3784	•	•	•	
•	•	•	•	•	John V Eriksson Group Inc	281-488-0018	•	•	•	•
•	•	•	•	•	Kimmons Security Services Inc [SOP]	281-679-0070	•	•	•	•
	•	•		•	Land Records of Texas	800-678-8016	•	•	•	
•	•	•	•		Mach 5 Couriers Inc [SOP]	800-593-2023	•	•	•	
•	•	•	•	•	PM Clinton International Investigation	866-686-6864	•	•	•	
•	•	•	•	•	Professional Civil Process (Austin) [SOP]	800-950-7493	•	•	•	•

DT	BK	CV	CR	PR	←Courts	Recording→	UC	RE	TX	VS
•	•	•	•		Spectrum Screening Inc	800-222-8199	•		•	
					Texas Abstract Services	866-290-3743		•	•	
•	•	•	•	•	The Research Staff Inc	800-822-3584	•	•	•	
•	•	•	•	•	Tyler-McLennon Choicepoint	512-334-6244	•	•	•	•

DT	BK	CV	CR	PR	←Courts	Franklin	Recording→	UC	RE	TX	VS
•	•	•		•	Abstracts/Trustees of Texas		888-452-0331	•	•	•	
•	•	•			Joe Gillenwater [SOP]		870-772-2923	•	•	•	
	•	•		•	Land Records of Texas		800-678-8016	•	•	•	
•	•	•	•	•	Tyler-McLennon Choicepoint		512-334-6244	•	•	•	•

DT	BK	CV	CR	PR	←Courts	Freestone	Recording→	UC	RE	TX	VS
•	•	•		•	Abstracts/Trustees of Texas		888-452-0331	•	•	•	
•	•	•	•	•	East Texas Professional Svcs [SOP]		903-928-0117			•	•
	•	•		•	Land Records of Texas		800-678-8016	•	•	•	

DT	BK	CV	CR	PR	←Courts	Frio	Recording→	UC	RE	TX	VS
•	•	•		•	Abstracts/Trustees of Texas		888-452-0331	•	•	•	
	•	•		•	Land Records of Texas		800-678-8016	•	•	•	

DT	BK	CV	CR	PR	←Courts	Gaines	Recording→	UC	RE	TX	VS
•	•	•		•	Abstracts/Trustees of Texas		888-452-0331	•	•	•	
•	•	•	•	•	Davick Services		800-658-6656	•	•	•	
	•	•		•	Land Records of Texas		800-678-8016	•	•	•	

DT	BK	CV	CR	PR	←Courts	Galveston	Recording→	UC	RE	TX	VS
•	•	•		•	Abstracts/Trustees of Texas		888-452-0331	•	•	•	
•	•	•			All State Document Services		888-246-8180	•	•	•	•
•	•	•		•	Amerititle Abstract & Research Inc		800-856-1228	•	•	•	
•	•	•	•	•	Asset Research Group		713-864-2536	•	•	•	•
•	•	•		•	BAST Research Services Inc		713-721-7077	•	•	•	
•	•	•	•	•	Compex Legal Services [SOP]		713-861-3900				•
•	•	•	•	•	Court Record Research Inc		800-552-3353	•	•	•	•
	•	•	•	•	Courthouse Specialists		800-925-4225	•	•	•	
		•	•		Criminal Background Investigations		979-848-0632				
•	•			•	DeedSearcher Title Research Services		281-375-8480	•	•	•	
•	•	•	•	•	Garza-McNamee Agency Inc		888-262-6221	•	•	•	
•	•	•	•	•	John V Eriksson Group Inc		281-488-0018	•	•	•	•
•	•	•	•	•	Kimmons Security Services Inc [SOP]		281-679-0070	•	•	•	•
	•	•		•	Land Records of Texas		800-678-8016	•	•	•	
•	•	•	•		Mach 5 Couriers Inc [SOP]		800-593-2023				
•	•	•	•	•	PM Clinton International Investigation		866-686-6864	•	•	•	
•	•	•	•	•	Professional Civil Process (Austin) [SOP]		800-950-7493	•	•	•	•
•	•	•	•		Spectrum Screening Inc		800-222-8199	•		•	
•		•	•		The Partnership		877-558-9928				
•	•	•	•	•	The Research Staff Inc		800-822-3584	•	•	•	
•	•	•	•	•	Tyler-McLennon Choicepoint		512-334-6244	•	•	•	•

DT	BK	CV	CR	PR	←Courts	Garza	Recording→	UC	RE	TX	VS
•	•	•		•	Abstracts/Trustees of Texas		888-452-0331	•	•	•	
•	•	•	•	•	Davick Services		800-658-6656	•	•	•	
	•	•		•	Land Records of Texas		800-678-8016	•	•	•	

DT	BK	CV	CR	PR	←Courts	Gillespie	Recording→	UC	RE	TX	VS
•	•	•		•	Abstracts/Trustees of Texas		888-452-0331	•	•	•	
		•	•	•	Fredericksburg Titles Inc		830-997-3852	•	•	•	
	•	•		•	Land Records of Texas		800-678-8016	•	•	•	

DT	BK	CV	CR	PR	←Courts	Glasscock	Recording→	UC	RE	TX	VS
•	•	•		•	Abstracts/Trustees of Texas		888-452-0331	•	•	•	
				•	Big Spring Abstract & Title Co Inc		432-267-1604		•	•	

DT	BK	CV	CR	PR	←Courts	Recording→	UC	RE	TX	VS
•	•	•	•	•	Davick Services	800-658-6656	•	•	•	
	•	•		•	Land Records of Texas	800-678-8016	•	•	•	

DT	BK	CV	CR	PR	←Courts GOLIAD	Recording→	UC	RE	TX	VS
•	•	•		•	Abstracts/Trustees of Texas	888-452-0331	•	•	•	
		•		•	Bedgood Abstract & Title Co (Goliad)	361-645-3145	•	•	•	
	•	•		•	Land Records of Texas	800-678-8016	•	•	•	

DT	BK	CV	CR	PR	←Courts GONZALES	Recording→	UC	RE	TX	VS
•	•	•		•	Abstracts/Trustees of Texas	888-452-0331	•	•	•	
		•	•		Crimecheck Research Services	281-288-6930				
	•	•		•	Land Records of Texas	800-678-8016	•	•	•	
•	•	•	•	•	Property Research & Documentation Service Inc	210-520-7884	•	•	•	•
		•	•	•	TexDirect	512-353-4257	•	•	•	
•	•	•	•	•	Tyler-McLennon Choicepoint	512-334-6244	•	•	•	•

DT	BK	CV	CR	PR	←Courts GRAY	Recording→	UC	RE	TX	VS
•	•	•		•	Abstracts/Trustees of Texas	888-452-0331	•	•	•	
	•	•		•	Land Records of Texas	800-678-8016	•	•	•	
•	•	•		•	Rollins Research Ltd	806-353-7886	•	•	•	

DT	BK	CV	CR	PR	←Courts GRAYSON	Recording→	UC	RE	TX	VS
•	•	•		•	Abstracts/Trustees of Texas	888-452-0331	•	•	•	
		•	•		Accu-Source Inc	214-637-4064				
•	•	•	•	•	Court & Public Records Service Inc	800-856-0585	•	•	•	•
			•		Dataprompt Corporation	214-390-2530				
•	•	•	•	•	DFW Court Services [SOP]	800-436-0516	•	•	•	
		•	•		Inquest Investigations, LLC	903-893-2020	•	•	•	
•		•	•		Kota Cornelius Kruse & Assoc	903-783-1883		•	•	
	•	•		•	Land Records of Texas	800-678-8016	•	•	•	
•	•	•	•	•	Mendenhall Information Services	940-696-0758	•	•	•	•
•	•	•	•	•	PADIC Inc [SOP]	940-665-6130	•	•	•	•
•	•	•	•	•	Quick Search	214-358-2840	•	•	•	•
•	•	•	•	•	Security Information Service Inc [SOP]	800-525-5747	•	•	•	•
					Pat Stephens	903-583-5215		•	•	
•	•	•	•	•	Super Search Inc [SOP]	800-687-5553	•	•	•	
•	•	•	•		Texsearch #A09479 [SOP]	903-786-4636	•	•	•	

DT	BK	CV	CR	PR	←Courts GREGG	Recording→	UC	RE	TX	VS
•	•	•		•	Abstracts/Trustees of Texas	888-452-0331	•	•	•	
		•	•		Accu-Source Inc	214-637-4064				
			•		Dataprompt Corporation	214-390-2530				
		•	•		Inquest Investigations, LLC	903-893-2020	•	•	•	
	•	•		•	Land Records of Texas	800-678-8016	•	•	•	
•	•	•	•		Texsearch #A09479 [SOP]	903-786-4636	•	•	•	
•	•	•	•	•	Tyler-McLennon Choicepoint	512-334-6244	•	•	•	•

DT	BK	CV	CR	PR	←Courts GRIMES	Recording→	UC	RE	TX	VS
•	•	•		•	Abstracts/Trustees of Texas	888-452-0331	•	•	•	
•	•			•	DeedSearcher Title Research Services	281-375-8480	•	•	•	
		•		•	Guaranty Title Co of Grimes County	936-873-2250	•	•	•	
	•	•		•	Land Records of Texas	800-678-8016	•	•	•	

DT	BK	CV	CR	PR	←Courts GUADALUPE	Recording→	UC	RE	TX	VS
•	•	•		•	Abstracts/Trustees of Texas	888-452-0331	•	•	•	
		•	•		Crimecheck Research Services	281-288-6930				
	•	•		•	Land Records of Texas	800-678-8016	•	•	•	
			•		PI Inc	800-359-5131				
•	•	•	•	•	Property Research & Documentation Service Inc	210-520-7884	•	•	•	•
		•	•	•	TexDirect	512-353-4257	•	•	•	
•	•	•	•		Texsearch #A09479 [SOP]	903-786-4636	•	•	•	

DT	BK	CV	CR	PR	←Courts	Recording→	UC	RE	TX	VS
•	•	•	•	•	Morris Todd [SOP]	210-673-4690	•	•	•	•
•	•	•	•	•	Tyler-McLennon Choicepoint	512-334-6244	•	•	•	•

DT	BK	CV	CR	PR	←Courts **HALE**	Recording→	UC	RE	TX	VS
•	•	•		•	Abstracts/Trustees of Texas	888-452-0331	•	•	•	
•	•	•	•	•	Davick Services	800-658-6656	•	•	•	
	•	•		•	Land Records of Texas	800-678-8016	•	•	•	

DT	BK	CV	CR	PR	←Courts **HALL**	Recording→	UC	RE	TX	VS
•	•	•		•	Abstracts/Trustees of Texas	888-452-0331	•	•	•	
	•	•		•	Land Records of Texas	800-678-8016	•	•	•	
		•	•	•	Security Abstract Co	806-874-3511	•	•	•	•

DT	BK	CV	CR	PR	←Courts **HAMILTON**	Recording→	UC	RE	TX	VS
•	•	•		•	Abstracts/Trustees of Texas	888-452-0331	•	•	•	
	•	•		•	Land Records of Texas	800-678-8016	•	•	•	

DT	BK	CV	CR	PR	←Courts **HANSFORD**	Recording→	UC	RE	TX	VS
•	•	•		•	Abstracts/Trustees of Texas	888-452-0331	•	•	•	
	•	•		•	Land Records of Texas	800-678-8016	•	•	•	

DT	BK	CV	CR	PR	←Courts **HARDEMAN**	Recording→	UC	RE	TX	VS
•	•	•		•	Abstracts/Trustees of Texas	888-452-0331	•	•	•	
	•	•		•	Land Records of Texas	800-678-8016	•	•	•	
•	•	•	•	•	Mendenhall Information Services	940-696-0758	•	•	•	•
•	•	•		•	Superior Process Svc [SOP]	888-230-2663		•	•	•
		•	•	•	T.A.B.B.S. Inv & Process Service [SOP]	580-477-3292	•	•	•	•

DT	BK	CV	CR	PR	←Courts **HARDIN**	Recording→	UC	RE	TX	VS
•	•	•		•	Abstracts/Trustees of Texas	888-452-0331	•	•	•	
•	•	•			All State Document Services	888-246-8180	•	•	•	•
•	•	•	•	•	ELH Contracting Inc Independent Land & Title Abstractor	409-832-5793	•	•	•	•
		•		•	Hooks Title & Abstract	409-246-3447	•	•	•	
	•	•		•	Land Records of Texas	800-678-8016	•	•	•	
•		•	•		The Partnership	877-558-9928				
•	•	•	•	•	The Research Staff Inc	800-822-3584	•	•	•	

DT	BK	CV	CR	PR	←Courts **HARRIS**	Recording→	UC	RE	TX	VS
•	•	•		•	Abstracts/Trustees of Texas	888-452-0331	•	•	•	
		•	•		Accu-Source Inc	214-637-4064				
•	•	•	•	•	Airborn Civil Process & Inv [SOP]	888-933-6863	•	•	•	•
•	•	•			All State Document Services	888-246-8180	•	•	•	•
•	•	•		•	Ameritite Abstract & Research Inc	800-856-1228	•	•	•	
•	•	•	•		Asset Control Inc	877-277-3812	•	•	•	•
•	•	•	•	•	Asset Research Group	713-864-2536	•	•	•	•
		•	•		Background Information Systems Inc	800-687-0894				
•	•	•		•	BAST Research Services Inc	713-721-7077	•	•	•	
•	•	•			Capitol Services Inc (Texas)	800-345-4647	•		•	
•	•	•	•	•	Compex Legal Services [SOP]	713-861-3900				•
•	•	•	•	•	Court Record Research Inc	800-552-3353	•	•	•	•
	•	•	•	•	Courthouse Specialists	800-925-4225	•	•	•	
			•		Dataprompt Corporation	214-390-2530				
•	•	•	•		DBU Investigations	281-564-9043	•		•	
•	•			•	DeedSearcher Title Research Services	281-375-8480	•	•	•	
•	•	•	•	•	DFW Court Services [SOP]	800-436-0516	•	•	•	
					Fox Hunt	713-772-8018	•	•	•	
•	•	•	•		G.A. Public Record Services Inc	800-760-2468				
•	•	•	•	•	Garza-McNamee Agency Inc	888-262-6221	•	•	•	
•	•	•	•		General Information Services	800-447-0798	•	•		
•	•	•	•		Hart & Associates Inc	866-429-4044			•	•
•	•	•	•	•	Houston Court Services Inc [SOP]	713-655-0555	•	•	•	•

DT	BK	CV	CR	PR	←Courts	Recording→	UC	RE	TX	VS
		•	•	•	Information Protective Services Inc (IPS) [SOP]	888-720-3784	•	•	•	
•	•	•	•	•	John V Eriksson Group Inc	281-488-0018	•	•	•	•
•	•	•	•	•	Kimmons Security Services Inc [SOP]	281-679-0070	•	•	•	•
	•	•		•	Land Records of Texas	800-678-8016	•	•	•	
•	•	•	•		Mach 5 Couriers Inc [SOP]	800-593-2023				
•	•	•	•	•	MS Document Services Inc	800-292-3868	•	•	•	•
			•		PI Inc	800-359-5131				
•	•	•	•	•	PM Clinton International Investigation	866-686-6864	•	•	•	
•	•	•	•	•	Professional Civil Process (Austin) [SOP]	800-950-7493	•	•	•	•
		•	•		Spearhead Research - On Target Information	512-295-7298				
•	•	•	•		Spectrum Screening Inc	800-222-8199	•		•	
					Texas Abstract Services	866-290-3743		•	•	
•	•	•	•		Texsearch #A09479 [SOP]	903-786-4636	•	•	•	
•		•	•		The Partnership	877-558-9928				
•	•	•	•	•	The Research Staff Inc	800-822-3584	•	•	•	
•	•	•	•	•	Tyler-McLennon Choicepoint	512-334-6244	•	•	•	•
•	•	•	•	•	Varoga & Shallett	713-522-0101	•	•	•	•
		•	•		Your Information Source Inc	800-644-9668				

DT	BK	CV	CR	PR	←Courts **HARRISON**	Recording→	UC	RE	TX	VS
•	•	•		•	Abstracts/Trustees of Texas	888-452-0331	•	•	•	
•	•	•	•	•	Court & Public Records Service Inc	800-856-0585	•	•	•	•
	•	•		•	Land Records of Texas	800-678-8016	•	•	•	
		•		•	M & M Title / Mitchell Co.	318-798-1198	•	•	•	
•	•	•	•	•	Tyler-McLennon Choicepoint	512-334-6244	•	•	•	•

DT	BK	CV	CR	PR	←Courts **HARTLEY**	Recording→	UC	RE	TX	VS
•	•	•		•	Abstracts/Trustees of Texas	888-452-0331	•	•	•	
		•		•	Hunter & Oelke	800-350-1288		•	•	
	•	•		•	Land Records of Texas	800-678-8016	•	•	•	
•	•	•		•	Rollins Research Ltd	806-353-7886	•	•	•	

DT	BK	CV	CR	PR	←Courts **HASKELL**	Recording→	UC	RE	TX	VS
•	•	•		•	Abstracts/Trustees of Texas	888-452-0331	•	•	•	
		•	•	•	Haskell Abstract & TItle Co	940-864-2604	•	•	•	•
	•	•		•	Land Records of Texas	800-678-8016	•	•	•	
•	•	•	•	•	Mendenhall Information Services	940-696-0758	•	•	•	•
•	•	•		•	Superior Process Svc [SOP]	888-230-2663		•	•	•

DT	BK	CV	CR	PR	←Courts **HAYS**	Recording→	UC	RE	TX	VS
•	•	•		•	Abstracts/Trustees of Texas	888-452-0331	•	•	•	
•	•	•	•	•	Americorp Research Inc	877-989-6850	•	•	•	•
•	•	•			Carma Austin	254-634-1701	•		•	
•		•	•	•	Bar Nunn Research Specialists	512-497-5584		•	•	
•		•		•	John Blackburn	210-867-0399	•	•	•	
•	•	•		•	Central Tejas Research & Title Services	512-469-6062	•	•	•	
		•	•		Crimecheck Research Services	281-288-6930				
					Executec Services	512-345-5402	•	•	•	
•	•	•	•	•	John C Dunaway & Company [SOP]	512-835-5888	•	•	•	•
	•	•		•	Land Records of Texas	800-678-8016	•	•	•	
•	•	•	•	•	MS Document Services Inc	800-292-3868	•	•	•	•
			•		PI Inc	800-359-5131				
•	•	•	•	•	Promesa Enterprises Inc	800-474-4420	•	•	•	•
•	•	•	•	•	Property Research & Documentation Service Inc	210-520-7884	•	•	•	•
•	•	•	•	•	Research Network	512-469-1740	•	•	•	•
•	•	•	•		Spectrum Screening Inc	800-222-8199	•	•	•	
		•	•	•	TexDirect	512-353-4257	•	•	•	
•	•	•	•		Texsearch #A09479 [SOP]	903-786-4636	•	•	•	
•	•	•	•	•	Tyler-McLennon Choicepoint	512-334-6244	•	•	•	•

DT	BK	CV	CR	PR	←Courts	HEMPHILL	Recording→	UC	RE	TX	VS
•	•	•		•	Abstracts/Trustees of Texas		888-452-0331	•	•	•	
	•	•		•	Land Records of Texas		800-678-8016	•	•	•	

DT	BK	CV	CR	PR	←Courts	HENDERSON	Recording→	UC	RE	TX	VS
•	•	•		•	Abstracts/Trustees of Texas		888-452-0331	•	•	•	
			•		Dataprompt Corporation		214-390-2530				
•	•	•	•	•	East Texas Professional Svcs [SOP]		903-928-0117			•	•
•	•	•	•	•	Investigative Concepts		903-677-9473				
	•	•		•	Land Records of Texas		800-678-8016	•	•	•	
		•		•	M & M Title / Mitchell Co		318-798-1198	•	•	•	
			•		Princeton Data Search Inc		469-474-1025		•	•	
•	•	•	•	•	Tyler-McLennon Choicepoint		512-334-6244	•	•	•	•

DT	BK	CV	CR	PR	←Courts	HIDALGO	Recording→	UC	RE	TX	VS
•	•	•		•	Abstracts/Trustees of Texas		888-452-0331	•	•	•	
•	•	•	•		Asset Control Inc		877-277-3812	•	•	•	•
	•	•		•	Land Records of Texas		800-678-8016	•	•	•	
		•	•	•	Jean Peck [SOP]		402-721-4143	•	•	•	•
•	•	•	•	•	Professional Civil Process (McAllen) [SOP]		800-880-4223	•	•	•	•
•	•	•	•	•	Record Finders		956-571-5378	•	•	•	•
•	•	•	•	•	Shawver & Associates		800-364-2333	•	•	•	•
					South Texas Title and Trustee Services		956-412-3413	•	•	•	
•	•	•	•		Texsearch #A09479 [SOP]		903-786-4636	•	•	•	
•	•	•	•	•	Tyler-McLennon Choicepoint		512-334-6244	•	•	•	•
•	•	•		•	Valley Abstract & Trustee Services		956-571-1119	•	•	•	

DT	BK	CV	CR	PR	←Courts	HILL	Recording→	UC	RE	TX	VS
•	•	•		•	Abstracts/Trustees of Texas		888-452-0331	•	•	•	
•	•	•	•	•	Attorney Civil Process Service [SOP]		254-755-6447				
		•	•		B & B Info Search		817-774-1310				
		•	•		Crimecheck Research Services		281-288-6930				
		•	•	•	Eastland Title Co		254-582-2762	•	•	•	•
	•	•		•	Land Records of Texas		800-678-8016	•	•	•	

DT	BK	CV	CR	PR	←Courts	HOCKLEY	Recording→	UC	RE	TX	VS
•	•	•		•	Abstracts/Trustees of Texas		888-452-0331	•	•	•	
•	•	•		•	Davick Services		800-658-6656	•	•	•	
	•	•		•	Land Records of Texas		800-678-8016	•	•	•	

DT	BK	CV	CR	PR	←Courts	HOOD	Recording→	UC	RE	TX	VS
•	•	•		•	Abstracts/Trustees of Texas		888-452-0331	•	•	•	
		•	•		B & B Info Search		817-774-1310				
•	•	•	•	•	Bray & Freeman LP [SOP]		817-596-9255	•	•	•	•
		•	•		Crimecheck Research Services		281-288-6930				
•	•	•	•	•	Info2go		817-656-1997	•	•	•	•
	•	•		•	Land Records of Texas		800-678-8016	•	•	•	
•	•	•	•	•	Mendenhall Information Services		940-696-0758	•	•	•	•
•	•	•	•	•	Super Search Inc [SOP]		800-687-5553	•	•	•	

DT	BK	CV	CR	PR	←Courts	HOPKINS	Recording→	UC	RE	TX	VS
•	•	•		•	Abstracts/Trustees of Texas		888-452-0331	•	•	•	
			•		Dataprompt Corporation		214-390-2530				
•		•	•		Kota Cornelius Kruse & Assoc		903-783-1883		•	•	
	•	•		•	Land Records of Texas		800-678-8016	•	•	•	
•	•	•	•	•	Tyler-McLennon Choicepoint		512-334-6244	•	•	•	•

DT	BK	CV	CR	PR	←Courts	HOUSTON	Recording→	UC	RE	TX	VS
•	•	•		•	Abstracts/Trustees of Texas		888-452-0331	•	•	•	
	•	•		•	Land Records of Texas		800-678-8016	•	•	•	

DT	BK	CV	CR	PR	←Courts		Recording→	UC	RE	TX	VS
•	•	•	•	•	Professional Civil Process (Austin) [SOP]		800-950-7493	•	•	•	•
•	•	•	•	•	The Research Staff Inc		800-822-3584	•	•	•	
					HOWARD						
•	•	•		•	Abstracts/Trustees of Texas		888-452-0331	•	•	•	
				•	Big Spring Abstract & Title Co Inc		432-267-1604		•	•	
			•		Dataprompt Corporation		214-390-2530				
•	•	•	•	•	Davick Services		800-658-6656	•	•	•	
	•	•		•	Land Records of Texas		800-678-8016	•	•	•	
					HUDSPETH						
•	•	•		•	Abstracts/Trustees of Texas		888-452-0331	•	•	•	
	•	•		•	Land Records of Texas		800-678-8016	•	•	•	
•	•	•	•	•	Legal Net Process Service [SOP]		915-532-7871	•		•	•
					HUNT						
•	•	•		•	Abstracts/Trustees of Texas		888-452-0331	•	•	•	
		•	•		Accu-Source Inc		214-637-4064				
•	•	•	•	•	Court & Public Records Service Inc		800-856-0585	•	•	•	•
			•		Dataprompt Corporation		214-390-2530				
	•	•		•	Land Records of Texas		800-678-8016	•	•	•	
			•		Princeton Data Search Inc		469-474-1025		•	•	
•	•	•	•	•	Quick Search		214-358-2840	•	•	•	•
•	•	•	•	•	Security Information Service Inc [SOP]		800-525-5747	•	•	•	•
					Pat Stephens		903-583-5215		•	•	
•	•	•	•	•	Taylor Research & Investigations [SOP]		972-991-5045	•	•	•	•
•	•	•	•	•	Tyler-McLennon Choicepoint		512-334-6244	•	•	•	•
					HUTCHINSON						
•	•	•		•	Abstracts/Trustees of Texas		888-452-0331	•	•	•	
	•	•		•	Land Records of Texas		800-678-8016	•	•	•	
	•	•	•	•	Payne Research & Sales		806-878-3195; mobil 806-886-3731			•	•
•	•	•		•	Rollins Research Ltd		806-353-7886	•	•	•	
					IRION						
•	•	•		•	Abstracts/Trustees of Texas		888-452-0331	•	•	•	
	•	•		•	Land Records of Texas		800-678-8016	•	•	•	
					JACK						
•	•	•		•	Abstracts/Trustees of Texas		888-452-0331	•	•	•	
•	•	•	•	•	Bray & Freeman LP [SOP]		817-596-9255	•	•	•	•
	•	•		•	Land Records of Texas		800-678-8016	•	•	•	
•	•	•	•	•	Mendenhall Information Services		940-696-0758	•	•	•	•
		•		•	Spiller Abstract		940-567-2271	•	•	•	
•	•	•		•	Superior Process Svc [SOP]		888-230-2663		•	•	•
					JACKSON						
•	•	•		•	Abstracts/Trustees of Texas		888-452-0331	•	•	•	
•	•	•			All State Document Services		888-246-8180	•	•	•	•
		•		•	Guaranty Abstract Co of Jackson County Inc		361-782-3591	•	•	•	
	•	•		•	Land Records of Texas		800-678-8016	•	•	•	
					JASPER						
•	•	•		•	Abstracts/Trustees of Texas		888-452-0331	•	•	•	
				•	Garland Smith Abstract Co		409-384-2571	•	•	•	•
	•	•		•	Land Records of Texas		800-678-8016	•	•	•	
					JEFF DAVIS						
•	•	•		•	Abstracts/Trustees of Texas		888-452-0331	•	•	•	
		•		•	Ellyson Abstract & Title Co of Brewster		432-837-5801	•	•	•	•
		•		•	Jeff Davis County Abstract Co.		432-426-3288	•	•	•	

DT	BK	CV	CR	PR	←Courts		Recording→	UC	RE	TX	VS
	•	•		•	Land Records of Texas	800-678-8016		•	•	•	

DT	BK	CV	CR	PR	←Courts	JEFFERSON	Recording→	UC	RE	TX	VS
•	•	•		•	Abstracts/Trustees of Texas	888-452-0331		•	•	•	
•	•	•		•	All State Document Services	888-246-8180		•	•	•	•
•	•	•	•	•	Compex Legal Services [SOP]	713-861-3900					•
•	•	•	•	•	ELH Contracting Inc Independent Land & Title Abstractor	409-832-5793		•	•	•	•
	•	•		•	Land Records of Texas	800-678-8016		•	•	•	
•	•	•	•		Mach 5 Couriers Inc [SOP]	800-593-2023					
•		•	•		The Partnership	877-558-9928					
•	•	•	•	•	The Research Staff Inc	800-822-3584		•	•	•	
•	•	•	•	•	Tyler-McLennon Choicepoint	512-334-6244		•	•	•	•

DT	BK	CV	CR	PR	←Courts	JIM HOGG	Recording→	UC	RE	TX	VS
•	•	•		•	Abstracts/Trustees of Texas	888-452-0331		•	•	•	
					Border Title Group	956-791-5810		•	•	•	
	•	•		•	Land Records of Texas	800-678-8016		•	•	•	

DT	BK	CV	CR	PR	←Courts	JIM WELLS	Recording→	UC	RE	TX	VS
•	•	•		•	Abstracts/Trustees of Texas	888-452-0331		•	•	•	
					Border Title Group	956-791-5810		•	•	•	
•	•	•	•	•	Condor Inv [SOP]	361-881-8977		•	•	•	•
•	•	•	•	•	Corpus Christi Court Services	361-887-8122		•	•	•	•
•	•	•	•	•	Brenda Kolle/Title Abstractor	361-852-8236		•	•	•	
	•	•		•	Land Records of Texas	800-678-8016		•	•	•	
•	•	•	•	•	Shawver & Associates	800-364-2333		•	•	•	•
					South Texas Title and Trustee Services	956-412-3413		•	•	•	
•	•	•	•	•	Texas Civil Process [SOP]	800-976-9595		•	•	•	•
•	•	•	•	•	Tyler-McLennon Choicepoint	512-334-6244		•	•	•	•

DT	BK	CV	CR	PR	←Courts	JOHNSON	Recording→	UC	RE	TX	VS
•	•	•		•	Abstracts/Trustees of Texas	888-452-0331		•	•	•	
		•	•		Accu-Source Inc	214-637-4064					
•	•	•	•	•	Atlantis Agency [SOP]	817-896-9337				•	•
		•	•		B & B Info Search	817-774-1310					
•	•	•	•	•	Bray & Freeman LP [SOP]	817-596-9255		•	•	•	•
•	•	•	•	•	Court & Public Records Service Inc	800-856-0585		•	•	•	•
		•	•		Crimecheck Research Services	281-288-6930					
			•		Dataprompt Corporation	214-390-2530					
•	•			•	DeedSearcher Title Research Services	281-375-8480		•	•	•	
•	•	•	•	•	Info2go	817-656-1997		•	•	•	•
	•	•		•	Land Records of Texas	800-678-8016		•	•	•	
•	•	•	•	•	Mendenhall Information Services	940-696-0758		•	•	•	•
•	•	•	•	•	Quick Search	214-358-2840		•	•	•	•
•	•	•	•	•	Security Information Service Inc [SOP]	800-525-5747		•	•	•	•
•	•	•	•	•	Segovia & Associates [SOP]	877-573-7833			•		•
•	•	•	•	•	Super Search Inc [SOP]	800-687-5553		•	•	•	
•	•	•	•	•	Taylor Research & Investigations [SOP]	972-991-5045		•	•	•	•
				•	Title Info	817-244-7757			•	•	

DT	BK	CV	CR	PR	←Courts	JONES	Recording→	UC	RE	TX	VS
•	•	•		•	Abstracts/Trustees of Texas	888-452-0331		•	•	•	
		•		•	Fisher/Jones Title Co (Anson)	325-823-3236		•	•	•	•
	•	•		•	Land Records of Texas	800-678-8016		•	•	•	
•	•	•	•	•	MS Document Services Inc	800-292-3868		•	•	•	•

DT	BK	CV	CR	PR	←Courts	KARNES	Recording→	UC	RE	TX	VS
•	•	•		•	Abstracts/Trustees of Texas	888-452-0331		•	•	•	
		•		•	Karnes Land Title Co Inc	830-780-2221		•	•	•	•
	•	•		•	Land Records of Texas	800-678-8016		•	•	•	

DT	BK	CV	CR	PR			UC	RE	TX	VS
•	•	•	•	•	Tyler-McLennon Choicepoint	512-334-6244	•	•	•	•

DT	BK	CV	CR	PR	←COURTS KAUFMAN	RECORDING→	UC	RE	TX	VS
•	•	•		•	Abstracts/Trustees of Texas	888-452-0331	•	•	•	
		•	•		Accu-Source Inc	214-637-4064				
•		•	•		CLUSO Inc	866-30-CLUSO			•	
•	•	•	•	•	Court & Public Records Service Inc	800-856-0585	•	•	•	•
			•		Dataprompt Corporation	214-390-2530				
	•	•		•	Land Records of Texas	800-678-8016	•	•	•	
•	•	•	•	•	Nell Watkins & Associates	972-226-8811	•	•	•	•
			•		Princeton Data Search Inc	469-474-1025		•	•	
•	•	•	•	•	Quick Search	214-358-2840	•	•	•	•
•	•	•	•	•	Security Information Service Inc [SOP]	800-525-5747	•	•	•	•
•	•	•	•	•	Taylor Research & Investigations [SOP]	972-991-5045	•	•	•	•
•	•	•	•		Texsearch #A09479 [SOP]	903-786-4636	•	•	•	
					TOB Public Records Research	214-358-4744	•	•	•	
•	•	•	•	•	Tyler-McLennon Choicepoint	512-334-6244	•	•	•	•
		•	•	•	Watkins Investigations [SOP]	972-926-6011	•	•	•	

DT	BK	CV	CR	PR	←COURTS KENDALL	RECORDING→	UC	RE	TX	VS
•	•	•		•	Abstracts/Trustees of Texas	888-452-0331	•	•	•	
	•	•		•	Land Records of Texas	800-678-8016	•	•	•	
•	•	•	•	•	Property Research & Documentation Service Inc	210-520-7884	•	•	•	•
•	•	•	•	•	Morris Todd [SOP]	210-673-4690	•	•	•	•
•	•	•	•	•	Tyler-McLennon Choicepoint	512-334-6244	•	•	•	•

DT	BK	CV	CR	PR	←COURTS KENEDY	RECORDING→	UC	RE	TX	VS
•	•	•		•	Abstracts/Trustees of Texas	888-452-0331	•	•	•	
•	•	•	•	•	Corpus Christi Court Services	361-887-8122	•	•	•	•
	•	•		•	Land Records of Texas	800-678-8016	•	•	•	

DT	BK	CV	CR	PR	←COURTS KENT	RECORDING→	UC	RE	TX	VS
•	•	•		•	Abstracts/Trustees of Texas	888-452-0331	•	•	•	
		•		•	Caprock Title Co	432-687-3232		•	•	
•	•	•	•	•	Davick Services	800-658-6656	•	•	•	
	•	•		•	Land Records of Texas	800-678-8016	•	•	•	

DT	BK	CV	CR	PR	←COURTS KERR	RECORDING→	UC	RE	TX	VS
•	•	•		•	Abstracts/Trustees of Texas	888-452-0331	•	•	•	
	•	•		•	Land Records of Texas	800-678-8016	•	•	•	
•	•	•	•	•	Property Research & Documentation Service Inc	210-520-7884	•	•	•	•
•	•	•	•	•	Morris Todd [SOP]	210-673-4690	•	•	•	•
•	•	•	•	•	Tyler-McLennon Choicepoint	512-334-6244	•	•	•	•

DT	BK	CV	CR	PR	←COURTS KIMBLE	RECORDING→	UC	RE	TX	VS
•	•	•		•	Abstracts/Trustees of Texas	888-452-0331	•	•	•	
	•	•		•	Land Records of Texas	800-678-8016	•	•	•	

DT	BK	CV	CR	PR	←COURTS KING	RECORDING→	UC	RE	TX	VS
•	•	•		•	Abstracts/Trustees of Texas	888-452-0331	•	•	•	
		•		•	Caprock Title Co	432-687-3232		•	•	
•	•	•	•	•	Davick Services	800-658-6656	•	•	•	
				•	Jones & Renfrow Abstracters	806-492-3573	•	•	•	•
	•	•		•	Land Records of Texas	800-678-8016	•	•	•	

DT	BK	CV	CR	PR	←COURTS KINNEY	RECORDING→	UC	RE	TX	VS
•	•	•		•	Abstracts/Trustees of Texas	888-452-0331	•	•	•	
	•	•		•	Land Records of Texas	800-678-8016	•	•	•	

DT	BK	CV	CR	PR	←COURTS KLEBERG	RECORDING→	UC	RE	TX	VS
•	•	•		•	Abstracts/Trustees of Texas	888-452-0331	•	•	•	

DT	BK	CV	CR	PR	←Courts	Recording→	UC	RE	TX	VS
•	•	•	•	•	Condor Inv [SOP]	361-881-8977	•	•	•	•
•	•	•	•	•	Corpus Christi Court Services	361-887-8122	•	•	•	•
			•		Dataprompt Corporation	214-390-2530				
		•	•	•	Information Protective Services Inc (IPS) [SOP]	888-720-3784	•	•	•	
•	•	•	•	•	Brenda Kolle/Title Abstractor	361-852-8236	•	•	•	
	•	•		•	Land Records of Texas	800-678-8016	•	•	•	
•	•	•	•	•	Shawver & Associates	800-364-2333	•	•	•	•
					South Texas Title and Trustee Services	956-412-3413	•	•	•	
•	•	•	•	•	Texas Civil Process [SOP]	800-976-9595	•	•	•	•
•	•	•	•	•	Tyler-McLennon Choicepoint	512-334-6244	•	•	•	•
DT	**BK**	**CV**	**CR**	**PR**	**←Courts** **Knox**	**Recording→**	**UC**	**RE**	**TX**	**VS**
•	•	•		•	Abstracts/Trustees of Texas	888-452-0331	•	•	•	
•	•	•	•	•	Davick Services	800-658-6656	•	•	•	
	•	•		•	Land Records of Texas	800-678-8016	•	•	•	
•	•	•	•	•	Mendenhall Information Services	940-696-0758	•	•	•	•
•	•	•		•	Superior Process Svc [SOP]	888-230-2663	•	•	•	•
DT	**BK**	**CV**	**CR**	**PR**	**←Courts** **La Salle**	**Recording→**	**UC**	**RE**	**TX**	**VS**
•	•	•		•	Abstracts/Trustees of Texas	888-452-0331	•	•	•	
					Border Title Group	956-791-5810	•	•	•	
	•	•		•	Land Records of Texas	800-678-8016	•	•	•	
DT	**BK**	**CV**	**CR**	**PR**	**←Courts** **Lamar**	**Recording→**	**UC**	**RE**	**TX**	**VS**
•	•	•		•	Abstracts/Trustees of Texas	888-452-0331	•	•	•	
		•	•		Accu-Source Inc	214-637-4064				
			•		Dataprompt Corporation	214-390-2530				
•		•	•		Kota Cornelius Kruse & Assoc	903-783-1883	•	•	•	
	•	•		•	Land Records of Texas	800-678-8016	•	•	•	
					Pat Stephens	903-583-5215		•	•	
•	•	•	•	•	Tyler-McLennon Choicepoint	512-334-6244	•	•	•	•
DT	**BK**	**CV**	**CR**	**PR**	**←Courts** **Lamb**	**Recording→**	**UC**	**RE**	**TX**	**VS**
•	•	•		•	Abstracts/Trustees of Texas	888-452-0331	•	•	•	
•	•	•	•	•	Davick Services	800-658-6656	•	•	•	
	•	•		•	Land Records of Texas	800-678-8016	•	•	•	
DT	**BK**	**CV**	**CR**	**PR**	**←Courts** **Lampasas**	**Recording→**	**UC**	**RE**	**TX**	**VS**
•	•	•		•	Abstracts/Trustees of Texas	888-452-0331	•	•	•	
•	•	•			Carma Austin	254-634-1701	•		•	
	•	•		•	Land Records of Texas	800-678-8016	•	•	•	
DT	**BK**	**CV**	**CR**	**PR**	**←Courts** **Lavaca**	**Recording→**	**UC**	**RE**	**TX**	**VS**
•	•	•		•	Abstracts/Trustees of Texas	888-452-0331	•	•	•	
	•	•		•	Land Records of Texas	800-678-8016	•	•	•	
•	•	•	•	•	Property Research & Documentation Service Inc	210-520-7884	•	•	•	•
DT	**BK**	**CV**	**CR**	**PR**	**←Courts** **Lee**	**Recording→**	**UC**	**RE**	**TX**	**VS**
•	•	•		•	Abstracts/Trustees of Texas	888-452-0331	•	•	•	
	•	•		•	Land Records of Texas	800-678-8016	•	•	•	
•		•		•	Lee County Land & Abstract	979-542-3636	•	•	•	
•	•	•	•	•	MS Document Services Inc	800-292-3868	•	•	•	•
DT	**BK**	**CV**	**CR**	**PR**	**←Courts** **Leon**	**Recording→**	**UC**	**RE**	**TX**	**VS**
•	•	•		•	Abstracts/Trustees of Texas	888-452-0331	•	•	•	
		•		•	Guaranty Title Co (Centerville)	903-536-2133	•	•	•	•
	•	•		•	Land Records of Texas	800-678-8016	•	•	•	
DT	**BK**	**CV**	**CR**	**PR**	**←Courts** **Liberty**	**Recording→**	**UC**	**RE**	**TX**	**VS**
•	•	•		•	Abstracts/Trustees of Texas	888-452-0331	•	•	•	
•	•	•			All State Document Services	888-246-8180	•	•	•	•

DT	BK	CV	CR	PR	←Courts	Recording→	UC	RE	TX	VS
		•	•		Don W Caskey	281-422-7527	•		•	
	•	•	•	•	Courthouse Specialists	800-925-4225	•	•	•	
•	•	•	•	•	ELH Contracting Inc Independent Land & Title Abstractor	409-832-5793	•	•	•	•
	•	•		•	Land Records of Texas	800-678-8016	•	•	•	
•	•	•	•	•	The Research Staff Inc	800-822-3584	•	•	•	
•	•	•	•	•	Tyler-McLennon Choicepoint	512-334-6244	•	•	•	•

DT	BK	CV	CR	PR	←Courts **LIMESTONE**	Recording→	UC	RE	TX	VS
•	•	•		•	Abstracts/Trustees of Texas	888-452-0331	•	•	•	
			•		Dataprompt Corporation	214-390-2530				
				•	Groesbeck Abstract & Title Co d/b/a Limestone County Title Company	254-729-3806	•	•	•	•
	•	•		•	Land Records of Texas	800-678-8016	•	•	•	

DT	BK	CV	CR	PR	←Courts **LIPSCOMB**	Recording→	UC	RE	TX	VS
•	•	•		•	Abstracts/Trustees of Texas	888-452-0331	•	•	•	
	•	•		•	Land Records of Texas	800-678-8016	•	•	•	

DT	BK	CV	CR	PR	←Courts **LIVE OAK**	Recording→	UC	RE	TX	VS
•	•	•		•	Abstracts/Trustees of Texas	888-452-0331	•	•	•	
•	•	•	•	•	Brenda Kolle/Title Abstractor	361-852-8236	•	•	•	
	•	•		•	Land Records of Texas	800-678-8016	•	•	•	
•	•	•	•	•	Texas Civil Process [SOP]	800-976-9595	•	•	•	•

DT	BK	CV	CR	PR	←Courts **LLANO**	Recording→	UC	RE	TX	VS
•	•	•		•	Abstracts/Trustees of Texas	888-452-0331	•	•	•	
	•	•		•	Land Records of Texas	800-678-8016	•	•	•	
•	•	•	•	•	Tyler-McLennon Choicepoint	512-334-6244	•	•	•	•

DT	BK	CV	CR	PR	←Courts **LOVING**	Recording→	UC	RE	TX	VS
•	•	•		•	Abstracts/Trustees of Texas	888-452-0331	•	•	•	
	•	•		•	Land Records of Texas	800-678-8016	•	•	•	
•	•	•		•	Stewart Title of Midland Inc	432-687-3355		•		

DT	BK	CV	CR	PR	←Courts **LUBBOCK**	Recording→	UC	RE	TX	VS
•	•	•		•	Abstracts/Trustees of Texas	888-452-0331	•	•	•	
			•		Dataprompt Corporation	214-390-2530				
•	•	•	•	•	Davick Services	800-658-6656	•	•	•	
	•	•		•	Land Records of Texas	800-678-8016	•	•	•	
•	•	•	•	•	Tyler-McLennon Choicepoint	512-334-6244	•	•	•	•
•	•	•	•	•	US Legal Support of Lubbock [SOP]	877-947-8500	•	•	•	•

DT	BK	CV	CR	PR	←Courts **LYNN**	Recording→	UC	RE	TX	VS
•	•	•		•	Abstracts/Trustees of Texas	888-452-0331	•	•	•	
•	•	•	•	•	Davick Services	800-658-6656	•	•	•	
	•	•		•	Land Records of Texas	800-678-8016	•	•	•	

DT	BK	CV	CR	PR	←Courts **MADISON**	Recording→	UC	RE	TX	VS
•	•	•		•	Abstracts/Trustees of Texas	888-452-0331	•	•	•	
	•	•		•	Land Records of Texas	800-678-8016	•	•	•	
		•		•	Landmark Title Co of Madison County	936-348-5618	•	•	•	

DT	BK	CV	CR	PR	←Courts **MARION**	Recording→	UC	RE	TX	VS
•	•	•		•	Abstracts/Trustees of Texas	888-452-0331	•	•	•	
	•	•		•	Land Records of Texas	800-678-8016	•	•	•	
		•		•	M & M Title / Mitchell Co	318-798-1198	•	•	•	
•	•	•	•	•	Tyler-McLennon Choicepoint	512-334-6244	•	•	•	•

DT	BK	CV	CR	PR	←Courts **MARTIN**	Recording→	UC	RE	TX	VS
•	•	•		•	Abstracts/Trustees of Texas	888-452-0331	•	•	•	
•	•	•	•	•	Davick Services	800-658-6656	•	•	•	
	•	•		•	Land Records of Texas	800-678-8016	•	•	•	
•	•	•		•	Stewart Title of Midland Inc	432-687-3355		•		

DT	BK	CV	CR	PR	←COURTS **MASON** RECORDING→		UC	RE	TX	VS
•	•	•		•	Abstracts/Trustees of Texas	888-452-0331	•	•	•	
•		•		•	First Mason Title Co	325-347-6388	•	•	•	•
	•	•		•	Land Records of Texas	800-678-8016	•	•	•	

DT	BK	CV	CR	PR	←COURTS **MATAGORDA** RECORDING→		UC	RE	TX	VS
•	•	•		•	Abstracts/Trustees of Texas	888-452-0331	•	•	•	
•	•	•			All State Document Services	888-246-8180	•	•	•	•
				•	Bay City Abstract & Title	979-245-6321	•	•	•	
•	•			•	DeedSearcher Title Research Services	281-375-8480	•	•	•	
	•	•		•	Land Records of Texas	800-678-8016	•	•	•	
•	•	•	•	•	The Research Staff Inc	800-822-3584	•	•	•	

DT	BK	CV	CR	PR	←COURTS **MAVERICK** RECORDING→		UC	RE	TX	VS
•	•	•		•	Abstracts/Trustees of Texas	888-452-0331	•	•	•	
		•	•	•	Border Legal Services [SOP]	830-773-0525			•	•
					Border Title Group	956-791-5810	•	•	•	
				•	Border Title Group	830-773-0555	•	•	•	
	•	•		•	Land Records of Texas	800-678-8016	•	•	•	

DT	BK	CV	CR	PR	←COURTS **MCCULLOCH** RECORDING→		UC	RE	TX	VS
•	•	•		•	Abstracts/Trustees of Texas	888-452-0331	•	•	•	
	•	•		•	Land Records of Texas	800-678-8016	•	•	•	

DT	BK	CV	CR	PR	←COURTS **MCLENNAN** RECORDING→		UC	RE	TX	VS
•	•	•		•	Abstracts/Trustees of Texas	888-452-0331	•	•	•	
•	•	•	•	•	Attorney Civil Process Service [SOP]	254-755-6447				
•	•	•			Carma Austin	254-634-1701	•		•	
•	•	•	•	•	BG Criminal Research	254-755-6808	•		•	
•		•		•	John Blackburn	210-867-0399	•	•	•	
		•	•		Crimecheck Research Services	281-288-6930				
•	•	•	•	•	Harvey Public Records Inc	254-662-6265	•	•	•	•
	•	•		•	Land Records of Texas	800-678-8016	•	•	•	
					Search Enterprises	254-752-2057		•	•	
•	•	•	•		Texsearch #A09479 [SOP]	903-786-4636	•	•	•	
•	•	•	•	•	Tyler-McLennon Choicepoint	512-334-6244	•	•	•	•

DT	BK	CV	CR	PR	←COURTS **MCMULLEN** RECORDING→		UC	RE	TX	VS
•	•	•		•	Abstracts/Trustees of Texas	888-452-0331	•	•	•	
	•	•		•	Land Records of Texas	800-678-8016	•	•	•	

DT	BK	CV	CR	PR	←COURTS **MEDINA** RECORDING→		UC	RE	TX	VS
•	•	•		•	Abstracts/Trustees of Texas	888-452-0331	•	•	•	
		•	•		Crimecheck Research Services	281-288-6930				
	•	•		•	Land Records of Texas	800-678-8016	•	•	•	
•	•	•	•	•	Property Research & Documentation Service Inc	210-520-7884	•	•	•	•
•	•	•	•	•	Morris Todd [SOP]	210-673-4690	•	•	•	•

DT	BK	CV	CR	PR	←COURTS **MENARD** RECORDING→		UC	RE	TX	VS
•	•	•		•	Abstracts/Trustees of Texas	888-452-0331	•	•	•	
	•	•		•	Land Records of Texas	800-678-8016	•	•	•	
		•	•	•	Ben Neel	325-396-2351	•	•	•	•

DT	BK	CV	CR	PR	←COURTS **MIDLAND** RECORDING→		UC	RE	TX	VS
•	•	•		•	Abstracts/Trustees of Texas	888-452-0331	•	•	•	
•	•	•	•	•	Davick Services	800-658-6656	•	•	•	
	•	•		•	Land Records of Texas	800-678-8016	•	•	•	
•	•	•	•		Permian Court Reporters Inc [SOP]	432-683-3032				
•	•	•		•	Stewart Title of Midland Inc	432-687-3355		•		
•	•	•	•		Texsearch #A09479 [SOP]	903-786-4636	•	•	•	
•	•	•	•	•	Tyler-McLennon Choicepoint	512-334-6244	•	•	•	•

Milam

DT	BK	CV	CR	PR	←Courts	Recording→	UC	RE	TX	VS
•	•	•		•	Abstracts/Trustees of Texas	888-452-0331	•	•	•	
•	•	•			Carma Austin	254-634-1701	•		•	
				•	Botts Title Co	254-697-6962	•	•	•	•
	•	•		•	Land Records of Texas	800-678-8016	•	•	•	
•	•	•	•	•	Tyler-McLennon Choicepoint	512-334-6244	•	•	•	•

Mills

DT	BK	CV	CR	PR	←Courts	Recording→	UC	RE	TX	VS
•	•	•		•	Abstracts/Trustees of Texas	888-452-0331	•	•	•	
	•	•		•	Land Records of Texas	800-678-8016	•	•	•	

Mitchell

DT	BK	CV	CR	PR	←Courts	Recording→	UC	RE	TX	VS
•	•	•		•	Abstracts/Trustees of Texas	888-452-0331	•	•	•	
•	•	•	•	•	Davick Services	800-658-6656	•	•	•	
	•	•		•	Land Records of Texas	800-678-8016	•	•	•	
•	•	•	•	•	MS Document Services Inc	800-292-3868	•	•	•	•

Montague

DT	BK	CV	CR	PR	←Courts	Recording→	UC	RE	TX	VS
•	•	•		•	Abstracts/Trustees of Texas	888-452-0331	•	•	•	
	•	•		•	Land Records of Texas	800-678-8016	•	•	•	
•	•	•	•	•	Mendenhall Information Services	940-696-0758	•	•	•	•
•	•	•		•	Superior Process Svc [SOP]	888-230-2663		•	•	•

Montgomery

DT	BK	CV	CR	PR	←Courts	Recording→	UC	RE	TX	VS
•	•	•		•	Abstracts/Trustees of Texas	888-452-0331	•	•	•	
•	•	•			All State Document Services	888-246-8180	•	•	•	•
•	•	•		•	Amerititle Abstract & Research Inc	800-856-1228	•	•	•	
•	•	•	•	•	Asset Research Group	713-864-2536	•	•	•	•
•	•	•		•	BAST Research Services Inc	713-721-7077	•	•	•	
•	•	•	•	•	Compex Legal Services [SOP]	713-861-3900				•
•	•	•	•	•	Court Record Research Inc	800-552-3353	•	•	•	•
		•	•	•	Courthouse Filings Inc	936-273-6427	•	•	•	•
	•	•	•	•	Courthouse Specialists	800-925-4225	•	•	•	
		•	•		Crimecheck Research Services	281-288-6930				
•	•			•	DeedSearcher Title Research Services	281-375-8480	•	•	•	
					Fox Hunt	713-772-8018	•	•	•	
•	•	•	•	•	Garza-McNamee Agency Inc	888-262-6221	•	•	•	
•	•	•	•	•	Houston Court Services Inc [SOP]	713-655-0555	•	•	•	•
•	•	•	•	•	John V Eriksson Group Inc	281-488-0018	•	•	•	•
•	•	•	•	•	Kimmons Security Services Inc [SOP]	281-679-0070	•	•	•	•
	•	•		•	Land Records of Texas	800-678-8016	•	•	•	
•	•	•	•		Mach 5 Couriers Inc [SOP]	800-593-2023				
		•	•	•	Metro Research & Inv	800-364-3590	•	•	•	•
•	•	•	•	•	PM Clinton International Investigation	866-686-6864	•	•	•	
•		•	•		The Partnership	877-558-9928				
•	•	•	•	•	The Research Staff Inc	800-822-3584	•		•	
•	•	•	•	•	Tyler-McLennon Choicepoint	512-334-6244	•	•	•	•

Moore

DT	BK	CV	CR	PR	←Courts	Recording→	UC	RE	TX	VS
•	•	•		•	Abstracts/Trustees of Texas	888-452-0331	•	•	•	
	•	•		•	Land Records of Texas	800-678-8016	•	•	•	
•	•	•		•	Rollins Research Ltd	806-353-7886	•	•	•	

Morris

DT	BK	CV	CR	PR	←Courts	Recording→	UC	RE	TX	VS
•	•	•		•	Abstracts/Trustees of Texas	888-452-0331	•	•	•	
•	•	•			Joe Gillenwater [SOP]	870-772-2923	•	•	•	
	•	•		•	Land Records of Texas	800-678-8016	•	•	•	
•	•	•	•	•	Tyler-McLennon Choicepoint	512-334-6244	•	•	•	•

DT	BK	CV	CR	PR	←COURTS	MOTLEY	RECORDING→	UC	RE	TX	VS
•	•	•		•	Abstracts/Trustees of Texas		888-452-0331	•	•	•	
•	•	•	•	•	Davick Services		800-658-6656	•	•	•	
				•	Jones & Renfrow Abstracters		806-492-3573	•	•	•	•
	•	•		•	Land Records of Texas		800-678-8016	•	•	•	

DT	BK	CV	CR	PR	←COURTS	NACOGDOCHES	RECORDING→	UC	RE	TX	VS
•	•	•		•	Abstracts/Trustees of Texas		888-452-0331	•	•	•	
		•	•	•	Community Title Co		936-559-7900	•	•	•	•
•		•	•	•	East Tex Records Research		936-824-3724	•	•	•	
•	•	•	•	•	Investigative Concepts		903-677-9473				
	•	•		•	Land Records of Texas		800-678-8016	•	•	•	
					Record Time Research		936-632-5150		•		
•	•	•	•	•	Tyler-McLennon Choicepoint		512-334-6244	•	•	•	•

DT	BK	CV	CR	PR	←COURTS	NAVARRO	RECORDING→	UC	RE	TX	VS
•	•	•		•	Abstracts/Trustees of Texas		888-452-0331	•	•	•	
		•	•		B & B Info Search		817-774-1310				
•	•	•	•	•	Court & Public Records Service Inc		800-856-0585	•	•	•	•
	•	•		•	Land Records of Texas		800-678-8016	•	•	•	
				•	Navarro County Abstract Co		903-874-3768		•	•	

DT	BK	CV	CR	PR	←COURTS	NEWTON	RECORDING→	UC	RE	TX	VS
•	•	•		•	Abstracts/Trustees of Texas		888-452-0331	•	•	•	
				•	Garland Smith Abstract Co		409-384-2571	•	•	•	•
	•	•		•	Land Records of Texas		800-678-8016	•	•	•	

DT	BK	CV	CR	PR	←COURTS	NOLAN	RECORDING→	UC	RE	TX	VS
•	•	•		•	Abstracts/Trustees of Texas		888-452-0331	•	•	•	
•	•	•	•	•	Davick Services		800-658-6656	•	•	•	
	•	•		•	Land Records of Texas		800-678-8016	•	•	•	
•	•	•	•	•	MS Document Services Inc		800-292-3868	•	•	•	•

DT	BK	CV	CR	PR	←COURTS	NUECES	RECORDING→	UC	RE	TX	VS
•	•	•		•	Abstracts/Trustees of Texas		888-452-0331	•	•	•	
		•	•		Accu-Source Inc		214-637-4064				
•	•	•	•	•	Brack Warren & Associates		361-884-8000	•	•	•	•
•	•	•	•	•	Condor Inv [SOP]		361-881-8977	•	•	•	•
•	•	•	•	•	Corpus Christi Court Services		361-887-8122	•	•	•	•
			•		Dataprompt Corporation		214-390-2530				
•	•			•	DeedSearcher Title Research Services		281-375-8480	•	•	•	
•	•	•	•	•	FYII Acct [SOP]		563-299-5683	•	•	•	•
		•	•	•	Inquest Investigations, LLC		903-893-2020	•	•	•	
•	•	•	•	•	Brenda Kolle/Title Abstractor		361-852-8236	•	•	•	
	•	•		•	Land Records of Texas		800-678-8016	•	•	•	
•	•	•	•	•	Professional Civil Process (Austin) [SOP]		800-950-7493	•	•	•	•
•	•	•	•	•	Shawver & Associates		800-364-2333	•	•	•	•
					South Texas Title and Trustee Services		956-412-3413	•	•	•	
•	•	•	•	•	Texas Civil Process [SOP]		800-976-9595	•	•	•	•
•	•	•	•		Texsearch #A09479 [SOP]		903-786-4636	•	•	•	
•	•	•	•	•	Tyler-McLennon Choicepoint		512-334-6244	•	•	•	•
		•	•		Your Information Source Inc		800-644-9668				

DT	BK	CV	CR	PR	←COURTS	OCHILTREE	RECORDING→	UC	RE	TX	VS
•	•	•		•	Abstracts/Trustees of Texas		888-452-0331	•	•	•	
	•	•		•	Land Records of Texas		800-678-8016	•	•	•	

DT	BK	CV	CR	PR	←COURTS	OLDHAM	RECORDING→	UC	RE	TX	VS
•	•	•		•	Abstracts/Trustees of Texas		888-452-0331	•	•	•	
•	•	•	•	•	Davick Services		800-658-6656	•	•	•	

DT	BK	CV	CR	PR	←Courts	Recording→	UC	RE	TX	VS
	•	•		•	Land Records of Texas	800-678-8016	•	•	•	
•	•	•		•	Rollins Research Ltd	806-353-7886	•	•	•	

DT	BK	CV	CR	PR	←Courts **Orange**	Recording→	UC	RE	TX	VS
•	•	•		•	Abstracts/Trustees of Texas	888-452-0331	•	•	•	
•	•	•			All State Document Services	888-246-8180	•	•	•	•
•	•	•	•	•	ELH Contracting Inc Independent Land & Title Abstractor	409-832-5793	•	•	•	•
	•	•		•	Land Records of Texas	800-678-8016	•	•	•	
•		•	•		The Partnership	877-558-9928				
•	•	•	•	•	The Research Staff Inc	800-822-3584	•	•	•	

DT	BK	CV	CR	PR	←Courts **Palo Pinto**	Recording→	UC	RE	TX	VS
•	•	•		•	Abstracts/Trustees of Texas	888-452-0331	•	•	•	
		•	•		B & B Info Search	817-774-1310				
•	•	•	•	•	Bray & Freeman LP [SOP]	817-596-9255	•	•	•	•
		•		•	Elliott & Waldron Abstr Co of Palo Pinto	940-325-6564	•	•	•	•
	•	•		•	Land Records of Texas	800-678-8016	•	•	•	
•	•	•	•	•	Mendenhall Information Services	940-696-0758	•	•	•	•
•	•	•	•	•	MS Document Services Inc	800-292-3868	•	•	•	•

DT	BK	CV	CR	PR	←Courts **Panola**	Recording→	UC	RE	TX	VS
•	•	•		•	Abstracts/Trustees of Texas	888-452-0331	•	•	•	
	•	•		•	Land Records of Texas	800-678-8016	•	•	•	
		•		•	M & M Title / Mitchell Co	318-798-1198	•	•	•	
•	•	•	•	•	Tyler-McLennon Choicepoint	512-334-6244	•	•	•	•

DT	BK	CV	CR	PR	←Courts **Parker**	Recording→	UC	RE	TX	VS
•	•	•		•	Abstracts/Trustees of Texas	888-452-0331	•	•	•	
		•	•		Accu-Source Inc	214-637-4064				
•	•	•	•	•	Atlantis Agency [SOP]	817-896-9337			•	•
		•	•		B & B Info Search	817-774-1310				
•	•	•	•	•	Bray & Freeman LP [SOP]	817-596-9255	•	•	•	•
			•		Dataprompt Corporation	214-390-2530				
•	•	•	•	•	Info2go	817-656-1997	•	•	•	•
	•	•		•	Land Records of Texas	800-678-8016	•	•	•	
•	•	•	•	•	Mendenhall Information Services	940-696-0758	•	•	•	•
•	•	•	•	•	MS Document Services Inc	800-292-3868	•	•	•	•
•	•	•	•	•	Segovia & Associates [SOP]	877-573-7833		•		•
•	•	•	•	•	Super Search Inc [SOP]	800-687-5553	•	•	•	
•	•	•	•	•	Taylor Research & Investigations [SOP]	972-991-5045	•	•	•	•
				•	Title Info	817-244-7757		•	•	
•	•	•	•	•	Tyler-McLennon Choicepoint	512-334-6244	•	•	•	•

DT	BK	CV	CR	PR	←Courts **Parmer**	Recording→	UC	RE	TX	VS
•	•	•		•	Abstracts/Trustees of Texas	888-452-0331	•	•	•	
•	•	•	•	•	Davick Services	800-658-6656	•	•	•	
		•	•	•	Farwell Abstract Co Inc	806-481-9992		•	•	
	•	•		•	Land Records of Texas	800-678-8016	•	•	•	

DT	BK	CV	CR	PR	←Courts **Pecos**	Recording→	UC	RE	TX	VS
•	•	•		•	Abstracts/Trustees of Texas	888-452-0331	•	•	•	
					Elliott & Waldron Abstract Co - Pecos	432-336-5214	•	•	•	
	•	•		•	Land Records of Texas	800-678-8016	•	•	•	

DT	BK	CV	CR	PR	←Courts **Polk**	Recording→	UC	RE	TX	VS
•	•	•		•	Abstracts/Trustees of Texas	888-452-0331	•	•	•	
	•	•		•	Land Records of Texas	800-678-8016	•	•	•	

DT	BK	CV	CR	PR	←Courts **Potter**	Recording→	UC	RE	TX	VS
•	•	•		•	Abstracts/Trustees of Texas	888-452-0331	•	•	•	
		•	•		Crimecheck Research Services	281-288-6930				

DT	BK	CV	CR	PR	Name	Phone	UC	RE	TX	VS
•	•	•	•	•	Davick Services	800-658-6656	•	•	•	
	•	•		•	Land Records of Texas	800-678-8016	•	•	•	
•	•	•	•	•	Patricia Chambers Inv [SOP]	806-359-5989	•	•	•	
•	•	•		•	Rollins Research Ltd	806-353-7886	•	•	•	
•	•	•	•		Texsearch #A09479 [SOP]	903-786-4636	•	•	•	
•	•	•	•	•	Tyler-McLennon Choicepoint	512-334-6244	•	•	•	•

DT	BK	CV	CR	PR	←Courts **PRESIDIO**	Recording→	UC	RE	TX	VS
•	•	•		•	Abstracts/Trustees of Texas	888-452-0331	•	•	•	
		•		•	Ellyson Abstract & Title Co of Brewster	432-837-5801	•	•	•	•
	•	•		•	Land Records of Texas	800-678-8016	•	•	•	
•	•	•	•	•	Presidio County Abstract	432-729-4264	•	•	•	

DT	BK	CV	CR	PR	←Courts **RAINS**	Recording→	UC	RE	TX	VS
		•		•	AAA Abstract & Title Co Inc (Texas) [SOP]	903-473-2233		•	•	
•	•	•		•	Abstracts/Trustees of Texas	888-452-0331	•	•	•	
	•	•		•	Land Records of Texas	800-678-8016	•	•	•	
•	•	•	•	•	Tyler-McLennon Choicepoint	512-334-6244	•	•	•	•

DT	BK	CV	CR	PR	←Courts **RANDALL**	Recording→	UC	RE	TX	VS
•	•	•		•	Abstracts/Trustees of Texas	888-452-0331	•	•	•	
		•	•		Crimecheck Research Services	281-288-6930				
•	•	•	•	•	Davick Services	800-658-6656	•	•	•	
	•	•		•	Land Records of Texas	800-678-8016	•	•	•	
•	•	•	•	•	Patricia Chambers Inv [SOP]	806-359-5989	•	•	•	
•	•	•		•	Rollins Research Ltd	806-353-7886	•	•	•	
•	•	•	•		Texsearch #A09479 [SOP]	903-786-4636	•	•	•	
•	•	•	•	•	Tyler-McLennon Choicepoint	512-334-6244	•	•	•	•

DT	BK	CV	CR	PR	←Courts **REAGAN**	Recording→	UC	RE	TX	VS
•	•	•		•	Abstracts/Trustees of Texas	888-452-0331	•	•	•	
	•	•		•	Land Records of Texas	800-678-8016	•	•	•	
•	•	•		•	Stewart Title of Midland Inc	432-687-3355		•		

DT	BK	CV	CR	PR	←Courts **REAL**	Recording→	UC	RE	TX	VS
•	•	•		•	Abstracts/Trustees of Texas	888-452-0331	•	•	•	
	•	•		•	Land Records of Texas	800-678-8016	•	•	•	
		•		•	Real County Title Co	830-232-5303	•	•	•	

DT	BK	CV	CR	PR	←Courts **RED RIVER**	Recording→	UC	RE	TX	VS
•	•	•		•	Abstracts/Trustees of Texas	888-452-0331	•	•	•	
•	•	•			Joe Gillenwater [SOP]	870-772-2923	•	•	•	
•		•	•		Kota Cornelius Kruse & Assoc	903-783-1883		•	•	
	•	•		•	Land Records of Texas	800-678-8016	•	•	•	
•	•	•	•	•	Tyler-McLennon Choicepoint	512-334-6244	•	•	•	•

DT	BK	CV	CR	PR	←Courts **REEVES**	Recording→	UC	RE	TX	VS
•	•	•		•	Abstracts/Trustees of Texas	888-452-0331	•	•	•	
	•	•		•	Land Records of Texas	800-678-8016	•	•	•	
•	•	•		•	Stewart Title of Midland Inc	432-687-3355		•		

DT	BK	CV	CR	PR	←Courts **REFUGIO**	Recording→	UC	RE	TX	VS
•	•	•		•	Abstracts/Trustees of Texas	888-452-0331	•	•	•	
•	•	•	•	•	Condor Inv [SOP]	361-881-8977	•	•	•	•
•	•	•	•	•	Brenda Kolle/Title Abstractor	361-852-8236	•	•	•	
	•	•		•	Land Records of Texas	800-678-8016	•	•	•	
•	•	•	•	•	Shawver & Associates	800-364-2333	•	•	•	•
•	•	•	•	•	Texas Civil Process [SOP]	800-976-9595	•	•	•	•
•	•	•	•	•	Tyler-McLennon Choicepoint	512-334-6244	•	•	•	•

DT	BK	CV	CR	PR	←Courts	**Roberts**	Recording→	UC	RE	TX	VS
•	•	•		•	Abstracts/Trustees of Texas		888-452-0331	•	•	•	
	•	•		•	Land Records of Texas		800-678-8016	•	•	•	
•	•	•		•	Rollins Research Ltd		806-353-7886	•	•	•	

DT	BK	CV	CR	PR	←Courts	**Robertson**	Recording→	UC	RE	TX	VS
•	•	•		•	Abstracts/Trustees of Texas		888-452-0331	•	•	•	
•	•	•			Carma Austin		254-634-1701	•		•	
		•		•	Guaranty Title Co of Robertson County Inc		979-828-4688	•	•	•	•
	•	•		•	Land Records of Texas		800-678-8016	•	•	•	

DT	BK	CV	CR	PR	←Courts	**Rockwall**	Recording→	UC	RE	TX	VS
•	•	•		•	Abstracts/Trustees of Texas		888-452-0331	•	•	•	
		•	•		Accu-Source Inc		214-637-4064				
					David C Bayoud		214-824-9944		•		
•		•	•		CLUSO Inc		866-30-CLUSO			•	
•	•	•	•	•	Court & Public Records Service Inc		800-856-0585	•	•	•	•
•	•	•	•	•	CRRG Inc		800-687-9030	•	•	•	•
			•		Dataprompt Corporation		214-390-2530				
•	•	•	•	•	Info2go		817-656-1997	•	•	•	•
	•	•		•	Land Records of Texas		800-678-8016	•	•	•	
•	•	•	•	•	Nell Watkins & Associates		972-226-8811	•	•	•	•
			•		Princeton Data Search Inc		469-474-1025		•	•	
•	•	•	•	•	Quick Search		214-358-2840	•	•	•	•
•	•	•	•	•	Security Information Service Inc [SOP]		800-525-5747	•	•	•	•
•	•	•	•	•	Taylor Research & Investigations [SOP]		972-991-5045	•	•	•	•
•	•	•	•		Texsearch #A09479 [SOP]		903-786-4636	•	•	•	
					TOB Public Records Research		214-358-4744	•	•	•	
•	•	•	•	•	Tyler-McLennon Choicepoint		512-334-6244	•	•	•	•
		•	•	•	Watkins Investigations [SOP]		972-926-6011	•	•	•	

DT	BK	CV	CR	PR	←Courts	**Runnels**	Recording→	UC	RE	TX	VS
•	•	•		•	Abstracts/Trustees of Texas		888-452-0331	•	•	•	
	•	•		•	Land Records of Texas		800-678-8016	•	•	•	
•	•	•	•	•	MS Document Services Inc		800-292-3868	•	•	•	•
		•	•	•	Surety Title Co of Ballinger		325-365-5713	•	•	•	•

DT	BK	CV	CR	PR	←Courts	**Rusk**	Recording→	UC	RE	TX	VS
•	•	•		•	Abstracts/Trustees of Texas		888-452-0331	•	•	•	
•		•	•	•	East Tex Records Research		936-824-3724	•	•	•	
	•	•		•	Land Records of Texas		800-678-8016	•	•	•	
		•		•	M & M Title / Mitchell Co		318-798-1198	•	•	•	
•	•	•	•	•	Tyler-McLennon Choicepoint		512-334-6244	•	•	•	•

DT	BK	CV	CR	PR	←Courts	**Sabine**	Recording→	UC	RE	TX	VS
•	•	•		•	Abstracts/Trustees of Texas		888-452-0331	•	•	•	
	•	•		•	Land Records of Texas		800-678-8016	•	•	•	

DT	BK	CV	CR	PR	←Courts	**San Augustine**	Recording→	UC	RE	TX	VS
•	•	•		•	Abstracts/Trustees of Texas		888-452-0331	•	•	•	
	•	•		•	Land Records of Texas		800-678-8016	•	•	•	

DT	BK	CV	CR	PR	←Courts	**San Jacinto**	Recording→	UC	RE	TX	VS
•	•	•		•	Abstracts/Trustees of Texas		888-452-0331	•	•	•	
	•	•	•	•	Courthouse Specialists		800-925-4225	•	•	•	
		•	•		Cheryl A Hayes		936-520-1036	•	•	•	
	•	•		•	Land Records of Texas		800-678-8016	•	•	•	

DT	BK	CV	CR	PR	←Courts	**San Patricio**	Recording→	UC	RE	TX	VS
•	•	•		•	Abstracts/Trustees of Texas		888-452-0331	•	•	•	
•	•	•	•	•	Condor Inv [SOP]		361-881-8977	•	•	•	•

DT	BK	CV	CR	PR	←Courts	Recording→	UC	RE	TX	VS
•	•	•	•	•	Corpus Christi Court Services	361-887-8122	•	•	•	•
•	•	•	•	•	FYII Acct [SOP]	563-299-5683	•	•	•	•
•	•	•	•	•	Brenda Kolle/Title Abstractor	361-852-8236	•	•	•	
	•	•		•	Land Records of Texas	800-678-8016	•	•	•	
•	•	•	•	•	Shawver & Associates	800-364-2333	•	•	•	•
•	•	•	•	•	Texas Civil Process [SOP]	800-976-9595	•	•	•	•
•	•	•	•	•	Tyler-McLennon Choicepoint	512-334-6244	•	•	•	•

DT	BK	CV	CR	PR	←Courts **San Saba**	Recording→	UC	RE	TX	VS
•	•	•		•	Abstracts/Trustees of Texas	888-452-0331	•	•	•	
	•	•		•	Land Records of Texas	800-678-8016	•	•	•	

DT	BK	CV	CR	PR	←Courts **Schleicher**	Recording→	UC	RE	TX	VS
•	•	•		•	Abstracts/Trustees of Texas	888-452-0331	•	•	•	
					Benton Abstract & Title Co	325-853-2631	•	•	•	
	•	•		•	Land Records of Texas	800-678-8016	•	•	•	

DT	BK	CV	CR	PR	←Courts **Scurry**	Recording→	UC	RE	TX	VS
•	•	•		•	Abstracts/Trustees of Texas	888-452-0331	•	•	•	
•	•	•	•	•	Davick Services	800-658-6656	•	•	•	
	•	•		•	Land Records of Texas	800-678-8016	•	•	•	
•	•	•	•	•	MS Document Services Inc	800-292-3868	•	•	•	•
•				•	Snyder Abstract & Title Co Inc	325-573-6339	•	•	•	

DT	BK	CV	CR	PR	←Courts **Shackelford**	Recording→	UC	RE	TX	VS
•	•	•		•	Abstracts/Trustees of Texas	888-452-0331	•	•	•	
		•		•	Albany Abstract Co	325-762-3077	•	•	•	•
	•	•		•	Land Records of Texas	800-678-8016	•	•	•	
•	•	•	•	•	MS Document Services Inc	800-292-3868	•	•	•	•

DT	BK	CV	CR	PR	←Courts **Shelby**	Recording→	UC	RE	TX	VS
•	•	•		•	Abstracts/Trustees of Texas	888-452-0331	•	•	•	
	•	•		•	Land Records of Texas	800-678-8016	•	•	•	
		•		•	M & M Title / Mitchell Co	318-798-1198	•	•	•	
•	•	•	•	•	Tyler-McLennon Choicepoint	512-334-6244	•	•	•	•

DT	BK	CV	CR	PR	←Courts **Sherman**	Recording→	UC	RE	TX	VS
•	•	•		•	Abstracts/Trustees of Texas	888-452-0331	•	•	•	
	•	•		•	Land Records of Texas	800-678-8016	•	•	•	

DT	BK	CV	CR	PR	←Courts **Smith**	Recording→	UC	RE	TX	VS
•	•	•		•	Abstracts/Trustees of Texas	888-452-0331	•	•	•	
•	•	•	•	•	Court & Public Records Service Inc	800-856-0585	•	•	•	•
			•		Dataprompt Corporation	214-390-2530				
•	•	•	•	•	East Texas Professional Svcs [SOP]	903-928-0117			•	•
	•	•		•	Land Records of Texas	800-678-8016	•	•	•	
		•		•	M & M Title / Mitchell Co	318-798-1198	•	•	•	
	•	•		•	Smith County Title Co	903-581-6400	•	•	•	
•	•	•	•	•	Tyler-McLennon Choicepoint	512-334-6244	•	•	•	•

DT	BK	CV	CR	PR	←Courts **Somervell**	Recording→	UC	RE	TX	VS
•	•	•		•	Abstracts/Trustees of Texas	888-452-0331	•	•	•	
		•	•		B & B Info Search	817-774-1310				
		•	•		Crimecheck Research Services	281-288-6930				
	•	•		•	Land Records of Texas	800-678-8016	•	•	•	
•	•	•	•	•	Mendenhall Information Services	940-696-0758	•	•	•	•
•	•	•	•	•	Super Search Inc [SOP]	800-687-5553	•	•	•	

DT	BK	CV	CR	PR	←Courts **Starr**	Recording→	UC	RE	TX	VS
•	•	•		•	Abstracts/Trustees of Texas	888-452-0331	•	•	•	
	•	•		•	Land Records of Texas	800-678-8016	•	•	•	

DT	BK	CV	CR	PR	Name	Phone	UC	RE	TX	VS
•	•	•	•	•	Professional Civil Process (McAllen) [SOP]	800-880-4223	•	•	•	•
•	•	•	•	•	Shawver & Associates	800-364-2333	•	•	•	•

DT	BK	CV	CR	PR	←Courts STEPHENS	Recording→	UC	RE	TX	VS
•	•	•		•	Abstracts/Trustees of Texas	888-452-0331	•	•	•	
	•	•		•	Land Records of Texas	800-678-8016	•	•	•	
•	•	•	•	•	MS Document Services Inc	800-292-3868	•	•	•	•
					Stephens County Abstract	254-559-9089	•	•	•	

DT	BK	CV	CR	PR	←Courts STERLING	Recording→	UC	RE	TX	VS
•	•	•		•	Abstracts/Trustees of Texas	888-452-0331	•	•	•	
	•	•		•	Land Records of Texas	800-678-8016	•	•	•	
				•	Sterling Title Co	325-378-2405	•	•	•	

DT	BK	CV	CR	PR	←Courts STONEWALL	Recording→	UC	RE	TX	VS
•	•	•		•	Abstracts/Trustees of Texas	888-452-0331	•	•	•	
		•		•	Caprock Title Co	432-687-3232		•	•	
				•	Consolidated Abstract Co	940-989-3566	•	•	•	•
•	•	•	•	•	Davick Services	800-658-6656	•	•	•	
	•	•		•	Land Records of Texas	800-678-8016	•	•	•	

DT	BK	CV	CR	PR	←Courts SUTTON	Recording→	UC	RE	TX	VS
•	•	•		•	Abstracts/Trustees of Texas	888-452-0331	•	•	•	
	•	•		•	Land Records of Texas	800-678-8016	•	•	•	
				•	Ben Neel	325-396-2351	•	•	•	•

DT	BK	CV	CR	PR	←Courts SWISHER	Recording→	UC	RE	TX	VS
•	•	•		•	Abstracts/Trustees of Texas	888-452-0331	•	•	•	
•	•	•	•	•	Davick Services	800-658-6656	•	•	•	
	•	•		•	Land Records of Texas	800-678-8016	•	•	•	
•	•	•		•	Rollins Research Ltd	806-353-7886	•	•	•	

DT	BK	CV	CR	PR	←Courts TARRANT	Recording→	UC	RE	TX	VS
•	•	•		•	Abstracts/Trustees of Texas	888-452-0331	•	•	•	
		•	•		Accu-Source Inc	214-637-4064				
		•		•	Ameristar Information Network	800-920-9270		•	•	•
•	•	•	•	•	ASA (Attorney Service Associates) [SOP]	972-394-1175	•	•	•	•
•	•	•	•		Asset Control Inc	877-277-3812	•	•	•	•
•	•	•	•	•	Atlantis Agency [SOP]	817-896-9337			•	•
•	•	•	•	•	Attorney's Service Bureau of Texas [SOP]	888-522-5297	•	•	•	•
		•	•		Background Information Systems Inc	800-687-0894				
					David C Bayoud	214-824-9944		•		
•	•	•	•	•	Bray & Freeman LP [SOP]	817-596-9255	•	•	•	•
•		•	•		CLUSO Inc	866-30-CLUSO			•	
•	•	•	•	•	Court & Public Records Service Inc	800-856-0585	•	•	•	•
		•	•		Crimecheck Research Services	281-288-6930				
•	•	•	•	•	CRRG Inc	800-687-9030	•	•	•	•
•	•	•	•		Data Screen Inc	817-294-7671	•			
			•		Dataprompt Corporation	214-390-2530				
•	•	•	•	•	DFW Court Services [SOP]	800-436-0516	•	•	•	
•		•	•		FP Resources	866-989-8999				
•	•	•	•		G.A. Public Record Services Inc	800-760-2468				
•	•	•	•		General Information Services	800-447-0798	•	•		
•	•	•	•		Hart & Associates Inc	866-429-4044			•	•
•	•	•	•	•	Info2go	817-656-1997	•	•	•	•
		•	•		Inquest Investigations, LLC	903-893-2020	•	•	•	
•	•	•	•	•	Kimmons Security Services Inc [SOP]	281-679-0070	•	•	•	•
	•	•		•	Land Records of Texas	800-678-8016	•	•	•	
•	•	•	•		Lone Star Inv & Recovery Inc	800-887-3890	•	•	•	•
•	•	•	•	•	Mendenhall Information Services	940-696-0758	•	•	•	•

DT	BK	CV	CR	PR	←Courts	Recording→	UC	RE	TX	VS
•	•	•	•		Minco Research	817-834-6744		•		
•	•	•	•	•	MS Document Services Inc	800-292-3868	•	•	•	•
•	•	•	•	•	PADIC Inc [SOP]	940-665-6130	•	•	•	•
•	•	•	•	•	Professional Civil Process (Austin) [SOP]	800-950-7493	•	•	•	•
•	•	•	•	•	Quick Search	214-358-2840	•	•	•	•
•	•	•	•	•	Reliable Courier [SOP]	214-637-4800			•	•
•	•	•	•		Research Specialists [SOP]	800-771-7547				
•	•	•	•	•	Security Information Service Inc [SOP]	800-525-5747	•	•	•	•
•	•	•	•	•	Segovia & Associates [SOP]	877-573-7833		•		•
		•	•		Spearhead Research - On Target Information	512-295-7298				
•	•	•	•		Spectrum Screening Inc	800-222-8199	•		•	
•	•	•	•	•	Super Search Inc [SOP]	800-687-5553	•	•	•	
•	•	•	•	•	Taylor Research & Investigations [SOP]	972-991-5045	•	•	•	•
		•	•		Tex Research	817-472-5997				
•	•	•	•	•	Texas Industrial Security Inc	214-634-2791			•	
•	•	•	•	•	Texas Subpoena & Process Svc [SOP]	800-717-3463	•	•	•	•
•	•	•	•		Texsearch #A09479 [SOP]	903-786-4636	•	•	•	
				•	Title Info	817-244-7757		•	•	
					TOB Public Records Research	214-358-4744	•	•	•	
•	•	•	•	•	Tyler-McLennon Choicepoint	512-334-6244	•	•	•	•
		•	•		Your Information Source Inc	800-644-9668				
DT	**BK**	**CV**	**CR**	**PR**	**←Courts**	**Taylor** / **Recording→**	**UC**	**RE**	**TX**	**VS**
•	•	•		•	Abstracts/Trustees of Texas	888-452-0331	•	•	•	
				•	Big Country Title	325-698-9195	•	•	•	•
	•	•		•	Land Records of Texas	800-678-8016	•	•	•	
•	•	•	•	•	MS Document Services Inc	800-292-3868	•	•	•	•
DT	**BK**	**CV**	**CR**	**PR**	**←Courts**	**Terrell** / **Recording→**	**UC**	**RE**	**TX**	**VS**
•	•	•		•	Abstracts/Trustees of Texas	888-452-0331	•	•	•	
	•	•		•	Land Records of Texas	800-678-8016	•	•	•	
DT	**BK**	**CV**	**CR**	**PR**	**←Courts**	**Terry** / **Recording→**	**UC**	**RE**	**TX**	**VS**
•	•	•		•	Abstracts/Trustees of Texas	888-452-0331	•	•	•	
		•		•	Brownfield Abstract & Title Co	806-637-9595	•	•	•	
•	•	•	•	•	Davick Services	800-658-6656	•	•	•	
	•	•		•	Land Records of Texas	800-678-8016	•	•	•	
DT	**BK**	**CV**	**CR**	**PR**	**←Courts**	**Throckmorton** / **Recording→**	**UC**	**RE**	**TX**	**VS**
•	•	•		•	Abstracts/Trustees of Texas	888-452-0331	•	•	•	
	•	•		•	Land Records of Texas	800-678-8016	•	•	•	
•	•	•	•	•	Mendenhall Information Services	940-696-0758	•	•	•	•
•	•	•		•	Superior Process Svc [SOP]	888-230-2663		•	•	•
DT	**BK**	**CV**	**CR**	**PR**	**←Courts**	**Titus** / **Recording→**	**UC**	**RE**	**TX**	**VS**
•	•	•		•	Abstracts/Trustees of Texas	888-452-0331	•	•	•	
•	•	•			Joe Gillenwater [SOP]	870-772-2923	•	•	•	
•		•	•		Kota Cornelius Kruse & Assoc	903-783-1883		•	•	
	•	•		•	Land Records of Texas	800-678-8016	•	•	•	
		•		•	Titus County Title Company	903-577-0333	•	•	•	•
•	•	•	•	•	Tyler-McLennon Choicepoint	512-334-6244	•	•	•	•
DT	**BK**	**CV**	**CR**	**PR**	**←Courts**	**Tom Green** / **Recording→**	**UC**	**RE**	**TX**	**VS**
•	•	•		•	Abstracts/Trustees of Texas	888-452-0331	•	•	•	
		•	•		Accu-Source Inc	214-637-4064				
	•	•		•	Land Records of Texas	800-678-8016	•	•	•	
•	•	•	•	•	MS Document Services Inc	800-292-3868	•	•	•	•
•	•	•	•	•	Surety Title Co of San Angelo	325-658-7588	•	•	•	•
•	•	•	•		Texsearch #A09479 [SOP]	903-786-4636	•	•	•	
•	•	•	•	•	Tyler-McLennon Choicepoint	512-334-6244	•	•	•	•

DT	BK	CV	CR	PR	←Courts	Travis	Recording→	UC	RE	TX	VS
•	•	•		•		Abstracts/Trustees of Texas	888-452-0331	•	•	•	
•		•	•			American Background Checks	512-497-7988	•		•	
•	•	•	•	•		Americorp Research Inc	877-989-6850	•	•	•	•
•	•	•		•		Ameritile Abstract & Research Inc	800-856-1228	•	•	•	
		•	•			Background Information Systems Inc	800-687-0894				
•		•	•	•		Bar Nunn Research Specialists	512-497-5584		•	•	
•		•		•		John Blackburn	210-867-0399	•	•	•	
•	•	•	•	•		Blumberg Excelsior Corporate Svcs Inc (Texas)	800-252-3050	•	•	•	•
•	•	•				Capitol Services Inc (Texas)	800-345-4647	•		•	
•	•	•		•		Central Tejas Research & Title Services	512-469-6062	•	•	•	
•	•	•	•	•		Corporation Service Company - CSC	800-927-9800	•	•	•	•
•	•	•	•	•		Countywide Research Services [SOP]	512-922-1676 cell	•	•	•	•
•	•	•	•	•		Court & Public Records Service Inc	800-856-0585	•	•	•	•
•	•	•	•	•		CPS (Capitol Process Service) [SOP]	800-856-0216	•	•	•	•
		•	•			Crimecheck Research Services	281-288-6930				
			•			Dataprompt Corporation	214-390-2530				
•	•			•		DeedSearcher Title Research Services	281-375-8480	•	•	•	
•	•	•	•	•		DFW Court Services [SOP]	800-436-0516	•	•	•	
						Executec Services	512-345-5402	•	•	•	
•	•	•	•			G.A. Public Record Services Inc	800-760-2468				
•	•	•	•	•		John C Dunaway & Company [SOP]	512-835-5888	•	•	•	•
•	•	•	•	•		Kimmons Security Services Inc [SOP]	281-679-0070	•	•	•	•
	•	•		•		Land Records of Texas	800-678-8016	•	•	•	
•	•	•	•	•		Lawyer's Aid Service	877-474-2112	•	•	•	•
•	•	•	•	•		MS Document Services Inc	800-292-3868	•	•	•	•
•	•	•	•	•		Professional Civil Process (Austin) [SOP]	800-950-7493	•	•	•	•
•	•	•	•	•		Profile Information Services	512-472-9380	•	•	•	•
•	•	•	•	•		Promesa Enterprises Inc	800-474-4420	•	•	•	•
•	•	•	•	•		Property Research & Documentation Service Inc	210-520-7884	•	•	•	•
•	•	•	•	•		Research N More	512-868-5828	•	•	•	•
•	•	•	•	•		Research Network	512-469-1740	•	•	•	•
		•	•			Spearhead Research - On Target Information	512-295-7298				
•	•	•				Spectrum Screening Inc	800-222-8199	•		•	
•	•	•	•	•		Sterling Research	512-670-9334	•	•	•	•
•	•	•	•	•		Taylor Research & Investigations [SOP]	972-991-5045	•	•	•	•
•	•	•	•	•		Texsearch #A09479 [SOP]	903-786-4636	•	•	•	
•	•	•	•	•		The Nemesis Group [SOP]	800-918-8343	•	•	•	•
•	•	•	•	•		Tyler-McLennon Choicepoint	512-334-6244	•	•	•	•
•	•	•	•	•		Weeks and Associates LLC [SOP]	512-472-9989	•		•	•
		•	•			Your Information Source Inc	800-644-9668				

DT	BK	CV	CR	PR	←Courts	Trinity	Recording→	UC	RE	TX	VS
•	•	•		•		Abstracts/Trustees of Texas	888-452-0331	•	•	•	
						East Texas Public Records	936-632-7385		•		
	•	•		•		Land Records of Texas	800-678-8016	•	•	•	
		•		•		Trinity County Abstract	936-642-1698	•	•	•	

DT	BK	CV	CR	PR	←Courts	Tyler	Recording→	UC	RE	TX	VS
•	•	•		•		Abstracts/Trustees of Texas	888-452-0331	•	•	•	
	•	•		•		Land Records of Texas	800-678-8016	•	•	•	
•	•	•	•	•		Professional Civil Process (Austin) [SOP]	800-950-7493	•	•	•	•

DT	BK	CV	CR	PR	←Courts	Upshur	Recording→	UC	RE	TX	VS
•	•	•		•		Abstracts/Trustees of Texas	888-452-0331	•	•	•	
			•			Dataprompt Corporation	214-390-2530				
	•	•		•		Land Records of Texas	800-678-8016	•	•	•	
•	•	•	•	•		Tyler-McLennon Choicepoint	512-334-6244	•	•	•	•

DT	BK	CV	CR	PR	←COURTS UPTON RECORDING→		UC	RE	TX	VS
•	•	•		•	Abstracts/Trustees of Texas	888-452-0331	•	•	•	
	•	•		•	Land Records of Texas	800-678-8016	•	•	•	
		•		•	Southwest Abstract & Title Co	432-693-2242	•	•	•	

DT	BK	CV	CR	PR	←COURTS UVALDE RECORDING→		UC	RE	TX	VS
•	•	•		•	Abstracts/Trustees of Texas	888-452-0331	•	•	•	
	•	•		•	Land Records of Texas	800-678-8016	•	•	•	

DT	BK	CV	CR	PR	←COURTS VAL VERDE RECORDING→		UC	RE	TX	VS
•	•	•		•	Abstracts/Trustees of Texas	888-452-0331	•	•	•	
	•	•		•	Land Records of Texas	800-678-8016	•	•	•	
		•		•	Southwest Abstract Co Inc	830-775-8508	•	•	•	•

DT	BK	CV	CR	PR	←COURTS VAN ZANDT RECORDING→		UC	RE	TX	VS
•	•	•		•	Abstracts/Trustees of Texas	888-452-0331	•	•	•	
•	•	•	•	•	Court & Public Records Service Inc	800-856-0585	•	•	•	•
		•	•		Crimecheck Research Services	281-288-6930				
			•		Dataprompt Corporation	214-390-2530				
•	•	•	•	•	East Texas Professional Svcs [SOP]	903-928-0117			•	•
		•	•	•	Elliott & Waldron Abstract Co - Canton	903-567-4127	•	•	•	•
	•	•		•	Land Records of Texas	800-678-8016	•	•	•	
			•		Princeton Data Search Inc	469-474-1025		•	•	
•	•	•	•	•	Taylor Research & Investigations [SOP]	972-991-5045	•	•	•	•
•	•	•	•	•	Tyler-McLennon Choicepoint	512-334-6244	•	•	•	•

DT	BK	CV	CR	PR	←COURTS VICTORIA RECORDING→		UC	RE	TX	VS
•	•	•		•	Abstracts/Trustees of Texas	888-452-0331	•	•	•	
•	•	•			All State Document Services	888-246-8180	•	•	•	•
•	•	•	•	•	Condor Inv [SOP]	361-881-8977	•	•	•	•
			•		Dataprompt Corporation	214-390-2530				
•	•			•	DeedSearcher Title Research Services	281-375-8480	•	•	•	
	•	•		•	Land Records of Texas	800-678-8016	•	•	•	
•	•	•	•	•	Shawver & Associates	800-364-2333	•	•	•	•
•	•	•	•	•	Tyler-McLennon Choicepoint	512-334-6244	•	•	•	•

DT	BK	CV	CR	PR	←COURTS WALKER RECORDING→		UC	RE	TX	VS
•	•	•		•	Abstracts/Trustees of Texas	888-452-0331	•	•	•	
•	•	•			All State Document Services	888-246-8180	•	•	•	•
	•	•	•	•	Courthouse Specialists	800-925-4225	•	•	•	
		•	•		Crimecheck Research Services	281-288-6930				
•	•			•	DeedSearcher Title Research Services	281-375-8480	•	•	•	
	•	•		•	Land Records of Texas	800-678-8016	•	•	•	
•	•	•	•	•	PM Clinton International Investigation	866-686-6864	•	•	•	
•	•	•	•	•	Tyler-McLennon Choicepoint	512-334-6244	•	•	•	•

DT	BK	CV	CR	PR	←COURTS WALLER RECORDING→		UC	RE	TX	VS
•	•	•		•	Abstracts/Trustees of Texas	888-452-0331	•	•	•	
•	•	•			All State Document Services	888-246-8180	•	•	•	•
•	•	•	•	•	Asset Research Group	713-864-2536	•	•	•	•
	•	•	•	•	Courthouse Specialists	800-925-4225	•	•	•	
•	•			•	DeedSearcher Title Research Services	281-375-8480	•	•	•	
•	•	•	•	•	Garza-McNamee Agency Inc	888-262-6221	•	•	•	
	•	•		•	Land Records of Texas	800-678-8016	•	•	•	
•	•	•	•		Mach 5 Couriers Inc [SOP]	800-593-2023				
•	•	•	•	•	PM Clinton International Investigation	866-686-6864	•	•	•	
•	•	•	•	•	The Research Staff Inc	800-822-3584	•	•	•	

DT	BK	CV	CR	PR	←COURTS WARD RECORDING→		UC	RE	TX	VS
•	•	•		•	Abstracts/Trustees of Texas	888-452-0331	•	•	•	

DT	BK	CV	CR	PR	Name	Phone	UC	RE	TX	VS
	•			•	Land Records of Texas	800-678-8016	•	•	•	
		•		•	Pioneer-Ward County Abstract Co	432-943-5561	•	•	•	

DT	BK	CV	CR	PR	←COURTS WASHINGTON RECORDING→		UC	RE	TX	VS
•	•	•		•	Abstracts/Trustees of Texas	888-452-0331	•	•	•	
•	•	•		•	All State Document Services	888-246-8180	•	•	•	•
				•	Botts Title Co	254-697-6962	•	•	•	•
•	•			•	DeedSearcher Title Research Services	281-375-8480	•	•	•	
	•	•		•	Land Records of Texas	800-678-8016	•	•	•	

DT	BK	CV	CR	PR	←COURTS WEBB RECORDING→		UC	RE	TX	VS
•	•	•		•	Abstracts/Trustees of Texas	888-452-0331	•	•	•	
					Border Title Group	956-791-5810	•	•	•	
•	•	•	•	•	Condor Inv [SOP]	361-881-8977	•	•	•	•
			•		Dataprompt Corporation	214-390-2530				
	•	•		•	Land Records of Texas	800-678-8016	•	•	•	
•	•	•	•	•	Shawver & Associates	800-364-2333	•	•	•	•

DT	BK	CV	CR	PR	←COURTS WHARTON RECORDING→		UC	RE	TX	VS
•	•	•		•	Abstracts/Trustees of Texas	888-452-0331	•	•	•	
•	•	•		•	All State Document Services	888-246-8180	•	•	•	•
	•	•		•	Land Records of Texas	800-678-8016	•	•	•	

DT	BK	CV	CR	PR	←COURTS WHEELER RECORDING→		UC	RE	TX	VS
•	•	•		•	Abstracts/Trustees of Texas	888-452-0331	•	•	•	
	•	•		•	Land Records of Texas	800-678-8016	•	•	•	

DT	BK	CV	CR	PR	←COURTS WICHITA RECORDING→		UC	RE	TX	VS
•	•	•		•	Abstracts/Trustees of Texas	888-452-0331	•	•	•	
•	•			•	DeedSearcher Title Research Services	281-375-8480	•	•	•	
	•	•		•	Land Records of Texas	800-678-8016	•	•	•	
•	•	•	•	•	Mendenhall Information Services	940-696-0758	•	•	•	•
•	•	•		•	Superior Process Svc [SOP]	888-230-2663		•	•	•
•	•	•	•	•	Texas Detective.com [SOP]	940-592-7000	•	•	•	•
•	•	•	•		Texsearch #A09479 [SOP]	903-786-4636	•	•	•	

DT	BK	CV	CR	PR	←COURTS WILBARGER RECORDING→		UC	RE	TX	VS
•	•	•		•	Abstracts/Trustees of Texas	888-452-0331	•	•	•	
			•		Dataprompt Corporation	214-390-2530				
		•	•	•	King Investigations Inc	580-477-1676	•	•	•	
	•	•		•	Land Records of Texas	800-678-8016	•	•	•	
•	•	•	•	•	Mendenhall Information Services	940-696-0758	•	•	•	•
•	•	•		•	Superior Process Svc [SOP]	888-230-2663		•	•	•
	•	•	•	•	T.A.B.B.S. Inv & Process Service [SOP]	580-477-3292	•	•	•	•
•	•	•	•	•	Texas Detective.com [SOP]	940-592-7000	•	•	•	•

DT	BK	CV	CR	PR	←COURTS WILLACY RECORDING→		UC	RE	TX	VS
•	•	•		•	Abstracts/Trustees of Texas	888-452-0331	•	•	•	
•		•	•		American Background Checks	512-497-7988	•		•	
	•	•		•	Land Records of Texas	800-678-8016	•	•	•	
•	•	•	•	•	Professional Civil Process (McAllen) [SOP]	800-880-4223	•	•	•	•
					South Texas Title and Trustee Services	956-412-3413	•	•	•	
•	•	•		•	Valley Abstract & Trustee Services	956-571-1119	•	•	•	

DT	BK	CV	CR	PR	←COURTS WILLIAMSON RECORDING→		UC	RE	TX	VS
•	•	•		•	Abstracts/Trustees of Texas	888-452-0331	•	•	•	
		•		•	American Abstract & Title Co Inc	254-526-9525	•	•	•	•
•	•	•	•	•	Americorp Research Inc	877-989-6850	•	•	•	•
•	•	•			Carma Austin	254-634-1701	•		•	
		•	•		Background Information Systems Inc	800-687-0894				
•		•	•	•	Bar Nunn Research Specialists	512-497-5584		•	•	

DT	BK	CV	CR	PR	Retriever	Phone	UC	RE	TX	VS
•		•		•	John Blackburn	210-867-0399	•	•	•	
•	•	•		•	Central Tejas Research & Title Services	512-469-6062	•	•	•	
•	•	•	•	•	Countywide Research Services [SOP]	512-922-1676 cell	•	•	•	•
•	•	•	•	•	CPS (Capitol Process Service) [SOP]	800-856-0216	•	•	•	•
		•	•		Crimecheck Research Services	281-288-6930				
•	•			•	DeedSearcher Title Research Services	281-375-8480	•	•	•	
					Executec Services	512-345-5402	•	•	•	
•	•	•	•	•	John C Dunaway & Company [SOP]	512-835-5888	•	•	•	•
	•	•		•	Land Records of Texas	800-678-8016	•	•	•	
•	•	•	•	•	MS Document Services Inc	800-292-3868	•	•	•	•
•	•	•	•	•	Promesa Enterprises Inc	800-474-4420	•	•	•	•
•	•	•	•	•	Property Research & Documentation Service Inc	210-520-7884	•	•	•	•
•	•	•	•	•	Research N More	512-868-5828	•	•	•	•
•	•	•	•	•	Research Network	512-469-1740	•	•	•	•
		•	•		Spearhead Research - On Target Information	512-295-7298				
•	•	•	•		Spectrum Screening Inc	800-222-8199	•		•	
•	•	•	•	•	Sterling Research	512-670-9334	•	•	•	•
•	•	•	•	•	Taylor Research & Investigations [SOP]	972-991-5045	•	•	•	•
•	•	•	•		Texsearch #A09479 [SOP]	903-786-4636	•	•	•	
•	•	•	•	•	The Nemesis Group [SOP]	800-918-8343	•	•	•	•
•	•	•	•	•	Tyler-McLennon Choicepoint	512-334-6244	•	•	•	•
•	•	•	•	•	Weeks and Associates LLC [SOP]	512-472-9989	•		•	•

DT	BK	CV	CR	PR	←COURTS WILSON RECORDING→		UC	RE	TX	VS
•	•	•		•	Abstracts/Trustees of Texas	888-452-0331	•	•	•	
		•	•		Crimecheck Research Services	281-288-6930				
	•	•		•	Land Records of Texas	800-678-8016	•	•	•	
•	•	•	•	•	Property Research & Documentation Service Inc	210-520-7884	•	•	•	•
•	•	•	•	•	Tyler-McLennon Choicepoint	512-334-6244	•	•	•	•

DT	BK	CV	CR	PR	←COURTS WINKLER RECORDING→		UC	RE	TX	VS
•	•	•		•	Abstracts/Trustees of Texas	888-452-0331	•	•	•	
	•	•		•	Land Records of Texas	800-678-8016	•	•	•	
•	•	•		•	Stewart Title of Midland Inc	432-687-3355		•		

DT	BK	CV	CR	PR	←COURTS WISE RECORDING→		UC	RE	TX	VS
•	•	•		•	Abstracts/Trustees of Texas	888-452-0331	•	•	•	
		•	•		Accu-Source Inc	214-637-4064				
		•	•		B & B Info Search	817-774-1310				
•	•	•	•	•	Bray & Freeman LP [SOP]	817-596-9255	•	•	•	•
		•	•		Crimecheck Research Services	281-288-6930				
			•		Dataprompt Corporation	214-390-2530				
•	•	•	•	•	Info2go	817-656-1997	•	•	•	•
	•	•		•	Land Records of Texas	800-678-8016	•	•	•	
•	•	•	•	•	Mendenhall Information Services	940-696-0758	•	•	•	•
•	•	•	•	•	Segovia & Associates [SOP]	877-573-7833		•		•
•	•	•	•	•	Super Search Inc [SOP]	800-687-5553	•	•	•	

DT	BK	CV	CR	PR	←COURTS WOOD RECORDING→		UC	RE	TX	VS
•	•	•		•	Abstracts/Trustees of Texas	888-452-0331	•	•	•	
			•		Dataprompt Corporation	214-390-2530				
	•	•		•	Land Records of Texas	800-678-8016	•	•	•	
•	•	•	•	•	Tyler-McLennon Choicepoint	512-334-6244	•	•	•	•

DT	BK	CV	CR	PR	←COURTS YOAKUM RECORDING→		UC	RE	TX	VS
•	•	•		•	Abstracts/Trustees of Texas	888-452-0331	•	•	•	
•	•	•	•	•	Davick Services	800-658-6656	•	•	•	
	•	•		•	Land Records of Texas	800-678-8016	•	•	•	
					Yoakum County Abstract Co	806-456-2615		•	•	

DT	BK	CV	CR	PR	←COURTS YOUNG	RECORDING→	UC	RE	TX	VS
•	•	•		•	Abstracts/Trustees of Texas	888-452-0331	•	•	•	
	•	•		•	Land Records of Texas	800-678-8016	•	•	•	
•	•	•	•	•	Mendenhall Information Services	940-696-0758	•	•	•	•

DT	BK	CV	CR	PR	←COURTS ZAPATA	RECORDING→	UC	RE	TX	VS
•	•	•		•	Abstracts/Trustees of Texas	888-452-0331	•	•	•	
					Border Title Group	956-791-5810	•	•	•	
	•	•		•	Land Records of Texas	800-678-8016	•	•	•	

DT	BK	CV	CR	PR	←COURTS ZAVALA	RECORDING→	UC	RE	TX	VS
•	•	•		•	Abstracts/Trustees of Texas	888-452-0331	•	•	•	
		•	•	•	Border Legal Services [SOP]	830-773-0525			•	•
					Border Title Group	956-791-5810	•	•	•	
	•	•		•	Land Records of Texas	800-678-8016	•	•	•	
					Zavala County Abstract Co Inc	830-374-3218		•	•	

[SOP] = PERFORMS SERVICE OF PROCESS

COURT RECORDS

CODE	GOVERNMENT AGENCY	TYPE OF INFORMATION
DT	US District Court	Federal civil and criminal cases
BK	Bankruptcy Court	United States bankruptcy cases
CV	Civil Court	Municipal, county and state level civil cases
CR	Criminal Court	Municipal, county and state level criminal cases
PR	Probate Court	Wills and estate cases

COUNTY RECORDS - RECORDINGS

CODE	GOVERNMENT AGENCY	TYPE OF INFORMATION
UC	UCC Filing Office	Uniform Commercial Code and other personal property liens
RE	Real Estate Recording Office	Real property transactions and liens
TX	Tax Filing Office(s)	Federal and state tax liens, judgment liens
VS	Vital Records Office	Vital statistics—birth, death, marriage, divorce

= PRRN Member. *A retriever you can trust!*

Utah

COURT RECORDS RETRIEVED — **RECORDING RECORDS RETRIEVED**

DT	BK	CV	CR	PR	←COURTS	BEAVER	RECORDING→	UC	RE	TX	VS
•	•	•		•	D W Moore & Assoc Inc		801-266-6585	•	•	•	•
		•		•	Security Title of Beaver County		435-438-2354	•	•	•	

DT	BK	CV	CR	PR	←COURTS	BOX ELDER	RECORDING→	UC	RE	TX	VS
•	•	•	•	•	All-Search		800-227-3152	•	•	•	•
•	•	•		•	D W Moore & Assoc Inc		801-266-6585	•	•	•	•
		•	•	•	Mower Services [SOP]		888-317-7458	•	•	•	
•	•	•	•	•	Quick Data Services Inc		800-720-6167	•	•	•	•
		•		•	The Home Abstract & Title Co Inc		800-699-7861	•	•	•	
		•	•		Wasatch Inv Inc [SOP]		800-970-8220				

DT	BK	CV	CR	PR	←COURTS	CACHE	RECORDING→	UC	RE	TX	VS
•	•	•	•	•	All-Search		800-227-3152	•	•	•	•
•	•	•		•	D W Moore & Assoc Inc		801-266-6585	•	•	•	•
		•	•	•	Hickman Land Title		800-365-7760	•	•	•	•
		•	•	•	Mower Services [SOP]		888-317-7458	•	•	•	
•	•	•	•	•	Quick Data Services Inc		800-720-6167	•	•	•	•
					Reliance Abstract Company UT		800-207-1523	•	•	•	
		•	•		Wasatch Inv Inc [SOP]		800-970-8220				

DT	BK	CV	CR	PR	←COURTS	CARBON	RECORDING→	UC	RE	TX	VS
•	•	•		•	D W Moore & Assoc Inc		801-266-6585	•	•	•	•
		•	•	•	Southeastern Utah Title		435-637-4455	•	•	•	•

DT	BK	CV	CR	PR	←COURTS	DAGGETT	RECORDING→	UC	RE	TX	VS
•	•	•		•	D W Moore & Assoc Inc		801-266-6585	•	•	•	•

DT	BK	CV	CR	PR	←COURTS	DAVIS	RECORDING→	UC	RE	TX	VS
•	•	•	•	•	All-Search		800-227-3152	•	•	•	•
•	•	•	•	•	Beehive Attorney Svc [SOP]		800-779-0379	•	•	•	•
•	•	•		•	D W Moore & Assoc Inc		801-266-6585	•	•	•	•
•	•	•	•	•	DataTrace Inv Inc, PI# 100008 [SOP]		800-748-5335	•	•	•	•
•	•	•	•	•	Quick Data Services Inc		800-720-6167	•	•	•	•
					Reliance Abstract Company UT		800-207-1523	•	•	•	
		•		•	The Home Abstract & Title Co Inc		800-699-7861	•	•	•	
		•	•		Wasatch Inv Inc [SOP]		800-970-8220				

DT	BK	CV	CR	PR	←COURTS	DUCHESNE	RECORDING→	UC	RE	TX	VS
•	•	•	•	•	All-Search		800-227-3152	•	•	•	•
•	•	•		•	D W Moore & Assoc Inc		801-266-6585	•	•	•	•
		•	•	•	Sunrise Title Co		800-244-1644	•	•	•	•

DT	BK	CV	CR	PR	←COURTS	EMERY	RECORDING→	UC	RE	TX	VS
•	•	•		•	D W Moore & Assoc Inc		801-266-6585	•	•	•	•
		•	•	•	Southeastern Utah Title		435-637-4455	•	•	•	•

DT	BK	CV	CR	PR	←COURTS	GARFIELD	RECORDING→	UC	RE	TX	VS
•	•	•		•	D W Moore & Assoc Inc		801-266-6585	•	•	•	•
		•	•	•	Security Title Co of Garfield County		435-676-8808	•	•	•	•

DT	BK	CV	CR	PR	←Courts	Grand	Recording→	UC	RE	TX	VS
•	•	•		•	D W Moore & Assoc Inc		801-266-6585	•	•	•	•
		•	•	•	Southeastern Utah Title		435-637-4455	•	•	•	•

DT	BK	CV	CR	PR	←Courts	Iron	Recording→	UC	RE	TX	VS
•	•	•		•	D W Moore & Assoc Inc		801-266-6585	•	•	•	•

DT	BK	CV	CR	PR	←Courts	Juab	Recording→	UC	RE	TX	VS
•	•	•	•	•	All-Search		800-227-3152	•	•	•	•
•	•	•		•	D W Moore & Assoc Inc		801-266-6585	•	•	•	•
		•	•	•	Juab Title & Abstract Co		435-623-0387	•	•	•	

DT	BK	CV	CR	PR	←Courts	Kane	Recording→	UC	RE	TX	VS
•	•	•		•	D W Moore & Assoc Inc		801-266-6585	•	•	•	•
		•	•	•	Southern Utah Title Co		435-644-5891	•	•	•	•

DT	BK	CV	CR	PR	←Courts	Millard	Recording→	UC	RE	TX	VS
•	•	•		•	D W Moore & Assoc Inc		801-266-6585	•	•	•	•
		•	•	•	Juab Title & Abstract Co		435-623-0387	•	•	•	
		•	•	•	Utah Title & Abstract		435-896-5429	•	•	•	

DT	BK	CV	CR	PR	←Courts	Morgan	Recording→	UC	RE	TX	VS
•	•	•	•	•	All-Search		800-227-3152	•	•	•	•
•	•	•		•	D W Moore & Assoc Inc		801-266-6585	•	•	•	•
•	•	•	•	•	Quick Data Services Inc		800-720-6167	•	•	•	•
		•		•	The Home Abstract & Title Co Inc		800-699-7861	•	•	•	

DT	BK	CV	CR	PR	←Courts	Piute	Recording→	UC	RE	TX	VS
•	•	•		•	D W Moore & Assoc Inc		801-266-6585	•	•	•	•
		•	•	•	Security Title Co of Garfield County		435-676-8808	•	•	•	•
		•	•	•	Utah Title & Abstract		435-896-5429	•	•	•	

DT	BK	CV	CR	PR	←Courts	Rich	Recording→	UC	RE	TX	VS
•	•	•		•	D W Moore & Assoc Inc		801-266-6585	•	•	•	•
		•	•	•	Hickman Land Title		800-365-7760	•	•	•	•
		•	•	•	Mower Services [SOP]		888-317-7458	•	•	•	

DT	BK	CV	CR	PR	←Courts	Salt Lake	Recording→	UC	RE	TX	VS
•	•	•	•	•	All-Search		800-227-3152	•	•	•	•
•	•	•	•	•	Beehive Attorney Svc [SOP]		800-779-0379	•	•	•	•
•	•	•		•	D W Moore & Assoc Inc		801-266-6585	•	•	•	•
•	•	•	•	•	DataTrace Inv Inc, PI# 100008 [SOP]		800-748-5335	•	•	•	•
•	•	•	•	•	Quick Data Services Inc		800-720-6167	•	•	•	•
					Reliance Abstract Company UT		800-207-1523	•	•	•	
•	•	•	•		Secure Data Corporation		801-595-1510	•		•	
		•	•		Wasatch Inv Inc [SOP]		800-970-8220				
			•		Western Reporting		800-466-1996				

DT	BK	CV	CR	PR	←Courts	San Juan	Recording→	UC	RE	TX	VS
		•	•		Attorney Service New Mexico [SOP]		505-326-7486				
•	•	•		•	D W Moore & Assoc Inc		801-266-6585	•	•	•	•
		•	•	•	Southeastern Utah Title		435-637-4455	•	•	•	•

DT	BK	CV	CR	PR	←Courts	Sanpete	Recording→	UC	RE	TX	VS
				•	Central Utah Title		435-835-1111	•	•	•	
•	•	•		•	D W Moore & Assoc Inc		801-266-6585	•	•	•	•
		•	•	•	Juab Title & Abstract Co		435-623-0387	•	•	•	

DT	BK	CV	CR	PR	←Courts	Sevier	Recording→	UC	RE	TX	VS
•	•	•		•	D W Moore & Assoc Inc		801-266-6585	•	•	•	•
		•	•	•	Utah Title & Abstract		435-896-5429	•	•	•	

DT	BK	CV	CR	PR	←Courts SUMMIT	Recording→	UC	RE	TX	VS
•	•	•	•	•	All-Search	800-227-3152	•	•	•	•
•	•	•	•	•	Beehive Attorney Svc [SOP]	800-779-0379	•	•	•	•
•	•	•		•	D W Moore & Assoc Inc	801-266-6585	•	•	•	•
•	•	•	•	•	Quick Data Services Inc	800-720-6167	•	•	•	•

DT	BK	CV	CR	PR	←Courts TOOELE	Recording→	UC	RE	TX	VS
•	•	•	•	•	All-Search	800-227-3152	•	•	•	•
•	•	•	•	•	Beehive Attorney Svc [SOP]	800-779-0379	•	•	•	•
•	•	•		•	D W Moore & Assoc Inc	801-266-6585	•	•	•	•
•	•	•	•	•	Quick Data Services Inc	800-720-6167	•	•	•	•
		•	•		Wasatch Inv Inc [SOP]	800-970-8220				

DT	BK	CV	CR	PR	←Courts UINTAH	Recording→	UC	RE	TX	VS
•	•	•	•	•	All-Search	800-227-3152	•	•	•	•
•	•	•		•	D W Moore & Assoc Inc	801-266-6585	•	•	•	•
		•	•	•	Sunrise Title Co	800-244-1644	•	•	•	•

DT	BK	CV	CR	PR	←Courts UTAH	Recording→	UC	RE	TX	VS
•	•	•	•	•	All-Search	800-227-3152	•	•	•	•
•	•	•	•	•	Beehive Attorney Svc [SOP]	800-779-0379	•	•	•	•
•	•	•		•	D W Moore & Assoc Inc	801-266-6585	•	•	•	•
•	•	•	•	•	DataTrace Inv Inc, PI# 100008 [SOP]	800-748-5335	•	•	•	•
•	•	•	•	•	Quick Data Services Inc	800-720-6167	•	•	•	•
					Reliance Abstract Company UT	800-207-1523	•	•	•	
		•	•		Wasatch Inv Inc [SOP]	800-970-8220				

DT	BK	CV	CR	PR	←Courts WASATCH	Recording→	UC	RE	TX	VS
•	•	•	•	•	All-Search	800-227-3152	•	•	•	•
•	•	•		•	D W Moore & Assoc Inc	801-266-6585	•	•	•	•
•	•	•	•	•	Quick Data Services Inc	800-720-6167	•	•	•	•

DT	BK	CV	CR	PR	←Courts WASHINGTON	Recording→	UC	RE	TX	VS
•	•	•	•	•	All-Search	800-227-3152	•	•	•	•
•	•	•		•	D W Moore & Assoc Inc	801-266-6585	•	•	•	•

DT	BK	CV	CR	PR	←Courts WAYNE	Recording→	UC	RE	TX	VS
•	•	•		•	D W Moore & Assoc Inc	801-266-6585	•	•	•	•
		•	•	•	Utah Title & Abstract	435-896-5429	•	•	•	

DT	BK	CV	CR	PR	←Courts WEBER	Recording→	UC	RE	TX	VS
•	•	•	•	•	All-Search	800-227-3152	•	•	•	•
•	•	•	•	•	Beehive Attorney Svc [SOP]	800-779-0379	•	•	•	•
•	•	•		•	D W Moore & Assoc Inc	801-266-6585	•	•	•	•
•	•	•	•	•	Quick Data Services Inc	800-720-6167	•	•	•	•
					Reliance Abstract Company UT	800-207-1523	•	•	•	
		•		•	The Home Abstract & Title Co Inc	800-699-7861	•	•	•	
		•	•		Wasatch Inv Inc [SOP]	800-970-8220				

Editor's Tip: In the interest of compiling a concise index with less than 5,000 pages, the Local Retrievers County Index does not indicate counties where a firm provides document retrieval services using hired correspondents and non-employees. Correspondent Relationships are indicated in the Retriever Profiles.

Vermont

COURT RECORDS RETRIEVED | **RECORDING RECORDS RETRIEVED**

DT	BK	CV	CR	PR	←COURTS ADDISON	RECORDING→	UC	RE	TX	VS
					Horizons Unlimited	617-696-6397		•	•	
•	•	•	•	•	New England Recovery Inc	800-922-7376	•	•	•	•
•	•	•	•	•	Vermont Land Records Research	802-985-9723	•	•	•	

DT	BK	CV	CR	PR	←COURTS BENNINGTON	RECORDING→	UC	RE	TX	VS
					Horizons Unlimited	617-696-6397		•	•	
•	•	•	•	•	New England Recovery Inc	800-922-7376	•	•	•	•
		•			Title Search Services Inc	802-867-4447	•	•	•	•
•	•	•	•	•	Vermont Land Records Research	802-985-9723	•	•	•	

DT	BK	CV	CR	PR	←COURTS CALEDONIA	RECORDING→	UC	RE	TX	VS
•	•	•	•	•	Countryside Paralegal Services	802-888-2150	•	•	•	•
					Horizons Unlimited	617-696-6397		•	•	
•	•	•	•	•	New England Recovery Inc	800-922-7376	•	•	•	•
•	•	•	•	•	Vermont Land Records Research	802-985-9723	•	•	•	

DT	BK	CV	CR	PR	←COURTS CHITTENDEN	RECORDING→	UC	RE	TX	VS
					Horizons Unlimited	617-696-6397		•	•	
•	•	•	•	•	Inquisitive Research Corporation	732-321-0041	•	•	•	•
•	•	•	•	•	New England Recovery Inc	800-922-7376	•	•	•	•
•	•	•	•	•	Vermont Land Records Research	802-985-9723	•	•	•	
		•	•		VPS [SOP]	802-496-6863				

DT	BK	CV	CR	PR	←COURTS ESSEX	RECORDING→	UC	RE	TX	VS
•	•	•	•	•	Countryside Paralegal Services	802-888-2150	•	•	•	•
					Horizons Unlimited	617-696-6397		•	•	
•	•	•	•	•	New England Recovery Inc	800-922-7376	•	•	•	•
•	•	•	•	•	Vermont Land Records Research	802-985-9723	•	•	•	

DT	BK	CV	CR	PR	←COURTS FRANKLIN	RECORDING→	UC	RE	TX	VS
•	•	•	•	•	Countryside Paralegal Services	802-888-2150	•	•	•	•
					Horizons Unlimited	617-696-6397		•	•	
•	•	•	•	•	New England Recovery Inc	800-922-7376	•	•	•	•
•	•	•	•	•	Vermont Land Records Research	802-985-9723	•	•	•	

DT	BK	CV	CR	PR	←COURTS GRAND ISLE	RECORDING→	UC	RE	TX	VS
					Horizons Unlimited	617-696-6397		•	•	
•	•	•	•	•	New England Recovery Inc	800-922-7376	•	•	•	•
•	•	•	•	•	Vermont Land Records Research	802-985-9723	•	•	•	

DT	BK	CV	CR	PR	←COURTS LAMOILLE	RECORDING→	UC	RE	TX	VS
•	•	•	•	•	Countryside Paralegal Services	802-888-2150	•	•	•	•
					Horizons Unlimited	617-696-6397		•	•	
•	•	•	•	•	New England Recovery Inc	800-922-7376	•	•	•	•
•	•	•	•	•	Vermont Land Records Research	802-985-9723	•	•	•	

DT	BK	CV	CR	PR	←COURTS ORANGE	RECORDING→	UC	RE	TX	VS
					Horizons Unlimited	617-696-6397		•	•	
•	•	•	•	•	New England Recovery Inc	800-922-7376	•	•	•	•
•	•	•	•	•	Vermont Land Records Research	802-985-9723	•	•	•	

DT	BK	CV	CR	PR	←COURTS ORLEANS	RECORDING→	UC	RE	TX	VS
•	•	•	•	•	Countryside Paralegal Services	802-888-2150	•	•	•	•
					Horizons Unlimited	617-696-6397		•	•	
•	•	•	•	•	New England Recovery Inc	800-922-7376	•	•	•	•
•	•	•	•	•	Vermont Land Records Research	802-985-9723	•	•	•	

DT	BK	CV	CR	PR	←COURTS RUTLAND	RECORDING→	UC	RE	TX	VS
					Horizons Unlimited	617-696-6397		•	•	
•	•	•	•	•	Inquisitive Research Corporation	732-321-0041	•	•	•	•
•	•	•	•	•	New England Recovery Inc	800-922-7376	•	•	•	•
		•			Title Search Services Inc	802-867-4447	•	•	•	•
•	•	•	•	•	Vermont Land Records Research	802-985-9723	•	•	•	

DT	BK	CV	CR	PR	←COURTS WASHINGTON	RECORDING→	UC	RE	TX	VS
					Horizons Unlimited	617-696-6397		•	•	
•	•	•	•	•	New England Recovery Inc	800-922-7376	•	•	•	•
•	•	•	•	•	Vermont Land Records Research	802-985-9723	•	•	•	
		•	•		VPS [SOP]	802-496-6863				

DT	BK	CV	CR	PR	←COURTS WINDHAM	RECORDING→	UC	RE	TX	VS
					Horizons Unlimited	617-696-6397		•	•	
•	•	•	•	•	Margaret H Knoras	802-885-4375	•	•	•	•
•	•	•	•	•	New England Recovery Inc	800-922-7376	•	•	•	•
		•			Title Search Services Inc	802-867-4447	•	•	•	•
•	•	•	•	•	Vermont Land Records Research	802-985-9723	•	•	•	

DT	BK	CV	CR	PR	←COURTS WINDSOR	RECORDING→	UC	RE	TX	VS
					Horizons Unlimited	617-696-6397		•	•	
•	•	•	•	•	Margaret H Knoras	802-885-4375	•	•	•	•
		•	•		MSI Inv [SOP]	603-298-8060				
•	•	•	•	•	New England Recovery Inc	800-922-7376	•	•	•	•
		•			Title Search Services Inc	802-867-4447	•	•	•	•
•	•	•	•	•	Vermont Land Records Research	802-985-9723	•	•	•	

Editor's Tip: Remember the first rule about public record searching-- Simply because your state or county has certain rules, regulations and practices regarding the accessibility and content of public records, does not mean that another state or county adheres to the same rules.

Virginia

COURT RECORDS RETRIEVED — **RECORDING RECORDS RETRIEVED**

DT	BK	CV	CR	PR	←COURTS	ACCOMACK	RECORDING→	UC	RE	TX	VS
		•	•	•	Judith Ayres		757-336-5313	•	•	•	•
		•	•		Innovative Enterprises Inc		888-777-9435				

DT	BK	CV	CR	PR	←COURTS	ALBEMARLE	RECORDING→	UC	RE	TX	VS
		•		•	Blue Ridge Title, Div of Chicago Title Ins Co		434-295-7196	•	•	•	
		•			E Title & Abstract LLC		540-727-0515	•	•	•	
					Fact Finders Ltd		866-672-0666	•	•	•	
		•	•		Innovative Enterprises Inc		888-777-9435				
					Johnson Title & Abstract Inc		540-368-8104	•	•	•	

DT	BK	CV	CR	PR	←COURTS	ALEXANDRIA	RECORDING→	UC	RE	TX	VS
•	•	•	•	•	ALIASS [SOP]		800-747-0820	•	•	•	•
•	•	•	•	•	Alliance Legal Services Inc [SOP]		703-644-8571	•	•	•	•
		•		•	Amarisearch Inc		703-267-6827	•	•	•	
•	•	•	•	•	CorpAssist Inc - DC Office		800-438-2996	•	•	•	•
•	•	•	•	•	Enterprise Title Company Inc		703-351-8066	•	•	•	•
					Estate Title & Escrow Inc		703-385-5850	•	•	•	
				•	Examiner's Title LC		703-491-0805	•	•		
•	•	•		•	Federal Research Corporation [SOP]		800-846-3190	•	•	•	•
•	•	•	•	•	Fitzgerald Servaites Inc		202-257-7775	•	•	•	•
•	•	•	•	•	Infoline Inc		888-284-4581	•	•	•	•
•	•	•	•	•	InfoNation (Virginia) Inc [SOP]		888-346-9090	•	•	•	
		•	•		Innovative Enterprises Inc		888-777-9435				
•	•	•	•	•	Mohr Information Services LLC		540-678-8775	•	•	•	
•	•	•	•		National Background Inv Inc		800-798-0079			•	
•	•	•	•		OneSource, Inc		540-450-2250		•	•	
		•		•	Boyd F Plumley, BA, M.S.L.S.		703-522-4363		•		•
•	•	•	•	•	Richmond Group International [SOP]		703-494-4645			•	•
•	•	•	•		Security Consultants Inc		202-686-3953			•	
•	•	•	•		Wieder Young & Assoc Inc		301-681-7206	•		•	

DT	BK	CV	CR	PR	←COURTS	ALLEGHANY	RECORDING→	UC	RE	TX	VS
		•	•		Innovative Enterprises Inc		888-777-9435				
•	•	•	•	•	Law Offices of Joan C Singleton		540-839-5009	•	•	•	•

DT	BK	CV	CR	PR	←COURTS	AMELIA	RECORDING→	UC	RE	TX	VS
		•	•	•	Dominion Abstract & Title Agency		804-794-9037	•	•	•	
		•	•		Innovative Enterprises Inc		888-777-9435				
•	•	•		•	UCC Retrievals, Inc [SOP]		804-559-5919	•	•	•	

DT	BK	CV	CR	PR	←COURTS	AMHERST	RECORDING→	UC	RE	TX	VS
		•	•	•	Berry & Maddox		434-263-4886	•	•	•	•
		•	•		Innovative Enterprises Inc		888-777-9435				

DT	BK	CV	CR	PR	←COURTS	APPOMATTOX	RECORDING→	UC	RE	TX	VS
		•	•		Innovative Enterprises Inc		888-777-9435				

DT	BK	CV	CR	PR	←COURTS	ARLINGTON	RECORDING→	UC	RE	TX	VS
•	•	•	•	•	ALIASS [SOP]		800-747-0820	•	•	•	•
•	•	•	•	•	Alliance Legal Services Inc [SOP]		703-644-8571	•	•	•	•

DT	BK	CV	CR	PR	←Courts	Recording→	UC	RE	TX	VS
		•		•	Amarisearch Inc	703-267-6827	•	•	•	
•	•	•	•		Capitol District Information [SOP]	800-494-5225	•		•	
•	•	•	•	•	CorpAssist Inc - DC Office	800-438-2996	•	•	•	•
•	•	•	•	•	Enterprise Title Company Inc	703-351-8066	•	•	•	•
					Estate Title & Escrow Inc	703-385-5850	•	•	•	
				•	Examiner's Title LC	703-491-0805	•	•		
•	•	•		•	Federal Research Corporation [SOP]	800-846-3190	•	•	•	•
•	•	•	•	•	Fitzgerald Servaites Inc	202-257-7775	•	•	•	•
•	•	•	•	•	Infoline Inc	888-284-4581	•	•	•	•
•	•	•	•	•	InfoNation (Virginia) Inc [SOP]	888-346-9090	•	•	•	
		•	•		Innovative Enterprises Inc	888-777-9435				
•	•	•	•	•	Investigative Consultants Inc	202-237-1500	•	•	•	•
•	•	•	•	•	Mohr Information Services LLC	540-678-8775	•	•	•	
•	•	•	•		National Background Inv Inc	800-798-0079			•	
•	•	•	•		OneSource, Inc	540-450-2250		•	•	
		•		•	Boyd F Plumley, BA, M.S.L.S.	703-522-4363		•		•
•	•	•	•	•	Richmond Group International [SOP]	703-494-4645			•	•
•	•	•	•		Security Consultants Inc	202-686-3953			•	
•	•	•	•	•	Washington Document Service (DC)	800-728-5201	•	•	•	•
DT	BK	CV	CR	PR	←Courts **AUGUSTA**	Recording→	UC	RE	TX	VS
		•	•		Innovative Enterprises Inc	888-777-9435				
DT	BK	CV	CR	PR	←Courts **BATH**	Recording→	UC	RE	TX	VS
		•	•		Innovative Enterprises Inc	888-777-9435				
•	•	•	•	•	Law Offices of Joan C Singleton	540-839-5009	•	•	•	•
DT	BK	CV	CR	PR	←Courts **BEDFORD**	Recording→	UC	RE	TX	VS
		•	•	•	Deeds Inc	540-563-5699	•	•	•	
		•	•		Innovative Enterprises Inc	888-777-9435				
		•	•		Innovative Enterprises Inc	888-777-9435				
DT	BK	CV	CR	PR	←Courts **BLAND**	Recording→	UC	RE	TX	VS
		•	•		Innovative Enterprises Inc	888-777-9435				
					New Century Title	276-223-1207		•	•	
DT	BK	CV	CR	PR	←Courts **BOTETOURT**	Recording→	UC	RE	TX	VS
				•	Betsy Biesenbach	540-982-7892	•	•	•	
		•	•	•	Deeds Inc	540-563-5699	•	•	•	
		•	•		Innovative Enterprises Inc	888-777-9435				
DT	BK	CV	CR	PR	←Courts **BRISTOL**	Recording→	UC	RE	TX	VS
		•	•		Innovative Enterprises Inc	888-777-9435				
DT	BK	CV	CR	PR	←Courts **BRUNSWICK**	Recording→	UC	RE	TX	VS
		•	•	•	Autten Barrett & Whitby	434-634-2167	•	•		
		•	•		Innovative Enterprises Inc	888-777-9435				
DT	BK	CV	CR	PR	←Courts **BUCHANAN**	Recording→	UC	RE	TX	VS
		•	•		Innovative Enterprises Inc	888-777-9435				
DT	BK	CV	CR	PR	←Courts **BUCKINGHAM**	Recording→	UC	RE	TX	VS
		•	•		Innovative Enterprises Inc	888-777-9435				
•	•	•		•	UCC Retrievals, Inc [SOP]	804-559-5919	•	•	•	
DT	BK	CV	CR	PR	←Courts **BUENA VISTA**	Recording→	UC	RE	TX	VS
		•	•		Innovative Enterprises Inc	888-777-9435				
DT	BK	CV	CR	PR	←Courts **CAMPBELL**	Recording→	UC	RE	TX	VS
		•	•		Innovative Enterprises Inc	888-777-9435				

DT	BK	CV	CR	PR	←Courts CAROLINE	Recording→	UC	RE	TX	VS
		•		•	Amarisearch Inc	703-267-6827	•	•	•	
					Fact Finders Ltd	866-672-0666	•	•	•	
•	•	•	•	•	Greater Richmond Abstract & Title Inc	804-266-2101	•	•	•	
		•	•		Innovative Enterprises Inc	888-777-9435				
					Johnson Title & Abstract Inc	540-368-8104	•	•	•	
		•			Margene Libertino Inc	540-785-9930	•	•	•	
•	•	•		•	UCC Retrievals, Inc [SOP]	804-559-5919	•	•	•	

DT	BK	CV	CR	PR	←Courts CARROLL	Recording→	UC	RE	TX	VS
		•	•		Innovative Enterprises Inc	888-777-9435				

DT	BK	CV	CR	PR	←Courts CHARLES CITY	Recording→	UC	RE	TX	VS
•	•	•	•	•	Greater Richmond Abstract & Title Inc	804-266-2101	•	•	•	
		•	•		Innovative Enterprises Inc	888-777-9435				
•	•	•		•	UCC Retrievals, Inc [SOP]	804-559-5919	•	•	•	

DT	BK	CV	CR	PR	←Courts CHARLOTTE	Recording→	UC	RE	TX	VS
		•	•		Innovative Enterprises Inc	888-777-9435				
					VA Abstract & Title Agency	434-941-2569		•	•	

DT	BK	CV	CR	PR	←Courts CHARLOTTESVILLE	Recording→	UC	RE	TX	VS
		•		•	Blue Ridge Title, Div of Chicago Title Ins Co	434-295-7196	•	•	•	
					Fact Finders Ltd	866-672-0666	•	•	•	
		•	•		Innovative Enterprises Inc	888-777-9435				
					Johnson Title & Abstract Inc	540-368-8104	•	•	•	

DT	BK	CV	CR	PR	←Courts CHESAPEAKE	Recording→	UC	RE	TX	VS
•	•	•	•		Data-Tec Research Inc	757-424-3606				
•	•	•	•		Dominion Record Search	757-566-8233	•	•	•	•
		•	•		Innovative Enterprises Inc	888-777-9435				
•	•	•	•		Research & Retrieval Services Inc	757-463-0030	•	•	•	

DT	BK	CV	CR	PR	←Courts CHESTERFIELD	Recording→	UC	RE	TX	VS
		•	•	•	Dominion Abstract & Title Agency	804-794-9037	•	•	•	
•	•	•	•	•	Greater Richmond Abstract & Title Inc	804-266-2101	•	•	•	
		•	•		Innovative Enterprises Inc	888-777-9435				
•	•	•	•	•	Mohr Information Services LLC	540-678-8775	•	•	•	
•	•	•	•	•	The Pettit Company	800-752-6158	•	•	•	
•	•	•		•	UCC Retrievals, Inc [SOP]	804-559-5919	•	•	•	

DT	BK	CV	CR	PR	←Courts CLARKE	Recording→	UC	RE	TX	VS
					Estate Title & Escrow Inc	703-385-5850	•	•	•	
		•	•		Innovative Enterprises Inc	888-777-9435				
•	•	•	•		OneSource, Inc	540-450-2250		•	•	
		•		•	Shenandoah Title Services Inc	540-667-1393	•	•	•	

DT	BK	CV	CR	PR	←Courts CLIFTON FORGE	Recording→	UC	RE	TX	VS
		•	•		Innovative Enterprises Inc	888-777-9435				
•	•	•	•	•	Law Offices of Joan C Singleton	540-839-5009	•	•	•	•

DT	BK	CV	CR	PR	←Courts COLONIAL HEIGHTS	Recording→	UC	RE	TX	VS
•	•	•	•	•	Greater Richmond Abstract & Title Inc	804-266-2101	•	•	•	
		•	•		Innovative Enterprises Inc	888-777-9435				
•	•	•	•	•	The Pettit Company	800-752-6158	•	•	•	
•	•	•		•	UCC Retrievals, Inc [SOP]	804-559-5919	•	•	•	

DT	BK	CV	CR	PR	←Courts COVINGTON	Recording→	UC	RE	TX	VS
		•	•		Innovative Enterprises Inc	888-777-9435				
•	•	•	•	•	Law Offices of Joan C Singleton	540-839-5009	•	•	•	•

DT	BK	CV	CR	PR	←Courts	CRAIG	Recording→	UC	RE	TX	VS
		•	•			Innovative Enterprises Inc	888-777-9435				

DT	BK	CV	CR	PR	←Courts	CULPEPER	Recording→	UC	RE	TX	VS
		•	•			Atlantic Title & Research	540-439-1800	•	•	•	
		•				E Title & Abstract LLC	540-727-0515	•	•	•	
						Fact Finders Ltd	866-672-0666	•	•	•	
		•	•			Innovative Enterprises Inc	888-777-9435				
						Raines Record Research Inc	540-937-2005		•		•

DT	BK	CV	CR	PR	←Courts	CUMBERLAND	Recording→	UC	RE	TX	VS
		•	•			Innovative Enterprises Inc	888-777-9435				
•	•	•		•		UCC Retrievals, Inc [SOP]	804-559-5919	•	•	•	

DT	BK	CV	CR	PR	←Courts	DANVILLE	Recording→	UC	RE	TX	VS
		•	•			Innovative Enterprises Inc	888-777-9435				

DT	BK	CV	CR	PR	←Courts	DICKENSON	Recording→	UC	RE	TX	VS
		•	•			Innovative Enterprises Inc	888-777-9435				

DT	BK	CV	CR	PR	←Courts	DINWIDDIE	Recording→	UC	RE	TX	VS
•	•	•	•	•		Greater Richmond Abstract & Title Inc	804-266-2101	•	•	•	
		•	•			Innovative Enterprises Inc	888-777-9435				
•	•	•		•		UCC Retrievals, Inc [SOP]	804-559-5919	•	•	•	

DT	BK	CV	CR	PR	←Courts	EMPORIA	Recording→	UC	RE	TX	VS
		•	•	•		Autten Barrett & Whitby	434-634-2167	•	•		
		•	•			Innovative Enterprises Inc	888-777-9435				

DT	BK	CV	CR	PR	←Courts	ESSEX	Recording→	UC	RE	TX	VS
		•	•			Innovative Enterprises Inc	888-777-9435				
•	•	•	•	•		Investigative Consultants Inc	202-237-1500	•	•	•	•
•	•	•		•		UCC Retrievals, Inc [SOP]	804-559-5919	•	•	•	

DT	BK	CV	CR	PR	←Courts	FAIRFAX	Recording→	UC	RE	TX	VS
•	•	•	•	•		ALIASS [SOP]	800-747-0820	•	•	•	•
•	•	•	•	•		Alliance Legal Services Inc [SOP]	703-644-8571	•	•	•	•
		•		•		Amarisearch Inc	703-267-6827	•	•	•	
		•	•			Atlantic Title & Research	540-439-1800	•	•	•	
•	•	•	•	•		CorpAssist Inc - DC Office	800-438-2996	•	•	•	•
•	•	•	•	•		Enterprise Title Company Inc	703-351-8066	•	•	•	•
						Estate Title & Escrow Inc	703-385-5850	•	•	•	
				•		Examiner's Title LC	703-491-0805	•	•		
•	•	•		•		Federal Research Corporation [SOP]	800-846-3190	•	•	•	•
•	•	•	•	•		Fitzgerald Servaites Inc	202-257-7775	•	•	•	•
		•	•			For The Record In Virginia	703-862-9105			•	
•	•	•	•	•		Hylind Search Company Inc (Maryland) [SOP]	888-449-5463	•	•	•	•
•	•	•	•	•		Infoline Inc	888-284-4581	•	•	•	•
•	•	•	•	•		InfoNation (Virginia) Inc [SOP]	888-346-9090	•	•	•	
		•	•			Innovative Enterprises Inc	888-777-9435				
		•	•			Innovative Enterprises Inc	888-777-9435				
•	•	•	•	•		Investigative Consultants Inc	202-237-1500	•	•	•	•
•	•	•	•			Investigative Research Specialists LLC [SOP]	866-298-9601				
•	•	•	•	•		Mohr Information Services LLC	540-678-8775	•	•	•	
•	•	•	•			National Background Inv Inc	800-798-0079			•	
•	•	•	•			OneSource, Inc	540-450-2250		•	•	
		•		•		Boyd F Plumley, BA, M.S.L.S.	703-522-4363		•		•
•	•	•	•	•		Richmond Group International [SOP]	703-494-4645			•	•
•	•	•	•			Security Consultants Inc	202-686-3953			•	
•	•	•	•	•		Washington Document Service (DC)	800-728-5201	•	•	•	•
•	•	•	•			Wieder Young & Assoc Inc	301-681-7206	•		•	

DT	BK	CV	CR	PR	←Courts — FAIRFAX CITY (see also Fairfax County)	Recording→	UC	RE	TX	VS
•	•	•	•	•	ALIASS [SOP]	800-747-0820	•	•	•	•
•	•	•	•	•	CorpAssist Inc - DC Office	800-438-2996	•	•	•	•
		•	•		For The Record In Virginia	703-862-9105			•	
•	•	•	•	•	Investigative Consultants Inc	202-237-1500	•	•	•	•
•	•	•	•	•	Mohr Information Services LLC	540-678-8775	•	•	•	
•	•	•	•		National Background Inv Inc	800-798-0079			•	
•	•	•	•		OneSource, Inc	540-450-2250		•	•	
•	•	•	•	•	Richmond Group International [SOP]	703-494-4645			•	•

DT	BK	CV	CR	PR	←Courts — FALLS CHURCH (see also Arlington County)	Recording→	UC	RE	TX	VS
•	•	•	•	•	Enterprise Title Company Inc	703-351-8066	•	•	•	•
		•	•		Innovative Enterprises Inc	888-777-9435				
•	•	•	•		National Background Inv Inc	800-798-0079			•	
•	•	•	•		OneSource, Inc	540-450-2250		•	•	

DT	BK	CV	CR	PR	←Courts — FAUQUIER	Recording→	UC	RE	TX	VS
•	•	•	•	•	ALIASS [SOP]	800-747-0820	•	•	•	•
		•		•	Amarisearch Inc	703-267-6827	•	•	•	
		•	•		Atlantic Title & Research	540-439-1800	•	•	•	
		•			E Title & Abstract LLC	540-727-0515	•	•	•	
					Estate Title & Escrow Inc	703-385-5850	•	•	•	
				•	Examiner's Title LC	703-491-0805	•	•		
					Fact Finders Ltd	866-672-0666	•	•	•	
•	•	•		•	InfoNation (Virginia) Inc [SOP]	888-346-9090	•	•	•	
		•	•		Innovative Enterprises Inc	888-777-9435				
•	•	•	•		Investigative Research Specialists LLC [SOP]	866-298-9601				
		•		•	Boyd F Plumley, BA, M.S.L.S.	703-522-4363				•
					Raines Record Research Inc	540-937-2005		•		•
		•	•	•	Rutledge Title Research LLC	540-903-1481	•	•	•	

DT	BK	CV	CR	PR	←Courts — FLOYD	Recording→	UC	RE	TX	VS
		•		•	Deeds Inc	540-563-5699	•	•	•	
		•	•		Innovative Enterprises Inc	888-777-9435				

DT	BK	CV	CR	PR	←Courts — FLUVANNA	Recording→	UC	RE	TX	VS
		•		•	Blue Ridge Title, Div of Chicago Title Ins Co	434-295-7196	•	•	•	
					Fact Finders Ltd	866-672-0666	•	•	•	
		•	•		Innovative Enterprises Inc	888-777-9435				
•	•	•		•	UCC Retrievals, Inc [SOP]	804-559-5919	•	•	•	

DT	BK	CV	CR	PR	←Courts — FRANKLIN	Recording→	UC	RE	TX	VS
		•	•	•	Deeds Inc	540-563-5699	•	•	•	
		•	•		Innovative Enterprises Inc	888-777-9435				

DT	BK	CV	CR	PR	←Cts — FRANKLIN CITY (see also Southampton & Isle of Wight)	Recording→	UC	RE	TX	VS
		•	•		Innovative Enterprises Inc	888-777-9435				

DT	BK	CV	CR	PR	←Courts — FREDERICK	Recording→	UC	RE	TX	VS
•	•	•	•	•	InfoNation (Virginia) Inc [SOP]	888-346-9090	•	•	•	
		•	•		Innovative Enterprises Inc	888-777-9435				
•	•	•	•	•	Investigative Consultants Inc	202-237-1500	•	•	•	•
•	•	•	•	•	Mohr Information Services LLC	540-678-8775	•	•	•	
•	•	•	•		OneSource, Inc	540-450-2250		•	•	
		•		•	Shenandoah Title Services Inc	540-667-1393	•	•	•	

DT	BK	CV	CR	PR	←Courts — FREDERICKSBURG	Recording→	UC	RE	TX	VS
		•		•	Amarisearch Inc	703-267-6827	•	•	•	
					Amcor Title LLC	540-752-2246	•	•	•	
					Fact Finders Ltd	866-672-0666	•	•	•	
•	•	•	•	•	InfoNation (Virginia) Inc [SOP]	888-346-9090	•	•	•	

DT	BK	CV	CR	PR	←Courts	Recording→	UC	RE	TX	VS
		•	•		Innovative Enterprises Inc	888-777-9435				
					Johnson Title & Abstract Inc	540-368-8104	•	•	•	
		•			Margene Libertino Inc	540-785-9930	•	•	•	
		•	•	•	Rutledge Title Research LLC	540-903-1481	•	•	•	

DT	BK	CV	CR	PR	←Courts **GALAX**	Recording→	UC	RE	TX	VS
		•	•		Innovative Enterprises Inc	888-777-9435				

DT	BK	CV	CR	PR	←Courts **GILES**	Recording→	UC	RE	TX	VS
		•	•		Innovative Enterprises Inc	888-777-9435				

DT	BK	CV	CR	PR	←Courts **GLOUCESTER**	Recording→	UC	RE	TX	VS
					Hixson Enterprises	757-898-9865; cell-876-0018	•	•	•	
		•	•		Innovative Enterprises Inc	888-777-9435				
•	•	•		•	UCC Retrievals, Inc [SOP]	804-559-5919	•	•	•	

DT	BK	CV	CR	PR	←Courts **GOOCHLAND**	Recording→	UC	RE	TX	VS
•	•	•	•	•	Greater Richmond Abstract & Title Inc	804-266-2101	•	•	•	
		•	•		Innovative Enterprises Inc	888-777-9435				
•	•	•		•	UCC Retrievals, Inc [SOP]	804-559-5919	•	•	•	

DT	BK	CV	CR	PR	←Courts **GRAYSON**	Recording→	UC	RE	TX	VS
		•	•		Innovative Enterprises Inc	888-777-9435				

DT	BK	CV	CR	PR	←Courts **GREENE**	Recording→	UC	RE	TX	VS
		•		•	Blue Ridge Title, Div of Chicago Title Ins Co	434-295-7196	•	•	•	
					Fact Finders Ltd	866-672-0666	•	•	•	
		•	•		Innovative Enterprises Inc	888-777-9435				
					Johnson Title & Abstract Inc	540-368-8104	•	•	•	

DT	BK	CV	CR	PR	←Courts **GREENSVILLE**	Recording→	UC	RE	TX	VS
		•	•	•	Autten Barrett & Whitby	434-634-2167	•	•		
		•	•		Innovative Enterprises Inc	888-777-9435				

DT	BK	CV	CR	PR	←Courts **HALIFAX**	Recording→	UC	RE	TX	VS
		•	•		Innovative Enterprises Inc	888-777-9435				

DT	BK	CV	CR	PR	←Courts **HAMPTON**	Recording→	UC	RE	TX	VS
•	•	•	•		Data-Tec Research Inc	757-424-3606				
•	•	•	•		Dominion Record Search	757-566-8233	•	•	•	•
		•	•		Innovative Enterprises Inc	888-777-9435				
•	•	•	•	•	Nikki A O'Connell	757-877-8469	•	•	•	
•	•	•	•		Research & Retrieval Services Inc	757-463-0030	•	•	•	

DT	BK	CV	CR	PR	←Courts **HANOVER**	Recording→	UC	RE	TX	VS
		•		•	Amarisearch Inc	703-267-6827	•	•	•	
		•	•	•	Dominion Abstract & Title Agency	804-794-9037	•	•	•	
•	•	•	•	•	Greater Richmond Abstract & Title Inc	804-266-2101	•	•	•	
		•	•		Innovative Enterprises Inc	888-777-9435				
•	•	•	•	•	Mohr Information Services LLC	540-678-8775	•	•	•	
•	•	•	•	•	The Pettit Company	800-752-6158	•	•	•	
•	•	•		•	UCC Retrievals, Inc [SOP]	804-559-5919	•	•	•	

DT	BK	CV	CR	PR	←Courts **HARRISONBURG**	Recording→	UC	RE	TX	VS
		•	•		Innovative Enterprises Inc	888-777-9435				
•	•	•	•	•	Doris Pye [SOP]	540-433 8134	•	•	•	•

DT	BK	CV	CR	PR	←Courts **HENRICO**	Recording→	UC	RE	TX	VS
		•		•	Amarisearch Inc	703-267-6827	•	•	•	
		•	•	•	Dominion Abstract & Title Agency	804-794-9037	•	•	•	
•	•	•	•	•	Greater Richmond Abstract & Title Inc	804-266-2101	•	•	•	
		•	•		Innovative Enterprises Inc	888-777-9435				

DT	BK	CV	CR	PR				UC	RE	TX	VS
•	•	•	•	•		Mohr Information Services LLC	540-678-8775	•	•	•	
•	•	•	•	•		The Pettit Company	800-752-6158	•	•	•	
•	•	•		•		UCC Retrievals, Inc [SOP]	804-559-5919	•	•	•	

DT	BK	CV	CR	PR	←Courts	**Henry**	Recording→	UC	RE	TX	VS
		•	•			Innovative Enterprises Inc	888-777-9435				

DT	BK	CV	CR	PR	←Courts	**Highland**	Recording→	UC	RE	TX	VS
		•	•			Innovative Enterprises Inc	888-777-9435				
•	•	•	•	•		Law Offices of Joan C Singleton	540-839-5009	•	•	•	•

DT	BK	CV	CR	PR	←Courts	**Hopewell**	Recording→	UC	RE	TX	VS
•	•	•	•	•		Greater Richmond Abstract & Title Inc	804-266-2101	•	•	•	
		•	•			Innovative Enterprises Inc	888-777-9435				
•	•	•	•	•		The Pettit Company	800-752-6158	•	•	•	
•	•	•		•		UCC Retrievals, Inc [SOP]	804-559-5919	•	•	•	

DT	BK	CV	CR	PR	←Courts	**Isle of Wight**	Recording→	UC	RE	TX	VS
						Carr Title	757-647-7873				
		•	•			Innovative Enterprises Inc	888-777-9435				
•	•	•	•			Research & Retrieval Services Inc	757-463-0030	•	•	•	

DT	BK	CV	CR	PR	←Courts	**James City**	Recording→	UC	RE	TX	VS
•	•	•	•			Data-Tec Research Inc	757-424-3606				
•	•	•	•			Dominion Record Search	757-566-8233	•	•	•	•
						Hixson Enterprises	757-898-9865; cell-876-0018	•	•	•	
		•	•			Innovative Enterprises Inc	888-777-9435				
•	•	•	•	•		Nikki A O'Connell	757-877-8469	•	•	•	
•	•	•	•			Research & Retrieval Services Inc	757-463-0030	•	•	•	

DT	BK	CV	CR	PR	←Courts	**King and Queen**	Recording→	UC	RE	TX	VS
						Hixson Enterprises	757-898-9865; cell-876-0018	•	•	•	
		•	•			Innovative Enterprises Inc	888-777-9435				
•	•	•		•		UCC Retrievals, Inc [SOP]	804-559-5919	•	•	•	

DT	BK	CV	CR	PR	←Courts	**King George**	Recording→	UC	RE	TX	VS
						Fact Finders Ltd	866-672-0666	•	•	•	
		•	•			Innovative Enterprises Inc	888-777-9435				
						Johnson Title & Abstract Inc	540-368-8104	•	•	•	
		•				Margene Libertino Inc	540-785-9930	•	•	•	
•	•	•		•		UCC Retrievals, Inc [SOP]	804-559-5919	•	•	•	

DT	BK	CV	CR	PR	←Courts	**King William**	Recording→	UC	RE	TX	VS
•	•	•	•	•		Greater Richmond Abstract & Title Inc	804-266-2101	•	•	•	
		•	•			Innovative Enterprises Inc	888-777-9435				
•	•	•		•		UCC Retrievals, Inc [SOP]	804-559-5919	•	•	•	

DT	BK	CV	CR	PR	←Courts	**Lancaster**	Recording→	UC	RE	TX	VS
		•	•			Innovative Enterprises Inc	888-777-9435				

DT	BK	CV	CR	PR	←Courts	**Lee**	Recording→	UC	RE	TX	VS
		•	•			Innovative Enterprises Inc	888-777-9435				

DT	BK	CV	CR	PR	←Courts	**Lexington**	Recording→	UC	RE	TX	VS
		•	•			Innovative Enterprises Inc	888-777-9435				

DT	BK	CV	CR	PR	←Courts	**Loudoun**	Recording→	UC	RE	TX	VS
•	•	•	•	•		ALIASS [SOP]	800-747-0820	•	•	•	•
		•		•		Amarisearch Inc	703-267-6827	•	•	•	
		•	•			Atlantic Title & Research	540-439-1800	•	•	•	
•	•	•	•	•		CorpAssist Inc - DC Office	800-438-2996	•	•	•	•
•	•	•	•	•		Enterprise Title Company Inc	703-351-8066	•	•	•	•

DT	BK	CV	CR	PR	Retriever	Recording	UC	RE	TX	VS
					Estate Title & Escrow Inc	703-385-5850	•	•	•	
				•	Examiner's Title LC	703-491-0805	•	•		
•	•	•		•	Federal Research Corporation [SOP]	800-846-3190	•	•	•	•
•	•	•	•	•	Fitzgerald Servaites Inc	202-257-7775	•	•	•	•
•	•	•	•	•	Infoline Inc	888-284-4581	•	•	•	•
•	•	•	•	•	InfoNation (Virginia) Inc [SOP]	888-346-9090	•	•	•	
		•	•		Innovative Enterprises Inc	888-777-9435				
•	•	•	•		Investigative Research Specialists LLC [SOP]	866-298-9601				
•	•	•	•	•	Mohr Information Services LLC	540-678-8775	•	•	•	
•	•	•	•		OneSource, Inc	540-450-2250		•	•	
		•		•	Boyd F Plumley, BA, M.S.L.S.	703-522-4363		•		•

DT	BK	CV	CR	PR	←Courts LOUISA	Recording→	UC	RE	TX	VS
		•		•	Blue Ridge Title, Div of Chicago Title Ins Co	434-295-7196	•	•	•	
		•			E Title & Abstract LLC	540-727-0515	•	•	•	
					Fact Finders Ltd	866-672-0666	•	•	•	
		•	•		Innovative Enterprises Inc	888-777-9435				
					Johnson Title & Abstract Inc	540-368-8104	•	•	•	
•	•	•		•	UCC Retrievals, Inc [SOP]	804-559-5919	•	•	•	

DT	BK	CV	CR	PR	←Courts LUNENBURG	Recording→	UC	RE	TX	VS
		•	•		Innovative Enterprises Inc	888-777-9435				

DT	BK	CV	CR	PR	←Courts LYNCHBURG	Recording→	UC	RE	TX	VS
		•	•		Innovative Enterprises Inc	888-777-9435				

DT	BK	CV	CR	PR	←Courts MADISON	Recording→	UC	RE	TX	VS
					Fact Finders Ltd	866-672-0666	•	•	•	
		•	•		Innovative Enterprises Inc	888-777-9435				
					Johnson Title & Abstract Inc	540-368-8104	•	•	•	

DT	BK	CV	CR	PR	←Courts MANASSAS	Recording→	UC	RE	TX	VS
•	•	•	•	•	CorpAssist Inc - DC Office	800-438-2996	•	•	•	•
		•	•		Innovative Enterprises Inc	888-777-9435				
•	•	•	•	•	Investigative Consultants Inc	202-237-1500	•	•	•	•

DT	BK	CV	CR	PR	←Courts MANASSAS CITY	Recording→	UC	RE	TX	VS
•	•	•	•		OneSource, Inc	540-450-2250				

DT	BK	CV	CR	PR	←Courts MANASSAS PARK	Recording→	UC	RE	TX	VS
		•	•		Innovative Enterprises Inc	888-777-9435				
•	•	•	•	•	Investigative Consultants Inc	202-237-1500	•	•	•	•
•	•	•	•		OneSource, Inc	540-450-2250		•	•	

DT	BK	CV	CR	PR	←Courts MARTINSVILLE	Recording→	UC	RE	TX	VS
		•	•		Innovative Enterprises Inc	888-777-9435				

DT	BK	CV	CR	PR	←Courts MATHEWS	Recording→	UC	RE	TX	VS
		•	•		Innovative Enterprises Inc	888-777-9435				
•	•	•		•	UCC Retrievals, Inc [SOP]	804-559-5919	•	•	•	

DT	BK	CV	CR	PR	←Courts MECKLENBURG	Recording→	UC	RE	TX	VS
		•	•		Innovative Enterprises Inc	888-777-9435				

DT	BK	CV	CR	PR	←Courts MIDDLESEX	Recording→	UC	RE	TX	VS
		•	•		Innovative Enterprises Inc	888-777-9435				
•	•	•		•	UCC Retrievals, Inc [SOP]	804-559-5919	•	•	•	

DT	BK	CV	CR	PR	←Courts MONTGOMERY	Recording→	UC	RE	TX	VS
		•	•	•	Deeds Inc	540-563-5699	•	•	•	
•	•	•		•	Federal Research Corporation [SOP]	800-846-3190	•	•	•	•
		•	•		Innovative Enterprises Inc	888-777-9435				

DT	BK	CV	CR	PR	←Courts	NELSON	Recording→	UC	RE	TX	VS
		•	•	•		Berry & Maddox	434-263-4886	•	•	•	•
		•		•		Blue Ridge Title, Div of Chicago Title Ins Co	434-295-7196	•	•	•	
		•	•			Innovative Enterprises Inc	888-777-9435				

DT	BK	CV	CR	PR	←Courts	NEW KENT	Recording→	UC	RE	TX	VS
•	•	•	•	•		Greater Richmond Abstract & Title Inc	804-266-2101	•	•	•	
						Hixson Enterprises	757-898-9865; cell-876-0018	•	•	•	
		•	•			Innovative Enterprises Inc	888-777-9435				
•	•	•		•		UCC Retrievals, Inc [SOP]	804-559-5919	•	•	•	

DT	BK	CV	CR	PR	←Courts	NEWPORT NEWS	Recording→	UC	RE	TX	VS
•	•	•	•			Data-Tec Research Inc	757-424-3606				
•	•	•	•			Dominion Record Search	757-566-8233	•	•	•	•
		•	•			Innovative Enterprises Inc	888-777-9435				
•	•	•	•	•		Nikki A O'Connell	757-877-8469	•	•	•	
•	•	•	•			Research & Retrieval Services Inc	757-463-0030	•	•	•	

DT	BK	CV	CR	PR	←Courts	NORFOLK	Recording→	UC	RE	TX	VS
•	•	•	•			Data-Tec Research Inc	757-424-3606				
•	•	•	•			Dominion Record Search	757-566-8233	•	•	•	•
		•	•			Innovative Enterprises Inc	888-777-9435				
•	•	•	•			Research & Retrieval Services Inc	757-463-0030	•	•	•	

DT	BK	CV	CR	PR	←Courts	NORTHAMPTON	Recording→	UC	RE	TX	VS
		•	•	•		Judith Ayres	757-336-5313	•	•	•	•
		•	•			Innovative Enterprises Inc	888-777-9435				

DT	BK	CV	CR	PR	←Courts	NORTHUMBERLAND	Recording→	UC	RE	TX	VS
		•	•			Innovative Enterprises Inc	888-777-9435				

DT	BK	CV	CR	PR	←Courts	NORTON	Recording→	UC	RE	TX	VS
		•	•			Innovative Enterprises Inc	888-777-9435				

DT	BK	CV	CR	PR	←Courts	NOTTOWAY	Recording→	UC	RE	TX	VS
		•	•			Innovative Enterprises Inc	888-777-9435				
•	•	•		•		UCC Retrievals, Inc [SOP]	804-559-5919	•	•	•	

DT	BK	CV	CR	PR	←Courts	ORANGE	Recording→	UC	RE	TX	VS
		•				E Title & Abstract LLC	540-727-0515	•	•	•	
						Estate Title & Escrow Inc	703-385-5850	•	•	•	
						Fact Finders Ltd	866-672-0666	•	•	•	
		•	•			Innovative Enterprises Inc	888-777-9435				
						Johnson Title & Abstract Inc	540-368-8104	•	•	•	

DT	BK	CV	CR	PR	←Courts	PAGE	Recording→	UC	RE	TX	VS
		•	•			Innovative Enterprises Inc	888-777-9435				
		•		•		Shenandoah Title Services Inc	540-667-1393	•	•	•	

DT	BK	CV	CR	PR	←Courts	PATRICK	Recording→	UC	RE	TX	VS
		•	•			Innovative Enterprises Inc	888-777-9435				

DT	BK	CV	CR	PR	←Courts	PETERSBURG	Recording→	UC	RE	TX	VS
•	•	•	•	•		Greater Richmond Abstract & Title Inc	804-266-2101	•	•	•	
		•	•			Innovative Enterprises Inc	888-777-9435				
•	•	•	•	•		The Pettit Company	800-752-6158	•	•	•	
•	•	•		•		UCC Retrievals, Inc [SOP]	804-559-5919	•	•	•	

DT	BK	CV	CR	PR	←Courts	PITTSYLVANIA	Recording→	UC	RE	TX	VS
		•	•			Innovative Enterprises Inc	888-777-9435				

DT	BK	CV	CR	PR	←Courts	POQUOSON	Recording→	UC	RE	TX	VS
•	•	•	•			Dominion Record Search	757-566-8233	•	•	•	•

DT	BK	CV	CR	PR	Name	Phone	UC	RE	TX	VS
		•	•		Innovative Enterprises Inc	888-777-9435				

DT	BK	CV	CR	PR	←Courts **Portsmouth**	Recording→	UC	RE	TX	VS
•	•	•	•		Data-Tec Research Inc	757-424-3606				
		•	•		Innovative Enterprises Inc	888-777-9435				
•	•	•	•		Research & Retrieval Services Inc	757-463-0030	•	•	•	

DT	BK	CV	CR	PR	←Courts **Powhatan**	Recording→	UC	RE	TX	VS
		•	•	•	Dominion Abstract & Title Agency	804-794-9037	•	•	•	
•	•	•	•	•	Greater Richmond Abstract & Title Inc	804-266-2101	•	•	•	
		•	•		Innovative Enterprises Inc	888-777-9435				
•	•	•	•	•	The Pettit Company	800-752-6158	•	•	•	
•	•	•		•	UCC Retrievals, Inc [SOP]	804-559-5919	•	•	•	

DT	BK	CV	CR	PR	←Courts **Prince Edward**	Recording→	UC	RE	TX	VS
		•	•		Innovative Enterprises Inc	888-777-9435				

DT	BK	CV	CR	PR	←Courts **Prince George**	Recording→	UC	RE	TX	VS
•	•	•		•	Federal Research Corporation [SOP]	800-846-3190	•	•	•	•
•	•	•	•	•	Greater Richmond Abstract & Title Inc	804-266-2101	•	•	•	
		•	•		Innovative Enterprises Inc	888-777-9435				
•	•	•	•	•	Richmond Group International [SOP]	703-494-4645			•	•
•	•	•		•	UCC Retrievals, Inc [SOP]	804-559-5919	•	•	•	

DT	BK	CV	CR	PR	←Courts **Prince William**	Recording→	UC	RE	TX	VS
•	•	•	•	•	ALIASS [SOP]	800-747-0820	•	•	•	•
		•		•	Amarisearch Inc	703-267-6827	•	•	•	
		•	•		Atlantic Title & Research	540-439-1800	•	•	•	
•		•	•	•	Bob Lessemun Investigations Inc [SOP]	703-580-6611	•	•	•	•
•	•	•	•	•	CorpAssist Inc - DC Office	800-438-2996	•	•	•	•
•	•	•	•	•	Enterprise Title Company Inc	703-351-8066	•	•	•	•
					Estate Title & Escrow Inc	703-385-5850	•	•	•	
				•	Examiner's Title LC	703-491-0805	•	•		
•	•	•		•	Federal Research Corporation [SOP]	800-846-3190	•	•	•	•
•	•	•	•	•	Fitzgerald Servaites Inc	202-257-7775	•	•	•	•
•	•	•	•	•	Infoline Inc	888-284-4581	•	•	•	•
•	•	•	•	•	InfoNation (Virginia) Inc [SOP]	888-346-9090	•	•	•	
		•	•		Innovative Enterprises Inc	888-777-9435				
•	•	•	•	•	Investigative Consultants Inc	202-237-1500	•	•	•	•
•	•	•	•		Investigative Research Specialists LLC [SOP]	866-298-9601				
•	•	•	•	•	Mohr Information Services LLC	540-678-8775	•	•	•	
•	•	•	•		National Background Inv Inc	800-798-0079			•	
•	•	•	•		OneSource, Inc	540-450-2250		•	•	
		•		•	Boyd F Plumley, BA, M.S.L.S.	703-522-4363		•		•
•	•	•	•		Security Consultants Inc	202-686-3953			•	
•	•	•	•		Wieder Young & Assoc Inc	301-681-7206	•		•	

DT	BK	CV	CR	PR	←Courts **Pulaski**	Recording→	UC	RE	TX	VS
		•	•		Innovative Enterprises Inc	888-777-9435				

DT	BK	CV	CR	PR	←Courts **Radford**	Recording→	UC	RE	TX	VS
		•	•		Innovative Enterprises Inc	888-777-9435				

DT	BK	CV	CR	PR	←Courts **Rappahannock**	Recording→	UC	RE	TX	VS
		•	•		Innovative Enterprises Inc	888-777-9435				
					Raines Record Research Inc	540-937-2005		•		•

DT	BK	CV	CR	PR	←Courts **Richmond County**	Recording→	UC	RE	TX	VS
•	•	•	•		CourtEXPRESS (DC) [SOP]	800-542-3320				
		•	•		Innovative Enterprises Inc	888-777-9435				
		•	•		Innovative Enterprises Inc	888-777-9435				

DT	BK	CV	CR	PR	←Courts	Richmond City	Recording→	UC	RE	TX	VS
		•	•	•	Dominion Abstract & Title Agency		804-794-9037	•	•	•	
•	•	•		•	Federal Research Corporation [SOP]		800-846-3190	•	•	•	•
•	•	•	•	•	Greater Richmond Abstract & Title Inc		804-266-2101	•	•	•	
•	•	•	•	•	Mohr Information Services LLC		540-678-8775	•	•	•	
•	•	•	•	•	The Pettit Company		800-752-6158	•	•	•	
•	•	•	•	•	UCC Retrievals, Inc [SOP]		804-559-5919	•	•	•	
•	•	•	•	•	Washington Document Service (DC)		800-728-5201	•	•	•	•

DT	BK	CV	CR	PR	←Courts	Roanoke County	Recording→	UC	RE	TX	VS
				•	Betsy Biesenbach		540-982-7892	•	•	•	
		•	•	•	Deeds Inc		540-563-5699	•	•	•	
		•	•		Innovative Enterprises Inc		888-777-9435				
		•	•		Innovative Enterprises Inc		888-777-9435				

DT	BK	CV	CR	PR	←Courts	Roanoke City	Recording→	UC	RE	TX	VS
				•	Betsy Biesenbach		540-982-7892	•	•	•	
		•	•	•	Deeds Inc		540-563-5699	•	•	•	

DT	BK	CV	CR	PR	←Courts	Rockbridge	Recording→	UC	RE	TX	VS
		•	•		Innovative Enterprises Inc		888-777-9435				

DT	BK	CV	CR	PR	←Courts	Rockingham	Recording→	UC	RE	TX	VS
		•	•		Innovative Enterprises Inc		888-777-9435				
•	•	•	•	•	Doris Pye [SOP]		540-433 8134	•	•	•	•

DT	BK	CV	CR	PR	←Courts	Russell	Recording→	UC	RE	TX	VS
		•	•		Innovative Enterprises Inc		888-777-9435				

DT	BK	CV	CR	PR	←Courts	Salem	Recording→	UC	RE	TX	VS
				•	Betsy Biesenbach		540-982-7892	•	•	•	
		•	•	•	Deeds Inc		540-563-5699	•	•	•	
		•	•		Innovative Enterprises Inc		888-777-9435				

DT	BK	CV	CR	PR	←Courts	Scott	Recording→	UC	RE	TX	VS
		•	•		Innovative Enterprises Inc		888-777-9435				

DT	BK	CV	CR	PR	←Courts	Shenandoah	Recording→	UC	RE	TX	VS
		•	•		Innovative Enterprises Inc		888-777-9435				
		•		•	Shenandoah Title Services Inc		540-667-1393	•	•	•	

DT	BK	CV	CR	PR	←Courts	Smyth	Recording→	UC	RE	TX	VS
		•	•		Innovative Enterprises Inc		888-777-9435				

DT	BK	CV	CR	PR	←Courts	South Boston	Recording→	UC	RE	TX	VS
		•	•		Innovative Enterprises Inc		888-777-9435				

DT	BK	CV	CR	PR	←Courts	Southampton	Recording→	UC	RE	TX	VS
					Carr Title		757-647-7873				
		•	•		Innovative Enterprises Inc		888-777-9435				
•	•	•		•	UCC Retrievals, Inc [SOP]		804-559-5919	•	•	•	

DT	BK	CV	CR	PR	←Courts	Spotsylvania	Recording→	UC	RE	TX	VS
		•		•	Amarisearch Inc		703-267-6827	•	•	•	
					Amcor Title LLC		540-752-2246	•	•	•	
		•			E Title & Abstract LLC		540-727-0515	•	•	•	
					Estate Title & Escrow Inc		703-385-5850	•	•	•	
					Fact Finders Ltd		866-672-0666	•	•	•	
•	•	•	•	•	InfoNation (Virginia) Inc [SOP]		888-346-9090	•	•	•	
		•	•		Innovative Enterprises Inc		888-777-9435				
					Johnson Title & Abstract Inc		540-368-8104	•	•	•	
		•			Margene Libertino Inc		540-785-9930	•	•	•	

DT	BK	CV	CR	PR	←Courts		Recording→	UC	RE	TX	VS
		•		•	Boyd F Plumley, BA, M.S.L.S.		703-522-4363		•		•
		•	•	•	Rutledge Title Research LLC		540-903-1481	•	•	•	

DT	BK	CV	CR	PR	←Courts	STAFFORD	Recording→	UC	RE	TX	VS
		•		•	Amarisearch Inc		703-267-6827	•	•	•	
					Amcor Title LLC		540-752-2246	•	•	•	
		•	•		Atlantic Title & Research		540-439-1800	•	•	•	
•	•	•	•	•	Enterprise Title Company Inc		703-351-8066	•	•	•	•
					Estate Title & Escrow Inc		703-385-5850	•	•	•	
					Fact Finders Ltd		866-672-0666	•	•	•	
•	•	•		•	Fitzgerald Servaites Inc		202-257-7775	•	•	•	•
•	•	•	•	•	InfoNation (Virginia) Inc [SOP]		888-346-9090	•	•	•	
		•	•		Innovative Enterprises Inc		888-777-9435				
					Johnson Title & Abstract Inc		540-368-8104	•	•	•	
		•			Margene Libertino Inc		540-785-9930	•	•	•	
		•		•	Boyd F Plumley, BA, M.S.L.S.		703-522-4363		•		•
		•	•	•	Rutledge Title Research LLC		540-903-1481	•	•	•	

DT	BK	CV	CR	PR	←Courts	STAUNTON	Recording→	UC	RE	TX	VS
		•	•		Innovative Enterprises Inc		888-777-9435				

DT	BK	CV	CR	PR	←Courts	SUFFOLK	Recording→	UC	RE	TX	VS
•	•	•	•		Data-Tec Research Inc		757-424-3606				
•	•	•	•		Dominion Record Search		757-566-8233	•	•	•	•
		•	•		Innovative Enterprises Inc		888-777-9435				
•	•	•	•		Research & Retrieval Services Inc		757-463-0030	•	•	•	

DT	BK	CV	CR	PR	←Courts	SURRY	Recording→	UC	RE	TX	VS
					Carr Title		757-647-7873				
		•	•		Innovative Enterprises Inc		888-777-9435				

DT	BK	CV	CR	PR	←Courts	SUSSEX	Recording→	UC	RE	TX	VS
		•	•		Innovative Enterprises Inc		888-777-9435				
•	•	•		•	UCC Retrievals, Inc [SOP]		804-559-5919	•	•	•	

DT	BK	CV	CR	PR	←Courts	TAZEWELL	Recording→	UC	RE	TX	VS
		•	•		Innovative Enterprises Inc		888-777-9435				

DT	BK	CV	CR	PR	←Courts	VIRGINIA BEACH	Recording→	UC	RE	TX	VS
•	•	•	•		Data-Tec Research Inc		757-424-3606				
•	•	•	•		Dominion Record Search		757-566-8233	•	•	•	•
		•	•		Innovative Enterprises Inc		888-777-9435				
•	•	•	•		Research & Retrieval Services Inc		757-463-0030	•	•	•	

DT	BK	CV	CR	PR	←Courts	WARREN	Recording→	UC	RE	TX	VS
•	•	•	•	•	Enterprise Title Company Inc		703-351-8066	•	•	•	•
		•	•		Innovative Enterprises Inc		888-777-9435				
		•		•	Shenandoah Title Services Inc		540-667-1393	•	•	•	

DT	BK	CV	CR	PR	←Courts	WASHINGTON	Recording→	UC	RE	TX	VS
		•	•		Innovative Enterprises Inc		888-777-9435				

DT	BK	CV	CR	PR	←Courts	WAYNESBORO	Recording→	UC	RE	TX	VS
		•	•		Innovative Enterprises Inc		888-777-9435				

DT	BK	CV	CR	PR	←Courts	WESTMORELAND	Recording→	UC	RE	TX	VS
		•	•		Innovative Enterprises Inc		888-777-9435				
•	•	•		•	UCC Retrievals, Inc [SOP]		804-559-5919	•	•	•	

DT	BK	CV	CR	PR	←Courts	WILLIAMSBURG	Recording→	UC	RE	TX	VS
•	•	•	•		Data-Tec Research Inc		757-424-3606				
•	•	•	•		Dominion Record Search		757-566-8233	•	•	•	•

DT	BK	CV	CR	PR	←Courts	Recording→	UC	RE	TX	VS
					Hixson Enterprises	757-898-9865; cell-876-0018	•	•	•	
		•	•		Innovative Enterprises Inc	888-777-9435				
•	•	•	•		Research & Retrieval Services Inc	757-463-0030	•	•	•	

DT	BK	CV	CR	PR	←Courts	WINCHESTER	Recording→	UC	RE	TX	VS
		•	•		Innovative Enterprises Inc		888-777-9435				
•	•	•	•	•	Mohr Information Services LLC		540-678-8775	•	•	•	
•	•	•	•		OneSource, Inc		540-450-2250		•	•	
		•		•	Shenandoah Title Services Inc		540-667-1393	•	•	•	

DT	BK	CV	CR	PR	←Courts	WISE	Recording→	UC	RE	TX	VS
		•	•		Innovative Enterprises Inc		888-777-9435				

DT	BK	CV	CR	PR	←Courts	WYTHE	Recording→	UC	RE	TX	VS
		•	•		Innovative Enterprises Inc		888-777-9435				

DT	BK	CV	CR	PR	←Courts	YORK	Recording→	UC	RE	TX	VS
•	•	•	•		Data-Tec Research Inc		757-424-3606				
•	•	•	•		Dominion Record Search		757-566-8233	•	•	•	•
					Hixson Enterprises		757-898-9865; cell-876-0018	•	•	•	
		•	•		Innovative Enterprises Inc		888-777-9435				
•	•	•	•	•	Nikki A O'Connell		757-877-8469	•	•	•	
•	•	•	•		Research & Retrieval Services Inc		757-463-0030	•	•	•	

Editor's Tip: This section of the directory is not organized to promote search firms that are statewide, regional, or national in coverage. A limited list of larger firms who are PRRN members is listed in the back of the book. Screening companies are included

An expanded resource of search firms, distributors, and screening firms is BRB Publication's website at www.brbpub.com. Click the "Find A Vendor" tab. Both sources contain information on firms that use online resources to obtain public record index information.

= PRRN Member. *A retriever you can trust!*

Virgin Islands

COURT RECORDS RETRIEVED — **RECORDING RECORDS RETRIEVED**

DT	BK	CV	CR	PR	←COURTS	ST. CROIX	RECORDING→	UC	RE	TX	VS
•	•	•	•	•	Dennis R Sheraw & Associates Inc [SOP]		800-967-6379	•	•	•	•
•	•	•	•		GPS & Assoc (Florida)		866-813-8131	•		•	•

DT	BK	CV	CR	PR	←COURTS	ST. JOHN	RECORDING→	UC	RE	TX	VS
•	•	•	•	•	Dennis R Sheraw & Associates Inc [SOP]		800-967-6379	•	•	•	•
•	•	•	•		GPS & Assoc (Florida)		866-813-8131	•		•	•

DT	BK	CV	CR	PR	←COURTS	ST. THOMAS	RECORDING→	UC	RE	TX	VS
•	•	•	•	•	Dennis R Sheraw & Associates Inc [SOP]		800-967-6379	•	•	•	•
•	•	•	•		GPS & Assoc (Florida)		866-813-8131	•		•	•

Editor's Tip: Only Call a Retriever For the Records They Retrieve. If you call for a criminal record from a retriever who only does work at the recorder's office, then you are wasting your time and the retriever's time.

[SOP] = PERFORMS SERVICE OF PROCESS

COURT RECORDS

CODE	GOVERNMENT AGENCY	TYPE OF INFORMATION
DT	US District Court	Federal civil and criminal cases
BK	Bankruptcy Court	United States bankruptcy cases
CV	Civil Court	Municipal, county and state level civil cases
CR	Criminal Court	Municipal, county and state level criminal cases
PR	Probate Court	Wills and estate cases

COUNTY RECORDS

CODE	GOVERNMENT AGENCY	TYPE OF INFORMATION
UC	UCC Filing Office	Uniform Commercial Code and other personal property liens
RE	Real Estate Recording Office	Real property transactions and liens
TX	Tax Filing Office(s)	Federal and state tax liens, judgment liens
VS	Vital Records Office	Vital statistics—birth, death, marriage, divorce

Washington

COURT RECORDS RETRIEVED — **RECORDING RECORDS RETRIEVED**

DT	BK	CV	CR	PR	←COURTS ADAMS	RECORDING→	UC	RE	TX	VS
		•			AM-PM Services [SOP]	509-765-1776	•	•	•	•
•	•	•	•		ASAP Legal Messenger [SOP]	253-640-1312		•		
•	•	•	•	•	Trident Investigative Service Inc [SOP]	888-277-3238	•	•	•	•
•	•	•	•	•	Washington Court Records Svc	509-448-5012	•	•	•	•

DT	BK	CV	CR	PR	←COURTS ASOTIN	RECORDING→	UC	RE	TX	VS
•	•	•	•	•	Gem State Inv [SOP]	208-746-4152	•	•	•	•
•	•	•	•		Ryan Myers	208-882-6678	•	•	•	
					Rat Dog Research LLC	208-765-4598	•	•	•	
•	•	•	•	•	Trident Investigative Service Inc [SOP]	888-277-3238	•	•	•	•
•	•	•	•	•	Washington Court Records Svc	509-448-5012	•	•	•	•

DT	BK	CV	CR	PR	←COURTS BENTON	RECORDING→	UC	RE	TX	VS
		•	•	•	Information Retrieval Services (Washington)	800-769-3051	•	•	•	
•	•	•	•	•	Pronto Process & Messenger Svc [SOP]	509-547-1122	•	•	•	
•	•	•	•	•	Trident Investigative Service Inc [SOP]	888-277-3238	•	•	•	•
•	•	•	•	•	Washington Court Records Svc	509-448-5012	•	•	•	•

DT	BK	CV	CR	PR	←COURTS CHELAN	RECORDING→	UC	RE	TX	VS
		•			AM-PM Services [SOP]	509-765-1776	•	•	•	•
•	•	•	•		ASAP Legal Messenger [SOP]	253-640-1312		•		
		•	•		Patterson Inv Inc [SOP]	509-884-7531				
•	•	•	•	•	Trident Investigative Service Inc [SOP]	888-277-3238	•	•	•	•
•	•	•	•	•	Washington Court Records Svc	509-448-5012	•	•	•	•

DT	BK	CV	CR	PR	←COURTS CLALLAM	RECORDING→	UC	RE	TX	VS
•	•	•	•	•	Trident Investigative Service Inc [SOP]	888-277-3238	•	•	•	•
•	•	•	•	•	Washington Court Records Svc	509-448-5012	•	•	•	•

DT	BK	CV	CR	PR	←COURTS CLARK	RECORDING→	UC	RE	TX	VS
•	•	•	•	•	Barrister Support Service [SOP]	503-246-8934				
•	•	•	•	•	Burton Professional Services [SOP]	360-254-0878	•	•	•	•
•	•	•	•	•	CICS Employment Services LLC [SOP]	800-660-0507	•	•	•	
•	•	•	•	•	Data Research Inc (Oregon)	800-992-1983	•	•	•	
		•			Frank Paine Records Search & Retrieval	888-739-8760	•	•	•	
•	•	•	•	•	Lawyer's Legal Service LLC [SOP]	800-224-7911	•	•	•	•
		•	•		Prospective Renters Verification Svc	503-655-0888	•	•	•	•
•	•	•	•	•	Quik Check Records	503-876-6477	•	•	•	•
		•		•	Timely Documents	360-944-1082	•	•	•	
•	•	•	•	•	Trident Investigative Service Inc [SOP]	888-277-3238	•	•	•	•
•	•	•	•		Vancouver Legal Messengers Inc [SOP]	888-695-3654	•	•	•	•
•	•	•	•	•	Washington Court Records Svc	509-448-5012	•	•	•	•

DT	BK	CV	CR	PR	←COURTS COLUMBIA	RECORDING→	UC	RE	TX	VS
•	•	•	•	•	Pronto Process & Messenger Svc [SOP]	509-547-1122	•	•	•	
•	•	•	•	•	Trident Investigative Service Inc [SOP]	888-277-3238	•	•	•	•

DT	BK	CV	CR	PR	←COURTS COWLITZ	RECORDING→	UC	RE	TX	VS
•	•	•	•	•	Burton Professional Services [SOP]	360-254-0878	•	•	•	•
		•			Frank Paine Records Search & Retrieval	888-739-8760	•	•	•	

DT	BK	CV	CR	PR	←Courts	Recording→	UC	RE	TX	VS
•	•	•	•	•	Lawyer's Legal Service LLC [SOP]	800-224-7911	•	•	•	•
•	•	•	•	•	Trident Investigative Service Inc [SOP]	888-277-3238	•	•	•	•
•	•	•	•		Vancouver Legal Messengers Inc [SOP]	888-695-3654	•	•	•	•
•	•	•	•	•	Washington Court Records Svc	509-448-5012	•	•	•	•
DT	**BK**	**CV**	**CR**	**PR**	**←Courts DOUGLAS**	**Recording→**	**UC**	**RE**	**TX**	**VS**
		•			AM-PM Services [SOP]	509-765-1776	•	•	•	•
•	•	•	•		ASAP Legal Messenger [SOP]	253-640-1312		•		
		•	•		Patterson Inv Inc [SOP]	509-884-7531				
•	•	•	•	•	Trident Investigative Service Inc [SOP]	888-277-3238	•	•	•	•
•	•	•	•	•	Washington Court Records Svc	509-448-5012	•	•	•	•
DT	**BK**	**CV**	**CR**	**PR**	**←Courts FERRY**	**Recording→**	**UC**	**RE**	**TX**	**VS**
•	•	•	•	•	Trident Investigative Service Inc [SOP]	888-277-3238	•	•	•	•
•	•	•	•	•	Washington Court Records Svc	509-448-5012	•	•	•	•
DT	**BK**	**CV**	**CR**	**PR**	**←Courts FRANKLIN**	**Recording→**	**UC**	**RE**	**TX**	**VS**
		•			AM-PM Services [SOP]	509-765-1776	•	•	•	•
		•	•	•	Information Retrieval Services (Washington)	800-769-3051	•	•	•	
•	•	•	•	•	Pronto Process & Messenger Svc [SOP]	509-547-1122	•	•	•	
•	•	•	•	•	Trident Investigative Service Inc [SOP]	888-277-3238	•	•	•	•
•	•	•	•	•	Washington Court Records Svc	509-448-5012	•	•	•	•
DT	**BK**	**CV**	**CR**	**PR**	**←Courts GARFIELD**	**Recording→**	**UC**	**RE**	**TX**	**VS**
•	•	•	•	•	Gem State Inv [SOP]	208-746-4152	•	•	•	•
•	•	•	•	•	Trident Investigative Service Inc [SOP]	888-277-3238	•	•	•	•
•	•	•	•	•	Washington Court Records Svc	509-448-5012	•	•	•	•
DT	**BK**	**CV**	**CR**	**PR**	**←Courts GRANT**	**Recording→**	**UC**	**RE**	**TX**	**VS**
		•			AM-PM Services [SOP]	509-765-1776	•	•	•	•
		•	•		Patterson Inv Inc [SOP]	509-884-7531				
•	•	•	•	•	Trident Investigative Service Inc [SOP]	888-277-3238	•	•	•	•
•	•	•	•	•	Washington Court Records Svc	509-448-5012	•	•	•	•
DT	**BK**	**CV**	**CR**	**PR**	**←Courts GRAYS HARBOR**	**Recording→**	**UC**	**RE**	**TX**	**VS**
•	•	•	•	•	ABC Legal Services Inc [SOP]	800-736-7295	•	•	•	•
		•			Frank Paine Records Search & Retrieval	888-739-8760	•	•	•	
•	•	•	•	•	Trident Investigative Service Inc [SOP]	888-277-3238	•	•	•	•
•	•	•	•	•	Washington Court Records Svc	509-448-5012	•	•	•	•
DT	**BK**	**CV**	**CR**	**PR**	**←Courts ISLAND**	**Recording→**	**UC**	**RE**	**TX**	**VS**
•	•	•	•	•	ABC Legal Services Inc [SOP]	800-736-7295	•	•	•	•
		•	•		Diligenz Inc	800-858-5294	•		•	
		•	•	•	Madrona Research Inc	360-647-8126	•	•	•	•
		•			Mask Research Services	425-377-1780	•	•	•	
•	•	•	•	•	Trident Investigative Service Inc [SOP]	888-277-3238	•	•	•	•
•	•	•	•	•	Washington Court Records Svc	509-448-5012	•	•	•	•
DT	**BK**	**CV**	**CR**	**PR**	**←Courts JEFFERSON**	**Recording→**	**UC**	**RE**	**TX**	**VS**
		•	•		Diligenz Inc	800-858-5294	•		•	
					Jefferson Title Co	306-385-2000		•	•	
•	•	•	•	•	Quik Check Records	503-876-6477	•	•	•	•
•	•	•	•	•	Trident Investigative Service Inc [SOP]	888-277-3238	•	•	•	•
•	•	•	•	•	Washington Court Records Svc	509-448-5012	•	•	•	•
DT	**BK**	**CV**	**CR**	**PR**	**←Courts KING**	**Recording→**	**UC**	**RE**	**TX**	**VS**
•	•	•	•	•	ABC Legal Services Inc [SOP]	800-736-7295	•	•	•	•
•	•	•	•	•	Absolute Abstracting	206-335-7837	•	•	•	•
•	•	•	•		ASAP Legal Messenger [SOP]	253-640-1312		•		
•	•	•	•	•	Attorneys' Information Bureau Inc	206-622-1909	•	•	•	•
•	•	•	•		Confidential Services & Investigations [SOP]	360-981-1657		•	•	

DT	BK	CV	CR	PR	Retriever	Phone	UC	RE	TX	VS
		•	•		Diligenz Inc	800-858-5294	•		•	
•	•	•	•	•	Wesley W Ewart, PI [SOP]	800-646-1143	•	•	•	•
					HK Partners Research	808-291-2071	•	•	•	•
		•	•	•	Information Retrieval Services (Washington)	800-769-3051	•	•	•	
•	•	•	•		McGowan & Clark Inv [SOP]	425-396-5680	•	•	•	•
					Miller & Assoc Information Services Inc	253-752-5500	•	•	•	
•	•	•	•	•	N W Legal Support Inc [SOP]	800-729-9426	•		•	•
•	•	•	•	•	Personal Background Inv, Inc	800-949-9982				
•	•	•	•	•	Quik Check Records	503-876-6477	•	•	•	•
•	•	•	•	•	Seattle Process Service Inc [SOP]	800-842-8913				
•	•	•	•	•	Select Information Business Services	425-444-7877	•	•	•	•
		•	•		Sumpter & Associates LLC	925-671-7755	•	•	•	•
•	•	•	•	•	Trident Investigative Service Inc [SOP]	888-277-3238	•	•	•	•
•	•	•	•		Unisearch Inc (Washington)	800-722-0708	•		•	•
•	•	•	•	•	Washington Court Records Svc	509-448-5012	•	•	•	•

DT	BK	CV	CR	PR	←Courts **Kitsap** Recording→		UC	RE	TX	VS
•	•	•	•	•	ABC Legal Services Inc [SOP]	800-736-7295	•	•	•	•
•	•	•	•	•	Absolute Abstracting	206-335-7837	•	•	•	•
•	•	•	•		ASAP Legal Messenger [SOP]	253-640-1312		•		
•	•	•	•	•	Attorneys' Information Bureau Inc	206-622-1909	•	•	•	•
•	•	•	•		Confidential Services & Investigations [SOP]	360-981-1657		•	•	
					Miller & Assoc Information Services Inc	253-752-5500	•	•	•	
•	•	•	•	•	Personal Background Inv, Inc	800-949-9982				
•	•	•	•	•	Trident Investigative Service Inc [SOP]	888-277-3238	•	•	•	•
•	•	•	•	•	Washington Court Records Svc	509-448-5012	•	•	•	•

DT	BK	CV	CR	PR	←Courts **Kittitas** Recording→		UC	RE	TX	VS
		•			AM-PM Services [SOP]	509-765-1776	•	•	•	•
•	•	•		•	Legal Couriers Inc [SOP]	888-450-9453	•	•	•	•
•	•	•	•	•	Trident Investigative Service Inc [SOP]	888-277-3238	•	•	•	•
•	•	•	•	•	Washington Court Records Svc	509-448-5012	•	•	•	•

DT	BK	CV	CR	PR	←Courts **Klickitat** Recording→		UC	RE	TX	VS
•	•	•	•	•	Trident Investigative Service Inc [SOP]	888-277-3238	•	•	•	•
•	•	•	•		Vancouver Legal Messengers Inc [SOP]	888-695-3654	•	•	•	•
•	•	•	•	•	Washington Court Records Svc	509-448-5012	•	•	•	•

DT	BK	CV	CR	PR	←Courts **Lewis** Recording→		UC	RE	TX	VS
•	•	•	•	•	ABC Legal Services Inc [SOP]	800-736-7295	•	•	•	•
		•	•		Diligenz Inc	800-858-5294	•		•	
		•			Frank Paine Records Search & Retrieval	888-739-8760	•	•	•	
•	•	•	•	•	Quik Check Records	503-876-6477	•	•	•	•
•	•	•	•	•	Trident Investigative Service Inc [SOP]	888-277-3238	•	•	•	•
•	•	•	•		Unisearch Inc (Washington)	800-722-0708	•		•	•
•	•	•	•	•	Washington Court Records Svc	509-448-5012	•	•	•	•

DT	BK	CV	CR	PR	←Courts **Lincoln** Recording→		UC	RE	TX	VS
		•			AM-PM Services [SOP]	509-765-1776	•	•	•	•
•	•	•	•	•	Trident Investigative Service Inc [SOP]	888-277-3238	•	•	•	•
•	•	•	•	•	Washington Court Records Svc	509-448-5012	•	•	•	•

DT	BK	CV	CR	PR	←Courts **Mason** Recording→		UC	RE	TX	VS
•	•	•	•	•	ABC Legal Services Inc [SOP]	800-736-7295	•	•	•	•
•	•	•	•	•	Trident Investigative Service Inc [SOP]	888-277-3238	•	•	•	•
•	•	•	•		Unisearch Inc (Washington)	800-722-0708	•		•	•
•	•	•	•	•	Washington Court Records Svc	509-448-5012	•	•	•	•

DT	BK	CV	CR	PR	←Courts **Okanogan** Recording→		UC	RE	TX	VS
		•	•		Patterson Inv Inc [SOP]	509-884-7531				
•	•	•	•	•	Trident Investigative Service Inc [SOP]	888-277-3238	•	•	•	•

DT	BK	CV	CR	PR	←Courts		Recording→	UC	RE	TX	VS
•	•	•	•	•	Washington Court Records Svc		509-448-5012	•	•	•	•

DT	BK	CV	CR	PR	←Courts	**Pacific**	Recording→	UC	RE	TX	VS
•	•	•	•	•	Trident Investigative Service Inc [SOP]		888-277-3238	•	•	•	•
•	•	•	•		Vancouver Legal Messengers Inc [SOP]		888-695-3654	•	•	•	•
•	•	•	•	•	Washington Court Records Svc		509-448-5012	•	•	•	•

DT	BK	CV	CR	PR	←Courts	**Pend Oreille**	Recording→	UC	RE	TX	VS
•	•	•	•	•	Trident Investigative Service Inc [SOP]		888-277-3238	•	•	•	•
•	•	•	•	•	Washington Court Records Svc		509-448-5012	•	•	•	•

DT	BK	CV	CR	PR	←Courts	**Pierce**	Recording→	UC	RE	TX	VS
•	•	•	•	•	ABC Legal Services Inc [SOP]		800-736-7295	•	•	•	•
•	•	•	•	•	Absolute Abstracting		206-335-7837	•	•	•	•
•	•	•	•		ASAP Legal Messenger [SOP]		253-640-1312		•		
•	•	•	•	•	Attorneys' Information Bureau Inc		206-622-1909	•	•	•	•
•	•	•	•		Confidential Services & Investigations [SOP]		360-981-1657		•	•	
		•	•		Diligenz Inc		800-858-5294	•		•	
		•			Frank Paine Records Search & Retrieval		888-739-8760	•		•	
•	•	•	•	•	Hoover Professional Investigations [SOP]		253-272-5090	•	•	•	•
•	•	•	•		McGowan & Clark Inv [SOP]		425-396-5680	•	•	•	•
					Miller & Assoc Information Services Inc		253-752-5500	•	•	•	
•	•	•	•	•	N W Legal Support Inc [SOP]		800-729-9426	•		•	•
•	•	•	•	•	Personal Background Inv, Inc		800-949-9982				
•	•	•	•	•	Quik Check Records		503-876-6477	•	•	•	•
•	•	•	•	•	Seattle Process Service Inc [SOP]		800-842-8913				
•	•	•	•	•	Select Information Business Services		425-444-7877	•	•	•	•
•	•	•	•	•	Trident Investigative Service Inc [SOP]		888-277-3238	•	•	•	•
•	•	•	•		Unisearch Inc (Washington)		800-722-0708	•		•	•
•	•	•	•	•	Washington Court Records Svc		509-448-5012	•	•	•	•

DT	BK	CV	CR	PR	←Courts	**San Juan**	Recording→	UC	RE	TX	VS
		•	•		Paper Chase [SOP]		360-378-3345				
•	•	•	•	•	Trident Investigative Service Inc [SOP]		888-277-3238	•	•	•	•
•	•	•	•	•	Washington Court Records Svc		509-448-5012	•	•	•	•

DT	BK	CV	CR	PR	←Courts	**Skagit**	Recording→	UC	RE	TX	VS
•	•	•	•	•	ABC Legal Services Inc [SOP]		800-736-7295	•	•	•	•
		•	•		Diligenz Inc		800-858-5294	•		•	
		•	•	•	Fourth Corner Network Inc [SOP]		800-321-2455	•	•	•	•
		•	•	•	Information Retrieval Services (Washington)		800-769-3051	•	•	•	
		•	•	•	Madrona Research Inc		360-647-8126	•	•	•	•
•	•	•	•	•	Quik Check Records		503-876-6477	•	•	•	•
•	•	•	•	•	Trident Investigative Service Inc [SOP]		888-277-3238	•	•	•	•
•	•	•	•		Unisearch Inc (Washington)		800-722-0708	•		•	•
•	•	•	•	•	Washington Court Records Svc		509-448-5012	•	•	•	•

DT	BK	CV	CR	PR	←Courts	**Skamania**	Recording→	UC	RE	TX	VS
•	•	•	•	•	Burton Professional Services [SOP]		360-254-0878	•	•	•	•
•	•	•	•	•	Lawyer's Legal Service LLC [SOP]		800-224-7911	•	•	•	•
•	•	•	•	•	Trident Investigative Service Inc [SOP]		888-277-3238	•	•	•	•
•	•	•	•		Vancouver Legal Messengers Inc [SOP]		888-695-3654	•	•	•	•
•	•	•	•	•	Washington Court Records Svc		509-448-5012	•	•	•	•

DT	BK	CV	CR	PR	←Courts	**Snohomish**	Recording→	UC	RE	TX	VS
•	•	•	•	•	ABC Legal Services Inc [SOP]		800-736-7295	•	•	•	•
•	•	•	•	•	Absolute Abstracting		206-335-7837	•	•	•	•
•	•	•	•		ASAP Legal Messenger [SOP]		253-640-1312		•		
•	•	•	•	•	Attorneys' Information Bureau Inc		206-622-1909	•	•	•	•
		•	•		Diligenz Inc		800-858-5294	•		•	
		•	•	•	Information Retrieval Services (Washington)		800-769-3051	•	•	•	

DT	BK	CV	CR	PR	←Courts	Recording→	UC	RE	TX	VS
•	•	•	•		McGowan & Clark Inv [SOP]	425-396-5680	•	•	•	•
					Miller & Assoc Information Services Inc	253-752-5500	•	•	•	
•	•	•	•	•	N W Legal Support Inc [SOP]	800-729-9426	•		•	•
•	•	•	•	•	Personal Background Inv, Inc	800-949-9982				
•	•	•	•	•	Quik Check Records	503-876-6477	•	•	•	•
•	•	•	•	•	Seattle Process Service Inc [SOP]	800-842-8913				
•	•	•	•	•	Select Information Business Services	425-444-7877	•	•	•	•
		•	•		Sumpter & Associates LLC	925-671-7755	•	•	•	•
•	•	•	•	•	Trident Investigative Service Inc [SOP]	888-277-3238	•	•	•	•
•	•	•	•		Unisearch Inc (Washington)	800-722-0708	•		•	•
•	•	•	•	•	Washington Court Records Svc	509-448-5012	•	•	•	•

DT	BK	CV	CR	PR	←Courts **SPOKANE**	Recording→	UC	RE	TX	VS
•	•	•	•	•	A & A Attorney Services Inc [SOP]	509-325-0001	•	•	•	•
					Rat Dog Research LLC	208-765-4598	•	•	•	
•	•	•	•	•	Trident Investigative Service Inc [SOP]	888-277-3238	•	•	•	•
•	•	•	•	•	Washington Court Records Svc	509-448-5012	•	•	•	•

DT	BK	CV	CR	PR	←Courts **STEVENS**	Recording→	UC	RE	TX	VS
					Rat Dog Research LLC	208-765-4598	•	•	•	
		•	•	•	Stevens County Title	509-684-4589	•	•	•	
•	•	•	•	•	Trident Investigative Service Inc [SOP]	888-277-3238	•	•	•	•
•	•	•	•	•	Washington Court Records Svc	509-448-5012	•	•	•	•

DT	BK	CV	CR	PR	←Courts **THURSTON**	Recording→	UC	RE	TX	VS
•	•	•	•	•	ABC Legal Services Inc [SOP]	800-736-7295	•	•	•	•
•	•	•	•	•	Absolute Abstracting	206-335-7837	•	•	•	•
•	•	•	•	•	AccuFacts Research Corporation	800-898-5583	•		•	
•	•	•	•	•	Attorneys' Information Bureau Inc	206-622-1909	•	•	•	•
		•	•		Diligenz Inc	800-858-5294	•		•	
•	•	•	•	•	Fairchild Record Search Ltd	800-547-7007	•		•	•
		•			Frank Paine Records Search & Retrieval	888-739-8760	•	•	•	
					Miller & Assoc Information Services Inc	253-752-5500	•	•	•	
•	•	•	•	•	Personal Background Inv, Inc	800-949-9982				
•	•	•	•	•	Quik Check Records	503-876-6477	•	•	•	•
•	•	•	•	•	Select Information Business Services	425-444-7877	•	•	•	•
•	•	•	•	•	Trident Investigative Service Inc [SOP]	888-277-3238	•	•	•	•
•	•	•	•		Unisearch Inc (Washington)	800-722-0708	•		•	•
•	•	•	•	•	Washington Court Records Svc	509-448-5012	•	•	•	•

DT	BK	CV	CR	PR	←Courts **WAHKIAKUM**	Recording→	UC	RE	TX	VS
•	•	•	•	•	Trident Investigative Service Inc [SOP]	888-277-3238	•	•	•	•
•	•	•	•		Vancouver Legal Messengers Inc [SOP]	888-695-3654	•	•	•	•

DT	BK	CV	CR	PR	←Courts **WALLA WALLA**	Recording→	UC	RE	TX	VS
•	•	•	•	•	Pronto Process & Messenger Svc [SOP]	509-547-1122	•	•	•	
•	•	•	•	•	Trident Investigative Service Inc [SOP]	888-277-3238	•	•	•	•
		•		•	Walla Walla Title Co	509-525-8660	•	•	•	•
•	•	•	•	•	Washington Court Records Svc	509-448-5012	•	•	•	•

DT	BK	CV	CR	PR	←Courts **WHATCOM**	Recording→	UC	RE	TX	VS
•	•	•	•	•	ABC Legal Services Inc [SOP]	800-736-7295	•	•	•	•
		•	•		Diligenz Inc	800-858-5294	•		•	
		•	•	•	Fourth Corner Network Inc [SOP]	800-321-2455	•	•	•	•
		•	•	•	Madrona Research Inc	360-647-8126	•	•	•	•
•	•	•	•	•	Trident Investigative Service Inc [SOP]	888-277-3238	•	•	•	•

DT	BK	CV	CR	PR	←Courts **WHITMAN**	Recording→	UC	RE	TX	VS
•	•	•	•	•	Gem State Inv [SOP]	208-746-4152	•	•	•	•
•	•	•	•		Ryan Myers	208-882-6678	•	•	•	
•	•	•	•	•	Trident Investigative Service Inc [SOP]	888-277-3238	•	•	•	•

DT	BK	CV	CR	PR	←Courts		Recording→	UC	RE	TX	VS
•	•	•	•	•	Washington Court Records Svc		509-448-5012	•	•	•	•

DT	BK	CV	CR	PR	←Courts	Yakima	Recording→	UC	RE	TX	VS
		•	•	•	Information Retrieval Services (Washington)		800-769-3051	•	•	•	
•	•	•		•	Legal Couriers Inc [SOP]		888-450-9453	•	•	•	•
•	•	•	•	•	Trident Investigative Service Inc [SOP]		888-277-3238	•	•	•	•
•	•	•	•	•	Washington Court Records Svc		509-448-5012	•	•	•	•

[SOP] = Performs service of process

Court Records

CODE	Government Agency	Type of Information
DT	US District Court	Federal civil and criminal cases
BK	Bankruptcy Court	United States bankruptcy cases
CV	Civil Court	Municipal, county and state level civil cases
CR	Criminal Court	Municipal, county and state level criminal cases
PR	Probate Court	Wills and estate cases

County Records - Recordings

CODE	Government Agency	Type of Information
UC	UCC Filing Office	Uniform Commercial Code and other personal property liens
RE	Real Estate Recording Office	Real property transactions and liens
TX	Tax Filing Office(s)	Federal and state tax liens, judgment liens
VS	Vital Records Office	Vital statistics—birth, death, marriage, divorce

= PRRN Member. *A retriever you can trust!*

Editor's Tip: At the back of this directory is a short list of search firms who are Public Record Retriever Network "Associate Members." These Associate Members utilize retrievers to obtain documents outside their local area of coverage. The Associate Members are statewide, regional, or national in scope, and are not listed in the county sections.

West Virginia

COURT RECORDS RETRIEVED | **RECORDING RECORDS RETRIEVED**

DT	BK	CV	CR	PR	←COURTS BARBOUR	RECORDING→	UC	RE	TX	VS
•	•	•		•	The Croson Agency	304-343-1564	•	•	•	
•	•	•	•	•	DMI [SOP]	304-842-2946	•	•	•	•
					Liberty Record Search Inc	304-863-5542	•	•	•	
•		•	•	•	RLS Inc [SOP]	304-472-8800	•	•	•	•
•	•	•	•	•	Vanhorn & Vanhorn Inc [SOP]	304-623-1362	•	•	•	•

DT	BK	CV	CR	PR	←COURTS BERKELEY	RECORDING→	UC	RE	TX	VS
•	•	•		•	The Croson Agency	304-343-1564	•	•	•	
					Liberty Record Search Inc	304-863-5542	•	•	•	
					Paralegal Services (Berkeley Springs)	304-676-5550	•	•	•	
		•	•		PAT Research	304-725-4845			•	

DT	BK	CV	CR	PR	←COURTS BOONE	RECORDING→	UC	RE	TX	VS
•	•	•	•	•	American Investigations [SOP]	304-343-3346	•	•	•	•
•	•	•		•	The Croson Agency	304-343-1564	•	•	•	
					Liberty Record Search Inc	304-863-5542	•	•	•	

DT	BK	CV	CR	PR	←COURTS BRAXTON	RECORDING→	UC	RE	TX	VS
•	•	•		•	The Croson Agency	304-343-1564	•	•	•	
					Liberty Record Search Inc	304-863-5542	•	•	•	
•		•	•	•	RLS Inc [SOP]	304-472-8800	•	•	•	•

DT	BK	CV	CR	PR	←COURTS BROOKE	RECORDING→	UC	RE	TX	VS
•	•	•		•	The Croson Agency	304-343-1564	•	•	•	
					Liberty Record Search Inc	304-863-5542	•	•	•	

DT	BK	CV	CR	PR	←COURTS CABELL	RECORDING→	UC	RE	TX	VS
•	•	•	•	•	American Investigations [SOP]	304-343-3346	•	•	•	•
•	•	•		•	The Croson Agency	304-343-1564	•	•	•	
•		•	•	•	Daniel Agency	606-324-6029	•	•	•	•
					Liberty Record Search Inc	304-863-5542	•	•	•	
		•	•		West Virginia Records Research	304-633-6964				
•	•	•	•	•	Whiting Background & Legal Services	304-372-6499			•	•

DT	BK	CV	CR	PR	←COURTS CALHOUN	RECORDING→	UC	RE	TX	VS
•	•	•	•	•	Accu-Check Information Services	304-375-4802	•		•	•
•	•	•		•	The Croson Agency	304-343-1564	•	•	•	
					Liberty Record Search Inc	304-863-5542	•	•	•	
•		•	•	•	RLS Inc [SOP]	304-472-8800	•	•	•	•

DT	BK	CV	CR	PR	←COURTS CLAY	RECORDING→	UC	RE	TX	VS
•	•	•		•	The Croson Agency	304-343-1564	•	•	•	
					Liberty Record Search Inc	304-863-5542	•	•	•	
•	•	•	•	•	Whiting Background & Legal Services	304-372-6499			•	•

DT	BK	CV	CR	PR	←COURTS DODDRIDGE	RECORDING→	UC	RE	TX	VS
•	•	•	•	•	Accu-Check Information Services	304-375-4802	•		•	•
•	•	•		•	The Croson Agency	304-343-1564	•	•	•	
•	•	•	•	•	DMI [SOP]	304-842-2946	•	•	•	•
					Liberty Record Search Inc	304-863-5542	•	•	•	
•		•	•	•	RLS Inc [SOP]	304-472-8800	•	•	•	•
•	•	•	•	•	Vanhorn & Vanhorn Inc [SOP]	304-623-1362	•	•	•	•
•	•	•	•	•	Whiting Background & Legal Services	304-372-6499			•	•

DT	BK	CV	CR	PR	←Courts FAYETTE	Recording→	UC	RE	TX	VS
•	•	•	•	•	Accu-Check Information Services	304-375-4802	•		•	•
•	•	•		•	The Croson Agency	304-343-1564	•	•	•	
					Liberty Record Search Inc	304-863-5542	•	•	•	
•	•	•	•	•	Whiting Background & Legal Services	304-372-6499			•	•

DT	BK	CV	CR	PR	←Courts GILMER	Recording→	UC	RE	TX	VS
•	•	•		•	The Croson Agency	304-343-1564	•	•	•	
					Liberty Record Search Inc	304-863-5542	•	•	•	
•		•	•	•	RLS Inc [SOP]	304-472-8800	•	•	•	•

DT	BK	CV	CR	PR	←Courts GRANT	Recording→	UC	RE	TX	VS
•	•	•		•	The Croson Agency	304-343-1564	•	•	•	

DT	BK	CV	CR	PR	←Courts GREENBRIER	Recording→	UC	RE	TX	VS
•	•	•	•	•	Accu-Check Information Services	304-375-4802	•		•	•
•	•	•		•	The Croson Agency	304-343-1564	•	•	•	
					Liberty Record Search Inc	304-863-5542	•	•	•	

DT	BK	CV	CR	PR	←Courts HAMPSHIRE	Recording→	UC	RE	TX	VS
•	•	•		•	The Croson Agency	304-343-1564	•	•	•	

DT	BK	CV	CR	PR	←Courts HANCOCK	Recording→	UC	RE	TX	VS
•	•	•		•	The Croson Agency	304-343-1564	•	•	•	
					Liberty Record Search Inc	304-863-5542	•	•	•	

DT	BK	CV	CR	PR	←Courts HARDY	Recording→	UC	RE	TX	VS
•	•	•		•	The Croson Agency	304-343-1564	•	•	•	

DT	BK	CV	CR	PR	←Courts HARRISON	Recording→	UC	RE	TX	VS
•	•	•		•	The Croson Agency	304-343-1564	•	•	•	
•	•	•	•	•	DMI [SOP]	304-842-2946	•	•	•	•
					Liberty Record Search Inc	304-863-5542	•	•	•	
•		•	•	•	RLS Inc [SOP]	304-472-8800	•	•	•	•
•	•	•	•	•	Vanhorn & Vanhorn Inc [SOP]	304-623-1362	•	•	•	•

DT	BK	CV	CR	PR	←Courts JACKSON	Recording→	UC	RE	TX	VS
•	•	•	•	•	Accu-Check Information Services	304-375-4802	•		•	•
•	•	•	•	•	American Investigations [SOP]	304-343-3346	•	•	•	•
•	•	•		•	The Croson Agency	304-343-1564	•	•	•	
					Liberty Record Search Inc	304-863-5542	•	•	•	
•	•	•	•	•	Whiting Background & Legal Services	304-372-6499			•	•

DT	BK	CV	CR	PR	←Courts JEFFERSON	Recording→	UC	RE	TX	VS
•	•	•	•	•	Accu-Check Information Services	304-375-4802	•		•	•
•	•	•		•	The Croson Agency	304-343-1564	•	•	•	
					Liberty Record Search Inc	304-863-5542	•	•	•	
		•	•		PAT Research	304-725-4845			•	

DT	BK	CV	CR	PR	←Courts KANAWHA	Recording→	UC	RE	TX	VS
•	•	•	•	•	Accu-Check Information Services	304-375-4802	•		•	•
•	•	•	•	•	American Investigations [SOP]	304-343-3346	•	•	•	•
•	•	•		•	The Croson Agency	304-343-1564	•	•	•	
•		•	•	•	Daniel Agency	606-324-6029	•	•	•	•
					Liberty Record Search Inc	304-863-5542	•	•	•	
		•	•		West Virginia Records Research	304-633-6964				
•	•	•	•	•	Whiting Background & Legal Services	304-372-6499			•	•

DT	BK	CV	CR	PR	←Courts LEWIS	Recording→	UC	RE	TX	VS
•	•	•		•	The Croson Agency	304-343-1564	•	•	•	
•	•	•	•	•	DMI [SOP]	304-842-2946	•	•	•	•
					Liberty Record Search Inc	304-863-5542	•	•	•	
•		•	•	•	RLS Inc [SOP]	304-472-8800	•	•	•	•
•	•	•	•	•	Vanhorn & Vanhorn Inc [SOP]	304-623-1362	•	•	•	•

DT	BK	CV	CR	PR	←Courts	Lincoln	Recording→	UC	RE	TX	VS
•	•	•	•	•	American Investigations [SOP]		304-343-3346	•	•	•	•
•	•	•		•	The Croson Agency		304-343-1564	•	•	•	
•		•	•	•	Daniel Agency		606-324-6029	•	•	•	•
					Liberty Record Search Inc		304-863-5542	•	•	•	

DT	BK	CV	CR	PR	←Courts	Logan	Recording→	UC	RE	TX	VS
•	•	•		•	The Croson Agency		304-343-1564	•	•	•	
					Liberty Record Search Inc		304-863-5542	•	•	•	
•		•	•	•	RLS Inc [SOP]		304-472-8800	•	•	•	•

DT	BK	CV	CR	PR	←Courts	Marion	Recording→	UC	RE	TX	VS
•	•	•		•	The Croson Agency		304-343-1564	•	•	•	
•	•	•	•	•	DMI [SOP]		304-842-2946	•	•	•	•
					Liberty Record Search Inc		304-863-5542	•	•	•	
•		•	•	•	RLS Inc [SOP]		304-472-8800	•	•	•	•
•	•	•	•	•	Vanhorn & Vanhorn Inc [SOP]		304-623-1362	•	•	•	•

DT	BK	CV	CR	PR	←Courts	Marshall	Recording→	UC	RE	TX	VS
•	•	•		•	The Croson Agency		304-343-1564	•	•	•	
					Liberty Record Search Inc		304-863-5542	•	•	•	

DT	BK	CV	CR	PR	←Courts	Mason	Recording→	UC	RE	TX	VS
•	•	•		•	The Croson Agency		304-343-1564	•	•	•	
•	•	•	•	•	DMI [SOP]		304-842-2946	•	•	•	•
					Liberty Record Search Inc		304-863-5542	•	•	•	
		•		•	Paralegal Services Point Pleasant		304-675-4008	•	•	•	

DT	BK	CV	CR	PR	←Courts	McDowell	Recording→	UC	RE	TX	VS
•	•	•		•	The Croson Agency		304-343-1564	•	•	•	
					Liberty Record Search Inc		304-863-5542	•	•	•	
•		•	•	•	RLS Inc [SOP]		304-472-8800	•	•	•	•

DT	BK	CV	CR	PR	←Courts	Mercer	Recording→	UC	RE	TX	VS
•	•	•		•	The Croson Agency		304-343-1564	•	•	•	
					Liberty Record Search Inc		304-863-5542	•	•	•	

DT	BK	CV	CR	PR	←Courts	Mineral	Recording→	UC	RE	TX	VS
•	•	•		•	The Croson Agency		304-343-1564	•	•	•	

DT	BK	CV	CR	PR	←Courts	Mingo	Recording→	UC	RE	TX	VS
•	•	•	•	•	Accu-Check Information Services		304-375-4802	•		•	•
•	•	•		•	The Croson Agency		304-343-1564	•	•	•	
					Liberty Record Search Inc		304-863-5542	•	•	•	

DT	BK	CV	CR	PR	←Courts	Monongalia	Recording→	UC	RE	TX	VS
•	•	•		•	The Croson Agency		304-343-1564	•	•	•	
•	•	•	•	•	DMI [SOP]		304-842-2946	•	•	•	•
					Liberty Record Search Inc		304-863-5542	•	•	•	
•		•	•	•	RLS Inc [SOP]		304-472-8800	•	•	•	•

DT	BK	CV	CR	PR	←Courts	Monroe	Recording→	UC	RE	TX	VS
•	•	•		•	The Croson Agency		304-343-1564	•	•	•	
					Liberty Record Search Inc		304-863-5542	•	•	•	

DT	BK	CV	CR	PR	←Courts	Morgan	Recording→	UC	RE	TX	VS
•	•	•		•	The Croson Agency		304-343-1564	•	•	•	
					Liberty Record Search Inc		304-863-5542	•	•	•	
					Paralegal Services (Berkeley Springs)		304-676-5550	•	•	•	

DT	BK	CV	CR	PR	←Courts	Nicholas	Recording→	UC	RE	TX	VS
•	•	•	•	•	Accu-Check Information Services		304-375-4802	•		•	•
•	•	•		•	The Croson Agency		304-343-1564	•	•	•	
					Liberty Record Search Inc		304-863-5542	•	•	•	
•	•	•	•	•	Whiting Background & Legal Services		304-372-6499			•	•

DT	BK	CV	CR	PR	←Courts	Ohio	Recording→	UC	RE	TX	VS
•	•	•		•	The Croson Agency		304-343-1564	•	•	•	
•	•	•	•	•	Confidential Services [SOP]		800-752-4581	•	•	•	•
					Liberty Record Search Inc		304-863-5542	•	•	•	

DT	BK	CV	CR	PR	←Courts	Pendleton	Recording→	UC	RE	TX	VS
•	•	•		•	The Croson Agency		304-343-1564	•	•	•	

DT	BK	CV	CR	PR	←Courts	Pleasants	Recording→	UC	RE	TX	VS
•	•	•	•	•	Accu-Check Information Services		304-375-4802	•		•	•
•	•	•		•	The Croson Agency		304-343-1564	•	•	•	
					Liberty Record Search Inc		304-863-5542	•	•	•	

DT	BK	CV	CR	PR	←Courts	Pocahontas	Recording→	UC	RE	TX	VS
•	•	•		•	The Croson Agency		304-343-1564	•	•	•	
					Liberty Record Search Inc		304-863-5542	•	•	•	

DT	BK	CV	CR	PR	←Courts	Preston	Recording→	UC	RE	TX	VS
•	•	•		•	The Croson Agency		304-343-1564	•	•	•	
•	•	•	•	•	DMI [SOP]		304-842-2946	•	•	•	•
					Liberty Record Search Inc		304-863-5542	•	•	•	
•		•	•	•	RLS Inc [SOP]		304-472-8800	•	•	•	•

DT	BK	CV	CR	PR	←Courts	Putnam	Recording→	UC	RE	TX	VS
•	•	•	•	•	American Investigations [SOP]		304-343-3346	•	•	•	•
•	•	•		•	The Croson Agency		304-343-1564	•	•	•	
					Liberty Record Search Inc		304-863-5542	•	•	•	
		•	•		West Virginia Records Research		304-633-6964				
•	•	•	•	•	Whiting Background & Legal Services		304-372-6499			•	•

DT	BK	CV	CR	PR	←Courts	Raleigh	Recording→	UC	RE	TX	VS
•	•	•	•	•	Accu-Check Information Services		304-375-4802	•		•	•
•	•	•		•	The Croson Agency		304-343-1564	•	•	•	
					Liberty Record Search Inc		304-863-5542	•	•	•	
•	•	•	•	•	Whiting Background & Legal Services		304-372-6499			•	•

DT	BK	CV	CR	PR	←Courts	Randolph	Recording→	UC	RE	TX	VS
•	•	•		•	The Croson Agency		304-343-1564	•	•	•	
•	•	•	•	•	DMI [SOP]		304-842-2946	•	•	•	•
					Liberty Record Search Inc		304-863-5542	•	•	•	
•		•	•	•	RLS Inc [SOP]		304-472-8800	•	•	•	•

DT	BK	CV	CR	PR	←Courts	Ritchie	Recording→	UC	RE	TX	VS
•	•	•	•	•	Accu-Check Information Services		304-375-4802	•		•	•
•	•	•		•	The Croson Agency		304-343-1564	•	•	•	
•	•	•	•	•	DMI [SOP]		304-842-2946	•	•	•	•
					Liberty Record Search Inc		304-863-5542	•	•	•	
			•		Professional Services of America Inc		304-485-1278				
•		•	•	•	RLS Inc [SOP]		304-472-8800	•	•	•	•

DT	BK	CV	CR	PR	←Courts	Roane	Recording→	UC	RE	TX	VS
•	•	•	•	•	Accu-Check Information Services		304-375-4802	•		•	•
•	•	•		•	The Croson Agency		304-343-1564	•	•	•	
					Liberty Record Search Inc		304-863-5542	•	•	•	
•	•	•	•	•	Whiting Background & Legal Services		304-372-6499			•	•

DT	BK	CV	CR	PR	←Courts	Summers	Recording→	UC	RE	TX	VS
•	•	•		•	The Croson Agency		304-343-1564	•	•	•	
					Liberty Record Search Inc		304-863-5542	•	•	•	

DT	BK	CV	CR	PR	←Courts	Taylor	Recording→	UC	RE	TX	VS
•	•	•		•	The Croson Agency		304-343-1564	•	•	•	
					Liberty Record Search Inc		304-863-5542	•	•	•	
•		•	•	•	RLS Inc [SOP]		304-472-8800	•	•	•	•
•	•	•	•	•	Vanhorn & Vanhorn Inc [SOP]		304-623-1362	•	•	•	•

DT	BK	CV	CR	PR	←Courts	Tucker	Recording→	UC	RE	TX	VS
•	•	•		•		The Croson Agency	304-343-1564	•	•	•	
•		•	•	•		RLS Inc [SOP]	304-472-8800	•	•	•	•

DT	BK	CV	CR	PR	←Courts	Tyler	Recording→	UC	RE	TX	VS
•	•	•	•	•		Accu-Check Information Services	304-375-4802	•		•	•
•	•	•		•		The Croson Agency	304-343-1564	•	•	•	
•	•	•	•	•		DMI [SOP]	304-842-2946	•	•	•	•
						Liberty Record Search Inc	304-863-5542	•	•	•	

DT	BK	CV	CR	PR	←Courts	Upshur	Recording→	UC	RE	TX	VS
•	•	•		•		The Croson Agency	304-343-1564	•	•	•	
•	•	•	•	•		DMI [SOP]	304-842-2946	•	•	•	•
						Liberty Record Search Inc	304-863-5542	•	•	•	
•		•	•	•		RLS Inc [SOP]	304-472-8800	•	•	•	•
•	•	•	•	•		Vanhorn & Vanhorn Inc [SOP]	304-623-1362	•	•	•	•

DT	BK	CV	CR	PR	←Courts	Wayne	Recording→	UC	RE	TX	VS
•	•	•		•		The Croson Agency	304-343-1564	•	•	•	
•		•	•	•		Daniel Agency	606-324-6029	•	•	•	•
						Liberty Record Search Inc	304-863-5542	•	•	•	
		•	•			West Virginia Records Research	304-633-6964				

DT	BK	CV	CR	PR	←Courts	Webster	Recording→	UC	RE	TX	VS
•	•	•		•		The Croson Agency	304-343-1564	•	•	•	
•	•	•	•	•		Whiting Background & Legal Services	304-372-6499			•	•

DT	BK	CV	CR	PR	←Courts	Wetzel	Recording→	UC	RE	TX	VS
•	•	•	•	•		Accu-Check Information Services	304-375-4802	•		•	•
•	•	•		•		The Croson Agency	304-343-1564	•	•	•	
						Liberty Record Search Inc	304-863-5542	•	•	•	

DT	BK	CV	CR	PR	←Courts	Wirt	Recording→	UC	RE	TX	VS
•	•	•	•	•		Accu-Check Information Services	304-375-4802	•		•	•
•	•	•		•		The Croson Agency	304-343-1564	•	•	•	
						Liberty Record Search Inc	304-863-5542	•	•	•	
•	•	•	•	•		Whiting Background & Legal Services	304-372-6499			•	•

DT	BK	CV	CR	PR	←Courts	Wood	Recording→	UC	RE	TX	VS
•	•	•	•	•		Accu-Check Information Services	304-375-4802	•		•	•
•	•	•		•		The Croson Agency	304-343-1564	•	•	•	
•	•	•	•	•		DMI [SOP]	304-842-2946	•	•	•	•
						Liberty Record Search Inc	304-863-5542	•	•	•	
			•			Professional Services of America Inc	304-485-1278				
		•	•			West Virginia Records Research	304-633-6964				
•	•	•	•	•		Whiting Background & Legal Services	304-372-6499			•	•

DT	BK	CV	CR	PR	←Courts	Wyoming	Recording→	UC	RE	TX	VS
•	•	•		•		The Croson Agency	304-343-1564	•	•	•	
						Liberty Record Search Inc	304-863-5542	•	•	•	

Wisconsin

DT	BK	CV	CR	PR	←Courts	County / Retriever	Recording→	UC	RE	TX	VS
						ADAMS					
				•		Boles-Wallner Abstract & Title	715-423-6940	•	•	•	
						Central Wisconsin Title	608-297-2789		•	•	
						ASHLAND					
•	•	•		•		Phillips Land Title Co Inc	715-339-2230	•	•	•	
						BARRON					
		•		•		Guaranty Title Services Inc	715-235-3393	•	•	•	
						BAYFIELD					
						Wisconsin Title Washburn	715-373-2412		•	•	
						BROWN					
•	•	•	•	•		Attorney's Process & Inv Services [SOP]	800-236-5202	•	•	•	•
•	•	•	•	•		Backgrounds Plus [SOP]	920-457-7355	•	•	•	•
		•		•		Bay Title & Abstract Inc	920-431-6100	•	•	•	
						Document Search Services	800-526-2157		•		
•	•	•	•	•		Lowery Professional Services Corp [SOP]	920-830-2114	•	•	•	•
						BUFFALO					
		•	•			Advanced Private Inv [SOP]	608-785-2744				
	•			•		The Title Co Inc (Eau Claire)	800-848-4853	•	•	•	
						BURNETT					
						Burnett County Abstract Co	715-349-2269	•	•	•	
						CALUMET					
•	•	•	•	•		Attorney's Process & Inv Services [SOP]	800-236-5202	•	•	•	•
		•		•		Bay Title & Abstract Inc	920-431-6100	•	•	•	
						Document Search Services	800-526-2157		•		
						CHIPPEWA					
		•	•			Chippewa Valley Civil Process [SOP]	715-289-3922				
	•			•		The Title Co Inc (Eau Claire)	800-848-4853	•	•	•	
						CLARK					
				•		Boles-Wallner Abstract & Title	715-423-6940	•	•	•	
	•			•		The Title Co Inc (Eau Claire)	800-848-4853	•	•	•	
						COLUMBIA					
•	•	•		•		Priority Records Search LLC	608-544-9991	•	•	•	•
						CRAWFORD					
•	•			•		The Title Co Inc (Prairie Du Chien WI)	888-918-4853	•	•	•	
						DANE					
•	•	•	•	•		Attorney's Process & Inv Services [SOP]	800-236-5202	•	•	•	•
		•		•		Bay Title & Abstract Inc	920-431-6100	•	•	•	
•	•	•	•	•		Dane County Legal Notice [SOP]	800-720-6871	•	•	•	
						Document Search Services	800-526-2157		•		
•	•	•	•	•		Gregg Inv, Inc of Madison [SOP]	800-866-1976	•			•
•	•	•	•			Infotrack Information Services Inc	800-275-5594	•	•	•	

DT	BK	CV	CR	PR	←Courts		UC	RE	TX	VS
•	•	•	•	•	Paul C Klumb Agency LLC [SOP]	414-254-1335	•	•	•	•
•	•	•		•	Priority Records Search LLC	608-544-9991	•	•	•	•
	•	•	•	•	Southeast Wisconsin Process & Inv Inc [SOP]	262-650-8904	•	•	•	•

DT	BK	CV	CR	PR	←Courts **Dodge**	Recording→	UC	RE	TX	VS
					Document Search Services	800-526-2157		•		
•	•	•	•		Infotrack Information Services Inc	800-275-5594	•	•	•	
•	•	•	•	•	Paul C Klumb Agency LLC [SOP]	414-254-1335	•	•	•	•
	•	•	•	•	Southeast Wisconsin Process & Inv Inc [SOP]	262-650-8904	•	•	•	•

DT	BK	CV	CR	PR	←Courts **Door**	Recording→	UC	RE	TX	VS
•	•	•	•	•	Attorney's Process & Inv Services [SOP]	800-236-5202	•	•	•	•
		•		•	Bay Title & Abstract Inc	920-431-6100	•	•	•	
					Document Search Services	800-526-2157		•		

DT	BK	CV	CR	PR	←Courts **Douglas**	Recording→	UC	RE	TX	VS
•	•	•	•	•	Abstract & Title Services of Carlton Inc [SOP]	888-331-3966	•	•	•	•
					Document Search Services	800-526-2157		•		

DT	BK	CV	CR	PR	←Courts **Dunn**	Recording→	UC	RE	TX	VS
					Dunn County Abstract & Title Inc	800-628-5727		•	•	
		•		•	Guaranty Title Services Inc	715-235-3393	•	•	•	
	•			•	The Title Co Inc (Eau Claire)	800-848-4853	•	•	•	

DT	BK	CV	CR	PR	←Courts **Eau Claire**	Recording→	UC	RE	TX	VS
		•	•		Chippewa Valley Civil Process [SOP]	715-289-3922				
	•			•	The Title Co Inc (Eau Claire)	800-848-4853	•	•	•	

DT	BK	CV	CR	PR	←Courts **Florence**	Recording→	UC	RE	TX	VS
		•		•	Florence County Abstract	715-528-3272	•	•	•	•
		•	•		PI & Shadow Security [SOP]	800-626-7578				
		•	•		Superior Title & Abstract	906-774-9010	•	•	•	

DT	BK	CV	CR	PR	←Courts **Fond du Lac**	Recording→	UC	RE	TX	VS
		•		•	Bay Title & Abstract Inc	920-431-6100	•	•	•	
					Document Search Services	800-526-2157		•		
	•	•	•	•	Southeast Wisconsin Process & Inv Inc [SOP]	262-650-8904	•	•	•	•

DT	BK	CV	CR	PR	←Courts **Forest**	Recording→	UC	RE	TX	VS
		•	•		PI & Shadow Security [SOP]	800-626-7578				

DT	BK	CV	CR	PR	←Courts **Grant**	Recording→	UC	RE	TX	VS
•	•			•	The Title Co Inc (Prairie Du Chien WI)	888-918-4853	•	•	•	

DT	BK	CV	CR	PR	←Courts **Green**	Recording→	UC	RE	TX	VS
		•	•	•	Ekum Abstract & Title	608-328-8221	•	•	•	
•	•	•	•	•	Gregg Investigations Inc of Janesville [SOP]	800-866-1976	•		•	•
•	•	•	•	•	Stewart & Associates Inc [SOP]	800-442-3807	•	•	•	•

DT	BK	CV	CR	PR	←Courts **Green Lake**	Recording→	UC	RE	TX	VS
		•	•	•	Green Lake Title & Abstract Co	920-294-6070	•	•	•	•

DT	BK	CV	CR	PR	←Courts **Iowa**	Recording→	UC	RE	TX	VS
					Iowa County Title	608-935-3834		•	•	

DT	BK	CV	CR	PR	←Courts **Iron**	Recording→	UC	RE	TX	VS
		•		•	Iron Title & Abstract Co	906-932-6340	•	•	•	

DT	BK	CV	CR	PR	←Courts **Jackson**	Recording→	UC	RE	TX	VS
		•	•		Advanced Private Inv [SOP]	608-785-2744				
				•	Boles-Wallner Abstract & Title	715-423-6940	•	•	•	

DT	BK	CV	CR	PR	←COURTS **JEFFERSON**	RECORDING→	UC	RE	TX	VS
					Document Search Services	800-526-2157		•		
•	•	•	•	•	Gregg Inv, Inc of Madison [SOP]	800-866-1976	•			•
•	•	•	•		Infotrack Information Services Inc	800-275-5594	•	•	•	
•	•	•	•	•	Paul C Klumb Agency LLC [SOP]	414-254-1335	•	•	•	•
	•	•	•	•	Southeast Wisconsin Process & Inv Inc [SOP]	262-650-8904	•	•	•	•

DT	BK	CV	CR	PR	←COURTS **JUNEAU**	RECORDING→	UC	RE	TX	VS
				•	Boles-Wallner Abstract & Title	715-423-6940	•	•	•	

DT	BK	CV	CR	PR	←COURTS **KENOSHA**	RECORDING→	UC	RE	TX	VS
		•	•	•	AGH Professional Inv [SOP]	262-884-4688		•		•
•	•	•	•	•	Attorney's Process & Inv Services [SOP]	800-236-5202	•	•	•	•
					Document Search Services	800-526-2157		•		
•	•	•	•	•	ESI Associates [SOP]	262-652-6361	•	•	•	•
•	•	•	•		Infotrack Information Services Inc	800-275-5594	•	•	•	
•	•	•	•	•	Myhre Process [SOP]	414-271-9574	•		•	•
•	•	•	•	•	Paul C Klumb Agency LLC [SOP]	414-254-1335	•	•	•	•
		•	•	•	PeopleSearch	877-835-1983	•	•	•	•
		•	•	•	Search Associates Two Great Minds	414-321-3375	•	•	•	
	•	•	•	•	Southeast Wisconsin Process & Inv Inc [SOP]	262-650-8904	•	•	•	•
		•	•		Wisconsin Employee & Renter Check (WERC)	414-967-9342				

DT	BK	CV	CR	PR	←COURTS **KEWAUNEE**	RECORDING→	UC	RE	TX	VS
•	•	•	•	•	Attorney's Process & Inv Services [SOP]	800-236-5202	•	•	•	•
		•		•	Bay Title & Abstract Inc	920-431-6100	•	•	•	
					Document Search Services	800-526-2157		•		

DT	BK	CV	CR	PR	←COURTS **LA CROSSE**	RECORDING→	UC	RE	TX	VS
		•	•		Advanced Private Inv [SOP]	608-785-2744				
•	•			•	The Title Co Inc (La Crosse)	800-788-4853	•	•	•	

DT	BK	CV	CR	PR	←COURTS **LAFAYETTE**	RECORDING→	UC	RE	TX	VS
		•	•	•	Ekum Abstract & Title	608-328-8221	•	•	•	
		•		•	Lafayette County Abstract	608-776-3338	•	•	•	

DT	BK	CV	CR	PR	←COURTS **LANGLADE**	RECORDING→	UC	RE	TX	VS
		•	•		PI & Shadow Security [SOP]	800-626-7578				

DT	BK	CV	CR	PR	←COURTS **LINCOLN**	RECORDING→	UC	RE	TX	VS
		•	•		PI & Shadow Security [SOP]	800-626-7578				

DT	BK	CV	CR	PR	←COURTS **MANITOWOC**	RECORDING→	UC	RE	TX	VS
•	•	•	•	•	Attorney's Process & Inv Services [SOP]	800-236-5202	•	•	•	•
•	•	•	•	•	Backgrounds Plus [SOP]	920-457-7355	•	•	•	•
		•		•	Bay Title & Abstract Inc	920-431-6100	•	•	•	
					Document Search Services	800-526-2157		•		
		•		•	Evans Title Companies	920-684-1261	•	•	•	•

DT	BK	CV	CR	PR	←COURTS **MARATHON**	RECORDING→	UC	RE	TX	VS
				•	Boles-Wallner Abstract & Title	715-423-6940	•	•	•	
		•	•		PI & Shadow Security [SOP]	800-626-7578				

DT	BK	CV	CR	PR	←COURTS **MARINETTE**	RECORDING→	UC	RE	TX	VS
•	•	•	•	•	Attorney's Process & Inv Services [SOP]	800-236-5202	•	•	•	•
		•		•	Bay Title & Abstract Inc	920-431-6100	•	•	•	
					Document Search Services	800-526-2157		•		
		•	•		Superior Title & Abstract	906-774-9010	•	•	•	

DT	BK	CV	CR	PR	←COURTS **MARQUETTE**	RECORDING→	UC	RE	TX	VS
					Central Wisconsin Title	608-297-2789		•	•	

DT	BK	CV	CR	PR	←Courts MENOMINEE	Recording→	UC	RE	TX	VS
		•		•	Bay Title & Abstract Inc	920-431-6100	•	•	•	

DT	BK	CV	CR	PR	←Courts MILWAUKEE	Recording→	UC	RE	TX	VS
•	•	•	•	•	Attorney's Process & Inv Services [SOP]	800-236-5202	•	•	•	•
•	•	•	•	•	Backgrounds Plus [SOP]	920-457-7355	•	•	•	•
					Document Search Services	800-526-2157		•		
•	•	•	•	•	ESI Associates [SOP]	262-652-6361	•	•	•	•
•	•	•	•		Infotrack Information Services Inc	800-275-5594	•	•	•	
•	•	•	•		Interstate Reporting Co Inc (IRC) [SOP]	262-251-6590	•		•	
•	•	•	•	•	Klitzke & Assoc Inc/Klitzke Services Group	262-521-9502	•	•	•	•
•	•	•	•	•	Myhre Process [SOP]	414-271-9574	•		•	•
•	•	•	•	•	Paul C Klumb Agency LLC [SOP]	414-254-1335	•	•	•	•
		•	•	•	Search Associates Two Great Minds	414-321-3375	•	•	•	
	•	•	•	•	Southeast Wisconsin Process & Inv Inc [SOP]	262-650-8904	•	•	•	•
		•	•		Wisconsin Employee & Renter Check (WERC)	414-967-9342				

DT	BK	CV	CR	PR	←Courts MONROE	Recording→	UC	RE	TX	VS
		•	•		Advanced Private Inv [SOP]	608-785-2744				

DT	BK	CV	CR	PR	←Courts OCONTO	Recording→	UC	RE	TX	VS
•	•	•	•	•	Attorney's Process & Inv Services [SOP]	800-236-5202	•	•	•	•
		•		•	Bay Title & Abstract Inc	920-431-6100	•	•	•	

DT	BK	CV	CR	PR	←Courts ONEIDA	Recording→	UC	RE	TX	VS
		•	•		PI & Shadow Security [SOP]	800-626-7578				

DT	BK	CV	CR	PR	←Courts OUTAGAMIE	Recording→	UC	RE	TX	VS
•	•	•	•	•	Attorney's Process & Inv Services [SOP]	800-236-5202	•	•	•	•
		•		•	Bay Title & Abstract Inc	920-431-6100	•	•	•	
					Document Search Services	800-526-2157		•		
					Fox Cities Title Co	920-731-5494		•	•	
•	•	•	•	•	Lowery Professional Services Corp [SOP]	920-830-2114	•	•	•	•
		•	•	•	Wisconsin Title of Shawano Inc	715-823-3600	•	•	•	

DT	BK	CV	CR	PR	←Courts OZAUKEE	Recording→	UC	RE	TX	VS
•	•	•	•	•	Attorney's Process & Inv Services [SOP]	800-236-5202	•	•	•	•
					Document Search Services	800-526-2157		•		
•	•	•	•		Infotrack Information Services Inc	800-275-5594	•	•	•	
•	•	•	•		Interstate Reporting Co Inc (IRC) [SOP]	262-251-6590	•		•	
•	•	•	•	•	Klitzke & Assoc Inc/Klitzke Services Group	262-521-9502	•	•	•	•
•	•	•	•	•	Myhre Process [SOP]	414-271-9574	•		•	•
•	•	•	•	•	Paul C Klumb Agency LLC [SOP]	414-254-1335	•	•	•	•
		•	•	•	Search Associates Two Great Minds	414-321-3375	•	•	•	
	•	•	•	•	Southeast Wisconsin Process & Inv Inc [SOP]	262-650-8904	•	•	•	•
		•	•		Wisconsin Employee & Renter Check (WERC)	414-967-9342				

DT	BK	CV	CR	PR	←Courts PEPIN	Recording→	UC	RE	TX	VS
					Dunn County Abstract & Title Inc	800-628-5727		•	•	
	•			•	The Title Co Inc (Eau Claire)	800-848-4853	•	•	•	

DT	BK	CV	CR	PR	←Courts PIERCE	Recording→	UC	RE	TX	VS
		•	•	•	St Croix Valley Title Services Inc	715-425-1519	•	•	•	
	•			•	The Title Co Inc (Eau Claire)	800-848-4853	•	•	•	

DT	BK	CV	CR	PR	←Courts POLK	Recording→	UC	RE	TX	VS
					Guaranty Title Services Osceola	888-620-7243	•	•	•	

DT	BK	CV	CR	PR	←Courts PORTAGE	Recording→	UC	RE	TX	VS
				•	Boles-Wallner Abstract & Title	715-423-6940	•	•	•	

DT	BK	CV	CR	PR	←Courts	PRICE	Recording→	UC	RE	TX	VS
•	•	•		•		Phillips Land Title Co Inc	715-339-2230	•	•	•	

DT	BK	CV	CR	PR	←Courts	RACINE	Recording→	UC	RE	TX	VS
		•	•	•		AGH Professional Inv [SOP]	262-884-4688		•		•
•	•	•	•	•		Attorney's Process & Inv Services [SOP]	800-236-5202	•	•	•	•
						Document Search Services	800-526-2157		•		
•	•	•	•	•		ESI Associates [SOP]	262-652-6361	•	•	•	•
•	•	•	•			Infotrack Information Services Inc	800-275-5594	•	•	•	
•	•	•	•			Interstate Reporting Co Inc (IRC) [SOP]	262-251-6590	•		•	
•	•	•	•	•		Myhre Process [SOP]	414-271-9574	•		•	•
•	•	•	•	•		Paul C Klumb Agency LLC [SOP]	414-254-1335	•	•	•	•
		•	•	•		Search Associates Two Great Minds	414-321-3375	•	•	•	
	•	•	•	•		Southeast Wisconsin Process & Inv Inc [SOP]	262-650-8904	•	•	•	•
		•	•			Wisconsin Employee & Renter Check (WERC)	414-967-9342				

DT	BK	CV	CR	PR	←Courts	RICHLAND	Recording→	UC	RE	TX	VS
•	•			•		The Title Co Inc (Prairie Du Chien WI)	888-918-4853	•	•	•	
				•		Wisconsin Title of Richland Center Inc	800-236-4596	•	•	•	•

DT	BK	CV	CR	PR	←Courts	ROCK	Recording→	UC	RE	TX	VS
•	•	•	•	•		Gregg Investigations Inc of Janesville [SOP]	800-866-1976	•		•	•
•	•	•	•	•		Stewart & Associates Inc [SOP]	800-442-3807	•	•	•	•

DT	BK	CV	CR	PR	←Courts	RUSK	Recording→	UC	RE	TX	VS
						Sawyer County Abstract & Title	715-634-9444	•	•	•	

DT	BK	CV	CR	PR	←Courts	SAUK	Recording→	UC	RE	TX	VS
•	•	•		•		Priority Records Search LLC	608-544-9991	•	•	•	•

DT	BK	CV	CR	PR	←Courts	SAWYER	Recording→	UC	RE	TX	VS
						Sawyer County Abstract & Title	715-634-9444	•	•		

DT	BK	CV	CR	PR	←Courts	SHAWANO	Recording→	UC	RE	TX	VS
•	•	•	•	•		Attorney's Process & Inv Services [SOP]	800-236-5202	•	•	•	•
		•		•		Bay Title & Abstract Inc	920-431-6100	•	•	•	
		•	•	•		Wisconsin Title of Shawano Inc	715-823-3600	•	•	•	

DT	BK	CV	CR	PR	←Courts	SHEBOYGAN	Recording→	UC	RE	TX	VS
•	•	•	•	•		Backgrounds Plus [SOP]	920-457-7355	•	•	•	•
		•	•	•		Search Associates Two Great Minds	414-321-3375	•	•	•	
	•	•	•	•		Southeast Wisconsin Process & Inv Inc [SOP]	262-650-8904	•	•	•	•

DT	BK	CV	CR	PR	←Courts	ST. CROIX	Recording→	UC	RE	TX	VS
•	•	•	•	•		Capitol Lien Records & Research [SOP]	800-845-4077	•	•	•	•
		•		•		Guaranty Title Services Inc	715-235-3393	•	•	•	
		•	•	•		St Croix Valley Title Services Inc	715-425-1519	•	•	•	
•	•	•	•	•		Twin Cities Research	651-714-0002	•	•	•	•

DT	BK	CV	CR	PR	←Courts	TAYLOR	Recording→	UC	RE	TX	VS
		•	•	•		Gowley Abstract	715-748-4790	•	•	•	

DT	BK	CV	CR	PR	←Courts	TREMPEALEAU	Recording→	UC	RE	TX	VS
		•	•			Advanced Private Inv [SOP]	608-785-2744				
•	•			•		The Title Co Inc (La Crosse)	800-788-4853	•	•	•	

DT	BK	CV	CR	PR	←Courts	VERNON	Recording→	UC	RE	TX	VS
		•	•			Advanced Private Inv [SOP]	608-785-2744				
•	•	•		•		The Title Co Inc (Viroqua)	800-538-4853	•	•	•	

DT	BK	CV	CR	PR	←Courts	VILAS	Recording→	UC	RE	TX	VS
		•		•		Northern Title of Vilas County	715-479-6459	•	•	•	
		•	•			PI & Shadow Security [SOP]	800-626-7578				

DT	BK	CV	CR	PR	←COURTS WALWORTH	RECORDING→	UC	RE	TX	VS
•	•	•	•	•	Gregg Investigations Inc of Janesville [SOP]	800-866-1976	•		•	•
•	•	•	•		Infotrack Information Services Inc	800-275-5594	•	•	•	
•	•	•	•	•	Klitzke & Assoc Inc/Klitzke Services Group	262-521-9502	•	•	•	•
•	•	•	•	•	Myhre Process [SOP]	414-271-9574	•		•	•
•	•	•	•	•	Paul C Klumb Agency LLC [SOP]	414-254-1335	•	•	•	•
		•	•	•	Search Associates Two Great Minds	414-321-3375	•	•	•	
	•	•	•	•	Southeast Wisconsin Process & Inv Inc [SOP]	262-650-8904	•	•	•	•
		•	•		Wisestart Information Services	262-723-7881				

DT	BK	CV	CR	PR	←COURTS WASHBURN	RECORDING→	UC	RE	TX	VS
					Sawyer County Abstract & Title	715-634-9444	•	•	•	

DT	BK	CV	CR	PR	←COURTS WASHINGTON	RECORDING→	UC	RE	TX	VS
					Document Search Services	800-526-2157		•		
•	•	•	•		Infotrack Information Services Inc	800-275-5594	•	•	•	
•	•	•	•		Interstate Reporting Co Inc (IRC) [SOP]	262-251-6590	•		•	
•	•	•	•	•	Klitzke & Assoc Inc/Klitzke Services Group	262-521-9502	•	•	•	•
•	•	•	•	•	Myhre Process [SOP]	414-271-9574	•		•	•
•	•	•	•	•	Paul C Klumb Agency LLC [SOP]	414-254-1335	•	•	•	•
		•	•	•	Search Associates Two Great Minds	414-321-3375	•	•	•	
	•	•	•	•	Southeast Wisconsin Process & Inv Inc [SOP]	262-650-8904	•	•	•	•
		•	•		Wisconsin Employee & Renter Check (WERC)	414-967-9342				

DT	BK	CV	CR	PR	←COURTS WAUKESHA	RECORDING→	UC	RE	TX	VS
•	•	•	•	•	Attorney's Process & Inv Services [SOP]	800-236-5202	•	•	•	•
					Document Search Services	800-526-2157		•		
•	•	•	•		Infotrack Information Services Inc	800-275-5594	•	•	•	
•	•	•	•		Interstate Reporting Co Inc (IRC) [SOP]	262-251-6590	•		•	
•	•	•	•	•	Klitzke & Assoc Inc/Klitzke Services Group	262-521-9502	•	•	•	•
•	•	•	•	•	Myhre Process [SOP]	414-271-9574	•		•	•
•	•	•	•	•	Paul C Klumb Agency LLC [SOP]	414-254-1335	•	•	•	•
		•	•	•	Search Associates Two Great Minds	414-321-3375	•	•	•	
	•	•	•	•	Southeast Wisconsin Process & Inv Inc [SOP]	262-650-8904	•	•	•	•
		•	•		Wisconsin Employee & Renter Check (WERC)	414-967-9342				

DT	BK	CV	CR	PR	←COURTS WAUPACA	RECORDING→	UC	RE	TX	VS
		•		•	Bay Title & Abstract Inc	920-431-6100	•	•	•	
		•	•	•	Wisconsin Title of Shawano Inc	715-823-3600	•	•	•	

DT	BK	CV	CR	PR	←COURTS WAUSHARA	RECORDING→	UC	RE	TX	VS
				•	Boles-Wallner Abstract & Title	715-423-6940	•	•	•	

DT	BK	CV	CR	PR	←COURTS WINNEBAGO	RECORDING→	UC	RE	TX	VS
•	•	•	•	•	Attorney's Process & Inv Services [SOP]	800-236-5202	•	•	•	•
		•		•	Bay Title & Abstract Inc	920-431-6100	•	•	•	
					Document Search Services	800-526-2157		•		
•	•	•	•	•	Lowery Professional Services Corp [SOP]	920-830-2114	•	•	•	•

DT	BK	CV	CR	PR	←COURTS WOOD	RECORDING→	UC	RE	TX	VS
				•	Boles-Wallner Abstract & Title	715-423-6940	•	•	•	

Editor's Tip: Remember the first rule about public record searching: Simply because your state or county has certain rules, regulations and practices regarding the accessibility and content of public records, does not mean that another state or county adheres to the same rules.

Wyoming

COURT RECORDS RETRIEVED | **RECORDING RECORDS RETRIEVED**

DT	BK	CV	CR	PR	←COURTS	COUNTY	RECORDING→	UC	RE	TX	VS
						ALBANY					
•	•	•		•	Daniel E Peel		970-484-1542	•	•	•	
						BIG HORN					
		•		•	Heritage Escrow LLC		307-765-9399	•	•	•	•
		•	•		Process Service of Wyoming [SOP]		307-266-1979				
						CAMPBELL					
					See adjoining counties for retrievers or contact court or recording office.						
						CARBON					
		•	•		Process Service of Wyoming [SOP]		307-266-1979				
						CONVERSE					
		•	•		Process Service of Wyoming [SOP]		307-266-1979				
						CROOK					
					First American Title Co of Crook Cty		307-283-1844	•	•	•	
						FREMONT					
		•	•		Process Service of Wyoming [SOP]		307-266-1979				
						GOSHEN					
					First American Torrington		307-532-5642		•	•	
						HOT SPRINGS					
		•	•		Process Service of Wyoming [SOP]		307-266-1979				
						JOHNSON					
		•	•		Process Service of Wyoming [SOP]		307-266-1979				
						LARAMIE					
•	•	•		•	Daniel E Peel		970-484-1542	•	•	•	
						LINCOLN					
		•	•		Bontecou Inv Services [SOP]		307-733-2637				
		•		•	Land Title Co		800-289-9920		•	•	
						NATRONA					
•	•	•		•	Daniel E Peel		970-484-1542	•	•	•	
		•		•	Petroleum Title Service Inc		307-235-6237	•	•	•	
		•	•		Process Service of Wyoming [SOP]		307-266-1979				
						NIOBRARA					
		•	•		Process Service of Wyoming [SOP]		307-266-1979				
						PARK					
		•	•		Bontecou Inv Services [SOP]		307-733-2637				
		•	•	•	Grizzly Inv Services [SOP]		307-587-8395	•	•	•	
						PLATTE					
					First American Wheatland		307-322-2133		•	•	
						SHERIDAN					
•	•	•		•	Daniel E Peel		970-484-1542	•	•	•	

DT	BK	CV	CR	PR	←Courts		Recording→	UC	RE	TX	VS
•		•		•	Sheridan County Title		307-672-6478	•	•	•	

DT	BK	CV	CR	PR	←Courts	SUBLETTE	Recording→	UC	RE	TX	VS
		•	•		Bontecou Inv Services [SOP]		307-733-2637				

DT	BK	CV	CR	PR	←Courts	SWEETWATER	Recording→	UC	RE	TX	VS
•	•	•	•	•	Pioneer National Title Insurance		307-875-9833	•	•	•	

DT	BK	CV	CR	PR	←Courts	TETON	Recording→	UC	RE	TX	VS
		•	•		Bontecou Inv Services [SOP]		307-733-2637				
		•	•	•	Bontecou Investigative Services Inc [SOP]		307-733-2637	•	•	•	
		•		•	Land Title Co		800-289-9920		•	•	

DT	BK	CV	CR	PR	←Courts	UINTA	Recording→	UC	RE	TX	VS
					Uinta Title		307-789-1777		•	•	

DT	BK	CV	CR	PR	←Courts	WASHAKIE	Recording→	UC	RE	TX	VS
		•	•		Process Service of Wyoming [SOP]		307-266-1979				

DT	BK	CV	CR	PR	←Courts	WESTON	Recording→	UC	RE	TX	VS
					Weston County Title		307-746-2001		•	•	

[SOP] = PERFORMS SERVICE OF PROCESS

COURT RECORDS

CODE	GOVERNMENT AGENCY	TYPE OF INFORMATION
DT	US District Court	Federal civil and criminal cases
BK	Bankruptcy Court	United States bankruptcy cases
CV	Civil Court	Municipal, county and state level civil cases
CR	Criminal Court	Municipal, county and state level criminal cases
PR	Probate Court	Wills and estate cases

COUNTY RECORDS - RECORDINGS

CODE	GOVERNMENT AGENCY	TYPE OF INFORMATION
UC	UCC Filing Office	Uniform Commercial Code and other personal property liens
RE	Real Estate Recording Office	Real property transactions and liens
TX	Tax Filing Office(s)	Federal and state tax liens, judgment liens
VS	Vital Records Office	Vital statistics—birth, death, marriage, divorce

= PRRN Member. *A retriever you can trust!*

Local Document Retriever Profiles

Information Found In The Retriever Profiles Section

The 2600 retriever profiles that follow are listed in alphabetical order. Individuals are listed by last name; companies are listed by the first letter of the company name.

Each Profile Contains...

- Retriever name, with PRRN logo if they are a PRRN Member in 2004
- Address
- Telephone number, including 800/888/877 number if available
- Fax number
- World Wide Web site address; email
- Summary of types of records retrieved
- Local retrieval area—a list of counties they service directly
- Other geographic areas serviced through correspondents
- When established
- Project turnaround times
- Billing and payment terms
- If they perform service of process
- Additional information, including special areas of expertise

Although the usual billing practices used by each of the retrieval companies are indicated, no information about actual pricing is included. Fees are subject to private negotiation and depend on the type and extent of any given project.

Hints and Tips on Using the Retriever Profiles Section

Alphabetical Rules

Individual names are alphabetized by last name first, unless the name appears as part of a company name, in which case it is alphabetized by the first letter of the company name.

If the word "The" appears to be a definitive connected part of the company name, you may find the company in the "T" section.

Branch offices of larger retriever firms are listed individually. Usually the firm name is followed by the branch office name or locale in parenthesis, along with that branch's corresponding retrieval area.

Read for Specialties and Expertise

Each retriever was given the opportunity to submit a twenty-five word statement indicating what they do best. Take a moment and read this statement before calling a retriever. This will give you a much better idea of their service and expertise.

Listed at the end of this section are PRRN Associate Members who offer regional or national search or screening services only.

Some Retrievers Are Mobile

Don't be alarmed if you don't get a live person when calling a retriever. Many retrievers are on the job at the local courthouse or recorder's office. Some may carry a cell phone. As a general rule, retrievers will return calls as they are able. We provide all the telephone numbers for each entry in this Profile section. The previous section—the Index—only had the main telephone number.

Only Call a Retriever for the Records They Retrieve

Remember to review which categories of public record are retrieved by the company prior to making a telephone call. For example, a company may only search and retrieve real estate records at the recorder's office, but no court record retrieval. If you call for a criminal record from a retriever who only does work at the recorder's office, then you are wasting your time and the retriever's time.

Consider the Coverage Area

Your public record request should be done on time, although reasonable variations may be expected for remote counties and for county offices that have long, internal turnaround times. Generally, you should never expect to incur a correspondent fee when selecting a retriever listed in the County Index.

As some retriever companies are also screening firms or search firms, you should always ask if they also offer services on a regional, statewide or national basis, or electronically.

How to Decide Which Retriever to Hire

If you are not sure how to chose a competent retriever or whether you should hire a local document retriever or hire a online service/gateway, we have provided helpful charts at the front of this directory.

A

A & A Attorney Services Inc
621 W Mallon Ave #505, Spokane, WA 99201-2181
Phone: 509-325-0001 **Fax:** 509-328-3226
aaattysv@earthlink.net

Types of Records Retrieved: Civil, criminal and probate courts; Federal courts; Real Estate; Tax liens/Judgments; UCC records; Vital records

Local Retrieval Area: WA-Spokane. **Correspondent Relationships:** statewide.

Add'l Information: Established 1979. Normal turnaround time- 48 hours. Projects billed by number of names searched. 1st project may require prepayment. They perform service of process.

A & A Legal Service Inc
1541 Bayshore Hwy, Burlingame, CA 94010-1602
Phone: 650-697-9431 **Fax:** 650-697-4640
www.aalegalservice.com **email:** general@aalegalservice.com

Types of Records Retrieved: Civil, criminal and probate courts; Federal courts; Real Estate; Tax liens/Judgments; UCC records; Vital records

Local Retrieval Area: CA-Alameda, Contra Costa, Marin, San Francisco, San Mateo, Santa Clara. **Correspondent Relationships:** nationwide.

Add'l Information: Established 1978. Normal turnaround time- 2-3 days. Expedited service available. Projects billed by the hour. They charge by mile and/or per copy. 1st project may require prepayment. Credit cards accepted. A & A Legal Service Inc is accurate, trustworthy and reliable. Their researchers are well trained and keep updated on court procedures. A licensed PI in CA. They perform service of process.

A & A Screening Solutions LLC
PO Box 608, 80 St Michael St #303, Mobile, AL 36601
Phone: 877-999-9318; 251-432-6100 **Fax:** 877-999-9319; 251-432-6103
www.aaverify.com **email:** rbw@aaverity.com

Types of Records Retrieved: Civil, criminal and probate courts; Federal courts; UCC records; Tax liens/Judgments.

Local Retrieval Area: AL-Baldwin, Mobile. **Correspondent Relationships:** nationwide. Online with the AL Court system.

Add'l Information: Established 1996. Normal turnaround time- same day to 72 hours. Projects billed by number of names searched. 1st project may require prepayment. Credit cards accepted. Payment terms can be net 30 days. They specialize in criminal record retrieval, civil and criminal investigations, service of process, pre-employment screening and tenant screening. They serve process all along the Gulf Coast in AL and MS. A licensed PI in AL. They perform service of process.

A & C Research
6185 Magnolia Ave #257, Riverside, CA 92506-2524
Phone: 951-301-6956 **Fax:** 951-301-6823
AandCResearch@aol.com

Types of Records Retrieved: Civil and criminal courts.

Local Retrieval Area: CA-Orange, Riverside, San Bernadino

Add'l Information: Established 2001. Normal turnaround time- 24 hours. Projects billed by number of names searched. Will bill weekly or bi-monthly with a net 30 days. They have over 15 years combined experience.

A & J Research Inc
1609 Clydesdale Dr, Lewisville, TX 75067
Phone: 972-221-7744 **Fax:** 972-219-5801
ajresearch@comcast.net

Types of Records Retrieved: Real Estate, UCCs, Tax liens/Judgments

Local Retrieval Area: TX-Collin, Dallas, Denton

Add'l Information: Established 2003. Normal turnaround time- 24-48 hours. Projects billed by number of names searched. Monthly billing, each order invoiced. A & J specializes in real estate document retrievals and filings in Dallas and North Dallas area.

A & M Attorney Services Inc
4647 Long Beach Blvd #D2, Long Beach, CA 90805-6976
Phone: 562-426-8306 **Fax:** 562-426-6384

Types of Records Retrieved: Civil, criminal, probate courts; Federal courts

Local Retrieval Area: CA-Los Angeles, Orange

Add'l Information: Established 1959. Normal turnaround time- 1-4 days. Projects billed by the hour. Credit cards accepted. They specialize in process service. They perform service of process.

A & S Abstracting
1602 Little Cake Rd, Columbia, KY 42728
Phone: 270-250-1203 **Fax:** 270-384-4805

Types of Records Retrieved: Real Estate; Tax liens/Judgments

Local Retrieval Area: KY-Adair

Add'l Information: Established 2003. 1st project may require prepayment. They specialize in real estate.

A All State Tracers Company
6180C Hixson Pike #105, Hixson, TN 37343-3030
Phone: 423-605-0155 **Fax:** 423-842-8011
cham7854_@bellsouth.net

Types of Records Retrieved: Civil, criminal and probate courts; Federal courts; Real Estate; Tax liens/Judgments; UCC records; Vital records.

Local Retrieval Area: AL-De Kalb, Jackson; GA-Bartow, Catoosa, Chattooga, Cherokee, Clayton, Cobb, Dawson, De Kalb, Douglas, Floyd, Forsyth, Fulton, Gilmer, Gordon, Gwinnett, Henry, Murray, Paulding, Pickens, Polk, Whitfield; TN-Bedford, Bledsoe, Blount, Bradley, Cannon, Coffee, Davidson, De Kalb, Franklin, Grundy, Hamilton, Knox, Lincoln, Loudon, McMinn, Marion, Meigs, Monroe, Roane, Rutherford, Sequatchie, Van Buren, Warren, White, Williamson. **Correspondents:** nationwide.

Add'l Information: Established 1990. Normal turnaround time- 24-72 hours. Projects billed by number of names searched. 1st project may require prepayment. Credit cards accepted. They specialize in real estate, mortgages, UCCs, suits, Tax liens/Judgments, corporate document filing, skiptracing & asset information. They perform title searches & current owner searches. Also performs criminal searches in 6 TN counties.

A California Process & Attorney Svc
206 S "D" St, San Bernardino, CA 92401
Phone: 909-381-5185 **Fax:** 909-885-5199
www.youbeenserved.com **email:** stephanie@youbeenserved.com

Types of Records Retrieved: Civil, criminal and probate courts; Federal courts; Real Estate; Tax liens/Judgments; UCC records; Vital records

Local Retrieval Area: CA-Los Angeles, Orange, Riverside, San Bernardino. **Correspondent Relationships:** nationwide.

Add'l Information: Established 1985. Normal turnaround time- 1-3 days. Projects billed by the hour. 1st project may require prepayment. They specialize in civil and real estate searches, process service and all attorney support services, including mobile photocopying and notary service. They perform service of process.

A Data Source
7909 Walerga Rd #112-205, Antelope, CA 95843
Phone: 916-726-4636 **Fax:** 916-726-4902
adatas@aol.com

Types of Records Retrieved: Civil, criminal and probate courts; Federal courts; Real Estate; UCC records; Vital records

Local Retrieval Area: CA-Placer, Sacramento. **Correspondent Relationships:** nationwide.

Add'l Information: Established 1996. Normal turnaround time- 24-48 hours. Credit cards accepted. They specialize in UCC, corporate, court and real property research, pre-employment screening, business and individual background profiles. Antelope, CA is located in Sacramento County.

A David Research

122 Calistoga Rd #243, Santa Rosa, CA 95409
Phone: 707-479-2779 **Fax:** 707-535-2040
office@workingthecourts.com

Types of Records Retrieved: Civil, criminal and probate courts; Real Estate; Tax liens/Judgments; UCC records; Vital records

Local Retrieval Area: CA-Napa, Sonoma. **Correspondent Relationships:** Kings, Madera, Merced, Tulore counties CA.

Add'l Information: Established 1991. Normal turnaround time- 24 hours. Projects billed by number of names searched. They have 14 years daily experience. Know who, what and exactly where to find it. Forensic searches done in both counties. 2,000,000/3,000,000 E & O insurance.

A Judicial Process Inc

191 University Blvd, PMB 338, Denver, CO 80206-4613
Phone: 800-317-9221; 303-860-0322

Types of Records Retrieved: Civil, criminal and probate courts; Federal courts; Real Estate; Tax liens/Judgments; UCC records; Vital records

Local Retrieval Area: CO-Boulder, Denver. **Correspondent Relationships:** NAPPS members in all states.

Add'l Information: Established 1987. Normal turnaround time- 24 hours. Projects billed by number of names searched. Projects billed by the hour. All projects require prepayment. They specialize in process service and court record retrieval. Licensed PI in CO. They perform service of process.

A P Legal Support Services

2522 N Calvert St, Baltimore, MD 21218
Phone: 800-273-9928; 410-366-9109 **Fax:** 410-366-9403
www.aplegalsupport.com **email:** ap2522@aol.com

Types of Records Retrieved: Civil, criminal and probate courts; Federal courts; Real Estate; Tax liens/Judgments; UCC records; Vital records

Local Retrieval Area: MD-Anne Arundel, Baltimore, Baltimore City, Carroll, Harford, Howard, Montgomery, Prince George's

Add'l Information: Established 1969. Normal turnaround time- 24-48 hours. Expedited service available. Projects billed by the hour. 1st project may require prepayment. They perform service of process.

A Public Record Expert Inc

5028 Lakehurst Ct, Palmetto, FL 34221
Phone: 941-504-7734 **Fax:** 941-723-3989
www.aprei.com **email:** david@aprei.com

Types of Records Retrieved: Civil, criminal and probate courts; Federal courts; Real Estate; Tax liens/Judgments; UCC records

Local Retrieval Area: FL-Charlotte, De Soto, Hardee, Hillsborough, Manatee, Pinellas, Sarasota. **Correspondent Relationships:** Virginia.

Add'l Information: Established 2001. Normal turnaround time- 12-48 hours. Projects billed by number of names searched. Bulk rate discounts are available. Payment net 30 days. They specialize in UCCs, tax liens, judgments, pending suits, mortgage retrievals and title searches. They are a notary & certified signing agent.

A Public Record Search Inc

424 N Vermont St, Covington, LA 70433
Phone: 985-892-5194 **Fax:** 985-898-0837
lds@skycom1.com

Types of Records Retrieved: Civil, criminal and probate courts; Real Estate; Tax liens/Judgments; UCC records

Local Retrieval Area: LA-St. Tammany Parish. **Correspondent Relationships:** Jefferson, Livingston, Orleans, St Bernard, St Charles, Tangipahoa, Washington parishes.

Add'l Information: Established 1960. Normal turnaround time- 5 working days. Fee basis will vary by type of project. 1st project may require prepayment. They specialize in document retrieval, metes and bounds, lot and block abstracting, property tax research and ownerships.

A Scott Broadhurst Associates

12 Main St, Dover, MA 02030
Phone: 617-536-3486 **Fax:** 508-785-2852

Types of Records Retrieved: Civil, criminal and probate courts; Federal courts; Real Estate; Tax liens/Judgments; UCC records

Local Retrieval Area: MA-Essex, Middlesex, Norfolk, Suffolk, Worcester

Add'l Information: Established 1988. Normal turnaround time- 24-48 hours. Expedited service is available. Projects billed by number of names searched. They specialize in real estate, current owner, mortgage and assignement searches and document retrieval as well as UCC and court record searches. They are fully insured.

A Short Abstract Co

PO Box 657, Cavalier, ND 58220
Phone: 701-265-4176 **Fax:** 701-265-4176

Types of Records Retrieved: Real Estate; Tax liens/Judgments

Local Retrieval Area: ND-Pembina

Add'l Information: Established 1920. Normal turnaround time- 1-2 weeks depending on the order. Fee basis will vary by type of project. 1st project may require prepayment. Out-of-state orders require prepayment. They specialize in title searches and abstracts of title.

A Total Search Solution

6357 S Gray Ct, Littleton, CO 80123
Phone: 303-738-9955 **Fax:** 303-738-9656
www.atssgroup.com **email:** orders@atssgroup.com

Types of Records Retrieved: Real Estate; Tax liens/judgments; UCC records

Local Retrieval Area: CO-Arapahoe, Denver, Douglas, Jefferson

Add'l Information: Established 2003. Normal turnaround time- 48-72 hours. Projects billed by number of names searched. Will invoice semi-monthly. They specialize in premier real estate information solutions. They offer a full line of title services.

A Very Private Eye Inc

4589 Southfield Ave, Orlando, FL 32812
Phone: 407-273-6646 **Fax:** 407-658-2555
www.averyprivateeye.com **email:** crahn@intellistar.net

Types of Records Retrieved: Civil, criminal and probate courts; Federal courts; Real Estate; Tax liens/Judgments; UCC records; Vital records

Local Retrieval Area: FL-Brevard, Lake, Orange, Osceola, Polk, Seminole

Add'l Information: Established 1996. Normal turnaround time- 24 hours. Projects billed by the hour. 1st project may require prepayment. Credit cards accepted. They specialize in electronic sweeps, backgrounds, intelligence, covert equipment, domestics, locates, formal government wiretapping export. They are 25 year law enforcement veterans. They cover all of Central FL, both civil and criminal investigations. A licensed PI in FL. They perform service of process.

A Wright Resource

PO Box 26593, Macon, GA 31221-6593
Phone: 478-757-9371 **Fax:** 478-757-4913
AWrightResource@aol.com

Types of Records Retrieved: Civil and criminal courts; Federal courts

Local Retrieval Area: AL-Jefferson; GA-Bibb. **Correspondent Relationships:** statewide.

Add'l Information: Established 2000. Normal turnaround time- 24-48 hours. Projects billed by number of names searched. 1st project may require prepayment. They specialize in civil and criminal searches.

A.D.I. Investigative

323 6th St, Marysville, CA 95901
Phone: 530-743-4245 **Fax:** 530-743-4250

Types of Records Retrieved: Civil, criminal and probate courts; Real Estate; Tax liens/Judgments; Vital records

Local Retrieval Area: CA-Butte, Colusa, Sutter, Yuba

Add'l Information: Established 1990. Normal turnaround time- 1-2 days. Projects billed by the hour. 1st project may require prepayment. They specialize in SOP and record retrieval. Insured. Celebrating 11th year serving Yuba, Sutter, Butte, and eastern Colusa counties. A licensed PI in CA. They perform service of process.

A.G.O. Legal Process Service

PO Box 16143, Las Cruces, NM 88004
Phone: 505-526-4303 **Fax:** 505-526-4303

Types of Records Retrieved: Civil, criminal and probate courts; Real Estate; Tax liens/Judgments; UCC records; Vital records

Local Retrieval Area: NM-Dona Ana, Grant, Hidalgo, Lincoln, Luna; TX-El Paso

Add'l Information: Established 1992. Normal turnaround time- 1-4 days. Expedited service available. Projects billed by the hour. All projects require prepayment. They perform service of process.

A/M Investigations

25 Congress St, Portland, ME 04101
Phone: 207-838-3111 **Fax:** 207-772-5455 nmmpi007@verizon.net

Types of Records Retrieved: Federal courts

Local Retrieval Area: ME-Cumberland. **Correspondent Relationships:** Maine, with personal service to Androscoggin, Aroostock, Franklin, Hancock, Lincoln, Oxford, Penobsot, Picataquis, Sagadahoc, Somerset, Waldo, Washington, York counties.

Add'l Information: Established 1988. Normal turnaround time- 24-48 hours for nearby counties; northern counties require more. Projects billed by the hour. All projects require prepayment. Many searches require fees to Clerk up front. Specialize in process service throughout Maine, 1 mile from civil and federal courthouse in Cumberland, Kennebec, Androscoggin, Sagadahoc, York, Knox and Waldo. Call for rates. A licensed PI in ME. They perform service of process.

A1 Cleveland Service Agency Inc

PO Box 93447, Cleveland, OH 44101-5447
Phone: 888-212-5614; **Fax:** 888-212-0896;
www.clevelandservice.com **email:** phil@clevelandservice.com

Types of Records Retrieved: Civil, criminal and probate courts; Federal courts; Real Estate; Tax liens/Judgments; UCC records; Vital records

Local Retrieval Area: OH-Cuyahoga, Lake

Add'l Information: Established 2000. Normal turnaround time- 1-3 business days. Expedited service available. Projects billed by the hour. All projects require prepayment. Credit cards accepted. They specialize in "Getting the job done right". They are prior military and law enforcement professionals providing superior legal support services to Northeast Ohio. A licensed PI in OH. They perform service of process.

A1 Inv

PO Box 357, 114 N West St #205, Lima, OH 45802
Phone: 419-229-1955 **Fax:** 419-229-2872
www.a1investigations.net **email:** p.wainscott@a1investigations.net

Types of Records Retrieved: Civil and criminal courts

Local Retrieval Area: OH-Allen, Auglaize, Hancock, Hardin, Mercer, Putnam, Van Wert

Add'l Information: Established 2003. All projects require prepayment. They also provide skiptracing, private investigations, and is a examiner and consultant for computerize voice stress analyzer. A licensed PI in OH. They perform service of process.

A-1 Unisource Screening & Information

8280 Utica Ave, Rancho Cucamonga, CA 91730
Phone: 800-525-6972; 909-980-3311 **Fax:** 909-980-5566
www.unisourcescreening.com **email:** info@unisourcescreening.com

Types of Records Retrieved: Civil and criminal courts; Federal courts

Local Retrieval Area: CA-Alameda, El Dorado, Glenn, Kern, Los Angeles, Orange, Riverside, Sacramento, San Bernardino, San Diego, San Francisco, San Mateo, Santa Barbara, Ventura. **Correspondent Relationships:** nationwide.

Add'l Information: Established 1986. Normal turnaround time- 24-72 hours. Projects billed by number of names searched. They conduct drug testing and background screening nationally. With over 14 years investigative experience, they are dedicated to "Providing Safe Environments" for employers and employees nationally.

AAA Abstract & Title Co Inc (Texas)

PO Box 38, 1 Planter St, Emory, TX 75440
Phone: 903-473-2233 **Fax:** 903-474-9483
rca@verizon.net

Types of Records Retrieved: Civil courts; Probate courts; Real Estate; Tax liens/Judgments

Local Retrieval Area: TX-Rains

Add'l Information: Established 1965. Normal turnaround time- variable depending on project. Fee basis varies by type of transaction. 1st project may require prepayment. They perform service of process.

AAA Abstract Co Inc (Oklahoma)

118 W Olive St, Stilwell, OK 74960
Phone: 918-696-2770 **Fax:** 918-696-5869
nfarrier@intellex.com

Types of Records Retrieved: Civil, criminal and probate courts; Federal courts; Real Estate; Tax liens/Judgments; UCC records; Vital records

Local Retrieval Area: OK-Adair

Add'l Information: Established 1965. Normal turnaround time- 1-10 days. Projects billed by number of records located. All projects require prepayment. Personal checks are accepted. They specialize in abstracts by photocopies of actual documents, increasing accuracy of abstract and usefulness to examining attorney. They also do closings.

AAA Process Servers Inc

2075 S University Blvd #184, Denver, CO 80210-4300
Phone: 800-293-6098; **Fax:** 719-573-1089
www.coloradoprocessservers.com **email:** service@coloradoprocessservers.com

Types of Records Retrieved: Civil, criminal and probate courts; Federal courts; Real Estate; UCC records

Local Retrieval Area: CO-Adams, Arapahoe, Boulder, Denver, Douglas, El Paso, Jefferson

Add'l Information: Established 1993. Normal turnaround time- 24 hours to 1 week. Projects billed by number of names searched. Projects billed by number of records located. Projects billed by the hour. 1st project may require prepayment. Personal checks are accepted. They specialize in process service, location of people, court retrieval, photo copying, skip tracing and court filings. They also have offices in Boulder, CO and Colorado Springs, CO.

AAA Process Service Inc

PO Box 21788, St Louis, MO 63109-0788
Phone: 888-350-5809; 314-351-7979 **Fax:** 314-752-5785
www.havepaperswilltravel.com **email:** andersonispy@aol.com

Types of Records Retrieved: Civil, criminal and probate courts; Federal courts; Real Estate; Tax liens/Judgments; UCC records Vital records

Local Retrieval Area: IL-Madison, Monroe, St. Clari; MO-Franklin, Jefferson, St. Charles, St Louis City, St. Louis. **Correspondent Relationships:** statewide.

Add'l Information: Established 1998. Normal turnaround time- 3-5 days. Expedited service available. Projects billed by the hour. All projects require prepayment. Credit cards accepted. A licensed PI in MO. They perform service of process.

AAA Search Excellence Inc

3099 Deltona Blvd, Spring Hill, Fl 34606
Phone: 352-688-6751 **Fax:** 352-666-1449

Types of Records Retrieved: Civil courts; Probate courts; Real Estate; Tax liens/Judgments; UCC records

Local Retrieval Area: FL-Bay, Citrus, Hernando, Okaloosa, Pasco, Walton

Add'l Information: Established 1994. Normal turnaround time- 24-48 hours. Projects billed by number of names searched. They provide document retrievals, current owner searches, full searches and document filings. Call for full information. Has 24-48 hour turnaround. Other counties serviced.

AAA VTS Investigations

79 W Monroe St #1122, Chicago, IL 60603
Phone: 800-203-4160; 312-782-7361 **Fax:** 312-782-2838
www.pichicago.com **email:** lisah@pichicago.com

Types of Records Retrieved: Civil, criminal and probate courts; Federal courts; Real Estate; Tax liens/Judgments; UCC records; Vital records

Local Retrieval Area: IL-Cook, De Kalb, Du Page, Kane, Kendall, Lake, McHenry, Will. They also retrieve from Federal Archive Center in Chicago

Add'l Information: Established 1980. Normal turnaround time- 24-48 hours. Rush service accepted. Projects billed by number of names searched. Credit cards accepted. Personal checks accepted. Formerly VTS, they are a licensed, insured Illinois detective agency providing document retrieval in Chicago metro area since 1979. They cover all of Northern IL. Cook county experts. Has a daily standing appointment at Chicago Federal Archives Ctr. A licensed PI in IL. They perform service of process.

AAABackgroundchex.com - Eleda Luther

15642 Poppyseed Lane, Canyon Country, CA 91387-1850
Phone: 661-250-8254 **Fax:** 661-250-8253
www.aaabackgroundchex.com **email:** eleda@earthlink.net

Types of Records Retrieved: Civil, criminal and probate courts; Federal courts; Tax liens/Judgments; UCC records

Local Retrieval Area: CA-Los Angeles, Ventura

Add'l Information: Established 1992. Normal turnaround time- 1-5 days. They cannot guarantee any specific turnaround time for felony/misdemeanor searches in Los Angeles. All felony/misdemeanor searches are done by the court. To perform this job legally and safely requires that they submit all names to the court. Projects billed by number of names searched. 1st project may require prepayment. Will invoice weekly or monthly depending on volume. Accept Pay Pal. They specialize in criminal background checks. They also do upper civil, federal criminal, federal civil, and probate. Turnaround for these searches is usually 24 hours. They also provide mortgage verification service.

Aaron Anderson Agency

PO Box 2065, Escondido, CA 92033-2065
Phone: 760-751-0101 **Fax:** 760-751-0599
apvti@yahoo.com

Types of Records Retrieved: Civil and criminal courts; Federal courts; Tax liens/Judgments

Local Retrieval Area: CA-San Diego. **Correspondent Relationships:** nationwide.

Add'l Information: Established 1993. Normal turnaround time- 1-2 days. Projects billed by number of names searched. Monthly payment. They specialize in civil, criminal and workers' compensation. All searches are "hands on." Owner is a retired US Probation/Parole Officer now licensed as a California Private Investigator. A licensed PI in CA.

ABA Services

1156 W Thornbury Pl, Highlands Ranch, CO 80129
Phone: 720-344-1259 **Fax:** 720-344-1265
karl-long@comcast.net

Types of Records Retrieved: Civil and criminal courts; Federal Courts; Real Estate; Tax liens/Judgments; UCC records

Local Retrieval Area: CO-Adams, Arapahoe, Boulder, Denver, Douglas, Elbert, Jefferson

Add'l Information: Established 2004. Normal turnaround time- 24-72 hours. Projects billed by number of names searched. Payment due net 15 days. A complete court retrieval research and document retrieval services.

ABC Inv

3820 Neal Ave, Kingman, AZ 86401
Phone: 928-757-4370 **Fax:** 928-757-4407

Types of Records Retrieved: Civil, criminal and probate courts; Real Estate; Tax liens/Judgments; UCC records.

Local Retrieval Area: AZ-Mohave

Add'l Information: Established 1973. Normal turnaround time- 24-48 hours. Expedited service available. Projects billed by number of names searched. They specialize in attorney services. A licensed PI in AZ. They perform service of process.

ABC Investigators Inc

PO Box 62167, Lafayette, LA 70596
Phone: 800-738-7300; 307-783-6131 **Fax:** 337-783-7070
www.abcinvestigators.com **email:** pete@abcinvestigators.com

Types of Records Retrieved: Civil, criminal and probate courts; Federal courts; Real Estate; Tax liens/Judgments; UCC records

Local Retrieval Area: LA-Acadia Parish, Jefferson Davis Parish, Lafayette Parish, St. Landry Parish, Vermilion Parish. **Correspondent Relationships:** nationwide.

Add'l Information: Established 1982. Normal turnaround time- same week. Projects billed by the hour. 1st project may require prepayment. They are a certified legal investigative firm, a CLI. A licensed PI in LA. They perform service of process.

ABC Legal Services Inc

910 5th Ave, Seattle, WA 98104-1137
Phone: 800-736-7295; 206-839-1195 **Fax:** 800-536-0797;
www.abclegal.com **email:** research@abclegal.com

Types of Records Retrieved: Civil, criminal and probate courts; Federal courts; Real Estate; Tax liens/Judgments; UCC records; Vital records

Local Retrieval Area: WA-Grays Harbor, Island, King, Kitsap, Lewis, Mason, Pierce, Skagit, Snohomish, Thurston, Whatcom. **Correspondent Relationships:** nationwide.

Add'l Information: Established 1974. Normal turnaround time- 1-2 days. Billing depends on the nature of the project. Credit cards accepted. They will also invoice. Personal checks are accepted. They are online with SCOMIS, PACER and CourtLink, which allows them instant access to court index records. A licensed PI in WA. They perform service of process.

ABC Services Inc

15 S Park Ave, Le Center, MN 56057
Phone: 507-357-6320 **Fax:** 507-357-6056
tba@frontiernet.net

Types of Records Retrieved: Civil and criminal courts; Federal courts, Real Estate, Tax liens/Judgments; UCC records

Local Retrieval Area: MN-all counties (may exempt far northern counties). **Correspondent Relationships:** statewide.

Add'l Information: Established 1991. Normal turnaround time- 8-24 hours. Projects billed by number of names searched. Monthly billing. They have been in business for over 10 years; the owner was deputy court administrator for six years. They also offer statewide unlawful detainers. Will retrieve real estate, UCC, and tax lien records for select counties.

Abeln Abstract & Title Co

PO Box 92, 47 W 7th St, Dubuque, IA 52004-0092
Phone: 563-582-7148 **Fax:** 563-582-5298

Types of Records Retrieved: Civil courts; Probate courts; Real Estate; Tax liens/Judgments; UCC records; Vital records

Local Retrieval Area: IA-Dubuque

Add'l Information: Established 1890. Normal turnaround time- 2-3 days. Projects billed by number of names searched. A charge for time is also included. They specialize in real estate and personal lien searches.

Aberdeen Inv, Inc

172 Wolverine Cr, Thunder Bay, ON P7C 5Z2
Phone: 807-626-4074 **Fax:** 807-475-6915 rperkins@tbaytel.net

Types of Records Retrieved: Civil courts; Probate courts; Real Estate; Tax liens/Judgments

Local Retrieval Area: CANADA-Ontario, Thunder Bay

Add'l Information: Established 1981. Normal turnaround time- 24 hours. Projects billed by the hour. Payment due upon receipt of invoice. They specialize in Thunder Bay, Ontario, and northwestern Ontario. They are a full service investigation company that services all of Northwestern

Ontario. In business since 1981. A licensed PI in ONTARIO, CANADA. They perform service of process.

Abess/Cyberdix

PO Box 5943, Stockton, CA 95205
Phone: 877-594-0498; 209-942-1110 **Fax:** 877-594-0498;
www.employeescreening.net **email:** russpi@sbcglobal.net

Types of Records Retrieved: Civil and criminal courts; Probats courts; Federal courts; Tax liens/Judgments; UCC records; Vital records

Local Retrieval Area: CA-El Dorado, Placer, Sacramento, San Joaquin, Yolo, Yuba. **Correspondent Relationships:** nationwide, 74 foreign countries.

Add'l Information: Established 1986. Normal turnaround time- 1 day. Projects billed by number of names searched. Fees negotiated with volume. 1st project may require prepayment. Credit cards accepted. They specialize in pre-employment background checks, criminal and civil investigations. Registered process server, licensed investigator. Principal is an ex-federal investigator/police officer. A licensed PI in CA. They perform service of process.

Able Atlanta Research

3904 N Darid Hills Rd, Decatur, GA 30033
Phone: 404-502-2024 **Fax:** 770-987-3782

Types of Records Retrieved: Civil and criminal courts; UCC records; Tax liens/Judgments.

Local Retrieval Area: GA-Barrow, Clayton, De Kalb, Fulton, Gwinnett, Hall, Henry, Rockdale, Walton. **Correspondent Relationships:** Cobb, Cherokee, Forsyth.

Add'l Information: Established 2003. Normal turnaround time- 24-48 hours. Projects billed by number of names searched. Will bill 30 days net.

Absolute Abstracting

19656 SE 260th St, Covington, WA 98042
Phone: 206-335-7837 **Fax:** 253-520-4981
www.hometown.aol.com/aabstracting/myhomepage/profile.html **email:** aabstracting@aol.com

Types of Records Retrieved: Civil, criminal and probate courts; Federal courts; Real Estate; Tax liens/Judgments; UCC records; Vital records

Local Retrieval Area: WA-King, Kitsap, Pierce, Snohomish, Thurston

Add'l Information: Established 2001. Normal turnaround time- 24-hours. Same day in many cases. 1st project may require prepayment. All work in performed by experienced abstractors. A quality product with timely results.

Abstract & Data Search Services

513 E McKinley Ave, Mishawaka, IN 46545
Phone: 888-457-5344; 574-256-5344 **Fax:** 574-256-7350
datasearch@ameritech.net

Types of Records Retrieved: Civil and criminal courts; Probate; Federal courts; UCC records; Real Estate; Tax liens/Judgments

Local Retrieval Area: IN-Elkhart, LaPorte, Marion, Marshall, Porter, St Joseph

Add'l Information: Established 1988. Normal turnaround time- same or next day. Bill monthly and special arrangements are avaiable. 1st project may require prepayment. Their main objectives are solid communications, consistent turnaround times and top quality research.

Abstract & Guaranty Co

812 Manvel Ave, Chandler, OK 74834-3858
Phone: 405-258-1244 **Fax:** 405-258-1657

Types of Records Retrieved: Civil courts; Probate courts; Real Estate; Tax liens/Judgments; UCC records

Local Retrieval Area: OK-Lincoln

Add'l Information: Established 1900. Normal turnaround time- 48 hours. Fee basis will vary by the type of project. All projects require prepayment.

Abstract & Title Co

PO Box 369, 67 Central Ave S, Beach, ND 58621-0369
Phone: 701-872-4531 **Fax:** 701-872-4531

Types of Records Retrieved: Civil, criminal and probate courts; Real Estate; Tax liens/Judgments; UCC records

Local Retrieval Area: ND-Golden Valley

Add'l Information: Established 1912. Normal turnaround time- 3-5 days. Projects billed by number of names searched. 1st project may require prepayment. They specialize in titles, abstracts and title insurance work.

Abstract & Title Co

PO Box 182, Albion, IL 62806
Phone: 618-445-2554 **Fax:** 618-445-2938

Types of Records Retrieved: Civil, criminal and probate courts; Real Estate; Tax liens/Judgments; UCC records

Local Retrieval Area: IL-Alexander, Clark, Clay, Clinton, Coles, Crawford, Cumberland, Edgar, Edwards, Effingham, Franklin, Gallatin, Hamilton, Jackson, Jasper, Jefferson, Johnson, Lawrence, Marion, Massac, Perry, Pope, Pulaski, Randolph, Richland, Saline, Union, Wabash, Washington, Wayne, White, Williamson. **Correspondent Relationships:** Gibson and Posey counties IN.

Add'l Information: Established 1974. Normal turnaround time- 36 hours. Projects billed by number of names searched. Terms: net 15-30 days. They specialize in all the above services along with real estate closings, disbursing monies, full real estate searches and preparation of Complete Abstracts of Title in all listed counties.

Abstract & Title Guaranty Co

326 5th Ave S, Clinton, IA 52732-4511
Phone: 563-243-2027 **Fax:** 563-243-6108
atgc@abstractco.com

Types of Records Retrieved: Civil, criminal and probate courts; Real Estate; Tax liens/Judgments; UCC records; Vital records

Local Retrieval Area: IA-Clinton, Jackson

Add'l Information: Established 1893. Normal turnaround time- 2-3 days. Expedited service available. Fee basis varies by type of transaction.

Abstract & Title Inc

PO Box 246, 413 D St, Fairbury, NE 68352
Phone: 402-729-2771 **Fax:** 402-729-6366
abstractandtitle@netscape.net

Types of Records Retrieved: Real Estate; Tax liens/judgments; UCC records

Local Retrieval Area: NE-Clay, Fillmore, Gage, Jefferson, Saline, Seward, Thayer

Add'l Information: Established 1964. Normal turnaround time- 24 hours. Projects billed by number of names searched. Projects billed by number of records located. Fee basis is per description of one ownership. 1st project may require prepayment. They specialize in abstracting, title insurance, closing and research. They have been in business over 30 years and have a 100-year title plant.

Abstract & Title Services Inc

503 W Main, PO Box 26, Anamosa, IA 52205
Phone: 319-462-4828 **Fax:** 319-462-4958

Types of Records Retrieved: Civil, criminal and probate courts; Real Estate; Tax liens/Judgments; UCC records; Vital records

Local Retrieval Area: IA-Jones

Add'l Information: Established 1857. Normal turnaround time- 1-5 days. Projects billed by number of names searched. Projects billed by the hour. All projects require prepayment.

Abstract & Title Services of Carlton Inc

PO Box 556, 199 Chestnut, Carlton, MN 55718
Phone: 888-331-3966; 218-384-3450 **Fax:** 218-384-3451
www.abstracttitle.net **email:** info@abstracttitle.net

Types of Records Retrieved: Civil, criminal and probate courts; Federal courts; Real Estate; Tax liens/Judgments; UCC records; Vital records

Local Retrieval Area: MN-Aitkin, Carlton, St. Louis; WI-Douglas

Add'l Information: Established 1993. Normal turnaround time- 24 hours depending on travel time. Projects billed by number of names searched. Projects billed by the hour. 1st project may require prepayment. They specialize in real estate & searches for UCC, court judgment, tax lien, probate records & bankruptcy docs. Access US Bankruptcy & judgment records in Duluth. Licensed closers & abstractors. Special orders OK. Aiken cty office phone- 877-751-5528. They perform service of process.

Abstract &Title Co

PO Box 720, 299 N Main St, Watford City, ND 58854-0720
Phone: 701-842-3366 **Fax:** 701-444-2709
abstract@rtc.com

Types of Records Retrieved: Civil courts; Probate courts; Real Estate; Tax liens/Judgments; UCC records; Vital records

Local Retrieval Area: ND-McKenzie

Add'l Information: Established 1954. Normal turnaround time- variable depending on project. Projects billed by number of names searched. Projects billed by the hour. 1st project may require prepayment. Personal checks are accepted.

Abstract Art Inc

PO Box 1749, Clinton, NC 28329
Phone: 910-592-2972 **Fax:** 910-592-4942

Types of Records Retrieved: Real Estate; Tax liens/Judgments; UCC records; Vital records

Local Retrieval Area: NC-Cumberland, Harnett, Johnston, Sampson, Wayne

Add'l Information: Established 1995. Normal turnaround time- 24 hours. Projects billed by number of names searched. 1st project may require prepayment.

Abstract Associates of Lancaster Inc

1903 Lititz Pike, Lancaster, PA 17601-3805
Phone: 717-581-5841 **Fax:** 717-581-5845
www.abstractassociates.com **email:** bstull@abstractassociates.com

Types of Records Retrieved: Probate courts; Real Estate; Tax liens/Judgments; UCC records; Vital records

Local Retrieval Area: PA-Berks, Chester, Dauphin, Lancaster, Lebanon, York. **Correspondent Relationships:** nationwide.

Add'l Information: Established 1992. Normal turnaround time- 1 week. Expedited service available. Fee basis will vary by the type of project. 1st project may require prepayment. They specialize in deed and lien searches, financing statements, document retrieval. They perform service of process.

Abstract Enterprises Inc

628 Spruce St, Scranton, PA 18503
Phone: 570-963-5290 **Fax:** 570-983-0093

Types of Records Retrieved: Civil courts; Probate courts; Real Estate; Tax liens/Judgments; UCC records; Vital records

Local Retrieval Area: PA-Lackawanna

Add'l Information: Established 1990. Normal turnaround time- 3 days. Fee basis will vary by the type of project.

Abstract One

3 Rolling Acres, Dagsboro, DE 19939-9647
Phone: 302-732-9027 **Fax:** 302-732-9029
abstractone@cb.com

Types of Records Retrieved: Civil, criminal and probate courts; Real Estate; Tax liens/Judgments; UCC records; Vital records

Local Retrieval Area: PA-York. **Correspondent Relationships:** nationwide

Add'l Information: Established 1986. Normal turnaround time- 24-48 hours. Projects billed by number of names searched. Projects billed by the hour. Fee basis will vary by the type of project. 1st project may require prepayment. Terms: net 30 days. They specialize in lien searches (one or more owner property reports), criminal checks, UCC reports, judgments and full title searches.

Abstracting & Legal Research Inc

PO Box 127, Alexandria, LA 71309-0127
Phone: 318-473-9979 **Fax:** 318-449-9739
www.alrinc-la.com **email:** alrinc@cox-internet.com

Types of Records Retrieved: Civil, criminal and probate courts; Federal courts; Real Estate; Tax liens/Judgments; UCC records; Vital records

Local Retrieval Area: LA-Allen Parish, Avoyelles Parish, Evangeline Parish, Grant Parish, Natchitoches Parish, Rapides Parish, Sabine Parish, St. Landry Parish, Vernon Parish. **Correspondent Relationships:** statewide.

Add'l Information: Established 1989. Normal turnaround time- 48 hours for direct parishes and over 48 hours for the remainder of state. Projects billed by number of names searched. Projects billed by the hour. 1st project may require prepayment. They specialize in parish records.

Abstractor Associates Inc

18044 13 Mile Rd #200, Roseville, MI 48066
Phone: 586-778-7554 **Fax:** 586-778-9730
michele@abstractorassociates.com

Types of Records Retrieved: Civil courts; Probate courts; Federal courts; Real Estate; Tax liens/Judgments; UCC records; Vital records

Local Retrieval Area: MI-Macomb, St. Clair, Washtenaw, Wayne. **Correspondent Relationships:** Oakland, Genesee, Lapeer, Saginaw, Shiawasee.

Add'l Information: Established 1990. Normal turnaround time- 24-48 hours. Expedited service available. Projects billed by number of names searched. Projects billed by the hour. They specialize in title research (current owner to full 60 year searches). They also do asset lien searches, litigation research, and document retrieval.

Abstracts by Godail

251 Florida Blvd #212, Baton Rouge, LA 70801
Phone: 800-660-7318; 225-343-0351 **Fax:** 800-660-7469; 225-343-1341

Types of Records Retrieved: Civil courts; Probate courts; Federal courts; Real Estate; Tax liens/Judgments; UCC records

Local Retrieval Area: LA-Ascension Parish, Assumption Parish, East Baton Rouge Parish, Livingston Parish, Pointe Coupee Parish, Rapides Parish, St. Landry Parish, West Baton Rouge Parish. **Correspondent Relationships:** statewide.

Add'l Information: Normal turnaround time- 1-2 days. Projects billed by the hour. 1st project may require prepayment. They have been established for over 22 years. Covers all Louisiana at added cost.

Abstracts of McIntosh County Inc

PO Box 154, Ashley, ND 58413-0154
Phone: 701-288-3618 **Fax:** 701-288-3508
grosslo@drtel.net

Types of Records Retrieved: Civil, criminal and probate courts; Real Estate; Tax liens/Judgments; UCC records; Vital records

Local Retrieval Area: ND-McIntosh

Add'l Information: Established 1984. Normal turnaround time- 1-3 days. Projects billed by number of names searched. Projects billed by number of records located. 1st project may require prepayment. They specialize in researching all records on file in the county offices. They have many records in-house.

Abstracts/Trustees of Texas

PO Box 9932, Austin, TX 78766
Phone: 888-452-0331; 512-340-0331 **Fax:** 888-452-3442; 512-340-0226
www.atotx.com **email:** orders@xspediusmail.net

Types of Records Retrieved: Civil courts; Probate courts; Federal courts; Real Estate; Tax liens/Judgments; UCC records

Local Retrieval Area: TX-all counties

Add'l Information: Established 1986. Normal turnaround time- 24-72 hours. Projects billed by number of names searched. Fees vary depending upon volume. 1st project may require prepayment. They specialize in property searches and foreclosures.

Abstrax

2022 Cliff Dr, PMB 178, Santa Barbara, CA 93109
Phone: 805-965-9858 **Fax:** 805-965-0913
www.west.net/~abstrax **email:** abstrax@west.net

Types of Records Retrieved: Civil, criminal and probate courts; Federal courts; Real Estate; Tax liens/Judgments; UCC records; Vital records

Local Retrieval Area: CA-San Luis Obispo, Santa Barbara, Ventura

Add'l Information: Established 1993. Normal turnaround time- 24-48 hours. Projects billed by number of names searched. Contract services available. 1st project may require prepayment. Terms: net 45 days.

Acadia Legal Support

PO Box 191, Frankfort, ME 04438-0191
Phone: 207-223-5285 **Fax:** 207-223-3904

Types of Records Retrieved: Civil, criminal and probate courts; Federal courts; Real Estate; Tax liens/Judgments

Local Retrieval Area: ME-Hancock, Penobscot, Waldo

Add'l Information: Established 1997. Normal turnaround time- 1-2 days. Expedited service available. Projects billed by number of names searched. 1st project may require prepayment. They perform service of process.

ACBS

5910 Hamilton Blvd, Allentown, PA 18106
Phone: 866-530-2227; **Fax:** 610-530-5646
www.acbsi.com **email:** info@acbsi.com

Types of Records Retrieved: Civil and criminal courts; Real Estate; Tax liens/Judgments; UCC records

Local Retrieval Area: PA-Carbon, Lehigh, Northampton, Schuylkill. **Correspondent Relationships:** statewide in PA, NJ.

Add'l Information: Established 1929. Normal turnaround time- 24-36 hours. Projects billed by number of records located. Credit cards accepted. Will file/record documents. Will invoice monthly. Their real estate department has a comprehensive selection of business and real estate search reports and flood certification reports with life of loan, accessible via Internet ordering.

Access Information

234 Columbine St #310, Denver, CO 80206-4711
Phone: 800-827-7607; 303-778-7677 **Fax:** 303-778-7691
www.access-information.com **email:** ai@access-information.com

Types of Records Retrieved: Civil, criminal and probate courts; Federal courts; Real Estate; Tax liens/Judgments; UCC records; Vital records

Local Retrieval Area: CO-Arapahoe, Boulder, Broomfield, Denver, Douglas, Jefferson. **Correspondent Relationships:** most of Colorado and nationwide.

Add'l Information: Established 1981. Normal turnaround time- same or next day. Projects billed by the hour. 1st project may require prepayment. Credit cards accepted. They specialize in document research and retrieval, as well as court monitoring and insurance records.

Access Information & Retrievals

PO Box 52132, Boston, MA 02205
Phone: 617-306-1547 **Fax:** 781-871-6662
www.aircorp.org **email:** rgreen@aircorp.org

Types of Records Retrieved: Civil courts; Federal courts; Real Estate; Tax liens/Judgments; UCC records

Local Retrieval Area: MA-Essex, Middlesex, Norfolk, Plymouth, Suffolk

Add'l Information: Established 2003. Normal turnaround time- 24-48 hours. Projects billed by number of names searched. Will invoice. They specialize in UCC, Tax liens/Judgments & suits. They also provide mortgage retrieval & title research throughout Eastern Massachusetts.

Access Information Services Inc

1773 Western Ave, Albany, NY 12203
Phone: 800-388-1598; 518-452-1873 **Fax:** 800-388-1599; 518-452-0822
accessin@sprynet.com

Types of Records Retrieved: Civil and criminal courts; Federal courts; Real Estate; Tax liens/Judgments; UCC records

Local Retrieval Area: NY-Albany, Rensselaer, Saratoga, Schenectady. **Correspondent Relationships:** nationwide.

Add'l Information: Established 1994. Normal turnaround time- 24-36 hours. Projects billed by number of names searched. 1st project may require prepayment. Credit cards accepted. They specialize in UCC preparation, filing and searching. Will search any public record nationwide. They perform service of process.

Access Louisiana Inc

400 Travis St #504, Shreveport, LA 71101
Phone: 800-489-5620; 318-227-9730 **Fax:** 800-705-8953; 318-222-3053

Types of Records Retrieved: Civil courts; Probate courts; Federal courts; Real Estate; Tax liens/Judgments; UCC records

Local Retrieval Area: LA-Bienville, Bossier, Caddo, Claiborne, DeSoto, Red River, Webster. **Correspondent Relationships:** Louisiana, Texas, Florida extensively.

Add'l Information: Established 1991. Normal turnaround time- 24-48 hours. Projects billed by number of names searched. They offer a discount for volume. Personal checks are accepted. They provide registered agent services for Louisiana and all corp services and filings with the Sec. of State. They are online with the UCC system and corporate database with the Sec. of State. Registered agent services for Louisiana.

Access Research

PO Box 33325, San Diego, CA 92163
Phone: 800-456-9613; 619-231-8947 **Fax:** 619-231-9338
www.accessresearchsd.com **email:** newrequest@accessresearchsd.com

Types of Records Retrieved: Civil, criminal and probate courts; Federal courts; Tax liens/Judgments; UCC records; Vital records

Local Retrieval Area: CA-Alameda, Fresno, Kern, Los Angeles, Orange, Riverside, Sacramento, San Bernardino, San Diego, San Francisco, San Joaquin, San Luis Obispo, San Mateo, Santa Barbara, Ventura. **Correspondent Relationships:** nationwide.

Add'l Information: Established 1995. Normal turnaround time- 24-48 hours. Projects billed by number of names searched. Credit cards accepted. Terms are net 30 days. Past due invoices are subject to late fees. They are a nationwide public record provider and pre-employment screening firm, specializing in wholesale public records. All research in CA is performed by "hands on" researchers at the courthouse. Members of PRRN, NPRRA, BBB & NAPBS.

Access RI Public Information

741 Westminster St #204, Providence, RI 02903
Phone: 877-999-7474; 401-421-5700 **Fax:** 401-421-5701
www.ri-pi.com **email:** access@ri-pi.com

Types of Records Retrieved: Civil, criminal and probate courts; Federal courts; Tax liens/Judgments; UCC records; Vital records.

Local Retrieval Area: RI-Bristol, Kent, Newport, Providence, Washington

Add'l Information: Established 1994. Normal turnaround time- 24 hours or same-day service. Projects billed by the hour. 1-hr minimum on most jobs. 1st project may require prepayment. They specialize in comprehensive personal background and corporate due diligence profiling as well as document procurement and document filing. A licensed PI in RI.

Accessible Document Retrieval

525 N Fulton St, Fresno, CA 93728-3401
Phone: 559-779-5491 **Fax:** 559-443-0073
loveystoys@hotmail.com

Types of Records Retrieved: Civil, criminal and probate courts; Federal courts; Real Estate; Tax liens/Judgments; UCC records; Vital records

Local Retrieval Area: CA-Fresno, Madera

Add'l Information: Established 1992. Normal turnaround time- 24 hours, except weekends, holidays. Some archived courts records may take longer. Projects billed by number of names searched. Fee basis varies by type of project. Per agreement. They specialize in all types of court records research and county recorder's records located in Fresno County, and Madera County, CA. All work is "hands on" from actual public records.

Accountable Process Servers Inc

PO Box 588, Cambridge, MN 55008-0588
Phone: 763-689-4190 **Fax:** 763-689-4191
lynxamanda@cs.com

Types of Records Retrieved: Civil, criminal and probate courts; Federal courts; Real Estate; Tax liens/Judgments

Local Retrieval Area: MN-Anoka, Chisago, Hennepin, Isanti, Ramsey, Sherburne, Washington

Add'l Information: Established 1986. Normal turnaround time- 1-2 days. Projects billed by number of names searched. 1st project may require prepayment. Will invoice; terms net 30 days. They specialize in real estate records and process serving. Cell number is 612-991-7849. They perform service of process.

Accu-Check Information Services

PO Box 1002, Parkersburg, WV 26102
Phone: 304-375-4802 **Fax:** 304-375-2018
accucheck@charter.net

Types of Records Retrieved: Civil, criminal and probate courts; Federal courts; UCC records; Tax liens/Judgments; Vital records

Local Retrieval Area: OH-Athens, Gallia, Jefferson, Meigs, Monroe, Morgan, Noble, Putnam, Washington. WV-Calhoun, Doddridge, Fayette, Greenbrier, Jackson, Kanawha, Mingo, Nicholas, Pleasants, Raleigh, Ritchie, Roane, Tyler, Wetzel, Wirt, Wood

Add'l Information: Established 1999. Normal turnaround time- 24-48 hours. Expedited service available. Projects billed by number of names searched. 1st project may require prepayment. Monthly billing. Accu-Check Information Services is owned and operated by professional record researcher of over 10 years experience. They believe their clients deserve excellent and accurate customer service.

AccuFacts Research Corporation

PO Box 514, Olympia, WA 98507-0514
Phone: 800-898-5583; 360-956-3990 **Fax:** 800-473-0148; 360-956-1398
www.accufactsresearch.com **email:** cynthia@accufactsresearch.com

Types of Records Retrieved: Civil, criminal and probate courts; Federal courts; Tax liens/Judgments; UCC records

Local Retrieval Area: WA-Thurston. **Correspondent Relationships:** nationwide.

Add'l Information: Established 1994. Normal turnaround time- 4 hours. Projects billed by number of names searched. Charges are per jurisdiction/per name searched. Terms: net 30 days. They specialize in obtaining Superior Court records at all counties in Washington, and UCC and corporate services nationwide. Online access to US District & Bankruptcy courts nationwide.

Accurate Background Check

PO Box 1864, Ocala, FL 34478
Phone: 877-611-2277; 352-291-1155 **Fax:** 877-913-2277; 352-854-8917
www.accuratebackgroundcheck.com **email:** LolaGonzalez@AccurateBackgroundCheck.com

Types of Records Retrieved: Civil, criminal and probate courts; Federal courts; Real Estate; Tax liens/Judgments; Vital records

Local Retrieval Area: FL-all counties. **Correspondent Relationships:** statewide.

Add'l Information: Established 1999. Normal turnaround time- 24 hours. Projects billed by number of names searched. 1st project may require prepayment. They specialize in criminal, misdemeanor civil searches, drug screening, credit reports, tenant screening, polygraphs & investigations. Their staff includes a licensed PI.They also do workers compensation searches, fingerprinting & retrieval. A licensed PI in FL.

Accurate Background Inc

20988 Bake Pky #104, Lake Forest, CA 92630
Phone: 800-784-3911; 949-609-0155 **Fax:** 800-784-3593; 949-609-0166
www.accuratebackground.com **email:** caldrich@accuratebackground.com

Types of Records Retrieved: Civil and criminal courts; Federal courts; Tax liens/Judgments; UCC records

Local Retrieval Area: CA-Los Angeles, Orange, Riverside, San Bernardino, San Diego, San Francisco, San Mateo, Santa Clara, Ventura; AZ-Maricopa; NV-Clark. **Correspondent Relationships:** nationwide.

Add'l Information: Established 1997. Normal turnaround time- 24-48 hours. Projects billed by number of names searched. Credit cards accepted. Credit accounts accepted. They are a national wholesaler of criminal and civil court searches for pre-employment screeners. Online computer ordering and electronic transfers are featured.

Accurate Confidential Research Inc

12973 SW 112th St #317, Miami, FL 33186
Phone: 305-386-6677 **Fax:** 305-383-2514
accurate247@aol.com

Types of Records Retrieved: Civil, criminal and probate courts; Federal courts; Real Estate; Tax liens/Judgments; UCC records; Vital records

Local Retrieval Area: FL-Broward, Dade, Palm Beach. **Correspondent Relationships:** nationwide.

Add'l Information: Established 1984. Normal turnaround time- 24 hours. Projects billed by number of names searched. Payment terms are net 30 days. 1st project may require prepayment. Credit cards accepted. They do all of their court/real estate research ON-SITE. They use old fashioned methods for accuracy; can retrieve any document. They use microfilm, microfiche and ledger books. A licensed PI in FL.

Accurate Records Research LLC

1801 Todd Way, Meridian, ID 83642
Phone: 208-888-2857 **Fax:** 208-288-4371
recresrch@cableone.net

Types of Records Retrieved: Civil and criminal courts; Federal courts; Real Estate; Tax liens/Judgments; UCC records

Local Retrieval Area: ID-Ada, Bannock, Bear Lake, Bingham, Blaine, Boise, Bonner, Bonneville, Boundary, Canyon, Cassia, Clearwater, Fremont, Gem, Gooding, Idaho, Jefferson, Jerome, Kootenai, Latah, Lewis, Lincoln, Madison, Minidoka, Nez Perce, Payette, Twin Falls, Washington. **Correspondent Relationships:** Bingham, Bonner. Bonneville, Canyon, Gem, Bannock, Kootenai, Madison, Nevada, Churchill, Clark, Elko, Humboldt, Lander.

Add'l Information: Established 1998. Normal turnaround time- 24-48 hours. Projects billed by number of names searched. Net 30 days. They specialize in criminal background checks and current owner searches.

Accurate Search Corporation

217 E Houston St 5th Fl, New York, NY 10002
Phone: 212-228-1850 **Fax:** 212-228-0114
www.accuratesearches.com **email:** maria@accuratesearches.com

Types of Records Retrieved: Civil courts; Federal courts; Real Estate; Tax liens/Judgments; UCC records

Local Retrieval Area: NY-Bronx, Kings, New York, Queens, Richmond

Add'l Information: Established 2003. Normal turnaround time- 24-48 hours. Projects billed by number of names searched. All projects require prepayment. Accurate Search Corp will guarantee superior service in the New York City area abstracting and record retrieval industry. Twenty years experience and a great team of qualified abstractors.

Accurate Source.com Inc

1205 Jess Dr, Oakville, Ontario, CANADA L6J 7N6
Phone: 800-978-8950; 905-829-0755 **Fax:** 800-404-4677;
www.accuratesource.com **email:** info@accuratesource.com

Types of Records Retrieved: Civil and criminal courts; Driver Records & Abstracts; SINs, Reference checks.

Local Retrieval Area: Canada-Alberta, British Columbia, Manitoba, New Brunswick, Newfoundland, Northwest Territories, Nova Scotia, Ontario, Prince Edward, Saskatchewan, Yukon. **Correspondent Relationships:** Canada.

Add'l Information: Established 1995. Normal turnaround time- 48-72 hours. Projects billed by number of names searched. Credit cards accepted. Payment due net 15-30 days. They are a public records retrieval and service corp engaged in providing private sector wholesale prices and service in research for entire Canada, including driver records/abstracts, SINs, ref checks.

Accurate Source.com Inc

PO Box 3488, Fullerton, CA 92831
Phone: 800-978-8950; 714-449-0961 **Fax:** 800-978-8951; 714-449-9581
www.accuratesource.com **email:** info@accuratesource.com

Types of Records Retrieved: Civil, criminal and probate courts; Federal courts; Real Estate; Tax liens/Judgments; UCC records; Vital records

Local Retrieval Area: CA-Los Angeles, Orange, Riverside, San Bernardino, San Diego, Santa Clara, Ventura. **Correspondent Relationships:** statewide and Canada.

Add'l Information: Established 1995. Normal turnaround time- 12-48 hours. Projects billed by number of names searched. Credit cards accepted. Payment terms are net 15-30 days. They are a public records retrieval and services company providing the private sector with wholesale prices and exceptional service. They perform service of process.

AccuScreen Systems

1038 Main St, Baton Rouge, LA 70802
Phone: 800-383-6476; 225-343-8378 **Fax:** 225-383-6445
www.accuscreensystems.com **email:** bruce@accuscreensystems.com

Types of Records Retrieved: Civil and criminal courts; Federal district

Local Retrieval Area: LA-East Baton Rouge Parish, West Baton Rouge Parish. **Correspondent Relationships:** LA parishes of St. Tammany, Lafayette, Rapides.

Add'l Information: Established 1974. Normal turnaround time- 2 days. Projects billed by number of names searched. 1st project may require prepayment. Monthly billing available. They specialize in criminal background checks, investigative services, pre-employment screening and drug testing. A licensed PI in LA. They perform service of process.

AccuSearch Inc

2338 W Royal Palm Rd, Suite J, Phoenix, AZ 85021-9339
Phone: 800-462-7019; 602-249-3466 **Fax:** 602-249-0821
www.accusearch.biz **email:** info@accusearch.biz

Types of Records Retrieved: Civil, criminal and probate courts; Federal courts; Real Estate; Tax liens/Judgments; UCC records

Local Retrieval Area: AZ-Maricopa. **Correspondent Relationships:** nationwide for criminal records. Exclusive AZ statewide network.

Add'l Information: Established 1989. Normal turnaround time- 24-48 hours. Projects billed by number of names searched. 1st project may require prepayment. Credit cards accepted. Payment terms are net 30 days. Checks accepted. A licensed PI firm searching all Arizona records - criminal, civil MVR, bankruptcy, property, liens, judgments. State and county UCC searches and filing. Corporate document retrieval and filing. A licensed PI in AZ.

Accu-Source Inc

8585 Stemmons #M26, Dallas, TX 75247
Phone: 214-637-4064 **Fax:** 817-887-1603
www.accu-source.com **email:** sales@accu-source.com

Types of Records Retrieved: Civil and criminal courts

Local Retrieval Area: TX-Bexar, Collin, Dallas, Denton, Grayson, Gregg, Harris, Hunt, Johnson, Kaufman, Larmar, Nueces, Parker, Rockwall, Tarrant, Tom Green, Wise. **Correspondent:** nationwide (for criminal).

Add'l Information: Established 1986. Normal turnaround time- 24-48 hours for local counties, usually less than 2 hrs. Projects billed by number of names searched. 1st project may require prepayment. Credit cards accepted. Terms are net 30 days. Pay Pal payments are also accepted. They specialize in pre-employment background processing, automated plate and VIN searches. Please note their fast turnaround times and online services on criminal records and credit header searches.

AccuTech Legal Support Services

PO Box 12037, San Diego, CA 92101
Phone: 800-275-7189; 619-232-9905 **Fax:** 619-232-5928
accubob1@msn.com

Types of Records Retrieved: Civil, criminal and probate courts; Federal courts; Real Estate; Tax liens/Judgments; UCC records; Vital records

Local Retrieval Area: CA-San Diego. **Correspondent Relationships:** statewide.

Add'l Information: Established 1986. Normal turnaround time- 1-4 days. Projects billed by number of names searched. Projects billed by number of records located. 1st project may require prepayment. Credit cards accepted. Terms: net 30 days. Mastercard and Visa accepted. They specialize in court research and record retrieval. A general attorney service and can scan documents to CD-ROM. They perform service of process.

Ace Background Check Inc

6267 Caribou Dr, Clinton, OH 44216
Phone: 800-731-9221; 330-882-4284 **Fax:** 330-882-4292
www.acebackground.com **email:** jabologa@msn.com

Types of Records Retrieved: Civil and criminal records; Federal courts; Real Estate; Tax liens/Judgments; UCC records; Vital records.

Local Retrieval Area: OH-all counties

Add'l Information: Established 2002. Normal turnaround time- 24-72 hours. Expedited service available. Projects billed by number of names searched. Credit cards accepted. Will invoice net 30 days. With the mission of providing their clients with the most accurate, affordable background information available, Ace offers one-stop search to extensive employment, tenant, or character profile screenings both locally and nationally.

Ace Data Service

2476 Tradewinds Dr, Dunedin, FL 34698-2034
Phone: 727-735-9311 **Fax:** 727-736-4531
rpolo2@tampabay.rr.com

Types of Records Retrieved: Civil and criminal courts; Federal courts; Real Estate; Tax liens/Judgments; UCC records; Vital records

Local Retrieval Area: FL-Hillsborough, Pasco, Pinellas. **Correspondent Relationships:** statewide.

Add'l Information: Normal turnaround time- 24-48 hours. Accept checks, money orders, addressed to Ace Data & checks payable to Ace Data Service. They specialize in hands on retrieval, easy to read reports and savings for multiple searches. 25% discount for first time customers. They perform service of process.

ACME Research

44272 Rail Rd, Guthrie, MN 56461-9728
Phone: 218-224-3239 **Fax:** 218-224-4005
acme@paulbunyan.net

Types of Records Retrieved: Civil, criminal and probate courts; Federal courts; Real Estate; Tax liens/Judgments; UCC records; Vital records

Local Retrieval Area: MN-Beltrami, Cass, Hubbard

Add'l Information: Established 1991. Normal turnaround time- 72 hours. Projects billed by the hour. 1st project may require prepayment. Personal checks accepted. They specialize in personal injury investigation. A licensed PI in MN. They perform service of process.

Acme Research

Michigan City, IN 46360
Phone: 219-878-9950 **Fax:** 219-878-9950

Types of Records Retrieved: Criminal courts

Local Retrieval Area: IN-Elkhart, Marshall, St Joseph. **Correspondent Relationships:** Adams County, IL for criminal records only.

Add'l Information: Established 1989. Normal turnaround time- 24 hours. Projects billed by number of names searched. 1st project may require prepayment. Will bill established customers on 15th and end of month. Their work is very accurate with fast turnaround time; is a paralegal and has been in county gov.t, ran for county clerk. Fax contact suggested.

ACMS Process Service

PO Box 26604, Tucson, AZ 85726
Phone: 520-629-0303 **Fax:** 520-628-8339
acms2serve@cox.net

Types of Records Retrieved: Civil, criminal and probate courts; Federal courts; Real Estate; Tax liens/Judgments; UCC records; Vital records

Local Retrieval Area: AZ-Cochise, Graham, Pima, Pinal, Santa Cruz. **Correspondent Relationships:** Cochise and Graham counties AZ.

Add'l Information: Established 1975. Normal turnaround time- 2-3 days. Expedited service available. Projects billed by number of names searched. 1st project may require prepayment. ACMS Process Service prides itself in its customer service and customer satisfaction. They are fast efficient and professional. They perform service of process.

ACS Legal Search

5905 Whitney Way, Rex, GA 30273
Phone: 770-474-3195 **Fax:** 770-474-3825

Types of Records Retrieved: Civil and criminal courts

Local Retrieval Area: GA-Clayton, De Kalb, Henry

Add'l Information: Established 2001. Normal turnaround time- 24 hours. Projects billed by number of names searched. 1st project may require prepayment. ACS Legal Search goes to the courthouse in the counties listed to search and retrieve documents.

Action Abstracts

6304 Greenspring Ave, Baltimore, MD 21209
Phone: 410-358-7162 or 410-493-6344 **Fax:** 410-358-2142
titles@actionabstracts.com

Types of Records Retrieved: Real Estate; Tax liens/Judgments

Local Retrieval Area: MD-Baltimore. **Correspondent Relationships:** statewide.

Add'l Information: Established 1995. Normal turnaround time- 1-2 days. Projects billed by number of names searched. They specialize in document retrieval statewide and title abstracts in Baltimore county. Fully insured, thorough and on time.

Action Legal Support Services

5528 N Palm #123, Fresno, CA 93704
Phone: 559-432-3337 **Fax:** 559-432-1140
www.actionlegalsupport.com **email:** action@attitude.com

Types of Records Retrieved: Civil, criminal and probate courts; Federal courts

Local Retrieval Area: CA-Fresno, Kern, Madera, Merced, Stanislaus, Tulare. **Correspondent Relationships:** Fresno, Kern, Kings, Madera, Merced, Stanislaus, Tulare counties CA.

Add'l Information: Established 1968. Normal turnaround time- within 1 week. Projects billed by number of names searched. Projects billed by number of records located. Projects billed by the hour. 1st project may require prepayment. They have more than 35 years in business and are members of CAPPS and NAPPS. They perform service of process.

Action Professional Services

115 E 11th #212, Sioux Falls, SD 57104
Phone: 888-335-3090; 605-335-3090 **Fax:** 605-335-0739
http://action.business-direct.com/ **email:** action@willinet.net

Types of Records Retrieved: Civil and criminal courts; Real Estate; Tax liens/Judgments; UCC records

Local Retrieval Area: SD-Lincoln, Minnehaha

Add'l Information: Established 1983. Normal turnaround time- 4 days. Projects billed by number of names searched. 1st project may require prepayment. Credit cards accepted. They specialize in service of process and collections. They perform service of process.

Action Services & Research Inc

25 Falconer St #2, North Tonawanda, NY 14120
Phone: 877-553-7504; 716-692-5032 **Fax:** 716-692-5039
www.actionservicesandresearch.com **email:** mike@actionservicesandresearch.com

Types of Records Retrieved: Civil, criminal and probate courts; Federal courts; Real Estate; Tax liens/Judgments; UCC records; Vital records

Local Retrieval Area: NY-Erie, Niagara. **Correspondent Relationships:** New York.

Add'l Information: Established 1985. Normal turnaround time- 1-2 days depending on project. Projects billed by number of names searched. 1st project may require prepayment. Credit cards accepted. At Action Services we know our business and progressively work at being the best, so you're the best. They perform service of process.

Active Detective Bureau Inc

4239 Hamilton Ave, Cincinnati, OH 45223
Phone: 800-405-4006; 513-541-6600 **Fax:** 513-541-6690
www.cbpgs.com/adb

Types of Records Retrieved: Civil, criminal and probate courts; Federal courts; Real Estate; Tax liens/Judgments; Vital records

Local Retrieval Area: KY-Boone, Campbell, Kenton; OH-Butler, Clermont, Hamilton, Warren

Add'l Information: Established 1976. Normal turnaround time- 2-3 days. Expedited service available. Projects billed by number of records located. Projects billed by the hour. 1st project may require prepayment. Process service requires pre-payment. They specialize in legal service of process, investigative services & commercial & domestic surveillance. A licensed PI in OH & IN. They perform service of process.

AD Services (ADS)

38750 Paseo Padre Pky #A1, Fremont, CA 94536-6169
Phone: 800-827-9101; 510-795-1111 **Fax:** 510-793-2222

Types of Records Retrieved: Civil, criminal and probate courts; Real Estate; Tax liens/Judgments; Vital records

Local Retrieval Area: CA-Alameda, Contra Costa, San Joaquin, San Mateo, Santa Clara, Stanislaus

Add'l Information: Established 1972. Normal turnaround time- 2-5 days. Projects billed by the hour. All individuals must prepay, all companies are invoiced. They specialize in process servicing. They perform service of process.

Adair County Abstract Company

230 Public Square, PO Box 86, Greenfield, IA 50849
Phone: 800-798-6129; 641-743-6129 **Fax:** 641-743-6129

Types of Records Retrieved: Civil courts; Probate courts; Real Estate; Tax liens/Judgments; UCC records

Local Retrieval Area: IA-Adair

Add'l Information: Established 1875. Normal turnaround time- 1-2 days. They charge a flat rate per project.

Adams County Abstract Co

PO Box 790, Hettinger, ND 58639
Phone: 701-567-2224 **Fax:** 701-567-2910

Types of Records Retrieved: Real Estate; Tax liens/judgments; UCC records

Local Retrieval Area: ND-Adams

Add'l Information: Established 1907. Normal turnaround time- 7-10 days full title. Fee basis will vary by the amount of time to perform the search. 1st project may require prepayment. They will also invoice. They specialize in title and mineral searches.

Adams Freelance Title

1875 Kentucky Hwy 1781, Waynesburg, KY 40489
Phone: 606-365-8108 **Fax:** 606-365-8108

Types of Records Retrieved: Real Estate; Tax Lliens/judgments

Local Retrieval Area: KY-Rockcastle

Add'l Information: Established 1997. 1st project may require prepayment. She specializes in real estate.

Adams Investigations

PO Box 42052, Des Moines, IA 50323
Phone: 888-844-0624; 515-523-1081 **Fax:** 775-703-1689
www.investigatorlady.com **email:** Nic@investigatorlady.com

Types of Records Retrieved: Civil, criminal and probate courts; Federal courts; Real Estate; Tax liens/Judgments; UCC records; Vital records

Local Retrieval Area: IA-Dallas, Polk. **Correspondent Relationships:** O'Brien, Sioux counties IA.

Add'l Information: Established 1995. Normal turnaround time- 24-48 hours. Projects billed by number of names searched. Projects billed by the hour. All projects require prepayment. Credit cards accepted. They specialize in location of people and assets, fraud detection, witness location, identity theft, legal research, hidden assets, witness interviews, fraud and insurance. A licensed PI in IA. They perform service of process.

Adams Land Title (Hastings)

PO Box 1347, 209 W 9th St #E, Hastings, NE 68901
Phone: 402-463-4198 **Fax:** 402-463-6480
superfoot@navix.net

Types of Records Retrieved: Probate courts; Federal courts; Real Estate; Tax liens/Judgments

Local Retrieval Area: NE-Adams, Buffalo, Clay, Hall, Kearney, Nuckolls, Webster. **Correspondent Relationships:** Nebraska.

Add'l Information: Established 1979. Normal turnaround - 1 week. Projects billed by number of records located. 1st project may require prepayment.

Adams Title Agency

179 Clairmont Dr, Painesville, OH 44077
Phone: 440-951-8296 **Fax:** 440-354-5139

Types of Records Retrieved: Civil courts; Real Estate, Tax liens/Judgments; UCC records

Local Retrieval Area: OH-Lake

Add'l Information: Established 1983. Normal turnaround time- within 24 hours. Projects billed by number of names searched. Projects billed by number of records located. All projects require prepayment. Terms: net 30 days. A licensed insurance specialist and escrow officer, she has 27-years experience in the area. Additional phone is 440-357-0280.

Stephen J Addison

3010 Longfellow Ave, Hazel Creest, IL 60429-1718
Phone: 708-335-9179 **Fax:** 708-335-9179
fourtyfathomz1@juno.com

Types of Records Retrieved: Civil, criminal and probate courts; Real Estate; Tax liens/Judgments; UCC records; Vital records

Local Retrieval Area: IL-Cook, Kankakee

Add'l Information: Established 2004. Normal turnaround time- less than 30 days. Projects billed by number of names searched. Projects billed by number of records located. All projects require prepayment. Specialize in executive protection, subpoena services, pre-employment screening, video surveillance, missing persons and insurance fraud. A licensed PI in IL.

Adit Research Inc

3512 35th Ave S, Minneapolis, MN 55406
Phone: 888-721-5220; 612-721-5220 **Fax:** 612-721-5224
aditresearch@yahoo.com

Types of Records Retrieved: Civil, criminal and probate courts; Federal courts; Real Estate; Tax liens/Judgments; UCC records; Vital records

Local Retrieval Area: MN-Anoka, Carver, Chisago, Dakota, Hennepin, Ramsey, Scott, Sherburne, Stearns, Washington. **Correspondent Relationships:** Blue Earth, Brown, Freeborn, Jackson, LeSueur, McLeod, Mille Lacs, Mower, Nicollet, Rice, Rock, Sibley, St. Louis, Steele, Waseca MN counties.

Add'l Information: Established 2002. Normal turnaround time- 24-48 hours. Projects billed by number of names searched. 1st project may require prepayment. Formerly known as Access Information Svcs, they specialize in document retrieval, UCC, state and federal tax liens, real estate and civil and criminal background checks.

ADM & Associates Inc

132 Windward Cr, Vincent, AL 35178
Phone: 800-242-5999; 205-525-5260 **Fax:** 205-525-4289
admasso2@centurytel.net

Types of Records Retrieved: Criminal Courts, Federal Cou;rts

Local Retrieval Area: AL-Jefferson, St Clair

Add'l Information: Established 1993. Normal turnaround time- 1 day. Projects billed by number of names searched. 1st project may require prepayment. ADM specializes in criminal record research for Alabama, Birmingham Municipal, and Alabama Federal Courts; these searches are returned next morning. A licensed PI in AL.

Advance Real Estate Services LLC

10996 Welsh Run Rd, Greencastle, PA 17225
Phone: 717-328-5062 **Fax:** 717-328-5062
www.advancerealestateservices.com **email:** advanceres@yahoo.com

Types of Records Retrieved: Civil courts; Real Estate; Tax liens/Judgments.

Local Retrieval Area: PA-Adams, Cumberland, Franklin, Fulton

Add'l Information: Established 2003. Normal turnaround time- 24-48 hours. 60-years searches 3-5 days. Projects billed by number of names searched. Will invoice. ARES provides accurate real estate property searches from document retrieval to full 60 year searches. Quick turnaround and customized searches help meet each clients needs.

Advanced Background Check Inc

1221 Wilmington Av #211, Dayton, OH 45420
Phone: 888-264-4018; 937-296-9585 **Fax:** 800-414-6212; 937-296-9608
www.abcheck.com **email:** dmachowsky@abcheck.com

Types of Records Retrieved: Civil, criminal and probate courts; Federal courts; Real Estate; Tax liens/Judgments; UCC records; Vital records; Mortgages and deeds

Local Retrieval Area: OH-Butler, Cuyahoga, Delaware, Franklin, Hamilton, Lorain, Lucas, Montgomery, Summitt, Warren. **Correspondent Relationships:** nationwide.

Add'l Information: Established 1993. Normal turnaround time- 24-48 hours. Projects billed by number of names searched. 1st project may require prepayment. Credit cards accepted. They specialize in civil, criminal, federal and probate court searches. Also real estate, Tax liens/Judgments, UCC records and vital records.

Advanced Background Services

PO Box 17162, Indianapolis, IN 46217
Phone: 317-884-4600 **Fax:** 317-884-4601
www.advancedbackground.com **email:** info@advancedbackground.com

Types of Records Retrieved: Civil and criminal courts; Federal courts. Real estate, Tax liens/Judgments.

Local Retrieval Area: IN-Allen, Lake, Johnson, Marion. St Joseph. **Correspondent Relationships:** nationwide.

Add'l Information: Established 2000. Normal turnaround time- 24-48 hours. Depending on size of request. 1st project may require prepayment. Advanced Background Svcs specializes in all levels of criminal record searches - metro, county, state, federal. Their expert services also include reports on SSNs, driver records, civil court and bankruptcy. Will do real estate & liens Marion county only.

Advanced Data Technology Inc

955 Greene St, Augusta, GA 30901
Phone: 800-426-5265; 706-823-6261 **Fax:** 706-823-6288
adti@mcbusa.com

Types of Records Retrieved: Civil courts; Federal courts; Real Estate; Tax liens/Judgments

Local Retrieval Area: GA-Bibb, Chatham, Columbia, Richmond; SC-Aiken, Charleston, Greenville, Richland. **Correspondent Relationships:** GA, SC.

Add'l Information: Established 1991. Normal turnaround time- 1-2 days. Projects billed by number of names searched. 1st project may require prepayment.

Advanced Investigations Inc

24 NW Racetrack Rd, Ft Walton, FL 32547
Phone: 850-863-3997 **Fax:** 850-864-1733
rjboycepi@yahoo.com

Types of Records Retrieved: Civil, criminal and probate courts; Federal courts; Real Estate; Tax liens/Judgments; UCC records; Vital records

Local Retrieval Area: FL-Franklin, Gadsden, Jefferson, Leon, Liberty, Okalossa, Santa Rosa, Wakulla, Walton. **Correspondent Relationships:** Okaloosa County.

Add'l Information: Established 1982. Normal turnaround time- 3 working days. Corporate filings may be done same day. Expedited service available. Projects billed by the hour. Incurred expenses will be added to the fee. All projects require prepayment. Credit cards accepted. They require a retainer until the client becomes established. They specialize in criminal and civil case work/investigations, process service (CPS 1st & 2nd Circuit Fla.), people locates and asset locates. A licensed PI in FL. They perform service of process.

Advanced Private Inv

PO Box 3024, 2107 Main St, La Crosse, WI 54601
Phone: 608-785-2744 **Fax:** 608-784-0149
www.advancedprivateinvestigations.com **email:** mark@advancedprivateinvestigations.com

Types of Records Retrieved: Civil and criminal courts

Local Retrieval Area: WI-Buffalo, Jackson, La Crosse, Monroe, Trempealeau, Vernon

Add'l Information: Established 2001. Normal turnaround time- 2 days. 1st project may require prepayment. They also provide court filings, subpoena preparation, photocopying, skiptracing, and private investigations. A licensed PI in WI, MN. They perform service of process.

Advanced Surveillance Group Inc

40 Macomb Pl #201, Mount Clemens, MI 48043-5615
Phone: 888-677-9700; 586-493-0300 **Fax:** 586-783-3939
www.asginvestigations.com **email:** info@asginvestigations.com

Types of Records Retrieved: Civil, criminal and probate courts; Federal courts; Real Estate; UCC records; Vital records

Local Retrieval Area: MI-Genesee, Macomb, Oakland, Wayne. **Correspondent Relationships:** Manistee, Mason, Lake, Oceana, Muskegon counties OR.

Add'l Information: Established 1995. Normal turnaround time- 48 hours. Projects billed by number of names searched. Projects billed by number of records located. 1st project may require prepayment. Credit cards accepted. They are in most state, federal and county offices within Metro-Detroit almost daily. Very competitive prices. They perform service of process.

Advanced Title

2343 Croydon Rd, Sebring, FL 33870-1526
Phone: 863-471-6334 **Fax:** 863-382-7677

Types of Records Retrieved: Real Estate

Local Retrieval Area: FL-Highlands. **Correspondent Relationships:** Polk and Hardee counties.

Add'l Information: Established 1989. Normal turnaround time- 3 days. Fee basis will vary by the type of project. Billed when search performed, terms are net 30 days.

Advanced Title & Closing Services (CT)

7 Jacop Dr, Uncasville, CT 06382
Phone: 888-443-4592 (Pager); 860-848-7964 **Fax:** 775-307-8750
www.advancedtitle.freeservers.com **email:** advtitlect@aol.com

Types of Records Retrieved: Probate courts; Real Estate; Tax liens/Judgments; UCC records; Vital records

Local Retrieval Area: CT-Hartford, Middlesex, New Haven. **Correspondent Relationships:** statewide.

Add'l Information: Established 1998. Normal turnaround time- 24-48 hours. Projects billed by number of names searched. Projects billed by number of records located. They specialize in document retrievals, mortgage/deed searches, current owner searches, recording updates, 2 owner searches and PMM searches.

Advantage Background Services Inc

3888 Pearl Rd, Cleveland, OH 44109
Phone: 800-355-2650; 216-635-2638 **Fax:** 440-842-9123
absbackgrounds@aol.com

Types of Records Retrieved: Civil and criminal courts; Federal courts

Local Retrieval Area: CA-Alameda, San Francisco, Santa Clara; OH-Butler, Cuyahoga, Geauga, Hamilton, Lake, Montgomery, Summit. **Correspondent Relationships:** CA, OH, FL, NC, TX, VA, WI.

Add'l Information: Established 2000. Normal turnaround time- 48-72 hours. Projects billed by number of names searched. 1st project may require prepayment. They specialize in retrieving court copies and also offer the following services; workers compensation, motor vehicle reports, education and employment verifications.

Advantage Research Corporation

1000 C Shady Grove Rd, Hot Springs, AR 71901
Phone: 501-262-5575 **Fax:** 800-262-0013
www.advantageresearchcorp.com
email: search@advantageresearchcorp.com

Types of Records Retrieved: Civil and criminal courts; Federal district court; UCC records; Real Estate.

Local Retrieval Area: AR-all counties

Add'l Information: Normal turnaround time- 24 hours. Projects billed by number of names searched. Credit cards accepted. Payment terms are net 30 days. They perform service of process.

AEGIS Consulting & Inv Inc

3420 Mountain Meadows Rd, Helena, MT 59601
Phone: 888-742-3447; 406-458-5369 **Fax:** 406-458-5369
http://aegisinvestigations.com **email:** lswaegis@aol.com

Types of Records Retrieved: Civil, criminal and probate courts; Federal courts; Tax liens/Judgments; UCC records; Vital records

Local Retrieval Area: MT-Broadwater, Cascade, Gallatin, Jefferson, Lewis and Clark, Missoula, Yellowstone. **Correspondent Relationships:** statewide; they do almost all of their statewide work themselves.

Add'l Information: Established 1995. Normal turnaround time- 24-48 hours. Federal records take a maximum of 2 days. Projects billed by number of names searched. 1st project may require prepayment. Credit cards accepted. Please call to establish account. They specialize in fraud & private investigations, public records searches/retrieval, registered agent representation, public record filing, pre-employment screening (MT), background & asset investigations & litigation support. Licensed/bonded in MT & WA. A licensed PI in MT, WA.

Agency-One Inv

1332 Ashley Square, Winston-Salem, NC 27103
Phone: 800-557-5500; 336-760-4000 **Fax:** 336-760-4155
www.a1investigations.com **email:** a1investigations@aol.com

Types of Records Retrieved: Civil and criminal courts; Federal courts; Real Estate; Tax liens/Judgments; UCC records; Vital records

Local Retrieval Area: NC-Davidson, Davie, Forsyth, Guilford, Rockingham, Rowan, Stokes, Surry, Yadkin

Add'l Information: Established 1977. Normal turnaround time- 48 hours. Projects billed by the hour. All projects require prepayment. Credit cards accepted. They will also invoice. They specialize in criminal, civil judgment, probate and property searches. A licensed PI in NC, SC. They perform service of process.

AGH Professional Inv

PO Box 085133, Racine, WI 53408
Phone: 262-884-4688 **Fax:** 262-884-4689
aghpi@wirr.com

Types of Records Retrieved: Civil, criminal and probate courts; Real Estate; Vital records

Local Retrieval Area: WI-Kenosha, Racine

Add'l Information: Established 1992. Normal turnaround time- 48 hours. Projects billed by the hour. 1st project may require prepayment. They specialize in skiptracing and public records. A licensed PI in WI. They perform service of process.

Ahern Research

Box 662, Mountain Ranch, CA 95246
Phone: 209-754-9709 **Fax:** 209-754-9031
dahern@mcn.org

Types of Records Retrieved: Civil, criminal and probate courts; Federal courts; Real Estate; Tax liens/Judgments; UCC records; Vital records

Local Retrieval Area: CA-Calaveras, Shasta

Add'l Information: Established 2003. All projects require prepayment. Credit cards accepted. They are a background checking firm located in Redding and Mountain Ranch, CA. They offer a broad range of this and related services.

AIM3 Research

39 W 120 Preston Cir, Geneva, IL 60134
Phone: 630-631-6531 **Fax:** 630-208-7961
aim3research@yahoo.com

Types of Records Retrieved: Real Estate

Local Retrieval Area: IL-Cook, DuPage, Kane, Kendall

Add'l Information: Established 1986. Normal turnaround time- 4-5 business days. Projects billed by number of names searched. Standard invoice method. They are highly motivated and reliable covering the 4 collar counties to include Chicago.

Airborn Civil Process & Inv

PO Box 131381, Houston, TX 77219
Phone: 888-933-6863; 713-523-0471 **Fax:** 713-523-9112
www.claimyourmoney.net **email:** tillman@pdisinc.com

Types of Records Retrieved: Civil, criminal and probate courts; Federal courts; Real Estate; Tax liens/Judgments; UCC records; Vital records, Voter registration records

Local Retrieval Area: TX-Brazos, Fort Bend, Harris

Add'l Information: Established 1998. Normal turnaround time- 24 hours. Projects billed by the hour. All projects require prepayment. Credit cards accepted. When you need diligence, call them. They are your local hands on document retrievers. A licensed PI in TX. They perform service of process.

Al Bernardi Backgrounds Process Svc

PO Box 1272, Manhattan, KS 66505
Phone: 785-456-8821 **Fax:** 785-456-8821
albpi@wamego.net

Types of Records Retrieved: Civil and criminal courts; Real Estate; Tax liens/Judgments, UCC records

Local Retrieval Area: KS-Dickinson, Geary, Riley

Add'l Information: Established 1996. Normal turnaround time- 24 hours. Projects billed by number of names searched. Invoices at the end of the month. They perform service of process.

AL McLeroy Inv

PO Box 5052, 5601 Remington Way (72916), Ft. Smith, AR 72913
Phone: 479-484-0444 **Fax:** 479-484-0444

Types of Records Retrieved: Civil, criminal and probate courts; Federal District courts; Real Estate; UCC records; Vital records

Local Retrieval Area: AR-Benton, Carroll, Crawford, Madison, Sebastian, Washington. **Correspondent Relationships:** Western AR, Eastern OK.

Add'l Information: Established 1968. Normal turnaround time- 48 hours. Expedited service available. Projects billed by the hour. 1st project may require prepayment. A licensed PI in AR. They perform service of process.

Al Smith Private Inv

PO Box 5079, Lakeland, FL 33807
Phone: 863-295-1375 **Fax:** 863-534-9483 alsmith@gate.net

Types of Records Retrieved: Civil, criminal and probate courts; Real Estate; Tax liens/Judgments; UCC records; Vital records

Local Retrieval Area: FL-Hardee, Highlands, Polk. **Correspondent Relationships:** nationwide.

Add'l Information: Established 1989. Normal turnaround time- 24 hours. Projects billed by the hour. 1st project may require prepayment. Credit cards accepted. Al Smith is a 260yr veteran of county law enforcement and private investigations. General investigations provided in addition to document retrieval. A licensed PI in FL. They perform service of process.

AlaDocs Inc

911 2nd Ave N, Birmingham, AL 35203
Phone: 205-251-8200 **Fax:** 205-251-9007
www.aladocs.com **email:** rick@aladocs.com

Types of Records Retrieved: Probate Courts, Real Estate, Tax liens/Judgments, UCC records

Local Retrieval Area: AL-all counties. **Correspondents:** statewide.

Add'l Information: Established 2001. Normal turnaround time- 1-3 days. Projects billed by number of names searched. Terms are net 30 with approved credit. They specialize in real estate filings and document retrieval, also UCC and probate courts records.

Alaska Public Records Search LLC

PO Box 210587, 8200 Pioneer Dr (99504), Anchorage, AK 99521-0587
Phone: 800-808-5105; 907-333-5105 **Fax:** 907-333-5155
www.alaskapublicrecords.com **email:** info@alaskapublicrecords.com

Types of Records Retrieved: Civil and criminal courts; Federal courts; Real Estate; Tax liens/Judgments; UCC records

Local Retrieval Area: AK-Aleutian Islands East & West, Anchorage Borough, Bristol Bay Borough, Fairbanks North Star, Juneau, Kenai Peninsula, Lake And Peninsula, Matanuska Susitna, North Slope, Valdez-Cordova. **Correspondent Relationships:** statewide and nationwide.

Add'l Information: Established 1993. Normal turnaround time- 24-72 hours. Projects billed by number of names searched. 1st project may require prepayment. Credit accounts accepted, terms are net 15 days. They specialize in UCC, asset/lien, litigation, real property, corporate, filing services, licensing/registrations. They cover all federal, state and county level agencies in Alaska. They are registered agents. A licensed PI in AK. They perform service of process.

Albany Abstract Co

PO Box 817, Albany, TX 76430
Phone: 325-762-3077 **Fax:** 325-762-2102

Types of Records Retrieved: Civil courts; Probate courts; Real Estate; Tax liens/Judgments; UCC records; Vital records

Local Retrieval Area: TX-Shackelford

Add'l Information: Established 1922. Normal turnaround time- up to 1 week. Fee basis will vary by the type of project. All projects require prepayment.

Albert Lea Abstract Co

205 S Washington Ave, Albert Lea, MN 56007
Phone: 507-373-9001 **Fax:** 507-373-2528 alac@smig.net

Types of Records Retrieved: Probate courts; Real Estate; Tax liens/Judgments; UCC records; Vital records

Local Retrieval Area: MN-Freeborn, Mower

Add'l Information: Established 1976. Normal turnaround time- 2 days. Projects billed by number of names searched. All projects require prepayment. They specialize in title searching, closings and 1031 exchanges.

Albright Abstract & Title Guaranty

PO Box 467, Newkirk, OK 74647
Phone: 800-522-1251; 580-362-2525 **Fax:** 580-362-3390

Types of Records Retrieved: Civil courts; Probate courts; Real Estate; Tax liens/Judgments

Local Retrieval Area: OK-Kay

Add'l Information: Established 1899. Normal turnaround time- 2-5 days. Fee is determined on a "per name plus time" basis. 1st project may require prepayment. Payment due upon delivery. They specialize in title insurance statewide, abstracts and lien reports.

Aldridge & Associates

PO Drawer 90, Smithville, MS 38870-0090
Phone: 662-651-7376 **Fax:** 662-651-6060
jerryaldridge@yahoo.com

Types of Records Retrieved: Civil, criminal and probate courts; Federal courts; Real Estate; Tax liens/Judgments; UCC records; Vital records

Local Retrieval Area: AL-Lamar; MS-Calhoun, Chickasaw, Clay, Itawamba, Lee, Lowndes, Monroe, Pontotoc, Union

Add'l Information: Established 1997. Normal turnaround time- 48 hours. Projects billed by number of names searched. Projects billed by the hour. 1st project may require prepayment. They specialize in criminal court records, background screening, real estate, legal service of process, notary signing agent, private investigations, probate & pre-employment/tenant screening. They also offer attorney services. A licensed PI in MS. They perform service of process.

Alfalfa Guaranty Abstract Co

201 S Grand Ave., PO Box 224, Cherokee, OK 73728
Phone: 580-596-3394 **Fax:** 580-596-3395

Types of Records Retrieved: Civil courts; Probate courts; Real Estate; Tax liens/Judgments; UCC records; Vital records

Local Retrieval Area: OK-Alfalfa

Add'l Information: Established 1989. Normal turnaround time- 1-2 days. Projects billed by the hour. If amount is over $500.00, payment is made before abstracter leaves office.

ALIASS

10560 Main St #405, Fairfax, VA 22030
Phone: 800-747-0820; 703-934-6777 **Fax:** 703-383-3246
www.american-legal.com **email:** aals@american-legal.com

Types of Records Retrieved: Civil, criminal and probate courts; Federal courts; Real Estate; Tax liens/Judgments; UCC records; Vital records

Local Retrieval Area: DC-District of Columbia; MD-Montgomery, Prince George's; VA-Alexandria City, Arlington, Fairfax, Fairfax City, Fauquier, Loudoun, Prince William. **Correspondent Relationships:** Maryland and Virginia.

Add'l Information: Established 1998. Normal turnaround time- 2 days. Projects billed by the hour. 1st project may require prepayment. Credit cards accepted. Personal checks are accepted. They do service of process for the entire Metropolitan DC area, MD, VA and courthouse research. A licensed PI in VA. They perform service of process.

All American Document Services

521 S Andrews Ave #16, Ft Lauderdale, FL 33301
Phone: 954-761-7292 **Fax:** 954-761-7294
www.allamericandocs.com **email:** customerservice@allamericandocs.com

Types of Records Retrieved: Civil, criminal and probate courts; Federal courts; Real Estate; Tax liens/Judgments; UCC records; Vital records

Local Retrieval Area: FL-Broward, Dade, Palm Beach. **Correspondent Relationships:** Tampa, FL.

Add'l Information: Established 1996. Normal turnaround time- 72 hours. Expedited service available. Projects billed by number of names searched. Projects billed by number of records located. Projects billed by the hour. 1st project may require prepayment. All American's services include current owner searches, judgments, liens, bankruptcy and civil/criminal searches at county/state/federal levels. They provide experienced, accurate and honest service.

All American Research LLC

PO Box 2321, 608 Dexter Dr, Dunedin, FL 34697
Phone: 800-215-7958; 727-734-3302 **Fax:** 727-736-0693
scieszla@tampabay.rr.com

Types of Records Retrieved: Civil, criminal and probate courts; Federal courts; Real Estate; Tax liens/Judgments; UCC records; Vital records

Local Retrieval Area: FL-Hillsborough, Pasco, Pinellas. **Correspondent Relationships:** nationwide and Canada.

Add'l Information: Established 2002. Normal turnaround time- 12-24 hours. 24-48 hr expedited service available. Projects billed by number of names searched. Invoiced on 1st & 15th of each month. All American Research LLC conducts searches of various public records and provides the requester with information and /or specific documents in a timely manner.

All Penn Abstract Co

15 Public Square #200, Wilkes-Barre, PA 18701
Phone: 570-823-5410 **Fax:** 570-822-2774

Types of Records Retrieved: Probate courts; Real Estate; Tax liens/Judgments; UCC records

Local Retrieval Area: PA-Luzerne.

Add'l Information: Established 1987. Normal turnaround time- 7 to 10 days. They charge a flat rate per project. They specialize in real estate, closings and property searches.

All Phase Reports

11266 W Hillsborough Ave #201, Tampa, FL 33635-9762
Phone: 813-885-9822 **Fax:** 813-885-9822

Types of Records Retrieved: Civil, criminal and probate courts; Federal courts; Real Estate; Tax liens/Judgments; UCC records; Vital records

Local Retrieval Area: FL-Hillsborough, Pasco, Pinellas, Polk. **Correspondent Relationships:** Broward, Dade, Lee, Orange, Osceola counties.

Add'l Information: Established 1992. Normal turnaround time- 24-48 hours. Expedited service available. Fees are per name per court. Fees can be negotiated per project. First 4 payments required to establish "Good Will" to pay. A paralegal owned/operated company using expertise/technology searching both online and manual data. A recent addition, All Phase Investigations & Reports is a full service private investigation firm. A licensed PI in FL. They perform service of process.

All Search Title Co

PO Box 544, Grayson, KY 41143
Phone: 606-474-4253 **Fax:** 606-474-2615

Types of Records Retrieved: Real Estate; Tax liens/Judgments

Local Retrieval Area: KY-Bath, Boyd, Carter, Elliott, Fleming, Floyd, Greenup, Johnson, Lawrence, Lewis, Martin, Mason, Menifee, Montgomery, Morgan, Rowan

Add'l Information: Established 1985. Normal turnaround time- 48 hours. Will do monthly billings. 1st project may require prepayment. They specialize in real estate title searches and also perform witness closings.

All State Document Services

2418 N Krenek, Crosby, TX 77532
Phone: 888-246-8180; 281-462-2730 **Fax:** 888 236 0863; 281-462-2731
tjmatt@aol.com

Types of Records Retrieved: Civil courts; Federal courts; Real Estate; Tax liens/Judgments; UCC records; Vital records

Local Retrieval Area: TX-Austin, Brazoria, Brazos, Calhoun, Chambers, Colorado, Fort Bend, Galvaston, Hardin, Harris, Jackson, Jefferson, Liberty, Matagorda, Montgomery, Orange, Victoria, Walker, Waller, Washington, Wharton. **Correspondent Relationships:** nationwide.

Add'l Information: Established 1998. Normal turnaround time- 24-48 hours. Projects billed by number of names searched. 1st project may require prepayment. Credit cards accepted. Invoice monthly. All State Documents established in 1998, the owner is a 20 year plus record research & retrieval individual. Has professionalism and accurate knowledge of research provided for state & county needs.

All The Facts

2620 Centenary Blvd Bldg 2 #210, Shreveport, LA 71104
Phone: 866-401-5676; 318-222-5676 **Fax:** 318-425-8524
www.all-the-facts.com **email:** allfacts@xspedius.net

Types of Records Retrieved: Civil, criminal and probate courts; Federal courts; Real Estate; Tax liens/Judgments; UCC records; Vital records

Local Retrieval Area: LA-Bossier, Caddo. **Correspondent Relationships:** statewide for criminal; Texas; Miller county AR. Call for extended list.

Add'l Information: Established 1995. Normal turnaround time- 6-12 hours. Out of area: 24-48 hours. Projects billed by number of names searched.

Billing is monthly. Terms are net 30 days. They also provide sex offender information as well as medicare/medicaid fraud, GSA list of excluded persons, pre-employment, pre-leasing credit reports, private investigations and 24 hour mobile notary services. A licensed PI in LA. They perform service of process.

All-American Attorney Services

4617 Sycamore St, Dallas, TX 75204

Phone: 800-838-9044; 214-220-0226 **Fax:** 214-855-1237

Types of Records Retrieved: Civil, criminal and probate courts; Federal courts; Real Estate; Tax liens/Judgments; UCC records; Vital records

Local Retrieval Area: CA-Los Angeles; TX-Dallas. **Correspondent Relationships:** nationwide.

Add'l Information: Established 1975. Normal turnaround time- call for turnaround time. Projects billed by number of names searched. Projects billed by the hour. 1st project may require prepayment. Credit cards accepted. Visa and Mastercard accepted They specialize in hard-to-do service of process, celebrity and other special circumstance services. They perform service of process.

Allen Abstract & Title

West Side Court Sq, Alton, MO 65606

Phone: 417-778-6665

Types of Records Retrieved: Real estate; Tax liens/Judgments

Local Retrieval Area: MO-Oregon

Add'l Information: 1st project may require prepayment. They specialize in Oregon County real estate related records.

Alliance Legal Services Inc

PO Box 523078, Springfield, VA 22152-5080

Phone: 703-644-8571 **Fax:** 703-644-8572

www.alliancelegalservices.com **email:** alliance.express@verizon.net

Types of Records Retrieved: Civil, criminal and probate courts; Federal courts; Real Estate; Tax liens/Judgments; UCC records; Vital records

Local Retrieval Area: VA-Arlington, Alexandria, Fairfax. **Correspondent Relationships:** Washington DC and Maryland.

Add'l Information: Established 1993. Normal turnaround time- 24-72 hours depending on agency where records are stored. Projects billed by the hour. 1st project may require prepayment. They provide private investigations and process serving, including filings and document retrieval. A licensed PI in VA. They perform service of process.

Alliance Title & Escrow Corp

78 N Main, PO Box 644, Driggs, ID 83422

Phone: 800-214-1418; 208-354-2285 **Fax:** 208-354-2811

Types of Records Retrieved: Federal courts; Real Estate; Tax liens/Judgments; UCC records

Local Retrieval Area: ID-Teton

Add'l Information: Fees vary by type of project. Alliance Title & Escrow Corp has 21 offices throughout Idaho.

Allied Inv Services

PO Box 5012, Anderson, SC 29623-5012

Phone: 800-302-0861; 864-231-8446 **Fax:** 864-224-3175

www.alliedinvestigative.com **email:** bonnie@alliedinvestigative.com

Types of Records Retrieved: Civil and criminal courts.

Local Retrieval Area: SC-Anderson

Add'l Information: Established 2002. 1st project may require prepayment. They also provide court filings, photocopying, skiptracing, private investigations, and research on questioned documents. A licensed PI in SC. They perform service of process.

Allington International

19885 Detroit Rd #314, Cleveland, OH 44116-1815

Phone: 866-729-8555; **Fax:** 866-470-0506;

Types of Records Retrieved: Civil, criminal and probate courts; Federal courts; Real Estate; Tax liens/Judgments; UCC records; Vital records

Local Retrieval Area: OH-Ashtabula, Cuyahoga, Geauga, Lake, Lorain, Medina, Stark, Summit, Trumbull. **Correspondent Relationships:** nationwide.

Add'l Information: Established 1989. Normal turnaround time- 2 business days. Projects billed by number of names searched. 1st project may require prepayment. Credit cards accepted. Terms: net 30 days. They specialize in employment screening programs, private investigations, drug testing, criminal and court record searches, MVR information, workers' compensation claims, shopping services, security consulting, due diligence investigations. A licensed PI in OH. They perform service of process.

All-Search

1108 E South Union Av, Midvale, UT 84047-2904

Phone: 800-227-3152; 801-984-8160 **Fax:** 801-984-8170

www.all-search.com **email:** brad@all-search.com

Types of Records Retrieved: Civil, criminal and probate courts; Federal courts; Real Estate; Tax liens/Judgments; UCC records; Vital records

Local Retrieval Area: UT-Box Elder, Cache, Davis, Duchesne, Juab, Morgan, Salt Lake, Summit, Tooele, Uintah, Utah, Wasatch, Washington, Weber. **Correspondent Relationships:** nationwide and Canada.

Add'l Information: Established 1983. Normal turnaround time- 1-2 days for Utah; 1-4 days nationwide. Projects billed by number of names searched. Credit cards accepted. Will invoice. They specialize in corporate document retrieval and corporate filings. All liens searched, all jurisdictions. They also are a registered agent for Utah corporations. Also, complete real estate research.

Allstate Real Estate Service

PO Box 515, Grimes, IA 50111-0515

Types of Records Retrieved: Real Estate; Tax liens/Judgments; UCC records; Probate courts

Local Retrieval Area: IA-Dallas, Polk

Add'l Information: Established 1995. Normal turnaround time- 24-72 hours. Projects billed by number of names searched. Fee basis varies by project; mileage & volume are factored. All projects require prepayment. They specialize in current owner real estate, title searches, UCC, tax liens, also civil, criminal, judgments, litigation searches, document retrieval and searches.

Alma Abstract & Title Co

310 N State St, Alma, MI 48801

Phone: 989-463-8325 **Fax:** 989-463-2363

www.almaabstract.com **email:** dedicated@almaabstract.com

Types of Records Retrieved: Probate courts; Real Estate; Tax liens/Judgments; UCC records; Vital records

Local Retrieval Area: MI-Gratiot, Montcalm

Add'l Information: Established 1980. Normal turnaround time- 1 week. Fee basis will vary by type of project. They specialize in real estate.

Alpha Attorney Service

1010 2nd Ave #120B, San Diego, CA 92101-4961

Phone: 619-235-8008 **Fax:** 619-235-0580

Types of Records Retrieved: Civil, criminal and probate courts; Federal courts; Real Estate; Tax liens/Judgments; UCC records; Vital records

Local Retrieval Area: CA-San Diego

Add'l Information: Established 1990. Normal turnaround time- 1-2 days. Projects billed by number of names searched. They specialize in process serving, records search, copy service, rush filings and fax filings. They perform service of process.

Alpha Court Records & Research

1326 Osceola Ave, St Paul, MN 55105

Phone: 651-699-2222 **Fax:** 651-699-9004

miriamleone@worldnet.att.net

Types of Records Retrieved: Civil and criminal courts; Federal courts; Tax liens/Judgments; UCC records

Local Retrieval Area: MN-Anoka, Benton, Blue Earth, Brown, Carlton, Carver, Chisago, Dakota, Dodge, Faribault, Goodhue, Hennepin, Isanti, Itasca, Kanabec, Kandiyohi, Le Sueur, Martin, McLeod, Mille Lacs, Nicollet, Pine, Ramsey, Renville, Scott, Sherburne, Sibley, Washington, Wright

Add'l Information: Established 1992. Normal turnaround time- same day or following day. Work assigned by 11AM (CT) will be returned same day. Projects billed by number of names searched. Credit cards accepted. Terms: net 30 days. They have specialized in criminal background searches (felonies, misdemeanors & alcohol/drug-related traffic) since 1992. They also perform civil litigation & judgment searches, tax liens, document retrieval, Federal District & Bankruptcy court searches.

Alpha Information Inc

10153 Riverside Dr #590, Tuluca Lake, CA 91602
Phone: 800-900-1471; **Fax:** 800-900-1488;
kbanks@alphainformation.com

Types of Records Retrieved: Criminal courts

Local Retrieval Area: CA-Fresno, Los Angeles, Marin, Orange, Riverside, San Bernardino, San Diego, Santa Clara, Ventura. **Correspondent Relationships:** San Luis Obispo, San Francisco counties CA.

Add'l Information: Established 1991. Normal turnaround time- 24-36 hours. Projects billed by number of names searched. Will invoice two times monthly. They have over 10 years experinece and have their own researchers going to courts daily. They do large volume searches.

Alpha Omega USA Information Brokers LLC

1055 W College Ave #148, Santa Rosa, CA 95401
Phone: 866-636-6342; **Fax:** 866-326-6342;
www.alphaomegausa.com **email:** usa@alphaomegausa.com

Types of Records Retrieved: Civil and criminal courts

Local Retrieval Area: CA-Placer. **Correspondent Relationships:** nationwide.

Add'l Information: Normal turnaround time- 48-72 hours. Projects billed by number of names searched. They provide nationwide criminal records for pre-employment. They perform service of process.

Alpha Record Search & Retrieval

PO Box 2116, Toluca Lake, CA 91610
Phone: 323-851-5701 **Fax:** 323-851-6611
finderjm@pacbell.net

Types of Records Retrieved: Civil, criminal and probate courts; Federal courts; Real Estate; Tax liens/Judgments; UCC records; Vital records

Local Retrieval Area: CA-Los Angeles

Add'l Information: Established 1997. Normal turnaround time- per agreement. Expedited service available. Fees are by mutually agreed terms and vary by assignment. 1st project may require prepayment. They specialize in complicated, unusual assignments. They have over 20 years experience with all public record file systems in the 5-county area. A licensed PI in CA.

Alpha-Omega Investigations

3307 S College Ave #200-8, Ft Collins, CO 80525
Phone: 866-510-8200; 970-282-8200 **Fax:** 970-282-8803
www.alpha-omega-investigations.com **email:** alpha-omega@qwest.net

Types of Records Retrieved: Civil, criminal and probate courts; Federal courts; Real Estate; Tax liens/Judgments; UCC records; Vital records

Local Retrieval Area: CO-Boulder, Larimer, Weld

Add'l Information: Established 1990. Normal turnaround time- 48 hours. Expedited service available. Projects billed by number of names searched. 1st project may require prepayment. Credit cards accepted. Will invoice PRRN members. They have a record retrieval service available in Larimer, Weld and Boulder counties. Statewide Colorado available through state association. They perform service of process.

AlphaOmega USA Info Brokers LLC

4120 Douglas Blvd #142, Granite Bay, CA 95746
Phone: 866-636-6342; **Fax:** 866-326-6342;
www.alphaomegausa.com **email:** usa@alphaomegausa.com

Types of Records Retrieved: Civil and criminal courts

Local Retrieval Area: CA-Placer, Sacramento, Sonoma. **Correspondent Relationships:** nationwide.

Add'l Information: Normal turnaround time- 48-72 hours. Projects billed by number of names searched. 1st project may require prepayment. They provide nationwide criminal records for pre-employment. Other information research provided on a case by case basis. Call above phone number for information.

Alstate Process Service Inc

60 Burt Dr, Deer Park, NY 11729
Phone: 631-667-1800 **Fax:** 631-667-0302
www.alstateprocessservice.com **email:** diana@alstateprocessservice.com

Types of Records Retrieved: Civil, criminal and probate courts; Federal courts; Real Estate; Tax liens/Judgments; UCC records; Vital records

Local Retrieval Area: NY-Bronx, Kings, Nassau, New York, Queens, Richmond, Suffolk. **Correspondent Relationships:** statewide.

Add'l Information: Established 1980. Normal turnaround time- 48 hours. Fee basis will vary by the type of project. Will bill. A licensed PI in NY. They perform service of process.

Alternative Investigative & Attorney Services

7657 Winnetka Ave #545, Canoga Park, CA 91306
Phone: 888-457-1314; 818-402-0800 **Fax:** 818-341-8804
www.irwinsaltz.com **email:** altinv1000@aol.com

Types of Records Retrieved: Civil, criminal and probate courts; Federal courts; Real Estate; Tax liens/Judgments; UCC records; Vital records

Local Retrieval Area: CA-Los Angeles, Orange, San Bernardino, Riverside, Ventura

Add'l Information: Established 1992. Normal turnaround time- 24 hours depending on the court. Projects billed by the hour. Charge by volume. 1st project may require prepayment. Discounts for volume. They have "FLAT FEE" service of process, no attemp/mileage on routine work, specialize in real estate loan documents. Is a "traveling" notary public-statewide document signing. A licensed PI in CA. They perform service of process.

AM Search & Retrieve

336 E Perry St, Versailles, IN 47042-9478
Phone: 812-689-0672 **Fax:** 812-689-5832

Types of Records Retrieved: Civil, criminal and probate courts; Real Estate; Tax liens/Judgments; UCC records

Local Retrieval Area: IN-Dearborn, Jefferson, Ohio, Ripley

Add'l Information: Established 1994. Normal turnaround time- less than 48 hours. Projects billed by number of names searched. 1st project may require prepayment. They specialize in criminal background checks, UCC searches, current owner real estate searches and MVR record checks.

Amarisearch Inc

4085 Chain Bridge Rd #G5, Fairfax, VA 22030-4111
Phone: 703-267-6827 **Fax:** 703-267-6825
www.amarisearch.com **email:** info@amarisearch.com

Types of Records Retrieved: Civil courts; Probate courts; Real Estate; Tax liens/Judgments; UCC records

Local Retrieval Area: VA-Alexandria, Arlington, Caroline, Fairfax, Fauquier, Fredericksburg, Hanover, Henrico, Loudoun, Prince William, Spotsylvania, Stafford. **Correspondent Relationships:** Metro Atlanta, GA; Metro Richmond, VA.

Add'l Information: Established 2001. Normal turnaround time- 24-48 hours. Projects billed by number of names searched. Also charged by property address. They will invoice monthly.

Amcor Title LLC

69 Boundary Dr, Stafford, VA 22556
Phone: 540-752-2246 **Fax:** 540-752-4271
RDACRDAC@Adelphia.net

Types of Records Retrieved: Real Estate; Tax liens/judgments; UCC records

Local Retrieval Area: VA-Fredericksburg, Spotsylvania, Stafford

Add'l Information: Established 2001. Normal turnaround time- 24-48 hours. Payment due upon receipt, net 30 days. Searches include: Current and full owner searches, UCC/judgments, document retrievals, recordings, updates, courthouse research needs, quick turnaround time and highest efficiency, competitively priced.

American Abstract

91-101 Broadway #11, Greenlawn, NY 11740
Phone: 631-262-1826 **Fax:** 631-262-1927
www.nationalabstract.com **email:** info@nationalabstract.com

Types of Records Retrieved: Federal courts; Real Estate; Tax liens/Judgments; UCC records; Vital records

Local Retrieval: NY-Bronx, Kings, Nassau, New York, Queens, Richmond, Suffolk, Westchester. **Correspondent Relationships:** nationwide.

Add'l Information: Established 1996. Normal turnaround time- 24-48 hours. Projects billed by number of names searched. 1st project may require prepayment. Payment terms are net 30 days. Located on Long Is, NY, they provide a large nationwide network of real estate services.

American Abstract & Title

814 Avenue F, Fort Madison, IA 52627-2817
Phone: 319-372-8110 **Fax:** 319-372-2628

Types of Records Retrieved: Civil courts, Probate courts; Real Estate; Tax liens/Judgments; UCC records; Vital records

Local Retrieval Area: IA-Lee

Add'l Information: Established 1978. Normal turnaround time- variable. Projects billed by number of names searched. Fee may be based per year searched.

American Abstract & Title Co Inc

322 E Ave C, Killeen, TX 76541
Phone: 254-526-9525 **Fax:** 254-526-9518
staff@americanabstract.org

Types of Records Retrieved: Civil courts; Probate courts; Real Estate; Tax liens/Judgments; UCC records; Vital records

Local Retrieval Area: TX-Bell, Coryell, Williamson. **Correspondent Relationships:** statewide.

Add'l Information: Normal turnaround time- 5-7 days. Fee basis will vary by the type of project. All projects require prepayment. They specialize in closing loans including commercial and single family (1-4 family).

American Abstract Company

PO Box 15565, 138 W Main, Purcell, OK 73080
Phone: 405-527-7575 **Fax:** 405-527-7574

Types of Records Retrieved: Civil courts; Probate courts; Real Estate; Tax liens/Judgments; UCC records

Local Retrieval Area: OK-McClain

Add'l Information: Normal turnaround time- 1-2 days. Projects billed by number of names searched. Projects billed by number of records located. Projects billed by the hour. Credit cards accepted.

American Abstractors Inc

PO Box 97, Broomall, PA 19008
Phone: 610-353-5375 **Fax:** 610-356-3245
www.american.investigators.biz **email:** nathanlautar@comcast.net

Types of Records Retrieved: Civil, criminal and probate courts; Federal courts; Real Estate; Tax liens/judgements; UCC records; Vital records

Local Retrieval Area: PA-Chester, Delaware, Lancaster, Montgomery, Philadelphia

Add'l Information: Established 1999. Normal turnaround time- 24-48 hours. Projects billed by number of names searched. Projects billed by number of records located. 1st project may require prepayment. Formerly known as American Abstractors. A licensed PI in PA, DE. They perform service of process.

American Background Checks

8508 Cockney Dr, Austin, TX 78748
Phone: 512-497-7988 **Fax:** 512-282-3813
abchecks@austin.rr.com

Types of Records Retrieved: Civil and criminal courts; Federal District courts; Tax liens/Judgments; UCC records

Local Retrieval Area: TX-Travis, Williamson. **Correspondent Relationships:** nationwide.

Add'l Information: Established 1998. Normal turnaround time- 24-48 hours. Projects billed by number of names searched. clients billed monthly; 30 days net. They specialize in wholesale criminal and civil searches in TX and the US. Has 20 years legal experience. A licensed PI in TX.

American Detective Agency

5350 S Western #500, Oklahoma City, OK 73109
Phone: 800-219-9120; 405-636-4222 **Fax:** 405-632-7667
www.americanpi.net

Types of Records Retrieved: Civil, criminal and probate courts; Federal courts; Real Estate; Tax liens/Judgments; UCC records; Vital records

Local Retrieval Area: OK-Canadian, Cleveland, Oklahoma. **Correspondent Relationships:** TX, MO, KS.

Add'l Information: Normal turnaround time- 24 hours. Projects billed by number of names searched. Projects billed by the hour. 1st project may require prepayment. Credit cards accepted. They specialize in full service investigating with emphasis on criminal defense, insurance and workers compensation. A licensed PI in OK, TX. They perform service of process.

American Heritage Abstract

104 N Lincoln St #A, Desloge, MO 63601
Phone: 573-431-1359 **Fax:** 573-431-2137
ahaco@charter.net

Types of Records Retrieved: Civil courts; Probate courts; Real Estate; Tax liens/Judgments; UCC records

Local Retrieval: MO-Bollinger, Iron, Madison, St. Francois, Washington

Add'l Information: Established 1986. Normal turnaround time- 1 week. Projects billed by number of names searched. Projects billed by number of records located. Projects billed by the hour. Personal checks are accepted. They specialize in title insurance and land title searches.

American Investigations

1120 Main St, Charleston, WV 25302-1108
Phone: 304-343-3346 **Fax:** 304-343-2211

Types of Records Retrieved: Civil, criminal and probate courts; Federal courts; Real Estate; Tax liens/Judgments; UCC records; Vital records

Local Retrieval Area: WV-Boone, Cabell, Jackson, Kanawha, Lincoln, Putnam

Add'l Information: Normal turnaround time- 2 days. Projects billed by the hour. A licensed PI in WV. They perform service of process.

American Legal Services

225 S Civic Dr #216, Palm Springs, CA 92262
Phone: 760-323-5445 **Fax:** 760-323-5509
als@amlegal.net

Types of Records Retrieved: Civil, criminal and probate courts; Federal courts; Real Estate; Tax liens/Judgments

Local Retrieval: CA-Riverside. **Correspondent Relationships:** nationwide.

Add'l Information: Established 1991. Normal turnaround time- 24-48 hours. Projects billed by number of names searched. Projects billed by number of records located. Projects billed by the hour. They also charge per page if they do any copies. 1st project may require prepayment. They specialize in record document photocopying and process serving. Can retrieve records from the Joshua Tree Branch in San Bernardino County. They perform service of process.

American Legal Solution Inc

7060 Nova Dr #107, Davie, FL 33317
Phone: 954-986-5442 **Fax:** 954-987-0945
americanlegal@mfire.com

Types of Records Retrieved: Civil, criminal and probate courts; Federal courts; Real Estate; Tax liens/Judgments; UCC records; Vital records

Local Retrieval Area: FL-Broward, Dade, Palm Beach. **Correspondent Relationships:** nationwide, Canada, Puerto Rico.

Add'l Information: Established 2002. Normal turnaround time- 24-48 hours. Projects billed by number of names searched. Projects billed by number of records located. Projects billed by the hour. 1st project may require prepayment. Credit cards accepted. American Legal Solutions takes pride in their work and understands the very importance of research and retrieval of proper documents in a timely manner and they also perform extensive research. Process Service designated by Broward Sheriff's office.

American Research Unlimited Inc

5676 County Rd 120, Carthage, MO 64836
Phone: 417-358-6494 **Fax:** 417-359-5734
amru@ecarthage.com

Types of Records Retrieved: Civil, criminal and probate courts; Federal courts; Real Estate; Tax liens/Judgments; UCC records; Vital records

Local Retrieval Area: KS-Bourbon, Cherokee, Crawford, Labette; MO-Barton, Bates, Cedar, Christian, Greene, Jasper, Lawrence, McDonald, Newton, Vernon

Add'l Information: Established 1984. Normal turnaround time- 1-2 days. They charge a flat rate per search. Personal checks accepted. Will bill regular clients. They have 10 years experience in public records research. Very timely turnaround with a staff of experienced researchers; competitive prices. They perform service of process.

American Title & Abstract Specialists Inc

412 N Kansas, Liberal, KS 67901
Phone: 620-624-9111 **Fax:** 620-624-6610
www.amtitles.com **email:** amt@swko.net

Types of Records Retrieved: Civil, criminal and probate courts; Real Estate; Tax liens/Judgments; UCC records; Vital records

Local Retrieval Area: KS-Haskell, Seward, Stevens

Add'l Information: Established 1995. Normal turnaround time- 1-3 days. Fee basis varies by type of transaction. 1st project may require prepayment. They specialize in title ins, abstracting and closings. They give prompt & efficient service. They write for First American Title & Commonwealth.

American Title & Escrow of Big Horn County

409 N Center Ave, Hardin, MT 59034
Phone: 406-665-3797 **Fax:** 406-665-1099 hardin@amtitlemontana.com

Types of Records Retrieved: Civil courts; Probate courts; Real Estate; Tax liens/Judgments; UCC records

Local Retrieval Area: MT-Big Horn. **Correspondent Relationships:** southeastern Montana.

Add'l Information: Normal turnaround time- up to 5 days. Expedited service available. Projects billed by the hour. They specialize real estate and title searches.

American Title & Escrow of Musselshell County

226 Main St, PO Box 838, Roundup, MT 59072
Phone: 406-323-3165 **Fax:** 406-323-3311
www.amtitlemontana.com **email:** roundup@amtitlemontana.com

Types of Records Retrieved: Real Estate; Tax liens/judgments; UCC records

Local Retrieval Area: MT-Musselshell

Add'l Information: Established 1988. Normal turnaround time- 3-5 days. Fee basis varies by type of transaction.

American Title Company of Lenawee

142 N Winter St, Adrian, MI 49221-2043
Phone: 517-263-4040 **Fax:** 517-265-2533 atcl@tc3net.com

Types of Records Retrieved: Real Estate; Tax liens/Judgments; UCC records; Vital records

Local Retrieval Area: MI-Lenawee

Add'l Information: Established 1979. Normal turnaround time- 1 week. Fee basis will vary by type of project. They specialize in real estate.

American-First Abstract Co

111 E Comanche St, Norman, OK 73069
Phone: 405-321-7577 **Fax:** 405-321-3833
chawkins@americanfirst.com

Types of Records Retrieved: Civil courts; Probate courts; Real Estate; Tax liens/Judgments; UCC records **Local Retrieval Area:** OK-Cleveland

Add'l Information: Established 1969. Normal turnaround time- 3-5 days. Fee basis will vary by the type of project. 1st project may require prepayment. They specialize in real estate title searches.

Americorp Research Inc

2700 Pecan St West #427, Pflugerville, TX 78660
Phone: 877-989-6850; 512-989-6854 **Fax:** 877-989-6852; 512-989-6858
anne@capitollien.com

Types of Records Retrieved: Civil, criminal and probate courts; Federal courts; Real Estate; Tax liens/Judgments; UCC records; Vital records

Local Retrieval Area: TX-Bastrop, Bell, Burnet, Caldwell, Comal, Hays, Travis, Williamson. **Correspondent Relationships:** nationwide.

Add'l Information: Established 1999. Normal turnaround time- 24-48 hours. Projects billed by number of records located. All projects require prepayment. Credit cards accepted. They specialize in Secretary of State Texas UCCs and corporate filings. Filings can be faxed for same day filing.

Ameristar Information Network

2720 N Stemmons Fwy #300, Dallas, TX 75207
Phone: 800-920-9270; 214-634-9270 **Fax:** 800-920-9271; 214-634-9271

Types of Records Retrieved: Civil courts; Probate courts; Real Estate; Tax liens/Judgments; Vital records

Local Retrieval Area: TX-Collin, Dallas, Denton, Tarrant. **Correspondent Relationships:** nationwide for property research.

Add'l Information: Established 1989. Normal turnaround time- 24-72 hours. Projects billed by number of names searched.

Ameritite Abstract & Research Inc

6300 Hillcroft #114, Houston, TX 77081
Phone: 800-856-1228; 713-772-7870 **Fax:** 713-772-7922
www.atitle.net **email:** kmorris@atitle.net

Types of Records Retrieved: Civil courts; Probate courts; Federal courts; Real Estate; Tax liens/Judgments; UCC records

Local Retrieval Area: TX-Brazoria, Collin, Dallas, Denton, Fort Bend, Galveston, Harris, Montgomery, Travis. **Correspondent Relationships:** Texas.

Add'l Information: Normal turnaround time- 24-48 hours. 1st project may require prepayment.

Amma H General Ltd

PO Box 226, Beaufort, SC 29901-0226
Phone: 843-263-5677 or 843-525-9890 **Fax:** 843-525-6923
ammagen1@yahoo.com

Types of Records Retrieved: Civil, criminal and probate courts; Real Estate; Tax liens/Judgments; UCC records

Local Retrieval Area: SC-Beaufort, Hampton, Jasper

Add'l Information: Established 1986. Normal turnaround time- 48 hours. Projects billed by number of names searched. 1st project may require prepayment. Amma H General has been a leader in the R.A.C.E. for the past 15 years. Each clients assignment is treated with reliability, accuracy, confidentiality and expediency.

AM-PM Services

PO Box 1776, Moses Lake, WA 98837
Phone: 509-765-1776 **Fax:** 509-766-5776

Types of Records Retrieved: Civil courts; Real Estate; Tax liens/Judgments; UCC records; Vital records

Local Retrieval Area: WA-Adams, Chelan, Douglas, Franklin, Grant, Kittitas, Lincoln

Add'l Information: Established 1977. Normal turnaround time- 3 days or less. Projects billed by the hour. One hour minimum. Mileage is at 42 cents per mile. 1st project may require prepayment. Money orders and cashier checks accepted. Special orders may require downpayment. They specialize in process serving and document retrieval, and will go to the Canadian border. They perform service of process.

Analytical Inspection Services

720 Canton St, Jefferson, LA 70121

Phone: 504-832-0869 **Fax:** 504-832-0869

Types of Records Retrieved: Civil and criminal courts; Federal courts; Real Estate; UCC records

Local Retrieval Area: LA-Jefferson Parish, Orleans Parish. **Correspondent Relationships:** St. Tammany Parish, St. Charles Parish, Plaquemine Parish, St. Bernard Parish.

Add'l Information: Established 1993. Normal turnaround time- 24-48 hours. Projects billed by number of names searched. 1st project may require prepayment. Payment due upon completion. They specialize in felony, misdemeanor and civil searches. They can also handle property searches, real estate tax searches, deed claims and investigations. Contact office for fees and turnaround times for abstract work.

Anchorage & Matzu Process Svc

PO Box 212041, Anchorage, AK 99521-2041

Phone: 907-258-3211 **Fax:** 907-279-0754 arturos@alaska.net

Types of Records Retrieved: Civil, criminal and probate courts; Bankruptcy court, UCC records.

Local Retrieval Area: AK-Anchorage, Fairbanks North Star, Kenai Peninsula, Kodiak Island, Valdez-Cordova. **Correspondent Relationships:** Eagle River, Wasilla, Palmer, Chugiak, Eklutna, Girdwood, Bird Creek, Hope, North Pole.

Add'l Information: Established 1087. Normal turnaround time- 3-5 days. Expedited service available. Projects billed by number of names searched. They specialize in process service in south central Alaska. A licensed PI in AK. They perform service of process.

Anderson Abstract Co

PO Box 8, Tekamah, NE 68061-0008

Phone: 402-374-1476 **Fax:** 402-374-1478

randerson@huntel.net

Types of Records Retrieved: Civil, criminal and probate courts; Real Estate; Tax liens/Judgments; UCC records

Local Retrieval Area: NE-Burt

Add'l Information: Established 1905. Normal turnaround time- 2 days. Projects billed by number of names searched. plus copies, etc. Payment due upon receipt of invoice. They have provided record search, title insurance and abstracting services for over 90 years. In the Nebraska 402 area code, you may dial (800) 246-1476.

Anderson County Abstract Co

PO Box 847, 519 N Church St, Palestine, TX 75802

Phone: 903-729-5871 **Fax:** 903-729-1160

Types of Records Retrieved: Real Estate; Tax liens/judgments; UCC records

Local Retrieval Area: TX-Anderson

Add'l Information: Established 1900. Normal turnaround time- 1 week to 10 days. Fee basis varies by type of transaction. 1st project may require prepayment. They specialize in title policies and abstracting. They specialize in marriage/divorce and death searches.

H Ray Anderson

618 F Ave, Lawton, OK 73501

Phone: 580-355-4450 **Fax:** 580-250-1482

hraypi@aol.com

Types of Records Retrieved: Civil, criminal and probate courts; Federal courts; Real Estate; Tax liens/Judgments; UCC records

Local Retrieval Area: OK-Comanche, Cotton, Jefferson, Stephens, Tillman. **Correspondent Relationships:** Comanche, Cotton, other SW Okla. areas.

Add'l Information: Established 1990. Normal turnaround time- 24 hours. Projects billed by the hour. Criminal searches are a flat rate. Credit cards accepted. Personal checks are accepted. He specializes in workers' compensation, defense, personal injuries, custody and asset searches. A licensed PI in OK.

Katie Anderson

PO Box 90585, Tucson, AZ 85752

Phone: 520-405-8737 **Fax:** 520-844-1759

katieand@earthlink.net

Types of Records Retrieved: Civil and criminal courts.

Local Retrieval Area: AZ- Cochise, Gila, Graham, Greenlee, LaPaz, Maricopa, Pima, Pinal, Santa Cruz, Yuma. **Correspondent Relationships:** statewide.

Add'l Information: Established 1992. Normal turnaround time- within 24 hours of ordering. Projects billed by number of names searched. 1st project may require prepayment. She specializes in felony, misdemeanor, and civil cases in Arizona.

Andrews Agency Inc

736-B N Magnolia Ave, Orlando, FL 32803-3809

Phone: 407-649-2085 **Fax:** 407-649-3053

Types of Records Retrieved: Civil, criminal and probate courts; Federal courts; Real Estate; Tax liens/Judgments; UCC records; Vital records

Local Retrieval Area: FL-Brevard, Lake, Orange, Osceola, Seminole, Volusia

Add'l Information: Established 1983. Normal turnaround time- 24 hours. Projects billed by the hour. Credit cards accepted. Mastercard, Visa, American Express and Discover accepted. They specialize in process serving. A licensed PI in FL. They perform service of process.

Sharron Andrews

230 Grant St, Independence, CA 93526

Phone: 760-878-2038 **Fax:** 760-878-2471

Types of Records Retrieved: Civil, criminal and probate courts; Real Estate; Tax liens/Judgments; UCC records; Vital records

Local Retrieval Area: CA-Inyo

Add'l Information: Established 1978. Normal turnaround time- 1-2 days. Projects billed by the hour. 1st project may require prepayment. She will invoice companies.

Ankeny Allied Title Services LLC

2020 W 1st St, Ankeny, IA 50021-2404

Phone: 515-964-8868 **Fax:** 515-964-8897

sales@ankenyallied.com

Types of Records Retrieved: Civil courts; Federal District courts; Real Estate; Tax liens/Judgments; UCC records; Vital records

Local Retrieval Area: IA-Boone, Dallas, Jasper, Madison, Marion, Marshall, Polk, Story, Warren. **Correspondent Relationships:** statewide.

Add'l Information: Established 2003. Normal turnaround time- 24-72 hours. Projects billed by number of names searched. 1st project may require prepayment. They provide research and document retrieval in Iowa, specializing in current owner searches, title searches. UCC, tax liens, bankruptcy, civil and vital records.

Annette Sanders Research

637 Edenderry Dr, Vacaville, CA 95688-8552

Phone: 707-449-3620 **Fax:** 707-449-3655

netsand@compuserve.com

Types of Records Retrieved: Civil and criminal courts

Local Retrieval Area: CA-Napa, Solano

Add'l Information: Established 1996. Normal turnaround time- 4-24 hours. Projects billed by number of names searched. Will customize billing method. Will invoice monthly. She offer fast, accurate service; she lives minutes from the court house and can return results faster than others. Has been a researcher for 9 years.

Apex Information & Research Inc (AIR)

PO Box 814, Simonton, TX 77476-0814
Phone: may no longer be in business
Types of Records Retrieved: Real Estate; Tax liens/Judgments; UCC records
Local Retrieval Area: TX-Fort Bend, Harris, Montgomery. **Correspondent Relationships:** Texas.
Add'l Information: Established 1991. Normal turnaround time- 24-48 hours. Projects billed by number of names searched. Projects billed by the hour. Fees are per report. 1st project may require prepayment. Terms: net 15 days. They specialize in foreclosure reports, ownership and lien reports, survey adjoiners, document retrieval, environmental 50 year title searches and background checks, also telecommunciatins. Will file documents in Harris and Ft Bend counties only.

Apex Research

417 15th St SW, Albuquerque, NM 87104
Phone: 505-275-0848 **Fax:** 505-293-1037
apexsearch@msn.com
Types of Records Retrieved: Civil and criminal courts; Federal Courts; UCC records; Real Estate, Tax liens/Judgments.
Local Retrieval Area: NM-Bernalillo, Sandoval, Santa Fe, Valencia
Add'l Information: Established 2003. Normal turnaround time- 24-48 hours. Projects billed by number of names searched. 30-day billing cycle. They take pride in their fast, accurate searches with 24-hr turnaround time in most cases.

Applecheeks Research Ltd

3310 Pitkin Rd, Martinsville, IN 47756
Phone: 765-349-8371 **Fax:** 765-349-8371
dalefaye@yahoo.com
Types of Records Retrieved: Real Estate; Tax liens/judgments; UCC records
Local Retrieval Area: IN-Monroe, Morgan
Add'l Information: Established 1997. Normal turnaround time- 24 hours. Invoices are billed at the end of each month.

Applicant Insight Ltd

PO Box 458, New Port Richey, FL 34656-0458
Phone: 800-771-7703; **Fax:** 800-890-6454;
www.ainsight.com
Types of Records Retrieved: Civil and criminal courts; Federal courts; UCC records
Local Retrieval Area: FL-Pasco, Pinellas. **Correspondent Relationships:** nationwide, hands-on.
Add'l Information: Established 1990. Normal turnaround time- 1-3 business days. Projects billed by number of names searched. Credit cards accepted. Invoiced monthly. They do in-depth interviews of the supervisor to whom the applicant reported. Statewide, they have an interactive web site for orders and retrievals at www.ainsight.com. A licensed PI in FL.

Applicant Profile Services

6720 Hickman Rd, Windsor Heights, IA 50322
Phone: 515-727-7964 **Fax:** 515-727-7965
www.applicantprofileservices.com **email:** info@applicantprofileservices.com
Types of Records Retrieved: Civil, criminal and probate courts; Federal courts; Real Estate; Tax liens/Judgments; UCC records
Local Retrieval Area: IA-all counties
Add'l Information: Established 1993. Normal turnaround time- 24-48 hours. Projects billed by number of names searched. Credit cards accepted. They specialize in pre-employment screening, real estate title search work, current owner searches, document retrieval, and mortgage recordings. Also provides skiptracing services, tenant background checks, asset recovery.

Applied Research & Investigation

3818 4th Ave, Beaver Falls, PA 15010
Phone: 800-594-0008; 724-847-1116 **Fax:** 724-847-7268
michael.yaria@verizon.net
Types of Records Retrieved: Civil, criminal and probate courts
Local Retrieval Area: OH-Columbiana; PA-Allegheny, Beaver
Add'l Information: Established 2001. Normal turnaround time- 1-2 days. Projects billed by number of names searched. 1st project may require prepayment. They are a comprehensive pre-employment screening service focused on healthcare, manufacturing and engineering/technical fields. Reference available.

APSCREEN Inc

2043 Westcliff Dr #300, Newport Beach, CA 92660
Phone: 800-277-2733; 949-646-4003 **Fax:** 888-277-2733; 949-646-5160
www.apscreen.com **email:** tomlawson@apscreen.com
Types of Records Retrieved: Civil, criminal and probate courts; Federal courts; Real Estate; Tax liens/Judgments; UCC records; Vital records
Local Retrieval Area: CA-Kern, Los Angeles, Orange, Riverside, San Bernardino, San Diego, Santa Barbara, Ventura. **Correspondent Relationships:** worldwide.
Add'l Information: Established 1980. Normal turnaround time- 24-48 hours. Projects billed by number of names searched. Credit cards accepted. They specialize in asset searches, document retrieval, research, fraud examinations, due diligence, permissible purpose credit reporting (licensed credit bureau), expert testimony, employment/tenant screening.

Arbor Abstracting Co

403 Wayne St, Bethany, PA 18431
Phone: 570-253-0472 **Fax:** 570-253-6214
titleins@ptd.net
Types of Records Retrieved: Civil, criminal and probate courts; Real Estate; Tax liens/Judgments; UCC records
Local Retrieval Area: PA-Pike, Wayne
Add'l Information: Established 1983. Normal turnaround time- 24-48 hours. Expedited service available. They charge a flat rate per project. Payment expected upon presentation of file. They specialize in real estate, title insurance and settlement services. They will file/record UCC and real estate documents on behalf of clients in Wayne County only.

Arbuckle Searches

1003 N King, Harrisonville, MO 64701
Phone: 816-550-9106 **Fax:** 815-642-9147
Types of Records Retrieved: Real Estate
Local Retrieval Area: MO-Cass, Johnson
Add'l Information: Established 2001. Normal turnaround time- 24-48 hours. Projects billed by number of names searched. They have over 2 years experience with record retreivals, provides mortgage/single property searches with a 24-48 hours turnaround time.

ARC Document Research Inc

180 W Washington St #600, Chicago, IL 60602
Phone: 312-346-4895 **Fax:** 312-346-4947
www.arcdocumentresearchinc.net **email:** arcdocs@aol.com
Types of Records Retrieved: Real Estate; Tax liens/Judgments; UCC records
Local Retrieval Area: IL-Cook, Du Page, Kane, Lake, McHenry, Sangamon. Will, Winnebago. **Correspondent Relationships:** Illinois.
Add'l Information: Established 1997. Normal turnaround time- 48-72 hours. Projects billed by number of names searched. 1st project may require prepayment. They specialize in real estate searches.

Archives Retrieval Service of GA

85 Highland Park Way, Sharpsburg, GA 30277
Phone: 770-252-5510 **Fax:** 770-252-1542 arsdocuments@aol.com
Types of Records Retrieved: Civil, criminal and probate courts; Federal courts; Real Estate; Tax liens/Judgments; UCC records; Vital records
Local Retrieval Area: GA-Cherokee, Clayton, Coweta, DeKalb, Fayette, Fulton, Gwininett, Henry. **Correspondent Relationships:** Georgia.
Add'l Information: Established 1998. Normal turnaround time- 24-48 hours. Projects billed by number of records located. They specialize in professional research in bankruptcy, civil and criminal courts, real estate and tax liens, judgments and vital records.

Arenae Abstract & Title Co
PO Box 727, Standish, MI 48658-0727
Phone: 989-846-6560 **Fax:** 989-846-6633

Types of Records Retrieved: Civil, criminal and probate courts; Real Estate; Tax liens/Judgments; UCC records; Vital records

Local Retrieval Area: MI-Arenac

Add'l Information: Normal turnaround time- up to 1 week. Projects billed by the hour. All projects require prepayment. They specialize in title insurance.

Argus Services Inc
330 S Wells St #514, Chicago, IL 60606-7103
Phone: 800-297-3377; 312-922-6766 **Fax:** 312-786-9508
ops@argus-services.com

Types of Records Retrieved: Civil, criminal and probate courts; Federal courts; Tax liens/Judgments; Vital records.

Local Retrieval Area: IL-Cook, De Kalb, Du Page, Kane, Kendall, Lake, McHenry, Will, Winnebago. **Correspondent Relationships:** all counties in the US for criminal records.

Add'l Information: Established 1991. Normal turnaround time- 24 hours; same day available in Chicago metro area. Projects billed by number of names searched. Projects billed by the hour. Net 20 days. 1st project may require prepayment. Credit cards accepted. They are located in downtown Chicago 1/2 block from the Federal Building and four blocks from Cook County offices. They are a licensed private detective agency in Illinois, offering many kinds of criminal checks in the Chicago area. A licensed PI in IL. They perform service of process.

Arizona Abstractors
16021 N Lake Forest Dr, Sun City, AZ 85351
Phone: 602-989-3428 **Fax:** 623-875-9092 codutcher@aol.com

Types of Records Retrieved: Real Estate; Tax liens/judgments; UCC records

Local Retrieval Area: AZ-Maricopa

Add'l Information: Established 2004. Normal turnaround time- 24-48 hours. Expedited service available. Projects billed by number of names searched. Payment terms are net 30 days. They specialize in quality-timely searches, judgments, tax liens, updates, UCC's, 40 year, O & E, two owner, etc. They are a 30 year member of NAR.

Arizona Express Attorney Services
PO Box 25426, Phoenix, AZ 85002-5426
Phone: 602-616-1715 **Fax:** 602-532-7877
http://arizonaexpress.com **email:** sam@arizonaexpress.com

Types of Records Retrieved: Civil, criminal and probate courts; Federal courts; Real Estate; Tax liens/Judgments; UCC records; Vital records

Local Retrieval Area: AZ-Maricopa

Add'l Information: Established 1995. Normal turnaround time- 48 hours. Projects billed by number of names searched. Credit cards accepted. Credit cards accepted thru PayPal. They specialize in service of process, asset searches, skiptracing, and court filings as well as public record retrieval. A licensed PI in AZ. They perform service of process.

Arizona Research & Retrieval Services Inc
24810 S Lakewood Dr, Chandler, AZ 85248
Phone: 888-500-7767; 480-802-5918 **Fax:** 602-532-7764
www.azretrieval.com **email:** info@azretrieval.com

Types of Records Retrieved: Civil, criminal and probate courts; Federal courts; Real Estate; Tax liens/Judgments; UCC records; Vital records

Local Retrieval Area: AZ-Apache, Cochise, Coconino, Gila, Graham, Greenlee, La Paz, Maricopa, Mohave, Navajo, Pima, Pinal, Santa Cruz, Yavapai, Yuma; NV-Clark. **Correspondent Relationships:** statewide AZ.

Add'l Information: Established 1998. Normal turnaround time- 24-48 hours. Expedited service available. Projects billed by number of names searched. 1st project may require prepayment. Terms are net 15 days. They specialize in research and retrieval of county/federal court and county recorder records throughout AZ and in Clark County (Las Vegas) NV. A licensed PI in AZ (pending).

Arkansas Corporate Research & Service Co
323 Center St #1202, Little Rock, AR 72201
Phone: 501-374-3843 **Fax:** 501-374-3836 acrsc@swbell.net

Types of Records Retrieved: Civil and criminal courts; Federal Courts; UCC records.

Local Retrieval Area: AR-Faulkner, Lonoke, Pulaski, Lonoke. **Correspondent Relationships:** statewide.

Add'l Information: Established 1995. 1st project may require prepayment. They provide court record and UCC services for entire state of Arkansas.

Victoria J Armes
263 Whippoorwill Rd, Mooresville, NC 28117
Phone: 704-663-4085 **Fax:** 704-663-7801
crazyarmes@alltel.net

Types of Records Retrieved: Real Estate; Tax liens/judgments; UCC records

Local Retrieval Area: NC-Cabarrus, Catawba, Iredell, Lincoln, Rowan. **Correspondent Relationships:** Durham, Johnston, Orange, Wake counties.

Add'l Information: Established 1985. Normal turnaround time- 24 hours. Projects billed by number of names searched. 1st project may require prepayment. She specializes in real estate title searches.

Armstrong Document Retrieval
8711 Rosewood Dr, Prairie Village, KS 66207-2223
Phone: 913-341-1991 **Fax:** 913-341-1667
armdoc@kc.rr.com

Types of Records Retrieved: Civil and criminal courts; Federal courts; Real Estate; Tax liens/Judgments; UCC records

Local Retrieval Area: KS-Johnson, Wyandotte; MO-Clay, Jackson, Platte

Add'l Information: Established 1988. Normal turnaround time- 24-48 hours. Projects billed by number of names searched. 1st project may require prepayment. Prepayment required if copy charges are over $50.00. They do daily document retrieval from the two Federal Archives in K.C., one of which has closed case files from New York and New Jersey.

Arrow Background Svcs LLC
3510 Newland Rd, Baltimore, MD 21218
Phone: 410-243-8301 **Fax:** 410-243-8302 arrowbackground@verizon.net

Types of Records Retrieved: Civil and criminal courts; Federal courts, Tax liens/Judgments

Local Retrieval Area: MD-Anne Arundel, Baltimore, Baltimore City, Carroll, Harford, Howard, Montgomery, Prince George's. **Correspondent Relationships:** statewide, including eastern shore.

Add'l Information: Established 1995. Normal turnaround time- 24 hours. Projects billed by number of names searched. 1st project may require prepayment. They specialize in court record retrievals and Maryland State Department of Assessment and Taxation retrievals and filings.

ASA (Attorney Service Associates)
PO Box 116874, Carrollton, TX 75011
Phone: 972-394-1175 **Fax:** 972-492-4552
www.asainfo.com **email:** ron@asainfo.com

Types of Records Retrieved: Civil, criminal and probate courts; Federal courts; Real Estate; Tax liens/Judgments; UCC records; Vital records

Local Retrieval Area: TX-Collin, Dallas, Denton, Tarrant. **Correspondent Relationships:** Excellent statewide system of correspondents.

Add'l Information: Established 1991. Normal turnaround time- 24-48 hours. Expedited service available. Projects billed by number of names searched. Terms: net 15 days, 5% late fee. They specialize in county record research & document retireval. Licensed PI in TX. They perform service of process.

ASAP Legal Messenger
6824 W 19th St #215, Tacoma, WA 98466
Phone: 253-640-1312
andyigor@ix.netcom.com

Types of Records Retrieved: Civil and criminal courts; Federal courts; Real Estate

Local Retrieval Area: WA-Adams, Chelan, Douglas, King, Kitsap, Pierce, Snohomish. **Correspondent Relationships:** Washington and Oregon.

Add'l Information: Established 1990. Normal turnaround time- 3 days. Projects billed by number of names searched. 1st project may require prepayment. They perform service of process.

ASAP Process Service

PO Box 607, 230 E 1st Ave, Lisbon, IA 52253
Phone: 877-455-2490; 319-455-2490 **Fax:** 319-455-5041
rcook10672@aol.com

Types of Records Retrieved: Civil, criminal and probate courts; Federa courts; Real Estate; Vital records

Local Retrieval Area: IA-Benton, Black Hawk, Buchanan, Cedar, Clinton, Dubuque, Delaware, Des Moines, Henry, Iowa, Jackson, Jefferson, Johnson, Jones, Linn, Muscatine, Scott

Add'l Information: Established 1996. Normal turnaround time- 3-4 days. Expedited service available. Projects billed by the hour. All projects require prepayment. They also provide court filings, subpoena preparation, photocopying, and skiptracing. They perform service of process.

ASAP Process Services

3115 Northington Ct, Florence, AL 35630
Phone: 256-766-9805 **Fax:** 256-740-5530
www.serveanyone.com **email:** info@serveanyone.com

Types of Records Retrieved: Civil, criminal and probate courts; Federal courts; Real Estate; UCC records; Vital records

Local Retrieval Area: AL-Colbert, Cullman, Franklin, Jefferson, Lauderdale, Lawrence, Limestone, Marion, Morgan, Shelby, Winston; MS-Lauderdale, Tishomingo; TN-Davidson, Giles, Hardin, Lawrence

Add'l Information: Established 1999. Normal turnaround time- 1-3 days. Expedited service available. Projects billed by number of records located. All projects require prepayment. Cellphone # 256-335-8133. A licensed PI in AL. They perform service of process.

ASAP Services

25504 E 219th St, Pleasant Hill, MO 64080
Phone: 816-540-2901 **Fax:** 816-540-2915
asapserviceskc@kcweb.net

Types of Records Retrieved: Civil courts; Probate courts; Federal courts; Real Estate; Tax liens/Judgments

Local Retrieval Area: MO-Cass, Clay, Jackson. **Correspondent Relationships:** Platte, Bates, MO; Johnson & Wyandotte, KS counties.

Add'l Information: Established 1998. Normal turnaround time- 24 hours. Projects billed by number of names searched. 1st project may require prepayment. They specialize in residential and real estate abstracting along with Federal District and Bankruptcy courts.

Ascension Title Services Inc

PO Box 117, Gonzales, LA 70707 (311 E Cornerview, Prairieville, 70769)
Phone: 225-647-8051 **Fax:** 225-647-8064
ascensiontitle@ats.brcoxmail.com

Types of Records Retrieved: Civil courts; Probate courts; Real Estate; Tax liens/Judgments; UCC records

Local Retrieval Area: LA-Ascension Parish, Iberville Parish, St. James Parish. **Correspondent Relationships:** statewide.

Add'l Information: Established 1992. Normal turnaround time- 2-3 days. Fee basis varies by type of transaction. 1st project may require prepayment.

Ashley Abstract Co

113 W Main St, PO Box 365, Ashley, ND 58413
Phone: 701-288-3584 **Fax:** 701-288-2110

Types of Records Retrieved: Civil courts; Real Estate; Tax liens/Judgments; UCC records; Vital records

Local Retrieval Area: ND-McIntosh

Add'l Information: Established 1901. Normal turnaround time- 24 hours. Projects billed by number of names searched. Projects billed by number of records located. All projects require prepayment.

ASK Services Inc

336 S High St, Columbus, OH 43215
Phone: 888-416-1313; **Fax:** 734-983-9041
www.ask-services.com **email:** publicrecords@ask-services.com

Types of Records Retrieved: Civil and criminal courts; Federal courts; Real Estate; Tax liens/Judgments; UCC records

Local Retrieval Area: OH-Cuyahoga, Delaware, Fairfield, Franklin, Hamilton, Licking, Lucas, Madison. **Correspondent Relationships:** MI, IN, NC & SC.

Add'l Information: Established 2000. Normal turnaround time- 24-48 hours. Projects billed by number of names searched. Credit cards accepted. They specialize in real property/title searches as well as criminal, civil, UCC and tax lien searches in all counties. A licensed PI in MI, NC.

ASK Services Inc (Indiana)

136 E Market St, Indianapolis, IN 43204
Phone: 888-416-1313; **Fax:** 734-983-9041
www.ask-services.com **email:** publicrecords@ask-services.com

Types of Records Retrieved: Civil and criminal courts; Federal courts; Real Estate; UCC records; Tax liens/Judgments

Local Retrieval Area: IN-Elkhart, Hamilton, Hendricks, Johnson, Lake, LaPorte, Marion, Morgan, Porter, St Joseph. **Correspondent Relationships:** nationwide.

Add'l Information: Established 2000. Normal turnaround time- 24-48 hours. Projects billed by number of names searched. Credit cards accepted. They specialize in criminal, civil and bankruptcy searches as well as UCC, tax liens searches and filings in all counties. They also do expedited real property/title searches. A licensed PI in MI, NC.

ASK Services Inc (Michigan)

42180 Ford Rd, Canton, MI 48187
Phone: 888-416-1313; **Fax:** 734-983-9041
www.ask-publicrecords.com **email:** ask@ask-services.com

Types of Records Retrieved: Civil, criminal and probate courts; Federal courts; Real Estate; Tax liens/Judgments; UCC records; Vital records

Local Retrieval Area: MI-all counties. **Correspondent Relationships:** nationwide.

Add'l Information: Established 1985. Normal turnaround time- 24-48 hours. Expedited service available. Projects billed by number of names searched. Projects billed by the hour. Credit cards accepted. They specialize in statewide civil, criminal & bankruptcy searches. UCC, tax lien searches and filings at all counties. They also do expedited real property/title searches. A licensed PI in MI.

ASK Services Inc (North Carolina)

5 W Hargett St #803, Raleigh, NC 27601-1357
Phone: 888-416-1313; **Fax:** 734-983-9041
www.ask-services.com **email:** publicrecords@ask-services.com

Types of Records Retrieved: Civil, criminal and probate courts; Federal courts; Real Estate; Tax liens/Judgments; UCC records; Vital records

Local Retrieval Area: NC-Cabarrus, Chatham, Cumberland, Durham, Guilford, Harnett, Johnston, Mecklenburg, Orange, Wake, Wayne. **Correspondent Relationships:** nationwide.

Add'l Information: Established 1998. Normal turnaround time- 24-48 hours. Expedited service available. Projects billed by number of names searched. Projects billed by the hour. Credit cards accepted. They specialize in civil, criminal and bankruptcy searches, also UCC, tax liens searches and filings for all counties covered. Will complete expedited real property/title searches. A licensed PI in MI.

Asset Control Inc

1300 Fulton Pl #300, Denton, TX 76201
Phone: 877-277-3812; 940-891-1919 **Fax:** 877-277-3829;
www.assetcontrol.net **email:** info@assetcontrol.net

Types of Records Retrieved: Civil and criminal courts; Federal courts; Real Estate; Tax liens/Judgments; UCC records; Vital records

Local Retrieval Area: DC-Washington; IL-Cook; TX-Bexar, Collin, Dallas, Denton, Harris, Hidalgo, Tarrant. **Correspondent Relationships:** nationwide.

Add'l Information: Established 1994. Normal turnaround time- 24-48 hours. Projects billed by number of names searched. Credit cards accepted. Net 30 days on monthly bills. A licensed PI in TX.

Asset Protection Associates Inc

PO Box 310, Little Switzerland, NC 28749
Phone: 828-765-9359 **Fax:** 828-765-9369
www.asset-protectionassociates.com **email:** swilson@asset-protectionassociates.com

Types of Records Retrieved: Civil and criminal courts; Real Estate

Local Retrieval Area: NC-Mitchell, Yancey

Add'l Information: Established 1978. Normal turnaround time- 24-48 hours. Expedited service available at add'l charge. Projects billed by number of names searched. Projects billed by number of records located. Projects billed by the hour. 1st project may require prepayment. Will invoice. They are a full service investigative firm serving the business, legal and financial communities since 1978. A licensed PI in NC.

Asset Protection Inv, Inc

PO Box 2426, Beaufort, SC 29902
Phone: 843-525-9664 **Fax:** 843-521-4667
i@charter.net

Types of Records Retrieved: Civil, criminal and probate courts; Real Estate; Tax liens/Judgments

Local Retrieval Area: SC-Beaufort, Colleton, Hampton, Jasper

Add'l Information: Established 1995. Normal turnaround time- 48-72 hours. Expedited service available. Projects billed by the hour. A licensed PI in SC, GA. They perform service of process.

Asset Research Group

2121 Tannehill #2057, Houston, TX 77008
Phone: 713-864-2536 **Fax:** 713-864-8932
assetresearch@aol.com

Types of Records Retrieved: Civil, criminal and probate courts; Federal courts; Real Estate; Tax liens/Judgments; UCC records Vital records

Local Retrieval Area: TX-Brazoria, Fort Bend, Galveston, Harris, Montgomery, Waller

Add'l Information: Established 1986. Normal turnaround time- 2 days. Expedited service available. Projects billed by the hour. Will invoice. They specialize in locating missing persons, background checks, interviewing (in person), courthouse searches and/or retrieval of records. Also alanysis of assets. A licensed PI in TX.

ASSIST International

101 W 29th St, New York, NY 10001
Phone: 800-382-7747; 212-244-2074 **Fax:** 212-594-1939
www.assistintl.net **email:** assistnyc@aol.com

Types of Records Retrieved: Civil, criminal and probate courts; Federal courts; Real Estate; Tax liens/Judgments; UCC records; Vital records

Local Retrieval Area: NY-Bronx, Kings, New York, Orange, Putnam, Queens, Richmond, Rockland, Suffolk, Westchester. **Correspondent Relationships:** nationwide.

Add'l Information: Established 1981. Normal turnaround time- immediate to 5 days. Projects billed by number of names searched. They are a full service investigation agency specializing in locates, investigations and surveillance. Online computer searches are available. A licensed PI in NJ, NY. They perform service of process.

Assist Investigations

1223 Wilshire Blvd #943, Santa Monica, CA 90403
Phone: 310-451-2204 **Fax:** 310-395-7355
www.assistinvestigations.com **email:** btb@assistinvestigations.com

Types of Records Retrieved: Civil, criminal and probate courts; Federal courts; Real Estate; Tax liens/Judgments; UCC records; Vital records

Local Retrieval Area: CA-Los Angeles, Orange

Add'l Information: Established 1998. Normal turnaround time- 24-72 hours. Projects billed by number of names searched. Projects billed by the hour. 1st project may require prepayment. Will invoice. They have over 15 years experience conducting public record research in Southern CA. They specialize in real estate documents and court records research. A licensed PI in CA, Lic# 21703..

Associated Abstracting Services of MN

PO Box 39047, Edina, MN 55439
Phone: 612-819-6115 **Fax:** 952-842-0812

Types of Records Retrieved: Civil courts; Federal courts; Real Estate; Tax liens/Judgments; UCC records

Local Retrieval Area: MN-Anoka, Benton, Blue Earth, Carver, Chisago, Hennepin, Isanti, LaSueur, McLeod, Mille Lacs, Nicollet, Ramsey, Rice, Scott, Sherburne, Stearns, Steele, Waseca, Wright

Add'l Information: Established 1985. Normal turnaround time- 24-48 hours. Projects billed by number of names searched. 1st project may require prepayment. Terms: net 30 days. Orders must be received by 6 AM to be completed on same day.

Associated Attorney Services

123 W Padre St #1, Santa Barbara, CA 93105
Phone: 805-898-0022 **Fax:** 805-898-0012

Types of Records Retrieved: Civil, criminal and probate courts; Federal courts; Real Estate; Tax liens/Judgments; UCC records; Vital records

Local Retrieval Area: CA-Santa Barbara. **Correspondent Relationships:** California.

Add'l Information: Established 1965. Normal turnaround time- 24 hours. Projects billed by number of names searched. Projects billed by number of records located. 1st project may require prepayment. They specialize in process service. They perform service of process.

Associated Investigative Services Inc

30 S 9th St, Allentown, PA 18102
Phone: 610-351-9911 **Fax:** 610-351-9913
www.associnv.com **email:** aisinc@rcn.com

Types of Records Retrieved: Civil, criminal and probate courts; Federal courts; Real Estate; Tax liens/Judgments; UCC records

Local Retrieval Area: PA-Lehigh, Monroe, Northampton

Add'l Information: Established 1995. Normal turnaround time- 48 hours. Projects billed by number of names searched. Credit cards accepted. They specialize in being a full service investigative agency serving the Lehigh Valley (Allentown) Bethlehem/Eastern area of PA. They are licensed, bonded and insured. A licensed PI in PA. They perform service of process.

Associated Peninsula Title & Abstract Co

945 First St, PO Box 516, Menominee, MI 49858
Phone: 906-863-7871 **Fax:** 906-863-1363
cindybehnke@menomineeabstract.com

Types of Records Retrieved: Civil, criminal and probate courts; Real Estate; Tax liens/Judgments; UCC records; Vital records

Local Retrieval Area: MI-Menominee

Add'l Information: Established 1970. Normal turnaround time- 2-3 days. Projects billed by the hour. $120.00 minimum for Title Insurance; $50.00 minimum for searches. 1st project may require prepayment. Terms: net 30 days. They specialize in title insurance, title searches (letter reports), closings and escrows.

Associated Professional Services

PO Box 4068, New Bedford, MA 02740-4068
Phone: 800-849-7870; 508-995-5901 **Fax:** 508-998-4926
asscprosvc@verizonmail.com

Types of Records Retrieved: Civil, criminal and probate courts; Federal courts; Real Estate; Tax liens/Judgments; UCC records; Vital records

Local Retrieval Area: MA-Barnstable, Bristol, Plymouth. **Correspondent Relationships:** Rhode Island.

Add'l Information: Established 1979. Normal turnaround time- 24-48 hours. 1st project may require prepayment. They are a private investigation firm.

Their retrieval unit is dedicated to record retrieval and exist as an adjunct to our core services. A licensed PI in MA. They perform service of process.

Associated Services

PO Box 5437, Harrisburg, PA 17110
Phone: 717-938-1550 **Fax:** 717-938-5546
www.assocservlimited.com **email:** assocser1@aol.com

Types of Records Retrieved: Civil and criminal courts; Federal courts; Real Estate; Tax liens/Judgments; UCC records

Local Retrieval Area: PA-Cumberland, Dauphin, York. **Correspondent Relationships:** Lancaster county PA.

Add'l Information: Established 1989. Normal turnaround time- 24-48 hours. Fee basis varies by project. Net 30 days. They specialize in criminal background checks, current owner searches, civil and UCC searches, service of process and court filings. They perform service of process.

Associated Title Company Inc

717 S Main St, Princeton, IL 61356
Phone: 800-713-4224; 815-872-9601 **Fax:** 815-872-4701
www.associatedtitle.net **email:** atc@mtco.com

Types of Records Retrieved: Civil, criminal and probate courts; Real Estate; Tax liens/Judgments; UCC records; Vital records

Local Retrieval Area: IL-Bureau, Putnam

Add'l Information: Established 1969. Normal turnaround time- 1 day for status checks of real estate records; 1-2 weeks for title insurance orders. Projects billed by number of names searched. Monthly billing. They specialize in title insurance, title reports, lien searches and criminal searches.

Assured Inquiries LLC

PO Box 87, 19 Bunker Hill Rd, New Castle, DE 19720-0087
Phone: 888-644-0004; 302-324-1190 **Fax:** 302-324-0177
www.assuredinquiries.com **email:** louis.dempsey@verizon.net

Types of Records Retrieved: Civil, criminal and probate courts; Federal courts

Local Retrieval Area: DE-New Castle

Add'l Information: Established 2002. Normal turnaround time- 3 business days. Expedited service available. 1st project may require prepayment. Credit cards accepted. They provide general investigative services including pre-employment screening and security consultation in Delaware. Over 31 years experience in law enforcement and corporate security management. A licensed PI in DE. They perform service of process.

Assured Realty

2nd & Norwegian St, Pottsville, PA 17901
Phone: 570-622-1366 **Fax:** 570-622-4216

Types of Records Retrieved: Civil courts; Probate courts; Real Estate; Tax liens/Judgments; UCC records

Local Retrieval Area: PA-Schuylkill

Add'l Information: Established 1984. Normal turnaround time- variable depending on search. Charges vary depending on type of search. 1st project may require prepayment. Assured Realty takes pride in its experienced staff and over 25 years in business - providing real estate title search and title insurance services.

Assured Title Company

611 Westridge, O'Fallon, MO 63366
Phone: 636-240-0833 **Fax:** 636-240-0786
www.assuredtitle.net

Types of Records Retrieved: Civil, criminal and probate courts; Real Estate; Tax liens/Judgments; UCC records

Local Retrieval Area: MO-Lincoln, Montgomery, St. Charles, Warren. **Correspondent Relationships:** St. Louis, Pike, Camden, Miller, Ralls, MO counties.

Add'l Information: Established 1977. Normal turnaround time- 5 working days. Projects billed by number of names searched. They specialize in record searching for title insurance and real estate closings.

ATACO Inc

228 W Gay St, West Chester, PA 19380
Phone: 800-220-2039; 610-436-6510 **Fax:** 610-436-8112
www.atlantictitleabstract.com **email:** edougherty@landam.com

Types of Records Retrieved: Real Estate

Local Retrieval Area: PA-Berks, Bucks, Chester, Delaware. **Correspondent Relationships:** Pennsylvania and Delaware.

Add'l Information: Established 1987. Normal turnaround time- 2-3 days for lien searches, up to 2 weeks for all other searches. Expedited service available. Fee basis will vary by the type of project. They specialize in real estate and abstracting.

Atlanta Attorney Services

5825 Glenridge Dr NE Bldg 1 #209, Atlanta, GA 30328
Phone: 800-804-4078; 404-303-7899 **Fax:** 404-303-7890
www.aaslegal.com **email:** info@aaslegal.com

Types of Records Retrieved: Civil, criminal and probate courts; Federal courts; Tax liens/Judgments; UCC records

Local Retrieval Area: GA-Clayton, Cobb, De Kalb, Forsyth, Fulton, Gwinnett. **Correspondent Relationships:** nationwide.

Add'l Information: Established 1996. Normal turnaround time- 48 hours. Expedited service available. Projects billed by number of names searched. Projects billed by the hour. Credit cards accepted. They specialize in court searches, document retrieval, service of process, court filings and bankruptcy services. They perform service of process.

Atlanta Legal Services Inc

3070 Presidential Pky #148, Atlanta, GA 30340-3712
Phone: 877-302-4136; 404-876-8098 **Fax:** 404-876-8099
www.atlantalegalservices.com **email:** info@atlantalegalservices.com

Types of Records Retrieved: Civil and criminal courts; Probats courts; Federal courts; Real Estate; Tax liens/Judgments; UcC records; Vital records

Local Retrieval Area: GA-Clayton, Cobb, De Kalb, Douglas, Forsyth, Fulton, Gwinnett, Paulding, Rockdale

Add'l Information: Established 1993. Normal turnaround time- 24 hours. Expedited service available. Projects billed by number of names searched. Projects billed by the hour. Flat rate per county (plus) time if over 30 minutes. 1st project may require prepayment. Credit cards accepted. Will invoice. They are a full ligitation support service, providing process service, record retrieval and research and court filings. A licensed PI in GA. They perform service of process.

Atlanta Title Abstractors

3410 Bold Springs Rd, Monroe, GA 30656
Phone: 770-267-2727 **Fax:** 770-267-6554

Types of Records Retrieved: Civil courts; Probate courts; Federal courts; Real Estate; Tax liens/Judgments; UCC records

Local Retrieval Area: GA-Barrow, Clark, Clayton, Cobb, De Kalb, Douglas, Fayette, Fulton, Gwinnett, Hall, Jackson, Madison, Morgan, Newton, Oconee, Oglethorpe, Rockdale, Spalding. **Correspondent Relationships:** IN, SC, FL, NJ, AL, MS, TN, GA.

Add'l Information: Established 1985. Normal turnaround time- 48 hours. Projects billed by number of names searched. 1st project may require prepayment. They specialize in current owner of property, full owner of property, UCC by name, probate of name, civil by full name and tax liens by name/address.

Atlantic Investigations

315 W Ponce de Leon Ave, Suite 800, Decatur, GA 30030
Phone: 800-216-9877; 404-378-0700 **Fax:** 404-378-1030
www.atlanticinvestigations.com **email:** jasonbeeker@aol.com

Types of Records Retrieved: Civil, criminal and probate courts; Federal courts; Real Estate; Tax liens/Judgments; UCC records; Vital records

Local Retrieval Area: GA-De Kalb. **Correspondent Relationships:** Georgia.

Add'l Information: Established 1963. Normal turnaround time- 2-7 days. Projects billed by the hour. 1st project may require prepayment. Credit cards accepted. Visa and Mastercard accepted. They have provided investigative services for more than 40 years. Services include extensive database access and surveillance. A licensed PI in GA. They perform service of process.

Atlantic Title & Research

6184 Library Ln, Bealeton, VA 22712
Phone: 540-439-1800 **Fax:** 540-439-1700
www.atlantictitleandresearch.com **email:** talkmac@aol.com

Types of Records Retrieved: Civil and criminal courts; Real Estate, Tax liens/Judgments, UCC records

Local Retrieval Area: VA-Culpeper, Fairfax, Fauquier, Loudoun, Prince William, Stafford. **Correspondent Relationships:** statewide.

Add'l Information: Established 2002. Normal turnaround time- 24-48 hours. Projects billed by number of names searched. 1st project may require prepayment. Credit cards accepted. Terms agreed on individual basis They specialize in civil and criminal courts, real estate, Tax liens/Judgments and UCC records. They have nearly 20 years of experience.

Atlantis Agency

2700 Meadowview Dr, Arlington, TX 76016-1427
Phone: 817-896-9337 **Fax:** 817-492-9030 sdrrissler@yahoo.com

Types of Records Retrieved: Civil, criminal and probate courts; Federal courts; Tax liens/Judgments; Vital records

Local Retrieval Area: TX-Dallas, Johnson, Parker, Tarrant

Add'l Information: Established 2000. Normal turnaround time- 24 hours. Projects billed by the hour. They specialize in process service, legal research, courier service and record retrieval. They perform service of process.

Atlas Abstract Co

125 N Broadway, Holdenville, OK 74848
Phone: 405-379-3311 **Fax:** 405-379-3349

Types of Records Retrieved: Civil courts; Probate courts; Real Estate; Tax liens/Judgments; UCC records

Local Retrieval Area: OK-Hughes

Add'l Information: Established 1904. Normal turnaround time- varied by project. They specialize in Hughes county real estate.

Atlas Research Services Inc

13843 Mt View Pl, Sylmar, CA 91342
Phone: 818-362-0140 **Fax:** 818-833-0870 atlasrsch@aol.com

Types of Records Retrieved: Civil and criminal courts; Federal courts

Local Retrieval Area: CA-Fresno, Kern, Los Angeles, Orange, Riverside, San Bernardino, San Diego, Santa Barbara, Siskiyou, Ventura. **Correspondent Relationships:** all of California.

Add'l Information: Established 1996. Normal turnaround time- 24-48 hours. Charge by number of records located after 5 recorded cases. Credit cards accepted. Terms: net 25 days. They specialize in criminal background investigations. Online ordering available.

Atoka Abstract Co Inc

308 E Court St, Atoka, OK 74525
Phone: 580-889-7316 **Fax:** 580-889-7317

Types of Records Retrieved: Real Estate; Tax liens/judgments; UCC records

Local Retrieval Area: OK-Atoka

Add'l Information: Established 1977. Normal turnaround time- variable depending on project. Projects billed by the hour.

ATT Investigations Inc

PO Box 25831, Fort Lauderdale, FL 33320
Phone: 800-733-4405; 954-733-4005 **Fax:** 954-677-0562
customerservice@attloss.com

Types of Records Retrieved: Civil, criminal and probate courts; Federal courts; Real Estate; Tax liens/Judgments; UCC records; Vital records

Local Retrieval Area: FL-Broward, Dade, Hillsborough, Lake, Marion, Orange, Osceola, Palm Beach, Pasco, Pinellas, Seminole, Volusia. **Correspondent Relationships:** nationwide.

Add'l Information: Established 1994. Normal turnaround time- 2-3 days. Projects billed by number of names searched. Projects billed by number of records located. Credit cards accepted. They provide extensive public record retrieval in all courts and recorders offices. A licensed PI in FL.

ATT Loss Prevention Inc

PO Box 1681, Torrington, CT 06790
Phone: 860-496-1472 **Fax:** 860-482-0377
customerservice@attloss.com

Types of Records Retrieved: Civil, criminal and probate courts; Federal courts; Real Estate; Tax liens/Judgments; UCC records; Vital records

Local Retrieval Area: CT-Fairfield, Hartford, Litchfield, Middlesex, New Haven, New London, Tolland, Windham. **Correspondent Relationships:** nationwide.

Add'l Information: Established 1994. Normal turnaround time- 2-3 days. Will bill depending on the nature of the project. 1st project may require prepayment. Credit cards accepted. They provide extensive public record retrieval in all courts, recorders offices and motor vehicle records.

Attorney Civil Process Service

425 Austin Ave #2102, Waco, TX 76701
Phone: 254-755-6447 **Fax:** 254-754-4050

Types of Records Retrieved: Civil, criminal and probate courts; Federal courts

Local Retrieval Area: TX-Bell, Bosque, Falls, Hill, McLennan

Add'l Information: Established 1986. Normal turnaround time- 2-3 days. Projects billed by number of names searched. All projects require prepayment. They specialize in service of process, court records search, skiptracing and videotape depositions. They perform service of process.

Attorney Service Bureau

PO Box 382, Pomona, NY 10970
Phone: 845-638-1323

Types of Records Retrieved: Civil, criminal and probate courts; Federal courts; Real Estate; Tax liens/Judgments; UCC records; Vital records

Local Retrieval Area: NY-Orange, Rockland, Westchester. **Correspondent Relationships:** nationwide.

Add'l Information: Established 1990. Normal turnaround time- 7 working days. Same day service available. Projects billed by number of names searched. Projects billed by number of records located. Projects billed by the hour. All projects require prepayment. They specialize in Tri-State Metro-Mid Hudson areas of NY, NJ and CN. They serve process service and public record investigations. A licensed PI in NY. They perform service of process.

Attorney Service New Mexico

418 W Broadway #A, Farmington, NM 87401
Phone: 505-326-7486 **Fax:** 505-326-3492
mduncan@co.san-juan.nm.us

Types of Records Retrieved: Civil and criminal courts

Local Retrieval Area: AZ-Apache; CO-Archuleta, La Plata, Montezuma; NM-Cibola, McKinley, Rio Arriba, San Juan; UT-San Juan

Add'l Information: Established 2000. All projects require prepayment. They also provide court filings, subpoena preparation, photocopying, and skiptracing. The specialize in Indian reservations in the Four Corners area. They perform service of process.

Attorney Service of California-Monterey

270 El Dorado St, Monterey, CA 93940
Phone: 888-306-2194 **Fax:** 831-465-9632

Types of Records Retrieved: Civil, criminal and probate courts; Real Estate; Tax liens/Judgments; UCC records; Vital records

Local Retrieval Area: CA-Monterey

Add'l Information: Established 1972. Normal turnaround time- 1-2 days. Projects billed by number of names searched. 1st project may require prepayment. They perform service of process.

Attorney Service of California-Salinas
PO Box 220, Watsonville, CA 95077
Phone: 888-306-2194 **Fax:** 831-465-9632
Types of Records Retrieved: Civil, criminal and probate courts; Real Estate; Tax liens/Judgments; UCC records; Vital records
Local Retrieval Area: CA-Monterey, Santa Cruz
Add'l Information: Established 1972. Normal turnaround time- 1-2 days. Projects billed by number of names searched. 1st project may require prepayment. They perform service of process.

Attorney Service of California-Santa Cruz
PO Box 1436, Santa Cruz, CA 95060
Phone: 888-306-2194; **Fax:** 831-465-9632
Types of Records Retrieved: Civil, criminal and probate courts; Real Estate; Tax liens/Judgments; UCC records; Vital records
Local Retrieval Area: CA-Monterey, Santa Cruz. **Correspondent Relationships:** nationwide.
Add'l Information: Established 1972. Normal turnaround time- 1-2 days. Expedited service available. Projects billed by number of names searched. Projects billed by the hour. They specialize in process service and investigations and court research. Also has an office in Watsonville. They perform service of process.

Attorney Service of Merced
PO Box 2351, 833 W 22nd St (95340), Merced, CA 95344
Phone: 209-383-3233 **Fax:** 209-383-0311
Types of Records Retrieved: Civil, criminal and probate courts; Federal courts; Real Estate; Tax liens/Judgments; UCC records; Vital records
Local Retrieval Area: CA-Madera, Mariposa, Merced, San Joaquin, Stanislaus
Add'l Information: Established 1982. Normal turnaround time- up to 3 days. Projects billed by number of names searched. 1st project may require prepayment. Credit cards accepted. They specialize in process serving. They perform service of process.

Attorney Service of San Luis Obispo
860 Walnut St, San Luis Obispo, CA 93401
Phone: 850-543-8919 **Fax:** 850-541-4450
Types of Records Retrieved: Civil, criminal and probate courts; Federal courts; Real Estate; Tax liens/Judgments; UCC records; Vital records
Local Retrieval Area: CA-San Luis Obispo, Santa Barbara. **Correspondent Relationships:** statewide.
Add'l Information: Projects billed by number of names searched. varies depending on project. 1st project may require prepayment. They specialize in document management and litigation support. They perform service of process.

Attorney Services of Kentucky
2815 Taylorsville Rd, Louisville, KY 40205
Phone: 502-327-6677 **Fax:** 502-412-1955
Types of Records Retrieved: Civil, criminal and probate courts; Federal courts; Real Estate; Tax liens/Judgments; UCC records; Vital records
Local Retrieval Area: KY-Bullitt, Fayette, Franklin, Hardin, Jefferson, Kenton, Meade, Nelson, Oldham, Shelby. **Correspondent Relationships:** Clark, Floyd, Hancock counties IN.
Add'l Information: Established 1993. Normal turnaround time- 24 hours. Projects billed by the hour. 1st project may require prepayment. They specialize in witness and defendant locates, asset searches, records research, KY employment search and driver's licenses. They perform service of process.

Attorney Services of Northeast Ohio
40 E Buchtel Ave, Akron, OH 44308
Phone: 800-804-7787; 330-376-8100 **Fax:** 330-376-0110
www.courtreportersinc.com **email:** reporters@compuserve.com
Types of Records Retrieved: Civil, criminal and probate courts; Federal courts; Real Estate; Tax liens/Judgments
Local Retrieval Area: OH-Cuyahoga, Geauga, Lake, Lorain, Mahoning, Medina, Portage, Stark, Summit, Trumbull, Wayne
Add'l Information: Established 1972. Normal turnaround time- variable depending on project. Projects billed by the hour. 1st project may require prepayment. After 20 years experience, they can often times advise of local procedures or acquire documents quickly, while others less experienced might not be as successful. They specialize in accomplishing rush, priority, same day orders. They perform service of process.

Attorney Subpoena Services
27 Glen St #9B, Stoughton, MA 02072
Phone: 877-786-5374 **Fax:** 781-344-6357
Types of Records Retrieved: Civil, criminal and probate courts; Federal courts; Real Estate; Tax liens/Judgments; UCC records; Vital records
Local Retrieval Area: MA-all counties. **Correspondents:** nationwide.
Add'l Information: Established 1994. Normal turnaround time- 24-48 hours. Fees vary on job performed They perform service of process.

Attorney's Aid Inc of Sacramento
PO Box 1203, Sacramento, CA 95812
Phone: 888-443-3915; 916-443-3915 **Fax:** 916-325-2555
Types of Records Retrieved: Civil, criminal and probate courts; Federal courts; Real Estate; UCC records; Vital records
Local Retrieval Area: CA-Alameda, Contra Costa, El Dorado, Fresno, Placer, Sacramento, San Joaquin, Shasta, Sonoma, Stanislaus, Sutter, Yolo. **Correspondent Relationships:** statewide.
Add'l Information: Established 1974. Normal turnaround time- 2 days. Projects billed by the hour. Prepayment required if you are not with a law firm/private attorney or insurance company. They specialize in document reproduction, onsite and in-house. They perform service of process.

Attorney's Diversified Services-Bakersfield
701 H St, Bakersfield, CA 93304
Phone: 800-842-6334; 661-323-2377 **Fax:** 661-323-3376
www.attorneysdiversified.com **email:** rallison@attorneysdiversified.com
Types of Records Retrieved: Civil, criminal and probate courts; Federal courts; Tax liens/Judgments; UCC records
Local Retrieval Area: CA-Kern
Add'l Information: Normal turnaround time- routine 72 hours. Projects billed by number of names searched. Projects billed by the hour. 1st project may require prepayment. Credit cards accepted. They specialize in document management and litigation support. Perform service of process.

Attorney's Diversified Services-Fresno
741 N Fulton St, Fresno, CA 93728
Phone: 800-842-2695; 559-233-1475 **Fax:** 559-486-4119
www.attorneysdiversified.com
Types of Records Retrieved: Civil, criminal and probate courts; Federal courts; Real Estate; Tax liens/Judgments; UCC records; Vital records
Local Retrieval Area: CA-Fresno, Inyo, Kings, Madera, Mariposa, Merced, Mono, Monterey, San Benito, Santa Cruz, Tulare
Add'l Information: Normal turnaround time- routine 72 hours. Projects billed by number of names searched. Projects billed by the hour. 1st project may require prepayment. Credit cards accepted. They specialize in document management and litigation support. Perform service of process.

Attorney's Diversified Services-Modesto
342 Burney St, Modesto, CA 95354
Phone: 800-473-0273; 209-576-0273 **Fax:** 209-576-0238
www.attorneysdiversified.com
Types of Records Retrieved: Civil, criminal and probate courts; Federal courts; Real Estate; Tax liens/Judgments; UCC records; Vital records
Local Retrieval Area: CA-Stanislaus, Tuolumne. **Correspondent Relationships:** nationwide.
Add'l Information: Established 1969. Normal turnaround time- routine 72 hours. Projects billed by number of names searched. Projects billed by the hour. 1st project may require prepayment. Credit cards accepted. They specialize in document management and litigation support. They perform service of process.

Attorney's Diversified Services-Oakland

3640 Grand Ave #211, Oakland, CA 94610
Phone: 800-800-6788; 510-835-9176 **Fax:** 510-835-0510
www.attorneysdiversified.com

Types of Records Retrieved: Civil, criminal and probate courts; Federal courts; Real Estate; Tax liens/Judgments; UCC records; Vital records

Local Retrieval Area: CA-Alameda, Contra Costa

Add'l Information: Normal turnaround time- routine 72 hours. Projects billed by number of names searched. Projects billed by the hour. 1st project may require prepayment. Credit cards accepted. They specialize in document management and litigation support. Perform service of process.

Attorney's Diversified Services-Redding

2395 Bechelli Lane #C, Redding, CA 96002
Phone: 800-473-1228; 530-241-1228 **Fax:** 530-241-1508
www.attorneysdiversified.com

Types of Records Retrieved: Civil, criminal and probate courts; Federal courts; Real Estate; Tax liens/Judgments; UCC records; Vital records

Local Retrieval Area: CA-Butte, Del Norte, Glenn, Lassen, Modoc, Plumas, Shasta, Siskiyou, Tehama, Trinity

Add'l Information: Normal turnaround time- routine 72 hours. Projects billed by number of names searched. Projects billed by the hour. 1st project may require prepayment. Credit cards accepted. They specialize in document management and litigation support. Perform service of process.

Attorney's Diversified Services-Sacramento

1424 21st St, (Corporate Office), Sacramento, CA 95814
Phone: 800-266-4624; 916-441-4396 **Fax:** 916-443-1162
www.attorneysdiversified.com **email:** g_singley@yahoo.com

Types of Records Retrieved: Civil, criminal and probate courts; Federal courts; Real Estate; Tax liens/Judgments; UCC records; Vital records

Local Retrieval Area: CA-Alpine, Colusa, El Dorado, Nevada, Placer, Sacramento, Sierra, Solano, Sutter, Yolo, Yuba

Add'l Information: Normal turnaround time- routine 72 hours. Projects billed by number of names searched. Projects billed by the hour. 1st project may require prepayment. Credit cards accepted. They specialize in document management and litigation support. Perform service of process.

Attorney's Diversified Services-San Diego

2535 Camino Del Rio S #324, San Diego, CA 92108
Phone: 800-566-9501; 619-839-3400 **Fax:** 619-839-3414
www.attorneysdiversified.com

Types of Records Retrieved: Civil, criminal and probate courts; Federal courts; Real Estate; Tax liens/Judgments; UCC records; Vital records

Local Retrieval Area: CA-Imperial, Los Angeles, Orange, Riverside, San Diego. **Correspondent Relationships:** statewide.

Add'l Information: Normal turnaround time- routine 72 hours. Projects billed by number of names searched. Projects billed by the hour. 1st project may require prepayment. Credit cards accepted. They specialize in document management and litigation support. Perform service of process.

Attorney's Diversified Services-San Francisco

1453 Mission St #510, San Francisco, CA 94103
Phone: 800-775-3455; 415-437-6177 **Fax:** 415-437-6175
www.attorneysdiversified.com

Types of Records Retrieved: Civil, criminal and probate courts; Federal courts; Real Estate; Tax liens/Judgments; UCC records; Vital records

Local Retrieval Area: CA-San Francisco, San Mateo, Santa Clara. **Correspondent Relationships:** statewide.

Add'l Information: Established 1969. Normal turnaround time- routine 72 hours. Projects billed by number of names searched. Projects billed by the hour. 1st project may require prepayment. Credit cards accepted. They specialize in document management and litigation support. They perform service of process.

Attorney's Diversified Services-Santa Rosa

2421 Mendocino Ave 2nd Fl, Santa Rosa, CA 95403
Phone: 800-473-5455; 707-545-5455 **Fax:** 707-545-5454
www.attorneysdiversified.com

Types of Records Retrieved: Civil, criminal and probate courts; Federal courts; Real Estate; Tax liens/Judgments; UCC records; Vital records

Local Retrieval: CA-Humboldt, Lake, Marin, Mendocino, Napa, Sonoma

Add'l Information: Normal turnaround time- routine 72 hours. Projects billed by number of names searched. Projects billed by the hour. All projects require prepayment. Credit cards accepted. Due upon receipt of invoice. They specialize in document management and litigation support. They perform service of process.

Attorney's Diversified Services-Stockton

845 N California St, Stockton, CA 95202
Phone: 800-343-2108; 209-948-6110 **Fax:** 209-948-0806
www.attorneysdiversified.com

Types of Records Retrieved: Civil, criminal and probate courts; Federal courts; Real Estate; Tax liens/Judgments; UCC records; Vital records

Local Retrieval Area: CA-Amador, Calaveras, San Joaquin

Add'l Information: Normal turnaround time- routine 72 hours. Projects billed by number of names searched. Projects billed by the hour. 1st project may require prepayment. Credit cards accepted. They specialize in document management and litigation support. They perform service of process.

Attorney's Diversified Services-Ventura

1363 Donlon St #1, Ventura, CA 93003
Phone: 800-933-8014; 805-644-8014 **Fax:** 805-658-6336
www.attorneysdiversified.com

Types of Records Retrieved: Civil, criminal and probate courts; Federal courts; Real Estate; Tax liens/Judgments; UCC records; Vital records

Local Retrieval Area: CA-Los Angeles, San Luis Obispo, Santa Barbara, Ventura

Add'l Information: Normal turnaround time- routine 72 hours. Projects billed by number of names searched. Projects billed by the hour. 1st project may require prepayment. Credit cards accepted. They specialize in document management and litigation support. They perform service of process.

Attorneys' Information Bureau Inc

516 3rd Ave, C603 King County Courthouse, Seattle, WA 98104
Phone: 206-622-1909 **Fax:** 206-622-2911
attysinfob@aol.com

Types of Records Retrieved: Civil, criminal and probate courts; Federal courts; Real Estate; Tax liens/Judgments; UCC records; Vital records

Local Retrieval Area: WA-King, Kitsap, Pierce, Snohomish, Thurston. **Correspondent Relationships:** statewide.

Add'l Information: Established 1923. Normal turnaround time- 24 hours, same day is available for a higher fee. Fee basis varies by type of transaction. 1st project may require prepayment. Credit cards accepted. They can search all of Washington court records through an online system.

Attorneys Messenger Svc

PO Box 15363, 1407 S Vista Ave, Boise, ID 83715
Phone: 208-345-2905 **Fax:** 208-345-8740

Types of Records Retrieved: Civil, criminal and probate courts; Federal courts; Real Estate; Tax liens/Judgments; UCC records; Vital records

Local Retrieval Area: ID-Ada, Canyon, Elmore, Gem, Owyhee. **Correspondent Relationships:** statewide.

Add'l Information: Established 1977. Normal turnaround time- 1-3 days. Expedited service available. Flat fee. 1st project may require prepayment. They perform a variety of services at reasonable rates including skiptracing. They perform service of process.

Attorneys' Personal Services

433 Bishop St NW #I, Atlanta, GA 30318
Phone: 800-245-0122; 404-872-1200 **Fax:** 404-872-4578
www.aps-ga.com **email:** esmith@aps-ga.net

Types of Records Retrieved: Civil, criminal and probate courts; Federal courts; Real Estate; Tax liens/Judgments; UCC records; Vital records

Local Retrieval Area: GA-Clayton, Cobb, De Kalb, Fulton, Gwinnett. **Correspondent Relationships:** Georgia.

Add'l Information: Established 1983. Normal turnaround time- same day. Projects billed by the hour. A mileage fee is also added. 1st project may require prepayment. They specialize in court research and process service. They also go to the Federal Records Center. A licensed PI in GA. They perform service of process.

Attorney's Process & Inv Services

205 Doty St #202, Green Bay, WI 54301
Phone: 800-236-5202; 920-435-8317 **Fax:** 920-436-7585
api@api-inc.com

Types of Records Retrieved: Civil, criminal and probate courts; Federal courts; Real estate; Tax liens/Judgments; UCC records; Vital records.

Local Retrieval Area: WI-Brown, Calumet, Dane, Door, Kenosha, Kewaunee, Manitowoc, Marinette, Milwaukee, Oconto, Outgamie, Ozaukee, Racine, Shawano, Waukesha, Winnebago. **Correspondent Relationships:** statewide in Wisconsin.

Add'l Information: Established 1975. Normal turnaround time- 72 hours. Expedited service available. Projects billed by number of records located. 1st project may require prepayment. They specialize in Eastern Wisconsin; they have branch offices in Milwaukee and elsewhere. A licensed PI in WI. They perform service of process.

Attorney's Process & Research Service Inc

1 Columbia Pl 1st Fl, Albany, NY 12207
Phone: 800-640-7863; 518-465-8951 **Fax:** 518-465-0449

Types of Records Retrieved: Civil courts; Federal courts; Tax liens/Judgments; UCC records; Vital records

Local Retrieval Area: NY-Albany, Columbia, Erie, Greene, Monroe, Onondaga, Rensselaer, Schenectady, Warren, Washington. **Correspondent Relationships:** statewide.

Add'l Information: Established 1977. Normal turnaround time- same day or next day. Projects billed by the hour. 1st project may require prepayment. They specialize in document retrieval throughout the state of New York, court record research, nationwide service of process and state agency, personal and corporate records. A licensed PI in NY. They perform service of process.

Attorney's Service Bureau of Texas

900 Jackson St #750, Dallas, TX 75202
Phone: 888-522-5297; 214-522-5297 **Fax:** 214-393-0210
asb-texas@sbcglobal.net

Types of Records Retrieved: Civil, criminal and probate courts; Federal courts; Real Estate; Tax liens/Judgments; UCC records; Vital records

Local Retrieval Area: TX-Collin, Dallas, Denton, Tarrant. **Correspondent Relationships:** nationwide and Canada.

Add'l Information: Established 1986. Normal turnaround time- same day to 24 hours. Expedited service available. Projects billed by number of names searched. Projects billed by number of records located. Projects billed by the hour. 1st project may require prepayment. With established credit will invoice. They have extensive experience in all state, federal & county courts including Bankruptcy Courts, and all Secretary of State records, and have long term experience with all Federal Records Centers & National Archives facilities. They perform service of process.

Attorneys' Service Limited

931 W Julian St, San Jose, CA 95126
Phone: 408-293-9111 **Fax:** 408-293-9568

Types of Records Retrieved: Civil, criminal and probate courts; Federal courts; Real Estate; Tax liens/Judgments; UCC records; Vital records

Local Retrieval Area: CA-Alameda, San Francisco, San Mateo, Santa Clara

Add'l Information: Established 1965. Normal turnaround time- 2 hours. Fees are based on a flat rate plus expenses. They specialize in researching fictitious business names. They perform service of process.

Attorneys Services & Legal Inv

936 2nd Ave, Columbus, GA 31901
Phone: 706-322-3554 **Fax:** 706-322-0182 attysvclglinv@aol.com

Types of Records Retrieved: Civil and criminal courts; Federal courts; Real Estate; UCC records; Vital records

Local Retrieval Area: AL-Barbour, Chambers, Lee, Russell; GA-Chattahoochee, Harris, Marion, Muscogee, Talbot, Taylor

Add'l Information: Established 1992. Normal turnaround time- 24-48 hours. Expedited service available. Projects billed by number of names searched. First project requires prepayment. A licensed PI in GA. They perform service of process.

Attorney's Services Inc

400 W Capitol #1248, Little Rock, AR 72201
Phone: 888-376-6267; 501-376-2300 **Fax:** 501-376-7925
myersas@swbell.net

Types of Records Retrieved: Civil, criminal and probate courts; Federal courts; Real Estate; Tax liens/Judgments; UCC records; Vital records

Local Retrieval: AR-Pulaski. **Correspondent Relationships:** nationwide.

Add'l Information: Established 1963. Normal turnaround time- 1 week. Expedited service available. Projects billed by the hour. All projects require prepayment. Terms: net 30 days. They specialize in records research/retrieval, process service, courier service, general private investigation, expert consultation/witness (investigative techniques and negligent security). A licensed PI in AR. They perform service of process.

Attorney's Title Co

PO Box 407, Concordia, KS 66901-0407
Phone: 785-243-1357 **Fax:** 785-243-1359
www.condraylaw.com **email:** condraylaw@condraylaw.com

Types of Records Retrieved: Civil, criminal and probate courts; Real Estate; Tax liens/Judgments; UCC records

Local Retrieval Area: KS-Clay, Cloud, Mitchell, Ottawa, Republic, Washington

Add'l Information: Established 1989. Normal turnaround time- 2-3 days. Projects billed by the hour. 1st project may require prepayment. They provide quality searches in a timely manner. The searcher is a full time title insurance representative and record retriever.

Attorney's Title Ins. Fund Inc

2355 Stanford Ct, Naples, FL 34112
Phone: 239-774-2627 **Fax:** 239-774-0063
www.thefund.com **email:** mmiller@thefund.com

Types of Records Retrieved: Civil courts; Real Estate; Tax liens/Judgments; UCC records; Vital records

Local Retrieval Area: FL-Collier

Add'l Information: Established 1955. Normal turnaround time- 1-3 days. Fee basis will vary by the type of project. 1st project may require prepayment. Formerly Lawyers' Abstract Service Inc, they specialize in land records and title information.

Auburn Abstract & Title Company LLC

910 13th St, Auburn, NE 68305
Phone: 402-274-4321 **Fax:** 402-274-4323

Types of Records Retrieved: Probate courts; Real Estate; Tax liens/Judgments; UCC records

Local Retrieval Area: NE-Nemaha. **Correspondent Relationships:** Richardson and Johnson counties.

Add'l Information: Established 1925. Normal turnaround time- 1-2 days. Projects billed by number of names searched. All projects require prepayment. They prefer prepay request, but will invoice. Personal checks are accepted.

Audrain County Title Co

PO Box 599, Mexico, MO 65265
Phone: 573-581-5136 **Fax:** 573-581-8752
acac@audraincountyabstract.com

Types of Records Retrieved: Civil courts; Probate courts; Real Estate; Tax liens/Judgments; UCC records

Local Retrieval Area: MO-Audrain

Add'l Information: Established 1895. Normal turnaround time- 2-3 days. Terms: net 30 days from date of billing. They specialize in real estate searches.

Eileen Augatis

731 Washington Ave, Woodbury, NJ 08096

Phone: 609-472-6513 **Fax:** 856-845-3060

www.title1stnj.com **email:** title1st@comcast.net

Types of Records Retrieved: Civil and criminal courts; Real Estate; Tax liens/Judgments; UCC records

Local Retrieval Area: NJ-Camden, Gloucester

Add'l Information: Established 1986. Normal turnaround time- 24-48 hours. Projects billed by number of names searched. Invoices by month or by job. They provide fast reliable "hands-on" servicing of property & foreclosure searches, county level UCC's, criminal and civil record searches. They are E & O insured.

Aurico Inv LLC

116 W Eastman #101, Arlington Heights, IL 60004

Phone: 847-255-1852 **Fax:** 847-255-1896

www.auricoinvestigations.com **email:** investigate@aurico.com

Types of Records Retrieved: Civil, criminal and probate courts; Federal courts; Real Estate; Tax liens/Judgments; UCC records; Vital records

Local Retrieval Area: IL-Cook, Du Page. **Correspondent Relationships:** nationwide and international.

Add'l Information: Established 1994. Normal turnaround time- 48-72 hours. Expedited service available. Projects billed by number of names searched. Projects billed by the hour. They specialize in corporate, legal, insurance, personal investigation services, criminal and civil investigations, surveillance, security consulting, protective services and public records research. A licensed PI in IL. They perform service of process.

Aurora County Abstract

PO Box 443, Plankinton, SD 57368

Phone: 605-942-7558 **Fax:** 605-942-7558

Types of Records Retrieved: Real Estate; Tax liens/Judgments

Local Retrieval Area: SD-Aurora

Add'l Information: Established 2000. 1st project may require prepayment. They specialize in real estate.

AuSable Valley Abstract & Title Co

PO Box 548, Mio, MI 48647

Phone: 989-826-3385 **Fax:** 989-826-3385

Types of Records Retrieved: Real Estate; Tax liens/Judgments; UCC records

Local Retrieval Area: MI-Crawford, Ogemaw, Oscoda

Add'l Information: Established 1984. Normal turnaround time- 5 working days. Projects billed by number of records located. 1st project may require prepayment.

Carma Austin

PO Box 10364, Killeen, TX 76547-0364

Phone: 254-634-1701 **Fax:** 254-634-1588

carma4tx@aol.com

Types of Records Retrieved: Civil courts; Federal courts; Tax liens/Judgments; UCC records

Local Retrieval Area: TX-Bastrop, Bell, Brazos, Burleson, Burnet, Caldwell, Coryell, Falls, Hays, Lampasas, McLennan, Milam, Robertson, Williamson

Add'l Information: Established 1996. Normal turnaround time- 48 hours. Projects billed by number of names searched. 1st project may require prepayment. Over 12 years experience. Most counties done next day.

Autauga Abstract

140 W Main St, Prattville, AL 36067

Phone: 334-361-0606 **Fax:** 334-361-8402

Types of Records Retrieved: Probate courts; Real Estate; Tax liens/Judgments; UCC records

Local Retrieval Area: AL-Autauga, Elmore

Add'l Information: Established 1975. Normal turnaround time- 24-48 hours. Projects billed by the hour. 1st project may require prepayment. Personal checks are accepted.

Autten Barrett & Whitby

314 S Main St, Emporia, VA 23847

Phone: 434-634-2167 **Fax:** 434-634-3798

lwabw@telpage.net

Types of Records Retrieved: Civil, criminal and probate courts; Real Estate; UCC records

Local Retrieval Area: VA-Brunswick, Emporia City, Greensville

Add'l Information: Established 1977. Normal turnaround time- 2 days. Projects billed by the hour. 1st project may require prepayment. He is a trial lawyer.

AV Investigations Inc

PO Box 95, Geneva, IL 60134

Phone: 630-443-3617 **Fax:** 630-443-3618

www.avInvestigations.com **email:** tvincent@ameritech.net

Types of Records Retrieved: Civil, criminal and probate courts; Real Estate; Tax liens/Judgments; UCC records; Vital records

Local Retrieval Area: IL-Du Page, Kane, Kendall. **Correspondent Relationships:** nationwide.

Add'l Information: Established 1998. Normal turnaround time- 24-48 hours. Projects billed by number of names searched. 1st project may require prepayment. They specialize in pre-employment background screening, process serving, skiptracing, general investigations and document retrieval. A licensed PI in IL. They perform service of process.

Avalon Information Services

194 135th St, Deer Park, WI 54007

Phone: 715-554-0890 **Fax:** 715-269-5347

avaloninfo@amerytel.net

Types of Records Retrieved: Civil and criminal courts; Real Estate; Tax liens/Judgments; UCC records; Vital records; Bureau of Criminal Apprehension records

Local Retrieval Area: MN-Anoka, Carver, Dakota, Hennepin, Ramsey, Scott, Sherburne, Washington

Add'l Information: Established 1998. Normal turnaround time- same day. Projects billed by number of names searched. Terms are net 30 days. They specialize in criminal and civil searches, also document retrieval, all public records, and real estate land searches.

Avalon/Tracy Bowers

1821 Emerald Bay Dr, Reno, NV 89521

Phone: 775-853-3003 **Fax:** 775-853-3007

Types of Records Retrieved: Civil, criminal and probate courts; Federal courts; Real Estate; Tax liens/Judgments; UCC records; Vital records

Local Retrieval Area: NV-Carson City, Churchill, Douglas, Humboldt, Lyon, Pershing, Storey, Washoe

Add'l Information: Established 1996. Normal turnaround time- 24 hours. Expedite service available. Projects billed by number of names searched. 1st project may require prepayment. Payment due net 30 days. They conduct Nevada searches, retrievals and filings on all types and they also offer a mobile notary public and signing agent service.

Avritt & Avritt

PO Box 671, 103 W Main St, Lebanon, KY 40033

Phone: 270-692-4270 **Fax:** 270-692-0520

Types of Records Retrieved: Civil courts; Probate courts; Real Estate; Tax liens/Judgments; UCC records; Vital records

Local Retrieval Area: KY-Marion

Add'l Information: Established 1980. Normal turnaround time- 3-4 days. Projects billed by the hour. 1st project may require prepayment.

Ronald J Axelrod

PO Box 275, Morris Plains, NJ 07950-0275
Phone: 973-538-4606 **Fax:** 973-267-4606

Types of Records Retrieved: Probate courts; Real Estate; Tax liens/Judgments; UCC records

Local Retrieval Area: NJ-Morris, Somerset. **Correspondent Relationships:** Sussex, Bergen, Warren counties.

Add'l Information: Established 1979. Normal turnaround time- variable; contact office to discuss time frame. The first job may require a prepayment. We are a 3rd generation company since 1979, that specializes in title searches, title abstracts & judgment searches along with boundary/location deeds & filing of original documents.The Somerset Cty office # is 908-722-4606. Pager #973-203-4606.

Axess Maine Co

697 Cushing Rd, Cushing, ME 04563-3121
Phone: 207-594-2641 **Fax:** 207-594-2641
axessmaine@aol.com

Types of Records Retrieved: Civil, criminal and probate courts; Federal courts; Real Estate; Tax liens/Judgments; UCC records; Vital records

Local Retrieval Area: ME-Kennebec, Knox, Lincoln, Somerset, Waldo

Add'l Information: Established 2000. Normal turnaround time- 2-3 business days. Projects billed by number of names searched. Projects billed by number of records located. Projects billed by the hour. All projects require prepayment. Additional charge per page & delivery. They specialize in civil, criminal, federal & probate court records, county, city & town recorder records, MVR's, criminal records & real estate. They perform service of process.

Axis Research Inc

900 Old Roswell Lakes Parkway #310, Roswell, GA 30076
Phone: 678-795-1005 **Fax:** 678-795-1002
www.axisresearch.com **email:** axisrinc@bellsouth.net

Types of Records Retrieved: Civil, criminal and probate courts; Federal courts; Real Estate; Tax liens/Judgments; UCC records; Vital records

Local Retrieval Area: GA-Bartow, Cherokee, Clayton, Cobb, De Kalb, Douglas, Fayette, Forsyth, Fulton, Gwinnett, Hall, Henry, Paulding, Pickens, Spalding; NC-Cabarrus, Catawba, Gaston, Lincoln, Mecklenburg, Rowan, Union. **Correspondent Relationships:** Delaware, North Carolina.

Add'l Information: Established 1992. Normal turnaround time- 24-48 hours. Projects billed by number of names searched. Will bill for searches. They specialize in UCC, Federal and State tax liens and judgment searches. They have access to Federal Archives. Also Corporate Secretary of State filing and retrieval. Cell phone- 770-560-5808. They perform service of process.

Jerry Axton

12216 Clark Bayou Rd, Moss Point, MS 39562
Phone: 228-475-1739 **Fax:** 228-475-4822
axton@datasync.com

Types of Records Retrieved: Civil, criminal and probate courts; Real Estate; Tax liens/Judgments; UCC records

Local Retrieval Area: MS-George, Hancock, Harrison, Jackson

Add'l Information: Established 2000. Normal turnaround time- 24-48 hours. Projects billed by number of names searched. Terms are net 30 days. He specializes in civil, criminal checks, property, probate, ltax and judgments. He is also a process server. Retrieves documents, case law decisions, and files in 6 counties. Researches case histories for publishers and legal professionals. They perform service of process.

Judith Ayres

3487 Accomack St, Chincoteague Island, VA 23336
Phone: 757-336-5313 **Fax:** 757-336-1357
jhayres@verizon.net

Types of Records Retrieved: Civil, criminal and probate courts; Real Estate; Tax liens/Judgments; UCC records; Vital records

Local Retrieval Area: MD-Somerset, Wicomico, Worcester; VA-Accomack, Northampton. **Correspondent Relationships:** Norfolk, Virginia Bch, VA.

Add'l Information: Established 1991. Normal turnaround time- 24-48 hours. Expedited service available. Fee basis will vary by type of project. 1st project may require prepayment. She specializes in real estate, UCC searches, criminal and litigation. She also performs searches from the 1600's to the present. Her pager (and voice number) is 757-990-0314.

B

B & B Info Search
4400 Ascot Dr, Cleburne, TX 76033
Phone: 817-774-1310 **Fax:** 817-517-7295
bbinfo@direcway.com

Types of Records Retrieved: Civil, criminal and probate courts.

Local Retrieval Area: TX-Bosque, Ellis, Erath, Hill, Hood, Johnson, Navarro, Palo Pinto, Parker, Somervell, Wise. **Correspondent Relationships:** Anderson, Freestone counties.

Add'l Information: Established 1996. Normal turnaround time- 48 hours. Projects billed by number of names searched. Volume discount with multiple counties. Billed by 1st of month, payment by 15th of month. They have 25 years of professional Law Enforcement experience. A criminal research specialist. A licensed PI in TX.

B & B Investigative Services
11 Whitman Blvd, Englishtown, NJ 07726
Phone: 732-446-7482 **Fax:** 732-446-3886

Types of Records Retrieved: Civil and criminal courts

Local Retrieval Area: NJ-Essex, Hudson, Mercer, Middlesex, Monmouth, Ocean, Somerset, Union

Add'l Information: Established 1995. Normal turnaround time- 24 hours. Projects billed by number of names searched. Will bill monthly. They specialize in the New Jersey area. They expedite with 100% accuracy.

B & B Reporting Inc
PO Box 191, 106 W Laurel, Scottsboro, AL 35768
Phone: 256-574-2524 **Fax:** 256-259-4323
www.bbreporting.com **email:** adminstrator@bbreporting.com

Types of Records Retrieved: Civil, criminal and probate courts; Federal courts; Real Estate; Tax liens/Judgments; UCC records; Vital records

Local Retrieval Area: AL-Calhoun, De Kalb, Jackson, Madison, Marshall; TN-Shelby. **Correspondent Relationships:** Alabama, nationwide.

Add'l Information: Established 1985. Normal turnaround time- 1 day. Projects billed by number of names searched. 1st project may require prepayment. They will also invoice monthly. They specialize in state and federal court searches and criminal and civil searches nationwide. They preform MVR's nationwide, in Canada and Puerto Rico. They perform service of process.

B & G Ltd of Hollidaysburg
416 Allegheny St, Hollidaysburg, PA 16648-2026
Phone: 814-695-8414 **Fax:** 814-695-8496

Types of Records Retrieved: Civil, criminal and probate courts; Real Estate; Tax liens/Judgments; UCC records

Local Retrieval Area: PA-Bedford, Blair, Cambria, Centre, Clearfield, Huntingdon

Add'l Information: Established 1984. Normal turnaround time- 24-48 hours. Projects billed by number of names searched. 1st project may require prepayment. They specialize in real estate and abstracting.

B & J/Barristers' Aide Inc
PO Box 88, Eugene, OR 97440
Phone: 541-687-0747 **Fax:** 541-687-0429
www.barristersaide.com

Types of Records Retrieved: Civil, criminal and probate courts; Federal courts; Vital records

Local Retrieval Area: OR-Lane

Add'l Information: Established 1976. Normal turnaround time- next day. Projects billed by number of names searched. Projects billed by the hour. Charges will include costs. 1st project may require prepayment. They perform service of process.

B & R Services for Professionals
235 S 13th St, Philadelphia, PA 19107
Phone: 800-503-7400; 215-546-7400 **Fax:** 215-985-0169
fredb@concentric.net

Types of Records Retrieved: Civil, criminal and probate courts; Federal courts; Real Estate; Tax liens/Judgments; UCC records; Vital records

Local Retrieval Area: PA-Bucks, Chester, Delaware, Montgomery, Philadelphia. **Correspondent Relationships:** Dauphin.

Add'l Information: Established 1967. Normal turnaround time- 24-48 hours. Projects billed by number of names searched. Projects billed by number of records located. Projects billed by the hour. 1st project may require prepayment. They specialize in court filings, record retrieval, process service, court reporting and private investigation. A licensed PI in PA. They perform service of process.

Background Information Services
1800 30th St #204, Boulder, CO 80301
Phone: 303-442-3960 **Fax:** 303-442-1004
www.bisi.com **email:** john@bisi.com

Types of Records Retrieved: Civil and criminal courts; Federal courts; UCC

Local Retrieval: CO-Boulder. **Correspondent Relationships:** nationwide.

Add'l Information: Established 1988. Normal turnaround time- 1 day for MVRs. In-state CBI is 1 day. Database results are immediate. Projects billed by number of names searched. Terms: net 15 to 30 days. They have their own database of civil, criminal (nationwide), domestic relations, UCC, Secretary of State and Department of Revenue records. They also specialize in pre-employment and tenant screening as well as MVRs, credit checks, workers compensation.

Background Information Systems Inc
10501 N Central Expy #309, Dallas, TX 75231
Phone: 800-687-0894; 214-360-9122 **Fax:** 800-600-1408; 214-360-0775
www.backgroundsystems.com **email:** beverly@natcrime.com

Types of Records Retrieved: Civil and criminal courts

Local Retrieval Area: TX-Bexar, Collin, Dallas, Denton, Harris, Tarrant, Travis, Williamson. **Correspondent Relationships:** nationwide, especially in 375 counties nearby.

Add'l Information: Established 1980. Normal turnaround time- 24 hours. Payment due upon receipt of invoice. Formerly National Crime Reporting Systems, now BIS provides high-quality, reliable pre-employment and background screening to national corporate clients and well over 100 independent school districts and municipalities. A licensed PI in TX.

Background Research Agency Inc
1820 Hwy 20 #132-188, PO Box 1850 (30012), Conyers, GA 30013
Phone: 770-788-1885 **Fax:** 770-788-1277
gasearches@aol.com

Types of Records Retrieved: Civil, criminal and probate courts; Tax liens/Judgments; UCC records

Local Retrieval Area: GA-141 of 159 counties. **Correspondent Relationships:** nationwide.

Add'l Information: Established 1998. Normal turnaround time- 24-48 hours. Projects billed by number of names searched. Terms are net 30 days. They provide criminal, civil and tax lien research in numerous counties in GA. All research is accurate, hands-on and generally returned within 24-48 hours. A licensed PI in GA.

Backgrounds Express LLC
55 N 3rd St, Memphis, TN 38103-2304
Phone: 888-811-4667; 901-578-3287 **Fax:** 888-811-4668; 901-578-7889
expressBE@aol.com

Types of Records Retrieved: Civil and criminal courts; Federal courts

Local Retrieval Area: TN-Shelby

Add'l Information: Established 1991. Normal turnaround time- same day. Projects billed by number of names searched. Projects billed by the hour. 1st project may require prepayment. Credit cards accepted. They specialize in pre-employment and tenant investigations. They visit Memphis government agencies once daily and maintain a database of forcible detainer cases. A licensed PI in TN. They perform service of process.

Backgrounds Plus

PO Box 624, Sheboygan, WI 53082-0624
Phone: 920-457-7355 **Fax:** 920-457-7355

Types of Records Retrieved: Civil, criminal and probate courts; Federal courts; Real Estate; Tax liens/Judgments; UCC records; Vital records

Local Retrieval Area: WI-Brown, Manitowoc, Milwaukee, Sheboygan

Add'l Information: Established 1993. Normal turnaround time- same day is ordered before 3PM, otherwise 24 hours. Projects billed by number of records located. They do research for private investigators, attorneys and business firms. A licensed PI in WI. They perform service of process.

Judy J Badon/Public Records Specialists

10928 Ansley Ave, Baton Rouge, LA 70816
Phone: 225-291-5537 **Fax:** 225-291-5856
jjbad@bellsouth.net

Types of Records Retrieved: Civil, criminal and probate courts; Federal Bankruptcy courts; Mortgages; Tax liens/Judgments; UCC records

Local Retrieval Area: LA-East Baton Rouge, West Baton Rouge Parish

Add'l Information: Established 1995. Normal turnaround time- 24 hours-3 business days. Projects billed by the hour. Terms are net 15 days. (30 day credit on approval). 1st project may require prepayment. They specialize in filings, search & retrieval, criminal, civil, judgments, tax liens, bankruptcy, CDV's & one/last owner property searches. They also collect judgments, tax liens, bankruptcies, mortgages, etc), by the record or name.

Badzmierowski Services

139 Mechanic St #7, Rellingham, MA 02019
Phone: 508-498-3583 **Fax:** 508-966-4101
www.badzmierowskiservices.com **email:** badzmierowskiservices@comcast.net

Types of Records Retrieved: Civil, criminal and probate courts; Federal courts; Real Estate; Tax liens/Judgments; UCC records; Vital records

Local Retrieval Area: MA-Barnstable, Berkshire, Bristol, Dukes, Essex, Franklin, Hampden, Hampshire, Middlesex, Nantucket, Norfolk, Plymouth, Suffolk, Worcester

Add'l Information: Established 1991. Normal turnaround time- 24-72 hours. Projects billed by number of names searched. Projects billed by number of records located. Projects billed by the hour. They specialize in civil and criminal courts, probate courts, federal courts, registry of deeds, tax liens, UCC records, vital records, asset research and civil and federal subpoenas. A licensed PI in MA. They perform service of process.

Virginia Balentine

5600 Critchlow Rd SE, Elizabeth, IN 47117
Phone: 812-737-2871 **Fax:** 314-228-1494
vkbalentine@seidata.com

Types of Records Retrieved: Real Estate

Local Retrieval Area: IN-Clark, Floyd, Harrison, Jackson, Jefferson, Jennings, Scott. **Correspondent Relationships:** Bullitt, Shelby, Meade, Nelson counties KY.

Add'l Information: Established 1998. Normal turnaround time- 24/48 hours. Projects billed by number of names searched. Projects billed by number of records located. based on type of project. She collects data for comparible land sales, deeds, mortgages, licenses, building permits, land contracts, private mortgages and trust deeds - Commercial/Residential/private held notes, picks up copies of documents and new home lists & names.

Balkin Library & Information Services

295 Hurstbourne Rd, Rochester, NY 14609
Phone: 585-482-1506 **Fax:** 585-654-5235
www.balkininfo.com **email:** rbalkin@balkininfo.com

Types of Records Retrieved: Civil, criminal and probate courts; Federal courts; Real Estate, Tax liens/Judgments; UCC records

Local Retrieval Area: NY-Monroe. **Correspondent Relationships:** surrounding counties: Wayne, Ontario, Livingston, Genesee & Orleans.

Add'l Information: Established 1978. Normal turnaround time- 72 hours. Projects billed by the hour. 1st project may require prepayment. Credit cards accepted. Credit cards accepted through PayPal. Servicing corporations, law firms, and consulting since 1978, they provide full public records services, document delivery as well as research. They provide access to online and printed resources.

Banko Document Retrieval

100 S 5th St #300, Minneapolis, MN 55402-1237
Phone: 800-969-2377; 619-232-9999 **Fax:** 800-486-2377; 619-232-9998
www.banko.com

Types of Records Retrieved: Federal courts (Bankruptcy only)

Local Retrieval Area: CA-Los Angeles, San Diego; FL-Dade; Also covers the boroughs of New York (Bronx, Booklyn, Kings, Manhatten, Queens and Staten Island). **Correspondent Relationships:** every Federal bankruptcy court in the US, including Puerto Rico and Virgin Islands.

Add'l Information: Established 1989. Normal turnaround time- 2-5 days. Projects billed by number of names searched. Accounts are set-up and invoices are sent. They offer online ordering and delivery, order confirmation, shipping logs, status reports, and saving completed orders for up to 60 days (unless original copy is sent). Does death certificate searches.

Banta Abstract Co

108 E Washington St, PO Box 240, Osceola, IA 50213-0240
Phone: 641-342-2029 **Fax:** 641-342-2029

Types of Records Retrieved: Real Estate; Tax liens/Judgments

Local Retrieval Area: IA-Clarke

Add'l Information: Established 1869. Normal turnaround time- 3 days. They charge a flat rate per project. 1st project may require prepayment. They specialize in real estate title.

Bar Nunn Research Specialists

1204 Parker Pl, Cedar Park, TX 78613
Phone: 512-497-5584 **Fax:** 512-260-1079
debbienunn2001@austin.rr.com

Types of Records Retrieved: Civil and riminal courts; Probate courts; Federal District court; Real Estate; Tax liens/Judgments

Local Retrieval Area: TX-Bell, Hays, Travis, Williamson

Add'l Information: Established 2002. Normal turnaround time- 24 hours or less. Projects billed by number of names searched. Payment due net 30 days. She is an independent contractor.

Barbour Title Co

216 E 9th Ave, Winfield, KS 67156
Phone: 866-379-0430; 620-221-0430 **Fax:** 866-379-2839; 620-221-2839
www.barbourtitle.com **email:** firstcontact@barbourtitle.com

Types of Records Retrieved: Civil, criminal and probate courts; Real Estate; Tax liens/Judgments; UCC records; Vital records

Local Retrieval Area: KS-Cowley, Sumner

Add'l Information: Established 1915. Normal turnaround time- 24-48 hours. Projects billed by number of names searched. 1st project may require prepayment. Associated with Rogers Abstract and Title Co, 620-326-7460, 116 E Harvey St, Wellington. KS 67152

Barefoot Private Investigations

1011 E Morehead St #110, Charlotte, NC 28204-2890
Phone: 704-377-1000 **Fax:** 704-343-9226
www.barefootpi.com **email:** barefoot@barefootpi.com

Types of Records Retrieved: Civil, criminal and probate courts; Federal courts; Real Estate; Tax liens/Judgments; UCC records

Local Retrieval Area: NC-Gaston, Mecklenburg

Add'l Information: Established 1986. Normal turnaround time- 48 hours. Projects billed by number of names searched. Projects billed by number of records located. Projects billed by the hour. 1st project may require prepayment. Credit cards accepted. They specialize in all types of private investigative work, including courthouse research, surveillance, personal injury and criminal defense. A licensed PI in NC, SC. They perform service of process.

James M Barnes Jr

PO Box 639, Marion, AL 36756
Phone: 334-683-6060 **Fax:** 334-683-9242
Types of Records Retrieved: Civil, criminal and probate courts; Real Estate; Tax liens/Judgments; UCC records; Vital records
Local Retrieval Area: AL-Perry
Add'l Information: Established 1983. Normal turnaround time- 3 days. Fee basis will vary by the type of the project. 1st project may require prepayment. Terms: net 30 days. He is an attorney in general practice. They perform service of process.

Barney Abstract & Title Co

PO Box 546, 2222 2nd Ave #100 (68847), Kearney, NE 68848
Phone: 308-234-5548 **Fax:** 308-236-9240
Types of Records Retrieved: Civil courts; Probate courts; Real Estate; Tax liens/Judgments; UCC records; Vital records
Local Retrieval Area: NE-Buffalo
Add'l Information: Established 1888. Normal turnaround time- up to 2 weeks. Fee basis varies by type of transaction.

Barnone Bailbonds & Investigations

PO Box 2632, 104 S Broad St, Globe, AZ 85502
Phone: 800-607-8200; 928-425-3270 **Fax:** 928-425-3270
haughhbarmone@aol.com
Types of Records Retrieved: Civil, criminal and probate courts; Real Estate; Tax liens/Judgments; UCC records; Vital records
Local Retrieval Area: AZ-Gila
Add'l Information: Established 2000. Normal turnaround time- can be hours. Projects billed by number of records located. Needs retainer. They are a bailbond and private investigations company. A licensed PI in AZ. They perform service of process.

Barrett Title Co

PO Box 467, Baxter Springs, KS 66713-0467
Phone: 620-856-3531 **Fax:** 620-856-3408
Types of Records Retrieved: Civil, criminal and probate courts; Real Estate; Tax liens/Judgments; UCC records; Vital records
Local Retrieval Area: KS-Cherokee
Add'l Information: Established 1994. Normal turnaround time- 48-72 hours. Projects billed by number of names searched. They are a law office and title company.

Barrister Support Service

8700 SW 26th #L, Portland, OR 97219
Phone: 503-246-8934 **Fax:** 503-246-0098
Types of Records Retrieved: Civil, criminal and probate courts; Federal courts
Local Retrieval Area: OR-Clackamas, Multnomah, Washington; WA-Clark. **Correspondent Relationships:** nationwide.
Add'l Information: Established 1983. Normal turnaround time- 7-10 days. Expedited service available. Projects billed by the hour. 1st project may require prepayment. They specialize in service of process. They perform service of process.

Barry County Abstract & Title

PO Box 427, Cassville, MO 65625
Phone: 417-847-3224 **Fax:** 417-847-3118
bcat@mo-net.com
Types of Records Retrieved: Probate courts; Real Estate; Tax liens/Judgments; UCC records
Local Retrieval Area: MO-Barry
Add'l Information: Established 1935. Normal turnaround time- 5-10 days. Expedited service available. Projects billed by number of names searched. 1st project may require prepayment. They have the only complete set of real estate records for Barry County and take pride in the services they provide.

Barry Shuster Information Svcs, Div of Search-It

PO Box 79578, North Dartmouth, MA 02747
Phone: 877-852-2507; 508-999-5436 **Fax:** 877-852-7531; 508-990-2655
ucclien@rcn.com
Types of Records Retrieved: Civil, criminal and probate courts; Federal courts; Real Estate; Tax liens/Judgments; UCC records; Vital records
Local Retrieval Area: FL-Palm Beach; MA-Barnstable, Berkshire, Bristol, Dukes, Essex, Franklin, Hampden, Hampshire, Middlesex, Nantucket, Norfolk, Plymouth, Suffolk, Worcester; RI-Bristol, Kent, Newport, Providence, Washington. **Correspondent Relationships:** nationwide.
Add'l Information: Established 1981. Normal turnaround time- same day to 1 week. Projects billed by number of names searched. Fee basis will vary by jurisdiction. 1st project may require prepayment. Payment due upon receipt of completed work. They specialize in property searches & state/federal tax liens. They also provide UCC. Litigation and judgments, motor vehicle & pre-employment record retrieval, as well as resident agent services in MA & RI.

Cindy Bartkis

RR 1 Box 137 H, Susquehanna, PA 18847
Phone: 570-756-3093 **Fax:** 570-756-2560
Types of Records Retrieved: Civil, criminal and probate courts; Real Estate; Tax liens/Judgments; UCC records; Vital records
Local Retrieval Area: PA-Susquehanna
Add'l Information: Established 1985. Normal turnaround time- 48 hours. Projects billed by number of names searched. Projects billed by number of records located. She specializes in real estate record searches.

Barton County Abstract & Title Co

2010 Forest, Great Bend, KS 67530-4093
Phone: 620-793-3781 **Fax:** 620-793-5475
Types of Records Retrieved: Civil courts; Probate courts; Real Estate; Tax liens/Judgments; UCC records
Local Retrieval Area: KS-Barton
Add'l Information: Established 1874. Normal turnaround time- 24-48 hours. Projects billed by the hour. 1st project may require prepayment. They specialize in title insurance and special ownership searches.

Barton County Title Co

122 W 10th St, Lamar, MO 64759
Phone: 417-682-3100 **Fax:** 417-682-3975
Types of Records Retrieved: Civil, criminal and probate courts; Real Estate; Tax liens/Judgments; UCC records; Vital records
Local Retrieval Area: MO-Barton
Add'l Information: Established 1989. Normal turnaround time- about one week. Fee basis will vary by the type of project.

BAST Research Services Inc

405 Main #524, Houston, TX 77002
Phone: 713-721-7077 **Fax:** 713-721-7747
www.bastresearch.com **email:** bast@mail.bastresearch.com
Types of Records Retrieved: Civil courts; Probate courts; Federal courts; Real Estate; Tax liens/Judgments; UCC records
Local Retrieval Area: TX-Brazoria, Fort Bend, Galveston, Harris, Montgomery. **Correspondent Relationships:** nationwide.
Add'l Information: Established 1993. Normal turnaround time- 24-48 hours; 3-5 days for 50 year and asset searches. Expedited service available. Fees will vary by the type of search. 1st project may require prepayment. They specialize in real estate title, ownership/lien reports for home equity/improvement lending & 50 year chain of title searches for environmental site assessments; UCC, tax lien, judgment & litigation searches, mortgage/assignment & document research.

Batman-Sayers Abstract & Title Co

1013 6th St, Nevada, IA 50201
Phone: 515-382-4127 **Fax:** 515-382-4358

Types of Records Retrieved: Real Estate; Tax liens/judgments; UCC records
Local Retrieval Area: IA-Story
Add'l Information: Normal turnaround time- 3-5 days. Fee basis will vary by the type of project. They specialize in real estate title.

Baxter County Abstract Co
617 S Baker, Mountain Home, AR 72653
Phone: 870-425-8989 **Fax:** 870-425-9080
bxtitle@mtnhome.com

Types of Records Retrieved: Probate courts; Real Estate
Local Retrieval Area: AR-Baxter
Add'l Information: Established 1982. Normal turnaround time- 5 days. Expedited service available. Fee basis will vary by type of project. 1st project may require prepayment. Payment due within 10 days of service. They specialize in real estate, abstracts, and title insurance.

Timothy & Sara Baxter
500 Lansdale Ave, San Francisco, CA 94127-1618
Phone: 415-333-5402 **Fax:** 415-333-6244
www.baxterresearch.net **email:** timothy@baxterresearch.net

Types of Records Retrieved: Civil and criminal courts; Federal courts
Local Retrieval Area: CA-Alameda, Contra Costa, Marin, Monterey, San Francisco, San Mateo, Santa Clara, Santa Cruz, Sonoma. **Correspondent Relationships:** Cook, Los Angeles, Napa, Monterey, Placer, Sacramento, Santa Cruz, Santa Clara, Solano, Yolo, San Joaquin, Kings, Fresno, Tulare, Madera, Lake, Kern, Ventura counties CA.
Add'l Information: Established 1993. Normal turnaround time- 24 hours. Projects billed by number of names searched. Credit cards accepted. They bill monthly with a net 30 days. They are experienced California researchers. Timely, competent, responsive. Official records only, hands on, in the courts daily. Secure web access.

Bay Area Records
544 Golden Gate Ave, Mezz., San Francisco, CA 94102
Phone: 888-934-3848; 415-440-9100 **Fax:** 415-440-9200
www.bayarearecords.com **email:** commune@probusresearch.com

Types of Records Retrieved: Civil, criminal and probate courts; Federal courts; Real Estate; Tax liens/Judgments; UCC records
Local Retrieval Area: CA-Alameda, Contra Costa, Marin, San Francisco, San Mateo, Santa Clara, Solano. **Correspondent Relationships:** most California counties.
Add'l Information: Established 1985. Normal turnaround time- same day to 2 days. Projects billed by number of names searched. Hourly charge for special projects. 1st project may require prepayment. Terms: net 30 days. They specialize in complex litigation case file, regulatory, business and library research. They also provide fax filings and super rush research and document retrievals. They perform service of process.

Bay Area Search Inc
PO Box 973, Safety Harbor, FL 33695
Phone: 727-724-5995 **Fax:** 727-724-8363
bayareasearch@prodigy.net

Types of Records Retrieved: Civil, criminal and probate courts; Federal courts; Real Estate; Tax liens/Judgments; UCC records; Vital records
Local Retrieval Area: FL-Hillsborough, Pasco, Pinellas
Add'l Information: Established 1986. Normal turnaround time- 24-48 hours. Projects billed by number of names searched. Projects billed by the hour. They are proudly celebrating 17 years of service in the Tampa Bay area providing clients with fast, quality research at reasonable prices. Pager number 727-468-5246.

Bay City Abstract & Title
2228 Ave G, Bay City, TX 77414-5003
Phone: 979-245-6321 **Fax:** 979-245-1323
Types of Records Retrieved: Probate courts; Real Estate; Tax liens/Judgments; UCC records
Local Retrieval Area: TX-Matagorda
Add'l Information: Established 1936. Normal turnaround time- 14 days. Projects billed by number of names searched. 1st project may require prepayment.

Bay County Abstract Co
612 Adams St, Bay City, MI 48708-5832
Phone: 989-895-9910 **Fax:** 989-895-5631
Types of Records Retrieved: Probate courts; Real Estate; Tax liens/Judgments; UCC records
Local Retrieval Area: MI-Arenac, Bay, Clare, Gladwin, Huron, Isabella, Lapeer, Midland, Sanilac, Saginaw, Tuscola
Add'l Information: Established 1974. Normal turnaround time- 3-4 days. Fee basis will vary by type of project. They require out of town clients to prepay. They specialize in real estate searches.

Bay State Corporate Services Inc
6 Beacon St #510, Boston, MA 02108
Phone: 617-742-8484 **Fax:** 617-742-8482
www.baystatecorp.com **email:** scryan@baystatecorp.com

Types of Records Retrieved: Civil courts; Probate courts; Real Estate; Tax liens/Judgments; UCC records; Vital records
Local Retrieval: MA-Suffolk. **Correspondent Relationships:** nationwide.
Add'l Information: Established 1998. Normal turnaround time- 24 hours. Expedited service available. Projects billed by number of names searched. Terms are net 30 days. They are located one block from the MA SOS and within minutes of Boston city clerk, US District court, US Bankruptcy court and all Suffolk county government offices.

Bay Title & Abstract Inc
345 S Monroe Ave, Green Bay, WI 54301
Phone: 920-431-6100 **Fax:** 920-431-6101
www.baytitle.com

Types of Records Retrieved: Civil courts; Probate courts; Real Estate; Tax liens/Judgments; UCC records
Local Retrieval Area: WI-Brown, Calumet, Dane, Door, Fond du Lac, Kewaunee, Manitowoc, Marinette, Menominee, Oconto, Outagamie, Shawano, Waupaca, Winnebago. **Correspondent Relationships:** Manitowoc county.
Add'l Information: Normal turnaround time- 24 hours. Projects billed by number of names searched. Personal checks are accepted.

Bayou Investigations Inc
PO Box 92825, Lafayette, LA 70509
Phone: 800-256-9009; 337-235-2322 **Fax:** 337-232-0365
www.bayouinvestigations.com **email:** steve@bayouinvestigations.com

Types of Records Retrieved: Civil/criminal courts; Federal courts; UCCs
Local Retrieval Area: LA-Acadia Parish, Evangeline Parish, Iberia Parish, Jefferson Davis Parish, Lafayette Parish, St. Landry Parish, St. Martin Parish, St. Mary Parish, Vermilion Parish. **Correspondent Relationships:** Louisiana.
Add'l Information: Established 1986. Normal turnaround time- 72 hours. Projects billed by the hour. They specialize in research, investigations, surveillance, process service and video depositions. A licensed PI in LA. They perform service of process.

David C Bayoud
6207 Bryan Parkway, Dallas, TX 75214
Phone: 214-824-9944 **Fax:** 214-824-4350
mbayoud@aol.com

Types of Records Retrieved: Real Estate
Local Retrieval Area: TX-Collin, Dallas, Denton, Ellis, Rockwall, Tarrant
Add'l Information: Established 1981. Normal turnaround time- 24 hours. Projects billed by number of names searched. Projects billed by number of records located. 1st project may require prepayment.

Bayshore Research & Retrieval
15890 Walter Breton Dr, Morgan Hill, CA 95037
Phone: 408-776-1544 **Fax:** 408-778-4455
info@bayshoreresearch.com

Types of Records Retrieved: Civil, criminal and probate courts; Federal courts; Real Estate; Tax liens/Judgments; UCC records; Vital records

Local Retrieval Area: CA-San Mateo, Santa Clara

Add'l Information: Established 1987. Normal turnaround time- approximately 24 hours. Projects billed by number of names searched. Monthly billing available. They customize their services & prices to fit the specific needs of each of their clients. Super rushes and requests for large copy/document retrieval jobs are welcomed. Large volume requests are accepted. Recordings/Filings done daily. They perform service of process.

Bearak Reports
1257 Worcester Rd #308, Framingham, MA 01701
Phone: 800-331-5677; 508-788-6660 **Fax:** 508-788-6642
www.bearak.com **email:** info@bearak.com

Types of Records Retrieved: Civil, criminal and probate courts; Federal courts; Real Estate; Tax liens/Judgments; UCC corporate records; Vital records

Local Retrieval Area: MA-Barnstable, Berkshire, Bristol, Essex, Franklin, Hampshire, Middlesex, Norfolk, Plymouth, Suffolk, Worcester. **Correspondent Relationships:** nationwide.

Add'l Information: Established 1992. Normal turnaround time- 1-5 business days. Expedite service available. Projects are billed at a flate rate or time and expenses. 1st project may require prepayment. Credit cards accepted. Terms: net 30 days with credit approval. They specialize in nationwide asset searches, public record research, retrieval services and pre-employment screening services. Will retrieve DMV and Criminal records.

Leslie Bearce
1075 Capistrano Ct, San Luis Obispo, CA 93405
Phone: 805-541-2615 **Fax:** 805-541-2615
leslieb930@aol.com

Types of Records Retrieved: Civil, criminal and probate courts; Real Estate; Tax liens/Judgments; UCC records; Vital records

Local Retrieval Area: CA-San Luis Obispo

Add'l Information: Established 1995. Normal turnaround time- 24-48 hours. Projects billed by number of names searched.

Beauregard Abstract Co
104 W 2nd St, PO Box 280, DeRidder, LA 70634
Phone: 337-463-7090 **Fax:** 337-463-7094

Types of Records Retrieved: Probate courts; Real Estate; Tax liens/Judgments; UCC records

Local Retrieval Area: LA-Beauregard Parish

Add'l Information: Established 1913. Normal turnaround time- 24 hours. Projects billed by number of names searched. 1st project may require prepayment. Terms: net 30 days. They have a tract index covering entire Beauregard Parish real estate, and have all records on microfilm, with last 10 years on computer.

Beaver County Abstract Co
PO Box 928, 118 Douglas St, Beaver, OK 73932
Phone: 580-625-4423 **Fax:** 580-625-3643

Types of Records Retrieved: Civil courts; Probate courts; Real Estate; Tax liens/Judgments; UCC records; Vital records

Local Retrieval Area: OK-Beaver

Add'l Information: Established 1979. Normal turnaround time- 3-4 days. Projects billed by the hour.

Beckham County Abstract
PO Box 80, Sayre, OK 73662
Phone: 580-928-3143 **Fax:** 580-928-5000

Types of Records Retrieved: Civil, criminal and probate courts; Real Estate; Tax liens/Judgments; UCC records; Vital records

Local Retrieval Area: OK-Beckham

Add'l Information: Established 1907. Normal turnaround time- 1 week. Projects billed by number of names searched. Projects billed by number of records located. Projects billed by the hour. 1st project may require prepayment. Personal checks are accepted. They specialize in situations affecting mineral or surface matters in Beckham County.

Bedgood Abstract & Title Co (Goliad)
PO Box 12, 325 S Market St, Goliad, TX 77963
Phone: 361-645-3145 **Fax:** 361-645-3256
www.bedgoodtitle.com

Types of Records Retrieved: Civil courts; Probate courts; Real Estate; Tax liens/Judgments; UCC records

Local Retrieval Area: TX-Goliad

Add'l Information: Established 1987. Normal turnaround time- 1-2 days. Fee basis will vary by the type of project. 1st project may require prepayment. They also have offices in Port lavaca, Port O'Connor, and Victoria.

Bedgood Abstract & Title Co (Port Lavaca)
PO Box 143, 416 E Railroad Ave, Port Lavaca, TX 77979
Phone: 361-552-6761 **Fax:** 361-575-7581
www.bedgoodtitle.com

Types of Records Retrieved: Civil courts; Probate courts; Real Estate; Tax liens/Judgments; UCC records

Local Retrieval Area: TX-Calhoun

Add'l Information: Established 1897. Normal turnaround time- 1-2 days. Fee basis will vary by the type of project. 1st project may require prepayment. They also have offices in Goliad, Port O'Connor, and Victoria.

Beehive Attorney Svc
4956 W 6200 S #A547, Salt Lake City, UT 84118-6703
Phone: 800-779-0379; **Fax:** 800-966-2838;
beehiveattorney@hotmail.com

Types of Records Retrieved: Civil and criminal courts, Probate courts; Federal courts; Real Estate; Tax liens/Judgments; UCC records; Vital records.

Local Retrieval Area: UT-Davis, Salt Lake, Summit, Tooele, Utah, Weber

Add'l Information: Established 1982. Normal turnaround time- 1-3 days. Projects billed by number of names searched. 1st project may require prepayment. Credit cards accepted. They specialize in the populated counties arround Salt Lake area. They perform service of process.

Bell Investigative Services Inc
PO Box 848395, Pembroke Pines, FL 33084
Phone: 954-454-4859 **Fax:** 954-458-8493
bell_inv@bellsouth.net

Types of Records Retrieved: Civil, criminal and probate courts; Federal courts; Real Estate; Tax liens/Judgments; UCC records; Vital records

Local Retrieval Area: FL-Brevard, Broward, Collier, Dade, Hillsborough, Lee, Martin, Orange, Palm Beach, Pinellas, Seminole, St Lucie, Volusia

Add'l Information: Established 1997. Normal turnaround time- same day to 36 hours. Projects billed by number of names searched. 1st project may require prepayment. Payment due by 15th of month. They specialize in background investigations for the purposes of pre-employment screening and secret shopper, executive protection, surveillance, and other services. A licensed PI in FL.

Bent County Abstract & Title
PO Box 183, Las Animas, CO 81054
Phone: 719-456-0381 **Fax:** 719-456-0791

Types of Records Retrieved: Real Estate; Tax liens/Judgments

Local Retrieval Area: CO-Bent, Prowers

Add'l Information: Established 1902. Normal turnaround time- 3-5 days. Fee basis will vary by the type of project. They specialize in ownership and encumbrance reports, title insurance, and abstract updates.

Bentley Title Co
PO Box 104, Hermitage, MO 65668
Phone: 417-745-6626 **Fax:** 417-745-6160
bentleytitle@yahoo.com

Types of Records Retrieved: Real Estate; Tax liens/Judgments; UCC records
Local Retrieval Area: MO-Hickory
Add'l Information: Established 1890. Normal turnaround time- 3-5 days. Fee basis varies by type of transaction. A $75.00 cancellation fee applies.

Benton Abstract & Title Co
106 W Redwood, Eldorado, TX 76936
Phone: 325-853-2631
Types of Records Retrieved: Real Estate; Tax liens/judgments; UCC records
Local Retrieval Area: TX-Schleicher
Add'l Information: Established 1916. Normal turnaround time- 1-2 days. Fee basis varies by type of transaction. 1st project may require prepayment. They have their own complete set of land title records covering Schleicher county, in digital form available over the internet.

Benton County Abstract & Title Co Inc
PO Box 346, 202 N Madison Ave, Fowler, IN 47944
Phone: 765-884-1140 **Fax:** 765-884-0839
Types of Records Retrieved: Civil courts; Probate courts; Real Estate; Tax liens/Judgments; UCC records
Local Retrieval Area: IN-Benton
Add'l Information: Established 1989. Normal turnaround time- 3-5 days. Fee basis will vary by the type of project. They specialize in insured closings, title insurance and abstracting.

Benton County Abstract Co
PO Box 128, 411 Dewey St, Foley, MN 56329-0128
Phone: 320-968-7278 **Fax:** 320-968-6487
Types of Records Retrieved: Civil courts; Probate courts; Federal courts; Real Estate; Tax liens/Judgments; UCC records; Vital records
Local Retrieval Area: MN-Benton
Add'l Information: Established 1911. Normal turnaround time- same day. Projects billed by number of names searched. Projects billed by number of records located. Personal checks are accepted. They specialize in owners encumbrance reports, abstracting and name searches.

Benton County Title Co
112 E. 4th St, Vinton, IA 52349
Phone: 319-472-2369 **Fax:** 319-472-2360
www.bctco.com **email:** cjuhl@bctco.com
Types of Records Retrieved: Civil, criminal and probate courts; Real Estate; Tax liens/Judgments; UCC records
Local Retrieval Area: IA-Benton
Add'l Information: Established 1863. Normal turnaround time- 2 days. Projects billed by number of names searched. 1st project may require prepayment. They are a title company providing searches and abstracts in real estate, including liens and taxes, escrow closing and appraisals.

Bergman Records Access
988 Stearns Dr #1, Los Angeles, CA 90048
Phone: 323-939-1632 **Fax:** 310-481-6720
jscottbergman@sbcglobal.net
Types of Records Retrieved: Civil, criminal and probate courts; Federal courts; Real Estate; Tax liens/Judgments; UCC records; Vital records
Local Retrieval Area: CA-Los Angeles, Orange. **Correspondent Relationships:** San Francisco, CA; Las Vegas, NV.
Add'l Information: Established 1997. Normal turnaround time- 24 hours. Projects billed by number of names searched. Projects billed by the hour. 1st project may require prepayment. They specialize in all around reliable and accurate support in public record and asset information acquisition. A pager number to reach them is 323-969-6690. They perform service of process.

Berry & Maddox
PO Box 354, Lovingston, VA 22949
Phone: 434-263-4886 **Fax:** 434-263-4285
Types of Records Retrieved: Civil, criminal and probate courts; Real Estate; Tax liens/Judgments; UCC records; Vital records
Local Retrieval Area: VA-Amherst, Nelson
Add'l Information: Established 1983. Normal turnaround time- 2 days. Projects billed by the hour. 1st project may require prepayment.

Best Legal Services Inc
1617 JFK Blvd #1045, Philadelphia, PA 19103
Phone: 800-562-9620; 215-567-7777 **Fax:** 215-561-4546
Types of Records Retrieved: Civil and criminal courts; Federal courts; Real Estate; Tax liens/Judgments; UCC records; Vital records
Local Retrieval Area: NJ-Burlington, Camden, Gloucester; PA-Berks, Bucks, Chester, Dauphin, Delaware, Lancaster, Montgomery, Philadelphia. **Correspondent Relationships:** Lehigh, Allegheny, Lancaster, Dauphin, Luzerne, York counties PA.
Add'l Information: Established 1981. Normal turnaround time- 2 days. Projects billed by number of names searched. 1st project may require prepayment. Will invoice. They specialize in serving legal papers, document filings, skiptracing and provide access to the Federal Record Ctr in Philadelphia for states of PA, MD, DE, DC and VA. They provide nationwide service through their correspondent relationship with NAPPS. They perform service of process.

Bettendorf Abstract Co
1987 Spruce Hills Dr, Bettendorf, IA 52722
Phone: 563-359-3646 **Fax:** 563-359-3647
Types of Records Retrieved: Civil, criminal and probate courts; Real Estate; Tax liens/Judgments; UCC records; Vital records
Local Retrieval Area: IA-Scott
Add'l Information: Established 1982. Normal turnaround time- up to 7 days. Projects billed by the hour. 1st project may require prepayment. They specialize in real estate and abstracting. They perform service of process.

Bexar Professional
8065 Callaghan Rd #605, San Antonio, TX 78230
Phone: 210-228-0083 **Fax:** 210-228-0066
bexarpro@swbell.net
Types of Records Retrieved: Civil, criminal and probate courts; Federal courts; Real Estate; Tax liens/Judgments; UCC records; Vital records
Local Retrieval Area: TX-Bexar. **Correspondent Relationships:** Texas.
Add'l Information: Established 1987. Normal turnaround time- same day to next day. Projects billed by number of names searched. Projects billed by number of records located. Projects billed by the hour. 1st project may require prepayment. They specialize in process service. They perform service of process.

BG Criminal Research
PO Box 294, Kaufman, TX 75142
Phone: 254-755-6808 **Fax:** 254-753-5980
www.bgcrimresearch.com **email:** billie@bgcrimresearch.com
Types of Records Retrieved: Civil, criminal and probate courts; Federal courts; Tax liens/Judgments; UCC records
Local Retrieval Area: TX-Bell, Coryell, McLennan
Add'l Information: Established 1994. Normal turnaround time- 24 to 48 hours. Projects billed by number of names searched. Will bill every two weeks or monthly. They specialize in criminal record information. A licensed PI in TX.

Betsy Biesenbach
1948 Belleville Rd SW, Roanoke, VA 24015
Phone: 540-982-7892 **Fax:** 540-982-7892
Types of Records Retrieved: Probate courts; Real Estate; Tax liens/Judgments; UCC records
Local Retrieval Area: VA-Botetourt, Roanoke, Roanoke City, Salem City
Add'l Information: Established 1986. Normal turnaround time- 24 hours for Roanoke City, Roanoke County and Salem City, and 48 hours for all others. Projects billed by number of names searched. Projects billed by number of records located. She specializes in title examinations and document retrieval.

Big Country Title

400 Pine St #765, Abilene, TX 79601
Phone: 325-698-9195 **Fax:** 325-698-1864

Types of Records Retrieved: Probate courts; Real Estate; Tax liens/Judgments; UCC records; Vital records

Local Retrieval Area: TX-Callahan, Taylor

Add'l Information: Normal turnaround time- 2 days. Projects billed by number of names searched. 1st project may require prepayment. They specialize in divorce and death searches, title insurance and abstracting.

Big Spring Abstract & Title Co Inc

208 W 3rd St, Big Spring, TX 79720
Phone: 432-267-1604 **Fax:** 432-267-1815
tpaige@moutonlaw.com

Types of Records Retrieved: Probate courts; Real Estate; Tax liens/Judgments

Local Retrieval Area: TX-Glasscock, Howard

Add'l Information: Established 1986. Normal turnaround time- 2-3 days. Fee basis will vary by the type of project. 1st project may require prepayment.

Bill Greenberg Special Services Inc

18450 NE 2nd Ave, Miami, FL 33179-4426
Phone: 888-770-9008; 305-770-4437 **Fax:** 800-770-4496; 786-248-3000
http://bgss.com **email:** bill@bgss.com

Types of Records Retrieved: Civil, criminal and probate courts; Federal courts; Real Estate; Tax liens/Judgments; UCC records; Vital records; Property records

Local Retrieval Area: FL-Broward, Charlotte, Dade, Escambia, Hillsborough, Palm Beach, Pasco, Pinellas, Polk, Seminole, Volusia. **Correspondent Relationships:** Florida.

Add'l Information: Established 1987. Normal turnaround time- 8-24 hours. Projects billed by number of names searched. Projects billed by the hour. All projects require prepayment. Credit cards accepted. They specialize in the service of legal papers, current owner and other property searches, investigation, surveillance and document retrieval. A licensed PI in FL. They perform service of process.

Billings County Abstract

PO Box 187, Madora, ND 58645
Phone: 701-623-4344 **Fax:** 701-623-4896

Types of Records Retrieved: Real Estate; Tax liens/Judgments

Local Retrieval Area: ND-Billings

Add'l Information: 1st project may require prepayment. They specialize in real estate.

Birthcertificate.com

601 Van Ness Av #E, San Francisco, CA 94102
Phone: 888-934-3848; 415-440-9100 **Fax:** 415-440-9200
www.birthcertificate.com **email:** commune@probusresearch.com

Types of Records Retrieved: Vital Records

Local Retrieval Area: CA-Alameda, Contra Costa, Marin, San Francisco, San Mateo, Santa Clara. **Correspondent Relationships:** nationwide.

Add'l Information: Established 1985. Normal turnaround time- same day to 2 days. Projects billed by number of names searched. Hourly charge for special projects. 1st project may require prepayment. Terms: net 30 days. They specialize in nationwide vital records retrieval. The company provides direct service in the Bay area counties.

Bismarck Title Co

PO Box 1811, 421 N 4th St, Bismarck, ND 58502
Phone: 701-222-4247 **Fax:** 701-221-3039
www.bismarcktitle.com **email:** Julie@BismarckTitle.com

Types of Records Retrieved: Civil, criminal and probate courts; Real Estate; Tax liens/Judgments; UCC records

Local Retrieval Area: ND-Burleigh, Morton, Stark. **Correspondent Relationships:** abstract companies throughout North Dakota.

Add'l Information: Established 1987. Normal turnaround time- 24 hours for verbal, 48 hours for paper. Fee basis is per base rate plus name.

Bison Security Group

3402 - 8 St. SE, Calgary, Alberta, Canada, CAN T2G 2S7
Phone: 800-661-2245; 403-262-4545 **Fax:** 403-266-3827
www.bsgcorp.com **email:** info@bsgcorp.com

Types of Records Retrieved: Civil and criminal courts; Real Estate; Tax liens/Judgments; Vital records

Local Retrieval Area: CANADA-Alberta. **Correspondent Relationships:** Edmonton, Red Deer, Lethbridge, Alberta; also in British Columbia, Western Canada.

Add'l Information: Established 1980. Normal turnaround time- 24-48 hours, if local. Projects billed by number of names searched. Projects billed by the hour. All projects require prepayment. They specialize in due diligence, corporate/commercial crime investigations, loss prevention, insurance, polygraph. They perform service of process.

Bi-State Title Search (Div of Bi-State Ind.)

105 Concord Plaza #201, St Louis, MO 63128
Phone: 866-450-7399; **Fax:** 314-843-1238
www.bistate.info **email:** bsts@bistate.info

Types of Records Retrieved: Criminal courts; Probate courts; Real Estate; Tax liens/Judgments; UCC records

Local Retrieval Area: IL-Bond, Jersey, Madison, Monroe, St. Clair; KS-Atchison, Douglas, Franklin, Jefferson, Johnson, Leavenworth, Miami, Wyandotte; MO-Buchanan, Bates, Cass, Clay, Clinton, Crawford, Franklin, Gasconade, Henry, Jackson, Jefferson, Lafayette, Lincoln, Johnson, Montgomery, Pike, Platte, Ray, St. Charles, Ste. Genevieve, St. Francios, St. Louis, St. Louis City, Warren, Washington. **Correspondent Relationships:** remainder of Missouri, Kansas, Illinois.

Add'l Information: Established 2000. Normal turnaround time- 24-48 hours. Projects billed by number of names searched. Invoice montly. Missouri company now growing into Illinois and Kansas. A licensed PI in MO.

Bit O' Blarney

9835 Rolling Meadows Ln, Salinas, CA 93907
Phone: 831-663-6945 **Fax:** 831-663-1119
mja@bitoblarney.com

Types of Records Retrieved: Civil and criminal courts

Local Retrieval Area: CA-Monterrey

Add'l Information: Established 1999. Normal turnaround time- 1-2 days. Fee basis depends upon type of project. 1st project may require prepayment. They specialize in backgrounding, court and real estate record retrieval, and cats.

Bitterroot Research

PO Box 1422, Hamilton, MT 59840
Phone: 406-363-4408 **Fax:** 406-363-4408

Types of Records Retrieved: Real Estate; Tax liens/Judgments; UCC records

Local Retrieval Area: MT-Ravalli

Add'l Information: Established 1993. Normal turnaround time- 1-5 days. Projects billed by number of names searched. Projects billed by the hour. 1st project may require prepayment. They specialize in water rights, mineral rights and easements.

Black Hawk County Abstract Co

614 Sycamore St, Waterloo, IA 50703-4726
Phone: 319-291-4000 **Fax:** 319-291-3929
order@blackhawkabstract.com

Types of Records Retrieved: Civil courts; Probate courts; Real Estate; Tax liens/Judgments; UCC records

Local Retrieval Area: IA-Black Hawk

Add'l Information: Established 1878. Normal turnaround time- 24-48 hours. Projects billed by number of names searched. Projects billed by the hour. Fees negotiated with volume. 1st project may require prepayment. They specialize in complete real estate title searches, current ownership and lien reports within 24 hours with few exceptions on any real estate within Black Hawk county.

John Blackburn

PO Box 50263, Austin, TX 78763
Phone: 210-867-0399 **Fax:** 707-885-3658
www.johnblackburn.net **email:** john03@flash.net

Types of Records Retrieved: Civil courts; Probate courts; Federal district courts; UCC records, Real Estate, Tax liens/Judgments

Local Retrieval Area: TX-Bell, Bexar, Bosque, Hays, McLennan, Travis, Williamson. **Correspondent Relationships:** Blanco, Burnette, Caldwell, Comal, Falls, Guadalupe, Johnson, Kerr, Lampasas, Lee, Limestone, Somervell.

Add'l Information: Established 1995. Normal turnaround time- 24-48 hours. Projects billed by number of names searched. Invoices once a month.

Blaine County Abstract

PO Box 368, 100 W Main, Watonga, OK 73772
Phone: 580-623-7248 or 7257 **Fax:** 580-623-7268
bca@watonga.net

Types of Records Retrieved: Civil courts; Probate courts; Real Estate; Tax liens/Judgments; UCC records

Local Retrieval Area: OK-Blaine

Add'l Information: Normal turnaround time- 1 week. Projects billed by rate schedules. Personal checks are accepted. They specialize in abstracts, title insurance, closings, deed preparation and record searches.

Blaine County Title Co

PO Box 1328, 411 Ohio St, Chinook, MT 59523
Phone: 406-357-3884 **Fax:** 406-357-2884
bctitle@ttc-cmc.net

Types of Records Retrieved: Civil, criminal and probate courts; Real Estate; Tax liens/Judgments; UCC records; Vital records

Local Retrieval Area: MT-Blaine

Add'l Information: Normal turnaround time- 3 days. Projects billed by the hour. 1st project may require prepayment.

Allen J Blazinski

PO Box 2036, Dayton, OH 45401-2036
Phone: 937-475-4370 **Fax:** 937-222-3285

Types of Records Retrieved: Civil, criminal and probate courts; Federal courts; Real Estate; Tax liens/Judgments; UCC records; Vital records

Local Retrieval Area: OH-Greene, Miami, Montgomery, Preble

Add'l Information: Established 1986. Normal turnaround time- 48-72 hours for real estate records; 72 hours for all others. Fee basis will vary by the type of project. He specializes in title work.

Sallie Blount

509 N Rogers St, Waxahachie, TX 75165
Phone: 972-824-1414 **Fax:** 972-689-3645
sallieblount@sbcglobal.net

Types of Records Retrieved: Civil and criminal courts.

Local Retrieval Area: TX-Ellis

Add'l Information: Established 1999. Normal turnaround time- 2 to 2 1/2 days. Projects billed by number of names searched. Invoice monthly; terms net 30 days. She provides civil and criminal records in less than 3 days. Other services are available on a as needed basis, including county recorder records. A licensed PI in TX.

Blue Line Investigations

6600 Stage Rd #107, PMB 602, Bartlett, TN 38134
Phone: 901-266-7100 **Fax:** 901-266-7121
blueln1@bellsouth.net

Types of Records Retrieved: Criminal courts

Local Retrieval Area: AR-Crittendon, Pulaski; MS-Desoto, Marshall, Oktibbeha, Panola, Tate, Tunica; TN-Dyer, Fayette, Henderson, Lauderdale, Obion, Shelby, Tipton, Weakley. **Correspondent Relationships:** nationwide researcher network who perform criminal background checks.

Add'l Information: Established 1996. Normal turnaround time- same day for Shelby County, TN; 48 hours for other counties. Projects billed by number of names searched. Terms: net 30 days. Specializes in the Memphis area, including AR, MS as well as TN. A licensed PI in TN.

Blue Marble Logistics LLC

800 King St, Wilmington, DE 19801
Phone: 302-661-4390 **Fax:** 302-661-4398
www.bluemarblelog.com **email:** research@bluemarblelog.com

Types of Records Retrieved: Civil and criminal courts; Federal courts; Real Estate; Tax liens/Judgments; UCC records

Local Retrieval Area: DE-Kent, New Castle; PA-Chester, Delaware, Philadelphia. **Correspondent Relationships:** Sussex, DE, and nationwide.

Add'l Information: Established 2003. Normal turnaround time- 24 hours. Expedited service available. Projects billed by number of names searched. 1st project may require prepayment. Credit cards accepted. They focus on detail, accuracy, and quick turnaround times. Documents can be scanned and emailed for speed and convenience. They perform service of process.

Blue Ridge Title, Div of Chicago Title Ins Co

218 5th St NE, Charlottesville, VA 22902
Phone: 434-295-7196 **Fax:** 434-979-7208
whiteb@ctt.com

Types of Records Retrieved: Civil courts; Probate courts; Real Estate; Tax liens/Judgments; UCC records

Local Retrieval Area: VA-Albemarle, Charlottesville City, Fluvanna, Greene, Louisa, Nelson. **Correspondent Relationships:** Augusta, Orange, Madison counties VA.

Add'l Information: Established 1973. Normal turnaround time- 1-2 days in Albemarle; 3-5 days in other counties. Fee basis varies by type of transaction. 1st project may require prepayment. They specialize in real estate and title searches.

Bluegrass Investigations LLC

PO Box 1043, Georgetown, KY 40324
Phone: 502-316-5776 **Fax:** 502-867-7495
cbowman@bluegrass.net

Types of Records Retrieved: Civil, criminal and probate courts; Federal courts; Real Estate; Tax liens.judgments; UCC records; Vital records

Local Retrieval Area: KY-Fayette, Franklin, Scott, Woodford

Add'l Information: Established 2003. Normal turnaround time- 2-3 days. Expedited service available. Projects billed by the hour. 1st project may require prepayment. They specialize in litigation support, Federal & State, criminal & civil, criminal defense investigation, background investigation and witness location KY wide court records. A licensed PI in KY. They perform service of process.

Blumberg Excelsior Corporate Services Inc

52 S Pearl St, 2nd Fl, Albany, NY 12207
Phone: 800-999-0850; 518-436-0855 **Fax:** 800-835-7137;
www.blumberg.com **email:** slb@blumb.com

Types of Records Retrieved: Civil, criminal and probate courts; Federal courts; Real Estate; Tax liens/Judgments; UCC records; Vital records

Local Retrieval Area: NY-Albany, Columbia, Greene, Rensselaer, Schenectady. **Correspondent Relationships:** nationwide and international.

Add'l Information: Established 1972. Normal turnaround time- 24 hours. Projects billed by number of names searched. 1st project may require prepayment. Credit cards accepted. They specialize in corporate filings, document retrieval, trademark searches and filings and litigation and lien packages. They perform service of process.

Blumberg Excelsior Corporate Svcs Inc (NYC)

62 White St, 2nd Fl, New York, NY 10013
Phone: 800-221-2972; 212-431-5000 **Fax:** 888-692-9256;
www.blumberg.com **email:** slb@blumb.com

Types of Records Retrieved: Tax liens/Judgments; UCC records

Local Retrieval Area: NY-Bronx, Kings, New York, Queens, Richmond. **Correspondent Relationships:** nationwide.

Add'l Information: Established 1975. Normal turnaround time- 1-2 days. Projects billed by number of names searched. 1st project may require prepayment. Credit cards accepted. House accounts available. They specialize in trademark, copyright, nationwide and international incorporation services. Will search for and file UCC documents.

Blumberg Excelsior Corporate Svcs Inc (Texas)

814 San Jacinto Blvd #303, Austin, TX 78701
Phone: 800-252-3050; 512-478-6620 **Fax:** 512-478-0001
www.blumberg.com **email:** blumberg@texas.net

Types of Records Retrieved: Civil, criminal and probate courts; Federal courts; Real Estate; Tax liens/Judgments; UCC records; Vital records

Local Retrieval Area: TX-Travis. **Correspondent Relationships:** nationwide.

Add'l Information: Established 1975. Normal turnaround time- 24 hours. Projects billed by number of names searched. Projects billed by number of records located. 1st project may require prepayment. Credit cards accepted. They specialize in research, retrieval and filing of any type of public record.

Bob Lessemun Investigations Inc

4893 Prince William Pky #201, Woodbridge, VA 22192
Phone: 703-580-6611 **Fax:** 703-670-8668
www.lessemun.com **email:** blessemun@yahoo.com

Types of Records Retrieved: Civil, criminal and probate courts; Federal district courts; Real Estate; Tax liens/Judgments; UCC records; Vital records

Local Retrieval Area: VA-Prince William. **Correspondent Relationships:** Alexandria, Arlington, Fairfax, Winchester counties VA.

Add'l Information: Established 1999. Normal turnaround time- 24 hours. Projects billed by number of names searched. 1st project may require prepayment. He is a licensed private investitgator operating throughout Northern VA with 38 years investigative experience specializing in crime, domestic, civil, process serving, tracing missing persons and deadbeats. He is professional and dedicated. A licensed PI in VA. They perform service of process.

Bob Prins Associates

401 Ardmore, Waterloo, IA 50701
Phone: 319-232-4752 **Fax:** 319-236-2249

Types of Records Retrieved: Civil and criminal courts; Real Estate; Tax liens/Judgments

Local Retrieval Area: IA-Black Hawk

Add'l Information: Established 1989. Normal turnaround time- 2 days. Projects billed by number of names searched. They charge by the hour after 1 hour per name. Net 30 days. They specialize in document retrieval. Serving the industry since 1989.

Bodo PI

PO Box 943, Bullhead City, AZ 86430
Phone: 877-381-7009 **Fax:** 877-381-7009
www.BodoPI.com **email:** bodocook67@earthlink.net

Types of Records Retrieved: Civil, criminal and probate courts; Federal courts; Real Estate; Tax liens/Judgments; UCC records; Vital records

Local Retrieval Area: AZ-Mohave; NV-Clark (Goes to Bullhead City, AZ and Laughlin, NV). **Correspondent Relationships:** nationwide.

Add'l Information: Established 1979. Normal turnaround time- 24 hours. Projects billed by the hour. Will invoice, payment terms are net 30 days. Credit cards accepted. They are a full service investigative agency specializing in background inquires, asset inquiries and locate inquires-nationwide. A licensed PI in AZ, CA, NV. They perform service of process.

Todd Boehr

133 East De la Guerra St #150, Santa Barbara, CA 93101
Phone: 805-452-7579 **Fax:** 805-456-3813
www.crimicheck.com

Types of Records Retrieved: Civil and criminal courts

Local Retrieval Area: CA-Santa Barbara, Ventura

Add'l Information: Established 1991. Normal turnaround time- usually same day. Projects billed by number of names searched. 1st project may require prepayment. Terms: net 30 days. Specializing in Santa Barbara and Ventura court and county records. He has been providing research and retrieval services since 1993.

Boerger Investigative Services LLC

1350 W 5th Ave #330, Columbus, OH 43212
Phone: 877-754-8295; 614-481-0777 **Fax:** 614-481-0778
www.ohioprocessserver.com

Types of Records Retrieved: Civil, criminal and probate courts; Federal courts; Real Estate; Tax liens/Judgments; UCC records; Vital records

Local Retrieval Area: OH-Athens, Cuyahoga, Delaware, Fairfield, Franklin, Lake, Licking, Madison, Marion, Richland, Stark, Summit, Union, Wyandot

Add'l Information: Established 1998. Normal turnaround time- 48-72 hours. Expedited service available. Projects billed by number of names searched. All projects require prepayment. Credit cards accepted. They are a full-service litigation support and investigative agency serving all of Ohio. Prompt, efficient and professional service with process service and records retrieval within 48 hours. A licensed PI in OH. They perform service of process.

Boles-Wallner Abstract & Title

214 W Grand Ave, Wisconsin Rapids, WI 54495-0575
Phone: 715-423-6940 **Fax:** 715-423-6912

Types of Records Retrieved: Probate courts; Real Estate; Tax liens/Judgments; UCC records

Local Retrieval Area: WI-Adams, Clark, Jackson, Juneau, Marathon, Portage, Waushara, Wood

Add'l Information: Established 1987. Normal turnaround time- 48 hours. Projects billed by number of records located. 1st project may require prepayment.

Bollinger Attorney Service

PO Box 3296, Palm Springs, CA 92263-3296
Phone: 760-329-2504 **Fax:** On Request
http://home.att.net/~DennisBollinger **email:** dennisbollinger@worldnet.att.net

Types of Records Retrieved: Civil, criminal and probate courts; Real Estate; Tax liens/Judgments; UCC records; Vital records

Local Retrieval Area: CA-Imperial, Riverside, San Bernardino. **Correspondent Relationships:** worldwide.

Add'l Information: Established 1972. Normal turnaround time- 24 hours. Expedited service available. Projects billed by number of records located. 1st project may require prepayment. They specialize in court filings, investigations, process serving-evasive, record searches from all agencies and paralegal JD services. Other phone numbers 760-778-0610 & 818-902-6009 (pagers). They perform service of process.

Bollinger County Abstract Co

PO Box 889, Marble Hill, MO 63764
Phone: 573-238-2823 **Fax:** 573-238-2819
bocoabst@hotmail.com

Types of Records Retrieved: Civil, criminal and probate courts; Real Estate; Tax liens/Judgments; UCC records

Local Retrieval Area: MO-Bollinger

Add'l Information: Established 1907. Normal turnaround time- 7-10 days. Projects billed by the hour. 1st project may require prepayment. Payment acceptance may vary. They specialize in land title and geographic land locations. They also do real estate closing.

Bombet Cashio & Associates

11220 N Harrells Ferry Rd, Baton Rouge, LA 70816
Phone: 800-256-5333; 225-275-0796 **Fax:** 225-272-3631
www.bombet.com **email:** buddy@bombet.com

Types of Records Retrieved: Civil, criminal and probate courts; Federal courts; Real Estate; Tax liens/Judgments; UCC records; Vital records

Local Retrieval Area: LA-Ascension, East Baton Rouge, Iberville, Jefferson, Orleans, St. Charles, St. John the Baptist, St. Tammany, West Baton Rouge parishes. **Correspondent Relationships:** worldwide.

Add'l Information: Established 1967. Normal turnaround time- 24-48 hours. Projects billed by the hour. Net 30 days. All projects require prepayment. Credit cards accepted. They specialize in general investigations, research and process service. They have been in business since 1967. Have staff statewide. A licensed PI in LA. They perform service of process.

Bon Homme Title Co

PO Box 276, Tyndall, SD 57066
Phone: 605-589-3572 **Fax:** 605-589-3093

Types of Records Retrieved: Real Estate; Tax liens/Judgments

Local Retrieval Area: SD-Bon Homme

Add'l Information: 1st project may require prepayment. They specialize in real estate.

Bonafide Research Services

9135-A Reseda Blvd #146, Northridge, CA 91324
Phone: 818-349-3955 **Fax:** 818-349-3255
zbonafide@aol.com

Types of Records Retrieved: Civil and criminal courts; Federal courts; Tax liens/Judgments; UCC records; Vital records

Local Retrieval Area: CA-Fresno, Los Angeles, Orange, Santa Barbara, Ventura. **Correspondent Relationships:** California.

Add'l Information: Established 1998. Normal turnaround time- 24-48 hours. Projects billed by number of names searched. Terms: net 30 days.

Bond Title

102 E Main, Greenville, IL 62246
Phone: 618-664-1872 **Fax:** 618-664-1873

Types of Records Retrieved: Civil courts; Probate courts; Real Estate; Tax liens/Judgments; UCC records; Vital records

Local Retrieval Area: IL-Bond, Clinton, Fayette, Macoupin, Madison, Montgomery, St. Clair

Add'l Information: Established 1870. Normal turnaround time- Nov. to March- 1-2 days. April to October- 1 week. Projects billed by number of names searched. 1st project may require prepayment. Credit cards accepted. They have been in business since 1870 and they have copies of Abstracts from Bond county on record there in their office.

Bontecou Inv Services

PO Box 2448, 350 E Broadway, Jackson, WY 83001
Phone: 307-733-2637

Types of Records Retrieved: Civil and criminal courts.

Local Retrieval Area: WY-Lincoln, Park, Sublette, Teton. **Correspondent Relationships:** statewide.

Add'l Information: Established 1988. 1st project may require prepayment. They also provice court filings, subpoena preparation, photocopying, skiptracing, private investigations. They perform service of process.

Bontecou Investigative Services Inc

PO Box 2448, 350 E Broadway, Jackson, WY 83001
Phone: 307-733-2637 **Fax:** 307-733-5873
www.wyominginvestigator.com **email:** bisinc@earthlink.net

Types of Records Retrieved: Civil, criminal and probate courts; Real Estate; Tax liens/Judgments; UCC records

Local Retrieval Area: WY-Teton

Add'l Information: Established 1884. Normal turnaround time- 3-5 business days. Projects billed by number of names searched. Projects billed by the hour. 1st project may require prepayment. They specialize in background searches civil litigation, investigation & surveillance and process service. A licensed PI in WY. They perform service of process.

Boone County Abstract Co

814 8th St, Boone, IA 50036
Phone: 515-432-3633 **Fax:** 515-432-3634

Types of Records Retrieved: Civil, criminal and probate courts; Real Estate; Tax liens/Judgments; UCC records; Vital records

Local Retrieval Area: IA-Boone

Add'l Information: Normal turnaround time- up to 1 week. Projects billed by number of names searched. They specialize in real estate.

Border Legal Services

909 Austin St, Eagle Pass, TX 78852-5205
Phone: 830-773-0525 **Fax:** 830-757-1069
borderlegalprocess@yahoo.com

Types of Records Retrieved: Civil, criminal and probate courts; Tax liens/Judgments; Vital records.

Local Retrieval Area: TX-Maverick, Dimmit, Zavala

Add'l Information: Established 1997. Normal turnaround time- 2 days. Projects billed by the hour. 1st project may require prepayment. They also do business under the name of "Professional Civil Process." They perform service of process.

Border Title Group

5810 San Bernardo Ave, Laredo, TX 78041
Phone: 956-791-5810 **Fax:** 956-791-5555
www.bordertitle.com **email:** batco@bordertitle.com

Types of Records Retrieved: Real Estate; Tax liens/judgments; UCC records

Local Retrieval Area: TX-Brooks, Dimmit, Jim Hogg, Jim Wells, La Salle, Maverick, Webb, Zapata, Zavala

Add'l Information: Normal turnaround time- 7-10 working days.. Fee basis varies according to the type of project. All projects require prepayment. They have a branch office at 6019 McPherson Rd in McPherson, 956-717-8339, also offices in Crystal City, Carrizo Springs, Eagle Pass, and Alice.

Border Title Group

1000 Crown Ridge Blvd, Eagle Pass, TX 78852
Phone: 830-773-0555 **Fax:** 830-773-6886

Types of Records Retrieved: Probate courts; Real Estate; Tax liens/Judgments; UCC records

Local Retrieval Area: TX-Maverick

Add'l Information: Established 1992. Normal turnaround time- 3-4 days. Projects billed by number of names searched. All projects require prepayment.

Border Title Group, FKA Elliott & Waldron Abstract

PO Box 248, Carrizo Springs, TX 78834
Phone: 830-876-2926 **Fax:** 830-876-5077
www.bordertitle.com **email:** ballen@bordertitle.com

Types of Records Retrieved: Real Estate; Tax liens/judgments; UCC records

Local Retrieval Area: TX-Dimmit. **Correspondent Relationships:** They have offices in Laredo, Alice, Eagle Pass, Carrie Springs, Crystal City. Also have correspondents in Webb, LaSalle, Jim Wells, Jim Hogg, Zapata, Brooks, Dimmit, Maverick and Zavala.

Add'l Information: Established 1955. Normal turnaround time- 1-5 days. Fee basis will vary by the type of project. 1st project may require prepayment. Border Title Group is a computerized title plant with an imaged database of the counties they are active in. For a fee their plant can be accessed through www.bordertitle.com.

Bosic & Bosic

PO Box 1024, Huntington Beach, CA 92647-1024
Phone: 951-788-1988

Types of Records Retrieved: Civil, criminal and probate courts; Real Estate; Tax liens/Judgments; Vital records

Local Retrieval Area: CA-Orange, Riverside, San Bernardino. **Correspondent Relationships:** Los Angeles and San Diego counties, but can retrieve records throughout most of CA.

Add'l Information: Established 1980. Normal turnaround time- 1-2 days. Projects billed by the hour. 1st project may require prepayment. A licensed PI in CA. They perform service of process.

M V Bostick Jr

6521 Barfield Rd, PO Box 20002, Macon, GA 31205
Phone: 478-781-9344 **Fax:** 478-781-9682

Types of Records Retrieved: Probate courts; Real Estate; Tax liens/Judgments

Local Retrieval Area: GA-Baldwin, Bibb, Bleckley, Crawford, Jones, Lamar, Macon, Monroe, Peach, Pulaski, Putman, Taylor, Twiggs, Upson, Wilkinson

Add'l Information: Normal turnaround time- 24-36 hours. 1st project may require prepayment. They specialize in real estate title examinatioins, deed/affidavit preparation and title abstracts.

Botts & Assoc

2537 Spring Place Rd, Cleveland, TN 37323
Phone: 423-595-2692 **Fax:** 423-472-0211
aebotts@aol.com

Types of Records Retrieved: Civil and criminal courts; Federal courts; Real Estate; UCC records; Tax liens/Judgments; Vital records.

Local Retrieval Area: TN-Bradley, Loudon, McMinn, Meigs, Monroe, Polk, Rhea. **Correspondent Relationships:** statewide.

Add'l Information: Established 1994. Normal turnaround time- 3 days. Expedited service available. Projects billed by the hour. 1st project may require prepayment. They provide professional investigations, service of process as well as record checks. A licensed PI in TN. They perform service of process.

Botts Title Co

300 E 1st St, Cameron, TX 76520
Phone: 254-697-6962 **Fax:** 254-697-2952

Types of Records Retrieved: Probate courts; Real Estate; Tax liens/Judgments; UCC records; Vital records

Local Retrieval Area: TX-Austin, Burleson, Colorado, Fayette, Milam, Washington

Add'l Information: Normal turnaround time- 2-5 days. Fees vary by project. 1st project may require prepayment. They are familiar with all records maintained at the county courthouse. The sell title insurance.

Brabston Legal Inv Inc

PO Box 91711, Mobile, AL 36691-1711
Phone: 251-666-5666 **Fax:** 251-661-8807
www.survsol.com/bli.htm **email:** twb@survsol.com

Types of Records Retrieved: Civil, criminal and probate courts; Federal courts; Real Estate; Tax liens/Judgments; UCC records

Local Retrieval Area: AL-Baldwin, Clarke, Mobile. **Correspondent Relationships:** Alabama.

Add'l Information: Established 1986. Normal turnaround time- 2-3 days. Projects billed by number of names searched. 1st project may require prepayment. They are online with Alabama State Judicial Computer and Florida Department of Law Enforcement. A licensed PI in AL, FL. They perform service of process.

Brack Warren & Associates

PO Box 297, Corpus Christi, TX 78403-0297
Phone: 361-884-8000 **Fax:** 361-884-8002
bwarren@intcomm.net

Types of Records Retrieved: Civil, criminal and probate courts; Federal courts; Real Estate; Tax liens/Judgments; UCC records; Vital records

Local Retrieval Area: TX-Nueces. **Correspondent Relationships:** statewide.

Add'l Information: Established 1976. Normal turnaround time- 1-2 days. Expedited service available. Projects billed by the hour. All projects require prepayment. They specialize in investigative services. They have 35 years experience.

Bradley Enterprises LLC

7716 Mary Eve Rd, Shreveport, LA 71106-6015
Phone: 318-868-4906 **Fax:** 318-219-3000
bellcla@aol.com

Types of Records Retrieved: Civil, criminal and probate courts; Federal courts; Real Estate; Tax liens/Judgments; UCC records

Local Retrieval Area: LA-Bossier Parish, Caddo Parish

Add'l Information: Established 1993. Normal turnaround time- 24-48 hours. Projects billed by number of names searched. Projects billed by number of records located. Projects billed by the hour. Terms are net 15 days. Terms: net 15 days. They specialize in oil and gas searches, real estate titles, abstracts, criminal and bankruptcy court searches.

Branda Agency

PO Box 781444, Wichita, KS 67278
Phone: 800-310-8174; 316-634-0000 **Fax:** 316-636-4406
www.effectivedetective.com **email:** dbranda@aol.com

Types of Records Retrieved: Civil, criminal and probate courts; Federal courts; Real Estate; Tax liens/Judgments; UCC records; Vital records

Local Retrieval Area: KS-Butler, Harvey, KingmanReno, Sedgwick, Sumner

Add'l Information: Established 1983. Normal turnaround time- county court records in 48 hours; federal records depend on nature of file. Projects billed by number of names searched. All projects require prepayment. Visit the web site for additional services. A licensed PI in KS. They perform service of process.

Attorney Leonard Brashear

PO Box 677, Hyden, KY 41749
Phone: 606-672-3577 **Fax:** 606-672-2142

Types of Records Retrieved: Civil, criminal and probate courts; Real Estate; Tax liens/Judgments; UCC records

Local Retrieval Area: KY-Leslie

Add'l Information: Established 1982. Normal turnaround time- up to 1 week. Projects billed by the hour. All projects require prepayment.

Jerry M Braud

1312 Park Dr, Thibodaux, LA 70301
Phone: 985-447-1227 **Fax:** 985-447-1227

Types of Records Retrieved: Civil, criminal and probate courts; Real Estate; Tax liens/Judgments; UCC records

Local Retrieval Area: LA-Lafourche Parish

Add'l Information: Normal turnaround time- 1-2 days. Projects billed by the hour. 1st project may require prepayment. Will invoice. She has been in business for over 40 years. She specializes in real estate, mineral and all public record searches.

Bray & Freeman LP

PO Box 123991, Ft. Worth, TX 76121
Phone: 817-596-9255 **Fax:** 817-534-4955
georgebray@charter.net

Types of Records Retrieved: Civil, criminal and probate courts; Federal courts; Real Estate; Tax liens/Judgments; UCC records; Vital records

Local Retrieval Area: TX-Collin, Dallas, Denton, Hood, Jack, Johnson, Palo Pinto, Parker, Tarrant, Wise. **Correspondent Relationships:** national and international.

Add'l Information: Established 1992. Normal turnaround time- 3 days. Projects billed by the hour. 1st project may require prepayment. They specialize in personnel matters for corporation. Several areas they cover are internal theft, fraud, drug use and thefts. They work complex domestic issues and with automobile dealerships. They also do due diligence and asset searches. A licensed PI in TX. They perform service of process.

Bremer County Abstract Co

218 E Bremer Ave, Waverly, IA 50677
Phone: 319-352-2710 **Fax:** 319-352-0675

Types of Records Retrieved: Civil courts; Federal District courts; Probate courts; Real Estate; Tax liens/Judgments; UCC records; Vital records

Local Retrieval Area: IA-Bremer

Add'l Information: Normal turnaround time- 3 days. Projects billed by number of names searched. Fee may also be based per claim. All projects require prepayment.

Bridge Service Corp

277 Broadway #510, New York, NY 10007-2001
Phone: 800-225-2736; 212-267-8600 **Fax:** 888-267-8680; 212-267-8687
www.bridgeservice.com **email:** info@bridgeservice.com

Types of Records Retrieved: Civil courts; Probate courts; Federal courts; Real Estate; Tax liens/Judgments; UCC records

Local Retrieval Area: NY-Bronx, Kings, New York, Queens. **Correspondent Relationships:** nationwide.

Add'l Information: Established 1994. Normal turnaround time- 1-3 days. Expedited service available. Projects billed by number of names searched. Projects billed by the hour. 1st project may require prepayment. Credit cards accepted. They specialize in all filing and search services in 4 of the 5 counties which comprise New York City in all courts, agencies and government offices.

Brill Title Company

240 W Main Plaza, West Plains, MO 65775
Phone: 417-256-2951 **Fax:** 417-256-0284

Types of Records Retrieved: Civil courts; Probate courts; Real Estate; Tax liens/Judgments; UCC records

Local Retrieval Area: MO-Howell

Add'l Information: Normal turnaround time- 2-3 days. Projects billed by number of names searched. They specialize in title insurance.

Broadmoor Research Consultants

PO Box 38421, Colorado Springs, CO 80937-8421
Phone: 719-205-1177 **Fax:** 719-475-0569
brc.inc@adelphia.net

Types of Records Retrieved: Civil and criminal courts: Probate courts; Real Estate; Tax liens/Judgments: UCC records; Vital records

Local Retrieval Area: CO-El Paso, Fremont, Teller. **Correspondent Relationships:** statewide.

Add'l Information: Established 1984. Normal turnaround time- 24-48 hours. Expedited service available. Projects billed by the hour. 1st project may require prepayment. A full service, well networked investigations & HR consulting firm. They focus on judgments/asset recovery and child welfare. Owner is a former president of State PI Assoc and former school board member. They perform service of process.

J Stephen Broadway

310 Market St E, Fayetteville, TN 37334-3024
Phone: 931-433-5979 **Fax:** 931-433-7297

Types of Records Retrieved: Civil, criminal and probate courts; Real Estate; Tax liens/Judgments; UCC records; Vital records

Local Retrieval: TN-Franklin, Giles, Lawrence, Lincoln, Marshall, Moore

Add'l Information: Established 1982. Normal turnaround time- 2-3 days. Charges vary depending on type of search. 1st project may require prepayment.

Cory Brooks

3047 Cribbens, Boise, ID 83713
Phone: 208-376-3312 **Fax:** 208-377-3760

Types of Records Retrieved: Civil and criminal courts; Federal District courts; Tax liens/Judgments; UCC records

Local Retrieval Area: ID-Ada, Canyon. **Correspondent Relationships:** Elsewhere in Idaho.

Add'l Information: Established 1989. Normal turnaround time- 24-48 hours. Projects billed by number of names searched. Projects billed by the hour. Fees vary by type of search required. 1st project may require prepayment. Monthly invoice or by prior agreement. Formerly operated by Kathy Bess, Cory specializes in the combined use of public records, computer databases, court record retrieval, UCC searching and filing, bankruptcy and DMV. They perform service of process.

Brown County Abstract Co (Nebraska)

127 W 3rd St, Ainsworth, NE 69210
Phone: 402-387-2718 **Fax:** 402-387-2342

Types of Records Retrieved: Civil courts; Probate courts; Real Estate; Tax liens/Judgments; UCC records

Local Retrieval Area: NE-Blaine, Brown, Keya Paha, Rock

Add'l Information: Established 1981. Normal turnaround time- 2-7 days. Fee basis includes a charge by the hour; there is a minimum. Payment due upon service. Will charge fee if cancelled. They specialize in title certificates and title insurance.

Brown County Abstract Co (Texas)

201 S Broadway St, Brownwood, TX 76801
Phone: 325-646-6591 **Fax:** 325-643-5086

Types of Records Retrieved: Civil courts; Probate courts; Real Estate; Tax liens/Judgments; UCC records

Local Retrieval Area: TX-Brown

Add'l Information: Normal turnaround time- 1 week. Projects billed by the hour. There is a possibility of a retainer required. 1st project may require prepayment. There is a possiblity of a retainer required. They specialize in oil and gas searches.

Brown County Title Co

108 S 7th St, Hiawatha, KS 66434
Phone: 785-742-4194 **Fax:** 785-742-7103

Types of Records Retrieved: Civil, criminal and probate courts; Real Estate; Tax liens/Judgments; UCC records

Local Retrieval Area: KS-Brown

Add'l Information: Established 1991. Normal turnaround time- 5-10 days. Projects billed by number of names searched. 1st project may require prepayment.

Brownfield Abstract & Title Co

305B W Broadway, Brownfield, TX 79316
Phone: 806-637-9595 **Fax:** 806-637-7560
bfldabst@aol.com

Types of Records Retrieved: Civil courts; Probate courts; Real Estate; Tax liens/Judgments; UCC records

Local Retrieval Area: TX-Terry

Add'l Information: Established 1985. Normal turnaround time- 2-3 days. It may average 1-2 weeks for difficult tracts. Projects billed by number of records located. Projects billed by the hour. Personal checks are accepted. They specialize in abstracts of title, title insurance and closing services. They also have complete computerized services.

Brule County Abstract Co

PO Box 378, Chamberlain, SD 57325
Phone: 605-734-4275 **Fax:** 605-734-4275

Types of Records Retrieved: Civil courts; Probate courts; Real Estate; Tax liens/Judgments

Local Retrieval Area: SD-Brule, Jackson, Lyman. **Correspondent Relationships:** nationwide.

Add'l Information: Normal turnaround time- up to 2 weeks. Fee basis varies by type of transaction. They specialize in land records. They will file/record real estate documents on behalf of clients on a same or next day basis.

Dan & Jackie Buck

162 Anthony Rd, Glen Gardner, NJ 08826
Phone: 908-537-2475 **Fax:** 908-537-2978

Types of Records Retrieved: Civil, criminal and probate courts; Real Estate; Tax liens/Judgments; UCC records; Vital records

Local Retrieval Area: NJ-Hunterdon, Morris, Somerset

Add'l Information: Established 1979. Normal turnaround time- 24-48 hours. Projects billed by number of records located. 1st project may require prepayment. Subsequent projects are individually invoiced. They are fourth generation title searchers with more than 24 years experience.

Bucks Legal Services Inc

PO Box 1197, Yardley, PA 19067-9197
Phone: 888-512-8257; 215-493-8544 **Fax:** 267-200-0885
www.buckslegal.com **email:** walt@buckslegal.com

Types of Records Retrieved: Civil, criminal and probate courts; Federal courts; Real Estate; Tax liens/Judgments; UCC records; Vital records

Local Retrieval Area: PA-Bucks, Mongtomery. **Correspondent Relationships:** Philadelphia, PA; Mercer, NJ.

Add'l Information: Established 1998. Normal turnaround time- 24-48 hours. Projects billed by number of names searched. Monthly or individual search billing available. 1st project may require prepayment. Credit cards accepted. They are able to retrieve records in southeast PA or NJ. Documents can be copied or scanned. Returns can be faxed, mailed or emailed. Also searches the NARA and Philadelphia federal courts. They perform service of process.

Budget Document Retrieval & Info. Svc

215 W Grape St #15, San Diego, CA 92101-1935
Phone: 866-805-6288; 619-235-6288 **Fax:** 866-805-6288; 619-235-6288
budgetretrieval@cs.com

Types of Records Retrieved: Civil and criminal courts; Federal courts; Real Estate; Tax liens/Judgments; UCC records; Vital records

Local Retrieval Area: CA-San Diego

Add'l Information: Established 1991. Normal turnaround time- 24-48 hours. Projects billed by number of names searched. 1st project may require prepayment. They are dedicated to saving clients time and money by providing the documents and information needed to make informed business decisions.

Buffalo County Abstract

PO Box 57, Chamberlain, SD 57325
Phone: 605-734-6891

Types of Records Retrieved: Real Estate; Tax liens/Judgments

Local Retrieval Area: SD-Buffalo

Add'l Information: Established 1884. 1st project may require prepayment. They specialize in real estate.

Buffalo Employment Screening LLC

PMB350, 333 S State St #V, Lake Oswego, OR 97034
Phone: 888-884-6860; 503-699-3340 **Fax:** 503-699-3336
www.bfloscreen.com **email:** info@bfloscreen.com

Types of Records Retrieved: Criminal courts

Local Retrieval Area: OR-Benton, Clackamas, Lane, Linn, Marion, Multnomah, Polk, Washington, Yamhill. **Correspondent Relationships:** nationwide.

Add'l Information: Established 1993. Normal turnaround time- next business day. Projects billed by number of names searched. Terms: net 30 days. They specialize in pre-employment screening, SSN validation, and overseeing drug screening nationwide.

Buffalo Land Abstract Inc

103 N Kemp Ave, Tishomingo, OK 73460
Phone: 800-631-1880; 580-371-9375 **Fax:** 580-371-2771

Types of Records Retrieved: Civil courts; Probate courts; Real Estate; Tax liens/Judgments; UCC records

Local Retrieval Area: OK-Johnston

Add'l Information: Established 1989. Normal turnaround time- 2-5 days. They charge per page or per certificate. They specialize in closings and title insurance.

B Scott Buffington

PO Box 745, 115 Main St, Magee, MS 39111
Phone: 601-849-4267 **Fax:** 601-849-9600

Types of Records Retrieved: Real Estate; Tax liens/Judgments; UCCs

Local Retrieval Area: MS-Covington, Forrest, Jefferson Davis, Lamar, Simpson, Smith

Add'l Information: Normal turnaround time- 1-2 days. Fee basis varies by type of transaction. 1st project may require prepayment. He is in general practice.

Burnett County Abstract Co

25084 State Rd 35, Siren, WI 54872-9002
Phone: 715-349-2269 **Fax:** 715-349-7604

Types of Records Retrieved: Real Estate; Tax liens/Judgments; UCC records

Local Retrieval Area: WI-Burnett

Add'l Information: Established 1906. Normal turnaround time- 3 days. Projects billed by number of names searched. Projects billed by number of records located. Projects billed by the hour. Will invoice with a prepaid deposit. They specialize in real estate title searches.

Burr Investigation

PO Box 6486, Boise, ID 83707
Phone: 800-582-5441; 208-342-3463 **Fax:** 208-342-8097
76233.475@compuserve.com

Types of Records Retrieved: Civil, criminal and probate courts; Federal courts; Real Estate; Tax liens/Judgments; UCC records; Vital records

Local Retrieval Area: ID-Ada, Adams, Blaine, Boise, Canyon, Cassia, Elmore, Gem, Gooding, Minidoka, Owyhee, Twin Falls, Valley. **Correspondent Relationships:** nationwide and international.

Add'l Information: Established 1975. Normal turnaround time- several days. Projects billed by the hour. All projects require prepayment. They have 25 years combined law enforcement and investigative experience. A licensed PI in ID-Ada. They perform service of process.

Burton Professional Services

PO Box 820861, Vancouver, WA 98682
Phone: 360-254-0878 **Fax:** 360-250-6390
www.burtonprofessional.com **email:** sam@burtonprofessional.com

Types of Records Retrieved: Civil, criminal and probate courts; Federal courts; Real Estate; Tax liens/Judgments; UCC reocrds; Vital records

Local Retrieval Area: OR-Clackamas, Multnomah, Washington; WA-Clark, Cowlitz, Skamania. **Correspondent Relationships:** Pacific, WA county; Clatsop, Columbia counties OR.

Add'l Information: Established 2002. Normal turnaround time- 24-48 hours. Expedited service available. Projects billed by number of names searched. Also trip fee plus copy charges. 1st project may require prepayment. Credit cards accepted. They specialize in document retrieval, investigations and business support services. Also do court document filing, forclosure postings and field services. They are local process servers. A licensed PI in WA, OR. They perform service of process.

Burtschi Bros & Co

PO Box 8, Vandalia, IL 62471
Phone: 618-283-2102 **Fax:** 618-283-2768
lisasmithbb@sbcglobal.net

Types of Records Retrieved: Real Estate; Tax liens/judgments; UCC records

Local Retrieval Area: IL-Fayette. **Correspondent Relationships:** Fayette County, IL.

Add'l Information: Established 1894. Normal turnaround time- 24 hours. Projects billed by number of names searched. 1st project may require prepayment.

Business Connections

810 Main St, Red Bluff, CA 96080
Phone: 530-527-6262 **Fax:** 530-529-2645
www.bcconnects.com **email:** business@bcconnects.com

Types of Records Retrieved: Civil and criminal courts; Federal courts; Tax liens/Judgments; UCC records; Vital records

Local Retrieval Area: CA-Butte, Fresno, Glenn, Merced, Modoc, Shasta, Tehama. **Correspondent Relationships:** California except Tulare, Alpine, San Luis Obispo, Colusa, Sierra.

Add'l Information: Normal turnaround time- 24-48 hours. Projects billed by number of names searched. Credit cards accepted. Terms are net 30 days. They specialize in deeds, bankruptcies, liens, UCCs-fixture judgments and building permit searches. They also do service of process in Tehama County only. They perform service of process.

Business Intelligence Inc

350 S Oyster Bay Rd, Syosset, NY 11791
Phone: 516-938-1525 x107 **Fax:** 516-938-0010
www.businessintell.com **email:** info@businessintell.com

Types of Records Retrieved: Civil, criminal and probate courts; Federal courts; Real Estate; Tax liens/Judgments; UCC records; Vital records

Local Retrieval Area: NY-Kings, Nassau, New York, Queens, Suffolk, Westchester. **Correspondent Relationships:** nationwide.

Add'l Information: Established 1998. Normal turnaround time- 48 hours. Projects billed by number of names searched. 1st project may require prepayment. Credit cards accepted. Business Intelligence Inc provides full-service due diligence, employment screening, litigation support, computer system intelligence, special research and public record retrieval, usually of business information. A licensed PI in NY. Perform service of process.

Business Maven LLC

PO Box 270082, Louisville, CO 80027
Phone: 303-725-2668 **Fax:** 413-581-9234
www.businessmaven.com **email:** wolff@businessmaven.com

Types of Records Retrieved: Civil, criminal and probate courts; Federal courts; Real Estate; Tax liens/Judgments; UCC records; Vital records

Local Retrieval Area: CO-Adams, Boulder, Broomfield, Denver, Jefferson. **Correspondent Relationships:** statewide. Also Wyoming on special projects.

Add'l Information: Established 2002. Normal turnaround time- 24 hours. Projects billed by the hour. 1st project may require prepayment. Business Maven LLC provides research and investigation services for attorneys, businesses and nonprofits. Expertise in federal, state and local public records research, FOIA and Open Records Act.

Business Research Services

PO Box 31976, Knoxville, TN 37923-1976
Phone: 800-608-4636; 865-531-6620 **Fax:** 877-864-3463; 865-531-6621
bisinfo@bellsouth.net

Types of Records Retrieved: Civil, criminal and probate courts; Federal courts; Real Estate; Tax liens/Judgments; UCC records; Vital records

Local Retrieval: TN-Knox. **Correspondent Relationships:** nationwide.

Add'l Information: Established 1990. Normal turnaround time- 1-3 days. Fee is per name, per court. 1st project may require prepayment. Terms: net 15 days. They specialize in civil and criminal record searches, secretary of state records, patent and trademark registrations, MVR records, UCC filings, real property records, consumer and business credit reports. A licensed PI in FL, TN.

Business Services Group of CT LLC

1924 Straits Turnpike, PO Box 57, Middlebury, CT 06762
Phone: 203-758-2493 **Fax:** 203-841-1002
www.bsgctsearch.com **email:** bsgct@snet.net

Types of Records Retrieved: Civil courts; Federal courts; Real Estate; Tax liens/Judgments; UCC records

Local Retrieval Area: CT-Fairfield, Hartford, Litchfield, Middlesex, New Haven, New London, Tolland

Add'l Information: Established 2003. Normal turnaround time- 2-5 business days. Expedited service available. Projects billed by number of names searched. 1st project may require prepayment. BSG is a full service title abstracting and document filing and retreival company, providing fast, dependable service and competative prices.

Butcher & Associates Ltd

311 E Thayer Ave #119, Bismarck, ND 58501
Phone: 701-224-1541 **Fax:** 701-224-1097
www.northdakotapi.com **email:** wtb@northdakotapi.com

Types of Records Retrieved: Civil, criminal and probate courts; Federal courts; Real Estate; Tax liens/Judgments; UCC records; Vital records

Local Retrieval Area: MN-Clay; ND-Burleigh, Cass, Morton. **Correspondent Relationships:** North Dakota and nationwide.

Add'l Information: Established 1982. Normal turnaround time- 24-48 hours. Projects billed by number of names searched. Fee basis varies by type of transaction. 1st project may require prepayment. They are former FBI agents that specialize in private investigations, pre-employment screening & state & county record retrieval. Voter registration records are only avaliable for Clay County, MN. Criminal & UCC records are available for all of ND. A licensed PI in ND. They perform service of process.

Butler County Abstract & Title Inc

111 N Main St, Poplar Bluff, MO 63901
Phone: 573-686-1495 **Fax:** 573-686-3804

Types of Records Retrieved: Civil courts; Probate courts; Real Estate; Tax liens/Judgments; UCC records

Local Retrieval Area: MO-Butler

Add'l Information: Normal turnaround time- 1-3 days. Projects billed by number of names searched. Projects billed by number of records located. 1st project may require prepayment. Personal checks are accepted.

C

C & S Research

450 Harding Rd, Yuba City, CA 95993-5116
Phone: 530-415-3161 **Fax:** 530-673-0264

Types of Records Retrieved: Civil, criminal and probate courts; Federal courts; Real Estate; Tax liens/Judgments; UCC records; Vital records

Local Retrieval Area: CA-Alameda, Butte, Colusa, Contra Costa, El Dorado, Mendocino, Nevada, Placer, Plumas, Sacramento, Shasta, Sierra, Sutter, Tehama, Yolo, Yuba. **Correspondent Relationships:** Northern California.

Add'l Information: Established 1997. Normal turnaround time- 12-36 hours. Projects billed by number of names searched. Projects billed by number of records located. Will bill once or twice per month, Their goal is to give their clients fast and accurate service at a quality price. In Law enforcement and record searching since 1988. Visits all courts daily.

C W Lynn Abstract Co Inc

121 N 7th St, Salina, KS 67401
Phone: 785-823-3706 **Fax:** 785-823-7922

Types of Records Retrieved: Civil courts; Probate courts; Real Estate; Tax liens/Judgments; UCC records

Local Retrieval Area: KS-Saline

Add'l Information: Established 1867. Normal turnaround time- 2-3 days. Charges vary by purchase price or mortgage amount. They specialize in title insurance.

C.C.I.

PO Box 2383, Fargo, ND 58108
Phone: 701-235-4842

Types of Records Retrieved: Civil, criminal and probate courts; Federal courts; Real Estate; Tax liens/Judgments; UCC records

Local Retrieval Area: MN-Clay; ND-Cass

Add'l Information: Established 1995. Normal turnaround time- 48 hours. Projects billed by number of names searched. Payment due upon receipt by client. They specialize in civil, criminal, insurance investigation and surveillance. A licensed PI in ND. They perform service of process.

Cal Info Inc

4750 41st St NW #5, Washington, DC 20016
Phone: 202-537-8901 **Fax:** 202-537-8902
http://calinfo.net **email:** admin@calinfo.net

Types of Records Retrieved: Civil, criminal and probate courts; Federal courts

Local Retrieval Area: DC-District of Columbia. **Correspondent Relationships:** nationwide.

Add'l Information: Established 1987. Normal turnaround time- same day. Projects billed by the hour. 1st project may require prepayment. Credit cards accepted. They specialize in research and document retrieval service with offices in Washington, DC and Los Angeles, CA, 213-687-8710.

Cal Info Inc

316 W 2nd St #1102, Los Angeles, CA 90012
Phone: 213-537-8901 **Fax:** 213-537-8902
www.calinfo.net **email:** calinfola@aol.com

Types of Records Retrieved: Civil, criminal and probate courts; Federal courts; Real Estate; Tax liens/Judgments; UCC records; Vital records

Local Retrieval Area: CA-Los Angeles, Orange. **Correspondent Relationships:** nationwide.

Add'l Information: Established 1957. Normal turnaround time- same day. Projects billed by the hour. 1st project may require prepayment. Credit cards accepted. They are a research and retrieval firm whose expertise includes law, business, government documents and the sciences with offices in Los Angeles, CA and Washington, DC.

Cal Search

PO Box 9552, San Diego, CA 92169
Phone: 858-488-7572 **Fax:** 858-488-7592
www.calsearch.com **email:** calsearch@san.rr.com

Types of Records Retrieved: Civil, criminal and probate courts; Federal courts; Tax liens/Judgments; UCC records; Vital records

Local Retrieval Area: CA-Alameda, Butte, Contra Costa, Fresno, Los Angeles, Marin, Merced, Monterey, Orange, Riverside, Sacramento, San Bernardino, San Diego, San Francisco, San Mateo, Santa Barbara, Santa Clara, Santa Cruz, Stanislaus, Ventura. **Correspondent Relationships:** nationwide.

Add'l Information: Established 1995. Normal turnaround time- 24-48 hours. Expedited service available. Projects billed by number of names searched. Payment due net 30 days. They specialize in fast and accurate background research & Document retrieval in every CA county. Also specialize in criminal, civil, federal, tax liens, judgments, probate and bankruptcy.

Cal Title-Search Inc

1005 12th St #E, Sacramento, CA 95814
Phone: 800-482-1497; 916-448-1397 **Fax:** 916-448-1698
caltitlesearch@hotmail.com

Types of Records Retrieved: Civil courts; Probate courts; Federal courts; Real Estate; Tax liens/Judgments; UCC records; Vital records

Local Retrieval Area: CA-Sacramento. **Correspondent Relationships:** nationwide.

Add'l Information: Established 1979. Normal turnaround time- 24 hours for state records, 2-3 days for county records. Projects billed by number of names searched. 1st project may require prepayment.

California Backgrounds

7010 N Marks #103 PMB 295, Fresno, CA 93711
Phone: 559-274-9784 **Fax:** 559-274-9038

Types of Records Retrieved: Criminal courts

Local Retrieval Area: CA-Fresno, Kern, Kings, Madera, San Joaquin, Tulare

Add'l Information: Established 1998. Normal turnaround time- 24 hours. Projects billed by number of names searched. Payment due upon receipt of monthly invoice. All requests are processed at the courts public access. No databases used.

California Criminal Research

4195 Chino Hills Pky #317, Chino Hills, CA 91709
Phone: 909-445-7288 **Fax:** 775-854-0081
www.calcriminalresearch.com **email:** info@calcriminalresearch.com

Types of Records Retrieved: Civil, criminal and probate courts

Local Retrieval Area: CA-Los Angeles, Orange, San Diego

Add'l Information: Established 1989. Normal turnaround time- 24 hours or less. Projects billed by number of names searched. All projects require prepayment. Since 1989, CCR has specialized in criminal record searches, civil and probate courts for Southern California. All work completed within 24 hours. Professional staff and highest standards and accuracy in the industry. They perform service of process.

Callahan Lawyers Service

50 Main St, (POB 632, 07602), Hackensack, NJ 07601
Phone: 877-767-2245; 201-489-2245 **Fax:** 201-489-8093
www.processandbail.com **email:** dan@processandbail.com

Types of Records Retrieved: Civil, criminal and probate courts; Federal courts; Vital records

Local Retrieval Area: NJ-Bergen, Essex, Hudson, Morris, Passaic, Sussex. **Correspondent Relationships:** Morris and Hudson.

Add'l Information: Established 1963. Normal turnaround time- 2-3 days. Expedited service available. Fee basis is per job. 1st project may require prepayment. Credit cards accepted. Large enough to serve you, small enough to care. In business since 1965. They perform service of process.

Kerry H Callahan

7110 Vice President, Baton Rouge, LA 70817
Phone: 225-752-8750 **Fax:** 225-751 7544
kerrycal@juno.com

Types of Records Retrieved: Civil, criminal and probate courts; Federal courts; UCC records; Vital records

Local Retrieval: LA-Ascension, East Baton Rouge, Iberville, Livingston, West Baton Rouge. **Correspondent Relationships:** St. James, LA.

Add'l Information: Established 1992. Normal turnaround time- 24 hours. Projects billed by number of names searched. 1st project may require prepayment. Does invoice every 30 days. She specializes in criminal & civil hands on searches. Turnaround is usually 24 hours. Pulls hard case files for case file information. Does not rely on computer information. She searches the US Middle District Federal Courts. They perform service of process.

Camp County Land Abstract Co

PO Box 99, 202 Jefferson St, Pittsburg, TX 75686-0099
Phone: 903-856-3676 **Fax:** 903-856-0470

Types of Records Retrieved: Civil courts; Probate courts; Real Estate; UCC records; Vital records

Local Retrieval Area: TX-Camp

Add'l Information: Established 1981. Normal turnaround time- 1-7 days. Fee basis will vary by the type of project. 1st project may require prepayment. They specialize in land searches, title policies, and real estate closings.

Campbell Abstract Co

7 NW 2nd St, PO Box 425, Buffalo, MN 55313-0425
Phone: 763-682-1252 **Fax:** 763-682-5810
karen@campbellabstract.com

Types of Records Retrieved: Civil courts; Probate courts; Federal courts; Real Estate; Tax liens/Judgments

Local Retrieval Area: MN-Wright

Add'l Information: Established 1925. Normal turnaround time- 2-3 days. Projects billed by number of names searched. Projects billed by number of records located. 1st project may require prepayment. Terms: net 30 days. They specialize in abstracts of title, owners and encumbrances and tract checks.

Campbell Abstract Inc

417 N 8th St, Garden City, KS 67846-5302
Phone: 620-275-7441 **Fax:** 620-275-8658
www.gardencity.net/campbell **email:** campbell@gcnet.com

Types of Records Retrieved: Civil courts; Probate courts; Real Estate; Tax liens/Judgments; UCC records

Local Retrieval Area: KS-Finney

Add'l Information: Established 1978. Normal turnaround time- 1-3 days. Projects billed by the hour. 1st project may require prepayment.

Campbell County Abstract & Title

PO Box 315, Herreid, SD 57632
Phone: 605-437-2222 **Fax:** 605-437-2222
Types of Records Retrieved: Real Estate; Tax liens/Judgments
Local Retrieval Area: SD-Campbell
Add'l Information: Established 1920. 1st project may require prepayment. They specialize in real estate.

Cape Girardeau County Abstract & Title

PO Box 878, Cape Girardeau, MO 63702-0878
Phone: 573-335-5890 **Fax:** 573-335-6381
Types of Records Retrieved: Civil courts; Probate courts; Federal District courts; Real Estate; Tax liens/Judgments; UCC records
Local Retrieval Area: MO-Cape Girardeau
Add'l Information: Established 1903. Normal turnaround time- 3 days. Projects billed by number of names searched. Projects billed by number of records located. They specialize in land title record searches title insurance, escrow and complete closing services.

Capital City Assurance Group

300 W Osborn Rd #409, Phoenix, AZ 85013
Phone: 602-728-0100 **Fax:** 602-728-0500
www.ccaginvestigations.com **email:** ccag@ccaginvestigations.com
Types of Records Retrieved: Civil, criminal and probate courts; Federal courts; Real Estate; Tax liens/Judgments; Vital records
Local Retrieval Area: AZ-Maricopa. **Correspondent Relationships:** nationwide.
Add'l Information: Established 1995. Normal turnaround time- 48 hours or less. Expedited service available. Projects billed by number of names searched. 1st project may require prepayment. Billed weekly with 15 day net. They provide service without limitations in a timely and reader friendly manner, to include criminal history checks as well as employment verificaitons. A licensed PI in AZ.

Capital Connection

417 E Virginia St #1, Tallahassee, FL 32301
Phone: 850-224-8870 **Fax:** 800-342-8062; 850-222-1222
www.mycapitalconnection.com **email:** mycapitalconnection@yahoo.com
Types of Records Retrieved: Civil and criminal courts; Federal courts; Real Estate; Tax liens/Judgments; UCC records
Local Retrieval Area: FL-Gadsden, Jefferson, Leon, Wakulla. **Correspondent Relationships:** nationwide.
Add'l Information: Established 1983. Normal turnaround time- 1-2 days. Projects billed by number of names searched. 1st project may require prepayment. Credit cards accepted. Will bill service companies, attorneys and CPA's. Filing, retrieval and corporate supply company specializing in 1 day incorporations, registered agent service, UCC searches, complete corporate book and out of state retrievals. They perform service of process.

Capital Inv Services Inc

3127 SW Huntoon #12, Topeka, KS 66604
Phone: 800-633-7136; 785-232-1515 **Fax:** 785-232-9170
www.cis-pi.com
Types of Records Retrieved: Civil and criminal courts.
Local Retrieval Area: KS-Dickinson, Douglas, Ellsworth, Franklin, Geary, Harvey, Jackson, Jefferson, Lyon, Marion, McPherson, Osage, Pottawatomie, Rice, Riley, Saline, Shawnee, Wabaunsee. **Correspondent Relationships:** all of NE Kansas.
Add'l Information: 1st project may require prepayment. They also provide court filings, photocopying, and private investigations. Licensed PI in KS.

Capitol City Network

1191 Spruce Tree Cir, Sacramento, CA 95831
Phone: 916-395-2917 **Fax:** 916-429-2823
www.capitolcitynetwork.bizonthe.net **email:** ccnis@sbcglobal.net
Types of Records Retrieved: Civil, criminal and probate courts; Federal courts; Real Estate; Tax liens/Judgments; UCC records; Vital records
Local Retrieval Area: CA-Sacramento. **Correspondents:** nationwide.
Add'l Information: Established 1985. Normal turnaround time- 2-24 hours. Fee basis varies by type of transaction. 1st project may require prepayment. They specialize in legislative analysis/bill tracking and asset searches. They do all Secretary of State filings for California. Obtain all business defendant filings for Sacramento County daily. Check web site for info.

Capitol Corporate Services

815 N 1st Ave #4, Phoenix, AZ 85003
Phone: 800-255-4052; 602-254-4489 **Fax:** 800-752-0098; 602-258-5833
www.capitolservices.com **email:** capserv@capitolservices.com
Types of Records Retrieved: Federal courts; Tax liens/Judgments, UCC and Corporate records
Local Retrieval Area: AZ-Maricopa
Add'l Information: Established 1985. Normal turnaround time- 1-2 days. Projects billed by number of names searched. 1st project may require prepayment. Credit cards accepted. They specialize in UCC searches and filings, corporation document filings and retrieval as well as county tax lien, judgment and pending litigation searches.

Capitol Corporate Services Inc (AZ)

815 N 1st Ave #4, Phoenix, AZ 85003
Phone: 800-255-4052; 602-254-4489 **Fax:** 800-752-0098; 602-258-5833
www.capitolservices.com **email:** tlukas@capitolservices.com
Types of Records Retrieved: Civil courts; Probate courts; Federal courts; Tax liens/Judgments; UCC & corporate records
Local Retrieval Area: AZ-Maricopa. **Correspondent Relationships:** Arizona, nationwide.
Add'l Information: Normal turnaround time- 24 hours in Maricopa, 2-4 days in other Arizona counties. Projects billed by number of names searched. They sometimes charge by the hour depending on search. 1st project may require prepayment. Credit cards accepted. They specialize in UCC, tax lien and judgments searches and corporate document filing, retrieval and registered agent services.

Capitol Corporate Services Inc (California)

455 Capitol Mall Complex #217, Sacramento, CA 95814
Phone: 800-327-4842; 916-444-6787 **Fax:** 800-770-1332; 916-444-6178
www.capitolservices.com **email:** tsartell@capitolservices.com
Types of Records Retrieved: Civil courts; Federal courts; Tax liens/Judgments; UCC & corporate records
Local Retrieval Area: CA-Sacramento. **Correspondents:** nationwide.
Add'l Information: Established 1996. Normal turnaround time- next day. Projects billed by number of names searched. 1st project may require prepayment. Credit cards accepted. They specialize in UCC searches and filings, corporation document filing and retrieval and registered agent services.

Capitol Corporate Services Inc (Louisiana)

8550 United Plaza Blvd, Bldg 2, #305, Baton Rouge, LA 70809
Phone: 800-408-1262; 225-922-4693 **Fax:** 888-234-5859; 225-922-4694
www.capitolservices.com **email:** info-batonrouge@capitolservices.com
Types of Records Retrieved: Civil courts; Federal courts; Tax liens/Judgments; UCC and corporate records
Local Retrieval Area: LA-East Baton Rouge Parish. **Correspondent Relationships:** nationwide.
Add'l Information: Established 1996. Normal turnaround time- within 24 hours. Projects billed by number of names searched. 1st project may require prepayment. Credit cards accepted. They do except check payments. They are a public research company specializing in Lien searches. Also provides corporate records from Secretary of State.

Capitol Corporate Services Inc (Nevada)

202 S Minnesota, Carson City, NV 89703
Phone: 800-899-0490; 775-884-0490 **Fax:** 888-231-4790; 775-884-0493
www.capitolservices.com **email:** mellis@capitolservices.com
Types of Records Retrieved: Tax liens/Judgments; UCCs; corporate records

Local Retrieval Area: NV-Carson City. **Correspondent Relationships:** nationwide.

Add'l Information: Established 1991. Normal turnaround time- 1-2 days for the listed counties; 3-5 days for network counties. Next day for state records. Projects billed by number of names searched. 1st project may require prepayment. Credit cards accepted. They specialize in UCC searches and filings, corporation document filings and retrieval as well as county tax lien, judgment and pending litigation searches.

Capitol District Information

471 H St NW #LWR, Washington, DC 20001-2617
Phone: 800-494-5225; 202-265-1516 **Fax:** 800-494-7512; 202-265-5006
www.capitoldistrict.com **email:** info@capitoldistrict.com

Types of Records Retrieved: Civil and criminal courts; Federal courts; Tax liens/Judgments; UCC records

Local Retrieval Area: DC-District of Columbia; MD-Montgomery, Prince George's; VA-Arlington. **Correspondent Relationships:** nationwide.

Add'l Information: Established 1988. Normal turnaround time- 2-48 hours. Projects billed by number of names searched. Projects billed by the hour. Credit accounts available. Call for price/time quote. 1st project may require prepayment. Credit cards accepted. Will invoice most companies. They specialize in research/retrieval of legal/financial documents at federal, state and local levels. Emphasis on federal courts and agencies. Also offer services at federal libraries (Library of Congress and National Library of Medicine). They perform service of process.

Capitol Lien Records & Research

1010 Dale St, St Paul, MN 55117-5603
Phone: 800-845-4077; 651-488-0100 **Fax:** 800-845-4080; 651-488-0200
www.capitollien.com **email:** tony@capitollien.com

Types of Records Retrieved: Civil, criminal and probate courts; Federal courts; Real Estate; Tax liens/Judgments; UCC records; Vital records

Local Retrieval Area: MN-all counties; WI-St. Croix. **Correspondent Relationships:** nationwide.

Add'l Information: Established 1990. Normal turnaround time- 1-3 days. Projects billed by number of names searched. Projects billed by number of records located. 1st project may require prepayment. Credit cards accepted. Terms: net 30 days after first order. Personal checks are accepted. They have access to UCC electronic filings online for all 50 states. They perform service of process.

Capitol Services (California)

926 J St #919, Sacramento, CA 95814
Phone: 916-443-0657 **Fax:** 916-443-1908
www.cutredtape.com **email:** capserve@cwo.com

Types of Records Retrieved: UCC records

Local Retrieval Area: CA-Sacramento

Add'l Information: Established 1982. Normal turnaround time- 3-4 working days. 1st project may require prepayment. Credit cards accepted. They provide document filing and retrieval at the California Secretary of State's office in Sacramento.

Capitol Services Inc (New York)

40 Colvin Ave #200, Albany, NY 12206
Phone: 800-662-0171; 518-453-0171 **Fax:** 800-662-0275; 518-453-0275
www.capitolservices.com **email:** lfrank@capitolservices.com

Types of Records Retrieved: Federal courts; Tax liens/Judgments; UCC & corporate records

Local Retrieval Area: NY-Albany, Rensselaer. **Correspondent Relationships:** nationwide.

Add'l Information: Established 1993. Normal turnaround time- next day. Projects billed by number of names searched. 1st project may require prepayment. Credit cards accepted. They are a full service UCC and corporate search and filing service.

Capitol Services Inc (Texas)

800 Brazos #1100, Austin, TX 78701
Phone: 800-345-4647; 512-474-8377 **Fax:** 800-432-3622; 512-476-3678
www.capitolservices.com **email:** jrobinson@capitolservices.com

Types of Records Retrieved: Civil courts; Federal courts; Tax liens/Judgments; UCC & corporate records

Local Retrieval Area: TX-Dallas, Harris, Travis. **Correspondent Relationships:** nationwide.

Add'l Information: Established 1978. Normal turnaround time- next day. Projects billed by number of names searched. 1st project may require prepayment. Credit cards accepted. They specialize in UCC, tax lien, judgment and pending litigation searches, expedited UCC filings and corporation document filing and retrieval.

Caprock Title Co

511 W Ohio Ave #100, Midland, TX 79701
Phone: 432-687-3232 **Fax:** 432-687-3240
caprock@apex2000.net

Types of Records Retrieved: Civil courts; Probate courts; Real Estate; Tax liens/Judgments

Local Retrieval Area: NM-Eddy, Lea; TX-Dickens, Kent, King, Stonewall. **Correspondent Relationships:** West Texas, Southeast, New Mexico.

Add'l Information: Established 1984. Normal turnaround time- up to 1 week. Fee basis will vary by the type of project. 1st project may require prepayment. They specialize in oil & gas, mineral interests and working interests.

Capstone Title Services

720 Energy Center Blvd #504, Northport, AL 35473
Phone: 205-759-1105 **Fax:** 205-759-1106

Types of Records Retrieved: Probate courts; Real Estate; Tax liens/Judgments; UCC records

Local Retrieval Area: AL-Bibb, Dallas, Fayette, Greene, Hale, Pickens, Tuscaloosa, Walker

Add'l Information: Established 1986. Normal turnaround time- 1-2 days. Projects billed by number of names searched. Fee basis may vary on length of search. 1st project may require prepayment. Personal checks are accepted. Credit accounts are not accepted. They specialize in title insurance, limited title searches, UCCs, judgments, probate, loan closings.

Carbon County Abstract & Title

PO Box 787, 105 N Broadway, Red Lodge, MT 59068
Phone: 406-446-1090 **Fax:** 406-446-1091
www.ccatco.com **email:** ccatco@montana.net

Types of Records Retrieved: Real Estate; Tax liens/judgments; UCC records

Local Retrieval Area: MT-Carbon

Add'l Information: Established 1981. Normal turnaround time- 2-3 days. Fees vary by project.

Caribbean Investigative Network

31 Victoria St, Hamilton, Bermuda, BER MN10
Phone: 441-292-2626 **Fax:** 441-292-8341
www.carib.bm **email:** carib@ibl.bm

Types of Records Retrieved: Probate courts; Real Estate; Vital records

Local Retrieval Area: Bermuda. **Correspondent Relationships:** Caribbean Islands-Aruba, Anquilla, Antiqua, British Virgin Island, Bahamas, Barbados, Cayman Islands, Curacao, Dominica, Grenada, Jamaica, Montserrat, Nevis, St Lucia, St Kitts, St Vencent, Trinidad, Turks & Caicos Islands.

Add'l Information: Established 1982. Normal turnaround time- 5 business days. Projects billed by number of names searched. A licensed PI in BER. They perform service of process.

Carly J Carman Abstracting Service

2046 Independence Sq, Iuka, MS 38852-1006
Phone: 662-423-5923 **Fax:** 662-423-1410 carly-carman@yahoo.com

Types of Records Retrieved: Civil courts; Probate courts; Real Estate, Tax liens/Judgments; UCC records

Local Retrieval Area: MS-Alcorn, Prentiss, Tishomingo

Add'l Information: Established 1997. Normal turnaround time- 24-48 hours. Projects billed by number of records located. 1st project may require prepayment. They specialize in retrieval of real estate records and in performing current owner/possessory abstract of title searches. They perform service of process.

Carmona & Associates

PO Box 992600, Redding, CA 96001
Phone: 530-246-1010 **Fax:** 530-246-1313

Types of Records Retrieved: Civil and criminal courts; Real Estate; Tax liens/Judgments; UCC records; Vital records

Local Retrieval Area: CA-Shasta, Siskiyou, Tehama

Add'l Information: Established 1988. Normal turnaround time- 2-3 days. Expedited service available. Projects billed by number of names searched. Projects billed by the hour. 1st project may require prepayment. They specialize in insurance defence investigations. A licensed PI in CA. They perform service of process.

Carolina Investigative Research (SC)

106D Fountain Brook Circle, Cary, NC 27511
Phone: 800-328-8981; 919-460-7799 **Fax:** 919 460 5338
www.cir-nc.com **email:** ann@cir-nc.com

Types of Records Retrieved: Civil, criminal and probate courts; Federal courts; Real Estate; Tax liens/Judgments; UCC records; Vital records

Local Retrieval Area: SC-Abbeville, Anderson, Cherokee, Florence, Greenville, Greenwood, Lancaster, Laurens, Richland, Spartanburg, York. **Correspondent Relationships:** NC, SC, GA, AL, FL, TN, VA.

Add'l Information: Established 1998. Normal turnaround time- 24-48 hours. Projects billed by number of names searched. 1st project may require prepayment. Credit cards accepted. They specialize in public record searches including criminal, civil, federal, real estate, UCCs, pre-employment and tenant screening. A licensed PI in NC, SC.

Carolina Investigative Research Inc

106D Fountain Brook Circle, Cary, NC 27511
Phone: 800-328-8981; 919-460-7799 **Fax:** 919-460-5338
www.cir-nc.com **email:** ann@cir-nc.com

Types of Records Retrieved: Civil, criminal and probate courts; Real Estate; Tax liens/Judgments; UCC records; Vital records

Local Retrieval Area: NC-Buncombe, Chatham, Cumberland, Durham, Harnett, Hoke, Johnston, Lee, Moore, Wake. **Correspondent Relationships:** nationwide, specializing in GA, NC, SC, AL, FL, TN, VA.

Add'l Information: Established 1998. Normal turnaround time- 48 hours. Projects billed by number of names searched. 1st project may require prepayment. Credit cards accepted. They are licensed private investigators who specialize in employment screening. They also perform all types of public record searches, including all types of real estate searches. A licensed PI in NC, SC. They perform service of process.

Carr Title

26433 Collosse Rd, Carrsville, VA 23315
Phone: 757-647-7873 **Fax:** 757-569-0486

Types of Records Retrieved: Real Estate' Tax liens/Judgments

Local Retrieval Area: VA-Isle of Wight, Southampton, Surry

Add'l Information: 1st project may require prepayment. They specialize in real estate.

Carroll Abstract Co

4 W Benton St, Carrollton, MO 64633
Phone: 660-542-1364 **Fax:** 660-542-1764

Types of Records Retrieved: Civil and criminal courts; Probate court; Real Estate; Tax liens/Judgments

Local Retrieval Area: MO-Carroll

Add'l Information: Established 1904. 1st project may require prepayment. They specialize in court records and real estate.

Carson & Associates Research, Inc

5915 Trammell Rd #Q12, Morrow, GA 30260-1371
Phone: 404-610-7181 or 608-8300 **Fax:** 404-608-0035

Types of Records Retrieved: Civil and criminal courts

Local Retrieval Area: GA-Carroll, Cherokee, Clayton, Cobb, De Kalb, Douglas, Fayette, Fulton, Gwinnett, Muscogee. **Correspondent Relationships:** statewide.

Add'l Information: Established 1992. Normal turnaround time- 2 days. Projects billed by number of names searched. Payment due within 30 days of billing. They specialize in record retrieval from county, state and superior courts and criminal and civil background checks for pre-employment screening since 1992. They perform service of process.

Carter Investigations

PO Box 492, Pocatello, ID 83204-0492
Phone: 208-232-3592 **Fax:** 208-232-0444
carterpi@msn.com

Types of Records Retrieved: Civil, criminal and probate courts; Federal courts; Real Estate; Tax liens/Judgments; UCC records; Vital records

Local Retrieval Area: ID-Bannock, Bingham, Bonneville, Power. **Correspondent Relationships:** Northern Idaho.

Add'l Information: Established 1988. Normal turnaround time- 24-48 hours. Projects billed by number of names searched. 1st project may require prepayment. Payment method negotiable. They specialize in child custody, domestic work, insurance, process serving and repossessions. They perform service of process.

Casa De Search Inc

9 Carlito Rd, Santa Fe, NM 87505
Phone: 800-757-0220; 505-466-4455 **Fax:** 800 743 6217; 505-466-4464
casasearch@aol.com

Types of Records Retrieved: Civil, criminal and probate courts; Federal Courts; Real Estate; Tax liens.judgments; UCC records

Local Retrieval Area: NM-Bernalillo, Dona Ana, Los Alamos, San Juan, Sandoval, Santa Fe

Add'l Information: Normal turnaround time- 24-48 hours. Projects billed by number of names searched. 1st project may require prepayment. They search civil and criminal records. They provide corporate retrieval & filing services as well as current owner searches, UCC & Tax liens/Judgments searches. They search all courts as well as registrations & titles for MVD.

Case Services Inc

PO Box 2343, South Bend, IN 46680
Phone: 877-291-6868; 574-291-0480 **Fax:** 574-291-0855
www.casepi.com **email:** casey@casepi.com

Types of Records Retrieved: Civil, criminal and probate courts; Federal courts; Real Estate; Tax liens/Judgments; UCC records; Vital records

Local Retrieval Area: IN-Elkhart, La Porte, Marshall, St Joseph; MI-Berrien, Cass. **Correspondent Relationships:** nationwide.

Add'l Information: Established 1986. Normal turnaround time- 48-hour rush service available. Projects billed by number of names searched. 1st project may require prepayment. Credit cards accepted. They are a full service investigative agency specializing in attorney litigation investigations, and corporate background investigations, fraud investigations and security assessment. Also does pre-employment screening. A licensed PI in IN. They perform service of process.

Don W Caskey

702 N Circle, Baytown, TX 77520
Phone: 281-422-7527 **Fax:** 281-422-7527

Types of Records Retrieved: Civil and criminal courts; Tax liens/Judgments; UCC records

Local Retrieval Area: TX-Chambers, Liberty

Add'l Information: Established 1992. Normal turnaround time- 24-48 hours. Projects billed by number of names searched. Due upon receipt of statement. Visits courthouses daily. Includes docket book searches. Serving Chambers & Liberty counties since 1991. Will retrieve bankruptcy court records from Texas Eastern Division.

Cass County Abstract Co (North Dakota)

PO Box 826, Fargo, ND 58107
Phone: 701-232-3341 **Fax:** 701-232-7851
Types of Records Retrieved: Real Estate; Tax liens/Judgments; UCC records
Local Retrieval Area: MN-Clay; ND-Cass
Add'l Information: Established 1910. Normal turnaround time- 2 days. Fee basis will vary by type of search. They specialize in real estate.

Cass County Abstract Co Inc (Iowa)

518 Chestnut St, Atlantic, IA 50022
Phone: 712-243-2136 **Fax:** 712-243-4360
Types of Records Retrieved: Civil, criminal and probate courts; Real Estate; Tax liens/Judgments; UCC records; Vital records
Local Retrieval Area: IA-Cass
Add'l Information: Normal turnaround time- 1-10 days. Fee basis will vary by the type of project.

M B Cassell

PO Box 235, Finley, ND 58230-0235
Phone: 701-524-1961 **Fax:** 701-524-1961
Types of Records Retrieved: Civil courts; Real Estate; Tax liens/Judgments
Local Retrieval Area: ND-Steele
Add'l Information: Established 1890. Normal turnaround time- 1-3 days. Projects billed by number of names searched. Projects billed by number of records located.

Cassia County Abstract Co

PO Box 548, Burley, ID 83318
Phone: 208-678-8347 **Fax:** 208-678-8348
ccatitle@pmt.org
Types of Records Retrieved: Probate courts; Real Estate; Tax liens/Judgments; UCC records
Local Retrieval Area: ID-Cassia
Add'l Information: Established 1904. Normal turnaround time- 5 days. Projects billed by the hour. All projects require prepayment. They specialize in title insurance and real estate closing.

Cattaraugus Abstract Corp

406 Erie St, Little Valley, NY 14755
Phone: 800-559-1242; 716-938-9109 **Fax:** 716-938-6259
Types of Records Retrieved: Civil courts; Probate courts; Real Estate; Tax liens/Judgments; UCC records
Local Retrieval Area: NY-Cattaraugus
Add'l Information: Established 1964. Normal turnaround time- 48 hours. Projects billed by number of names searched.

Centennial Abstract of Pratt

126 E 3rd St, Pratt, KS 67124-2710
Phone: 620-672-5928 **Fax:** 620-672-7334
Types of Records Retrieved: Civil courts; Probate courts; Real Estate; Tax liens/Judgments; UCC records
Local Retrieval Area: KS-Pratt. **Correspondent Relationships:** Barber, Kiowa, Stafford counties KS.
Add'l Information: Established 1984. Normal turnaround time- 3-5 days. Projects billed by number of names searched. 1st project may require prepayment. They specialize in real estate records, also civil & probate court record retrieval.

Centennial Coverages Inc (Colorado)

PO Box 441433, 16748 C E Smoky Hill Rd #227 (80015-2492), Aurora, CO 80044-1433
Phone: 800-338-8221; 303-400-3990 **Fax:** 303-400-3322
centennial@speakeasy.net
Types of Records Retrieved: Civil, criminal and probate courts; Federal courts; Real Estate; Tax liens/Judgments; UCC records; Vital records
Local Retrieval Area: CO-Adams, Arapahoe, Boulder, Denver, Douglas, El Paso, Elbert, Jefferson, Larimer. **Correspondent Relationships:** nationwide.
Add'l Information: Established 1986. Normal turnaround time- 2-10 days. Projects billed by number of names searched. Projects billed by number of records located. Projects billed by the hour. Fee is by the hour on chain-of-title. 1st project may require prepayment. Terms: net 10 days. They specialize in real estate searches, UCC searches, skiptracing, civil and criminal court searches, asset investigations, real estate chain-of-title, investigative background reports and nationwide UCC article 9 work.

Centennial Title & Abstract Co

G4137 Fenton Road, Burton, MI 48529
Phone: 810-238-5100 **Fax:** 810-238-5270
www.centennialtitle.com **email:** ctac@centennialtitle.com
Types of Records Retrieved: Probate courts; Real Estate; Tax liens/Judgments; UCC records
Local Retrieval Area: MI-Genesee. **Correspondent Relationships:** Saginaw County.
Add'l Information: Established 1980. Normal turnaround time- 3-4 days. Fee basis will vary by the project. 1st project may require prepayment. They specialize in real estate transactions.

Central Arkansas Title

212 S Main St, Malvern, AR 72104
Phone: 501-332-3770 **Fax:** 501-337-0729
www.centralarkansastitle.com **email:** shodge@centralarkansastitle.com
Types of Records Retrieved: Real Estate; Tax liens/Judgments; UCC records; Vital records
Local Retrieval Area: AR-Hot Spring
Add'l Information: Established 1983. Normal turnaround time- 3 days. Projects billed by number of names searched. Fee basis will vary by the type of project. 1st project may require prepayment. They specialize in real estate records.

Central Carolina Process Service

2834 Montclair Cir, Sanford, NC 27330
Phone: 919-776-7584 **Fax:** 919-776-7584
Types of Records Retrieved: Civil, criminal and probate courts; Federal courts; Real Estate; Tax liens/Judgments; UCC records; Vital records
Local Retrieval Area: NC-Alamance, Anson, Caswell, Chatham, Cumberland, Durham, Franklin, Granville, Guilford, Harnett, Hoke, Johnston, Lee, Montgomery, Moore, Orange, Person, Randolph, Richmond, Robeson, Rockingham, Sampson, Scotland, Stanly, Vance, Wake, Warren, Wayne, Wilson
Add'l Information: Established 1992. Normal turnaround time- 3-4 days. Expedited service available. Fees vary by project. All projects require prepayment. They perform service of process.

Central Indiana Paralegal Service Inc

55 Monument Cir #1424, Indianapolis, IN 46204
Phone: 317-636-1311 **Fax:** 800-321-1600; 317-636-1426
www.cips1.com **email:** cips1@cips1.com
Types of Records Retrieved: Civil courts; Probate courts; Federal courts; Tax liens/Judgments; UCC records
Local Retrieval Area: IN-Marion. **Correspondent Relationships:** Indiana.
Add'l Information: Established 1992. Normal turnaround time- 2-3 days. Projects billed by number of names searched. Terms: net 30 days. They specialize in public record research and document filing & retrieval at Indiana Secretary of State and Indiana Counties, plus all federal, state, & local government offices located in Marion County.

Central Legal Services

PO Box 150, Bend, OR 97709-0150
Phone: 800-599-8133; 541-389-8133 **Fax:** 541-388-5033
mlong@empnet.com
Types of Records Retrieved: Civil, criminal and probate courts; Real Estate; Tax liens/Judgments; UCC records; Vital records

Local Retrieval Area: OR-Crook, Deschutes, Jefferson

Add'l Information: Established 1977. Normal turnaround time- 48 hours. Expedited service available. Projects billed by number of names searched. Remit upon invoice. They will file/record UCC and real estate documents on behalf of clients on a same or next day basis in Deschutes County only. PI license# 1998022. A licensed PI in OR. They perform service of process.

Central New York Abstract Corp

PO Box 268, 24 Elizabeth St, Utica, NY 13503
Phone: 315-724-1614 **Fax:** 315-724-0563

Types of Records Retrieved: Civil courts; Probate courts; Real Estate; Tax liens/Judgments; UCC records

Local Retrieval Area: NY-Cayuga, Herkimer, Madison, Oneida

Add'l Information: Established 1904. Normal turnaround time- 1-2 days for reports; 1-2 weeks for abstracts. Projects billed by number of names searched. Projects billed by number of records located. 1st project may require prepayment.

Central Tejas Research & Title Services

807 Brazos #607, Austin, TX 78701
Phone: 512-469-6062 **Fax:** 512-469-6053
centraltejas@austin.rr.com

Types of Records Retrieved: Civil courts; Probate courts; Federal courts; Real Estate; Tax liens/Judgments; UCC records

Local Retrieval Area: TX-Bastrop, Caldwell, Hays, Travis, Williamson

Add'l Information: Established 2004. Normal turnaround time- 24-48 hours. Projects billed by number of names searched. Payment due net 30 days. They specialize in document retrieval, document filings, probate & bankruptcy courts; historical deed chains, owner lien encumbrance reports, easements, restrictions & right of ways, Deed of Trust assignment and other real estate related research.

Central Utah Title

PO Box 37, 140 N Main St, Manti, UT 84642
Phone: 435-835-1111 **Fax:** 435-835-8824
centuttitle@manti.com

Types of Records Retrieved: Real Estate; Tax liens/judgments; UCC records

Local Retrieval Area: UT-Sanpete

Add'l Information: Established 1983. Normal turnaround time- 1 week. Projects billed by number of names searched. They specialize in escrow closings.

Central Valley Records Service Inc

2101 Ottawa Ct, Modesto, CA 95356
Phone: 209-524-3849 **Fax:** 209-525-8786
cvrs@sbcglobal.net

Types of Records Retrieved: Civil and criminal courts; Federal Bankruptcy courts; Tax liens/Judgments; UCC records; Vital records

Local Retrieval Area: CA-Merced, San Joaquin, Stanislaus. **Correspondent Relationships:** Tuolumne and Mariposa counties CA.

Add'l Information: Established 1989. Normal turnaround time- 24 hours in Stanislaus & San Joaquin; 24-48 hours in Merced County. Projects billed by number of names searched. Monthly billing available.

Central Wisconsin Title

PO Box 117, Montello, WI 53949
Phone: 608-297-2789 **Fax:** 608-297-9387

Types of Records Retrieved: Real Estate; Tax liens/Judgments

Local Retrieval Area: WI-Adams, Marquette

Add'l Information: Established 1993. 1st project may require prepayment. They specialize in real estate.

Cerro Gordo Abstract Co

10 N Washington #300, Mason City, IA 50401
Phone: 641-423-1145 **Fax:** 641-423-0289

Types of Records Retrieved: Civil, criminal and probate courts; Federal courts; Real Estate; Tax liens/Judgments; UCC records; Vital records

Local Retrieval Area: IA-Cerro Gordo

Add'l Information: Normal turnaround time- 1-2 days. Projects billed by number of names searched. Fee basis may also be per description. They specialize in real estate.

Certified Process & Information Services

1058 W 36th Pl, Yuma, AZ 85365-4583
Phone: 928-341-0756 **Fax:** 928-783-1230
locator@cybertrails.com

Types of Records Retrieved: Civil, criminal and probate courts; Federal courts; Real Estate; Tax liens/Judgments; UCC records; Vital records.

Local Retrieval Area: AZ-Yuma

Add'l Information: Established 1996. Normal turnaround time- 2-3 days. Projects billed by number of names searched. Projects billed by the hour. All projects require prepayment. They specialize in skiptracing as well as document retrieval. A licensed PI in AZ. They perform service of process.

Cestero & Co Inc

PO Box 194511, San Juan, PR 00919-4511
Phone: 888-764-7229; 787-764-7229 **Fax:** 787-766-0881
www.puertoricoproserve.com **email:** rcestero@coqui.net

Types of Records Retrieved: Civil, criminal and probate courts; Federal courts; UCC records; Tax liens/Judgments

Local Retrieval Area: All of Puerto Rico

Add'l Information: Established 1994. Normal turnaround time- 48-72 hours. Projects billed by the hour. 1st project may require prepayment. Mr. Reinaldo E. Cestero is a licensed private investigator who provides Asset Identification, Service of Process, Accident and Civil case investigations. He is bilingual and provides reports in English or Spanish. Document retrieval is also provided. A licensed PI in PR. Perform service of process.

Cfacts

650 Smithfield St #1850, Pittsburgh, PA 15222
Phone: 800-233-4747; 412-232-3232 **Fax:** 800-332-2317; 412-232-0903
www.cfacts.com **email:** inquire@cfacts.com

Types of Records Retrieved: Civil courts; Probate courts; Federal courts; Real Estate; Tax liens/Judgments; UCC records

Local Retrieval Area: PA-Allegheny, Beaver, Butler, Washington, Westmoreland. **Correspondent Relationships:** nationwide.

Add'l Information: Established 1984. Normal turnaround time- 48 hours. Projects are billed by the number of addresses searched. Terms aret 15 days. Cfacts offers a full complement of title & closing services. They emphasize single-source convenience, local resources and personalized attention. They have been in operation since 1984.

Chaffee Title-Abstract Co

225 "G" St, Salida, CO 81201
Phone: 719-539-2215 **Fax:** 719-539-2588
chaffeetitle@amigo.net

Types of Records Retrieved: Real Estate; Tax liens/judgments; UCC records

Local Retrieval Area: CO-Chaffee

Add'l Information: Established 1968. Normal turnaround time- 3 days. Fee basis will vary by the type of project. They specialize in real estate searching.

Chambers Investigations

606 49th St W, Bradenton, FL 34209
Phone: 800-792-1107; 941-747-7265 **Fax:** 941-798-2074
slipinn@aol.com

Types of Records Retrieved: Civil, criminal and probate courts; Real Estate; Tax liens/Judgments; UCC records; Vital records

Local Retrieval Area: FL-Manatee, Sarasota. **Correspondent Relationships:** nationwide.

Add'l Information: Established 1982. Normal turnaround time- 24 hours. Projects billed by the hour. All projects require prepayment. Credit cards accepted. Mastercard, Visa accpeted. They specialize in private investigations and intelligence information such as bank accounts, non-public phones, cellular and hidden assets. They perform service of process.

Charles F Edgar & Associates Inc
2724 10th Ave SW, Huntsville, AL 35805-4136
Phone: 256-539-7761 **Fax:** 256-539-7768
cfea@cfedgar.com

Types of Records Retrieved: Civil, criminal and probate courts; Federal courts; Real Estate; Tax liens/Judgments; UCC records

Local Retrieval Area: AL-34 Counties; TN-10 Counties

Add'l Information: Established 1974. Normal turnaround time- 1-2 days. Projects billed by number of names searched. Terms: net 30 days. For over 20 years this firm handles civil and criminal investigations, surveillance, background investigations, public record checks, video depositions and process services. A licensed PI in AL. They perform service of process.

Charles Jones Inc
PO Box 8488, Trenton, NJ 08650-8488
Phone: 800-792-8888; 609-538-1000 **Fax:** 800-883-0677; 609-883-0677
www.charlesjones.com **email:** info@charlesjones.com

Types of Records Retrieved: Civil courts; Probate courts; Federal courts; Real Estate; Tax liens/Judgments; UCC records

Local Retrieval Area: NJ-Atlantic, Bergen, Burlington, Camden, Cape May, Cumberland, Essex, Gloucester, Hudson, Hunterdon, Mercer, Middlesex, Monmouth, Morris, Ocean, Passaic, Salem, Somerset, Sussex, Union, Warren. **Correspondent Relationships:** Mid-Atlantic states.

Add'l Information: Established 1911. Normal turnaround time- 1-10 days. Projects billed by number of names searched. Projects billed by number of records located. 1st project may require prepayment. Credit cards accepted. Charles Jones has been an info services leader for over 90 years. Services include statewide lien searches and certified patriot name searches.

Charley's Legal Angels
1283 Lake Arrowhead Station, Wateska, GA 30183
Phone: 770-310-4047 **Fax:** 770-720-9701

Types of Records Retrieved: Civil, criminal and probate courts; Federal courts; Real Estate; Tax liens/Judgments; UCC records; Vital records

Local Retrieval Area: GA-Bartow, Cherokee, Cobb, De Kalb, Fulton, Gwinnett. **Correspondent Relationships:** Clayton, Douglas, Forsythe, Henry counties GA.

Add'l Information: Established 1994. Normal turnaround time- 24 hours for Gwinnett and Cobb counties, 24-48 hours for Cherokee, Fulton and De Kalb counties. Expedited service available. Projects billed by number of names searched. Terms: net 30 days. They specialize in criminal checks for pre-employment screening, process serving, document retrieval, legal research, bankruptcy services and online research. Skiptracing and investigations services are also available. A licensed PI in GA. They perform service of process.

Charlson & Wilson Bonded Abstractors
1213 Hylton Heights Rd #121, Manhatton, KS 66502
Phone: 785-537-2900 **Fax:** 785-537-2904
info@charlsonandwilson.com

Types of Records Retrieved: Civil courts; Probate courts; Real Estate; Tax liens/Judgments; UCC records

Local Retrieval Area: KS-Riley. **Correspondent Relationships:** Pottawatomie County, KS.

Add'l Information: Normal turnaround time- 3-5 days. Projects billed by the hour. All projects require prepayment. The specialize in any kind of title search.

Chautauqua County Abstract Co inc
121 W Main St, Sedan, KS 67361
Phone: 620-725-3215 **Fax:** 620-725-5569

Types of Records Retrieved: Civil, criminal and probate courts; Real Estate; Tax liens/Judgments; UCC records; Vital records

Local Retrieval Area: KS-Chautauqua

Add'l Information: Established 1994. Normal turnaround time- 2-3 days. Fee basis varies by type of transaction. 1st project may require prepayment. They specialize in abstract and title searching.

Cheboygan Title
228 N Main St, Cheboygan, MI 49721
Phone: 866-627-7150; 231-627-3131 **Fax:** 231-627-5191

Types of Records Retrieved: Real Estate; Tax liens/Judgments; UCC records; Vital records

Local Retrieval Area: MI-Cheboygan

Add'l Information: Normal turnaround time- 2-5 days. Fee basis will vary by type of project. 1st project may require prepayment. They specialize in land title searches. They purchased the former Cheboygan Straits Area Title company in 2004.

Check - Pointe, Inc
2309 Plymouth Ln, Cuyahoga Falls, OH 44221
Phone: 330-923-5930 **Fax:** 330-923-5296
check-point@neo.rr.com

Types of Records Retrieved: Civil, criminal and probate courts; Federal courts; Tax liens/Judgments; UCC records

Local Retrieval Area: OH-Portage, Summit. **Correspondent Relationships:** Northeast OH counties.

Add'l Information: Established 1994. Normal turnaround time- same day. Projects billed by number of names searched. Billing can also depend on type of search. 1st project may require prepayment. Payment due upon receipt of invoice. As "Investigative Information" specialists, they can retrieve a wide variety of information in a timely and accurate manner. "Hands-on" document retrieval since 1994. 10 year anniversary in 2004!

Checkered Past Inc
PO Box 1369, Lafayette, IN 47905
Phone: 765-474-3905 **Fax:** 765-474-3795
checkeredpastinc@hotmail.com

Types of Records Retrieved: Civil and criminal courts; Real Estate; Tax liens/Judgments; UCC records

Local Retrieval Area: IN-Boone, Hamilton, Hendricks, Tippecanoe

Add'l Information: Established 1997. Normal turnaround time- 24-48 hours. Projects billed by number of names searched. They specialize in civil and criminal courts; driving records, real estate, tax liens and UCC records.

Cherokee Capitol Abstract Title & Closing
107-109 E Delaware St, Tahlequah, OK 74464
Phone: 918-456-8851 **Fax:** 918-456-8322
ccabst@swbell.net

Types of Records Retrieved: Civil, criminal and probate courts; Real Estate, Tax liens/Judgments; UCC records; Vital records

Local Retrieval Area: OK-Cherokee

Add'l Information: Established 1903. Normal turnaround time- within same day of request. Projects billed by number of records located. 1st project may require prepayment. Lenders may send loan documents via fax at 918-456-7681.

Chesapeake Services
PO Box 470, 202 Anchor Ln., Chester, MD 21619
Phone: 800-834-7938; 410-643-3731 **Fax:** 410-643-4814
tony@friend.ly.net

Types of Records Retrieved: Civil, criminal and probate courts; Real Estate; Tax liens/Judgments; UCC records; Vital records

Local Retrieval Area: MD-Anne Arundel, Caroline, Kent, Queen Anne's, Talbot

Add'l Information: Established 1983. Normal turnaround time- 24-48 hours. Projects billed by number of names searched. Charge by hour for research work. 1st project may require prepayment. Payment net 30 days. They have access to a statewide Court computer system. They can communicate with accounts through Internet e-mail online with State Motor Vehicle Administrations. A licensed PI in MD. They perform service of process.

Cheyenne County Abstract
1024 Jackson St, Sidney, NE 69162
Phone: 308-254-5636 **Fax:** 308-254-6159

cheycoabs@qwest.net

Types of Records Retrieved: Civil courts; Probate courts; Federal courts; Real Estate; Tax liens/Judgments; UCC records

Local Retrieval Area: NE-Cheyenne

Add'l Information: Established 1907. Normal turnaround time- 3-5 days. Projects billed by number of records located.

Cheyenne County Abstract Co

PO Box 9, 130 S 1st E, Cheyenne Wells, CO 80810

Phone: 719-767-5585 **Fax:** 719-767-5029

Types of Records Retrieved: Probate courts; Real Estate; Tax liens/Judgments; UCC records

Local Retrieval Area: CO-Cheyenne

Add'l Information: Established 1907. Normal turnaround time- up to 1 week. Projects billed by number of names searched. Projects billed by the hour. Terms: net 30 days. They specialize in real estate title.

Chicagoland Detective Services Inc

2223 W Lyndale Dr, Chicago, IL 60647-3205

Phone: 877-426-4278; 312-661-0702 or 773-772-2651 **Fax:** 312-661-0734 or 773-772-7319

www.falconpi.com **email:** falconpi@aol.com

Types of Records Retrieved: Civil, criminal and probate courts; Federal courts; Real Estate; Tax liens/Judgments; UCC records; Vital records

Local Retrieval Area: IL-Cook, Du Page, Kane, Lake. **Correspondent Relationships:** nationwide.

Add'l Information: Established 1988. Normal turnaround time- 2 days. Projects billed by the hour. 1st project may require prepayment. Credit cards accepted. Formerly Don C Haworth & Assoc, they provide record retrievals as well as investigation services to the business, insurance, and legal communities. A licensed PI in IL. They perform service of process.

Chilvers Abstract & Title Co

PO Box 204, Pierce, NE 68767

Phone: 402-329-4525 **Fax:** 402-329-4845

Types of Records Retrieved: Probate courts; Real Estate; Tax liens/Judgments; UCC records

Local Retrieval Area: NE-Pierce

Add'l Information: Normal turnaround time- 1-3 days. Fee bases is a flat rate and per record. They specialize in title insurance.

Darlene Chiota

PO Box 1849, Erie, PA 16507-0849

Phone: 814-454-7589 **Fax:** 814-454-7589

Types of Records Retrieved: Civil and criminal courts; Federal courts; Real Estate; Tax liens/Judgments; UCC records

Local Retrieval Area: PA-Erie

Add'l Information: Established 1982. Normal turnaround time- 24-48 hours. Turnaround time is up to 1 week for title searches. Projects billed by number of names searched. Projects billed by number of records located. She requests prepayment for copies, but will invoice for services. She specializes in current owner searches and criminal records.

Chippewa Valley Civil Process

PO Box 188, Chippewa Falls, WI 54729

Phone: 715-289-3922 **Fax:** 715-289-3992

Types of Records Retrieved: Civil and criminal courts

Local Retrieval Area: WI-Chippewa, Eau Claire

Add'l Information: Established 1998. 1st project may require prepayment. Specializing in process service, they also provide court filings, photocopying and skiptracing. They perform service of process.

Choctaw County Abstract & Title

PO Box 636, Hugo, OK 74743

Phone: 580-326-9616 **Fax:** 580-326-6782

Types of Records Retrieved: Civil courts; Probate courts; Real Estate; Tax liens/Judgments; UCC records

Local Retrieval Area: OK-Choctaw

Add'l Information: Established 1978. Normal turnaround time- 1 week. Fee basis will vary by the type of project. 1st project may require prepayment. Clients may make payments upon receipt.

Chouteau County Abstract Co

Box 578, Fort Benton, MT 59442

Phone: 406-622-3221

Types of Records Retrieved: Civil courts; Probate courts; Real Estate; Tax liens/Judgments; UCC records

Local Retrieval Area: MT-Chouteau

Add'l Information: Normal turnaround time- 2-4 days. Projects billed by the hour.

Chreyton Research

145 Larchwood Dr, Painesville Township, OH 44077

Phone: 440-354-0316 **Fax:** 440-354-2677

lms5301@sbcglobal.net

Types of Records Retrieved: Civil, criminal and probate courts; Federal courts; Real Estate; Tax liens/Judgments; UCC records; Vital records

Local Retrieval Area: OH-Geauga, Lake

Add'l Information: Established 2004. Normal turnaround time- 24 hours or less. Expedited service available. Projects billed by number of names searched. Will invoice, payment due net 30 days.

CICS Employment Services LLC

1135 N Widow Creek Rd, Otis, OR 97368

Phone: 800-660-0507; **Fax:** 888-247-3683; 541-994-7159

www.cicsecurity.com **email:** goodwin@harborside.com

Types of Records Retrieved: Civil, criminal and probate courts; Federal courts; Real Estate; Tax liens/Judgments; UCC records

Local Retrieval Area: OR-Clackamas, Lane, Lincoln, Marion, Multnomah, Washington: WA-Clark. **Correspondent Relationships:** Oregon, Utah, Colorado, Washington counties.

Add'l Information: Established 1995. Normal turnaround time- 24 hours or same day. Projects billed by number of names searched. Projects billed by number of records located. They specialize in criminal background checks and also provide DMV reports, real estate information and document retrieval. A licensed PI in OR. They perform service of process.

Citizen's Title Co

104 E Race Ave, Searcy, AR 72143

Phone: 501-268-5571 **Fax:** 501-268-7378

Types of Records Retrieved: Civil, criminal and probate courts; Real Estate; Tax liens/Judgments; UCC records

Local Retrieval Area: AR-White

Add'l Information: Established 1963. Normal turnaround time- up to 1 week. Fee basis will vary by type of project. 1st project may require prepayment. They specialize in land title and title insurance.

City Abstract

PO Box 257, Scottsbluff, NE 69363

Phone: 308-632-4021 **Fax:** 308-635-2896

Types of Records Retrieved: Real Estate; Tax liens/Judgments

Local Retrieval Area: NE-Banner, Scotts Bluff

Add'l Information: Established 1984. 1st project may require prepayment. They specialize in real estate.

Civil Claims Service

PO Box 33898, Juneau, AK 99803

Phone: 907-364-2714 **Fax:** 907-364-2313

tshanley@gci.net

Types of Records Retrieved: Civil, criminal and probate courts; Federal courts; Real Estate; Tax liens/Judgments; UCC records

Local Retrieval Area: AK-Haines, Juneau, Ketchikan Gateway, Sitka, Skagway-Hoonah-Angoon, Wrangell-Petersburg

Add'l Information: Established 1982. Normal turnaround time- 24-48 hours. Expedited service available. The billing method is dependant on nature of the job. They specialize in civil process service, investigations, and repossessions. A licensed PI in AK. They perform service of process.

CJRS

23 W Central Entrance #341, Duluth, MN 55811-3433

Phone: 866-758-7903; 218-310-1914 **Fax:** 866-758-7903; cjrs@innoport.com

Types of Records Retrieved: Civil, criminal and probate courts; Federal courts; Real Estate; Tax liens/Judgments; UCC records; Vital records

Local Retrieval Area: MN-Douglas, St. Louis. **Correspondent Relationships:** statewide.

Add'l Information: Established 2004. Normal turnaround time- 2 days. Expedited service available. Projects billed by number of names searched. 1st project may require prepayment. Payment through PayPal. CJRS provides public record retrieval searches to businesses and law firms in the Twin Ports region, electronic retrieval available nationwide as possible.

Clarifacts Inc

130 N Central Ave #309, Phoenix, AZ 85004

Phone: 800-318-0553; 602-258-8858 **Fax:** 602-258-7177

www.clarifacts.com **email:** kevin@clarifacts.com

Types of Records Retrieved: Civil and criminal courts

Local Retrieval Area: AZ-Maricopa

Add'l Information: Established 2001. Normal turnaround time- 24-48 hours. Projects billed by number of names searched. Monthly billings. Professional, reliable researchers located just blocks from the courthouse of the nation's 4th most-populated county. A licensed PI in AZ.

Clark Abstract & Title Co

PO Box 253, Clark, SD 57225

Phone: 605-532-3812 **Fax:** 605-532-3812

Types of Records Retrieved: Probate courts; Real Estate; Tax liens/Judgments; UCC records; Vital records

Local Retrieval Area: SD-Clark

Add'l Information: Established 1980. Normal turnaround time- 2-3 days. Fee basis varies by type of transaction. Payment due on delivery. Abstracts of title, title insurance and title reports are our main business.

Clark County Abstract & Title Co Inc

310 Clay St, Arkadelphia, AR 71923

Phone: 870-246-2821 **Fax:** 870-246-9501

Types of Records Retrieved: Civil, criminal and probate courts; Real Estate; Tax liens/Judgments; UCC records

Local Retrieval Area: AR-Clark

Add'l Information: Established 1907. Normal turnaround time- 3 days. Expedited service available. Projects billed by number of names searched. Projects billed by number of records located. Projects billed by the hour. Fee basis will vary by type of project. 1st project may require prepayment.

Clarke Investigations Inc

1405 Ridgecrest Rd, Edmond, OK 73013

Phone: 405-844-7300 **Fax:** 405-844-8196

clarkeinvestigations@hotmail.com

Types of Records Retrieved: Civil, criminal and probate courts; Federal courts; Real Estate; Tax liens/Judgments; UCC records; Vital records

Local Retrieval Area: OK-Bryan, Caddo, Canadian, Carter, Cherokee, Cleveland, Comanche, Creek, Custer, Delaware, Dewey, Ellis, Garfield, Garvin, Grady, Greer, Harmon, Harper, Jackson, Jackson, Kay, Kingfisher, Kiowa, Lincoln, Logan, Mayes, McClain, Muskogee, Noble, Oklahoma, Okmulgee, Payne, Roger Mills, Rogers, Texas, Tillman, Tulsa, Wagoner, Washington, Woodward. **Correspondent Relationships:** statewide.

Add'l Information: Established 1996. Normal turnaround time- 24-48 hours. Projects billed by number of names searched. Will invoice monthly. They specialize in aircraft ownership and pilot licensing nationwide and also do Oklahoma DMV histories and license plate registrations. They also do work for abstractors. Daily, hands-on service to all Oklahoma counties. A licensed PI in OK. They perform service of process.

Brad Clarkson

PO Box 582, Maryville, IL 62062

Phone: 618-344-0656 **Fax:** 618-344-0656

http://clarksondiversified.com **email:** clarkson@clarksondiversified.com

Types of Records Retrieved: Civil and criminal courts: Probate courts; Federal courts; Real Estate; Tax liens/Judgments; UCC records; Vital records

Local Retrieval Area: IL-Madison, St. Clair; MO-St. Charles, St. Louis, St. Louis City

Add'l Information: Established 1993. Normal turnaround time- 1-3 days, depending on court. Expedited service available. Projects billed by number of names searched. 1st project may require prepayment. Credit cards accepted. Paypal accepted. He specializes in civil and criminal courts, Eastern Missouri & Southern Illinois Federal courts, real estate, tax liens, UCC records and probate.

Clay County Abstract Co

403 Center Ave #600, Moorhead, MN 56560-1975

Phone: 218-233-1358 **Fax:** 218-233-1359

Types of Records Retrieved: Civil courts; Probate courts; Federal courts; Real Estate; Tax liens/Judgments; UCC records

Local Retrieval Area: MN-Clay; ND-Cass. **Correspondent Relationships:** Becker, Otter Tail, Norman, Polk, Red Lake, Wilkin, Mahnomen, Marshall, Kittson, Roseau counties.

Add'l Information: Established 1832. Normal turnaround time- 5-10 days. Projects billed by number of names searched. Personal checks are accepted. They are across the river from Fargo, North Dakota. They perform service of process.

Clay County Title

12 Austin St, Vermillion, SD 57069

Phone: 605-624-2068

Types of Records Retrieved: Real Estate; Tax liens/Judgments.

Local Retrieval Area: SD-Clay

Add'l Information: 1st project may require prepayment. They specialize in real estate.

Clayton County Abstract Co

126 S Main, Elkader, IA 52043

Phone: 563-245-1430 **Fax:** 563-245-1490

abstract@alpinecom.net

Types of Records Retrieved: Civil, criminal and probate courts; Real Estate; Tax liens/Judgments; UCC records; Vital records

Local Retrieval Area: IA-Clayton

Add'l Information: Established 1878. Normal turnaround time- 24-48 hours. Fee basis will vary by the type of project.

Clayton Title Services Inc

PO Box 327, 8 Main St, Clayton, NM 88415

Phone: 505-374-9789 **Fax:** 505-374-8381

Types of Records Retrieved: Civil courts; Probate courts; Real Estate; Tax liens/Judgments; UCC records; Vital records

Local Retrieval Area: NM-Union

Add'l Information: Established 1978. Normal turnaround time- 5-10 days. Fee basis will vary by the type of project. 1st project may require prepayment. They specialize in abstracts, title insurance, closings, oil and gas searches, mineral searches.

Clear Creek-Gelpin Abstract & Title Corp

PO Box 545, 619 5th St, Georgetown, CO 80444
Phone: 303-569-2391 **Fax:** 303-569-2670
www.ccgat.com **email:** rjonas@ccgat.com

Types of Records Retrieved: Real Estate

Local Retrieval Area: CO-Clear Creek, Gilpin

Add'l Information: Established 1966. Normal turnaround time- 3-5 days. Fee basis will vary by the type of project. 1st project may require prepayment. They specialize in real estate and title matters.

Clear Title Co

140 S Washington St, La Grange, TX 78945-2629
Phone: 979-968-5885 **Fax:** 979-968-6082
www.cleartitlecompany.com **email:** cleartitle@cmaaccess.com

Types of Records Retrieved: Civil, criminal and probate courts; Real Estate; Tax liens/Judgments; UCC records; Vital records

Local Retrieval Area: TX-Fayette

Add'l Information: Normal turnaround time- up to 1 week as court is not computerized. Fee basis will vary by the type of project. 1st project may require prepayment.

Cleveland & Carl Inv

PO Box 5358, Central Point, OR 97502-0054
Phone: 800-888-6629; 541-535-6005 **Fax:** 541-535-3411
gcwrightjr@aol.com

Types of Records Retrieved: Civil, criminal and probate courts; Federal courts; Real Estate; Tax liens/Judgments; UCC records; Vital records

Local Retrieval Area: CA-Siskiyou; OR-Jackson, Josephine, Klamath, Lane, Polk. **Correspondent Relationships:** statewide and California.

Add'l Information: Established 1983. Normal turnaround time- up to 3 days. Expedited service available. Projects billed by number of names searched. Projects billed by the hour. 1st project may require prepayment. Will bill for established clients. A licensed PI in OR, CA.. They perform service of process.

Clinton Abstract Co Inc

519 Gary Blvd, Clinton, OK 73601
Phone: 580-323-3025 **Fax:** 580-323-0524

Types of Records Retrieved: Civil courts; Probate courts; Real Estate; Tax liens/Judgments; UCC records

Local Retrieval Area: OK-Custer

Add'l Information: Established 1941. Normal turnaround time- 2 days. Copy charges will be added to the fee. Personal checks are accepted.

Clovis Title & Abstract Ltd

420 Mitchell St, Clovis, NM 88101
Phone: 505-762-4403 **Fax:** 505-762-4404

Types of Records Retrieved: Civil, criminal and probate courts; Federal courts; Real Estate; Tax liens/Judgments; UCC records

Local Retrieval Area: NM-Curry

Add'l Information: Established 1908. Normal turnaround time- 24 hours to 2 days. Projects billed by number of names searched. Personal checks are accepted. They specialize in title searches, abstracts of title, title insurance, lien searches and criminal searches. They also do loan closing on new loans or refinances. They also search for financing statements in Curry County, NM.

CLUSO Inc

PO Box 227503, Dallas, TX 75222-7503
Phone: 866-30-CLUSO; 214-999-1140 **Fax:** 214-853-4423
www.cluso.com **email:** sales@cluso.com

Types of Records Retrieved: Civil and criminal courts; Federal Courts; Tax liens/Judgments.

Local Retrieval Area: TX- Dallas, Kaufman, Rockwall, Tarrant. **Correspondent Relationships:** nationwide.

Add'l Information: Established 1999. Normal turnaround time- 24-hours. 1st project may require prepayment. CLUSO Inc provides courthouse research for the Dallas/Ft. Worth area every day. They also offer national and international background services, including pre-employment and tenant screening.

CMS (Consumer Marketing Services)

6500 New Venture Gear Dr, East Syracuse, NY 13057
Phone: 800-388-1365; 315-476-8414 **Fax:** 315-476-7945
www.cmsinfonet.com **email:** j.decuffa@cmsinfonet.com

Types of Records Retrieved: Civil, criminal and probate courts; Federal courts; Real Estate; Tax liens/Judgments; UCC records

Local Retrieval Area: NY-Albany, Broome, Cayuga, Chemung, Chenango, Columbia, Cortland, Delaware, Dutchess, Erie, Fulton, Genesee, Greene, Herkimer, Jefferson, Livingston, Madison, Monroe, Montgomery, Niagara, Oneida, Onondaga, Ontario, Orange, Orleans, Oswego, Otsego, Putnam, Rensselaer, St Lawrence, Saratoga, Schenectady, Schoharie, Schuyler, Seneca, Steuben, Sullivan, Tioga, Tompkins, Ulster, Wayne, Westchester, Wyoming, Yates. **Correspondent Relationships:** nationwide.

Add'l Information: Established 1987. Normal turnaround time- 24-48 hours. Expedited service available. Fees depend on type of search performed. 1st project may require prepayment. Credit cards accepted. Terms: net 30 days. CMS specializes in all functions of abstract/document retrieval within the county, state and federal levels. There are 22 CMS branch offices throughout New York.

CMS Information Services

PO Box 1001, Buffalo, NY 14205
Phone: 716-812-2587
aa262@ustrackers.com

Types of Records Retrieved: Real Estate; Tax liens/Judgments; UCC records; Vital records

Local Retrieval Area: NY-Erie, Monroe, Niagara

Add'l Information: Established 1999. Normal turnaround time- 72 hours. Projects billed by the hour. 1st project may require prepayment.

CMT Abstract

380 Catherine St, Somerville, NJ 08876
Phone: 908-722-6565 **Fax:** 908-722-5011
staff@cmtabstract.com

Types of Records Retrieved: Probate courts; Real Estate; Tax liens/Judgments; UCC records

Local Retrieval Area: NJ-Somerset

Add'l Information: Established 1986. Normal turnaround time- 24 hours. Fee basis will vary by type of project. They perform title, judgments, and UCC searches, and property searches at the county level.

CN Search LLC

239 Baileyville Rd, Middlefield, CT 06455
Phone: 860-349-3772 **Fax:** 860-349-8581
cnsearchct@comcast.net

Types of Records Retrieved: Civil and criminal courts; Federal courts; Tax liens/Judgments; UCC records

Local Retrieval Area: CT-Fairfield, Hartford, Litchfield, Middlesex, New Haven, New London, Tolland, Windham. **Correspondent Relationships:** nationwide and Canada.

Add'l Information: Established 1986. Normal turnaround time- 24 hours for courts; other times vary with jurisdiction. Projects billed by number of names searched. 1st project may require prepayment. Payment due upon receipt of invoice. Perform UCC, corporate searches and record retrieval. Visits Sec of State daily. Will search courts statewide.

Coast to Coast Abstracting

1525 Dilbeck Dr, Spring Hill, FL 34610
Phone: 352-442-1500 **Fax:** 727-856-9524
shwatt@tampabay.rr.com

Types of Records Retrieved: Probate courts; Real Estate; Tax liens/Judgments; UCC records

Local Retrieval: FL-Citrus, Hernando, Hillsborough, Pasco, Polk, Sumter

Add'l Information: Established 2004. Normal turnaround time- 24-48 hours. Billed according to search or services ordered. Will invoice. They specialize in document retrieval & recordings; also bringdowns, current owner & full searches. They have 6 years experience.

Coast to Coast Research Network

PO Box 7018, Loudon, NH 03307
Phone: 603-783-8034 **Fax:** 603-783-8038
jlectcrn@aol.com

Types of Records Retrieved: Civil, criminal and probate courts; Federal Courts; Real Estate; Tax liens/Judgments; UCC records; Vital records

Local Retrieval Area: NH-all counties

Add'l Information: Established 1999. Normal turnaround time- 24-72 hours. Projects billed by number of names searched. Terms are net 30 days. They specialize in UCC, corporate searches, property title updates on current owner, tax liens, voter registration and real estate assessment records found in towns and cities, also criminal and civil searches in all courts.

Coastal Office Dimensions

PO Box 10612, Pensacola, FL 32524-0612
Phone: 850-484-8098 **Fax:** 850-484-4583
CoastalSGL@aol.com

Types of Records Retrieved: Civil, criminal and probate courts; Federal courts; Real Estate; Tax liens/Judgments; UCC records; Vital records

Local Retrieval Area: FL-Escambia, Monroe, Santa Rosa

Add'l Information: Established 1995. Normal turnaround time- 24-48 hours. Projects billed by number of names searched. Projects billed by number of records located. 1st project may require prepayment. They specialize in pre-employment searches, including felony and misdemeanor, federal criminal and federal civil.

Coastal Research

PO Box 7343, Arroyo Grande, CA 93421
Phone: 805-710-4926 **Fax:** 805-473-1431
coastalresearch1@aol.com

Types of Records Retrieved: Civil and criminal courts; Real Estate; Tax liens/Judgments

Local Retrieval Area: CA-San Luis Opispo, Santa Barbara. **Correspondent Relationships:** statewide.

Add'l Information: Established 2004. Normal turnaround time- 24-48 hours. Projects billed by number of names searched. 1st project may require prepayment. Credit cards are accepted. They personally go to courthouses on daily basis. They also perform credit checks.

Coit Enterprises

2560 Newport Ave #A, Omaha, NE 68112-3326
Phone: 402-451-0462 **Fax:** 402-451-3949
www.terrycoit.com **email:** terry@terrycoit.com

Types of Records Retrieved: Civil, criminal and probate courts; Federal courts; Real Estate; Tax liens/Judgments

Local Retrieval Area: IA-Mills, Pottawattamie; NE-Dodge, Douglas, Sarpy, Washington

Add'l Information: Established 1994. Normal turnaround time- next day for Douglas, Pottawattamie, and Sarpy counties; 2-7 business days for others counties. Projects billed by number of names searched. Also, by jurisdiction. Will bill monthly. Professional, personalized service provided by the owners. Not all services/retrievals listed are available in all counties.

Coke County Abstract Co

PO Box 69, 3 E 6th St, Robert Lee, TX 76945
Phone: 325-453-2049 **Fax:** 325-453-2345

Types of Records Retrieved: Civil, criminal and probate courts; Real Estate; Tax liens/Judgments; UCC records; Vital records

Local Retrieval Area: TX-Coke

Add'l Information: Established 1938. Normal turnaround time- 1-2 days. Fee basis will vary by the type of project. 1st project may require prepayment.

Coleman County Title Co

PO Box 865, 108 W Liveoak St, Coleman, TX 76834-0865
Phone: 325-625-4628 **Fax:** 325-625-4417

Types of Records Retrieved: Probate courts; Real Estate; Tax liens/Judgments; UCC records

Local Retrieval Area: TX-Coleman

Add'l Information: Normal turnaround time- up to 5 days. Projects billed by the hour. 1st project may require prepayment.

Colfax County Title & Abstract Co

1109 C St, Schuyler, NE 68661
Phone: 402-352-2027 **Fax:** 402-352-2027

Types of Records Retrieved: Civil courts; Probate courts; Real Estate; Tax liens/Judgments; UCC records

Local Retrieval Area: NE-Butler, Colfax. **Correspondent Relationships:** nationwide.

Add'l Information: Established 1988. Normal turnaround time- 2 days. Projects billed by number of names searched. 1st project may require prepayment. Personal checks are accepted.

Collective Intelligence Inc

14622 Ventura Blvd #419, Sherman Oaks, CA 91403
Phone: 800-436-1969; 818-904-0655 **Fax:** 818-901-7745
www.collintel.com **email:** erika@collintel.com

Types of Records Retrieved: Civil, criminal and probate courts; Federal courts; Vital records

Local Retrieval Area: CA-Los Angeles, Orange, Riverside, San Bernardino, San Diego, San Luis Obispo, Santa Barbara, Ventura. **Correspondent Relationships:** statewide.

Add'l Information: Established 2001. Normal turnaround time- 24-48 hours. Projects billed by number of names searched. Projects billed by the hour. Credit cards accepted. A private investigation/research company providing on-site record search & retrieval. They offer expedient & accurate results with services available at the county, state & federal levels. Prices vary by area & service. A licensed PI in CA.

Collier Abstracts Inc

107 N Main St, Smith Center, KS 66967-0254
Phone: 785-282-3351 **Fax:** 785-282-3351

Types of Records Retrieved: Civil courts; Probate courts; Real Estate; Tax liens/Judgments; UCC records

Local Retrieval Area: KS-Smith

Add'l Information: Established 1930. Normal turnaround time- up to 1 week. Fee basis varies by type of transaction. They request prepayment from out of state clients, but will invoice established customers.

Collier Connections

309 Co Rd 530, Jackson, MO 63755
Phone: 573-833-6349 **Fax:** 573-833-6166

Types of Records Retrieved: Real Estate; Tax liens/Judgments

Local Retrieval Area: MO-Bollinger, Cape Girardeau, Perry, Scott, St. Francois, Ste. Genevieve, Stoddard

Add'l Information: Established 2000. Normal turnaround time- 24-48 hours. Projects billed by number of names searched. They invoice 2 weeks to 30 day net. The principal of the company has worked 10 years at the Cape Girardeau County Recorder's Office. She is very skilled in land records & retrieval services. Cell # is 573-576-3035. She has done document retrieval and current owner searches for last 4 years.

Colonial Valley Abstract Co

216 E Market St #1, York, PA 17403
Phone: 717-848-2871 **Fax:** 717-845-6161
cva@blazenet.net

Types of Records Retrieved: Real Estate; Tax liens/judgments; UCC records

Local Retrieval Area: PA-Adams, Franklin, Lancaster, York

Add'l Information: Normal turnaround time- 5 days. Fee basis will vary by the type of project. 1st project may require prepayment. They specialize in real estate.

Colorado County Abstract Co

PO Box 428, 315 Walnut St, Columbus, TX 78934
Phone: 979-732-2213 **Fax:** 979-732-6096

Types of Records Retrieved: Real Estate; Tax liens/judgments; UCC records

Local Retrieval Area: TX-Colorado

Add'l Information: Normal turnaround time- 2-3 days. Fee basis will vary by the type of project. 1st project may require prepayment.

Colorado Records Search Inc

5025 S Federal Blvd, Englewood, CO 80110
Phone: 800-645-7712; 303-797-6831 **Fax:** 800-988-2303; 303-797-8329
colorecord@aol.com

Types of Records Retrieved: Civil, criminal and probate courts; Federal courts; Real Estate; Tax liens/Judgments; UCC records; Vital records

Local Retrieval Area: CO-Adams, Arapahoe, Archuleta, Baca, Boulder, Broomfield, Cheyenne, Clear Creek, Delta, Denver, Douglas, Eagle, El Paso, Elbert, Fremont, Garfield, Gilpin, Gunnison, Jefferson, La Plata, Larimer, Las Animas, Mesa, Montezuma, Montrose, Morgan, Ouray, Park, Pitkin, Pueblo, Rio Grande, Routt, San Miguel, Teller, Weld. **Correspondent Relationships:** statewide and elsewhere.

Add'l Information: Established 1986. Normal turnaround time- 24-48 hours. Projects billed by number of names searched. They specialize in public record retrieval. They perform service of process.

Colorado Records Sooner

3210 Huron Peak Ave, Superior, CO 80027
Phone: 303-494-2132 **Fax:** 303-494-2133
sooner93@aol.com

Types of Records Retrieved: Civil courts; Federal courts; Real Estate, Tax liens/Judgments; UCC records; Vital records

Local Retrieval Area: CO-Adams, Arapahoe, Boulder, Broomfield, Denver, Douglas, El Paso, Grand, Jefferson, Larimer, Weld

Add'l Information: Established 1993. Normal turnaround time- 24 hours or less. Projects billed by number of names searched. 1st project may require prepayment. They specialize in limited title/O&E reports, document retrieval and recordings with or without date.

Colton & Associates Inc

PO Box 15433, Clearwater, FL 33766-5433
Phone: 800-704-6699; 727-789-0485 **Fax:** 727-734-8413
www.intelligencesource.com **email:** gregg@intelligencesource.com

Types of Records Retrieved: Civil, criminal and probate courts; Federal courts; Real Estate; Tax liens/Judgments; UCC records; Vital records

Local Retrieval Area: FL-Hillsborough, Pasco, Pinellas, Sarasota. **Correspondent Relationships:** nationwide for criminal and civil records only.

Add'l Information: Established 1988. Normal turnaround time- 2 business days. Projects billed by number of names searched. 1st project may require prepayment. Terms: net 10 days. They specialize in statewide criminal histories for CO, FL and TX as well as loss prevention, claims investigations, employment screening, process service, and business intelligence. A licensed PI in FL. They perform service of process.

Comanche Abstract & Title Co

120 E Main, PO Box 41, Coldwater, KS 67029
Phone: 620-582-2125 **Fax:** 620-582-2125

Types of Records Retrieved: Civil, criminal and probate courts; Real Estate; Tax liens/Judgments; UCC records

Local Retrieval Area: KS-Comanche

Add'l Information: Established 1950. Normal turnaround time- 7-10 days. Projects billed by number of names searched. Projects billed by number of records located. Personal checks are accepted. They specialize in title searches, ownership, mineral interest, leasehold, oil and gas searches, and certificates of title and abstracts.

Comanche County Abstract Co

PO Box 747, 106 N Austin St, Comanche, TX 76442
Phone: 325-356-2564 **Fax:** 325-356-3066

Types of Records Retrieved: Civil, criminal and probate courts; Real Estate; Tax liens/Judgments; UCC records; Vital records

Local Retrieval Area: TX-Comanche

Add'l Information: Normal turnaround time- 2-5 days. Fee basis will vary by type of project. 1st project may require prepayment.

Commercial Process Serving Inc

674 County Sq Dr #107, Ventura, CA 93003
Phone: 800-382-0088; 805-650-9291 **Fax:** 805-658-8170
www.comproserve.net

Types of Records Retrieved: Civil, criminal and probate courts

Local Retrieval Area: CA-Santa Barbara, Ventura. **Correspondent Relationships:** Los Angeles, Orange, Santa Barbara, San Bernardino, Riverside, San Diego counties.

Add'l Information: Established 1992. Normal turnaround time- varied, depending on project. Projects billed by the hour. 1st project may require prepayment. Personal checks accepted. They specialize in court filings, fax filings, process serving and deposition interpreting (English/Spanish). They perform service of process.

Commonwealth Inv Agency

3431 Kathleen Ave, Allentown, PA 18103-7916
Phone: 610-433-2325 **Fax:** 610-821-8627
www.commonwealthdetectives.com **email:** info@commonwealthdetectives.com

Types of Records Retrieved: Civil, criminal and probate courts; Federal courts; Real Estate; Tax liens/Judgments; UCC records; Vital records

Local Retrieval Area: PA-Berks, Bucks, Lehigh, Northampton

Add'l Information: Normal turnaround time- 1-3 days. Projects billed by the hour. 1st project may require prepayment. They are a full service private investigations firm. A licensed PI in PA. They perform service of process.

Community Title Co

302 N University Dr, Nacogdoches, TX 75961
Phone: 936-559-7900 **Fax:** 936-559-7977
www.communitytitle.com

Types of Records Retrieved: Civil, criminal and probate courts; Real Estate; Tax liens/Judgments; UCC records; Vital records

Local Retrieval Area: TX-Angelina, Nacogdoches. **Correspondent Relationships:** San Augustine and Sabine counties.

Add'l Information: Normal turnaround time- up to 1 week. Projects billed by the hour. 1st project may require prepayment. Payment due upon receipt of bill. Formerly East Texas Title & Abstract Co. Now has a branch office in Lutkin, 936-634-1600.

Comparable Sales Research

7 N Cascade #C, Montrose, CO 81401
Phone: 970-249-2118 **Fax:** 970-249-6482
lynnv@montrose.net

Types of Records Retrieved: Real Estate; Tax liens/judgments; UCC records

Local Retrieval Area: CO-Delta, Montrose, Ouray. **Correspondent Relationships:** Gunnison county CO.

Add'l Information: Established 1991. Normal turnaround time- 24 to 36 hours. Projects billed by number of records located. 1st project may require prepayment. They have available a comprehensive comparable sales database. They can tailor a commercial, single family or vacant comparable report for you for the 3 counties they serve. Several types of reports & statistical reports are available. Call for info.

Compass Investigations

408 S Andrews Ave #205, Ft Lauderdale, FL 33301
Phone: 954-527-5722 **Fax:** 954-527-4451
www.compassinvestigations.net **email:** sheri@compassinvestigations.net

Types of Records Retrieved: Civil, criminal and probate courts; Federal courts; Real Estate; Tax liens/Judgments; UCC records; Vital records

Local Retrieval Area: FL-Broward, Dade, Palm Beach. **Correspondent Relationships:** Florida.

Add'l Information: Established 1986. Normal turnaround time- same day. Projects billed by number of names searched. Projects billed by the hour. 1st project may require prepayment. They specialize in record research, surveillance and process service. Their office is located next to the courthouse. A licensed PI in FL. They perform service of process.

Compex Legal Services

2040 North Loop W #200, Houston, TX 77018-8113
Phone: 713-861-3900 **Fax:** 713-864-0439
www.compexlegal.com **email:** cservice@compexlegal.com

Types of Records Retrieved: Civil, criminal and probate courts; Federal courts; Vital records

Local Retrieval Area: TX-Fort Bend, Galveston, Harris, Jefferson, Montgomery. **Correspondent Relationships:** Bexar, Cameron, Dallas, Hidalgo, Jefferson, Tarrant.

Add'l Information: Established 1974. Normal turnaround time- 2-3 days. Projects billed by number of records located. Projects billed by the hour. All projects require prepayment. Formerly MRS Datascope Inc, they specialize in record retrieval for pretrial discovery, complete litigation support services, court reporters and legal video. They also do business and medical searches. They perform service of process.

🏛Complete Corporate Services of Alaska

PO Box 33735, 4009 Diane Rd, Juneau, AK 99803
Phone: 907-790-4956 **Fax:** 907-790-4954

Types of Records Retrieved: Civil, criminal and probate courts; Federal courts; Real Estate; Tax liens/Judgments; UCC records

Local Retrieval Area: AK-Anchorage, Haines, Juneau, Ketchikan Gateway, Prince of Wales-Outer Ketchikan, Sitka, Skagway-Hoonah-Angoon, Wrangell-Petersburg Boroughs. **Correspondent Relationships:** Alaska.

Add'l Information: Established 1991. Normal turnaround time- same day for most records. Fee basis will vary by the type of project. All projects require prepayment. They also will accept personal checks. Located in the capitol city, they specialize in searches at the State level also at UCC central. Does searches and recording of corporat records. They also provide service to Southern Alaska They perform service of process.

Compu-Fact Research Inc

4 Silkrose Ct, St Peters, MO 63376-7769
Phone: 636-477-1115, 618-239-0677 **Fax:** 636-477-1115
compufact@hotmail.com

Types of Records Retrieved: Civil, criminal and probate courts; Real Estate; Tax liens/Judgments; UCC records

Local Retrieval Area: IL-Madison, St. Clair; MO-Greene. **Correspondent Relationships:** IL-Cook, Kankakee, Madison, Sangamon; MO-St. Louis; NE-Dawes, Douglas, Lancaster.

Add'l Information: Established 1994. Normal turnaround time- 1-2 days. Projects billed by number of names searched. 1st project may require prepayment. They specialize in public record retrieval. Another office number is 314-291-3308.

Concord Commercial Services

5213 Streamwood Ln, Plano, TX 75093
Phone: 972-931-7431 **Fax:** 267-295-8632
mrude@sbcglobal.net

Types of Records Retrieved: Real Estate

Local Retrieval Area: IL-Cook; TX-Collin, Dallas. **Correspondent Relationships:** nationwide.

Add'l Information: Established 1994. Normal turnaround time- 24-48 hours. Projects billed by number of names searched.

🏛Concord Search & Retrieval Inc

10 Ferry St #420, Concord, NH 03301
Phone: 877-273-1119; 603-856-0087 **Fax:** 877-647-5734; 603-856-0099
www.concordsandr.com **email:** gac@concordsandr.mv.com

Types of Records Retrieved: Civil, criminal and probate courts; Federal courts; Real Estate; Tax liens/judgment; UCC records; Vital records.

Local Retrieval Area: NH-Belknap, Hillsborough, Merrimack, Rockingham. **Correspondent Relationships:** nationwide.

Add'l Information: Established 2002. Normal turnaround time- 24-48 hours. Projects billed by number of names searched. Will invoice. They provide fast reliable UCC, tax lien, litigation and real property searches in New Hampshire.

Condello Associates, Accusearch

5082 E Hampden Ave #157, Denver, CO 80222
Phone: 888-756-9687; 303-756-9687 **Fax:** 303-758-5486
www.coloradoinvestigations.com **email:** acusearch9@aol.com

Types of Records Retrieved: Civil and crimnial courts; Probate courts; Federal courts; Real Estate; Tax liens/Judgments; UCC records; Vital records

Local Retrieval Area: CO-Adams, Arapahoe, Boulder, Broomfield, Denver, Jefferson, Larimer, Weld.. **Correspondent Relationships:** statewide.

Add'l Information: Established 1978. Normal turnaround time- 48 hours. Expedited service available. Projects billed by number of names searched. Projects billed by number of records located. Projects billed by the hour. All projects require prepayment. Credit cards accepted. Payment terms are net 30 days. They specialize in locating individuals, process service, court record research/retrieval and general investigation for the legal community and general public nationwide. In business since 1978. A licensed PI in CO. They perform service of process.

Condor Inv

PO Box 181293, 317 Peoples St #400, Corpus Christi, TX 78480-1293
Phone: 361-881-8977 **Fax:** 361-884-1658

Types of Records Retrieved: Civil, criminal and probate courts; Federal courts; Real Estate; Tax liens/Judgments; UCC records; Vital records

Local Retrieval Area: TX-Aransas, Bee, Brooks, Calhoun, Duval, Jim Wells, Kleberg, Nueces, Refugio, San Patricio, Victoria, Webb. **Correspondent Relationships:** Nueces, San Patricio, Aransas, Jim Wells, Duval, Kleberg.

Add'l Information: Established 1987. Normal turnaround time- 24-48 hours. Projects billed by the hour. 1st project may require prepayment. Credit cards accepted. They specialize in service of civil process. They also have investigators available for background, surveillance, statements and skiptracing. A licensed PI in TX. They perform service of process.

Confi-Chek

1821 Q St, Sacramento, CA 95814
Phone: 800-821-7404; 916-443-4822 **Fax:** 800-758-5859; 916-443-7420
www.confi-chek.com

Types of Records Retrieved: Civil, criminal and probate courts; Federal courts; Real Estate; Tax liens/Judgments; UCC records; Vital records

Local Retrieval Area: CA-Sacramento. **Correspondent Relationships:** via national online data.

Add'l Information: Established 1987. Normal turnaround time- same day if online. Projects billed by number of names searched. 1st project may require prepayment. Credit cards accepted. They specialize in online services and people locator information. They also do National credit header titles and judgments. A licensed PI in CA.

🏛Confidential Background Services

1344 Westminster Place, Birmingham, AL 35235
Phone: 205-853-4535 **Fax:** 205-853-4535

Types of Records Retrieved: Civil, criminal and probate courts; Federal courts; Real Estate; Tax liens/Judgments; UCC records; Vital records

Local Retrieval Area: AL-Jefferson, Shelby, St Clair. **Correspondent Relationships:** statewide in criminal, traffic, civil.

Add'l Information: Established 1986. Normal turnaround time- 24 hours. Projects billed by number of names searched. 1st project may require prepayment. They specialize in law enforcement background, state licensed. Also pre-law degree. Do pre-employment screening. All inquiries kept strictly confidential. Authorized to get state criminal record searches covering a 10 year period. A licensed PI in AL. Perform service of process.

Confidential Investigations

455 Linden St, Allentown, PA 18102
Phone: 610-821-9112 **Fax:** 610-481-9419
worldwideci@aol.com

Types of Records Retrieved: Civil and criminal courts; Federal courts; Real Estate; Tax liens/Judgments; UCC records; Vital records

Local Retrieval Area: PA-Berks, Carbon, Lehigh, Monroe, Northampton. **Correspondent Relationships:** nationwide.

Add'l Information: Established 1988. Normal turnaround time- 24 hours. Projects billed by the hour. 1st project may require prepayment. Invoice net 30 days. They specialize in commercial crime, theft fraud, workers' compensation and background checks. A licensed PI in PA & NJ. They perform service of process.

Confidential Service Group

c/o 17320 Tulsa St, Granada Hills, CA 91344
Phone: 877-799-9197; 818-832-1016

Types of Records Retrieved: Civil, criminal and probate courts; Federal courts; Real Estate; Tax liens/Judgments; UCC records; Vital records

Local Retrieval Area: CA-Los Angeles. **Correspondent Relationships:** TN and TX.

Add'l Information: Established 1992. Normal turnaround time- 48 hours to 5 days. Projects billed by number of names searched. All projects require prepayment. Non-refundable retainer required. They specialize in private investigations and executive personnel security. They have over 20 years experience in high profile executive security. Parent company is Executive Security & Investigations.

Confidential Services

1156 Alum Creek Dr, Columbus, OH 43209-2715
Phone: 800-752-4581; 614-552-4646 **Fax:** 614-252-5359

Types of Records Retrieved: Civil, criminal and probate courts; Federal courts; Real Estate; Tax liens/Judgments; UCC records; Vital records

Local Retrieval Area: OH-Athens, Clermont, Cuyahoga, Delaware, Franklin, Hamilton, Lucas, Medina; WV-Ohio. **Correspondent Relationships:** nationwide.

Add'l Information: Established 1988. Normal turnaround time- 24-72 hours. Projects billed by number of names searched. Projects billed by number of records located. Projects billed by the hour. 1st project may require prepayment. Credit cards accepted. They specialize in unsolved criminal cases, child custody/endangerment, skiptracing, locate services and complete asset protection throughout Ohio. They are the largest full service agency in Ohio. They also do process service nationwide. A licensed PI in OH. They perform service of process.

Confidential Services & Investigations

2600 Randal Way #11-204, Silverdale, WA 98383
Phone: 360-981-1657 **Fax:** 360-697-5785

Types of Records Retrieved: Civil and criminal courts; Federal courts; Real Estate; Tax liens/Judgments

Local Retrieval Area: WA-King, Kitsap, Pierce

Add'l Information: Established 2004. Normal turnaround time- 3-5 business days. Projects billed by number of names searched. Credit cards accepted. CST is a full service private investigation agency licensed in WA, offering a full range of investigative and legal support services. A licensed PI in WA. They perform service of process.

Jeanetta, Conner

1765 Beckham Rd, Smith Grove, KY 42171
Phone: 270-746-4465 **Fax:** 270-563-4112

Types of Records Retrieved: Real Estate; Tax liens/Judgments

Local Retrieval Area: KY-Barren, Metcalfe, Warren

Add'l Information: Established 1997. 1st project may require prepayment. She specializes in real estate.

Consolidated Abstract Co

PO Box 569, Aspermont, TX 79502
Phone: 940-989-3566 **Fax:** 940-989-2032

Types of Records Retrieved: Probate courts; Real Estate; Tax liens/Judgments; UCC records; Vital records

Local Retrieval Area: TX-Stonewall

Add'l Information: Normal turnaround time- 1-2 days. Fee basis will vary by the type of project. 1st project may require prepayment.

Contemporary Realty Solutions Inc

1056 W Jericho Turnpike, Smithtown, NY 11787
Phone: 631-979-5677 **Fax:** 631-979-1042
www.contemporaryrealty.com **email:** jgirardi@contemporaryrealty.com

Types of Records Retrieved: Real Estate; Tax liens/judgments; UCC records

Local Retrieval Area: NY-Nassau, Suffolk. **Correspondent Relationships:** nationwide.

Add'l Information: Established 1999. Normal turnaround time- 2-3 days. Projects billed by number of names searched. Terms are net 30 days.

Kathy Coonts

12408 E 41st, Independence, MO 64055
Phone: 816-833-0417 **Fax:** 816-833-2957
gkcoonts@aol.com

Types of Records Retrieved: Real Estate, Tax liens/Judgments

Local Retrieval Area: MO-Jackson

Add'l Information: Established 1997. Normal turnaround time- 24 hours. She provides real estate & title searches, mortgage & loan details, state & county lien information. Also provides assessor & tax information, ownership information, document retreival and real estate filings. All information is kept confidential.

Nina N Cooper

620 Fulmar Dr, Suisun City, CA 94585
Phone: 707-428-5712 **Fax:** 707-428-5712
ninacooper_research@comcast.net

Types of Records Retrieved: Civil, criminal and probate courts; Tax liens/Judgments; Vital records

Local Retrieval Area: CA-Butte, Napa, Nevada, Sacramento, Sierra, Solano, Sutter, Yolo, Yuba. **Correspondent Relationships:** Napa and North CA.

Add'l Information: Established 1999. Normal turnaround time- 24-48 hours. Projects billed by number of names searched. Payment terms are net 30 days. They specialize in cirminal, civil and probate records. County recorder records inclusive of vital records, tax liens, UCC and voter registration, serving above counties in CA. Offering personalized service for reliability, accuracy and expediancy.

Copper Range Abstract & Title Co

707 Shelden Ave, Houghton, MI 49931
Phone: 906-482-7903 **Fax:** 906-482-7977
www.copperrangetitle.com **email:** crat@portup.com

Types of Records Retrieved: Probate courts; Federal courts; Real Estate; Tax liens/Judgments; UCC records; Vital records

Local Retrieval Area: MI-Houghton, Keweenaw

Add'l Information: Established 1977. Normal turnaround time- 2 days. Fee basis will vary by type of project. They specialize in real estate.

Corley Research

1642 N Lake Dr, Lexington, SC 29072
Phone: 803-951-3350 **Fax:** 803-358-6594
corkyfamily4@alltel.net

Types of Records Retrieved: Civil and criminal courts

Local Retrieval Area: SC-Lexington, Richland

Add'l Information: Established 2004. Normal turnaround time- 24 hours. Projects billed by number of names searched. All projects require prepayment. Corley research is a courthouse researcher specializing in county criminal records.

Cornell Abstract Co

1811 Hill Ave, Spirit Lake, IA 51360
Phone: 712-336-3845 **Fax:** 712-336-1402
www.cornellabstract.com **email:** info@cornellabstract.com

Types of Records Retrieved: Probate courts; Real Estate; Tax liens/Judgments; UCC records

Local Retrieval Area: IA-Dickinson

Add'l Information: Established 1947. Normal turnaround time- variable depending on project. Fee basis will vary by the type of project. They specialize in real estate.

Cornerstone Title Research

5114 Cabin Lake Dr, San Antonio, TX 78244
Phone: 210-661-2357 **Fax:** 305-704-3866
ctr@satx.rr.com

Types of Records Retrieved: Civil, criminal and probate courts; Real Estate; Tax liens/Judgments; UCC records; Vital records

Local Retrieval Area: TX-Bexar, Comal. **Correspondent Relationships:** Atascosa, Bandera, Bastrop, Brazoria, Caldwell, Callahan, Cameron, Cooke, Frio, Guadalupe, Hays, Hidalgo, Jones, Kendall, Lubbock, Hockley, Medina, Real, Starr, Taylor, Throckmorton, Travis, Uvalde, Willacy, Williamson, Wilson counties in TX.

Add'l Information: Established 1996. Normal turnaround time- 1-2 days. Projects billed by number of names searched. Projects billed by the hour. 1st project may require prepayment. They specialize in quality, affordable abstracting and public records retrieval and they support the survey industry with deed research and 50-year chains of title.

CorpAmerica Inc

30 Old Rudnick Ln, Dover, DE 19901
Phone: 888-736-4300; 302-736-4300 **Fax:** 302-736-5620

Types of Records Retrieved: Civil and criminal courts; Real Estate; Tax liens/Judgments; UCC records

Local Retrieval Area: DE-Kent, New Castle, Sussex. **Correspondent Relationships:** nationwide.

Add'l Information: Established 1989. Normal turnaround time- 1-2 days depending upon state systems time frame. Projects billed by number of names searched. 1st project may require prepayment. Credit cards accepted. Credit cards are subject to 5% rush fee. They specialize in forming corporations and providing registered agent service in all states and in retrieving SOS records. Complete UCC and public records services for Delaware, including MVR records. Now part of Lexis-Nexis Document Solutions.

CorpAssist Inc - DC Office

1090 Vermont Ave NW #910, Washington, DC 20005
Phone: 800-438-2996; 202-371-8090 **Fax:** 202-371-1945
www.corpassist.com **email:** corpdc@aol.com

Types of Records Retrieved: Civil, criminal and probate courts; Federal courts; Real Estate; Tax liens/Judgments; UCC records; Vital records

Local Retrieval Area: DC-District of Columbia; MD-Montgomery, Prince George's; VA-Alexandria City, Arlington, Fairfax, Fairfax City, Loudoun, Manassas City, Prince William. **Correspondent Relationships:** nationwide (National Registered Agents, Inc).

Add'l Information: Established 1992. Normal turnaround time- 24-48 hours. Projects billed by number of names searched. Projects billed by the hour. 1st project may require prepayment. Terms: net 15 days for service companies. They provide research services at all federal agencies and courts in addition to the traditional UCCs, tax liens, judgments, real estate, judgments, etc. They also provide Registered Agent services worldwide.

CorpAssist Inc - Baltimore

11 East Chase St #9E, Baltimore, MD 21202
Phone: 800-536-9778; 410-539-5370 **Fax:** 410-539-5848
www.corpassist.com **email:** kerry@corpassist.com

Types of Records Retrieved: Civil and criminal courts; Federal courts; Real Estate; Tax liens/Judgments; UCC records

Local Retrieval Area: MD-Anne Arundel, Baltimore, Baltimore City, Howard. **Correspondent Relationships:** nationwide (National Registered Agents, Inc).

Add'l Information: Established 1992. Normal turnaround time- 24-72 hours. Projects billed by number of names searched. Projects billed by number of records located. Net 15 days. 1st project may require prepayment. Credit cards accepted. They provide research at the Federal level, state level and listed county level. They specialize in registered agent services on a nationwide basis. They are affiliated with National Registered Agents Inc. They do not do commercial real estate research.

Corporate Access Inc

236 E 6th Ave, Tallahassee, FL 32303
Phone: 800-969-1666; 850-222-2666 **Fax:** 850-222-1666
www.user.talstar.com/cai **email:** cai@talstar.com

Types of Records Retrieved: Civil, criminal and probate courts; Federal courts; Real Estate; Tax liens/Judgments; UCC records; Vital records

Local Retrieval Area: FL-Bay, Calhoun, Franklin, Gadsden, Gulf, Jefferson, Leon, Liberty, Wakulla; GA-Thomas. **Correspondent Relationships:** nationwide.

Add'l Information: Established 1994. Normal turnaround time- 24-48 hours. Projects billed by number of names searched. 1st project may require prepayment. Credit cards accepted. Corporate Access will file and retrieve anything that is publicly available. They perform service of process.

Corporate Research Solutions Inc

12631 E Imperial Hwy #F-226, Santa Fe Springs, CA 90670
Phone: 800-486-0757; 562-465-0020 **Fax:** 800-486-0859; 562-465-0068
www.crslink.com **email:** sprewitt@crslink.com

Types of Records Retrieved: Civil and criminal courts; Federal courts; Real Estate; Tax liens/Judgments; UCC records; Vital records

Local Retrieval Area: CA-Los Angeles, Orange. **Correspondent Relationships:** nationwide.

Add'l Information: Established 2002. Normal turnaround time- 24 hours. Expedited service available. Projects billed by number of names searched. Will invoice after completion of project. They are a full service company providing public record research, filing services and document retrievals. They provide personalized and consistent service.

Corporate Screening Services

16530 Commerce Ct, Cleveland, OH 44130
Phone: 800-229-8606; 440-816-0500 **Fax:** 440-243-4204
www.corporate-screening.com **email:** tfeher@corporatescreening.com

Types of Records Retrieved: Civil, criminal and probate courts; Federal courts; UCC records

Local Retrieval Area: OH-Cuyahoga, Lake, Lorain, Medina. **Correspondent Relationships:** nationwide.

Add'l Information: Established 1987. Normal turnaround time- 24-72 hours. Projects billed by number of names searched. Credit cards accepted. Bill monthly. They specialize in screening of UCC and court records in the Cleveland area. A licensed PI in OH.

Corporation Service Co - CSC (New York City)

1133 Avenue of the Americas #3100, New York, NY 10036-6710
Phone: 800-221-0770; 212-299-9100 **Fax:** 212-299-9102
www.incspot.com

Types of Records Retrieved: Civil, criminal and probate courts; Federal courts; Real Estate; Tax liens/Judgments; UCC records; Vital records

Local Retrieval Area: NY-Kings, New York, Queens. **Correspondent Relationships:** nationwide.

Add'l Information: Established 1899. Normal turnaround time- 1-2 days. Projects billed by number of names searched. 1st project may require prepayment. They are part of the CSC network of offices, specializing in UCC and corporate matters. They relocated from the WTC in late 2001.

Corporation Service Company - CSC

2711 Centerville Rd #400, Wilmington, DE 19808-1645
Phone: 800-927-9800; 302-636-5400 **Fax:** 302-636-5454
www.incspot.com **email:** selias@cscinfo.com

Types of Records Retrieved: Civil, criminal and probate courts; Federal courts; Real Estate; Tax liens/Judgments; UCC records; Vital records

Local Retrieval Area: DC-District of Columbia; DE-Kent, New Castle, Sussex; FL-Leon; IL-Cook, Sangamon; MA-Suffolk; NJ-Mercer; NV-Carson City; NY-Albany; OR-Marion; PA-Dauphin; TX-Travis. **Correspondent Relationships:** nationwide.

Add'l Information: Established 1899. Normal turnaround time- 24-48 hours. Projects billed by number of names searched. They also charge by index. 1st project may require prepayment. Credit cards accepted. Wilmington, DE is the corporate headquarters of the national network of CSC offices. They have been doing business since 1899.

Corpus Christi Court Services

PO Box 147, Corpus Christi, TX 78403
Phone: 361-887-8122 **Fax:** 361-887-0335 skanth@swbell.net

Types of Records Retrieved: Civil, criminal and probate courts; Federal courts; Real Estate; Tax liens/Judgments; UCC records; Vital records

Local Retrieval Area: TX-Aransas, Duval, Jim Wells, Kenedy, Kleberg, Nueces, San Patricio. **Correspondent Relationships:** most Texas counties and the United States.

Add'l Information: Established 1986. Normal turnaround time- 36 hours or less. 2-hour expedited service available. Projects billed by number of names searched. Projects billed by the hour. 1st project may require prepayment. They specialize in personalized and professional processing of your document filing, retrieval and research requests. They are locally owned and operated for 17 years.

Thomas E Corsi

52 Edna Pl, Buffalo, NY 14218-1326
Phone: 716-863-7797 **Fax:** 716-828-1620 tcorsi@msn.com

Types of Records Retrieved: Real Estate

Local Retrieval Area: NY-Genesee, Cattaraugus, Chautanqua, Erie, Livingston, Niagara, Orleans, Wyoming. **Correspondent Relationships:** Steuben county.

Add'l Information: Established 1996. Normal turnaround time- 24-48 hours. Projects billed by number of names searched. Will invoice. Terms, net 30 days. They speciazlie in current owner/last owner/property reports and institutional lender/two-owner searches. Forte is quick turnaround time.

Corson County Land and Title

PO Box 287, McIntosh, SD 57641
Phone: 605-273-4513

Types of Records Retrieved: Real Estate; Tax liens/Judgments

Local Retrieval Area: SD-Corson

Add'l Information: Established 1981. 1st project may require prepayment. They specialize in real estate.

Cottonwood County Abstract Company

900 3rd Ave, PO Box 336 (56101-0336), Windom, MN 56101
Phone: 507-831-1504 **Fax:** 507-831-3675

Types of Records Retrieved: Real Estate; Tax liens/Judgments

Local Retrieval Area: MN-Cottonwood

Add'l Information: Established 1965. Normal turnaround time- variable depending on project. Expedited service available for add'l charge. Projects billed by number of names searched. Projects billed by number of records located. All projects require prepayment. Personal checks are accepted. They specialize in abstracting, name searches, judgment searches, tax and bankruptcy searches.

Countryside Paralegal Services

13 Depot Street Extension, Hyde Park, VT 05655
Phone: 802-888-2150 **Fax:** 802-888-2183
jmcountryside@aol.com

Types of Records Retrieved: Civl and criminal courts; Probate courts; Federal courts; Real Estate; Tax liens/Judgments; UCC records; Vital records.

Local Retrieval Area: VT-Caledonia, Essex, Franklin, Lamoille, Orleans. **Correspondent Relationships:** statewide.

Add'l Information: Normal turnaround time- 48-72 hours. Projects billed by number of names searched. Projects billed by the hour. 1st project may require prepayment.

County Courthouse Retrieval

PO Box 532288, Indianapolis, IN 46253
Phone: 765-485-0233

Types of Records Retrieved: Civil, criminal and probate courts; Real Estate; Tax liens/Judgments; UCC records; Vital records

Local Retrieval Area: IN-Benton, Boone, Hamilton, Hendricks, Montgomery, Tippecanoe

Add'l Information: Established 2002. Normal turnaround time- 1-2 business days. Projects billed by number of names searched. 1st project may require prepayment. Payment due 30 days net for existing clients. They specialize in real property current owner title searches and mortgage & deed retrieval at the county courthouse level. Bulk orders may qualify for discounted rate.

County House Research Inc

42 S 15th St #1710, Philadelphia, PA 19102
Phone: 866-594-1177; 215-717-7433 **Fax:** 866-872-7610; 215-717-7437
www.countyhouseresearch.com **email:** info@countyhouseresearch.com

Types of Records Retrieved: Civil and criminal courts; Federal courts; Tax liens/Judgments

Local Retrieval Area: NJ-Atlantic, Bergen, Camden, Essex, Passiac; PA-Allegheny, Beaver, Berks, Clarion, Cumberland, Dauphin, Delaware, Mercer, Monroe, Northampton, Philadelphia, Tioga, Venango, Westmoreland, York. **Correspondent Relationships:** DE, DC, GA, ME, MA, NC, RI, SC.

Add'l Information: Established 1996. Normal turnaround time- 24-48 hours. Most counties searched daily. Projects billed by number of names searched. 1st project may require prepayment. Credit cards accepted. Payments due net 30 days. They specialize in same day searches, using the Flexible Research System technology and with the abilities of "FRS Connect" can provide direct access to their services. Can do all counties in NJ and most counties in PA.

County Seat Abstract

17 W Main St, Johnstown, NY 12095
Phone: 518-762-3011 **Fax:** 518-762-3011

Types of Records Retrieved: Civil, criminal and probate courts; Real Estate; Tax liens/Judgments; UCC records

Local Retrieval Area: NY-Fulton, Hamilton, Montgomery. **Correspondent Relationships:** New York.

Add'l Information: Established 1986. Normal turnaround time- 3-5 days. Projects billed by the hour. They specialize in title insurance searches.

County Wide Abstract & Title Co Inc

PO Box 98, (4 S Elm St), Dexter, MO 63841
Phone: 573-624-2436 **Fax:** 573-624-5376
countywd@midwest.net

Types of Records Retrieved: Probate courts; Real Estate; Tax liens/Judgments; UCC records

Local Retrieval Area: MO-Stoddard

Add'l Information: Established 1972. Normal turnaround time- 2 days. Projects billed by number of records located. 1st project may require prepayment. Serving Stoddard county for 30-plus years.

Countywide Research Services

30111 Carmel Bay Ct, Georgetown, TX 78628
Phone: 512-922-1676 cell **Fax:** 512-869-8185
ramona.batts@verizon.net

Types of Records Retrieved: Civil, criminal and probate courts; Federal courts; Real Estate; Tax liens/Judgments; UCC records; Vital records

Local Retrieval Area: TX-Travis, Williamson

Add'l Information: Established 1997. Normal turnaround time- 24-48 hours. Expedited service available. Projects billed by number of names searched. 1st project may require prepayment. They specialize in current property searches & lien searches, 50 year chain or title searches, preforeclosure title searches, STLs, FTLs, AJs, UCCs, criminal & civil litigation and asset searches. They offer notary. The office phone is 512-863-2007. A licensed PI in TX. They perform service of process.

Court & Public Records Service Inc

708 Creekview Ct, Mesquite, TX 75181
Phone: 800-856-0585; 469-726-9500 **Fax:** 469-726-9501
www.courtsystem.com

Types of Records Retrieved: Civil, criminal and probate courts; Federal courts; Real Estate; Tax liens/Judgments; UCC records; Vital records; Corporate records

Local Retrieval Area: TX-Bexar, Collin, Cooke, Dallas, Denton, Ellis, Fannin, Grayson, Harrison, Hunt, Johnson, Kaufman, Navarro, Rockwall, Smith, Tarrant, Travis, Van Zandt. **Correspondent Relationships:** nationwide.

Add'l Information: Established 1989. Normal turnaround time- 1-3 days. Projects are billed at a flat fee per search. 1st project may require prepayment. Terms: net 10 days and COD. They specialize in all public records especially court records and real estate records. The President has had in excess of 25 years of paralegal experience.

Court Data Research Services

PO Box 1184, Tulsa, OK 74101
Phone: 918-745-2231 **Fax:** 918-745-2234
jphager1@mindspring.com

Types of Records Retrieved: Civil, criminal and probate courts; Federal courts; Real Estate; Tax liens/Judgments; UCC records

Local Retrieval Area: OK-Rogers, Tulsa. They also offer criminal and real estate searches in Creek county. **Correspondent Relationships:** Oklahoma.

Add'l Information: Established 1981. Normal turnaround time- 24 hours. Projects billed by number of names searched. Projects billed by the hour. Flat rate available per court also. Hands on court work and copy (document) retrieval. 1st project may require prepayment. Payment due upon receipt of invoice. They specialize in court searches, title, criminal, bankruptcy searches and federal/USDC searches.

Court Data Search

6 Sycamore Way, Mt Arlington, NJ 07856
Phone: 973-770-1170 **Fax:** 973-770-1170

Types of Records Retrieved: Civil and criminal courts; Federal courts

Local Retrieval Area: NJ-Bergen, Essex, Hudson, Middlesex, Monmouth, Morris, Passaic, Somerset, Sussex, Union

Add'l Information: Established 1987. Normal turnaround time- 48 hours. Projects billed by number of names searched. They specialize in criminal and civil judgment checks.

Court Explorers Inc

111 John Street, #645, New York, NY 10038
Phone: 212-608-1585 **Fax:** 212-608-1586
www.courtexplorers.com **email:** tcollins@courtexplorers.com

Types of Records Retrieved: Civil, criminal and probate courts; Federal courts; Real Estate; Tax liens/Judgments; UCC records; Vital records

Local Retrieval Area: NY-Bronx, Dutchess, Kings, Nassau, New York, Orange, Queens, Richmond, Suffolk, Westchester. **Correspondent Relationships:** nationwide.

Add'l Information: Established 1995. Normal turnaround time- 1-3 days. Projects billed by number of names searched. 1st project may require prepayment. Credit cards accepted. They specialize in all public record searches. They perform service of process.

Court Process Service & Document Retrieval

2506 E Platte Ave Ste #10, Colorado Springs, CO 80909
Phone: 800-898-8662; 719-650-7761 **Fax:** 719-471-3111
www.courtprocess.net **email:** cps188@qwest.net

Types of Records Retrieved: Civil, criminal and probate courts; Federal courts; Real Estate; Tax liens/Judgments; UCC records; Vital records

Local Retrieval Area: CO-Arapahoe, Denver, El Paso, Pueblo, Teller

Add'l Information: Established 1998. Normal turnaround time- 4-5 days. Expedited service available. Projects billed by the hour. All projects require prepayment. Credit cards accepted. Will invoice after established work of 6 months. They specialize in service of process, general investigations, video stakeouts and record retrievals. They perform service of process.

Court Process Service & Investigations

3333 S Wadsworth Blvd #B-104, Denver, CO 80227
Phone: 800-898-8662; **Fax:** 719-471-3111
www.courtprocess.net

Types of Records Retrieved: Civil, criminal and probate courts; Federal courts; Real Estate; Tax liens/Judgments; UCC records; Vital records

Local Retrieval Area: CO-Adams, Arapahoe, Boulder, Chaffee, Clear Creek, Denver, Douglas, Eagle, Gunnison, Jefferson, Lake, Park, Summitt

Add'l Information: Established 1998. Normal turnaround time- 4-5 days. Expedited service available. Projects billed by the hour. All projects require prepayment. Credit cards accepted. Will invoice after established work of 6 months. They specialize in service of process, general investigations, video stakeouts and record retrievals. A licensed PI in CO. They perform service of process.

Court Record Consultants

11024 Balboa Blvd PMB 128, Granada Hills, CA 91344-5007
Phone: 818-366-1906 **Fax:** 818-366-1985
inchhipicb@earthlink.net

Types of Records Retrieved: Civil, criminal and probate courts; Federal courts; Real Estate; Tax liens/Judgments; UCC records; Vital records

Local Retrieval Area: CA-Alameda, Contra, Costa, Fresno, Kern, Los Angeles, Marin, Monterey, Orange, Riverside, Sacramento, San Benito, San Bernardino, San Diego, San Francisco, San Luis Obispo, Santa Barbara, Santa Clara, Stanislaus, Ventura. **Correspondents:** statewide.

Add'l Information: Established 1985. Normal turnaround time- 1-3 days. Projects billed by number of names searched. Projects billed by the hour. 1st project may require prepayment. Credit cards accepted. They specialize in pre-employment screening, private investigation and real estate research. A licensed PI in CA. They perform service of process.

Court Record Research Inc

405 Main St #550, Houston, TX 77002-1876
Phone: 800-552-3353; 713-227-3353 **Fax:** 888-395-8055; 713-236-1970
www.courtrecords.com **email:** angela@courtrecords.com

Types of Records Retrieved: Civil, criminal and probate courts; Federal courts; Real Estate; Tax liens/Judgments; UCC records; Vital records

Local Retrieval Area: TX-Brazoria, Fort Bend, Galveston, Harris, Montgomery. **Correspondent Relationships:** Walker, Waller, Wharton, Chambers counties TX.

Add'l Information: Established 1974. Normal turnaround time- 1-3 days. Harris county same day service available. Expedited service available. Projects billed by the hour. Will also work on retainer. 1st project may require prepayment. Credit cards accepted. They specialize in obtaining copies of documents for pending and closed court cases from federal, state and local courts. They also perform real estate oriented searches, and they are licensed private investigators. A licensed PI in TX.

Court Services of Iowa Inc

980 NE 134th Ave, Alleman, IA 50007
Phone: 515-965-5722 **Fax:** 515-965-5674
kroberts@prairieinet.net

Types of Records Retrieved: Civil courts; Real Estate; Tax liens/Judgments; UCC records

Local Retrieval Area: IA-all counties. **Correspondents:** statewide.

Add'l Information: Established 2002. Normal turnaround time- 24-48 hours. Expedited service available. Projects billed by number of names searched. They invoice per search completed. They have been business since 2002, and have 2 full-time and 3 part-time searchers on staff. Rush orders accepted at no extra charge.

CourtCheckers

315 W Los Olivos St #8, Santa Barbara, CA 93105
Phone: 805-898-7084 **Fax:** 805-898-7094 courtcheckers@cox.net

Types of Records Retrieved: Civil, criminal and probate courts; Federal courts; Real Estate; Tax liens/Judgments; UCC records; Vital records

Local Retrieval Area: CA-San Luis Obispo, Santa Barbara, Ventura

Add'l Information: Established 1994. Normal turnaround time- 24 hours. Monthly billing. They specialize in 24-hour turnaround, accurate and professional filing as well as research and information retrieval. They perform service of process.

Courtesy Title

PO Box 493, Jamestown, KY 42629
Phone: 270-343-4486 **Fax:** 270-343-4487

Types of Records Retrieved: Real Estate; Tax liens/Judgments

Local Retrieval Area: KY-Russell

Add'l Information: Established 2000. 1st project may require prepayment. They specialize in real estate.

CourtEXPRESS (CA)

205 S Broadway #1023, Los Angeles, CA 90012
Phone: 800-766-3320; **Fax:** 213-680-7813
www.courtexpress.com **email:** lsolancho@courtexpress.com

Types of Records Retrieved: Civil, criminal and probate courts; Federal courts; Real Estate; Tax liens/Judgments; UCC records; Vital records

Local Retrieval Area: CA-Los Angeles, Orange, Sacramento, San Diego, San Francisco, San Mateo, Santa Clara. **Correspondents:** nationwide.

Add'l Information: Established 1981. Normal turnaround time- same or next day. Projects billed by the hour. 1st project may require prepayment. Credit cards accepted. Mastercard, Visa accepted. They specialize in obtaining legal and financial documents from any source in the country. Provide online name/case searching and docket sheets.

CourtEXPRESS (DC)

701 Pennsylvania Ave NW #C100, Washington, DC 20004
Phone: 800-542-3320; 202-737-7111 **Fax:** 202-737-3324
www.courtexpress.com **email:** info@courtexpress.com

Types of Records Retrieved: Civil and criminal courts; Federal courts; Supreme Court records

Local Retrieval Area: CA-Los Angeles; DC-District of Columbia; MD-Montgomery; NY-New York; VA-Arlington, Fairfax, Richmond. **Correspondent Relationships:** nationwide.

Add'l Information: Established 1979. Normal turnaround time- 24-48 hours. Projects billed by the hour. Credit cards accepted. They specialize in online searches and ordering of documents from any court USA court and from government agencies and various international courts. Also specialize in case monitoring and Freedom of Information Act requests. They perform service of process.

Courthouse Abstractors

PO Box 1172, Cumming, GA 30028
Phone: 770-271-9002 **Fax:** 877-726-8950;
deedog@bellsouth.net

Types of Records Retrieved: Civil courts; Federal courts; Real Estate; Tax liens/Judgments; UCC records

Local Retrieval Area: GA-Bartow, Cherokee, Clayton, Cobb, Dawson, De Kalb, Douglas, Fayette, Forsyth, Fulton, Gordon, Gwinnett, Hall, Lumpkin, Paulding, Pickens and Whitfield

Add'l Information: Established 1997. Normal turnaround time- 24-48 hours. Projects billed by number of names searched. They specialize in servicing surrounding metro Atlanta counties and North Georgia.

Courthouse Concepts Inc

16 W Center, Fayetteville, AR 72701
Phone: 877-750-3660; 479-582-3660 **Fax:** 877-750-7379; 479-582-3662
www.courthouseconcepts.com

Types of Records Retrieved: Civil, criminal and probate courts; Federal courts; Real Estate; Tax liens/Judgments; UCC records; Vital records

Local Retrieval Area: AR-Benton, Carroll, Conway, Crawford, Faulkner, Franklin, Johnson, Madison, Pope, Pulaski, Sebastian, Washington. **Correspondent Relationships:** nationwide.

Add'l Information: Established 2000. Normal turnaround time- 24 hours. Projects billed by number of names searched. Will invoice monthly. They specialize in information retrieval to include current owner, document retrieval, criminal, civil and application screening.

Courthouse Connections

3109 Hawk St, San Diego, CA 92103-5304
Phone: 619-692-3538 **Fax:** 619-692-0931 eplouff@cox.net

Types of Records Retrieved: Civil, criminal and probate courts; Federal courts; Real Estate; Tax liens/Judgments; UCC records; Vital records

Local Retrieval Area: CA-San Diego

Add'l Information: Established 1996. Normal turnaround time- 24-48 hours. Projects billed by number of names searched. Projects billed by number of records located. Payment terms are net 30 days. They are dedicated to keeping their clients satisfied with performance done as efficiently as possible in a timely manner.

Courthouse Filings Inc

544 Shenondoah Pk, Conroe, TX 77302
Phone: 936-273-6427 **Fax:** 936-273-2067
courthousefilings@hotmail.com

Types of Records Retrieved: Civil, criminal and probate courts; Tax liens/Judgments; UCC records; Vital records

Local Retrieval Area: TX-Montgomery

Add'l Information: Established 2001. Normal turnaround time- 24 hours. All orders received by noon are processed that day. Projects billed by number of records located. A family owned business specializing in providing owner research and document retrieval on a 24 hours turnaround basis in Montgomery County, Texas.

Courthouse Specialists

9800 Northwest Fwy, Ste 400, Houston, TX 77092
Phone: 800-925-4225; 713-683-0491 **Fax:** 713-683-0493
www.courth.com **email:** orders@courth.com

Types of Records Retrieved: Civil, criminal and probate courts; Bankruptcy courts; Real Estate; Tax liens/Judgments; UCC records

Local Retrieval Area: TX-Brazoria, Chambers, Fort Bend, Galveston, Harris, Liberty, Montgomery, San Jacinto, Walker, Waller. **Correspondent Relationships:** nationwide.

Add'l Information: Established 1982. Normal turnaround time- 24-48 hours. Projects billed by number of names searched. Projects billed by the hour. 1st project may require prepayment. Credit cards accepted. They specialize in chain of title, ownership searches, lien searches, 50-year environmental searches, expert testimony and educational instruction with proprietary databases.

CourthouseData

PO Box 3446, 525 S School Ave #100, Fayetteville, AR 72702
Phone: 479-582-0900 **Fax:** 479-582-5862
www.courthousedata.com **email:** info@courthousedata.com

Types of Records Retrieved: Civil, criminal and probate courts; Federal courts; Real Estate; Tax liens/Judgments; UCC records; Vital records

Local Retrieval Area: AR-all counties; MS-Bolivar, Coahoma, DeSoto, Tate, Tunica; OK-Adair, Cleveland, Creek, Craig, Cherokee, Delaware, Lincoln, Mayes, McIntosh, Muskogee, Nowata, Oklahoma, Okmulgee, Okfuskee, Osage, Ottawa, Payne, Pawnee, Pittsburg, Rogers, Tulsa, Wagoner, Washington

Add'l Information: Established 2001. Normal turnaround time- same day or within 48 hours. Projects billed by number of names searched. Projects billed by number of records located. Agreement required for a title plant subscription. 1st project may require prepayment. Credit cards accepted. All major credit cards and all orders can be placed online and delivered online. CourthouseData is a real estate information services company that has imaged and indexed over 5 million public records. They provide fast, accurate public record and title research throughout Arkansas, Oklahoma & Mississippi.

Coyne Search Service Inc

300 Pond St 2nd Fl, Bristol, PA 19007
Phone: 215-781-3722 **Fax:** 215-781-3724

Types of Records Retrieved: Civil, criminal and probate courts; Federal courts; Real Estate; Tax liens/Judgments; UCC records; Vital records

Local Retrieval Area: NJ-Burlington, Camden, Mercer; PA-Bucks, Chester, Delaware, Montgomery, Philadelphia

Add'l Information: Established 1984. Normal turnaround time- 24-48 hours. They charge per name and per index. Monthly billing can be arranged for certain services. Billed upon completion. They retrieve records from the US Coast Guard-Philadelphia, Federal Records Center and the New Jersey Superior Court Record Center.

Coyote

17890 Fantail Cir, Reno, NV 89506
Phone: 775-972-6530 **Fax:** 775-972-6683
cltvcoyote@aol.com

Types of Records Retrieved: Federal courts; Real Estate; Tax liens/Judgments; UCC records

Local Retrieval Area: NV-Washoe. **Correspondents:** statewide.

Add'l Information: Established 1998. Normal turnaround time- 24 hours. Projects billed by number of names searched. All projects require prepayment. Monthly billing is available for established clients.

CPS (Capitol Process Service)

PO Box 1323, Georgetown, TX 78627
Phone: 800-856-0216; 512-930-7378 **Fax:** 512-863-7477
austincps@cox-internet.com

Types of Records Retrieved: Civil, criminal and probate courts; Federal courts; Real Estate; Tax liens/Judgments; UCC records; Vital records

Local Retrieval Area: TX-Travis, Williamson. **Correspondent Relationships:** nationwide.

Add'l Information: Established 1988. Normal turnaround time- 24 hours. Fees are charged by case. They perform service of process.

Crawford County Abstract Co (Iowa)

PO Box 277, 1317 Broadway, Denison, IA 51442
Phone: 712-263-5626 **Fax:** 712-263-8773

Types of Records Retrieved: Civil, criminal and probate courts; Real Estate; Tax liens/Judgments; UCC records; Vital records

Local Retrieval Area: IA-Crawford

Add'l Information: Established 1993. Normal turnaround time- 1-3 days. Projects billed by number of names searched. Projects billed by number of records located. Terms: net 30 days.

Crawford County Abstract Co Inc (Arkansas)

424 Main Street (PO Box 426), Van Buren, AR 72956
Phone: 479-474-2711 **Fax:** 479-474-2954
crawfordcountyabstract@hotmail.com

Types of Records Retrieved: Civil, criminal and probate courts; Real Estate; Tax liens/Judgments

Local Retrieval Area: AR-Crawford

Add'l Information: Established 1972. Normal turnaround time- 2 days. Projects billed by number of names searched. They specialize in real estate.

Crawford County Title Co

600 W Washington St, Cuba, MO 65453-1221
Phone: 573-885-6470 **Fax:** 573-885-2758
wepllc@fidnet.com

Types of Records Retrieved: Real Estate; Tax liens/Judgments

Local Retrieval Area: MO-Crawford. **Correspondent Relationships:** Franklin, Dent, Phelps, Gasconade counties MO.

Add'l Information: Established 1967. Normal turnaround time- 1 week. Fee basis varies by type of transaction.

Crawford Cty Title, Roscommon Cty Title

PO Box 581, Grayling, MI 49738
Phone: 989-348-9832 **Fax:** 989-348-7511
mferrigan@landcoenterprises.com

Types of Records Retrieved: Real Estate; Tax liens/Judgments; UCC records

Local Retrieval Area: MI-Crawford, Roscommon

Add'l Information: Established 1971. Normal turnaround time- up to 1 week. Fee basis will vary by the type of project. All projects require prepayment. They require a prepayment for all out of area transactions. They specialize in title insurance. Additional phone is 517-821-4544 and Fax: 517-821-3844.

Creative Services Inc

87 Columbia Ave, Cranston, RI 02905
Phone: 800-227-0002; 508-339-5451 **Fax:** 508-339-2352
www.creativeservices.com **email:** jgootkind@creativeservices.com

Types of Records Retrieved: Criminal courts

Local Retrieval Area: RI-Bristol, Kent, Newport, Providence, Washington

Add'l Information: Established 1972. Normal turnaround time- 24-48 hours. Projects billed by number of names searched. Projects are billed semi-monthly. They excel in their ability to understand clients needs and provide customized reporting, superior customer service and comprehensive and factual data, meeting all time lines. Licensed PI in MA, RI, CT, FL, NJ.

Credit Bureau of Connecticut Inc

600 Saw Mill Rd, PO Box 26775, West Haven, CT 06516-0966
Phone: 800-922-0002; 203-931-2000 **Fax:** 203-931-2075
www.cbct.com **email:** asimeone@cbct.com

Types of Records Retrieved: Real Estate; Tax liens/Judgments

Local Retrieval Area: CT-Fairfield, Hartford, Litchfield, Middlesex, New Haven, New London, Tolland, Windham. **Correspondent Relationships:** Rhode Island, Massachusetts.

Add'l Information: Established 1929. Normal turnaround time- 3 business days. Payable upon receipt. 1st project may require prepayment. Payment by check accepted. They are a major supplier of title searches, appraisals, document recording and retrieval, flood certification, credit reporting and collection services to the financial industry. For info, add extension #248 to phone number.

Credit Bureau of Eudora Inc (CBE)

PO Box 545, Eudora, KS 66025-0545
Phone: 785-542-1771 **Fax:** 785-542-1661
www.ksrental.com **email:** cbe@sunflower.com

Types of Records Retrieved: Civil, criminal and probate courts; Real Estate; Tax liens/Judgments; UCC records

Local Retrieval Area: KS-Douglas, Leavenworth, Shawnee. **Correspondent Relationships:** Kansas and nationwide.

Add'l Information: Established 1993. Normal turnaround time- 24-48 hours. Expedited service available. Projects billed by number of names searched. Projects billed by the hour. All projects require prepayment retainer or credit card on website. CBEspecializes in rent-screens, skiptraces, research & document retrieval. They daily update their specialized regional/local databases and have a sex offender database for 24 states. The principal is a licensed private investigator. A licensed PI in KS. They perform service of process.

Credit Bureau of Valley City

PO Box 912, 135 Fourth St NW, Valley City, ND 58072
Phone: 701-845-3912 **Fax:** 701-845-0220
cbvcmen@daktel.com

Types of Records Retrieved: Civil, criminal and probate courts; Real Estate; Tax liens/Judgments; UCC records; Vital records

Local Retrieval Area: ND-Barnes

Add'l Information: Established 1990. Normal turnaround time- 2-3 days. Fee basis will vary by the type of project. 1st project may require prepayment. They request that all out of county clients prepay.

Credit Control Inc/Resource Confidential

500 S Salina #102, Syracuse, NY 13202
Phone: 800-886-7407; 315-475-4191 **Fax:** 315-484-3389
www.creditneeds.com **email:** n.bernardo@creditneeds.com

Types of Records Retrieved: Civil, criminal and probate courts; Federal courts; Real Estate; Tax liens/Judgments; UCC records; Vital records

Local Retrieval Area: NY-Albany, Broome, Fulton, Herkimer, Madison, Oneida, Onondaga, Oswego, Rensselaer, Saratoga, Schenectady, Warren, Washington. **Correspondent Relationships:** nationwide. The also offer service to southern New York including NYC.

Add'l Information: Established 1990. Normal turnaround time- 24-48 hours. Projects billed by number of names searched. Credit cards accepted. Will bill bi-monthly. Whatever your paticular search requirements might be, they have the experienced staff to provide you with the specific results you need. They perform service of process.

Credit Lenders Service Agency Inc

PO Box 508, Cherry Hill, NJ 08003
Phone: 856-787-9005 **Fax:** 800-648-0401;
www.creditlenders.com **email:** keithm@creditlenders.com

Types of Records Retrieved: Federal courts; Real Estate; Tax liens/Judgments; UCC records

Local Retrieval Area: NJ-Bergen, Burlington, Camden, Mercer, Middlesex, Morris, Ocean, Somerset; PA-Lackawanna, Monroe, Pike, Wayne. **Correspondent Relationships:** nationwide.

Add'l Information: Established 1983. Normal turnaround time- 24-48 hours. Projects billed by number of names searched. Projects billed by number of records located. 1st project may require prepayment. They specialize in real estate searching. They are also a title company.

Credit Plus Solutions Group

2491 Paxton St, PO Box 67533, Harrisburg, PA 17106
Phone: 800-344-3125; 717-236-8061 **Fax:** 800-526-8962; 717-233-6116
www.cpsg.com **email:** creditplus@cpsg.com

Types of Records Retrieved: Civil, criminal and probate courts; Federal courts; Real Estate; Tax liens/Judgments; UCC records

Local Retrieval Area: PA-Adams, Berks, Cumberland, Dauphin, Franklin, Fulton, Juniata, Lancaster, Lebanon, Lehigh, Mifflin, Montgomery, Perry, York. **Correspondent Relationships:** PA, MD, NJ, DE, OH.

Add'l Information: Established 1922. Normal turnaround time- 24-48 hours. Expedited service available. Charges are by products ordered. Credit cards accepted. End of the month invoicing available. All major credit cards accepted. They specialize in present owner searches, flood certificates, criminal checks, bankruptcy searches, county and state UCC searches, census tract, mortgage filings and real estate appraisals. Email for property product-propertyrequests@cpsg.com. They perform service of process.

Credit Services LLC

PO Box 72739, Fairbanks, AK 99707
Phone: 907-456-1749 **Fax:** 907-456-6203
c.stephen@creditservicesllc.com

Types of Records Retrieved: Civil, criminal and probate courts; Federal courts

Local Retrieval Area: AK-Fairbanks North Star Borough

Add'l Information: Established 1982. Normal turnaround time- 24-48 hours. Fee basis depends upon the type of search. 1st project may require prepayment. They require prepay from individuals only. They specialize in process serving. They perform service of process.

Crime Checkers

PO Box 57, Dixon Springs, TN 37057
Phone: 615-735-0010 **Fax:** 615-735-0081
crimchckrs@aol.com

Types of Records Retrieved: Civil and criminal courts; Tax liens/Judgments; UCC records

Local Retrieval Area: TN-Rutherford, Wilson

Add'l Information: Established 1995. Normal turnaround time- 24 hours. Projects billed by number of names searched. 1st project may require prepayment. Credit cards accepted thru PayPal.

Crimecheck Research Services

PO Box 8333, The Woodlands, TX 77387-8333
Phone: 281-288-6930 **Fax:** 281-296-8261
crimecheckresearchsvcs2003@yahoo.com

Types of Records Retrieved: Civil and criminal courts.

Local Retrieval Area: TX-Angelina, Atascosa, Bandera, Bell, Bosque, Brazos, Caldwell, Collin, Comal, Ellis, Gonzales, Guadalupe, Hays, Hill, Hood, Johnson, McLennan, Medina, Montgomery, Potter, Randall, Somervell, Tarrant, Travis, Van Zandt, Walker, Williamson, Wilson, Wise. **Correspondent Relationships:** nationwide.

Add'l Information: Established 1995. Normal turnaround time- 24-48 hours. Projects billed by number of names searched. Payment due upon receipt of invoice. They specialize in criminal and civil record research and pre-employment screening.

Criminal Background Investigations

PO Box 2363, Angleton, TX 77516
Phone: 979-848-0632 **Fax:** 979-549-0695
sramsower@sbcglobal.net

Types of Records Retrieved: Civil and criminal courts.

Local Retrieval Area: TX-Brazoria, Galveston. **Correspondent Relationships:** Fort Bend counties TX.

Add'l Information: Established 1992. Normal turnaround time- if faxed over by 8 AM, 24 hours same day. Projects billed by number of names searched. Monthly billing for NAPBS members. Will invoice monthly. Started researching criminal records in 1992. Visits the courthouse daily and obtains all information from the courthouse. Does not use search engines. 24-hr turnaround. They are a foundiing member of NAPBS.

Criminal Information Network Inc

PO Box 54961, Cincinnati, OH 45254
Phone: 888-923-0271; 513-474-8800 **Fax:** 513-474-8801

Types of Records Retrieved: Civil and criminal courts

Local Retrieval Area: KY-Boone, Campbell, Kenton; OH-Clermont, Hamilton. **Correspondent Relationships:** nationwide.

Add'l Information: Normal turnaround time- 24 hours. Projects billed by number of names searched. Will invoice bi-monthly. They specialize in accurate crimnal records and MVRs from KY, and also OH and other state MVRs.

Criminal Record Research Services

404 W South St, Carlisle, PA 17013
Phone: 717-249-7053 **Fax:** 717-249-9397
dawn@planetcable.net

Types of Records Retrieved: Criminal records

Local Retrieval Area: PA-Cambria, Cumberland, Franklin, Westmoreland

Add'l Information: Established 1995. Normal turnaround time- 95% of searches completed in less than 8 hours. Projects billed by number of names searched. 1st project may require prepayment. With 10 years experience, they provide a reliable, fast turnaround service for clients. They understand the importance every search as degreed, seasoned HR professionals.

Crisp & Associates

PO Box 31070, Savannah, GA 31410
Phone: 912-898-9973 **Fax:** 912-898-5044
www.crispandassociates.com **email:** jwcrisp@bellsouth.net

Types of Records Retrieved: Civil, criminal and probate courts; Federal courts; Tax liens/Judgments; UCC records

Local Retrieval Area: GA-Bryan, Chatham, Effingham, Liberty

Add'l Information: Established 1992. Normal turnaround time- 48 hours. They specialize in process service and investigations. A licensed PI in GA, SC. They perform service of process.

Crockett County Abstract Co

PO Drawer E, 1108 Ave E, Ozona, TX 76943
Phone: 325-392-2232 **Fax:** 325-392-2839

Types of Records Retrieved: Real Estate; Tax liens/judgments; UCC records

Local Retrieval Area: TX-Crockett

Add'l Information: Normal turnaround time- 2-3 days. Fee basis will vary by the type of project. 1st project may require prepayment.

The Croson Agency

804 Monmouth St, St Albans, WV 25177
Phone: 304-343-1564 **Fax:** 304-727-1353

Types of Records Retrieved: Civil courts; Probate courts; Federal courts; Real Estate; Tax liens/Judgments; UCC records

Local Retrieval Area: WV-all counties.

Add'l Information: Established 1958. Normal turnaround time- generally same day. Search may take 24-48 hours. For faster service, please fax your order for fee quote. No work will begin until they receive your final approval via fax. They accept no verbal orders. Projects billed by number of names searched. Hands on searches in remote WV counties are available at an hourly rate plus expenses. 1st project may require prepayment. Accounts closed if invoice not paid in 30 days. Serving the legal profession since 1958. She is a retired private investigator. Former Real Estate Agent. Fifteen minutes from the WV State Capitol, USDC and Bankruptcy court. Fax request to 304-727-1353 for price quote and TAT.

David Cross

PO Box 70, Albany, KY 42602
Phone: 606-387-6638 **Fax:** 606-387-6639

Types of Records Retrieved: Civil and criminal courts; Real estate; Tax liens/Judgments

Local Retrieval Area: KY-Clinton

Add'l Information: Established 1984. 1st project may require prepayment. He is an attorney and performs searches on a very limited basis.

Laura Cross

4859 Geranium, Oakland, CA 94619
Phone: 510-336-0865 **Fax:** 510-336-9688
crosslaura@hotmail.com

Types of Records Retrieved: Civil and criminal courts; Federal courts; Tax liens/Judgments; Vital records

Local Retrieval Area: CA-Alameda, Contra Costa. **Correspondent Relationships:** Marin, San Francisco, San Mateo, Santa Clara counties CA.

Add'l Information: Established 1994. Normal turnaround time- 24 hours but often same day service. Projects billed by number of names searched. Terms: net 30 days.

Crow Wing County Abstract Co

PO Box 378, Brainerd, MN 56401
Phone: 218-829-7368 **Fax:** 218-829-8586

Types of Records Retrieved: eal Estate; Tax liens/Judgments; UCC records

Local Retrieval Area: MN-Crow Wing

Add'l Information: Established 1915. Normal turnaround time- 2-7 days. Projects billed by number of names searched. Projects billed by the hour. They specialize in land title.

CRRG Inc

204 Westview Terrace, Arlington, tx 76013
Phone: 800-687-9030; 817-459-0075 **Fax:** 800-687-7658; 817-459-1388

Types of Records Retrieved: Civil, criminal and probate courts; Federal courts; Real Estate; Tax liens/Judgments; UCC records; Vital records

Local Retrieval Area: TX-Collin, Dallas, Denton, Ellis, Rockwall, Tarrant. **Correspondent Relationships:** nationwide.

Add'l Information: Established 1994. Normal turnaround time- same day if order in by 10AM. Projects billed by number of names searched. 1st project may require prepayment. Credit cards accepted. Invoice monthly. They are a national search firm, specializing in every kind of courthouse research in every county in the country. A licensed PI in TX.

Crummey Investigations Inc

PO Box 510130, Melbourne Beach, FL 32951-0130
Phone: 321-724-0518 **Fax:** 321-728-0274
www.crummey-p-i.com **email:** bev@cfl.rr.com

Types of Records Retrieved: Civil, criminal and probate courts; Real Estate; Tax liens/Judgments; UCC records; Vital records

Local Retrieval Area: FL-Brevard, Indian River, Orange

Add'l Information: Established 1985. Normal turnaround time- 24 hours. Projects billed by the hour. 1st project may require prepayment. Credit cards accepted. Personal checks are accepted. They specialize in missing persons. A licensed PI in FL. They perform service of process.

Crutchfield & Associates

415 N Camden Dr, Beverly Hills, CA 90210
Phone: 818-349-4836 **Fax:** 818-349-4856
www.pi4stars.com **email:** pi4stars@pacbell.net

Types of Records Retrieved: Civil and criminal courts; Real Estate; Tax liens/Judgments; UCC records

Local Retrieval Area: CA-Los Angeles, Orange, San Bernardino, San Diego, Ventura. **Correspondent Relationships:** nationwide, Mexico, Canada.

Add'l Information: Established 1978. Normal turnaround time- 24 hours to 1 month depending on court. Projects billed by number of names searched. Fees depend on case file activity. 1st project may require prepayment. They specialize in criminal background checks, surveillance, driving records, credit checks with a signed release and asset searches. A licensed PI in CA. They perform service of process.

Crystal Clear Copy Service

8241 Mesa Ave, Oakhill, CA 92345
Phone: 760-947-5699 **Fax:** 760-949-1389
chubla1@yahoo.com

Types of Records Retrieved: Civil courts; Probate courts; Vital records

Local Retrieval Area: CA-Orange, Riverside, San Bernardino. **Correspondent Relationships:** statewide.

Add'l Information: Established 1990. Normal turnaround time- 10 days. Expedited service available. Fee basis will vary by the type of project. They specialize in photocopy. They perform service of process.

CSRA Background Verification Inc

519 Pleasant Home Rd #C-2, Augusta, GA 30907
Phone: 706-869-8882 **Fax:** 706-869-9689
www.csrabv.com **email:** charles@csrabv.com

Types of Records Retrieved: Civil, criminal and probate courts; Federal courts; Real Estate; Tax liens/Judgments; UCC records

Local Retrieval Area: GA-Burke, Columbia, McDuffie, Richmond; SC-Aiken. **Correspondent Relationships:** Georgia counties Jefferson, Johnson, Washington, Glassock, Hancock, Warren, Lincoln, Taliaferro & Wilkes.

Add'l Information: Established 1993. Normal turnaround time- 12-48 hours. Projects billed by number of names searched. 1st project may require prepayment. Bills monthly. They specialize in pre-employment background checks and current owner/title searches. They provide a full array of courthouse records retrieval.

Cumberland Research

162 Langford Rd, Carthage, TN 37030
Phone: 615-735-6558 **Fax:** 615-735-6558
cmbrr@earthlink.net

Types of Records Retrieved: Civil and criminal courts; Real Estate; Tax liens/Judgments; UCC records

Local Retrieval Area: TN-Macon, Smith, Sumner, Trousdale

Add'l Information: Established 2000. Normal turnaround time- 24 hours. Projects billed by number of names searched. 1st project may require prepayment. They specialize in criminal and civil searches in Macon, Smith, Sumner, and Trousdale counties in TN. Results usually in 24 hours.

Cumberland Title

43 Ashley Dr, Liberty, KY 42539
Phone: 606-787-8743

Types of Records Retrieved: Real Estate; Tax liens/Judgments

Local Retrieval Area: KY-Taylor

Add'l Information: 1st project may require prepayment. They specialize in real estate.

Current River Abstract

129 State St, Doniphan, MO 63935
Phone: 573-996-2907 **Fax:** 573-996-2909

Types of Records Retrieved: Real Estate; Tax liens/Judgments

Local Retrieval Area: MO-Ripley

Add'l Information: Established 1993. 1st project may require prepayment. They specialize in real estate.

Currier Abstract Company

PO Box 540, Artesia, NM 88211-0540
Phone: 505-746-9823 **Fax:** 505-746-9661

Types of Records Retrieved: Civil courts; Probate courts; Real Estate; Tax liens/Judgments; UCC records

Local Retrieval Area: NM-Eddy

Add'l Information: Established 1940. Normal turnaround time- 1 week. Fee basis will vary by the type of project. Land title business in Eddy County, NM.

Cygneture Title Inc

1401 Excelsior Rd N, Baxter, MN 56425-9659
Phone: 218-828-0122 **Fax:** 218-828-0873

Types of Records Retrieved: Criminal courts; Probate courts; Real Estate; Tax liens/Judgments; UCC records

Local Retrieval Area: MN-Cass, Crow Wing, Morrison, Todd, Wadena

Add'l Information: Established 1988. Normal turnaround time- 1-10 days depending on types of records retrieved. Fee basis will vary by type of project. 1st project may require prepayment. They will also invoice. They specialize in real estate.

Cynthia H Miller, Paralegal

931 Watch Creek Dr, Cincinnati, OH 45230
Phone: 513-368-2855 **Fax:** 513-624-0858
cctn.cincy@off.res.com

Types of Records Retrieved: Civil courts; Real Estate; Tax liens/Judgments; UCC records

Local Retrieval Area: OH-Butler, Clermont, Hamilton, Warren

Add'l Information: Established 1990. Normal turnaround time- 2-3 days. Projects billed by number of names searched. Terms are net 30 days. She specializes in searching records for UCC's, federal, state, civil suits and judgments, obtains copies and file documents. Is also insured.

D

D & B Legal Services Inc

PO Box 7471, Overland Park, KS 66207
Phone: 913-963-1279 **Fax:** 913-385-9992
billpowell@kc.rr.com

Types of Records Retrieved: Civil, criminal and probate courts; Federal courts; Real Estate; Tax liens/Judgments; UCC records; Vital records

Local Retrieval Area: KS-Johnson, Wyandotte; MO-Cass, Clay, Jackson, Platte. **Correspondent Relationships:** Shawnee, Douglas counties, KS; Johnson, LaPayene counties, MO.

Add'l Information: Established 2000. Normal turnaround time- 24 hours. Projects billed by number of names searched. 1st project may require prepayment. D & B Legal Services, they have been in the legal field for 22 years and know their way around the courts. A licensed PI in KS, MO. They perform service of process.

D D Hamilton Title Co

PO Box 11, Marshfield, MO 65706
Phone: 417-859-2078 **Fax:** 417-859-2020

Types of Records Retrieved: Civil courts; Probate courts; Real Estate; Tax liens/Judgments; UCC records

Local Retrieval Area: MO-Webster, Wright

Add'l Information: Established 1893. Normal turnaround time- 48 hours. Projects billed by number of names searched. Projects billed by number of records located. They specialize in land title and civil judgments.

D K Abstract

2095 W Vanhook St, Milan, TN 38358
Phone: 731-686-9373/9363 **Fax:** 731-686-9309

Types of Records Retrieved: Civil, criminal and probate courts; Federal courts; Real Estate; Tax liens/Judgments; UCC records; Vital records

Local Retrieval Area: TN-Benton, Carroll, Chester, Crockett, Decatur, Dyer, Fayette, Gibson, Hardeman, Hardin, Haywood, Henderson, Henry, Humphreys, Lake, Lauderdale, McNairy, Madison, Obion, Perry, Stewart, Tipton, Weakley

Add'l Information: Established 1989. Normal turnaround time- 48 hours. They charge by search. Personal checks are accepted. They do bankruptcy searches in Madison County only.

D W Moore & Assoc Inc

4849 S State St #2, Salt Lake City, UT 84107-4821
Phone: 801-266-6585 **Fax:** 801-266-6031
www.dwmoore.com **email:** david@dwmoore.com

Types of Records Retrieved: Civil courts; Probate courts; Federal courts; Real Estate; Tax liens/Judgments; UCC records; Vital records

Local Retrieval Area: UT-Beaver, Box Elder, Cache, Carbon, Daggett, Davis, Duchesne, Emery, Garfield, Grand, Iron, Juab, Kane, Millard, Morgan, Piute, Rich, Salt Lake, San Juan, Sanpete, Sevier, Summit, Tooele, Uintah, Utah, Wasatch, Washington, Wayne, Weber

Add'l Information: Established 1987. Normal turnaround time- 3-5 days. Projects billed by the hour. They specialize in research and historical investigation, environmental review and education services. Also offers geneological services

D.G.I. LLC

8444 Kingston Dr, PO Box 1182, Newburgh, IN 47630
Phone: 812-853-3222 **Fax:** 812-853-3222
http://members.sigecom.net/dgi **email:** dgi@sigecom.net

Types of Records Retrieved: Civil and criminal courts; Federal courts; Tax liens/Judgments; UCC records; Vital records

Local Retrieval Area: IN-Gibson, Posey, Spencer, Vanderburgh, Warrick; KY-Henderson. **Correspondent Relationships:** nationwide.

Add'l Information: Established 1993. Normal turnaround time- 48 hours. Expedited service available for add'l fee. Projects billed by number of names searched. Projects billed by the hour. 1st project may require prepayment. Terms: net 10 days. They specialize in general investigations, surveillance, photographic's and time-lapse video, accident reconstruction; serving Metro Evansville, IN. They will do other nearby counties on demand. A pager number is: 812-467-9220. A licensed PI in IN. They perform service of process.

Daggett Abstract Co

PO Box 389, Marianna, AR 72360

Phone: 870-295-3434 **Fax:** 870-295-3445

dlawfirmjd@aol.com

Types of Records Retrieved: Civil, criminal and probate courts; Real Estate; Tax liens/Judgments; UCC records

Local Retrieval Area: AR-Lee

Add'l Information: Established 1873. Normal turnaround time- 1 day to 1 week. Fee basis will vary by type of project. All projects require prepayment. Credit cards accepted. Visa accepted. They specialize in title search and land ownership.

Daily Journal Corporation

915 E 1st St, Los Angeles, CA 90012

Phone: 800-952-5232; 213-229-5300 **Fax:** 213-680-3682

www.dailyjournal.com **email:** searches@dailyjournal.com

Types of Records Retrieved: Civil, criminal and probate courts; Federal courts; Real Estate; Tax liens/Judgments; UCC records.

Local Retrieval Area: CA-Los Angeles, Orange, Riverside, San Bernardino, San Diego, Ventura. **Correspondent Relationships:** California.

Add'l Information: Established 1888. Normal turnaround time- 3-5 business days. Expedited service available. Projects billed by number of names searched. 1st project may require prepayment. Fees due upon receipt of invoice. They will record legal notices and coordinate publication of legal notices. They will also file/record UCC documents, also FBN searches, and credit cards are accepted

Dakota County Abstract Co

1250 N Hwy 55, Hastings, MN 55033

Phone: 651-437-5600 **Fax:** 651-437-8876

www.dcatitle.com

Types of Records Retrieved: Probate courts; Real Estate; Tax liens/Judgments; UCC records

Local Retrieval Area: MN-Dakota. **Correspondent Relationships:** Minnesota.

Add'l Information: Established 1957. Normal turnaround time- 1-5 days. Projects billed by number of names searched. Projects billed by number of records located. All projects require prepayment. They will also invoice. They specialize in title searches.

Dana Caughey Document Retrieval Svc

115 Lincoln Pky, East Peoria, IL 61611

Phone: 309-694-4407 **Fax:** 309-694-4528

Types of Records Retrieved: Civil, criminal and probate courts; Federal courts; Real Estate; Tax liens/Judgments; UCC records

Local Retrieval Area: IL-Peoria, Tazewell, Woodford. **Correspondent Relationships:** Woodford, Mason, Fulton counties IL.

Add'l Information: Established 1998. Normal turnaround time- 24-48 hours. Expedited service available. Projects billed by number of names searched. Monthly or Bi-Weekly billing. They specialize in criminal/civil searches at county and Federal levels, real estate, UCC, and Tax liens/Judgments.

Dane County Legal Notice

139 W Wilson St #106, Madison, WI 53703

Phone: 800-720-6871; 608-251-1181 **Fax:** 608-251-8999

Types of Records Retrieved: Civil, criminal and probate courts; Federal courts; Tax liens/Judgments; UCC records

Local Retrieval Area: WI-Dane

Add'l Information: Established 1977. Normal turnaround time- 24-48 hours. Projects billed by number of names searched. Projects billed by the hour. Hourly plus mileage anywhere in WI. Will extend credit to PRRN members. They specialize in process service and records retrieval. A licensed PI in WI. They perform service of process.

Daniel Agency

PO Box 342, Ashland, KY 41105

Phone: 606-324-6029 **Fax:** 606-324-6029

Types of Records Retrieved: Civil, criminal and probate courts; Federal District courts; Real Estate; Tax liens/Judgments; UCC records; Vital records

Local Retrieval Area: KY-Boyd, Carter, Elliott, Floyd, Greenup, Johnson, Lawrence, Martin, Morgan, Pike, Rowan; WV-Cabell, Kanawha, Lincoln, Wayne

Add'l Information: Established 1981. Normal turnaround time- 2-3 days. Projects billed by the hour. 1st project may require prepayment. The company is a multi-faceted real estate research and consulting firm providing abstracts of title, right-of-way & easement acquisition, appraisals, real estate & mineral acquisition and leasing and acquisition investigation. They are bonded.

Darren J Harper & Associates

5000 W Esplanade Ave #196, Metairie, LA 70006

Phone: 800-962-4907; 504-888-5262 **Fax:** 504-341-1966

x1212djh@yahoo.com

Types of Records Retrieved: Civil courts; Federal courts; Real Estate; Tax liens/Judgments

Local Retrieval Area: LA-Jefferson, Orleans. **Correspondent Relationships:** East Baton Rouge, LA.

Add'l Information: Established 1990. Normal turnaround time- 4 days. Projects billed by the hour. Will invoice. They perform service of process.

Data Reporting Corp

330 Roberts St #203, East Hartford, CT 06108-3654

Phone: 800-570-7750; 860-282-0685 **Fax:** 800-672-8635; 860-290-3731

Types of Records Retrieved: Civil, criminal and probate courts; Federal courts; Real Estate; Tax liens/Judgments; UCC records

Local Retrieval Area: CT-Fairfield, Hartford, Litchfield, Middlesex, New Haven, New London, Tolland, Windham. **Correspondent Relationships:** nationwide.

Add'l Information: Normal turnaround time- same day to 3-5 days. Projects billed by the hour. Has flat rate by entity name. 1st project may require prepayment. They perform service of process.

Data Research Inc (Oregon)

8130 SW Beaverton Hillsdale Hwy, Portland, OR 97225-1845

Phone: 800-992-1983; 503-296-0760 **Fax:** 800-992-1984; 503-296-0766

mail@drius.com

Types of Records Retrieved: Civil, criminal and probate courts; Federal courts; Real Estate; Tax liens/Judgments; UCC records

Local Retrieval Area: OR-Benton, Clackamas, Columbia, Coos, Crook, Curry, Deschutes, Douglas, Hood River, Jackson, Jefferson, Klamath, Lane, Lincoln, Linn, Marion, Multnomah, Polk, Wasco, Washington, Yamhill; WA-Clark. **Correspondent Relationships:** nationwide.

Add'l Information: Established 1989. Normal turnaround time- 24-72 hours. Projects billed by number of names searched. They specialize in records retrieval/research and filings/recordings at the state and county levels, all corporate work and state and federal litigation.

Data Screen Inc

PO Box 16839, Fort Worth, TX 76162

Phone: 817-294-7671 **Fax:** 817-294-0773

datascreen@mesh.net

Types of Records Retrieved: Civil and criminal courts; Federal courts; UCC records

Local Retrieval Area: TX-Tarrant. **Correspondent Relationships:** statewide and nationwide.

Add'l Information: Established 1991. Normal turnaround time- 24-48 hours. Projects billed by number of names searched. Will bill clients. For over 14 years they have specialized in criminal record checks, MVRs and North Texas Federal Records facility access as well as statewide checks and services throughout Texas, and the nation. A licensed PI in TX.

Data-Find

PO Box 575, Glasco, NY 12432
Phone: 845-246-3263 **Fax:** 845-247-0126
tschirmer@hvc.rr.com

Types of Records Retrieved: Civil, criminal and probate courts; Real Estate; Tax liens/Judgments; UCC records

Local Retrieval Area: NY-Ulster

Add'l Information: Established 1996. Normal turnaround time- 48 hours. Projects billed by number of names searched. Projects billed by number of records located. 1st project may require prepayment. Payment due upon receipt. They specialize in previous owner and tax searches for Ulster County.

Datalink Investigative Services

PO Box 755, White Pine, TN 37890
Phone: 865-674-0030 **Fax:** 865-674-0076
dis@planetc.com

Types of Records Retrieved: Civil and criminal courts

Local Retrieval Area: TN-Cocke, Hamblen, Jefferson

Add'l Information: Established 1998. Normal turnaround time- 24-48 hours. Projects billed by number of names searched. 1st project may require prepayment. Invoice on a monthly basis. They do civil service of process in the East Tennessee area, also insurance and general investigations, attorney support. A licensed PI in TN. They perform service of process.

Dataprompt Corporation

6919 Santa Fe Ave, Dallas, TX 75223-1124
Phone: 214-390-2530 **Fax:** 214-320-1575
dataprompt@msn.com

Types of Records Retrieved: Criminal courts

Local Retrieval Area: TX-Anderson, Bee, Bexar, Bowie, Brazos, Collin, Cooke, Coryell, Dallas, Denton, Erath, Fannin, Grayson, Gregg, Harris, Henderson, Hopkins, Howard, Hunt, Johnson, Kaufman, Kleberg, Lamar, Limestone, Lubbock, Nueces, Parker, Rockwall, Smith, Tarrant, Travis, Upshur, Van Zandt, Victoria, Webb, Walbarger, Wise, Wood. **Correspondent Relationships:** statewide.

Add'l Information: Established 1993. Normal turnaround time- next day. Projects billed by number of names searched. Terms: net 30 days. They specialize in criminal and eviction record data on a per name basis or in a full database format. A licensed PI in TX.

DataSearch

PO Box 3195, Clarksville, TN 37043
Phone: 931-645-2562 **Fax:** 931-645-1173
gibbsdatasearch@charter.net

Types of Records Retrieved: Criminal courts; Tax liens/Judgments

Local Retrieval Area: TN-Cheatham, Montgomery, Robertson, Stewart

Add'l Information: Established 1999. Normal turnaround time- 24-48 hours in Montgomery. 1 day per week in Stewart County. Projects billed by number of names searched. Invoices at the end of the month. She has been doing research since 1999.

DataSearch Inc

PO Box 15406, Sacramento, CA 95851
Phone: 800-452-3282; 916-925-3282 **Fax:** 916-922-5199
datasearch@sbcglobal.net

Types of Records Retrieved: Civil, criminal and probate courts; Federal courts; Real Estate; Tax liens/Judgments; UCC records; Vital records

Local Retrieval Area: CA-El Dorado, Los Angeles, Orange, Riverside, Sacramento, San Bernardino, San Diego. **Correspondent Relationships:** nationwide.

Add'l Information: Established 1930. Normal turnaround time- 24-48 hours. Projects billed by number of names searched. 1st project may require prepayment. Credit cards accepted. They specialize in UCC, Corporate, LP, LLC and business name filing and document retrieval services. They have access to DMV (nationwide), courthouse records and county recorder records.

Data-Search of Arkansas

PO Box 21042, Little Rock, AR 72221
Phone: 501-868-4814 **Fax:** 501-868-4815
wilmax@alltel.net

Types of Records Retrieved: Civil and criminal courts. Federal courts, UCC records.

Local Retrieval Area: AR-Faulkner, Garland, Jackson, Jefferson, Lee, Lonoke, Ouachita, Pulaski, Saline, White. **Correspondent Relationships:** Arkansas.

Add'l Information: Established 1981. Normal turnaround time- 24-48 hours. Projects billed by number of names searched. Terms are net 30 days. 1st project may require prepayment. Same day turnaround in most cases.

Data-Tec Research Inc

4024 Tanglewood Tr, Chesapeake, VA 23325-2252
Phone: 757-424-3606 **Fax:** 757-424-3615
ljvanderhoff@cox.net

Types of Records Retrieved: Civil and criminal courts; Federal courts

Local Retrieval Area: VA-Chesapeake City, Hampton City, James City, Newport News, Norfolk, Portsmouth, Suffolk, Virginia Beach; Williamsburg, York. **Correspondent Relationships:** Virginia.

Add'l Information: Established 1987. Normal turnaround time- 12-48 hours. Projects billed by number of names searched. 1st project may require prepayment. Personal checks accepted. They specialize in court record searches in southeast Virginia, also tax liens and judgments in above counties except for James City and York.

DataTrace Inv Inc, PI# 100008

PO Box 95322, South Jordan, UT 84095-0322
Phone: 800-748-5335; 801-253-2400 **Fax:** 801-253-2478
www.datatraceonline.com **email:** scott@datatraceonline.com

Types of Records Retrieved: Civil, criminal and probate courts; Federal courts; Real Estate; Tax liens/Judgments; UCC records; Vital records

Local Retrieval Area: UT-Davis, Salt Lake, Utah. **Correspondent Relationships:** statewide and nationwide.

Add'l Information: Established 1983. Normal turnaround time- 24-48 hours. Expedited service available. Projects billed by number of names searched. Projects billed by the hour. Credit cards accepted. Service agreement required for billing. They specialize in public record research, asset, background & skiptracing, criminal record checks & pre-employment screening. They have instant criminal record checks & nationwide database & public record searches available on their web site. A licensed PI in UT. They perform service of process.

Davick Services

PO Box 1274, Shallowater, TX 79363-1274
Phone: 800-658-6656; 806-832-4349 **Fax:** 512-233-1768
www.davickservices.com **email:** dbloys@door.net

Types of Records Retrieved: Civil, criminal and probate courts; Federal courts; Real Estate; Tax liens/Judgments; UCC records

Local Retrieval Area: NM-Curry, DeBaca, Lea, Quay, Roosevelt; TX-Andrews, Armstrong, Bailey, Borden, Briscoe, Castro, Cochran, Cottle, Crosby, Dawson, Deaf Smith, Dickens, Ector, Fisher, Floyd, Gaines, Garza, Glassock, Hale, Hockley, Howard, Kent, King, Knox, Lamb, Lubbock, Lynn, Martin, Midland, Mitchell, Motley, Nolan, Oldham, Parmer, Potter, Randall, Scurry, Stonewall, Swisher, Terry, Yoakum

Add'l Information: Established 1989. Normal turnaround time- 24-48 hours. Projects billed by number of names searched. 1st project may require prepayment. Personal checks accepted. They provide fast, accurate public records research into Lubbock County, TX and 37 surrounding counties. Licensed, insured and experienced. A licensed PI in TX.

David Lung & Assoc

2977 Hwy K, #119, Ofallon, MO 63366
Phone: 888-477-2664; 636-262-1082 **Fax:** 636-272-1803
www.davelung.com **email:** dave@davelung.com

Types of Records Retrieved: Civil and criminal courts

Local Retrieval Area: MO-Franklin, Jefferson, Lincoln, St. Charles, St. Louis, Warren

Add'l Information: Established 1994. 1st project may require prepayment. They also provide court filings, skiptracing, private investigation and bank account info. They perform service of process.

David Smith Detective Agency

3018 Hill Creek Dr, Augusta, GA 30909
Phone: 877-793-9426; 706-793-8279
davidp3407@aol.com

Types of Records Retrieved: Civil, criminal and probate courts; Federal courts; Tax liens/Judgments; UCC records

Local Retrieval Area: GA-Burke, Columbia, Jefferson, Lincoln, McDuffie, Richmond; SC-Aiken, Edgefield, Saluda

Add'l Information: Established 1975. Normal turnaround time- 1-2 days. Expedited service available. A licensed PI in GA, SC. They perform service of process.

Daviess County Land Title LLC

106 N Market St, Gallatin, MO 64640
Phone: 660-663-2155 **Fax:** 660-663-2156

Types of Records Retrieved: Civil courts; Probate courts; Real Estate; Tax liens/Judgments; UCC records

Local Retrieval Area: MO-Caldwell, Clinton, Daviess, DeKalb

Add'l Information: Established 1972. Normal turnaround time- 3 days. Projects billed by number of records located. 1st project may require prepayment. They specialize in real estate searches. Will not perform civil court record searches in Davies County.

Davis and Assoc.

PO Box 1023, Pryor, OK 74362
Phone: 918-825-5223 **Fax:** 918-825-5273

Types of Records Retrieved: Civil and criminal courts

Local Retrieval Area: OK-Craig, Delaware, Mayes, Rogers

Add'l Information: Established 1995. 1st project may require prepayment. They also provide court filings, skiptracing, and private investigations A licensed PI in OK. They perform service of process.

Dawes County Abstract Co

PO Box 70, Chadron, NE 69337
Phone: 308-432-4840 **Fax:** 308-432-4338
dcat@panhandle.net

Types of Records Retrieved: Probate courts; Real Estate; Tax liens/Judgments; UCC records

Local Retrieval Area: NE- Dawes, Sheridan, Sioux

Add'l Information: Established 1982. Normal turnaround time- 3 days. Projects billed by number of names searched. 1st project may require prepayment. They specialize in title insurance and oil and gas reports. They will file/record UCC and real estate documents on behalf of clients on a same or next day in Dawes and Sheridan counties only.

Lori A Day

1047 Donal Dr, Mansfield, OH 44907
Phone: 419-544-4740 **Fax:** 419-756-4369
luvmycrv@aol.com

Types of Records Retrieved: Civil, criminal and probate courts; Real Estate; Tax liens/Judgments; UCC records

Local Retrieval Area: OH-Richland

Add'l Information: Established 1990. Normal turnaround time- 24-48 hours. Projects billed by number of names searched. Invoices at the end of the month. She specializes in all real estate research. Also does court checks but is very selective on criminal. Is insured.

DBU Investigations

7814 Soledad Dr, Houston, TX 77083-4977
Phone: 281-564-9043 **Fax:** 281-494-0951
www.dbuinvestigations.com **email:** dbu@dbuinvestigations.com

Types of Records Retrieved: Civil and criminal courts; Federal courts; Tax liens/Judgments; UCC records

Local Retrieval Area: TX-Harris. **Correspondent Relationships:** nationwide.

Add'l Information: Established 2000. Normal turnaround time- 24-72 hours. Credit cards accepted. They specialize in access to criminal records: felony & misdemeanor information. They also offer civil/family records, including a wide variety of lawsuits, tax, divorce & paternity case information & general investigations. A licensed PI in TX.

DCW & Associates

7400 Center Ave #209, Huntington Beach, CA 92647
Phone: 800-899-0442; 714-892-0442 **Fax:** 714-892-3543
www.dcwpi.com **email:** dwilliams@dcwpi.com

Types of Records Retrieved: Civil, criminal and probate courts; Federal courts; Real Estate; Tax liens/Judgments; UCC records; Vital records

Local Retrieval Area: CA-Los Angeles, Orange, Riverside, San Bernardino, San Diego, Santa Barbara. **Correspondent Relationships:** CA-Kern, Ventura; NV-Las Vegas, TX- Dallas, CO-Denver, Durango.

Add'l Information: Established 1987. Normal turnaround time- 24-48 hours. Projects billed by number of names searched. Projects billed by the hour. 1st project may require prepayment. Credit cards accepted. They specialize in competitor intelligence, records retrieval/research, aviation security, business counter intelligence, surveillance and corporate investigations. They are former federal agents and air marshal's. A licensed PI in CA. They perform service of process.

DDI Inc

218 W Pike St, Covington, KY 41011
Phone: 866-954-3000; 859-431-3011 **Fax:** 866-431-1541; 859-392-8583
www.ddi-incorporated.com **email:** sales@ddi-incorporated.com

Types of Records Retrieved: Civil, criminal and probate courts; Federal courts; Real Estate; Tax liens/Judgments; UCC records; Vital records

Local Retrieval Area: IN-Dearborn; KY-Boone, Campbell, Kenton; OH-Hamilton. **Correspondent Relationships:** IN, KY, OH, TN, MS.

Add'l Information: Established 1997. Normal turnaround time- 24-30 hours. Expedited service available. Projects billed by number of names searched. 1st project may require prepayment. Credit cards accepted. They are a licensed registered and insured company that provides regional access to county courts. They are a FRS user and Clearstar user. A licensed PI in KY, OH. They perform service of process.

DDR (Delaware Document Retrieval)

4 East 7th St, Wilmington, DE 19801
Phone: 800-343-1742; 302-658-9971 **Fax:** 302-658-9951
www.parcelsinc.com **email:** info@parcelsinc.com

Types of Records Retrieved: Civil, criminal and probate courts; Federal courts; Real Estate; Tax liens/Judgments; UCC records

Local Retrieval Area: DE-Kent, New Castle, Sussex. **Correspondent Relationships:** Philadelphia, PA.

Add'l Information: Established 1981. Normal turnaround time- same day. Projects billed by number of names searched. 1st project may require prepayment. Credit cards accepted. Visa, Mastercard and American Express accepted. They specialize in any type of search, document retrieval, filings, service of process, Secretary of State work and CD-rom briefs. They visit SOS, DMV, and Supreme Court regularly. Second web address is www.virtualdocket.com. They perform service of process.

De Baca Abstract Inc

PO Drawer 330, 811 N 4th, Fort Sumner, NM 88119
Phone: 505-355-2431 **Fax:** 505-355-2850
debacabstract@plateautel.net

Types of Records Retrieved: Civil courts; Probate courts; Real Estate; UCC records

Local Retrieval Area: NM-De Baca

Add'l Information: Established 1917. Normal turnaround time- 1 week. Projects billed by number of names searched. Projects billed by number of records located. 1st project may require prepayment.

Dealey Abstract & Title Company

311 West Ave, Holdrege, NE 68949
Phone: 308-995-4622 **Fax:** 308-995-6103

Types of Records Retrieved: Probate courts; Real Estate; Tax liens/Judgments; UCC records

Local Retrieval Area: NE-Phelps

Add'l Information: Established 1986. Normal turnaround time- 24-48 hours. Fee basis will vary by type of project.

Decatur County Abstract

308 State St, Atwood, KS 67730-9719
Phone: 785-626-3885 **Fax:** 785-626-9481

Types of Records Retrieved: Civil, criminal and probate courts; Real Estate; Tax liens/Judgments; UCC records; Vital records

Local Retrieval Area: KS-Decatur, Rawlins

Add'l Information: Established 1985. Normal turnaround time- 1-3 days. Projects billed by number of records located. Projects billed by the hour. Personal checks are accepted. They specialize in real estate titles and title insurance.

Deception Control Inc

1835 S Perimeter Rd #125, Fort Lauderdale, FL 33309
Phone: 800-776-1660; 954-771-6900 **Fax:** 954-776-7687
www.deception.com **email:** dci@deception.com

Types of Records Retrieved: Civil and criminal courts; Real Estate; Tax liens/Judgments; Vital records

Local Retrieval Area: FL-Broward, Dade, Palm Beach. **Correspondent Relationships:** nationwide.

Add'l Information: Established 1975. Normal turnaround time- 24-72 hours. Projects billed by number of names searched. 1st project may require prepayment. They specialize in pre-employment screening of employees to include retrieval, drug screening, polygraph testing & application verification. They now have a Windows-based system which makes them easy to access for pre-employment screening. A licensed PI in FL.

Decker Document Retrieval

814 S Covell Ave, Sioux Falls, SD 57104
Phone: 605-336-8402 **Fax:** 605-336-8402 *51

Types of Records Retrieved: Civil, criminal and probate courts; Federal courts; Real Estate; Tax liens/Judgments; UCC records; Vital records

Local Retrieval Area: SD-Brookings, Lincoln, Minnehaha

Add'l Information: Established 1987. Normal turnaround time- 24-48 hours. Projects billed by number of names searched.

Deeds Inc

3738 Williamson Rd, Roanoke, VA 24012
Phone: 540-563-5699 **Fax:** 540-362-7833
gail@deedsinc.com

Types of Records Retrieved: Civil, criminal and probate courts; Real Estate; Tax liens/Judgments; UCC records

Local Retrieval Area: VA-Bedford, Botetourt, Floyd, Franklin, Montgomery, Roanoke, Roanoke City, Salem City. **Correspondent Relationships:** Richmond.

Add'l Information: Established 1991. Normal turnaround time- 24-48 hours unless otherwise states. Projects billed by number of names searched. Trip fees to outside counties are charged. Terms: net 30 days. They specialize in title work, document retrieval, UCC retrieval and tax liens. NOTE: Bedford City title records are located in Bedford County, Please confirm exact location of search prior to request for work.

Deeds Plus Abstract Services Inc

PO Box 114, Wyalusing, PA 18853
Phone: 570-746-3844 **Fax:** 570-746-3699
www.lesliewizelman.com

Types of Records Retrieved: Real Estate; Tax liens/Judgments; UCC records

Local Retrieval Area: PA-Bradford

Add'l Information: Established 1983. Normal turnaround time- 24-48 hours depending on project and workload. Projects billed by number of names searched. Terms are net 10 days, after which interest accrues. 1st project may require prepayment. Credit cards accepted. They specialize in complete real estate and mortgage closings, including the issuing of title insurance. Closings and settlements are completed promptly and professionally with quality service.

DeedSearcher Title Research Services

4407 FM 1489, Brookshire, TX 77423
Phone: 281-375-8480 **Fax:** 281-375-8481
deedsearcher@aol.com

Types of Records Retrieved: Probate courts; Federal courts; Real Estate; Tax liens/Judgments; UCC records

Local Retrieval Area: TX-Bell, Brazoria, Brazos, Calhoun, Colorado, Coryell, Dallas, Fort Bend, Calveston, Grimes, Harris, Johnson, Matagorda, Montgomery, Nueces, Travis, Victoria, Walker, Waller, Washington, Wichita, Williamson. **Correspondent Relationships:** Texas.

Add'l Information: Established 1994. Normal turnaround time- 6-24 hours. Projects billed by number of names searched. Terms are net 30 days. They specialize in providing expedient real estate property searches statewide with a commitment to accuracy and complete customer satisfaction. They have competitive fees and have a 24 hour FAX. Document copies provided with every order.

Deines Inc

5850 Sky Pointe Dr #1046, Las Vegas, NV 89130-4959
Phone: 702-453-9859 **Fax:** 702-437-1558
deines_inc@yahoo.com

Types of Records Retrieved: Civil, criminal and probate courts; Federal courts; Real Estate; Tax liens/Judgments; UCC records

Local Retrieval Area: NV-Clark

Add'l Information: Established 1999. Normal turnaround time- 24 hours. Projects billed by number of names searched. Payments due net 30 days. They specialize in fast document filing and retrieval of most types of documents located in Clark County, NV. Has been in business since 1999.

Deister Ward & Witcher

2812 1st Ave N #318, Petroleum Bldg, Billings, MT 59101
Phone: 800-443-7874; 406-248-6481 **Fax:** 406-248-6478
www.dwwtitles.com **email:** dwwtitles@dwwtitles.com

Types of Records Retrieved: Civil courts; Probate courts; Real Estate; Tax liens/Judgments; UCC records; Vital records

Local Retrieval Area: MT-Yellowstone

Add'l Information: Established 1952. Normal turnaround time- 24 hours days. Out of county can be done in 1 week. Charges vary per service. They specialize in abstracts of title and mineral title research and O&E reports.

Delaware Attorney Services

2000 Pennsylvania Ave #207, Wilmington, DE 19806
Phone: 800-457-9560; 302-429-0657 **Fax:** 302-429-0656

Types of Records Retrieved: Civil and criminal courts; Federal courts; Real Estate; Tax liens/Judgments; UCC records; Vital records

Local Retrieval Area: DE-Kent, New Castle, Sussex

Add'l Information: Established 1985. Normal turnaround time- 2-5 days. Expedited service available. Projects billed by number of names searched. Terms: net 30 days. They specialize in skiptracing and process service. They perform service of process.

Delaware County Abstract Co (Iowa)

304 E Main St, Manchester, IA 52057
Phone: 563-927-4858 **Fax:** 563-927-1028
dcabstract@iowatelecom.net

Types of Records Retrieved: Civil, criminal and probate courts; Real Estate; Tax liens/Judgments; UCC records; Vital records

Local Retrieval Area: IA-Delaware

Add'l Information: Established 1906. Normal turnaround time- 1-2 days. Projects billed by number of names searched. Projects billed by the hour. They request prepayment from individuals, but will invoice businesses and established customers. They specialize in real estate lien searches.

Delaware County Abstract Co (Oklahoma)

330 N 5th St, Jay, OK 74346
Phone: 918-253-4425 **Fax:** 918-253-6224

Types of Records Retrieved: Civil courts; Probate courts; Real Estate; Tax liens/Judgments; UCC records

Local Retrieval Area: OK-Delaware

Add'l Information: Established 1907. Normal turnaround time- 2-3 days. Fee basis is determined per search. They specialize in title insurance and will also do divorce searches.

Delmarva Abstractors

4 Kiowa Rd, PO Box 376, Cambridge, MD 21613
Phone: 410-228-6044 **Fax:** 410-228-6044

Types of Records Retrieved: Civil and criminal; Probate courts; Real Estate; Tax liens/Judgments; UCC records

Local Retrieval Area: MD-Caroline, Dorchester, Queen Anne's, Talbot

Add'l Information: Normal turnaround time- 24-48 hours. Projects billed by number of names searched. They specialize in title searches. They perform service of process.

Delta County Title Co

PO Box 127, Cooper, TX 75432
Phone: 903-395-4116 **Fax:** 903-395-2106
delta_title@hotmail.coom

Types of Records Retrieved: Civil, criminal and probate courts; Real Estate; Tax liens/Judgments; UCC records; Vital records

Local Retrieval Area: TX-Delta

Add'l Information: Established 1914. Normal turnaround time- variable depending on project. Projects billed by the hour. 1st project may require prepayment. They have an attorney on staff. They perform service of process.

Kathleen Demmitt

3006 S Bannock St #408, Englewood, CO 80110
Phone: 303-781-0605 **Fax:** 303-781-0605
searcher10@mail.com

Types of Records Retrieved: Civil, criminal and probate courts; Federal courts; Vital records

Local Retrieval Area: CO-Denver

Add'l Information: Established 1998. Normal turnaround time- 24-48 hours. Projects billed by number of names searched. 1st project may require prepayment. She specializes in probate and federal and county criminal record searches.

Richard Demoody

PO Box 71, Delaware Water Gap, PA 18327
Phone: 570-350-0105

Types of Records Retrieved: Civil and criminal courts; US District Court; Tax liens/Judgments

Local Retrieval Area: PA-Monroe, Pike

Add'l Information: Established 2003. Normal turnaround time- 2-3 days. Negotiable, usually court costs plus time All projects require prepayment. They specialize in locates, skiptracing, investigations as well as local document retrieval.

Dennis R Sheraw & Associates Inc

5131 Estate Welcome, Christiansted, St Croix, VI 00820-4962
Phone: 800-967-6379; 340-773-3110 **Fax:** 340-773-3113
www.islands.vi/~sheraw **email:** sheraw@islands.vi

Types of Records Retrieved: Civil, criminal and probate courts; Federal courts; Real Estate; Tax liens/Judgments; UCC records; Vital records

Local Retrieval Area: VI-St. Croix, St. John, St. Thomas. Call for availability of other Caribbean islands. **Correspondent Relationships:** nationwide.

Add'l Information: Established 1983. Normal turnaround time- 1 week. Projects billed by the hour. 1st project may require prepayment. They specialize in civil investigation for attorneys and insurance companies. They cover the entire Caribbean. A licensed PI in Virgin Islands. They perform service of process.

Dennis S Carley and Associates Inc

1030 Winton Ct, Lancaster, OH 43130-3468
Phone: 1-866-689-6899; 740-689-6899 **Fax:** 740-689-6899
www.carleyinvestigations.com

Types of Records Retrieved: Civil and criminal courts; Federal courts

Local Retrieval Area: OH-Athens, Fairfield, Franklin, Hocking, Licking, Perry, Pickaway

Add'l Information: Established 2000. Normal turnaround time- 48-72 hours. Projects billed by number of names searched. 1st project may require prepayment. They are a full service private investigation firm. They do complete public records retrieval, including state and local law enforcement records and service of process. A licensed PI in OH. They perform service of process.

DeReign & DeReign Attorneys at Law

PO Box 108, Caruthersville, MO 63830-0108
Phone: 573-333-4666 **Fax:** 573-333-2641
dereign@semo.net

Types of Records Retrieved: Civil courts; Probate courts; Real Estate; Tax liens/Judgments; UCC records

Local Retrieval Area: MO-Pemiscot

Add'l Information: Established 1930. Normal turnaround time- 1-3 days. Fee basis will vary by the type of project. They specialize in title probate.

Desha Abstract & Title Co LLC

PO Box 261, McGehee, AR 71654
Phone: 870-222-5001 **Fax:** 870-222-5504
smithanddrake@ipa.net

Types of Records Retrieved: Civil, criminal and probate courts; Real Estate; Tax liens/Judgments; UCC records

Local Retrieval Area: AR-Desha

Add'l Information: Established 1930. Normal turnaround time- 1 week. Projects billed by the hour. 1st project may require prepayment. They specialize in real estate, civil judgments and probate. They will file/record real estate documents on behalf of clients.

DeSoto Abstract & Title Co (FL)

11 N Polk Ave, Arcadia, FL 34266
Phone: 863-494-3656 **Fax:** 863-494-3481

Types of Records Retrieved: Civil, criminal and probate courts; Real Estate; Tax liens/Judgments; UCC records; Vital records

Local Retrieval Area: FL-De Soto. **Correspondent Relationships:** Charlotte, Lee, Hardee counties.

Add'l Information: Established 1889. Normal turnaround time- 3-5 days. Projects billed by number of records located. They specialize in title insurance and O & E searches.

Detailed Investigations

PO Box 5, Winslow, NJ 08095
Phone: 609-338-3088 **Fax:** 609-704-2980
febbo@comcast.net

Types of Records Retrieved: Criminal courts

Local Retrieval Area: NJ-Atlantic, Bergen, Burlington, Camden, Cape May, Cumberland, Essex, Gloucester, Hudson, Hunterdon, Mercer, Middlesex, Monmouth, Morris, Ocean, Passaic, Salem, Somerset, Sussex, Union, Warren

Add'l Information: Established 1985. Normal turnaround time- 24-36 hours. Projects billed by number of names searched. He is a sole proprietership since 1985. He does all types of PI investigations and criminal record retrievals. A licensed PI in NJ.

Deuel County Abstract Co (Nebraska)

171 Vincent Ave, Chappell, NE 69129
Phone: 308-874-2212 **Fax:** 308-874-3491
wpllaw@lakemac.net

Types of Records Retrieved: Civil courts; Probate courts; Real Estate; Tax liens/Judgments

Local Retrieval Area: NE-Cheyenne, Deuel, Garden, Keith, Kimball, Morrill, Scotts Bluff

Add'l Information: Normal turnaround time- 3-4 days. Charges may vary depending on projects. They are an attorneys' office, they can provide real estate closing services if needed. They perform service of process.

Deuel County Abstract Co (South Dakota)

PO Box 737, Clear Lake, SD 57226-0737
Phone: 605-874-8597 **Fax:** 605-874-8598
dcabstco@itctel.com

Types of Records Retrieved: Civil, criminal and probate courts; Real Estate; Tax liens/Judgments; UCC records; Vital records

Local Retrieval Area: SD-Deuel

Add'l Information: Established 1889. Normal turnaround time- 10 days. Fee basis will vary by the type of project. All projects require prepayment. They specialize in title insurance.

Devine & Co Inc

PO Box 1149, Minot, ND 58702
Phone: 701-852-6800 **Fax:** 701-852-6806
devine@minot.ndak.net

Types of Records Retrieved: Probate courts; Federal District courts; Real Estate; Tax liens/Judgments.

Local Retrieval Area: ND-Ward. **Correspondent Relationships:** 22 other counties; NW North Dakota.

Add'l Information: Established 1903. Normal turnaround time- 1-2 days. Projects billed by number of names searched. Abstracting has per item charge. All projects require prepayment. They will also invoice. They specialize real estate closings, title insurance, title searches, title memorandums and abstracts.

Dewey County Abstract Co

PO Box 157, Taloga, OK 73667
Phone: 580-328-5556 **Fax:** 580-328-5484

Types of Records Retrieved: Civil, criminal and probate courts; Federal courts; Real Estate; Tax liens/Judgments; UCC records

Local Retrieval Area: OK-Dewey

Add'l Information: Established 1896. Normal turnaround time- less than 1 week. Projects billed by number of names searched. Projects billed by the hour. Fee basis will vary by the type of project.

DFW Court Services

PO Box 50071, Dallas, TX 75250
Phone: 800-436-0516; 214-747-1756 **Fax:** 888-318-8569; 214-747-1758
www.dfwcourtservices.com **email:** dfwcourt@yahoo.com

Types of Records Retrieved: Civil, criminal and probate courts; Federal courts; Real Estate; Tax liens/Judgments; UCC records

Local Retrieval Area: TX-Bexar, Collin, Dallas, Denton, Grayson, Harris, Tarrant, Travis. **Correspondent Relationships:** statewide.

Add'l Information: Established 1993. Normal turnaround time- 24 hours for Tarrant and Dallas Counties, 48-72 hours for all other counties. Expedited service available. Projects billed by number of names searched. Credit cards accepted. They specialize in all public records on county, state and federal basis, including document retrieval and court filings in these courts. They also have extensive experience with the Federal Record Center and National Archive facility. A licensed PI in TX. Perform service of process.

Diablo Consulting Services

4060 E Monte Vista, Tucson, AZ 85712
Phone: 520-323-1951 **Fax:** 520-323-1951

Types of Records Retrieved: Civil, criminal and probate courts; Federal courts; Real Estate; Tax liens/Judgments; UCC records Vital records

Local Retrieval Area: AZ-Pima

Add'l Information: Established 2002. Normal turnaround time- 24-72 hours. Projects billed by the hour. 1st project may require prepayment. Estimates per job basis. They specialize in researching property records for individuals and pre-employment screening for companies. Doing business in Pima County only.

Dickey County Abstract & Title

PO Box 339, Ellendale, ND 58436
Phone: 701-349-3450 **Fax:** 701-349-2453

Types of Records Retrieved: Civil, criminal and probate courts; Federal courts; Real Estate; Tax liens/Judgments; UCC records; Vital records

Local Retrieval Area: ND-Dickey

Add'l Information: Established 1961. Normal turnaround time- variable depending on project. Projects billed by number of names searched. Fee basis will vary by the type of project. Payment due upon delivery of invoice.

George L Dickinson

PO Box 1761, Chicago, IL 60690
Phone: 708-307-4792 **Fax:** 708-799-2247
gdickinson@earthlink.net

Types of Records Retrieved: Civil and criminal courts; Federal courts

Local Retrieval Area: IL-Cook. **Correspondent Relationships:** DeKalb, DuPage, Kane, Lake, McHenry counties IL.

Add'l Information: Established 1986. Normal turnaround time- 24 hours. Projects billed by number of names searched. Projects billed by the hour. 1st project may require prepayment. Net 30 days. They also perform workers' comp record searches.

DIG Research Inc

1475 Cherry St #303, Denver, CO 80220
Phone: 720-941-9959 **Fax:** 720-941-9969
digresearch@yahoo.com

Types of Records Retrieved: Civil, criminal and probate courts; Federal courts; Real Estate; Tax liens/Judgments; UCC records; Vital records

Local Retrieval Area: CO-Adams, Arapahoe, Broomfield, Denver, Douglas, Jefferson

Add'l Information: Established 2001. Normal turnaround time- 24-48 hours. 1st project may require prepayment. Credit cards accepted. DIG Research provides the most through cost effective, timely public record retrieval and service of process. We have an experienced staff who are knowledgable professionals.

Diligent Detective Agency Inc

PO Box 581, Clifton, IL 60927
Phone: 877-694-3332; 815-694-3332 **Fax:** 815-694-3351
glenn@stelle.net

Types of Records Retrieved: Civil, criminal and probate courts; Federal courts; Real Estate; Tax liens/Judgments; Vital records

Local Retrieval Area: IL-Champaign, Ford, Iroquois, Kankakee, Vermilion

Add'l Information: Established 1991. Normal turnaround time- 48 hours. Expedited service available. Projects billed by number of names searched. Projects billed by number of records located. 1st project may require prepayment. A licensed PI in IL. They perform service of process.

Diligenz Inc

6500 Harbour Heights Pky, Mukilteo, WA 98275
Phone: 800-858-5294; **Fax:** 800-345-6059;
www.diligenz.com **email:** chritg@diligenz.com

Types of Records Retrieved: Civil and criminal courts; Tax liens/Judgments; UCC records

Local Retrieval Area: WA-Island, Jefferson, King, Lewis, Pierce, Skagit, Snohomish, Thurston, Whatcom. **Correspondent Relationships:** nationwide.

Add'l Information: Established 1991. Normal turnaround time- 24 hours. Projects billed by number of names searched. Credit cards accepted. They specialize in UCC searches and filing, also Corporate Good Standing searches, Federal/state Tax liens/Judgments, corporate document retrieval, Bankruptcy searches, business credit reports, litigation searches, flood determinations.

Direct Corporate Services Inc

12043 Warwick Cr., Parish, FL 34219
Phone: 800-783-7904; **Fax:** 941-776-9812
directcorp@tampabay.rr.com

Types of Records Retrieved: Civil, criminal and probate courts; Federal courts; Real Estate; Tax liens/Judgments; UCC records

Local Retrieval Area: FL-Alachua, Bay, Brevard, Broward, Charlotte, Collier, DeSoto, Escambia, Flagler, Hendry, Hernando, Hillsborough, Indian River, Lake, Lee, Leon, Manatee, Marion, Martin, Miami-Dade, Monroe, Okaloosa, Okeechobee, Orange, Osceola, Palm Beach, Pasco, Pinellas, Polk, Santa Rosa, Sarasota, Seminole, St Lucie, Sumter, Volusia, Walton. **Correspondent Relationships:** statewide.

Add'l Information: Established 1985. Normal turnaround time- 24-48 hours. Expedited service available. Projects billed by number of names searched. 1st project may require prepayment. Terms: net 30 days. They specialize in complete research for UCC, federal and state tax liens, judgments and litigation. They also do bulk projects and current owner searches. Title searches are done in Pinellas and Hillsborough counties only.

DiSearch

3417 Quail Ridge Ln, Matthews, NC 28104
Phone: 704-846-6335 **Fax:** 704-846-8178
disearch99@carolina.rr.com

Types of Records Retrieved: Civil courts; Probate courts; Real Estate; Tax liens/Judgments; UCC records; Vital records

Local Retrieval Area: NC-Mecklenburg, Union. **Correspondent Relationships:** statewide.

Add'l Information: Established 1999. Normal turnaround time- 1-2 days. Projects billed by number of names searched. 1st project may require prepayment. Payment due net 30 days. They specialize in property/real estate. They are a professional hands-on service in all local courts as well as NC Western District of the Federal Court.

Divide Abstract Co

109 S Main St, Crosby, ND 58730
Phone: 701-965-6352, 701-965-2222

Types of Records Retrieved: Real Estate; Tax liens/Judgments

Local Retrieval Area: ND-Divide

Add'l Information: Established 1900. 1st project may require prepayment. They specialize in real estate.

Divine Eye Investigations

2707 Franklin St, Michigan City, IN 46360
Phone: 219-872-5204 **Fax:** 219-872-5205

Types of Records Retrieved: Civil, criminal and probate courts; Real Estate; Tax liens/Judgments; UCC records Vital records

Local Retrieval Area: IN-La Porte, Porter

Add'l Information: Established 2004. Normal turnaround time- 5-10 business days. Expedited service available. Projects billed by number of names searched. 1st project may require prepayment. They provide process service, background, fraud, UCC and employment investigations. They also provide surveillance, skip tracing and judgment recoveries. A licensed PI in IN. They perform service of process.

DJ Records

PO Box 753597, Memphis, TN 38175-3597
Phone: 901-795-6450 **Fax:** 901-362-8320
JLucyDJR@aol.com

Types of Records Retrieved: Criminal courts

Local Retrieval Area: TN-Shelby

Add'l Information: Established 1996. Normal turnaround time- 24 hours. Projects billed by number of names searched. Will bill once a month.

DL Inv & Attorney Support

3507 N Central #203, Phoenix, AZ 85012
Phone: 602-285-9901 **Fax:** 602-285-0445

Types of Records Retrieved: Civil, criminal and probate courts; Federal courts; Real Estate; Tax liens/Judgments; UCC records; Vital records

Local Retrieval Area: AZ-Maricopa. **Correspondent Relationships:** Pinal, Pima, Coconino counties AZ.

Add'l Information: Established 1994. Normal turnaround time- 24 hours. Projects billed by number of names searched. Projects billed by number of records located. Projects billed by the hour. 1st project may require prepayment. Payment due upon completion of work. A licensed PI in AZ. They perform service of process.

DLS (Demovsky Lawyer Service - Albany)

100 State St #220, Albany, NY 12207
Phone: 518-449-8411 **Fax:** 518-449-2467

Types of Records Retrieved: Civil, criminal and probate courts; Federal courts; Real Estate; Tax liens/Judgments; UCC records

Local Retrieval Area: NY-Albany, Rensselaer, Schenectady. **Correspondent Relationships:** nationwide.

Add'l Information: Established 1983. Normal turnaround time- 72 hours. Projects billed by the hour. Charges may be varied depending on project. First project requires prepayment. They specialize in corporate law. They perform service of process.

DLS (Demovsky Lawyer Service - New York)

401 Broadway #510, New York, NY 10013
Phone: 800-443-1058; 212-925-1220 **Fax:** 212-941-0235
www.dlsny.com **email:** info@dlsny.com

Types of Records Retrieved: Civil, criminal and probate courts; Federal courts; Real Estate; Tax liens/Judgments; UCC records; Vital records

Local Retrieval Area: NJ-Bergen, Essex; NY-Bronx, Kings, Nassau, New York, Queens, Richmond, Rockland, Westchester. **Correspondent Relationships:** New York, New Jersey, Connecticut, also nationally, internationally.

Add'l Information: Established 1983. Normal turnaround time- 24 hours. Projects billed by the hour. 1st project may require prepayment. They specialize in detail-oriented personal service. Can retrieve MVRs nationwide, as well as specializing in NY They perform service of process.

DLS Background Services Inc

30141 Antelope Rd PMB #231, Menifee, CA 92584
Phone: 951-301-8584 **Fax:** 951-672-2234
dlsbackground@comcast.net

Types of Records Retrieved: Civil and criminal courts; Federal courts; Tax liens/Judgments; UCC records

Local Retrieval Area: CA-Mariposa, Placer, Plumas, San Bernardino, San Diego, Santa Clara, Shasta, Tehama, Tulare, Tuolumne. **Correspondent Relationships:** nationwide.

Add'l Information: Established 1998. Normal turnaround time- 24-48 hours. Projects billed by number of names searched. 1st project may require prepayment. Credit cards accepted. They specialize in criminal and civil record research throughout the whole State of California with nationwide correspondence; other searches available include MVR report and employment/education verification. Offers quick and thorough turnaround.

DMI

413 High St #300, Bridgeport, WV 26330
Phone: 304-842-2946 **Fax:** 304-842-5826
www.dmiauctions.com **email:** dmi@dmiauctions.com

Types of Records Retrieved: Civil, criminal and probate courts; Federal courts; Real Estate; Tax liens/Judgments; UCC records; Vital records

Local Retrieval Area: WV-Barbour, Doddridge, Harrison, Lewis, Marion, Mason, Monongalia, Preston, Randolph, Ritchie, Tyler, Upshur, Wood. **Correspondent Relationships:** West Virginia.

Add'l Information: Established 1978. Normal turnaround time- 24-48 hours. Projects billed by number of names searched. Credit cards accepted. They perform service of process.

Shelly and James Dobler

207 Bob Hayes Rd, Jonesboro, TN 37659
Phone: 423-753-4885

Types of Records Retrieved: Civil and criminal courts

Local Retrieval Area: TN-Carter, Sullivan, Unicoi, Washington

Add'l Information: Established 2000. 1st project may require prepayment. They specialize in civil and criminal court records.

Doc Hunters

812 Pinellas St, Clearwater, FL 33756-3429
Phone: 727-518-6700 **Fax:** 727-518-6886
www.dochunters.com **email:** orders@dochunters.com

Types of Records Retrieved: Real Estate; Current Owner Searches; UCC records, Tax liens/Judgments

Local Retrieval Area: FL-Hillsborough, Pinellas. **Correspondent Relationships:** Nationwide, especially in FL, IL, IN, MD, MI, NM, PA.

Add'l Information: Established 2001. Normal turnaround time- 3-5 days. Projects billed by number of names searched. Doc Hunters specializes in current owner searches and all forms of real estate and mortgage document retrieval and also filing in FL, IL, IN, MD, MI, NM, PA.

Doc*U*Search Inc

PO Box 777, Concord, NH 03302-0777
Phone: 800-332-3034; 603-224-2871 **Fax:** 877-524-3034; 603-224-2794
www.docusearchinc.com **email:** mlc@docusearchinc.com

Types of Records Retrieved: Civil, criminal and probate courts; Federal courts; Real Estate; Tax liens/Judgments; UCC records; Vital records

Local Retrieval Area: NH-Belknap, Carroll, Cheshire, Coos, Grafton, Hillsborough, Merrimack, Rockingham, Strafford, Sullivan. **Correspondent Relationships:** nationwide, as well as Carroll, Cheshire, Coos, Grafton, Strafford, Sullivan counties in NH.

Add'l Information: Established 1977. Normal turnaround time- variable depending on county. Fee basis will vary by type of search. Credit accounts accepted. They specialize in UCC, corporate, court documents, tax lien, current owner, and specific mortgage/assignment searches in all New England states.

Docu-File Inc

3015 E Skelly Dr #253, Tulsa, OK 74015
Phone: 877-742-4994; 918-742-4994 **Fax:** 800-722-8889; 918-742-4228

Types of Records Retrieved: Real Estate; Tax liens/Judgments; UCC records; Vital records

Local Retrieval Area: OK-Creek, Rogers, Tulsa. **Correspondent Relationships:** nationwide.

Add'l Information: Established 1997. Normal turnaround time- 24 hours. Projects billed by number of names searched. 1st project may require prepayment. They specialize in real estate record checks, including 40 years searches. They also do oil and gas related title work. They have 20 years experience in title business.

Document Depot Express

18738 Jersey Ave, Artesia, CA 90701
Phone: 562-860-2907, 706-2031 **Fax:** 562-865-8207, 865-7000
docdepotexpress@aol.com

Types of Records Retrieved: Real Estate; Tax liens/Judgments; Vital records

Local Retrieval Area: CA-Los Angeles, Orange, Riverside, San Bernardino, San Diego. **Correspondent Relationships:** Southern California.

Add'l Information: Established 1999. Normal turnaround time- 24 hours. Projects billed by number of names searched. All projects require prepayment. Payment terms are net 30 days. They specialize in real estate record research, document retrieval, current owner and deed reports.

Document Hunters LLC

PO Box 10986, Fort Wayne, IN 46855
Phone: 260-760-5703 **Fax:** 530-504-8086
www.documenthunters.com **email:** info@documenthunters.com

Types of Records Retrieved: Civil and criminal courts; Real Estate

Local Retrieval Area: IN-Adams, Allen, De Kalb, Huntington, Noble, Wells, Whitley

Add'l Information: Established 2003. Normal turnaround time- 24-48 hours. Expedited service available. Projects billed by number of names searched. 1st project may require prepayment. They are a publicrecords search firm serving central and northern Indiana.

Document Recording & Retrieval Services

55 S Valle Verde #235-192, Henderson, NV 89012
Phone: 702-558-6207 **Fax:** 702-617-9548
www.drrsvcs.com **email:** customerservice@drrsvcs.com

Types of Records Retrieved: Real Estate; Tax liens/Judgments; UCC records; Vital records

Local Retrieval Area: NV-Clark, Washoe. **Correspondent Relationships:** nationwide.

Add'l Information: Established 2000. Normal turnaround time- 48 hours. Projects billed by number of names searched. 1st project may require prepayment. They specialize in document recording of assignments in all recording districts. They do expedient retrieval of records nationwide.

Document Research Service

6002 E Cambridge Av, Scottsdale, AZ 85257
Phone: 480-947-5493 **Fax:** 480-947-5496
jjohn32@juno.com

Types of Records Retrieved: Real Estate; Tax liens/Judgments; UCC records; Vital records

Local Retrieval Area: AZ-Maricopa

Add'l Information: Established 1999. Normal turnaround time- 24-48 hours, depending upon project. Projects billed by number of names searched. Or, per project or report. Payment due upon receipt. They specialize in current owner/mortgage abstracts and obtaining local and nationwide police reports. A licensed PI in AZ.

Document Retrieval Inc

6307 Red Haven Rd, Columbia, MD 21045-4475
Phone: 443-995-7488 **Fax:** 410-312-9989
a_carels@yahoo.com

Types of Records Retrieved: Real Estate

Local Retrieval Area: MD-Anne Arundel, Baltimore, Baltimore City, Calvert, Carroll, Cecil, Charles, Frederick, Harford, Howard, Mongtomery, Prince George's, Queen Annes, St Marys

Add'l Information: Established 1999. Normal turnaround time- 24-48 hours if electronic, 3-5 days if courthouse retrieval. Projects billed by number of names searched. 1st project may require prepayment. Document Retrieval Inc started in 1999. They specialize in land record recording and retrieval, but will pull legal documents as well. They have the ability to pull records from home as well as from the courthouses. Also a process server. They perform service of process.

Document Retrieval Network Inc

351 Elm St, Falmouth, KY 41040
Phone: 859-654-2890 **Fax:** 859-654-2892
www.docret.com **email:** arindel@docret.com

Types of Records Retrieved: Real Estate; Tax liens/judgments; UCC records

Local Retrieval Area: KY-Boone, Campbell, Fayette, Grant, Harrison, Jefferson, Kenton, Pendleton; NY-Bronx, Kings, Nassau, Queens, Suffolk; OH-Butler, Clermont, Hamilton, Montgomery, Warren. **Correspondent Relationships:** OH, NY, NJ, PA, KY, WV, ME, CT & MA.

Add'l Information: Established 1999. Normal turnaround time- 24-48 hours. Projects billed by number of names searched. 1st project may require prepayment. They specialize in high volume real estate document retrieval and title searches.

Document Retrieval Service

PO Box 276, Oklahoma City, OK 73101
Phone: 877-902-9377; 405-235-3653 **Fax:** 877-903-9377; 405-235-2691
www.drsok.com **email:** steve@drsok.com

Types of Records Retrieved: Civil and criminal courts; Federal courts; Real Estate; Tax liens/Judgments; UCC records; Vital records; Corporate filings; Secretary of State documents

Local Retrieval Area: OK-77 counties. **Correspondents:** statewide.

Add'l Information: Established 1970. Normal turnaround time- 24 hours Oklahoma County and Secretary of State, all other counties 48 hours or more. Projects billed by number of names searched. Payment is due on receipt. They specialize in corporate retrieval and filings at the Secretary of State. They also search all (77) counties in Oklahoma for UCC filings, State and Federal tax liens, pending suits and judgments as well as real property searches.

Document Search Services

422 Memory Ct, Green Bay, WI 54301
Phone: 800-526-2157; 920-437-6040 **Fax:** 800-981-9502; 920-437-6045
shinegb@aol.com

Types of Records Retrieved: Real Estate

Local Retrieval Area: WI-Brown, Calumet, Dane, Dodge, Door, Douglas, Fond du Lac, Jefferson, Kenosha, Kewaunee, Manitowoc, Marinette, Milwaukee, Outagamie, Ozaukee, Racine, Washington, Waukesha, Winnebago. **Correspondent Relationships:** statewide.

Add'l Information: Normal turnaround time- 3-5 days. Projects billed by number of names searched. Bill within 15-30 days. They specialize in providing document retrieval of mortgage and assignment copies in all Wisconsin counties.

Document Services

1003 K St NW #200, Washington, DC 20001-4425
Phone: 202-637-0362 **Fax:** 202-637-0169

Types of Records Retrieved: Civil, criminal and probate courts; Federal courts; Real Estate; Tax liens/Judgments; UCC records; Vital records

Local Retrieval Area: District of Columbia. **Correspondent Relationships:** nearby DC areas.

Add'l Information: Normal turnaround time- 48-72 hours. Projects billed by number of names searched. Projects billed by the hour. They are primarily an abstracting company, and provides full services, including surrounding DC area.

Documents 5280

12555 Forest View St, Broomfield, CO 80020
Phone: 303-438-8967 **Fax:** 303-438-8180
documents5280@msn.com

Types of Records Retrieved: Real Estate; Tax liens/judgments; UCC records

Local Retrieval Area: CO-Adams, Arapahoe, Boulder, Broomfield, Denver, Douglas, Jefferson

Add'l Information: Established 2004. Normal turnaround time- 24-72 hours. Expedited service available. Projects billed by number of names searched. Payment due-net 30 days. Invoice sent with each job. They specialize in real estate document search/retrieval in the Metro Denver area. Expect professional and accurate work completed on time and at a fair rate.

DocumentServe Express

1800 3rd Ave #612, Rock Island, IL 61201
Phone: 309-786-2220 **Fax:** 309-786-2221
www.documentserve.com **email:** documentserve@mchsi.com

Types of Records Retrieved: Civil, criminal and probate courts; Federal courts; Real Estate; Tac liens/judgments; UCC records; Vital records

Local Retrieval Area: IA-Scott; IL-Rock Island

Add'l Information: Established 1997. Normal turnaround time- 48-72 hours. Expedited service available. records searched. 1st project may require prepayment. Credit cards accepted. Please call to schedule service and payment. DocumentServe Express specialize in motor vehicle registration and drivers licenses as well as court services. Is a division of Russwurn Services Ltd, a licensed Private Detective/Investigation service. They service Illinois and Iowa. A licensed PI in IA, IL. They perform service of process.

Docu-Search California

14252 Culver Dr #A802, Irvine, CA 92604
Phone: 800-466-9450; 714-836-8664 **Fax:** 888-466-9459; 714-836-8871

Types of Records Retrieved: Civil, criminal and probate courts; Federal courts; Real Estate; Tax liens/Judgments; UCC records; Vital records

Local Retrieval Area: CA-Los Angeles, Orange, Riverside, San Bernardino. **Correspondent Relationships:** statewide.

Add'l Information: Established 1990. Normal turnaround time- 1-3 days. Projects billed by number of names searched. 1st project may require prepayment.

Doc-U-Search Hawaii

1188 Bishop St #2212, Honolulu, HI 96813
Phone: 808-523-1200 **Fax:** 808-533-3686

Types of Records Retrieved: Civil and criminal courts; Federal courts; Real Estate; Tax liens/Judgments; UCC records

Local Retrieval Area: HI-Hawaii, Honolulu, Kalawao, Kauai, Maui

Add'l Information: Established 1986. Normal turnaround time- 2 days. Expedited service available. Projects billed by number of names searched. 1st project may require prepayment. They perform service of process.

Docu-Search of Washington DC

630 Indiana Ave NW 2nd Fl, Washington, DC 20004-2905
Phone: 202-737-5707 **Fax:** 202-737-5708

Types of Records Retrieved: Civil, criminal and probate courts; Federal courts; Real Estate; Tax liens/Judgments; UCC records; Vital records

Local Retrieval Area: DC-District of Columbia, MD-Montgomery

Add'l Information: Established 1991. Normal turnaround time- 48 hours. Fee depends upon type of project. 1st project may require prepayment. They specialize in real estate searches, land tax liens, and UCC in the city of Washington, DC. A cell phone contact number for the company is 202-276-0119.

DocuSearch Services

1036 Shady Fork Rd, Chattanooga, TN 37421
Phone: 423-894-2425 **Fax:** 423-894-3572
hendersonlarry@juno.com

Types of Records Retrieved: Real Estate; Tax liens/Judgments; UCC records

Local Retrieval Area: GA-Chattooga, Murray, Walker; TN-Marion, Polk

Add'l Information: Established 1996. Normal turnaround time- 24-48 hours. Projects billed by number of names searched. Perfer 30-60 payment cycles. They are a document retrieval resource pledging timeliness and accuracy.

Docutech Information Services Inc

580 E Town St #131, Columbus, OH 43215-4872

Phone: 800-361-3310; 614-221-4625 **Fax:** 800-445-3308; 614-221-4658

Types of Records Retrieved: Civil, criminal and probate courts; Federal courts; Real Estate; Tax liens/Judgments; UCC records; Vital records

Local Retrieval Area: OH-Clark, Fairfield, Fayette, Franklin, Jackson, Licking, Montgomery, Muskingum, Pickaway, Pike, Ross. **Correspondent Relationships:** Ohio. They do not charge correspondence fees.

Add'l Information: Established 1991. Normal turnaround time- 24-48 hours. Projects billed by number of names searched. Payment due upon invoice. They specialize in UCC searches, liens, suits, judgment searches, asset searches, record retrieving, probate, domestic relations and bankruptcy.

Docx

1111 Alderman Dr #350, Alpharetta, GA 30005

Phone: 866-729-8099; **Fax:** 770-753-2730

www.docx.com **email:** docxacct@docx.com

Types of Records Retrieved: Real Estate; UCC records

Local Retrieval Area: GA-Cobb, De Kalb, Fulton. **Correspondent Relationships:** nationwide contractors every county nationwide.

Add'l Information: Normal turnaround time- 3-5 business days. Projects billed by number of names searched. 1st project may require prepayment. Payment due upon receipt for established clients. They offer image delivery, certified copies, online ordering, 1 day turnaround on "information only" requests, and online status reporting.

Dolores Dios Title Abstractor

59 Crescent Ave, Totowa, NJ 07512-2305

Phone: 201-207-0628 **Fax:** 973-837-1594

Types of Records Retrieved: Probate courts; Real Estate; Tax liens/Judgments; UCC records

Local Retrieval Area: NJ-Bergen, Essex, Hudson, Middlesex, Monmouth, Morris, Ocean, Passaic, Somerset, Susses, Union

Add'l Information: Established 1974. Normal turnaround time- 3 days. Projects billed by number of names searched. Projects billed by number of records located. 1st project may require prepayment. Payment due upon receipt. She specializes in court record searches, real estate and environmental searches, foreclosures and tax sales. Voice mail: 973-837-1959.

Dominion Abstract & Title Agency

PO Box 72607, Richmond, VA 23235

Phone: 804-794-9037 **Fax:** 804-379-6232

saabgirl1@netzero.com

Types of Records Retrieved: Civil, criminal and probate courts; Real Estate; Tax liens/Judgments; UCC records

Local Retrieval Area: VA-Amelia, Chesterfield, Hanover, Henrico, Powhatan, Richmond City

Add'l Information: Established 1985. Normal turnaround time- 24-48 hours. Projects billed by number of names searched. 1st project may require prepayment.

Dominion Record Search

2416 Little Creek Dam Rd, Toano, VA 23168

Phone: 757-566-8233 **Fax:** 757-566-8291

joan.hanchey@verizon.net

Types of Records Retrieved: Civil and criminal courts; Federal courts; Real Estate; Tax liens/Judgments; UCC records; Vital records

Local Retrieval Area: VA-Chesapeake, Hampton, James City, Newport News, Norfolk, Poquoson, Suffolk, Virginia Beach, Williamsburg, York

Add'l Information: Established 2001. Normal turnaround time- 24 hours. Projects billed by number of names searched. End of the month billing cycle. Dominion Record Search represents the Old Dominion state in the greater Hampton Roads and Tidewater areas. Requests are searched in civil courts, federal courts, district and circuit courts.

Lorina Dominquez

209 N 1st, Carlsbad, NM 88220

Phone: 505-887-3489 **Fax:** 505-887-3489

Types of Records Retrieved: Civil and criminal courts.

Local Retrieval Area: NM-Eddy

Add'l Information: Normal turnaround time- 1-2 days. 1st project may require prepayment. Her cell phone is 505-361-0015. She specializes in criminal court records, also civil.

Don Martin & Assoc.

1315 Homs Ave #A, Kokemo, IN 46902

Phone: 765-452-1760 **Fax:** 765-236-1770

www.indianapi.com **email:** dmartin@indianapi.com

Types of Records Retrieved: Civil and criminal courts.

Local Retrieval Area: IN-Cass, Grant, Howard, Miami, Tipton, Wabash

Add'l Information: Established 2003. Normal turnaround time- 3-5 days. 1st project may require prepayment. They also provide court filings, court record retrieval, skiptracing and private investigations. A licensed PI in IN. They perform service of process.

Larry R Dorning PC

111 W Main St, Hohenwald, TN 38462-1404

Phone: 931-796-5959 **Fax:** 931-796-5950

Types of Records Retrieved: Real Estate; Tax liens/Judgments; UCC records

Local Retrieval Area: TN-Hickman, Lawrence, Lewis, Maury, Perry, Wayne

Add'l Information: Established 1975. Normal turnaround time- 48 hours. Charges vary depending on type of search. He specializes in real estate record searches. He will file documents in Lewis County only.

Dotter Abstract & Associates

506 Main St, Walsenburg, CO 81089

Phone: 719-738-1730 **Fax:** 719-738-1012

Types of Records Retrieved: Real Estate; Tax liens/Judgments; UCC records; Vital records

Local Retrieval Area: CO-Huerfano, Las Animas

Add'l Information: Established 1982. Normal turnaround time- 2-3 days. Fee basis will vary by the type of project. 1st project may require prepayment. They specialize in real estate title and insurance.

Dora Doty

106 Ruggles Ave, St Clairsville, OH 43950

Phone: 740-695-4917 **Fax:** 740-699-0676

Types of Records Retrieved: Civil, criminal and probate courts; Real Estate; Tax liens/Judgments; UCC records; Vital records

Local Retrieval Area: OH-Belmont, Guernsey, Harrison, Jefferson, Monroe, Noble

Add'l Information: Established 1990. Normal turnaround time- 24-48 hours. Projects billed by number of names searched. She specializes in title and lien work. She has 30 years experience.

Douglas County Abstract & Title Co

PO Box 97, Ava, MO 65608

Phone: 417-683-4701 **Fax:** 417-683-5980

Types of Records Retrieved: Civil, criminal and probate courts; Real Estate; Tax liens/Judgments

Local Retrieval Area: MO-Douglas

Add'l Information: Established 1950. Normal turnaround time- 5 working days. Fee basis will vary by type of project.

Douglas County Abstract Co

117 7th Ave E, Alexandria, MN 56308-1807
Phone: 320-763-3426 **Fax:** 320-762-2455
dcac@rea-alp.com

Types of Records Retrieved: Civil courts; Probate courts; Real Estate; Tax liens/Judgments

Local Retrieval Area: MN-Douglas, Pope. **Correspondent Relationships:** statewide.

Add'l Information: Normal turnaround time- 1 week. Projects billed by number of names searched. Charges vary depending on project. 1st project may require prepayment. They also invoice. They specialize in abstracts, closings and title insurance.

Douglas County Abstract Co Inc

PO Box 167, 110 E Sale St, Tuscola, IL 61953
Phone: 217-253-3214 **Fax:** 217-253-3022

Types of Records Retrieved: Probate courts; Real Estate; Tax liens/Judgments; UCC records

Local Retrieval Area: IL-Douglas

Add'l Information: Established 1896. Normal turnaround time- 1-3 days. Projects billed by the hour. 1st project may require prepayment. They are Chicago Title agents.

Douglas County Title Co (Oregon)

629 SE Main St, Roseburg, OR 97470
Phone: 541-672-3388 **Fax:** 541-672-8110
www.douglascountytitle.com **email:** lorries@douglascountytitle.com

Types of Records Retrieved: Civil, criminal and probate courts; Real Estate; Tax liens/Judgments; UCC records; Vital records

Local Retrieval Area: OR-Douglas

Add'l Information: Established 1879. Normal turnaround time- 2-3 days. Projects billed by the hour. All projects require prepayment. They specialize in real estate and escrow collections.

Douglas County Title Inc (South Dakota)

PO Box 310, 722 Main St, Armour, SD 57313
Phone: 605-724-2235 **Fax:** 605-724-2419

Types of Records Retrieved: Civil courts; Probate courts; Real Estate; Tax liens/Judgments

Local Retrieval Area: SD-Douglas

Add'l Information: Established 1953. Normal turnaround time- 4 days. Fee basis varies by type of transaction. They specialize in abstracts and title insurance. They also file/record real estate documents on behalf of clients on a same or next day basis.

Dr Dave's Docs

PO Box 251183, Glendale, CA 91225
Phone: 818-246-3087 **Fax:** 818-265-5006
dhatch1@earthlink.net

Types of Records Retrieved: Real Estate

Local Retrieval Area: CA-Los Angeles, Orange, Riverside, San Bernardino, San Diego, Santa Barbara, Ventura

Add'l Information: Established 1999. Normal turnaround time- 24-72 hours. Projects billed by number of names searched. 1st project may require prepayment. Terms are net 30 days. Will do walk-in recording of documents.

Drake Land Title Co

167 W Main, PO Box 998, Warsaw, MO 65355-0998
Phone: 660-438-5188 **Fax:** 660-438-6644
drakeland@earthlink.net

Types of Records Retrieved: Civil, criminal and probate courts; Real Estate; Tax liens/Judgments; UCC records

Local Retrieval Area: MO-Benton

Add'l Information: Established 1886. Normal turnaround time- variable depending on project. Projects billed by number of names searched. 1st project may require prepayment. They specialize in title insurance.

Drew County Abstract & Title Co

PO Box 533, Monticello, AR 71657
Phone: 870-367-6607 **Fax:** 870-367-6560 drewabst@ccc-cable.net

Types of Records Retrieved: Real Estate

Local Retrieval Area: AR-Drew

Add'l Information: Established 1982. Fee basis will vary by type of project. All projects require prepayment. They specialize in title insurance.

DRS Information Services

1333 Clock Ave., Redlands, CA 92374
Phone: 909-792-6466 **Fax:** 909-792-6434
drsinfo@dslextreme.com

Types of Records Retrieved: Civil and criminal courts.

Local Retrieval Area: CA-San Bernardino. **Correspondent Relationships:** Southern California.

Add'l Information: Established 1994. Normal turnaround time- 24-36 hours. 1st project may require prepayment. They special in court research - criminal and civil - in San Bernardino County. Over 10 years experience.

Duke City Process Service & Inv

PO Box 16166, Albuquerque, NM 87191-6166
Phone: 505-275-0994 **Fax:** 505-275-7327

Types of Records Retrieved: Civil and criminal courts; Probte courts; Federal courts; Real Estate; Tax liens/Judgments; Vital Records

Local Retrieval Area: NM-Bernallio, Sandoval, Valencia. **Correspondent Relationships:** statewide.

Add'l Information: Established 1980. Normal turnaround time- 3-4 days. Expedited service available. Projects billed by the hour. 1st project may require prepayment. Threee decades of experience in New Mexico's economic center. A licensed PI in NM. They perform service of process.

Dunn County Abstract & Title Inc

815 7th St E, Menomonie, WI 54751
Phone: 800-628-5727; 715-235-0875 **Fax:** 715-235-9690
dcat@wwt.net

Types of Records Retrieved: Real Estate; Tax liens/Judgments

Local Retrieval Area: NC-Mitchell

Add'l Information: Established 1940. Normal turnaround time- 1-2 days for Dunn county. For Pepin county 1 week to 10 days. Fee basis varies by type of transaction. 1st project may require prepayment. They specialize in title work and closings.

E

E Title & Abstract LLC

10831 Dutch Hollow Rd, Rixeyville, VA 22737
Phone: 540-727-0515 **Fax:** 540-727-0519
etitleabstract@aol.com

Types of Records Retrieved: Civil courts; Real Estate; Tax liens/Judgments; UCC records

Local Retrieval Area: VA-Albemarle, Culpeper, Fauquier, Louisa, Orange, Spotsylvania

Add'l Information: Established 2003. Normal turnaround time- 24-48 hours. Projects billed by number of names searched. Will invoice with a net 10 days. E Title & Abstract is a quality title research company in the North Central area of Virginia committed to being of service.

Eagle Communications

4568 Mayfield Rd #213, Cleveland, OH 44121
Phone: 216-297-3200 **Fax:** 216-297-3203
www.wingsinfonet.com **email:** miker@wingsinfonet.com

Types of Records Retrieved: Civil, criminal and probate courts; Federal courts; Real Estate; Tax liens/Judgments; UCC records; Vital records

Local Retrieval Area: OH-Ashtabula, Cuyahoga, Franklin, Geauga, Hamilton, Lake, Lorain, Mahoning, Portage, Stark, Summit, Trumbull. **Correspondent Relationships:** all 88 Ohio counties; most counties nationwide; Canada, Puerto Rico.

Add'l Information: Established 1990. Normal turnaround time- 24-48 hours. Projects billed by number of names searched. Billing dependent on type of search. Terms: net 10 days. They specialize in felony/misd., civil, UCCs, lien searches, pre-employment screening, real estate/owner/asset searches, business & individual background screenings/profiles. They file/record UCC and real estate docs for clients in Cuyahoga & Lake only. They perform service of process.

EAGLE i Communications

7800 Lonesome Harbor Ave, Las Vegas, NV 89131-5001
Phone: 702-658-3912 **Fax:** 702-658-4860
eagleicomm@cox.net

Types of Records Retrieved: Civil courts; Probate courts; Federal courts; Real Estate; Tax liens/Judgments; UCC records

Local Retrieval Area: CA-Los Angeles, Orange; NV-Clark. **Correspondent Relationships:** statewide.

Add'l Information: Established 1996. Normal turnaround time- 24-72 hours. Projects billed by number of names searched. Terms: net 30 days. They specialize in civil litigation, UCCs, liens and all recorded documents as well as retrieval from the US Bankruptcy Central District of California & US District Court, Central District. Also includes Clark County, NV.

Earlene Y Speer Law Offices

PO Box 310, Altamont, TN 37301
Phone: 931-692-2368 **Fax:** 931-692-2367

Types of Records Retrieved: Civil, criminal and probate courts; Real Estate; Tax liens/Judgments; UCC records; Vital records

Local Retrieval Area: TN-Grundy

Add'l Information: Established 1989. Normal turnaround time- 2 days. Projects billed by number of names searched. 1st project may require prepayment. They specialize in title and UCC searches.

East Arkansas Title Co

PO Box 408, Helena, AR 72342-0408
Phone: 870-338-8306 **Fax:** 870-338-8307

Types of Records Retrieved: Civil courts; Probate courts; Real Estate; Tax liens/Judgments; UCC records

Local Retrieval Area: AR-Phillips

Add'l Information: Established 1937. Normal turnaround time- 3-5 days. Projects billed by the hour. 1st project may require prepayment.

East Tex Records Research

5901 Glengary Rd, Lufkin, TX 75901-9764
Phone: 936-824-3724 **Fax:** 936-824-3724
www.masterwebs.com/eastex **email:** eastexrecords@yahoo.com

Types of Records Retrieved: Civil, criminal and probate courts; Federal Disctrict courts; Real Estate; Tax liens/Judgments; UCC records

Local Retrieval Area: TX-Angelina, Nacogdoches, Rusk. **Correspondent Relationships:** most of East and Central Texas areas.

Add'l Information: Established 1994. Normal turnaround time- 2-36 hours, most CV/CR orders rec'd by e-mail or by 10 AM are completed on same day. Expedited service available. Projects billed by number of names searched. Terms are net 30 days. Credit cards accepted. Terms net 30 days. Accurate and timely reports result from concerted attention to detail & over 17 years experience. Searches are performed "hands on" at the courts (including USDC TX East Div.) not by databases. Cell phone # 936-414-1193.

East Texas Professional Svcs

PO Box 253, Tennessee Colony, TX 75861
Phone: 903-928-0117 **Fax:** 903-928-0117

Types of Records Retrieved: Civil and criminal courts, Probate courts; Federal courts; Tax liens/Judgments; Vital records.

Local Retrieval Area: TX-Anderson, Cherokee, Freestone, Handerson, Smith, Van Zandt

Add'l Information: Established 1999. Normal turnaround time- 24 hours. Projects billed by the hour. All projects require prepayment. They specialize in notary services and service of process as well as document retrieval. They perform service of process.

East Texas Public Records

PO Box 152555, Lufkin, TX 75915
Phone: 936-632-7385 **Fax:** 936-632-7385
meredithsmith@consolidated.net

Types of Records Retrieved: Real Estate

Local Retrieval Area: TX-Angelina, Trinity

Add'l Information: Established 1997. Normal turnaround time- 24-72 hours. Projects billed by number of names searched. Will invoice. They specialize in real estate searches. They have been in business since 1997. Fax is same as phone.

Eastern Oregon Title Inc

PO Box 1084, 1601 Adams Ave, La Grande, OR 97850
Phone: 541-963-8561 **Fax:** 541-963-2391
www.eotitle.com **email:** eotitle@uwtc.net

Types of Records Retrieved: Civil and criminal courts; Real Estate; Tax liens/Judgments; UCC records

Local Retrieval Area: OR-Union

Add'l Information: Established 1974. Normal turnaround time- 3-4 days. Projects billed by the hour. 1st project may require prepayment. Terms: net 30 days. They specialize in title, escrow and collections.

Eastland Title Co

PO Box 680, 69 W Franklin St, Hillsboro, TX 76645
Phone: 254-582-2762 **Fax:** 254-582-2760
eastlandtitle@hillsboro.net

Types of Records Retrieved: Civil, criminal and probate courts; Real Estate; Tax liens/Judgments; UCC records; Vital records

Local Retrieval Area: TX-Hill

Add'l Information: Established 1898. Normal turnaround time- up to 1 week. Fee basis will vary by the type of project. Prepayment requirement on first project for title searches.

Eaton Abstract Company

122 S Van Buren St, Newton, IL 62448
Phone: 618-783-8474 **Fax:** 618-783-3199

Types of Records Retrieved: Civil, criminal and probate courts; Real Estate; Tax liens/Judgments; UCC records

Local Retrieval Area: IL-Jasper

Add'l Information: Established 1941. Normal turnaround time- 24-48 hours. Projects billed by number of names searched. Projects billed by number of records located. 1st project may require prepayment. They specialize in complete title service searches.

Donna Eccles

4207 Thompson Rd, Sulphur, LA 76665
Phone: 337-558-6627 **Fax:** 337-558-6627
deccles4207@aol.com

Types of Records Retrieved: Criminal records at the District Court only.

Local Retrieval Area: LA-Calcasieu

Add'l Information: Established 1996. Normal turnaround time- 24-48 hours. 1st project may require prepayment. Specializes in criminal searches in Calcasieu Parish; all searches confidential.

Ed Knight Information Service

6651 Cameron Rd, Morrow, GA 30260
Phone: 800-282-6418; **Fax:** 800-282-6416;
www.edknight.com **email:** ekis@edknight.com

Types of Records Retrieved: Civil and criminal courts; Federal courts; Real Estate; Tax liens/Judgments; UCC records

Local Retrieval Area: GA-Clayton, Henry. **Correspondent Relationships:** Georgia statewide.

Add'l Information: Established 1972. Normal turnaround time- 1-2 days. Projects billed by number of names searched. 1st project may require prepayment. Payment due net 30 days from invoice. They specialize in lien searches in metropolitan Atlanta, but will drive to any county in Georgia for a reasonable fee. They are online with the Georgia Clerks Authority.

Eddy County Abstract Co

116 N Canyon St, Carlsbad, NM 88220
Phone: 800-348-1232; 505-887-2828 **Fax:** 505-887-0824

Types of Records Retrieved: Civil courts; Probate courts; Real Estate; Tax liens/Judgments; UCC records

Local Retrieval Area: NM-Eddy. **Correspondent Relationships:** worldwide.

Add'l Information: Established 1891. Normal turnaround time- 12-24 hours. Fees depend on type of service. They specialize in loan closing and mineral searches, and are fully computerized.

Edgar County Title Co

206 W Washington St, Paris, IL 61944
Phone: 217-465-5821 **Fax:** 217-463-7265
www.tigerpaw.com/ect **email:** edgar.county.title.co@tigerpaw.com

Types of Records Retrieved: Civil courts; Probate courts; Real Estate; Tax liens/Judgments; UCC records; Vital records

Local Retrieval Area: IL-Edgar

Add'l Information: Established 1977. Normal turnaround time- 1-5 days. Projects billed by number of names searched. Billing upon completion.

Edith Wiggins & Marvin Singer

1725 Taylor St #A, San Francisco, CA 94133
Phone: 415-771-9369 **Fax:** 415-441-8519
www.mesinger.com **email:** maemsi@mesinger.com

Types of Records Retrieved: Civil, criminal and probate courts; Federal courts; Tax liens/Judgments; UCC records

Local Retrieval Area: CA-San Francisco, San Mateo

Add'l Information: Normal turnaround time- 1 day or less. Projects billed by number of names searched. Terms: net 30 days. They provide criminal pre-employment background checks and a variety of public record search services.

Edmunds County Abstract Co

PO Box 128, Ipswich, SD 57451-0128
Phone: 605-426-6041 **Fax:** 605-426-6400

Types of Records Retrieved: Civil courts; Probate courts; Real Estate; Tax liens/Judgments

Local Retrieval Area: SD-Edmunds

Add'l Information: Established 1929. Normal turnaround time- 3-5 days. Projects billed by number of names searched. Projects billed by number of records located. Projects billed by the hour. All projects require prepayment.

Edna Yerks Abstracts

103 Brand Rd, Toms River, NJ 08753
Phone: 732-349-9747 **Fax:** 732-240-0950

Types of Records Retrieved: Criminal courts

Local Retrieval Area: NJ-Ocean

Add'l Information: Established 1984. Normal turnaround time- 24-48 hours. Projects billed by number of names searched. She specializes in criminal record searching.

EHS Research Services

253 Garth Rd, Scarsdale, NY 10583
Phone: 914-472-5848 **Fax:** 914-725-3613
ehsshap316@cs.com

Types of Records Retrieved: Civil, criminal and probate courts; Federal courts; Real Estate; Tax liens/Judgments; UCC records

Local Retrieval Area: NY-New York, Putnam, Rockland, Westchester

Add'l Information: Established 1992. Normal turnaround time- 48-72 hours. Projects billed by the hour. They specialize in locating people and assets. A licensed PI in NY. They perform service of process.

Ekum Abstract & Title

PO Box 263, 912 18th Ave (53566), Monroe, WI 53566-0263
Phone: 608-328-8221 **Fax:** 608-328-8223
www.ekum.com **email:** ekum@ekum.com

Types of Records Retrieved: Civil, criminal and probate courts; Real Estate; Tax liens/Judgments; UCC records

Local Retrieval Area: WI-Green, Lafayette. **Correspondent Relationships:** Lafayette county WI.

Add'l Information: Established 1897. Normal turnaround time- 1-2 days. Projects billed by number of names searched. They specialize in real estate and maintain their own in-house records of real estate in tract indexes. All other county records are 1 block away.

Elder & Ryan Abstracts LLC

30 Courthouse Sq #403, Rockville, MD 20850
Phone: 301-854-1200 **Fax:** 301-854-1212
jamie@elderabstracts.com

Types of Records Retrieved: Civil, criminal and probate courts; Federal courts; Real Estate; Tax liens/Judgments; UCC records; Vital records

Local Retrieval Area: MD-Montgomery

Add'l Information: Established 1985. Normal turnaround time- 6-24 hours. Projects billed by number of names searched. Payment due net 30 days. They specialize in title abstracts and local document retrieval.

ELH Contracting Inc, Independent Land & Title Abstractor

PO Box 35, Dayton, TX 77535
Phone: 409-832-5793 **Fax:** 409-866-3546
leehill@sbcglobal.net

Types of Records Retrieved: Civil, criminal and probate courts; Federal courts; Real Estate; Tax liens/Judgments; UCC records; Vital records

Local Retrieval Area: TX-Chambers, Hardin, Jefferson, Liberty, Orange

Add'l Information: Established 1989. Normal turnaround time- 24-48 hours. Projects billed by number of names searched. Invoices at the end of month. They specialize in civil and criminal records, probate, Tax liens/Judgments, real estate, UCCs, vital records, dba/assumed names, abstracting and general retrieval and filings.

Elk County Abstract & Title Co

PO Box 458, 144 E Randolph, Howard, KS 67349-0458
Phone: 620-374-2500 **Fax:** 620-374-2555

Types of Records Retrieved: Civil, criminal and probate courts; Real Estate; Tax liens/Judgments; UCC records; Vital records

Local Retrieval Area: KS-Elk

Add'l Information: Established 1900. Normal turnaround time- 1-2 days. Fee basis varies by type of transaction. All projects require prepayment. They specialize in title insurance and abstracts.

Elliott & Waldron Abstr Co of Palo Pinto

403 S Oak Ave, Mineral Wells, TX 76067
Phone: 940-325-6564 **Fax:** 940-325-1036
elliottwaldron@cox-internet.com

Types of Records Retrieved: Civil courts; Probate courts; Real Estate; Tax liens/Judgments; UCC records; Vital records

Local Retrieval Area: TX-Palo Pinto

Add'l Information: Normal turnaround time- 2 days. Fee basis will vary by the type of project. 1st project may require prepayment.

Elliott & Waldron Abstract Co - Canton

681 W Dallas St, Canton, TX 75103
Phone: 903-567-4127 **Fax:** 903-567-1757
ellwalco@vzinet.com

Types of Records Retrieved: Civil, criminal and probate courts; Real Estate; Tax liens/Judgments; UCC records; Vital records

Local Retrieval Area: TX-Van Zandt. **Correspondent Relationships:** Dallas, Kaufman, Rains, Smith, Wood, Rockwell, Hunt counties.

Add'l Information: Established 1960. Normal turnaround time- 1-3 days. Fee basis will vary by the type of project. Payment due upon completion. They are fast and accurate. They specialize in title examination, real estate closing and title policy issues.

Elliott & Waldron Abstract Co - Pecos

PO Box 490, 306 S Nelson St, Fort Stockton, TX 79735-0490

Phone: 432-336-5214 **Fax:** 432-336-7869

Types of Records Retrieved: Real Estate; Tax liens/Judgments; UCC records

Local Retrieval Area: TX-Pecos

Add'l Information: Normal turnaround time- up to 1 week. Fee basis will vary by the type of project. 1st project may require prepayment.

Elliott & Waldron Title & Abstract

1819 N Turner #B, Hobbs, NM 88240

Phone: 505-393-7706 **Fax:** 505-393-7725

www.ewtitle.com **email:** ew@ewtitle.com

Types of Records Retrieved: Civil courts; Probate courts; Real Estate; Tax liens/Judgments; UCC records

Local Retrieval Area: NM-Lea

Add'l Information: Established 1979. Normal turnaround time- variable depending on project. Fee basis will vary by type of project. Terms: net 30 days.

Ellis County Abstract & Title Co

110 E 12th St, Hays, KS 67601

Phone: 785-625-2316 **Fax:** 785-625-6349

Types of Records Retrieved: Civil, criminal and probate courts; Real Estate; Tax liens/Judgments; UCC records; Vital records

Local Retrieval Area: KS-Ellis, Rooks

Add'l Information: Normal turnaround time- 2-3 days. Projects billed by number of names searched. They specialize in abstract, title insurance and certificates.

Ellyson Abstract & Title Co of Brewster

PO Box 418, Alpine, TX 79830

Phone: 432-837-5801 **Fax:** 432-837-3509

Types of Records Retrieved: Civil courts; Probate courts; Real Estate; Tax liens/Judgments; UCC records; Vital records

Local Retrieval Area: TX-Brewster, Jeff Davis, Presidio

Add'l Information: Normal turnaround time- 2 days. Fee basis will vary by the type of project. 1st project may require prepayment.

Elman Resources

546 Orange Dr #12, Altamonte Springs, FL 32701

Phone: 407-834-5344 **Fax:** 407-834-6748

caelman@aol.com

Types of Records Retrieved: Civil and criminal courts

Local Retrieval Area: FL-Lake, Marion, Orange, Osceola, Seminole, Volusia. **Correspondent Relationships:** Martin, Polk, Brevard, Monroe, Palm Beach, Hernando, Lake Marion, Hillsborough, Pinellas, Duval, Flagler, Lee, Pasco, Sarasota, St Johns.

Add'l Information: Established 1997. Normal turnaround time- 24-48 hours. Projects billed by number of names searched. 1st project may require prepayment. Formerly Elman Searches, they specialize in criminal and civil searches. Requests accepted via fax, phone or email. Initial project guaranteed satisfaction.

EL-RU Inc

670 Roland Manor Dr, Dacula, GA 30019

Phone: 770-963-8023 **Fax:** 770-682-1885

goodolboy@att.net

Types of Records Retrieved: Civil, criminal and probate courts; Federal courts; Real Estate; Tax liens/Judgments; UCC records; Vital records

Local Retrieval Area: GA-Banks, Barrow, Cherokee, Clarke, Clayton, Cobb, Dawson, DeKalb, Forsyth, Fulton, Gwinnett, Hall, Henry, Jackson, Lumpkin, Newton, Oconee, Oglethorpe, Pickens, Rockdale, Walton, White

Add'l Information: Normal turnaround time- 12-24 hours. Projects billed by number of names searched. They specialize in UCC searches and filing, tax liens, suits, judgments, employee checks, court records retrieval and mortgage searches. Registered agent for the State of Georgia. A licensed PI in GA.

Elson & Fulton Abstractors

203 NE Idaho St, Leon, IA 50144

Phone: 641-446-4621 **Fax:** 641-446-4888

enf@grm.net

Types of Records Retrieved: Civil, criminal and probate courts; Real Estate; Tax liens/Judgments; UCC records; Vital records

Local Retrieval Area: IA-Decatur

Add'l Information: Established 1875. Normal turnaround time- 1-2 days. Fee basis varies by type of transaction. Payment due on completion of work.

Emerald Coast Protective Services Inc

PO Box 9949, Panama City Beach, FL 32417

Phone: 877-234-6252; 850-234-6252 **Fax:** 850-234-8006

www.emeraldpi.net **email:** rpeak@knology.net

Types of Records Retrieved: Civil, criminal and probate courts; Federal courts; Real Estate; Tax liens/Judgments; UCC records; Vital records

Local Retrieval Area: FL-Bay, Gulf, Jackson, Walton. **Correspondent Relationships:** statewide.

Add'l Information: Established 1997. Normal turnaround time- 48 hours. Projects billed by the hour. 1st project may require prepayment. Credit cards accepted. They provide investigative services for Northwest Florida in civil process service and foreclosure sales. A licensed PI in FL. They perform service of process.

Emmons County Abstract & Title

PO Box 428, Linton, ND 58552

Phone: 701-254-4261 **Fax:** 701-254-4261

Types of Records Retrieved: Real Estate; Tax liens/judgments; UCC records

Local Retrieval Area: ND-Emmons

Add'l Information: Established 1963. Normal turnaround time- 1-5 days. Fee basis will vary by the type of project. Terms: net 30 days. They specialize in title searches and abstracting.

Employee Screening Inc

PO Box 2414, Largo, FL 33779

Phone: 727-581 1147 **Fax:** 727-581-1106

jpolivick@ij.net

Types of Records Retrieved: Civil, criminal and probate courts; Real Estate; Tax liens/Judgments

Local Retrieval Area: FL-Manatee, Pinellas. **Correspondent Relationships:** South Carolina.

Add'l Information: Established 1998. Normal turnaround time- 24-48 hours. Projects billed by number of names searched. They specialize in retrievals for attorneys, title companies and employers.

Employmentscreening.com

1463D Gravel Pike, PO Box 177, Perkiomenville, PA 18074-0177

Phone: 215-234-0700 **Fax:** 215-234-0905

www.accufax.cc

Types of Records Retrieved: Civil and criminal courts; Federal courts; Real Estate; Tax liens/Judgments; UCC records; Vital records

Local Retrieval Area: DE-Kent, New Castle, Sussex; NJ-all counties; PA-all counties; MD-all counties. **Correspondent Relationships:** nationwide.

Add'l Information: Established 1986. Normal turnaround time- 12-24 hours. Projects billed by number of names searched. Fees are by county searched. 1st project may require prepayment. They specialize in a full service program for all facets of employment screening. They also do motor vehicle records, UCC, civil litigation and property research.

English Research Services

3631 107th St #208, Riverside, CA 91501
Phone: 951-328-9995 **Fax:** 951-328-9997
calenglish8@verizon.net

Types of Records Retrieved: Civil, criminal and probate courts; Federal courts; Real Estate; Tax liens/Judgments; UCC records; Vital records

Local Retrieval Area: CA-Los Angeles, Orange, Riverside, San Bernardino. **Correspondent Relationships:** West Los Angeles, CA.

Add'l Information: Established 2003. Normal turnaround time- 24 hours. Expedited service available. Projects billed by number of names searched. Projects billed by number of records located. Projects billed by the hour. 1st project may require prepayment. Credit cards accepted. Terms are net 30 days. The specialize in research and retrieval from all county, state and federal agencies and archives. Daily filing provided in Riverside County. Orders accepted by email at calenglish8@verizon.net.

Enterprise Title Company Inc

4343 Lee Hwy #202, Arlington, VA 22207-3241
Phone: 703-351-8066 **Fax:** 703-351-8069
ncc-1701@pressroom.com

Types of Records Retrieved: Civil, criminal and probate courts; Federal courts; Real Estate; Tax liens/Judgments; UCC records

Local Retrieval Area: DC-District of Columbia; VA-Alexandria City, Arlington, Fairfax, Falls Church City, Loudoun, Prince William, Stafford, Warren. **Correspondent Relationships:** statewide.

Add'l Information: Established 1984. Projects billed by number of names searched. Projects billed by the hour. Charges depends on search. 1st project may require prepayment. They also provide research in the federal agencies in Washington, DC, such as the Library of Congress, the Patent & Trademark Office, and the SEC and US Archives.

Jo Ann Entwisle

16340 West 143rd St, Lockport, IL 60441
Phone: 815-838-2871 **Fax:** 815-838-2037
joentwisle@aol.com

Types of Records Retrieved: Criminal courts

Local Retrieval Area: IL-Will

Add'l Information: Established 1996. Normal turnaround time- 24-48 hours. Projects billed by number of names searched.

Equisearch

PO Box 21838, (410 Kingswood Dr, 40502), Lexington, KY 40522-1838
Phone: 859-268-1206 **Fax:** 859-268-1206

Types of Records Retrieved: Civil courts; Federal courts; Real Estate; Tax liens/Judgments; UCC records

Local Retrieval Area: KY-Anderson, Bourbon, Boyle, Clark, Fayette, Franklin, Garrard, Jessamine, Lincoln, Madison, Mercer, Montgomery, Scott, Woodford. **Correspondent Relationships:** Kentucky.

Add'l Information: Established 1987. Normal turnaround time- 24-48 hours. Projects billed by number of names searched. Fee basis will vary by type of project. 1st project may require prepayment. Payment due upon completion of job. They specialize in KY Secretary of state records and Eastern Dist. KY federal court records, as well as 14 eastern KY county courts.

Equity Process Management

PO Box 4906, Missoula, MT 59806
Phone: 888-721-3337; 406-721-3337 **Fax:** 406-721-0372
www.equityprocess.com **email:** equity@centric.net

Types of Records Retrieved: Civil, criminal and probate courts; Federal courts; Tax liens/Judgments; UCC records; Vital records

Local Retrieval Area: MT-Cascade, Deer Lodge, Flathead, Gallatin, Hill, Lake, Lewis & Clark, Missoula, Powell, Ravalli, Silver Bow. **Correspondent Relationships:** statewide.

Add'l Information: Established 1992. Normal turnaround time- 1-3 days. Expedited service available. Projects billed by the hour. 1st project may require prepayment. Credit cards accepted. They specialize in no limits on servicing the clients needs. Licensed PI in MT. Perform service of process.

Equity Title Search

137 N Larchmont #545, Los Angeles, CA 90004
Phone: 323-965-0759 **Fax:** 323-965-1247
email@equitytitlesearch.com

Types of Records Retrieved: Civil, criminal and probate courts; Real Estate; Vital records

Local Retrieval Area: CA-Alameda, Los Angeles, Orange, Riverside, San Francisco. **Correspondent Relationships:** Florida, New Jersey, Illinois, Colorado.

Add'l Information: Established 1973. Normal turnaround time- 24 hours. Expedited service available. Fees vary by complexity of the project. 1st project may require prepayment. They specialize in locating people and assets. A licensed PI in CA. They perform service of process.

ESI Associates

723 58th St #101, Kenosha, WI 53140
Phone: 262-652-6361 **Fax:** 262-658-4610
esi_assoc@hotmail.com

Types of Records Retrieved: Civil, criminal and probate courts; Federal courts; Real Estate; Tax liens/Judgments; UCC records; Vital records, Voter retistration records

Local Retrieval Area: WI-Kenosha, Milwaukee, Racine. **Correspondent Relationships:** Walworth, Waukeska counties WI.

Add'l Information: Established 1983. Normal turnaround time- 24 hours. Projects billed by number of records located. 1st project may require prepayment. Credit cards accepted. They have 20 years experience in real estate, criminal, civil and document retrieval. A licensed PI in WI. They perform service of process.

Espanola Abstract Co

PO Box 1282, 224 Los Alamos Hiway, Espanola, NM 87532
Phone: 505-753-2248 **Fax:** 505-753-4392

Types of Records Retrieved: Civil courts; Probate courts; Real Estate; Tax liens/Judgments; UCC records; Vital records

Local Retrieval Area: NM-Rio Arriba. **Correspondent Relationships:** courtesy closings throughout New Mexico.

Add'l Information: Established 1947. Normal turnaround time- 10-14 days. Charges vary depending on project. Payment is due upon delivery. They are the only local title company with records dating back to county's inception. They will file UCC and real estate documents on behalf of clients twice a week.

Esquire Assist Ltd

225 South St, Harrisburg, PA 17101
Phone: 717-232-9398 **Fax:** 717-232-6248
esquire-assist@worldnet.att.net

Types of Records Retrieved: Civil, criminal and probate courts; Federal courts; Real Estate; Tax liens/Judgments; UCC records; Vital records

Local Retrieval Area: PA-Dauphin. **Correspondent Relationships:** statewide for judgments/liens and UCC searches.

Add'l Information: Established 1988. Normal turnaround time- 1-3 days, most within 24 hours. Projects billed by number of names searched. 1st project may require prepayment. They specialize in corporation bureau filings which includes corporations, LLC's, LLP's, LP's and UCC filings.

Esquire Express Inc

1501 NW 29th St, Miami, FL 33142
Phone: 800-439-8744; 305-530-9580 **Fax:** 305-530-8414
www.esquireexpress.com **email:** esqexpress@aol.com

Types of Records Retrieved: Civil, criminal and probate courts; Federal courts; Real Estate; Tax liens/Judgments; UCC records; Vital records

Local Retrieval Area: FL-Broward, Dade, Palm Beach. **Correspondent Relationships:** Leon, Gadsden, Escambia, Santa Rosa, Hillsborough, Pinellas and nationwide.

Add'l Information: Established 1990. Normal turnaround time- 24 hours. Expedited service available. Projects billed by the hour. 1st project may require prepayment. Credit cards accepted. Mastercard, Visa and American Express accepted. They specialize in civil, criminal, bankruptcy and public records retrieval throughout South Florida. Courier service. A licensed PI in FL. They perform service of process.

Essex County Paralegals Inc

900 Cummings Center #417T, Beverly, MA 01915
Phone: 800-922-4752; 978-921-5300 **Fax:** 800-928-4752; 978-921-5398
don@essexparalegals.com

Types of Records Retrieved: Civil courts; Probate courts; Federal courts; Real Estate; Tax liens/Judgments; UCC records

Local Retrieval Area: MA-Essex, Middlesex, Suffolk, Worcester

Add'l Information: Established 1995. Normal turnaround time- 24-72 hours. Fees are per subject/jurisdiction. 1st project may require prepayment. Terms: net 30 days. They specialize in real estate current owner searches, UCC, tax liens, judgments and corporate document filing and retrieval. They also have microfiche Library of State UCC filings.

Estate Title & Escrow Inc

4041 University Dr #302, Fairfax, VA 22030
Phone: 703-385-5850 **Fax:** 703-385-1016
www.estatetitle.com **email:** michele@estatetitle.com

Types of Records Retrieved: Real Estate; Tax liens/Judgments; UCC records

Local Retrieval Area: DC-District of Columbia; VA-Alexandria City, Arlington, Clarke, Culpeper, Fairfax, Fauquier, Loudoun, Prince William, Spotsylvania, Stafford. **Correspondent Relationships:** Virginia and Maryland.

Add'l Information: Established 1984. Normal turnaround time- 2-3 days. Payment due upon receipt of invoice. Payment due upon reciept of invoice. They specialize in providing title evidence in real estate transactions, tax liens and other liens, UCC and court records. They are a full service title insurance company and agent who underwrites through several major underwriters.

Estherville Abstract Co

119 N 6th St, Estherville, IA 51334-2228
Phone: 712-362-3148 **Fax:** 712-362-8042
evabstco@mchsi.com

Types of Records Retrieved: Civil, criminal and probate courts; Real Estate; Tax liens/Judgments; UCC records; Vital records

Local Retrieval Area: IA-Emmet

Add'l Information: Established 1937. Normal turnaround time- 2 days. They charge a flat rate per search. They specialize in abstracting and real estate transactions.

Kim Estrada

665 Creekside Dr, Prescott, AZ 86303
Phone: 928-443-0779 **Fax:** 928-445-4437
azestrada@msn.com

Types of Records Retrieved: Civil, criminal and probate courts; Real Estate; Tax liens/Judgments; UCC records

Local Retrieval Area: AZ-Yavapai

Add'l Information: Established 1995. Normal turnaround time- 24-48 hours. Projects billed by number of names searched. Specializing in criminal, civil, UCC, tax lien, judgment searches, and property searches usually within 24 hours. All searches done in person at courthouse/recorder.

Etna Abstract Corp

PO Box 462, 63 E Main St, Malone, NY 12953
Phone: 518-483-7204 **Fax:** 518-483-7204

Types of Records Retrieved: Probate courts; Real Estate; Tax liens/Judgments; UCC records

Local Retrieval Area: NY-Franklin

Add'l Information: Established 1977. Normal turnaround time- 1-2 weeks. Projects billed by number of names searched. Projects billed by number of records located. Fee basis will vary per abstract. All projects require prepayment. They specialize in abstracts of title.

Euchner Research LLC

270 Switch Rd #7, Calhoun, GA 30701
Phone: 678-614-1816 **Fax:** 706 625 9151
johneuchner@earthlink.net

Types of Records Retrieved: Civil, criminal and probate courts; Real Estate; Tax liens/Judgments/UCC records; Vital records

Local Retrieval Area: GA-Bartow, Floyd, Gordon

Add'l Information: Established 2002. Normal turnaround time- 24 hours. Projects billed by number of names searched. Payment due net 30 days. They are a research and retrieval firm specializing in public records searches and retrieval for the banking, mortgage, investigative and legal industries.

Eufaula Abstract & Title Co Inc

PO Box 548, Eufaula, OK 74432
Phone: 918-689-2241 **Fax:** 918-689-2248

Types of Records Retrieved: Real Estate; Tax liens/judgments; UCC records

Local Retrieval Area: OK-McIntosh

Add'l Information: Normal turnaround time- 10-12 working days after receipt of order. Projects billed by the hour. They specialize in abstracting and title insurance.

Euler Abstract & Title Co

PO Box 326, 137 S Main, Troy, KS 66087
Phone: 785-985-3562 **Fax:** 785-985-2322

Types of Records Retrieved: Civil, criminal and probate courts; Real Estate; Tax liens/Judgments

Local Retrieval Area: KS-Doniphan

Add'l Information: Established 1895. Normal turnaround time- 3 days. Fee basis varies by type of transaction. They specialize in abstracting and title insurance and own a title plant which includes all land title records for Doniphan County. They have been in business for over 40 years. Their staff includes 3 attorneys. They perform service of process.

Evans Title Companies

PO Box 6, 823 Jay St, Manitowoc, WI 54221
Phone: 920-684-1261 **Fax:** 920-684-6581
www.firstam.com **email:** tkunesh@firstam.com

Types of Records Retrieved: Civil courts; Probate courts; Real Estate; Tax liens/Judgments; UCC records; Vital records

Local Retrieval Area: WI-Manitowoc. **Correspondent Relationships:** Outagamie, Winnebago, Calumet, Waupaca, Portage, Brown, Shawano, Marquette, Waushara, Green Lake.

Add'l Information: Established 1898. Normal turnaround time- 2-3 days. Projects billed by number of names searched. 1st project may require prepayment.

Everhart & Everhart Abstractors

PO Box 37, Toledo, IL 62468
Phone: 217-849-2671 **Fax:** 217-849-2671
everhart@rr1.net

Types of Records Retrieved: Real Estate; Tax liens/Judgments; UCC records

Local Retrieval Area: IL-Clark, Coles, Cumberland, Effingham

Add'l Information: Established 1881. Normal turnaround time- 3-4 days. Projects billed by number of names searched. Projects billed by number of records located. Projects billed by the hour. Personal checks are accepted. They specialize in title insurance and abstracts, and also perform judgment/lien, UCC and other record searches. There may be additional charges for Clark County searches due to distance from their home office.

Wesley W Ewart, PI

PO Box 95828, Seattle, WA 98145
Phone: 800-646-1143; 425-646-1143 **Fax:** 425-454-2611
http://wesleyewart.aiass.org **email:** on-point@worldnet.att.net

Types of Records Retrieved: Civil, criminal and probate courts; Federal courts; Real Estate; Tax liens/Judgments; UCC records; Vital records

Local Retrieval Area: WA-King. **Correspondent Relationships:** statewide

Add'l Information: Established 1995. Normal turnaround time- 1 week. Projects billed by the hour. 1st project may require prepayment. They specialize in process service, surveillance and witness location. A licensed PI in WA. They perform service of process.

Thomas E Ewinger Jr

3900 Old Tasso Rd NE, Cleveland, TN 37312-5827
Phone: 423-614-5290 **Fax:** 423-614-5299

Types of Records Retrieved: Probate courts; Real Estate; Tax liens/Judgments; UCC records; Vital records.

Local Retrieval Area: TN-Anderson, Bledsoe, Blount, Bradley, Hamilton, Knox, Loudon, Marion, McMinn, Meigs, Monroe, Polk, Rhea, Roane, Sequatchie

Add'l Information: Established 1979. Normal turnaround time- 24-48 hours. Projects billed by number of names searched. All projects require prepayment. They specialize in title abstracts, deed copies, updates, recordings, current owner & 20 year and 30 years searches.

Examiner's Title LC

1427 Admiral Dr, Woodbridge, VA 22192
Phone: 703-491-0805 **Fax:** 703-497-0408
pyianilos@aol.com

Types of Records Retrieved: Probate courts; Real Estate; UCC records

Local Retrieval Area: VA-Alexandria, Arlington, Fairfax, Fauquier, Loudoun, Prince William. **Correspondent Relationships:** Frederick, City of Winchester, Culpeper, Stafford counties, VA.

Add'l Information: Established 1997. Normal turnaround time- 24-48 hours. Same day turnaround in many cases. Projects billed by number of names searched. Call for info on regular invoicing, payment terms. They perform document retrieval for current owner searches (as well as regular title searches) for the local neighboring counties of Northern Virginia. They can e-mail their reports to clients as they wish.

Excel Abstract Services

238 S Richard St, Bedford, PA 15522-1741
Phone: 814-623-5213 **Fax:** 814-623-1602
excelabstract@earthlink.net

Types of Records Retrieved: Civil and criminal courts; Federal courts; Real Estate; Tax liens/Judgments; UCC records

Local Retrieval Area: PA-Bedford, Blair, Fulton, Huntingdon. **Correspondent Relationships:** Cambria, Somerset, Indiana, Clearfield.

Add'l Information: Established 1960. Normal turnaround time- 24 hours. Expedited service available. Fees based on type of report. Terms: net 30 days. They specialize in property reports, current owner searches, title searches, lien searches, criminal searches and closings.

EX-CEL Inv

PO Box 22124, St Petersburg, FL 33742
Phone: 800-317-7626; 727-527-5440
www.ex-celpi.com **email:** excel@digital.net

Types of Records Retrieved: Civil, criminal and probate courts; Federal courts; Real Estate; Tax liens/Judgments; UCC records; Vital records

Local Retrieval Area: FL-Hillsborough, Pinellas. **Correspondent Relationships:** Pasco and Hernando.

Add'l Information: Established 1974. Normal turnaround time- 48 hours. Projects billed by number of names searched. Projects billed by the hour. Copy expenses added to the fee. All projects require prepayment. Terms: net 15 days. They specialize in process service, background checks, locates and video surveillance. They also do traffic and boat record searches. A licensed PI in FL. They perform service of process.

Excel Search Inc

6704 Mountain Lake Ln, Cumming, GA 30040
Phone: 770-844-1201 **Fax:** 770-205-2623
excelsearch@adelphia.net

Types of Records Retrieved: Civil, criminal and probate courts; Federal courts; Real Estate; Tax liens/Judgments; UCC records; Vital records

Local Retrieval Area: GA-Barrow, Bibb, Butts, Cherokee, Clarke, Clayton, Cobb, Dawson, De Kalb, Forsyth, Fulton, Greene, Gwinnett, Hall, Henry, Jackson, Jasper, Lamar, Madison, Monroe, Morgan, Newton, Oconee, Oglethorpe, Putnam, Rockdale, Spalding, Walton. **Correspondent Relationships:** Georgia.

Add'l Information: Established 1982. Normal turnaround time- 12-48 hours. Projects billed by number of names searched. Fees for some counties can vary. A rush request may make rate higher. Bill upon completion. They specialize in UCC searches and filing, tax liens, suits, judgments, court records retrieval and mortgage searches.

Executec Services

6404 Sumac Dr, Austin, TX 78731
Phone: 512-345-5402 **Fax:** 512-345-3932
www.ExecutecServices.com

Types of Records Retrieved: Real Estate; Tax liens/judgments; UCC records

Local Retrieval Area: TX-Hays, Travis, Williamson. **Correspondent Relationships:** various Texas counties.

Add'l Information: Established 1989. Normal turnaround time- 24-48 hours. Projects billed by number of names searched. 1st project may require prepayment. They specialize in property records including warranty and trust deeds, assignments, liens, foreclosures, plats, etc. They only do document filing in Travis County.

Executive Attorney Service Inc

201 N Figueroa St #535, Los Angeles, CA 90012
Phone: 213-482-6680 **Fax:** 213-482-6688
www.EASSITE.com **email:** Silvia@eassite.com

Types of Records Retrieved: Civil, criminal and probate courts; Federal courts; Real Estate; Tax liens/Judgments; UCC records; Vital records

Local Retrieval Area: CA-Los Angeles, Orange, Riverside, San Bernardino, Ventura

Add'l Information: Established 1966. Normal turnaround time- variable depending on project. Projects billed by number of names searched. Projects billed by the hour. 1st project may require prepayment. Credit cards accepted. They specialize in service of writs, court filing, service of process, skiptracing and small claims. They perform service of process.

Executive Investigative Services

PO Box 13308, Overland Park, KS 66282-3308
Phone: 800-764-9484; 913-764-9484 **Fax:** 913-764-6972

Types of Records Retrieved: Civil and criminal courts; Federal courts; Real Estate; Tax liens/Judgments; UCC records

Local Retrieval Area: KS-Franklin, Douglas, Johnson, Leavenworth, Miami, Wyandotte; MO-Clay, Platte. **Correspondent Relationships:** Miami, Douglas, Leavenworth, Fraknlin, Anderson, Jefferson, Atchison, Geary counties in Kansas.

Add'l Information: Established 1990. Normal turnaround time- 1-2 days. Projects billed by the hour. 1st project may require prepayment. They serve an area within 100 miles of Kansas City, Either side of the KS or MO state line. Call for price quote. They perform service of process.

E-Z Messenger Attorney Service Inc

10 W Madison, Phoenix, AZ 85003
Phone: 800-380-8081; 602-258-8081 **Fax:** 602-258-8864
www.e-zmessenger.com **email:** ronezell@e-zmessenger.com

Types of Records Retrieved: Civil and criminal couts; Probate courts; Federal courts; UCC records; Vital records

Local Retrieval Area: AZ-Maricopa

Add'l Information: Established 1973. Normal turnaround time- 48 hours. Expedited service available. Projects billed by number of names searched. All projects require prepayment. A licensed PI in AZ. They perform service of process.

E-Z Messenger Attorney Service Inc

65 E Pennington St, Tucson, AZ 85701
Phone: 800-264-8436; 520-623-8436 **Fax:** 520-624-1819
www.e-zmessenger.com **email:** ronezell@e-zmessenger.com

Types of Records Retrieved: Civil, criminal and probate courts; Federal courts; Real Estate; Tax liens/Judgments; UCC records

Local Retrieval Area: AZ-Cochise, Pima, Santa Cruz

Add'l Information: Established 1973. Normal turnaround time- 48 hours. Expedited service available. Projects billed by number of names searched. Projects billed by the hour. All projects require prepayment. They are a full attorney service. They also have offices in Phoenix and Mesa to cover Maricopa County (state capitol/Phoenix) A licensed PI in AZ. They perform service of process.

F

Fact Finders Ltd

125 Chapman St, Orange, VA 22960

Phone: 866-672-0666; 540-717-5214 (Cell) **Fax:** 877-561-2423;

http://factfindersltd.com **email:** theperfectsearch@cs.com

Types of Records Retrieved: Real estate; Tax liens/Judgments; UCC records

Local Retrieval Area: VA-Albemarle, Caroline, Charlottesville, Culpeper, Fauquier, Fluvanna, Fredericksburg, Greene, Louisa, King George, Madison, Orange, Spotsylvania, Stafford

Add'l Information: Established 2001. Normal turnaround time- less than 72 hours. Projects billed by number of names searched. Fees dependant on volume. Payment due upon receipt of invoice. A family owned and operated business, they promise their searches will be timely and efficient. Also offering signature settlement services.

Fact Finders of Nebraska

609 S Ash, North Platte, NE 69101

Phone: 308-534-8956 **Fax:** 308-534-5884

2newport@nque.com

Types of Records Retrieved: Civil, criminal and probate courts; Real Estate; Tax liens/Judgments; UCC records; Vital records

Local Retrieval Area: NE-Adams, Buffalo, Cheyenne, Dawson, Hall, Kearney, Lincoln, Phelps, Red Willow. **Correspondent Relationships:** Custer, Frontier, Logan, Gosper, Perkins counties NE.

Add'l Information: Established 1997. Normal turnaround time- 1-3 working days. Charge billed per name per county. Terms are net 30 days. Monthly billing. Fact Finders provides personal services. They do go to the courthouses and have an excellent working relationship with all employees of the courthouse.

Fairbanks Title Agency

714 3rd Ave, Fairbanks, AK 99701

Phone: 907-456-6626 **Fax:** 907-452-5406

Types of Records Retrieved: Real Estate; Tax liens/Judgments

Local Retrieval Area: AK-Barrow, Fairbanks Recording District, Fort Gibbon, Kotzebue, Manley Hot Springs, Mount McKinley, Nenana, Nome, Nulato, Rampart

Add'l Information: Established 1976. Normal turnaround time- 24 hours. Projects billed by the hour. All projects require prepayment. They specialize in title insurance searches and escrow closings in Fairbanks Recording District and statewide.

Fairchild Record Search Ltd

PO Box 1368, 3400 Capitol Blvd S #101 (98501), Olympia, WA 98507

Phone: 800-547-7007; 360-786-8775 **Fax:** 800-433-3404; 360-943-6656

www.recordsearch.com **email:** renee@recordsearch.com

Types of Records Retrieved: Civil, criminal and probate courts; Federal courts; Tax liens/Judgments; UCC records; Vital records

Local Retrieval Area: WA-Thurston. **Correspondent Relationships:** nationwide and Canada.

Add'l Information: Established 1980. Normal turnaround time- 1-2 days. Projects billed by number of names searched. 1st project may require prepayment. Credit cards accepted. They will file/record UCC documents on behalf of clients on a same or next day basis. They are a registered agent service.

Fairview Abstract Co

PO Box 60, Fairview, OK 73737

Phone: 580-227-4524 **Fax:** 580-227-3607

Types of Records Retrieved: Civil, criminal and probate courts; Real Estate; Tax liens/Judgments; UCC records; Vital records

Local Retrieval Area: OK-Major

Add'l Information: Established 1917. Normal turnaround time- 1 week. Projects billed by the hour. Terms: net 30 days. They specialize in abstracting, title insurance and escrow closings.

Faith to Faith Legal Productions

23944 Taylor St, Plaquemine, LA 70761

Phone: 225-685-0008 **Fax:** 225-685-0009

f2flp@bellsouth.net

Types of Records Retrieved: Civil, criminal and probate courts; Federal courts; Real Estate; Tax liens/Judgments; UCC records.

Local Retrieval Area: LA-Ascension, Assumption, East Baton Rouge, Iberville, Livingston, Pointe Coupee, West Baton Rouge. **Correspondent Relationships:** East Feliciana, West Feliciana.

Add'l Information: Established 1995. Normal turnaround time- 24-48. Expedited service available. Projects billed by number of names searched. Net 30 days. They specialize in the areas of document retrievals, abstracting, real estate notarial closings, and federal criminal and civil background checks.

Faithful Abstract

2 Broad St, Elizabeth, NJ 07201

Phone: 908-351-9398 **Fax:** 908-351-4618

Types of Records Retrieved: Civil courts; Probate courts; Real Estate; Tax liens/Judgments; UCC records

Local Retrieval Area: NJ-Ocean, Union

Add'l Information: Established 1980. Normal turnaround time- 1-5 days. Fee basis will vary by the type of project. 1st project may require prepayment. They have more than 20 years of abstract and title experience.

Falcon Research & Settlement

4181 Brookville St, Hawthorn, PA 16230

Phone: 800-828-4081; 814-365-5455 **Fax:** 814-365-5019

www.falconsettlement.com **email:** customerservice@falconsettlement.com

Types of Records Retrieved: Civil and criminal courts; Federal Bankruptcy courts; Real Estate; Tax liens/Judgments; UCC records

Local Retrieval Area: PA-Armstrong, Butler, Cameron, Clarion, Clearfield, Crawford, Elk, Forest, Indiana, Jefferson, McKean, Mercer, Potter, Venango, Warren

Add'l Information: Established 1986. Normal turnaround time- up to 1 week. Projects billed by number of names searched. Fee basis will vary by the type of project. Will invoice at the end of the month. They have served the real estate and banking business for over 20 years with quick turnaround times and thorough top quality work in Western Pennsylvania.

Fall River Abstract Co

141 S Chicago St, PO Box 908, Hot Springs, SD 57747

Phone: 605-745-5187 **Fax:** 605-745-5482 frtitlco@gwtc.net

Types Records Retrieved: Probate courts; Real Estate; Tax liens/Judgments

Local Retrieval Area: SD-Fall River, Shannon

Add'l Information: Established 1943. Normal turnaround time- 24-48 hours. Projects billed by the hour. Terms are net 30 days after billing. 1st project may require prepayment.

Fallon County Abstractor

PO Box 827, Baker, MT 59313
Phone: 406-778-2422 **Fax:** 406-778-3466
Types of Records Retrieved: Real Estate; Tax liens/Judgments
Local Retrieval Area: MT-Fallon
Add'l Information: Established 1913. 1st project may require prepayment. They specialize in real estate.

Falls County Title Co Inc

122 Bridge St, Marlin, TX 76661-2829
Phone: 254-883-2112 **Fax:** 254-883-6260
Types of Records Retrieved: Civil courts; Probate courts; Real Estate; Tax liens/Judgments; UCC records; Vital records
Local Retrieval Area: TX-Falls
Add'l Information: Established 1995. Normal turnaround time- 2-3 weeks. Fee basis will vary by the type of project. All projects require prepayment.

Lisa Farris

1219 Walker Rd, Goodlettsville, TN 37072
Phone: 615-859-7135 **Fax:** 615-859-3982
farris05@bellsouth.net
Types of Records Retrieved: Civil, criminal and probate courts; Federal courts; Real Estate; Tax liens/Judgments; UCC records; Vital records
Local Retrieval Area: TN-Sumner
Add'l Information: Established 1999. Normal turnaround time- 24 hours. Projects billed by the hour. Will invoice. She is a paralegal with a BS in addition to a paralegal certification from an ABA approved school. She performs any kind of record retrieval. They perform service of process.

FarVision Consulting Title Co

4751 Rte 10, Barboursville, WV 25504
Phone: 304-733-5086 **Fax:** 304-733-5087
Types of Records Retrieved: Real Estate; Tax liens/Judgments
Local Retrieval Area: KY-Boone, Bracken
Add'l Information: Established 1993. 1st project may require prepayment. They specialize in real estate.

Farwell Abstract Co Inc

402 3rd St, Farwell, TX 79325
Phone: 806-481-9992 **Fax:** 806-481-9060
Types of Records Retrieved: Civil, criminal and probate courts; Real Estate; Tax liens/Judgments
Local Retrieval Area: TX-Bailey, Parmer
Add'l Information: Established 1907. Normal turnaround time- 72 hours. Projects billed by the hour. They specialize in title insurance.

Faxxon Legal Information Services Inc

1 W Old State Capitol Plaza #805, Myers Bldg, Springfield, IL 62701
Phone: 800-932-9966; 217-522-3280 **Fax:** 800-229-7028; 217-522-3570
www.faxxon.com **email:** wjstokes@faxxon.com
Types of Records Retrieved: Civil, criminal and probate courts; Federal courts; Real Estate; Tax liens/Judgments; UCC records; Vital records
Local Retrieval Area: IL-Sangamon. **Correspondent Relationships:** nationwide, especially Central IL area.
Add'l Information: Established 1995. Normal turnaround time- 24 hours. Projects billed by number of names searched. 1st project may require prepayment. Credit cards accepted. An expert in the field of public record searching since 1982, they specialize in IL state records - Sec of State, UCCs, etc. Also specialize in real estate and personal abstracting.

Fayette Professional Services

56 E Main St, Uniontown, PA 15401
Phone: 412-439-1450 **Fax:** 412-439-3460
fayette1@attglobal.net
Types of Records Retrieved: Real Estate; Tax liens/judgments; UCC records
Local Retrieval Area: PA-Fayette, Greene, Washington, Westmoreland
Add'l Information: Established 1976. Normal turnaround time- same day in Fayette County only. Fee basis will vary by type of project. Terms: net 30 days. Specialize in real estate closing (witness only). They take pride in their excellent service. Same day or 24-hour return of reports.

Federal Research Corporation

1030 15th St NW #920, Washington, DC 20004
Phone: 800-846-3190; **Fax:** 202-783-0145
www.federalresearch.com
Types of Records Retrieved: Civil courts; Probate courts; Federal courts; Real Estate; Tax liens/Judgments; UCC records; Vital records
Local Retrieval Area: DC-District of Columbia; MD-Anne Arundel, Baltimore, Baltimore City, Harford, Howard, Montgomery, Prince George's; VA-Alexandria City, Arlington, Fairfax, Loudoun, Prince William, Richmond City. **Correspondent Relationships:** nationwide.
Add'l Information: Established 1985. Normal turnaround time- 3-5 days. Expedited service available. Fee may be based per index. Federal searches are per hour. Credit cards accepted. Visa, Mastercard and American Express accepted In addition to nationwide UCC and corporate searches, they specialize in intellectual property searches and filings, document authentication, federal agency and Library of Congress work, also copyright/trademarks. Federal agent services. Performs service of process.

R L Ferrelle

PO Box 30752, Savannah, GA 31410
Phone: 912-786-6577 **Fax:** 912-786-6577
mudbank4@earthlink.net
Types of Records Retrieved: Civil and criminal courts; Federal courts
Local Retrieval Area: GA-Chatham, Effingham
Add'l Information: Established 1996. Normal turnaround time- 24-48 hours. Projects billed by number of names searched. Terms are net 30 days. They specialize in being prompt, reliable, accurate with 7 years of experience. Phone calls returned promptly. Also do hospital liens.

Ferret Diversified Services Inc

PO Box 661, 2057 Greenbay Rd, Highland Park, IL 60035
Phone: 847-266-7666 **Fax:** 847-266-0860
www.ferretdiv.com **email:** ferretdiv@aol.com
Types of Records Retrieved: Civil and criminal courts
Local Retrieval Area: IL-Adams, Carroll, Champaign, Coles, Cook, De Kalb, Du Page, Henry, Jackson, Jo Daviess, Kane, Kendall, Lake, Lee, Logan, Madison, Mercer, Ogle, Pike, Rock Island, Sangamon Stephenson, Union, Whiteside, Will, Winnebago. **Correspondent Relationships:** nationwide.
Add'l Information: Established 1997. Normal turnaround time- same day if received by 1 PM CST. Payment due net 15 days. They specialize in providing criminal background information and other screening services. A licensed PI in IL.

Fidelifacts

42 Broadway, New York, NY 10004
Phone: 800-678-0007; **Fax:** 800-509-8496; 212-248-5619
www.fidelifacts.com **email:** norton@fidelifacts.com
Types of Records Retrieved: Civil, criminal and probate courts; Federal courts; Real Estate; Tax liens/Judgments; UCC records; Vital records
Local Retrieval Area: NJ-Atlantic, Bergen, Burlington, Camden, Cape May, Cumberland, Essex, Gloucester, Hudson, Hunterdon, Mercer, Middlesex, Monmouth, Morris, Ocean, Passaic, Salem, Somerset, Sussex, Union, Warren; NY-Bronx, Dutchess, Kings, Nassau, New York, Orange, Putnam, Queens, Richmond, Rockland, Suffolk, Ulster, Westchester. **Correspondent Relationships:** nationwide.
Add'l Information: Established 1956. Normal turnaround time- 2-10 days. Projects billed by number of names searched. 1st project may require prepayment. They specialize in criminal records checks and credit checks plus employment background investigations nationwide. A licensed PI in NJ, NY.

Fidelity Abstract & Title Co

PO Box 247, 115 N Main, Howard, SD 57349
Phone: 605-772-5632 **Fax:** 605-772-5648
fatc@alliancecom.net

Types of Records Retrieved: Civil courts; Probate courts; Real Estate; Tax liens/Judgments; UCC records

Local Retrieval Area: SD-Miner

Add'l Information: Established 1947. Normal turnaround time- depends on nature of project. Projects billed by the hour. 1st project may require prepayment. They specialize in title insurance and abstracting. Faxing them is suggested.

Fidelity Home Abstract Inc

3 Landmark Ctr, East Stroudsburg, PA 18301
Phone: 800-224-5601; 570-424-5600 **Fax:** 570-424-9860

Types of Records Retrieved: Civil courts; Probate courts; Real Estate; Tax liens/Judgments; UCC records

Local Retrieval Area: PA-Carbon, Monroe, Northampton, Pike, Wayne. **Correspondent Relationships:** Nebraska and Pennsylvania.

Add'l Information: Normal turnaround time- 10 days. Expedited service available. Projects billed by number of records located. Terms: net 30 days. They specialize in abstracting.

Financial Dimensions

1400 Lebanon Church Rd, Pittsburgh, PA 15236
Phone: 800-858-9808; 412-650-1700 **Fax:** 800-858-9810;
www.financialdimensions.com **email:** bill@financialdimensions.com

Types of Records Retrieved: Civil and criminal courts; Federal courts; Real Estate; Tax liens/Judgments; UCC records

Local Retrieval Area: PA-Allegheny. **Correspondent Relationships:** nationwide.

Add'l Information: Established 1986. Normal turnaround time- 24-48 hours. Projects billed by number of names searched. They invoice monthly. They specialize in mortgage document retrieval, recording and servicing nationwide.

Fink Abstract Co

PO Box 418, 622 Madison St, Fredonia, KS 66736
Phone: 620-378-2351 **Fax:** 620-378-4425

Types of Records Retrieved: Civil courts; Probate courts; Real Estate; Tax liens/Judgments; UCC records; Vital records

Local Retrieval Area: KS-Wilson

Add'l Information: Established 1904. Normal turnaround time- 2-3 days. Fee basis varies by type of transaction. 1st project may require prepayment.

Finley Abstract & Title Co

PO Box 397, 309 Jefferson Street, Oskaloosa, KS 66066
Phone: 785-863-2271 **Fax:** 785-863-2065

Types of Records Retrieved: Civil courts; Probate courts; Real Estate; Tax liens/Judgments; UCC records

Local Retrieval Area: KS-Jefferson

Add'l Information: Established 1889. Normal turnaround time- 2-3 days. Projects billed by the hour. 1st project may require prepayment.

Finney Land Co

PO Box 2471, Durango, CO 81302
Phone: 970-259-5691 **Fax:** 970-259-4279
Finney@frontier.net

Types of Records Retrieved: Civil, criminal and probate courts; Federal courts; Real Estate; Tax liens/Judgments; UCC records; Vital records

Local Retrieval Area: CO-Archuleta, La Plata, Montezuma

Add'l Information: Established 1988. Normal turnaround time- 1-2 days. Projects billed by the hour. Payment due upon receipt, no work done until last job paid. 1st project may require prepayment. They specialize in oil and gas.

Margaret Fiorillo

151 N Vermillion St #4, Paxton, IL 60957-1381
Phone: 217-379-3359

Types of Records Retrieved: Civil and criminal courts; Real Estate; Tax liens/Judgments; UCC records; Vital records

Local Retrieval Area: IL-Ford

Add'l Information: Established 1994. Normal turnaround time- 24 hours. Projects billed by number of names searched. She specializes in criminal record searches. They perform service of process.

First Abstract & Loan Co

601 W Main, Cherokee, IA 51012
Phone: 712-225-3612 **Fax:** 712-225-1033

Types of Records Retrieved: Civil, criminal and probate courts; Real Estate; Tax liens/Judgments; UCC records

Local Retrieval Area: IA-Cherokee

Add'l Information: Established 1950. Normal turnaround time- 2 weeks. Fee basis will vary by type of project.

First American Title & Escrow (Libby)

120 W 6th St, Libby, MT 59923
Phone: 800-282-5630; 406-293-3721 **Fax:** 406-293-3723

Types of Records Retrieved: Civil, criminal and probate courts; Real Estate; Tax liens/Judgments; UCC records; Vital records

Local Retrieval Area: MT-Lincoln

Add'l Information: Established 1990. Normal turnaround time- next day. Fee basis varies by type of transaction.

First American Title & Escrow (Polson)

PO Box 910, 210 2nd St E, Polson, MT 59860
Phone: 800-331-2349; 406-883-5258 **Fax:** 406-883-3056
cs.polson.mt@firstam.com

Types of Records Retrieved: Civil, criminal and probate courts; Real Estate; Tax liens/Judgments; UCC records

Local Retrieval Area: MT-Lake

Add'l Information: Established 1975. Normal turnaround time- next day. Fee basis varies by type of transaction. Will bill.

First American Title Co

PO Box 54, 106 E Wallace St, Virginia City, MT 59755
Phone: 800-570-5337; 406-843-5337 **Fax:** 406-843-5431
alongfellow@firstam.com

Types of Records Retrieved: Real Estate

Local Retrieval Area: MT-Madison

Add'l Information: Established 1922. Normal turnaround time- 1-3 days. Projects billed by the hour. 1st project may require prepayment.

First American Title Co (Colorado)

102 Grand Ave #B, Delta, CO 81416-2058
Phone: 970-874-8286 **Fax:** 970-874-4762

Types of Records Retrieved: Real Estate; Tax liens/judgments; UCC records

Local Retrieval Area: CO-Delta, Montrose, Ouray

Add'l Information: Established 1985. Normal turnaround time- 3-5 days. Fee basis will vary by the type of project. Terms: net 30 days. They specialize in title insurance and full closing services.

First American Title Co (Thomspon Falls)

Box 850, 1211 Main St, Thompson Falls, MT 59873
Phone: 406-827-3591 **Fax:** 406-827-3848

Types of Records Retrieved: Civil courts; Probate courts; Real Estate; Tax liens/Judgments; UCC records

Local Retrieval Area: MT-Sanders

Add'l Information: Normal turnaround time- 3-5 days. Projects billed by the hour. 1st project may require prepayment.

First American Title Co of Crook Cty

PO Box 190, Sundance, WY 82729-0190
Phone: 307-283-1844 **Fax:** 307-283-1855

lfoster@firstam.com

Types of Records Retrieved: Real Estate; Tax liens/Judgments; UCC records

Local Retrieval Area: WY-Crook

Add'l Information: Established 1981. Normal turnaround time- 1-2 days. Projects billed by number of names searched. Projects billed by the hour. 1st project may require prepayment. They specialize in title insurance, abstracts and certificates of titles. Will search civil and probate courts in connection with real estate only.

First American Title Co of Montana Inc

304 N Kendrick Ave, Glendive, MT 59330-1716
Phone: 406-365-5482 **Fax:** 406-365-5835
mherring@firstam.com

Types of Records Retrieved: Civil courts; Probate courts; Real Estate; Tax liens/Judgments; UCC records

Local Retrieval Area: MT-Dawson, McCone

Add'l Information: Normal turnaround time- 1 week or less. Projects billed by number of names searched. Project billed according to amount of mortgage, etc.

First American Title Ins Co

2233 Lee Rd #101, Winter Park, FL 32789
Phone: 407-740-7131 **Fax:** 407-691-5300
www.firstam.com

Types of Records Retrieved: Civil courts; Probate courts; Federal courts; Real Estate; Tax liens/Judgments; UCC records; Vital records

Local Retrieval Area: FL-Brevard, Duval, Flagler, Lake, Marion, Orange, Osceola, Polk, Seminole, Volusia

Add'l Information: Established 1883. Normal turnaround time- 3 working days. Projects billed by the hour. They specialize in serving Central Florida and have a computer database of real estate for Orange, Seminole, Lake, Osceola and Volusia counties.

First American Title Insurance Company (IL)

351 Sabella St, Central IL Division, Pekin, IL 61554
Phone: 309-347-6126 **Fax:** 309-347-4523

Types of Records Retrieved: Civil courts; Probate courts; Real Estate; Tax liens/Judgments; UCC records; Vital records

Local Retrieval Area: IL-Cass, Fulton, Mason, Menard, Schuyler

Add'l Information: Established 1948. Normal turnaround time- recording same day received; 5 working days for searches. Expedited service available. Projects billed by number of names searched. They are a full service title company. They also prepare documents, closings, search of real estate records and circuit clerk records.

First American Title Insurance of Oregon

454 Commercial St, Coos Bay, OR 97420
Phone: 800-235-0119; 541-269-0119 **Fax:** 541-269-0470

Types of Records Retrieved: Civil courts; Probate courts; Real Estate; Tax liens/Judgments; UCC records; Vital records

Local Retrieval Area: OR-Coos. **Correspondent Relationships:** courtesy signing throughout Oregon.

Add'l Information: Normal turnaround time- 1-2 days. Projects billed by the hour. Their hourly rate varies. 1st project may require prepayment. They specialize in title insurance and escrow services.

First American Title Mineral County

305 W 3rd Ave, Superior, MT 59872
Phone: 406-822-3391 **Fax:** 406-822-3396

Types of Records Retrieved: Real Estate; Tax liens/Judgments

Local Retrieval Area: MT-Mineral. **Correspondent Relationships:** nationwide.

Add'l Information: They specialize in real estate.

First American Title of Preston

PO Box 148, 28 W Oneida St, Preston, ID 83263
Phone: 208-852-2810 **Fax:** 208-852-2811

Types of Records Retrieved: Civil courts; Probate courts; Real Estate; Tax liens/Judgments; UCC records; Vital records

Local Retrieval Area: ID-Franklin

Add'l Information: Established 1996. Normal turnaround time- 1-2 days. Projects billed by the hour.

First American Torrington

PO Box 59, Torrington, WY 82240
Phone: 307-532-5642 **Fax:** 307-532-3001

Types of Records Retrieved: Real Estate; Tax liens/Judgments

Local Retrieval Area: WY-Goshen

Add'l Information: Established 1977. 1st project may require prepayment. They specialize in real estate.

First American Wheatland

PO Box 722, Wheatland, WY 82201
Phone: 307-322-2133 **Fax:** 307-322-2213

Types of Records Retrieved: Real Estate; Tax liens/Judgments

Local Retrieval Area: WY-Platte

Add'l Information: Established 1992. 1st project may require prepayment. The specialize in real estate.

First Choice Research

6151 Miramar Pky #307, Miramar, FL 33023
Phone: 954-964-1260 **Fax:** 954-964-8283
www.firstchoiceresearch.com **email:** jloriga@firstchoicers.com

Types of Records Retrieved: Civil, criminal and probate courts; Federal courts; Real Estate; Tax liens/Judgments; UCC records

Local Retrieval Area: FL-all counties.

Add'l Information: Established 1995. Normal turnaround time- 24-48 hours. Projects billed by number of names searched. End of month billing. They specialize in record retrieval, criminal, civil, federal, UCC searches, judgments/liens, mortgage & assignment retrieval and nationwide criminal search. A licensed PI in FL.

First Choice Title Service LLC

23 Bussing Ct, Timonium, MD 21093-2009
Phone: 410-252 3803 **Fax:** 775-942-1874
firstchoicetitle@comcast.net

Types of Records Retrieved: Real Estate

Local Retrieval Area: DC-Washington; MD-Allegany, Anne Arundel, Baltimore County, Baltimore City, Calvert, Caroline, Carroll, Cecil, Charles, Dorchester, Frederick, Garrett, Harford, Howard, Kent, Montgomery, Prince George, Queen Anne's, Summerset, St. Mary's, Talbot, Washington, Wicomico, Worchester

Add'l Information: Established 1996. Normal turnaround time- 24-72 hours. Projects billed by number of names searched. 1st project may require prepayment. They pride themselves in their thorough work and quick request turnaround time. They cover all of Maryland and Washington, DC in a timely dependable manner. Cell phone # is 410-960-6493.

First Coast Inv

PO Box 10673, Jacksonville, FL 32247
Phone: 904-398-4076 **Fax:** 904-346-0329
jakiseer1@iwon.com

Types of Records Retrieved: Civil, criminal and probate courts; Federal courts; Tax liens/Judgments; Vital records

Local Retrieval Area: FL-Clay, Duval, Nassau. **Correspondent Relationships:** Miami and Orlando.

Add'l Information: Established 1979. Normal turnaround time- 24-48 for criminal records. Fees are based on a county schedule. Surviellance required deposit. They specialize in background investigations and Motor Vehicle Record checks. A licensed PI in FL. They perform service of process.

First Gunnison Title & Escrow

113 E Georgia, Gunnison, CO 81230
Phone: 800-530-9598; 970-641-4600 **Fax:** 970-641-4071
www.firstgunnison.com **email:** service@firstgunnison.com

Types of Records Retrieved: Real Estate; Tax liens/Judgments

Local Retrieval Area: CO-Gunnison, Hinsdale

Add'l Information: Established 1994. Normal turnaround time- 24 hours. Projects billed by the hour. 1st project may require prepayment. They specialize in real estate records. 21st century technology with a small town touch.

First Idaho Title Co

469 Washington, Montpelier, ID 83254
Phone: 208-847-1300 **Fax:** 208-847-1314
fitc@dcdi.net

Types of Records Retrieved: Civil courts; Probate courts; Real Estate; Tax liens/Judgments; UCC records

Local Retrieval Area: ID-Bear Lake

Add'l Information: Established 1980. Normal turnaround time- 1 week. Fees vary by project.

First Insurance Agency of Hoxie Inc

700 Main St, Hoxie, KS 67740-0108
Phone: 800-569-0198; 785-675-3252 **Fax:** 785-675-3811
econard@ruraltel.net

Types of Records Retrieved: Civil, criminal and probate courts; Federal courts; Real Estate; Tax liens/Judgments; UCC records

Local Retrieval Area: KS-Decatur, Gove, Graham, Sheridan, Thomas. **Correspondent Relationships:** Gove, Thomas, Decatur counties KS.

Add'l Information: Established 1976. Normal turnaround time- 1 day for Sheridan County; 2-3 days for surrounding counties. Projects billed by number of records located. Projects billed by the hour. Personal checks are accepted. They specialize in record searches.

First Investigative Consultants, PI# 6949

3043 Foothill Blvd #6, La Cresenta, CA 91214
Phone: 800-900-4342; 818-957-1958 **Fax:** 800-842-4004; 818-957-4910
www.fic-ca.com **email:** infosvcs@earthlink.net

Types of Records Retrieved: Civil, criminal and probate courts; Federal courts; Real Estate; Tax liens/Judgments; UCC records; Vital records

Local Retrieval Area: CA-Los Angeles, Orange, Riverside, San Bernardino, San Diego, Ventura. **Correspondent Relationships:** California.

Add'l Information: Established 1977. Normal turnaround time- 24-72 hours. Projects billed by number of names searched. Projects billed by the hour. Fee basis depends on type of search. 1st project may require prepayment. Credit cards accepted. Terms: net 30 days. They specialize in insurance investigations, pre-trial preparation, attorney services (service of process), information services, locate investigations, backgrounds, fraud, workers' compensation, surveillance. A licensed PI in AZ, CA, NV.

First Mason Title Co

PO Box 1219, 100 Broad St, Mason, TX 76856
Phone: 325-347-6388 **Fax:** 325-347-5418

Types of Records Retrieved: Civil courts; Probate courts; Federal courts; Real Estate; Tax liens/Judgments; UCC records; Vital records

Local Retrieval Area: TX-Mason

Add'l Information: Normal turnaround time- 2-5 days. Projects billed by the hour. Charges may also be a set fee depending on the project. All projects require prepayment.

First Montana Title

879 Main St, Forsyth, MT 59327
Phone: 406-356-2011 **Fax:** 406-356-2220

Types of Records Retrieved: Real Estate; Tax liens/Judgments

Local Retrieval Area: MT-Rosebud, Treasure. **Correspondent Relationships:** statewide.

Add'l Information: Established 1940s. 1st project may require prepayment. They specialize in real estate.

First Securities Corp in Aurora

1220 L St, Aurora, NE 68818
Phone: 402-694-6926 **Fax:** 402-694-6927

Types of Records Retrieved: Civil, criminal and probate courts; Real Estate; Tax liens/Judgments; UCC records; Vital records

Local Retrieval Area: NE-Hamilton

Add'l Information: Established 1932. Normal turnaround time- 3-4 days. Fee basis varies by type of transaction. Terms: net 30 days. They specialize in title searches.

First State Abstract

101 E Front St #101, Lonoke, AR 72086-3237
Phone: 501-676-2486 **Fax:** 501-676-2444

Types of Records Retrieved: Civil courts; Probate courts; Real Estate; Tax liens/Judgments; UCC records

Local Retrieval Area: AR-Lonoke

Add'l Information: Established 1953. Normal turnaround time- 3-4 days. Fee basis will vary by type of project. All projects require prepayment. They specialize in title insurance.

DeAnne Fisher

PO Box 625, Mercer, PA 16137-0625
Phone: 724-699-5528 **Fax:** 724-662-5932

Types of Records Retrieved: Civil, criminal and probate courts; Real Estate; Tax liens/Judgments; UCC records

Local Retrieval Area: PA-Mercer

Add'l Information: Established 1998. Normal turnaround time- 28-48 hours. Projects billed by number of names searched. Projects billed by number of records located. Will bill upon completion. She is an independent paralegal with over 12 years of experience. She specializes in title searches, lien checks and criminal/civil record checks. 2nd phone number 724-662-5933.

Robin Fisher Paralegal

c/o Executive Title, Somerset, KY 42501
Phone: 606-219-1700

Types of Records Retrieved: Real Estate

Local Retrieval Area: KY-Pulaski

Add'l Information: 1st project may require prepayment. She specializes in real estate.

Fisher/Jones Title Co (Anson)

PO Box 149, 1312 Commercial Ave, Anson, TX 79501
Phone: 325-823-3236 **Fax:** 325-823-3224

Types of Records Retrieved: Civil, criminal and probate courts; Real Estate; Tax liens/Judgments; UCC records; Vital records

Local Retrieval Area: TX-Jones

Add'l Information: Established 1901. Normal turnaround time- 1-2 days. Fee basis will vary by the type of project. 1st project may require prepayment. Their main office is in Roby in Fisher County.

Fisher/Jones Title Co (Roby)

PO Box 428, W Hiway 180, Roby, TX 79543
Phone: 325-776-2471 **Fax:** 325-776-2886

Types of Records Retrieved: Civil, criminal and probate courts; Real Estate; Tax liens/Judgments; UCC records; Vital records

Local Retrieval Area: TX-Fisher

Add'l Information: Established 1901. Normal turnaround time- 1-2 days. Fee basis will vary by the type of project. 1st project may require prepayment.

Fitzgerald Servaites Inc

7308 Langsford Ct, Springfield, VA 22153
Phone: 202-257-7775 **Fax:** 703-912-4840
www.fsiresearch.com **email:** fsiresearch@aol.com

Types of Records Retrieved: Civil, criminal and probate courts; Federal courts; Real Estate; Tax liens/Judgments; UCC records; Vital records

Local Retrieval Area: DC-District of Columbia; MD-Montgomery, Prince George's; VA-Alexandria City, Arlington, Fairfax, Loudoun, Prince William, Stafford

Add'l Information: Established 1997. Normal turnaround time- 24 hours. Projects billed by number of names searched. Projects billed by the hour. All projects are invoiced. They specialize in providing accurate, expeditious litigation research within the Washington, DC metropolitan region.

Judith A Fitzgerald

421 Manono St, Kailua, HI 96734
Phone: 808-263-2120 **Fax:** 808-263-5823
heyjude831@aol.com

Types of Records Retrieved: Civil, criminal and probate courts; Federal courts; Real Estate; Tax liens/Judgments; UCC records

Local Retrieval Area: HI-Hawaii, Honolulu, Kauai, Maui

Add'l Information: Established 1982. Normal turnaround time- variable depending on project. Projects billed by the hour. Terms: net 30 days. She specializes in real property asset searches and lien searches statewide, is a certified Real Estate Appraiser and a certified polygraph examiner. Court record searches for Oahu only (City and county of Honolulu) and criminal convictions statewide.

FLA Search Company

PO Box 5346, Lake Worth, FL 33466
Phone: 561-969-6594 **Fax:** 561-641-7516

Types of Records Retrieved: Civil courts; Probate courts; Federal courts; Real Estate; Tax liens/Judgments; UCC records; Vital records

Local Retrieval Area: FL-Broward, Dade, Martin, Palm Beach, St. Lucie. **Correspondent Relationships:** statewide.

Add'l Information: Established 1985. Normal turnaround time- 24 hours. Projects billed by number of names searched. Terms: net 30 days. Specializes in current owner searches, does criminal searches in Broward and Palm Beach counties only. They search financing statements, judgments, state and federal taxliens in all Florida Counties.

Flagler County Abstract Co

PO Box 398, Bunnell, FL 32110
Phone: 386-437-4151 **Fax:** 386-437-1913
www.flaglercountyabstract.com **email:** fcac@flaglercountyabstract.com

Types of Records Retrieved: Probate courts; Real Estate; Tax liens/Judgments; UCC records

Local Retrieval Area: FL-Flagler, St. Johns, Volusia

Add'l Information: Established 1917. Normal turnaround time- 24 hours. Projects billed by number of names searched. All projects require prepayment. They have been established since 1917 and specialize in titles. Another address for their website is www.fcac.earthmax.net. They perform service of process.

Fleischmann Research

PO Box 1592, Cypress, CA 90630
Phone: 714-229-5938 **Fax:** 714-826-6714
fleischmannrrch@aol.com

Types of Records Retrieved: Criminal courts

Local Retrieval Area: CA-Los Angeles, Orange, Riverside, San Bernardino. **Correspondent Relationships:** nationwide.

Add'l Information: Established 1994. Normal turnaround time- 24-48 hours. Projects billed by number of names searched. Projects iinvoiced twice a month. They do background checks including employment verification, driving records, credit histories, criminal record checks, education verification, professional licensing, etc.

Fleming Attorney Service

PO Box 3882, Phoenix, AZ 85030
Phone: 800-776-3301; 602-253-1155 **Fax:** 602-253-5841
www.flemingattorneyservices.com **email:** admin@flemingattorneyservices.com

Types of Records Retrieved: Civil, criminal and probate courts; Federal courts; Real Estate; Tax liens/Judgments; UCC records

Local Retrieval Area: AZ-Maricopa. **Correspondent Relationships:** statewide.

Add'l Information: Established 1964. Normal turnaround time- next day for court searches; 2-3 days for UCC and tax records. Projects billed by number of names searched. Projects billed by the hour. 1st project may require prepayment. They specialize in process servicing, asset searches, and skiptracing. A licensed PI in AZ. They perform service of process.

Glenn A Fleming

PO Box 772, Belle Chasse, LA 70037
Phone: 504-393-0988 **Fax:** 504-433-5101

Types of Records Retrieved: Civil and criminal courts; Real Estate; Tax liens/Judgments; UCC records

Local Retrieval Area: LA-Plaquemines Parish

Add'l Information: Established 1990. Normal turnaround time- 1-3 days. Fee basis varies by type of transaction. 1st project may require prepayment. He specializes in real estate transfer searches, mortgage searches, tax searches and title abstracts.

Flink Findzum Lawyers Service

31 Pleasant Pl, Oceanport, NJ 07757
Phone: 800-380-5434; 732-219-5433 **Fax:** 732-219-5466
mpagan4750@aol.com

Types of Records Retrieved: Civil and criminal courts; Federal courts; Real Estate; Tax liens/Judgments; UCC records; Vital records

Local Retrieval Area: NJ-Atlantic, Bergen, Burlington, Camden, Cape May, Cumberland, Essex, Gloucester, Hudson, Hunterdon, Mercer, Middlesex, Monmouth, Morris, Ocean, Passaic, Salem, Somerset, Sussex, Union, Warren

Add'l Information: Established 1987. Normal turnaround time- 1-2 days. Expedited service available. Projects billed by number of names searched. Projects billed by number of records located. Projects billed by the hour. 1st project may require prepayment. They perform service of process.

Florence County Abstract

PO Box 86, Florence, WI 54121
Phone: 715-528-3272 **Fax:** 715-528-4707

Types of Records Retrieved: Civil courts; Probate courts; Real Estate; Tax liens/Judgments; UCC records; Vital records

Local Retrieval Area: WI-Florence

Add'l Information: Established 1950. Normal turnaround time- 24-48 hours. Projects billed by number of names searched. They have the a complete in-house tract index and judgment index to serve Florence County.

Florida Filing & Search Services Inc

1333 N Duval St, Tallahassee, FL 32303
Phone: 800-435-9371; 850-668-4318 **Fax:** 850-668-3398
www.floridafiling.com **email:** paul@floridafiling.com

Types of Records Retrieved: Civil courts; Federal courts; Tax liens/Judgments; UCC records

Local Retrieval Area: FL-Gadsden, Jefferson, Leon, Wakulla. **Correspondent Relationships:** nationwide.

Add'l Information: Established 1990. Normal turnaround time- 24-48 hours. Projects billed by number of names searched. Will use PayPal. They specialize in UCC, state and federal tax liens, judgments, pending suits & corporate document filing & retrieval. Registered agent services.

Florida Information Associates Inc

PO Box 11144, Tallahassee, FL 32302-3144
Phone: 850-878-0188 **Fax:** 850-656-2126
etfia@earthlink.net

Types of Records Retrieved: Civil courts; Federal courts

Local Retrieval Area: FL-Leon

Add'l Information: Established 1985. Normal turnaround time- 2-3 days. Expedited service available. Projects billed by number of names searched. Projects billed by the hour. They offer flexible charging for large requests. 1st project may require prepayment. They research and retrieve for state executive, judicial & legislative agencies at the state capital, including legislative intent, corporations, UCC, motor vehicle records, regulatory/licensure agencies and administrative proceedings.

Florida Records Research

1200 Lastrada Ln, Naples, FL 34103
Phone: 239-435-1189 **Fax:** 239-435-1089
Leedmc@earthlink.net

Types of Records Retrieved: Civil, criminal and probate courts; Federal courts; Real Estate; Tax liens/Judgments; UCC records; Vital records

Local Retrieval Area: FL-Collier, Hendry, Lee

Add'l Information: Established 1980. Normal turnaround time- 24-48 hours, may vary. Projects billed by number of names searched. Projects billed by the hour. Depends upon the project. 1st project may require prepayment. They are a fully experienced examiner in business for over 20 years. Researches counties is Southwest Florida. Also do locations and social security number traces, etc. Is experienced, insured and professional.

Florida Research & Filing Services Inc

1211 Circle Dr, Tallahassee, FL 32301
Phone: 850-656-6446 **Fax:** 850-942-6446
www.myfloridaresearch.com **email:** lydia@myfloridaresearch.com

Types of Records Retrieved: Civil courts; Federal courts; Real Estate; Tax liens/Judgments; UCC records

Local Retrieval Area: FL-Leon. **Correspondent Relationships:** nationwide.

Add'l Information: Established 2003. Normal turnaround time- 24 hours. Projects billed by number of names searched. 1st project may require prepayment. Will file/record documents. They specialize in corporate document retrieval/filings, registered agent services and UCC, tax liens, judgments and pending litigation searches. Over 10 years experience.

Margaret Flowers

3640 N. Woodford, Decatur, IL 62526
Phone: 217-877-2105 **Fax:** 217-877-2105
marghappy@insightbb.com

Types of Records Retrieved: Civil and criminal courts

Local Retrieval Area: IL-De Witt, Logan, Macon, Moultrie, Sangamon

Add'l Information: Established 1994. Normal turnaround time- 24 hours. Projects billed by number of names searched. She will bill monthly.

Folks Finders Ltd

PO Box 880, RR 1, Neoga, IL 62447
Phone: 800-277-3318; 217-895-2524 **Fax:** 800-476-0782; 217-895-2418
www.pimall.com/folkfinders/folkfind.htm **email:** wehuntum@aol.com

Types of Records Retrieved: Civil, criminal and probate courts; Federal courts; Real Estate; Tax liens/Judgments; UCC records; Vital records

Local Retrieval Area: IL-Coles, Cumberland, Effingham, Moultrie, Shelby. **Correspondent Relationships:** nationwide.

Add'l Information: Established 1974. Normal turnaround time- 24-48 hours depending on type of inquiry. Projects billed by number of names searched. Two or more earns volume discounts. Copying costs added. 1st project may require prepayment. Credit cards accepted. Payment due upon receipt of invoice; Same day faxed. They specialize in "no find - no fee" searches and locates. nationwide and in 92 foreign countries. A licensed PI in KY.

For The Record In Virginia

9105 Lyon Park, Burke, VA 22015
Phone: 703-862-9105 **Fax:** 703-323-6385
dzigninglady1@yahoo.com

Types of Records Retrieved: Civil and criminal courts; Tax liens/Judgments

Local Retrieval Area: VA-Fairfax, Fairfax City

Add'l Information: Established 1989. Normal turnaround time- daily for primary Fairfax area; 2 days for correspondent areas. Expedited service available. Projects billed by number of names searched. Projects billed by the hour. Fee basis varies by type of project. Will accept check payments. 1st project may require prepayment. Continual monthly projects invoiced; searches and verifications invoiced. They specialize in background/pre-employment, criminal searches, federal/state tax lien information, new business listings filed with the court, judgments and document prepared retrieval. A licensed PI in VA.

For The Record Inc

2711 Kittrell Dr, Raleigh, NC 27608
Phone: 919-783-7766 **Fax:** 919-571-9933
www.myftr.com **email:** info@myftr.com

Types of Records Retrieved: Civil and criminal courts; Federal courts

Local Retrieval Area: NC-Wake. **Correspondent Relationships:** nationwide.

Add'l Information: Established 1996. Normal turnaround time- same day if received before 11AM EST. Projects billed by number of names searched. Monthly billing. They specialize in electronic searching of all 100 NC counties, featuring a direct link to the statewide criminal court computer system by computer terminals located in the Wake County courthouse.

For The Record Title & Court Services

12614 Grand Teton Dr, Bakersfield, CA 93312
Phone: 661-703-9610 **Fax:** 661-589-1895
my4therecord@bak.rr.com

Types of Records Retrieved: Civil courts; Probate courts; Real Estate; Tax liens/Judgments; UCC records; Vital records

Local Retrieval Area: CA-Kern. **Correspondent Relationships:** statewide.

Add'l Information: Established 1995. Normal turnaround time- 24-48 hours. Expedited service available. Projects billed by number of names searched. 1st project may require prepayment. Terms are net 30. They specialize in title searches, judgments/liens and document recording/filing. They can do signups and notary. A mobile phone to reach them is 661-703-9610.

Forbes Public Research Inc

114 Seaman Ave, Castleton, NY 12033
Phone: 518-732-2841 **Fax:** 518-732-2849
www.forbespublicresearch.com **email:** eforbespublicr@nycap.rr.com

Types of Records Retrieved: Civil courts; Federal courts; Real Estate; Tax liens/Judgments; UCC records

Local Retrieval Area: MA-Berkshire, Hampden, Hampshire; NY-Albany, Rensselaer, Saratoga, Schenectady, Warren. **Correspondent Relationships:** nationwide.

Add'l Information: Established 2000. Normal turnaround time- 24-48 hours. Expedited service available. Projects billed by number of names searched. 1st project may require prepayment. Payment due within 30 days. They are known to be one of the fastest and most economical public research teams in litigation and real estate. Will also search Mass. at town court level. Provides records from bankruptcy and US District Courts nationwide.

Ford Abstract Corp

221 N Franklin St, Greensburg, IN 47240
Phone: 812-663-2190 **Fax:** 812-663-2190

Types of Records Retrieved: Civil courts; Probate courts; Real Estate; Tax liens/Judgments; UCC records

Local Retrieval Area: IN-Decatur. **Correspondent Relationships:** Rush, Franklin, Ripley IN counties.

Add'l Information: Established 1940. Normal turnaround time- 5 days. They charge a flat rate.

Fort Enterprises Process Srv & Investigation

PO Box 56589, North Pole, AK 99705
Phone: 907-488-7766 **Fax:** 907-451-0132
fepsi@gci.net

Types of Records Retrieved: Civil, criminal and probate courts; Federal courts; Real Estate; Tax liens/Judgments; UCC records; Vital records

Local Retrieval Area: AK-Fairbanks North Star Borough. **Correspondent Relationships:** statewide.

Add'l Information: Established 1984. Normal turnaround time- 2 days to 2 weeks. Projects billed by number of names searched. Projects billed by number of records located. Projects billed by the hour. Also bill by monthly retainer and special arrangements. 1st project may require prepayment. Monthly billing to approved credit. They specialize in field work and locating persons who are not "in the system". Exercises proper care and diligence in retrieval and researching public records. A licensed PI in AK. They perform service of process.

Fort Lauderdale-Miami Courthouse Research

4796 SW 110th Ave, Ft Lauderdale, FL 33328
Phone: 954-434-6819 **Fax:** 954-434-5862

Types of Records Retrieved: Real Estate; Tax liens/judgments; UCC records

Local Retrieval Area: FL-Broward, Clay, Nassau, Orange, Palm Beach

Add'l Information: Established 1991. Normal turnaround time- 24 hours. Projects billed by number of names searched. Billing every 2 weeks. Their title services cover Broward, Clay, Nassau and Orange counties. They provide title reports and current owner reports. They have 13 years experience, are accurate and timely.

Foster County Abstract & Title

105 10th Ave N, Carrington, ND 58421
Phone: 701-652-3164 **Fax:** 701-652-3165

Types of Records Retrieved: Civil courts; Probate courts; Real Estate; Tax liens/Judgments; UCC records; Vital records

Local Retrieval Area: ND-Foster. **Correspondent Relationships:** statewide.

Add'l Information: Established 1962. Normal turnaround time- 1-2 weeks. Projects billed by number of records located. 1st project may require prepayment.

Foster Inv

PO Box 863, Normal, IL 61761
Phone: 800-526-0307; 309-862-3473 **Fax:** 309-862-0197
www.fosterinvestigations.com **email:** mark@fosterinvestigations.com

Types of Records Retrieved: Civil and criminal courts, Probate courts; Real Estate; Tax liens/Judgments; UCC records; Vital records.

Local Retrieval Area: IL-McLean

Add'l Information: Established 1994. Normal turnaround time- 1-2 days. Fee varies according to the nature of the project. 1st project may require prepayment. They offer more than nine years experience in their area. A licensed PI in IL. They perform service of process.

Four Corners Abstract

370 East Ave, Rochester, NY 14604
Phone: 800-724-3668; 716-454-2263 **Fax:** 716-454-6163
www.fourcornersabstract.com **email:** samw@fourcornersabstract.com

Types of Records Retrieved: Probate courts; Real Estate; Tax liens/Judgments; UCC records

Local Retrieval Area: NY-Albany, Broome, Cayuga, Chenango, Columbia, Delaware, Erie, Fulton, Genesee, Greene, Herkimer, Livingston, Madison, Monroe, Montgomery, Niagara, Oneida, Onondaga, Ontario, Orleans, Oswego, Rensselaer, Saratoga, Schenectady, Sececa, Tioga, Wayne, Yates. **Correspondent Relationships:** nationwide.

Add'l Information: Established 1980. Normal turnaround time- 3-5 working days. Fees are calculated on a per order basis. 1st project may require prepayment. They specialize in title insurance.

Fourth Corner Network Inc

110 Prospect St, Bellingham, WA 98225-4402
Phone: 800-321-2455; 360-671-2455 **Fax:** 888-861-0287; 360-734-1286
www.4thcorner.com **email:** robin@4thcorner.com

Types of Records Retrieved: Civil, criminal and probate courts; Real Estate; Tax liens/Judgments; UCC records; Vital records

Local Retrieval Area: WA-Skagit, Whatcom

Add'l Information: Established 1978. Normal turnaround time- 1-3 days for Whatcom County; 2-5 days for Skagit County. Fee basis depends upon the type of project. Credit cards accepted. Terms: net 30 days. They specialize in a wide variety of record retrieval, filings, etc. A licensed PI in WA. They perform service of process.

Fowler Abstract & Title Inc

110 N Main, Wakeeney, KS 67672
Phone: 785-743-6422 **Fax:** 785-743-5769
fowler@ruraltel.net

Types of Records Retrieved: Civil, criminal and probate courts; Real Estate; Tax liens/Judgments; UCC records; Vital records

Local Retrieval Area: KS-Trego. **Correspondent Relationships:** Ness, Gove, Graham counties KS.

Add'l Information: Established 1975. Normal turnaround time- 1-2 days. Projects billed by the hour. Personal checks are accepted.

Fox Cities Title Co

PO Box 2547, Appleton, WI 54912-2547
Phone: 920-731-5494 **Fax:** 920-731-5493
foxcitiestitle@new.rr.com

Types of Records Retrieved: Real Estate; Tax liens/Judgments

Local Retrieval Area: WI-Outagamie. **Correspondent Relationships:** Winnebago county WI.

Add'l Information: Established 1978. Normal turnaround time- 7-10 days. Projects billed by number of names searched. 1st project may require prepayment. Personal checks are accepted. They are a full service title insurance company with on-site legal staff and a licensed real estate broker, specializing in "for sale by owner" transactions.

Fox Hunt

PO Box 742342, Houston, TX 77274
Phone: 713-772-8018 **Fax:** 713-772-8774
www.foxhuntland.com **email:** bryan@foxhuntland.com

Types of Records Retrieved: Real Estate; Tax liens/judgments; UCC records

Local Retrieval Area: TX-Brazoria, Fort Bend, Harris, Montgomery

Add'l Information: Established 1982. Normal turnaround time- 24-48 hours. Projects billed by number of names searched. 1st project may require prepayment. They are in their 22nd year of business. They pride themselves in being able to customize their service to fit their client's needs.

FOX Investigations, Research & Legal Svcs

1333 S Eliot St, Denver, CO 80219
Phone: 877-369-3698; 303-216-0339 **Fax:** 303-216-0208
www.foxinvestigations.com **email:** fox@foxinvestigations.com

Types of Records Retrieved: Civil, criminal and probate courts; Federal courts; Real Estate; Tax liens/Judgments; UCC reocrds; Vital records

Local Retrieval Area: Co-Adams, Arapahoe, Boulder, Broomfield, Denver, Douglas, Jefferson

Add'l Information: Established 2003. Normal turnaround time- 3-5 days. Expedited service available. Projects billed by the hour. 1st project may require prepayment. Credit cards accepted. They specialize in civil, criminal, probate, federal courts, real estate, Tax liens/Judgments, UCC records, corporate filings, Federal Records Center documents and National Archive records. Have excellent communications and great follow-up. They perform service of process.

FP Resources

4100 Spring Valley #250, Dallas, TX 75224
Phone: 866-989-8999; 972-991-8999 **Fax:** 972-702-0776

Types of Records Retrieved: Civil and criminal courts; Federal courts

Local Retrieval Area: TX-Collin, Dallas, Denton, Tarrant. **Correspondent Relationships:** nationwide.

Add'l Information: Normal turnaround time- 24-48 hours. Projects billed by number of names searched. Billings go out weekly for searches done the previous week. They specialize in many different pre-employment searches. They have a web based program. Their prices are very competitive and they have a quick turnaround time.

Frank Paine Records Search & Retrieval

1000 NE Rhoades St, Winlock, WA 98596
Phone: 888-739-8760; 360-785-0477 **Fax:** 360-785-9937
frankpaine@netscape.net

Types of Records Retrieved: Civil courts; Real Estate; Tax liens/Judgments; UCC records

Local Retrieval Area: WA-Clark, Cowlitz, Grays Harbor, Lewis, Pierce, Thurston

Add'l Information: Established 1998. Normal turnaround time- 24-48 hours. Projects billed by number of names searched. Net 10 days. They specialize in current owner search for property, last vesting deed, legal description, parcel number, CPEN mortgages, assignments, judgments, liens, land improvement values and taxes.

Franklin Civil Process
2661 Jack Rd, Chambersburg, PA 17201
Phone: 717-263-0041 **Fax:** 717-263-6423
Types of Records Retrieved: Civil, criminal and probate courts; Federal courts; Real Estate; Tax liens/Judgments; UCC records; Vital records.
Local Retrieval Area: PA-Adams, Cumberland, Franklin, Fulton, Huntingdon, Juniata, Mifflin, Perry. **Correspondents:** statewide.
Add'l Information: Established 1991. Normal turnaround time- 48 hours. Expedited service available. Projects billed by the hour. 1st project may require prepayment. In business since 1991. A licensed PI in PA. They perform service of process.

Franklin County Abstract Co (Iowa)
121 1st Ave NE, Hampton, IA 50441
Phone: 641-456-4551 **Fax:** 641-456-2359
Types of Records Retrieved: Civil, criminal and probate courts; Real Estate; Tax liens/Judgments; UCC records; Vital records
Local Retrieval Area: IA-Franklin
Add'l Information: Established 1979. Normal turnaround time- 2-3 days. Fee basis varies by type of transaction.

Franklin Investigations LLC
PO Box 473026, Aurora CO 80047
Phone: 720-371-0212 **Fax:** 303-337-7844 jimfranklin@comcast.net
Types of Records Retrieved: Civil, criminal and probate courts; Federal Courts; Real Estate; Tax liens/Judgments; UCC records; Vital records
Local Retrieval Area: CO-Adams, Arapahoe, Denver, Douglas, Jefferson
Add'l Information: Established 2004. Normal turnaround time- 48-72 hours. Will expedite. Projects are billed by the number of names searches. Terms - net 14 days. 1st project may require prepayment. Specializes in lititgation, investigations, real estate, corporate, filing svcs, licensing/registrations. They perform service of process.

Fraser Abstracting
141 N Main St #203, Brewer, ME 04412
Phone: 207-947-6344 **Fax:** 207-990-3843
fraserabst@aol.com
Types of Records Retrieved: Probate courts; Real Estate; Tax liens/ judgments; UCC records
Local Retrieval Area: ME-Hancock, Penobscot, Piscataquis, Waldo
Add'l Information: Established 1989. Normal turnaround time- 48 hours. Projects billed by the hour. 1st project may require prepayment. Statements due upon receipt.

Frazee Abstract & Title Co
301 N Main, Syracuse, KS 67878
Phone: 800-736-7832; 316-384-7828 **Fax:** 316-384-7828
frazee1@pld.com
Types of Records Retrieved: Civil, criminal and probate courts; Real Estate; Tax liens/Judgments; UCC records; Vital records
Local Retrieval Area: KS-Grant, Hamilton, Kearny, Stanton
Add'l Information: Established 1979. Normal turnaround time- 1 day for Hamilton County, 2 days for Stanton and Grant counties and 3 days for Kearney County. Projects billed by number of names searched. Payment due on receipt of statement. They will file/record UCC and real estate documents on behalf of clients on a same or next day basis in Hamilton and Grant counties only.

Frazier & Associates
308 S School St, Ukiah, CA 95482-4826
Phone: 707-462-8559 **Fax:** 707-462-8579
sfrazier@pacific.net
Types of Records Retrieved: Civil, criminal and probate courts; Tax liens/Judgments; UCC records; Vital records
Local Retrieval Area: CA-Mendocino. **Correspondents:** nationwide.
Add'l Information: Established 1988. Normal turnaround time- 2-3 days. Expedited service available for an additional charge. Projects billed by number of names searched. Projects billed by the hour. 1st project may require prepayment. Credit cards accepted. Visa, MC, AmEx and Discover accepted. They specialize in public record searches, fax filings and other attorney support services.

Fred Phillips Research Inc
10945 Chardonnay Pl, San Diego, CA 92131-1509
Phone: 858-735-3431 **Fax:** 858-777-5537
bestresearch@aol.com
Types of Records Retrieved: Civil, criminal and probate courts; Federal Disctrict courts
Local Retrieval Area: CA-San Diego
Add'l Information: Established 1994. Normal turnaround time- 12-48 hours. Projects billed by number of names searched. Pay after names are searched. They specialize in criminal and civil records research that is fast, reliable, efficient and reasonably prices. Serving the San Diego County area.

Fredericksburg Titles Inc
203 W Austin St, Fredericksburg, TX 78624
Phone: 830-997-3852 **Fax:** 830-997-0193
www.fredericksburgtitles.com/ **email:** fbgtitle@ktc.com
Types of Records Retrieved: Civil, criminal and probate courts; Real Estate; Tax liens/Judgments; UCC records
Local Retrieval Area: TX-Gillespie
Add'l Information: Established 1986. Normal turnaround time- 1-10 days depending on project. Fee basis will vary by the type of project. All projects require prepayment. Specialize in title searches and lien searches.

Freelance Abstracting Svc
507 W Third St, Iuka, MS 38852
Phone: 662-424-3636 **Fax:** 662-423-2048
youngjan@bellsouth.net
Types of Records Retrieved: Civil, criminal and probate courts; Federal courts; Real Estate; Tax liens/Judgments; UCC records; Vital records
Local Retrieval Area: AL-Colbert; MS-Alcorn, Benton, Itawamba, Lafayette, Lee, Marshall, Monroe, Pontotoc, Prentiss, Tishomingo, Tippah, Union; TN-Hardin
Add'l Information: Established 1988. Normal turnaround time- 1-2 days. Projects billed by number of names searched. Fee basis depends upon type of project. 1st project may require prepayment. Payment due upon completion. Independent title abstractor & record retriever. Company provides hands-on professional title searches & abstracts, public record retrievals, witness loan closings, foreclosures & other real estate services. They have over 18 years hands on experience. They perform service of process.

Freelance Legal Secretary
911 W 8th #204, Anchorage, AK 99501
Phone: 907-278-8855 **Fax:** 907-276-8967
Types of Records Retrieved: Civil, criminal and probate courts; Federal courts; Real Estate; Vital records
Local Retrieval Area: AK-Anchorage Borough
Add'l Information: Established 1981. Normal turnaround time- 1-2 days under normal circumstances. Projects billed by number of names searched. Fee basis will vary by the type of project. 1st project may require prepayment. They specialize in court record retrieval, researching court records and probate in civil arena.

Irene Friend
406 Old Hwy 11, Beattyville, KY 41311
Phone: 606-464-2638 **Fax:** 606-464-2638
Types of Records Retrieved: Real Estate; Tax liens/Judgments; UCC records
Local Retrieval Area: KY-Breathitt, Estill, Lee, Owsley, Powell, Wolfe
Add'l Information: Established 1985. Normal turnaround time- 1-2 days. Fee basis varies by type of transaction. All projects require prepayment. She specializes in researching coal, oil, and mineral rights.

Fritcher Abstract Co
605 Cayuga St, Storm Lake, IA 50588
Phone: 712-732-2732 **Fax:** 712-732-2444
Types of Records Retrieved: Civil, criminal and probate courts; Federal district court; Real Estate; Tax liens/Judgments; UCC records; Vital records
Local Retrieval Area: IA-Buena Vista
Add'l Information: Established 1942. Normal turnaround time- up to 4 days. Fee basis is "per search". Terms: net 30 days.

Frontier Private Process Service (Flagstaff)
PO Box 1863, Flagstaff, AZ 86002
Phone: 800-711-8511; 928-774-8501 **Fax:** 928-779-1044
Types of Records Retrieved: Civil, criminal and probate courts; Real Estate; Tax liens/Judgments; UCC records
Local Retrieval Area: AZ-Coconino. **Correspondent Relationships:** Arizona.
Add'l Information: Established 1963. Normal turnaround time- 48 hours. Projects billed by number of names searched. 1st project may require prepayment. They specialize in process serving, skiptracing, and record retrieval. A licensed PI in AZ. They perform service of process.

Frontier Private Process Service (Phoenix)
1145 W McDowell Rd, Phoenix, AZ 85007
Phone: 800-860-0858; 602-258-0022 **Fax:** 602-258-9550
www.frontierpps.com **email:** receptionist@frontierpps.com
Types of Records Retrieved: Civil, criminal and probate courts; Federal courts; Real Estate; Tax liens/Judgments; UCC records; Vital records
Local Retrieval Area: AZ-Maricopa. **Correspondent Relationships:** Arizona.
Add'l Information: Established 1963. Normal turnaround time- 48 hours; recorders may take 1 week. Projects billed by number of names searched. 1st project may require prepayment. They specialize in process service, skiptracing, record retrieval, court and probate bonds. A licensed PI in AZ.

Peg Fuoti
35 English Lane, Egg Harbor Twp, NJ 08234
Phone: 609-625-9401 **Fax:** 609-653-8066
Types of Records Retrieved: Real Estate; Tax liens/Judgments; UCC records
Local Retrieval Area: NJ-Atlantic
Add'l Information: Established 1980. Normal turnaround time- 2-7 days. Fee basis will vary by the type of project. She specializes in title searches. They will file/record real estate documents on behalf of clients.

Furnas Valley Title
PO Box 776, Oxford, NE 68967
Phone: 308-824-3304 **Fax:** 308-824-3342
Types of Records Retrieved: Real Estate; Tax liens/Judgments
Local Retrieval Area: NE-Furnas
Add'l Information: Established 2002. 1st project may require prepayment. They specialize in real estate.

Future Security Concepts
16217 W 144th St, Olathe, KS 66062
Phone: 800-398-3051; 913-782-1766 **Fax:** 913-782-5281
www.futuresecurityconcepts.com **email:** joe@netprofithosting.com
Types of Records Retrieved: Civil and criminal courts; Federal courts; Tax liens/Judgments; UCC records
Local Retrieval Area: KS-Douglas, Johnson, Sedgwick, Shawnee, Wyandotte. **Correspondent Relationships:** all Texas, Kansas.
Add'l Information: Established 1993. Normal turnaround time- within 24 hours. Expedited service available. Projects billed by number of names searched. Billing at end of month. They specialize in criminal searches by name in all Kansas and Texas counties. They can do criminal searches nationwide by county; all for pricing. They specialize in criminal searches nationwide.

FYI Screening Inc
PO Box 29698, Columbus, OH 43229
Phone: 800-809-2419; 614-890-9908
www.fyiscreening.com **email:** info@fyiscreening.com
Types of Records Retrieved: Criminal courts.
Local Retrieval Area: OH-Franklin. **Correspondent Relationships:** nationwide.
Add'l Information: Established 1994. Normal turnaround time- 2-3 business days. Projects billed by number of names searched. All projects require prepayment. Credit cards accepted. They are a licensed investigation company and specialize in on-site criminal background searches. They deliver timely, accurate information and adhere to the highest professional standards. A licensed PI in OH.

FYII Acct
226 Sandpiper Dr, Portland, TX 78374
Phone: 563-299-5683 **Fax:** 703-991-7411
research@fyii.org
Types of Records Retrieved: Civil, criminal and probate courts; Federal courts; Real Estate; Tax liens/Judgments; UCC records; Vital records; Votor registration records
Local Retrieval Area: IA-Cedar, Johnson, Linn, Muscatine, Polk, Scott; IL-Rock Island; TX-Nueces, San Patricio. **Correspondent Relationships:** Iowa and nationwide.
Add'l Information: Established 2001. Normal turnaround time- same day or 24 hours. Projects billed by number of names searched. Invoices 1st of each month. They specialize in criminal and background checks. They have low prices and quick turnaround time. They perform service of process.

G

G & H Abstract
PO Box 121, Ellsworth, KS 67439
Phone: 800-640-7390; 785-472-3491 **Fax:** 785-472-4767
Types of Records Retrieved: Civil, criminal and probate courts; Tax liens/Judgments
Local Retrieval Area: KS-Ellsworth
Add'l Information: Established 1973. Normal turnaround time- 2-3 days. Fee basis varies by type of transaction. 1st project may require prepayment.

G & L Research Associates
PO Box 11765, Jacksonville, FL 32239
Phone: 904-743-4116 **Fax:** 904-743-0022
www.glresearch.com **email:** glresearch@comcast.net
Types of Records Retrieved: Civil and criminal courts; Federal courts; Real Estate; Tax liens/Judgments; UCC records
Local Retrieval Area: FL-Clay, Duval, Nassau, St. Johns
Add'l Information: Established 1996. Normal turnaround time- 24-48 hours. Projects billed by number of names searched. Terms: net 30 days. They specialize in 4 part UCC, tax lien and judgments searches, also expedited criminal background checks.

G.A. Public Record Services Inc
3200W Pleasant Run Rd #420, Lancaster, TX 75146
Phone: 800-760-2468; 469-727-0457 **Fax:** 800-669-1642; 469-727-0461
www.gaprs.com **email:** webinquires@gaprs.com
Types of Records Retrieved: Civil and criminal courts; Federal courts
Local Retrieval Area: NY-Bronx, Erie, Kings, New York, Queens, Suffolk; TX-Collin, Dallas, Denton, Harris, Tarrant, Travis. **Correspondent Relationships:** nationwide.

Add'l Information: Established 1989. Normal turnaround time- 24-72 hours. Projects billed by number of names searched. Credit cards accepted. Since 1993, they have specialized in on-site, county level criminal record searches nationwide. A licensed PI in TX.

Gadsden Abstract Co

120 S Madison St, Quincy, FL 32351
Phone: 850-627-6811 **Fax:** 850-627-6440

Types of Records Retrieved: Civil courts; Probate courts; Real Estate; Tax liens/Judgments

Local Retrieval Area: FL-Gadsden

Add'l Information: Established 1967. Normal turnaround time- 1-5 days. Projects billed by number of names searched. Projects billed by the hour. They specialize in real estate.

Ginger Galloway

PO Box 233, Cedarville, OH 45314
Phone: 937-241-8442 **Fax:** 937-766-9873
crthseservs@yahoo.com

Types of Records Retrieved: Civil, criminal and probate courts; Real Estate; Tax liens/Judgments; UCC records

Local Retrieval Area: OH-Champaign, Clark, Clinton, Fayette, Greene, Highland, Madison

Add'l Information: Normal turnaround time- 24-72 hours for real estate records and 72 hours for all others. She specializes in title exams.

Gamble Legal Research

302 Timberhill Ct, Knoxville, TN 37922
Phone: 865-966-3364 **Fax:** 865-966-8260 ferretoutinfo@charter.net

Types of Records Retrieved: Civil and criminal courts; Federal courts; Tax liens/Judgments; UCC records

Local Retrieval Area: TN-Anderson, Blount, Knox, Loudon, Roane, Sevier

Add'l Information: Established 2000. Normal turnaround time- 12-48 hours. Projects billed by number of names searched. Will bill monthly, payment due net 30 days. She has 7 years experience, having owned her own business for 4 years. She provides accurate, expediant results and stays in close commumication with her customers.

Gamma Investigative Research Inc

PO Box 10981, Fairfield, NJ 07004-6981
Phone: 800-878-9393; 973-227-1415 **Fax:** 973-882-0960
www.priveye.com **email:** gamma@priveye.com

Types of Records Retrieved: Civil, criminal and probate courts; Federal courts; Real Estate; Tax liens/Judgments; UCC records

Local Retrieval Area: NJ-Bergen, Hudson, Passaic, Sussex, Union, Warren. **Correspondent Relationships:** nationwide.

Add'l Information: Established 1981. Normal turnaround time- 24-48 hours. The online is almost immediate. Projects billed by the hour. 1st project may require prepayment. They access New Jersey courts and state criminal through online systems. They also specialize in field investigations, skiptraces, background, asset investigations and surveillance. A licensed PI in NJ. They perform service of process.

Catherine J Garbus

PO Box 504, Tunkhannock, PA 18657
Phone: 570-836-6749 **Fax:** 570-836-8894

Types of Records Retrieved: Civil, criminal and probate courts; Real Estate; Tax liens/Judgments; UCC records; Vital records

Local Retrieval Area: PA-Wyoming. **Correspondent Relationships:** Susquehanna and Lackawannock.

Add'l Information: Established 1987. Normal turnaround time- 24 hours. Projects billed by number of names searched. Charges vary depending on type of search. 1st project may require prepayment. Monthly billing.

Daniel E Gardner, dba SCIPRIS

430 S Dunn St #213, Bloomington, IN 47401
Phone: 812-335-0746 **Fax:** 812-335-0746
scipris@sbcglobal.net

Types of Records Retrieved: Civil, criminal and probate courts; Real Estate; Tax liens/Judgments; UCC records; Vital records

Local Retrieval Area: IN-Monroe

Add'l Information: Established 1995. Normal turnaround time- 24-48 hours. Projects billed by number of names searched. Payment due upon completion of project. Now known as South Central IN Public Record Information Svc, they specialize in criminal felony and misdemeanor records, current owner searches, title searches, abstracting and service of process.

Garland Smith Abstract Co

PO Box 329, 132 E Lamar St, Jasper, TX 75951
Phone: 409-384-2571 **Fax:** 409-384-4762

Types of Records Retrieved: Probate courts; Real Estate; Tax liens/Judgments; UCC records; Vital records

Local Retrieval Area: TX-Jasper, Newton

Add'l Information: Established 1908. Normal turnaround time- 48 hours. Fees vary by project.

Garza-McNamee Agency Inc

PO Box 19893, Houston, TX 77224-9893
Phone: 888-262-6221; 713-465-9877 **Fax:** 713-932-1973
vmcnameec@sbcglobal.net

Types of Records Retrieved: Civil, criminal and probate courts; Federal courts; Real Estate; Tax liens/Judgments; UCC records

Local Retrieval Area: TX-Brazoria, Chambers, Fort Bend, Galveston, Harris, Montgomery, Waller. **Correspondent Relationships:** Dallas, Tarrant, Travis counties TX.

Add'l Information: Established 1981. Normal turnaround time- maximum 3 working days. Expedited service available if agreed in advance. Projects billed by number of names searched. Projects billed by the hour. "Standard" reports by name, otherwise by the hour. Invoiced and net 30 days. They specialize in mortgage company updates, full title searches, real property problem analysis, other misc searches for people or corporations in Texas.

Brenda L Gaskill

34 Buttermilk Way, Buzzards Bay, MA 02532
Phone: 508-759-3156 **Fax:** 508-759-0303
blgaskill@aol.com

Types of Records Retrieved: Civil, criminal and probate courts; Real Estate; Tax liens/Judgments; UCC records, Vital records

Local Retrieval Area: MA-Barnstable, Bristol, Plymouth

Add'l Information: Established 2004. Normal turnaround time- 2-3 business days. Projects billed by number of names searched. 1st project may require prepayment. She started her small business in 2004. She will provide reliable service in court record retrieval, real estate, tax liens but not limited to the above.

Gates Land Title Corp

222 W Van Buren St, Columbia City, IN 46725
Phone: 260-244-5127 **Fax:** 260-244-7423

Types of Records Retrieved: Civil courts; Probate courts; Real Estate; Tax liens/Judgments; UCC records; Vital records

Local Retrieval Area: IN-Whitley

Add'l Information: Established 1908. Normal turnaround time- 1 week. Fee basis varies by type of transaction.

Marcia A Gazoorian

PO Box 53, Worcester, MA 01613-0053
Phone: 508-754-9503 **Fax:** 508-754-9503
magparalegal@verizon.net

Types of Records Retrieved: Civil courts; Probate courts; Federal courts; Real Estate; Tax liens/Judgments; UCC records

Local Retrieval Area: MA-Worcester

Add'l Information: Established 1990. Normal turnaround time- 2 days. Expedited service available. Projects billed by number of names searched. Projects billed by the hour. 1st project may require prepayment. Requires immediate reimbursement of costs expended. She specializes in document search and investigation at Worcester Bankruptcy Court. Offering paralegal services since 1976.

G-Docs Inc

311 W Main St, Festus, MO 63028
Phone: 636 937 9440 **Fax:** 636 937 9460
www.g-docs.net **email:** stephm@g-docs.net

Types of Records Retrieved: Federal Bankruptcy courts; Real Estate; Tax liens/Judgments; UCC records

Local Retrieval Area: MO-Jefferson, Lincoln, Pulaski, St. Charles, St. Louis, St. Louis City, Washington. **Correspondent Relationships:** nationwide.

Add'l Information: Normal turnaround time- 24-48 hours. Projects billed by number of names searched. 1st project may require prepayment. They specialize in document retrieval and current owner searches throughout Missouri and across the US. They offer expert 30-years searches. Preparation and recording of releases, assignments, etc.

Gem State Inv

2012 Powers Dr, Lewiston, ID 83501-6154
Phone: 208-746-4152 **Fax:** 208-746-5078

Types of Records Retrieved: Civil, criminal and probate courts; Federal courts; Real Estate; Tax liens/Judgments; UCC records; Vital records

Local Retrieval Area: ID-Benewah, Clearwater, Idaho, Latah, Lewis, Nez Perce; WA-Asotin, Garfield, Whitman. **Correspondent Relationships:** Northern Idaho and Eastern Washington.

Add'l Information: Established 1981. Normal turnaround time- variable depending on project. Fee basis varies by type of transaction. 1st project may require prepayment. They specialize in insurance fraud. A licensed PI in ID. They perform service of process.

Genco Services

PO Box 16334, Baton Rouge, LA 70893
Phone: 225-216-9595 **Fax:** 225-216-9593
http://gencoservices.org **email:** gensvc@aol.com

Types of Records Retrieved: Civil, criminal and probate courts; Federal courts; Real Estate; Tax liens/Judgments; UCC records; Vital records

Local Retrieval Area: LA-East Baton Rouge, Iberville Parish, West Baton Rouge Parish. **Correspondent Relationships:** Mississippi County MO.

Add'l Information: Established 1987. Normal turnaround time- 24-48 hours. Expedited service available. Charges are by name and court searched, plus copy expenses. 1st project may require prepayment. They perform service of process.

General Corporate Inv - GCI

PO Box 2657, Cincinnati, OH 45201
Phone: 800-735-7992; 859-491-5341 **Fax:** 859-491-5420
www.gcicorp.net **email:** gciadmin@gcicorp.net

Types of Records Retrieved: Civil, criminal and probate courts; Federal courts; Real Estate; Tax liens/Judgments; UCC records; Vital records

Local Retrieval Area: KY-Boone, Campbell, Kenton; OH-Butler, Clermont, Hamilton, Montgomery, Warren. **Correspondent Relationships:** Ohio, Kentucky, Indiana.

Add'l Information: Established 1982. Normal turnaround time- 2 days. Projects billed by the hour. 1st project may require prepayment. They specialize in surveillance, activity, background and asset checks, financial investigations, subrogation, locations and pre-employment. A licensed PI in OH, KY, IN, TN. They perform service of process.

General Information Services

PO Box 749032, Dallas, TX 75374
Phone: 800-447-0798; 214-265-8817 **Fax:** 214-265-7572
www.geninfo.com **email:** dbartley@geninfo.com

Types of Records Retrieved: Civil and criminal courts; Federal courts; Real Estate; UCC records

Local Retrieval Area: TX-Collin, Dallas, Denton, Harris, Tarrant. **Correspondent Relationships:** California, Colorado, New York, Ohio, South Carolina.

Add'l Information: Established 1966. Normal turnaround time- 24-48 hours. Projects billed by number of names searched. Will invoive monthly. They specialize in pre-employment background investigations, criminal record research, credit and MVR reports and mortgage/title services. A licensed PI in TX.

General Investigations LLC

171 SE 125th, Warrensburg, MO 64093
Phone: 660-747-8900 **Fax:** 815-301-9620
jrgentry@earthlink.net

Types of Records Retrieved: Civil, criminal and probate courts; Real Estate; Tax liens/Judgments; UCC records; Vital records

Local Retrieval Area: MO-Benton, Henry, Johnson, Pettis, Saline. **Correspondent Relationships:** Cass, Carroll, St. Clair, Bates, Camden, Cedar, Saline counties MO.

Add'l Information: Established 1997. Normal turnaround time- next day. Projects billed by number of names searched. 1st project may require prepayment. Net 15 days. He has a masters degree in criminal justice and a real estate license. They perform service of process.

General Services

1645 S La Cienega Blvd, Los Angeles, CA 90035
Phone: 310-859-1122 **Fax:** 310-859-1123

Types of Records Retrieved: Civil and criminal courts; Real Estate

Local Retrieval Area: CA-Los Angeles, Orange, Riverside, San Bernardino, Santa Barbara, Ventura. **Correspondent Relationships:** statewide.

Add'l Information: Established 1974. Normal turnaround time- 2-3 days. Projects billed by number of names searched. Projects billed by the hour. They are also a mobile photo copy business. Perform service of process.

Geo G Smith & Son Inc

108 E Morrison, Fayette, MO 65248
Phone: 660-248-2467 **Fax:** 660-248-3731

Types of Records Retrieved: Civil, criminal and probate courts; Real Estate; Tax liens/Judgments; UCC records; Vital records

Local Retrieval Area: MO-Howard

Add'l Information: Established 1915. Normal turnaround time- 1-5 days. Projects billed by number of names searched. Fee may also be based per page. 1st project may require prepayment. Personal checks are accepted. They specialize in abstracting and title insurance.

Georgia Bankruptcy Services

3242 Henderson Mill Rd #3, Atlanta, GA 30341
Phone: 770-908-9133 **Fax:** 770-496-0169

Types of Records Retrieved: Federal courts

Local Retrieval Area: GA-Bibb, Fulton, Muscogee. **Correspondent Relationships:** nationwide bankruptcy.

Add'l Information: Established 1998. Normal turnaround time- 2-3 business days. Expedited service available. Projects billed by number of names searched. 1st project may require prepayment. Credit cards accepted. They are a nationwide document retrieval service. They specialize in retrieval of bankruptcy, district court records and records from the federal archives.

GHI Abstracting Inc

110 Jardin Cir, Highland, IL 62249
Phone: 618-971-5780 or 618-654-7253 **Fax:** 618-654-1741
getdocs@charter.net

Types Records Retrieved: Real Estate; Tax liens/Judgments; UCC records

Local Retrieval Area: IL-Madison, St. Clair

Add'l Information: Established 2002. Normal turnaround time- 24-48 hours. Projects billed by number of names searched. Payment within 30 days of service. She specializes best prices for property searches ranging from document pulls to 40 year searches, also performs witness closings.

GHS Inc - Record Research

3019 63rd Ave N, Brooklyn Center, MN 55429
Phone: 763-566-2125 **Fax:** 763-566-2588

Types of Records Retrieved: Civil and criminal courts; US District court; Real Estate; Tax liens/Judgments

Local Retrieval Area: MN-all counties. **Correspondent Relationships:** statewide.

Add'l Information: Established 1998. Normal turnaround time- 24-48 hours. Projects billed by number of names searched. 1st project may require prepayment. Provides mortgage svcs in Anoka, Blue Earth, Brown, Carver, Chisago, Cottonwood, Dakota, Freeborn, Goodhue, Hennepin, Lesueur, Mower, Niccollette, Olmsted, Ramsey, Rice, Scott, Sherburne, Sibley, Waseca, Washington. Also, vital records from some counties.

Connie Giandalia

18850 Wigwam Pl, Independence, MO 64056
Phone: 816-217-1849 **Fax:** 816-796-1130

Types of Records Retrieved: Civil courts; Probate courts; Federal courts; Real Estate; Tax liens/Judgments; UCC records

Local Retrieval Area: KS-Wyandotte; MO-Clay, Jackson

Add'l Information: Established 2003. Normal turnaround time- 24-48 hours. Projects billed by number of names searched. 1st project may require prepayment. Credit cards accepted. She specializes in real estate, probate and federal courts, Tax liens/Judgments, filing/recording documents, document retrieval and notary services. Has 20 years experience in the mortgage industry.

Gietzen & Associates Inc

1302 N Marion St, Tampa, FL 33602-2917
Phone: 813-223-3233 **Fax:** 813-223-9717
www.gietzen.com

Types of Records Retrieved: Civil, criminal and probate courts; Federal courts; Real Estate; Tax liens/Judgments

Local Retrieval Area: FL-Hillsborough, Pasco, Pinellas, Polk. **Correspondent Relationships:** nationwide.

Add'l Information: Established 1990. Normal turnaround time- 1 day. Projects billed by the hour. 1st project may require prepayment. Credit cards accepted. They specialize in financial and general investigations, process and court reporting. A licensed PI in FL. They perform service of process.

Joe Gillenwater

1415 Mangan, Texarkana, AR 71854
Phone: 870-772-2923 **Fax:** 870-773-0108

Types of Records Retrieved: Civil courts; Federal courts; Real Estate; Tax liens/Judgments; UCC records

Local Retrieval Area: AR-Columbia, Hempstead, Howard, Lafayette, Little River, Miller, Nevada; TX-Bowie, Cass, Franklin, Morris, Red River, Titus

Add'l Information: Established 1993. Normal turnaround time- 24-48 hours. Projects billed by number of names searched. Fees are plus mileage and copy charge. 1st project may require prepayment. Terms: net 20 days. He will file/record UCC documents on behalf of clients. They perform service of process.

Gion Law Office

PO Box 101, Regent, ND 58650-0101
Phone: 701-563-4354 **Fax:** 701-563-4497

Types of Records Retrieved: Civil, criminal and probate courts; Real Estate; Tax liens/Judgments; UCC records; Vital records

Local Retrieval Area: ND-Adams, Bowman, Grant, Hettinger, Slope, Stark

Add'l Information: Established 1980. Normal turnaround time- 5-7 days. Projects billed by the hour. 1st project may require prepayment. They specialize in general law practice.

Roger Gladden Law Office

208 W Clarke St, Oxford, GA 30054
Phone: 404-550-0749 **Fax:** 770-550-0749
rglad1@juno.com

Types of Records Retrieved: Civil, criminal and probate courts; Real Estate; Tax liens/Judgments; UCC records

Local Retrieval Area: GA-Newton, Rockdale, Walton

Add'l Information: Established 1977. Normal turnaround time- 1-3 days. Projects billed by number of names searched. Projects billed by number of records located. 1st project may require prepayment. They specialize in criminal and civil searches in Newton, Rockdale and Walton counties. They perform service of process.

Gladwin County Abstract Company

PO Box 736, 320 W Cedar St, Gladwin, MI 48624
Phone: 989-426-7411 **Fax:** 989-426-2411
www.titlepeople.com **email:** info@titlepeople.com

Types of Records Retrieved: Probate courts; Real Estate; Tax liens/Judgments; UCC records

Local Retrieval Area: MI-Bay, Clare, Gladwin, Midland, Ogemaw, Roscommon. **Correspondent Relationships:** Clare, Roscommon, Ogemon counties MI.

Add'l Information: Established 1877. Normal turnaround time- 1 week unless requested sooner. Projects billed by number of names searched. Projects billed by number of records located. 1st project may require prepayment. Personal checks are accepted. They specialize in closings, searches, abstracts, excrow services, and 1031 exchanges.

Howard Glass

PO Box 9784, Marina Del Rey, CA 90291
Phone: 310-827-8473 **Fax:** 310-827-8913
howarddglass@aol.com

Types of Records Retrieved: Civil, criminal and probate courts; Federal courts

Local Retrieval Area: CA-Los Angeles, Orange, Riverside

Add'l Information: Established 1987. Normal turnaround time- 24-48 hours. Expedited service available. Projects billed by number of names searched. Projects billed by number of records located. Projects billed by the hour. 1st project may require prepayment. Regular clients billed on monthly basis. He provides court record research and retrieval in Southern California. High and low volume accounts as well as unique or difficult projects welcome.

Global Inv Agency

1240 Nebo Rd, Madisonville, KY 42431
Phone: 800-597-2812; 270-825-1515 **Fax:** 270-825-1575
captd@onebox.com

Types of Records Retrieved: Civil and criminal courts.

Local Retrieval Area: KY-Caldwell, Christian, Crittenden, Henderson, Hopkins, McLean, Muhlenberg, Todd, Webster

Add'l Information: Established 2002. All projects require prepayment. They also provide court filings, photocopying, skiptracing, private investigations, accident investigations, and workers' comp data. They perform service of process.

Global Securities Information

419 7th St NW #300, Washington, DC 20004
Phone: 202-628-1155 **Fax:** 202-628-1133

Types of Records Retrieved: Civil, criminal, probate courts & Federal courts

Local Retrieval Area: DC-District of Columbia. **Correspondent Relationships:** NY, CA, IL, TX, MD, VA, DE, PA, FL, TN.

Add'l Information: Established 1988. Normal turnaround time- same day. Projects billed by the hour. They specialize in document retrieval from all federal and state courts and government agencies, specifically SEC filings.

Global Title Reporting Services Inc

3376 S Eastern Ave #184, Las Vegas, NV 89109
Phone: 702-248-0593 **Fax:** 702-248-5475
www.globaltrs.com **email:** jorlov@globaltrs.com

Types of Records Retrieved: Real Estate; Tax liens/Judgments; UCC records

Local Retrieval: NV-Clark. **Correspondent Relationships:** nationwide.

Add'l Information: Established 2002. Normal turnaround time- 24-72 hours. Projects billed by number of names searched. Net 30 days. They are a full-service company specializing in nationwide current owner reports; errors and omission coverage; 24-72 hour turnarounds.

Teresa L Godman

PO Box 5032, Quincy, IL 62305
Phone: 217-223-4186

Types of Records Retrieved: Civil and criminal courts

Local Retrieval Area: IL-Adams

Add'l Information: Established 1994. Normal turnaround time- 24-48 hours. Minimum fee required. Will bill.

Linda Gonzales

PO Box 345, Tucson, AZ 85702
Phone: 520-603-6360 **Fax:** 520-670-0034
Lygonz@hotmail.com

Types of Records Retrieved: Civil, criminal and probate courts; Federal courts; Real Estate; Tax liens/Judgments; UCC records; Vital records

Local Retrieval Area: AZ-Pima

Add'l Information: Established 1988. Normal turnaround time- 24 hours. Projects billed by number of names searched. She specializes in criminal name searches for employment screening, insurance, etc.

John Gordon

214 Kilmer Ln SE, Winter Haven, FL 33884
Phone: 863-224-4377 **Fax:** 863-324-8442
www.johngordon.net **email:** gunnygordon@hotmail.com

Types of Records Retrieved: Civil, criminal and probate courts; Real Estate; Tax liens/Judgments; UCC records; Vital records

Local Retrieval Area: FL-Polk

Add'l Information: Established 1998. Normal turnaround time- 24-48 hours. Projects billed by the hour. 1st project may require prepayment. They specialize in court record and real estate record retrieval in Polk County. They perform service of process.

Gotcha Legal Process Service Inc

PO Box 1525, Stony Brook, NY 11790-0878
Phone: 800-698-2748; 631-751-1450 **Fax:** 631-751-0974
skorin@servem.com

Types of Records Retrieved: Civil, criminal and probate courts; Federal courts; Real Estate; Tax liens/Judgments; UCC records

Local Retrieval Area: NY-Nassau, Suffolk. **Correspondent Relationships:** nationwide and international.

Add'l Information: Established 1989. Normal turnaround time- 4 hours to 2 days. Projects billed by the hour. 1st project may require prepayment. They perform service of process.

Gowley Abstract

PO Box 326, Medford, WI 54451
Phone: 715-748-4790 **Fax:** 715-748-6826

Types of Records Retrieved: Civil and criminal courts; Probate court; Real Estate; Tax liens/Judgments; UCC records

Local Retrieval Area: WI-Taylor

Add'l Information: Established 1931. 1st project may require prepayment. They specialize in court records and real estate.

GPS & Assoc (Florida)

PO Box 1465, Zephyrhills, FL 33539-1465
Phone: 866-813-8131; **Fax:** 866-813-8132;
www.gpsassociatesinc.com **email:** backgrounds@gpsassociatesinc.com

Types of Records Retrieved: Civil and criminal courts; Federal courts; Tax liens/Judgments; UCC records; Vital records

Local Retrieval Area: FL-Citrus, Dade, Hernando, Hillsborough, Palm Beach, Pasco, Pinellas, Polk, Orange; VI-St. Croix, St. John, St. Thomas; Puerto Rico. **Correspondent Relationships:** nationwide, Puerto Rico, Guam, Virgin Islands.

Add'l Information: Established 1991. Normal turnaround time- 24-48 hours. Projects billed by number of names searched. They will invoice every 30 days. They specialize in background screening and document retrieval as a nationwide pre-employment service. Specialities include VI driving and criminal records, and Puerto Rico. Also do investigative work. A licensed PI in FL, TN.

Graham Abstract Co

PO Box 276, 202 Washington Ave E, Albia, IA 52531
Phone: 641-932-7156 **Fax:** 641-932-3280

Types of Records Retrieved: Civil, criminal and probate courts; Real Estate; Tax liens/Judgments; UCC records; Vital records

Local Retrieval Area: IA-Monroe

Add'l Information: Established 1982. Normal turnaround time- 2-3 days. Fee basis will vary by the type of project. 1st project may require prepayment.

Graham Abstract Co

121 W 2nd St, Portales, NM 88130
Phone: 505-356-8505 **Fax:** 505-356-8508
grahamtitle@yucca.net

Types of Records Retrieved: Civil courts; Probate courts; Federal courts; Real Estate; Tax liens/Judgments; UCC records

Local Retrieval Area: NM-Roosevelt

Add'l Information: Established 1998. Normal turnaround time- 1-5 days. Fee basis will vary by the type of project. They specialize in escrow, title insurance, closings, mineral searches and escrow collection services.

Grand Forks Abstract & Title Co

PO Box 6326, Grand Forks, ND 58206-6326
Phone: 701-772-3484 **Fax:** 701-795-1957
orderdesk@gfabstract.com

Types of Records Retrieved: Civil courts; Real Estate; Tax liens/Judgments; UCC records

Local Retrieval Area: ND-Grand Forks, MN-Pennington

Add'l Information: Established 1930. Normal turnaround time- 48 hours. Projects billed by number of names searched. 1st project may require prepayment. They specialize in title insurance and abstracting.

Grand Traverse Title Co

116 Boardman Ave, Traverse City, MI 49684
Phone: 231-946-5686 **Fax:** 231-929-5486
www.gttitle.com

Types of Records Retrieved: Probate courts; Real Estate; Tax liens/Judgments; UCC records

Local Retrieval Area: MI-Grand Traverse. **Correspondent Relationships:** Antrim, Kalkaska counties MI.

Add'l Information: Established 1927. Normal turnaround time- 2-3 days. Fee basis will vary by type of project. 1st project may require prepayment. They specialize in title insurance.

Grand Valley Associates

PO Box 2932, Grand Junction, CO 81502
Phone: 970-256-9300 **Fax:** 970-257-7174
www.grandvalleyassociates.com

Types of Records Retrieved: Civil, criminal and probate courts; Real Estate; Tax liens/Judgments; UCC records

Local Retrieval Area: CO-Delta, Garfield, Mesa, Montrose

Add'l Information: Established 1993. Projects billed by number of names searched. Projects billed by the hour. 1st project may require prepayment. Credit cards accepted. They specialize in investigations, process serving and collections. They perform service of process.

Grant County Abstract & Title Co

210 E 5th Ave, Milbank, SD 57252
Phone: 605-432-5461 **Fax:** 605-432-7517

gctitle@tnics.com

Types of Records Retrieved: Civil courts; Probate courts; Real Estate; Tax liens/Judgments; UCC records

Local Retrieval Area: SD-Grant

Add'l Information: Established 1909. Normal turnaround time- 1 week to 10 days. Projects billed by number of records located. All projects require prepayment. They specialize in real estate titles.

Grant County Abstract Co (Indiana)

200 S Washington, Marion, IN 46952
Phone: 765-664-7371 **Fax:** 765-664-0766

Types of Records Retrieved: Civil courts; Probate courts; Real Estate; Tax liens/Judgments; UCC records

Local Retrieval Area: IN-Grant

Add'l Information: Established 1946. Normal turnaround time- variable depending on project. Projects billed by number of names searched. Projects billed by the hour. They specialize in title insurance.

Grant County Abstract Co (Oklahoma)

PO Box 25, Medford, OK 73759
Phone: 580-395-2854 **Fax:** 580-395-2854

Types of Records Retrieved: Civil courts; Probate courts; Real Estate; Tax liens/Judgments; UCC records

Local Retrieval Area: OK-Grant

Add'l Information: Established 1893. Normal turnaround time- 1-2 days. Projects billed by number of records located. 1st project may require prepayment.

K Maxwell Graves Jr

PO Box 607, Meadville, MS 39653
Phone: 601-384-2733 **Fax:** 601-384-5568
mgraves@telepak.net

Types of Records Retrieved: Civil, criminal and probate courts; Real Estate; Tax liens/Judgments; UCC records

Local Retrieval Area: MS-Franklin. **Correspondent Relationships:** adjacent counties.

Add'l Information: Normal turnaround time- 1 working day. Projects billed by the hour. They accept personal checks. He specializes in general law practice. They perform service of process.

Graystone Investigations Inc

PO Box 5091, Macon, GA 31208-5091
Phone: 478-743-5551 **Fax:** 478-743-5121
graystoneinv@aol.com

Types of Records Retrieved: Civil, criminal and probate courts; Federal courts; Real Estate; Tax liens/Judgments; UCC records; Vital records

Local Retrieval Area: GA-Bibb, Crawford, Forsyth, Houston, Jones, Monroe, Peach. **Correspondent Relationships:** Kentucky, Indiana, Tennessee, South Carolina, Georgia, Florida, Alabama.

Add'l Information: Established 1991. Normal turnaround time- 3-5 days. Projects billed by the hour. Fees will include mileage when applicable. 1st project may require prepayment. They specialize in background investigation, surveillance, and defense case searches. A licensed PI in GA, FL, TN. KY, AL, & SC. They perform service of process.

Great Divide Title

390 Boulder Dr #100, Pagosa Springs, CO 81147-9889
Phone: 970-731-7700 **Fax:** 970-731-7740
gdtpagosa@yahoo.com

Types of Records Retrieved: Probate courts; Real Estate; Tax liens/Judgments; UCC records

Local Retrieval Area: CO-Archuleta

Add'l Information: Established 1980. Normal turnaround time- 3 days to 1 week. Projects billed by the hour. Out of town clients are charged a setup fee and must prepay. They specialize in real estate and title matters.

Great Northern Title & Abstract Inc

155 W Baraga #201, Marquette, MI 49855
Phone: 906-228-6100 **Fax:** 906-228-4015

Types of Records Retrieved: Probate courts; Real Estate; Tax liens/Judgments; UCC records

Local Retrieval Area: MI-Marquette

Add'l Information: Established 1983. Normal turnaround time- 1 week. Projects billed by the hour. 1st project may require prepayment. They specialize in title insurance and abstracts of title.

Greater Richmond Abstract & Title Inc

4807 Hermitage Rd #204, Richmond, VA 23227-3335
Phone: 804-266-2101 **Fax:** 804-266-2810

Types of Records Retrieved: Civil, criminal and probate courts; Federal courts; Real Estate; Tax liens/Judgments; UCC records

Local Retrieval Area: VA-Caroline, Charles City, Chesterfield, Colonial Heights, Dinwiddie, Goochland, Hanover, Henrico, Hopewell, King William, New Kent, Petersburg, Powhatan, Prince George, Richmond City

Add'l Information: Established 1997. Normal turnaround time- 12-24 hours. Projects billed by number of names searched. Invoice after projects are completed. They perform title examinations from current owners top full title searches. Retrieve all documents of public record from criminal records to insurance rate filing.

Green Lake Title & Abstract Co

533 Mill St, Green Lake, WI 54941
Phone: 920-294-6070 **Fax:** 920-294-3630
gltitle@voyager.net

Types of Records Retrieved: Civil, criminal and probate courts; Real Estate; Tax liens/Judgments; UCC records; Vital records

Local Retrieval Area: WI-Green Lake. **Correspondent Relationships:** Fond du Lac, Marquette & Waushara counties, WI.

Add'l Information: Established 1984. Normal turnaround time- 1-2 days. Fee basis varies by type of transaction. 1st project may require prepayment.

Greene County Abstract Company Inc

102 S Wilson Ave, Jefferson, IA 50129
Phone: 515-386-2191 **Fax:** 515-386-4509

Types of Records Retrieved: Civil, criminal and probate courts; Real Estate; Tax liens/Judgments; UCC records; Vital records

Local Retrieval Area: IA-Greene

Add'l Information: Established 1900. Normal turnaround time- 1-7 days. Projects billed by number of names searched. Projects billed by number of records located. Fee may also be based on a combination of valuation and clerical. All projects require prepayment.

Greer Guaranty Abstract Co

111 N Oklahoma Ave, Mangum, OK 73554
Phone: 580-782-3121 **Fax:** 580-782-3121

Types of Records Retrieved: Civil courts; Probate courts; Real Estate; Tax liens/Judgments; UCC records; Vital records

Local Retrieval Area: OK-Greer

Add'l Information: Established 1900. Normal turnaround time- 1-2 days. Charges are set fees.

Gregg Investigations Inc of Janesville

PO Box 669, 210 Dodge St, Janesville, WI 53547-0669
Phone: 800-866-1976; 608-755-1976 **Fax:** 608-755-5853
www.gregginvestigations.com **email:** lisa@gregginvestigations.com

Types of Records Retrieved: Civil, criminal and probate courts; Federal courts; Tax liens/Judgments; UCC records; Vital records

Local Retrieval Area: WI-Rock, Green, Walworth

Add'l Information: Established 1979. Normal turnaround time- same day. Projects billed by number of names searched. Projects billed by the hour. Credit cards accepted. Their specialty is "Information Services". They also work with DOT records, boats, city directory library, bartenders and bowlers. Will not search real estate records in Green County. A licensed PI in WI & IL. They perform service of process.

Gregg Inv, Inc of Madison
PO Box 6155, 6320 Monona Dr, Madison, WI 53716-0155
Phone: 800-866-1976; 608-256-1074 **Fax:** 800-377-5853; 608-755-5853
www.gregginvestigations.com **email:** lisa@gregginvestigations.com

Types of Records Retrieved: Civil, criminal and probate courts; Federal courts; UCC records; Vital records

Local Retrieval Area: WI-Dane, Jefferson. **Correspondent Relationships:** Wisconsin.

Add'l Information: Established 1979. Normal turnaround time- same day. Projects billed by number of names searched. Projects billed by the hour. Credit cards accepted. They specialize in "Information Services". They also work with DOT records, boats, city directory, library, bartenders and bowlers. A licensed PI in WI, IL. They perform service of process.

Gregg Inv, Inc of Rockford
PO Box 6340, Rockford, IL 61125-1340
Phone: 800-377-1976; 608-755-1976 **Fax:** 800-377-5853; 608-755-5853
www.gregginvestigations.com **email:** lisa@gregginvestigations.com

Types of Records Retrieved: Civil, criminal and probate courts; Federal courts; Real Estate; Tax liens/Judgments; UCC records; Vital records

Local Retrieval Area: IL-Boone, Stephenson, Winnebago. **Correspondent Relationships:** Wisconsin.

Add'l Information: Established 1999. Normal turnaround time- same day. Projects billed by number of names searched. Credit accounts accepted. They specialize in "Information Services" near Rockford, IL, with offices in So. WI at Madison & Janesville. A licensed PI in IL, WI. They perform service of process.

Gregory Abstract & Title Co Inc
124 W Main, Osborne, KS 67473
Phone: 785-346-5445 **Fax:** 785-346-5446

Types of Records Retrieved: Civil, criminal and probate courts; Real Estate; Tax liens/Judgments; UCC records

Local Retrieval Area: KS-Osborne

Add'l Information: Established 1930. Normal turnaround time- 12-24 hours or less. Projects billed by number of names searched. Payment due upon receipt of requested information.

Gregory County Title Co
PO Box 352, Burke, SD 57523
Phone: 605-775-2943 **Fax:** 605-775-2943

Types of Records Retrieved: Civil, criminal and probate courts; Real Estate; Tax liens/Judgments; UCC records; Vital records

Local Retrieval Area: SD-Gregory

Add'l Information: Established 1949. Normal turnaround time- 10 days. Fee basis will vary by the type of project. All projects require prepayment. They specialize in real estate.

Joe C Griffin
PO Box 237, Ackerman, MS 39735
Phone: 662-285-6080 **Fax:** 662-285-6089
jgriffin@telapex.com

Types of Records Retrieved: Civil, criminal and probate courts; Real Estate; Tax liens/Judgments; UCC records; Vital records

Local Retrieval Area: MS-Choctaw

Add'l Information: Established 1979. Normal turnaround time- 1-2 days. Projects billed by the hour. 1st project may require prepayment. He specializes in marriage/divorce and property searches.

Grissom & Associates
2210 E Highland Ave #104, San Bernardino, CA 92404
Phone: 800-861-6483; 909-863-9073

Types of Records Retrieved: Civil, criminal and probate courts; Real Estate; Tax liens/Judgments; UCC records; Vital records

Local Retrieval Area: CA-Riverside, San Bernardino

Add'l Information: Established 1982. Normal turnaround time- 24 hours. Longer for criminal archive information. Projects billed by the hour. 1st project may require prepayment. They can also get records in Guadalajara, Mexico. They perform service of process.

Grizzly Inv Services
800 South Fork Rd, Cody, WY 82414
Phone: 307-587-8395 **Fax:** 307-587-5855
grizly@wtp.net

Types of Records Retrieved: Civil, criminal and probate courts; Real Estate; Tax liens/Judgments; UCC records

Local Retrieval Area: WY-Park

Add'l Information: Established 1997. Normal turnaround time- 72 hours. 1st project may require prepayment. They also provide private investigation services. A licensed PI in WY. They perform service of process.

Groesbeck Abstract & Title Co d/b/a Limestone County Title Company
PO Box 127, Groesbeck, TX 76642
Phone: 254-729-3806 **Fax:** 254-729-5655
www.limestonetitle.com **email:** service@limestonetitle.com

Types of Records Retrieved: Probate courts; Real Estate; Tax liens/judgments; UCC records; Vital records

Local Retrieval Area: TX-Limestone. **Correspondents:** statewide.

Add'l Information: Established 1892. Normal turnaround time- 3-4 days. Fee basis will vary by the type of project. 1st project may require prepayment. They specialize in real property records.

Grue Abstract Co
PO Box 559, Webster, SD 57274
Phone: 605-345-3891 **Fax:** 605-345-4051

Types of Records Retrieved: Civil courts; Probate courts; Real Estate; Tax liens/Judgments; UCC records; Vital records

Local Retrieval Area: SD-Day

Add'l Information: Normal turnaround time- 5-10 days. Fee basis will vary by the type of project. They specialize in land title.

GSB Communications & Inv
PO Box 7033, Fullerton, CA 92834
Phone: 866-472-2666; 866-472-2666 **Fax:** 866-472-2666; 866-472-2666
www.garybrummond.com **email:** gsbcomm2000@aol.com

Types of Records Retrieved: Civil and criminal courts; Federal courts; Real Estate; Tax liens/Judgments; UCC records; Vital records

Local Retrieval Area: CA-Los Angeles, Orange. **Correspondent Relationships:** Ventura, San Bernardino, Riverside, San Diego counties.

Add'l Information: Established 1998. Normal turnaround time- 24-48 hours. Expedited service available. Projects billed by the hour. 1st project may require prepayment. GSB communications & investigations provides subpoena service (specialize in evasive types), background investigations, public records research and surveillance. Utilizes virtual office capabilites to communicate. A licensed PI in CA. They perform service of process.

Guaranty Abstract Co (Colorado)
PO Box 859, 311 S Main St, Lamar, CO 81052
Phone: 719-336-3261 **Fax:** 719-336-8106

Types of Records Retrieved: Probate courts; Real Estate; Tax liens/Judgments; UCC records

Local Retrieval Area: CO-Bent, Prowers

Add'l Information: Established 1927. Normal turnaround time- 1-3 days. Fee basis is determined on "per name/description" or "flat rate." 1st project may require prepayment. They specialize in real estate and title matters.

Guaranty Abstract Co (Silverton)
PO Box 718, 415 Main St, Silverton, TX 79257
Phone: 806-823-2354 **Fax:** 806-823-2354

Types of Records Retrieved: Civil courts; Probate courts; Real Estate; Tax liens/Judgments; UCC records

Local Retrieval Area: TX-Briscoe

Add'l Information: Normal turnaround time- 2-3 days. Projects billed by the hour. 1st project may require prepayment.

Guaranty Abstract Co of Jackson County Inc

116 W Main, Edna, TX 77957

Phone: 361-782-3591 **Fax:** 361-782-3649

Types of Records Retrieved: Civil courts; Probate courts; Real Estate; Tax liens/Judgments; UCC records

Local Retrieval Area: TX-Jackson

Add'l Information: Established 1992. Normal turnaround time- 24-48 hours. Fees vary by project.

Guaranty Abstract of Stigler

PO Box 278, 101 E Main St, Stigler, OK 74462

Phone: 918-967-8876 **Fax:** 918-967-2191

Types of Records Retrieved: Civil courts; Probate courts; Real Estate; Tax liens/Judgments; UCC records

Local Retrieval Area: OK-Haskell

Add'l Information: Normal turnaround time- 1 week. 2 weeks on abstracts. Projects billed by the hour. All projects require prepayment. They specialize in land records.

Guaranty Land Title

2000 Forum Blvd #5, Columbia, MO 65203-5460

Phone: 573-874-4912 **Fax:** 573-874-4916 www.guarantytitle.com

Types of Records Retrieved: Civil courts; Probate courts; Real Estate; Tax liens/Judgments; UCC records; Vital records

Local Retrieval Area: MO-Audrain, Boone, Caldwell, Callaway, Camden, Chariton, Clinton, Cole, Cooper, Crawford, Daviess, DeKalb, Dent, Howard, Laclede, Livingston, Macon, Maries, Miller, Moniteau, Monroe, Morgan, Osage, Pettis, Phelps, Pulaski, Randolph, Saline, St. Louis, St. Louis City

Add'l Information: Established 1991. Normal turnaround time- next day to 2 days. Projects billed by number of names searched. 1st project may require prepayment. They specialize in land title searches and UCC searches in 30 key Missouri counties. Centralized ordering and billing.

Guaranty Title Co (Centerville)

PO Box 449, Centerville, TX 75833

Phone: 903-536-2133 **Fax:** 903-536-7643

Types of Records Retrieved: Civil courts; Probate courts; Real Estate; Tax liens/Judgments; UCC records; Vital records

Local Retrieval Area: TX-Leon. **Correspondent Relationships:** statewide.

Add'l Information: Normal turnaround time- up to 1 week. Fee basis will vary by the type of project. 1st project may require prepayment.

Guaranty Title Co (New Mexico)

108 N Canyon, PO Box 430, Carlsbad, NM 88221-0430

Phone: 505-887-3593 **Fax:** 505-885-5204

www.guarantytitlenm.com **email:** docs@guarantytitlenm.com

Types of Records Retrieved: Civil courts; Probate courts; Real Estate; Tax liens/Judgments; UCC records

Local Retrieval Area: NM-Eddy

Add'l Information: Established 1940. Normal turnaround time- 1 week. Fee basis will vary by the type of project. The same family has owned and operated this business in Eddy County for over 60 years.

Guaranty Title Co of Grimes County

PO Box 290, Anderson, TX 77830

Phone: 936-873-2250 **Fax:** 936-873-2056

Types of Records Retrieved: Civil courts; Probate courts; Real Estate; Tax liens/Judgments; UCC records

Local Retrieval Area: TX-Grimes

Add'l Information: Normal turnaround time- 2-3 weeks. Fee basis will vary by the type of project. 1st project may require prepayment.

Guaranty Title Co of Robertson County Inc

PO Box 481, Franklin, TX 77856

Phone: 979-828-4688 **Fax:** 979-828-3803

Types of Records Retrieved: Civil courts; Probate courts; Real Estate; Tax liens/Judgments; UCC records; Vital records

Local Retrieval Area: TX-Robertson

Add'l Information: Established 1975. Normal turnaround time- up to 1 week. Fee basis will vary by the type of project. 1st project may require prepayment.

Guaranty Title Services Inc

PO Box 69, Menomonie, WI 54751-0069

Phone: 715-235-3393 **Fax:** 715-235-0624

www.titleservice.com

Types of Records Retrieved: Civil courts; Probate courts; Real Estate; Tax liens/Judgments; UCC records

Local Retrieval Area: WI-Barron, Dunn, St Croix. **Correspondent Relationships:** Fond du Lac, Marathon, Door, Dodge, Green Lake, Polk counties WI.

Add'l Information: Established 1885. Normal turnaround time- 24 hours. Projects billed by number of names searched. Projects billed by number of records located. 1st project may require prepayment. Personal checks accepted.

Guaranty Title Services Osceola

PO Box 126, Osceola, WI 54020

Phone: 888-620-7243; 715-294-2624 **Fax:** 715-755-3535

www.titleservice.com **email:** gtsosceola@titleservice.com

Types of Records Retrieved: Real Estate; Tax liens/Judgments; UCC records

Local Retrieval Area: WI-Polk. **Correspondent Relationships:** Burnett, Barron, St. Croix, Pierce.

Add'l Information: Established 1882. Normal turnaround time- 2-7 days. Projects billed by number of names searched. Projects billed by number of records located. Payment due upon receipt. Formerly known as Oakey & Oakey Abstract Co, they specialize in DOT searches for new road set ups, title searches and full abstracting.

Guardian Inv & Doc Svcs, TPI Court Svcs, dba L & L Paper Chase

637 N 3rd Ave #8, Phoenix, AZ 85003-4532

Phone: 888-268-6162; 602-257-0897 **Fax:** 602-257-1038

www.guardian-ids.com **email:** info@guardian-ids.com

Types of Records Retrieved: Civil, criminal and probate courts; Federal courts; Real Estate; Tax liens/Judgments; UCC records

Local Retrieval Area: AZ-Maricopa

Add'l Information: Established 1998. Normal turnaround time- 24-48 hours. Expedited service available. Projects billed by number of names searched. They will do 30 day billing. Formerly Arizona One Investigations, they specialize in pre-employment criminal histories and bankruptcy records. Also retrieve marriage and divorce records in Arizona. A licensed PI in AZ.

Jerry Guffey

62 Public Square, Leitchfield, KY 42754

Phone: 270-259-4828 **Fax:** 270-259-8161

Types of Records Retrieved: Probate courts; Real Estate; Tax liens/Judgments; UCC records; Vital records

Local Retrieval Area: KY-Breckenridge, Butler, Edmonson, Grayson, Hardin, Hart, Ohio

Add'l Information: Established 1975. Normal turnaround time- 3-5 days. Expedited service available. Projects billed by number of names searched. Will mail statement with findings. He specializes in real estate searches.

Gulf Coast Records

10985 Peppertree Ln, Port Richey, FL 34668
Phone: 727-580-4873 **Fax:** 727-863-6396 gulfcoastrecords@verizon.net

Types of Records Retrieved: Civil, criminal and probate courts; Federal courts; Real Estate, Tax liens/Judgments; UCC records; Vital records

Local Retrieval Area: FL-Hernando, Hillsborough, Manatee, Pasco, Pinellas, Polk, Sarasota

Add'l Information: Established 1996. Normal turnaround time- 24 hours. Projects billed by number of names searched. 1st project may require prepayment. They specialize in criminal and civil record checks. They also perform current owner searches and obtain mortgage documents.

Guthrie County Abstract

110 N 4th St, PO Box 39, Guthrie Center, IA 50115
Phone: 641-332-2339 **Fax:** 641-232-2340 abstrct@netins.net

Types of Records Retrieved: Civil courts; Probate courts; Real Estate; Tax liens/Judgments; UCC records; Vital records

Local Retrieval Area: IA-Guthrie

Add'l Information: Established 1954. Normal turnaround time- 1-2 days. Fee basis varies by type of transaction. 1st project may require prepayment.

Guzman Title Research Inc

4726 Oakley Rd, North Port, FL 34288-2359
Phone: 941-423-5310 **Fax:** 941-423-5320 sandyguz@sunline.net

Types of Records Retrieved: Real Estate; Tax liens/judgments; UCC records

Local Retrieval Area: FL-Charlotte, De Soto, Lee, Sarasota

Add'l Information: Established 1988. Normal turnaround time- 24 hours. Projects billed by number of names searched. Projects billed by the hour. Fees depend on type of service requested. They specialize in real estate title reports, UCC searches, judgments, liens, US tax liens and real estate tax information. The owner has more than 30 years experience.

H

H S Black Abstractor Inc

PO Box 717, 415 Commerce St, Childress, TX 79201
Phone: 940-937-3681 **Fax:** 940-937-3682

Types of Records Retrieved: Civil courts; Probate courts; Real Estate; Tax liens/Judgments; UCC records; Vital records

Local Retrieval Area: TX-Childress

Add'l Information: Established 1920. Normal turnaround time- 2-3 days. Fee basis will vary by the type of project.

Haakon County Abstract Co

Box 40, Philip, SD 57567-0040
Phone: 605-859-2461 **Fax:** 605-859-3461

Types of Records Retrieved: Real Estate; Tax liens/judgments; UCC records

Local Retrieval Area: SD-Haakon. **Correspondent Relationships:** Pennington, Jackson, Stanley counties SD.

Add'l Information: Established 1999. Normal turnaround time- 2-3 days. Projects billed by the area searched. 1st project may require prepayment. Personal checks are accepted. Credit accounts not accepted. They specialize in real estate title searches for abstracts or title insurance.

Ken Haave PI

7715 SW 86th St #106, Miami, FL 33143-7251
Phone: 305-710-7409 **Fax:** 253-323-8202 gsretrieval@aol.com

Types of Records Retrieved: Civil, criminal and probate courts; Federal courts; Real Estate; Tax liens/Judgments; UCC records; Vital records

Local Retrieval Area: FL-Broward, Dade, Palm Beach

Add'l Information: Established 2002. Normal turnaround time- within 72 hours. Projects billed by number of names searched. Will invoice. Formerly Global Search & Retrieval Inc, he can also fulfill your surveillance and skiptracing needs. A licensed PI in FL.

Haber Investigations

1702-H Meridian Ave #333, San Jose, CA 95125
Phone: 800-382-6333; 408-978-2325 **Fax:** 408-266-1119
haberpeye@earthlink.net

Types of Records Retrieved: Civil, criminal and probate courts; Federal courts; Real Estate; Tax liens/Judgments; UCC records; Vital records

Local Retrieval Area: CA-Santa Clara. **Correspondents:** worldwide.

Add'l Information: Established 1987. Normal turnaround time- 2 hours. Projects billed by number of names searched. All projects require prepayment. Terms: net 30 days. He has 30 years police and investigative experience, a law degree and a criminology degree, and teaches a hands-on workshop. A licensed PI in CA. They perform service of process.

Hale Investigative Services/Process

PO Box 720426, (6564 Bayboro Ct), Orlando, FL 32872-0426
Phone: 800-882-5137; 407-275-6969 **Fax:** 407-275-9171
www.hale-pi.com **email:** halepi@hale-pi.com

Types of Records Retrieved: Civil, criminal and probate courts; Federal courts; Real Estate; Tax liens/Judgments; UCC records; Vital records

Local Retrieval Area: FL-Brevard, Lake, Orange, Osceola, Polk, Seminole, Volusia. **Correspondent Relationships:** statewide.

Add'l Information: Established 1985. Normal turnaround time- 24-48 hours. Expedited service available. Projects billed by number of names searched. They do individual considerations. Credit cards accepted. Checks accepted, upon approval They specialize in surveillance and counter electronic surveillance. They investigate civil, criminal, domestic and industrial cases, also property, tax searches. They also have a division that can serve legal documents anywhere in the US or Florida. A licensed PI in FL. They perform service of process.

Haley Title Co Inc

PO Box 454, Ottawa, KS 66067
Phone: 785-242-2457 **Fax:** 785-242-6830

Types of Records Retrieved: Civil, criminal and probate courts; Real Estate; Tax liens/Judgments; UCC records **Local Retrieval Area:** KS-Franklin

Add'l Information: Established 1945. Normal turnaround time- 1-2 days. Fee basis varies by type of transaction.

Hamilton & Johnson Abstract Inc

PO Box 85, Wahoo, NE 68066
Phone: 402-443-3081 **Fax:** 402-443-4120

Types of Records Retrieved: Probate courts; Real Estate; Tax liens/Judgments; UCC records **Local Retrieval Area:** NE-Saunders

Add'l Information: Established 1962. Normal turnaround time- 24 business hours. Projects billed by number of names searched.

Sue P Hamm

PO Box 46, Aurora, NC 27806
Phone: 252-322-5015 **Fax:** 252-322-7205

Types of Records Retrieved: Civil courts; Real Estate; Tax liens/Judgments; UCC records; Vital records

Local Retrieval Area: NC-Beaufort, Craven, Lenoir, Pamlico, Pitt

Add'l Information: Established 1990. Normal turnaround time- 24-48 hours. Fee basis will vary by the type of project. She specializes in real estate, civil action and lien searches. Cell phone is 252-635-7694.

Hancock County Abstract Co

130 E 8th St, Garner, IA 50438
Phone: 641-923-2454 **Fax:** 641-923-3381

Types of Records Retrieved: Probate courts; Real Estate; Tax liens/Judgments; UCC records **Local Retrieval Area:** IA-Hancock

Add'l Information: Established 1903. Normal turnaround time- 2-3 days. Projects billed by number of records located.

Hand County Abstract & Title Co

PO Box 368, 116 E 3rd St, Miller, SD 57362
Phone: 605-853-2194 **Fax:** 605-853-3606
Types of Records Retrieved: Real Estate; Tax liens/judgments; UCC records
Local Retrieval Area: SD-Hand
Add'l Information: turnaround time- 1 week. Projects billed by the hour.

Hannaford Abstract & Title Co

222 E Main St, Marion, KS 66861
Phone: 620-382-2130 **Fax:** 620-382-2253
Types of Records Retrieved: Civil, criminal and probate courts; Real Estate; Tax liens/Judgments; UCC records; Vital records
Local Retrieval Area: KS-Marion
Add'l Information: Established 1871. Normal turnaround time- 3 days. Projects billed by number of names searched. Fee basis varies by type of transaction. 1st project may require prepayment. They specialize in title insurance, title searches, escrow closings and certificates of title.

Sharon K Hannaman Abstracter

PO Box 246, Blue Earth, MN 56013
Phone: 507-526-5144
Types of Records Retrieved: Real Estate; Tax liens/Judgments
Local Retrieval Area: MN-Faribault
Add'l Information: Established 1990. Normal turnaround time- 1-2 weeks. Projects billed by number of names searched. Projects billed by number of records located. 1st project may require prepayment.

Harbor City Research Inc

201 N Charles St #900, Baltimore, MD 21201-4113
Phone: 800-445-6029; 410-539-0400 **Fax:** 800-331-1566; 410-659-0517
www.hcrsearch.com **email:** orders@hcrsearch.com
Types of Records Retrieved: Civil courts; Probate courts; Federal courts; Real Estate; Tax liens/Judgments; UCC records
Local Retrieval Area: MD-Anne Arundel, Baltimore, Baltimore City, Harford, Howard, Montgomery, Prince George's. **Correspondent Relationships:** nationwide.
Add'l Information: Established 1985. Normal turnaround time- 1-2 days. Projects billed by number of names searched. Projects billed by number of records located. 1st project may require prepayment.

Hardin County Abstract Company

Main Street Courthouse, PO Box 158, Elizabethtown, IL 62931
Phone: 618-287-7944 **Fax:** 618-287-7833 kim@shawneelink.com
Types of Records Retrieved: Civil, criminal and probate courts; Real Estate; Tax liens/Judgments; Local UCC records; Vital records
Local Retrieval Area: IL-Hardin County. **Correspondent Relationships:** Pope County.
Add'l Information: Established 1920. Normal turnaround time- 3 days or less. Projects billed by number of names searched. Projects billed by number of records located. 1st project may require prepayment. They are issuing agents for Chicago Title Insurance Co. in Hardin and Pope counties. Other services provided--real estate closings and document filing.

Harding County Abstract

202 4th St West, Buffalo, SD 57720
Phone: 605-375-3422
Types of Records Retrieved: Real Estate; Tax liens/Judgments
Local Retrieval Area: SD-Harding
Add'l Information: 1st project may require prepayment. They specialize in real estate.

Dudley P Hardy PA (Bradford Title Service)

PO Drawer 1030, Starke, FL 32091
Phone: 904-964-4747 **Fax:** 904-964-2304
Types of Records Retrieved: Civil courts; Probate courts; Real Estate; Tax liens/Judgments; UCC records
Local Retrieval Area: FL-Bradford. **Correspondent Relationships:** Union, Clay, Alachua counties FL.

Add'l Information: Established 1910. Normal turnaround time- 2-3 days depending on the project. Projects billed by number of records located. Payment due upon receipt of invoice.

Harlan County Abstract

PO Box 695, Alma, NE 68920
Phone: 308-928-2343 **Fax:** 308-928-2612
Types of Records Retrieved: Real estate; Tax liens/Judgments
Local Retrieval Area: NE-Harlan
Add'l Information: Established 1969. 1st project may require prepayment. They specialize in real estate.

Harmon Legal Process Service

PO Box 1794, Jefferson City, MO 65102
Phone: 573-635-6690 **Fax:** 573-635-2339 jchdrs@aol.com
Types of Records Retrieved: Ciriminal courts; Federal Disctrict courts
Local Retrieval Area: MO-Boone, Callaway, Cole, Miller, Morgan, Osage
Add'l Information: Established 1978. Normal turnaround time- 1 day. Projects billed by number of names searched. Projects billed by number of records located. Credit cards accepted. Billed monthly. They specialize in statewide criminal searches and public record retrieval. They will file/record UCC documents on behalf of clients on a same or next day basis, also summons and subpoenas. Can do entire state of criminal records thru MSHP-CRID. They perform service of process.

Nancy Harris

1820 California Ave, Las Curces, NM 88001
Phone: 877-461-6700; 505-647-0290 **Fax:** 928-437-1215
believe58@juno.com
Types of Records Retrieved: Civil and criminal courts; Federal District courts; Real Estate; Tax liens/Judgments; UCC records
Retrieval area NM-Dona Ana, Los Alamos, Rio Arriba, San Miguel, SantaFe
Add'l Information: Normal turnaround time- 24-48 hours. Projects billed by number of names searched. Projects billed by number of records located. Projects billed by the hour. 1st project may require prepayment. They specialize in real estate, title searches, criminal background searches, mortgage data, retrieval, judicial judgment assistance and locating missing persons. They also search in the Department of Insurance. They perform service of process.

Harrison County Title

14048 Main St, Bethany, MO 64424-1966
Phone: 660-425-3523 **Fax:** 660-425-6698
Types of Records Retrieved: Civil courts; Probate courts; Real Estate; Tax liens/Judgments; UCC records **Local Retrieval Area:** MO-Harrison
Add'l Information: Established 1947. Turnaround time- variable depending on project. Fee varies depending on project. Formerly known as Harrison County Abstract Co. They specialize in lien and real estate searches.

Harrison County Title & Guaranty

114 N 2nd Ave, Logan, IA 51546
Phone: 712-644-2703 **Fax:** 712-644-2557
Types of Records Retrieved: Civil, criminal and probate courts; Real Estate; Tax liens/Judgments
Local Retrieval Area: IA-Harrison
Add'l Information: Established 1981. Turnaround time- 1 week. Projects billed by number of records located. Payment due upon receipt of billing.

Harry W Hawley Inc

4 Court St, Delhi, NY 13753
Phone: 607-746-3860 **Fax:** 607-746-3339
www.hwhawleyrealty.com **email:** info@hwhawleyrealty.com
Types of Records Retrieved: Civil courts; Probate courts; Federal courts; Real Estate; Tax liens/Judgments; UCC records
Local Retrieval Area: NY-Delaware. **Correspondent Relationships:** Otesgo, Scoharie, Chenango counties.
Add'l Information: Normal turnaround time- 3-10 days. Fee basis will vary by type of project. Personal checks and/or cash is accepted. Credit accounts

are not accepted. They specialize in abstracts, appraisals, title searches, title insurance, witness closings and escrow services.

Hart & Associates Inc

PO Box 61060, Oklahoma City, OK 73146-1060
Phone: 866-429-4044; **Fax:** 877-446-3775;
www.hartassocinc.com **email:** hart@hartassocinc.com

Types of Records Retrieved: Civil and criminal courts; Federal courts; Tax liens/Judgments; Vital records

Local Retrieval Area: OK-Oklahoma; TX-Bexar, Collin, Dallas, Denton, Harris, Tarrant. **Correspondent Relationships:** nationwide.

Add'l Information: Established 1996. Normal turnaround time- 24-72 hours. Projects billed by number of names searched. Projects billed by number of records located. Projects billed by the hour. 1st project may require prepayment. Credit cards accepted. Net 30 days. They specialize in pre-employment screening as well as commercial, residential rental property screening. Services include employee drug testing, interviews, evaluations and profiles and document retrieval. A licensed PI in TX.

Harvey Public Records Inc

PO Box 11397, Waco, TX 76716
Phone: 254-662-6265 **Fax:** 254-662-6266
www.harveypublicrecords.com **email:** info@harveypublicrecords.com

Types of Records Retrieved: Civil, criminal and probate courts; Federal courts; Real Estate; Tax liens/Judgments; UCC records;Vital records

Local Retrieval Area: TX-Bell, McLennan

Add'l Information: Established 1984. Turnaround time- 24-48 hrs. Projects billed by number of names searched. They also do bankruptcy work.

Haskell Abstract & TItle Co

306 N 1st St, Haskell, TX 79521
Phone: 940-864-2604 **Fax:** 940-864-2840 hat@westtex.net

Types of Records Retrieved: Civil, criminal and probate courts; Real Estate; Tax liens/Judgments; UCC records; Vital records

Local Retrieval Area: TX-Haskell

Add'l Information: Turnaround time- 1-2 days. Fee basis will vary by the type of project. 1st project may require prepayment. They specialize in real estate closings, deed preparation, land/lien searches. They are a law office.

Haskell County Abstract & Title

109 S Inman, PO Box 636, Sublette, KS 67877
Phone: 620-675-2322 **Fax:** 620-675-2025

Types of Records Retrieved: Civil, criminal and probate courts; Real Estate; Tax liens/Judgments; UCC records; Vital records

Local Retrieval Area: KS-Haskell

Add'l Information: turnaround time- 2 days. Projects billed by number of names searched. Projects billed by the hour. Document filing/rec fees must accompany documents. They specialize in abstracts and title insurance.

Attorney John A Hatcher

101 W College St, Booneville, MS 38829
Phone: 662-728-9444 **Fax:** 662-728-9440

Types of Records Retrieved: Civil, criminal and probate courts; Real Estate; Tax liens/Judgments; UCC records; Vital records

Local Retrieval Area: MS-Prentiss. **Correspondents:** nationwide.

Add'l Information: Established 1992. Normal turnaround time- 1-2 days. Projects billed by the hour. 1st project may require prepayment. He is an attorney in general practice. They perform service of process.

Hatfield Process Service

1669 Jefferson, Kansas City, MO 64108
Phone: 816-842-9800 **Fax:** 816-842-9801
www.hatfieldprocess.com **email:** service@hatfieldprocess.com

Types of Records Retrieved: Civil, criminal and probate courts; Federal courts; Real Estate; Tax liens/Judgments; UCC records; Vital records

Local Retrieval Area: KS-Douglas, Johnson, Shawnee, Wyandotte; MO-Buchanan, Cass, Clay, Jackson, Platte. **Correspondent Relationships:** Boone, Cole counties.

Add'l Information: Established 1976. Normal turnaround time- 1-2 days. Expedited service available. Projects billed by the hour. 1st project may require prepayment. Hatfield Process Service (HPS) is one of Kansas City's oldest legal services firms. Only experienced investigators are used for their document research and retreival. Please visit www.hatfieldprocess.com. A licensed PI in KS, MO. They perform service of process.

William Patrick Hauser

PO Box 1900, Barbourville, KY 40906
Phone: 606-546-3811 **Fax:** 606-546-3050

Types of Records Retrieved: Real Estate; Tax liens/Judgments

Local Retrieval Area: KY-Knox

Add'l Information: Established 1979. 1st project may require prepayment. He is an attorney and performs searches on a very limited basis.

Hawaii Real Property Research

PO Box 622, Kaaawa, HI 96730
Phone: 808-396-7581 **Fax:** 808-396-4452
www.hawaiiresearch.com **email:** hawaiiresearch@hawaii.rr.com

Types of Records Retrieved: Probate courts; Federal courts; Real Estate; Tax liens/Judgments; UCC records; Vital records

Local Retrieval Area: HI-Hawaii, Honolulu, Kalawao, Kauai, Maui. **Correspondent Relationships:** statewide.

Add'l Information: Established 1995. Normal turnaround time- 48 hours. Expedited service available. Projects billed by number of names searched. Projects billed by number of records located. 1st project may require prepayment. Credit cards accepted. Escrow billing accepted. They specialize in real estate research, title records, (Bureau of Conveyance) tax office records, building permits, market research, and mailing lists.

Hawk Investigations

1647 Butler Plank Rd #12, Glenshaw, PA 15116-1704
Phone: 412-487-9274 **Fax:** 412-487-9260
www.hawk-investigations.com **email:** hawk17@earthlink.net

Types of Records Retrieved: Civil, criminal and probate courts; Federal courts; Real Estate; Tax liens/Judgments; UCC records; Vital records

Local Retrieval Area: PA-Allegheny, Armstrong, Beaver, Butler, Fayette, Indiana, Lawrence, Washington, Westmoreland

Add'l Information: Established 1989. Normal turnaround time- 2-3 days. Projects billed by the hour. 1st project may require prepayment. They specialize in record retrieval and all types of investigations in Pittsburgh and surrounding areas. March, 2005 they will be able to handle all of PA electronic connection to all county criminal records. A licensed PI in PA. They perform service of process.

Hawkins & Campbell Inc

800 N 4th St, Phoenix, AZ 85004
Phone: 602-452-1800 **Fax:** 602-271-4517
www.hawkinsandcampbell.com
email: tmacdonald@hawkinsandcampbell.com

Types of Records Retrieved: Civil, criminal and probate courts; Federal courts; Real Estate; Tax liens/Judgments; UCC records; Vital records

Local Retrieval Area: AZ-Maricopa. **Correspondent Relationships:** AZ.

Add'l Information: Established 1948. Normal turnaround time- 24 hours. Projects billed by the hour. 1st project may require prepayment. They specialize in litigation support, process serving, paper investigation, and skiptracing by licensed experienced professionals. A licensed PI in AZ. They perform service of process.

Hawkins & Ezinessenger Tucson Inc

PO Box 87185, 65 E Pennington (85701), Tucson, AZ 85754-7185
Phone: 520-628-9737 **Fax:** 520-624-9965
www.hawkinsandcampbell.com **email:** hctucson@att.net

Types of Records Retrieved: Civil, criminal and probate courts; Federal courts; Real Estate; Tax liens/Judgments; UCC records; Vital records

Local Retrieval Area: AZ-Pima. **Correspondents:** nationwide.

Add'l Information: Established 1948. Normal turnaround time- 24 hours. Projects billed by the hour. They specialize in service of process A licensed PI in AZ. They perform service of process.

Hayes Inv

325 Claypool-Alvaton Rd, Bowling Green, KY 42103
Phone: 270-781-7488 **Fax:** 270-781-7488 jkjwhayes@bellsouth.net

Types of Records Retrieved: Civil and criminal courts

Local Retrieval Area: KY-Allen, Barren, Butler, Edmonson, Logan, Simpson, Warren

Add'l Information: Established 2002. 1st project may require prepayment. They also provide court filings, subpoena preparation, photocopying, private investigations, witnesss locates, statements, pre-employment screening, surveillance and service of process. Performs service of process.

Cheryl A Hayes

50 Mirror Lake Ln, Coldspring, TX 77331
Phone: 936-520-1036 **Fax:** 936-377-4679 cherylahayes@eastex.net

Types of Records Retrieved: Civil and criminal courts; Real Estate; Tax liens/Judgments; UCC records **Local Retrieval Area:** TX-San Jacinto

Add'l Information: Normal turnaround time- 48 hours. Projects billed by number of names searched. Will invoice monthly. She began research in the Fall of 1998 in Montgomery County for public records research. Currently San Jacinto County is being served for criminal, property records, judgments, tax liens, UCC's and fixture filings.

Tommy Hayes

PO Box 748, McKee, KY 40447
Phone: 606-287-8891 **Fax:** 606-287-8428

Types of Records Retrieved: Real Estate

Local Retrieval Area: KY-Jackson

Add'l Information: Established 1987. 1st project may require prepayment. He specializes in real estate.

Hedlund Abstract

309 Fourth St, Hugo, CO 80821
Phone: 719-743-2353 **Fax:** 719-743-2349

Types of Records Retrieved: Civil Court; Real Estate; Tax liens/Judgments; older UCC records. **Local Retrieval Area:** CO-Lincoln

Add'l Information: Normal turnaround time- 1-2 days. 1st project may require prepayment. They are a title company.

Heartland Document Retrieval

9921 W 71st, Merriam, KS 66203
Phone: 888-221-2778 orders only; 913-362-6190 **Fax:** 888-221-2778 Fax orders only; 913-722-6367
www.heartlanddocuments.com **email:** patty@heartlanddocuments.com

Types of Records Retrieved: Real Estate; UCC records; Tax liens/judgments

Local Retrieval Area: KS-Douglas, Franklin, Johnson, Leavenworth, Miami, Shawnee, Wyandotte. **Correspondent Relationships:** KS and OK.

Add'l Information: Established 2000. Normal turnaround time- 48 hours for non-certified copies. Projects billed by number of names searched. Payment due net 30 days. They provide fast and accurate service in Kansas and Oklahoma. Specializes in current owner searches. Toll-free numbers are for orders only!

Heartland Information Services

PO Box 2918, Minneapolis, MN 55402
Phone: 800-967-1882; 612-371-9255 **Fax:** 800-695-9531; 612-371-9262
www.heartlandinfo.com **email:** skolar@heartlandinfo.com

Types of Records Retrieved: Civil, criminal and probate courts; Federal courts; Real Estate; Tax liens/Judgments; UCC records; Vital records

Local Retrieval Area: MN-Anoka, Carver, Dakota, Hennepin, Ramsey, Scott, Washington. **Correspondent Relationships:** nationwide.

Add'l Information: Established 1991. Normal turnaround time- 24-72 hours. Projects billed by number of names searched. Projects billed by the hour. Credit cards accepted. Terms: net 15 days. They are a licensed and bonded PI agency. A licensed PI in MN. Performs service of process.

Heartland Inv Inc

PO Box 1096, Murphysboro, IL 62966
Phone: 618-687-4900 **Fax:** 618-687-4805
www.heartlandinvestigations.com **email:** reagan618@mychoice.net

Types of Records Retrieved: Civil, criminal and probate courts; Federal courts; Real Estate; Tax liens/Judgments; UCC records; Vital records

Local Retrieval Area: IL-Franklin, Jackson, Jefferson, Massac, Randolph, Saline, Union, Williamson. **Correspondent Relationships:** nationwide.

Add'l Information: Established 1986. Normal turnaround time- 48 hours. Projects billed by the hour. 1st project may require prepayment. Credit cards accepted. They are a full service private detective agency specializing in fire cause/origin investigations, workers' compensation and personal injury. A licensed PI in IL. They perform service of process.

Heartland Recovery

PO Box 205, Wayne, NE 68787
Phone: 866-375-1730; 402-375-1730 **Fax:** 402-375-1168

Types of Records Retrieved: Civil and criminal courts.

Local Retrieval Area: NE-Wayne. **Correspondents:** Northeast Nebraska.

Add'l Information: Normal turnaround time- 1-2 days if in county, slightly longer if in nearby county. 1st project may require prepayment. They specialize is local court records in Nebraska.

Heartland Title Company

404 N Fisk, Brownwood, TX 76801
Phone: 325-646-0509 **Fax:** 325-643-5059 heartlandtitle@juno.com

Types of Records Retrieved: Probate courts; Real Estate; Tax liens/Judgments; UCC records; Mortgage records

Local Retrieval Area: TX-Brown

Add'l Information: Established 1975. Normal turnaround time- 5 days. Projects billed by number of names searched. Projects billed by the hour. 1st project may require prepayment. Their searches are made by attorneys with many years of experience.

Heather Gilbert Title Abstract & Closing Svc

501 W High St, Waynesburg, PA 15370
Phone: 724-998-5954 **Fax:** 724-627-7480 hlgilbert@alltel.net

Types of Records Retrieved: Civil, criminal and probate courts; Real Estate, Tax liens/Judgments; UCC records, Vital records

Local Retrieval Area: PA-Fayette, Greene, Washington

Add'l Information: Established 1999. Normal turnaround time- 24 hours. Projects billed by number of names searched. Projects billed by the hour. Payment due net 30 days. They specialize in being a full service title search company which includes surface, coal, oil and gas. Commercial searches available.

Hebert Land Services

PO Box 772, Poteau, OK 74953
Phone: 918-647-9524 **Fax:** 918-647-9522 jabear@classicnet.net

Types of Records Retrieved: Civil courts; Probate courts; Real Estate; Tax liens/Judgments; UCC records; Vital records

Local Retrieval Area: AR-Crawford, Franklin, Logan, Pope, Scott, Sebastian, Yell; OK-Haskell, Latimer, Le Flore, Pittsburg, Sequoyah. **Correspondent Relationships:** nationwide.

Add'l Information: Established 1981. Normal turnaround time- 1-2 days. Fee basis is determined "per hour/day". 1st project may require prepayment. They specialize in oil and gas.

Held Abstract & Title Co Inc

10 Railroad St, Williamsport, IN 47993-0068
Phone: 765-762-2457 **Fax:** 765-762-2458

Types of Records Retrieved: Civil, criminal and probate courts; Real Estate; Tax liens/Judgments; UCC records

Local Retrieval Area: IN-Benton, Fountain, Warren

Add'l Information: Established 1890. Normal turnaround time- 48 hours. Fee basis will vary by type of project. All projects require prepayment.

Helena Abstract & Title Co

PO Box 853, 6th & Fuller, Helena, MT 59624
Phone: 406-442-5080 **Fax:** 406-442-6179

Types of Records Retrieved: Civil courts; Probate courts; Federal courts; Real Estate; Tax liens/Judgments; UCC records; Vital records

Local Retrieval Area: MT-Lewis and Clark. **Correspondent Relationships:** statewide non-Real Estate.

Add'l Information: Established 1935. Normal turnaround time- 2-5 days. Fee basis varies by type of transaction. All projects require prepayment. They specialize in real estate searches.

Hempstead County Abstract & Title

401 S Washington, Hope, AR 71801
Phone: 870-777-2351 **Fax:** 870-777-6033 wrwpa@sbcglobal.net

Types of Records Retrieved: Civil, criminal and probate courts; Real Estate; Tax liens/Judgments; UCC records

Local Retrieval Area: AR-Hempstead

Add'l Information: Established 1891. Normal turnaround time- 1 week. Projects billed by number of records located. Credit accounts not accepted. They specialize in title insurance, land titles and abstracts.

Barbara K Henritze

807 Brooklawn Dr, Boulder, CO 80303-2729
Phone: 303-499-3750 barbara@henritze.com

Types of Records Retrieved: Civil, criminal and probate courts; Federal courts; Real Estate; Tax liens/Judgments; UCC records; Vital records

Local Retrieval Area: CO-Adams, Boulder, Broomfield, Denver, Jefferson

Add'l Information: Established 1986. Normal turnaround time- 2 days. Projects billed by the hour. 1st project may require prepayment. She specializes in 50 year environmental title chains.

Henry County Abstract Co (Iowa)

300 S Adams St, Mt Pleasant, IA 52641
Phone: 319-385-9017 **Fax:** 319-385-9017

Types of Records Retrieved: Civil, criminal and probate courts; Real Estate; Tax liens/Judgments; UCC records; Vital records

Local Retrieval Area: IA-Henry

Add'l Information: Established 1978. Normal turnaround time- 2-3 days. Fee basis will vary by the type of project. Billing upon completion.

Henry County Abstract Co (Missouri)

101 N Main St, Clinton, MO 64735
Phone: 800-748-7985; 660-885-6168 **Fax:** 660-885-3945

Types of Records Retrieved: Civil courts; Probate courts; Real Estate; Tax liens/Judgments; UCC records

Local Retrieval Area: MO-Henry

Add'l Information: Normal turnaround time- 2-5 days. Fee basis will vary by the type of project. They specialize in title searches and closings.

Heritage Escrow LLC

444 Greybull Ave, Greybull, WY 82426
Phone: 307-765-9399 **Fax:** 307-765-9599 hesjd00@tctwest.net

Types of Records Retrieved: Civil courts; Probate courts; Real Estate; Tax liens/Judgments; UCC records; Vital records

Local Retrieval Area: WY-Big Horn

Add'l Information: Established 1992. Normal turnaround time- 24-48 hours. Projects billed by number of names searched. Heritage Escrow LLC is a full service closing company that is expanding into title searches, ownership and encumbrance reports, title preliminary and soon offering title insurance.

Rick Hessig

404 Hidden Oak Way, Louisville, KY 40222-4894
Phone: 502-583-2453 **Fax:** 502-339-8828 rickhessig@aol.com

Types of Records Retrieved: Civil, criminal and probate courts; Federal courts; Tax liens/Judgments; UCC records; Vital records

Local Retrieval Area: KY-Jefferson; IN-Clark, Floyd. **Correspondent Relationships:** nationwide.

Add'l Information: Normal turnaround time- up to 1 week. Rush service available. A licensed PI in IN. They perform service of process.

Hettinger-Sioux County Abstractors Inc

Box 160, Mott, ND 58646
Phone: 701-824-3148 **Fax:** 701-824-3148

Types of Records Retrieved: Civil courts; Federal courts; Real Estate; Tax liens/Judgments; UCC records; Vital records

Local Retrieval Area: ND-Hettinger, Sioux

Add'l Information: Established 1989. Projects are billed by the amount of entries. They specialize in real estate title work.

Hickman Land Title

PO Box 386, Logan, UT 84323-0386
Phone: 800-365-7760; 435-752-0582 **Fax:** 435-752-0584
hlt@landtitleco.com

Types of Records Retrieved: Civil, criminal and probate courts; Real Estate; Tax liens/Judgments; UCC records; Vital records

Local Retrieval Area: UT-Cache, Rich

Add'l Information: Established 1904. Normal turnaround time- 1-2 days. Projects billed by the hour.

Attorney John O Hicks III

PO Box 64, 105 Main St, Calhoun, KY 42327
Phone: 270-273-5749 **Fax:** 270-273-9855

Types of Records Retrieved: Civil courts; Probate courts; Real Estate; Tax liens/Judgments; UCC records

Local Retrieval Area: KY-Daviess, McLean, Muhlenberg. **Correspondent Relationships:** statewide.

Add'l Information: Established 1977. Normal turnaround time- 2 days for McLean County and up to 1 week for Muhlenberg and Daviess counties. Fee basis varies by type of transaction. 1st project may require prepayment.

Hidalgo County Abstract

PO Box 188, Lordsburg, NM 88045
Phone: 505-542-9181 **Fax:** 505-542-9190 hcacinc@atnx.net

Types of Records Retrieved: Real Estate; Tax liens/Judgments

Local Retrieval Area: NM-Hidalgo

Add'l Information: Established 1962. Normal turnaround time- 1 week. Projects billed by number of names searched. A deposit is required. They specialize in land searches.

High Sierra Courier Service

100 Washington St #103, Reno, NV 89503
Phone: 877-812-8444; 775-322-8444 **Fax:** 775-322-4501
hscourier@softcom.net

Types of Records Retrieved: Civil, criminal and probate courts; Federal courts; Tax liens/Judgments; UCC records; Vital records

Local Retrieval Area: NV-Carson City, Douglas, Washoe

Add'l Information: Established 1996. Normal turnaround time- 3-5 days. Expedited service available. Flat fee and costs. 1st project may require prepayment. They perform service of process.

Hill County Title Co

PO Box 1688, 309 3rd St, Havre, MT 59501
Phone: 406-265-7624 **Fax:** 406-265-8385 title@hctc.havre.mt.us

Types of Records Retrieved: Civil courts; Probate courts; Real Estate; Tax liens/Judgments; UCC records; Vital records

Local Retrieval Area: MT-Hill

Add'l Information: Established 1890. Normal turnaround time- 2-3 days. Projects billed by the hour.

Hill-N-Dale Abstracters Inc

PO Box 547, 20 Scotchtown Ave, Goshen, NY 10924
Phone: 845-294-5110 **Fax:** 845-294-9581

Types of Records Retrieved: Real Estate

Local Retrieval Area: NY-Orange, Sullivan, Ulster

Add'l Information: Established 1959. Normal turnaround time- 2-3 days. Projects billed by number of names searched. They specialize in foreclosure searches, last owner searches, full searches and title insurance.

Hillsdale Title Co - Mid-State Title

32 E Bacon St, Hillsdale, MI 49242-1636
Phone: 517-437-7345 **Fax:** 517-439-1659

Types of Records Retrieved: Probate courts; Real Estate; Tax liens/Judgments; Vital records

Local Retrieval Area: MI-Branch, Hillsdale, Lenawee. **Correspondent Relationships:** adjoining counties.

Add'l Information: Normal turnaround time- up to 1 week. Fee basis will vary by type of project. They specialize in real estate and title research. They will file/record real estate documents on behalf of clients on a same or next day basis.

Hinsdale Title Co

PO Box 69, 0324 N Silver, Lake City, CO 81235
Phone: 970-944-2614 **Fax:** 970-944-4444
www.hinsdaletitle.com **email:** mail@hinsdaletitle.com

Types Records Retrieved: Probate courts; Real Estate; Tax liens/judgments

Local Retrieval Area: CO-Hinsdale

Add'l Information: Established 1978. Normal turnaround time- 3-5 days. Projects billed by the hour. 1st project may require prepayment. They specialize in real estate.

Hire Screening Inc

PO Box 210265, Chula Vista, CA 91921
Phone: 619-656-6068 **Fax:** 619-482-8042

Types of Records Retrieved: Civil and criminal courts; Federal courts; Tax liens/Judgments

Local Retrieval Area: CA-San Diego. **Correspondent Relationships:** nationwide.

Add'l Information: Established 1994. Normal turnaround time- 6-8 hours initial results; 24-48 hours hit results. Projects billed by number of names searched. 1st project may require prepayment. Large projects may require a down payment. They are a full service employment verification and screening company specializing in criminal record searches, credit information, credential and education verification, and reference checking. Rush service available with a turnaround time of 1-3 hours.

Hi-Tech Investigative

1209 Lincoln, Evansville, IN 47714
Phone: 812-477-1400 **Fax:** 812-477-6250

Types of Records Retrieved: Civil and criminal courts; Federal courts

Local Retrieval Area: IN-Gibson, Posey, Spencer, Vanderburgh, Warrick. **Correspondent Relationships:** Henderson, KY.

Add'l Information: Established 1976. Normal turnaround time- 24-48 hours. Projects billed by number of names searched. 1st project may require prepayment. Credit cards accepted. Terms: net 15 days. They are a full service investigative agency, investigations, drug testing, paper & pencil testing and record retrieval. A licensed PI in IN. Perform service of process.

Hixson Enterprises

800 Dandy Loop Rd, Yorktown, VA 23692
Phone: 757-898-9865; cell-876-0018 **Fax:** 757-872-4717
hixson@infionline.net

Types of Records Retrieved: Real Estate; Tax liens/judgments; UCC records

Local Retrieval Area: VA-Gloucester, James City, King & Queen, New Kent, Williamsburg, York. **Correspondent Relationships:** City of Williamsburg, Charles City, Isle of Wight, King & Queen, King William, Mathews, New Kent VA counties.

Add'l Information: Established 1990. Normal turnaround time- 1 day. Projects billed by number of names searched. Projects billed by the hour. Charges by the hour are for 60 year searches. Payment due upon presentation of statement. They specialize in old land records in York County and do some genealogy research. A cell phone number to reach them is 757-876-0018.

HK Partners Research

PO Box 622, Kaaawa, HI 96730
Phone: 808-291-2071 **Fax:** 808-396-4452 hkpresearch@hotmail.com

Types of Records Retrieved: Real Estate; Tax liens/Judgments; UCC records; Vital records

Local Retrieval Area: AZ-Maricopa, HI-Honolulu, WA-King

Add'l Information: Normal turnaround time- 5 business days. Expedited service available. Projects billed by number of names searched. Projects billed by number of records located. 1st project may require prepayment. Credit cards accepted. They specialize in real estate research, title records, HI Bureau of Conveyance tax office records, building permits, market research and mailing lists.

Hodgeman County Abstract & Title

PO Box 487, 112 E Bramley, Jetmore, KS 67854-0487
Phone: 620-357-8328 **Fax:** 620-357-6221

Types of Records Retrieved: Civil, criminal and probate courts; Real Estate; Tax liens/Judgments; UCC records

Local Retrieval Area: KS-Hodgeman

Add'l Information: Established 1973. Normal turnaround time- 1-2 days. Fee basis varies by type of transaction. All projects require prepayment. They specialize in closings, abstracts and title insurance.

Hogan Land Title Co

1605 E Sunshine St, Springfield, MO 65804-1312
Phone: 417-882-3000 **Fax:** 417-823-2620 www.hogantitle.com

Types of Records Retrieved: Civil courts; Probate courts; Real Estate; Tax liens/Judgments

Local Retrieval Area: MO-Christian, Dallas, Greene, Stone, Taney

Add'l Information: Established 1955. Normal turnaround time- 3 days. Fee basis varies by type of transaction. They will file/record real estate documents on behalf of clients on a same or next day basis. Also has offices in Ozark. Buffalo, and Branson.

Holden Abstract Co

PO Box 67, 202 W Wood St, Albany, MO 64402
Phone: 660-726-3417 **Fax:** 660-726-3487

Types of Records Retrieved: Civil courts; Probate courts; Real Estate; Tax liens/Judgments; UCC records

Local Retrieval Area: MO-Gentry

Add'l Information: Established 1868. Normal turnaround time- variable depending on project. Fee basis is per document. Payment must be paid in advance for the file/record of UCC and real estate documents. They specialize in title searches, abstracts and title insurance.

Holifield Investigation Agency

PO Box 8, 95 Main St, Bisbee, AZ 85603
Phone: 800-427-1294; 520-432-7364

Types of Records Retrieved: Civil, criminal and probate courts; Real Estate; Tax liens/Judgments **Local Retrieval Area:** AZ-Cochise

Add'l Information: Established 1998. Normal turnaround time- 24 hours. Projects billed by the hour. 1st project may require prepayment. They specialize in background investigations, insurance claims, missing persons, and surveillance. A licensed PI in AZ.

Hollenbeck Title Co

PO Box 215, Vienna, MO 65582
Phone: 573-422-3633 **Fax:** 573-422-3213

Types of Records Retrieved: Probate courts; Real Estate; Tax liens/Judgments; UCC records

Local Retrieval Area: MO-Maries

Add'l Information: Established 1893. Normal turnaround time- 48 hours. Projects billed by number of names searched. Projects billed by number of records located. 1st project may require prepayment.

Hollingsworth Court Reporting Inc

10761 Perkins Rd, Baton Rouge, LA 70810

Phone: 225-769-3386 **Fax:** 225-769-1814 www.public-records.com

Types of Records Retrieved: Civil, criminal and probate courts; Federal courts; Real Estate; Tax liens/Judgments

Local Retrieval Area: LA-East Baton Rouge. **Correspondent Relationships:** nationwide (criminal).

Add'l Information: Established 1983. Normal turnaround time- 5 days for major metropolitan areas and 15 days for outlying locations. Projects billed by number of names searched. 1st project may require prepayment. They specialize in derogatory information including tax liens, judgments and bankruptcies. An online database for ordering searches is available.

Home Abstract Co

PO Box 520, Martin, SD 57551

Phone: 605-685-6525 **Fax:** 605-685-6452

Types of Records Retrieved: Civil and criminal courts; Real Estate; Tax liens/Judgments **Local Retrieval Area:** SD-Bennett

Add'l Information: Established 1984. 1st project may require prepayment. They specialize in real estate.

Honolulu Information Service, Inc

1136 Union Mall #301, PO Box 2390 (96804), Honolulu, HI 96813

Phone: 808-524-4488 **Fax:** 808-524-4499

www.honinfo.com **email:** info@honinfo.com

Types of Records Retrieved: Civil, criminal and probate courts; Federal courts; Real Estate; Tax liens/Judgments; UCC records; Vital records

Local Retrieval Area: HI-Hawaii, Honolulu, Kauai, Maui. **Correspondent Relationships:** nationwide.

Add'l Information: Established 1982. Normal turnaround time- 48 hours. Expedited service available. Projects billed by number of names searched. 1st project may require prepayment. Credit cards accepted. Terms: net 10 days. Established in 1982, Honolulu Information Services Inc offers a full spectrum of public record filing, search, and retrieval services for the State of Hawaii. They perform service of process.

Hons Investigations

311 S 4th St #204, Grand Forks, ND 58201

Phone: 800-450-4667; 701-775-7704 **Fax:** 701-775-8062

www.honsinvestigations.com **email:** pi@honsinvestigations.com

Types of Records Retrieved: Civil and criminal courts

Local Retrieval Area: ND-Barnes, Bottineau, Bowman, Burleigh, Cass, Cavalier, Dickey, Dunn, Eddy, Emmons, Grand Forks, McLean, Mercer, Montrail, Morton, Pembina, Pierce, Ramsey, Richland, Stark, Stutsman, Walsh, Ward, Williams. **Correspondent Relationships:** statewide.

Add'l Information: Established 1992. Normal turnaround time- 24 hours. Projects billed by number of names searched. 1st project may require prepayment. Credit cards accepted. Volume discounts available. They do statewide criminal history checks through ND Bureau of Criminal Investigations with 1-2 day turnaround. A licensed PI in ND, MN. They perform service of process.

Hood & Whalen

137 E Pike St, Cynthiana, KY 41031

Phone: 859-234-4321 **Fax:** 859-234-4321

Types of Records Retrieved: Civil courts; Probate courts; Real Estate; Tax liens/Judgments; UCC records; Vital records

Local Retrieval Area: KY-Harrison. **Correspondent Relationships:** surrounding counties.

Add'l Information: Established 1984. Normal turnaround time- 3-4 days. Projects billed by the hour. 1st project may require prepayment. They are a general practice law firm.

Hooks Title & Abstract

PO Box 2190, Kountze, TX 77625

Phone: 409-246-3447 **Fax:** 409-246-3559

www.hookstitle.com **email:** hooks@hookstitle.com

Types of Records Retrieved: Civil courts; Probate courts; Real Estate; Tax liens/Judgments; UCC records **Local Retrieval Area:** TX-Hardin

Add'l Information: Established 1902. Normal turnaround time- 2-5 days. Fees vary by project. They have an in-house title plant.

Hoover Professional Investigations

3202 E "M", Tacoma, WA 98404-4027

Phone: 253-272-5090 **Fax:** 253-272-5090

hooverinvestigations@netzero.com

Types of Records Retrieved: Civil, criminal and probate courts; Federal courts; Real Estate; Tax liens/Judgments; UCC records; Vital records

Local Retrieval Area: WA-Pierce. **Correspondent Relationships:** King, Kitsap, Mason, Snohomish counties WA.

Add'l Information: Established 1964. Normal turnaround time- 1-7 days. Projects billed by the hour. 1st project may require prepayment. Specialize in all phases of investigations since 1964. Electronic debugging service and intelligence gathering. A licensed PI in WA. Performs service of process.

Horger Barnwell & Reid LLP

PO Drawer 329, 1459 Amelia St, Orangeburg, SC 29116

Phone: 803-531-3000 **Fax:** 803-531-3030 rhorger@hbrllp.com

Types of Records Retrieved: Civil courts; Probate courts; Federal courts; Real Estate; Tax liens/Judgments; UCC records; Vital records

Local Retrieval Area: SC-Bamberg, Calhoun, Dorchester, Orangeburg. **Correspondent Relationships:** statewide.

Add'l Information: Established 1950. Normal turnaround time- 2-3 days. Projects billed by the hour. 1st project may require prepayment. They do worker's comp and corporate law.

Horizons Unlimited

55 Valentine Rd, Milton, MA 02186-1027

Phone: 617-696-6397 **Fax:** 617-696-0460

www.hudrinc.com **email:** erica@hudrinc.com

Types of Records Retrieved: Real Estate; Tax liens/Judgments

Local Retrieval Area: CT-all counties; MA-all counties; ME-all counties; NH-all counties; RI-all counties; VT-all counties

Add'l Information: Established 1996. Normal turnaround time- 1-5 days. Expedited service available. Projects billed by number of records located. 1st project may require prepayment. Payment due net 30 days. They specialize in abstracting, name searches and document retrieval in all of CT, MA, ME, NH, VT, and RI.

Hornthal Riley Ellis & Maland

PO Box 220, 301 E Main St, Elizabeth City, NC 27907-0220

Phone: 252-335-0871 **Fax:** 252-335-4760 www.hrem.com

Types of Records Retrieved: Civil, criminal and probate courts; Federal courts; Real Estate; Tax liens/Judgments; UCC records; Vital records

Local Retrieval Area: NC-Camden, Chowan, Dare, Gates, Hertford, Pasquotank, Perquimans, Tyrrell, Washington

Add'l Information: Established 1900. Normal turnaround time- 48 hours. Projects billed by the hour. Fee basis varies by type of transaction. They are a full service law firm. They specialize in litigation, real estate, corporate practice and criminal practice. Outer Banks office, 252-441-0871.

Horvath Enterprises Inc

105 Park Ave, PO Box 52, Milaca, MN 56353

Phone: 320-982-3253 **Fax:** 320-982-2572 tph02@maxminn.com

Types of Records Retrieved: Civil and criminal courts; Tax liens/Judgments

Local Retrieval Area: MN-Anoka, Becker, Benton, Chisago, Clay, Douglas, Isanti, Kanabec, Mille Lacs, Morrison, Otter Tail, Pine, Sherburne, Stearns, Todd, Wadena, Washington, Wright

Add'l Information: Established 1994. Normal turnaround time- 1-2 days. Projects billed by number of names searched. 1st project may require prepayment. Will bill monthly. Pager number is 320-982-1601.

Hotopp Public Record Searches

4021 S Whitehorse Rd, Nashville, IN 47448
Phone: 812-342-2163 **Fax:** 812-342-6395 hotopp@hsonline.net

Types of Records Retrieved: Civil courts; Real Estate; Tax liens/Judgments; UCC records

Local Retrieval Area: IN-Bartholomew, Brown, Jackson, Johnson, Monroe. **Correspondent Relationships:** Marion County.

Add'l Information: Established 1999. Normal turnaround time- 24-48 hours. Projects billed by number of names searched. Projects billed by number of records located. 1st project may require prepayment. Billing upon search completion. In business since 1999, they are known for their fast turnaround, 24-28 hours in most cases.

Houston Court Services Inc

1201 Louisiana St #210, Houston, TX 77002-5609
Phone: 713-655-0555 **Fax:** 713-426-3422
www.mach5couriers.com **email:** info@mach5couriers.com

Types of Records Retrieved: Civil, criminal and probate courts; Federal courts; Real Estate; Tax liens/Judgments; UCC records; Vital records

Local Retrieval Area: TX-Brazoria, Brazos, Fort Bend, Harris, Montgomery. **Correspondent Relationships:** the Southern states.

Add'l Information: Established 1988. Normal turnaround time- 24-72 hours. Expedited service available. Projects billed by number of names searched. Credit cards accepted. Payment due upon receipt. They specialize in servicing legal documents and court record retrieval on a nationwide basis. They also provide courier/messenger service and same day and overnight service. A licensed PI in TX. They perform service of process.

Howard County Abstract & Title Co

115 S Park Pl, Cresco, IA 52136-1632
Phone: 563-547-4944 **Fax:** 563-547-5197

Types of Records Retrieved: Civil, criminal and probate courts; Real Estate; Tax liens/Judgments; UCC records; Vital records

Local Retrieval Area: IA-Howard

Add'l Information: Established 1972. Normal turnaround time- 1-2 days. Projects billed by number of names searched. File/record UCC and real estate documents on behalf of clients will be submitted with filing fees advanced. 1st project may require prepayment.

HR Plus

2902 Evergreen Pky #100, Evergreen, CO 80439
Phone: 800-332-7587; 303-670-8177 **Fax:** 303-670-8906
www.hrplus.com **email:** information@hrplus.com

Types of Records Retrieved: Criminal courts

Local Retrieval Area: CO-Denver, Larimer. **Correspondents:** nationwide.

Add'l Information: Established 1989. Normal turnaround time- 1-2 days. Expedited service available. Projects billed by number of names searched. Projects are billed monthly, net 10 days. They specialize in criminal record retrieval.

Hubbard-Kavanaugh Title Co

106 S Fisher, Versailles, MO 65084
Phone: 573-378-4411 **Fax:** 573-378-6385

Types of Records Retrieved: Civil courts; Probate courts; Real Estate; Tax liens/Judgments; UCC records; Vital records

Local Retrieval Area: MO-Morgan

Add'l Information: Normal turnaround time- 24 hours. Projects billed by number of records located. They specialize in land titles, only complete set of records outside of the county courthouse. Have been in business for over 125 years.

Huddleston & Huddleston Law Firm

PO Box 807, 309 W Main St, Warsaw, KY 41095
Phone: 859-567-2818 **Fax:** 859-567-2404

Types of Records Retrieved: Probate courts; Real Estate; Tax liens/Judgments; UCC records

Local Retrieval Area: KY-Gallatin

Add'l Information: Established 1980. Normal turnaround time- 2-3 days. Projects billed by the hour. He is the prosecuting attorney for the county.

Huffman Research

27520 E 15th St, Hayward, CA 94544
Phone: 510-537-4261 **Fax:** 510-217-3615
huffmanresearch@prodigy.net

Types of Records Retrieved: Civil and criminal courts

Local Retrieval Area: CA-Alameda

Add'l Information: Established 1995. Normal turnaround time- 24-48 hours. Projects billed by number of names searched. Payment terms are net 30 days. 1st project may require prepayment. They bill monthly. They specialize in prompt, efficient and thorough service at competitive prices. Volume rate discounts are available.

Huffmaster Associates Inc

1300 Combermere, Troy, MI 48083
Phone: 800-446-1515; 248-588-1600 **Fax:** 248-597-7075
www.huffmaster.com

Types of Records Retrieved: Civil, criminal and probate courts; Real Estate; Tax liens/Judgments; UCC records; Vital records

Local Retrieval Area: MI-Genesee, Lapeer, Livingston, Macomb, Monroe, Oakland, St. Clair, Washtenaw, Wayne

Add'l Information: Established 1962. Normal turnaround time- 1 week. Projects billed by number of names searched. Projects billed by the hour. 1st project may require prepayment. Will take a company purchase order number. They specialize in vehicle/asset tracking, locates, missing persons, business crimes, undercover investigations, legal support services, pre-employment and workers' compensation searches. A licensed PI in MI. They perform service of process.

Hughes Legal Support

7 Eva Ln, Cranston, RI 02921
Phone: 800-783-7690; 401-944-8980 **Fax:** 401-944-3314
www.rilegalsupport.com/ **email:** hughes_legal_support@usa.net

Types of Records Retrieved: Civil, criminal and probate courts; Federal courts; Real Estate; Tax liens/Judgments; UCC records

Local Retrieval Area: RI-Bristol, Kent, Newport, Providence, Washington. **Correspondent Relationships:** nationwide.

Add'l Information: Established 1982. Normal turnaround time- 1 business day. Projects billed by the hour. 1st project may require prepayment. They are a RI company providing litigation support and document retrieval to the RI community since 1982 They perform service of process.

Human Arts Consulting

6420 Escondido Dr #4C, El Paso, TX 79912
Phone: 800-493-2641; 915-751-1532 **Fax:** 915-751-1578
episb@aol.com

Types of Records Retrieved: Civil and criminal courts; Federal courts

Local Retrieval Area: TX-El Paso. **Correspondent Relationships:** nationwide and Canada.

Add'l Information: Established 1995. Normal turnaround time- 24-36 hours. Projects billed by number of names searched. Net 20 days. 1st project may require prepayment. They specialize in training in human resources management issues (e.g. sexual harassment prevention, management leadership, documenting employee behavior, team building). Also write policies & company handbooks for employees.

Hunter & Oelke

PO Box 792, Dalhart, TX 79022
Phone: 800-350-1288; 806-244-5632 **Fax:** 806-244-2863
hunterok@xit.net

Types of Records Retrieved: Civil courts; Probate courts; Real Estate; Tax liens/Judgments.

Local Retrieval Area: TX-Dallam, Hartley. **Correspondents:** statewide.

Add'l Information: Established 1977. Normal turnaround time- 3-4 days. Projects billed by the hour. 1st project may require prepayment. They specialize in Real Estate Law. They are a general practice law office. They will also file/record UCC documents on behalf of clients on a same or next day basis, and specialize in estate work.

Huron Shores Abstract & Title

206 S 3rd Street, Rogers City, MI 49779
Phone: 989-734-3344 **Fax:** 989-734-4920

Types of Records Retrieved: Probate courts; Real Estate; Tax liens/Judgments; UCC records

Local Retrieval Area: MI-Alpena, Presque Isle. **Correspondent Relationships:** Cheboygan and Montmorency counties MI.

Add'l Information: Established 1990. Normal turnaround time- 4 days. Fee basis will vary by the type of project. Terms: net 30 days. They specialize in title insurance, oil, gas and mineral research.

Huron Title Co

PO Box 563, Huron, SD 57350 **Phone:** 605-352-6157 **Fax:** 605-352-7354

Types of Records Retrieved: Civil courts; Probate courts; Real Estate; Tax liens/Judgments; UCC records **Local Retrieval Area:** SD-Beadle

Add'l Information: Established 1949. Normal turnaround time- 5-10 days. Fee basis will vary by the type of project. Payment due upon completion of order. They specialize in land title searches.

Huron Title Co (Michigan)

330 Michigan St, Port Huron, MI 48060
Phone: 800-878-4853; 810-987-2141 **Fax:** 810-987-1317
www.hurontitle.com

Types of Records Retrieved: Civil courts; Probate courts; Real Estate; Tax liens/Judgments; UCC records **Local Retrieval Area:** MI-St. Clair

Add'l Information: Established 1970. Normal turnaround time- 5 days. Fee basis will vary by type of project. 1st project may require prepayment. They specialize in real estate and title insurance.

Hylind Search Company Inc (Delaware)

304 S State St, Dover, DE 19901-6730
Phone: 888-243-6857; 302-744-9023 **Fax:** 888-243-6859; 302-744-9025
www.hylindsearch.com **email:** hylindde@concentric.net

Types of Records Retrieved: Civil, criminal and probate courts; Federal courts; Real Estate; Tax liens/Judgments; UCC records; Vital records

Local Retrieval Area: DE-Kent, New Castle, Sussex. **Correspondent Relationships:** nationwide.

Add'l Information: Established 2000. Normal turnaround time- 24-48 hours. Expedited service available. Projects billed by number of names searched. Invoicing available. They are a national search & filing service that specializes in searching, filing & document retrieval of corporate, UCC, real estate & resident agent services. Online agents for the State of DE & can perform same day searches & filings. They perform service of process.

Hylind Search Company Inc (Maryland)

245 W Chase St, Baltimore, MD 21201-4823
Phone: 888-449-5463; 410-468-3333 **Fax:** 888-597-7377; 410-468-0808
www.hylindsearch.com **email:** info@hylindsearch.com

Types of Records Retrieved: Civil, criminal and probate courts; Federal courts; Real Estate; Tax liens/Judgments; UCC records; Vital records

Local Retrieval Area: DC-Washington; MD-Allegany, Anne Arundel, Baltimore, Baltimore City, Calvert, Caroline, Carroll, Cecil, Charles, Dorchester, Frederick, Garrett, Harford, Howard, Kent, Montgomery, Prince George's, St Mary's, Talbot, Washington, Wicomico, Worcester; VA-Fairfax. **Correspondent Relationships:** nationwide.

Add'l Information: Established 1996. Normal turnaround time- 48 hours or less. Projects billed by number of names searched. Fees are per index searched. Credit cards accepted. Terms: net 30 days. They tailor their asset/lien searches to the client's needs. They offer competitive pricing & volume discounts. Online ordering & expedited services are available. They have a location in Dover, DE as well. They have a quick turnaround & reasonable fees. They perform service of process.

I

ICDI Inc

250 N Wymore Rd, Winter Park, FL 32789-3455
Phone: 407-622-2532 **Fax:** 407-622-2535 icdi@cfl.rr.com

Types of Records Retrieved: Civil courts; Probate courts; Federal courts; Real Estate; Tax liens/Judgments; UCC records

Local Retrieval Area: FL-Brevard, Orange, Osceola, Seminole, Volusia. **Correspondent Relationships:** Lake County FL.

Add'l Information: Established 1992. Normal turnaround time- 24-48 hours. Projects billed by number of names searched. 1st project may require prepayment. Payment due on receipt. They specialize in several counties online, and to counties physically in courthouse records.

Idaho Title & Trust Co

260 W Grand, PO Box 802, Arco, ID 83213
Phone: 208-527-8517 **Fax:** 208-527-3930 ittarco@atcnet.net

Types of Records Retrieved: Civil courts; Probate courts; Real Estate; Tax liens/Judgments; UCC records

Local Retrieval Area: ID-Butte

Add'l Information: Established 1987. Normal turnaround time- 48 hours. Fees vary by project. Only title company in Butte County, ID. They have been there since 1920. They perform service of process.

Idealogic

20 Eglinton Ave W #1300 Box 2006, Toronto, Ontario, Canada, M4R 1K8
Phone: 866-506-9900; 416-506-9900 **Fax:** 866-506-0700; 416-506-0700
www.idealogic.com **email:** ideal@idealogic.com

Types of Records Retrieved: Civil courts; Federal Bankruptcy courts; Real Estate; Tax liens/Judgments; UCC records; Vital records

Local Retrieval Area: CANADA-Ontario, Canada. **Correspondent Relationships:** provinces in Canada.

Add'l Information: Established 1980. Normal turnaround time- same or next day. Projects billed by number of names searched. Projects billed by the hour. 1st project may require prepayment. Credit cards accepted. They specialize in Canadian corporate information, civil and bankruptcy courts, motor vehicle, real estate, PPSA and trademark work for all provinces. They perform service of process.

IGB Associates Inc

1181 Shipwatch Circle, Tampa, FL 33602
Phone: 813-226-8810 **Fax:** 813-226-8710
Igrantbu@aol.com

Types of Records Retrieved: Civil, criminal and probate courts; Federal courts; Real Estate; Tax liens/Judgments; UCC records; Vital records

Local Retrieval Area: FL-Broward, Dade, Duval, Hillsborough, Manatee, Orange, Pasco, Pinellas, Polk, Sarasota. **Correspondents:** nationwide.

Add'l Information: Established 1993. Normal turnaround time- 24-48 hours. Projects billed by number of names searched. 1st project may require prepayment. Terms: net 10 days. They specialize in current owner & title searches, bankruptcy, US Federal courts, county courts, criminal searches and property searches. They can acquire Social Security, address verification and address changes. They carry E & O Insurance.

Ike L Hoy PE (Control Systems)

PO Box 5588, Destin, FL 32540
Phone: 850-259-4650 captcasino@aol.com

Types of Records Retrieved: Civil, criminal and probate courts; Federal courts; Real Estate; Tax liens/Judgments; UCC records; Vital records

Local Retrieval Area: AL-Baldwin, Covington, Escambia, Geneva, Mobile; FL-Bay, Holmes, Okaloosa, Santa Rosa, Walton, Washington. **Correspondent Relationships:** statewide.

Add'l Information: Established 1975. Normal turnaround time- 24-72 hours. If order is received in AM, will send in PM. Projects billed by number of names searched. Projects billed by number of records located. 1st project may require prepayment. Credit cards accepted. He is a registered professional engineer. He has 25 years in research and development and is a Florida notary public.

Iles & Bond Inc

210 W Clinton Ave, Oaklyn, NJ 08107

Phone: 856-854-9580 **Fax:** 856-854-9582 ilesandbond@comcast.net

Types of Records Retrieved: Criminal courts; UCC records; Real Estate

Local Retrieval Area: PA-Philadelphia

Add'l Information: Established 2000. Normal turnaround time- 4-6 hours. Fees negotiated with volume. They also offer records from the Department of Records. They have a 22-year library of county Dept. of Records data in-house on microfilm.

ILS Research

1512 N Church St, Route 309, Hazleton, PA 18202

Phone: 570-454-3535 **Fax:** 570-454-5436 dtedesco55@msn.com

Types of Records Retrieved: Civil, criminal and probate courts; Federal courts; Real Estate; Tax liens/Judgments; UCC records; Vital records

Local Retrieval Area: PA-Armstrong, Beaver, Bedford, Butler, Cambria, Cameron, Carbon, Clarion, Columbia, Crawford, Cumberland, Elk, Fayette, Forest, Greene, Indiana, Jefferson, Lackawanna, Lawrence, Luzerne, McKean, Schuylkill, Vernango, Warren, Westmoreland. **Correspondent Relationships:** Allegheny, Lehigh, Lycoming, Mercer, Monroe, Montour, Montgomery, Northumberland, Philadelphia, Susquehanna, Tioga, Union, Washington counties in PA,

Add'l Information: Established 1988. Normal turnaround time- 24-48 hours. Projects billed by number of names searched. Billing with each job completed. 1st project may require prepayment. Net 30 days. They specialize in criminal & civil background searches, real estate closings, current owner searches & document retrieval of estates, bankruptcies, UCCs, deeds & mortgages. They perform service of process.

In Search of Inc

247 Wayne Ave, Cliffside, NJ 07010

Phone: 201-224-3063 **Fax:** 201-224-0761 iso.search@verizon.net

Types of Records Retrieved: Civil, criminal and probate courts; Federal courts; Real Estate; Tax liens/Judgments; UCC records; Vital records

Local Retrieval Area: NJ-Bergen, Essex, Hudson, Passaic, Union

Add'l Information: Established 1992. Normal turnaround time- 24-48 hours. Projects billed by number of names searched. Terms are net 30 days. They specialize in fast reliable and cost-effective public information, retrieval and filing.

Incognito Services

234 Marshall St, Upstairs #3, Redwood City, CA 94063-1550

Phone: 650-363-9100 **Fax:** 650-363-9200

www.incognitoservices.com

Types of Records Retrieved: Civil and criminal courts; Real Estate

Local Retrieval Area: CA-San Mateo. **Correspondent Relationships:** California; the West Coast;, International.

Add'l Information: Established 1980. Normal turnaround time- 48 hours. Expedited service available. Projects billed by the hour. They add mileage and copy costs. 1st project may require prepayment. Credit cards accepted. They specialize in investigations, electronic countermeasures equipment and service, including covert video equipment, and installations. They also offer surety+bail, bail bond, notary public services and bail fugitive recovery services. A licensed PI in CA. They perform service of process.

Incorporating Services Ltd

3500 S DuPont Hwy, Dover, DE 19901

Phone: 800-346-4646; 302-531-0855 **Fax:** 302-531-3150

www.incserv.com **email:** admin@incserv.com

Types of Records Retrieved: Civil courts; Federal courts; Real Estate; Tax liens/Judgments; UCC records; Vital records

Local Retrieval Area: DE-Kent, New Castle, Sussex. **Correspondent Relationships:** nationwide and Canada.

Add'l Information: Established 1972. Normal turnaround time- 1-2 working days. Projects billed by number of names searched. Projects billed by number of records located. 1st project may require prepayment. Credit cards accepted. Certified checks, money orders or cash are accepted. Providing blue ribbon service for over 31 years, specializing in regestered agent services, corporate and UCC searches, retrievals and filings. Located in Dover, DE and providing nationwide services.

Independence County Abstract Co

150 S Broad St, Batesville, AR 72501

Phone: 870-793-3333 **Fax:** 870-793-3343

independence@cox-Internet.com

Types of Records Retrieved: Probate courts; Real Estate; Tax liens/Judgments; UCC records **Local Retrieval Area:** AR-Independence

Add'l Information: Established 1950. Normal turnaround time- 5-10 days. Expedited service available. Projects billed by the hour. A minimum charge also applies. They specialize in real estate.

Independent Abstract & Title

600 Whitehead St #203, Key West, FL 33040

Phone: 305-294-5105 **Fax:** 305-294-5354 intitle@bellsouth.net

Types of Records Retrieved: Civil, criminal and probate courts; Real Estate; Tax liens/Judgments; UCC records **Local Retrieval Area:** FL-Monroe

Add'l Information: Established 1984. Normal turnaround time- 48 hours. They charge a flat rate per project. 1st project may require prepayment. They specialize in title insurance.

Independent Abstracting Service Inc

9298 Central Ave NE #418, Blaine, MN 55434-4220

Phone: 763-792-6800 **Fax:** 763-792-6820 hmorgan@mcleodusa.net

Types of Records Retrieved: Probate courts; Real Estate; Tax liens/Judgments; UCC records; Vital records

Local Retrieval Area: MN-Anoka, Carver, Chisago, Dakota, Hennepin, Isanti, Ramsey, Scott, Sherburne, Washington, Wright. **Correspondent Relationships:** St. Louis County.

Add'l Information: Established 1986. Normal turnaround time- 3-5 days. Fee basis will vary by type of project. 1st project may require prepayment. They are a real estate services company providing document retrieval, ownership & encumbrance reports, lien reports, chain of title, absract updates and title insurance.

Independent Research Assoc

PO Box 677988, (359 Portstewart Dr, 32828), Orlando, FL 32867-7988

Phone: 407-832-8580 **Fax:** 407-823-8939 shanlina@aol.com

Types of Records Retrieved: Civil courts; Probate courts; Federal courts; Real Estate; Tax liens/Judgments; UCC records

Local Retrieval Area: FL-Brevard, Orange, Osceola, Seminole, Volusia

Add'l Information: Established 1979. Normal turnaround time- 24 hours. Projects billed by number of names searched. They specialize in rapid return of official records - UCCs, tax liens, etc.

Independent Research Inc

2963 Wyndwicke Dr, St Joseph, MI 49085

Phone: 269-429-9873 **Fax:** 269-429-5693

www.independent-inc.com **email:** marie@independent-inc.com

Types of Records Retrieved: Civil and criminal courts

Local Retrieval Area: MI-Berrien, Genesee, Ingham, Kalamazoo, Kent, Macomb, Oakland, Saginaw, Washtenaw, Wayne. **Correspondent Relationships:** nationwide for criminal information; all types in MI.

Add'l Information: Established 1990. Normal turnaround time- 1-3 days. Expedited service available. Projects billed by number of names searched. Projects billed by number of records located. 1st project may require prepayment. Credit accounts are payable net 30 days. They specialize in nationwide criminal in Michigan and numerous other states.

Independent Research LLC

12649 W Warren Ave, Lakewood, CO 80228
Phone: 303-969-8608 **Fax:** 303-969-9363
www.independentresearchofcolorado.com
email: searchcolorado@netscape.net

Types of Records Retrieved: Civil, criminal and probate courts; Federal courts; Real Estate; Tax liens/Judgments; UCC records; Vital records

Local Retrieval Area: CO-all counties. **Correspondents:** statewide.

Add'l Information: Established 1982. Normal turnaround time- 24 hours. Projects billed by number of names searched. 1st project may require prepayment. Terms: net 30-60 days. They offer discounts for multiple/similar names searched. They also provide E & O searches in all Colorado counties. They are online with Sec of State Statewide database for all UCCs - same day results with copies. Order via Internet or website.

Indepth Profiles Inc

4528 S Sheridan, #224, Tulsa, OK 74145
Phone: 800-364-8319; 918-610-0192 **Fax:** 800-416-9504; 918-610-1183
www.indepthprofiles.com **email:** sales@indepthprofiles.com

Types of Records Retrieved: Civil and criminal courts; Federal courts

Local Retrieval Area: OK-Tulsa. **Correspondent Relationships:** nationwide and Canada.

Add'l Information: Established 1985. Normal turnaround time- 24-72 hours. Projects billed by number of names searched. Credit cards accepted. They specialize in all phases of pre-employment screening, background investigations and criminal record retrieval. They are experts in TX, OK and AR, but also reach nationwide.

Infiniti Title Agency Inc

33 E Main St #2, Moorestown, NJ 08057
Phone: 609-727-0818 **Fax:** 856-727-5173 www.infinitytitle.com

Types of Records Retrieved: Real Estate; Tax liens/Judgments

Local Retrieval Area: NJ-Burlington. **Correspondent Relationships:** New Jersey, Eastern Pennsylvania.

Add'l Information: Established 1942. Normal turnaround time- 24 hours. Fee basis will vary by the type of project. Formerly known as Burlington County Abstract, they specialize in real estate records throughout New Jersey; now also in eastern PA.

Info Quest Inc

812 S Poplar Dr, Surfside Business Ctr, #8, Surfside Beach, SC 29587
Phone: 800-507-9628; 843-233-9675 **Fax:** 800-588-1152; 843-233-9676
alagrange@sc.rr.com

Types of Records Retrieved: Bankruptcy courts; Vital Records

Local Retrieval Area:SC-Georgetown, Horry. **Correspondents:** nationwide

Add'l Information: Established 1995. Turnaround time- 24-48 hours. Projects billed by number of names searched. Projects billed by number of records located. 1st project may require prepayment. Credit cards accepted. They specialize in criminal records retrieval, pre-employment background checks, rental background checks, credit reports, current owner searches, probate, mortgage and title. Nationwide pre-employment screening.

Info Search Inc

PO Box 40221, Indianapolis, IN 46240
Phone: 317-251-6290 **Fax:** 317-251-1755 info-search@prodigy.net

Types of Records Retrieved: Civil, criminal and probate courts; Federal courts; Real Estate; Tax liens/Judgments; UCC records; Vital records

Local Retrieval Area: IN-Hamilton, Hendricks, Marion

Add'l Information: Established 1996. Normal turnaround time- 24 hours (criminal); 24-36 (other). Projects billed by number of names searched. 1st project may require prepayment. Invoice net 30 days. They specialize in criminal, civil and bankruptcy court searches.

Info2go

5305 Grand Mesa Dr, Ft Worth, TX 76137
Phone: 817-656-1997 **Fax:** 817-656-3099
www.debsinfo2go.us **email:** deb@debsinfo2go.us

Types of Records Retrieved: Civil, criminal and probate courts; Federal courts; Real Estate; Tax liens/Judgments; UCC records; Vital records

Local Retrieval Area: TX-Collin, Dallas, Denton, Ellis, Hood, Johnson, Parker, Rockwall, Tarrant, Wise

Add'l Information: Established 2003. Projects billed by the hour. 1st project may require prepayment. Will accept PayPal. Info2go retrieves public records in the DFW area and manually searches newspapers and archives, including the Ft Worth NARA.

Infocite

3248 Chamberlain Cir, Ann Arbor, MI 48103
Phone: 734-665-6484 **Fax:** 734-665-3246 infocite1@yahoo.com

Types of Records Retrieved: Criminal courts; US District court; Real Estate; Tax liens/Judgments; Vital records

Local Retrieval Area: MI-Livingston, Macomb, Oakland, Washtenaw, Wayne. **Correspondent Relationships:** Real Estate only-Jackson, Ingham, Genesee counties.

Add'l Information: Established 1998. Normal turnaround time- 1-3 days. Expedited service available. Projects billed by number of names searched. 1st project may require prepayment. They specialize in mortgage/ASG/deed searches, criminal, and tax lien searches. Normal turnaround time- 24-48 hours; expedited service available for add'l charge.

InfoCorp Investigative Services LLC

PO Box 120, Lewis Center, OH 43035
Phone: 866-657-8003; 614-785-1669 **Fax:** 614-340-7179
www.infocorponline.com **email:** infocorpllc@aol.com

Types of Records Retrieved: Civil, criminal and probate courts; Federal courts; Tax liens/Judgments; UCC records; Vital records

Local Retrieval Area: OH-Delaware, Franklin. **Correspondents:** statewide.

Add'l Information: Established 2002. Normal turnaround time- 48-72 hours. Expedited service available. Projects billed by number of names searched. Credit cards accepted. Will invoice. They offer pre-employment screening, fingerprinting (manual & web check prints), public record research & retrieval, process svc, professional license, education verification, private investigation, surveillance, locates, notary assignments & field calls. A licensed PI in OH. They perform service of process.

Infoline Inc

601 Indiana Ave #615, Washington, DC 20004
Phone: 888-284-4581; 202-783-3538 **Fax:** 877-404-2262; 202-393-0933
www.infolineinc.com **email:** requests@infolineinc.com

Types of Records Retrieved: Civil, criminal and probate courts; Federal courts; Real Estate; Tax liens/Judgments; UCC records; Vital records

Local Retrieval Area: DC-District of Columbia; MD-Anna Arundel, Baltimore, Baltimore City, Calvert, Charles, Frederick, Howard, Montgomery, Prince George's; VA- Alexandria City, Arlington, Fairfax, Loudoun, Prince William. **Correspondent Relationships:** nationwide.

Add'l Information: Established 1989. Normal turnaround time- same day or by requested deadline. Credit cards accepted. Visa and Mastercard accepted. Infoline Inc specializes in research and retrieval from federal, state and bankruptcy courts as well as Capitol Hill and federal/state agencies. Case monitoring is available. They provide real & personal property abstracting svcs throughout MD, VA, & DC.

Infomax

PO Box 15744, Rio Rancho, NM 87174
Phone: 505-994-0370 **Fax:** 505-994-0338
www.infomaxnm.com **email:** request@infomaxnm.com

Types of Records Retrieved: Civil, criminal and probate courts; Federal courts; Real Estate; Tax liens/Judgments; UCC records; Vital records

Local Retrieval Area: NM-Bernalillo, Los Alamos, Sandoval, Santa Fe. **Correspondent Relationships:** New Mexico and nationwide.

Add'l Information: Established 1988. Normal turnaround time- 24-48 hours. Projects billed by number of names searched. 1st project may require prepayment. They specialize in lien and asset searches, background investigations, pre-employment screening and real property abstracting. A licensed PI in NM.

InfoNation (Virginia) Inc

10570 Main St #504, Fairfax, VA 22030
Phone: 888-346-9090; 703-278-9090 **Fax:** 703-278-9184
info4usa@aol.com

Types of Records Retrieved: Civil, criminal and probate courts; Federal courts; Real Estate; Tax liens/Judgments; UCC records

Local Retrieval Area: VA-Alexandria City, Arlington, Fairfax, Fauquier, Frederick, Fredericksburg City, Loudoun, Prince William, Spotsylvania, Stafford. **Correspondent Relationships:** nationwide.

Add'l Information: Established 1997. Normal turnaround time- 24-48 hours. Projects billed by the hour. Credit cards accepted. They specialize in skiptracing, asset location, courthouse research, real estate and pre-employment checks. They perform service of process.

InfoQuest of West Michigan LLC

PO Box 68402, Grand Rapids, MI 49516-8402
Phone: 616-581-2820 **Fax:** 888-949-9008; 616-949-9008
Infoquestwm@aol.com

Types of Records Retrieved: Civil and criminal courts

Local Retrieval Area: MI-Kent, Muskegon, Ottawa

Add'l Information: Established 1998. Normal turnaround time- 24 hours. Projects billed by number of names searched. 1st project may require prepayment.

InfoRetrieval Services

PO Box 268, Georgetown, DE 19947
Phone: 302-337-0548 **Fax:** 302-337-8730
www.inforetrieval.net **email:** info@inforetrieval.net

Types of Records Retrieved: Civil and crriminal courts

Local Retrieval Area: DE-Kent, New Castle, Sussex. **Correspondent Relationships:** MD, PA, NJ.

Add'l Information: Established 1993. Normal turnaround time- 24 hours. Projects billed by number of names searched. Fees vary by depth of search requested (standard search vs. pull and read entire file). Since 1993, specializing in service of process and complete in-depth criminal searches for attorneys/investigators with subject report/ copies of relevant sections of records. A licensed PI in DE, MD. They perform service of process.

Information Consultants Inc

PO Box 1282, Franklin, TN 37065
Phone: 866-473-9149; 615-595-9794 **Fax:** 877-684-0181;
www.informing1.com **email:** info@informing1.com

Types of Records Retrieved: Civil and criminal courts

Local Retrieval Area: TN-Williamson. **Correspondent Relationships:** Davidson, Rutherford, Maury, Wilson, Robertson, Sumner counties TN.

Add'l Information: Established 1997. Normal turnaround time- 24 hours. Projects billed by number of names searched. 1st project may require prepayment. They perform applicant background checks, public record searches and private investigations. A licensed PI in TN.

Information Inc

PO Box 382, Hermitage, TN 37076
Phone: 615-884-8000 **Fax:** 615-889-6492
http://hometown.aol.com/publicrecordstn **email:** InfomanTN@aol.com

Types of Records Retrieved: Civil and criminal courts; Federal district court; Vital records; Tax liens/Judgments

Local Retrieval Area: TN-Davidson

Add'l Information: Established 1991. Normal turnaround time- 2 hours - 72 hours. Expedited service available. Projects billed by number of names searched. 1st project may require prepayment. They operate a criminal database available online containing criminal history to 01/01/87. For a free demonstration, just call us.

Information Management Systems Inc

114 W Main St #202, (PO Box 2924), New Britain, CT 06050
Phone: 888-403-8347; 860-229-1119 **Fax:** 888-403-8402; 860-225-5524
www.imswebb.com **email:** infomat@aol.com

Types of Records Retrieved: Civil, criminal and probate courts; Federal courts; Real Estate; Tax liens/Judgments; UCC records; Vital records

Local Retrieval Area: CT-Fairfield, Hartford, Litchfield, Middlesex, New Haven, New London, Tolland, Windham. **Correspondent Relationships:** Domestic and International.

Add'l Information: Established 1989. Normal turnaround time- same day. Projects billed by number of names searched. Fees vary by project volume. Credit cards accepted. They specialize in public and business record retrieval and asset locates. They also provide nationwide background investigation, MVRs and due diligence services; criminal/civil records and more. Document retrieval and delivery. They perform service of process.

Information Network Associates Inc

5235 N Front St, Harrisburg, PA 17110-1717
Phone: 800-443-0824; 717-599-5505 **Fax:** 717-599-5507
www.ina-inc.com **email:** ina-inc@ina-inc.com

Types of Records Retrieved: Civil, criminal and probate courts; Federal courts; Real Estate; Tax liens/Judgments; UCC records; Vital records

Local Retrieval Area: PA-Cumberland, Dauphin, Lancaster, Lebanon, York. **Correspondent Relationships:** Pennsylvania.

Add'l Information: Established 1986. Normal turnaround time- 24-48 hours. Projects billed by number of records located. Credit cards accepted. Payment due upon receipt of invoice. They specialize in asset searches, state level searches, retrieving driving records and motor vehicle records. A licensed PI in PA. They perform service of process.

Information Protective Services Inc (IPS)

PO Box 800383, Houston, TX 77280
Phone: 888-720-3784; 713-460-8884 **Fax:** 713-460-9399

Types of Records Retrieved: Civil, criminal and probate courts; Real Estate; Tax liens/Judgments; UCC records

Local Retrieval Area: TX-Fort Bend, Harris, Kleberg. **Correspondent Relationships:** nationwide, especially in Texas.

Add'l Information: Established 1995. Normal turnaround time- 24-48 hours. Projects billed by number of names searched. Terms: net 30 days, with approved credit. They specialize in pre-employment screening and third party administrator for drug testing on a nationwide level. A licensed PI in TX. They perform service of process.

Information Reporting Services Inc

2101 Hennepin Ave #201, Minneapolis, MN 55405
Phone: 612-870-8770 **Fax:** 612-870-8765
www.inforeport.com **email:** dahl@inforeport.com

Types of Records Retrieved: Civil, criminal and probate courts; Federal courts; Tax liens/Judgments.

Local Retrieval Area: MN-Anoka, Blue Earth, Carver, Dakota, Goodhue, Hennepin, Olmsted, Ramsey, Scott, Washington, Winona, Wright. **Correspondent Relationships:** nationwide.

Add'l Information: Established 1989. Normal turnaround time- 24-48 hours. Projects billed by number of names searched. Monthly billing available. They specialize in background screening for corporations. Search capabilities include entire State of MN. Their searches are hands-on. Their results are typed, reviewed and returned to you the same day. A licensed PI in MN, WI. They perform service of process.

Information Retrieval Services (Washington)

15220 OK Mill Rd, Snohomish, WA 98290-4504
Phone: 800-769-3051; 425-334-2052 **Fax:** 425-397-6519
inforetrieval@comcast.net

Types of Records Retrieved: Civil, criminal and probate courts; Real Estate; Tax liens/Judgments; UCC records

Local Retrieval Area: WA-Benton, Franklin, King, Skagit, Snohomish, Yakima. **Correspondent Relationships:** California, Georgia.

Add'l Information: Established 1992. Normal turnaround time- 24-48 hours. Monthly billing statements. They have over 30 years combined experience in local courts. They are a small company with the ability to focus on your individual needs. Cell phone # 425-238-4622.

Information Search Inc

PO Box 33657, Palm Beach Gardens, FL 33420-3657
Phone: 561-624-5115 **Fax:** 561-694-8281
www.infohotline.com **email:** info@infohotline.com

Types of Records Retrieved: Civil, criminal and probate courts; Federal courts; Real Estate; Tax liens/Judgments; UCC records; Vital records

Local Retrieval Area: FL-Martin, Palm Beach, St. Lucie. **Correspondent Relationships:** Florida and nationwide.

Add'l Information: Established 1995. Normal turnaround time- 3 days. Call for expedited service. Call for pricing options. 1st project may require prepayment. Call for details. May negotiate for larger contracts. They source, discover, verify or retrieve critical information for clients in the solution of their business problems in addition to public records retrieval. Filing of documents requires prepayment. A licensed PI in FL. They perform service of process.

Information Services (Colorado)

PO Box 2085, Durango, CO 81302
Phone: 877-385-4897; 970-385-4897 **Fax:** 970-259-9454
www.frontier.net/~dkgis **email:** dkgis@frontier.net

Types of Records Retrieved: Real Estate; Tax liens/Judgments; UCC records; Vital records

Local Retrieval Area: CO-La Plata, Mesa

Add'l Information: Established 1995. Normal turnaround time- 24 hours. Projects billed by the hour. 1st project may require prepayment.

The Information Super Store

PO Box 5992, Scottsdale, AZ 85261-5992
Phone: 800-774-6585; 480-661-7964 **Fax:** 800-774-6586; 480-860-5755

Types of Records Retrieved: Civil, criminal and probate courts; Federal courts; Tax liens/Judgments; UCC records; Vital records

Local Retrieval Area: AZ-Coconino, Maricopa, Pima, Yavapai, Yuma. **Correspondent Relationships:** nationwide and Canada.

Add'l Information: Established 1994. Normal turnaround time- 1-3 days. Projects billed by number of names searched. 1st project may require prepayment. Credit cards accepted. Visa, Mastercard and Discover are accepted. They specialize in pre-employment screening, tenant/property management, asset searches, pre-trial preparation. A licensed PI in AZ.

Infotrack Information Services Inc

111 Deerlake Rd #105, Deerfield, IL 60015-4986
Phone: 800-275-5594; 847-444-1177 **Fax:** 800-275-5595; 847-444-1166
www.infotrackinc.com **email:** ed@infotrackinc.com

Types of Records Retrieved: Civil and criminal courts; Federal courts; Real Estate; Tax liens/Judgments, UCC records.

Local Retrieval Area: AZ-Maricopa, Pima, Pinal; FL-Broward, Charlotte, Collier, Duval, Escombia, Hillsborough, Indian River, Lake, Lee, Leon, Manatee, Dade, Nassau, Okaloosa, Orange, Osceola, Palm Beach, Pasco, Pinellas, Polk, Sarasota, Volusia, Walton; IL-Adams, Bond, Boone, Brown, Bureau, Calhoun, Carroll, Cass, Champaign, Christian, Clinton, Coles, Cook, Cumberland, De Kalb, De Witt, Douglas, Du Page, Edgar, Effingham, Fayette, Ford, Franklin, Fulton, Greene, Grundy, Hancock, Henderson, Henry, Iroquois, Jackson, Jefferson, Jersey, Jo Daviess, Johnson, Kane, Kankakee, Kendall, Knox, Lake, La Salle, Lee, Livingston, Logan, McDonough, McHenry, McLean, Macon, Macoupin, Madison, Marion, Marshall, Mason, Menard, Mercer, Monroe, Montgomery, Morgan, Moultrie, Ogle, Peoria, Perry, Piatt, Pike, Putnam, Randolph, Rock Island, St. Clair, Sangamon, Schuyler, Scott, shelby, Stark, Stephenson, Tazewell, Union, Vermilion, Warren, Washington, Whiteside, Will, Williamson, Winnebago, Woodford; MO-Franklin, Jefferson, Lincoln, St. Louis County, St. Louis City, Warren; WI-Dane, Dodge, Jefferson, Kenosha, Milwaukee, Ozaukee, Racine, Walworth, Washington, Waukesha. **Correspondent Relationships:** nationwide.

Add'l Information: Established 1990. Normal turnaround time- 1-2 days. Projects billed by number of names searched. Credit cards accepted. They specialize in pre-employment, tenant screening, title services, investigative, litigation support and wholesale criminal research. A licensed PI in IL.

Infotrackers Inc

800 N Rainbow Blvd #123, Las Vegas, NV 89107
Phone: 702-948-7055 **Fax:** 702-948-7056
http://infotrackersinc.com **email:** infotrackers@aol.com

Types of Records Retrieved: Civil, criminal and probate courts; Federal courts; Real Estate; Tax liens/Judgments; UCC records

Local Retrieval Area: NV-Clark

Add'l Information: Established 2002. Normal turnaround time- 2-5 hours for information w/o copies, 1-3 days for District Courts; 1 day for Recorders Office (plain copies); 1-3 weeks for certified copies. Projects billed by number of names searched. Projects billed by the hour. 1st project may require prepayment. Accepts checks by fax or phone. They provide the business community with personal records research, court research and investigative services. All requests are handled with prompt and professional response. A licensed PI in NV.

Innovative Enterprises Inc

12695 McManus Blvd., #4-B, Newport News, VA 23602
Phone: 888-777-9435; 757-875-9500 **Fax:** 888-777-9436; 757-877-4242
www.knowthefacts.com **email:** info@knowthefacts.com

Types of Records Retrieved: Civil and criminal courts

Local Retrieval Area: VA-all counties.. **Correspondents:** nationwide.

Add'l Information: Established 1996. Normal turnaround time- next business day. Expedited service available. Projects are billed on a per-search basis. 1st project may require prepayment. Credit cards accepted. Terms are net 30 days. Using their proprietary research database, they provide identifiers for 85% - 90% of the Virginia cases reported by their competitors as "name match only".

INPRO

14870 Granada Ave #323, Apple Valley, MN 55124-5514
Phone: 952-891-3617 **Fax:** 952-891-3618
www.inproinvestigations.com **email:** inproinvestigations@mac.com

Types of Records Retrieved: Civil and criminal courts; Federal courts; Tax liens/Judgments; UCC records; Vital records

Local Retrieval Area: MN-Carver, Dakota, Hennepin, Ramsey, Scott

Add'l Information: Established 1994. Normal turnaround time- 24-48 hours. Expedited service available. Projects billed by the hour. Credit cards accepted. Some projects may require prepayment. Terms: net 15 days. They specialize in providing prompt and professional investigative search and retrieval services. A licensed PI in MN, WI. Performs service of process.

Inquest

PO Box 54063, San Jose, CA 95154-0063
Phone: 408-395-1300 **Fax:** 408-395-8466
www.inquestscreening.com **email:** info@inquestscreening.com

Types of Records Retrieved: Civil and criminal courts

Local Retrieval Area: CA-Alameda, Contra Costa, Sacramento, San Mateo, Santa Clara, Santa Cruz. **Correspondent Relationships:** nationwide.

Add'l Information: Established 1999. Normal turnaround time- 2-48 hours. Projects billed by number of names searched. Terms: net 30 days. Inquest is a full service pre-employment screening company that specializes in criminal records retrieval in the Silicon Valley, CA.

InQuest Agency Inc

645 G St #590, Anchorage, AK 99501
Phone: 907-272-2201 **Fax:** 907-272-2090
www.inquestagency.com **email:** todd@inquestagency.com

Types of Records Retrieved: Civil, criminal and probate courts; Federal courts; Real Estate; Tax liens/Judgments; UCC records; Vital records.

Local Retrieval Area: AK-Anchorage, Fairbanks North Star, Matanuska Susitna. **Correspondent Relationships:** statewide.

Add'l Information: Established 1984. Normal turnaround time- 24-48 hours. Expedited service available. Projects billed by the hour. 1st project may require prepayment. Alaska's only statewide company to offer process service, court record retrieval, investigative services. Central coverage area includes Anchorage, Fairbanks, Eagle River, Palmer, Wasilla and Matanuska-Susitna borough. Has a Fairbanks office. A licensed PI in AK. They perform service of process.

Inquest Investigations, LLC

1201 W Washington St, Sherman, TX 75092
Phone: 903-893-2020 **Fax:** 903-892-6211
www.inquestinvestigations.com **email:** inquest@texoma.net

Types of Records Retrieved: Civil and criminal courts; Real Estate; Tax liens/Judgments; UCC records

Local Retrieval Area: TX-Collin, Dallas, Denton, Grayson, Gregg, Nueces, Tarrant. **Correspondent Relationships:** nationwide.

Add'l Information: Established 1998. Normal turnaround time- 24-72 hours. Projects billed by number of names searched. They specialize in criminal, civil, property and tax background research as well as nationwide MVR and credit history information. A licensed PI in TX.

Inquisitive Research Corporation

167 Main St, Metuchen, NJ 08840-2744
Phone: 732-321-0041 **Fax:** 732-321-0085
www.iqresearch.com **email:** info@iqresearch.com

Types of Records Retrieved: Civil, criminal and probate courts; Federal courts; Real Estate; Tax liens/Judgments; UCC records; Vital records

Local Retrieval Area: NJ-all counties; NY-Bronx, Kings, Nassau, New York, Queens, Richmond, Suffolk, Westchester; PA-Bucks, Chester, Delaware, Montgomery, Northampton, Philadelphia; VT-Chittenden, Rutland. **Correspondent Relationships:** NY, PA & VT.

Add'l Information: Established 1992. Normal turnaround time- 24-48 hours. Projects billed by number of names searched. 1st project may require prepayment. Credit cards accepted. Their specialities are: mortgage/assignment document retrieval/research in NJ, NY, PA & VT. Documents are e-mailed back fast!

Insured Titles Inc

1724 Fairview Av, Missoula, MT 59806
Phone: 406-728-7900 **Fax:** 406-728-5892
www.insuredtitles.com **email:** info@insuredtitles.com

Types of Records Retrieved: Probate courts; Real Estate; Tax liens/Judgments; UCC records

Local Retrieval Area: MT-Missoula. **Correspondent Relationships:** Missoula County MT.

Add'l Information: Established 1975. Normal turnaround time- 3-5 days. Projects billed by number of names searched. They specialize in real estate record searches, also title and escrow closings.

Integrity Abstracting

410 8th Ave, Crystal City, MO 63019-1503
Phone: 314-807-6359 **Fax:** 636-937-1177
integrity1000@sbcglobal.net

Types of Records Retrieved: Civil courts; Probate courts; Real Estate; Tax liens/Judgments; UCC records

Local Retrieval Area: MO-Franklin, Jefferson, St. Charles, St. Louis, St. Louis City

Add'l Information: Established 2000. Normal turnaround time- 24 hours. Expedited service available. Projects billed by number of names searched. Projects billed by number of records located. Bills monthly/semi-monthly. They are dedicated to quick, accurate customer service in title searches and document retrieval. They offer exclusive cooperation with interested companies. Does criminal record searches on a limited basis.

Integrity Check LLC

2250 E Chemise Dr, Meridian, ID 83642
Phone: 877-887-1226; 208-887-1226 **Fax:** 877-887-3934; 208-887-9801
www.integritycheckllc.com **email:** scompton@integritycheckllc.com

Types of Records Retrieved: Civil, criminal and probate courts; Federal courts; Real Estate; Tax liens/Judgments; UCC records; Vital records

Local Retrieval Area: ID-Ada, Boise, Canyon, Elmore, Gem. **Correspondent Relationships:** statewide.

Add'l Information: Established 2004. Normal turnaround time- 24-48 hours. Projects billed by number of names searched. 1st project may require prepayment. They are a full service background investigation and document retrieval company servicing Idaho and the northwest. They are experienced and professional. A licensed PI in ID.

Integrity Records Access

325 S 3rd St, PMB 184, Las Vegas, NV 89101
Phone: 702-296-9145 **Fax:** 702-441-7008 integrityra@cox.net

Types of Records Retrieved: Civil, criminal and probate courts; Federal courts; Real Estate; Tax liens/Judgments; UCC records; Vital records

Local Retrieval Area: NV-Clark. **Correspondents:** nationwide.

Add'l Information: Established 1996. Normal turnaround time- 24-48 hours. Projects billed by number of names searched. Projects billed by the hour. If extensive searches, it moves to hourly charges. 1st project may require prepayment. Terms: net 30 days. They specialize in state & federal court research & retrieval, also filing & searching at recorders' offices across the US. They provide retrieval services from the Federal Records Ctr in Laguna Niguel, CA. Extensive contacts throughout the Southwest.

Intelysis Corp (Ziegler & Assoc.)

1230 Parkway Ave, #304, West Trenton, NJ 08628
Phone: 800-489-1239; 609-538-0508 **Fax:** 609-637-9403
www.intelysis.com **email:** dziegler@intelysis.com

Types of Records Retrieved: Civil and Criminal courts; Real Estate; UCC records; Vital records

Local Retrieval Area: NJ-Mercer. **Correspondent Relationships:** nationwide, Canada, International (criminal records).

Add'l Information: Established 1995. Normal turnaround time- 10 business days for statewide criminal records; other records 2 days. Projects billed by number of names searched. 1st project may require prepayment. Credit cards accepted. They specialize in statewide criminal searches, computer forensics, fire/arson/explosion investigations, international searches and employee screening. They do Canadian wide criminal record searches. A licensed PI in NJ, PA.

Intercoastal Research & Inv

PO Box 1133, Little River, NC 29566
Phone: 843-280-4461 **Fax:** 843-280-2828
www.ncresearcher.com **email:** ncresearcher@sc.rr.com

Types of Records Retrieved: Civil and criminal courts

Local Retrieval Area: NC-Alamance, Brunswick, Columbus, Durham, Granville, Johnston, Mecklenburg, New Hanover, Orange, Wake; SC-Horry. **Correspondent Relationships:** nationwide.

Add'l Information: Established 1996. Normal turnaround time- 24 hours or less. Projects billed by number of names searched. Will invoice monthly. They specialize in criminal records and MVR records nationwide. Will supply court computer print-outs of hits if requested. Since 1995, they have specialized in on-site, county and statewide criminal & civil record searches. Reasonable rates. A licensed PI in NC & SC.

Inter-County Abstract

926 Court St, Honesdale, PA 18431-1871
Phone: 570-253-4734 **Fax:** 570-253-1359

Types of Records Retrieved: Civil courts; Real Estate

Local Retrieval Area: PA-Wayne. **Correspondent Relationships:** Lackawanna.

Add'l Information: Established 1979. Normal turnaround time- 1 week. Projects billed by number of names searched. Charges are also based on title insurance. All projects require prepayment. They specialize in information certificates for real estate abstracts.

International Investigators Inc

3216 N Pennsylvania St, Indianapolis, IN 46205-3414
Phone: 800-403-8111; 317-925-1496 **Fax:** 317-926-1177
www.internationalinvestigators.com **email:** info@iiiweb.net

Types of Records Retrieved: Civil, criminal and probate courts; Federal courts; Real Estate; Tax liens/Judgments; UCC records; Vital records

Local Retrieval Area: IN-Boone, Hamilton, Hancock, Hendricks, Johnson, Marion, Shelby. **Correspondents:** nationwide & international.

Add'l Information: Established 1960. Normal turnaround time- 1-4 days. Projects billed by the hour. 1st project may require prepayment. Credit cards accepted. They specialize in international insurance fraud, loss prevention, corporate request and attorney assistance. Also do skiptracing, investigations, surveillance, countermeasures sweeps and covert video systems. A licensed PI in IN. They perform service of process.

International Research Bureau Inc (IRB)

PO Box 14189, Tallahassee, FL 32317
Phone: 866-620-4636; 850-878-5437 **Fax:** 800-814-7714;
www.irb-online.com **email:** darrellg@irb-online.com

Types of Records Retrieved: Criminal courts; Real Estate; UCC records

Local Retrieval Area: FL-Leon. **Correspondent Relationships:** nationwide.

Add'l Information: Established 1986. Normal turnaround time- variable depending on project. Expedited service available. Projects billed by number of names searched. 1st project may require prepayment. Credit cards accepted. Personal checks are accepted. They specialize in background searches (driving records, criminal histories, workers comp claims), asset searches (vehicles, property, boats, aircraft, corporate, UCC) and instant nationwide locate product. They do civil and criminal searches nationwide. A licensed PI in FL.

Interquest Information Services

PO Box 2082, Cape Girardeau, MO 63702
Phone: 800-455-1655; 573-339-1505 **Fax:** 573-332-2786
www.interqst.com **email:** tina@interqst.com

Types of Records Retrieved: Civil and criminal courts; Federal courts; Real Estate; Tax liens/Judgments; UCC records; Vital records

Local Retrieval Area: MO-Cape Girardeau. **Correspondents:** nationwide.

Add'l Information: Established 1989. Normal turnaround time- 24-72 hours. Projects billed by number of names searched. 1st project may require prepayment. Credit cards accepted. Terms: net 30 days for established accounts. They specialize in employment screening, drug & tenant screening, skiptracing, and general information research for business, industrial and legal use.

Interstate Reporting Co Inc (IRC)

W177N9886 Rivercrest Dr #106, Germantown, WI 53022-4500
Phone: 262-251-6590 **Fax:** 262-251-0929 ircinc@execpc.com

Types of Records Retrieved: Civil and criminal courts; Federal courts; Tax liens/Judgments; UCC records

Local Retrieval Area: WI-Milwaukee, Ozaukee, Racine, Washington, Waukesha

Add'l Information: Established 1984. Normal turnaround time- 48 hours. Projects billed by number of names searched. 1st project may require prepayment. They specialize in locate/subrogation, pre-employment background reports, insurance fraud and worker's compensation investigations. A licensed PI in WI. They perform service of process.

Intracoastal Detective Agency Inc

1511 E Commercial Blvd #81, Fort Lauderdale, FL 33334
Phone: 954-564-5455 **Fax:** 954-564-1415
www.legalinvestigators.com **email:** Ladygumshoe@legalinvestigators.com

Types of Records Retrieved: Civil, criminal and probate courts; Federal courts; Real Estate; Tax liens/Judgments; UCC records; Vital records

Local Retrieval Area: FL-Broward, Dade, Palm Beach. **Correspondent Relationships:** nationwide.

Add'l Information: Established 1997. Normal turnaround time- 1-2 days. Expedited service available. Projects billed by the hour. 1st project may require prepayment. Credit cards accepted. They specialize in courthouse searches of all public records and quick and efficient searches. A licensed PI in FL.

Intra-Lex Investigations Inc

505 6th St #202, Sioux City, IA 51101
Phone: 712-233-1639 **Fax:** 712-255-1127 ili@willinet.net

Types of Records Retrieved: Civil, criminal and probate courts; Federal courts; Real Estate; Tax liens/Judgments; UCC records

Local Retrieval Area: IA-Monona, Plymouth, Sioux, Woodbury; NE-Dakota, Dixon, Douglas, Sarpy, Thurston; SD-Union. **Correspondent Relationships:** other counties in Nebraska.

Add'l Information: Established 1983. Normal turnaround time- 24 hours. Projects billed by number of names searched. Projects billed by the hour. Mileage charges will be added. A miminum fee applies. Payment in full 30 days from date of service. They are a full line investigation agency, multi-state licensed, bonded and insured. A licensed PI in IA, NE. They perform service of process.

Intricate Solutions Inc

1525 Highway 53 East, Dawsonville, GA 30534
Phone: 866-640-5210; 706-265-6235 **Fax:** 706-265-6234
www.4ebi.com **email:** tanderson@4ebi.com

Types of Records Retrieved: GA-Criminal history records.

Local Retrieval Area: GA-Dawson, Lumpkin. **Correspondents:** nationwide.

Add'l Information: Established 2001. Normal turnaround time- guaranteed 24-hr return. Projects billed by number of names searched. Will bill to accepted clients. EBI - Employee Background Investigators - provides criminal records for Dawson and Lumpkin counties, also Georgia (also MT, NM, RI, WA, WI) statewide criminal history, with signed release.

Introspect Investigations USA Inc

752A Hempstead Turnpike #205, Franklin Square, NY 11010
Phone: 800-847-7177; 516-292-4130 **Fax:** 516-292-4135
www.introspectusa.com **email:** introusa@aol.com

Types of Records Retrieved: Civil, criminal and probate courts; Federal courts; Real Estate; Tax liens/Judgments; UCC records, Voter records

Local Retrieval Area: NY-Kings, Nassau, New York, Queens. **Correspondent Relationships:** nationwide.

Add'l Information: Established 1984. Normal turnaround time- 3 days. Expedited service available. Projects billed by number of names searched. 1st project may require prepayment. They specialize in public record research, background investigations, asset investigations, pre-employment screening, DMV records and general investigations. Special request considered. A licensed PI in NY. They perform service of process.

Investigate-Claims.com

8 Tudor Ct, Buffalo, NY 14068
Phone: 716-689-6577 **Fax:** 716-689-4721
www.investigate-claims.com **email:** ferraribuffalony@att.net

Types of Records Retrieved: Civil, criminal and probate courts; Federal courts; Real Estate; Tax liens/Judgments; UCC records; Vital records

Local Retrieval Area: NY-Erie, Niagara. **Correspondent Relationships:** nationwide network of retrievers.

Add'l Information: Established 1978. Normal turnaround time- 3-5 business days; expedited service by request. Can perform NY statewide court record search in 24 hours. Projects billed by number of names searched. Projects billed by the hour. All projects require prepayment. Credit cards accepted. Net due 30 days for insurance companies. AMBest co-rated them as Qualified Spec. Investigator. They are a Licensed PI and Independent Adjuster. Also is notary public. Operates PublicRecordWorld.com and www.investigate-claims.com. Online direct to NY MVRs. A licensed PI in NY. They perform service of process.

Investigations LLC

1161 S Meridian Ave #104, Wichita, KS 67213-1936
Phone: 800-658-1688; 316-262-1721 **Fax:** 316-262-3189

Types of Records Retrieved: Civil, criminal , Federal, probate courts

Local Retrieval Area: KS-Butler, Harvey, Kingman, Reno, Sedgwick, Sumner. **Correspondent Relationships:** statewide.

Add'l Information: Established 1983. Normal turnaround time- 24-48 hours. Projects billed by number of names searched. Charges are case-by-case. They specialize in trial preparation, lawyer support, criminal and license checks and asset investigations. A licensed PI in KS. They perform service of process.

Investigative Concepts

PO Box 2279, Athens, TX 75751
Phone: 903-677-9473 **Fax:** 903-677-9493
www.investigativeconcepts.com **email:** carolyn@investigativeconcepts.com

Types of Records Retrieved: Civil, criminal, probate courts; Federal courts

Local Retrieval Area: TX-Anderson, Henderson, Nacogdoches. **Correspondent Relationships:** TX, MD, AZ, NV, OK, KY.

Add'l Information: Established 1996. Normal turnaround time- 24-48 hours. Projects billed by number of names searched.

Investigative Consultant Service

3337 Earhart Rd, Mt Juliet, TN 37122
Phone: 615-885-1126 **Fax:** 615-885-1641
phillipdsutton@bellsouth.net

Types of Records Retrieved: Civil and criminal courts; Probatge courts; Federal courts; UCC records; Vital records

Local Retrieval Area: TN-Davidson, Wilson

Add'l Information: Established 1997. Normal turnaround time- 3 days or less, depending on type of search performed. Billing methed varies by type of searches and volume. 1st project may require prepayment. Credit cards accepted. In addition to record retrieval, they provide background investigations for pre-employment, employee theft cases, also copyright investigations. A licensed PI in TN.

Investigative Consultants Inc

2020 Pennsylvania Ave NW #813, Washington, DC 20006
Phone: 202-237-1500 **Fax:** 202-237-8642
www.icioffshore.com **email:** dberlin@icioffshore.com

Types of Records Retrieved: Civil, criminal and probate courts; Federal courts; Real Estate; Tax liens/Judgments; UCC records; Vital records

Local Retrieval Area: DC-District of Columbia; MD-Howard, Montgomery, Prince George's; VA-Arlington, Essex, Fairfax, Fairfax City, Frederick, Manassas City, Manassas Park City, Prince William. **Correspondent Relationships:** nationwide.

Add'l Information: Established 1977. Normal turnaround time- 4 hours to 4 days. Projects billed by the hour. Retainer of 80% of all fees is required. All projects require prepayment. Wire transfers and firm checks only. They specialize in assisting attorneys who practice in the field of complex federal and state litigation. A licensed PI in DC, WI.

Investigative Information Inc

27852 Ashland Ave, Harrison Township, MI 48045
Phone: 586-491-6125 **Fax:** 586-783-5242 vojo8665@juno.com

Types of Records Retrieved: Civil and criminal courts; Real estate; Tax liens/Judgments

Local Retrieval Area: MI-Genesee, Macomb, Oakland, Saginaw, St. Clair, Wayne. **Correspondent Relationships:** Saginaw, Genesee, St Clair counties MI.

Add'l Information: Established 1997. Normal turnaround time- 24-48 hours. Projects billed by number of names searched. Billed monthly. They provide investigative information on criminal and civil litigation in the Detroit Metropolitan area; clients receive accurate information and fast turnaround.

Investigative Legal Services Inc

PO Box 3551, Orlando, FL 32802-3551
Phone: 888-426-7436; 407-426-7433 **Fax:** 407-426-6968
www.processfl.com **email:** donatils@aol.com

Types of Records Retrieved: Civil, criminal and probate courts; Federal courts; Real Estate; Tax liens/Judgments; UCC records; Vital records

Local Retrieval Area: FL-Lake, Orange, Osceola, Seminole. **Correspondent Relationships:** nationwide including Puerto Rico.

Add'l Information: Established 1992. Normal turnaround time- 5 days. Projects billed by the hour. 1st project may require prepayment. Personal checks are accepted. He was a practicing trial lawyer for over 30 years. A licensed PI in FL. They perform service of process.

Investigative Research Consultants Inc

191 N Wacker Dr #2350, Chicago, IL 60606
Phone: 888-578-8600; 312-578-8600 **Fax:** 888-578-1320; 630-681-9243
www.irc-web.com **email:** brad@irc-web.com

Types of Records Retrieved: Civil and criminal courts

Local Retrieval Area: IL-Cook, Du Page. **Correspondents:** statewide.

Add'l Information: Established 1996. Normal turnaround time- 24 hours. Projects billed by number of names searched. 1st project may require prepayment. Credit cards accepted. A licensed PI in IL. They perform service of process.

Investigative Research Specialists LLC

PO Box 903, Bristow, VA 20136
Phone: 866-298-9601; **Fax:** 703-852-3886
www.corporateresearchers.com **email:** lwz@corporateresearchers.com

Types of Records Retrieved: Civil and criminal courts; Federal courts

Local Retrieval Area: VA-Fairfax, Fauquire, Loudoun, Prince William

Add'l Information: Established 1991. Normal turnaround time- 3-5 business days. Projects billed by the hour. 1st project may require prepayment. Credit cards accepted. They provide public record research and investigative due diligence to attorneys, investors and corporations. A licensed PI in VA. They perform service of process.

Investigative Resources

PO Box 70209, Staten Island, NY 10307-0209
Phone: 718-317-0043. 212-571-2500 **Fax:** 718-967-0688
joepiny@yahoo.com

Types of Records Retrieved: Civil and criminal courts; Federal courts; Real Estate; Tax liens/Judgments; UCC records

Local Retrieval Area: NY-Bronx, Kings, Nassau, New York, Queens, Richmond, Suffolk, Westchester. **Correspondent Relationships:** the Northeast.

Add'l Information: Established 1978. Normal turnaround time- as soon as 4 hours. Emergency Expedited service available. Billing depends upon volume. 1st project may require prepayment. They specialize in locating Department of Motor Vehicle records within one hour. They also have a 2nd office. A licensed PI in NY. They perform service of process.

Investigative Solutions

PO Box 250, Atwater, OH 44201-0250
Phone: 330-947-2911 **Fax:** 330-947-2799
moore.dennis@sbcglobal.net

Types of Records Retrieved: Civil, criminal and probate courts; Federal courts; Tax liens/Judgments; UCC records; Vital records

Local Retrieval Area: OH-Ashland, Ashtabula, Columbiana, Cuyahoga, Erie, Geauga, Holmes, Huron, Lake, Lorain, Mahoning, Medina, Ottawa, Portage, Sandusky, Stark, Summit, Trumbull, Tuscarawas, Wayne. **Correspondent Relationships:** nationwide.

Add'l Information: Established 1987. Normal turnaround time- 1-7 days. Billing is generally based upon the type of search requested. Volume discounts available. 1st project may require prepayment. They specialize in polygraph.

Investigative Surveillance Group

PO Box 1732, Murfreesboro, TN 37133
Phone: 615-895-0268 **Fax:** 615-893-7892
www.courthousesearch.com **email:** sales@courthousesearch.com

Types of Records Retrieved: Civil, criminal and probate courts; Federal courts; Real Estate; Tax liens/Judgments; UCC records; Vital records

Local Retrieval Area: TN-Davidson, Rutherford, Wilson. **Correspondent Relationships:** elsewhere in the state. Established 1999.

Add'l Information: Accept credit cards. How proejects are billed depends on the nature of the project. 1st project may require prepayment. They can assist you in any way; feel free to contact them. A licensed PI in TN.

InVision Research

5253 W Troy Ave, Fresno, CA 93722-2375
Phone: 559-432-3053 **Fax:** 559-451-0821 bonita200@juno.com

Types of Records Retrieved: Criminal courts

Local Retrieval Area: CA-Fresno, Kern, Kings, Madera, Placer, Sacramento, San Francisco, San Joaquin, San Mateo, Santa Barbara, Tulare, Ventura, Yolo

Add'l Information: Established 1999. Normal turnaround time- 24 hours or less. Projects billed by number of names searched. 1st project may require prepayment. Bills monthly. They specialize in performing searches personally. This includes pre-employment and tenant screening.

Iosco County Abstract Office Ltd

432 W Lake St, Tawas City, MI 48764-0420
Phone: 989-362-3231 **Fax:** 989-362-7844

Types of Records Retrieved: Civil courts; Probate courts; Real Estate; Tax liens/Judgments; UCC records; Vital records

Local Retrieval Area: MI-Iosco

Add'l Information: Established 1869. Normal turnaround time- 5 working days or less. Projects billed by number of names searched. Projects billed by number of records located. Projects billed by the hour. 1st project may require prepayment. A setup fee is required for abstracts and searches only. Personal checks are accepted. They specialize in title insurance and closings.

Iowa County Abstract Company

PO Box 226, Marengo, IA 52301
Phone: 319-642-7321 **Fax:** 319-642-1231

Types of Records Retrieved: Civil, criminal and probate courts; Real Estate; Tax liens/Judgments; UCC records **Local Retrieval Area:** IA-Iowa

Add'l Information: Established 1914. Normal turnaround time- 2-3 days for personal lien searches, and 3-4 days for a full written search. Fee basis is per transaction. Personal checks are accepted.

Iowa County Title

141 N Iowa St, Dodgeville, WI 53533
Phone: 608-935-3834 **Fax:** 608-935-1965

Types of Records Retrieved: Real Estate; Tax liens/Judgments

Local Retrieval Area: WI-Iowa

Add'l Information: Established 1954. 1st project may require prepayment. They specialize in real estate.

Iowa Title & Guaranty Co

115 S 2nd St, #4 Park Plaza Bldg, Maquoketa, IA 52060
Phone: 563-652-6081 **Fax:** 563-652-3544

Types of Records Retrieved: Civil courts; Probate courts; Real Estate; Tax liens/Judgments; UCC records; Vital records

Local Retrieval Area: IA-Jackson

Add'l Information: Established 1952. Normal turnaround time- 1-3 days. Fee basis will vary by the type of project.

Iowa Title & Realty Co

101 N Main St, Charles City, IA 50616-2014
Phone: 641-228-1515 **Fax:** 641-228-7538

Types of Records Retrieved: Probate courts; Real Estate; Tax liens/Judgments; UCC records; Vital records

Local Retrieval Area: IA-Floyd

Add'l Information: Normal turnaround time- 1-7 days. Fee basis will vary by the type of project. 1st project may require prepayment.

Iowa Title Co

312 1st St SE, Cedar Rapids, IA 52401
Phone: 319-365-1478 **Fax:** 319-365-1340 www.iowatitle.com

Types of Records Retrieved: Civil, criminal and probate courts; Federal courts; Real Estate; Tax liens/Judgments; UCC records; Vital records

Local Retrieval Area: IA-Linn. **Correspondent Relationships:** statewide.

Add'l Information: Established 1867. Normal turnaround time- 24-48 hours. Fee basis varies by type of transaction. They request prepayment from individuals, but will invoice companies. Iowa Title Co, formerly United Title Services Inc, specialize in abstracts, flood and credit.

IPS Investigations Inc

PO Box 24272, Knoxville, TN 37933-2272
Phone: 865-689-7732 **Fax:** 865-675-1574
www.ipsinvestigations.com **email:** ipsinvestigations@tds.net

Types of Records Retrieved: Civil, criminal and probate courts; Federal courts; Tax liens/Judgments; UCC records

Local Retrieval Area: TN-Anderson, Blount, Knox, Loudon, Sevier. **Correspondent Relationships:** Davidson county TN.

Add'l Information: Established 1988. Normal turnaround time- 1-2 days. Projects billed by the hour. 1st project may require prepayment. IPS Investigations has been in business since 1988. They perform civil/criminal investigations, process service, surveillance and person/records locates. A licensed PI in TN. They perform service of process.

Iron Title & Abstract Co

205 Harrison St, Ironwood, MI 49938
Phone: 906-932-6340 **Fax:** 906-932-4350

Types of Records Retrieved: Civil courts; Probate courts; Real Estate; Tax liens/Judgments; UCC records

Local Retrieval Area: MI-Gogebic; WI-Iron

Add'l Information: Established 1937. Normal turnaround time- 1-2 days. Fee basis varies by type of transaction. All projects require prepayment.

Terri Irwin

4383 Warmstone Path, Douglasville, GA 30135
Phone: 770-920-9957 **Fax:** 770-920-3772 irwint@bellsouth.net

Types of Records Retrieved: Civil, criminal and probate courts; Tax liens/Judgments **Local Retrieval Area:** GA-Douglas

Add'l Information: Established 1998. Normal turnaround time- 24 hours. Projects billed by number of names searched. Monthly billing. She specializes in 7-year superior court searches, felony and misdemeanor. Guarantees next day turnaround. Specialzing in Douglas County for 6 years.

Isabella County Abstract

209 E Broadway, Mt Pleasant, MI 48858
Phone: 989-773-3241 **Fax:** 989-773-6221
www.ibttitle.com **email:** isabellaabstract@ibttitle.com

Types of Records Retrieved: Real Estate; Tax liens/judgments; Vital records

Local Retrieval Area: MI-Clare, Isabella, Mecosta, Montcalm

Add'l Information: Established 1930. Normal turnaround time- 1 week. Projects billed by number of records located. Personal checks are accepted. They occasionally do civil and criminal court record searches.

Itasca County Abstract Co

430 NE 3rd Av, Grand Rapids, MN 55744
Phone: 218-326-9601 **Fax:** 218-326-4348 annsmith@firstam.com

Types of Records Retrieved: Civil courts; Probate courts; Real Estate; Tax liens/Judgments; UCC records; Vital records

Local Retrieval Area: MN-Itasca

Add'l Information: Established 1927. Normal turnaround time- 24 hours for name and UCC searches. 5 to 10 days for owner's and encumbrance reports and abstracts. Projects billed by number of names searched. Projects billed by number of records located. 1st project may require prepayment. Personal checks are accepted. They specialize in complete title service.

Izard County Abstract Co

PO Box 579, Hiway 9 and 69, Melbourne, AR 72556

Phone: 870-368-4818 **Fax:** 870-368-5511

Types of Records Retrieved: Probate courts; Real Estate; Tax liens/Judgments; UCC records **Local Retrieval Area:** AR-Izard

Add'l Information: Normal turnaround time- 3-5 days. Fee basis will vary by the type of project. They specialize in real estate.

J

J & A Land Searching

3588 S Lexus Ave, Springfield, MO 65807-8688

Phone: 417-887-1049 **Fax:** 417-887-1049

jandalandsearch@sbcglobal.net

Types of Records Retrieved: Real Estate; Tax liens/judgments; UCC records

Local Retrieval Area: MO-Greene

Add'l Information: Established 1997. Normal turnaround time- 24 hours. Projects billed by number of names searched. They specialize in current owner searches, institutional searches, and full searches with a very quick turnaround time.

J & J Enterprises - MO

10012 Steamboat Run, Jefferson City, MO 65101

Phone: 573-395-4205 **Fax:** 573-395-3378 J2ent@aol.com

Types of Records Retrieved: Civil and criminal courts; Federal District Court; Real Estate; Tax liens/Judgments; UCC records

Local Retrieval Area: MO-Boone, Callaway, Cole, Gasconade, Laclede, Maries, Miller, Osage, Phelps, Pulaski

Add'l Information: Established 1996. Normal turnaround time- 24-48 hours. Projects billed by number of names searched. Billing by job or monthly. Credit cards accepted. They specialize in Missouri state criminal searches and current owner searches. Federal criminal records retrieved from MO East & West Districts. They perform service of process.

J & J Research

7507 Red Fox Trail, Shreveport, LA 71129

Phone: 318-686-3109 **Fax:** 318-688-8232 jmurray@sport.rr.com

Types of Records Retrieved: Civil and criminal courts; Federal courts; UCC records

Local Retrieval Area: LA-Bossier District/Parish, Caddo District/Parrish. **Correspondent Relationships:** nationwide.

Add'l Information: Established 1994. Normal turnaround time- 12-24 hours. Projects billed by number of names searched. Bills clients monthly. Billed per request. They also do searches in the Shreveport City Court, Bossier City Court and Western District Federal Court. They provide "hands-on" record searches opposed to data base related, for more accurate record retrieval. A licensed PI in LA.

J B Data & Research, LLC

502 S 19th Ave #103, Bozeman, MT 59718-6827

Phone: 406-585-3323 **Fax:** 406-585-3323

www.eEllis.Net/JBData.htm **email:** jbdata@eellis.net

Types of Records Retrieved: Civil, criminal and probate courts; Real Estate; Tax liens/Judgments; UCC records

Local Retrieval Area: MT-Beaverhead, Broadwater, Cascade, Fergus, Flathead, Gallatin, Lewis & Clark, Madison, Missoula, Park, Ravalli, Sanders, Silver Bow, Yellowstone. **Correspondent Relationships:** Call for availability of service to all other Montana counties.

Add'l Information: Established 1999. Normal turnaround time- 24-48 hours. Projects billed by number of names searched. Projects billed by number of records located. 1st project may require prepayment. They do property searches for larger counties in Montana, along with criminal/civil, judgment, and other searches. Collects bulk civil records in 55 counties.

J C Humphrey Abstract Co

217 W Broadway, PO Box 1641 (73702), Enid, OK 73701

Phone: 580-237-3136 **Fax:** 580-237-1948

www.enidabstract.com **email:** toddh@enidabstract.com

Types of Records Retrieved: Civil courts; Probate courts; Real Estate; Tax liens/Judgments; UCC records

Local Retrieval Area: OK-Garfield. **Correspondent Relationships:** Grant County, Oklahoma.

Add'l Information: Established 1930. Normal turnaround time- 1-2 days. Projects billed by number of records located. 1st project may require prepayment. They specialize in abstracting.

J H L Enterprises

7775 York Rd, Parma, OH 44130

Phone: 440-845-2823 **Fax:** 440-845-2823 j.belter@worldnet.att.net

Types of Records Retrieved: Civil and criminal courts; Federal courts; Tax liens/Judgments; UCC records

Local Retrieval Area: OH-Cuyahoga, Medina, Wayne

Add'l Information: Established 1988. Normal turnaround time- 24-48 hours. Projects billed by number of names searched. 1st project may require prepayment. Will invoice monthly. They specialize in civil, criminal, UCC, tax liens and US District and Bankruptcy court searches.

Jackson County Abstract Co

PO Box 756, Altus, OK 73521

Phone: 580-482-1235 **Fax:** 580-482-9180

www.jacksoncountyabstractok.com

Types of Records Retrieved: Civil courts; Probate courts; Real Estate; Tax liens/Judgments; UCC records

Local Retrieval Area: OK-Jackson

Add'l Information: Established 1948. Normal turnaround time- variable depending on project. Projects billed by the hour. 1st project may require prepayment. They specialize in abstracts.

Jackson County Land Title Services, Inc

508 3rd St, Newport, AR 72112

Phone: 870-523-8976 **Fax:** 870-523-3969

Types of Records Retrieved: Civil courts; Probate courts; Real Estate; Tax liens/Judgments; UCC records

Local Retrieval Area: AR-Jackson

Add'l Information: Established 1960. Normal turnaround time- up to 10 days. Projects billed by the hour. They specialize in real estate abstracting and title insurance.

Jackson Research Associates

536 N Westmoreland Dr. #4, Orlando, FL 32787

Phone: 877-654-9988; 407-944-4422 **Fax:** 407-944-4444

www.criminalscreening.com **email:** jra@criminalscreening.com

Types of Records Retrieved: Civil and criminal courts

Local Retrieval Area: FL-Orange, Osceola. **Correspondent Relationships:** Florida.

Add'l Information: Established 1998. Normal turnaround time- 24-48 hours. Projects billed by number of names searched. 1st project may require prepayment. Credit cards accepted. There is a $25.00 application fee for new members. Then billed monthly. They provide employee and tenant screening at wholesale prices. They provide criminal, credit, drug screening, driving records and much more. Online ordering capabilites.

Jacobs & Associates CPD Inc

901 East Wood St, Decatur, IL 62521

Phone: 800-445-1675; 217-429-2711 **Fax:** 217-429-2718

Types of Records Retrieved: Civil, criminal and probate courts; Federal courts; Real Estate; Tax liens/Judgments; UCC records; Vital records

Local Retrieval Area: IL-Champaign, Coles, De Witt, Douglas, Logan, McLean, Macon, Mason, Moultrie, Piatt, Sangamon, Shelby. **Correspondent Relationships:** nationwide by ex-FBI agents.

Add'l Information: Established 1970. Normal turnaround time- 1-3 days. Same day if received by noon central time. Projects billed by number of names searched. Terms: net 30 days. They specialize in forensic sciences, criminal and civil investigations and process service. A licensed PI in IL. They perform service of process.

JAK Abstract

PO Box 416, 413 2nd Street, Belvidere, NJ 07823
Phone: 908-475-3344 **Fax:** 908-689-2147

Types of Records Retrieved: Civil courts; Real Estate

Local Retrieval Area: NJ-Warren

Add'l Information: Established 1996. Normal turnaround time- 3-10 days. Fee basis will vary by type of project. They will file/record real estate documents on behalf of clients.

James F Havill Attorney at Law PC

401 E South St, Washington, IN 47501
Phone: 812-254-0050 **Fax:** 812-254-7633

Types of Records Retrieved: Civil courts; Probate courts; Real Estate; Tax liens/Judgments; UCC records; Vital records

Local Retrieval Area: IN-Daviess. **Correspondent Relationships:** Knox, Martin, Pike counties.

Add'l Information: Established 1971. Normal turnaround time- 1 week to 10 days. Personal checks are accepted. They specialize in title opinions, abstracts and title insurance.

James M Sweeney & Associates Inc

320 Leclaire St, Davenport, IA 52801-1721
Phone: 800-494-5922; 563-323-5922 **Fax:** 563-323-5441
www.inquirehire.com **email:** inbox@inquirehire.com

Types of Records Retrieved: Civil, criminal and probate courts; Federal courts; Tax liens/Judgments; UCC records; Vital records

Local Retrieval Area: IA-Scott; IL-Rock Island. **Correspondent Relationships:** nationwide.

Add'l Information: Established 1994. Normal turnaround time- 24-48 hours. Projects billed by number of names searched. Payment due upon receipt. They specialize in criminal checks in state and federal courts, drivers' licenses, workers' compensation records, bankruptcy and reference checks. An alternate web address is www.sweeneyinc.com. A licensed PI in IA, IL. They perform service of process.

Janke Abstract Co

PO Box 114, St Paul, NE 68873
Phone: 308-754-4251 **Fax:** 308-754-4444 carolyn@cornhusker.net

Types of Records Retrieved: Civil courts; Probate courts; Real Estate; Tax liens/Judgments; UCC records

Local Retrieval Area: NE-Greeley, Hall, Howard, Merrick, Nance, Sherman. **Correspondent Relationships:** Howard, Merrick, Greeley, Hall counties.

Add'l Information: Established 1980. Normal turnaround time- 2-3 days. Projects billed by number of names searched. Projects billed by number of records located. Projects billed by the hour. 1st project may require prepayment. They specialize in real estate.

Jay County Abstract Company Inc

125 W Main St, Portland, IN 47371
Phone: 260-726-4303 **Fax:** 260-726-4395

Types of Records Retrieved: Civil courts; Probate courts; Real Estate; Tax liens/Judgments; UCC records; Vital records **Local Retrieval Area:** IN-Jay

Add'l Information: Established 1897. Normal turnaround time- 5-6 working days. Fee basis will vary by type of project. Billing is made when work is completed. All projects require prepayment. They will also invoice. They specialize in real estate searches.

Jay Portland Abstract Inc Co

PO Box 1237, Portland, IN 47371
Phone: 260-726-6466 **Fax:** 260-726-6627

Types of Records Retrieved: Civil courts; Probate courts; Real Estate; Tax liens/Judgments; UCC records; Vital records **Local Retrieval Area:** IN-Jay

Add'l Information: Established 1978. Normal turnaround time- 5 days. Projects billed by number of names searched. Projects billed by the hour. All projects require prepayment. They will also invoice. They specialize in abstracting and title insurance.

Jean Randall Process Service

561 Louis Dr, Novato, CA 94945
Phone: 415-897-2361 **Fax:** 415-897-2305

Types of Records Retrieved: Civil, criminal and probate courts; Real Estate; Tax liens/Judgments; UCC records

Local Retrieval Area: CA-Marin

Add'l Information: Established 1978. Normal turnaround time- 1 day. Projects billed by number of names searched. 1st project may require prepayment. Personal checks accepted. She also specializes in fictitious business name filing searches. They perform service of process.

Jeff City Filing Inc

222 E Dunklin #102, Jefferson City, MO 65101
Phone: 573-634-3894 **Fax:** 573-634-5159
jeffcityfiling@earthlink.net

Types of Records Retrieved: Civil, criminal and probate courts; Real Estate; Tax liens/Judgments; UCC records; Vital records; Corporate filing and retrieval with Mo. Sec. of State.

Local Retrieval Area: MO-Cole

Add'l Information: Established 1986. Normal turnaround time- 24-48 hours. Projects billed by number of names searched. Terms: net 30 days. They specialize in filing & recording legal instruments with local & Missouri Supreme Courts, "walking through" filings with state agencies, UCC searches, MVRs, tax clearances/rescissions, corporate filings/retrieval. A registered agent for corporations. They perform service of process.

Jeff Davis County Abstract Co

PO Box 813, State Hiway 17, Fort Davis, TX 79734
Phone: 432-426-3288 **Fax:** 432-426-3844

Types of Records Retrieved: Civil courts; Probate courts; Real Estate; Tax liens/Judgments; UCC records

Local Retrieval Area: TX-Jeff Davis. **Correspondent Relationships:** adjoining counties.

Add'l Information: Normal turnaround time- 2 days. Projects billed by the hour. 1st project may require prepayment. They specialize in title work.

Jefferson County Abstract

122 N Court St, Fairfield, IA 52556-2811
Phone: 641-472-5052 **Fax:** 641-472-1944 jeffcoab@lisco.com

Types of Records Retrieved: Civil, criminal and probate courts; Real Estate; Tax liens/Judgments; UCC records; Vital records

Local Retrieval Area: IA-Jefferson. **Correspondent Relationships:** Van Buren County IA.

Add'l Information: Established 1800. Normal turnaround time- 1-2 days. Fee basis varies by type of transaction. 1st project may require prepayment. Specializes in complete land records, updated daily in Jefferson County.

Jefferson Title Co

PO Box 256, 2205 Washington St, Port Townsend, WA 98368
Phone: 306-385-2000 **Fax:** 306-385-6967

Types of Records Retrieved: Real Estate; Tax liens/Judgments.

Local Retrieval Area: WA-Jefferson

Add'l Information: Normal turnaround time- 1-2 days. 1st project may require prepayment. They have real estate records on hand.

Jerauld County Abstract Co Inc

Box 341, 210 E Main St, Wessington Springs, SD 57382
Phone: 605-539-1541 **Fax:** 605-539-1541

Types of Records Retrieved: Civil courts; Probate courts; Real Estate; Tax liens/Judgments; UCC records; Vital records

Local Retrieval Area: SD-Jerauld

Add'l Information: Normal turnaround time- variable depending on project. Projects billed by number of records located. Specializes in title insurance and abstracting.

Jess Barker Document Research/Retrieval

209A S Macoupin St, Gillespie, IL 62033-1605
Phone: 888-316-3773; 217-839-3219 **Fax:** 877-522-7537; 217-839-2901
www.documentresearch.biz

Types of Records Retrieved: Civil, criminal and probate courts; Federal courts; Real Estate; Tax liens/Judgments; UCC records; Vital records

Local Retrieval Area: IL-Macoupin, Madison, Sangamon, St. Clair; MO-Jackson, St Charles, St Louis. **Correspondent Relationships:** Illinois.

Add'l Information: Established 1993. Normal turnaround time- 24-48 hours. Fees are per name per index searched. They specialize in real estate current owner searches. They also do UCC, Lien and court record searches. The principal has an M.A. in Legal Studies focusing on law-related research and writing. Current owner searches/call for quote.

JG Weiss Research & Retrieval

5433 S Dorchester #1-N, Chicago, IL 60615
Phone: 773-241-6923 **Fax:** 773-241-5012 jgweiss@sbcglobal.net

Types of Records Retrieved: Civil, criminal and probate courts; Federal courts; Real Estate; Tax liens/Judgments; UCC records; Vital records

Local Retrieval Area: IL-Cook, DuPage, Kane, Lake, McHenry, Will

Add'l Information: Established 1997. Normal turnaround time- 24 hours. Expedited service available. Projects billed by number of names searched. Projects billed by number of records located. Projects billed by the hour. Projects are billed by the type of job done. 1st project may require prepayment. They specialize in title/property reports, document retrieval, judgments/liens and document recording. Competitive fees. Has E & O Insurance. No subcontracting. Has 6 years experience.

Jireh Business Information Solutions Inc

8775 Norwin Ave PMB 194, North Huntingdon, PA 15642-2744
Phone: 724-863-7270 **Fax:** 724-863-7271
www.jbizinfo.com **email:** info@jkizinfo.com

Types of Records Retrieved: Civil courts; Probate courts; Real Estate, Tax liens/Judgments

Local Retrieval Area: PA-Armstrong, Beaver, Bedford, Blair, Butler, Cambria, Fayette, Greene, Indiana, Lawrence, Somerset, Washington, Westmoreland

Add'l Information: Established 2001. Projects billed by number of names searched. Projects billed by number of records located. Projects billed by the hour. They will bill monthly. Terms are net 30 days w/10 day grace period. They furnish land title information, public records research and background screening services in ten southwestern PA counties. Professionalism, integrity and confidentiality are their highest priorities.

JM Search Services Inc

7787 SW 86th St #102-E, Miami, FL 33143
Phone: 800-393-7563; 305-273-7766 **Fax:** 305-273-8855
jamie.milton@prodigy.net

Types of Records Retrieved: Civil, criminal and probate courts; Federal courts; Real Estate; Tax liens/Judgments; UCC records

Local Retrieval Area: FL-Broward, Dade, Palm Beach

Add'l Information: Established 1991. Normal turnaround time- 24-48 hours. Expedited service available. Projects billed by number of names searched. Projects billed by the hour. Payment due upon receipt of invoice. They specialize in asset/lien, due diligence, civil/criminal, US District Ct, bankruptcy and real property searches. They also perform historical and biographical research for news publications and organizations. Will file documents in Dade County only.

John C Dunaway & Company

PO Box 202102, Austin, TX 78720
Phone: 512-835-5888 **Fax:** 512-835-2136
www.dunawaypi.com **email:** texaspi@swbell.net

Types of Records Retrieved: Civil, criminal and probate courts; Federal courts; Real Estate; Tax liens/Judgments; UCC records; Vital records

Local Retrieval Area: TX-Bastrop, Hays, Travis, Williamson. **Correspondent Relationships:** nationwide and Canada.

Add'l Information: Established 1978. Normal turnaround time- 24-48 hours. Projects billed by number of names searched. They bill at the end of the month. They are a full service investigations company assisting employers by helping them avoid potential claims exposure and to better evaluate the risks inherent when hiring personnel. A licensed PI in TX. They perform service of process.

John E Jones Jr Land Title & Appraisal

PO Box 105, (231 S Broad St), Metter, GA 30439
Phone: 912-685-3047 **Fax:** 912-685-3393 bandt@pineland.net

Types of Records Retrieved: Probate courts; Federal courts; Real Estate; Tax liens/Judgments; UCC records; Vital records

Local Retrieval Area: GA-Candler. **Correspondent Relationships:** Eastern and Southern Georgia.

Add'l Information: Established 1982. Normal turnaround time- 1-4 days. Expedited service available. Projects billed by number of names searched. Fee basis will vary by type of search plus costs of copies. 1st project may require prepayment. They specialize in appraisal, title, UCC, lien and judgment, federal court, and bankruptcy searches. Can do appraisals in adjoining or nearby counties.

John H Rider Abstracts of Title

300 W Marion, POB 256, Corydon, IA 50060
Phone: 641-872-1966 **Fax:** 641-872-2468

Types of Records Retrieved: Civil, criminal and probate courts; Real Estate; Tax liens/Judgments; UCC records **Local Retrieval Area:** IA-Wayne

Add'l Information: Normal turnaround time- 2-3 days. Fee basis varies by type of transaction. 1st project may require prepayment.

John Roberson Inv

746 Hwy 314, Fayetteville, GA 30214
Phone: 800-325-0914; 770-461-8958 **Fax:** 770-461-0119

Types of Records Retrieved: Civil, criminal and probate courts; Federal courts; Real Estate; Tax liens/Judgments; UCC records; Vital records

Local Retrieval Area: GA-Clayton, Cobb, Coweta, De Kalb, Fayette, Fulton, Gwinnett, Henry, Spalding. **Correspondent Relationships:** nationwide.

Add'l Information: Established 1984. Normal turnaround time- 2 days. Projects billed by the hour. 1st project may require prepayment. Payment due upon receipt. They are a specialist and experts in skiptrace and asset location. They perform service of process.

John V Eriksson Group Inc

1203 El Dorado, Houston, TX 77062
Phone: 281-488-0018 **Fax:** 281-488-0018 Jerik1@aol.com

Types of Records Retrieved: Civil, criminal and probate courts; Federal courts; Real Estate; Tax liens/Judgments; UCC records; Vital records

Local Retrieval Area: TX-Brazoria, Fort Bend, Galveston, Harris, Montgomery. **Correspondent Relationships:** Travis, Williamson, Hayes, Bexar counties TX.

Add'l Information: Established 1996. Normal turnaround time- 1-2 days. Projects billed by number of names searched. Projects billed by the hour. Fee basis varies by type of project. 1st project may require prepayment. They specialize in background and asset searches. Licensed Private Investigator, and Certified Fraud Examiner. A licensed PI in TX.

Johnson County Abstract

PO Box 627, Vienna, IL 62995-0627
Phone: 618-658-3721 **Fax:** 618-658-3700

Types of Records Retrieved: Civil courts; Probate courts; Real Estate; Tax liens/Judgments; UCC records; Vital records

Local Retrieval Area: IL-Johnson. **Correspondent Relationships:** Williamson, Pope, Union counties.

Add'l Information: Established 1800. Normal turnaround time- 2-3 business days. Projects billed by number of records located. Personal checks are accepted. They specialize in title insurance through Chicago Title Insurance Company.

Johnson Title & Abstract Inc
410 Westwood Office Park, Fredricksburg, VA 22401
Phone: 540-368-8104 **Fax:** 540-368-8105
johnsontitle@aol.com

Types of Records Retrieved: Real Estate; Tax liens/judgments; UCC records

Local Retrieval Area: VA-Albemarle, Caroline, Charlottesville, Fredericksburg City, Greene, King George, Louisa, Madison, Orange, Spotsylvania, Stafford

Add'l Information: Established 1993. Normal turnaround time- 24-48 hours. Projects billed by number of names searched. Payment due upon receipt of title work. She performs witness closings.

Johnston & Associates
PO Box 1183, Albertville, AL 35950-0019
Phone: 256-572-4967 **Fax:** 815-377-6850
http://paralegalone.tripod.com **email:** jeffjohnson1977@msn.com

Types of Records Retrieved: Civil, criminal and probate courts; Federal courts; Real estate; Tax liens/Judgments; UCC records

Local Retrieval Area: AL-Etowah, Jefferson, Madison, Marshall

Add'l Information: Established 2000. Normal turnaround time- 24-48 hours. Projects billed by number of names searched. 10-day billing. They specialize in full-service paralegal services and document retrieval and real estate title abstracting.

Jones & Associates Inc
1611 S Utica Av, PMB 117, Tulsa, OK 74104-4909
Phone: 918-583-4779 **Fax:** 918-587-8571 jones007@cox.net

Types of Records Retrieved: Civil, criminal and probate courts; Federal courts; Real Estate; Tax liens/Judgments; UCC records

Local Retrieval Area: OK-Tulsa. **Correspondents:** Oklahoma.

Add'l Information: Established 1976. Normal turnaround time- 24-72 hours. Projects billed by number of names searched. Projects billed by number of records located. Projects billed by the hour. All projects require prepayment. They specialize in private investigation, process service, medical research, document retrieval, and legal research. A licensed PI in OK. They perform service of process.

Jones & Renfrow Abstracters
802 9th, Heatly Building, Paducah, TX 79248
Phone: 806-492-3573 **Fax:** 806-492-3574

Types of Records Retrieved: Probate courts; Real Estate; Tax liens/Judgments; UCC records; Vital records

Local Retrieval Area: TX-Cottle, King, Motley

Add'l Information: Established 1910. Normal turnaround time- 1-2 days. Fee basis will vary by the type of project. 1st project may require prepayment.

Jones Abstract & Title Co Inc
313 Warren St, Huntington, IN 46750
Phone: 866-356-5663; 260-356-2122 **Fax:** 260-356-4533
www.jonesabstract.com **email:** jonesabstract@jonesabstract.com

Types of Records Retrieved: Civil courts; Probate courts; Real Estate; Tax liens/Judgments; UCC records

Local Retrieval Area: IN-Huntington. **Correspondent Relationships:** most of the state through an alliance of title companies, also Ohio, Kentucky, Wisconsin.

Add'l Information: Established 1877. Normal turnaround time- 3-5 days. Fee basis will vary by the type of project. 1st project may require prepayment. They specialize in title searching.

Jones County Abstract
PO Box 508, Murdo, SD 57559
Phone: 605-669-3004 **Fax:** 952-960-0090

Types of Records Retrieved: Real Estate; Tax liens/Judgments.

Local Retrieval Area: SD-Murdo

Add'l Information: 1st project may require prepayment. They specialize in real estate.

JR Investigations
PO Box 4175, Des Moine, IA 50333
Phone: 515-288-4682 **Fax:** 515-288-3295
www.jrinvestigations.com **email:** vixxenn@msn.com

Types of Records Retrieved: Civil, criminal and probate courts; Federal courts; Real Estate; Tax liens/Judgments; UCC records; Vital records

Local Retrieval Area: IA-Jasper, Madison, Polk, Warren. **Correspondent Relationships:** statewide.

Add'l Information: Established 1987. Normal turnaround time- 24 hours. 1st project may require prepayment. Billed at end of the month. They specialize in pre-employment screening, workers' compensation, surveillance, accident investigations, process service and real estate research/abstracting. A licensed PI in IA. They perform service of process.

JRW Documents & Lien Services LLC
PO Box 5491, Yuma, AZ 85366
Phone: 928-314-3993 **Fax:** 928-314-0951 Cell phone: 928-210-8804
jrwdocs@aol.com

Types of Records Retrieved: Federal Courts; Real Estate; Tax liens/Judgments; UCC records

Local Retrieval Area: AZ-Yuma; They also retrieve bankruptcy records for LaPaz and Mohave counties

Add'l Information: Established 2000. Normal turnaround time- 24-48 hours. Projects billed by number of names searched. Net 30 days. Require payment for first time customers.

Juab Title & Abstract Co
PO Box 246, Nephi, UT 84648
Phone: 435-623-0387 **Fax:** 435-623-1000
www.juabtitle.com **email:** tina@juabtitle.com

Types of Records Retrieved: Civil, criminal and probate courts; Real Estate; Tax liens/Judgments; UCC records

Local Retrieval Area: UT-Juab, Millard, Sanpete

Add'l Information: Established 1935. Normal turnaround time- 1-2 days. Charges vary according to project. All projects require prepayment. They specialize in real estate. They will file/record UCC and real estate docs on behalf of clients on a same or next day basis in Juab County ONLY.

Judd Law Office
PO Box 415, Burkesville, KY 42717
Phone: 270-864-3144 **Fax:** 270-864-3144

Types of Records Retrieved: Real Estate; Tax liens/Judgments

Local Retrieval Area: KY-Cumberland

Add'l Information: 1st project may require prepayment. They specialize in real estate.

Judicial Research & Retrieval (Ft Lauderdale)
1 E Broward Blvd #106, Ft Lauderdale, FL 33301
Phone: 954-832-0111 **Fax:** 954-832-0993 www.judicialresearch.com

Types of Records Retrieved: Civil, criminal and probate courts; Federal courts; Real Estate; Tax liens/Judgments; UCC records; Vital records

Local Retrieval Area: FL-Broward. **Correspondents:** nationwide.

Add'l Information: Normal turnaround time- 24-48 hours. Projects billed by number of names searched. Projects billed by the hour. 1st project may require prepayment. Credit cards accepted. They specialize in civil litigation, public records and bankruptcy. A licensed PI in FL.

Judicial Research & Retrieval Svcs (Georgia)
70 Spring St SW, Atlanta, GA 30303
Phone: 800-529-1338; **Fax:** 404-522-9600 www.judicialresearch.com

Types of Records Retrieved: Criminal courts; Probate courts; Federal courts; Real Estate; Tax liens/Judgments; UCC records; Vital records

Local Retrieval Area: GA-Clayton, Cobb, De Kalb, Fulton, Gwinnett. **Correspondent Relationships:** nationwide.

Add'l Information: Normal turnaround time- 24-48 hours. Projects billed by number of names searched. Projects billed by the hour. 1st project may require prepayment. Credit cards accepted. They specialize in civil litigation, public records, and bankruptcy.

Judicial Research & Retrieval (Jacksonville)

126 W Adams #505, Jacksonville, FL 32202
Phone: 904-356-9110 **Fax:** 904-356-9455
www.judicialresearch.com

Types of Records Retrieved: Civil, criminal and probate courts; Federal courts; Real Estate; Tax liens/Judgments; UCC records; Vital records

Local Retrieval Area: FL-Duval, Nassau, St. Johns. **Correspondent Relationships:** nationwide.

Add'l Information: Established 1996. Normal turnaround time- 24-48 hours. Projects billed by number of names searched. Projects billed by the hour. 1st project may require prepayment. Credit cards accepted. They specialize in civil litigation, public records and bankruptcy.

Judicial Research & Retrieval Svcs (Miami)

17 NW Miami Ct, Miami, FL 33128-1829
Phone: 800-529-6226; 305-379-3900 **Fax:** 305-379-4460
www.judicialresearch.com

Types of Records Retrieved: Civil, criminal and probate courts; Federal courts; Real Estate; Tax liens/Judgments; UCC records; Vital records

Local Retrieval Area: FL-Dade, Escambia, Gadsden, Lee, Leon. **Correspondent Relationships:** nationwide.

Add'l Information: Established 1996. Normal turnaround time- 24-48 hours. Projects billed by number of names searched. Projects billed by the hour. 1st project may require prepayment. Credit cards accepted. They specialize in civil litigation, public records and bankruptcy. A licensed PI in FL. They perform service of process.

Judicial Research & Retrieval Svcs (Orlando)

62 W Washington St, Orlando, FL 32801
Phone: 407-999-7717 **Fax:** 407-999-5220
www.judicialresearch.com

Types of Records Retrieved: Civil, criminal and probate courts; Federal courts; Real Estate; Tax liens/Judgments; UCC records; Vital records

Local Retrieval Area: FL-Orange, Osceola, Seminole. **Correspondent Relationships:** nationwide.

Add'l Information: Established 1996. Normal turnaround time- 24-48 hours. Projects billed by number of names searched. Projects billed by the hour. 1st project may require prepayment. Credit cards accepted. They specialize in civil litigation, public records and bankruptcy. A licensed PI in FL.

Judicial Research & Retrieval (Palm Beach)

328 Banyan Blvd #D, West Palm Beach, FL 33401
Phone: 561-659-7677 **Fax:** 561-659-6061
www.judicialresearch.com

Types of Records Retrieved: Civil, criminal and probate courts; Federal courts; Real Estate; Tax liens/Judgments; UCC records; Vital records

Local Retrieval Area: FL-Palm Beach, St Lucie. **Correspondent Relationships:** nationwide.

Add'l Information: Normal turnaround time- 24-48 hours. Projects billed by number of names searched. Projects billed by the hour. 1st project may require prepayment. Credit cards accepted. They specialize in civil litigation, public records and bankruptcy.

Judicial Research & Retrieval Svcs (Tampa)

711 N Florida Ave #227, Tampa, FL 33602
Phone: 813-228-7200 **Fax:** 813-228-7400
www.judicialresearch.com

Types of Records Retrieved: Civil, criminal and probate courts; Federal courts; Real Estate; Tax liens/Judgments; UCC records; Vital records

Local Retrieval Area: FL-Hillsborough, Pasco, Pinellas, Polk. **Correspondent Relationships:** nationwide.

Add'l Information: Established 1996. Normal turnaround time- 24-48 hours. Projects billed by number of names searched. Projects billed by the hour. 1st project may require prepayment. Credit cards accepted. They specialize in civil litigation, public records and bankruptcy.

Justifacts Credential Verification Inc

8085 Saltsburg Rd #100, Pittsburgh, PA 15239
Phone: 800-356-6885; 412-798-4790 **Fax:** 412-798-5249
www.justifacts.com **email:** ayoder@justifacts.com

Types of Records Retrieved: Criminal records

Local Retrieval Area: PA-Allegheny, Armstrong, Butler, Westmoreland. **Correspondent Relationships:** nationwide.

Add'l Information: Established 1984. Normal turnaround time- 24-48 hours. Projects billed by number of names searched. Will invoice monthly. They are a nationwide background information service specializing in comprehensive personnel profiles. They verify employment, credit, driving, education, workers' compensation, criminal/civil records and professional licenses.

JV & Associates

595 Piedmont Ave #320-149, Atlanta, GA 30808
Phone: 877-716-6668; **Fax:** 770-234-6994
www.jvandassociates.com **email:** halea729@aol.com

Types of Records Retrieved: Civil, criminal and probate courts; Federal courts; Real Estate; Tax liens/Judgments; UCC records; Vital records

Local Retrieval Area: GA-Cobb, De Kalb, Fulton

Add'l Information: Established 2002. Normal turnaround time- 2 business days. Expedited service available. Projects billed by the hour. Prepayment is required for 1st hour of service. Call JV & Associates for all your public record research needs. They perform service of process.

K

Kamber Agency

247 N Main St #126, Fort Bragg, CA 95437
Phone: 707-961-5464 **Fax:** 707-961-1581
kkamber@adelphia.net

Types of Records Retrieved: Civil, criminal and probate courts; Real Estate; Tax liens/Judgments; Vital records

Local Retrieval Area: CA-Mendocino

Add'l Information: Established 2000. Normal turnaround time- 5 days. Expedited service available at add'l charge. Projects billed by the hour. 1st project may require prepayment. Credit cards accepted. PayPal accepted. Private investigation specializing in criminal defense, civil litigation support, insurance defense, missing persons & public record retrieval. A licensed PI in CA #15517.

Kansas Investigative Services Inc

970 N Santa Fe, Wichita, KS 64214
Phone: 888-889-3340; 316-267-1356 **Fax:** 316-267-5476
kisinc@swbell.net

Types of Records Retrieved: Civil, criminal and probate courts; Federal courts; Real Estate; Tax liens/Judgments; UCC records; Vital records

Local Retrieval Area: KS-Butler, Reno, Sedgwick

Add'l Information: Established 1976. Normal turnaround time- 2 hours for criminal and civil records, 4-24 hours for real estate in Sedgwick; 1-3 days for Butler or Reno. Projects billed by number of names searched. Projects billed by the hour. Charges are by the trip. Flat fees are available for all searches. 1st project may require prepayment. They also service surrounding Kansas counties on 1-2 weekly trips. Sedgwick County searched daily, both A.M. and P.M. Toll-free number is available 24 hours. A licensed PI in KS. They perform service of process.

Karnes Land Title Co Inc

108 N Panna Maria Ave, Karnes City, TX 78118
Phone: 830-780-2221 **Fax:** 830-780-2236

Types of Records Retrieved: Civil courts; Probate courts; Real Estate; Tax liens/Judgments; UCC records; Vital records

Local Retrieval Area: TX-Karnes. **Correspondent Relationships:** adjoining counties.

Add'l Information: Normal turnaround time- 1 week. Fee basis will vary by the type of project. 1st project may require prepayment.

KasparNet LLC

3613 Reserve Commons Dr, Medina, OH 44256-8179
Phone: 800-886-7534; 330-725-7534 **Fax:** 800-845-1610; 330-722-4969
www.kasparassociates.com **email:** larryc@kasparassociates.com

Types of Records Retrieved: Civil courts; Probate courts; Bankruptcy courts; Real Estate; Tax liens/Judgments; UCC records

Local Retrieval Area: OH-Cuyahoga, Medina, Portage, Summit. **Correspondent Relationships:** statewide.

Add'l Information: Established 1980. Normal turnaround time- 24-72 hours. Projects billed by number of names searched. They will invoice. Formerly known as Kaspar & Associates Inc, they specialize in real estate title research in all 88 Ohio counties.

Kaufman Information Resources Inc

14 Scenic Dr, Dayton, NJ 08810-1495
Phone: 732-438-1967 **Fax:** 732-438-1971
kaufmaninc@aol.com

Types of Records Retrieved: Civil courts; Federal courts; Real Estate; Tax liens/Judgments; UCC records; Vital records

Local Retrieval Area: NJ-Mercer, Middlesex, Monmouth, Somerset, Union. **Correspondent Relationships:** New Jersey.

Add'l Information: Established 1995. Normal turnaround time- 3 days. Projects billed by number of names searched. 1st project may require prepayment. Terms: net 30 days. They specialize in UCC, corporate records, state and federal tax liens, and federal, state, county and local courts and retrieve records from Department of Treasury.

KC Court Research Inc

PO Box 4288, Olathe, KS 66063
Phone: 913-239-8995 **Fax:** 913-239-9606
kccourt@kc.rr.com

Types of Records Retrieved: Civil, criminal and probate courts; Federal courts; Real Estate; Tax liens/Judgments; UCC records

Local Retrieval Area: KS-Johnson, Wyandotte; MO-Jackson

Add'l Information: Established 1999. Normal turnaround time- 48 hours. Projects billed by number of names searched. 1st project may require prepayment. net 30 days. They specialize in Johnson & Wyandotte Counties, also Kansas Federal Courts and Missouri Western District statewide. They also specialize in all document retrieval from federal records center in Lee's Summit and Kansas City, MO.

Keating & Walker

1 Beekman St #406, New York, NY 10038
Phone: 800-466-2730; 212-964-6444 **Fax:** 212-964-5508
www.keatingandwalker.com **email:** johnwalker@keatingandwalker.com

Types of Records Retrieved: Civil courts; Probate courts; Federal courts

Local Retrieval Area: NY-Bronx, Kings, Nassau, New York, Queens, Richmond, Westchester. **Correspondent Relationships:** nationwide.

Add'l Information: Established 1992. Normal turnaround time- 24 hours. Projects billed by number of names searched. 1st project may require prepayment. They specialize in the NY city and suburban NYC area. They perform service of process.

Kellerman Investigations Ltd

21 Kingsley Way, Glen Carbon, IL 62034-1551
Phone: 888-402-6662; 618-288-6662; 618-410-3943 (Cell) **Fax:** 618-288-6668
www.kellermaninvestigations.com/ **email:** klaxon_greg1@yahoo.com

Types of Records Retrieved: Civil, criminal and probate courts; Federal courts

Local Retrieval Area: IL-Champaign, De Kalb, Kendall, Madison, Sangamon, St. Clair, Will, Winnebago. **Correspondent Relationships:** statewide.

Add'l Information: Established 1987. Normal turnaround time- less that 8 business hours. Projects billed by number of names searched. They are adjacent to the Madison County Courthouse in Illinois making their turnaround time reliably fast. Licensed and insured investigative agency, licence #'s 115-001758/117-001201. They perform service of process.

Keppler Legal Research

768 W Celeste Ave, Fresno, CA 93704-1813
Phone: 559-431-1358 **Fax:** 559-431-1358
mikekeppler@hotmail.com

Types of Records Retrieved: Civil and criminal courts; Federal courts

Local Retrieval Area: CA-Fresno, Kings, Madera, Tulare

Add'l Information: Established 1992. Normal turnaround time- 24 hours. Projects billed by number of names searched. Invoices on the 15th of each month. They specialize in criminal and civil research, bankruptcy, and federal civil.

Kern Attorney Service Inc

533 N Glendale Blvd #101, Los Angeles, CA 90026
Phone: 213-483-4900 **Fax:** 213-483-7777

Types of Records Retrieved: Civil, criminal and probate courts; Federal courts; Real Estate; Tax liens/Judgments; Vital records

Local Retrieval Area: CA-Los Angeles, Orange, Riverside, San Bernardino, San Diego, Ventura

Add'l Information: Established 1971. Normal turnaround time- 1-3 days. Expedited service available. Projects billed by number of names searched. All projects require prepayment. Credit cards accepted. They will file/record real estate documents on behalf of clients. They perform service of process.

Kevin W McClain Inv Ltd

PO Box 1434, Centralia, IL 62801
Phone: 877-532-1152; 618-532-1152 **Fax:** 618-545-0375
www.wespy4u2.com **email:** ispy4u@accessus.net

Types of Records Retrieved: Civil, criminal and probate courts; Federal courts; Real Estate; Tax liens/Judgments; UCC records; Vital records

Local Retrieval Area: IL-Clinton, Cook, Effingham, Franklin, Jefferson, Madison, Marion, St. Clair, Washington, Williamson. **Correspondent Relationships:** nationwide.

Add'l Information: Established 1994. Normal turnaround time- 24-48 hours. Expedited service available. Projects billed by number of names searched. Projects billed by number of records located. Projects billed by the hour. 1st project may require prepayment. Credit cards accepted. They are a full service investigative agency, specializing in civil, criminal, workers compensation, process serving, nationwide background checks and online access in IL statewide in criminal history. They have a paralegal on staff. A licensed PI in IL. They perform service of process.

Keystone Intelligence Network Inc

1704 Locust St, Philadelphia, PA 19103
Phone: 215-545-1111 **Fax:** 215-545-1773
truthfinder@compuserve.com

Types of Records Retrieved: Civil, criminal and probate courts; Federal courts; Real Estate; Tax liens/Judgments; UCC records; Vital records

Local Retrieval Area: PA-Montgomery, Philadephia; NJ-Camden, Gloucester

Add'l Information: Normal turnaround time- 1 day. Projects billed by the hour. 1st project may require prepayment. Credit cards accepted. They are a private investigating firm, performing various services for clients such as law firms & private individuals.

Kidder County Abstract Co

114 Mitchell Ave S, Box 108, Steele, ND 58482
Phone: 701-475-2432

Types of Records Retrieved: Real Estate; Tax liens/Judgments; UCC records

Local Retrieval Area: ND-Kidder

Add'l Information: Normal turnaround time- 2 days. Projects billed by number of names searched. Payment due upon receipt of invoice.

Kiefer Title Co

21 S Main St, Perryville, MO 63775-2522
Phone: 573-547-7755 **Fax:** 573-547-7788
ktcmary@powrup.net

Types of Records Retrieved: Probate courts; Real Estate; Tax liens/Judgments

Local Retrieval Area: MO-Perry

Add'l Information: Established 1991. Normal turnaround time- 1 week. They charge a flat rate per project. 1st project may require prepayment.

Kimmons Security Services Inc

2000 Dairy Ashford #300, Houston, TX 77077-5737
Phone: 281-679-0070 **Fax:** 281-679-0080
www.kimmonssecurity.com **email:** houston@kimmonssecurity.com

Types of Records Retrieved: Civil, criminal and probate courts; Federal courts; Real Estate; Tax liens/Judgments; UCC records; Vital records

Local Retrieval Area: TX-Brazoria, Dallas, Fort Bend, Galveston, Harris, Montgomery, Tarrant, Travis. **Correspondent Relationships:** most Texas counties and many counties nationwide.

Add'l Information: Established 1982. Normal turnaround time- 24-48 hours. Projects billed by number of names searched. Projects billed by the hour. 1st project may require prepayment. Credit cards accepted. Personal checks are accepted. Billing after each assignment. They specialize in asset investigations and public record searches. They also have nationwide capabilities for multitude of information databanks. They are an investigative and security company. A licensed PI in TX. They perform service of process.

King Investigations Inc

PO Box 113, Altus, OK 73521
Phone: 580-477-1676 **Fax:** 580-477-1828
www.audiostream.net/kinginvestigations **email:** kinginv@direcway.com

Types of Records Retrieved: Civil, criminal and probate courts; Real Estate; Tax liens/Judgments; UCC records

Local Retrieval Area: OK-Comanche, Greer, Harmon, Jackson, Kiowa, Tillman; TX-Wilbarger. **Correspondent Relationships:** They will only do real estate searches in Comache and Tillman counties OK; Wilbarger in TX.

Add'l Information: Established 1996. Normal turnaround time- 48 hours. Projects billed by number of names searched. 1st project may require prepayment. They specialize in locates, pre-employment, background information, real estate searches, civil-criminal searches and market research. A licensed PI in OK.

Vickie King Paralegal

PO Box 1340, Whitley City, KY 42653
Phone: 606-376-5931 **Fax:** 606-376-4401

Types of Records Retrieved: Real Estate

Local Retrieval Area: KY-Mc Creary

Add'l Information: Established 1994. 1st project may require prepayment. She sepcializes in real estate.

Patrick King

4538 Halifax Rd, El Monte, CA 91731-1539
Phone: 626-452-0838 **Fax:** 626-452-0838
kilgore211@juno.com

Types of Records Retrieved: Civil courts; Probate courts; Federal courts; Real Estate; Tax liens/Judgments; Vital records

Local Retrieval Area: CA-Los Angeles

Add'l Information: Established 1990. Normal turnaround time- 1 day. Projects billed by number of names searched. 1st project may require prepayment. They perform service of process.

Kingman Abstract & Title Co Inc

221 N Main, Kingman, KS 67068
Phone: 620-532-2011 **Fax:** 620-532-5383

Types of Records Retrieved: Civil courts; Probate courts; Real Estate; Tax liens/Judgments

Local Retrieval Area: KS-Kingman

Add'l Information: Established 1889. Normal turnaround time- 24-48 hours. Projects billed by the hour. They specialize in title insurance, escrow and closings. They will file/record real estate documents on behalf of clients.

King-Reed & Assoc Ltd

85 Scarsdale Rd #309, Toronto, ON M3B 2R2
Phone: 877-695-6575; 416-449-8677 **Fax:** 416-449-9889
www.king-reed.com **email:** king@king-reed.com

Types of Records Retrieved: Civil courts; Probate courts; Federal courts; Tax liens/Judgments; UCC records; Vital records

Local Retrieval Area: CANADA-Ontario, Toronto. **Correspondent Relationships:** affiliates across Canada for national service through Investigations Canada.

Add'l Information: Established 1984. Projects billed by number of names searched. Projects billed by the hour. 1st project may require prepayment. They specialize in due diligence inquiries, full record searches, surveillance, general investigations. Has 10 offices in Ontario.

Kings Title & Abstract Co (Anderson)

223 W 9th St, Anderson, IN 46016-1366
Phone: 800-317-1515; 765-643-3019 **Fax:** 765-644-0362
www.kingstitle.com **email:** anderson@kingstitle.com

Types of Records Retrieved: Civil courts; Probate courts; Real Estate; Tax liens/Judgments; UCC records

Local Retrieval Area: IN-Madison

Add'l Information: Established 1974. Normal turnaround time- 24-48 hours. Projects billed by number of names searched. Projects billed by number of records located. Projects billed by the hour. 1st project may require prepayment. They specialize in right of way and railroad research.

Kings Title & Abstract Co (Marion)

201 W 3rd St, Marion, IN 46952
Phone: 800-662-1299; 765-662-1111 **Fax:** 765-662-2018
www.kingstitle.com **email:** marion@kingstitle.com

Types of Records Retrieved: Civil courts; Probate courts; Real Estate; Tax liens/Judgments; UCC records

Local Retrieval Area: IN-Grant. **Correspondent Relationships:** surrounding counties.

Add'l Information: Established 1974. Normal turnaround time- 24-48 hours. Projects billed by number of names searched. Projects billed by number of records located. Projects billed by the hour. 1st project may require prepayment. They specialize in right of way and railroad research.

Kings Title & Abstract Co (Muncie)

1901 W McGalliard Rd, Muncie, IN 47304-2212
Phone: 800-294-1566; 765-288-1566 **Fax:** 765-288-1642
www.kingstitle.com **email:** muncie@kingstitle.com

Types of Records Retrieved: Civil courts; Probate courts; Real Estate; Tax liens/Judgments; UCC records

Local Retrieval Area: IN-Delaware

Add'l Information: Established 1974. Normal turnaround time- 24-48 hours. Projects billed by number of names searched. Projects billed by number of records located. Projects billed by the hour. 1st project may require prepayment. They specialize in railroad research.

Kings Title & Abstract Co (Richmond)

100 S 5th St, Richmond, IN 47374-4223
Phone: 800-757-7762; 765-962-6541 **Fax:** 765-966-3719
www.kingstitle.com **email:** richmond@kingstitle.com

Types of Records Retrieved: Civil courts; Probate courts; Real Estate; Tax liens/Judgments; UCC records

Local Retrieval Area: IN-Wayne

Add'l Information: Established 1961. Normal turnaround time- 24-48 hours. Projects billed by number of names searched. Projects billed by number of records located. Projects billed by the hour. 1st project may require prepayment. They specialize in right of way and railroad research.

Kings Title & Abstract Co (Rushville)

111 W 3rd St, Rushville, IN 46173-1839
Phone: 877-932-5757; 765-932-5757 **Fax:** 765-932-2168
www.kingstitle.com **email:** rushville@kingstitle.com

Types of Records Retrieved: Civil courts; Probate courts; Real Estate; Tax liens/Judgments; UCC records

Local Retrieval Area: IN-Rush. **Correspondent Relationships:** statewide.

Add'l Information: Established 1974. Normal turnaround time- 24-48 hours. Projects billed by number of names searched. Projects billed by number of records located. Projects billed by the hour. 1st project may require prepayment. They are the area's leader in title & closing services.

Kings Title & Abstract Co (Shelbyville)

1 Howard St, Shelbyville, IN 46176-2616
Phone: 317-398-0424 **Fax:** 317-392-0174
www.kingstitle.com **email:** shelbyville@kingstitle.com

Types of Records Retrieved: Civil courts; Probate courts; Real Estate; Tax liens/Judgments; UCC records

Local Retrieval Area: IN-Hancock, Shelby

Add'l Information: Established 1974. Normal turnaround time- 24-48 hours. Projects billed by number of names searched. Projects billed by number of records located. Projects billed by the hour. 1st project may require prepayment. They specialize in right of way and railroad research.

Kings Title & Abstract Co (Winchester)

125 S Main St, PO Box 25, Winchester, IN 47394
Phone: 800-280-6322; 765-584-9882 **Fax:** 765-584-2302
www.kingstitle.com **email:** winchester@kingstitle.com

Types of Records Retrieved: Civil courts; Probate courts; Real Estate; Tax liens/Judgments; UCC records

Local Retrieval Area: IN-Randolph. **Correspondent Relationships:** Jay and Darke counties OH.

Add'l Information: Established 1970. Normal turnaround time- 24-48 hours. Projects billed by number of names searched. Payment due upon project completion. They specialize in right of way, railroad research, title and abstracts research and insured escrow closings.

Kings Title & Closing Services

1111 Broad St, New Castle, IN 47362
Phone: 800-860-2990; 765-593-2167 **Fax:** 765-593-2168
www.kingstitle.com **email:** newcastle@kingstitle.com

Types of Records Retrieved: Civil courts; Probate courts; Real Estate; Tax liens/Judgments; UCC records

Local Retrieval Area: IN-Allen, Blackford, Decatur, Delaware, Fayette, Franklin, Grant, Henry, Jay, Madison, Randolph, Rush, Shelby, Wayne. **Correspondent Relationships:** Indiana.

Add'l Information: Established 1974. Normal turnaround time- 24-48 hours. Projects billed by the hour. 1st project may require prepayment. They specialize in utility right of way/railroad research. They service the entire state with searches, title insurance, and closings.

Kiowa County Abstract Co

PO Box 128, 1304 Goff, Eads, CO 81036
Phone: 719-438-5811 **Fax:** 719-438-5926

Types of Records Retrieved: Real Estate; Tax liens/judgments; UCC records

Local Retrieval Area: CO-Kiowa

Add'l Information: Established 1907. Normal turnaround time- 1-2 days. Fee basis will vary by the type of project. They specialize in real estate title.

Kiowa County Abstract Company

108 E 4th St, Hobart, OK 73651
Phone: 580-726-5283 **Fax:** 580-726-3545 kcac@itlnet.net

Types of Records Retrieved: Civil courts; Probate courts; Real Estate; Tax liens/Judgments; UCC records

Local Retrieval Area: OK-Kiowa

Add'l Information: Established 1901. Normal turnaround time- variable depending on project. Projects billed by number of names searched. Projects billed by number of records located. Projects billed by the hour. They will accept personal checks. They are a full title service company.

Jimmie Kirby

185 Trisdale Ln, Gainesboro, TN 38562
Phone: 931-858-8786 **Fax:** 931-858-8786

Types of Records Retrieved: Civil and criminal courts; Real estate; Tax liens/Judgments.

Local Retrieval Area: TN-Clay, Fentress, Jackson, Overton, Putnam, Smith, White, Wilson

Add'l Information: Normal turnaround time- 1-2 days usually. 1st project may require prepayment. Specializes in NE Tennessee.

Terry Kirkland

215 Walnut St, Monticello, KY 42633
Phone: 606-348-8645

Types of Records Retrieved: Real Estate; Tax liens/Judgments

Local Retrieval Area: KY-Wayne

Add'l Information: Established 1992. 1st project may require prepayment. Terry specializes in real estate.

KJK Abstract Co

38 Alpine Way, Raritan, NJ 08869
Phone: 908-725-6336 **Fax:** 908-253-9228

Types of Records Retrieved: Real Estate; Tax liens/judgments; UCC records

Local Retrieval Area: NJ-Somerset

Add'l Information: Established 1985. Normal turnaround time- 5-10 days. Fee basis will vary by type of project. They specialize in real estate searches.

Klitzke & Assoc Inc/Klitzke Services Group

PO Box 144, Genessee Depot, WI 53127-0144
Phone: 262-521-9502 **Fax:** 262-521-9503
www.klitzke.biz **email:** kklitzke@wi.rr.com

Types of Records Retrieved: Civil, criminal and probate courts; Federal courts; Real Estate; Tax liens/Judgments; UCC records; Vital records

Local Retrieval Area: WI-Milwaukee, Ozaukee, Walworth, Washington, Waukesha

Add'l Information: Established 1994. Normal turnaround time- 24-48 hours. Projects billed by number of names searched. Credit cards accepted. $2.00 per page for copies. Statewide criminal record searches in 50 states and in more that 120 foreign countries. Also driver records, asset searches and locate people. More that 15,000 conficential databases. Licensed PI in WI.

KLK Research

51 Eldorado Dr, Moscow Mills, MO 63362
Phone: 636-366-7055 **Fax:** 636-356-4557
www.klkresearch.com **email:** keith@klkresearch.com

Types of Records Retrieved: Civil, criminal and probate courts; Federal courts; Vital records

Local Retrieval Area: IL-St Clair; MO-St Charles, St Louis, St Louis City

Add'l Information: Established 1998. Normal turnaround time- 24 hours. Projects billed by number of names searched. 1st project may require prepayment. They specialize in criminal and civil background searches for pre-employment, and tenant screening. Also, will do court filings and other litigation support services.

Judi Knecht

4817 Bowfield Dr, Antioch, TN 37013
Phone: 615-832-8255 **Fax:** 615-833-3082
judi_knecht@comcast.net

Types of Records Retrieved: Real Estate

Local Retrieval Area: TN-Davidson, Montgomery, Madison, Rutherford, Sumner, Williamson, Wilson

Add'l Information: Established 2002. Normal turnaround time- 24-48 hours. Projects billed by number of names searched. 1st project may require prepayment. She provides current-owner searches that are accurate and prompt, at reasonable rates

Charles M Kneisley

1602 Sewanee Dr, West Columbia, SC 29169-6054

Phone: 803-936-1200 **Fax:** 803-936-1201 ckneisley@sc.rr.com

Types of Records Retrieved: Civil, criminal and probate courts; Federal courts; Real Estate; Tax liens/Judgments; UCC records

Local Retrieval Area: SC-Lexington, Richland. **Correspondent Relationships:** Sumter, Kershaw, Orangeburg, Charleston, Calhoun, Aiken counties.

Add'l Information: Established 1990. Normal turnaround time- 24-48 hours. Projects billed by number of names searched. Monthly billing. They specialize in retrieving statewide criminal histories from the SC Law Enforcement Division. They have been in business for 13 years.

Margaret H Knoras

23 East Lane, Springfield, VT 05156

Phone: 802-885-4375 **Fax:** 802-885-2405

peggyk@vermontel.net

Types of Records Retrieved: Civil, criminal and probate courts; Federal courts; Real Estate; Tax liens/Judgments; UCC records; Vital records

Local Retrieval Area: VT-Windham, Windsor. **Correspondent Relationships:** statewide.

Add'l Information: Established 1996. Normal turnaround time- 48 hours. Projects billed by number of names searched.

Know It All Background Research Svcs Inc

3655 Hulmeville Rd #303, Bensalem, PA 19020

Phone: 888-281-9535; 215-245-1975 **Fax:** 215-638-8071

www.screenmyapplicants.com **email:** inquiry@screenmyapplicants.com

Types of Records Retrieved: Civil and criminal courts

Local Retrieval Area: De-Kent, New Castle, Sussex; NJ-Burlington, Camden, Cumberland, Essex, Union; PA-Allegheny, Beaver, Bucks, Delaware, Lehigh, Luzerne, Northampton, Philadelphia, York. **Correspondent Relationships:** nationwide.

Add'l Information: Established 1999. Normal turnaround time- 24-48 hours. Projects billed by number of names searched. 1st project may require prepayment. They are a nationwide employment screening and public records research firm dedicated to providing outstanding customer service and quick, accurate results.

Brenda Kolle/Title Abstractor

4145 Montego Dr, Corpus Christi, TX 78411

Phone: 361-852-8236 **Fax:** 361-882-9987

Types of Records Retrieved: Civil, criminal and probate courts; Federal courts; Real Estate; Tax liens/Judgments; UCC records

Local Retrieval Area: TX-Aransas, Jim Wells, Kleberg, Live Oak, Nueces, Refugio, San Patricio

Add'l Information: Established 1990. Normal turnaround time- 48-72 hours. 2-hour Expedited service available. Projects billed by number of names searched. 1st project may require prepayment. Terms: net 10 days. Will fax invoice. They also specialize in oil & gas records research, 60 year environmental title chains, real estate owner searches. Personalized courier and notary service. Document filing service available in Nueces County and San Patricio County.

Kolling & Associates

3576 W FR 182, Brookline, MO 65619

Phone: 417-889-4092 **Fax:** 417-889-4026 coachmkoll@aol.com

Types of Records Retrieved: Civil, criminal and probate courts; Federal courts; Real Estate; Tax liens/Judgments; UCC records; Vital records

Local Retrieval Area: MO-Christian, Greene. **Correspondent Relationships:** nationwide.

Add'l Information: Established 1997. Normal turnaround time- 24-36 hours or less. Projects billed by number of names searched. 1st project may require prepayment. Credit cards accepted. Requires pre-paid check. He specializes in criminal record checks statewide and county, credit reports, MVRs (all 50 states), educational employment, and license verifications, as well as tracing, verification, and finding SSNs.

Kossuth Abstract & Title Co

113 N Hall St, Algona, IA 50511-2318

Phone: 515-295-3745 **Fax:** 515-295-7633

Types of Records Retrieved: Civil courts; Probate courts; Real Estate; Tax liens/Judgments

Local Retrieval Area: IA-Kossuth

Add'l Information: Established 1850. Normal turnaround time- 2-3 days.

Kota Cornelius Kruse & Assoc

PO Box 6422, Paris, TX 75461

Phone: 903-783-1883 **Fax:** 903-783-3968

Types of Records Retrieved: Civil and criminal courts; Federal District courts; Real Estate; Tax liens/Judgments

Local Retrieval Area: TX-Delta, Fannin, Grayson, Hopkins, Lamar, Red River, Titus; OK-Choctaw. **Correspondent Relationships:** nationwide.

Add'l Information: Established 2003. Normal turnaround time- 1-3 days. Expedited service available. Projects billed by number of names searched. Projects billed by the hour. 1st project may require prepayment. They are experienced in judgment recovery, researching assets, liens, judgments, UCCs; bankruptcy, DBA's, skiptracing, marriage, divorce, criminal records and more.

Kotner Abstract & Title

1333 B Locust St, Eldorado, IL 62930

Phone: 618-273-7611 **Fax:** 618-273-7611

Types of Records Retrieved: Civil courts; Probate courts; Real Estate; Tax liens/Judgments; UCC records

Local Retrieval Area: IL-Saline

Add'l Information: Established 1978. Normal turnaround time- 24 hours. Projects billed by number of names searched. Projects billed by number of records located. Projects billed by the hour. He specializes in title abstracts and title insurance in Saline County. He is a policy issuing agent for 1st American Title and Nat. Land Title Insurance Companies. Will file/record UCC and real estate documents for clients in Saline County only.

Krayer Detective Agency Inc

107 N Apple St, Dunmore, PA 18512

Phone: 800-249-3704; 570-347-5754 **Fax:** 570-347-4913

www.krayerdetective.com **email:** krayer@aol.com

Types of Records Retrieved: Civil and criminal courts

Local Retrieval Area: PA-Bradford, Columbia, Lackawanna, Luzerne, Monroe, Pike, Susquehanna, Wayne, Wyoming

Add'l Information: Established 1987. 1st project may require prepayment. They also provide court filings, subpoena preparation, skiptracing, private investigations, and repossessions. A licensed PI in PA. They perform service of process.

Kroes Detective Agency

7301 E 22nd St, Tucson, AZ 85710

Phone: 800-249-0694; 520-886-8397 **Fax:** 877-428-6939; 520-886-0949

jimkroes@cs.com

Types of Records Retrieved: Civil, criminal and probate courts; Federal courts; Real Estate; Tax liens/Judgments; UCC records

Local Retrieval Area: AZ-Pima. **Correspondent Relationships:** nationwide.

Add'l Information: Established 1970. Normal turnaround time- 24-48 hours. Projects billed by number of names searched. 1st project may require prepayment. They have 24 years experience, knowledge and equipment in debugging services. They also perform pre-employment screening, all types of investigation and process serving. A licensed PI in AZ. They perform service of process.

Kroll Background America

1900 Church St #400, Nashville, TN 37203
Phone: 800-697-7189; 615-320-9800 **Fax:** 800-845-2183; 615-321-9585
https://www.baionline.net **email:** moutlaw@krollworthode.com

Types of Records Retrieved: Criminal courts; Real Estate; Tax liens/Judgments

Local Retrieval Area: TN-Davidson, Rutherford; MD-Baltimore, Baltimore City, Carroll, Harford. **Correspondent Relationships:** nationwide. Kroll offices: Hampstead MD (800-673-9089) and Nashville TN (800-697-7189).

Add'l Information: Established 1983. Normal turnaround time- 24 hours in Maryland, other areas 3-5 days. Projects billed by number of names searched. Will bill monthly. They specialize in pre-employment background investigations, including criminal records nationwide, MVRs, credit histories and reference checking. Maryland statewide criminal records within 24 hours; TN statewide convictions only searches. A licensed PI in FL, MD, TN.

Kroll Document Filing & Retrieval Services

1900 Church St #400, Nashville, TN 37203
Phone: 800-324-2050; 615-321-2050 **Fax:** 800-788-0835; 615-329-3343
www.baionline.net

Types of Records Retrieved: Civil, criminal and probate courts; Federal courts; Real Estate; Tax liens/Judgments; UCC records; Vital records

Local Retrieval Area: TN-Cheatham, Davidson, Robertson, Rutherford, Sumner, Williamson, Wilson. **Correspondent Relationships:** nationwide.

Add'l Information: Established 1979. Normal turnaround time- 1-3 days. Projects billed by number of names searched. 1st project may require prepayment. Credit cards accepted. They specialize in corporate work, state and county UCC, tax liens, judgments and real property. Visits TN Secretary of State daily. They perform service of process.

KY Data Search Inc

1374 Ouerbacker Ct, Louisville, KY 40208
Phone: 502-637-4658 **Fax:** 502-637-4495
springbooks@insightbb.com

Types of Records Retrieved: Civil courts; Federal courts; Real Estate; Tax liens/Judgments

Local Retrieval Area: IN-Clark, Floyd; KY-Bullitt, Franklin, Hardin, Henry, Jefferson, Meade, Nelson, Oldham, Shelby, Spencer

Add'l Information: Established 1989. Normal turnaround time- 48 hours. Projects billed by number of names searched. Terms: net 30 days. Formerly Kentucky Data Search, they specialize in current owner searches, UCCs, lien searches and litigation searches.

KY Search & Retrieval Services

1413 Pine Meadow Rd, Lexington, KY 40504
Phone: 859-252-6874 **Fax:** 859-231-0808

Types of Records Retrieved: Civil courts; Federal courts; Real Estate; Tax liens/Judgments; UCC records

Local Retrieval Area: KY-Anderson, Boone, Bourbon, Boyle, Campbell, Clark, Fayette, Fleming, Franklin, Garrard, Grant, Harrison, Jessamine, Kenton, Laurel, Lincoln, Madison, Mercer, Montgomery, Scott, Woodford

Add'l Information: Established 1990. Normal turnaround time- 48-72 hours. Projects billed by number of names searched. Payment by check only. They provide public record searches at federal, locat and KY SOS specializing in UCC/Tax/Corporate records.

Kyle & Kyle (Michelle Kyle)

7015 Eagle View Ct, St Louis, MO 63129
Phone: 314-846-7728 **Fax:** 314-846-9925
kylenkyleri@aol.com

Types of Records Retrieved: Civil, criminal and probate courts; Federal courts; Real Estate; Tax liens/Judgments; UCC records

Local Retrieval Area: MO-St. Charles, St. Louis, St. Louis City

Add'l Information: Established 1987. Normal turnaround time- 24-48 hours. Projects billed by number of names searched. Will Bill. They specialize in court records, judgments, pre-employment screening, UCCs and tax lien records. Sixteen years experience in the area.

L

L & J Research

PO Box 211874, Chula Vista, CA 91921-1874
Phone: 619-829-2083 **Fax:** 619-397-5594
ljresearch@cox.net

Types of Records Retrieved: Civil and criminal courts; Federal courts; Tax liens/Judgments; UCC records; Vital records

Local Retrieval Area: CA-San Diego

Add'l Information: Established 1995. Normal turnaround time- 24-48 hours. Check or money order only accepted. Invoice on the 1st & 15th of each month. They specialize in public record retrieval at all court levels.

L Fay Hedden Abstract Office Inc

214 N 7th St, Vincennes, IN 47591-2114
Phone: 812-882-5273 **Fax:** 812-882-9886

Types of Records Retrieved: Civil courts; Probate courts; Real Estate; Tax liens/Judgments; UCC records; Vital records

Local Retrieval Area: IN-Knox

Add'l Information: Established 1939. Normal turnaround time- 5-10 days. Projects billed by number of names searched. Projects billed by number of records located. They specialize in real estate title.

L L Lesko Inc

1072 SE Floresta Dr, Port St Lucie, FL 34983
Phone: 772-879-2625 **Fax:** 800-944-9811; 772-879-0068
www.leskotitle.com **email:** iva@adelphia.net

Types of Records Retrieved: Real Estate; Tax liens/judgments; UCC records

Local Retrieval Area: FL-Brevard, Indian River, Martin, Palm Beach, St. Lucie

Add'l Information: Established 1996. Normal turnaround time- within 24 hours. Projects billed by number of names searched. 1st project may require prepayment. Terms: net 30 days. They specialize in title and abstract research, O/E reports, title search reports, UCCs.

Deborah Labhart

320 N Kirscher Ln, Placentia, CA 92870
Phone: 714-993-0185 **Fax:** 714-993-5264
deborahlabhart@sbcglobal.net

Types of Records Retrieved: Civil and criminal courts

Local Retrieval Area: CA-Orange. **Correspondent Relationships:** San Diego, Riverside, San Bernardino counties CA.

Add'l Information: Established 1981. Normal turnaround time- 24-48 hours. Projects billed by number of names searched. Payment is net 30 days. She specializes in background screening information and civil and criminal court records.

Lacey Pioneer Abstract Company Inc

PO Box 788, Anadarko, OK 73005
Phone: 405-247-5152 **Fax:** 405-247-5777
lacey-pioneer@classicnet.net

Types of Records Retrieved: Civil, criminal and probate courts; Real Estate; Tax liens/Judgments; UCC records; Vital records

Local Retrieval Area: OK-Caddo

Add'l Information: Established 1901. Normal turnaround time- 1-2 days. Projects billed by number of names searched. Personal checks are accepted. They specialize in closings, title insurance and title searches. They also prepare abstract of titles.

LaCrosse Abstract & Title LLC
110 W 8th, PO Box 636, La Crosse, KS 67548
Phone: 800-256-6911; 785-222-2712 **Fax:** 785-222-3340
stull1@gbta.net

Types of Records Retrieved: Civil, criminal and probate courts; Real Estate; Tax liens/Judgments; UCC records

Local Retrieval Area: KS-Rush

Add'l Information: Established 1994. Normal turnaround time- up to 1 week. Fee basis varies by type of transaction.

Lafayette County Abstract
330 Main St, Darlington, WI 53530
Phone: 608-776-3338 **Fax:** 608-776-4798
www.lafayettecountytitle.com

Types of Records Retrieved: Civil courts; Probate courts; Real Estate; Tax liens/Judgments; UCC records

Local Retrieval Area: WI-Lafayette

Add'l Information: Normal turnaround time- 1-2 days. Fee basis varies by type of transaction. All projects require prepayment. They specialize in abstracts, title insurance and closing service.

Lafayette County Abstract & Title Inc
PO Box 943, 113 E 3rd St, Lewisville, AR 71845
Phone: 870-921-4263 **Fax:** 870-921-5262 lafabs@aol.com

Types of Records Retrieved: Civil, criminal and probate courts; Real Estate; Tax liens/Judgments; UCC records; Vital records

Local Retrieval Area: AR-Lafayette

Add'l Information: Established 1939. Normal turnaround time- 1 week. Projects billed by the hour. They accept personal checks. They specialize in anything to do with real estate.

Lafayette County Land Title Co
1007 Franklin Ave, Lexington, MO 64067
Phone: 660-259-4631 **Fax:** 660-259-3142

Types of Records Retrieved: Probate courts; Real Estate

Local Retrieval Area: MO-Lafayette

Add'l Information: Established 1860. Normal turnaround time- 2-3 days. Fee basis will vary by type of project. They specialize in real estate title.

Sue Ellen Lagneaux
9 Carlito Rd, Santa Fe, NM 87508
Phone: 505-466-4061 **Fax:** 505-466-4061

Types of Records Retrieved: Real Estate

Local Retrieval Area: NM-Bernalillo, Sandoval, Santa Fe

Add'l Information: Established 1990. Normal turnaround time- 24-48 hours. Projects billed by number of names searched. 1st project may require prepayment. Will invoice. She is an independent contractor, has extensive experience in providing real estate research for current owner and current deed searches. A licensed PI in NM.

LaGrange Title Company
127 W Spring, LaGrange, IN 46761
Phone: 260-463-3232 **Fax:** 260-463-3232 lagrangetitle@earthlink.net

Types of Records Retrieved: Civil courts; Probate courts; Real Estate; Tax liens/Judgments; UCC records **Local Retrieval Area:** IN-LaGrange

Add'l Information: Established 1947. Normal turnaround time- 3 business days. Projects billed by number of names searched.

Lake County Abstract & Title Co
314 1st St E, Polson, MT 59860
Phone: 800-823-6225; 406-883-6226 **Fax:** 406-883-2586
www.lctitles.com **email:** info@lctitles.com

Types of Records Retrieved: Civil courts; Probate courts; Real Estate; Tax liens/Judgments; UCC records; Vital records

Local Retrieval Area: MT-Lake

Add'l Information: Established 1923. Normal turnaround time- 3 days. Projects billed by the hour.

Lake County Abstract Co
PO Box 913, 131 W 5th St, Leadville, CO 80461
Phone: 719-486-2688 **Fax:** 719-486-8352

Types of Records Retrieved: Probate courts; Real Estate; Tax liens/Judgments; UCC records; Vital records

Local Retrieval Area: CO-Lake

Add'l Information: Established 1965. Normal turnaround time- 1 week to 10 days. Fee basis will vary by the type of project. 1st project may require prepayment. They specialize in real estate title searches.

Lake County Abstract Co Inc
830 N Michigan Ave #501, Po Box 369, Baldwin, MI 49304
Phone: 231-745-3432 **Fax:** 231-745-7660
www.lcac.com **email:** leeannr@lcac.com

Types of Records Retrieved: Civil, criminal and probate courts; Real Estate; Tax liens/Judgments; UCC records; Vital records

Local Retrieval Area: MI-Lake, Osceola

Add'l Information: Established 1913. Normal turnaround time- up to 1 week. Expedited service available. Fee basis will vary by type of project. They will invoice. They specialize in real estate.

Lake Michigan Title Co
11 W Main St, Hartford, MI 49057
Phone: 269-637-8595 **Fax:** 269-637-1857

Types of Records Retrieved: Probate courts; Real Estate; Tax liens/Judgments; UCC records

Local Retrieval Area: MI-Allegan, Van Buren

Add'l Information: Normal turnaround time- up to 1 week. Fee basis will vary by the type of project. They specialize in title insurance.

LaMoure County Abstract Co
PO Box 596, 103 S Main St, LaMoure, ND 58458-0596
Phone: 701-883-4246 **Fax:** 701-883-4246 abstract@drtel.net

Types of Records Retrieved: Real Estate; Tax liens/Judgments

Local Retrieval Area: ND-La Moure

Add'l Information: Established 1900. Normal turnaround time- 2-5 days. Fee basis will vary by type of project. 1st project may require prepayment. They specialize in abstracts of title and title memorandums.

Land Grant Title Group Inc
420 S 2nd St, Elkhart, IN 46516
Phone: 888-563-4768; 574-295-1620 **Fax:** 888-563-4760; 574-295-8302
www.mylandgrant.com **email:** wecare@mylandgrant.com

Types of Records Retrieved: Civil courts; Probate courts; Federal courts; Real Estate; Tax liens/Judgments; UCC records

Local Retrieval Area: IN-Elkhart, Kosciusko, LaGrange, Marshall, St Joseph. **Correspondent Relationships:** LaGrange and Marion counties IN.

Add'l Information: Established 1996. Normal turnaround time- 3 business days. Projects billed by number of names searched. Projects billed by number of records located. 1st project may require prepayment. They will also invoice. They specialize in title insurance, land record searches and escrow closings.

Land Records of Texas
1945 Walnut Hill Ln, Irving, TX 75038
Phone: 800-678-8016; 972-580-8575 **Fax:** 800-678-8017; 972-518-2412
www.fntic.com/services/l_records.htm **email:** jakins@fnf.com

Types of Records Retrieved: Civil courts; Probate courts; Bankruptcy court; Real Estate; Tax liens/Judgments; UCC records

Local Retrieval Area: TX-all counties. **Correspondents:** nationwide.

Add'l Information: Established 1983. Turnaround time- 1-5 days. Projects billed by the hour. 1st project may require prepayment. They specialize in pre-foreclosure reports, trustee services and current owner searches.

Land Title & Abstract

247 W Cedar Ave, Gladwin, MI 48624
Phone: 989-426-0011 **Fax:** 989-426-7141

Types of Records Retrieved: Probate courts; Real Estate; Tax liens/Judgments; UCC records; Vital records

Local Retrieval Area: MI-Clare, Gladwin. **Correspondents:** nationwide.

Add'l Information: Established 1987. Normal turnaround time- 2-3 days. Fee basis may vary by the type of project. 1st project may require prepayment. They specialize in title insurance and closings.

Land Title Co

PO Box 651, Jackson, WY 83001
Phone: 800-289-9920; 307-733-4713 **Fax:** 307-733-6186
landtitle@onewest.net

Types of Records Retrieved: Civil courts; Probate courts; Real Estate; Tax liens/Judgments

Local Retrieval Area: WY-Lincoln, Teton. **Correspondents:** statewide.

Add'l Information: Normal turnaround time- 1-2 days. Projects billed by number of names searched. Net 30 days.

Land Title Corp

501 Cedar St, Tipton, IA 52772
Phone: 563-886-6915 **Fax:** 563-886-1238

Types of Records Retrieved: Civil, criminal and probate courts; Real Estate; Tax liens/Judgments; UCC records; Vital records

Local Retrieval Area: IA-Cedar

Add'l Information: Established 1987. Normal turnaround time- up to 3 days. Fee basis will vary by the type of project. 1st project may require prepayment. Payment due upon completion.

Land Title Guarantee Co

533 E Hopkins, Aspen, CO 81611
Phone: 970-925-1678 **Fax:** 970-925-6243
www.ltgc.com **email:** dharris@ltgc.com

Types of Records Retrieved: Real Estate; Tax liens/Judgments; UCC records; Vital records

Local Retrieval Area: CO-Pitkin

Add'l Information: Established 1993. Normal turnaround time- 2 days. Projects billed by number of records located. Projects billed by the hour. All projects require prepayment.

Land Title Inc

1900 Silver Lake Rd #200, New Brighton, MN 55112
Phone: 651-638-1900 **Fax:** 651-638-1994

Types of Records Retrieved: Civil courts; Real Estate; Tax liens/Judgments; UCC records

Local Retrieval Area: MN-Anoka, Chisago, Dakota, Hennepin, Ramsey, Washington. **Correspondent Relationships:** statewide.

Add'l Information: Established 1985. Normal turnaround time- 2-3 days. Projects billed by number of names searched. Personal checks accepted. They specialize in distressed property and foreclosure information.

Land Title of America Group

3700 US Hwy 1 S, St Augustine, FL 32086-7150
Phone: 904-797-9600 **Fax:** 904-794-4744
www.titlecompany.tv **email:** patti@ltoag.com

Types of Records Retrieved: Probate courts; Real Estate; Tax liens/Judgments; UCC records; Vital records

Local Retrieval Area: FL-Clay, Duval, Flagler, Nassau, Putnam, St. Johns

Add'l Information: Established 1979. Normal turnaround time- variable depending on project. Fee basis will vary by the type of project. They specialize in real estate title work.

Landlord Secure Assoc (L.S.A.) Process Serve & Legal Svcs

41 Watchung Plaza #131, Montclair, NJ 07042-4117
Phone: 973-332-4016 **Fax:** 973-833-0251
www.landlordsecure.com **email:** info@landlordsecure.com

Types of Records Retrieved: Civil, criminal and probate courts; Federal courts; Real Estate; Tax liens/Judgments; UCC records; Vital records

Local Retrieval Area: NJ-Bergen, Essex, Hudson, Mercer, Middlesex, Morris, Passaic, Union. **Correspondent Relationships:** nationwide.

Add'l Information: Established 1999. Normal turnaround time- 1-5 days. Projects billed by the hour. All projects require prepayment. Credit cards accepted. They specialize in pre-employment and tenant screening, process service, court filings, legal research, skiptracing, notary service and fingerprinting. They perform service of process.

Landmark Abstract & Information Svcs

PO Box 504, Hernando, MS 38632
Phone: 901-268-3200 **Fax:** 662-429-1634
www.landmarkabstract.com **email:** bill.garrett@mac.com

Types of Records Retrieved: Probate courts; Real Estate; Tax liens/Judgments; UCC records

Local Retrieval Area: MS-DeSoto. **Correspondent Relationships:** Tate, Marshall, Tunica, Hinds, Rankin, Madison counties MS.

Add'l Information: Established 1991. Normal turnaround time- 24-48 hours. Projects billed by number of names searched. Projects billed by the hour. 1st project may require prepayment.

Landmark Title Co of Madison County

PO Box 160, Madisonville, TX 77864
Phone: 936-348-5618 **Fax:** 936-348-5604

Types of Records Retrieved: Civil courts; Probate courts; Real Estate; Tax liens/Judgments; UCC records **Local Retrieval Area:** TX-Madison

Add'l Information: Normal turnaround time- 2-4 days. Fee basis will vary by the type of project. 1st project may require prepayment.

Landmark Title Inc (Clovis NM)

PO Box 1326, 117 E 4th St, Clovis, NM 88102-1326
Phone: 505-763-3904 **Fax:** 505-763-6610 landmark@plateautel.net

Types of Records Retrieved: Civil courts; Probate courts; Real Estate; Tax liens/Judgments; UCC records

Local Retrieval Area: NM-Curry

Add'l Information: Established 1989. Normal turnaround time- 48 hours. Projects billed by number of names searched. 1st project may require prepayment. Will invoice.

Landmark Title Roswell

PO Box 1476, 109 W 3rd St, Roswell, NM 88202
Phone: 505-622-5340 **Fax:** 505-622-5346 ltr@drn.com

Types of Records Retrieved: Civil courts; Probate courts; Real Estate; Tax liens/Judgments; UCC records

Local Retrieval Area: NM-Chaves

Add'l Information: Established 1992. Normal turnaround time- variable depending on project. Fee basis will vary by the type of project. 1st project may require prepayment.

Landmark Title Service

10315 E Grand River, Brighton, MI 48116
Phone: 810-227-1733 **Fax:** 810-227-1570
landmark@covad.net

Types of Records Retrieved: Civil courts; Probate courts; Real Estate; Tax liens/Judgments; UCC records; Vital records

Local Retrieval Area: MI-Livingston, Oakland, Washtenaw

Add'l Information: Normal turnaround time- 3 days. Fee basis will vary by the type of project. 1st project may require prepayment. They specialize in title insurance and escrow closings.

LaPeer County Abstract & Title Co Inc
194 W Nepessing St, LaPeer, MI 48446-2145
Phone: 810-664-9951 **Fax:** 810-664-8331
Types of Records Retrieved: Probate courts; Real Estate; Tax liens/Judgments; UCC records; Vital records
Local Retrieval Area: MI-Lapeer
Add'l Information: Established 1940. Normal turnaround time- 1 week. Projects billed by number of names searched. Projects billed by number of records located. They specialize in real estate.

LaPrade Services Inc
PO Box 5218, 31 Corlies Ave, Poughkeepsie, NY 12602-5218
Phone: 845-473-0468 **Fax:** 845-473-1667
Types of Records Retrieved: Civil, criminal and probate courts; Real Estate; Tax liens/Judgments; UCC records; Vital records
Local Retrieval Area: NY-Dutchess, Orange, Putnam, Ulster. **Correspondent Relationships:** Westchester, NYC, Long Island, Sullivan, Rockland counties.
Add'l Information: Established 1985. Normal turnaround time- 2-4 days. Expedited service available. Fee basis will vary by the type of project. They may require a retainer. They have the county contract for social services and handle 200 court papers a week. They perform service of process.

Margaret Laratta
95 Blossom Dr, Toms River, NJ 08753
Phone: 732-349-1301 **Fax:** 732-341-7224
Types of Records Retrieved: Probate courts; Real Estate; Tax liens/Judgments; UCC records
Local Retrieval Area: NJ-Ocean
Add'l Information: Established 1967. Normal turnaround time- 1-2 days. Projects billed by number of names searched. Projects billed by the hour. They will invoice. Their alternate fax number is 732-929-1058.

Larson Abstract Co
PO Box 387, Little Falls, MN 56345
Phone: 320-632-5667 **Fax:** 320-632-4583
Types of Records Retrieved: Probate courts; Real Estate; Tax liens/Judgments; UCC records; Vital records
Local Retrieval Area: MN-Morrison
Add'l Information: Established 1923. Normal turnaround time- 10 days. Fee basis will vary by type of project. All projects require prepayment. They will also invoice. They specialize in real estate.

LaSalle Process Servers LP
29 S LaSalle St #956, Chicago, IL 60603
Phone: 800-815-3801; 312-263-0620 **Fax:** 312-263-0622
www.lasalleprocessservers.com **email:** info@lasalleprocessservers.com
Types of Records Retrieved: Civil, criminal and probate courts; Federal courts; Real Estate; Tax liens/Judgments; UCC records; Vital records
Local Retrieval Area: IL-Cook, Du Page, kane, Lake, McHenry, Will. **Correspondent Relationships:** Other counties in Illinois.
Add'l Information: Established 1944. Normal turnaround time- same day to 1 day. If archives need to be searched, time averages 1-2 weeks. Projects billed by the hour. Copy expenses will be added to the fee. 1st project may require prepayment. Process service is their speciality. Check out their website for services provided. They perform service of process.

Lassen Inv Services
PO Box 997, Susanville, CA 96130
Phone: 530-251-2399 **Fax:** 530-251-5494 johncapi@yahoo.com
Types of Records Retrieved: Civil and criminal courts
Local Retrieval Area: CA-Lassen, Modoc, Plumas, Sierra
Add'l Information: Established 1994. Normal turnaround time- 2-3 days. Projects billed by the hour. Credit cards accepted. A licensed PI in CA. They perform service of process.

Helen Lattus
PO Box 96, Woodland Mills, TN 38271
Phone: 731-884-9994 **Fax:** 731-884-2774
Types of Records Retrieved: Civil courts; Probate courts; Federal courts; Real Estate; Tax liens/Judgments; UCC records
Local Retrieval Area: KY-Fulton, Hickman, TN-Benton, Carroll, Crockett, Dyer, Gibson, Haywood, Henry, Lake, Lauderdale, Madison, Obion, Stewart, Tipton, Weakley
Add'l Information: Established 1991. Normal turnaround time- 1-2 days. Projects billed by number of names searched. She specializes in real estate title searches.

Law In Motion
560 Ash St, San Diego, CA 92101
Phone: 619-232-1291 **Fax:** 619-232-0910
Types of Records Retrieved: Civil, criminal and probate courts; Federal courts; Real Estate; Tax liens/Judgments; UCC records; Vital records
Local Retrieval Area: CA-San Diego. **Correspondent Relationships:** California.
Add'l Information: Established 1988. Normal turnaround time- 3-4 days. Expedited service available. Projects billed by the hour. Some cases require fees in advance. 1st project may require prepayment. Terms: net 10 days. They also work with the Assessor's office and search fictitious business name. They perform service of process.

Noel D Law Jr
450 W 7th St #141, Tulsa, OK 74119
Phone: 918-599-0988 **Fax:** 918-599-0986
lbitsy009@sbcglobal.net
Types of Records Retrieved: Real Estate; UCC records
Local Retrieval Area: OK-Canadian, Cherokee, Cleveland, Craig, Creek, Delaware, Grady, Lincoln, Logan, Mayes, McClain, Muskogee, Noble, Nowata, Oklahoma, Okmulgee, Osage, Ottawa, Pawnee, Payne, Rogers, Tulsa, Wagoner, Washington
Add'l Information: Established 1995. Normal turnaround time- 24-48 hours. Projects billed by number of names searched. They specialize in title searches. Has over 20 years experience. Business is across the street from Tulsa County Courthouse.

Lawrence County Title
1300 15th St, PO Box 612, Lawrenceville, IL 62439
Phone: 618-943-4464 **Fax:** 618-943-4299 lct1@shawneelink.net
Types of Records Retrieved: Civil, criminal and probate courts; Real Estate; Tax liens/Judgments; UCC records; Vital records
Local Retrieval Area: IL-Crawford, Lawrence, Richland, Wabash
Add'l Information: Established 1988. Normal turnaround time- 24-48 hours for liens and judgment searches, and 1 to 2 weeks for abstracts and title insurance. Projects billed by number of names searched. Projects billed by number of records located. Projects billed by the hour. A charge per page and length of period (years) searched will be added to the fee. Some clients are required to pay a retainer. Personal checks are accepted. They will file/record UCC and real estate documents on behalf of clients on a same or next day basis in Lawrence County only.

Lawyers' Abstract Co
220 S Main St, Holly Point #A, Butler, PA 16001
Phone: 724-283-3510 **Fax:** 724-283-2258
Types of Records Retrieved: Civil courts; Probate courts; Real Estate; Tax liens/Judgments; UCC records
Local Retrieval Area: PA-Armstrong, Butler, Westmoreland. **Correspondent Relationships:** Lawrence, Mercer, Crawford, Clarion, Beaver, Westmoreland, Armstrong counties.
Add'l Information: Normal turnaround time- 2-14 days. Projects billed by the hour. They will also invoice. 1st project may require prepayment. They will also invoice. Personal checks are accepted. They specialize in title searching and title insurance. The company is owned by Butler County Lawyers and has been in business since 1965. They have the only title plant in Butler County.

Lawyer's Aid Service
408 W 17th St, PO Box 848 (78767), Austin, TX 78701
Phone: 877-474-2112; **Fax:** 877-474-4218;
MainDesk@Lawyersaidservice.com

Types of Records Retrieved: Civil, criminal and probate courts; Federal courts; Real Estate; Tax liens/Judgments; UCC records; Vital records

Local Retrieval Area: TX-Travis. **Correspondent Relationships:** major Texas counties.

Add'l Information: Established 1980. Normal turnaround time- 24 hours. Projects billed by the hour. Payment terms are net 10 days, pay simultaneously if large fees are advanced. They specialize in retrievals and filings in virtually all federal, state, local agencies and courts in Austin, plus corporate outfits and registered agent service.

Lawyers Filing SVCS of Southeastern PA Inc

4 Staterd #308, Media, PA 19063
Phone: 888-490-0409; 610-565-2620 **Fax:** 610-872-3635
lawyersfiling@comcast.net

Types of Records Retrieved: Civil, criminal and probate courts; Federal courts; Real Estate; Tax liens/Judgments; UCC records; Vital records

Local Retrieval Area: DE-New Castle; PA-Berks, Bucks, Chester, Delaware, Montgomery, Philadelphia

Add'l Information: Established 2003. Normal turnaround time- 24-72 hours. Projects billed by the hour. All projects require prepayment. Credit cards accepted. They specialize in comprehensive legal support.

Lawyers Investigating Svc

PO Box 8479, Portland, ME 04104
Phone: 888-244-5685; 207-775-5685 **Fax:** 207-893-1475
www.lawyersinvestigatingservice.com **email:** aeglis@aol.com

Types of Records Retrieved: Civil, criminal and probate courts; Federal courts; Real estate; Tax liens/Judgments; UCC records; Vital records.

Local Retrieval Area: ME-Androscoggin, Cumberland, Kennebec, Lincoln, Oxford, Sagadahoc, York. **Correspondent Relationships:** statewide in Maine.

Add'l Information: Established 1975. Normal turnaround time- 2-3 days. Expedited service available. Projects billed by number of names searched. Projects billed by the hour. 1st project may require prepayment. They are a full-service nationally-recognized investigative agency, licensed, bonded, and insured. A licensed PI in ME. They perform service of process.

Lawyer's Legal Service LLC

3301 SW Barbur Blvd #200, PO Box 9007 (97207), Portland, OR 97239
Phone: 800-224-7911; 503-224-7911 **Fax:** 503-224-9611
www.lawyerslegalservice.com **email:** lls@easystreet.com

Types of Records Retrieved: Civil, criminal, and Probate courts; Federal courts; Real Estate; Tax liens/Judgments; UCC records; Vital records

Local Retrieval Area: OR-Clackamas, Clatsop, Columbia, Hood River, Marion, Multnomah, Washington, Yamhill; WA-Clark, Cowlitz, Skamania. **Correspondent Relationships:** Oregon and Southwest Washington.

Add'l Information: Established 1982. Normal turnaround time- 1st attempt within 4 days; 3 attempts within 10 days. Expedited service available. Projects billed by number of names searched. Projects billed by number of records located. Projects billed by the hour. 1st project may require prepayment. Payment in advance for first time requests; 15 days net on all accounts. Their process services include rush and difficult services. Commission for out-of-state subpoenas in all OR counties. Specialties include investigations, document retrieval, and on or off site photocopy. Established in 1982. A licensed PI in OR. They perform service of process.

Lawyer's Resource

415 Washington St. #108, Waukegan, IL 60085
Phone: 888-909-7112; 847-263-9214 **Fax:** 847-263-1676
www.lawyersresource.net **email:** wendy@lawyersresource.net

Types of Records Retrieved: Civil, criminal and probate courts; Real Estate; Tax liens/Judgments; UCC records; Vital records

Local Retrieval Area: IL-Lake

Add'l Information: Established 1996. Normal turnaround time- 24 hours, often same day. Projects billed by number of names searched. Projects billed by the hour. 1st project may require prepayment. Credit cards accepted. They conduct criminal, civil & property-related searches, document retrieval and court filings daily. They collect court data weekly to be used for marketing purposes. They service high-volume accounts without compromising quality or turnaround time.

Lee County Land & Abstract

PO Drawer 1039, 200 S Grimes, Giddings, TX 78942
Phone: 979-542-3636 **Fax:** 979-542-5604

Types of Records Retrieved: Civil courts; Probate courts; Federal courts; Real Estate; Tax liens/Judgments **Local Retrieval Area:** TX-Lee

Add'l Information: Established 1906. Normal turnaround time- 2-3 days. Fee basis will vary by the type of project. 1st project may require prepayment.

Leelanau Title Co

PO Box 10, Suttons Bay, MI 49682
Phone: 231-271-6191 **Fax:** 231-271-3516

Types of Records Retrieved: Probate courts; Real Estate; Tax liens/Judgments; UCC records **Local Retrieval Area:** MI-Leelanau

Add'l Information: Established 1970. Normal turnaround time- 2-3 days. Fee basis will vary by transactions. 1st project may require prepayment. They specialize in real estate, title searches, and abstracts.

Legal 1 Document Retrieval

102 Royal Park Dr #1A, Oakland Park, FL 33309
Phone: 954-733-8934 **Fax:** 954-535-1875
http://adolfofc.tripod.com/legal1doc/ **email:** legal1doc@msn.com

Types of Records Retrieved: Civil, criminal and probate courts; Federal courts; Real Estate; Tax liens/Judgments; UCC records; Vital records

Local Retrieval Area: FL-Broward, Dade, Orange, Palm Beach, Seminole, Volusia. **Correspondent Relationships:** Volusia, Seminole, Orange, Hillsbourgh, Pinellas, Lee counties FL.

Add'l Information: Established 1998. Normal turnaround time- 24-48 hours. Projects billed by number of names searched. They perform the research, abstracting searches, recordings and document retrieval from most of the public records in South Florida. They also have a reliable network along Florida's east coast. They perform service of process.

Legal Abstract Co

301 E 2nd St, Muscatine, IA 52761
Phone: 563-263-3171 **Fax:** 563-263-5206 legalabstractco@machlink.com

Types of Records Retrieved: Civil courts; Probate courts; Real Estate; Tax liens/Judgments; UCC records; Vital records

Local Retrieval Area: IA-Muscatine

Add'l Information: Established 1937. Normal turnaround time- up to 1 week. Fee basis will vary by the type of project. Have been serving Muscatine for over 50 years with computerized record keeping.

Legal Beagles Inc

PO Box 886, New Castle, DE 19720
Phone: 800-743-9897; 302-322-9897 **Fax:** 302-322-8418
legalbegls@aol.com

Types of Records Retrieved: Civil, criminal and Probate courts; Federal courts; Real Estate; Tax liens/Judgments; UCC records; Vital records

Local Retrieval Area: DE-New Castle

Add'l Information: Established 1992. Normal turnaround time- 48 hours or less. Projects billed by number of names searched. 1st project may require prepayment. Service of Process always requires prepayment. They specialize in public records research; majority of research is criminal records searches for pre-employment screening. They perform service of process.

Legal Couriers Inc

PO Box 825, Yakima, WA 98907-0825
Phone: 888-450-9453; 509-453-1134 **Fax:** 509-575-6680
legalcouriers@yahoo.com

Types of Records Retrieved: Civil courts; Probate courts; Federal courts; Real Estate, Tax liens/Judgments; UCC records; Vital records

Local Retrieval Area: WA-Kittitas, Yakima. **Correspondent Relationships:** nationwide.

Add'l Information: Established 1966. Normal turnaround time- 24 hours. Projects billed by number of names searched. They will bill clients. They preform the following services: process service, document retrieval, skiptracing, federal fax filings, document research, monitoring of trustee sales, full attorney services. They have 35 years of experience. They perform service of process.

Legal Couriers Inc

PO Box 825, Yakima, WA 98902
Phone: 888-450-9453; 509-453-1134 **Fax:** 509-575-6680
rugscott@yahoo.com

Types of Records Retrieved: Civil, criminal and Probate courts; Federal courts; Real Estate; Tax liens/Judgments; UCC records; Vital records

Local Retrieval Area: WA-Yakima. **Correspondent Relationships:** nationwide, Canada, Mexico, Puerto Rico, New Zealand, Australia, U.K.

Add'l Information: Established 1965. Normal turnaround time- 24-48 hours. Expedited service available. They charge flat fee plus copies. Will invoice law firms and other companies. After 20 years experience - they can often times advise of local precedures or acquire documents quickly, while others less experienced might not. They perform service of process.

Legal Data Resources

2816 W Summerdale, Chicago, IL 60625
Phone: 800-735-9207; 773-561-2468 **Fax:** 773-561-2488
www.ldrsearch.com **email:** legaldat@theramp.net

Types of Records Retrieved: Civil, criminal and probate courts; Federal courts; Real Estate; Tax liens/Judgments; UCC records; Vital records

Local Retrieval Area: IL-Cook, Du Page, Lake, Will. **Correspondent Relationships:** nationwide.

Add'l Information: Established 1990. Normal turnaround time- 24 hours. Projects billed by number of names searched. Personal checks are accepted. They specialize in criminal background checks, service of process, pre-employment screening and skiptracing. Does daily service to the Federal Record Center in Chicago. They perform service of process.

Legal Document Search & Signing Services

882 Cascade Dr, Sunnyvale, CA 94087
Phone: 408-483-0061 **Fax:** 408-973-7261
legaldocs4u@comcast.net

Types of Records Retrieved: Civil and criminal courts; Tax liens/Judgments; Vital records

Local Retrieval Area: CA-San Mateo, Santa Clara

Add'l Information: Established 2000. Normal turnaround time- 24-48 hours. Expedited service available. Projects billed by the hour. All projects require prepayment. They specialize in self-help legal documents, prompt and accurate public record research and loan signing services. They are a bonded legal document assistant in Santa Clara County. They perform service of process.

Legal Eagle Inc / Eagle Search & Service

17330 W Center Rd #110-310, Omaha, NE 68130-2392
Phone: 402-342-4427 **Fax:** 402-691-8824
LegalEagleWMR@cox.net

Types of Records Retrieved: Civil, criminal and probate courts; Federal courts; Real Estate; Tax liens/Judgments; UCC records; Vital records

Local Retrieval Area: IA-Pottawattamie; NE-Douglas, Sarpy. **Correspondent Relationships:** Washington, Cass, Saunders counties NE.

Add'l Information: Established 1986. Normal turnaround time- 24-48 hours. Projects billed by number of names searched. 1st project may require prepayment. They have been in business since 1986, Statewide Neb. criminal history checks, they also handle all your document filing needs. Notary on staff. They perform service of process.

Legal Ease Inc

407 Vine St #102, Cincinnati, OH 45202-2806
Phone: 800-519-6331; 513-621-1017 **Fax:** 513-251-1403
paulapi5@aol.com

Types of Records Retrieved: Civil, criminal and probate courts; Federal courts; Real Estate; Tax liens/Judgments; UCC records; Vital records.

Local Retrieval Area: OH-Clermont, Darke, Greene, Hamilton, Montgomery, Preble, Warren. **Correspondent Relationships:** Ohio and nationwide.

Add'l Information: Established 1996. Normal turnaround time- 1 day or same day service. Projects billed by number of names searched. All projects require prepayment. Legal Ease provides court record retrieval, filings, process service, and investigative research to clients nationwide. They perform service of process.

Legal Express

15 S Weber #D, Colorado Springs, CO 80903
Phone: 719-578-0407 **Fax:** 719-635-9802
www.legalexpressco.homestead.com **email:** legalexpressco@hotmail.com

Types of Records Retrieved: Civil, criminal and probate courts; Real Estate; Tax liens/Judgments; Vital records

Local Retrieval Area: CO-El Paso, Teller

Add'l Information: Established 1967. Normal turnaround time- 2 working days. Projects billed by number of names searched. They perform service of process.

Legal Investigations

8612 Malmaison Way, Knoxville, TN 37923-7142
Phone: 865-970-4444 tedhembree@aol.com

Types of Records Retrieved: Civil, criminal and probate courts; Federal courts; Real Estate; UCC records

Local Retrieval Area: TN-Knox. **Correspondent Relationships:** other counties in TN.

Add'l Information: Established 1982. Normal turnaround time- 1-3 working days. Projects billed by the hour. 1st project may require prepayment. They specialize in personal injury investigation searches and automotive safety. All East Tennessee served on a per case basis. They perform service of process.

Legal Net Process Service

1013 Montana Ave, El Paso, TX 79902
Phone: 915-532-7871 **Fax:** 915-533-8039

Types of Records Retrieved: Civil, criminal and probate courts; Federal courts; Tax liens/Judgments; UCC records; Vital records

Local Retrieval Area: NM-Dona Ana; TX-El Paso, Hudspeth

Add'l Information: Established 1992. Normal turnaround time- 1 day in El Paso; 2-3 days in other counties. Projects billed by number of names searched. Fee basis will vary by the type of project. 1st project may require prepayment. They perform service of process.

Legal Recording of Rochester Inc

16 E Main St #6, Rochester, NY 14614-1803
Phone: 585-232-6710 **Fax:** 585-232-1475
legalrecording@myexcel.com

Types of Records Retrieved: Civil, criminal and probate courts; Federal courts; Real Estate; Tax liens/Judgments; UCC records

Local Retrieval Area: NY-Monroe

Add'l Information: Established 1970. Normal turnaround time- 24-48 hours. Projects billed by number of names searched. Projects billed by number of records located. 1st project may require prepayment. Credit cards accepted. Cost of copies and disbursements for filing fees require prepayment. They specialize in real property tax searches for lenders, criminal searches and real estate DBA searches, as well as civil court record retrieval.

Legal Research Associates Inc

PO Box 3091, Tustin, CA 92781-3091
Phone: 714-734-9337 **Fax:** 714-734-9441
http://legalresearchassociates.com **email:** lratim@cox.net

Types of Records Retrieved: Civil, criminal and probate courts; Federal courts; Real Estate; Tax liens/Judgments; UCC records; Vital records

Local Retrieval Area: CA-Los Angeles, Orange, Riverside, San Bernardino. **Correspondent Relationships:** nationwide.

Add'l Information: Established 1993. Normal turnaround time- 24-48 hours. Projects billed by number of names searched. Projects billed by number of records located. Projects billed by the hour. All projects require prepayment. Credit cards accepted. Will bill bi-weekly or monthly. They perform service of process.

Legal Research Service LLC

PO Box 66128, Mobile, AL 36660
Phone: 251-432-1006 **Fax:** 251-471-5588
jhbcli@comcast.net

Types of Records Retrieved: Civil, criminal and probate courts; Federal courts; Tax liens/Judgments; UCC records; Vital records

Local Retrieval Area: AL-Baldwin, Clarke, Escambia, Mobile, Monroe, Washington. **Correspondent Relationships:** Jefferson, Montgomery, Tuscaloosa, Shelby counties AL.

Add'l Information: Established 1995. Normal turnaround time- 1-3 days. Expedited service available. Projects billed by the hour. 1st project may require prepayment. They specialize in full service investigative firm for plaintiff and well as defense. Also do process service and document retrieval. A licensed PI in AL. They perform service of process.

Legal Research Services

1373 Rosevalley Rd, Dover, DE 19904
Phone: 302-672-9411 **Fax:** 302-672-9277
collenaw@yahoo.com

Types of Records Retrieved: Civil and criminal courts; Real Estate; Tax liens/Judgments; UCC records; Vital records

Local Retrieval Area: DE-Kent, New Castle, Sussex

Add'l Information: Established 1993. Normal turnaround time- 24-36 hours. Projects billed by number of names searched. 1st project may require prepayment. Needs deposit for first time and big orders.

Legal Support Services-II

19 Nickel Pl, Spearfish, SD 57783
Phone: 800-583-0365; 605-642-7146 **Fax:** 605-642-5941
ohstormie@rushmore.com

Types of Records Retrieved: Civil, criminal and probate courts; Federal courts; Real Estate; Tax liens/Judgments; UCC records; Vital records

Local Retrieval Area: SD-Brown, Butte, Lawrence, Meade, Minnehaha, Pennington,. **Correspondent Relationships:** South Dakota.

Add'l Information: Established 1980. Normal turnaround time- 24-48 hours. Projects billed by number of names searched. They specialize in record searches and filings in all federal, state and county agencies in South Dakota, including Secretary of State.

LegalEase Inc

139 Fulton St #1013, New York, NY 10038
Phone: 800-393-1277; 212-393-9070 **Fax:** 212-393-9796
www.legaleaseinc.com **email:** info@legaleaseinc.com

Types of Records Retrieved: Civil courts; Probate courts; Federal courts; Tax liens/Judgments

Local Retrieval Area: NY-Bronx, Kings, Nassau, New York, Queens, Westchester. **Correspondent Relationships:** nationwide.

Add'l Information: Established 1985. Normal turnaround time- 24-72 hours. Expedited service available. Projects billed by number of names searched. Projects billed by the hour. Volume searches will be charged by the hour. 1st project may require prepayment. Credit cards accepted. They specialize in document retrieval (federal and state courts) online information retrieval, and public record research. Rush service a specialty. They perform service of process.

Legalese

1754 36th St, Sacramento, CA 95816-6613
Phone: 916-453-2860 **Fax:** 916-453-2875
jeffs@cwo.com

Types of Records Retrieved: Civil, criminal and probate courts; Federal courts; Real Estate; Tax liens/Judgments; UCC records; Vital records

Local Retrieval Area: CA-El Dorado, Placer, Sacramento, San Joaquin, Sutter, Yolo, Yuba. **Correspondent Relationships:** California

Add'l Information: Established 1980. Normal turnaround time- 2 days. Projects billed by number of names searched. 1st project may require prepayment. They specialize in UCC, corporation and county records. They perform service of process.

LegalNet Inc

2510 W 237th St #110, Torrance, CA 90505
Phone: 888-530-3100; 310-530-2200 **Fax:** 310-530-1014
www.legalnetinc.com

Types of Records Retrieved: Civil, criminal and probate courts; Federal courts; Real Estate; Tax liens/Judgments; UCC records; Vital records

Local Retrieval Area: CA-Los Angeles, Orange. **Correspondent Relationships:** Ventura, San Diego, Riverside, San Bernardino.

Add'l Information: Established 1971. Normal turnaround time- routine 72 hours. Expedited service available. Projects billed by number of names searched. Projects billed by the hour. All projects require prepayment. Credit cards accepted. Generally a process server and mobile copy service, their standard service includes all Courts in LA and Orange Counties. Premium service includes San Bernardino, Riverside, Ventura and San Diego Counties. They perform service of process.

LegalTrieve Information Services

18 Oliver St #204, North Easton, MA 02356
Phone: 508-238-4227 **Fax:** 508-238-4678
legaltrieve@email.msn.com

Types of Records Retrieved: Civil, criminal and probate courts; Federal courts; Real Estate; Tax liens/Judgments; UCC records

Local Retrieval Area: MA-Bristol, Essex, Middlesex, Norfolk, Plymouth, Suffolk. **Correspondent Relationships:** nationwide.

Add'l Information: Established 1995. Normal turnaround time- 1-3 business days. Projects billed by number of names searched. 1st project may require prepayment. Large projects require prepayment. Payment due upon receipt for smaller projects. They specialize in public record research, document retrieval and asset searches.

LegalWorks Inc

PO Box 435, Clinton, NY 13323-0435
Phone: 800-853-6756; 315-737-9800 **Fax:** 315-737-0055
http://legal-works.com **email:** gregg@legal-works.com

Types of Records Retrieved: Civil, criminal and probate courts; Federal courts; Real Estate; Tax liens/Judgments; UCC records; Vital records

Local Retrieval Area: NY-Herkimer, Madison, Oneida

Add'l Information: Established 1982. Normal turnaround time- 24 hours. Projects billed by number of names searched. 1st project may require prepayment. They specialize in proficient expertise, progressive technologies and premier service via integrity, diligence and timeliness. They perform service of process.

Lehr's Process Service

1017 SW 86th Way, Gainesville, FL 32607-4949
Phone: 352-331-1010 **Fax:** 352-332-3895
www.lehrsprocessservice.com **email:** steve@lehrsprocessservice.com

Types of Records Retrieved: Civil, criminal and probate courts; Federal District courts; Real Estate; Tax liens/Judgments; UCC records; Vital records; Votor registration records

Local Retrieval Area: FL-Alachua, Marion

Add'l Information: Established 1994. Normal turnaround time- 24-72 hours. Projects billed by number of names searched. Will invoice due to cost of copies. They perform service of process.

Len Page Paralegal/Research Services

PO Box 50805, New Bedford, MA 02745
Phone: 508-967-2504 **Fax:** 775-514-1742
www.lpprs.com **email:** len.page@lpprs.com

Types of Records Retrieved: Civil, criminal and probate courts; Federal courts; Real Estate; Tax liens/Judgments; UCC records; Vital records

Local Retrieval Area: MA-Barnstable, Bristol, Norfolk, Plymouth. **Correspondent Relationships:** Suffolk, Dukes, MA counties.

Add'l Information: Established 2003. Normal turnaround time- 24-72 hours. Projects billed by number of names searched. Projects billed by number of records located. Projects billed by the hour. LPPRS being a provider to the legal community, conducts research, filings and retrieval of pertinent information from public resources. LPPRS prides itself in providing excellent quality work.

Lenmark Personal Services

PO Box 211, Eureka, MO 63025
Phone: 636-677-3831 **Fax:** 636-677-3831 Trailhorse1@Juno.com

Types of Records Retrieved: Civil, criminal and probate courts; Federal courts; Real Estate

Local Retrieval Area: MO-Franklin, Jefferson, St. Charles, St. Louis. **Correspondent Relationships:** St Louis, MO extended area.

Add'l Information: Established 1977. Normal turnaround time- 48 hours or less. Billing method depends on project. Rural counties are 50 miles to courthouse, basic rates will be higher because of fluctuating gas prices. 1st project may require prepayment. They specialize in credit and collection services. They will perform record retrieval in outlying counties, away from the St. Louis area, though rates are slightly higher than urban charges. They perform service of process.

Lenow International Inc

PO Box 3092, 1503 Union Ave #210 (38104), Memphis, TN 38173-0092
Phone: 901-726-0735 **Fax:** 901-725-4079
www.lenowintl.nu **email:** nlenow@compuserve.com

Types of Records Retrieved: Civil, criminal and probate courts; Federal courts; Tax liens/Judgments; UCC records; Vital records

Local Retrieval Area: MS-De Soto; TN-Shelby. **Correspondent Relationships:** statewide.

Add'l Information: Established 1977. Normal turnaround time- 24 hours. Projects billed by the hour. 1st project may require prepayment. They specialize in locating records when limited information is available. A licensed PI in TN. They perform service of process.

Dawn Curran Letcher

125 Main St, Carlisle, KY 40311
Phone: 859-289-3745 **Fax:** 859-289-3746

Types of Records Retrieved: Real Estate; Tax liens/Judgments

Local Retrieval Area: KY-Carlisle

Add'l Information: Established 1991. 1st project may require prepayment. Will file/record documents. They preform real estate services on a limited basis only.

Lewis County Abstract (Idaho) d/b/a Lewis County Title

PO Box 36, Nezperce, ID 83543
Phone: 208-937-2621 **Fax:** 208-937-2621
dmjjd@camasnet.com

Types of Records Retrieved: Civil, criminal and probate courts; Real Estate; Tax liens/Judgments

Local Retrieval Area: ID-Lewis

Add'l Information: Established 1911. Normal turnaround time- 1-2 days. Fee basis will vary by the type of project. They specialize in providing title insurance. Also legal and accounting available.

Lewis County Abstract (Missouri)

329 Lewis St, Canton, MO 63435
Phone: 573-288-4461 **Fax:** 573-288-4463

Types of Records Retrieved: Probate courts; Real Estate; Tax liens/Judgments; UCC records

Local Retrieval Area: MO-Lewis

Add'l Information: Established 1920. Normal turnaround time- 24 hours. Projects billed by number of records located. Personal checks are accepted.

Lexington Title Corp

301 Gibson Rd, Lexington, SC 29072
Phone: 803-957-1243 **Fax:** 803-957-9359

Types of Records Retrieved: Civil courts; Probate courts; Real Estate; Tax liens/Judgments; UCC records

Local Retrieval Area: SC-Aiken, Calhoun, Edgefield, Fairfield, Kershaw, Lexington, Newberry, Orangeburg, Richland, Saluda

Add'l Information: Established 1985. Normal turnaround time- 24-48 hours. Fee basis varies by type of transaction. Terms: net 15 days. They specialize in title abstracts and title insurance.

Margene Libertino Inc

11609 Bend Bow Dr, Fredericksburg, VA 22407-7491
Phone: 540-785-9930 **Fax:** 540-785-9933

Types of Records Retrieved: Civil courts; Real Estate; Tax liens/Judgments; UCC records

Local Retrieval Area: VA-Caroline, Fredericksburg City, King George, Spotsylvania, Stafford

Add'l Information: Established 1991. Normal turnaround time- 24-48 hours. Projects billed by number of names searched. Payment due upon receipt of invoice. Her pager number is 540-372-2165, 370-9228.

Liberty Corporate Services Inc

1040 Rock-N-Creek Rd, Leesville, SC 29070
Phone: 888-875-1280; 803-604-0264 **Fax:** 888-875-4223; 803-604-0834
libertycorp@starband.net

Types of Records Retrieved: Civil court; Probate Courts; fEderal Courts; Real Estate; UCC records; Tax liens/Judgments.

Local Retrieval Area: SC-all counties EXCEPT Allendale, Bamberg, Barnwell, Clarendon, Dillon, Edgefield, Marlboro, Williamsburg, Union. **Correspondent Relationships:** nationwide.

Add'l Information: Established 1995. Normal turnaround time- 1-5 days. Fee basis is by name and location by county. Credit accounts are accepted. They are a full service company with a UCC/Corporate division. Their real esate division handles filings, lost mortgage retrievals, and land record searches.

Liberty Record Search Inc

PO Box 3456, Parkersburg, WV 26101
Phone: 304-863-5542 **Fax:** 304-863-5670
www.libertyrecordsearch.com **email:** lrsinc@casinternet.net

Types of Records Retrieved: Real Estate; Tax liens/Judgments; UCC records

Local Retrieval Area: OH-Athens, Carroll, Columbiana, Gallia, Jefferson, Meigs, Washington; WV-Barbour, Berkeley, Boone, Braxton, Brooke, Cabell, Calhoun, Clay, Doddridge, Fayette, Gilmer, Greenbrier, Hancock, Harrison, Jackson, Jefferson, Kanawha, Lewis, Lincoln, Logan, McDowell, Marion, Marshall, Mason, Mercer, Mingo, Monongalia, Monroe, Morgan, Nicholas, Ohio, Pleasants, Pocahontas, Preston, Putnam, Raleigh, Randolph, Ritchie, Roane, Summers, Taylor, Tyler, Upshur, Wayne, Wetzel, Wirt, Wood, Wyoming

Add'l Information: Established 1992. Normal turnaround time- 24-48 hours depending on county of search. Projects billed by number of names searched. Billed monthly with net due the 15th. They specialize in property searches.

Liberty Record Search of NJ Inc

470 Ridgedale Ave #3, East Hanover, NJ 07936
Phone: 973-887-8808 **Fax:** 973-887-8801
lrsnj@optonline.net

Types of Records Retrieved: Civil courts; Probate courts; Real Estate; Tax liens/Judgments; UCC records

Local Retrieval Area: NJ-Atlantic, Bergen, Cumberland, Burlington, Camden, Cape May, Essex, Gloucester, Hudson, Hunterdon, Mercer, Middlesex, Monmouth, Morris, Ocean, Passaic, Salem, Somerset, Sussex, Union, Warren. **Correspondent Relationships:** statewide.

Add'l Information: Established 1996. Normal turnaround time- 24-48 hours. Projects billed by number of names searched. Monthly billing; net due by the 15th. The specialize in expert service with quick turnaround in all of New Jersey.

LIDA Credit Agency Inc

450 Sunrise Hwy, Rockville Centre, NY 11570
Phone: 516-678-4600 **Fax:** 516-678-4611

Types of Records Retrieved: Civil, criminal and probate courts; Federal courts; Real Estate; Tax liens/Judgments; UCC records; Vital records

Local Retrieval Area: NY-Nassau, Queens, Suffolk. **Correspondent Relationships:** nationwide.

Add'l Information: Established 1920. Normal turnaround time- 8-48 hours. Projects billed by number of records located. All projects require prepayment. Credit cards accepted. They specialize in public record research, background reports, commercial and individual, credit reports and general investigations. A licensed PI in NY. They perform service of process.

Lighthouse Information Service LLC

PO Box 242, 1025 Rose Creek Dr #620-212, Woodstock, GA 30189, Baxley, GA 31513
Phone: 912-367-5900; 678-574-5795 **Fax:** 912-366-9978; 770-529-2755
www.lighthouseinfoserv.com **email:** ebpeacock@lighthouseinfoserv.com

Types of Records Retrieved: Civil, criminal and probate courts; Real Estate; Tax liens/Judgments; UCC records; Vital records

Local Retrieval Area: GA-Bartow, Cherokee, Cobb, Fulton, Pickens

Add'l Information: Established 1998. Normal turnaround time- 24-48 hours. Projects billed by number of names searched. Projects billed by the hour. 1st project may require prepayment. Formerly G & P Holdings, they do document retrieval, abstracting, criminal/civil work throughout GA, NC and SC,

specializing in asset location, current address identification, judgment recovery/collection, and process service. They perform service of process.

Lightning Legal Services LLC

PO Box 9132, Albany, NY 12209
Phone: 518-463-1049 **Fax:** 518-463-3681
www.lightninglegal.info **email:** kgunner@lightninglegal.info

Types of Records Retrieved: Probate courts; Federal courts; Tax liens/Judgments; UCC records; Vital records

Local Retrieval Area: NY-Albany, Rensselaer, Saratoga, Schenectady. **Correspondent Relationships:** nationwide.

Add'l Information: Established 1993. Normal turnaround time- variable. Billing method depends on project. 1st project may require prepayment. Will file/record documents. They specialize in corporate services, including the preparation & filing of corporate documents in NY & other states. They have prompt reliable document filing and retrieval. Also NY UCC, tax lien searches, death records, and DMV. They perf20orm service of process.

Lightning Records Inc

341 Emmons, Wyandotte, MI 48192
Phone: 734-285-2495 **Fax:** 734-285-2809
lightning_records@yahoo.com

Types of Records Retrieved: Federal District courts; Real Estate; Tax liens/Judgments; UCC records

Local Retrieval Area: MI-Oakland, Washtenaw, Wayne

Add'l Information: Established 2001. Normal turnaround time- 24-48 hours. Projects billed by number of names searched. Call for payment information. This company is operated by an abstractor with over 13 years of experience in South East Michigan. Fast turnaround; reasonable prices.

Lincoln Abstract Co

PO Box 37, Star City, AR 71667
Phone: 870-628-3144 **Fax:** 870-628-3348
lincolnabstract@centurytel.net

Types of Records Retrieved: Real Estate; Tax liens/judgments; UCC records

Local Retrieval Area: AR-Lincoln. **Correspondent Relationships:** Bradley, Cleveland, Drew, Desha, Jefferson counties AR.

Add'l Information: Established 1930. Normal turnaround time- 48 hours. Projects billed by the hour. Billed by the job. All projects require prepayment. They are experts at Lincoln County, AR record books. They have the only title plant in Lincoln County, AR.

Lincoln County Abstract & Title Co (NM)

PO Box 2335, Ruidoso, NM 88355-2335
Phone: 800-635-4692; 505-258-5959 **Fax:** 505-258-9010
www.ruidoso.net/title **email:** lcatc@zianet.com

Types of Records Retrieved: Civil courts; Probate courts; Real Estate; Tax liens/Judgments; UCC records **Local Retrieval Area:** NM-Lincoln

Add'l Information: Established 1989. Normal turnaround time- variable depending on project. Projects billed by number of names searched. Projects billed by number of records located. They specialize in title insurance.

Lincoln Home Title (KS)

113 S 5th St, Lincoln, KS 67455
Phone: 785-524-4228 **Fax:** 785-524-3042
www.landhometitle.com

Types of Records Retrieved: Civil courts; Probate courts; Real Estate; Tax liens/Judgments; UCC records

Local Retrieval Area: KS-Lincoln

Add'l Information: Established 1935. Normal turnaround time- 2-3 days. Fee basis varies by type of transaction. 1st project may require prepayment. Formerly Lincoln County Abstract & Title Co.

Lincoln Inv Inc DBA Bay Point Legal Svc

820 Park Row #652, Salinas, CA 93901
Phone: 831-422-3007 **Fax:** 831-455-0848
baypointlegal@comcast.net

Types of Records Retrieved: Civil, criminal and probate courts; Real Estate; Tax liens/Judgments; UCC records Vital records

Local Retrieval Area: CA-Monterey. **Correspondent:** statewide.

Add'l Information: Established 1997. Normal turnaround time- 72 hours. Expedited service available. Projects billed by number of names searched. Projects billed by number of records located. Projects billed by the hour. 1st project may require prepayment. They are a full service investigative firm. They also are a full scale process service and document retrieval and research company. A licensed PI in CA. They perform service of process.

Lincoln Trail Title

2935 Dolphine #101, Elizabethtown, KY 42701
Phone: 270-765-5566 **Fax:** 270-769-3267

Types of Records Retrieved: Real Estate; Tax liens/Judgments

Local Retrieval Area: KY-Larue

Add'l Information: Established 1984. 1st project may require prepayment. They specialize in real estate.

Lincoln Trail Title Services Inc

PO Box 111, 2935 Dolphin Dr, Elizabethtown, KY 42702
Phone: 270-765-5566 **Fax:** 270-769-3267

Types of Records Retrieved: Civil courts; Probate courts; Real Estate; Tax liens/Judgments; UCC records

Local Retrieval Area: KY-Hardin

Add'l Information: Established 1986. Normal turnaround time- 3-5 days. Projects billed by the hour. 1st project may require prepayment.

Lincoln-Evans Advanced Land & Title

203 N 2nd Ave, Ozark, MO 65721-7450
Phone: 417-581-8251 **Fax:** 417-581-8280

Types of Records Retrieved: Real Estate; Tax liens/Judgments; UCC records

Local Retrieval Area: MO-Christian, Greene, Taney

Add'l Information: Established 1993. Normal turnaround time- 3 days. Projects billed by number of names searched. Projects billed by number of records located. They will accept cashiers checks. Terms are net 30 days. They specialize in title and escrow closings. The phone number for their Taney and Greene, MO office is 417-889-1818.

Lindsey and Suyak Inv LLC

PO Box 9537, Owensboro, KY 42302

Phone: 270-281-0213 **Fax:** 270-281-0311

Types of Records Retrieved: Civil, criminal and probate courts; Federal District courts; Real Estate, Tax liens/Judgments; UCC records

Local Retrieval Area: KY-Daviess, Hancock, Ohio

Add'l Information: Established 2001. Normal turnaround time- 24 hours. Projects billed by the hour. Occasionally there is a mileage charge. Will invoice net 20 days. They are a one-member LLC able to do investigations, surveillance and record checks. Will serve process. Has a BS degree in Criminal Justice and is retired Navy (legal). A licensed PI in KY. They perform service of process.

Linn County Abstract Co

PO Box 98, 108 S 5th St, Mound City, KS 66056

Phone: 888-795-2949; 913-795-2949 **Fax:** 913-795-2449

smitty1gar@earthlink.net

Types of Records Retrieved: Civil, criminal and probate courts; Real Estate; Tax liens/Judgments; UCC records **Local Retrieval Area:** KS-Linn

Add'l Information: Established 1973. Normal turnaround time- 1 day. Basis for fees varies by project.

Linn County Title

118 N Main St, Burkfield, MO 64628

Phone: 660-258-2260 **Fax:** 660-258-7287

Types of Records Retrieved: Real Estate; Tax liens/Judgments

Local Retrieval Area: MO-Linn

Add'l Information: Established 1976. 1st project may require prepayment. They specialize in real estate.

Liquori Investigations

6539 Turtlemound Rd, New Smyrna Beach, FL 32169

Phone: 386-423-4235 **Fax:** 386-428-9110 wliquori@cfl.rr.com

Types of Records Retrieved: Civil, criminal and probate courts; Federal courts; Real Estate; Tax liens/Judgments; UCC records; Vital records

Local Retrieval Area: FL-Orange, Seminole, Volusia

Add'l Information: Established 1987. Normal turnaround time- 24-48 hours. Projects billed by number of names searched. 1st project may require prepayment. A licensed PI in FL.

LLG Enterprises

911 N Birch Ct, Oak Grove, MO 64075

Phone: 816-443-2396 **Fax:** 816-433-2397

lgraves@llgenterprises.net

Types of Records Retrieved: Criminal courts; Federal courts

Local Retrieval Area: KS-Douglas, Johnson, Leavenworth, Sedgwick, Shawnee, Wyandotte; MO-Barton, Boone, Buchanan, Callaway, Clay, Cole, Franklin, Greene, Howell, Montgomery, Osage, Perry, Platte, St. Charles, Taney, Vernon. **Correspondent Relationships:** Kansas and Missouri statewide criminal record repository.

Add'l Information: Established 1997. Normal turnaround time- 24-36 hours. Projects billed by number of names searched. Projects billed by the hour. 1st project may require prepayment. End of month billing due in 14 days. They specialize in hands-on county criminal and civil research, also federal criminal/civil and bankruptcy research. They have access to the Federal Archives for KS, MO, NE, IA, NY, NJ, PR & VI. They visit each courthouse daily. 24-hour turnaround.

Locke-Neosho Abstracts Inc

PO Box 178, 219 S Main, Erie, KS 66733

Phone: 620-244-3641 **Fax:** 620-244-3234

Types of Records Retrieved: Civil courts; Probate courts; Real Estate; Tax liens/Judgments; UCC records

Local Retrieval Area: KS-Neosho

Add'l Information: Established 1992. Normal turnaround time- up to 1 week. Fee basis varies by type of transaction. They request prepayment from out of area clients.

Logan County Abstract Co

Box C, Napoleon, ND 58561 **Phone:** 701-754-2200

Types of Records Retrieved: Civil courts; Real Estate; Tax liens/Judgments; UCC records **Local Retrieval Area:** ND-Logan

Add'l Information: Normal turnaround time- 1-2 days. Projects billed by number of records located.

Logan Registration Service Inc

PO Box 161644, Sacramento, CA 95816

Phone: 916-457-5787 **Fax:** 800-524-4111; 916-457-5789

www.loganreg.com **email:** joan@loganreg.com

Types of Records Retrieved: UCCs, Corporate records

Local Retrieval Area: CA-Sacramento. **Correspondent Relationships:** state of California; nationwide DMV records.

Add'l Information: Established 1976. Normal turnaround time- 24-48 hours. Online immediately. Projects billed by number of names searched. Terms: net 30 days. Court records are online only. They specialize in all types of California DMV records, online and manual access. Also, manual retrieval of UCC and Sec of State records . They also obtain DMV records from most of the US.

Lone Star Inv & Recovery Inc

PO Box 701688, Dallas, TX 75370

Phone: 800-887-3890; 972-774-0037 **Fax:** 972-774-9612

Types of Records Retrieved: Civil and criminal courts; Probate coursts; Federal courts; Real Estate; Tax liens/Judgments; UCC and vital records

Local Retrieval Area: TX-Collin, Dallas, Denton, Tarrant. **Correspondent Relationships:** Travis and Williamson counties TX.

Add'l Information: Established 1996. Normal turnaround time- 24-48 hours. May search by either number of names or by number of records located. 1st project may require prepayment. Will bill. They are a licensed private investigator with 25-plus years banking/financial experience, and record research and asset lien searches. A licensed PI in TX.

Lone Star Legal

340 Division St, San Francisco, CA 94103-4810

Phone: 415-255-8550 **Fax:** 415-255-8549

www.lonestarlegal.com **email:** jay@lonestarlegal.com

Types of Records Retrieved: Civil, criminal and probate courts; Federal courts; Real Estate; Tax liens/Judgments; UCC records; Vital records

Local Retrieval Area: CA-Alameda, San Francisco, San Mateo

Add'l Information: Established 1989. Normal turnaround time- 2 days. Projects billed by the hour. 1st project may require prepayment. Credit cards accepted. They specialize in complex and routine court research, complete litigation copying and on-site copying. Large volume specialists. We also offer scanning, imaging and digital printing.

Lorain County Title Co

424 Middle Ave, Elyria, OH 44035

Phone: 440-284-5100 **Fax:** 440-284-5161

www.lctc.com **email:** lctc@lctc.com

Types of Records Retrieved: Civil courts; Probate courts; Federal courts; Real Estate; Tax liens/Judgments; UCC records; Vital records

Local Retrieval Area: OH-Cuyahoga, Erie, Lorain

Add'l Information: Established 1952. Normal turnaround time- 3 days. Projects billed by number of names searched. Fee basis varies by type of transaction. 1st project may require prepayment. Payment due upon delivery, terms are net 10 days.

Lord Investigations, LLC

PO Box 2509, Eagle, ID 83616-9118
Phone: 208-939-4040 **Fax:** 208-422-0480
lordinvestigative@msn.com

Types of Records Retrieved: Civil, criminal and probate courts; Federal courts; UCC records

Local Retrieval Area: ID-Ada, Boise, Canyon, Elmore, Gem, Valley, Washington

Add'l Information: Established 1990. Normal turnaround time- 72 hours. Projects billed by the hour. They specialize in civil and criminal investigations (plaintiff and defense), sub rosa surveillance, locates and security consulting. . A licensed PI in ID & UT. Perform service of process.

Los Angeles County Document Services Inc

1914 N Verdugo Rd #6, Glendale, CA 91208
Phone: 818-241-1990 **Fax:** 818-550-1509 glenn@ladocs.biz

Types of Records Retrieved: Real Estate; Tax liens/Judgments

Local Retrieval Area: CA-Los Angeles, Orange, Riverside, San Bernardino, San Diego, Ventura

Add'l Information: Established 2001. Normal turnaround time- 24 hours. Projects billed by number of names searched. Payment due net 30 days. They specialize in 100% accurate title/current owner searches. They do document retrieval and recordings in Los Angeles, San Bernardino, Riverside, Orange, San Diego and Ventura counties.

Loss Prevention Associates Inc

9550 Warner Ave #250, Fountain Valley, CA 92708
Phone: 714-593-2323 **Fax:** 714-593-2383
www.lpassociates.com **email:** bkelsheimer@lpassociates.com

Types of Records Retrieved: Civil, criminal, probate courts; Federal courts

Local Retrieval Area: CA-Los Angeles, Orange, Riverside, San Bernardino, San Diego. **Correspondent Relationships:** nationwide.

Add'l Information: Established 1995. Normal turnaround time- 24-48 hours. Projects billed by number of names searched. Credit cards accepted. Will bill monthly/bi-monthly. Loss Prevention Associates is a nationwide leader in security consulting, investigations and pre-employment/tenant background screening. They can provide their clients a decisive advantage in the business world. A licensed PI in CA.

Lowery Professional Services Corp

1809 N Linwood Ave, Appleton, WI 54914-2404
Phone: 920-830-2114

Types of Records Retrieved: Civil, criminal and probate courts; Federal courts; Real Estate; Tax liens/Judgments; UCC records; Vital records

Local Retrieval Area: WI-Brown, Outagamie, Winnebago

Add'l Information: Established 1985. Normal turnaround time- 1-4 days depending on project. Expedited service available. Projects billed by number of names searched. Projects billed by number of records located. 1st project may require prepayment. They provide physical searches and retrieval of public records at city, county, state and federal locations. They also provide court filings and service of documents, skip tracing, property verification, pre-employment screenings and database searches. They perform service of process.

Lowry Document Service

2384 Statler Terrace, Deltona, FL 32738
Phone: 386-789-6193 **Fax:** 386-789-3801 milow4@joimail.com

Types of Records Retrieved: Civil, criminal and probate courts; Real Estate; Tax liens/Judgments; UCC records; Vital records

Local Retrieval Area: FL-Flagler, Orange, Seminole, Volusia

Add'l Information: Established 1995. Normal turnaround time- 24-48 hours. Projects billed by number of names searched. They have a paralegal background and have a notary service.

LT Marketing LLC

PO Box 530934, Livonia, MI 48153-0934
Phone: 313-361-2468 **Fax:** 313-361-5857 ltmarketing001@yahoo.com

Types of Records Retrieved: Criminal courts; Federal Bankruptcy courts

Local Retrieval Area: MI-Oakland, Wayne

Add'l Information: Established 1987. Normal turnaround time- same day in Wayne County; 24-48 hours elsewhere. Projects billed by number of names searched. Same day results in Wayne County MI if received by 10 AM; 24 hours otherwise. All returns come with docket printout and summary explanation from the official MI penal code book. Also does statewide felony & misdemeanor records in Michigan.

Lueken Document Research Inc

9864 Diamond Point Dr, St Louis, MO 63123
Phone: 314-631-5928 **Fax:** 314-638-8082 LuekenDoc@earthlink.net

Types of Records Retrieved: Civil, criminal and probate courts; Federal courts; Real Estate; Tax liens/Judgments; UCC records; Vital records

Local Retrieval Area: MO-St. Louis, St. Louis City

Add'l Information: Established 1983. Normal turnaround time- next day. Same day for filings. Projects billed by number of names searched. They specialize in checks for EPA and ERISA liens.

Lutek Investigations LLC

PO Box 161, Hartford, CT 06141
Phone: 860-729-3310 **Fax:** 860-216-1754
www.lutekpi.com **email:** sitek@lutekpi.com

Types of Records Retrieved: Civil and criminal courts; Federal District courts; Real Estate; Tax liens.judgments; UCC records; Vital records

Local Retrieval Area: CT-Hartford, Middlesex, Tolland. **Correspondent Relationships:** New Haven, Fairfield, CT counties.

Add'l Information: Established 2002. Normal turnaround time- within 48 hours. Expedited service available. Projects billed by number of names searched. Projects billed by the hour. 1st project may require prepayment. They are a full service detective agency available to retrieve records within their work territory. A licensed PI in CT. They perform service of process.

Lyman County Title Co

PO Box 187, Kennebec, SD 57544
Phone: 605-869-2269 **Fax:** 605-869-2236

Types of Records Retrieved: Civil courts; Probate courts; Real Estate; Tax liens/Judgments; UCC records

Local Retrieval Area: SD-Lyman

Add'l Information: Normal turnaround time- up to 2 weeks. Fee basis varies by type of transaction. They specialize in land records.

Lynch Abstracting

PO Box 129, Bloomfield, IA 52537
Phone: 641-664-3188 **Fax:** 641-664-3186

Types of Records Retrieved: Civil, criminal and probate courts; Real Estate; Tax liens/Judgments; Vital records

Local Retrieval Area: IA-Davis

Add'l Information: Established 1975. Normal turnaround time- 3-4 days. Fee basis will vary by the type of project. They specialize in title searches on real estate and personal lien searches in Davis County.

Lynne J Cox Paralegal

1631 Fisher St, Munster, IN 46321
Phone: 800-510-3009; 219-838-1890 **Fax:** 800-510-3009; 219-838-1890
LegaLynne1@msn.com

Types of Records Retrieved: Civil, criminal and probate courts; Federal courts; Real Estate; Tax liens/Judgments; UCC records

Local Retrieval Area: IL-Cook; IN-Lake. **Correspondent Relationships:** Lake, DeKalb, DuPage, Kane, Kendall, McHenry, IL; Porter, LaPorte, Marion, IN.

Add'l Information: Established 1997. Normal turnaround time- 24-48 hours. Projects billed by number of names searched. As trained and credentialed paralegals, they provide on-site court and county record searches which are accurate, timely and meet the highest legal and ethical standards.

Lyon County Title Co Inc

109 S Marshall St, Rock Rapids, IA 51246
Phone: 712-472-3758 **Fax:** 712-472-3758

Types of Records Retrieved: Probate courts; Real Estate; Tax liens/Judgments **Local Retrieval Area:** IA-Lyon

Add'l Information: Normal turnaround time- 1-3 days. Fee basis will vary by the type of project. 1st project may require prepayment.

M

M & D Records Research

648 Forsythe, Toledo, OH 43605
Phone: 419-693-5649 **Fax:** 419-693-4211
mdrecordsresearch@buckeye-express.com

Types of Records Retrieved: Civil, criminal and probate courts; Federal courts; Real Estate; Tax liens/Judgments; UCC records; Vital records

Local Retrieval Area: OH-Lucas, Wood

Add'l Information: Established 1990. Normal turnaround time- 24-48 hours. Projects billed by number of names searched. Projects billed by number of records located. Charges are quoted by job.

M & J Abstractors

416 Hillcrest Ct, Lansing, KS 66043
Phone: 913-727-3588 **Fax:** 913-351-0175
jmenzel1@kc.rr.com

Types of Records Retrieved: Civil courts; Probate courts; Federal Distrcit courts; Real Estate, Tax liens/Judgments, UCC records

Local Retrieval Area: KS-Johnson, Leavenworth; MO-Clay, Jackson, Platte

Add'l Information: Established 1999. Normal turnaround time- 24-72 hours. Projects billed by number of names searched. 1st project may require prepayment. They specialize in accurate searches in a timely manner. Please feel free to contact their company with any questions.

M & M Legal Services

PO Box 364, La Grande, OR 97850
Phone: 541-963-8219 **Fax:** 541-963-8219

Types of Records Retrieved: Civil, criminal and probate courts; Real Estate; Tax liens/Judgments; Vital records

Local Retrieval Area: OR-Baker, Union, Wallowa

Add'l Information: Established 1979. Normal turnaround time- 1 day for Union County; 1-2 days for Baker County; 4 days for Wallowa County. Projects billed by the hour. They request prepayment from out of state clients, but will invoice established customers. A licensed PI in OR. They perform service of process.

M & M Search Service

17 W Jefferson St #007, Rockville, MD 20850-4201
Phone: 301-251-9545 **Fax:** 301-251-6785
www.mandmsearchservice.com **email:** info@mandmsearchservice.com

Types of Records Retrieved: Civil courts; Probate courts; Federal courts; Real Estate; Tax liens/Judgments; UCC records; Vital records

Local Retrieval Area: DC-District of Columbia; MD-Montgomery, Prince George's. **Correspondent Relationships:** DC area.

Add'l Information: Established 1985. Normal turnaround time- 8 hours for court records and UCCs. Full 60-year real estate search: 2 to 3 days. They charge by the hour for Commercial searches only. They charge by the property or address 1st project may require prepayment. Credit cards accepted. A full-service real estate title and abstract company, they specialize in real estate and UCC searches.

M & M Title / Mitchell Co

2412 E 70th St, Shreveport, LA 71105
Phone: 318-798-1198 **Fax:** 318-798-1191

Types of Records Retrieved: Civil courts; Probate courts; Real Estate; Tax liens/Judgments; UCC records

Local Retrieval Area: LA-Bienville Parish, Bossier Parish, Caddo Parish, Claiborne Parish, De Soto Parish, Lincoln Parish, Webster Parish; TX-Cass, Harrison, Henderson, Marion, Panola, Rusk, Shelby, Smith. **Correspondent Relationships:** Southern Louisiana.

Add'l Information: Established 1960. Normal turnaround time- variable, depending on project. Projects billed by the hour. 1st project may require prepayment. Formerly DeSoto Abstract, they specialize in oil, gas and environmental assessment.

M & M Title Services

42 Inkberry Tr, Narraqansett, RI 02882
Phone: 413-374-0158 **Fax:** 401-284-0101 mbmann1@juno.com

Types of Records Retrieved: Probate courts; Real Estate; Tax liens/Judgments; UCC records

Local Retrieval Area: MA-Franklin, Hampden, Hampshire, Worcester

Add'l Information: Established 1976. Normal turnaround time- 24-48 hours. Projects billed by number of names searched. 1st project may require prepayment. She is a real estate title abstractor, document retrieval of records at Registry of Deeds and probate abstracting.

M C Associates

766 Robinhood Dr, Newark, OH 43055
Phone: 740-366-1922 **Fax:** 740-366-1922 mmcordova@yahoo.com

Types of Records Retrieved: Civil, criminal and probate courts; Federal courts; Real Estate; Tax liens/Judgments; UCC records; Vital records

Local Retrieval Area: OH-Delaware, Fairfield, Franklin, Hamilton, Knox, Licking, Montgomery, Muskingum, Pickaway, Ross, Union

Add'l Information: Established 1994. Normal turnaround time- 24-48 hours. Expedited service available. Projects billed by number of names searched. They specialize in real property searches, document retrieval, real property tax, and property ownership verification. They also do federal and state tax liens, mortgages and judgments. They perform service of process.

M L Cozart Copy Service (dba: Quality Business Information)

PO Box 580666, Elk Grove, CA 95758-0012
Phone: 916-691-9685 **Fax:** 916-691-9645 qbinfocoy@aol.com

Types of Records Retrieved: Civil and criminal courts

Local Retrieval Area: CA-Amador, Calaveras, El Dorado, Napa, Placer, Sacramento, San Joaquin, Solano, Stanislaus, Yolo; NV-Washoe. **Correspondent Relationships:** Butte, Glenn, Lassen, Merced, Plumas, Shasta, Siskiyou, Sutter, Tehama, Tuolumne, Yuba, Fresno, Tulare, Kings, Madera, Monterrey, Santa Cruz, San Benito, San Luis Obispo, Sonoma, Humboldt, Mariposa, Nevada, San Diego, other counties in CA, OR & WA.

Add'l Information: Established 1991. Normal turnaround time- 24-48 hours. Projects billed by number of names searched. Customers are billed at the end of the month. They have over fifty years experience in court record retrieval. Many counties are searched by state licensed private investigators A licensed PI in CA (dba: Quality Business Information).

M R Search Co LLC

PO Box 692, Barnegat, NJ 08005
Phone: 732 462 6108 **Fax:** 732-210-0424
www.mrsearchcompany.com **email:** markruss@comcast.net

Types of Records Retrieved: Probate courts; Real Estate; UCC records

Local Retrieval Area: NJ-Monmouth, Ocean

Add'l Information: Normal turnaround time- same day. They specialize in complex projects in Momnouth and Ocean Counties. They offer same day service on all searches except for time intensive projects. Guaranteed service. All searches are done same day or it's free.

Mach 5 Couriers Inc

1201 Louisiana #210, Houston, TX 77002

Phone: 800-593-2023; 713-754-8239, 713-754-8244 **Fax:** 713-655-1219

www.mach5couriers.com **email:** james@mach5couriers.com

Types of Records Retrieved: Civil and criminal courts; Federal courts

Local Retrieval Area: TX-Brazoria, Chambers, Fort Bend, Galveston, Harris, Jefferson, Montgomery, Waller

Add'l Information: Established 1985. Normal turnaround time- 24-48 hours. 1st project may require prepayment. They also specialize in courier service, 24/7. They perform service of process.

MacIntire & Associates (Tucson)

531 W Plata #200, Tucson, AZ 85705

Phone: 800-641-2737; 520-622-2737 **Fax:** 888-882-5205; 520-792-2764

www.macintireandassociates.com

email: info@macintireandassociates.com

Types of Records Retrieved: Civil, criminal and probate courts; Federal courts; Tax liens/Judgments; UCC records

Local Retrieval Area: AZ-Cochise, Maricopa, Pima. **Correspondent Relationships:** nationwide and international.

Add'l Information: Established 1979. Normal turnaround time- 48 hours. Expedited service available. Projects billed by number of names searched. Projects billed by the hour. Prepayment required for volume requests. 1st project may require prepayment. Credit cards accepted. Payment is a flat fee and due upon completion. They have extensive background in criminal defense, personal injury, surveillance and employment screening services. A licensed PI in AZ.

Mackinac Abstract & Title

291 Stockbridge, PO Box 322, St Ignace, MI 49781

Phone: 906-643-7452 **Fax:** 906-643-0026

Types of Records Retrieved: Probate courts; Real Estate; Tax liens/Judgments **Local Retrieval Area:** MI-Chippewa, Luce, Mackinac

Add'l Information: Established 1979. Normal turnaround time- 7-10 business days. Fee basis will vary by type of project. They specialize in real estate and tax record searches, title insurance and abstracts of title.

Macon County Title

PO Box 562, Macon, MO 63552-0562

Phone: 660-385-6474 **Fax:** 660-385-6629

Types of Records Retrieved: Civil courts; Probate courts; Real Estate; Tax liens/Judgments; UCC records; Vital records

Local Retrieval Area: MO-Macon

Add'l Information: Normal turnaround time- next day. Projects billed by number of names searched. Formerly A Verne Baker Abstract Co, they specialize in title searches.

Madrona Research Inc

PO Box 29001, Bellingham, WA 98228

Phone: 360-647-8126 **Fax:** 360-650-0819

marlenesmi@comcast.net

Types of Records Retrieved: Civil, criminal and probate courts; Real Estate; Tax liens/Judgments; UCC records; Vital records

Local Retrieval Area: MT-Gallatin; WA-Island, Skagit, Whatcom

Add'l Information: Established 1994. Normal turnaround time- 24 hours. They specialize in court access, including approved access as a confidential intermediary service to sealed adoption records. They also provide real estate owner reports and lien/judgment searches on a regular basis.

Maggie M & Associates

2 Bordeaux Ct, Petaluma, CA 94954

Phone: 707-778-7304 **Fax:** 707-762-3282

maggiemassoc@comcast.ent

Types of Records Retrieved: Civil courts; Federal courts; Real Estate; Tax liens/Judgments; UCC records **Local Retrieval Area:** CA-Sonoma

Add'l Information: Established 1996. Normal turnaround time- 24-48 hours. Projects billed by number of names searched. 1st project may require prepayment. She specializes in UCC, tax liens, judgments and bulk real estate and new business filings in most bay area counties. Page her for rush orders (707-541-9253).

Magic P I & Security Inc

PO Box 19938, Kalamazoo, MI 49019-0938

Phone: 800-362-4388; 269-381-7772 **Fax:** 269-381-2324

dmagett@aol.com

Types of Records Retrieved: Civil, criminal and probate courts; Real Estate; Tax liens/Judgments; UCC records; Vital records

Local Retrieval Area: MI-Barry, Berrien, Calhoun, Cass, Kalamazoo, St Joseph, Van Buren

Add'l Information: Established 1983. Normal turnaround time- 48-72 hours. Projects billed by the hour. 1st project may require prepayment. They specialize in civil process and private investigations. A licensed PI in MI. They perform service of process.

Mahaska Title - Johnson Abstract Co

121 High Ave E, Oskaloosa, IA 52577

Phone: 641-673-5666 **Fax:** 641-673-9224

www.mtja.net **email:** mtja@mtja.net

Types of Records Retrieved: Civil, criminal and probate courts; Real Estate; Tax liens/Judgments; UCC records; Vital records

Local Retrieval Area: IA-Mahaska

Add'l Information: Established 1980. Normal turnaround time- 1-2 days. Also billed according to assessed value and flat rates. 1st project may require prepayment. The Mahaska Title Johnson Abstract staff has 80+ years of experience and provides the best service in Mahaska County. Also includes full service closing department.

Mahnomen County Abstract Co

103 E Monroe Ave, Mahnomen, MN 56557

Phone: 218-935-5227 **Fax:** 218-935-5227*51

Types of Records Retrieved: Real Estate

Local Retrieval Area: MN-Mahnomen

Add'l Information: Established 1987. Normal turnaround time- 48 hours. Projects billed by number of names searched. Projects billed by number of records located. Will send invoice. They specialize in title searches, owner and encumbrance reports, registered property abstracts and continuation of existing abstracts and preparation of new abstracts.

Maine Public Record Services

PO Box 514, Moody, ME 04054

Phone: 207-646-9065 **Fax:** 207-646-9065 mepub@verizon.net

Types of Records Retrieved: Civil, criminal and probate courts; Federal District courts; Real Estate; Tax liens/Judgments; UCC records

Local Retrieval Area: ME-Cumberland, York; NH-Strafford

Add'l Information: Established 1993. Normal turnaround time- 24-48 hours. Terms net 30 days. They specialize in document retrieval, current owner reports, recording/bringdown services and UCC searchs. All services provided in Maine. Call or email for services provided in NH. Retainer programs available.

Mainline Researchers Inc

PO Box 741, 213 S Center St (15931), Ebensburg, PA 15931-0741

Phone: 814-472-7913 **Fax:** 814-472-7936

Types of Records Retrieved: Civil and criminal courts; Real Estate; Tax liens/Judgments; UCC records

Local Retrieval Area: PA-Cambria. **Correspondent Relationships:** most counties in Western Pennsylvania.

Add'l Information: Established 1971. Normal turnaround time- 24 hours. 60 year title searches take longer. Projects billed by number of names searched. Charges vary depending on type of search. Billed monthly; terms are net 10 days.

Majestic Research Services Inc

1290 Kennestone Cir Bldg D #213, Marietta, GA 30066
Phone: 678-355-5393 **Fax:** 678-355-6762

Types of Records Retrieved: Probate courts, Real Estate, Tax liens/Judgments; UCC records

Local Retrieval Area: GA-Bartow, Cherokee, Clayton, Cobb, Coweta, DeKalb, Douglas, Fulton, Fayette, Gwinnett, Henry, Paulding

Add'l Information: Established 2000. Normal turnaround time- 24-48 hours. Projects billed by number of names searched. Payment terms net 30 days.

Johanna E Malki

11041 NE 10th Ave, Biscayne Park, FL 33161
Phone: 305-899-0273 **Fax:** 305-899-2092 bdrfl@mindspring.com

Types of Records Retrieved: Civil courts; Probate courts; Federal courts; Real Estate; Tax liens/Judgments; UCC records

Local Retrieval Area: FL-Broward, Dade, Palm Beach

Add'l Information: Established 1995. Normal turnaround time- 24-48 hours. Projects billed by number of names searched. 1st project may require prepayment. She is a Notary Public in the State of Florida since 1971.

Malloy & Company Inc dba Judicial Courier

34 W Franklin, Tucson, AZ 85701
Phone: 520-792-0250 **Fax:** 520-917-0520
www.judicialcouries.com **email:** craig@judicialcouries.com

Types of Records Retrieved: Civil, criminal and probate courts; Federal courts; Real Estate; Tax liens/Judgments; UCC records; Vital records

Local Retrieval Area: AZ-Pima. **Correspondent Relationships:** statewide.

Add'l Information: Established 1987. Normal turnaround time- 48 hours. Expedited service available. Projects billed by the hour. 1st project may require prepayment. They specialize in process serving, court running and skip tracing. They perform service of process.

Management Information Services

1836 W 25th St #2A, Cleveland, OH 44113-3152
Phone: 216-241-4282 **Fax:** 216-241-3227
www.managementinfoservices.com
email: mis@managementinfoservices.com

Types of Records Retrieved: Civil and criminal courts; US District courts

Local Retrieval Area: OH-Ashtabula, Cuyahoga, Geauga, Lake, Lorain. **Correspondent Relationships:** nationwide.

Add'l Information: Established 1995. Normal turnaround time- 1-4 days. Projects billed by number of names searched. Net 30 days. They specialize in pre-employment screening. Services include: criminal checks, employment verification and Ohio drivers license.

Manistee Abstract & Title Co

63 Maple St, Manistee, MI 49660
Phone: 231-723-3397 **Fax:** 231-723-5382

Types of Records Retrieved: Civil, criminal and probate courts; Real Estate; Tax liens/Judgments; UCC records; Vital records

Local Retrieval Area: MI-Manistee

Add'l Information: Established 1947. Normal turnaround time- 3-5 days. Fee basis will vary by type of project. All projects require prepayment. They will also invoice. They specialize in real estate.

Patsy Maranville

PO Box 707, Benkelman, KS 69021
Phone: 785-426-2725 pmm@bwtelcom.com

Types of Records Retrieved: Civil, criminal and probate courts.

Local Retrieval Area: KS-Cheyenne; NE-Chase, Dundy, Hitchcock

Add'l Information: Normal turnaround time- 2 days. Projects billed by number of names searched. All projects require prepayment. She specializes court records in remote SW Nebraska and far NW Kansas area near Kansas/Nebraska border.

Marias Title Company

PO Box 589, Shelby, MT 59474-0589
Phone: 406-434-5156 **Fax:** 406-434-5157 title@3rivers.net

Types of Records Retrieved: Civil courts; Probate courts; Real Estate; Tax liens/Judgments; UCC records; Vital records

Local Retrieval Area: MT-Liberty, Toole

Add'l Information: Established 1915. Normal turnaround time- 8 days. Projects billed by the hour. All projects require prepayment. They will file/record UCC and real estate documents on behalf of clients if filing fees are included with the request, payable to the County.

Maricopa Research

12467 W Palm Ln, Avondale, AZ 85323
Phone: 623-935-0572 **Fax:** 623-535-4197 lilmel89@yahoo.com

Types of Records Retrieved: Civil courts; Federal Bankruptcy courts; Real Estate; Tax liens/Judgments; UCC records; Vital records

Local Retrieval Area: AZ-Maricopa

Add'l Information: Established 1999. Normal turnaround time- 3-5 days. Projects billed by the hour. 1st project may require prepayment.

Marietta Abstract Co

PO Box 287, 305 W Main St, Marietta, OK 73448
Phone: 580-276-2231 **Fax:** 580-276-2771

Types of Records Retrieved: Civil courts; Probate courts; Real Estate; Tax liens/Judgments; UCC records; Vital records

Local Retrieval Area: OK-Love

Add'l Information: Established 1906. Normal turnaround time- varied by project. Projects billed by the hour. All projects require prepayment.

Marilyn Smolinsky & Associates

705 Battalion Dr, Stony Point, NY 10980-2447
Phone: 845-634-5770 **Fax:** 845-634-5791
marilynsmolinsky@aol.com

Types of Records Retrieved: Civil, criminal and probate courts; Real Estate; UCC records

Local Retrieval Area: NY-Rockland

Add'l Information: Established 1988. Normal turnaround time- 24 hours. Projects billed by number of names searched. Payment due upon delivery. They specialize in property searches for title insurance companies. They perform title and witness only closings, document retrieval and filings. In business since 1988.

Marion County Abstract Co (Arkansas)

PO Box 388, Yellville, AR 72687
Phone: 870-449-4218 **Fax:** 870-449-4220

Types of Records Retrieved: Civil, criminal and probate courts; Real Estate; Tax liens/Judgments; UCC records **Local Retrieval Area:** AR-Marion

Add'l Information: Established 1967. Normal turnaround time- 24-72 hours. Fee basis will vary by type of project. All projects require prepayment. They have more than 35 years experience in real estate.

Marion County Abstract Co (Missouri)

PO Box 2, Palmyra, MO 63461
Phone: 800-952-5314; 573-769-2212 **Fax:** 573-769-4916
harla@marioncountyabstract.com

Types of Records Retrieved: Civil, criminal and probate courts; Real Estate; Tax liens/Judgments; UCC records; Vital records

Local Retrieval Area: IL-Adams, Hancock, Pike; MO-Clark, Lewis, Macon, Marion, Monroe, Pike, Ralls, Shelby

Add'l Information: Established 1900. Normal turnaround time- 4-5 days. Fee basis will vary by the type of project. Invoice sent with report. Payment due upon completion They specialize in title insurance, title searches and abstracting.

Marion County Title Services

303 S 2nd St, Knoxville, IA 50138-2212
Phone: 641-842-3518 **Fax:** 641-842-3528

Types of Records Retrieved: Civil, criminal and probate courts; Real Estate; Tax liens/Judgments; UCC records; Vital records

Local Retrieval Area: IA-Marion

Add'l Information: Established 1902. Normal turnaround time- 1-2 days. Fee basis varies by type of transaction. 1st project may require prepayment.

Theresa Marrinan

117 Cross Main, Springfield, KY 40069
Phone: 859-336-5425 **Fax:** 859-336-5408

Types of Records Retrieved: Real Estate; Tax liens/Judgments

Local Retrieval Area: KY-Washington

Add'l Information: 1st project may require prepayment. She specializes in real estate; works on a limited basis only. After hours phone: 859-336-3581

Marshall County Abstract Co

PO Box 50, Madill, OK 73446
Phone: 580-795-7388 **Fax:** 580-795-7389

Types of Records Retrieved: Real Estate

Local Retrieval Area: OK-Carter, Johnston, Marshall

Add'l Information: Established 1920. Normal turnaround time- 2 days. Fee basis will vary by the type of project. 1st project may require prepayment. They only retrieve court records from Johnston, Marshall and Love counties.

Marshall County Abstract Company

23 S Center St, Marshalltown, IA 50158-2850
Phone: 641-752-5358 **Fax:** 641-754-1763

Types of Records Retrieved: Civil, criminal and probate courts; Federal courts; Real Estate; Tax liens/Judgments; UCC records; Vital records

Local Retrieval Area: IA-Marshall

Add'l Information: Established 1950. Normal turnaround time- 2 days. Fee basis will vary by type of project.

Marshall Land & Title Co Inc

PO Box 898, Britton, SD 57430
Phone: 605-448-5796 **Fax:** 605-448-2894
mlt@venturecomm.net

Types of Records Retrieved: Civil, criminal and probate courts; Real Estate; Tax liens/Judgments; UCC records; Vital records

Local Retrieval Area: SD-Marshall

Add'l Information: Established 1894. Normal turnaround time- 3-4 days. Fee basis is based on evaluation of project. 1st project may require prepayment. They specialize in abstracts, title insurance, and real estate transaction closings.

Martin Abstract Co (Warren)

PO Box 970, Warren, AR 71671
Phone: 870-226-7487 **Fax:** 870-226-2685

Types of Records Retrieved: Civil, criminal and probate courts; Real Estate; Tax liens/Judgments; UCC records

Local Retrieval Area: AR-Bradley, Cleveland

Add'l Information: Established 1965. Normal turnaround time- up to 7 days. Projects billed by number of names searched. 1st project may require prepayment. Credit cards accepted. They specialize in title insurance and record checks.

Martin Title & Closing Services

602 Dequeen St, Mena, AR 71953
Phone: 479-394-1963 **Fax:** 479-394-1995

Types of Records Retrieved: Civil, criminal and probate courts; Real Estate; Tax liens/Judgments; UCC records **Local Retrieval Area:** AR-Polk

Add'l Information: Established 1904. Normal turnaround time- 2-3 days. Fee basis will vary by the type of project. 1st project may require prepayment.

Marx Information Service Inc

118 1/2 N Woodland Blvd. #2, Deland, FL 32720
Phone: 386-740-7122 **Fax:** 386-734-3613
marxinfo@bellsouth.net

Types of Records Retrieved: Civil, criminal and probate courts; US District Court; UCC records; Real Estate; Vital Records; Tax liens/Judgments

Local Retrieval Area: FL- Volusia. **Correspondent Relationships:** Florida statewide.

Add'l Information: Established 1996. Normal turnaround time- 24 hours on average. Billing depends on quantity. 1st project may require prepayment. They also cover all of Florida.

Mary Lindsey Research

11643 Pride Port Hudson Rd, Zachary, LA 70791
Phone: 225-654-6576 **Fax:** 225-658-0029 maryblindsey@cs.com

Types of Records Retrieved: Civil courts; Federal courts

Local Retrieval Area: LA-East Baton Rouge, West Baton Rouge, West Feliciana

Add'l Information: Established 1984. Normal turnaround time- 24 hours. Projects billed by the hour. 1st project may require prepayment. She is a research librarian who specializes in online database, Internet, and library research. She can provide LA state agency records, e.g.. DEQ, Dept of Natural Resources, and LA Public Service Commission.

Maryland Abstract Services LLC

9928 Old Ocean City Blvd #9, Berlin, MD 21811-1170
Phone: 410-641-2298 **Fax:** 410-641-0437 marylandabstract@aol.com

Types of Records Retrieved: Civil courts; Real Estate; Tax liens/Judgments; UCC records

Local Retrieval Area: MD-Anne Arundel, Baltimore, Baltimore City, Calvert, Caroline, Carroll, Cecil, Charles, Dorchester, Frederick, Harford, Howard, Kent, Montgomery, Prince George's, Queen Anne's, St Mary's Somerset, Talbot, Washington, Wicomico, Worcester. **Correspondent Relationships:** Maryland. Delaware, New Jersey, all Northern Virginia counties.

Add'l Information: Established 1994. Normal turnaround time- 1-3 days. Prices vary by type of search. Commercial searches are charged by the hour. 1st project may require prepayment. Payment due when records are sent. They specialize in residential and commercial title searches, also document retrievals, UCCs, and judgment searches. Fast turnaround and competitive prices.

Maryland Research & Abstract Co

25 W Chesapeake Ave #214, Baltimore, MD 21204-4820
Phone: 410-823-1944 **Fax:** 410-823-7254 mrac@radicus.net

Types of Records Retrieved: Civil courts; Probate courts; Real Estate; UCC records

Local Retrieval Area: MD-Baltimore, Harford

Add'l Information: Established 1989. Normal turnaround time- 1 week. Projects billed by number of names searched. Fee may be charged per property. They specialize in real estate title searches.

Mask Research Services

PO Box 1499, Granite Falls, WA 98252
Phone: 425-377-1780 **Fax:** 360-691-2078
stemarkl@msn.com

Types of Records Retrieved: Civil courts; Real Estate; Tax liens/Judgments; UCC records

Local Retrieval Area: WA-Island

Add'l Information: Established 2000. Normal turnaround time- 48 hours. Projects billed by number of names searched. Projects billed by number of records located. Fees negotiated with volume. They specialize in real estate current ownership.

Mason County Abstract & Title Inc

5734 W Deren Rd, Ludington, MI 49431-9795
Phone: 231-843-2645 **Fax:** 231-843-3305
Types of Records Retrieved: Real Estate; Tax liens/judgments; UCC records
Local Retrieval Area: MI-Mason
Add'l Information: Established 1892. Normal turnaround time- variable depending on project. Projects billed by number of names searched. Projects billed by number of records located. Projects billed by the hour. They specialize in searches covering real estate in Mason County, MI.

Massachusetts Document Retrieval

PO Box 529, North Easton, MA 02356-0529
Phone: 617-249-0323 **Fax:** 800-699-0249;
www.mass-doc.com **email:** services@mass-doc.com
Types of Records Retrieved: Probate courts; Vital records
Local Retrieval Area: MA-Middlesex, Suffolk
Add'l Information: Established 1997. Normal turnaround time- varied with request, project, size/scope; usually 24-48 hours. Projects billed by number of names searched. Projects billed by the hour. All projects require prepayment. Specialize in heir researching, vital records research including divorce, missing persons and genealogical projects. Other search services include wills/probate and naturalization records.

Masscourtresearch

328 Blue Hills Pky, Milton, MA 02186
Phone: 617-696-2178 **Fax:** 617-696-7814
www.masscourtresearch.com **email:** masscourt.research@verizon.net
Types of Records Retrieved: Civil and criminal courts; Federal courts; Tax liens/Judgments
Local Retrieval Area: MA-Middlesex, Suffolk
Add'l Information: Established 1995. Normal turnaround time- 48 hours. 30 day billings. They are hands-on court researcher at the Superior Courts and all District courts in Suffolk and Middlesex counties.

Massey Abstract Inc

PO Box 211, Covington, IN 47932-0211
Phone: 765-793-3451 **Fax:** 765-793-0668
lmassey@masseyabstract.com
Types of Records Retrieved: Civil courts; Probate courts; Real Estate; Tax liens/Judgments; UCC records
Local Retrieval Area: IN-Fountain, Vermillion, Warren
Add'l Information: Established 1950. Normal turnaround time- 5 working days. Projects billed by number of names searched. 1st project may require prepayment. They specialize in title searches.

Master File Inc

7925 Clayton Road #200, St Louis, MO 63117
Phone: 866-242-0469; 314-862-6049 **Fax:** 314-863-8300
www.masterfile-stlouis.com **email:** sjw@mail.mastserfile-stlouis.com
Types of Records Retrieved: Civil courts; Probate courts; Federal courts; Real Estate; Tax liens/Judgments; UCC records
Local Retrieval Area: IL-Madison, St. Clair; MO-Jefferson, St. Charles, St. Louis, St. Louis City. **Correspondent Relationships:** MO and Southern IL.
Add'l Information: Established 1991. Normal turnaround time- 24-36 hours. Projects billed by number of names searched. Projects billed by number of records located. Projects billed by the hour. Terms are net 15 days. 1st project may require prepayment. Credit cards accepted. Terms: net 30 days. They specialize in court and recorder searches. They perform service of process.

Matrix Info Services

4348 Carter Creek #103, Bryan, TX 77802
Phone: 979-846-3593 **Fax:** 979-846-7005
charlesstipe90@hotmail.com
Types of Records Retrieved: Civil and criminal courts, Probate courts; Federal courts; Real Estate; Tax liens/Judgments; UCC records; Vital records.
Local Retrieval Area: TX-Brazos
Add'l Information: Established 1994. Normal turnaround time- 2-3 days. Expedited service available. Projects billed by number of names searched. 1st project may require prepayment. Credit cards accepted. In business in the same area for 10 years. They perform service of process.

Mayes County Abstract

PO Box 967, Pryor, OK 74362
Phone: 918-825-3074 **Fax:** 918-825-3571
Types of Records Retrieved: Civil courts; Probate courts; Real Estate; Tax liens/Judgments; UCC records; Vital records
Local Retrieval Area: OK-Mayes
Add'l Information: Established 1910. Normal turnaround time- 1-2 days. Projects billed by the hour.

William (Bill) H Maynard

144 Stuart Rd NE PMB 289, Cleveland, TN 37312
Phone: 423-472-9858 **Fax:** 423-614-5484
Types of Records Retrieved: Real Estate; Tax liens/Judgments; UCC records
Local Retrieval Area: TN-Blount, Bradley, Hamilton, Knox, Loudon, McMinn, Meigs, Monroe, Polk, Rhea, Roane
Add'l Information: Established 1997. Normal turnaround time- 24-48 hours. Projects billed by number of records located. Payment due at time of invoicing or monthly statement. They service southeast Tennessee for Real Estate. 11 counties along the I-75 corridor from Hamilton to Knox counties. Specialize in current owner and full (30-40 year) searches. Cell number is 423-715-5310.

MBE

4080 Hampshire Ct, Allentown, PA 18104
Phone: 610-395-2202 **Fax:** 610-530-7198 maronercol@rcn.com
Types of Records Retrieved: Criminal courts
Local Retrieval Area: PA-Berks, Bucks, Lehigh, Montgomery, Northampton, Philadelphia. **Correspondent Relationships:** New Jersey.
Add'l Information: Established 1997. Normal turnaround time- 24 hours. Projects billed by number of names searched. Will bill monthly.

MBK Consulting

60 N Harding Rd, Columbus, OH 43209-1524
Phone: 614-239-8977 **Fax:** 614-239-0599
www.mbkcons.com **email:** mbkcons@netexp.net
Types of Records Retrieved: Probate courts; Federal courts; Real Estate; Tax liens/Judgments; UCC records; Vital records
Local Retrieval Area: OH-Franklin. **Correspondent Relationships:** other counties in Ohio.
Add'l Information: Established 1991. Normal turnaround time- 24-48 hours. Projects billed by number of names searched. Project rates available. 1st project may require prepayment. Large projects require prepayment. They specialize in historical and genealogical research as well as general public record retrieval. They also do title examinations.

McAllister & Associates Inc

16 Northtown Dr #200-D, PO Box 12082 (39236-2082), Jackson, MS 39211
Phone: 601-977-0406 **Fax:** 601-977-8464
Types of Records Retrieved: Civil, criminal and probate courts; Federal courts; Real Estate; Tax liens/Judgments; UCC records; Vital records
Local Retrieval Area: MS-Hinds, Madison, Rankin, Warren. **Correspondent Relationships:** Mississippi.
Add'l Information: Established 1979. Normal turnaround time- variable depending on project. Projects billed by the hour. 1st project may require prepayment. They will also invoice. They are a general investigative agency. A licensed PI in MS. They perform service of process.

McBrayer McGinnis Leslie & Kirkland

PO Box 280, Main & Harrison St, Greenup, KY 41144
Phone: 606-473-7303 **Fax:** 606-473-9003
brucemac@zoominternet.net

Types of Records Retrieved: Civil, criminal and probate courts; Federal courts; Real Estate; Tax liens/Judgments; UCC records; Vital records

Local Retrieval Area: KY-Boyd, Carter, Fayette, Franklin, Greenup, Lawrence, Lewis

Add'l Information: Established 1960. Normal turnaround time- 2 days. Projects billed by the hour. Or, billing by arrangement. Credit cards accepted. Net 30 days.

McCarthy Abstract Co

PO Box 528, O'Neill, NE 68763
Phone: 402-336-2860 **Fax:** 402-336-4489

Types of Records Retrieved: Probate courts; Real Estate; Tax liens/Judgments; UCC records

Local Retrieval Area: NE-Boyd, Holt, Wheeler

Add'l Information: Established 1983. Normal turnaround time- 3-5 days in Holt county. Projects billed by the hour. 1st project may require prepayment. They specialize in real estate records, abstracts, title insurance, and real estate closings.

McCook County Abstract & Title Ins

PO Box 506, Salem, SD 57058
Phone: 605-425-2612 **Fax:** 605-425-3277

Types of Records Retrieved: Civil, criminal and probate courts; Real Estate; Tax liens/Judgments; UCC records; Vital records

Local Retrieval Area: SD-McCook

Add'l Information: Established 1900. Normal turnaround time- 1 week. Fee basis is set by state law. All projects require prepayment. They specialize in title insurance.

McCormick Detective Agency

PO Box 444, Breckenridge, CO 80424
Phone: 970-453-6378 **Fax:** 970-453-6852 mda444brek@aol.com

Types of Records Retrieved: Civil and criminal courts; Real Estate; Tax liens/Judgments; UCC records

Local Retrieval Area: CO-Clear Creek, Lake, Park, Summit. **Correspondent Relationships:** Denver, CO.

Add'l Information: Established 1977. Normal turnaround time- 1 day. Projects billed by the hour. Will bill at the first of the month. They specialize in trial preparation for civil and criminal cases. A licensed PI in CO. They perform service of process.

McCoy Investigations (CAPI# 18621)

PO Box 174, Carmichael, CA 95609
Phone: 800-287-6789; 916-481-3525 **Fax:** 916-481-5293
www.mccoyinvestigations.com

Types of Records Retrieved: Civil and criminal courts; Federal courts

Local Retrieval Area: CA- Sacramento. **Correspondents:** nationwide.

Add'l Information: Established 1993. Normal turnaround time- 24-72 hours. Projects billed by number of records located. 1st project may require prepayment. They specialize in screening services for the business community, nationwide. They use "On-Hands" researchers to check criminal records nationwide. Provides driving records, SS traces, credit reports, employment verification, education and civil. A licensed PI in CA.

McDaniel & Associates Inc

PO Box 3871, Montgomery, AL 36109 **Phone:** 334-312-0781

Types of Records Retrieved: Civil, criminal and probate courts; Federal courts; Real Estate; Tax liens/Judgments; UCC records

Local Retrieval Area: AL-Autauga, Elmore, Montgomery. **Correspondent Relationships:** Elmore, Macon, Lee, Dallas, Russell counties AL.

Add'l Information: Established 1985. Normal turnaround time- 1-3 days. Expedited service available. Projects billed by the hour. 1st project may require prepayment. A licensed PI in AL. They perform service of process.

Sherry McDowell

PO Box 10, Broadus, MT 59317
Phone: 406-436-2885 **Fax:** 406-436-2885

Types of Records Retrieved: Civil, criminal and probate courts

Local Retrieval Area: MT-Powder River

Add'l Information: Established 2000. 1st project may require prepayment. She specializes in court records.

McGinley Search & File Service Corp

722 Bristol Ct, Greenwood, IN 46143-3161
Phone: 317-807-0760 **Fax:** 317-807-0767
www.mcginleyfilesearch.com **email:** bmcginley@mcginleyfilesearch.com

Types of Records Retrieved: Civil courts; Federal courts; Real Estate; Tax liens/Judgments; UCC records

Local Retrieval Area: IN-all counties. **Correspondents:** statewide.

Add'l Information: Established 1992. Normal turnaround time- 24-72 hours. Projects billed by number of names searched. From Indianapolis, they specialize in assisting various professionals in filing, searching and retrieval of documents in all local, county, state and district offices statewide. They do not search criminal indexes. A licensed PI in IN.

McGowan & Clark Inv

7810 Fairway Ave SE #1201, Snoqualmie, WA 98065-9020
Phone: 425-396-5680 **Fax:** 425-396-5681
raymcgowan@attbi.com

Types of Records Retrieved: Civil and criminal courts; Federal courts; Real Estate; Tax liens/Judgments; UCC records; Vital records; Property records

Local Retrieval Area: WA-King, Pierce, Snohomish. **Correspondent Relationships:** statewide.

Add'l Information: Established 1993. Normal turnaround time- 24 hours. Expedited service available. Projects billed by number of names searched. Terms: net 30 days. For 10 years they have been accessing all of Washington's public records through physical retrieval, courthouse & county databases, along with online access. They perform service of process.

McGuire Research Associates

107 Danielson Pike, Scituate, RI 02857
Phone: 401-647-7881 **Fax:** 401-647-4693
lmcguire12@cox.net

Types of Records Retrieved: Civil courts; Probate courts; Federal courts; Real Estate; Tax liens/Judgments; UCC records

Local Retrieval Area: RI-Bristol, Kent, Newport, Providence, Washington. **Correspondent Relationships:** Bristol County MA.

Add'l Information: Established 1989. Normal turnaround time- 24 hours at state agencies, 24-48 hours at town offices. Projects billed by number of names searched. Terms: net 30 days. They specialize in filings in Rhode Island, at the state or town level. They cover all thirty-nine (39) towns.

McHenry County Abstract & Title Co

PO Box 420, Towner, ND 58788
Phone: 701-537-5723 **Fax:** 701-537-5723

Types of Records Retrieved: Civil, criminal and probate courts; Federal courts; Real Estate; Tax liens/Judgments; UCC records

Local Retrieval Area: ND-McHenry, Sheridan

Add'l Information: Established 1986. Normal turnaround time- 24 hours. Fee basis varies by the type of project 1st project may require prepayment. They specialize in title abstracting and document retrieval.

McHugh Abstract Co

PO Box 151, Langdon, ND 58249
Phone: 701-256-2851 **Fax:** 701-256-2852

Types of Records Retrieved: Civil courts; Federal courts; Real Estate; Tax liens/Judgments; UCC records; Vital records

Local Retrieval Area: ND-Cavalier

Add'l Information: Established 1970. Normal turnaround time- 2-5 days. Fee based on nature of project.

McIver Abstract & Title Co

317 NW Front St, Ashdown, AR 71822
Phone: 870-898-3502 **Fax:** 870-898-5560

Types of Records Retrieved: Real Estate

Local Retrieval Area: AR-Little River

Add'l Information: Established 1930. Normal turnaround time- 3-4 days. Fee basis will vary by type of project. 1st project may require prepayment. They specialize in real estate and title work.

McKesson Title Corp

407 N Center St, Plymouth, IN 46563
Phone: 800-261-8437; 574-936-2555 **Fax:** 574-935-5515
http://mckessontitle.com **email:** info@mckessontitle.com

Types of Records Retrieved: Real Estate; Tax liens/judgments; UCC records

Local Retrieval Area: IN-Elkhart, Fulton, Kosciusko, La Porte, Marshall, Pulaski, St Joseph, Starke

Add'l Information: Established 1919. Normal turnaround time- varied; rush service available on request. Fees vary depending on project. Personal or cashier checks are accepted. They specialize in title insurance and escrow closings, 1031 tax exchanges and home owners insurance. They are celebrating the 85th year in business, being the oldest family-owned title company in Indiana. A licensed PI in IN.

McLean County Abstract Inc

PO Box 370, 615 Main Ave, Washburn, ND 58577
Phone: 701-462-3244 **Fax:** 701-462-8444

Types of Records Retrieved: Civil, criminal and probate courts; Federal courts; Real Estate; Tax liens/Judgments; UCC records; Vital records

Local Retrieval Area: ND-McLean

Add'l Information: Established 1991. Normal turnaround time- 2 weeks. Fee basis will vary by type of project. All projects require prepayment. They will also invoice.

McQueen Abstract Company

PO Box 549, 521 S Main, Hugoton, KS 67951
Phone: 620-544-2311 **Fax:** 620-544-8029 glen@pld.com

Types of Records Retrieved: Civil, criminal and probate courts; Real Estate; Tax liens/Judgments

Local Retrieval Area: KS-Stevens

Add'l Information: Normal turnaround time- 3-5 days. Projects billed by the hour.

Meade County Title

PO Box 520, 121 E Carthage, Meade, KS 67864
Phone: 620-873-2756 **Fax:** 620-873-2756

Types of Records Retrieved: Civil courts; Probate courts; Real Estate; Tax liens/Judgments; UCC records

Local Retrieval Area: KS-Meade. **Correspondent Relationships:** Clark County KS.

Add'l Information: Established 1966. Normal turnaround time- 2-3 days. Fee basis varies by type of transaction. 1st project may require prepayment. Payment due upon receipt of report.

Meade County Title Co

PO Box 221, Ashland, KS 67831
Phone: 800-725-7802; **Fax:** 620-635-2716

Types of Records Retrieved: Civil courts; Probate courts; Real Estate; Tax liens/Judgments; UCC records; Vital records

Local Retrieval Area: KS-Clark

Add'l Information: Normal turnaround time- 2-3 days. Fee basis varies by type of transaction. 1st project may require prepayment.

Medina Retrieval Service

271 NE 45th St, Ft Lauderdale, FL 33334
Phone: 954-560-9077 **Fax:** 954-958-0871
www.mrssearch.com **email:** gmedina@mrssearch.com

Types of Records Retrieved: Civil, criminal and probate courts; Federal courts; Real Estate

Local Retrieval Area: FL-Broward, Dade, Palm Beach. **Correspondent Relationships:** Leon County, FL.

Add'l Information: Established 2002. Normal turnaround time- 1-2 days dependant on time request is received and availability of documents. Expedited service available for $25 charge. Projects billed by the hour. 1st project may require prepayment. Credit cards accepted. Will bill major firms. They are a legal document retrieval service for Broward, Miami-Dade and Palm Beach counties. They focus on Federal and State/County courts.

Medlin Research Company

PO Box 159, Louisburg, KS 66053-0159
Phone: 913-206-4615 **Fax:** 913-837-4975 wtmedlin@yahoo.com

Types of Records Retrieved: Civil, criminal and probate courts; Federal courts; Real Estate; Tax liens/Judgments; UCC records

Local Retrieval Area: KS-Johnson, Miami; MO-Cass. **Correspondent Relationships:** Platte, Clay counties MO.

Add'l Information: Established 1999. Normal turnaround time- 24-36 hours. Projects billed by number of names searched. Payment due at the end of the month. They offer criminal, civil, UCC, tax liens, Federal criminal and bankruptcy searches. They also do current owner searches on property (residential only). Pager # is 913-259-1626.

Meier Inv

PO Box 36203, Des Moines, IA 50315
Phone: 515-205-2738 **Fax:** 515-243-1932 meierc@juno.com

Types of Records Retrieved: Civil, criminal and probate courts; Federal courts; Real Estate; Tax liens/Judgments; UCC records, Vital records

Local Retrieval Area: IA-Appanoose, Monroe, Polk, Warren; MO-Putnam

Add'l Information: Established 1999. Normal turnaround time- 24-48 hours. Projects billed by the hour. All projects require prepayment. They specialize in location people, assets, witness location, legal research, hidden assets, surveillance and process service. A licensed PI in IA. They perform service of process.

Jesse Melcher, Attny

PO Box 345, Mt Olivet, KY 41064
Phone: 606-724-5322 **Fax:** 606-724-2612

Types of Records Retrieved: Real Estate; Tax liens/Judgments

Local Retrieval Area: KY-Robertson

Add'l Information: Established 1999. 1st project may require prepayment. He specializes in real estate.

MEM Consulting

1083 N Collier Blvd #137, Marco Island, FL 34145
Phone: 239-394-2893 **Fax:** 239-394-1893
mmosser1@earthlink.net

Types of Records Retrieved: Civil, criminal and probate courts; Federal Courts; Real Estate; Tax liens/Judgments; UCC records; Vital records

Local Retrieval Area: FL-Collier. **Correspondent Relationships:** Lee, FL county.

Add'l Information: Established 1998. Normal turnaround time- 24-72 hours. Projects billed by number of names searched. 1st project may require prepayment. She is a private investigation company that performs civil and criminal record retrieval. A licensed PI in FL. Performs service of process.

Menard Title & Abstract Co Inc

121 Court St, Clarendon, AR 72029
Phone: 870-747-3712 **Fax:** 870-747-5488

Types of Records Retrieved: Civil, criminal and probate courts; Real Estate; Tax liens/Judgments; Vital records

Local Retrieval Area: AR-Monroe

Add'l Information: Normal turnaround time- up to 2 weeks. Fee basis will vary by the type of project. They specialize in real estate and title insurance.

Mendenhall Information Services

4245 Kemp Blvd #304, Wichita Falls, TX 76308
Phone: 940-696-0758 **Fax:** 940-689-8408
mendenhallsvcs@aol.com

Types of Records Retrieved: Civil, criminal and probate courts; Federal courts; Real Estate; Tax liens/Judgments; UCC records; Vital records

Local Retrieval Area: TX-Archer, Baylor, Childress, Clay, Collin, Cooke, Dallas, Denton, Erath, Foard, Grayson, Hardeman, Haskell, Hood, Jack, Johnson, Knox, Montague, Palo Pinto, Parker, Somervell, Tarrant, Throckmorton, Wichita, Wilbarger, Wise, Young; OK-Comanche, Cotton, Jackson, Stephens, Tillman

Add'l Information: Established 1999. Projects billed by number of names searched. 1st project may require prepayment.

Mendo-Lake Paralegals

435 N Main St, Lakeport, CA 95453
Phone: 707-263-8755 **Fax:** 707-263-0298 mlp@pacific.net

Types of Records Retrieved: Civil, criminal and probate courts; Real Estate; Tax liens/Judgments; UCC records; Vital records

Local Retrieval Area: CA-Lake

Add'l Information: Established 1988. Normal turnaround time- 2-3 days. Projects billed by number of names searched. 1st project may require prepayment. Will bill established clients. They specialize in real property research.

Mercer County Abstract Co Inc

PO Box 1003, Hazen, ND 58545
Phone: 701-748-2190 **Fax:** 701-748-5956

Types of Records Retrieved: Civil courts; Real Estate; Tax liens/Judgments

Local Retrieval Area: ND-Mercer. **Correspondent Relationships:** North Dakota.

Add'l Information: Established 1991. Normal turnaround time- 2 days. Projects billed by number of names searched. 1st project may require prepayment. They specialize in title insurance, title searches, closing search title memos, abstracts, closings and oil & gas searches.

Mercury Service Inc

PO Box 46196, Station D, Vancouver, BC, Canada, CAN V6J 5G5
Phone: 604-228-9993 **Fax:** 604-224-8682

Types of Records Retrieved: Civil courts; Probate courts; Federal courts; Real Estate; UCC records

Local Retrieval Area: CANADA-British Columbia, Canada. **Correspondent Relationships:** Alberta, Ontario, Quebec provinces.

Add'l Information: Established 1972. Normal turnaround time- 4 hours on database searches; 24 hours for "hand" searches. Projects billed by number of names searched. Projects billed by the hour. 1st project may require prepayment. They specialize in business backgrounds (individuals and companies), accident investigation (legal), forensic photography and tracing people. A licensed PI in British Columbia.

Merkel Abstract & Title

216 N Broadway, PO Box 767, Hartington, NE 68739-0767
Phone: 402-254-3547 **Fax:** 402-254-3547

Types of Records Retrieved: Probate courts; Federal courts; Real Estate

Local Retrieval Area: NE-Cedar

Add'l Information: Established 1991. Normal turnaround time- 2-4 days. Projects billed by number of names searched. Projects billed by number of records located. 1st project may require prepayment.

Merlins Data Research

178 Golf Club Dr, Longwood, FL 32779-4697
Phone: 888-434-6337; 407-869-5394 **Fax:** 407-869-9002
www.merlinsreports.com **email:** wefindem@cfl.rr.com

Types of Records Retrieved: Civil, criminal and probate courts; Federal courts; Real Estate; Tax liens/Judgments; UCC records; Vital records

Local Retrieval Area: FL-Brevard, Indian River, Lake, Martin, Orange, Osceola, Seminole, St. Lucie, Volusia. **Correspondents:** nationwide.

Add'l Information: Established 1992. Normal turnaround time- 24-48 hours. Projects billed by number of names searched. Payment due net 10 days. 1st project may require prepayment. Credit cards accepted. They specialize in civil, real estate and criminal searches. Based in the Orlando area, they cover all of Florida counties at courthouse level. They cover the entire state. Orlando and Central Florida their specialty.

Merola Services

PO Box 54, Michigan City, IN 46361-0054
Phone: 219-878-9699 **Fax:** 800-272-7717; 219-878-9698
www.merolaservices.com **email:** info@merolaservices.com

Types of Records Retrieved: Civil and criminal courts; Federal courts; Real Estate; Tax liens/Judgments; UCC records; Vital records

Local Retrieval Area: NY-Albany, Onondaga. **Correspondent Relationships:** FL, OH, CT. They access the entire eastern seaborad for DMV records.

Add'l Information: Established 1988. Normal turnaround time- same day to 2 days. Projects billed by number of names searched. 1st project may require prepayment. Credit cards accepted. Payment due upon receipt. They specialize in retrieval of certified documents at NYS DMV (and elsewhere EC), insurance (auto-nationwide) and police reports, asset searches, background & pre-employment searches as well as civil and criminal searches at the state and federal level.

Merola Services (Indiana)

PO Box 54, Michigan City, IN 46361
Phone: 219-878-9699 **Fax:** 219-878-9698
www.merolaservices.com **email:** info@merolaservices.com

Types of Records Retrieved: Civil and criminal courts; Federal courts; Real Estate; Tax liens/Judgments; UCC records; Vital records

Local Retrieval Area: IN-La Porte. **Correspondent Relationships:** FL, OH, CT. They access the entire eastern seaborad for DMV records.

Add'l Information: Established 1988. Normal turnaround time- same day to 2 days. Projects billed by number of names searched. 1st project may require prepayment. Credit cards accepted. Payment due upon receipt. They specialize in retrieval of certified documents at NYS DMV (and elsewhere EC), insurance (auto-nationwide) and police reports, asset searches, background & pre-employment searches as well as civil and criminal searches at the state and federal level.

Merritt & Henry LLC

155 S Main St, Madison, GA 30650
Phone: 706-342-9668 **Fax:** 706-342-9843

Types of Records Retrieved: Civil, criminal and probate courts; Real Estate; Tax liens/Judgments; UCC records

Local Retrieval Area: GA-Greene, Morgan, Putnam

Add'l Information: Established 1987. Normal turnaround time- 48 hours. Projects billed by number of names searched. Projects billed by the hour. All projects require prepayment. Credit cards accepted. Personal checks accepted. He specializes in real estate searches. He also does file/record UCC and real estate documents of behalf of clients on same or next day basis in Morgan.

Metro Clerking Inc

134 N La Salle #1005, Chicago, IL 60602
Phone: 312-263-2977 **Fax:** 312-263-2985 sferrari@comcast.net

Types of Records Retrieved: Civil, criminal and probate courts; Federal courts; Real Estate; Tax liens/Judgments; UCC records; Vital records

Local Retrieval Area: IL-Cook, Du Page, Kane, Lake, McHenry, Will

Add'l Information: Established 1985. Normal turnaround time- 24 hours. Expedited service available. Projects billed by number of names searched. 1st project may require prepayment. They have an attorney on staff to cover court matters in State & Federal Courts. They also do searches in the Federal Records Center, in Chicago, which houses archived District Court files from MI, WI, OH, IN, IA and IL. Will do IL workers' comp searches.

Metro Legal Services

330 S 2nd Ave #150, Minneapolis, MN 55401
Phone: 800-488-8994; 612-332-0202 **Fax:** 612-332-5215
www.metrolegal.com **email:** service@metrolegal.com

Types of Records Retrieved: Civil, criminal and probate courts; Federal courts; Real Estate; Tax liens/Judgments; UCC records; Vital records

Local Retrieval Area: MN-Anoka, Carver, Dakota, Hennepin, Ramsey, Scott, Sherburne, Washington, Wright

Add'l Information: Established 1969. Normal turnaround time- 24 hours. Expedited service available. Projects billed by number of names searched. 1st project may require prepayment. They have a trained staff of over 100, they are uniquely capable of providing document retrievals, public record searches and filing in the State of Minnesota. A licensed PI in MN. They perform service of process.

Metro Research & Inv

219 Sunset Blvd, Conroe, TX 77303
Phone: 800-364-3590; 936-441-2294 **Fax:** 800-364-3506; 936-539-1236
metro@wt.net

Types of Records Retrieved: Civil, criminal and probate courts; Real Estate; Tax liens/Judgments; UCC records; Vital records

Local Retrieval Area: TX-Montgomery

Add'l Information: Established 1990. Normal turnaround time- 24 hours. Projects billed by number of names searched. Projects billed by number of records located. Projects billed by the hour. 1st project may require prepayment. They a full service investigative firm specializing in discrimination investigations and harrassment investigations in the workplace. Also conduct all aspects of civil and criminal investigations including real property and tax research. A licensed PI in TX.

Metropolis Group

10061 Riverside Dr #230, Toluca Lake, CA 91602
Phone: 818-240-1332 **Fax:** 818-240-1421 liesel36@pacbell.net

Types of Records Retrieved: Civil and criminal courts; Federal courts

Local Retrieval Area: CA-Los Angeles, San Diego, Ventura. **Correspondent Relationships:** nationwide.

Add'l Information: Established 1994. Normal turnaround time- 48 hours. Projects billed by number of names searched. Projects billed by the hour. Charge by number in criminal searches; hourly for document retrieval. Credit cards accepted. Will bill once account is established and agreement signed. Normal turnaround is 1-2 days. Volume discounts. Searches can be returned via web or fax. Quality research in a timely efficient manner since 1995. A licensed PI in CA.

Metropolitan Title Co (Hastings)

629 W State St #202, Hastings, MI 49058
Phone: 269-945-9447 **Fax:** 269-945-5350
www.metropolitantitle.com/branches/branch.asp?BranchID=9

Types of Records Retrieved: Civil, criminal and probate courts; Real Estate; Tax liens/Judgments; UCC records; Vital records

Local Retrieval Area: MI-Barry

Add'l Information: Established 1989. Normal turnaround time- 3 days. Fee basis will vary by the type of project. They specialize in real estate title work.

Michael Anderson Company

25972 Novi Rd, Novi, MI 48375
Phone: 800-992-9936; 248-596-9711 **Fax:** 800-992-9937; 248-596-9719
MichaelAnderson@ameritech.net

Types of Records Retrieved: Civil, criminal and probate courts; Federal courts; Real Estate; Tax liens/Judgments; UCC records; Vital records

Local Retrieval Area: MI-Livingston, Macomb, Oakland, Washtenaw, Wayne. **Correspondent Relationships:** statewide.

Add'l Information: Established 1997. Normal turnaround time- 24-48 hours. Projects billed by number of names searched. Will invoice upon completion of order. They are professional, dependable and confidential. Also offer pre-employment screening and statewide searching for corporate information, UCCs, MVRs and real estate.

Michael B Fixman & Associates

72 Hancock St, PO Box 83, Everett, MA 02149
Phone: 800-434-9626; 617-387-1100
www.constableservices.com **email:** fixy@comcast.net

Types of Records Retrieved: Civil, criminal and probate courts; Federal courts; Real Estate; Tax liens/Judgments; UCC records; Vital records

Local Retrieval Area: MA-Essex, Middlesex, Suffolk. **Correspondent Relationships:** Massachusetts and other New England states upon request.

Add'l Information: Established 1957. Normal turnaround time- 1 day. Projects billed by the hour. All projects require prepayment. Personal checks are accepted. He is a private detective licensed in MA and NH, a process server and a licensed/bonded constable. A licensed PI in MA, NH. They perform service of process.

Michael's Legal Research

PO Box 2558, Darien, GA 31305
Phone: 912-269-5532 **Fax:** 912-437-3510 mcgrathbus@earthlink.net

Types of Records Retrieved: Real Estate

Local Retrieval Area: GA-Brantley, Camden, Glynn, Long, McIntosh

Add'l Information: Established 1998. Normal turnaround time- 24-48 hours (primary); 48-72 hours (secondary). Billed by the type of real estate abstract, ie full, limited or update. Residential and commercial real estate title abstracting, full searches. Developer & limited recordation of documents, document retrieval, liens and judgment searches in McIntosh & Glenn counties only. They are a member of NALA.

Michiana Searches Inc

28916 Kehres St, Elkhart, IN 46514-9563
Phone: 574-266-4652, 574-536-7135 **Fax:** 574-266-8399
conduit2me@comcast.net

Types of Records Retrieved: Civil courts; Real Estate; Tax liens/Judgments; UCC records

Local Retrieval Area: IN-Elkhart, St Joseph

Add'l Information: Established 1993. Normal turnaround time- no more than 48 hours unless notified. Projects billed by number of names searched. Terms: net 10 days. She specializes in foreclosures, UCC, court record searching and real estate/ title searches.

Michigan Search Company

181 Helen St, Garden City, MI 48135-2787
Phone: 734-427-7224 **Fax:** 734-427-1218 Michigansearchco@aol.com

Types of Records Retrieved: Civil courts; Federal courts; Real Estate; Tax liens/Judgments; UCC records

Local Retrieval Area: MI-Allegan, Barry, Berrien, Branch, Calhoun, Cass, Dickinson, Eaton, Genesee, Grand Traverse, Hillsdale, Ingham, Isabella, Jackson, Kalamazoo, Kent, Kivingston, Macomb, Midland, Oakland, Ottawa, Saginaw, St Joseph, Van Buren, Wayne, Washtenaw, Wexferd. **Correspondent Relationships:** Allegan, Barry, Berrien, Branch, Calhoun, Cass, Dickinson, Eaton, Genesee, Grand Traverse, Hillsdale, Ingham, Isabella, Jackson, Kalamazoo, Kent, Livingston, Macomb, Midland, Oakland, Ottawa, Saginaw, St Joseph, Van Buren, Wayne, Washtenaw, Wexferd.

Add'l Information: Established 1992. Normal turnaround time- 48 hours. Expedited service available. Projects billed by number of names searched. They specialize in UCC & lien searches, civil record checks, good standings, name reservations and corporate documents.

Mid-America Reporting Co LLC

PO Box 145, Nesbit, MS 38651-0145
Phone: 662-487-0932 **Fax:** 662-487-0934
www.marcinfo.com **email:** customerservice@marcinfo.com

Types of Records Retrieved: Civil, criminal and probate courts; Real Estate; Tax liens/Judgments; UCC records; Vital records

Local Retrieval Area: MS-De Soto, Panola, Tate, Tunica. **Correspondent Relationships:** statewide.

Add'l Information: Normal turnaround time- typically 24-48 hours. Fees vary depending upon request. Mid-America Reporting Company, LLC., specializes in on-site court searches, document retrieval and filings.

Midland Title and Abstract Co

2816 Jefferson Ave, Midland, MI 48640

Phone: 989-839-1003 **Fax:** 989-895-0580

Types of Records Retrieved: Civil courts; Probate courts; Federal courts; Real Estate; Tax liens/Judgments; UCC records; Vital records

Local Retrieval Area: MI-Isabella, Midland

Add'l Information: Established 1987. Normal turnaround time- 2-3 days. Fee basis will vary by the type of project. They require out of town clients to prepay. They specialize in title insurance.

Mid-South Legal Services

PO Box 610008, 215 Richard Arrington Jr Blvd N #505, Birmingham, AL 35261

Phone: 205-326-0900 **Fax:** 205-326-0600

Types of Records Retrieved: Civil, criminal and probate courts; Federal courts; Tax liens/Judgments; UCC records; Vital records

Local Retrieval Area: AL-Jefferson, Shelby, St Clair, Talladega, Tuscaloosa, Walker

Add'l Information: Established 1983. Normal turnaround time- 24-48 hours. Projects billed by number of names searched. Projects billed by number of records located. Projects billed by the hour. Fees vary depending upon request. They specialize in process service, document retrieval, and skiptracing. They perform service of process.

Mid-South Subpoena Service

100 N Main #413, Memphis, TN 38103

Phone: 800-737-8542; 901-528-9116 **Fax:** 901-528-9118

subpoena@aol.com

Types of Records Retrieved: Civil, criminal and probate courts; Federal courts

Local Retrieval Area: TN-Fayette, Hardeman, Lauderdale, Madison, Shelby, Tipton. **Correspondent Relationships:** West Tennessee.

Add'l Information: Established 1982. Normal turnaround time- 2-3 days. Expedited service available. Projects billed by the hour. 1st project may require prepayment. They also are a notary service. They perform service of process.

Midstate Legal Support Services

PO Box 7, Utica, NY 13503

Phone: 315-797-8609 **Fax:** 315-797-0270

Types of Records Retrieved: Civil, criminal and probate courts; Federal courts; Real Estate; Tax liens/Judgments; UCC records; Vital records

Local Retrieval Area: NY-Oneida

Add'l Information: Established 1984. Normal turnaround time- 72 hours. Projects billed by number of names searched. Projects billed by number of records located. 1st project may require prepayment. Invoicing is available. They specialize in judgment enforcement, process service, auto repossessions, foreclosure bidding and bank repossenssions (homes secured, etc). They perform service of process.

Midwest Abstract Co

40 S Main #600, Dayton, OH 45402

Phone: 800-606-9488; 937-228-2292 **Fax:** 937-228-0640

midwestabstract2@netzero.net

Types of Records Retrieved: Real Estate; Tax liens/judgments; UCC records

Local Retrieval Area: OH-Montgomery. **Correspondent Relationships:** Miami, Darke, Clark, Preble, Warren, Butler, Clermont, Green counties.

Add'l Information: Established 1984. Normal turnaround time- 5-7 days. Projects billed by number of names searched. The fee basis is per examination. They specialize in "ALL" real estate title examinations.

Midwest Backgrounds Inc

101 N Park Ave #200, Herrin, IL 62948

Phone: 618-942-8808 **Fax:** 618-942-8810

www.mbiworldwide.com **email:** info@mbiworldwide.com

Types of Records Retrieved: Criminal courts; Federal courts

Local Retrieval Area: IL-Franklin, Williamson. **Correspondent Relationships:** nationwide.

Add'l Information: Established 1998. Normal turnaround time- 24-72 hours. Projects billed by number of names searched. All projects require prepayment. Credit cards accepted. They specialize in employee screening. Orders may be placed via fax, secure website, mail, phone or email.

Midwest Data Search

2350 Watertown Rd, Orono, MN 55356

Phone: 952-475-2002 **Fax:** 952-475-5483 deanodata@netzero.net

Types of Records Retrieved: Real Estate; Tax liens/judgments; UCC records

Local Retrieval Area: MN-Anoka, Carver, Hennepin, Scott, Sherburne, Wright

Add'l Information: Established 2002. Normal turnaround time- 24-48 hours. Projects billed by number of names searched. Payment is net 30 days.

Mid-West Investigations

PO Box 755, Mustang, OK 73064-0755

Phone: 800-359-5410; 405-636-1976 **Fax:** Call before faxing

Types of Records Retrieved: Civil, criminal and probate courts; Federal courts; Real Estate; Tax liens/Judgments; UCC records; Vital records

Local Retrieval Area: OK-Canadian, Cleveland, Oklahoma. **Correspondent Relationships:** Oklahoma, Texas.

Add'l Information: Established 1984. Normal turnaround time- 24-48 hours. Projects billed by number of names searched. 1st project may require prepayment. Service and application agreement may be required. They specialize in insurance fraud, asset locating, collections, skiptracing, process serving, and public & private record retrieval. A licensed PI in OK. They perform service of process.

Midwest Investigative Services Inc

6077 Far Hills Ave #215, Dayton, OH 45459-1923

Phone: 800-227-9740; 937-433-9903 **Fax:** 937-433-9918

misi@earthlink.net

Types of Records Retrieved: Civil and criminal courts; Federal courts; Vital records

Local Retrieval Area: OH-Greene, Miami, Montgomery, Warren

Add'l Information: Established 1989. Normal turnaround time- 1-3 days. Expedited service available. Projects are billed by court search. They will invoice. They specialize in pre-employment screening, civil and criminal investigations, process service, corporate investigations, locator service, witness interview, fires, arson and explosions. A licensed PI in OH. They perform service of process.

Steven P Mielke

116 E Market St, Celina, OH 45822

Phone: 419-586-2323 **Fax:** 419-586-2154 mielkelaw@yahoo.com

Types of Records Retrieved: Civil, criminal and probate courts; Real Estate; Tax liens/Judgments; UCC records

Local Retrieval Area: OH-Auglaize, Mercer, Vanwert

Add'l Information: Normal turnaround time- 3 days. Fee basis will vary by type of project. 1st project may require prepayment. They specialize in real estate record searches.

Mike Moore Inv

PO Box 2401, Visalia, CA 93279

Phone: 559-636-1057 **Fax:** 559-636-1088 bigmike2401@sbcglobal.net

Types of Records Retrieved: Civil and criminal courts; Real Estate; Tax liens/Judgments; UCC records; Vital records

Local Retrieval Area: CA-Kings, Tulare

Add'l Information: Established 1988. Normal turnaround time- 24 hours. Projects billed by number of names searched. Personal checks are accepted. They specialize in process serving and investigation. A licensed PI in CA. They perform service of process.

Mill Creek Investigation Agency PC

992 Cottage St NE, Salem, OR 97301

Phone: 877-378-1581; 503-378-1581 **Fax:** 503-585-4384

tnlinv@comcast.net

Types of Records Retrieved: Civil, criminal and probate courts; Real Estate

Local Retrieval Area: OR-Marion, Polk

Add'l Information: Established 1990. Normal turnaround time- 2 days if information is furnished by 3:00 pm. Projects billed by number of names searched. 1st project may require prepayment. The Mill Creek Investigation Agency engages in public record reseach and litigation support in civil and criminal cases in Oregon courts. A licensed PI in OR.

Mill Creek Title Service

PO Box 911, Plainfield, IN 46168

Phone: 317-714-7190 **Fax:** 317-539-6804

www.millcreektitle.com **email:** dave@millcreektitle.com

Types of Records Retrieved: Real Estate; Tax liens/Judgments; UCC records; Vital records.

Local Retrieval Area: IN-Boone, Carroll, Clinton, Fountain, Hendricks, Johnson, Monroe, Montgomery, Morgan, Owen, Parke, Putnam, Tippecanoe, Vermillion, Warren

Add'l Information: Established 2002. Normal turnaround time- 1-2 days. Rush "immediate service" available. 1st project may require prepayment. Will file/record documents. Mill Creek is a local title company servicing central and western counties in Indiana. 24-48 hr turnaround times, E&O insurance, and competitive prices.

Millennial Investigative Agency

10604 Quail Ridge Dr, St Augustine, FL 32095

Phone: 888-299-7574; 904-819-9700 **Fax:** 904-826-1071

www.stevenkbrown.com

Types of Records Retrieved: Civil, criminal and probate courts; Federal courts; Real Estate; Tax liens/Judgments; UCC records; Vital records

Local Retrieval Area: FL-Clay, Duval, St. Johns. **Correspondent Relationships:** Putnam and Nassau counties FL.

Add'l Information: Established 1984. Normal turnaround time- 48 hours. Expedited service available. Projects billed by number of names searched. All projects require prepayment. Credit cards accepted. They specialize in retrieval of all public records available, criminal, civil, filings, recordings, bankruptcy and federal. They have been in business for 20 years. Formerly Brown, Plance & Assoc. A licensed PI in FL.

Miller & Assoc Information Services Inc

6001 N Westgate Blvd, Tacoma, WA 98406-2526

Phone: 253-752-5500 **Fax:** 253-752-5538 orderdesk@millerinfo.com

Types of Records Retrieved: Real Estate; Tax liens/judgments; UCC records

Local Retrieval Area: WA-King, Kitsap, Pierce, Snohomish, Thurston. **Correspondent Relationships:** Skagit and Whatcom counties WA.

Add'l Information: Established 1996. Normal turnaround time- 6-12 business hours. Charges are per address/name. Terms: net 30 days. They specialize in current owner searches. All research is supervised by a senior title researcher with 25 years experience. Company carries E & O insurance.

Miller & Johnson PLLC

PO Box 49, 766 W King St, Boone, NC 28607

Phone: 828-264-1125 **Fax:** 828-262-3544

Types of Records Retrieved: Civil courts; Probate courts; Real Estate; Tax liens/Judgments; UCC records

Local Retrieval Area: NC-Ashe, Avery, Watauga

Add'l Information: Established 1988. Normal turnaround time- 2 days. Projects billed by the hour. 1st project may require prepayment. They specialize in real estate, foreclosures, corporations and estate planning.

Miller Abstract & Title Co

401 E 4th St #101, PO Box 107, Minden, NE 68959

Phone: 308-832-0969 **Fax:** 308-832-0969 millerabstract@yahoo.com

Types of Records Retrieved: Probate courts; Real Estate; Tax liens/Judgments; UCC records

Local Retrieval Area: NE-Kearney. **Correspondent Relationships:** Phelps, Franklin, Buffalo counties.

Add'l Information: Established 1991. Normal turnaround time- 1-4 days. Fee basis is per search. Personal checks are accepted. They specialize in title insurance, abstracting and limited title reports.

Miller Abstracts

2555 Monroeville Blvd, Monroeville, PA 15146

Phone: 412-607-4952 **Fax:** 412-824-7141 hope314@msn.com

Types of Records Retrieved: Civil, criminal and probate courts; Federal courts; Real Estate; Tax liens/Judgments; UCC records; Vital records

Local Retrieval Area: PA-Allegheny, Washington, Westmoreland

Add'l Information: Established 2003. Normal turnaround time- 1-3 days for title searches, document retrieval 1 day. Expedited service available for $.50 surcharge. Projects billed by number of names searched. 1st project may require prepayment. She is an independent abstractor with 7 years experience. Accurate title search reports that are easy to understand. Immediate cell phone access during business hours. Professional liability insurance.

G Scott Miller

103 N Union St #A, Delaware, OH 43015-1709

Phone: 740-363-1324 **Fax:** 740-548-5443 gsm@rrohio.com

Types of Records Retrieved: Civil courts; Probate courts; Real Estate; Tax liens/Judgments; UCC records

Local Retrieval Area: OH-Delaware

Add'l Information: Established 1985. Normal turnaround time- 24 hours. Fee basis will vary by the type of project. He is an attorney.

Gail L Miller

208 N Commercial, Mankato, KS 66956

Phone: 785-378-3128 **Fax:** 785-378-3543

Types of Records Retrieved: Civil, criminal and probate courts; Tax liens/Judgments

Local Retrieval Area: KS-Jewell, Republic

Add'l Information: Established 1987. Normal turnaround time- 1-7 days. Projects billed by the hour. Personal checks are accepted. Credit accounts are not accepted.

Mills & Associates

35 Boyce Rd, Pine Bush, NY 12566

Phone: 845-744-4243 **Fax:** 845-744-6469 smills@hvc.rr.com

Types of Records Retrieved: Civil and criminal courts; Federal courts; Real Estate; Tax liens/Judgments; UCC records

Local Retrieval Area: NY-Dutchess, Erie, Nassau, Orange, Putnam, Rockland, Suffolk, Westchester. **Correspondent Relationships:** statewide.

Add'l Information: Established 1991. Normal turnaround time- 24-48 hours. Projects billed by number of names searched. 1st project may require prepayment. They offer MVR retrieval for 44 states. Also NY statewide criminal searches.

Mimbres Valley Abstract & Title Co

PO Drawer 2849, 920 N Diamond Ave (88030), Deming, NM 88031

Phone: 505-546-8896 **Fax:** 505-546-9697 mvat@zianet.com

Types of Records Retrieved: Civil, criminal and probate courts; Real Estate; Tax liens/Judgments; UCC records; Vital records

Local Retrieval Area: NM-Luna

Add'l Information: Normal turnaround time- 2-5 days. Fee basis is determined per name or per legal description. They specialize in title searches.

Minco Research

5425 Mallory Dr, Fort Worth, TX 76117

Phone: 817-834-6744 **Fax:** 817-834-6744

http://members.aol.com/minco99 **email:** mlme@juno.com

Types of Records Retrieved: Civil and criminal courts; Federal courts; Real Estate

Local Retrieval Area: TX-Tarrant

Add'l Information: Established 1999. Normal turnaround time- 4 days. Projects billed by the hour. All projects require prepayment. They specialize in Genealogy Record Searches.

Minor Services Inc - Excel Legal Search

4886 Woodhurst Way, Stone Mountain, GA 30088

Phone: 770-987-0942, 770-789-8543 **Fax:** 770-987-8884

pat4142@bellsouth.net

Types of Records Retrieved: Civil and criminal courts; Tax liens/Judgments; UCC records

Local Retrieval Area: GA-Clayton, De Kalb, Fulton, Gwinnett, Hall, Henry, Rockdale. **Correspondent Relationships:** Forsyth, Cherokee, Cobb, Barrow, Paulding.

Add'l Information: Established 1992. Normal turnaround time- 24-48 hours. Projects billed by number of names searched. Often known as simply Excel Legal Search, they specialize in efficient affordable service and quick turnaround. Voice mail phone number is 770-987-0942 or 770-789-8543.

Missaukee Title Co

PO Box 480, Lake City, MI 49651

Phone: 231-839-4563 **Fax:** 231-839-5642

missaukee_title@chartermi.net

Types of Records Retrieved: Real Estate

Local Retrieval Area: MI-Missaukee

Add'l Information: Established 1980. Normal turnaround time- 2 day Expedited service available. Projects billed by number of records located. 1st project may require prepayment.

Mississippi County Abstract & Loan Co

105 E Court St, Charleston, MO 63834

Phone: 573-683-4671 **Fax:** 573-683-6898

Types of Records Retrieved: Civil courts; Probate courts; Real Estate; Tax liens/Judgments

Local Retrieval Area: MO-Mississippi

Add'l Information: Established 1974. Normal turnaround time- 3-5 days. Fee basis will vary by type of project. 1st project may require prepayment. They specialize in title insurance.

Mitchell County Abstract Co

519 Main St, Osage, IA 50461

Phone: 641-732-4571 **Fax:** 641-732-5550

abstract@osage.net

Types of Records Retrieved: Civil, criminal and probate courts; Real Estate; Tax liens/Judgments; UCC records

Local Retrieval Area: IA-Mitchell

Add'l Information: Established 1945. Normal turnaround time- 3-5 days. They charge a flat rate per project. All projects require prepayment.

Mitchell McNutt & Sams PA

PO Box 7120, Tupelo, MS 38802

Phone: 662-842-3871 **Fax:** 662-842-8450 www.mitchellmcnutt.com

Types of Records Retrieved: Civil courts; Probate courts; Federal courts; Real Estate; Tax liens/Judgments; UCC records; Vital records

Local Retrieval Area: MS-Alcorn, Lafayette, Lee, Lowndes, Pontotoc, Union

Add'l Information: Established 1902. Normal turnaround time- 1-2 days. Projects billed by the hour. They specialize in insurance investigations.

MJT Research

3902 N US 35, LaPorte, IN 46350

Phone: 219-326-7637 **Fax:** 219-325-9083

mjtslater@csinet.net

Types of Records Retrieved: Civil and criminal courts; Federal courts; Real Estate; Tax liens/Judgments; UCC records; Vital records

Local Retrieval Area: IN-Elkhart, Lake, La Porte, Marshall, Porter, St Joseph. **Correspondent Relationships:** Knox, Clark, Floyd, Vigo, Putnam, Monroe counties IN. They can retrieve criminal records from nearly all IN counties.

Add'l Information: Established 1994. Normal turnaround time- 48 hours or less. Projects billed by number of names searched. They specialize in criminal background screening but can do any public record searches.

MLQ Attorney Services

2110 Powers Ferry Rd #305, Atlanta, GA 30339

Phone: 800-446-8794; 770-984-7007 **Fax:** 800-984-7049; 770-984-7049

www.mlqattorneyservices.com **email:** mmarks@mlqattorneyservices.com

Types of Records Retrieved: Civil, criminal and probate courts; Federal courts; Real Estate; Tax liens/ judgments; UCC records; Vital records

Local Retrieval Area: DC-Washington; GA-Cobb, De Kalb, Fulton, Gwinnett; MD-Anne Arundel, Mongtomery, Prince George's. **Correspondent Relationships:** nationwide.

Add'l Information: Established 1982. Normal turnaround time- 24-48 hours. Expedited service available. Projects billed by the hour. 1st project may require prepayment. Credit cards accepted. MLQ Attorney Services is a one stop legal support service. UCC, title document retriever and service of process. They perform service of process.

MO Data Inc

1152 S 20th St, Ozark, MO 65721-7363

Phone: 417-299-2469 **Fax:** 417-485-2251 modatainc@yahoo.com

Types of Records Retrieved: Civil courts; Real Estate; Tax liens/Judgments; UCC records

Local Retrieval Area: MO-Christian, Greene, Stone, Taney, Webster

Add'l Information: Established 1996. Normal turnaround time- 24-48 hours. Projects billed by number of names searched. 1st project may require prepayment. They specialize in current owner and refinance searches. Would prefer customers to use email as primary contact, but fax can also be used as secondary contact number.

Models with Brains

3000 F Danville Blvd #408, Alamo, CA 94507

Phone: 925-838-3899 **Fax:** 925-215-8402

Cherie@modelswithbrains.com

Types of Records Retrieved: Real Estate; Tax liens/judgments; UCC records

Local Retrieval Area: CA-Alameda, Contra Costa, Placer, Sacramento, San Francisco, San Mateo, Santa Clara, Solano. **Correspondent Relationships:** Pima county, AZ; counties of CA.

Add'l Information: Established 1998. Normal turnaround time- 48 hours. Projects billed by number of names searched. 1st project may require prepayment. Credit cards accepted. With over 7 years experience, they provide fast, accurate, reliable service as well as affordable pricing.

Mohave County Process Service

PO Box 4357, Kingman, AZ 86402-4357

Phone: 800-692-5881; 928-692-9088 **Fax:** 928-757-9088

process@citlink.net

Types of Records Retrieved: Civil and criminal courts; Tax liens/Judgments

Local Retrieval Area: AZ-Mohave

Add'l Information: Established 1993. Normal turnaround time- 24 hours. Projects billed by number of names searched. 1st project may require prepayment. They specialize in process service. Also do skip tracing nationwide electronically. They perform service of process.

Mohr Information Services LLC

31 S Braddock St, Winchester, VA 22601-4144

Phone: 540-678-8775 **Fax:** 540-678-1696

www.mohrinformation.com **email:** orders@mohrinformation.com

Types of Records Retrieved: Civil, criminal and probate courts; Federal courts; Real Estate; Tax liens/Judgments; UCC records

Local Retrieval Area: DC-District of Columbia; FL-Hernando, Hillsborough, Pasco, Pinellas, Polk; MD-Anne Arundel, Baltimore, Baltimore City, Frederick, Howard, Montgomery, Prince George's, Washington; VA-Alexandria City, Arlington, Chesterfield, Fairfax, Fairfax City, Frederick, Hanover, Henrico, Loudoun, Prince William, Richmond City, Winchester City

Add'l Information: Established 1992. Normal turnaround time- 24-48 hours. Projects billed by number of names searched. Will submit an invoice upon completion of research requested and require prompt payment. They specialize in criminal, civil, UCC, judgments, and property searches. Most research completed within 24 hours. Quality research, very reasonable. A licensed PI in VA, FL.

Molly Ply Investigations

PO Box 61, Redfield, AR 72132
Phone: 501-397-2620 **Fax:** 501-397-2620
www.mollyplyinvestigations.com **email:** mollyply@cei.net

Types of Records Retrieved: Civil, criminal and probate courts; Tax liens/Judgments; UCC records

Local Retrieval Area: AR-Jefferson, Pulaski

Add'l Information: Established 1997. Normal turnaround time- 24-48 hours. Rush service available. Projects billed by number of names searched. 1st project may require prepayment. Credit cards accepted. She specializes in criminal record searches, also skiptraces, domestics, adoptions, locates, surveillance. Cell phone # 501-416-9385. A licensed PI in AR.

Monroe County Abstract & Title Co Inc

229 N Main St, Paris, MO 65275
Phone: 660-327-4109 **Fax:** 660-327-4331
hendlaw@dstream.net

Types of Records Retrieved: Civil, criminal and probate courts; Real Estate; Tax liens/Judgments; UCC records

Local Retrieval Area: MO-Monroe. **Correspondent Relationships:** Ralls, Marion, Shelby counties MO.

Add'l Information: Established 1900. Normal turnaround time- 3 days. Projects billed by number of names searched. A fee for the length of the search may also be added to the per name charge. They provide complete title service, abstracting, title insurance, document preparation, escrow and closings.

Monroe County Title Co

PO Box 188, 231 S Main St, Waterloo, IL 62298
Phone: 618-939-8292 **Fax:** 618-939-3931

Types of Records Retrieved: Real Estate

Local Retrieval Area: IL-Monroe

Add'l Information: Established 1930. Normal turnaround time- 5 days. Projects billed by number of names searched. Personal checks are accepted. They specialize in insured real estate title searches.

Monroe Title Insurance Corp (Albany)

Albany County Courthouse, 16 Eagle St, Rm 128A #5, Albany, NY 12207
Phone: 800-966-6763; 518-462-6566 **Fax:** 518-462-0625
www.monroetitle.com/offices.asp?office=albany
email: comments@monroetitle.com

Types of Records Retrieved: Federal courts; Real Estate; Tax liens/Judgments; UCC records

Local Retrieval Area: NY-Albany, Rensselaer

Add'l Information: Established 1922. Normal turnaround time- 48 hours. Projects billed by number of names searched. Projects billed by number of records located. 1st project may require prepayment. Credit cards accepted. They have 20 offices statewide. The 800 number is direct to their state customer service administrator.

Monroe Title Insurance Corp (Rochester)

47 W Main St, Rochester, NY 14614
Phone: 800-966-6763; 585-232-2070 **Fax:** 585-232-4988
www.monroetitle.com

Types of Records Retrieved: Probate courts; Federal courts; Real Estate; Tax liens/Judgments; UCC records

Local Retrieval Area: NY-Albany, Allegany, Broome, Cayuga, Chemung, Erie, Fulton, Genesee, Herkimer, Livingston, Madison, Monroe, Montgomery, Niagara, Oneida, Onondaga, Ontario, Orleans, Oswego, Otsego, Rensselaer, Saratoga, Schenectady, Schoharie, Schuyler, Seneca, Steuben, Tioga, Tompkins, Warren, Washington, Wayne, Wyoming, Yates. **Correspondent Relationships:** NY-Cattaraugus, Chautauqua, Chenango, Clinton, Columbia, Cortland, Delaware, Essex, Franklin, Greene, Hamilton, Jefferson, Lewis, St. Lawrence counties.

Add'l Information: Established 1922. Normal turnaround time- 48 hours. Projects billed by number of names searched. Projects billed by number of records located. All projects require prepayment. Credit cards accepted. They will also invoice.

Montana Abstract & Title Co

2961 Nevada Ave, Butte, MT 59701-1116
Phone: 406-533-0433 **Fax:** 406-533-0430 mtabstract@aol.com

Types of Records Retrieved: Civil, criminal and probate courts; Federal courts; Real Estate; Tax liens/Judgments; UCC records; Vital records

Local Retrieval Area: MT-Deer Lodge, Granite, Silver Bow

Add'l Information: Established 1902. Normal turnaround time- variable with each project. Projects billed by the hour. They specialize in title insurance.

Montana Abstract Co Inc

PO Box 128, Scobey, MT 59263
Phone: 406-487-5961

Types of Records Retrieved: Civil courts; Probate courts; Federal courts; Real Estate; Tax liens/Judgments; Vital records

Local Retrieval Area: MT-Daniels

Add'l Information: Established 1982. Normal turnaround time- 1 week. Projects billed by number of records located. Projects billed by the hour. 1st project may require prepayment. They specialize in title insurance and abstract updating.

Montezuma-Dolores Title Co

236 W North St, Cortez, CO 81321
Phone: 970-565-8491 **Fax:** 970-565-7050 mdtitle@charter.net

Types of Records Retrieved: Real Estate; Tax liens/judgments; UCC records

Local Retrieval Area: CO-Dolores, Montezuma

Add'l Information: Normal turnaround time- 5-7 days. Projects billed by the hour. Personal checks are accepted. They specialize in real estate title searches.

Montgomery County Abstract & Title Co

106 N Sturgeon St, Montgomery City, MO 63361
Phone: 573-564-2298 **Fax:** 573-564-6158

Types of Records Retrieved: Civil, criminal and probate courts; Real Estate; Tax liens/Judgments; UCC records

Local Retrieval Area: MO-Montgomery

Add'l Information: Established 1950. Normal turnaround time- 5-10 days. Fee basis will vary by the type of project. They will invoice. They maintain a complete set of in-house record books for Montgomery County.

Montgomery County Abstract Co

PO Box 743, Independence, KS 67301-0743
Phone: 620-331-1440 **Fax:** 620-331-4760

Types of Records Retrieved: Civil; Probate courts; Real Estate; Tax liens/Judgments; UCC records

Local Retrieval Area: KS-Montgomery

Add'l Information: Established 1940. Normal turnaround time- 1-2 days. Fee basis varies by type of transaction. 1st project may require prepayment.

Montgomery Investigative Services

12073 Tech Rd, Silver Spring, MD 20904
Phone: 800-410-4404; 301-384-7777 **Fax:** 301-680-8966
mis@aol.com

Types of Records Retrieved: Civil and criminal courts; Federal courts; Real Estate

Local Retrieval Area: MD-Montgomery, Prince George's. **Correspondent Relationships:** nationwide, especially all MD counties.

Add'l Information: Established 1981. Normal turnaround time- 24-48 hours. Projects billed by number of names searched. Projects billed by the hour. Mileage expenses are added to the fee. Payment is required within 30 days of invoice. They reserve the right to require pre-payment. A licensed PI in MD, PA, VA, DE, DC. They perform service of process.

Moody County Abstract Co

218 2nd Ave E, Flandreau, SD 57028
Phone: 605-997-3723 **Fax:** 605-997-3872

Types of Records Retrieved: Civil courts; Probate courts; Real Estate; Tax liens/Judgments; UCC records

Local Retrieval Area: SD-Moody

Add'l Information: Established 1900. Normal turnaround time- 1 week. Fee basis will vary by the type or project. 1st project may require prepayment. They specialize in title insurance and record searches.

Moon Abstract Co

421 Commercial St, Emporia, KS 66801
Phone: 620-342-1917 **Fax:** 620-342-6888

Types of Records Retrieved: Civil courts; Probate courts; Real Estate; Tax liens/Judgments; UCC records

Local Retrieval Area: KS-Lyon. **Correspondent Relationships:** Chase, Coffey, Greenwood, Morris, Osage.

Add'l Information: Established 1934. Normal turnaround time- "as soon as possible" for Lyon County and 1 week for other counties served. Projects billed by number of names searched. Projects billed by number of records located. Fee basis varies by type of transaction. Statement sent when order completed. They specialize in long term escrow holdings, title insurance, closings and searches.

Attorney Reed Moore Jr

PO Box 235, 109 2nd St, Tompkinsville, KY 42167
Phone: 270-487-6262 **Fax:** 270-487-8000
reedmoorejr@mcksi.com

Types of Records Retrieved: Civil courts; Probate courts; Real Estate; Tax liens/Judgments; UCC records

Local Retrieval Area: KY-Barren, Monroe

Add'l Information: Established 1981. Normal turnaround time- 2-3 days. Fee basis varies by type of transaction. 1st project may require prepayment.

Moore Mowdy & Youngblood

PO Box 540, Atoka, OK 74525-0540
Phone: 580-889-5656 **Fax:** 580-889-7149 mylf@mail.atoka.net

Types of Records Retrieved: Real Estate

Local Retrieval Area: OK-Atoka, Bryan, Coal, Johnston, Pushmataha

Add'l Information: Established 1953. Normal turnaround time- 48 hours. Projects billed by the hour. They specialize in probate and real estate record searches.

Moore Title & Escrow Inc

1215 E Hoffer St, Kokomo, IN 46902-5728
Phone: 888-289-1301; 765-459-3183 **Fax:** 765-459-3188
www.mooretitle.com **email:** mte@mooretitle.com

Types of Records Retrieved: Civil courts; Probate courts; Real Estate; Tax liens/Judgments; UCC records; Vital records

Local Retrieval Area: IN-Howard, Tipton

Add'l Information: Established 1899. Normal turnaround time- 2-3 days. Fee basis varies by type of transaction. They have a branch office in Tipton, 800-845-9644, 765-675-2704, 118 W Madison.

Conrad Mord

PO Drawer 311, Tylertown, MS 39667
Phone: 601-876-2611 **Fax:** 601-876-4379

Types of Records Retrieved: Civil, criminal and probate courts; Real Estate; Tax liens/Judgments; UCC records; Vital records

Local Retrieval Area: MS-Pike, Walthall

Add'l Information: Normal turnaround time- 1 day in Walthall; 2-3 days in other counties. Projects billed by the hour. 1st project may require prepayment. He is an attorney in general practice, including real estate and family law.

Morgan/Brooks Resources Inc

115 E Travis St #1140, San Antonio, TX 78205-1606
Phone: 210-476-0500 **Fax:** 210-476-0503

Types of Records Retrieved: Probate courts; Federal Courts; Real Estate; Tax liens/Judgments; UCC records.

Local Retrieval Area: TX-Bexar, Comal

Add'l Information: Established 1991. Normal turnaround time- 24-48 hours; 50-year and asset searches take 3-5 days. Projects billed by the hour. 1st project may require prepayment. Morgan/Brooks has more than 40 years experience in title research, providing timely, accurate and detailed title information to a variety of businesses.

Morrilton Abstract Co

110 S Chestnut #C, Morrilton, AR 72110
Phone: 501-354-2611 **Fax:** 501-354-4634

Types of Records Retrieved: Civil courts; Probate courts; Real Estate; Tax liens/Judgments; UCC records **Local Retrieval Area:** AR-Conway

Add'l Information: Normal turnaround time- 1 week. Fee basis will vary by the type of project. All projects require prepayment. They will also invoice. They specialize in title and real estate research.

Morris Hills Abstract Co

44 Washington St, Morristown, NJ 07960
Phone: 973-267-0450 **Fax:** 973-267-0981

Types of Records Retrieved: Probate courts; Real Estate; Tax liens/Judgments; UCC records

Local Retrieval Area: NJ-Morris

Add'l Information: Established 1965. Normal turnaround time- up to 2 weeks. Projects billed by the hour. They specialize in title insurance.

Melissa F Morris

10854 US Highway 29, Andalusia, AL 36420
Phone: 334-222-1986 **Fax:** 334-222-1986
cmmorris@alaweb.com

Types of Records Retrieved: Civil courts; Probate courts; Real Estate; Tax liens/Judgments; UCC records

Local Retrieval Area: AL-Conecuh, Covington, Escambia

Add'l Information: Established 1996. Normal turnaround time- 24-48 hours. Projects billed by number of names searched. 1st project may require prepayment. She specializes in real estate, UCC, lien and judgment searches. She has over 10 years experience as an assistant to a Real Estate Attorney.

Morrissey Morrissey & Dalluge

PO Box 597, Tecumseh, NE 68450
Phone: 402-335-3344 **Fax:** 402-335-3345

Types of Records Retrieved: Real Estate

Local Retrieval Area: NE-Johnson

Add'l Information: Established 1960. Normal turnaround time- 1 week. Projects billed by the hour. 1st project may require prepayment. Credit cards accepted. They specialize in probate and real estate.

Mosley Abstract & Title Insurance Co

PO Box 2124, Fort Smith, AR 72902
Phone: 479-782-3054 **Fax:** 479-782-5432
www.mosleyabst.com

Types of Records Retrieved: Real Estate; Tax liens/Judgments

Local Retrieval Area: AR-Crawford, Franklin, Sebastian

Add'l Information: Established 1953. Normal turnaround time- 2 days. Projects billed by number of names searched. Fee basis varies by type of project. All projects require prepayment. They specialize in real estate.

Alice S Mosley
PO Box 164 (35570 CR 39 N), Stapleton, AL 36578
Phone: 251-937-8468 **Fax:** 251-580-0292
alicemosle@aol.com

Types of Records Retrieved: Civil, criminal and probate courts; Federal courts; Real Estate; Tax liens/Judgments; UCC records

Local Retrieval Area: AL-Baldwin. **Correspondent Relationships:** Mobile and Baldwin counties AL.

Add'l Information: Established 1981. Normal turnaround time- 24-36 hours. Projects billed by number of names searched. 1st project may require prepayment. They can search any Alabama county online for criminal and civil cases. They perform service of process.

Mountain States Title Services
1975 Oro Fino Gulch, Helena, MT 59624
Phone: 406-443-0521 **Fax:** 406-443-7973 harwellco@aol.com

Types of Records Retrieved: Civil and criminal courts; Real Estate; Tax liens/Judgments; UCC records

Local Retrieval Area: MT-Broadwater, Jefferson, Lewis and Clark, Powell

Add'l Information: Established 1981. Normal turnaround time- 24-48 hours. Projects billed by number of names searched. Special billing for oil, gas and mineral reports. 1st project may require prepayment. They specialize is mineral reports, oil & gas reports, ownership & encumbrance reports, and right-of-way title reports.

Mountain View Abstract Co
PO Box 130, Mountain View, AR 72560
Phone: 870-269-8410 **Fax:** 870-269-6901

Types of Records Retrieved: Civil courts; Probate courts; Real Estate; Tax liens/Judgments; UCC records **Local Retrieval Area:** AR-Stone

Add'l Information: Established 1947. Normal turnaround time- 1-2 weeks. Fee basis will vary by the type of project. All projects require prepayment. They will invoice. They specialize in real estate and title work.

Mountrail County Abstract & Title Co
PO Box 519, Stanley, ND 58784
Phone: 701-628-2886

Types of Records Retrieved: Civil courts; Probate courts; Federal courts; Real Estate; Tax liens/Judgments; UCC records

Local Retrieval Area: ND-Burke, McKenzie, Mountrail, Ward, Williams

Add'l Information: Established 1972. Normal turnaround time- 1-5 days. Fee basis will vary by type of project.

Mower Services
PO Box 2041, Pocatello, ID 83206
Phone: 888-317-7458; 208-237-0116 **Fax:** 208-238-5705

Types of Records Retrieved: Civil, criminal and probate courts; Real estate; Tax liens.judgments; UCC records.

Local Retrieval Area: ID-Blaine; UT-Box Elder, Cache, Rich. **Correspondent Relationships:** statewide.

Add'l Information: Established 1994. Normal turnaround time- 1-5 days. Expedited service available. Projects billed by number of records located. 1st project may require prepayment. They specialize in foreclosure notices and process service. They perform service of process.

Mozark Investigations
PO Box 61, 10891 State Route BB, Rolla, MO 65402
Phone: 866-308-1411; 573-308-1411 **Fax:** 573-368-4307
www.mozark.com **email:** bobjones@mozark.com

Types of Records Retrieved: Civil, criminal and probate courts; Real Estate; Tax liens/Judgments; UCC records; Vital records

Local Retrieval Area: MO-Camden, Carter, Crawford, Dent, Franlin, Gasconade, Iron, Maries, Miller, Phelphs, Pulaski, Reynolds, Shannon, St. Francois, Texas, Washington

Add'l Information: Established 1997. Normal turnaround time- 3-5 days. Expedited service available. Projects billed by number of names searched. Projects billed by number of records located. Projects billed by the hour. All projects require prepayment. Credit cards accepted. Also provides services related to investigations, bail bonds, collections, accredited/certified computer investigations, national and special criminal records. A licensed PI in MO. They perform service of process.

Mr Holmes Inv
PO Box 3176, Jackson, MS 39207-3176
Phone: 601-859-7955 **Fax:** 601-859-0455 mrholmes@netdoor.com

Types of Records Retrieved: Civil, criminal and probate courts; Federal courts; Real Estate; Tax liens/Judgments; UCC records; Vital records

Local Retrieval Area: MS-Hinds, Madison, Rankin

Add'l Information: Established 1990. Normal turnaround time- 24-30 hours. Projects billed by number of names searched. Projects billed by the hour. All projects require prepayment. They specialize in criminal, civil, liens (state tax, judgments & federal tax), federal, criminal & civil courts, bankruptcy court and UCCs (state & county level) in the above listed counties in MS each day. They perform service of process.

MS Document Services Inc
707 West Ave #204, Austin, TX 78765
Phone: 800-292-3868; 512-474-8973 **Fax:** 800-292-2103; 512-474-1639
www.msdocs.com **email:** mindy@msdocs.com

Types of Records Retrieved: Civil, criminal and probate courts; Federal courts; Real Estate; Tax liens/Judgments; UCC records; Vital records

Local Retrieval Area: NY-Jefferson, Monroe, Onondaga, Oswego; TX-Bastrop, Bexar, Blanco, Brown, Burnet, Caldwell, Callahan, Coleman, Collin, Comal, Comanche, Dallas, Denton, Eastland, Fisher, Hays, Harris, Jones, Lee, Mitchell, Nolan, Palo Pinto, Parker, Runnels, Scurry, Shackelford, Stephens, Tarrant, Taylor, Tom Green, Travis, Williamson. **Correspondent Relationships:** Texas and New York.

Add'l Information: Established 1997. Normal turnaround time- varied. Some documents retrieved immediately; most 24-48 hours. Projects billed by number of names searched. 1st project may require prepayment. Specialize in abstracting, insurance, and filing services in New York, Texas, and throughout the Federal Court System. Prompt, accurate service, built to your needs. Get substancial savings in time and money for Travis County Texas and Texas Sec of State.

MSI Inv
PO Box 5342, West Lebanon, NH 03784
Phone: 603-298-8060 **Fax:** 603-298-6080
www.msipi.com **email:** msi@vermontel.net

Types of Records Retrieved: Civil and criminal records

Local Retrieval Area: NH-Belknap, Cheshire, Grafton, Sullivan; VT-Windsor. **Correspondent Relationships:** NH, VT.

Add'l Information: Established 1984. Normal turnaround time- 24-72 hours. Projects billed by number of names searched. 1st project may require prepayment. They specialize in criminal and civil record retrieval daily from Vermont and New Hampshire county courts. A licensed PI in NH, VT. They perform service of process.

MT Corporate Services
407 E King St, PO Box 1165, East Helena, MT 59635
Phone: 406-227-7665 **Fax:** 406-227-7991 mtcorpserv@aol.com

Types of Records Retrieved: Civil, criminal and probate courts; Federal courts; Real Estate; Tax liens/Judgments; UCC records; Vital records

Local Retrieval Area: MT-Broadwater, Lewis & Clark

Add'l Information: Established 1999. Normal turnaround time- 24-48 hours. Projects billed by number of names searched. Will advance costs not exceeding $25.00. Terms are net 30 days. They can assst with Montanan contractor and insurance licensing and obtain insurance good standing certificates. Serve as corporate registered agent. Cell phone 406-431-3353.

Mt Pleasant Abstract & Title Inc

116 Court St #A, Mt Pleasant, MI 48858
Phone: 989-773-3651 **Fax:** 989-773-0751
palexander@mtpleasantabstract.com

Types of Records Retrieved: Civil courts; Probate courts; Real Estate; Tax liens/Judgments; UCC records

Local Retrieval Area: MI-Clare, Gladwin, Gratiot, Isabella, Mecosta, Midland, Montcalm, Newaygo, Osceola

Add'l Information: Normal turnaround time- 1 week. Fee basis will vary by type of project. They specialize in real estate and title insurance.

David Mulberry

4050 Lakespur Circle S, Palm Beach Gardens, FL 33410
Phone: 800-704-1287; 561-624-0526 **Fax:** 561-624-0576
www.PalmBeachPI.com **email:** david@palmbeachpi.com

Types of Records Retrieved: Civil, criminal and probate courts; Federal courts; Real Estate; Tax liens/Judgments; UCC records; Vital records

Local Retrieval Area: FL-Palm Beach. **Correspondent Relationships:** Florida.

Add'l Information: Established 1979. Normal turnaround time- variable, depending on project. Projects billed by the hour. 1st project may require prepayment. Credit cards accepted. He is a private investigator and certified process server with over 30 years of investigative experience. A licensed PI in FL. They perform service of process.

Mulholland Investigations & Security

221 E Adams St, Jacksonville, FL 32202
Phone: 904-354-7989 **Fax:** 904-354-7922
www.mulhollandinvestigation.com **email:** miscwork@bellsouth.net

Types of Records Retrieved: Civil, criminal and probate courts; Federal courts; Real Estate; Tax liens/Judgments; UCC records; Vital records

Local Retrieval Area: FL-Baker, Clay, Duval, Nassau, St. Johns

Add'l Information: Normal turnaround time- 24-48 hours. Projects billed by number of names searched. Projects billed by the hour. Credit cards accepted. Only Visa and Mastercard accepted. Their offices are 2 blocks from the Duval County Courthouse, 3 from the sheriff's office, and walking distance to Middle Dist. of Florida Federal courthouse. A licensed PI in FL. They perform service of process.

Mullen Abstract Co

PO Box 567, 119 SW 2nd St, Walnut Ridge, AR 72476
Phone: 870-886-2452 **Fax:** 870-886-5929

Types of Records Retrieved: Civil, criminal and probate courts; Real Estate; Tax liens/Judgments; UCC records **Local Retrieval Area:** AR-Lawrence

Add'l Information: Established 1975. Normal turnaround time- 3-5 days. Fee basis will vary by the type of project. They specialize in real estate abstracting and title insurance

Donna Mundwiller

118 E 4th St, Hermann, MO 65041
Phone: 573-486-2925 **Fax:** 573-486-2059

Types of Records Retrieved: Civil, criminal and probate courts; Real Estate; Tax liens/Judgments; UCC records; Vital records

Local Retrieval Area: MO-Gasconade

Add'l Information: Established 1965. Normal turnaround time- variable depending on project. Projects billed by the hour. All projects require prepayment. She specializes in genealogy searches.

Murray County Abstract Inc

1020 W 2nd, Sulphur, OK 73086
Phone: 800-687-2988; 580-622-5294 **Fax:** 580-622-2866
murraycoabstract@cableone.net

Types of Records Retrieved: Civil courts; Probate courts; Real Estate; Tax liens/Judgments; UCC records

Local Retrieval Area: OK-Murray

Add'l Information: Established 1935. Normal turnaround time- 24 hours. Projects billed by the hour. 1st project may require prepayment. They specialize in abstracting, title insurance, escrow closings and title reports.

Musselman Abstract Co

PO Box 1072, 216 E 4th St, Bartlesville, OK 74005
Phone: 918-336-6410 **Fax:** 918-336-4880
www.musselmanabstract.com **email:** mussabst@fullnet.net

Types of Records Retrieved: Civil courts; Probate courts; Real Estate; Tax liens/Judgments; UCC records

Local Retrieval Area: OK-Washington

Add'l Information: Established 1907. Normal turnaround time- 24 hours. Fee basis will vary by the type of project.

Mutual Abstract Corporation

132 Nassau St #812, New York, NY 10038
Phone: 212-964-4686 **Fax:** 212-385-0758
rshul@aol.com

Types of Records Retrieved: Bankryuptcy Courts; Tax liens/Judgments; Real Estate; UCC records

Local Retrieval Area: NY-Bronx, Kings, Nassau, New York, Queens, Westchester. **Correspondent Relationships:** nationwide.

Add'l Information: Established 1964. Normal turnaround time- 2-4 days. Expedited service available. Projects billed by number of names searched. 1st project may require prepayment. They specialize in cooperative apartment lien searches, UCC searching and filing. They also search mechanics liens, tax liens and pending suits.

Myaer & Co Inc

PO Box 189, Mohall, ND 58761
Phone: 701-756-6487 **Fax:** 701-756-6186

Types of Records Retrieved: Real Estate; Tax liens/judgments; UCC records

Local Retrieval Area: ND-Renville

Add'l Information: Established 1996. Normal turnaround time- 10 days. Fee basis will vary by type of project.

Myers Investigations Inc

8144 Madison Ave, Indianapolis, IN 46227
Phone: 800-788-8018; 317-865-1006 **Fax:** 317-882-7204
www.myerspi.com **email:** dmyers@myerspi.com

Types of Records Retrieved: Civil and criminal courts; Tax liens/Judgments; UCC records; Vital records

Local Retrieval Area: IN-Bartholomew, Boone, Delaware, Hamilton, Hancock, Hendricks, Johnson, Madison, Marion, Monroe, Putnam, Shelby. **Correspondent Relationships:** Indiana, Kentucky, Ohio, Michigan.

Add'l Information: Established 1995. Normal turnaround time- 24 hours or less. Projects billed by number of names searched. 1st project may require prepayment. Net 10 days after pre-paid case. They specialize in legal investigations, locates, process service, background investigations, and witness interviews. A licensed PI in IN. They perform service of process.

Carrie J Myers

866 Conestoga Dr, Moscow, ID 83843
Phone: 208-883-7963 **Fax:** 208-883-7963 myersmtp@turbonet.com

Types of Records Retrieved: Civil and criminal courts; Federal courts, Real Estate, Tax liens/Judgments; UCC records

Local Retrieval Area: ID-Latah

Add'l Information: Established 1998. Normal turnaround time- 24 hours. Projects billed by number of names searched. Payment due within one month of job completion.

Ryan Myers

215 E Henley St #301, Moscow, ID 83843
Phone: 208-882-6678 **Fax:** 208-883-7963 ryanmyers@tvrbonet.com

Types of Records Retrieved: Civil anc criminal courts; Federal courts; Real Estate; Tax liens/Judgments; UCC records

Local Retrieval Area: ID-Nez Perce; WA-Asotin, Whitman

Add'l Information: Established 1999. Normal turnaround time- 48 hours. Projects billed by number of names searched. Payment due within 30 days of completion.

Myhre Process

740 N Plankinton Ave, Milwaukee, WI 53203
Phone: 414-271-9574 **Fax:** 414-271-4018

Types of Records Retrieved: Civil, criminal and probate courts; Federal courts; Tax liens/Judgments; UCC records; Vital records

Local Retrieval Area: WI-Kenosha, Milwaukee, Ozaukee, Racine, Walworth, Washington, Waukesha. **Correspondent Relationships:** Wisconsin.

Add'l Information: Established 1971. Normal turnaround time- usually same day; maximum 1 day. Projects billed by the hour. Fee may include incurred costs. 1st project may require prepayment. They specialize in process serving repossession, skiptracing & notary. Performs service of process.

N

N F Field Abstract Co

PO Box 697, Fergus Falls, MN 56538
Phone: 218-736-6844 **Fax:** 800-736-5988; 218-736-5988
www.nffield.com

Types of Records Retrieved: Civil courts; Probate courts; Real Estate; Tax liens/Judgments; UCC records

Local Retrieval Area: MN-Otter Tail

Add'l Information: Established 1910. Normal turnaround time- 5-10 days. Projects billed by number of names searched. Fee may also be based per entry. All projects require prepayment. They will also invoice. They specialize in title insurance and closings.

N W Legal Support Inc

526 Yale Ave N #A, Seattle, WA 98109-5550
Phone: 800-729-9426; 206-223-9426 **Fax:** 206-223-9475
www.nwlegal.com **email:** evennes@nwlegal.com

Types of Records Retrieved: Civil, criminal and probate courts; Federal courts; Tax liens/Judgments; UCC records; Vital records

Local Retrieval Area: WA-King, Pierce, Snohomish. **Correspondent Relationships:** Washington.

Add'l Information: Established 1989. Normal turnaround time- 48 hours. Projects billed by the hour. 1st project may require prepayment. Credit cards accepted. Terms: net 10 days. They do process service, and provide messenger services. They perform service of process.

NACM/Colorado

777 S Wadsworth Blvd Bldg 2-100, Lakewood, CO 80226-4300
Phone: 800-451-7868; 303-837-1280 **Fax:** 303-830-7808
www.nacmcolorado.com **email:** sharenl@nacmcolorado.com

Types of Records Retrieved: UCC records

Local Retrieval Area: CO-Denver

Add'l Information: Established 1996. Normal turnaround time- 3-4 hours. Projects billed by number of names searched. Projects billed by number of records located. All projects require prepayment. Credit cards accepted. They are a credit reporting association that can provide business and corporate information for KS, NE, NM, AZ, CO, MT, and WY

Nancy Durbin Process Service

PO Box 1341, Salem, IL 62881
Phone: 618-548-8296 **Fax:** 618-548-4908

Types of Records Retrieved: Civil, criminal and probate courts; Federal courts; Real Estate; Tax liens/Judgments; UCC records; Vital records

Local Retrieval Area: IL-Clay, Clinton, Fayette, Jefferson, Marion

Add'l Information: Established 1994. Normal turnaround time- 1-3 days. Expedited service available. Projects billed by the hour. 1st project may require prepayment. Cell # 618-267-0472; Pager # 618-325-3229. A licensed PI in IL. They perform service of process.

National Abstract

7659 N State St, Lowville, NY 13367
Phone: 800-535-3477; 315-376-3911 **Fax:** 315-376-8305
nac1@telenet.net

Types of Records Retrieved: Civil courts; Probate courts; Real Estate; Tax liens/Judgments; UCC records

Local Retrieval Area: NY-Lewis. **Correspondent Relationships:** Herkimer, Jefferson, Oneida, St Lawrence counties.

Add'l Information: Established 1920. Normal turnaround time- 24 hours for court records, taxes and UCC's, and 24-48 hours for real estate searches. Projects billed by number of names searched. They specialize in title insurance.

National Background Inv Inc

PO Box 966, Stevensville, MD 21666
Phone: 800-798-0079; 410-604-6200 **Fax:** 877-472-4676; 410-604-2496
www.nationalbackground.com **email:** research@nationalbackground.com

Types of Records Retrieved: Civil and criminal courts; Federal courts; Tax liens/Judgments

Local Retrieval Area: DE-all counties; MD-Allegany, Anne Arundel, Baltimore, Baltimore City, Calvert, Caroline, Carroll, Cecil, Charles, Dorchester, Frederick, Garrett, Harford, Howard, Kent, Montgomery, Prince George's, Queen Anne's, St Mary's Somerset, Talbot, Washington, Wicomico, Worcester; NJ-Atlantic, Bergen, Berlington, Camden, Cape May, Cumberland, Essex, Gloucester, Hudson, Hunterdon, Mercer, Middlesex, Monmouth, Morris, Ocean, Passaic, Salem, Somerset, Sussex, Union, Warren; VA-6 counties near DC; DC-District of Columbia. **Correspondent Relationships:** nationwide.

Add'l Information: Established 1996. Normal turnaround time- 24-48 hours. Projects billed by number of names searched. Credit cards accepted. Terms: net 15 days. They are a regional firm with collective team experience of over 30 years in public record retrieval, including title searching.

National Background Reports Inc

PO Box 752295, Memphis, TN 38175-2295
Phone: 901-526-4654 **Fax:** 901-526-4753

Types of Records Retrieved: Civil, criminal and probate courts; Federal courts; Real Estate; Tax liens/Judgments; UCC records; Vital records

Local Retrieval Area: AR-Crittenden; MS-De Soto; TN-Fayette, Shelby, Tipton. **Correspondent Relationships:** nationwide.

Add'l Information: Established 1983. Normal turnaround time- same day on criminal searches. Projects billed by number of names searched. Projects billed by number of records located. Monthly invoicing available. They conduct research in any designated court or governmental agency nationwide and specialize in providing criminal background reports for pre-employment and tenant screening in Shelby, TN county. They also provide Online services via the Internet. A licensed PI in TN.

National Corporate Research Ltd

615 S Dupont Hwy, Dover, DE 19901-4517
Phone: 800-483-1140; 302-734-1450 **Fax:** 302-734-1476
www.nationalcorp.com **email:** info@nationalcorp.com

Types of Records Retrieved: Civil courts; Federal courts; Real Estate; Tax liens/Judgments; UCC records

Local Retrieval Area: DE-Kent. **Correspondents:** nationwide.

Add'l Information: Established 1994. Normal turnaround time- next day. Projects billed by number of names searched. 1st project may require prepayment. AMEX cards accepted. They invoice for each indices and jurisdiction searched. They specialize in UCC and corporate searches at the Delaware Secretary of State office, to which they are connected online.

National Data Retrieval

174 Mark St, Bristol, CT 06010
Phone: 860-589-6716 **Fax:** 860-589-2564

Types of Records Retrieved: Civil and criminal courts; Federal courts; Real Estate, UCC records, Tax liens/Judgments.

Local Retrieval Area: CT-Hartford

Add'l Information: Established 2002. Normal turnaround time- depends per case. Expedited service available. Projects billed by number of names searched. Projects billed by the hour. 1st project may require prepayment. Credit cards accepted. In addtition to CT MVRs and 8 Connecticut counties, they also provide asset recovery searches. Call for the basic rate for each county; volume discounts available.

National Document Filing & Retrieval Inc

2601 N 3rd St #202, Phoenix, AZ 85004
Phone: 800-829-5578; 602-274-5578 **Fax:** 800-837-5573; 602-274-5573
www.natldoc.com **email:** werelistening@natldoc.com

Types of Records Retrieved: Civil, criminal and probate courts; Federal courts; Real Estate; Tax liens/Judgments; UCC records

Local Retrieval Area: AZ-Maricopa. **Correspondent Relationships:** Arizona, nationwide.

Add'l Information: Established 1985. Normal turnaround time- same day to 48 hours. Projects billed by number of names searched. Projects billed by the hour. 1st project may require prepayment. Credit cards accepted. Net 30 days, or as agreed to. National Document Filing & Retrieval is a nationwide public record company specializing in the retrieval and filing of county and state documents. They are a licensed private investigative firm. A licensed PI in AZ.

National Information Access Bureau (NIAB)

PO Box 30326, Honolulu, HI 96820
Phone: 800-787-6422; 808-455-2900 **Fax:** 808-455-2951
www.publicrecords-hawaii.com **email:** brendadey@earthlink.net

Types of Records Retrieved: Civil and criminal courts; Federal courts; Real Estate; Vital records

Local Retrieval Area: HI-Honolulu. **Correspondents:** statewide.

Add'l Information: Established 1995. Normal turnaround time- 24-48 hours. Projects billed by number of names searched. 1st project may require prepayment. They specialize in criminal background histories and MVRs.

National Information Agency

3206 S Hopkins Ave #240, Titusville, FL 32780
Phone: 321-543-9381 **Fax:** 321-383-8929
www.infoagency.com **email:** search@infoagency.com

Types of Records Retrieved: Civil, criminal and probate courts; Federal bankruptcy courts; Real Estate; Tax liens/Judgments; UCC & Vital records

Local Retrieval Area: FL-Brevard. **Correspondent Relationships:** nationwide.

Add'l Information: Established 1998. Normal turnaround time- 1-2 days. Expedited service available. Projects billed by the hour. 1st project may require prepayment. Credit cards accepted. NIA specializes in record retrieval, foreclosure representation, process service, civil and criminal, probate, real estate, Tax liens/Judgments, vital records and property records. A licensed PI in FL. They perform service of process.

National Inv Services Inc

1325 W Sunshine St, PMB 228, Springfield, MO 65807-2344
Phone: 417-831-2500 **Fax:** 417-831-4710

Types of Records Retrieved: Civil, criminal and probate courts; Federal courts; Real Estate; Tax liens/Judgments; UCC records; Vital records

Local Retrieval Area: MO-Barry, Barton, Cedar, Christian, Dade, Dallas, Douglas, Greene, Hickory, Jasper, Laclede, Lawrence, McDonald, Miller, Newton, Ozark, Phelps, Polk, Stone, Taney, Vernon, Webster, Wright

Add'l Information: Established 1989. Normal turnaround time- 2 days. Projects billed by number of names searched. 1st project may require prepayment. They specialize in record retrieval and process serving in 23 MO counties. They perform service of process.

National Pre-Employment Research

PO Box 2272, Stockbridge, GA 30281
Phone: 770-389-6607 **Fax:** 770-389-5297 nationalpr@bellsouth.net

Types of Records Retrieved: Civil and Criminal courts

Local Retrieval Area: GA-Appling, Baldwin, Bibb, Bleckley, Brantley, Bryan, Bulloch, Burke, Butts, Canden, Chatham, Clarke, Columbia, Coweta, Effingham, Evans, Glascock, Glynn, Greene, Habersham, Henry, Jasper, Lamar, Laurens, Liberty, McDuffie, McIntosh, Madison, Marion, Meriwether, Monroe. Morgan, Muscogee, Newton, Oconee, Peach, Pierce, Pike, Putnam, Richmond, Rockdale, Spakding, Talbot, Taliaferro, Tattnall, Taylor, Troup, Twiggs, Upson, Walton, Ware, Wayne; TN-Carter, Cumberland, Davidson, Fayette, Franklin, Giles, Hawkins, Haywood, Lauderdale, Lawrence, Lewis, Marion, Maury, McMinn, Meigs, Morgan, Polk, Sevier, Tipton, Union. **Correspondent Relationships:** nationwide.

Add'l Information: Established 2002. Payment method may depend on nature of job. 1st project may require prepayment. National Pre-Employment Research has 10 years experience in the pre-employment area. They specialize in criminal record information in the South, and driver information across the nation. They also provide locates. They perform service of process.

National Research Associates Inc

2138 Silas Deane Hwy #102, Rocky Hill, CT 06067-2317
Phone: 860-529-3006 **Fax:** 860-529-4375

Types of Records Retrieved: Civil, criminal and probate courts; Federal courts; Real Estate; Tax liens/Judgments; UCC records; Vital records

Local Retrieval Area: CT-Fairfield, Hartford, Litchfield, Middlesex, New Haven, New London, Tolland, Windham. **Correspondent Relationships:** nationwide, Canada, Puerto Rico.

Add'l Information: Established 1982. Normal turnaround time- 24-48 hours. Projects billed by number of names searched. 1st project may require prepayment.

National Search Solutions LLC

3736 Braewood Cir, Las Vegas, NV 89120
Phone: 702-431-9100 **Fax:** 702-431-9120 marc248@cox.net

Types of Records Retrieved: Real Estate; Tax liens/Judgments; UCC records; Vital records **Local Retrieval Area:** NV-Clark

Add'l Information: Established 1999. Normal turnaround time- 12-24 hours. Projects billed by number of names searched. 1st project may require prepayment. They offer the quickest turn-around, along with accurate information and lowest prices. "Need we say more?"

National Service Information Inc (Indiana)

320 N Meridian #817, Indianapolis, IN 46204
Phone: 317-266-0040 **Fax:** 317-266-8453
www.nsii.net **email:** search@nsii.net

Types of Records Retrieved: Civil, criminal and probate courts; Federal courts; Real Estate; Tax liens/Judgments; UCC records; Vital records

Local Retrieval Area: IN-Boone, Hamilton, Hancock, Hendricks, Johnson, Madison, Marion, Morgan, Shelby. **Correspondent Relationships:** IN, OH, KY and nationwide.

Add'l Information: Established 1989. Normal turnaround time- 1-3 days. Fee basis varies by project. They are online with Ohio and Indiana Secretary of State databases and can provide microfilm copies. They also perform corporate work. They perform service of process.

National Service Information Inc (Ohio)

145 Baker St, Marion, OH 43302
Phone: 800-235-0337; 740-387-6806 **Fax:** 800-382-1256; 740-382-1256
www.nsii.net **email:** search@nsii.net

Types of Records Retrieved: Civil, criminal and probate courts; Federal courts; Tax liens/Judgments; UCC records; Vital records

Local Retrieval Area: KY-Franklin; OH-Cuyahoga, Delaware, Franklin, Hamilton, Lucas, Marion, Montgomery, Summit. **Correspondent Relationships:** Ohio, Indiana, Kentucky, nationwide.

Add'l Information: Established 1989. Normal turnaround time- 1-3 days. Fee basis will vary by type of project. They are online with OH and IN Secretary of State databases and can provide microfilm copies. They also perform corporate work and maintain online databases (w/images) of UCC/Corporate for CA, IN, OH, & PA.

Nationwide Court Services Inc

3340 Veterans Hwy, Bohemia, NY 11716
Phone: 888-941-1234; 631-981-4400 **Fax:** 631-981-5514
www.nationwidecourtservice.com **email:** arlene2324@aol.com

Types of Records Retrieved: Civil, criminal and probate courts; Federal courts; Real Estate; Tax liens/Judgments; UCC records; Vital records

Local Retrieval Area: NY-Bronx, Dutchess, Kings, Nassau, New York, Orange, Putnam, Queens, Richmond, Rockland, Suffolk, Westchester. **Correspondent Relationships:** nationwide.

Add'l Information: Established 1994. Normal turnaround time- 2 days. Fee basis depends on type of project. 1st project may require prepayment. Will bill; terms net 30 days. They specialize in foreclosure litigation and service of process. They have a satellite office in Brooklyn Heights (718-625-5194). They perform service of process.

Nationwide Environmental Title Research

2055 E Rio Salada Pky, Tempe, AZ 85281
Phone: 800-324-4956; 480-967-6752 **Fax:** 480-966-9422
www.netronline.com **email:** brett@netronline.com

Types of Records Retrieved: Real Estate

Local Retrieval Area: AZ-Coconino, Maricopa, Mohave, Pima, Pinal, Yavapai. **Correspondent Relationships:** nationwide.

Add'l Information: Established 1993. Normal turnaround time- 5-7 days. Flat fee per project is available. Credit cards accepted. Terms: net 10 days. They specialize in providing historical property information (environmental title searches) throughout the country, to satisfy one of the requirements for the land owner defense to CERCLA liability.

Nationwide Information Services Inc

52 James Street, Albany, NY 12207
Phone: 800-873-3482; 518-449-8429 **Fax:** 800-234-8522;
nis@broadviewnet.net

Types of Records Retrieved: Civil, criminal and probate courts; Federal courts; Real Estate; Tax liens/Judgments; UCC records; Vital records; Corporate filings

Local Retrieval Area: NY-Albany. **Correspondent Relationships:** nationwide.

Add'l Information: Established 1980. Normal turnaround time- 24-48 hours. Expedited service available. Projects billed by number of names searched. 1st project may require prepayment. Credit cards accepted. They perform service of process.

Navarro County Abstract Co

PO Box 685, Corsicana, TX 75151
Phone: 903-874-3768 **Fax:** 903-874-6204

Types of Records Retrieved: Probate courts; Real Estate; Tax liens/Judgments

Local Retrieval Area: TX-Navarro

Add'l Information: Normal turnaround time- variable depending on project. Fee basis will vary by type of project.

NC Corporate Connection Inc

2605 Scribe Ct, Raleigh, NC 27615
Phone: 888-844-8360; 919-844-3360 **Fax:** 919-844-8364
krozar@nc.ri.com

Types of Records Retrieved: Civil courts; Probate courts; Federal courts; Real Estate; Tax liens/Judgments; UCC records; Vital records

Local Retrieval Area: NC-Alamance, Cabarrus, Catawba, Chatham, Durham, Franklin, Gaston, Granville, Harnett, Johnston, Lincoln, Mecklenburg, Nash, Orange, Rowan, Union, Wake. **Correspondent Relationships:** nationwide.

Add'l Information: Established 1999. Normal turnaround time- 24-48 hours. Projects billed by number of names searched. Will invoice for all projects. They specialize in civil and criminal court, probate courts, federal courts, superior courts, liens/judgments, UCC, vital records and last owner searches. They also do Secretary of State filings and searches.

Nebraska Title Company

629 Court St, Beatrice, NE 68310
Phone: 402-228-2233 **Fax:** 402-228-4543

Types of Records Retrieved: Civil courts; Probate courts; Federal courts; Real Estate; Tax liens/Judgments; UCC records

Local Retrieval Area: NE-Gage. **Correspondent Relationships:** Lancaster county NE.

Add'l Information: Established 1948. Normal turnaround time- 36 hours. Projects billed by number of names searched. 1st project may require prepayment.

Ben Neel

PO Box 355, Menard, TX 76859
Phone: 325-396-2351 **Fax:** 325-396-2047

Types of Records Retrieved: Civil, criminal and probate courts; Real Estate; Tax liens/Judgments; UCC records; Vital records

Local Retrieval Area: TX-Menard, Sutton. **Correspondent Relationships:** Menant Concho, Kimble, Mason, Schleicher, Tom Green, McCulloch, Sutton, Stephens.

Add'l Information: Established 1984. Normal turnaround time- 1-2 days. Projects billed by number of names searched. Projects billed by number of records located. Projects billed by the hour. Charges by the hour are $100.00/hr. All projects require prepayment. He is a lawyer.

Nell Watkins & Associates

6417 Faircove Circle, Garland, TX 75043
Phone: 972-226-8811 **Fax:** 972-226-8811
nellw@ticnet.com

Types of Records Retrieved: Civil, criminal and probate courts; Federal courts; Real Estate; Tax liens/Judgments; UCC records; Vital records

Local Retrieval Area: TX-Dallas, Kaufman, Rockwall. **Correspondent Relationships:** nationwide.

Add'l Information: Established 1994. Normal turnaround time- 24-48 hours. Projects billed by number of names searched. In Dallas county, charge by houry rate. They specialize in background, asset and locate investigations. 25 years experience in court record research/retrieval. Licensed PI in TX.

Nelson County Abstract

206 Main St, Lakota, ND 58344
Phone: 701-247-2221 **Fax:** 701-247-2221

Types of Records Retrieved: Real Estate; Tax liens/Judgments

Local Retrieval Area: ND-Nelson

Add'l Information: Established 2002. 1st project may require prepayment. They specialize in real estate.

Nemaha County Abstract & Title Co

402 Main St #C, Seneca, KS 66538
Phone: 785-336-2137 **Fax:** 785-336-2537

Types of Records Retrieved: Civil courts; Probate courts; Real Estate; Tax liens/Judgments; UCC records; Vital records

Local Retrieval Area: KS-Nemaha

Add'l Information: Established 1994. Normal turnaround time- 1-2 days. Fee basis varies by type of transaction. 1st project may require prepayment.

Joe Y Nerio

1832 Cordova Av, Colton, CA 92324
Phone: 909-824-9358 **Fax:** 909-824-8012

Types of Records Retrieved: Civil, criminal and probate courts; Federal courts; Vital records

Local Retrieval Area: CA-Riverside, San Bernardino. **Correspondent Relationships:** Los Angeles, Orange counties, CA.

Add'l Information: Established 1994. Normal turnaround time- 1-3 days. Projects billed by number of names searched. Projects billed by the hour. 1st project may require prepayment. He specializes in criminal record searches.

Net Check Investigations

26523 N Huntswood Ln, Santa Clarita, CA 91387
Phone: 888-638-2432; 661-250-3188 **Fax:** 661-250-3198
netcheck@earthlink.net

Types of Records Retrieved: Civil, criminal and probate courts; Federal courts; Real Estate, UCC records

Local Retrieval Area: CA-Los Angeles, Orange

Add'l Information: Established 1997. Normal turnaround time- 24-48 hours. Projects billed by number of names searched. Will invoice monthly. They specialize in criminal, civil, property record searches in one to three days. Volume discounts. Also does surveillance, behavioral assessments, profiling, pre-employment, domestic violence/stalking prevention. A licensed PI in CA, AZ.

Tim Neuroth

PO Box 484, Webster City, IA 50595-0484
Phone: 515-832-3156 **Fax:** 515-832-9153

Types of Records Retrieved: Civil, criminal and probate courts; Real Estate; Tax liens/Judgments; UCC records; Vital records

Local Retrieval Area: IA-Hamilton

Add'l Information: Established 1989. Normal turnaround time- 1-2 days. Projects billed by the hour. 1st project may require prepayment. He will accept personal checks.

Nevada Land Services

PO Box 1608, 363 Erie Main St, Tonopah, NV 89049
Phone: 800-233-4999; 775-482-5641 **Fax:** 775-482-8935

Types of Records Retrieved: Real Estate; Tax liens/Judgments; UCC records

Local Retrieval Area: NV-Churchill, Esmeralda, Eureka, Humboldt, Lander, Lincoln, Mineral, Nye, Pershing

Add'l Information: Established 1990. Normal turnaround time- 10 days. Projects billed by number of names searched. Personal checks are accepted.

New Century Title

583 W Main St, Witheville, VA 24382
Phone: 276-223-1207 **Fax:** 276-223-1807

Types of Records Retrieved: Real Estate; Tax liens/Judgments

Local Retrieval Area: VA-Bland

Add'l Information: Established 1999. 1st project may require prepayment. They specialize in real estate.

New England Abstract LLC

8 Pine Glen Terrace, Wallingford, CT 06492
Phone: 203-265-0256 **Fax:** 815-301-8506 john_a_harlow@sbcglobal.net

Types of Records Retrieved: Civil, criminal and probate courts; Federal district courts; Real Estate; Tax liens/Judgments; UCC & Vital records

Local Retrieval Area: CT-Fairfield, Hartford, Litchfield, Middlesex, New Haven, New London, Tolland, Windham

Add'l Information: Established 2002. Normal turnaround time- 24-48 hours. Expedited service available. Projects billed by number of names searched. Billing done on client terms. They are a locally-owned and operated title search and document retrieval firm covering all of CT. Search and pricing options available upon inquiry. A licensed PI in CT.

New England Recovery Inc

PO Box 1025, Barre, VT 05641
Phone: 800-922-7376; 802-433-6111 **Fax:** 802-433-6742

Types of Records Retrieved: Civil, criminal and probate courts; Federal courts; Real Estate; Tax liens/Judgments; UCC records; Vital records

Local Retrieval Area: VT-Addison, Bennington, Caledonia, Chittenden, Essex, Franklin, Grand Isle, Lamoille, Orange, Orleans, Rutland, Washington, Windham, Windsor

Add'l Information: Established 1985. Normal turnaround time- 2-4 days. They charge a base fee and per hour. They also charge extra for the copy charges. 1st project may require prepayment. Will discuss with clients terms for billings. They specialize in hidden asset searches and location of missing persons. A licensed PI in NH, VT.

New Information Court Research

22737 Barton Rd #162, Grand Terrace, CA 92313
Phone: 909-514-1595 **Fax:** 909-514-1595
inforsch@dslextreme.com

Types of Records Retrieved: Civil and criminal courts; Federal Courts; UCC records; Tax liens/Judgments

Local Retrieval Area: CA-Riverside, San Bernardino. **Correspondent Relationships:** Orange, Los Angeles counties.

Add'l Information: Established 1997. Normal turnaround time- 24 hours. Projects billed by number of names searched. 1st project may require prepayment. Terms net 30 days. They specialize in civil and criminal court background checks

New Road Research

362 New Road, Laurens, NY 13796
Phone: 607-432-8911 **Fax:** 607-432-2104 research@dmcom.net

Types of Records Retrieved: Civil, criminal and probate courts; Federal Courts; Real Estate; Tax liens/Judgments

Local Retrieval Area: NY-Chenango, Delaware, Otsego. **Correspondent Relationships:** statewide, with quick return.

Add'l Information: Normal turnaround time- 24 hours; slightly longer for other counties in NY. 1st project may require prepayment. New Road performs hands on felony background checks locally, also land, civil and criminal records; also felony and misdemeanor statewide searches.

Newell & Associates Inc

PO Box 1624, Meridian, MS 39302
Phone: 601-693-7700 **Fax:** 601-483-7954 newellcan@aol.com

Types of Records Retrieved: Civil and criminal courts; Real Estate; Tax liens/Judgments; UCC records

Local Retrieval Area: MS-Attala, Clarke, Clay, Jasper, Kemper, Lauderdale, Leake, Lee, Lowndes, Monroe, Neshoba, Newton, Noxubee, Oktibbeha, Webster, Winston. **Correspondent Relationships:** statewide.

Add'l Information: Established 2000. Normal turnaround time- 24 hours if received before 10:00 AM. Projects billed by number of names searched. 1st project may require prepayment. Must pre-pay for process service. Newell & Associates Inc is a service support company that is motivated to provide accurate, expedient customer service. Performs service of process.

NH Background Investigations LLC

PO Box 1064, Nashua, NH 03061
Phone: 603-598-4106 **Fax:** 603-598-4108
www.preemploymentsearch.com **email:** rod@preemploymentsearch.com

Types of Records Retrieved: Civil, criminal and probate courts; Federal courts; Real Estate; Tax liens/Judgments; UCC records; Vital records

Local retrieval area: MA-Middlesex, Suffolk; NH-Hillsborough, Merrimack

Add'l Information: Established 1994. Normal turnaround time- 12-24 hours. Projects billed by number of names searched. Credit cards accepted. Clients are billed monthly. They specialize in pre-employment screening, criminal record searches, background investigations and corporate due-diligence reports. They are a subsidiary of Gagnon & Wendt, A NH PI Agency. A licensed PI in NH.

Jake Nichols

PO Box 441, Plentywood, MT 59254
Phone: 406-765-1651, 406-765-1806 **Fax:** 406-765-1651

Types of Records Retrieved: Real Estate; Tax liens/Judgments

Local Retrieval Area: MT-Daniels, Roosevelt, Sheridan

Add'l Information: Established 1957. Normal turnaround time- variable depending on project. Projects billed by the hour. 1st project may require prepayment. He specializes in mineral searches.

Nisonger Abstracting Services

8174 Sunbonnet Dr, Fair Oaks, CA 95628
Phone: 916-965-6544 **Fax:** 916-975-9489
www.faqsforyou.com **email:** info@faqsforyou.com

Types of Records Retrieved: Real Estate; Tax liens/Judgments; UCC records

Local Retrieval Area: CA-El Dorado, Placer, Sacramento, Yolo

Add'l Information: Established 2004. Normal turnaround time- 24-48 hours. Expedited service available for extra charge. Projects billed by number of names searched. Projects billed by number of records located. 1st project may require prepayment. Payment due net 30 days.

NNBS Inc

730 N Broadway #B, Knoxville, TN 37917
Phone: 865-633-5079 **Fax:** 865-637-1556
http://anytimeservices.com **email:** dossier@anytimeservices.com

Types of Records Retrieved: Probate courts; Real Estate; Tax liens/Judgments; UCC records

Local Retrieval Area: TN-Anderson, Blount, Jefferson, Knox, Loudon, Roane, Sevier, Union. **Correspondent Relationships:** Kentucky and Tennessee, areas of Georgia and Indiana.

Add'l Information: Established 2001. Normal turnaround time- 24-48 hours. Projects billed by number of names searched. Projects billed by the hour. They only charge by the hour on probate and will searches. Credit cards accepted. Discounts for volume/monthly orders. Credit cards accepted through Paypal. Formerly Nesbit & Nesbit Business Svcs, they provide service throughout Tennessee and Kentucky.

Nodaway County Abstract Co

501 N Market St, Maryville, MO 64468-1616
Phone: 660-582-2332 **Fax:** 660-582-8145
mail@nodabstract.com

Types of Records Retrieved: Civil courts; Probate courts; Real Estate; Tax liens/Judgments; UCC records; Vital records

Local Retrieval Area: MO-Nodaway, Worth

Add'l Information: Established 1980. Normal turnaround time- 1 day. Projects billed by number of names searched. They specialize in complete searches of land records.

Nor-Cal Court Research

PO Box 246, Orland, CA 95963
Phone: 530-865-3525 **Fax:** 530-865-8066
lefdalbarbara@snowcrest.net

Types of Records Retrieved: Civil and criminal courts

Local Retrieval Area: CA-Butte, Glenn, Humboldt, Shasta, Tehama. **Correspondent Relationships:** Oregon, Washington.

Add'l Information: Established 1997. Normal turnaround time- 12-24 hours. Projects billed by number of names searched. Terms are net 30 days. They specialize in court record retrieval.

Norcal Public Records Service

21430 Perimeter Rd, Grass Valley, CA 95949
Phone: 800-252-0910; 530-889-5865 **Fax:** 530-885-0662

Types of Records Retrieved: Civil and criminal courts; Real Estate; Tax liens/Judgments; UCC records

Local Retrieval Area: CA-Nevada, Placer, Sonoma. **Correspondent Relationships:** other California counties.

Add'l Information: Established 1993. Normal turnaround time- 1-3 days. Projects billed by number of names searched. Terms: net 15 days. They are specialist in county court, federal court, and county recorder research. Fax ordering is encouraged. Reports are faxed back at no charge.

North American Security Solutions

2844 E River Rd, Dayton, OH 45439-1538
Phone: 888-898-6277; 937-890-4300 **Fax:** 937-890-4301
www.nassinc.com **email:** jhuber@nassinc.com

Types of Records Retrieved: Civil and criminal courts; Federal courts; Real Estate; Tax liens/Judgments

Local Retrieval Area: OH-Clark, Darke, Greene, Miami, Montgomery, Preble

Add'l Information: Established 1997. Normal turnaround time- 1-2 days. Projects billed by the hour. Credit cards accepted. A licensed PI in OH.

North Country Process Inc

PO Box 101126, Anchorage, AK 99510
Phone: 907-274-2023 **Fax:** 907-274-2823

Types of Records Retrieved: Civil and criminal courts, Probate courts; Federal courts, UCC records, Real Estate, Tax liens/Judgments.

Local Retrieval Area: AK-Anchorage, Fairbanks North Star, Kenai Peninsula, Ketchikan Gateway, Matanuska Susitna

Add'l Information: Established 1987. Normal turnaround time- 1-2 days. Expedited service available. Projects billed by the hour. All projects require prepayment. Their hands-on coverage includes these communities: Anchorage, Ft Richardson, Elmendorf AFB, Eagle River, Chugiak, Wasilla, Palmer, Talkeetna, Big Lake, Kenai, Soldotna, Nikiski, Seward, Homer, Fairbanks, North Pole, Ketchikan, Eilesen AFB and Girdwood. They perform service of process.

North Florida Abstract & Title Company

PO Box 838, Monticello, FL 32345
Phone: 850-997-2670 **Fax:** 850-997-3412 nfabstract@cs.com

Types of Records Retrieved: Civil, criminal and probate courts; Real Estate; Tax liens/Judgments; UCC records; Vital records

Local Retrieval Area: FL-Jefferson

Add'l Information: Established 1972. Normal turnaround time- 1 week. Fee basis will vary by the type of project. Specializes in real estate searches.

North Louisiana Title Co Inc

1126 Plaza Blvd, Monroe, LA 71201
Phone: 800-515-7715; 318-323-3838 **Fax:** 318-330-9390

Types of Records Retrieved: Civil, criminal and probate courts; Federal courts; Tax liens/Judgments; Real Estate; UCC records.

Local Retrieval Area: LA-Bienville, Bossier, Caddo, Caldwell, Catahoula, Claiborne, Concordia, East Carroll, Franklin, Grant, Jackson, La Salle, Lincoln, Madison, Morehouse, Ouachita, Rapides, Richland, Tensas, Union, Webster, West Carroll, Winn

Add'l Information: Normal turnaround time- 1-3 days. Fee will vary by type of search. All projects require prepayment. They specialize in title searches.

North Missouri Title

PO Box 787, Kirksville, MO 63501
Phone: 660-665-4711 **Fax:** 660-627-0625

Types of Records Retrieved: Real Estate; Tax liens/Judgments

Local Retrieval Area: MO-Adair

Add'l Information: 1st project may require prepayment. They specialize in real estate.

North Pacific Legal

PO Box 193, 895 Commercial Ave, Coos Bay, OR 97420
Phone: 541-888-5118 **Fax:** 541-269-5294

Types of Records Retrieved: Civil, criminal and probate courts

Local Retrieval Area: OR-Coos

Add'l Information: Established 1987. Normal turnaround time- variable depending on project. Projects billed by the hour. They specialize in process service and trustee sales. They perform service of process.

North Vernon Abstract Co Inc

PO Box 368, North Vernon, IN 47265
Phone: 812-346-2259 **Fax:** 812-346-6056 nvabstract@seidata.com

Types of Records Retrieved: Civil courts; Probate courts; Real Estate; Tax liens/Judgments; UCC records

Local Retrieval Area: IN-Jennings. **Correspondent Relationships:** Jackson, Jefferson, Scott, Ripley Bartholonew & Decatur counties.

Add'l Information: Established 1969. Normal turnaround time- variable, depending on project. Projects billed by number of names searched. Personal checks accepted.

North Winds Inv Inc

PO Box 1654, Rogers, AR 72757
Phone: 800-530-4514; 479-925-1612 **Fax:** 479-925-2819
nwi@cox-internet.com

Types of Records Retrieved: Civil, criminal and probate courts; Federal courts; Real Estate; Tax liens/Judgments; UCC records; Vital records

Local Retrieval Area: AR-Benton, Crawford, Pulaski, Sebastian, Washington. **Correspondent Relationships:** Arkansas.

Add'l Information: Established 1986. Normal turnaround time- 2-3 days. Projects billed by the hour. 1st project may require prepayment. They specialize in worker's compensation, liability surveillance, skiptracing, fire cause and origin, product liability, background searches and complete asset searches as well as polygraph exams and process service. A licensed PI in AR, MO, MS, OK, TN. They perform service of process.

Northeast Colorado Title Co LLC

206 N 3rd St, PO Box 110, Sterling, CO 80751
Phone: 970-522-7130 **Fax:** 970-522-7382
northeast_colorado_title@hotmail.com

Types of Records Retrieved: Civil and criminal courts; Real Estate; Tax liens/Judgments; UCC records

Local Retrieval Area: CO-Logan

Add'l Information: Established 1996. Normal turnaround time- 48 hours. Projects billed by number of names searched. 1st project may require prepayment.

Northeast Investigations Inc

201 W Genesee St #200, Fayetteville, NY 13066
Phone: 888-796-1051; 315-682-1160 **Fax:** 315-682-1157
www.nei-cny.com **email:** jcalver945@aol.com

Types of Records Retrieved: Civil, criminal and probate courts; Federal courts; Real Estate; Tax liens/Judgments; UCC records; Vital records

Local Retrieval Area: NY-Albany, Broome, Cayuga, Cortland, Erie, Herkimer, Jefferson, Lewis, Madison, Monroe, Oneida, Onondaga, Oswego. **Correspondent Relationships:** most of NY State, including Albany and Erie counties.

Add'l Information: Established 1989. Normal turnaround time- 3-4 days to 1 week. Projects billed by number of names searched. Projects billed by the hour. 1st project may require prepayment. Credit cards accepted. Will take checks upon assignment for new customers. They are a full service company, specializing in investigations. They offer the insurance fraud hotline via their toll-free number. Record retrieval and trial preparation work a speciality. A licensed PI in NY. They perform service of process.

Northeast Nebraska Court Research

Box 842, 1007 Tenth St, Stanton, NE 68779
Phone: 402-439-2469 **Fax:** 402-439-2468 nncr_carla@yahoo.com

Types of Records Retrieved: Civil, criminal and probate courts; Real Estate; Tax liens/Judgments; Vital records

Local Retrieval Area: NE-Cuming, Dodge, Madison, Pierce, Saunders, Stanton, Wayne

Add'l Information: Established 1994. Normal turnaround time- 24 hours, sometimes less. Projects billed by number of names searched. Trip charges for Cuming, Pierce, and Wayne counties. Monthly billing. They specialize in same day turnarounds. Services also include state/federal tax liens, property searches, and delinquent tax lien lists. Can do 20 counties for property searches.

Northeast Nebraska Title & Escrow

PO Box 991, Norfolk, NE 68702-0991
Phone: 402-371-1221 **Fax:** 402-371-7800

Types of Records Retrieved: Civil courts; Probate courts; Real Estate; Tax liens/Judgments; UCC records; Vital records

Local Retrieval Area: NE-Knox, Madison, Pierce

Add'l Information: Established 1990. Normal turnaround time- 1-3 days. Fee basis is a flat rate and per record. They specialize in title insurance.

Northern Arizona Inv

PO Box 1326, Flagstaff, AZ 86002
Phone: 800-657-2747; 928-779-2823 **Fax:** 928-779-1044
nai@flagstaff.az.us

Types of Records Retrieved: Civil, criminal and probate courts; Real Estate; Tax liens/Judgments; UCC records

Local Retrieval Area: AZ-Coconino, Navajo

Add'l Information: Established 1989. Normal turnaround time- 24-48 hours in Coconino County; 48-72 hours in Navajo County. Projects billed by number of names searched. 1st project may require prepayment. They specialize in skiptracing, process serving and civil and criminal investigations. A licensed PI in AZ. They perform service of process.

Northern Intermountain Security Inc

PO Box 4793, Ketchum, ID 83340
Phone: 208-726-2705 **Fax:** 208-726-5802

Types of Records Retrieved: Civil, criminal and probate courts; Real Estate; Tax liens/Judgments; UCC records; Vital records

Local Retrieval Area: ID-Blaine, Twin Falls. **Correspondent Relationships:** Jerome, Lincoln, Gooding counties ID.

Add'l Information: Established 1994. Normal turnaround time- 24 hours. Expedited service available. Projects billed by number of records located. They perform service of process.

Northern Title of Vilas County

Box 877, Eagle River, WI 54521
Phone: 715-479-6459 **Fax:** 715-477-2515
www.northerntitleinc.com

Types of Records Retrieved: Civil courts; Probate courts; Real Estate; Tax liens/Judgments; UCC records

Local Retrieval Area: WI-Vilas

Add'l Information: Established 1975. Normal turnaround time- 2 days. Projects billed by number of names searched. Standard fees are charged for searches. They specialize in title, closing and escrow services.

Northshore Paralegal Services Inc

130 Centre St, Danvers, MA 01923
Phone: 800-883-6020; 978-750-6020 **Fax:** 888-844-8135; 978-750-8135
www.nsps.com **email:** jostiguy@nsps.com

Types of Records Retrieved: Civil, criminal and probate courts; Federal courts; Real Estate; Tax liens/Judgments; UCC and corporate records; Vital records

Local Retrieval Area: MA-Barnstable, Berkshire, Bristol, Essex, Franklin, Hampden, Hampshire, Middlesex, Nantucket, Norfolk, Plymouth, Suffolk, Worcester. **Correspondent Relationships:** nationwide.

Add'l Information: Established 1987. Normal turnaround time- 1-2 business days. Expedited service available. Projects billed by number of names searched. 1st project may require prepayment. Payment due upon receipt of report/invoice. They specialize in current owner searches, corporate retrieval and filings, resident agent, court searches, UCC retrieval and filings on state and town levels.

Northwest Abstract & Title Inc

PO Box 1265, Williston, ND 58802
Phone: 800-798-6723; 701-774-8829 **Fax:** 701-774-9004

Types of Records Retrieved: Civil courts; Real Estate; Tax liens/Judgments; UCC records

Local Retrieval Area: ND-Burke, Dunn, Williams

Add'l Information: Established 1987. Normal turnaround time- 3 days. Projects billed by the hour. 1st project may require prepayment. They specialize in abstracts, title insurance, real estate closings, escrow services and oil and gas titles.

NR&C

175 Lancaster St #221, Portland, ME 04101-2400
Phone: 207-791-2852 **Fax:** 207-791-2858
www.nationwideresearch.com **email:** nrcinfo@maine.rr.com

Types of Records Retrieved: Civil, criminal and probate courts; Federal courts; Real Estate; Tax liens/Judgments; UCC records

Local Retrieval Area: ME-Cumberland, Franklin, Kennebec, Oxford, York; NH-Carroll, Cheshire, Hillsborough, Merrimack, Rockingham. **Correspondent Relationships:** nationwide and international.

Add'l Information: Established 1997. Normal turnaround time- 24-48 hours. Projects billed by the hour. They specialize in litigation monitoring services, national bankruptcy info, due diligence and document retrieval.

NU West Investigations

5717 W Glendale Ave, Glendale, AZ 85301
Phone: 623-937-9676 **Fax:** 623-937-8706
www.nuwestinvestigations.com **email:** royce_fowler@hotmail.com

Types of Records Retrieved: Civil, criminal and probate courts; Federal courts; Real Estate; Tax liens/Judgments; UCC records; Vital records

Local Retrieval Area: AZ-Maricopa

Add'l Information: Established 1996. Normal turnaround time- 48 hours. Expedited service available. Projects billed by the hour. All projects require prepayment. Credit cards accepted. An investigative firm with full service, process service, fingerprinting, photographs, mystery shopping, court document retrieval, surveillance, background checks, debuggings and locates. They perform service of process.

NW Missouri Information Services

PO Box 8222, St Joseph, MO 64508-6334
Phone: 816-233-4779 **Fax:** 816-233-6934
nwmis@csimokan.com

Types of Records Retrieved: Civil, criminal and probate courts; Federal courts; Real Estate; Tax liens/Judgments; UCC records; Vital records

Local Retrieval Area: MO-Andrew, Atchison, Buchanan, Clay, Clinton, DeKalb, Holt, Jackson, Nodaway, Platte

Add'l Information: Established 1980. Normal turnaround time- 1-4 days depending on county. Projects billed by number of names searched. Fee basis will vary by the type and location (distance) of project. 1st project may require prepayment. They specialize in real estate, civil and criminal records as well as process service and missing persons. Northwest Missouri Info Svcs performs the document retrieval; phone is 816-233-4779. Orders are NOT accepted by e-mail. A licensed PI in KS, MO. They perform service of process.

Jerome Nye

830 N St, Eureka, CA 95501 **Phone:** 707-442-9542 **Fax:** 707-442-9542

Types of Records Retrieved: Civil and criminal courts; Real Estate; Tax liens/Judgments; UCC records; Vital records

Local Retrieval Area: CA-Humboldt

Add'l Information: Established 2001. Normal turnaround time- 24-36 hours. Expedited service available. Projects billed by number of names searched. 1st project may require prepayment. He specializes in public records research, retrieval, reporting and recording.

O

O H Vivell Title Co

506 N Main St, Carrollton, IL 62016-0031
Phone: 217-942-3733 **Fax:** 217-942-3207 ohvivell@earthlink.net

Types of Records Retrieved: Civil, criminal and probate courts; Real Estate; Tax liens/Judgments; UCC records; Vital records

Local Retrieval Area: IL-Greene. **Correspondent Relationships:** Calhoun.

Add'l Information: Established 1891. Normal turnaround time- variable depending on project. Projects billed by number of records located. 1st project may require prepayment.

Oberdier Search Services

5191 Wyandot Rd, Nevada, OH 44849
Phone: 740-225-3057 **Fax:** 740-465-5308 crtrnr1@aol.com

Types of Records Retrieved: Civil courts; Probate courts; Real Estate; Tax liens/Judgments; UCC records

Local Retrieval Area: OH-Crawford, Delaware, Hardin, Marion, Morrow, Union, Wyandot. **Correspondent Relationships:** state of Ohio.

Add'l Information: Established 1992. Normal turnaround time- 24-72 hours. Projects billed by number of names searched. Terms: net 30 days. She specializes in UCCs, federal and state tax liens, judgments, fixture filings, single property searches and delinquent tax information. Document retrieval of court records available. Filing of UCCs, mortgages & deeds are also available.

Rosemary O'Brien

8207 17th Ave, Adelphi, MD 20783
Phone: 301-434-4044; Cell-301-807-1809 **Fax:** 301-434-9144
irishroi@aol.com

Types of Records Retrieved: Civil, criminal and probate courts; Federal courts; Real Estate; Tax liens/Judgments; UcC records; Vital records

Local Retrieval Area: MD-Anne Arundel, Montgomery, Prince George's

Add'l Information: Established 2000. Normal turnaround time- 3-5 days. Expedited service available. Hourly rate charged plus costs with a minimum of 1/2 hours. All projects require prepayment. She is an independent paralegal, provide legal servcies for attorneys, ie, physically search & retrieve documents from various state & county & federal offices. Pager # is 301-426-8045. They perform service of process.

Nikki A O'Connell

155 Princess Margaret Dr, Newport News, VA 23602
Phone: 757-877-8469 **Fax:** 757-877-8469 searchvasenikki@aol.com

Types of Records Retrieved: Civil, criminal and probate courts; Federal courts; Real Estate; Tax liens/Judgments; UCC records

Local Retrieval Area: VA-Hampton, James City, Newport News, York

Add'l Information: Normal turnaround time- 24-48 hours. Projects billed by number of names searched. Fees also determined by number of indexes. Personal checks accepted. She specializes in UCC, judgment, tax liens, suits & property/title searches. She also does credit & construction reporting & document filings. Would consider search requests for Gloucester, Isle of Wight, Norfolk, Virginia Beach & Surry counties.

Ogemaw County Abstract Co

111 N 3rd St, West Branch, MI 48661
Phone: 989-345-0110 **Fax:** 989-345-2907

Types of Records Retrieved: Real Estate; Tax liens/Judgments

Local Retrieval Area: MI-Ogemaw

Add'l Information: Established 1902. Normal turnaround time- 3-5 business days. Projects billed by number of names searched. Or, charge by legal descriptions 1st project may require prepayment. Pre-payment required for searches. In business since 1902, they have the records in their office to provide fast and efficient service.

Ogemaw Title Co

PO Box 384, West Branch, MI 48661
Phone: 989-345-7240 **Fax:** 989-345-4777

Types of Records Retrieved: Civil, criminal and probate courts; Real Estate; Tax liens/Judgments; UCC records; Vital records

Local Retrieval Area: MI-Arenac, Ogemaw

Add'l Information: Established 1987. Normal turnaround time- up to 1 week. Expedited service available. Fee basis will vary by the type of project. They request prepay on out of area transactions. They specialize in title insurance and closing.

Ohio Title

250 S Prospect St, Ravenna, OH 44266
Phone: 330-297-7003 **Fax:** 330-296-9644

Types of Records Retrieved: Civil courts; Probate courts; Real Estate; Tax liens/Judgments; UCC records; Vital records

Local Retrieval Area: OH-Portage

Add'l Information: Established 1954. Normal turnaround time- 24 hours for most searches, and full real estate title searches average 3 working days. Fee basis will vary by type of project. Personal checks are accepted.

Okeechobee Abstract & Title Ins Inc

207 NW 2nd St, Okeechobee, FL 34972-4115
Phone: 863-763-3710 **Fax:** 863-763-3787

Types of Records Retrieved: Civil, criminal and probate courts; Real Estate; Tax liens/Judgments; UCC records

Local Retrieval Area: FL-Glades, Okeechobee. **Correspondent Relationships:** Palm Beach, Martin, St. Lucie, Broward, Dade, Monroe counties.

Add'l Information: Established 1943. Normal turnaround time- same day for name and UCC searches; 2-3 days for real estate commitments. Projects billed by number of names searched. They are a family owned company that has been in business for over 50 years.

Okfusee Abstract & Title Co

320 W Broadway St, Okemah, OK 74859
Phone: 918-623-0565 **Fax:** 918-623-4022

Types of Records Retrieved: Civil courts; Probate courts; Real Estate; Tax liens/Judgments; UCC records; Vital records

Local Retrieval Area: OK-Okfuskee

Add'l Information: Established 1991. Normal turnaround time- 2-3 days. Projects billed by the hour.

Oklahoma Court Explorers

PO Box 2453, Muskogee, OK 74402
Phone: 918-360-4798 **Fax:** 918-687-1899 jgann74401@yahoo.com

Types of Records Retrieved: Civil, criminal and probate courts; Federal courts; Real Estate; Tax liens/Judgments; UCC records

Local Retrieval Area: OK-Cherokee, Mayes, McIntosh, Muskogee, Rogers, Tulsa, Wagoner

Add'l Information: Normal turnaround time- 24-48 hours. Projects billed by number of names searched. 1st project may require prepayment.

Theresa Olaires

12 Eastwind Dr, Buena Park, CA 90621
Phone: 714-595-4729 **Fax:** 714-670-2156 tolairesresearch@yahoo.com

Types of Records Retrieved: Civil, criminal and probate courts; Federal courts; Real Estate; Tax liens/Judgments; UCC records; Vital records

Local Retrieval Area: CA-Orange

Add'l Information: Established 2001. Normal turnaround time- same day to 24 hours. Orders received after 10AM requesting same day turnaround is considered rush. Projects billed by number of names searched. Will charge by the hour on special projects. 1st project may require prepayment. Terms are net 15 days. They specialize in servicing other search companies in their document filings, UCCs, tax liens, judgments, property and all types of litigation searches. All searches are performed in person.

Oliver County Abstract

Box 105, Center, ND 58530
Phone: 701-794-3496 **Fax:** 701-794-3476

Types of Records Retrieved: Civil courts; Probate courts; Federal courts; Real Estate; Tax liens/Judgments; UCC records

Local Retrieval Area: ND-Oliver

Add'l Information: Established 1910. Normal turnaround time- variable depending on project. Projects billed by the hour. A base rate is charged in addition to the hourly rate. 1st project may require prepayment. Professional credit extended to clients whose accounts are current. They specialize in title abstracts, lien searches and title memorandums.

Olson & Humboldt County Abstract

PO Box 276, 503 Sumner Ave, Humboldt, IA 50548
Phone: 515-332-1593 **Fax:** 515-332-3672

Types of Records Retrieved: Civil, criminal and probate courts; Real Estate; Tax liens/Judgments; UCC records; Vital records

Local Retrieval Area: IA-Humboldt

Add'l Information: Established 1975. Normal turnaround time- 7-10 days. Projects billed by number of names searched. Fee basis depends upon type of project. 1st project may require prepayment. They specialize in title searches.

Omni Data Retrieval Inc

20890 Kenbridge Ct, Lakeville, MN 55044
Phone: 952-985-7220 **Fax:** 952-985-7211
www.omnidataretrieval.com **email:** sales@omnidataretrieval.com

Types of Records Retrieved: Civil and criminal courts; US District Court; Tax liens/Judgments

Local Retrieval Area: MN-all counties. **Correspondent Relationships:** nationwide.

Add'l Information: Normal turnaround time- 24 hours. Payment due net 15 days from date of invoice. Credit cards accepted. They specialize in criminal background searches.

On the Record Inc

700 Youngstown-Warren Rd, Niles, OH 44446
Phone: 330-652-4109 **Fax:** 330-652-4283

Types of Records Retrieved: Civil, criminal and probate courts; Federal courts; Real Estate; Tax liens/Judgments; UCC records; Vital records

Local Retrieval Area: OH-Ashland, Ashtabula, Belmont, Carroll, Columbiana, Cuyahoga, Erie, Geauga, Harrison, Holmes, Huron, Jefferson, Lake, Lorain, Mahoning, Medina, Portage, Richland, Stark, Summit, Trumbull, Tuscarawas, Wayne. **Correspondent Relationships:** Ohio.

Add'l Information: Established 1999. Normal turnaround time- 24-48 hours. Charge by search type. Specialize in title abstracting, current owner (42-60 years), pre judicial reports, UCCs & document retrieval. They also have a commercial real estate div & pre-employment div. Title attorneys are on staff. They have add'l offices in Kent & Cleveland.

One Legal

504 Redwood Blvd #223, Novato, CA 94947
Phone: 800-938-8815; 415-491-0606 **Fax:** 415-491-0562
www.onelegal.com **email:** support@onelegal.com

Types of Records Retrieved: Civil, criminal and probate courts; Federal courts; Real Estate; Tax liens/Judgments; UCC records; Vital records

Local Retrieval Area: CA-Alameda, Contra Costa, Fresno, Imperial, Kern, Kings, Los Angeles, Madera, Marin, Merced, Monterey, Napa, Orange, Placer, Riverside, Sacramento, San Bernardino, San Diego, San Francisco, San Joaquin, San Luis Obispo, San Mateo, Santa Barbara, Santa Clara, Santa Cruz, Solano, Sonoma, Stanislaus, Tulare, Ventura, Yolo. **Correspondent Relationships:** California, nationwide generally.

Add'l Information: Established 1990. Normal turnaround time- 3-5 days. Projects billed by the hour. Credit cards accepted. Formerly Fax & File Legal Services Inc, they specialize in filing court documents the same day and process service. They have 17 branches throughout California. They perform service of process.

Oneida Valley Abstract

PO Box 29, Court St, Wampsville, NY 13163
Phone: 315-363-1444 **Fax:** 315-363-9547

Types of Records Retrieved: Probate courts; Real Estate; Tax liens/Judgments; UCC records

Local Retrieval Area: NY-Madison

Add'l Information: Established 1986. Normal turnaround time- 48 hours. Fee basis will vary by years searched. Personal checks are accepted.

OneSource, Inc

121 E Piccadilly St #100, Winchester, VA 22601
Phone: 540-450-2250 **Fax:** 540-450-2254
www.onesourcescreening.com **email:** info@onesourcescreening.com

Types of Records Retrieved: Civil and criminal courts; Federal courts; Real Estate; Tax liens/Judgments

Local Retrieval Area: Prince George's; VA-Alexandria, Arlington, Clarke, Fairfax, Fairfax City, Falls Church City, Frederick, Loudoun, Manassas City, Manassas Park City, Prince William, Winchester; DC-Washington. **Correspondent Relationships:** nationwide.

Add'l Information: Established 2000. Normal turnaround time- 24 hours or less. Projects billed by number of names searched. Fees negotiated with volume. 1st project may require prepayment. They specialize in court research and document retrieval in the mid-atlantic area. All research completed with in 24 hours. Very competitive pricing.

Onistagrawa Abstracting Corp

PO Box 777, Middleburgh, NY 12122-0777

Phone: 518-827-8088 **Fax:** 518-827-6566 oaccorp@midtel.net

Types of Records Retrieved: Civil, criminal and probate courts; Real Estate; Tax liens/Judgments; UCC records

Local Retrieval Area: NY-Columbia, Delaware, Fulton, Greene, Montgomery, Otsego, Schenectady, Schoharie

Add'l Information: Established 1987. Normal turnaround time- 1-3 days for current owner, judgments, probate and simple deed/mortgage searches. Full abstracts take 1-5 days. Projects billed by number of names searched. The fee basis for real estate is figured on a per parcel basis.

Oplinger Abstract & Title Inc

PO Box 133, 155 Euclid St, Olivet, SD 57052

Phone: 605-387-2335 **Fax:** 605-387-2337

Types of Records Retrieved: Civil, criminal and probate courts; Real Estate; Tax liens/Judgments; UCC records; Vital records

Local Retrieval Area: SD-Hutchinson

Add'l Information: Established 1948. Normal turnaround time- 5 days. Projects billed by the hour. All projects require prepayment.

Orange Abstractor Services Co

222 Greenwich Ave, Goshen, NY 10924

Phone: 845-294-3331 **Fax:** 845-294-8748 ngill2@hvc.rr.com

Types of Records Retrieved: Civil, criminal and probate courts; Federal courts; Real Estate; Tax liens/Judgments; UCC records

Local Retrieval Area: NY-Orange

Add'l Information: Established 1984. Normal turnaround time- 1-14 days. Fee basis will vary by type of project. Terms: net 30 days.

Orange County Abstract & Title Co Inc

204 E Main St, Paoli, IN 47454

Phone: 812-723-3044 **Fax:** 812-723-3044

Types of Records Retrieved: Civil courts; Probate courts; Real Estate; Tax liens/Judgments; UCC records **Local Retrieval Area:** IN-Orange

Add'l Information: Established 1974. Normal turnaround time- 24-72 hours. Projects billed by number of names searched. Projects billed by the hour. 1st project may require prepayment. Personal checks accepted. They specialize in title searches and lien searches. They have been in business for 30 years.

Orange Paper Placers Inc

26 Scotchtown Ave, PO Box 22, Goshen, NY 10924

Phone: 845-294-7810 **Fax:** 845-294-3511

Types of Records Retrieved: Civil, criminal and probate courts; Real Estate; Tax liens/Judgments; UCC records; Vital records

Local Retrieval Area: NY-Dutchess, Orange, Putnam, Rockland, Sullivan, Ulster

Add'l Information: Established 1976. Normal turnaround time- 7 days. Expedited service available. Projects billed by number of names searched. All projects require prepayment. They specialize in court services, getting judges signatures on court documents, etc. They perform service of process.

Origin Information & Services Inc (GA)

233 Mitchell St SW, Suite 550, Atlanta, GA 30303

Phone: 800-315-3492; 404-524-8400 **Fax:** 800-315-3493; 404-524-8807

www.origininformation.com **email:** origin@origininformation.com

Types of Records Retrieved: Civil, criminal and probate courts; Federal courts; Real Estate; Tax liens/Judgments; UCC records

Local Retrieval Area: GA-all counties. **Correspondents:** nationwide.

Add'l Information: Established 1996. Normal turnaround time- 24 hours in Metro Atlanta; 1-3 days in other counties. Projects billed by number of names searched. They specialize in public records research and corporate document preparation.

Origin Information & Services Inc (NC)

16 W Martin St #407, Raleigh, NC 27601-2931

Phone: 800-940-1755; 919-856-0315 **Fax:** 919-856-0316

www.origininformation.com **email:** origin@origininformation.com

Types of Records Retrieved: Civil and criminal courts; Federal courts; Real Estate; Tax liens/Judgments; UCC records

Local Retrieval Area: NC-all counties. **Correspondent Relationships:** North Carolina and nationwide.

Add'l Information: Established 1996. Normal turnaround time- 24-48 hours. Projects billed by number of names searched. They specialize in public record retrieval and filing in the state of North Carolina.

Orion Research Services Inc

1266 W Paces Ferry Rd NW #589, Atlanta, GA 30327

Phone: 800-975-0865; 770-457-4776 **Fax:** 877-287-9244; 770-451-7944

www.orionresearch.com **email:** info@orionresearch.com

Types of Records Retrieved: Civil, criminal and probate courts; Federal courts; Tax liens/Judgments; UCC records; Vital records

Local Retrieval Area: GA-Clayton, Cobb, De Kalb, Fulton, Gwinnett. **Correspondent Relationships:** nationwide and international.

Add'l Information: Established 1997. Normal turnaround time- 24-48 hours. Projects billed by number of names searched. Projects billed by the hour. 1st project may require prepayment. Credit cards accepted. They specialize in all court searches and nationwide warrant searches, DMV records and will work closely with companies to provide customized services. They service Georgia statewide. A licensed PI in GA.

Dora Orum

4782 E Fountain Way, Fresno, CA 93726

Phone: 559-251-5193 **Fax:** 559-456-3833

Types of Records Retrieved: Civil, criminal and probate courts; Federal courts; Real Estate; Tax liens/Judgments; UCC records; Vital records

Local Retrieval Area: CA-Fresno

Add'l Information: Established 1986. Normal turnaround time- 1-2 days. Fee basis is per search. 1st project may require prepayment. She specializes in abstracting and public record searching in superior or federal court, which includes fictitious business name searches. Second contact person is Loretta Reyna at 559-253-0963; Fax 559-253-0363.

Oscoda County Abstract Inc

PO Box 127, Mio, MI 48647

Phone: 989-826-5832 **Fax:** 989-826-3294

Types of Records Retrieved: Civil courts; Probate courts; Real Estate; Tax liens/Judgments; UCC records **Local Retrieval Area:** MI-Oscoda

Add'l Information: Established 1978. Normal turnaround time- 24 hours. Fee basis depends upon type of project. All projects require prepayment. They specialize in title insurance.

William J O'Shea, PI

17895 Rt 37, West Frankfort, IL 62896

Phone: 618-937-3895 **Fax:** 618-937-2805 osheas@midwest.net

Types of Records Retrieved: Civil, criminal and probate courts; Federal courts; Tax liens/Judgments; Vital records

Local Retrieval Area: IL-Franklin, Williamson. **Correspondent Relationships:** Southern IL area.

Add'l Information: Established 1983. Normal turnaround time- 24-48 hours. Projects billed by number of names searched. All projects require prepayment. Credit cards accepted. Volume billing available. He specializes in insurance investigation, video/still photography, process service, skiptracing, and So. IL Federal District Court records. A licensed PI with 17 years experience, also 20 years experience with the Chicago Police Dept. A licensed PI in IL. They perform service of process.

Otoe County Title Co

PO Box 488, Nebraska City, NE 68410

Phone: 402-873-5501 **Fax:** 402-873-5622

Types of Records Retrieved: Civil, criminal and probate courts; Real Estate; Tax liens/Judgments; UCC records

Local Retrieval Area: NE-Cass, Nemaha, Otoe

Add'l Information: Established 1965. Normal turnaround time- 1-2 days. They charge a flat fee per project. 1st project may require prepayment. They specialize in title records.

Otsego County Abstract Co

120 E Main St, Gaylord, MI 49735

Phone: 989-732-5765 **Fax:** 989-732-7288

Types of Records Retrieved: Civil, criminal and probate courts; Real Estate; Tax liens/Judgments; UCC records; Vital records

Local Retrieval Area: MI-Otsego

Add'l Information: Normal turnaround time- 7-10 days. Expedited service available. Fee basis will vary by type of project. 1st project may require prepayment. They specialize in oil & gas abstracts and research.

Ouren Title Inc

1009 7th St, PO Box 229, Harlan, IA 51537-0229

Phone: 712-755-2174 **Fax:** 712-755-3865 ourentitleinc@harlannet.com

Types of Records Retrieved: Probate courts; Real Estate; Tax liens/Judgments; Vital records

Local Retrieval Area: IA-Shelby

Add'l Information: Established 1895. Normal turnaround time- 24 hours. Projects billed by number of names searched. Projects billed by number of records located. Payment due upon receipt of billing. They specialize in preparing abstracts record ownership and lien reports. Can retrieve bankruptcy records if recorded in Recorders Office.

Owens & Associates Inv

2245 San Diego Ave #225, San Diego, CA 92110-2942

Phone: 800-297-1343; 619-297-1343 **Fax:** 619-297-7622

www.owenspi.com **email:** wayne@owenspi.com

Types of Records Retrieved: Civil, criminal and probate courts; Federal courts; Real Estate; Tax liens/Judgments; UCC records; Vital records

Local Retrieval Area: CA-San Diego. **Correspondents:** nationwide.

Add'l Information: Established 1988. Normal turnaround time- 24-48 hours. Projects billed by the hour. 1st project may require prepayment. Credit cards accepted. They specialize in on-site criminal and civil searches nationwide. Worldwide full service investigations by former FBI agents and other law enforcement officers. A licensed PI in AZ, CA. They perform service of process.

Ozark Inv

3761 Spencer Creek Rd, Camdenton, MO 65020

Phone: 888-685-5366; 573-346-5366 **Fax:** 417-532-9728

Types of Records Retrieved: Civil and criminal courts

Local Retrieval Area: MO-Benton, Camden, Dallas, Hickory, Laclede, Miller, Morgan, Pulaski

Add'l Information: Established 1996. 1st project may require prepayment. The also provide court record retrieval, and private investigations They perform service of process.

P

P & A Research Service

10155 June Rd, St James, LA 70086

Phone: 225-268-2777 **Fax:** 225-746-0561

mtcalvary1785@bellsouth.net

Types of Records Retrieved: Civil and criminal courts; Federal courts; Real Estate; Tax liens/Judgments; UCC records

Local Retrieval Area: LA-Ascension, Lafourche

Add'l Information: Established 1994. Normal turnaround time- 12-24 hours; same day for Asension if received by 4 PM. 1st project may require prepayment. Credit cards accepted. Invoice on a monthly basis. They specialize in civil and criminal investigations, pre-employment screening and record retrieval. They are also a process server along the Louisiana area. They perform service of process.

P.S.P.S. Legal Support Services Inc

PO Box 520155, Winthrop, MA 02152

Phone: 617-846-7130 **Fax:** 617-846-1017

ILQQK4DOE@worldnet.att.net

Types of Records Retrieved: Civil, criminal and probate courts; Federal courts; Real Estate; Tax liens/Judgments; UCC records; Vital records; Votor registration records

Local Retrieval Area: MA-Essex, Middlesex, Suffolk. **Correspondent Relationships:** Norfolk and Plymouth counties MA

Add'l Information: Established 1995. Normal turnaround time- 2 days. Projects billed by number of names searched. Projects billed by the hour. fees negotiated with volume. 1st project may require prepayment. Credit cards accepted. They specialize in background investigaitons, real estate due diligence, RE title abstracts, rule 4c process service and all manner of protective services. A licensed PI in MA. They perform service of process.

PAC Research

1840 41st Ave 102-243, Capitola, CA 95010

Phone: 831-475-7780 **Fax:** 831-475-7781 peggy@pacresearch.net

Types of Records Retrieved: Civil and criminal courts; Federal courts; Tax liens/Judgments; UCC records; Vital records

Local Retrieval Area: CA-Santa Clara, Santa Cruz

Add'l Information: Established 1997. Normal turnaround time- 24-48 hours. Projects billed by number of names searched. Projects billed by number of records located. Additional charge for over 5 cases. Fee basis depends upon type of project. Terms net 30 days. End of month billing They are a family operation that provides quick turnaround, accurate results, and exceptional personalized service.

Walter J Pace

125 Linden St, Everett, MA 02149

Phone: 617-389-6730 **Fax:** 617-389-5936

Types of Records Retrieved: Civil and criminal courts

Local Retrieval Area: MA-Middlesex, Suffolk

Add'l Information: Established 1996. Normal turnaround time- 24-48 hours. Projects billed by number of names searched. Terms are net 30 days. He specializes in criminal and civil court record searches.

Pacific Corporate & Title Services (Sacramento)

914 S St, Sacramento, CA 95814

Phone: 800-230-4988; 916-558-4988 **Fax:** 800-230-2217; 916-441-2217

www.paccorp.com **email:** info@paccorp.com

Types of Records Retrieved: Civil courts; Probate courts; Federal courts; Real Estate; Tax liens/Judgments; UCC records; Vital records

Local Retrieval Area: CA-Alameda, Contra Costa, El Dorado, Fresno, Los Angeles, Marin, Monterey, Napa, Orange, Placer, Riverside, Sacramento, San Bernardino, San Diego, San Francisco, San Joaquin, San Mateo, Santa Clara, Santa Cruz, Solano, Sonoma, Stanislaus, Yolo. **Correspondent Relationships:** nationwide.

Add'l Information: Established 1987. Normal turnaround time- 1-2 days. Projects billed by number of names searched. 1st project may require prepayment. Credit cards accepted. Terms: Net 30 days for clients. They specialize in UCC, title and publishing and filing services. They also have 10 branch offices throughout California. They are registered agents.

Pacific NW Title of Alaska

3201 C St #110, Anchorage, AK 99503

Phone: 907-561-5122 **Fax:** 907-261-2275

www.aktitle.com **email:** info@aktitle.com

Types of Records Retrieved: Real Estate; Tax liens/Judgments

Local Retrieval Area: AK-Anchorage, Bethel, Bristol Bay, Iliamna, Kvichak, Valdez-Cordova. **Correspondent Relationships:** statewide.

Add'l Information: Normal turnaround time- 24 hours. Projects billed by the hour. All projects require prepayment. They also have a branch in Eagle River, 907-696-5426.

Pacific Photocopy & Research (Ft. Lauderdale)

33 NE 2nd St #207, Ft Lauderdale, FL 33301-1036
Phone: 954-764-5646 **Fax:** 954-764-5447
www.pacificphotocopy.com **email:** Legal@pacificphotocopy.com

Types of Records Retrieved: Civil, criminal and probate courts; Federal courts; Real Estate; Tax liens/Judgments; UCC records; Vital records

Local Retrieval Area: FL-Broward. **Correspondents:** nationwide.

Add'l Information: Established 1972. Normal turnaround time- 2 days, 1 day, and Same Day options available. Fee basis will vary by the type of project. 1st project may require prepayment. Credit cards accepted. They specialize in bankruptcy court records as well as records in all departments of the circuit court.

Pacific Photocopy & Research (Jacksonville)

33 NE 2nd St #207, Ft Lauderdale, FL 33301-1036
Phone: 904-355-1062 **Fax:** 904-355-0958
www.pacificphotocopy.com **email:** Legal@pacificphotocopy.com

Types of Records Retrieved: Civil, criminal and probate courts; Federal courts; Real Estate; Tax liens/Judgments; UCC records; Vital records

Local Retrieval Area: FL-Baker, Bradford, Citrus, Clay, Columbia, Duval, Flagler, Hamilton, Marion, Nassau, Putnam, St Johns, Sumter, Suwannee, Union. **Correspondent Relationships:** nationwide.

Add'l Information: Established 1972. Normal turnaround time- 1 hour to availability of the file. Projects billed by number of names searched. Projects billed by number of records located. Projects billed by the hour. Fee basis will vary by the type of project. All projects require prepayment. They specialize in bankruptcy court records. They perform service of process.

Pacific Photocopy & Research (Miami)

33 N 2nd St #207, Fort Lauderdale, FL 33301
Phone: 305-371-7694 **Fax:** 305-371-9657
www.pacificphotocopy.com **email:** Legal@pacificphotocopy.com

Types of Records Retrieved: Civil, criminal and probate courts; Federal courts; Real Estate; Tax liens/Judgments; UCC records; Vital records

Local Retrieval Area: FL-Dade, Highlands, Indian River, Martin, Monroe, Okeechobee, St. Lucie. **Correspondents:** Florida and nationwide.

Add'l Information: Established 1972. Normal turnaround time- 1 hour to availability of the file. Fee basis will vary by the type of project. 1st project may require prepayment. Credit cards accepted. They specialize in bankruptcy court records.

Pacific Photocopy & Research (Orlando)

129-9 Los Alamitos Ct, Orlando, FL 32837-6333
Phone: 407-425-7234 **Fax:** 407-425-7218
www.pacificphotocopy.com **email:** Legal@pacificphotocopy.com

Types of Records Retrieved: Civil, criminal and probate courts; Federal courts; Real Estate; Tax liens/Judgments; UCC records; Vital records

Local Retrieval Area: FL-Orange, Osceola, Seminole. **Correspondent Relationships:** nationwide.

Add'l Information: Established 1972. Normal turnaround time- same or next day. Fee basis will vary by the type of project. 1st project may require prepayment. Credit cards accepted. They specialize in bankruptcy court records.

Pacific Photocopy & Research (Pensacola)

33 NE 2nd St #207, Fort Lauderdale, FL 33301
Phone: 850-435-3183 **Fax:** 850-435-3185
www.pacificphotocopy.com **email:** Legal@pacificphotocopy.com

Types of Records Retrieved: Civil, criminal and probate courts; Federal courts; Real Estate; Tax liens/Judgments; UCC records; Vital records

Local Retrieval Area: FL-Bay, Escambia, Okaloosa, Santa Rosa, Walton, Washington. **Correspondent Relationships:** nationwide.

Add'l Information: Established 1972. Normal turnaround time- 24-48 hours depending on availability of file. Fee basis will vary by type of project. 1st project may require prepayment. Credit cards accepted. They specialize in bankruptcy court records and Federal court records as well as all County court records, including civil and criminal. Performs service of process.

Pacific Photocopy & Research (Tampa)

33 NE 2nd St #207, Ft Lauderdale, FL 33301
Phone: 813-221-6828 **Fax:** 813-221-6678
www.pacificphotocopy.com **email:** Legal@pacificphotocopy.com

Types of Records Retrieved: Civil, criminal and probate courts; Federal courts; Real Estate; Tax liens/Judgments; UCC records; Vital records

Local Retrieval Area: FL-Charlotte, Collier, Desoto, Glades, Hardee, Hendry, Hernando, Hillsborough, Lee, Manatee, Pasco, Pinellas, Polk, Sarasota. **Correspondent Relationships:** nationwide.

Add'l Information: Established 1982. Normal turnaround time- 1 hour to availability of the file. Fee basis will vary by the type of project. 1st project may require prepayment. Credit cards accepted. They specialize in bankruptcy court records.

Pacific Photocopy & Research (W. Palm Beach)

33 NE 2nd St #207, Fort Lauderdale, FL 33301
Phone: 561-832-3878 **Fax:** 561-832-8035
www.pacificphotocopy.com **email:** Legal@pacificphotocopy.com

Types of Records Retrieved: Civil, criminal and probate courts; Federal courts; Real Estate; Tax liens/Judgments; UCC records; Vital records

Local Retrieval Area: FL-Palm Beach. **Correspondents:** nationwide.

Add'l Information: Established 1972. Normal turnaround time- 1 hour to availability of the file. Fee basis will vary by type of project. 1st project may require prepayment. Credit cards accepted. They specialize in bankruptcy court records.

Pacific Research & Retrieval Inc

28 N 1st St #700, San Jose, CA 95113-1210
Phone: 800-222-7040; 408-295-6800 **Fax:** 408-295-6895
pacrsch@aol.com

Types of Records Retrieved: Civil, criminal and probate courts; Federal courts; Real Estate; Tax liens/Judgments; UCC records; Vital records

Local Retrieval Area: CA-Alameda, San Francisco, San Mateo, Santa Clara, Santa Cruz. **Correspondent Relationships:** nationwide.

Add'l Information: Established 1992. Normal turnaround time- 24 hours, but specializes in 1-2 hour service. Projects billed by number of names searched. Projects billed by the hour. Fees negotiable with volume. 1st project may require prepayment. Credit cards accepted. Payment due net 30 days. They specialize in 1-2 HR rushes, also difficult document intensive research assignments, large copy or file is "unavailable" jobs. Regular and fax filings in state and federal courts. They perform service of process.

Pacificsearch & Information

656 5th Ave #C, San Diego, CA 92101
Phone: 619-702-3334 **Fax:** 619-702-3336

Types of Records Retrieved: Civil, criminal and probate courts; Federal courts; Real Estate; Tax liens/Judgments; UCC records; Vital records

Local Retrieval Area: CA-Los Angeles, Orange, San Diego. **Correspondent Relationships:** Los Angeles and Orange counties.

Add'l Information: Established 1997. Normal turnaround time- 24 hours. Projects billed by number of names searched.

PADIC Inc

1609 E Broadway, Gainesville, TX 76240
Phone: 940-665-6130 **Fax:** 940-665-7486
www.padic.com **email:** padic@ntin.net

Types of Records Retrieved: Civil, criminal and probate courts; Federal courts; Real Estate; Tax liens/Judgments; UCC records; Vital records

Local Retrieval Area: TX-Collin, Cooke, Dallas, Denton, Ellis, Grayson, Tarrant. **Correspondent Relationships:** nationwide.

Add'l Information: Established 1991. Normal turnaround time- 48 hours. Projects billed by number of names searched. 1st project may require prepayment. They specialize in document retrieval, asset searches, environmental investigations, surveillance, witness location and statements, computer database research and insurance defense investigation. A licensed PI in TX. They perform service of process.

Page County Abstract & Title Company

118 N 16th St, PO Box 180, Clarinda, IA 51632
Phone: 712-542-3613 **Fax:** 712-542-2629

Types of Records Retrieved: Civil courts; Probate courts; Real Estate; Tax liens/Judgments; UCC records

Local Retrieval Area: IA-Page

Add'l Information: Established 1989. Normal turnaround time- 48 hours. Fee basis will vary by the type of project. Personal checks are accepted. They specialize in searching county records and abstracting RE titles.

Page-Hawkeye Legal Services

2731 Douglas Ave, Des Moines, IA 50310
Phone: 515-276-3984 **Fax:** 515-271-0664 pagepi@msn.com

Types of Records Retrieved: Civil and criminal courts

Local Retrieval Area: IA-Dallas, Greene, Jasper, Madison, Mahaska, Marion, Polk, Story, Warren. **Correspondent Relationships:** nationwide.

Add'l Information: Established 2001. Normal turnaround time- 24 hours. 1st project may require prepayment. Pre-payment of private parties, invoice to attorneys, other investigators & process servers. They also provide court filings, skiptracing, and private investigations. They have 16 years of experience, full time office staff. A licensed PI in IA. They perform service of process.

Pallorium Inc

PO Box 155, Brooklyn, NY 11230
Phone: 212-969-0286 **Fax:** 212-858-5720
www.pallorium.com **email:** pallorium@pallorium.com

Types of Records Retrieved: Civil, criminal and probate courts; Real Estate; Tax liens/Judgments; Vital records

Local Retrieval Area: NY-Bronx, Kings, Nassau, New York, Queens, Richmond, Suffolk, Westchester. **Correspondent Relationships:** San Antonio and Los Angeles. Also Toronto, Canada, Hong Kong, Bangkok, Thailand, all of Israel.

Add'l Information: Established 1980. Normal turnaround time- 1-3 days. Projects billed by the hour. 1st project may require prepayment. Terms: net 30 days. They maintain an online investigative support system with criminal, voter, credit, MVR, corporate telephone & other records. They also maintain an online network of 850+ investigative agencies. They have offices in USA, Canada, Israel and Hong Kong. A licensed PI in CA, LA, NY, TX. They perform service of process.

Palmer & Murrie Abstract Co Inc

PO Box 337, Marion, IL 62959
Phone: 618-993-3866 **Fax:** 618-993-3015

Types of Records Retrieved: Probate courts; Real Estate; Tax liens/Judgments; UCC records; Vital records

Local Retrieval Area: IL-Franklin, Jefferson, Johnson, Massac, Saline, Union, Williamson. **Correspondent Relationships:** Union and Jackson counties.

Add'l Information: Established 1962. Normal turnaround time- 5-6 working days. Projects billed by number of names searched. Projects billed by number of records located. Projects billed by the hour. Personal checks are accepted.

Palmer Abstract Inc

19 1st Ave NW, Waukon, IA 52172
Phone: 563-568-3488 **Fax:** 563-568-5055

Types of Records Retrieved: Civil, criminal and probate courts; Real Estate; Tax liens/Judgments; UCC records; Vital records

Local Retrieval Area: IA-Allamakee

Add'l Information: Established 1925. Normal turnaround time- 48 hours. Projects billed by number of names searched. Projects billed by number of records located. Projects billed by the hour.

Palmer Inv Services

PO Box 10760, Prescott, AZ 86304-0760
Phone: 800-280-2951; 928-778-2951 **Fax:** 800-215-7049; 928-445-7204
www.palmerinvestigative.com **email:** magnum@cableone.net

Types of Records Retrieved: Civil and criminal courts; Federal courts; Probate courts; Real Estate; Tax liens/Judgments; UCC records

Local Retrieval Area: AZ-Yavapai. **Correspondent Relationships:** Coconino, Maricopa, Mohave counties AZ. Can retrieve adoption records.

Add'l Information: Established 1980. Normal turnaround time- 48 hours. Expedited service available. Document retrieval is charged by the hour; per name for initial search. All projects require prepayment. Credit cards accepted. Regular clients may arrange for credit. They specialize in investigations, legal process serving and drug and alcohol testing. They can retrieve UCC, recorder and Secretary of State records. A licensed PI in AZ. They perform service of process.

Palo Alto County Abstract Co

1009-1011 Broadway St, Emmetsburg, IA 50536
Phone: 712-852-4313 **Fax:** 712-852-4313

Types of Records Retrieved: Civil, criminal and probate courts; Real Estate; Tax liens/Judgments; UCC records; Vital records

Local Retrieval Area: IA-Palo Alto

Add'l Information: Established 1800. Normal turnaround time- variable depending on project. Fee basis will vary by the type of project.

Palo Verde Research

15260 Shamrock Dr, Ft Myers, FL 33912
Phone: 239-481-9434 **Fax:** 239-481-9890
paloverderesearch@comcast.net

Types of Records Retrieved: Civil, criminal and probate courts; Real Estate; Tax liens/Judgments; UCC records; Vital records

Local Retrieval Area: FL-Charlotte, Collier, Hendry, Lee

Add'l Information: Established 1993. Normal turnaround time- 24-48 hours. Projects billed by number of names searched. 1st project may require prepayment. They specialize in real estate records.

Paper Chase

PO Box 2331, 690 Larson St, Friday Harbor, WA 98250
Phone: 360-378-3345 **Fax:** 360-378-3345 paperchase@centurytel.net

Types of Records Retrieved: Civil and criminal courts

Local Retrieval Area: WA-San Juan

Add'l Information: Established 1993. Normal turnaround time- 1-2 days. Fee basis varies by type of transaction. 1st project may require prepayment. Located in the county seat of Friday Harbor, we offer a variety of courthouse services as well as county wide service of process. They perform service of process.

Paper Trail Information Services Inc

PO Box 4715, Lafayette, IN 47905
Phone: 765-471-4999 **Fax:** 765-471-2666
papertrailinfo@aol.com

Types of Records Retrieved: Civil and criminal courts; Real Estate; Tax liens/Judgments; UCC records

Local Retrieval Area: IN-Boone, Hamilton, Hendricks, Putnam, Tippecanoe

Add'l Information: Established 2003. Normal turnaround time- 24-48 hours. Expedited service available. Projects billed by number of names searched. 1st project may require prepayment. They specialize in criminal and civil courts, UCC searches, real estate records and tax liens.

Paragon Document Research Inc

PO Box 65216, St Paul, MN 55165
Phone: 800-892-4235; 651-222-6844 **Fax:** 800-847-7369; 651-222-2281
www.banc.com/pdrstore **email:** pdrinc@qwest.net

Types of Records Retrieved: Civil, criminal and probate courts; Federal courts; Real Estate; Tax liens/Judgments; UCC records; Vital records

Local Retrieval Area: MN-Anoka, Carver, Dakota, Hennepin, Ramsey, Scott, St Louis, Stearns, Washington, Wright. **Correspondent Relationships:** nationwide (state and county level), Canada, International.

Add'l Information: Established 1990. Normal turnaround time- 24-48 hours. Expedited service available. Projects billed by number of names searched. Projects billed by the hour. 1st project may require prepayment. Will bill clients on a monthly basis. They specialize in notification letter processing, UCC e-filing, corporate documents and registered agent services nationwide. They offer nationwide MVR service/real property searches and background profiles. A licensed PI in WI, MN. They perform service of process.

Paragon Property Services

12482 W Ken Caryl Ave #B1-136, Littleton, CO 80127
Phone: 866-697-6156; 303-697-6156 **Fax:** 303-697-1856
angelamuirhead@comcast.net

Types of Records Retrieved: Real Estate; Tax liens/judgments; UCC records

Local Retrieval Area: CO-Arapahoe, Boulder, Denver, Douglas, Jefferson. **Correspondent Relationships:** nationwide.

Add'l Information: Established 2001. Normal turnaround time- 24-48 hours. 1st project may require prepayment. Paragon Property Services specializes in current owner searches, recording in CO and nationwide and document retrieval. Fast turnaround, competitive pricing and many years experience in commercial banking, mortgage and title research industries.

Paralegal Enterprises Inc

401 W First St #2-D, Greenville, NC 27835
Phone: 252-758-6622 **Fax:** 252-758-6622

Types of Records Retrieved: Civil courts; Probate courts; Real Estate; Tax liens/Judgments; UCC records; Vital records

Local Retrieval Area: NC-Greene, Pitt

Add'l Information: Established 1991. Normal turnaround time- 48 hours. Projects billed by number of names searched. Projects billed by the hour. Fee basis will vary with portions of tracts of land. 1st project may require prepayment. They specialize in real estate searches.

Paralegal Field Research Service

330 Clematis St #209, West Palm Beach, FL 33401
Phone: 800-256-7459; 561-832-5770 **Fax:** 561-832-1857
www.pfrsinvestigations.com **email:** shapka@bigfoot.com

Types of Records Retrieved: Civil, criminal and probate courts; Federal courts; Real Estate.

Local Retrieval Area: FL-Palm Beach. **Correspondent Relationships:** Florida.

Add'l Information: Established 1989. Normal turnaround time- variable depending on project. Projects billed by number of names searched. Projects billed by number of records located. Projects billed by the hour. All projects require prepayment. They specialize in criminal investigations and mitigation investigations (Capital cases). Mobile phone # is: 561-714-8255. A licensed PI in FL. They perform service of process.

Paralegal Resource Center Inc

4 Faneuil Hall Marketplace, Boston, MA 02109
Phone: 866-742-1939; 617-742-1939 **Fax:** 617-742-1417
www.paralegalboston.com **email:** prc@paralegalboston.com

Types of Records Retrieved: Civil, criminal and probate courts; Federal courts; Real Estate; Tax liens/Judgments; UCC records; Vital records; Corporate documents

Local Retrieval Area: MA-Essex, Middlesex, Norfolk, Plymouth, Suffolk, Worcester. **Correspondent Relationships:** outside Greater Boston and New England.

Add'l Information: Established 1976. Normal turnaround time- 1-3 business days. Expedited service available. Projects billed by number of names searched. Projects billed by number of records located. Projects billed by the hour. 1st project may require prepayment. They specialize in UCC, corporate records, state & federal tax lien searches & document retrieval of all court records at all Massachusetts courthouses & public records at state agencies. They also provide permanent & temporary paralegal staffing.

Paralegal Services (Berkeley Springs)

1039 Martinsburg Rd., Berkeley Springs, WV 25411
Phone: 304-676-5550 **Fax:** 304-258-4287

Types of Records Retrieved: Real Estate; Tax liens/judgments; UCC records

Local Retrieval Area: WV-Berkeley, Morgan

Add'l Information: Established 1989. Normal turnaround time- 24-48 hours. Expedited service available. Projects billed by number of names searched. 1st project may require prepayment. They will bill monthly. They specialize in real estate title work, with 17 years of experience. They also assist in civil and criminal litigation, trial preparation and summarizing depositions.

Paralegal Services Inc

PO Box 118, 100 Hillcrest Dr, Marion, NC 28752
Phone: 828-606-8297 **Fax:** 828-659-2502 unc45mom@aol.com

Types of Records Retrieved: Civil, criminal and probate courts; Federal courts; Real Estate; Tax liens/Judgments; UCC records; Vital records

Local Retrieval Area: NC-Buncombe, Henderson, McDowell, Mitchell, Polk, Rutherford

Add'l Information: Established 1995. Normal turnaround time- 6-12 hours. Projects billed by number of names searched. Terms are net 30 days. Above phone number is the primary number (cell number) and the other local number is 828-659-3508.

Paralegal Services of Buffalo

112 Franklin St, Buffalo, NY 14202
Phone: 716-822-3279 **Fax:** 716-853-0184
www.paralegalservicesofbuffalo.com **email:** para@adelphia.net

Types of Records Retrieved: Civil, criminal and probate courts; Federal courts; Real Estate; Tax liens/Judgments; UCC records; Vital records

Local Retrieval Area: NY-Erie, Niagara. **Correspondents:** nationwide.

Add'l Information: Established 1976. Normal turnaround time- 1 day. Projects billed by number of names searched. 1st project may require prepayment. They specialize in criminal records, civil searches, real estate related and document retrieval in all courts. They also retrieve DMV insurance, title and license information.

Paralegal Services of North Carolina Inc

120 Penmarc Dr #118, Raleigh, NC 27603
Phone: 919-821-7762 **Fax:** 919-832-6378
www.psnc.net **email:** psnc@bellsouth.net

Types of Records Retrieved: Civil, criminal and probate courts; Federal courts; Real Estate; Tax liens/Judgments; UCC records; Vital records

Local Retrieval Area: NC-Alamance, Chatham, Cumberland, Durham, Franklin, Guilford, Harnett, Johnston, Nash, Orange, Wake, Wayne. **Correspondent Relationships:** statewide.

Add'l Information: Established 1988. Normal turnaround time- 1-3 days. Projects billed by number of names searched. Invoice due in 30 days. 1st project may require prepayment. They specialize in real property, asset/lien searches, probate and process service, and Secretary of State information searches. They cover every county in North Carolina either hands on or by agent. A licensed PI in NC. They perform service of process.

Paralegal Services Point Pleasant

RR 2 Box 65, Point Pleasant, WV 25550-4775
Phone: 304-675-4008 **Fax:** 304-675-4008

Types of Records Retrieved: Civil courts; Probate courts; Real Estate; Tax liens/Judgments; UCC records

Local Retrieval Area: WV-Mason

Add'l Information: Established 1992. Normal turnaround time- 24-48 hours. Projects billed by number of names searched. Net 10 days from receipt of invoice. They specialize in Real Estate.

Parasearch Inc

222 Jefferson Blvd, Warwick, RI 02888
Phone: 401-732-2490 **Fax:** 800-739-7740; 401-739-7708
www.para-search.com **email:** richd@para-search.com

Types of Records Retrieved: Civil, criminal and probate courts; Federal courts; Real Estate; Tax liens/Judgments; UCC records

Local Retrieval Area: RI-Kent, Newport, Providence, Washington. **Correspondent Relationships:** nationwide.

Add'l Information: Established 1987. Normal turnaround time- 24-48 hours. Projects billed by number of names searched. 1st project may require prepayment. Terms: net 30 days. They specialize in UCC searches, state, cities, towns corporate document filings and procurement.

Parasec (California)

640 Bercut Dr #A, Sacramento, CA 95814
Phone: 800-533-7272; 916-441-1001 **Fax:** 800-603-5868; 916-447-6091
www.parasec.com **email:** parasec@parasec.com

Types of Records Retrieved: Civil, criminal and probate courts; Federal courts; Real Estate; Tax liens/Judgments; UCC records; Vital records

Local Retrieval Area: CA-Los Angeles, Orange, Sacramento. **Correspondent Relationships:** nationwide.

Add'l Information: Established 1977. Normal turnaround time- 24-72 hours. Projects billed by number of names searched. Projects billed by number of records located. Projects billed by the hour. Credit cards accepted. Personal checks are accepted. They specialize in UCC, corporate, limited partnership, real estate and litigation. They are qualified to do business in all 50 states & act as Agent for Service of Process in all states. They perform service of process.

Parasec (Nevada)

318 N Carson St, #208, Carson City, NV 89701
Phone: 888-972-7273; 775-883-0104 **Fax:** 888-886-7168; 775-883-0340
www.parasec.com **email:** ngaches@parasec.com

Types of Records Retrieved: Civil courts; Tax liens/Judgments; UCC records; Vital records

Local Retrieval Area: NV-all counties. **Correspondents:** nationwide.

Add'l Information: Established 1996. Normal turnaround time- 24-72 hours. Projects billed by number of names searched. VISA, MC, AMEX only. 1st project may require prepayment. Credit cards accepted. They specialize in all Nevada document filing and retrieval, but will not file or retrive real estate documents, only UCCs.

Parker Legal Services

1379 E Riviera Dr, Mobile, AL 36605
Phone: 251-476-7464 **Fax:** 251-473-7309 wkp1@aol.com

Types of Records Retrieved: Civil, criminal and probate courts; Federal courts; Real Estate; Tax liens/Judgments; UCC records; Vital records

Local Retrieval Area: AL-Baldwin, Mobile; FL-Escambia; MS-Jackson

Add'l Information: Established 1995. Normal turnaround time- 24-48 hours. Projects billed by number of names searched. Projects billed by number of records located. 1st project may require prepayment. They specialize in legal research, process service, civil and criminal investigations as well as loss prevention and process service. A licensed PI in FL. They perform service of process.

Parrish Research

1447 Alabama St, Navarre, FL 32566-7100
Phone: 850-936-1240 **Fax:** 850-939-7282
parrishresearch@mchsi.com

Types of Records Retrieved: Civil, criminal and probate courts; Federal courts; Real Estate; Tax liens/Judgments; UCC records; Vital records

Local Retrieval Area: AL-Baldwin, Coffee, Dale, Geneva, Henry, Houston, Mobile; FL-Bay, Escambia, Holmes, Jackson, Okaloosa, Santa Rosa, Walton, Washington

Add'l Information: Established 1999. Normal turnaround time- 12 hours. Projects billed by number of records located. Payment due when project completed.

Parsley Enterprises Inc

4527 S 450 W, Trafalgar, IN 46181
Phone: 317-878-9979 **Fax:** 317-878-5514 parcelli@aol.com

Types of Records Retrieved: Civil courts; Real Estate; Tax liens/Judgments

Local Retrieval Area: IN-Bartholmew, Brown, Decatur, Hancock, Jackson, Jennings, Johnson, Marion, Scott, Shelby

Add'l Information: Normal turnaround time- 24-hours. Projects billed by number of names searched. 1st project may require prepayment. They specialize in mortgage and assignment retrieval.

Pasco Records Check Inc

PO Box 7616, Wesley Chapel, FL 33544
Phone: 813-991-5719 **Fax:** 813-991-5829

Types of Records Retrieved: Civil and criminal courts

Local Retrieval Area: FL-Bay, Columbia, Hillsborough, Martin, Nassau, Orange, Palm Beach, Pasco, Pinellas, St. Lucie, Union, Walton. **Correspondent Relationships:** Florida.

Add'l Information: Established 2002. Normal turnaround time- 24-48 hours. Projects billed by number of names searched. Credit cards accepted. Casual requests allowed. Their team of experienced "hands on researchers" will ensure that your search requests are handled and researched with great care.

Past Records Inc

120 Glenridge Rd, East Aurora, NY 14052
Phone: 716-805-0418 **Fax:** 716-805-0417 pastrecordsinc@aol.com

Types of Records Retrieved: Criminal courts; Federal courts

Local Retrieval Area: NY-Erie, Niagara

Add'l Information: Established 1999. Normal turnaround time- 24-72 hours. Projects billed by number of names searched. They specialize in felony convictions and bankruptcy.

PAT Research

PO Box 305, Charlestown, WV 25414
Phone: 304-725-4845 **Fax:** 304-728-3969 patdickeus@aol.com

Types of Records Retrieved: Civil and criminal courts; Tax liens/judgments.

Local Retrieval Area: WV-Berkeley, Jefferson

Add'l Information: Normal turnaround time- 1-2 days. Projects billed by number of names searched. Monthly billing available. They specialize in local court records.

Patricia Chambers Inv

6666 Amarillo Blvd W Studio #2, Amarillo, TX 79106
Phone: 806-359-5989 **Fax:** 806-258-7635
pchambers@wtrt.net

Types of Records Retrieved: Civil, criminal and probate courts; Federal courts; Real Estate; Tax liens/Judgments; UCC records

Local Retrieval Area: TX-Deaf Smith, Potter, Randall

Add'l Information: Established 1990. Normal turnaround time- 24 hours, exception on Holidays. Projects billed by number of names searched. 1st project may require prepayment. Billed monthly. They have been business since 1990. Conduct civil, criminal & background investigations. They provide public record searches made in person at county, district, and federal levels. TALI & NALI member. A licensed PI in TX. They perform service of process.

Patrick Investigative Services Inc

6542 Hypoluxo Rd #361, Lake Worth, FL 33467
Phone: 800-700-2958; 561-964-3434 **Fax:** 561-868-4969
www.pisnoops.com **email:** patrick@pisnoops.com

Types of Records Retrieved: Civil, criminal and probate courts; Federal courts; Real Estate; Tax liens/Judgments; UCC records; Vital records

Local Retrieval Area: FL-Broward, Dade, Palm Beach. **Correspondent Relationships:** state of Florida.

Add'l Information: Established 1994. Normal turnaround time- 48-72 hours. Projects billed by number of names searched. Fees based on number of names searched/location. 1st project may require prepayment. They specialize in complete investigative services offering 40 years of investigative experience in public and private sectors. Licensed PI in FL.

Pat's Information Services

8500 New Hampshire Ave #221, Silver Spring, MD 20903
Phone: 202-285-2116
www.valuableresearch.com **email:** pis@valuableresearch.com

Types of Records Retrieved: Civil and criminal courts; Federal courts; Tax liens.judgments.

Local Retrieval Area: DC-Washington; MD-Howard, Montgomery, Prince George

Add'l Information: Normal turnaround time- 1-3 days. 1st project may require prepayment. PIS works with individuals and businesses in need of research assistance. They provide our clients with quality, professional, and valuable information service at very affordable rates.

Patterson Inv Inc

PO Box 893, Wenatchee, WA 98807
Phone: 509-884-7531 **Fax:** 509-884-7531

Types of Records Retrieved: Civil and criminal courts

Local Retrieval Area: WA-Chelan, Douglas, Grant, Okanogan

Add'l Information: Established 1994. 1st project may require prepayment. They also provide court filings, photocopying, skiptracing, private investigations, and asset searches. A licensed PI in WA. They perform service of process.

Paul C Klumb Agency LLC

6688 N Shawmoors Dr, Chenequa, WI 53029
Phone: 414-254-1335 **Fax:** 888-755-6415; pklumb@msn.com

Types of Records Retrieved: Civil, criminal and probate courts; Federal courts; Real Estate; Tax liens/Judgments; UCC records; Vital records

Local Retrieval Area: WI-Dane, Dodge, Jefferson, Kenosha, Milwaukee, Ozaukee, Racine, Walworth, Washington, Waukesha. **Correspondent Relationships:** national and international.

Add'l Information: Established 1994. Normal turnaround time- 48 hours. Expedited service available. Projects billed by number of names searched. Projects billed by the hour. 1st project may require prepayment. Credit cards accepted. They prefer payment by credit card. Specializes in competitive intelligence, municipal records, hidden assets, informal business relationships, video GPS or electronic surveillance and digital imaging. Also, he is certified for paint inspection and risk assessor. E&O insured. Notary. A licensed PI in WI. They perform service of process.

Paul Maisano Designs

6770 Berwick Dr, Clarkston, MI 48346
Phone: 248-625-6366 **Fax:** 248-625-5098
www.paulmaisanodesigns.com **email:** vickey@paulmaisanodesigns.com

Types of Records Retrieved: Criminal and Civil Courts; Probate Courts; Federal Courts; Real estate, Tax liens/Judgments, UCC Records.

Local Retrieval Area: MI-Bay, Calhoun, Clinton, Eaton, Genesee, Ingham, Jackson, Kalamazoo, Kent, Lapeer, Livingston, Macomb, Monroe, Oakland, Ottawa, Saginaw, Shiawassee, St. Clair, Washtenaw, Wayne. **Correspondent Relationships:** statewide, also Indiana, Ohio.

Add'l Information: Established 2001. Normal turnaround time- 24-48 hours. Projects billed by number of names searched. Will file/record documents. Net 10 days after bill. They provide public record document retrieval for all of MI including current owner, UCC & fixtures, tax liens, and judgments. They also do filings. Any volume. Accurate, reliable results.

Pawnee County Abstract Co

637 G St, Pawnee City, NE 68420
Phone: 402-852-2035 **Fax:** 402-852-2035

Types of Records Retrieved: Civil, criminal and probate courts; Real Estate; Tax liens/Judgments; UCC records

Local Retrieval Area: NE-Pawnee

Add'l Information: Established 1976. Normal turnaround time- variable depending on project. Projects billed by number of names searched. Projects billed by number of records located.

Payne Research & Sales

PO Box 214, Stinnett, TX 79083
Phone: 806-878-3195; mobil 806-886-3731 **Fax:** 806-878-3723
rpayne@hutchinsoncnty.com

Types of Records Retrieved: Civil, criminal and probate courts; Federal Bankruptcy courts; Tax liens/Judgments; Vital records

Local Retrieval Area: TX-Hutchinson

Add'l Information: Established 2000. Normal turnaround time- 24 hours. Expedited service available. Projects billed by number of names searched. Billings at the 1st of the month. Has access to District court 24 hours a day. Charges per name; if copies are requested there is a $1.00 per page charge.

PC Abstracting

2821 Whispering Hills, Chester, NY 10918
Phone: 845-699-6107 **Fax:** 845-464-5907 pcabstracting@yahoo.com

Types of Records Retrieved: Civil and criminal courts; Real Estate; Tax liens/Judgments; UCC records

Local Retrieval Area: NY-Dutchess, Orange, Rockland, Sullivan, Ulster, Westchester

Add'l Information: Established 1999. Normal turnaround time- 24 hours. Projects billed by number of names searched. 1st project may require prepayment. They are friendly, fast reliable with reasonable rates.

PDQ Legal Services Inc

7720 E Evans Rd #107, Scottsdale, AZ 85260
Phone: 480-556-6660 **Fax:** 480-556-6661
www.pdqlegal.com **email:** fmadanick@pdqlegal.com

Types of Records Retrieved: Civil and criminal courts

Local Retrieval Area: AZ-Apache, Cochise, Coconino, Gila, Graham, Greenlee, LaPaz, Maricopa, Mohave, Navajo, Pima, Pinal, Santa Cruz, Yavapai, Yuma. **Correspondent Relationships:** statewide.

Add'l Information: Established 1996. Normal turnaround time- 24 hours. Possible same day if received by 9am MST. Projects billed by number of names searched. They specialize in a fast, true prehire program that included speed, accuracy & economy. Their goal is to win your confidence daily through the quality & timeliness of each & every background request. They have researchers in the courthouse daily. A licensed PI in AZ. They perform service of process.

Pearl Information Services

110 Park St, Portland, ME 04101
Phone: 207-775-5889 **Fax:** 207-775-5883
www.pearlinformation.com **email:** pearl@maine.rr.com

Types of Records Retrieved: Civil, criminal and probate courts; Federal courts; Real Estate; Tax liens/Judgments; UCC records; Vital records

Local Retrieval Area: ME-Androscoggin, Cumberland, Kennebec, Knox, Sagadahoc, York

Add'l Information: Established 2000. Normal turnaround time- 48-72 hours. Expedited service available. Projects billed by number of names searched. Projects billed by the hour. 1st project may require prepayment. Credit cards accepted. They provide business research including competitive intelligence, asset searches, corporate profiles, employment screening and due diligence.

Jean Peck

1735 N Park Ave, Fremont, NE 68025
Phone: 402-721-4143 **Fax:** 402-753-9255

Types of Records Retrieved: Civil, criminal and probate courts; Real Estate; Tax liens/Judgments; UCC records; Vital records

Local Retrieval Area: NE-Dodge, Saunders, Washington; TX-Hidalgo (from Nov-April [956-381-9203])

Add'l Information: Established 1996. Normal turnaround time- 24 hours. Projects billed by number of names searched. Statements sent end of month. They perform service of process.

Becky Petro

1209 W Cottage Grove Ave, Bloomington, IN 47404
Phone: 812-335-1185 **Fax:** 812-335-1185 mmouse@kiva.net

Types of Records Retrieved: Civil and criminal courts; UCC records

Local Retrieval Area: IN-Monroe

Add'l Information: Established 1990. Normal turnaround time- 8-24 hours. Expedited service available. She invoices twice a month. She worked in the Monroe County Clerks Office for 13 1/2 years with misdeameanor division. Pride in her work, honesty and the best turnaround time.

Richard Peek Jr Attny

PO Box 8, Smithland, KY 42081
Phone: 270-928-4523 **Fax:** 270-928-2717

Types of Records Retrieved: Real Estate; Tax liens/Judgments

Local Retrieval Area: KY-Livingston

Add'l Information: Established 1974. 1st project may require prepayment. He specializes in real estate.

Daniel E Peel

1209 Robertson St, Fort Collins, CO 80524
Phone: 970-484-1542 **Fax:** 970-484-1544 danpeel@comcast.net

Types of Records Retrieved: Civil courts; Probate courts; Federal courts; Real Estate; Tax liens/Judgments; UCC records

Local Retrieval Area: CO-Larimer, Weld; WY-Albany, Laramie, Natrona, Sheridan; other CO and WY counties are available by arrangment. **Correspondent Relationships:** various correspondents in Rocky Mt. region.

Add'l Information: Established 1982. Normal turnaround time- 24-48 hours, or by arrangement. Net 30 days. They specialize in current owner searches in CO, WY and OR. Other searches by arraingement.

Pelican Land & Abstract Co Inc

PO Box 608, (1117 Kirkman St), Lake Charles, LA 70601
Phone: 337-436-3419 **Fax:** 337-439-3451
pelicantitle@cox-internet.com

Types of Records Retrieved: Civil, criminal and probate courts; Federal courts; Real Estate; Tax liens/Judgments; UCC records; Vital records

Local Retrieval Area: LA-Beauregard Parish, Calcasieu Parish, Cameron Parish, Jefferson Davis Parish

Add'l Information: Established 1992. Normal turnaround time- variable depending on project. Fee basis will vary by the type of project. 1st project may require prepayment. They specialize in oil, gas and leasing research and in residential and commercial abstracts of title and right-of-way research.

Pellish & Pellish Attorneys at Law

809 W Market St, Pottsville, PA 17901
Phone: 570-622-2338 **Fax:** 570-622-2339
www.pellishlaw.com **email:** pellishlaw@mindspring.com

Types of Records Retrieved: Civil, criminal and probate courts; Real Estate; Tax liens/Judgments; UCC records; Vital records

Local Retrieval Area: PA-Schuylkill

Add'l Information: Normal turnaround time- 1-14 days. Projects billed by the hour. 1st project may require prepayment. Personal checks are accepted. They specialize in assured, accurate and prompt service. They are an experience staff.

Penncorp Service Group Inc

600 N 2nd St #500, Harrisburg, PA 17101
Phone: 800-544-9050; 717-234-2300 **Fax:** 800-264-1137; 717-238-8232
penncorp@ezonline.com

Types of Records Retrieved: Civil courts; Probate courts; Federal courts; Real Estate; Tax liens/Judgments; UCC records; Vital records

Local Retrieval Area: PA-Cumberland, Dauphin. **Correspondent Relationships:** nationwide and Canada.

Add'l Information: Established 1987. Normal turnaround time- 24 hours. If certification is needed, allow 3-7 days. Projects billed by number of names searched. Credit cards accepted. Personal checks accepted. They specialize in working with the Pennsylvania State Corp. Bureau and Dept. of Transportation. State search requests are completed within 24 hours or less.

Pennington County Abstract Co

PO Box 508, Thief River Falls, MN 56701
Phone: 218-681-2527 **Fax:** 218-681-2528

Types of Records Retrieved: Civil, criminal and probate courts; Real Estate; Tax liens/Judgments; Vital records

Local Retrieval Area: MN-Pennington

Add'l Information: Normal turnaround time- variable depending on project. Fee basis will vary by type of project. All projects require prepayment. They will also invoice.

Penninsula Title & Abstract Corp

15 S 4th St, Crystal Falls, MI 49920
Phone: 906-875-6618 **Fax:** 906-875-4382

Types of Records Retrieved: Real Estate; Tax liens/judgments; UCC records

Local Retrieval Area: MI-Iron, Ontonagon

Add'l Information: Established 1974. Normal turnaround time- 1 day. Fee basis will vary by type of project. All projects require prepayment. They specialize in real estate.

PeopleSearch

PO Box 873, Waukegan, IL 60079
Phone: 877-835-1983; 847-360-0360 **Fax:** 847-623-3501
www.hirescreen.com **email:** searchpeople@covad.net

Types of Records Retrieved: Civil, criminal and probate courts; Real Estate; Tax liens/Judgments; UCC records; Vital records

Local Retrieval Area: IL-Lake, McHenry; WI-Kenosha

Add'l Information: Established 1995. Normal turnaround time- 24 hours. Usually same day. Projects billed by number of names searched. 1st project may require prepayment. Credit cards accepted. They have 30 years genealogical research experience, adoption research and do skiptracing, missing relatives, etc, as well as 13+ years of background/courthouse research. Principal of company is a Confidential Intermediary for State of Illinois.

Peregrine Investigation & Research

PO Box 3601, Boulder, CO 80307-3601
Phone: 303-324-7442 **Fax:** 303-499-9834
pmclean@cris.com

Types of Records Retrieved: Civil, criminal and probate courts; Federal courts; Real Estate; Tax liens/Judgments; UCC records; Vital records

Local Retrieval Area: CO-Adams, Arapaho, Boulder, Denver, Douglas, Jefferson, Weld. **Correspondent Relationships:** Larimer, Pagosa, Weld, El Paso counties.

Add'l Information: Established 1979. Normal turnaround time- 1-2 days. Projects billed by number of names searched. Projects billed by the hour. 1st project may require prepayment. They specialize in real estate research and document retrieval. They find those who default on consumer and commercial loans and in background and asset searches. They perform service of process.

Perkins County Abstract Co

PO Box 157, Bison, SD 57620
Phone: 605-244-5544 **Fax:** 605-244-5544

Types of Records Retrieved: Civil, criminal and probate courts; Real Estate; Tax liens/Judgments; UCC records

Local Retrieval Area: SD-Perkins

Add'l Information: Established 1949. Normal turnaround time- 2 weeks. Will provide expedited service. Projects billed by number of names searched. Projects billed by the hour. 1st project may require prepayment. They specialize in abstracts and title insurance.

Permian Court Reporters Inc

605 W Texas Ave, Midland, TX 79701
Phone: 432-683-3032 **Fax:** 432-683-5324

Types of Records Retrieved: Civil and criminal courts; Federal courts

Local Retrieval Area: TX-Ector, Midland

Add'l Information: Established 1974. Normal turnaround time- 2 days. Projects billed by number of names searched. Projects billed by the hour. 1st project may require prepayment. Odessa customers may call 432-620-9887. They perform service of process.

Shirley Perrone

9722 Deerpath Circle, Marcy, NY 13403
Phone: 315-733-6126 **Fax:** 315-733-7333

Types of Records Retrieved: Civil, criminal and probate courts; Federal courts; Tax liens/Judgments

Local Retrieval Area: NY-Oneida

Add'l Information: Established 1991. Normal turnaround time- 24 hours. Projects billed by number of names searched. Monthly billing available. Thirteen years experience as a record retriever. He provides federal court services in Northern District of NY. He provides county court services in Oneida County Court.

Marilyn Person

819 W 3rd, Pierre, SD 57501
Phone: 605-224-8168 **Fax:** 605-945-2440 personnj@pie.mideo.net

Types of Records Retrieved: Civil, criminal and probate courts; Federal courts; Tax liens/Judgments; UCC records; Vital records; Good Standings at State Level; Secretary of State Filings

Local Retrieval Area: SD-Hughes, Stanley, Sully. **Correspondent Relationships:** Lincoln, Minnehaha & Penington.

Add'l Information: Established 1980. Normal turnaround time- 24-48 hours. Projects billed by number of names searched. Fees are based upon project. They will invoice. She acts as registered agent for corporations. She will do any type of filings or searches needed at the state level at State Capitol in Pierre, SD.

Personal Background Inv, Inc

945 Tacoma Ave South #F, Tacoma, WA 98402
Phone: 800-949-9982; 253-597-4999 **Fax:** 253-272-9482
pbiinc@harbornet.com

Types of Records Retrieved: Civil, criminal, probate courts; Federal courts

Local Retrieval Area: WA-King, Kitsap, Pierce, Snohomish, Thurston. **Correspondent Relationships:** statewide.

Add'l Information: Established 1990. Normal turnaround time- 24-48 hours for most records. Fee basis varies by type of transaction. 1st project may require prepayment. Will invoice business accounts. They specialize in pre-employment screening. They have direct online capabilities for several northwest states, and statewide access in several others, also national SSN, DMV and credit.

Pete Costanzo Private Inv

5130 E Charleston Blvd #5 PMB 70, Las Vegas, NV 89142-1034
Phone: 702-459-1640 **Fax:** 702-459-4723

Types of Records Retrieved: Civil, Criminal, Probate Courts; Federal Courts; Real Estate, UCC records; Tax liens/Judgments

Local Retrieval Area: NV-Clark

Add'l Information: Established 1999. Normal turnaround time- 1-2 days. Projects billed by number of records located. 1st project may require prepayment. They specialize in general private investigations and locates. A licensed PI in NV.

Marilyn Peterson

810 S Pinkham St, Visalia, CA 93292
Phone: 800-401-5356; 559-732-2135 **Fax:** 559-635-4612
amstarlet@aol.com

Types of Records Retrieved: Civil courts; Probate courts; Real Estate; Tax liens/Judgments; UCC records; Vital records

Local Retrieval Area: CA-Kings, Tulare

Add'l Information: Established 1987. Normal turnaround time- 24 hours or less. Projects billed by number of names searched. Projects billed by the hour. 1st project may require prepayment. Net 30 days She is a certified notary public and will travel to handle loan documents and other signings in her area. Will retrieve large scale record orders in Fresno and Kern Counties. They perform service of process.

Petroleum Title Service Inc

3603 Hawthorne Ave, Casper, WY 82604
Phone: 307-235-6237 **Fax:** 307-577-4966

Types of Records Retrieved: Civil courts; Probate courts; Real Estate; Tax liens/Judgments; UCC records

Local Retrieval Area: WY-Natrona. **Correspondents:** statewide.

Add'l Information: Established 1962. Normal turnaround time- 1 week. Mileage expenses will be added to the fee. All billing is done on per case basis. They prepare abstracts of title, title certificates and any research pertaining to title information on surface, minerals, research for ownership for probates, leasehold checks or any type of title research across the State of Wyoming.

Sheila Pettit

469 Old Stagecoach Rd, Carrollton, GA 30116
Phone: 770-832-9273 **Fax:** 770-830-9301 pettit_s@bellsouth.net

Types of Records Retrieved: Civil and criminal courts; Real Estate; Tax liens/Judgments; UCC records

Local Retrieval Area: GA-Carroll, Coweta, Heard, Haralson

Add'l Information: Normal turnaround time- 24 hours. Projects billed by number of names searched. Will invoice monthly. She has been working in deed room for almost 4 years. She collects real estate, criminal, civil, liens & UCCs. She has a 24 hours turnaround time unless weather or courthouse closing prevents it.

PFC Information Services Inc

6114 LaSalle Ave #638, Oakland, CA 94611
Phone: 510-653-5061 **Fax:** 510-653-0842
www.pfcinformation.com **email:** lpeterson@pfcinformation.com

Types of Records Retrieved: Civil, criminal and probate courts; Federal courts; Real Estate; Tax liens/Judgments; UCC records; Vital records

Local Retrieval Area: CA-Alameda, San Francisco. **Correspondent Relationships:** Marin, Santa Clara, Contra Costa, San Mateo.

Add'l Information: Established 1987. Normal turnaround time- 24 hours. Projects billed by number of names searched. Projects billed by the hour. Credit cards accepted. Personal checks are accepted. They specialize in asset searches, corporate profiles, locating people, employment screening, competitor intelligence and due diligence research.

PHB Minerals

PO Box 50216, 838 Senora Av, Billings, MT 59105
Phone: 406-248-8838 **Fax:** 406-248-8838 phbeddow@bresnan.net

Types of Records Retrieved: Civil, criminal and probate courts; Federal District courts; Real Estate; Tax liens/Judgments; UCC & Vital records

Local Retrieval Area: MT-Yellowstone. **Correspondent Relationships:** Wyoming & Montana as needed.

Add'l Information: Established 1978. Normal turnaround time- 48 hours depending on travel time. Projects billed by number of names searched. Projects billed by the hour. Travel expenses are added for outlying counties. 1st project may require prepayment. Payment due upon delivery. Travel billed for outlying counties. Invoice net 15 days. They specialize in current owner, encumbrance reports, complete memorandum of title, mineral search, civil and criminal record search and retrieval of records.

Phelps Investigation & Employer Services

PO Box 9147, Mesa, AZ 85214-9147
Phone: 800-347-9918; 480-807-9799 **Fax:** 800-494-7950; 480-807-5530
one_slypi@msn.com

Types of Records Retrieved: Civil, criminal and probate courts; Federal courts; Real Estate; Tax liens/Judgments; UCC records

Local Retrieval Area: AZ-Maricopa. **Correspondents:** statewide.

Add'l Information: Established 1986. Normal turnaround time- 24-48 hours. Expedited service available. Projects billed by number of names searched. Projects billed by number of records located. 1st project may require prepayment. They specialize in general investigations, pre-employment screening and retrieving state and county records. A licensed PI in AZ.

Philip D Smith & Associates

338 Harris Hill Rd., Buffalo, NY 14221
Phone: 716-631-2100 **Fax:** 716-632-7838
www.pdsainc.com **email:** smith@pdsainc.com

Types of Records Retrieved: Civil and criminal courts; Federal courts; Tax liens/Judgments; UCC records

Local Retrieval Area: NY-Erie, Monroe, Niagara

Add'l Information: Established 1986. Normal turnaround time- 48 hours. Projects billed by the hour. 1st project may require prepayment. They specialize in the Buffalo NY area. A licensed PI in NY. They perform service of process.

Phillips County Abstract Co

53 South 2 East, Malta, MT 59538 **Phone:** 406-654-1413

Types of Records Retrieved: Real Estate; Tax liens/Judgments

Local Retrieval Area: MT-Phillips

Add'l Information: 1st project may require prepayment. They specialize in real estate.

Phillips Land Title Co Inc

174 N Avon Ave, Phillips, WI 54555
Phone: 715-339-2230 **Fax:** 715-339-4975

Types of Records Retrieved: Civil courts; Probate courts; Federal courts; Real Estate; Tax liens/Judgments; UCC records

Local Retrieval Area: WI-Ashland, Price. **Correspondent Relationships:** Ashland County WI.

Add'l Information: Established 1978. Normal turnaround time- 2 days. Fee basis varies by type of transaction. 1st project may require prepayment.

Phoenix Document Service Inc

12600 Seminole Blvd #A-3, Largo, FL 33778
Phone: 727-581-2552 **Fax:** 727-581-2589
www.phoenixdocumentservice.com **email:** kurt@phoenixdocumentservice.com

Types of Records Retrieved: Civil courts; Federal courts, Real Estate; Tax liens/ judgments; UCC records

Local Retrieval Area: FL-Alachua, Baker, Bay, Brevard, Charlotte, Citrus, Collier, Dade, Escambia, Flagler, Hernando, Highlands, Hillsborough, Indian River, Lake, Lee, Leon, Manatee, Marion, Martin, Monroe, Nassau, Okaloosa, Orange, Palm Beach, Pasco, Pinellas, Polk, Putnam, St. Johns, St. Lucie, Santa Rosa, Sarasota, Seminole, Volusia, Walton; NJ-Bergen, Essex, Middlesex, Monmouth, Morris, Ocean, Passiac, Union. **Correspondent Relationships:** check website for extended areas.

Add'l Information: Established 2000. Normal turnaround time- 24 hours. Projects billed by number of names searched. Will invoice client. They are a full service public records research & retrieval company. They have been serving the needs of the settlement & title industry since 2000. Let their friendly staff assist you today.

Phoenix Research Inc

100 Lyming Farm Rd, Mt Orab, OH 45154
Phone: 800-260-1092; **Fax:** 800-260-3997;
www.hrliability.com **email:** bbrown@hrliability.com

Types of Records Retrieved: Criminal courts

Local Retrieval Area: IN-Dearborn; KY-Boone, Campbell, Kenton, Union; OH-Butler, Clermont, Hamilton, Warren. **Correspondents:** nationwide.

Add'l Information: Established 1997. Normal turnaround time- 48-72 hours. Projects billed by number of names searched. Use their software and receive a discount. Volume discounts available. 1st project may require prepayment. Credit cards accepted. Prepayment discount available. Credit card required for NY O.C.A. search requests. They specialize in criminal record histories, training seminars, public speaking and due diligence issues. They are published authors on background investigations and privacy issues. They are a wholesale company and don't provide retail screening svcs.

Photo Abstract Co

22 E Central Ave, Miami, OK 74354
Phone: 918-542-1871 **Fax:** 918-542-9748

Types of Records Retrieved: Civil courts; Probate courts; Real Estate; Tax liens/Judgments; UCC records; Vital records

Local Retrieval Area: OK-Ottawa

Add'l Information: Established 1917. Normal turnaround time- 1-3 days. Projects billed by number of records located. They will file/record real estate documents on behalf on clients.

PI & Shadow Security

PO Box 1499, Rhinelander, WI 54501
Phone: 800-626-7578; 715-369-5944 **Fax:** 715-369-2405

Types of Records Retrieved: Civil and criminal courts.

Local Retrieval Area: WI-Forest, Florence, Langlade, Lincoln, Marathon, Oneida, Vilas. **Correspondent Relationships:** Eau Claire, La Crosse.

Add'l Information: Established 2000. 1st project may require prepayment. Specializing in process service, they also provide court filings, photocopying, skiptracing, and private investigations. A licensed PI in WI. They perform service of process.

PI Inc

PO Box 1584, Sequin, TX 78155
Phone: 800-359-5131; 210-655-2513 **Fax:** 800-730-0050; 210-655-5818
edward@ays4u.net

Types of Records Retrieved: Criminal courts

Local Retrieval Area: TX-Bexar, Caldwell, Comal, Guadalupe, Harris, Hays

Add'l Information: Established 1965. Normal turnaround time- 24-48 hours. Projects billed by number of names searched. Net 30 days; invoice weekly. They specialize in criminal records and pre-employment screening. We can retrieve MVR records in any state. A licensed PI in TX.

Pickard & Associates Inc

PO Box 473, Wenham, MA 01984
Phone: 978-468-4118 **Fax:** 978-468-3582
www.pickardassociates.com **email:** don@pickardassociates.com

Types of Records Retrieved: Civil, criminal and probate courts; Federal courts; Real Estate; Tax liens/Judgments; UCC records; Vital records

Local Retrieval Area: MA-Essex. **Correspondent Relationships:** nationwide.

Add'l Information: Established 1992. Normal turnaround time- 2-5 days. Fees will vary by type of project. 1st project may require prepayment. They are a private investigative firm specializing in asset research and background investigations on a nationwide basis. A licensed PI in MA.

Pierce County Abstract

216 S Main Ave, Rugby, ND 58368
Phone: 701-776-7777 **Fax:** 701-776-7777

Types of Records Retrieved: Civil courts; Probate courts; Real Estate; Tax liens/Judgments; UCC records

Local Retrieval Area: ND-Pierce

Add'l Information: Normal turnaround time- 2 weeks. Fee basis will vary by type of project. There is a set fee for abstracting.

PII Inc

1337 Wadash Ave, Springfield, IL 62704
Phone: 217-483-8845 **Fax:** 217-483-5491
www.piidetective.com **email:** pennell@piidetective.com

Types of Records Retrieved: Civil and criminal courts, Probate courts; Federal courts; Real Estate; Tax liens/Judgments; UCC & Vital records.

Local Retrieval Area: IL-Adams, Cass, Christian, Coles, Effingham, Logan, Macon, Macoupin, Mason, Menard, Montgomery, Morgan, Moultrie, Sangamon, Scott, Shelby

Add'l Information: Established 1991. Normal turnaround time- 2-3 days. Expedited service available. Projects billed by the hour. 1st project may require prepayment. Credit cards accepted. PII is a retired police officer with a solid background working with public records. A licensed PI in IL. They perform service of process.

Pinnacle Records

4000 Faxon Ave, Memphis, TN 38122-5217
Phone: 901-324-9163 **Fax:** 901-324-4685

Types of Records Retrieved: Civil and criminal records

Local Retrieval Area: TN-Shelby

Add'l Information: Established 1997. Normal turnaround time- same day in many cases. Projects billed by number of names searched. Fee basis depends upon type of project. Formerly Looksee Records, they specialize in background searches for both felonies and misdemeanors.

Pioneer Abstract Co

PO Box 1100, 113 S Wewoka Ave, Wewoka, OK 74884
Phone: 405-257-3351 **Fax:** 405-257-3358

Types of Records Retrieved: Civil, criminal and probate courts; Real Estate; Tax liens/Judgments; UCC records; Vital records

Local Retrieval Area: OK-Seminole

Add'l Information: Established 1937. Normal turnaround time- 1-3 days. Fee basis is determined on a per hour or per name plus service charge basis. They specialize in county records.

Pioneer Abstract Co of McAlester Inc

PO Box 926, 101 E Carl Albert Pky (74501), McAlester, OK 74502
Phone: 918-423-0817 **Fax:** 918-423-1202

Types of Records Retrieved: Civil courts; Probate courts; Real Estate; Tax liens/Judgments

Local Retrieval Area: OK-Pittsburg

Add'l Information: Normal turnaround time- 3 days. Projects billed by the hour. 1st project may require prepayment. Credit cards accepted. They specialize in real estate closings & title insurance.

Pioneer National Title Insurance

122 W Railroad Ave, Green River, WY 82935
Phone: 307-875-9833 **Fax:** 307-875-5025
pioneertitle@sweetwaterhsa.com

Types of Records Retrieved: Civil, criminal and probate courts; Federal courts; Real Estate; Tax liens/Judgments; UCC records

Local Retrieval Area: WY-Sweetwater

Add'l Information: Established 1982. Normal turnaround time- 24-48 hours. Projects billed by number of names searched. Payment due upon receipt of invoice. They specialize in full complete of title services including closings and escrows.

Pioneer-Ward County Abstract Co

PO Box 1639, 407 N Allen Ave, Monahans, TX 79756
Phone: 432-943-5561 **Fax:** 432-943-3716

Types of Records Retrieved: Civil courts; Probate courts; Real Estate; Tax liens/Judgments; UCC records

Local Retrieval Area: TX-Ward

Add'l Information: Normal turnaround time- 2-3 days. Projects billed by the hour. 1st project may require prepayment.

Pipestone County Abstract Co LLC

PO Box 335, Pipestone, MN 56164
Phone: 507-825-5833 **Fax:** 507-825-5833

Types of Records Retrieved: Civil, criminal and probate courts; Real Estate; Tax liens/Judgments; UCC records

Local Retrieval Area: MN-Pipestone

Add'l Information: Established 1995. Normal turnaround time- 2-3 days. Projects billed by number of names searched. Projects billed by number of records located. They specialize in real estate recordings and complete abstracting. They also offer closing services.

Pittsburgh Information & Research Co

PO Box 99181, Pittsburgh, PA 15233
Phone: 412-766-3832 **Fax:** 412-761-5391 oinvsvc@aol.com

Types of Records Retrieved: Civil, criminal and probate courts; Federal courts; Real Estate; Tax liens/Judgments; UCC records; Vital records

Local Retrieval Area: PA-Allegheny, Armstrong, Beaver, Blair, Butler, Cambria, Centre, Clarion, Crawford, Dauphin, Erie, Fayette, Greene, Indiana, Lawrence, Mercer, Somerset, Venango, Washington, Westmoreland. **Correspondent Relationships:** Pennsylvania.

Add'l Information: Established 1984. Normal turnaround time- 24-48 hours for verbal report. Fees are by name/index. 1st project may require prepayment. Terms: net 30 days. They specialize in complete coverage of every jurisdiction contained within Pennsylvania, including federal and state offices. A licensed PI in PA. They perform service of process.

Platte County Title & Escrow Co

PO Box 946, 2511 15th St, Columbus, NE 68602
Phone: 402-563-4519 **Fax:** 402-564-0588

Types of Records Retrieved: Civil, criminal and probate courts; Real Estate; Tax liens/Judgments; UCC records; Vital records

Local Retrieval Area: NE-Platte. **Correspondent Relationships:** Boone, Nance, Butler, Merrick counties.

Add'l Information: Normal turnaround time- 1 week. Fee basis varies by type of transaction. They specialize in escrow closings.

Platte Title Co

PO Box 788, Platte, SD 57369 **Phone:** 605-337-3824

Types of Records Retrieved: Real Estate; Tax liens/Judgments

Local Retrieval Area: SD-Charles Mix

Add'l Information: 1st project may require prepayment. They specialize in real estate.

PLM Court Research

PO Box 2903, Ranchos De Taos, NM 87557
Phone: 505-758-4467 **Fax:** 505-758-4629 Nica@LaPlaza.org

Types of Records Retrieved: Civil and criminal records, Probate records

Local Retrieval Area: NM-Taos

Add'l Information: Established 2001. Normal turnaround time- 24-48 hours. Projects billed by number of names searched. 1st project may require prepayment. They specialize in court searches in the Taos area. They perform service of process.

Boyd F Plumley, BA, M.S.L.S.

214 N George Mason Dr #1, Arlington, VA 22203-2934
Phone: 703-522-4363

Types of Records Retrieved: Civil/Probate courts; Real Estate; Vital records

Local Retrieval Area: MD-Montgomery; VA-Alexandria, Arlington, Fairfax, Fauquier, Loudoun, Prince William, Spotsylvania; Stafford

Add'l Information: Established 1969. Normal turnaround time- 5-7 business days. Projects billed by the hour. May charge for expenses. All projects require a deposit. They specialize in probate, vital, land, and military records, also maps (L of C) and manuscripts (L of C). They also do cemetery research, telephone numbers and addresses (residences).

Plymouth County Abstract

126 Central Ave SE, Le Mars, IA 51031
Phone: 712-546-4564 **Fax:** 712-546-4124

Types of Records Retrieved: Probate courts; Real Estate; Tax liens/Judgments; UCC records

Local Retrieval Area: IA-Plymouth

Add'l Information: Normal turnaround time- 2-7 days. Fee basis will vary by type of project. Personal checks are accepted.

PM Clinton International Investigation

7201 Westview, Houston, TX 77055
Phone: 866-686-6864; 713-686-6864 **Fax:** 713-686-6891
pm.clinton@houston.rr.com

Types of Records Retrieved: Civil, criminal and probate courts; Federal courts; Real Estate; Tax liens/Judgments; UCC records

Local Retrieval Area: TX-Brazoria, Chambers, Fort Bend, Galveston, Harris, Montgomery, Walker, Waller

Add'l Information: Established 1988. Normal turnaround time- 1-3 days. Expedited service available. Projects billed by number of names searched. Projects billed by the hour. All projects require prepayment. Credit cards accepted. They are a results oriented firm. They work for some of the largest firms in the US to the smallest. They give all their clients 110%. A licensed PI in TX.

Poindexter & Associates Inc

PO Box 37284, Raleigh, NC 27627
Phone: 800-373-2804; 919-859-5294 **Fax:** 919-834-7039
www.poindexter-associates.com
email: DetectiveOne@poindexter-associates.com

Types of Records Retrieved: Civil, criminal and probate courts; Federal courts; Real Estate; Tax liens/Judgments; UCC records; Vital records

Local Retrieval Area: NC-Chatham, Cumberland, Durham, Franklin, Granville, Harnett, Johnston, Rowan, Vance, Wake, Warren. **Correspondent Relationships:** DC, NC, VA.

Add'l Information: Established 1995. Normal turnaround time- 24-48 hours. Projects billed by the hour. 1st project may require prepayment. Credit cards accepted. They have a direct T1 connection to NC statewide criminal, civil and dmv records with instantaneous access. They are licensed detective agencys in NC, VA & DC. A licensed PI in NC, VA, DC & FL.. They perform service of process.

Poinsett County Abstract Co

409 Court St, Harrisburg, AR 72432
Phone: 870-578-5914 **Fax:** 870-578-5808

Types of Records Retrieved: Civil, criminal and probate courts; Real Estate; Tax liens/Judgments; UCC records **Local Retrieval Area:** AR-Poinsett

Add'l Information: Established 1912. Normal turnaround time- 1 week. Fee basis will vary by the type of project. They are a full service title company.

Maureen H Poole

PO Box 1664, Spring Hill, TN 37174-1664
Phone: 931-294-2988 **Fax:** 931-294-3032 sankar2@bellsouth.net

Types of Records Retrieved: Civil courts; Probate courts; Federal courts; Real Estate; Tax liens/Judgments; UCC records

Local Retrieval Area: TN-Bedford, Coffee, Davidson, Franklin, Giles, Hickman, Lawrence, Lewis, Lincoln, Marshall, Maury, Moore, Rutherford, Wayne, Williamson, Wilson; AL-Colbert, Cullman, Franklin, Jackson, Lauderdale, Limestone, Madison, Marion, Morgan, Winston. She will search other AL and TN counties upon request. **Correspondent Relationships:** can provide statewide services on request.

Add'l Information: Established 1998. Normal turnaround time- 24-48 hours. Expedited service available. Projects billed by number of names searched. Fees vary with type of search. Terms: net 30 days. They also will do searches in other north Alabama and south central Tennessee counties on request. Filing services, notary, and closing services available.

Pottawatomie County Abstract Co

PO Box 218, Westmoreland, KS 66549-0218
Phone: 785-457-3441 **Fax:** 785-457-3612 pottcoab@kansas.net

Types of Records Retrieved: Civil courts; Probate courts; Real Estate; Tax liens/Judgments; UCC records; Vital records

Local Retrieval Area: KS-Pottawatomie

Add'l Information: Normal turnaround time- 2-3 days. Fee basis varies by type of transaction. 1st project may require prepayment. They will file/record UCC and real estate documents on behalf of clients, if they did the closings or title work.

Potter & Co

PO Box 650, White Sulphur Springs, MT 59645
Phone: 406-547-3355 **Fax:** 406-547-3445

Types of Records Retrieved: Civil, criminal and probate courts; Real Estate; Tax liens/Judgments; UCC records; Vital records

Local Retrieval Area: MT-Meagher

Add'l Information: Established 1922. Normal turnaround time- 1 week. Projects billed by hour. They specialize in real estate and land title work.

Potter County Land & Abstract Inc

PO Box 203, Gettysburg, SD 57442
Phone: 605-765-2858 **Fax:** 605-765-2252

Types of Records Retrieved: Civil, criminal and probate courts; Real Estate; Tax liens/Judgments; Vital records

Local Retrieval Area: SD-Potter

Add'l Information: Established 1884. Normal turnaround time- 5 days. Projects billed by the hour. All projects require prepayment. They specialize in real estate.

Cynthia Potthoff

187 McLaren Dr N, Sycamore, IL 60178
Phone: 815-895-9527 **Fax:** 815-895-1775 cindypotthoff@comcast.net

Types of Records Retrieved: Civil, criminal and probate courts

Local Retrieval Area: IL-De Kalb, Kane, Kendall

Add'l Information: Established 1997. Normal turnaround time- within 24 hours. Projects billed by number of names searched.

Powell's Backtracking

4427 Dodt St, New Orleans, LA 70126
Phone: 504-242-7700 **Fax:** 504-242-7061 powellbt@bellsouth.net

Types of Records Retrieved: Civil/criminal courts; Federal District courts

Local Retrieval Area: LA-Jefferson Parish, Orleans Parish, St. Bernard Parish, St. Tammany Parish

Add'l Information: Established 1995. Normal turnaround time- 24-36 hours. Fees are per court search or per property. 1st project may require prepayment. Payment due upon billing. They specialize in criminal and civil searches. A licensed PI in LA. They perform service of process.

Powers Abstract Co Inc

PO Box 707, 635 Delaware St, Perry, OK 73077
Phone: 580-336-4068 **Fax:** 580-336-4060

Types of Records Retrieved: Civil, criminal and probate courts; Federal courts; Real Estate; Tax liens/Judgments; UCC records

Local Retrieval Area: OK-Noble

Add'l Information: Established 1971. Normal turnaround time- 5-7 days. Fee basis will vary by the type of project. 1st project may require prepayment. They specialize in real estate and titles.

Poweshiek Abstract Co Inc

PO Box 683, 833 Main St, Grinnell, IA 50112
Phone: 641-236-8668 **Fax:** 641-236-0614

Types of Records Retrieved: Civil, criminal and probate courts; Federal courts; Real Estate; Tax liens/Judgments; UCC records; Vital records

Local Retrieval Area: IA-Poweshiek

Add'l Information: Established 1950. Normal turnaround time- 1 business week. Projects billed by number of names searched. 1st project may require prepayment.

Prairie Abstract & Title

203 S Logan Ave, Terry, MT 59349
Phone: 406-635-5472 **Fax:** 406-635-5472

Types of Records Retrieved: Civil, criminal and probate courts; Real Estate; Tax liens/Judgments; UCC records; Vital records

Local Retrieval Area: MT-Prairie

Add'l Information: Established 1915. Normal turnaround time- 2-3 days. Projects billed by the hour. 1st project may require prepayment.

Pre-Check, The Pre-Check Company

14701 Detroit Ave #LL70, PO Box 711264, Lakewood, OH 44107
Phone: 800-268-2435; 216-226-7700 **Fax:** 216-226-0777
www.pre-check.com **email:** info@pre-check.com

Types of Records Retrieved: Civil and criminal courts; US Federal District courts

...val Area: OH-Astabula, Cuyahoga, Franklin, Hamilton, Lake, ...n, Lucas, Mahoning. Montgomery, Summit. **Correspondent Relationships:** nationwide.

Add'l Information: Established 1992. Normal turnaround time- 2-4 days. Projects billed by number of names searched. Credit cards accepted. Net 30 days. They specialize in comprehensive pre-employment background checks, offer comprehensive drug testing solutions, including 90-day hair tests, alcohol & oral fluids for "under the influence" detection.

Precision Quest

PO Box 6088, Marion, OH 43302
Phone: 740-383-3753 **Fax:** 740-383-5543
precisionquest@adelphia.net

Types of Records Retrieved: Civil, criminal and probate courts; Real Estate; Tax liens/Judgments; UCC records

Local Retrieval Area: OH-Crawford, Delaware, Franklin, Marion, Morrow, Union

Add'l Information: Established 1997. Normal turnaround time- 24 hours. Projects billed by number of names searched. Payment terms net 30 days. They specialize in current owner searches, UCC, criminal, mortgage, suits, judgments and Federal & State tax liens. They perform service of process.

Precision Research & Information

PO Box 3162, Quail Valley, CA 92587
Phone: 951-244-8118 **Fax:** 951-244-8777 pricalif@msn.com

Types of Records Retrieved: Civil, criminal and probate courts; Federal courts; Tax liens/Judgments; UCC recordsl; Vital records

Local Retrieval Area: CA-Riverside, San Bernardino

Add'l Information: Established 1995. Normal turnaround time- 12-24 hours. Projects billed by number of names searched. Payment terms are net 30 days. All searches are conducted at the county seat. Record retrieval depends upon the location of file.

Preferred Land Title

PO Box 708, Farmington, MO 63640
Phone: 800-310-6721; 573-756-6721 **Fax:** 573-756-0519

Types of Records Retrieved: Probate courts; Real Estate; Tax liens/Judgments; UCC records

Local Retrieval Area: MO-Madison, St. Francois, Ste. Genevieve, Washington

Add'l Information: Established 1906. Normal turnaround time- 3-5 working days. Projects billed by number of names searched. Projects billed by the hour. Fee basis is per chain of title. All projects require prepayment. Personal checks are accepted. They maintain complete geographical indexed title plants for each county they do business in.

Premier Corporate Services MN

590 Park St #6, St Paul, MN 55103-1846
Phone: 800-227-1256; 651-225-9500 **Fax:** 800-227-1263; 651-225-9579
www.premiercorp.com **email:** sueb@premiercorp.com

Types of Records Retrieved: Civil courts; Federal courts; Real Estate; Tax liens/Judgments; UCC records

Local Retrieval Area: MN-Hennepin, Ramsey. **Correspondent Relationships:** nationwide.

Add'l Information: Established 1991. Normal turnaround time- 48 hours. Projects billed by number of names searched. Credit cards accepted. Formerly Unisearch Inc (Minnesota) they specialize in Minnesota but can certainly obtain corporate and other documents nationwide.

Premiere Investigations

767 S State Rd 7 #22-C, Margate, FL 33068
Phone: 954-974-1139 **Fax:** 954-956-7508
www.premierepi.com **email:** info@pinvestigations.com

Types of Records Retrieved: Civil, criminal and probate courts; Federal courts; Real Estate; Tax liens/Judgments; UCC records; Vital records

Local Retrieval Area: FL-Broward, Dade, Palm Beach

Add'l Information: Established 1997. Normal turnaround time- 2-5 days. Expedited service available. Projects billed by number of names searched. Projects billed by the hour. 1st project may require prepayment. They specialize in domestic cases, accident investigations, worker's comp, surveillance, insurance fraud, locates (skiptrace), witness statements, asset and background searches, and process service. Se habla espanol. A licensed PI in FL. They perform service of process.

PreSearch Background Services

PO Box 50134, Colorado Springs, CO 80949-0134
Phone: 719-533-1880 **Fax:** 719-260-7172 or 719-535-0223
presearch@adelphia.net

Types of Records Retrieved: Civil, criminal and probate courts; Real Estate; Tax liens/Judgments; UCC records

Local Retrieval Area: CO-El Paso. **Correspondent Relationships:** nationwide.

Add'l Information: Established 1995. Normal turnaround time- 24-48 hours. Invoiced monthly for services rendered. Presearch Background Services specializes in hands-on document retrieval for El Paso county, CO. Normal turnaround time is 24 hours. They company also provides criminal & civil retrieval services in all CO statewide courts, with access to online sources.

Presidio County Abstract

PO Box 1357, 212 N Highland Ave, Marfa, TX 79843
Phone: 432-729-4264 **Fax:** 432-729-3286 psabstract@christophers.net

Types of Records Retrieved: Civil, criminal and probate courts; Federal courts; Real Estate; Tax liens/Judgments; UCC records

Local Retrieval Area: TX-Presidio

Add'l Information: Normal turnaround time- 1-2 days. Projects billed by the hour. All projects require prepayment. They specialize in escrow closings, title searches and abstracting.

Deloris Presley

309 N Pine St, Brewton, AL 36426
Phone: 888-544-8006; **Fax:** 251-867-2968

Types of Records Retrieved: Civil courts; Probate courts; Federal courts; Real Estate; Tax liens/Judgments; UCC records; Vital records

Local Retrieval Area: AL-Clarke, Conecuh, Covington, Escambia, Monroe

Add'l Information: Established 1996. Normal turnaround time- 24-48 hours. Fees are by type of projects. Terms: net 30 days. She specializes in title searches, UCC, lien & judgments and mineral reports. She has worked for 20 years with the same Title and Abstract Company.

Presque Isle Title Inc

283 N 3rd St, Rogers City, MI 49779
Phone: 989-734-2816 **Fax:** 989-734-3896

Types of Records Retrieved: Civil courts; Probate courts; Real Estate; Tax liens/Judgments; UCC records

Local Retrieval Area: MI-Presque Isle

Add'l Information: Normal turnaround time- 48-72 hours. Fee basis will vary by type of project. All projects require prepayment. They specialize in title/mortgage insurance.

Prestige Legal Services

14620 N Nebraska Ave #101A, Tampa, FL 33613
Phone: 800-784-7572; 813-264-1889 **Fax:** 813-264-5539
www.plsprocess.com **email:** dean@plsprocess.com

Types of Records Retrieved: Civil, criminal and probate courts; Federal courts; Real estate; Tax liens/Judgments; UCC records; Vital records.

Local Retrieval Area: FL-Citrus, Hernando, Hillsborough, Pasco, Pinellas, Sumter. **Correspondent Relationships:** Florida.

Add'l Information: Established 1991. Normal turnaround time- 24-48 hours. Projects billed by the hour. Credit cards accepted. Will invoice. They have over 30 years experience. A licensed PI in FL. Performs service of process.

Prewitt-Rogers Abstract Co

203 E Hale Ave, Osceola, AR 72370
Phone: 870-563-2137 **Fax:** 870-563-3558

Types of Records Retrieved: Civil courts; Probate courts; Real Estate; Tax liens/Judgments; UCC records

Local Retrieval Area: AR-Mississippi. **Correspondent Relationships:** Chickasawba district of Mississippi County.

Add'l Information: Established 1923. Normal turnaround time- 2-5 days. Projects billed by number of names searched. Projects billed by number of records located. Personal checks are accepted. They specialize in abstracts of title and title insurance.

Primetime Research Inc

83 Hanover St #8, Manchester, NH 03101
Phone: 866-737-2714; 603-666-4687 **Fax:** 866-621-0754; 603-621-0754
www.ptrionline.com **email:** lschofield@primetimeresearch.com

Types of Records Retrieved: Civil and criminal courts

Local Retrieval Area: MA-Essex, Franklin, Hampden, Hampshire, Middlesex, Norfolk, Suffolk, Worcester; NH-Belknap, Cheshire, Hillsborough, Merrimack, Rockingham, Strafford; RI-Bristol, Kent, Newport, Providence, Washington

Add'l Information: Established 1998. Normal turnaround time- 8-48 hours. (8AM EST cutoff). Projects billed by number of names searched. Terms are net 30 days. Formerly Primetime Research Inc, they specialize in customer service, they also are web enabled and insured.

Princess McDonald Process & Record Retrieval

1000 Ridge Ave, West Monroe, LA 71291-5222
Phone: 318-323-8566 **Fax:** 318-396-6573

Types of Records Retrieved: Civil and criminal courts; Federal District courts; Vital records

Local Retrieval Area: LA-Lincoln, Madison, Morehouse, Ouachita, Richland, Union

Add'l Information: Established 1970. Normal turnaround time- 2 days. Expedited service available. Projects billed by number of names searched. All projects require prepayment. They perform service of process.

Princeton Data Search Inc

PO Box 1162, Kaufman, TX 75142
Phone: 469-474-1025 **Fax:** 972-932-2217
www.princetondatasearch.net **email:** pds@princetondatasearch.net

Types of Records Retrieved: Criminal courts; Real Estate; Tax liens/Judgments

Local Retrieval Area: TX-Collin, Dallas, Ellis, Henderson, Hunt, Kaufman, Rockwall, Van Zandt. **Correspondent Relationships:** TX and LA.

Add'l Information: Established 2001. Normal turnaround time- 24-48 hours. Criminal records are billed monthly. They obtain felony and misdemeanor records in person for almost all of the counties served, with a quick turnaround time and low price. They also complete document retrievals and current owner searches.

Priority One Messenger Service

99 S Cameron St, PO Box 454, Harrisburg, PA 17108-0454
Phone: 800-444-1365; 717-257-1365 **Fax:** 717-232-6772

Types of Records Retrieved: Civil and criminal courts; Federal courts; Real Estate; Tax liens/Judgments; UCC records

Local Retrieval Area: PA-Cumberland, Dauphin, York

Add'l Information: Established 1986. Normal turnaround time- 48-72 hours. Projects billed by number of names searched. Projects billed by number of records located. 1st project may require prepayment. They specialize in retrieval of UCC, federal and state tax liens and judgments, also criminal pre-employment records for Cumberland, Dauphin and York counties, PA. Also specialize in motor vehicle pre-employment searches in 24-48 hours. They perform service of process.

Priority Plus Investigations

PO Box 518, China Grove, NC 28023
Phone: 704-857-7222 **Fax:** 704-857-7222

Types of Records Retrieved: Civil, criminal and probate courts; Federal Courts; Real Estate; Tax liens/Judgments; UCC records; Vital records

Local Retrieval Area: NC-Cabarrus, Davidson, Davie, Forsyth, Iredell, Mecklenburg, Rowan, Stanly, Yadkin

Add'l Information: Established 2000. Normal turnaround time- 2-3 days. Projects billed by number of names searched. 1st project may require prepayment. They are a full service private investigative agency. A licensed PI in NC.

Priority Process Service

Rt 1 Box 51, Newberry, IN 47449
Phone: 866-464-2192; 812-863-4129 **Fax:** 812-863-4130
www.angelfire.com/in/HIS **email:** jimhart@smithville.net

Types of Records Retrieved: Civil and criminal courts; Real Estate; Tax liens/Judgments; UCC records

Local Retrieval Area: IN-Daviess, Greene, Knox, Lawrence, Martin, Monroe, Owen, Sullivan. **Correspondent Relationships:** Brown, Daviess, Greene, Lawrence, Martin, Monroe, Orange, Owen, Sullivan Vigo, Pike, Dubois counties, IN.

Add'l Information: Established 1983. Normal turnaround time- 2 days. Expedited service available. Projects billed by number of names searched. Monthly invoice (due within 30 days). They specialize in process serving and document retrieval. A licensed PI in IN. They perform service of process.

Priority Records Search LLC

S8386 Hemlock Rd, North Freedom, WI 53951-9760
Phone: 608-544-9991 **Fax:** 608-544-9941
www.priorityrecordssearch.com **email:** prsllc@chorus.net

Types of Records Retrieved: Civil courts; Probate courts; Federal courts; Real Estate; Tax liens/Judgments; UCC records; Vital records

Local Retrieval Area: WI-Columbia, Dane, Sauk. **Correspondent Relationships:** statewide, nationwide.

Add'l Information: Established 2001. Normal turnaround time- 24-48 hours. Expedited service available. Projects billed by number of names searched. Payment due upon receipt. Their business is a records search and retrieval service. They have all the resources to give accurate and timely responses to their clients and customers, with personal attention and professional confidentiality.

Pro Facto Inc

9300 Batesville Pike, Jacksonville, AR 72076
Phone: 501-988-5340 **Fax:** 501-988-5874 profacto@aol.com

Types of Records Retrieved: Civil and criminal courts; Federal courts; Real Estate; Tax liens/Judgments; UCC records

Local Retrieval Area: AR-Faulkner, Hot Spring, Lonoke, Pulaski, Saline

Add'l Information: Established 1989. Normal turnaround time- 1-2 days. Expedited service available. Fee basis will vary by the type of search. Will invoice by project or monthly. They specialize in quick turnaround and good communication with clients. They have provided quality searches and retrieval services since 1989.

Pro Search Inc

91 Dora St, Stamford, CT 06902
Phone: 203-348-6994 **Fax:** 203-348-6994

Types of Records Retrieved: Real Estate; Tax liens/judgments; UCC records

Local Retrieval Area: CT-Fairfield. **Correspondent Relationships:** Connecticut.

Add'l Information: Established 1988. Normal turnaround time- 3-5 days. Projects billed by number of names searched. They also have a cell phone number: (203) 969-5566.

Probus Research

601 Van Ness Ave #E, San Francisco, CA 94102
Phone: 888-934-3848; 415-440-9100 **Fax:** 415-440-9200
www.probusresearch.com **email:** commune@probusresearch.com

Types of Records Retrieved: Civil, criminal and probate courts; Federal courts; Real Estate; Tax liens/Judgments; UCC records; Vital records

Local Retrieval Area: CA-Alameda, Contra Costa, Marin, San Francisco, San Mateo, Santa Clara. **Correspondent Relationships:** most California counties.

Add'l Information: Established 1985. Normal turnaround time- same day to 2 days. Projects billed by number of names searched. Charge by the hour on special projects. 1st project may require prepayment. Terms: net 30 days for established clients. They specialize in complex litigation case file, regulatory, business and library research. They also provide fax filings and super rush research and document retrievals. They perform service of process.

Process Service Network

10010 Canaga Ave #B6, Chatsworth, CA 91311-0959
Phone: 800-417-7623; 818-772-4795 **Fax:** 818-772-4798
www.processnet1.com **email:** processnet@sbcglobal.net

Types of Records Retrieved: Civil, criminal and probate courts; Federal courts; Real Estate; Tax liens/Judgments; Vital records

Local Retrieval Area: CA-Los Angeles, Orange, Riverside, San Bernardino, Ventura. **Correspondent Relationships:** Kern, Santa Barbara, San Diego counties California.

Add'l Information: Established 1978. Normal turnaround time- 1 day. Projects billed by number of names searched. All projects require prepayment. Credit cards accepted. Visa, Mastercard and American Express accepted. They specialize in court filings, document retrieval, hard-to-serve process, and international service of process. They perform service of process.

Process Service of Wyoming

224 South Park, Casper, WY 82601
Phone: 307-266-1979 **Fax:** 307-265-7747
www.wyomingprocessserver.com **email:** rtate@trib.com

Types of Records Retrieved: Civil and criminal courts.

Local Retrieval Area: WY-Big Horn, Carbon, Converse, Fremont, Hot Springs, Johnson, Natrona, Niobrara, Washakie. **Correspondent Relationships:** statewide.

Add'l Information: Established 2001. 1st project may require prepayment. They also provide court filing, subpoena preparation, photocopying, skiptracing, private investigations. They perform service of process.

Process Serving Unlimited

1832 Gippy Lane, PO Box 1884 (29402), Charleston, SC 29407
Phone: 843-728-2732 **Fax:** 843-766-0618

Types of Records Retrieved: Civil and criminal courts; US District courts

Local Retrieval Area: SC-Berkeley, Charleston

Add'l Information: Established 1984. Normal turnaround time- 2 days. Projects billed by number of names searched. Projects billed by the hour. 1st project may require prepayment. Will file documents in Charleston County only. Call before faxing. They perform service of process.

ProCom Services Corp

PO Box 202, Springfield, IL 62705
Phone: 217-744-4013 **Fax:** 217-544-1005
www.pro-comservices.com **email:** cbsiprocom@aol.com

Types of Records Retrieved: Civil, criminal and probate courts; Federal courts; Tax liens/Judgments; UCC records; Vital records

Local Retrieval Area: IL-Sangamon. **Correspondent Relationships:** Sangamon, IL.

Add'l Information: Established 1924. Normal turnaround time- 24 hours. Projects billed by number of names searched. 1st project may require prepayment. Monthly billing available. Specializing in collection services, mortgage reporting, tenant screening and employment screening.

Professional Choice Services

32055 Tiboe Plaza, Springfield, LA 70462
Phone: 225-294-3703 **Fax:** 225-294-7499
www.professionalchoiceservices.com **email:** bethbordelon@bellsouth.net

Types of Records Retrieved: Civil, criminal and probate courts; Real Estate; Tax liens/Judgments; UCC records; Vital records

Local Retrieval Area: LA-Livingston, St Tammany, Tangipahoa

Add'l Information: Established 1995. Normal turnaround time- 48 hours. Expedited service available. Projects billed by the hour. 1st project may require prepayment. They specialize in document recording, retrieval and research services. Notary public certified signing agent.

Professional Civil Process (Austin)

510 S Congress #110, Austin, TX 78704-1246
Phone: 800-950-7493; 512-477-3500 **Fax:** 512-477-8700
www.pcpusa.com **email:** austin@pcpusa.net

Types of Records Retrieved: Civil, criminal and probate courts; Federal courts; Real Estate; Tax liens/Judgments; UCC records; Vital records

Local Retrieval Area: TX-Austin, Bexar, Cameron, Dallas, Denton, El Paso, Fort Bend, Galveston, Harris, Houston, Nueces, Tarrant, TravisTyler. **Correspondent Relationships:** Texas.

Add'l Information: Established 1978. Normal turnaround time- 2-3 days. Expedited service available. Projects billed by the hour. 1st project may require prepayment. They have expanded their business to cover all Texas. They perform service of process.

Professional Civil Process (McAllen)

4307 N 10th St #G-2, McAllen, TX 78504-3019
Phone: 800-880-4223; 956-630-4223 **Fax:** 956-630-4182

Types of Records Retrieved: Civil, criminal and probate courts; Federal courts; Real Estate; Tax liens/Judgments; UCC records; Vital records

Local Retrieval Area: TX-Cameron, Hidalgo, Starr, Willacy. **Correspondent Relationships:** Texas.

Add'l Information: Established 1992. Normal turnaround time- 5 working days. Expedited service available. Projects billed by the hour. All projects require prepayment. Credit cards accepted. They will invoice to NAPPS members only. Their specialties include medical records. They perform service of process.

Professional Courier Service

124 Lyon NW, Grand Rapids, MI 49503
Phone: 616-451-4445 **Fax:** 616-451-4459

Types of Records Retrieved: Civil and criminal courts; Federal courts; UCC records; Vital records **Local Retrieval Area:** MI-Kent

Add'l Information: Established 1978. Normal turnaround time- 24-48 hours. Expedited service available. Projects billed by the hour. A flat fee is also charged in addition to the per hour fee. 1st project may require prepayment. Credit cards accepted.

Professional Paralegal Services Inc

PO Drawer 427, 72 N Main St, Watkinsville, GA 30677
Phone: 706-310-1166 **Fax:** 706-310-1167 gaparalegalsvc@aol.com

Types of Records Retrieved: Civil and criminal courts

Local Retrieval Area: GA-Baldwin, Barrow, Clarke, Elbert, Greene, Hancock, Jasper, Jones, Madison, Morgan, Oconee, Oglethorpe, Putnam, Walton, Wilkinson

Add'l Information: Established 2003. All projects require prepayment. They also provide skiptracing, court filings, and court records retrieval. They perform service of process.

Professional Process Service LLC

105 Haddad Rd, Waterbury, CT 06708
Phone: 888-712-7378; 203-753-7378 **Fax:** 203-573-8835
www.professionalprocess.com **email:** stup46@aol.com

Types of Records Retrieved: Civil, criminal and probate courts; Federal courts; Real Estate; Tax liens/Judgments; UCC records; Vital records

Local Retrieval Area: CT-Fairfield, Hartford, Litchfield, Middlesex, New Haven, New London, Tolland, Windham

Add'l Information: Established 1992. Normal turnaround time- 24-48 hours. Projects billed by the hour. Will invoice. They are a full service legal support company. They specialize in process serving, document retrieval and notary mortgage closing. They perform service of process.

Professional Services of America Inc

601 Avery St #500, Parkersburg, WV 26101
Phone: 304-485-1278 **Fax:** 304-485-9286
www.psa-inc.com **email:** jzotti@psa-inc.com

Types of Records Retrieved: Criminal courts

Local Retrieval Area: IL-Cook, Du Page; WV-Ritchie, Wood

Add'l Information: Established 1989. Normal turnaround time- 48 hours areas served. Projects billed by number of names searched. 1st project may require prepayment. They specialize in criminal background checks and social security number trace. They are also a staffing, screening and outsourcing services company.

Professional Services of New Mexico Inc

PO Box 51554, Albuquerque, NM 87181

Phone: 505-271-2291 **Fax:** 505-271-2313 tnprofse@nm.net

Types of Records Retrieved: Criminal courts; Probate courts; Federal courts

Local Retrieval Area: NM-Bernalillo, Sandoval

Add'l Information: Established 1989. Normal turnaround time- 48 hours. Projects billed by number of names searched. Projects billed by the hour. 1st project may require prepayment. They specialize in search and retrieval of public records.

Profile Information Services

816 Congress Ave #1280, Austin, TX 78701

Phone: 512-472-9380 **Fax:** 512-472-9551

www.profileinfo.com **email:** profileinfo@sbcglobal.net

Types of Records Retrieved: Civil, criminal and probate courts; Federal courts; Real Estate; Tax liens/Judgments; UCC records; Vital records

Local Retrieval Area: TX-Travis; TN-Blount, Knox, Loudon, Monroe, Roane, Travis. **Correspondent Relationships:** nationwide and Canada.

Add'l Information: Established 1993. Normal turnaround time- 48-72 hours. Projects billed by number of names searched. 1st project may require prepayment. They specialize in background verification, asset searches, and corporate, personal financial verification and fraud investigations. Owner Herbert J Cleveland is a certified fraud examiner and PI. A licensed PI in TN.

Promesa Enterprises Inc

5316 W Highway 290 #500, Austin, TX 78735

Phone: 800-474-4420; 512-891-6060 **Fax:** 512-891-6161

www.integratedscreening.com **email:** info@promesa.com

Types of Records Retrieved: Civil, criminal and probate courts; Federal courts; Real Estate; Tax liens/Judgments; UCC records; Vital records

Local Retrieval Area: TX-Bastrop, Hays, Travis, Williamson. **Correspondent Relationships:** nationwide.

Add'l Information: Established 1994. Normal turnaround time- 24-72 hours. Projects billed by number of names searched. Projects billed by the hour. 1st project may require prepayment. Terms: net 30 days. They specialize in pre-employment screening, which includes criminal & civil litigation, also litigation support, pre & post lending decision making, and asset search/verification for individuals nationwide. A licensed PI in TX.

Pronto Process & Messenger Svc

PO Box 1194, 114 N 5th Ave, Pasco, WA 99301

Phone: 509-547-1122 **Fax:** 509-547-5472 pmessen896@aol.com

Types of Records Retrieved: Civil, criminal and probate courts; Federal courts; Real Estate; Tax liens/Judgments; UCC records

Local Retrieval Area: WA-Benton, Columbia, Franklin, Walla Walla

Add'l Information: Established 1982. Normal turnaround time- 1-2 days. Expedited service available. Projects billed by number of names searched. 1st project may require prepayment. They perform service of process.

Property Research & Documentation Svc Inc

106 E Brandon, San Antonio, TX 78209

Phone: 210-520-7884 **Fax:** 210-520-7885 PropResearch@aol.com

Types of Records Retrieved: Civil, criminal and probate courts; Federal courts; Real Estate; Tax liens/Judgments; UCC records; Vital records

Local Retrieval Area: TX-Atascosa, Bandera, Bexar, Caldwell, Comal, DeWitt, Gonzales, Guadalupe, Hays, Kendall, Kerr, Lavaca, Medina, Travis, Williamson, Wilson. **Correspondent Relationships:** Bell, Cameron, Hidalgo, Nueces counties.

Add'l Information: Established 1988. Normal turnaround time- 24-48 hours. Projects billed by number of names searched. Projects billed by the hour. 1st project may require prepayment. Terms: net 15 days for new clients, otherwise net 30. They specialize in subject/adjoiner research for surveyors/engineers; 50 year chains-of titles for environmental assessments, Phase I; city, county, state & federal abstracting, retrieval & recording services. Now with offices in Gonzales & San Antonio.

Property Research Associates

2907 Unity Tree Dr, Edgewater, FL 32141

Phone: 386-423-0258 **Fax:** 386-423-0419

www.praterra.com **email:** nmarangoni@cfl.rr.com

Types of Records Retrieved: Real Estate; Tax liens/judgments; UCC records

Local Retrieval Area: FL-Volusia. **Correspondents:** nationwide.

Add'l Information: Established 1999. Normal turnaround time- 24-48 hours. Projects billed by number of names searched. Terms: net 30 days. Based in Florida, they specialize in O & E, current owner, property searches in TX and FL.

ProSearch

69333 County Rd 384, South Haven, MI 49090-7771

Phone: 888-585-6473; 269-544-4665 **Fax:** 888-585-6475; 269-544-4668

office@prosearchinfo.com

Types of Records Retrieved: Civil, criminal and probate courts; Federal courts; Real Estate; Tax liens/Judgments; UCC records; Vital records

Local Retrieval Area: MI-Allegan, Berrien, Cass, Kalamazoo, Kent, Ottawa, St. Joseph, Van Buren. **Correspondent Relationships:** nationwide for criminal searches.

Add'l Information: Established 1996. Normal turnaround time- 24 hours. Projects billed by number of names searched. Terms: net 15 days. They specialize in title and property searches & closings, civil and criminal searches and document retrieval. Expedited services and volume discounts available; call for details and charges. Notary Public.

Pro-Serv Process Service

451 Middle Rd, Fairfield, ME 04937

Phone: 207-453-2331 **Fax:** 207-453-2331

proserv@adelphia.net

Types of Records Retrieved: Service of process only.

Local Retrieval Area: ME-Kennebec, Somerset

Add'l Information: Established 1990. Normal turnaround time- 3-5 days. Expedited service available. They specialize in Service of Process. They perform service of process.

Prospective Renters Verification Svc

PO Box 69, Eagle Creek, OR 97022-0069

Phone: 503-655-0888 **Fax:** 503-655-0900

Types of Records Retrieved: Civil and criminal courts; Real Estate; Tax liens/Judgments; UCC records; Vital records

Local Retrieval Area: OR-Multnomah; WA-Clark. **Correspondent Relationships:** Oregon and Washington.

Add'l Information: Established 1991. Normal turnaround time- 2 hours or less. Projects billed by number of names searched. Monthly billing available. Subscription agreement required. They specialize in tenant and employee screening.

Pro-Tech Investigations LLC

PO Box 6133, Laurel, MS 39441-6133

Phone: 877-685-5655; 601-649-3800 **Fax:** 601-649-3899

www.proinvestigating.com **email:** jcsj@bellsouth.net

Types of Records Retrieved: Civil, criminal and probate courts; Federal courts; Real Estate; Tax liens/Judgments; UCC records

Local Retrieval Area: MS-Clarke, Covington, Forrest, Greene, Hancock, Harrison, Jasper, Jefferson Davis, Jones, Lamar, Marion, Pearl River, Perry, Smith, Stone, Wayne

Add'l Information: Established 1997. Normal turnaround time- 24 hours. Projects billed by number of names searched. Net 30 days. They specialize in pre-employment screening, background checks, records research, property searches, property abstracting, notary services, document retrieval. Coast office# 228-475-5520/Fax 228-475-5551. licensed PI in MS.

PRP Research

25 Colonial Circle, Cartersville, GA 30120
Phone: 770-769-9794 **Fax:** 770-769-9180 prpresearch@hotmail.com

Types of Records Retrieved: Civil, criminal and probate courts; Federal Bankruptcy courts; Real Estate; Tax liens/Judgments; UCC records

Local Retrieval Area: GA-Cobb, Fulton. **Correspondents:** nationwide.

Add'l Information: Established 2001. Normal turnaround time- 24-48 hours. Projects billed by number of names searched. Payment terms are net 30 days. They are a full service court retrieval network. Results are quality work received in a timely manner.

Prudential Associates

11 N Washington St #350, Rockville, MD 20850-4229
Phone: 800-726-7723; 301-590-1200 **Fax:** 301-590-1201
www.usainvestigators.com **email:** jks@usainvestigators.com

Types of Records Retrieved: Civil, criminal and probate courts; Federal courts; Real Estate; UCC records; Vital records

Local Retrieval Area: MD-Montgomery, Prince George's, Washington. **Correspondent Relationships:** Virginia.

Add'l Information: Established 1973. Normal turnaround time- 7-10 days. Projects billed by number of names searched. Projects billed by the hour. 1st project may require prepayment. Credit cards accepted. They specialize in full service private investigations, security consulting, and process service firms. A licensed PI in MD, DC, VA. Performs service of process.

PST Abstracting Inc

38 Ivy Rd, Rocky Point, NY 11778
Phone: 631-744-0759 **Fax:** 631-744-7120 pstabstracting@aol.com

Types of Records Retrieved: Civil Courts; Probate courts; Federal courts; Real Estate; Tax liens/Judgments; UCC records

Local Retrieval Area: NY-Nassau, Suffolk

Add'l Information: Established 1995. Normal turnaround time- less than 48 hours. Projects billed by number of names searched. Discounts given for muliple searches ordered. A full service information and retrieval corp that includes records, UCC, mortgages, deeds, judgments, etc. They have an excellent turnaround time.

Public Chex Inc

5245 Keith Bridge Rd, Cumming, GA 30041
Phone: 770-889-5662 **Fax:** 770-889-1132 pchex@adelphia.net

Types of Records Retrieved: Civil and criminal courts; Federal courts; Real Estate; Tax liens/Judgments; UCC records

Local Retrieval Area: GA-Bartow, Cherokee, Cobb, Dawson, De Kalb, Forsyth, Fulton, Gwinnett, Hall

Add'l Information: Established 1999. Normal turnaround time- 24-36 hours. Projects billed by number of names searched.

Public Information Resource

PO Box 509, Readfield, ME 04355-0509
Phone: 800-675-6350; 207-685-3500 **Fax:** 207-685-3338
keepar@adelphia.net

Types of Records Retrieved: Real Estate; Tax liens/Judgments; UCC records; Vital records

Local Retrieval Area: ME-Androscoggin, Cumberland, Franklin, Kennebec, Knox, Lincoln, Oxford, Penobscot, Sagadahoc, Somerset, Waldo, York. **Correspondent Relationships:** Maine and New Brunswick, Canada.

Add'l Information: Established 1985. Normal turnaround time- same day to 48 hours. Projects billed by number of names searched. Projects billed by the hour. 1st project may require prepayment. Personal checks are accepted. They take UCC-11's to the State Department daily. They file UCCs, articles of incorporation, annual reports and obtain Certificates of Good Standing. (CGS).

Public Record Services

PO Box 11565, Montgomery, AL 36111
Phone: 334-262-0350 **Fax:** 334-613-0289
m.gewin@worldnet.att.net

Types of Records Retrieved: Civil, criminal and probate courts; Federal courts; Real Estate; Tax liens/Judgments; UCC records; Vital records

Local Retrieval Area: AL-Autauga, Baldwin, Barbour, Bibb, Blount, Bullock, Butler, Calhoun, Chambers, Cherokee, Chilton, Choctaw, Clarke, Clay, Cleburne, Coffee, Colbert, Conecuh, Coosa, Covington, Crenshaw, Cullman, Dale, Dallas, De Kalb, Elmore, Escambia, Etowah, Fayette, Franklin, Geneva, Greene, Hale, Henry, Houston, Jackson, Jefferson, Lamar, Lauderdale, Lawrence, Lee, Limestone, Lowndes, Macon, Madison, Marengo, Marion, Marshall, Mobile, Monroe, Montgomery, Morgan, Perry, Pickens, Pike, Randolph, Russell, St Clair, Shelby, Sumter, Talladega, Tallapoosa, Tuscaloosa, Walker, Washington, Wilcox, Winston. **Correspondent Relationships:** statewide.

Add'l Information: Established 1974. Projects billed by number of names searched. Projects billed by the hour. The only Alabama firm covering all record sources. They perform service of process.

Public Records Abstract

142 Koenig Rd, Bernville, PA 19506
Phone: 484-256-6416 **Fax:** 610-488-1834

Types of Records Retrieved: Civil and criminal courts; Federal Courts; Real Estate; Tax liens/Judgments; UCC records; Vital records

Local Retrieval Area: PA-Berks

Add'l Information: Established 1998. Normal turnaround time- 24-48 hours. They will invoice bi-monthly. They specialize in all courthouse records.

Public Records Info Service

PO Box 91109, Tucson, AZ 85752
Phone: 520-321-8015 **Fax:** 520-575-8644 perhach@earthlink.net

Types of Records Retrieved: Civil and criminal courts

Local Retrieval Area: AZ-Coconino, Maricopa, Pima; NV-Clark

Add'l Information: Established 1989. Normal turnaround time- 24-48 hours. Projects billed by number of names searched. Will bill at end of month.

Public Records Research

403-C N Jefferson Ave, Cookeville, TN 38501
Phone: 931-520-8902 **Fax:** 931-520-1911 shawngp@excite.com

Types of Records Retrieved: Civil, criminal and probate courts; Federal courts; Real Estate; Tax liens/Judgments; UCC records; Vital records

Local Retrieval Area: TN-Cumberland, DeKalb, Overton, Putnam. **Correspondent Relationships:** Van Buren, Warren, White counties TN.

Add'l Information: Established 1997. Normal turnaround time- 1-3 days. Projects billed by number of names searched. 1st project may require prepayment.

Public Records Research Inc (Florida)

11350 178th Rd No, Jupiter, FL 33478
Phone: 561-746-0850 **Fax:** 561-745-2450 publicrr@adelphia.net

Types of Records Retrieved: Civil, criminal and probate courts; Federal courts; Real Estate; Tax liens/Judgments; UCC records

Local Retrieval Area: FL-Palm Beach

Add'l Information: Established 1986. Normal turnaround time- 48 hours. Projects billed by number of names searched. Projects billed by number of records located. Projects billed by the hour. 1st project may require prepayment. They have over 30 years experience searching court records. They are very customer orientated and very knowledgable and have reasonable rates.

Pulaski County Abstract Company

232 Main St, Miller City, IL 62962
Phone: 618-748-9233 **Fax:** 618-748-9233

Types of Records Retrieved: Civil courts; Probate courts; Real Estate; Tax liens/Judgments; UCC records; Vital records

Local Retrieval Area: IL-Pulaski

Add'l Information: Established 1960. Normal turnaround time- 2-14 days. Fee basis will vary by complexity and time of the job. Personal checks are accepted. They specialize in real estate transactions and court records.

Pure Again

37861 Town Hall, Harrison Township, MI 48045

Phone: 586-465-4359 **Fax:** 586-465-5727 steve@totheworld.com

Types of Records Retrieved: Criminal courts (Macomb county only); Real Estate; Tax liens/Judgments; UCC records

Local Retrieval Area: MI-Genessee, Lapeer, Livingston, Macomb, Oakland, Washtenaw, Wayne

Add'l Information: Established 1995. Normal turnaround time- 24-48 hours. Expedited service available. Projects billed by number of names searched. They take pride in everything they do. They work efficiently and exactly. Has been a record retriever for 7 years without complaints. Also does commercial searches in Wayne County. Cellphone is 586-484-3241.

Purintun Abstract

103 Second St SE, De Smet, SD 57231 **Phone:** 605-854-3401

Types of Records Retrieved: Real Estate; Tax liens/Judgments

Local Retrieval Area: SD-Kingsbury

Add'l Information: 1st project may require prepayment. He specializes in real estate.

Pushmataha County Abstract Co

Box 849, Antlers, OK 74523

Phone: 580-298-3189 **Fax:** 580-298-2322

Types of Records Retrieved: Civil courts; Probate courts; Real Estate; Tax liens/Judgments

Local Retrieval Area: OK-Pushmataha

Add'l Information: Established 1988. Normal turnaround time- 3-7 days. Projects billed by number of names searched. Projects billed by number of records located. Projects billed by the hour. All projects require prepayment. They specialize in abstracting and title insurance.

Putnam County Abstract

PO Box 303, 103 S 16th St, Unionville, MO 63565

Phone: 660-947-3105 **Fax:** 660-947-3105

Types of Records Retrieved: Real Estate; Tax liens/judgments; UCC records

Local Retrieval Area: MO-Putnam, Sullivan

Add'l Information: Established 1967. Normal turnaround time- 1 week. Fee basis varies by type of transaction.

Doris Pye

250 Hartman Dr, Harrisonburg, VA 22802

Phone: 540-433 8134 **Fax:** 540-433 8134 dapye@adelphia.net

Types of Records Retrieved: Civil, criminal and probate courts; Federal courts; Real Estate; Tax liens/Judgments; UCC records; Vital records

Local Retrieval Area: VA-Harrisonburg City, Rockingham

Add'l Information: Established 1991. Normal turnaround time- 48 hours. Projects billed by number of names searched. 1st project may require prepayment. Please fax all requests to 540-433-8134. They specialize in ABA certified paralegal services, jury consulting, process service, and document retrieval. You may also email to dapye@adelphia.net. A licensed PI in VA. They perform service of process.

Q

Quality Abstractors Inc

129 W Patrick St #11, Frederick, MD 21701

Phone: 301-695-9329 **Fax:** 301-695-5016

www.quality-titles.com **email:** orders@quality-titles.com

Types of Records Retrieved: Civil, criminal and probate courts; Real Estate; Tax liens/Judgments; UCC records

Local Retrieval Area: MD-Frederick, Washington. **Correspondent Relationships:** Washington County MD.

Add'l Information: Established 1966. Normal turnaround time- 1-14 days. Projects billed by number of names searched. Personal checks are accepted. They have been in the land title abstracting business for more than 25 years. They are the largest abstracting company in Frederick County, MD.

Quality Business Information

PO Box 2645, Elk Grove, CA 95759

Phone: 916-684-0444 **Fax:** 916-684-4950

qbinfocoy@aol.com

Types of Records Retrieved: Civil and criminal courts; Federal courts; Real Estate; Tax liens/Judgments. Vital records

Local Retrieval Area: CA-El Dorado, Nevada, Placer, Sacramento, Yolo; NV-Washoe. **Correspondent Relationships:** statewide.

Add'l Information: Established 1989. Normal turnaround time- 48 hours. Projects billed by number of names searched. Terms: net 30-60 days. No databases are used. Researchers personally go to all courthouses on a daily basis. Many counties researched by private investigators. They have over 50 years experience with court research. A licensed PI in CA.

Quality Research Service Inc

814 Barbara Dr, Craig, CO 81625

Phone: 970-824-4144 (Cell 970-629-0388) **Fax:** 970-824-4144

bjohnson@gct21.net

Types of Records Retrieved: Real Estate; Tax liens/Judgments; UCC records; Title search for mineral ownership

Local Retrieval Area: CO-Moffat, Rio Blanco, Routt. **Correspondent Relationships:** Routt, Rio Blanco counties CO.

Add'l Information: Established 2002. Normal turnaround time- 24-36 hours. Results returned by fax. Projects billed by number of names searched. Payment due within 30 days. They specializes in searches, document retrieval, county loan closings, document filings & oil & gas minerals search. Also provided title searches for mineral ownership. She is a retired county clerk with 24 years experience. Cell phone# is 970-629-0388.

Queen City Paralegal

3901 Belfast Ave, Cincinnati, OH 45236-1633

Phone: 513-984-4345 **Fax:** 513-984-4342 gayle_lunken@hotmail.com

Types of Records Retrieved: Civil courts

Local Retrieval Area: OH-Clermont, Hamilton, Montgomery, Warren

Add'l Information: Established 1993. Normal turnaround time- 24-48 hours. Will bill monthly or per project. They specialize in 42 year and current owner real estate searches, as well as E.P.A. (environmental) and commercial title examinations. They also have loan closing availability.

Quest & Assoc Inc

2517 Wenzell Ave, Pittsburgh, PA 15222

Phone: 412-563-1007 **Fax:** 412-563-6869

lquest78820@earthlink.net

Types of Records Retrieved: Civil, criminal and probate courts; Federal courts; Real Estate; Tax liens/Judgments; UCC records

Local Retrieval Area: PA-Allegheny. **Correspondent Relationships:** PA.

Add'l Information: Established 1990. Normal turnaround time- 24-72 hours. Projects billed by number of names searched. Billed last business day of month. They specialize in all public record searches.

Quest Discovery Service

2025 Gateway Place #330, San Jose, CA 95110
Phone: 408-441-7000 **Fax:** 408-441-7070
www.questds.com **email:** cbracamontes@questds.com

Types of Records Retrieved: Civil courts; Probate courts; Federal courts; Real Estate; Tax liens/Judgments; UCC records; Vital records

Local Retrieval Area: CA-all counties. **Correspondent Relationships:** Nevada and nationally.

Add'l Information: Established 1989. Normal turnaround time- 5-10 days. Projects billed by number of names searched. Projects billed by number of records located. Projects billed by the hour. 1st project may require prepayment. Terms: net 30 days. Formerly Valley Copy Svc. An attorney service with 8 branch offices, they prepare subpoenas, serve process and copy medical employment and other records throughout CA. They perform service of process.

Quest Research (Arkansas)

101 S Spring St #220, Little Rock, AR 72201
Phone: 501-374-4712 **Fax:** 501-374-3029
www.questresearch.info **email:** questark@sprynet.com

Types of Records Retrieved: Civil, criminal and probate courts; Federal courts; Real Estate; Tax liens/Judgments; UCC records; Vital records

Local Retrieval Area: AR-Arkansas, Ashley, Bradley, Calhoun, Chicot, Clark, Cleveland, Columbia, Conway, Dallas, Desha, Drew, Faulkner, Garland, Grant, Hot Spring, Howard, Jefferson, Lafayette, Lee, Lincoln, Little River, Lonoke, Miller, Monroe, Montgomery, Nevada, Ouachita, Perry, Pike, Polk, Prairie, Pulaski, Saline, Sevier, Union. **Correspondent Relationships:** statewide, AR, TX, OK, MO, TN, KY, MS, AL, GA, FL.

Add'l Information: Established 1982. Normal turnaround time- 1-3 days. Projects billed by number of names searched. Projects billed by number of records located. 1st project may require prepayment. Payment due upon receipt of invoice. They specialize in corporate retrieval, filing service, lien searches title searches, and document retrieval. They provide these services in all 75 Arkansas counties through a combination of employees and correspondents. Established in 1982.

Quick Data Services Inc

50 W 3900 S #2B, Salt Lake City, UT 84107
Phone: 800-720-6167; 801-268-4407 **Fax:** 800-720-6168; 801-268-4415
lquick@quickdatastaff.com

Types of Records Retrieved: Civil, criminal and probate courts; Federal courts; Real Estate; Tax liens/Judgments; UCC records; Vital records

Local Retrieval Area: UT-Box Elder, Cache, Davis, Morgan, Salt Lake, Summit, Tooele, Utah, Wasatch, Weber. **Correspondents:** statewide.

Add'l Information: Established 1995. Normal turnaround time- same day or next day. Expedited service available. Projects billed by number of names searched. 1st project may require prepayment. Terms: net 30 days. They specialize in state level UCC searches & filings, corporate document filing and registered agent services. They also do county level UCC, tax lien and judgment searches, property reports and certified copy retrieval.

Quick Search

4155 Buena Vista St, Dallas, TX 75204-7518
Phone: 214-358-2840 **Fax:** 214-358-6057
www.quicksi.com **email:** dwolter@quicksi.com

Types of Records Retrieved: Civil, criminal and probate courts; Federal courts; Real Estate; Tax liens/Judgments; UCC records; Vital records

Local Retrieval Area: TX-Collin, Dallas, Denton, Ellis, El Paso, Fannin, Grayson, Hunt, Johnson, Kaufman, Rockwall, Tarrant. **Correspondent Relationships:** nationwide.

Add'l Information: Established 1991. Normal turnaround time- 4-72 hours. Projects billed by number of names searched. Credit cards accepted. Terms: net 30 days. They specialize all types of retrieval. Check their website at www.quicksi.com. The website features a PASSWORD-PROTECTED online system where you may place orders and retrieve results. A licensed PI in TX.

Quick Search Title Services

3420 Elm St, St Charles, MO 63301
Phone: 636-723-1888 **Fax:** 636-896-0287 qusearch@aol.com

Types of Records Retrieved: Civil, criminal and probate courts; Rederal Courts; Real Estate; Tax liens/Judgments; UCC records; Vital records.

Local Retrieval Area: MO-St. Charles, St. Louis City, St. Louis. **Correspondent Relationships:** Franklin, Jefferson, Lincoln counties.

Add'l Information: Established 1995. Normal turnaround time- 6-8 hours. Quick Search Title Svcs offers quick and accurate title search services with superior customer service.

Quickfacts

134 Hill St, Woodstock, IL 60098
Phone: 815-236-8874 **Fax:** 815-206-5679 Melissamv@ameritech.net

Types of Records Retrieved: Criminal courts

Local Retrieval Area: IL-McHenry. **Correspondent Relationships:** Illinois.

Add'l Information: Established 1993. Normal turnaround time- 24-48 hours. Projects billed by number of names searched. Will invoice with a net 30 days. Melissa Flavin specializes in local court criminal cases and does civil searches incidentally. Has more that 10 years experience in public record document retrieval and research.

Quik Check Records

PO Box 440, Willamina, OR 97396-0440
Phone: 503-876-6477 **Fax:** 503-876-6877 qcrclp@msn.com

Types of Records Retrieved: Civil, criminal and probate courts; Federal courts; Real Estate; Tax liens/Judgments; UCC records; Vital records

Local Retrieval Area: OR-Benton, Clackamas, Lane, Lincoln, Linn, Marion, Multnomah, Polk, Tillamook, Washington, Yamhill; WA-Clark, Jefferson, King, Lewis, Pierce, Skagit, Snohomish, Thurston. **Correspondent Relationships:** OR, WA, also affiliates in CA, NV.

Add'l Information: Established 1996. Normal turnaround time- same day/24 hours for civil/criminal records; other searches 24-48 hours. Projects billed by number of names searched. Terms net 15 days of invoice. They specialize in civil and criminal research, current owner searches, mortgage retrievals. They copy medical records from physicians, hospitals and clinics. They are online to Washington and Oregon records statewide.

Quinn and Woodall Attnys

PO Box 1549, Cadiz, KY 42211
Phone: 270-522-3481 **Fax:** 270-522-3483

Types of Records Retrieved: Real Estate; Tax liens/Judgments

Local Retrieval Area: KY-Trigg

Add'l Information: 1st project may require prepayment. They specialize in real estate; is a law firm. They preform search services on a limited basis.

Quirk Associates

368 Washington St, Dedham, MA 02026
Phone: 781-326-1202 **Fax:** 781-326-0916

Types of Records Retrieved: Probate courts; Real Estate; Tax liens/Judgments; UCC records; Vital records

Local Retrieval Area: MA-Middlesex, Norfolk, Suffolk. **Correspondent Relationships:** Plymouth, Essex, Bristol counties.

Add'l Information: Established 1988. Normal turnaround time- within 1 week. The fee basis will vary with the type of search. They specialize in real estate record searches.

R

R & B Research & Recording Inc

208 S Blvd #A, Evanston, IL 60202
Phone: 847-477-7510 **Fax:** 847-492-9241
rbresearch@sbcglobal.net

Types of Records Retrieved: Real Estate; UCC records

Local Retrieval Area: IL-Cook, DuPage, Kane, Lake, McHenry, Will. **Correspondent Relationships:** statewide.

Add'l Information: Established 2002. Normal turnaround time- 1-3 days. Projects billed by number of names searched. payment due net 30 days. They are a document retrieval/recording company. They provide quick turnaround in the Chicago land area. Also provide coverage for State of IL.

R & D Research Services

108 Central Ave NW, Orange City, IA 51041
Phone: 712-737-8741 **Fax:** 712-737-8629
www.certifiedabstractandtitle.com **email:** vanroeke@frontiernet.net

Types of Records Retrieved: Civil, criminal and probate courts; Federal courts; Real Estate; Tax liens/Judgments; UCC records; Vital records

Local Retrieval Area: IA-Buena Vista, Cherokee, Clay, Dickinson, Lyon, O'brien, Osceola, Plymouth, Sioux, Woodbury. **Correspondent Relationships:** nationwide.

Add'l Information: Established 1999. Normal turnaround time- 24-48 hours. Projects billed by number of names searched. All projects require prepayment. They specialize in far northwest Iowa counties. Also abstracting, appraisals, mortgage broker and witness closing. A licensed PI in IA. They perform service of process.

R & R Search Inc

24 Lowell Mason Rd, Medfield, MA 02052
Phone: 508-359-2400 **Fax:** 508-359-7682
www.randrsearch.com **email:** orders@randrsearch.com

Types of Records Retrieved: Civil, criminal and probate courts; Federal courts; Real Estate; Tax liens/Judgments; UCC records; Vital records

Local Retrieval Area: MA-Barnstable, Berkshire, Bristol, Dukes, Essex, Franklin, Hampden, Hampshire, Middlesex, Nantucket, Norfolk, Plymouth, Suffolk, Worcester. **Correspondent Relationships:** nationwide.

Add'l Information: Established 1997. Normal turnaround time- 24-48 hours. Projects billed by number of names searched. 1st project may require prepayment. They specialize in MA and nationwide public record research, document retrieval, filing services, UCC searches, corporate document retrieval, court searches, tax lien searches and real property searches.

R A Heales & Associates Ltd

7935 E Prentice Ave #301, Englewood, CO 80111
Phone: 800-225-7043; 303-721-6300 **Fax:** 303-721-6340
www.heales-pi.com

Types of Records Retrieved: Civil, criminal and probate courts; Federal courts; Real Estate; Tax liens/Judgments; UCC records; Vital records

Local Retrieval Area: CO-Adams, Arapahoe, Boulder, Denver, Douglas, El Paso, Jefferson. **Correspondent Relationships:** Minnesota and Colorado.

Add'l Information: Established 1974. Normal turnaround time- 2-3 days. Projects billed by the hour. 1st project may require prepayment. Credit cards accepted. Personal checks are accepted. Also has offices in Minneapolis and Cross Lake Minnesota. Is Past President of Prof. PI Association of Colorado; served on Board of Directors of the NCISS.

R Miller & Associates LLC

PO Box 40579, Albuquerque, NM 87196
Phone: 800-395-1992; 505-345-4100 **Fax:** 505-345-4374
www.rmalocate.com **email:** rma@rmalocate.com

Types of Records Retrieved: Civil, criminal and probate courts; Federal courts; Real Estate; Tax liens/Judgments; UCC records; Vital records

Local Retrieval Area: NM-Bernalillo, Sandoval, Valencia

Add'l Information: Established 1982. Normal turnaround time- 24 hours in Bernalillo county; 72 hours in Sandoval and Valencia counties. Projects billed by number of names searched. Projects billed by the hour. They have been a established PI agency that has access to ALL New Mexico records in person and online. Will accept other investigative assignments. Santa Fe office phone is 505-984-9100 A licensed PI in NM. They perform service of process.

Raban's Record Search & Inv

PO Box 1105, St Johns, AZ 85936
Phone: 928-337-4250 **Fax:** 928-337-4250

Types of Records Retrieved: Civil, criminal and probate courts; Real Estate; Tax liens/Judgments; UCC records

Local Retrieval Area: AZ-Apache

Add'l Information: Established 1992. Normal turnaround time- 24 hours; guaranteed 48. Projects billed by number of names searched. 1st project may require prepayment. They specialize in Apache County AZ. They perform service of process.

Raines Record Research Inc

10072 Dulaney Rd, Rixeyville, VA 22737
Phone: 540-937-2005 **Fax:** 540-937-3848
rainesrecordrsch@aol.com

Types of Records Retrieved: Real Estate; Vital records

Local Retrieval Area: VA-Culpeper, Fauquier, Rappahannock

Add'l Information: Established 2000. Normal turnaround time- 24-48 hours. Fees negotiated with volume. They specialize in document retrieval and abstracting and get them to clients as soon as possible. Services include vital records, deeds, wills, judgments, and UCC searches.

RAM Services

PO Box 8356, Newport Beach, CA 92658-8356
Phone: 714-792-2860 **Fax:** 714-792-2860 ramservices@pacbell.net

Types of Records Retrieved: Civil, criminal and probate courts; Federal courts; Real Estate; Tax liens/Judgments; UCC records; Vital records

Local Retrieval Area: CA-Orange

Add'l Information: Established 1983. Normal turnaround time- 24 hours to 2 weeks. A licensed PI in CA. They perform service of process.

Ramsey Paralegal/Process

18 S Bradley Branch Rd #12, Arden, NC 28704
Phone: 828-687-9974 **Fax:** 828-687-9998 draml2@hotmail.com

Types of Records Retrieved: Civil, criminal and probate courts; Federal courts; Real Estate; Tax liens/Judgments; UCC records; Vital records

Local Retrieval Area: NC-Buncombe, Burke, Cherokee, Cleveland, Haywood, Henderson, Jackson, Macon, Madison, McDowell, Polk, Rutherford, Swain, Transylvania, Yancey

Add'l Information: Established 1989. Normal turnaround time- 1-2 days. Expedited service available. Fee varies. 1st project may require prepayment. They specialize in data searches, locate persons, SOP & record retrievals and buys mortgage and business notes. They perform service of process.

Ranger Recovery

PO Box 1184, Woodstock, NY 12498
Phone: 845-679-2957 **Fax:** 845-336-5480
http://ronsafe.webjogger.net **email:** rangerrecovery@yahoo.com

Types of Records Retrieved: Civil, criminal and probate courts; Real Estate; Tax liens/Judgments; UCC records; Vital records

Local Retrieval Area: NY-Ulster. **Correspondent Relationships:** Greene, Dutchess, Columbia, DE counties.

Add'l Information: Established 1986. Normal turnaround time- less than 1 week. Projects billed by number of names searched. Projects billed by number of records located. Projects billed by the hour. 1st project may require prepayment. A licensed PI in NY. They perform service of process.

Ransom County Title Co

PO Box 511, 7 Fourth Ave W, Lisbon, ND 58054
Phone: 701-683-5511 **Fax:** 701-683-5511
Types of Records Retrieved: Real Estate; Tax liens/Judgments
Local Retrieval Area: ND-Ransom
Add'l Information: Established 1953. Normal turnaround time- 1 week. Projects billed by number of names searched. Projects billed by number of records located. Fee basis will vary by the type of project. 1st project may require prepayment.

Rapid Document Service

211 S Lincoln Way, Galt, CA 95632
Phone: 209-745-0999 **Fax:** 800-225-0036; 209-745-0908
dseitz@softcom.net
Types of Records Retrieved: Civil, criminal and probate courts; Federal courts; Real Estate; Tax liens/Judgments; UCC records; Vital records
Local Retrieval Area: CA-Alameda, Amador, Calaveras, Contra Costa, El Dorado, Fresno, Madera, Marin, Merced, Napa, Placer, Sacramento, San Francisco, San Joaquin, San Mateo, Santa Clara, Solano, Stanislaus, Sutter, Yolo. **Correspondent Relationships:** Putnam and White counties, TN.
Add'l Information: Established 2001. Normal turnaround time- 12-48 hours. Projects billed by number of names searched. They invoice monthly. They specialize in felony, misdemeanor and civil searches.

Rapid Documents

2512 Dave Dietz Dr, Cookville, TN 38506
Phone: 931-372-6948 **Fax:** 931-372-2948
dseitz@softcom.net
Types of Records Retrieved: Civil, criminal and probate courts; Real Estate; Tax liens/Judgments; UCC records; Vital records
Local Retrieval Area: TN-Putnam, White
Add'l Information: Normal turnaround time- 12-48 hours. Projects billed by number of names searched.

Rapid Record Retrieval

PO Box 677, Monument Beach, MA 02553-0677
Phone: 508-759-8622 **Fax:** 508-759-9657
lori@rapidrecordretrieval.com
Types of Records Retrieved: Civil and criminal courts
Local Retrieval Area: MA-Barnstable, Bristol, Norfolk, Plymouth; RI-Bristol, Kent, Newport, Providence, Washington. **Correspondent Relationships:** New Hampshire.
Add'l Information: Established 1999. Normal turnaround time- 2 business days. Projects billed by number of names searched. 1st project may require prepayment. Terms: net 15 days.

Rapid Research

2625 Alcatraz Ave #171, Berkeley, CA 94705
Phone: 510-883-1602 **Fax:** 888-726-9040
jimdammann@earthlink.net
Types of Records Retrieved: Civil and criminal courts
Local Retrieval Area: CA-Alameda, San Mateo. **Correspondent Relationships:** California.
Add'l Information: Established 1994. Normal turnaround time- 1 day. Projects billed by number of names searched. They specialize in criminal records for pre-employment screening companies; courts are visited daily.

RASCAL

28465 Old Town Front St #318, Temecula, CA 92590
Phone: 951-693-0165 **Fax:** 951-693-4056
Types of Records Retrieved: Civil courts; Probate courts; Real Estate; Tax liens/Judgments
Local Retrieval Area: CA-Riverside, San Diego. **Correspondent Relationships:** Los Angeles, Orange, Ventura, San Bernardino, Riverside, San Diego.
Add'l Information: Established 1988. Normal turnaround time- 1-5 days. Projects billed by number of names searched. Projects billed by the hour. 1st project may require prepayment. They accept personal checks. They specialize in service of process in those "hard to reach" places. They also specialize in "search and serves." They perform service of process.

Rat Dog Research LLC

204 Bruce Dr, Coeur D' Alene, ID 83814
Phone: 208-765-4598 **Fax:** 208-666-8872 ratdogresearch@hotmail.com
Types of Records Retrieved: Real Estate; Tax liens/judgments; UCC records
Local Retrieval Area: ID-Bonner, Boundary, Clearwater, Kootenai, Latah, Nez Perce; WA-Asotin, Spokane, Stevens. **Correspondent Relationships:** Ada, Bannock, Benewah, Bingham, Bonner, Bonneville, Boundary, Canyon, Cassia, Fremont, Gem, Gooding, Idaho, Jefferson, Jerome, Kootenai, Latah, Lewis, Lincoln, Madison, Minidoka, Nez Perce, Owyhee, Payette, Twin Falls, Washington.
Add'l Information: Established 1996. Normal turnaround time- 24 hours. Projects billed by number of names searched. Monthly billing. They specialize in searches in northern Idaho and eastern Washington State. They offer over 20 years of mortgage underwriting experience.

Ray County Land Title

203 W Main, Richmond, MO 64085
Phone: 816-470-6500 **Fax:** 816-554-9707
Types of Records Retrieved: Real Estate; Tax liens/Judgments
Local Retrieval Area: MO-Ray
Add'l Information: Established 1997. 1st project may require prepayment. They specialize in real estate.

RBI Inc Joliet

100 S Larkin Av, Joliet, IL 60436
Phone: 800-724-8366; 815-741-1742 **Fax:** 815-741-1751
www.rbiinc.net **email:** rbiincor@juno.com
Types of Records Retrieved: Criminal courts; Probate courts; Federal courts; Real Estate; Tax liens/Judgments; UCC records; Vital records
Local Retrieval Area: IL-Cook, Du Page, Grundy, Kane, Kankakee, La Salle, Lake, Will. **Correspondent Relationships:** nationwide.
Add'l Information: Established 1976. Normal turnaround time- 3 working days. Projects billed by the hour. All projects require prepayment. Credit cards accepted. Established clients billed. They specialize in asset searches, skiptracing, and investigations. Branch offices in Cook, LaSalle, and Kankakee counties. A licensed PI in IL. They perform service of process.

RBI Inc Ottawa

500 State St, Ottawa, IL 61350
Phone: 815-228-3694 **Fax:** 815-434-5162 rossradke@hotmail.com
Types of Records Retrieved: Civil and criminal courts.
Local Retrieval Area: IL-Bureau, De Kalb, Lee, Marshall. **Correspondent Relationships:** Will, Grundy, Kendall, Kankakee, La Salle, Livingston, Cook, DuPage, Kane, Lake.
Add'l Information: Established 2001. 1st project may require prepayment. They also provide court filings, skiptracing, subpoenas, photocopying, and private investigations. A licensed PI in IL. They perform service of process.

RCC & Associates Inc

PO Box 201, N Grafton, MA 01536
Phone: 508-839-3234 **Fax:** 508-839-0199
rccsearch@aol.com
Types of Records Retrieved: Civil, criminal and probate courts; Federal courtsTax liens/Judgments
Local Retrieval Area: MA-Middlesex, Suffolk, Worcester
Add'l Information: Established 1999. Normal turnaround time- 24 hours. Projects billed by number of names searched. Payment due net 30 days. They are a retrieval company offering services with the highest level of integrity and quality.

Real County Title Co

PO Box 298, Leakey, TX 78873
Phone: 830-232-5303 **Fax:** 830-232-5399

Types of Records Retrieved: Civil courts; Probate courts; Real Estate; Tax liens/Judgments; UCC records

Local Retrieval Area: TX-Real

Add'l Information: Normal turnaround time- 1-2 days. Fee basis will vary by the type of project. They specialize in title insurance, title runs and real estate closings.

Real Data

204 Jordan St, Jefferson City, MO 65109-1239
Phone: 573-893-4898 **Fax:** 573-893-6282

Types of Records Retrieved: Civil courts; Federal District courts; Real Estate; Tax liens/Judgments

Local Retrieval Area: MO-Audrain, Boone, Callaway. Camden, Cole, Cooper, Crawford, Gasconade, Maries, Marion, Morgan, Osage, Pettis, Phelps, Pulaski, Ralls, Randolph

Add'l Information: Established 1984. Normal turnaround time- 48 hours. Projects billed by number of names searched. Fee basis will vary per county. They specialize in residential real estate searches and document retrievals.

Real Estate Data Inc

3073 Rt 148, Marion, IL 62959-8878
Phone: 618-964-1907 **Fax:** 618-964-1366

Types of Records Retrieved: Civil courts; Probate courts; Real Estate; Tax liens/Judgments; UCC records

Local Retrieval Area: IL-Franklin, Johnson, Williamson

Add'l Information: Established 1982. Normal turnaround time- 3 days. Projects billed by number of names searched. They specialize in real estate searches and issuance of title policies.

Real Estate Loan Services

5751 Uptain Rd #524, Chattanooga, TN 37411-5675
Phone: 423-855-0581 **Fax:** 423-894-3184
www.rels-corp.com

Types of Records Retrieved: Civil courts; Probate courts; Real Estate; Tax liens/Judgments; UCC records

Local Retrieval Area: TN-Bledsoe, Bradley, Grundy, Hamilton, McMinn, Marion, Meigs, Monroe, Polk, Rhea, Sequatchie. **Correspondent Relationships:** Georgia.

Add'l Information: Normal turnaround time- 24-72 hours. Projects billed by number of records located. 1st project may require prepayment. They specialize in title openings and closing.

Real Estate Loan Services of TN Inc

1100 Kermit Dr #204, Nashville, TN 37217
Phone: 800-475-2334; 615-367-2300 **Fax:** 615-399-9491

Types of Records Retrieved: Civil courts; Probate courts; Federal courts; Real Estate; Tax liens/Judgments; UCC records

Local Retrieval Area: TN-Cannon, Cheatham, Cumberland, Davidson, DeKalb, Dickson, Fentress, Giles, Hickman, Houston, Humphreys, Jackson, Lawrence, Lewis, Macon, Marshall, Maury, Montgomery, Overton, Perry, Pickett, Putnam, Robertson, Rutherford, Smith, Stewart, Sumner, Trousdale, Wayne, White, Williamson, Wilson. **Correspondent Relationships:** Kentucky and Alabama.

Add'l Information: Established 1975. Normal turnaround time- 24-48 hours. Projects billed by number of records located. Fees are based on the number of property addresses searched. All projects require prepayment. They specialize in appraisals, property reports, commitments for title insurance, closing documents (prepared, closing, escrow service, foreclosure sales) and other courthouse related services.

Real Land Abstract Inc

3545 Wolf Rd, Taylor Mill, KY 41015
Phone: 859-291-1140 **Fax:** 859-291-0112

Types of Records Retrieved: Civil and criminal courts; Real Estate; Tax liens/Judgments

Local Retrieval Area: KY-Boone, Bracken, Campbell, Carroll, Grant, Kenton, Mason, Owen, Pendleton, Trimble

Add'l Information: Established 2003. 1st project may require prepayment. Will file/record documents. They specialize in real estate.

Real Property Resources

8015 Mountain Road Pl, NE #105, Albuquerque, NM 87110
Phone: 505-232-3555 **Fax:** 505-294-3244
realpropertyresources@msn.com

Types of Records Retrieved: Civil and Probate courts; Real Estate; Tax liens/Judgments; UCC records.

Local Retrieval Area: NM-Bernalillo, Cibola, Los Alamos, McKinley, Sandoval, Santa Fe, Valencia,. **Correspondent Relationships:** nationwide.

Add'l Information: Established 1999. Normal turnaround time- 48 hours or less for current owner searches. Projects billed by number of names searched. Billing is included in delivery of all orders. Their services include but are not limited to real estate research, document retrieval, generation of title reports, document filing, retrieval of taxes & assessments, etc.

Reality Check Inc

PO Box 2233, East Peoria, IL 61611-2233
Phone: 309-699-1846 **Fax:** 309-699-5862
realitychecksrus@hotmail.com

Types of Records Retrieved: Criminal courts; Federal courts; Real Estate

Local Retrieval Area: IL-De Kalb, Kane, Kankakee, Kendall, McHenry, Peoria, Tazewell, Will

Add'l Information: Established 1998. Normal turnaround time- 24-48 hours. Projects billed by number of names searched. Will do monthly invoicing. They specialize in federal civil and criminal searches. They also do MVR searches. They have quality and accurate researching at low prices.

Realty Settlement Inc

915 Liberty St, Meadville, PA 16335
Phone: 814-336-1802 **Fax:** 814-336-5881

Types of Records Retrieved: Civil courts; Real Estate; Tax liens/Judgments; UCC records

Local Retrieval Area: PA-Crawford, Mercer, Venango

Add'l Information: Normal turnaround time- up to 7 days. Fee basis will vary by the type of project. They specialize in title insurance.

Realty Title Co Inc

517 W Janeaux St, Lewistown, MT 59457
Phone: 406-538-8176 **Fax:** 406-538-5184 rtc@midrivers.com

Types of Records Retrieved: Civil, criminal and probate courts; Real Estate; Tax liens/Judgments; UCC records; Vital records

Local Retrieval Area: MT-Fergus, Judith Basin, Petroleum

Add'l Information: Established 1890. Normal turnaround time- 2-3 days. Projects billed by the hour. They specialize in title insurance and long-term escrows.

Recon Investigative Services

112 Palm Ave, Pass Christian, MS 39571
Phone: 228-452-0120 **Fax:** 228-452-5709 diarecon@cs.com

Types of Records Retrieved: Civil and criminal coruts; Probate courts; Federal courts; Tax liens/Judgments; UCC records; Vital records

Local Retrieval Area: MS-George, Hancock, Harrison, Jackson, Pearl River, Stone

Add'l Information: Established 1994. Normal turnaround time- 1-2 days. Expedited service available. Projects billed by number of names searched. 1st project may require prepayment. They specialize in a full line of PI services. A licensed PI in MS. They perform service of process.

Record Access

321 1/2 E 1st St #207, Los Angeles, CA 90012-3923
Phone: 888-621-1491; 213-617-1828 **Fax:** 213-617-1887
recordaccess@yahoo.com

Types of Records Retrieved: Civil, criminal and probate courts; Federal courts; Tax liens/Judgments; UCC records

Local Retrieval Area: CA-Los Angeles, Orange. **Correspondent Relationships:** nationwide.

Add'l Information: Established 1996. Normal turnaround time- same to next day. Projects billed by number of names searched. Projects billed by the hour. 1st project may require prepayment. They specialize in name searches in all government offices and research of public records and documents.

Record Data Inc (Arkansas)

1501 Huron Ln, Little Rock, AR 72211

Phone: 501-223-0949 **Fax:** 501-223-0944

Types of Records Retrieved: Civil courts; Probate courts; Federal courts; Real Estate; Tax liens/Judgments; UCC records

Local Retrieval Area: AR-all counties. **Correspondent Relationships:** Tennessee.

Add'l Information: Established 1986. Normal turnaround time- variable depending upon search requirements. Fee basis varies by project. Formerly Wilson & Associates, RDI provides accurate, timely real estate records retrieval statewide in Arkansas and Tennessee.

Record Data Inc (Tennessee)

100 Winners Circle #110, Brentwood, TN 37027

Phone: 615-221-0021 **Fax:** 615-221-0053

Types of Records Retrieved: Civil courts; Probate courts; Federal courts; Real Estate; Tax liens/Judgments; UCC records

Local Retrieval Area: TN-all counties. **Correspondent Relationships:** Arkansas.

Add'l Information: Established 1986. Normal turnaround time- variable depending on search. Fee basis will vary with type of search. Formerly Wilson & Associates, RDI provides accurate, timely real estate records retrieval statewide in Arkansas and Tennessee.

Record Finders

PO Box 3242, Brownsville, TX 78523

Phone: 956-571-5378 **Fax:** 956-350-5120

Types of Records Retrieved: Civil, criminal and probate courts; Federal courts; Real Estate; Tax liens/Judgments; UCC records; Vital records

Local Retrieval Area: TX-Cameron, Hidalgo

Add'l Information: Established 1998. Normal turnaround time- 24-48 hours. Projects billed by number of names searched. Charge is per index when multiple indexes are searched. Will bill per order or at end of month, They specialize in 50 year chain of title searches.

Record Information Services

PO Box 894, Elburn, IL 60119

Phone: 630-557-1000 **Fax:** 630-557-1001

www.public-record.com **email:** jmetcalf@public-record.com

Types of Records Retrieved: Civil and criminal courts; Federal ourts; Probate; Real Estate; Tax liens/Judgments; UCC records; Vital records

Local Retrieval Area: IL-Cook, De Kalb, Du Page, Kane, Kendall, Lake, McHenry, Will

Add'l Information: Established 1993. Normal turnaround time- 24 hours. Fees are on project by project basis. All projects require prepayment. Credit cards accepted. They specialize in bankruptcies, judgments, foreclosures, new businesses, homeowners lists, criminal, misdemeanors, felonies, foreclosure sales, building permits, state & federal tax liens, DUIs, divorce, mortgages, foreclosures & property tax liens.

Record Retrieval of Indianapolis

2516 E 17th St, Indianapolis, IN 46218-4302

Phone: 317-383-1306 **Fax:** 317-383-1306

www.angelfire.com/in4/alvinesper **email:** alvinesper2000@yahoo.com

Types of Records Retrieved: Civil, criminal and probate courts; Federal courts; Real Estate; Tax liens/Judgments; UCC records; Vital records

Local Retrieval Area: IN-Marion. **Correspondents:** nationwide.

Add'l Information: Established 1992. Normal turnaround time- 24-48 hours. Projects billed by number of names searched. Projects billed by the hour. All projects require prepayment. They specialize in service of process and record retrieval, investigations. A licensed PI in IN. They perform service of process.

Record Retrieval Services Inc

PO Box 264, Allen, TX 75013-0005

Phone: 877-527-5355; 972-527-5355 **Fax:** 866-527-5266; 972-527-5266

rrsinc@comcast.net

Types of Records Retrieved: Civil and criminal courts; Real Estate

Local Retrieval Area: TX-Collin, Dallas. **Correspondent Relationships:** Texas statewide, also nationwide.

Add'l Information: Established 1996. Normal turnaround time- 24-48 hours. Projects billed by number of names searched. Credit cards accepted. Invoice monthly. They specialize in fast, accurate, competitively-priced in-person searches at the court house or title plants. They are a licensed PI, real estate broker and property/casualty agent with general liability and errors & omissions insurance. A licensed PI in TX.

Record Search America Inc

5527 Kendall St, Boise, ID 83704

Phone: 208-375-1906 **Fax:** 208-322-5469

www.researchforyou.com **email:** sby@researchforyou.com

Types of Records Retrieved: Probate courts; Federal courts; Real Estate; Tax liens/Judgments; UCC records

Local Retrieval Area: ID-all counties. **Correspondent Relationships:** Idaho (for court records), 17 counties in Nevada, 36 counties in Oregon, 18 counties in Utah, 30 counties in MT, 38 counties in Washington.

Add'l Information: Established 1991. Normal turnaround time- 24 hours. Projects billed by number of names searched. 1st project may require prepayment. Credit cards accepted. They have trained Land Title Researcher in every county for ID, NV, OR, MT, UT and WA to do real estate searches, within a 24 hour turnaround time. They have a private investigation license and can obtain Idaho DMV and criminal court records A licensed PI in ID.

Record Time Research

6072 Lotus Ln, Lufkin, TX 75904

Phone: 936-632-5150 **Fax:** 936-632-5150

elbel@cox-internet.com

Types of Records Retrieved: Real Estate

Local Retrieval Area: TX-Angelina, Nacogdoches. **Correspondent Relationships:** Angelina County TX.

Add'l Information: Established 1998. Normal turnaround time- 24-48 hours. They specialize in current owner searches conducted in several East TX counties. Call for more information.

Record-Check Services Inc

4515 Poplar #327, Memphis, TN 38117

Phone: 800-530-7226; 901-761-9979 **Fax:** 901-761-3409

lisalyon00@hotmail.com

Types of Records Retrieved: Civil, criminal and probate courts; Federal courts; Real Estate; Tax liens/Judgments; UCC records; Vital records

Local Retrieval Area: MS-Benton, De Soto, Marshall; TN-Fayette, Shelby, Tipton. **Correspondent Relationships:** nationwide and Puerto Rico. They routinely search all of TN, KY, MS, MO, AL.

Add'l Information: Established 1985. Normal turnaround time- 1-3 days. Expedited service available. Projects billed by number of names searched. Projects billed by the hour. Fees depend on type of search. 1st project may require prepayment. They specialize in multi-state and multi-county projects. They have a combined 55 years of real estate experience in-house.

Records Quest

1607 S Ironton St, Aurora, CO 80012

Phone: 303-369-0693 **Fax:** 303-755-0597 danballan@comcast.net

Types of Records Retrieved: Real Estate; Tax liens/Judgments; UCC records; Vital records

Local Retrieval Area: CO-Adams, Arapahoe, Boulder, Broomfield, Denver, Douglas, El Paso, Jefferson, Larimer, Mesa, Weld

Add'l Information: Established 1999. Normal turnaround time- 4 hours. Projects billed by number of names searched. Will invoice. They specialize in 24 hours or less document retrieval. O & E. Recording and e-mail capabilities. They have competitive rates and can handle high volume. He has 11 years experience.

Records Research & Retrieval

7777 E Via Sonrisa, Scottsdale, AZ 85258-4125
Phone: 602-574-2781 **Fax:** 480-951-1790 sldoucette@earthlink.net

Types of Records Retrieved: Civil, criminal and probate courts; Bankruptcy court; Real Estate; Tax liens/Judgments; UCC records; Vital records

Local Retrieval Area: AZ-Maricopa

Add'l Information: Established 1995. Normal turnaround time- 24-48 hours. Projects billed by number of names searched. 1st project may require prepayment.

Records Research Inc (California)

PO Box 19300, Sacramento, CA 95819
Phone: 800-952-5766; **Fax:** 800-870-6877;
www.recordsresearch.com **email:** tech@recordsresearch.com

Types of Records Retrieved: MVR; Secretary of State; Civil and criminal courts; UCC records; Real Estate; Tax liens/Judgments.

Local Retrieval Area: CA-Sacramento

Add'l Information: Established 1981. Normal turnaround time- varied depending on state. Check website for details. Projects billed by number of names searched. They specialize in instant retrieval of California MVRs. Other states are also available.

Records Research Inc (Nebraska)

PO Box 6169, 6003 Old Cheney Rd (68516), Lincoln, NE 68506
Phone: 402-476-3869, 402-323-3828 (direct line) **Fax:** 402-476-0635
fharwick@nebtitlelincoln.com

Types of Records Retrieved: Civil courts; Federal courts; Real Estate; Tax liens/Judgments; UCC records.

Local Retrieval Area: NE-Lancaster. **Correspondents:** statewide.

Add'l Information: Established 1981. Normal turnaround time- 24 hours to 48 hours. Projects billed by number of names searched. 1st project may require prepayment. They specialize in UCC searches statewide as well as corporate filings. They perform service of process.

Records Research of Knoxville

7725 Devonshire Dr, Knoxville, TN 37919
Phone: 865-693-3589 **Fax:** 865-693-5716
recordsresearchknox@comcast.net

Types of Records Retrieved: Civil and criminal courts; Federal courts; Real Estate; Tax liens/Judgments; UCC records

Local Retrieval Area: TN-Anderson, Blount, Knox, Sevier, Union

Add'l Information: Established 1996. Normal turnaround time- 24-48 hours. Projects billed by number of names searched. Projects billed by the hour. 1st project may require prepayment. Billing schedule may be applicable. They specialize in criminal searches and civil searches, local & federal. They have an excellent turnaround time.

Records Research of Mesa County

935 Bader Dr, Grand Junction, CO 81501
Phone: 866-321-6611; 970-241-6470 **Fax:** 970-241-6282
www.gardnerbusiness.com **email:** asgardner@gardnerbusiness.com

Types of Records Retrieved: Civil, criminal and probate courts; Federal courts; Real Estate; Tax liens/Judgments; UCC records; Vital records

Local Retrieval Area: CO-Mesa

Add'l Information: Established 1996. Normal turnaround time- 24-48 hours. Projects billed by the hour. Credit cards accepted. Will invoice customers meeting their standards. They specialize in routine research and investigations as well as those that others cannot accomplish. Primary investigator has an LLB and PE. They perform service of process.

Records Retrieval Service

5505 Old US 23 #450, Brighton, MI 48114
Phone: 810-220-0810 **Fax:** 810-220-0910 dnidz@hotmail.com

Types of Records Retrieved: Civil, criminal and probate courts; Federal courts; Real Estate; Tax liens/Judgments; UCC records; Vital records

Local Retrieval Area: MI-Bay, Calhoun, Genesee, Ingham, Kalamazoo, Kent, Livingston, Macomb, Midland, Monroe, Oakland, Ottawa, Saginaw, Washtenaw, Wayne. **Correspondent Relationships:** statewide.

Add'l Information: Established 1997. Normal turnaround time- 1-3 days. Projects billed by number of names searched. They provide court research for criminal and civil histories through direct contact with the courts. They will file documents in Genesee, Livingston, and Washtenaw Counties only. They are capable of providing statewide county and state searches.

Records Search & Report Svc

PO Box 82, Hominy, OK 74035
Phone: 918-885-4724 **Fax:** 918-885-4049 rcrdsrchrprtsrvc@aol.com

Types of Records Retrieved: Probate courts; Federal courts; Real Estate; Tax liens/Judgments; UCC record; Vital records.

Local Retrieval Area: OK-Adair, Cherokee, Craig, Creek, Delaware, Haskell, Kay, Lincoln, Logan, Mayes, McIntosh, Muskogee, Noble, Nowata, Okfuskee, Okmulgee, Osage, Ottawa, Pawnee, Payne, Rogers, Sequoyah, Tulsa, Wagoner, Washington. **Correspondent Relationships:** Oklahoma.

Add'l Information: Established 2003. Normal turnaround time- 24-48 hours. Projects may be billed by the hour or by number of names searched. 1st project may require prepayment. They specialize in ownership of surface, minerals, oil & gas lease holds, real estate, also liens/judgments and record retrieval.

RecordSearch Inc

4301 Chaucer Ln, Columbus, OH 43220
Phone: 614-457-6836 **Fax:** 614-457-5843

Types of Records Retrieved: Civil courts; Probate courts; Real Estate; Tax liens/Judgments; UCC records

Local Retrieval Area: OH-Franklin

Add'l Information: Established 1990. Normal turnaround time- 24-48 hours. Projects billed by number of names searched. Projects billed by number of records located. Projects billed by the hour. 1st project may require prepayment. Terms are net 30 days. They specialize mostly in the following: real estate searches, current owner, back title and full. They carry E & O Insurance.

Reda's Attorney Service

70 Osborne Ave, Mount Sinai, NY 11766
Phone: 631-331-0700 **Fax:** 631-474-0592 search01@optonline.net

Types of Records Retrieved: Real Estate; Tax liens/judgments; UCC records

Local Retrieval Area: NY-Suffolk

Add'l Information: Established 1986. Normal turnaround time- 24 hours for Suffolk County and 48 hours for Nassau County. Expedited service available. Projects billed by number of names searched. Fee basis will vary by the type of search. 1st project may require prepayment. They specialize in title and variance searches.

Redi-Info Information Services

PO Box 12145, Oklahoma City, OK 73157
Phone: 888-320-6805; **Fax:** 888-320-6805;
www.redi-info.com **email:** customerservice@redi-info.com

Types of Records Retrieved: Civil and criminal courts.

Local Retrieval Area: OK-Beckham, Blaine, Bryan, Canadian, Cherokee, Cleveland, Comanche, Cotton, Craig, Creek, Custer, Delaware, Garfield, Garvin, Grant, Haskell, Hughes, Kay, Kingfisher, Lincoln, Mayes, McClain, Muskogee, Noble, Oklahoma, Ottawa, Pawnee, Payne, Pottawatomie, Rogers, Seminole, Sequoyah, Texas, Tulsa, Wagoner, Washita. **Correspondent Relationships:** nationwide.

Add'l Information: Established 1992. Normal turnaround time- 24-48 hours. Projects billed by number of names searched. Account billing.

Red's Rapid Research

1148 Miller Ct, Rio Dell, CA 95562
Phone: 707-764-8836 **Fax:** 707-764-8811
www.redsrapidresearch.com **email:** wendy@redsrapidresearch.com

Types of Records Retrieved: Civil, criminal and probate courts; Real Estate; Tax liens/Judgments; UCC records, Vital records

Local Retrieval Area: CA-Del Norte, Humboldt

Add'l Information: Established 1998. Normal turnaround time- 24 hours. Expedited service available. Projects billed by number of names searched. Payment terms are net 30. Performing hands on record searches daily, Red's Rapid Research provides the most-accurate and up-to-date information with the fastest possible turnaround time.

David Reed

315 W 4th St, Emporium, PA 15834
Phone: 814-486-9327 **Fax:** 814-486-0464 reeddavidjohn@yahoo.com

Types of Records Retrieved: Civil, criminal and probate courts; Real Estate; Tax liens/Judgments; UCC records; Vital records

Local Retrieval Area: PA-Cameron, Elk, McKean, Potter

Add'l Information: Established 1980. Normal turnaround time- 24-48 hours. Fee is determined by an established schedule. 1st project may require prepayment. Requests that individuals prepay, but will invoice attorneys and companies. He specializes in oil and gas ownership searches. They perform service of process.

Regier Title Co

129 E Broadway #100, Newton, KS 67114
Phone: 316-283-2750 **Fax:** 316-283-5680

Types of Records Retrieved: Civil courts; Probate courts; Real Estate; Tax liens/Judgments; UCC records

Local Retrieval Area: KS-Harvey

Add'l Information: Normal turnaround time- 2-3 days. Fee basis varies by type of transaction. 1st project may require prepayment.

Registry Research

PO Box 448, South Egremont, MA 01258
Phone: 413-528-3919 **Fax:** 413-528-0907

Types of Records Retrieved: Probate courts; Real Estate

Local Retrieval Area: MA-Berkshire

Add'l Information: Established 1988. Normal turnaround time- 2 weeks. Projects billed by the hour. 1st project may require prepayment. A downpayment is required. They specialize in title abstracts and historical or genealogical documentation in Southern Berkshire.

Reliable Abstract

PO Box 141, Locus Grove, GA 30248
Phone: 678-614-0715 **Fax:** 770-898-1596
www.reliableabstractcompany.com
email: bene@reliableabstractcompany.com

Types of Records Retrieved: Civil courts; Probate courts; Real Estate; Tax liens/Judgments

Local Retrieval Area: GA-Butts, Henry, Jasper, Putnam, Spalding. **Correspondent Relationships:** in other Central Georgia counties.

Add'l Information: Established 1998. Normal turnaround time- 24-48 hours. Projects billed by number of names searched. 1st project may require prepayment. Due upon completion of project. They specialize in full and limited title searches.

Reliable Courier

2797 Irving Blvd #110, Dallas, TX 75207-2310
Phone: 214-637-4800 **Fax:** 214-637-4803 courier2@swbell.net

Types of Records Retrieved: Civil, criminal and probate courts; Federal courts; Tax liens/Judgments; Vital records

Local Retrieval Area: TX-Dallas, Ellis, Tarrant

Add'l Information: Established 1990. Normal turnaround time- 2 days. Projects billed by the hour. Credit cards accepted. A licensed PI in TX. They perform service of process.

Reliable Document Retrieval Inc

2111 20th St, Sacramento, CA 95818
Phone: 916-438-3000 **Fax:** 916-438-3001
www.reliabledocs.com **email:** orders@reliabledocs.com

Types of Records Retrieved: US District courts

Local Retrieval Area: CA-El Dorado, Placer, Sacramento, Yolo. **Correspondent Relationships:** CA statewide, OR, WA, NV, TX, UT, AZ.

Add'l Information: Established 1998. Normal turnaround time- 1-3 days. Projects billed by number of names searched. Fee basis depends upon type of project. 1st project may require prepayment. Terms are net 30 days. They specialize in real estate research, document retrieval & current owner. Secretary Of State, walk-in recordings in 7 states, US District Court.

Reliable Title Co of NH

PO Box 84, Epsom, NH 03234
Phone: 603-798-5230 **Fax:** 603-798-5231
www.nhtitle.com **email:** dave@nhtitle.com

Types of Records Retrieved: Probate courts; Real Estate; Tax liens/Judgments; UCC records

Local Retrieval Area: NH-Rockingham

Add'l Information: Established 1990. Normal turnaround time- 24 hours. Projects billed by number of names searched. Will invoice for services. They offer full abstract services in Rockingham County, from current owner searches to commercial projects, from asset searches to document recordings.

Reliable Title Search Inc

1165 S US Highway 1 #16, Fort Pierce, FL 34950
Phone: 772-489-9650 **Fax:** 772-489-9651

Types of Records Retrieved: Real Estate; Tax liens/Judgments; UCC records

Local Retrieval Area: FL-Indian River, Martin, Okeechobee, Palm Beach, St. Lucie

Add'l Information: Established 1995. Normal turnaround time- 24 hours. Projects billed by number of names searched. Will invoice.

Reliance Abstract Company AZ

70 S Val Vista Dr #605, Gilbert, AZ 85296
Phone: 800-207-1523; 480-926-6312 **Fax:** 800-207-1526; 480-926-6311
relianceabstract@yahoo.com

Types of Records Retrieved: Real Estate; Tax liens/judgments; UCC records

Local Retrieval Area: AZ-Maricopa, Mohave, Pima, Pinal, Yavapai. **Correspondent Relationships:** statewide.

Add'l Information: Established 1982. Normal turnaround time- 24 hours. Expedited service available Projects billed by number of names searched. Projects billed by number of records located. Payment due upon receipt of product or service. They specialize in land records research & reports, current owner searches, deed reports, deed of trust, assignments & reconveyance research & retrieval, UCC research & retrieval and document recording & filing.

Reliance Abstract Company UT

1275 N University Ave #8, Provo, UT 84604
Phone: 800-207-1523; 801-375-1800 **Fax:** 800-207-1526; 801-371-0514
relianceabstract@yahoo.com

Types of Records Retrieved: Real Estate; Tax liens/judgments; UCC records

Local Retrieval Area: UT-Cache, Davis, Salt Lake, Utah, Weber. **Correspondent Relationships:** statewide.

Add'l Information: Established 1982. Normal turnaround time- 24 hours. Expedited service available. Projects billed by number of names searched. Projects billed by number of records located. Payment due upon receipt of product or service. They specialize in land records research and reports, current owner searches, deed reports, deed of trust, assignments & reconveyance research & retrieval, UCC research & retrieval and document recording & filing.

Reliance Title Services

725 S Clinton St, Iowa City, IA 52244
Phone: 319-354-6505 **Fax:** 319-354-9705
kstoner@reliancetitle.com

Types of Records Retrieved: Civil, criminal and probate courts; Real Estate; Tax liens/Judgments; UCC records; Vital records

Local Retrieval Area: IA-Johnson

Add'l Information: Established 1987. Normal turnaround time- 24 hours for court searches, and 2 working days for real estate.

Relyea Services Inc

1524 Central Av, Albany, NY 12205
Phone: 800-854-4111; **Fax:** 800-854-4112 relyeaserv@aol.com

Types of Records Retrieved: Civil, criminal and probate courts; Federal courts; Real Estate; Tax liens/Judgments; UCC records; Vital records

Local Retrieval Area: NY-Albany, Rensselaer, Saratoga, Schenectady. **Correspondent Relationships:** every court in the nation.

Add'l Information: Established 1991. Normal turnaround time- same day. Projects billed by number of names searched. They specialize in court record retrieval, UCC searching and filing and corporate work. They perform service of process.

Reno/Carson Messenger Service Inc

185 Martin St, Reno, NV 89509-2827
Phone: 800-222-4249; 775-322-2424 **Fax:** 775-322-3408
www.renocarson.com **email:** pete1@callat6.com

Types of Records Retrieved: Civil, criminal and probate courts; Federal courts; Real Estate; Tax liens/Judgments; UCC records; Vital records

Local Retrieval Area: NV-Carson City, Churchill, Douglas, Lyon, Storey, Washoe. **Correspondent Relationships:** Northern Nevada; El Dorado and Placer, CA counties.

Add'l Information: Established 1982. Normal turnaround time- 24 hours to 3 days. Projects billed by number of names searched. Projects billed by number of records located. Projects billed by the hour. 1st project may require prepayment. Credit cards accepted. They specialize in process service. They perform service of process.

Renville County Abstract Co

PO Box 86, Olivia, MN 56277
Phone: 320-523-5328 **Fax:** 320-523-5321

Types of Records Retrieved: Probate courts; Real Estate; Tax liens/Judgments; Vital records

Local Retrieval Area: MN-Redwood, Renville

Add'l Information: Established 1988. Normal turnaround time- 2 days. Fee basis will vary by type of project. 1st project may require prepayment. Payment due on receipt of work. They specialize in real estate title searches.

Research & Abstract Associates

PO Box 61888, Ft Myers, FL 33906
Phone: 239-337-5354 **Fax:** 239-337-5653
flresearch@aol.com

Types of Records Retrieved: Civil, criminal and probate courts; Real Estate, Tax liens/Judgments; UCC records; Vital records.

Local Retrieval Area: FL-Broward, Charlotte, Collier, De Soto, Glades, Hardee, Hendry, Hernando, Hillsborough, Highlands, Lee, Manatee, Pasco, Pinellas, Sarasota. **Correspondent Relationships:** Southern Florida.

Add'l Information: Normal turnaround time- 24 hours. The specialize in far southwestern Florida.

Research & Investigative Associates

PO Box 1321, Eureka, CA 95502
Phone: 707-444-8767 **Fax:** 815-352-0701 talletec@pacbell.net

Types of Records Retrieved: Civil, criminal and probate courts; Real Estate; Tax liens/Judgments; UCC records; Vital records

Local Retrieval Area: CA-Del Norte, Humboldt

Add'l Information: Established 1983. Normal turnaround time- 48 hours for verbal request; 5 days on complex requests. Projects billed by the hour. 1st project may require prepayment. A 50% retainer is required. Personal checks are accepted. They specialize in investigation, locates and trial preparation. They are a full service agency. A licensed PI in CA. They perform service of process.

Research & Retrieval Inc

1301 Manhattan Av #E, Hermosa Beach, CA 90254
Phone: 800-707-8771; 310-798-8100 **Fax:** 310-798-9394
http://researchandretrieval.com **email:** order@researchandretrieval.com

Types of Records Retrieved: Civil, criminal and probate courts; Federal courts; Real Estate; Tax liens/Judgments; UCC records

Local Retrieval Area: CA-Los Angeles, Orange, Riverside, Sacramento, San Bernardino, San Diego, San Francisco, Santa Clara. **Correspondent Relationships:** nationwide.

Add'l Information: Established 1990. Normal turnaround time- same day to 24 hours. Projects billed by number of names searched. Terms are net 30 days. They specialize in providing public record research & document retrieval from all county, state and federal agencies & archives. Same day service at no extra cost. You can order via email-order@researchandretrieval.com.

Research & Retrieval Services Inc

703 Woodbox Dr, Virginia Beach, VA 23462
Phone: 757-463-0030 **Fax:** 757-463-0040
www.researchandretrievals.com **email:** dbeloff@cox.net

Types of Records Retrieved: Civil and criminal courts; Federal courts; Real Estate; Tax liens/Judgments; UCC records

Local Retrieval Area: VA-Chesapeake, Hampton, Isle of Wight, James City, Newport News, Norfolk, Portsmouth, Suffolk, Virginia Beach, Williamsburg, York

Add'l Information: Established 1995. Normal turnaround time- 24-48 hours. Projects billed by number of names searched. Projects billed by number of records located. 1st project may require prepayment. Payment due upon receipt of job. They specialize in knowing the many idiosyncrasies of each individual courthouse.

Research & Revisions Etc

1200 E Stuart St #50, Ft Collins, CO 80525-1137
Phone: 970-484-0176 laileenb@aol.com

Types of Records Retrieved: Civil courts; Real Estate; Tax liens/Judgments

Local Retrieval Area: CO-Larimer, Weld

Add'l Information: Established 1991. Normal turnaround time- 2-3 days. Projects billed by the hour. Payment for minimum charge (1 hour) in advance.

Research and Title Services Inc

2123 Pioneer Ave, Cheyenne, WY 82001
Phone: 800-584-9190; 307-638-4853; cell:640-8314 **Fax:** 307-634-0502
www.researchandtitle.com **email:** etia@lonetree.com

Types of Records Retrieved: Civil, criminal and probate courts; Federal courts; Real Estate; Tax liens/Judgments; UCC records; Corporate docs and filings.

Local Retrieval Area: WY-Albany, Laramie. **Correspondent Relationships:** court clerks throughout Wyoming.

Add'l Information: Established 1989. Normal turnaround time- 24-48 hours; civil and criminal records search times vary. Projects billed by number of names searched. also will charge by project. 1st project may require prepayment. Personal checks are accepted. They provide corporate filings & document retrieval (state level), county document retrieval, UCC, criminal & civil searches statewide, also MVR titles and plate searches (Laramie & Albany Ctys) and any type of misc research available to the public.

Research Associates

27999 Clemens Rd, Cleveland, OH 44145
Phone: 800-225-9693; 440-892-1000 **Fax:** 440-892-9439
www.raiglobal.com **email:** info@raiglobal.com

Types of Records Retrieved: Civil, criminal and probate courts; Federal courts; Real Estate; Tax liens/Judgments; UCC records; Vital records

Local Retrieval Area: OH-Cuyahoga, Lorain, Lake, Summit

Add'l Information: Normal turnaround time- 5-7 days. 1st project may require prepayment.

Research By Request Inc

3949 Fighting Creek Dr, Powhatan, VA 23139
Phone: 804-598-4121 **Fax:** 804-598-4374

Types of Records Retrieved: Civil and criminal courts; Federal Courts; Tax liens/Judgments; UCC records; Vital records

Local Retrieval Area: VA-Amelia, Chesterfield, Goochland, Henrico, Powhatan, Richmond City

Add'l Information: Established 1999. Projects billed by number of names searched. They will bill. The principal of the company has 18 years of experience through InfoSearch, Prentice Hall Legal & Financial Services, and Corporation Service Company. They perform service of process.

The Research Connection Inc of NH

1 Old Loudon Rd, Concord, NH 03301-7810
Phone: 800-540-5064; 603-226-8600 **Fax:** 603-228-6440
www.theresearchconnection.com

Types of Records Retrieved: Civil and criminal courts; Federal courts; Real Estate; Tax liens/Judgments; UCC records; Vital records

Local Retrieval Area: NH-Belknap, Carroll, Cheshire, Coos, Grafton, Hillsborough, Merrimack, Rockingham, Strafford, Sullivan

Add'l Information: Established 1989. Normal turnaround time- 3-5 business days. Projects billed by number of names searched. 1st project may require prepayment. They specialize in obtaining UCC/tax lien and corporate searches at the secretary of state's office, and town and county searching. Can reach Vermont locales bordering on NH. They perform service of process.

Research Express

3055 Crawfordville Hwy, Crawfordville, FL 32327
Phone: 850-926-5665 **Fax:** 850-926-4166

Types of Records Retrieved: Real Estate

Local Retrieval Area: FL-Bay, Calhoun, Columbia, Dixie, Franklin, Gadsden, Gilchrist, Gulf, Hamilton, Holmes, Jackson, Jefferson, Lafayette, Leon, Liberty, Madison, Suwannee, Taylor, Union, Wakulla, Washington

Add'l Information: Established 1996. Normal turnaround time- 24 hours. Expedited service available. 1st project may require prepayment. Terms: net 30 days. They specialize in property searches. They also perform witness location, closings after property search and mortgage recordings. The cellular phone number is 850-926-5665.

Research For You

10929 Firestone Blvd #158, Norwalk, CA 90650
Phone: 626-974-4484 **Fax:** 626-974-4934
srchlady12@yahoo.com

Types of Records Retrieved: Civil, criminal and probate courts; Federal courts; Real Estate; Tax liens/Judgments; UCC records; Vital records

Local Retrieval Area: CA-Los Angeles, Orange

Add'l Information: Established 1996. Normal turnaround time- 24 hours. Projects billed by number of names searched. 1st project may require prepayment. Terms: net 30 days. They specialize in locating documents from only partial information in courts and county offices. Same day fax results available. All research is performed in-person.

Research Information Consultants

4939 Fuller Dr, Columbus, OH 43214
Phone: 614-286-6303 **Fax:** 614-430-0104 lpahdopony@aol.com

Types of Records Retrieved: Civil, criminal and probate courts; Real Estate; Tax liens/Judgments; UCC records

Local Retrieval Area: OH-Delaware, Franklin, Madison, Marion, Morrow, Union

Add'l Information: Established 1996. Normal turnaround time- 48 hours. Projects billed by number of names searched. 1st project may require prepayment. They offer over 15 years experience in document retreival, archaeology/surveying research & title abstracts. E & O insurance guaranteed on all title work.

Research Information Services LLC

2741 39th St, Topeka, KS 66617
Phone: 800-522-3884; 785-235-6767 **Fax:** 800-327-6987; 785-235-1919
www.ristoday.com **email:** ris@ristoday.com

Types of Records Retrieved: Civil and criminal courts; Federal courts; Tax liens/Judgments; UCC records

Local Retrieval Area: KS-all counties. **Correspondents:** nationwide.

Add'l Information: Established 1960. Normal turnaround time- 48 hours. Projects billed by number of names searched. Will invoice monthly or by project. Specializing in criminal background checks for over 40 years.

Research N More

PO Box 2623, Georgetown, TX 78627-2623
Phone: 512-868-5828 **Fax:** 512-868-5847
http://researchnmore.7p.com **email:** jrusseau@stic.net

Types of Records Retrieved: Civil, criminal and probate courts; Federal courts; Real Estate; Tax liens/Judgments; UCC records; Vital records

Local Retrieval Area: TX-Bell, Burnet, Travis, Williamson

Add'l Information: Normal turnaround time- 24-48 hours. Projects billed by number of names searched. Projects billed by the hour. All projects require prepayment. They also provide comprehensive reports, foreclosure research, new business mailing lists and more.

Research Network

807 Brazos #312, Austin, TX 78701
Phone: 512-469-1740 **Fax:** 512-469-9305
researchnetwork@austin.rr.com

Types of Records Retrieved: Civil, criminal and probate courts; Federal courts; Real Estate; Tax liens/Judgments; UCC records; Vital records

Local Retrieval Area: TX-Bastrop, Hays, Travis, Williamson

Add'l Information: Established 1997. Normal turnaround time- same day to 36 hours. Projects billed by number of names searched. Projects billed by the hour. Flat fees are charged on certain searches. 1st project may require prepayment. They specialize in all public records, including criminal, property and state record searches. A licensed PI in TX.

Research North Inc of Alpena

537 W Chisholm #400, Alpena, MI 49707-0637
Phone: 888-876-1010; **Fax:** 888-876-1401;
www.researchnorth.com **email:** info@researchnorth.com

Types of Records Retrieved: Civil, criminal and probate courts; Federal courts; Real Estate; Tax liens/Judgments; UCC records; Vital records

Local Retrieval Area: MI-Alpena, Presque Isle

Add'l Information: Established 1981. Normal turnaround time- 24-48 hours. Projects are billed by time and material. All projects require prepayment. They specialize in investigative services for the insurance industry, legal community and business and industrial groups. Performs service of process.

Research North Inc of Marquette

220 W Washington #320, Marquette, MI 49855-4331
Phone: 888-876-1010; **Fax:** 888-876-1401;
www.researchnorth.com **email:** info@researchnorth.com

Types of Records Retrieved: Civil, criminal and probate courts; Federal courts; Real Estate; Tax liens/Judgments; UCC records; Vital records

Local Retrieval Area: MI-Delta, Marquette

Add'l Information: Established 1981. Normal turnaround time- 24-48 hours. Projects billed by the hour. Projects are billed by time and material. All projects require prepayment. They specialize in investigative services for the insurance industry, legal community and business and industrial groups. A licensed PI in MI, OH and WI. They perform service of process.

Research North Inc of Petoskey

207 Michigan, Petoskey, MI 49770-2607
Phone: 888-876-1010; **Fax:** 888-876-1401;
www.researchnorth.com **email:** info@researchnorth.com

Types of Records Retrieved: Civil, criminal and probate courts; Federal courts; Real Estate; Tax liens/Judgments; UCC records; Vital records

Local Retrieval Area: MI-Charlevoix, Emmet. **Correspondent Relationships:** Alpena, Grand Traverse, Ingham, Marquette counties, MI.

Add'l Information: Established 1981. Normal turnaround time- 24-48 hours. Projects are billed by time and material. All projects require prepayment. They specialize in investigative services for the insurance industry, legal community and business as well as industrial groups. A licensed PI in MI, OH and WI. They perform service of process.

Research North Inc of Traverse City

207 Michigan St (Corporate Office), Pitoskey, MI 49770
Phone: 888-876-1010; **Fax:** 888-876-1401;
www.researchnorth.com **email:** info@researchnorth.com

Types of Records Retrieved: Probate courts; Federal courts

Local Retrieval Area: MI-Grand Traverse, Leelanau

Add'l Information: Established 1981. Normal turnaround time- 24-48 hours. Projects are billed by time and material All projects require prepayment. They specialize in investigative services for the insurance industry, legal community and business and industrial groups. A licensed PI in MI. They perform service of process.

Research Specialists

PO Box 997, Destin, FL 32540-0097
Phone: 800-771-7547; 850-654-7352 **Fax:** 888-522-3600; 850-654-7353
www.rsi-pi.com **email:** rsi1dallas@aol.com

Types of Records Retrieved: Civil and criminal courts; Federal courts

Local Retrieval Area: TX-Dallas, Tarrant. **Correspondent Relationships:** Collin, Denton, Travis, Bexar counties TX.

Add'l Information: Established 1988. Normal turnaround time- 1-2 days. Projects billed by number of names searched. All projects require prepayment. They specialize in any type of research or investigation, offering criminal and civil searches in all Texas counties. A licensed PI in TX. They perform service of process.

Research Specialists & Investigators

PO Box 3536, Eagle, CO 81631
Phone: 970-331-7712 **Fax:** 303-845-8748
www.eaglecountyrsi.com **email:** retrieve@vale.net

Types of Records Retrieved: Civil, criminal and probate courts; Federal courts; Real Estate; Tax liens/Judgments; UCC records; Vital records

Local Retrieval Area: CO-Eagle. **Correspondents:** nationwide.

Add'l Information: Established 1966. Normal turnaround time- 24 hours to 2 weeks depending on the records. Projects billed by number of names searched. Projects billed by number of records located. Projects billed by the hour. All projects require prepayment. Has been in business since 1966. They are the only full time background public records company in CO. Do tenant screeing, employment screening & service of process. Also the web post of CO process servers directory. They perform service of process.

Research Specialists Inc

16 Denise Dr, Thornton, PA 19373
Phone: 610-358-2507 research@icdc.com

Types of Records Retrieved: Civil and criminal courts; Federal courts; Tax liens/Judgments; UCC records

Local Retrieval Area: DE-Kent, New Castle, Sussex; PA-Chester, Delaware, Montgomery

Research Unlimited LLC

PO Box 86075, Tucson, AZ 85754
Phone: 520-624-7024 **Fax:** 520-770-0807 suzyatresearch@aol.com

Types of Records Retrieved: Civil, criminal and probate courts; Federal courts; Real Estate; Tax liens/Judgments; UCC records; Vital records

Local Retrieval Area: AZ-Pima, Cochise, Santa Cruz

Add'l Information: Established 1992. Normal turnaround time- 24 hours. Projects billed by number of names searched. They specialize in real estate records, superior court record retrieval and background searches in the Tucson and Pima county areas.

Researchers Ltd

RR 3 Box 205, Frankford, DE 19945-9551
Phone: 302-238-7442 **Fax:** 302-238-7462

Types of Records Retrieved: Civil, criminal and probate courts; Real Estate; Tax liens/Judgments; UCC records

Local Retrieval Area: DE-Sussex. **Correspondent Relationships:** DE-Kent, New Castle; MD-Worchester, Wicomico, Somerset.

Add'l Information: Established 1990. Normal turnaround time- 1-48 hours for document retrieval, 3-7 days for title searches and 24-48 hours for current owner property searches. Projects billed by number of names searched. All projects require prepayment. They specialize in document retrieval and current owner property searches.

ResearchSource for Hard-to-Find Information

1255 New Hampshire Ave NW #521, Washington, DC 20036-2352
Phone: 202-778-0002 **Fax:** 202-331-1585
www.researchsource.com **email:** crichter@researchsource.com

Types of Records Retrieved: Civil courts; Federal courts; National Archives.

Local Retrieval Area: DC-Washington

Add'l Information: Established 1996. Normal turnaround time- 24 hours for Federal filings. Projects billed by the hour. 1st project may require prepayment. Payment due upon receipt of invoice. Specializes in research and retrieval at all US district, appellate and special courts (Tax & Federal Claims), regulatory agencies. Also the Library of Congress, National Archives and Patent Office.

Resource Management Specialists

1508 JF Kennedy Dr #206-2, Bellevue, NE 68005
Phone: 877-476-3337; 402-682-9305 **Fax:** 877-314-2110; 402-682-0016
www.rmspecialists.com **email:** rms@rmspecialists.com

Types of Records Retrieved: Criminal courts

Local Retrieval Area: NE-Douglas, Sarpy. **Correspondents:** nationwide.

Add'l Information: Established 1998. Normal turnaround time- 24-48 hours. Projects billed by number of names searched. Will invoice. They specialize in fast accurate criminal court records retrieval in both felony and misdemeanor searches.

Resource Reporting Ltd

30 Courthouse Sq #G-3, Rockville, MD 20850
Phone: 877-279-0298; 301-838-9200 **Fax:** 301-838-7095
processmd@aol.com

Types of Records Retrieved: Civil, criminal and probate courts; Federal courts; Real Estate; Tax liens/Judgments; UCC records

Local Retrieval Area: MD-Frederick, Montgomery, Washington. **Correspondent Relationships:** Maryland.

Add'l Information: Established 1983. Normal turnaround time- 24-72 hours. Projects billed by the hour. Projects are also billed by a flat rate. 1st project may require prepayment. They specialize in document retrieval, investigative services, genealogical research, document retrieval, asset identification, surveillance, real property title current owner searches, database information research & service of process in MD, VA, DC, PA. A licensed PI in MD. They perform service of process.

Reynolds Professional Service Inc

725 E Trade St #215, Charlotte, NC 28202
Phone: 800-814-8662; 704-338-1775 **Fax:** 704-338-1686
www.reynoldsprofessionalservice.com **email:** reynoldsproserv@mindspring.com

Types of Records Retrieved: Civil and criminal courts; Federal courts; Vital records

Local Retrieval Area: NC-Cabarrus, Cleveland, Davidson, Gaston, Iredell, Lincoln, Mecklenburg, Rowan, Stanly; SC-York. **Correspondent Relationships:** North Carolina.

Add'l Information: Established 1990. Normal turnaround time- 48 hours. Projects billed by the hour. 1st project may require prepayment. They specialize in process serving and location of missing witnesses and defendants, private investigation, mystery shopping, and they perform filing and issuance services applicable to state and federal courts. A licensed PI in NC, PI#2216. They perform service of process.

RFYI (Research For Your Information)

320 Bluebird Rd, Covington, TN 38019
Phone: 901-475-1276 **Fax:** 901-475-1277
dab_01@hotmail.com

Types of Records Retrieved: Civil, criminal and probate courts; Federal courts; Real Estate; Tax liens/Judgments; UCC records; Vital Records

Local Retrieval Area: TN-Crockett, Fayette, Gibson, Haywood, Lauderdale, Obion, Shelby, Tipton

Add'l Information: Established 1998. Normal turnaround time- 24-48 hours. Projects billed by number of names searched. They have a 30 day billing cycle. RFYI will meet your research needs; accuracy, timely and with integrity. A hands-on research firm providing up-to-the-minute information.

Richardson Abstract Co Inc

521 Marsh St, Kinsley, KS 67547
Phone: 620-659-2592 **Fax:** 620-659-2730
susanploger@sbcglobal.net

Types of Records Retrieved: Civil courts; Probate courts; Real Estate; Tax liens/Judgments; UCC records

Local Retrieval Area: KS-Edwards

Add'l Information: Normal turnaround time- same day. Projects billed by the hour. Personal checks are accepted. They specialize in title insurance and abstracts.

Richland County Abstract Co

123 N 3rd St, Wahpeton, ND 58074
Phone: 701-642-3781 **Fax:** 701-642-3852
richlandabstract@702com.net

Types of Records Retrieved: Civil, criminal and probate courts; Real Estate; Tax liens/Judgments; UCC records; Vital records

Local Retrieval Area: MN-Wilkin; ND-Richland, Sargent. **Correspondent Relationships:** North Dakota and Minnesota.

Add'l Information: Established 1922. Normal turnaround time- 1 week or less. Projects billed by number of names searched. 1st project may require prepayment. They specialize in real estate records, taxes, judgments and UCC searches.

Richmond Group International

2230C Tackets Mill Dr, Woodbridge, VA 22192-3012
Phone: 703-494-4645 **Fax:** 703-497-2578
www.richmondgroupintl.com **email:** jmattiaccio@richmondgroupintl.com

Types of Records Retrieved: Civil, criminal and probate courts; Federal courts; Tax liens/Judgments; Vital records; International criminal records

Local Retrieval Area: DC-all counties; TX-Dallas; VA-Alexandria, Arlington, Fairfax, Fairfax City, Prince George. **Correspondent Relationships:** nationwide and over 250 countries.

Add'l Information: Established 1992. Normal turnaround time- 1-2 days in USA, 5-10 days International. Projects billed by number of names searched. Credit cards accepted. They specialize in M & A/due diligence investigations, employment screeing, and international background investigations. They also have offices in Dallas, Miami, Chicago, Mexico and U.K. A licensed PI in VA, TX & Mexico. Performs service of process.

Ridgerunner Record Search Inc

2201 Holly, Fayetteville, AR 72703-1214
Phone: 479-443-4928 **Fax:** 479-251-1955

Types of Records Retrieved: Civil and criminal courts; Federal courts; Tax liens/Judgments; UCC records

Local Retrieval Area: AR-Benton, Washington

Add'l Information: Established 1990. Normal turnaround time- same day to 24 hours. Projects billed by number of names searched. Individual company billing. Ridgerunner Record Search Inc is a public record search and retrieval service with background search experience of 44 years.

Right On Time Documents Inc

622 Belgium Dr, Hermitage, TN 37076
Phone: 615-885-8672 **Fax:** 615-884-1368
rotdocuments@earthlink.net

Types of Records Retrieved: Real Estate; UCC records

Local Retrieval Area: TN-Cheatham, Davidson, Dickson, Hamilton, Knox, Montgomery, Robertson, Rutherford, Shelby, Sullivan, Sumner, Williamson, Wilson. **Correspondent Relationships:** statewide.

Add'l Information: Established 2000. Normal turnaround time- 24-48 hours; rural counties 72 hours. Projects billed by number of names searched. 1st project may require prepayment. This company's products include retrieval of Deeds of Trust, chain of assignments, releases, walk in recordings, current owner searches and bring down report with recording. They have excellent turnaround time.

Rigoli Searches

12038 W 58th Ter #A, Shawnee, KS 66216
Phone: 913-908-8863 **Fax:** 815-346-3443 rigoli@sbcglobal.net

Types of Records Retrieved: Civil and criminal courts; Real Estate; Tax liens/Judgments; UCC records

Local Retrieval Area: KS-Johnson, Leavenworth; MO-Clay, Platte. **Correspondent Relationships:** Eastern Kansas or Western Missouri.

Add'l Information: Established 2004. Normal turnaround time- 24-48 hours. Projects billed by number of names searched. Will invoice. They provide accurate and prompt abstracting services including current owner searches, UCC/FLS/SLS, document retrieval and walk-in recordings.

Ringgold County Abstract Co Inc

107 E Adams St, Mt Ayr, IA 50854-1620
Phone: 641-464-3902 **Fax:** 641-464-2265

Types of Records Retrieved: Civil, criminal and probate courts; Real Estate; Tax liens/Judgments; UCC records; Vital records

Local Retrieval Area: IA-Ringgold

Add'l Information: Established 1986. Normal turnaround time- 3-5 days. Fee basis will vary by the type of project. 1st project may require prepayment.

Rio Grande Mineral Title

PO Box 489, 580 Columbia Ave, Del Norte, CO 81132
Phone: 719-657-3366 **Fax:** 719-657-2395
rgmt@fone.net

Types of Records Retrieved: Real Estate; Tax liens/judgments; UCC records

Local Retrieval Area: CO-Mineral, Rio Grande. **Correspondent Relationships:** Saguach, Alamosa, Conejos, CO counties.

Add'l Information: Established 1893. Normal turnaround time- 48 hours. Projects billed by number of names searched. Personal checks accepted.

RIQ and Associates Inc

PO Box 494, 473 Eaglestone Dr, Castle Rock, CO 80104
Phone: 720-529-5736 **Fax:** 720-529-8120
riq_company@msn.com

Types of Records Retrieved: Civil and criminal courts; Federal district courts; Real Estate; Tax liens/Judgments; UCC records; Vital records

Local Retrieval Area: CO-Adams, Arapahoe, Boulder, Broomfield, Clear Creek, Denver, Douglas, El Paso, Elbert, Fremont, Gilpin, Jefferson, Larimer, Puelbo, Teller, Weld. **Correspondent Relationships:** Arizona, Colorado.

Add'l Information: Established 2002. Normal turnaround time- 24-48 hours. Projects billed by number of records located. 1st project may require prepayment. Quanity discounts available. He specializes in public record search and retrieval in accurate and timely manner. Also do real estate closings.

Risk Assessment Group

PO Box 27443, Tempe, AZ 85285

Phone: 866-777-1114; 480-777-1114 **Fax:** 866-777-0004; 480-777-3776

www.riskassessmentgroup.com/index.asp **email:** brad@ragrp.com

Types of Records Retrieved: Criminal courts

Local Retrieval Area: AZ-Maricopa. **Correspondents:** nationwide.

Add'l Information: Established 1985. Normal turnaround time- same day. Projects billed by number of names searched. Bill monthly. A licensed PI in AZ, #0105006.

Risk Mitigation Services Inc

404 W Avalon Ave #103, Muscle Shoals, AL 35661

Phone: 866-633-9339; 256-383-1180 **Fax:** 866-633-9309; 256-314-0488

riskms@bellsouth.net

Types of Records Retrieved: Civil, criminal and probate courts; Federal courts; Real Estate; Tax liens/Judgments; UCC records; Vital records

Local Retrieval Area: AL-Colbert, Cullman, Franklin, Lauderdale, Lawrence, Limestone, Madison, Morgan

Add'l Information: Established 1999. Normal turnaround time- less than 24 hours. Projects billed by number of names searched. Monthly billing. They perform service of process.

RJI Services Inc

2219 W Olive Blvd #295, Burbank, CA 91506

Phone: 800-344-4754; 818-846-5038 **Fax:** 818-846-5977

www.rji.com **email:** rafael@rji.com

Types of Records Retrieved: Civil, criminal and probate courts; Federal courts; Real Estate; Tax liens/Judgments; UCC records; Vital records

Local Retrieval Area: CA-Alameda, Contra Costa, Los Angeles, Orange, Riverside, San Diego, San Francisco, Ventura. **Correspondent Relationships:** nationwide.

Add'l Information: Established 1988. Normal turnaround time- 1-3 days. Projects billed by number of names searched. Terms: net 30 days. They specialize in hands on research and record retrieval of criminal, civil, UCC, tax liens and bankruptcy records at the local and federal courts. A full service investigative company. A licensed PI in CA. They perform service of process.

RLS Inc

PO Box 974, Buckhannon, WV 26201

Phone: 304-472-8800 **Fax:** 304-472-8837

Types of Records Retrieved: Civil, criminal and probate courts; Federal courts; Real Estate; Tax liens/Judgments; UCC records; Vital records

Local Retrieval Area: WV-Barbour, Braxton, Calhoun, Doddridge, Gilmer, Harrison, Lewis, Logan, McDowell, Marion, Monongalia, Preston, Randolph, Ritchie, Taylor, Tucker, Upshur. **Correspondent Relationships:** West Virginia.

Add'l Information: Established 1974. Normal turnaround time- 2 days to 3 weeks based on county requested. Contract prices upon request. They specialize in real estate, oil, gas and coal records and also serve as private investigators. They perform service of process.

Roberts County Title

516 2nd Ave East, Sisseton, SD 57262

Phone: 605-698-7272 **Fax:** 605-698-7890

Types of Records Retrieved: Real Estate; Tax liens/Judgments

Local Retrieval Area: SD-Roberts

Add'l Information: Established 1954. 1st project may require prepayment. They specialize in real estate.

Rocksprings Abstract & Title Co

PO Box 1062, 116 N Wells St, Rocksprings, TX 78880

Phone: 830-683-2185 **Fax:** 830-683-4185

Types of Records Retrieved: Civil courts; Probate courts; Real Estate; Tax liens/Judgments; UCC records; Vital records

Local Retrieval Area: TX-Edwards

Add'l Information: Established 1930. Normal turnaround time- variable depending on project. Fee basis will vary by the type of project. 1st project may require prepayment.

Rogers County Abstract Co

PO Box 38, 119 S Missouri Ave (74017), Claremore, OK 74018

Phone: 918-341-0525 **Fax:** 918-341-0637

Types of Records Retrieved: Civil courts; Probate courts; Real Estate; Tax liens/Judgments; UCC records; Vital records

Local Retrieval Area: OK-Rogers

Add'l Information: Established 1907. Normal turnaround time- 3-4 days. Fee basis will vary by the type of project. They specialize in title insurance and closings.

Rogers Inv & Research

PO Box 1825, Carlsbad, CA 92018

Phone: 800-935-6654; 760-434-4044 **Fax:** 760-434-1641

www.rogersinvestigations.com **email:** brogers@rogersinvestigations.com

Types of Records Retrieved: Civil, criminal and probate courts; Federal courts; Real Estate; Tax liens/Judgments; UCC records; Vital records

Local Retrieval Area: CA-Orange, San Diego

Add'l Information: Established 1981. Normal turnaround time- 24 hours. Projects billed by number of names searched. Projects billed by number of records located. Projects billed by the hour. 1st project may require prepayment. Credit cards accepted. They specialize in research, surveillance and counter measures. A licensed PI in CA. They perform service of process.

Rolette County Abstract Inc

PO Box 549, Rolla, ND 58367

Phone: 701-477-3149 **Fax:** 701-477-0375 abstract@utma.com

Types of Records Retrieved: Civil, criminal and probate courts; Real Estate; Tax liens/Judgments; UCC records; Vital records

Local Retrieval Area: ND-Rolette

Add'l Information: Established 1902. Normal turnaround time- 1-2 weeks. Fee basis will vary by the type of project.

Rollins Research Ltd

6412 Alpine Lane, Amarillo, TX 79109

Phone: 806-353-7886 **Fax:** 806-353-7886 rollinsresearch@cox.net

Types of Records Retrieved: Civil courts; Probate courts; Federal courts; Real Estate; Tax liens/Judgments; UCC records

Local Retrieval Area: TX-Armstrong, Carson, Castro, Dallam, Deaf Smith, Donley, Gray, Hartley, Hutchinson, Moore, Oldham, Potter, Randall, Roberts, Swisher

Add'l Information: Established 1987. Normal turnaround time- 24-72 hours for Potter and Randall Counties; 24-120 hours for all other counties. Projects billed by number of names searched. Add'l mileage charges may be applied for local court record searches in counties other than Potter & Randall. 1st project may require prepayment. She specializes in title runs for foreclosures or second liens, UCC, asset searches and home equity loans. Does criminal record searches in Potter and Randall counties only.

Roosevelt County Abstract Co Inc

PO Box 176, Wolf Point, MT 59201

Phone: 406-653-2800 **Fax:** 406-653-2803

Types of Records Retrieved: Civil courts; Probate courts; Real Estate; Tax liens/Judgments; UCC records

Local Retrieval Area: MT-Roosevelt

Add'l Information: Established 1919. Normal turnaround time- 4 days. Projects billed by the hour. Billing mailed with completed job. They specialize in title insurance.

Susan K Rosenbaum

PO Box 4, Genoa, NE 68640-0004
Phone: 888-459-8700; 402-560-6759 **Fax:** 888-459-8700; rosenbaumsusan@msn.com

Types of Records Retrieved: Civil and criminal courts; Tax liens/Judgments

Local Retrieval Area: NE-Antelope, Boone, Buffalo, Butler, Colfax, Dodge, Hall, Hamilton, Howard, Knox, Lancaster, Madison, Merrick, Nance, Pierce, Platte, Polk, Saunders, Seward, York

Add'l Information: Established 1989. Normal turnaround time- 24-48 hours. Invoice monthly or per search.

Betty M Rowell, CLA

6672 College Ave, Blackshear, GA 31516
Phone: 912-449-0849 **Fax:** 912-449-0849

Types of Records Retrieved: Civil courts; Probate courts; Real Estate; Tax liens/Judgments; UCC records

Local Retrieval Area: GA-Brantley, Pierce, Ware

Add'l Information: Established 1991. Normal turnaround time- 24-48 hours. Projects billed by number of names searched. She specializes in real estate matters. She will file/record UCC and real estate documents on behalf of clients in Ware & Pierce Counties only.

Royal Title Services

108 N Lebanon St, Lebanon, IN 46052
Phone: 800-773-7279; 765-482-2270 **Fax:** 765-483-3549
www.royaltitle.com **email:** lebanon@royaltitle.com

Types of Records Retrieved: Civil and criminal courts; Real Estate; Tax liens/Judgments; UCC records; Vital records

Local Retrieval Area: IN-Boone. **Correspondent Relationships:** Indiana.

Add'l Information: Established 1950. Normal turnaround time- 24-48 hours. Projects billed by number of names searched. They specialize in title searching and closings.

Rucar Business Information Center

100 Gran Bolevar Paseos #112 MSC 369, San Juan, PR 00926-5955
Phone: 787-645-1659 **Fax:** 787-293-1071
rub_00926@hotmail.com

Types of Records Retrieved: Civil and criminal courts; Federal courts; Real Estate; Tax liens/Judgments; UCC records; Vital records

Local Retrieval Area: Puerto Rico. **Correspondent Relationships:** Puerto Rico.

Add'l Information: Established 1998. Normal turnaround time- 10 days or less. Projects billed by number of names searched. 1st project may require prepayment. The specialize in all types of records, insurance inspections, claims process and medical record copies. The perform phone insurance inspections or face to face. Process claims and have a surveillance department . A licensed PI in PR.

David M Rumancik

1681 Cadbury St NW, Massillon, OH 44646
Phone: 330-837-7737 **Fax:** 330-837-7737
venariyy@aol.com

Types of Records Retrieved: Civil, criminal and probate courts; Real Estate; Tax liens/Judgments; UCC records

Local Retrieval Area: OH-Carroll, Holmes, Stark, Summit, Trumbull, Tuscarawas, Wayne; PA-Crawford, Mercer, Venango

Add'l Information: Established 1979. Normal turnaround time- 24 hours and up depending on the service requested. Fee depends on type of search. All projects require prepayment. He specializes in real estate titles, oil & gas titles, oil & gas research, easement & right of way research for utility companies, criminal & misdemeanor background checks on individuals for employment purposes and lien searches.

Runnymeade Research Inc

20 South Tollgate Rd, Owings Mills, MD 21117
Phone: 410-998-9886 **Fax:** 443-431-0217
www.runnymeaderesearch.com **email:** runnymeadesearch@aol.com

Types of Records Retrieved: Real Estate

Local Retrieval Area: MD-Baltimore, Baltimore City, Howard. **Correspondent Relationships:** statewide in Maryland.

Add'l Information: Established 2001. Normal turnaround time- 3-5 days. Expedited service available. Projects billed by number of names searched. Payment due upon receipt. The offer accurate, fast, personal service at their guaranteed lowest cost in Maryland. All new clients will receive their first order "Free". Call for details.

Rus B Robison & Associates Inc

PO Box 720560, Oklahoma City, OK 73172-0560
Phone: 877-721-2295; 405-721-2295 **Fax:** 405-722-2422
www.robisonpi.com **email:** rbr@robisonpi.com

Types of Records Retrieved: Civil, criminal and probate courts; Federal courts; Real Estate; Tax liens/Judgments; UCC records; Vital records

Local Retrieval Area: OK-Canadian, Cleveland, McClain, Oklahoma

Add'l Information: Established 1972. Normal turnaround time- 1-2 business days. Projects billed by number of names searched. Projects billed by the hour. 1st project may require prepayment. Will accept immediate bank account payments, but not credit cards, through Pay Pal. They have numerous legal proprietary databases for added access. A licensed PI in OK. They perform service of process.

Russell Abstract

PO Box 6, Greenfield, MO 65661
Phone: 417-637-2414 **Fax:** 417-637-2214

Types of Records Retrieved: Probate courts; Real Estate; Tax liens/Judgments

Local Retrieval Area: MO-Dade

Add'l Information: Established 1850. Normal turnaround time- 3-5 business days. Fee basis will vary by type of project. 1st project may require prepayment. They specialize in title searches; title plant dating back to 1849. Also do real estate escrow closings and title insurance.

Russell-Surles Title Inc

337 Market St, Baird, TX 79504
Phone: 325-854-1115 **Fax:** 325-854-1459

Types of Records Retrieved: Civil, criminal and probate courts; Real Estate; Tax liens/Judgments; UCC records

Local Retrieval Area: TX-Callahan

Add'l Information: Normal turnaround time- variable depending on project. Projects billed by number of names searched. Personal checks are accepted.

Rutledge Title Research LLC

19 W Briar Dr, Stafford, VA 22556
Phone: 540-903-1481 **Fax:** 540-752-9239
rutledgetitle@adelphia.net

Types of Records Retrieved: Civil, criminal and probate courts; Real Estate; Tax liens/Judgments; UCC records

Local Retrieval Area: VA-Fauquier, Fredericksburg, Spotsylvania, Stafford. **Correspondent Relationships:** Culpeper, King, George, Caroline, Prince William, VA.

Add'l Information: Established 2003. Normal turnaround time- 24 hours. Same day if request is early AM. Projects billed by number of names searched. Projects billed by number of records located. Payment due on delivery. Specializes in real estate research with 20 years experience. Current owner info or full searches. Daily access land, civil, criminal, tax and assessment records.

Ryco Information Services Inc

7591 Morgan Rd #1, Liverpool, NY 13090
Phone: 800-240-7926; 315-461-8308 **Fax:** 315-461-8395
www.rycoinfo.com **email:** order@rycoinfo.com

Types of Records Retrieved: Probate courts; Real Estate; Tax liens/Judgments; UCC records

Local Retrieval Area: NY-Onondaga. **Correspondents:** statewide.

Add'l Information: Established 1992. Normal turnaround time- 24-48 hours. Projects billed by number of names searched. Net 30 days. They specialize in property searches from last owners to full searches including tax and bankruptcy searches.

S

S & S Public Record Retrievers

7 Georgetown Dr, Amherst, NH 03031
Phone: 603-672-7179 **Fax:** 603-672-6005
www.ssrecordretrievers.com **email:** info@ssrecordretrievers.com

Types of Records Retrieved: Civil, criminal and probate courts; Bankruptcy courts; Real Estate/Mortgage; UCC records; Tax liens/Judgments; Vital records

Local Retrieval Area: NH-Hillsborough, Merrimack

Add'l Information: Established 2002. Normal turnaround time- 1-10 business days depending on court searched. Projects billed by number of names searched. 1st project may require prepayment. They retrieve civil, criminal, probate records from all Hillsborough county courts and some Merrimack county courts; bankruptcy records from Hillsborough Superior Courts, mortgage records.

Sac County Abstract Co

420 Main, PO Box 98, Sac City, IA 50583
Phone: 712-662-7317 **Fax:** 712-662-4090 mgreen@pionet.net

Types of Records Retrieved: Civil, criminal and probate courts; Real Estate; Tax liens/Judgments; UCC records; Vital records

Local Retrieval Area: IA-Sac

Add'l Information: Normal turnaround time- 2-3 days. Fee basis will vary by the type of project. 1st project may require prepayment.

Sacandaga Abstract Corp

8 Fremont St, Gloversville, NY 12078
Phone: 518-773-2828 **Fax:** 518-725-9875

Types of Records Retrieved: Probate courts; Real Estate; Tax liens/Judgments; UCC records

Local Retrieval Area: NY-Fulton, Montgomery

Add'l Information: Established 1986. Normal turnaround time- 1-7 days. Projects billed by number of names searched. Projects billed by number of records located. 1st project may require prepayment. Personal checks are accepted. Their company offers fast and efficient abstracing work at reasonable prices.

Alice E Sackman

10617 N Ash St, Hayden, ID 83835
Phone: 208-964-0209 **Fax:** 208-762-3397
thesackmans@juno.com

Types of Records Retrieved: Civil and criminal courts; Federal Bankruptcy courts; Real Estate; Tax liens/Judgments; UCC records

Local Retrieval Area: ID-Kootenai

Add'l Information: Established 1998. Normal turnaround time- 24 hours. Projects billed by number of names searched. Projects billed by number of records located. 1st project may require prepayment. They specialize in high quality, accurate work delivered within 24 hours at an affordable price. Also specialize in databases, mailing lists and fore-closure reports. Been in buisness since 1998.

Saguache County Abstract & Investment

309 4th St, Saguache, CO 81149
Phone: 719-655-2611 **Fax:** 719-655-2326

Types of Records Retrieved: Civil, criminal and probate courts; Federal courts; Real Estate; Tax liens/Judgments; UCC records; Vital records

Local Retrieval Area: CO-Saguache

Add'l Information: Established 1905. Normal turnaround time- 2-5 days. Projects billed by number of records located. Out of state clients prepay, in-state terms are net 30 days. They specialize in all related title insurance company searches and closings.

Salem Title Corporation

54 Courthouse Sq, Salem, IN 47167
Phone: 812-883-5806 **Fax:** 812-883-5229 damaudlin@Yahoo.com

Types of Records Retrieved: Real Estate; Tax liens/judgments; UCC records

Local Retrieval Area: IN-Clark, Crawford, Floyd, Harrison, Jackson, Lawrence, Orange, Scott, Washington

Add'l Information: Established 1954. Normal turnaround time- 1 day for judgment or UCC searches, and 3-5 days for complete title searches. Fee basis will vary by the type of project. 1st project may require prepayment. Personal checks are accepted. They maintain a title plant in their office. They are a full service title company.

Salyer & Assoc.

114 W Main, McArthur, OH 45651
Phone: 740-596-5291 **Fax:** 740-596-3700

Types of Records Retrieved: Civil, criminal and probate courts; Real Estate; Tax liens/Judgments; UCC records; Vital records

Local Retrieval Area: OH-Jackson, Vinton. **Correspondent Relationships:** Athens, Hocking, Meigs counties Ohio.

Add'l Information: Normal turnaround time- variable depending on search. Charges vary depending on the type of search. They are attorneys and specialize in real estate record searches.

San Diego Attorney Service Inc

3776 4th Ave, San Diego, CA 92103
Phone: 619-236-9585 **Fax:** 619-236-9136

Types of Records Retrieved: Civil, criminal and probate courts; Federal courts; Real Estate; Tax liens/Judgments; UCC records; Vital records

Local Retrieval Area: CA-Los Angeles, Orange, Riverside, San Bernardino, San Diego. **Correspondent Relationships:** California.

Add'l Information: Established 1970. Normal turnaround time- same day, if requested. Projects billed by number of records located. Projects billed by the hour. 1st project may require prepayment. Credit cards accepted. Terms: net 30 days, once approved. They perform service of process.

San Juan County Abstract & Title

111 N Orchard Ave, Farmington, NM 87401
Phone: 505-325-2808 **Fax:** 505-327-7483
www.sanjuantitle.com **email:** admin@sanjuantitle.com

Types of Records Retrieved: Civil, criminal and probate courts; Real Estate; Tax liens/Judgments; UCC records; Vital records

Local Retrieval Area: NM-San Juan

Add'l Information: Established 1946. Normal turnaround time- 1-3 days. Fee basis will vary by the type of project. A minimum fee is involved. Payment due upon delivery of order.

Sanborn County Realty & Title

PO Box 127, 207 S Dumont Ave, Woonsocket, SD 57385-0127
Phone: 605-796-4417 **Fax:** 605-796-4248 scrtmpp@santel.net

Types of Records Retrieved: Civil courts; Probate courts; Real Estate; Tax liens/Judgments

Local Retrieval Area: SD-Sanborn

Add'l Information: Established 1982. Normal turnaround time- 7-10 days. The fee basis is a flat fee. 1st project may require prepayment. Personal checks and cash are accepted. They specialize in abstracts and title insurance. They also search liens and real estate taxes. They also have a real estate closing service. They will file/record real estate documents of behalf of clients.

Sandhills Abstracting

218 N Main St, Gordon, NE 69343
Phone: 308-282-0715 **Fax:** 308-282-0715
cginkens@broncs.net

Types of Records Retrieved: Civil, criminal and probate courts; Real Estate; Tax liens/Judgments; UCC records; Vital records

Local Retrieval Area: NE-Cherry, Sheridan

Add'l Information: Established 1987. Normal turnaround time- 1 week. Projects billed by number of names searched. Projects billed by number of records located. Projects billed by the hour. Personal checks are accepted. They specialize in records from Sheridan County, but will provide service to Cherry county for add'l fee.

Sandhills Title

PO Box 181, Valentine, NE 69201
Phone: 402-376-2639 **Fax:** 402-376-1180

Types of Records Retrieved: Civil, criminal and probate courts; Real Estate; Tax liens/Judgments

Local Retrieval Area: NE-Brown, Cherry, Keya Paha, Thomas

Add'l Information: Established 1995. Normal turnaround time- 1-2 days in Cherry County; other counties up to 1 week. Projects billed by number of names searched. Projects billed by the hour. 1st project may require prepayment. They specialize in record and title searches. Will file documents in Cherry County only.

Sargents Title Co

625 S Grand Traverse St, Flint, MI 48502
Phone: 810-767-2355 **Fax:** 810-767-2430
www.sargentstitle.com

Types of Records Retrieved: Real Estate

Local Retrieval Area: MI-Genesee. **Correspondent Relationships:** 21 counties in SE Michigan area.

Add'l Information: Established 1968. Normal turnaround time- 3-5 days. Projects billed by the hour. Fee basis depends upon type of project. They specialize in title insurance.

SAS Associates Inc

1423 Brown St, Bettendorf, IA 52722
Phone: 800-373-0727; 563-359-0408 **Fax:** 563-359-0830
www.sasassociates.com **email:** sas@netexpress.net

Types of Records Retrieved: Civil, criminal and probate courts; Federal courts; Tax liens/Judgments; UCC records

Local Retrieval Area: IA-Clinton, Jackson, Johnson, Linn, Muscatine, Polk, Scott; IL-Henry, Mercer, Rock Island, Whiteside. **Correspondent Relationships:** statewide and IL, MN, WS.

Add'l Information: Established 1984. Normal turnaround time- 3-4 days. Projects billed by number of names searched. Projects billed by the hour. 1st project may require prepayment. Credit cards accepted. Net 10 days upon receipt of invoice. They specialize in investigations for attorneys, business & insurance companies, including workers compensation, also mystery shopping, missing person locating, employment backgrounds and consulting. A licensed PI in IA, IL. They perform service of process.

Sathre Title & Abstracting Inc

315 5th St NW #2, Bemidji, MN 56601-3021
Phone: 218-751-4565 **Fax:** 218-751-7991
title@paulbunyan.net

Types of Records Retrieved: Real Estate; Tax liens/Judgments; UCC records

Local Retrieval Area: MN-Beltrami

Add'l Information: Established 1914. Normal turnaround time- variable depending on project. Fee basis will vary by type of project. They specialize in real estate and property reports.

Sawyer County Abstract & Title

PO Box 169, Hayward, WI 54843
Phone: 715-634-9444 **Fax:** 715-634-9445
www.sawyercountytitle.com **email:** sawyercountytitle@centurytel.net

Types of Records Retrieved: Real Estate; Tax liens/judgments; UCC records

Local Retrieval Area: WI-Rusk, Sawyer, Washburn

Add'l Information: Normal turnaround time- 48 hours. Projects billed by number of names searched. Projects billed by number of records located. Projects billed by the hour. Personal checks are accepted.

SCC Information Services Inc

PO Box 494, Lexington, SC 29071
Phone: 803-957-1243 **Fax:** 803-957-9359 menlow@alltel.net

Types of Records Retrieved: Civil courts; Probate courts; Real Estate; Tax liens/Judgments; UCC records

Local Retrieval Area: SC-Aiken, Edgefield, Lexington, Newberry, Saluda

Add'l Information: Established 1995. Normal turnaround time- 24-48 hours. Projects billed by number of names searched. Projects billed by number of records located. Terms: net 30 days.

Schaeffer Papers

100 N Main #220B, Memphis, TN 38103
Phone: 800-848-6119; 901-725-9555 **Fax:** 901-578-7424
schaefferpapers@mindspring.com

Types of Records Retrieved: Civil, criminal and probate courts; Federal courts; Real Estate; Tax liens/Judgments; UCC records; Vital records

Local Retrieval Area: AR-Crittenden; MS-De Soto, Tunica; TN-Blount, Davidson, Dyer, Fayette, Knox, Madison, Shelby, Sumner, Tipton. **Correspondent Relationships:** Fayette, Tipton, Lauderdale, Dyer counties.

Add'l Information: Established 1988. Normal turnaround time- 24-72 hours. Projects billed by number of names searched. Projects billed by number of records located. Projects billed by the hour. Incurred expenses will be added to the fee. By the hour fees are for out of county or state. Flat fee charged for Shelby County Service of Process. All projects require prepayment. Personal checks are accepted. They specialize in civil court matters and process service. They are also abstractors. They perform service of process.

Schillinger & Keith Abstract & Settlement

840 Philadelphia St #201, Indiana, PA 15701
Phone: 800-275-2959; 724-465-9520 **Fax:** 724-465-9583
snkinc@adelphia.net

Types of Records Retrieved: Civil, criminal and probate courts; Real Estate; Tax liens/Judgments; UCC records

Local Retrieval Area: PA-Indiana

Add'l Information: Established 1993. Normal turnaround time- 24 hours. Charges vary depending on type of search. They do monthly invoicing. Due within 10 days of billing. They are a title insurance agent for Stewart Title Ins. Co. and Lawyers Title Ins Co.

Kathleen Schloesser

403 Wayne St, Bethany, PA 18431
Phone: 570-253-5368 **Fax:** 570-253-6214 titleins@ptd.net

Types of Records Retrieved: Civil and criminal courts; Real Estate; Tax liens/Judgments; UCC records

Local Retrieval Area: PA-Wayne

Add'l Information: Established 1981. Normal turnaround time- 24 hours. Projects billed by number of names searched. Net 5 days. She specializes in real estate searches, current owner, 60 year and real estate closings.

Jacqueline Schoeneberg

2848 S Quail Av, Springfield, MO 65807
Phone: 417-889-6390 **Fax:** 417-882-8973 schonanny@aol.com

Types of Records Retrieved: Criminal courts

Local Retrieval Area: MO-Greene

Add'l Information: Established 1999. Normal turnaround time- 24 hours. Projects billed by number of names searched. Monthly billing. They do daily hands one service with a 24 hour turnaround.

Paul Scholtes

PO Box 1262, West Palm Beach, FL 33402
Phone: 561-385-8163 **Fax:** 561-745-4404

Types of Records Retrieved: Civil, criminal and probate courts; Federal courts; Real Estate; Tax liens/Judgments; UCC records; Vital records

Local Retrieval Area: FL-Palm Beach. **Correspondent Relationships:** Broward, Dade, Martin, Palm Beach, St. Lucie counties FL.

Add'l Information: Established 1990. Normal turnaround time- variable depending on project. Projects billed by the hour. All projects require prepayment. They specialize in private investigating, process serving and most other legal services. A licensed PI in FL. They perform service of process.

Scotland County Abstract & Title Inc

205 E Monroe St, Memphis, MO 63555

Phone: 660-465-7052 **Fax:** 660-465-7452 scat@nemr.com

Types of Records Retrieved: Probate courts; Real Estate; Tax liens/Judgments

Local Retrieval Area: MO-Clark, Knox, Schuyler, Scotland

Add'l Information: Established 1981. Normal turnaround time- 3 days. Projects billed by number of records located. They specialize in title insurance and title searches.

Scott Abstract

220 N Dewey St, North Platte, NE 69101

Phone: 308-532-8535 **Fax:** 308-532-6559

Types of Records Retrieved: Civil, criminal and probate courts; Real Estate; Tax liens/Judgments; UCC records; Vital records

Local Retrieval Area: NE-Frontier, Hayes, Hooker, Lincoln, Logan, McPherson, Thomas

Add'l Information: Established 1984. Normal turnaround time- 3 days for Lincoln County, and longer for other counties. Fee basis varies by type of transaction. They will file/record UCC and real estate documents on behalf of clients on a same or next day basis in Lincoln county only.

Scott County Abstract & Title Co Inc

310 Court St, Scott City, KS 67871

Phone: 620-872-3470 **Fax:** 620-872-7105 sc@wbsnet.org

Types of Records Retrieved: Civil courts; Probate courts; Federal courts; Real Estate; Tax liens/Judgments; UCC records; Vital records

Local Retrieval Area: KS-Scott

Add'l Information: Established 1972. Normal turnaround time- 24-48 hours. Projects billed by number of names searched. 1st project may require prepayment. Personal checks are accepted.

Scott Investigation

PO Box 7704, St Cloud, MN 56302

Phone: 800-357-7862; 320-363-7559 **Fax:** 320-363-8512

piscott@aol.com

Types of Records Retrieved: Civil, criminal and probate courts; Real Estate; Tax liens/Judgments; UCC records; Vital records

Local Retrieval Area: MN-Benton, Stearns. **Correspondent Relationships:** Central Minnesota.

Add'l Information: Established 1992. Normal turnaround time- 24-48 hours. Expedited service available. Projects billed by the hour. 1st project may require prepayment. They are a full service private detective agency specializing in personal injury, background checks, skip tracing and process service. A licensed PI in MN. They perform service of process.

Screencorp Inc

4859 E Skinner Dr, Cave Creek, AZ 85331

Phone: 602-739-7289 **Fax:** 480-515-9895

www.pre-employmentscreens.com

email: email@pre-employmentscreens.com

Types of Records Retrieved: Criminal courts

Local Retrieval Area: AZ-Maricopa. **Correspondents:** nationwide.

Add'l Information: Established 1994. Normal turnaround time- 24-36 hours. Projects billed by number of names searched. Will do monthly invoicing. They do pre-employment background checks provided to client companies on job applicants. This is all they do. They have a rapid turnaround, very affordable pricing and comprehensive information. A licensed PI in AZ.

Search & Find

PO Box 1053, LaGrange, GA 30241

Phone: 706-884-9801 **Fax:** 706-812-9407

www.search-and-find-usa.com **email:** snf1996@aol.com

Types of Records Retrieved: Civil and criminal courts; Tax liens/Judgments

Local Retrieval Area: GA-Catoosa, Clayton, Coweta, Fayette, Harris, Heard, Henry, Muscogee, Rockdale, Troup, Walker. **Correspondent:** statewide.

Add'l Information: Normal turnaround time- 24-48 hours. Projects billed by number of names searched. 1st project may require prepayment. Credit cards accepted. They have been in business since 1994. Their staff is there to care for all your needs in the area of criminal & civil research.

Search & Genealogy Services

281 Glenn Rd, Murphysboro, IL 62966

Phone: 618-529-1024

www.sgservices.bravepages.com **email:** timjuli@earthlink.net

Types of Records Retrieved: Civil, criminal and probate courts; Real Estate; Tax liens/Judgments; UCC records; Vital records

Local Retrieval Area: IL-Jackson, Perry, Union

Add'l Information: Established 2000. Normal turnaround time- next day in most cases. Expedited service available. Projects billed by number of names searched. Projects billed by the hour. 1st project may require prepayment. Credit cards accepted. Search & Genealogy Services retreives documents in-person in several southern Illinois counties, conducts nationwide people searches, ocates missing heirs and conducts genealogical research.

Search Arkansas

1724 Big Springs Rd, Onia, AR 72663

Phone: 888-875-2553; 870-746-4297 **Fax:** 870-746-4070

farmlady@mvtel.net

Types of Records Retrieved: Probate courts; Real Estate; Tax liens/Judgments; UCC records

Local Retrieval Area: AR-Cleburne, Faulkner, Independence, Stone, White

Add'l Information: Established 1997. Normal turnaround time- 24-48 hours. Projects billed by number of names searched. Projects billed by number of records located. Also, per search. Terms: net 30 days from invoice date. They specialize in title searches, real estate searches, UCC searches, tax liens, deed and mortgage retrievals and filings.

Search Associates Two Great Minds

7740 W Forest Home Ave, Greenfield, WI 53220-3386

Phone: 414-321-3375 **Fax:** 414-321-3377

twogreatminds@ameritech.net

Types of Records Retrieved: Civil, criminal and probate courts; Real Estate; Tax liens/Judgments; UCC records

Local Retrieval Area: WI-Kenosha, Milwaukee, Ozaukee, Racine, Sheboygan, Walworth, Washington, Waukesha

Add'l Information: Established 1991. Normal turnaround time- 24-48 hours. Projects billed by number of names searched. Fee depends on type of search. 1st project may require prepayment. Now known as Two Great Minds, they specialize in real estate title searches, letter/title reports, in-home loan closings, days, nights and weekends. A licensed PI in WI.

Search Company International

1535 Grant St #140, Denver, CO 80203-1843

Phone: 800-727-2120; 303-863-1800 **Fax:** 800-956-1200; 303-863-7767

www.searchcompanyintl.com **email:** find-it@searchcompanyintl.com

Types of Records Retrieved: Civil, criminal and probate courts; Federal courts; Real Estate; Tax liens/Judgments; UCC records; Corporate filings; Federal Records Center documents

Local Retrieval Area: CO-Adams, Arapahoe, Boulder, Broomfield, Delta, Denver, Douglas, Eagle, El Paso, Elbert, Fremont, Garfield, Jefferson, Larimer, Mesa, Pueblo, Teller, Weld. **Correspondent Relationships:** nationwide.

Add'l Information: Established 1979. Normal turnaround time- 24-48 hours. Projects billed by number of names searched. 1st project may require prepayment. Credit cards accepted. Personal checks are accepted. They are online with Colorado's Secretary of State. They have the Secretary of State microfilm library and all CO UCC filings. They specialize in UCC, lien, property, litigation (state/fed), corporate filing. They can e-mail results. They perform service of process.

Search Company of North Dakota LLC

1008 E Capitol Ave, Bismarck, ND 58501-1930
Phone: 701-223-1848 **Fax:** 701-223-1850
www.searchcompanynd.com **email:** michael@searchcompanynd.com

Types of Records Retrieved: Civil, criminal and probate courts; Federal courts; Real Estate; Tax liens/Judgments; UCC records; Vital records

Local Retrieval Area: ND-Burleigh, Cass, Morton. **Correspondent Relationships:** North Dakota.

Add'l Information: Established 1984. Normal turnaround time- 24-72 hours. Projects billed by number of names searched. They have 16 years of public record experience in North Dakota at the city, county, state and federal levels. They also provide registered agent services. A licensed PI in ND. They perform service of process.

Search Enterprises

2914 Windsor Ave, Waco, TX 76708
Phone: 254-752-2057 **Fax:** 254-752-8201
vrgnweb@aol.com

Types of Records Retrieved: Real Estate; Tax liens/Judgments

Local Retrieval Area: TX-Bell, Bosque, Coryell, Falls, McLennan

Add'l Information: Established 1986. Normal turnaround time- 24-96 hours. Projects billed by number of names searched. 1st project may require prepayment. Terms: 30 days net. They specialize in real estate, environmental, and other public record research. They do a full title report (real property only) from last owner forward. Their report includes complete deed info, all open liens, 10 year state & fed tax lien check, etc.

Search International Inc

22 Commonwealth Av, Erlanger, KY 41018-1798
Phone: 859-342-0456 **Fax:** 859-342-0457

Types of Records Retrieved: Civil and criminal courts; Federal courts; Real Estate; Tax liens/Judgments; UCC records

Local Retrieval Area: KY-Boone, Campbell, Grant, Kenton, Pendleton; OH-Clermont, Hamilton

Add'l Information: Established 1995. Normal turnaround time- 24-48 hours. Projects billed by number of names searched. 1st project may require prepayment. They specialize in felony, misdemeanor, UCC searches, civil, tax liens. They also cover federal courts in Southwest Ohio. They are court research specialists.

Search Network Ltd (Iowa)

2 Corporate Pl, Suite 210, 1501 42nd St, West Des Moines, IA 50266
Phone: 800-383-5050; 515-223-1153 **Fax:** 800-383-5060; 515-223-2814
www.searchnetworkltd.com **email:** lharken@searchnetworkltd.com

Types of Records Retrieved: Civil courts; Federal courts; Real Estate; Tax liens/Judgments; UCC records

Local Retrieval Area: IA-Polk. **Correspondent Relationships:** nationwide and Canada.

Add'l Information: Established 1965. Normal turnaround time- same day for state UCC; County; 2-4 days. Projects billed by number of names searched. Projects billed by the hour. 1st project may require prepayment. Terms: net 30 days. They specialize in UCC lien filing and search services, also corporate document filings and retrieval. Onsite UCC database for Iowa and Kansas.

Search Network Ltd (Kansas)

700 SW Jackson #100, Topeka, KS 66603
Phone: 800-338-3618; 785-235-5777 **Fax:** 785-235-5788
www.searchnetworkltd.com **email:** lharken@searchnetworkltd.com

Types of Records Retrieved: Civil courts; Federal courts; Real Estate; Tax liens/Judgments; UCC records; Vital records

Local Retrieval Area: KS-Shawnee. **Correspondent Relationships:** nationwide, especially Kansas, Missouri.

Add'l Information: Established 1965. Normal turnaround time- same day for state UCC; County; 2-4 days. Projects billed by number of names searched. 1st project may require prepayment. Terms: net 30 days. They specialize in corporate & UCC lien filing and retrieval. They are online with Kansas for UCC records, and provide an onsite database for Kansas and Iowa from their Iowa office. They have correspondents in all KS counties

Search NY Inc

111 John St, 6th Fl, New York, NY 10038
Phone: 212-608-2546 **Fax:** 212-566-5901
www.searchnyinc.com **email:** pnuzio@searchnyinc.com

Types of Records Retrieved: Civil, criminal and probate courts; Federal courts; Real Estate; Tax liens/Judgments; UCC records; Vital records

Local Retrieval Area: NY-Bronx, Dutchesss, Kings, Nassau, New York, Orange, Queens, Richmond, Rockland, Suffolk, Westchester. **Correspondent Relationships:** nationwide.

Add'l Information: Established 1983. Normal turnaround time- 24-72 hours. Projects billed by number of names searched. 1st project may require prepayment. They specialize in all public record searches. They perform service of process.

Search One Services

6746 Axtel Dr, Columbus, OH 43110-8429
Phone: 614-834-5603 **Fax:** 614-834-5605
searchone@sbcglobal.net

Types of Records Retrieved: Civil courts; Federal courts; Real Estate; Tax liens/Judgments; UCC records

Local Retrieval Area: OH-Cuyahoga, Delaware, Fairfield, Franklin, Greene, Hamilton, Licking, Miami, Pickaway. **Correspondent Relationships:** Cuyahoya, Summit, Stark & Miami counties.

Add'l Information: Established 1996. Normal turnaround time- same day to 48 hours. Projects billed by number of names searched. Terms: net 30 days. They search UCCs, tax liens, judgments, federal and bankruptcy courts. They do document retrievals and Franklin filings; No correspondent fees. Rapid Franklin County service.

Search Services

116 Byron Pl, Raleigh, NC 27609
Phone: 919-781-9997 **Fax:** 919-781-3706 searchsvcs@yahoo.com

Types of Records Retrieved: Civil courts; Federal courts; Tax liens/Judgments; UCC records

Local Retrieval Area: NC-Durham, Wake

Add'l Information: Established 1978. Normal turnaround time- 24-48 hours. Projects billed by number of names searched. Terms are net 30 days. Record research specialist in the Raliegh, NC area. They perform service of process.

Searcher Girls

PO Box 8573, Hamilton, NJ 08650-0573
Phone: 800-292-2757; **Fax:** 800-292-2858; 1search@optonline.net

Types of Records Retrieved: Civil, criminal and probate courts; Federal courts; Real Estate; Tax liens/Judgments; UCC records; Vital records

Local Retrieval Area: NJ-Atlantic, Bergen, Burlington, Camden, Cape May, Cumberland, Essex, Gloucester, Hudson, Hunterdon, Mercer, Middlesex, Monmouth, Morris, Ocean, Passiac, Salem, Somerset, Sussex, Union, Warren. **Correspondent Relationships:** nationwide.

Add'l Information: Established 1995. Normal turnaround time- 24-48 hours. Projects billed by number of names searched. Projects billed by the hour. Credit accounts are accepted. They assist attorneys who practice in the field of complex federal and state litigation and develop computer programs and solutions.

Searches by SKW

14355 Bradford Ct, Waverly, NE 68462

Phone: 402-786-2184 **Fax:** 402-786-2185 skw3@alltel.net

Types of Records Retrieved: Civil and criminal courts; Federal District courts; Tax liens/Judgments

Local Retrieval Area: NE-Lancaster

Add'l Information: Established 1995. Normal turnaround time- 24-48 hours. Projects billed by number of names searched. 1st project may require prepayment. They specialize in background checks by name for misdemeanor or felony judgments. Also can check for state or federal tax liens.

Searching Registration Service

PO Box 15824, Sacramento, CA 95852-1824

Phone: 800-488-0238; 916-452-8231 **Fax:** 800-488-0231; 916-451-2322

Types of Records Retrieved: Real Estate; UCC records; Vital records

Local Retrieval Area: CA-Sacramento

Add'l Information: Established 1946. Projects billed by number of names searched. 1st project may require prepayment. Terms: net 10 days. They specialize in driver/license and vehicle registration searches.

SearchLink LLC

299 Commonwealth Ave, Buffalo, NY 14216

Phone: 716-873-8315 **Fax:** 716-873-2534

www.searchlink.org **email:** searchlink@searchlink.org

Types of Records Retrieved: Civil, criminal and probate courts; Federal courts; Real Estate; Tax liens/Judgments; UCC records

Local Retrieval Area: NY-all counties. **Correspondents:** nationwide.

Add'l Information: Established 1991. Normal turnaround time- 24-48 hours. Projects billed by number of names searched. Terms: net 30 days. Formerly NY Criminal Search, they specialize in criminal record searches in Erie, Monroe, Niagara and Westchester Counties, also UCC searches, tax liens and judgments. Can do any search statewide.

Searchtec

211 N 13th St #600, Philadelphia, PA 19107

Phone: 877-2SEARCH; 215-963-0888 x191 **Fax:** 215-851-8775

www.searchtec.com **email:** info@searchtec.com

Types of Records Retrieved: Civil courts; Probate courts; Federal courts; Real Estate; Tax liens/Judgments; UCC records

Local Retrieval Area: NJ-Burlington, Camden, Gloucester, Mercer; PA-Bucks, Chester, Delaware, Montgomery, Philadelphia. **Correspondent Relationships:** nationwide.

Add'l Information: Established 1990. Normal turnaround time- 24-48 hours. Charge by product. Credit cards accepted. They specialize in public record searches, corp svcs appraisals, title ins & settlements, witness closings & filing records. They combine advanced technology with a knowledgeable staff to provide svcs to those in the legal, real estate, etc. industries.

Searchtec (Carolinas)

2 Office Park Ct #103, Columbia, SC 29223

Phone: 800-528-8790; 803-699-6130 **Fax:** 800-542-7499; 803-699-6178

www.searchtec.com **email:** shatcher@searchtec.com

Types of Records Retrieved: Civil, criminal and probate courts; Federal courts; Real Estate; Tax liens/Judgments; UCC records; Vital records

Local Retrieval Area: NC-78 counties; SC-all counties. **Correspondent Relationships:** nationwide.

Add'l Information: Established 1990. Normal turnaround time- 24 hours - 3 days. Projects billed by number of names searched. 1st project may require prepayment. Terms: net 15 days. Formerly National Data Access Corp, their quality work is surpassed only by their superb customer service. Recently acquired by SearchTec, Inc their combined companies make them a leader in their industry. Has office in Raleigh, NC at 4208 Six Forks Rd. They perform service of process.

SearchWorks Inc

6917 W 76th St, Overland Park, KS 66204

Phone: 913-383-0940 **Fax:** 913-383-8561

Types of Records Retrieved: Civil courts; Federal courts; Real Estate; Tax liens/Judgments; UCC records

Local Retrieval Area: KS-Douglas, Johnson, Wyandotte; MO-Cass, Clay, Jackson, Johnson, Platte

Add'l Information: Established 1989. Normal turnaround time- 2 days. Projects billed by number of names searched. Payment due net 30 days. They specialize in real estate; current-owner forward showing open liens and UCC, tax liens, and litigation.

Seattle Process Service Inc

157 Yesler Way #500, Seattle, WA 98104-2588

Phone: 800-842-8913; 206-748-9890 **Fax:** 206-748-5189

www.seattleprocessservice.com **email:** seattleprocess@qwest.net

Types of Records Retrieved: Civil, criminal and probate courts; Federal courts. **Local Retrieval Area:** WA-King, Pierce, Snohomish

Add'l Information: Established 1980. Normal turnaround time-approximately 5 business days. Projects billed by the hour. 1st project may require prepayment. Independent process serving company in downtown Seattle; has routine coverage in the Greater Seattle Metropolitan area. Nig enough to get the job done and small enough to offer personalized attention. They perform service of process.

Secrest Legal Services

4515 Prentice St #102, Dallas, TX 75206

Phone: 214-696-3959 **Fax:** 214-696-5377 abbey2@aol.com

Types of Records Retrieved: Civil, criminal and probate courts; Federal courts; Real Estate; Tax liens/Judgments; UCC records

Local Retrieval Area: TX-Dallas. **Correspondent Relationships:** nationwide and Canada.

Add'l Information: Established 1992. Normal turnaround time- 24 hours. Projects billed by number of names searched. 1st project may require prepayment. They specialize in UCC, county and federal court searches. Filing mortgages and assignment of liens in mass quantity is also a service provided. Owner operated and managed.

Secretarial Outsource Services

1303 Catherine St, Pekin, IL 61554

Phone: 309-347-3736 **Fax:** 309-347-4571

Types of Records Retrieved: Civil and criminal courts

Local Retrieval Area: IL-Tazewell

Add'l Information: Established 1992. Normal turnaround time- 24 hours. Projects billed by number of names searched. 1st project may require prepayment.

Secure Data Corporation

508 E South Temple #A28, Salt Lake City, UT 84102-1018

Phone: 801-595-1510 **Fax:** 801-595-8366

Types of Records Retrieved: Civil and criminal courts; Federal courts; Tax liens/Judgments; UCC records

Local Retrieval Area: UT-Salt Lake

Add'l Information: Established 1997. Normal turnaround time- 24-48 hours. Projects billed by number of names searched. All projects require prepayment. They specialize in pre-employment screening.

Securitech Inc

8230 E Broadway #E-10, Tucson, AZ 85710

Phone: 800-805-4473; 520-721-0305 **Fax:** 520-721-7706

www.localscreening.com **email:** isa@localscreening.com

Types of Records Retrieved: Civil, criminal and probate courts; Federal courts; Tax liens/Judgments; UCC records; Vital records

Local Retrieval Area: AZ-Pima. **Correspondent Relationships:** Apache, Cochise, Gila, Maricopa, Pinal, Yuma counties AZ.

Add'l Information: Established 1993. Normal turnaround time- same day to 3 days. Expedited service available. Projects billed by number of names searched. 1st project may require prepayment. Specializes in retrieval of records from county, state and federal agencies. Securitech also provides tenant and employment screening services. A licensed PI in AZ.

Security Abstract & Title Co

510 Main St, Miles City, MT 59301

Phone: 406-234-3415 **Fax:** 406-234-3447

Types of Records Retrieved: Civil courts; Probate courts; Real Estate; Tax liens/Judgments; UCC records

Local Retrieval Area: MT-Custer. **Correspondent Relationships:** Carter and Garfield.

Add'l Information: Established 1929. Normal turnaround time- as much as 2 weeks. Projects billed by the hour. 1st project may require prepayment. They specialize in title insurance.

Security Abstract & Title Inc

114 N 1st Ave, Winterset, IA 50273

Phone: 515-462-1691 **Fax:** 515-462-3927

Types of Records Retrieved: Civil, criminal and probate courts; Federal courts; Real Estate; Tax liens/Judgments; UCC records; Vital records

Local Retrieval Area: IA-Madison

Add'l Information: Established 1901. Normal turnaround time- 2-5 days. Projects billed by number of names searched. Projects billed by the hour. 1st project may require prepayment. Will also visit federal courts for Madison County related information.

Security Abstract Co

PO Box 673, 222 S Sully, Clarendon, TX 79226

Phone: 806-874-3511 **Fax:** 806-874-3298

Types of Records Retrieved: Civil, criminal and probate courts; Real Estate; Tax liens/Judgments; UCC records; Vital records

Local Retrieval Area: TX-Armstrong, Donley, Hall. **Correspondent Relationships:** statewide.

Add'l Information: Established 1987. Normal turnaround time- 2-3 weeks. Projects billed by number of names searched. They specialize in extensive property reports.

Security Abstract Co (Arkansas)

101 N Washington, Magnolia, AR 71753

Phone: 870-234-1291 **Fax:** 870-234-5590

secabco@seark.net

Types of Records Retrieved: Civil courts; Probate courts; Real Estate; Tax liens/Judgments; UCC records

Local Retrieval Area: AR-Columbia. **Correspondent Relationships:** Union County AR.

Add'l Information: Normal turnaround time- 2-3 days for civil, criminal and UCC searches, 5-7 days for real estate and probate. Fee basis will vary by the type of project. They specialize in title insurance.

Security Abstract Co (Missouri)

305 Main, New Madrid, MO 63869

Phone: 573-748-2372 **Fax:** 573-748-2376 jvann@sheltonbbs.com

Types of Records Retrieved: Civil, criminal and probate courts; Real Estate; Tax liens/Judgments; Vital records

Local Retrieval Area: MO-New Madrid

Add'l Information: Established 1945. Normal turnaround time- 1 week or less. Projects billed by number of names searched. All projects require prepayment. Personal checks are accepted.

Security Abstract Company

214 E Washington St, Norton, KS 67654-2150

Phone: 785-877-2141 **Fax:** 785-877-2185

Types of Records Retrieved: Civil, criminal and probate courts; Real Estate; Tax liens/Judgments; UCC records; Vital records

Local Retrieval Area: KS-Norton

Add'l Information: Established 1949. Normal turnaround time- 24 hours. Projects billed by the hour. Payment due on completion of project. They specialize in abstracts, title insurance, home loans and investments.

Security Consultants Inc

5020 45th St NW, Washington, DC 20016-4043

Phone: 202-686-3953 **Fax:** 202-686-0264

www.dcbackground.com **email:** sci@dcbackground.com

Types of Records Retrieved: Civil and criminal courts; Federal courts; Tax liens/Judgments

Local Retrieval Area: DC-District of Columbia; MD-Anne Arundel, Baltimore, Harford, Howard, Montgomery, Prince George's; VA-Alexandria, Arlington, Fairfax, Prince William

Add'l Information: Established 1992. Normal turnaround time- 3 hours in DC; 12 hours in other jurisdictions. Projects billed by number of names searched. Terms: net 30 days. They specialize in on-site searches in the Washington, DC-Baltimore-Northern Virginia metro area. Owner/Mgr Ken Hurley is a former CIA Station Chief, experienced in directing complex investigations.

Security Enforcement Inc

PO Box 279, Oceanside, NY 11572

Phone: 800-924-2896 (NY); 516-678-0344 **Fax:** 516-678-7134

www.securityenforcementinc.net

email: securityenforcementinc@hotmail.com

Types of Records Retrieved: Civil, criminal and probate courts; Federal courts; Real Estate; Tax liens/Judgments; UCC records; Vital records

Local Retrieval Area: NY-Nassau, Suffolk. **Correspondent Relationships:** Westchester, Kings, Queens, Richmond, New York City.

Add'l Information: Established 1986. Normal turnaround time- variable, depending on project. 1st project may require prepayment. Personal checks accepted. They specialize in the NYC metro area. A licensed PI in NY. They perform service of process.

Security Essentials LLC

29525 Chagrin Blvd #318, Pepper Pike, OH 44122

Phone: 216-839-0700 **Fax:** 216-839-0600 purban1@msn.com

Types of Records Retrieved: Civil and criminal courts; Federal courts; Tax liens/Judgments

Local Retrieval Area: OH-Cuyahoga, Geauga, Lake, Summit

Add'l Information: Established 1997. Normal turnaround time- 24-48 hours. Expedited service available. Projects billed by number of names searched. 1st project may require prepayment. Terms are net 10 days. They conduct background investigations on persons and businesses. Forms in compliance with the Fair Credit Reporting Act are provided to clients at no cost. Expect professional and thorough service. A licensed PI in OH.

Security First Title Co

205 W Stephenson, Freeport, IL 61032

Phone: 815-235-2900 **Fax:** 815-235-9955

www.securityfirsttitlecompany.com **email:** sec1title@aol.com

Types of Records Retrieved: Civil and criminal courts; Probate anf Bankruptcy courts; Real Estate; Tax liens/Judgments; UCC records

Local Retrieval Area: IL-Boone, Carroll, Jo Daviess, Lee, Ogle, Stephenson, Whiteside, Winnebago

Add'l Information: Established 1999. Normal turnaround time- 48 hours. Projects billed by number of names searched. Projects billed by number of records located. They specialize in Northwestern Illinois.

Security Information Service Inc

8585 N Stemmons Fwy #M-28, Dallas, TX 75247

Phone: 800-525-5747; 214-637-4055 **Fax:** 214-637-1443

www.SecurityInfoService.com **email:** Larry@SecurityInfoService.com

Types of Records Retrieved: Civil, criminal and probate courts; Federal courts; Real Estate; Tax liens/Judgments; UCC records; Vital records

Local Retrieval Area: TX-Collin, Cooke, Dallas, Denton, Ellis, Grayson, Hunt, Johnson, Kaufman, Rockwall, Tarrant. **Correspondent Relationships:** nationwide and international.

Add'l Information: Established 1967. Normal turnaround time- 1-3 days. Projects billed by number of names searched. Projects billed by number of records located. Projects billed by the hour. All projects require prepayment. Credit cards accepted. They specialize in security consulting, investigations and loss prevention. They also have experience in theft by fraud/embezzlement, due diligence/financial risk analysis, litigation/legal support, conflict of interest/bribery, kickbacks, etc. A licensed PI in TX. They perform service of process.

Security Land Title Co

607 1st Ave West, Box 113, Spencer, IA 51301
Phone: 712-262-1074 **Fax:** 712-262-1082 sltc@ncn.net

Types of Records Retrieved: Civil, criminal and probate courts; Real Estate; Tax liens/Judgments; UCC records

Local Retrieval Area: IA-Clay

Add'l Information: Established 1858. Normal turnaround time- variable depending on project. They charge a flat fee.

Security Search & Abstract Co Inc

926 Pine St, Philadelphia, PA 19107
Phone: 800-345-9494; 215-592-0660 **Fax:** 800-343-4284; 215-592-1277
www.securitysearchabstract.com
email: abarone@securitysearchabstract.com

Types of Records Retrieved: Civil courts; Federal courts; Real Estate; Tax liens/Judgments; UCC records

Local Retrieval Area: DE-New Castle; NJ-Monmouth, Ocean; PA- Berks, Bucks, Chester, Delaware, Lancaster, Lehigh, Montgomery, Northhampton, Philadelphia, Schuylkill. **Correspondent Relationships:** nationwide.

Add'l Information: Established 1962. Normal turnaround time- 24-48 hours. Projects billed by number of names searched. 1st project may require prepayment. They are a nationwide full service public records research company with title plants in Philadelphia, Bucks, Chester, Delaware and Montgomery counties.

Security Services Inc (SSI)

1009 N Sheridan Rd, Peoria, IL 61606
Phone: 800-383-4312; 309-674-4321 **Fax:** 309-674-9357

Types of Records Retrieved: Civil and criminal courts; Federal courts

Local Retrieval Area: IL-Fulton, Knox, Marshall, McLean, Peoria, Stark, Tazewell, Woodford

Add'l Information: Established 1957. Normal turnaround time- 1-3 working days. Projects billed by the hour. Established clients are billed by the hour plus expenses. 1st project may require prepayment. A licensed PI in IL. They perform service of process.

Security Title Canon City

804 Main St, Canon City, CO 81212-3741
Phone: 800-526-7805; 719-276-1438 **Fax:** 719-269-3353

Types of Records Retrieved: Real Estate; Tax liens/Judgments

Local Retrieval Area: CO-Custer, Fremont. **Correspondents:** statewide.

Add'l Information: Normal turnaround time- 1-2 days. Projects billed by number of names searched. 1st project may require prepayment. They specialize in real estate and title matters.

Security Title Co of Garfield County

PO Box 177, Panguitch, UT 84759
Phone: 435-676-8808 **Fax:** 435-676-2421
sectitle@color-country.net

Types of Records Retrieved: Civil, criminal and probate courts; Real Estate; Tax liens/Judgments; UCC records; Vital records

Local Retrieval Area: UT-Garfield, Piute

Add'l Information: Established 1978. Normal turnaround time- 3-5 days. Projects billed by the hour. They specialize in recreational properties.

Security Title Miles City

PO Box 1588, 510 Main St, Miles City, MT 59301
Phone: 800-728-5022; 406-234-3415 **Fax:** 406-234-3447

Types of Records Retrieved: Real Estate; Tax liens/Judgments

Local Retrieval Area: MT-Carter, Custer, Garfield. **Correspondent Relationships:** statewide.

Add'l Information: Established 1984. 1st project may require prepayment. They specialize in real estate.

Security Title of Beaver County

5 S Main St, Beaver, UT 84713
Phone: 435-438-2354 **Fax:** 435-438-5805

Types of Records Retrieved: Civil courts; Probate courts; Real Estate; Tax liens/Judgments; UCC records

Local Retrieval Area: UT-Beaver

Add'l Information: Established 1977. Normal turnaround time- 24 hours. Projects billed by number of names searched. All projects require prepayment.

Sedgwick County Title Co

114 W 1st St, Julesburg, CO 80737
Phone: 970-474-2696 **Fax:** 970-474-2293

Types of Records Retrieved: Real Estate; Tax liens/judgments; UCC records

Local Retrieval Area: CO-Sedgwick

Add'l Information: Established 1993. Normal turnaround time- 24 hours. Projects billed by number of names searched. All projects require prepayment. They specialize in closings and notary services. They also do O & E's, mineral searches and title searches.

Carol Seewald

6101 Sequioa Rd NW #A6, Albuquerque, NM 87120
Phone: 505-831-5713 **Fax:** 505-831-5713

Types of Records Retrieved: Civil couts; Federal courts; Real Estate; Tax liens.judgments; UCC records

Local Retrieval Area: NM-Bernalillo, Sandoval, Santa Fe, Valencia

Add'l Information: Normal turnaround time- 24-48 hours. Projects billed by number of names searched. 1st project may require prepayment.

Segars & Holly

1231 Curtis Dr, Iuka, MS 38852
Phone: 662-423-1006 **Fax:** 662-423-1091

Types of Records Retrieved: Civil, criminal and probate courts; Real Estate; Tax liens/Judgments; UCC records; Vital records

Local Retrieval Area: MS-Alcorn, Prentiss, Tishomingo

Add'l Information: Established 1992. Normal turnaround time- 1-2 days. Fee basis varies by type of project. 1st project may require prepayment. Payment due upon receipt fo statement. He is an attorney in general and real estate practice. They perform service of process.

Segovia & Associates

2020 E Pioneer Pky #100 PMB 5, Arlington, TX 76010-6806
Phone: 877-573-7833; 817-538-7236 **Fax:** 877-221-6008; 817-548-9591
www.segoviaandassociates.com **email:** info@segoviaandassociates.com

Types of Records Retrieved: Civil, criminal and probate courts; Federal courts; Real Estate; Vital records

Local Retrieval Area: TX-Collin, Dallas, Denton, Ellis, Johnson, Parker, Tarrant, Wise. **Correspondent Relationships:** Johnson, Parker, Wise, Ellis, Denton counties TX; TX Sec of State.

Add'l Information: Established 1996. Normal turnaround time- 24 hours or less. Projects billed by number of names searched. All projects require prepayment. Credit cards accepted. Check by Telephone/Fax They specialize in service of process, document retrieval, legal and courthouse research and photocopying. Former private investigator with ten (10) years experience in the industry. They perform service of process.

Select Information Business Services

12025 215th Pl SE, Snohomish, WA 98296
Phone: 425-444-7877 **Fax:** 253-540-1824
www.selectinfobiz.com **email:** cbowers@selectinfobiz.com

Types of Records Retrieved: Civil, criminal and probate courts; Federal courts; Real Estate; Tax liens/Judgments; UCC records; Vital records.

Local Retrieval Area: WA-King, Pierce, Snohomish, Thurston. **Correspondent Relationships:** statewide.

Add'l Information: Established 2003. Normal turnaround time- 24-72 hours. 1st project may require prepayment. They provide intelligent information on real property, litigation, and screening support. Over 20-yrs experience; efficient and professional.

Select Research

PO Box 2346, Bakersfield, CA 93303
Phone: 661-301-7979 **Fax:** 661-326-0361
ahashim@assurancedevelopment.com

Types of Records Retrieved: Civil, criminal and probate courts; Federal Bankruptcy courts; Real Estate; Tax liens/Judgments; Vital records

Local Retrieval Area: CA-Kern

Add'l Information: Established 2004. Normal turnaround time- same day, 3 hours. Projects billed by number of names searched. Projects billed by number of records located. Will invoice. They handle probate, background checks, document recording and retrieval. They also specialize in locating individuals, heirs, property and general tax assor information.

Serunian Inv

211 Marginal Way, PMB 114, Portland, ME 04101
Phone: 207-773-2660 **Fax:** 207-773-4369

Types of Records Retrieved: Civil and criminal courts

Local Retrieval Area: ME-Cumberland, York

Add'l Information: Established 1985. Normal turnaround time- 24 hours. Projects billed by number of names searched. 1st project may require prepayment. They specialize in public record retrieval, private investigator/detective, service of process, notary public, pre-employment screening, mystery shopper and background investigations. Criminal searches a specialty; in business since 1985. A licensed PI in ME. They perform service of process.

Service Abstract Company of Randolph County

208 E Everett St, Pocahontas, AR 72455
Phone: 870-892-4538 **Fax:** 870-892-0302
servabst@cox-Internet.com

Types of Records Retrieved: Civil, criminal and probate courts; Federal courts; Real Estate; Tax liens/Judgments; UCC records; Vital records

Local Retrieval Area: AR-Randolph

Add'l Information: Established 1979. Normal turnaround time- variable depending on project. Projects billed by number of records located. Projects billed by the hour. Fee basis will vary by the type of project. Personal checks accepted. They specialize in title insurance, abstracts and loan closings. A licensed PI in AR. They perform service of process.

Services For Lawyers

221 N Olive St, Media, PA 19063
Phone: 610-566-9165 **Fax:** 610-566-9166
lawyerserv@aol.com

Types of Records Retrieved: Civil, criminal and probate courts; Federal courts; Real Estate; Tax liens/Judgments; Vital records

Local Retrieval Area: PA-Chester, Delaware, Montgomery. **Correspondent Relationships:** Philadelphia, Wilmington, Bucks County, southern New Jersey.

Add'l Information: Established 1990. Normal turnaround time- 24-48 hours. Billing method depends on project. 1st project may require prepayment. They specialize in criminal searches, civil searches, litigation file review & status reports, document retrieval. Also, statistical information on jury & bench verdicts, and arbitration awards. Located next to the Delaware County courthouse. They perform service of process.

Services Rendered Inc

7186 Manchester Rd, St Louis, MO 63143
Phone: 888-434-8200; 314-644-3955 **Fax:** 314-645-4291
www.lgr-sri.com **email:** larry@lgr-sri.com

Types of Records Retrieved: Civil, criminal and probate courts; Federal courts; UCC records; Vital records

Local Retrieval Area: IL-Madison, Monroe, St Clair; MO-Franklin, Jefferson, St Charles, St Louis City, St Louis. **Correspondent Relationships:** nationwide in USA, also in Europe, Canada, Australia.

Add'l Information: Established 1989. Normal turnaround time- 3 day; 24-hr. rush service and 48-hr. priority service available. Projects billed by number of names searched. 1st project may require prepayment. They specialize in finding individuals and their assets. They perform service of process.

Services Rendered Inc

7186 Manchester Rd, St. Louis, MO 63143
Phone: 314-644-3955 **Fax:** 314-645-4291
www.lgr-sri.com **email:** larry@lgr-sri.com

Types of Records Retrieved: Civil and criminal courts.

Local Retrieval Area: MO-Bollinger, Butler, Cape Girardeau, Dunklin, Mississippi, New Madrid, Pemiscot, Perry, Scott, Stoddard

Add'l Information: Established 1994. All projects require prepayment. They also provide court filings, photocopying, skiptracing, private investigations and asset searches. They perform service of process.

Servico Inc

283 Washington Ave, Albany, NY 12206
Phone: 518-463-4179 **Fax:** 518-463-3752
www.servico.com **email:** inc@servico.com

Types of Records Retrieved: Civil, criminal and probate courts; Tax liens/Judgments; UCC records; Corporate records

Local Retrieval Area: NY-Albany, Schenectady. **Correspondent Relationships:** New York.

Add'l Information: Established 1924. Normal turnaround time- 1-5 business days. Projects billed by number of names searched. Credit cards accepted. They require prepayment for corporation filings. A licensed PI in NY. They perform service of process.

Seva Services

501 W Broadway #A231, San Diego, CA 92101
Phone: 858-490-9009 **Fax:** 858-490-9009 triguru@fda.net

Types of Records Retrieved: Civil, criminal and probate courts; Federal courts; Real Estate; Tax liens/Judgments; Vital records

Local Retrieval Area: CA-San Diego. **Correspondent Relationships:** Alameda, Los Angeles, Orange, Riverside, San Bernadino, San Francisco, San Mateo, Santa Cruz, Santa Barbara, Santa Clara, Ventura counties.

Add'l Information: Established 1990. Normal turnaround time- 24 hours to 4 days. Projects billed by number of records located. Charges depend on volume and response requirements. 1st project may require prepayment. Terms: net 30 days. They specialize in indexing, title abstracts, news media, employment, large-volume civil and unlawful detainer searches.

Seve Company

PO Box 14286, Charleston, SC 29422
Phone: 843-762-4520 **Fax:** 843-762-4593
www.sevecompany.com **email:** info@sevecompany.com

Types of Records Retrieved: Civil, criminal and probate courts; Federal courts; Real Estate; Tax liens/Judgments; UCC records; Vital records

Local Retrieval Area: SC-Berkeley, Charleston, Dorchester. **Correspondent Relationships:** statewide.

Add'l Information: Established 2002. Normal turnaround time- 48-72 hours. Projects billed by number of names searched. Terms are net 30 days. They are a South Carolina public records and document research and retrieval company.

Seyfried Support Services

PO Box 2882, Carmichael, CA 95609-2882
Phone: 916-359-5275 **Fax:** 916-359-5276 seycheck@surewest.net

Types of Records Retrieved: Civil, criminal and probate courts; Federal courts; Real Estate; Tax liens/Judgments; UCC records; Vital records

Local Retrieval Area: CA-El Dorado, Placer, Sacramento, Sutter, Yolo, Yuba. **Correspondent Relationships:** Stanislaus, San Joaquin, Merced counties CA.

Add'l Information: Established 1991. Normal turnaround time- 24 hours. Projects billed by number of names searched. Will do monthly billings. They specialize in rapid turnaround. They are an experienced and accurate data retriever.

Seyler Retrieval

36 S Shore Dr, Springfield, MA 01118-1247
Phone: 413-782-9907/348-3667 **Fax:** 413-782-9907
seylersnj@msn.com

Types of Records Retrieved: Civil and criminal courts; US district courts

Local Retrieval Area: MA-Franklin, Hampden, Hampshire

Add'l Information: Established 1997. Normal turnaround time- 24 hours if docket copy clears, 48 hours if docket copy required. Projects billed by number of names searched. 1st project may require prepayment. Will invoice monthly. They are a small emerging retrieval company offering excellent personal prompt and reliable service at flexible pricing. Also do mass housing and small claims searches.

Shadow Trackers Investigative Svcs Inc

912 N Main, Meridian, ID 83642
Phone: 208-895-0074 **Fax:** 208-884-8257
www.shadowtrackers.com **email:** ron@shadowtrackers.com

Types of Records Retrieved: Civil and criminal courts; Federal courts; Tax liens/Judgments

Local Retrieval Area: ID-Ada, Bannock, Canyon, Gem, Latah, Payette. **Correspondent Relationships:** nationwide.

Add'l Information: Established 1992. Normal turnaround time- 72 hours or less. 24 hours for Ada County. Projects billed by number of names searched. 1st project may require prepayment. Credit cards accepted. They are a full service PI firm. Voted leading PI firm in USA by PI Magazine. They perform service of process.

Shannon County Abstract Co

PO Box 334, 108 Pine, Eminence, MO 65466
Phone: 573-226-3331 **Fax:** 573-226-3751

Types of Records Retrieved: Civil courts; Probate courts; Real Estate; Tax liens/Judgments; UCC records **Local Retrieval Area:** MO-Shannon

Add'l Information: Normal turnaround time- 1-2 weeks. Fee basis will vary by the type of project. They specialize in real estate.

Sharp County Abstract Co Inc

PO Box 81, Ash Flat, AR 72513
Phone: 870-994-7314 **Fax:** 870-994-2880

Types of Records Retrieved: Civil, criminal and probate courts; Real Estate; Tax liens/Judgments; UCC records **Local Retrieval Area:** AR-Sharp

Add'l Information: Established 1896. Normal turnaround time- 10 days. Expedited service available. Fee basis will vary by the type of project. They specialize in title insurance, escrow and closings.

Sharp Law Office

PO Box 906, Mt Vernon, IL 62864
Phone: 618-242-0246 **Fax:** 618-242-8950 tsharp@lotsharp.com

Types of Records Retrieved: Real Estate; Tax liens/Judgments

Local Retrieval Area: IL-Franklin, Jefferson, Marion, Williamson

Add'l Information: Established 1974. Normal turnaround time- 3-5 days. Projects billed by the hour. They specialize in real estate searches.

Shaw Investigations

PO Box 828, Yreka, CA 96097
Phone: 530-841-0255 **Fax:** 530-841-0255 billshaw@snowcrest.com

Types of Records Retrieved: Civil and criminal courts

Local Retrieval Area: CA-Siskiyou

Add'l Information: Established 1998. Normal turnaround time- 24 hours. Projects billed by the hour. All projects require prepayment. They specialize in criminal background. A licensed PI in CA. They perform service of process.

Shawver & Associates

6262 Weber Rd #112, Corpus Christi, TX 78413-4030
Phone: 800-364-2333; 361-880-8968 **Fax:** 361-880-8971
www.stxpi.com **email:** dshawver@stxpi.com

Types of Records Retrieved: Civil, criminal and probate courts; Federal courts; Real Estate; Tax liens/Judgments; UCC records; Vital records

Local Retrieval Area: TX-Aransas, Bee, Brooks, Cameron, Duval, Hidalgo, Jim Wells, Kleberg, Nueces, Refugio, San Patricio, Starr, Victoria, Webb. **Correspondent Relationships:** Texas.

Add'l Information: Established 1986. Normal turnaround time- 2 days for areas within a 50 mile radius. Projects billed by the hour. 1st project may require prepayment. They specialize in finding the missing, litigation support, and insurance fraud investigations. A licensed PI in TX.

Parri Shebley

766 Violet Ln, Vacaville, CA 95687
Phone: 707-448-5018 **Fax:** 707-448-5103 parri@neteze.com

Types of Records Retrieved: Civil and criminal courts; US District court

Local Retrieval Area: CA-Sacramento, Solano, Yolo. **Correspondent Relationships:** statewide.

Add'l Information: Established 2002. Normal turnaround time- 3-5 business days. Projects billed by number of records located. 1st project may require prepayment. They will same searches for criminal or civil. Also offers litigation service of process. They perform service of process.

Shelby County Land Title Corp

PO Box 473, 236 E Main St, Shelbyville, IL 62565
Phone: 217-774-2623 **Fax:** 217-774-3702

Types of Records Retrieved: Civil, criminal and probate courts; Real Estate; Tax liens/Judgments; UCC records; Vital records

Local Retrieval Area: IL-Shelby

Add'l Information: Established 1920. Normal turnaround time- 2 days. Projects billed by number of records located. Payment due after work is completed. They specialize in mortgage closings.

Shenandoah Title Services Inc

2113 Valley Ave, Winchester, VA 22601-2753
Phone: 540-667-1393 **Fax:** 540-667-0464 titles@shentel.net

Types of Records Retrieved: Civil courts; Probate courts; Real Estate; Tax liens/Judgments; UCC records

Local Retrieval Area: VA-Clarke, Frederick, Page, Shenandoah, Warren, Winchester City

Add'l Information: Established 1988. Normal turnaround time- 3-5 days. Expedited service available. Fee basis will vary by type of project. They specialize in real estate searches.

Shepp Johnman & Associates Inv

2723 37 Ave NE #121, Calgary, Alberta, Canada, CAN T1Y 5R8
Phone: 877-258-9073; 403-250-8947 **Fax:** 403-250-9205
www.sheppjohnman.com **email:** roger_maslen@compuserve.com

Types of Records Retrieved: Civil and criminal courts

Local Retrieval Area: CANADA-Alberta. **Correspondent Relationships:** British Columbia, Canada.

Add'l Information: Established 1975. Projects billed by the hour. All projects require prepayment. They specialize in record retrieval in Calgary and southern Alberta. A licensed PI in Alberta, BC. They perform service of process.

Sheridan County Title

23 S Main St, Sheridan, WY 82801
Phone: 307-672-6478 **Fax:** 307-672-8310

Types of Records Retrieved: Civil courts; Probate courts; Federal courts; Real Estate; Tax liens/Judgments; UCC records

Local Retrieval Area: WY-Sheridan

Add'l Information: Established 1976. Normal turnaround time- 2 days. Projects billed by the hour. 1st project may require prepayment.

Sherlock Research

PO Box 2629, Akron, OH 44309
Phone: 330-882-4690 **Fax:** 330-882-4686

Types of Records Retrieved: Civil, criminal and probate courts; Federal courts; Real Estate; Tax liens/Judgments; UCC records; Vital records

Local Retrieval Area: OH-Cuyahoga, Medina, Portage, Stark, Summit, Wayne

Add'l Information: Established 1989. Normal turnaround time- 1 week upon payment. Expedited service available. Projects billed by number of names searched. Projects billed by number of records located. Projects billed by the hour. Down payment up front, balance due upon completion. They are coroner trained investigative reporter owned firm. They can find in Ohio, midwest, northeast, DC. Will interview officials for cases. Good at assets location.

Valerie Shickel

42 Book Hill Rd, Essex, CT 06426
Phone: 860-767-2269 **Fax:** 860-767-7621
vshickel@netscape.net

Types of Records Retrieved: Civil courts; Probate courts; Real Estate; Tax liens/Judgments; UCC records; Vital records

Local Retrieval Area: CT-Middlesex, New Haven, New London

Add'l Information: Established 1984. Normal turnaround time- 24-48 hours. Fees are based on a per search basis. 1st project may require prepayment. Billed by project. She specializes in 40 to 60 year land and probate record searches and document retrieval in Middlesex and New London Counties.

Shore One Title Abstract Services

403 N Main St, PO Box 537, Hurlock, MD 21643
Phone: 410-943-8637 **Fax:** 410-943-0028

Types of Records Retrieved: Civil, criminal and probate courts; Real Estate; Tax liens/Judgments; UCC records

Local Retrieval Area: MD-Caroline, Dorchester, Talbot. **Correspondent Relationships:** Eastern Shore counties.

Add'l Information: Established 1996. Normal turnaround time- 24-48 hours. Fee basis will vary with type of search. Payment due upon completion/settlement. They specialize in title searches, full searches, and P and J's.

Simmons Agency Inc

190 High St 2nd Fl, Boston, MA 02210
Phone: 800-237-8230; 508-771-4477 **Fax:** 508-771-5353
www.simmonsagency.com **email:** simmons.agency@verizon.net

Types of Records Retrieved: Civil, criminal and probate courts; Federal courts; Real Estate; Tax liens/Judgments; UCC records; Vital records.

Local Retrieval Area: MA-Barnstable, Middlesex, Norfolk, Plymouth, Suffolk. **Correspondent Relationships:** Essex, Hampden, Worcester counties MA.

Add'l Information: Established 1937. Normal turnaround time- 1-3 days. Projects billed by the hour. 1st project may require prepayment. They are experienced private investigators capable of performing in-depth background and due diligence investigations. Many areas covered, see the web site. A licensed PI in MA.

Faith Simpson

20663 Becky Dr, McCalla, AL 35111
Phone: 205-381-0788 **Fax:** 205-477-6708
faithsroe@aol.com

Types of Records Retrieved: Probate courts; Real Estate; Tax liens/Judgments; UCC records

Local Retrieval Area: AL-Jefferson. **Correspondent Relationships:** Shelby and Tuscaloosa counties AL.

Add'l Information: Established 1994. Normal turnaround time- 48 hours. Projects billed by number of names searched. 1st project may require prepayment. Will bill weekly or monthly. Will also send bill with returned documents on report. She specializes in probate, UCC, tax liens, real estate, mortgage and deed, assignment retrieval, property reports, estate, wills, voter registration and notary search. Cell phone number is 205-381-0788. Email is faithsroe@aol.com.

SingleSource Services Corp

2320 S 3rd St #7, Jacksonville Beach, FL 32250
Phone: 800-713-3412; 904-241-1821 **Fax:** 877-835-5787; 904-241-0601
www.singlesourceservices.com **email:** checkit@singlesourceservices.com

Types of Records Retrieved: Civil and criminal courts; Tax liens/Judgments; UCC records

Local Retrieval Area: FL-Duval. **Correspondent Relationships:** especially North Carolina, Ohio, Texas, Georgia, New Jersey, Delaware, South Carolina, Virginia, Tennessee, Kentucky, also national and international.

Add'l Information: Established 1993. Normal turnaround time- 48 hours requested; most results in 24 hours or less. Projects billed by number of names searched. Fees vary according to work type and volume. 1st project may require prepayment. Terms: net 30 days. They also feature web-based applicant tracking, employee assessments and full-service background screening. Researchers deal directly with the client. Hirs system and payroll. A licensed PI in FL.

Law Offices of Joan C Singleton

PO Box 116, Courthouse Rd, Warm Springs, VA 24484
Phone: 540-839-5009 **Fax:** 540-839-2986

Types of Records Retrieved: Civil, criminal and probate courts; Federal courts; Real Estate; Tax liens/Judgments; UCC records; Vital records

Local Retrieval Area: VA-Alleghany, Bath, Clifton Forge City, Covington City, Highland

Add'l Information: Established 1985. Normal turnaround time- 24 hours. Projects billed by the hour.

Skimerhorn Inv

444 N Jackson Ave, Bradley, IL 60915
Phone: 815-933-0843 **Fax:** 815-933-0843 jskinvestigation@aol.com

Types of Records Retrieved: Civil, criminal and probate courts; Real Estate; Tax liens/Judgments; UCC records; Vital records

Local Retrieval Area: IL-Kankakee

Add'l Information: Established 1990. Normal turnaround time- 1-2 days. Expedited service available. Fees are per name searched, per class of record. Process service on case-by-case basis per paper served, per name. 1st project may require prepayment. May be billed monthly. They specialize in skiptracing, asset searches and conduct missing person checks. They also specialize in lis pendens, misc. liens, mechanics liens, judgments and civil & criminal investigations. A licensed PI in IL. They perform service of process.

Bobbie Slice

541 Chapin Rd, Chapin, SC 29036
Phone: 803-932-7013 **Fax:** 803-932-7254 bslice@bellsouth.net

Types of Records Retrieved: Civil and criminal courts; Real Estate; Tax liens/Judgments; UCC records

Local Retrieval Area: SC-Lexington, Newberry, Richland

Add'l Information: Established 2000. Normal turnaround time- 24 hours. Projects billed by number of names searched. Will bill monthly. They specialize in court record research and information and document retrieval. Professional and accurate reporting. No outsourcing or online databases used, does physical searches.

Slover Investigations

PO Box 6515, Chandler, AZ 85246-6515
Phone: 480-917-3708 **Fax:** 480-917-2603
www.sloverpi.com **email:** sloverpi@msn.com

Types of Records Retrieved: Civil, criminal and probate courts; Federal courts; Tax liens/Judgments; UCC records

Local Retrieval Area: AZ-Maricopa

Add'l Information: Established 1988. Normal turnaround time- 1-2 days. Projects billed by number of names searched. Projects billed by the hour. 1st project may require prepayment. They specialize in criminal records checks, motor vehicle, watercraft and aircraft searches, skiptracing, personal injury, asset, background, and pre-employment investigations. A licensed PI in AZ.

Smith County Title Co

5040 Kinsey Dr, Tyler, TX 75703
Phone: 903-581-6400 **Fax:** 903-581-6445
Types of Records Retrieved: Civil courts; Probate courts; Real Estate; Tax liens/Judgments; UCC records
Local Retrieval Area: TX-Smith
Add'l Information: Established 1923. Normal turnaround time- 1-3 days. Projects billed by number of names searched. Projects billed by the hour. Personal checks accepted. Formerly Smith County Title Co.

Cheryl Smith

692 New Liberty Rd, New Bern, NC 28562
Phone: 252-633-3890 **Fax:** 252-633-3890
Types of Records Retrieved: Real Estate; UCC records
Local Retrieval Area: NC-Craven, Jones, Pamlico
Add'l Information: Established 1986. Normal turnaround time- 1-3 days. Projects billed by the hour. Personal checks are accepted. She specializes in title examinations.

SMS Searches

109 Huntleigh Forest Dr, St Louis, MO 63122
Phone: 314-691-1593 **Fax:** 314-965-8531
smssrchs@sbcglobal.net
Types of Records Retrieved: Civil and criminal courts; Probate; Federal Courts; Real Estate; UCC records; Vital Records; Tax liens/Judgments
Local Retrieval Area: MO-St Charles, St Louis County, St Louis City
Add'l Information: Established 1996. Normal turnaround time- 8-48 hours. Fee basis varies by project. Net 30 days. They specialize in current owner to 45 years ownership for real estate; deed reports; recordings, signature signing by notary, all document retrieval. Criminal & civil searches.

Snoop For You

1326 S Kline St, Lakewood, CO 80232
Phone: 303-985-5521 **Fax:** 303-985-5521
pwlameris@comcast.net
Types of Records Retrieved: Civil, criminal and probate courts; Federal courts; Real Estate; Tax liens/Judgments; UCC records; Vital records
Local Retrieval Area: CO-Adams, Arapahoe, Boulder, Clear Creek, Denver, Douglas, Jefferson, Summit, Weld
Add'l Information: Established 2004. Projects billed by the hour. 1st project may require prepayment. Credit cards accepted. Depends on client. They specialize in pre-employment screening, small claims recovery, background checking, public record retrieval and filing services.

Snyder Abstract & Title Co Inc

1816 26th St, Snyder, TX 79549
Phone: 325-573-6339 **Fax:** 325-573-8112
satco1@sbcglobal.net
Types of Records Retrieved: Probate courts; Federal District courts; Real Estate; Tax liens/Judgments; UCC records
Local Retrieval Area: TX-Borden, Scurry
Add'l Information: Normal turnaround time- 2-3 days. Fee basis will vary by the type of project. 1st project may require prepayment. They provide title insurance, abstracts, abstractor's certificates and searches.

Somerset Abstract Co Ltd

PO Box 374, Somerset, PA 15501
Phone: 814-445-9525 **Fax:** 814-443-2255
Types of Records Retrieved: Civil courts; Real Estate; Tax liens/Judgments; UCC records
Local Retrieval Area: PA-Somerset
Add'l Information: Normal turnaround time- up to 1 week. Fee basis is per transaction. They specialize in real estate.

Leslie or Mike Sosa

100 Frazer Ct, Folsom, CA 95630-7718
Phone: 916-984-7654 **Fax:** 916-984-0910
www.pub-info.com **email:** leslie@pub-info.com
Types of Records Retrieved: Real Estate; Tax liens/judgments; UCC records
Local Retrieval Area: CA-El Dorado, Marin, Merced, Monterey, Placer, Sacramento, San Benito, San Francisco, San Mateo, Santa Clara, Santa Cruz, Solano
Add'l Information: Established 1977. Normal turnaround time- 24 hours. Projects billed by number of names searched. 1st project may require prepayment. Large copy orders may require prepayment. They have 23 years of experience in providing fast and accurate reports, specializing in title searches.

Source

PO Box 88, Cookeville, TN 38503
Phone: 800-678-8774; **Fax:** 800-537-3297;
www.sourceresources.com **email:** info@sourceresources.com
Types of Records Retrieved: Civil, criminal and probate courts; Federal courts; Real Estate; Tax liens/Judgments; UCC records
Local Retrieval Area: TN-Cumberland, DeKalb, Jackson, Macon, Overton, Putnam, Roane, Smith, White. **Correspondent Relationships:** nationwide.
Add'l Information: Established 1985. Normal turnaround time- 1-7 working days. Projects billed by number of names searched. All projects require prepayment. Credit cards accepted. They specialize in extended court filings and searches for New Jersey, Pennsylvania and New York. They also search public record information on individuals and businesses. A licensed PI in TN. They perform service of process.

Source Documents & Information Inc

404 S Dr Martin Luther King Jr Ave, Clearwater, FL 33756
Phone: 727-447-8844 **Fax:** 727-447-8414
www.sourcedocsinfo.com **email:** Sam@sourcedocsinfo.com
Types of Records Retrieved: Real Estate; Tax liens/judgments; UCC records
Local Retrieval Area: FL-Brevard, Broward, Dade, Hernando, Hillsborough, Manatee, Orange, Palm Beach, Pasco, Pinellas, Polk, Sarasota. **Correspondent Relationships:** statewide in FL, GA, NC, SC, MD, VA, Washington, DC.
Add'l Information: Established 1999. Normal turnaround time- 1-5 days. Expedited 1-day service available. Projects billed by number of names searched. Payment upon order completion. They specialize in document retrieval of mortgages, deeds, assignments, satisfactions, liens, etc. Will provide photocopy, certified copies or recording info. Walk-in recordation service. Offers current owner searches in FL, GA, VA & MD.

South Central Title Agency Inc

35096 Kenai Spur Hwy, Soldotna, AK 99669
Phone: 907-262-4494 **Fax:** 907-262-3925 sctitle@alaska.net
Types of Records Retrieved: Real Estate; Tax liens/Judgments
Local Retrieval Area: AK-Kenai Peninsula, Seward. **Correspondent Relationships:** statewide.
Add'l Information: Normal turnaround time- 24 hours. Projects billed by the hour. All projects require prepayment.

South Eastern Data

127 Monticello St #1, Somerset, KY 42501
Phone: 606-679-1688 **Fax:** 606-679-6557
Types of Records Retrieved: Real Estate; Tax liens/Judgments
Local Retrieval Area: KY-Whitley
Add'l Information: Established 1984. 1st project may require prepayment. They specialize in real estate.

South Florida Legal Services of Naples

PO Box 8456, Naples, FL 34101
Phone: 239-332-7000 **Fax:** 239-337-2100 sflsnaples@aol.com
Types of Records Retrieved: Civil and criminal courts; Probate court; Federal courts; Real Estate; Tax liens/Judgments; Vital records.

Local Retrieval Area: FL-Charlotte, Collier, Hendry, Lee. **Correspondent Relationships:** Florida and nationwide.

Add'l Information: Established 1992. Normal turnaround time- 2 days. Expedited service available. Fee is based on the nature of the search. 1st project may require prepayment. The specialize in the area of Ft Myers, Florida. A licensed PI in FL. They perform service of process.

South Florida Title Research Inc dba SFTR

13822 Wellington Trace, #121, Wellington, FL 33414-8553
Phone: 866-398-7387; **Fax:** 866-329-7387;
www.sftr.net **email:** info@sftr.net

Types of Records Retrieved: Civil, criminal and probate courts; Federal courts; Real Estate; Tax liens/Judgments; UCC records

Local Retrieval Area: FL-Broward, Dade, Martin, Palm Beach. **Correspondent Relationships:** statewide.

Add'l Information: Established 1987. Normal turnaround time- 24 hours. Projects billed by number of records located. net 30 days. They specialize in current owner searches and environmental searches (statewide). Main office is located at 12527 Central Ave Minneapolis, MN 55434.

South Plains Abstract Co

PO Box 418, 408 N 1st St, LaMesa, TX 79331
Phone: 806-872-3023 **Fax:** 806-872-2904

Types of Records Retrieved: Real Estate; Tax liens/Judgments; UCC records

Local Retrieval Area: TX-Dawson

Add'l Information: Normal turnaround time- 2 days. Fee basis will vary by the type of project. All projects require prepayment.

South Ridge Abstract & Title Co

229 S Commerce Ave, Sebring, FL 33870
Phone: 863-385-2521 **Fax:** 863-382-6438 sratseb@ct.net

Types of Records Retrieved: Civil courts; Probate courts; Real Estate; Tax liens/Judgments; UCC records

Local Retrieval Area: FL-Highlands

Add'l Information: Established 1948. Normal turnaround time- 7-10 working days. Projects billed by number of names searched. 1st project may require prepayment. Invoice sent with results. They maintain an in-house title plant.

South Texas Title and Trustee Services

530 Lake Dr, Harlingen, TX 78550
Phone: 956-412-3413 **Fax:** 956-412-0103 mmedley@rgv.rr.com

Types of Records Retrieved: Real Estate; Tax liens/judgments; UCC records

Local Retrieval Area: TX-Cameron, Hidalgo, Jim Wells, Kleberg, Nueces, Willacy

Add'l Information: Established 1993. Normal turnaround time- 24 hours. Projects billed by number of names searched. Payment due upon receipt. Formerly Valley Court Services, they are an experienced company specializing in title abstracting and trustee sales for Cameron, Hidalgo, Jim Wells Nueces and Kleberg counties.

Southeast Arizona Legal Support

PO Box 43, Bisbee, AZ 85603
Phone: 520-432-9032 **Fax:** 520-432-9032
www.lashlaroue.com **email:** laroue@cableone.net

Types of Records Retrieved: Civil, criminal and probate courts; Real Estate; Tax liens/Judgments; UCC records

Local Retrieval Area: AZ-Cochise

Add'l Information: Established 1992. Normal turnaround time- 24 hours. Projects billed by number of names searched. 1st project may require prepayment. Projects billed 30 days net. They specialize in criminal and civil case support, background investigations, and are a licensed private investigator. A licensed PI in AZ.

Southeast Nebraska Abstract

1524 Stone St, Falls City, NE 68355
Phone: 402-245-4222 **Fax:** 402-245-3859

Types of Records Retrieved: Civil, criminal and probate courts; Real Estate; Tax liens/Judgments; UCC records

Local Retrieval Area: NE-Richardson

Add'l Information: Established 1973. Normal turnaround time- 24-48 hours. Fee basis will vary by the type of project. Depends on project.

Southeast Wisconsin Process & Inv Inc

419 N Grand Ave, Waukesha, WI 53186
Phone: 262-650-8904 **Fax:** 262-650-8921
sewiprocess@wi.rr.com

Types of Records Retrieved: Civil, criminal and probate courts; Federal Bankruptcy courts; Real Estate; Tax liens/Judgments; UCC & Vital records

Local Retrieval Area: WI-Dane, Dodge, Fond du Lac, Jefferson, Kenosha, Milwaukee, Ozaukee, Racine, Sheboygan, Walworth, Washington, Waukesha. **Correspondent Relationships:** statewide.

Add'l Information: Established 1992. Normal turnaround time- 2-3 days. Expedited service available. Projects billed by the hour. 1st project may require prepayment. They offer instant email notification and status by the web. A licensed PI in WI. They perform service of process.

Southeastern Utah Title

PO Box 855, Price, UT 84501
Phone: 435-637-4455 **Fax:** 435-637-4459
www.southeasttitle.com **email:** setitle@emerytelcom.net

Types of Records Retrieved: Civil, criminal and probate courts; Real Estate; Tax liens/Judgments; UCC records; Vital records

Local Retrieval Area: UT-Carbon, Emery, Grand, San Juan

Add'l Information: Established 1949. Normal turnaround time- 24 hours. Fee basis will vary by the type of project. 1st project may require prepayment.

Southern Abstract & Title Co

PO Box 507, 16 NW Martin Luthur King Ave, Idabel, OK 74745
Phone: 580-286-2288 **Fax:** 580-286-7885

Types of Records Retrieved: Civil courts; Probate courts; Real Estate; Tax liens/Judgments; UCC records; Vital records

Local Retrieval Area: OK-McCurtain

Add'l Information: Normal turnaround time- 2-3 weeks. Projects billed by the hour. Fee is also determined per abstract. Clients pay before searches are released.

Southern California Strategic Research

249 N Brand Blvd #314, Glendale, CA 91023
Phone: 323-257-4472 **Fax:** 323-257-8613 weplatz@aol.com

Types of Records Retrieved: Civil, criminal and probate courts; Federal courts; Real Estate; Tax liens/Judgments; UCC records; Vital records

Local Retrieval Area: CA-Los Angeles, Orange, Riverside, San Bernardino, Santa Barbara, Ventura. **Correspondent Relationships:** statewide.

Add'l Information: Established 2003. Normal turnaround time- 1-3 days for index; 1-7 days for documents depending on the courts. Projects billed by the hour. Special flat rates for bulk searches are available. Retainer is required. Association of individually licensed private investigators with over 60 years combines experience in investigations throughout southern California. Due diligence, litigation support and backgorund investigations. A licensed PI in CA.

Southern Courthouse Ventures

PO Box 81483, 2078 Beechwood Dr, Conyers, GA 30013
Phone: 678-413-4697 **Fax:** 678-413-4626 jimreyscv@aol.com

Types of Records Retrieved: Civil courts; Federal Bankruptcy courts; Real Estate; Tax liens/Judgments; UCC records

Local Retrieval Area: GA-Baldwin, Banks, Barrow, Bartow, Bibb, Butts, Carroll, Catoosa, Chattooga, Cherokee, Clarke, Clayton, Cobb, Coweta, Crawford, Dade, Dawson, DeKalb, Dougals, Elbert, Fannin, Fayette, Floyd, Forsyth, Franklin, Fulton, Gilmer, Gordon, Greene, Gwinnett, Habersham, Hall, Hancock, Haralson, Hart, Harris, Heard, Henry, Houston, Jackson, Jasper, Jones, Lamar, Lincoln, Lumpkin, Madison, Meriwether, Monroe, Morgan, Murray, Muscogee, Newton, Oconee, Oglethorpe, Paulding, Peach, Pickens, Pike, Polk, Putnam, Rabun, Rockdale, Spalding, Stephens,

Taliaferro, Towns, Troup, Twiggs, Union, Upson, Walton, Walker, White, Whitfield, Wilkes. **Correspondent Relationships:** Cherokee, Cobb, Floyd, Dawson, Whitfield counties.

Add'l Information: Established 1990. Normal turnaround time- 24-48 hours. Charge by number of searches requested. Some projects require prepayment. Terms: net 30 days. They do hand delivered filings. Three major bankruptcy courts covered. Statewide index access and 24 hours service available upon request.

Southern Land & Title LLC

406 S 2nd St, Gadsden, AL 35901
Phone: 256-543-1361 **Fax:** 256-543-1377 solandtitle@microxl.com

Types of Records Retrieved: Civil courts; Probate courts; Federal courts; Real Estate; Tax liens/Judgments; UCC records

Local Retrieval Area: AL-Calhoun, Cherokee, Cleburne, De Kalb, Etowah, Jefferson, Madison, Marshall, Randolph, St Clair, Shelby, Talladega. **Correspondent Relationships:** Alabama, Georgia and Tennessee.

Add'l Information: Established 1998. Normal turnaround time- 48 hours. Projects billed by number of names searched. Payment due upon completion. They provide comprehensive research and service in the public document retrieval business. They provide UCC, tax lien, judgment and litigation searches. They also provide deed, mortgages and tax assessment information on real estate transactions.

Southern Montana Abstract & Title

PO Box 390, 15 S Idaho St, Dillon, MT 59725
Phone: 406-683-4445 **Fax:** 406-683-4393

Types of Records Retrieved: Civil courts; Probate courts; Real Estate; Tax liens/Judgments; UCC records; Vital records

Local Retrieval Area: MT-Beaverhead

Add'l Information: Established 1917. Normal turnaround time- 5 days. Fee basis varies by type of transaction.

Southern Process Service

2000 Whittle Springs Rd, Knoxville, TN 37917
Phone: 865-525-3124 **Fax:** Call First
www.southernprocess.com **email:** jim@southernprocess.com

Types of Records Retrieved: Civil, criminal and probate courts; Federal courts; Real Estate

Local Retrieval Area: TN-Knox

Add'l Information: Established 1993. Normal turnaround time- 48 hours or less; same day service for an add'l fee. Projects billed by number of names searched. Will invoice attorneys only. 1st project may require prepayment. They are court appointed and bonded for service of process and can also retrieve automobile registration records in TN. They perform service of process.

Southern Research Company

2850 Centenary Blvd, Shreveport, LA 71104
Phone: 888-772-6953; 318-227-9700 **Fax:** 318-424-1801
www.southernresearchinc.com **email:** background@southernresearchinc.com

Types of Records Retrieved: Civil, criminal and probate courts; Federal courts; Real Estate; Tax liens/Judgments; UCC records

Local Retrieval Area: LA-Bossier Parish, Caddo Parish. **Correspondent Relationships:** Louisiana and nationwide.

Add'l Information: Established 1956. Normal turnaround time- same day to 48 hours. Clients are normally billed by the number of names searched per court. Special projects are billed by the hour. 1st project may require prepayment. They specialize in employment & tenant screening, localized court documents & field investigation searches. Since inception the firm has focused on providing premium general investigative & fact finding assignments for diverse clientele throughout the US. A licensed PI in LA. They perform service of process.

Southern Research Enterprises

24 Jeffery Ln NE, Cartersville, GA 30121
Phone: 770-387-9439 **Fax:** 770-387-0664 nena@sre-abstractor.com

Types of Records Retrieved: Civil, criminal and probate courts; Federal courts; Real Estate; Tax liens/Judgments; UCC records, Vital records

Local Retrieval Area: GA-Bartow, Catoosa, Chattooga, Cherokee, Cobb, Coweta, Dade, Dawson, Douglas, Fannin, Floyd, Fulton, Gilmer, Gordon, Lumpkin, Murray, Paulding, Pickens, Walker, Whitfield;. **Correspondent Relationships:** statewide.

Add'l Information: Established 2001. Normal turnaround time- 24-48 hours. Expedited service available. Projects billed by number of names searched. Projects billed by number of records located. Projects are billed by the number of addresses or legal descriptions. 1st project may require prepayment. Will provide monthly billing with proof of estimated cost. Can invoice individual jobs. They specialize in real estate record retrieval, all secure forms from current to 150 years, federal/state tax liens, UCC and judgments. Fast, accurate and reliable; has E&O coverage. Will go the extra mile.

Southern Utah Title Co

44 N Main St #1, Kanab, UT 84741
Phone: 435-644-5891 **Fax:** 435-644-8136
www.titlesearch.net **email:** sutico@xpressweb.com

Types of Records Retrieved: Civil, criminal and probate courts; Real Estate; Tax liens/Judgments; UCC records; Vital records

Local Retrieval Area: UT-Kane

Add'l Information: Established 1948. Normal turnaround time- 1 week or less. Fee basis will vary by the type of project. All projects require prepayment.

Southwest Abstract & Title Co

PO Box 13, 1006 Rankin Ave, Rankin, TX 79778
Phone: 432-693-2242 **Fax:** 432-693-2249

Types of Records Retrieved: Civil courts; Probate courts; Real Estate; Tax liens/Judgments; UCC records **Local Retrieval Area:** TX-Upton

Add'l Information: Established 1915. Normal turnaround time- 2-3 days. Fee basis will vary by the type of project.

Southwest Abstract & Title Co

PO Box 1149, 902 SW D Ave (73501), Lawton, OK 73502
Phone: 405-355-3680 **Fax:** 405-248-1849 swatco@sirinet.net

Types of Records Retrieved: Civil courts; Probate courts; Real Estate; Tax liens/Judgments; UCC records; Vital records

Local Retrieval Area: OK-Comanche

Add'l Information: Normal turnaround time- 2-4 days. Fee basis will vary by the type of project. They specialize in title insurance.

Southwest Abstract & Title Company

PO Box 559, Bowman, ND 58623
Phone: 701-523-2922 **Fax:** 701-523-2922 swabstract1@ndsupernet.com

Types of Records Retrieved: Civil courts; Probate courts; Federal courts; Real Estate; Tax liens/Judgments; UCC records

Local Retrieval Area: ND-Bowman, Slope

Add'l Information: Normal turnaround time- 1-3 days. Projects billed by the hour. 1st project may require prepayment. Prepayment dependant on job. They specialize in abstracting, title search, title insurance and closings. They have 24 years experience in the business.

Southwest Abstract Co Inc

PO Box 1175, Del Rio, TX 78841
Phone: 830-775-8508 **Fax:** 830-775-9183
www.southwestabstract.com **email:** requests@southwestabstract.com

Types of Records Retrieved: Civil courts; Probate courts; Real Estate; Tax liens/Judgments; UCC records; Vital records

Local Retrieval Area: TX-Val Verde

Add'l Information: Established 1910. Normal turnaround time- 2 days. Projects billed by number of names searched. Fee basis will vary by the type of project. All projects require prepayment.

Southwestern Title & Abstract Co

711 E 1st St, Ogallala, NE 69153
Phone: 308-423-2611 **Fax:** 308-284-8319

Types of Records Retrieved: Civil, criminal and probate courts; Real Estate; Tax liens/Judgments; UCC records; Vital records

Local Retrieval Area: NE-Chase, Dundy, Hitchcock, Keith, Red Willow. **Correspondent Relationships:** Perkins, Hayes, Keith counties.

Add'l Information: Established 1969. Normal turnaround time- 2 days. Projects billed by the hour. They accept personal checks. They specialize in title insurance and real estate.

Sparks Searches

1286 S Riverbend Ct, Nixa, MO 65714
Phone: 417-725-4851 **Fax:** 417-725-7765 gjs1286@aol.com

Types of Records Retrieved: Real Estate; Tax liens/Judgments

Local Retrieval Area: MO-Christian, Douglas, Greene, Stone, Taney

Add'l Information: Established 1995. Normal turnaround time- 12-24 hours. Projects billed by number of names searched.

Spearhead Research - On Target Information

116 Taylor's Cove, Buda, TX 78610
Phone: 512-295-7298 **Fax:** 512-295-7308
spearheadresearch@austin.rr.com

Types of Records Retrieved: Civil and criminal courts

Local Retrieval Area: TX-Bexar, Harris, Tarrant, Travis, Williamson. **Correspondent Relationships:** statewide.

Add'l Information: Established 1998. Normal turnaround time- 24 to 48 hours most request results returned. Expedited service available. Projects billed by number of names searched. Invoices are sent monthly with a net 30 days. Research work is done hands-on - very accurate and detailed. Excellent turnaround times. All 254 Texas counties covered by experienced researchers.

Spears & Jones Attorneys

113 S Market St, Benton, AR 72015
Phone: 501-315-5335 **Fax:** 501-315-6475 spearsandjones2@yahoo.com

Types of Records Retrieved: Civil, criminal and probate courts; Real Estate; Tax liens/Judgments; UCC records

Local Retrieval Area: AR-Grant, Saline

Add'l Information: Established 2000. Normal turnaround time- 48-72 hours. Projects billed by number of names searched. 1st project may require prepayment. They also do real estate title searches with tax info and witness closings.

Special Inv Inc

984 Logan St #1, Noblesville, IN 46060
Phone: 317-773-7900 **Fax:** 317-773-3752
www.indianainvestigator.com
email: investigator@indianainvestigator.com

Types of Records Retrieved: Civil and criminal courts, Probate courts; Federal courts; Real Estate; Tax liens/Judgments; UCC & Vital records.

Local Retrieval Area: IN-Boone, Hamilton, Marion

Add'l Information: Established 1996. Normal turnaround time- 3-5 days. Expedited service available. Projects billed by the hour. They specialize in insurance, civil/domestic matters, service of process as well as document retrieval. A licensed PI in IN. They perform service of process.

Special Private Inv Inc

72 Indian Lakes NE, Sparta, MI 49345
Phone: 800-577-3783; 616-887-8574 **Fax:** 616-887-8775
spi@iserv.net

Types of Records Retrieved: Probate courts; Federal courts

Local Retrieval Area: MI-Kent

Add'l Information: Established 1989. Normal turnaround time- 2 days for civil cases and probate. Projects billed by the hour. 1st project may require prepayment. They specialize in vehicle and driver license registrations for the State of Michigan and statewide criminal conviction searches. A licensed PI in MI. They perform service of process.

Specialized Investigations

14530 Delano St, Van Nuys, CA 91411
Phone: 800-714-3728; 818-909-9607 **Fax:** 818-782-3012
www.specialpi.com **email:** si@specialpi.com

Types of Records Retrieved: Civil, criminal and probate courts; Federal courts; Real Estate; Tax liens/Judgments; UCC records; Vital records

Local Retrieval Area: CA-Los Angeles. **Correspondent Relationships:** Kern, Riverside, San Bernardino, San Diego, Santa Barbara, Orange, Ventura counties in California.

Add'l Information: Established 1982. Normal turnaround time- 1-7 working days. Projects billed by number of names searched. Projects billed by the hour. Can charge a flat rate if discussed beforehand. 1st project may require prepayment. Credit cards accepted. Terms: net 30 days. They specialize in insurance fraud, surveillance, background checks, asset searches, trial preparation and skiptracing as well as labor and employment law investigations. A licensed PI in CA. They perform service of process.

Specialty Services

8491 Hospital Dr, PMB 151, Douglasville, GA 30134
Phone: 770-942-8264 **Fax:** 770-942-5355

Types of Records Retrieved: Civil and criminal courts; Federal courts; Real Estate; Tax liens/Judgments; UCC records

Local Retrieval Area: GA-Caroll, Cobb, Coweta, De Kalb, Douglas, Fulton, Paulding. **Correspondent Relationships:** Alabama.

Add'l Information: Established 1991. Normal turnaround time- 24-72 hours. Projects billed by number of names searched. Projects billed by the hour. Billed monthly, due upon receipt (late fees after 30 days). They specialize in record retrieval from county, state and federal courts. Criminal and civil backgrounds for pre-employment screening, litigation support, insurance fraud investigation assistance, asset reports, UCC searches, etc. They perform service of process.

Spectrum Screening Inc

PO Box 685055, Austin, TX 78768-5055
Phone: 800-222-8199; 512-459-2181 **Fax:** 512-459-2182
stacey@spectrumscreening.net

Types of Records Retrieved: Civil and criminal courts; Federal courts; Tax liens/Judgments; UCC records

Local Retrieval Area: TX-Bexar, Collin, Dallas, Denton, Fort Bend, Galveston, Harris, Hays, Tarrant, Travis, Williamson. **Correspondent Relationships:** statewide in TX, GA, MO, VA, NC, TN, AL, AR, KY, CA, CO.

Add'l Information: Established 1992. Normal turnaround time- 24-72 hours depending on the project. Projects billed by number of names searched. 1st project may require prepayment. They specialize in criminal/civil/federal court research.

SPI

5650 S Archer, Chicago, IL 60638 **Phone:** 773-581-1400 **Fax:** 773-581-6900

Types of Records Retrieved: Civil and criminal courts; Federal courts

Local Retrieval Area: IL-Cook, DuPage, Will. **Correspondents:** nationwide

Add'l Information: Established 1983. Normal turnaround time- 24-48 hours. Projects billed by number of names searched. Fees negotiated with volume. 1st project may require prepayment. Security Professionals Inc specialize in pre-employment screening, Illinois drivers' abstracts, social security verification, criminal background checks and workers' compensation checks. They perform service of process.

SPI

72 Indian Lakes Rd, Sparta, MI 49345
Phone: 800-577-3783; 616-887-5261 **Fax:** 616-887-8775 spi@iserv.net

Types of Records Retrieved: Probate courts; Federal courts

Local Retrieval Area: MI-Kent

Add'l Information: Established 1990. 1st project may require prepayment. They also provide court filings, photocopying as well as computer searches of MI Sec of State records. A licensed PI in MI. They perform service of process.

Spiller Abstract

122 E Belknap, PO Box I, Jacksboro, TX 76458
Phone: 940-567-2271 **Fax:** 940-567-3999

Types of Records Retrieved: Civil courts; Probate courts; Real Estate; Tax liens/Judgments; UCC records

Local Retrieval Area: TX-Jack

Add'l Information: Established 1888. Normal turnaround time- 3 days to 1 week. Fees vary by project. They specialize in real estate records.

Spink County Abstract

502 N Main St, Redfield, SD 57469 **Phone:** 605-472-2011

Types of Records Retrieved: Real Estate; Tax liens/judgements

Local Retrieval Area: SD-Spink

Add'l Information: 1st project may require prepayment. They specialize in real estate.

Springdale Realty

PO Box 40, Ord, NE 68862
Phone: 308-728-3569 **Fax:** 308-728-3587

Types of Records Retrieved: Real estate; Tax liens/Judgments

Local Retrieval Area: NE-Valley

Add'l Information: Established 2001. 1st project may require prepayment. They specialize in real estate.

Spyglass Pre-Employment Specialist

PO Box 528499, Chicago, IL 60652-8499
Phone: 773-581-0180 **Fax:** 773-581-0181
spyglasspreemployment@comcast.net

Types of Records Retrieved: Civil, criminal and probate courts; Federal courts; Real Estate; Tax liens/Judgments; UCC records; Vital records

Local Retrieval Area: IL-Cook, Du Page, Kane, Lake, Will. **Correspondent Relationships:** surrounding counties.

Add'l Information: Established 1992. Normal turnaround time- 24-48 hours. Projects billed by number of names searched. They will bill monthly. They are a licensed detective agency. They take a one on one relationship with each client. No client is to small or big for us. A licensed PI in IL. They perform service of process.

SRA Inv Inc

2372 Hwy 80 W #B, Jackson, MS 39204
Phone: 800-530-7115 x4197; 228-214-9927 **Fax:** 228-214-9978
srainves@sra-inc.net

Types of Records Retrieved: Civil and criminal courts

Local Retrieval Area: MS-George, Hancock, Harrison, Jackson, Pearl River, Stone

Add'l Information: Established 2000. All projects require prepayment. They also provide court filings, subpoena preparation, skiptracing, and private investigations. They perform service of process.

SRS Private Inv Inc

52 Mission Cir #122, PMB 152, Santa Rosa, CA 95409
Phone: 707-537-1091 **Fax:** 707-537-1095 srspi@prodigy.net

Types of Records Retrieved: Civil, criminal and probate courts; Real Estate; Tax liens/Judgments; UCC records; Vital records

Local Retrieval Area: CA-Sonoma

Add'l Information: Established 1980. Normal turnaround time- 3 days. Expedited service available. Projects billed by the hour. 1st project may require prepayment. Credit cards accepted. They specialize in full range investigative services that include backgrounds, locates, asset searches, security surveys, witness statements and much more. A licensed PI in CA. They perform service of process.

SRT Investigations

PO Box 35403, Tulsa, OK 74153
Phone: 800-499-0472; 918-481-6045 **Fax:** 918-491-9774
srtinv@msn.com

Types of Records Retrieved: Civil, criminal and probate courts; Federal courts; Real Estate; Tax liens/Judgments; UCC records

Local Retrieval Area: OK-Creek, Logan, Muskogee, Nowata, Oklahoma, Okmulgee, Osage, Rogers, Tulsa, Wagoner, Washington. **Correspondent Relationships:** statewide.

Add'l Information: Established 1987. Normal turnaround time- 24 hours. Projects billed by number of names searched. Projects billed by the hour. 1st project may require prepayment. They specialize in record searches, title searches, chain of owner searches. Offer a 24 hour turnaround time on most searches. A licensed PI in OK.

St Croix Valley Title Services Inc

109 N Main St, PO Box 750, River Falls, WI 54022
Phone: 715-425-1519 **Fax:** 715-425-2569

Types of Records Retrieved: Civil, criminal and probate courts; Real Estate; Tax liens/Judgments; UCC records

Local Retrieval Area: WI-Pierce, St. Croix

Add'l Information: Normal turnaround time- 1-2 days. Fee basis varies by type of transaction. 1st project may require prepayment.

St Joseph County Abstract Office Inc

PO Box 217, Centreville, MI 49032
Phone: 269-467-6075 **Fax:** 269-467-4314

Types of Records Retrieved: Civil, criminal and probate courts; Real Estate; Tax liens/Judgments; UCC records; Vital records

Local Retrieval Area: MI-Cass, St. Joseph

Add'l Information: Normal turnaround time- 3 days. Projects billed by the hour. They specialize in title and real estate.

St Paul Abstract & Title

710 Howard Ave, St Paul, NE 68873
Phone: 308-754-4922 **Fax:** 308-754-4922 sdecamp@cornhusker.net

Types of Records Retrieved: Probate courts; Federal courts; Real Estate; Tax liens/Judgments

Local Retrieval Area: NE-Adams, Buffalo, Hall, Howard

Add'l Information: Established 1991. Normal turnaround time- 24-48 hours. Bill per search jobs. All projects are billed and payable within 2 weeks.

ST Sayers & MS Chiarkas

250 Market St, Sunbury, PA 17801
Phone: 570-286-9831 **Fax:** 570-286-8774

Types of Records Retrieved: Civil, criminal and probate courts; Real Estate; Tax liens/Judgments

Local Retrieval Area: PA-Montour, Northumberland, Union. **Correspondent Relationships:** Pennsylvania.

Add'l Information: Established 1975. Normal turnaround time- 24-48 hours. Projects billed by number of names searched. Charges vary depending on type of search. All searches are insured against errors and omissions.

St Vrain Resources

11939 Manchester Rd #264, St Louis, MO 63131
Phone: 314-645-1710 **Fax:** 314-645-1707

Types of Records Retrieved: Civil, criminal and probate courts; Federal courts; Real Estate; Tax liens/Judgments; Vital records

Local Retrieval Area: MO-Jefferson, Franklin, St. Louis, St. Louis City, St Charles

Add'l Information: Established 1984. Normal turnaround time- 24-72 hours. Projects billed by the hour. Charge by the mile also. 1st project may require prepayment. They specialize in conducting investigation, research and documentation, especially US military records and federal district court of appeals searches. A licensed PI in MO. They perform service of process.

Stafford County Abstract & Title Co

PO Box 265, 205 E 4th Ave, St John, KS 67576
Phone: 620-549-3579 **Fax:** 620-549-6594

Types of Records Retrieved: Civil courts; Probate courts; Real Estate; Tax liens/Judgments; UCC records; Vital records

Local Retrieval Area: KS-Stafford

Add'l Information: Established 1933. Normal turnaround time- up to 1 week. Projects billed by the hour. Payment due at time of completion of work. They specialize in courthouse and record searches.

Jamie D Stallings

1104 Pebble Creek Court East, Antioch, TN 37013
Phone: 615-781-2323 **Fax:** 615-781-6821
mrsstallings@aol.com

Types of Records Retrieved: Federal courts; Real Estate; Tax liens/Judgments; UCC records

Local Retrieval Area: TN-Anderson, Carroll, Cheatham, Davidson, Dickson, Hamilton, Knox, Montgomery, Robertson, Rutherford, Shelby, Sumner, Washington, Williamson, Wilson. **Correspondents:** statewide.

Add'l Information: Established 1997. Normal turnaround time- 24-48 hours. Projects billed by number of names searched. Net 30 day invoicing. They have over 12 years experience in public records and the title industry. They offer quick turnarounds, typed reports and optional e-mailed reports.

Stan Duby Investigations

PO Box 208, Salinas, CA 93902
Phone: 800-953-0435; 831-675-0435 **Fax:** 831-675-8552
pvti@sbcglobal.net

Types of Records Retrieved: Civil, criminal and probate courts; Tax liens/Judgments; UCC records; Vital records

Local Retrieval Area: CA-Monterey, San Benito, Santa Cruz. **Correspondent Relationships:** nationwide.

Add'l Information: Established 1992. Normal turnaround time- 24-48 hours. Projects billed by number of names searched. 1st project may require prepayment. Payments are net 20 days. They are licensed investigators specializing in background checks and locates. A licensed PI in CA. They perform service of process.

Stanton Co Abstract

PO Box 86, Stanton, NE 68779
Phone: 402-439-2142 **Fax:** 402-439-2145

Types of Records Retrieved: Civil, criminal and probate courts; Real Estate; Tax liens/Judgments; UCC records; Vital records

Local Retrieval Area: NE-Madison, Pierce, Stanton

Add'l Information: Established 1981. Normal turnaround time- 1-3 days. Fee basis is flat rate plus per record and mileage. Payment due upon receipt of invoice. They specialize in title insurance, title searches, abstracts, closings and escrows.

Star Group Services

2058 N Mills Ave #620, Claremont, CA 91711
Phone: 909-625-8810 **Fax:** 951-233-5366
www.stargroupservices.com **email:** lepage21@aol.com

Types of Records Retrieved: Civil and criminal courts; Federal Courts; Real Estate; Tax liens/Judgments; UCC records

Local Retrieval Area: CA-Los Angeles, Orange, San Bernardino. **Correspondent Relationships:** statewide.

Add'l Information: Established 2004. Normal turnaround time- 7-10 days. Expedited service available. Projects billed by the hour. All projects require prepayment. Credit cards accepted. They are a full service private investigation firm. A licensed PI in CA.

Star Security & Inv

7034 Indianapolis Blvd, Hammond, IN 46324
Phone: 219-554-0100 **Fax:** 219-554-0101
www.starsecurity.org **email:** staray@aol.com

Types of Records Retrieved: Civil and criminal courts; Federal courts; Real Estate; Tax liens/Judgments; UCC records; Vital records

Local Retrieval Area: IN-Jasper, Lake, La Porte, Newton, Porter

Add'l Information: Established 1989. Normal turnaround time- 2-3 days. Expedited service available. Fees vary. Credit cards accepted. Will invoice. A licensed PI in IN. They perform service of process.

Starke County Abstract Title & Guaranty

14 E Washington St, Knox, IN 46534
Phone: 574-772-3733 **Fax:** 574-772-7603

Types of Records Retrieved: Civil, criminal and probate courts; Real Estate; Tax liens/Judgments; UCC records **Local Retrieval Area:** IN-Starke

Add'l Information: Established 1876. Normal turnaround time- 3-5 days. Fee basis will vary by type of project. They specialize in record searching.

State Capital Title & Abstract Co

830 Bear Tavern Rd, Trenton, NJ 08628-1020
Phone: 800-876-8994; 609-771-4301 **Fax:** 609-771-0821
www.statecapital.net **email:** info@statecapital.net

Types of Records Retrieved: Federal Courts

Local Retrieval Area: NJ-Mercer

Add'l Information: Established 1925. Normal turnaround time- 24-48 hours. Will invoice monthly. They are the oldest and largest provider of certified corporate searches in NJ. They provide full filing services in Trenton and comprehensive foreclosure services.

State Information Bureau

842 E Park Ave #B, Tallahassee, FL 32301
Phone: 800-881-1742; 850-561-3990 **Fax:** 800-948-1543; 850-561-3995
www.stateinformationbureau.com **email:** armadillo@nxus.com

Types of Records Retrieved: Civil, criminal and probate courts; Federal courts; Real Estate; Tax liens/Judgments; UCC records

Local Retrieval Area: FL-Gadsden, Jefferson, Leon, Wakulla. **Correspondent Relationships:** major counties in Florida.

Add'l Information: Established 1986. Normal turnaround time- 24-48 hours for Leon County. Fee basis will vary by type of project. 1st project may require prepayment. They are a licensed private investigative agency that specializes in obtaining information from state records. Licensed PI in FL.

Statewide Recovery Inc

PO Box 6513, Great Falls, MT 59406
Phone: 406-761-4843 **Fax:** 406-452-1365 repoplus@montana.com

Types of Records Retrieved: Civil and criminal courts

Local Retrieval Area: MT-Cascade, Chouteau, Flathead, Glacier, Hill, Pondera, Teton, Toole

Add'l Information: Established 2994. All projects require prepayment. They also provide court filings, photocopying, and collections/repossessions. They perform service of process.

Statewide Recovery Inc

PO Box 6513, Great Falls, MT 59406
Phone: 406-761-4843 **Fax:** 406-452-1365

Types of Records Retrieved: Civil, criminal and probate courts; Federal District courts; Real Estate; Tax liens/Judgments; UCC & Vital records

Local Retrieval Area: MT-Cascade, Lewis & Clark

Add'l Information: Established 1987. Normal turnaround time- 3-5 days. Expedited service available. Projects billed by number of names searched. Projects billed by number of records located. Projects billed by the hour. 1st project may require prepayment. They perform service of process.

Staton Abstract & Title Co

PO Box 168, 516 Washington St, Chillicothe, MO 64601
Phone: 660-646-1421 **Fax:** 660-646-1441

Types of Records Retrieved: Civil courts; Probate courts; Real Estate; Tax liens/Judgments; UCC records; Vital records

Local Retrieval Area: MO-Livingston

Add'l Information: Established 1890. Normal turnaround time- 3 days. Fee basis varies by type of transaction.

Steele County Abstract Co

PO Box 413, 125 W Bridge St, Owatonna, MN 55060
Phone: 507-451-6487 **Fax:** 507-444-6262

Types of Records Retrieved: Civil and criminal courts; Real Estate; Tax liens/Judgments; UCC records

Local Retrieval Area: MN-Steele

Add'l Information: Established 1984. Normal turnaround time- 4 days. Projects billed by number of names searched. 1st project may require prepayment.

Steele Investigation Agency

PO Box 1635, Bradenton, FL 34206-1635
Phone: 941-758-5890 **Fax:** 941-755-1100 sia@fali.com

Types of Records Retrieved: Civil, criminal and probate courts; Real Estate; Tax liens/Judgments; UCC records; Vital records

Local Retrieval Area: FL-Manatee, Sarasota. **Correspondent Relationships:** nationwide.

Add'l Information: Established 1981. Normal turnaround time- 3 days. Expedited service available. Projects billed by the hour. 1st project may require prepayment. They specialize in online Florida records, and are a full service investigative agency including, but not limited to asset location, criminal, civil, background, video, photograph, missing persons and surveillance. A licensed PI in FL. They perform service of process.

Steelman Abstracting Co

PO Box 544, Salem, MO 65560
Phone: 573-729-6183 **Fax:** 573-729-1042
steelabs@fident.com

Types of Records Retrieved: Civil courts; Probate courts; Real Estate; Tax liens/Judgments

Local Retrieval Area: MO-Dent

Add'l Information: Normal turnaround time- 2 weeks. Projects billed by number of records located. 1st project may require prepayment. They specialize in title insurance.

Stehlik Law Office

653 G St, Pawnee City, NE 68420
Phone: 402-852-2973 **Fax:** 402-852-2940
www.stehliklaw.com **email:** stehliklaw@stehliklaw.com

Types of Records Retrieved: Civil, criminal and probate courts; Real Estate; Tax liens/Judgments; UCC records

Local Retrieval Area: NE-Pawnee

Add'l Information: Established 1971. Normal turnaround time- 24 hours. Projects billed by the hour. Personal checks are accepted. They specialize in general law and abstracting.

Stephens County Abstract

100 N Baylor, Cook Building, Breckenridge, TX 76424
Phone: 254-559-9089 **Fax:** 254-559-8935

Types of Records Retrieved: Real Estate; Tax liens/judgments; UCC records

Local Retrieval Area: TX-Stephens

Add'l Information: Established 1895. Normal turnaround time- 2 days. Fee basis will vary by the type of project. All projects require prepayment.

Stephens County Abstract Co

919 W Main St, Duncan, OK 73533
Phone: 580-255-2525 **Fax:** 580-255-3844

Types of Records Retrieved: Civil courts; Probate courts; Real Estate; Tax liens/Judgments; UCC records

Local Retrieval Area: OK-Stephens

Add'l Information: Established 1907. Normal turnaround time- 4-5 days. Fee basis is per page and time. Payment due when service is delivered.

Pat Stephens

605 Agnew, Bonham, TX 75418
Phone: 903-583-5215 **Fax:** 903-640-0206

Types of Records Retrieved: Real Estate; Tax liens/Judgments

Local Retrieval Area: OK-Bryan; TX-Collin, Fannin, Grayson, Hunt, Lamar. **Correspondent Relationships:** OK, TX.

Add'l Information: Normal turnaround time- 2-3 days. Projects billed by number of names searched. Projects billed by number of records located. She specializes in abstracting deeds and also 50 year title commercial searches and foreclosure sale documents.

Sterling Pacific Inv Ltd

794 Fort St, PO Box 38033, Victoria, BC V8W 3N2
Phone: 250-652-0541 **Fax:** 250-652-0851
www.sterlingpacificinv.bc.ca **email:** spi@pacificcoast.net

Types of Records Retrieved: Civil, criminal and probate courts

Local Retrieval Area: CANADA-British Columbia. **Correspondent Relationships:** across Canada.

Add'l Information: Established 1988. Projects billed by the hour. 1st project may require prepayment. They specialize in court record retrieval and insurance claims in Victoria and the Vancouver Island area. A licensed PI in British Columbia. They perform service of process.

Sterling Research

14303 Richard Walker Blvd, Austin, TX 78728
Phone: 512-670-9334 **Fax:** 512-670-9334 grocamora@austin.rr.com

Types of Records Retrieved: Civil, criminal and probate courts; Federal courts; Real Estate; Tax liens/Judgments; UCC records; Vital records

Local Retrieval Area: TX-Bell, Travis, Williamson. **Correspondent Relationships:** statewide.

Add'l Information: Established 2002. Normal turnaround time- 24-48 hours. Projects billed by number of names searched. 1st project may require prepayment. They specialize in UCCs, fixtures, State & Federal tax liens, judgments, civil, criminal, bankruptcy, vital statistics, driving records, corporate and UCC fillings.

Sterling Title Co

609 4th St, PO Box 2, Sterling City, TX 76951
Phone: 325-378-2405 **Fax:** 325-378-2405 sharicope@aol.com

Types of Records Retrieved: Probate courts; Real Estate; Tax liens/Judgments; UCC records

Local Retrieval Area: TX-Sterling

Add'l Information: Established 1992. Normal turnaround time- 2-3 days. Projects billed by number of names searched. Projects billed by the hour. All projects require prepayment.

Stevens County Title

PO Box 349, 280 S Oak St, Colville, WA 99114
Phone: 509-684-4589 **Fax:** 509-684-5448

Types of Records Retrieved: Civil, criminal and probate courts; Real Estate; Tax liens/Judgments; UCC records

Local Retrieval Area: WA-Stevens

Add'l Information: Normal turnaround time- 24-48 hours. Projects billed by the hour. 1st project may require prepayment. They specialize in title searches.

Stewart & Associates Inc

308 W State St, Stewart Sq #175, Rockford, IL 61101
Phone: 800-442-3807; 815-235-3807 **Fax:** 815-235-1290
www.bwstewart.com **email:** brians@bwstewart.com

Types of Records Retrieved: Civil, criminal and probate courts; Federal courts; Real Estate; Tax liens/Judgments; UCC records; Vital records

Local Retrieval Area: IL-Boone, Carroll, De Kalb, JoDaviess, Lee, Ogle, Stephenson, Whiteside, Winnebago; WI-Green, Rock. **Correspondent Relationships:** statewide.

Add'l Information: Established 1987. Normal turnaround time- 1-2 business days. Projects billed by number of names searched. Projects billed by number of records located. Projects billed by the hour. Fees negotiated with volume. 1st project may require prepayment. Credit cards accepted. They are an Illinois, Iowa, and Wisconsin licensed private detective agency that specializes in investigative services, records and background services. A licensed PI in IL, IA, WI. They perform service of process.

Stewart Title of Arkansas

200 E Central, Bentonville, AR 72712
Phone: 479-273-2111 **Fax:** 479-273-9247
www.stewart.com **email:** jay.hubert@stewart.com

Types of Records Retrieved: Civil courts; Probate courts; Real Estate; Tax liens/Judgments; UCC records

Local Retrieval Area: AR-Benton, Washington

Add'l Information: Established 1893. Normal turnaround time- 3 days for UCC and taxes and 5 days for real estate. Projects billed by the hour. Flat fee for closing. All projects require prepayments or down payments. They specialize in title insurance and escrow services to include 1099's.

Stewart Title of Midland Inc

206 N Main St, Midland, TX 79701
Phone: 432-687-3355 **Fax:** 432-687-3358
www.stewartmidland.com **email:** chejones@stewart.com

Types of Records Retrieved: Civil courts; Probate courts; Federal courts; Real Estate

Local Retrieval Area: TX-Culberson, Loving, Martin, Midland, Reagan, Reeves, Winkler

Add'l Information: Established 1986. Normal turnaround time- variable depending on project. Projects billed by number of names searched. Projects billed by number of records located. Projects billed by the hour. 1st project may require prepayment. They will also invoice. Personal checks are accepted. They specialize in title examinations, mineral take off and name searches, abstracts and title insurance.

Stillwater Abstract

PO Box 806, 21 N 4th St, Columbus, MT 59019
Phone: 406-322-5216 **Fax:** 406-322-4465

Types of Records Retrieved: Civil courts; Probate courts; Real Estate; Tax liens/Judgments; UCC records **Local Retrieval Area:** MT-Stillwater

Add'l Information: Normal turnaround time- 2-3 days. Fee basis depends on the project.

Donna Stovall

28 Solitaire Rd, Rocky Point, NY 11778
Phone: 631-744-5834 **Fax:** 631-744-9379 Jett1005@aol.com

Types of Records Retrieved: Civil and criminal courts; Real Estate; Tax liens/Judgments; UCC records

Local Retrieval Area: NY-Suffolk

Add'l Information: Established 1986. Normal turnaround time- 24-48 hours. Fee basis will vary by type of project. 1st project may require prepayment. Will bill monthly. She also does judgment searches. They perform service of process.

Strander Abstract Inc

PO Box 622, Crookston, MN 56716
Phone: 218-281-1191 **Fax:** 218-281-3212 strander@rrv.net

Types of Records Retrieved: Civil courts; Real Estate; Tax liens/Judgments; UCC records **Local Retrieval Area:** MN-Polk

Add'l Information: Established 1886. Normal turnaround time- 1 week. Projects billed by number of names searched. All projects require prepayment.

Street Abstract Co

PO Box 306, 118 N Main, Yates Center, KS 66783
Phone: 620-625-2421 **Fax:** 620-625-3631

Types of Records Retrieved: Civil, criminal and probate courts; Real Estate; Tax liens/Judgments; UCC records

Local Retrieval Area: KS-Allen, Coffey, Greenwood, Neosho, Wilson, Woodson

Add'l Information: Established 1964. Normal turnaround time- 48 hours. Fee basis varies by type of transaction. 1st project may require prepayment.

Street Legal Research

235 W Rio Rd, Lincoln, NE 68505-2561
Phone: 402-476-9505 **Fax:** 402-476-9506 lo22150@inebraska.com

Types of Records Retrieved: Civil, criminal and probate courts; Federal courts; Vital records

Local Retrieval Area: NE-Cass, Douglas, Lancaster. **Correspondent Relationships:** statewide.

Add'l Information: Established 2000. Normal turnaround time- 24-48 hours or less. Projects billed by number of names searched. Billing statement done monthly. They offer confidential searching.

Marge Strein

PO Box 132, Taylor, PA 18517
Phone: 570-457-3939 **Fax:** 570-457-3939 marg25@netscape.com

Types of Records Retrieved: Real Estate; Tax liens/Judgments.

Local Retrieval Area: PA-Lackawanna, Luzerne

Add'l Information: Normal turnaround time- 24-48 hours. 1st project may require prepayment. Her database includes real estate searches include assignments, deed copies, mortgages, ownership verification or info extracted from deed in the Lackawanna County area of PA. Also, she specializes in civil/criminal for state, county and federal records.

Strother-Wilbourn Land Title Co

308 E Market Ave, Searcy, AR 72143
Phone: 501-268-8273 **Fax:** 501-268-3275
www.strotherwilbourn.com **email:** wtitle@cablelynx.com

Types of Records Retrieved: Civil courts; Probate courts; Real Estate; Tax liens/Judgments; UCC records

Local Retrieval Area: AR-White

Add'l Information: Established 1918. Normal turnaround time- 5-10 days. Fee basis will vary by the type of project. They specialize in title insurance.

Stutsman County Abstract

223 3rd Ave SW, Jamestown, ND 58401
Phone: 701-252-4870 **Fax:** 701-252-4960 abstract@daktel.com

Types of Records Retrieved: Real Estate; Tax liens/judgments; UCC records

Local Retrieval Area: ND-La Moure, Stutsman. **Correspondent Relationships:** working relationship with all ND abstract companies.

Add'l Information: Established 1901. Normal turnaround time- 2-5 days. Fee basis will vary by type of project. 1st project may require prepayment.

Suburban Record Research

12 Main St, Dover, MA 02030
Phone: 617-536-3486 **Fax:** 508-785-2852

Types of Records Retrieved: Civil, criminal and probate courts; Federal courts; Real Estate; Tax liens/Judgments; UCC records

Local Retrieval Area: MA-Essex, Middlesex, Norfolk, Suffolk, Worcester

Add'l Information: Established 1982. Normal turnaround time- 24-48 hours. Expedited service available. Projects billed by number of names searched. They specialize in real estate, current owner, mortgage and assignment searches and document retrieval as well as UCC and court record searches. They are fully insured.

Sugarbaker Investigations

PO Box 15498, Brooksville, FL 34604
Phone: 800-720-2567; 352-684-9388 **Fax:** 800-720-2567; 352-684-9173
www.sugarb.com **email:** sugarbaker@bellsouth.net

Types of Records Retrieved: Civil, criminal and probate courts; Federal courts; UCC records; Vital records

Local Retrieval Area: FL-Broward, Dade, Hernando, Hillsborough, Manatee, Marion, Orange, Pasco, Pinellas, Polk, Sarasota, Seminole, Volusia. **Correspondent Relationships:** nationwide.

Add'l Information: Established 1985. Normal turnaround time- 24-48 hours. Projects billed by the hour. 1st project may require prepayment. They specialize in automobile product liability and general litigation support. They have been in business for 19 years. They retrieve records from all states in the USA, also in Canada. A licensed PI in FL.

Sullivan County Abstract Co

217 E 3rd St, Milan, MO 63556
Phone: 660-265-3744 **Fax:** 660-265-4908 scac@nemr.net

Types of Records Retrieved: Civil, criminal and probate courts; Federal courts; Real Estate; Tax liens/Judgments; UCC records; Vital records

Local Retrieval Area: MO-Sullivan. **Correspondent Relationships:** Putnam, Grundy, Linn, Adair counties.

Add'l Information: Established 1975. Normal turnaround time- 2 days. Fee basis will vary by the type of project. All projects require prepayment. They specialize in title insurance.

SumData

1203 Ranch Rd, McPherson, KS 67460
Phone: 620-241-5448 **Fax:** 620-241-5448
sumdata@southwind.net

Types of Records Retrieved: Civil and criminal courts; Federal courts; Probate courts; Real Estate; Tax liens/Judgments; UCC records; Vital records

Local Retrieval Area: KS-Harvey, Marion, McPherson, Reno, Saline

Add'l Information: Established 2004. Normal turnaround time- 24-48 hours. Projects billed by number of names searched. 1st project may require prepayment. They specialize in retrieval of public real estate records, UCC's, judgments/tax liens & bankruptcy in Central Kansas. Criminal background searches in McPherson & Saline County, KS.

Summit Documents

PO Box 1603, Owensboro, KY 42301
Phone: 270-281-5406 **Fax:** 270-281-5406

Types of Records Retrieved: Civil, criminal and probate courts; Federal courts; Real Estate; Tax liens/Judgments; UCC records; Vital records

Local Retrieval Area: IN-Perry, Spencer, Warrick; KY-Daviess, Hancock, Henderson, Ohio, Webster

Add'l Information: Established 1995. Normal turnaround time- 24-48 hours. Projects billed by number of names searched. Projects billed by the hour. They specialize in local court and KY Federal Court record retrieval in the Owensboro area, both Kentucky and Indiana; offers a variety of investigative services as well.

Sumpter & Associates LLC

4425-C Treat Blvd #298, Concord, CA 94521
Phone: 925-671-7755 **Fax:** 925-671-2095
www.sumpterassociates.com **email:** sales@sumpterassociates.com

Types of Records Retrieved: Civil and criminal courts; Real Estate; Tax liens/Judgments; UCC records; Vital records

Local Retrieval Area: CA-Alameda, Contra Costa, Solano; WA-King, Snohomish. **Correspondent Relationships:** Oregon, Washington

Add'l Information: Established 2001. Normal turnaround time- 24-48 hours. Projects billed by number of names searched. They have over 16 years in the public record search and retrival business. They also provide corporate, ficititious name, and MVR records.

Sunrise Title Co

550E 200 N #118-3, Roosevelt, UT 84066
Phone: 800-244-1644; 435-722-2257 **Fax:** 435-722-2258

Types of Records Retrieved: Civil, criminal and probate courts; Real Estate; Tax liens/Judgments; UCC records; Vital records

Local Retrieval Area: UT-Duchesne, Uintah

Add'l Information: Normal turnaround time- 1 week to 10 days for mineral searches and 3 days for others. Projects billed by the hour. They specialize in real estate.

Sunshine Research Inc

1501 S Pinellas Ave #3H, Tarpon Springs, FL 34689
Phone: 888-786-1242; 727-939-9039 **Fax:** 888-785-7451; 727-934-2939
www.sunshineresearch.com **email:** info@sunshineresearch.com

Types of Records Retrieved: Civil and criminal courts; Federal District courts; UCC records

Local Retrieval Area: FL-Hillsborough, Pasco, Pinellas, Manatee. **Correspondent Relationships:** LA-Jefferson, Orleans; NY-Kings, Queens, Richmond, Suffolk, Nassau, New York City.

Add'l Information: Established 1997. Normal turnaround time- 24 hours. Projects billed by number of names searched. 1st project may require prepayment. Credit cards accepted. They are a fully Internet-based, full-service pre-employment screening firm. They offer nationwide searches. A licensed PI in FL.

Sunstate Research Associates Inc

143 Whetherbine Way W, Tallahassee, FL 32301
Phone: 800-621-7234; **Fax:** 850-656-5454

Types of Records Retrieved: Civil courts; Federal courts; Tax liens/Judgments; UCC records

Local Retrieval Area: FL-Gadsden, Jefferson, Leon, Wakulla. **Correspondent Relationships:** Pinellas and Hillsborough counties.

Add'l Information: Established 1990. Normal turnaround time- same or next day for Secretary of State; 1-3 days for remainder of their service area. Projects billed by number of names searched. 1st project may require prepayment. Personal checks are accepted. They specialize in filing and retrieval of UCC documents from the FL Secured Transaction Registry and corporate documents from the Florida Secretary of State. They also search federal and state tax liens and judgment files with the SOS.

Super Search Inc

1245 Hurstview Dr #209, Hurst, TX 76053
Phone: 800-687-5553; 817-268-3224 **Fax:** 800-687-5554; 817-285-9956
www.callsupersearch.com **email:** eturner@callsupersearch.com

Types of Records Retrieved: Civil, criminal and probate courts; Federal courts; Real Estate; Tax liens/Judgments; UCC records

Local Retrieval Area: TX-Collin, Dallas, Denton, Ellis, Erath, Grayson, Hood, Johnson, Parker, Somervell, Tarrant, Wise. **Correspondent Relationships:** statewide.

Add'l Information: Established 1990. Normal turnaround time- 1-2 days. Projects billed by number of names searched. 1st project may require prepayment. Credit cards accepted. They specialize in court research, including retrieval from the Federal Records Center serving Texas, Oklahoma, Arkansas and Louisiana. They will file UCC and real estate documents in Dallas, Tarrant, Collin and Denton counties, TX. A licensed PI in TX. They perform service of process.

Superior Information Services, LLC

PO Box 8787, Trenton, NJ 08650-0787
Phone: 800-848-0489; 609-883-7000 **Fax:** 609-883-1413
www.superiorinfo.com **email:** lmartin@superiorinfo.com

Types of Records Retrieved: Civil courts; Federal courts; Tax liens/Judgments; UCC records

Local Retrieval Area: NJ-all counties

Add'l Information: Established 1987. Normal turnaround time- 3-5 business days depending on location. Service fee by case or file. Credit cards accepted. In addition to their online judgment database, Superior provides direct hands-on access to case documents in all federal and state courts located in NJ, and UCC documents filed at the state & county levels in NJ. They also offer NJ corporate services.

Superior Process Svc

409 E Summit Ave, Electra, TX 76360
Phone: 888-230-2663; 940-495-2663 glenthe5@aol.com

Types of Records Retrieved: Civil courts, Probate courts; Federal courts; Real Estate; Tax liens/Judgments; Vital records.

Local Retrieval Area: TX-Archer, Baylor, Clay, Foard, Hardeman, Haskell, Jack, Knox, Montague, Throckmorton, Wichita, Wilbarger. **Correspondent Relationships:** statewide in Texas.

Add'l Information: Established 1990. Normal turnaround time- 2-4 days. Expedited service available. Projects billed by number of names searched. 1st project may require prepayment. They perform service of process.

Superior Subpoena Service

126 S Wood Ave, PO Box 2002 (07036), Linden, NJ 07036
Phone: 800-862-5660; 908-862-5660 **Fax:** 908-486-0332

Types of Records Retrieved: Civil, criminal and probate courts; Federal courts; Real Estate; Tax liens/Judgments; UCC records

Local Retrieval Area: NJ-Essex, Hudson, Middlesex, Union. **Correspondent Relationships:** New Jersey.

Add'l Information: Established 1978. Normal turnaround time- variable depending on project. Expedited service available. Projects billed by the hour. Billed by job also. 1st project may require prepayment. They can access almost all records in most of NJ. The principle of the company is also a constable. They also do service of process, summons & complaints, subpeonas, etc. They perform service of process.

Superior Title & Abstract

PO Box 766, Iron Mountain, MI 49801-0766
Phone: 906-774-9010 **Fax:** 906-774-8994
www.superiortitleabstract.com **email:** sta@superiortitleabstract.com

Types of Records Retrieved: Civil and criminal courts; Real Estate; Tax liens/Judgments; UCC records

Local Retrieval Area: MI-Dickinson, Menominee; WI-Florence, Marinette. **Correspondents:** all counties in the Michigan upper penisula.

Add'l Information: Established 1975. Normal turnaround time- 2 days. Projects billed by number of names searched. Projects billed by number of records located. Projects billed by the hour. The specialize in real estate and title work. Phone for the Marinette office is 715-735-6100; phone for Menominee office is 706-864-0052.

Surette Investigations

PO Box 116, Litchfield, ME 04350
Phone: 207-268-3419 **Fax:** 207-268-3420
kevin@suretteinvestigations.com

Types of Records Retrieved: Civil, criminal and probate courts; Real Estate; Tax liens/Judgments; UCC records; Vital records

Local Retrieval Area: ME-Androscoggin, Kennebec, Lincoln, Sagadahoc; MA-Essex, Middlesex. **Correspondent Relationships:** Massachusetts and New Hampshire.

Add'l Information: Established 1992. Normal turnaround time- 24-48 hours. Expedited service available. Projects billed by number of names searched. Flat rate. 1st project may require prepayment. They specialize in full service security consulting and investigations. A licensed PI in ME, MA, NH. They perform service of process.

Surety Title Co

PO Box 551, 523 Central Av, New Rockford, ND 58356
Phone: 701-947-2446 **Fax:** 701-947-2443

Types of Records Retrieved: Civil courts; Probate courts; Real Estate; Tax liens/Judgments; UCC records

Local Retrieval Area: ND-Benson, Eddy, Griggs

Add'l Information: Established 1925. Normal turnaround time- 5 days. Fee basis will vary by the type of project. Payment is based on individual basis.

Surety Title Co of Ballinger

PO Box 31, 803 Hutchings, Ballinger, TX 76821-0031
Phone: 325-365-5713 **Fax:** 325-365-3897

Types of Records Retrieved: Civil, criminal and probate courts; Real Estate; Tax liens/Judgments; UCC records; Vital records

Local Retrieval Area: TX-Runnels. **Correspondent Relationships:** add'l offices in Kendall, San Angelo, San Saba, Kimble, Real, Concho, Tom Green counties.

Add'l Information: Normal turnaround time- 1-2 days. Fee basis will vary by the type of project. 1st project may require prepayment.

Surety Title Co of Eden

PO Box 1328, 113 Market St, Eden, TX 76837-1328
Phone: 325-869-7081 **Fax:** 325-869-5426 info@suretytitle.com

Types of Records Retrieved: Civil, criminal and probate courts; Real Estate; Tax liens/Judgments; UCC records; Vital records

Local Retrieval Area: TX-Concho. **Correspondent Relationships:** add'l offices in Kendall, San Angelo, San Saba, Kimble, Real, Runnels, Tom Green counties.

Add'l Information: Normal turnaround time- 1-2 days. Fee basis will vary by the type of project. 1st project may require prepayment.

Surety Title Co of San Angelo

136 W Twohig, San Angelo, TX 76903
Phone: 325-658-7588 **Fax:** 325-655-3743

Types of Records Retrieved: Civil, criminal and probate courts; Federal courts; Real Estate; Tax liens/Judgments; UCC records; Vital records

Local Retrieval Area: TX-Tom Green. **Correspondent Relationships:** various Texas counties including offices in Kendall, San Angelo, San Saba, Kimble, Real, Concho, Runnels counties.

Add'l Information: Established 1886. Normal turnaround time- 1-2 days. Fee basis will vary by the type of project. 1st project may require prepayment. They have a fully equipped title plant with three abstractors.

Sutherlin Associated Services

300 Carlsbad Village Dr #108A-354, Carlsbad, CA 92008-2999
Phone: 800-217-1555; 760-433-1555 **Fax:** 760-433-6155
www.sutherlinassociated.com **email:** sutherlinassoc3@aol.com

Types of Records Retrieved: Civil, criminal and probate courts; Federal courts; Real Estate; Tax liens/Judgments; UCC records

Local Retrieval Area: CA-San Diego. **Correspondent Relationships:** network affiliations nationwide.

Add'l Information: Established 1986. Normal turnaround time- 24-48 hours. Expedited service available. Charges are by the number of names searched or hourly depending on project. Credit cards accepted. They do bi-monthly invoicing, terms are net 15 days. Prepayment is required for some projects. They are licensed private investigators since 1986, doing nationwide background checks and pre-employment screening, workplace investigations, due diligence and witness locations/statements. A licensed PI in CA.

Sweet Grass Title Co

118 W 1st Ave, PO Box 1067, Big Timber, MT 59011
Phone: 406-932-4888 **Fax:** 406-932-5378

Types of Records Retrieved: Civil courts; Probate courts; Real Estate; Tax liens/Judgments

Local Retrieval Area: MT-Golden Valley, Sweet Grass, Wheatland

Add'l Information: Established 1960. Normal turnaround time- variable depending on project. Fee basis varies by type of transaction. They provide title insurance and related products, mineral reports and abstracts and closing services.

Kathy Swenson, PI

36250 Cross St, Pearl River, LA 70452-5962
Phone: 985-863-8151 **Fax:** 985-863-3603 swensonkoo7@bellsouth.net

Types of Records Retrieved: Civil, criminal and probate courts; Real Estate; Tax liens/Judgments; UCC records

Local Retrieval Area: LA-St. Tammany Parish

Add'l Information: Established 1986. Normal turnaround time- 24-48 hours. She specializes in current owner searches, court filing of documents, criminal record searches, felony record searches statewide in Louisiana. Also does nationwide felony searches (only) nationwide. Has been in business for 18+ years. A licensed PI in LA.

SWF Private Inv

1049 Waterside St, Pt Charlotte, FL 33952
Phone: 941-764-9156 **Fax:** 941-764-6200
www.swfpi.com **email:** jimg@swfpi.com

Types of Records Retrieved: Civil and criminal courts; Probate coruts; Real Estate, Tax liens/Judgments; UCC records; Vital records

Local Retrieval Area: FL-Charlotte, De Soto, Lee, Sarasota. **Correspondent Relationships:** nationwide.

Add'l Information: Established 2000. Normal turnaround time- 1-3 days turnaround; 48-hour guaranteed expedited service. Dependant on number of searches and method of search. 1st project may require prepayment. Terms negotiable. Will accept check by fax. Willing to go the extra mile, they also provide security and private eye services as well as pre-employment and tenant screening. A licensed PI in FL. They perform service of process.

Swift Attorney Service

500 Allerton St #105, Redwood City, CA 94063
Phone: 800-987-9438; 650-364-9612 **Fax:** 650-364-3305
www.swiftattorneyservice.com **email:** swiftattysvc@hotmail.com

Types of Records Retrieved: Civil, criminal and probate courts; Federal courts; UCC records; Real Estate; Tax liens/Judgments; Vital records

Local Retrieval Area: CA-Alameda, Contra Costa, San Mateo, Santa Clara, San Francisco. **Correspondent Relationships:** statewide.

Add'l Information: Established 1976. Normal turnaround time- call for turnaround time. Projects billed by number of names searched. Projects billed by number of records located. Projects billed by the hour. 1st project may require prepayment. Additional services include medical records, locates, skiptraces, writ services and private investigations. A licensed PI in CA. They perform service of process.

SWP Searches

119 S Hopkins, Grand Haven, MI 49417
Phone: 616-847-6989 **Fax:** 616-850-9802 spyle@i2k.com

Types of Records Retrieved: Civil, criminal and probate courts; Federal courts; Real Estate; Tax liens/Judgments; UCC records; Vital records

Local Retrieval Area: MI-Allegan, Kent, Muskegon, Ottawa

Add'l Information: Established 1998. Normal turnaround time- 24-48 hours. Projects billed by number of names searched. 1st project may require prepayment. Specialize in any type of search. Performs service of process.

Synerfax Inc

460 State St #301, Rochester, NY 14608
Phone: 800-245-3013; 585-546-1640 **Fax:** 585-546-1683
www.synerfax.com **email:** charlie@synerfax.com

Types of Records Retrieved: Criminal courts

Local Retrieval Area: NY-Erie, Monroe, Niagara, Onondaga, Ontario, Wayne. **Correspondent Relationships:** nationwide.

Add'l Information: Established 1997. Normal turnaround time- same day. Projects billed by number of names searched. Payment due upon receipt of invoice. They are an information services company, providing pre-employment background checking services for human resources. Specializing in criminal record searches in Monroe, Ontario, Wayne, Erie, Niagara and Onondaga counties in NY.

Dona Szymaszek

22032 Chestnut Ridge, Kildeer, IL 60047
Phone: 847-540-7425 **Fax:** 847-438-4980 tomszymaszek@aol.com

Types of Records Retrieved: Civil and criminal courts; Probate; Real Estate; Tax liens/Judgments; UCC records; Vital records

Local Retrieval Area: IL-Lake, McHenry

Add'l Information: Established 1999. Normal turnaround time- 24 hours. Expedited service available. Projects billed by number of names searched. 1st project may require prepayment. She is a paralegal with five (5) years experience in document retrieval and searches in the Circuit Courts and County Recorders of Lake and McHenry counties in Illinois.

T

T D Wolfson & Associates

PMB 207 - 5021 Vernon Ave S #207, Edina, MN 55436-2102
Phone: 952-920-9645 **Fax:** 952-920-5280 twolfson@qwest.net

Types of Records Retrieved: Civil and criminal courts; Federal bankruptcy; Tax liens/Judgments; UCC records; Vital records

Local Retrieval Area: MN-Anoka, Carver, Dakota, Hennepin, Ramsey, Scott, Washington. **Correspondents:** nationwide and Canada.

Add'l Information: Established 1968. Normal turnaround time- 24-36 hours. Projects billed by number of names searched. 1st project may require prepayment. They are a full service licensed private investigative agency. A licensed PI in MN. They perform service of process.

T.A.B.B.S. Inv & Process Service

1509 N Main - PMB 112, Altus, OK 73521
Phone: 580-477-3292 **Fax:** 580-477-3257
www.tabbs.net **email:** tonya@tabbs.net

Types of Records Retrieved: Civil, criminal and probate courts; Real Estate; Tax liens/Judgments; UCC records; Vital records

Local Retrieval Area: OK-Comanche, Greer, Harmon, Jackson, Kiowa, Tillman; TX-Hardeman, Wilbarger. **Correspondent Relationships:** Oklahoma City, Norman; all 77 counties in Oklahoma.

Add'l Information: Established 1999. Normal turnaround time- 24-72 hours. Projects billed by number of records located. Credit cards accepted. They specialize in locates, pre-employment, background, workman's comp, criminal/civil courts, insurance fraud, domestic, child custody, civil, process service and public record retrieval. A licensed PI in OK. They perform service of process.

Tactical Private Inv

PO Box 12457, Lake Charles, LA 70611
Phone: 800-779-4893; 337-855-6470 **Fax:** 337-855-0168
www.tacticalpi.8m.com **email:** spyguytwo@aol.com

Types of Records Retrieved: Civil, criminal and probate courts; Federal courts; Real Estate; Tax liens/Judgments; UCC records; Vital records

Local Retrieval Area: LA-Calcasieu. **Correspondent Relationships:** Lafayette, Baton Rouge, Orleans parishes LA.

Add'l Information: Established 1989. Normal turnaround time- 1-2 days. Expedited service available. Projects billed by the hour. All projects require prepayment. They are a Louisiana's premier investigative firm. A licensed PI in LA. They perform service of process.

Talone & Associates

423 S 15th St, Philadelphia, PA 19146
Phone: 800-553-5189; 215-546-6080 **Fax:** 215-546-2412

Types of Records Retrieved: Civil, criminal and probate courts; Federal courts; Real Estate; Tax liens/Judgments; UCC records; Vital records

Local Retrieval Area: NJ-Burlington, Camden, Gloucester; PA-Bucks, Chester, Delaware, Lancaster, Lehigh, Montgomery, Philadelphia. **Correspondent Relationships:** surrounding NJ and PA counties.

Add'l Information: Established 1987. Normal turnaround time- 2-3 days. Projects billed by number of names searched. Projects billed by the hour. Charge by hour if it is a protracted search. 1st project may require prepayment. Terms: net 30 days. They specialize in prompt, professional service, with expedited same/next day service available. A licensed PI in NJ, PA. They perform service of process.

Tama County Abstract

PO Box 2, 123 W High St, 123 W High St, Toledo, IA 52342
Phone: 888-561-9061; 641-484-4386 **Fax:** 641-484-5449

Types of Records Retrieved: Civil, criminal and probate courts; Federal courts; Real Estate; Tax liens/Judgments; UCC records; Vital records

Local Retrieval Area: IA-Tama

Add'l Information: Established 1949. Normal turnaround time- 1-2 days. Fee basis varies by type of transaction. If accounts are paid in a timely fashion, they won't require prepayment.

Tammy L Listen Investigations

3950 Connie Ln, Edmond, OK 73634
Phone: 405-340-4843 **Fax:** 405-340-9610 tllisten@aol.com

Types of Records Retrieved: Civil and criminal courts; Federal courts; Real Estate; Tax liens/Judgments; UCC records; Vital records

Local Retrieval Area: OK-Caddo, Canadian, Cleveland, Grady, Lincoln, Logan, McClain, Oklahoma, Pottawatomie. **Correspondent Relationships:** statewide.

Add'l Information: Established 1996. Normal turnaround time- 24-48 hours. Expedited service available. Projects billed by number of names searched. Will invoice. This is a one person company, service oriented, with a bachelor's degree in educaiton. She takes her work very serious and prides herself in doing the best job possible. Female owned. A licensed PI in OK. They perform service of process.

Taya Gordon Research

PO Box 514, Hull, GA 30646
Phone: 706-546-6598 **Fax:** 706-369-9733

Types of Records Retrieved: Civil, criminal and probate courts; Real Estate; Tax liens/Judgments; UCC records

Local Retrieval Area: GA-Clarke, Jackson, Madison, Oconee, Oglethorpe

Add'l Information: Established 1999. Normal turnaround time- 24-48 hours. Projects billed by number of names searched. 1st project may require prepayment. She specializes in document retrieval, title exams, witness/notary closings, also offering certified copies and reasonable rates.

Taylor Abstract & Title Inc

PO Box 305, 114 W 5th St, Larned, KS 67550
Phone: 620-285-2026 **Fax:** 620-285-2753

Types of Records Retrieved: Civil, criminal and probate courts; Real Estate; Tax liens/Judgments; UCC records

Local Retrieval Area: KS-Pawnee, Stafford

Add'l Information: Established 1896. Normal turnaround time- 2 days; Stafford county may take longer. Fee basis varies by type of transaction. 1st project may require prepayment. They specialize in abstract and title insurance.

Taylor Research & Investigations

7417 Whispering Pines Dr, Dallas, TX 75248-3061
Phone: 972-991-5045 **Fax:** 972-503-3302
www.dallasprivateeye.com **email:** jhtj@swbell.net

Types of Records Retrieved: Civil, criminal and probate courts; Federal courts; Real Estate; Tax liens/Judgments; UCC records; Vital records

Local Retrieval Area: TX-Bell, Collin, Dallas, Denton, Ellis, Hunt, Johnson, Kaufman, Parker, Rockwall, Tarrant, Travis, Van Zandt, Williamson. **Correspondent Relationships:** TX, LA, OK.

Add'l Information: Established 1992. Normal turnaround time- 24 hours. Projects billed by the hour. 1st project may require prepayment. Credit cards accepted. They are a full service investigative and research company with expeditious, efficient results. They perform service of process.

Teeters Abstract & Title Co

PO Box 645, 517 Main, Goodland, KS 67735
Phone: 785-890-7138 **Fax:** 785-890-6644

Types of Records Retrieved: Civil courts; Probate courts; Real Estate; Tax liens/Judgments; UCC records

Local Retrieval Area: KS-Sherman

Add'l Information: Established 1885. Normal turnaround time- 2 days. 1st project may require prepayment. They specialize in real estate searches.

TENSTAR Corporation (Baton Rouge)

10985 N Harrell's Ferry Rd #200, Baton Rouge, LA 70816
Phone: 800-864-5154; 225-928-3877 **Fax:** 225-273-8987
www.tenstarcorporation.com **email:** tenstarco@aol.com

Types of Records Retrieved: Civil, criminal and probate courts; Federal courts; Real Estate; Tax liens/Judgments; UCC records; Vital records

Local Retrieval Area: LA-Ascension, Avoyelles, Concordia, East Baton Rouge, East Feliciana, Iberville, Livingston, Pointe Coupee, St. Helena, West Baton Rouge, West Feliciana. **Correspondent Relationships:** Louisiana and Mississippi statewide.

Add'l Information: Established 1989. Normal turnaround time- 48 hours. Expedited service available for add'l fee. Projects billed by number of names searched. Projects billed by the hour. Flat rates apply to some services. 1st project may require prepayment. Credit cards accepted. Personal checks and bank wires accepted. They specialize in research, retrieval, recording, corporate services, notary services, abstracting, process service, litigation support, paralegal services, court reporting, investigations, risk management & claims adjusting. All services are statewide. A licensed PI in LA. They perform service of process.

TENSTAR Corporation (Crowley)

607 N Parkerson Ave, Crowley, LA 70527
Phone: 800-960-2214; 337-839-1833 **Fax:** 337-839-8120
www.tenstarcorporation.com **email:** tenstarco@aol.com

Types of Records Retrieved: Civil, criminal and probate courts; Federal courts; Real Estate; Tax liens/Judgments: UCC records; Vital records

Local Retrieval Area: LA-Acadia, Jefferson Davis. **Correspondent Relationships:** Louisiana, Missouri

Add'l Information: Established 1989. Normal turnaround time- 48 hours. 24-hour Expedited service available for an extra charge. Projects billed by number of names searched. Projects billed by the hour. 1st project may require prepayment. Credit cards accepted. Flat rates apply to some services. Personal checks and bank wires accepted. They specialize in research, retrieval, recording, corporate services, notary services, abstracting, process service, litigation support, paralegal services, court reporting, investigations, risk management & claims adjusting. All services are statewide. A licensed PI in LA. They perform service of process.

TENSTAR Corporation (Jackson)

6069 Old Canton Rd #580, Jackson, MS 39211
Phone: 800-864-5154; **Fax:** 225-273-8987
www.tenstarcorporation.com **email:** tenstarco@aol.com

Types of Records Retrieved: Civil, criminal and probate courts; Federal courts; Real Estate; Tax liens/Judgments; UCC records; Vital records

Local Retrieval Area: MS-Copiah, George, Hancock, Harrison, Hinds, Jackson, Jones, Madison, Rankin, Simpson, Warren, Yazoo. **Correspondent Relationships:** Lousiana and Mississippi statewide.

Add'l Information: Established 1989. Normal turnaround time- 48 hours. 24-hour Expedited service available for an extra charge. Projects billed by number of names searched. Projects billed by the hour. Flat rates apply to some services. Credit cards accepted. Personal checks and bank wires accepted. They specialize in research, retrieval, recording, corporate services, notary services, abstracting, process service, litigation support, paralegal services, court reporting, investigations, risk management & claims adjusting. All services are statewide. A licensed PI in LA. They perform service of process.

TENSTAR Corporation (Main Office)

PO Box 82535, Lafayette, LA 70598
Phone: 800-960-2214; 337-839-1833 **Fax:** 337-839-8120
www.tenstarcorporation.com **email:** tenstarco@aol.com

Types of Records Retrieved: Civil, criminal and probate courts; Federal courts; Real Estate; Tax liens/Judgments; UCC records; Vital records

Local Retrieval Area: LA-Allen, Beauregard, Calcasieu, Caldwell, Cameron, Catahoula, East Carroll, Evangeline, Franklin, Grant, Iberia, Jackson, La Salle, Lafayette, Lincoln, Madison, Morehouse, Ouachita, Rapides, Richland, St. Landry, St. Martin, St. Mary, Tensas, Union, Vermilion, Vernon, West Carroll, Winn. **Correspondent Relationships:** Lousiana and Mississippi statewide.

Add'l Information: Established 1989. Normal turnaround time- 48 hours. 24-hour Expedited service available for an extra charge. Projects billed by number of names searched. Projects billed by the hour. Flat rates apply to some services. Credit cards accepted. Personal checks and bank wires accepted. They specialize in research, retrieval, recording, corporate services, notary services, abstracting, process service, litigation support, paralegal services, court reporting, investigations, risk management & claims adjusting. All services are statewide. A licensed PI in LA. They perform service of process.

TENSTAR Corporation (New Orleans)

650 Poydras St #1400, New Orleans, LA 70130
Phone: 800-856-8515; 504-524-4267 **Fax:** 504-524-9727
www.tenstarcorporation.com **email:** tenstarco@aol.com

Types of Records Retrieved: Civil, criminal and probate courts; Federal courts; Real Estate; Tax liens/Judgments; UCC records; Vital records

Local Retrieval Area: LA-Assumption, Jefferson, Lafourche, Orleans, Plaquemines, St. Bernard, St. Charles, St. James, St. John the Baptist, St. Tammany, Tangipahoa, Terrebonne, Washington. **Correspondent Relationships:** Louisiana and Mississippi statewide.

Add'l Information: Established 1989. Normal turnaround time- 48 hours. Expedited service available. Projects billed by number of names searched. Projects billed by the hour. Flat rates apply to some services. 1st project may require prepayment. Credit cards accepted. They specialize in research, retrieval, recording corporate services, notary services, abstracting, process service, litigation support, paralegal services, court reporting, investigations, risk management & claims adjusting. All services are statewide. A licensed PI in LA. They perform service of process.

TENSTAR Corporation (Shreveport)

6658 Youree Dr #22, Shreveport, LA 71105
Phone: 800-960-2214; **Fax:** 337-839-8120
www.tenstarcorporation.com **email:** tenstarco@aol.com

Types of Records Retrieved: Civil, criminal and probate courts; Federal courts; Real Estate; Tax liens/Judgments; UCC records; Vital records

Local Retrieval Area: LA-Bienville, Bossier, Caddo, Claiborne, DeSoto, Natchitoches, Red River, Sabine, Webster. **Correspondent Relationships:** Lousiana and Mississippi statewide.

Add'l Information: Normal turnaround time- 48 hours. 24-hour Expedited service available for an extra charge. Projects billed by number of names searched. Projects billed by the hour. Flat rates apply to some services. Credit cards accepted. Personal checks and bank wires accepted. They specialize in research, retrieval, recording, corporate services, notary services, abstracting, process service, litigation support, paralegal services, court reporting, investigations, risk management & claims adjusting, All services are statewide. A licensed PI in LA.

TENSTAR Corporation (Tupelo)

1020 N Gloster St, Tupelo, MS 38801
Phone: 800-864-5154; **Fax:** 225-273-8987
www.tenstarcorporation.com **email:** tenstarco@aol.com

Types of Records Retrieved: Civil, criminal and probate courts; Federal courts; Real Estate; Tax liens/Judgments; UCC records; Vital records

Local Retrieval Area: MS-Chickasaw, Itawamba, Lee, Monroe, Pontotoc, Prentiss, Tippah, Union. **Correspondent Relationships:** Lousiana and Mississippi statewide.

Add'l Information: Established 1989. Normal turnaround time- 48 hours. 24-hour Expedited service available for an extra charge. Projects billed by number of names searched. Projects billed by the hour. Flat rates apply to some services. Credit cards accepted. Personal checks and bank wires accepted. They specialize in research, retrieval, recording, corporate services, notary services, abstracting, process service, litigation support, paralegal services, court reporting, investigations, risk management & claims adjusting. All services are statewide. A licensed PI in LA. They perform service of process.

Territorial Title

PO Box 987, 919 Douglas Ave, Las Vegas, NM 87701
Phone: 505-425-3563 **Fax:** 505-425-9637
www.territorialtitle.com **email:** questions@territorialtitle.com

Types of Records Retrieved: Probate courts; Real Estate; Tax liens/Judgments; UCC records; Vital records

Local Retrieval Area: NM-Guadalupe, Mora, San Miguel

Add'l Information: Normal turnaround time- 1 week for San Miguel, 4 weeks for Mora, and 2 weeks for Guadalupe. Projects billed by the hour. They specialize in title insurance and closings.

Teter Security Assoc Inc

PO Box 8212, Saginaw, MI 48608
Phone: 800-726-5959; **Fax:** 517-781-7103 gatpi@aol.com

Types of Records Retrieved: Civil, criminal and probate courts; Federal courts; Tax liens/Judgments

Local Retrieval Area: MI-Bay, Midland, Saginaw

Add'l Information: Established 1983. Normal turnaround time- 48 hours. Projects billed by number of names searched. 1st project may require prepayment. They specialize in pre-employment investigations, background investigations, surveillance, and records research. A licensed PI in MI.

Tex Research

5225 Rio Bravo Dr, Arlington, TX 76017
Phone: 817-472-5997 **Fax:** 817-466-2889
ddgwills@aol.com

Types of Records Retrieved: Civil and criminal courts

Local Retrieval Area: TX-Collin, Tarrant. **Correspondent Relationships:** Texas.

Add'l Information: Established 1999. Normal turnaround time- 24-48 hours. Projects billed by number of names searched. Billed 1st of month, payment due net 15 days. They specialize in criminal and civil record searches. Collin & Tarrant County records can be returned same day.

Texas Research

2301 Austin Ave, Brownwood, TX 76801
Phone: 325-646-2890 **Fax:** 325-646-3035 elling40@hotmail.com

Types of Records Retrieved: Civil, criminal and probate courts; Real Estate, Tax liens/Judgments; UCC records.

Local Retrieval Area: courts: TX-Brown. **Real estate only:** Brown, Callahan. Coleman, Comache, Eastland, McCulloch, Mills, San Saba.

Add'l Information: Normal turnaround time- 24 hours for civil and criminal records; all other records 2-3 days. Projects billed by number of names searched. Fee varies dependent on type of search. Other area counties available on a special order basis. Specializes in courts in Brown County but also retrieves real estate in Central Texas counties.

Texas Abstract Services

412 Main St #250, Houston, TX 77002
Phone: 866-290-3743; 713-221-1757 **Fax:** 713-221-1756

Types of Records Retrieved: Real Estate; Tax liens/Judgments

Local Retrieval Area: TX-Fort Bend, Harris. **Correspondents:** nationwide.

Add'l Information: Established 1985. Normal turnaround time- 1-3 days. Flat fee per order, quoted in advance. 1st project may require prepayment. They are a full service abstract company, specializing in searches for home equity and home improvement loans, right-of-ways, oil and gas research as well as environmental property assessments.

Texas Civil Process

1650 S Brownlee Blvd, Corpus Christi, TX 78404
Phone: 800-976-9595; 361-887-9595 **Fax:** 361-887-9597
bddeel.tcp@interconnect.net

Types of Records Retrieved: Civil, criminal and probate courts; Federal courts; Real Estate; Tax liens/Judgments; UCC records; Vital records

Local Retrieval Area: TX-Aransas, Bee, Duval, Jim Wells, Kleberg, Live Oak, Nueces, Refugio, San Patricio. **Correspondent Relationships:** Bexar, Travis, Harris, Tarrant, Dallas, McMillian, Cameron, Hidalgo, Williamson, Taylor.

Add'l Information: Established 1980. Normal turnaround time- 24-48 hours. Projects billed by number of names searched. 1st project may require prepayment. Invoices are net 30 days. They specialize in process service, record research and skiptracing. Licensed private investigator on staff. A licensed PI in TX. They perform service of process.

Texas Detective.com

PO Box 851, Iowa Park, TX 76367
Phone: 940-592-7000 **Fax:** 940-592-1013
www.texasdetective.com **email:** records@texasdetective.com

Types of Records Retrieved: Civil, criminal and probate courts; Federal courts; Real Estate; Tax liens/Judgments; UCC records; Vital records

Local Retrieval Area: TX-Archer, Clay, Wichita, Willbarger. **Correspondent Relationships:** nationwide.

Add'l Information: Established 1996. Normal turnaround time- 72 hours. Expedited service available. Projects billed by number of names searched. All projects require prepayment. Credit cards accepted. PayPal payments accepted. They are a licenced private investigator (#A10709) who takes care of your needs. For peace of mind leave the search to them. A licensed PI in TX. They perform service of process.

Texas Industrial Security Inc

703 McKinney Ave #106, Dallas, TX 75202-1003
Phone: 214-634-2791 **Fax:** 214-634-2793
www.txsecurity.com **email:** dclines@sbcglobal.net

Types of Records Retrieved: Civil, criminal and probate courts; Federal courts; Tax liens/Judgments

Local Retrieval Area: TX-Bexar, Dallas, Tarrant

Add'l Information: Normal turnaround time- 2-5 days. Projects billed by number of records located. Projects billed by the hour. All projects require $100.00 retainer fee per case. They specialize in criminal, civil and domestic cases. Also do background investigation and surviellance.

Texas Subpoena & Process Svc

PO Box 496508, Garland, TX 75049
Phone: 800-717-3463; 972-303-6282 **Fax:** 972-303-1128
www.texassubpoena.com **email:** keith@texassubpoena.com

Types of Records Retrieved: Civil, criminal and probate courts; Federal courts; Real Estate; Tax liens/Judgments; UCC records; Vital records

Local Retrieval Area: TX-Collin, Dallas, Tarrant. **Correspondent Relationships:** Texas.

Add'l Information: Established 1990. Normal turnaround time- 24 hours. Projects billed by the hour. All projects require prepayment. Credit cards accepted. They specialize in investigations, service of process and document retrieval. A licensed PI in TX. They perform service of process.

TexDirect

1021 Eden Estates Dr, New Braunfels, TX 78132
Phone: 512-353-4257 **Fax:** 512-353-0731 mproue@centurytel.net

Types of Records Retrieved: Civil, criminal and probate courts; Real Estate; Tax liens/Judgments; UCC records

Local Retrieval Area: TX-Bexar, Caldwell, Comal, Gonzales, Guadalupe, Hays. **Correspondent Relationships:** statewide.

Add'l Information: Established 1998. Normal turnaround time- 24 hours. Projects billed by number of names searched. Will invoice. They are a dependable and thorough research company. They do hands-on work and results within 24-48 hours. Your direct connection to Texas public records.

Texsearch #A09479

2895 Gage Rd, Sherman, TX 75092-4950
Phone: 903-786-4636 **Fax:** 903-786-3363
www.texsearch.com **email:** texsearch@simple.net

Types of Records Retrieved: Civil and criminal courts; Federal courts; Real Estate; Tax liens/Judgments; UCC records

Local Retrieval Area: TX-Bell, Bexar, Cameron, Collin, Comal, Cooke, Dallas, Denton, Ector, Fannin, Grayson, Gregg, Guadalupe, Harris, Hays, Hidalgo, Kaufman, Mclennan, Midland, Nueces, Potter, Randall, Rockwall, Tarrant, Tom Green, Travis, Wichita, Williamson. **Correspondent Relationships:** statewide.

Add'l Information: Established 1997. Normal turnaround time- 24 hours or less. Projects billed by number of names searched. They accept payments via PayPal (www.paypal.com) and bill monthly. 1st project may require prepayment. Billed monthly payable 30 days net. A licensed investigative company that specializes in public record retrieval in any TX county, at county, state level. Services include court record searches, real estate, asset/lien, property ownership, motor vehicle ownership & driving records. A licensed PI in TX. They perform service of process.

Thalken Title Co

PO Box 307, 520 N Spruce, Ogallala, NE 69153
Phone: 308-284-3972 **Fax:** 308-284-6802

Types of Records Retrieved: Civil courts; Real Estate; Tax liens/Judgments; UCC records

Local Retrieval Area: NE-Arthur, Chase, Cherry, Deuel, Garden, Grant, Keith, Perkins, Sheridan. **Correspondent Relationships:** Banner, Cheyenne, Kimbal, Morrill counties NE.

Add'l Information: Established 1962. Normal turnaround time- 1 day for Keith; 2-5 days for the other counties. Fee basis varies by type of transaction. 1st project may require prepayment. They specialize in title insurance searches. Will file/record real estate documents if fees are attached and made out to correct county clerk.

The Amherst Group

4804 Arlington Ave #A, Riverside, CA 92504
Phone: 800-521-0237; 951-785-5777 **Fax:** 951-785-5888
www.amherst-group.com **email:** amherst@pe.net

Types of Records Retrieved: Civil, criminal and probate courts; Federal courts; Real Estate; Tax liens/Judgments; UCC records; Vital records

Local Retrieval Area: CA-Alameda, Contra Costa, Imperial, Los Angeles, Marin, Napa, Orange, Riverside, Sacramento, San bernardino, San Diego, San Francisco, Santa Barbara, Santa Clara, Sonoma, Ventura. **Correspondent Relationships:** nationwide.

Add'l Information: Established 1982. Normal turnaround time- 24-48 hours. Projects billed by number of names searched. Credit cards accepted. Terms: net 20 days. They specialize in national criminal, credit and motor vehicle records. They also have a national service offering background checks, tenant screening and general information services.

The Copy Shop of Aberdeen

115B E Commerce St, Aberdeen, MS 39730
Phone: 662-369-4428 **Fax:** 662-369-4112 copyshop@aberdeen.ms

Types of Records Retrieved: Civil courts; Federal courts

Local Retrieval Area: MS-Monroe

Add'l Information: Established 2001. Normal turnaround time- Same day. Expedited service available, add 10%. Projects billed by number of records located. Projects billed by the hour. 1st project may require prepayment. Credit cards accepted. Their primary focus is copy service (plus color), including litigation copying. Owner is former legal secretary (3 years) and medical researcher (18 years).

The Daily Report

310 H St, Bakersfield, CA 93304-2914
Phone: 800-803-6127; 661-322-3226 **Fax:** 661-322-9084
www.thedailyreport.com **email:** annem@thedailyreport.com

Types of Records Retrieved: Civil courts; Probate courts; Real Estate; Tax liens/Judgments; UCC records; Vital records

Local Retrieval Area: CA-Kern

Add'l Information: Established 1907. Normal turnaround time- 2 days. Projects billed by the hour. Credit cards accepted. They specialize in legal advertising. They also search at the municipal court level, superior court and county recorder's office. The web site offers a searchable database with up-to-date information at www.thedailyreport.com.

The Discovery Group Inc

1595 Main St, Southhaven, MS 38671
Phone: 662-280-1576 **Fax:** 662-280-1607 jf1534@aol.com

Types of Records Retrieved: Civil, criminal and probate courts; Federal courts; Tax liens/Judgments; UCC records; Vital records

Local Retrieval Area: AR-Crittenden; MS-De Soto, Lafayette, Marshall, Tate, Tunica; TN-Shelby. **Correspondent Relationships:** nationwide.

Add'l Information: Established 1996. Normal turnaround time- 24-48 hours. 1st project may require prepayment. Credit cards accepted. They specialize fast, reliable record searching services. Full service in all types of record retrieval. A licensed PI in TN. They perform service of process.

The Docket Clerk

141 Hoskins Rd, SimsBury, CT 06070
Phone: 866-758-2683; 860-658-2683 **Fax:** 860-658-2646
www.thedocketclerk.com **email:** admin@thedocketclerk.com

Types of Records Retrieved: Civil, criminal and probate courts; Federal courts; Real Estate; Tax liens/Judgments; UCC records; Vital records

Local Retrieval Area: CT-all counties. **Correspondents:** nationwide.

Add'l Information: Established 1999. Normal turnaround time- same day/24 hours. Projects billed by number of names searched. 1st project may require prepayment. Terms are net 30 days. They specialize in researching and obtaining publicly filed documents, performing due diligence, litigation/judgment searches, background investigations and pre-employment services. They also provide nationwide document retrieval and brokering svcs.

The Fatman Intl Private Detective Svc

6638 Cascade Rd SE, Grand Rapids, MI 49546-6896
Phone: 616-949-1790 **Fax:** 616-949-4800
www.fatmanpi.com **email:** superprivateye@prodigy.net

Types of Records Retrieved: Civil, criminal and probate courts; Federal courts; Real Estate; Tax liens/Judgments; UCC records; Vital records

Local Retrieval Area: MI-Barry, Calhoun, Kent, Ottawa. **Correspondent Relationships:** worldwide.

Add'l Information: Established 1955. Normal turnaround time- 1-2 days. Fee basis varies by type of transaction. 1st project may require prepayment. They ask for a retainer. They specialize in investigations. They have an office in Europe, located in Wassenaar, The Netherlands. A licensed PI in MI. They perform service of process.

The Gordon Company of Colby

450 N Franklin, Colby, KS 67701-0489
Phone: 785-462-7555 **Fax:** 785-462-2099
ggordon@we.rr.com

Types of Records Retrieved: Civil, criminal and probate courts; Real Estate; Tax liens/Judgments; UCC records

Local Retrieval Area: KS-Thomas

Add'l Information: Established 1885. Normal turnaround time- 24 hours. Projects billed by number of names searched. Projects billed by number of records located. Projects billed by the hour. Personal checks are accepted. Will invoice at time of provided service. They specialize in title insurance searches, abstracts, certificates of title and appraisals.

The Henry Agency

7527 Farm Gate Dr, Charlotte, NC 28215
Phone: 704-526-5030 **Fax:** 704-536-6010
piworking@aol.com

Types of Records Retrieved: Civil, criminal and probate courts; Federal District courts; Real Estate; Tax liens/Judgments; UCC records; Vital records

Local Retrieval Area: NC-Cabarrus, Gaston, Iredell, Lincoln, Mecklenburg, Stanly, Union. **Correspondent Relationships:** statewide and SC.

Add'l Information: Established 1981. Normal turnaround time- 2 days. Expedited service available. Projects billed by number of names searched. All projects require prepayment. They specialize in general investigations, record retrieval and SOP. A licensed PI in NC. They perform service of process.

The Home Abstract & Title Co Inc

2380 Washington Blvd #200, Ogden, UT 84401
Phone: 800-699-7861; 801-621-7861 **Fax:** 801-621-7850

Types of Records Retrieved: Civil courts; Probate courts; Real Estate; Tax liens/Judgments; UCC records

Local Retrieval Area: UT-Box Elder, Davis, Morgan, Weber

Add'l Information: Established 1908. Normal turnaround time- 48 hours. Projects billed by number of names searched. 1st project may require prepayment. Terms: net 15 days. Personal checks are accepted. They specialize in title insurance and escrow closing service. They have a Utah certified residential appraiser of counsel.

The Legal Source Attorney Services

PO Box 1542, Chico, CA 95927
Phone: 800-786-8163; 530-895-8163 **Fax:** 530-891-6616

Types of Records Retrieved: Civil and criminal courts.

Local Retrieval Area: CA-Butte, Colusa, Glenn, Lassen, Nevada, Plumas, Sacramento, Shasta, Sutter, Tehama, Yuba. **Correspondent Relationships:** California, Nevada, Oregon.

Add'l Information: Established 1980. Normal turnaround time- 7 to 15 days for remote counties. Expedited service available. Projects billed by number of records located. Charge is by location and by the page. 1st project may require prepayment. Terms: net 30 days. They prepare subpoenas to retrieve and photocopy records. They are a registered process server and certified notary public. also specialize in workers' comp records.

The McDowell Agency Inc

1714 University Ave W, St Paul, MN 55104
Phone: 651-644-3880 **Fax:** 651-644-3877
www.mcdowellagency.com **email:** kmf@mcdowellagency.com

Types of Records Retrieved: Civil, criminal and probate courts; Federal courts; Real Estate; Tax liens/Judgments; UCC records; Vital records

Local Retrieval Area: MN-Dakota, Hennepin, Ramsey, Washington

Add'l Information: Established 1984. Normal turnaround time- 24-72 hours. Projects billed by number of names searched. Credit cards accepted. Volume discounts. They are a full service licensed private detective agency with over 20 years of experience, specializing in pre-employment screening and courthouse record retrieval. A licensed PI in MN. They perform service of process.

The Nemesis Group

15021 Haley Hole, Austin, TX 78728-4456
Phone: 800-918-8343; 512-246-2288 **Fax:** 512-238-6935

Types of Records Retrieved: Civil, criminal and probate courts; Federal courts; Real Estate; Tax liens/Judgments; UCC records; Vital records

Local Retrieval Area: TX-Travis, Williamson. **Correspondent Relationships:** Bexar, Ector, El Paso, Galveston, Garza, Harris, Hidalgo, Hockley, Lubbock, Midland, Lynn, Potter, Terry TX.

Add'l Information: Established 1994. Normal turnaround time- 72 hours. Projects billed by number of names searched. 1st project may require prepayment. They specialize in worker's compensation, fraud, government, theft & basic investigations. A licensed PI in TX. They perform service of process.

The Paper Chase - CO

PO Box 520, Greeley, CO 80632 **Phone:** 970-350-1008 **Fax:** 970-352-1828

Types of Records Retrieved: Civil, criminal and probate courts; Federal courts; Real Estate; Tax liens/Judgments; UCC records; Vital records.

Local Retrieval Area: CO-Adams, Boulder, Larimer, Logan, Morgan, Weld

Add'l Information: Established 1988. Normal turnaround time- 24-48 hours. Projects billed by the hour. They specialize in counties north of Denver. They perform service of process.

The Partnership

411 E Crosstimbers, Houston, TX 77022
Phone: 877-558-9928; 713-695-9928 **Fax:** 877-914-6671; 713-697-6671
jmbrum@swbell.net

Types of Records Retrieved: Civil and criminal courts; US District court/

Local Retrieval Area: TX-Galveston, Hardin, Harris, Jefferson, Montgomery, Orange

Add'l Information: Established 1979. Normal turnaround time- 24-48 hours. They invoice once a month. They specialize in criminal and civil county court records. Mobile phone is 713-825-9953. A licensed PI in CA.

The Pettit Company

12807 Rossmere Ct, Midlothian, VA 23113
Phone: 800-752-6158; 804-379-2462 **Fax:** 800-236-2859; 804-379-3217
www.pettitcompany.com **email:** orders@pettitcompany.com

Types of Records Retrieved: Civil, criminal and probate courts; Federal courts; Real Estate; Tax liens/Judgments; UCC records

Local Retrieval Area: VA-Chesterfield, Colonial Heights City, Hanover, Henrico, Hopewell City, Petersburg City, Powhatan, Richmond City. **Correspondent Relationships:** nationwide.

Add'l Information: Established 1994. Normal turnaround time- 1-2 days. Projects billed by number of names searched. Terms: net 30 days. They specialize in providing quick, accurate and inexpensive personal service. They also offer filing services nationwide. Call to discuss special needs.

The Public Record Source

PO Box 6212, Peoria, AZ 85385-6212
Phone: 623-773-3997 **Fax:** 623-773-2861
azsherri@aol.com

Types of Records Retrieved: Civil, criminal and probate courts; Tax liens/Judgments; UCC records; Vital records

Local Retrieval Area: AZ-all counties. **Correspondents:** nationwide.

Add'l Information: Established 1997. Normal turnaround time- 24 hours. Projects billed by number of names searched. 1st project may require prepayment. They specialize in public record research, have been doing research since 1985. A licensed PI in AZ pending.

The R M Jaqua Abstract Co

Box 665, St Francis, KS 67756
Phone: 785-332-3041 **Fax:** 785-332-2595

Types of Records Retrieved: Civil, criminal and probate courts; Federal courts; Real Estate; Tax liens/Judgments; UCC records

Local Retrieval Area: KS-Cheyenne

Add'l Information: Established 1886. Normal turnaround time- within 48 hours. Projects billed by number of names searched. Personal checks accepted.

The Records Reviewer Inc

243 Wimbledon Lake Dr, Plantation, FL 33324-2445
Phone: 305-934-4920 **Fax:** 954-252-2245 recrev@bellsouth.net

Types of Records Retrieved: Civil, criminal and probate courts; Federal courts; Real Estate; Tax liens/Judgments; UCC records; Vital records

Local Retrieval Area: FL-Broward, Dade, Palm Beach. **Correspondent Relationships:** Apopka, Hillsborough, Pinellas, Osceola, Orange, most other FL counties.

Add'l Information: Established 1984. Normal turnaround time- 48 hours or less. Expedited service available. Projects billed by number of names searched. They may bill by the 1/4 hour. 1st project may require prepayment. They specialize in bankruptcy, environmental searches, criminal searches current owner searches and due diligence. They also record documents in Dade, Broward and Palm Beach, Fl counties.

The Research Staff Inc

5718 Hewitt St, Houston, TX 77092-5125
Phone: 800-822-3584; 713-688-3584 **Fax:** 713-688-1121
www.researchstaffonline.com **email:** sales@researchstaffonline.com

Types of Records Retrieved: Civil, criminal and probate courts; Federal courts; Real Estate; Tax liens/Judgments; UCC records

Local Retrieval Area: TX-Austin, Brazoria, Brazos, Chambers, Fort Bend, Galveston, Hardin, Harris, Houston, Jefferson, Liberty, Matagorda, Montgomery, Orange, Waller. **Correspondent Relationships:** Texas.

Add'l Information: Established 1985. Normal turnaround time- 24-48 hours. Expedited service available. Projects billed by number of names searched. 1st project may require prepayment. Credit cards accepted. They specialize in property reports (all kinds), specific name searches, UCC, T/L, A/J, business closings, asset searches and courts (all levels). Will design reports for special projects.

The Right Search Inc

810 E Aldrich, MPB 413, Bolivar, MO 65613
Phone: 417-852-7097 **Fax:** 417-852-1200 tlwright1@alltel.net

Types of Records Retrieved: Civil, criminal and probate courts; Federal courts; Real Estate; Tax liens/Judgments; UCC records; Vital records

Local Retrieval Area: MO-Benton, Camden, Cedar, Christian, Dallas, Greene, Hickory, Laclede, Lawrence, Polk, St. Clair, Stone, Taney, Webster

Add'l Information: Established 1998. Normal turnaround time- same day/24 hours depending on when request received. Invoices monthly. They do title searches & have been in business for 10 years with 4 employees. They offer excellent turnaround time. They do UCC Federal & State tax liens, current owner, deed reports, 40 year, document retrieval; licensed & E&O covered.

The Searchers

PO Box 842, Chiefland, FL 32644
Phone: 352-493-0101 **Fax:** 352-493-8004
searchers_34602@yahoo.com

Types of Records Retrieved: Real Estate; Tax liens/judgments; UCC records

Local Retrieval Area: FL-Alachua, Bradford, Citrus, Clay, Hernando, Lake, Levy, Marion, Pasco, Sumter, Volusia

Add'l Information: Established 2000. Normal turnaround time- 24-36 hours. Projects are billed by the type of search requested. 1st project may require prepayment. They do full title search, current owner, deed reports and document retrieval. Also do tax liens, judgment and UCC searches at reasonable fees.

The TarTec Corporation

PO Box 742139, Riverdale, GA 30274-1338
Phone: 678-479-0942 **Fax:** 770-478-1207
www.home.comcast.net/~tartec/web/html/view.cgi-home.html
email: tartec@comcast.net

Types of Records Retrieved: Civil, criminal and probate courts; Real Estate; Tax liens/Judgments; UCC records

Local Retrieval Area: GA-Clayton, Fulton

Add'l Information: Established 2003. Normal turnaround time- 2 days. Projects billed by number of names searched. Projects billed by number of records located. 1st project may require prepayment. Presently preforming document retrievals of criminal cases for defendants and plantiffs, Security Guard services (armed and unarmed and background pre-screenning. A licensed PI in GA.

The Title Co Inc (Eau Claire)

3408 Oakwood Mall Dr, Eau Claire, WI 54701
Phone: 800-848-4853; 715-838-2800 **Fax:** 877-838-2810; 715-838-2810
www.titleco.com **email:** mike@titleco.com

Types of Records Retrieved: Probate courts; Real Estate; Tax liens/Judgments; UCC records

Local Retrieval Area: WI-Buffalo, Chippewa, Clark, Dunn, Eau Claire, Pepin, Pierce. **Correspondent Relationships:** WI, MN, IA.

Add'l Information: Established 1985. Normal turnaround time- variable, depending on project. Projects billed by number of names searched. Title insurance search fees are preset. 1st project may require prepayment. Credit cards accepted. Visa, MasterCard and Discover are accepted. They specialize in title insurance and title reports.

The Title Co Inc (Iowa)

PO Box 256, Sibley, IA 51249-0256
Phone: 712-754-2284 **Fax:** 712-754-3195 titleco@hickorytech.net

Types of Records Retrieved: Probate courts; Federal District courts; Real Estate; Tax liens/Judgments; UCC records

Local Retrieval Area: IA-Osceola

Add'l Information: Established 1967. Normal turnaround time- 1-3 days. Fee basis will vary by the type of project. 1st project may require prepayment. They specialize in abstracts.

The Title Co Inc (La Crosse)

PO Box 578, La Crosse, WI 54602-0578
Phone: 800-788-4853; 608-791-2000 **Fax:** 888-791-2015; 608-791-2015
www.titleco.com **email:** mike@titleco.com

Types of Records Retrieved: Probate courts; Federal courts; Real Estate; Tax liens/Judgments; UCC records

Local Retrieval Area: MN-Houston; WI-La Crosse, Trempealeau. **Correspondent Relationships:** Wisconsin and Iowa.

Add'l Information: Normal turnaround time- variable, depending on project. Projects billed by number of names searched. Title insurance fees are preset. 1st project may require prepayment. Credit cards accepted. They are branch office that visits both WI and MN, and specialize in title insurance and reports.

The Title Co Inc (Prairie Du Chien WI)

PO Box 408, 124 E Blackhawk Ave, Praire Du Chien, WI 53821
Phone: 888-918-4853; 608-326-7330 **Fax:** 877-918-4853; 608-326-7631
www.titleco.com **email:** mike@titleco.com

Types of Records Retrieved: Probate courts; Federal courts; Real Estate; Tax liens/Judgments; UCC records

Local Retrieval Area: IA-all counties with a few exceptions; WI-Crawford, Grant, Richland

Add'l Information: Normal turnaround time- variable, depending on project. Projects billed by number of names searched. Title insurance search fees are preset. 1st project may require prepayment. Credit cards accepted. They specialize in title insurance and reports in SE Wisconsin and all of Iowa.

The Title Co Inc (Viroqua)

210 N Main St, Viroqua, WI 54665
Phone: 800-538-4853; 608-637-3700 **Fax:** 877-637-3700; 608-637-3799
www.titleco.com **email:** mike@titleco.com

Types of Records Retrieved: Civil courts; Probate courts; Federal courts; Real Estate; Tax liens/Judgments; UCC records

Local Retrieval: WI-Vernon. **Correspondent Relationships:** WI, MN, IA.

Add'l Information: Normal turnaround time- variable, depending on project. Projects billed by number of names searched. Title insurance search fees are preset. 1st project may require prepayment. Credit cards accepted. They specialize in title insurance and reports.

The Wright Group

200 N Harbor Blvd #205, Anaheim, CA 92805
Phone: 877-847-0431; 714-687-1190 **Fax:** 714-687-1194

Types of Records Retrieved: Civil and criminal courts; Federal courts; Real Estate; Tax liens/Judgments; UCC records; Vital records

Local Retrieval Area: CA-Los Angeles, Orange, Riverside, San Bernardino, San Diego. **Correspondent Relationships:** nationwide.

Add'l Information: Established 1993. Normal turnaround time- 24 hours. Projects billed by number of names searched. All projects require prepayment. They are a full service investigations firm with concentration in pre-employment screening & business background checks. A licensed PI in CA. They perform service of process.

Thomas Legal Support Service

PO Box 1450, 258 SW 10th St, Newport, OR 97365
Phone: 541-265-2233 **Fax:** 541-265-5853 tai-pi@pioneer.net

Types of Records Retrieved: Civil and criminal records

Local Retrieval Area: OR-Lane (coastal areas-Florence), Lincoln, Tillamook

Add'l Information: Established 2001. 1st project may require prepayment. They also provide court filings, photocopying, skiptracing, and private investigations. For Lane county, they serve only the Pacific coast area. A licensed PI in OR. They perform service of process.

Thomas Research Services (Donna Thomas)

1019 Tekamah Ln, Papillion, NE 68046
Phone: 402-339-7291 **Fax:** 402-339-0051

Types of Records Retrieved: Civil and criminal courts; Federal courts; Tax liens/Judgments; UCC records

Local Retrieval Area: IA-Harrison, Mills, Pottawattamie; NE-Cass, Douglas, Otoe, Sarpy, Washington. **Correspondent Relationships:** Audubon, Cass, Davis, Dodge, Shelby & Saunders counties IA.

Add'l Information: Established 1993. Normal turnaround time- 24-48 hours. Expedited service available. Projects billed by number of names searched. Personal checks accepted. Special interest of genealogy. She is compiling a book on Audubon county, IA cemetery inscriptions, and performs research for maiden and other married names. She also goes to the federal building in Douglas County. They perform service of process.

Julie L Thomas

7645 N Crestview Rd, Stillman Valley, IL 61084
Phone: 815-234-4172 **Fax:** 815-234-4172
julieilresearch@rockford.com

Types of Records Retrieved: Civil and criminal courts

Local Retrieval Area: IL-Boone, De Kalb, Jo Daviess, Kane, Kendall, Ogle, Stephenson, Winnebago. **Correspondent Relationships:** Dupage, Lake, McHenry, Will counties IL.

Add'l Information: Established 1994. Normal turnaround time- same day if requested before 8AM CST in most cases. Projects billed by number of names searched. Will bill at end of month. Will file UCC & real estate documents in Boone, Ogle, Stephenson, and Winnebago counties only, on same or next day basis.

Thompson & Hollingsworth PA

116 E 2nd St, Forest, MS 39074
Phone: 601-469-3411 **Fax:** 601-469-3020

Types of Records Retrieved: Civil, criminal and probate courts; Real Estate; Tax liens/Judgments; UCC records; Vital records

Local Retrieval Area: MS-Scott, Smith

Add'l Information: Established 1947. Normal turnaround time- 1 day. Projects billed by the hour. 1st project may require prepayment. They are in general practice. They specialize in marriage/divorce searches.

Deborah W Thompson

PO Box 3787, Clearlake, CA 95422
Phone: 917-309-4830 **Fax:** 966-387-2280 abstractordeb@yahoo.com

Types of Records Retrieved: Real Estate; Tax liens/judgments; UCC records

Local Retrieval Area: NY-Bronx, Kings, New York, Queens, Westchester

Add'l Information: Established 2003. Normal turnaround time- 24-48 hours. Expedited service available. Projects billed by number of names searched. Negotiable. They pride themselves on delivering accurate and speedy service with a smile. Providing document retrieval, current owner searches. Ask about their other services.

Three Rivers Title Co

727 Clinton St #100, Fort Wayne, IN 46802-1801
Phone: 260-424-2929 **Fax:** 260-424-0037 www.ilts.net

Types of Records Retrieved: Civil courts; Probate courts; Real Estate; Tax liens/Judgments; UCC records; Vital records

Local Retrieval Area: IN-Bartholomew, Boone, Clinton, De Kalb, Hamilton, Hancock, Henry, Huntington, Johnson, Kosciusko, Lagrange, Madison, Marion, Morgan, Noble, Steuben, Wabash, Wells, Whitley

Add'l Information: Established 1978. Normal turnaround time- 2-3 days. Fee basis varies by type of transaction.

Ticor Title Roseburg

PO Box 59, Roseburg, OR 97470
Phone: 800-660-1146; 541-673-1146 **Fax:** 541-673-2118
www.ticortitlenw.com

Types of Records Retrieved: Civil, criminal and probate courts; Real Estate; Tax liens/Judgments; UCC records

Local Retrieval Area: OR-Douglas

Add'l Information: Established 1985. Normal turnaround time- 2-3 days. 1st project may require prepayment. Formerly Key Title, they specialize in real estate, title insurance, escrow services, 1031 exchanges, lender insurance and escrow collections.

Timely Documents

15406 NE 47th Circle, Vancouver, WA 98682-6093
Phone: 360-944-1082 **Fax:** 360-944-1083
timelydocuments@comcast.net

Types of Records Retrieved: Civil courts; Probate courts; Real Estate; Tax liens/Judgments; UCC records

Local Retrieval Area: OR-Clackamas, Multnomah, Washington; WA-Clark. **Correspondent Relationships:** Oregon, Washington, Idaho.

Add'l Information: Established 2001. Normal turnaround time- 1-4 days. Projects billed by number of names searched. As contract bidded. They perform accurate, reliable real estate and court records searches of all types in most counties in Oregon and Washington states. They specialize in research, retrieval and recording.

Tippecanoe Title Services Inc

415 Columbia St, Lafayette, IN 47901
Phone: 888-423-2457; 765-423-2457 **Fax:** 765-742-0194
www.tiptitle.com **email:** tts@tiptitle.com

Types of Records Retrieved: Probate courts; Real Estate; Tax liens/Judgments; UCC records

Local Retrieval Area: IN-Benton, Boone, Carroll, Cass, Clinton, Fountain, Hamilton, Hendricks, Howard, Jasper, Marion, Montgomery, Newton, Parke, Tippecanoe, Vermillion, Warren, White

Add'l Information: Established 1987. Normal turnaround time- 3-4 days for Tippecanoe; 5-7 days for other counties. Projects billed by the hour. They specialize in land title insurance, real estate closings and title searches.

Title Abstracts & Document Services

9 Spyglass Dr, Aiken, SC 29803
Phone: 803-649-2500 **Fax:** 803-649-2500
deannaromeo@gforcecable.com

Types of Records Retrieved: Civil, criminal and probate courts; Federal courts; Real Estate; Tax liens/Judgments; UCC records; Vital records

Local Retrieval Area: SC-Aiken, Barnwell, Edgefield

Add'l Information: Established 1990. Normal turnaround time- 24-48 hours. Projects billed by number of names searched. 1st project may require prepayment. Invoices monthly. Their company offers professional & detail perfect work. All reports are typed out on computer for easier reading and understanding.

Title Company of Denver

2200 S Valley Hwy #B, Denver, CO 80222-5035
Phone: 303-369-5443 **Fax:** 303-369-2071
www.tcod.com

Types of Records Retrieved: Real Estate; Tax liens/Judgments

Local Retrieval Area: CO-Adams, Arapahoe, Boulder, Broomfield, Denver, Douglas, El Paso, Elbert, Jefferson, Larimer, Weld

Add'l Information: Established 1994. Normal turnaround time- 7 days. Retainer and fee agreement required prior to searches. They specialize in title underwriting and legal services.

The Title Company

PO Box 1304, 213 E 4th Ave, Mitchell, SD 57301
Phone: 605-996-4900 **Fax:** 605-996-3270

Types of Records Retrieved: Civil courts; Real Estate; Tax liens/Judgments.

Local Retrieval Area: SD-Davison, Hanson

Add'l Information: Established 1800s. 1st project may require prepayment. They specialize in real estate.

Title Court Service

1305 Franklin St #501, Oakland, CA 94612
Phone: 510-763-0975 **Fax:** 510-763-0802
www.titlecourt.com **email:** titlecourt@att.net

Types of Records Retrieved: Civil courts; Probate courts; Federal courts; Real Estate; Tax liens/Judgments; UCC records; Vital records

Local Retrieval Area: CA-all counties. **Correspondent Relationships:** statewide; all US Bankruptcy Courts.

Add'l Information: Established 1978. Normal turnaround time- 24-48 hours. Projects billed by number of names searched. 1st project may require prepayment. Credit cards accepted. They specialize in court research and document retrieval in all the CA counties, document recordings, building and safety permits and current owner searches.

Title Express Inc

4940 Davy Crockett Pky, Morristown, TN 37813
Phone: 423-587-9886 **Fax:** 423-587-5682
titleexpress@charter.net

Types of Records Retrieved: Civil, criminal and probate courts; Real Estate; Tax liens/Judgments; UCC records

Local Retrieval Area: TN-Claiborne, Cocke, Greene, Hamblen, Hancock, Hawkins, Jefferson, Sevier. **Correspondent Relationships:** Washington County.

Add'l Information: Established 1996. Normal turnaround time- 48 hours. Projects billed by number of names searched. 1st project may require prepayment. They specialize in real estate title examinations and UCC searches.

Title Guaranty & Trust of Chattanooga

617 Walnut St, Chattanooga, TN 37402
Phone: 423-266-5751 **Fax:** 423-266-4167

Types of Records Retrieved: Civil courts; Probate courts; Federal courts; Real Estate; Tax liens/Judgments; UCC records

Local Retrieval Area: AL-Cherokee, De Kalb, Houston; GA-Catoosa, Chattooga, Dade, Fannin, Gilmer, Gordon, Murray, Walker, Whitfield; TN-Bledsoe, Bradley, Coffee, Franklin, Grundy, Hamilton, Loudon, McMinn, Marion, Meigs, Monroe, Polk, Rhea, Sequatchie, Van Buren,. **Correspondent Relationships:** nationwide.

Add'l Information: Established 1887. Normal turnaround time- 2 days. Projects billed by the hour. 1st project may require prepayment. They specialize in title insurance. They have a second office at: 7042 Lee Hwy #102, Chattanooga, TN 37321 (423-892-7914, fax 423-855-1288).

Title Info

4614 Ridge North Rd, Ft. Worth, TX 76126
Phone: 817-244-7757 **Fax:** 817-244-7455

Types of Records Retrieved: Probate courts; Real Estate; Tax liens/Judgments

Local Retrieval Area: TX-Collin, Dallas, Denton, Johnson, Parker, Tarrant. **Correspondent Relationships:** Ellis, Ft. Bend, Harris, Hood, Travis, Williamson counties Texas.

Add'l Information: Established 1985. Normal turnaround time- 24 hours. Projects billed by number of names searched. Net 30 days. They specialize in property searches, environmental chains of title, judgment and tax lien searches.

Title Professionals Inc

2610 Buffaloe Rd, Garner, NC 27529-5132
Phone: 919-779-7065 **Fax:** 919-662-7907

Types of Records Retrieved: Civil and criminal courts; Real Estate; Tax liens/Judgments; UCC records; Vital records

Local Retrieval Area: NC-Chatham, Durham, Franklin, Granville, Harnett, Johnston, Orange, Vance, Wake. **Correspondent Relationships:** Cabarrus, Cumberland, Davidson, Guilford, Iredell, Rowan, Stanley counties NC.

Add'l Information: Normal turnaround time- 24 hours. Projects billed by number of names searched. Payment due upon receipt. They specialize in real estate and 24 hour turnaround time for most services. Eleven years legal experience.

Title Runners

3083 1/2 Calle Mariposa, Santa Barbara, CA 93105-2740
Phone: 805-569-6939 **Fax:** 805-569-6962 hancey@silcom.com

Types of Records Retrieved: Bankruptcy Court; Real Estate; Tax liens/Judgments; UCC records; Vital records

Local Retrieval Area: CA-Santa Barbara, Ventura. **Correspondent Relationships:** San Luis Obispo, Kern, Fresno counties CA.

Add'l Information: Established 1988. Normal turnaround time- 24-48 hours. Expedited service available. Projects billed by number of names searched. Projects billed by the hour. Fees depend on the type of search. Projects estimates over $300.00 require 50% prepayment of estimated final cost, otherwise payment is net 30 days of invoice date. They specialize in title searches for 50 year environmental chains, parcel validity studies, lot book reports, lien searches and court research.

Title Search

5433 S Dorchester, Chicago, IL 60637
Phone: 773-655-4142 **Fax:** 773-241-5012 gtones@sbcglobal.net

Types of Records Retrieved: Civil courts; Probate courts; Federal courts; Real Estate; Tax liens/Judgments; UCC records; Vital records

Local Retrieval Area: IL-Cook

Add'l Information: Established 1997. Normal turnaround time- 24 hours. Projects are billed by the type of job. They specialize in accurate reporting, document retrieval, title searches, property reports and do high volume work. Have competitive prices.

Title Search Services Inc

2349 West Rd, Dorset, VT 05251
Phone: 802-867-4447 **Fax:** 802-867-5506
www.vermontlandrecords.com **email:** annieg@sover.net

Types of Records Retrieved: Civil courts; Real Estate; Tax liens/Judgments; UCC records; Vital records

Local Retrieval Area: VT-Bennington, Rutland, Windham, Windsor. **Correspondent Relationships:** Addison, Chittenden, Grand Isle, Essex, Caledonia, Franklin, Lamoille, Orange, Washington, Orleans, VT.

Add'l Information: Established 1997. Normal turnaround time- 24-48 hours. Projects billed by number of names searched. Projects billed by the hour. 1st project may require prepayment. Please visit my web site, www.vermontlandrecords.com, for more information on the complete services they provide for the State of VT. They are the VT independent title abstractors' league. They also perform "full" 40-year title searches for VT attorneys.

Titles of Dakota Inc (Dupree)

PO Box 100, Dupree, SD 57623-0100
Phone: 605-365-5247 **Fax:** 605-365-5248 tidak@dakota2k.net

Types of Records Retrieved: Civil, criminal and probate courts; Real Estate; Tax liens/Judgments; UCC records

Local Retrieval Area: SD-Dewey, Ziebach. **Correspondent Relationships:** Dewey, Stanley, Sully counties SD.

Add'l Information: Normal turnaround time- 1 week. Fee basis will vary by the type of project. They specialize in title insurance and abstracting.

Titles of Dakota Inc (Fort Pierre)

PO Box 278, Fort Pierre, SD 57532-0278
Phone: 800-794-2725; 605-223-2727 **Fax:** 605-223-9237
tidak@dakota2k.net

Types of Records Retrieved: Probate courts; Real Estate; Tax liens/Judgments; UCC records

Local Retrieval Area: SD-Stanley, Sully. **Correspondent Relationships:** Ziebach, Dewey, Hyde, Sully counties SD.

Add'l Information: Normal turnaround time- 1 week. Fee basis will vary by the type of project. They specialize in title insurance and abstracting.

Titles of Dakota Inc (Onida)

PO Box 167, Onida, SD 57564-0167
Phone: 605-258-2291 **Fax:** 605-223-9237

Types of Records Retrieved: Real Estate; Tax liens/Judgments

Local Retrieval Area: SD-Sully. **Correspondent Relationships:** Stanley, Dewey, Hyde, Ziebach counties South Dakota.

Add'l Information: Normal turnaround time- 1 week. Fee basis will vary by the type of project. 1st project may require prepayment. They specialize in loan closings, escrow services, abstracts, and title insurance.

Titles of Dakota Inc (Timber Lake)

PO Box 402, Timber Lake, SD 57656-0402
Phone: 605-365-5247 **Fax:** 605-365-5248

Types of Records Retrieved: Civil, criminal and probate courts; Real Estate; Tax liens/Judgments; UCC records; Vital records

Local Retrieval Area: SD-Dewey. **Correspondent Relationships:** Ziebach, Sully, Stanley counties SD.

Add'l Information: Normal turnaround time- 1 week. Fee basis will vary by the type of project. They specialize in title insurance and abstracting.

Titleworks

6 Reeders Village Dr, Helena, MT 59601-9684
Phone: 406-442-4450 **Fax:** 406-442-4450 titleworks@hotmail.com

Types of Records Retrieved: Civil courts; Real Estate; Tax liens/Judgments; UCC records

Local Retrieval Area: MT-Broadwater, Cascade, Deer Lodge, Jefferson, Lewis and Clark, Powell

Add'l Information: Established 1994. Normal turnaround time- 24-48 hours. Projects billed by number of names searched. Projects billed by the hour. Terms: net 30 days. They specialize in real estate searching, including ownership and encumbrance reports, lot book reports, mortgage searches, title searches, document retrieval & loan closings. Custom orders accepted. Cell # 406-431-1389.

Titus County Title Company

103 N Madison Ave, Mt Pleasant, TX 75455
Phone: 903-577-0333 **Fax:** 903-577-1666

Types of Records Retrieved: Civil courts; Probate courts; Real Estate; Tax liens/Judgments; UCC records; Vital records

Local Retrieval Area: TX-Titus

Add'l Information: Established 1992. Normal turnaround time- 2-3 days. Fee basis will vary by the type of project. 1st project may require prepayment.

TJM & Associates

65 Norfield Rd, Weston, CT 06883
Phone: 800-749-4254; 203-227-8360 **Fax:** 203-221-0852
tjma@optonline.net

Types of Records Retrieved: Civil, criminal and probate courts; Federal courts; Real Estate; Tax liens/Judgments; UCC records; Vital records

Local Retrieval Area: CT-Fairfield, Hartford, Litchfield, Middlesex, New Haven

Add'l Information: Established 1988. Normal turnaround time- 24-48 hours. Expedited service available. Projects billed by number of names searched. Project fees available for large projects. 1st project may require prepayment.

TOB Public Records Research

4430 Shady Hill, Dallas, TX 75229
Phone: 214-358-4744 **Fax:** 214-358-4489 jeantom10@earthlink.net

Types of Records Retrieved: Real Estate; Tax liens/judgments; UCC records

Local Retrieval Area: TX-Collin, Dallas, Denton, Ellis, Kaufman, Rockwall, Tarrant. **Correspondent Relationships:** Bexar, Harris, Jefferson, Orange, Hardin, Vanzandt, Hunt, Navarro, TX counties.

Add'l Information: Established 1994. Normal turnaround time- 3-5 days. Billed by the job-1 fee. Payment due net 30 days. Specializes in per form 50 year chain for cell tower leases, commercial deed searches & property search for home equity loans, current owner updates and property searches.

Toby Nason Detective & Security Agency

44 Main St, Waterville, ME 04901
Phone: 207-873-7512 **Fax:** 207-872-2436

Types of Records Retrieved: Civil, criminal, probate courts; Federal courts

Local Retrieval Area: ME-Androscoggin, Aroostook, Cumberland, Franklin, Hancock, Kennebec, Knox, Lincoln, Oxford, Penobscot, Piscataquis, Sagadahoc, Somerset, Waldo, Washington, York

Add'l Information: Established 1962. Normal turnaround time- 24 hours. Projects billed by the hour. All projects require prepayment. They can visit any county in Maine upon request. A licensed PI in ME, FL. They perform service of process.

Morris Todd

323 Cable St, San Antonio, TX 78227-3268
Phone: 210-673-4690 **Fax:** 210-674-5508 MTodd143@msn.com

Types of Records Retrieved: Civil, criminal and probate courts; Federal courts; Real Estate; Tax liens/Judgments; UCC records; Vital records

Local Retrieval Area: TX-Atascosa, Bandera, Bexar, Comal, Guadalupe, Kendall, Kerr, Medina

Add'l Information: Normal turnaround time- all counties searched daily. Most results returned same day. Projects billed by number of names searched. Will bill monthly. Mr. Todd has over 29 years experience with Equifax, and retired as a Claims Director. They also offer abstracting services. They perform service of process.

Toma Abstract Inc

410 Broad St, Hazelton, PA 18201-6107
Phone: 570-454-7899 **Fax:** 570-454-5999

Types of Records Retrieved: Civil courts; Probate courts; Real Estate; Tax liens/Judgments; UCC records.

Local Retrieval Area: PA-Carbon, Columbia, Luzerne, Monroe, Montour, Schuylkill

Add'l Information: Established 1990. Normal turnaround time- never more than 2 weeks. Projects billed by number of names searched. Projects billed by the hour. They specialize in title searching and title insurance.

Top Flight Solutions

550 N McCarren Blvd, Sparks, NV 89431
Phone: 775-887-6645 **Fax:** 775-331-3086
tfgalaxy@pacbell.net

Types of Records Retrieved: Civil, criminal and probate courts; Federal courts; Real Estate, Tax liens/Judgments; UCC records; Vital records

Local Retrieval Area: NV-Carson City, Churchill, Douglas, Storey, Washoe. **Correspondent Relationships:** Las Vegas, Clark, Washoe counties NV.

Add'l Information: Established 1997. Normal turnaround time- 2-3 days. Expedited service available. Projects billed by number of names searched. Discounts for volume requests. Will invoice, net is 30 days. May require prepay if certifications in Los Angeles county is requested. They are familiar with all types of public records since 1992.

Torri's Legal Services

PO Box 18647, Washington, DC 20036
Phone: 800-990-7378; 202-296-0222 **Fax:** 202-296-4584
www.torrilegalservices.com **email:** tlsnc@erols.com

Types of Records Retrieved: Civil, criminal and probate courts; Federal courts

Local Retrieval Area: DC-District of Columbia; MD-Baltimore City. **Correspondent Relationships:** nationwide.

Add'l Information: Established 1991. Normal turnaround time- 1 day. Expedited service available. Projects billed by number of names searched. Projects billed by number of records located. Projects billed by the hour. 1st project may require prepayment. They specialize in skiptracing, process serving, asset searches, filing and court house record research. They also service numerous counties in Maryland and the Baltimore area. A licensed PI in DC. They perform service of process.

Total Access

PO Box 2368, Clovis, CA 93613
Phone: 559-325-1169 **Fax:** 559-325-2910 or 559-298-3902
www.yourtotalaccess.com **email:** darrylynn@yourtotalaccess.com

Types of Records Retrieved: Civil and criminal Courts; Federal Bankruptcy courts; Tax liens/Judgments; UCC records; Vital records

Local Retrieval Area: CA-Alameda, Fresno, Kings, Madera, Napa, Sonoma, Tulare

Add'l Information: Established 1996. Normal turnaround time- if received by 9:00AM PT, returned by 7PM PT. Expedited service (via phone 4 hours) available. Projects billed by number of names searched. Invoices bi-monthly or monthly. They have served employers and background reporting agencies for 9 years. Their timeliness is only second to their accuracy. Pre-employment criminal is their speciality.

Town & Country Abstract Co (Arkansas)

102 W War Eagle Ave, Huntsville, AR 72740
Phone: 479-738-2055 **Fax:** 479-738-1747

Types of Records Retrieved: Probate courts; Real Estate; Tax liens/Judgments; UCC records

Local Retrieval Area: AR-Madison

Add'l Information: Established 1977. Normal turnaround time- 1-2 days. Fee basis will vary by the type of project. 1st project may require prepayment. They specialize in title insurance.

Town & Country Abstract Co (Missouri)

101 S Main, Huntsville, MO 65259
Phone: 660-277-3467 **Fax:** 660-277-3939

Types of Records Retrieved: Civil courts; Probate courts; Real Estate; Tax liens/Judgments; UCC records

Local Retrieval Area: MO-Randolph. **Correspondents:** nationwide.

Add'l Information: Established 1929. Normal turnaround time- 24-48 hours. Projects billed by number of names searched. Projects billed by the hour. 1st project may require prepayment. Personal checks are accepted. They have the only complete set of land records for Randolph County, MO.

Towner County Abstract Co

PO Box 265, Cando, ND 58324
Phone: 701-968-3006 **Fax:** 701-968-3009

Types of Records Retrieved: Real Estate; Tax liens/Judgments

Local Retrieval Area: ND-Towner

Add'l Information: Established 1991. Normal turnaround time- 2 weeks. Projects billed by number of records located. Fee basis is per entry. 1st project may require prepayment.

TPQ Associates

1136 Pine Grove Dr, Alpharetta, GA 30004
Phone: 770-475-0743 **Fax:** 770-740-2088 Phussing@bellsouth.net

Types of Records Retrieved: Civil and criminal courts; Real Estate; Tax liens/Judgments; UCC records

Local Retrieval Area: GA-Clayton, Cobb, DeKalb, Forsyth, Fulton, Gwinnett, Hall

Add'l Information: Established 1999. Normal turnaround time- 24 hours. Projects billed by number of names searched. Payment terms are net 30 days. They are honest, accurate and reliable.

Trace Investigations

PO Box 2603, Bloomington, IN 47402
Phone: 812-334-8857 **Fax:** 812-334-2274
www.traceinvestigations.com **email:** dcjcli@insightbb.com

Types of Records Retrieved: Civil, criminal and probate courts; Real Estate; Tax liens/Judgments; UCC records; Vital records

Local Retrieval Area: IN-Monroe. **Correspondent Relationships:** Indiana for legal investigations and service of process.

Add'l Information: Established 1990. Normal turnaround time- 24-48 hours. Type of search determines billing. 1st project may require prepayment. Terms: net 30 days. Credit cards by Pay Pal accepted. They specialize in legal investigations, service of process, public record retrieval and skiptracing. They retrieve Indiana MVRs online. Requests must comply with permissible purposes pursuant to the DPPA. A licensed PI in IN, #PD58900651. They perform service of process.

Trace Unlimited

5917 E Pima St #A, Tucson, AZ 85712-4352
Phone: 520-299-0015 **Fax:** 520-751-1615

Types of Records Retrieved: Civil, criminal and probate courts; Federal courts; Real Estate; Tax liens/Judgments; UCC records; Vital records

Local Retrieval Area: AZ-Maricopa, Pima. **Correspondent Relationships:** Maricopa county.

Add'l Information: Established 1992. Normal turnaround time- 2 days. Tucson municipal averages 5 days. Projects billed by the hour. 1st project may require prepayment. They specialize in skiptracing, locating individuals and DMV records. They perform service of process.

Tracers International (Albany)

146 Barrett St #148, Schenectady, NY 12305-2004
Phone: 800-872-2377; 518-453-2560 **Fax:** 518-453-3009
www.tracers.com **email:** info@pecoraro.com

Types of Records Retrieved: Civil, criminal and probate courts; Federal courts; Real Estate; Tax liens/Judgments; UCC records; Vital records

Local Retrieval Area: NY-Albany, Erie, Monroe, Onondaga, Rensselaer, Saratoga, Warren, Washington. **Correspondent Relationships:** NY, all 5 boroughs, Long Island.

Add'l Information: Established 1973. Normal turnaround time- 48-72 hours. Projects billed by number of names searched. 1st project may require prepayment. They specialize in elusive information worldwide including assets discovery and current whereabouts/locates. A licensed PI in NY. They perform service of process.

Tracers International (New York)

305 Madison Ave #449, New York, NY 10001
Phone: 800-872-2377; **Fax:** 877-66-FAXUS;
www.tracers.com **email:** info@tracers.com

Types of Records Retrieved: Civil, criminal and probate courts; Federal courts; Real Estate; Tax liens/Judgments; UCC records; Vital records

Local Retrieval Area: NY-Bronx, Kings, Nassau, New York, Putnam, Queens, Richmond, Rockland, Suffolk, Westchester. **Correspondent Relationships:** Albany, NY; capital region.

Add'l Information: Established 1973. Normal turnaround time- 48-72 hours. Projects billed by number of names searched. 1st project may require prepayment. Credit cards accepted. They specialize in elusive information worldwide including assets discovery and current whereabouts/locates. A licensed PI in NY. They perform service of process.

Tracers International (Schenectady)

146-148 Barrett St #100, Schenectady, NY 12301
Phone: 800-872-2377; 518-370-3463 **Fax:** 518-374-0335
www.tracers.com **email:** info@tracers.com

Types of Records Retrieved: Civil, criminal and probate courts; Federal courts; Real Estate; Tax liens/Judgments; UCC records; Vital records

Local Retrieval Area: NY-Rensselaer, Saratoga, Schenectady, Schoharie. **Correspondent Relationships:** Orange, Dutchess, Rockland, Bronx, New York, Queens, Nassau, Suffolk, Ulster.

Add'l Information: Established 1973. Normal turnaround time- 3-5 days. Projects billed by number of names searched. 1st project may require prepayment. Credit cards accepted. They specialize in elusive information worldwide. They also do skiptracing and asset discovery and current whereabouts/locations. A licensed PI in NY. Performs service of process.

Track' Um Private Investigations

PO Box 4, Wilkesboro, NC 28651
Phone: 336-903-1700 **Fax:** 336-903-1701
www.agentboss.com **email:** Hayden@CarolinaPI.com

Types of Records Retrieved: Civil, criminal and probate courts; Federal courts; Real Estate; Tax liens/Judgments; UCC records; Vital records

Local Retrieval Area: NC-Alexander, Alleghany, Ashe, Caldwell, Catawba, Iredell, Surry, Watauga, Wilkes, Yadkin

Add'l Information: Established 1997. Normal turnaround time- 2 days. Projects billed by the hour. 1st project may require prepayment. They specialize in domestic investigations, process service, record retrieval, locate investigations and insurance investigations. A licensed PI in NC. They perform service of process.

Tracy Cuevas Record Retrieval

3511 Tony Ln, Shephardsville, KY 40165-8926
Phone: 502-957-6459 **Fax:** 502-957-6479 tcuevas007@aol.com

Types of Records Retrieved: Civil and criminal courts; Tax liens/Judgments

Local Retrieval Area: KY-Bullitt, Fayette, Hardin, Jefferson, Nelson, Oldham; IN-Clark, Floyd. **Correspondent Relationships:** nearby Louisville, KY area and IN.

Add'l Information: Established 1992. Normal turnaround time- 24-48 hours. Projects billed by number of names searched. Fee basis varies upon volume. Monthly billing. They have 9 years experience in background research and information retrieval, with an average 24 hour turnaround time. Specializes in 7-year felony-misdemeanor searches on circuit and district levels. Pager #: 502-672-1505. Cell #: 502-673-1033. A licensed PI in KY.

Traill County Abstract

PO Box 69, Hillsboro, ND 58045
Phone: 701-636-4880 **Fax:** 701-636-4880

Types of Records Retrieved: Real Estate; Tax liens/Judgments

Local Retrieval Area: ND-Traill

Add'l Information: Established 1995. 1st project may require prepayment. They specialize in real estate.

Trax

17 Joy St, Barrington, RI 02806 **Phone:** 401-245-3004 **Fax:** 401-245-9443

Types of Records Retrieved: Civil, criminal and probate courts; Federal courts; Real Estate; Tax liens/Judgments; UCC records; Vital records

Local Retrieval Area: RI-Bristol, Kent, Newport, Providence, Washington

Add'l Information: Established 1983. Normal turnaround time- 24 hours. Expedited service available. Projects billed by number of names searched. Terms are net 30 days. 1st project may require prepayment. Terms: net 14 days. Established in 1983. Licensed PI RI State Constable. Skip tracing, asset research, ALL courts researched, title/abstract research (real estate) and national MVR records (trace plate & VIN). Also photographs and measurments of accident locations. A licensed PI in RI. They perform service of process.

Treasure Coast Abstract & Title Ins Co

401 S Indian River Dr, Fort Pierce, FL 34950
Phone: 772-461-7190 **Fax:** 772-468-8461

Types of Records Retrieved: Probate courts; Real Estate; Tax liens/Judgments; UCC records

Local Retrieval Area: FL-Indian River, Martin, Okeechobee, St. Lucie

Add'l Information: Established 1905. Normal turnaround time- 7 days. Fee basis will vary by the type of project. They specialize in residential and commercial title searches. They will file/record UCC and real estate documents on behalf of clients if part of a closing.

Trenton Abstract

203 E 9th #E, Trenton, MO 64683
Phone: 660-359-2100 **Fax:** 660-339-7115

Types of Records Retrieved: Real Estate; Tax liens/Judgments

Local Retrieval Area: MO-Daviess, Grundy, Livingston, Mercer

Add'l Information: Established 1869. 1st project may require prepayment. They specialize in real estate.

Tri County Inv

1122 Briarwood Pl, Salinas, CA 93901
Phone: 831-758-3124 **Fax:** 831-758-0655 bettylyn@redshift.com

Types of Records Retrieved: Civil, criminal and probate courts; Real Estate; Tax liens/Judgments; UCC records; Vital records

Local Retrieval Area: CA-Monterey, San Benito, Santa Cruz

Add'l Information: Established 1987. Normal turnaround time- 24 hours. Projects billed by number of names searched. Monthly billing. They specialize in court record searches and document retrieval of records in the Monterey, Santa Cruz and San Benito, CA area. Cell # 831-594-8639.

Tri County Title & Escrow Co

258 N State St, Osceola, NE 68651
Phone: 402-747-2141 **Fax:** 402-747-2151 tri@alltel.net

Types of Records Retrieved: Probate courts; Federal courts; Real Estate; Tax liens/Judgments; UCC records

Local Retrieval Area: NE-Platte, Polk

Add'l Information: Established 1983. Normal turnaround time- 1 week. Fee basis varies by type of transaction. 1st project may require prepayment. They specialize in title insurance searches.

Triad Consultants

314 Caledonia St #B, Sausalito, CA 94965-1902
Phone: 415-332-4400 **Fax:** 415-332-4405 info@triadcon.com

Types of Records Retrieved: Civil and criminal courts

Local Retrieval Area: CA-Alameda, San Francisco, San Mateo, Santa Clara. **Correspondent Relationships:** nationwide and international.

Add'l Information: Established 1980. Normal turnaround time- 48 hours or less. Projects billed by number of names searched. Credit cards accepted. Billing payable net 30 days. They specialize in pre-employment screening and all types of background investigations. A licensed PI in CA.

Triad Inv

PO Box 913, Bentonville, AR 72712
Phone: 800-400-7582; 479-636-3155 **Fax:** 479-636-1916

triadinv@earthlink.net

Types of Records Retrieved: Civil, criminal and probate courts; Federal courts; Real estate; Tax liens/Judgments; UCC records; Vital records.

Local Retrieval Area: AR-Benton, Carroll, Crawford, Madison, Sebastian, Washington. **Correspondent Relationships:** Arkansas.

Add'l Information: Established 1990. Normal turnaround time- 2-4 days. Expedited service available. Projects billed by the hour. 1st project may require prepayment. The also specialize in insurance investigations, workers' comp, and skiptracing A licensed PI in AR, OK, LA. They perform service of process.

Tri-County Abstract & Title Guaranty

921 1st St N, St Cloud, MN 56303
Phone: 800-892-2399; 320-253-2096 **Fax:** 320-253-4536

Types of Records Retrieved: Real Estate; UCC records; Tax liens/Judgments

Local Retrieval Area: MN-Benton, Mille Lacs, Morrison, Sherburne, Stearns, Wright. **Correspondent Relationships:** statewide.

Add'l Information: Established 1973. Normal turnaround time- 1-10 business days. Projects billed by number of names searched. Projects billed by number of records located. Personal checks are accepted. They do abstracting in six counties, have 2 licensed abstractors, and store records for 5 counties.

Tri-County Land Title

110 S Jefferson St, Berne, IN 46711
Phone: 260-589-3139 **Fax:** 260-589-3130

Types of Records Retrieved: Civil courts; Probate courts; Real Estate; Tax liens/Judgments; UCC records; Vital records

Local Retrieval Area: IN-Adams, Blackford, Jay, Wells

Add'l Information: Established 1986. Normal turnaround time- 1-5 days. Projects billed by number of records located. All projects require prepayment. They specialize in real estate closings and title insurance.

Tri-County Legal Process Service

PO Box 309, 64060 Old Bend-Redmond Hwy #2, Bend, OR 97709
Phone: 800-600-6315; 541-317-5680 **Fax:** 541-317-0143
www.pjprocessplus.com **email:** pjhelikson@pjprocessplus.com

Types of Records Retrieved: Civil and criminal courts

Local Retrieval Area: OR-Crook, Deshutes, Jefferson

Add'l Information: Established 1991. 1st project may require prepayment. They also provide photocopying, skiptracing, DMV, assessor records and background checks. They perform service of process.

Tri-County Process Serving

417 W Fort St, Boise, ID 83702
Phone: 800-473-3454; 208-344-4132 **Fax:** 208-338-1530
tcps@rmci.net

Types of Records Retrieved: Civil, criminal and probate courts; Federal courts; Real Estate; Tax liens/Judgments; UCC records

Local Retrieval Area: ID-Ada, Boise, Canyon, Elmore, Gem, Payette, Valley. **Correspondent Relationships:** Twin Falls, Gooding, Jerome, Bonneville, Madison, Jefferson, Power, most counties in northern Idaho.

Add'l Information: Established 1976. Normal turnaround time- variable depending on project. Projects billed by number of names searched. They specialize in process service and skiptracing. They perform service of process.

Tri-County Title Abstracts Inc

1003 K St NW #215, Washington, DC 20001
Phone: 202-737-6116 **Fax:** 202-737-6117
tricountytitle@verizon.net

Types of Records Retrieved: Civil courts; Probate courts; Real Estate; Tax liens/Judgments; UCC records

Local Retrieval Area: DC-District of Columbia. **Correspondent Relationships:** Montgomery county MD.

Add'l Information: Established 1993. Normal turnaround time- 48-72 hours. Projects billed by number of names searched. Projects billed by number of records located. They charge per transaction for title searches. 1st project may require prepayment. They specialize in UCC, real estate, title searches, judgments, liens, court records, corporate standing and all research activities related to document retrieval and recording.

TRI-County Title LLC

PO Box 128, Washington, MO 63090
Phone: 636-239-7800 **Fax:** 636-239-4002

Types of Records Retrieved: Civil, criminal and probate courts; Real Estate; Tax liens/Judgments; UCC records

Local Retrieval Area: MO-Franklin

Add'l Information: Established 1983. Normal turnaround time- 7 working days. Fee basis will vary by type of project. Fee may be based per tract of land and/or per owner as required. 1st project may require prepayment. Payment due upon receipt. They specialize in title insurance, closings and title searches.

Trident Investigative Service Inc

PO Box 1950, Renton, WA 98057-1950
Phone: 888-277-3238; 206-772-9646 **Fax:** 206-772-9647
www.tridentseattle.com **email:** mike@tridentseattle.com

Types of Records Retrieved: Civil, criminal and probate courts; Federal courts; Real Estate; Tax liens/Judgments; UCC records; Vital records

Local Retrieval Area: WA-Adams, Asotin, Benton, Chelan, Clallam, Clark, Columbia, Cowlitz, Douglas, Ferry, Franklin, Garfield, Grant, Grays Harbor, Island, Jefferson, King, Kitsap, Kittitas, Klickitat, Lewis, Lincoln, Mason, Okanogan, Pacific, Pend Oreille, Pierce, San Juan, Skagit, Skamania, Snohomish, Spokane, Stevens, Thurston, Wahkiakum, Walla Walla, Whatcom, Whitman, Yakima. **Correspondents:** nationwide.

Add'l Information: Established 1991. Normal turnaround time- 1-2 days. Projects billed by the hour. Fee varies depending on type of search. 1st project may require prepayment. Credit cards accepted. They specialize in investigative and data research. A licensed PI in OR, WA. They perform service of process.

Trinity County Abstract

PO Box 249, Groveton, TX 75845
Phone: 936-642-1698 **Fax:** 936-642-1697
trinitycoabst@yahoo.com

Types of Records Retrieved: Civil courts; Probate courts; Real Estate; Tax liens/Judgments; UCC records

Local Retrieval Area: TX-Trinity

Add'l Information: Established 1981. Normal turnaround time- 5-10 working days. Commitments and land searches take 15 working days. Projects billed by number of names searched. 1st project may require prepayment. Personal checks are accepted. Payment upon completion. They specialize in land title searches and title insurance.

Tripp & Todd Title Company

134 E 3rd St, Winner, SD 57580-1804
Phone: 605-842-0334 **Fax:** 605-842-3088 tttco@gwtc.net

Types of Records Retrieved: Civil courts; Probate courts; Real Estate; Tax liens/Judgments; UCC records; Vital records

Local Retrieval Area: SD-Todd, Tripp

Add'l Information: Established 1994. Normal turnaround time- 5 business days. Fee basis will vary by the type of project. 1st project may require prepayment.

TriState Courier

827 King St, Wilmington, DE 19801
Phone: 800-783-0945; 302-654-4264 **Fax:** 302-654-3479
www.tristatecourier.com **email:** docs@tristatecourier.com

Types of Records Retrieved: Civil, criminal and probate courts; Federal courts; Real Estate; Tax liens/Judgments; UCC records

Local Retrieval Area: DE-New Castle. **Correspondent Relationships:** NY, TX, FL, CA, DC, MS, MO, OH & TN.

Add'l Information: Established 1993. Normal turnaround time- 24-48 hours. Expedited service available. Projects billed by number of names searched. 1st project may require prepayment. Credit cards accepted. They specialise in the fastest service offered in New Castle county. TriState is reliable, honest and accurate. They perform service of process.

Triwest Investigative Services

1441 Huntington Dr, #1930, South Pasadena, CA 91030
Phone: 323-254-5151 **Fax:** 323-258-1627 triwest@adelphia.net

Types of Records Retrieved: Civil, criminal and probate courts; Federal courts; Tax liens/Judgments; Vital records

Local Retrieval Area: CA-Los Angeles. **Correspondent Relationships:** southern and Bay area of California; also Oregon; Texas; Florida.

Add'l Information: Established 1995. Normal turnaround time- 24-48 hours. Projects billed by the hour. 1st project may require prepayment. They specialize in corporate and personal due diligence. They have a library of public record indices and proprietary databases to support complex research. A licensed PI in CA. They perform service of process.

Troy Title Co LLC

15 Ellis Ave, Troy, MO 63379-1151
Phone: 636-528-2220 **Fax:** 636-528-3953
www.troytitle.com **email:** janet@troytitle.com

Types of Records Retrieved: Civil courts; Probate courts; Real Estate; Tax liens/Judgments

Local Retrieval Area: MO-Lincoln, Montgomery, Pike, Warren. **Correspondent Relationships:** St Charles County MO.

Add'l Information: Established 1985. Normal turnaround time- 2-3 days. Projects billed by number of names searched. Personal checks are accepted. Specialize in real estate title searches, closings and construction escrows.

Trumbull County Abstract Co

PO Box 1268, 174 N Park Ave, Warren, OH 44482
Phone: 330-399-1891 **Fax:** 330-399-1892 tcac@usawebnet.net

Types of Records Retrieved: Probate courts; Real Estate; Tax liens/Judgments

Local Retrieval Area: OH-Trumbull

Add'l Information: Established 1898. Normal turnaround time- 3 days. Charges vary by project. All projects require prepayment. They specialize in abstracting and real estate title.

TSI - Title Services Inc

7 Woodstone Plza #7, Hattiesburg, MS 39402-8342
Phone: 800-736-9331; 601-264-3500 **Fax:** 601-264-6622

Types of Records Retrieved: Civil, criminal and probate courts; Real Estate; Tax liens/Judgments; UCC records

Local Retrieval Area: MS-Covington, Forrest, Greene, Jefferson Davis, Jones, Lamar, Marion, Pearl River, Perry, Stone, Walthall, Wayne

Add'l Information: Normal turnaround time- 2 days in Forrest county; 3 days all other counties. Fee basis varies by type of transaction. 1st project may require prepayment. Term are net 30 days. A Mississippi residential and commercial title company, they specialize in real estate transactions. Visit their web site.

Taylor Tucker

PO Box 7, Louisville, MS 39339
Phone: 662-773-9254 **Fax:** 662-773-9255 ttucker@telapex.com

Types of Records Retrieved: Civil courts; Probate courts; Real Estate; Tax liens/Judgments; UCC records; Vital records

Local Retrieval Area: MS-Winston

Add'l Information: Normal turnaround time- 2 days. Projects billed by the hour. 1st project may require prepayment. He is an attorney in general practice.

Turner County Abstract

205 N Main St, Parker, SD 57053
Phone: 605-297-5555

Types of Records Retrieved: Real Estate; Tax liens/Judgments.

Local Retrieval Area: SD-Turner

Add'l Information: 1st project may require prepayment. They specialize in real estate.

Barbara Tweedle

PO Box 9, Rosedale, MS 38769
Phone: 662-759-3048, 662-759-3762 **Fax:** 662-759-3467

Types of Records Retrieved: Civil, criminal and probate courts; Real Estate; Tax liens/Judgments; UCC records

Local Retrieval Area: MS-Bolivar

Add'l Information: Normal turnaround time- 1-2 days. Projects billed by number of names searched. All projects require prepayment. She specializes in records at the Rosedale courts. A fax number is available upon request.

Twenty Four Hour Record Retriever & Abstract Inc

1598 Liberty St, Oswego, NY 13126
Phone: 800-294-3740; 315-342-8363 **Fax:** 800-451-5028; 315-342-9058
www.24hourrecordandabstract.com
email: twentyfourhourrr@earthlink.net

Types of Records Retrieved: Civil, criminal and probate courts; Federal Bankruptcy courts; Real Estate; Tax liens/Judgments; UCC records

Local Retrieval Area: NY-Cayuga, Jefferson, Monroe, Onondaga, Oswego

Add'l Information: Established 2003. Normal turnaround time- 24 hours-court records, 24-48 hours-Real Estate searches. Expedited service available. Projects billed by number of names searched. Invoiced weekly, monthly, or per order. They provide timely, quality service for county court records, real estate searches, abstracts, bankruptcy and lien searches. Criminal records available within 24 hours and title insurance underwritten by Land America & First American Title Ins Co. They perform service of process.

Twin Cities Research

PO Box 28636, St Paul, MN 55128
Phone: 651-714-0002 **Fax:** 651-714-0003
twincitiesresearch@hotmail.com

Types of Records Retrieved: Civil, criminal and probate courts; Federal courts; Real Estate; Tax liens/Judgments; UCC records; Vital records

Local Retrieval Area: MN-Anoka, Carver, Chisago, Dakota, Goodhue, Hennepin, Isanti, Kanabec, Lesueur, McLeod, Pine, Ramsey, Scott, Sherburne, Sibley, Washington, Wright; WI-St Croix

Add'l Information: Established 1989. Normal turnaround time- 24-48 hours. Projects billed by number of names searched. Projects are billed by the type of research required. 1st project may require prepayment. They do invoice monthly. They have been serving the Twin Cities metro area for the past 15 years. Their service includes all matters of public record, but they will do their best to meet any research needs you may have. A cell phone number to reach them is 612-840-9846.

Twin City Title Co Inc

PO Box 2791, Texarkana, TX 75504
Phone: 903-793-7671 **Fax:** 903-792-2847

Types of Records Retrieved: Civil courts; Probate courts; Real Estate; Tax liens/Judgments; UCC records

Local Retrieval Area: TX-Bowie

Add'l Information: Normal turnaround time- 7 days. Projects billed by the hour. All projects require prepayment.

Twin Oaks Research

4814 W Woodlawn St, Dunnellon, FL 34433
Phone: 352-465-7844 **Fax:** 352-465-7846
m-hoffman@juno.com

Types of Records Retrieved: Civil and criminal courts, Probate courts, Real Estate; Tax liens/Judgments; UCC records

Local Retrieval Area: FL-Alachua, Citrus, Levy. **Correspondent Relationships:** Levy, Marion, Hernando counties FL.

Add'l Information: Established 1997. Normal turnaround time- 24 hours. Projects billed by number of names searched. They limit their geographical coverage in order to provide excellent local service. If its public record, they will find it!

Tyler-McLennon Choicepoint

701 Brazos St #500, Austin, TX 78701

Phone: 512-334-6244 www.tyler-mclennon.com

Types of Records Retrieved: Civil, criminal and probate courts; Federal courts; Real Estate; Tax liens/Judgments; UCC records; Vital records

Local Retrieval Area: TX-Anderson, Aransas, Austin, Bandera, Bastrop, Bee, Bell Bexar, Bowie, Brazoria, Brazos, Burnet, Caldwell, Calhoun, Cameron, Camp, Cass, Cherokee, Collin, Comal, Coryell, Dallas, Delta, Denton, Ector, Ellis, El Paso, Fort Bend, Franklin, Galveston, Gonzales, Gregg, Gaudalupe, Harris, Harrison, Hays, Henderson, Hidalgo, Hopkins, Hunt, Jefferson. Jim Wells, Karnes, Kaufman, Kendall, Kerr, Kleberg, Lamar, Liberty, Llano, Lubbock, McLennan, Marion, Midland, Milam, Montgomery, Morris, Nacogdoches, Nueces, Panola, Parker, Potter, Rains, Randall, Red River, Refugio, Rockwell, Rusk, San Patricio, Shelby, Smith, Tarrant, Titus, Tom Green, Travis, Upshur, Van Zandt, Victoria, Walker, Williamson, Wilson, Wood; IL-Cook, De Kalb, Du Page, Kane, Kendall, Lake, Madison, McHenry, St. Clair, Will; MO-St. Louis, St. Louis City. **Correspondent Relationships:** Iowa, Missouri, Wisconsin, Indiana, Texas, Oklahoma, Mississippi, Louisiana, Illinois.

Add'l Information: Established 1988. Normal turnaround time- 24-72 hours. Projects billed by number of names searched. Projects billed by the hour. Terms: net 30 days. They specialize in all types of county courthouse, Federal courthouse, criminal, Secretary of State searches, DPS and Texas Dept. of Insurance searches. Also active in IL, IN, IA, MO, and WS.

U

UCC Direct Services

187 Wolf Rd, Suire 101, Albany, NY 12205

Phone: 800-342-3676; 518-434-4020 **Fax:** 518-434-1521

www.intercountyclearance.com **email:** rvanko@uccdirect.com

Types of Records Retrieved: Civil courts; Federal courts; Real Estate; Tax liens/Judgments; UCC records; Secretary of State records

Local Retrieval Area: NY-Albany. **Correspondents:** nationwide.

Add'l Information: Established 1935. Normal turnaround time- 2-3 days. Projects billed by number of names searched. Fee may be based on location searched. 1st project may require prepayment. Credit cards accepted. They have provided public record retrieval services since 1935; offering services including UCC/lien and corporate document search, retrieval, preparation and filing.

UCC Retrievals, Inc

7288 Hanover Green Dr, Mechanicsville, VA 23111

Phone: 804-559-5919 **Fax:** 804-559-5920

www.uccretrievals.com **email:** traci@uccretrievals.com

Types of Records Retrieved: Civil courts; Probate courts; Federal courts; Real Estate; Tax liens/Judgments; UCC records

Local Retrieval Area: VA-Amelia, Buckingham, Caroline, Charles City, Chesterfield, Colonial Heights, Cumberland, Dinwiddie, Essex, Fluvanna, Gloucester, Goochland, Hanover, Henrico, Henry, Hopewell, King and Queen, King George, King William, Louisa, Mathews. Middlesex, New Kent, Nottoway, Petersburg, Powhatan, Prince George, Richmond, Southampton, Sussex, Westmoreland. **Correspondents:** statewide.

Add'l Information: Established 1989. Normal turnaround time- 48 hours. They offer same or next day service at Secretary of State's office for searches and corporate filings. Projects billed by number of names searched. They specialize in all Virginia Counties and Secretary of State, for research, retrieval and filing of public records throughout Virginia. They are located in the capitol. They perform service of process.

UCC Search Inc

1012 Marquez Pl #106B, PO Box 9315 (87504-9315), Santa Fe, NM 87505

Phone: 800-453-9404; 505-983-4228 **Fax:** 800-642-6382; 505-983-1169

uccsearchinc@msn.com

Types of Records Retrieved: Civil and criminal courts; Federal courts; Real Estate; Tax liens/Judgments; UCC records

Local Retrieval Area: NM-Santa Fe. **Correspondent Relationships:** New Mexico.

Add'l Information: Established 1985. Normal turnaround time- 2 days. Projects billed by number of names searched. Terms: net 30 days. 1 1/2% per month interest for late payment. They specialize in customer satisfaction and quick turnaround. They also retrieve corporate records at the state level and file corporate paperwork.

Uinta Title

1048 Main St, Evanston, WY 82930

Phone: 307-789-1777 **Fax:** 307-789-8549

Types of Records Retrieved: Real Estate; Tax liens/Judgments

Local Retrieval Area: WY-Uinta

Add'l Information: Established 1960. 1st project may require prepayment. They specialize in real estate.

Union Abstract Co

200 N Jefferson Ave #214, El Dorado, AR 71730

Phone: 870-863-6053 **Fax:** 870-864-0094

Types of Records Retrieved: Civil courts; Probate courts; Real Estate; Tax liens/Judgments; UCC records **Local Retrieval Area:** AR-Union

Add'l Information: Established 1940. Normal turnaround time- 1 day. Projects billed by the hour. All projects require prepayment.

Union County Abstract & Title Co

PO Box 40, Elk Point, SD 57025-0040

Phone: 605-356-3180 **Fax:** 605-356-3112

Types of Records Retrieved: Civil, criminal and probate courts; Real Estate; Tax liens/Judgments; UCC records; Vital records

Local Retrieval Area: SD-Union

Add'l Information: Established 1940. Normal turnaround time- 24-48 hours. Projects billed by the hour. Fee for copies additional. They specialize in title searches, lien searches, abstracting and title insurance. They are a licensed abstractor for Union County, South Dakota.

Union County Title Co

1 W Union St, Liberty, IN 47353-1349

Phone: 765-458-7148 **Fax:** 765-458-6331 unioncountytitle@aol.com

Types of Records Retrieved: Civil courts; Real Estate; Tax liens/Judgments; UCC records

Local Retrieval Area: IN-Fayette, Franklin, Union, Wayne; OH-Butler, Preble. **Correspondent Relationships:** elsewhere in Indiana.

Add'l Information: Established 1994. Normal turnaround time- 24 hours. Projects billed by number of names searched. Invoices are done at the end of the month.

Union-Speer Abstract Co

22 S Park St, Sapulpa, OK 74066

Phone: 918-224-4540 **Fax:** 918-224-4549

Types of Records Retrieved: Civil courts; Probate courts; Real Estate; Tax liens/Judgments; UCC records

Local Retrieval Area: OK-Creek

Add'l Information: Established 1960. Normal turnaround time- variable depending on project. Fee basis is per page.

Unisearch Inc (California)

1903 21st St, Sacramento, CA 95814-6813
Phone: 800-769-1864; 916-456-4111 **Fax:** 800-769-1868; 916-456-4068
www.unisearch.com

Types of Records Retrieved: Civil and criminal courts; Federal courts; Tax liens/Judgments; UCC records

Local Retrieval Area: CA-Sacramento. **Correspondent Relationships:** statewide, also WA, OR, OH; affiliates with National Registered Agents.

Add'l Information: Established 1995. Normal turnaround time- 1-2 days. Projects billed by number of names searched. 1st project may require prepayment. Credit cards accepted. Payment due net 30 days. They specialize in searching, filing and retrieving public documents nationwide. An extensive range of UCC/Lien and Corporate services to the legal, financial and business community in all 50 states as well as internationally.

Unisearch Inc (Nevada)

9900 Wilbur May Pky #705, Reno, NV 89521
Phone: 800-260-1131; 775-851-4500 **Fax:** 800-260-8118; 775-851-1330
www.unisearch.com **email:** vickij@unisearch.com

Types of Records Retrieved: Civil, criminal and probate courts; Federal courts; Tax liens/Judgments; UCC records; Vital records

Local Retrieval Area: NV-Carson City, Douglas, Washoe. **Correspondent Relationships:** nationwide with affiliates of National Registered Agents.

Add'l Information: Established 1991. Normal turnaround time- 1-2 days. Projects billed by number of names searched. Projects billed by number of records located. Credit cards accepted. Online access to over 40 states' records and UCC records on microfilm for 12 states. A licensed PI in NV.

Unisearch Inc (Ohio)

2545 Hilliard Rome Rd PMB 232, Hilliard, OH 43026-9471
Phone: 877-208-7783; 614-853-3355 **Fax:** 877-440-5104; 614-878-3264
www.unisearch.com **email:** amya@unisearch.com

Types of Records Retrieved: Civil courts; Federal courts; Tax liens/Judgments; UCC records

Local Retrieval Area: OH-Franklin. **Correspondent Relationships:** all states, counties nationwide.

Add'l Information: Established 1991. Normal turnaround time- 24-48 hours. Projects are billed per name searched. Credit cards accepted. They have offices in 7 states and are online to over 30 state offices, and have UCC microfilm for 12 states. They also obtain corporate documents nationwide.

Unisearch Inc (Oregon)

3533 Fairview Industrial Dr SE, Salem, OR 97302-1155
Phone: 800-554-3113; 503-399-9500 **Fax:** 800-554-3114; 503-378-7870
www.unisearch.com **email:** lorettam@unisearch.com

Types of Records Retrieved: Civil courts; Tax liens/Judgments; UCC records

Local Retrieval Area: OR-Marion. **Correspondents:** nationwide.

Add'l Information: Established 1991. Normal turnaround time- 1-2 days. Projects billed by number of names searched. Copy costs and disbursements are added to the search charge. Credit cards accepted. They specialize in UCC, corporate and registered agent services throughout the United States. They also search/retrieve/file documents with the Oregon Secretary of State.

Unisearch Inc (Washington)

1780 Barnes Blvd SW, Tumwater, WA 98512-0410
Phone: 800-722-0708; 360-956-9500 **Fax:** 800-531-1717; 360-956-9504
www.unisearch.com **email:** wendyb@unisearch.com

Types of Records Retrieved: Civil and criminal courts; Federal courts; Tax liens/Judgments; UCC records; Vital records

Local Retrieval Area: WA-King, Lewis, Mason, Pierce, Skagit, Snohomish, Thurston. **Correspondent Relationships:** nationwide.

Add'l Information: Established 1991. Normal turnaround time- 24-48 hours. Projects billed by number of names searched. Copy costs and disbursements are added to search charge. Credit cards accepted. They have online access to over 30 states' records. They have microfilm for 12 states. A licensed PI in NV.

United Attorneys' Services

601 University Ave #134, Sacramento, CA 95825
Phone: 916-457-3000

Types of Records Retrieved: Civil, criminal and probate courts; Federal courts; Real Estate; Tax liens/Judgments; UCC records; Vital records

Local Retrieval Area: CA-Placer, Sacramento, San Joaquin, Yolo. **Correspondent Relationships:** Solano, El Dorado, Nevada counties.

Add'l Information: Established 1980. Normal turnaround time- 4 days. Projects billed by number of names searched. Personal checks are accepted.

United Legal Services

217 N Harvey #102, Oklahoma City, OK 73102
Phone: 888-232-8432; 405-232-8432 **Fax:** 405-232-8442
alongi100@aol.com

Types of Records Retrieved: Civil, criminal and probate courts; Federal courts; Real Estate; Tax liens/Judgments; UCC records

Local Retrieval Area: OK-Canadian, Cleveland, Grady, Lincoln, Logan, McClain, Oklahoma, Pottawatomie. **Correspondent Relationships:** Oklahoma.

Add'l Information: Established 1970. Normal turnaround time- 48 hours for close counties. Contract areas average 3-4 days. Projects billed by the hour. 1st project may require prepayment. Personal checks are accepted. They perform service of process.

Universal Background Screening

4000 N Central Ave #1000, Phoenix, AZ 85012
Phone: 602-263-8033 **Fax:** 602-274-3551
www.universalbackground.com **email:** info@universalbackground.com

Types of Records Retrieved: Criminal courts

Local Retrieval Area: AZ-Maricopa. **Correspondents:** statewide.

Add'l Information: Normal turnaround time- 24-48 hours. Projects billed by number of names searched. 1st project may require prepayment. Terms are net 30 days. They specialize in criminal court searches and drug screening; nationwide court searches available. A licensed PI in AZ.

Universal Information Research

PO Box 8154, Mission Hills, CA 91346
Phone: 800-363-9813; 818-894-6226 **Fax:** 888-307-3433; 818-894-0868
www.piagency.com **email:** piagency@piagency.com

Types of Records Retrieved: Civil, criminal and probate courts; Federal courts; Real Estate; UCC records; Vital records

Local Retrieval Area: CA-Alameda, Los Angeles, Marin, Orange, Riverside, San Bernardino, San Diego, San Francisco, Santa Clara, Ventura. **Correspondent Relationships:** Ventura, Marin, Alameda, Santa Clara, San Francisco, also nationwide.

Add'l Information: Established 1994. Normal turnaround time- 48-72 hours. Projects billed by the hour. They do monthly billings. Credit cards accepted. Mastercard, Visa and American Express accepted. They are a full service company. They specialize in court record searches and subpoena files. They also take statements, conduct activity checks and do surveillance. A licensed PI in CA. They perform service of process.

Upper State Title Corp

PO Box 2205, Anderson, SC 29625-2205
Phone: 864-260-4649 **Fax:** 864-231-8419

Types of Records Retrieved: Probate courts; Real Estate; Tax liens/Judgments; UCC records; Vital records

Local Retrieval Area: SC-Abbeville, Anderson, Greenville, Greenwood, Laurens, McCormick, Oconee, Pickens, Spartanburg

Add'l Information: Normal turnaround time- 2-3 days. Projects billed by number of names searched. Projects billed by number of records located. Projects billed by the hour. All projects require prepayment.

Upstate Investigations

2418 Hwy 72 / 221 East, Greenwood, SC 29649
Phone: 864-277-0757 **Fax:** 253-322-9230
www.UpstateInvestigations.com **email:** wbensel@InfoAve.net

Types of Records Retrieved: Civil and criminal courts; Tax liens/Judgments

Local Retrieval Area: SC-Abbeville, Greenwood, McCormick

Add'l Information: Established 1995. Normal turnaround time- 24-48 hours. Projects billed by number of names searched. 1st project may require prepayment. They are an all around investigative agency. A licensed PI in SC. They perform service of process.

Urban Abstract Inc

6727 Eagle Creek Dr, Liberty Township, OH 45011
Phone: 513-755-8527 **Fax:** 513-755-8591 2black.cats@fuse.net

Types of Records Retrieved: Civil courts; Probate courts; Real Estate; UCC records

Local Retrieval Area: OH-Butler, Hamilton, Warren

Add'l Information: Established 1984. Normal turnaround time- 24-48 hours. Projects billed by number of names searched. 1st project may require prepayment. She specializes in current owner, 42 year, 62 year and commercial real estate searches.

Urban Title Search Services

609 W Main St, Ashland, OH 44805
Phone: 419-289-0437 **Fax:** 419-282-0437

Types of Records Retrieved: Civil, criminal and probate courts; Real Estate; Tax liens/Judgments; UCC records; Vital records

Local Retrieval Area: OH-Ashland, Holmes, Richland, Wayne

Add'l Information: Normal turnaround time- 24-48 hours. Projects billed by number of names searched. 1st project may require prepayment.

US Background Screening Inc

638 Lindero Canyon Rd #136, Oak Park, CA 91377
Phone: 866-777-1322; **Fax:** 866-777-1323;
www.usbscorp.net **email:** andrew@usbscorp.net

Types of Records Retrieved: Civil and criminal courts

Local Retrieval Area: CA-Los Angeles. **Correspondents:** nationwide.

Add'l Information: Established 1947. Normal turnaround time- 48 hours. Projects billed by number of names searched. 1st project may require prepayment. Credit cards accepted. Will invoice bi-monthly. They are a wholesale Felony and Misdemeanor research firm. They conduct research in every county in US. They service many of the largest background screening companies in the US. Statewide searches are available in addition to the county levels.

US Corporate Services

380 Jackson St #418, St Paul, MN 55101-3899
Phone: 800-327-1886; 651-227-7575 **Fax:** 800-603-0266; 651-225-9244
www.uscorpserv.com **email:** info@uscorpserv.com

Types of Records Retrieved: Civil courts; Probate courts; Federal courts; Real Estate; Tax liens/Judgments; UCC records; Vital records

Local Retrieval Area: MN-Anoka, Carver, Dakota, Hennepin, Ramsey, Scott, Sherburne, Washington, Wright. **Correspondents:** nationwide.

Add'l Information: Established 1966. Normal turnaround time- 24-72 hours. Projects billed by number of names searched. Will invoice monthly. They specialize in handling the needs of credit and banking professionals as they pertain to UCCs and the requisite due diligence associated with lending. Also has an office in Portland, OR.

US Document Retrieval Service Inc

225 Broadway, 8th Floor, New York, NY 10007
Phone: 800-595-0145; 212-528-0777 **Fax:** 800-595-3261; 212-528-1620
www.usretrieval.com **email:** robin@usretrieval.com

Types of Records Retrieved: Civil, criminal and probate courts; Federal courts; Real Estate; Tax liens/Judgments; Vital records

Local Retrieval Area: NJ-Atlantic, Bergen, Camden, Essex, Hudson, Middlesex, Monmouth, Morris, Ocean, Union; NY-Bronx, Kings, Nassau, Orange, Queens, Richmond, Rockland, Suffolk, Westchester. **Correspondent Relationships:** nationwide.

Add'l Information: Established 1998. Normal turnaround time- within 24 hours. Projects billed by the hour. 1st project may require prepayment. Credit cards accepted. Payment due upon receipt. They specialize in complex research and retrieval in all state & federal courts, including New York, New Jersey, and lower Connecticut. Eighteen years experience with the NY state court system.

US Legal Support of Lubbock

PO Box 11564, Lubbock, TX 79408
Phone: 877-947-8500; 806-747-8500 **Fax:** 806-741-0947
ayoung4927@aol.com

Types of Records Retrieved: Civil, criminal and probate courts; Real Estate; Tax liens/Judgments; UCC records; Vital records

Local Retrieval Area: TX-Lubbock. **Correspondent Relationships:** a network within Texas.

Add'l Information: Established 1988. Normal turnaround time- 1-3 days. Fee basis varies by type of transaction. 1st project may require prepayment. They have process servers who will do record retrieval, filing, court searches, and more. Call for quote. They perform service of process.

USIS - Commercial Services

PO Box 8366, Missoula, MT 59807
Phone: 800-331-9175 x2433; 406-728-0001 **Fax:** 406-728-0006
www.diligence.com **email:** sherri.taylor@usis-csd.com

Types of Records Retrieved: Civil, criminal and probate courts; Federal courts; Real Estate; Tax liens/Judgments; UCC records; Vital records

Local Retrieval Area: MT-Missoula. **Correspondent Relationships:** nationwide, Canada, Puerto Rico, Guam, Virgin Is. They have direct correspondence with over 4,000 record retrievers.

Add'l Information: Established 1994. Normal turnaround time- averages 36 hours. Projects billed by number of names searched. Credit cards accepted. They offer both billing and prepaid accounts. Volume pricing offered. Formerly known as Due Diligence, this research firm specializes in nationwide criminal records, plus over 40 other services. Orders accepted via web, proprietary software, fax, email, data transfer. A licensed PI in MT.

Utah Title & Abstract

PO Box 337, 109 E 200 N, Richfield, UT 84701
Phone: 435-896-5429 **Fax:** 435-896-6095 uttitle@xmission.com

Types of Records Retrieved: Civil, criminal and probate courts; Real Estate; Tax liens/Judgments; UCC records

Local Retrieval Area: UT-Millard, Piute, Sevier, Wayne

Add'l Information: Established 1981. Normal turnaround time- as much as 2-3 weeks. Projects billed by the hour. All projects require prepayment.

V

V & A Research LLC

6198 Co Rd 33, Skipperville, AL 36374
Phone: 334-774-7092 **Fax:** 334-774-7092

Types of Records Retrieved: Probate courts; Real Estate; Tax liens/Judgments; UCC records

Local Retrieval Area: AL-Coffee, Dale, Geneva, Henry, Houston

Add'l Information: Established 1995. Normal turnaround time- 24-48 hours. If search takes longer, will notify client. Fees based upon type of search requested. Payment due upon receipt of invoice. They research probate, tax, real estate, marriage and estate records, specializing in title searches, UCC/lien searches, updates and document recordings.

VA Abstract & Title Agency

PO Box 752, Concord, VA 24538
Phone: 434-941-2569 **Fax:** 434-376-7295

Types of Records Retrieved: Real Estate; Tax liens/Judgments

Local Retrieval Area: VA-Charlotte

Add'l Information: Established 1994. 1st project may require prepayment. They specialize in real estate.

Valley Abstract & Trustee Services

1408 Palm Valley Dr East, Harlingen, TX 78552

Phone: 956-571-1119 **Fax:** 956-412-1117

valleyabstract@aol.com

Types of Records Retrieved: Civil courts; Probate courts; Federal courts; Real Estate; Tax liens/Judgments; UCC records

Local Retrieval Area: TX-Cameron, Hidalgo, Willacy

Add'l Information: Established 1998. Normal turnaround time- 24-48 hours. Projects billed by number of names searched. They specialize in providing quality title abstracting (focusing on foreclosure work) and trustee services in the Rio Grande Valley of TX.

Valley County Abstract Company

431 2nd Ave S, Glasgow, MT 59230

Phone: 406-228-2350 **Fax:** 406-228-2350

Types of Records Retrieved: Civil, criminal and probate courts; Real Estate; Tax liens/Judgments; UCC records; Vital records

Local Retrieval Area: MT-Valley

Add'l Information: Established 1950. Normal turnaround time- variable depending on project. Projects billed by the hour. They specialize in mineral searches and title insurance.

Valley Security Inc

3136 Hwy 70, Thatcher, AZ 85552

Phone: 928-428-2142 **Fax:** 928-428-6653

Types of Records Retrieved: Civil and criminal courts

Local Retrieval Area: Az-Cochise, Graham, Greenlee

Add'l Information: Established 2000. 1st project may require prepayment. They provide document retrieval and messenger service to and from attorneys and courts. They do not service Southern Cochise County. They perform service of process.

Valley Title Services Inc

PO Box 141, 306 W Pike St, Vevay, IN 47043

Phone: 812-427-2135 **Fax:** 812-427-2139

Types of Records Retrieved: Civil courts; Probate courts; Real Estate; Tax liens/Judgments; UCC records

Local Retrieval Area: IN-Switzerland

Add'l Information: Normal turnaround time- normally 36-48 hours.

Valverde Abstract Co Inc

PO Box 5, 304 Main St, Center, NE 68724

Phone: 402-288-4466 **Fax:** 402-288-4426

Types of Records Retrieved: Civil, criminal and probate courts; Real Estate; Tax liens/Judgments

Local Retrieval Area: NE-Knox

Add'l Information: Established 1987. Normal turnaround time- 48 hours. Projects billed by the hour. 1st project may require prepayment.

Van Buren Abstract Co

PO Box 218, 405 Dodge St, Keosauqua, IA 52565

Phone: 319-293-7760 **Fax:** 319-293-6431

Types of Records Retrieved: Civil, criminal and probate courts; Real Estate; Tax liens/Judgments; UCC records; Vital records

Local Retrieval Area: IA-Van Buren

Add'l Information: Established 1930. Normal turnaround time- 2-3 days. Fee basis will vary by the type of project. 1st project may require prepayment.

Van Buren County Abstract Office

207 Paw Paw St, Paw Paw, MI 49079

Phone: 269-657-4250 **Fax:** 269-657-3207 vbcao@aol.com

Types of Records Retrieved: Civil, criminal and probate courts; Real Estate; Tax liens/Judgments; UCC records; Vital records

Local Retrieval Area: MI-Van Buren

Add'l Information: Established 1800. Normal turnaround time- 2-3 days. Expedited service available. Fee basis will vary by type of project. All projects require prepayment. They specialize in real estate matters.

Laura Vance

7313 Hiway 522, Totz, KY 40870

Phone: 606-574-1912, 606-273-2460 cell **Fax:** 606-573-7912

Types of Records Retrieved: Real Estate; Tax liens/Judgments

Local Retrieval Area: KY- Harlan

Add'l Information: Established 2001. 1st project may require prepayment. She specializes in real estate.

Vancouver Legal Messengers Inc

1612 Columbia St #A, Vancouver, WA 98660

Phone: 888-695-3654; 360-695-3654 **Fax:** 360-695-3894

www.vanlegal.com **email:** vlm@vanlegal.com

Types of Records Retrieved: Civil and criminal courts; Federal courts; Real Estate; Tax liens/Judgments; UCC records; Vital records

Local Retrieval Area: OR-Clackamas, Multnomah, Washington; WA-Clark, Cowlitz, Klickitat, Pacific, Skamania, Wahkiakum. **Correspondent Relationships:** worldwide.

Add'l Information: Established 1995. Normal turnaround time- 2-3 days. Expedited service available. Projects billed by number of names searched. Projects billed by the hour. 1st project may require prepayment. VLM can file legal documents with local, state and federal court systems, also deliver documents to the County Clerk, Auditor, Recorder or other municipal offices. They perform service of process.

Vanhorn & Vanhorn Inc

PO Box 1742, Clarksburg, WV 26302

Phone: 304-623-1362 **Fax:** 304-623-1363

www.vanhornpi.com **email:** info@vanhornpi.com

Types of Records Retrieved: Civil, criminal and probate courts; Federal courts; Real Estate; Tax liens/Judgments; UCC records; Vital records; Votor registration records

Local Retrieval Area: WV-Barbour, Doddridge, Harrison, Lewis, Marion, Taylor, Upshur. **Correspondent Relationships:** Roanoke, VA.

Add'l Information: Established 1979. Normal turnaround time- 1-3 days. Projects billed by number of names searched. Fees negotiated with volume. 1st project may require prepayment. They specialize in civil and criminal courts, probate courts, federal courts, real estate, tax liens and judgments, UCC records, vital records and votor registration records. A licensed PI in VA, WV.. They perform service of process.

Varoga & Shallett

3303 Louisiana #240, Houston, TX 77006

Phone: 713-522-0101 **Fax:** 713-522-0440

Types of Records Retrieved: Civil, criminal and probate courts; Federal courts; Real Estate; Tax liens/Judgments; UCC records; Vital records

Local Retrieval Area: TX-Harris. **Correspondent Relationships:** Alameda, Contra Costa, Marin, San Francisco, San Mateo, Santa Clara counties CA.

Add'l Information: Established 1995. Normal turnaround time- 1 day. Projects billed by the hour. They specialize in search strategy design as well as drafting and monitoring FOIA and Open Records Act requests.

VeriCORP, Inc

PO Box 436054, Louisville, KY 40253-6054

Phone: 800-416-2769; 502-254-1497 **Fax:** 502-254-5288

www.vericorp.org **email:** gdewitt@vericorp.org

Types of Records Retrieved: Criminal courts

Local Retrieval Area: KY-Fayette, Jefferson, Oldham, Shelby. **Correspondent Relationships:** national and worldwide.

Add'l Information: Established 1996. Normal turnaround time- 24-36 hours. Projects billed by number of names searched. 1st project may require prepayment. Credit cards accepted. Invoice terms are net 15 days. Full-service company with electronic data communication capability. Provides Windows-based software for clients; either modem to modem or Internet order/delivery. Automated processing system available for screening companies; also for court resesearchers. A licensed PI in KY.

Verified Credentials Inc

20890 Kenbridge Ct, Lakeville, MN 55044
Phone: 800-473-4934; 952-985-7200 **Fax:** 952-985-7218
www.verifiedcredentials.com

Types of Records Retrieved: Civil, criminal and probate courts; Federal courts; Real Estate; Tax liens/Judgments; UCC records; Vital records

Local Retrieval Area: MN-Anoka, Carver, Chisago, Dakota, Goodhue, Hennepin, Ramsey, Rice, Scott, Sherburne, Stearns, Washington, Wright. **Correspondent Relationships:** nationwide.

Add'l Information: Established 1984. Normal turnaround time- 24 hours. Projects billed by number of names searched. Credit cards accepted. They specialize in employment background screening. They have 20 years of criminal record searching experience.

VeriQuest Inc

3837 Northdale Blvd #162, Tampa, FL 33624-1841
Phone: 813-948-4889 **Fax:** 813-949-9599
customerservice@veriquestiq.com

Types of Records Retrieved: Civil and criminal courts.

Local Retrieval Area: FL-Broward, Dade, Duval, Hernando, Hillsborough, Leon, Manatee, Orange, Pasco, Pinellas, Polk, Sarasota. **Correspondent Relationships:** nationwide.

Add'l Information: Normal turnaround time- 24 - 72 hours. Online ordering available. Projects billed by number of names searched. 1st project may require prepayment. Veriquest also offers national services for background screening as well as the hands on record retrieval services to the Florida counties listed here.

Veritas Information Services

9 Alton St, Arlington, MA 02474
Phone: 781-643-7811 **Fax:** 781-643-1136
www.veritasinfo.com **email:** michael@veritasinfo.com

Types of Records Retrieved: Real Estate; Genealogical Searches

Local Retrieval Area: MA-Middlesex, Norfolk, Suffolk. **Correspondent Relationships:** Essex, Barnstable, Bristol, Worcester counties.

Add'l Information: Established 1994. Normal turnaround time- 48 hours; longer for real estate. Projects billed by the hour. 1st project may require prepayment. They specialize in real estate title examinations, including resolution of lost or disputed ownerships.

Vermont Land Records Research

460 Acorn Ln, Shelburne, VT 05482-6395
Phone: 802-985-9723
www.vermontlandrecords.com **email:** ddf@together.net

Types of Records Retrieved: Civil, criminal and probate courts; Federal courts; Real Estate; Tax liens/Judgments; UCC records

Local Retrieval Area: VT-Addison, Bennington, Caledonia, Chittenden, Essex, Franklin, Grand Isle, Lamoille, Orange, Orleans, Rutland, Washington, Windham, Windsor

Add'l Information: Established 1995. Normal turnaround time- 48 hours. Projects billed by the hour. They specialize in real estate/land records. They file documents in Chittenden County only.

Vin Lunney Inv

140 Bay View Ave, Bristol, RI 02809
Phone: 401-253-6052 **Fax:** 401-253-6052
vinlunney@yahoo.com

Types of Records Retrieved: Civil, criminal and probate courts; Real Estate; Vital records

Local Retrieval Area: RI-all counties. **Correspondent Relationships:** Los Angeles, Sacramento, Ventura counties CA, and Manhattan, NY.

Add'l Information: Established 1997. Normal turnaround time- 48 hours. Projects billed by number of names searched. They specialize in civil court, real estate and title services (Providence county only), DMV License plates only (RI, FL, OH, TX only). Nationwide SSN search & verification, judgment recovery and skiptracing. A licensed PI in RI.

Vinita Title Co

PO Box 306, Vinita, OK 74301
Phone: 918-256-2617 **Fax:** 918-256-3412
www.vinitatitle.com **email:** vtc@vinitatitle.com

Types of Records Retrieved: Real Estate; Tax liens/Judgments; UCC records; Vital records

Local Retrieval Area: OK-Craig

Add'l Information: Established 1972. Normal turnaround time- 48 hours. Projects billed by number of names searched. All projects require prepayment.

Vinson Detective Agency

955 Howard, New Orleans, LA 70113
Phone: 800-441-7899; 504-529-2260 **Fax:** 504-524-2039
www.vinsonguard.com **email:** dcampo@i-55.com

Types of Records Retrieved: Civil and criminal courts; Federal courts; Real Estate; Tax liens/Judgments; UCC records

Local Retrieval Area: LA-Ascension, Bossier, Caddo, Calcasieu, East Baton Rouge, Iberia, Iberville, Jefferson, Lafayette, Lafourche, Orleans, Ouachita, Plaquemines, Rapides, St. Bernard, St. Charles, St. John the Baptist, St. Landry, St. Mary, St. Tammany, Terrebonne, West Baton Rouge

Add'l Information: Established 1963. Normal turnaround time- 3-5 days. Projects billed by number of names searched. 1st project may require prepayment. Credit cards accepted. A licensed PI in LA. They perform service of process.

Vinson Detective Agency

2531 Lafayette Plaza Dr #C, Albany, GA 31707
Phone: 800-404-6698; 229-883-2144 **Fax:** 229-435-9577
www.vinsonguard.com **email:** vgs_ga@bellsouth.net

Types of Records Retrieved: Civil and criminal courts; Federal Bankruptcy courts; Real Estate; Tax liens/Judgments; UCC records; Vital records

Local Retrieval Area: GA-Baker, Colquitt, Dougherty, Lee, Thomas, Tift, Worth

Add'l Information: Established 1963. Normal turnaround time- 3-5 days. Projects billed by number of names searched. 1st project may require prepayment. Credit cards accepted. A licensed PI in GA. They perform service of process.

Vinson Detective Agency AL

2158 Government St, Mobile, AL 36606
Phone: 800-438-6072; 251-476-8231 **Fax:** 251-476-8239
www.vinsonguard.com **email:** mobile@vinsonguard.com

Types of Records Retrieved: Civil and criminal courts; Federal courts

Local Retrieval Area: AL-Baldwin, Clarke, Conecuh, Escambia, Jefferson, Mobile, Monroe, Washington

Add'l Information: Normal turnaround time- 3-5 days. Projects billed by number of names searched. 1st project may require prepayment. Credit cards accepted. They perform service of process.

Vinson Detective Agency TN

2008 E Magnolia Ave, Knoxville, TN 37917
Phone: 888-525-5047; 865-525-5047 **Fax:** 865-525-7960
www.vinsonguard.com **email:** vgs_vivian@bellsouth.net

Types of Records Retrieved: Civil, criminal and probate courts; Federal courts; Real Estate; Tax liens/Judgments; UCC records; Vital records

Local Retrieval Area: TN-Anderson, Blount, Jefferson, Knox, Sevier

Add'l Information: Normal turnaround time- 3-5 days. Projects billed by number of names searched. 1st project may require prepayment. Credit cards accepted. They perform service of process.

Vio-Com-Data Research

6295 N Anna St, Fresno, CA 93710-5305
Phone: 559-438-1058 **Fax:** 559-438-1158
Kricha4634@aol.com

Types of Records Retrieved: Civil, criminal and probate courts; Federal courts; Real Estate; Tax liens/Judgments; UCC records; Vital records

Local Retrieval Area: CA-Fresno, Kern, Kings, Madera, Tulare, Ventura. **Correspondent Relationships:** nationwide.

Add'l Information: Established 1996. Normal turnaround time- 24 hours in Fresno and Madera; 48 hours for other counties. Projects billed by number of names searched. Monthly billing available. Terms are net 45 days. They have over 30 years experience in criminal research. Low prices and best service, can beat any other prices in the area. Cell number is 559-974-1961.

VISTA Inc

29516 Southfield Rd, Southfield, MI 48076-2029
Phone: 248-559-3500 **Fax:** 248-559-4757
www.vistapi.com **email:** gporter@vistapi.com

Types of Records Retrieved: Civil, criminal and probate courts; Federal courts; Real Estate; Tax liens/Judgments; UCC records; Vital records

Local Retrieval Area: MI-Macomb, Monroe, Oakland, Washtenaw, Wayne. **Correspondent Relationships:** Michigan.

Add'l Information: Established 1976. Normal turnaround time- 1-2 weeks depending on the county. Projects billed by number of names searched. Projects billed by the hour. 1st project may require prepayment. May require retainer if not affiliated with national PI organization. They specialize in defense sub rosa. They also have the capability to retrieve documents in most European venues. A licensed PI in MI. They perform service of process.

Robert Vollrath

PO Box 010068, Miami, FL 33101-0068
Phone: 305-343-9344 **Fax:** 305-444-1563
www.robertvollrath.com **email:** robvoll@bellsouth.net

Types of Records Retrieved: Civil, criminal and probate courts; Federal courts; Real Estate; Tax liens/Judgments; UCC records; Vital records

Local Retrieval Area: FL-Dade

Add'l Information: Established 1983. Normal turnaround time- 1 week. Projects billed by the hour. All projects require prepayment. He is a licensed private investigator who specializes in process service. A licensed PI in FL. They perform service of process.

VPS

311 Hiddenwood Rd, Fayston, VT 05673
Phone: 802-496-6863 **Fax:** 802-496-6865
vpsdcain@madriver.com

Types of Records Retrieved: Civil and criminal courts.

Local Retrieval Area: VT-Chittenden, Washington

Add'l Information: Established 1997. All projects require prepayment. They also provide court filings, subpoena preparation, photocopying, skiptracing, videography, photography, and state public record searches. They perform service of process.

W

W P Mortensen & Associates

PO Box 2619, Dublin, CA 94568
Phone: 925-828-6440 www.seek-truth.net

Types of Records Retrieved: Civil, criminal and probate courts; Federal courts; Real Estate; Tax liens/Judgments; UCC records; Vital records

Local Retrieval Area: CA-Alameda, Contra Costa

Add'l Information: Established 1992. Normal turnaround time- 1 week. Expedited service avalaible. Projects billed by the hour. 1st project may require prepayment. They specialize in background investigations, due diligence, locates, skiptrace, process service, theft and competitive intelligence investigations. They are a California licensed private investigation agency (PI# 18794), and notary public. A licensed PI in CA. They perform service of process.

W.E. Works Office/Attorney Support

2373 Apache Dr, Bishop, CA 93514
Phone: 760-873-3788 **Fax:** 760-873-4208
www.weworks.com/wwnpage2.html **email:** weworks98@yahoo.com

Types of Records Retrieved: Civil and criminal courts; Bankruptcy court; Real Estate; Tax liens/Judgments; Vital records

Local Retrieval Area: CA-Inyo, Mono

Add'l Information: Established 1997. Normal turnaround time- 1-2 days. Expedited service available. Projects billed by the hour. 1st project may require prepayment. They have a mobile photocopier and are a mobile Notary Public; certified notary signing agent. Member of CAPPS, NAPPS, NNA. They perform service of process.

Wabash Valley Abstract Co Inc

PO Box 1350, 2 1/2 N Broadway #203, Peru, IN 46970
Phone: 765-472-4351 **Fax:** 765-472-4352 www.wvaco.com

Types of Records Retrieved: Civil courts; Probate courts; Real Estate; Tax liens/Judgments; UCC records

Local Retrieval Area: IN-Miami

Add'l Information: Established 1929. Normal turnaround time- 5-7 days. Projects billed by number of records located. Payments are also based on the premium and search time.

Wabasha County Abstract Co

100 W Main St, Wabasha, MN 55981
Phone: 651-565-3391 **Fax:** 651-565-4558 wababst@wabasha.net

Types of Records Retrieved: Civil courts; Probate courts; Federal courts; Real Estate; Tax liens/Judgments; UCC records; Vital records

Local Retrieval Area: MN-Wabasha

Add'l Information: Established 1976. Normal turnaround time- 1 week. Projects billed by number of names searched. Payment upon receipt of invoice. They specialize in posting abstract of title, preparing owner & encumbrance reports, name searches, real estate tax searches, preparation of new abstracts and research of real estate records.

Wagoner County Abstract Co

PO Box 188, 219 E Cherokee, 74467, Wagoner, OK 74477
Phone: 918-485-2215 **Fax:** 918-485-9162 avcfi@aol.com

Types of Records Retrieved: Civil courts; Probate courts; Real Estate; Tax liens/Judgments; UCC records

Local Retrieval Area: OK-Wagoner

Add'l Information: Established 1907. Normal turnaround time- 2-3 days. Projects billed on per case basis. Personal checks and cash are accepted. They have serviced Wagoner County since 1907.

Wakeman Process Service Inc

22283 Main Street, Hayward, CA 94541
Phone: 510-886-7667 **Fax:** 510-886-1523
wakeman_process@hotmail.com

Types of Records Retrieved: Civil, criminal and probate courts; Federal courts; Real Estate; Tax liens/Judgments; UCC records; Vital records

Local Retrieval Area: CA-Alameda, Contra Costa, Marin, San Francisco, San Mateo, Santa Clara, Solano. **Correspondent Relationships:** nationwide.

Add'l Information: Established 1967. Normal turnaround time- 3-5 business days depending on size of job. Projects billed by number of names searched. Projects billed by number of records located. 1st project may require prepayment. All records copied on microfilm copier and reproduced according to request. Also offer subpoena preparation and service. They perform service of process.

Walla Walla Title Co

PO Box 1058, 102 W Main St #100, Walla Walla, WA 99362
Phone: 509-525-8660 **Fax:** 509-529-4716

Types of Records Retrieved: Civil courts; Probate courts; Real Estate; Tax liens/Judgments; UCC records; Vital records

Local Retrieval Area: WA-Walla Walla

Add'l Information: Established 1970. Normal turnaround time- 1-2 days. Fee basis is determined on "per job". Out of area clients are asked to prepay. They specialize in real estate matters.

Walsh Inv Services

PO Box 524, Fishkill, NY 12524-0524
Phone: 888-438-9757; 845-896-3566 **Fax:** 845-896-3584
www.walshinvestigative.com **email:** hwalsh@walshinvestigative.com

Types of Records Retrieved: Civil, criminal and probate courts; Federal courts; Real Estate; Tax liens/Judgments; UCC records; Vital records

Local Retrieval Area: NY-Columbia, Dutchess, Orange, Putnam, Rockland, Sullivan, Ulster, Westchester. **Correspondent Relationships:** New York County, Long Island, Albany.

Add'l Information: Established 1988. Normal turnaround time- 1-2 days. Expedited service available. Projects billed by the hour. 1st project may require prepayment. They specialize in all types of record retrieval and all types of searches performed. A licensed PI in NY. They perform service of process.

Walworth County Abstract & Title

PO Box 418, Selby, SD 57472-0418
Phone: 605-649-7772 **Fax:** 605-649-7204

Types of Records Retrieved: Civil courts; Probate courts; Real Estate; Tax liens/Judgments; UCC records

Local Retrieval Area: SD-Walworth

Add'l Information: Established 1895. Normal turnaround time- 2 days. Projects billed by number of records located.

Ward Abstracting Svcs

95 Ridgeview Court, Roanoke Rapids, NC 27870
Phone: 252-535-3440 **Fax:** 252-537-7437 mhl1959@aol.com

Types of Records Retrieved: Civil, criminal and probate courts; Real Estate; Tax liens/Judgments; UCC records; Vital records.

Local Retrieval Area: NC-Halifax, Northampton, Warren. **Correspondent Relationships:** They may search nearby counties upon request such as Edgecombe, Nash, Franklin, Vance, others.

Add'l Information: Established 1986. Normal turnaround time- 24 hours; most performed the same day. Projects billed by number of names searched. All projects require prepayment. Has 25 years experience in courthouse real estate serches and record searches that include civil, probate, UCC, vitals, tax liens and real estate.

Larry M Warner

PO Box 601, Crossville, TN 38557
Phone: 931-484-1611 **Fax:** 931-484-4509

Types of Records Retrieved: Criminal courts; Real Estate; Tax liens/Judgments

Local Retrieval Area: TN-Clay, Cumberland, Fentress, Overton, Pickett, Putnam, White

Add'l Information: Established 1974. Normal turnaround time- 1-2 days. Fee basis will vary with type of search. He is an attorney. For real estate, they can only provide records from Cumberland county.

Warren County Abstract Company

215 W Salem Ave, Indianola, IA 50125-2420
Phone: 515-961-7479 **Fax:** 515-961-7470

Types of Records Retrieved: Probate courts; Real Estate; Tax liens/Judgments; UCC records; Vital records

Local Retrieval Area: IA-Warren

Add'l Information: Established 1970. Normal turnaround time- 24 hours for most abstract continuations and 1 week for title abstracts. Projects billed by number of names searched. Projects billed by number of records located. Personal checks are accepted.

Wasatch Inv Inc

2375 West 5800 South, Roy, UT 84067
Phone: 800-970-8220; 801-773-8220 **Fax:** 801-773-8229

Types of Records Retrieved: Civil and criminal courts.

Local Retrieval Area: UT-Box Elder, Cache, Davis, Salt Lake, Tooele, Utah, Weber

Add'l Information: Established 2003. 1st project may require prepayment. The also provide court filings, subpoena preparation, photocopying, skiptracing, private and fire investigations. A licensed PI in UT. They perform service of process.

Washington County Title Co

158 Main Ave, PO Box 397, Akron, CO 80720
Phone: 970-345-2256 **Fax:** 970-345-2953

Types of Records Retrieved: Real Estate; Tax liens/judgments; UCC records

Local Retrieval Area: CO-Washington

Add'l Information: Established 1887. Normal turnaround time- 1 week. Projects billed by number of names searched. Terms are net 30 days. 1st project may require prepayment. Title insurance and abstracting.

Washington Court Records Svc

PO Box 30291, Spokane, WA 99223
Phone: 509-448-5012 **Fax:** 509-448-8221

Types of Records Retrieved: Civil, criminal and probate courts; Federal courts; Real Estate; Tax liens/Judgments; UCC records; Vital records

Local Retrieval Area: WA-Adams, Asotin, Benton, Chelan, Clallam, Clark, Cowlitz, Douglas, Ferry, Franklin, Garfield, Grant, Grays Harbor, Island, Jefferson, King, Kitsap, Kittitas, Klickitat, Lewis, Lincoln, Mason, Okanogan, Pacific, Pend Orielle, Pierce, San Juan, Skagit, Skamania, Snohomish, Spokane, Stevens, Thurston, Walla Walla, Whitman, Yakima; OR-Baker, Benton, Clackamas, Clatsop, Columbia, Coos, Crook, Curry, Deschutes, Douglas, Gilliam, Grant, Harney, Hood River, Jackson, Jefferson, Josephine, Klamath, Lake, Lane, Lincoln, Linn, Malheur, Marion, Morrow, Multnomah, Polk, Sherman, Tillamook, Umatilla, Union, Wallowa, Washington, Wheeler, Yamhill; MT-Beaverhead, Blaine, Broadwater, Carbon, Carter, Cascade, Dawson, Fergus, Flathead, Gallatin, Wibaux. **Correspondent Relationships:** WA, MT, ID, OR.

Add'l Information: Normal turnaround time- negotiable. Projects billed by number of names searched. Projects billed by the hour. bill twice monthly unless otherwise arranged. They have nearly 20 years experience, they take pride in accurate service in a timely manor, using efficient, dependable researchers. Nationwide correspondence are abundant.

Washington Document Service (DC)

1023 15th St NW 12th Floor, Washington, DC 20005
Phone: 800-728-5201; 202-628-5200 **Fax:** 800-385-3823; 202-626-7628
www.wdsdocs.com **email:** wdsdocs@worldnet.att.net

Types of Records Retrieved: Civil, criminal and probate courts; Federal courts; Real Estate; Tax liens/Judgments; UCC records; Vital records

Local Retrieval Area: DC-District of Columbia; MD-Montgomery; VA-Arlington, Fairfax, Richmond City. **Correspondent Relationships:** nationwide and Canada.

Add'l Information: Established 1979. Normal turnaround time- same day. Projects billed by the hour. 1st project may require prepayment. Credit cards accepted. Visa, Mastercard and American Express accepted. They specialize in court research and obtaining documents nationwide including the Supreme Court and all state, federal and bankruptcy courts. They also search public agencies including the Securities and Exchange Commission. Case monitoring available.

Washington Document Services (NY)

299 Broadway #320, New York, NY 10007
Phone: 800-422-2776; 212-267-9600 **Fax:** 800-537-1711; 212-267-9665
www.wdsdocs.com **email:** wdsdocs@worldnet.att.net

Types of Records Retrieved: Civil, criminal and probate courts; Federal courts; Tax liens/Judgments; UCC records

Local Retrieval Area: NY-Bronx, Dutchess, Kings, Nassau, New York, Queens, Richmond, Rockland, Suffolk, Westchester; NJ-all counties. **Correspondent Relationships:** Connecticut, Vermont, upstate New York, nationwide.

Add'l Information: Established 1979. Normal turnaround time- same day or requested deadline. Projects billed by the hour. 1st project may require prepayment. Credit cards accepted. They specialize in complex research and retrieval of all aspects of court documents. They deal directly with county and federal courts and archives in New York and New Jersey. Case monitoring available.

Washita Valley Abstract Co

PO Box 458, Chickasha, OK 73023
Phone: 405-224-6111 **Fax:** 405-222-4429

Types of Records Retrieved: Civil courts; Probate courts; Real Estate; Tax liens/Judgments; UCC records

Local Retrieval Area: OK-Grady

Add'l Information: Normal turnaround time- 3-4 days. Fee basis is per page and time. They specialize in complete abstracting, title insurance and loan closing services. Also do mineral ownership.

Watertown Title & Escrow Co

PO Box 1444, 20 S Maple St, Watertown, SD 57201
Phone: 605-886-8406 **Fax:** 605-882-3473
www.watertowntitle.com

Types of Records Retrieved: Probate courts; Real Estate; Tax liens/Judgments; UCC records; Vital records

Local Retrieval Area: SD-Codington

Add'l Information: Normal turnaround time- 2-5 days. Fee basis varies by type of transaction.

Watkins Investigations

746 Colonel Dr #2E, Garland, TX 75043
Phone: 972-926-6011 **Fax:** 972-926-6022 rlw@myexcel.com

Types of Records Retrieved: Civil, criminal and probate courts; Real Estate; Tax liens/Judgments; UCC records

Local Retrieval Area: TX-Dallas, Kaufman, Rockwall

Add'l Information: Established 1999. Normal turnaround time- 24-48 hours. Invoice monthly. They specialize in background investigations, public record research, locates, asset investigations, process service, surveillance. A licensed PI in TX. They perform service of process.

Kathi Watson

PO Box 45, Canton, NC 28716
Phone: 828-648-5830 **Fax:** 828-648-0060
mycroft111@yahoo.com

Types of Records Retrieved: Civil, criminal and probate courts; Real Estate; Tax liens/Judgments; UCC records; Vital records

Local Retrieval Area: NC-Haywood, Jackson. **Correspondent Relationships:** Western NC depending on nature of project.

Add'l Information: Established 1978. Normal turnaround time- 24-48 hours. Projects billed by number of names searched. All projects require prepayment. Credit cards accepted. PayPal.com is used for Credit Card use. She specializes in real estate and title searches. Other counties available depending on need and cost.

Wayne County Abstract

103 Sycamore St, Greenville, MO 63944
Phone: 573-224-3616 **Fax:** 573-224-3196

Types of Records Retrieved: Real estate; Tax liens/Judgments.

Local Retrieval Area: MO-Wayne

Add'l Information: 1st project may require prepayment. They specialize in any real estate-related records.

We Search ReSearch Inc

PO Box 125, 316 N Main St (46710), Avilla, IN 46710
Phone: 800-251-8167; 260-897-2336 **Fax:** 260-897-3988 or 260-897-4489

Types of Records Retrieved: Civil, criminal and probate courts; Federal courts; Real Estate; Tax liens/Judgments; UCC records

Local Retrieval Area: IN-Adams, Allen, Benton, Blackford, Boone, Carroll, Cass, Clinton, De Kalb, Delaware, Elkhart, Fayette, Fountain, Fulton, Grant, Hamilton, Hancock, Hendricks, Henry, Howard, Huntington, Jasper, Jay, Johnson, Kosciusko, La Porte, LaGrange, Lake, Madison, Marion, Marshall, Miami, Montgomery, Newton, Noble, Porter, Pulaski, Randolph, Rush, Shelby, St Joseph, Starke, Steuben, Tippecanoe, Tipton, Union, Wabash, Warren, Wayne, Wells, White, Whitley

Add'l Information: Established 1997. Normal turnaround time- 24-48 hours. Projects billed by number of records located. Will invoice on a monthly basis, except when requested a different billing method. They specialize in felony and misdemeanor searches, civil charge searches, UCC, mortgages, judgments, tax liens, deed searches and bankruptcy searches. They have been in service for 10 years.

Weber Abstract Co

PO Box 263, Madison, SD 57042
Phone: 605-256-4640 **Fax:** 605-256-3835
www.weberabstract.com **email:** info@weberabstract.com

Types of Records Retrieved: Civil courts; Probate courts; Real Estate; Tax liens/Judgments; UCC records; Vital records

Local Retrieval Area: SD-Lake

Add'l Information: Established 1949. Normal turnaround time- 1 day to 2 weeks. Fee basis is set by law. 1st project may require prepayment. They specialize in title work.

David V Weber, Attorney

PO Box 211149, Martinez, GA 30917-1149
Phone: 706-860-8160 **Fax:** 706-860-1568 dvweber@bellsouth.net

Types of Records Retrieved: Real Estate

Local Retrieval Area: GA-Burke, Columbia, Richmond

Add'l Information: Established 1976. Normal turnaround time- usually up to 3 days. Fee basis will vary by the type of project. He specializes in title searches.

Webster County-Butler & Rhodes Abstract

628 Central Ave, Fort Dodge, IA 50501-3812
Phone: 515-573-3341 **Fax:** 515-573-8806

Types of Records Retrieved: Civil, criminal and probate courts; Real Estate; Tax liens/Judgments; UCC records; Vital records

Local Retrieval Area: IA-Webster

Add'l Information: Normal turnaround time- 1-2 days. Fee basis will vary by the type of project. 1st project may require prepayment.

Webster's Research Inc

PO Box 7565, Rapid City, SD 57709
Phone: 605-718-5472 **Fax:** 605-718-3914
lwebster@rushmore.com

Types of Records Retrieved: Civil, criminal and probate courts; Federal courts; Real Estate; Tax liens/Judgments; UCC records; Vital records

Local Retrieval Area: SD-Butte, Custer, Fall River, Lawrence, Meade, Pennington. **Correspondent Relationships:** statewide.

Add'l Information: Established 2000. Normal turnaround time- 24-48 hours. Projects billed by number of names searched. Invoice with the job, payment due within 30 days. They specialize in real estate, record searches and filing in all federal, state and county agencies in South Dakota, including Secretary of State.

Weeks and Associates LLC

316 W 12th St #308, Austin, TX 78701
Phone: 512-472-9989 **Fax:** 512-494-1133
www.carlweeks.com **email:** cw@carlweeks.com

Types of Records Retrieved: Civil, criminal and probate courts; Federal courts; Tax liens/Judgments; UCC records; Vital records

Local Retrieval Area: TX-Travis, Williamson. **Correspondent Relationships:** Dallas, Harris, Bexar, Tarrant, TX counties.

Add'l Information: Established 1992. Normal turnaround time- 2 business days. Expedited service available. Projects billed by number of names searched. All projects require prepayment. Credit cards accepted. They specialize in full service legal support, document service records from all State of TX agencies, medical & business records, depostion by written questions and business records affidavit. A licensed PI in TX. They perform service of process.

Weissinger & Hunter

PO Box 215, Rolling Fork, MS 39159
Phone: 662-873-6258 **Fax:** 662-873-6903

Types of Records Retrieved: Civil, criminal and probate courts; Real Estate; Tax liens/Judgments; UCC records; Vital records

Local Retrieval Area: MS-Issaquena, Sharkey

Add'l Information: Normal turnaround time- 2 days. Projects billed by the hour. 1st project may require prepayment. They are a law firm that will do public record searching.

Welch & Ekman

PO Box 107, 321 Briggs Ave S #2, Park River, ND 58270
Phone: 701-284-7833 **Fax:** 701-284-7832

Types of Records Retrieved: Civil, criminal and probate courts; Real Estate; Tax liens/Judgments; UCC records; Vital records

Local Retrieval Area: ND-Cavalier, Walsh

Add'l Information: Established 1992. Normal turnaround time- 1 day. Projects billed by the hour.

Welliver & Associates LLC

22431 Antonio Pky #B160-435, Rancho Santa Margarita, CA 92688
Phone: 800-569-5677; 949-459-5919 **Fax:** 949-459-5922
www.4quicksearch.com **email:** welliver@4quicksearch.com

Types of Records Retrieved: Criminal courts; Federal courts

Local Retrieval Area: CA-Los Angeles, Orange, Riverside, San Bernardino, San Diego. **Correspondent Relationships:** nationwide.

Add'l Information: Established 1989. Normal turnaround time- 24 hours. Projects billed by number of names searched. Credit cards accepted. They specialize in retail loss prevention, internal theft, investigations and bank account searches (judgments required). A licensed PI in CA. They perform service of process.

Wells Abstract Co

119 S 10th, PO Box 732, Hannibal, MO 63401
Phone: 573-221-0644 **Fax:** 573-221-7303

Types of Records Retrieved: Civil courts; Probate courts; Real Estate; Tax liens/Judgments; UCC records

Local Retrieval Area: MO-Audrain, Knox, Lewis, Macon, Marion, Monroe, Ralls, Randolph, Shelby

Add'l Information: Established 1900. Normal turnaround time- 2 days. Projects billed by number of records located. Personal checks accepted.

Wells County Abstract

523 Railroad St South, Fessenden, ND 58438 **Phone:** 701-547-3433

Types of Records Retrieved: Real Estate; Tax liens/Judgments

Local Retrieval Area: ND-Wells

Add'l Information: 1st project may require prepayment. They specialize in real estate.

Weltner Law Office

PO Box 303, Mankato, KS 66956
Phone: 785-378-3172 **Fax:** 785-378-3203
rweltmer@uscenter.net

Types of Records Retrieved: Civil, criminal and probate courts; Real Estate; UCC records; Tax liens/Judgments.

Local Retrieval Area: KS-Jewell. **Correspondent Relationships:** Mitchell, Republic, Smith counties KS.

Add'l Information: Normal turnaround time- 24 hours. Projects billed by the hour. They accept personal checks. They also operate Weltner Abstract and Title Ins. Co. which specializes in title searches, abstracts, and title insurance. They have been in business over 65 years.

West Central Abstracting Co

202 Junius Ave, Fergus Falls, MN 56537
Phone: 218-736-5685 **Fax:** 218-739-4610 westcen@prtel.com

Types of Records Retrieved: Probate courts; Real Estate; Tax liens/Judgments; UCC records; Vital records

Local Retrieval Area: MN-Otter Tail

Add'l Information: Established 1988. Normal turnaround time- 3-5 days. Fee basis is per entry.

West Coast MCI

PO Box 627, Martinez, CA 94553
Phone: 925-372-8909

Types of Records Retrieved: Civil, criminal and probate courts; Federal courts; Real Estate; Tax liens/Judgments; UCC records; Vital records

Local Retrieval Area: CA-Contra Costa, Solano. **Correspondent Relationships:** the bay area of Northern California.

Add'l Information: Established 1982. Normal turnaround time- 24-48 hours. Projects billed by the hour. 1st project may require prepayment. They specialize in hands-on searching and investigation since 1982. A licensed PI in CA. They perform service of process.

West Virginia Records Research

PO Box 2222, Huntington, WV 25722
Phone: 304-633-6964 **Fax:** 304-697-0996
www.wvrecords.com **email:** william.alan@worldnet.att.net

Types of Records Retrieved: Civil and criminal courts

Local Retrieval Area: WV-Cabell, Kanawha, Putnam, Wayne, Wood. **Correspondent Relationships:** Fayette, Raleigh, Boone, Pleasnts, Jackson, Roane counties, WV.

Add'l Information: Established 1998. Normal turnaround time- 24-36 hours. Projects billed by number of names searched. Net 15 days. Regular clients billed monthly. They specialize in protecting clients from costly mistakes. Reliable and accurate, they provide background checks from court records. Discount rates available. Go online: www.wvrecords.com.

Westchester Court Services-Fox Advertising Inc

199 Main St, 10th Fl, White Plains, NY 10601
Phone: 914-948-5200 **Fax:** 914-948-5501

Types of Records Retrieved: Civil, criminal and probate courts; Federal courts; Tax liens/Judgments; UCC records

Local Retrieval Area: NY-Rockland, Westchester. **Correspondent Relationships:** New York City, Queens, King, Bronx, Brooklyn, Staten Island, Long Island.

Add'l Information: Established 1937. Normal turnaround time- variable, depending on project. Projects billed by number of records located. They retrieve records in only Rockland and Westchester Counties but do filings in Dutchess, Orange, Putnam, Rockland, Sullivan, Ulster, Westchester. They perform service of process.

Western Attorney Services

75 Columbia Sq, San Francisco, CA 94103-4099
Phone: 415-487-4140 **Fax:** 415-864-6238

Types of Records Retrieved: Civil, criminal and probate courts; Federal courts

Local Retrieval Area: CA-Alameda, Contra Costa, Marin, Monterey, San Francisco, San Mateo, Santa Clara, Solano, Sonoma. **Correspondent Relationships:** nationwide.

Add'l Information: Normal turnaround time- same day. Fee basis is per hour and a distance charge. 1st project may require prepayment. They specialize in civil case record searches.

Western Kentucky Title

1135 Tennevue, Paducah, KY 42003
Phone: 270-898-9666 **Fax:** 270-898-9667

Types of Records Retrieved: Real Estate; Tax liens/Judgments

Local Retrieval Area: KY-Ballard, Calloway, Carlisle, Graves, Marshall, McCracken

Add'l Information: Established 1994. 1st project may require prepayment. They specialize in real estate. A second office is in Murray, KY call 270-759-3760.

Western Nebraska Inv

PO Box 401, North Platte, NE 69103-0401
Phone: 308-534-9003 **Fax:** 308-696-0009
wni804@kdsi.net

Types of Records Retrieved: Civil and criminal courts

Local Retrieval Area: NE-Custer, Dawson, Keith, Lincoln, Perkins

Add'l Information: Established 2003. 1st project may require prepayment. They also provide photocopying, skiptracing, private investigations and interviews. Covers central and western Nebraska. A licensed PI in NE. They perform service of process.

Western Reporting

PO Box 1348, Draper, UT 84020-1348
Phone: 800-466-1996; 801-281-2000 **Fax:** 800-351-4558; 801-281-2005
www.westernreporting.com **email:** customerservice@westernreporting.com

Types of Records Retrieved: Criminal court, Criminal Court, Probate

Local Retrieval Area: UT-Salt Lake. **Correspondent Relationships:** Western US.

Add'l Information: Established 1993. Normal turnaround time- 4-24 hours. Projects billed by number of names searched. 1st project may require prepayment. Set up accounts of check by phone. They are a screening firm, they do tenant, employment and business screening statewide and nationally. They have reports that include criminal, credit, eviction, bad check and all verifications.

Weston County Title

PO Box 548, New Castle, WY 82701
Phone: 307-746-2001 **Fax:** 307-746-2217

Types of Records Retrieved: Real Estate; Tax liens/Judgments

Local Retrieval Area: WY-Weston

Add'l Information: Established 1996. 1st project may require prepayment. They specialize in real estate.

Wetherill Law Office

215 Main St, Rockport, IN 47635
Phone: 812-649-2221 **Fax:** 812-649-2222
wethlaw@psci.net

Types of Records Retrieved: Civil, criminal and probate courts; Real Estate; Tax liens/Judgments; UCC records; Vital records

Local Retrieval Area: IN-Spencer

Add'l Information: Established 1970. Normal turnaround time- variable depending on search. Charges vary with the type of record. They specialize in record searches, deeds and title insurance. They have 30+ years experience.

Wheels of Justice Inc

657 Mission St #502, San Francisco, CA 94105
Phone: 800-649-1198; 415-546-6000 **Fax:** 888-649-1199; 415-546-6199
www.proserver.com **email:** woj@proserver.com

Types of Records Retrieved: Civil, criminal and probate courts; Federal courts; Real Estate; Tax liens/Judgments; UCC records; Vital records

Local Retrieval Area: CA-Alameda, Contra Costa, Marin, San Francisco, San Mateo, Santa Clara. **Correspondent Relationships:** nationwide.

Add'l Information: Established 2000. Normal turnaround time- 24-48 hours. Expedited service available. Projects billed by number of names searched. Projects billed by the hour. 1st project may require prepayment. They are a San Francisco based litigation support company with an experienced staff. They offer court research, court filings, service of process and skiptracing. They perform service of process.

Whiteside Abstract & Title Insurance

132 N State St, St Ignace, MI 49781
Phone: 906-643-9292 **Fax:** 906-643-9806 whiteside@sault.com

Types of Records Retrieved: Probate courts; Real Estate; Tax liens/Judgments; UCC records

Local Retrieval Area: MI-Mackinac

Add'l Information: Normal turnaround time- 3-10 days. Fee basis will vary by type of project. 1st project may require prepayment. They specialize in real estate and title insurance.

Whiting Background & Legal Services

HC 88 Box 72B, Statts Mill, WV 25279
Phone: 304-372-6499 **Fax:** 304-372-6812 patonaw@yahoo.com

Types of Records Retrieved: Civil, criminal and probate courts; Federal courts; Tax liens/Judgments; Vital records

Local Retrieval Area: WV-Cabell, Clay, Doddridge, Fayette, Jackson, Kanawha, Nicholas, Putnam, Raleigh, Roane, Webster, Wirt, Wood

Add'l Information: Established 2001. Normal turnaround time- 24 hours. Projects billed by number of names searched. Will invoice monthly. They have been in business for 4 years and have 23 years of legal experience. They have an excellent reputation for accuracy and result timeliness.

Wieder Young & Assoc Inc

PO Box 2114, Silver Spring, MD 20915-2114
Phone: 301-681-7206 **Fax:** 301-593-1583 wyai@comcast.net

Types of Records Retrieved: Civil and criminal courts; Federal courts; Tax liens/Judgments; UCC records

Local Retrieval Area: MD-Anne Arundel, Baltimore, Baltimore City, Calvert, Carroll, Charles, Frederick, Harford, Howard, Montgomery, Prince George's, Washington; VA-Alexandria City, Fairfax, Prince William

Add'l Information: Established 1990. Normal turnaround time- 1-2 days. Projects billed by number of names searched. Terms: net 15 days.

The Wilki Group Inc

256 E Cherry Cove Ln, Round Lake Beach, IL 60073
Phone: 847-356-8546 **Fax:** 847-356-8641
www.thewilkigroup.com **email:** tom@thewilkigroup.com

Types of Records Retrieved: Real Estate; Tax liens/Judgments; UCC records

Local Retrieval Area: IL-Cook, De Kalb, Du Page, Grundy, Kane, Kendall, Lake, McHenry, Will

Add'l Information: Established 2002. Normal turnaround time- 24 hours. Projects billed by number of names searched. 1st project may require prepayment. Credit cards accepted. The Wilki Group is a public record retreival/court filing company that services Northeastern IL.

Wilkin County Abstract

PO Box 910, Wahpeton, ND 58044
Phone: 701-642-3781 **Fax:** 701-642-3852 richlandabstract@702com.net

Types of Records Retrieved: Civil, criminal and probate courts; Real Estate; Tax liens/Judgments; UCC records

Local Retrieval Area: MN-Wilkin. **Correspondent Relationships:** Traverse, Stevens, Ottertail, Grant, Clay counties MN.

Add'l Information: Established 1922. Normal turnaround time- 1 week or less. Projects billed by number of names searched. They are escrow agents and title insurance agents representing Old Republic and Stewart Title Insurance Company as well as Chicago Title.

William C Brown & Co

631 Walnut St, Reading, PA 19601
Phone: 610-373-1516 **Fax:** 610-373-7360
Wm.C.Brown@juno.com

Types of Records Retrieved: Civil, criminal and probate courts; Real Estate; Tax liens/Judgments; UCC records

Local Retrieval Area: PA-Berks

Add'l Information: Established 1972. Normal turnaround time- 1-2 days. Fee basis will vary by the type of project. 1st project may require prepayment. They specialize in title searches.

William Olmsted Inv

2443 Fair Oaks Blvd #72, Sacramento, CA 95825-7684
Phone: 916-484-6465

Types of Records Retrieved: Civil, criminal and probate courts; Federal courts; Real Estate; Tax liens/Judgments; UCC records; Vital records

Local Retrieval Area: CA-El Dorado, Placer, Sacramento, San Joaquin, Sutter, Yolo, Yuba. **Correspondent Relationships:** California.

Add'l Information: Established 1983. Normal turnaround time- variable depending on project. Expedited service available. Projects billed by the hour. Mileage and expenses will be added to the hourly charge. 1st project may require prepayment. They specialize in investigations including civil, assets and background searches. They also do real estate, insurance and mortgage insurance fraud. A licensed PI in CA.

George Williams

PO Box 63, 113 A Main St, Quitman, MS 39355
Phone: 601-776-2111 **Fax:** 601-776-2112

Types of Records Retrieved: Civil, criminal and probate courts; Real Estate; Tax liens/Judgments; UCC records

Local Retrieval Area: MS-Clarke

Add'l Information: Normal turnaround time- 2-3 days. Projects billed by the hour. 1st project may require prepayment. He is an attorney.

Williamson Abstract Co

110 Public Square, Greenfield, IA 50849
Phone: 641-743-2175 **Fax:** 641-743-6201

Types of Records Retrieved: Real Estate; Tax liens/Judgments; UCC records; Vital records

Local Retrieval Area: IA-Adair

Add'l Information: Established 1960. Normal turnaround time- 2-5 days. Fee basis will vary by the type of search. Will file/record documents. They require a retainer and will accept personal checks. They specialize in abstract and real estate searches.

John Wilmot

PO Box 68, Athens, GA 30603
Phone: 706-546-7411 **Fax:** 706-354-4177
thewilmotcompany@hotmail.com

Types of Records Retrieved: Civil, criminal and probate courts; Real Estate; Tax liens/Judgments; UCC records; Vital records

Local Retrieval Area: GA-Clarke. **Correspondent Relationships:** Clayton, Cobb, DeKalb, Fulton, Gwinnett, Cherokee, Douglas, Fayette, Henry, Rockdale, Muscogee, plus all Georgia counties.

Add'l Information: Established 1979. Normal turnaround time- 24-48 hours. Projects billed by number of names searched. They are a complete title company and will provide personalized, in-depth service.

Wilson Abstract Co

215 W Washington, Macomb, IL 61455
Phone: 309-833-2049 **Fax:** 309-833-5311
wlnabst@macomb.com

Types of Records Retrieved: Probate courts; Real Estate; Tax liens/Judgments; UCC records; Vital records

Local Retrieval Area: IL-Fulton, Hancock, Henderson, McDonough, Schuyler, Warren

Add'l Information: Normal turnaround time- 2 days for a judgment search; 4 days for title work. Projects billed by the hour. Travel expenses will be included in the fee. All projects require prepayment. They have been in business for over 54 years.

Todd Wilson PC

PO Box 325, Elwood, NE 68937
Phone: 308-785-2550 **Fax:** 308-785-2852

Types of Records Retrieved: Civil and criminal courts; Probate; Real Estate; Tax lines/judgments

Local Retrieval Area: NE-Gosper

Add'l Information: Established 1998. 1st project may require prepayment. They specialize in court and real estate records.

Wisconsin Employee & Renter Check (WERC)

4141 N Bartlett Ave, Milwaukee, WI 53211
Phone: 414-967-9342 **Fax:** 414-967-9346
www.wercinc.com **email:** aaronswerc@yahoo.com

Types of Records Retrieved: Civil and criminal courts.

Local Retrieval Area: WI-Kenosha, Milwaukee, Ozaukee, Racine, Washington, Waukesha. **Correspondent Relationships:** subcontractors statewide.

Add'l Information: Established 1993. Normal turnaround time- 24-48 hours. Projects billed by number of names searched. 1st project may require prepayment. Credit cards accepted. Net 30 days after receipt of invoice. Formerly Cryaar Inv, they specialize in statewide criminal background checks and renter checks. Turnaround time is 24-48 hours.

Wisconsin Title of Richland Center Inc

PO Box 436, 161 N Central Ave, Richland Center, WI 53581
Phone: 800-236-4596; 608-647-4596 **Fax:** 608-647-8033

Types of Records Retrieved: Probate courts; Real Estate; Tax liens/Judgments; UCC records; Vital records

Local Retrieval Area: WI-Richland

Add'l Information: Normal turnaround time- 1-2 days. Fee basis varies by type of transaction. 1st project may require prepayment.

Wisconsin Title of Shawano Inc

110 W North Water St, New London, WI 54961-1208
Phone: 715-823-3600 **Fax:** 715-823-9100
www.wititleinc.com **email:** clintonville@wititleinc.com

Types of Records Retrieved: Civil, criminal and probate courts; Real Estate; Tax liens/Judgments; UCC records

Local Retrieval Area: WI-Outagamie, Shawano, Waupaca. **Correspondent Relationships:** Ashland, Fond du Lac, Appleton, Richland Center, Stevens Point, Washburn, Wausau, Waupaca, WI.

Add'l Information: Normal turnaround time- 1-2 days. Fee basis varies by type of transaction. 1st project may require prepayment. They specialize in quality service with a fast and accurate turnaround time.

Wisconsin Title Washburn

PO Box 205, Washburn, WI 54891
Phone: 715-373-2412 **Fax:** 715-373-5551

Types of Records Retrieved: Real Estate; Tax liens/Judgments

Local Retrieval Area: WI-Bayfield

Add'l Information: Established 1994. 1st project may require prepayment. They specialize in real estate.

Wisestart Information Services

PO Box 497, Elkhorn, WI 53121
Phone: 262-723-7881 **Fax:** 262-723-7884 info@wisestart.com

Types of Records Retrieved: Civil and criminal courts.

Local Retrieval Area: IL-Du Page, Kane, Lake, McHenry; WI-Walworth. **Correspondent Relationships:** nationwide.

Add'l Information: Established 1994. Normal turnaround time- 24-36 hours. Expedited service available. Projects billed by number of names searched. Projects billed by number of records located. 1st project may require prepayment. They specialize in employment and tenant screening nationwide. A licensed PI in WI.

WNC Search Service

PO Box 637, Candler, NC 28715
Phone: 828-768-0062 **Fax:** 828-665-9701
xstchn@bellsouth.net

Types of Records Retrieved: Civil and Criminal courts; Federal courts; Real Estate; Tax liens/Judgments; UCC records

Local Retrieval Area: NC-Buncombe, Haywood, Henderson, Madison, McDowell, Polk, Rutherford, Transylvania, Yancey

Add'l Information: Established 2001. Normal turnaround time- 48-72 hours. Projects billed by number of names searched.

Woelfel & Assoc Inc

2010 Mall St #C2, Collinsville, IL 62234
Phone: 888-297-7180; 618-345-3411 **Fax:** 618-345-9337
www.woelfelassociates.com **email:** woelfel@woelfelassociates.com

Types of Records Retrieved: Civil, criminal and probate courts; Federal courts; Real estate; Tax liens/Judgments; UCC records.

Local Retrieval Area: IL-Adams, Bond, Calhoun, Clay, Clinton, Fayette, Jersey, Macoupin, Madison, Marion, Randolph, St. Clair; MO-St Charles, St Louis

Add'l Information: Established 1995. Projects billed by the hour. 1st project may require prepayment. They are a fully service agency, offering civil and criminal investigation as well as surveillance, process service and skiptracing. A licensed PI in IL. They perform service of process.

Elaine Wolf

561 Village Sq, Hazelwood, MO 63042
Phone: 314-731-1839 **Fax:** 314-731-1464 werica28@aol.com

Types of Records Retrieved: Civil, criminal, probate courts; Federal Courts

Local Retrieval Area: MO-St. Louis, St. Louis City

Add'l Information: Established 1995. Normal turnaround time- 24-48 hours; 1-day expedited service available. Projects billed by number of names searched. She specializes in civil and criminal record searches, including the Federal District Court/Eastern District of Missouri. She also does bankruptcies, and National Labor Relations Board filings, and will consider any projects not listed here.

Kathy Wolken

7540 N Camino Sin Vacas, Tucson, AZ 85718-1298
Phone: 520-544-4228 **Fax:** 520-219-8171 kwolken@comcast.net

Types of Records Retrieved: Civil, criminal and probate courts; Federal courts; Tax liens/Judgments.

Local Retrieval Area: AZ-Pima

Add'l Information: Established 1993. Normal turnaround time- less that 24 hours excluding weekends and holidays. They bill monthly. A licensed PI in AZ.

Wood & Tait Inc

PO Box 6180, 64-5249 Kauakea Rd, Kamuela, HI 96743
Phone: 800-774-8585; 808-885-5090 **Fax:** 888-630-0500; 808-885-5622
www.woodtait.com **email:** jwood@woodtait.com

Types of Records Retrieved: Civil, criminal and probate courts; Federal courts; Real Estate

Local Retrieval Area: HI-Hawaii, Honolulu, Kauai, Maui. **Correspondent Relationships:** close relationships with search firms nationwide.

Add'l Information: Established 1984. Normal turnaround time- 2-3 working days. Customized pricing offered. 1st project may require prepayment. Credit cards accepted. All major credit cards accpeted. They specialize Private investigations in finding property tax records, business registrations, professional and occupational licenses and bankruptcies. A licensed PI in HI. They perform service of process.

Woodard & Bohse Law Office

121 W 3rd St, Dover, OH 44622
Phone: 330-343-8848 or 8849 **Fax:** 330-343-3496

Types of Records Retrieved: Civil, criminal and probate courts; Real Estate; Tax liens/Judgments; UCC records; Vital records

Local Retrieval: OH-Carroll, Coshocton, Harrison, Holmes, Tuscarawas

Add'l Information: Established 1945. Normal turnaround time- 1 week. Projects billed by number of records located. Projects billed by the hour. 1st project may require prepayment. They will accept personal checks. They specialize in real estate, accounts receivable, probate and estates. They perform service of process.

Woods County Abstract Corp

PO Box 686, Alva, OK 73717
Phone: 580-327-1746 **Fax:** 580-327-1780

Types of Records Retrieved: Civil, criminal and probate courts; Real Estate; Tax liens/Judgments; UCC records

Local Retrieval Area: OK-Woods

Add'l Information: Normal turnaround time- 1-5 days. Fee basis will vary by the type of project. They specialize in title work, special certificates and abstracting.

Woodward County Abstract Co

PO Box 508, Woodward, OK 73802
Phone: 580-256-3344 **Fax:** 580-256-4530

Types of Records Retrieved: Civil courts; Probate courts; Real Estate; Tax liens/Judgments; UCC records

Local Retrieval Area: OK-Harper, Woodward

Add'l Information: Normal turnaround time- 2-3 days. They specialize in abstracts of title and title insurance.

Worcester Record Search

4 Jill Circle, Shrewsbury, MA 01545
Phone: 508-842-7282 **Fax:** 508-842-2236 wrsearch@aol.com

Types of Records Retrieved: Civil, criminal and probate courts; Federal courts; Real Estate; Tax liens/Judgments; UCC records; Vital records

Local Retrieval Area: MA-Franklin, Hampden, Hampshire, Worcester

Add'l Information: Established 1992. Normal turnaround time- 24 hours. Projects billed by number of names searched. They specialize in Central MA and Pioneer Valley. They also file, search, abstract and retrieval of public records in each court, land registry and municipal office in four counties.

World Class Inv

PO Box 510549, Melbourne Beach, FL 32951-0549
Phone: 321-728-0641 **Fax:** 321-728-0818 DianaPI@aol.com

Types of Records Retrieved: Civil, criminal and probate courts

Local Retrieval Area: FL-Brevard. **Correspondents:** nationwide.

Add'l Information: Established 1988. Normal turnaround time- 2-3 days. Projects billed by number of names searched. 1st project may require prepayment. Credit cards accepted. They specialize in law probate, pre-employment, civil & criminal information gathering. A licensed PI in FL. They perform service of process.

Worth County Abstract Co Inc

736 Central Ave, PO Box 64, Northwood, IA 50459
Phone: 641-324-1761 **Fax:** 641-324-1761

Types of Records Retrieved: Civil, criminal and probate courts; Real Estate; Tax liens/Judgments; Vital records

Local Retrieval Area: IA-Worth

Add'l Information: Established 1901. Normal turnaround time- 1-3 days. Projects billed by the hour. 1st project may require prepayment.

Wright County Title Co

221 N Talcott Ave, Mountain Grove, MO 65711-1758
Phone: 417-926-6163 **Fax:** 417-926-6166 wctc@getgoin.net

Types of Records Retrieved: Civil courts; Probate courts; Real Estate; Tax liens/Judgments; UCC records

Local Retrieval Area: MO-Douglas, Wright

Add'l Information: Established 1989. Normal turnaround time- 1-2 weeks. Projects billed by number of names searched. 1st project may require prepayment. They specialize in real estate records, chains of title and encumbrances.

Wright Research

PO Box 1590, Caldwell, ID 83606
Phone: 208-455-2450 **Fax:** 208-455-2462
wrightresearch@direcway.com

Types of Records Retrieved: Civil, criminal and probate courts; Tax liens/Judgments; UCC records; Vital records

Local Retrieval Area: ID-Ada, Canyon

Add'l Information: Established 1997. Normal turnaround time- same day guaranteed 24 hours. Projects billed by number of names searched. Will do the work and bill the company at the end of the month.

X-Y-Z

XL Professional Services Inc

3776 4th Ave, San Diego, CA 92103-4203
Phone: 619-232-7874 **Fax:** 619-232-7882

Types of Records Retrieved: Civil, criminal and probate courts; Federal courts; Real Estate; Tax liens/Judgments; UCC records; Vital records

Local Retrieval Area: CA-Los Angeles, Riverside, San Diego. **Correspondent Relationships:** nationwide.

Add'l Information: Established 1989. Normal turnaround time- 1-3 days. Projects billed by number of names searched. Projects billed by number of records located. Projects billed by the hour. 1st project may require prepayment. Payment due upon receipt on work. They specialize in civil court research, filing of court documents & service of process. They also deal with workers compensation, County Recorders & Court of Appeals & family law at Superior & Municipal Court levels. They can do this nationwide. They perform service of process.

Xpedite Wholesale Criminal Research

3091 W Galbraith Rd #308, Cincinnati, OH 45239
Phone: 800-325-3609; 513-522-8764 **Fax:** 513-728-4411
www.xpediteonline.com **email:** tirvin@xpediteonline.com

Types of Records Retrieved: Civil & criminal courts; US District courts

Local Retrieval Area: KY-Boone, Campbell, Kenton; OH-Butler, Clermont, Franklin, Hamilton, Warren. **Correspondent Relationships:** nationwide and international.

Add'l Information: Established 1988. Normal turnaround time- 24-48 hours. Projects billed by number of names searched. 1st project may require prepayment. Credit cards accepted. They specialize in criminal research.

XpertSearch Inc

PO Box 403, Flagler Beach, FL 32136
Phone: 732-229-6688 **Fax:** 775-248-6436
www.xpertsearch.com **email:** research@xpertsearch.com

Types of Records Retrieved: Criminal and Probate courts; Federal courts; Real Estate; Tax liens/Judgments; UCC records; Vital records

Local Retrieval Area: FL-Flagler, Orange, Seminole, St. Johns, Volusia; NJ-Monmouth, Ocean. **Correspondent Relationships:** nationwide and international.

Add'l Information: Normal turnaround time- 24-48 hours. Projects billed by number of names searched. Credit cards accepted. They specialize in criminal research and pre-employment screening, but are capable of retrieving any public record of any kind nationwide or worldwide.

Yahnke Professional Svs & Investigations

2112 W Galena Blvd #8-235, Aurora, IL 60506
Phone: 630-966-9774 **Fax:** 630-966-9774 toni@ypsandI.com

Types of Records Retrieved: Civil, criminal and probate courts; Real Estate; Tax liens/Judgments; UCC records; Vital records

Local Retrieval Area: ID-Ada, Canyon

Add'l Information: Established 2004. Normal turnaround time- 24-48 hours. Projects billed by number of names searched. Most projects require prepayment. They specialize in process service, first run papers (free if not served) court records search, skiptracing, surveillance, private investigations. Is a licensed PI in IL. They perform service of process.

Yoakum County Abstract Co

PO Box 457, Plains, TX 79355
Phone: 806-456-2615 **Fax:** 806-456-2625
ycoabst@hiplains.net

Types of Records Retrieved: Real Estate; Tax liens/Judgments

Local Retrieval Area: TX-Yoakum

Add'l Information: Established 1984. Normal turnaround time- 2-3 days. Fee basis varies by type of project.

York County Title Co

PO Box 572, 608 N Grant Ave, York, NE 68467
Phone: 402-362-4405 **Fax:** 402-362-4421
www.yorkcountytitleco.com **email:** vziegler@alltel.net

Types of Records Retrieved: Civil, criminal and probate courts; Real Estate; Tax liens/Judgments; UCC records

Local Retrieval Area: NE-York

Add'l Information: Established 1969. Normal turnaround time- 24 hours. Fee basis varies by type of transaction. Project may require prepayment. They will file UCC and real estate documents if prepaid.

Beth Young

1012 Lumber Ave, Elliott, IA 51532
Phone: 712-767-2510 **Fax:** 712-767-2510 jon_beth@netins.net

Types of Records Retrieved: Criminal courts; Real Estate; Tax liens/Judgments

Local Retrieval Area: IA-Cass, Montgomery

Add'l Information: Established 1995. Normal turnaround time- 48 hours. Projects billed by number of names searched. 1st project may require prepayment. They also do title and abstract searches.

William R Young

PO Box 4172, Eddyville, KY 42038
Phone: 270-388-0807 **Fax:** 270-388-0307

Types of Records Retrieved: Criminal and civil courts; Probate courts; Real Estate; Tax liens/Judgments

Local Retrieval Area: KY-Lyon

Add'l Information: Established 1984. 1st project may require prepayment. He specializes in court records and real estate.

Your Information Source Inc

PO Box 441237, Houston, TX 77244
Phone: 800-644-9668; 281-497-3770 **Fax:** 800-644-9189; 281-558-5288
service@yourinformationsource.com

Types of Records Retrieved: Civil and criminal courts

Local Retrieval Area: TX-Bexar, Dallas, Denton, Harris, Nueces, Tarrant, Travis. **Correspondent Relationships:** statewide.

Add'l Information: Established 1997. Normal turnaround time- 24-48 hours. Projects billed by number of names searched. 1st project may require prepayment. All projects require preauthorization or prepayment. They are a full service pre-employment company that specializes in Texas: they offer drug testing, MVR's, credit and all other employee related data. They have fast, efficient and credible services. A licensed PI in TX.

Zap! Courier Service

90 S Swan St, Albany, NY 12210
Phone: 518-449-3361 **Fax:** 518-449-1332 zapalbany@aol.com

Types of Records Retrieved: Civil courts; Federal courts

Local Retrieval Area: NY-Albany, Rensselaer, Saratoga, Schenectady. **Correspondent Relationships:** New York City and Washington, DC.

Add'l Information: Established 1977. Normal turnaround time- 24 hours depending on court turnaround. Projects billed by number of names searched. Projects billed by the hour. They work closely with the Public Service Commission, Department of State, Insurance Department and New York State Legislature.

John A Zapf II

PO Box 1006, 628 W Broad St, Bethlehem, PA 18016-1006
Phone: 610-868-5101 **Fax:** 610-691-1216 jazapf@verizon.net

Types of Records Retrieved: Civil courts; Probate courts; Real Estate; Tax liens/Judgments; UCC records

Local Retrieval Area: PA-Lehigh, Northampton

Add'l Information: Established 1976. Normal turnaround time- 48 hours. Projects billed by number of names searched. They specialize in real estate title searches and abstracts as well as current owner searches.

Zavala County Abstract Co Inc

123 E Uvalde St, Crystal City, TX 78839
Phone: 830-374-3218 **Fax:** 830-374-3947

Types of Records Retrieved: Real Estate; Tax liens/Judgments

Local Retrieval Area: TX-Zavala

Add'l Information: Established 1958. Normal turnaround time- up to 1 week. Fee basis will vary by the type of project. 1st project may require prepayment.

Zero Investigations Inc

2816 E 51st St #300, Tulsa, OK 74105-1743
Phone: 866-400-9376; 918-492-7741 **Fax:** 918-492-7677
www.zeroinvestigationsinc.com **email:** info@zeroinvestigationsinc.com

Types of Records Retrieved: Civil, criminal and probate courts; Federal courts; Real Estate; Tax liens/Judgments; UCC records; Vital records

Local Retrieval Area: OK-Creek, Rogers, Tulsa. **Correspondent Relationships:** nationwide correspondent network.

Add'l Information: Established 2000. Normal turnaround time- 24-48 hours. Projects billed by number of names searched. Credit cards accepted. They specialize in nationwide employment screening services, process service and document retrieval. Private investigations, drug & alcohol testing, hari follical, DNA paternity testing and instant drug testing products. A licensed PI in OK. They perform service of process.

Zook Search Inc - NYC

285 22nd St #2, Brooklyn, NY 11215
Phone: 718-369-3879 **Fax:** 718-369-0849
www.zooksearch.com **email:** ny@zooksearch.com

Types of Records Retrieved: Civil, criminal and probate courts; Federal courts; Real Estate; Tax liens/Judgments; UCC records

Local Retrieval Area: NY-Kings, New York, Queens

Add'l Information: Established 1997. Normal turnaround time- 24 hours. Projects billed by number of names searched. Payment is net 30 days. Accurate and efficient document retrieval and filing services. They strive for 24 hours turnaround on all orders and happy clients.

Zook Search Inc - California

5431 California St #11, San Francisco, CA 94118
Phone: 415-387-1029 **Fax:** 415-387-1030
www.zooksearch.com **email:** ca@zooksearch.com

Types of Records Retrieved: Civil, criminal and probate courts; Federal courts; Real Estate; Tax liens/Judgments

Local Retrieval Area: CA-Alameda, San Francisco

Add'l Information: Established 1997. Normal turnaround time- 24 hours. Projects billed by number of names searched. 1st project may require prepayment. Accurate and efficient document retrieval and filing services. They strive for 24 hour turnaround on all orders and happy clients.

Zook Search Inc - Colorado

2925 Josephine St, Denver, CO 80205
Phone: 303-292-5138 **Fax:** 303-294-0483
www.zooksearch.com **email:** co@zooksearch.com

Types of Records Retrieved: Civil courts; Probate courts; Federal courts; Real Estate; Tax liens/Judgments; UCC records

Local Retrieval Area: CO-Adams, Arapahoe, Boulder, Denver, Jefferson

Add'l Information: Established 1997. Normal turnaround time- 24 hours. Projects billed by number of names searched. Payment is net 30 days. Accurate and efficient document retrieval and filing services. They strive for 24 hour turnaround on all orders and happy clients.

Public Record Retriever Network 2005 Associate Members

(Includes PRRN Members not Listed in the Local Retrievers Section)

The following companies are PRRN Associate Members who provide statewide or regional services, either as a search firm or screening firm such as pre-employment screening or tenant screening company. For local retrievers companies, see the previous sections. Many local document retrieval companies who are standard PRRN members are also search firms or screening firms, and they can be found in these previous sections. Search firms and screening firms can also be found at www.brbpub.com and www.publicrecordsources.com.

The BRB book *Public Records Online* contains listing on hundreds of additional companies that offer online or other electronic access to public record information.

2005 PRRN Member Search Firms, Distributors, Publishers, Gateways, Database Companies

ADAM Safeguard

PO Box 1210, Toms River, NJ 08754

Phone: 800-722-2326, 732-286-0800 **Fax:** 732-286-9201

www.adamsafeguard.com email: dld@adamsafeguard.com

Founded: 1973 **Memberships:** IALEIA, IACP, PRRN

Clientele Restrictions: Agreement required.

Pre-Employment Screening Services: Credit Reports, Drug Testing - Outsourced, Workers Compensation History, Criminal Records, Education/Employment, Licenses/Registrations/Permits

Special Distribution Methods to Client: Dial-Up (Other than Internet), Email

ADAM Safeguard is the only company to provide a "How-to" book to all registered clients. The owner of ADAM Safeguard is co-author of "25 Essential Lessons in Employee Management" and "Don't Hire a Crook!" ADAM Safeguard conducts pre-employment background checks for all types of businesses. Ordering is processed by fax, phone, and mail as well as HireCheck software for direct access via modem.

ADM & Associates Inc

132 Windward Cr, Vincent, AL 35178

Phone: 800-242-5999, 205-525-5260 **Fax:** 205-525-4289

admasso2@centurytel.net

Founded: 1993 **Memberships:** AMA, ALA

Clientele Restrictions: Casual requesters permitted.

Applications: Background Info - Individuals, Legal Compliance, Employment Screening, Fraud Prevention/Detection

ADM & Assoc. Products & Information Categories:

Criminal Information, Driver and/or Vehicle (AL)

Foreign Country Information (Intl)

Pre-Employment and Tenant Screening Services: Criminal Records, Local Document Retrieval, MVRs

Special Distribution Methods to Client: Email, Microfilm/Microfiche

ADM specializes in criminal record research for Alabama, Birmingham Municipal, and Alabama Federal Courts; these searches are returned next morning.

Allied Data Research

PO Box 473, Elverta, CA 95626-0473

Phone: 888-378-2641

www.alliedresearch.net email: support@alliedresearch.net

Founded: 2003 **Memberships:** PRRN, SHRM

Clientele Restrictions: Casual requesters permitted.

Applications: Background Info - Business, Background Info - Individuals, Employment Screening, Locating People/Businesses, Tenant Screening

Products & Information Categories:

Credit Information, Workers Compensation (US)

Driver and/or Vehicle (US, AR, CA, CO, GA, MI, OH, WA)

Criminal Information, Licenses/Registrations/Permits, Litigation/Judgments/Tax Liens, Vital Records (US, CA)

Education/Employment, Tenand History (US, CA)

Pre-Employment Screening Services: Credit Reports, Criminal Records, Education/Employment, Former Employer Interviews, Licenses/Registrations/Permits, Local Document Retrieval, MVRs

Tenant Screening Services: Credit Reports, Criminal Records, Forcible Detainer Check, Former Landlord Interviews

Special Distribution Methods to Client: Dial-Up (Other than Internet), FTP, Gateway via Another Online Service, Software

Allied Data Research provides nationwide background checks, emplyment screening, criminal records, drug testing, driving records, and other business-related services for employers. Open 6AM-6PM M-F, Sat. 8AM-5PM.

Background Information Services Inc

24500 Chagrin Blvd #315, Beachwood, OH 44122

Phone: 800-235-3954, 216-514-2800

www.employeescreen.com email: jmorris@employeescreen.com

Branch Offices: Cleveland, OH **Founded:** 1999
Memberships: ASIS, SHRM, PRRN **Clientele Restrictions:** Casual requesters permitted, agreement required

Applications: Background Info - Individuals, Employment Screening

Products & Information Categories:

Criminal Information, Litigation/Judgments/Tax Liens (US. OH)
Credit Information, Driver and/or Vehicle, Education/Employment, Workers Compensation (US)

Pre-Employment Screening Services: Bankruptcy, Local Document Retrieval, Credit Reports, Profile/Aptitude Testing, Criminal Records, MVRs, Drug Testing - In House

Tenant Screening Services: Credit Reports, Local Document Retrieval, Criminal Records, MVRs

Special Distribution Methods to Client: Email, Gateway via Another Online Service, Internet, Software

Background Information Services Inc. has access to criminal records in over 3500 counties, all 50 states, and delivers results to clients in 24-72 hours. Helps develop a program to complement your existing hiring practices. Pre-employment screening and background check packages also include verification of education and employment, credit reports, driving records, civil records and other types of information.

Comprehensive Information Services

PO Box 79007, Pittsburgh, PA 15216

Phone: 800-454-8725, 412-561-3003

www.cisonline.com email: srafferty@cisonline.com

Founded: 1991 **Memberships:** PRRN **Clientele Restrictions:** Casual requesters permitted; agreement required.

Applications: Background Info - Business, Employment Screening, Fraud Prevention/Detection, General Business Information, Background Info - Individuals

Products & Information Categories:

Bankruptcy, Corporate/Trade Name Data, Credit Information, Criminal Information, Education/Employment (US, PA)
Licenses/Registrations/Permits, Litigation/Judgments/Tax Liens, Uniform Commercial Code, Workers Compensation (US, PA)
Driver and/or Vehicle (US, PA)

Special Distribution Methods to Client: Email, Internet

CIS is a leader in the background screening industry, providing an array of services to assist in the hiring process. They will customize requests to include any service component; requests can be sent using various means, including fax, phone, oe electronic delivery. With one of the most advanced automated systems in the industry, they utilize a wide variety of tracking systems, customer driven reports, flexible invoicing procedures, as well as error-free record diagnosis and SSN verification systems, all professionally investigated.

eChase LLC

17897 E Cranberry, Parker, CO 80139

Phone: 303-884-8002 **Fax:** 303-840-0829

www.ehcasedata.com email: jim@echasedata.com

Founded: 2003 **Clientele Restrictions:** Agreement required.

Applications: Background Info - Individuals, Employment Screening, Fraud Prevention/Detection, Locating People/Businesses, Tenant Screening

Products & Information Categories:

Criminal Info, Addresses/Telephone Numbers, Tenant History (US, CO)

Special Distribution Methods to Client: Email, Gateway via Another Online Service, Internet

eChase includes social fraud identifier with every search. Includes the OFLAC database with every search criminal search. Eviction data for 25 states; criminal for 44 states; SOR for 44 states. Competitive prices and volume discounts. Their XML gateway makes it easy to perform searches. If you do not have a website, eChase can build one for you.

Ekeholm & Assoc LLC

PO Box 145, Lebanon, GA 30146

Phone: 770-720-8343

www.screensafecheck.com email: info@screensafecheck.com

Founded: 1998 **Memberships:** ACFE, NCISS, NAPBS, PRRN
Clientele Restrictions: Signed services agreement required.

Applications: Background Info - Business, Background Info - Individuals, Employment Screening, Locating People/Businesses, Tenant Screening

Products & Information Categories:

Addresses/Telephone Numbers, Credit Information, Driver and/or Vehicle, Tenant History, SEC/Other Financial (US)
Criminal Information, Education/Employment, Licenses/Registrations/Permits, Real Estate/Assessor, Litigation/Judgments/Tax Liens (US, GA)

Proprietary Databases or Gateways:
Gateway Name: Criminal Records
‣ Criminal Information (US, GA)
Gateway Name: Credit History
‣ Credit Information (US)
Gateway Name: MVR
‣ Driver and/or Vehicle (US)
Gateway Name: Identity Trace
‣ Education/Employment (US, GA)

Pre-Employment Screening Services: Credit Reports, Criminal Records, Drug Testing - In House, Education/Employment, Licenses/Registrations/Permits, MVRs

Tenant Screening Services: Credit Reports, Criminal Records, Forcible Detainer Check, Litigation/Judgments

Special Distribution Methods to Client: Internet

Georgia-based, Ekeholm is a licensed and bonded, private investigative firm that provides investigative and background screening services for the legal, business, professional communities, and qualified individuals. Kirsti Ekeholm is the Manager and Licensed Private Investigator.

Employment Screening Resources

7110 Redwood Blvd Ste C, Novato, CA 94945

Phone: 888-999-4474, 415-898-0044

www.ESRcheck.com email: esr@ESRcheck.com

Founded: 1996 **Memberships:** SHRM, PRRN
Clientele Restrictions: Must be ongoing account

Pre-Employment Screening Services: Drug Testing - Outsourced, Credit Reports, Former Employer Interviews, Workers Compensation History

Special Distribution Methods to Client: Email, Internet

Employment Screening Resources (ESR) combines investigative, legal and public record research experience to provide pre-employment background reports to human resources and security departments. ESR provides services nationally as well as to California employers who need to comply with complicated California regulations. In compliance with the Fair Credit Reporting Act, ESR reports highlight and summarize important information, not merely providing raw data or computer printouts. The status of all reports is available in real time, 24/7 on the secured ESRnet online reporting system. ESR offers support, training and consultation in safe hiring procedures as well as HR help desk. ESR also offers a turnaround time guarantee.

Ernst Publishing Co, LLC

PO Box 318, Clarksville, NY 12041

Phone: 800-345-3822

www.ernstpublishing.com email: lrcanier@ernst.cc

Parent Company: Ernst Publishing Company, LLC
Founded: 1992 **Memberships:** AIIP, SIIA, NPRRA, PRRN
Clientele Restrictions: None reported

Applications: Lending/Leasing, Legal Compliance, Filing/Recording Documents, General Business Information, Real Estate Transactions
Proprietary Databases or Gateways:
Database Name: Uniform Commercial Code Filing Guide
- Uniform Commercial Code Filing Guide (US)

Database Name: Real Estate Recording Guide
- Real Estate/Assessor (US)

Special Distribution Methods to Client: Database, Internet, Publication/Directory

The Uniform Commercial Code Filing Guide™ is a practical "How To" reference for the preparation, filing and searching of Article 9 Financing Statements nationwide. This Guide provides information re: fees, forms, facts for all 4,316 filing jurisdictions and is designed for the high-volume filer. Included are sections hosting the Model Act, Filing Fundamentals, Purchase Money Secured Interest and Definitions. Subscription is annual with quarterly updates; a newsletter is provided in non-updating months. The new Revised Article 9 Alert assists filers and searchers to function in the new Revision environment. They also publish the Real Estate Recording Guide and National Release Guide and offer a database and web-based product, National Online Mortgage Assistance Database Program.

GA Public Record Services Inc

8035 ERL Thornton Fwy #415, Dallas, TX 75228

Phone: 214-320-9836 **Fax:** 214-320-2992

www.gaprs.com email: wbarnes@gaprs.com

Parent Company: Greet America **Founded:** 1989
Memberships: ASIS, SHRM, NPRRA, NTPIA, PRRN
Clientele Restrictions: Casual requesters permitted

Applications: Employment Screening, Background Info - Individuals, Fraud Prevention/Detection, Tenant Screening, Litigation

Products & Information Categories:

Criminal Information, Litigation/Judgments, Bankruptcy (US)

Special Distribution Methods to Client: Email, Internet

Since 1993, GA Public Record Services has specialized in on-site, county level criminal record searches, primarily for pre-employment screening purposes. GA also provides information for corporate due diligence, security consultants, insurance investigations, risk management as well as the applications listed above. GA searches nationwide and access court records in over 1,800 counties every month; over 2,800 counties are searched each year. GA will usually return reports within 24 to 72 hours. 55% is completed within 24 hours. Efficient internet, password-protected access provides a responsible method of information communication. Quality is the primary focus - providing information you can trust.

Merlin Information Services

215 S Complex Dr, Kalispell, MT 59901

Phone: 800-367-6646, 406-755-8550 **Fax:** 406-755-8568

www.merlindata.com email: Support@merlindata.com

Founded: 1991 **Memberships:** ACA, CAC, CAPPS, NARM, SCRIA, NCSEA **Clientele Restrictions:** Casual requesters permitted

Applications: Locating People/Businesses, Asset/Lien Searching/Verification, Background Info - Business, Collections, Fraud Prevention/Detection
Proprietary Databases or Gateways:
Database Name: Merlin Cross Directory
- Addresses/Telephone #s, Credit Data, Driver and/or Vehicle, Vital Records, Voter Registration (US)

Gateway Name: National FlatRate, Collector's FlatRate
- Civil/Criminal Indexes, UCC, Aviation/Vessels, MVRs, Real Estate/Assessor, Litigation/Judgments/Tax Liens, Addresses/Telephone #s, Corp./Trade Name Data, SSN, Bankruptcy, Credit Information, Licenses/Registration/Permits, Vital Records, Voter Regis. (US)

Gateway Name: Merlin Super Header
- Addresses/Telephone #s, SSNs, Credit Information, Vital Statistics (US)

Gateway Name: QuikInfo.net FlatRate
- Civil/Criminal (CA), UCC, Aviation/Vessels, Real Estate/Assessor, Criminal Data, Driver and/orVehicle, Wrokers' Comp, Addresses/Telephone Numbers, Corporation/Trade Name Data, SSN, Bankruptcy, Licenses/Registration/Permits, Vital Records, Voter Registration (US)

Database Name: Nat'l Fictitious Business Names
- Corporation/Trade Names, Addresses/Telephone #s (CA, US)

Database Name: CA Criminal Indexes, CA Brides/Grooms, CA Birth/Death Indexes, many other CA databases
- UCC (Filing Index), Civil/Criminal Indexes, Vital Records, Licenses/Reg./Permits, Real Estate/Assessor, Litigation/Judgments/Tax Liens, Wills/Probate (CA)

Gateway Name: Link to America, DOB File
- Addresss/Phone #s, Credit Data, Driver and/or Vehicle, Real Estate/Assessor, Vital Statistics, Voter Registration (US)

Database Name: Nat'l People Finder/Credit Headers/Criminal/Property
- Addresses/Phone #s, Real Estate/Assessor, Litigation/Judgments/Tax Liens, Criminal Data, Credit Data, Vital Statistics (US)

Special Distribution Methods to Client: CD-ROM, Dial-Up (Other than Internet), Internet, Magnetic Tape

Merlin Information Services provides access to public records on the Internet. Their search and retrieval site and their software assists in obtaining results not found through traditional access. Merlin's extensive California databases are the most current and complete available. Their wide selection of national databases such as The Merlin Cross-Directory, Link to America, and Nat'l FlatRate rounds out their extensive skiptracing and investigative tools, helping you locate people, assets, neighbors, and associates.

Motznik Information Services

8301 Briarwood St #100, Anchorage, AK 99518-3332

Phone: 907-344-6254 **Fax:** 907-344-1759

www.motznik.com email: lori@motznik.com

Founded: 1974 **Memberships:** NFIB, PRRN
Clientele Restrictions: Casual requesters permitted

Applications: Direct Marketing, Locating People/Businesses, Real Estate Transactions, Government Document Retrieval, Filing/Recording Documents
Proprietary Databases or Gateways:
Database Name: Motznik Online Svc
- Addresses/Telephone Numbers, Bankruptcy, Licenses/Registrations/Permits, Litigation/Judgments/Tax Liens, Criminal Information, Corporate/Trade Name Data, Uniform Commercial Code, Real Estate/Assessor, Voter Registration and Driver and/or Vehicle (AK)
- Vessels (AK, US)

Special Distribution Methods to Client: CD-ROM, Database, Dial-Up (Other than Internet), Disk, Email, FTP, Lists/Labels, Magnetic Tape

Formerly Motznik Computer Services, they offer a comprehensive online information research system that provides access to a wide selection of Alaska public files. Their files are cumulative and, in some cases, is the only source for many historical records dating back to 1972. Motznik also provides mailing lists and reports for analysis. Has most CDS files for Alaska. Many of their current databases are for sale and can be delivered in many formats.

Owens OnLine Inc

6501 N Himes Ave #104, Tampa, FL 33614

Phone: 800-745-4656, 813-877-2008 **Fax:** 813-877-1826

www.owens.com email: email@owens.com

Founded: 1992 **Clientele Restrictions:** Casual requesters permitted

Applications: Background Info - Business, Background Info - Individuals, Collections, Competitive Intelligence, Employment Screening

Products & Information Categories:

Criminal Information, Bankruptcy, Education/Employment, Vital Records, Voter Registration (US, itl)
Uniform Commercial Code (US)

Proprietary Databases or Gateways:

Gateway Name: Owens OnLine
- Credit Information (US, Itl)

Gateway Name: Owens OnLine
- Foreign Country Information (Itl)

Special Distribution Methods to Client: Email, FTP, Internet

Owens OnLine specializes in international background checks and credit reports on businesses and individuals, and in international criminal checks. They provide worldwide coverage and also offer FreeDirectories.com where over 1 billion people, companies, and public records can be found free of charge.

Public Record Research System

PO Box 27869, Tempe, AZ 85285

Phone: 800-929-3811, 480-829-7475

www.brbpub.com email: brb@brbpub.com

Parent Company: BRB Publications Inc

Founded: 1989 **Memberships:** PRRN, NAPBS
Clientele Restrictions: Casual requesters permitted

Applications: General Business Information, Government Document Retrieval, Risk Management, Locating People/Businesses, Competitive Intelligence

Proprietary Databases or Gateways:

Database Name: PRRS
- Addresses/Telephone Numbers, Legislation/Regulations (US)

Special Distribution Methods to Client: CD-ROM, Database, Disk, Internet, Lists/Labels, Publication/Directory

The Public Record Research System is a series of in-depth databases formatted into books, CDs and online. BRB is recognized as the nation's leading research and reference publisher of public record related information. The principals of the parent company are directors of the Public Record Retriever Network, the nation's largest organization of public record professionals. Over 26,000 government and private enterprises are analyzed in-depth regarding regulations and access of public records and public information. The Public Record Research System (PRRS) is available on CD, the Internet and as a customized database.

Search First Information Services

2741 Bryan Dairy Rd, Largo, FL 33777

Phone: 888-807-3272, 727-549-8866

www.searchfirst.com email: debbie@searchfirst.com

Founded: 1991 **Memberships:** PRRN, SHRM, BNI
Clientele Restrictions: Contractual agreement required.

Pre-Employment Screening Services: Credit Reports, Criminal Records, Drug Testing - In House, Education/Employment, Former Employer Interviews, Licenses/Registrations/Permits, MVRs

Tenant Screening Services: Credit Reports, Criminal Records, Forcible Detainer Check, MVRs

Special Distribution Methods to Client: Email, Internet

Search First Information Services is a pre-employment screening company-serving customers throughout the United States. Primary location is in the Tampa, Florida area and maintains a sales office in Los Angeles and Akron, Ohio. They specialize in pre-employment and employee screening. A strategic partners with Alcohol and Substance Abuse Programs; A.S.A.P. provides drug screening and drug free workplace programs designed for specific hiring and workplace environments.

United Screening Services Corp.

4343 W Flagler St #350, Miami, FL 33134

Phone: 800-731-2139, 305-774-1711

www.unitedscreening.com email: robert@unitedscreening.com

Memberships: ASIS, NAA, SHRM, NAPBS, CAI, PRRN
Clientele Restrictions: End-user agreement required.

Pre-Employment Screening Services: Credit Reports, Criminal Records, Education/Employment, Former Employer Interviews, Licenses/Registrations/Permits, MVRs, Workers' Compensation History

Tenant Screening Services: Credit Reports, Criminal Records, Forcible Detainer Check, MVRs

United Screening Services is a full-service business-to-business background screening company specializing in tenant/resident screening, pre-employment screening and drug testing. Through their extensive network of private and governmental databases and agency relationships, they are able to provide clients with in-depth background screening in 50 states and worldwide. Their team has combined experience in the credit, verification, and screening industry of over 30 years.

PRRN - The Public Record Retriever Network

PRRN - The Public Record Retriever Network - is the largest membership organization representing professionals in the public record industry. With more than 750 members in 50 states, Puerto Rico, Canada and elsewhere in North America retrieving documents from local government agencies in over 2,000 counties, boroughs, parishes and provinces, PRRN Members are recognized as the nation's leaders in local public record searching and document retrieval.

Only PRRN Members are listed by state on two Internet sites that receive over 18,000 hits per month. Visit www.brbpub.com/prrn or www.publicrecordsources.com.

Who Is Eligible For Membership?

Any firm eligible to be listed in *The Directory of Local Court and County Record Retrievers* is eligible for annual membership. Once a member, your continued membership depends on your maintaining the standards expressed in the Code of Professional Conduct and Terms of Membership.

What is PRRN's Mission?

The mission of PRRN is to promote development within the public document retrieval industry of—

- Standards of professional conduct, and
- Improved marketing and sales practices

What is the PRRN Code of Public Record Retriever Standards?

Members of PRRN commit their organization to a set standard Record Retrieval and of Professional Conduct. These standards are summarized starting on page 654.

The Benefits of PRRN Membership

New Business Opportunities

The PRRN Membership roster is strongly promoted to business entities that use public records and hire public record retrievers. For example:

PRRN Members are exclusively profiled on the *Public Record Research System*, a CD-Rom and Internet subscription product. A county or state query will show exclusively PRRN members at: www.brbpub.com/prrn and www.publicrecordsources.com

The PRRN Member listings are prominently featured in *The Directory of Local Court and County Record Retrievers*.

Network With Other Professionals

PRRN Members can rely upon the assurance and pledge from other PRRN members when looking for a record retriever to service a client need outside of their local retrieval area. The PRRN **member logo** can be used in member's advertising and promotional materials.

The **PRRN Membership Kit** that each member receives includes a printed roster of all members. Throughout the year PRRN members may view or download the updated roster from the web site.

The PRRN Directors **monitor problems or disputes** members may have with other members or non-members.

Educational Benefits

PRRN Members receive the Public Record Retrieval Industry Standards Manual (PRRISM). This 32-page document is a training aid and is full of useful information regarding:

- Taking the order, preparing the report
- Standards, guaranties, and disclaimers
- Pricing and invoicing, how to handle billing and receivables problems

PRRN Members receive the PRRN newsletter, SOURCES. This newsletter features articles relevant to the public record retrieval industry, and how to increase your business or to operate more efficiently.

Throughout the year, PRRN members are notified when events affect the business public record retrievers. The directors monitor legislation and get involved when necessary to lobby legislative committees and licensing boards.

PRRN Members will receive a 10% discount on single book purchases from BRB Publications.

Features of the PRRN Members Only Web Page

Search for a PRRN Member. You can find a PRRN member by searching in a specific county or by state. This is the same service open to the general public, and a source of new business for many members.

Download PRRN Forms For Your New Client and Credit Needs. You can download three important PRRN-approved forms. (Sample forms are included in this package.)

- New Account/Credit Application – For a Business
- New Account/Credit Application – For an Individual
- Personal Guarantee Authorization to Release Information

The forms are available on the web site in either MS Word or PDF. You can modify the MS Word forms by adding your company information and logo, or editing the text, or you can print the PDF versions and paste your address or logo onto the forms. Also, the PRRN Logo can be downloaded from this location. You can use the PRRN logo on any forms or your company advertising pieces.

Download Current Roster of PRRN Members. This is a PDF file of approximately 70 pages. The roster is updated weekly, adding new members and making changes as necessary. You are free to download and print the file, or simply scroll through and view the state by state listings. You may keep it on your computer system as a viewable PDF file.

Download Memos and Newsletters. Previous editions of Sources and copies of email memos can be found here.

The Bulletin Board. The PRRN Bulletin Board is a forum to help PRRN members with particular questions or needs. Once a topic or "discussion" is initiated, all additional member comments are saved and viewable. We ask that you please identify yourself when you participate. We want to make this site as easy and functional as possible and are very interested in your feedback and comments, if you have the time and interest.

By the way, the PRRN Members Bulletin Board is NOT meant to promote or market services. Members attempting to use the Bulletin Board as a means of self-promotion will have their passwords deleted by the Directors.

Terms of Membership in PRRN

PRRN is a service by BRB Publications, Inc. for the purpose of promoting standards in the retrieval industry. The principals of BRB, Carl Ernst and Michael Sankey, serve as the Directors of PRRN.

PRRN members agree to follow the highest standards of ethics and conduct in all their dealings with other members and with clients. These standards not only include those explicitly listed in the Code of Professional Conduct, but also include such matters as paying invoices to other firms in a timely fashion and not accepting projects which members are not competent to complete correctly or in a timely manner.

The members of PRRN may communicate with the Directors at any time, using the Retriever Satisfaction Survey or any other means, concerning problems or disputes with other members or with clients. The Directors may, at their sole discretion, use such information to inform members about such disputes, including but not limited to failure to pay invoices and failure to complete project on time or correctly. At the request of any member, the Directors may mediate disputes among members.

Once you are a PRRN Member, your continued membership depends on your maintaining the standards expressed in the Code of Professional Conduct and the Terms of Membership. The Directors of PRRN may, at their sole discretion and without notice, cancel the membership of any member that, in their opinion, has not met the spirit of these terms. Fees will not be returned upon cancellation of membership.

Members agree explicitly not to hold the Directors or any other members liable in any way for reporting or taking action on problems or disputes communicated to them in good faith.

Public Record Retriever Network

PRRN Code of Public Record Retriever Standards

The Public Record Retriever Network (PRRN) has set as part of its mission a goal of establishing industry standards for public record retrieval. These standards will apply to all members within the part of the industry they serve.

1. Definitions

In order to establish standards, it is first necessary to make certain that all retrievers are using a common language. The industry segments for the purpose of this Code of Standards are defined as follows:

Public Record Retriever (PRR)—PRRs search specific requested categories of public records, usually in order to obtain documentation for legal compliance, lending, hiring, screening, or litigation support. The retriever or his/her personnel goes directly to the agency to look up the information. A retriever may be relied upon for strong knowledge in a local area, whereas a search generalist has a breadth of knowledge and experience in a wider geographic range. A PRR may also be known as an **Abstractor**.

PRRs do not review or interpret the results or issue reports in the sense that investigators or CRA's do. Instead PRRs return copies of documents if requested, and/or report the findings of their searches. A search will usually involve some form of manual intervention, which may include on-site access to a courthouse or other government agency, but which may be automated to some extent, such as access to PACER or another agency with direct access web-based indexes.

Beyond the local coverage of most PRRs, **Retriever Companies** are a type of PRR that offers record retrieval services on a state, regional or a national basis. **Retriever Companies** use a network of retrievers and/or correspondents. When the term PRR is used in this document, the term is also meant to include Retriever Companies. When a local PRR is hired by another PRR or Retriever Company, the PRR may also be known as an **Independent Contractor.**

Retail Screening Companies—Companies that provide background checks use public records and other information to prepare an overall report about a subject for an end-user (e.g. employer or property owner). When a Screening Company performs services for employers or property owners, it must comply with the **Federal Fair Credit Reporting Act (FCRA),** under which the Screening Company is considered to be a **Consumer Reporting Agency (CRA).**

There are several types of Screening Companies. The two with which we are primarily concerned are:

Employment Screener—Provides applicant and employee background screening services to employers.

Tenant Screener—Provides tenant background screening services to property owners.

It is the responsibility of the Retail Screening Company to Review the Results of public record research to determine what is Reportable to the End-User.

Retail Search Firms—These Search Firms furnish public records to a variety of clients as an intermediary, or to end-users. Search firms obtain public records from numerous sources including Wholesale Distributors and Gateways (see below), government sources, PRRs, and other search firms.

Wholesale Distributors—Automated public record firms combine public sources of bulk data and/or provide online access to supply information to retail Screening Companies.

Primary Distributors include companies that collect or buy public record information from its original source and reformat the information in some useful way, usually to create a proprietary database of information.

Another type of Distributor is a **Gateway**. Gateways provide their customers with seamless, automated access to other Distributors' data or to government sources. Gateways thus provide "one-stop shopping" for multiple geographic areas and/or categories of information. Companies can be both Primary Distributors and Gateways.

Private Investigators—PIs use public records as tools rather than as ends in themselves, in order to create an overall, comprehensive "picture" of an individual or company for a particular purpose. PIs interpret the information they have gathered in order to identify further investigation tracks. They summarize their results in a report compiled from all the sources used. Many Private Investigators also provide FCRA-compliant employment and tenant screening services as well as public record retrieval. In addition, an investigator may be licensed and may perform the types of services traditionally thought of as detective work, such as surveillance.

More **Industry Terms:**

FCRA—The federal Fair Credit Reporting Act and related FTC rules.

Subject—The applicant or employee about whom background information is being gathered.

Customer—Direct customer or client of a PRR or a Retriever Company, but not an End-User.

End-User—The entity that ultimately ends up with the search results (e.g. the customer of the attorney, title company, or the employer or property owner customer of a Screening Company).

Result—An item of information obtained that may pertain to a Subject.

Negative or Derogatory Information—Information unearthed during the performance of public record retrieval that could be classified as adverse to the Subject under FCRA or other law.

Review—To look at Results obtained from other sources for the purpose of determining whether the information is Reportable to an end-user. PRRs do not perform a review; their clients do.

Reportable—This term refers to which Results can be reported to an end-user, after a Review. The standard for what is "Reportable" is whether the information complies with applicable law, such as the FCRA. PRRs do not determine what is Reportable.

Identifiers—Facts about the Subject used to analyze a public record for the purpose of determining if the record is about the Subject. Examples are full name, DOB, SSN, sex, address, and hair color.

Matching Logic—Using the Identifiers given with a search request in order to determine if the record found does, in fact, belong to the Subject. Retail Screening Companies are always responsible to determine the level of matching logic that will meet FCRA rules before reporting a Result. Stricter matching logic should be applied to Negative or Derogatory Information. Three levels of matching logic are: **Partial Name Match Logic**—Matching Logic that requires only a partial match of the Subject's name to a Result; **Name Match Only**—Results of a search that uses the full Subject name as a match; **Strict Match Logic**—Match logic that requires a minimum of two and when possible three Subject Identifiers before reporting.

Match—A Result that the Matching Logic of the Retail Screening Company determines is about the Subject.

2. General Standard

A Public Record Retriever (PRR) shall work diligently and use reasonable care in the performance of this work, in order to provide the highest possible level of service and accuracy. All searches will be conducted directly by the PRR or by researchers that are under its direct and immediate supervision and control. Order taking follows standard, written procedures that assure the Customer has provided complete and accurate Identifiers to the PRR. **Report preparation is standardized to include all the information taken on the order as well as a clear explanation of the Results and the procedures, as outlined in *Section 7.*** *Reporting the Logistics of the Search,* used in obtaining them. **Report preparation does not include a determination of what is Reportable to a Customer's client or end-user.** Disclaimers are used appropriately to put the Customer on notice about the extent of any guaranties and the constraints on obtaining information from government agencies. Pricing and invoicing methods are understandable and ethical.

3. Legal Compliance

The PRR agrees to perform public record searches in a manner consistent with that prescribed by the local, state, or federal offices and courts in which it searches. A PRR also agrees the searches will be performed legally in the manner prescribed by said offices and courts. At no time will the PRR obtain or convey to a Customer any information that was obtained through illegal or unethical means. A PRR agrees to obtain any business license that is required under applicable local city or county laws or regulations.

4. Timeliness

A PRR agrees that public record search services provided for the Customer are to be completed in an agreed upon time frame from receipt of each individual search requested by the Customer. Unless otherwise agreed with the Customer, the PRR begins the search as soon as possible after the receipt of the order, and immediately transmits any Results obtained to the Customer. In the event that there is a delay caused by the need of a court clerk to obtain files, the PRR will track the progress daily, make all necessary effort to obtain the information as soon a possible, and keep the Customer informed.

5. Performing the Search

The PRR uses only the most current, official, due-diligence-compliant source from the government agency when conducting a search. If not, the PRR will disclose the fact up front to the Customer. The PRR will fully divulge the source of information (i.e., court clerk, online service, correspondent, etc.), and the manner in which the search was conducted, (i.e. microfiche, court computer, submission to the clerk, etc.).

The following pertains to performing a search of an individual Subject name:

A. In searching a common name on an index with no DOBs or other comparable ID, the PRR should use reasonable care to investigate any name matches or near name matches listed on the index with no middle initial. If such cannot be eliminated as a match by a clerk check or other valid means, the PRR should pull and examine the files in question to search for more Identifiers. If this further examination is not reasonable to do, then the PRR must inform the Customer.

B. The Customer determines the minimum scope of each search, and the PRR should never assume a default depth of the search. If the timeframe to be researched has not been transmitted with the request, or if it is not mutually agreed upon in writing, the PRR should seek clarification from the Customer prior to performing the research.

C. For every Subject name to search in each court requested and unless instructions are given otherwise, the PRR is expected to search at least 7 years, but not less than the depth of records readily available at that court or per specific request, and do so without spending additional access fees unless specifically authorized to spend those fees. **In all cases, all history possibly relating to the Subject, regardless of the age of the record, disposition or offense, must be reported, unless otherwise agreed with the Customer.** Thus, if a default 7-year search is requested, and 12 years are available at no additional court cost in the same index, a 12-year history is expected, unless prior instruction given. In that same court, if an additional 20 years is available by searching through ledger books, that search is not performed unless the Customer separately authorizes such a search. In a different court, if only 5 years are available on a public index and the remaining years are in ledger books or only through the court staff, the PRR is expected to search whatever source and record material is required to deliver the depth of search, unless otherwise specified by the Customer, up to the default minimum of 7 years.

D. The PRR recognizes a "Name Match Only" record report constitutes a problem for the Customer in that it presents an uncertainty. As such, the PRR must give best efforts in searching for any type of ID on the record. If none can be found, the name should not be cleared; rather the PRR will submit to the Customer a "Name Match Only" report including an express statement that no Identifiers of any kind could be found in the file or agency database. In addition, if the PRR determines in its judgement that a record with only a partial name match may in fact be about the Subject, the PRR is encouraged to report the record as a "Name Match Only" record. In other words, the basic reporting rule for a PRR to follow is: **let the Customer decide what is reportable to the End-User.**

6. Reporting the Search

The PRR will report the search results in a clear, concise, legible manner that can be easily understood by the Customer. This includes refraining from the use of locally acceptable abbreviations that may not be understood outside the area.

The PRR will refrain from passing on any record information they themselves do not understand until the PRR gets any such data clarified and understood before including that data in a report.

The PRR will report only verifiable facts that can be substantiated by available court records. The researcher should refrain from guessing at or "dubbing in" key case information.

The PRR will report the existence of any additional records found in the course of research that may match to the Subject, unless instructions otherwise given. This holds true regardless of the record's location, and regardless of whether it is listed under an alias.

The PRR will report the existence of any AKA's or other ID variations found in the course of research on any given Subject.

In reporting on a record where the name or ID given to search differs in any way from that which was found in the court or government office, the PRR should include a statement acknowledging this discrepancy so there is no question as to whether it was intentional or accidental.

Reporting Results to a CRA—It is not the responsibility of the PRR or the Retriever Company to Review the Results of a search to determine what information is Reportable per the FCRA to a CRA. The PRR reports the results of a search to the CRA; the CRA determines what is Reportable to the End-User.

7. Reporting the Logistics of the Search

The PRR agrees to supply as part of each public record search the following information:

A. Full name of subject, property address checked, and other Identifiers as supplied by the Customer.

B. Specific agency(s), name(s) and indices checked.

C. Date the search was completed.

D. The period the research covers, meaning how far back the records in the file, index or database go AND the through date (date through which records have been posted, that is, the currency of records) on the government office system.

Logistics of results in the event a criminal record is located at a court—In the event a criminal record is found and in addition to the information specified above, the PRR agrees to provide the following information, if known:

A. Exact full name as listed in docket or index, and the docket or index number.

B. All Identifiers listed in docket or index including address, date of birth, SSN, or any other relatable Identifier.

C. The original charges and date of charge listed in docket or index.

D. The final disposition as listed in docket or index, including conviction charge, level of charge (felony, misdemeanor, indictable, violation, petty misdemeanor, etc), all sentencing information listed and any subsequent and pertinent information pertaining to the docket or index.

E. If requested in advance by the Customer and possible to obtain, the actual code sections that were charged as well as any relevant subsequent history (i.e. expunged, pardoned, dismissed, etc.).

F. If requested in advance by the Customer and possible to obtain, the PRR will request and provide copies of the court records and/or documents that support the information reported above. The PRR and Customer will determine, in advance, a reasonable pricing scheme for those copies.

8. Correcting Information

In the event a PRR discovers that information was given to a Customer in error, it is the absolute professional obligation of the PRR to correct any mistake or error as soon as humanly possible despite any embarrassment or difficulty it may create. All parties should understand that mistakes and errors are always possible when it comes to public records despite taking every reasonable effort to be factual and correct, but that the failure to correct the errors if and when discovered is a gross violation of a researcher's ethical duties.

9. Audits

Retriever Companies and Search Firms will conduct various procedures to audit their the PRRs they use and advise their Customers of the general nature of those procedures. Retriever Companies and PRRs acknowledge that Customers reserve the right to periodically send names that are known to have "hits," or to direct identical searches to multiple PRRs, in order to test the PRR and to establish that the Customer has exercised due diligence in the selection of a PRR. A Customer will not advise a Retriever Company or PRR ahead of time when a test is being conducted.

10. Confidentiality

The PRR agrees that all information provided by the Customer shall be maintained by the PRR in strict confidence and disclosed only to individuals whose duties reasonably relate to the legitimate business purposes for which the information is submitted. The PRR will not sell or otherwise distribute to third parties any information received, except as otherwise required by law or agreed upon in writing between the PRR and the Customer.

MEMBER Public Record Retriever Network

Code of Professional Conduct

The Public Record Retriever Network (PRRN) Code consists of ten guidelines according to which each member of the Network conducts its business.

Competency Guidelines

The Competency Guidelines refer to each of the types of records a PRRN member is proficient in retrieving

1. We know where each type of local public record is maintained.
2. We access these agencies regularly.
3. We understand the contents of the documents we retrieve.
4. We search records ourselves in those agencies that do not conduct searches for the public.
5. We maintain good relationships with agency personnel.

Customer Service Guidelines

The Customer Service Guidelines refer to the way in which each member of PRRN is expected to serve its clients.

1. We return calls promptly.
2. We complete projects as promised.
3. We explain our charges in advance.
4. We will expedite results, on request.
5. We will explain how agencies maintain their records, on request.

PRRN

Public Record Research Network Annual Membership Fees

The annual fee for PRRN membership is based on the number of counties you service hands-on on a regular basis. The fee is $10.00 per county. The minimum fee is $25.00. The maximum fee is $200.00.

A PRRN "Associate Membership" - available to search firms, screening firms, and other public record-related companies that do not retrieve county or court documents in person - is available for $39.00 per year.

For details, or for a PRRN application, or to join using a credit card over the phone, contact BRB Publications, PO Box 27869, Tempe AZ 85285
Phone: 800-929-3811 • Fax: 800-929-4981
www.brbpub.com and www.brbpub.com/PRRN

The Public Record Research System

Now on CD-Rom and the Internet!

The most comprehensive and up-to-date resource for accessing public records directly from the government agency or institution that houses them. Including:

- County Courts
- State Agencies
- State Occupational Licensing Agencies
- US Bankruptcy Courts
- US District Courts
- Federal Record Centers
- County Recording Offices
- Colleges & Universities
- Trade Schools
- Local Record Retrievers
  Members of the Public Record Retriever Network (PRRN)
- Also includes *The County Locator* – County/City/ZIP Code Cross Indexes

Visit the FREE Demo at www.publicrecordsources.com

Retriever Satisfaction Survey

We want to make sure that the Document Retrievers profiled in this book meet the expectations of their clientele. We are especially interested in knowing whether a PRRN member is living up to the commitment represented by the Code of Standards and Professional Conduct.

Therefore, we are providing a separate survey form for you to communicate to us your experience, positive or negative, with Document Retrievers. This form, known as *The Retriever Satisfaction Survey*, appears on the next page. To request a copy of this form, call 800-929-3811. You may choose to have it faxed or mailed to you.

Negative comments will be held in confidence by BRB Publications. Based on your input, we reserve the right to exclude from future editions any firms who fail to maintain an acceptable standard of professional conduct.

Retriever Satisfaction Survey

for readers of the 2005 *Directory of Local Court and County Record Retrievers*

Instructions

1. Make a copy of this form so you can use it again.
2. Report exceptional (good or bad) service you received from a public record retriever.
3. Enter all information that you think useful in assessing the performance of the retriever. The source of negative comments will be kept in confidence.
4. **FAX to Michael Sankey, Pres., BRB Publications, 1-800-929-3810.**

Date: ____________________ This is a ☐ positive report or a ☐ negative report.

Your Name	
Company	
Address	
City, State, ZIP	
Telephone Number	
Type of Company (Why you use retrievers)	

Retrieval Firm Name	
Address	
City, State, ZIP	
Telephone Number	

Summarize Your Favorable Comments or Negative Concerns:

____

____

____

____

____

____

General Questions about the Retrieval Firm:

Please answer Yes, No, Usually, or DK (for don't know) based upon your experience with this firm:

Is this firm a member of the Public Record Retriever Network? .... ______
How many times have you used this firm during the past six months? .... ______
Is the firm knowledgeable about the kinds of information it retrieves for you? .... ______
Is the firm always available when you need their services? .... ______
Does the firm perform within the turnaround times stated in our publication? .... ______
Will this firm expedite work on request? .... ______
Does this firm access all the agencies marked for it in the County Index? .... ______
Is billing timely and accurate? .... ______
Does this firm cover all the counties listed in its profile? .... ______
Is all the information in this company's profile accurate? .... ______
If not, what information is wrong?

____

____

____

If you cannot fax, then mail to BRB Publications, PO Box 27869, Tempe, AZ 85285

Notes

If you are not included in this book...

If you are a document retriever, you need to be listed in this book. What's more, it is a free listing. Here is what you need to be included in the next issue.

On the facing page is a blank questionnaire where you provide your company information and details about your record retrieval services, coverage area, and any related services you may provide such as document filing/recording, process service, investigative services, or more. *

A retriever is a company, branch office, or individual that meets the following criterion: you or employees under your direct supervision go to court offices, courts, or other government agencies on a regular basis to search public records or retrieve documents.

Public Record Retriever Application Instructions

Section 1. Local Retrieval Area In this section, list ONLY the county names where you or your FICA employees regularly visit in person. The purpose here is to present your company as an expert for a given area and not merely someone who can "get anything from anywhere." (For counties where you use another retriever - a "correspondent" - or where you use an online source to access records, these can be mentioned in Section 6.)

If you list more than 20 counties, please attach a statement to your profile explaining how you cover all these counties, for example, "we have twenty employees in cars" or "we do a circuit every two days." To avoid complaints, we need you to provide us with evidence that your true employees are regularly visiting - in person - those counties. 1099 people are not included. We may need to call to discuss this.

Sections 2-5. Profile Items Let us know the types of records you can retrieve in person; if or when you require prepayment; if you are licensed PI; your standard billing and payment methods. These details enhance your profile and should cut down on nuisance calls.

Section 6. Expanded Coverage Retrieval Area This is where you can indicate the geographic region if you use other retrievers, correspondents, sub-contractors, etc. Typical answers are "statewide" or listing the counties, states, foreign countries, etc. Here you can show coverage with 1099 people.

Section 7. Your 25-word Company Description Here you can describe your company's special features, advantages to clients, or other important facts - in 25 words or less. Typical items to mention are specialized services, online databases you may use, length of your experience, etc. One exception: we cannot print information about your rates. If you are not sure what to include, say what you do best.

Fill out the questionnaire, review, then return it either by fax or mail as soon as possible to BRB Publications. If you have questions, feel free to call BRB Publications at 800-929-3811.

---

* In addition to your free listing in this book, if you also wish to become a member of the PRRN (Public Record Retriever Network), please indicate so on your questionnaire. Details about PRRN membership and PRRN membership fees are on previous pages. Only PRRN members are featured on BRB websites that receive over 18,000 hits per month and appear in other packaged products sold to large public record provider companies. In short, as a PRRN member you will receive greater exposure. With more than 750 members in 50 states and elsewhere in North America retrieving documents from local government agencies in over 2,000+ counties, boroughs, parishes and provinces, PRRN Members are recognized as the nation's leaders in local public record searching and document retrieval.

Local Court & County Record Retriever Book

Retriever & Abstractor Questionnaire

New ___________

Office us only: ☐ Access ☐Q&A ☐ Cert ☐ Kit

Basic Information About Your Company

List full company name. ☐ Check here to be included as a PRRN member*

Contact Name ______________________ Telephone: ______________

Firm Name ______________________ Toll Free Phone ______________

Address ______________________ Local Fax ______________

City ______________ State____ Zip__________ Toll-free Fax ______________

Web address ______________________ Cell phone ______________

Email (your best email address for contacting you) ______________________

In what year did you start doing business? __________ If you perform litigation Service of Process, check here ☐

1. Local Retrieval Area

List ONLY the COUNTIES where YOUR wage-earning employees retrieve records IN-PERSON. (Do NOT list online or electronic retrieval here. Do NOT list third parties or 1099 people here)

2. TYPES of Records You Retrieve IN-PERSON

A. County Court Records

☐ Civil ☐ Criminal ☐ Probate

B. Federal Court Records

☐ US District ☐ Bankruptcy

C. County Recorded Records

☐ UCCs ☐ Real Estate ☐ Tax Liens/Judgments ☐ Vital Records

D. Other Services

☐ You can file/record documents for clients ☐ You are a licensed PI (in what state(s):

3. Usual Turnaround Time for Document Retrieval

Explain turnaround times in days or hours; also expedited services:

4. Billing Methods

☐ Bill by # of names searched ☐ Bill by the hour ☐ Bill by # or records located

5. Payment Terms

☐ All projects require prepayment ☐ First project may require prepayment

☐ Will accept credit cards Other payment terms: ______________________

6. Extended Services

Extended services using correspondents, independent contractors or others not under your direct control

☐ Yes, we can conduct services beyond our local area (using correspondents) If you use correspondents, list their counties/states/nationwide:

☐ Check this box if you offer electronic record retrieval on a statewide/regional/national basis.

7. 25-word Company Description

Describe your company, services, and special features in 25 words or less.

Questionnaire completed by: ______________________ Date: ______________

FAX to 800-929-4981 or mail to BRB Publications, PO Box 27869, Tempe AZ 85285

BRB Publications, PO Box 27869, Tempe AZ 85285 Phone: 800-929-3811 www.brbpub.com

* to become a PRRN member and receive add'l benefits, a PRRN member application and payment must be included. See PRRN section

IT'S CARVED IN STONE...
"NOBODY KNOWS MORE
ABOUT INVESTIGATIVE
DATA THAN WE DO!"
INFORMATION SERVICES
MERLIN
Online Public Record & Skiptracing Databases
www.merlindata.com • 800-367-6646

PI
journal of professional investigators
magazine
Investigating
Workplace
VIOLENCE

PI
journal of professional investigators
magazine
MISSING
OR
ABDUCTED?

PI
magazine
Secrets of Successful Fugitive Apprehension
Big Brother or Big Ideas?
Evidence on Computers: Getting Rid of it, Getting it Back
WITNESS
INTERVIEWS
and STATEMENTS

PI
journal of professional investigators
magazine
When
INFORMANTS...
become TARGETS
INSURANCE FRAUD:
INTERVIEWING ADOLESCENTS AND YOUNG ADULTS
SKIP TRACING: A REFRESHER

PI
magazine
PRETEXT
A TOOL...OR TROUBLE?
THE FTC'S DEFINITION
GARBOLOGY
CARBON MONOXIDE
RETURN TO SENDER